List of Re

(Continued on inside back cover)

IRWIN'S
BUSINESS LAW

Concepts, Analysis, Perspectives

Elliot I. Klayman
The Ohio State University

John W. Bagby
Pennsylvania State University

Nan S. Ellis
Loyola College—Maryland

Burr Ridge, Illinois
Boston, Massachusetts
Sydney, Australia

IRWIN LEGAL STUDIES IN BUSINESS SERIES

Barnes/Dworkin/Richards
LAW FOR BUSINESS, 5/e, 1994

Blackburn/Klayman/Malin
THE LEGAL ENVIRONMENT OF BUSINESS,
5/e, 1994

Dworkin
CONTRACT LAW TUTORIAL SOFTWARE, 1993

Klayman/Bagby/Ellis
IRWIN'S BUSINESS LAW, 1994

Metzger/Mallor/Barnes/Bower/Phillips
*BUSINESS LAW AND THE REGULATORY
ENVIRONMENT*, 8/e, 1992

McAdams
LAW, BUSINESS, AND SOCIETY, 3/e, 1992

McCarty/Bagby
THE LEGAL ENVIRONMENT OF BUSINESS,
2/e, 1993

Richards
LAW FOR GLOBAL BUSINESS, 1994

Tucker/Henkel
*THE LEGAL AND ETHICAL ENVIRONMENT
OF BUSINESS*, 1992

About the Authors

Elliot I. Klayman is Associate Professor of Legal Environment at The Ohio State University College of Business. He received his Juris Doctor degree from the University of Cincinnati and his L.L.M. degree from Harvard Law School. Professor Klayman is the Associate Director of the Center for Real Estate Education and Research at The Ohio State University, and is the Managing Editor of the *Journal of Legal Studies Education*. He is the coauthor of Irwin's *Legal Environment of Business*, scheduled for publication in 1994.

John W. Bagby is Professor of Business Law at Pennsylvania State University. Professor Bagby has taught business law, business organizations, regulation, real estate law, securities regulations, and commercial law to undergraduates and MBAs and has served as Staff Editor for the *American Business Law Journal*. He received his Juris Doctor degree from the University of Tulsa. Professor Bagby is the coauthor of another Irwin title, *The Legal Environment of Business*, which was published in 1993.

Nan S. Ellis is Associate Professor of Law and Social Responsibility at Loyola College in Maryland. She received her Juris Doctor degree from The Ohio State University and is a member of the Academy of Legal Studies in Business. Professor Ellis is the author of numerous articles on commercial law and was Staff Editor of the *American Business Law Journal*.

Senior sponsoring editor:	Craig Beytien
Developmental editors:	Karen E. Perry and Lara Feinberg
Marketing manager:	Robb Linsky
Project editor:	Rebecca Dodson
Production manager:	Diane Palmer
Designer:	Michael Warrell
Art coordinator:	Mark Malloy
Compositor:	Carlisle Communications, Ltd.
Typeface:	10/12 Times Roman
Printer:	Von Hoffmann Press

Library of Congress Cataloging-in-Publication Data

Klayman, Elliot I.
    Irwin's business law : concepts, analysis, perspectives / Elliot
I. Klayman, John W. Bagby, Nan S. Ellis.
       p.   cm. — (Irwin legal studies in business series)
    Includes index.
    ISBN 0-256-09178-1
    Instructor's Edition: ISBN 0-256-14889-9
    1. Commercial law—United States.   2. Business enterprises—United
States.   3. Trade regulation—United States.   I. Bagby, John W.
II. Ellis, Nan S.   III. Title.   IV. Title: Business law.   V. Series:
Irwin legal studies in business.
    KF889.K53   1994
    346.73'07 — dc20
    [347.3067]   93–5994

Printed in the United States of America
1 2 3 4 5 6 7 8 9 0 VH 0 9 8 7 6 5 4 3

KLAYMAN

To my mother Lillian, who fought the good fight; my father, Samuel, who sought and found a better place; my wife, Joyce, my best friend; and my children, Seth, my pride, and Rhena, my joy with love.

BAGBY

To my children Julia and Jack, my wife Robin, and my parents Emmett and Lucinda with love.

ELLIS

To my parents Marionlee and Irwin Teitelbaum and my children Joey, Michael, and Andy Ellis with love.

Preface

Irwin's Business Law is, in some respects, a traditional business law book, designed for business law and legal environment courses. However, this book is distinguishable by its use of a critical thinking approach. This approach imparts the skills necessary for conceptualizing, synthesizing, integrating, and analyzing. Simply, it incorporates pedagogical tools designed to help the instructor teach and the student think. The critical thinking method is carefully defined and explained in the Unit I Overview starting on page 1.

Cognitive skills must be learned and honed through exercise. One of the biggest gaps in elementary through higher education is the lack of critical thinking skills. There are a number of reasons for this lack. First, many courses do not readily lend themselves to critical thinking but rather invite regurgitation of the material learned. Second, instructors have not had experience with imparting critical thinking skills because the textbooks on the market, for the most part, do not support that approach. Third, the status quo of traditional memorization and ''spit back the facts'' approaches tend to perpetuate themselves.

The study of law is particularly suited to a critical thinking approach to learning. This book capitalizes on that opportunity and employs a consistent critical thinking theme throughout. It challenges the student to learn concepts not as an end but as a means to thinking analytically, exhaustively, and pragmatically. It exercises the various cognitive functions of the student, challenging him or her to solve problems, examine alternatives, and question answers and solutions.

CRITICAL THINKING INQUIRIES

Each chapter begins with a Chapter Outline and Critical Thinking Inquiries. These inquiries are designed to highlight the questions the student should be able to address intelligently after studying the chapter. They are questions that *identify, compare and contrast, analyze, distinguish,* and *criticize*. They function as an overview of the chapter by readying the student for the next pedagogical encounter: the Managerial Perspective.

MANAGERIAL PERSPECTIVE

One criticism of business law texts is that they are not made consistently relevant to the business context. In response, each chapter of this text opens with a business scenario, and from a managerial point of view challenges

the student to study the chapter to answer the questions that follow. The opening scenario is then integrated throughout the chapter by using the same characters for various illustrations and examples. This feature of the book keeps the focus on the business relationship. It places the student in the mind of the manager, and serves to motivate and challenge the student to delve into the chapter so that alternatives may be explored and the best solution to the question found.

CASES

Chapters contain a number of edited law cases designed to illustrate principles and trends discussed in the text. The cases open with a concise summary of the facts followed by relevant portions of the opinion in the court's language. The opinions are edited so that the significant material is retained. Cases are selected on the basis of their teachability, factual patterns, and ease of understanding. Because the controversies underlying cases and their resolution are ideal contexts to develop thinking skills, critical thinking questions follow each case.

READINGS

Chapters contain selected readings designed to illustrate trends, policies, or some significant contemporary issue in the law. These readings offer a scholarly perspective to the student, opening understanding to new thought and approaches. The readings are drawn from law journals, newspapers, business periodicals, and other appropriate sources. Each reading is followed by thought questions to reinforce critical thinking skills.

BOLDFACE TERMS

The authors have selected terms and concepts necessary to build a critical thinking mode. These terms are set in boldface in each chapter and are also defined in the glossary.

FIGURES

Throughout the book, concepts are illustrated in figures consisting of tables, charts, and illustrations. These figures help the student grasp the concepts necessary for analyses and application.

END–OF–CHAPTER QUESTIONS

The end-of-chapter questions contain a mix of actual and hypothetical cases, critical thinking, and policy questions. They are intended to test the student's ability to assimilate and integrate the material contained within the chapter.

ORGANIZATION AND CONTENT

The book is divided into four units: The Legal Environment, Commercial Transactions, Business Organizations, and Regulation of Business. Each unit contains an overview that ties together the material within the unit. The units are further broken down into 13 parts, which are in turn separated into 54 chapters. Special effort has been made to shape the book to meet the curriculum accrediting standards of the American Assembly of the Collegiate Schools of Business (AACSB), whose guidelines suggest the inclusion of ''(1) ethical and global issues, (2) the influence of political, social, legal, and regulatory environmental and technological issues, and (3) the impact of demographic diversity on organizations.'' A chapter on Ethics Analysis, an entire section on Corporate Social Responsibility, and a chapter on International Sales Transactions, in addition to one on International Law, satisfies the first criterion. Moreover, ethical and global issues are integrated throughout the text. To meet the second criterion, we have selected a wide array of cases that blend and impact historical, political, social, regulatory, and technological issues in a legal setting. Finally, the third criterion is satisfied by the array of topics contained in the Business Organizations unit.

APPENDIXES

The full text of the U.S. Constitution and excerpts from the Uniform Commercial Code are contained in the appendixes to the book.

SUPPLEMENTS

To aid the instructor in the preparation and teaching of the materials within this book, a number of helpful supplements are provided. First, there is a teaching-ready instructor's manual, which contains a chapter by chapter outline tied to the sequence of the material. The outline restates and answers every question posed, briefs every case and reading, and offers suggested tips to the instructor on how to teach and approach the material. The outline may be easily used as lecture notes for the instructor. Other ancillary materials include:

- Student study guide.
- Test bank.
- Computerized test bank.
- Teletests.
- Transparencies.
- Videos.
- LEXIS/NEXIS.

ACKNOWLEDGMENTS

We wish to recognize a number of people without whom this book would not be a reality. Richard O. Nathan contributed much of the thought and materials to this book in its early development. R. Michael Smith lent his expertise to the Administrative Law chapter and shaped its presentation. Steven B. Dow lent support and expertise on the commercial law chapters. Colleagues in Business Logistics and International Business at Pennsylvania State University were also helpful, including Joe Cauinato, Evelyn Thomalick, Lisa Williams, Gene Tyworth, John C. Spyehalski, Jeff Sharp, Matthew Walker, Rich Young, and Prasad Padmanabhan. Colleagues in Law and Social Responsibility at Loyola University—Maryland also deserve credit, including John Gray, Tim Brown, Andrea Giampetro, and Jim O'Hara.

Joyce Reichman Klayman, Sandra Yoakam, Jan Tate, and Helen Monk assisted greatly in manuscript preparation. Maryanne Herbst and Heidi Dayhoff tended to a number of administrative tasks related to this book.

In our commitment to craft a textbook and supplemental package that reflects how an instructor teaches business law, we sought the help of many of our peers from colleges and universities throughout the country. We wish to express our gratitude and indebtedness to all of the following, who either reviewed the manuscript or participated in various focus groups. These individuals represent a variety of educational institutions—state colleges, universities, and junior colleges—with varying needs, but a universal desire for a text that challenges students to think, comprehend, and apply legal principles to business:

H. Theodore Noell, *University of Notre Dame*
Mary Jane Dundas, *Arizona State University*
Theodore M. Dinges, *Longview Community College*
Donald L. Carper, *California State University—Sacramento*
Gene Marsh, *University of Alabama*
O. E. Elmore, *Texas A&M University*
Penny Herrickhoff, *Mankato State University*
Carol Rasnic, *Virginia Commonwealth University*
Barbara Danos, *Southeastern Louisiana University*
Elisabeth Crocker, *University of Arkansas*
Barbara George, *California State University—Long Beach*
Greg Mosier, *Oklahoma State University*
Marlene Swerdlow, *Lamar University*

J. David Lofton, *University of Southwestern Louisiana*
Charles Stowe, *Sam Houston State University*
Michael Garrison, *North Dakota State University*
Jack Hires, *Valparaiso University*
Lara Short, *Middle Tennessee State University*
Mike Litka, *University of Akron*
Roger Reinsch, *Emporia State University*
Susan Willey, *University of Wisconsin—La Crosse*
Sandford Searlman, *Adirondack Community College*
Marsha Hass, *College of Charleston*
Luis Aranda, *Arizona State University*
Laura Pincus, *DePaul University*
Dawn Bennett-Alexander, *University of Georgia—Athens*
Marc Lampe, *University of San Diego*
William Greenspan, *University of Bridgeport*
Janice Loutzenhiser, *California State University—San Bernardino*
Ernest W. King, *University of Southern Mississippi*
John Collins, *Syracuse University*
David Fisher, *North Central College*
Brian G. Sullivan, *Western Kentucky University*
John C. Bost, *San Diego State University*
Jeffrey M. Sharp, *Pennsylvania State University*
Prasad Padmanabhan, *Pennsylvania State University*
Rodolfo A. Camacho, *Oregon State University*
Melanie Havens, *California State University—Northridge*

Carol Docan, *California State University—Northridge*
Douglas Gordon, *Arapahoe Community College*
Lynda J. Oswald, *University of Michigan*
Edward C. Goldberg, *West Virginia State University*
Arthur J. Marinelli, *Ohio University*
James E. MacDonald, *Weber State University*
William H. Walker, *Indiana University—Purdue University*
Mitchell Povsner, *Moraine Valley Community College*
William C. Honey, *Auburn University at Montgomery*
Lisa K. Mayer, *University of Wisconsin—Oshkosh*
Donald Wiesner, *University of Miami*
Michael W. Pustay, *Texas A&M University*
Dr. L. M. Alberto, *University of South Florida*
Larry D. Strate, *University of Nevada—Las Vegas*
Ed Kaminski, *University of Central Florida*
Clark Wheeler, *Santa Fe Community College*
Adley M. Shulman, *Humboldt State University*
E. Eugene Arthur, *Rockhurst College*
Georgia Holmes, *Mankato State University*
Franklin Strier, *California State University—Dominquez Hills*
John Wheeler, *University of Virginia*

In addition, we want to give a standing ovation to the following Irwin personnel who were instrumental in producing this work: Jerry Saykes, Craig Beytien, Karen Perry, Lara Feinberg, Becky Dodson, Diane Palmer, Michael Warrell, and Mark Malloy.

Contents in Brief

Contents

UNIT II
COMMERCIAL TRANSACTIONS, 213

Part III Contract Law, 215

Chapter 11
Introduction to Contracts, 216

Chapter 12
The Agreement, 230

Chapter 13
Capacity and Genuine Assent, 248

Unit I

The Legal Environment

■

PART 1 THE LEGAL SYSTEM
PART 2 PRIVATE LAW

OVERVIEW: DEVELOPING CRITICAL THINKING SKILLS THROUGH BUSINESS LAW STUDY

Irwin's Business Law integrates the critical thinking approach in the belief that education should promote thinking, not merely rote memorization of facts. Critical thinking skills enable students to become independent learners, so it is particularly appropriate in the study of business law for several reasons. Legal rules frequently change, so managers are better equipped with an understanding of the legal process. Managers better serve their constituencies with a thorough understanding of the issues and policy-making process underlying lobbying, lawmaking, regulation, and litigation. Critical thinking skills also promote informed and intelligent business decisions.

Irwin's Business Law presents business law as a culmination of historical, social, political, and economic forces that have a strong impact on the legal and regulatory environment of business. Business law study is an ideal context in which to build critical thinking skills. Traditional law study and pedagogy naturally use critical thinking approaches and the critical thinking inquiries fundamental to legal analysis.

Irwin's Business Law presents all the traditional materials normally found in business law texts. However, this text does not just focus on rote—asking you to simply repeat what you just read. Questions are cast to require you to think about the text, cases, and readings. The au-

dience is often required to (1) *analyze* by stating why something is true, (2) *integrate* by explaining the relationship between two concepts (e.g., compare and contrast), (3) *evaluate* by ascertaining why something is not true, and (4) *discover* reasoning flaws in others' arguments and reasoning processes.

Critical thinking is not just criticism. Instead, it requires the audience to probe into the reasons, logic, and weight of evidence others use. Careful analysis accepts well-supported and reasoned arguments but rejects poorly supported or reasoned arguments. To perform these important tasks you must understand a speaker's or author's issue, conclusion, and reasoning. Next, you must evaluate the link between the author's reasons and the conclusion the reasons actually support. These are methodical and systematic critical thinking inquiries that enable you to answer the question "Should I accept this conclusion for these reasons?"

While critical thinking is not always easy at first, it usually produces good results. You probably engage in critical thinking every day without referring to it as such. However, practice is needed to sharpen critical thinking skills. A brief how-to explanation of performing critical thinking inquiry follows and will help the critical thinker to approach any advocacy, reading, or class lecture with care.

ISSUE, AUTHOR'S CONCLUSION, AND SUPPORTING REASONS

Before evaluating the quality of an argument, the issue and conclusion must be identified. **Issues** are the primary subject of the controversy. The **conclusion** represents the author's judgment about that issue based on the author's evidence. Some conclusions are **descriptive**: The author attempts to explain how the world *is*. Other conclusions are **prescriptive** or **normative**: The author advocates how the world *ought* to be. Forthright authors clearly identify the issue in the title, opening sentence, or paragraph. The issue is also restated in terms of the author's conclusion. Conclusions are often preceded by *indicator words* that move you from the body of the argument to the author's ultimate point. Look for indicator words or phrases such as *thus, therefore, as a result*, or *it follows that*. Sometimes, however, the issue and conclusion may be obscured by complex arguments or emotional pleas wrapped in manipulative advocacy (e.g., *sophistry*). Concealed conclusions are sometimes inferred from the author's solution at the end of the logical flow or chain of reasoning.

Next, identify the reasons or evidence the author offers. **Reasons** are statements given in support of the conclusion by way of facts, examples, evidence, analogies, or beliefs. Reasons are often preceded by indicator words or phrases such as *because, the fact is, as a result of, by reason of, due to, in view of, on account of*, or *thanks to*. Reasons answer *why* the audience should accept the author's conclusion. Practice by reading the following passage and identifying the issue, conclusion, and reasons.

Example

Businesses are paying increasingly more in legal judgments and insurance premiums. Every year these costs rise dramatically. American business cannot remain competitive in international markets if it must continue absorbing these unreasonable costs. American business needs some protection, such as a statutory cap on the amounts juries award for pain and suffering damages. These caps do not limit the amount an injured plaintiff can recover for medical costs and out-of-pocket expenses. Only noneconomic awards need be limited by damage caps. It is only fair that these caps protect business from the unpredictable and unreasonable jury verdicts that are unrelated to the injured plaintiff's actual injuries. Thus, state legislatures should impose statutory caps on pain and suffering awards.

Issue: Desirability of statutory caps on plaintiff's noneconomic damages.

Conclusion: Statutory caps must be imposed on pain and suffering awards to protect American business.

Reasons: 1. American business will become unable to compete in international markets with continued high damage awards and insurance premiums.

2. Statutory damage caps need not limit an injured plaintiff's recovery of economic damages — only of noneconomic damages.

3. Juries award unreasonable damages.

Only after the issue, conclusion, and reasons are located can the audience evaluate the quality of evidence and determine if the reasons really support the conclusion. The following inquiries form the crux of critical thinking.

LOCATE AMBIGUITY

The next step is to locate **ambiguous words** because they create misunderstanding. Is the author attaching the same meaning to ambiguous words as the audience? First, look for *key terms* central to the author's issue, conclusion, or reasons that might have alternative meanings. If you easily find an alternative meaning, there is probably ambiguity. Ambiguity is significant if the author's argument changes by substituting an alternate reasonable meaning. When the author and the audience use different meanings, the author's message is too easily distorted. Good authors clearly define ambiguous terms and clarify ambiguity when questioned by their audience.

Some ambiguity is inevitable, particularly where the author and the audience have varied backgrounds. Some laws are intentionally left vague to fit new situations "within the spirit" of the law's original intent. For example, *insider trading* is a term purposefully left vague so that new variations of the practice are more easily prohibited. *Sophistry* is the intentional use of ambiguity to mislead an audience.

Look carefully at the author's intended meaning. For example, an author might attempt to persuade you that *affirmative action* is discriminatory, unfair, and unethical. However, the author's reasoning might only support the narrower view of the unfavorability of *quotas*, which are only one type of affirmative action. Sometimes, ambiguity is clarified by examining the context of the expression because this usually suggests the author's intended meaning. However, not every ambiguity is important to critical thinking. When ambiguities appear in the link between the conclusion and the reasons, they cause the greatest misunderstanding. Now, reread the preceding example about damage caps for ambiguous terms that affect the link between the author's reasons and conclusion.

The example has several ambiguities. While rising litigation costs are the reason given for needing caps, the author provides no benchmark for the alleged cost increases. Are the increases due to inflation or do they consume an increasing percentage of sales, assets, or GDP? Does business receive other value for its legal and insurance costs, such as preventative legal advice and risk management? The damage cap advocated as a solution to the litigation cost problem is ambiguous because the cap amount is not indicated. An audience might accept the conclusion if the cap were set at $500,000, but maybe not if it were $50. The "noneconomic damage" classification is unclear. Does it include punitive damages, pain and suffering, and hedonic damages (pleasures of life)? Could pain and suffering be restated in an economic value? Evidence about trends in each damage category would help the audience accept or reject the author's argument. Critical thinkers must be alert to such ambiguities.

EVALUATING THE EVIDENCE

Authors support conclusions with reasons they base on evidence alleged to be fact. Such arguments are often quite convincing because factually based claims have an air of certainty. **Facts** are descriptive statements about past events or current conditions. Factual claims come from examples, empirical research, analogies, metaphors, or from appeals to authority. However, factual evidence may be misleading if the facts are not systematically gathered. A critical thinker inquires into the quality of factual evidence used to support any conclusion by routinely asking the author to "show me."

Sampling

Survey results and empirical studies are types of factual evidence used to support conclusions. It is often difficult to measure characteristics about entire populations. Studies following the scientific method permit inferences from results of a smaller subgroup. These *sample* results are then presumed to accurately reflect the same proportion of those characteristics in the whole population. Results of scientific research using the *sampling technique* may be validly generalized to the whole population, but only if the author's evidence is gathered according to the scientific method.

Researchers using the scientific method gather data under *controlled conditions* to minimize any inaccuracy introduced by extraneous factors. Scientific research uses *objective evidence* so that other competent researchers using the same methodology can try to reproduce similar results. This is called *verifiable data* and it means the study is *replicable*. Such research should clearly state the methodology used, the assumptions made, and the results produced to clarify the study's implications.

The scientific method requires the use of a **representative sample** before generalizations about the larger population are valid. This avoids using a biased sample. A sample is representative if it is sufficiently large, broad, and random to permit generalization to the larger population. For example, if a researcher studied American law by generalizing from a sample of only northeastern states, this might not be representative of laws in western or southern states. Differences in the historical, economic, and social forces that produced the laws are different among these regions. Therefore, before accepting the results of sample evidence, ensure that the sample is representative. Is it sufficiently large and broad? Beware of statements such as "two out of three dentists surveyed. . . ." Sufficiently unbiased samples are broad enough to include all the critical characteristics of the target population. Samples should be selected randomly—that is, chosen by chance—to prevent any systematic bias.

Evaluating Statistical Flaws

When statistical evidence is used, look for impressively large numbers, misleading percentages, and ambiguous averages. Conclusions based on statistical averages (mean, mode, and median) provide no information about the **variance**, disparity, or spread between the top and the bottom values. Averages can lose some significance if the sample is not *normally distributed*. The average may be misleading without an indication of how widely dispersed most of the data is on either side of the mean. Students are generally exposed to statistical testing in business statistics courses.

GENERATING RIVAL HYPOTHESES AND CONCLUSIONS

When the author offers support for a causal connection, the critical thinker should search for an alternative connection. **Causation** is the relationship between the reasons given and the author's conclusion. For example, the author might argue that condition B resulted every time event A occurred. The author urges the audience to accept that A caused B. However, consider the more obvious alternatives: condition B might cause event A, or both A and B might be caused by another condition, C.

Before beginning the research, a good researcher develops a **hypothesis** to project the chain of reasoning and improve control over the collection of evidence. However, the author's evidence may also be consistent with other conclusions. Critical thinkers generate **rival hypotheses** or **alternative conclusions** to evaluate the author's conclusion. For example, consider the tax policy debate when a recession follows a tax increase. Some people argue tax increases slow the economy. However, the impact of the business cycle or the oil cartel's price increase are reasonable alternative hypotheses to explain a recession that may only appear to be caused by a tax increase.

Create rival hypotheses by initially ignoring the author's hypothesis. Next, search for another hypothesis consistent with the author's evidence such as in the tax policy example. The development of highly probable rival hypotheses casts doubt on both the author's hypothesis and conclusion. Rival hypotheses should be independently tested for soundness, logic, and consistency with the critical thinker's personal knowledge.

EVALUATING ANALOGIES

Analogies are used as reasons to support arguments, particularly in legal reasoning from precedent. Reasoning by **analogy** compares two things to find their shared characteristics. An author using analogical reasoning first claims that the two things compared are similar in some respects. Second, the author then implies that the two things must surely share other similarities. Third, the author asserts some fact about the familiar thing so that this fact can also be asserted by analogy about the unfamiliar thing.

Analogical reasoning can be quite persuasive. Analogies help resolve problems when seemingly different things share numerous fundamental similarities that are relevant to how they are treated. However, an analogy can provide weak or misleading evidence if the two things have fundamental differences. In evaluating analogical reasoning, carefully examine both the similarities and differences between the two things compared. If there are few similarities, the analogy may be only weak evidence, at best. If there are fundamental and relevant differences, the analogy may actually be misleading. However, numerous, fundamental, and relevant similarities suggest strong evidence by analogy. Try to weaken the author's analogies by generating competing yet plausible analogies that contradict the author's conclusions.

REASONING ERRORS AND LOGICAL FALLACIES

The reasoning process usually involves several steps: the author makes assumptions, states premises, assembles evidence, constructs logical syllogisms, and produces a conclusion or recommendations. However, many authors make errors in this reasoning process. Critical thinkers should hunt for common logical fallacies before accepting the author's position. Authors who intentionally use fallacious reasoning engage in **sophistry**, the art of using superficially plausible but fallacious arguments to deceive the audience.

Watch for several common fallacies that can be persuasive to an uncritical audience. An author may attempt a **diversion** of the audience's attention away from the real issue or away from the author's weaker arguments, assumptions, or logic. One method is to switch similar words and thereby make a hidden but weak analogy. For example, a political critic might charge that a person who belongs to the Republican political party does not believe in democracy. This argument commits the diversionary fallacy of directly relating the similar words *Democratic Party* with the *democratic* form of government.

The author's use of emotional language can cause feelings of guilt and anger or arouse other passions that distract from the author's weak argument. Emotional pleas are hidden diversions that change the subject, enabling the author to avoid defending faulty reasoning. The **glittering generality** is a glib expression that evokes an emotional response that may divert the audience's attention from seeking more concrete facts.

Another fallacious reasoning technique is to draw attention to personal characteristics of known persons involved in a controversy. An **appeal to authority** or *testimonial* is the author's implicit claim the audience should accept evidence or conclusions from a respected expert. Uncritical thinkers may be unduly swayed by the fact that a respected person holds a particular opinion or urges its acceptance. An appeal to authority is fallacious if the authority's reputation is used to support claims unrelated to the authority's expertise, such as when a celebrity makes a false product testimonial. However, such appeals can provide valid evidence if the authority is well qualified, has sole access to the facts, and is unbiased.

The **ad populum argument** encourages acceptance of attitudes held by a whole group the audience may wish to emulate. By contrast, negative references to a person, group, or institution the audience may not like is fallacious *name calling,* the **ad hominem abusive** fallacy. Ad hominem arguments are valid only when they clearly show the attacked person is self-interested or biased. You should carefully evaluate the personal conflicts of interest and believability of any person or group whom the author appeals to or attacks.

Authors may create irreconcilable conflicts to force the audience to accept the author's argument. A **false dilemma** is a conflict created between the author's reasoning and reasoning used by the author's opposition. There are seldom only two choices possible in any controversy. Some authors weaken the arguments of their opposition by extending those arguments to absurd lengths. Critical analysis reveals when the author is misrepresenting the opposition.

Circular reasoning or *begging the question* is the fallacy of supporting a conclusion by restating it as evidence simply disguised in different words. For example, an argument to regulate an undesirable type of conduct because it is bad is circular reasoning because the evidence that it is "bad" is identical to its label as "undesirable."

Remain sensitive to some common types of poor quality evidence. **Anecdotes** are unscientifically gathered personal experiences that neither prove nor disprove an author's generalization. Some authors urge the audience to make a **hasty generalization** by "jumping to the author's conclusion" based on thin, biased, or still incomplete evidence.

VALUE CONFLICTS AND DESCRIPTIVE ASSUMPTIONS

The author's assumptions may affect the movement of reasoning from the evidence to the conclusions. The reasons given often support the conclusions only if the audience assumes things the author expects them to take for granted. Such presumptions are invisible links in the author's reasoning that the critical thinker must discover.

Value Assumptions

Values are abstract, normative ideas that form the foundation on which decisions are made. People variously value concepts such as honesty, freedom of choice, productivity, individuality, fairness, equality of condition, equality of opportunity, innovation, self-reliance, hard work, justice, excellence, tradition, logic, order, obedience, equality, patriotism, competition, cooperation, and efficiency among others. These values, however, are often in conflict for an author, a listener or reader, or between opposing advocates.

Authors rarely state their value assumptions because this might divert attention from their conclusions. Critical thinkers must ascertain the author's unexpressed value assumptions, particularly any assumption that links the reasons to the conclusion. Identify the value assumption of the author and then identify the values of the audience or opposing advocates to determine if there is a *value conflict*. Many audiences willingly accept an author's con-

clusion only if they share the author's value priorities. For example, an author might argue for the continued interpretation of a law on the basis of precedent and strict constructionism. This argument makes a hidden value assumption that tradition is most important. However, an audience that values justice over tradition might reject the author's argument if the laws in question seemed unjust to some group in society. Read the following excerpt to identify the value assumptions of the author and reader and the resulting value conflict. Also state the issue, reasons, conclusion, ambiguities, and reasoning flaws and generate a rival hypothesis.

Example

Government should strengthen worker safety protections. The Occupational Safety and Health Administration (OSHA) does not protect workers adequately. Potential profits from tolerating unsafe working conditions are greater than the potential fines. Employers' violations are seldom detected. OSHA must increase its fines and inspections. This is the only way to protect the employee.

Author's Value Assumption: Sanctity of life and health; priority given to worker safety.

Value Conflict: Sanctity of life versus productivity and free choice. Readers valuing laissez-faire, efficiency, productivity, or competitiveness more will probably actively search for the author's hidden value assumptions and then probably reject the whole argument.

Descriptive Assumptions

Look for the author's unstated factual beliefs. Ask yourself whether there are hidden facts that must be true in order for the reasons stated to support the conclusion. An audience should accept the author's argument only if the audience shares such hidden **descriptive assumptions** with the author. Critical thinkers can try to identify the author's perspective to simulate their reasoning and biases. Identifying the author's opponents helps find the author's likely ideologies and assumptions. Now, reread the OSHA example above to identify descriptive assumptions.

The author makes several descriptive assumptions. First, the author assumes that increased governmental regulation will protect employees. Next, the author assumes that employee injuries are caused by employer "misconduct" rather than worker error. Further, the author assumes that worker injury is caused by the employer's desire for greater profit. These descriptive assumptions may be untrue, so they should be analyzed separately.

CONCLUDING COMMENTS ON CRITICAL THINKING

This introduction to critical thinking provides an idea of the type of analyses possible throughout this text. Each critical thinking inquiry may not be applicable in all instances. However, evaluating the author's reasons and logic are nearly always important. Because this text emphasizes critical thinking in the public policy realm, the reader should pay particular attention to discovering the issue, the author's biases and hidden assumptions, and ambiguities. The critical thinking inquiries are summarized in the accompanying concept summary. Additional information on critical thinking is available from several recognized critical thinking guides or your instructor.

Critical Thinking Inquiries

Critical Thinking Inquiry	Definition	Function in Critical Analysis	Critical Thinking Tips
Issue	Subject or controversy addressed in author's expression	Essential to understanding points under discussion	May be obscured in complex or poorly composed expression or author's sophistry
Conclusion	Author's answer to the issue under controversy	Summary of author's slant or logical direction; the precise point advocated for audience's acceptance	Look for indicator words: *therefore, thus, as a result, it follows that*
Reasons	Statements of facts, evidence, analogies, or beliefs used to support a conclusion	Answers why audience should accept author's conclusion; relationship of reasons to conclusion is focus of critical thinking inquiry	Look for indicator words: *because, the fact is, as a result of, by reason of, due to, in view of, on account of, thanks to*
Ambiguities	Words or phrases susceptible to alternate meanings	Often inevitable given the imprecision of language; good authors prevent much ambiguity; sophists use them to manipulate opinion	Evaluate key terms in issue, conclusion, and reasons; examine context meaning; request author clarification; substitute alternate meaning to test whether conclusion changes
Statistical Flaws	Failure in rigor of scientific method; nonrepresentative or biased sample; uncontrolled conditions; research method not replicable; deceptive but impressive large numbers; misleading percentages; ambiguous averages; unknown variance	Factual-based claims misleading if statistical flaws in empirical evidence; sampling often a practical necessity	Demand author "show me"; use personal experience or others' studies as benchmark for comparison; examine controlled conditions; search for sample bias
Rival Hypotheses and Conclusion	Alternate hypotheses consistent with author's reasons or conclusion; alternate conclusion consistent with author's reasons or hypothesis	Author's reasoning weakened by rival hypotheses or conclusions; generated easily because rivals may be more accurate than author's reasoning	Initially ignore author's hypothesis, then author's conclusion; use personal experience to search for alternate explanations consistent with author's conclusion, then generate alternate conclusions consistent with author's reasons

Critical Thinking Inquiry	Definition	Function in Critical Analysis	Critical Thinking Tips
Analogies	Similarities between different things, suggesting that other similarities exist	Can provide convincing reasons, particularly when scientifically gathered evidence is missing or difficult to collect; law uses analogy significantly; most people accept analogy; however, weak analogies can be misleading	Carefully examine both the similarities and differences between two things compared: analogy is weak reason if differences predominate; may be good reason if similarities predominate; generate competing yet plausible analogies to weaken author's analogies
Reasoning Errors and Logical Fallacies	Analytical flaws that weaken or contradict author's reasoning:	Fallacious argument misleads the reader	Be vigilant; always look for all these fallacies
	• **Diversions** lure reader from critical thinking • **Glittering generalities** divert and evoke emotion	Diversions and glittering generalities obscure reasons, assumptions, and analogies or evoke emotion	
	• **Appeals to authority** urge acceptance of accepted person's views	Appeals to authority are fallacious if unrelated to authority's expertise	
	• **Ad hominem abusive** attacks person or group	Ad hominem is invalid reason unless person attacked is biased	
	• **Circular reasoning** simply restates conclusion as evidence	Circular reasoning disguises conclusion as reasons by begging the question	
	• **False dilemma** raises conflict between reasoning of author and author's opposition	False dilemma incorrectly forces misbelief that there are only two choices	
Value Assumptions	Unstated fundamental normative beliefs—honesty, excellence, tradition, self-reliance—implicit in author's reasoning	Some value assumptions are inevitable; they appear to strengthen conclusions with weak factual support; usually not clearly stated but hidden in value-laden terms	Look for value-laden phrases and normative tone of author's reasons or how author moves from incomplete or unconvincing reasons to partially unsupported conclusion; confront hidden value assumptions explicitly
Descriptive Assumptions	Unstated factual beliefs implicit in author's reasoning	Some descriptive assumptions inevitable, so expression has to make the writing or speech manageable in size; seem to strengthen conclusions until confronted by reader	Look for hidden descriptive assumptions used as missing links in logic; identify author's background or bias to suggest any type of hidden assumption

Part I

The Legal System

■

Chapter 1

The Legal System

■

CRITICAL THINKING INQUIRIES

As you read this chapter, you should be able to address the following:

- In what ways does law serve a positive purpose?
- Compare and contrast authoritative and nonauthoritative sources of law.
- Why is it necessary to classify law into different categories?
- Compare and contrast law and morality.
- Describe what a world without lawyers would be like.

MANAGERIAL PERSPECTIVE

Robert Bonn has just been elevated from a middle-level manager in production to general manager of Toys 'n Stuff, a medium-sized company that manufactures and distributes children's toys. Bonn has a certain disdain for the legal system and lawyers. This is based in part on some negative experiences both he and his family had with lawyers representing an adversary and in part on the fact that he did poorly in his business law course in college. He was overheard saying, ''The first thing we do is to get rid of our legal staff. They just tell you what you can't do, and you can't understand their gobbledygook anyway.''

- What dangers does Bonn's attitude present?
- What do you suggest Bonn do?

As Bonn will soon learn, business managers come into contact with law on a daily basis. They are regularly confronted with contracts and the need to comply with government regulations. At times, they may come into conflict in their business relations, necessitating legal help. This legal involvement brings managers like Bonn in touch with legal jargon and lawyers. Hence, it behooves the manager to be conversant with lawyers and the legal system.

To gain an appreciation of law and to be effective as a manager, it is necessary to have some understanding of the legal system—the purposes of law, sources of law, classification of law, the interplay of law and morality, and the place and function of lawyers. This chapter covers these topics. The knowledge gained from this chapter will provide a foundation for the areas of law covered in this book relevant to Bonn and others.

PURPOSES OF LAW

Everywhere we go, our lives interact with the law. Simply driving to school, we confront a host of traffic laws. The gas we put in our cars is regulated by law from the oil well to the gas pump. The credit card we use to pay for the gas is governed by consumer credit legislation.

When we purchase a new car, contracts, products liability, advertising, and labeling laws govern our purchase. The car dealership itself is subject to various employment, consumer credit, and safety laws.

Law also impacts business and business decisionmaking. Many recent surveys of business executives disclose that a chief concern for the coming decade is the legal environment within which business operates. From contracts to products liability to international marketing and new technologies to our environment, the law is the overriding factor in the businessperson's mind.

Beginning students of law are often asked to write a definition of ''law'' on the first day of class. Common responses are ''a set of rules,'' ''a rule of order,'' and ''a code of rights and responsibilities.'' This entire chapter is devoted to providing some preliminary answers to the question, ''What is law?''

Law, first of all, is designed to *maintain the social order* by responding to disruptions. The disruption may involve a criminal act, in which case the state or sovereign will prosecute the wrongdoer. Or, it may involve a private grievance, in which case

legal remedies are available through state-provided forums.

Law also *promotes rational decisionmaking* by helping people plan the future with some confidence. Because of law, individuals can spend large amounts of time and money developing a new product, confident that trademark, patent, or copyright laws will protect them when the product is marketed. A person inclined to steal someone else's work may be dissuaded from doing so by the threat of law. Thus, law helps people predict future legal consequences and base their decisions on such predictions.

A third function of law is to *shape social behavior.* To the extent that people respect its authority, law teaches what is right and wrong. Activities once considered moral, such as racial discrimination or physically striking one's spouse, will be deemed immoral by many people if the activity is illegal. Similarly, activities formerly considered immoral, such as alcohol use, gambling, or abortion, will be considered moral by many if they are deemed legal.

SOURCES OF LAW

Where do we find the law? The law can be found in a variety of legal source books contained in law libraries. These may be divided between primary and secondary sources of law.

Primary (authoritative) sources consist of the statements of various governmental units or officials who have power to make law. **Secondary** (nonauthoritative) sources consist of the writings of legal experts (such as law professors), religious or philosophic ideas, moral principles, social customs, and laws from other countries or states. Both types will be examined (see Figure 1–1).

Primary Sources

Primary sources consist of constitutions, treaties, statutes, administrative regulations, ordinances, court rules, executive orders, and case law. The following sections briefly describe each of these primary sources of law.

Constitutions

The U.S. Constitution, drafted in 1787, is the oldest written **constitution** in the world and serves as a model for emerging democracies in Eastern Europe. (See Appendix A.) It has been amended 27 times

Figure 1–1   Sources of Law

Primary	Example	Secondary	Example
Constitutions	U.S. Constitution	Legal treatises	Prosser on Torts
Treaties	North American Treaty on Free Trade	Legal periodicals	*Harvard Law Review*
Statutes	State statute designating how property of a decedent is to pass when there is no will	*Restatements*	*Restatement of Contracts*
Regulations	Federal Reserve Board regulation prohibiting creditors from inquiring about the gender of an applicant	Laws from other jurisdictions	Laws of Canada
Ordinances	City health codes	Religious ideas	The Bible
Court rules	Federal Rules of Civil Procedure	Philosophic ideas	Kant
Executive orders	Presidential order requiring federal contractors to engage in affirmative action	Moral principles	Do unto others as you would have them do unto you
Case law	*Marbury v. Madison*	Social customs	The customs of the Hopi Indians

since its adoption and serves as the supreme law of the land. All law, from whatever source, that contravenes the U.S. Constitution is unconstitutional and must be declared invalid by a court. Particular provisions of the U.S. Constitution are discussed fully in Chapter 4.

Every state has a constitution. These are not merely mirror images of the U.S. Constitution. However, they often include provisions similar to those in the U.S. Constitution concerning basic government organization and individual rights. They often contain specific provisions concerning, for example, workers' compensation, school districts, civil service employment, and lotteries. Thus, state constitutions tend to be longer and more detailed than the federal constitution.

The Supremacy Clause in the U.S. Constitution declares that federal law is superior in authority to state law. State constitutions, however, serve as the highest state law of an individual state.

Treaties

Another type of federal legislation is the **treaty.** Treaties may be concluded only by the president with the concurrence of two thirds of the U.S. senators present. States may not enter into compacts with foreign nations. Treaties not only have a sig-

nificant impact on our relationship with foreign governments but may significantly impact domestic policy as well. Thus, if the United States concludes an arms or trade treaty, many local businesses will be affected. As federal law, treaties have superior authority over all conflicting state law.

Statutes

Federal **statutes,** passed by Congress and signed by the president, are part of the supreme law of the land. In recent years, federal regulatory authority has been significantly expanded through statutes into areas formerly governed primarily by state or local law. These areas include crime prevention, civil rights, employment law, consumer protection, and environmental law. Unit IV of this book discusses specific areas of this federal regulatory expansion.

State legislatures likewise enact statutes in many of these areas. In addition, state statutes tend to exclusively govern real property law, family law, and insurance law.

Both state and federal statutes are separately compiled into **codes.** These codes organize statutes by subject matter. The federal code containing congressional statutes is known as the U.S. Code.

In recent years, a uniform laws movement has gained momentum. This move has caused state legislatures to adopt statutes patterned on a suggested model drafted by lawyers, judges, and law professors. The popularity of uniform laws is due in large part to the great interstate movement of goods and people that has taken place in the past 50 years. Companies doing business across the country have traditionally been governed by a wide variety of conflicting laws. The most important uniform law, separately enacted by all 50 state legislatures,[1] is the Uniform Commercial Code. (See Appendix B.) The Uniform Commercial Code will be discussed in Unit II of this book, which deals with contract law, sales, and negotiable instruments.

Administrative Regulations

Administrative agencies exist at every level of government—federal, state, and local. More than 90 federal administrative agencies, such as the Internal Revenue Service or the Securities and Exchange Commission, promulgate **regulations** governing both business and private activities. These rules are enacted pursuant to a legislative grant of authority. When validly enacted, they are superior to all state law. Federal administrative regulations are arranged in a code called the *Code of Federal Regulations*. Chapter 5 discusses federal administrative law in more detail.

State and municipal agencies likewise enact many different rules and regulations governing economic and private activities in the particular locale. A uniform act governing the procedures for adopting these regulations, called the *Revised Model State Administrative Procedure Act,* has been adopted in many states.

Ordinances

Local units of government, such as municipalities, enact legislation called **ordinances** that are subject to the state's constitution and federal law. Many of these ordinances deal with the organization and administration of the municipality. Others concern the regulation of private behavior, such as health ordinances covering restaurants and hotels or criminal ordinances covering traffic or parking offenses.

Court Rules and Executive Orders

Nonlegislative branches of government, such as a court or the executive branch (a president, governor, or mayor), may enact laws. Courts commonly enact rules of procedure governing the way a case will proceed through the court. These ''rules of court'' prescribe, among other things, the way a case is filed, the trial process, the rendering of the jury's verdict, and the filing of appeals. The best-known court rules are the *Federal Rules of Civil Procedure* promulgated by the U.S. Supreme Court. These govern the procedures to be followed in all federal courts. State supreme courts likewise have prescribed rules governing the practice in state courts. Procedural rules will be described more fully in Chapter 3.

The president, as the head of the executive branch of government, has the power to issue **executive orders** governing the administration of that branch. With the growth of administrative agencies within the executive department (they collectively employ over 2 million people), these executive orders have grown in importance. One significant executive order, for example, requires certain contractors doing business with the government to have written affirmative action policies. Since over $1 trillion of services and goods are sold to the government each year, this order has a huge impact on the conduct of American business. Likewise, governors and mayors may generally issue executive orders affecting the administration of state or municipal agencies, respectively.

Case Law

Legislation of all types requires interpretation and application to particular facts and disputes. **Case law**, or judge-made law, is the written opinion of a judge or judicial officer who decides a dispute by applying and interpreting legislation or prior case decisions. (See Chapter 6 for the methods of this interpretation and application.) These judicial officers may be judges in a federal or state court.

The decisions of judges in a court are collected in various books called **reporters.**[2] These decisions

---

[1]The Uniform Commercial Code, which governs commercial transactions such as the sale of goods, commercial paper, bank deposits, and secured transactions, has been substantially enacted in every American jurisdiction.

[2]Since 1887, the West Publishing Company has published all the opinions of the highest appellate state and federal courts as well as some intermediate appellate and trial courts. These decisions are published in four federal reporters, two state report-

become precedents for deciding future disputes. A **precedent** is a prior judicial decision on a similar factual or legal issue. The particular relation of a precedent to a current dispute is discussed in Chapter 6.

Secondary Sources

Secondary sources of law are not binding on judges but may be persuasive. Well-known, nonauthoritative sources include **treatises** on various subjects, such as Corbin on contracts and Wright on federal courts. These treatises are often cited as the ultimate statement of law by judges. A treatise is simply an exposition of case law and legislation by a learned scholar.

Another secondary source is a **legal periodical.** The function of a legal periodical is the "recording and criticizing of doings of legislators and judges, discussions of current case law, narration of lives of eminent lawyers, and the scientific study of jurisprudence."[3] When a law school publishes a legal periodical, it is generally called a law "review" or law "journal."

A third important set of secondary sources are the various **Restatements** of Law. The *Restatements* are attempts by various legal scholars, judges, and lawyers to reduce the mass of unorganized judicial opinions into clear and precise statements of principles. The *Restatements* thus read like a codification of the case law. There are *Restatements* on such legal subjects as agency, contracts, landlord and tenant law, property, and torts. These sections cited by courts become law in the jurisdiction.

CLASSIFICATION OF LAW

Since the days of the Roman Empire, the process of classifying law has been part of legal studies. Like any science, to enhance understanding, law may be classified according to certain common traits.

Procedural and Substantive Law

Procedural law governs the method by which a legal right is enforced. **Substantive law** governs the existence and definition of those rights. Although this distinction between substantive and procedural law will be more fully explored in Chapter 3, the following discussion should prove helpful at this point.

A person who has been injured may turn to the legal system for a remedy. Obviously, not all injuries are redressed by the legal system. For example, a firm may lose customers because a competing business opens in town, but no legal remedy is available to the injured party. Whether the legal system provides a remedy for an injury is a question of substantive law. If the substantive law does provide a legal remedy, that injured party has a *cause of action*. The injured party must then enforce this cause of action provided by the substantive law. The mechanics, or the ways to enforce a cause of action, such as filing a lawsuit and arguing a case, are questions of procedural law.

Federal and State Law

The U.S. Constitution balanced the opposing theories of states' rights and central government in a federal system of dualism. This system distributes power between a central national government and individual state governments. Law may be classified according to its origin as federal (national) law or state law. Each part of government has its own court system. There is a federal court system. There is also an entirely separate state court system for each of the 50 states. As mentioned earlier, where a conflict exists between these two competing powers, the Constitution's Supremacy Clause makes federal law supreme over state law.

Federal courts are often called on to decide cases based on a state's laws. In such cases, the federal court will employ federal procedural law concerning the mechanics of the lawsuit and the state's substantive law to decide the nature and definition of the injured party's cause of action. This is known as the *Erie* doctrine because it was first decided in *Erie v. Tompkins,* a U.S. Supreme Court case.[4]

---

ers (California and New York), and seven regional reporters. Regional reporters contain decisions of courts from several states. Some states publish reporters for their particular courts.

[3]F. Hicks, *Materials and Methods of Legal Research,* 210 (3rd rev. ed. 1942).

---

[4]*Erie R.R. Co. v. Tompkins,* 304 U.S. 64 (1938).

Figure 1–2   Civil and Criminal Actions Compared

	Civil	Criminal
Person initiating the action	Plaintiff	Sovereign
Person against whom the action is filed	Defendant	Defendant
Rights vindicated	Individual rights	Societal rights
Remedy sought	Damages, injunction, specific performance	Fine, imprisonment, death
Burden of persuasion	Preponderance of the evidence	Beyond a reasonable doubt
Constitutional protections	Few	Many

Civil and Criminal Law

Many legal actions brought in this country are non-criminal cases in which a private party seeks a remedy against another private party. These noncriminal actions are called **civil actions.** The person who is injured and initiates the lawsuit is called the **plaintiff.** The person against whom the civil action is brought is called the **defendant.** Civil and criminal actions are contrasted in Figure 1–2.

In a civil suit, the plaintiff typically seeks **damages**—that is, some monetary amount from the defendant to compensate for the injury to the plaintiff's person, property, or rights. In certain cases, the plaintiff may seek an **injunction,** which is a court order that forbids the defendant to do some act. To illustrate the difference between damages and an injunction, suppose a factory produces noxious fumes that drift onto the Algurs's property, making the family members sick. The Algurs could seek damages as compensation for their injuries, but the ongoing nuisance would continue. They might, in addition, seek a court injunction ordering the factory to stop its pollution. Another remedy is an order of **specific performance.** This directs a person to do something, for example, perform a contract according to its specifications.

To win a civil action, a plaintiff generally must be able to convince the judge or jury that his or her version of the facts is more likely true than not. This burden requires proof by a **preponderance** (by the greater weight) of the evidence. If the persuasive force of the evidence is in equipoise—that is, equally balanced between the plaintiff and defendant—the plaintiff will lose. Since the plain-

tiff must tip the balance in favor of his or her version of the case, the plaintiff is said to have the **burden of proof** (see Figure 1–3).

A **criminal action** is very different from a civil action. In a criminal action, the public is deemed to be the injured party, rather than an individual. The person initiating a criminal action is thus the government, typically through a district attorney, prosecutor, or attorney general. The action must be based on the violation of a specific provision of the federal, state, or local penal code.

One aim of the criminal law is to punish violators of society's penal codes. Thus, the remedy sought is not damages to compensate for an injury, but imprisonment, a fine, or death. The state must persuade the trier of the case that the accused defendant is guilty **beyond a reasonable doubt.** This is the highest standard of proof known to the law, requiring **acquittal**—that is, a legal determination of innocence—if a reasonable doubt remains concerning the defendant's guilt.

A host of constitutional protections surround a criminal action. These include the right to state-appointed counsel if the criminal defendant is indigent and imprisonment may result, the right to a speedy trial, the right to release on bail, the right of the accused not to take the witness stand, the presumption of innocence, and the exclusion of evidence obtained in an illegal manner.

Subject Matter Classification

Additionally, the law can be subdivided into subjects. Some of the major topical classifications include:

Figure 1–3   Burden of Proof

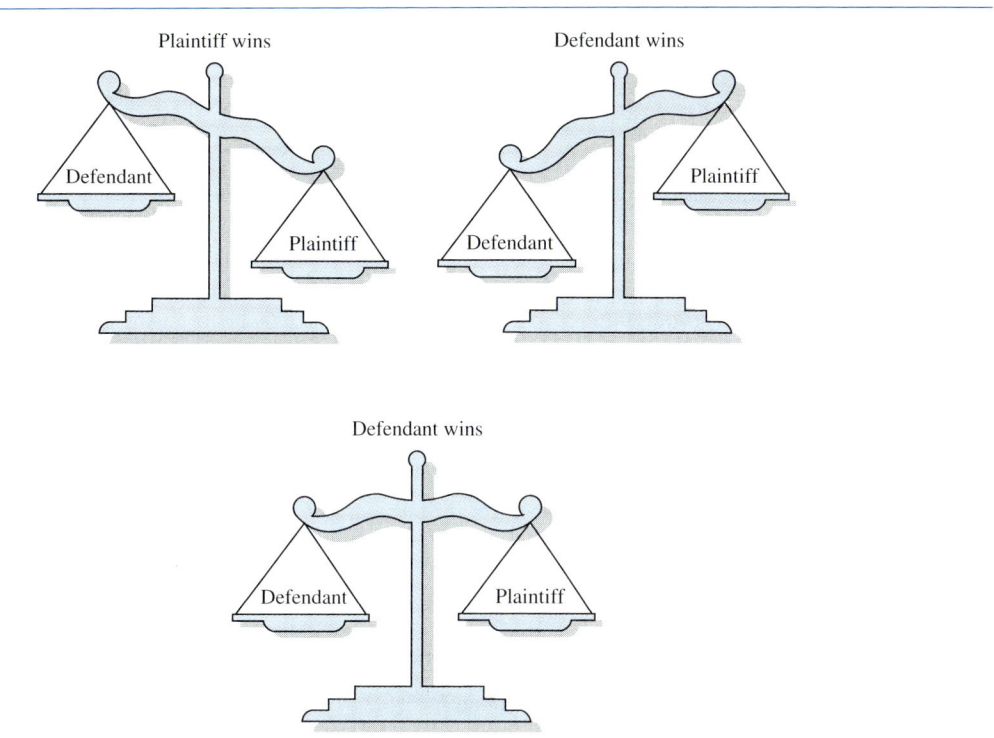

- *Tort law*—involving civil wrongs such as injuries to one's property, person, business, or reputation.
- *Contract law*—concerning enforceability and performance of voluntary agreements.
- *Commercial law*—including bankruptcy, commercial paper, secured transactions, and sales law.
- *Property law*—including the law of real property, personal property, wills, trusts, and estates.
- The law of *business associations*—including the law of corporations, partnerships, agency, and sole proprietorships.
- *Family law*—including the law of domestic relations and juvenile law.
- *Public law* or *regulatory law*—including the regulation of public utilities, taxation, antitrust, workers' compensation, labor, securities, consumer protection, and environmental law.

More than a dozen major subject matter classifications could easily be added to this list.

The Common Law

Common law has a number of different meanings. It may refer to the system of law derived from England as contrasted with the law of continental Europe. Common law may be used in a different sense to refer to certain judicial decisions of English courts, as contrasted with decisions made by the chancellor in courts of equity. Finally, common law may refer to decisions by courts, as opposed to laws enacted by legislatures.

Common Law and Civil Law

Legal systems may be grouped into various families depending on their common history and structure. The two basic families that arose on the European continent and spread to other countries trace their roots either to England or to the law of the Roman Empire. The former is called a common law country; the latter, a civil law country.

Civil law countries generally organize their legal systems around codes. These codes may be traced back in history to classical Roman law and particularly to Emperor Justinian's great Corpus Juris Civilis compiled in the sixth century in Constantinople. These codes were revived and reapplied during the Middle Ages. The fundamental idea of the civil law is that all law is contained in a code adopted by the legislature. Civil law judges turn to the Code's comprehensive dictates to resolve disputes. Their method of reasoning is deductive, from broad general principles in the codes to particular cases.

Countries that have been most influenced by Roman law are found in Western Europe—Germany, France, Spain, and Italy. Through French and Spanish colonial influence, civil law spread to South America and Africa. It remains influential in the various parts of North America that were settled by the French or Spanish, particularly Louisiana and the southwestern states, Quebec, and Mexico.[5]

The one country in Western Europe that did not adopt the Roman civil law was England. This country's primary source of law was not found in legislative codes but in judicial case precedents. The method of reasoning was inductive—from particular cases to general principles—rather than deductive as in civil law countries. Although England and the countries it influenced, such as the United States, Canada, and Australia, do have codes, common law lawyers look at both case law and codes to answer legal questions.

Of course, many legal systems do not fit neatly under either of these two classifications. Some have been heavily influenced by religious law, such as Islam or Hinduism, and some by Marxist socialism. The main focus of this book is naturally on common law in the U.S. with notable differences found in major world nations mentioned from time to time.

Common Law and Equity

Medieval England had three courts—the King's Bench, Exchequer, and the Court of Common Pleas—that administered law that was "common" to all the country. By contrast, other courts had merely local or countywide jurisdiction. The law of these three courts thus became known as the common law. The common law courts developed a series of **writs** that were requests to the court to intervene in a dispute. These writs became the bases of modern causes of action such as tort and breach of contract.

It was in the common law courts that the jury system developed as a check on judicial power. The common law courts were, however, inadequate in several ways. First, suit could not be brought unless the cause of action fit within the technical confines of one of the writs. Second, the common law rapidly developed technical and rigid procedures for initiating and maintaining a suit. Finally, these courts had only the power to award money damages as remedies. They had no power to issue any other orders, such as injunctive remedies or specific performance.

Alongside common law courts, the Chancery Court, called a court of **equity,** developed in the Middle Ages to address these deficiencies. The head of the Chancery Court, the chancellor, was originally a clergyman, as were his subordinates. Their major source of law was not case precedents but church canon law and conscience. The Chancery Court, in general, tended to have a less formal system of procedure than was found at common law. Thus, litigants found it easier to bring suits there. Not confined to writs or technical law, it made decisions to do substantial justice, without the aid of a jury system. At equity, litigants could seek an injunction or specific performance as a remedy. The damage remedy was only available through the common law courts.

Today, law and equity have merged in most states and with few exceptions are not administered in separate courts in the United States. Nevertheless, many of the historic distinctions between law and equity remain. Of chief importance is the rule that an equitable remedy is available only where damages are an inadequate remedy. The other major distinction is that a jury trial generally is available for causes of action that would have been tried in the common law courts, but not for those that would have been heard in the Chancery Court. Finally, precedent is more applicable to law actions, whereas the outcome of equity actions is more determined by doctrines of fairness called **equitable maxims.**

Common Law and Statutes

Common law is often used as a shorthand for the law developed by courts. This is to be distinguished from the law made by the various legislatures or

---

[5]Civil law should not be confused with the previously mentioned civil action. By civil *law* we mean the law of a place that is derived from Roman law. By civil *actions* we mean noncriminal actions.

Congress. Common law, used in this sense, is synonymous with **adjudication** (the process of deciding a case), as opposed to legislation. Generally, when this book refers to a *common law principle,* it will be using the term in the sense of precedents drawn from case law, as opposed to rules specified in legislation.

Thus, contract principles derived from case law are called common law principles. These are distinguished from principles found in legislative enactments such as the Uniform Commercial Code.

LAW AND MORALITY

Laws have a moral component. They are affected and shaped by our moral values. In our culture, as in most, there are laws against stealing, murdering, and raping. Laws also influence what we think about certain conduct. How immoral we perceive driving while intoxicated to be may turn on how stiff the penalty is for violating such a law. Hence, law and morality are interrelated. Any comprehensive discussion of this question would fill a textbook in itself; only the barest generalities can thus be discussed in an introductory chapter.

First, in any complex, highly organized society many laws will be enacted that do not have a readily identifiable moral component. For example, the government may wish to preserve the value of free trade by lowering import taxes or tightening antitrust laws. Or the government may choose to place a ceiling on the price of domestically produced crude oil. Such laws have chiefly economic factors in view—free competition and conservation.

Second, even if a moral component is readily identifiable, competing values may mitigate against imposing a law. For example, lying is considered immoral by most standards. Yet, the enforcement of a legal prohibition against all lying is too problematic and administratively expensive. How would it be discovered? Would family members report one another? Would government become so intrusive as to destroy democratic ideals? Still, lying in certain situations, such as on an income tax return or while under oath in court, is definitely illegal.

Other reasons a law is not enacted against immoral behavior may include the lack of a consensus concerning the rightness or wrongness of the behavior. Without a popular consensus, the law is often flouted, and this leads to doubt concerning the legitimacy of other laws. For example, widespread disapproval of a law prohibiting alcohol consumption may encourage citizens to violate that law and disrespect other laws. Further, the value of self-determination in personally choosing one's own behavior often weighs against the enactment of a law with a moral component. Thus, state legislatures refuse to enact laws against tobacco consumption even though these laws would surely reduce the number of deaths. These laws would be viewed as overly intrusive to individual freedom.

Third, it is commonly asserted that law imposes a minimum level of decency below which human beings may not fall. Morality often calls for heroic, self-sacrificial acts and points forward to ideals. To illustrate this difference, there is no generally recognized legal duty to render aid to a stranger in danger. Yet common morality compels people to go beyond the law and to act as good Samaritans on behalf of another. In this respect, consider the following case.

SOLDANO v. O'DANIELS
190 Cal. Rptr. 310 (Cal. App. 1983)

Darrell Soldano was shot and killed at the defendant's Happy Jack's Saloon. The defendant, O'Daniels, owns and operates the Circle Inn, an eating establishment located across the street from Happy Jack's.

On the date of the shooting, a patron of Happy Jack's Saloon came into the Circle Inn and informed a Circle Inn employee-bartender that a man (Darrell) had been threatened at Happy Jack's. He requested that the employee either call the police or allow him to use the Circle Inn phone to place the call. The employee refused both requests.

The plaintiff, Darrell's son, sued for wrongful death. The suit was dismissed, and the plaintiff appealed to the Court of Appeals.

ANDREEN, Judge

Does a business establishment incur liability for wrongful death if it denies use of its telephone to a good samaritan who explains an emergency situation occurring . . . and wishes to call the police?

There is a distinction well rooted in the common law, between action and nonaction. "The fact that the actor realizes or should realize that action on his part is necessary for another's aid or protection does not of itself impose upon him a duty to take action."

Defendant argues that the request that its employee call the police is a request that it do something. He points to the established rule that one who has not created a peril ordinarily does not have a duty to take affirmative action to assist an imperiled person. It is urged that the alternative request of the patron from Happy Jack's Saloon that he be allowed to use defendant's telephone so that he personally could make the call is again a request that the defendant do something—assist another to give aid.

The refusal of the law to recognize the moral obligation of one to aid another when he is in peril and when such aid may be given without danger and at little cost in effort has been roundly criticized.

It is time to reexamine the common law rule of nonliability . . . in the special circumstances of the instant case.

The Supreme Court has identified certain factors to be considered in determining whether a duty is owed to third persons. These factors include: "the foreseeability of harm to the plaintiff, the degree of certainty that the plaintiff suffered injury, the closeness of the connection between the defendant's conduct and the injury suffered, the moral blame attached to the defendant's conduct, the policy of preventing future harm, the extent of the burden to the defendant and consequences to the community of imposing a duty to exercise care with resulting liability for breach, and the availability, cost, and prevalence of insurance for the risk involved."

We examine those factors in reference to this case. (1) The harm to the decedent was abundantly foreseeable; it was imminent. The employee was expressly told that a man had been threatened. The employee was a bartender. As such he knew it is foreseeable that some people who drink alcohol in the milieu of a bar setting are prone to violence. (2) The certainty of decedent's injury is undisputed. (3) There is arguably a close connection between the employee's conduct and the injury: the patron wanted to use the phone to summon the police to intervene. The employee's refusal to allow the use of the phone prevented this anticipated intervention. If permitted to go to trial, the plaintiff may be able to show that the probable response time of the police would have been shorter than the time between the prohibited telephone call and the fatal shot. (4) The employee's conduct displayed a disregard for human life that can be characterized as morally wrong: he was callously indifferent to the possibility that Darrell Soldano would die as the result of his refusal to allow a person to use the telephone. Under the circumstances before us the bartender's burden was minimal and exposed him to no risk: all he had to do was allow the use of the telephone. It would have cost him or his employer nothing. It could have saved a life. (5) Finding a duty in these circumstances would promote a policy of preventing future harm. A citizen would not be required to summon the police but would be required, in circumstances such as those before us, not to impede another who has chosen to summon aid. (6) We have no information on the question of the availability, cost, and prevalence of insurance for the risk, but note that the liability which is sought to be imposed here is that of employee negligence, which is covered by many insurance policies. (7) The extent of the burden on the defendant was minimal, as noted.

Many citizens simply "don't want to get involved." No rule should be adopted which would require a citizen to open up his or her house to a stranger so that the latter may use the telephone to call for emergency assistance. . . . It does not follow, however, that use of a telephone in a public portion of a business should be refused for a legitimate emergency call. Imposing liability for such a refusal would not subject innocent citizens to possible attack by the "good samaritan," for it would be limited to an establishment open to the public during times when it is open to business, and to places within the establishment ordinarily accessible to the public. Nor would a stranger's mere assertion that an "emergency" situation is occurring create the duty to utilize an accessible telephone because the duty would arise if and only if it were clearly conveyed that there exists an imminent danger of physical harm.

We conclude that the bartender owed a duty to the plaintiff's decedent to permit the patron from Happy Jack's to place a call to the police or to place the call himself.

It bears emphasizing that the duty in this case does not require that one must go to the aid of another. That is not the issue here. The employee was not the good samaritan intent on aiding another. The patron was.

The possible imposition of liability on the defendant in this case is not a global change in the law. It is but a slight departure from the "morally questionable" rule of nonliability for inaction absent a special relationship.

We conclude there are sufficient . . . issues to permit the case to go to trial and therefore reverse.

Case Questions

1. In what way does this case extend the common law? Is this a case of "legislating morality"? Explain.

2. What language does the court use that is emotionally persuasive?

3. Does the plaintiff now win? Explain.

4. Construct a scenario where denial of the use of the phone to a good Samaritan would not result in liability.

5. Would the result be different in this case if the victim came into the Circle Inn, bleeding to death, and requested use of the phone? Explain.

There is a spectrum of opinion concerning the precise relationship of law's interaction with morality. At one end of the spectrum is the Austrian scholar Hans Kelsen, who sought to purify the law of "all extraneous elements"[6] such as ethics, ideals, and theories of justice. Law, according to Kelsen, is simply a body of norms created by the sovereign.

In the spectrum's middle, one might place John Stuart Mill, who, in a famous treatise, wrote "the only purpose for which power can be rightfully exercised over any member of a civilized community, against his will, is to prevent harm to others."[7] Mill was not arguing against the legitimate, indeed necessary, overlapping of law and morality. He merely sought to confine law to a sphere he considered proper, so as to preserve personal liberty.

At the spectrum's other end, Sir Patrick Devlin asserts first that there are few human behaviors that affect only the actor. For example, cocaine abuse concerns the actor's family, the actor's employer, and perhaps the public as well. Second, Devlin suggests that society consists of a shared morality and will disintegrate if that morality is attacked. Thus, polygamy will affect society's value of monogamy. Devlin argues that society may pass laws to protect its morality just as it passes laws to protect its national security.

Different cultures produce differing concepts of morality—what is right and wrong. This diversity is reflected in the United States, where people from a wide variety of cultures locate; hence, our legal system is often challenged to adjudicate tough cases where people have breached laws in the United States that would have been widely accepted in their community of origin. This legal clash of cultures is discussed in the following article.

[6]Kelsen, *The Pure Theory of Law*, 50 L.Q. Rev. 474 (1934).

[7]J. S. Mill, *On Liberty*, 8 (Oxford University Press: 1946).

---

*Legal Clash of Cultures**

As police investigations, lawyer case loads and judicial dockets begin to reflect the burgeoning Asian immigrant and refugee population in the United States, lawyers, judges and

---

*Source: Spencer Sherman, New York Law Publishing Co., *The National Law Journal* (Aug. 5, 1985). Reprinted with permission.

law-enforcement officials are going through a severe bout of culture shock, complete with a list of legal problems as difficult to untangle as a Japanese movie with Korean subtitles.

At times the cases are merely amusing. Sergeant Marvin Reyes of the Fresno, Calif[ornia], police department tells of a fellow officer who stopped the car of an Indochinese refugee as it lurched and jerked through an intersection.

After a difficult period of sign language and rough translations, Sergeant Reyes says, the officer determined that the refugee, following exactly what he had been told, had come to a full stop every time the light turned red. It was late at night and the signal was blinking.

"We get these kinds of misunderstandings of the small types of laws all the time," Sergeant Reyes says.

Sometimes, however, the clash of a foreign culture with the American legal system has its roots in tragedy.

Fumiko Kimura is at the center of one such case. . . . Ms. Kimura took her children on a long bus ride from her suburban Los Angeles home to the beach in Santa Monica, Calif[ornia]. Once at the bus stop near the shore, she abandoned the baby stroller. Carrying daughter Yuri, 6 months old, while holding 4-year-old son, Kazutaka, by the hand, Ms. Kimura walked into the sea.

Distraught after learning her husband had been supporting a mistress, Ms. Kimura was attempting to commit oyako-shinju—parent-child suicide—to rid herself of shame.

Ms. Kimura was saved by passersby, but her two children drowned. She was charged with first-degree murder, a crime potentially carrying the death penalty. But, as 4,000 members of the Japanese community in Los Angeles explained in a petition to the Los Angeles County district attorney, what Ms. Kimura did would not be considered murder in Japan.

This petition, asking the prosecutor to apply "modern Japanese law" to the case, asserted that "the roots of her Japanese culture" directed Ms. Kimura's acts. In her native land she would be charged at most with involuntary manslaughter "resulting in a light, suspended sentence, probation and supervised rehabilitation," the petition said.

The case, says Deputy District Attorney Lauren L. Weis, "is very, very difficult," but she rejects the use of Japanese law. Ms. Kimura's background should be taken into account in considering her mental state at the time of the crime, but murder must be considered murder in the United States and not mitigated by legal or cultural standards from other countries, says Ms. Weis, the prosecutor in the case.

"You're treading on such shaky ground when you decide something based on a cultural thing because our society is made up of so many different cultures. It is very hard to draw the line somewhere, but they are living in our country and people have to abide by our laws or else you have anarchy," Ms. Weis says. American law, she adds, "ought to be able to handle it—hopefully."

Under American law, Ms. Kimura had the requisite intent and premeditation to be convicted of murder, Ms. Weis believes. "She left the stroller at the bus stop. She knew she was not going to need it because she had planned what she was going to do," says the prosecutor.

Thought Questions

1. Should there be a "cultural defense" in criminal cases? What would be the consequences?
2. Are there any other defenses that might aid Ms. Kimura? Explain.
3. Is our legal system equipped to handle cases involving cultural anomalies? Explain. Is there a solution?

STRATEGIC PLANNING OF LEGAL SERVICES

Business experts for years have emphasized the importance of strategic planning for various areas of a business. Unfortunately, very little is spoken about planning for the legal aspects of the business. The relationship between the businessperson and the lawyer continues to look very much like the firefighter syndrome. Just as the firefighter is often called only when the fire is blazing out of control and the damage is already done, so businesspersons often consult attorneys only after a legal problem has reached epidemic proportions.

Strategic planning of the legal service component of a business goes beyond viewing the lawyer as someone who can help to resolve a dispute or a problem that has already occurred. Strategic planning is hindered by those like Bonn in our opening scenario who feel lawyers are hurdles and naysayers to every proposed business plan. The lawyer needs to understand the business environment and goals of the business. The business manager needs to understand the legal concepts that are developing within the firm's business environment as well as the creative ways lawyers may be employed.

The following sections discuss where lawyers work and what lawyers do and are designed to further explain the strategic planning of a business firm's legal environment.

Where Lawyers Work

The United States has approximately 1 million lawyers, more lawyers in total and by percentage of the population than any other country in the world. The law as a profession is growing at twice the rate of the population every 20 years.

Almost 70 percent of all lawyers work for private law firms. The vast majority of these practice law on their own or in firms of fewer than 10 lawyers. There are, however, many large law firms. The average size of the largest 250 law firms is 175 lawyers. As one might expect, the largest firms are almost entirely located in major cities, near the offices of their business clients. Although most law firms are located in one city, some larger firms have branches in several cities. The largest firms often have branch offices overseas as well.

The next largest employer of lawyers is private industry, with Fortune 500 companies, banking, and insurance as the major sources of corporate employment. About 10 percent are employed as **in-house counsel** for corporations. In-house simply means that these lawyers are paid staff of the corporation and do not work for a law firm.

This trend toward hiring attorneys as in-house staff or expanding their existing staff rather than hiring out work to private law firms is occurring for several reasons. First, spiraling costs for legal services have caused corporations to take some work inside to control expenses. For example, Xerox Corporation reduced outside legal expenses from $26 million to $5 million in five years by bringing work in-house.

Second, in-house counsel typically understands the corporation and its personnel and business objectives better than outside counsel. A lawyer working for a corporation also understands its management style, its history, and the broader issues concerning the industry. Thus, in-house advice will often prove to be more practical, less legalistic, and more finely tuned to the particular corporation's need than would be the advice of outside counsel. Because of in-house lawyers' understanding of the business, much of their advice may be used in a creative way to actually help formulate corporate strategy.

Third, corporations are increasingly recognizing that much of their legal practice must be in the area of **preventive law.** This means that company strategies must be structured to avoid future legal problems. The distinction between preventive lawyering and the typical dispute-centered model is chronological. Dispute-centered lawyering is representation after a problem develops. Preventive lawyering focuses on problems that might arise in the future and attempts to avoid them by smart legal planning. As part of this preventive approach, many firms have employed a **legal audit,** analogous to the annual financial audit performed by accountants. A legal audit examines such things as compliance with equal employment, products liability, labor, and antitrust laws, as well as documents such as leases, contracts, form letters, catalogs, advertisements, and packaging forms. In short, a legal audit involves an internal investigation that can provide advance knowledge of potential legal problems and assist in shaping an appropriate response, while reducing overall legal costs.

Despite the enormous value of in-house attorneys, **outside counsel** is still needed, even by cor-

Figure 1–4   Where Lawyers Work

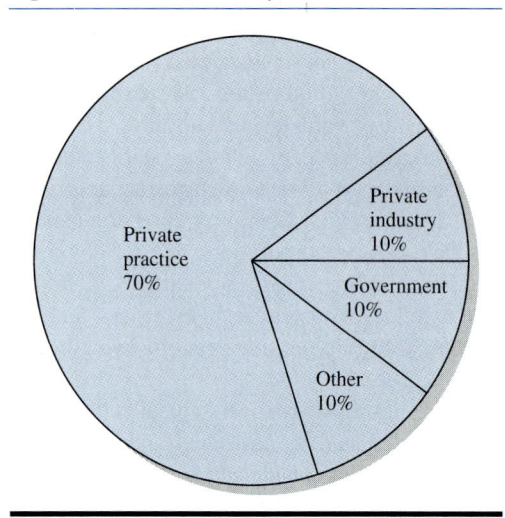

porations with large in-house staffs. Some legal matters call for expertise beyond that of the in-house staff—matters not so regularly practiced in-house to permit adequate efficiencies. Investigation of corporate mismanagement, particularly concerning possible criminal or ethical violations, also requires the objectivity of outside help. Finally, outside counsel is normally retained whenever a lawsuit is contemplated. Few in-house staffs actually take a matter to trial, preferring to rely instead on experienced trial lawyers. This is particularly so if the lawsuit is in another area where local attorneys are familiar with that locale's courts, procedures, and judges.

Another large employer of lawyers is government, with almost 10 percent of all lawyers working for federal, state, and local governments. The rest of the practicing lawyers are employed as judges, support personnel for courts, or for nonbusiness associations such as trade unions, public defender's offices, special interest lobbying groups, and law professors (see Figure 1–4).

Roles of a Lawyer

Counseling, advocacy, and the lawyer's role as a lobbyist are of chief importance to the study of business law. Each will be separately considered.

The Lawyer as Counselor

The lawyer is a counselor-at-law. As counselor, the lawyer practices preventive law, predicting and an-

ticipating any legal difficulties that might result from a client's proposed course of action. In this role, the lawyer asks how a court or other governmental body would view a client's actions in the event of some future controversy.

As counselor, the law is not the only concern of the lawyer. The client must be confronted as a whole person, not simply as a legal issue. Since legal problems do not arise in a vacuum, the lawyer must understand the client's related problems—ethical, personal, family, and business—to give complete advice. Therefore, many clients discuss a wide range of nonlegal issues with their lawyers, who often become trusted friends and confidants.

The Lawyer as Advocate

An advocate represents a client's interests. Such representation can occur by *enforcing* a client's rights through such a simple matter as issuing a warning. For years, the Coca-Cola Company has aggressively enforced its right to exclusively use the name *Coke* by issuing warnings to businesses to refrain, upon the threat of a lawsuit, from selling another cola product in response to a buyer's request for "Coke."

Such representation can additionally occur through *negotiation* with an adversary to settle an existing dispute. For example, Toys 'n Stuff, the company in our opening scenario, may have a tax problem. Rather than proceed to litigation, a lawyer, acting as Toys 'n Stuff's advocate, might negotiate a settlement with the Internal Revenue Service. Similarly, negotiation and settlement of existing claims often involve disputes with insurance companies after an accident or in the employment setting after a strike or employer lockout.

Of course, negotiation and settlement is not always possible, and some cases must proceed to trial. The lawyer, according to a canon of professional responsibility, is to represent clients zealously within the bounds of the law. This requires an attorney to present a client's case in court in the light most favorable to the client; at the same time, the lawyer must not mislead a court by knowingly using false evidence.

The Lawyer as Lobbyist

Lawyers have a variety of roles in shaping legislative decisions and public opinion. On the one hand, about 50 percent of Congress is made up of lawyers. On the other, lawyers make up a sizable percentage of the paid professional **lobbyists** who attempt to influence the decisions of lawmakers. In many ways, the same advocacy skills of persuading, informing, and negotiation used by lawyers in a lawsuit are used by lawyer-lobbyists before legislative bodies.

Lobbyists serve many very important functions in a democratic society by expressing the needs of their constituents. They may awaken an awareness of a broader national concern in the legislator's mind in place of a more parochial self-interest. Lobbyists also keep public officials abreast of the issues by supplying such officials with factual information and necessary research. Lobbyists also help to popularize important issues by disseminating information to the public. They define issues and important arguments in support of their position, and in some cases actually draft proposed legislation.

To keep lobbying within bounds, there are many regulations prohibiting bribery and other forms of corruption. An important statute regulating lobbying is the *Federal Regulation of Lobbying Act,* which requires all paid lobbyists to register with the clerks of the House of Representatives and the Senate. The registration statement contains information such as the lobbyist's name and address, the name and address of the person or interest the lobbyist represents, and all terms of compensation.

Strategic planning of legal services involves, therefore, an appreciation of the many roles that an attorney can play to assist the business firm in achieving its goals by employing a lawyer in broader ways. The firm can better respond to legal trends affecting its business and indeed, in some cases, creatively influence those trends toward its advantage.

END–OF–CHAPTER QUESTIONS

1. Why is it important to possess a basic understanding of "the law?" Do you think that law fulfills its purposes? Explain.

2. Why are some sources of law considered more authoritative than others?

3. What do you think is meant by this saying: "The law is a seamless web"?

4. What is the relationship between law and morality? Discuss.

5. To what does "strategic planning of the legal services component of a business"

refer? How does it differ from the traditional view businesspersons have of lawyers?

6. The United States has approximately 1 million lawyers. In contrast, Japan, which has about half the population of the United States has roughly 12,500 lawyers. Whereas there is one practicing attorney for every 300 Americans, there is only one attorney for every 10,000 Japanese citizens. How do you explain this stark contrast? Do you think that Americans experience more justice than Japan? Less harmony? Is it a healthier sign for a society to have few or many attorneys? Discuss.

7. Three men were exploring caves when a cave-in occurred, precluding their safe exit. Using their CB radio they called for help. Excavation work began, but the victims knew that the rescue team would not be able to reach them for at least five days. Air was thinning and the victims had no food. Knowing of their fate, the victims decided to draw straws to see who would be "sacrificed" so that the other two could live. The one who drew the short straw thereafter objected. However, the plan was carried out and the remaining two survived by eating the flesh of the deceased one. Several days later the two men were rescued. Should the survivors be prosecuted for murder? Explain. What additional information would you like to have?

8. A man was involved in an adulterous relationship with his mistress. She became distraught and took poison in an attempted suicide. The man did nothing to render aid. Should he have a legal duty to do so? A moral duty? Explain. See *People v. Beardsley,* 113 N.W. 1128 (Mich. 1907).

9. Many sociological studies have been done indicating that women are treated differently than men in many areas of American society. Should "the law" intervene to change this situation? Why or why not? What is the best way to legally change this if you think that law should

intervene? By court decision? Legislation? Constitutional amendment? Justify your answer. See *Frontiero v. Richardson*, 411 U.S. 677 (1973).

10. A criminal defendant stood trial for murder. He felt that he had a better chance if he could show that the victim was shot in self-defense. He told his lawyer at first that he had not seen a gun in the hands of the victim, but later wished to testify that he had seen a gun. His lawyer told him that if he insisted on testifying, the lawyer would notify the court that the testimony was perjury and would personally testify against the defendant. The defendant did not testify and was convicted. What dilemma did the lawyer face in this case? Do you agree with the way in which he resolved it? Explain. See *Nix v. Whiteside*, 475 U.S. 157 (1986).

Chapter 2

Ethical Analysis

■

Critical Thinking Inquiries

As you read this chapter, you should be able to address the following:

- Analyze the following statement: ''The organizational environment creates a unique set of challenges for one seeking to make the right decision within a business.''
- How do Kant's two formulations of the categorical imperative relate to each other?
- Consider the plight of the homeless as Rawls might. As Nozick might.
- Compare and contrast law and ethics.

Managerial Perspective

Joe was hired as a foreman in a plant that manufactured airplane parts that were sold both to commercial airlines and to the government. He soon discovered that employee time cards were ''doctored'' so that training and idle time were charged to government contracts. Work done on projects that were overbudgeted was routinely charged to other projects. Joe's boss told Joe to alter his employee time cards.*

- Should Joe alter the time cards?
- How should Joe decide what to do?
- What factors are relevant to Joe's decision?

---

*Source: Marianne Moody Jennings, ''The Changing Time Cards,'' *Case Studies in Business Ethics* (Minneapolis / St. Paul: West Publishing Co., 1993), p. 95.

The opening scenario for this chapter illustrates the kinds of questions facing managers, especially middle managers. Ethics plays a role in these day-to-day decisions. Most people, like Joe, want to do the ''right'' thing. However, the right thing is not always easy to determine. How should Joe decide what to do? Further, the environment in some organizations may create obstacles to acting ethically, and the ''price'' to be paid for acting ethically may be great—for example, lost promotions or raises.

Two related ethical issues will be considered in this text. First, this chapter will provide an overview of ethical treatment, specifically with regard to individual ethics. How should individuals behave? Second, ethical behavior by corporations (corporate social responsibility) will be considered in Chapter 54. In addition, ethical considerations will be integrated in each chapter.

NATURE OF ETHICS

To properly examine individual ethical behavior, one must understand the concept of ethics. How does one determine whether certain behavior is ethical or unethical?

Simply stated, **ethics** are principles of conduct that enable one to decide whether an activity is morally right or wrong. The study of ethics is the study of theories by which the ''rightness'' and ''wrongness'' of behavior is judged. While the terms *ethical* and *moral* are often used interchangeably, morality is the set of beliefs through which individuals and communities determine the positive or negative value of their actions and establish long-term value goals for individual achievement. Ethics is a critical study of the nature and foundations for morality, the logic of moral arguments and the meanings of moral terms, normative ethics, which compares and evaluates different foundations for a coherent moral system; and applied ethics, which uses the results of metaethical and normative ethical research to understand and resolve dilemmas encountered in the practice of business and the professions.

A related concept is that of **values.** Values are ideas of importance to individuals. The following are examples of values: freedom of choice, tradition, order, honesty, harmony, individualism, excel-lence, justice, competition, cooperation, and productivity. Values are often in conflict even within an individual. To illustrate, a person may place priority on both productivity and worker safety. In a meatpacking plant, the value placed on productivity might encourage the plant owner to speed up processing, but the value placed on worker safety might encourage the plant owner to slow down processing.

A **value system** or **ideology** is a coherent, systematic statement of values. It is the foundation on which decisions are made. Capitalism is a value system or ideology.

Nature of an Ethical Dilemma

An ethical dilemma is a clash of beliefs or values involving questions of how people should live their lives and how they should treat others. In the meatpacking plant value conflict, the plant owner's decision with respect to the speed of processing is an ethical dilemma. The decision involves a struggle between two values, both of which are recognized as important by the plant owner. Ethical dilemmas almost always involve tradeoffs. The plant owner must balance competing interests and obligations to shareholders, employees, and consumers.

An ethical dilemma is more than a decision of how to allocate money (should we spend money on books for illiterate inner-city children or on a safety device to protect workers?). It is also more than a decision about whether to act within the limits of the law (should we engage in insider trading?). The ethical dilemma in the example exists because of the value conflict within the plant owner.

Business/Organizational Ethics

Business ethics considers what is right or wrong behavior in a business context. There is not one set of rules for what is morally right in one's personal life and another set for what is right in business activities. However, the organizational environment creates a unique set of challenges for one seeking to make the right decision within a business.

Read the following parable and ask yourself to what extent the individual decisions were influenced by group dynamics.

≋

The Parable of the Sadhu†

Buzz McCoy, his friend Stephen and their guide, Pasang, were halfway through a 60-day Himalayan hike. Anxious to cross a pass through the mountains before the sun melted the ice steps and forced them to turn back, they met a New Zealander carrying the near naked body of a sadhu—an Indian holy man. He had found the sadhu lying on the ice suffering from hypothermia. Because the New Zealander wanted to get across the pass, he gave the sadhu to Buzz's group. Buzz, Stephen and Pasang quickly clothed the sadhu. Buzz noticed a group of Japanese climbers below and with little thought took a number of porters and set off across the pass.

Stephen took the sadhu down the mountain to the Japanese hikers and returned to Buzz's group. He left the sadhu sitting by the side of the trail throwing rocks. Stephen believed that the sadhu would not make it safely to shelter and that he would probably die.

■ ■ ■

Bowen H. McCoy

For many of the following days and evenings Stephen and I discussed and debated our behavior toward the sadhu. Stephen is a committed Quaker with deep moral vision. He said, "I feel that what happened with the sadhu is a good example of the breakdown between the individual ethic and the corporate ethic. No one person was willing to assume ultimate responsibility for the sadhu. Each was willing to do his bit just so long as it was not too inconvenient. When it got to be a bother, everyone just passed the buck to someone else and took off. Jesus was relevant to a more individualistic stage of society, but how do we interpret his teaching today in a world filled with large, impersonal organizations and groups?

I defended the larger group, saying, "Look, we all cared. We all stopped and gave aid and comfort. Everyone did his bit. The New Zealander carried him down below the snow line. I took his pulse and suggested we treat him for hypothermia. You and the Swiss gave him clothing and got him warmed up. The Japanese gave him food and water. The Sherpas carried him down to the sun and pointed out the easy trail toward the hut. He was well enough to throw rocks at a dog. What more could we do?"

"You have just described the typical affluent Westerner's response to a problem. Throwing money—in this case food and sweaters—at it, but not solving the fundamentals," Stephen retorted.

"What would satisfy you?" I said. "Here we are, a group of New Zealanders, Swiss, Americans, and Japanese who have never met before and who are at the apex of one of the most powerful experiences of our lives. Some years the pass is so bad no one gets over it. What right does an almost naked pilgrim who chooses the wrong trail have to disrupt our lives? Even the Sherpas had no interest in risking the trip to help him beyond a certain point."

Stephen calmly rebutted, "I wonder what the Sherpas would have done if the sadhu had been a well-dressed Nepali, or what the Japanese would have done if the sadhu had been a well-dressed Asian, or what you would have done, Buzz, if the sadhu had been a well-dressed Western woman."

"Where, in your opinion," I asked instead, "is the limit of our responsibility in a situation like this? We had our own well-being to worry about. Our Sherpa guides were unwilling to jeopardize us or the porters for the sadhu. No one else on the mountain was willing to commit himself beyond certain self-imposed limits."

■ ■ ■

The Individual versus the Group Ethic

Despite my arguments, I felt and continue to feel guilt about the sadhu. I had literally walked through a classic moral dilemma without fully thinking through the consequences. My excuses for my actions include a high adrenaline flow, a super-ordinate goal, and a once-in-a-lifetime opportunity—factors in the usual corporate situation, especially when one is under stress.

Real moral dilemmas are ambiguous, and many of us hide right through them, unaware that they exist. When, usually after the fact, someone makes an issue of them, we tend to resent his or her bringing it up. Often, when the full import of what we have done (or not done) falls on us, we dig into a defensive position from which it is very difficult to emerge. In rare circumstances we may contemplate what we have done from inside a prison.

Had we mountaineers been free of physical and mental stress caused by the effort and the high altitude, we might have treated the sadhu differently. Yet isn't stress the real test of personal and corporate values? The instant decisions executives make under pressure reveal the most about personal and corporate character.

Among the many questions that occur to me when pondering my experience are: What are the practical limits of moral imagination and vision? Is there a collective or institutional ethic beyond the ethics of the individual? At what level of effort or commitment can one discharge one's ethical responsibilities?

Not every ethical dilemma has a right solution. Reasonable people often disagree; otherwise there would be no dilemma. In a business context, however, it is essential that managers agree on a process for dealing with dilemmas.

The sadhu experience offers an interesting parallel to business situations. An immediate response was mandatory. Failure to act was a decision in itself. Up on the mountain we could not resign and submit our resumes to a headhunter. In contrast to philosophy, business involves action and implementation—getting things done. Managers must come up with answers to problems based on what they see and what they allow to influence their decision-making process. On the mountain, none of us but Stephen realized the true dimensions of the situation we were facing.

■ ■ ■

I see the current interest in corporate culture and corporate value systems as a positive response to Stephen's pessimism about the decline of the role of the individual in large organizations. Individuals who operate from a thoughtful set of personal values provide the foundation for a corporate culture. A corporate tradition that encourages freedom of inquiry, supports personal values, and reinforces a focused sense of direction can fulfill the need for individuality along with the prosperity and success of the group. Without such corporate support, the individual is lost.

That is the lesson of the sadhu. In a complex corporate situation, the individual requires and deserves the support of the group. If people cannot find such support from their organization, they don't know how to act. If such support is forthcoming, a person has a stake in the success of the group, and can add much to the process of establishing and maintaining a corporate culture. It is management's challenge to be sensitive to individual needs, to shape them, and to direct and focus them for the benefit of the group as a whole.

For each of us the sadhu lives. Should we stop what we are doing and comfort him; or should we keep trudging up toward the high pass? Should I pause to help the derelict I pass on the street each night as I walk by the Yale club en route to Grand Central Station? Am I his brother? What is the nature of our responsibility if we consider ourselves to be ethical persons? Perhaps it is to change the values of the group so that it can, with all its resources, take the other road.

Thought Questions

1. Why do you think everyone was willing to do something to help the sadhu but no one was willing to take complete responsibility for seeing to the sadhu's safety? What is the parallel to decisionmaking within an organization?

2. Buzz says: "On the mountain, none of us but Stephen realized the true dimensions of the situation we were facing." Is there a parallel to corporate decisionmaking?

3. What is the lesson of the parable?

What is it about an organization that allows people within that organization to make choices that they might not make in the individual context? Was it something about the group that allowed Buzz to leave the sadhu, while as an individual he might have rescued the sadhu? What within the corporate organization allowed executives at A H. Robins to market the Dalkon Shield knowing that it was defective? What within the corporate organization allowed the executives at Ford Motor Company to market the Pinto knowing that it was defective? Read the following essay, where an answer and a solution are suggested.

*The Corporate Apology**

Imagine that your two teenage daughters and your niece were burned to death in a Ford Pinto when it was hit from behind by an auto as they slowed to pull off the highway. The impact shoved the gas tank onto the rear axle where it split open, gushing fuel into the passenger compartment. At the trial against Ford, the prosecution introduces a Ford study revealing . . . management's decision was rather straightforward: pay the less costly probable judgments for the burn deaths, and keep the design the same.

The results of this event, and ones like it, are the awful deaths that could have been prevented, the heart-shuddering grief of family and friends, and an onerous lawsuit against an organization that is today one of America's most profitable companies — as well as a plea by concerned observers of such events that we somehow address this problem through courses in ethics.

In the current offering of business ethics courses, the textbooks provide a mild critique of what I call the surface problems: the misplaced emphasis on the values of corporate efficiency and profit. But the heart of the problem is deeper. It lies in understanding the structure

*Source: Art Wolfe, "The Corporate Apology." Reprinted from *Business Horizons,* (March–April 1990). Copyright 1990 by the Foundation for the School of Business at Indiana University. Used with permission.

of the environment in which the committee at Ford saw death and destruction to be preferable to a design change. In short, if we assume that the managers at Ford are reasonable, intelligent, and humane like you and me, what arrangements of people, institutions, and ideas could cause them to make the decision they made? Once we believe we have the answer, the next question is, what can be done to change matters so that these decisions are not repeated?

Stating exactly what caused the Ford managers to decide the way they did is by no means simple, but I believe there are two fundamental facets of our business environment that must be acknowledged and changed before this type of event ceases. The first is obvious and needs little elaboration. It is that our business environment is dominated by very large corporations where thousands of employees and managers interact and make decisions that affect us all. Many, if not most, of the business ethics cases take place within the large American corporation, or involve it in some crucial capacity. The high-level decision makers in these institutions are far removed from the impact of their decisions. As with our pilots who dropped bombs ''in the mountains'' in Vietnam, the victims of their corporate actions are out of sight and mind.

This first facet, then, is one of physical distance, or proximity. The Ford managers could read ''180 burn deaths'' on the paper in front of them, but the people that would die would be ''out there'' somewhere beyond the misty periphery of their consequences. These deaths just did not mean much to them. However, the cost of the change was more immediate; it would probably affect the reputation of their department; perhaps it would even affect them directly. So, they would rather plant bombs on some remote highway than disturb an operational design for which they had direct responsibility.

The second facet of the problem is not so obvious and needs some elaboration. It involves the metaphor managers use (mostly unconsciously) to give meaning to their business activities. This metaphor is a residue of the manner in which most managers are taught business-related skills.

Implicit in almost all instruction in colleges of business today is that business is game-like. The rhetoric of business leaders, business professors and public opinion makers is that of a game. In business, managers think and speak about winners, losers, offensive strategies, defensive postures, corporations gaining ground or losing ground, striking out or scoring or hitting it out of the park, and on and on.

This game-like view of life is intensified in course after course for the two years it takes to get a business degree. Students are trained to understand the business environment by seeing humans as units and then assigning a number to the unit studied; the numbers are then accumulated and either assigned another symbol or directly plugged into some formula or model.

■ ■ ■

So it is not surprising that the managers and designers at Ford made the decision not to correct the design of the Pinto. They were removed from the impact of their decisions. They were trained to view human beings as units or numerical symbols of some sort. Their moral sensitivities were attuned to winning. These elements in the business environment contributed to the Ford managers' belief that they could become winners by choosing dollars over lives.

■ ■ ■

Let us return to the decision made by Ford to find a solution to the problems as I have defined them. What sort of approach can we find that is consistent with the fact that our business environment is the way it is? The approach should close the distance between the decision maker and those suffering the impact of the decision, and it should reveal, in the making of a decision—especially one that trades lives for dollars—that the lives are very real people like you, and me, and your imagined deceased daughters. How are we to do this? We must make the circumstances in which business decisions are made compellingly human by making business managers literally feel the impact of their decisions. But how is this to be accomplished?

I believe that in addition to compelling the corporation to pay a money judgment that is intended as a form of compensation for an unintentional wrong, the agents of the corporation responsible for the decision that resulted in the wrongful death should be forced to apologize in person to the relatives of the deceased.

■ ■ ■

How might offering an apology help close the distance between the decision makers and those affected, and help to confront a system of knowledge that tends to trivialize our humanity? Philosophers and psychologists have pointed out that the chief moral constraint on humans is not in the formalized law, but in our everyday activity; it is our ability to see ourselves as the recipient of our own actions. Basically, there is a form of the Golden Rule at work in our culture. We treat other people (when we can see them or know of their presence) as we would want to be treated. When someone else unintentionally but negligently hurts us, we expect a form of reparation, and the legal system provides this in the form of a money judgment. But, human to human, does the money judgment ever provide full reparation? At the very least, we should expect a mild form of reparation to our moral sensitivities, which are always affected when our body is wrongfully harmed. It seems to me the existence of the idea of an apology in our culture serves to assuage the feelings of the one hurt. But, equally important, it is also a conscious acknowledgment by the wrongdoers that they have acted wrongly, or that someone within their control has acted wrongly.

■ ■ ■

Thought Questions

1. What descriptive assumption does Wolfe make about corporate executives?

2. Do you agree that business is taught as a game? Think back to your business courses. Offer two pieces of anecdotal evidence to support or refute Wolfe's position.

3. Do you think that the apology proposed by Wolfe would work to minimize misconduct by individuals within the corporate environment? How, in Wolfe's view, does the apology address the two fundamental facets of the business environment that allow individuals to make unethical decisions?

Moral Reasoning Process

Acting ethically within a business environment is made more difficult when there is conflict between one's individual notions of morality and those of the group. To some extent, this is illustrated by the Parable of the Sadhu.

In order to carefully consider the ethical nature of a question, rather than "walk[ing] through a classical moral dilemma without fully thinking through the consequences," as McCoy did in the parable, one must engage in a process of moral reasoning. The moral reasoning process is one of moving from premise to conclusion. Christopher Stone[1] suggests that this entails the following deliberate cognitive process.

---

[1]Christopher D. Stone, *Where the Law Ends: The Social Control of Corporate Behavior* (New York: Harper Collins, 1975).

Reflection   Ethical people do not immediately follow their first impulse.

Perception   Ethical people look for the morally significant features of their environment: harm and benefit.

Accountability   Ethical people accept accountability for their actions.

Weigh and consider consequences   Ethical people consider the consequences of their action.

Desire to do "the right thing"   Ethical people want to act ethically.

Justification   Ethical people must be prepared to justify their actions. No matter what ethical theory individuals accept, they must be willing to give reasons for their actions and to "generalize."

For example, let's return to the opening scenario and apply this moral reasoning process.

Reflection   First, Joe must decide to apply the moral reasoning process.

Perception   Joe must recognize that there are ethical as well as legal and economic constraints. He must gather information before he makes a decision. Is what he is being asked to do illegal? Who is being harmed by altering the time cards? What is the extent of the harm? Who benefits? Are there alternative ways to achieve this benefit?

Accountability   Joe must be willing to accept responsibility for his decision. He must recognize that he is making a decision—he is not just "following orders."

Weigh and Consider Consequences   Joe must determine the consequences for each alternative. Even though this is often difficult in an ethical dilemma because the consequences are frequently uncertain, Joe must consider the extended consequences of each alternative course of action.

Desire to Do the Right Thing   Regardless of the ethical theory chosen, Joe must want to act ethically. He must consciously apply the facts gathered to the ethical theory chosen and reach a suggested course of action.

Justification   Again, no matter what ethical theory Joe chooses, he must be prepared to justify his ac-

tion. Would Joe be willing to have everyone act as he has under these circumstances?

Application of this moral reasoning process to an ethical dilemma is consistent with the critical thinking process outlined in the unit opener. Critical thinking better enables Joe to undertake this moral reasoning process. He can better identify the issues, analyze and evaluate information, and reach a reasoned conclusion by using critical thinking skills.

Individuation

To be able to make ethical decisions in light of the organizational pressures to do otherwise requires an understanding of one's personal value system separate from that of the organization. A process of group socialization begins to occur almost immediately when an individual joins an organization. Both loyalty to the organization and a desire to become a team player are inducements to this process. However, unless one is careful, this can result in a loss of one's own values and ethics and lead to the adoption of one set of behavior for the business environment and another for personal life.

In order to guard against a sacrifice of one's own values, each person must engage in what Carl Jung calls the process of individuation. Individuation, as applied to the business environment, is the process by which individuals see themselves separate from the beliefs and values of the organization. To some extent, this chapter is designed to aid in the beginning of that process.

NORMATIVE PHILOSOPHY

For hundreds of years, philosophers have been wrestling with the question of how to judge behavior as right or wrong. There is behavior on which there is near consensus: Murder is wrong, lying is wrong. But why are these behaviors wrong? How is rightness and wrongness measured? Various alternative philosophies have been offered.

Cultural Relativism

Cultural relativism is the belief that there is no universal standard by which to judge morality. Actions are moral if they are in conformity with the **mores** (the traditions and customs) of a *culture*. The same act might be right in one society and wrong in another. For example, we believe that it is wrong to kill our aged parents, but some Eskimo cultures believed that it was right. Therefore, under relativism, such killing was unethical in our culture but ethical in the Eskimo culture.

Objections to Relativism

The doctrine of cultural relativism has been seriously criticized on a number of grounds. First, if one accepts the concept of relativism, there is no universal way to determine right or wrong. Second, whether mores really determine the rightness of an action has been questioned. Third, the relativist ignores the fact that what appears to be the same act might really be a different act in one culture because the consequences or the motives might be different. For example, the aged Eskimo was killed to stop the rest of the family from starving. This might be ethical because of the consequences (saving the many) or because of the motive (to protect the family), rather than because it is the norm. Fourth, certain actions accepted in some societies, such as slavery and the treatment of Jews in Nazi Germany, are thought to be so morally repugnant as to invalidate the whole theory. Last, it is suggested that cultural relativism never adequately defines the culture or the mores. What if a small group holds different views from the majority in a culture? Should the mores of the smaller group or the larger group be recognized?

Consider the following:

1. Is the ethical nature of a bribe affected by whether the bribe is paid in this country or internationally? How would a relativist answer this question?
2. Analyze the following statement: "If you believe in cultural relativism, you do not believe that there is one guiding principle by which to judge the rightness or wrongness of an action."

Egoism

Perhaps the simplest answer to the question of how people should behave is offered by the ethical egoist. The ethical egoist believes that people *should* act only in their own self-interest, to maximize pleasure and minimize pain.

Figure 2–1   Psychological Egoism

There is in reality nothing desired except happiness. Whatever is desired otherwise then as a means to some end beyond itself, and ultimately to happiness, is desired as itself a part of happiness, and is not desired for itself.

Source: John Stuart Mill, *Utilitarianism*.

Related to ethical egoism is the theory of psychological egoism. The psychological egoist, epitomized by Thomas Hobbes (1588–1679) and Jeremy Bentham (1748–1832), believes that people are motivated solely by a desire to maximize pleasure and minimize pain—that people act only in their own self-interest (see Figure 2–1). This theory *describes* what the psychological egoist sees as reality—it does not prescribe what is desirable behavior.

Objections to Egoism

Some people disagree with the theory of psychological egoism. In other words, some believe that people are capable of acting in other than self-interest. They question the scientific basis of the theory because there is no empirical evidence to support psychological egoism.

Consider the following:

1. Compare ethical egoism and psychological egoism.
2. Do you believe that everyone acts only in self-interest? Can you give examples of altruistic behavior?
3. Compare egoism and relativism.
4. How would Joe in our opening scenario resolve his dilemma under egoism and relativism?

Utilitarianism

Utilitarianism is a **teleological** or **consequentialist** theory advanced by philosophers such as Jeremy Bentham and John Stuart Mill (1806–1873). To a utilitarian thinker, motive is irrelevant. The rightness or wrongness of an action is judged by the goodness or badness of its *consequences* (see Figure 2–2). Actions are right if they tend to promote happiness; actions are wrong if they tend to promote unhappiness. The right action is the alternative that benefits the most people, weighing the happiness to

Figure 2–2   Utilitarianism

Greatest good for the greatest number.

be achieved for society minus the unhappiness, considering both immediate and long-term costs and benefits. In other words, a right action achieves the greatest good for the greatest number.

Objections to Utilitarianism

Philosophers have raised a number of objections to utilitarianism. First, the theory of utilitarianism concentrates only on the consequences and ignores how those consequences are achieved. In other words, the ends justify the means.

Second, problems with measurement are ignored by utilitarianism. For example, it is difficult to measure the benefit of one choice over another. If both Alice and Bob apply for the same job, how does one measure the benefit of hiring one over the other? Similarly, some costs and benefits are difficult to measure. For example, how does one put a value on human life or health? How could Ford Motor Company measure the value of a burn victim and compare it to the costs of redesign? Further, it is often difficult to predict long-term costs and benefits. Last, it is sometimes difficult to determine what to count as a cost and what to count as a benefit.

Third, utilitarianism ignores rights and justice concerns. It is asserted that utilitarianism is incapable of respecting certain rights that should not be violated. For example, assume that your evil uncle will die in six months. During this six months, he will continue to operate the factory that he owns in a manner that intentionally harms workers and the surrounding community. Under a utilitarian analysis, the "right" decision is to murder your uncle, saving the greater number from harm. Opponents to utilitarianism believe that your uncle's rights are not considered by this analysis. Murder is wrong irrespective of the harm it prevents. Further, they assert that the doctrine ignores the fact that the benefits and costs are not borne by the same persons. Under a utilitarian analysis, a great benefit to the majority justifies an extreme burden placed on a small group. Consider the following:

1. How does the doctrine of psychological egoism relate to the theory of utilitarianism?

Figure 2–3   Kant: Categorical Imperative, First Formulation

An action is morally right for a person in a certain situation if and only if the person's reason for carrying out the action is a reason that he or she would be willing to have every person act on, in any similar situation.

Source: Manuel G. Velasquez, *Business Ethics, Concepts and Cases* (Englewood Cliffs, N.J.: Prentice-Hall, 1988), p. 91.

Figure 2–4   Categorical Imperative

Universalizability	The person's reasons for acting must be reasons that everyone could act on.
Reversibility	The person's reasons for acting must be reasons that he or she would be willing to have others use, even as a basis of how they treat him or her.

Source: Velasquez, p. 91.

2. How might a utilitarian thinker respond to the preceding objections to utilitarianism?

3. How would a utilitarian thinker resolve the dilemma outlined in the opening scenario?

Kant

Under a **deontological** theory, the rightness or wrongness of an action is determined by the *intentions* of the person making the decisions, not by the consequences of the action. Immanuel Kant (1724–1804) believed that to be ethical, actions must be motivated by a sense of *duty,* — that is, by a desire to behave ethically. Kant called these moral duties **categorical imperatives.** He offered two formulations of the categorical imperative. Under the first formulation, the tests of **universalizability** and **reversibility** determine the moral worth of an action (see Figure 2–3). Actions are right only if individuals would be willing to be treated as they are treating others (reversibility); actions are right only if the motives for the action are motives that we would be willing to have all act on (universalizability) (see Figure 2–4). For example, if I intend to make a promise without keeping it, I must be willing to have all make promises without keeping them, including promises made to me. Because this destroys the notion of a promise, it is right to keep promises.

Figure 2–5   Kant: Categorical Imperative, Second Formulation

An action is morally right for a person if and only if in performing the action, the person does not use others merely as a means for advancing his or her own interests, but also both respects and develops their capacity to choose freely for themselves.

Source: Velasquez, p. 93.

Under Kant's second formulation of the categorical imperative, all human beings should be treated as ends, not means toward some objective (see Figure 2–5).

Objections to Kantian Philosophy

Philosophers have raised a number of objections to Kantian theory. It is seen as imprecise or vague. What does it mean to say that we should act out of "duty"? Duty to what? Further, it ignores the fact that rights and duties may be in conflict and offers no suggestion as to how to examine the relative importance of the rights and duties in conflict.

Consider the following:

1. Use Kantian philosophy to examine the opening scenario.
2. Compare and contrast the utilitarian paradigm with the Kantian paradigm.
3. Relate Kantian philosophy to the golden rule.

Distributive Justice

Theories of distributive justice consider the distribution of limited commodities and burdens. Almost everyone agrees that *similar* individuals should be treated similarly. The disagreements come when determining which differences between individuals warrant different treatment. Five different views of distributive justice will be briefly examined (see Figure 2–6).

Egalitarian

The egalitarian believes that no differences justify inequalities in the distribution of benefits and burdens. Under this theory, all should share equally. This theory is criticized because it ignores that humans are different in many respects—in ability, need, and effort.

Figure 2–6   Theories of Distributive Justice

Egalitarian	Equal shares
Capitalist justice	Contribution
Socialism	Ability and needs
John Rawls's philosophy	Fairness
Entitlement	Historical

Figure 2–7   Rawls—Justice as Fairness

- Veil of ignorance.
- The original position.

Capitalist Justice

The capitalist believes that contribution, measured either by work effort or productivity, should be the deciding factor in allocating benefits and burdens. This theory is criticized because of the difficulties in evaluating effort and contribution and because it ignores needs.

Socialism

The socialist believes that burdens should be distributed according to abilities and that benefits should be distributed according to needs. Such sharing is designed to mirror the family. Socialist theory is criticized because there is no relationship between the worker's effort and the benefit received. Therefore, there is little incentive to work, which can lead to stagnating economies and declining productivity. Further, critics assert that the family model is unrealistic because human nature is self-interested and competitive.

Justice as Fairness

Alternatively, the philosopher John Rawls believes that in order for a distribution of benefits and burdens to be just, it must be fair. Rawls proposes that actions that distribute benefits and burdens are just if they are principles that would have been chosen by people ignorant of their own abilities, preferences, and social position in the state of nature (see Figure 2–7). He suggests two principles that would be considered fair by people in this state of nature (the original position) ignorant of their status in society (the veil of ignorance).

First, under the **liberty principle,** each person's civil liberties, such as the right to vote and free speech, are equal and must be protected from invasion by others. Second, under the **difference principle,** Rawls believes that people ignorant of their position would accept social and economic inequalities only if they benefit all, including the least advantaged. This principle stresses the importance of equal opportunities in training and education. Rawls believes that a distribution is just if it is consistent with both the liberty and the difference principle.

Critics of this theory argue alternatively that the original position is not a useful concept for choosing moral principles and that those in the original position would not choose Rawls's principles.

Justice as Entitlement

This theory of distributive justice is best illustrated by the philosopher Robert Nozick. Nozick believes that the most basic right is the right to be free from the coercion of others. A belief that people must be free to choose what to do with their own labor and the products of their labor is fundamental to this theory (see Figure 2–8). Nozick measures justice by a historical reference: A distribution is just if all are *entitled* to the holdings that they possess under the distribution. Under this view,

Figure 2–8   Nozick—Justice as Entitlement

From each as they choose, to each as they are chosen.

government should leave people free to choose and protect the liberty of the individual to make these choices.

The major objection to this theory is that the value of freedom of choice is given priority over all other values without justification. It is claimed that this theory ignores the needs of the disadvantaged.

Consider the following:

1. Compare and contrast the theories of distributive justice with Kantian ethics.

2. Is Rawls or Nozick more consistent with theories of capitalist justice?

Because issues of distributive justice naturally lead to discussions about distribution of wealth, questions of poverty are often considered. Read the following essay and ask yourself which principle of distributive justice is being advocated.

Lifeboat Ethics: The Case against Helping the Poor*

Environmentalists use the metaphor of the earth as a ''spaceship'' in trying to persuade countries, industries and people to stop wasting and polluting our natural resources. Since we all share life on this planet, they argue, no single person or institution has the right to destroy, waste, or use more than a fair share of its resources.

But does everyone on earth have an equal right to an equal share of its resources? The spaceship metaphor can be dangerous when used by misguided idealists to justify suicidal policies for sharing our resources through uncontrolled immigration and foreign aid. In their enthusiastic but unrealistic generosity, they confuse the ethics of a spaceship with those of a lifeboat.

■ ■ ■

If we divide the world crudely into rich nations and poor nations, two thirds of them are desperately poor, and only one third comparatively rich, with the United States the wealthiest of all. Metaphorically each rich nation can be seen as a lifeboat full of comparatively rich people. In the ocean outside each lifeboat swim the poor of the world, who would like to get in, or at least to share some of the wealth.

*Source: Garrett Hardin, ''Lifeboat Ethics: The Case against Helping the Poor,'' *Psychology Today,* (September 1974). Reprinted with permission from *Psychology Today* magazine. Copyright © 1974 (Sussex Publishers, Inc.).

■ ■ ■

Adrift in a Moral Sea

So here we sit, say 50 people in our lifeboat. To be generous, let us assume it has room for 10 more, making a total capacity of 60. Suppose the 50 of us in the lifeboat see 100 others swimming in the water outside, begging for admission to our boat or for handouts. We have several options: we may be tempted to try to live by the Christian ideal of being ''our brother's keeper,'' or by the Marxist ideal of ''to each according to his needs.'' Since the needs of all in the water are the same, and since they can all be seen as ''our brothers,'' we could take them all into our boat, making a total of 150 in a boat designed for 60. The boat swamps, everyone drowns. Complete justice, complete catastrophe.

Since the boat has an unused excess capacity of 10 more passengers, we could admit just 10 more to it. But which 10 do we let in? How do we choose? Do we pick the best 10, the neediest 10, ''first come, first served''? And what do we say to the 90 we exclude? If we do let an extra 10 into our lifeboat, we will have lost our ''safety factor,'' an engineering principle of critical importance. For example, if we don't leave room for excess capacity as a safety factor in our country's agriculture, a new plant disease or a bad change in the weather could have disastrous consequences.

Suppose we decide to preserve our small safety factor and admit no more to the lifeboat. Our survival is then possible, although we shall have to be constantly on guard against boarding parties.

While this last solution clearly offers the only means of our survival, it is morally abhorrent to many people. Some say they feel guilty about their good luck. My reply is simple: ''Get out and yield your place to others.'' This may solve the problem of the guilt-ridden person's conscience, but it does not change the ethics of the lifeboat. The needy person to whom the guilt-ridden person yields his place will not himself feel guilty about his good luck. If he did, he would not climb aboard. The net result of conscience-stricken people giving up their unjustly held seats is the elimination of that sort of conscience from the lifeboat.

■ ■ ■

The Tragedy of the Commons

The fundamental error of spaceship ethics, and the sharing it requires, is that it leads to what I call ''the tragedy of the commons.'' Under a system of private property, the men who own property recognize their responsibility to care for it, for if they don't they will eventually suffer. A farmer, for instance, will allow no more cattle in a pasture than its carrying capacity justifies. If he overloads it, erosion sets in, weeds take over, and he loses the use of the pasture.

If the pasture becomes a commons open to all, the right of each to use it may not be matched by a corresponding responsibility to protect it. Asking everyone to use it with discretion will hardly do, for the considerate herdsman who refrains from overloading the commons suffers more than a selfish one who says his needs are greater. If everyone would restrain himself, all would be well; but it takes only one less than everyone to ruin a system of voluntary restraint. In a crowded world of less than perfect human beings, mutual ruin is inevitable if there are no controls. This is the tragedy of the commons.

■ ■ ■

[The author here outlines the Food for Peace program of the World Food Bank.]

Learning the Hard Way

What happens if some organizations or countries budget for accidents and others do not? If each country is solely responsible for its own well-being, poorly managed ones will suffer.

But they can learn from experience. They may mend their ways, and learn to budget for infrequent but certain emergencies. For example, the weather varies from year to year, and periodic crop failures are certain. A wise and competent government saves out of the production of the good years in anticipation of bad years to come. Joseph taught this policy to Pharaoh in Egypt more than 2,000 years ago. Yet the great majority of governments in the world today do not follow such a policy. They lack either the wisdom or the competence, or both. Should those nations that do manage to put something aside be forced to come to the rescue each time an emergency occurs among the poor nations?

"But it isn't their fault!" some kindhearted liberals argue. "How can we blame the poor people who are caught in an emergency? Why must they suffer for the sins of their governments?" The concept of blame is simply not relevant here. The real question is, what are the operational consequences of establishing a world food bank? If it is open to every country every time a need develops, slovenly rulers will not be motivated to take Joseph's advice. Someone will always come to their aid. Some countries will deposit food in the world food bank, and others will withdraw it. There will be almost no overlap. As a result of such solutions to food shortages emergencies, the poor countries will not learn to mend their ways, and will suffer progressively greater emergencies as their populations grow.

Population Control the Crude Way

On the average, poor countries undergo a 2.5 percent increase in population each year; rich countries, about 0.8 percent. Only rich countries have anything in the way of food reserves set aside, and even they do not have as much as they should. Poor countries have none. If poor countries received no food from the outside, the rate of their population growth would be periodically checked by crop failures and famines. But if they can always draw on a world food bank in time of need, their population can continue to grow unchecked, and so will their "need" for aid. In the short run, a world food bank may diminish that need, but in the long run it actually increases the need without limit.

■ ■ ■

A world food bank is thus a commons in disguise. People will have more motivation to draw from it than to add to any common store. The less provident and less able will multiply at the expense of the abler and more provident, bringing eventual ruin upon all who share in the commons.

■ ■ ■

Pure Justice versus Reality

Without a true world government to control reproduction and the use of available resources, the sharing ethic of the spaceship is impossible. For the foreseeable future, our survival demands that we govern our actions by the ethics of a lifeboat, harsh though they may be. Posterity will be satisfied with nothing less.

Thought Questions

1. What is the purpose of Hardin's lifeboat metaphor?
2. Analyze the following statement: "Under a system of private property, the men and women who own property recognize their responsibility to care for it, for if they don't they will eventually suffer."

3. Analyze the following statement: "Hardin would be more likely to agree with Nozick than Rawls."

4. How might Hardin respond to the question of how to help the poor domestically?

Figure 2–9   Law and Ethics Overlap

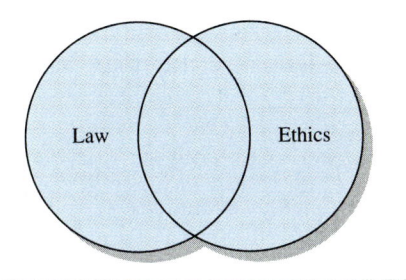

Figure 2–10   Jurisprudence Theories of Law

Natural law	Law as right and wrong
Positivism	Law as rules
Historical theories of law	Law as customs
Sociological jurisprudence	Law as balancing competing claims
Legal realism	Law as reality
Law and economics	Law explained by economic theory

ETHICS AND THE LAW

There are obvious similarities between law and ethics. That is why ethics is discussed in a book on law. Both law and ethics prescribe guidelines for individual behavior. Law certainly reflects society's values and customs. Law is a way of enforcing the behavior that society determines is ethical.

As Figure 2–9 illustrates, the overlap between law and ethics is not complete. First, some laws have no moral or ethical basis. For example, we have a law requiring that we drive on the right-hand side of the street. It is necessary that we be consistent, but there is no *moral* reason for this rule.

Second, some laws may be considered immoral. For example, the laws requiring segregation were immoral. Many, such as Martin Luther King, Jr., believed that ethical behavior required "civil disobedience" to these laws. In other words, ethical behavior required *disobeying* the law.

Third, many ethical principles are not mandated by law. For example, there is no general law against lying. Another example involves the duty to rescue. Assume that you are walking on the beach and see someone struggling in the water and calling for help. In spite of the fact that you are an excellent swimmer, there is no legal obligation for you to attempt to aid the swimmer. Many of us would recognize an ethical obligation. In this category of cases, one might consider the law to be a "floor" below which ethical behavior cannot fall.

Last, it is important to recognize that the nature of law and ethics differs. Law is generally negative: "Thou shalt not . . ." Ethics, on the other hand, is generally positive: "You should . . ."

Theories of Jurisprudence

Jurisprudence is often defined as the philosophy of the law. It seeks to answer such questions as what is law, and what should be the law? As in any branch of philosophy, people differ in their ideas concerning the correct way to answer fundamental questions. In legal philosophy, these differences are grouped in various "schools" of jurisprudence according to certain common traits. Within those schools of jurisprudence, legal philosophers may differ, but there is enough commonality to group these views together. The examination of a few of these schools will help the student to understand the philosophical presuppositions undergirding the cases in this book.

Figure 2–10 summarizes the various theories discussed in this chapter.

Natural Law—Law as Right and Wrong

Natural law is the oldest philosophy of law in Western civilization. With its roots in ancient Greece, it has an impressive list of adherents throughout the ages. These include the Greek philosopher Aristotle (384–322 B.C.), the Roman orator Cicero (106–43 B.C.), the great medieval theologian and philosopher

St. Thomas Aquinas (1224–1274), the father of international law Hugo Grotius (1583–1645), and the political philosopher who most directly influenced the conception of government at the time of the American Revolution, John Locke (1632–1704). There are, in addition, contemporary proponents of natural law.

Natural law philosophers believe:

- In the conception of a ''higher law'' or a law above the law of Man. (The source of this higher law is variously posited as God, human reason, or human nature.)
- That this higher law is immutable (it does not change).
- That this higher law is universally binding on all persons at all times.

Language in the Declaration of Independence is a classic enunciation of the natural law philosophy. In its second paragraph, we read:

We hold these truths to be self-evident, that all men are created equal, that they are endowed by their creator with certain unalienable rights; that among these are life, liberty and the pursuit of happiness. That to secure these rights, Governments are instituted among Men, deriving their powers from the consent of the governed.

Such key natural rights concepts as the equality of all people, the supremacy of the Creator's laws even over rulers, and the self-evident nature of truth are found here. Critics of natural law reject the existence of universally binding ideals that never change. They argue that it makes the law inflexible, not apt to accommodate a changing society. They further reject the possibility of discovering these ideals, finding them far from self-evident.

Positivism—Law as Rules

Positivism is a relatively new philosophy of law propounded first by an Englishman named John Austin (1790–1859). It was further developed by the Austrian Hans Kelsen (1881–1973) and the contracts theoretician Professor Arthur Corbin (1874–1967). It remains the dominant theory of law in England and the Commonwealth nations.

Austin separated positive law from other types of law such as divine law and rules of morality. By positive law, Austin simply meant ''the aggregate of rules established by political superiors.'' These were laws of people to people, not God to people. Such laws were rules prescribed by a sovereign and not rules of custom prescribed by the general public. Positive law is concerned with law as it is, not as it ought to be. As sovereign commands, positive law provides threats for its breach.

Positive law has been criticized because of its sharp distinction between law and morality. It is morality that often informs and shapes the law. Further, by denying the universaiity of various norms, the positive law approach has no platform from which to challenge the laws of dictatorships or totalitarian governments.

Historical Theories of Law—Law as Custom

Borrowing from the evolutionary philosophies of Hegel, who taught that truth is a process of dynamic development (as opposed to being revealed once for all time), the historical school envisions law as a process of evolutionary development as well. Law, according to the historical school, is built on the accumulation of customs of a certain people and culture. Just as language, art, and music are products of a certain nation's customs, so is law. To understand law properly, one must engage in historical research, tracing the development of a nation's customs and attitudes.

This evolutionary theory of law was first proposed by a German, Karl von Savigny (1779–1861), who was much influenced by Hegel. Another proponent, Sir Henry Maine (1822–1888), an English legal scholar, borrowed profusely from Charles Darwin's evolutionary theory. Maine found in law primitive ideas that died over time. He also found common traits among different cultures' legal systems.

Historical jurisprudence has been praised for its commitment to historical research and the perception of development in law. It has been criticized, however, for its philosophic indebtedness to one particular theory of knowledge—evolution—and for promoting nationalism by placing so much weight on a nation's customs and unique history.

Sociological Jurisprudence—Law as Balancing Competing Claims

Sociological jurisprudence is in large measure the product of one man, Roscoe Pound (1870–1964), who published more articles and books about American law than anyone else—almost 1,000 in all. Of course, many others influenced Pound and were in turn influenced by his phenomenal productivity.

Pound saw law as an attempt to balance competing social interests — that is, the various claims or desires of human beings, either individually or as groups. For example, a wife in Georgia filed criminal charges against her husband for rape.[2] The law has had a longstanding policy preventing actions by family members against one another. This policy is designed to promote the social interest of harmony within marriages and families. Yet the law has also promoted a competing policy, freedom from acts of aggression against one's person. In upholding the husband's conviction for rape, the Georgia Supreme Court found the social interest of the family to be subordinate to the wife's individual interest in this case.

Sociological jurisprudence, according to Pound, is also concerned with studying the actual social effects of legal institutions and doctrines. It is not enough to simply enact a law against drunk driving. Follow-up must be done to see whether this particular legal rule in fact reduces the number of drunk drivers. Second, sociological jurisprudence stresses the social purpose or the end that the law serves, rather than its sanction. Enhancing a particular individual interest, such as protection from drunk drivers, is thus more important to Pound than punishing the drunk driver.

Sociological jurisprudence has been praised for articulating clearly the various social interests that law must explicitly attempt to balance. Criticism has resulted from its tendency to be overly pragmatic, concerned only with law if it is practically useful as opposed to being normative or achieving some ideal. Second, it is asserted that a balance of interests is impossible without some objective standard against which to quantify the competing interests. Pound does not supply us with this standard. Judges' own value systems must therefore be the criteria by which the interests are weighed, relativizing the whole notion of law to a matter of individual preference.

Legal Realism — Law as Reality

With the rise of behaviorist psychology and psychoanalysis, a certain level of cynicism concerning the objectivity of the legal system was created. The chief proponents of realism were Karl Llewellyn (1893–1961) and Judge Jerome Frank (1889–

1957). Realists are more varied in their thinking than any other school mentioned heretofore. Only a few generalities may be stated with any confidence.

Law, according to the realists, was not some "brooding omnipresence in the sky"[3] or some neatly fitted together system of rules. To understand law, one must examine the particular response of a judge to a given set of facts. Law is "what officials do about a dispute."[4] Thus, the announced reasoning of a judge in a particular case is less important than the decision, since (according to the realists) his or her reasons are often rationalizations bolstering a decision already made. Logic alone does not account for a decision.

At its best, legal realism focuses students on the particular facts of a case and the process of decisionmaking as important items of study. At its worst, realism becomes nihilistic, making law senseless and utterly relative.

Law and Economics — Law Explained by Economic Theory

The attempt to explain or analyze legal rules by economics has a distinguished history. Adam Smith analyzed the laws of inheritance through such a method in the 18th century, and John Stuart Mill applied economic analysis to the laws of landlord-tenant relations in the 19th century. Recently, the attempt both to explain law and to predict the results of a dispute by economic theory has been spreading. Fueled by the free market theories associated with the University of Chicago, influential law professors turned judges such as Richard Posner, Robert Bork, and Antonin Scalia are now leading a movement called law and economics.

The key concept by which law is analyzed through economic theory is *efficiency*. "Efficiency means exploiting economic resources in such a way that value — human satisfaction as measured by aggregate consumer willingness to pay for goods — is maximized."[5]

To illustrate efficiency, if an object is worth $10 to A and $20 to B, a law that prohibits A from selling the object to B would be inefficient (since both A and B would be better off by a sale of the object for $15). Likewise, appropriate deterrents for

[2]*Warren v. State,* 54 U.S.L.W. 2284 (December 12, 1985).

[3]E. Patterson, *Jurisprudence,* 26–27 (1953).

[4]Llewellyn, *The Bramble Bush,* 3 (1930).

[5]R. Posner, *Economic Analysis of the Law,* 10 (2d ed. 1977).

crimes can be assessed by an efficiency argument, assuming a rational computation of potential punishments versus potential gains by the lawbreaker.

Consider each of the schools of jurisprudence and how a judge adopting a particular school would decide the following case.

REGINA v. DUDLEY & STEPHENS
14 Q.B.D. 273 (Queens Bench) 1884

On July 5, 1884, Dudley, Stephens, Brooks and a boy were forced to cast off in a lifeboat in a storm 1,600 miles from the Cape of Good Hope. They had no water and little food. On July 24, when they had been without food for several days, Dudley suggested to Stephens and Brooks that they should cast lots to see who would be killed to save the rest. Brooks refused. Dudley and Stephens decided that instead of drawing lots, the boy should be killed. On the next day, Dudley slit the boy's throat while he was in the bottom of the boat weakened by famine and unable to resist. The boy did not consent to be killed. The three men then ate the boy for the next four days. They were rescued on the fourth day. If they had not eaten the boy, they would not have lived to be rescued. The boy would probably have died before them. The survivors were charged with murder.

LORD COLERIDGE, Chief Justice

The real question in the case [is] whether killing under the circumstances set forth in the verdict be or be not murder. The contention that it could be anything else was, to the minds of us all, both new and strange. First, it is said that it follows from various definitions of murder in books of authority, which definitions imply, if they do not state, the doctrine, that in order to save your own life you may lawfully take away the life of another, when that other is neither attempting nor threatening yours, nor is guilty of any illegal act whatever towards you or any one else. But if these definitions be looked at they will not be found to sustain this contention.

It is clear that the doctrine contended for receives no support from the great authority of Lord Hale. It is plain that in his view the necessity which justified homicide is that only which has always been and is now considered a justification. Lord Hale regarded the private necessity which justified the taking of life of another for the safeguard of one's own to be what is commonly called "self-defence."

But if this could be even doubtful upon Lord Hale's words, Lord Hale himself has made it clear. For in the chapter in which he deals with the exemption created by compulsion or necessity he thus expresses himself, "If a man be desperately assaulted and in peril of death, and cannot otherwise escape unless, to satisfy his assailant's fury, he will kill an innocent person then present, the fear and actual force will not acquit him of the crime and punishment of murder, if he commit the act, for he ought rather to die himself than kill an innocent; but if he cannot otherwise save his own life the law permits him in his own defence to kill the assailant."

We exclude from our consideration all the incidents of war. We are dealing with a case of private homicide, not one imposed upon men in the service of their sovereign and in the defence of their country. Now it is admitted that the deliberate killing of this unoffending and unresisting boy was clearly murder, unless the killing can be justified by some well-recognized excuse admitted by the law. It is further admitted that there was in this case no such excuse, unless the killing was justified by what has been called "necessity." But the temptation to the act which existed here was not what the law has ever called necessity. Nor is this to be regretted. Though law and morality are not the same, and many things may be immoral which are not necessarily illegal, yet the absolute divorce of law from morality would be of fatal consequence; and such divorce would follow if the temptation to murder in this case were to be held by law an absolute defence of it. It is not so. To preserve one's life is generally speaking a duty, but it may be the plainest and the highest duty to sacrifice it. It is not needful to point out the awful danger of admitting the principle which has been contended for. Who is to be the judge of this sort of necessity? By what measure is the comparative value of lives to be measured? Is it to be strength, or intellect, or what? It is plain that the principle leaves to him who is to profit by it to determine the necessity which will justify him in deliberately taking another's life to save his own. In this case the weakest, the youngest, the most unresisting, was chosen. Was it more necessary to kill him than one of the grown men? The answer must be ''no''.

It is quite plain that such a principle once admitted might be made the legal cloak for unbridled passion and atrocious crime. There is no safe path for judges to tread but to ascertain the law to the best of their ability and to declare it according to their judgment; and if in any case the law appears to be too severe on individuals, to leave it to the Sovereign to exercise that prerogative of mercy which the Constitution has intrusted to the hands fittest to dispense it.

It must not be supposed that in refusing to admit temptation to be an excuse for crime it is forgotten how terrible the temptation was; how awful the suffering; how hard in such trials to keep the judgment straight and the conduct pure. We are often compelled to set up standards we cannot reach ourselves, and to lay down rules which we could not ourselves satisfy. But a man has no right to declare temptation to be an excuse, though he might himself have yielded to it, nor allow compassion for the criminal to change or weaken in any manner the legal definition of the crime. It is therefore our duty to declare that the prisoners' act in this case was wilful murder, that the facts as stated in the verdict are no legal justification of the homicide; and to say that in our unanimous opinion the prisoners are upon this special verdict guilty of murder. The Court then proceeded to pass sentence of death on the prisoners.

Case Questions

1. With which of the jurisprudential schools does the author of this opinion most likely identify?

2. Do you think that the defendants were guilty of murder? Why? With which of the jurisprudential schools do you most identify?

END–OF–CHAPTER QUESTIONS

1. How are the collective interests of humankind protected under utilitarianism?

2. Do you think that our laws represent the collective moral judgments of society? Explain.

3. What assumptions does Kant make about the way people behave? How would this assumption differ from the assumptions made by a utilitarian thinker?

4. Jeane Kirkpatrick said: ''It might be possible . . . for government to equalize income, but not equality of opportunity, for that would require eliminating inequalities of beauty, strength, health, intelligence, size and talent'' (Jeane J. Kirkpatrick, *Dictatorships and Double Standards* [New York: Simon & Schuster and the American Enterprise Institute, 1982], 15). With which view of distributive justice would she most likely agree?

5. Rawls's difference principle is based on an ''original agreement to share in the benefits of the distribution of natural talents and abilities, . . . to alleviate as far as possible the arbitrary handicaps resulting from our initial starting places in society'' (John Rawls, ''Distributive Justice,'' in *Issues in Moral Philosophy*, ed. T. Donaldson [New York: McGraw-Hill, 1986], p. 81). What assumptions does Rawls make about how our initial starting places in society are determined?

6. Rawls relies on the government to ensure that the distribution is just. Specifically, if ''law and government act effectively to keep markets competitive, resources fully employed, property and wealth widely distributed over time and to maintain the appropriate social minimum, then if there is equality of opportunity underwritten by education for all, the resulting distribution will be just'' (Rawls, ''Distributive Justice,'' p. 82). How would Robert Nozick respond to Rawls's concept of a social minimum?

7. A distinction has been made recently between the deserving and the nondeserving poor. The nondeserving poor are gener-

ally thought of as chronically poor because of choices that they have made. For example, alcoholics, the mentally ill, and third-generation welfare recipients are considered to be nondeserving poor by many. Deserving poor are those temporarily out of work. Do you think that this distinction has any validity? What does your answer say about your view of distributive justice? Which writers would distinguish between the deserving and the nondeserving poor: Rawls? Nozick? Hardin?

8. Jim comes on a group of military and 20 Indians lined up against a wall. The military is about to shoot the Indians. Jim is told that because he is a guest, he may select one Indian to be killed. If he accepts, the other Indians will be freed. If he does not, all 20 will be shot. What should Jim do? From Bernard Williams, ''A Critique of Utilitarianism,'' in *Utilitarianism: For and Against*.)

9. Your wife is near death from a rare blood disease. There is a drug that will cure her, but you cannot afford it. The drugstore in town charges $2,000 for a small dose of the drug even though it pays only $200 for it. The drugstore will not sell it to you on credit. Should you steal it? Does it make a difference if it is against the law to steal the drug? Would your answer be any different if the person in need of the drug was a stranger rather than your wife? Based on ''The Heinz case.''

10. You are the owner of a small company. You employ 20 people who conduct telephone sales for your product. You believe that a number of these employees are making personal phone calls during office hours. You are considering monitoring their phones to increase productivity. Is this ethical? What are the issues? Should you notify your employees that their phones are monitored? Explain the analysis necessary to answer this question.

Chapter 3

Civil Process and Dispute Resolution

∎

CRITICAL THINKING INQUIRIES

As you read this chapter, you should be able to address the following:

- What is the origin of the adversary system, and why does it play such an important role in modern civilization?
- What are the problems with the dual federal/state court system? Is there an alternative that would streamline that system and economize our resources?
- What are the nonmonetary considerations when deciding whether to sue or settle a case short of suit?
- Are there preventive techniques that society can invoke to reduce conflict?
- Who are the players in society that are affected by lawsuits? How would you calculate the impact on them?
- Suggest a comprehensive model that would be an alternative to the traditional judicial resolution of conflict.

MANAGERIAL PERSPECTIVE

Infra Disposal Corporation is a waste treatment plant that operates in most states. It receives solid waste from customers, then treats and disposes of the wastes. Slater Stockton is vice president of the corporation's legal relations department. One component of his job is to keep track of the corporation's litigation and to make policy recommendations and specific suggestions regarding the various cases. Currently, there are 43 lawsuits that involve Infra Disposal. On one particular day, Stockton formulated the following questions that needed answers, rather quickly.

- Should we sue Planetguard, a customer who is six months overdue on paying an invoice?
- In what state should we sue Algorithims, a land dump that has breached a contract?
- Should we accept the $100,000 settlement offer in the case against us involving a hazardous spill?
- What can the company do to promote ways other than litigation to resolve disputes?

Figure 3-1   A Typical State Court Structure

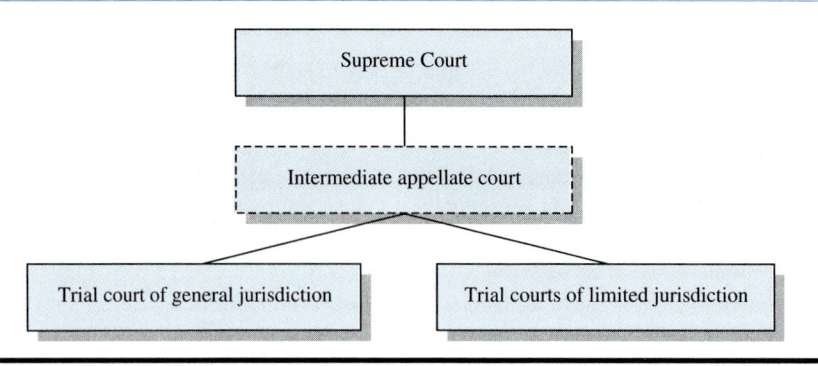

We live in a litigious society in which courts are called on to resolve conflict. Business comes into conflict with competitors, suppliers, consumers, and government, as Stockton well knows. The management of conflict is part of business' business. Managers are called on to make decisions based primarily on cost-benefit analyses. Should we sue? Should we settle, and if so for how much? Are there alternatives to the traditional court suits that would better serve the company's purpose? How can we prevent conflict? In order to answer these and other hard questions, businesspeople need to know about the courts, the judicial process, and alternatives to litigation. This chapter is designed to inform the reader about these most important matters.

THE ADVERSARY SYSTEM

The **adversary system** is characteristic of the American legal system. Our legal system places the responsibility of bringing the suit, and producing evidence, on the parties to the civil lawsuit (the plaintiff and the defendant). The burden is on the parties or their attorneys to investigate, to ask questions, and to raise objections. The court functions as an impartial arbiter of the controversy.

Since the parties are interested in the outcome of the case, they have the incentive to do a thorough job. This, in turn, will enable the court to reach a decision based on full information and a complete range of arguments.

Critics of the adversary system point out that victory may reflect considerations other than the merits of the case. Thus, one side may simply be "outmaneuvered" due to a lack of skill or financial power. Although this is true in some cases, it is not the norm.

The adversary system is not the only system employed in the Western world. Continental Europe (France, Germany, and Russia) employs the **inquisitorial system.** In that system, judges take an active role in the litigation, ask questions at trial, and conduct independent investigations of the case.

COURT STRUCTURE

In the United States, we have a dual court system: state and federal. Each will be carefully examined.

State

The typical state court system (see Figure 3-1) consists of trial courts and appellate courts. There are two types of trial courts — **trial courts of general jurisdiction** and **trial courts of limited jurisdiction.** Trial courts of general jurisdiction are empowered to hear a wide variety of cases. They can, for example, hear criminal cases, probate cases, divorce cases, and accident cases. Trial courts of general jurisdiction are labeled common pleas courts, county courts, or even supreme courts, depending on the state where they are located.

In contrast, courts of limited jurisdiction are restricted in the types of cases they can hear. For example, some courts are not empowered to hear felony cases; others are restricted to juvenile cases or to civil cases under a certain dollar amount. The small claims court is a court of limited jurisdiction that has gained in popularity over the years. It is a court that hears civil matters that do not exceed a monetary ceiling — for example, $1,000 or $5,000. In this court, the rules of evidence are relaxed, the parties ordinarily appear without attorneys, and the cases are tried

Figure 3–2   Federal Court Structure

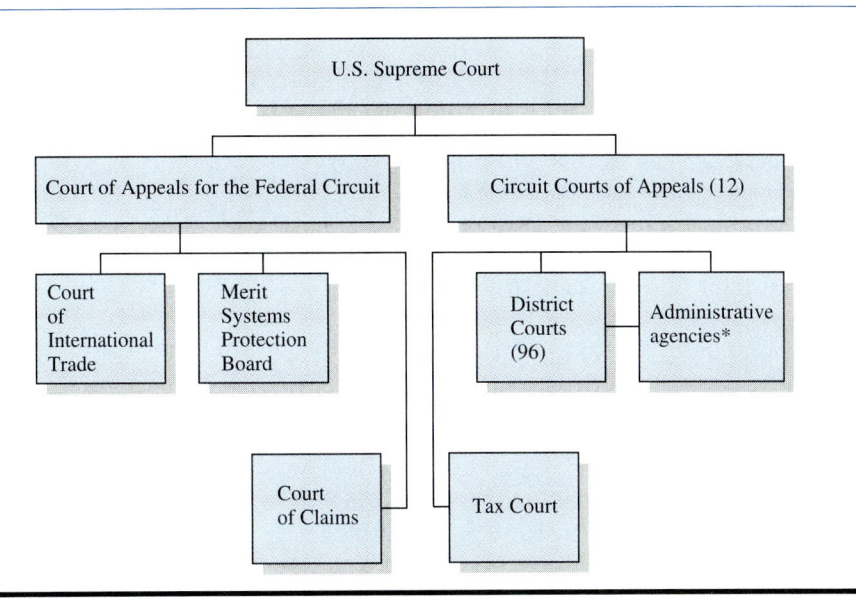

quickly. Trial courts of limited jurisdiction are commonly called municipal, chancery, or mayor's courts, depending on the state where they are located.

Every state has at least one appellate court. The more populous states have two tiers of appellate courts—an intermediate appellate court and an appellate court of last resort. Intermediate appellate courts hear appeals directly from the states' trial courts. Ordinarily, parties who are dissatisfied with the judgment of the trial court have an automatic right of appeal to the intermediate appellate court. The highest appellate court of the state is the court of last resort. It hears cases on appeal from trial courts in states where there is no intermediate court of appeals. When there is an intermediate court of appeals within the jurisdiction, the highest appellate court ordinarily reviews that court's decisions as a matter of discretion, referred to as review by **certiorari**. Finally, parties who are unhappy with the decision in the highest appellate court may petition by certiorari the U.S. Supreme Court to review the case when it involves a constitutional issue.

Federal

The federal court system is patterned closely after the state systems (see Figure 3–2). The trial courts are called district courts. There are 96 district courts located throughout the United States, its territories,

and possessions. A federal district court may hear only those cases entrusted to it by the legislative grant of Congress or the U.S. Constitution. The federal district court has exclusive jurisdiction over federal criminal prosecutions. It also has jurisdiction over cases involving **federal questions** and **diversity of citizenship.** Federal question cases involve those "arising under the Constitution, laws or treaties of the United States." They essentially require that the suit involve a substantial federal basis. For example, a suit alleging sex discrimination contrary to Title VII of the federal Civil Rights Act of 1964 involves a substantial federal question and thus may be brought in the federal district court. In some federal question cases, Congress permits the plaintiff to elect to sue in the state court or the federal court.

Diversity of citizenship cases involve a citizen of one state suing a citizen of another state where the amount in controversy exceeds $50,000. In these cases, the federal district court has **concurrent jurisdiction** with the state courts. This means that the plaintiff may elect to sue in the federal district court or the state trial court. In some cases, where the plaintiff sues in the state court, the defendant may remove the case to the federal district court. This is referred to as the federal district court's **removal jurisdiction.** In a diversity of citizenship case, the federal district court applies its own procedural law and the substantive law of the state where the court is located or where the most significant contacts of the controversy occurred.

For purposes of diversity jurisdiction, a corporation is both a citizen in the state where it is incorporated and where it has its principal place of business. Assume, for example, that Infra Disposal Corporation is incorporated under the laws of Delaware and has its principal place of business in Michigan. Twenty citizens of Ohio and one citizen of Michigan join together to sue Infra Disposal for injuries sustained when Infra Disposal dumped mercury in the waterways. Each plaintiff-resident complains of injury greater than $50,000. Plaintiffs cannot sue in the federal courts under diversity of citizenship since one plaintiff is a citizen of the same state (Michigan) as Infra Disposal, Inc. They will either have to resort to a state court or drop the Michigan citizen from their suit.

There are 13 circuit courts of appeal. They hear appeals from the district courts located within their circuit. They also hear appeals from the U.S. Tax court and administrative agencies. The U.S. Supreme Court is the highest court within the federal judicial hierarchy. It reviews cases by certiorari from the circuit courts of appeal and from the highest courts of the states. Since it can hear only about 150 cases a year, it normally grants certiorari just for cases involving constitutional issues of widespread concern. In a few cases designated by the U.S. Constitution, the U.S. Supreme Court acts as a court of original jurisdiction—that is, a trial court. Examples of these cases include when a state sues another state or a citizen sues a foreign government official.

MECHANICS OF A LAWSUIT

The decision to bring a legal action is not an easy one. Some of the decisions are essentially questions of law, such as whether the law will entertain such an action; the admissibility of evidence; the availability of defenses; and the selection of a court. For these, the parties must rely on well-selected, competent attorneys. Other decisions, including the cost of an action in terms of effort, time, money, and one's image, rest primarily on the judgment of the person contemplating the suit. This decision should be made with input from legal counsel.

Once the decision to file a lawsuit has been reached, it must be filed in an appropriate court. Appropriateness is a product of three factors: jurisdiction, venue, and strategy.

Jurisdiction

Jurisdiction is the authority or power of a court to decide a particular case. Once a court has jurisdiction over a defendant, it has the power to enter a judgment against a defendant who loses or fails to defend. This judgment may be a money judgment and may be enforced in any jurisdiction where the defendant has property. To render a decision in a case, the court must have both jurisdiction over the subject matter of the dispute and over the defendant's person or property.

Subject Matter Jurisdiction

A court has **subject matter jurisdiction** over a case if it has the power to hear the particular type of case. For example, a court legislatively empowered with exclusive jurisdiction to hear domestic relations cases does not have subject matter jurisdiction to hear probate cases. Two sovereigns, the states and the federal government, exercise simultaneous power over some cases involving the same subject matter jurisdiction. Figure 3–3 illustrates overlapping subject matter jurisdiction of the federal and state courts. This overlapping authority is called **concurrent jurisdiction.** Some areas are exclusively within the sphere of either the state or the federal courts. This is known as **exclusive jurisdiction.**

Personal Jurisdiction

A court generally has **personal jurisdiction** over defendants who have a presence in the state. Historically, physical presence was required. The plaintiff needed to find the defendant within the state's boundaries and serve the defendant with notice of the suit in a document called a **summons.**

The territorial limitation on jurisdiction was adequate so long as people and products did not move around too much. Two changes in our country, however, signaled the obsolescence of the rigid territorial concept. First, automobile accidents between nonresident travelers and local residents became frequent occurrences. The nonresident traveler responsible for the accident would return home (perhaps several thousand miles away) and escape the reach of the state where the accident occurred. Second, as products increasingly moved in interstate commerce, litigation resulted between nonresident manufacturers and resident consumers. But because the nonresident manufacturer was located beyond the territorial bounds of the consumer's home state, suit

Figure 3–3   Subject Matter Jurisdiction

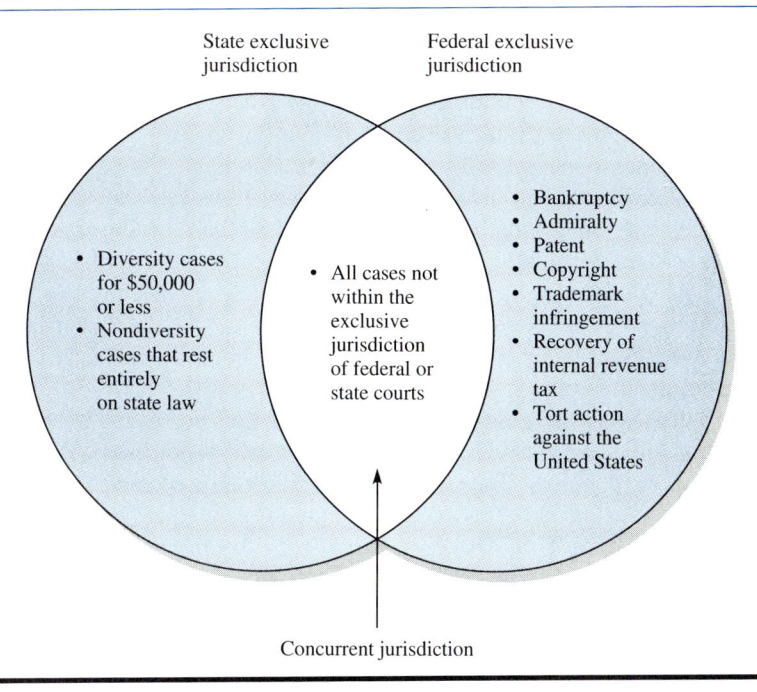

State exclusive jurisdiction

Federal exclusive jurisdiction

- Diversity cases for $50,000 or less
- Nondiversity cases that rest entirely on state law

- All cases not within the exclusive jurisdiction of federal or state courts

- Bankruptcy
- Admiralty
- Patent
- Copyright
- Trademark infringement
- Recovery of internal revenue tax
- Tort action against the United States

Concurrent jurisdiction

could not be brought in the consumer's locality even though the wrong arguably occurred there. Instead, the consumer had to travel to the manufacturer's place of residence to file suit.

To deal with the problem of increasing numbers of nonresident defendants, states passed **long-arm statutes** designed to reach out across boundaries and "pull" nonresident defendants back into the forum state, the state where the plaintiff is suing. The due process constitutional provision, however, limits the reach of a state's long-arm statute. To be subject to suit consistent with constitutional due process, the nonresident citizen or corporation must have certain "minimum contacts" with the forum state. One reason for the limitation of "minimum contacts" is that it is unfair to require a nonresident hundreds or thousands of miles away from his or her home to defend a lawsuit if that nonresident had no real contact with the place of trial. For example, assume Alan, an Ohio resident who is visiting Hawaii for the first time, gets into a fight with Bob, a Hawaiian waiter in Hawaii. Alan returns to Ohio and files a civil suit against Bob in Ohio. Since Bob had no "minimum contacts" with Ohio, it would be unfair to force him to defend the case in Ohio. Minimum contacts with a state have been found, however, where a nonresident regularly transacts business in the state, causes injury in the state, owns real property in the state, or sells insurance within the state.

The following case discusses the due process requirement of minimum contacts with the forum state.

BURGER KING CORPORATION v. RUDZEWICZ
471 U.S. 462 (1985)

Burger King, a Florida corporation, has its principal offices in Florida. It has over 3,000 outlets throughout the United States and foreign countries. It conducts most of its business through the "Burger King System," a franchise operation. It licenses its franchises to use its trademarks and service marks for 20 years. Franchisees lease restaurant facilities from Burger King Corporation and acquire information about "standards specifications, procedures, and methods for operating a Burger King Restaurant.'' Franchisees also receive a variety of other assistance in marketing and management.

Franchisees initially pay Burger King $40,000 and also agree to pay monthly royalties, promotional fees, and rentals. The franchisee also agrees to submit to Burger King's detailed rigid standards, which promote uniformity and quality control.

The contracts specify that the franchise relationship is governed by Florida law and require all payment and notices to be sent to its Miami, Florida, headquarters. Headquarters works directly with its franchisees to solve major problems. However, day-to-day monitoring occurs through regional offices that report directly to the Miami headquarters.

John Rudzewicz and Brian MacShara, Michigan citizens, jointly applied for a franchise through Burger King's Birmingham, Michigan, office. The application was forwarded to Miami and an agreement was entered into whereby Rudzewicz and MacShara were to assume operation of a facility in Michigan. Rudzewicz obligated himself personally to future payments exceeding $1 million.

After some initial prosperity, patronage declined and Rudzewicz and MacShara fell behind in their monthly payments. Eventually, headquarters terminated the franchise and ordered vacation of the premises. Rudzewicz and MacShara refused and continued to operate the franchise.

Burger King sued in the U.S. District Court for the Southern District of Florida and invoked Florida's long-arm statute to obtain personal jurisdiction. The district court concluded that it had jurisdiction and found that Rudzewicz and MacShara breached their franchise agreements and infringed Burger King's trademarks and service marks. Judgment was entered against Rudzewicz and MacShara in the amount of almost $229,000. Rudzewicz appealed to the Eleventh Circuit Court of Appeals, which reversed the judgment and held that the district court did not have personal jurisdiction over him. The U.S. Supreme Court granted certiorari.

BRENNAN, Justice

Jurisdiction . . . may not be avoided merely because the defendant did not physically enter the forum State. Although territorial presence frequently will enhance a potential defendant's affiliation with a State and reinforce the reasonable foreseeability of suit there, it is an inescapable fact of modern commercial life that a substantial amount of business is transacted solely by mail and wire communications across state lines, thus obviating the need for physical presence within a State in which business is conducted. So long as a commercial actor's efforts are ''purposefully directed'' toward residents of another State, we have consistently rejected the notion that an absence of physical contacts can defeat personal jurisdiction there.

Once it has been decided that a defendant purposefully established minimum contacts within the forum State, these contacts may be considered in light of other factors to determine whether the assertion of personal jurisdiction would comport with ''fair play and substantial justice.'' Thus courts in ''appropriate case[s]'' may evaluate ''the burden on the defendant,'' ''the forum State's interest in adjudicating the dispute,'' ''the plaintiff's interest in obtaining convenient and effective relief,'' ''the efficient resolution of controversies,'' and the ''shared interest of the several States in furthering fundamental substantive social policies.''

In this case, no physical ties to Florida can be attributed to Rudzewicz other than MacShara's brief training course in Miami. Rudzewicz did not maintain offices in Florida and, for all that appears from the record, has never even visited there. Yet this franchise dispute grew directly out of ''a contract which has a substantial connection with the State.'' Eschewing the option of operating an independent local enterprise, Rudzewicz deliberately ''reach[ed] out beyond'' Michigan and negotiated with a Florida corporation for the purchase of a long-term franchise and the manifold benefits that would derive from affiliation with a nationwide organization. Upon approval, he entered into a carefully structured 20-year relationship that envisioned continuing and wide-reaching contacts with Burger King in Florida. In light of Rudzewicz's voluntary acceptance of the long-term and exacting regulation of his business from Burger King's Miami headquarters, the "quality and nature" of his relationship to the company in Florida can in no sense be viewed as "random," "fortuitous," or "attenuated." Rudzewicz's refusal to make the contractually required payments in Miami, and his continued use of Burger King's trademarks and confidential business information after his termination, caused foreseeable injuries to the corporation in Florida. For these reasons it was, at the very least, presumptively reasonable for Rudzewicz to be called to account there for such injuries.

. . . Because Rudzewicz established a substantial and continuing relationship with Burger King's Miami headquarters, received fair notice from the contract documents and the course of dealing that he might be subject to suit in Florida and has failed

to demonstrate how jurisdiction in that forum would otherwise be fundamentally unfair, we conclude that the District Court's exercise of jurisdiction . . . did not offend due process. . . . Judgment reversed.

Case Questions

1. What issue does this case present?
2. Is the test of "minimum contacts" as defined by the court a workable one? Analyze. Is there a way of quantifying minimum contacts so that there may be more certainty in this area of the law? Explain.
3. Alter a fact that would change the result in this case.
4. What could the franchisee have done to avoid litigating disputes in Florida?

In Rem Jurisdiction

A court that has jurisdiction over the subject matter and over a "thing," usually property, possesses **in rem jurisdiction.** To have jurisdiction over property, the property must be within the boundaries of the state. In contrast to *in personam* jurisdiction, the court need not obtain personal service over the defendant to decide the case in an *in rem* action. However, only rights concerning the property can be adjudicated; for example, in a case involving the ownership rights to a parcel of land, a court with only in rem jurisdiction cannot subject an out-of-state litigant to pay damages.

Venue

Sometimes several courts will have jurisdiction over a legal dispute sufficient to give them the authority to adjudicate the case. Still, the local forum chosen must not only have jurisdiction, it must also be convenient for the parties to litigate there. This second stipulation is called the **venue** requirement. Generally, venue statutes demand that jurisdiction only be exercised by a local court in the place where all the plaintiffs or all the defendants reside, or in the place where the claim arose, or where the real property in dispute is located. More than one court may have proper venue; hence, a plaintiff may "venue shop" in order to select a court the plaintiff perceives would be most favorably disposed to its case. Some-

times a defendant may seek a change of venue based, for example, on bias due to widespread publicity within the venue. And, unlike jurisdiction, a failure to object to venue may be deemed a consent to have the case heard in that locality.

Strategy

The strategic selection of a court is often a more complex matter than the determination of jurisdiction or venue. Both a state court and a federal court may have concurrent jurisdiction over a claim. In which court should the plaintiff choose to institute a suit? One factor considered in choosing an appropriate court is time. One court's calendar may be much more crowded than another's, which is an important consideration when time is of the essence. (However, some litigants view delay as favorable; hence, they may have an incentive to make such forum selections based on that consideration.)

Procedural rules also vary from one court to another. This is true of the requirement for jury verdicts. Some courts allow for majority jury verdicts, while others require unanimity. A plaintiff with a weak case may opt for the court with the majority rule. Additionally, different states have different **statutes of limitation**—that is, time periods within which a particular suit must be lodged. This may be a critical factor when selecting a state in which to sue.

Figure 3–4   Stages of a Lawsuit

Pleading stage	Discovery stage		Trial stage	Appellate stage
Complaint	Deposition	Written interrogatories	Voir dire	Filing the appeal
Answer	Request for admissions	Production of documents	Opening statements	Submission of briefs
Reply			Cases in chief	Arguing the case
	Request for physical examination		Arguments	Decision of the court
	Request for mental examination		Instruction to jury	
			Verdict	
			Judgment	

STAGES OF A LAWSUIT

Few people really want to litigate. Often, a person is covered by insurance and the dispute is settled by the insurance company out of court. Other times, the parties themselves, or through their attorneys, are able to arrive at a negotiated settlement. However, when a party has been injured and negotiations for settlement break down, there is little alternative but to initiate a lawsuit. Not every lawsuit is accompanied by the drama and suspense displayed in popular television or motion picture depictions. In fact, most lawsuits, though important to the litigants, are dull to the general public.

Since business operates in an environment where the potential for civil litigation looms large, it behooves the businessperson to be familiar with the nature of a lawsuit. The lawsuit may be divided into four stages: the pleading stage, the discovery stage, the trial stage, and the appellate stage (see Figure 3–4).

Pleading Stage

The lawsuit begins when a plaintiff files a **complaint** against a defendant. The complaint is the first pleading. It contains a concise statement of the facts that constitute the basis for legal action against the defendant. It also contains a demand for money or some other type of relief. Allegations within the complaint are broken down into paragraphs, as illustrated in Figure 3–5.

The complaint is ordinarily served — that is, physically delivered — on the defendant, along with a summons, notifying the defendant of the suit. The defendant is required to respond to the charges. Should the defendant fail to respond within the prescribed time, the court may enter a **default judgment** in favor of the plaintiff.

Historically, the service of the complaint and the summons required the placing of the documents in the hands of the defendant. Professional process servers were called on to engage in creative means to serve defendants bent on escaping service. However, both federal and state rules of civil procedure permit alternative or substituted forms of service in addition to personal service. These present less hardship to the process servers but nonetheless are designed to notify the defendant of the lawsuit. Residential service permits the papers to be left with a responsible person at the defendant's residence. Certified mail service, evidenced by the defendant signing the receipt for the mail, is also permitted in most jurisdictions. In a few cases, publication in a newspaper within the jurisdiction may be an appropriate way to obtain service, particularly when the defendant is purposefully absent from the jurisdiction to evade service.

Figure 3–5   Complaint

UNITED STATES DISTRICT COURT
SOUTHERN DISTRICT OF OHIO

Ellis Quentin
981 Indianola
Columbus, Ohio 43211,   Civil Action No. 94–3001
         Plaintiff

         v.   COMPLAINT

Infra Disposal Corporation
801 South Ave.
Hurdle, Missouri 50911,
         Defendant
Plaintiff alleges that:

1.   Plaintiff is a citizen of the State of Ohio and defendant is a corporation incorporated under the laws of the State of Missouri and has its principal place of business in Missouri. The matter in controversy exceeds fifty thousand ($50,000) dollars exclusive of interest and costs.
2.   On or about March 1, 1994, plaintiff and defendant entered into a written contract in Columbus, Ohio, whereby defendant agreed to employ plaintiff at a sum of forty-five thousand ($45,000) dollars each year.
3.   On September 1, 1994, defendant did dismiss plaintiff from its employ.
4.   As a result of said dismissal defendant did breach the contract.
5.   As a result, plaintiff has incurred injury in the amount of $1 million ($1,000,000) dollars.
Wherefore plaintiff demands judgment against defendant in the amount of $1 million ($1,000,000) dollars, interest and costs of court.

_____

Michael Walsh
Attorney for Plaintiff
5293 Poplarwood Rd
Columbus, Ohio

Figure 3–6   Answer

UNITED STATES DISTRICT COURT
SOUTHERN DISTRICT OF OHIO

Ellis Quentin
981 Indianola
Columbus, Ohio 43211,   Civil Action No. 94–3001
         Plaintiff

         v.   ANSWER AND
                         COUNTERCLAIM

Infra Disposal Corporation
801 South Ave.
Hurdle, Missouri 50911,
         Defendant

In answer to plaintiff's Complaint defendant:

1.   Admits paragraphs 1–3 contained in plaintiff's complaint.
2.   Denies paragraphs 4–5 contained in plaintiff's complaint.
         FIRST DEFENSE
3.   Plaintiff fails to state a cause upon which relief may be granted.
         SECOND DEFENSE
4.   Plaintiff was dismissed for just cause.
         COUNTERCLAIM
5.   Defendant incorporates paragraphs 1–3 contained in plaintiff's complaint into this counterclaim and makes them a part hereof.
6.   Plaintiff wrongfully converted defendant's monies to his own use in the amount of twelve thousand ($12,000) dollars.
Wherefore defendant prays that plaintiff's complaint be dismissed and that the court render judgment on the defendant's counterclaim in the amount of twelve thousand ($12,000) dollars, interest and costs of court.

_____

Gerald Howell
Attorney for Defendant
1900 Nineteenth Ave.
Missuagua, Missouri

The second pleading is the **answer** (see Figure 3–6). It is filed with the court by the defendant and a copy is sent to the plaintiff. The answer may admit or deny allegations in the complaint or may avoid responding to particular allegations if the defendant lacks sufficient information to form an opinion on the allegation's truth.

The defendant may have defenses to the plaintiff's complaint, which should be stated in the answer. As noted previously, one defense may be that the complaint is filed too late and thus is barred by the statute of limitations. Another defense, which is raised in Figure 3–6, is that the complaint fails to state a cause of action on which relief may be

granted — that is, the law does not recognize a claim under the facts as alleged.

A defendant may also include a **counterclaim** in the answer. A counterclaim asserts an independent cause of action the defendant claims against the plaintiff. The counterclaim is, in effect, a new suit against the plaintiff. It may be relevant to the subject matter of the complaint, as is the counterclaim in the answer in Figure 3–6, or it may be based on facts unrelated to the plaintiff's complaint. When a counterclaim is included in the answer, the plaintiff must file a **reply,** a third pleading that is, in effect, the

Figure 3–7   Reply

UNITED STATES DISTRICT COURT
SOUTHERN DISTRICT OF OHIO

Ellis Quentin
981 Indianola
Columbus, Ohio 43211,   Civil Action No. 94–3001
              Plaintiff
         v.   REPLY
Infra Disposal Corporation
801 South Ave.
Hurdle, Missouri 50911,
              Defendant

In reply to defendant's Counterclaim plaintiff admits paragraph number 5 and denies each and every other allegation contained in defendant's Counterclaim.

Wherefore plaintiff requests that defendant's Counterclaim be dismissed at defendant's costs.

_____
Michael Walsh
Attorney for Plaintiff
5293 Poplarwood Rd
Columbus, Ohio

Figure 3–8   Motions

	Pleading	Discovery	Trial
Motion to dismiss	X		
Motion to strike	X		
Motion to make definite and certain	X		
Motion for judgment on the pleading	X		
Motion for summary judgment		X	
Motion for sanctions		X	
Motion for directed verdict			X
Motion for judgment n.o.v.			X
Motion for new trial			X

plaintiff's response to the counterclaim contained in the answer. A sample reply appears in Figure 3–7. The effect of these three pleadings — complaint, answer, and reply — is to define and narrow the areas of dispute.

Pretrial Motions

Each party wants to win the lawsuit as early as possible. The earlier the suit is resolved, the less time and money will be expended. To resolve the dispute early, the defendant may interpose a **motion to dismiss** (see Figure 3–8). This motion attacks the plaintiff's complaint. One ground for attack may be that the court lacks jurisdiction to hear the case; thus, the complaint should be dismissed. Or, a motion to dismiss might assert that, even if the plaintiff proves the allegations in the complaint, no grounds for recovery exist. This is a motion to dismiss for failure to state a claim on which relief may be granted, discussed previously as a defense included in the defendant's answer. Either party may file a **motion to strike** material in the pleadings that is irrelevant.

After all the pleadings are filed, either party may move for a **motion for judgment on the pleadings.** This motion will be granted if it is clear from the pleadings that there is no genuine factual dispute; hence, a trial becomes unnecessary because it is obvious as a matter of law who should prevail.

Pretrial Settlement

One of the jobs of a lawyer is to assess the settlement value of a lawsuit at any given time. There are various formulas for assessing the value; each has its limitations because there is some subjectivity and speculation in selecting the numbers. Nonetheless, the following formula is illustrative. The settlement value of a lawsuit is the probability of winning multiplied times the damages the party would win if successful, reduced by the amount of savings if settled now, as opposed to going to trial. This may be expressed:

$$V = (P \times D) - S$$

where

$$V = \text{Settlement value}$$
$$P = \text{Probability of winning}$$
$$D = \text{Damages}$$
$$S = \text{Savings}$$

Assume that the plaintiff's lawyer assesses the damages to the plaintiff, who was fired from her job, wrongfully at $300,000. The lawyer also evaluates the probability of recovery at 75 percent, and the savings in attorney fees of not going to trial as

Figure 3-9   Sample Excerpt from Deposition

Defendant's attorney:	What are your complaints concerning the house you purchased?
Plaintiff:	There are cracks in the foundation and every time it rains, water gushes into the basement.
Defendant's attorney:	Any other complaints?
Plaintiff:	Yes, the living room is sinking.
Defendant's attorney:	Did you inspect the property before you bought it?
Plaintiff:	Yes, I did.
Defendant's attorney:	Was anyone else with you when you inspected the property?
Plaintiff:	Just my husband.
Defendant's attorney:	What type of work does your husband do?
Plaintiff:	What's the difference?
Defendant's attorney:	Please answer the question.
Plaintiff:	He is a building contractor.

$25,000. Substituting these values in the preceding formula, if settled now, we arrive at the following settlement value of the case:

$$V = (.75 \times 300,000) - 25,000$$
$$V = \$200,000$$

Discovery Stage

If the case is neither settled nor dismissed during the pleading stage, the parties will exercise their right to discover the opponent's case through the various tools of discovery. The federal courts permit a broad range of discovery, prompting many states to do likewise by patterning their rules of civil procedure after the federal rules.

The purposes of discovery include helping to narrow and define the areas of disagreement in a lawsuit, exposing fraudulent claims, and preserving testimony for trial. One of the most important functions of discovery is to encourage pretrial settlements. As a party discovers the opponent's case, he or she will be in a better position to evaluate the worth of his or her own claim or defense. The bulk of the civil process is consumed by discovery. One antitrust case brought by the U.S. government against IBM generated millions of pages of documents through discovery before the government ultimately dismissed the suit. Some observers charge that such excessive discovery imposes social costs on litigants, often coercing settlement of baseless claims.

Six basic devices are used in discovery: the deposition, written interrogatories, requests for admissions, production of documents, and requests for mental and physical examination. A party may desire to use one or more of these "tools."

Deposition

A **deposition** is sworn testimony taken before trial from the plaintiff, the defendant, or a witness by certified reporters. In many respects, it is conducted in the same manner as the examination of a witness at trial—it is done under oath and is subject to cross-examination. The deposition, however, normally takes place in the office of the attorney representing the party who has called for the deposition. The deposition may be videotaped, recorded, or transcribed by a stenographer. It is made in question-and-answer form (see Figure 3-9).

Written Interrogatories

A deposition may be very costly. The stenographer must be paid to transcribe the deposition; attorneys and witnesses must be present. In contrast, written questions, called **interrogatories,** may be prepared by the attorney and submitted by mail to the opponent for response under oath. The opponent will usually have 20 to 30 days to respond in writing to the questions, depending on the rules of the jurisdiction. Written interrogatories do have their drawbacks. Responses to the interrogatories will be less spontaneous than at a deposition because the responding party has more time to formulate answers to the questions. Further, the attorney asking the questions will not be face to face with the witness and cannot pose "on the spot," follow-up questions to probe revealing answers more deeply. Another limitation of this form of discovery is that it may be sent only to a party to the lawsuit and not to other witnesses. Nonetheless, the minimal cost of written interrogatories justifies their initial use; a follow-up deposition may be used. The following case establishes still another limitation placed on the use of written interrogatories.

SLATNICK v. LEADERSHIP HOUSING SYSTEMS

368 So.2d 78 (Fla. App. 1979)

The plaintiff, Slatnick, propounded written interrogatories to the defendant during the discovery stage of the lawsuit. The defendant, Leadership Housing Systems, objected to answering the interrogatories, because they were voluminous. The trial court upheld those objections and the plaintiff appealed.

LETTS, Judge

The propounded interrogatories are composed of 2,300 legal size pages in small type (without excessive space between questions) and include such choice samples as:

"State fully and in detail the load carried by *each* steel pipe column located within (each) apartment . . . or state fully and in detail the equation method used by designers stated in answer to prior interrogatories to calculate that loa(d)."

This question alone, relative to 18 condominium buildings, might take a week to answer. It is difficult to imagine how the author of these particular interrogatories could have possibly conjured up a more oppressive and burdensome collection.

[Florida Rules of Civil Procedure] permit discovery regarding any matter *reasonably* calculated to lead to the discovery of admissible evidence. The contents of the subject interrogatories are in our opinion unreasonable.

The petitioner also contends that the trial judge was in error, because he failed to consider the merits of each and every one of the interrogatories separately, and cites *Watkins v. Mother's Auto Sales, Inc.* . . . as authority that each must receive separate consideration. It is true that in *Watkins* the court stated that it *had* meticulously reviewed all the interrogatories, but we do not construe this as a holding that it must always do so. For the trial judge, in this instance, to review and hear argument on all these interrogatories would be impossible, unless he were to accept it as an exclusive line of work for weeks.

Thus the court, armed with judicial discretion, may determine that the matter at issue does not require such extensive discovery and that for counsel or the court to have to examine and specify each irrelevant, repetitious, or immaterial question would constitute an undue burden and would be an extraordinary waste of judicial time and effort.

"The excessive number of interrogatories of a drag-net nature, which not only are unduly burdensome and oppressive, but seek information irrelevant to the fundamental issue in this suit, constitute an abuse of the interrogatory Rule. They are inconsistent with the spirit and purpose of the Rules."

Finally, in the hearing held on the objections, the moving party offered to open up his records to the appellants' attorney and let her go to the warehouse, where they are stored, to obtain the answers for herself. . . . We agree this might be an acceptable alternative, however the task may prove as arduous as cleaning the Augean stables (see the Seven Labors of Hercules). Affirmed.

Case Questions

1. What is the possible motivation of Slatnick in asking such extensive questions?

2. Should the decision be different if all the questions were relevant? Explain.

3. Should the length of time it would take the court to review the interrogatories be a reason for ruling that the interrogatories are oppressive? Analyze.

4. Formulate a list of considerations that would be important in determining the quantity of interrogatories permissible.

Figure 3–10   Sample Request for Admission

Do you admit that the document attached to these Requests for Admissions and marked as Exhibit #2 is a true and genuine specimen of a check that bears your indorsement?

Requests for Admissions

Requests for admissions, as a discovery tool, are a modification of the written interrogatory device. Instead of asking open-ended questions, the party is asked simply to admit or deny a statement. It is used most effectively when eliciting admissions from a party concerning a document (see Figure 3–10). Obtaining admissions to the authenticity of documents saves time and the trouble and costs of proving their authenticity at trial.

Production of Documents

Often, accounting records, business reports, correspondence, and other data or objects relevant to the case may be under the control of an opposing party to the lawsuit. Either party may discover these documents by making a formal request to produce the document(s).

A request for production of documents must be carefully worded. Too narrow a request, such as "Produce the contract dated September 1, 1993, between the plaintiff and defendant" would not produce other contracts the parties made. On the other hand, a request for "all documents" might result in a truckload of irrelevant material that would burden the requestor, or such a burdensome request might be disallowed by the court.

Physical and Mental Examinations

When a party is suing for personal injury, medical proof is required. A defendant may desire to have an independent professional examine the plaintiff to counter evidence of an alleged injury. Under the rules of discovery, the defendant is entitled to have a doctor physically examine the plaintiff and may also choose any doctor to accomplish the examination. When a person's mental condition or capacity is at issue, a request for a mental examination may be proper.

Sanctions

Failure to comply with discovery requests may result in court-imposed sanctions. If a party refuses to answer a proper question at a deposition or to respond to written interrogatories, the opponent may secure an order from the court compelling a response. The court has the power to order the uncooperative party to pay the opponent's costs of seeking the order, including attorney fees. If a party fails to admit to the genuineness of a document pursuant to a Request for Admissions, and the opponent proves its genuineness at trial, the court has the power to order the party to pay the reasonable expense incurred in making the proof, including attorney fees. Failure to comply with a court's order to respond to discovery may result in even more drastic consequences. The court may enter judgment against the disobedient party.

Summary Judgment

During or after discovery, it may become clearer whether a party can prove allegations made in the pleading. The pleadings are comparable to a skeleton. The facts elicited from discovery are like the flesh. Without the "flesh," a litigant's suit cannot survive. It is easy to make statements in the pleadings, but backing up allegations with factual proof is often more difficult.

A motion for summary judgment is proper to test the factual sufficiency of the pleadings. This motion requests the court to consider the pleadings and material outside the pleadings, for example, discovery responses (see Figure 3–8). The **movant** (the party making the motion) argues that there is no genuine factual dispute, and hence the case must be decided on the law.

Assume that the plaintiff, Infra Disposal Corporation, alleges in its complaint that defendant, General Ocean, "met with other companies and conspired to fix prices, and engaged in other antitrust activities, all designed to drive Infra Disposal Corporation out of business." General Ocean denies the allegation in its answer. The president of General Ocean testifies under oath at a deposition stating that "at no time did General Ocean or any agents on its behalf fix prices nor did it intend to drive Infra Disposal out of business." General Ocean then moves for summary judgment. If Infra Disposal fails to raise any factual issue or present any documentation suggesting the price-fixing scheme, the court will grant defendant's motion since there is no genuine factual dispute. The defendant will win as a matter of law.

Trial Stage

A pretrial conference may be conducted in the judge's chambers. Normally, only the attorneys for the parties are permitted to attend. At the conference, the judge inquires whether discovery is completed and whether the parties are ready for trial. If so, a trial date is set. Some judges spend the bulk of the time at the conference in an attempt to narrow and clarify the issues for trial. Others focus on settlement.

Most judges are very "docket conscious" and generally desire the parties to settle the case before trial. Many cases settle at the pretrial conference or "on the courthouse steps" just before, or even as, the trial unfolds. Only a small precentage of suits that are instituted actually go to trial.

Voir Dire

A trial starts with the **voir dire** — the examination and selection of prospective jurors. Depending on the local law, a jury may consist of anywhere from 1 to 12 members. Each side will attempt to select jurors favorable to its cause. Many courts permit the attorneys, in collaboration with their clients, to question prospective jurors to ascertain their biases — that is, whether they can genuinely arrive at a decision based only on the facts and the law. In some jurisdictions, the parties are passive during voir dire while the judge does the questioning.

Each side will have an opportunity to exercise challenges against prospective jurors for cause. A **challenge for cause** will be granted if the judge believes that the prospective juror has a sympathy or prejudice that would prevent that person from rendering a just verdict. There are also certain statutory grounds for excusing a juror for cause — for example, if the juror is related to one of the parties or has a financial interest in the outcome of the case.

In addition to an unlimited number of challenges for cause, each side has a limited number of **peremptory challenges** depending on the jurisdiction and the type of trial. A peremptory challenge automatically excuses a prospective juror. The challenger need not show any cause whatsoever for the challenge. After jurors are selected, they are sworn, and the parties begin their opening statements.

Opening Statements

Opening statements are usually made first by the plaintiff, followed by the defendant. The opening statement is not evidence. It is like an opening paragraph in an essay in that it provides the jury with an overview of what the evidence will show. The evidence is presented during the next stage, called the **case in chief.**

Cases in Chief

After opening statements, the trial continues with the plaintiff presenting evidence. Evidence consists of witnesses' testimony and exhibits. Witnesses may be expert or nonexpert. Nonexpert witnesses can only testify about what they perceived. For example, a nonexpert cannot testify that "I believe Mr. Button suffered cerebral injury," but a nonexpert could describe personal observations about Mr. Button's condition: "He was in a wheelchair, his speech was slurred, his face contorted, and his arms flayed randomly." By contrast, an expert witness may render opinion testimony regarding his or her area of expertise.

After the plaintiff questions a witness, the defendant is given an opportunity to cross-examine that witness. During cross-examination, it is proper to "lead" the witness. A leading question contains facts suggesting the answer, as for example, "Is it true that you informed the defendant that you signed the contract on July 21?"

During cross-examination, the opposing attorney may attempt to show that the witness is not telling the truth by asking questions that probe into bias, an inconsistency in the witness's testimony, or a faulty memory. The attorney will also try to draw out testimony favorable to his or her own client. After cross-examination of a witness, the plaintiff's attorney will have limited freedom to ask the witness questions (re-direct examination). Similarly, thereafter, the defendant has limited freedom to inquire of the witness (re-cross examination).

Exhibits may also be introduced in evidence during the case in chief. Exhibits may consist of documents such as contracts, bills, receipts, or other physical evidence such as guns, clothing, or a car fender.

After the plaintiff has completed the case in chief, the defendant may respond by introducing testimony and exhibits. Sometimes during the defendant's case in chief new evidence arises covering matters not introduced during the plaintiff's case in chief. The plaintiff is then given an opportunity to rebut that evidence.

The defendant, in turn, may rebut new matters raised by the plaintiff. Theoretically, arguments could go back and forth in this manner forever. The judge, of course, has discretion to set sensible limitations on this process.

Lawyers raise **objections** in an attempt to block the admission of evidence. **Rules of evidence**, which govern the admissibility of evidence, will control the judge's ruling on such objections. These rules serve several purposes. First, they are designed to assist the fact finder in arriving at the truth. Therefore, evidence that is inherently unreliable is excluded. This is the rationale for the exclusion of **hearsay evidence**—out-of-court statements offered in court to prove the truth of the statement.

The reason hearsay is generally excluded is that hearsay statements are neither made under oath nor may the declarant even be available for cross-examination. Nonetheless, some types of hearsay evidence are considered more reliable; hence, these are admissible as an exception to the hearsay rule. Examples of admissible hearsay include statements made by persons on their deathbeds (dying declarations) or, as the next case indicates, certain research studies.

ELLIS v. INTERNATIONAL PLAYTEX, INC.
745 F.2d 292 (4th Cir. 1984)

Margaret Ellis, a user of Playtex tampons, died unexpectedly while using the tampons. Her husband, Jefferey, convinced that she had died from toxic shock syndrome (TSS), sued International Playtex, Inc., the manufacturer of the tampons. The case was tried by a jury, which found in favor of the defendant, International Playtex, Inc. Jefferey appealed to the U.S. Court of Appeals contending that the court committed error by refusing to admit into evidence toxic shock syndrome studies carried out by the Center for Disease Control (CDC) and various state health departments, offered in an attempt to prove the causative link between tampon use and TSS.

ERVIN, Judge

Toxic shock syndrome was first identified in 1978, but it was not until 1980 that the symptoms of the disease were linked to menstruation. Faced with a rapid and severe outbreak of a novel disease, the federal government and a group of state health agencies undertook a series of studies designed to isolate the cause of the disease. The CDC and Tri-State reports at issue here were among the first of these epidemiological studies. Focusing on a pool of TSS cases that had been reported to state health officials, the CDC and the state health departments of Wisconsin, Minnesota, and Iowa administered a questionnaire to a selected group of the TSS victims and to a control group. The studies revealed that the vast majority of TSS victims had recently used some type of tampon. Playtex tampons were among those that TSS victims reported having used.

Fed.R.Evid. 803 (8) (C) states that the following are not excluded by the hearsay rule:

> records, reports, statements, or data compilations, in any form, of public offices or agencies, setting forth . . . factual findings resulting from an investigation made pursuant to authority granted by law, unless the sources of information or other circumstances indicate lack of trustworthiness.

The rule is premised on "the assumption that a public official will perform his duty properly and the unlikelihood that he will remember details independently of the record." "Admissibility in the first instance" is assumed because of the reliability of the public agencies usually conducting the investigation, and "their lack of any motive for conducting the studies other than to inform the public fairly and adequately." This is not to say that a report containing the findings of a public agency, made pursuant to an investigation authorized by law, is always admissible. To the contrary, if "sufficient negative factors are present" to indicate the report is not trustworthy, it should not be admitted. . . . The factors that may be used to determine admissibility include: (1) the timeliness of the investigation; (2) the special skill or experience of the official; and (3) possible motivation problems. But the burden is on the party opposing admission to demonstrate that the report is not reliable.

We do not believe scientific reports should be treated any differently from other public findings of fact under a Fed.R.Evid. 803 (8) (C) analysis. Indeed, in this instance the rationale behind the rule argues strongly for admission of the contested studies. First, both studies were carried out by public offices "pursuant to authority granted by law."

Second, the studies possess ample indicia of trustworthiness. The CDC and the state health departments of Minnesota, Iowa, and Wisconsin are highly skilled in the study of epidemiology. Both the CDC and the state health departments use uniform procedures and methods in their epidemiology studies that are widely accepted by their peers. Data is not reported . . . unless it is statistically significant. We find nothing in the record that would lead us to doubt the reliability of those procedures as they were applied in this particular instance. Furthermore, there is no conceivable motive for carrying out the studies in any other manner than to inform the public fairly and accurately. At the time the studies were undertaken, TSS had become an epidemic of significant proportion. There is no reason to believe that the CDC and Tri-State group approached this epidemic with anything but the professional impartiality they regularly apply to similar public crises. . . . Finally, the studies were clearly timely.

In our view, Playtex's concern about the methodology of the studies should have been addressed to the relative weight accorded the evidence and not its admissibility. This position, we believe, is consistent with the rationale behind the 803 (8) (C) exception. Although the rule is designed to assume the admissibility of a report in the absence of affirmative indicia of untrustworthiness, there is no indication that Congress intended for the reports to escape searching examination. Allowing the jury to evaluate the reports after careful cross-examination and the presentation of expert testimony, therefore, serves both of these functions well; it permits admission without sacrificing scrutiny.

Because we believe that the exclusion of the CDC and Tri-State reports prejudiced the outcome of the Trial, the matter is remanded for a new trial consistent with this opinion.

Case Questions

1. What issue does this case present?
2. What is the reason for excluding hearsay? What is the reason for including hearsay?
3. What other exceptions to the hearsay rule should exist? What about business records? Explain.
4. What attacks could Playtex have made against the reliability and trustworthiness of the report?
5. Would you favor abolishing the hearsay evidence rule, admitting all relevant hearsay, and permitting the trier of the fact to determine the value to be assigned to the specific hearsay? Analyze.

Evidence that would unfairly prejudice jury members or arouse their passion is also excludable. For example, in a case in which the plaintiff is suing a train company for damages suffered when the company's train failed to warn of its approach, any attempt to parade a severed limb before the jury would be met with a sustainable objection. The victim's injury can be adequately proved without a gruesome and prejudicial display of the limb, obviously designed to appeal to the passion of the jurors.

A second purpose of rules of evidence is to expedite the trial. The admission of evidence not germane to the issues wastes time and judicial resources; therefore, it is excludable. Finally, society's desire to protect certain privacy values may result in exclusion. Although a confession to an attorney may present truthful and relevant evidence, such confession is privileged and normally cannot be introduced into evidence if the client objects. In the same light, evidence that is seized in violation of a person's constitutional right to be free from unreasonable search and seizures is excludable.

Closing Arguments

When both sides have ''rested'' their case, each party through his or her attorney has an opportunity to make a summation or closing argument to the jury. Each attorney uses the argument to persuade the jury that, on the basis of the evidence, his or her side should prevail. During this time, the attorneys highlight the favorable evidence and attempt to discredit the evidence presented by the opponent. The argument is not evidence. It is designed to help the jury draw conclusions on the basis of the evidence presented. After the closing arguments by the parties, the judge instructs the jury on the law.

Instructions to the Jury

The jurors are normally not experts on the law that governs the case. That is why the judge must instruct them on the proper law to apply. After the voir dire, the jurors are sworn to apply the law as instructed by the judge. They have no discretion regarding this matter, even if they do not think the law is just. After the judge's instructions, the jury retires to deliberate in the jury room. There they will discuss the testimony and the exhibits and determine what testimony to believe and which version of the case to accept. The jurors are the experts on "finding the truth." They must apply the truth as they find it to the law as the judge instructed them and then render a verdict.

Verdict and Judgment

Jury verdicts may be general or special. A **general verdict** is simply a finding for the plaintiff or defendant. If there is a finding for the plaintiff, the verdict will also grant the plaintiff damages. Sometimes **special interrogatories** are submitted to the jury at the time jurors are instructed by the judge. Special interrogatories are questions that the jury is required to answer; for example, "Was the defendant negligent?"

The judge is informed when the jury comes to a verdict. The parties and the jury reconvene in the courtroom, and the verdict is announced. Thereafter, the judge enters judgment on the verdict.

Trial Motions

Just as certain motions were proper during the pleading and discovery stage, other motions can be interposed at trial (see Figure 3–8). The most common ones at this stage include a motion for **directed verdict** and a **motion for judgment non obstante verdicto (n.o.v.),** sometimes referred to as a motion for **judgment nonwithstanding the verdict.** The motion for directed verdict may be made by either party at the conclusion of the opponent's case in chief. The motion requests the judge to enter a verdict in favor of the movant on the grounds that reasonable minds cannot differ on the basis of the evidence. If the judge agrees, then the case will not "go to the jury" but will instead be decided "as a matter of law" in favor of the movant. Assume that in a products liability case plaintiff fails to present any evidence to support her allegation that the defendant manufactured a defective product that caused plaintiff's injury. In such a case, it would be proper for the court to grant defendant's motion for a directed verdict.

The motion for judgment notwithstanding the verdict is made after the verdict but before the judgment. The party who is the subject of the unfavorable jury verdict argues that the verdict should be discounted because the case should never have gone to the jury in the first place since, on the evidence, reasonable minds could not differ. This motion affords the judge an opportunity to correct a previous error in denying the party's motion for directed verdict.

Finally, either party may make a motion for a new trial, and the party who loses that motion may appeal to a higher court.

Appellate Stage

The party who loses at the trial level may appeal the cause to an appropriate appellate court on the grounds that an error was committed in the trial court. The party appealing the decision is called the **appellant**. The party responding to the appeal is called the **appellee**. No witnesses testify in the appeals court, and no jury is present. Normally, three appellate judges hear the parties' counsel argue why the lower court decision should either be affirmed or reversed. The appellate judges, additionally, have the benefit of the lower court record of trial testimony and the exhibits that were received into evidence. They review the court record to determine whether the lower court made an error during the trial. Lower court judges may err when they improperly rule on motions and the admissibility of evidence or when they incorrectly instruct the jury.

ALTERNATIVE DISPUTE RESOLUTION

The increasing number of lawsuits filed each year results in court congestion and delay. It is not unusual for the final resolution of a civil case to take three or more years. The queue after pleadings are filed in some California civil courts can delay start of a trial by as much as five years.

The cost of litigation is also increasing. All legal services are expensive. Taxpayers also bear indirect costs because judges, court personnel, and jurors must all be paid.

Many people have become disillusioned with the traditional approach to dispute resolution through litigation. Alternative methods of solving disputes may be one of the biggest challenges facing society in the years ahead. Some alternative approaches have been employed with satisfaction and are discussed here.

Mediation

Sometimes the parties to a dispute can negotiate and resolve their differences themselves. This, of course, is the ideal. However, when a dispute arises, those who are involved are often blinded by their own point of view. A **mediator** may be helpful to facilitate a settlement. A mediator is a third party whose role is to aid in resolving the conflict. The mediator should be objective and a person in whom both parties have confidence and respect.

Mediation avoids the technical aspects of litigation as well as its high cost and delay. However, the mediator does not have the power to impose a resolution—only to suggest, advise, and attempt to bring the parties to a mutual settlement of the dispute. Oftentimes, mediators are able to promote settlement by sensitizing each party to the other's position and helping them come to a rational compromise.

Mediators have been used in marital, labor, and international disputes. They are particularly suitable for parties who have an ongoing relationship. In contrast to the alienation often caused by litigation, mediation often helps to resolve the dispute quickly and promote reconciliation between the parties.

Minitrial

The **minitrial** proceeding is a combination of both mediation and negotiation. Both disputing parties agree to briefly present their evidence and argue their case before observers, who then make recommendations based on how a court might rule. Managerial officers of each disputing company may then negotiate a settlement based on the strength of the parties' presentations and the recommendations of observers. Although the minitrial does not necessarily produce a settlement, it offers the parties a great incentive to do so because the cost involved is far less than the cost of litigation. In the event there is no settlement, the parties are practiced and better equipped to prepare their case for litigation.

Arbitration

Like mediation, arbitration has traditionally been viewed as a quicker and less costly way of resolving a dispute than litigation. Unlike mediation, the third party, called an **arbitrator,** has the power to render a decision.

Arbitrators are impartial third parties who hear evidence and arguments, and then render a decision. Technical rules of discovery and evidence are not generally employed and the proceedings are more informal than court proceedings. However, there is a clear trend for arbitration to adopt many litigation-like procedures. Arbitration awards are generally more private than judicial judgments, since arbitration results are not ordinarily a matter of public record. Arbitration may be held anywhere and anytime as agreed by the parties, whereas procedural rules dictate more strictly the place and time of litigation.

Arbitrators are often chosen because of their expertise in an area. For example, an automotive engineer may be selected for a dispute involving the condition of an automobile engine.

More and more contracts include arbitration clauses. An **arbitration clause** contains an agreement to submit any dispute arising under the contract to arbitration. Such a clause may require each party to select an arbitrator and those two arbitrators to select a third. Clearly, arbitration is a favorable trend in the law.

A variation of the arbitration procedure is the **rent-a-judge**. Retired judges and others offer their services for pay to disputants. The rent-a-judge process uses a modified trial court procedure. By state law, as in California, the rent-a-judge's decision has the full force of law. The advantages are that it avoids the delays and publicity of traditional litigation.

---

 *Can We Talk? Mediation Gains in Law Disputes**

To many Americans it's almost a ritual. Two parties get into a dispute, hire lawyers to press their claims and the battle lines harden. The result: ''We'll see you in court.''

---

*Source: Bill Richards, *The Wall Street Journal,* May 14, 1985. Reprinted with permission.

But more individuals and businesses are seeking alternatives to the lawyer-and-litigation route. Two that are growing more popular are mediation and arbitration, which can settle most disputes — from consumer complaints to accident and assault cases — usually for much less time and money.

The organizations providing these services, many of which are free, include the Better Business Bureau, the American Arbitration Association and the nearly 200 Neighborhood Justice Centers nationwide that are sponsored by local bar associations. . . .

Disgruntled Owners

The services are particularly useful for some of the most common consumer complaints. The Better Business Bureau, for example, which last year mediated about 240,000 such disputes, runs an automobile arbitration program that gives disgruntled car owners a chance to negotiate their differences with manufacturers at no cost. Arbitrators rule on the disputes within 10 days; automakers have agreed to accept the decisions, but consumers aren't held to them.

An arbitrator in Chicago recently awarded Joseph Doyle $1,250 of his requested $2,500 after the businessman spent two hours recounting his fruitless efforts to get General Motors Corp. to repaint his peeling . . . Cadillac for the third time. ''The legal folderol of suing GM would have been so expensive it wouldn't have been worth the effort,'' Mr. Doyle says. Ten domestic and foreign auto makers participate in the program. (Chrysler Corp. and Ford Motor Co. run their own, separate arbitration programs.)

Insurance Claims

Settling disputed insurance claims is another area where mediation or arbitration services are useful. Last year the American Arbitration Association inaugurated a service and handled nearly 1,000 disputes. Some 20 insurance companies now refer disputed claims to the association's 26 regional offices for arbitration. The claims, ranging from fallen-tree damage to false arrest, tend to run between $10,000 and $51,000 each and usually take about a half-day to settle instead of the years it might take in court. Either the claimant or the insurer can initiate the arbitration at a usual cost of $150 to $225 each.

Using a mediation or arbitration service isn't always a good idea. Experienced mediators say that for the process to work well, both parties should be able to make a good case for their positions. If one party doesn't have enough evidence or isn't skilled at presenting it, they recommend court, where lawyers and judges may better produce a fair decision. ''Mediation is a bargaining process,'' says Joan Hall, a lawyer on the board of the Chicago Neighborhood Justice Center. ''You have to make sure you have the chips to bargain with.''

Complicated Disputes

But in the majority of cases, even complicated disputes, with lawyers often taking part, mediation can still be cheaper and quicker. Terrance Jordan, a Chicago lawyer, recently represented a client charged with assault during a neighborhood dispute. His client filed a countersuit. Instead of taking the case to trial, a judge recommended that both squabblers go to the Neighborhood Justice Center.

After a four-hour mediation session, conducted in Spanish and English, the neighbors agreed to stop fighting and patch up their differences. In return, the charges were dropped.

Mr. Jordan, who sat in on the mediation, says the case could have cost his client as much as $4,000 in fees if it had gone to trial. ''I had no idea this kind of procedure existed,'' he says, ''but I highly recommend it.''

Thought Questions

1. Would it be possible to eliminate our court system and substitute mediation and arbitration in its place? Analyze.
2. What can businesses do to promote mediation and arbitration?
3. Under what circumstances is mediation effective? Arbitration? When are they ineffective?

END–OF–CHAPTER QUESTIONS

1. What values are served by the jury system? What are the disadvantages? Should the jury system be replaced with another? Discuss.

2. Should values other than truth-seeking and efficiency be aims of the rules of evidence? Explain.

3. List the factors that should be considered before appealing a case.

4. Do you think that the adversary system is an efficient model for the resolution of conflicts? Can you propose a just alternative?

5. The plaintiff, a Cleveland, Ohio, corporation, entered into a subcontracting agreement with the defendant, a Minnesota Corporation with its principal place of business in Fort Smith, Arkansas. The contract was for marine dredging in Peoria, Illinois. Negotiations regarding this contract took place at the defendant's home office and in Tampa, Florida. The contract was then mailed to the plaintiff's headquarters in Cleveland. In addition, several phone calls were made by the plaintiff to the defendant from the plaintiff's Cleveland office, and one meeting with the defendant's vice president took place in Columbus, Ohio. Has the defendant made itself subject to suit in Ohio pursuant to Ohio's long-arm statute by virtue of its contacts with the plaintiff in Ohio? See *Capital Dredge and Dock Corporation v. Midwest Dredging Co.*, 573 F.2d 377 (6th Cir. 1978).

6. Harry and Kay Robinson purchased a new Audi automobile from Seaway Volkswagen in New York. The Robinsons, who lived in New York at the time, left the state for a new home in Arizona. As they passed through Oklahoma, another car struck their Audi in the rear, causing a fire and injuring Kay and her two children. Seaway, a retail dealer, is incorporated and has its principal place of business in New York. Seaway does not do any business in Oklahoma, neither does it ship or sell any products to that state, nor does it do any advertising calculated to reach people in Oklahoma. The Robinsons seek to invoke Oklahoma's long-arm statute and sue Seaway in Oklahoma. May the Oklahoma court assert jurisdiction over Seaway? Explain. See *Worldwide Volkswagen Corp. v. Woodson*, 444 U.S. 286 (1980).

7. The plaintiffs sued Johns-Manville seeking damages for injuries as a result of exposure to asbestos. The plaintiffs contended that Johns-Manville knew asbestos was hazardous to health long before exposing the plaintiffs to the danger. They seek to prove this by introducing three depositions and one sworn statement taken of witnesses in another case. Those witnesses are unavailable to testify because they are now dead. What rule of evidence must plaintiffs hurdle to have the evidence admitted? What arguments can plaintiff make in favor of the evidence's introduction? See *Beckwith v. Bethlehem Steel*, 185 N.J. Super. 50, 447 A2d 207 (1982).

8. Inez Daviess sued Globe Indemnity Co. for $1,000 to recover on a policy indemnifying her against robbery of jewelry. Daviess's unrebutted testimony was essentially as follows: "In response to my doorbell ringing, I opened the door and a

man with a handkerchief over his face threatened me with a gun and demanded I hand over my jewelry, which I did. I gave him a diamond bracelet, sapphires, diamonds, and a solitaire with diamonds around it and onyx. About five months later, I found all of the jewelry that was taken from me, except a diamond ring, in my mailbox.''

Daviess was unable to describe the alleged robber except to say that ''he was a medium-sized man wearing a cap.'' She lived on a principal thoroughfare in Louisville, Kentucky, and the alleged robbery took place in the afternoon. The defendant presented no evidence to rebut Daviess's testimony. Should the trial court grant Daviess's motion for directed verdict? Explain. See *Globe Indemnity Co. v. Daviess*, 243 Ky. 356, 47 S.W. 990 (1932).

9. The plaintiff sued the defendant, a cab company, for injuries sustained while the plaintiff was a passenger in a taxicab allegedly owned by defendant. During the trial, the defense counsel objected to the admission of certain records of the Bos-

ton police department and requested permission to be heard ''at the bench.'' The following dialogue in the presence of the jury ensued:

The court: No, no, no, no, no, no. What do you want to hide from the jury?

Counsel: Judge, with all due respect to the court, I didn't say I wanted to hide anything from the jury.

The court: Well, why do you want to see me at the bench?

The jury returned a verdict in favor of the plaintiff. Should the case be reversed on appeal if the jury heard the court's comments? What if the jury did not hear the court's comments?

10. Frank Andrews has purchased a prefabricated house from Megabuilders Craftsman. Andrews has had many problems with the house, and he is contemplating suing. There is a clause within the purchase contract that gives Andrews the right to elect to arbitrate his disputes. What factors should Andrews consider when making the decision to litigate or arbitrate?

Chapter 4

Constitutional Law and Individual Liberties

■

CRITICAL THINKING INQUIRIES

As you read this chapter, you should be able to address the following:

- Compare and contrast ''state action'' and ''private action.''
- Compare and contrast the various tests of equal protection.
- Compare and contrast procedural due process and substantive due process.
- When is taking not a ''taking'' under the Constitution?
- Analyze: ''All speech is protected.''
- Why do certain searches of businesses not require a warrant in order to satisfy the Constitution?
- Is the intent of the framers of the U.S. Constitution being met today in the area of individual liberties?

MANAGERIAL PERSPECTIVE

Ross Allen is the director of the Research Institute of Industry University, a small private university. The university does a lot of government contract work in the area of labor and human resources research. The federal government is the major source of funding and leases the land to the university for $1 a year. Additionally, the university is involved in a number of joint projects with the government in the area of smoking in the workplace.

Ross had a course in political science that dealt with the Constitution and how government works. His boss wants answers to a number of questions so that the company can develop sound and relevant policies.

- Is the Equal Protection Clause and the Due Process Clause of the Constitution applicable to our university?
- What type of safeguards and protections must we give to students who engage in alleged scholarly and research misconduct before disciplining them?
- What limitations, if any, can we put on speech at the university?

Constitutional law is not confined to the courthouses but is relevant to our lives and businesses. This chapter introduces the large body of law referred to as constitutional law. It is essential for Ross Allen and other people to understand this subject since it is the foundation of our relationship to government. Although every state has a constitution, the focus in this chapter is on the U.S. Constitution. The chapter first defines constitutional law, then examines the "state action" requirement, and finally explores the relationship of the government to the individual in the areas of equal protection, due process, taking property, free speech, and searches and seizures.

DEFINING CONSTITUTIONAL LAW

"We must never forget . . .," thundered Chief Justice John Marshall, "that it is a Constitution we are expounding."[1] Despite the popularity of this quotation, it is not obvious what meaning should be assigned to the term **constitution.** What is the Constitution? Does the Constitution change, so that today's definition may be different from tomorrow's? Or is it simply a fixed document set for all time and displayed in the National Archives? Constitutional law is derived from the U.S. Supreme Court's interpretation of the Constitution. Constitutional law may be characterized as all of the following:

- The supreme law of the land.
- A brake limiting the power of government.
- Judge-made law.

Supreme Law of the Land

Unlike the British constitution, which is not written, the U.S. Constitution is a written document. The chief distinction between the British and American constitutions is not, however, their form but the relationship between the constitutions and ordinary acts of the legislature. The authority of the legislative branch of government in Great Britain, called Parliament, is higher than the constitution. Parliament may overturn its provisions. This is not the case with the U.S. Constitution.

The American system created two levels of law: (1) the Constitution, unalterable by ordinary legislation, and (2) statutory law, capable of change through the normal legislative process. The Constitution was intended to be "the law above the law." This was recognized early by the U.S. Supreme Court in *Marbury v. Madison.*[2] That case held the Constitution to be the supreme law of the land. Every congressional act contrary to the Constitution must be struck down as unconstitutional, as must state laws that transgress the Constitution.

A Brake Limiting Power

To control the abuse of power by the government, the constitutional framers adopted federalism, a division of powers between the states and the national government. A second division of power among the three branches of the national government is often called our system of *checks and balances.* The Constitution structurally imposes the maxim on our government: "You may cover whole skins of parchment with limitations, but power alone can limit power." Figure 4–1 lists instances of power limiting power in our Constitution.

Judge-Made Law

The Constitution sets up a framework for our government, yet even the supreme law of the land must be interpreted. The Constitution is silent about who is to supply such interpretation. The early case of *Marbury v. Madison* broke this silence by declaring that it is within the special province and duty of the judiciary to interpret the Constitution.

The power of judicial review—the authority of the Supreme Court to declare an act of a coordinate branch of government or a state government unconstitutional—remains a fundamental principle of American constitutional law. Thus, the Constitution is what the judges say it is. Whether the framers of the Constitution intended to grant such authority to the judiciary is the subject of scholarly debate. As a practical matter, it is clear that constitutional law is now essentially judge-made law and more particularly, U.S. Supreme Court–made law.

Those who want the Supreme Court to move society along in small increments urge the Court to exercise its judicial review power with reservation. These are the conservatives who opt for

---

[1] *McCulloch v. Maryland,* 17 U.S. (4 Wheat.) 316, 407 (1819).

[2] 5 U.S. (1 Cranch) 137 (1803).

Figure 4–1   Constitutional Limitations of Power

Power	Limitation	Concept
National government	States	Federalism: The relationship between the national government and state or local governments.
Senate	House	Bicameralism: A division of the legislature into two chambers. Example: One chamber of Congress, acting alone, may not veto a decision of the executive branch.
Congress	President	Checks and balances: The power of one coordinate branch of the national government to limit the power of another branch. Example: Bills passed by Congress must be presented to the president for signature or veto.
Congress	Courts	Judicial review: The power of the Supreme Court to determine the constitutionality of the acts of coordinate branches of government. Example: The Supreme Court determines that an act of Congress conflicts with the constitutional guaranty of free speech and voids the act.
President	Senate	Treaty power: Two-thirds of the Senate must consent to a treaty before it is ratified. Example: The Senate rejects an arms control treaty negotiated by the president with Russia.
Representatives	People	Representative democracy: Individual legislators are chosen by the people to represent their varied interests in the legislature. Example: Voting districts must be set so that all who participate in an election have an equal vote.
People	Electoral college	Democratic ideals: The president is elected by the electoral college which is elected by the people.
Senate	People	Direct representation: Since the passage of the Seventeenth Amendment in 1913, senators are directly elected by the people of each state.

judicial restraint. In contrast, others believe that greater change is needed to cure society's ills and that the Court should be at the forefront of that change. These are the liberals who opt for judicial activism.

When the Supreme Court interprets the Constitution, it is as if its decision is being typed right onto the parchment that is preserved at the National Archives. Constitutional law is, therefore, the text and amendments to the Constitution combined with the Court's interpretation of the text and amendments (see Figure 4–2). Like the text and amendments, the Court's constitutional interpretation cannot be altered by anything short of a constitutional amendment or a reinterpretation by the Supreme Court.

REQUIREMENT OF STATE ACTION

Constitutional protections apply only when the government is in some way involved in a case. The Constitution was not designed to protect people against other people. It was, however, designed to protect against the abridgement of various rights by the government or one clothed with governmental authority. To illustrate, the Constitution does not restrain someone from telling another person to stop talking. It does restrain the government, however, from telling an individual to stop talking. This would be an infringement on free speech. Similarly, the Constitution does not protect one against racial or religious prejudice from another

---

Figure 4–2   Structure of the Constitution

I. Text	Article I	Legislative powers of congress
	Article II	Executive powers of the president
	Article III	Judicial power of the courts
	Article IV	Relationship among the several states
	Article V	Amendment provisions
	Article VI	Miscellaneous provisions
	Article VII	Ratification of the Constitution

II. Amendments   An amendment must be ratified by three fourths of the state legislatures after being approved by two thirds of the Congress. There have been 27 amendments. Of chief importance to businesspersons are the following amendments:

First Amendment	Freedom of speech
Fourth Amendment	Freedom from unreasonable searches and seizures
Fifth Amendment	Takings Clause
Fourteenth Amendment	Due Process Clause
	Equal Protection Clause

III. Judicial Interpretations   The U.S. Supreme Court is the final interpreter of the U.S. Constitution.   .

---

individual. It does, however, prohibit the government from practicing or participating in such prejudice. This requirement that the government be involved in the deprivation of one's rights before the Constitution applies is called the **state action** requirement.

Government Participation in Private Action

In most cases, state action is clearly present or absent. Thus, a government agent inspecting a manufacturing plant for alleged safety violations and a city prohibiting the posting of billboard advertisements are clearly acts involving state action.

State action is more difficult to discern in cases where the person or organization who allegedly violates the Constitution is not working for the government. Can a private actor's conduct ever be considered state action? Sometimes, the government directly encourages or supports the private actor's conduct through subsidies, government contracts, and other forms of aid, as is the case for Industry University in our opening scenario. At other times, the government, through licensing or regulation, is merely a passive participant in the private actor's conduct. How involved must the government be in the private actor's conduct before constitutional protection attaches? The following case seeks to answer this quesion by considering the factors necessary to find state action.

BURTON v. WILMINGTON PARKING AUTHORITY
365 U.S. 715 (1961)

The plaintiff, Burton, was denied service at the defendant's restaurant solely because he was a member of the Negro race. The defendant, Wilmington Parking Authority, was a lessee at a parking building that was owned and operated by an agency created by the State of Delaware. Burton sued the Wilmington Parking Authority in the Delaware Chancery Court, claiming his Fourteenth Amendment right to equal protection was violated. The judge granted Burton's motion for summary judgment but was reversed on appeal by the Delaware Supreme Court. Burton appealed that decision to the U.S. Supreme Court.

CLARK, Justice

. . . It is clear . . . that ''[i]ndividual invasion of individual rights is not the subject-matter of the [Fourteenth] amendment,'' . . . and that private conduct abridging individual rights does no violence to the Equal Protection Clause unless to some significant extent the State in any of its manifestations has been found to have become involved in it. . . . To fashion and apply a precise formula for recognition of state responsibility under the Equal Protection Clause is an ''impossible task'' which ''this Court has never attempted.''. . . Only by sifting facts and weighing circumstances can the nonobvious involvement of the State in private conduct be attributed its true significance.

. . . The land and [restaurant] building were publicly owned. As an entity, the building was dedicated to ''Public uses'' in performance of the Authority's essential governmental functions.'' The costs of land acquisition, construction, and maintenance are defrayed entirely from donations by the City of Wilmington, from loans and revenue bonds and from the proceeds of rentals and parking services out of which the loans and bonds were payable. . . . The commercially leased areas were not surplus state property, but constituted a physically and financially integral and, indeed, indispensable part of the State's plan to operate its project as a self-sustaining unit. Upkeep and maintenance of the building, including necessary repairs, were responsibilities of the Authority and were payable out of public funds. It cannot be doubted that the peculiar relationship of the restaurant to the parking facility in which it is located confers on each an incidental variety of mutual benefits. Guests of the restaurant are afforded a convenient place to park their automobiles, even if they cannot enter the restaurant directly from the parking area. Similarly, its convenience for diners may well provide additional demand for the Authority's parking facilities. . . . Neither can it be ignored, especially in view of [the restaurant's] affirmative allegation that for it to serve Negroes would injure its business, that profits earned by discrimination not only contribute to, but also are indispensable elements in, the financial success of a governmental agency.

Addition of all these activities, obligations and responsibilities of the Authority, the benefits mutually conferred, together with the obvious fact that the restaurant is operated as an integral part of a public building devoted to a public parking service, indicates that degree of state participation and involvement in discriminatory action which it was the design of the Fourteenth Amendment to condemn. It is irony amounting to grave injustice that in one part of a single building, erected and maintained with public funds by an agency of the State to serve a public purpose, all persons have equal rights, while in another portion, also serving the public, a Negro is a second-class citizen, . . . because of his race, without rights and unentitled to service, but at the same time fully enjoys equal access to nearby restaurants in wholly privately owned buildings. As the Chancellor [the title of the judge in the Delaware court] pointed out, in its lease with [the restaurant,] the Authority could have affirmatively required it to discharge the responsibilities under the Fourteenth Amendment imposed upon the private enterprise as a consequence of state participation. But no State may effectively abdicate its responsibilities by either ignoring them or by merely failing to discharge them whatever the motive may be. It is of no consolation to an individual denied the equal protection of the laws that it was done in good faith. Certainly the conclusions drawn in similar cases by the various Courts of Appeals do not depend upon such a distinction. By its inaction, the Authority, and through it the State, has not only made itself a party to the refusal of service, but has elected to place its power, property and prestige behind the admitted discrimination. The State had so far insinuated itself into the position of interdependence with [the restaurant] that it must be recognized as a joint participant in the challenged activity, which, on that account, cannot be considered to have been so ''purely private'' as to fall without the scope of the Fourteenth Amendment. . . . Specifically defining the limits of our inquiry, what we hold today is that when a State leases public property in the manner and for the purpose shown to have been the case here, the prescriptions of the Fourteenth Amendment must be complied with by the lessee as certainly as though they were binding covenants written into the agreement itself.

The judgment of the Supreme Court of Delaware is reversed and the cause remanded for further proceedings consistent with this opinion.

Case Questions

1. What is the issue in this case?
2. Identify the facts that make this a state action case.

3. Do you agree that state action was involved in the defendant lessee's refusal to serve the plaintiff? Analyze.

4. Can inactivity by the state suffice to fulfill the state action requirement of the Fourteenth Amendment? Analyze.

The Public Function Doctrine

There is another line of state action cases that do not involve governmental participation, aid, or contacts with the private actor. Under what has become known as the **public function doctrine,** where the private actor exercises a power that is traditionally and exclusively reserved to the government, the private actor's conduct will be considered state action. For example, where a private corporation owns and operates an entire city, the corporation is treated like the government, and its actions are limited by the Constitution. By way of contrast, running a nursing home or a shopping center do not involve the assumption of public functions by private actors. These functions are not subject to constitutional limitations.

DEPRIVATION OF INDIVIDUAL LIBERTIES

Once state action is found, the Court must next consider whether there has been a deprivation of rights that the Constitution protects. For businesses, the constitutional protections of major concern are:

- Equal Protection Clause.
- Due Process Clause.
- Takings Clause.
- Guaranty of free speech.
- Protection against unreasonable searches and seizures.

Equal Protection Clause

The Fourteenth Amendment to the U.S. Constitution states in part: ''No state [shall] . . . deny to any person within its jurisdiction the equal protection of the laws.'' The purpose of this clause is to guarantee the basic principles of justice that similarly situated people should be treated similarly by the government. The clause applies any time the government classifies individuals or businesses. There are three different tests applied to equal protection cases (see Figure 4–3).

The Rational Basis Test

Almost every attempt by the government to regulate a business involves some line drawing. For example, a state may prohibit the sale of milk that is three weeks old. Milk 21 days old must then be thrown out while milk 20 days and 23 hours old could be sold. Where a law involves economic matters, the Supreme Court requires that any classification must rationally relate to a legitimate governmental objective. The test of economic classifications is therefore a very relaxed one in which the court defers to the judgment of the Congress or the state legislature. Under the **rational basis test** if any rational basis for the classification can be found, the economic regulation will be upheld as constitutional. The following case involving a woman who was discharged from the military because she was homosexual illustrates the application of the rational basis test.

PRUITT v. CHENEY
963 F.2d 1160 (9th Cir. 1992)

The appellant, Dusty Pruitt, served in the U.S. Army, rising to the rank of captain. She left active military service to seek ordination as a Methodist minister, which she obtained. She remained in the reserves and was notified of her selection for promotion to major.

It then came to the attention of the army that Pruitt was a lesbian and that she twice went through ''marriage ceremonies'' to other women. The military suspended her promotion and then honorably discharged her for being a practicing homosexual. On appeal, the federal district court dismissed her action. She appealed to the 9th Circuit Court of Appeals.

Figure 4–3   Three Tests for Equal Protection

Legislative Classification	Name of Test	Required Connection with Governmental Interest	Importance of Government's Interest
1. Economic Alienage-based restrictions for government jobs Age	Rational basis—almost complete deference to the legislature	Rationally relate	Legitimate
2. Gender	Intermediate—some deference to the legislature	Substantially relate	Important
3a. Suspect classifications: Race Religion National origin Alienage 3b. Ability to exercise fundamental rights: Voting Interstate travel Procreation	Strict scrutiny—wholly independent decision by the judiciary; almost no deference to the legislature	Necessarily relate	Compelling

CANBY, Judge

The Army does not contend that Pruitt has failed to allege that she was discriminated against because of her homosexuality. Instead, the Army argues that its right to discharge homosexual servicepersons is so firmly supported in the law that any equal protection claim that Pruitt has asserted or might assert is legally insufficient on its face.

The Army first relies on *Beller v. Middendorf,* in which we upheld the discharge from the Navy of three enlisted persons who had engaged in homosexual acts. In analyzing the Navy's actions under a due process standard, we held that there were several grounds on which the regulation could be upheld: "The Navy can act to protect the fabric of military life, to preserve the integrity of the recruiting process, to maintain the discipline of personnel in active service, and to insure the acceptance of men and women in the military, who are sometimes stationed in foreign countries with cultures different from our own."

Beller, however, is distinguishable. . . . [T]he servicepersons in that case were discharged for homosexual conduct, not homosexual status. Pruitt

does not dispute that the Army can discharge members for at least certain kinds of homosexual conduct, but she alleges that she was discharged for her status, with no evidence of conduct. . . .

Finally, one of the justifications offered by the Navy in *Beller* was the tension "between known homosexuals and other members who 'despise/detest homosexuality.'" To the degree that *Beller* may thus have rested on prejudice of others against homosexuals themselves, rather than on disapproval of specific acts of criminal conduct, its reasoning is undercut by *Palmore v. Sidoti.* In *Palmore,* the Supreme Court struck down a denial of custody of a child based on social disapproval of the interracial marriage of her mother. In so ruling, the Court said: "The Constitution cannot control such prejudices but neither can it tolerate them. Private biases may be outside the reach of the law, but the law cannot, directly or indirectly, give them effect." *Cleburne* made clear that this principle is not confined to instances of racial discrimination reviewed under strict scrutiny.

The next case upon which the government principally relies is *High Tech Gays v. Defense Indus. Security Clearance Office.* . . . In *High Tech Gays,* homosexual defense workers brought an equal protection challenge to the practice of the Department of Defense of routinely subjecting homosexuals to expanded investigations and adjudications prior to granting them security clearances. We rejected the contention that a classification of homosexuals was entitled to strict scrutiny, and instead required that the Department of Defense policy have a rational basis. We then found that the Department's policy had a rational basis because foreign intelligence agencies had been shown to target homosexuals as potentially vulnerable to compromise.

High Tech Gays will not, however, do the service the government asks of it. It is true that we found the discrimination against homosexuals in that case to have a rational basis, but it is clear that we applied the type of "active" rational basis review employed by the Supreme Court in *City of Cleburne v. Cleburne Living Center, Inc.* In *Cleburne,* the Supreme Court held that the City had failed to show a rational basis for its requirement that homes for the mentally retarded obtain a special permit, when other care and multiple-dwelling facilities needed no such permit. Relying on *Palmore,* the Court specifically rejected the legitimacy of relying on opposition to the home by neighbors. "Mere negative attitudes, or fear, unsubstantiated by factors which are properly cognizable in a zoning proceeding, are not permissible bases for treating a home for the mentally retarded differently from apartment houses, multiple dwellings, and the like. The Court observed that "this record does not clarify how, in this connection, the characteristics of the intended occupants of the . . . home rationally justify denying to those occupants what would be permitted to groups occupying the same site for different purposes."

In *High Tech Gays,* we relied on *Cleburne* and performed the same type of review to see whether the government had established on the record a rational basis for the challenged discrimination. The government submitted, and we reviewed declarations of officials that explained the practice of foreign intelligence agencies (notably the KGB) to target homosexuals. The declarations referred to and incorporated expert testimony to the same effect. Finally, we rejected as insufficient the plaintiffs' affidavits attempting to establish that the KGB's policy of targeting homosexuals was irrational; we ruled that the Department was entitled to take the KGB's practices into account even if they were irrational.

It is clear, then, that in *High Tech Gays,* upon plaintiffs' showing of discrimination, we required the government to establish on the record that its policy had a rational basis. The Supreme Court imposed the same requirement in *Cleburne.* Neither case supports the contention of the Army here that its far more rigid discrimination against homosexuals should be held to be rational as a matter of law, without any justification in the record at all. We have before us only a complaint that has been dismissed for failure to state a claim. After *Palmore, Cleburne* and *High Tech Gays,* we cannot say that the complaint is insufficient on its face. Assuming that Pruitt supports her allegations with evidence, we will not spare the Army the task, which those cases imposed, of offering a rational basis for its regulation, nor will we deprive Pruitt of the opportunity to contest that basis.

. . . The district court erred . . . in dismissing Pruitt's action on the ground that her complaint failed to state a claim for relief. . . . We reverse the judgment of dismissal, and remand for further appropriate proceedings, including those directed toward determining whether the Army's discrimination is rationally related to a permissible governmental purpose.

Case Questions

1. What issue does this case present?

2. What arguments might the government make that discrimination against homosexuals in the military has a rational basis? What are the counterarguments?

3. Are there any other constitutional arguments that Pruitt could make? Enumerate.

Strict Scrutiny Test

There are certain cases where the courts strictly scrutinize the government action and require the government to show that its purposes are overriding or compelling. When government classifies people on some "suspect" basis such as race, religion, or national origin, the court requires that the classification be necessary or mathematically relate to a compelling governmental interest. No statute has passed this very strict test since 1945.

The court also strictly reviews cases in which the government attempts to classify people in terms of their ability to exercise fundamental rights such as voting, the right to travel, or the right to procreate. Where the government burdens these fundamental rights, it must show that its burden is justified by an interest of compelling or overriding importance. This is known as the **strict scrutiny test.**

Intermediate Test

A middle level of review between strict scrutiny and the rational basis test, referred to as the **intermediate test,** has been applied to classifications based on gender. The court in these cases requires the classification to substantially relate to an important government objective. In *Mississippi University for Women v. Hogan,* the plaintiff, a male, applied for admission to the nursing program at the Mississippi University for Women (MUW),[3] a school that limited its enrollment to women. Although he was otherwise qualified, the plaintiff was denied admission solely because of his sex. The plaintiff alleged that

his right to equal protection had been violated. The U.S. Supreme Court agreed with him. Justice O'Connor said:

> Rather than compensate for discriminatory barriers faced by women, MUW's policy of excluding males from admission to the School of Nursing tends to perpetuate the steryotyped view of nursing as an exclusively women's job. By assuring that Mississippi allots more openings in its state-supported nursing schools to women than it does to men, MUW's admissions policy lends credibility to the old view that women, not men, should become nurses, and makes the assumption that nursing is a field for women a self-fulfilling prophecy.

■ ■ ■

Thus, considering both the asserted interest and the relationship between the interest and the methods used by the State, we conclude that the State has fallen far short of establishing the ''exceedingly persuasive justification'' needed to sustain the gender-based classification. Accordingly, we hold that MUW's policy of denying males the right to enroll for credit in its School of Nursing violates the Equal Protection Clause of the Fourteenth Amendment.

The following article makes a case for gender- and race-based reverse discrimination—discrimination against males and racial majorities.

[3]458 U.S. 718 (1982).

*Justice and Reverse Discrimination**

I shall adumbrate four aims in view of which a comprehensive social program of reverse discrimination may be justified. These are worthy goals which, were there no serious countervailing considerations, should surely be sufficient to justify preferential treatment.

1. *To ensure that past discrimination against females and blacks does not continue.* It takes some societies a long time to cease, finally and completely, patterns of injustice that have prevailed for generations. Legislative acts and constitutional amendments often simply do not do the job. A comprehensive, tightly administered social program involving reverse discrimination in hiring would help bring past and continuing injustice to a halt. Blacks and females may feel, quite understandably, that in order for them not to be discriminated *against* they must be discriminatingly *favored.*

2. *To offer, officially and explicitly, a symbolic denunciation of our racist and sexist past.* A program of reverse discrimination, suitably touted and carefully advertised, might serve well as such a symbol. Among other benefits, such a program could have the salutary effect of encouraging victims to work hard to offset the often sadly debilitating consequences of injustice. Further, this gesture might represent a confession of past wrong and a resolution to be more just. Employers might be encouraged voluntarily to stop discriminating against blacks and females.

*Source: Hardy E. Jones, ''Justice and Reverse Discrimination,'' 48 UMKC Law Rev. 506 (1980). Reprinted with permission.

3. *To provide role models for victimized blacks and females.* One good way for persons to shake off the shackles of past injustice is to become aware of others, relevantly similar to them, who have good jobs. By noting quite directly that these others are succeeding in respectable positions, persons may be encouraged to proceed vigorously in pursuit of satisfying careers for themselves.

4. *To compensate victims of discrimination by preferring them over beneficiaries of injustice.* It seems only just to give those who have been treated unjustly extra benefits and, in this way, to make some effort toward "evening the score." Those who benefit directly from the preferential treatment may not have been discriminated against, but they may have suffered from previous unjust acts toward their ancestors. The effects of past discriminatory acts may have deprived them of the wealth, education, health, and employment essential to equal-opportunity competition. The white males to be discriminated against may not have perpetrated the injustices, but many have greatly benefited from them. So it seems proper that they now be deprived of still further fruits, in the form of jobs, of past acts of unjust discrimination. This position may be buttressed by reflection on how people have come to have the qualifications they possess. The better-qualified white males might have been far less qualified had they not reaped the benefits of an unjust system which favored them at every turn. And the now lesser-qualified blacks and females might have been much better qualified if they and their ancestors had received equal, fair treatment from the start. The meritocratic view holds that persons deserved jobs on the basis of merit or ability—whatever their qualifications now happen to be. The position set out here rejects this "meritocracy of present qualifications." What is also relevant is how people have gotten qualifications and what their qualifications would have been in certain crucial aspects if their histories had been different.

The notion employed here may be thought of as "counterfactual meritocracy." On this view, people are deserving, at least within certain limits, of jobs on the basis of what their qualifications would have been if they had been neither victims nor beneficiaries of past injustice. The future qualifications of job applicants, as well as present and "what would have been" qualifications, are relevant. If a presently lesser-qualified person, a victim of past injustice, can increase his level of competence by being offered the position, then there is some reason for preferring him to a beneficiary of past injustice whose future qualifications will become no higher.

Thought Questions

1. Is reverse discrimination moral? Analyze.
2. How can one prove past discrimination? Is statistical underrepresentation one method? Is this method reliable?
3. Is reparation to a group as opposed to an individual just?
4. How would counterfactual meritocracy be shown?

Due Process Clause

The Fourteenth Amendment also acts as a bar against a state's deprivation or impairment of "any person's life, liberty, or property without due process of law." The Fifth Amendment similarly restricts the federal government from depriving these interests without **due process** of law.

The Due Process Clause applies to "persons." The Supreme Court has interpreted "person" to mean not only human beings, but also corporations and other business entities. As such, they are entitled to due process. The unborn and municipalities, however, have not been held to be persons under the Due Process Clause. Thus, they are not entitled to the Constitution's protection.

There are two aspects to the Due Process Clause according to the Supreme Court. First, the government may not deprive a person of these interests without following certain procedures. The evaluation of the fairness of the procedures followed by the government and the process due a person is the subject of the first aspect of due process. This is called **procedural due process.** When, however, the Court considers the substance of certain legislation and determines that the legislature's power is constitutionally limited, it is concerned with the second aspect of due process called **substantive due process.**

Procedural Due Process

Procedural due process breaks down into the questions: How much procedure is due and when are procedures due? Many procedures may be due persons when the government acts to deprive them of life, liberty, or property. Persons are entitled to, for example, timely and adequate notice detailing the reasons for a proposed action; an effective opportunity to defend by confronting and cross-examining witnesses; presentation of evidence and arguments; the right to an attorney; an impartial decisionmaker; and an appeal.

Not every case of a government's interference with a person's interests requires *all* of the above listed procedures. The precise combination of procedures due in a particular case will be determined by balancing the importance of the person's interest against the government's need for efficient action. A person who might be seriously injured by the government's action is entitled to more procedures than someone facing relatively minor injuries. Thus, all the procedures are required in a criminal trial where the defendant faces the loss of liberty. On the other hand, a student who is accused of academic misconduct at a state university or one where there is significant governmental participation and involvement such as in Industry University is entitled to fewer procedures since the potential consequences of such accusations are less serious than imprisonment. The extensiveness of procedures due is weighed against the government's need to act efficiently. Sometimes, the government must act swiftly to prevent injury to the public. For example, the Food and Drug Administration can order tainted drugs off the market before affording a corporation all of the procedures mentioned in this section.

The government must provide procedures to persons only when it impairs life, liberty, or property.

Many of the due process cases involving life center on the procedures due a person before the death penalty can be imposed for a capital offense. The issue of life has also arisen in the context of recent medical technologies.

The U.S. Supreme Court appears to have recognized a constitutional right of a person to refuse food and hydration when there is no reasonable medical hope of recovery from a vegetative state. However, the court noted that there must be a balance of that right of the patient against the state interest of protecting life.[4] These "life and death" matters continue to be fleshed out in the courts. Many states have enacted living will statutes, affording people an opportunity to clearly express their interests in this regard in a formal instrument that will be respected (see Chapter 10).

Liberty not only includes physical liberty—that is, freedom from imprisonment or involuntary civil commitment to a mental hospital—but also much of the Bill of Rights (see Figure 4–4). These rights, incorporated into the Due Process Clause through the word *liberty,* will be discussed in the next section under Substantive Due Process.

Property is a very difficult term to define in modern society, for it no longer merely embraces the ownership of land or personal property such as stocks or jewelry. Many of a person's financial interests now include pensions, social security, medical benefits, welfare, governmental employment, public education, and a variety of licenses. The Supreme Court formerly considered these benefits to be mere privileges that could be withdrawn by the government without any procedures. The distinction between rights and privileges has now largely collapsed. Since the 1970s, each of these interests has been described as a statutory entitlement, a form of property. If a person meets the minimum standard necessary to be entitled to the benefit, the governmental benefit cannot be taken away without due process.

Substantive Due Process

When the Court considers the fairness of a legislative act, rather than the procedures due a person to enforce the act, it is concerned with substantive due process. In earlier days of this country, the limit on the government's power was found in the unwritten law of

---

[4]*Cruzan v. Director, Missouri Dep't of Health,* 497 U.S. 261 (1990).

Figure 4–4	Bill of Rights
Amendment	**Content**
First	No state religion Freedom of religion Freedom of speech Freedom of press Freedom of assembly Right to petition government
Second	Right to bear arms
Third	Right to refuse housing to soldiers in peacetime
Fourth	Freedom from unreasonable searches and seizures Warrants issued only on probable cause
Fifth	Right against being tried twice for the same offense Privilege against self-incrimination Due process Eminent domain
Sixth	Right to speedy trial in criminal cases Right to confront witnesses Right to subpoena witnesses Right to counsel
Seventh	Right to jury trial in civil cases when amount exceeds $20
Eighth	No excessive bail No cruel and unusual punishment
Ninth	Enumeration of rights shall not deny those retained by people
Tenth	All powers not delegated are reserved to the states or people

"nature and nature's God." When this "law above the law" was violated by the legislature, the Declaration of Independence declared the appropriate remedy to be revolution. Another more restrained remedy is to have the courts void the legislative act.

Beginning in the 1890s, the Supreme Court declared that the term *liberty* in the Fourteenth Amendment included liberty of contract. According to the Supreme Court (up until 1937), the Due Process Clause limited government's power to interfere in the marketplace or with a person's ability to contract freely. By injecting the word *liberty* with the economic theory prevalent at the time—laissez-faire capitalism—the Court used the Due Process Clause to invalidate over 175 state statutes, including many maximum hour, minimum wage, and employment safety statutes.

The court backed away from this economic use of the Due Process Clause during the Depression. In 1937, enraged that so many of his economic plans were struck down by the Supreme Court, President Roosevelt proposed that six additional justices be added to the court. Though unsuccessful in "packing" the court with friendly justices, his threat caused the Court to abandon the economic theories that were limiting legislation designed to create jobs and stimulate the economy.

Despite the demise of economic limits on legislation, the Court still employs the Due Process Clause as a higher law to substantively limit a legislature's power. Incorporated in the word *liberty* today are most of the Bill of Rights and other rights that are so ingrained in our tradition as to be fundamental.

The Bill of Rights (the first 10 amendments to the Constitution) were by their terms only applicable to the federal government. By incorporating the Bill of Rights into the 14th Amendment Due Process Clause, the Supreme Court has declared a substantive limit on a state's power to abridge constitutional rights.

The Due Process Clause was further utilized by the Supreme Court in the 1970s to invalidate legislation that limited a woman's liberty to have an abortion and an individual's liberty to use contraceptives. Thus, although governmental power to enact legislation is no longer limited by economic theories, there are many other liberties that still substantively limit state legislation.

Takings Clause

To achieve certain desirable common goals such as building highways, schools, and bridges, the government must take private property from landowners. Property rights in things other than land also may be invaded by the government. The government's power to take private property is called the power of **eminent domain.** To protect landowners and others from the federal government's invasion of their property rights, the framers of the Constitution included in the Fifth Amendment a Takings Clause. This clause reads:

[N]or shall private property be taken for public use without just compensation.

The Fifth Amendment Takings Clause has also been made applicable to the states through the Fourteenth Amendment Due Process Clause.

Three issues arise in eminent domain cases. First, has the government taken *property?* Many regulations, though impairing the value of private property, do not rise to the level of taking. The government may impose zoning limits or building codes on a landowner without any compensation for the devaluation of the land. The city of St. Paul, for instance, passed a zoning ordinance that prohibited the erection of high-rise buildings in a certain area. Since the land could not be used most profitably, the private landowners contended that the city, through its zoning ordinance, had ''taken'' their land and they were entitled to be justly compensated. The court, however, held that no taking occurred despite the property's devaluation. How serious the devaluation must be before an ordinance will be consid-

ered a taking is a matter of much judicial debate. It is clear, however, that zoning ordinances may not be ''hidden'' exercises of eminent domain powers. Some zoning ordinances are mere shams and require the government to justly compensate landowners for a taking.

The second issue that arises in the eminent domain cases is whether the private property has been taken for a *public use.* This requirement has been broadly construed by the Supreme Court to include any taking for the ''benefit of the health, safety and welfare of the citizens.'' Since this encompasses most of what the government wishes to do anyway, few recent cases have limited the eminent domain power by this requirement that the land be taken for a public use. In fact, even the taking of property to be resold to a private company that will create jobs and generate new taxes has been deemed ''for public use.''

The third issue that arises in eminent domain cases is how much compensation is due a property owner when his or her land is taken. The Fifth Amendment requires *just compensation.* The standard normally applied is one of market value, based upon the highest and best use of the property. This usually necessitates an appraisal.

The following case concerning pamphlet distribution in a private shopping center involves Takings Clause considerations.

PRUNEYARD SHOPPING CENTER v. ROBINS
447 U.S. 74 (1980)

The appellant, PruneYard, is a privately owned shopping center in the city of Campbell, California. It covers approximately 21 acres. Five acres are devoted to parking, while the remaining 16 acres are occupied by walkways, plazas, sidewalks, and buildings that contain more than 65 specialty shops, 10 restaurants, and a movie theater. The PruneYard is open to the public. It has a policy not to permit any visitor or tenant to engage in any publicly expressive activity, including the circulation of petitions, that is not directly related to its commercial purposes. This policy has been strictly enforced in a nondiscriminatory fashion.

The appellees are high school students who sought to solicit support for their opposition to a United Nations resolution against ''Zionism.'' On a Saturday afternoon, the students set up a card table in a corner of PruneYard's central courtyard. They distributed pamphlets and asked passersby to sign petitions, which were to be sent to the president and members of Congress. Their activity was peaceful and orderly and so far as the record indicates, was not objected to by PruneYard's patrons.

Soon after the appellees had begun soliciting signatures, a security guard informed them that they would have to leave because their activity violated PruneYard regulations. The guard suggested that they move to the public sidewalk at the PruneYard's perimeter. The appellees immediately left the premises and later filed a lawsuit in the California Superior Court of Santa Clara County. They sought to enjoin appellants from denying them access to the PruneYard for the purpose of circulating their petitions.

The Superior Court held that appellees were not entitled under either the federal or California Constitution to exercise their asserted rights on the shopping center property. The California Court of Appeal affirmed.

The California Supreme Court reversed, holding that the California Constitution protects ''speech and petitioning, reasonably exercised, in shopping centers even when the centers are privately owned.'' It concluded that the appellees were entitled to conduct their activity on PruneYard property. A petition for certiorari to the U.S. Supreme Court was granted.

REHNQUIST, Justice

Appellants . . . contend that a right to exclude others underlies the Fifth Amendment guarantee against the taking of property without just compensation and the Fourteenth Amendment guarantee against the deprivation of property without due process of law.

It is true that one of the essential sticks in the bundle of property rights is the right to exclude others. And here there has literally been a ''taking'' of the right to the extent that the California Supreme Court has interpreted the State Constitution to entitle its citizens to exercise free expression and petition rights on shopping center property. But it is well established that ''not every destruction or injury to property by governmental action has been held to be a 'taking' in the constitutional sense. Rather, the determination whether a state law unlawfully infringes a landowner's property in violation of the Taking Clause requires an examination of whether the restriction on private property 'force[s]' some people alone to bear public burdens which, in all fairness and justice, should be borne by the public as a whole. This examination entails inquiry into such factors as the character of the governmental action, its economic impact, and its interference with reasonable investment-backed expectations. When 'regulation goes too far it will be recognized as a taking.' ''

Here the requirement that appellants permit appellees to exercise state-protected rights of free expression and petition on shopping center property clearly does not amount to an unconstitutional infringement of appellants' property rights under the Taking Clause. There is nothing to suggest that preventing appellants from prohibiting this sort of activity will unreasonably impair the value or use of their property as a shopping center. The PruneYard is a large commercial complex that covers several city blocks, contains numerous separate business establishments, and is open to the public at large. The decision of the California Supreme Court makes it clear that the PruneYard may restrict expressive activity by adopting time, place, and manner regulations that will minimize any interference with its commercial functions. Appellees were orderly, and they limited their activity to the common areas of the shopping center. In these circumstances, the fact that they may have ''physically invaded'' appellants' property cannot be viewed as determinative. A State is, of course, bound by the Just Compensation Clause of the Fifth Amendment, but here applicants have failed to demonstrate that the ''right to exclude others'' is so essential to the use or economic value of their property that the state-authorized limitations of it amounted to a ''taking.'' [The California Supreme Court decision was affirmed.]

Case Questions

1. What is the issue in this case?
2. Does *PruneYard* hold that anyone has the constitutional right to distribute leaflets in a shopping center? Analyze.
3. Why did the court hold that depriving the shopping center of the right to exclude those exercising speech was not a violation of the Takings Clause? Under what circumstances might a deprivation be deemed to interfere with ''reasonable investment-backed expectations''?
4. Analyze: ''Here the requirement that appellants permit appellees to exercise *state-protected rights* of free expression and petition on shopping center property clearly does not amount to an unconstitutional infringement of appellants' property rights under the Taking Clause.''

First Amendment

The First Amendment to the Constitution protects associational interests, speech, the press, assembly, and worship and permits petitioning the government. Perhaps it was not accidental that these ''fundamental concepts of ordered liberty'' were located in the First Amendment.

Several reasons have been suggested for the Constitution's protection of free speech. The colonists wished to check the power of the central government by guaranteeing people the liberty to openly criticize its faults.

Another theory is the marketplace theory of free speech. The test of a product is its acceptance in the competition of the market. Likewise, under this theory, the best test of truth is the power of the thought to be accepted in the marketplace's competition of ideas. The notion is that only in a society in which all ideas are allowed to be freely expressed will the best and truest ideas be accepted by the people. Others point to the value of free speech for promoting individual potential and its importance to a democracy.

Despite the variety of theories used to support free speech, it is abundantly clear that the First Amendment has never been absolute. Substantial areas of speech are not protected by the First Amendment. Obscenity statutes, if properly drawn, are constitutionally permissible. The government may also regulate the time, place, and manner of speech. For example, under an antinoise statute, a city could prohibit a roving sound truck from blaring its message at 4 A.M. in the morning. In addition, the government can restrain speech if it presents a clear and present danger of physical harm. Further, where the government has a compelling or overriding interest, such as protecting secret CIA information important to our national security, it may impinge on one's right to free speech. Finally, according to the Supreme Court, **commercial speech** enjoys less protection than political speech.

Advertisements of a product such as pharmaceuticals or a service such as legal services have been held to be commercial speech. Thus, a state may regulate attorney solicitations of clients in ways that would be impermissible if applied to pure speech.

Corporations enjoy the same free speech rights as other citizens. The following case discusses the commercial speech doctrine in the context of a law prohibiting certain advertisements by gambling casinos.

POSADAS DE PUERTO RICO ASSOCIATES v. TOURISM COMPANY
478 U.S. 328 (1986)

In 1948, Puerto Rico legalized certain forms of casino gambling. This law (amended several times since) prohibited the advertisement of gambling parlors within Puerto Rico. In 1978, the appellant, Posadas de Puerto Rico, was fined twice by the agency charged with enforcing the antiadvertisement law, the Tourism Company, for violating the law. The appellant challenged the law, claiming it violated the appellant's First Amendment free speech rights. The Superior Court of Puerto Rico determined that the law as applied to the appellant was constitutional. The Puerto Rico Supreme Court affirmed. The U.S. Supreme Court granted certiorari to review this judgment.

REHNQUIST, Justice

Because this case involves the restriction of pure commercial speech which does ''no more than propose a commercial transaction'' . . . our First Amendment analysis is guided by the general principles identified in *Central Hudson Gas and Electric Corp. v. Public Service Commission*. . . . Under *Central Hudson*, commercial speech receives a limited form of First Amendment protection so long as it concerns a lawful activity and is not misleading or fraudulent. Once it is determined that the First Amendment applies to the particular kind of commercial speech at issue, then the speech may be restricted only if the government's interest in doing so is substantial, the restrictions directly advance the government's asserted interest, and the restrictions are no more extensive than necessary to serve that interest.

The particular kind of commercial speech at issue here, namely, advertising of casino gambling aimed at the residents of Puerto Rico, concerns a lawful activity and is not misleading or fraudulent, at least in the abstract. We must therefore proceed to the three remaining steps of the *Central Hudson* analysis in order to determine whether Puerto Rico's advertising restrictions run afoul of the First Amendment. The first of these three steps involves an assessment of the strength of the government's interest in restricting the speech. The interest at stake in this case, as determined by the Superior Court, is the reduction of demand for casino gambling by the residents of Puerto Rico. Appellant acknowledged the existence of this interest in its letter to the Tourism Company. ("The legislators wanted the tourists to flock to the casinos to gamble, but not our own people.") The Tourism Company's brief before this Court explains the legislature's belief that "[e]xcessive casino gambling among local residents . . . would produce serious harmful effects on the health, safety and welfare of the Puerto Rico citizens, such as the disruption of moral and cultural patterns, the increase in local crime, the fostering of prostitution, the development of corruption, and the infiltration of organized crime." These are some of the very same concerns, of course, that have motivated the vast majority of the 50 States to prohibit casino gambling. We have no difficulty in concluding that the Puerto Rico Legislature's interest in the health, safety, and welfare of its citizens constitutes a "substantial" government interest.

The last two steps of the *Central Hudson* analysis basically involve a consideration of the "fit" between the legislature's ends and the means chosen to accomplish those ends. Step three asks the question whether the challenged restrictions on commerical speech "directly advance" the government's asserted interest. In the instant case, the answer to this question is clearly "yes." The Puerto Rico Legislature obviously believed, when it enacted the advertising restrictions at issue here, that advertising of casino gambling aimed at the residents of Puerto Rico would serve to increase the demand for the product advertised. We think the legislature's belief is a reasonable one.

Appellant argues, however, that the challenged advertising restrictions are underinclusive because other kinds of gambling such as horse racing, cockfighting, and the lottery may be advertised to the residents of Puerto Rico. Appellant's argument is misplaced for two reasons. First, whether other kinds of gambling are advertised in Puerto Rico or not, the restrictions on advertising of casino gambling "directly advance" the legislature's interest in reducing demand for games of chance. . . . Second, the legislature's interest, as previously identified, is not necessarily to reduce demand for all games of chance, but to reduce demand for casino gambling. According to the Superior Court, horse racing, cockfighting, "picas," or small games of chance at fiestas, and the lottery "have been traditionally part of the Puerto Rican's roots," so that "the legislation could have been more flexible than in authorizing more sophisticated games which are not so widely sponsored by the people." In other words, the legislature felt that for Puerto Ricans the risks associated with casino gambling were significantly greater than those associated with the more traditional kinds of gambling in Puerto Rico. In our view, the legislature's separate classification of casino gambling, for purposes of the advertising ban, satisfies the third step of the *Central Hudson* analysis.

We also think it clear . . . that the challenged statute and regulations satisfy the fourth and last step of the *Central Hudson* analysis, namely, whether the restrictions on commercial speech are no more extensive than necessary to serve the government's interest. The narrowing constructions of the advertising restrictions announced by the Superior Court ensure that the restrictions will not affect advertising of casino gambling aimed at tourists, but will apply only to such advertising when aimed at the residents of Puerto Rico. Appellant contends, however, that the First Amendment requires the Puerto Rico Legislature to reduce demand for casino gambling among the residents of Puerto Rico not by suppressing commercial speech that might *encourage* such gambling, but by promulgating additional speech designed to *discourage* it. We reject this contention. We think it is up to the legislature to decide whether or not such a "counterspeech" policy would be as effective in reducing the demand for casino gambling as a restriction on advertising. The legislature could conclude, as it apparently did here, that residents of Puerto Rico are already aware of the risks of casino gambling, yet would nevertheless be induced by widespread advertising to engage in such potentially harmful conduct. . . .

In short, we conclude that the statute and regulations at issue in this case, as construed by the Superior Court, pass muster under each prong of the *Central Hudson* test. We therefore hold that the Supreme Court of Puerto Rico properly rejected appellant's First Amendment claim.

For the foregoing reasons, the decision of the Supreme Court of Puerto Rico that, as construed by the Superior Court, section 8 of the Games of Chance Act of 1948 and the implementing regulations do not facially violate the First Amendment or the due process or equal protection guarantees of the Constitution, is affirmed.

Case Questions

1. Could the appellants have asserted any constitutional violations other than the First Amendment? Explain.

2. Why does the First Amendment provide less protection for commercial speech than non-commercial speech?

3. When can the government regulate commercial speech? How can the government regulate speech?

4. Identify the court's language that holds the ordinance to be a violation of the First Amendment?

Fourth Amendment

The Fourth Amendment to the Constitution prohibits unreasonable searches and seizures and provides that search warrants be issued only on a finding of probable cause by the government. With the growth of administrative agencies, an increasing number of businesses have been subjected to administrative inspection. These might include an inspection by an agent of the Occupational Safety and Health Administration (OSHA) to determine if a business is complying with health and safety regulations. Or an inspector from the U.S. Environmental Protection Agency might wish to inspect the premises of a business to check its compliance with the Clean Air Act or Clean Water Act. The issue arises whether such inspectors must obtain a search warrant before they may enter on the land of an employer without consent.

In 1978, the landmark ruling of *Marshall v. Barlow's Inc.* held the Fourth Amendment applicable to administrative investigations. In that case, the attempted warrantless search of an electrical and plumbing installation business by an OSHA inspector was held violative of the Fourth Amendment proscription against "unreasonable searches and seizures."[5] However, searches of businesses that are traditionally highly regulated, such as firearms merchants and pawn brokers, have less of an expectancy of privacy, and under certain circumstances warrantless searches are constitutional. (See *New York v. Burger* in Chapter 5.)

END–OF–CHAPTER QUESTIONS

1. Compare the American constitutional system and the British constitutional system.

2. Comment on the following:
   a. "It should not be up to the courts to determine when life begins."
   b. "The Second Amendment to the Constitution prohibits gun control."
   c. "The First Amendment Establishment of Religion Clause would prevent the government from giving financial support to private religious schools."

3. What values are served by the Equal Protection Clause? Does this clause require equal opportunities and/or equal results?

4. What arguments can be made in favor of an activist approach to interpreting the Constitution? What arguments can be made in favor of judicial restraint?

5. The plaintiff, Irvis, was refused service by Moose Lodge because he was black. Irvis brought an action alleging an equal protection violation. State action was claimed to be present because the lodge was licensed by the Pennsylvania Liquor Authority. Is the state action requirement met here? See *Moose Lodge v. Irvis*, 407 U.S. 163 (1972).

6. A state zoning statute provided that no low-rent housing projects could be developed in any community until approved by a majority of voters in a community refer-

---

[5]*Marshall v. Barlow's, Inc.*, 436 U.S. 307 (1978).

endum. Should a classification based on one's wealth be tested by the economic classification test or the racial classification test? See *James v. Valtierra,* 402 U.S. 137 (1971). What about a city zoning ordinance that excludes group homes for the mentally retarded unless a special use permit is granted? What test of equal protection should apply? Would this city ordinance pass this test? See *City of Cleburne v. Cleburne Living Center,* 473 U.S. 432 (1985).

7. The Hawaii state legislature passed a Land Reform Act (LRA) giving the Hawaii Housing Authority the right to condemn certain leased property to "effectuate the public purposes." It then acquired the land, giving just compensation to the owners. The purpose behind the LRA was to break up concentrated land ownership that was responsible for "skewing the State's residential [housing] . . . market, inflating land prices, and injuring the public tranquility and welfare." May the state legislature do this without running afoul of the Takings Clause of the Fifth Amendment as made applicable to the states through the Fourteenth Amendment? Analyze. See *Hawaii Housing Authority v. Midkiff,* 467 U.S. 229 (1984).

8. A public utility was prohibited by a regulatory agency from including pronuclear advertising in its bills to consumers. Is the advertising commercial speech? Would such a prohibition violate the First Amendment? What arguments could be raised in defense of the prohibition? See *Central Hudson Gas & Electric Corp. v. Public Service Commission of New York,*

447 U.S. 557 (1980). What about the reverse—that is, *requiring* a utility to place consumer group announcements in its billing envelopes? Is a statutory requirement to disseminate the views of an opponent a violation of the First Amendment? See *Pacific Gas and Electric Co. v. Public Utilities Commission of California,* 475 U.S.1 (1986).

9. A rule of the Minnesota Agricultural Society, a government corporation that operates the public state fair, prohibits the distribution of any merchandise or printed material unless it is from a licensed location on the fairgrounds. Space in the fairgrounds is rented in a nondiscriminatory manner on a first-come, first-served basis. The International Society for Krishna Consciousness, Inc. (ISCON), maintains that the rule violates its First Amendment rights to distribute religious literature and solicit donations. Is ISCON correct? Analyze. *Lee Heffron v. International Society for Krishna Consciousness, Inc.,* 452 U.S. 640 (1981).

10. A California regulatory scheme permitted the warrantless search of child day-care facilities, including private homes that are used as day-care centers at any time of day. Day-care centers are heavily regulated in California. The concern of the legislature was to protect the health and safety of children by eliminating such hazards as overcapacity, accessibility to poisonous materials, open pools, and sexual abuse. Is the California warrantless search scheme constitutional as applied to private homes? See *Rush v. Obledo,* 756 F.2d 713 (9th Cir. 1985).

Chapter 5

Administrative Agencies

CRITICAL THINKING INQUIRIES

As you read this chapter, you should be able to address the following:

- How does the U.S. Constitution impact the administrative agency process?
- Analyze the impact of the following acts on administrative agencies:
  —Administrative Procedures Act.
  —Freedom of Information Act.
  —Government in Sunshine Act.
  —Privacy Act.
- Compare and contrast the three major administrative agency functions.
- Analyze judicial review of administrative agency action.

MANAGERIAL PERSPECTIVE

Toys 'n Shop is a national manufacturer and distributor of children's toys. The Consumer Product Safety Commission (CPSC) has become aware that a number of toddlers have been injured or have died when they were caught in the lid of a toy chest. The CPSC has proposed a rule that would ban toy chests with lids. Toys 'n Shop is aware of the proposed rule and strongly opposes it.

- What should Toys 'n Shop do?
- What arguments against the ban can be made?
- What are the CPSC's alternatives?

Businesses need to be smart when it comes to government regulations. Many, like Toys 'n Shop, keep an eye on proposed government regulations and quickly respond to them. In fact, business and industry should have learned the lesson that failure to self-regulate results in more government regulation.

The more traditional sources of the law are: legislative, executive, and judicial. Quite recently, in terms of American political history, there has emerged an additional source of law—the administrative agency. Constituting the "fourth branch" of government, the administrative branch is the principal tool by which governments (both federal and state) regulate the activities of businesses and citizens.

The pervasiveness of agency influence on business cannot be understated. Some of the common areas of regulation within the workplace include:

- The manufacture and sale of various consumable foods and drugs by the Food and Drug Administration (FDA).
- The impact of industrial activities on air, water, and soil by the Environmental Protection Agency (EPA).
- Stock-trading practices, shareholders' rights, and actions by the Securities and Exchange Commission (SEC).
- Safety concerns in the workplace by the Occupational Health and Safety Administration (OSHA).
- The obligation to pay taxes, regulated by the Internal Revenue Service (IRS).

The goal of this chapter is to present the constitutional underpinnings of the administrative agency and its limitations, functions, and powers.

CONSTITUTIONAL BACKGROUND OF THE ADMINISTRATIVE AGENCY

The American Republic was intentionally placed on the two-tiered foundation composed of state and federal governmental powers. The federal power was expressly divided into three departments: executive, legislative, and judicial. This separation of powers idea was first set forth in the Utopian writings of Baron Montesque and strongly asserted in the *Federalist* papers by James Madison, Alexander Hamilton, and John Jay.

The framers of the Constitution, most of whom had business experience, were aware of the effects that disruptions to peaceful commerce entailed. These disruptions had plagued Europe and were brought about by wars based on everything from religious enmity to disagreements among monarchs. Consequently, the framers sought to ensure peaceful transition of power from one generation to the next.

The separation of governmental powers, with the attendant checks and balances one on the other, was intended to keep the individuals in one branch of government from assuming a preeminent position over the others and ultimately the federal government (see Figure 4–1 on page 75).

Checks and Balances

Article I of the U.S. Constitution requires every bill passed by the House and Senate to be signed into law by the president and, if vetoed, to be repassed by two thirds of Congress. In 1980, Congress passed the Federal Trade Commission Improvements Act, which permitted Congress to veto Federal Trade Commission trade regulation rules without prior approval or signature by the president. A similar congressional veto of executive action (without signature by the president) was also enacted pursuant to the Immigration and Naturalization Act. However, the Supreme Court, in *Immigration and Naturalization Service v. Chadha,*[1] struck down this Congressional procedure as an unconstitutional violation of the principle of checks and balances. The Court in *Chadha* stated:

It is beyond doubt that lawmaking was a power *to be shared* by both Houses and the President. . . . Presentment to the President and the Presidential veto were considered so imperative that the draftsmen took special pains to assure that these requirements could not be circumvented.

Preemption

Article VI, clause 2, establishes what is known as the **Supremacy Clause:** The Constitution, laws, and treaties of the United States are to be considered the supreme law of the land. Thus, where a federal law and a state law come into conflict, the federal law prevails. The **preemption doctrine** derives from this clause and, briefly summarized, states that

---

[1] 462 U.S. 919 (1983).

whenever federal regulation of a subject area is so pervasive, it is considered that Congress did not intend that the states create supplemental laws. Accordingly, the state laws are considered unconstitutional due to Congress's preemption of the area. Thus, federally created administrative agencies are usually considered to have preeminent authority within those areas subject to their regulation.

An excellent example of the preemption doctrine is presented by the decision of the U.S. Supreme Court in *Burbank v. Lockheed Air Terminal, Inc.*[2] In that case, the municipal government of Burbank, California, prohibited jets from taking off at the Burbank airport between 11 P.M. and 7 A.M. The Court, after reviewing federal law in the area, concluded as follows:

> The pervasive control [of noise] . . . under the . . . [Noise Control] Act seems to us to leave no room for local curfews or other local controls. . . . The interdependence of factors requires a uniform and exclusive system of federal regulation if the congressional objectives . . . are to be fulfilled.

Creation of an Administrative Agency

Most agencies are created by the legislature, which must authorize the expenditure of funds without which an agency could not hire employees, lease or construct office space, or generally incur operating expenses. Constraints on elected officials do not permit individual legislators to do more than govern in the quite general sense. It thus becomes necessary for legislative bodies to make specific delegations of authority to bodies created to act as instrumentalities of the legislature. The same rationale applies to agencies created by the executive branch of government.

In order for the legislative branch to create an administrative agency, it must possess constitutional enumerated power to regulate the specific area. Perhaps the most important of the enumerated powers of Congress with respect to the relationship between administrative agencies and businesses is the **Commerce Clause.** Under the Commerce Clause, Congress has the power ''To regulate Commerce . . . among the several States.'' Based on this clause, the Supreme Court recognized that Congress has the power to regulate any activity that affects interstate commerce. In a world that is shrinking rapidly,

hardly any activity does not affect interstate commerce in some way. Hence, Congress is permitted to regulate such industries as communications, transportation, securities, real estate and manufacturing. Even civil rights and prostitution have been held to be within the meaning of commerce.

The enactment of the law creating an agency is called **enabling legislation.** Enabling legislation usually determines the purpose and scope of activity within which the agency is to function. The enabling provisions ordinarily are phrased in quite general terms, which of course allows the agency to exercise considerable discretion in implementing the legislative mandate.

Enabling legislation establishes the agency and delegates in intelligible terms the area within which the agency is to regulate. In addition, it typically includes provisions that the head of the agency shall be appointed by the executive branch; that the agency's actions are subject to judicial review; and that the agency must act according to the provisions of the Administrative Procedures Act.

ADMINISTRATIVE PROCEDURES ACT

Congress enacted the Administrative Procedures Act (APA) in 1946. This Act provides that all federal agencies are required to comply with its provisions unless specifically exempted by the agency's enabling legislation or a subsequent statute. For example, the APA is made expressly inapplicable to military commissions, the Congress, and the entire judicial branch.

The APA was intended to provide for uniformity, impartiality, and fairness in the administrative process. As a comprehensive statute, it was intended to provide for all phases of agency activity. It serves as an agency's rule book.

The federal APA also functions as a model act for state legislatures, and has had a wide impact similar to that of such model acts as the Uniform Commercial Code and the Uniform Partnership Act. Almost all states have adopted it, either wholly or in part, for the regulation of that state's agencies.

FREEDOM OF INFORMATION ACT

From the very beginning, there has been a concern about the secrecy with which agencies operate. Initially, agencies were not required to divulge their

---

[2] 411 U.S. 624 (1973).

activities to the public. Obviously, such secrecy effectively barred the public from meaningful participation at any level, whether for the purpose of criticism or approval. Without information, lobbying activity to obtain legislative changes of specific agency activities was hampered.

Congress, in 1966, passed the **Freedom of Information Act (FOIA).** Its purpose was "to enable the public to have sufficient information in order to be able, through the electoral process, to make intelligent, informed choices with respect to the nature, scope, and procedure of federal government activities."

Procedures under FOIA

Any member of the public may send a letter to the director of an agency in order to request information. The letter need only set forth the requested information and need not follow any particular format. The agency has 10 days in which to respond. It may state its intention to release the information and thereafter promptly do so. It may also deny access to the requested information, in which event the person seeking the information can appeal to the agency by letter. The agency must respond within 20 days. If it

---

Figure 5–1   FOIA Exemptions

1. National security and foreign policy.
2. Internal personnel rules and practices.
3. Subsequent statutory provisions.
4. Trade secrets and commercial and/or financial information.
5. Letters and reports stating opinions that are part of internal deliberations.
6. Protection from unwarranted invasions of privacy.
7. Law enforcement records and investigative reports.
8. Records of financial institutions.
9. Oil well information.

---

does not, or if its response is to deny the request, then the person may file a lawsuit in the nearest U.S. district court, seeking disclosure.

Exemptions under FOIA

Agencies may refuse to provide information requested if they are able to demonstrate any of nine exemptions which are listed in Figure 5–1. The following case illustrates the extent of the "invasion of privacy" exemption.

DEPARTMENT OF STATE v. RAY
112 Sup.Ct. 541 (1991)

The secretary of the State Department obtained assurances from the Haitian government that it would not prosecute Haitians intercepted by the United States and returned to Haiti. The State Department, the petitioner, thereafter monitored that assurance by interviewing Haitian returnees. The respondents, Haitian nationals, sought political asylum for the Haitians on the basis that they would face persecution on returning home. They sought copies of the State Department's interview reports under the Freedom of Information Act (FOIA). They received 17 documents from which the names and other identifying information were removed. The State Department cited FOIA exemption 6, which exempts "personnel and medical files . . . which constitute a clearly unwarranted invasion of personal privacy." The District Court ordered the State Department to produce the excised material. The Court of Appeals affirmed, finding that the returnees' privacy interests were outweighed by the public interest. On petition by the State Department, the U.S. Supreme Court granted certiorari.

STEVENS, Justice

The Freedom of Information Act was enacted to facilitate public access to Government documents. The statute was designed "to pierce the veil of administrative secrecy and to open agency action to the light of public scrutiny." Consistent with this purpose, as well as the plain language of the Act, the strong presumption in favor of disclosure places the burden on the agency to justify the withholding of any requested documents.

. . . The question in this case is whether the Government has discharged its burden of demonstrating that the disclosure of the contents of the interviews with the Haitian returnees adequately served the statutory purpose and that the release of the information identifying the particular interviewees would constitute a clearly unwarranted invasion of their privacy.

. . . [T]he text of the exemption requires the court to balance ''the individual's right of privacy'' against the basic policy of opening ''agency action to the light of public scrutiny.'' The District Court and the Court of Appeals properly began their analysis by considering the significance of the privacy interest at stake. We are persuaded, however, that several factors, when considered together, make the privacy interest more substantial than the Court of Appeals recognized.

First, the Court of Appeals appeared to assume that respondents sought only the names and addresses of the interviewees. But respondents sought—and the District Court ordered that the Government disclose—the unredacted interview summaries. As the Government points out, many of these summaries contain personal details about particular interviewees. Thus, if the summaries are released without the names redacted, highly personal information regarding marital and employment status, children, living conditions, and attempts to enter the United States, would be linked publicly with particular, named individuals.

In addition, disclosure of the unredacted interview summaries would publicly identify the interviewees as people who cooperated with a State Department investigation of the Haitian Government's compliance with its promise to the United States Government not to prosecute the returnees. The Court of Appeals failed to acknowledge the significance of this fact. As the State Department explains, disclosure of the interviewees' identities could subject them or their families to embarrassment in their social and community relationships. More importantly, this group of interviewees occupies a special status: they left their homeland in violation of Haitian law and are protected from prosecution by their government's assurance to the State Department. Although the Department's monitoring program indicates that that assurance has been fulfilled, it nevertheless remains true that the State Department considered the danger of mistreatment sufficiently real to necessitate that monitoring program.

We are also persuaded that the Court of Appeals gave insufficient weight to the fact that the interviews had been conducted pursuant to an assurance of confidentiality. We agree that such a promise does not necessarily prohibit disclosure, but it has a special significance in this case. Not only is it apparent that an interviewee who had been given such an assurance might have been willing to discuss private matters that he or she would not otherwise expose to the public—and therefore would regard a subsequent interview by a third party armed with that information as a special affront to his or her privacy—but, as discussed above, it is also true that the risk of mistreatment gives this group of interviewees an additional interest in assuring that their anonymity is maintained.

Finally, we cannot overlook the fact that respondents plan to make direct contact with the individual Haitian returnees identified in the reports. As the Court of Appeals properly recognized, the intent to interview the returnees magnifies the importance of maintaining the confidentiality of their identities.

Although the interest in protecting the privacy of the redacted information is substantial, we must still consider the importance of the public interest in its disclosure. For unless the invasion of privacy is ''clearly unwarranted,'' the public interest in disclosure must prevail. As we have repeatedly recognized, FOIA's basic policy of ''full agency disclosure unless information is exempted under clearly delineated statutory language'' . . . focuses on the citizens' right to be informed about ''what government is up to.'' Thus, the Court of Appeals properly recognized that the public interest in knowing whether the State Department has adequately monitored Haiti's compliance with its promise not to prosecute returnees is cognizable under FOIA. We are persuaded, however, that this public interest has been adequately served by disclosure of the redacted interview summaries and that disclosure of the unredacted documents would therefore constitute a clearly unwarranted invasion of the interviewees' privacy. The Judgement of the Court of Appeals is reversed.

Case Questions

1. What is the issue in this case?
2. What additional information might be derived from further interviews with the Haitian returnees that would be helpful to the respondents?

3. Under what circumstances would the revelation of the returnees' names outweigh the privacy interests?

4. Are there any other avenues that respondents may have utilized to obtain the desired information?

Under the regulations of various agencies, businesses must submit information to agencies. Agencies require such information because the key to effective regulation is access to relevant information. However, once information is submitted to the administrative agency, it becomes subject to the FOIA and may be obtained by a competitor unless it fits one of the exemptions.

GOVERNMENT IN SUNSHINE ACT

When government operates in secrecy, there is an appearance of evil. To avoid that appearance, Congress passed the **Government in Sunshine Act. The act requires, with some exemptions, that all meetings of an independent agency be open to the public.** It does not mandate public voice and participation but does afford citizens a presence.

PRIVACY ACT

The **Privacy Act protects the confidentiality of ''private'' information accumulated by federal government agencies.** Many states have adopted similar legislation. The act restricts the right of an agency to disclose certain information about persons without their consent. There are a number of exceptions; for example, no consent is necessary to release information required under FOIA or to agency employees who need the information to perform their duties.

Under the act, agencies may not gather unnecessary information about individuals. During the 1950s and 1960s, the head of the FBI ordered a number of telephones of private citizens tapped and citizens surveiled. Some of these invasions were for purely personal reasons. The act prohibits this type of abuse of power. Individuals, under the act, have a right to request their files and have them corrected if in error.

FUNCTION AND POWER OF ADMINISTRATIVE AGENCIES

The way in which agencies carry out their mandate, as well as the particular organizational form that the

agency adopts, usually develops from the kind of task set before the agency. However, there are generally three ways in which the agency function becomes an exercise of power over those who are the objects of their mandate. Not surprisingly, these functions mirror the powers of the three branches of government. Thus, agencies primarily engage in **rulemaking** (legislative power) and **adjudication** (judicial power). Within the context of both functions, agencies provide **enforcement** actions— investigations and prosecutions (executive power). The nature of the function engaged in directly determines what rights a business may possess, both during the proceeding and in subsequent challenges to the result of the proceeding. Precisely defining the particular function also determines what procedures the agency must comply with in order to safeguard such rights (see Figure 5–2).

Agency Action: Rulemaking

The purpose of **rulemaking** is to administer an act or program created by the legislature. An agency is usually empowered by the legislature to create substantive legislation in its particular area of regulation. The agency also may promulgate various kinds of procedural standards applicable to those who bring matters before the agency.

In addition to the requirements or grants of power contained in the agency's enabling legislation, the APA sets forth the requirements for rulemaking. It divides the rulemaking process into three categories of procedures: (1) those rules that require informal rulemaking procedures; (2) those that require formal rulemaking procedure; (3) those exempted from formal or informal rulemaking procedures. Any rule that has a legally binding force and effect on those regulated must be created according to either the formal or informal rulemaking procedures.

Informal Rulemaking

Most rules that have the force of law are created under **informal rulemaking** procedures, ordinarily referred to as **notice and comment rulemaking.** This process requires that before an agency issues a

Figure 5–2   Types of Rulemaking

	Informal	Formal	Hybrid	Negotiation
Publication of Notice of Proposed Rule	X	X	X	
Written Comments	X			
Hearing		X	X	
Publication of Final Rule	X	X	X	

legislative-type rule, it must provide notice of the proposed rule to all "interested persons" or by publication in the *Federal Register*. An opportunity to comment on the proposed rule must also be given. The comment requirement is usually satisfied by soliciting written submissions, although sometimes a hearing is scheduled. The notice requirement allows businesses such as Toys 'n Shop to carefully observe the regulatory activities of those administrative agencies with which they are directly concerned. A final rule must then be published in the *Federal Register* no less than 30 days prior to its effective date and must be accompanied by a statement of basis and purpose. Comments may be written or, if a hearing is provided, oral. The comments themselves may include scientific data or facts, views held, or simply arguments for or against the proposed rule. The comments then become part of the record, which forms the basis of the formulation of the rule. Obviously, such material may accumulate by the roomful where the proposed rule will have a wide impact on a variety of interest groups. Where these procedures are not fully observed, businesses adversely affected by the final rule issued may challenge the rule's legal effect on the basis of inadequate notice and/or that the final rule differed substantially from the proposed rule.

Formal Rulemaking

Formal rulemaking is a more elaborate procedure than informal rulemaking. As a consequence, it is much less utilized in the rulemaking process. The formal rulemaking process begins, as with informal rulemaking, by notice of a proposed rule in the Federal Register. Thereafter, the process shifts to a man-

datory hearing. The agency is required to provide an evidentiary hearing, with formal presentations and cross-examination, presided over by a hearing officer of the agency. This process has been fairly criticized as unduly cumbersome for the rulemaking process. The APA requires application of formal rulemaking only when the agency's enabling statute specifically mandates it.

Hybrid Rulemaking

Hybrid rulemaking involves a blend of informal and formal rulemaking requirements. The process requires notice and a hearing. However, the hearing is not as extensive as that provided in formal adjudications. Cross-examination of witnesses is eliminated.

Rulemaking by Negotiation

Businesses and regulatory agencies have a degree of distrust for one another. Also, rulemaking by any process can become both cumbersome and expensive. Therefore, creating a rule by negotiation, whereby agency members and business representatives come together to decide the contents of a rule, is viewed as a preferable solution.

While a promising development for the future, negotiated rulemaking has a number of difficulties that impede widespread use. Under the APA, *all* interested persons have the right to notice and comment on proposed rules. It is physically impossible for an agency to have face-to-face access with all interested persons. Also, in order for negotiations to work, both sides must possess power to affect the other. If one side has the upper hand, it has no need to negotiate.

The most successful negotiated rulemaking is accomplished between trade associations and agencies. Usually, trade associations provide an arena of debate and consensus among those engaged in a particular range of activities. The agency may suggest the need for reforming activities, hinting that more formal action will follow. The trade association then engages in self-regulation and develops a set of internal guidelines. The agency thereafter accepts the industry's self-regulation. In addition, Congress is increasingly providing for negotiated rulemaking by authorizing the creation of advisory panels to make recommendations of proposed rules to agencies.

Agency Action: Adjudication

Agency **adjudication** is the primary means utilized by agencies to enforce their mandates. This process is a trial-like proceeding, and is adversarial in nature. Agency adjudication may be the basis for granting licenses, conferring benefits, or removing either. It is often the tool used to force compliance with a particular statute or regulation. Failure to comply with occupational health and safety requirements, environmental standards, tax regulations, building codes, or hiring guidelines are some of the more common bases for encounters between businesses and agencies on the adjudicatory level. Agency adjudications are of two types: formal and informal.

Formal Adjudication

Formal adjudication requires near trial-type procedures and is therefore quite expensive. These procedures include rights to notice, counsel, and information of the basis for the action; an unbiased decisionmaker; an opportunity to present evidence and to know opposing evidence; the right to cross-examine adverse witnesses; and a written decision, based only on the submitted evidence. On the other hand, trial-type procedural requirements, such as the rules of evidence, are relaxed and are overlooked to the extent that they hinder access to information.

Extensive discovery is permitted during a formal adjudicatory process. The parties are afforded the usual discovery techniques provided under the rules of civil procedure such as depositions (interviews with witnesses), interrogatories (written questions submitted to a party), and, usually, compulsory pro-

cess (subpoena power) over both documents and individuals. Additionally, any information that the agency possesses may be obtained by the business either through subpoena power or under the Freedom of Information Act. Discovery is expensive and time-consuming and is a principal reason why formal adjudication is disfavored.

The APA requires an independent decisionmaker, who is usually the administrative law judge (ALJ). Crucially, this judge's independence from the agency must be structured into the hearing system. Thus, although technically agency employees, their pay is not dependent on agency evaluations. They are assigned cases on a rotation basis that cannot be circumvented by the agency without a demonstration that the ALJ is unavailable or equally compelling reasons. No agency employee who has power to investigate or prosecute an action may have any authority over an ALJ. Combination in a single individual of the prosecution-investigation function with the decisionmaking function in one person is prohibited.

Although contacts by the ALJ with such agency employees are not prohibited, any agency attempt to influence the ALJ's decision may become a basis for overturning the decision. Likewise, an **ex parte** communication—that is, usually an off-the-record conversation with the ALJ by some individual interested in the outcome of the proceeding—is strictly prohibited.

Although the ALJ submits findings of fact and conclusions of law, the ALJ usually is not the ultimate decisionmaker; instead, the ALJ is responsible for the creation of a record from which the agency ultimately judges the issues. After the hearing, the ALJ issues a determination that must be based on the record. The agency may adopt or reject this decision. However determined, the final decision must be based on evidence set forth within the record. The decision of the agency is then subject to judicial review.

Informal Adjudication

The vast majority of public agency adjudications are of the informal variety and encompass the more common interactions between individuals and an area of government. Public high school discipline, termination of employment at a public university, and termination of welfare or social security are all variations of informal adjudication. Agencies are free to include or exclude those elements of trial proceedings as they deem necessary. This has resulted in a variety of procedures that couple trial-type procedures with other resolution techniques such as conferences or written exchanges. There are, however, three elements that are common to all informal adjudications: notice, an opportunity to participate, and disclosure of reasons for the decision.

The U.S. Constitution's Due Process Clause and the body of decisions that interpret it determine how much process is due to individuals in such proceedings. As observed from an analysis of the following case, the amount of formalized hearing requirements is determined by a flexible analysis that focuses on the impact of the agency action on the person adversely affected.

MATHEWS v. ELDRIDGE
424 U.S. 319 (1976)

Cash benefits are provided to workers during periods in which they are completely disabled under the disability insurance benefits program created by the Social Security Act. Respondent, Eldridge, was awarded disability benefits. Some four years later Eldridge completed a questionnaire, indicating that his condition had not improved and identifying the medical sources from whom he had recently received treatment. After considering these reports and other information, the state agency informed Eldridge by letter that his disability had ceased. This determination was accepted by the Social Security Administration (SSA).

Eldridge commenced an action challenging the constitutional validity of the administrative procedures. In support of his contention that due process requires a predetermination hearing, Eldridge relied exclusively on the U.S. Supreme Court decision in *Goldberg v. Kelly,* which established a right to an "evidentiary hearing" prior to termination of welfare benefits.

The District Court concluded that the administrative procedures pursuant to which Eldridge's benefits were terminated abridged his right to procedural due process. The Court of Appeals for the Fourth Circuit affirmed. The case was appealed to the U.S. Supreme Court.

POWELL, Judge

The issue in this case is whether the Due Process Clause of the Fifth Amendment requires that prior to the termination of Social Security disability benefit payments the recipient be afforded an opportunity for an evidentiary hearing.

. . . "[D]ue process is flexible and calls for such procedural protection as the particular situation demands." More precisely, our prior decisions indicate that identification of the specific dictates of due process generally requires consideration of three distinct factors: First, the private interest that will be affected by the official action; second, the risk of an erroneous deprivation of such interest through the procedures used, and the probable value, if any, of additional or substitute procedural safeguards; and finally, the Government's interest, including the

function involved and the fiscal and administrative burdens that the additional or substitute procedural requirement would entail.

. . . Eligibility for disability benefits, in contrast [to welfare benefits], is not based upon financial need. Indeed, it is wholly unrelated to the worker's income or support from many other sources, such as earnings of other family members, workmen's compensation awards, tort claims awards, savings, private insurance, public or private pensions, veterans' benefits, food stamps, public assistance, or the "many other important programs, both public and private, which contain provisions for disability payments affecting a substantial portion of the work force. . . ."

An additional factor to be considered here is the fairness and reliability of the existing pretermination procedures, and the probable value, if any, of additional procedural safeguards. . . . In order to remain eligible for benefits the disabled worker must demonstrate by means of ''medically acceptable clinical and laboratory diagnostic techniques,'' that he is unable ''to engage in any substantial gainful activity by reason of any *medically determinable* physical or mental impairment. . . .'' This is a more sharply focused and easily documented decision than the typical determination of welfare entitlement. In the latter case, a wide variety of information may be deemed relevant, and issues of witness credibility and veracity often are critical to the decisionmaking process. . . .

By contrast, the decision whether to discontinue disability benefits will turn, in most cases, upon ''routine, standard, and unbiased medical reports by physician specialists,'' concerning a subject whom they have personally examined.

The detailed questionnaire which the state agency periodically sends the recipient identifies with particularity the information relevant to the entitlement decision, and the recipient is invited to obtain assistance from the local SSA office in completing the questionnaire. More important, the information critical to the entitlement decision usually is derived from medical sources, such as the treating physician. Such sources are likely to be able to communicate more effectively through written documents than are welfare recipients or the lay witnesses supporting their cause. . . .

A further safeguard against mistake is the policy of allowing the disability recipient's representative full access to all information relied upon by the state agency. In addition, prior to the cutoff of benefits the agency informs the recipient of its tentative assessment, the reasons therefor, and provides a summary of the evidence that it considers most relevant. Opportunity is then afforded the recipient to submit additional evidence or arguments, enabling him to challenge directly the accuracy of information in his file as well as the correctness of the agency's tentative conclusions.

In striking the appropriate due process balance the final factor to be assessed is the public interest. . . . We only need say that experience with the constitutionalizing of government procedures suggests that the ultimate additional cost in terms of money and administrative burden would not be insubstantial.

We conclude that an evidentiary hearing is not required prior to the termination of disability benefits and that the present administrative procedures fully comport with due process.

The judgment of the Court of Appeals is *Reversed*.

Case Questions

1. What is the issue in this case?
2. Analyze: ''Due process is flexible and calls for such procedural protection as the particular situation demands.''
3. Identify the applicable law that supports the court's holding.
4. Is this decision consistent with *Goldberg v. Kelly?* Analyze.
5. ''Eligibility for disability benefits . . . is not based on need.'' Criticize.

Agency Action: Enforcement

Administrative agencies perform functions of the executive power. Agency enforcement officers all have authority to investigate—that is, gather information about those regulated—to ensure that they have complied with established standards. As such, they have power to issue agency subpoenas prior to an adjudicatory proceeding, thereby obtaining access to documents and data. Agencies invariably compel the regular filing of answers to question-filled documents. The answers supplied serve as trip wires to enforcement action.

Some businesses, by virtue of the industry engaged in, are subject to a higher degree of agency scrutiny. In particular, the regulatory agency may have been granted a greater degree of power to observe their activities, enter their premises, and compel production of information. Such power has created a quandary since it would seem to contravene various constitutionally guaranteed protections. Moreover, as the following case illustrates, the information obtained from these searches may be the basis of a criminal prosecution.

NEW YORK v. BURGER
482 US 691 (1987)

Joseph Burger, respondent, owns a junkyard. His business consists of dismantling automobiles and selling their parts. Officers entered the junkyard pursuant to section 415–a5 in order to conduct an inspection. They determined that Burger was in possession of stolen vehicles and parts and arrested him.

At the trial, Burger moved to suppress the evidence on the ground that section 415–a5 is unconstitutional. The court overruled the motion. The New York Court of Appeals reversed. On petition by the State of New York, the U.S. Supreme Court granted certiorari.

BLACKMAN, Judge

This case presents the question whether the warrantless search of an automobile junkyard, conducted pursuant to a statute authorizing such a search, falls within the exception to the warrant requirement for administrative inspections of pervasively regulated industries. The case also presents the question whether an otherwise proper administrative inspection is unconstitutional because the ultimate purpose of the regulatory statute pursuant to which the search is done—the deterrence of criminal behavior—is the same as that of penal laws, with the result that the inspection may disclose violations not only of the regulatory statute but also of the penal statutes.

The Court long has recognized that the Fourth Amendment's prohibition on unreasonable searches and seizures is applicable to commercial premises, as well as to private homes. An owner or operator of a business thus has an expectation of privacy in commercial property, which society is prepared to consider to be reasonable. This expectation exists not only with respect to traditional police searches conducted for the gathering of criminal evidence but also with respect to administrative inspections designed *to enforce regulatory statutes*. An expectation of privacy in commercial premises, however, is different from, and indeed less than, a similar expectation in an individual's home. This expectation is particularly attenuated in commercial property employed in ''closely regulated'' industries.

Because the owners or operator of commercial premises in a ''closely regulated'' industry has a reduced expectation of privacy, the warrant and probable-cause requirements, which fulfill the traditional Fourth Amendment standard of reasonable-ness for a government search . . . have lessened application in this context. Rather, we conclude that, as in other situations of ''special need'' . . . where the privacy interests of the owner are weakened and the government interests in regulating particular businesses are concomitantly heightened, a warrantless inspection of commercial premises may well be reasonable within the meaning of the Fourth Amendment.

This warrantless inspection, however, even in the context of a pervasively regulated business, will be deemed to be reasonable only so long as three criteria are met. First, there must be a ''substantial'' government interest that informs the regulatory scheme pursuant to which the inspection is made.

Second, the warrantless inspections must be ''necessary to further [the] regulatory scheme.''

Finally, ''the statute's inspection program, in terms of the certainty and regularity of its application, [must] provid[e] a constitutionally adequate substitute for a warrant.'' In other words, the regulatory statute must perform the two basic functions of a warrant: it must advise the owner of the commercial premises that the search is being made pursuant to the law and has a properly defined scope, and it must limit the discretion of the inspecting officers.

In addition, in defining how a statute limits the discretion of the inspectors, we have observed that it must be ''carefully limited in time, place, and scope.''

Searches made pursuant to section 415-a, in our view, clearly fall within this established exception to the warrant requirement for administrative inspections in ''closely regulated'' businesses. . . .

Accordingly, in light of the regulatory framework governing his business and the history of regulation of related industries, an operator of a junkyard engaging in vehicle dismantling has a reduced expectation of privacy in this "closely regulated" business.

The New York regulatory scheme satisfies the three criteria necessary to make reasonable warrantless inspections pursuant to section 415-a5. First, the State has a substantial interest in regulating the vehicle-dismantling and automobile-junkyard industry because motor vehicle theft has increased in the State and because the problem of theft is associated with this industry.

Second, regulation of the vehicle-dismantling industry reasonably serves the State's substantial interest in eradicating automobile theft.

Moreover, the warrantless administrative inspections pursuant to section 415-a5 "are necessary to further [the] regulatory scheme."

Similarly, in the present case, a warrant requirement would interfere with the statute's purpose of deterring automobile theft accomplished by identifying vehicles and parts as stolen and shutting down the market in such items. Because stolen cars and parts often pass quickly through an automobile junkyard, "frequent" and "unannounced" inspections are necessary in order to detect them. In sum, surprise is crucial if the regulatory scheme aimed at remedying this major social problem is to function at all.

Third, section 415-a5 provides a "constitutionally adequate substitute for a warrant." The statute informs the operator of a vehicle dismantling business that inspections will be made on a regular basis. Thus, the vehicle dismantler knows that the inspections to which he is subject do not constitute discretionary acts by a government official but are conducted pursuant to statute.

Finally, the "time, place, and scope" of the inspection is limited, to place appropriate restraints upon the discretion of the inspecting officers. The officers are allowed to conduct an inspection only "during [the] regular and usual business hours." The inspections can be made only of vehicle-dismantling and related industries.

Nor do we think that this administrative scheme is unconstitutional simply because, in the course of enforcing it, an inspecting officer may discover evidence of crimes, besides violations of the scheme itself.

The discovery of evidence of crimes in the course of an otherwise proper administrative inspection does not render that search illegal or the administrative scheme suspect.

Accordingly, the judgment of the New York Court of Appeals is reversed and the case is remanded to that court for further proceedings not inconsistent with this opinion.

Case Questions

1. What is the issue in this case?
2. Analyze the potential scope of this decision; that is, to what other trades or occupations might it be applied?
3. Analyze: "By choosing to engage in this occupation, one automatically becomes subject to the administrative regulations permitting inspections."
4. How may the needs of agencies be reconciled to the warrant requirements? Is there a better solution than that of the Court's opinion?
5. In what ways might the decision in this case lead to abuse?

JUDICIAL REVIEW OF AGENCY ACTION

Agency action is ordinarily subject to judicial review. The aggrieved must have exhausted administrative remedies and have standing.

Exhaustion

Agencies are presumed to be expert in the area that has been delegated to them. For this reason, the law requires that a party exhaust the administrative remedies before instituting a suit. A case would not be considered ripe for judicial review until each appeal within an administrative agency is exhausted. Assume, for example, that a state bureau of unemployment compensation denies compensation to a discharged employee, contending that she was fired for just cause. Before the discharged employee can appeal to a court to overturn the ruling, she would have to continue to work through the state bureau's internal appeal process (see Figure 5–3).

Figure 5–3   Exhaustion of Administrative Remedies:
A Hypothetical Administrative Agency

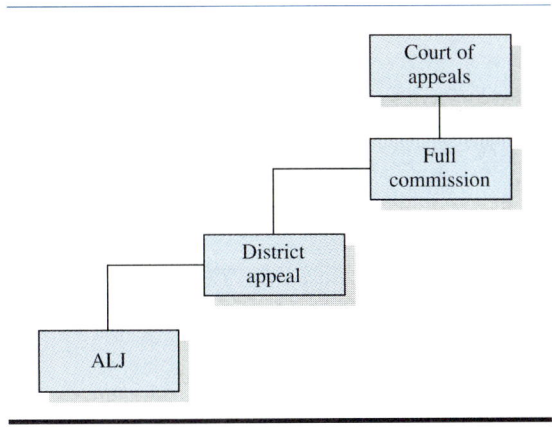

Figure 5–4   Scope of Review

Scope of Review	When Used	Deference to Agency Decision
De Novo	Incomplete records Statutory mandate	None
Substantial Evidence on the Record	Adjudications Formal rulemaking	Great
Arbitrary and Capricious	Informal rulemaking	Greatest

Standing

The U.S. Constitution limits the jurisdiction of the federal courts to "cases or controversies." Cases or controversies are limited to those persons who have legal standing to sue. In order to have legal standing, one must have a personal stake in the outcome of the controversy.

In challenging an agency action, a party must first show an injury. An injury is not confined to an economic one but may include other injuries such as one shown by environmentalists who suffer specific injury when wilderness land is reallocated for commercial purposes. Second, a party challenging an agency action must show that the injury falls within the zone of interests protected by the law that the action allegedly thwarts. To meet the zone of interest test, there must be a relationship between the type of injury the complainant sustains and the purpose of the statute. For example, assume that a business seeks to challenge an environmental reallocation of wilderness land on the basis that the business will be hurt. Assume, further, a federal statute states that wilderness lands will be preserved for environmental enjoyment. Although injury may occur, this would be outside the zone of interests since the purpose of such statute is environmental and not to promote or protect competition. On the other hand, an environmental club's objection that it would be deprived of the use of the wilderness land for backpacking would be within the zone of interests since the statute is clearly for preserving wilderness lands for environmental enjoyment.

Scope of Review

Assuming that an aggrieved party has exhausted the administrative remedies and has standing, that person may seek judicial review of an administrative ruling. In the federal system, most administrative appeals are reviewed by the federal court of appeals. In a few exceptions—for example, review of social security benefits decisions—the case is reviewed by the federal district court.

Generally, there are three types of review: de novo, substantial evidence on the record, and arbitrary and capricious standard of review (see Figure 5–4). The enabling legislation controls the type of review. In the absence of specification in the enabling legislation, the Administrative Procedures Act governs the type of review.

De novo review is the exceptional type of review. It involves a new hearing with no deference to the administrative agency decision. It will be accorded to those types of administrative decisions where there is a decision but no record to review. **Substantial evidence on the record review** affords more deference to the administrative agency. In cases where there is a well-developed record—for example, in formal rulemaking and adjudication proceedings—this type of review upholds the administrative agency decision if there is a substantial basis for the decision. Finally, the **arbitrary and capricious standard of review** commits to the agency the greatest deference by upholding the decision as long as it is not irrational—arbitrary and capricious. This type of standard is ordinarily required when reviewing informal rulemaking. The following article expresses the reality of the judicial scope of review.

"new trial" in courts

*Separated Powers and Positive Political Theory: The Tug of War over Administrative Agencies**

The problem facing courts is both subtle and complex. On the one hand, it would seem clear that courts should scrutinize agency deliberations with great care, granting little, if any, deference and generally hindering agency efforts to promulgate rules. This is because administrative agencies, like legislatures, are subject to substantial interest group influence. . . .

On the other hand, close judicial scrutiny of agency decisions may facilitate rather than impede interest group activities. Building a modicum of delay into the process of administrative agency rulemaking benefits poorly organized groups by providing them with the time necessary both to learn about proposed actions by administrative agencies and to galvanize [them] into an effective political coalition to respond to those proposals. Courts have imposed a variety of requirements on the process of administrative rulemaking that result in the imposition of this modicum of delay. For example, the judicially imposed requirement of notice and comment periods, the requirement that agencies provide interested parties with the right to participate in an elaborate paper hearing process that generates a documentary record, and the requirement that agencies articulate the basis and purpose of their decisions all create the sort of delay that can help to even the playing field between relatively diffuse, poorly organized groups, and highly organized, well-financed special interests.

■ ■ ■

By contrast, however, the extraordinary delay that results from constant reversals of agency decisions can benefit highly organized groups relative to poorly organized groups because the comparative advantage of the highly organized groups lies in their ability to retain their cohesiveness over a long period of time. Thus, while a delay in agency rulemaking from two days to two months probably serves the public interest by permitting a more diverse set of interests to become involved in the process, an extension of the rulemaking process from two months to 2 (or 10) years probably is contrary to the public interest because it has the opposite effect.

Consistent with a public-interest oriented view of the judiciary, courts have erected a complex legal infrastructure to govern agency rulemaking that incorporates some, but not too much, delay into the regulatory process. In interpreting the Administrative Procedures Act (APA), courts ''have built on the opportunity for comment and 'concise general statement' requirements . . . to transform notice and comment procedures into a far more elaborate 'paper hearing' process that generates a documentary record and an elaborate agency opinion as the basis for 'hard look' judicial review.'' Thus, the overall portrait of administrative law that emerges is deference, coupled with delay. . . .

■ ■ ■

Thus, while courts generally defer to administrative agencies' decisions, courts have acted in a variety of subtle but effective ways to drive a wedge between Congress and administrative agencies, thereby fulfilling their role in the constitutional scheme of raising the decision costs of government so as to make law more public-regarding. . . .

■ ■ ■

Often the decisions promulgated by an agency will be a better reflection of Congress' will than Congress' own articulation of its intentions due to the public interest rhetoric that

*Source: Jonathan R. Macey, ''Separated Powers and Positive Political Theory: The Tug of War over Administrative Agencies,'' 80 Geo. Wash. L.J. 671 (1992). Reprinted with permission.

accompanies an initial statutory enactment. Such public interest rhetoric may belie an underlying naked preference for a special interest group. This rhetoric may be ignored by the agency, but it will not be ignored by the courts. Ironically, courts will view the agency's construction as invalid on the principle that Congress retains the ultimate power to make law. Because courts take Congress at its word when it declares that a statute was enacted to serve the public interest, courts often will thwart the will of Congress by invalidating an agency order that is inconsistent with Congress' formally articulated public interest justification for a delegation to an agency.

In addition to the court's persistent willingness . . . to find an agency's interpretation to be inconsistent with Congress' unambiguous intentions, . . . courts may decline to defer to agency decisions that are ''unreasonable.'' While the term ''reasonable'' suggests that courts will give agencies ''considerable latitude,'' the reasonableness requirement imposes a meaningful constraint on Congress' ability to enact wealth transfers costlessly.

The reasonableness inquiry should probably be seen as similar to the inquiry into whether the agency's decision is ''arbitrary'' or ''capricious'' within the meaning of the APA. That inquiry requires the agency to give a detailed explanation of its decision by reference to factors that are relevant under the governing statute.

The requirement that agencies make detailed explanations of their decisions has two consequences. First, it undermines the ability of Congress to use agency resources to stifle poorly organized interests' efforts to monitor and control the behavior of administrative agencies. Second, the requirement that agencies make detailed explanations of their actions lowers the costs to poorly organized groups of finding out about what agencies are doing. Absent such a requirement, only highly organized, well-funded groups would have access to the administrative process. Thus, even if courts do not often find that administrative agencies have acted unreasonably, the requirement that agencies give a detailed explanation of their actions makes it more difficult for Congress to hide special interest legislation by promulgating statutes that involve vague delegations to administrative agencies. Further, requiring agencies to make detailed explanations makes it difficult for Congress to structure an agency so that it is likely to be captured by powerful special interests.

Thought Questions

1. Can you identify any defects in the author's logic?
2. Do you believe that courts consciously attempt to orchestrate their review of administrative decisions so as to neutralize special interest group power? Analyze.

END–OF–CHAPTER QUESTIONS

1. What constitutional problems do the existence of administrative agencies present?
2. Name the federal acts that impact administrative agencies. What are their functions? Is there any overlap?
3. How might business avoid government regulation?
4. Assume that the rulemaking functions of administrative agencies are suspended. How might this affect the administrative process?
5. Analyze: ''Courts should review all administrative actions de novo.''
6. Develop a scenario where a person comes into contact with all four branches of government.
7. Congress created a federal agency to ''do all things necessary to restore the economy.'' The agency promulgated a rule requiring businesses to extend leaves of absence for illnesses up to two weeks per year with pay to any employee. Analyze the constitutionality of the administrative action.

8. Prison inmates were sentenced to death by lethal injection. They complained to the Food and Drug Administration alleging that the use of certain drugs for such purpose violated the Food, Drug, and Cosmetic Act. Do the inmates have standing? Analyze. See *Heckler v. Chaney,* 470 U.S. 821 (1985).

9. The Consumer Product Safety Commission is considering establishing standards for swimming pool slides to reduce the risk of paralysis from accidents in the use of slides. As a manufacturer of slides, write a comment letter to the Commission to express your views. See *Aqua Slide 'N' Dive v. CPSC,* 569 F. 2d 831 (5th Cir. 1978).

10. The Federal Trade Commission is charged with supervising the marketplace for "unfair and deceptive advertising" and is authorized to bring enforcement action against those deceptive advertisers. The FTC is aware of a company that engaged in "bait and switch" tactics — luring consumers into the store with one item and switching them to a higher price item by disparaging the first item. Should the FTC promulgate a rule against bait and switch techniques or should it proceed directly against the advertiser by adjudication? Analyze. Are there other options? Explain.

Chapter 6

Legal Reasoning

■

CRITICAL THINKING INQUIRIES

As you read this chapter, you should be able to address the following:

- What role does precedent play in our judicial system? In what way does it influence society?
- Might judicial decisionmaking be replaced by a process whereby a computer applies precedent and arrives at a decision? What would be the advantages of such a system? What would be the disadvantages?
- Compare and contrast case law and statutes.
- What are the impediments to accurately deriving a legislature's intent?
- Why might a judges' philosophy of interpreting the U.S. Constitution be different from that of interpreting statutes or cases?

MANAGERIAL PERSPECTIVE

Carolyn Seabright is a real estate broker in the firm of Seabright Associates. The firm is in bankruptcy due in large part to lawsuits and enormous judgments rendered against it. Seabright wishes that she would have taken more time to understand the legal reasoning process and to have more meaningful communications with her attorneys. In particular, she wishes she would have gained familiarity with the answers to the following questions:

- How can we predict the legal outcome of our brokerage practices?
- How can we know how the language within a statute or constitution will be interpreted?

It is the job of a lawyer to predict how a court will decide a case. Lawyers are familiar with legal reasoning—the ways in which a judge goes about making decisions. For this reason, a lawyer can predict with varying accuracy the outcome of a case. With an understanding of legal reasoning, lawyers advise their clients. Oftentimes, a lawyer's advice to his or her client does not coincide with what the client wants to hear. This gulf in communication between lawyers and business clients is due in part to a client's unfamiliarity with the process of legal reasoning—why judges do what they do. This chapter is an attempt to bridge that gap between lawyers and their business clients. Understanding how judges interpret cases, statutes, and the constitution should equip managers to better understand the basis of a lawyer's advice, and hence, to make smart decisions, averting costly legal battles.

INTERPRETATION OF CASES

The common law is the product of judicial decision-making. When judges decide a case, they are, in effect, making law. For this reason, common law is sometimes referred to as case law or judge-made law. It derives from decisions of courts applying customs and usages to resolve a conflict and is based on reason and justice. Common law is the backbone of the judicial decisionmaking process. Although today, most of our substantive laws are statutory in nature, still the laws of torts, contracts, and agency are largely governed by common law precedent. Additionally, statutory interpretation by courts places a common law gloss over the legislation. Finally, many statutes are merely codification of the older common law rules.

Stare Decisis

Stare decisis is a doctrine in the law that literally means "let the decision stand." It is from this doctrine that we derive the rule of **precedent.** Judges are expected to decide cases on the basis of principles of law formulated in past cases. These principles serve as precedent for future cases.

Because of the significance of precedent, judges and lawyers alike are intent on searching for past cases that are substantially similar to the case before them. This search leads them to Regional and Federal Reporters (bound volumes) that contain all the official decisions of state and federal courts. There are seven primary regional reporters: Northeast, Northwest, Southeast, Southwest, Southern, Atlantic, and Pacific. Federal district court cases are reported in the Federal Supplement; federal court of appeals cases are reported in the Federal Reporter; and the U.S. Supreme court reports its decisions in U.S. Reports.

Lawyers are trained in various methods designed to research the law. Over the last decade legal research has entered the computer age. Two computerized law services have added a new dimension to legal research. WestLaw and Lexis/Nexis are computerized data banks of full text cases, statutes, scholarly articles and other law materials. They have centralized the plethora of legal materials and placed them at the fingertips of the researcher, thus making legal materials more accessible and the search more efficient.

A judge who ignores precedent may be reversed by a higher court. Sometimes a judge will find a case that is on "all fours"—that is, a case previously decided whose fact pattern is virtually identical to the case before the court. Other times, the closest cases that exist may differ slightly on the facts, but not enough to justify a different application.

Assume, for example, that a case arises in a jurisdiction that presents the following facts: Hillary Max, a real estate broker, represented Pinkas Taylor, who was interested in selling his residence. Max located Anton Duncan, an interested buyer. Although Max knew that the house was infiltrated with termites, she failed to inform Duncan. Duncan purchased the house, and after he became aware of the termite infestation, he sued Max. The case ascended to the highest court within the jurisdiction, which found for the plaintiff, reasoning that Max breached an obligation to inform Duncan of the termite inspection.

Now assume a future case arises involving Seabright Associates and its real estate salesperson, who knowingly fails to inform a buyer that the house is shifting due to an infirm foundation.

Clearly, an infirm foundation and termites are different. Nonetheless, this distinction would not justify a different result. In both cases, a real estate broker willfully failed to inform a buyer of a hidden defect that would likely cause damage. Logic would not distinguish the cases or compel a different result.

The **holding** of a case is the principle of law for which the case stands. Cases will usually also give the underlying rationale for the holding. Sometimes, a judge will include additional reasoning not necessary to decide the case. This reasoning is called **dicta** and is not binding on a future court. For example, assume that in the case involving Seabright Associates the court in its opinion said: "We believe that fairness demands that brokers be held to the highest degree of responsibility and that they be strictly liable for injury to buyers caused by hidden defects, regardless of the brokers' knowledge of their existence." This statement is dictum since it goes beyond the facts of the case and deals with a hypothetical involving an *unintentional* failure to inform. A holding concerning *unintentional* failures to inform must await a future case where the parties will have an opportunity to muster their respective arguments; and where the future court has the benefit of a full hearing on the issue. Dictum does not have precedential value.

Stare decisis is binding. It requires a decision on an issue of law to be followed by the same court and by all lower courts in that jurisdiction in future cases that arise. For example, the Supreme Court of Texas is bound to follow its own previous decisions. All lesser ranked courts in Texas are also bound to follow decisions of higher ranked courts in Texas. Texas and other state courts are also bound to follow U.S. Supreme Court decisions on issues involving the interpretation of federal law. Cases decided by courts of other states are not binding precedent, although they may be persuasive.

Figure 6–1 Benefits of Stare Decisis

- Promotes certainty.
- Promotes fairness.
- Promotes efficiency.

It is through the application of stare decisis that the common law has evolved. Stare decisis has several benefits (see Figure 6–1). The doctrine promotes certainty in the law. By examining precedent cases, a lawyer can make a reasonable prediction as to the outcome of a case involving a given set of facts. Based on this prediction, a lawyer can advise clients accordingly. This ability to predict with a fair degree of accuracy reduces uncertainty, and hence results in less conflict and litigation.

By requiring substantially similar cases to be treated the same, the doctrine also promotes fairness or evenhandedness. This application avoids feelings of injustice that would arise if different litigants were treated differently given the same facts.

Finally, stare decisis promotes efficiency. There should be no need for judges to "reinvent the wheel." When an issue of law is settled by the judicatory process, it would be wasteful for a court to invest the time again in reconsidering that principle of law.

The following excerpt from a former U.S. Supreme Court justice should add clarity to this discussion of stare decisis.

*The Nature of the Judicial Process**

The work of deciding cases goes on every day in hundreds of courts throughout the land. . . . What is it that I do when I decide a case? To what sources of information do I appeal for guidance? In what proportions do I permit them to contribute to the result? In what proportions ought they to contribute? If a precedent is applicable, how do I reach the rule that will make a precedent for the future? If I am seeking logical consistency, the symmetry of the legal structure, how far shall I seek it? At what point shall the quest be halted by some discrepant custom, by some consideration of the social welfare, by my own or the common standards of justice and morals? Into that strange compound which is brewed daily in the caldron of the courts, all these ingredients enter in varying proportions. I am not concerned to inquire whether judges ought to be allowed to brew such a compound at all. I take judge-made law as one of the existing realities of life. There, before us, is the brew. . . . The elements have not come together by chance.

---

*Source: Benjamin Cardozo, *The Nature of the Judicial Process* (New Haven, Conn.: Yale University Press, 1921). Reprinted by permission.

■ ■ ■

Before we can determine the proportions of a blend, we must know the ingredients to be blended. Our first inquiry should therefore be: Where does the judge find the law which he embodies in his judgment? There are times when the source is obvious. The rule that fits the case may be supplied by the constitution or by statute. If that is so, the judge looks no farther. . . . We reach the land of mystery when constitution and statute are silent, and the judge must look to the common law for the rule that fits the case. . . .

The first thing he does is to compare the case before him with the precedents, whether stored in his mind or hidden in the books. . . . Back of precedents are the basic juridical conceptions which are the postulates of judicial reasoning, and farther back are the habits of life, the institutions of society, in which those conceptions had their origin, and which, by a process of interaction, they have modified in turn. Nonetheless, in a system so highly developed as our own, precedents have so covered the ground that they fix the point of departure from which the labor of the judge begins. Almost invariably, his first step is to examine and compare them. If they are plain and to the point, there may be need of nothing more. *Stare decisis* is at least the everyday working rule of our law. . . . [T]he work of deciding cases in accordance with precedents that plainly fit them is a process similar in its nature to that of deciding cases in accordance with a statute. It is a process of search, comparison, and little more. Some judges seldom get beyond that process in any case. Their notion of their duty is to match the colors of the case at hand against the colors of many sample cases spread out upon their desk. The sample nearest in shade supplies the applicable rule. . . . It is when the colors do not match, when the references in the index fail, when there is no decisive precedent, that the serious business of the judge begins. He must then fashion law for the litigants before him. In fashioning it for them, he will be fashioning it for others. . . .

■ ■ ■

. . . [T]he problem which confronts the judge is in reality a twofold one: he must first extract from the precedents the underlying principle, the *ratio decidendi*; he must then determine the path or direction along which the principle is to move and develop, if it is not to wither and die.

The first branch of the problem is the one to which we are accustomed to address ourselves more consciously than to the other. Cases do not unfold their principles for the asking. They yield up their kernel slowly and painfully. . . .

■ ■ ■

. . . "If a group of cases involves the same point, the parties expect the same decision. It would be a gross injustice to decide alternate cases on opposite principles. If a case was decided against me yesterday when I was defendant, I shall look for the same judgment today if I am plaintiff. To decide differently would raise a feeling of resentment and wrong in my breast; it would be an infringement, material and moral, of my rights." Everyone feels the force of this sentiment when two cases are the same. Adherence to precedent must then be the rule rather than the exception if litigants are to have faith in the evenhanded administration of justice in the courts. A sentiment like in kind, though different in degree, is at the root of the tendency of precedent to extend itself along the lines of logical development. No doubt the sentiment is powerfully reinforced by what is often nothing but an intellectual passion for . . . symmetry of form and substance.

Thought Questions

1. What is the "brew" of which Justice Cardozo speaks? Are there components of the brew that the judge has not mentioned? Explain.

2. Do you think Justice Cardozo was content to "compare the colors" of cases and mechanically achieve a result? Explain.

3. What is the function of stare decisis?

4. What does the justice mean when he states: "Cases do not unfold their principles for the asking. They yield up their kernel slowly and painfully"?

Following Precedent

Courts are bound by tradition and even duty to follow precedent. Sometimes this obligation places a judge in a dilemma. The judge desires to do what is fair and right in adjudicating the controversy and to stay true to personal conscience. The judge also seeks to apply stare decisis for the policy reasons previously discussed. It is when these two considerations diverge that the dilemma arises. The following case illustrates this dilemma.

FELDER v. BUTLER
438 A.2d 494 (Md. 1981)

Felder and others (plaintiffs-appellants) were injured when Hawkins, while under the influence of alcohol, drove her car across the lane of oncoming traffic and collided with the appellant's vehicle. Hawkins had been drinking at a bar owned by Butler. The plaintiffs sued Butler, claiming that he should not have served alcohol to Hawkins since she was already "visibly intoxicated." Under Maryland criminal law, this conduct by Butler, if proven, would be a misdemeanor. Maryland had no similar civil statute, and the prior decision of *State v. Hatfield* held that bar owners such as Butler had no liability in these cases. Based on *Hatfield,* the lower court dismissed the case. The plaintiffs appealed to the Court of Appeals.

MURPHY, Chief Judge

The issue in this case is whether, in light of changes evolving in the common law since our decision in *State v. Hatfield* (1951), Maryland should now recognize a right of action in tort against a licensed vendor of intoxicating beverages for injuries negligently caused by an intoxicated patron to an innocent third party.

In *State v. Hatfield* . . . Maryland adopted the early common law rule that an innocent third party did not have a cause of action against a vendor of alcoholic beverages for injuries suffered as a result of the intoxication of the vendor's patron. . . .

In so holding, the Court in *Hatfield* noted that statutes existed in some states, although not in Maryland, creating a civil cause of action for damages against one selling alcohol to an intoxicated person who, as a result of such intoxication, negligently causes injury to innocent persons. The Court said that apart from statute, no cases existed which held "a seller of intoxicating liquor . . . liable for a tort of the buyer who drank the liquor." . . .

The appellants correctly point out that in the 30 years since *Hatfield* was decided, a number of jurisdictions have departed from the early common law rule and have imposed civil liability, independent of statute, upon sellers of alcoholic beverages for damages caused by their intoxicated patrons. They urge that we abandon *Hatfield* and adopt the rationale of the new trend of cases which, applying traditional negligence principles, recognizes a cause of action brought against a tavern owner by a party injured as a result of negligent acts of a patron of the tavern to whom alcoholic beverages were sold while the patron was under the influence of intoxicating liquors.

A number of other [states] have followed the [trend] in imposing civil liability upon vendors of intoxicating liquors for damages caused by their intoxicated customers. Applying common law principles . . . these [courts] recognize a civil right of action against a seller of alcoholic beverages where the patron's intoxication is shown to have been either apparent, visible, obvious, or actual and was so known to the tavern owner or his employees, or should have been known had due care been exercised. . . .

Of course, the common law is not static. Its life and heart is its dynamism—its ability to keep pace with the world while constantly searching for just and fair solutions to pressing societal problems like that presented by the senseless carnage occurring on our highways, due in no small measure to the drinking driver. The common law is, therefore, subject to modification by judicial decision in light of changing conditions or increased knowledge where this Court finds that it is a vestige of the past, no longer suitable to the circumstances of our people. Indeed, we have not hesitated to adopt a new course of action by judicial decision where we have concluded that course was compelled by changing circumstances. Although of great importance, we have not construed the doctrine of stare decisis to prevent us from changing a rule of law if we are convinced that the rule has become unsound in the circumstances of modern life.

Although empowered to change common law rules in light of changed conditions, the Court has always recognized that declaration of public policy is normally the function of the legislative branch of government. The Court has therefore declined to alter a common law rule in the face of indications that to do so would be contrary to the public policy of the State, as declared by the General Assembly of Maryland. Whether Maryland should abandon the rule in *Hatfield* and align itself with the new trend of cases which impose civil liability upon vendors of alcoholic beverages for the torts of their inebriated patrons depends ultimately upon which line of authorities, all things considered, best serves the societal interest and need. That determination clearly impacts on the development of the law relating to the dispensing and consumption of alcoholic beverages, a subject long pervasively regulated by the legislature. . . . This state of the statutory law of Maryland has remained unchanged since *Hatfield* was decided 30 years ago.

In determining the public policy of the State, courts consider, as a primary source, statutory or constitutional provisions. Therefore, since the legislature has not yet created . . . liability by statute, we decline, for now, to join the new trend of cases. . . . Nevertheless, the legislature may wish to consider reexamining the *Hatfield* rule to determine if the public policy of the State continues to favor a rule which, in any and all circumstances, precludes consideration of whether the sale of intoxicating liquor to an inebriated tavern patron may be a proximate cause of subsequent injury caused to others by the intoxicated customer. We, therefore, find no error in the judgment of the lower court.

DAVIDSON, Judge, Dissenting

In my view, it is common knowledge that the problems associated with drunk driving have presently reached massive proportions. Just and fair solutions additional to those presently existing are required if societal interests are to be protected and preserved. . . . In light of changing conditions, I am convinced that the common law rule has become unsound in the circumstances of modern life. I would hold that a cause of action exists against licensed vendors of intoxicating liquors for the tortious acts of minor or intoxicated patrons to whom they sell alcoholic beverages in violation of Maryland Code.

Case Questions

1. Do you agree that legislative inaction was an indication of the public policy of the state regarding the issue of tavern owners' liability to third parties? Explain.

2. What effect do you think departing from the rule of *State v. Hatfield* would have on the drunk-driving problem in Maryland? Explain.

3. Under what circumstances would the majority have been willing to join the dissent? Explain.

4. Contrast the difference in judicial philosophy of the majority and the dissent.

5. Was this case decided on the basis of legal logic or fairness? Explain.

Overruling Precedent

Stare decisis promotes certainty in the law. However, the law must also contain a degree of flexibility. The judiciary maintains this flexibility in decisionmaking by exercise of the **power to overrule** precedent. When the reason for the rule initially laid down is no longer consistent with logic, justice, or fairness, a court may depart from stare decisis. For example, in *Plessy v. Ferguson*,[1] the U.S. Supreme Court announced a decision that laid down the rule of law that "separate but equal facilities for blacks and whites is constitutional." Fifty-eight years later, in *Brown v. Board of Education*,[2] the High Court was called upon to reexamine the issue. It could

[1]163 U.S. 537 (1896).
[2]347 U.S. 483 (1954).

have applied stare decisis, followed *Plessy,* and reasoned that it is constitutional for public school boards to segregate educational facilities for blacks and whites as long as the facilities are equal. An enlightened court recognized that the rule announced in *Plessy* was unsupported by logic, justice, or reason. Consequently, it overruled *Plessy,* and held that separate public educational facilities for blacks and whites were not constitutional.

A court may also overrule precedent if the economic, political, sociological, and/or technological climate has changed. Where circumstances have changed such that the reason for the rule is no longer valid, then the rule should not be blindly followed. Society is organic—ever changing—and the law should not be entombed in stare decisis for posterity when reason demands otherwise. The following case illustrates the power of a court to depart from stare decisis and overrule precedent.

ENGHAUSER MFG. CO. v. ERIKSSON ENGINEERING LTD.
451 N.E.2d 228 (Ohio 1983)

Enghauser Manufacturing Co., appellant, sued the city of Lebanon, alleging that it had negligently planned, designed, and constructed a new bridge and roadway that resulted in the flooding of Enghauser's abutting industrial property.

Enghauser was awarded $91,000 in damages against the city. The trial court judge set that verdict aside. The judgment was affirmed by the court of appeals, which determined that the suit was barred by the doctrine of sovereign immunity—that the government cannot be sued. The Supreme Court of Ohio granted Enghauser's petition for certiorari.

BROWN, Justice

The case presents this court with the question of whether the doctrine of governmental immunity from tort liability for municipalities should be sustained in Ohio. With the limitations set forth in this opinion, this court overrules *Dayton v. Pease* (1854) wherein the sovereign immunity doctrine was extended to encompass local governmental units, and all other decisions which support this doctrine, and holds that immunity from tort liability heretofore judicially conferred upon local governmental units is hereby abrogated. Henceforth, so far as municipal governmental responsibility for torts is concerned, the rule is liability—the exception is immunity.

The abolition of this doctrine in Ohio is long overdue. There are probably few tenets of American jurisprudence which have been so unanimously berated as the governmental immunity doctrine. A quick review of Ohio case law reveals that this court has many times had the matter under consideration.

Various reasons have been assigned for perpetuation of the doctrine of municipal immunity from liability for torts. The reason adduced most frequently to support the doctrine is that "if there is to be a departure from the rule the policy should be declared and the extent of liability fixed by the legislature." This type of argument begs the question of the desirability of the doctrine and relegates the whole problem to a discussion of who should change the doctrine.

In Ohio, there is no doubt that the municipal immunity doctrine was judicially created. Inasmuch as it is a judicially created doctrine, it may be judicially abolished.

Having established that this doctrine is a creature of the courts, this court not only has the power but the duty and responsibility to evaluate the doctrine of municipal immunity in light of reason, logic, and the actions, functions and duties of a municipality in the 20th century in order to determine whether it should adhere to its own rule of municipal tort immunity.

The courts which have adhered to the rule cite few reasons for that position, other than the longevity of the doctrine and its firmly established position. It is commonly accepted that the doctrine by which municipal corporations are held immune from liability in tort originated with the case of *Russell v. Men of Devon* (1788), wherein the immunity was supported because (1) since the group was unincorporated, there was no fund from which the judgment could be paid and (2) "it is better that an individual should sustain an injury than that the public should suffer an inconvenience."

In scarifying the second justification for immunity as set forth in *Russell, supra,* the Supreme Court of New Hampshire stated . . . as follows:

"That an individual injured by the negligence of the employees of a municipal corporation should bear his loss himself as advocated in the *Russell* case, *supra,* instead of having it borne by the public treasury to which he and all other citizens contribute, offends the basic principles of equality of burdens and of elementary justice. It is foreign to the spirit of our constitutional guarantee that every subject is entitled to a legal remedy for injuries he may receive in his person or property. . . . It is also contrary to the basic concept of the law of torts that liability follows negligence and that individual corporations are responsible for the negligence of their agents, servants and employees in the course of their employment." . . .

The other justification for immunity set forth in *Russell* has likewise lost its validity and vitality. The widespread availability and use of insurance or other modern funding methods render an argument based on economics invalid. Further, there is no empirical data to support the fear that governmental functions would be curtailed as a result of imposing liability for tortious conduct.

Even though the reasons behind the municipal immunity doctrine have vanished and its construction renders an injustice to all people wronged by the local governmental unit or its agents, it has been suggested that the rule be retained because of the principle of *stare decisis*.

As to the fundamental nature and the importance of *stare decisis,* there is no doubt. It lies at the heart of the common law. By this rule, our society has preserved the best of the wisdom and the morality of past ages. Wisdom and morality, however, are not immutable universals of the scholastic philosophers; they are to be modified by each new generation.

When, however, a rule of law is judge-made, and the reasons for its use have vanished, the court should not perpetuate it until petrification. A rule that has outlived its usefulness should be changed. Greater justification is needed for a rule of law than that it has been part of the common law for a few hundred years.

For the foregoing reasons, this court holds that the trial court erred in granting the motion for judgment notwithstanding the verdict based on the applicability of the doctrine of municipal immunity and the jury verdict awarding damages to the appellant is hereby reinstated.

Judgment reversed.

Case Questions

1. Was *Russell v. Men of Devon* controlling precedent on *Enghauser*? Explain. Can *Russell* be distinguished from the facts of *Enghauser*? Explain.

2. Do you think that it is more appropriate for the legislature to abolish municipal immunity than for the court? Explain.

3. How would you characterize a society that shields government from liability? How would you characterize one that does not? Compare and contrast.

4. What is the primary reason that the court departed from *stare decisis*?

When a court overrules precedent, it announces a new rule of law. The new rule becomes precedent and can be relied on for future conduct and when deciding future cases. When researching cases, judges and lawyers often look in a book of citations published by *Shephards* to determine whether a case has been overruled. This research procedure is referred to as ''Shephardizing'' a case. Few things in the legal practice are more embarrassing to a lawyer than citing a case to a judge that has been overruled.

Distinguishing Precedent

The process of distinguishing precedent is a subtle art that is developed by judges and lawyers after years of training and experience. When distinguishing precedent, a judge will carefully compare past cases with the case before it. The comparison is based on the facts and the underlying reasons for the principle of law. If the prior case is substantially similar on the facts, then its holding will control the case under consideration. On the other hand, if the cases are not substantially similar, the prior case will not serve as precedent. To illustrate, assume a case involving a nonprofit hospital that is sued because its employees were careless in treating a patient. Assume further that the common law of the state is that charitable institutions are immune from suit. In a reasoned opinion, the court overrules the charitable immunity doctrine and holds that the hospital is not immune from suit. Now assume that a case involving a similar set of facts arises, but instead of a hospital it involves a synagogue. Is a synagogue like a hospital? A court would examine the underlying rationale for overruling charitable immunity for hospitals to see if it is equally applicable to synagogues. In looking at the ''colors of the cases'' a court might reason:

Hospital	Synagogue
• Employs *large* professional staff at *good* salaries.	• Employs *small* staff at *modest* salaries.
• Dependent on *paying* patients and medical insurance payments.	• Dependent on *voluntary* donations.
• Malpractice premiums passed on through payment systems.	• Liability premiums reduce limited charitable budget.

Hence, a court may conclude that, for purposes of immunity, synagogues need to be treated differently than hospitals; synagogues may still need the protection of the doctrine as they are generally ''char-

Figure 6-2 Judicial Decisionmaking

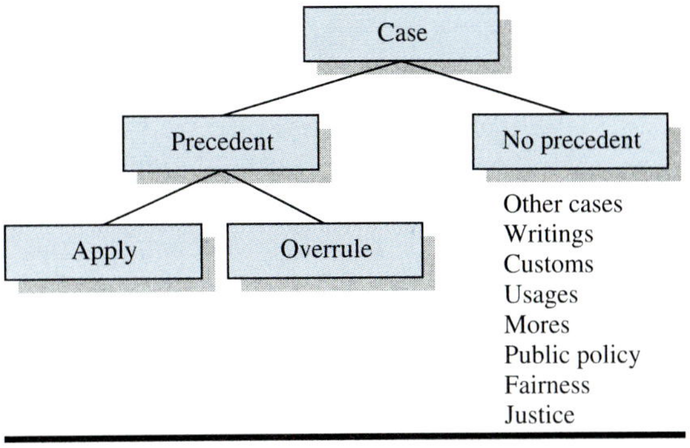

itable'' while hospitals behave more like businesses. On the other hand, other courts may focus on the similarity of the two cases:

- Both involve charities.
- Both may insure against liability.
- It is no fairer to deprive an injured plaintiff recovery in a synagogue than in a hospital.

The process of distinguishing precedent may lead some courts to one result and other courts to an opposite result depending on how exhaustively they analyze similarities and differences and how strongly they view the various public policies involved.

Absence of Precedent

When there is no precedent within the jurisdiction, a judge must still decide the case (see Figure 6-2). Such a case is referred to as a **case of first impression** or a **novel case**. In deciding such a case, the court may look to similar cases decided in other states or other common law countries like England. These cases are not binding but may be persuasive. The court may also look to scholarly writings, customs, usages, community mores, and public policy. Fairness and justice are ideals that also influence a judge's decisionmaking process. Once the case is decided, it becomes precedent for future cases. The primary responsibility of the court is to adjudicate the case before it. A court, however, cannot neglect the impact the decision will have on future cases.

The following case illustrates the manner in which a court decides a case in the absence of precedent.

E.I. DUPONT DENEMOURS & CO. v. CHRISTOPHER
431 F.2d 1012 (5th Cir. 1970)

Rolfe and Gary Christopher were hired by an unknown third party to take aerial photographs of an incomplete methanol production facility of E.I. duPont deNemours & Co., Inc. (DuPont). They took 16 photos and delivered them to the third party. DuPont discovered the Christophers' activities and contacted them requesting disclosure of the name of their client. The Christophers refused to disclose the information.

DuPont filed suit alleging "that the Christophers had wrongfully obtained photographs revealing DuPont's trade secrets which they then sold to the undisclosed third party. It maintained that it had developed a method for making synthetic methanol—a trade secret—and that photographs of the area would permit a skilled person to discover the secret process.

DuPont sought damages and an injunction preventing future photographing. The Christophers answered by maintaining that DuPont failed to state a claim on which relief could be granted—that there was no right in Texas to protect trade secrets acquired through industrial espionage. During a deposition, the Christophers refused to disclose the name of the third party. DuPont filed a motion with the court to compel an answer.

The court granted DuPont's motion to compel disclosure, and then granted the Christophers' motion for an immediate appeal to obtain a review of the court's finding that DuPont had stated a claim on which relief could be granted.

GOLDBERG, Judge

This is a case of first impression, for the Texas courts have not faced this precise factual issue. . . . The Christophers argued both at trial and before this court that they committed no "actionable wrong" in photographing the DuPont facility and passing these photographs on to their client because they conducted all of their activities in public airspace, violated no government aviation standard, did not breach any confidential relation, and did not engage in any fraudulent or illegal conduct. . . .

It is true, as the Christophers assert, that the previous trade secret cases have contained one or more of these elements. However, we do not think that the Texas courts would limit the trade secret protection exclusively to these elements. On the contrary . . . the Texas Supreme Court specifically adopted the [following] rule:

One who discloses or uses another's trade secret, without a privilege to do so, is liable to the other if . . . he discovered the secret by improper means.

The question remaining, therefore, is whether aerial photography of plant construction is an improper means of obtaining another's trade secret. We conclude that it is and that the Texas courts would so

hold. The Supreme Court of that state has declared that "the undoubted tendency of the law has been to recognize and enforce higher standards of commercial morality in the business world." That court has quoted with approval articles indicating that the *proper* means of gaining possession of a competitor's secret process is "through inspection and analysis" of the product in order to create a duplicate. . . .

We think, therefore, that the Texas rule is clear. One may use his competitor's secret process if he discovers the process by reverse engineering applied to the finished product; one may use a competitor's process if he discovers it by his own independent research; but one may not avoid these labors by taking the process from the discoverer without his permission at a time when he is taking reasonable precautions to maintain its secrecy. To obtain knowledge of a process without spending the time and money to discover it independently is *improper* unless the holder voluntarily discloses it or fails to take reasonable precautions to ensure its secrecy.

In the instant case the Christophers deliberately flew over the DuPont plant to get pictures of a process which DuPont had attempted to keep secret. The Christophers delivered their pictures to a third party who was certainly aware of the means by which they had been acquired and who may be planning to use the information contained therein to manufacture methanol by the DuPont process. The third party has a right to use this process only if he obtains this knowledge through his own research efforts, but thus far all information indicates that the third party has gained this knowledge solely by taking it from Du-Pont at a time when DuPont was making reasonable efforts to preserve its secrecy. . . .

In taking this position we realize that industrial espionage of the sort here perpetrated has become a popular sport in some segments of our industrial community. However, our devotion to freewheeling industrial competition must not force us into accepting the law of the jungle as the standard of morality expected in our commercial relations. Our tolerance of the espionage game must cease when the protections required to prevent another's spying cost so much that the spirit of inventiveness is dampened. Commercial privacy must be protected from espionage which could not have been reasonably anticipated or prevented. We do not mean to imply, however, that everything not in plain view is within the protected vale, nor that all information obtained through every extra optical extension is forbidden. Indeed, for our industrial competition to remain healthy there must be breathing room for observing a competing industrialist. A competitor can and must shop his competition for pricing and examine his products for quality, components, and methods of manufacture. Perhaps ordinary fences and roofs must be built to shut out incursive eyes, but we need not require the discoverer of a trade secret to guard against the unanticipated, the undetectable, or the unpreventable methods of espionage now available.

In the instant case DuPont was in the midst of constructing a plant. Although after construction the finished plant would have protected much of the process from view, during the period of construction the trade secret was exposed to view from the air. To require DuPont to put a roof over the unfinished plant to guard its secret would impose an enormous expense to prevent nothing more than a schoolboy's trick. We introduce here no new or radical ethic since our ethos has never given moral sanctity to piracy. The marketplace must not deviate far from our mores. We should not require a person or corporation to take unreasonable precautions to prevent another from doing that which he ought not do in the first place. Reasonable precautions against predatory eyes we may require, but an impenetrable fortress is an unreasonable requirement, and we are not disposed to burden industrial inventors with such a duty in order to protect the fruits of their efforts. ''Improper'' will always be a word of many nuances, determined by time, place, and circumstances. We therefore need not proclaim a catalogue of commercial improprieties. Clearly, however, one of its commandments does say ''thou shall not appropriate a trade secret through deviousness under circumstances in which countervailing defenses are not reasonably available.''

[Affirmed.]

Case Questions

1. What issue does this case present?

2. What sources of law does the court use to come to its conclusion?

3. Write a paragraph focusing on the moral impact of the Christophers' actions. Write another paragraph focusing on the economic impact of their actions.

4. How do you distinguish this case from a case where a person purchases methanol from a competitor and then through reverse chemical engineering discovers the secret process?

5. Would the result have been different if the Christophers had been traveling in a commercial airliner 30,000 feet high and drew pictures of what they saw? Explain.

INTERPRETATION OF STATUTES

Statutes are enacted by legislative bodies. Congress, consisting of the Senate and the House of Representatives, is the federal legislative body. It was created by the U.S. Constitution. Each state also has a similar legislative body, as do cities and townships, normally established by a constitution or charter. Legislators are elected by their constituents and vote on the passage of statutes or ordinances.

Figure 6–3   Contrast: Case Law and Statutes

Case Law	Statutes
Judges	Legislators
Mandatory	Discretionary
General class	Specific class
Retroactive	Prospective

Statutes Contrasted with Case Law

Statutes may be contrasted with case law, as shown in Figure 6–3. Judges decide cases, whereas legislators pass statutes. When a case comes before a court, the judge must decide the case. Legislators, in contrast, do not have to pass a law. Consequently, the legislative process is often slower and more deliberate than the judicial process, although this is not true in every case. The common law is found in cases and its principles must be extracted from judges' opinions. In that sense, common law decisions are more general than statutes, which contain specific provisions intended to govern a particular problem. A case is decided to adjudicate the right of the parties before the court. Of course, it serves as precedent on all future litigants. In contrast, a statute is passed to impact a large class of the public; it applies to individuals as well. Finally, common law decisions have retroactive effect—that is, they apply as precedent to situations that arose before the case was decided. This is true because judges, when deciding cases, are deemed to announce the law that already exists. In order to mitigate the hardship on those who otherwise relied, a court sometimes announces that its decision will apply only to future litigants. Statutes usually apply only prospectively—that is, to situations in the future.

Enacting Statutes

The procedure for passage of a statute is formal and involves a series of steps. Legislation ordinarily begins with the introduction of a **bill,** the legislative proposal. Federal bills are introduced into the Senate or House by an individual senator or representative or by a group of legislators whose names may be attached to the proposed legislation (e.g., the Sherman Act). The bill is then referred to an appropriate committee or committees that specialize in such matters for detailed consideration. The committee may kill the bill by inaction, or it may send it to a subcommittee or consider it itself. Some bills are subjected to public hearings where those who have a particular interest in the subject matter will be called on to testify before the committee or subcommittee. Eventually, the committee may discuss the bill, mark it up, rewrite it, and send it along with a report to the respective house of Congress for consideration. After floor debates on the bill, it may be sent back to the committee for further study, or it may be voted on. If passed, it will then be sent to the other house of Congress to be afforded similar process.

Sometimes a similar bill is introduced into both Houses at the same time. Differences between the similar bills considered by both houses of Congress may necessitate a joint conference committee, which will attempt to resolve the differences and forge a compromise bill acceptable to both houses. When that is accomplished, the bill will be sent back to each house for vote. If both houses pass the compromise bill, then it is sent to the president for signature. The president may sign it into law or do nothing, in which case it will become law in 10 days ''unless the Congress by their Adjournment prevent its Return, in which Case it shall not be a Law'' (**pocket veto**). If the president vetoes the legislation, it can become law only if the full Congress overrides the veto by a two-thirds majority vote.

State statutes become law in a similar way. For details of a state's specific procedure, each state's constitution must be consulted. Most recently, there has been a resurgence in the move among states to adopt uniform state laws. The National Conference on Uniform State Laws, and the American Law Institute, two private organizations, have proposed legislation throughout the years for adoption by the states' legislatures. Some of the more well-known uniform acts widely adopted among the states are the Uniform Commercial Code (UCC), the Uniform Partnership Act (UPA), and the Uniform Limited Partnership Act (ULPA). Even though states adopt the same legislative language, each state, through its judiciary, must still interpret its own statute. Hence, states may interpret the same language differently.

Deriving Legislative Intent

The process of interpreting a statute involves a quest to find the will of the legislature. It is this ''will,'' or legislative intent, that controls the interpretation of a statute. Statutes must be interpreted because it is difficult at one point in time to adequately define permitted/prohibited actions that clearly encompass the wide array of future factual patterns relevant to the statute. The judicial branch has developed rules of statutory construction designed to find the legislative intent. **Textual analysis** and **contextual analysis** are the two primary methods of ascertaining this legislative intent.

Textual Analysis

When interpreting statutes, a judge will first look to the text of the statute. More specifically, the court will focus on the particular statutory word or phrase under consideration. It will then apply the plain meaning of the language. This application should yield the intent of the legislature; the legislature is presumed to have intended the plain meaning derived from the word usage. Hence, words are assigned their obvious meaning. Consider, for example, a statute that states in part, "No person shall import peaches, mangos, plums, or any other fruit into the United States." Obviously, peaches, pears, and plums may not be imported under this statute. What about watermelons? If the statute is applicable here, the watermelons would have to fall under the "any other fruit" language. Remember, however, we are attempting to find the will of the legislative body. Under a common rule of textual interpretation called **ejusdem generis,** the general catchall clause at the end of the list will be controlled by the preceding specific items. Here, the general clause "any other fruit" is preceded by items that are all fruits with pits. Under *ejusdem generis,* "any other fruit" may be confined to fruits with pits and hence would not include watermelons. Here, the legislature certainly did not mean to prohibit all fruit imports. This *ejusdem generis* rule of interpretation is calculated to determine the spirit and intent of the legislature.

What if a corporation desired to import peaches into the United States? Is a corporation a person or are "persons" confined to individuals? When looking for the definition of a word, help may come from examining other sections within the statute. For example, a section within the statute that defines person as "any individual, partnership, corporation, or organization" would be dispositive of the issue.

Another rule of construction aiding a court in a textual analysis interpretation is **expressio unius est exclusio alterius**—the enumeration of specific items excludes the inclusion of others. For example,

consider a statute stating that an agency shall have the power to "entertain complaints, hold hearings, decide cases, and issue cease and desist orders." In the absence of other language in the statute, application of the Latin maxim would lead a court to conclude that the agency lacks the power to "make rules" because rulemaking is not listed and no catchall phrase is included at the end.

Contextual Analysis

In most instances, application of plain-meaning interpretation disposes of the question. However, in two types of cases, interpretation will require resort to the context.

First, words may be *ambiguous,* with no help provided from other portions of the text. What is a motor vehicle? Does it include an airplane, a motorboat, and a riding lawnmower? What does it mean to "enlarge an existing cemetery"? Would the addition of a noncontiguous branch cemetery constitute enlargement? These and other questions may arise, necessitating further inquiry into the context of the law's passage.

The legislature is presumed to be rational. Consequently, if application of a plain meaning results in an *absurdity,* then the context must be examined. For example, assume that a statute states, "No person shall carry a weapon into a nuclear power plant." Now assume the president of the United States is visiting a power plant and his security officers accompany him with weapons. Are they in violation of this statute? Under a plain-meaning interpretation, the answer would be yes. However, this results in an absurdity. Consequently, we must delve deeper into the context.

Sources for Contextual Analyses Numerous sources may be consulted when engaging in a contextual analysis (see Figure 6–4). The circumstances under which the statute was passed and the evil it was intended to remedy may be particularly helpful. If we know, for example, that a law was passed to protect the wages of laborers from employer-coerced kickbacks, then the law would not apply to the activities of union leaders.

The legislative history of the statute is probably the most important and often used method employed when trying to derive the intent of the legislature from a contextual perspective. The U.S. Congress preserves its legislative history in the *Congressional Record,* and it is also reported in other publications.

Figure 6–4   Legislative Sources for Contextual Analysis

- Committee and subcommittee reports.
- Committee and subcommittee hearings.
- Congressional debates.
- Sponsor's remarks.
- Legislative counsel reports.
- Executive department comments.
- Joint conference reports.

Committee reports and hearings, analysis of bills by legislative counsel and executive departments, and congressional debates on the House and Senate floors are examined in the search for the legislature's will. Of course, it is an oversimplification to say that there is one unified will. Legislation is a process involving compromise and accommodation, and various interpretations may be placed on the same language by different legislators. Sometimes, the compromise process results in a term or phrase being consciously general, to allow for a selective interpretation. At other times, legislators attempt to "strategize" a particular result. Hence, when examining the legislative record, the judge must be careful not to be "taken in" by preorchestrated legislative manipulation techniques by individuals or interest groups filling the record with biased material.

The *Congressional Record* includes more than the materials actually considered by Congress. Leg-islators are permitted to edit their remarks and insert material not presented. In the case of one hearing involving the fiscal budgets of the Departments of Labor and Health, Education, and Welfare, one half the 4,500-page record published as hearings were never part of the actual hearings. Also, the legislative debate opens up opportunity for "friendly colloquy" involving preplanned dialogue by legislators designed to settle the intent in a way favorable to their whim and constituents. Courts are mindful of this and assign little or no weight to such attempts. Courts assign different weight to different legislative materials. For example, greater weight is given to the sponsor's remarks or a committee chairperson's remarks than to an opponent's remarks. But even here, many judges are reluctant to routinely defer to a committee report, recognizing that the details contained in the report rarely come to the attention of the house enacting the bill.

Most state and local legislatures do not maintain as extensive a legislative record as Congress. Nonetheless, courts are called on to find the state legislature's will, which may necessitate resort to the context. Comparisons to language in other statutes of the state, judicial constructions of similar statutes in other states, and national debates for uniform statutes may provide help.

Finally, as the next case illustrates, even when the statutory language speaks plain and clear, courts often buttress their conclusion with contextual support.

TENNESSEE VALLEY AUTHORITY v. HILL
437 U.S. 153 (1978)

Section 4 of the Endangered Species Act (Act) authorizes the Secretary of the Interior (Secretary) to declare a species of life endangered. Section 7 of the Act requires federal departments and agencies to take action to ensure that the existence of "endangered species" is not threatened. Pursuant to the statute, the Secretary listed the snail darter as an endangered species. The Secretary determined that the snail darter lived only in a portion of the Little Tennessee River and that completion of the Tellico Dam by the Tennessee Valley Authority (TVA) would result in the destruction of the snail darter's critical habitat. Consequently, the Secretary declared that all federal agencies must take necessary actions to ensure that the snail darter's habitat would not be altered.

Hill and others (respondents) brought an action in the Federal district court seeking to stop completion of the dam. The district court dismissed the complaint, contending that Congress, by continued appropriation of monies for the TVA project, did not intend the Act to apply in this case. The Court of Appeals reversed. The U.S. Supreme Court granted certiorari.

BURGER, Chief Justice

One would be hard pressed to find a statutory provision whose terms were any plainer than those in section 7 of the Endangered Species Act. Its very words affirmatively command all federal agencies "to *insure* that actions *authorized, funded, or carried out* by them do not *jeopardize* the continued existence" of an endangered species or "*result* in the destruction or modification of habitat of such species. . . ."

Concededly, this view of the Act will produce results requiring the sacrifice of the anticipated benefits of the project and of many millions of dollars in public funds. But examination of the language, history, and structure of the legislation under review here indicates beyond doubt that Congress intended endangered species to be afforded the highest of priorities.

. . . By 1973, when Congress held hearings on what would later become the Endangered Species Act of 1973, it was informed that species were still being lost at the rate of about one per year . . . and "the pace of disappearance of species" appeared to be "accelerating." Moreover, Congress was also told that the primary cause of this trend was something other than the normal process of natural selection:

"[M]an and his technology has [sic] continued at an ever-increasing rate to disrupt the natural ecosystem. This has resulted in a dramatic rise in the number and severity of the threats faced by the world's wildlife. The truth in this is apparent when one realizes that half of the recorded extinctions of mammals over the past 2,000 years have occurred in the most recent 50-year period." 1973 House Hearings 202 (statement of Assistant Secretary of the Interior).

. . . Typifying these sentiments is the Report of the House Committee on Merchant Marine and Fisheries on H.R. 37, a bill which contained the essential features of the subsequently enacted Act of 1973; in explaining the need for the legislation, the Report stated:

"Who knows, or can say, what potential cures for cancer or other scourges, present or future, may lie locked up in the structures of plants which may yet be undiscovered, much less analyzed?"

In shaping legislation to deal with the problem thus presented, Congress started from the finding that "[t]he two major causes of extinction are hunting and destruction of natural habitat." S. Rep. No. 93–307, p. 2 (1973). Of these twin threats, Congress was informed that the greatest was destruction of natural habitats; see 1973 House Hearings 236 (statement of Associate Deputy Chief for National Forest System, Department of Agriculture). . . . Witnesses recommended, among other things, that Congress require all land-managing agencies "to avoid damaging critical habitat for endangered species and to take positive steps to improve such habitat." 1973 House Hearings 241 (statement of Director of Michigan Department of Natural Resources). Virtually every bill introduced in Congress during the 1973 session responded to this concern by incorporating language similar, if not identical, to that found in the present section 7 of the Act. These provisions were designed, in the words of an administration witness, "for the first time [to] *prohibit* [a] federal agency from taking action which does jeopardize the status of endangered species." Hearings on S. 1592 and S. 1983 before the Subcommittee on Environment of the Senate Committee on Commerce . . . (statement of Deputy Assistant Secretary of the Interior). . . .

Section 7 of the Act, which of course is relied upon by respondents in this case, provides a particularly good gauge of congressional intent. . . . [T]his provision had its genesis in the Endangered Species Act of 1966, but that legislation qualified the obligation of federal agencies by stating that they should seek to preserve endangered species only "*insofar as is practicable and consistent with the[ir] primary purposes.* . . ." Likewise, every bill introduced in 1973 contained a qualification similar to that found in the earlier statutes. . . .

What is very significant in this sequence is that the final version of the 1973 Act carefully omitted all of the reservations described above. In the bill which the Senate initially approved (S. 1983), however, the version of the current section 7 merely required federal agencies to "carry out such programs *as are practicable* for the protection of species listed. . . ." S. 1983, section 7(a). By way of contrast, the bill that originally passed the House . . . contained a provision which was essentially a mirror image of the subsequently passed section 7 — indeed all phrases which might have qualified an agency's responsibilities had been omitted from the bill . . . . Resolution of this difference in statutory language . . . was the task of a Conference Committee. The Conference Report . . . basically adopted the Senate bill, S. 1983; but the conferees rejected the Senate version of section 7 and adopted the stringent, mandatory language in H.R. 37. While the Conference Report made no specific reference to this choice of provisions, the House manager of the bill, Representative Dingell, provided an interpretation of what the Conference bill would require, making it clear that the mandatory provisions of section 7 were not casually or inadvertently included. . . .

In passing the Endangered Species Act of 1973, Congress was also aware of certain instances in which exceptions to the statute's broad sweep would be necessary. Thus . . . U.S.C. section 1539 (1976 ed.), creates a number of limited "hardship exemptions," none of which would even remotely apply to the Tellico Project. In fact, there are no exemptions in the Endangered Species Act for federal agencies, meaning that under the maxim *expressio unius est exclusio alterius* . . . we must presume that these were the only "hardship cases" Congress intended to exempt.

Here we are urged to view the Endangered Species Act "reasonably," and hence shape a remedy "that accords with some modicum of common sense and the public weal." . . . [However] Congress has spoken in the plainest of words, making it abundantly clear that the balance has been struck in favor of affording endangered species the highest of priorities, thereby adopting a policy which it described as "institutionalized caution."

[The Court of Appeals decision is affirmed.]

Case Questions

1. Make the best arguments you can to arrive at an opinion that dissents from the majority opinion.

2. List the various pieces of legislative history relied on by the court. Which should be given the most weight? Which should be given the least weight?

3. Estimate the costs to the parties and society as a result of this lawsuit.

4. Why do you think that Congress continued to authorize funds for the project even after it was aware of the snail darter?

5. What other avenues were open to Congress to ensure the completion of the TVA project?

INTERPRETATION OF THE CONSTITUTION

The U.S. Constitution is the foundational document for the establishment of the federal government. Its contents are discussed in Chapter 4. Each state also has a constitution establishing government and specifying powers of state and local governments. Any law that violates a constitutional provision is deemed to be unconstitutional and hence invalid. The task of interpreting the constitution resides in the judiciary.

The rules of constitutional interpretation are not unlike those employed in interpreting statutes. The plain meaning of the wording as understood at the time the provision was enacted is employed. When there is no plain meaning, the search for the meaning of a particular clause necessitates an examination of the constitutional history regarding the provision.

The Constitution is a dynamic document intended to survive the long term. As such, the framers of the Constitution were consciously general in their selection of certain language. Terms such as *due process, unreasonable searches and seizures,* and *just com-*pensation are examples. The U.S. Supreme Court is the final authority on the meaning of these and other constitutional provisions. The way in which a judge interprets the constitutional language is often a matter of judicial philosophy. Differing philosophies lead to different results when interpreting the same constitutional provision. There are several theories of constitutional interpretation. The current battle, however, rages between the strict constructionists and the broad constructionists.

Strict constructionists adhere very closely to the text of the constitution and the intent of its framers. They hold true to the belief that the Constitution contains value choices that are to be the guide to its interpretation. Constitutional decisionmaking, then, is restricted by the intent of the framers and should not be a search for extended goals and values not contained within the original text or its spirit. Strict interpretists point out that the Constitution is too "fragile" to be tampered with by using it as a political platform. It is the foundation, and sets up delicate balances among the branches of government. Hence, constitutional interpretation should not turn on one's politics, for this would encourage an appointment of judges based on loyalty to party politics rather than on legal ability. Strict constructionists believe society is served best in the long run by rigidly adhering to ''principled decisions'' mandated by the values contained within the Constitution. Strict constructionism lies in sharp contrast to broad constructionism.

Broad constructionists take the position that the court may refer to values external to the Constitution in decisionmaking. They point out that the intent of the framers is basically unknowable. Since the framers couched constitutional language in general terms, they conclude, it is fair to treat the Constitution as an organic document designed to facilitate ''social advancement'' for society. Broad constructionists are often accused of being result oriented — achieving a desired result by post hoc rationale and fitting the Constitution to justify the result.

The battle between the strict constructionists and the broad Constructionists continues to rage. Since the members of the U.S. Supreme Court change, the philosophy of the court is subject to change. Under the ''Warren court'' era in the 1950s and 1960s, a broad constructionism led to sweeping reforms, especially in the area of expanding individual liberties. An example of broad constructionism versus strict constructionism may be seen in the U.S. Supreme Court's adoption of the exclusionary rule for unreasonable searches and seizures. The rule states that any evidence that is discovered as a result of an unconstitutional search and seizure may not be used as evidence in a court of law — that is, it must be suppressed. This is an example of a broad constructionist application. The strict constructionist would see this as making law rather than interpreting it, since there is no ''suppression'' requirement to be found in the Constitution. The post–Warren court decisions have, to some extent, stemmed the tide of ''social reform'' by turning to a more strict constructionist mode.

END–OF–CHAPTER QUESTIONS

1. ''Cultural mores are sources of law.'' Analyze this statement. Give an example of such a custom that is strongly ingrained in any society.

2. There is a tension that occurs between the principle of following precedent and the principle of overruling precedent. Following precedent makes the law rigid. Overruling precedent gives a quality of flexibility to law. What is the proper balance between these two competing principles?

3. A statute reads ''all toothbrushes, hairbrushes, lint brushes, and other brushes are subject to health inspection codes of this state.'' What about a paintbrush? Analyze.

4. Describe what a society would be like without a legislative branch of government. How would the judicial branch of government fill the void? Explain.

5. Fitzer attended a camp operated by Greater Greenville South Carolina Young Men's Christian Association. While there, Fitzer was injured as a result of the camp's negligence. In a suit filed by Fitzer's parents for their son's injury, the camp defended by asserting the charitable immunity doctrine, which was the rule in the jurisdiction. What are the arguments in favor of overruling the doctrine? What are the arguments in favor of adhering to the doctrine in this case? See *Fitzer v. Greater Greenville South Carolina Young Men's Christian Ass'n,* 282 S.E.2d 230 (S.C. 1981).

6. The common law rule currently in the state, and announced as early as 1852 in *Kent v. Broad,* is that a minor can avoid his or her contracts. More specifically, a minor who seeks to avoid a contract must return the property received and then he or she is entitled to a return of the money or property he or she had given. Assume that a case arises in the state involving Eddie, a 17-year-old minor, who is married with two children. Eddie entered into a contract with Used Car Lot and bought a 1978 Ford station wagon for $2,000. Eddie used the car primarily to go back and forth to work. One day, on his way to work, Eddie crashed into a wall, seriously damaging his Ford. The auto was totaled and Eddie did not have collision insurance coverage. Eddie instituted suit seeking to disavow the contract. The case is before the Supreme Court of the State. Do you think that the court should overrule *Kent v. Broad*? Explain your answer. Do you think

the court should modify *Kent*? Explain. Can this case be distinguished from *Kent*? See *Kiefer v. Howe Motors, Inc.*, 158 N.W. 2d 288 (Wis. 1968).

7. Geary is employed by a company that refines oil for resale. Geary was told by his boss to participate in a price-fixing scheme, which he refused to do. As a result, he was fired. He had no employment contract with the company. Geary sued the company for wrongful discharge. The case was unprecedented. What are the options open to the court? If the court finds in favor of Geary, what principle of law should it announce? See *Geary v. United States Steel Corp.*, 319 A.2d 174 (Pa. 1975).

8. The Medical School of the University of California at Davis had two admissions programs: regular and special. Those in the general admissions program were not admitted if their undergraduate grade-point averages were below 2.5. Applicants under the special admissions program included blacks and other minorities who were "economically and/or educationally disadvantaged." These applicants did not have to meet the 2.5 grade-point average to be considered for admission. Sixteen slots were held open to be filled by special admissions candidates. Bakke, a white male, applied to the Medical School and was rejected. Special applicants were admitted with lower grade-point averages. Title VI of the Civil Rights Act of 1964 provides that "[n]o person . . . shall, on the ground of race, color, or national origin, be excluded from participating in . . . or be subjected to discrimination under any program receiving Federal financial assistance." Bakke filed suit alleging that he was the subject of discrimination in violation of Title VI. Would Title VI apply to whites? Where would you look to make that determination? See *University of California Regents v. Bakke*, 438 U.S. 265 (1978).

9. Congress passed the following statute:

> Be it enacted by the Senate and House of Representatives of the United States of America in Congress assembled, That from and after the passage of this act it shall be unlawful for any person, company, partnership, or corporation, in any manner whatsoever, to prepay the transportation, or in any way assist or encourage the importation or migration of any alien or aliens, any foreigner or foreigners, into the United States, its Territories, or the District of Columbia, under contract or agreement . . . made previous to the importation or migration of such alien or aliens, foreigner or foreigners, to perform labor or service of any kind in the United States, its Territories, or the District of Columbia.

Exempt from the statute were "professional actors, artists, lecturers, singers, and domestic servants." The Holy Trinity Church entered into an agreement with Warren, a pastor in England, to pastor the church. Warren immigrated to the United States and began pastoring. Under a plain-meaning interpretation of the statute, is the Holy Trinity Church guilty of violating the statute? Analyze. Can you make an argument for considering the context? Explain. See *Holy Trinity Church v. United States,* 143 U.S. 457 (1892).

10. The Fourteenth Amendment to the Constitution states: "Nor shall any state deprive any person of life, liberty, or property without due process of law, nor deny to any person within its jurisdiction the equal protection of its laws." Yick Wo, a Chinese citizen, was denied a license to operate a laundry. Yick Wo contends he is being deprived of "equal protection of the laws." Does the Fourteenth Amendment apply to him since he is a noncitizen of the United States? What questions would you want answered in order to come to a conclusion? See *Yick Wo. v. Hopkins*, 118 U.S. 356 (1886).

Part II

Private Law

Chapter 7

Intentional Wrongs: Business Crimes and Torts

■

CRITICAL THINKING INQUIRIES

As you read this chapter, you should be able to address the following:

- Extract the common elements of business crimes.
- Compare and contrast torts against persons, property, and competition.
- What is the relationship between business crimes and torts?
- Compare and contrast defenses to intentional torts.

MANAGERIAL PERSPECTIVE

Clarence Barker is the new chief legal counsel to Chemical Designs, a large ''think tank'' operation that produces specialized computer software. In an attempt to prevent problems before they occur, he spends the bulk of his time keeping up with the recent legal developments that might affect his company. Over the years, Chemical Designs has been embroiled in numerous criminal and civil prosecutions involving such matters as bribery, computer wrongdoing, misappropriation of trade secrets, invasion of privacy, and wrongful discharge. Barker is working on a comprehensive policy and procedures manual that he hopes will cut drastically the instances of crimes and torts. Mr. Barker needs to know:

- What business crimes and torts should be included in the manual?
- What is the best way to educate the managers and employees so that the company will be in a preventive mode?

This chapter is intended to help businesspeople like Barker. Thus far, you have been exposed to the foundations of law. In this chapter, we begin an in-depth look at substantive areas of law—those that create duties, rights, and obligations on individuals and business organizations. The chapter is divided into criminal wrongs and intentional civil wrongs. The distinction between a crime and a civil wrong was discussed and illustrated in Chapter 1. Both of these wrongs may be committed by and against businesses. Chapter 8 is devoted to other civil wrongs.

BUSINESS CRIMES

Business crimes cost American business $50 billion a year. Business crimes are associated with some type of business activity (see Figure 7–1). Job positions and business activity enhance the opportunity to commit certain crimes. For example, a real estate broker is in a strategic position to wrongfully take clients' monies; an accountant for a business firm is in a position to cheat on income tax returns for the business; a lobbyist who works for a trade association has many potential opportunities to bribe public officials. In other instances, the business itself is an illegal venture. Houses of prostitution, distribution of illegal drugs and liquor, gambling, and illegal exporting of goods are examples.

Figure 7–1   Business Crimes

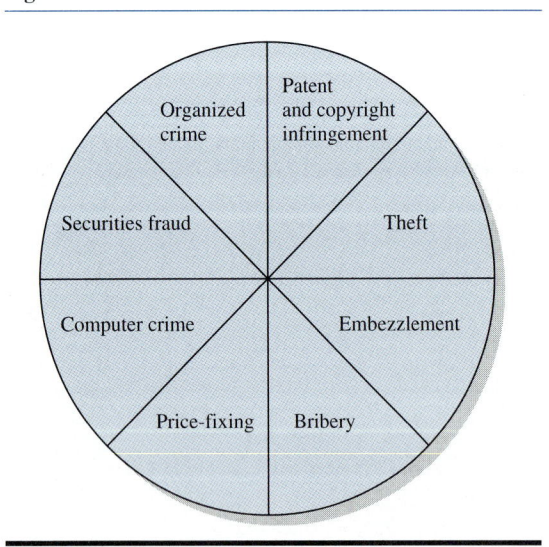

Business crimes have several features that make them distinct from other crime. First, these crimes are often difficult to detect, because the method of their commission is so interconnected with normal commercial behavior and because the crime may consist of a very complex series of steps. Second, business crimes, in contrast to other crimes, more often involve individuals who are economically successful and who appear to be upright, law-abiding citizens. Third, the economic clout of those who commit business crimes often enables them to muster strong legal defenses. Prosecutors overburdened with large caseloads are often forced to forgo lengthy trials and instead plea bargain for lesser offenses.

Business crimes come in an endless variety. Four in particular are very common: embezzlement, bribery, racketeering, and computer crimes.

Embezzlement

Embezzlement occurs when a person wrongfully appropriates property entrusted to him or her. For embezzlement to occur, the wrongdoer must first come into lawful possession of the property. This crime is different from ordinary theft, usually referred to as **larceny.** Larceny is the wrongful taking of another's property. With larceny, the wrongdoer is never in lawful possession of the property. To clarify the distinction, consider the following two hypothetical examples.

- W. B. Harris is employed as a janitor with Chemical Designs. One evening while in the comptroller's office, he opens the petty cash drawer and pockets $50. This constitutes larceny.
- Alice Brown is a stockbroker. Ralph, a customer, gives Alice $50 to be deposited in Ralph's brokerage account. Alice receives the money and instead, appropriates it to her own use. This constitutes embezzlement.

The key difference in the two preceding examples is that in the first case, the janitor was never in lawful possession of the monies; in the second case, the stockbroker was in lawful possession before the unlawful taking took place.

Each state has laws making embezzlement a crime. Because embezzlement involves a breach of trust, it usually carries greater penalties than larceny.

Bribery

Bribery is the offering or receiving of anything of value to influence official action. Bribing federal officials is a federal crime. In addition, states have laws that make it a crime to bribe anyone. **Commercial bribery** is a form of bribery. It occurs when bribery is used to acquire sensitive information from a competitor—for example, customer lists, new product lines, unpatented secrets, or expansion plans.

In the United States, widespread bribery of public officials came to light when the Watergate Special Prosecution Force uncovered numerous illegal campaign contributions. Abscam, a sting operation, used decoys to film transactions of federal legislators taking bribes. This resulted in passage of federal and state laws known as **anticorrupt practice acts.** These acts typically limit the amount of campaign contributions and require strict reporting and disclosure. In 1977 Congress passed the **Foreign Corrupt Practices Act**, which makes it a crime to bribe an official of another country. Violation of the law carries a penalty up to $1 million for companies and up to $10,000 and five years' imprisonment for individuals. ''Grease'' payments to a foreign official to speed up the governmental process (as opposed to influencing an official to decide favorably) are not, however, prohibited by the act. (See a fuller discussion in Chapter 44.) The following excerpt highlights the dilemma of the American businessperson operating in foreign countries.

*Big Profits in Big Bribery**

At a table in Mexico City's Camino Real Hotel, a foreign businessman and a middle-ranking government official are talking quietly in a corner. Midway through the conversation, the foreigner casually places an envelope on a chair next to him. When the foreigner rises to leave, the envelope remains behind. The government official slips it into his coat pocket a few minutes later and departs.

That is the way all too much of the world's most important business is done these days. From the shrewdly sophisticated kickback schemes of the Middle East and Latin America, to the virtual Mafia-style and shakedowns of sub-Saharan Africa and Indonesia, the universal game of bribery in the pursuit of profit goes on and on.

Is this a game that U.S. businessmen should be allowed, and even encouraged to play? Or should they instead be compelled to wash their hands of it entirely, leaving the spoils to competitors in other lands? Those are some of the difficult questions that were addressed . . . when the General Accounting Office released a detailed study of the impact on American business of the 1977 Foreign Corrupt Practices Act.

The act sprang from the nation's Watergate-era revulsion at the global bribery excesses of such well-known American companies as Lockheed, Northrop and Gulf Oil. During the mid-1970s those companies, and others, made headlines almost weekly as sensational disclosures surfaced about their roles in paying megabuck bribes to high foreign officials to clinch deals.

In an effort to stop such corruption, revelations of which rocked the government of Takeo Miki in Japan and disgraced Prince Bernhard in The Netherlands, the Foreign Corrupt Practices Act made it a criminal offense to pay bribes of any sort to foreign officials to secure or retain business abroad. . . . The legislation also set up accounting procedures designed to make it virtually impossible for companies to disguise such ''sensitive payments'' or to hide them elsewhere in the corporate books.

*Source: *Time*, ''Big Profits in Big Bribery,'' March 16, 1981, p. 58. Reprinted with permission.

There is little doubt that the passage of the 1977 act has made U.S. businessmen think twice about bribing abroad. At Lockheed Corp., whose very name was synonymous with payoffs and freebies for foreign officials in the 1970s, the company now no longer picks up even hotel bills for customers visiting its California headquarters for contract talks.

By contrast, "caution" to some U.S. companies simply means figuring out clever new bribery schemes that are harder to spot. One way is to join up with a foreign company that is not prohibited from making the necessary payments, and let it do the dirty work instead.

The major problem of any law on bribery is that in much of the less-developed world what some Westerners might regard as commercial corruption of government and business has always been looked upon as an inescapable fact of everyday life. The stylized arrangements for giving and taking payments are often perfectly normal and legal under local law and custom.

Corruption exists, and probably always will, in this obviously imperfect world. But should the U.S. participate in it? Bribery on the global scale that is now occurring is costly, saps political vitality and can eventually undermine a people's trust in government. . . .

. . . [T]he current American law is riddled with complicating ambiguities and shortcomings. Many of the problems arise from confusion over what constitutes a bribe. So-called grease payments, such as fees to get low-level civil servants to perform their bureaucratic duties of stamping documents and processing licenses, are specifically permitted on the grounds that petty corruption is unavoidable almost anywhere. But there is a large gray area between that sort of bureaucratic paper shuffling and the discretionary authority of local officials to withhold approval for a project or license, and thereby extort not $50 or $100, but perhaps $10,000 or even $500,000 from a victimized company.

American businessmen also complain that the complex law keeps them out of many profitable deals. Says Robert Malott, chairman of Chicago's FMC Corp., a leading manufacturer of chemicals and machinery: "The law has American export companies thoroughly confused. We simply cannot get clarification on what is legal and what is not."

Thought Questions

1. How do you answer the question, "Should U.S. businesspersons be allowed to bribe officials in countries where it is acceptable?"

2. In what ways are U.S. businesspersons at a disadvantage when doing business in other countries? What can they do short of bribery to overcome those difficulties?

3. What problems do you see with the Foreign Corrupt Practices Act? Should it be repealed? Modified? Explain.

Racketeering and Organized Crime

Organized crime and racketeering involve a structure of individuals who provide illegally obtained goods and services. These individuals use the profits from their activities to expand to other legal and illegal enterprises. Often they seek to corrupt political officials for the purpose of protecting or furthering their illegal activities.

To combat organized crime, Congress in 1970 enacted the **Racketeer Influenced and Corrupt Organizations Act** (RICO). The primary thrust of the act was the removal of organized Mafia-type crime from the business community. However, its application has been extended to reach unorganized criminal activity as well.

RICO makes it a crime to acquire or operate an *enterprise* by a *pattern of racketeering*. The enterprise includes partnerships, corporations, or even an informal association of persons. It may be a legal or illegal enterprise. Private businesses, foreign and domestic corporations, labor organizations, government agencies, drug dealers, and pornographers have all been found to be enterprises. The offender must additionally be involved in a pattern of racketeering. One act does not create a pattern. The statute requires at least two acts within 10 years. The so-called predicate acts are mentioned within the statute and include such crimes as murder, arson, bribery, extortion, illegal drug dealing, embezzlement, and securities fraud. Prosecutions under RICO have been particularly successful against businesspeople engaging in securities and insurance fraud schemes and filtering money gained from illegal operations through legal business enterprises.

Penalties for violation of RICO include fines of up to twice the gross profits of the enterprise and imprisonment of 20 years. RICO also provides for seizure and forfeiture of the property related to the enterprise. In addition to criminal prosecutions under RICO, the act provides for civil damage suits by those injured as a result of a violation of RICO. Treble damages are recoverable. (For a fuller discussion of RICO see Chapter 44.)

Computer Crime

Computer technology has revolutionized major segments of our society, not the least of which is the business world. With the advent of computers and computerized database systems, a new type of crime has emerged—**computer crime.** A computer crime is any illegal act requiring knowledge of computer technology.

There are two distinct classes of computer crimes. First, a computer may be used as a *tool of a crime,* as in cases of embezzlement and fraud. For example, an employee familiar with the computer system in a bank may, by use of the computer, access depositors' accounts and thereby withdraw monies. In one case involving an insurance fraud, employees of an insurance company used computers to manufacture insurance policies issued to fictitious insureds so that the company could resell the policies and avert a cash flow problem. Before the scam was uncovered, stockholders in the company sustained monumental losses. Several company officials responsible for the crime served jail terms.[1]

The second class of computer crimes are those where the computer is the *object of a crime*. Massive quantities of computer information can be stored on microchips the size of a pinhead. This data is valuable. Like other property, it is subject to sabotage and destruction. However, more subtle means of erasure and destruction exist. Programs designed to erase existing data can be written and introduced into the system. The modification or elimination of customer accounts, product codes, inventory data, and other financial information could cause a company considerable damage. Moreover, theft may be achieved through unauthorized entry into a computer system by use of an illegally obtained password. Computer time may also be the subject of theft.

Computer crime is a type of crime that often can only be detected by one who has been specifically trained and skilled in computer technology. For this reason, the FBI and state police are giving special training to selected law enforcement officers. And more and more states are adopting legislation to prohibit all facets of computer crimes.

TORTS

Tort derives its name from the Latin word *tortus,* which means twisted. A tort is the legal term assigned to twisted, or wrongful, conduct. It was previously defined simply as a civil wrong. A more comprehensive definition of a tort is a civil wrong (other than a breach of contract) for which a court will provide a remedy.

A tort is not a crime, although the same conduct may give rise to both a tort and a crime. A crime constitutes an offense against society. One who commits a crime is subject to criminal prosecution and punishment. The purpose of a criminal proceeding is to protect the public. The action is not directly concerned with compensating the victim of the crime. In contrast, a civil action in tort is instituted by a victim. Tort law is designed to compensate an injured party for wrongs.

A tort is different from a breach of a contract. The law of contracts is yet another substantive area of law, which is treated in great detail in Chapters 11 through 18. A contract involves an agreement between parties. Consequently, it arises by operation of the parties who establish the terms of the agreement. A breach of contract occurs when one party deviates from the terms of that agreement or contract. In contrast, a tort occurs when a party deviates from a standard imposed by the law. It does not matter that the wrongdoer did not consent to that standard of conduct. Breach of that standard results in a tort.

---

[1]These cases arose out of the Equity Funding scandal that occurred in the late 1960s and early 1970s.

Figure 7–2   Tort Spectrum

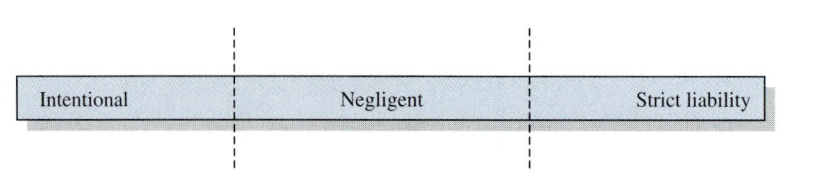

Torts may be classified in various ways. One way of classifying torts is according to the gravity of fault of the tortfeasor (wrongdoer)—the degree of wrongfulness of the conduct. Figure 7–2 divides torts along a culpability spectrum into three distinct classifications. On the far left are **intentional torts**—those accomplished with a mind to injure. The perpetrators of these types of torts intend to do harm. The torts in the middle of the spectrum are characterized as **negligent torts.** The tort of negligence involves a less culpable mind than that involved in intentional torts. Nonetheless, when a careless act results in injury to another, the law requires that the victim be compensated.

On the far right are the least culpable types of torts—**strict liability.** Here, the law imposes a duty even on persons whose wrongdoing is minimal or nonexistent. For example, strict liability, discussed in Chapters 8 and 23, is applied to those who handle ultrahazardous materials or sell defective products. Law and society have determined that certain conduct should result in absolute liability regardless of culpability.

The following materials concentrate on intentional torts. Negligence and strict liability torts are the subject of Chapter 8.

INTENTIONAL TORTS

Intentional torts are committed with a desire to interfere with another's interest. The intent necessary to establish the tort does not require a desire to do harm; it requires only that the defendant commit a voluntary act knowing that it is substantially certain to injure the plaintiff. Since the actor's conduct is most culpable, the law allows for the greatest damages. Not only may the plaintiff recover ordinary damages to compensate for the injury but **punitive damages** as well—those intended to punish the defendant, deter others from such antisocial wrongs, and compensate the victim for wounded sensibilities.

Figure 7–3 categorizes the intentional torts as torts against (1) persons, (2) property, and (3) competition/employment.

Torts against Persons

Torts against persons include battery, assault, false imprisonment, intentional infliction of emotional distress, defamation, and invasion of privacy.

Battery

A **battery** is the intentional offensive touching of another. A classical illustration of a battery occurs when one person strikes another. A battery may, however, be less aggravated. Assume that a chiropractor advises a patient that she is in need of a spinal adjustment. The patient consents to have her thoracic (back) area adjusted but not her cervical (neck) area. While adjusting the thoracic area, the chiropractor intentionally adjusts the cervical portion of the patient's spine. This amounts to a battery. Any unwanted touching of the body is considered a battery, even if it proves beneficial.

Under the doctrine of **transferred intent,** an act done with the intention of harming one person that actually harms another constitutes a battery. Suppose that Henry, chairman of the board of Chemical Designs, intending to strike Ralph with the gavel at a board meeting, throws it for that purpose but the gavel instead strikes Jim who is in back of Ralph. Henry's intent to cause bodily harm to Ralph will be transferred to Jim, who will have an action against Henry in battery.

Unpermitted contacts with things that are attached to the person also constitute a battery. Thus, the offensive contact with another's clothing, flicking one's hat, kicking another's cane, or even intentionally bumping a car carrying a passenger all constitute batteries. And, the victim does not have to be aware of the battery at the time of occurrence. An unwanted kiss imposed on a sleeping person or an

Figure 7–3 Intentional Torts — Classification

Against Person	**Against Property**	**Against Competition/Employment**
Battery	Trespass	Interference with economic relations
Assault	Conversion	Appropriation of trade secrets
False imprisonment	Injurious falsehood	Wrongful discharge
Infliction of emotional distress		
Defamation		
Invasion of privacy		

unconsented operation on an anesthetized patient may constitute a battery if the requisite intent is present.

Assault

Intentionally placing a person in apprehension of a battery constitutes an **assault.** It is not necessary that there be physical contact for an assault to occur. Aiming a gun, loaded or unloaded, at a person, raising one's fist as if to strike another, or lunging at a person in a hostile manner are all assaults even if the threatened action fails to result in actual physical contact.

It is not necessary that the victim be placed in fear; anticipation of harm is enough. Thus, the holder of a black belt in karate may be the target of an assault even if he is too courageous to be fearful. However, the victim must be aware of the threatening conduct and must actually feel threatened. Thus, one who points a gun at a person who is sleeping has not committed an assault.

One who commits an assault must have an apparent present ability to carry out the threat. Assume that Randal waves a real-looking toy pistol at Jennifer in a threatening manner. Though Randal has no *real* ability to harm Jennifer, the gun *appeared* to endanger Jennifer. This constitutes an assault. As-sume, however, that Randal who was in California, phoned Jennifer, who was in New York, and threatened to "blow your brains out." Without an apparent present ability to carry out the threat, there is no civil assault.

False Imprisonment

The tort of **false imprisonment** is the intentional confinement of another. The confinement does not have to be an incarceration in prison or within walls or bars. False imprisonment may occur in a room, an automobile, or even a city. The tort involves a restriction on one's freedom to move. However, the restriction must be complete. Merely obstructing one exit from a building when another reasonable means of exit exists does not constitute false imprisonment.

No false imprisonment exists unless a person is conscious and aware of the confinement. However, the detention need not be lengthy. A detention for a few minutes or even a moment will support the tort of false imprisonment, although the greater the time, the greater the damages. False imprisonment may be accomplished by force or threats of force. However, the restraint must be against the will of the plaintiff, and a voluntary relinquishment of freedom will not constitute false imprisonment, as illustrated by the following case.

FANIEL v. CHESAPEAKE & POTOMAC TELEPHONE CO.
404 A.2d 147 (D.C. Ct. App. 1979)

Essie Faniel (appellant) was employed as a keypunch operator by American Telephone and Telegraph Co. (AT&T). Her supervisor requested her to step into a conference room. There, an AT&T security supervisor informed Faniel that "routine testing had revealed excessive electronic resistance on her line, suggesting the presence of an unauthorized telephone installation. She admitted to having three unauthorized phones and signed a statement to that effect. She was then informed that it would be necessary to take a trip to her home to recover the equipment. Faniel did not object because "I just assumed that I had to go." Faniel was driven to her home by her supervisor and the security officer. They made one stop to pick up another security man.

When the foursome arrived at Faniel's house, they were greeted by her husband. The telephone company employees recovered the equipment and then left. Faniel received a 30-day suspension from work.

Faniel sued AT&T and Chesapeake & Potomac Telephone Company of Maryland, a subsidiary of AT&T, for false imprisonment. The jury found for Faniel and awarded her $7,000. The judge granted defendants' motion for judgment notwithstanding the verdict and set aside the award. Faniel appealed the trial court decision.

GALLAGHER, Judge

False imprisonment is defined, in this jurisdiction, as the restraint by one person of the physical liberty of another without consent or legal justification. The threshold question in this false imprisonment action is necessarily, whether a detention of appellant occurred.

As appellant's counsel conceded at trial, any unlawful confinement took place during the automobile trip, not the initial questioning episode. The security officer was entitled to question Mrs. Faniel, an employee, on the employer's premises, about a violation of company policy, without incurring liability for false imprisonment. . . . Here, [the] brief questioning of Mrs. Faniel was directed toward investigation and explanation of suspicious circumstances, and terminated immediately upon admission of wrongdoing. . . . Under the facts of this case . . . we cannot say that a detention occurred, even during the subsequent trip to appellant's home for further investigation and for recovery of the unauthorized equipment.

To constitute imprisonment, the restraint of appellant's freedom of movement by appellees must have been total. Appellant's movements could be restrained, of course, even in a traveling automobile, if she was compelled to go along against her will. The driver of a car imprisons an unwilling passenger by restraining the passenger's liberty.

However, it is not enough for plaintiff to feel "mentally restrained" by the actions of the defendant. The evidence must establish a restraint against the plaintiff's will, as where she yields to force, to the threat of force or to the assertion of authority. Although plaintiff may submit to a confinement without resistance, if the submission is voluntary, as where an accused voluntarily accompanies his accusers to vindicate himself, then no false imprisonment occurs.

Submission to the mere verbal direction of another, unaccompanied by force or threats of any character does not constitute false imprisonment. Similarly, fear of losing one's job, although a powerful incentive, does not render involuntary the behavior induced.

Appellant's testimony at trial indicates that she did not accompany the telephone employees because of threats, either of force or prosecution. She did not at any point object or attempt to leave the car. . . .

. . . Absent evidence that appellant accompanied the other employees against her will, we cannot say she was imprisoned or unlawfully detained by appellees. Indeed, it cannot be false imprisonment where the "prisoner" voluntarily submits, without proof of duress or force legally sufficient to vitiate the apparent consent. Appellant failed to demonstrate, however, the absence of lawful consent, part of the definition of false imprisonment.

. . . Mrs. Faniel testified that she never consented to the detour to pick up the C&P security officers, and expressed concern during the ride, about the unfamiliar route. Nonetheless, Mrs. Faniel did not object, or manifest a desire to leave the car at that point, so as to negate her prior consent and convert her into an unwilling passenger on the trip to her home to recover the company equipment.

We conclude that the evidence, viewed most favorably to appellant, was insufficient as a matter of law to establish false imprisonment. Therefore, the judgment . . . for appellees was properly granted.

Case Questions

1. Do you believe that a jury of reasonable people could have come to a verdict in favor of Faniel? Why is this question important in this case?

2. To what limits may an employer go to interrogate an employee about misconduct? Construct a scenario for this case that would exceed that limit.

3. Do you think that a "mental restraint" may ever satisfy the elements of a false imprisonment? Explain.

4. What additional facts would you like to know to render an opinion in this case?

Police officers are authorized to effect an arrest under certain circumstances: when an officer possesses a warrant or has reasonable cause to believe a suspect has committed a crime. An unlawful arrest, however, results in false imprisonment and is often referred to as false arrest. Additionally, false arrest may result when one was lawfully arrested but detained beyond lawful limits, as, for example, a refusal to release a prisoner even after the required bond for release is posted.

In recent years, many states have passed laws giving shopkeepers and their agents the authority to detain people they reasonably believe have stolen goods from their store. These laws permit a reasonable detention for the time necessary to contact law enforcement officers to effect an arrest. Any detention beyond a reasonable time, or in an unreasonable manner, results in false imprisonment.

Intentional Infliction of Emotional Distress

In order to recover for the tort of **intentional infliction of emotional distress,** the plaintiff must show outrageous misconduct that results in severe emotional distress. These requirements make recovery very difficult. For example, in one case,[2] a creditor attempting to collect a debt and knowing that the debtor had heart problems nonetheless made repeated phone calls to the debtor, even at the hospital; told others that the debtor was writing bad checks, which was not technically true; and pretended to inventory the debtor's property in attempts to intimidate. Nonetheless, these actions were not considered a tortious intentional infliction of emotional distress.

Defamation

Communications that injure another's reputation may be actionable under the tort of **defamation.** Defamation occurs when a communication tends to hold one up to contempt or ridicule, or to cause the victim to be shunned or avoided. It is defamatory to falsely say that a person has attempted suicide, is immoral, or refuses to pay just debts. These accusations tend to affect reputation by diminishing the victim's esteem in the eyes of others.

Any living person may be the target of defamation. Corporations, partnerships, and unincorporated associations may also be defamed.

Some communications are obviously defamatory; others are defamatory because of the circumstances surrounding the communication. For example, accusing one of burning down his house is not obviously defamatory since a person has a right to destroy his or her own property. However, if the innuendo is that the person burned his house in order to collect insurance proceeds, this would constitute defamation.

A claim of defamation must be based on communication to someone other than the person defamed. If, for example, Polly accuses Rolly of selling horsemeat, no defamation occurs if only Rolly hears the communication.

When defamation is published orally it is considered **slander;** when it is published in any permanent form it is considered **libel.** Libelous communication may include writings, pictures, signs, and statues. Dissemination by videocassette tapes would also appear to fall under the class of libel.

Generally, in order to recover for slander, one must show that actual money damages resulted from the slander. Actual monetary loss may be shown by proof of loss of a contract, employment, or customers. This rule, however, is not applicable in cases of libel. Generally, one may recover for libelous publication on a showing of monetary or nonmonetary damages. Nonmonetary damages may include, for example, mental anguish or humiliation. However, there are four types of slander, referred to as **slander per se,** where, like libel, the plaintiff need not show

---

[2]*Public Finance Corp. v. Davis,* 360 N.E. 2d 765 (Ill. 1976).

actual monetary loss to recover. They are accusing a person of (1) a serious crime that involves moral turpitude, (2) having a loathsome disease (such as leprosy or a sexually transmitted disease), (3) an act that adversely affects the victim's business reputation, and (4) sexual immorality. In any of these exceptions, it is sufficient to show nonmonetary harm in order to recover.

Several defenses to defamation exist. Truth is a defense. A defendant who proves the truth of the accusation will not be found liable for defamation. In most jurisdictions, the defendant's motives are not material as long as the publication is true.

Certain persons have an absolute privilege to defame when their communications occur within the scope of the discharge of their duties. These include judges and others involved in the judicial process, legislators, and those within the executive branch of government. The law affords these government officials great latitude so that they will not be hampered by a stifling of their communications (or the threat of suits) in the performance of their jobs.

Some situations give rise to a qualified (conditional) privilege to defame. Where a party has a right or a duty to publish matter to a person who has a special interest to receive it, a qualified privilege arises. Former employers have a qualified privilege to communicate information about a former employee to prospective employers. Persons communicating to proper authorities for the prevention or detection of crimes similarly enjoy a qualified privilege. In these cases, even though the communication is defamatory, the communicator will not be guilty of defamation unless there is a malicious motive attached to it.

Defamation may be accomplished quite innocently, negligently, or maliciously. Where, however, the plaintiff is a public figure, there must be proof that the statements were made with **actual malice**—knowledge of falsity or in reckless disregard of the truth. This requirement regarding public figures—those who are within the public focus—is an attempt to balance the constitutional right of free speech and press with the plaintiff's reputational interest.

Invasion of Privacy

Recognition of a legal right to be let alone arose in the late 19th century. Initially, it was a reaction to the tendency of the press to snoop and pry into the private affairs of public figures. Today, decisions upholding a right to privacy generally fall within one of four categories:

- Intrusion.
- Public disclosure of private facts.
- False light.
- Appropriation.

Intrusion occurs when a person's privacy is physically invaded. The invasion must be of the type that is offensive to a reasonable person. An illegal wiretap of one's home constitutes such an intrusion.

Many employers today require employees to submit to drug-detection tests as a device for screening employees. This raises invasion of privacy questions. However, most courts find drug testing in the workplace to be lawful as long as:

- The drug test is conducted at a time reasonably contemporaneous with the employee's work time.
- The purpose for monitoring is the concern for employee performance or safety.
- The employee receives notice of the adoption of a drug-testing program.

Public disclosure of private facts arises when information, private in character, is exposed to the public gaze. Publishing in a newspaper the fact that one does not pay his or her debts violates this category of invasion of privacy. Employers often gather detailed private information about their employees. Release of true but private and embarrassing information about an employee constitutes public disclosure of private facts. The following case involves an alleged invasion of privacy within the workplace.

BEARD v. AKZONA, INC.
517 Supp. 128 (E.D. 1981)

Stella Beard and her husband William worked at Akzona. William suspected that Stella and Bosma, another Akzona employee, were having a romantic affair. William informed his supervisor, Holt, and the site manager at the plant, Benning, of his suspicions. Benning called a meeting with Swann, Bosma's immediate supervisor, and Davis and Avery, personnel officers at the plant. They decided that Benning should confront Bosma with the story. Bosma denied the charge.

William then tapped his own phone and recorded incriminating conversations between Stella and Bosma. He shared the tapes with Benning, who listened to the tapes and discussed the situation with management personnel within the company.

Bosma and Stella were terminated. Stella, the plaintiff, sued the defendant, Akzona, for damages. She claimed invasion of privacy. The jury awarded her a judgment of $80,000. Akzona filed a motion for judgment notwithstanding the verdict.

TAYLOR, Judge

(a) Invasion of Privacy
Plaintiff claims that she is entitled to recovery of the jury's verdict on the basis of the defendant corporation's invasion of her privacy. There is no doubt that the tort of invasion of privacy has been recognized by the Tennessee Courts.

(1) Intrusion
Having been cited to no Tennessee cases explicitly defining this aspect of invasion of privacy, we defer to the statement of the law contained in *Restatement (Second) of Torts,* section 652B. That section provides:

> One who intentionally intrudes, physically or otherwise, upon the solitude or seclusion of another or his private affairs or concerns, is subject to liability to the other for invasion of his privacy, if the intrusion would be highly offensive to a reasonable person.

The tort "consists solely of an intentional interference with [the plaintiff's] interest in solitude or seclusion. . . ." This "intrusion" type of claim represents the purest form of invasion of privacy. Clearly the crux of plaintiff's claim must be that the defendant—here, the corporation—intentionally invaded her solitude or seclusion. Whether the information gained by reason of the intrusion was ever publicized is irrelevant to this form of invasion of privacy.

Assuming that a wiretap on the plaintiff's telephone constitutes a sufficient intrusion to give rise to liability there is no proof in the record that the defendant Akzona, Inc., had anything whatsoever to do with the actual interception of any of plaintiff's conversations with Bosma. In fact, plaintiff alleges in her complaint that it was her husband and not the defendant who placed the wiretap on her telephone. There was no evidence that he did so in his capacity as an agent or employee of the defendant.

Plaintiff maintains that Benning's . . . phone call to William to tell him to bring the tapes was itself an act of intrusion sufficient to give rise to the defendant's liability. We cannot agree. Benning's call was in response to several prior calls from William informing Benning of the existence of the tapes and of their contents. His call to William in no way constituted an intentional intrusion into the solitude or seclusion of Stella; nor, for that matter, did his mere act of listening to taped conversations obtained wholly independently by a third party.

The record is devoid of any proof that the defendant in this case, Akzona, Inc., at any time *itself* intentionally intruded upon plaintiff's solitude or seclusion, or that it ordered or authorized any such intrusion by any employee or agent acting in that capacity. Plaintiff's claim of intrusion cannot, therefore, support the jury's verdict.

(b) Publicity Given to Private Facts
At trial, plaintiff also relied on the type of invasion of privacy involving undue publicity of purely private matters. Again, we turn to the *Restatement (Second) of Torts* for guidance. Section 652D provides:

> One who gives publicity to a matter concerning the private life of another is subject to liability to the other for invasion of his privacy, if the matter publicized is of a kind that (a) would be highly offensive to a reasonable person, and (b) is not of legitimate concern to the public.

We assume that the private facts surrounding plaintiff's relations with a fellow employee were both highly offensive and not a legitimate concern to the general public. The question is whether the evidence shows the kind and extent of publicity that can give rise to liability.

The interest protected by the tort is the plaintiff's right to be free from unwanted *publicity*. Thus essential to recovery is a showing of a *public disclosure* of private facts. Communication to a single individual or to a small group of people, absent breach of contract, trust, or other confidential relationship, will not give rise to liability.

With all conflicts resolved in plaintiff's favor, the evidence shows that, at most, Benning disclosed the information contained in the tapes to only five individuals; Swann, Avery, Davis, Givens and Coley. As stated above, all of these people were management employees of the defendant corporation, and all had some job-related connection to at least one of the parties involved. We hold that plaintiff has not shown the extent of publicity necessary to give rise to liability for invasion of her privacy.

For the reasons stated, it is ORDERED that the defendant's motion for judgment notwithstanding the verdict be, and the same hereby is, granted.

Case Questions

1. What is the issue in this case?
2. Was Stella's husband guilty of intrusion? Explain.
3. Do you believe Akzona had a good reason for firing Stella? Explain.
4. Write a dissenting opinion that holds that Akzona's acts were an invasion of privacy.

False light in the public's eye arises when one publishes false material designed to make a person look bad. Signing a political candidate's name to a scandalous campaign flyer in order to undermine the candidate's credibility is an example. It is akin to the tort defamation. Often, there is an overlap, and the same facts may give rise to an action for both invasion of privacy and defamation.

Appropriation occurs when a person's name, picture, or other likeness is used for commercial advantage without the person's consent. A company that places a person's picture on its cereal box without consent in order to sell cereal would be liable for appropriation. Similarly, impersonating another for the purpose of gain constitutes appropriation. The law recognizes this type of misconduct as a form of "stealing one's identity" and affords a person a remedy against the appropriator. In *Carson v. Here's Johnny Portable Toilets, Inc.*,[3] a company used a well-known talk show host's introductory phrase, "Here's Johnny," to market its merchandise. The court held that the use of the phrase was a commercial exploitation that constituted invasion of privacy.

Torts against Property

Torts against property include trespass, conversion, and injurious falsehood.

Trespass to Realty

Trespass is the intentional invasion of another's real property, without authorization; the intent need not

be a matter of conscious wrongdoing. **Real property** is land and the immovable items attached to it. Houses, garages, barns, growing crops, trees, and grass are all examples of real property (see Chapter 9). The clearest example of a trespass to realty is the direct physical invasion of another's land by walking across it. The traditional view regarding trespass is that there must be an actual tangible invasion. Consequently, the projection of light, noise, and vibrations are not deemed by the majority of courts to constitute a trespass. Such invasions may, however, amount to an unreasonable interference constituting the tort—**nuisance.**

Real property ownership extends above and below the land. How high above and how far below is the subject of debate. Some states draw the line of extension to the actual use of the land. Other jurisdictions extend the limit to effective or potential use of the land. All courts have rejected the old English view that a person owns the soil "upwards into heaven and downward to perdition."

A technical trespass occurs even if no damage results except for a few blades of grass trampled under. In such a case, **nominal damages**, for example, $1, is the appropriate remedy. Nominal damages are designed to recognize an injury to one's rights where no significant economic harm is present. If the trespass is recurrent, an injunction ordering the defendant to cease from such action may be proper.

Conversion

Conversion is the intentional taking of another's personal property as distinguished from real property. **Personal property** is movable and may consist

---

[3] 698 F.2d 831 (6th Cir. 1983).

of such tangible items as wedding rings, refrigerators, and firewood (see Chapter 9). Intangible items such as checks, stocks, and accounts receivable may also be the subject of conversion. As with the action of trespass, intent does not have to be a matter of conscious wrongdoing. Mistake will not constitute a defense, so one who receives stolen goods and continues to exercise dominion over the goods commits conversion even if unaware that the goods were stolen. However, the wrongful taking must be of a serious nature.

Those factors important in the determination of seriousness include the duration of time the defendant has exercised control over the property, the defendant's motive, and the harm done. Therefore, it is not conversion for a parking lot garage attendant to innocently delay the return of the plaintiff's automobile for 15 minutes without harm to the plaintiff. However, if the delay amounts to a month with ill motive, coupled with a refusal to surrender the property, there is a conversion.

Conversion may be committed in a number of ways. Acquisition of the property without justification is one way. This may be the result of theft or fraud or even mistake if the continued possession is serious. Refusal to surrender goods, lawfully acquired, to the rightful owner may also constitute conversion. For example, one who comes into possession of stolen goods unwittingly becomes a converter for refusal to surrender the goods to the lawful owner.

The proper remedy in the event of conversion is either a forced sale of the property with the proceeds awarded to the plaintiff, or, at the plaintiff's election, the return of the goods.

Injurious Falsehood

Injurious falsehood is a tort that arises when the plaintiff's property is disparaged. This is to be distinguished from defamation, which arises when the plaintiff's reputation is injured. Assume, for example, that Ron falsely accuses Chemical Designs of going out of business. This comment may tend to disparage Chemical Designs' business and deter people from doing business there. This disparagement to the business may constitute injurious falsehood.

Originally, injurious falsehood was confined to false statements affecting one's ownership interest in real property. For example, a false accusation that the plaintiff is not the true owner of property might inhibit the ability of the owner to sell the property. The tort was later expanded to include aspersions cast on the title to personal property. Disparagement of the quality of goods is also actionable. In one case, the defendant falsely charged that the plaintiff's manure was inferior to three other manures.[4] This accusation was deemed an injurious falsehood. In an injurious falsehood suit, the plaintiff must prove that the accusation was false and malicious and that it caused money damages.

Torts against Competition and Employment Relations

Torts against competition and employment relations include interference with economic relations, appropriation of trade secrets, and wrongful discharge.

Interference with Economic Relations

Intentionally interfering with another's contract is a tort. An English case decided in 1853 illustrates the tort of contractual interference.[5] A prominent opera singer was under contract to sing for a definite period of time at a theater. A competitor of the theater, knowing of the contractual relationship, nevertheless persuaded the singer to break her contract. The court held the defendant's conduct tortious. A more recent interference with economic relations resulted in a $10.5 billion judgment. In that case, a court found that Texaco, Inc., improperly acquired Getty Oil knowing that a contract existed for Pennzoil to acquire Getty.

Liability for interference with contractual relations extends beyond existing contracts to potential contracts. The tort of interference with prospective relations protects against such conduct as impeding the opportunity of obtaining employment, employees, or customers. For example, intentionally diverting customers from a shop by destroying a walkway or erecting a "closed" sign on the premises is tortious conduct. By contrast, competing vigorously for another's competitors does not constitute a tort. Attempts to increase business by undercutting a competitor's price promotes free enterprise and that alone cannot be the basis of tort liability. However, where the price-cutting motive is to drive another

---

[4] *Western Counties Manure Co. v. Lawes Chemical Manure Co.*, 9 L.R. 218 (Ex 1874).

[5] *Lumley v. Guy,* 118 Eng. Rep. 749 (1853).

out of business, competition is not promoted but destroyed. Hence, a court found tortious misconduct in a case where a defendant opened a barbershop with a malicious intent to drive the rival out of business rather than make profit.[6] Consider the following case, which involves alleged tortious interference directed toward a golf club.

---

[6]*Tuttle v. Buck,* 119 N.W. 946 (Minn. 1890).

CHEMAWA COUNTRY GOLF v. WNUK
402 N.E.2d 1069 (Mass. App. Ct. 1980)

Lorraine and Stephen Wnuk own a 25-acre residential property on Cushman Road. A golf course opened up across the road, which was purchased by Chemawa Country Golf (Chemawa). Lorraine Wnuk lodged several complaints about the noise emanating from pool parties lasting into the early morning hours.

Chemawa expanded its facilities around the swimming pool and sought to cut a new driveway entrance to its parking lot near the Wnuk's home. The Wnuks responded by a series of complaints to governmental agencies alleging zoning violations, health violations, and unlawful activities. Over a four-year period, the Wnuks appeared 14 times before the town planning board and addressed 20 written communications to it about Chemawa's activities. As a result, the town revoked Chemawa's license to have live music on the premises and to serve alcoholic beverages after 11 P.M.

On one occasion, Lorraine Wnuk parked her car near the pool and blew her horn 20 minutes at a time; she played loud music and clanged garbage can tops together to annoy Chemawa's members.

Chemawa sued the Wnuks for tortious interference with contractual relations. A jury returned a verdict of $15,000 for Chemawa against the Wnuks. After the verdict, the Wnuks moved for a judgment notwithstanding the verdict. The trial court judge denied the motion. The Wnuks appealed to the Appeals Court of Massachusetts.

KASS, Judge

In the instant case the plaintiff charges no disruption of a particular contract, rather it complains of interference with prospective contractual relations. This is a recognized extension of the more typical tort . . . which includes in the field of potential harm "any other relations leading to potentially profitable contracts." It is not necessary that the prospective relation be expected to be reduced to a formal binding contract.

As we have previously noted, it is an essential element of the tort that the defendant act without justifiable cause. The jury could have found that the purpose of Lorraine's repetitive activity was to obstruct the functioning of Chemawa's country club rather than to protect her own property rights.

It is also of the essence in an action for wrongful interference with contractual relationships that the plaintiff suffer damages as a consequence of the defendant's conduct, and those damages cannot be speculative or conjectural losses. We find the record barren of any evidence on which the jury might have found that Chemawa was damaged by Wnuk's conduct. Chemawa's principal officer, Raymond Bourque, testified that Chemawa lost club members because of the blighting effect of construction work in progress which was delayed by the Wnuks' lawsuits. Bourque also testified to time lost from work and legal expenses because of these proceedings. . . . With regard to the balance of Lorraine's activities concerning Chemawa, nothing is established other than that it was intensely irritating. Chemawa is a corporation which has no heart to ache or ulcer to bleed and, in any event, it is not vexation but interference with beneficial relations with third parties which must be established. The only tangible item of loss placed in evidence—

$310 of expenses incident to a delay arising from an unwarranted complaint to the police made by Lorraine—concerned land which did not belong to Chemawa, but to Bourque. . . . The only club members who testified concerning Lorraine's activities remained as members. No evidence tied the loss of members or green fees to Lorraine's conduct. . . . On the other hand, there was evidence that an unrelated shooting incident had occurred at the club and . . . it is at least as likely that Chemawa lost members for that quite different reason.

For this reason, the motion for judgment notwithstanding the verdict should have been allowed. On the evidence, without weighing the credibility of the witnesses or substituting the court's judgment of facts for that of the jury, there is but one conclusion as to the verdict that can be reached. Judgment reversed.

Case Questions

1. What is the issue that this case presents?
2. Why was Chemawa not complaining of conduct that disrupted existing contracts? Of what was Chemawa specifically complaining?
3. Has Lorraine Wnuk committed any other tort? Explain.
4. Modify the facts of this case so that Chemawa recovers.

Appropriation of Trade Secrets

Free competition promotes creative innovation. Inventors attempt to find new ways of doing work more efficiently. Authors seek to embody their books, dramas, lectures, and computer programs in publishable form. Federal laws provide protection for inventors and authors through patent and copyright laws (see Chapter 48). These federal laws carefully define what is protected and provide penalties for patent and copyright infringement—the unauthorized use of the protected material.

Some businesses prefer not to seek protection through patent and copyright law, perhaps because this would require them to make the invention or material public. Additionally, not all inventions and information are subject to federal statutory protection under the patent and copyright laws. Nevertheless, the common law in most jurisdictions provides protection against misappropriation of trade secrets (See Chapter 48). A **trade secret** is any formula, pattern, device, or compilation of information that is used in one's business and that gives one a competitive advantage over others. Trade secrets may be customer lists, chemical processes, and computer data. To be considered a trade secret, the owner must take reasonable precautions to maintain its secrecy. When the secret is obtained through improper means—for example, when an employee discloses secret information—the law affords a remedy (see *E. I. du Pont de Nemours & Co. v. Christopher* on page xx). The remedy may be in the form of an injunction and/or damages.

Wrongful Discharge

Torts are the product of common law, and the common law changes as society changes. From this dynamism, new torts emerge. One of the newer torts to be recognized is **wrongful discharge.** Traditionally, in the absence of protection by a contract, a statute, or a union, an employer was free to discharge an employee for any cause. This was the plight of most workers, who were aptly designated at-will employees. Recently, however, many courts have cut away at the principle of "discharge for any cause" and have afforded an employee a remedy in tort for wrongful discharge. (A more complete discussion of the erosion of the employment-at-will doctrine is found in Chapter 49.) Wrongful discharge may occur when, for example, an employer retaliates against an employee who fails to abide by employer instructions to commit an illegal act. For example, a court has held that a tortious wrong occurs when an employer discharges an employee for refusing to fix prices contrary to law.[7] Courts have also extended protection to employees who are discharged because they claim a right, such as workers' compensation, or for performing a public duty, for example, serving on a jury. More recently, **whistle-blowers**—those who inform the government that their employer is committing an illegal act—are gaining protection from discharge.

---

[7]*Tameny v. Richfield Co.,* 164 Cal. Rptr. 839 (Cal. Sup. Ct. 1980).

Figure 7–4   Intentional Torts: Defenses

Defense	Characteristic	Example
Mistake	Honest belief	Striking another under an honest misimpression that it is necessary for protection
Consent	Voluntary and specific	Informed consent to gall bladder surgery
Self-defense	Use of force proportionate to occasion	Defending against force or threat of force
Necessity	Emergency	Chased on another's property by a bulldog

The common thread among the decisions that recognize wrongful discharge as a tort is an employer discharge in bad faith and against public policy.

DEFENSES TO INTENTIONAL TORTS

Some intentional torts are defensible by a showing that the defendant was lawfully permitted to commit the wrong. These defenses are based on the policy that social justice will best be served by permitting the defendant's conduct. The more common defenses are mistake, consent, self-defense, and necessity (see Figure 7–4).

Mistake

The commission of an intentional tort may be negated by **mistake.** Where it appears necessary for the defendant to act quickly to protect a right, mistake will be a good defense against a tort action. For example, assume that Walter and Barry are engaged in a heated argument over business matters. Walter suddenly thrusts his hand into his breastpocket. Thinking that Walter is about to pull out a gun, Barry lunges at Walter's arm and immobilizes it. It turns out that, in fact, Walter was only reaching in his pocket for a handkerchief. Nonetheless, Barry's honest belief will be a good defense against a charge of battery.

Mistake, however, will not be a proper defense in every case. There is no defense just because one trespasses on the land of another or converts property mistakenly. Unlike battery, in these cases, it is not usually necessary for the defendant to act quickly to protect a right.

Consent

Consent negates intentional torts. A plaintiff who invites conduct cannot usually complain later. One who insists, "take my property," for example, may not later complain that the property was converted. Consent may also be implied from the plaintiff's conduct. Holding out an arm to be vaccinated, puckering up for a kiss, and stepping into a ring with boxing gloves are all displays of consent.

Even with consent, however, a tort may result if an individual exceeds the agreed-on terms. Inviting someone to come onto property and stay for a night is consent for the night. Any stay past that time will be a trespass. A consent to engage in a mutual fist fight does not constitute consent to be kicked or sliced with a knife. A football player impliedly consents to be tackled and even roughed up during the game. However, an intentional striking of a player, not in the course of play, arising out of anger and frustration, is beyond consent.

Consent to surgical operations is a defense to a battery claim. In cases when there is no time to gain a patient's consent because he or she is unconscious, then consent is *implied in law*. For example, when a patient is brought into a hospital emergency room, unconscious and unidentified, it is permissible to perform tests to diagnose the problem and if life is threatened, even to perform heroic measures to save the patient. Some states have "good Samaritan" statutes that protect a person who acts in good faith when going to the medical aid of another.

Self-Defense

The law affords a person the right to use force proportionate to the occasion necessary for self-protection. Verbal provocation, however, is insufficient to justify force. There must be an overt threat of physical force before self-defense is appropriate. Even then, force must be reasonable under the circumstances. The amount of force may not be greater than necessary to ward off the assailant. Deadly force can be used to meet deadly force. Thus, it is a permissible act of self-defense to use a gun against another who is attacking with a knife.

Generally, it is not appropriate to use a gun against another who is threatening with a fist. Resistance with a deadly weapon is justified only when there is a reasonable fear of loss of life or grave bodily harm.

The use of deadly force to protect oneself does not extend to the protection of property, as illustrated by the following case.

KATKO v. BRINEY
183 N.W.2d 657 (Iowa 1971)

The Brineys owned an uninhabited farmhouse. For about 10 years, there were a series of trespasses on the property by people who vandalized the premises. To stop the unlawful intrusions, the Brineys boarded up the windows and posted ''no trespass'' signs outside. Still, the incidents continued. The Brineys responded with more drastic measures. They attached a 20-gauge shotgun to an iron bed in the farmhouse bedroom, pointing the barrel at the bedroom door. It was wired so that when anyone broke into the farmhouse and turned the doorknob of the bedroom, the shotgun would go off. The gun could not be seen from the outside.

Katko knew of the premises. He had invaded it on a prior occasion and had stolen antique bottles and fruit jars. On a second trip to the Briney property, Katko and a companion entered the house through a window. When Katko opened the bedroom door, the shotgun went off and he was struck in the right leg above the ankle bone, blowing a part of his leg away.

Katko was hospitalized for 40 days; his leg was in a cast for about a year; and he wore a special brace for another year. Additionally, Katko suffered a permanent shortening of the leg.

Katko sued the Brineys, seeking damages for willful and wanton injuries inflicted on him. The jury returned a verdict against the defendants in the amount of $30,000. The defendants appealed the case to the Supreme Court of Iowa.

MOORE, Chief Judge

The primary issue presented here is whether an owner may protect personal property in an unoccupied, boarded-up farm house against trespassers and thieves by a spring gun capable of inflicting death or serious injury.

We are not here concerned with a man's right to protect his home and members of his family. Defendant's home was several miles from the scene of the incident to which we refer. . . .

Plaintiff testified he knew he had no right to break and enter the house with intent to steal bottles and fruit jars therefrom. He further testified he had entered a plea of guilty to larceny in the nighttime of property of less than $20 value from a private build-ing. He stated he had been fined $50 and costs and paroled during good behavior from a 60-day jail sentence. Other than minor traffic charges this was plaintiff's first brush with the law. On this civil case appeal it is not our prerogative to review the disposition made of the criminal charge against him.

Instruction 6 stated: ''An owner of premises is prohibited from willfully or intentionally injuring a trespasser by means of force that either takes life or inflicts great bodily injury; and therefore a person owning a premise is prohibited from setting out 'spring guns' and like dangerous devices which will likely take life or inflict great bodily injury, for the purpose of harming trespassers. The fact that the trespasser may be acting in violation of the law does not change the rule. The only time when such conduct of setting a 'spring gun' or a like dangerous device is justified would be when the trespasser was committing a felony of violence or a felony punishable by death, or where the trespasser was endangering human life by his act.''

The overwhelming weight of authority, both textbook and case law, supports the trial court's statement of the applicable principles of law.

In *Hooker v. Miller* . . . we held defendant vineyard owner liable for damages resulting from a spring gun shot although plaintiff was a trespasser and there to steal grapes. . . . ''This court has held that a mere trespass against property other than a dwelling is not a sufficient justification to authorize the use of a deadly weapon by the owner in its defense; and that if death results in such a case it will be murder, though the killing be actually necessary to prevent the trespass. . . . [T]respassers and other inconsiderable violators of the law are not to be visited by barbarous punishments or prevented by inhuman inflictions of bodily injuries.''

The facts in *Allison v. Fiscus* . . . are very similar to the case at bar. There plaintiff's right to damages was recognized for injuries received when he feloniously broke a door latch and started to enter defendant's warehouse with intent to steal. As he entered[,] a trap of two sticks of dynamite buried under the doorway by defendant owner was set off and plaintiff seriously injured. The court held the question whether a particular trap was justified as a use of reasonable and necessary force against a tres-

passer engaged in the commission of a felony should have been submitted to the jury. The Ohio Supreme Court recognized plaintiff's right to recover punitive . . . damages. . . .

In addition to civil liability many jurisdictions hold a land owner criminally liable for serious injuries or homicide caused by spring guns or other set devices. . . .

In Wisconsin, Oregon and England the use of spring guns and similar devices is specifically made unlawful by statute.

Case Questions

1. Why was this not deemed to be a simple case of self-defense? Would there have been a different result if the Brineys were occupying the farmhouse? Explain.

2. What measures short of a spring gun were available to the Brineys?

3. What if the Brineys had placed two German shepherds within the premises? Would they be liable if the dogs injured a trespasser? What if they placed boa constrictor snakes within the premises? Any different result?

4. Formulate a rule that you feel is fair regarding defense of property located at uninhabited premises.

5. How is Katko's wrong of trespass reconciled with Briney's wrong of setting up the spring gun?

Closely related to the issue of self-defense is the right to defend others. Early common law limited the right to go to another's defense to family members. Since then, it has been extended to nonfamily members, and in many states the privilege extends to strangers. Here, the intervenor must use reasonable force under the circumstances. States are split on the consequences where a third party intervenes based on a reasonable mistake as to the necessity for taking action. Assume, for example, that Pam mistakenly thinks Claude attacked Seville, when in fact Seville had attacked Claude. Pam goes to Seville's ''aid'' and injures Claude. A slight majority of the states hold that the intervenor ''steps into the shoes'' of the person he or she is defending. In this case, since Pam was the real aggressor, Pam would be

liable for the injury to Claude. A minority of courts hold that the intervention is lawful as long as the mistake was reasonable.

Necessity

Under some circumstances, necessity justifies conduct otherwise tortious. For example, someone who dynamites a building to stop a fire that threatens the community acts out of a public necessity. In such a case, the actor is not liable to the owner for the damage.

When an act is purely for a self-interest, however, the privilege is more limited. For example, trespassing over another's property because of a blocked highway is not justified if another route is available. However, the privilege extends to a great emergency even if it involved only a private necessity. For example, going on another's land to escape from a mad dog or mooring a ship in another's dock to avoid a storm present sufficient types of emergencies to negate trespass. However, the privilege here does not extend to the destruction of the owner's land. In that case, the actor is required to pay for any damage caused by the trespass.

END–OF–CHAPTER QUESTIONS

1. What are the main differences between torts and crimes? What are the similarities? Give an illustration where one act gives rise to both a tort and a crime.

2. Name each intentional tort discussed in this chapter. For each one, create a hypothetical factual pattern to illustrate tortious conduct within a business environment.

3. Should the tort of abusive discharge be expanded to include all discharges without just cause? Explain.

4. Carol Kobeck worked the 11:30 P.M. to 7:30 A.M. shift at Nabisco bakery. On the evening of April 21, instead of reporting to work, unbeknownst to her husband, she spent the night at the home of her lover. When her husband called the bakery, he was told that she had not reported to work. The following day, Mr. Kobeck went to the bakery and spoke to the assistant personnel manager, who confirmed that his wife had not reported to work the night before. The personnel manager also showed him attendance records revealing that there were other occasions when she had missed work. Kobeck confronted his wife with his suspicions that she was seeing another man. She denied it. He then committed suicide. Carol Kobeck sued her employer, alleging that it invaded her privacy by sharing private information with her husband. How do you think the court ruled? Explain. See *Kobeck v. Nabisco, Inc.* 305 S.E. 183 (Ga. App. 1983).

5. Lambertson was employed by Armour & Co. Boslet was a meat inspector for the U.S. Department of Agriculture. While Lambertson was unloading a truckload of meat, Boslet jumped on his back, screamed boo, pulled Lambertson's wool stocking hat over his eyes, and began to ride him piggyback. As a result, Lambertson fell forward and struck his face on some meathooks. He sustained severe injuries to his mouth and teeth. Boslet had no intention to injure Lambertson. Has Boslet committed a battery? Explain. See *Lambertson v. United States,* 528 F.2d 441 (2nd Cir. 1976).

6. Sapp worked for Western Union Telegraph Co. as the manager of a telegraph office. Western Union was under contract with Hill to keep his clock in repair. Mr. Hill's wife reported to Sapp over the phone that the clock needed repair. She went to the office and found Sapp behind a counter. The counter was four feet, two inches high. It was wide enough so that Sapp reaching over the counter could just reach his fingers to the outer edge of the counter. When Mrs. Hill asked Sapp when he was going to fix the clock, he said, "If you will come back here and let me love and pet you, I will fix your clock." He reached for Mrs. Hill with his hand and she jumped back. Was a tort committed? Analyze. See *Western Union Telegraph Co. v. Hill,* 150 So. 709 (Ala. Ct. App. 1933).

7. Rouse went to Russell-Vaughn Ford, Inc., to discuss trading in his Falcon for a new Ford. He went back a second and third time. The third time, a salesman asked Rouse for the keys to his Falcon. He turned them over. Rouse then decided he did not wish to trade in his car. He asked for a return of the keys. All the employees denied knowing where the keys were and they laughed as if the matter was a big joke. Rouse called the police. After a policeman arrived, a salesman threw him the keys stating that "they just wanted to see him cry a while." What tort if any has Russell-Vaughn Ford, Inc., or its employees committed? Analyze. To what damages, if any, is Rouse entitled? See *Russell-Vaughn Ford, Inc. v. Rouse,* 206 S.2d 371 (Ala. 1968).

8. Edward Vantine Studios (Vantine) contracted with Iowa State University to photograph sororities and fraternities on the campus. A sales manager for Fraternal Composite Service (Composite) met with officers of the fraternities and sororities in an attempt to sign them to photographing contracts. The officers told the sales representative that they had existing contracts with Vantine. The sales manager suggested that they investigate the legality of those contracts and on subsequent visits signed contracts for 12 houses that had been covered by contract with Vantine. Eleven of those contracts contained a provision whereby Composite agreed to pay any legal costs or fees as a result of the breach of contract with Vantine. Is Composite liable for any tort? Explain. See *Edward Vantine Studios, Inc. v. Fraternal Composite Service, Inc.*, 373 N.W.2d 512 (Iowa Ct. App. 1985).

9. Touissaint worked for Blue Cross & Blue Shield as a manager. When hired he was told that he would continue with the company as long as he did his job. The company's personnel policy manual stated that after the probationary period, employees would only be terminated for just cause. After five years with the company, Touissaint was fired without just cause. Would he be successful in a suit for wrongful discharge? Explain. See *Touissaint v. Blue Cross & Blue Shield*, 292 N.W.2d 880 (Mich. 1980).

10.
Mr. and Mrs. John Fenton own a home adjoining a golf course operated by Quaboag Country Club. The ninth fairway adjoins the western boundary of the Fenton's home. An average of 250 golf balls land on the Fenton's property annually. Sixteen panes of glass in the Fenton's house have been broken by stray golf balls over the years. When a sand trap was added to the ninth hole, affairs worsened. The Fenton's Doberman dog was struck by a flying golf ball. Mr. Fenton has been struck by a misdirected golf ball. A family steak cookout has been interrupted by a misangled ball. On one occasion, a ball bearing the greeting "Hi, Johnnie" plummeted to the Fenton's abode. Several hostile incidents have occurred. One player ventured on the Fenton's property to retrieve a ball and wound up swinging his club at the dog and raising it at Mr. Fenton. What torts, if any, have been committed? How would you assess the Fenton's damages? What alternatives do you suggest for remedying the problem? See *Fenton v. Quaboag Country Club, Inc.*, 233 N.E. 2d 216 (Sup. Jud. Ct. Mass. 1968).

Chapter 8

Negligence and Strict Liability

■

CRITICAL THINKING INQUIRIES

As you read this chapter, you should be able to address the following:

- Compare and contrast the tort of negligence with the tort of strict liability.
- What are the shortcomings of the negligence theory of recovery?
- What are the shortcomings of the strict liability theory of recovery?
- What alternatives to our traditional tort system can you suggest?

MANAGERIAL PERSPECTIVE

Cart Hill is the manager of Methanol, Inc., a plant that produces and stores synthetic phosphate. The plant is located near a major waterway and adjacent to a farming community. Recently, a number of environmentalists have moved into the vicinity of the plant. They are protesting the presence of the plant. Hill is very concerned about liability issues in case of a phosphate leak or spill.

- What is the potential liability of Methanol, Inc.?
- What tort theories should concern Hill?
- What defenses may be available to Methanol, Inc., in the event it is sued as a result of damage caused by a phosphate leak or spill?
- What precautions should Hill take to minimize potential liability?

Cart Hill is looking ahead as do successful managers. They familiarize themselves with the laws that may be applicable to their companies. They look for trends in the law in those areas to help them better manage the present and avoid future pitfalls. Two major substantive areas of torts — negligence and strict liability — impact business. These areas are often the subject of large settlements or jury verdicts, and high costs of insurance can have the effect of bankrupting an otherwise sound company. Because of this, there is much talk of needed tort reform. Cart Hill and others will benefit from the discussion of negligence, strict liability, and alternatives to the traditional tort system treated in this chapter.

NEGLIGENCE

Negligence very simply is carelessness. Everyone is negligent from time to time, but fortunately most negligence does not cause harm to others.

A person is responsible for his or her negligent acts that cause injury to another. In some cases, the negligence of one person is imputed to another. This is the case when an employee's negligence causes injury to another while operating within the scope of employment. The employer in such a case would be deemed liable, under the doctrine of **respondeat superior** (let the master respond). For example, assume that while delivering methanol for Methanol, Inc., the driver of the truck, an employee, negligently strikes and damages a guardrail on the highway. Under the doctrine of respondeat superior, Methanol, Inc., will be liable for the damage. If, however, the driver was not acting within the scope of employment — for example, if the accident happened on the way to a bar — Methanol, Inc., would not be held responsible.

Negligence is a tort that encompasses a wide variety of conduct. In order to establish the tort of negligence (see Figure 8–1), a plaintiff must prove:

- A duty owing to plaintiff.
- Breach of that duty.
- Proximate cause.
- Injury.

Duty Owing

The law imposes a duty on people to exercise a standard of care to avoid injury to another. For example, doctors owe a duty of care to their patients;

Figure 8–1   Elements of Negligence

Elements of Negligence	Basis
Duty owing	Reasonable care
Breach of duty	Reasonable person standard
Proximate cause	Causation in fact Foreseeability
Injury	Person or property

operators of motor vehicles owe a duty of care to passengers and pedestrians; and product distributors owe a duty of care to their customers.

The law also determines the degree of care that is required. Certain activities oblige one to use greater care than others. In many jurisdictions, for example, operators of common carriers such as buses, trains, and airplanes, owe a duty of extraordinary care to their passengers. Most activities, however, are subject to the standard of ordinary care. To measure that care, the law creates a standard — the care of a **reasonable person** under the circumstances. The reasonable person always does what is right under the circumstances by exercising prudent care, skill, and judgment. The reasonable person standard is a sliding standard that is tapered to a person's age, training, and profession. Hence, a minor is held to the standard of a reasonably prudent minor, and a brain surgeon, to a reasonably prudent brain surgeon.

Breach of Duty

Negligent conduct results when a person's conduct falls short of the reasonable person's. This constitutes a breach of duty. For example, a doctor who fails to properly diagnose an enlarged appendix when presented with all the textbook symptoms of the condition has breached a duty owing to the patient; an operator of a motor vehicle who fails to yield the right of way to a pedestrian at a crosswalk has breached a duty to the pedestrian; and a manufacturer of wine who carelessly turns the wrong nozzle, resulting in the release of acid instead of wine into a bottle it distributes, has breached a duty of care to its customers.

It is the plaintiff's burden to prove that the defendant breached a standard of care. Ordinarily, the question is for the trier of the facts (jury or judge) who, on the basis of all the evidence presented, determines whether the defendant's conduct falls short of the reasonable person's. The following case, involving an employer's handling of personnel records, examines the question of a breach of a duty owing.

■

QUINONES v. UNITED STATES
492 F.2d 1269 (3d Cir. 1974)

Quinones, the plaintiff, was employed by the federal government for eight years as a law enforcement agent. His service was exemplary and he received grade promotions, commendations, and awards. He resigned from his position for personal reasons. Thereafter, he sought new employment with other law enforcement agencies and educational institutions. His applications were all refused because of statements made by his past employer indicating that he was not a fit law enforcement officer and was the subject of disciplinary action.

Quinones instituted suit against his former employer seeking compensation for injury sustained as a result of the government's negligent failure to maintain complete and adequate records of his exceptional performance on the job. The Federal District Court, applying the law of the state of Pennsylvania, dismissed the claim. Quinones appealed to the Third Circuit Court of Appeals.

ALDISERT, Judge

■ ■ ■

Plaintiff argues that the law imposes a duty on an employer to use due care in maintaining an employee's work history once it has undertaken the task of such recordkeeping and that injury to the ex-employee's reputation is foreseeable when an employer disseminates such information to prospective employers. For its part, the government argues: "In the instant case, there is present no tort principle which makes an employer's failure to compile and maintain complete employment records actionable."

. . . Conduct is negligent "if the harmful consequences could reasonably have been foreseen and prevented by the exercise of reasonable care." Restated, the act of negligence consists of the existence of a legal duty and a breach thereof. "The judge . . . is to draw his inspiration from consecrated principles. He is not to yield to spasmodic sentiment, to vague and unregulated benevolence. He is to exercise a discretion informed by tradition, methodized by analogy, disciplined by system. . . ." Mindful of these precepts we turn to elementary principles set forth in Section 285 *Restatement (Second) of Torts:* The standard of conduct of a reasonable man may be

(a) established by a legislative enactment or administrative regulation which so provides, or

(c) established by judicial decision.

First, we note that federal administrative regulations govern the establishment, maintenance and disclosure of personnel records of executive department employees like plaintiff. . . .

Moreover, 5 [Code of Federal Regulation] (section) 294.702, mandates what information may be made available to a prospective employer of a Government employee or former Government employee. Definite restrictions as to dissemination of employment information are imposed. . . . Since the regulations contemplate the dissemination of information to prospective employers and impose certain safeguards, a risk of injury to an employee's reputation is contemplated. Thus, it follows that there arises a corresponding duty to use reasonable care in maintaining the accuracy of the records. By finding that the United States does owe plaintiff a duty of reasonable care in the maintenance of his personnel folder, we do not indicate the precise bounds of the government's duty, nor intimate that the duty is breached merely by permitting inaccurate information to be filed or by failing to file pertinent information. Questions of breach of duty and causation, as well as possible defenses to the action in negligence, will be considered by the district court on remand in the processing of plaintiff's claim.

Alternatively, we have endeavored to ascertain whether a standard of conduct for the employer can be said to have been established by Pennsylvania judicial decision. While our research has uncovered no precise precedent covering the facts of this case, we know, at least, that the employer would be required to confront the doctrine that one who gratuitously assumes to render a service obligates himself to proceed with due care. . . . "When an agency of the United States voluntarily undertakes a task, it can be held to have accepted the duty of performing that task with due care."

Having due regard for those principles of tort law followed by the Pennsylvania Supreme Court, we are persuaded that the state courts would recognize a duty of the defendant personal to the plaintiff to use due care in keeping and maintaining employment records, and that for breach of that duty, plaintiff may have a cause of action if he is injured thereby and if the defendant's breach was the proximate cause of his injury. We do nothing more than continue "in the tradition of spinning out applications of accepted precedents. . . .

The judgment of the district court will be reversed.

Case Questions

1. What practical problems confront the employer in a large business who is attempting to maintain accurate personnel files?
2. What is the first sentence in the opinion that tips you off as to the way the court is going to rule? Why?
3. Restate the decision of the court as a syllogism.
4. What type of controls should an employer implement to protect against misrepresenting an employee's work record?

Res Ipsa Loquitur

Breach of a duty of a standard of care may be proved by circumstantial evidence. A banana peel found on a supermarket floor, black, flattened, and dry, would give rise to an inference that it was there for a long enough time that management should have discovered it. Akin to this concept of circumstantial evidence is **res ipsa loquitur,** which literally means, "the thing speaks for itself." This rule of evidence helps the plaintiff in a negligence action survive a motion to dismiss and thus have the case decided by the jury based on the evidence. It establishes an inference that the defendant breached a standard of care and was thus negligent. Res ipsa loquitur may be invoked when (1) an event occurs that ordinarily does not happen in the absence of negligence and (2) the instrumentality causing the injury was within the exclusive control of the defendant. Assume, for example, a barrel of flour rolls out of the defendant's warehouse and strikes a passing pedestrian. Ordinarily, this event would not occur unless someone was negligent. And, since the barrel was within the exclusive control of the warehouse-defendant, res ipsa loquitur would be applicable. Similarly, elevators do not ordinarily fall, boilers do not explode, and foreign objects are not found in sealed food containers unless someone is negligent. Res ipsa loquitur raises an inference of negligence under each of these circumstances.

Res ipsa loquitur does not absolutely establish negligence; it merely sets up a presumption of negligence that the defendant may rebut by offering credible proof to negate the defendant's negligence. In the example involving a barrel of flour, the defendant might rebut the presumption by proof that the warehouse was closed and vandals broke in and released the barrel on the street.

Violation of a Statute — Exam question

The plaintiff's necessity to prove a breach of a standard of conduct may be aided by a statute. In some cases, a breach of a statute gives rise to negligence, termed **negligence per se.** Negligence per se arises only when (1) the plaintiff is within the class of persons intended to be protected by the statute, (2) the plaintiff suffers the type of harm the statute was intended to prevent, and (3) the breach of the statute caused the injury.

Statutes requiring druggists to clearly label poisons are for the benefit of the public. Additionally, they are intended to prevent injury that occurs when a person is mistaken about a package's contents. Here, a broad class is within the intended scope of protection. Some statutes intend only protection for a narrow class of persons. For example, a statute requiring guardrails on conveyor belts in factories may be designed only for the protection of employees. A visitor to the plant who is injured by the conveyor belt could not invoke the negligence per se doctrine. Likewise, a statute that prohibits trains from blocking intersections during certain hours may be intended to prevent delays of traffic. Personal injury sustained as a result of a violation of the statute is outside the harm the statute was intended to prevent.

Proximate Cause

Proximate cause is a third ingredient the plaintiff must prove to establish the tort of negligence. Proximate cause may be broken down into causation in fact and foreseeability.

Causation in Fact

Causation in fact is established when the plaintiff proves that the defendant's conduct was a substantial factor in contributing to the plaintiff's injury. Causation in fact simply answers the question: Did the defendant's conduct actually cause the plaintiff's harm? One who sets a fire at home may *cause* injury to an adjacent building. The failure to erect a fence around a swimming pool may be the cause of a child drowning in the pool. But a person's conduct or omission is not a cause of injury if the harm would have happened anyway—as, for example, when an improperly constructed house is leveled by an earthquake that would have leveled it even if the house were properly constructed.

The burden of proof regarding causation is on the plaintiff. However, there are exceptions. One exception is when two negligent acts occur close in time and only one of the acts causes injury. For example, assume that two defendants, while hunting, negligently shoot at the plaintiff. The plaintiff is only struck by one bullet, which, according to the evidence, could have been discharged by either hunter's gun. Only one person has caused the harm here, but the law places the burden on both defendants. To defeat liability for the entire harm, the burden shifts to the defendant to prove that his or her conduct did not in fact cause the harm.

Foreseeability

Causation in fact is not the end of the determination of proximate cause. All events can be traced back historically to original or remote causes. Ultimately, one could blame Adam and Eve for all our woes. But the policy of the law limits the defendant's responsibility to immediate or foreseeable harm as opposed to remote or unforeseeable harm. The question then posed is whether, at the time of the imprudent act or omission, the consequences of injury were reasonably foreseeable. Assume, for example, that an employee of Methanol, Inc., the company in our opening scenario, carelessly threw a rock that hit a can that fell over and dropped on a load of wastes destined to be incinerated; assume, further, that the can tripped a wire in the incinerator that caused a short that two days later resulted in an explosion that damaged some nearby barns. Is the employee liable for the damage to the barns on the basis of negligence? The answer is no, since at the time the employee threw the rock, it was not reasonably foreseeable that the chain of events causing damage to the barn would occur. What if the rock struck and injured a co-employee passing by? Here, liability would attach, since the resulting injury is within the foreseeable consequences of throwing the rock. The next case illustrates proximate cause in the context of medical malpractice.

CHRYSTAL v. THE HAWKES HOSPITAL
598 N.E. 2d 1174 (Ohio App. 1991)

Chrystal, the plaintiff, underwent breast reduction surgery to alleviate back pain. In anticipation of the surgery she had a unit of her blood drawn prior to surgery. A plastic surgeon, assisted by a resident, performed the surgery. Chrystal received a unit of her own blood. Thereafter, Dr. Cozzone, the defendant, ordered one more unit be given, in response to a drop in the plaintiff's hemoglobin level. Mt. Carmel Hospital did not screen the blood for the AIDS virus because it lacked the facilities to do so. Plaintiff thereafter tested positive for the AIDS virus.

Chrystal, the plaintiff-appellee, sued Mt. Carmel Hospital and Dr. Cozzone, the appellants, for medical malpractice for negligence in ordering the blood transfusion. The jury returned a verdict for the plaintiff and judgment was entered in her favor in the amount of $8,150,000. The defendants appealed to the Ohio Court of Appeals, contending that the trial court had failed to properly instruct the jury on remote cause.

BOWMAN, Judge

A defendant is not liable to one injured as the result of some unusual occurrence that cannot fairly be anticipated or foreseen and is not within the range of reasonable probability. Foreseeability of harm usually depends upon the defendant's knowledge. However, if an injury is the natural and probable consequence of a negligent act, and it is something that should have been foreseen in light of all of the attending circumstances, the injury is then the proximate result of the negligence. It is not necessary that the defendant should have anticipated the particular injury; it is sufficient that his act is likely to result in injury to someone.

There is nothing in the record before this court disclosing a state of facts whereby an ordinarily prudent physician should not have reasonably anticipated or foreseen that appellee could get AIDS, or any other disease associated with blood transfusions. As early as 1983 or 1984, Mt. Carmel held a symposium for their medical staff and hospital personnel which included a lecture on AIDS. At that time, it appeared that AIDS was spread in certain risk populations; however, it was noted that AIDS was also spread in a manner similar to Hepatitis B, which can be transmitted by blood.

Dr. Michael Greenburg, a hematologist from the Mount Sinai School of Medicine testified that, in January 1984, *The New England Journal of Medicine* published an article showing 18 cases where it was felt that AIDS had been transmitted by blood. By February 1985, the Communicable Disease Center reported that there were 120 cases where AIDS had been brought on by the transfusion of blood.

". . . [T]here would not be one physician who by 1985 would not know that AIDS could be transmitted by transfusion." Based on this evidence, it was foreseeable that if a person received a blood transfusion, one of the possible consequences of the transfusion was that the person could get AIDS.

This court finds that the trial court did not err in refusing to give the requested instruction on remote cause since the instruction was not specifically pertinent to an issue in the case. The court's general charge included all of the applicable law necessary to decide the case and, as such, it was sufficient to lead the jury in their decision-making process. The judgment of the trial court is affirmed.

Case Questions

1. What is the issue?
2. As to Dr. Cozzone, would there have been a different result if there had been a life-threatening demand that required Chrystal to have an immediate transfusion?
3. What if the hospital had used an AIDS screening device and it failed to discover the virus? Would there be a different result? Explain.
4. What should the doctor and the hospital have done to eliminate the risk of liability?

Injury

Finally, the plaintiff has the burden of proving **injury.** Without injury, there is no recovery. Injury may consist of damage to the defendant's property or person. For negligence, the defendant is entitled to compensation for this injury, referred to as **compensatory damages.** In the case of property damage, the plaintiff is entitled to an amount equal to the loss. For example, assume that as a result of the defendant's negligence, the plaintiff's car is damaged. The plaintiff would be entitled to the difference between what the auto was worth on the market before the damage and the amount it is worth on the market after the damage. Personal injury damages include medical expenses (doctor, hospital, and pharmaceutical bills) and other expenses associated with the defendant's negligence (e.g., loss of wages). Proper compensatory damages also include an amount to compensate the plaintiff for pain and suffering and psychological damages caused by the defendant's negligence.

Figure 8–2   Defenses

Defenses	Characteristic	Negligence	Strict Liability
Contributory negligence	Carelessness	Complete defense	No defense
Comparative negligence	Carelessness	Partial defense	No defense
Assumption of the risk	Voluntariness	Complete defense	Defense*

*Some states.

Courts differ, however, on the question of whether a bystander who witnesses an injury of another can recover damages for psychological trauma against the party who negligently causes the injury. Most courts hold that if the plaintiff was within the sphere of danger, recovery is proper. A number of courts extend liability to those outside the zone of danger if the injured party was a child or close relative of the plaintiff.

In most jurisdictions, the spouse of one who has a claim for negligence may also maintain a claim against the defendant for loss of the spouse's services and companionship, referred to as **loss of consortium.**

DEFENSES TO NEGLIGENCE

There are three main defenses to an action in negligence: contributory negligence, comparative negligence, and assumption of the risk (see Figure 8–2). Contributory negligence and assumption of the risk completely bar the plaintiff's recovery. Comparative negligence diminishes the plaintiff's award. In most states, the burden is on the defendant to establish the defense.

Contributory Negligence

Contributory negligence occurs when the plaintiff's own negligence is a contributing cause of his or her injury. The defense of contributory negligence, once established, is an absolute bar to plaintiff's recovery. In determining the existence of contributory negligence, the reasonable person standard is employed. The plaintiff is guilty of contributory negligence if he or she acts in a manner short of the reasonably prudent person. Assume, for example, that the plaintiff is struck by the defendant, who negligently operates a vehicle by running a red light.

The defendant may defeat recovery by showing, for example, that the plaintiff contributed to the accident by speeding.

Some jurisdictions do not distinguish between the relative fault of the parties. In those jurisdictions, however slight the plaintiff's negligence, the plaintiff is completely barred from recovery. Because of the harshness of the doctrine of contributory negligence, most states, by case decision or legislative enactment, have adopted comparative negligence.

Comparative Negligence

The majority of the states have departed from contributory negligence as a total bar to recovery. Instead, they have adopted **comparative negligence** whereby the plaintiff's recovery is diminished by the percentage he or she has contributed to the injury. This necessitates a jury verdict assessing the relative contribution of each party to the plaintiff's injury. There are two basic types of comparative negligence systems: modified and pure. Under most modified systems, the plaintiff may recover diminished damages if the plaintiff's contribution is not greater than the defendant's. Assume that the jury returns with the following findings:

Amount of plaintiff's damages	$50,000
Degree of plaintiff's negligence	55%
Degree of defendant's negligence	45%

Here, the plaintiff would be barred from recovery since the plaintiff's contribution (55 percent) is greater than that of the defendant (45 percent). If we switch the figures around so that the plaintiff's negligence was 45 percent and the defendant's 55 percent, we have a different result. The plaintiff would be entitled to recover $27,500 (55 percent × $50,000).

Figure 8–3   Negligence and Strict Liability: A Comparison

Tort	Basis	Application	Defenses
Negligence	Fault	All conduct	Contributory negligence Comparative negligence Assumption of the risk
Strict liability	Economics	Vicious animals Ultrahazardous activities Products	Assumption of the risk* Misuse of product

*Some states.

The second system of comparative negligence is called pure comparative negligence. In a jurisdiction that adopts the pure form, the plaintiff will recover an amount diminished by the plaintiff's contribution even if the plaintiff's contribution to his or her own injury is greater than that of the defendant. In the first example above, the plaintiff would recover $22,500 ($50,000 × 45%).

Assumption of the Risk

Assumption of the risk occurs when the plaintiff voluntarily assumes the risk of exposure to a known danger. Assumption of the risk completely bars plaintiff's recovery. There are two basic types of assumption of the risk: express and implied. Express assumption of the risk occurs when the plaintiff agrees in advance that the defendant is not liable for negligent conduct that injures the plaintiff. These types of agreements are often referred to as exculpatory clauses or waivers. They may be void as against public policy and are discussed more fully in Chapter 15. Implied assumption of the risk occurs when the plaintiff, with knowledge and appreciation of a particular risk, nonetheless voluntarily chooses to remain exposed to the risk.

Assumption of the risk is distinguishable from negligent conduct. The basis of assumption of the risk is consent. This is to be contrasted with contributory negligence, which is based on carelessness. Assume that Bill Bear has his brakes repaired at Friendly Garage. While operating the vehicle, Bear hears a screeching noise every time he applies the brakes. Thinking that it is nothing serious, he ignores the warning. When driving down the next hill, Bear is injured when the brakes fail to hold. Here, Bear was careless, for he should have known that the screeching noise indicated a problem with the brakes.

Under such circumstances, the reasonably prudent person would have investigated the problem before continuing to operate the vehicle. Bear was guilty of contributory negligence. Now assume that Bear, before approaching the downhill, applied his brakes and they were ineffective. Assume he could have pulled over. Nonetheless, aware of the risk, he decided to take the hill and was injured as a result. This is a case of assumption of the risk. Bear has, in effect, consented to assume the risk of injury.

Many states that have adopted comparative negligence have discarded assumption of the risk as a complete bar. In those jurisdictions, the facts underlying assumption of the risk are relevant in determining relative fault.

STRICT LIABILITY

Over the last 100 years, there have been a multitude of cases imposing liability even in the absence of intent or negligence. In these cases, the defendant is held strictly liable for harm regardless of the existence of moral blame (see Figure 8–3). **Strict liability** was first applied in the United States to the keeping of dangerous animals such as lions, tigers, elephants, and wolves. Owners of those animals who injure another are strictly liable. Some states have enacted statutes making owners of dogs or other domesticated animals strictly liable for harm done even though all precautions were taken to confine the animal.

Another group of cases impose strict liability on those engaging in abnormally dangerous activities. The English case of *Rylands v. Fletcher*[1] is an example. In that case, the defendants owned a mill.

---

[1] L.R. 3 E. & I. App. 330 (H.L. 1868).

They constructed a reservoir in order to supply the mill with water. The water broke through into a shaft of an abandoned coal mine and moved along connecting passages into the plaintiff's mine. The defendants themselves were free from personal blame, having hired contractors to do the construction work. Nevertheless, the House of Lords held that it was proper for the defendants to bear the liability for damages to the plaintiff's premises. In the United States, the principle of *Rylands v. Fletcher* was at first rejected but then widely accepted. It has been applied to such conditions and activities as use of explosives, blasting operations, phosphate mining, fumigation with cyanide gas, and erecting a dangerous dividing wall. The *Restatement (Second) of Torts* has adopted the principle of *Rylands v. Fletcher*, imposing liability for harm resulting from an abnormally dangerous activity even where the defendant has exercised the utmost care to prevent the harm. The *Restatement* lists six factors (a through f) in determining whether the activity is abnormally dangerous: existence of a high degree of risk of some

Figure 8–4 Factors Determining Abnormally Dangerous Activities

- Degree of risk.
- Likelihood of harm.
- Ability to eliminate risk.
- Common usage.
- Appropriateness of activity.
- Value to community.

harm to the person, land, or chattels of others; likelihood that the harm that results from it will be great; inability to eliminate the risk by the exercise of reasonable care; extent to which the activity is not a matter of common usage; inappropriateness of the activity to the place where it is carried on; and extent to which its value to the community is outweighed by its dangerous attributes (see Figure 8–4).

The following case discusses each of these factors within the context of a storage building for explosives.

YUKON EQUIPMENT v. FIREMAN'S FUND INS. CO.
585 P.2d 1206 (1978)

Yukon Equipment Co. (Yukon–petitioner) operated a storage warehouse for explosives in a suburban area. The warehouse, located on federal land, was 3,820 feet from the nearest building not used to store explosives. Thieves broke into the warehouse, set a prepared charge to cover up evidence of theft, and fled. The resulting explosion of 80,000 pounds of explosives damaged buildings within a 2-mile radius. An insurance company covering damaged buildings sued Yukon. The court found in favor of the insurance company, and Yukon appealed to the Supreme Court of Alaska.

MATTHEWS, Justice

Based in large part on the *Restatement (Second)*, petitioners argue that their use was not abnormally dangerous. Specifically they contend that their use of the [warehouse] for the storage of explosives was a normal and appropriate use of the area in question since the [warehouse] was situated on lands set aside by the United States for such purposes and was apparently located in compliance with applicable federal regulations. They point out that the storage served a legitimate community need for an accessible source of explosives for various purposes. . . .

If we were to apply the *Restatement (Second)*'s six factor test to the storage of explosives in this case we would be inclined to conclude that the use involved here was an abnormally dangerous one. Comment (f) to section 520 makes it clear that all of the factors need not be present for an activity to be considered abnormally dangerous:

In determining whether the danger is abnormal, the factors listed in clauses (a) to (f) of this Section are all to be considered, and are all of importance. Any one of them is not necessarily sufficient to itself in a particular case, and ordinarily several of them will be required for strict liability. On the other hand it is not necessary that each of them be present, especially if others weigh heavily.

The first three factors, involving the degree of risk, harm, and difficulty of eliminating the risk, are obviously present in the storage of 80,000 pounds of explosives in a suburban area. The fourth factor, that the activity not be a matter of common usage, is also met.

The fifth factor, inappropriateness of the activity, is arguably not present, for the storage did take place on land designated by the United States government for that purpose. However, the designation took place at a time when the area was less densely populated than it was at the time of the explosion. Likewise, the storage reserve was not entirely appropriate to the quantity of explosives stored because the explosion caused damage well beyond the boundaries of the reserve. The sixth factor, value to the community relates primarily to situations where the dangerous activity is the primary economic activity of the community in question. Thus comment (k) states that such factor applies

particularly when the community is largely devoted to the dangerous enterprise and its prosperity largely depends upon it. Thus the interests of a particular town whose livelihood depends upon such an activity as manufacturing cement may be such that cement plants will be regarded as a normal activity for that community notwithstanding the risk of serious harm from the emission of cement dust.

Since five of the six factors required by section 520 of the *Restatement (Second)* are met and the sixth is debatable, we would impose absolute liability here if we were to use that approach.

However, we do not believe that the *Restatement (Second)* approach should be used in cases involving the use or storage of explosives. Instead, we impos[e] absolute liability in such cases. The *Restatement (Second)* approach requires an analysis of degrees of risk and harm, difficulty of eliminating risk, and appropriateness of place, before absolute liability may be imposed. Such factors suggest a negligence standard. The six factor analysis may well be necessary where damage is caused by unique hazards and the question is whether the general rule of absolute liability applies, but in cases involving the storage and use of explosives we take that question to have been resolved by more than a century of judicial decisions.

The reasons for imposing absolute liability on those who have created a grave risk of harm to others by storing or using explosives are largely independent of considerations of locational appropriateness. We see no reason for making a distinction between the right of a homesteader to recover when his property has been damaged by a blast set off in a remote corner of the state, and the right to compensation of an urban resident whose home is destroyed by an explosion originating in a settled area. In each case, the loss is properly to be regarded as a cost of the business of storing or using explosives. Every incentive remains to conduct such activities in locations which are as safe as possible, because there the damages resulting from an accident will be kept to a minimum.

The next question is whether the intentional detonation of the storage [warehouse] was a superseding cause relieving petitioners from liability. . . . [A] superseding cause exists where ''after the event and looking back from the harm to the actor's negligent conduct, it appears to the court highly extraordinary that it would have brought about the harm.'' . . .

Prior to the explosion in question the petitioners' warehouse had been illegally broken into at least six times. Most of these entries involved the theft of explosives. Petitioners had knowledge of all of this.

Applying the standards . . . to these facts we find there to have been no superseding cause. The incendiary destruction of premises by thieves to cover evidence of theft is not so uncommon an occurrence that it can be regarded as highly extraordinary. Moreover, the particular kind of result threatened by the defendant's conduct, the storage of explosives, was an explosion at the storage site. . . . Absolute liability is imposed on those who store or use explosives because they have created an unusual risk to others. As between those who have created the risk for the benefit of their own enterprise and those whose only connection with the enterprise is to have suffered damage because of it, the law places the risk of loss on the former. When the risk created causes damage in fact, insistence that the precise details of the intervening cause be foreseeable would subvert the purpose of that rule of law. Reversed.

Case Questions

1. Do you agree with the court that the six-factor *Restatement* test establishes a negligence standard? Analyze.

2. What if the explosion occurred as a result of an airplane crashing into it? Would there be any different result? What about lightning striking it?

3. Consistent with this opinion, what other activities might be the subject of *absolute liability*?

4. How do you think this decision will affect owners and operators of storage warehouses for explosives?

More recently, strict liability has been extended into new fields. Probably the most extensive application today is in the area of products liability. Here, liability is imposed on the manufacturers and distributors of defective products regardless of their exercise of due care. Discussion of products liability is reserved for Chapter 23. The most widely cited reasons for extending strict liability into these areas are that (1) the supplier is in a better position to bear the cost of injury, (2) it will enhance safety, (3) it avoids proof problems the plaintiff would otherwise have to bear, and (4) it meets consumers' expectations. The strict liability ''explosion'' has not stopped at products but has been extended by a few courts to other areas such as leases and services.

Defenses to Strict Liability

The area of defenses to strict liability is somewhat clouded, and a more extensive discussion is reserved for Chapter 23, when strict liability is discussed within the context of products liability. Since strict liability is based more on economics than fault, ordinary negligence is not deemed sufficient to bar or reduce recovery. However, some jurisdictions do allow the defense of assumption of risk on the theory that this presents grossly unreasonable conduct, contributing to the plaintiff's injury. This conduct may have the effect of barring or reducing the plaintiff's recovery depending on the jurisdiction. For example, in our opening scenario, assume Methanol, Inc., is engaged in an abnormally dangerous activity, and that an explosion occurs. Those who have exposed themselves to the danger by moving near

the site may be deemed to have assumed the risk from an explosion in jurisdictions that recognize this as a defense to strict liability.

ALTERNATIVES TO TORT

Cries for tort reform ring loudly. The high cost of insurance is attributed, according to some, to large jury verdicts. For this reason, some states have passed legislation placing caps on liability awards for pain and suffering. Other states have liberalized defenses, shortened statutes of limitations, and removed strict liability as a cause of action for certain wrongs.

Tort law is based on the principle of awarding compensation to victims against a party at fault. Some states have abolished traditional aspects of tort law in automobile accident cases. They have substituted instead a no-fault system of compensation through insurance. Under such a system, a person injured in an automobile accident recovers from an insurer regardless of fault. Workers' compensation (discussed in Chapter 49), which has been in place in all states since the early 20th century, also operates on nontort principles. Under workers' compensation, a person who is injured on the job recovers from a fund regardless of fault.

A relevant question today is whether tort law should be abandoned in favor of a social system of insurance (such as workers' compensation) to compensate those injured in accidents, without regard to fault. The following article presents a case for supplanting tort law with such an alternative system.

 ### *Doing Away with Tort Law**

In the 1960s and early 1970s legal scholars debated exciting proposals to replace sections of tort law with compensation systems tailored to classes of accidents. The most pressing concern was a no-fault scheme to supplant auto-accident law. Initial legislative successes

*Source: Stephen Sugarman, ''Doing Away with Tort Law,'' 73 Cal. L. Rev. 548 (1985). Reprinted with permission.

encouraged reformers to grow increasingly bold in their proposals. However, they have not been able to retain center stage. In the political arena, the auto no-fault movement has ground to a halt. In academia, tort theory has captured the limelight. . . . It is time . . . to focus academic and political attention once more on doing away with ordinary tort actions for personal injury.

■ ■ ■

. . . [T]ort law is unlikely to promote more desirable behavior than that which would occur in its absence. . . . In the absence of convincing data on deterrence, there is no reason to conclude that tort law and its baggage yield a net social gain. Given its enormous administrative costs, it is reasonable to conclude that the system is operating in the ''red.'' . . . I am not advocating that society abandon behavior control, but rather that new non-torts approaches be tried. . . .

■ ■ ■

Over the past few decades, it has become increasingly popular to view victim compensation as the central purpose of tort law. This idea has particularly infected the courts, and it is easy to appreciate why courts find ''compensation'' so appealing. Appellate judges typically must choose between a single plaintiff who may have suffered greatly and a defendant who is a giant enterprise or is backed by an insurance company. Judges and juries realize that such defendants can readily absorb and widely distribute this loss. . . . At the same time, it often appears that the victim may not be able to absorb the loss very well; the financial burden of the accident may be crushing. Since courts usually do not have access to evidence of plaintiffs' collateral benefits, they play it safe and assume the worst—no health insurance, no sick leave, no Social Security. . . . Besides, even though a particular victim may be well off, courts formulate doctrine to protect other less fortunate victims.

In sum, given (a) the general compassion for accident victims, (b) the superior loss-spreading abilities of tort defendants, and (c) the activism of today's judiciary, tort law has become a dynamo for doling out compensation to meet a presumed need.

There are, however, serious shortcomings to this approach. No matter how passionately they wish to compensate victims, judges are stuck with the administrative apparatus of tort law, the rules of damages, and an obligation to maintain a modicum of fidelity to principles of private adjudication. Because of these constraints, tort law fails as a sensible general system for accident victim compensation.

Moreover, while some praise creative judicial expansions of the existing structure, one result is that tort law becomes harder to supplant. This is the familiar problem of the good being the enemy of the best. The need for a better approach to compensation becomes less urgent because at least some victims are helped. More important, vested interests entrench and multiply. As the system grows, the stakes increase, and these interests find more reasons to fight the displacement of tort. At the same time liberalizing tort law takes time, talent, and attention away from work on superior compensation plans.

■ ■ ■

My judgment is that the mammoth social costs of ordinary tort law, importantly including the socially undesirable behavior prompted by tort law, outweigh its benefits. Thus, were tort law for accidents repealed, society as a whole would gain. This seems especially so if one reasonably assumes that absent tort law new private compensation arrangements would emerge so as to alter considerably the background context against which tort law so operates. . . .

■ ■ ■

. . . Once we disengage mechanisms for compensation and accident avoidance, we can address income protection and medical expense reimbursement in the broader context of protection for the population at large. . . .

■ ■ ■

In general . . . all Americans should be assured both income for periods of nonwork and medical-expense protection commensurate with that provided by progressive employers. There are many ways to reach this goal. The government could play an exclusive or minor role, depending upon the extent of mandated employee benefits.

■ ■ ■

. . . In the scheme I'd prefer, the government would radically simplify that system. With responsibility divided for lost income, medical expenses, and rehabilitation costs, employers would pay for short-term benefits using enterprise revenues. An expanded social security system, funded by payroll and income taxes, would provide long-term benefits. Deterrence would be the domain of administrative agencies concerned exclusively with safety, the market, self-protection, and private morality. The regulatory agencies would be bolstered by new citizen participation roles. Actions in tort might remain for cases of intentional wrongdoing, and private injunction remedies would still be available to stop unreasonably dangerous activities. But we would do away with the core of modern tort law.

Thought Questions

1. Take a position defending the continuation of traditional tort principles.
2. Can you identify any flaws in the author's logic?
3. Fill in more detail about the system the author proposes.

≈

END–OF–CHAPTER QUESTIONS

1. Compare and contrast breach of duty and proximate cause.

2. Distinguish between causation in fact and foreseeability.

3. Do you think it is appropriate for a court, as opposed to a legislature, to adopt a comparative negligence standard? Explain.

4. Do you think strict liability should be extended to accountants and other professionals? Analyze.

5. What are your thoughts of a no-fault system of liability replacing our common law fault theory? Explain.

6. Derdiarian, employed by a subcontractor, was engaged in sealing a gas main. James Dickens suffered an epileptic seizure and lost consciousness while operating his motor vehicle near the work site. Dickens's automobile struck Derdiarian and threw him into the air. When he landed, he was splattered with 400 degree hot liquid enamel that was released from a kettle also struck by Dickens's automobile. Derdiarian's body was ignited into a fireball but he survived. He sued Felix Contracting Corporation (Felix), the general contractor (he also sued Dickens), claiming that Felix negligently failed to safeguard workers on the site by erecting a barrier around the site and posting warning signs to motorists. Discuss each of the elements of negligence and determine whether Derdiarian would prevail against Felix in a suit.

7. Simpson was a paying guest at the Econo-Lodge Motel. He was given room number 27. Simpson took a shower. After he finished his shower he pushed in the shower-bath control knob. The water from the shower knob stopped, but moments later a sudden burst of scalding hot water gushed out of the shower head, hitting him. While jumping to get away from the hot water, he fell on the tile floor and sustained injuries. In an action against the Econo-Lodge Motel, will the

doctrine of res ipsa loquitur help Simpson? Analyze. *Simpson v. Cotton*, 390 S.E. 2d 345 (N.C. App. 1990).

8. The jury returned with the following findings:

Plaintiff's damages	$100,000
Plaintiff's negligence	70%
Defendant's negligence	30%

What is the verdict in a jurisdiction that (1) does not adopt comparative negligence but applies the doctrine of contributory negligence, (2) adopts modified comparative negligence, (3) adopts pure comparative negligence?

9. Waste Technologies Industries (WTI) operates a hazardous waste incineration plant. It spews thousands of tons of toxic chemicals into the air annually. It has taken all known safety precautions and received all the appropriate licenses to operate. WTI is located within 400 yards of an elementary school. It sits within one mile of the populated portion of the local community. Members of the community are complaining that the chemicals are causing illnesses (including rare forms of cancer) to the citizens within the community. Under what tortious standard should WTI be judged? What would the citizens need to prove to recover for injury? Analyze.

10. Roth commercially grew grass seed on 55 acres of land near an interstate highway. After the harvest of the grass, Roth and a crew burned the field after plowing a protective strip around the perimeter. An unexpected whirlwind carried burning material from Roth's field to an adjacent landowner's field, causing over $8,000 damage. Is Roth liable for the damage? Under what theory? Explain. *Koos v. Roth*, 293 Or. 670, 652 P.2d 1255 (1982).

Chapter 9

Property

■

CRITICAL THINKING INQUIRIES

As you read this chapter, you should be able to address the following:

- Compare and contrast a lay definition of property with a legal definition of property.
- Compare and contrast personal property with real property.
- Analyze this statement: "The law of real and personal property should be unified."
- What new interferences with the use of real property can we anticipate as technology continues to advance?
- What would you change about our property law system if given the opportunity, and why?

MANAGERIAL PERSPECTIVE

Nicole Allen is the managing partner of Wacker & Sons Systems. On Monday, Allen is contacted by the building code inspector, who wants to investigate rumors of zoning violations at the main office building that the partnership owns. On Tuesday, she receives a call from the county property assessment office informing her that they are sending an appraiser to reassess the value of the partnership's factory building. On Wednesday, the firm's lawyer calls and wants to know how the partnership wants to transfer specific property. On Thursday, the company's insurance agent informs Allen that the "fixtures" in the plant that were destroyed in a recent fire were uninsured. On Friday, she learns that the city is contemplating taking the land on which the partnership's home office sits for use as a bird sanctuary.

With her feet on her desk and the eraser end of a pencil in her mouth, she thinks, "Why didn't I ever study about property in college?"

- What is the difference between real and personal property?
- What are the various ways of acquiring and transferring property?
- What is a fixture, and what is its significance?
- What legitimate restrictions may the government place on the use of property?

Figure 9–1   Bundle of Rights

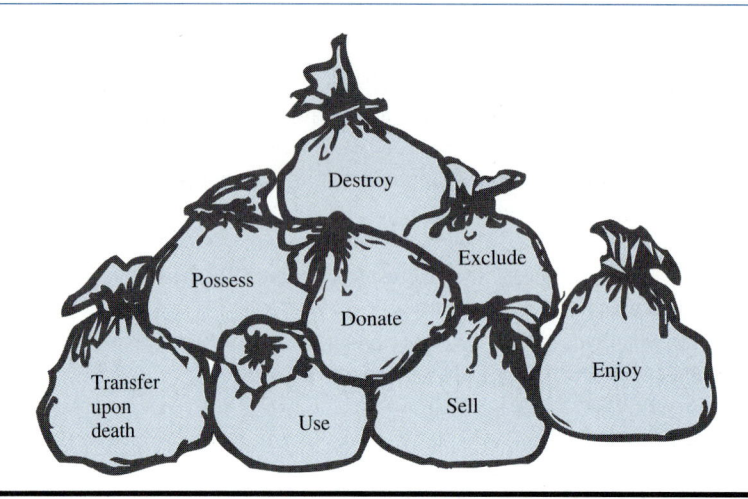

Managers such as Allen confront property issues daily, without realizing it. The concept of property is a slippery one. A mastery of this chapter is not a panacea for the woes confronting Allen this week; however, it does present the basics necessary for a working understanding of personal and real property.

DEFINING PROPERTY

Property is all around us. Every *thing* has certain physical properties in the scientific sense. However, we are concerned about property in the legal sense. Property, for our purposes, is concerned with legal relationships — the relation between things and people.

Property may consist of houses and trailers, puppies and gerbils, jewelry and clothing, stock and patents, and even jobs and pensions. What all these things have in common is that they are capable of being owned or possessed, and as such, the owner enjoys certain rights in the things. That is why at least one definition of property is simply a "bundle of rights." The owner of a sports car, for example, has a variety of rights in that car, including the right to sell, lease, and loan, the right to use it and to exclude others from its use, the right to give it away, and even the right to destroy it (see Figure 9–1).

With this in mind, a philosophical question may arise: Is everything property? Is the nearest star property? It certainly is in the physical sense; however, since no one may enjoy a bundle of rights in it, then it would not be considered property from a legal view. The following article suggests another way of looking at property.

 ### *The Concept of Property**

When a layman is asked to define "property," he is likely to say that "property" is something tangible, "owned" by a natural person (or persons), a corporation, or a unit of government. But such a response is inaccurate from a lawyer's viewpoint for at least two

*Source: Browder, Cunningham, & Smith, "The Concept of Property," *Basic Property Law* (St. Paul, Minn.: West Publishing, 1984). Reprinted by permission.

reasons: (1) it confuses ''property'' with the various subjects of ''property,'' and (2) it fails to recognize that even the subjects of ''property'' may be intangible.

■ ■ ■

The institution of ''private'' property, which has existed in most of Western Europe since the end of the Middle Ages and in the United States since its founding, has long been a subject of controversy among philosophers, political scientists, and economists. At least five different theories have been advanced to justify the institution of ''private'' property. These theories, briefly stated, are as follows: (1) the ''occupation'' theory—that the simple fact of occupation or possession of a thing justifies legal protection of the occupier's or possessor's claim to the thing; (2) the ''labor'' theory—that a person has a moral right to the ownership and control of things he produces or acquires through his or her labor; (3) the ''contract'' theory—that ''private'' property is the result of a contract between individuals and the community; (4) the ''natural rights'' theory—that the ''natural law'' dictates the recognition of ''private'' property; and (5) the ''social utility'' theory—that the law should promote the maximum fulfillment of human needs and aspirations, and that legal protection of ''private'' property does, in fact, promote such fulfillment.

The institution of ''private'' property has, of course, been the subject of vigorous criticism in the Western world from very early times. Such eminent philosophers as Plato and Sir Thomas More rejected ''private'' property and argued for ''communal'' property. More recently, Marx and Engels proposed the abolition of ''private'' property in the ''means of production'' and transfer of the ownership of the ''means of production'' to the State. Despite important modifications, the doctrines of Marx and Engels still provide the philosophical basis for the widespread transfer of ownership of the ''means of production'' to the State in . . . China, Vietnam, and other ''Communist'' nations. But even in the ''Communist'' nations ''private'' property has not been completely abolished. . . .

In recent years a number of American scholars have advanced an economic theory of property. Posner, e.g., asserts that ''the legal protection of property rights has an important economic function: to create incentives to use resources efficiently,'' and that there are three criteria of an efficient system of property rights:

1. Universality—i.e., ''all resources should be owned, or ownable, by someone, except resources so plentiful that everybody can consume as much of them as he wants without reducing consumption by anyone else.''

2. Exclusivity—to give owners an incentive to incur the costs required to make efficient use of resources owned by them.

3. Transferability—because, ''[i]f a property right cannot be transferred, there is no way of shifting a resource from a less productive to a more productive use through voluntary exchange.''

Posner's assertion that the legal protection of property rights performs the economic function of creating incentives to use resources efficiently is, of course, a normative proposition rather than a factual description of the way in which the rules of property law actually operate at any given time in a particular legal system. But—although neither the courts nor the legislatures have consistently been articulate on the point—it seems clear that the Anglo-American law of property has rarely lost sight of this normative proposition. Moreover, it seems likely that the future development of the Anglo-American law of property will be more explicitly based on that proposition.

It should be noted that much of the ''private'' property in the United States and Western Europe is held, at the present time, not by individuals directly, but by ''legal entities'' such as business corporations and religious corporations. Moreover, a good many things—both land and things other than land—are owned by governments.

Thought Questions

1. Explain why the authors object to characterizing property as things. Do you agree? Explain.
2. Which of the five theories do you adopt for justifying private property? Explain.
3. Do you agree with Posner's economic theory of property? Identify any criticisms against it.
4. Analyze "[T]hat the legal protection of property rights performs the economic function of creating incentives to use resources efficiently is, of course, a normative proposition rather than a factual description of the way in which the rules of property actually operate."

Property is ordinarily divided into two types: personal and real. Personal property is property that is generally movable—for example, furniture; real property is property that is immovable—for example, houses. This chapter will further explore the law of personal and real property.

PERSONAL PROPERTY

Personal property comes in a variety of shapes, sizes, and values. It may be as large as an elephant or as small as a safety pin. It may be as valuable as the Hope Diamond or as valueless as the pulp of a carrot.

Personal property is "personal" because it can move with the person. This is readily observable with clothing and jewelry. However, items such as refrigerators and boats, though personal property, are not as readily movable with the person. Nonetheless, they are "unattached," and this is one trait that distinguishes personal from real property.

Personal property may be divided into two categories: tangible and intangible. **Tangible personal property** is property that is capable of being touched, such as a briefcase or a nutcracker. By contrast, **intangible personal property** cannot be touched. Intangible property includes stocks, copyrights, goodwill of a business, and bank accounts. Each of these property rights may be evidenced by a writing—for example, by stock certificates, contracts, and savings passbooks—that represents the intangible property.

Acquisition of Personal Property

Personal property may be acquired in a number of ways. Often, acquisition occurs by purchase, gift, or inheritance. Sometimes property is acquired by find, by accession, or by confusion.

The most common way to acquire personal property is by purchase. Purchase is governed by contract law, treated in Chapters 11–18. Normally, the purchase of goods is evidenced by a bill of sale or a receipt for the goods. For small purchases, such as items purchased at a local pharmacy or supermarket, a cash register tape evidences purchase. However, for larger transactions, such as the sale of a business or major household furniture and appliances, a more detailed receipt (called a bill of sale), clearly specifying the items of sale is normal.

Gift

Another method of acquiring personal property is by gift. A gift occurs when a donor voluntarily gives property to a donee. At this point, title to the property vests in the donee. In order for a gift to be effective, three requirements must be met. First, there must be **donative intent**—that is, the donor must intend a present transfer of ownership of the property. Assume, for example, that Pinella says to Okra, "Take this stereo for me, and hold it until my return." Here, Pinella's intent is not to permanently transfer ownership but only to invest temporary custody of the stereo in Okra. There is no gift because donative intent is lacking. This is also the case if Pinella promises to give Okra her stereo "for your next birthday." A promise to give a gift in the future does not transfer ownership and is unenforceable. The donor must intend an immediate transfer, rather than a future transfer, in order for the transfer to be considered a gift.

Second, the donor must deliver the property to the donee. **Delivery** is a legal concept. It involves surrender of control over the property. Of course, a physical transfer of Pinella's stereo to Okra would satisfy this requirement. However, manual delivery is not always necessary or even feasible. Delivering the property to the donee's agent constitutes effective delivery. If, for example, Roy delivers a bouquet of flowers to Gloria's secretary (her agent) for Gloria, delivery occurs. And if the property is already in the possession of the donee, then there is no need to redeliver it to the donee.

Delivery may also occur by surrendering something to the donee that gives the donee control over the property. For example, Larkin surrenders the key to his storage locker to Harkness and says, "Here, the books in my locker are yours." Since Larkin has surrendered control over the locker by delivering the key, a valid transfer occurs. However, if the donor retains control over the property, no delivery results. Assume that Larkin had two keys to the storage locker and maintained control over one. Here, transfer to Harkness would not constitute effective delivery since Larkin still retains control over one key. The donor's surrender of control must be complete.

Intangible property may be delivered by surrendering control over the document that signifies the property. Hence, stock in a company may be delivered by transferring the stock certificate evidencing ownership of the stock.

Third, the donee must accept the gift. Although rare, a donee may refuse the gift, such as where the property is burdensome or not valuable.

Inheritance

Property may pass to heirs on a person's death. Property may be left to a designated person in a will, or it may pass under the laws of succession in the absence of a will. These concepts are thoroughly discussed in Chapter 10.

A type of gift similar to gift by inheritance is a **gift causa mortis**. This type of gift is made in contemplation of death from a particular disease or illness. However, it differs from a gift by will in that it does not have to conform to the formal statutory requirements of gifts by will. It need only conform to the requirements of a gift: donative intent, delivery, and acceptance. However, a gift causa mortis is distinguishable from an ordinary gift. The gift causa mortis is automatically revoked in the event the donor does not die from the particular illness or should the donee die before the donor.

Find

The common law established an elaborate set of rules, based on characterization of the found property, to resolve ownership of property found by a person. Wild animals were property that no one owned until they were caught. For example, two hunters may be stalking a wild deer. The first one to catch it is the lawful owner. A trespasser, however, cannot acquire title, and no title is acquired to a wild animal that has been taken in violation of law.

Another characterization of found property is **abandoned property**. Abandoned property is property discarded by the owner. The circumstances surrounding the presence of the property must be considered when determining whether that property is abandoned. An old refrigerator left in a dump yard is most certainly abandoned. By contrast, the same refrigerator left on the porch for several months by owners who are living in the house is not abandoned property. Abandoned property is acquired simply by taking possession. The finder of abandoned property has good title against the entire world, including the true owner. Trespassers, of course, cannot lawfully obtain title to abandoned property.

Lost and mislaid property are two other types of property that may be found. **Lost property** is property that is involuntarily left somewhere. **Mislaid property** is property that is voluntarily placed somewhere and forgotten. For example, a wallet found on the sidewalk is probably lost, whereas the same wallet found on the checkout counter at the local grocery store is probably mislaid. The owner of the premises is entitled to possession of mislaid property but must hold it in trust for the owner's benefit. This rule is predicated on the belief that one who has mislaid property will quite naturally, after remembering, call on the owner of the premises where the property was mislaid. The finder of lost property is entitled to possession of the property to be held in trust for the owner of the property. The following case involving found jewelry illustrates the importance of the distinction between lost and mislaid property.

RAY v. FLOWER HOSPITAL
439 N.E.2d 942 (Ohio Ct. App. 1981)

Karen Ray was a receptionist at Flower Hospital. She worked at the information desk greeting people who entered the main lobby of the hospital. There was a drawer for keeping lost and found property at the information desk. The drawer was locked and under the control of the receptionist. One evening, Ray noticed a soft-shell eyeglass case on the top of the information desk. The case contained (1) an opal ring with diamonds, (2) a diamond ring, (3) a ruby and a diamond ring, (4) a diamond and aquamarine ring, (5) a topaz pin, (6) a set of gold earrings, (7) a diamond necklace with a ruby or a garnet, (8) gold cuff links, and (9) one gold coin. Flower Hospital consulted the local police and the lost and found column of the *Toledo Blade*. No one claimed the jewelry.

Ray (appellee) filed a complaint seeking an order of the court requiring the court to order Flower Hospital (appellant) to return the property to her. Both Flower Hospital and Ray moved the court for summary judgment. The court granted Ray's motion, declaring her to be the owner of the property. Flower Hospital appealed to the Ohio Court of Appeals.

CONNORS, Judge

. . . [A]ppellant's brief is [based] upon the following . . . [argument]:

"The eyeglass case, having been found on top of the information desk of defendant hospital, should be deemed to be mislaid property and by law remain with the owner of the premises."

With respect to appellant's . . . argument . . . "mislaid property" [is defined] as follows:

"[P]roperty which the owner has involuntarily parted with through neglect, carelessness, or inadvertence, that is, property which the owner has unwittingly suffered to pass out of his possession and the whereabouts of which he has no knowledge.

"[A]rticles which are accidentally dropped in any public place, public thoroughfare, or street, are lost in the legal sense."

The substance then, of this court's analysis, must be a determination of whether the property in question is legally "lost" or legally "mislaid."

It is uncontroverted that the eyeglass case containing the jewels was found lying on the top of the information desk, not on the floor of the hospital in front of the information desk. Further, it cannot be presumed that the property was lost or abandoned from the mere passage of time, although this is another fact or circumstance to be taken into consideration in the particular case. Clearly, 15 years from the time the property was found would indicate that presumably the property was lost. However, another case indicates that four years is not an unreasonable time within which the owner can reclaim the property. Thus, the six months that elapsed in the case [at hand] from the time of discovery until the time that the appellee filed suit to ascertain the ownership of the property, did not create a presumption that the goods were either lost or mislaid.

The location in which the property was found in the case . . . however, does aid this court in its labeling the goods as lost or mislaid property. The jewels were secreted away in a soft-shell eyeglass case. They were not found strewn across the floor whereby anyone walking into the hospital could view them. Further, the eyeglass case containing the jewels in this case was laid down on the top of the information desk by someone, presumably the owner, or someone seeking their return to the true owner by turning the case in to the "lost and found" desk, and was not dropped by inadvertence, negligence or carelessness as would be the case of lost property. From all of the facts and circumstances of this particular case, this court finds that the property was mislaid, and, as such, should remain in possession of the hospital.

Thus, the trial court was in error in awarding possession and control of the goods to the appellee.

Judgment reversed.

Case Questions
1. Why was the property in the eyeglass case characterized as mislaid property? Do you agree? Explain.

2. What is the policy reason behind awarding the mislaid property to the owner of the premises as opposed to the finder? Do you believe it is a sensible rule? Explain.

3. Change the facts to make the property clearly lost instead of mislaid.

4. What if the mislaid property is never claimed by the true owner and the state does not have a statute for guidance. Who should be entitled to the property? Explain.

5. Construct a statute that would clearly specify the rights and responsibilities of the ''players'' involved in mislaid property.

Today, many states have modified these common law finding rules by finding statutes. Finding statutes detail the obligations of one who finds lost, mislaid, and abandoned property. They normally require that the finder turn over the property to a designated governmental official within a specified number of days. Failure to do so may result in criminal liability. The statutes also specify the finder's rights, which include the right to all or a portion of the property in the event it is not claimed by the owner within a specified time period — for example, one year.

Accession

Accession is a change or improvement to personal property by a nonowner. The question, in such a case, may arise: who owns the improved property, and is the improver entitled to compensation? The answer is determined by the circumstances. If the improvement occurs as a result of an agreement, the agreement controls.

In some cases, accession occurs without the owner's knowledge. Consider, for example, a case where a thief steals an automobile and installs a new engine, thus increasing the value of the car. Here, because the improver's actions were wrongful, the owner is entitled to the car with the new engine. The thief is, of course, not entitled to compensation. However, if a party innocently improves property owned by another, there may be a different result. For example, assume Ted purchases a motorcycle and then customizes it. Later, it is made known that the motorcycle was actually stolen and owned by someone other than Ted's seller. The owner would be entitled to a return of the cycle in its improved state. However, in most states, Ted would be entitled to compensation for the cost of improvements. In some states, he could recover the value of appreciation of the cycle due to the improvement.

In rare instances, title to the property may change as a result of an innocent accession. When one in good faith changes the nature of the property or greatly enhances the value of the property, that person may gain title to the property. Assume, for example, that Cooper, believing that he owns a quantity of lumber, uses it to build a tree house in his back yard. In fact, the lumber was owned by Hopson. Since the character of the lumber has been changed by transforming it into a tree house, title to the lumber changes to Cooper. Cooper, however, must compensate Hopson for the loss.

Confusion

Confusion results when property of different owners is commingled so that the owner's property cannot be identified. Normally, this occurs when the goods are fungible — that is, each item is virtually identical to the next — like oil, grain, and nails. If the confusion occurs by accident or by an act of a third party, the remedy is to simply separate the portions belonging to the owners. Assume, for example, Wacker & Sons Farming Systems and Booth both own feed corn and it is mistakenly intermingled in a silo. If Wacker & Sons had 100 tons and Booth 200 tons, it is relatively easy to separate the corn and return the right portions to each owner. Sometimes, commingling occurs by agreement. If Wacker & Sons and Booth agree to store their corn together in one silo, then the parties would jointly own the lot, Wacker & Sons having a one-third ownership interest and Booth a two-thirds ownership interest, the proportion of their contributions.

Finally, if confusion results due to negligence or willfulness, the party at fault bears the burden of proving exactly how much of the goods he or she owns. A failure of proof results in the innocent party receiving all the property.

REAL PROPERTY

Real property, also referred to as real estate, consists of land and anything permanently attached to it. Historically, real property was the chief source of

Figure 9–2   Real and Personal Property: A Comparison

	Real Property	**Personal Property**
Location	Fixed	Movable
Method of Transfer	Deed	Bill of sale
Taxes	Local	State
Laws	Primarily common law	Primarily statutory law

wealth. Because of its importance, a whole body of law grew up around it to protect the real property owner. As a result, the law of real property is distinguishable from the law of personal property in several respects (see Figure 9–2).

Real property passes by a written instrument of conveyance called a deed. Personal property does not pass by deed. Assume that Sally Seller conveys her house by deed to Bill Buyer. Items contained within the house include drapes, a refrigerator, and shag carpets. If these items are deemed to be personal property, they will not pass to Buyer by deed but will remain the property of Seller.

Second, the sale of personal property is controlled, in large part, by Article 2 of the Uniform Commercial Code, a statute adopted by every state, whereas real property is controlled, in large part, by the common law of contracts and real property. This distinction is discussed in Chapter 11.

Third, the laws of transfer of property upon death may differ depending on whether the property is real or personal. When a decedent dies without a will, some states provide for differing share distributions to beneficiaries depending on the characterization of the property. A surviving spouse may, for example, be entitled to a fixed percentage of the real property as compared to a different percentage of personal property.

Finally, tax and insurance consequences may differ depending on whether particular property is real or personal. For example, only real property should be valued for real property tax assessments. Further, when real property is insured, questions may arise as to whether a particular item is real or personal property. This determination is often made based on the law of fixtures.

Fixtures

Fixtures are items that were once personal property but have become real property by being annexed to land or buildings. The principal test in determining whether such an item is a fixture is the intent of the attacher. Did the owner of the house intend that the window air-conditioner unit become a permanent part of the structure? The answer may be very important when a sale of the house occurs. If the air conditioner is a fixture, then it passes to the buyer by the deed; if not, the seller retains title to the air conditioner and may remove it.

Difficulties arise when the intent of the affixer is not clear. In such case, other tests must be applied to settle the question, including affixation, adaptation, and relation.

Affixation

When an item has become affixed in such a manner that it would cause damage to the property if removed, it is generally considered a fixture. Consider, for example, chandeliers, kitchen cabinets, built-in stoves and dishwashers, wall-to-wall carpeting, and fences. All these items are attached to the realty in such a fashion that removal would result in damage. As such, they would be considered fixtures and would pass to the buyer of the house by deed.

Adaptation

Another influencing factor determining the characterization of an item is the extent that the item is particularly adapted for the realty. Take, for example, custom-made window screens particularly suitable for an odd-sized window. Or, consider a pair of multiton granite statues that are located on either side of the entrance to an elaborate multimillion dollar estate. Both these items could be removed without damage to the grounds. Nonetheless, because they are customized and fit the decor of the particular estate, they would be considered fixtures.

Relation

The relationship between the party who affixed the article and the claimant is relevant. The law favors buyers over sellers and tenants over owners. Consider the seller of a home who had affixed an air-conditioner unit to the window. A court might very well lean toward the buyer in finding that the unit was a fixture. However, under similar circumstances, assume that a tenant affixed the air conditioner. Upon the expiration of the term of the lease, it is very probable that a court, leaning toward the tenant, would find that the unit was personal property, thus permitting the tenant to remove it.

The following case involving a recreation park applies the tests of the law of fixtures to a ski chair lift.

LITTLE v. NATIONAL SERVICES INDUSTRIES, INC.
340 S.E. 2d 510 (N.C. 1986)

National Services Industries, Inc. (National), owns and operates Ghost Town in the Sky, a recreational park. National hired Goforth Industries, Inc. (Goforth), to repair and redesign the chair lift used to transport visitors from the parking lot to the park. Goforth redesigned and repaired the brake system, carriage tracks and wheels, and the concrete column footings.

While riding the chair lift, Tina Little was injured. She sued National, who in turn sued Goforth, alleging negligence in the redesign and repair of the chair lift. The trial court dismissed National's complaint against Goforth on the grounds that the repairs made to the chair lift were improvements to real property and thus barred by a statute of limitations requiring such actions to be commenced within six years. National appealed the decision to the North Carolina Court of Appeals.

MARTIN, Judge

The sole issue raised by this appeal relates to the status of National's chairlift as an "improvement to real property." If the chairlift is considered a part of the real property, G.S. 1–50(5) bars National's . . . claim, otherwise the statute has no application. . . .

G.S. 1–50(5) is a statute of repose which bars actions for personal injuries or property damages allegedly caused by defects in design, construction or repairs to real property unless the action is brought within six years from the completion of the work. Both National and Goforth agree that Goforth's work was completed more than six years before the initiation of this action. . . . Therefore, the resolution of this case depends upon whether there is any genuine issue of material fact as to the status of National's chairlift apparatus as an "improvement to real property."

National is the owner of the chairlift and of the premises upon which it is situated. Where the owner of the land and the owner of the chattel are the same person, annexation of the chattel to the realty gives rise to a presumption that the owner intended that the chattel become a part of the realty. Although the presumption may be rebutted by evidence of a contrary intention, the relationship of the parties to this controversy requires that the contrary intention be ascertainable from facts and circumstances reasonably apparent to Goforth. The burden of showing the contrary intention is upon the party claiming that the annexed chattel is personal property.

The characteristics of the chairlift and its relationship to National's land and its business are undisputed. The chairlift consists of towers, cables, tracks, wheels and other component parts, operated by electricity, and it is used to transport customers from National's parking lot at the highway to its recreational park at the top of the mountain. The nature of the annexed chattel and its use in connection with the business conducted on the realty is strong evidence of the intention with which it was attached to the realty.

The chairlift is appropriate to National's use of its land and it is apparently consistent with National's interest that the chairlift be treated as a part of the realty. Thus, to persons having no notice to the contrary, the nature of the chairlift and its use give the reasonable outward appearance that National intended that it be a part of the real property.

The manner in which the chattel is attached to the land also provides objective evidence of the intention of the party attaching it. In this case, the structure, or principal part of the chairlift system, is attached to National's property by means of steel tower legs bolted to poured concrete foundations. There is no question that the concrete footings were annexed to the real property; attachment of the tower legs to the concrete footings by bolts is also a sufficient actual annexation to the soil to show an intention that the chairlift system be a part of the real property. Where the principal part of the machinery is physically annexed to the realty, component parts thereof which are not physically annexed, but which, if removed, would not be useful other than as component parts of the machinery and the removal would leave the principal part useless, are considered to be annexed.

All of the external indicia of intent shown by the uncontested facts are consistent with an intention by National that the chairlift be made a part of the real property. National argues, however, that a genuine issue of fact as to its intention is created by its assertions as to the manner in which it treats the chairlift for tax purposes and as to the common practice with respect to chairlifts in the recreational park industry. We disagree. National's internal accounting treatment of the chairlift would evidence its subjective intention that the chairlift remain personalty. However, in the absence of some showing that Goforth had actual or constructive notice, this accounting practice would not ordinarily be ascertainable to third parties and would therefore not be relevant to the issue of National's intent. There was no showing that Goforth was engaged in the recreational park industry or familiar with practices among those who are.

. . . The judgment of the trial court must be affirmed.

Case Questions

1. Phrase the issue in this case as a single question.
2. Why is there so much concentration on the intent of the attacher when determining whether an item is a fixture?
3. What arguments did National make to support its contention that the chairlift is personal property? Do you agree with the court's rejection of these arguments? Analyze.
4. Under what circumstances might the chair lift have been considered personalty under an objective test of determining intent?

Intention

In order to avoid uncertainty, the parties should expressly agree on the characterization of an item. Thus, in a purchase contract for the sale of real property, the parties should specify what items are deemed fixtures. This intention will govern.

Trade Fixtures

Trade fixtures are those articles or appliances attached to leased buildings by a tenant in furtherance of a trade or business. They include, for example, barbers' chairs in a barbershop, bar stools in a bar, shelving and display freezers in a grocery store, and kitchen stoves and appliances in a restaurant. Trade fixtures are removable by the commercial tenant at the termination of the lease as long as any injury to the premises are remedied. Thus, even though an item is annexed to the property, it is removable by the tenant if it is a trade fixture.

Estates

The origin of American law regarding interests in real property is derived from English feudal rule dating back to the Norman conquest in 1066. Under feudalism, the king owned all the real estate and conferred status on his favored knights by investing them with estates; they, in turn, would entrust estates to loyal subjects. The estate holders owed a variety of obligations to their land grantors, including military service and rents. Today, in the United States, land is held privately and the feudal hierarchy no longer exists. However, remnants of the feudal system may be seen in some of the ancient terminology.

There are basically two types of interests in land—freehold estates and nonfreehold estates. **Nonfreehold estates** are leaseholds (leases)—those with a definite duration. **Freehold estates** are those held for an indefinite duration and include fee simples, fee tails, and life estates (see Figure 9–3).

Leases

A **lease** is a contract for the use of land or buildings. Ownership does not change, only occupancy. The one who leases property is termed the **lessor** or landlord. The one to whom the property is leased is called the **lessee** or tenant. Since a lease is a contract

Figure 9–3   Estates

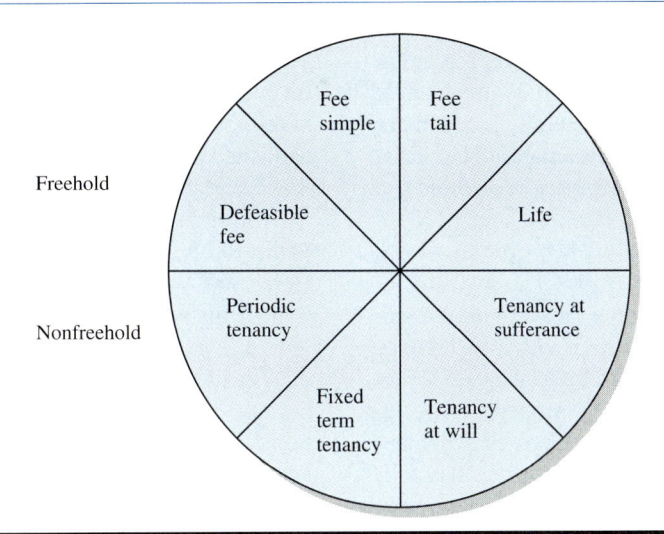

between the lessor and lessee, all of the requirements of a contract apply to leases. These requirements are covered in Chapters 11–18. The four common leases are the term tenancy, periodic tenancy, tenancy at will, and tenancy at sufferance.

A **term tenancy**, also known as an estate for years, has a definite beginning and ending date. To "Wacker & Sons for one year" is an example of language creating a term tenancy. At the end of the year, the tenancy automatically expires. No notice is necessary.

A **periodic tenancy** continues for successive periods of time until proper notice to terminate the tenancy is given by the landlord or the tenant. The periods are usually from week to week or month to month, but they may be any other periods. The formation of a periodic tenancy may occur by express agreement of the parties — for example, by contract "L leases to T from week to week beginning January 1." However, the periodic tenancies normally arise by implication when the landlord leases to the tenant without an agreement on the duration but requires rent to be paid periodically. If, for example, the rent is due monthly, then this would create a month-to-month tenancy.

Another way the periodic tenancy is created is when a tenant remains on the premises after the expiration of a term tenancy, with the permission of the landlord. The term tenancy is then converted into a periodic tenancy with the period determined by how often the rent is due.

Periodic tenancies are terminable by either party on proper notice. Proper notice is one full period's notice. Assume, for example, that Wacker & Sons, a landlord, and Stella, a tenant, entered into a month-to-month lease whereby rent is due on the first of each month. On February 10, Wacker & Sons gives notice to Stella to quit the premises March 10. This would be inadequate notice, since the notification must be given one full period prior to the periodic rental due date. Wacker & Sons would have to give notice by February 1 in order to give Stella a full month's notice before the rental due date. Some states have modified these common law rules to require a longer or shorter notice period.

A **tenancy at will** is exactly that. It continues until either party desires to terminate it. The tenancy at will may arise when parties enter into a defective lease, because of failure to comply with law. Or, it arises when parties enter into a lease where no term or rent is specified. At common law, no notice was required to terminate a tenancy at will. However, many states, by statute, require a minimum notice period.

A **tenancy at sufferance** is created when a person is wrongfully in possession of another's premises in the absence of a valid lease. The tenancy at sufferance arises when a term tenancy expires and the tenant refuses to leave the premises contrary to the landlord's will.

The tenant at sufferance is similar to, but different than, a trespasser. A trespasser enters the premises wrongfully and remains wrongfully. A tenant at sufferance enters the premises lawfully but remains wrongfully. The tenant at sufferance may be evicted at any time, while the trespasser may be arrested and criminally prosecuted.

Freehold Estates

The **fee simple absolute** is the most common ownership interest. It gives the owner virtually absolute rights in the property. The fee simple absolute owner may make unlimited use of the property, only restricted by state and local laws such as environmental or zoning requirements. The fee owner may sell, lease, or otherwise carve out lesser interests in the property, such as the life estate discussed shortly. The owner may transfer the property by will, or, if the owner dies without a will, the property passes to the next of kin as provided by state statute. In essence, the fee simple absolute estate owner possesses the greatest interest that private ownership in this country has to offer. A fee simple absolute is granted, in most states, by a deed conveyance stating, "To [name of grantee]."

A modification of the fee simple absolute is the **fee simple defeasible**, or defeasible fee. A defeasible fee is conditional and terminates upon the happening of a stated condition. The most notable conditions are those placed upon use of the property. Assume that Wacker & Sons deeds real property to a wildlife conservation organization "as long as the property is not used for hunting." The estate would terminate and revert back to Wacker & Sons in the event the prohibited behavior occurs. Under some circumstances, the reversion would be automatic; under others, the original grantor would have to institute a legal action to effectuate the reversion.

The **fee tail** estate, common in England during feudal times, limited the passing of an estate to lineal descendants. The common language transferring a fee tail would be "to [name of grantee] and the heirs of his body forever." This would have the effect of ensuring that the land grant remained in the family indefinitely. Upon the grantee's death, the property would descend to his or her child, and upon the death of that child, the property would descend to his or her child, ad infinitum. When

the lineage stopped because of no children, then the property reverted to the heirs of the original grantor.

The land under such a restriction is not very marketable, tying up land over generations in fractional interests in family members. As such, it is disfavored. Today, in the United States, many states have abolished the fee tail, and others have modified it so that the restriction may be easily removed.

A normal **life estate** conveys land "to my son, Seth, for his life, then to his children equally." Here, Seth would receive the property for the duration of his life, and afterwards it would go to the grantor's grandchildren equally in fee simple absolute. A life estate is an estate of indefinite duration, because no one knows the exact length of one's life. Sometimes, the life estate is based on the life of another—for example, "to A for the life of B." Here, A's estate will continue as long as B lives. Such an estate is called a life estate pour autre vie (for the life of another).

The life estate holder possesses an interest in the estate that he or she may sell, lease, or pledge as security to obtain a loan. However, the value of the estate is limited because it will terminate upon death. Because of this, life estates are not ordinarily very marketable.

Another type of life estate is one that arises as a result of marriage. It is called a dower interest, which is discussed more fully in Chapter 10. Dower is a life interest in one third of the lands that the decedent spouse owned during the marriage. It is a means of protecting the economic security of the surviving spouse. However, some states have abolished it in favor of other rights that guarantee the security of the surviving spouse, discussed in Chapter 10.

One who holds a life estate may not use the property in a manner that will impair its market value or use up its capital value. This is referred to as committing **waste**. The holder may not, for example, cut down all the standing timber and sell it without the permission of the **remainderman**—the person who will receive the property when the life estate terminates. The life estate holder may, however, cut down trees necessary to heat the property or to make repairs.

Concurrent Ownership

Real estate may be owned by more than one person at one time. There are a variety of ways to concurrently own real property. They include ten-

Figure 9–4   Concurrent Interests: A Comparison

	Tenancy in Common	Joint Tenancy	Tenancy by the Entirety	Community Property
Equal Interest Required	No	Yes	Yes	Yes
Survivorship	No	Yes	Yes	Yes*
Marriage Requirement	No	No	Yes	Yes
Passes to Heirs	Yes	No	No	Yes*

*One half of the community property.

ancy in common, joint tenancy, tenancy by the entirety, and community property ownership (see Figure 9–4).

Tenancy in Common

The most widely used form of concurrent ownership is the **tenancy in common**. Each tenant possesses an undivided right to the entire parcel. Ownership interests may be in any fraction; equal ownership is not required. Hence, assume that Alice, Brenda, and Carol own a parcel of land known as Breakacre as tenants in common; Carol owns one sixth, Brenda one third, and Alice one half. Each would have an equal right to possess the whole; however, upon sale by all the owners, each would receive her fractional interest multiplied by the sale price.

Upon death of any tenant in common, that tenant's interest passes to the tenant's heirs and not to the other cotenants. These heirs continue to hold the property as tenants in common with the other tenants. Suppose Brenda died, leaving two heirs, Evan and Farah, who share her property equally. Evan would own one sixth and Farah one sixth, and they would be tenants in common with each other and Carol and Alice.

Any tenant in common may sell his or her interest without the consent of the others. Assume, for example, that Alice sells her one half interest to Gladys. Gladys would now own a one-half interest as tenant in common along with the other cotenants.

Joint Tenancy

The **joint tenancy** is a form of concurrent ownership in which the estate passes to the surviving co-owner upon the death of the owner. Assume husband and wife own their home, Grandacre, as joint tenants. Upon the wife's death, the property will automatically pass to the husband. This survivorship feature distinguishes this type of ownership from the tenancy in common.

To create a joint tenancy, four features, called *unities*, must exist: possession, interest, time, and title. Unity of possession gives each cotenant an undivided interest in the whole. Unity of interest requires that each tenant hold the same fractional interest in the estate. Unity of time and title means that the parties took by the same instrument at the same time. The joint tenancy is severed by a break in any of these unities. For example, Carson and Anders hold Whiteacre as joint tenants. Carson sells his one-half interest to Billings. The unity of time and title has been broken. Billings and Anders would thus hold as tenants in common.

Tenancy by the Entirety

Tenancy by the entirety is a method by which husband and wife may own real property. It is similar to joint tenancy because the property passes to the survivor upon death of the cotenant. However, unlike the joint tenancy, it may not be severed by one tenant. In order to sever the tenancy by the entirety, both husband and wife must agree. Otherwise, it continues until death or divorce.

Because of the nature of the tenancy, creditors of one of the spouses may not ordinarily satisfy the debt out of the tenancy by the entirety. Thus, the tenancy by the entirety estate is often used to thwart creditors. As a result, many states have abolished it.

Community Property

Some states, including Idaho, Washington, Oregon, Texas, California, and Nevada, recognize the law of **community property**. Community property is a form of co-ownership between husband and wife, each of whom owns one half of all property acquired during the marriage as a result of the labor of either. This is true even if the property is held in the name of one spouse only.

Separate property is excluded from community property. Separate property is property each spouse brought into the marriage and property acquired by gift or inheritance during the marriage. In most of those states, real property that is purchased by a spouse with separate property funds is considered separate property. The law of community property varies among the community property states. Upon divorce in a community property state, the community property is divided equally; both parties are entitled to retain their separate property.

Transfer of Real Property

Real property may be transferred from one person to another by deed, inheritance, or by adverse possession.

Deed

The ordinary way to transfer real property is by **deed**. A deed is a written instrument that transfers title to realty. Deeds are used to transfer real property that is sold or that is the subject of a gift. Deeds usually include:

- The names of the grantor and the grantee.
- The legal description of the property.
- The interest that is being transferred.
- The signature of the grantor and the grantor's spouse.

Most states require that a deed be witnessed, notarized, and recorded.

There are a number of types of deeds. The most common deeds are the general warranty deed and the quitclaim deed. A **general warranty deed** con-

tains assurances that the grantor owns the property; the grantor has the right to convey the property; the property is free from encumbrances, such as mortgages; and the grantor will defend against claimants who contend that they have a superior title. In contrast, a **quitclaim deed** makes no warranties. It is often used in divorce cases, when one spouse is ordered to release his or her share in a home to the other spouse.

Inheritance

Real property, like personal property, may also be transferred by will. The testator may devise specific parcels of real property to specific persons; or, alternatively, the testator may devise all real property to specific persons. In such a case, a common clause within a will may read:

> All real property, wheresoever situate, that I may own at my death, I devise to my children equally, share and share alike.

As in the case of personal property, real property passes to the heirs of a decedent who has not made a will. The state laws of intestate succession discussed in Chapter 10 govern.

Adverse Possession

Under some circumstances, real property passes against the wishes of the grantor. This may occur by **adverse possession**. Adverse possession arises when all of the following occur:

- A person takes exclusive possession of the real property of another.
- The property is taken openly, not secretly.
- The possession continues for a period of time (ranging from 10 to 21 years, depending on the state).
- The possession is adverse — that is, against the interest of the owner.

When these elements occur, the adverse possessor gains an ownership interest in the property. The owner may stop this from happening by instituting a trespass suit (discussed in Chapter 7) against the adverse possessor before the requisite period of possession occurs. Assume, for example, that Wacker & Sons has been exercising exclusive control over a farmhouse that is owned by a neighbor. It does this even after numerous requests by the neighbor to cease doing so. After the requisite statutory period

Figure 9–5   Dimensions of Real Property

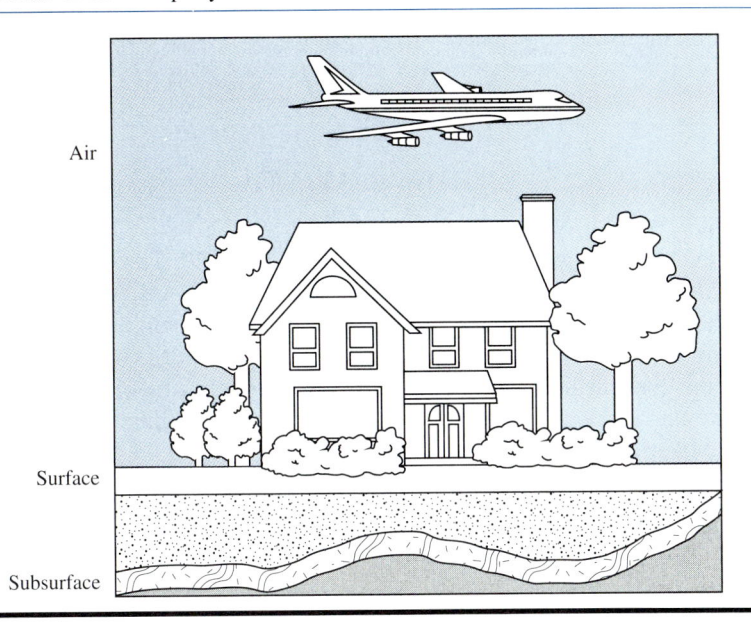

Air

Surface

Subsurface

of time—for example, 20 years—Wacker & Sons will gain the ownership interest in the property. There would be a different result, however, had Wacker & Sons merely used the farmhouse with the neighbor's permission.

Extent of Ownership Interest

Real property consists of land and the buildings attached to it. It also includes water, air, and subsurface space (see Figure 9–5).

Water

Streams, lakes, rivers, and other waterways flow on the surface of the earth. Those lands that are adjacent to surface waters are called **riparian lands**, and those who own such lands are referred to as riparian owners.

In the United States, there are two main theories that control water rights: riparianism and prior appropriation. **Riparianism** is the dominant theory and is applicable in all states east of the Mississippi and many other states. Riparian rights doctrine gives riparian owners equal use of the waters that abut their property. Most states allow these owners reasonable use of the water. Each riparian owner is entitled to use the water as long as it does not adversely affect another riparian owner. Thus, up-

stream riparian owners may make full use of the water, provided it does not unreasonably interfere with downstream riparian owners. A riparian owner may not dump wastes in the water and thus make it unusable for downstream owners.

The second doctrine is **prior appropriation**. It is applied in the western arid states. The essence of prior appropriation is "first come, first served." Those owners who first used the water have primary rights to the water and may have unlimited beneficial use of the water. The allocation of water in prior appropriation states is subject to administrative control. A system of permits is used to determine who has the right to appropriate the water.

Air

Traditionally, a landowner owned from the soil to the heavens above. However, with the advent of airplanes, this rule became impractical. To apply it rigidly would mean that airplanes above a property owner's land, no matter how high, were trespassing and subject to the owner's objection.

Today, courts, recognizing the need for efficient air transportation, have modified the traditional theory. The landowner owns the space above the property that is reasonably usable. It is reasonable to erect a large antenna on one's roof, and even a star platform on top of the highest tree. In fact, in one case, the court held that an airplane that made regular test flights 18 feet above the highest tree was an unreasonable invasion on the owner's airspace.

The following case involving "rights to the sun's rays" addresses the doctrine of reasonable use.

PRAH v. MARETTI
321 N.W.2d (Wis. 1982)

Glenn Prah, the plaintiff, is the owner of a solar-heated house. The solar system includes collectors on the roof that supply energy for heat and hot water. After Prah constructed his solar-heated house, Maretti, the defendant, purchased a lot adjacent to Prah's residence and began planning construction of a home. Prah informed Maretti that if the home were built according to the construction plans, it would "cause a shadowing effect on the solar collectors that would reduce the efficiency of the system and possibly damage the system." Nonetheless, Maretti began construction.

Prah sued Maretti, seeking to enjoin construction. The trial court denied the injunction and entered summary judgment in favor of Maretti. Prah appealed to the Supreme Court of Wisconsin.

ABRAHAMSON, Judge

This state has long recognized that an owner of land does not have an absolute or unlimited right to use the land in a way which injures the rights of others. The rights of neighboring landowners are relative; the uses by one must not unreasonably impair the uses or enjoyment of the other. When one landowner's use of his or her property unreasonably interferes with another's enjoyment of his or her property, that use is said to be a private nuisance.

The private nuisance doctrine has traditionally been employed in this state to balance the conflicting rights of landowners, and this court has recently adopted the analysis of private nuisance set forth in the *Restatement (Second) of Torts*. The *Restatement* defines private nuisance as "a nontrespassory invasion of another's interest in the private use and enjoyment of land." The phrase "interest in the private use and enjoyment of land" . . . is broadly defined to include any disturbance of the enjoyment of property. . . .

Although the defendant's obstruction of the plaintiff's access to sunlight appears to fall within the *Restatement*'s broad concept of a private nuisance as a nontrespassory invasion of another's interest in the private use and enjoyment of land, the defendant asserts that he has a right to develop his property in compliance with statutes, ordinances and private covenants without regard to the effect of such development upon the plaintiff's access to sunlight. In essence, the defendant is asking this court to hold that the private nuisance doctrine is not applicable in the instant case and that his right to develop his land is a right which is per se superior to his neighbor's interest in access to sunlight. This position is expressed in the maxim "cujus est solum, ejus est usque ad coelum et ad infernos," that is, the owner of land owns up to the sky and down to the center of the earth. The rights of the surface owner are, however, not unlimited.

Many jurisdictions in this country have protected a landowner from malicious obstruction of access to light (the spite fence cases) under the common law private nuisance doctrine. If an activity is motivated by malice it lacks utility and the harm it causes others outweighs any social values. . . .

This court's reluctance in the 19th and early part of the 20th century to provide broader protection for a landowner's access to sunlight was premised on three policy considerations. First, the right of landowners to use their property as they wished, as long as they did not cause physical damage to a neighbor, was jealously guarded.

Second, sunlight was valued only for aesthetic enjoyment or as illumination. Since artificial light could be used for illumination, loss of sunlight was at most a personal annoyance which was given little, if any, weight by society.

Third, society had a significant interest in not restricting or impeding land development. This court repeatedly emphasized that in the growth period of the 19th and early 20th centuries change is to be expected and is essential to property and that recognition of a right to sunlight would hinder property development. . . .

. . . These three policies are no longer fully accepted or applicable. They reflect factual circumstances and social priorities that are now obsolete.

First, society has increasingly regulated the use of land by the landowner for the general welfare.

Second, access to sunlight has taken on a new significance in recent years. In this case the plaintiff seeks to protect access to sunlight, not for aesthetic reasons or as a source of illumination but as a source of energy. Access to sunlight as an energy source is of significance both to the landowner who invests in solar collectors and to a society which has an interest in developing alternative sources of energy.

Third, the policy of favoring unhindered private development in an expanding economy is no longer in harmony with the realities of our society. The need for easy and rapid development is not as great today as it once was, while our perception of the value of sunlight as a source of energy has increased significantly.

Courts should not implement obsolete policies that have lost their vigor over the course of the years. The law of private nuisance is better suited to resolve landowners' disputes about property development . . . than is a rigid rule which does not recognize a landowner's interest in access to sunlight. . . .

Private nuisance law, the law traditionally used to adjudicate conflicts between private landowners, has the flexibility to protect both a landowner's right of access to sunlight and another landowner's right to develop land. Private nuisance law is better suited to

regulate access to sunlight in modern society and is more in harmony . . . than is an inflexible doctrine of non-recognition of any interest in access to sunlight across adjoining land.

We therefore hold that private nuisance law, that is, the reasonable use doctrine . . . is applicable to the instant case. Recognition of a nuisance claim for unreasonable obstruction of access to sunlight will not prevent land development or unduly hinder the use of adjoining land. . . . That obstruction of access to light might be found to constitute a nuisance in certain circumstances does not mean that it will be or must be found to constitute a nuisance under all circumstances. The result in each case depends on whether the conduct complained of is unreasonable.

Accordingly we hold that the plaintiff in this case has stated a claim under which relief can be granted. Nonetheless we do not determine whether the plaintiff in this case is entitled to relief. In order to be entitled to relief the plaintiff must prove the elements required to establish actionable nuisance, and the conduct of the defendant herein must be judged by the reasonable use doctrine. [Reversed and remanded.]

Case Questions

1. What is the issue that this case presents?
2. What factors should be relevant in determining whether a landowner's blockage of the sun is reasonable? Under what circumstances would it be unreasonable?
3. Assume that Maretti had complied with all building ordinances and that Prah had an electrical backup system. What should be the result? Explain.
4. Do you believe that this court adequately balanced the interests of the parties? Analyze.

Subsurface

In addition to the traditional perception that one's right in real property extended upward to the heavens, it also perceived rights extending downward to the center of the earth. This rule did not present great problems until technology for excavation markedly advanced and the demand for minerals such as coal, gas, and oil dramatically increased.

Two theories dominate U.S. law concerning mineral rights: ownership and nonownership. The ownership theory applies in most jurisdictions to solid minerals such as gold, coal, and limestone. These jurisdictions recognize that solid minerals are subject to absolute ownership. As such, these subsurface mineral rights may be held separately from the surface rights. Thus, an owner of real property may deed or lease mineral rights to another while still retaining ownership in surface and air rights. The owner of the mineral rights would be required to pay taxes on that property, even if the minerals are not extracted.

The ownership theory, though working well for solid minerals, is not feasible for nonsolid minerals such as oil and gas because of their migratory nature underground. That is why many states apply a nonownership theory to these minerals. Under such a theory, no one owns these minerals until they are extracted.

For oil, gas, and other minerals that travel underground, the rule of capture applies. In its pure sense, the rule of capture simply means the first one to bring the mineral to the surface is the owner. Oil, for example, flows to territorial boundaries in a reservoir or pool under the ground that may encompass many landowners' territory. The owner who is equipped with the most advanced "pumping" equipment might be able to drain the oil in one reservoir that formerly lay beneath several owners' property. Because of this apparent inequity, some judicial opinions and statutes have established rules in allocating oil and gas resources. These pooling and utilization rules differ from state to state, but in essence they require a fair allocation of minerals to those neighbors who own property above the minerals' basin.

Private Restrictions on Land Use

Few things in life are absolute. There always seem to be limitations. That is the case with ownership of real property. There are certain limitations imposed on one's use of land. Private restrictions on land usage include the law of restrictive covenants, easements, and nuisance.

Restrictive Covenants

Restrictive covenants are limitations included in the deed. Often, they are placed there by land developers who develop land into subdivisions. Certain restrictions are placed in the deeds for the benefit of the subdivision and to protect property owners against other owners whose use may tend to depreciate the value of the neighborhood. Such restrictions may limit usage to single-family dwellings and may prohibit parking vehicles on the lawn and erection of other buildings on the property.

Any homeowner in the subdivision may enforce the restrictive covenants against another by seeking a court injunction. And, the restrictive covenants normally "run with the land." That means that successor owners of the property continue to be bound by the restrictions imposed in the deed on their seller.

Restrictive covenants may be invalidated. In 1948, in *Shelley v. Kramer*, the U.S. Supreme Court refused to enforce a restrictive covenant in a deed that forbade the owner to sell to anyone of the "Negro race." The court found that for a court to enforce the covenant would be an unconstitutional denial of equal protection under the laws.

Changing neighborhoods may cause restrictive covenants to be unenforceable. Suppose a clause in the deeds to property in a neighborhood prohibits the erection of chain link fences. Assume that there currently exist scores of chain link fences throughout the neighborhood. Obviously, this restriction had not been enforced over the years. Consequently, enforcement of the restriction at this time would be senseless due to the widespread noncompliance and unenforcement of the covenant in the past.

Easements

An easement is a right of way across an owner's property. This right of way is an encumbrance that restricts the owner's usage.

There are basically two types of easements—an easement appurtenant and an easement in gross. **Easements appurtenant** normally involve two adjacent parcels of land—a dominant estate and a servient estate. The dominant estate enjoys a use of another's property, whereas the servient estate is burdened by the easement. In Figure 9–6, Parcel A is subject to an easement that Parcel B enjoys.

Easements appurtenant run with the land. Hence, if Parcel B is owned by Phil, then Phil would receive its benefit. Should Phil sell the property to Anders, then Anders would receive the benefit. The same is true for the owner of the servient estate. The burden runs with the land.

Easements appurtenant are created in a variety of ways. They may be created expressly by contract or deed. Another method of creation is by implication. Courts will imply an easement when, for example, a parcel is landlocked, and the owner cannot otherwise exit from the property. Hence, in Figure 9–6, if Parcel B was surrounded by trees and no roads,

Figure 9–6   Easements Appurtenant

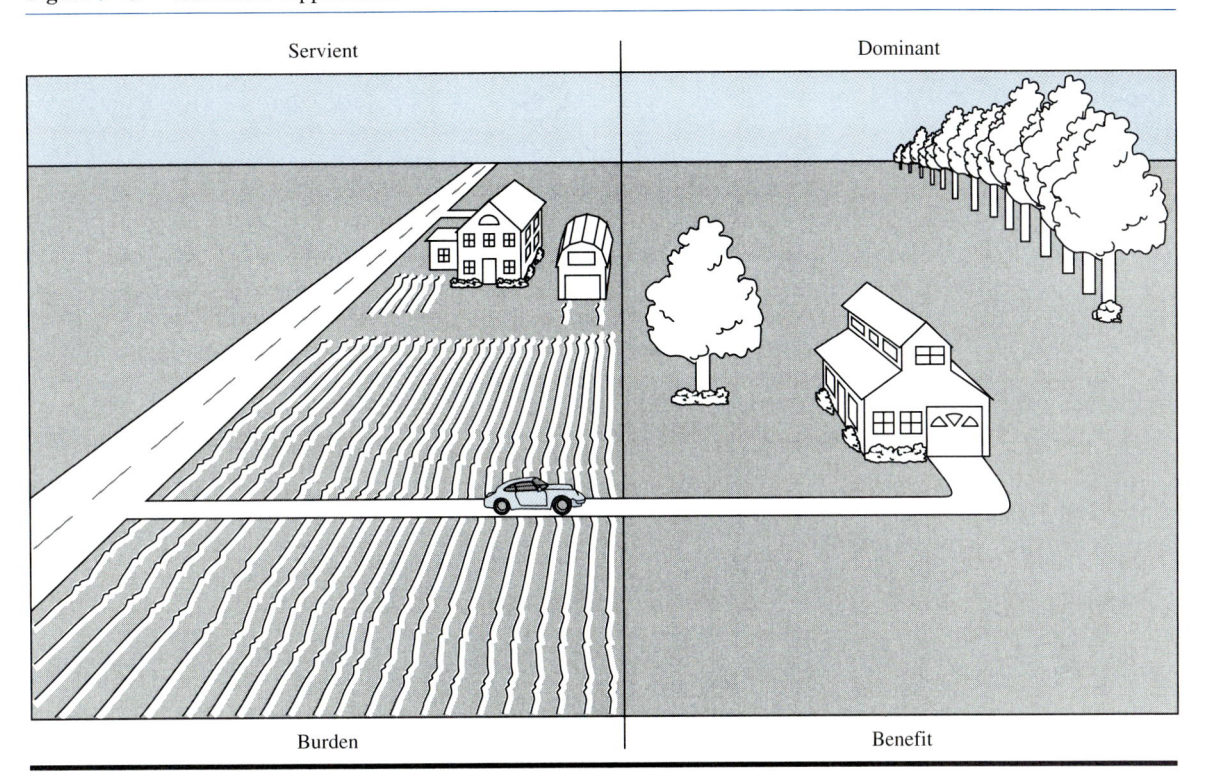

even in absence of an express easement, an easement by implication would exist.

Prescriptive easements, like adverse possession, occur by continuous wrongful use of another's property over a period of time. Different states require different lengths of adverse use; however, 20 years is normal. Assume that Zack has been traveling across his neighbor's property regularly for 20 years in order to take a shortcut to the bus stop. Although his neighbor has repeatedly warned Zack not to do this, Zack nonetheless continues. A prescriptive easement is thus created for the benefit of Zack. The neighbor could have avoided the easement by instituting a trespass suit against Zack for the wrongful invasion before the expiration of the 20-year time period. A court would order Zack to cease the trespass under threat of jail.

Easements in gross, in contrast to easements appurtenant, lack the requirement of adjacency. They directly benefit the easement holder. Commercial easements in gross include rights of way for utility maintenance and repair and for erection and maintenance of signs. Noncommercial easements in gross include, for example, the right to walk across someone's property to go the beach. While commercial easements in gross ordinarily run with the land, noncommercial easements in gross ordinarily do not (see Figure 9–7). Easements in gross may be created expressly or by prescription.

Nuisance

A **nuisance** is an unreasonable interference with the enjoyment of an owner's land. Generally, an owner has broad discretion to enjoy his or her property. But the law draws a line when that enjoyment interferes with the enjoyment of another's property. For example, homeowners may freely play their stereo, but they may not blast it loudly at 3:00 A.M. to the chagrin of a neighbor. This constitutes a nuisance. The same is true regarding release of noxious odors and unsightly messes. For example, a homeowner who burns treated wood that releases chemicals, or who stacks the front lawn with old car parts, may be guilty of creating a nuisance. Affected owners may sue for damages and an injunction prohibiting the nuisance.

Figure 9–7   Easements in Gross

Public Restrictions on Land Use

In addition to private restrictions on property use, there are governmental restrictions. These public restrictions of property use include zoning and environmental regulation.

Zoning

Zoning is the public regulation by a municipality of land uses within a zone. Areas are generally divided into residential, commercial, and industrial zones. Restrictions are then placed on building and activities within the zone. For example, residential zoning may place severe limitations on the size of the homes in relation to the size of the parcel, the type of structure, and the number of families per structure. Actually, many municipalities have expanded the three main zoning divisions to many more by narrowing the zones to, for example, single family (R-1), residential two family (R-2), condominiums

(R-3), office buildings (C-1), gas stations (C-2), light industry (C-3), medium industry (C-4), and so on.

The purpose of zoning is to create a comprehensive plan to maximize the welfare of the community. Since the 1960s, some communities have adopted new zoning approaches referred to as **planned unit developments** (PUDs). Instead of clustering all single-family units under one zone, light industry in another, and multiple housing complexes in another, PUDs allow for greater flexibility in the planning by permitting mixed uses within the development. The object is to provide a greater amount of open space. There is, of course, a trade-off. Density of living is sacrificed for nonliving space, which may consist of parks, bike trails, conservation areas, hunting lands, and natural lakes and lands. The key to an effective PUD is good planning and administration.

Environmental Regulation

Federal and state legislation has been enacted in efforts to preserve our environment from pollution and decay. These governmental regulations place restrictions on land use.

Congress enacted the National Environmental Policy Act (NEPA) in 1969. That act requires that all federal agencies file an environmental impact statement (EIS) for all actions that may have a significant effect on the environment. The EIS includes details about the effect of the proposed action on the environment and any alternatives to the proposed action. The EIS allows administrative decisionmakers to factor in the EIS data when making a decision. It does not otherwise require any special course of action by the decisionmaker.

Many states have also enacted statutes called little NEPAs. Although they are similar to the federal NEPA, they more often have an impact on private land developers than the federal NEPA. Developers need to obtain permits from the local governmental agencies. An application for such a permit may trigger the need to prepare an EIS. Developers may be required to assist in the preparation of the EIS by gathering the environmental information. Of course, this will become relevant when the local authority considers whether to grant the developing permit.

Other federal environmental statutes and regulations have an impact on private land usage. They include the Clean Air Act, the Clean Water Act, the Toxic Substances Control Act, the Resource Con-servation and Recovery Act, and the Noise Control Act. Additionally, states have enacted environmental legislation that affects permissible land use and decisionmaking. Environmental regulation is treated thoroughly in Chapter 51.

Eminent Domain

Under the law of **eminent domain**, federal, state, and local governments have the power to take private land for public purposes. This is permissible constitutionally as long as just compensation is paid for the property. Just compensation is the fair market value for the highest use of the property. When the parties cannot agree to an amount, the property owner is entitled to a jury determination of just compensation based on the testimony of experts.

Public use includes highways, parks, and airports. Courts have been liberal in recognizing public use and have found it in public housing and even redistribution of private land.

What constitutes a taking is not always an easy question. Of course, physical appropriation of the land, which naturally deprives the owner of use, is a taking. But less invasive measures have also been held to constitute a taking—for example, when the government makes test flights over dairy farmers' property, thus depriving the farmers of their livelihood, or passes regulations that significantly impede existing uses of the property. Zoning restrictions that leave the owner with no real use of the land are considered an exercise of eminent domain. The constitutional aspects of taking property were discussed in Chapter 4.

END–OF–CHAPTER QUESTIONS

1. What is property?
2. Compare and contrast lost, mislaid, and abandoned property.
3. Divide a parcel of real estate into as many different categories as you can.
4. Catherine Wagner and Robert Scherer lived together for about 15 years. They were involved in an automobile accident in which Wagner suffered injury. As a result, Wagner became very depressed and committed suicide by jumping off the roof of the apartment building where they lived. That morning, Wagner had received a check for $17,400 in satisfaction

of injuries she sustained in the automobile accident. She indorsed the check and left a note indicating she was willing the money to Scherer. The writing did not satisfy the requirements of a will. What arguments can you make that would entitle Scherer to the money? What are the counterarguments? See *Scherer v. Hyland*, 75 N.J. 127, 380 A.2d 698 (1977).

5. On July 9, 1776, a band of patriots, hearing news of the declaration of independence, toppled the equestrian statue of King George III. The statue was hacked apart and its pieces loaded onto wagons, to be delivered to a bullet-molding foundry to be cast into bullets. In the meantime, loyalists managed to steal back pieces of the statue, which were scattered about the Davis Swamp area in Wilton, Connecticut. Louis Miller entered the Davis Swamp area almost 200 years later. He trespassed on the owner's property, and with the aid of a metal detector discovered, 10 inches below the soil, a fragment of the King George III statue, 15 inches square and weighing 20 pounds. Miller agreed to sell the fragment of the statue to the Museum of the City of New York for $5,500. The owners of the property where the piece of the statue was found sought recovery of the fragment. Who should win? Explain. See *Fovoute v. Miller*, 407 A.2d 974 (Conn. 1978).

6. Western Ag Land Partners (WALP) was in the business of acquiring, leasing, and selling various parcels of irrigated farmland in Central Washington. The land was irrigated by center pivot irrigation systems (CPIS). These systems convey water through a long arm pipe moving in a circle around a pivot point. Water is pumped from its source and piped to a pivot point. The pivot point is constructed of a 6-cubic-yard concrete slab on which is bolted a metal structure. Through that structure, a vertical portion of the water supply line extends, called a riser pipe. The main arm of the system, which delivers water to the sprinkler heads, connects to this riser pipe through an elbow, cou-

pler, and rubber gasket. Finally, the main arm of the system sits on several wheeled towers 8 to 10 feet in height. The towers are controlled by timed electric motors. WALP leases the land and invests in the lessee the responsibility for operating the CPIS. The state of Washington seeks to assess a personal property tax on the CPIS systems. Will it be successful? What issues are raised? Analyze. See *Western Ag Land Partners v. State of Washington*, 716 P.2d 310 (Wash. App. 1986).

7. The Smiths deeded property to School District No. 35, the property to be used "only for school purposes." The property was used for school purposes for over 60 years and then ceased to be used for school purposes. What type of estate did the Smiths convey? Who owns the property? Explain. See *Roberts v. Rhodes*, 643 P.2d 116 (Kan. 1982).

8. While constructing a highway adjacent to the Balcome's real property, the South Carolina Department of Highways and Public Transportation dug to a depth of 20 to 25 feet and encountered groundwater. The Department redirected the water into a natural drainage ditch. As a result, the Balcome's 1.5-acre pond dropped 4 feet in depth. The Balcomes argue that their use and enjoyment of their property for agricultural and recreational purposes has been impaired. Do they have a remedy? Explain. See *South Carolina Dept. of Highways and Public Transp. v. Balcome*, 345 S.E.2d 762 (S.C. App. 1986).

9. The Nollans own a beachfront lot in Ventura County, California. One-quarter mile north of their property lies a public oceanside park with a public beach. Another public beach lies just 1,800 feet south of their lot. The beach portion of the Nollan property is separated from the rest of the lot by a concrete seawall. Originally, the Nollans leased the property with an option to buy. In turn, they rented it to vacationers. The property included a small bungalow, which eventually fell into disrepair and was no longer suitable to rent.

The Nollans' option to purchase was conditioned on their promise to demolish the bungalow and replace it. But under a California statute (California Public Resources Code), they were required to obtain a coastal development permit to do so. They applied for a permit to replace the structure with a three-bedroom house. The California Coastal Commission granted their permit subject to the condition that they allow the public an easement across a portion of their property so that it would be easier for the public to get to the public beaches and park.

The Nollans instituted an action in the Ventura County Superior Court seeking to invalidate the access condition. The court remanded the case to the Commission for a full hearing. On remand, the Commission found that the new house would increase blockage of the ocean view and would prevent the public "psychologically . . . from realizing a stretch of coastline exists nearby that they have every right to visit." The Commission also found that effects of the house plus other area development would "burden the public's ability to traverse to and along the shorefront."

The Nollans filed suit in the Superior Court, which directed that the permit condition be struck on the grounds that there was no adequate basis for determining that the replacement of the bungalow with the house would create a burden on public access to the sea. The Commission appealed to the California Court of Appeal, which reversed the Superior Court. The Nollans appealed that decision to the U.S. Supreme Court, arguing that the permit conditioned on an easement was a violation of the "Takings" clause of the U.S. Constitution requiring "just compensation." How do you think the High Court ruled? See *Nollan v. California Coastal Commission*, 483 U.S. 825 (1987).

10. You have a chance of creating a whole different system of landholding in a new settlement on a remote island in the South Pacific. Formulate the system.

Chapter 10

Estates and Trusts

■

CRITICAL THINKING INQUIRIES

As you read this chapter, you should be able to address the following:

- Compare and contrast distribution under a will and distribution when one dies without a will.
- Analyze the formalities for making a will.
- Compare and contrast the various types of wills.
- What is the purpose of court administration of an estate?
- What is the relationship of trusts and estates?

MANAGERIAL PERSPECTIVE

William Holler works at the First International Bank as a trustee and portfolio manager. He was a good friend of Amos Wabash and it was no surprise when Amos named Holler and First International Bank as executors of his estate and trustees of his trust. Amos had made some good business decisions in his life and he had a substantial portfolio. He had provided well for his family in his lifetime. While William was perusing the obituary column on Monday morning just before work, he was shocked to learn of his friend Amos's death.

- What were William's responsibilities as trustee?
- What are William's responsibilities now as executor?

William is not unlike myriads of people who one day find out that a friend or relative has died and that they are in some way legally related to the estate. In addition, the law provides for the establishment of trusts for the benefit of others. Trustees are necessary to fulfill the terms of the trusts. Both decedents' estates and trusts are the topic of this chapter.

INTESTATE DISTRIBUTION

No one gets out of this world alive. Consequently, it is prudent to think about providing for death by executing a will. The decedent who makes a will is called a **testator** and is said to have died testate. However, for one reason or another, not everybody dies with a will. One who dies without a will is said to have died **intestate.** When this occurs, state statutes must be consulted to determine to whom the estate passes. These state laws are commonly referred to either as **statutes of descent and distribution** or **intestate succession laws.** They, in effect, "write a will" for those who have failed to do so. They attempt to approximate the way a person would have wanted his or her property to descend. Figure 10–1 is an example of a state statute of descent and distribution.

It is a common fallacy that if you die without a will the property reverts to the state. Although once true in the early days of the Norman conquest in England, this concept met with great antagonism. The right of relatives to inherit is inherent in our system. Only when one dies and no relatives can be located does the estate **escheat** (revert) to the state. This, of course, is rare.

The intestacy statutes provide for the manner and order of distribution. Hence, upon death, the first inquiry for probate purposes is whether the decedent died with or without a will. If the decedent died without a will, then the state intestacy statute must be consulted to determine who gets what.

Per Stirpes Distribution

Most intestate succession laws provide for **per stirpes** distribution, referred to in some states as taking by right of representation. Per stirpes distribution means that a person takes the share of a deceased relative. Assume, for example that in our opening scenario, the decedent, Amos, died intestate leaving two children and the grandchild of a deceased child, as illustrated in Figure 10–2. Under the laws of intestate succession, in many jurisdictions, the two children would take one third of the estate each and the grandchild would take his or her deceased parent's share, or one third.

Per Capita Distribution

Under per capita distribution, lineal descendants share equally in the estate regardless of remoteness of relationship. Hence, consider a per capita distribution where a decedent leaves two children and two grandchildren of a deceased child. Each would take a one-fourth interest. In fact, some state statutes do provide for per capita distribution among those of equal degree. Under such a statute, if a person dies leaving no children but four grandchildren from deceased parents, each grandchild takes per capita or one fourth each without regard to their ancestor's share.

Order of Distribution

The statutes of descent and distribution show a high regard for spouses and children of the decedent. Some statutes leave it all to the spouse whereas others distribute the estate to the spouse and children. Still others give a certain initial sum to the surviving spouse and a fractional share of the remainder is distributed to the spouse and the children. In some states, the fractional share to the spouse is dependent on the number of children. For example, in Ohio, assume that a person dies leaving a spouse and two or more children. The spouse would be entitled to the first $60,000 plus one third of the remainder, and the children would divide the balance of the estate, two thirds, equally. However, if the decedent left a spouse and one child, then the spouse would take the first $60,000 and one half the remainder of the estate and the child would take the remaining one half of the estate.

Statutes usually provide for the detailed order of distribution, taking the various contingencies into consideration. The statutes specify the spouse and close blood relatives—for example, children, parents, and siblings. In most instances, except for the spouse, relatives by marriage do not inherit. In the event there are no specified relatives, then most statutes provide for the property to descend to the next of kin, which includes remote relatives—for example, cousins of various degrees. Sometimes these remote relatives are referred to as "laughing heirs"

Figure 10–1   Statute of Descent and Distribution

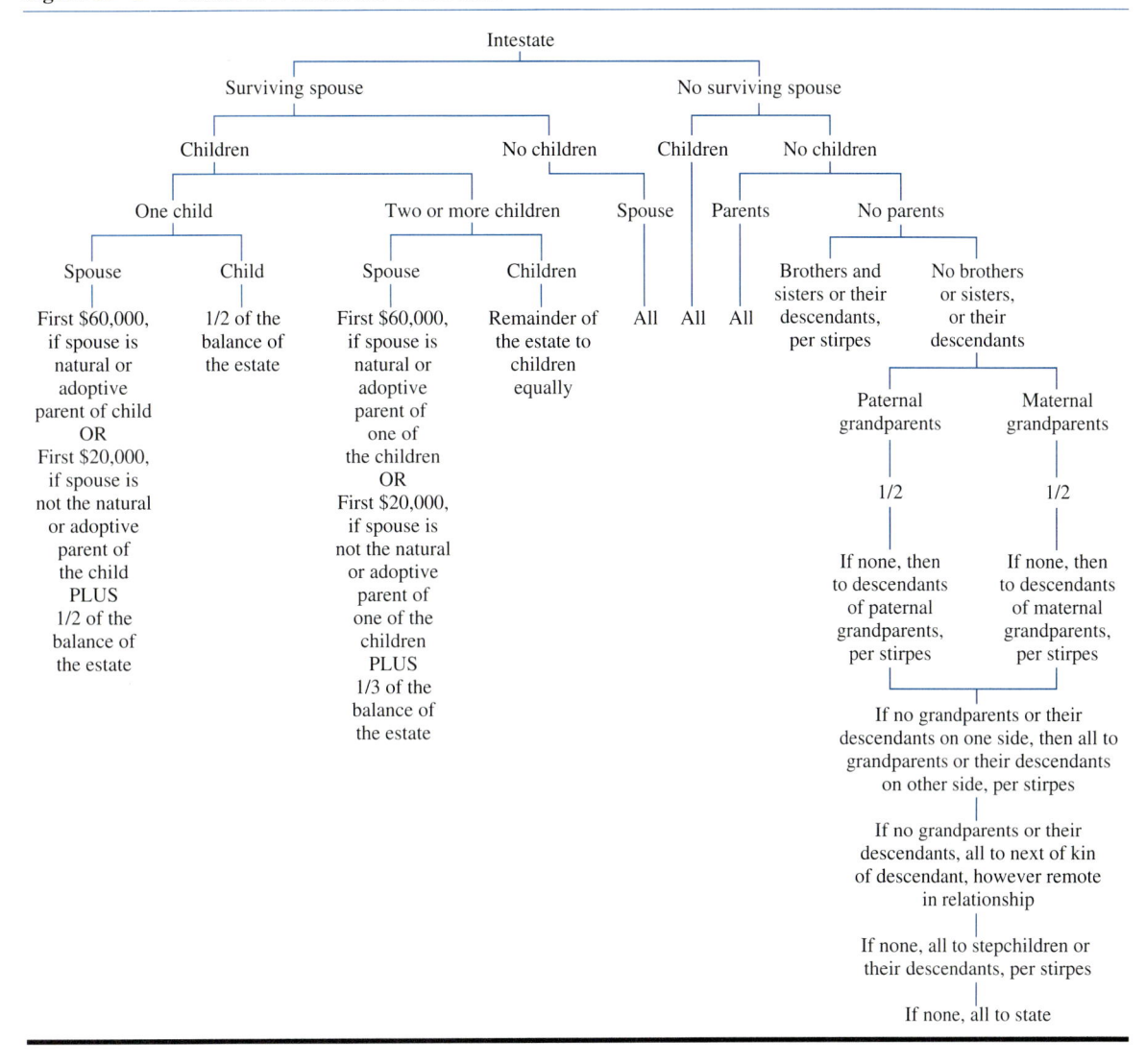

since they may not be close enough to grieve, yet they inherit. Some statutes provide that in the event that there are no next of kin, then stepchildren take. Others even provide that if there are neither kin nor stepchildren, then kin of a predeceased spouse take. In the event that no heirs are living, then the statutes provide that the property escheat to the state.

WILLS

In England, there was no right to distribute real property by will until the Statute of Wills was enacted in 1540. Real property was synonymous with

wealth and power. And the aristocracy lobbied successfully so that it would be kept in the family. However, as land became less distinguishable from personal property in connection with wealth, some freedom to will both real and personal property alike emerged.

A **will** is an instrument executed in accord with certain formalities that permits distribution of an owner's property according to the decedent's desire. A will is effective on death. Until then, it does not take effect and may be revoked. Wills, in order to be valid, must comply with certain formalities. The testator must have the capacity to make a will, and

Figure 10–2   Per Stirpes Distribution

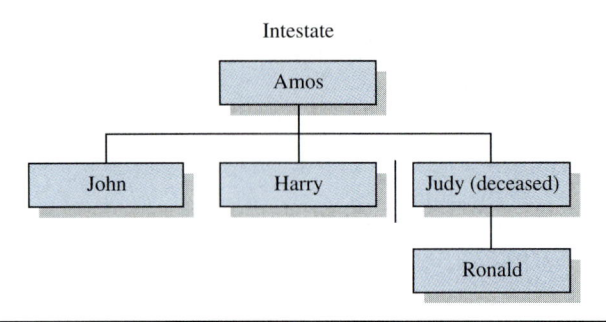

the will must be in writing, properly signed by the testator, and witnessed (see Figure 10–3 for a sample will).

Capacity

Most states require that a person be 18 years of age before making a will. Some states do not permit an incarcerated felon the right to make a will. All states require that the testator be of sound mind. This threshold is satisfied if the testator has the mental capacity to (1) know the extent of his or her property, (2) know and understand those who normally would inherit by way of relationship, and (3) formulate a plan for disposing of the property. These requirements are not designed to be a rigorous test but ones that all sound-minded persons can pass. One does not have to know the details and the specific value of his or her property. However, if a person is deluded by a mental disease such that his or her concept of dimensions, extent, and value is severely distorted, then this requirement would not be met.

Generally, one does not have to leave property to relatives in order to be considered of sound mind. A person may leave a child or parent or another relative out of the will because of a distaste for that person, or, not for a lack of love, but so that a more needy relative may get more. However, the decedent must have the capacity to understand relationships.

Finally, the testator does not have to pass the property in what appears to be a systematic, normal, and organized way. Leaving all one's property to a local humane society and nothing to relatives does not necessarily mean that the testator lacks capacity. The testator need only have the capacity to formulate a plan for disposing of the property. That plan may be as irrational as selecting the heirs randomly from the phone book.

Signed Writing

Wills, with one exception mentioned in the next section, must be in writing. Most wills are prepared by an attorney and neatly word processed. However, this is not necessary. Wills may be handwritten on scratch pads. They may make reference to other documents and incorporate those into the will. The normal will contains at least the following:

- Provision for repayment of all valid debts.
- Specification of the order of disposal of property.
- Appointment of an executor to fulfill the terms of the will and administer the estate.

In addition, a will may make specific provision for minor children, including the appointment of a guardian to supervise the person and property of the minors. Also, specific property—for example, heirlooms—may be designated to go to named beneficiaries.

Wills need to be signed by the testator at the end of the document. This cuts down on the possibility that someone will add to the document at a later time without the required formalities. It is a good idea for the testator to initial each page of the will as well.

The testator must sign with a mark. In most cases, this will be the testator's signature. However, it may be an initial or even an X, particularly if the testator cannot write. The key is that the testator intend the mark to be his or her signature. In some jurisdictions, it is legitimate for the testator to direct a person to sign the will on his or her behalf.

Figure 10-3 Will

LAST WILL AND TESTAMENT
OF
AVERY LANDMAN

I, AVERY LANDMAN of the City of Columbus, State of Ohio, being of full age and sound mind and memory, do make, publish and declare this to be my last will and testament, hereby revoking all wills and testamentary instruments by me made heretofore.

Item I. I direct that all my just debts and funeral expenses be paid out of my estate as soon as practicable after the time of my decease.

Item II. I request that I be interred at the cemetery near Sunset on West Broad Street with a preference to be buried near my father and mother.

Item III. I hereby devise the following: $1000 to the elders of Beth Messiah Congregation, Columbus, Ohio, in trust for its ministry on campuses.

Item IV. All the rest, residue and remainder of my property, real or personal, which I may own at the time of my decease, I hereby devise to my beloved wife, Sandra Landman, if she survives me, otherwise to my three children, Sam, Mary, and Shoshana, share and share alike per stirpes.

Item V. I make, nominate and appoint my beloved wife, Sandra Landman and my sister Mary Jane, or the survivor, as executor(s); otherwise, I appoint my beloved son, Sam. I give said executors all powers under the law including the power to sell without appraisal. I request that the executors serve without bond.

In testimony whereof, I, AVERY LANDMAN, hereunto set my hand at Columbus, Ohio, this *20th* day of *May,* 1994.

_____

AVERY LANDMAN

Signed by the said AVERY LANDMAN and by him acknowledged to be his last will and testament, before us and in our presence, and by us subscribed as attesting witnesses in his presence and in the presence of each other this *20th* day of *May,* 1994.

_____ Residing at _____
_____ Residing at _____

Witnesses

Most states require at least two witnesses. The witnesses must attest that the testator signed the will. Witnesses should not be a spouse or a person who may take under the will. In some states, this would either nullify the will, or the witness would be disqualified from taking under the will. Witnesses may be called on after the death of a decedent to give testimony that the testator actually did sign the will freely. However, this normally only occurs in the event of a will contest. A few states require the testator to publish the will. This amounts to the testator declaring to the witnesses that ''this is my last will and testament.''

Types of Wills

Three main types of wills exist: general, holographic, and oral.

General

The **general will,** sometimes known as the **statutory will,** is the most common form. It is the one that we have generally discussed requiring the statutory formalities that it be signed by the testator at the end and be attested by witnesses. The general will, in most states, is presumed to be regular if it has the signature of the testator and the requisite number of witnesses.

Holographic

Some jurisdictions recognize a **holographic will.** That is a will that lacks witnesses and has been written wholly in the hand of the testator and signed. It is arguable that this type of will, although lacking witnesses, is deemed reliable because it can be proved, if necessary, by handwriting analyses.

Oral

An **oral** or **nuncupative will** is sometimes referred to as a "foxhole will." Only a few states recognize it and most that do only permit the disposition of personal property under such a will. Death must be imminent for the testator, and there must be witnesses who are disinterested (do not inherit). In some states, the oral will must be reduced to writing, death must occur, and the writing presented within a specified period of time.

Amendment and Revocation of Wills

Just as wills are executed with formality, there is a certain formality required to amend or revoke a will. Wills may be amended by revoking an old will and executing a new one. The most common way of accomplishing this is by including express language in a new will that revokes the prior will. For example, the new will may "hereby revoke all testamen-

tary instruments previously made by me." Or, a prior will may simply be revoked by an act intended to revoke it. These acts include tearing it up, burning it, or mutilating it by writing canceled across its face. Sometimes, more than one will appears. If the wills are not inconsistent, then each will be given effect, as long as there is no indication that one has been revoked. However, if there are inconsistent provisions — for example, the same property is given to different people in the respective wills — then the most recent will prevails. When Howard Hughes, one of the wealthiest men in the United States at the time, died, there were over 300 wills presented to the court purporting to be his last will and testament. Some were obvious forgeries. The court was unable to determine which of the remaining was the real will, and hence determined that Mr. Hughes died without a will. The following case involves the determination of whether a testator whose will could not be found upon death had revoked it.

FEDER v. NATION OF ISRAEL
830 S.W.2d 449 (Mo. Ct. App. 1992)

Abram Sobol executed a will at his attorney's office and took possession of it. About two years later, he died. A diligent search was conducted but his will could not be located. The respondent, the Nation of Israel, the primary beneficiary under a photostatic copy of the will, filed an application for probate of a lost will. The appellants, the intestate heirs, challenged the application, claiming that since the original will could not be produced, Sobol had died intestate. A will contest ensued. A trial court ruled in favor of the respondent. That ruling was appealed to the Missouri Court of Appeals.

PUDLOWSKI, Judge

Under Missouri law, a will is presumed destroyed by the testator with intent to revoke if the will was last seen in possession of the testator prior to the testator's death and the will cannot be found after a diligent search was made therefore. Appellants assert to have established the presumption in two ways. First, Sobol took possession of the will after it was executed . . . and there was no evidence that any other person had possession of the will. Second, a diligent and thorough search of Sobol's effects, by the public administrator and his deputy, produced no will. We agree that appellants established the presumption that Sobol destroyed the will

because he last had possession of the will and the will could not be located subsequent to Sobol's demise.

This presumption, however, is rebuttable. Competent and satisfactory proof can be introduced to overcome it. It is for this reason that declarations of the decedent evincing the continued existence of the will, are properly received in evidence. Our task is to determine whether respondent rebutted the presumption by introducing not only competent but sufficient evidence for disappearance of the will inconsistent with revocation.

Respondent's evidence to rebut the presumption of revocation, comprised . . . the deposition testimony of two witnesses, Ms. Dodd and Mr. Weinberger. Ms. Dodd was friend, companion and housekeeper to Sobol for approximately 13 years. Ms. Dodd saw her name on Sobol's will just once, when he opened up a document which he said was his will, and asked her to look at her name, indicating she was named as a beneficiary. Ms. Dodd did not see the title to the document, any dates or signatures. Sobol informed Ms. Dodd that the bequest to her was $5,000 when in fact it was only $3,000. Thereafter, Sobol showed Ms. Dodd his will several times, but it was a folded piece of paper which he would remove from an envelope. The last she recalled of seeing the piece of paper which Sobol said was his will was a few days before his death. As a housekeeper, Ms. Dodd had almost daily contact with Sobol who frequently informed her of his desire to give his money to respondent. A copy of the will, located by the public administrator in Sobol's safe deposit box at Mercantile Bank, indicated the will had been altered by the deletion of the bequest to Ms. Dodd.

Based upon years of relationship and contact with Sobol, Mr. Weinberger testified that Sobol was a strong-willed individual. Prior to the execution of the will, Mr. Weinberger advised Sobol that if Sobol should die intestate, his estate would escheat to the State of Missouri. Mr. Weinberger testified that Sobol spoke with him several times, thereafter, in general terms about his desire to amend the will. Mr. Weinberger was unaware of any subsequent will that may have been drafted for Sobol, revoking the will in question, which respondent has offered.

A will is universally recognized as a sacred document. When the testator desires to dispose of his assets according to his will, a certain degree of care and caution in its preservation, is required. Where, as in the present case, no will is located subsequent to the testator's demise, despite a diligent search of his effects, the presumption is set in motion. Mere existence of decedent's statements of the continued existence of the will, is insufficient to overcome the presumption that a will, last seen in possession of the testator, and which cannot be found after a diligent search, is destroyed. . . . We believe that the testimony of Ms. Dodd and Mr. Weinberger, though competent, does not rise to the level of sufficient evidence capable of rebutting the presumption of revocation. What is required, and correctly so, is corroborating evidence, sufficient to justify the disappearance of the will inconsistent with revocation.

. . . [E]vidence that Sobol desired to give his estate to respondent, toward whom he harbored feelings of sympathy or affection, does not rise to the level of sufficient or corroborating evidence needed to overcome the presumption of revocation.

We reverse the judgment and remand for further proceedings consistent with our opinion.

Case Questions
1. What is the issue?
2. What do you think happened to the will?
3. By examining the facts, what fallacies do you see in appellants' reasoning? In respondent's reasoning?
4. How could this contest have been avoided?

Another common way of amending a will is by **codicil.** A codicil is an addendum to a will that amends or revokes a will. It must be executed with the same formalities as the will. A person cannot simply write an amendment to the will without attending to the formalities required by the state statute for the execution of wills. That usually means the testator must sign the codicil along with witnesses attesting to the signature of the testator. A codicil may be written at the end of the will or it may take the form of a separate instrument.

Some acts result in the revocation of a will automatically by operation of law. For example, in most states, divorce automatically revokes the portion of the will that leaves property to the ex-spouse. Some states will not enforce a will that predates a subsequent marriage.

Oftentimes, children are born after the making of a will. Because these children were not in existence at the time the will was made, they are not expressly mentioned. This fact will not cause a will to be revoked. These subsequently born children are referred to as **pretermitted heirs.** The law permits them to inherit an equal share with the other children. Hence, assume that in our opening scenario, after Amos executed his will, a new child was born. Assume there were two children at the time that Amos executed the will and that he left them each one fourth of the estate. The law in most states would distribute the one half of the estate the two children were to receive among the three children, so that each would receive one sixth of the estate. This same principle applies to those children whom the testator was unaware were in existence at the time—for example, those who the testator mistakenly thought had died.

ADMINISTRATION OF ESTATES

An estate must be administered or settled by an estate representative. The testator may name that representative in the will. A representative named in a will is called an **executor.** It is not unusual for a testator to name an alternative executor to provide for the contingency that the primary executor does not survive the decedent or is otherwise unqualified or unwilling to serve. When the decedent dies intestate, the court names an **administrator** to settle the estate. A special court called the probate or surrogate court supervises the administration or probate of the estate.

Probate

Probate is a proceeding establishing that the will is valid and genuine. However, the term has evolved to apply generally to the administration of a decedent's estate regardless of whether there is a will or not. Probate begins with the presentation of the will and/or the appointment of the executor or administrator. The person named in the will ordinarily is appointed executor, or in the case of intestacy, the surviving spouse or other close relative is appointed administrator. The court usually requires the representative to post a bond to protect the estate from wrongdoing, unless otherwise specified in the will or in the statute. If the will is regular on its face, then it will be admitted to probate with very little formality.

Responsibilities of the Representative

The representative must notify all interested parties of the death of the decedent and that the estate is being probated. Interested parties include all those named under the will and those that would otherwise inherit under the statute of descent and distribution. It is the responsibility of the executor to fulfill the wishes of the decedent as contained in the will. The executor or the administrator must administer the estate. Generally, this means:

- Pay all valid debts including funeral expenses and state and federal estate taxes.
- Prepare an inventory of the estate.
- Maintain and preserve the estate.
- Make distributions to those entitled to such under the will or the laws of intestate succession.
- Make accountings to the court.

To assist in the fulfillment of these duties, it is normal for the estate representative to hire an attorney.

Types of Probate

Probate proceedings are often costly, requiring attorneys, appraisers, and accountants. Additionally, representatives are entitled to fees for their work. Most states allow for a simpler form of probate when the value of an estate is under a certain amount. For example, California allows for a simplified short procedure when there is no real property and the value of the estate does not exceed $60,000. Some states allow for a relief of probate when the estate is very small.

Sometimes death cannot be proved, but a person has been absent for a long period of time. Most states permit the probate of an estate under such circumstances by providing for a presumption of death after a number of years—for example, five or seven.

When husband and wife die in a common accident, it may be difficult to ascertain who in fact died first, or the deaths may be very close together in time. The Uniform Simultaneous Death Act, adopted by many states, clarifies that under these circumstances each is presumed to have survived the other. This has the practical effect of avoiding double probate proceedings where the property would have to pass through both spouses' estates. Instead, each spouse's property passes to his or her beneficiaries.

Probate Contests

Probate may be contested for a variety of reasons. The will may not have been executed in accord with the statutory formalities. This results in the decedent's estate being administered under the laws of intestate succession. Another common ground for contesting a will is that it was signed under **duress.** Duress occurs when there is coercion by force or threat of force. Hence, a will that is signed unwillingly under threat of harm will not be deemed valid. Some contests occur because someone allegedly exercised **undue influence** over the testator.

These cases usually involve a trusted person, such as the decedent's nurse or a relative, who exercises dominion over the decedent. The elderly and dependent are particularly susceptible to undue persuasion. The following case illustrates a will contest grounded on lack of capacity and undue influence.

IN THE MATTER OF THE ESTATE OF FORRESTER

310 Ark. 639, 839 S.W. 2d 214 (1992)

Charlye Vera Forrester Davidson, decedent, died and left an estate in excess of $2 million. Davidson's estate had been managed by an attorney, Donald Goodner. In 1984, Goodner prepared a will that Davidson signed, appointing Goodner as executor and leaving the residue of her estate, after certain gifts, to Goodner. In 1985, Goodner prepared another will in which Goodner was named coexecutor and dropped as beneficiary in favor of Davidson's nephews, John and William Forrester.

The 1985 will, revoking the 1984 will, was admitted to probate, over the objections of the testator's nephew William Forrester, who alleged that the testator was of unsound mind and subject to undue influence at the time of executing the 1984 and 1985 wills. The case rose to the Supreme Court of Arkansas.

BROWN, Judge

I. Sound Mind

William Forrester now seeks to invalidate both the 1984 and 1985 wills on grounds of lack of testamentary capacity in an effort to have the estate pass by intestacy. In this effort, he presented evidence of the [testator's] developing dementia, aging diseases, and paranoid ideation regarding her house. There was also testimony that the [testator] suffered from near-total blindness.

The decedent's physician, Dr. Louis O. Lambiotte, testified that between 1960 and 1985, Mrs. Davidson began suffering from diseases associated with aging, including macular degeneration, arteriosclerosis, mild hypertension, abnormal glucose tolerance, a systolic murmur of the aortic valve, and paranoid ideation with reference to her house and the objects in it. He further testified that she always recognized him and knew where she was. In his view, "her delusional thinking . . . represented a slot of abnormality" which would not have prevented her from recognizing family members, and specifically her two nephews.

A psychiatrist, Dr. Joe H. Dorzab, who saw the decedent in April 1985, diagnosed her primary problem as deteriorating memory caused by either Alzheimer's . . . or multi-infarct dementia. Other witnesses described Mrs. Davidson as strong-willed, eccentric, and "nutty." Toward the end of her life, and in 1985, she was obsessed by the fact that someone was trying to lock her house and nail her door shut.

Our generally expressed rule for testamentary capacity is that the [testator] must be able to know the natural objects of her bounty and the extent of her property; to understand to whom the property is being given; and to realize those who are being excluded from the will.

In the present case, nothing before us suggests that the elements of mental competency were not present when Mrs. Davidson executed her 1985 will. No expert opinion contravenes her testamentary capacity on that date. On the contrary, three witnesses attested to her signature on the will, and none espoused the view that there was any unusual behavior on Mrs. Davidson's part or any problem concerning soundness of mind. Two witnesses in fact recall Mrs. Davidson specifically declaring that she was there to sign her will. Moreover, there was testimony that at the time Mrs. Davidson was aware of the property she owned by Lake Waldron and of her properties in Colorado and Texas.

Our probate law does not require that a [testator] mete out exact justice in the devise of her property. So long as she has the capacity to make a will, she may be unfair, eccentric, injudicious, or capricious in making distribution. Moreover, the fact that Mrs. Davidson was suffering ideation relative to her house and incipient dementia does not, in itself, establish an impairment of testamentary capacity.

Because there was insufficient proof that the [testator] lacked the requisite mental capacity to make a will on December 11, 1985, Forrester's contest must fail.

II. Undue Influence

Undue influence sufficient to void a will must not spring from natural affection but must result from fear and coercion so as to deprive a [testator] of free will and direct the benefits of the will to particular parties.

Undue influence is generally difficult of proof. It is generally exercised in secret, not openly, and, like a snake crawling upon a rock, it leaves no track behind it, but its sinister and insidious effect must be determined from facts and circumstances surrounding the testator, his physical and mental condition as shown by the evidence, and the opportunity of the beneficiary of the influenced bequest to mold the mind of the testator to suit his or her purposes.

Forrester asserts that the will was unjust and unnatural and is, therefore, invalid. He adduces the following authority to support his argument:

The expression ''unjust and unnatural will'' is usually applied when a testator leaves his estate, or a large portion of it, to strangers, to the exclusion of natural objects of his bounty without any apparent reason. A will cannot be said to be unnatural because a testator preferred one for whom she had developed a close and affectionate relationship, or when the natural objects of the testator's bounty are in no need of funds, aid or assistance.

We observe no strangers or unnatural beneficiaries under the will and no proof of coercion waged against Mrs. Davidson. Finally, though suspicions and theories abounded in this case, allegations of undue influence must be supported by proof. Here, the proof was deficient and the claim of undue influence cannot prevail.

Case Questions

1. What issues does this case present?
2. Why did the nephew desire to contest the will?
3. What argument, based on the facts, can you make that Davidson was of unsound mind?
4. What could Davidson have done to diminish the probability of a will contest?

Some states have enacted a predeath proceeding that makes a will virtually incontestable. The procedure involves a lawsuit instituted by the testator that gives all persons notice of the will executed by the testator. These persons then have an opportunity to come in and contest the will. Failure to do so means that they waive any right to do so in the future. If the court finds that the will is valid, then the testator can be assured that a successful contest will not occur after his or her death.

Estate Tax

Each state has its own system of estate taxes. Moreover, estates may be subject to federal inheritance taxes. There is a **unified tax credit** that exempts up to $600,000 of gifts (during lifetime) plus estate assets at death. However, the federal government also grants 100 percent marital and charitable exemptions. Hence, all estate property that goes to a

spouse or to a charity is free of estate tax. Finally, the federal tax laws permit a married couple to transfer up to $1.2 million to their children free of estate tax. The establishment of a testamentary trust discussed later in this chapter is a method of accomplishing this ''generation skipping'' tax benefit.

Alternatives to Probate

Because of the high cost of probate, the ''red tape,'' and because of its public nature, many look for suitable alternatives. Holding property jointly is an acceptable means of avoiding the probate of that property upon death. For example, assume that in our opening scenario, Amos had a savings account jointly held with his wife; and that he similarly holds his residence jointly with his wife with right of survivorship. These assets are not probatable. They would be transferred to the surviving spouse outside of probate. They may still be subject to estate tax.

However, they will not be tied up in probate but instead through simple paperwork and minimal cost vest in the survivor.

Life insurance with a designated beneficiary is not subject to probate. Therefore, the purchase of annuities or other insurance policies is a way of keeping property from the delays and expense of probate. Once again, they may be subject to estate taxes.

Giving away property is another way of divesting assets and shielding them from probate. The gifts may be subject to gift taxes; however, there is a liberal federal exemption for gifts—$10,000 annually, which does not count toward the unified credit discussed in the previous section. Finally, establishing a living trust, discussed later, avoids probate of the trust assets.

SPOUSAL PROTECTION

Public policy, and American law, based on historical precedent, place much emphasis on the protection of the family. Probate and other statutes protect the financial security of the family in several ways. We already examined the laws of intestate succession and noted how the spouse and the children share in the distribution of the estate. In addition, the law may give the spouse an elective share of the estate, provide for dower, homestead exemption, surviving spouse allowance, and a household and personal effects exemption. These rights all depend on whether a marriage exists.

Marriage

It is usually easy to determine or prove whether there is a valid marriage. Most marriages comply with the state statute that involves a ceremony and requires a marriage license. The probate court in the local jurisdiction keeps these records. However, some states recognize **common law marriages.** In those states, a ceremony or license is not necessary. There must however be:

- Cohabitation—an intent to live together as man and woman "until death do us part."
- Presentation—a holding out to the community as husband and wife.
- Acceptance—an acceptance within the community as husband and wife.
- Legality—no legal impediment to marriage such as one of the two being married to someone else.

There is no magic time that it takes to be married under the common law in those states that still recognize this form of marriage. When, however, it attaches, the marriage is no less valid than a statutory marriage and it takes a divorce to sever the bonds.

Dower

Dower is an historical right that gave a surviving wife one third of a life estate interest in real property. Today, those states that maintain dower rights apply them to surviving husbands as well. The dower interest applies to real property that the decedent-spouse owned during the marriage, which was conveyed out without the signature of the surviving spouse. The interest is an expectancy interest until the death of the owner-spouse. In order to claim dower, the spouse must survive the owner-spouse. Assume, for example, that Amos in our opening scenario owned Blueacre during the marriage and sold it or mortgaged it without the signature of his wife. His wife would have a dower interest on his death. Assume that the property was valued at $90,000 and that it has a rental value of $500 per month. Assume further that Amos's wife had a life expectancy of 10 years. What is the value of the dower interest? It is not one third of the value of the fee, which would be $30,000. It is one third of a life estate. One way of computing that would be to figure out the income produced from the property over the life of Amos's wife, and then take one third of that. Over the expected life of Amos's wife, the property would produce $60,000. Hence, the dower interest would be $20,000 or one third of the life estate. In many states, the spouses' right to elect to take against the will has replaced dower rights.

Elective Rights

A person is free to will property as he or she wishes. However, the law in many jurisdictions protects surviving spouses by affording them the option to elect to take against the will. Some states give the spouse an **elective share** of one third or one half; other states designate a share dependent on the number of children. For example, in Ohio, a surviving spouse with two or more children may elect to take a one-third share, whereas a surviving spouse with fewer than two children may elect a one-half share.

Many states require that the surviving spouse be notified in writing of the elective rights and be informed how much the spouse would receive under the will as opposed to taking an elective share. Then it is up to the spouse to choose. Assume that Amos in our opening scenario left $200,000 to his surviving spouse under the will. Assume further that the total value of the estate is $600,000, and that there is one child of the marriage. By electing to take against the will in Ohio, Amos's spouse would be entitled to $300,000. Although it would seem that a spouse would always elect the higher number, that is not always the case. By electing the lower amount, for example, the children may get more, which may be the desired end.

Mansion Rights

Many states provide what is referred to as **mansion rights.** A typical statute gives a surviving spouse the right to remain in the homestead for six months free from creditor interference. Some statutes permit the surviving spouse to take an amount of money in lieu of the mansion rights.

Widow's Allowance

Some states provide an allowance for the surviving widow during the first year or the term of probate. Probate often takes considerable time and the **widow's allowance** is intended to fill the gap between the time of death and distribution. States vary as to the amount (usually between $5,000 and $20,000), and sometimes a greater amount is given if minor children are in the home.

Household Exemption

States' creditor statutes usually afford **household exemptions.** These statutes have the effect of preventing general creditors who do not hold a security interest in specific property from seizing the property to satisfy the debt. Common exemptions include beds, clothing, and heating units. In addition, many statutes specify a sum of money—for example, $5,000—that is exempt from creditor attachment. These statutes are intended to afford persons a safety net—a minimal level of subsistence.

LIVING WILLS

Recently, a growing number of states have enacted **living will statutes.** These statutes give people the right to execute documents that direct doctors and family members on what to do when the person is in a medical state in which there is no reasonable expectation of recovery from extreme mental or physical disability. These are sometimes dubbed the "death with dignity" statutes. They permit the wishes of a person to be honored that no heroic measures be taken to preserve life under such circumstances and that medication, devices, and hydration be withheld (see Figure 10–4). However, as the following article points out, living wills are not without problems.

---

*Living Wills: Why a Patient's Last Wishes Are Not Always Respected**

Currently, approximately 10,000 Americans are in irreversible comas being kept alive by feeding tubes, respirators and other such technology. Many of these people are in a "persistent vegetative state," awake, yet not totally aware. Their bodies are stiff and contracted into a fetal position, and they are unable to eat, speak or recognize their loved ones. . . .

. . . Many states allow parents or guardians of a comatose patient to make decisions regarding the removal of life support, however, some states require that the wishes of the comatose patient, regarding removal of life support, be shown by clear and convincing evidence. A living will has been deemed to be such clear and convincing evidence.

---

*Source: Shelley Sheperd, "Why a Patient's Last Wishes Are Not Always Respected," 34 How.L.J.229 (1991). Reprinted with permission.

Figure 10–4   Living Will

STATE OF OHIO
LIVING WILL DECLARATION
OF
SHERMAN WILLIAMS

I, SHERMAN WILLIAMS, presently residing at Columbus, Ohio (The "Declarant"), being of sound mind and not under or subject to duress, fraud, or undue influence, intending to create a living will declaration under Chapter 2133 of the Ohio Revised Code, as amended from time to time, do voluntarily make known my desire that my dying shall not be artificially prolonged. If I am unable to give directions regarding the use of life-sustaining treatment when I am in a terminal condition or a permanently unconscious state, it is my intention that this living will declaration shall be honored by my family and physicians as the final expression of my legal right to refuse medical or surgical treatment. I am a competent adult who understands and accepts the consequences of such refusal and the purpose and effect of this document.

In the event I am in a terminal condition and/or a permanently unconscious state, I do hereby declare and direct that my attending physician shall:

1. Administer no life-sustaining treatment;

2. Withdraw such treatment if such treatment has commenced; and

3. Permit me to die naturally and provide me with only that care necessary to make me comfortable and to relieve my pain but not to postpone my death.

☐ _____ In addition if I have marked the foregoing box and have placed my initials on the line adjacent to it, I authorize my attending physician to withhold, or in the event that treatment has already commenced, to withdraw, the provision of artificially or technologically supplied nutrition and hydration, if I am in a permanently unconscious state and if my attending physician and at least one other physician who has examined me determine, to a reasonable degree of medical certainty and in accordance with the reasonable medical standards, that such nutrition or hydration will not or no longer will serve to provide comfort to me or alleviate my pain.

For purposes of this living will declaration:

(A) "Life-sustaining treatment" means any medical procedure, treatment, intervention, or other measure that, when administered, will serve principally to prolong the process of dying.

(B) "Terminal condition" means an irreversible, incurable, and untreatable condition caused by disease, illness, or injury to which, to a reasonable degree of medical certainty as determined in accordance with reasonable medical standards by my attending physician and one other physician who has examined me, both of the following apply:

(1) There can be no recovery, and

(2) Death is likely to occur within a relatively short time if life-sustaining treatment is not administered.

(C) "Permanently unconscious state" means a state of permanent unconsciousness that, to a reasonable degree of medical certainty as determined in accordance with reasonable medical standards by my attending physician and one other physician who has examined me, is characterized by both of the following:

(1) I am irreversibly unaware of myself and my environment and,

(2) There is a total loss of cerebral cortical functioning, resulting in my having no capacity to experience pain or suffering.

I understand the purpose and effect of this document and sign my name to this living will declaration after careful deliberation on August 15, 1994 at Columbus, Ohio.

_____

Declarant

I attest that the declarant signed or acknowledged this living will declaration in my presence, and that the declarant appears to be of sound mind and not under or subject to duress, fraud, or undue influence. I further attest that I am not the attending physician of the declarant, I am not the administrator of a nursing home in which the declarant is receiving care, and that I am an adult not related to the declarant by blood, marriage, or adoption.

Signature: _____   Residence address: _____
Print name: _____   _____
Date: _____

Signature: _____   Residence address: _____
Print name: _____   _____
Date: _____

■ ■ ■

A living will . . . is a document one drafts, while in good health, stating what if any, measures he or she wants employed to extend their life when they are dying. A living will is considered an informed medical consent statement authorizing the refusal or discontinuance of further medical treatment by artificial means or devices. Such consent is relied upon when or if a patient is terminally ill and no longer able to express their wishes. . . .

■ ■ ■

The increasing number of requests for living wills and related information illustrates that Americans are following the advice of experts in drafting living wills. However, there are cases which suggest that while living will statutes are in effect in most jurisdictions, the patient's wishes expressed in their living wills are not always followed.

Saunders v. New York, was one of the first cases in which a court failed to follow the patient's living will. In that case, the applicant and patient, Selma Saunders, was a 70 year old woman whose health was deteriorating from emphysema and lung cancer. Ms. Saunders prepared and executed a living will. She then petitioned the court, requesting that the living will take immediate effect. This case is different from most right-to-die cases in that the patient was not comatose when she petitioned the court to give her living will legal effect.

The New York Supreme Court held that the petitioner's living will "is evidence of the most persuasive quality and is a clear and convincing demonstration that while competent the petitioner clearly and explicitly expressed an informed, rational, and knowing decision to decline" life support. However, the court declined to declare the will valid because "only the legislature had the authority to enact a statute recognizing the validity of living wills". . . .

. . . While the court could not give the will in question legal effect, they did determine that a living will meets the clear and convincing standard necessary to terminate life support in a comatose patient. In essence, the court concludes that if a statute is enacted recognizing the validity of living wills, the court, in situations such as this, will have to consider the patient's wishes as expressed in their living will when deciding whether to terminate life support. [New York now has a living will statute]

In another case, however, the District Court of Appeals for Florida refused to follow the provisions set forth in the patient's living will, even though a living will statute had been enacted in that jurisdiction. In *In re Guardianship of Browning,* the comatose patient, Mrs. Estelle Browning, had prepared and executed a living will a year before she suffered a massive stroke and slipped into a permanent vegetative state. The patient's guardian sought to have a feeding tube removed because its insertion was against the patient's express wishes. The court refused to permit the removal of the patient's feeding tube because they felt the conditions of the will had not been met.

■ ■ ■

There were two reasons why the court would not grant withdrawal of the feeding tube. First, the court stated the statute would only allow the withdrawal of "life-prolonging procedures." Under the Florida statute, the term "life-prolonging procedures" does not include the provision of sustenance. Thus, even if her living will specified that she did not want her life prolonged with the insertion of a feeding tube, there would be no remedy because, under Florida law, a feeding tube involves the "provision of sustenance" and thus not considered to be a life-prolonging procedure.

Secondly, the living will specified that if she should have a "terminal condition" and be facing "imminent death," life sustaining procedures should then be removed. The Florida statutory definition of a "terminal condition" is "a condition caused by injury, disease or illness from which, to a reasonable degree of medical certainty, there can be no recovery and thus makes death imminent.'' The court reasoned that the patient's death was not imminent because she could live a substantial period of time with the feeding tube. In short, Florida law does not recognize a person's right to refuse nutrition and hydration. Therefore, her condition did not meet the statutory definition of terminal and thus does not fall within the parameters of the living will statute of Florida.

The basic problem with giving effect to living wills is that the ''vernacular of living wills—such phrases as 'terminally ill,' 'no reasonable expectation of recovery,' 'heroic measures' and 'life-prolonging procedures'—is so fuzzy and open to interpretation that doctors frequently are left with no clear idea of which measures the patient wants started, stopped or maintained.'' Thus, even if it is obvious that a comatose patient would want the life support withdrawn, doctors will continue to keep the patient alive because of the fear that state law will not support their interpretation of the living will. Sometimes it is advantageous for doctors to hesitate before removing life support. In Albany, New York, a judge authorized the removal of an 86 year old stroke patient's feeding tube. Before the tube was removed the patient regained consciousness and stated that she would like to wait before deciding whether she wanted the feeding tube removed. This situation is illustrative of the courts' apprehension about living wills.

Thought Questions

1. What is the gist of the author's point?
2. Analyze: ''There is a fundamental difference between the law and medicine regarding the meaning of life.''
3. How would you suggest avoiding the pitfalls of an unenforceable living will?
4. Draw up a model living will statute.

Health care proxies or **durable powers of attorney for health care** are closely related to living wills. The principal designates a particular proxy and invests in that person the authority and power to make medical decisions in the event that the principal is unable to do so. The proxy should be a person that fully understands the desire of the person.

TRUSTS

A **trust** is a legal device whereby property may be transferred to a trustee for the benefit of beneficiaries. The purpose of the trust may be for estate planning, avoidance of probate, tax advantages, and/or to facilitate management and control. A trust involves the settlor, the trustee, and the beneficiaries.

Parties to the Trust

The person who establishes the trust is referred to as the **settlor.** The settlor must be of sound mind and express a clear intention to establish a trust. Although in most instances the trust may be created orally, trusts are usually established by a written instrument. The settlor transfers property, called the **res,** to the trust. The property must be in existence. It may consist of tangible property such as real estate or intangible property such as shares of stock.

Normally, the settlor will name a **trustee,** which could be a person or a corporation, to administer the trust in accord with the settlor's instructions. If the settlor fails to name a trustee, then a court may do so. The trustee holds legal title to the property. The trustee is a fiduciary, held to the highest standard of care, which is owed to the **beneficiaries.** As such, the trustee must preserve the res, manage it prudently, and maintain accurate records. The trustee must act in accordance with the terms of the trust established by the settlor. Assume, for example, that the trust requires the income to go to one beneficiary and at the end of that person's life the remainder to another. This may require the trustee to determine what is income and what is principal. The trustee's determination will be final (so long as it is reasonable) if the trust instrument gives the trustee the power to make the determination. Otherwise, ordinary receipts from, for example, interest, rentals, and cash dividends are considered income. Extraordinary receipts such as proceeds from the sale of trust assets, stock dividends, and insurance proceeds are deemed principal. The trustee may not delegate trust duties.

The beneficiaries hold **equitable title** in the trust property. This means that they have the power to enforce the trust should the trustee breach its fiduciary responsibilities. The settlor may be a beneficiary.

Classification of Trusts

Trusts may be classified in various ways. There are living trusts and testamentary trusts. **Living trusts** are established during the lifetime of the settlor. For example, in our opening scenario, Amos may have established a living trust by placing $100,000 in trust, "the income to go to my children equally, with the remainder to them equally when the youngest one attains age 21." **Testamentary trusts** are established by a will and go into effect upon the settlor's death. For example, Amos could have established such a trust by designating in his will that "in the event my spouse fails to survive me, I place my estate in trust for the benefit of my children to share the income from the res, with the remainder to be distributed to the children equally when the youngest child reaches age 25."

Trusts may also be characterized as express trusts, implied trusts, or constructive trusts. **Express trusts** are those that are established by a clear expression of language. They include testamentary and living trusts. An **implied trust** is one that is created as a result of the circumstances. For example, assume that Amos gave $5,000 to an agent to purchase an automobile for him and that the automobile was placed in the name of the agent instead of in the name of Amos. A court would recognize an implied trust in favor of Amos and order the title changed. When fraud occurs, a court may impose another type of implied trust referred to as a **constructive trust.** For example, a constructive trust may be imposed on a person that has collected money on false pretenses. A court could order a constructive trust, designating the wrongdoer as trustee, to hold the monies in trust for the donors.

Trusts may be revocable or irrevocable. **Revocable trusts** give the settlor the option to revoke the trust, resulting in the property reverting back to the settlor. The disadvantage of the revocable trust is that the settlor will be taxed on the income produced by the trust. However, should the settlor die before revocation, the trust avoids probate. An **irrevocable trust** places the trust property beyond the control of the settlor. It normally cannot be terminated except by the consent of all the beneficiaries. As well as avoiding probate of these trust funds, the settlor may also avoid being taxed on the income produced by the property.

There are also special types of trusts including totten, blind, spendthrift, and charitable.

Totten Trust

The **totten trust** is a bank account in which the settlor deposits funds for the benefit of another. This type of trust is revocable simply by the settlor withdrawing the funds. However, should the settlor die before withdrawal, then the funds are vested in the named beneficiary.

Blind Trust

The **blind trust** is used almost exclusively by public officials who are required to avoid a conflict of interest in decisionmaking. In a blind trust, the settlor transfers investment funds to a trustee who makes investment decisions without consulting the settlor. In fact, the trustee will not inform the settlor of the specific holdings but instead will periodically inform the settlor of the income or loss of the trust.

Spendthrift Trust

Creditors of the beneficiary may attach the normal trust. However, the **spendthrift trust** is immune from creditor attachment. This may be used as a protective device to ensure that beneficiaries avoid "gambling" their trust away.

Charitable Trust

The **charitable trust** is established for a charitable purpose—religious, educational, relief of homelessness, or otherwise. The beneficiaries must be indefinite, as opposed to other types of trusts where the beneficiaries must be clearly ascertainable. A charitable trust may last in perpetuity, as opposed to other trusts where there are clear legal limits of duration imposed. Finally, the **cy pres doctrine** is applied to charitable trusts. Under this doctrine, instead of a trust failing when it is no longer possible to fulfill, the trust may continue by using the trust funds for a charity that closely approximates the original charity. Suppose, for example, that a charitable trust was established to feed the hungry of Somalia. If that can no longer be fulfilled because there are no longer any hungry in that country, then, under the cy pres doctrine, the trust funds could be used to feed the hungry elsewhere. The following case illustrates another approach to the cy pres doctrine.

IN RE FARROW
605 A.2d 1346 (Pa Super. 1992)

Malinda Farrow, settlor, executed a trust with the direction to pay income from the trust to named relatives, and the remainder to go to six charities: First Presbyterian Church, Moses Taylor Memorial Church, Geisinger Memorial Hospital, American Red Cross, Salvation Army, and Monmouth Memorial Hospital. When the named relatives died, Mellon Bank, the trustee, could not locate Moses Taylor Memorial Church.

The trustees instituted a cy pres proceeding to determine the appropriate beneficiary of the one sixth share of the trust. The court ordered that it be distributed equally to the five remaining beneficiaries. First Presbyterian Church appealed seeking the entire one sixth share.

DEL SOLE, Judge

The cy pres doctrine states in pertinent part that, ''if the charitable purpose for which an interest is conveyed shall be or become indefinite or impossible or impractical of fulfillment, . . . the court shall order an administration or distribution of the estate for a charitable purpose in a manner as nearly as possible to fulfill the intention of the conveyor. . . .'' The *Restatement*'s definition of the doctrine has also been cited in our case law. It states: ''If property is given in trust to be applied to a particular charitable purpose, and it is or becomes impossible or impracticable or illegal to carry out the particular purpose, and if the settlor manifested a more general intention to devote the property to charitable purposes, the trust will not fail but the court will direct the application of the property to some charitable purpose which falls within the general charitable intention of the settlor.''

The intention of the settlor must be derived from an examination of the entire will. In examining the entire will it is evident that the intention of the Settlor was to first benefit her family and then to benefit six named charities. None of the six designated charities were favored with a larger share than the others.

The application of the doctrine of cy pres requires the court to exercise its discretion in such a manner as to award the fund to a charity which most resembles the one the Settlor intended to benefit. To that end, it is necessary to examine the purposes and object of the defunct or non-existent organization, the locality that the charity intended to serve, and the nature of the population which was the intended object of the charitable gift.

In the instant case we cannot conduct a meaningful inquiry into these questions, because ''In the present case, we cannot 'study' and compare the Moses Taylor Church to the other named charities because the record is barren of evidence concerning the Moses Taylor Church.'' We do not know the corporate purposes of the Taylor Church, nor do we know its locale or the nature of the population served. Indeed, the only similarity between the lapsed beneficiary and Appellant, First Presbyterian, is the use of the term ''Church,'' and since we cannot know the nature or function of this defunct or non-existent Church, to decide this case based on the finding that it is closest to the name of the non-existent organization used by the settlor is error. In fact, in several cases in which the designated charity was defunct or ambiguously labelled in a testamentary or trust document, and the court applied the cy pres doctrine, the lapsed share did not go to any of the named beneficiaries, but to a charity not mentioned in the will or trust but which most nearly approximated the intention of the donor.

We also note that, ''[c]harities are favorites of the law and a gift, even for a specific charitable purpose, should be liberally construed whenever reasonably possible.'' We therefore endorse the Orphan's Court liberal construction of the Settlor's intent to benefit her favorite charities, although the gift was specifically made to the Taylor Church.

Furthermore, in conformance with the meaning of the doctrine of cy pres, which mandates that when a definite benefit cannot be performed in exact conformity to the scheme of the person or persons who have provided for it, it must be performed with as close approximation to that scheme as reasonably practicable, we find that the decree of the Orphan's Court equally dividing the Taylor Church's share of the residual estate among the five other residual beneficiaries, approximates the testator's express intention as nearly as possible and does no violence to it. Therefore, in the absence of any information concerning the Moses Taylor Memorial Church, Appellant has not met its burden of showing that the court has abused its discretion or committed an error of law, and we affirm the court's application of the doctrine of cy pres.

Case Questions

1. What is the issue?
2. What could First Presbyterian have produced to advance its cause?
3. Argue that the court did not apply the cy pres doctrine.
4. Did the court have other alternatives? Explain.

Modification and Termination of Trusts

A trust ends at the expiration of the stated term. Or, it will end when it is revoked by the settlor. An irrevocable trust may terminate upon the unanimous consent of the settlor and the beneficiaries. However, the death of the trustee does not result in a termination of the trust. In such event, a new trustee is appointed. A beneficiary may not unilaterally revoke a trust. However, under the doctrine of merger, a trust terminates when the settlor, the trustee, and the beneficiary are all the same person.

END–OF–CHAPTER QUESTIONS

1. Check the intestacy laws in your jurisdiction. For what reasons might you prefer to make a will?
2. Analyze the following statement: ''In the event that a person fails to make a will, all property should escheat to the state.''
3. Should a jurisdiction provide for holographic wills? Oral wills? If so, under what circumstances?
4. Compare and contrast the power to make living wills and physician-assisted suicide?
5. Explain when it would be advisable to establish each of the following trusts: totten, blind, and spendthrift.
6. Ray Holder desires to make a will. He has three living children and one deceased child who has three surviving children. Explain the difference in consequence should he design the will for per stirpes as opposed to per capita distribution. Assume that he drafted a will that stated ''all my property to be divided to my children equally, or to the survivor(s), share and share alike.'' How does that differ from per capita and per stirpes distribution?
7. Ivan Hoover prepared a will, leaving 25 percent of his estate to his wife and the remainder to his surviving siblings, equally. The state statute provides: ''No will in writing, and no clause thereof or devise therein, shall be revoked, except by a subsequent will, codicil, or declaration in writing, executed with like formalities, or by the testator destroying or canceling the same, or causing it to be done in his presence.'' Upon Ivan's death, it was found that the first page of the will, which had contained the disposition clauses, had been replaced by another page that left all his property to his wife. The rest of the will, including the signature and the witnesses' signatures, was intact as originally signed. Who gets

what? Analyze. See *Goode v. Estate of Hoover,* 828 S.W. 2d 558 (Tex. App. 1992).

8. A married woman owns a house ($200,000), stock ($100,000), money in a bank account ($50,000), a pension, life insurance, household furnishings, and personal effects ($30,000). Is it desirable for her to plan an estate in order to avoid probate? Explain. What other information would you like to know? What methods might she use to avoid probate?

9. Brauna Howman was 80 years old and feeble. She was particularly dependent on her nephew, Andrew, for her everyday existence. For the last three years, Andrew had been devoted to his aunt, taking her to the store, keeping her financial records, and generally helping her cope better with life. One day, he suggested she have a will prepared. After he took her to meet with a lawyer, she executed a will, leaving one half of her estate to Andrew. The other half of the estate she distributed equally to the humane society, her only cousin, and a friend from childhood. She had no other relatives. Howman died. Discuss whether undue influence is likely to be found. Who would most likely raise the issue? Why? What are the possible consequences should it be found that Howman was the victim of undue influence?

10. Williston Hanaby established a testamentary trust leaving all his property to the Society of Battered Women of Sarasota. Hanaby died leaving one son. The trustee was unable to locate any such Society. Hanaby's son maintains that the estate should go to him since the will fails and hence his father is deemed to have died intestate. Do you agree? Explain.

Unit II

Commercial Transactions

COMMERCIAL TRANSACTIONS

The present law of commercial transactions, both common law and the Uniform Commercial Code (UCC), has its origins in the 14th century law merchant of Europe. The law merchant is the body of law that developed from the system of rules, customs, and usages adopted by merchants and traders to regulate their transactions. Since commercial transactions can be viewed as specialized types of contracts, such as contracts for the sale of goods, or contracts for secured transactions, much of the law is contract law.

THE COMMERCIAL TRANSACTION

The commercial transaction is an entire puzzle with many pieces. The commercial transaction typically begins with a contract for the sale of goods. Assume Ben Buyer contracts to purchase 1,000 widgets from Sam Seller for $100,000. This is both a common law contract and a contract covered by Article 2 of the UCC. Sales contracts typically involve payment by check or promissory note for at least a portion of the purchase price. Assume that Ben gives Sam a check for $20,000, signing a promissory note

for the $80,000 remainder—in effect promising to pay the $80,000 in the future. The subject of commercial paper is governed by Article 3 of the UCC. If payment is made by a check processed by bank collection, that is regulated by Article 4 of the UCC as well as by federal regulation. If the goods are shipped or stored, the transaction typically involves a document of title, regulated by Article 7 of the UCC. Since the sale is on credit, Sam may require a security interest in some collateral. This is a secured transaction governed by Article 9 of the UCC. Alternatively, the entire transaction might have been structured around a letter of credit (either foreign or domestic). Letters of credit are regulated by Article 5 of the UCC. If the buyer is unable to pay for the goods, the creditor seeks to collect the debt. Thus, debtor-creditor law is oftentimes an integral part of the commercial transaction.

THE LAW

Contract law is generally common law, that is case law, rather than statutory law. As early as the late 19th century the need was perceived for uniformity in the regulation of commercial transactions. This led to the adoption of certain uniform statutes, for example the Uniform Negotiable Instruments Law in 1896 and the Uniform Sales Act in 1906. By 1940 the uniformity had been lost by different court interpretations between the states.

The UCC was enacted to simplify, modernize, and make uniform the law governing commercial transactions. It is in fact an ongoing process. The Permanent Editorial Board of the UCC continually evaluates the UCC and, when needed, proposes revisions. Further, the UCC was designed to permit the continued expansion of commercial practices through custom, usage, and the agreement of the parties. Thus, the Code provisions are often subject to modification by the parties and by usages of the trade. Similarly, the Code adopted a policy of ''open-drafting,'' designed, at least in part, to allow for continued expansion of commercial practices. For example, such phrases as *commercial reasonableness* and *good faith* appear throughout the Code. The use of these phrases allows for court interpretation to adjust to changing commercial practices.

The UCC is not a comprehensive commercial code. It incorporates the common law. The UCC provides in Section 1–103 that the provisions of the common law survive unless displaced by the provisions of the UCC.

Part III

Contract Law

■

Chapter 11

Introduction to Contracts

■

CRITICAL THINKING INQUIRIES

As you read this chapter, you should be able to address the following:

- Why has the nature of contract theory changed over time?
- How does the nature of contracts differ from the nature of torts?
- Analyze the need for classifying contracts.
- Evaluate: ''Morality should be sufficient to motivate us to keep our agreements.''

MANAGERIAL PERSPECTIVE

L&R, Inc. is a supplier of commercial grade plumbing supplies. It has dealt with plumbers and small companies for most of its corporate life. Recently, it has expanded significantly, and it now finds itself as a major player in the regional plumbing wholesale market. In the past, L&R has dealt with its customers on the basis of trust and a ''shake of the hand.'' Now, the company is faced with the need for more formal contractual relations. This necessitates a real knowledge of contract law and new policies.

Rosella Lieu, the chief executive officer, says, ''Let's just hire a few in-house attorneys.'' Dominic Santiago, the vice president of sales, suggests an intensive training program for employees that are involved in sales.

- Who is right—Lieu or Santiago?
- What are the rudiments of contract law with which sales employees should be familiar?

Figure 11–1   Historical Periods of Contract Theory

Period	Year	Characteristic	Features
Primitive	Pre-1000	Primitive	Gift exchanges Present change of status
Medieval	1000–1600	Feudalism	Specific performance Scrutinized for fairness
Postfeudal	1601–1900	Abuse of power	Enforced parties' will
Twentieth century	1901–present	Laissez-faire	Restrictions on freedom of contract

Contracts are the real glue that supports commercial transactions. Rosella Lieu and her sales force need to know a bit about contracts—for example, when a contract has been formed, when it is enforceable, and the consequences of breaching a contract. Additionally, the law of contracts is a foundation for understanding other areas of law, such as negotiable instruments, property, and antitrust laws.

This chapter presents the fundamentals of contract law. Like Lieu, students need to master the terminology and the basic concepts associated with contract law before examining the specifics of contract law. We begin by examining the nature of contract law and its sources. Then we consider the various ways in which a contract may be classified. We conclude by discussing the essential elements of a contract that will be the focus of the next seven chapters.

NATURE OF CONTRACTS

The nature of contract law can be discerned by examining its history, considering its definition, basis, and purpose, and comparing it with tort law.

History of Contracts

Contract law is not new (see Figure 11–1). It has developed over centuries and, as such, has been shaped over time by many civilizations. Still, its history may be outlined in four main periods, as suggested in the following excerpt.

*The Evolution of Contract Law**

Primitive Societies and Contracts (Pre–1000)

The existence of contract law in primitive societies is the subject of debate among anthropologists. Several features of typical exchanges in a primitive society do distinguish them from current notions of contract. In a fascinating study of exchanges among the Cheyenne Indians,[†] two university professors noted the following characteristics. Gift exchanges, rather than bargains, were the dominant means of trade, and the gift exchanges tended to take place along established family or community lines rather than with strangers. The exchanges

---

*Source: Richard Nathan, *The Evolution of Contract Law,* © Richard D. Irwin 1994. Reprinted with permission.

[†]K. N. Llewellyn and E. A. Hoebel, *The Cheyenne Way: Conflict and Case Law in Primitive Jurisprudence,* (1941).

were generally accompanied by formal ceremonies, that is, formal words and the exchange of gifts in the presence of witnesses. Finally, the exchange tended to look to a present change of status, for example, becoming a tribal chief, rather than a future commitment. The Cheyenne Indian's approach to exchanges is representative of other primitive cultures.

Medieval Society and Contracts (1000–1600)

Most obligations in medieval society were determined by a person's position or status in society. The feudal serf, for example, was obligated to render a certain portion of crops to the landlord. The landlord in turn provided protection to the serf against invading enemies.

The courts recognized contracts to the extent necessary to protect a property interest. Under a *title theory of exchange* a contract was perceived as transferring title to the specific property that was the subject of the contract. If a contracting party failed to deliver goods contracted for, the court, under the title theory, would order the goods delivered. This was the exclusive remedy. No damages would be awarded for the difference between the contract price and the market price.

Another feature of medieval contract traditions was that the courts scrutinized the agreement to determine whether the agreed price was just. If it was not, the court refused to enforce the agreement. Courts thus did not necessarily uphold business agreements as written, but instead were prone to impose their own sense of fairness.

Post-Feudal Society and Contracts (1601–1900)

As societal changes dismantled feudalism, the title theory of exchange collapsed. The new theory which supplanted it is commonly known as the *will theory*. Under the will theory, the courts enforced the declared will of the parties. Thus, if the parties decided to exchange a horse for a peppercorn, the courts would not substitute a ''just-price'' for the agreed upon price.

Several influences gave rise to this new theory. As Protestantism took hold in Europe, the notion of the autonomy of individuals was increasingly asserted. Liberty in all spheres, including the liberty to contract as one chose, was a necessary corollary of the new understanding of the individual. Further, post-feudal markets expanded as technological advances emerged, and society came to view governmental or court intrusion into individuals' freedom to contract as economically unwise. The ''invisible hand'' of the marketplace was held to be a better means of controlling the distribution of goods and services than legal interference.

Twentieth Century Contract Law (1901–present)

Laissez-faire capitalism brought with it social problems. In contract law parties with superior bargaining power were permitted to abuse those with less power. The corollary of enforcing the will of the parties meant that the weaker party was often presented with a ''take it or leave it'' offer and consequently was stuck with a bad bargain.

To curb abuses, courts and legislatures have increasingly restricted parties' freedom to contract. Labor and insurance agreements are two examples of contracts that are heavily regulated by legislatures. One statutory provision (UCC § 2-302) permits the courts to void any contract or term of a contract, involving the sale of goods, which the court considers unconscionable.

Thought Questions

1. Do you think that contract law shapes society or that society shapes contract law? Analyze.
2. What is the author's point? Does he support it well? Explain.
3. How might contract law evolve as we enter the 21st century, with its greater emphasis on technology, computerization, and speed of communication?

Definition of Contract

The word **contract,** at this point, probably conjures up an image of a very formal written document that is signed by two or more persons. Although this may be an accurate characterization of some contracts, it is a very limited view. Technically, a contract is "a promise or set of promises for the breach of which the law gives a remedy, or the performance of which the law in some way recognizes as a duty."[1] To fully understand this law textbook definition, the reader must already have some knowledge of contract law. Perhaps this formal definition will become more understandable after the entire unit on contracts is completed. Until then, it should suffice to define a contract as a promise or an agreement that the courts will enforce. This definition, of course, implies that the law will not enforce every promise or agreement.

Basis of Contract

A person should keep his or her promise. It is honorable to do so. Yet the law has never fashioned a remedy for every broken promise or agreement. Instead, the law has been willing to enforce those promises and agreements that justifiably arouse an expectation of performance. Casual comments such as "I'll meet you for lunch tomorrow" or "I'll give you a call tonight" are normally not the type of remarks that are the subject of great reliance and expectation. Although wounded feelings may result from the nonperformance, normally no great economic harm flows from such breaches. These types of arrangements are deemed social in nature, and the incentives to perform are best left to the consciences of the parties. Assume, for example, that Sue agrees to meet Jeff for a date, which is to in-

clude dinner and a movie. Jeff "stands Sue up" by failing to show for the date. A court would not offer a remedy to Sue for Jeff's nonperformance. The parties do not ordinarily intend for these casual social agreements to have legal consequences. On the other hand, assume that Sue hired Jeff as a bodyguard to protect her while she eats dinner and attends a movie. If Jeff fails to appear to perform the protective services for which he was hired, and Sue is injured as a result, a court would grant a remedy to Sue. This agreement is commercial in nature and is the type courts enforce.

Purpose of Contract Law

 Test Question

Contract law is designed to protect parties from liability for certain promises made. This initial function may be described as "freedom *from* contract." For example, as will be seen in future chapters within this Part, the law of contracts protects minors and the mentally incompetent.

Contract law serves another function as well. The second function of contract law might be described as "freedom *to* contract." Hardly a day passes that a person does not enter into a contract. Ordering lunch in a restaurant, writing checks to pay obligations, purchasing or selling property, and even agreements between two people to live together involve contracts. On a larger scale, businesses depend on contracts for their means of operation. As the executive officer in the opening scenario will soon learn, the business functions of financing, production, marketing, management, and personnel administration are based on the law of contracts.

Thus, the law of contracts serves a restrictive or a limiting function by protecting people from unwanted or illegal promises. Additionally, it provides a facilitating function for economic exchanges by adding the force of law to the moral compunction of fulfilling one's promises.

---

[1] *Restatement (Second) of Contracts* § 1.

Contract and Tort Distinguished

Torts and contracts are similar since both may be the basis of a civil action. However, there are distinctions. As we learned in Chapter 7, the law imposes certain duties on a person. A breach of such a duty, which proximately causes injury, amounts to a tort for which the law provides a remedy. By way of contrast, a contract arises not because of any duty imposed by law but because parties have entered into a "private piece of legislation" by which they have agreed to be bound. The obligations of the parties are self-imposed. Failure to comply amounts to a breach of contract for which the law provides a remedy in favor of the aggrieved party. Hence, a tort arises by operation of *law,* whereas a contract arises by operation of the *parties.*

SOURCES OF CONTRACT LAW

Lawyers must look to a body of law to advise their clients and to predict the outcome of a lawsuit. These sources of law include the common law and the Uniform Commercial Code (statutory law).

Common Law

The bulk of contract law is derived from the common law—judge-made law. The many judicial cases decided by judges form the primary source of law. Contract law, along with torts and property law, are the few remaining substantive areas that are more dependent on the common law than statutory law.

The common law, as discussed in a previous chapter, is based on the principle of *stare decisis.* This guiding principle, influencing judges to strictly apply the law of the past, suggests that contract law is static. However, the countervailing influences of the judicial tools—overruling, distinguishing precedent, and applying equity—discussed in Chapter 6, have all contributed to the evolution of contract law and its quest to meet the needs of modern society.

The common law of contracts is buried in a plethora of judicial opinions. Of course, no lawyer or judge has total recall of all opinions that shape the law. There are, however, legal digests, indexes, reporters, commentaries, and treatises that aid people interested in finding and understanding the law. Two noteworthy legal commentaries on contracts are authored by Professor Samuel Williston and Professor Arthur Corbin. They are scholarly treatises on contracts designed to simplify the law by extracting principles from the vast body of case law. These treatises have been very influential and are often cited "as law" by lawyers and judges.

In 1932, the American Law Institute (ALI), an organization of lawyers, judges, and law teachers, published a codelike work called the *Restatement of Contracts.* The *Restatement* is composed of the general rules of contract law as derived from case law. It is frequently cited authoritatively in legal literature and judicial cases.

The Uniform Commercial Code

The National Conference of Commissioners on Uniform State Law, an organization composed of appointees by various state governments, in collaboration with the American Law Institute, produced the Uniform Commercial Code (UCC or Code) in 1952 and recommended its adoption by the states. All states have now adopted the UCC.

The Uniform Commercial Code was enacted to serve three purposes:

1. *To bring commercial law in line with modern business practice.* In general, the UCC rejects archaic and outdated concepts in favor of modern commercial realities.
2. *To permit the expansion of trade.* The UCC rules tend to be flexible, preferring a liberal facilitation of the economy rather than a technical, straight-jacket approach.
3. *To make the laws of the various states uniform.* In dealing with the problem of 50 state laws and numerous court opinions, the drafters proposed a *uniform* commercial code. This principle of uniformity is especially important because the economy has moved from one based on local intrastate transactions to one based on interstate transactions.

There are limitations. Although its name would suggest otherwise, the UCC does not cover all commercial transactions. Topics not covered include transactions in real estate, employment contracts, bankruptcy, insurance contracts, and international transactions. Moreover, when federal law and the UCC conflict, federal law will govern because of the Constitution's Supremacy Clause. Even when the UCC covers a particular type of transaction, such as the sale of goods, it does not do so exhaustively. Common law principles still apply to the transaction unless a UCC provision specifically displaces the common law [UCC § 1–103]. The UCC has not been adopted in its *full form* by all states. Additionally, in some instances, different states have interpreted the same provision differently.

The Uniform Commercial Code is divided into nine substantive articles (see Figure 11–2). Each deals with a different type of transaction. Students of contract law are most concerned with Article 2 of the UCC, which covers transactions *in goods* only [UCC § 2–105]. Consequently, it is not explicitly applicable to real estate or service contracts. Because the UCC provides that certain implied warranties accompany the sale of goods (which warranties do not accompany the sale of services), the plaintiffs in the following case argued that a blood transfusion amounted to a sale of goods.

Figure 11–2   Uniform Commercial Code Articles

Article	Topic
1	General provisions
2	Sales
3	Commercial paper
4	Bank deposits and collections
5	Letters of credit
6	Bulk transfers
7	Documents of title
8	Investment securities
9	Secured transactions

LOVETT v. EMORY UNIVERSITY, INC.
156 S.E. 2d 923 (Ga. App. 1967)

Mildred Lovett underwent a blood transfusion at Emory University Crawford W. Long Memorial Hospital. As a result of "bad blood," she allegedly contracted serum hepatitis and died.

Lovett's family brought an action against Emory University, the owner and operator of the hospital, on the theory that the transfusion of blood was a "sale of goods" within the meaning of the Uniform Commercial Code. The Uniform Commercial Code provides that the seller of goods impliedly warrants that the goods are fit for their intended purpose, and Lovett's family contended that the defendant breached that warranty. The trial court disagreed and dismissed the action. The case was appealed to the Georgia Court of Appeals.

JORDAN, Judge

This is a case of novel impression in Georgia, in that the plaintiffs seek to show a cause of action for wrongful death based solely on the alleged breach of an implied warranty arising from the furnishing of blood by a hospital to a patient. After careful consideration of all aspects of the case, we are of the opinion that such a blood transfusion is an incidental part of the service furnished by a hospital in the course of medical treatment and is not a sales transaction under our [Uniform Commercial Code], even if the cost of the blood is specified as a separate item in the charges made. As to the Uniform Commercial Code Sales we think it is significant that the General

Assembly expressly provided that the "serving for value of food or drink . . . is a sale" of goods without expressly including other service-type transactions as covered by any implied warranty.

Various other jurisdictions have considered the issue of recovery for an injury or death caused by a blood transfusion under the theory of a breach of an implied warranty in the sale of the blood. These courts have generally refused to recognize the theory as affording any basis for recovery, adhering to the view that in a blood transfusion service predominates, and that even if a separate charge is made for the blood such charge is not indicative of a sale but is merely an incidental feature of the services rendered.

. . .[T]he New York Court of Appeals in the leading case determined that the transaction was a service and not a sale, and expressly rejected the theory of a breach of an implied warranty to support an action for injuries from serum hepatitis caused by a blood transfusion. Since that time other states, in identical or similar type cases usually involving hospitals as defendants, have followed the [lead] case. . . . [T]he Florida Court of Appeals, Second District, rejected what appears to have been the consistent view in other jurisdictions as shown above, and held that the furnishing of blood by a blood bank is a sale subject to an implied warranty in a serum hepatitis case but noted a distinction between a blood bank defendant and a hospital defendant by stating that a hospital supplied blood as part of its overall service, whereas a blood bank did not.

The court joins the overwhelming majority view that the furnishing of blood by a hospital in the course of treatment is not a sales transaction covered by an implied warranty under the Uniform Commercial Code or otherwise.

Judgment affirmed.

Case Questions

1. What is the issue in this case?
2. Why was it so important to determine whether the transfusion was a sale of goods?
3. With the advent of AIDS since this case, and the widespread use of blood screening designed to weed out AIDS-infected blood, should there be a different approach? A different result? Analyze.
4. Analyze: ''The courts should reason by analogy and adopt the principles of the Code even when a transaction is not covered by the Code.''

CLASSIFICATIONS OF CONTRACTS

Contract law, like any academic study, is better understood through classification. Just as the botanist classifies plants and the chemist elements, so too the lawyer classifies contracts.

Valid, Void, and Voidable

Contracts can be classified in a number of ways. One common approach is to classify contracts with reference to their enforceability. A **valid** contract is one that the courts will enforce by awarding a remedy in the event of a breach. A **void contract** is one that the courts will not enforce because it lacks the requisite elements. Since one essential element of a valid contract is that its purpose be legal, a contract for an illegal act would be void. The term *void contract* is really a misnomer since a contract that is void is really not a contract at all.

A **voidable** contract lies somewhere in between valid and void. If at least one party to a contract has the power either to avoid the responsibilities created by the contract or to treat the contract as binding, the contract is voidable. The most common example of a voidable contract is that entered into by a minor.

The law allows a minor who contracts to disaffirm the contract and treat it as void or to ratify it and treat it as valid (see Chapter 15).

Finally, some contracts are **unenforceable.** An unenforceable contract lacks certain formalities. Some types of contracts require a writing to be enforceable (see Chapter 16). Courts will refuse to grant contract relief to a party when the type of case requires a writing but no writing can be produced. And a contract that is otherwise valid may become unenforceable because the attempt to enforce it has not occurred in a timely manner.

Formal and Informal

Another way of classifying contracts is to distinguish between formal and informal ones. This distinction is largely a matter of historical importance. There are three types of **formal contracts.** The *contract under seal* is the least significant today. When parties entered into a solemn contract for which they expected performance, they would seal the contract with a signet of heated wax. Courts were prone to enforce contracts entered into with such formality. Today, contracts under seal are little more than an historical note. A second type of formal contract is the *recognizance*, a bond binding a person to do an act. An example of a recognizance would be an agreement before a court to pay a sum of money unless the recognizor, the person signing the recognizance, appeared in court on a fixed date. Finally, *negotiable instruments* are considered formal contracts. The most common form of negotiable instrument is a draft drawn on a bank, commonly known as a check. All contracts other than those under seal, recognizances, and negotiable instruments are **informal contracts.** Today, informal contracts are as enforceable as formal contracts if they meet the requirements discussed in the chapters to follow.

Unilateral and Bilateral

In every contract, at least one person makes a promise. This person is referred to as a **promisor.** The person to whom the promise is made is called the **promisee.** If only one promise is made, the contract is **unilateral** in nature. For example, Hillary says to Romanda, ''I will give you $10 if you cut my lawn tomorrow.'' Hillary is the promisor. She is bargaining for Romanda's act of cutting her lawn. If Romanda cuts Hillary's lawn ''tomorrow,'' then there is a unilateral contract. Here, we have a promise in exchange for an act. However, if Hillary said to Romanda, ''I promise to pay you $10 if you promise to cut my lawn tomorrow,'' a **bilateral** contract would arise when Romanda makes the requested return promise. Here, there would be two promises— a promise exchanged for a promise. In fact, both Hillary and Romanda would be promisors as well as promisees (see Figure 11–3).

Now, what if Hillary said to Romanda, as in the first example, ''I will give you $10 if you cut my lawn tomorrow,'' and Romanda immediately responded, ''I promise to cut your lawn tomorrow''? It appears that we have a bilateral contract since there are two promises. However, under traditional contract principles, no contract exists since Hillary was looking for an act and not a return promise. Romanda's attempt to accept Hillary's offer by giving Hillary a return promise instead of the sought after act would be ineffective. The Uniform Commercial Code has changed this result in the sale of goods area. Under the UCC, when a buyer orders goods, the seller can accept the offer *either* by shipping the goods—performance—or by promising to ship the goods—a return promise [UCC § 2–206(1)(b)]. Assume, for example, that a contractor ordered plumbing supplies from L&R, Inc. L&R

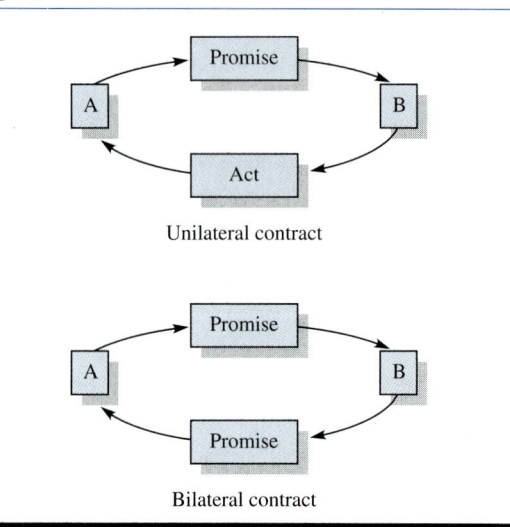

Figure 11–3   Unilateral and Bilateral Contracts

may accept the contractor's order by promising to deliver the order or simply by delivering the supplies. Thus, under the UCC, the distinction between unilateral and bilateral contracts has largely been eliminated.

Executed and Executory

Until the promises in a bilateral contract are performed, they are called **executory.** Assume, for example, that Phil Farmer and Sylvia Grocer enter into a contract whereby Farmer agrees to deliver and Grocer agrees to pay for 100 bushels of mungbeans at $4 per bushel. This bilateral contract is executory since neither party has performed his or her agreement. However, when Farmer delivers the bushels, his side of the contract will be executed. Likewise, when Grocer actually pays for the bushels of mungbeans as agreed, her side will be executed. A wholly **executed contract** occurs when each party has performed his or her side of the agreement (see Figure 11–4).

Oral and Written

Most contracts are oral. In fact, it would be impractical to put every contract in writing. Casual transactions at the grocery store and purchases from vending machines hardly justify the trouble of a writing. Generally, oral contracts are as enforceable as those in writing. However, certain agreements

Figure 11-4   Executory and Executed Contracts

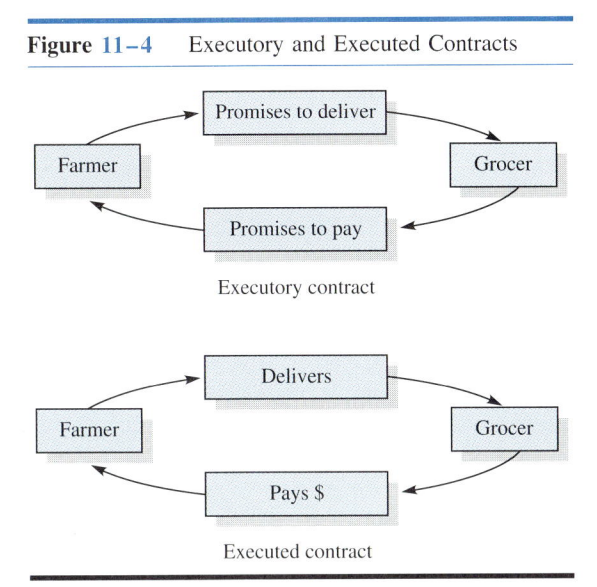

Executory contract

Executed contract

Figure 11-5   Express, Implied, and Quasi-Contracts: A Comparison

Contract Type	Expression	Agreement	Enforceable
Express	Yes	Yes	Yes
Implied	Yes	Yes	Yes
Quasi	No	No	Yes

require a writing to be enforceable. The sale of real estate is one such agreement. Agreements that require a writing to be enforceable are discussed in Chapter 16.

Express and Implied

Contracts may be express or implied (see Figure 11–5). **Express contracts** are those in which the agreement is manifested by words, either spoken or in writing. If words are not the vehicle for expressing agreement, the **contract is implied.** There are two types of implied contracts: implied in fact and implied in law. A contract **implied in fact** is inferred from the circumstances. For example, Jamie walks into a dry cleaners and drops off some clothing. When she returns to pick up her clean clothes she is expected to pay. Although no words were spoken, a true agreement can be inferred from the parties' conduct. Jamie will be required to pay for the cleaning.

Sometimes, serious questions arise as to whether a situation is an implied contract or simply a gratuitous undertaking. Assume, for example, that an elderly man, in need of help, advertises for someone to take care of his person and property. A young married couple responds to the advertisement and, pursuant to the elderly man's wishes, moves into his house and faithfully renders the requested duties until his death two years later. In the absence of any express agreement, the court must decide whether

the young couple volunteered their services for free or whether payment for services was expected based on an implied agreement. The answer, in such a case, often turns on a factual determination based on whether a reasonable person under the circumstances would have been justified in believing a contract for services existed.

The second type of implied contract consists of contracts **implied in law,** referred to as **quasi-contracts.** Under this theory, the court will construct a contract (even though one did not exist) to avoid unjust enrichment—an unfair windfall to a party. Generally, three elements must exist before the court will construct a contract without contractual assent:

- A benefit conferred on the defendant.
- Knowledge or appreciation of the benefit.
- Circumstances where it would be inequitable to permit the defendant to retain the benefit without paying for it.

To apply these elements, assume that Sandy moved into a neighborhood, taking up residence adjacent to Kenyon. Thinking that the fence separating Sandy and Kenyon's property belonged to Sandy, Sandy proceeds to sand and repaint it. At the same time, Kenyon watches from the window, knowing that Sandy is mistaken since the fence really belongs to Kenyon. In a suit by Sandy against Kenyon in quasi-contract, Sandy should be able to recover the value of the benefit conferred on Kenyon though there was no express or implied-in-fact contract on which to base an agreement. Sandy's conduct conferred a benefit on Kenyon. Kenyon knew about the benefit and it would be unfair to permit Kenyon to take advantage of Sandy's mistake and retain the benefit without payment. The following case further illustrates the principles found in implied-in-law contracts.

HURDIS REALTY, INC. v. TOWN OF NORTH PROVIDENCE
397 A.2d 896 (R.I. 1979)

The plaintiff, Hurdis Realty, Inc., owns a building situated at the corner of Charles Street and Mineral Spring Avenue in North Providence. Frank Hurdis, president of Hurdis Realty, was informed that the sewage was not flowing properly from the building. Hurdis employed a plumber who determined that the cause of the blockage was located past Hurdis Realty's property line, somewhere under Mineral Spring Avenue. Hurdis proceeded to the North Providence Town Hall where he requested that the town council president remedy the problem. The council president replied that before he could order any repair work, he needed a report from the sewer superintendent. The superintendent went to the site, but failed to observe a blockage.

Hurdis hired a private sewer contractor who located a blockage caused by a broken pipe. Hurdis obtained a permit to excavate a portion of Mineral Spring Avenue. The private contractor repaired the damaged pipe.

Hurdis Realty spent $4,773.29 to obtain the necessary repairs and presented its claim for reimbursement to the town council. The claim was not satisfied. Hurdis Realty sued the defendant, Town of North Providence, under a quasi-contract theory. The trial court held for Hurdis Realty. The case was appealed to the Supreme Court of Rhode Island.

DORIS, Justice

Unlike an express or implied-in-fact contract for which mutual assent is necessary, in an implied-in-law or quasi-contract, liability is implied by the law and arises from the facts and circumstances irrespective of any agreement or presumed intention. In such a case the intent of the parties is not dispositive. . . .

A municipality, no less than a private individual, may be liable upon the principle of unjust enrichment when it has enjoyed the benefit of work performed and when no statute forbids or limits its power to contract therefor. It is undisputed that municipalities have the power to enter into contracts with respect to their sewer systems. The defendant concedes that it had a duty to maintain its sewer systems. . . .

By statute defendant is empowered to assess users of the sewer system and utilize the revenues thereby derived for the maintenance of the sewer system. Even though it is subject to such an assessment, plaintiff was further required to expend its own funds to repair a damaged portion of the town's

sewer lines. In so doing, plaintiff clearly conferred a benefit upon the town and fulfilled what was essentially a municipal responsibility. The town, particularly the town council president and sewer superintendent, was fully aware of the repair work. Under these circumstances it would be manifestly inequitable for defendant to benefit from the fruits of plaintiff's labor without paying for the value of that benefit. Affirmed.

Case Questions

1. Should the doctrine of quasi-contract be applied against government? Why or why not?
2. Did the defendant, Town of North Providence, "appreciate the benefit"? Analyze.
3. What course of action should the defendant have taken after being informed of the sewage blockage?
4. Would the result have been any different if one of Hurdis Realty's full-time plumbers fixed the blockage? Why or why not?

ESSENTIALS OF A CONTRACT

We have already learned that the courts will not enforce every promise or agreement. An enforceable contract must contain certain ingredients. The basis of the contract is the *agreement*. Ordinarily, there must be a mutual manifestation of an intent to be bound by the parties. This requires an *offer* by an *offeror* and an *acceptance* by the *offeree*.

Figure 11–6   Contract Principles

Principle	Chapter
• Offer	12
• Acceptance	12
• Genuine assent	13
• Capacity	13
• Consideration	14
• Legality	15
• Writing requirement	16
• Third parties	17
• Remedies	18

Consideration is also an essential ingredient to a contract. It is a legal term that, in a contract context, has nothing to do with being nice. It is the value that is bargained for and given up by one party in exchange for value.

The parties must *genuinely assent* to the agreement. Agreements entered into because of fraud, duress, undue influence, misrepresentation, or mistake are voidable.

Only those parties who have the *capacity* may enter into contracts. Minors and those who are unable to understand the transaction do not have the full capacity to enter into binding agreements.

Legality of purpose is essential to the formation of a contract. An agreement to split the proceeds of a bank robbery is void.

Certain contracts require a *writing*. The absence of a writing in those cases makes the contract unenforceable.

Once these essential elements are present, the law will protect a party to the contract against the other party's breach by providing a *remedy*. Sometimes, *third parties* will have an interest in enforcing the contract.

Each of these contract principles is covered separately in the following seven chapters. (See Figure 11–6.)

END–OF–CHAPTER QUESTIONS

1. Compare the features of primitive exchanges with 20th-century conceptions. How do they differ? How does the medieval "just price" theory compare with 20th-century notions?

2. Why do we need contract law?

3. Compare and contrast:
   a. Voidable and void contracts.
   b. Formal and informal contracts.
   c. Unilateral and bilateral contracts.
   d. Executory and executed contracts.

4. Give an example of an implied-in-fact contract and an implied-in-law contract.

5. The Kappa Kega Beer sorority was planning a huge roast and invited the entire freshman class. Included within the invitations were RSVP cards. Since the sorority was having the event catered, it needed to know how many people would attend. The caterer was charging the sorority $12 a plate. One hundred and seven students responded positively to the RSVP. The sorority requested the caterer to prepare dinner for that number. In fact, only 85 students showed. Kappa Kega Beer was nonetheless required to pay for the 107 students. Does the sorority have an action for breach of contract against the 22 students who failed to show? Explain.

6. The plaintiff, Betty Epstein, went to a beauty show conducted by the defendant, Giannattasio, to receive a hair-coloring treatment. Giannattasio applied "Zotos 30-day Color." As a result of the treatment, Epstein suffered acute dermatitis and loss of hair. She sued Giannattasio under the theory that the Uniform Commercial Code is applicable and it provides for implied warranties that were breached by Giannattasio. Is Epstein right? Explain. See *Epstein v. Giannattasio*, 197 A.2d 342 (Conn. Sup. 1963).

7. Javins rented an apartment from First National Realty Corporation. First National filed an action seeking possession of Javins's apartment for nonpayment of rent. Javins defended alleging numerous defects in the apartment. The common law in the jurisdiction does not provide for an implied warranty that the apartment is fit for habitation. Give arguments for departing from stare decisis and recognizing such a

warranty. See *Javins v. First National Realty Corporation,* 428 F.2d 1071 (D.C. Cir. 1970).

8. Alan Anisgard, a professional tennis player, developed an idea for a tennis facility. Anisgard located a site for the facility, negotiated with the owner for a long-term lease, and expended other effort and incurred expenses in the amount of $10,000 in preparation for the project. Anisgard met William Feeley and discussed with him the details of his idea for developing a tennis facility and the work that he had done toward that end. He took Feeley to the property owner of the proposed site. Feeley introduced Anisgard to Bray, a wealthy investor, and later the three met to discuss the financial details of the enterprise. Feeley outlined the terms of the parties' agreement and submitted it to Anisgard for his signature. Anisgard failed to sign it because it included additional terms not previously discussed. Subsequently, Feeley and Bray decided to proceed with the project in partnership with each other and to exclude Anisgard. They formed Tamarack Tennis Associates, the name Anisgard had selected, and secured a long-term lease on the same site under the same terms Anisgard had proposed. Anisgard sued Feeley and Bray under theories of breach of an express and implied contract. What should the result be? Explain. See *Anisgard v. Bray,* 419 N.E. 2d 315 (Mass. Ct. App. 1981).

9. Peter Deskovick, Sr., was visited by his son Michael in the hospital. On various occasions, Peter led his son to believe that he was unable to afford the hospital expense. In response, Michael paid the hospital bills. After Peter's death, it became apparent that his estate was sufficient to pay the debts. Under what theories of recovery may Michael proceed against the executor of the estate of his father? Analyze. See *Deskovick v. Porzio,* 187 A. 2d 610 (N.J. 1963).

10. A surgeon employed by the plaintiff, CBS Surgical Group Inc. (CBS), amputated Marion Holt's leg, necessitating her confinement in a nursing home until her death. CBS received no payment for medical services. The defendant, Alfred Maringola, was a friend of Holt for years and took care of her financial affairs. CBS learned that Holt made a medicare claim based on surgeon's services, and that a check in the amount of $2,000 was sent to Holt, who turned it over to Maringola. Maringola kept the proceeds of the check. CBS sued Maringola for the $2,000 under a quasi-contract theory. Who should win and why? See *CBS Surgical Group, Inc. v. Holt,* 426 A.2d 819 (Conn. Sup. 555 1981).

Chapter 12

The Agreement

■

CRITICAL THINKING INQUIRIES

As you read this chapter, you should be able to address the following:

- Compare the objective standard of contractual assent with the subjective standard.
- Compare and contrast the various ways of terminating an offer.
- Under what circumstances might you want to make an offer irrevocable?
- How does the common law differ from the Uniform Commercial Code in respect to offers and acceptances?
- Analyze: ''The law of contractual agreement is based on common sense.''

MANAGERIAL PERSPECTIVE

Frances is the chief sales agent for Double C, Inc., a growing computer company that produces, markets, and sells computer hardware, and also services computers. Frances has had a number of unanswered legal questions about purchase contracts, but his superior says, ''Don't worry about it. If we get into trouble, we'll call our attorney.''

Some of those questions include:

- At what point have we entered into a contractual agreement with our customer?
- Are we bound to sell advertised computers at the advertised price even when we run out of them?
- Are there different contractual rules for the sale of our hardware than for the sale of our service contracts?
- What happens when there is an open term—for example, price, time of payment, or place of delivery? Does this nullify the agreement, and if not, how is the term supplied?
- Under what circumstances can a purchase order be revoked?

Answers to these questions are essential so Frances can operate his sales department knowledgeably and effectively. Knowledge about contract formation is basic to most business enterprises. Without the principles, businesses get into difficulty and wind up going to lawyers to extricate them. Remember, "an ounce of prevention is worth more than a pound of cure."

This chapter examines the process of agreement that includes the offer and the acceptance. As we examine the chapter, note that treatments are sometimes different depending on the subject matter. Transactions involving the sale of goods are covered by the Uniform Commercial Code (see Figure 12–1), while other contractual transactions are governed by the common law. This chapter, as well as the following contract chapters, contrast the two.

To form an agreement, the parties must assent to the same terms. The process of assenting to the same terms typically results from an initial promise or offer made by the **offeror** and the acceptance of that promise or offer by the **offeree.** When an offer and an acceptance occur, a contract is formed, provided that the other elements covered in Chapters 13 to 16 are also present.

Figure 12–1   Uniform Commercial Code Sections

Subject	UCC Sections
Contract formation	2–204(3)
Firm offer	2–205
Acceptances	2–206; 2–207
Output and requirements contracts	2–306
Gap fillers	2–305; 2–307; 2–308; 2–309; 2–310; 2–311
Auctions	2–308(3)

THE OFFER

An offer typically consists of a promise or a commitment by the offeror to do or refrain from doing something in the future. A valid offer contains a:

- Present intent by the offeror to contract.
- Reasonable definiteness and certainty concerning the material terms.
- Communication of the offer to the offeree.

Present Contractual Intent

In order for there to be a valid offer, there must be an apparent intent to contract. This element is examined in the context of offers made in jest, advertisements, preliminary negotiations, and auction sales.

Offers Made in Jest

Intent to contract by the offeror is measured objectively—that is, by the offeror's manifestations to the offeror, as opposed to subjectively—that is, what the offeror actually intended. It does no good for the offeror to claim that he or she was joking and did not intend to contract if it *appeared* to the offeree that the offeror was serious. On the other hand, if the offeree has reason to know that the offeror was joking, there is no offer. Thus, in one case, the defendant was held to have intended a joke and not an offer when he published the following advertisement in the newspaper's joke column: "Offer: $1,000 to anyone who provides me with the telephone number of the Western Union." Similarly, an offeror cannot claim that the offer was merely an expression of anger or exasperation if the offeror appeared to be serious. Consider these principles as you read the following case which illustrates the danger of carrying a good joke too far.

LUCY v. ZEHMER
84 S.E. 2d 516 (Va. 1954)

W. O. Lucy desired to purchase Zehmer's farm. Lucy visited Zehmer at Zehmer's restaurant. Lucy said to Zehmer, "I bet you wouldn't take $50,000 for that place." Zehmer replied, "Yes, I would too; you wouldn't give fifty." Lucy said he would and told Zehmer to write up an agreement to that effect. Zehmer took a restaurant check and wrote on the back of it,

''I do hereby agree to sell to W. O. Lucy the Ferguson Farm for $50,000 complete.'' At Lucy's urging Zehmer changed the wording to ''we'' because Zehmer's wife needed to sign it, too.

Lucy engaged an attorney to examine the title. The attorney reported favorably and Lucy wrote Zehmer stating that the title was satisfactory and that he was ready to pay the purchase price in cash. He asked Zehmer when he would be ready to close the deal. Zehmer replied by letter, asserting that he had never agreed or intended to sell.

W. O. Lucy and J. C. Lucy, complainants, instituted suit against A. H. Zehmer and Ida S. Zehmer, his wife, defendants, to have the contract enforced (specific performance). The court found for the Zehmers and the Lucys appealed to the Supreme Court of Virginia.

BUCHANAN, Judge

Zehmer . . . bought this farm more than 10 years ago for $11,000. He had had 25 offers, more or less, to buy it, including several from Lucy, who had never offered any specific sum of money. He had given them all the same answer, that he was not interested in selling it. On this Saturday night before Christmas it looked like everybody and his brother came by there to have a drink. He took a good many drinks during the afternoon and had a pint of his own. When he entered the restaurant around 8:30 Lucy was there and he could see that he was ''pretty high.'' He said to Lucy, ''Boy, you got some good liquor, drinking, ain't you?'' Lucy then offered him a drink.

After Zehmer had, as he described it, ''scribbled this thing off,'' Lucy said, ''Get your wife to sign it.'' Zehmer walked over to where she was and she at first refused to sign but did so after he told her that he ''was just needling him (Lucy), and didn't mean a thing in the world, that I was not selling the farm.'' Zehmer . . . reached and picked it up, ''and when I looked back again he had it in his pocket and he dropped a five dollar bill over there, and he said, 'Here is five dollars payment on it.' . . . I said, . . . that is beer and liquor talking. I am not going to sell you the farm.''

The defendants insist that the evidence was ample to support their contention that the writing sought to be enforced was prepared as a bluff or dare to force Lucy to admit that he did not have $50,000; that the whole matter was a joke; that the writing was not delivered to Lucy and no binding contract was ever made between the parties.

The record is convincing that Zehmer was not intoxicated to the extent of being unable to comprehend the nature and consequences of the instrument he executed, and hence that instrument is not to be invalidated on that ground.

In the field of contracts, as generally elsewhere, ''We must look to the outward expression of a person as manifesting his intention rather than to his secret and unexpressed intention. 'The law imputes to a person an intention corresponding to the reasonable meaning of his words and acts.' ''

The mental assent of the parties is not requisite for the formation of a contract. If the words or other acts of one of the parties have but one reasonable meaning, his undisclosed intention is immaterial except when an unreasonable meaning which he attaches to his manifestations is known to the other party.

So a person cannot set up that he was merely jesting when his conduct and words would warrant a reasonable person in believing that he intended a real agreement.

Whether the writing signed by the defendants and now sought to be enforced by the complainants was the result of a serious offer by Lucy and a serious acceptance by the defendants, or was a serious offer by Lucy and an acceptance in secret jest by the defendants, in either event it constituted a binding contract of sale between the parties.

There was no fraud, no misrepresentation, no sharp practice and no dealing between unequal parties. The farm had been bought for $11,000 and was assessed for taxation at $6,300. The purchase price was $50,000. Zehmer admitted that it was a good price.

The complainants are entitled to have specific performance of the contract. . . . The decree appealed from is therefore reversed and the cause is remanded for the entry of a proper decree requiring the defendants to perform the contract.

Case Questions

1. Zehmer repeatedly stated in his testimony that he and Lucy had ''a good many drinks.''

How would this assertion, if believed, help Zehmer's defense to this action?

2. Select out the facts favorable to Lucy. Select out the facts favorable to Zehmer.

3. Did the court conclude that Zehmer intended to sell his farm? Explain.

4. What is the difference between mental assent and mutual assent?

Advertisements

Suppose Double C, Inc., the computer company in our opening scenario, advertised "486 IBM-compatible computer, with 100 megabytes and monitor $2,000." Is this an offer? If it is, then the store would be contractually bound to sell these computers to any customer who came in and was willing to pay the stated price.

At common law, it was early settled that an ordinary advertisement was not an offer. The reason for this common law rule is that an advertiser makes no commitment to have an unlimited supply of the advertised merchandise. Without such a commitment to contract with any and all offerees, there can be no offer. Additionally, most advertisements are too indefinite to be considered an offer and thus do not contain language that a reasonable person would interpret as a promise. Courts have thus interpreted most advertisements as merely invitations to make an offer; the customer is the offeror and the advertiser is the offeree who can accept or reject the customer's offer.[1] Similar analysis applies to circulars, catalogs, and price quotations. Without a specific commitment to sell, coupled with specific terms, there is no offer.

This does not mean that an advertisement is never an offer. Some advertisements or price quotations are specific enough to indicate a commitment on the part of the advertiser to enter a contract if the customer assents to the terms. Thus, one court held the advertisement in the next column to be an offer that was accepted by the store's customer.[2]

Additionally, an advertisement to give a reward is normally considered an offer. Here, the offer—for example, "$500 for the return of my black-and-white lost Doberman Pinscher," is sufficiently definite to invite an acceptance by a return of the dog.

SATURDAY 9:00 A.M. *SHARP*

3 Brand New

FurCoats

Worth $100.00

FIRST COME • FIRST SERVED

$1 EACH

Preliminary Negotiations

Many contracts are the product of a long series of tentative negotiations, none of which constitute offers. The distinguishing feature between an offer and a preliminary negotiation is the notion of commitment. Statements made by both sides are often "feelers" and not commitments to be bound. Thus, "I would consider $5,000" or "I would not sell for less than $19,000" are not offers but rather invitations to make offers.

A statement of future intention, such as "I am going to sell my house for $50,000," is not an offer for the same reason—there is no present commitment or promise by the speaker.

Auction Sales

There are two types of auction sales—those "with reserve" and those "without reserve." In the auction **with reserve,** the auctioneer is merely inviting

---

[1] See e.g., *O'Keefe v. Lee Calan Imports, Inc.*, 262 N.E.2d 758 (Ill. App. 1970).

[2] *Lefkowitz v. Great Minneapolis Surplus Store,* 86 N.W.2d 689 (Minn. 1957).

bids or offers. Thus, the auctioneer might announce, "How much am I bid for this?" or start the bidding at a specified price. Once the bidders make offers, the auctioneer, like any offeree, may accept or reject a bid. Acceptance takes place when the auctioneer's hammer falls, or when it is announced, "Sold to the man with the cigar," or words to that effect. The auctioneer, however, is not compelled to sell the merchandise and may reject all bids.

If the auction, however, is **without reserve,** the auctioneer must sell the item to the highest bidder. The auctioneer may not withdraw the item, unless, of course, there are no bids. The Uniform Commercial Code establishes the presumption that auctions are with reserve unless the items are explicitly announced to be without reserve [UCC § 2–328(3)].

Definiteness and Certainty of Terms

An offer must be made in terms that are certain enough for a court to determine (1) whether a breach has occurred if the offer is accepted and (2) a remedy in the case of a breach. For example, if Double C, Inc., offers Rhesa $10 per hour if Rhesa will "work for the company for a week" and Rhesa accepts, has Rhesa breached the contract by refusing to do cleaning work? Or if Harlan offers to sell "several" Ping-Pong balls to Rhesa for $3 and Rhesa accepts Harlan's offer, has Harlan breached the contract if Harlan refuses to convey more than three Ping-Pong balls? The terms *work* in the first case and *several* in the second are so indefinite that a court could not determine if the contract had been breached.

Sometimes a breach has clearly occurred but the offer is so indefinite that there is no basis on which to award a *remedy*. Thus, in one case, the defendant offered to pay plaintiff "$40 a week plus *a fair share of the profits on January 1.*"[3] Although the company

was profitable, the defendant never paid the plaintiff anything beyond the agreed-on $40 a week. Some amount was obviously owing, but determining that amount would be pure conjecture by the court. There was, according to the court, "no basis upon which to assess the liability of the defendant."

However, outputs and requirements agreements are deemed sufficiently definite and are valid. An **outputs contract** is one in which the buyer agrees to purchase all the seller's "output" at a certain price. In a **requirements contract** the seller agrees to supply all the "requirements" of the buyer at a certain price. *The Restatement (Second) of Contracts* and UCC section 2–306 explicity uphold both outputs and requirements contracts.

Open Terms

Where the parties intend to be bound to a contract but have left one or more of the terms open for future determination, courts often find that there is both a definite offer and a contract. This is clearly the case where the term left out is relatively minor. Thus, if Hardy agrees to renovate a building for Double C, Inc., specifying everything in the plans except the type of paint to be used, the contract would not fail for indefiniteness.

If an offer specifies the major terms but fails to mention price, and it is clear that the parties intended to be contractually bound, most courts will imply that a reasonable price was intended. A reasonable price is ordinarily the market price, but it could be valued in some other way. For example, assume that Double C., Inc., desires to sell its stock, which is not listed on a stock exchange. An alternative way of valuing stock would be the book value of the company or its net worth divided by the total number of the shares of stock. When the parties do not specify a price and do not intend to be bound by their agreement, the courts will not fill in the missing price. The following case involves that very issue with respect to a "renewal of a lease."

---

[3] See *Varney v. Ditmars,* 111 N.E. 822 (N.Y. 1916).

MARTIN v. SCHUMACHER
417 N.E. 2d 541 (N.Y. 1981)

The landlord-appellant, Martin, leased a retail store to the tenant-respondent, Schumacher, for five years, at a rent graduated upwards from $500 per month to $650 per month for the last year. A renewal clause stated that "Tenant may renew this lease for an additional period of five years at annual rentals to be agreed upon.'' At the end of the five-year term Schumacher gave notice of a desire to renew. Martin refused to renew unless Schumacher agreed to $900, an amount well above the appraised rental value.

Schumacher sued, seeking specific performance. The trial court dismissed the action. Schumacher appealed to the Appellate Division, which reversed. Martin appealed to the New York Court of Appeals.

FUCHSBERG, Judge

We begin our analysis with the basic observation that, unless otherwise mandated by law (e.g., residential emergency rent control statutes), a contract is a private ''ordering'' in which a party binds himself to do, or not to do, a particular thing. This liberty is no right at all if it is not accompanied by freedom not to contract. The corollary is that, before one may secure redress in our courts because another has failed to honor a promise, it must appear that the promisee assented to the obligation in question.

It also follows that, before the power of law can be invoked to enforce a promise, it must be sufficiently certain and specific so that what was promised can be ascertained. Otherwise, a court, in intervening, would be imposing its own conception of what the parties should or might have undertaken, rather than confirming itself to the implementation of a bargain to which they have mutually committed themselves. Thus, definiteness as to material matters is of the very essence in contract law. Impenetrable vagueness and uncertainty will not do.

Dictated by these principles, it is rightfully well settled in the common law of contracts in this State that a mere agreement to agree, in which a material term is left for future negotiations, is unenforceable. This is especially true of the amount to be paid for the sale or lease of real property.

This is not to say that the requirement for definiteness in the case before us now could only have been met by explicit expression of the rent to be paid. The concern is with substance, not form. It certainly would have sufficed, for instance, if a methodology for determining rent was to be found within the four corners of the lease, for a rent so arrived at would have been the end product of agreement between the parties themselves. Nor would the agreement have failed for indefiniteness because it invited recourse to an objective extrinsic event, condition or standard on which the amount was made to depend.

But the renewal clause here in fact contains no such ingredients. Its unrevealing, unamplified language speaks to no more than ''annual rentals to be agreed upon.'' Its simple words leave no room for legal construction or resolution of ambiguity. Neither tenant nor landlord is bound to any formula. There is not so much as a hint at a commitment to be bound by the ''fair market rental value'' or the ''reasonable rent'' the Appellate Division would impose, much less any definition of either. Nowhere is there an inkling that either of the parties directly or indirectly assented, upon accepting the clause, to subordinate the figure on which it ultimately would insist, to one fixed judicially, as the Appellate Division decreed be done, or, for that matter, by an arbitrator or other third party.

For all these reasons, the order of the Appellate Division should be reversed, . . . and the orders of the Supreme Court, reinstated.

JASEN, Judge, Dissenting

While I recognize that the traditional rule is that a provision of renewal of a lease must be ''certain'' in order to render it binding and enforceable, in my view the better rule would be that if the tenant can establish its entitlement to renewal under the lease, the mere presence of a provision calling for renewal at ''rentals to be agreed upon'' should not prevent judicial intervention to fix rent at a reasonable rate in order to avoid a forfeiture. Therefore, I would affirm the order of the Appellate Division.

Case Questions

1. What is the issue this case presents?
2. For what reason do you think the parties included the renewal provision? Explain.
3. Compare and contrast the dissent's position with the majority?
4. How could the renewal provision have been altered to ensure that there was an enforceable agreement?

Figure 12-2	Open Terms under the Uniform Commercial Code	
Open Term	**Code §**	**Gap Filler**
Price	2-305	Reasonable
Method of delivery	2-307	Single lot
Place of delivery	2-308	Seller's place
Time for delivery	2-309	Reasonable
Time for payment	2-310	Upon delivery
Assortment of goods	2-311	Buyer's choice

Figure 12-3	Terminating the Offer
By Party	**By Law**
Rejection.	Lapse of time.
Counteroffer.	Death.
Revocation.	Incapacity.
	Destruction of subject matter.
	Supervening illegality.

The Code and Gap Fillers

UCC section 2-204(3) provides guidelines for determining whether an offer involving the sale or purchase of goods is definite.

UCC § 2-204(3). Formation in General

Even though one or more terms are left open a contract for sale does not fail for indefiniteness if the parties have intended to make a contract and there is a reasonably certain basis for giving an appropriate remedy.

If a major term is left out of the agreement, the UCC provides statutory guidance to help "fill in the gaps" (see Figure 12-2).

If a term is not omitted but is instead vague or ambiguous, construction of the term is aided by certain interpretive techniques. These include usage of trade (custom in the industry) [UCC § 1-205(2)] and course of dealing (past dealings between the contracting parties) [UCC § 1-205(1)].

Communication of the Offer

Because mutual assent to the terms of the offer is necessary to form an agreement, the offer must be communicated to the offeree before a contract may be formed. At times, an offeree may perform the requested act without knowing the offer. For example, if Double C, Inc., posts a reward offer of $250 for the return of its stolen computer, and Linda returns the computer without knowing of the offer, has Linda assented to the terms of this offer? The majority of states would say that Linda is not entitled to the reward by contract, either because the offer was not communicated to Linda or because Linda did not assent to its terms. On occasion, a court under these circumstances has awarded recovery on noncontract principles such as fairness or public policy.

Often, contractual provisions are found on railroad tickets, parking garage receipts, baggage checks, catalogs, or even on the merchandise itself. Courts generally have held that unless such terms are called to the attention of the offeree, the offeree is bound only by what he or she actually knew or would reasonably expect to find in the document. Under this rule, an unexpected limitation of liability clause on a coat check stub would be unenforceable unless it was specifically called to the customer's attention.

TERMINATING THE OFFER

Offers may be terminated in a number of ways (see Figure 12-3). Whether an offer is terminated is very important since the terminated offer cannot be accepted. Offers are terminated by rejection, lapse of time, revocation, death, incapacity, destruction of the subject matter, and intervening illegality.

Rejection and Counteroffer

Where an offeree rejects an offer, the original offer is terminated. A **rejection** is a manifestation of an intention not to accept an offer. After a rejection, the offeree may not then accept the original offer. For example, if Sally offers to sell Alan her car "the offer to be held open for a week," and Alan rejects the offer the next day, Alan has no power to accept the offer later in the week. Alan's purported "acceptance" after the rejection actually constitutes a new offer by Alan, termed a **counteroffer.** A counteroffer is a counterproposal made by the offeree that varies the terms of the original offer. It results in a rejection of the original offer and a new offer that the original offeror may accept or reject.

It is important to distinguish counteroffers from counterinquiries. To illustrate the difference between a counteroffer and a counterinquiry, assume Sally offers her car to Alan for $3,000 and Alan responds, "I'll give you $1,000 now and the remainder in 60 days." This constitutes a counteroffer that terminates Sally's offer. But if Alan responded "Won't you accept less?" or "Will you accept $2,500?" Alan's reply would be a counterinquiry and Sally's offer would still continue.

Lapse of Time

When the offer explicitly states that it will lapse at a certain time, then the offer is terminated after that point. If no time is stated, the offer is terminated after a *reasonable* time. What is reasonable depends on the facts and circumstances of each case. Where the parties bargain face to face, the offer ordinarily is terminated at the end of the conversation.

Where the offer is made by mail or telegram, reasonableness depends heavily on the subject matter involved in the transaction. If the value of the subject matter fluctuates rapidly (as in the case of commodity futures, for example), the offer would terminate after a short time. If the value is relatively stable (for example, an automobile engine), the offer would be deemed open for a longer time.

Revocation

Since an offer is merely a promise, and the offeree has ordinarily given nothing in exchange for the promise, the law permits the offeror to revoke the offer at any time prior to acceptance. This is so even if the offeror promised to keep the offer open for a longer time. (But see firm offers under the UCC discussed in this chapter on page 239.) For example, an offer to sell a car that states "such offer to be held open for 10 days" could still be revoked at any time before acceptance.

Offers may be directly or indirectly revoked. **Direct revocation** simply means that the offeror communicates an intention to revoke directly to the offeree. If the offer is made to the public through an advertisement, for example, it may be revoked through the same medium used for the original offer.

Indirect revocation results when, for example, the offeree learns from a third party that the offeror has done something inconsistent with the terms of the offer. Thus, if Batman offered to sell Robin his batmobile and Robin later learned that Batman sold the car to the Penguin, the original offer would be indirectly revoked.

As discussed in Chapter 11, offers to enter bilateral contracts are accepted by the offeree's return promise. The offer may be revoked at any time before the return promise is made. Offers to enter a unilateral contract are accepted by the offeree's performance of the requested act. This presents a problem since generally, an offeror may revoke an offer any time before there has been complete performance. To illustrate, assume that Diane (the offeree) has begun to paint Polo's (the offeror's) house. May Polo revoke his offer of payment for the paint job before Diane completes the job? The modern rule regarding offers to enter unilateral contracts is that once the offeree's performance *has begun,* the offeror may *not* revoke the offer. Diane would thus be protected from Polo's revocation of the offer of payment. The policy behind the modern rule is clear: An offeree who reasonably relies on an offer and, in reliance, begins performance, should be protected from a subsequent revocation of the offer. Any other rule would be unfair.

Death or Incapacity of the Offeror or Offeree

Death or incapacitation of the offeror or offeree *before* the offeree's acceptance terminates the offer. Thus, if Panda offered to sell her dishware to Bear, and Panda became mentally incapacitated before Bear accepts, the offer would be terminated. However, death or incapacitation after the contract is formed does not nullify the contract. Thus, if Panda became mentally incapacitated *after* Bear's acceptance, Bear could enforce the contract of sale against Panda's estate.

Destruction of the Subject Matter and Intervening Illegality

Destruction of the subject matter of the offer before acceptance terminates the offer. Thus, if Double C, Inc., offers its last 1995 model laser printer to Carol Customer and the printer is destroyed by fire before

Customer's acceptance, the offer is considered terminated. Intervening illegality will also automatically terminate the offer. Thus, if before Customer's acceptance, the sale becomes illegal due to, for example, a court injunction because of patent infringement, the offer automatically terminates.

MAKING THE OFFER IRREVOCABLE

Under certain circumstances, a party may desire to make an offer irrevocable. There are three ways for an offer to be made irrevocable. First, an offer may be rendered irrevocable if the offeror accepts something in exchange for a promise to keep the offer open. This type of agreement is called an **option**. An option is simply a continuing offer that the offeree may accept or reject within the stated time. An option contract is illustrated by the following hypothetical: Randy offers "to sell Peggy my Mercedes for $30,000, the offer to remain open for 30 days if Peggy pays me $200." If Peggy pays the $200, Randy may not revoke his offer to sell the car since Randy entered into a separate contract to keep the offer open. Peggy's payment is not considered a deposit but is instead a separate payment made for the privilege of having 30 days to consider Randy's offer.

Second, an offer may also be considered irrevocable under the UCC's **firm offer rule.** According to UCC section 2–205, if an offer:

- Is made by a merchant
- For the sale of goods
- In a signed writing, which promises to be held open for less than three months

then such offer will be considered irrevocable even if the offeree gives nothing in exchange for the offeror's promise to keep the offer open. The purpose of the firm offer rule is to give legal effect to a merchant's deliberate manifestation of an intent to keep an offer open. Consumers, in particular, often rely on such assurances by merchants. This firm offer rule, therefore, gives consumers a measure of protection.

Only the merchant-offeror must sign the writing. A **merchant** is one who regularly deals in the goods or has a particular expertise in the goods (UCC § 2–104–1). The offeree need not sign it. However, if the offer is presented on the offeree's form, the offeror must separately sign the firm offer section of the contract.

Finally, where the offeree begins to perform in reliance on the offer, the offer may be deemed irrevocable. For example, assume that Darren offers Helena $10,000 if Helena leaves her home and moves to Darren's farm to care for Darren. Darren cannot revoke this offer once Helena leaves her home, moves to Darren's farm, and begins to care for Darren.

ACCEPTANCE

An **acceptance** of an offer is a manifestation of assent to the terms of the offer made by an offeree in a manner invited or required by the offer. The following four prerequisites are necessary to the formation of an acceptance:

- An acceptance must involve a manifestation of assent.
- An acceptance must be to the terms of the offer.
- An acceptance must be by a proper offeree.
- An acceptance must be communicated in the manner authorized by the offer.

Manifestation of Assent

Contractual assent is measured by outward manifestations—that is, objectively—and not by inward subjective intent. One who manifests assent to an offer, in a fashion that reasonably appears to the offeror to be assent, will be held to the contract despite unexpressed reservations or an intended joke.

The offeree must manifest an assent in a manner that is clear and unequivocal. The offeror is entitled to know whether the offeree accepts the offer. Thus, if Melinda offers to sell her coffee maker to Bradley for $5 and Bradley responds, "I'll think about it" or "Your offer will receive my prompt attention," or "I think I may want it," there has been no clear manifestation of assent and no contract.

The general rule of contract law is that a person who signs an agreement manifests an assent to its terms, even if he or she did not read or understand the agreement. Courts have applied this rule even to illiterate persons who cannot read. The rule flows from the objective theory of contracts. A signature is a manifestation of assent, despite any subjective ignorance on the offeree's part. Of course, there are limitations to the rule that one is bound by what one signs. Fraud, coercion, insanity, and youth may all be raised by the offeree in defense.

In a growing body of case law, courts have found no manifestation of assent to provisions in a form contract presented to the offeree on a ''take it or leave it'' basis. As the following excerpt reflects, courts no longer give absolute freedom to contract but will examine the fairness of the transaction under certain circumstances.

Law, Social Change, and the Legalization of Management Practice*

This classical law of contract [strongly reflecting the influence of laissez-faire] made a lot of sense so long as its assumptions about the nature of transactions remained accurate. If most contracts were face-to-face transactions between parties with equal bargaining power and equal knowledge, why should the state intervene in the name of fairness? As time wore on, however, the stereotypical model became less descriptive of a growing percentage of transactions. Improved means of transportation and communication led to market expansion and a consequent decline in face-to-face transactions. Many contracts were between strangers for goods that the buyer had never seen. As manufacturing grew, goods became increasingly complex, and the organizations that made them increasingly large, to the detriment of both the equal knowledge and the equal bargaining power assumptions.

■ ■ ■

Classical contract law . . . began to evolve in the face of the fact that its laissez-faire premises were losing a substantial measure of their descriptive power. Many contracts clearly were not agreements between equals, and an increasingly complex economic system produced a variety of long-term, interdependent relationships (supplier-customer, manufacturer-distributor, franchisor-franchisee) that did not fit the laissez-faire model of discrete, one-time market transactions.

The most compelling development, however, was probably the widespread use of the preprinted form contract. Employed by large enterprises to standardize their transactions, minimize the discretion afforded their agents, and exploit disproportionate bargaining power, such contracts were very difficult to reconcile with the classical vision of contracts as the product of bargaining between equals. When one party dictates most of the terms of the ''contract,'' many of which the other party may not even read (or, in the case of insurance contracts, not even have the opportunity to read), let alone understand, before signing, can the result fairly be said to be the product of the wills of both parties?

Courts in the early to middle decades of this century wrestled with such questions without expressly addressing the fundamental issue of the impact of superior bargaining power and expertise on the quality of consent. Instead, they developed rules that allowed them to avoid ''unfair'' outcomes in some cases on other, less controversial grounds. While classical contract law tended to say that persons who signed contracts were bound by all of their terms, whether or not they were read or understood, the modern contract rule is that contract signers are only bound by terms that they have ''reasonable notice'' of. So terms in fine print, or on the back of the contract, or terms ''hidden'' under misleading headings, and so forth, could be judicially read out of the agreement. Likewise, the traditional rule of contract interpre-

*Source: Reprinted from Michael B. Metzger, ''Law, Social Change, and the Legalization of Management Practice,'' *Business Horizons* (Sept./Oct. 1990). Copyright 1990 by the Foundation for the School of Business at Indiana University. Used with permission.

tation that ''ambiguities'' in a written agreement are interpreted against its drafter took on new force in the age of the form contract, when the drafter was often the party with superior bargaining power whose attempts to exercise that power could be frustrated by interpretation.

Thought Questions

1. How does retreat from laissez-faire premises affect the doctrine of *caveat emptor* (let the buyer beware)?

2. How might a change in economics in the future affect further changes in contract law?

3. Analyze: ''Today there is a de facto laissez-faire theory of contracts because those who lack the power are not in a position to enforce their rights and hence those who have the power will dictate the terms.''

Silence

A manifestation of assent to an offer may be inferred from certain conduct. Thus, a nod of the head and a handshake in response to an offer to purchase one's baseball card collection for $500 would suffice as an acceptance. Without such accompanying conduct, however, *silence alone* will not ordinarily amount to an acceptance of an offer. For example, if an unsolicited letter is sent to Bradley with the following statement, ''If we do not hear from you within 30 days we will sign you up in the Bell Auto Club,'' Bradley's failure to reply cannot be construed as an acceptance of Bell's offer. Generally, an offeror does not have the power to create an acceptance from the offeree's silence.

Silence plus something else may amount to an acceptance. Where the parties have previously agreed that the offeree's silence will be construed as an acceptance, the offeree's failure to object will be a manifestation of assent. Many record and book clubs require the consumer (offeree) to agree that the consumer's failure to reject an offering of records or books will be construed as an acceptance.

Similarly, where a previous course of conduct leads a reasonable person to conclude that the offeree's silence is a manifestation of assent, a contract may result from the offeree's inaction. Consider this example: Double C, Inc. ships 50 boxes of computer paper to Fortune 500 Company on the first of every month for 10 months; on the 15th of the month 500 Company's bookkeeper mails payment to the wholesaler. This pattern has been the same for 10

months. Unless the company objects to another shipment, its silence results in a contract for sale of the 11th shipment.

Acceptance of the Terms of the Offer

To have an acceptance, the offeree must assent to the terms of the offer. This principle rests on the concept that the offeror is the master of the offer and is entitled to have the offer complied with according to its terms.

Where the offer requests acceptance by performance and not by a return promise, the common law rule is that assent can only be by performance. If Monroe posts an offer of a reward to anyone who furnishes information leading to the arrest and conviction of a certain kidnapper, Marie could not accept by *promising* to give such information. Only the act of furnishing the information would be assent to the offer's terms.

Similarly, if Monroe offers to pay Marie $200 ''if Marie will write to Monroe and promise to clear Monroe's land,'' Marie cannot accept by beginning to clear the land. The offer called for a return promise and cannot be accepted by beginning performance.

In cases involving a sale of goods, however, the UCC permits the offeree to choose acceptance by a return promise or prompt shipment [UCC § 2–206(b)]. Thus, if Monroe offers to purchase computer software from Double C, Inc., for $2,500, Double C., Inc. may accept either by promising to ship the software or by promptly shipping the software.

Acceptances Varying the Terms of the Offer

At common law, courts often stated that an acceptance had to be the *mirror image* of the offer. Any deviation, qualification, or addition between the offer and the purported acceptance caused the "acceptance" to operate as a counteroffer and a rejection.

Courts have held that certain assumptions are implied in the offer. Thus, assume Monroe offers to sell his house and land to Marie for $25,000. Marie responds, "I accept, provided you supply me with good title." This would be construed as an acceptance and not a counteroffer, since good title is reasonably implied within the offer.

The most radical departure from the common law mirror image rule is found in UCC section 2–207 (see Chapter 19). This section (like all others in UCC Article 2) only applies to the sale of goods.

UCC § 2–207. Additional Terms in Acceptance or Confirmation

(1) A definite and seasonable expression of acceptance or a written confirmation which is sent within a reasonable time operates as an acceptance even though it states terms additional to or different from those offered or agreed upon, unless acceptance is expressly made conditional on assent to the additional or different terms.

(2) The additional terms are to be construed as proposals for addition to the contract. Between merchants such terms become part of the contract unless:

(a) the offer expressly limits acceptance to the terms of the offer;

(b) they materially alter it; or

(c) notification of objection to them has already been given or is given within a reasonable time after notice of them is received.

(3) Conduct by both parties which recognizes the existence of a contract is sufficient to establish a contract for sale although the writings of the parties do not otherwise establish a contract. In such a case the terms of the particular contract consist of those terms on which the writings of the parties agree, together with any supplementary terms incorporated under any other provisions of this Act.

Analyzing UCC Section 2–207

The policy behind UCC Section 2–207 is to enhance commerce in a day in which much business is conducted by form contracts sent through the mails. Often, neither the buyer nor the seller pays attention to the non-negotiated form language that has been prepared by an attorney (or purchased from a stationery store). Thus, the parties are often unaware that the buyer's and seller's forms differ from one another in certain respects. A mechanical application of the mirror image rule defeats the parties' true intention—that is, to buy and sell goods despite form language differences. UCC Section 2–207 is thus designed to effectuate the parties' intention to complete a sale even when their forms differ.

Of course, if the offeree's response differs with respect to the price or the subject matter—"Send me shoes instead of radios"—such a radical deviation would be a counteroffer. In addition, UCC § 2–207 subsection 1 permits the offeree to demand that the deviating "acceptance" be expressly assented to by the offeror. If not assented to, there is no acceptance, and hence no contract.

In analyzing UCC section 2–207, we note several basic features:

1. *Subsection 1.* Subsection 1 eliminates the common law mirror image rule. Under UCC section 2–207(1) *a contract* exists even though the expression of acceptance states terms *additional to* or *different from* those in the offer. The mirror image rule, by way of contrast, holds the offeree's deviating response to be a rejection and a counteroffer.

2. *Subsection 2.* Since UCC section 2–207(1) states that a contract generally exists even if the acceptance deviates from the offer, what are *the terms* of the contract? Specifically, are the additional or different terms supplied by the offeree part of the contract? "Different" terms that contradict the offer apparently never become part of the contract unless accepted by the offeror. "Additional" terms (those added to the offer by the offeree) may become part of the contract depending on the status of the contracting parties.

a.   If a nonmerchant is one of the contracting parties, the offeree's additional terms are *not* part of the contract. Instead, these deviations are treated as proposals for future negotiations.

b.   On the other hand, if both contracting parties *are merchants,* then the additional terms *are* part of the contract unless the additional terms materially alter the contract, the offer expressly limits acceptance to its terms, or the offeror has already objected to the additional terms.

Figure 12–4   A UCC Section 2–207 Example

May 10: Form 1	May 15: Form 2	May 20: Goods Shipped	May 25: Defect Discovered
Buyer orders 200 widgets from seller Corporation at $10 a widget. No clause concerning arbitration is on the buyer's form.	Seller accepts buyer's order using seller's "acknowledgment form." On back of seller's form is a clause stating "all disputes must be submitted to binding arbitration."	Buyer accepts 200 widgets from seller at $10 a widget.	The widgets are found to be defective.

Issue: Must this dispute be submitted to binding arbitration?

Uniform Commercial Code Analysis

1. Seller's acknowledgment form was an acceptance despite seller's *addition* of an arbitration clause. A contract was formed on May 15.

2. Whether "binding arbitration" is part of the contract depends on the status of the parties:

   a. If either buyer or seller is a *nonmerchant,* the binding arbitration clause is not part of the contract. Buyer's form controls since seller's additional term was a "proposal for future negotiation."

   b. If both buyer and seller are *merchants,* then seller's arbitration provision would be part of the contract unless it was a material alteration. (Note: Courts have split concerning whether an arbitration clause is a material alteration. The trend is to find an arbitration clause *not* to be a material alteration. If such a trend is followed, the dispute would thus have to be submitted to binding arbitration.)

3. *Subsection 3.* If the seller expressly limits acceptance to his or her terms and no others, and the buyer expressly limits the offer to the buyer's terms and no others, a "battle of the forms" results. Although the two forms read together explicitly conflict, a contract is formed in this case under subsection 3, and the terms of the contract are the terms that are found in both buyer's and seller's forms plus provisions supplied by the Uniform Commercial Code—for example, the gap-filler provisions that were discussed earlier in this chapter (see Figure 12–4 for an example of the application of UCC § 2–207).

Acceptance by the Proper Offeree

The general rule is that an offer may only be accepted by the one to whom it is made. Thus, if Phillip makes an offer to Double C, Inc., Abacus Computers may not accept it. Nor can Double C, Inc., sell (assign) the offer to Abacus. (Note: As is discussed in Chapter 17, *contract* rights may be assigned; offers may not.) Offers made to corporations may be accepted by succeeding managers of the corporation, unless the promisor indicates that its offer is limited to the corporation's current management.

Communicating the Acceptance

Since the offeror is the master of the offer, the offeror may control the manner of its acceptance. If the offeror *explicitly limits* the manner of acceptance to one prescribed place, time, or manner, then the offeree must conform to those terms. Thus, if Leonard offers to sell his house to Gersten and says, "You must accept this by waving a green flag outside your window no later than 12:00 A.M., March 1," then Gersten is limited to accepting in this manner. Any other method of acceptance would be ineffective.

As a general rule, if an offer merely mentions a method of acceptance but does not specifically exclude all other methods, the offeree may accept by that method or another reasonable alternative. Thus, if Leonard's offer reads, "Accept this by return mail," Gersten may accept by another means that would reach Leonard within the same time as the mails.

Time When Acceptance Is Effective

Contract law has accorded acceptances a privilege not enjoyed by offers, rejections, or revocations. An acceptance of an offer to enter a bilateral contract is effective as soon as it is put out of the possession of the offeree, so long as the offeree uses the authorized means of acceptance. In contrast, offers, rejections, and revocations are effective only when actually received by the other party.

This out-of-possession privilege, sometimes called the **mailbox rule,** only arises if the offeree communicates the acceptance in an authorized manner. At common law, the authorized manner of acceptance was either the manner expressed in the offer, as in "*mail* me your acceptance," or if no manner was expressed, then the manner utilized by the offeror was implied as the authorized manner of acceptance. If the offer came by telegram, for instance, the implied authorized manner of acceptance was by telegram. If the offeree failed to use the authorized means of acceptance, either expressed or implied, the offeree forfeited the privilege of the out-of-possession rule. The time of the offeree's acceptance would then take place not upon dispatch, but upon receipt by the offeror.

The modern rule expands the out-of-possession privilege given to the offeree. In addition to the authorized means listed above, the modern rule authorizes the offeree to use *any reasonable medium* to communicate an acceptance. Thus, if the offer was mailed and did not express a preferred means of acceptance, the modern rule authorizes for acceptance the use of the mails and any other reasonable medium (for example, a telegram). What is reasonable depends on the speed and reliability of the means, custom in the industry, and prior dealings between the parties. In the following case, the out-of-possession rule was crucial to the plaintiff's case.

MORRISON v. THOELKE
155 So.2d 889 (Fla. Ct. App. 1963)

The Thoelkes, the appellees, own property. On November 26, the Morrisons, the appellants, executed a contract for the purchase of that property and mailed the contract to the Thoelkes. On November 27, the Thoelkes signed the contract and placed it in the mails addressed to the Morrisons' attorney. After mailing the contract but before its receipt, the Thoelkes called the Morrisons' attorney and canceled the contract. Nonetheless, the Morrisons recorded the contract.

Suit was filed. The lower court entered summary judgment for the Thoelkes. The basis of this decision was that the contract was canceled by the Thoelkes prior to its receipt by the Morrisons, and hence there was no legal contract binding on the parties. The case was appealed to the Florida Court of Appeals.

ALLEN, Judge

The question is whether a contract is complete and binding when a letter of acceptance is received, thus permitting repudiation prior to receipt. Appellants, of course, argue that posting the acceptance creates the contract; appellees contend that only receipt of the acceptance bars repudiation. The rule that a contract is complete upon deposit of the acceptance in the mails, hereinbefore referred to as "deposited acceptance rule". . . had its origin, insofar as the common law is concerned, in *Adams v. Lindsell*. In that case, the defendants had sent an offer to plaintiffs on September 2nd, indicating that they ex-

pected an answer "in course of post." The offer was misdirected and was not received and accepted until the 5th, the acceptance being mailed that day and received by defendant-offerors on the 9th. However, the defendants, who had expected to receive the acceptance on or before the 7th, sold the goods offered on the 8th of September. It was conceded that the delay had been occasioned by the fault of the defendants in initially misdirecting the offer.

The justification for the "deposited acceptance" rule proceeds from the uncontested premise of *Adams v. Lindsell* that there must be, both in practical and conceptual terms, a point in time when a contract is complete. In the formation of contracts (in one another's presence) this point is readily reached upon expressions of assent instantaneously communicated. In the formation of contracts (in the absence of one another) by post, however, delay in communication prevents concurrent knowledge of assents and some point must be chosen as legally significant.

Briefly, critics argue that the evident concern with risk occasioned by delay is premised on a time lag between mailing and delivery of a letter of acceptance, which lag, in modern postal systems is negligible. Opponents of the rule urge that if time is significant to either party, modern means of communication permit either party to avoid such delay as the post might cause. At the same time critics of the rule cannot deny that even in our time delay or misdirection of a letter of acceptance is not beyond the realm of possibility.

Opponents of the rule argue as forcefully that all of the disadvantages of delay or loss in communication which would potentially harm the offeree are equally harmful to the offeror. Why, they ask, should the offeror be bound by an acceptance of which he has no knowledge? Arguing specific cases, opponents of the rule point to the inequity of forbidding the offeror to withdraw his offer after the acceptance was posted but before he had any knowledge that the offer was accepted; they argue that to forbid the offeree to withdraw his acceptance, as in the instant case, scant hours after it was posted but days before the offeror knew of it, is unjust and indefensible. Too, the opponents argue, the offeree can always prevent the revocation of an offer . . . by buying an option.

In short, both advocates and critics muster persuasive argument. . . . [T]here must be a choice made, and such choice may, by the nature of things, seem unjust in some cases. Weighing the arguments with reference not to specific cases but toward a rule of general application and recognizing the general and traditional acceptance of the rule as well as the modern changes in effective long-distance communication, it would seem that the balance tips, whether heavily or near imperceptively, to continued adherence to the "Rule in *Adams v. Lindsell*." This rule, although not entirely compatible with ordered, consistent and sometime artificial principles of contract advanced by some theorists, is, in our view, in accord with the practical considerations and essential concepts of contract law. Outmoded precedents may, on occasion, be discarded and the function of justice should not be the perpetuation of error, but, by the same token, traditional rules and concepts should not be abandoned save on compelling ground.

In the instant case, an unqualified offer was accepted and the acceptance made manifest. Later, the offerees sought to repudiate their initial assent. Had there been a delay in their determination to repudiate permitting the letter to be delivered to appellant, no question as to the invalidity of the repudiation would have been entertained. As it were, the repudiation antedated receipt of the letter. However, adopting the view that the acceptance was effective when the letter of acceptance was deposited in the mails, the repudiation was equally invalid and cannot alone, support the summary [judgment] for appellees. [Reversed and remanded.]

Case Questions

1. Identify the issue.
2. Analyze the reason given by the court for the out-of-possession rule.
3. What arguments against the out-of-possession rule are raised by its opponents? Are these arguments sound? Analyze.

END–OF–CHAPTER QUESTIONS

1. Apply the objective and subjective theories of contract law to the following situations:
   a. An offer made in jest.
   b. A mistake in the transmission of the offer.
   c. A signature of acceptance on an unread form contract.

2. Analyze: "The differences between the law under the common law and under the UCC should be eliminated." How might this be accomplished?

3. Wilmington Mills Co. has made Davis Stores an offer to purchase 3,000 yards of #3 pile carpet at $7.50 a square yard. Davis is concerned that the offer might be revoked but needs time to obtain financing. How may this offer be made irrevocable?

4. While enroute from Rome to New York, defendant Alitalia's plane crashed, killing 13 passengers. A wrongful death action was brought on behalf of the passengers. Alitalia defended, claiming that its liability was limited due to a message on the passengers' tickets that read: "Each passenger should carefully examine this ticket, particularly the conditions on page 4." Page 4 stated in small print that the airline was limited in its liability to the payment of 125,000 francs for each passenger. Are the estates contractually bound to accept this amount? Explain. See *Lisi v. Alitalia-Linee Aeree Italiane,* 370 F.2d 508 (2d Cir 1966).

5. Defendant-employee Mettille was hired by the plaintiff, Pine River Bank, at a salary of $12,000 a year. The employment agreement was entirely oral. Nothing was said about the length of the employment term. Because of serious errors in job performance, Mettille was terminated after a year and a half. Mettille counterclaimed in a suit brought by Pine River (on an unrelated matter) claiming that the bank dismissed him in violation of certain provisions contained in an employee handbook that the employer had given to all its employees. Are provisions in an employee handbook an offer? If so, how are they accepted by an employee? See *Pine River Bank v. Mettille,* 333 N.W.2d 622 (Minn. 1983).

6. The plaintiff, Coastal Industries, Inc., brought suit against the defendant, Automatic Steam Products Corp. (Automatic), alleging that four commercial pressing machines that it bought were unworkable. Coastal sought damages in Federal District Court for breach of express and implied warranties. Automatic applied for a stay of the proceedings, alleging that the dispute was to be settled by arbitration according to the parties' contract. Coastal had ordered the machines by phone. The machines were delivered some time later with an invoice that contained a provision stating: "All controversies are committed to arbitration according to the rules of the American Arbitration Association." Is this arbitration clause part of the sales contract? Analyze. See *Coastal Industries, Inc. v. Automatic Steam Products Corp.,* 654 F.2d 375 (5th Cir. 1981).

7. The defendant, Evans, offered the plaintiff, Livingstone, a tract of land for $1,800. Livingstone wired back stating: "Send lowest cash price. Will give $1,600 cash." Evans replied to this by telegram as follows: "Cannot reduce price." Immediately upon receipt of this telegram, Livingstone "accepted" Evans's original offer. Is there a contract for the sale of the land? Which of these is the correct label for each telegram?: offer, acceptance, counteroffer, counterinquiry, rejection, or renewal of offer? See *Livingstone v. Evans,* 4 D.L.R. 769 (Alberta 1925).

8. Sullivan, the plaintiff, was a patient of O'Connor, the defendant, a plastic surgeon. Sullivan alleged that she entered into a contract with O'Connor wherein he promised to perform plastic surgery on her nose, enhance her beauty, and improve her appearance. In fact, she alleged the surgery disfigured and deformed her nose. Suit was brought alleging a breach of contract. What is the result? Analyze. See *Sullivan v. O'Connor,* 296 N.E.2d 183 (Mass. 1973).

9. The plaintiff, Hobbs, sent eel skins to the defendant, Massasoit Whip Co. (Massasoit), on four or five occasions. Each time they had been accepted by Massasoit and payment made. Thereafter, a number of skins were sent to Massasoit but not paid for, and after several months, the skins were destroyed. Hobbs brought an action for the price of the skins. Massasoit alleged that "silence is not an acceptance." Was there a contract for these eel skins? Explain. See *Hobbs v. Massasoit Whip Co.,* 33 N.E. 495 (Mass. 1890).

10. E. A. Coronis Assoc., the plaintiff, sent the following bid to M. Gordon Construction Co., the defendant, on a construction project:

We are pleased to offer:

All structural steel including steel girts and purlins. Both Buildings delivered and erected $155,413.50

All structural steel equipped with clips for wood girts & purlins. Both Buildings delivered and erected. 98,937.50

Note: This price is predicated on an erected price of .1175 per Lb. of steel and we would expect to adjust the price on this basis to conform to actual tonnage of steel used in the project.

Thank you very much for this opportunity to quote.

Very truly yours,
E.A. Coronis Associates
/s/ Arthur C. Pease

Is this a firm offer under the Uniform Commercial Code? Why or why not? See *E.A. Coronis Assoc. v. M. Gordon Const'n Co.*, 216 A.2d 246 (N.J. Super. 1966).

Chapter 13

Capacity and Genuine Assent

■

CRITICAL THINKING INQUIRIES

As you read this chapter, you should be able to address the following:

- Why are minors treated specially under the law of contracts?
- Compare and contrast a minor's contract for necessaries and one for nonnecessaries.
- Compare and contrast minority and incompetency.
- Analyze the elements of fraud.
- Compare and contrast duress and undue influence.
- Compare and contrast unilateral mistake and mutual mistake.

MANAGERIAL PERSPECTIVE

Decade Today Realtors is a large real estate brokerage firm that does business across the United States. One problem it has been experiencing of recent is an increase in litigation involvement. The percent of brokered transactions that wind up in court has increased threefold over the last 10 years. When this occurs, often Decade's broker fee is jeopardized and its personnel wind up spending time in court and sometimes have to hire their own attorneys. A study has shown that some of the litigation involves the capacity of minors and incompetents, but a greater number of suits involve fraud and mistake.

Decade Today, through its executives, is wondering what they can do about the problem. They have formulated some of the common questions that confront their personnel and are thinking of conducting some seminars on these critical issues.

- What are the consequences of contracting with a minor?
- What are the tests of competency to contract?
- What are the elements of fraud?
- How does duress and undue influence differ from fraud?
- What type of mistake will invalidate a contract?

Figure 13–1   Lack of Capacity and Assent

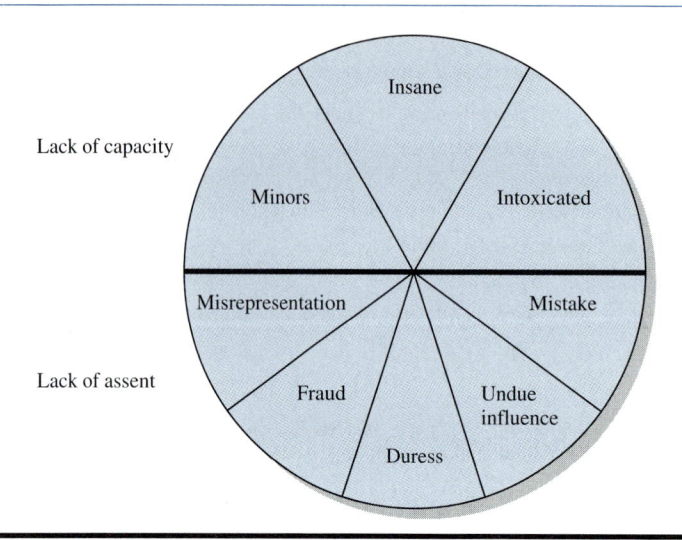

Those attending Decade Today Realtor's seminars will learn that a fundamental principle of contract law is that both parties must manifest assent to the transaction by words or conduct. This principle was examined in Chapter 12. Contract law, moreover, favors the finality of transactions. Contractual transactions should not be avoided when assent has been manifested. Nevertheless, at times, exceptions must be made to this presumption of finality.

For example, some incapacity, such as a mental disability or minority, may limit a person's ability to genuinely assent. Problems of assent other than a lack of capacity may also arise. For example, a mature person of sound mind may be induced to assent to the transaction by the other party's misrepresentations, wrongful threats, unfair persuasion, or mistake.

LEGAL CAPACITY

Historically, a number of classes of persons were either partially or totally incapacitated to assent to a transaction. These classes included minors, insane persons, intoxicated persons, married women, corporations, and Indians. Statutes in all states have given married women, corporations, and Indians capacity to contract. However, minors, the mentally incompetent, and, under limited circumstances, the intoxicated still suffer from contractual incapacity (see Figures 13–1 and 13–2).

Contracts with Minors

Minors or **infants** are those persons under a certain age—usually under 18, although there is some variation among the states. Minors are treated differently by the law than adults when it comes to capacity to contract. The reason most often given for this difference is the minor's need for protection from the consequences of immaturity.

Legal Effect of Minor's Contracts
A minor has only limited capacity to contract, and thus enters into voidable contracts. This means that a person may enter a valid contract with a minor, but the minor may later avoid contractual obligations by disaffirming the contract.

Disaffirmance occurs when a minor simply indicates an intention not to be bound to the contract and communicates that intention to the other party. Unlike many foreign jurisdictions, a minor in the United States may set aside a contract on the sole ground of minority.[1] A minor does not have to show that the contract was unfair, unwise, or improvident. In fact, a minor may disaffirm a contract entered during minority even after reaching the age of majority as long as it is done within a rea-

---

[1] In France, for example, in addition to showing minority, *lesion* (an injury or detriment) must be proven.

Figure 13–2   Incapacity

Incapacity	Contract Status	Exception	Condition for Disaffirmance/Voidance
Minority	Voidable	Misrepresentation of age	Return what consideration remains
Adjudicated Mentally Incompetent	Void	Ratified by guardian	Return what consideration remains
Actually Mentally Incompetent	Voidable	None	Return what remains and account for depreciation
Intoxicated Persons	Voidable	Valid if other party knows of intoxication	Return what remains and account for depreciation

sonable time thereafter.[2] No formal requirements need be met to disaffirm.[3]

Because an adult assumes a significant risk when contracting with a minor, it is advisable to require the minor to obtain a creditworthy adult **co-obligor** on any important obligation. The co-obligor is one who is obligated, along with the minor, to pay the debt. Even if the minor disaffirms, the adult co-obligor would still be liable on the entire debt.

Generally, a minor who disaffirms a contract is entitled to a full refund of any monies paid for the goods or services. The minor must, however, return

---

[2]A few contracts such as educational loans, military enlistments, bail bond, and child support obligations may not be disaffirmed under state or federal statutes. Some statutes also forbid the disaffirmance of certain banking and insurance transactions.

[3]Formal rules do apply to disaffirming contracts for the purchase and sale of land.

to the adult whatever is left of the goods. Most states do not require the minor to pay for depreciation or for the benefits derived from the contract. This is true even if the property is damaged or destroyed through the minor's negligence. To illustrate the majority rule, assume that Al, a minor, purchased an automobile for $5,000 and made a $2,000 down payment. Al disaffirmed the contract after driving negligently and damaging the car. Al would not be liable on the contract and he would also receive a full refund of his $2,000 payment without any subtraction for damages. In addition, Al would not have to pay for the benefits he received from using the car. The car dealer would be entitled to have the damaged car returned. Willful damage would, however, in most states, require the minor to pay for depreciation of the car.

The following case discusses the rule that a *minority* of states follow concerning a minor's liability on a contract that has been disaffirmed.

VALENCIA v. WHITE
647 P.2d 287 (Ariz. Ct. App. 1982)

White, the appellee, was a sophomore in high school (age 17 years) when his father established him in the trucking business. White hired drivers, secured jobs hauling produce, and managed the business. He was single and lived at home with his parents. He was furnished food, clothing, and housing by his parents during his minority.

Valencia, the appellant, owned a garage for the repair of motor vehicles, including large trucks and trailers. He serviced and repaired the appellee's equipment until disagreements occurred over replacement of an engine for White's truck. White disaffirmed the contract and refused to pay Valencia.

The trial court found that White's acts caused the damage to the engine. Nonetheless, citing principles of minor's rights to disaffirm contracts, it held in favor of White. Valencia appealed.

BIRDSALL, Judge

The appellant's . . . contention concerns the trial court's attempt to restore the parties to a "status quo" after disaffirmance. He argues that requiring him to return monies paid on the account and refusing to allow him any remuneration for the services performed was error. . . .

The trial court correctly recognized that the New Hampshire case of *Porter v. Wilson* . . . adopts a minority view that a minor who disaffirms a contract may be held liable for benefits received. . . .

The Court of Appeals of Ohio has observed that:

At a time when we see young persons between 18 and 21 years of age demanding and assuming more responsibilities in their daily lives; when we see such persons emancipated,[4] married, and raising families; when we see such persons charged with the responsibility for committing crimes; when we see such persons being sued in tort claims for acts of negligence; when we see such persons subject to military service; when we see such persons engaged in business and acting in almost all other respects as an adult, it seems timely to re-examine the case law pertaining to contractual rights and responsibilities of infants to see if the law as pronounced and applied by the courts should be redefined.

. . . Under the trial court's judgment in the instant case the appellant is not only precluded from recovering for parts and labor furnished the appellee in his going, successful business, [but] he is required to repay monies paid to him on account of those services. In return he is only permitted to retain a disassembled engine that was damaged by the appellee's acts.

No evidence suggests that the appellant took advantage of the appellee because of his age, lack of experience or judgment. Likewise no evidence suggests that the contract was disadvantageous to the appellee. . . .

In order to properly apply the rule in this case the trial court should have determined what benefits, if any, the minor actually received from the entire transaction. The only evidence presented in this regard is that the reasonable value of the parts and labor, including the Cummins engine, was $19,998.76. The parts and labor furnished the minor by the appellant were of benefit to him in that amount. The repair of the minor's business vehicles enabled him to successfully operate his trucking business. In addition to showing the profits from that business the evidence shows he purchased a pickup truck and a dragster from those profits. Obviously the parts and labor cannot be returned in kind to the appellant. Likewise the Cummins engine, having been damaged by acts attributable to the minor, cannot be returned in anywhere near the same condition as when it was acquired from the appellant.

We find that to restore both parties to a status quo, the disassembled engine and the other parts in the possession of the appellant should be returned to the appellee; that the appellee received benefits having a value to him of $19,998.76; that the $7,100 paid by the appellee should be credited against the value of the benefits, leaving a balance of $12,898.71 which the appellee must pay to the appellant.

We reverse and remand with directions to enter judgment in favor of the appellants and against the appellee, in that amount and to order the return of the engine and other parts to the appellee.

Case Questions

1. What is the issue in this case?
2. Do you think the court viewed this contract differently because it was entered for a business purpose? Explain. Why might the purpose of the contract matter?
3. Select out language that disparages the majority rule.
4. Which rule appears to render the more just result — the majority rule discussed previously in the text or the benefits rule employed in *Valencia*? Can you think of a third alternative?

---

[4]An emancipated minor is one who has been set free by his or her parents. These minors may contract as adults.

Contracts for Necessaries

A minor may disaffirm a contract for necessaries but must pay the reasonable value of the necessaries. What is necessary depends on the social position of the minor and his or her needs at the time. While food, clothing, shelter, and medical attention are usually considered necessary, the quality of these necessaries varies according to the social position of the minor. Simply stated, the law has historically found more expensive things necessary for the wealthy but not for the poor. As society places a higher priority on equality as a value, however, social position should carry less weight in determining whether something is a necessary.

Although a minor may still disaffirm a contract for necessaries, the minor will typically be liable for the *reasonable value* of the necessary. Thus, an action against the minor for the necessary good or service would be in quasi-contract rather than in contract (see Chapter 11 for this distinction). To illustrate, a minor disaffirms a contract for medical services costing $500 that are considered to be necessaries. Although the physician could not recover the contract price of the services, he or she could recover in quasi-contract for their reasonable value. Oftentimes, the contract price and the reasonable value are the same. Under quasi-contract, sums exceeding the contract price are not recoverable.

Misrepresentation of Age

Most states permit the minor to disaffirm the contract even in the case of a willful misrepresentation of age. Here, however, the minor must restore the adult party to the status quo. The status quo is the position the adult party would have been in if the contract had never been entered. To illustrate, suppose a minor enters a contract with a car dealer for the purchase of a car and willfully misrepresents her age. The cost to the dealer was $7,000 and the retail price to the minor was $9,000. The minor may disaffirm the contract but would be liable for the difference between the dealer's cost ($7,000) and the value of the car on the date of its return.

Other states permit the adult to sue the minor in a separate tort action for fraud after the minor disaffirms the contract. Finally, courts in a few states have found that the minor is legally prohibited from disaffirming the contract in the case of a willful misrepresentation.

Ratification of the Contract

A minor may ratify a contract upon reaching the age of majority. **Ratification** has the effect of accounting the contract as irrevocably valid. Ratification may not occur until the minor reaches the age of majority, since before that time, the ratification may itself be disaffirmed. Ratification of a contract entered during minority may occur in any one of three ways:

1. The former minor may *expressly ratify* the contract by clearly stating to the other party an intention to be bound by the contract.

2. The former minor may *implicitly ratify* the contract by selling the goods received, or completing payment or performance on the contract. Simply making a part payment after reaching the age of majority is, however, not a ratification.

3. The former minor may ratify by waiting *more than a reasonable time* after reaching the age of majority without disaffirming the contract. What is a reasonable time depends on the totality of the circumstances, including the nature of the subject matter and the extent to which the other party will be prejudiced by such a disaffirmance.

Contracts with the Mentally Incompetent

Contracts with the **mentally incompetent** such as the insane, senile, retarded, or temporarily delirious (from an accident, for example), follow similar rules as contracts involving minors. The transaction with the mentally infirm fall into one of two categories. A contract with a mentally incompetent who had a guardian[5] appointed prior to entering the transaction is void. This person has been **adjudicated insane.** The adjudication is treated as giving public notice of the person's incompetence to contract and the fact that control over that person's property has been wholly vested in a guardian.

If no guardian has been appointed over the incompetent, the transaction may be disaffirmed in the same manner as contracts involving minors if the contract is executory (unperformed). However, if the contract is executed — that is, fully performed — the incompetent person may only disaffirm the contract after restoring

---

[5]Guardianships over the property of an incompetent person are usually set up to maintain and preserve a person's estate.

the value taken from the competent party. This latter rule is designed to protect parties who do not know they are dealing with incompetent persons.

Like the minor, those actually mentally incompetent are liable in a quasi-contract action for the reasonable value of necessaries. Finally, like the minor, the incompetent may either ratify or disaffirm contracts upon regaining sanity or mental competence.

Courts vary widely in their definition of **incompetency.** Many states use the traditional cognitive test of mental competency. Under this test the issue

is whether the person is capable of *understanding* the nature and consequences of the transaction.

Some states employ a motivational test of incompetency. Perhaps the person understood the transaction but was operating under an *insane delusion* so that his or her actions could not be controlled. Other states consider the *fairness* of upholding the transaction. In short, the whole subject of mental incompetency is riddled with varying standards and contradictory applications, leading the authors of the following reading to propose a radical solution.

*From Contract to Status via Psychiatry**

Various and often inconsistent justifications are advanced for according special treatment to the contracts of incompetents. One of these is that, to be valid, contracts require "mutual assent"; hence, contracts that lack such assent should be void. Another is that since the aim of voiding the contracts of incompetents is to protect them from exploitation at the hands of the unscrupulous, contracts should be avoidable only by the weaker party. . . .

Still another reason for voiding the contracts of an adjudicated incompetent is to protect the freedom of the guardian in the proper management of the assets of [the] ward. However, that requires the improbable assumption that all contracts made by an incompetent will be disadvantageous. . . .

It is important to keep in mind, moreover, that, in practice, the party wishing to avoid a contract is usually not the alleged incompetent but a relative anxious to prevent what it considers a waste of assets. In a widely-quoted article on the public policies underlying the law of mental incompetency, Dr. Green recognizes this state of affairs, and asks, appropriately, "protection of whom?" His answers are: (1) Protection for society from the incompetent— the traditional justification for civil commitment; (2) Protection for the incompetent from society—the traditional justification for paternalistic legislation of all types; and (3) Protection for the family or dependents of the incompetent from . . . acts injurious to their welfare. A fourth category is conspicuous by its absence: Protection for the incompetent from members of [the ward's] family who, for reasons of their own, desire to curtail [the ward's] autonomy—or to remove [the ward] from society altogether. We must remember, in this connection, that a person declared incompetent is often deprived of rights to manage . . . property, and may in addition be civilly committed to a mental hospital for an indefinite period. . . . A basic policy decision must here be confronted. Will the interests of the incompetent and of society be better served by allowing some "undesirable" contracts to survive and be enforced, or is the sounder policy to continue to make void or voidable the contracts of the allegedly insane? Clearly, some interests of the incompetent are served if . . . allowed to avoid a contract, not unfair when made, but inconvenient when sought to be performed. However, in this area, no less than in torts, the other consequences of assuming the role of incompetent mental patient clearly tip the scales against this strategy for the "patient." Non-contracting parties, whether they be physicians or creditors should, of course, be denied the gambit of improving their lot by casting one of the contractors as insane.

---

*Source: G. Alexander & T. Szasz, "From Contract to Status via Psychiatry," 13 *Santa Clara Lawyer* 537, 546–547 (1973). Reprinted by permission.

In short, we favor doing away with the legal recognition of mental incompetency as a ground of avoiding contracts because we believe that this policy is most consistent with the traditional moral aims of Anglo-Saxon law, and especially contract law—namely, the expansion of the scope of individual self-determination and the protection of personal dignity; and because we cherish and support these values and rank them, on our own scale, higher than security or "mental health."

Thought Questions

1. What problems are there in attempting to merge psychiatry and law?
2. What is the authors' position? Do you agree? Analyze.
3. Who is injured by the current policy of voiding an incompetent's transactions? Who is helped?
4. Critique the last paragraph of the reading.

Because of the possibility of mental illness or disease interrupting a person's life, states permit a person to plan for that possibility by appointing an attorney in fact to attend to that person's affairs. In order for this appointment to be valid, it must be in the form of a formal written document called a **durable power of attorney.** The person must be of sound mind at the time of executing such a document (see Figure 13–3).

Contracts with Intoxicated Persons

A person so intoxicated as to not understand the nature and consequences of his or her actions may disaffirm the transaction, but only if the other party did not know of the intoxication. Such a situation is obviously rare. Nevertheless, chronic alcoholism or drug abuse may be treated as a form of mental illness and the rules discussed above concerning incompetency apply. In most cases, the other party obviously knows of the intoxication. If the intoxicated condition of a person is deliberately exploited for another's gain, then the issue is typically not one of contractual capacity but of misrepresentation, fraud, or undue influence. These problems are discussed in the remainder of this chapter (see Figure 13–4).

FRAUD

The law recognizes that some parties are induced to enter into a contract through misrepresentation of material facts. Misrepresentation may be innocent or

---

Figure 13–3   Durable Power of Attorney

I, _____ , being of sound mind and memory do designate my spouse, _____ , to act in my stead as attorney in fact, in the event I become mentally or physically incapacitated. In such event, I hearby entrust my spouse with all decisions including but not limited to the right to:

- the determination of medical treatment decisions
- access to my funds for my maintenance and support, including my checking and savings accounts and stock, bonds, mutuals, pension, and all other assets I may own
- sell my real property and use the proceeds for my maintenance and support

This power of attorney shall be in effect unless revoked by a writing.

_____   _____
Witness   Signed

_____
Witness

_____ appeared before me and signed this

Document this _____ day of _____ , 19 _____ .

_____

---

willful. Innocent misrepresentation of a material fact entitles an injured person to avoid the contract, or to rescind a contract already executed. Those who engage in willful misrepresentation commit **fraud,** and

Figure 13–4   Contractual Reality of Assent Defenses

Defense	Characteristic	Contract Status	Example
Innocent misrepresentation	Nonwillful misrepresentation	Voidable	Broker unknowingly represents that house is free from termites
Fraud	Willful misrepresentation	Voidable	Landlord knowingly misrepresents that apartment is electrically safe
Duress	Coercion	Voidable	Company under contract threatens to walk off job unless party pays additional sums of money
Undue influence	Dominion	Voidable	Nurse persuades patient to agree to sign contract for house
Mutual mistake	Both parties mistaken	Voidable	Both parties mistaken as to authenticity of art work
Unilateral mistake	One party mistaken	Generally valid	One party mistaken as to value of art work

the defrauded party is entitled to damages. To entitle a person to relief under fraud, the following four elements must be present:

- A *false assertion*.
- That is *fraudulent*.
- *Justifiable reliance* on the assertion.
- *Injury* suffered by the party.

False Assertions

To be a misrepresentation, there must first be "an assertion not in accordance with the facts." This false assertion may be due to a false statement, concealment, or the failure to disclose a fact.

False Statement

Traditionally, the common law granted relief for misstatements of *fact*, not false statements of opinion. A seller might lie about his or her opinion, calling a car "sharp" or "the best car for the money," and escape liability. But the seller could not lie about the facts — for example, whether "a new carburetor was installed last week" or even whether "a little old lady owned it and used it only to drive to church each Sunday." Facts can be proven by some amount of evidence; opinions cannot.

Nonetheless, the distinction between facts and opinions are often highly artificial. For example, is a statement that a car is in "mechanically perfect shape" a fact or an opinion? Recent cases reject the fact versus opinion distinction and permit recovery based on a false opinion under the following circumstances:

1. The opinion is given by a person who is in a position of trust or confidence to the recipient. For example, a family member or a lawyer or doctor who is in a relationship of trust is not permitted to misstate his or her opinion.

2. The opinion is given by a person who is claiming expert skill, judgment, or objectivity. For example, a jeweler or appraiser may not give false opinions to a person who is relying on the opinion.

3. The opinion is given by someone who has superior access to the facts. For example, a false opinion of a corporation's value by its chief financial officer would be a false assertion. A similar opinion by a shareholder would not be.

Concealment and Nondisclosure

False assertions can be made by conduct or even by silence under certain circumstances. A person may, for example, through conduct, *conceal* a condition and thereby prevent another from learning the truth. Thus, in one case involving the sale of a house, the seller concealed a hole in the floor made by termites by covering it with plywood and a throw rug.[6] This concealment constituted a false assertion.

As long as a person is not responsible for the other's ignorance of the truth through concealment or a false statement, there is generally no duty to speak. Thus, whereas concealment is a false assertion, simply not speaking (nondisclosure) is gener-

ally *not* held to be a false assertion. Exceptions to this general privilege of nondisclosure exist where a person has made a statement that was true when spoken, but subsequent events have made it no longer true. The person in such a case is under a duty to correct the former statement. There is likewise a duty to disclose all important facts where a relationship of trust and confidence exists between the parties.

As the following case points out, there are other exceptions to the rule of nondisclosure.

---

[6]*Hendrick v. Lynn*, 144 A.2d 147 (Del.Ch. 1958).

WEINTRAUB v. KROBATSCH
317 A.2d 68 (N.J. 1974)

Weintraub owned and occupied a six-year-old English townhome that she placed in the hands of a real estate broker (the Serafin Agency, Inc.) for sale. The Krobatsches examined the home while it was lit and found it suitable. They entered into a contract for the sale of the property for $42,500. The contract stated that the purchasers inspected the property and were fully satisfied with its physical condition, that no representations had been made, and that no responsibility was assumed by the seller as to the present or future condition of the premises.

Prior to closing, the purchasers entered the house, then unoccupied, and as they turned the lights on they were "astonished to see roaches literally running in all directions, up the walls, drapes, etc." On the following day, their attorney wrote a letter to Weintraub rescinding the contract.

Weintraub filed an action against the Krobatsches and the broker. There were opposing motions for summary judgment by the parties. The court granted summary judgment in favor of Weintraub and the Krobatches appealed to the New Jersey Supreme Court.

JACOBS, Judge

In *Obde v. Schlemeyer* . . . the defendants sold an apartment house to the plaintiff. The house was termite infested but that fact was not disclosed by the sellers to the purchasers who later sued for damages alleging fraudulent concealment. The sellers contended that they were under no obligation whatever to speak out. . . . The Supreme Court of Washington flatly rejected their contention, holding that . . . the sellers were under "a duty to inform the plaintiffs of the termite condition" of which they were fully aware. . . .

The attitude of the courts toward nondisclosure is undergoing a change and . . . it would seem that the object of the law in these cases should be to impose on parties to the transaction a duty to speak whenever justice, equity, and fair dealing demand it. . . . This duty to speak does not result from an implied representation by silence, but exists because a refusal to speak constitutes unfair conduct.

In *Sorrell v. Young* . . . the Court of Appeals of Washington recently applied the holding in *Obde v. Schlemeyer* . . . to a case where the sellers sold a residential lot to the buyers without disclosing that the lot had been filled. The buyers' evidence indicated the following: when the sellers originally acquired the lot it was below street grade and had been partially filled. They completed the filling and kept the lot until they considered it salable. At the time of the sale the fact that the land had been filled was not apparent. The sellers did not mention it at all and the buyers made no inquiry. The buyers sought a building permit and were told that expensive soil tests would be required, that piling would be necessary and that there was no assurance that a house could be built even if piling was installed. The court held that the buyers' evidence, if accepted, would support a right to rescind.

[T]he purchasers here were entitled to withstand the seller's motion for summary judgment. They should have been permitted to proceed with their efforts to establish by testimony that they were equitably entitled to rescind because the house was extensively infested in the manner described by them, the seller was well aware of the infestation, and the seller deliberately concealed or failed to disclose the condition because of the likelihood that it would defeat the transaction. . . .

If the trial judge finds such deliberate concealment or nondisclosure of the latent infestation not observable by the purchasers on their inspection, he will still be called upon to determine whether, in the light of the full presentation before him, the concealment or nondisclosure was of such significant nature as to justify rescission. Minor conditions which ordinary sellers and purchasers would reason-ably disregard as of little or no materiality in the transaction would clearly not call for judicial intervention.

. . . [W]e are satisfied that current principles grounded on justice and fair dealing, embraced throughout this opinion, clearly call for a full trial below; to that end the judgment entered in the Appellate Division is:

Reversed and Remanded.

Case Questions

1. What is the issue in this case?

2. Why did courts in the past hold that a seller of property had no duty to disclose defects in property that was being sold?

3. Is *Weintraub* distinguishable in any way from the cases on which it relies, specifically, *Obde v. Schlemeyer* and *Sorrell v. Young*? Analyze. Should the difference in facts result in a different legal result? Why or why not?

4. Extract the pertinent language from the court that specifies when the seller must disclose a defect. Is this sound? Analyze.

Fraudulent Assertions

The assertion, whether it is a misstatement, a concealment, or a nondisclosure, must be *fraudulent*. To be fraudulent, the person making the statement must either know the statement is not true or must make the statement in reckless disregard of the facts. To illustrate, assume a sales associate of Decade Today Realtors is asked whether a home she is selling is built on landfill. She asserts it is not, knowing the contrary is true. That would be a fraudulent assertion. It would likewise be a fraudulent assertion if, without knowing whether her statement was true, in face of rumors and without investigation, she asserted that it was not built on landfill when, in fact, it was.

Justifiable Reliance

The recipient of the fraudulent misrepresentation must *justifiably rely* on the misrepresentation. A person who knows the truth of the matter and enters the contract anyway cannot later avoid the contract on the ground of the misrepresentation. Here, there would be no reliance. An independent investigation by the recipient eliminates the recipient's reliance on the misrepresentation.

Recall that a person may rely on an opinion when the opinion is given by someone in a relationship of trust or claiming a special skill. In other cases, reliance on an opinion is unjustified.

Similar rules apply to reliance on a statement of law. Generally, people are presumed to know the law and may not justifiably rely on another's misrepresentation of the law. Where the parties are in a relationship of trust, or where the maker of the statement has unusual expertise, however, then the statement concerning the law may be relied on. To illustrate, a false statement is made concerning the legality of a certain financing scheme. If the statement of legality was made by *one of the parties* to a contract, it would not be justifiably relied on. In contrast, if the statement was made by a lawyer, or an accountant, then the recipient could successfully claim justifiable reliance.

Injury and Remedies

When the misrepresentation is fraudulent, the defrauded party may enforce the transaction and sue for damages. **Damages** typically include the plaintiff's loss of expected profit. Since fraudulent misrepresentations also constitute the tort of deceit, the defrauded party may seek punitive damages that are designed to punish the deceiver.

The defrauded party may, in the alternative, choose to avoid the transaction and sue in **restitution.** Restitution requires the deceiver to give back what the defrauded party has given. If the misrepresentation is innocent, then the defrauded party may merely avoid the transaction and sue for restitution. Remedies are discussed more thoroughly in Chapter 18.

DURESS

Duress results when one party coerces another to enter into a contract. Before the 18th century, a person could avoid obligation, claiming duress, only if assent was coerced by violence, the threat of violence, or imprisonment. Thus, if parties were induced to make contracts by the threat of harm to themselves or their families, their contracts would be voidable on the ground of duress.

Less extreme threats, involving the wrongful withholding of personal property, were added to the duress doctrine in the 18th century. In cases labeled ''duress of goods,'' where a person wrongfully refused to return another's goods without payment of an exorbitant sum, the coerced party could sue for a return of the coerced payment.

In the 19th and 20th centuries, even more subtle forms of economic pressure have permitted a coerced party relief under a doctrine called **economic duress.** Variety exists in courts' definitions of economic duress. The most frequently mentioned factors identified by courts in deciding a claim of economic duress are:

- The presence or absence of free will in making the agreement.
- Wrongful pressure applied by the coercing party.
- The availability of an alternative to agreeing to the coercing party's demands.
- The inequality of bargaining positions between the plaintiff and the defendant.
- The substantive fairness of the terms.

The following case involves some of these elements.

RICH & WHILLOCK, INC. v. ASHTON DEVELOPMENT, INC.
204 Cal.Rpt. 86 (Cal. Ct. App. 1984)

Rich & Whillock, Inc., signed a contract for excavating work at a price of $112,990 on a project run by Ashton Development, Inc. The price expressly excluded blasting costs. After encountering rock, Rich & Whillock, Inc., agreed to blast and remove the rock at an additional estimated cost of $60,000, ''but the actual cost may go higher.''

Rich & Whillock submitted a total bill of $192,000. Ashton refused to pay any additional costs beyond $50,000 and presented this offer to Rich & Whillock on a ''take it or leave it'' basis. After many protests, and a fear of bankruptcy if some payment was not received, Rich & Whillock agreed to the $50,000 payment and signed a release. Rich & Whillock then sued for the amount left unpaid under their contract, claiming the release was the product of economic duress. The trial court found against Rich & Whillock. The case was appealed to the California Court of Appeals.

WIENER, Judge

California courts have recognized the economic duress doctrine in private sector cases for at least 50 years. The doctrine is equitably based. . . . As it has evolved to the present day, the economic duress doctrine is not limited by early statutory and judicial expressions requiring an unlawful act in the nature of a tort or a crime. Instead, the doctrine now may come into play upon the doing of a wrongful act which is sufficiently coercive to cause a reasonably prudent person faced with no reasonable alternative to succumb to the perpetrator's pressure. The assertion of a claim known to be false or a bad faith threat to breach a contract or to withhold a payment may constitute a wrongful act for purposes of the economic duress doctrine. Further, a reasonably prudent person subject to such an act may have no reasonable alternative but to succumb when the only other alternative is bankruptcy or financial ruin.

The underlying concern of the economic duress doctrine is the enforcement in the marketplace of certain minimal standards of business ethics. Hard bargaining, ''efficient'' breaches and reasonable settlements of good faith disputes are all acceptable, even desirable, in our economic system. That system can be viewed as a game in which everybody wins, to one degree or another, so long as everyone plays by the common rules. Those rules are not limited to precepts of rationality and self-interest. They include equitable notions of fairness and propriety which preclude the wrongful exploitation of business exigencies to obtain disproportionate exchanges of value. Such exchanges make a mockery of freedom of contract and undermine the proper functioning of our economic system. The economic duress doctrine serves as a last resort to correct these aberrations when conventional alternatives and remedies are unavailing. . . .

Here, [Ashton] acted in bad faith when they refused to pay Rich & Whillock, Inc.'s final billing and offered instead to pay a compromise amount of $50,000. At the time of their bad faith breach and settlement offer, [Ashton] knew Rich & Whillock, Inc. was a new company overextended to creditors and subcontractors and faced with imminent bankruptcy if not paid its final billing. Whillock and Rich strenuously protested [Ashton's] coercive tactics, and succumbed to them only to avoid economic disaster to themselves and the adverse ripple effects of their bankruptcy on those to whom they were indebted. Under these circumstances, the trial court found the . . . agreement and . . . release were the products of economic duress. That finding is consistent with the legal principles discussed above and is supported by substantial evidence. Accordingly, the court correctly concluded Ashton Development, Inc. [was] liable for the $22,286.45 balance due under the contract.

Judgment affirmed.

Case Questions

1. What is the issue?
2. What policies is the court struggling to uphold in this case?
3. What is the doctrine of economic duress designed to do according to this court? Do you believe it is the function of courts to accomplish this particular goal? Explain.
4. Examine each of the elements of economic duress mentioned in the text. Cite facts to support those elements that are present in this case.

UNDUE INFLUENCE

Undue influence occurs when a person is persuaded to contract by one who exercises dominion over that person due to a special relationship of trust. Cases of undue influence involve the wrongful use of a dominant or superior psychological position to persuade a weaker person to assent to an agreement. For example, a suave nephew may persuade an elderly or ill aunt to agree to transfer her property by will or deed. Undue influence is distinguished from fraud inasmuch as no false assertion need be present in undue influence.

The line between duress and undue influence is not so bright. Typically, duress involves wrongful threats, while undue influence does not. Undue influence usually takes place in a setting of confidentiality and trust, so that one person believes another is acting in his or her best interests. Attorney-client, parent-child, husband-wife, or other family relationships are often involved in cases of undue influence. In contrast, duress is often found in a nonconfidential, arm's-length transaction.

MISTAKE

At times, assent is obtained by one or both parties' beliefs that are not in accord with the facts. These erroneous beliefs are mistakes. Depending on the seriousness of the **mistake**, the contract may or may not be voidable.

Mutual Mistake

Mutual mistake occurs when *both parties* to the contract are mistaken. Either party may avoid such a contract if two conditions are met: (1) the mistaken belief concerns a vital fact or an assumption on which the contract is based, and (2) the risk of the mistake's existence has not been assumed by the party seeking to avoid the contract.

Mistakes Concerning Vital Facts

When two parties enter a contract, they do so with certain basic assumptions. If the true state of affairs differs from these basic assumptions, the contract may be voidable. Basic assumptions include the *existence*, *nature*, or *value* of the subject matter to the contract. To illustrate, suppose Courtney contracts to sell Jansen a jigsaw for $500, located in A's shop. Unknown to either of them, the saw was stolen the night before. The contract would be voidable since the subject matter was gone. A similar result follows if, unknown to either party, the saw was not a jigsaw but rather was a band saw and could not be used for the buyer's intended purpose.

Another basic assumption concerns the *expression* of the parties' agreement. Sometimes, the parties differ fundamentally in their understanding of that expression. In one classic case, a seller agreed to sell cotton to arrive from Bombay on a ship named *Peerless*.[7] Two ships sailing from Bombay had that same name and they sailed at different times from the same port. The buyer had one ship and time in mind while the seller had another. The court held that the contract was voidable since the word *Peerless* was truly ambiguous.

Assumption of the Risk

The risk of a mistake regarding a "vital fact" must be one that has not been assumed by either party. The following case concerns the allocation of the risk of a mistake in value.

---

[7]*Raffles v. Wichelhaus*, 2 H.& C. 906 (1864).

ALUMINUM CO. OF AMERICA v. ESSEX GROUP, INC.
499 F. Supp 53 (W.D.Pa. 1980)

ALCOA and Essex entered into a written contract whereby ALCOA agreed to convert specified amounts of alumina supplied by Essex into aluminum for Essex. The price for each pound of aluminum converted was calculated by a complex formula that included three variable components, based on specific indices.

In the early years of the contract, the price formula yielded increases that were related to ALCOA's cost. But, due to actions beyond the parties' control, in later years, ALCOA's costs, mainly electricity, rose unforseeably beyond the indexed increase. ALCOA sought judicial relief.

TEITELBAUM, Judge

ALCOA initially argues that it is entitled to relief on the theory of mutual mistake. ALCOA contends that both parties were mistaken in their estimate of the suitability of the [index they chose for] ALCOA's non-labor production costs, and that their mistake is legally sufficient to warrant modification or avoidance of ALCOA's promise. . . . Essex . . . argues that ALCOA assumed or bore the risk of the mistake. . . .

Both Professor Corbin and the *Restatement* emphasize the limited place of the doctrine of mistake in the law of contracts. They, along with most modern commentators, emphasize the importance of contracts as devices to allocate the risks of life's uncertainties, particularly economic uncertainties. Where parties to a contract deliberately and expressly undertake to allocate the risk of loss attendant on those uncertainties between themselves or where they enter a contract of a customary kind which by common understanding, sense, and legal doctrine has the affect of allocating such risks, the commentators and the opinions are agreed that there is little room for judicial relief from resulting losses. . . . This is, in part, the function of the doctrine of assumption of the risk as a limitation of the doctrine of mistake. Whether ALCOA assumed the risk it seeks relief from is at issue in this case.

The *Restatements* and these cases reveal four facets of risk assumption and risk allocation under the law of mistake. First, a party to a contract may expressly assume a risk. If a contractor agrees to purchase and to remove 114,000 cubic yards of fill from a designated tract for the landowner at a set price ''regardless of subsurface soil and water conditions'' the contractor assumes the risk that subsurface water may make the removal unexpectedly expensive.

Customary dealing in a trade or common understanding may [also] lead a court to impose a risk on a party where the contract is silent.

Third, where neither express words nor some particular common understanding or trade usage dictate a result, the court must allocate the risk in some reasoned way. . . . A farmer who contracts to sell land may not escape the obligation if minerals are discovered which make the land more valuable. And in the case of the sale of fill stated above, if there is no express assumption of the risk of adverse conditions by the contractor, he may still bear the risk of losing his expected profits and suffering some out of pocket losses if some of the fill lies beneath the water table. . . . Contracts are generally to be enforced. Land sales are generally to be treated as final.

Fourth, where parties enter a contract in a state of conscious ignorance of the facts, they are deemed to risk the burden of having the facts turn out to be adverse, within very broad limits. Each party takes a calculated gamble in such a contract. Because information is often troublesome or costly to obtain, the law does not seek to discourage such contracts. Thus if parties agree to sell and purchase a stone which both know may be glass or diamond at a price which in some way reflects their uncertainty, the contract is enforceable whether the stone is in fact glass or diamond. If, by contrast, the parties both mistakenly believe it to be glass, [and it turns out to be a diamond] the case is said not to be one of conscious ignorance but one of mutual mistake. Consequently the vendor may void the contract.

Once courts recognize that supposed specific values lie, and are commonly understood to lie, within a penumbra of uncertainty, and that the range of probability is subject to estimation, the principle of conscious uncertainty requires reformulation. The proper question is not simply whether the parties to a contract were conscious of uncertainty with respect to a vital fact, but whether they believed that uncertainty was effectively limited within a designated range so that they would deem outcomes beyond that range to be highly unlikely. In this case the answer is clear. Both parties knew that the use of an objective price index injected a limited range of uncertainty into their projected return on the contract. Both had every reason to predict that the likely range of variation would not exceed 3 cents per pound. That is to say both would have deemed deviations yielding ALCOA . . . a return on its investment, work and risk of less than 1 cent a pound or of more than 7 cents a pound to be highly unlikely. Both consciously undertook a closely calculated risk rather than a limitless one. Their mistake concerning its calculation is thus fundamentally unlike the limitless conscious undertaking of an unknown risk which Essex now posits.

What has been said to this point suffices to establish that ALCOA is entitled to some form of relief due to mutual mistake of fact.

Case Questions

1. What vital fact was both ALCOA and Essex mistaken about?

2. What basic policy of contract law conflicts with the doctrine of mistake?

3. What is the traditional distinction courts have drawn between conscious and unconscious ignorance of the facts? Is the distinction justified? Explain. Why is this traditional distinction rejected in this case?

Unilateral Mistake

A **unilateral mistake** occurs when one party to the contract is mistaken and the other party is not. Although the cases are not uniform in their holdings concerning unilateral mistakes, a number of principles govern. Generally, unilateral mistake will not permit a party to avoid the contract. Under certain circumstances, however, unilateral mistake will give rise to a right to avoid. First, in order for the court to grant avoidance of a contact for a unilateral mistake:

- The mistake must concern a fact vital to the contract's performance.
- The risk of the mistake must not have been assumed by the party seeking to avoid the contract.

These conditions were previously discussed concerning mutual mistakes. In addition, one or more of the following conditions must be met if the unilateral mistake is to result in avoidance of the contract:

1. The nonmistaken party must have *reason to know* of the mistake. Suppose the mistake actually comes to a person's attention or that person has information on which to infer that a mistake exists. The person ought not to be able to take advantage of the mistake. To illustrate, assume that a general contractor takes bids on a job from various subcontractors. One subcontractor submits a mistaken bid. The subcontractor would be able to avoid the contract if the general contractor was either notified of the mistake or could infer a mistake when comparing this bid with other bids.

2. The nonmistaken party can be *restored to the status quo*. Using the example of the general contractor and subcontractor again, the contract may not be avoided if the general contractor has substantially changed his or her economic position in reliance on the subcontractor's mistaken bid. This would occur if the general contractor used the bid and entered another contract based on the bid. If, however, there has been no change in the economic position of the nonmistaken party, the contract may be avoided.

3. The mistake involves a *computational error* and not an error in judgment. Courts generally will not permit a person to escape a contract as a result of mistakes in appraising the labor or materials necessary to complete performance. However, if the mistake is of a routine sort—for example, in clerical computation—then the contract may be avoided. Perhaps the reason for this distinction is that clerical mistakes may be unavoidable, while the risk of judgment errors should be assumed by anyone who engages in business.

END–OF–CHAPTER QUESTIONS

1. What is the essential problem with assent in the following circumstances: minor's contract, misrepresentation, duress, undue influence, and mistake?

2. Compare the rules regarding persons who mistakenly deal with a minor on the assumption that he or she is an adult and persons who deal with a mentally incompetent person, mistakenly assuming that he or she is competent. Why is there a difference? Can such a difference in rules be logically justified?

3. Analyze: "Pay me more or I walk off the job." Under what circumstances would this constitute economic duress?

4. How would mistakes be treated under the subjective theory of contracts? Under the objective theory? Explain.

5. James Halbman, a minor, entered into an agreement with Michael Lemke whereby Lemke agreed to sell Halbman a 1968 Oldsmobile for $1,250. Halbman paid $1,000 cash and took possession of the car. Additional payments were made for five weeks until a connecting rod broke on the car. Halbman took the car in for repair at a cost of $637. Since Halbman never paid the bill, the garage removed the car's engine and transmission to satisfy the bill. The car was later vandalized. Halbman seeks to disaffirm the contract and recover the $1,100 he paid. May he disaffirm? If so, may he recover the full $1,100 or is recovery offset by the depreciation to the automobile? Analyze. See *Halbman v. Lemke*, 298 N.W.2d 562 (Wis. 1980).

6. From April to July, Faber, the plaintiff, was in the depressed phase of a bipolar disorder. Beginning in August, Faber engaged in a flurry of business transactions that included purchasing three expensive cars, attempting to convert his Long Beach bathhouse into a 12-story cooperative, purchasing property in the Catskills for $41,000, and entering a contract with the defendant, Sweet Style Manufacturing Corp., for the purchase of Sweet Style's property for $51,550. Faber sought to rescind the contract for the purchase of this property. Evidence was adduced at trial indicating that Faber understood what he was doing and that the contract was

not unfair. What must Faber prove to avoid the contract? See *Faber v. Sweet Style Manufacturing Corp.*, 242 N.Y.S.2d 743 (N.Y. Sup. Ct. 1963).

7. Stone, the plaintiff, purchased 14 art objects for $19,800. The seller contemporaneously appraised them at $275,800 and Stone applied for insurance in this amount. A question on the application for insurance asked, "Is there any other material fact within your knowledge, which should be submitted for consideration?" Stone answered no and never told the insurer the purchase price of the art objects or the source of the appraisal. A year later, the art objects were stolen during a burglary. Stone filed to recover the $275,800 and the defendant, Those Certain Underwriters at Lloyd's, London, responded, attempting to rescind the insurance policy. Who will succeed? Discuss fully. See *Stone v. Those Certain Underwriters at Lloyd's, London*, 401 N.E.2d 622 (Ill. App. 1980).

8. A single mother lived in a church-related home for eight weeks prior to relinquishing her child to the church agency for adoption placement. Although she sought to leave during the eight weeks, she was always persuaded to stay and receive additional counseling. She never received advice from an attorney concerning her right to retain the child and return to her home. May she revoke her relinquishment of her child to the agency? Analyze. See *In the Interest of Parry*, 641 P.2d 178 (Wash. App. 1982).

9. In 1970, the City Council of Duluth, Minnesota, rezoned a parcel of property from suburban to commercial. A restriction was placed on the property by the council, however, that only one building could be built on the property. That restriction was shown on zoning maps attached to the Duluth City Code. In 1976, the Campbell Soup Co. sold the parcel to Eikill. Eikill listed the property for sale in 1978, stating in his advertisement that the property was zoned commercial. When the plaintiff, Gartner, asked about the zoning, he was also told it was zoned commercial. Gartner never asked about any restrictions on the property and Eikill, the defendant, did not know they existed. After the purchase, Gartner learned of the restrictions and sought to rescind the contract since the land was worth one half of what he paid for it. May he rescind the contract? On what theory? Discuss. See *Gartner v. Eikill*, 319 N.W.2d 397 (Minn. 1982).

10. In 1977, the Pickles purchased a three-unit apartment building on a tract of land. Shortly after the sale, the county Board of Health condemned the property and prohibited human habitation on the premises due to the defective sewage system. The property was sold "as is." May the Pickles rescind the contract if neither party knew that the sewer was defective? On what theory? What if the seller knew the sewer was defective but was never asked? See *Lenawee County Bd. of Health v. Messerly*, 331 N.W.2d 203 (Mich. 1982).

Chapter 14

Consideration and Its Substitutes

■

CRITICAL THINKING INQUIRIES

As you read this chapter, you should be able to address the following:

- Analyze: "The contractual requirement of consideration is an ancient doctrine that has outlasted its usefulness."
- What is the purpose of the preexisting duty rule?
- Compare and contrast the laws of consideration and promissory estoppel.
- Under what conditions should the law enforce a person's promise?

MANAGERIAL PERSPECTIVE

Red Owl Stores assured Hoffman that if he raised $18,000 he would be granted a supermarket franchise under terms to be discussed at a later date. There was no agreement as to the details of the franchise arrangement. Hoffman followed Red Owl's recommendations and sold his bakery, purchased a grocery store to gain experience, resold the grocery though it was profitable, moved near to the place where the supermarket was to be located, and purchased the building site for the market. Red Owl then demanded that Hoffman raise an additional $13,000. Hoffman believed this to be unfair. Negotiations broke down.

Hoffman's wife tells him to walk away and "chalk it up to experience." Other advisers ridicule him for not "getting it in writing." Hoffman is heartbroken, exclaiming, "Am I without remedy?"

- What should Hoffman have done to avoid the predicament?
- Is Hoffman without remedy?

Figure 14–1   Consideration and Its Substitutes

Consideration	Promissory Estoppel	Writing
Act	Charitable subscriptions	UCC § 2–205 firm offer rule
Forbearance	Subcontractor's bids	UCC § 2–209 modification
Promise of act	Promise of employment fringes	UCC § 1–107 surrender of legal right
Promise of forbearance	Franchise promises of inducement	

Figure 14–2   Consideration Defined

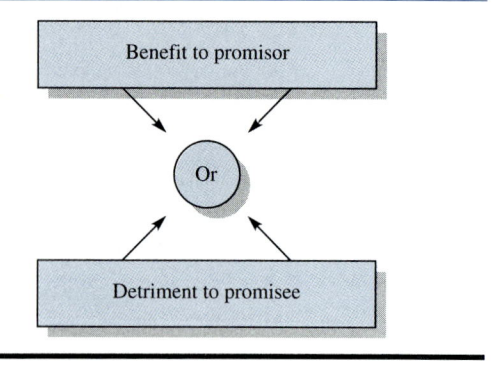

Hoffman finds himself in a predicament not unlike many managers and others because of a lack of knowledge about the area of contracts referred to as consideration and its substitutes.

Many promises are made every day. Some we make to ourselves in the form of personal resolutions—for example, to diet or to control our anger. Yet these imply no legal obligation. In general, the law is concerned about the effect of one's behavior in relation to others. Even so, not all promises made to others are legally binding.

This chapter explores one of the more technical aspects of contact law—the basis for holding a promisor legally responsible to fulfill a promise (see Figure 14–1). These bases are:

- Consideration.
- Promissory estoppel.
- Written obligation.

Even if one of the bases for holding a promisor legally responsible is present, the additional contract elements of an agreement, capacity, and legality discussed in Chapters 12, 15, and 16 must also be present for a contract to exist.

CONSIDERATION

Not every promise is enforceable. In England, only those contracts that were under seal were enforceable. These were the types of agreements that were

attended to with great deliberation. It took a serious mode to heat up the wax and embed it in the parties' signet rings and seal the written instrument with the rings' imprint. The seal has been abolished in the United States, but it has been replaced by the law of **consideration.** Consideration is one of the ingredients of a contract. It involves a benefit to a promisor or a detriment to a promisee bargained for and given over in exchange (see Figure 14–2). This is the glue that cements contracts by signaling to the courts that the necessary "value" is present to enforce the bargain. Simply stated, in order for consideration to be present:

- Something must be given for the promise that has a legal value consisting either of a benefit to the promisor or a detriment to the promisee.
- The something—the detriment or benefit—must be bargained for in exchange for the promise.

Legal Benefit or Detriment

The first element of consideration requires that the **promisee,** the one to whom the promise is made, suffer legal detriment *or* the **promisor,** the one making the promise, experience a legal benefit. Most cases include both a benefit to the promisor *and* a detriment to the promisee. Thus, if Faith does yard work for Elwin in exchange for Elwin's promise to pay $50, Faith has suffered a detriment (Faith's work) and Elwin has been benefited (by receiving yard work). Nevertheless, the requirement is stated in the alternative and at times the promisee may suffer a detriment without a corresponding benefit experienced by the promisor.

To meet the requirement of *legal* detriment, the promisee must do or promise to do what he or she is not legally obligated to do. Or, depending on the agreement, the promisee must refrain or promise to refrain from doing what he or she is legally privileged to do. Hence, assume that Red Owl promised to sell Hoffman a franchise for $30,000 (including other details) in return for Hoffman's promise to expend his best efforts to manage and promote the franchise. Hoffman has suffered a legal detriment since he has undertaken to do something that he was not otherwise required to do—expend his efforts on the franchise. Hoffman has also experienced a legal benefit since he is receiving something that he was not otherwise entitled to—a franchise. Similarly, Red Owl has experienced a corresponding legal detriment and legal benefit.

Doing an act in exchange for a promise occurs when the parties enter a unilateral contract. *Promising* to do something in exchange for the promisor's promise occurs when the parties enter a bilateral contract.

Legal detriment need not involve economic or financial loss. It is enough that the promisee refrains from exercising a right that he or she is legally privileged to exercise. The following case, illustrative of a legal detriment, involves a promise of $5,000 to a nephew in exchange for giving up certain ''vices.''

HAMER v. SIDWAY
27 N.E. 256 (N.Y. 1891)

William E. Story, Sr., made a promise to his nephew, William E. Story II: If the nephew would refrain from drinking, using tobacco, swearing, and playing cards or billiards for money until the nephew became 21 years of age, William, Sr., would pay him $5,000. The nephew assented and fully performed. When the nephew became 21 years old, he wrote his uncle informing him that he had complied.

The uncle died without having paid his nephew any portion of the $5,000 and interest. William Story II assigned (sold) his interest to Hamer, who sued William Story, Sr.'s estate. The trial court found in favor of the plaintiff, Hamer, and on appeal, it was reversed. Hamer appealed to New York's highest court.

PARKER, Judge

The defendant contends that the contract was without consideration to support it, and therefore invalid. He asserts that the promisee, by refraining from the use of liquor and tobacco, was not harmed, but benefited; that that which he did was best for him to do, independently of his uncle's promise—and insists that it follows that, unless the promisor was benefited, the contract was without consideration—a contention which, if well founded, would seem to leave open to controversy in many cases whether that which the promisee did or omitted to do was in fact of such benefit to him as to leave no consideration to support the enforcement of the promisor's agreement. Such a rule could not be tolerated, and is without foundation in the law. [Consideration is defined] as follows: ''A valuable consideration, in the sense of the law, may consist either in some right, interest, profit, or benefit accruing to the one party, or some forbearance, detriment, loss, or responsibility given, suffered, or undertaken by the other.'' Courts ''will not ask whether the thing which forms the consideration does in fact benefit the promisee or a third party, or is of any substantial value to any one. It is enough that something is promised, done, forborne, or suffered by the party to whom the promise is made as consideration for the promise made to him.''

''. . . 'Consideration' means not so much that one party is profiting as that the other abandons some legal right in the present, or limits his legal freedom of action in the future, as an inducement for the promise of the first.'' Now, applying this rule to the facts before us, the promisee used tobacco, occasionally drank liquor, and he had a legal right to do so. That right he abandoned for a period of years upon the strength of the promise of [his uncle] that for such forbearance he would give him $5,000. We need not speculate on the effort which may have been required to give up the use of those stimulants. It is sufficient that he restricted his lawful freedom of action within certain prescribed limits upon the faith of his uncle's agreement, and now, having fully performed the conditions imposed, it is of no moment whether such performance actually proved a benefit to the promisor, and the court will not inquire into it. . . . [The trial court decision in favor of plaintiff was reinstated.]

Case Questions

1. If it was illegal in New York to drink, smoke, gamble, or swear before the age of 21, would the nephew had suffered legal detriment? Explain.

2. Did the uncle, William E. Story, Sr., receive any legal benefit? Is this relevant? Explain.

3. Is there a better way of deciding this case without applying the law of consideration?

Figure 14–3   Sufficient and Insufficient Consideration

Sufficient Consideration	Insufficient Consideration
• Promises to perform an act.	• Gift.
• Promises to refrain.	• Past consideration.
• Refraining.	• Moral consideration.
• Acts.	• Preexisting duties.
	• Illusory promise.
	• Unconscionable agreements.

Sufficiency of Consideration

The detriment that is bargained for in exchange for the promise need not be the economic equivalent of the promise. As a general rule, courts will not inquire into the adequacy of the consideration. Any detriment, no matter how economically inadequate, will be considered sufficient consideration to support a promise (see Figure 14–3). Thus, in an old English case, surrendering a document of guaranty, which supposedly had value but turned out to be nothing more than a worthless scrap of paper, was consideration to support a promise of £10,000.[1] Similar exchanges of grossly unequal values have been upheld as binding contracts.

Exchanges of unequal value are upheld for several basic policy reasons. First, courts are not in a position to prescribe prices. The value of services, goods, or forbearance is better left to the market and the private action of the parties than the court's independent valuation. Second, because of the notion of freedom of contract, it has been held that parties of maturity and sound mind should be free to contract imprudently as well as prudently. Under this notion, courts should not interfere with a bargain freely made. Third, certainty of contractual obligations would be adversely affected if courts required that the ''value'' of the bargain be the reasonable equivalent or be determined by some other subjective standard.

Nevertheless, limitations are applied to the rule that the courts will not look into the adequacy of the consideration. If the disparity in value indicates that the transaction was merely a sham or a pretense for a gift, courts will find no consideration and no contract. Sham consideration is called **nominal consideration** and will not support a promise. This would be the case where a sum of money is exchanged for a lesser sum, or goods are exchanged for fewer goods of the same kind. For example, if Bentley promises to give Cynthia $300 in exchange for a nickel, the nickel is nominal consideration and will not support Bentley's promise (unless, of course, the nickel had greater value, perhaps because it was rare). A further limitation on this rule is found in the Uniform Commercial Code section 2–302. If the inadequacy is so severe that it is deemed *unconscionable* — that is, if ''it shocks the judicial conscience'' — the court may, in its discretion, refuse to enforce the agreement. The doctrine of unconscionability will be further explored in Chapter 15.

---

[1]*Haighs v. Brooks*, 10 A & E 309 (1839).

Forbearance to Sue

As a general rule, the surrender of a valid legal claim constitutes a legal detriment and will support a promise of payment for such surrender. For example, assume that in our opening scenario, Hoffman threatened to sue Red Owl, seeking $30,000 in damages. Assume further that Red Owl denied any liability but offered $15,000 in return for Hoffman surrendering his right to sue. If Hoffman's claim was valid, giving up his right to sue would be considered sufficient consideration. But what if Hoffman's claim was invalid—for example, because Red Owl has an adequate defense? It would seem that surrendering an invalid claim is not a detriment since a person is not giving anything up by failing to assert an invalid claim. Nevertheless, if success on the claim was doubtful because of uncertainty in the law or facts and the claimant is making the claim in *good faith*, courts generally hold that such surrender is legal detriment. Good faith, according to the Uniform Commercial Code, means "honesty in fact."

Requirement and Output Contracts

The early common law held that promises to purchase all of one's requirements or to deliver all one's output were illusory since a buyer may decide not to have requirements or a seller might decide not to produce any output. The law is clearly otherwise today. Thus, a contract in which Woodrow agrees to buy all the coal that Woodrow "requires" will be upheld, although a similar agreement to buy all the coal that Woodrow may "wish" is deemed illusory.

Both the *Restatement (Second) of Contracts* and the Uniform Commercial Code section 2–306 explicitly uphold such agreements. These contracts are commercially desirable since buyers and sellers often cannot predict their actual requirement or output due to contingencies of weather, raw materials availability, labor shortages, and the like. For example, the amount of coal that an electric company "requires" turns on weather conditions, industrial demands, and similar contingencies. Although demand cannot be fixed with complete certainty, it is not illusory.

To protect against unreasonable increases or decreases in the buyer's requirements or the seller's output due to price fluctuations in the market, the Uniform Commercial Code section 2–306 requires that requirements and outputs:

- Be exercised in good faith—that is, honestly and in a commercially reasonable manner.
- Not be disproportionate to a stated estimate.

Illusory Promises

An **illusory promise** is one that gives the illusion of a commitment by the promisor but in fact makes the promisor's performance entirely optional. For example, Douglas offers to supply as many bushels of tomatoes as Lydia may order from time to time. Lydia purports to accept this offer but has given no consideration since Lydia's acceptance merely creates an illusion of a commitment. Phrases such as, "as many as I may *wish* (or *want* or *desire*)," which leave performance to the unfettered discretion of the promisor, are illusory promises, not supported by consideration.

But if the promisor's discretion is limited by some objective standard, the promise is not illusory. Thus, if Douglas offers to sell "as many bushels of tomatoes as Lydia may want in the next six months, but not less than 300 bushels," and Lydia accepts, Lydia's acceptance is consideration to support Douglas's promise.

Courts exhibit a strong tendency toward upholding contracts even if the promise might seem to be illusory. Thus, recent cases have held that contracts do not contain an illusory promise even though they give one party a right to terminate the agreement at any time, with notice. It is enough that the promised freedom was limited in some way by the requirement of notice.

The Preexisting Duty Rule

When a person promises to do, or does what he or she is already legally obligated to do, that promise or performance is not a legal detriment. Similarly, if a person refrains from doing something that he or she is not legally privileged to do, such as smoking marijuana, such restraint would also not be a legal detriment.

Legal duties may arise by contract or by public law. Thus, if an FBI agent captures a kidnapper within the scope of his or her duty, the agent is not entitled to receive a reward, because this is part of the agent's job. Similarly, doing a job that one is already under contract to do is not consideration for a promise of additional compensation. Thus, if Cordelia is under contract to work for Caspar for one year at $25,000, Caspar's promise of a $5,000 bonus midway through the year is unenforceable unless, in return, Cordelia does something more than she is already legally obligated to do.

Part Payment of a Debt

When a debtor pays a lesser sum on the date the entire debt is due, that lesser payment is not consideration for a promise of release by the creditor. So if Josephine owes Caleb $100, due on June 1, and Caleb says "pay me $50 on June 1 and I will not sue you for the rest," Caleb's promise of no legal action is unsupported by consideration. Caleb may accept the $50 payment and sue for the rest.

Courts have distinguished between cases involving liquidated debts and those involving unliquidated debts. A **liquidated debt** is a debt that is undisputed in both existence and amount. The preexisting duty rule applies to liquidated debts. Promising to pay only part of an undisputed debt on the date it is due is not consideration for a promise of a release.

An **unliquidated debt,** by way of contrast, is one that is disputed either in amount or existence. Often, an unliquidated debt results from a tort claim. For example, suppose Mamie negligently smashes her car into Gordon's car. Mamie alleges that the damage she caused amounts to no more than $1,000. Gordon claims that the damage caused is closer to $3,000. An agreed compromise of this unliquidated debt is sufficient consideration. Thus, if Gordon promises to release Mamie from further legal obligation for $2,000, such a promise is supported by consideration.

Even if the debt is undisputed and certain, if the debtor does *anything* beyond what he or she was obligated to do, such performance is legal detriment to support a promise of a release by the creditor. Thus, if the debtor agrees to pay a day early, or in another place, or in a different medium, or even agrees to refrain from bankruptcy proceedings, such performance is sufficient to support a promise of discharge from the debt obligation.

The Check-Cashing Dilemma

Suppose Titus purchases a tractor from Charmagne for $80,000. Titus contends that the tractor delivered does not conform to the contract and is worth only $70,000. To avoid litigation, Titus issues a check for $75,000 as a compromise and marks the check "Paid in Full." If Charmagne cashes the check, is she barred from seeking any additional sums?

At common law, cashing a full payment check in this disputed situation leads to an **accord and satisfaction.** When a check marked paid in full is tendered for more than the buyer feels he owed, the buyer is offering an *accord*, a new agreement as a substitution for the old agreement. When the seller cashes the check, the seller accepts the accord and the new agreement is *satisfied*. Thus, an accord and satisfaction was worked and the seller could not sue for any additional amount.

Some courts and commentators are of the opinion that section 1–207 of the Uniform Commercial Code changed this common law result by allowing the check casher to qualify his or her indorsement.

UCC § 1–207. Performance or Acceptance under Reservation of Rights

A party who with explicit reservation of rights performs or . . . assents to performance in a manner demanded or offered by the other party does not thereby prejudice the rights reserved. Such words as "without prejudice," "under protest," or the like are sufficient.

Thus, using our hypothetical example, Charmagne could, according to some courts, cash the $75,000 "under protest" and still sue for the $5,000 Charmagne felt was owing. The trend, however, in recent cases, is to find that UCC section 1–207 did *not* change the common law.

Exceptions to the Preexisting Duty Rule

Courts have carved exceptions out of the preexisting duty rule. Perhaps this is because mature, consenting parties ought to be able to modify their contractual obligations as they see fit, even if no consideration is supplied.

One major exception concerns *unforeseen difficulties* that may arise during the course of the contract. In such a case, a modified agreement will be upheld even though it is unsupported by consideration. For example, suppose Roderick promises to pay Paula $50,000 to build a house on Roderick's property. Unknown to either of the parties, solid rock lies just below the surface, requiring expensive blasting. Roderick promises to pay Paula $15,000 for the additional expenses to be incurred in digging the foundation. Paula is doing only that which she was already legally obligated to do. Nevertheless, courts generally hold that Roderick is bound to pay the additional $15,000 under the modification agreement because of the unforeseen difficulty that was encountered in building. The following case further explores the unforeseen difficulty exception to the preexisting duty rule.

ANGEL v. MURRAY

322 A.2d 630 (R.I. 1974)

Maher provided the city of Newport with refuse collection services. He entered a five-year contract beginning in 1964, under which he was to receive $137,000 per year for collecting the refuse. Thereafter, Maher requested an additional $10,000 per year from the city council because there had been a substantial increase in the cost of collection due to an unanticipated increase of 400 new dwelling units. The city council agreed to pay him an additional $10,000. Maher made a similar request again because of a substantial increase in the quantity of refuse collection. The city council again agreed to pay an additional $10,000.

Angel brought suit against Murray, the director of finance of the city, alleging the council's payment of additional sums to Maher was illegal. The trial court found that each such $10,000 payment was made in violation of law and ordered Maher to repay the $20,000. Maher appealed to the Rhode Island Supreme Court.

ROBERTS, Judge

The primary purpose of the preexisting duty rule is to prevent what has been referred to as the ''hold-up game.'' A classic example of the ''hold-up game'' is found in *Alaska Packers' Ass'n. v. Domenico*. There 21 seamen entered into a written contract with Domenico to sail from San Francisco to Pyramid Harbor, Alaska. They were to work as sailors and fishermen out of Pyramid Harbor during the fishing season. The contract specified that each man would be paid $50 plus two cents for each red salmon he caught. Subsequent to their arrival at Pyramid Harbor, the men stopped work and demanded an additional $50. They threatened to return to San Francisco if Domenico did not agree to their demand. Since it was impossible for Domenico to find other men, he agreed to pay the men an additional $50. After they returned to San Francisco, Domenico refused to pay the men an additional $50. The court found that the subsequent agreement to pay the men an additional $50 was not supported by consideration because the men had a preexisting duty to work on the ship under the original contract, and thus the subsequent agreement was unenforceable.

The modern trend away from a rigid application of the preexisting duty rule is reflected by section 89D(a) of the American Law Institute's *Restatement (Second)* of the Law of Contracts, which provides: ''A promise modifying a duty under a contract not fully performed on either side is binding (a) if the modification is fair and equitable in view of circumstances not anticipated by the parties when the contract was made. . . .''

We believe that section 89D(a) is the proper rule of law and find it applicable to the facts of this case. It not only prohibits modifications obtained by coercion, duress, or extortion but also fulfills society's expectation that agreements entered into voluntarily will be enforced by the courts. Section 89D(a), of course, does not compel modification of an unprofitable or unfair contract; it only enforces a modification if the parties voluntarily agree and if (1) the promise modifying the original contract was made before the contract was fully performed on either side, (2) the underlying circumstances which prompted the modification were unanticipated by the parties, and (3) the modification is fair and equitable.

Having determined the voluntariness of this agreement, we turn our attention to the three criteria delineated above. . . . First, the modification was made . . . at a time when the five-year contract . . . had not been fully performed by either party. Second, although the . . . contract provided that Maher collect all refuse generated within the city, it appears this contract was premised on Maher's past experience that the number of refuse-generating units would increase at a rate of 20 to 25 per year. Furthermore, the evidence is uncontradicted that the 1967–1968 increase of 400 units "went beyond any previous expectation." Clearly, the circumstances which prompted the city council to modify the 1964 contract were unanticipated. Third, although the evidence does not indicate what proportion of the total this increase comprised, the evidence does indicate that it was a "substantial" increase. In light of this, we cannot say that the council's agreement to pay Maher the $10,000 increase was not fair and equitable in the circumstances. Reversed.

Case Questions

1. What is the issue this case presents?
2. Distinguish the "hold up" game from the unforeseeability exception to the preexisting duty rule.
3. How could Maher have provided for the unforeseeability within the contract?
4. Should the fair and equitable approach, as followed in this case, be applied to all contracts? Analyze.

The Code's Approach to the Preexisting Duty Rule

Another exception to the preexisting duty rule is found in Uniform Commercial Code section 2–209, which reads: "An agreement modifying a contract within this article needs no consideration to be binding." In effect, when the contract concerns the sale of goods, parties can modify their agreements without the constraint of the preexisting duty rule. For example, Emmet is an egg wholesaler and agrees to supply Viola with eggs for one year at $.60 a dozen. Due to increased fuel costs to heat Emmet's hen house, Emmet seeks to modify the agreement and obtain an additional $.10 a dozen midway through the contract term. Viola agrees to the price modification. Under the preexisting duty rule, courts would find that there was no consideration to support the modification. Emmet is doing nothing beyond his original obligation—that is, supplying eggs. But UCC section 2–209 dispenses with the need for consideration and would uphold the contract as modified.

The policy behind UCC section 2–209's elimination of the preexisting duty rule is straightforward. Requiring new consideration every time a change is made in the contract simply inhibits the free use of commercially desirable modifications. Under section 2–209, parties may rapidly readjust their ongoing contractual relationship by simple assent without actually having to give something in exchange for a promised modification. Of course, if the modification was agreed to because of coercion, such as, "Give me the $.10 a dozen extra or I may forget to make deliveries next week," such a coerced modification would be unenforceable.

Bargained-For Exchange

The second element of consideration is that the legal detriment must be *bargained for* as the price of the promise, act, or forbearance. The legal detriment suffered by the promisee must be bargained for and given up in exchange. Gifts and past consideration do not meet this requirement.

Gifts

At times, legal detriment is suffered but there is no consideration because the detriment was merely a condition for the receipt of a gift rather than the bargained-for price of a promise. For example, suppose Brent wishes to give a gift to his favorite niece Melody and writes the following note to Melody: "If you will go to Stacy's Department Store, a gift certificate in the amount of $300 is waiting for you in the women's department." Melody's trip to Stacy's would be legal detriment since Melody is doing something beyond her legal obligations. Nevertheless, this trip is not consideration since it was not sought as a trade or exchange for the promised gift certificate. The trip was merely a condition for Melody's receipt of a gift.

Past Consideration   *MISNAMED — IS NO CONSIDERATION*

Generally, a promise that is made *after* performance has been rendered will be viewed as a gift and not a contractual obligation. This is so because the performance was not sought as an exchange or as the price of the promise. The consideration necessary to support the promise is said to be **past consideration** and as such is insufficient to support a subsequent promise. For example, assume that Betty has decided to name her baby after her favorite Uncle Alfred and announces this choice to her uncle after the baby is named. Uncle Alfred's promise of $1,000 to Betty for naming the child is unsupported by consideration since the performance had already been rendered. It was thus not bargained for as the price of a promise.

In a few states, promises to pay for benefits previously received are sometimes enforceable as moral obligations to the extent necessary to prevent injustice. Although this is clearly not the rule in the majority of states, the influential *Restatement (Second) of Contracts* has adopted it, making it likely that this rule will gain wider acceptance. The following case is one where moral consideration was apparently sufficient to support a promise.

MCGOWIN v. MOBILE

4 So 2d 161 (Ala. 1941)

The plaintiff, Webb, was engaged in clearing the upper floor of one of the company's mills. While in the company's employ, he was dropping a 75-pound pine block from the upper floor to the ground. As he was dropping the block, he saw McGowin on the ground below, directly under where the block would fall. To prevent the block from striking McGowin, Webb held on to the block and fell with it to the ground below. The block did not strike McGowin but instead injured Webb. Webb was badly crippled for life and unable to do physical or mental labor.

As a result, McGowin agreed to care for Webb at the rate of $15 every two weeks until Webb's death. Shortly after McGowin's death, the payments stopped. Webb sued to recover the unpaid installments. The court dismissed the case and Webb appealed.

BRICKEN, Judge

The . . . appellant saved McGowin from death or grievous bodily harm. This was a material benefit to him of infinitely more value than any financial aid he could have received. Receiving this benefit, McGowin became morally bound to compensate appellant for the services rendered. Recognizing his moral obligation, he expressly agreed to pay appellant as alleged in the complaint and complied with this agreement up to the time of his death; a period of more than 8 years.

Had McGowin been accidentally poisoned and a physician, without his knowledge or request, had administered an antidote, thus saving his life, a subsequent promise by McGowin to pay the physician would have been valid. Likewise, McGowin's agreement as disclosed by the complaint to compensate appellant for saving him from death or grievous bodily injury is valid and enforceable.

Where the promisee cares for, improves, and preserves the property of the promisor, though done without his request, it is sufficient consideration for the promisor's subsequent agreement to pay for the service, because of the material benefit received.

. . . Any holding that saving a man from death or grievous bodily harm is not a material benefit sufficient to uphold a subsequent promise to pay for the service, necessarily rests on the assumption that saving life and preservation of the body from harm have only a sentimental value. The converse of this is true. Life and preservation of the body have material, pecuniary values, measurable in dollars and cents. Because of this, physicians practice their profession charging for services rendered in saving life and curing the body of its ills, and surgeons perform operations. The same is true as to the law of negligence, authorizing the assessment of damages in personal injury cases based upon the extent of the injuries, earnings, and life expectancies of those injured.

It is well settled that a moral obligation is a sufficient consideration to support a subsequent promise to pay where the promisor has received a material benefit, although there was no original duty or liability resting on the promisor.

The case at bar is clearly distinguishable from that class of cases where the consideration is a mere moral obligation or conscientious duty unconnected with receipt by promisor of benefits of a material or pecuniary nature. Here the promisor received a material benefit constituting a valid consideration for his promise.

. . . McGowin's express promise to pay appellant for the services rendered was an affirmance or ratification of what appellant had done raising the presumption that the services had been rendered at McGowin's request.

The . . . complaint show[s] that in saving McGowin from death or grievous bodily harm, appellant was crippled for life. This was part of the consideration of the contract. . . . McGowin was benefited. Appellant was injured. Benefit to the promisor or injury to the promisee is a sufficient legal consideration for the promisor's agreement to pay.

Reversed and remanded.

Case Questions

1. Was there really a detriment bargained for here? Analyze.
2. How can this case be criticized? [Note: Although the reasoning in *Webb* has by no means been adopted by the majority of states, the *Restatement (Second) of Contracts* section 86 has adopted its reasoning as a basis for enforcing a promise.]
3. Does this case actually recognize a type of moral consideration? Explain.

Figure 14-4   Elements of Promissory Estoppel

- Promise.
- Calculated to induce reliance.
- Justifiable reliance.
- Injury.
- Avoidance of injustice.

Figure 14-5   Consideration and Promissory Estoppel Compared

	Promise	Detriment	Bargained For
Consideration	Yes	Yes	Yes
Promissory estoppel	Yes	Yes	No

PROMISSORY ESTOPPEL

— Forcing a promise to be followed on. Enforceable.

In our opening scenario, the understanding between Red Owl Stores and Hoffman may have lacked consideration because the terms were indefinite and uncertain regarding the details of the franchise. However, there is in the law a substitute for consideration — **promissory estoppel.** When an agreement fails for lack of consideration, it may nonetheless be enforceable if the ingredients of promissory estoppel are present (see Figure 14-4). They are:

- A promise that induced the promisee's reliance.
- The promisor should have reasonably expected the promise to induce reliance or forbearance.
- The promisee actually relies on the promise to his or her injury.
- Injustice can be avoided only by enforcing the promise.

The reason the doctrine is called promissory estoppel is that if the elements mentioned above are present, the promisor is **estopped** — legally prohibited or barred — from denying the enforceability of the promise.

Promissory Estoppel Distinguished from Consideration

Promissory estoppel may be contrasted with the doctrine of consideration (see Figure 14-5). Recall that in the case of consideration, the legal detriment suffered by the promisee must be induced or bargained for by the promisor. Promissory estoppel presents a different situation. The legal detriment suffered by the promisee is induced by the promise but the promise is not bargained for and given over in exchange. There is no reciprocal relationship in promissory estoppel. Thus, assume that a philanthropist promises to give $200,000 to a university, and in reliance on the promise the university contracts to build a new building. The promisee's legal detriment (entering a contract with a construction firm) is induced by the promise. But, unlike the case of consideration, the promise was not induced by the legal detriment. The philanthropist-promisor only intended to make a gift, and did not bargain for a construction contract. In sum, promissory estoppel differs from consideration since, although a legal detriment is present in both cases, a bargained-for exchange exists only with respect to consideration.

Promissory Estoppel Applied

The doctrine of promissory estoppel is commonly applied in the case of charitable pledges, subcontractor's bids, and employment and franchise promises.

Charitable Pledges

When one makes a pledge to a charity, no consideration ordinarily exists. The pledge is tantamount to a promise to give a gift. Nonetheless, where the charity changes its position in justifiable reliance on the promise, courts are apt to enforce the pledge under the doctrine of promissory estoppel.

Subcontractor's Bid

Subcontractors make bids for jobs to general contractors. Those bids are incorporated into the contractor's overall bid. The subcontractor's bid is only an offer, and is not supported by consideration. Nonetheless, the doctrine of promissory estoppel prevents the subcontractor from withdrawing the bid once the contractor has relied on it by incorporating it within an overall bid and is awarded the contract.

Employment Promises

Courts have enforced promises in employment settings even where there is an absence of consideration. For example, an employer's promise of a pension to an employee that induces the employee to retire or to refrain from working during retirement would be enforceable under the doctrine of promissory estoppel. A fringe benefit plan instituted during an employee's contract term might also be enforceable as a contract under this doctrine, whereas the traditional application of consideration principles (under the preexisting duty rule) would defeat its enforceability.

Business Franchises

In the opening scenario, Red Owl made certain promises that Hoffman relied on. The agreement was probably too vague and indefinite for there to have been an enforceable agreement. Nonetheless, under the doctrine of promissory estoppel, a promise of a business franchise that induces a potential franchisee to take out a loan, move from his or her home, or expend money preparing to do business could not be withdrawn despite the absence of consideration.

WRITTEN OBLIGATIONS

Several statutes make a written promise enforceable despite the absence of consideration or detrimental reliance. In Chapter 12 on agreements, we learned that offers are generally revocable unless there is consideration to support an agreement not to revoke the offer (an option contract). We also learned that certain offers made by a merchant *in writing* are irrevocable under the Uniform Commercial Code's firm offer rule. Even if the offeree gives nothing in return to keep the offer open, the writing is a sufficient ground for making the offer firm under UCC section 2–205.

Contractual modifications are generally held to be unenforceable under the preexisting duty rule unless the promisee gives some consideration in exchange for the promise. Yet, under the Model Written Obligations Act and similar statutes adopted in some states, a modification is enforceable as long as it is *in writing*. The Uniform Commercial Code (section 2–209) employs a writing requirement as a substitute for consideration in most contractual modification cases as well.

Further, although the common law preexisting duty rule operates to make a waiver or renunciation of one's right to assert a legal claim invalid unless supported by consideration, UCC section 1–107 makes such a waiver or renunciation valid if it is signed and is in writing.

The following article suggests abolition of the doctrine of consideration and in its place, enforcement of all agreements in writing.

*Ought the Doctrine of Consideration to Be Abolished from the Common Law?**

I think the theory of consideration ought to find no place in our system of contract law. I do not stand alone in that opinion. . . . Sir William Holdsworth says that in its present form the doctrine of consideration is somewhat of an anachronism. He proposes as a practical reform that a contract should be enforced by law if either it is in writing or there is consideration. In that way a gratuitous promise would be enforced if there is written evidence.

I fear, however, that there is little prospect in the near future of the English law being completely changed in so vital a respect, though the practical reform suggested by Sir William may, perhaps, before very long be achieved. But there is a dead weight of legal conservatism to be overcome.

I often wonder what practical purpose is served by the doctrine of consideration in its present form. There is no public policy that I can see against enforcing gratuitous obligations. The most vital element of public policy in this regard is that people should keep their . . . word. In some cases, certainly, the judge or jury must be more particular about proof before a gratuitous obligation is enforced. We have, however, seen that the old rule of consideration does not dispense with proof of contractual intention, though it is generally strong evidence of that. But judges and juries can be trusted, I hope, to deal wisely where gratuitous promises are alleged. They have often to handle much more difficult questions of intention or mental state, *e.g.*, in cases of fraud or mistake. In adjudicating on a contract, they start with the objective basis of what the parties said or did, their words, written or spoken and their conduct: they have all the surrounding circumstances and relationships. There is no reason why they should be less successful in deciding if there is contractual intention than courts which know not consideration in our sense. The abolition of consideration would not affect the law relating to mistake, illegality, immorality, impossibility or failure of condition. In conclusion, I see no practical objections to the abolition of the doctrine, to counterbalance the reasoning on which I have advocated that it should be abolished.

Thought Questions

1. Do you agree that "there is no place for the theory of consideration in our system of law"? Why or why not?

2. Is there a public policy in the United States against enforcing gratuitous promises (i.e., promises without consideration)? Explain.

3. What problems would the author's proposal cause if adopted in the United States? Analyze.

---

*Source: Lloyd Wright, "Ought the Doctrine of Consideration to Be Abolished from the Common Law?" 49 Harv. Law Rev. 1225 (1930). Reprinted with permission.

END–OF–CHAPTER QUESTIONS

1. Why does the law not enforce every "truly intended" promise in a commercial setting? Why bother with the requirement of consideration or promissory estoppel?

2. What changes has the Uniform Commercial Code brought to the law of consideration?

3. Does the preexisting duty rule or the UCC rule regarding contract modifications adequately deal with the problem of co-

erced modifications, such as "agree to this modification or I'm walking off the job"? Analyze. Is there an approach that would better deal with this problem?

4. Does the word *legal* add anything to our understanding of detriment? Why does the law not focus on *actual* detriment rather than legal detriment?

5. Should courts as a matter of public policy focus on the adequacy of the consideration given in exchange for a promise? What changes would such a focus bring to the economy?

6. The plaintiff and the defendant were involved in an auto accident in which the plaintiff was severely injured. The defendant agreed to pay the plaintiff $21,000 for his injuries. In exchange, the plaintiff released the defendant from liability for this suit. Several weeks later, after contacting an attorney, the defendant learned that she had an absolute defense to any liability claim. She refused to pay the $21,000 and the plaintiff sued. Who would win this action? Discuss fully.

7. Consider the following hypothetical cases and determine whether the promises are supported by consideration. Label each promise as well.

   a. A and B agree that in consideration of $1 paid, B will give A $1,000 over the next six months. A pays the $1.

   b. A and B agree that B will purchase three motor scooters from A for $750 each. B is a minor and can avoid the terms of this contract.

   c. A and B agree that B will purchase from A all the "maple syrup that B may want in the next 6 months but no less than 30 gallons."

8. The defendant, Taylor, had assaulted his wife, who took refuge in the plaintiff's, Harrington's, house. The next day, Taylor gained access to the house and began another assault on his wife. Taylor's wife knocked him down with an axe, and was on the point of decapitating him while he was lying on the floor, when Harrington intervened and caught the axe as it was descending. The blow intended for Taylor fell on Harrington's hand, mutilating it badly, but saving Taylor's life. Thereafter, Taylor orally promised to pay Harrington her damages, but, after paying a small sum, failed to pay anything more. Harrington sued for the remainder of the damages. What are the obstacles here to Harrington's recovery? Is promissory estoppel present? Explain. See *Harrington v. Taylor*, 36 S. E. 2d 227 (N.C. 1945).

9. The plaintiff resided on public land. She received a letter from her brother encouraging her to move that stated: "If you will come down and see me, I will let you have a place to raise your family, and I have more open land than I can tend; [because] of your situation, and that of your family, I feel like I want you and the children to do well." The plaintiff moved to the defendant's property with her children, abandoning her home. Two years later, the defendant forced her to leave. Did the plaintiff suffer any legal detriment? Did the defendant gain any legal benefit? On what theory might the plaintiff succeed in this case? Analyze. See *Kirksey v. Kirksey*, 8 Ala. 131 (1845).

10. A bank robbery resulted in the posting of a reward offer of $1,500 for information leading to the arrest and conviction of the robbers. Among the claimants for the reward were bank employees who provided extremely useful information regarding the details of the crime and described the culprits fully. Two other claimants were state police officers who apprehended the robbers while on patrol. The last claimant was a deputy sheriff from Rockcastle County who assisted in the arrest, which took place in Polaski County, outside his jurisdiction. Who, if anyone, is entitled to the reward? State your reasons fully. See *Denney v. Reppert*, 432 S.W. 2d 647 (Ky. App. 1968).

Chapter 15

Illegal Agreements

■

CRITICAL THINKING INQUIRIES

As you read this chapter, you should be able to address the following:

- Analyze the ways in which the law discourages illegal agreements.
- Distinguish a legal risk-shifting agreement from an illegal wager.
- Compare and contrast a revenue-raising statute and a regulatory statute.
- Distinguish between legal and illegal restraints of trade.
- What are the relevant factors when determining whether an exculpatory clause is illegal?
- ''Consenting parties should be left to enter into unconscionable agreements.'' Critique.

MANAGERIAL PERSPECTIVE

Tennis Outlet is a franchisor of tennis shops. It is in the process of getting together with its attorney to redo its form franchisor/franchisee contracts. Tennis Outlet desires the following issues to be covered in the contract.

- Restricting the franchisee from competing against other Tennis Outlet stores in the event the franchise is terminated.
- Exempting the franchisor from liability in the event people are injured in conjunction with the franchisee's business.
- The terms, including financing charges, of the transaction.

The contract needs to be constructed in such a way as to avoid illegal provisions.

- How can Tennis Outlet legally prohibit franchisees from competing against it after termination of the franchise?
- Can Tennis Outlet protect itself against liability incurred by its franchisees?
- What is the consequence of terms within the contract deemed to be illegal?

Courts generally will not interfere with Tennis Outlet's right to contract. However, there are circumstances when some counter-balancing interests limit that right.

This chapter examines those circumstances when the courts limit the parties' freedom to contract. In Chapter 13 we learned that a bargain fails when the *process* of forming a contract is tainted with fraud, duress, undue influence, or some other problem of genuine assent. In this chapter, the *substance* of the agreement is scrutinized to see whether the law deems the agreement void due to illegality.

WHAT MAKES AN AGREEMENT ILLEGAL?

An agreement is deemed illegal for one of three reasons (see Figure 15–1). First, its enforcement may be prohibited by a *statute*. For example, statutes in most states prohibit certain gambling activities and performance of certain occupations without a license. An agreement made in violation of these statutes will be illegal.

Second, an agreement that is contrary to common law is deemed illegal. For example, the common law seeks to protect free competition, and therefore contracts in restraint of trade are strictly scrutinized.

Third, an agreement that violates public policy will also be deemed illegal. **Public policy** includes any standard of conduct that is generally accepted in the community. An agreement that falls short of the community's standards of morality, public safety, or public welfare is illegal even though these standards may not be expressly found in any statute. It is up to the courts to determine the scope of these community standards.

AGREEMENTS CONTRARY TO STATUTE

A wide variety of agreements may be deemed illegal by legislation. Agreements involving bribery, the obstruction of justice, perjury, racketeering, and other corrupting influences are widely dealt with by state and federal criminal laws. Further, manufacturers' contracts requiring retailers to sell goods for no less than a minimum price, called resale price maintenance contracts, are deemed illegal under Section 1 of the Sherman Act. (This and other antitrust violations are dealt with in Chapters 46 and 47.) Individual statutory schemes must be examined concerning each of these areas.

Charging an amount of interest beyond the legal limit, a practice called **usury,** is also regulated, chiefly by state statutes. States establish maximum interest rates that may be charged on various types of loans and credit arrangements. Any rates above the legal limit are usurious. In some states, the lender forfeits all interest. Other states allow the offender to collect the legal interest rate. A few states will not aid the offender to collect even the principal of the loan.

Both state and federal statutes prohibit gambling in certain contexts. Additionally, state licensing laws prohibit the practice of certain professions in the absence of a license. Each of these areas will be examined.

Wagering Agreements

All bargains contain some degree of risk. Yet, certain agreements require performance only on the happening of an *uncertain event*. Of these agreements performable on the happening of an uncertain event, some are legal and are referred to as risk-shifting agreements; others are illegal and are called **wagers.** A risk-shifting agreement simply shifts a risk from one person to another for a price. An illegal wager creates a new risk where none previously existed.

Most insurance contracts are examples of legal risk-shifting agreements. The contract does not create a risk where none previously existed. It is legal because it simply shifts the burden of loss due to a fire, death, accident, or other cause, from the insured to the insurance company.

Another common example of a legal risk-shifting agreement is an option or futures contract in which the buyer purchases an option to buy a commodity such as corn at a set price in the future. On July 1, for example, Zenos pays Rodney $1,000 in exchange for an option to buy Rodney's December corn at $2.80 a bushel. The buyer shifts the risk of a price increase to the seller. This practice, referred to as **hedging,** reduces the uncertainty of the consequences of a changing market and thus provides a valuable economic risk-shifting function.

An illegal wagering agreement occurs when the agreement itself creates the risk. Where Holly agrees to pay Damos $50 on the turn of a dice or the draw of a card, no risk is being shifted. The agreement creates an entirely new risk. Similarly, if Holly purchases insurance *on someone else's life* (with

Figure 15–1   Illegal Agreements

Illegal Agreements	Examples	Defenses
Contrary to statute	Wagering Licensing	Not at equal fault Excusable ignorance Severable
Contrary to common law	Covenant not to compete	Ancillary and reasonable
Contrary to public policy	Immoral Unconscionable	None

whom Holly had no financial or family relationship), the purchase would be an illegal wagering agreement. Holly is not shifting a risk previously belonging to her. Rather, the agreement is creating a wholly new risk, previously borne by neither Holly nor the insurance company. Thus, insurance agreements are not always legal. They may be illegal wagers if the beneficiary has no insurable interest[1] in the person or property.

The legality of lotteries, betting pools, pari-mutuel betting, or the award of prizes in certain contests varies with state laws.

Licensing and Registration Statutes

Statutes require people to have a license or registration before engaging in certain occupations. Otherwise, an agreement with the unlicensed businessperson is illegal. Sometimes, the licensing or registration statute clearly states that failure to comply with the statute's requirements renders all agreements made by the unlicensed person unenforceable. The court, then, is bound to carry out the legislature's will. At other times, the legislature has not made its will known. Where the legislature has not explicitly made its will known, the effect given an agreement with an unlicensed party turns in part on the legislature's purpose in enacting the statute. If the legislature's purpose was to protect the public from incompetence or fraud, operating without a license bars the unlicensed contractor from any recovery.

Such a protective statute is called a **regulatory statute.** If, on the other hand, the licensing law is simply a **revenue-raising statute** to boost the state's coffers, operating without a license does not render the contractor's agreements unenforceable.

The legislature's purpose in enacting the statute helps determine whether the statute is regulatory or revenue raising. If the applicant is required to pass a test measuring competence, complete a course of study, or serve an apprenticeship before being licensed, the statute is probably regulatory. In contrast, a licensing statute that requires everyone to pay a fee, without regard to competence, is probably a revenue-raising statute.

A stiff criminal penalty for operating without a license indicates that the legislature sought to protect the public by deterring unlicensed parties from engaging in these occupations. This statute is therefore likely to be regulatory. In contrast, little or no criminal penalty indicates that the statute was not intended as a deterrent and should be considered revenue raising (see Figure 15–2).

The following case considers whether an unlicensed plumber can recover under a contract for plumbing services.

Figure 15–2   Licensing Statutes

	Regulatory	Revenue Raising
Effect	Unenforceable	Enforceable
Violation	Stiff criminal penalty	Small fine
Purpose	Protect public	Raise revenue
Requirements	Test, skills, education	Fee

---

[1]An *insurable interest* means that the insured will suffer some economic loss if the property insured is damaged or destroyed. Concerning life insurance, the one purchasing the policy must have some reasonable expectation of benefit from the continuance of the insured's life (the person on whose life the policy is written).

GENE TAYLOR & SONS PLUMBING CO. v.
W & W CONSTRUCTION CO.

611 S.W.2d 572 (Tenn. 1981)

The plaintiff, Gene Taylor & Sons Plumbing Co., Inc. (Taylor), a subcontractor, was hired by the defendant, general contractor W & W Construction Co. (W & W), to do plumbing subcontracting work on a townhouse development. Taylor was not paid $18,891.12 as a final payment. W & W denied it owed this amount, in part because Taylor was not licensed in accordance with the Tennessee statute that required plumbers to be licensed. Taylor filed a complaint to enforce a mechanic's lien[2] against W & W. The chancellor dismissed the case. The Court of Appeals affirmed. The case was appealed to the Supreme Court of Tennessee.

DROWOTA, Justice

The issue in this case is whether a subcontractor not licensed . . . can recover against a licensed general contractor and a property owner under a subcontract agreement.

. . . At the time of entering into said contract . . . Plaintiff was not aware that a general contractor's license was required of it, nor was Plaintiff aware of said requirement at anytime during the performance of its contract. Plaintiff now has a general contractor's license which was acquired after the Complaint was filed in this case.

[In] *Santi v. Crabb* . . . the homeowner acted as his own general contractor and made an agreement with the plaintiff under which the plaintiff was to perform certain sheetrock work. The plaintiff was not licensed as a general contractor in his line of work as required by T.C.A. section 62–601. The plaintiff subsequently sued the homeowner for the value of his services, but this Court denied recovery. . . .

. . . In *Santi*, this Court has recognized the general rule regarding the effect of noncompliance with licensing statutes on the enforceability of contracts. Yet this rule is neither explicitly nor implicitly required by the licensing statute. The rule is a judicial creation designed to further the public policy behind the statute. As such, the general rule need not be applied inflexibly without regard to the facts in a particular case. . . .

. . . In the instant case, the appellant contends that the particular facts justify this Court in permit-

ting recovery. . . . With regard to the cause of action against the appellee W & W Construction Co., we agree.

In . . . *Santi*, the unlicensed contractors were suing the owner of the property where the work was to be done. In the instant case, the appellant contracted with and brought suit against a construction company licensed as a general contractor. Other courts have recognized that the policies that bar recovery against a member of the general public do not apply in suits against licensed professionals in the same business. . . .

In permitting recovery against W & W Construction Co. under a theory of quantum meruit [an amount equal to the reasonable value of the goods and services rendered], we do not intend to approve unlawful conduct or to enforce an illegal contract. The application of the *[Santi]* rule is unjust only with regard to the aspect of forfeiture when forfeiture is required neither by the licensing statute nor by the policy underlying that statute. In short, we merely avoid "unreasonable penalties and forfeitures."

Any recovery the appellant might have against W & W Construction Co. should be limited to actual expenses in the form of labor and materials expended on the project as shown by clear and convincing proof. These expenses should not include any amounts which constitute profit under the contract. In all events, recovery should be limited by the contract price unless the appellant can show by clear and convincing proof that labor and materials

---

[2]A mechanic's lien is a claim placed on the land or buildings of the property owner to secure payment of a debt for construction or other mechanical work done on the property.

were expended in addition to that required by the contract.

. . . This cause is remanded to the Chancellor for further proceedings in keeping with the opinion of this Court.

Case Questions

1. Identify the issue this case presents.

2. How do the facts in this case differ from those found in *Santi* cited in the opinion?

3. Analyze the impact of what the court decided.

Although there is a long-standing tradition of licensing to ''protect the public,'' the tradition is not without its critics. In the following excerpt, Nobel prize–winning economist Milton Friedman considers whether licensing statutes hurt the public more than they help.

---

*Capitalism and Freedom**

The most obvious social cost is that any one of these measures, whether it be registration, certification, or licensure, almost inevitably becomes a tool in the hands of a special producer group to obtain a monopoly position at the expense of the rest of the public. There is no way to avoid this result. One can devise one or another set of procedural controls designed to avert this outcome, but none is likely to overcome the problem that arises out of the greater concentration of producer than of consumer interest. The people who are most concerned with any such arrangement, who will press most for its enforcement and be most concerned with its administration, will be the people in the particular occupation or trade involved. They will inevitably press for the extension of registration to certification and of certification to licensure. Once licensure is attained, the people who might develop an interest in undermining the regulations are kept from exerting their influence. They who don't get a license, must therefore go into other occupations, and will lose interest. The result is invariably control over entry by members of the occupation itself and hence the establishment of a monopoly position. . . .

There is still another way in which licensure, and the associated monopoly in the practice of medicine, tend to render standards of practice low. I have already suggested that it renders the average quality of practice low by reducing the number of physicians, by reducing the aggregate number of hours available from trained physicians for more rather than less important tasks, and by reducing the incentive for research and development. It renders it low also by making it much more difficult for private individuals to collect from physicians for malpractice. One of the protections of the individual citizen against incompetence is protection against fraud and the ability to bring suit in the court against malpractice. Some suits are brought, and physicians complain a great deal about how much they have to pay for malpractice insurance. Yet suits for malpractice are fewer and less successful than they would be were it not for the watchful eye of the medical associations. It is not easy to get a physician to testify against a fellow physician when he faces the sanction of being denied the right to practice in an ''approved'' hospital. The testimony generally has to come from members of panels set up by medical associations themselves, always, of course, in the alleged interest of the patients.

---

*Source: Milton Friedman, *Capitalism and Freedom* (Chicago: University of Chicago Press, 1962). Reprinted with permission.

When these effects are taken into account, I am myself persuaded that licensure has reduced both the quantity and quality of medical practice; that it has reduced the opportunities available to people who would like to be physicians, forcing them to pursue occupations they regard as less attractive; that it has forced the public to pay more for less satisfactory medical service, and that it has retarded technological development both in medicine itself and in the organization of medical practice. I conclude that licensure should be eliminated as a requirement for the practice of medicine.

Thought Questions

1. Do you agree with the author that licensing renders the average quantity of medical practice low? What would be the consequences of no licensing? Explain.

2. Can you think of any alternatives to a licensing statute that might provide protection to the public from unqualified practitioners? Would these work as well as licensing?

3. Analyze whether Professor Friedman's argument would also apply to other license requirements — for example, gun or driver's licenses?

AGREEMENTS CONTRARY TO COMMON LAW

Deeply ingrained within the common law is a type of protectionism over free market competition and hence strict scrutiny of contracts in restraint of trade. In a sense, every business contract may be viewed as a restraint of trade since the parties are binding themselves to certain commitments and consequently remove themselves from the marketplace. For example, a company that contracts to purchase all the tennis equipment it needs from Tennis Outlet is no longer in the market to purchase the equipment elsewhere.

Despite this, the common law has singled out only certain agreements as *illegal* restraints of trade. Restraints of trade have been deemed illegal when they unreasonably restrain trade.

This section is concerned only with *judicially* created limits to an agreement restraining trade. Statutory limits found in federal antitrust laws are discussed in Chapters 46 and 47. Courts do not consider all agreements limiting competition or restricting a person's future employment opportunities illegal. Only *unreasonable* restraints are considered illegal. The courts use a rule of reason to balance the factors in a case. At times, the promisee's need for the restraint outweighs the harm caused to both the public and the promisor. Under these circumstances, the restraint will be deemed reasonable and legal. At

other times, the harm caused outweighs the promisee's need for the restraint, and it will thus be deemed unreasonable and illegal.

Ancillary and Primary Restraints

The common law has traditionally distinguished between ancillary restraints of trade, which are legal if reasonable, and primary restraints, which are illegal. An **ancillary restraint** is one that is secondary to a larger purpose of the agreement. Thus, in the sale of a business, the parties' primary purpose is the sale of the business. The agreement might include a clause that prohibits the seller from opening a similar business in the same locale for a period of time. This clause is ancillary and recognizes the buyer's need to prevent the seller from competing against the buyer at a time when the buyer is new and vulnerable. As long as such an ancillary restraint is limited to the purpose for which it is included, it will be deemed reasonable.

A **primary restraint** of trade is a restraint that is principal to the agreement and lessens competition. For example, assume two of Tennis Outlet's franchisees agree to divide up the market and not compete against each other. This agreement is a direct restraint on trade, harming the public without any legitimate counterbalancing need for protection on the part of the franchisees. Primary restraints are illegal.

Restraints of Trade in the Sale of a Business

A person who buys a business purchases certain assets: the location of the business, its stock in trade, its accounts, the building and its furnishings, and its goodwill. **Goodwill** refers to an intangible value of a business measured by reputation. The buyer desires to step into the seller's shoes and have the seller's customers continue business as they did with the seller. To protect this goodwill, the buyer may demand that the seller not compete with the buyer. Whether such a noncompetition clause is a reasonable restraint of trade is the subject of the next case.

WESTEC SECURITY SERVICES, INC. v. WESTINGHOUSE ELECTRIC CORP.
538 F.Supp. 108 (E.D. Pa. 1982)

The defendant, Westinghouse Electric Corp., was engaged in the residential security business through its ownership of Westinghouse Security Systems, Inc. (WSSI). By agreement, Westinghouse sold to the plaintiff, Westec Security Services, Inc. (Westec), all of the stock of WSSI. In the purchase agreement, Westinghouse agreed not to compete for 20 years against Westec in the United States in the sale of security systems.

Some 15 months after the sale, Westinghouse, two wholly owned subsidiaries of Westinghouse, and Teleprompter Corporation (Teleprompter) entered into a plan of acquisition and merger whereby Teleprompter became a wholly owned subsidiary of Westinghouse. Teleprompter's principal business was the operation of cable television franchises throughout the country; and it had recently begun to offer to the prospective subscribers of its cable television systems, a home security system and service.

Westec sued Westinghouse, contending that Teleprompter's involvement in the residential security business was barred under the terms of the Westec-Westinghouse covenant not to compete.

POLLAK, Judge

It now remains to determine whether enforcement of the covenant . . . would be reasonable. In determining whether a non-competition covenant's restraints are reasonable, courts have naturally focused on the extent of contested covenants, considering their extent along three different dimensions:

1. Types of Activities
The general rule is that the terms of a restrictive covenant can be no broader than is necessary "to protect the business sold," or the "good will purchased." Here the record of defendant's own statements appraising WSSI's performance and prospects makes it clear that defendant, while it still owned "the business sold," regarded WSSI's chief assets as (1) its capacity to offer, via its distributors, a total package of security systems and services to homeowners/consumers; and (2) its possession of the Westinghouse name and reputation and the recognition these "commodities" enjoyed among consumers. In keeping with this appraisal of WSSI's assets, defendant, sensibly, regarded its prime competitors in the home security market as including those companies which sold security systems to homeowners and offered to them installation, maintenance and monitoring services.

I conclude, therefore, that insofar as it embraces the activities of selling home security systems directly to the public and installing, servicing and monitoring such systems, the covenant not to compete is no broader than is reasonably necessary to protect plaintiff's legitimate interests.

2. The Covenant's Geographical Area
The covenant contains no express limit on the geographical extent of its operation. However, it is undisputed that the parties intended the covenant not to compete to cover the entire United States. . . .

The touchstone of "reasonableness" in scrutinizing the geographical reach of covenants not to compete ancillary to sales of businesses is this: The extent of such covenants must be "limited to the area of potential competition with the purchaser.'' Identifying a reasonably circumscribed geographical area within which this covenant may properly be enforced is a matter of some difficulty. I find two points of reference to be certain: (1) The ''area of potential competition'' in this case clearly embraces those localities or market areas in which Westec and its distributors currently operate; and (2) in light of the relatively limited number of markets in which plaintiff operates, the entire United States is far too broad an area in which to require defendant and Teleprompter to conform to the covenant's restraints. Such a requirement would impose hardship on defendant beyond the countervailing justification of being necessary to protect plaintiff's legitimate interests. However, it would be neither equitable nor a reasonable construction of the covenant to limit the covenant's geographical breadth to the markets currently served by plaintiff; for, . . . the business sold was one which both parties reasonably anticipated would expand into new markets during the lifetime of the covenant. Therefore, I conclude that plaintiff is entitled to the protection of the covenant, not only in its present markets but also in those market locales which it enters, via new distributors or otherwise, during the life of the covenant.

3. The Covenant's 20-Year Time Span

[I]n light of the contours of the covenant's restraints I find the 20-year extent contemplated by the covenant to be unreasonable.

In support of the 20-year provision, plaintiff contends that it needs 10 years in which to recoup a return on its investment and an additional 10-year period in which to make a profit. In a similar vein, plaintiff points to ''the amount of investment required to be made by a Westec distributor, and the time required to recapture that investment.'' Plaintiff's contentions ignore the limited purpose which animates the common law's tolerance of covenants not to compete. That purpose is to protect the buyer's interest in the good will purchased; it is not to permit one to purchase freedom from competition. Thus, the measure of reasonableness in this context has been articulated . . . as being ''the period required for the purchaser to establish his own customer following.'' . . .

In considering what would constitute a reasonable period within which plaintiff may establish its identity and ''customer following'' free from defendant's competition, I find from the record that one's ''good name'' in the field of providing security systems and services rests largely on one's reliability over time in providing maintenance and monitoring service. . . . In light of all the circumstances, I conclude that a restraint of 10 years, rather than the 20 years . . . represents a reasonable period of protection for plaintiff.

Accordingly, the public interest does not require that I forbear from enforcing the covenant [as modified].

Case Questions

1. What are the issues in the case?
2. What is a permissible purpose advanced by a covenant not to compete? What are impermissible purposes?
3. Is it proper for the court to ''legislate'' a new time scope? Why not 8 years or 12 years? Analyze.
4. Do you see any problems with the court's approach? Is there an alternative? Analyze.

Restraints of Trade in an Employment Contract

Similar rules apply to employment cases. Covenants not to compete are upheld as long as they are ancillary and reasonable. However, courts are more apt to uphold a clause that restrains trade ancillary to a contract for the sale of a business than a similar clause ancillary to an employment contract. Courts strictly scrutinize covenants not to compete, in employment agreements, for unreasonable harm to the employee.

This solicitude toward employees is due in part to the unequal bargaining power between employers and employees. The employee may sign an agreement limiting future employment opportunities simply to get the job. In contrast, the buyer and seller of a business usually stand on equal footing and both often hire attorneys to negotiate the agreement. In addition, limiting the use of postemployment restraints promotes the uninhibited flow of service, talent, and ideas essential to our economy. It should be noted that postemployment restraints are becoming increasingly common due to the high degree of mobility of the modern employee and the fear that confidential business information will pass to a new employer.

Remedies Available for Overbroad Restrictive Covenants

Courts have taken a variety of approaches in dealing with overbroad, and therefore illegal, restrictive covenants. Some courts simply deem the entire provision unenforceable. This approach may be unfair to purchasers who fairly negotiated admittedly overbroad covenants but now find themselves entirely without protection from their sellers' competition.

Other courts sever the offending provision, leaving the reasonable portions of the agreement intact. This process of severance is called the **blue pencil test.** This term originated from the courts' traditional use of a blue-leaded pencil when analyzing these agreements and marking out unreasonable provisions. It is illustrated in the following example. Assume that a restrictive covenant in a contract for the sale of a store is reasonable except for overbroad limitations on specified activities. The buyer only needs protection against the seller's subsequent sale of jewelry. The clause, however, reads: ''Seller agrees not to reestablish or reopen any business or trade involving the sale of jewelry, *silverware or china*. . . .'' Through the remedy of severance, the court could ''blue pencil,'' or delete, the offending restrictions on silverware or china. The other portion of the covenant regarding jewelry remains valid. The chief disadvantage of severance is that it works only if the overbroad clause is grammatically severable.

Where the offending clause cannot be severed, a court may reduce its overbroad language to a shorter duration or geographic area as it deems reasonable. This court-imposed alteration of the contract is called **reformation.** The majority of states now use the remedy of reformation, as did the court in *Westec*.

AGREEMENTS CONTRARY TO PUBLIC POLICY

Public policy is found in a state's constitution, statutes, common law, and general sense of societal values. Public policy bans contracts that are immoral and unconscionable. Contracts that run afoul of public policy are struck down by courts. For example, the New Jersey Supreme Court struck down a surrogate mother contract as against public policy.[3] In that case, Mary Beth Whitehead entered into an agreement with a married couple, William and Elizabeth Stern, whereby Mary Beth would be artificially impregnated with William's sperm and carry the offspring to term. Mary Beth further agreed to surrender the child to the Sterns, who were obligated to pay the medical bills plus $10,000. The court held that the contract offended public policy inasmuch as it is like child selling, it disregards the best interests of the child, it is degrading to the birth mother, and it benefits the rich over the poor. Not all states have found surrogate mother contracts of this nature to be illegal.

Agreements Detrimental to Morality

Courts are apt to declare an agreement illegal if it violates the community's notion of public morals. Since marriage is so firm an institution of American society, agreements detrimental to a marital relationship are illegal. For example, agreements that prohibit someone from getting married for an unreasonable period of time are illegal since they are harmful to the marital institution.

Consider how shifting standards of morality affected the court's decision regarding the legality of the following alleged agreement made between two unmarried persons living together.

---

[3]*In the Matter of Baby M*, 537 A.2d 1227 (N.J. 1988).

MARVIN v. MARVIN
557 P.2d 106 (Cal. 1976)

The plaintiff, Michelle Marvin, and the defendant, Lee Marvin, lived together for seven years without marrying; all property acquired during this period was taken in Lee's name. When Michelle sued to enforce a contract under which she was entitled to half the property and to support payments, the trial court granted judgment on the pleadings for Lee, thus leaving him with all property accumulated by the couple during their relationship.

Michelle contended that in October of 1964, she and Lee ''entered into an oral agreement'' that while ''the parties lived together they would combine their efforts and earnings and would share equally any and all property accumulated as a result of their efforts whether individual or combined.'' Furthermore, they agreed to ''hold themselves out to the general public as husband and wife'' and that ''plaintiff would further render her services as a companion, homemaker, housekeeper and cook to defendant.''

Shortly thereafter, Michelle agreed to ''give up her lucrative career as an entertainer [and] singer'' in order to ''devote her full time to defendant. . . .'' In return, Lee agreed to ''provide for all of plaintiff's financial support and needs for the rest of her life.''

Michelle alleges that she fulfilled her obligations under the agreement. During this period, the parties, as a result of their efforts and earnings, acquired in Lee's name substantial real and personal property, including motion picture rights worth over $1 million. In May of 1970, however, Lee compelled Michelle to leave his household. Support was discontinued shortly thereafter.

TOBRINER, Justice

During the past 15 years, there has been a substantial increase in the number of couples living together without marrying. Such nonmarital relationships lead to legal controversy when one partner dies or the couple separates. . . . We take this opportunity to resolve that controversy and to declare the principles which should govern distribution of property acquired in a nonmarital relationship.

Defendant first and principally relies on the contention that the alleged contract is so closely related to the supposed ''immoral'' character of the relationship between plaintiff and himself that the enforcement of the contract would violate public policy. He points to cases asserting that a contract between nonmarital partners is unenforceable if it is ''involved in'' an illicit relationship or made in ''contemplation'' of such a relationship. A review of the numerous California decisions concerning contracts between nonmarital partners, however, reveals that the courts have not employed such broad and uncertain standards to strike down contracts. The decisions instead disclose a narrower and more precise standard: a contract between nonmarital partners is unenforceable only *to the extent* that it *explicitly* rests upon the immoral and illicit consideration of meretricious sexual services.

In summary, we base our opinion on the principle that adults who voluntarily live together and engage in sexual relations are nonetheless as competent as any other persons to contract respecting their earnings and property rights. Of course, they cannot lawfully contract to pay for the performance of sexual services, for such a contract is, in essence, an agreement for prostitution and unlawful for that reason. But they may agree to pool their earnings and to hold all property acquired during the relationship in accord with the law governing community property; conversely, they may agree that each partner's earnings and the property acquired from those earnings remains the separate property of the earning partner. So long as the agreement does not rest upon illicit meretricious consideration, the parties may order their economic affairs as they choose, and no policy precludes the courts from enforcing such agreements.

We are aware that many young couples live together without the solemnization of marriage, in order to make sure that they can successfully later undertake marriage. This trial period, preliminary to marriage, serves as some assurance that the marriage will not subsequently end in dissolution to the harm of both parties.

The mores of the society have indeed changed so radically in regard to cohabitation that we cannot impose a standard based on alleged moral considerations that have apparently been so widely abandoned by so many. Lest we be misunderstood, however, we take this occasion to point out that the structure of society itself largely depends upon the institution of marriage, and nothing we have said in this opinion should be taken to derogate from that institution. The joining of the man and woman in marriage is at once the most socially productive and individually fulfilling relationship that one can enjoy in the course of a lifetime. Since we have determined that plaintiff's complaint states a cause of action for breach of an express contract . . . we must conclude that the trial court erred in granting defendant a judgment on the pleadings.

The judgment is reversed and the cause remanded for further proceedings consistent with the views expressed herein.

Case Questions

1. How does the court view the relationship between law and societal morality?

2. Do you agree with the court that granting a remedy in this case does *not* discourage marriage? Explain.

3. Can you identify any faulty assumptions or logic in the opinion?

4. What is the source of public policy according to the court? Is there any problem with this as the sole source of policy? Analyze.

California does not recognize common law marriage. Had California been a jurisdiction that recognized common law marriage, the Marvins would have been married and the break up and property dispute would have been settled in divorce court.

Today, there are a number of homosexuals who choose to live together in a state of ''marriage.'' Breakups often result in ''palimony'' suits, and a number of courts have recognized the enforceability of palimony agreements under similar rationale as in the Marvin case.

Unconscionable Agreements

The doctrine of freedom to contract is further limited by **unconscionable** contracts. Public policy dictates that these contracts be struck down. In some cases, exculpatory clauses fall under this class of contracts. An **exculpatory clause** is one that relieves a person from liability for his or her own negligence or wrongdoing (see Figure 15–3). These clauses will be deemed unconscionable and unenforceable when:

- The clause exempts an employer from liability to an employee.
- The clause exempts a public utility from liability for harm to the public in the provision of a public service.
- The clause exempts a manufacturer or dealer from liability for physical harm to a consumer.

A common thread running through each of these exemptions is a presumed inequality of bargaining power between the contracting parties. For example,

Figure 15–3   Exculpatory Clause

an employee may allow his or her employer to be exempt from liability simply to keep a job. A similar lack of genuine assent to an exculpatory clause may be present when dealing with the economic clout of a public utility or a common carrier.[4]

If the clause exempting the stronger party from liability results from free bargaining, it may be upheld. Suppose a common carrier offers a choice of cheaper service with a disclaimer of liability or more

---

Figure 15–4   Characteristics of Unconscionable Agreements

- Unequal bargaining position.
- Form contracts.
- Exploitation of disadvantaged and uneducated.
- Price of goods exceeds market value of goods.

---

expensive service with no disclaimer. The buyer freely chooses the cheaper service. The clause in such a case would be upheld (see Figure 15–4).

The following case considers the validity of an exculpatory clause in an action for negligent omission of a Yellow Pages advertisement.

[4]A common carrier is a transportation system that holds itself out as being willing to transport any passenger, so long as there is room. Examples would include taxis, buses, trains, and airline services.

DISCOUNT FABRIC HOUSE, INC. v. WISCONSIN TELEPHONE CO.
345 N.W.2d 417 (Wis. 1984)

After carrying the quarter-page advertising display correctly for three years, the telephone company omitted the plaintiff's long-standing trade name, Discount Fabric House, from the display ad. Discount Fabric House commenced an action against Wisconsin Telephone Co. to recover damages for business losses resulting from the telephone company's error in the directory.

The telephone company raised as a defense a disclaimer of liability clause contained in the advertising contract between Discount Fabric House and itself. This clause limited damages to the price of the advertisement. The advertising contract between the telephone company and Discount Fabric House is a form contract that the telephone company uses for all of its Yellow Pages advertising sales. None of the telephone company's employees or agents had the authority to alter any of the terms or provisions of the standard contract, nor had they ever done so. There was never any bargaining on either price or terms with any advertiser; each subscriber in the directory paid exactly the same for the same size listing or advertisement.

The jury determined that Discount Fabric House sustained $9,000 in business damages as a result of the omission of its trade name from its display advertisement. The judge ruled that the clause limiting liability was unconscionable and against public policy and granted judgment on the verdict. The decision was appealed.

The court of appeals reversed the judgment of the trial court. That case was appealed to the Supreme Court of Wisconsin.

STEINMETZ, Justice

The issue in the case is whether the relief from liability provision in the Wisconsin Telephone Company's yellow pages advertising contract is unconscionable and unenforceable as against the public policy of this state.

Some courts have held exculpatory clauses, as in this contract, not unconscionable since allowing damages for the telephone company's negligent acts in publishing the yellow pages would be delving in speculation. In *Willie v. Southwestern Bell Telephone Co.*, that court stated. . . .

"It would be virtually, if not completely, impossible to determine what portion of the business done by an advertiser is attributable to its use of 'Yellow Page' advertising. There are many factors which enter into periodic fluctuations in the volume of business done by a seller of goods. The purpose of the Limitation of Liability Clause is to protect the telephone company from the danger of verdicts primarily speculative in amount. This is not an unreasonable objective."

. . . The telephone company argues for the efficacy of the clause in that not being held economically responsible for its negligent acts in publishing the yellow pages keeps down the rate it charges ad subscribers. That would be an attribute of cost thrift acceptable to all commercial enterprises. In this argument there is an implied threat of advertising rates going up if the Telephone Company is subject to being held financially responsible for its negligent acts of publication. . . . We reject the threatened consequences theory as a criteria for deciding issues. . . . As long as such advertising has value, as it obviously does, there will be those in the public who will subscribe for it. The costs of the ads are only one factor in their attractive value to the public subscribers.

During oral argument, the telephone company admitted to a negligent error factor of 1 or 2 in 1,000 ads in the yellow pages which is .001 or .002, a noteworthy accomplishment which would be difficult to improve. The other 998 to 999 out of 1,000 ad subscribers will not be greatly offended economically if the risk is spread out so that the 1 or 2 out of 1,000 who are damaged due to the company's errors or omissions are not forced, due to the exculpatory clause, to bear their losses without recom-

pense. Also, during oral argument a statement was made by the telephone company attorney that the telephone company carries insurance of $85 million over the basic $1.5 million coverage. This exculpatory clause may have kept the company's insurance premiums down or may have been a bonus for its carrier, but if there is any effect on the rate for the ads, its direct effect in a true case of damages due to the company's neglect will not be an earth-shattering experience but rather one that is diluted many times.

"The Court is satisfied that the plaintiff did not have a meaningful choice, that the defendant had the bargaining power in a gross unbalanced manner in determining the terms and conditions in the directory advertisement which was an indispensable element of telephone service. The customer did not have a free choice nor did he have bargaining power."

This exculpatory clause in the modern commercial world is unconscionable and unenforceable since it is contrary to public policy.

The decision of the court of appeals is reversed.

Case Questions

1. What is the strongest argument Wisconsin Telephone advances in contending for the validity of the clause in this case?

2. Identify key facts that moved the court in favor of Discount Fabric House.

3. How does this decision affect the following basic contract principles:

   a. Freedom of contract.

   b. Certainty and stability in contractual relations.

   c. The requirement of mutual assent.

Discount Fabric suggests that certain contracts are unenforceable because the contract is unconscionable. The Uniform Commercial Code has codified the doctrine of unconscionability in section 2–302.

Several features of UCC section 2–302 should be noted. First, since this section is found in Article 2 of the UCC, it explicitly applies only to the sale of goods. Yet, as is illustrated in *Discount Fabric House,* the doctrine of unconscionability has not been limited to contracts for the sale of

UCC §2–302. Unconscionable Contract or Clause

(1) If the court as a matter of law finds the contract or any clause of the contract to have been unconscionable at the time it was made the court may refuse to enforce the contract, or it may enforce the remainder of the contract without the unconscionable clause, or it may so limit the application of any unconscionable clause as to avoid any unconscionable result.

goods but has overflowed into service contracts, leases, banking, insurance, and real estate contracts as well.

Unconscionability, according to section 2–302, is not determined by a jury but by the court (i.e., the judge). The doctrine of unconscionability permits judges to openly police agreements to ensure that they are fair and equitable. This open policing conflicts with traditional notions of freedom of contract in which parties may agree to unfair bargains.

A court is not limited to a single remedy if it finds the contract to be unconscionable. Rather, it can strike the entire contract, strike only the offending clause, or reform the clause to eliminate any unconscionable element.

Unconscionability has procedural and substantive aspects to it. By *procedural* aspects, we mean that there is something wrong with the way the contract was negotiated (though perhaps not quite so wrong as fraud or duress). Procedural problems indicate that the bargaining *process* was flawed so that one of the parties did not freely or knowingly enter the agreement. Perhaps the contract was orally negotiated in Spanish with a person who speaks only Spanish, yet the written version was in English. Or the agreement may be a form contract presented to a consumer by a merchant on a "take it or leave it" basis. The consumer had no opportunity for negotiation whatever.

By *substantive* aspects, we mean that the actual terms of the contract are unfair and oppressive. For example, the price may be wholly out of line with the market value of the goods. Or a contract clause may limit the buyer's access to normal legal remedies in the case of a dispute.

Some legal scholars have rejected the doctrine of unconscionability as being incompatible with the common law notion that mature parties should be free to make any contracts they wish, even foolish and unfair ones. They view unconscionability as a form of judicial paternalism. Others feel that courts may legitimately meddle with the parties' agreement but only when the bargaining process is flawed. To these scholars, if the contract is knowingly and freely entered, courts should not interfere with the substance of the agreement. Most legal scholars, however, accept the notion that some contracts are so unfair and oppressive that the judiciary cannot in good conscience enforce them. They would encourage courts to police both the substance of the agreement and the process of forming the agreement.

THE EFFECT OF ILLEGALITY

The general rule of contract law is that illegal agreements are unenforceable. **Unenforceability** means that the judicial machinery is unavailable to any party to an illegal transaction. A common law maxim addresses parties to an illegal contract: "the courts will leave the parties where it finds them." Suppose Tennis Outlet agrees with a franchisee to sell tennis balls made of a material that is illegal to market. Tennis Outlet delivers the balls, but the franchisee refuses to pay. The courts will be unavailable to the franchisor to enforce the agreement. This result may seem unfair since the franchisee is unjustly enriched, but the courts' refusal to render aid often deters the making of illegal contracts.

Courts will, however, aid a party to an illegal contract when that party is within the class of persons a statute was designed to protect. For example, suppose that for the sake of public safety a statute prohibits unlicensed contractors from doing electrical work on residential property. Steve, an unlicensed contractor, agrees to do electrical work on Richard's property for $500. Richard seeks to have the money returned to him after learning that Steve is unlicensed. Will the courts help him? The answer is yes. The statute was designed to penalize unlicensed contractors and *protect* consumers. Refusing to give Richard a remedy would defeat the statute's purpose by penalizing the person it was supposed to benefit.

For the same reason, if Steve did the work negligently and Richard sued Steve for the negligence, Steve could not assert his lack of a license as a defense. The statute was designed to protect consumers, not protect unlicensed contractors. Steve cannot turn Richard's shield of protection into a sword to be used against him.

Three doctrines provide relief based on an implied-in-law contract (quasi-contract) even though the bargain is illegal. These doctrines are called pari delicto, excusable ignorance, and severability. **Pari delicto** means equality of fault. Where the parties to an illegal contract are *not* in pari delicto—that is, not equally at fault—the party not equally in the wrong is entitled to restitution.[5] Thus, in one case,[6] a dairy-

---

[5]Restitution permits a party to be restored to the status quo, the position he or she would have been in had the contract not been entered. Thus, the value of the goods or services conferred on the defendant will be returned to the plaintiff.

[6]*Karpinski v. Collins*, 252 Cal. App. 711 (1967).

man was compelled to pay an illegal ''kickback'' to obtain a contract or go out of business. The court permitted the dairyman to recover the illegal payments that were coerced as a result of his extreme business necessity, holding that he was not in pari delicto with the extortioner.

A promisee's **excusable ignorance** of technical legislation or facts also may permit the promisee to recover damages even though the agreement is illegal. Recovery is possible only when the promisor knows of the illegality. In one case,[7] a general contractor hired a subcontractor to work on the city inspector's home. The subcontractor did not know that the work was an illegal bribe. The court permitted the subcontractor to recover from the general contractor.

A third situation permitting recovery (either for damages or restitution) on an illegal contract involves the doctrine of **severability.** Sometimes a contract can be separated into two parts, one of which is legal and enforceable, while the other is illegal and unenforceable. To illustrate, Kate offers Kerry $2,000 in exchange for Kerry's promise to type Kate's dissertation and to water Kate's marijuana plants. The contract may be severable and Kerry could recover a portion of the $2,000 for the legal promise Kerry made.

END–OF–CHAPTER QUESTIONS

1. Do you think it the proper function of a court to determine whether an agreement is moral or immoral? If not, who should make this determination?

2. What remedies might a court employ if it finds that a covenant not to compete is overbroad?

3. Are there good reasons for enforcing a revenue-raising statute and not enforcing an agreement made in violation of a licensing statute?

4. Define unconscionability. What problems does the doctrine of unconscionability pose for contract law? Do you think the doctrine's benefits outweigh its liabilities? Analyze.

5. Compare and contrast the doctrines that mitigate the harshness of the rule that the court leaves the parties to an illegal agreement where it finds them.

6. Donnelley, a commercial printer, set up a deferred compensation plan for its executives. The plan specified that a participant who competed directly with the firm within three years after leaving would forfeit all deferred compensation. Jack Briggs, a vice president of Donnelly, left the company and became president of a competing corporation. Briggs contended that the forfeiture provisions violated public policy as applied to his situation. Do you agree? Explain. Does the lack of a geographic limitation present a problem? See *Briggs v. R.R. Donnelley & Sons*, 589 F.2d 39 (1st Cir. 1978).

7. Herbert Vedder did contracting work on the home of Harry and Alice Spellman. At the time this work was performed, the plaintiffs were not licensed to do contracting work. A Washington statute read in part, ''It shall be unlawful for any person to submit any bid or do any work as a contractor until such person shall have been issued a certificate of registration by the state department of licenses. . . . A violation of this section shall be a misdemeanor.'' The Spellmans stopped payment on a $2,500 check claiming the contract was illegal. May Vedder recover on the check? Explain. Would the quasi-contract doctrine of pari delicto apply to this case? Explain. See *Vedder v. Spellman*, 480 P.2d 207 (Wash. 1971).

8. An attorney advised his client to lie under oath during a bankruptcy proceeding. Although the client was not charged with perjury, the lie did result in damages to others. An implied contract exists between a client and his or her attorney that an attorney will advise the client in the best way possible; this contract was clearly broken here. The client sued for damages. Can the client invoke the doctrine of in pari delicto and recover against the attorney? Explain. See *Evans v. Cameron*, 360 N.W.2d 25 (Wis. 1985).

---

[7]*Roylex, Inc. v. Avco Community Developers*, 559 S.W. 2d 833 (Tex. Civ. App. 1977).

9. A former franchisee of a national beauty pageant signed a contract that contained a covenant not to compete. According to the franchise agreement, the franchisee could not work for any other beauty pageant in any capacity for five years after leaving this franchise. The clause only referred to four neighboring states and prohibited the franchisee from working in teenage pageants only. If the franchisee later works for a teenage pageant in a neighboring state as a stage hand or judge, is there any recourse for the franchisor? Analyze. See *National Teenager Co. v. Scarborough*, 330 S.E.2d 711 (Ga. 1985).

10. Upon opening his account with a bank, a depositor signed an agreement to accept all of the bank's charges and policies. The depositor bounced a check and was charged $15 for processing fees. When he found that the actual processing fee was only 50 cents, he sued the bank, claiming the charge was unconscionably high. Will he win? Why or why not?

Chapter 16

Contracts in Writing

■

CRITICAL THINKING INQUIRIES

As you read this chapter, you should be able to address the following:

- What is the reason for requiring certain contracts to be evidenced by a writing? Is the reason still justified?
- Extract the common denominators of each of the transactions that require a written memorandum.
- How does the law mitigate the impact of the writing requirement?
- What is the parol evidence rule, and under what circumstances might it cause an injustice?
- What are the reasons behind the rules of interpreting contracts?

MANAGERIAL PERSPECTIVE

Richard Pace has just been promoted to supervisory administrator of Chief Construction Company, a small family-owned general contractor business. The company is involved in refurbishing old homes and supplying other contractors with building materials. It also has another related division, Chief Construction Financing (headed by Lisa Pace), that is involved in various aspects of consumer financing.

The Paces have, in the past, used some rough form contracts for their business agreements and, on occasion, entered into some oral contracts. Recently, they have been involved in litigation, and on a number of occasions technical issues involving the interpretation of contracts and the statute of frauds — requiring certain contracts to be evidenced by a writing — have arisen. The Paces need greater knowledge about what contracts need to be in writing, particularly:

- When is the statute of frauds applicable?
- What is required to satisfy the statute of frauds?
- What is the consequence of not satisfying the statute of frauds?
- When is it proper to look outside the written contract for additional terms of the contract?
- How are contracts interpreted?

Figure 16–1   Selected Contracts within the Statute of Frauds and Exceptions

Statute of Frauds	Exceptions
Suretyship agreements	Main purpose doctrine
Contracts for the sale of land	Part performance
Promises not perform-able within one year	Part performance
Contracts for the sale of goods for $500 or more	Specially manufactured goods Admissions Part performance Merchant's exception

This area of contracts in writing is an exception to the general rule that contracts need not be in writing. It is an area that businesses need to understand because of the drastic consequences of noncompliance. Some simple principles contained in this chapter will help businesses such as Chief Construction Company and its related concern.

This chapter covers the historical background of the writing requirement, the requirements of the writing, and the classes of contracts covered by the requirement. The chapter concludes with the rules and principles of interpreting the contract.

HISTORICAL BACKGROUND

In England, before the 14th century, oral promises could not be enforced in courts. As courts gradually began recognizing oral contracts as enforceable, perjured testimony became common. Witnesses often disagreed. Rules of evidence at the time prohibited the parties, their spouses, or anyone else interested in the outcome of a legal proceeding from testifying in court. This only aggravated the perjury problem. A merchant named in a breach of contract action, for example, had to sit silently while acquaintances and strangers falsely testified that the merchant orally agreed to sell certain goods.

To combat this problem, the English Parliament, in 1677, passed the Act for the Prevention of Fraud and Perjuries, commonly known as the statute of frauds. This statute denoted types of contracts that would be unenforceable unless evidenced by a signed writing (see Figure 16–1). Apparently these types of contracts were the most frequent subjects of abuse and fraud. The English statute of frauds was generally imported to the United States and adopted by state legislatures.

SATISFYING THE WRITING REQUIREMENT

The statute of frauds requires a writing as a means of preventing false testimony about the existence or nonexistence of a contract. But it serves other purposes as well. A writing is a more certain basis for evidencing the terms of a contract than a person's memory. Requiring a signed writing also cautions an individual about the seriousness of the transaction that is about to be undertaken. It is relatively easy to make a heedless oral promise. Adding formalities such as a handshake promotes additional deliberation and caution. Requiring a signature and a writing promotes even more deliberation.

The statute of frauds requires the enumerated classes of contracts to be evidenced by a signed writing. This writing may consist of a deed, note, letter, invoice, payroll card, statement of account, check, bill, or any other written memorandum evidencing the essential terms of the contract. The writing requirement may even be satisfied by a series of memoranda, such as several letters, evidencing the contract.

A **memorandum** must be sufficient for a court to determine the essential terms of the contract and the remedy on breach. The memorandum must ordinarily state:

- The names of the parties to the contract.
- A description of the property definite enough to identify the contract's subject matter.
- The essential terms of the contract such as warranties, credit terms, and time and place of payment.
- The price.
- A signature by the party against whom enforcement is sought.

The Uniform Commercial Code takes a more liberal approach to the memorandum requirement than the common law. For transactions involving the sale of goods, UCC section 2–201 requires only that the quantity of goods be written and that the writing indicate that the parties made a contract for sale.

Figure 16–2   Suretyship Agreement

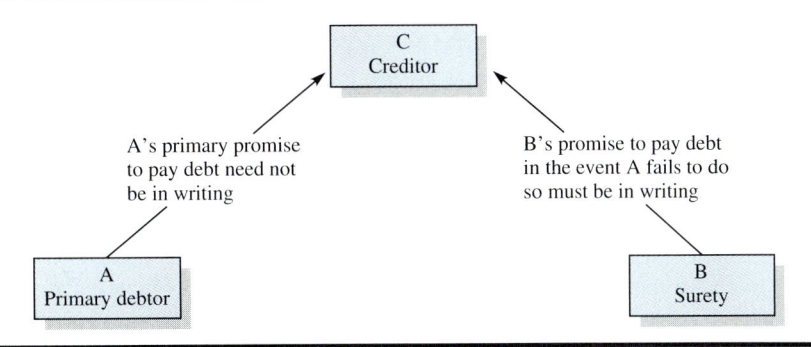

Price, warranty, payment terms, and other essential elements of the contract may be proven by oral testimony. Nor is there, under the Code, a need to name the parties to the contract. A signature by the party against whom enforcement is sought suffices. An invoice that states, "I agree to sell you 75 bushels of tomatoes, signed S. Seller," probably meets the memorandum requirements of the Code against S. Seller. However, it does not meet the more stringent requirements of a nongoods common law transaction.

CLASSES OF CONTRACT COVERED BY THE STATUTE OF FRAUDS

The following types of contracts covered by the statute of frauds are considered in this section: suretyship agreements, estate representative agreements, contracts for the sale of land, promises not to be performed within one year, contracts for the sale of goods, and other classes of contracts.

Suretyship Agreements

An agreement to answer for another's debt on condition that it is not paid by the original debtor is within the statute of frauds. This is called a **suretyship agreement.** In a suretyship agreement, there are

- Three parties.
- Two promises to pay.
- The second promise to pay is *conditional* on nonperformance of the first promise to pay.

For example, assume that Chief Construction Financing extends a loan to Homebuyer, and requires Homebuyer to have a third-party coguarantor on the loan as primarily liable along with Homebuyer. This would not be considered a suretyship agreement, and hence not covered by the statute. Although there are three parties, and two promises to pay, the third party is not conditionally liable but primarily liable. However, if the third party agrees to pay only in the event Homebuyer fails to pay, then we have a surety agreement within the statute that requires a writing; otherwise, the third party would not be liable (see Figure 16–2).

The Main Purpose Doctrine

Courts have carved out a major exception to the statute's writing requirement in cases of suretyship agreements. Where the surety's **main purpose** in making the agreement is to secure a business or economic self-advantage, an oral promise to pay the debt of another is enforceable. For example, suppose Nancy owes John $10,000. Nancy also owes Elliot $100,000. John is about to force Nancy into bankruptcy. If John were to do this, Elliot would suffer an economic loss since Nancy would be put out of business. Elliot therefore promises to guarantee Nancy's debt if John forgoes filing an involuntary bankruptcy petition. Elliot's main purpose in making this promise is to secure an economic benefit for himself. As such, an oral promise of suretyship would be enforceable as an exception to the statute under the main purpose doctrine.

The following case discusses the main purpose doctrine.

HOWARD M. SCHOOR ASSOCIATES, INC. v. HOLMDEL HEIGHTS CONST'N CO.

343 A 2d 401 (N.J. 1975)

The plaintiffs, two engineering and surveying firms, brought this action to recover amounts due for professional services rendered by them to the defendant, Holmdel Heights Construction Company. Holmdel Heights was insolvent and the suit proceeded, in effect, solely against the defendant Alan Sugarman. The plaintiffs claim that Sugarman, an attorney, personally undertook to pay for the services rendered. Sugarman defended on the factual ground that even had he made such a promise, it would be unenforceable under the statute of frauds since it was not in writing.

The trial judge found in favor of the plaintiffs and entered judgment against Sugarman in the amount of $24,105.30, together with interest. The Appellate Division reversed the judgment. The plaintiffs appealed to the New Jersey Supreme Court.

MOUNTAIN, Judge

It is conceded by everyone that the promise was not in writing, nor was there any written memorandum or note thereof. Defendant contends that the promise—again assuming it to have been made—obligated him only secondarily to pay the debt owed by Holmdel Heights Construction Company in the event it should default, and that as such it comes squarely within the purview of the statute. Plaintiffs argue that the promise was made largely if not principally for defendant's personal benefit, that it did not create a suretyship relationship but rather was an "original" promise resting upon consideration sought by defendant for his personal ends, and that this being so the promise is not controlled by the statute. This latter argument rests upon what is sometimes referred to as the "leading object or main purpose rule."

[I]n applying this rule, which we think expresses sound doctrine, it becomes important, and probably decisive, to determine what interest, purpose or object was sought to be advanced by defendant's promise to pay plaintiff's fees. . . . [D]efendant owned slightly more than 18 percent of the capital stock of Holmdel Heights Construction Company, for which he had paid $10,000. He was also attorney for the corporation and at the time of trial . . . was still owed $14,000 for services. Defendant, in the course of his testimony, agreed that had the corporation eventually been successful, the amount he would have received upon his investment, together with reasonably anticipated legal fees, would have been a substantial sum.

On the other hand, defendant was acting as counsel for the development corporation and presumably, in this capacity, was doing all he could to maintain its solvency and to further its best interests. The consideration that was sought and received from plaintiffs took the form of a continuing professional effort on their part to provide the developer with vital materials and data intended to become part of its submission to a finance agency in connection with its application for a substantial loan. Obviously this consideration would be of benefit both to defendant personally, even though indirectly, as well as to the client he served.

The leading object or main purpose rule has been set forth in the *Restatement of Contracts* in the following form:

Where the consideration for a promise that all or part of a previously existing duty of a third person to the promisee shall be satisfied is in fact or apparently desired by the promisor mainly for his own pecuniary or business advantage, rather than in order to benefit the third person, the promise is not within [the statute of frauds].

The interest of defendant, Sugarman, in inducing plaintiffs to undertake the work that they did seems obvious. His substantial pecuniary and business interest to be furthered is abundantly clear. On the other hand there is little to support the view that he meant to commit his personal assets to so considerable an extent only to further his client's interest. We have no difficulty in agreeing with the trial court and with the dissenting member of the Appellate Division that the consideration was *mainly* desired for his personal benefit.

Accordingly the judgment of the Appellate Division is reversed.

Case Questions

1. State the issue in this case.
2. Evaluate: ''If the promisor's main purpose is to secure a benefit for himself or herself, it is not a suretyship agreement at all.''
3. What if the motives of Sugarman were equally to benefit his client and himself? What is the result? Explain.
4. Is justice served here? Analyze.

Estate Representative Agreements

Another type of contract within the statute of frauds is a promise of a representative of an estate to personally pay a debt of the decedent. This requires a writing and protects the representative from being bound by an impulsive oral agreement to pay the decedent's debts. For example, assume an executor of an estate (see Chapter 10) makes an oral promise to the funeral home to pay the funeral expenses of the decedent. The agreement would be unenforceable against the executor since it is within the statute of frauds and not in writing.

Contracts for the Sale of Land

Generally, contracts for the sale of an interest in land are within the statute of frauds and require a writing. Interests in land are thoroughly treated in Chapter 9. They include the transfer of land and anything attached to it such as buildings. Most states, however, enforce short-term *oral* leases of one year or less duration.

Easements are interests in land. An **easement** is simply the right to use another's land. To be enforceable, the grant of an easement for the running of wires, railroads, pipes, cables, and roads across land must be in writing. Easements that arise by operation of law and not by the parties' agreement, however, need not be in writing. For example, a right of way may be implied from a land-locked piece of property to a roadway. No writing would be required in this case.

Mortgages are also considered a transfer of an interest in land. A **mortgage** secures repayment of a loan by taking a security interest in land and/or buildings. As such, it falls under the land prong of the statute of frauds and must therefore be in writing.

The Doctrine of Part Performance

Under what has become known as the doctrine of part performance, when a buyer relies on an oral promise to sell land and partly performs, the oral contract is enforceable. Courts examine the character of the buyer's performance in shaping a remedy. If the buyer has simply paid money in response to the seller's oral promise to sell land, the buyer is only entitled to a return of the money. If the buyer has actually made improvements on the land, such as building a house, the buyer is entitled to obtain the land through a decree of specific performance. Many cases obviously fall between the extremes of mere payment of money and actually going on the land and building a home. The following case discusses an in-between situation and the proper judicial remedy.

GEGG v. KIEFER

655 S.W.2d 834 (Mo. Ct. App. 1983)

Joseph P. Kiefer, appellant, and his wife, owned a 274-acre tract of land. Approximately 70 acres of this tract was farm land. Francis ''Franco'' Gegg, respondent, farmed the land as a tenant on a ''cash-rent'' basis.

Respondent attended to the upkeep of the Kiefer property. He maintained the gravel road, cleaned out the creek bed, cleared brush and weeds, and improved the land's drainage system. The farm's productivity increased considerably. Kiefer was pleased with his tenant's work and over the years on unspecified occasions told him, "Now, Franco, you take care of this land because someday it will be your own."

On one occasion, Kiefer stated: "Franco, now as soon as I get on my feet . . . I want to sell you this farm; as soon as I get on my feet we'll take care of this." He indicated to Kiefer that he would sell it for $45,000. Kiefer responded, "Well, that sounds good enough to me." Respondent visited a local banker in order to arrange a $45,000 loan. And, he went out and bought a corn planter.

Kiefer took ill and went to the hospital. While there he indicated that he "had turned everything over" to his nephew, William. Kiefer died having made no plans with his nephew to transfer his property to respondent.

Gegg sued the estate and the trial court found in his favor granting specific performance. The estate appealed.

PUDLOWSKI, Judge

Respondent urges us to believe that the totality of the evidence supported the trial court's finding of an oral contract and was sufficient to overcome the bar of the Statute of Frauds. The Statute of Frauds in Missouri provides:

No action shall be brought . . . upon any contract made for the sale of lands, . . . unless the agreement upon which the action shall be brought . . . shall be in writing and signed by the party to be charged therewith.

An oral contract to convey land falls within the literal ambit of the Statute of Frauds and so will not be enforced at law. However, equity will decree specific performance where a party has so far acted on the promise that to deny him the benefit of the agreement would be unjust. This resort to equity avails sparingly, and only upon clear and convincing proof of a definite agreement. The elements of proof required by equity for the specific performance of an oral contract to convey real estate . . . have been uniformly followed. . . .

(1) the alleged oral contract must be clear, explicit, and definite; (2) it must be proven as pleaded; (3) such contract cannot be established by conversations either too ancient on the one hand or too loose or casual upon the other; (4) the alleged oral contract must itself be fair, and not unconscionable; (5) the proof of the contract as pleaded must be such as to leave no reasonable doubt in the mind of the chancellor that the contract as alleged was in fact made, and that the full performance, so far as lies in the hands of the parties to perform, has been had; (6) and the work constituting performance must be such as is referable solely to the contract as sought to be enforced and not such as might be reasonably referable to some other and different con-

tract; (7) the contract must be one based upon an adequate and legal consideration, so that its performance upon the one hand, but not upon the other, would bespeak an unconscionable advantage and wrong, demanding in good conscience relief in equity; (8) proof of mere disposition to devise by will or convey by deed by way of gift, or as a reward for services, is not sufficient, but there must be shown a real contract to devise by will or convey by deed made before the acts of performance relied upon were had.

More recent Missouri cases have recognized the legal principal that oral promises to convey real estate may be enforced, where the plaintiff has partially performed, or has done other acts in reliance of such promises, and thereby has changed his position so materially "that to invoke the statute to deny the performer the benefit of the agreement would itself amount to a fraud." These cases seem to support relaxation of "full performance," the fifth requirement as set forth above.

. . . We note that there is no showing of part performance by respondent to require enforcement of the contract. The initial occupancy of the farm by respondent was as a tenant under an oral agreement to pay an annual cash rental and with the obligation to maintain the property. Work performed on the property was necessary to make it productive and as previously stated, such work was self-beneficial. The act of purchasing the corn planter was not dispositive of a specific act arising from the agreement to purchase Kiefer's property. At the time of purchase, respondent was farming two additional parcels of land. Furthermore, respondent told the dealer that he only "thought" he was going to keep the Kiefer property. The evidence which revealed that he *was* arranging to borrow $45,000 from the bank was merely tentative. . . .

It is the legislature and not Kiefer that has made the contract in this case unenforceable. We find no basis to remove this case from the operation of the statute of frauds.

The judgment is reversed.

Case Questions

1. What is the issue in this case?
2. Why was Gegg unable to recover? Under what circumstance could Gegg have recovered? Is the difference too subtle?
3. Distinguish the doctrine of part performance and promissory estoppel discussed in Chapter 14. Would Gegg have fared any better under the doctrine of promissory estoppel?
4. Do you agree with the court that it would be inappropriate to grant Gegg relief apart from a legislative amendment of the law? Analyze.

Promises Not to Be Performed within One Year

To protect against the problems resulting from the dimming of memories, the statute of frauds required a writing for any agreement that was not to be performed within the space of one year. A year, according to the *Restatement (Second) Contracts,* "ends at midnight of the anniversary of the day on which the contract is made." Thus, an oral contract entered at 6 P.M. on July 1, 1994 must be performable before midnight of July 1, 1995, to be enforceable.

As with the construction given other aspects of the statute of frauds, courts have narrowed the scope of the one-year provision. Generally, only those promises that by *the very terms* of the contract could not be performed (are not possibly performable) within one year are within the statute. Thus, a 13-month employment contract or a promise to deliver milk for two years would be within the statute. The very *terms* of the contract do not permit performance within a year.

However, if performance might possibly be completed within one year, despite the parties' expectations or actual subsequent events, the contract is outside the statute. For example, Chief Construction Corp. and Office Building, Inc., orally contract for the construction of an office building. The parties anticipate that construction will take sixteen months. The oral contract is nevertheless enforceable since it possibly, though improbably, could be performed within a year.

Many contracts are of uncertain duration because of a contingency in the contract that can discharge performance at any time. An employment contract "for life" is of uncertain duration. As long as the contingency that discharges performance could occur within one year, the contract is outside the statute and hence does not require a writing. Hence, the oral contract for employment would be outside of the statute since the contingency—the death of the person—could occur within a year.

Contracts for the Sale of Goods

Contracts for the sale of goods are within the statute of frauds if the price for the goods is $500 or more. In such a case, according to UCC section 2–201(1), there must be a writing sufficient to indicate that a contract for sale was made and the writing must be "signed[1] by the party against whom enforcement is sought."

UCC section 2–201 contains four exceptions to this writing requirement. These exceptions make *oral* contracts enforceable even when the price of the goods is $500 or more.

Specially Manufactured Goods

Contracts for goods that are to be **specially manufactured** for the buyer are enforceable even though not in writing. For this exception to apply, the goods must not be suitable for sale to others, must indicate they are for the buyer, and the seller must have made commitments toward their manufacture. To illustrate, a buyer orally agrees to purchase an $800 initial ring from a local jeweler. The jeweler carves a wax model, pours the cast, and then learns that the

---

[1] "Signed" includes any symbol executed or adopted by a party with present intention to authenticate a writing [UCC § 1–201(39)]. Thus, initials, a last name, or even an "X" may be a signing.

buyer wishes to repudiate the contract. This oral contract is enforceable under the ''specially manufactured'' goods exception to the statute of frauds since it meets the criteria listed above.

Admissions

Agreements that are *admitted* to by the party against whom enforcement is sought, in a pleading or testimony, are enforceable. Even without a writing, a defendant who admits in a deposition or in sworn testimony that an oral agreement existed will be bound by the admission.

Past Performance

Agreements concerning goods for which *payment has been made and accepted* are enforceable even without a writing. For example, suppose Chief Construction Corp. orally contracted with Ace Apartments to deliver 30 washers to the apartment building at $200 a washer. Ace paid $1,000 as a down payment, but now repudiates the oral agreement. Ace would be bound to the oral agreement, but only for the amount paid—that is, $1,000 (or five washers). Chief Construction could not enforce the remainder of the contract for the other 25 washers without a writing.

Agreements concerning goods that have been *received and accepted* are also enforceable even in the absence of a writing. Using the previous example, suppose Chief Construction delivered 10 of the 30 washers, and Ace accepted this delivery. Ace would be bound to pay for the 10 washers but no others.

Merchant Silence

A unique exception to the UCC's signature requirement is found in UCC section 2–201(2). Under the exception, a confirmation of an oral contract sent by one merchant to another that is received within a reasonable time will satisfy the requirements of the statute of frauds even though the recipient does not

Figure 16–3   Merchant's Exception to Statute of Frauds

- Both parties to the transaction must be merchants.
- The writing must be *in confirmation* of a contract.
- The writing must be sufficient to indicate that a contract for sale has been made.
- The writing must be received in a reasonable time.
- The recipient must have reason to know *of its contents.*
- The recipient must not have objected within 10 days of receipt.

sign the confirmation. The recipient, however, must have reason to know its contents and must not object within ten days of receipt (see Figure 16–3). This is treated in Chapter 19.

Other Classes of Contracts

Historically, courts have shown little sympathy for the statute and have narrowed its coverage considerably. At the same time, many state legislatures have added additional classes of contracts to the original statute, deeming these unenforceable unless evidenced by a signed writing. Three of these most commonly found statutes are:

- Statutes requiring a writing to enforce a debt discharged by bankruptcy proceedings or barred by the statute of limitations.
- Statutes requiring a writing to enforce a promise to pay a real estate broker's commission.
- Statutes requiring a writing to enforce a promise to leave property in a will.

To be safe, a person must examine a particular state's statutes to make sure that all writing requirements are complied with fully. A simple rule of thumb is this: ''When in doubt, put it in writing.'' The following reading, however, if accepted, would eliminate most provisions discussed in this chapter.

Abolishing the Statute of Frauds*

Perhaps the time has come for the death knell of the statute of frauds as we know it. Its origin dates back to 17th century England and was enacted as a reaction to fraud and deception that

*Source: Elliot Klayman, ''Abolishing the Statute of Frauds,'' ©Elliot Klayman 1993. Reprinted with permission.

accompanied a number of important transactions. Imported to the United States, it remains in essentially the same form today as it did over three centuries ago. . . . The statute presents pitfalls for the unwary and should be abolished to avoid the hypertechnicality of its application.

■ ■ ■

There are at least three compelling reasons why the statute should be abolished.

■ ■ ■

The exceptions that have grown up around the statute of frauds have all but eaten up its purpose. The part performance doctrine takes the contract out of the statute when the contract is partially executed. Although the degree of execution necessary to remove it from the statute is variable depending upon the jurisdiction, nonetheless, this exception swallows up a considerable number of the cases. The main purpose doctrine, admissions under oath, and specially manufactured goods, are other exceptions eating away at the rule. Then there is great liberality afforded by the courts in determining whether the writing requirement has been met. A memorandum may be woven together by various jottings and scribblings, whereas the testimony of witnesses are discounted. In reality, probably only few remain, that are deprived of the benefit of their bargain, because they do not have a sufficient writing to satisfy the statute. These are undoubtedly the unsophisticated who must suffer the loss.

Then secondly, there are many important types of contracts that are not governed by the statute. For example, a contract for employment for life would not be within the statute because it is performable within one year. A high technology consulting contract may fall outside of the statute even though it may involve millions of dollars, and great complexity. This is a form of discrimination against certain contracts with very little, if any, rationality for distinction.

Thirdly, there is the ethical component. Do we trust the parties to tell the truth when relating certain contracts and not others? Are not our judicial institutions set up to get at the truth, something juries are called upon to do everyday. The prudent business person will usually reduce contracts to writing. They have the resources to do so, staffs, and attorneys, the things the ''little guys'' lack.

■ ■ ■

Let's put everybody and every contract on equal footing and trust the system to weed out truth from fiction based upon credible evidence.

Thought Questions

1. What are the strong arguments of this article?
2. What are the weak arguments?
3. Is there any inconsistency in the author's arguments? Explain.
4. Can you make a case for requiring all executory contracts to be in writing in order to be enforceable?

THE PAROL EVIDENCE RULE

Once the parties do reduce their agreement to a writing, that writing will control over previous inconsistent expressions and understandings. Under the parol evidence rule, **parol evidence**—that is, evidence (either oral or written) that is outside or extrinsic to the writing—cannot be introduced into court to contradict or modify a later written agreement. The parol evidence rule does not require an agreement be in writing to be legally binding. The statute of frauds does that. The parol evidence rule merely states that *if an agreement is in writing,* certain evidence (parol) is excluded that would contradict the writing.

The parol evidence rule has no application to extrinsic or outside agreements made *after* the writing. It only applies to agreements made *prior* to the writing. To illustrate, Chief Construction Co. and Jeremy sign a written agreement for the sale and purchase of a refurbished house. Chief Construction orally warrants that the house is free of termites, although there is nothing in the agreement to this effect. If the house turns out to be infested with termites, may Jeremy introduce Chief Construction's oral promise of a warranty into evidence? The answer is probably not if the promise of a warranty was made *before* the sales agreement was reduced to writing. In contrast, if it was made after the writing, Jeremy may introduce the oral promise of a warranty.

The parol evidence rule only applies if the writing is *intended to be the final and complete expression of the parties' agreement.* A final and complete written expression is called a **total integration.** An incomplete expression is called a **partial integration.**

Prior agreements that *supplement* the writing by adding *consistent* additional terms are admissible as long as the writing is a *partial integration.* To illustrate a "consistent additional term," assume Chief Construction and Consumer agree in writing that Chief Construction is to convey a deed for Farmacre to Consumer, and Consumer will pay $40,000 "within 30 days of the signing of this agreement." Nothing is said in the writing about the place of delivery of the deed. Chief Construction may introduce into evidence a prior oral agreement that the deed and money were to be exchanged at its main office. This would be considered a consistent, additional term.

Previous agreements that *contradict* the writing are excluded by the parol evidence rule. Thus, if the writing says, "Goods to be delivered by January 15," and a prior oral agreement permits the goods to be delivered by January 30, the prior oral agreement is excluded. This is true even if the writing is only a partial integration.

The following court was called on to determine whether an oral addition to a written contract would be given effect.

MASTERSON v. SINE
436 P.2d 561 (Calif. 1968)

Dallas Masterson and his wife conveyed a ranch to Medora and Lu Sine. In the deed, they reserved to "the Grantors [the Mastersons] an option to repurchase the property on or before February 25, 1968." After the sale, Mr. Masterson was adjudged bankrupt and his trustee sought to enforce Masterson's option to repurchase the property.

At trial, the court determined that the parol evidence rule precluded the admission of extrinsic evidence offered by the defendants, Medora and Lu Sine, to show that the parties intended that the property be kept in the Masterson family. (Medora is Mr. Masterson's sister.) The court entered judgment for the Mastersons, declaring their right to exercise the option. The Sines appealed.

TRAYNOR, Chief Judge

When the parties to a written contract have agreed to it as an "integration"—a complete and final embodiment of the terms of an agreement—parol evidence cannot be used to add to or vary its terms. When only part of the agreement is integrated, the same rule applies to that part, but parol evidence may be used to prove elements of the agreement not reduced to writing.

The crucial issue in determining whether there has been an integration is whether the parties intended their writing to serve as the exclusive embodiment of their agreement. The instrument itself may help to resolve that issue. It may state, for example, that "there are no previous understandings or agreements not contained in the writing," and thus express the parties' "intention to nullify antecedent understandings or agreements." Any such collateral agreement itself must be examined, however, to determine whether the parties intended the subject of negotiation it deals with to be included in, excluded from, or otherwise affected by the writing. Circumstances at the time of the writing may also aid in the determination of such integration.

In formulating the rule governing parol evidence, several policies must be accommodated. One policy is based on the assumption that written evidence is more accurate than human memory. This policy, however, can be adequately served by excluding parol evidence of agreements that directly contradict the writing. Another policy is based on the fear that fraud or unintentional invention by witnesses interested in the outcome of the litigation will mislead the finder of facts.

Evidence of oral collateral agreements should be excluded only when the fact finder is likely to be misled. The rule must therefore be based on the credibility of the evidence. One such standard, adopted by section 240(1)(b) of the *Restatement of Contracts*, permits proof of a collateral agreement if it "is such an agreement as might *naturally* be made as a separate agreement by parties situated as were the parties to the written contract." . . . The draftsmen of the Uniform Commercial Code would exclude the evidence in still fewer instances: "If the additional terms are such that, if agreed upon, they would *certainly* have been included in the document in the view of the court, then evidence of their alleged making must be kept from the trier of fact."

The option clause in the deed in the present case does not explicitly provide that it contains the complete agreement and the deed is silent on the question of assignability [of the option]. Moreover, the difficulty of accommodating the formalized structure of a deed to the insertion of collateral agreements makes it less likely that all the terms of such an agreement were included. The statement of the reservation of the option might well have been placed in the recorded deed solely to preserve the grantors' rights against any possible future purchasers and this function could well be served without any mention of the parties' agreement that the option was personal. There is nothing in the record to indicate that the parties to this family transaction, through experience in land transactions or otherwise, had any warning of the disadvantages of failing to put the whole agreement in the deed. This case is one, therefore, in which it can be said that a collateral agreement such as that alleged "might naturally be made as a separate agreement." [Logically, then], the case is not one in which the parties "would certainly" have included the collateral agreement in the deed.

In the present case defendants offered evidence that the parties agreed that the option was not assignable in order to keep the property in the Masterson family. The trial court erred in excluding that evidence.

The judgment is reversed.

Case Questions

1. What issue does this case present?
2. Can you point to any language in the case that indicates that the judge is just constructing reasoning to achieve a predetermined result?
3. Analyze: "Evidence of oral collateral agreements should be excluded only when the fact finder is likely to be misled."
4. How could the parties have avoided a lawsuit?

THE INTERPRETATION OF CONTRACTS

Interpretation is the process of ascertaining the meaning of words used by parties to a written contract. Of course, words seldom have only one meaning. In any given case, the local or trade usage given a particular term may be quite different than its general meaning. To illustrate, a buyer orders from a seller 600 size 7 felt hats. In the felt industry, "felt" means not less than 80 percent felt cloth. In common usage, "felt" means 100 percent felt cloth. Should its general meaning or its meaning in this trade control?

Worse yet, terms within a particular contract may be inconsistent. For example, a printed form contract for the sale of a house may state: "The consideration shall include all window shades and curtains." Immediately below this printed form language the seller writes in pen: "seller to keep all curtains." Will the printed or the written term control?

Figure 16-4   Priorities for Interpreting Contracts

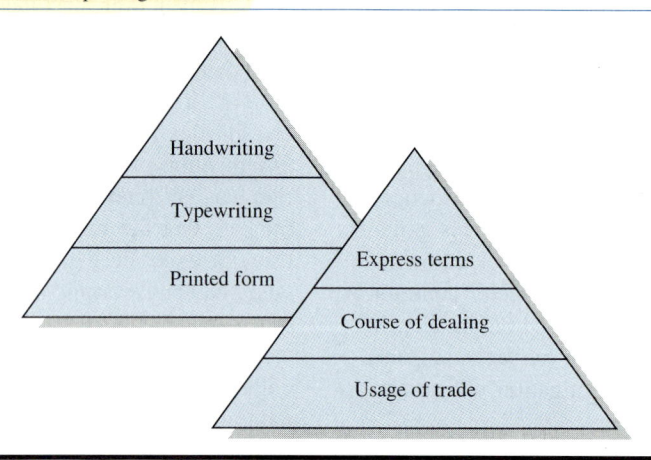

Courts have developed a number of rules that aid in interpreting an agreement. When a contract may be interpreted in two ways, one that renders it legal and the other illegal, the legal interpretation is preferred. The theory here is that the parties are presumed to enter into lawful enforceable contracts.

Language in a contract will be interpreted most strongly against the party drafting it, since that party is in the best position to avoid mistakes in its drafting and make the wording clear. To illustrate, an insurance policy drafted by an insurance company rendered it liable for damages arising from "*the use of the automobile.*" The insured used the automobile as a gun rest and he fired at some passing deer. A passenger in the car was killed when the bullet struck the top of the car and deflected downward. The insurance company argued against its liability, claiming "use" meant *only as a vehicle.* The court held for the insured stating that if the company intended this limitation, it ought to have more clearly drafted its policy contract.[2]

Words will be interpreted in the light of all surrounding circumstances prior to and contemporaneous with the writing. While the parol evidence rule bars *modifications* or *contradictions* of an integrated written agreement, most courts permit testimony of the surrounding circumstances to ascertain the *meaning* of the writing. Assume for example that

Chief Construction agrees to locate a "speculative home" for buyer. The surrounding circumstances, including the language of the industry, may be consulted to ascertain the meaning of speculative home. In addition, extraneous evidence will be admitted to prove fraud, duress, undue influence, and lack of capacity.

Sometimes the conflict between printed terms and typewritten or handwritten terms in a contract cannot be harmonized to give effect to all terms. In such a case, handwritten provisions prevail over typed provisions, and typed provisions prevail over printed provisions (see Figure 16-4).

The Uniform Commercial Code establishes the following hierarchy concerning the source of interpretation that prevails when terms conflict: express terms of a contract, prior course of dealing, and usage of trade, respectively (see Figure 16-4).

Course of dealing is the sequence of past conduct between the parties. It forms the basis for understanding or interpreting the contract. To illustrate, assume Trucker Transportation and Grocer, Inc. had previously contracted over the years concerning the sale of goods, and Trucker Transportation had always delivered the goods to Grocer's place of business. Trucker Transportation and Grocer enter a new contract for similar goods, and it simply states, "delivery to take place Oct. 5, 1994." A court would use the prior course of dealing to interpret "delivery" to mean delivery at Grocer's place of business. Usage of trade is simply the prevailing custom in the industry.

---

[2]See *Payne v Southern Guaranty Insurance Co.,* 282 S.E.2d 711 (Ga. App. 1981).

END–OF–CHAPTER QUESTIONS

1. England repealed most of the original statute of frauds in 1954. In contrast, many American state legislatures have added more types of contracts to those originally covered by the original statute. From a business and public policy perspective, which approach is sounder? Analyze.

2. What policies are served by the parol evidence rule? What are its drawbacks? Who is favored by strict adherence to the rule? Who is injured by strict adherence to the rule?

3. Which of the following agreements is within the statute of frauds? Justify your answer.
   a. The construction of a building estimated to take three years to build.
   b. The furnishing of accounting services ''so long as the promisee needs them.''
   c. An installment contract requiring 13 monthly deliveries.
   d. A contract for personal stationery with the purchaser's name and address engraved on it for a price of $200.

4. In the parable of the good Samaritan, Jesus of Nazareth tells of a person who is beaten, robbed, and left on the side of the road. Several people pass the person by but a Samaritan cares for him, taking the victim to a local inn and stating to the innkeeper: ''Take care of him, and whatever more you spend, when I return, I will repay you'' (Luke 10:35, *New American Standard Bible*). Is the Samaritan's oral promise enforceable? Explain.

5. An uncle orally promised his nephew that the uncle would will a certain piece of land to the nephew if the nephew would leave Greece and come to America. The nephew left Greece, settled his family in the United States, learned English, and worked on the land for a number of years. After the uncle died, the nephew learned that all the land was left to the uncle's widow. Does the nephew have any remedy? Explain. See *Tianetopoulous v. Margares* 98 N.W.2d 97 (Minn. 1959).

6. Wilson Floors entered a contract with Unit, Inc., to furnish and install floor materials in new apartments and an office building being built by Unit, Inc. Pittsburgh National Bank held mortgages on the buildings as security for construction loans made to Unit, Inc. Unit fell behind in payments to Wilson Floors and the latter threatened to walk off the job if it was not paid. Pittsburgh National Bank decided that guaranteeing the debt owed Wilson Floors would be cheaper than foreclosing on its mortgages and hiring a new contractor. Wilson Floors sued to enforce the bank's *oral* guaranty. Who should win? Analyze. See *Wilson Floors Co. v. Scioto Park, Ltd.*, 377 N.E.2d 514 (Ohio 1978).

7. The plaintiff, Wagers, and the defendant, Associated Mortgage Investors, exchanged a series of letters, negotiating a sale of land. The letters did not satisfy the statute but did lead Wagers, a real estate developer, to arrange financing for the transaction and prepare plans for the development. When the negotiations failed, Wagers sued for specific performance. With what result? See *Wagers v. Associated Mortgage Investors*, 577 P.2d 622 (Wash. App. 1978).

8. Adams & Co., Inc., orally agreed to sell a number of steel reinforcing rods for the Baker's, the defendant's, retaining wall. Half of the rods were specially manufactured for Baker. The rest of the rods came from Adam's stock but were altered to fit the project. Baker repudiated the contract and refused to pay Adams. Is this contract enforceable? Explain. See *Frank Adams & Co., Inc. v. Baker*, 439 N.E.2d 953 (Ohio 1981).

9. The plaintiff, Satterfield, was employed by the defendant, Missouri Dental Assoc., in 1944. Missouri Dental orally promised Satterfield that she would be employed until her retirement, which

could be at any time she decided. Satterfield told her employer that she planned to retire in 1981, but she retained the right to retire earlier. She was fired in 1979 and sued Missouri Dental. Is Missouri Dental's oral promise enforceable? Analyze. See *Satterfield v. Missouri Dental Assoc.*, 642 S.W.2d 110 (Mo. App. 1982).

10. The Plaintiff, Jaskey Finance & Leasing, signed a written contract with the defendant, Display Data Corp., buying a computer program designed by Display. The contract clearly stated that no express or implied warranties were made for the program. The contract also contained the following phrase: ''This contract contains the entire agreement between the parties.'' After the program malfunctioned, Jaskey sued for breach of warranty, claiming that Display orally promised that the system would be easy to use and would be virtually error-free. Should Jaskey win? See *Jaskey Finance & Leasing v. Display Data Corp.* 564 F. Supp. 160 (E.D. Pa. 1983).

Chapter 17

Third Parties

CRITICAL THINKING INQUIRIES

As you read this chapter, you should be able to address the following:

- Distinguish between intended third-party beneficiaries and unintended beneficiaries.
- Distinguish between third-party beneficiaries and assignees.
- Compare and contrast assignment of rights and delegation of duties.
- How does the assignment process facilitate commerce and business transactions?

MANAGERIAL PERSPECTIVE

Rolfe Hyde is a manager in the life and property division of Bright Life Insurance Co. He has been instructed to verify that policyholders of life and property insurance have an insurable interest in the life and property they are insuring. Although he does not completely understand why, he nonetheless complies.

Bright Life has been having some cash flow difficulty and is interested in selling some of its policies to generate more liquid cash. Nina Lauflin has been charged with checking into the various options.

- Explain to Hyde why it is important to verify that its insureds have an insurable interest.
- Evaluate the ways in which Bright Life can increase its cash flow by assigning its policies.

Figure 17–1   Third-Party Beneficiaries

	Creditor	**Donee**	**Incidental**
Intention	Yes	Yes	No
Consideration	Yes	No	No
Recovery	Yes	Yes	No

We have discussed, in previous chapters, the elements a contract must contain to be enforceable. Contracts are enforceable by the original parties to the contract—generally the offeror and offeree. However, under some special cases, a **third party**—one not an original party to the contract—may enforce the contract. This chapter focuses on those special cases by discussing the law of assignments and third-party beneficiaries.

An **assignment** occurs when one party transfers an interest in a contract to another party. Here, the party to whom the interest has been transferred has some rights under the contract even though not an original party to the contract. Closely akin to assignment of rights is delegation of duties, where one party delegates obligations to perform under a contract to another party.

A **third-party beneficiary,** although not a party to the contract, nonetheless receives a benefit as a result of a contract. We will see that some third-party beneficiaries may enforce the contract while others may not.

This area of assignments and third parties is not only peculiar to the insurance industry, but it extends to other businesses and industries. Hence, along with Rolfe Hyde and Nina Lauflin, businesspeople need a basic understanding of the law of assignments and third-party beneficiaries.

THIRD–PARTY BENEFICIARIES

There are three types of third-party beneficiaries: donee, creditor, and incidental (see Figure 17–1). Donee and creditor beneficiaries can enforce contracts to which they are not parties, while incidental beneficiaries may not. Donee and creditor beneficiaries are intended beneficiaries, in contrast to incidental beneficiaries who are unintended beneficiaries.

Donee Beneficiary

Donee beneficiaries are recipients of gift promises. They do not give up anything of value. For example, assume that Allison secures a promise from Brenda to pay Charles $100. Charles is a donee beneficiary. A common example of a donee beneficiary is a beneficiary under a life insurance policy.

Figure 17–2 depicts a life insurance contract between the Bright Life Insurance Co. and a father. Assume that the amount of the policy is for $1 million. The essence of the contract is that on the father's death, Bright Life will pay $1 million dollars to the father's designated beneficiary, which in this case is his daughter. The daughter is characterized as a donee beneficiary because she benefits from the contract though has not paid for the privilege. Now assume that the father dies and Bright Life refuses to pay the $1 million to the daughter. As a donee beneficiary, the daughter may institute suit against Bright Life to enforce the contract between it and her father.

Insurance contracts are a type of **indemnity contract.** Under a contract of indemnity one party (the indemnitor) agrees to protect another party (the indemnitee) in the event of loss. For example, assume that Dr. Herbert obtains a $1 million malpractice insurance policy from Bright Life covering patients

Figure 17–2   Donee Beneficiary

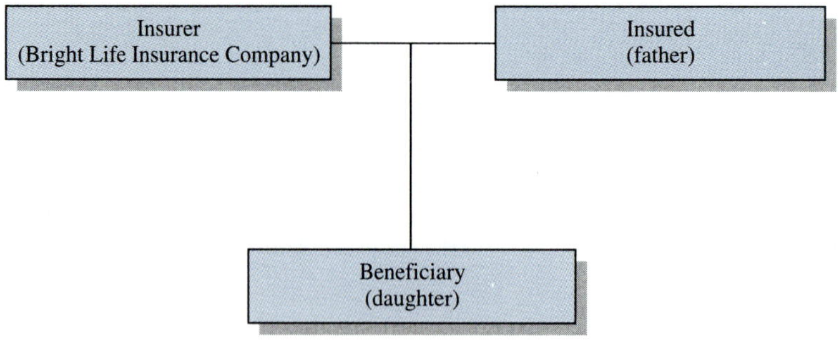

Figure 17–3 Donee Beneficiary

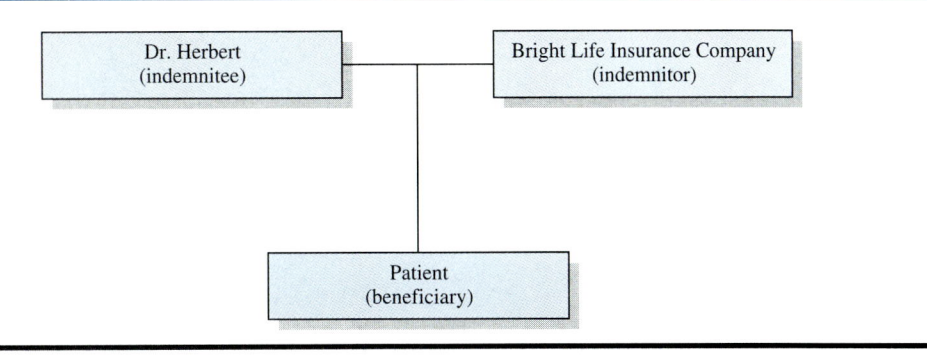

Figure 17–4 Creditor Beneficiary

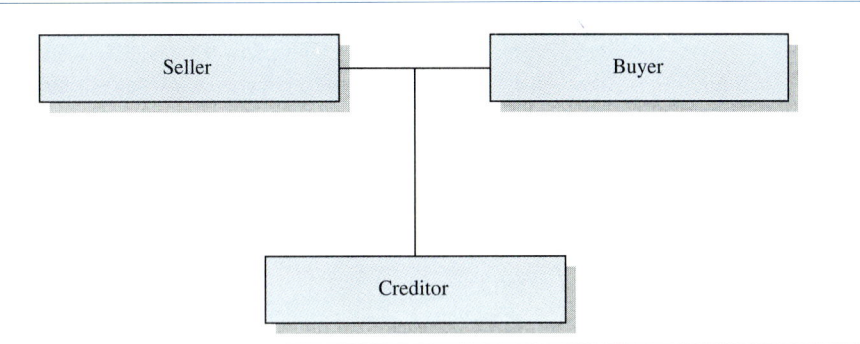

he may be liable to for injury. As illustrated in Figure 17–3, Bright Life is the indemnitor and Dr. Herbert is the indemnitee. Now assume that Rhonda, a patient, sues Dr. Herbert and obtains a judgment in the amount of $500,000. Rhonda is a third-party donee beneficiary of the contract. She may enforce the contract against Bright Life and require it to pay the $500,000.

Other contractual arrangements give rise to donee beneficiaries. For example, consider a separation agreement whereby a husband and wife agree that a portion of their assets will be distributed to specified parties, namely their children. Those specified parties are donee beneficiaries and are entitled to enforce the agreement.

Creditor Beneficiary

A **creditor beneficiary,** as distinguished from a donee beneficiary, is one who has given value (consideration). As illustrated in Figure 17–4, assume that a seller and a buyer enter into a contract for the purchase and sale of a business for a specified amount. Assume that the business is indebted to a creditor in the amount of $10,000. As part of the contract, the buyer agrees to assume the indebtedness. The creditor is a creditor beneficiary. The creditor may enforce the contract against the buyer in the event the buyer fails to abide by the agreement and pay $10,000 to the creditor. Of course, the creditor may also look to the seller for the $10,000.

Creditor beneficiary factual patterns may vary. *Lawrence v. Fox* is perhaps the most often cited case involving third-party beneficiaries.[1] In that case, Holly owed $300 to Lawrence. Holly loaned $300 to Fox, informing him that he (Holly) had agreed to pay Lawrence that sum the next day. Fox promised to pay the $300 to Lawrence the next day. Fox failed to pay the amount to Lawrence, who instituted suit against Fox. The court found that Lawrence was a creditor beneficiary entitled to enforce Fox's promise to him.

---

[1] 20 N.Y. 268 (1859).

Figure 17–5   Incidental Beneficiary

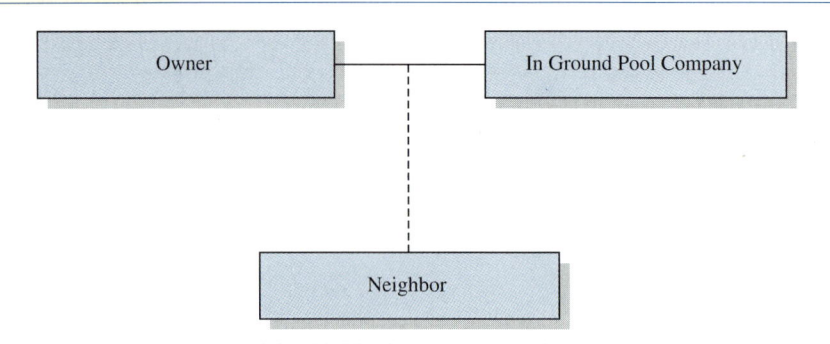

Suretyship agreements also fall under the category of third-party creditor beneficiaries. A **suretyship agreement** arises when one person agrees to answer for the debt of another. Assume that Craft Builders contracts to build an apartment complex for Harold. Craft Builders and A-1 Bonding (surety) enter into an agreement whereby A-1 Bonding promises that all of Craft Builder's debts for labor and materials on the house will be paid. This promise is called a **performance bond.** Craft then employs Plumbing Outlet to do the plumbing work and buys girders from Steel, Inc. Electrical Outlet and Steel, Inc., are creditor beneficiaries of A-1 Bonding's promise to Craft.

Incidental Beneficiary

An **incidental beneficiary** is not entitled to enforce a contract entered into between other parties. The incidental beneficiary is distinguished from the donee and creditor beneficiary in that he or she is not an *intended* beneficiary. Assume that, as illustrated by Figure 17–5, an owner and In Ground Pool Company enter into a contract whereby In Ground Pool Company agrees to construct a 25-meter in-ground pool at the owner's residence. The owner's neighbor is benefited by the construction. First, the neighbor's property value will probably increase since the neighborhood will be upgraded by the pool addition. Second, the neighbor, if on good terms with the owner, will get the benefit of using the owner's pool. In the event that In Ground Pool Company breaches the contract by failing to construct the pool, the owner, of course, may sue for damages. But the neighbor does not have such a right. Although the contract may benefit him, he is not an intended beneficiary. The parties to the contract did not contemplate the neighbor when they entered into the contract; that is, they did not contract for the purpose of benefiting the neighbor.

The following case involving a dispute arising out of a Big 10 basketball game illustrates the application of classical third-party beneficiary principles.

BAIN v. GILLISPIE
357 N.W. 2d 47 (Ia. Ct. App. 1984)

University of Iowa and Purdue were playing a Big 10 basketball game. James C. Bain, a referee, called a foul on a University of Iowa player. The foul resulted in a Purdue University player scoring on a foul shot, which gave Purdue the victory. Many University of Iowa fans believed the foul call to be in error and blasted Bain.

The Gillispies operated a novelty store specializing in University of Iowa sports memorabilia. The Gillispies began selling T-shirts that pictured a man with a rope around his neck, captioned ''Jim Bain Fan Club.''

Bain sued the Gillispies, who counterclaimed, alleging that they sustained damages as a result of Bain's bad call, which eliminated Iowa from the Big 10 Basketball Conference championship. This elimination allegedly hurt the potential market for the Gillispies' memorabilia. The Gillispies further maintained that they were beneficiaries of an employment contract between Bain and the Big 10 Athletic Conference. The trial court sustained Bain's motion for summary judgment, dismissing Gillispies' counterclaim. The Gillispies appealed to the Court of Appeals of Iowa.

SNELL, Judge

The trial court . . . found that there was no issue of material fact on the Gillispies' claim that they were beneficiaries under Bain's contract with the Big 10. Gillispies argue that until the contract is produced, there exists a question of whether they are beneficiaries. There is some question of whether there is a contract between Bain and the Big 10. In his response to interrogatories, Bain stated that he had no written contract with the Big 10, but that there was a letter which defined "working relationship." Although this letter was never produced and ordinarily we would not decide an issue without the benefit of examining the letter's contents, we nevertheless find the issue presently capable of determination. By deposition Gillispies answered that there was no contract between them and Bain, the Big 10 Athletic Conference, the University of Iowa, the players, coaches, or with any body regarding this issue. Thus, even if the letter were considered a contract, Gillispies would be considered third-party beneficiaries. Because Gillispies would not be privy to the contract, they must be direct beneficiaries to maintain a cause of action, and not merely incidental beneficiaries. A direct beneficiary is either a donee beneficiary or a creditor beneficiary. . . .

Gillispies make no claim that they are creditor beneficiaries of Bain, the Big 10 Athletic Conference, or the University of Iowa. "The real test is said to be whether the contracting parties intended that a third person should receive a benefit which might be enforced in the courts." It is clear that the purpose of any promise which Bain might have made was not to confer a gift on Gillispies. Likewise, the Big 10 did not owe any duty to the Gillispies such that they would have been creditor beneficiaries. If a contract did exist between Bain and the Big 10, Gillispies can be considered nothing more than incidental beneficiaries and as such are unable to maintain a cause of action.

Consequently, there was no genuine issue for trial which could result in Gillispies obtaining a judgment under a contract theory of recovery. The ruling of the trial court sustaining the summary judgment motion and dismissing the counterclaim is affirmed.

Case Questions
1. What is the issue in this case?
2. Would the result have been different if the Gillispies' store was owned by the University of Iowa? Explain.
3. How would the Gillispies argue a case in tort for negligence against Bain? Would they prevail? Why or why not?

Warranty Extension to Third Parties

The Uniform Commercial Code extends the right to sue for breach of express or implied warranty to nonparties to the contract. A **warranty** is a guarantee that a product conforms to certain standards. Warranties may be express or implied. An express warranty is one made orally or in writing and states, for example, "This automobile is new and guaranteed for 100,000 miles." Implied warranties arise out of obligations imposed by law. For example, the Uniform Commercial Code implies warranties of merchantability and fitness for a particular purpose. The implied warranty of merchantability means that the goods are fit for their intended purpose—for example, food is fit to eat and automobiles are suitable for travel. The implied warranty of fitness for a particular purpose states just that—the goods are suitable for the use the seller knows the buyer intends.

Figure 17–6   Typical Assignment

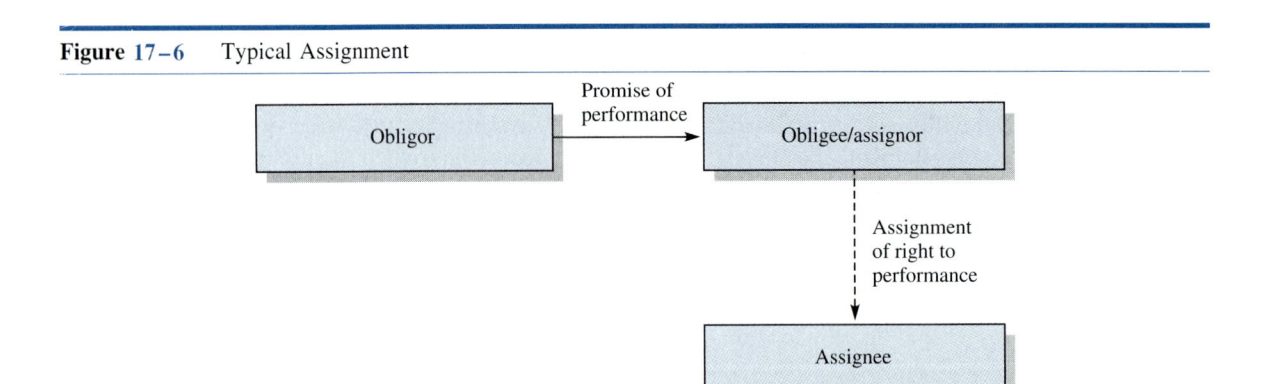

For example, if the seller knows that the buyer is purchasing boots for mountain climbing, there is an implied warranty that accompanies any boots so sold that they are fit for mountain climbing.

The drafters of the Code extend warranty protection to third parties by including legislative alternatives for states to select [UCC § 2–318]. Alternative A extends a seller's warranty to family, household members, and guests of the buyer. Alternative B extends the warranty to any person who may be reasonably expected to be exposed to the goods. This topic is treated in greater detail in Chapter 22.

Identity of Beneficiaries

It is not necessary for a third-party beneficiary to be specifically designated at the time of the contract. As long as the parties intend to confer a benefit on a third person, then the identity of the third person may await future determination. Assume, for example, that a life insurance policy names as beneficiaries the children who survive the insured. These third-party beneficiaries (children), if any, cannot be determined until the death of the insurer.

In many jurisdictions, a third party may be able to enforce a contract even without showing that the contract is exclusively for his or her benefit. In those jurisdictions, it is sufficient to show that the third party was a member of a class intended to be benefited. This may take the form of a contract to benefit the public. For example, assume that a municipality enters into a contract with Water Purifying Company to remove hard metals from the municipal water supply to prevent harm to the municipality's customers. Any customer would be an intended beneficiary and have a right to enforce the contract.

ASSIGNMENTS

An **assignment** occurs when one person transfers an interest in property to another. As illustrated in Figure 17–6, the typical assignment involves three parties: obligor, obligee/assignor, and assignee. The **obligor** is the one who is obligated to perform under the contract. The **obligee** is the one who has a right to receive performance. By transferring that right of performance, the obligee becomes an **assignor.** The **assignee** is the one to whom the right has been transferred and now is entitled to performance from the obligor. Assume, for example, that Alpha owes $1,000 to Beta. Beta has a right to receive the $1,000. Beta assigns that right to Gamma. Now Gamma has the right to receive the $1,000 from Alpha. Alpha is referred to as the obligor. Beta is the assignor. Gamma is the assignee (see Figure 17–7). Partial amounts of the debt may also be assigned. Beta may assign an amount less than the entire $1,000 to Gamma.

Form of Assignment

Assignments need not have a particular form. Words that indicate the assignor's intention to assign rights are sufficient to constitute an assignment. Some assignments, by statute, are required to be in writing. Any assignment of a subject covered by the statute of frauds (discussed in Chapter 16)—for example, real estate—must be in writing to be valid.

Generally, an assignment does not require consideration to be valid. If the assignee did not give consideration, however, the assignor may revoke the assignment any time before the obligor performs the contract. In contrast, if there is consideration, the

Figure 17–7   Assignment of a Debt

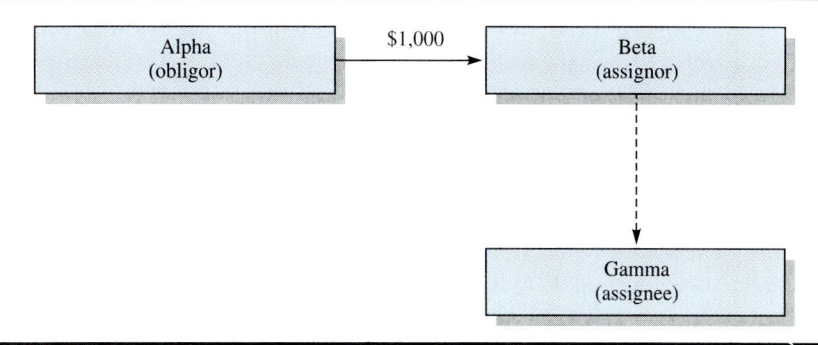

assignment is not revocable. Assume that our previous example involved a gratuitous assignment—Gamma did not give consideration. In such a case, Beta may revoke the assignment any time before Alpha pays the amount to Gamma.

Assignable Rights

Generally, any contract right is assignable as long as the assignment does not materially increase the burden of the obligor's performance. Since the assignment of monies does not ordinarily increase the obligor's burden, such rights are generally assignable. It is just as easy for Alpha to pay Beta as it is for Alpha to pay Gamma. However, an assignment of a right to receive delivery of goods may be ineffective if the assignee is more distant from the obligor than the assignor. In such a case, the burden and cost of delivery would be greater.

The right to accounts receivable is assignable. In fact, the assignment of accounts receivable is a common method of increasing the cash flow of a business. In a usual accounts receivable assignment, a creditor assigns (sells) its accounts receivable to a financing institute. This quite common practice is referred to as **factoring.** The financing institute pays the assignor a discounted lump sum amount for the right to receive future payment by the account debtors. Sometimes the assignment is made **without recourse.** Under such an assignment, the assignee assumes the risk of loss in the event the account debtor defaults. Under **with recourse** factoring, the assignor is usually required to buy back any bad accounts.

This system of factoring is used in the insurance industry, where it is usually referred to as **reinsurance.** Here, an insurance company assigns insurance policies to another insurer for a discounted lump-sum amount of money. The reinsurer (assignee) will be entitled to the ongoing premiums from the policyholders. This reinsurance, using assignment principles, is a way that Nina Lauflin, a manager in our opening scenario, may increase Bright Life's cash flow.

Some contracts expressly prohibit assignment. However, under the Uniform Commercial Code Section 9–318(4), any attempts by the account debtor and the assignor to prohibit assignment is ineffective. In other cases, the prohibition against assignment will be upheld if the parties' intent is clear. In a lease agreement, a prohibition against the tenant assigning the lease will not prohibit the tenant from subletting for a lesser period of time than remaining on the lease. For example, assume that a lessee and a lessor enter into a one-year lease and that a term included within the lease states: "Lessee agrees not to assign the lease without the written consent of the Lessor." This prohibition clause does not prevent the lessee from subletting without the lessor's consent for six months or any period less than that remaining on the lease. However, any assignment of the whole term remaining under the lease would require the lessor's written consent. Likewise, a clause within the lease prohibiting subletting will not prevent the tenant from assigning the right to occupy the premises to another for the remaining period of the lease. Under the Uniform Commercial Code, the prohibition of an assignment of "the contract" will be construed as prohibiting only the delegation of performance unless the circumstances otherwise indicate [UCC § 2–210(3)].

Some statutes prohibit the assignment of certain rights. For example, a number of states limit the assignment of future wages or prohibit them altogether. The purpose of this restriction is to protect the wage earner. Otherwise, wage assignments might seriously hamper the wage earner's ability to meet payment for necessities, which would lead to the necessity of public assistance.

Actions for torts are unassignable in many jurisdictions. In those jurisdictions, Henry cannot sell his right to sue Lyle in tort to Candace. Tort claims are deemed personal. However, there is an exception that permits an insured to assign tort rights to his or her insurer. Here, the insurer has a sufficient interest in the action so as to override any public policy against assignment. Assume that Bright Life Insurance Company insures its client against property damage incurred as a result of a collision. In return for coverage, the client agrees to assign to Bright Life any rights against third parties, who are responsible for damages. This assignment is deemed valid even in jurisdictions that fail to generally recognize the validity of the assignment of tort claims. In fact, the following makes a case for using the assignment of tort claims to insurers as a means of financing a system of no-fault insurance.

*A Canadian Proposal for No-Fault Benefits Financed by Assignments of Tort Rights**

For decades countless books, learned articles, empirical studies, and reports of government commissions of inquiry and law reform bodies have documented the vast deficiencies of traditional tort law as a means of dealing with personal injury. The delays and vagaries of tort have been laid bare in devastating fashion and the case for reform seems unanswerable. Yet even in the crisis area of automobile accidents change has been spasmodic at best, and in some jurisdictions non-existent or largely ineffectual. . . .

Until recently the road to reform has been seen as a matter of legislative action, and much of the effort has been directed at persuading legislators to take up the cause. The rather limited success in this regard has been attributed in many places to the power of the legal profession and, to a lesser extent, the insurance industry as lobbying forces. Lawyers have a clear vested interest in retaining the trial by combat inherent in the tort system. Insurance companies are understandably reluctant to embrace new ideas which may entail their abandoning systems and data built up over years of accumulated experience. . . .

The picture is not all bleak. In Canada and some U.S. jurisdictions substantial achievements have been made through the introduction of automobile no-fault insurance. But such achievements are far from universal, and calls to expand these initiatives to provide improved levels of benefits and to cover other categories of accidents have fallen on deaf legislative ears.

■ ■ ■

. . .[A] recent proposal . . . should be of interest not only in Ontario, but also in other Canadian provinces. . . . After two decades of involvement in reform efforts in the United States, the senior author has seen the impetus for legislative reform fade in that country. As a response he has developed a proposal for optional no-fault insurance which could be implemented voluntarily by insurers without an enabling statute. It would be available to consumers on an optional basis and would use rather than abolish the existing tort/liability-insurance system to assist in its implementation. The proposal calls for a preaccident assignment by the insured of any tort rights he may have in relation to his injury in return for agreed levels of guaranteed benefits which would be available regardless of the existence or practical enforceability of such tort rights.

Source: Jeffrey O'Connell and Craig Brown, ''A Canadian Proposal for No-Fault Benefits Financed by Assignments of Tort Rights,'' 33 Univ. of Toronto L. J., 434 (1983). Reprinted by permission.

■ ■ ■

No-fault insurance would be available from licensed insurers covering, up to agreed limits, wage loss, medical expenses (not covered by medicare), and perhaps other economic losses. Perils could be specified (for example, only automobile accidents or those arising from slips and falls), but it would be feasible to provide for any personal injury or death accidentally caused. A term of the policy would give the insurer an absolute preaccident assignment of any tort claims the insured would have against third parties in relation to any disability coming within the terms of the policy. This assignment would cover the full amount of such tort claims, including any amounts for non-pecuniary loss. Insurers would use these assigned rights to help finance no-fault benefits for all insureds, including those with no or minimal tort claims. In the case of serious injuries, economic loss would be compensated through periodic payments.

An insured who opted for an amount of no-fault cover which turned out to be lower than the value of tort rights which eventually accrued would still be entitled to the full amount of the tort recovery for . . . economic loss. This would be a term of the policy and, further, there would be no reduction for expenses incurred in obtaining full recovery from the tortfeasor. It is only the non-pecuniary loss portions of tort recoveries that would be retained by the insurer and used to offset the cost of guaranteed payments made to insureds having no or inadequate tort claims.

■ ■ ■

It is to be emphasized that the no-fault cover proposed herein is elective both from the perspective of insurers offering it and potential accident victims buying it. There is reason to believe that there is sufficient demand for a rational alternative to the tort system (from the potential victim's point of view) [and] that widespread acceptance could be expected.

Thought Questions

1. ''[S]ubstantial achievements have been made through the introduction of automobile no-fault insurance.'' How would you substantiate this statement?
2. What shortcomings do you see in the system the authors propose?
3. Are there reasons why this proposal would have less support in the United States than in Canada?
4. Analyze the last sentence of the reading.

Personal service contracts are not assignable. For example, a patient may not assign to another party the right to receive medical services. Most employment contracts are personal in nature and thus nonassignable. The following case illustrates the nonassignability of a personal service contract.

PETRY v. COSMOPOLITAN SPA INTERNATIONAL, INC.
641 S.W.2d 202 (Tenn. App. 1982)

Shirley Petry, appellant, contracted with Cosmopolitan (Spa) for a spa membership that, according to the terms of the contract, included ''processing, program counseling, and facilities usage. . . .'' The following exculpatory clause—attempting to relieve the spa from liability—was a term included within the contract:

Member represents that he or she is in good physical condition and able to use the equipment provided and to take the exercises recommended by Cosmopolitan. Member fully understands and agrees that in participating in one or more of the courses, or using the facilities maintained by Cosmopolitan, there is the possibility [of] accidental or other physical injury. Member further agrees to assume the risk of such injury and further agrees to indemnify Cosmopolitan from any and all liability to Cosmopolitan by either the member or third party as the result of the use by the member of the facilities and instructions as offered by Cosmopolitan.

Cosmopolitan sold the spa and assigned its rights to Holiday. Thereafter, Petry injured her back when an exercise machine collapsed under her. She sued Cosmopolitan and Holiday, appellees, for damages for personal injuries due to the appellees' negligence in maintaining the exercise machine in a dangerous condition.

Cosmopolitan and Holiday moved for summary judgment, arguing that (1) the exculpatory clause was a good bar to recovery and (2) the clause was assignable to Holiday. The trial court sustained the motion, and Petry appealed.

PARROTT, Judge

The Supreme Court of Tennessee held in *Empress Health and Beauty Spa, Inc. v. Turner* that an exculpatory clause of almost the exact type and wording as the one in this case was valid and enforceable. That case is both factually and legally on point with this one. The trial judge below correctly recognized this in his summary judgment opinion. Like the court below, we are compelled by the doctrine of stare decisis to follow this holding.

Appellant also contends that even if the exculpatory clause is valid, it does not protect appellee, Holiday, from liability because it could not be assigned. Again, we must disagree. The exculpatory clause in this contract was a right of appellee Cosmopolitan. Generally, contractual rights can be assigned:

(2) A contractual right can be assigned unless

(a) the substitution of a right of the assignee for the right of the assignor would materially change the duty of the obligor, or materially increase the burden or risk imposed on him by his contract, or materially impair his chance of obtaining return performance, or materially reduce its value to him, or

(b) the assignment is forbidden by statute or is otherwise inoperative on grounds of public policy, or

(c) assignment is validly precluded by contract.

None of the above exceptions to assignability can be successfully raised as to this exculpatory clause. Appellant contends that the assignment was invalid because the contract was of a personal nature and that she never consented to the assignment. We find this unpersuasive. This contract was primarily for the use of spa facilities and not of a personal nature. Beyond this, the exculpatory clause can only be viewed as a right of appellees, not appellant. Appellant had no right to consent to a transfer of a contractual right not her own. Appellant also claims that the contract contained language that prohibited assignment. We do not agree. The only language which remotely suggests a bar on transfer deals with either transfer of appellant's spa membership or the financial servicing of the contract.

It seems clear that the judge below was correct in his decision that appellant's suit was barred against appellee Holiday because it was appellee Cosmopolitan's assignee. That being the case, we must affirm the court below on this issue also. . . .

GODDARD, Judge

Concurring in Part and Dissenting in Part
I concur in the majority opinion insofar as it grants summary judgment in favor of Cosmopolitan Spa International, Inc., the original signator to the contract containing the exculpatory clause.

I do, however, respectfully dissent as to the dismissal of the assignee, Holiday Spa of Tennessee, Inc. . . . I do not believe that exculpatory clauses are or—perhaps more accurately—should be favored. It is my view such clauses should be strictly construed and the protection afforded thereby not assignable unless expressly authorized.

There is also a more narrow ground which I believe would justify a reversal. I am of the opinion that there is a disputed fact whether the Plaintiff comes within the exception set out in Subsection (a) of the *Restatement* cited in the majority opinion, in that both her affidavit and that of her mother show that she was induced to sign the agreement in part because of the representations of the personnel of the original contractor that they had had experience in the rehabilitative procedures that she sought in connection with her prior back injury. I believe it could be inferred that a change in personnel occurred from the time the assignment was made on January 1, . . . until the accident happened on February 25, and that, absent a showing that the personnel of the assignee corporation was equally skilled in supervising the Plaintiff's exercise and in maintaining the equipment, reasonable minds could differ as to whether the Plaintiff's risk was materially increased.

Case Questions

1. Why do you think Petry signed a contract containing the exculpatory clause?

2. What arguments could be made that the exculpatory clause is invalid?

3. Would it have made a difference if Petry had objected to the assignment immediately after the sale of the spa? Immediately before the sale of the spa? At the time of contracting?

4. What are the points of disagreement between the majority opinion and the dissent?

Rights of the Assignee

The assignee acquires the same rights to the contract as the assignor possessed. Sometimes it is said that the assignee "stands in the shoes of the assignor." The assignee is also subject to the same defenses that could be raised against the assignor—for example, fraud, misrepresentation, duress, undue influence, mistake, incapacity, lack of consideration, and breach of contract.

To illustrate, Hair Style, Inc., and Head Star entered into a contract for the sale of a business. Hair Style, Inc., assigned to Pro Care the right to receive the money. When Pro Care sought payment from Head Star under the assignment, Head Star refused to pay, alleging that Hair Style, Inc., induced it to enter the contract by making material misrepresentations about the financial condition of the business. These allegations, if provable, would be a successful defense against payment to Pro Care.

Notice of Assignments

When an assignment occurs, the obligor should be notified. Absence of notification does not invalidate the assignment but it may affect an assignee's rights. If the obligor pays the assignor before notification of

assignment occurs, the obligor will be discharged from paying the assignee. This means that the assignee will have to seek payment from the assignor, which may or may not be possible.

Another problem arises when the assignor makes more than one assignment of the same right. Assume, as illustrated in Figure 17–8, that an assignor, on February 1, assigned a right to receive $10,000 under a contract to Assignee 1. Although unlawful, the assignor, one month later, assigned the same right to Assignee 2. Assignee 1 gave notice of the assignment to the obligor on March 3, one day after Assignee 2 had given notice to the obligor. Who is entitled to the $10,000 from the obligor? Under the majority rule, the assignee who received the assignment first is entitled to the performance. In a state that follows the majority view, Assignee 1 would be entitled to the proceeds. In a minority of states, however, the assignee who gives notice first to the obligor is entitled to performance. In those states, the obligor would be obligated to pay Assignee 2. In either case, the assignee who is not entitled to performance from the obligor would have recourse against the assignor.

The following case illustrates the importance of being specific in the notice.

■

FIRST TRUST AND SAVINGS BANK OF GLENVIEW v. SKOKIE FEDERAL SAVINGS AND LOAN ASSOCIATION
466 N.E.2d 1048 (Ill. App. 1984)

Skokie Federal (Skokie) loaned Spanish Court II, Ltd. (Spanish Court) $2.4 million to construct a 32-unit condominium. Under the terms of the loan agreements, amounts were to

Figure 17–8   Successive Assignments

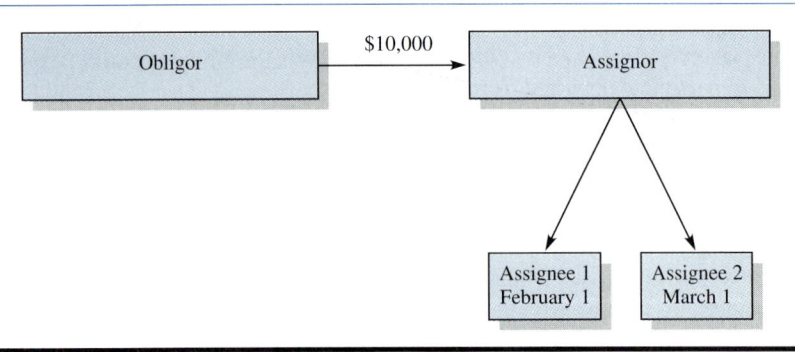

be disbursed to Spanish Court periodically as phases of the project were completed. Spanish Court secured an additional amount of $100,000 from First Trust needed to begin construction. This loan was secured by an assignment of the loan proceeds Spanish Court was to receive from Skokie. Skokie was aware of the assignment and the clause contained within the assignment stated in part:

I hereby authorize Skokie Federal Savings and Loan Association to . . . make all payouts . . . to The First Trust and Savings Bank.

Skokie Federal paid the loan proceeds directly to Spanish Court. After the final payment on the loan was made, First Trust made a demand on Skokie for the amounts due under the assignment. Skokie refused.

First Trust sued Skokie, seeking a determination that Skokie wrongfully paid funds directly to Spanish Court. The trial court found in favor of Skokie on the basis that Skokie did not receive explicit direction to pay First Trust. First Trust appealed to the Illinois Appellate Court.

MCGLOON, Judge

The sole issue presented for our determination is whether Skokie Federal, as the debtor of an account that had been assigned to First Trust, received sufficient notification that future payments should be made to the assignee to render it liable for continuing to disburse construction loan proceeds directly to Spanish Court.

Section 9–318(3) of the Uniform Commercial Code governs the situation in which a creditor has assigned its right to receive payments to another party. That section provides:

The account debtor is authorized to pay the assignor until the account debtor receives notification that the amount due or to become due has been assigned and that payment is to be made to the assignee. A notification which does not reasonably identify the rights assigned is ineffective. If requested by the account debtor, the assignee must seasonably furnish reasonable proof that the assignment has been made and unless he does so the account debtor may pay the assignor.

Section 9–318(3) has been interpreted as an express authorization for an account debtor to make payments to an assignor until the account debtor receives notification that the right to receive payments has been assigned and that the future payments are to be made to the assignee. Uniform Commercial Code Comment to section 9–218 further indicates that an account debtor may continue to pay the assignor even though the account debtor has knowledge of the assignment. The Illinois cases which rely on section 9-318(3) of the Code hold that enforcement of an assignee's rights under the assignment requires *both* notification of the assignment and a demand that future payments be made to the assignee. This holding is in accord with the plain language of the statute as clarified by Uniform Commercial Code Comment to section 9–318(3).

In the instant case, the assignment does not contain an explicit demand for Skokie Federal to make future disbursements of its construction loan proceeds to First Trust. The relevant language, which we have quoted above, merely ''authorizes'' Skokie Federal to direct the payout agent to make the disbursements to First Trust. Our review of the record supports the trial court's conclusion that, although Skokie Federal received notice of the existence of the assignment, it did not receive a demand that payments were to be made to First Trust. The uncontradicted affidavit of . . . an officer of Skokie Federal, states that Skokie Federal received no notification to pay any amount due under the assignment until after Skokie Federal made its final payment to Spanish Court. [On this issue the trial court decision is affirmed.]

Case Questions

1. Diagram the parties and the facts in this case.

2. As a loan officer of First Trust, what are your concerns about securing your loan with the proceeds of another loan?

3. Criticize the court's interpretation of UCC Section 9–318(3).

4. Can you think of a case where it would be the desire of the assignee to not receive the proceeds of an assignment?

5. Redraft the assignment to protect First Trust.

DELEGATION OF DUTIES

Every right under a contract usually involves a corresponding duty. For example, assume that Conroy and Ramos enter into a contract whereby Conroy agrees to draw up plans for a home for Ramos and Ramos agrees to pay a specified sum for the services. Conroy has a right to payment. Conroy has a corresponding duty to draw the plans. Ramos has a right to the plans. Ramos has a corresponding duty to pay Conroy. As long as Ramos consents to Conroy delegating his obligation to draw the plans to someone else, there is no problem. Questions arise, however, where the promisor delegates an obligation to another without the promisee's consent. Some duties are delegable, while others are not.

As in the case of assignments, those duties that involve personal services are not delegable without the promisee's consent. The example above involving the building contract is personal and hence, not delegable. Neither are the duties of babysitters, lawyers, or doctors delegable.

Those duties that are routine in character are, however, delegable without the consent of the promisee. These duties include impersonal contracts — for example, the duty to deliver newspapers or to spray lawns. Even here, however, the promisor is not released of its obligations under the contract. The promisor is still responsible for performance. Should the obligee fail to perform, the promisor would be liable.

An obligor and obligee must agree to an assignment. An agreement to ''assign all rights under the contract'' or similar wording constitutes both an assignment of rights and a delegation of duties [UCC § 2–210(4)].

END–OF–CHAPTER QUESTIONS

1. How do donee and creditor beneficiaries differ from incidental beneficiaries?

2. How does the Uniform Commercial Code affect the area of third parties?

3. Why are some contracts not assignable? Explain.

4. Explain the difference between assignment of rights and delegation of duties.

5. Jeffrey and Theresa Hines entered into a contract to purchase a dwelling from the Amoles. The contract was conditioned on a satisfactory termite report. The Amoles contracted with Able Pest Control to do the termite inspection. Able issued a report stating that there was no visible evidence of termite activity or damage. When the Hines moved into the house, they became aware of structural damage caused by termites. Do the Hines have any claim against Able? Explain. See *Hines v. Amole*, 448 N.E.2d 473 (Ohio App. 1982).

6. Chun owned scaffolding that he permitted Benge to use for various jobs. Benge's employee, Gonzales, was injured when the scaffolding on which he was standing collapsed while he was trimming a house. What additional information would you want to know in order to determine whether Gonzales could recover as a third-party beneficiary against Chun? See *Gonzales v. Kil Nam Chun*, 465 N.E.2d 727 (Ind. 1984).

7. A separation agreement between husband and wife included a term whereby the husband agreed to pay ''all reasonable college expenses'' for the children of the marriage who attended college. A divorce decree involving the parties approved the agreement and ordered its performance. Four children of the marriage attended college. Their father failed to perform pursuant to the terms of the agreement. Can the children enforce the agreement? Under what theory? See *Mitchell v. Combank/Winter Park*, 429 So.2d 1319 (Fla. App. 1983).

8. The Brays leased premises from the Days. The Brays operated a doughnut business on the premises. As part of the lease, it was agreed that ''Lessors will not compete with Lessees in the doughnut shop business, directly or indirectly, as employers, employees, or otherwise, within a radius of five miles from said business location for a period of five years from this date.'' The Brays sold the business and assigned the lease to Wanda Ball. May the Days compete against Ball? Explain. See *Ball v. Day*, 644 P.2d 649 (Or. App. 1982).

9. Beryl owed Adam $2,000. On February 4, Adam assigned the $2,000 due from Beryl to Seth. On March 1, Adam assigned the same $2,000 to Rhena. On April 1, Beryl paid Adam the $2,000. On April 2, Rhena notified Beryl of the assignment. On April 4, Seth notified Beryl of the assignment. What are Beryl's obligations to Seth and/or Rhena? Explain.

10. McDonald's granted a franchise to Copeland, authorizing him to operate a McDonald's restaurant in Omaha, Nebraska. McDonald's also granted Copeland the right to the first opportunity for any new McDonald's restaurants to be opened in the surrounding area. Copeland exercised this right of first refusal and opened five additional stores. Later, Copeland assigned all of his franchises and rights thereunder to Schupach, with McDonald's consent. Must McDonald's first offer any new franchises to Schupach before granting them to someone else? Analyze. See *Schupach v. McDonald's System, Inc.*, 264 N.W.2d 827 (Neb. 1978).

Chapter 18

Performance, Discharge, and Remedies

■

CRITICAL THINKING INQUIRIES

As you read this chapter, you should be able to address the following:

- Compare and contrast the various types of conditions to performance of a contract.
- Why does the law permit certain types of contracts to be fulfilled by substantial performance rather than perfect performance?
- Compare and contrast the ways in which a person is discharged from obligations under a contract.
- Compare and contrast the various types of contract remedies.

MANAGERIAL PERSPECTIVE

Ace Construction Company has been building homes for Sherwood Homes for a number of years. Most recently, it has been working on a building contract to build a community of 84 homes around a man-made lake. Problems have arisen:

1. The general project manager was in a serious accident and has been incapacitated.
2. High winds and soil stability problems are frustrating the work.
3. The cost of materials has increased beyond what was contemplated by the contract.

Ace has completed a number of the homes and a portion of the other homes and is thinking of bailing out of the rest of the contract.

- What are the consequences of Ace not completing the contract?
- What can Ace do to mitigate the harshness of any consequences?

In our competitive system, there are a myriad of unforeseeable factors beyond our control that make the difference between profitability and loss. Companies such as Ace are called on to make tough decisions in the face of these factors, such as a decision to cut losses today so that the business may survive tomorrow.

It is important for the manager to look beyond performance and be knowledgeable about the consequences of nonperformance so that at any given time, the manager may analyze the options. This chapter, the final in the Contracts Part, instructs on the legal consequences of contract performance, its breach, and available remedies.

CONDITIONS

Performance of a contract might not be required until a condition is satisfied. Or, performance may be excused on the happening of a condition. A **condition,** then, is an act or event that must occur before performance is required, or which causes a discharge of further performance.

The law traditionally classifies conditions in two ways. The first is the relationship of the time of the condition to the particular duty created or discharged. Here, conditions are classified as precedent, subsequent, or concurrent (see Figure 18–1). The second classification concerns the manner in which the condition is created: express, implied, or constructive.

Precedent Conditions

A **condition precedent** exists when a fact or event must occur before a contractual duty arises. To illustrate, Rita conditions the sale of her business to Harry "on Harry securing a loan of $30,000 by April 1." The event, securing the loan, is a condition precedent to Rita's duty to sell.

Subsequent Conditions

A **condition subsequent** exists when an event or act terminates an already existing duty. Often, insurers state that their duty to pay after a loss is discharged if the insured does not file a proof of loss within a certain period of time. The *Restatement (Second) of Contracts* has eliminated the distinction between conditions precedent and conditions subsequent and

treats conditions subsequent under the subject of discharge. Nevertheless, many courts still cling to the traditional classification scheme.

Concurrent Conditions

A **concurrent condition** is one in which two parties exchange their performances at the same time. If Bert agrees to sell his pig to Ralph for $30, the delivery of the pig to Ralph and the payment of the $30 to Bert are conditions for the other's performance. The typical informal contract involves concurrent conditions. Each performance is dependent on the other's performance.

Express Conditions

Conditions intended by the parties are **express conditions.** While no particular form of words is necessary to create an express condition, often such phrases as "on condition that," "provided that," "subject to," or "contingent on" will be used to create an express condition. The effect of creating an express condition is the law's requirement that the condition be literally fulfilled before a duty under the contract arises or continues. This strict compliance requirement is tempered by the common law doctrine of *de minimis non curat lex* (the law will not take account of trivial things). Thus, compliance will be satisfied if the express condition is breached by minor departures from the contract terms. To illustrate, if a living room measures 29 feet 11 inches rather than 30 feet as per an express condition in the contract, the express condition is nevertheless deemed fulfilled.

Conditions of Personal Satisfaction

Often, a contractual duty is conditioned on a party's "personal satisfaction." As a general rule, subjective satisfaction of a party governs only when the contract involves matters of personal taste or preference. To illustrate, if Rhonda agrees to paint Leona's portrait in exchange for $1,000 "subject to Leona's personal approval and satisfaction with the portrait," Leona would not have to pay Rhonda if Leona did not like the portrait. It would not matter that experts believed the portrait to be an excellent, even flattering, rendering. The only limitation on this rule is that the subjective opinion of a party be stated honestly.

Figure 18–1   Conditions

	Condition Precedent	**Condition Subsequent**	**Condition Concurrent**
Definition	Fact or event occurs before contractual duty arises	Fact or event terminates contractual obligation	Contractual obligation mutually dependant
Example	Sale of house conditioned on seller's relocation	Contractual obligation to employ worker ceases should worker smoke on the job	Sale of automobile for $10,000

Most contracts do not involve matters of personal taste or individual preference. Thus, even if the contract is conditioned on ''satisfaction'' or ''absolute satisfaction,'' the general test is objective, requiring only the satisfaction of a reasonable person. To illustrate, suppose August conditions her payment of $3,000 to Ace Construction for Ace's replacement of an old roof ''upon my complete satisfaction.'' August would have to pay Ace if a reasonable person would be satisfied with the roof replacement, even if August was not.

Many contracts, particularly in the construction industry, are conditioned on the satisfaction of a third party such as a named architect or engineer. Because this named expert is assumed to act with professional integrity and honesty, courts generally defer to that chosen expert's opinion.

Implied Conditions

An **implied condition** flows naturally from express conditions. For example, assume that a real estate purchase contract was expressly conditioned upon buyer obtaining financing. Implicit within this express condition, is that buyer will attempt to obtain financing within a reasonable period of time.

Constructive Conditions

A **constructive condition** is one implied by the law in order to do justice. Constructive conditions may be precedent or subsequent. For example, it is a constructive condition precedent that a specific heirloom that is the subject of a sale be in existence in order for the buyer to be required to perform by tendering the money for the heirloom. And, if the heirloom is in existence at the time of the contract, and before the contract is executed the heirloom is destroyed, the buyer will be discharged of the obligation to perform. The continued existence of the heirloom is a constructive condition subsequent.

PERFORMANCE

In most contracts, the law requires precise performance of the terms. For example, assume that a contract is entered into for the sale and purchase of a particular bicycle. All of the purchase price must be paid, and even a dollar short of the price would not fulfill the terms. Likewise, the specific bicycle contracted for must be tendered. However, when it comes to construction contracts, the law is more lenient. Construction contracts involve thousands of specifications, and it is understandably not always possible to perform exactly. For this reason, the courts have developed the doctrine of **substantial performance.** The following material treats this doctrine as well as other important issues related to performance of the contract.

Substantial Performance

Substantial performance occurs when a party has materially performed in all respects. There are various degrees to which a person may fail to comply with terms of a contract. If the failure to comply is deemed *material*, the injured party is completely discharged from having to carry out the contractual duties. To illustrate, an owner of property can immediately cease payment and cancel the contract if the contractor willfully departs from the blueprint specifications through a major change in design or materials.

If one's failure to perform is deemed insubstantial (immaterial), the injured party is still bound to the contract but may deduct the difference between what was contracted for and what was received. Using the previous example, if the materials differed in an insignificant way from the blueprints, the owner must still pay the builder despite the immaterial breach. Nonetheless, the breaching party (who substantially complied) is liable in damages for his or her immaterial breach.

Because the difference between a material and an immaterial breach creates such a difference in the nonbreaching party's duties (i.e., the party is discharged in the former case and bound in the latter), it is essential to distinguish between the two types of breaches. The following case discusses some of the factors used in deciding whether or not a breach is material. It also discusses the measure of damages to be applied for an immaterial breach.

ALASKA STATE HOUSING AUTHORITY v. WALSH & CO.
625 P.2d 831 (Ak. 1980)

The Alaska State Housing Authority (ASHA) contracted with Walsh and Co. for a roadway to be constructed. The specifications called for a 12-inch bed of wood chips to be covered by a mechanically crushed 12-inch layer of gravel. A dispute arose concerning the thickness of the layers applied by Walsh and the method of crushing the stone.

Walsh filed suit against ASHA for monies owed under the contract. ASHA filed a counterclaim for damages because of the alleged "deficiency" of Walsh's performance. The trial court found that Walsh had substantially performed and awarded a sum of money to Walsh. Both Walsh and ASHA appealed to the Alaska Supreme Court.

CONNER, Judge

[T]he doctrine of substantial performance permits recovery by a contractor who has substantially, though imperfectly, performed his contractual undertaking. In such circumstances, the contractor is entitled to recover the contract price, less the reasonable costs of remedying the defects in the work or materials. The initial burden of proving substantial performance is on the contractor. If his evidence shows substantial performance, the burden is then upon the owner to prove that certain deficiencies in the work require a [reduction in price]. As it applies here, the burden should be on ASHA to establish any [reduction in price] for deficiencies in performance of the work. Substantial performance is determined by considering such factors as the character of the performance that was promised, the purpose that the contract was meant to serve, and the extent to which any nonperformance by the contractor has defeated the purposes or ends which were meant to be achieved. This means that in many cases substantial performance becomes a matter of degree, to be determined by weighing a number of factors together.

In the case at bar the trial court stated: "in reaching the conclusion that Walsh did substantially perform its obligations I especially considered the ex-

tent of Walsh's performance, the lack of any willful noncompliance with the technical specifications, and the fact that the roadway as constructed has not required any inordinate or special maintenance by ASHA."

We now address ASHA's contention that the trial court erred in finding that there was substantial performance by Walsh. ASHA's argument is that the departures from the contract specifications were so grave that the owner was deprived of what it bargained for in that the road it received in its entirety averaged only 75 percent of the specified insulation depth, with a 2,000 foot section averaging only 40 percent of the design insulation depth.

However, the court had before it evidence that the road was substantially serving its intended purpose and did not require rebuilding. The evidence on this point consisted of both oral testimony and documentary evidence, from which inferences could be drawn both for and against a finding that Walsh had substantially performed. . . . We conclude that the trial court did not err in deciding that substantial performance had been rendered.

In cases of substantial performance, [damages] in construction should be measured either by the cost of correcting the deficiency or, if this would involve unreasonable economic waste, the difference in value between the project as contracted for and as received. ASHA estimates that it will cost $696,860 to bring the most deficient portion of the road into compliance with the contract. The court was not compelled to accept this estimate and could have properly found that the cost involved in re-building the road would constitute economic waste, but it could not merely award the value of the omit-ted materials as a proper alternative measure of damages.

The aim in assessing damages for deficiencies in performance should be to put the injured party in substantially as good a position as performance in accordance with the contract. The law recognizes, however, that sometimes actual reconstruction in compliance with the plans and specifications of the contract may be possible only at a cost that would be imprudent and unreasonable. In such cases, the court should consider alternative measures . . . which will substantially compensate the injured party for the deficiency in a less economically wasteful manner. For example, it may be possible to remedy the defect in the construction without having to tear down and rebuild. Although contro-verted, evidence was presented that the road as constructed by Walsh could be brought up to de-sign function without rebuilding by placing crushed gravel over the under-insulated areas of the road. If so, the cost of repairing the defect in this manner could provide the appropriate measure of damages. Alternatively, recovery could be measured by the reasonable maintenance costs for foreseeable addi-tional repair made necessary by the wood chip short-age. If, in the last analysis, the court is convinced that the defect cannot be remedied without economic waste, it must award ASHA the diminished value of the road due to the defect.

. . . [W]e remand to the superior court for a re-determination of the amount . . . owed to ASHA as a result of the wood chip deficiency.

Case Questions

1. What is the purpose of the doctrine of sub-stantial performance? Was it achieved in this case?

2. What factors did the court pinpoint in deter-mining whether ASHA substantially per-formed? Are there others that are relevant?

3. What measure of damages did the court suggest were proper in this case? Analyze. How do you believe the damages should be calculated?

Remedies for Substantial Performance

The whole subject of remedies will be more fully discussed later in this chapter. Even though a party has performed substantially, he or she has still breached, since something less than full perfor-mance has been given. Therefore, the breaching party is liable to the nonbreaching party for the dam-ages caused by the breach.

As mentioned in *Walsh*, the measure of damages will typically be the cost of repairing the defect or completing the unfinished part of the contract. If repairs would cause **economic waste**—that is, sub-stantial destruction of the property or unreasonable costs—then damages would be measured by the difference in value between the thing contracted for and the thing obtained. To illustrate, Home-owner contracts with Ace Construction for a 150-square-foot swimming pool for $25,000. The pool as built is only 125 square feet and is valued at $21,000. Homeowner is entitled to $4,000 dam-ages, since repairing the pool would create eco-nomic waste.

Some courts distinguish between willful and non-willful breaches. Where a willful breach occurs—for example, a builder walks off the job for no reason—the builder would be entitled to no re-covery in some jurisdictions and recovery under quasi-contract (the reasonable value of goods and services rendered) in other jurisdictions (see Fig-ure 18–2).

Remedies for a Material Breach

In the case of a material breach, it is clear that the breaching party often confers some benefit on the injured party. To illustrate, Ace Construction so neg-ligently constructs a home for Otto, the owner of the property, that its breach is considered material. Since Ace's performance is less than substantial, Ace may not recover on the contract for its expec-tation of profit.

Two doctrines may help Ace. It may recover in quasi-contract for the value of the unjust enrichment conferred on Otto (see Figure 18–2). Or, courts may find the building contract to be **divisible,** treat-

Figure 18–2   Recovery in Cases of Breach of Contract

	Immaterial Breach	**Material Breach**
Nonwillful Breach	Contract price minus cost to repair or Difference in value between the thing obtained and thing contracted for	Quasi-contract
Willful Breach	Quasi-contract	$0

ing it as if it were made up of several distinct parts. Ace might be permitted to recover for substantially performing part of the contract—for example, building the main dwelling—but be denied recovery for a material breach in its construction of the barn and garage. Whether a contract is divisible often depends on whether the subject matter can be easily separated. This concept of divisibility is further explored in this chapter in the section that discusses installment contracts. Nonetheless, if the material breach is willful, the builder is not entitled to recovery (see Figure 18–2).

Effect of Delay

The question often arises whether a delay in performance is to be treated as a material breach. Most modern authorities suggest that time is not "of the essence" since a short delay often does not matter to either party. Language contained in a form contract stating that "time is of the essence" will often not be determinative either. The key is whether the parties actually intended that this clause be given legal effect. Courts look not only at what the parties said but also at what they did in determining the actual scope of their contract.

One issue that often arises here is the effect of one party's regular acceptance of late payment despite a contractual provision that "time is of the essence" in payment. To illustrate, Vivian sells her home to Earl for $75,000. The contract provided for a down payment of $10,000 with monthly payments of $600 due the first of each month. A provision in the contract states that "time is of the essence" in payment. Earl regularly pays more than a week late and Vivian accepts the late payment without protest. Vivian's regular acceptance of late payment generally prevents Vivian from treating another late payment as a material breach. If Vivian wished to en-

force the "time is of the essence" clause, she would have to first give Earl a notice, specifically indicating that contrary to past practice, the clause would be strictly enforced in the future.

Anticipatory Repudiation

Any statement to the promisee that unequivocally expresses that the promisor is unwilling or unable to substantially perform his or her contractual duties is a **repudiation** and constitutes a breach. If the statement is made before the date due for performance, it is called an **anticipatory repudiation.** To illustrate, Violet agrees to transfer title to her home to Calvin on May 1. On March 1, Violet indicates that she will, in fact, not sell her home on May 1. In such a case, Calvin may treat the contract as breached and sue for damages immediately, without waiting for the date performance is due.

Performance of the Sales Contract

The rules that we have been examining have been mainly applicable in the nongoods area. The following material examines performance principles under the Code for the sale of goods. Treated in this area are the Code's perfect tender rule and its provisions on installment sales.

UCC § 2–601. Buyer's Rights on Improper Delivery

. . . if the goods or the tender of delivery [by the seller] fail in any respect to conform to the contract, the buyer may

   (a) reject the whole; or

   (b) accept the whole; or

   (c) accept any commercial unit or units and reject the rest.

The Perfect Tender Rule

A quick reading of UCC section 2–601 indicates that a seller must perfectly perform; anything less gives the buyer a right to reject.

There are exceptions, however, to this UCC perfect tender rule. First, the common law maxim *de minimis non curat lex* mentioned earlier in this chapter (the law will not cure trivial defects) applies to contracts for the sale of goods. Thus, in a contract for the sale of a car, if there are minor scratches in the paint or slight tears of the carpet, the buyer would not have a right to reject. Second, UCC section 2–508 gives a seller a right to remedy an imperfect tender. The third major exception to the perfect tender rule concerns installment contracts.

Installment Contracts

While a perfect tender (within the limits described above) is required when goods are tendered *in a single delivery,* a buyer may not reject for just "any defect" if the contract is an **installment contract.** An installment contract is a contract that "authorizes the delivery of goods in separate lots." To illustrate, if a wholesaler is to deliver 50 washers to a retailer, the washers to be delivered at a rate of five per month for the next 10 months, the contract would be an installment contract. In an installment contract, the buyer may reject any installment only if the defect "substantially impairs the value of that installment and cannot be cured."[1] Installment contracts are treated differently than single-delivery contracts because of the installment buyer's perceived bargaining strength. Since the seller must continue to deal with (and please) the installment buyer, the buyer does not need the drastic remedy of declaring a total breach for any slight nonconformity. Informal negotiations should straighten out most problems. In contrast, the single-delivery buyer is in a relatively weak bargaining position and needs the protection of the perfect tender rule since the seller does not have to deal with the buyer in the future.

Courts apply the traditional distinction of material and immaterial defects (insubstantial and substantial performance) to installment contracts for the sale of goods. If a seller's breach is material, the buyer may *reject* the goods and sue for damages for that one installment. The remainder of the contract continues. In contrast, if a seller's breach is immaterial, so that he or she substantially performs, the buyer *must pay* for the goods and seek damages for the breach.

DISCHARGE

A **discharge** releases the parties from their obligations under the contract. Normally, obligations are discharged when they are fully performed. Thus, a perfect tender discharges contractual duties concerning a sale of goods. Two other basic methods of discharge will be further explored — discharge resulting from a *change of circumstances* and discharge by the *assent of the parties.*

Discharge by a Change in Circumstances

Sometimes, after a contract is entered but before performance, circumstances change so radically that performance becomes impossible. For example, one of the parties to the contract may die or the subject matter of the contract may be destroyed. At other times, performance is possible but the purpose of one of the parties in entering the contract is now completely frustrated by the change of circumstances.

The basic rule to be employed in both cases is that a person may be discharged from contractual obligations when the change affects a basic assumption on which the contract is made; and the risk that this change would occur is not assumed by either party.

Death or Incapacity

Ordinarily, death or incapacity terminates an offer but does not discharge a contractual obligation. Thus, contracts for the sale of goods or real estate can normally be enforced against an obligor's estate. Often, however, the contract assumes the health or continued life of one of the contracting parties. In such a case, a substitute, such as the estate of the obligor, could not render adequate performance. To illustrate, a person may promise to perform personal services such as medical care or teaching. The death or incapacity of the doctor or teacher renders performance impossible. Contractual obligations under such circumstances would be discharged.

---

[1] UCC § 2–612(2).

Performance Prevented by Law

A basic assumption of parties to a contract is that their respective performances will continue to be lawful in the future. When a change in the law prevents or prohibits performance (and the risk of the change is not assumed by either party), performance is discharged. For example, suppose Ace Construction agreed to supply building materials to Xenos, a foreign nation. After declaring war on Xenos, Congress forbids all such sales. Ace would be discharged from its obligation due to this change in the law.

Destruction or Unavailability of Subject Matter

At times, the subject matter of the contract is destroyed or becomes unavailable before performance of the contract. The English case of *Taylor v. Caldwell*[2] is an excellent example of this means of discharging a contract. The plaintiff contracted for the use of defendant's music hall for a series of concerts. The music hall burned down before performance could be rendered. The defendant was discharged from its duty to perform due to the destruction of the subject matter essential to its performance.

Many contracts, particularly those involving the sale of goods and construction of buildings, ordinarily include provisions adjusting the price or allocating the risk of loss in case of the subject matter's destruction. When the risk is not allocated by contract or by a statute, the issue often becomes: who would have borne the risk of the subject matter's destruction if the parties had considered that possi-

bility? The answer to this question normally turns on who had control over the subject matter (such as a building) or who would more likely have insured against its loss. The party who controls the property or would have been more likely to have insured against its destruction will be deemed to bear the risk of its loss.

Commercial Impracticability

In the 1970s, as a result of historically unprecedented events such as oil embargoes, the rise of cartels, and double-digit inflation, many people who had entered long-term agreements for the sale or supply of goods faced serious economic problems. Prices for given commodities such as oil were based on traditionally reliable indexes such as the producer price index (PPI) that, in fact, failed to reflect the increase in production costs.[3] Many buyers likewise found themselves locked into contracts that did not adjust for industrywide technological advances and new governmental regulations.

When sellers and buyers were unable to informally work out a price adjustment in light of these market changes, they often sought judicial relief to either escape their contractual obligations or to reallocate the costs. The basic test used by courts, and embodied in UCC section 2–615, is whether the occurrence of this change of circumstances could have been foreseen by the obligor.

The following case discusses this foreseeability test.

---

[2]122 Eng. Rep. 309 (K.B. 1863).

[3]For example, the producer price index, based on some 2,800 products, rose 19 percent from 1973 to 1974, while the cost to produce a specific product such as ammonium nitrate explosives rose 300 percent. Basing prices on the PPI proved disastrous for many sellers.

MISSOURI PUBLIC SERVICE CO. v. PEABODY COAL CO.

583 S.W.2d 721 (Mo.1979)

In 1967, Peabody Coal entered into a 10-year supply contract with Public Service Corporation, a public utility. The contract provided for escalations in price to reflect the costs of labor, taxes, compliance with government regulations, and increase in transportation costs. The contract also included an inflation escalation clause based on the industrial commodities index published by the Department of Labor. Because of higher costs, Peabody attempted to negotiate a higher price per ton for the coal. Failing in that attempt Peabody declared its intention to discontinue coal shipments.

Public Service filed suit. The court entered a decree of specific performance in favor of Public Service Corporation. Peabody appealed.

SWOFFORD, Judge

Performance under the agreement was profitable for Peabody during the first two years of operation thereunder. Thereafter, production costs began to outpace the price adjustment features of the contract to the extent that . . . Peabody requested modification of the price adjustment features. Public Service rejected all proposed modifications in this area but did offer a modification to provide for an increase of $1 in the original cost per net ton. This proposal was rejected by Peabody.

. . . Peabody, by letter . . . mailed from its principal office in St. Louis, Missouri advised Public Service that upon the expiration of 60 days all coal shipments under the contract would cease, if the contract modifications were not agreed to by Public Service.

It is undisputed that Peabody possessed adequate coal supplies and ability to perform the contract. Rather, excuse from performance is claimed upon the basis of excessive economic loss under the agreement, absent modification; that excuse from performance was lawful upon the doctrine of ''commercial impracticability'' under Section 2–615.

Peabody claimed and the evidence tended to establish that the loss was occasioned largely because the escalation clause in the contract was based upon the Industrial Commodities Index which in years prior to the execution of the contract had been an accurate measure of inflation but had ceased to be an effective measure due to the . . . oil embargo, runaway inflation and the enactment of new and costly mine safety regulations. Public Service conceded a weakening of this significant function of the Industrial Commodities Index but introduced evidence, including admission by Peabody, that the events bringing this about were foreseeable at the time of the execution of the contract.

The comments accompanying [UCC section 2–615] treat it as dealing with the doctrine of ''commercial impracticability'' and central to this concept is that the doctrine may be applicable upon the occurrence of a supervening, unforeseen event not within the reasonable contemplation of the parties at the time the contract was made. Such occurrence must go to the heart of the contract.

. . . Peabody argues that in the resolution of this issue, only the contract in litigation should be considered by the court and that the factors of Peabody's financial conditions, experience in the production of coal, resources, availability of the raw material (coal reserves) and other factors should be disregarded. This argument is without merit and Peabody cites no authority in support thereof. Those factors have a direct bearing and evidentiary value in determining the question of foreseeability of the occurrence triggering the loss. A commercial, governmental or business trend affecting a contract's value which would be foreseeable to a party with wide experience and knowledge in the field and, perhaps, not to a party with less; a loss to a party with vast resources and ample supply of raw materials to perform a bad bargain would be less harmful than to a party without them; and, the application of the doctrine and the equitable principles inherent therein might call for relief in one instance and not another based upon these factors, and others, outside the strict confines of the contract itself.

The . . . claim made by Peabody alleged to bring it within the doctrine of ''commercial impracticability,'' is the . . . oil embargo. Such a possibility was common knowledge and had been thoroughly discussed and recognized for many years by our government, media economists and business, and the fact that the embargo was imposed during the term of the contract here involved was foreseeable. Peabody failed to demonstrate that this embargo affected its ability to secure oil and petroleum products necessary to its mining production albeit at inflated cost. In fact, as previously stated, this embargo can reasonably be said to have, at least indirectly, contributed to the market appreciation to the value of Peabody's coal reserves by forcing the market value of that alternative source of energy upward in this country.

It is apparent that Peabody did make a bad bargain and an unprofitable one under its contract with Public Service resulting in a loss, the cause and size of which is disputed. But this fact alone does not deal with either the ''basic assumption'' on which the contract was negotiated or alter the ''essential nature of the performance'' thereunder so as to constitute "commercial impracticability." The court below properly decreed specific performance.

The judgment is affirmed.

Case Questions

1. What is the issue in this case?
2. What does commercially impracticable mean? Why was the court not convinced that this contract was commercially impracticable?
3. What circumstances would have made this contract commercially impracticable?
4. Certain contractual clauses have been used to attempt to deal with changes in circumstances. Consider the drawbacks and benefits of the following clauses:

- *Force majeure clauses,* which excuse the seller from performance for events beyond his or her control such as fires, floods, war, civil strife, strikes, shortages of raw materials, and the like.
- *Price escalator clauses,* in which the parties may identify the principle components of the seller's fixed and variable cost such as raw materials, labor, overhead, depreciation, and taxes, and provide for a rise in the costs based on certain indexes.
- *Cost plus contracts,* in which the buyer agrees to pay a certain profit to the seller above the seller's actual costs.
- *Gross inequities clauses,* in which the seller and buyer agree to correct, by mutual assent, any gross inequity that arises from unusual economic conditions not contemplated by the parties.

Frustration of Purpose

Many contracts are neither impossible nor impracticable to perform. Nevertheless, a party may seek relief from his or her duty to perform when a change of circumstances makes the sought-for consideration valueless.

Suppose Ted agreed to rent Lisa's terrace to view the inauguration of the U.S. president. Due to an unusually cold day in Washington, D.C., the inauguration took place indoors. Although Ted was still entitled to use the terrace, his purpose in renting it would be frustrated. Hence, Ted would be excused from his duty to rent the terrace.

Two things are required before relief will be granted. First, the promisor's purpose in entering the contract must be totally frustrated. If subsidiary purposes, such as making money, may still be achieved, the contract will not be excused. Second, the frustrating event must not be foreseeable. The doctrine of frustration of purpose is discussed in the following reading.

---

*Henry's Lost Spectacle and Hutton's Lost Speculation: A Classic Riddle Solved?**

In *Henry,* rooms at 56A Pall Mall were let to the defendant for 26 and 27 June 1902. The rooms overlooked the route of processions associated with the coronation of King Edward VII which were scheduled to take place on the two days in question. In *Hutton,* the plaintiffs agreed to put their boat, the *Cynthia,* at the disposal of the defendant on 28 and 29 June 1902, "for the purpose of viewing the naval review and for a day's cruise round the fleet." On those two days a royal naval review was scheduled to take place at Spithead, again in connection with the coronation. Due to the unexpected illness of the King neither the processions nor the naval review took place, although the fleet remained anchored at Spithead on 28 and 29 June. In both cases the defendants argued that the contracts were frustrated. In *Henry,* the Court of Appeal held that there was frustration; in *Hutton* they refused to accede to the plea of frustration. Moreover, to compound the puzzle as to why the cases were decided differently, the Court of Appeal on each occasion comprised the same three judges. . . .

---

*Source: Roger Brownsword, "Henry's Lost Spectacle and Hutton's Lost Speculation: A Classic Riddle Solved," 129 *Solicitors Journal* 860 (1985). Reprinted with permission.

Points of View

There are, in principle, four views that can be taken about the decisions given in *Henry* and *Hutton*. These are as follows: (i) Both cases were decided correctly; (ii) *Henry* was right but *Hutton* was wrong; (iii) *Henry* was wrong, but *Hutton* was right; and (iv) both cases were decided incorrectly. . . . A typical student reaction to the cases is exactly that *Henry* was right, but *Hutton* was wrong, because there, too, the contract should have been held to have been frustrated. . . .

Points of Argument

Defenders of view (i) have expended a great deal of effort in seeking a persuasive reconciliation of the two cases. . . . To put a long story shortly, there are three leading arguments canvassed in defence of view (i), in defence of a plausible reconciliation. First, it is said that the room in *Henry* had some special quality that the boat in *Hutton* lacked. . . . The point is that the room (with a view) no more and no less than the boat (in the vicinity of Spithead) was a limited commodity, and whatever was special about the room was equally special about the boat, although neither was unique.

A second argument is that the purpose of the contract in *Henry* was to view the processions, whereas the purpose in *Hutton* was merely to have a boat. Now, the well known difficulty with this line is that the purpose of viewing the processions was merely implicit in *Henry* (although there was clear background evidence of this intention as the rooms were advertised as windows to view the coronation processions), whereas, in *Hutton*, the contract expressly referred to the purpose as being to view the naval review and to cruise round the fleet. If the coronation celebrations were at the foundation of the contract in *Henry*, then this seems to be so . . . in *Hutton*. So this will not do either.

Finally, a third argument begins by taking it that in both contracts the coronation celebrations were at the heart of the contractual understanding. The difference between the two cases is then seen to be a matter of degree. In *Henry* the non occurrence of the processions deprived the defendant of substantially the whole benefit of the contract; in *Hutton* the cancellation of the naval review still left the defendant with a significant part of the contracted consideration, namely, the chance to use the boat to see the fleet (which, it will be remembered, stayed anchored at Spithead). It is this third argument which is generally offered by defenders of view (i) as the best available, even if it is perhaps a bit slippery and leaves something to be desired. This argument is the best of the conventional reconciliations, but it is not the best available for the simple reason that it misses the most significant feature of the cases.

''Consumer Disappointment''

The image conjured up by the conventional presentation of the two cases, and unquestionably the view that students tend to adopt, is that the cases are to be understood in terms of relative consumer disappointment. In *Henry* the defendant would have been totally disappointed by the loss of the processions; in *Hutton* the loss of the naval review was a disappointment, but there was some compensation in that the fleet was still in the area. This, the writer suggests, is badly wrong and the source of the confusion. For, although it depicts *Henry* correctly enough, it totally misrepresents the position in *Hutton*. The defendant in *Hutton*, as the textbooks note, was hiring the *Cynthia* with a view to taking out a party. Were these friends? Hardly, for, as the textbooks again note but perhaps do not sufficiently emphasize, the defendant in *Hutton* . . . was intending to take out paying passengers. In short, Hutton was dealing in the course of business. . . . The essential feature of *Hutton* was that the defendant was acting in a business capacity, entering into a commercial speculation; whereas, in *Henry,* the defendant was not acting in any business capacity whatsoever. Accordingly, if we return to the imagery of relative disappointment, we see that the cases are distinguishable not by virtue of exhibiting different degrees of disappointment but rather different kinds of disappointment. In *Henry* the disappointment was of the private consumer kind. But, not so in *Hutton,* for the defendant there suffered commercial disappointment, a disappointment of a very different order. Hutton's loss was not that he did not see the naval review, merely the fleet; presumably, he did not care very much about this either way. His loss was a loss of a material rather than a cultural kind. What he lost was the opportunity to cash in on the naval review to the extent anticipated. In short, while Henry lost on the spectacle, Hutton lost on the speculation.

■ ■ ■

Definitely and Decidedly Correct

. . . To complete the case for the defence of view (i) it must be shown that *Henry,* too, was correctly decided. Once again, Lord Radcliffe's approach holds the key and suggests that *Henry* was right. The reason for this is that the defendant in *Henry* could fairly say that the contract for the letting of the rooms was radically different once the processions were cancelled. The suite of chambers on the third floor at 56A Pall Mall may well have had a delightful aspect, but without the procession they were of no interest to Henry. What was being purchased was a real consumer opportunity, not a ''white elephant'' and not a *commercial* opportunity. The radical differences lay in consumer disappointment, not in economic loss. In the light of modern policy objectives, there seems no reason why the courts should disallow frustration in the context of a non business agreement where there is a clear failure of a condition precedent to performance. On the contrary, frustration should be employed to prevent unjust enrichment in such circumstances.

Thought Questions

1. What does the author suggest is the basis for distinguishing between *Henry* and *Hutton?*
2. Are there any flaws in the author's reasoning? Make the argument that *Henry* and *Hutton* were decided incorrectly.
3. Should people be able to escape their contractual obligations simply because their purpose in entering the contract was frustrated? Analyze.

Discharge by Assent

The preceding sections discussed various ways that a contractual obligation might be discharged through a change of circumstances. Obligations may also be discharged by agreement of the parties through mutual rescission, accord and satisfaction or novation.

Mutual Rescission   *Both parties agreeing not to perform*

When a bilateral contract has not yet been performed, the parties may enter a new contract in which each surrenders his or her rights against the other. This is called a **mutual rescission.** To illustrate, Harvey promised to pay Priscilla $500 in exchange for Priscilla's promise to paint Harvey's house. Before performance, Harvey surrenders his rights under the old contract in exchange for Priscilla's surrender of her rights. The old contract is mutually rescinded.

If the contract has been partly performed, the issue, in cases not involving the sale of goods, will be whether there was consideration given for the performing party's release of the other party. In such cases, if there is consideration, the release will be

Figure 18–3   Accord and Satisfaction—Substituted Performance

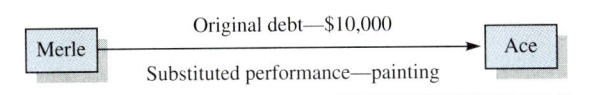

Figure 18–4   Novation—Substituted Parties

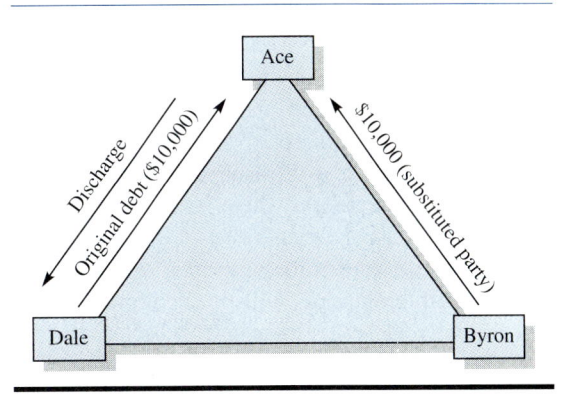

upheld. In cases involving the sale of goods, UCC section 2–209 permits a rescission without consideration.

Accord and Satisfaction

An **accord and satisfaction** is another way of effectuating a discharge by agreement. An accord and satisfaction occurs when a party agrees to accept a substituted performance in place of the other's original duty. Thus, if Merle owed Ace Construction $10,000, the debt could be satisfied by a mutual agreement of a substituted performance from Merle—for example, painting Ace's office building (see Figure 18–3).

Novation

A novation is still another manner of discharge by agreement. Unlike an accord and satisfaction, which requires a substituted *performance*, a **novation** involves a substitution *of parties*. In a novation, by the agreement of all the parties, a third party is substituted for one of the original parties. To illustrate, Dale owes Ace Construction $10,000. By agreement, Ace agrees to accept Byron's promise to pay the $10,000 and to discharge Dale from Dale's duty to pay. Dale's duty is extinguished. Ace may now look only to Byron for payment. Ace would be apt to agree to a novation if Byron is at least as creditworthy as Dale, the original debtor (see Figure 18–4).

A novation differs from an *assignment*, discussed in Chapter 17, since an assignment does not require either the knowledge or assent of the obligee. Moreover, in an assignment, the obligor is still liable under the original contract. To illustrate, Thelma owes Cliff (the obligee) $1,000. By an agreement between Thelma and Nellie, Thelma (the obligor) delegates her duty to pay. Cliff is not required to assent to this delegation. Thelma is not discharged until Nellie pays. As a general rule, then, debtors prefer novations to assignments since a novation discharges the debtor from any further obligation under the contract.

REMEDIES

Where performance is not discharged, any failure to perform amounts to a breach for which the law provides **remedies**. Remedies may involve money, restitution, or specific performance.

Damages — *Monetary*

As a general rule, **damages** for a breach of contract are designed to place the victim in the same economic position he or she would have occupied had the contract been fully performed. There are limits on the losses that contract law deems recoverable as damages, as the following section discusses.

Limitations on Damages

A person may not recover for *all* losses flowing from a breach. One limit is found in the rule that a nonbreaching party must make reasonable efforts to **mitigate** (that is, minimize) **damages**. This "duty to mitigate" is a commonsense requirement that forbids persons from sitting idly back and allowing losses to pile up. To illustrate the mitigation limit, assume that Marlene, a plumber, negligently repairs Barry's basement pipes, causing water to leak into Barry's basement. Barry discovers the leak, knows how to shut the water main off, but does nothing to stop it. Barry may not recover for the losses that could have been avoided through his reasonable efforts. The following case involving the wrongful firing of a gymnastics coach illustrates the duty to mitigate damages.

WILLSON v. BOARD OF TRUSTEES

Lexis 6303 (Ohio Ct. App. 1991)

Michael Willson, the Ohio State University gymnastics coach, was informed by Jim Jones, the athletic director, that his coaching contract would not be renewed for the upcoming academic year. Willson was given the option to resign or be reassigned to the ticket office at the same salary, where he could sell football tickets and reevaluate his career goals.

A dispute arose as to whether Willson had already entered into a contract with the University for the upcoming year. The University then officially informed Willson that he was terminated. Willson sued for breach of contract and the jury found for him but awarded only $1 on the basis that Willson failed to mitigate his damages by accepting other employment. Willson moved for a judgment notwithstanding the verdict, which the court granted, awarding him damages in the amount of his unpaid salary of $37,119.06. The defendant, the Board of Trustees of The Ohio State University appealed to the Ohio Court of Appeals.

BOWMAN, Judge

. . . Jones and the Board [of Trustees] assert that the trial court erred in granting Willson's motion for judgment notwithstanding the verdict on the issue of contract damages. Jones and the Board assert that ample evidence was presented by which the jury could conclude that Willson failed to use ordinary effort to obtain similar employment and mitigate damages and, thus, the award of $1 for breach of contract was well within the jury's discretion.

. . . [T]he usual remedy in a breach of contract case for wrongful discharge is to pay the injured party the difference between any wages due under the contract from the date of discharge until the contract term expires. That amount is to be reduced by any wages the employee earned in subsequent employment. A party seeking to recover such compensation is required to mitigate damages; however, a wrongfully discharged employee need only accept similar employment in mitigation. The party must use ordinary care to obtain similar employment and the employee's exercise of due diligence should be considered in light of available employment opportunities. The employer has the burden of proof on the issue of mitigation of damages.

In this case, the jury found that Willson had entered into an employment agreement for the position of men's gymnastics coach at OSU for the 1988–89 academic year, that Jones and the Board breached the employment agreement and that Willson, in the exercise of ordinary diligence, could have found, or was offered, similar employment in the same vicin-

ity. . . . The jury did not award Willson any lost fringe benefits. . . .

This court agrees with the trial court that reasonable minds could not reach different conclusions regarding Willson's attempts to find comparable employment. The evidence presented at trial was that the only comparable employment, head gymnastics coach at the intercollegiate level, was at Michigan State University and the United States Naval Academy. The evidence shows that Willson applied for both of these positions and that Jones recommended that he be interviewed for these positions. Regardless, Willson not only was not hired for either of these positions, he was not even interviewed for them. In addition, there was evidence that Willson attempted to obtain employment in other areas of gymnastics, but that he was unsuccessful in those endeavors as well.

This court agrees with the trial court that the position which Willson was offered in the OSU ticket office does not constitute comparable employment to that of head men's gymnastics coach. If that were the case, then an athletic ticket office employee could be offered the head coaching position of the men's gymnastics team. Accordingly, the trial court properly granted Willson's motion for judgment notwithstanding the verdict on the issue of contract damages.

Case Questions

1. What is the issue this case presents?
2. What is the purpose of the mitigation of damage rule?

3. What if Jones offered Willson an assistant gymnastics coach position at the same salary? Must Willson accept the position to mitigate damages? What is a ''comparable position''?

4. What if there was a private gymnastics club that offered Willson a job at a comparable salary teaching gymnastics to children? Would he be required to mitigate his damages by accepting the position? Analyze.

5. Assume that Willson accepted a position unrelated to coaching or gymnastics. Must the amount he received be deducted from the damage award? Explain.

In addition to mitigating damages, another limitation on recovery is the rule that damages must be established with a reasonable degree of certainty. This *certainty* limitation does not demand calculations that are mathematically precise. Damages from the breach of an *output contract,* for example, can be recovered although they are not mathematically certain. Nevertheless, damages may not be awarded on a purely speculative basis. This certainty limitation has, therefore, often been used to deny recovery for the lost profits of a new business resulting from a breach, since these losses would be too uncertain.

A third rule limits recovery for damages to those that are either *foreseeable* to the breaching party or would naturally flow from the breach. This limitation is often referred to as the rule in *Hadley v. Baxendale,*[4] for it was this 1854 English decision that laid down this limitation. The rule in *Hadley* may be divided into two parts. First, the aggrieved party may recover those damages that ''may fairly and reasonably be considered . . . to arise naturally . . . from such breach of contract itself.'' Thus, if a machine part for a lathe is not delivered on time, the aggrieved party can naturally be expected to have to rent a lathe and thus lose the rental value of the lathe for the period of delay. Second, in addition, damages may be recovered if the breaching party had reason to know of any additional damages that might flow as a probable result of the breach. Using the prior illustration, if the breaching party had reason to know that no substitute machine was available, that party would be liable in addition for the lost profits resulting from the delay. The following case applies the rule of *Hadley v. Baxendale* to a modern setting.

---

[4]156 Eng. Rep. 145 (1854).

PRUTCH v. FORD MOTOR COMPANY
618 P.2d 657 (Colo. 1980)

Carl and Sam Prutch, the plaintiffs, purchased a tractor, plow, disc harrow, and hay baler from Baldridge Implement Company. The Prutches contend that they suffered crop damages as a result of defects in those farm implements.

The Prutches sued Baldridge and the manufacturer of the farm equipment, Ford Motor Company, for breach of express and implied warranties. The trial resulted in a verdict in favor of the Prutches against Ford Motor Co. in the amount of $60,200. Ford appealed. The court of appeals overturned the jury verdict. The Prutches appealed to the Supreme Court of Colorado.

BY THE COURT

Ford contends that it cannot be charged with the crop damages incurred by the Prutches. Colorado law authorizes consequential damages for ''[a]ny loss resulting from general or particular requirements and needs of which the seller at the time of contracting had reason to know and which could not reasonably be prevented. . . .'' The court of appeals noted that the Colorado statutory scheme rejects the ''tacit agreement'' test that would permit consequential damages only if the seller specifically contemplated or actually assumed the risk of such damages. . . . Rather, as the court of appeals observed, recovery of consequential damages is determined by the test of ''foreseeability'' of consequences.

Ford would have us construe ''foreseeability'' to generate liability only if a manufacturer had some prior actual knowledge as a basis for anticipating damage. But the defendant, in trying to add the ingredient of ''prior knowledge'' to the ''foreseeability'' concept, confuses ''foreseeable'' with ''actually foreseen.'' A standard that would require actual ''prior knowledge'' by defendant would impose liability only upon proof that the defendant actually foresaw consequential damages. Such a test would be excessively restrictive. The statutory ''reason to know'' standard, in our view, triggers liability for consequences that may not have been actually foreseen but which were foreseeable.

A manufacturer knowing that its products will be used for crop production reasonably can be expected to foresee that defects in those products may cause crop losses. In such circumstances, therefore, the manufacturer should not escape liability by arguing that it did not actually foresee probable consequences which it should have foreseen. [The court of appeals judgment is reversed and the jury verdict reinstated.]

Case Questions

1. What is the issue in this case?
2. What was the nature of Ford's breach? Does the common law or the UCC govern this contract? Why?
3. Identify the test of foreseeability the court discusses. Analyze.
4. Does the court adopt an objective or subjective test of foreseeability? Cite language of the court to support your view.

Compensatory Damages

The most common type of damages granted for a breach of contract is **compensatory damages.** These are designed to put the injured party in as good a position as he or she would have been in had the contract not been breached. Generally, an injured party will be able to recover an amount that compensates for his or her disappointed expectations. Sometimes this is called the *benefit of the bargain,* the amount he or she would have gained had the contract been performed.

A basic formula for calculating damages is:

Benefit of the bargain = (Loss in value + Incidental damages + Consequential damages) − (Costs avoided)

Loss of Value   The loss of value to the nonbreaching party caused by the breach varies, of course, with the subject matter of the contract. Examples include the cost of repairing faulty construction, the difference in cost of purchasing comparable goods in the marketplace, the loss of royalties from a nonpublished book, or the additional cost of hiring new help when an employee wrongfully quits.

Incidental Damages   Incidental damages are the costs that the nonbreaching party incurs to obtain substituted performance. Illustrative of incidental damages are phone calls, salesperson's commissions, employment agency or brokerage fees, and automobile expenses to procure substituted goods.

Consequential Damages   Consequential damages are injuries to the person or property that the breaching party *has reason to know* would result from the breach. These may include injuries to a person due to defective products or the loss of future sales resulting from the nondelivery of goods or a machine to a business. The *Prutch* case and the rule in *Hadley v. Baxendale* were concerned with limiting the amount of consequential damages that would flow from a breach.

Costs Avoided   Costs avoided are subtracted from the sum of loss in value, incidental damages, and consequential damages. Costs avoided are the amount the nonbreaching party did *not* incur because of the breach.

To illustrate, Sam, the seller of a large grist mill that cost $25,000, wrongfully repudiates his contract to sell the mill to Ben, the buyer. Ben incurred $1,000 in sales commissions, phone calls, and delivery charges in buying another grist mill. The new mill cost $30,000. In addition, Ben lost two valu-

Figure 18–5   Computation of Damages

Loss in value (in this case, the difference in cost of the new and old mills).	$ 5,000
Incidental damages (the costs incurred to buy a substitute mill).	1,000
Consequential damages (the lost contracts that the seller had reason to know would result from the breach).	10,000
	$16,000
Costs avoided (the amount saved by the cheaper foundation).	−2,000
Total damage	$14,000

able contracts for grinding grain (he told seller about these). These contracts would have produced $10,000 in profits. The new mill requires a cheaper foundation, saving Ben $2,000 in building costs. Ben's damages would be calculated by the basic formula as shown in Figure 18–5.

Agreed Damages

Parties may agree to a contractual clause that fixes damages according to some formula in case of a breach. This avoids the necessity of having to prove damages and is particularly useful where damages may be uncertain.

Certain agreed damage clauses are unenforceable. Courts refuse to uphold clauses that are designed to penalize or punish a breaching party as opposed to estimating possible damages if a breach occurs. Thus, courts distinguish two types of clauses: invalid **penalty clauses** and valid **liquidated damages** clauses.

The most important criteria in distinguishing the two clauses is the rule that the agreed damages must not be unreasonably disproportional to any anticipated loss. To illustrate, assume that Elliot agrees to deliver a computer to his friend Joyce on March 1. The contract contains a clause stating: "Elliot agrees to pay Joyce $1,000 per day for any delay in delivering the computer." This is probably an invalid penalty clause since there appears to be no reasonable relationship between the damages agreed on ($1,000) and the damages expected in case of a breach.

Forfeiture clauses provide that, in the case of a breach, a certain amount will be forfeited, such as an entire security deposit for breaching a rental

agreement. This will be considered an invalid penalty, unless the forfeited amount is a good faith attempt to reasonably fix damages according to an anticipated loss.

Nominal Damages

A small sum of money characterized as **nominal damages** is awarded when there is a breach of contract that results in no damages or an inability to prove damages. The amount may be as low as $1. Nominal damages may be important since it is a determination of who wins, and court costs are normally assessed against the losing party.

Punitive Damages

Damages may also be designed to punish the breaching party. These are called **punitive damages** and will normally be awarded in contract cases only in the exceptional circumstances in which a contract breach also constitutes a tort. To illustrate, a mechanic agrees to fix Casey's car, but in breach of his contract sells Casey's car to Maxine, a good faith purchaser, for value. The mechanic, in addition to breaking the contract, committed the tort of conversion and could be subject to punitive damages. Additionally, awards of punitive damages are proper when insurance companies breach their agreements in bad faith.

Restitution

Restitution is an alternative to measuring damages by the benefit of the bargain rule discussed in the section on compensatory damages. Restitution merely requires a person to disgorge or pay back the value of the benefit received. The aim of restitution is to restore the parties to the status quo, the position they would have been in were the contract *never* entered. In contrast, the benefit of the bargain rule is designed to put the parties in the position they would be in if the contract was fully performed.

The measure of damages for restitution is the amount by which a person is "unjustly enriched." This is normally calculated to be the cost of obtaining similar services elsewhere. Restitution is often available when a contract fails because of some illegality, a breach, or a failure to comply with the statute of frauds. Restitution is also available when there is no agreement and a party sues in quasi-contract (see Chapter 11).

Specific Performance

A court may order **specific performance** as an alternative to the award of damages for breach of a contract. Specific performance is performance of that which is required by the contract—for example, to convey title to a piece of property or to supply utilities to a business. It is an equitable remedy, designed to do justice where the legal remedy of damages is not adequate to protect a person's interest.

Generally, an order of specific performance is unavailable to enforce contracts for the sale of goods. This is because a damage award permits a buyer to purchase similar goods in the marketplace or compensates a seller for any loss suffered by the buyer's breach. If, however, the goods are unique and could not be readily obtained in the marketplace, specific performance of the contract is the appropriate remedy. Heirlooms, antiques, and art objects might therefore be the subject of an order of specific performance.

Contracts for the sale of land are generally subject to an order for specific performance. Damages are inadequate since every parcel of land is considered unique. Aggrieved purchasers can find no available substitute in the marketplace. Aggrieved sellers of land are also able to obtain specific performance for the purchase price.

Contracts for personal services are generally not enforceable by an order of specific performance. Courts are reluctant to impose on unwilling employees a situation similar to involuntary servitude.[5]

END–OF–CHAPTER QUESTIONS

1. What criteria would be likely indicators of a material breach?

2. Distinguish between commercial impracticability and frustration of purpose.

3. How does a novation differ from an accord and satisfaction? From an assignment?

4. What is the reason for classifying conditions as precedent, subsequent, and concurrent? As express and constructive?

5. The plaintiff, Tolstoy Construction Co., a contractor, promised to build the defendant, Minter, a homeowner, ''a real nice house'' for $21,500. Various difficulties were encountered: the carport was visibly out of plumb, areas of wood were left unpainted, there was no insulation, doors and windows were misaligned, cracks appeared in the kitchen tile, there was no light switch in one bathroom, and water leaked through the floor due to improper installation of a water heater. Did the contractor substantially perform on the contract? Why or why not? What remedies are available to Minter? To Tolstoy? See *Tolstoy Construction Co. v. Minter*, 143 Cal. Rptr. 570 (Ct. App. 1978).

6. An importer of sewing machines brought an action seeking to be excused from performance of its contract due to commercial impracticability. The importer's costs had doubled due to a dramatic devaluation of the dollar in relation to the Swiss franc. The contract called for an increase or decrease of price based on changes in the cost of insurance, freight, handling, broker or port fees, or similar charges but did not explicitly mention exchange rate fluctuations. Three weeks before the contract was executed, there was a 7 percent devaluation of the dollar in relation to the Swiss franc. Should the importer be excused from performance due to commercial impracticability? Justify your answer. See *Bernina Distributors, Inc. v. Bernina Sewing Machine Co.*, 646 F.2d 434 (10th Cir. 1981).

7. The defendant, Cannarella, purchased a large quantity of fish from the plaintiff, Jay Cee Fish Co., and was indebted to Jay Cee for approximately $8,900. Jay Cee was contacted by Cannarella, and advised that Cannarella was selling his business to Boan. Shortly thereafter, Boan began making payments to Jay Cee on Cannarella's account. Jay Cee regularly accepted these checks but then sued Cannarella for an amount allegedly still owing on his debt. What is Jay Cee's best defense? What is the probable result in

---

[5]Involuntary servitude is a condition whereby an employee is compelled against his or her will to work for an employer by threats of imprisonment, violence, or other coercive tactics.

this case? See *Jay Cee Fish Co. v. Cannarella*, 279 F. Supp. 67 (D.S.C. 1968).

8. Schatz Distributing Co, Inc., the plaintiff, purchased a computer from Olivetti Corp., the defendant, under a lease-purchase agreement. Schatz was promised that it would ''never outgrow'' the system. Schatz was unable to get the computer working. Numerous contacts and repairs failed to correct the problem. Olivetti knew that Schatz had borrowed the money to purchase the computer. Schatz had to purchase another computer from another company, and incurred finance charges, programming fees, electrical wiring expenses, and maintenance fees. What items may Schatz be compensated for in this case? Classify each component of his damages. See *Schatz Distributing Co., Inc. v. Olivetti Corp.*, 647 P.2d 820 (Kan. App. 1982).

9. The plaintiff entered into a contract to purchase a Corvette automobile from the defendant for $15,000. The car was one of a limited edition (approximately 6,000 cars were manufactured). Offers on the car varied from $14,000 to $28,000. What remedies are available to the buyer in the event the seller breaches the contract?

10. In a commercial sales contract, a clause provided that in the event of buyer's breach, ''the seller may recover the reasonable value of attorney's fees.'' This was assumed to be 30 percent of any amount actually recovered against the buyer in a breach of contract suit. If buyer breached, would this clause be enforceable? Justify your answer in light of UCC section 2–718(1). See *Equitable Lumber Corp. v. Ipa Land Development Corp.*, 344 N.E.2d 391 (N.Y. 1976).

Part IV

Sales

■

Chapter 19

Sales Contract: Nature and Formation

■

CRITICAL THINKING INQUIRIES

As you read this chapter, you should be able to address the following:

- Explain the relationship between the scope of common law contracts and Article 2.
- Explain the relationship between the common law approach to indefiniteness and the Article 2 approach.
- Evaluate the following statement: ''An offer can be revoked at any time before acceptance even if the offeror has promised to keep the offer open for a specified period of time.''
- Evaluate the following statement: ''In order to create a contract, the acceptance must be the mirror image of the offer.''
- Compare the common law and the Code approach to the requirement of a writing under the statute of frauds.

MANAGERIAL PERSPECTIVE

Jan is responsible for selling china for China Chefs. She receives an order for 100 place settings at $20 per setting from The Place Downstairs, a new restaurant. The order gives Jan 10 days within which to return an acceptance form and includes an acknowledgment form. Jan returns an acceptance form prepared for China Chefs agreeing to furnish the place settings for the price quoted in the purchase order.

- If the purchase order and the acceptance form contain different terms, does a contract exist?
- If neither form mentions delivery terms, is there a contract? Must China Chefs deliver the china at its expense?
- If China Chefs wants to increase its price to $25 and The Place Downstairs agrees to the contract modification, is the contract enforceable?

Creating binding contracts to sell goods is the most fundamental and common managerial objective in doing business. Even the service industry is involved indirectly in various aspects of sales contracts: auditing, shipping, loading and handling, inspection, insurance, financing, document preparation and transfer, repossession, and equipment purchase. Given the pervasive impact of all phases of goods sales on business, a good working knowledge of the Uniform Commercial Code is essential for all managers.

Managers conversant with nuances of the Code may exploit opportunities to reduce the risk of transactions and thereby minimize costs to their firm. This chapter addresses essential managerial concerns about how and when contract obligations are created. Additionally, managers will learn what contract terms are implied by the Code and how to override them with separately negotiated terms. Managers must become familiar with the special obligations placed on merchants in negotiating and performing contracts for the sale of goods.

INTRODUCTION

The law of sales is a subset of the law of contracts. The common law of contracts, discussed in Chapters 11 through 17, is applicable to the law of sales unless displaced by the Uniform Commercial Code [UCC § 1–103]. Therefore, the general contract law elements (offer and acceptance, consideration, legality, and capacity) apply to sales contracts. However, Article 2 modifies the common law somewhat by making sales contracts easier to form and by reducing the formalities required at common law.

Scope of Article 2

The law of sales, for transactions within the United States, is contained in Uniform Commercial Code (UCC) Article 2. Article 2 has been adopted in 49 of the 50 states, in all states but Louisiana. Article 2 governs all "transactions in goods" [UCC § 2–102]. However, for practical purposes, coverage is limited to contracts for the sale of goods. A **sale** is the passing of title from the seller to the buyer for a price [UCC § 2–106(1)]. This includes both present sales and contracts to sell goods in the future. Contracts for leases of goods are governed by UCC Article 2A.

Goods are all things that are movable at the time of identification to the contract for sale [UCC § 2–105(1)]. Specifically excluded from the definition of goods are investment securities, certain intangibles, and money in which the price is to be paid. The sale of money is considered a contract for the sale of goods only when the money is being treated as a commodity, as in a coin collection, not when it is the method of payment. Goods also include the unborn young of animals and growing crops. Both are frequently sold and the sale contract is typically negotiated before birth or harvest.

UCC § 2–105. Definitions

(1) ''Goods'' means all things . . . which are moveable at the time of identification to the contract for sale other than the money in which the price is to be paid, investment securities and things in action.

Perhaps the best way to understand what is a "good" is to consider what is not included in the definition. Essentially, Article 2 applies to transactions involving almost everything but *services* and *real property.* For example, Article 2 applies to a transaction where Ben Buyer contracts to buy a car from Sam Seller, but not where Ben contracts to buy a piece of real property from Sam. Similarly, Article 2 applies where Ben Buyer contracts to buy a used television set from his next-door neighbor, but not where that same neighbor agrees to repair Ben's television. Unfortunately, this distinction is not always easy to make.

Distinguishing Goods from Services

If The Place Downstairs hires Sam Seller to sell and install equipment, does Article 2 apply? Is it the sale of a good or a service? It is obviously the sale of both the equipment and its installation. The fact that the agreement involves a substantial amount of labor does not automatically exclude it from Article 2 coverage. Services often are a major factor in contracts for the sale of goods. Agreements for the sale of goods with services *incidentally* provided are covered by the Code. By contrast, agreements *primarily* for the provision of services with an incidental sale of goods are not covered by the Code. This test is not always easy to apply to a particular fact situation. Using this test, courts have disagreed about whether blood furnished in a blood transfusion or hair dye applied by a beautician are goods. Use this test in analyzing the following case, which raises the question of whether a contract to design and provide computer software was the contract for the sale of goods.

MICRO-MANAGERS, INC. v. GREGORY
147 Wis. 2d 500, 434 N.W.2d 91 (1988)

Gregory entered into a contract with Micro-Managers, Inc. (MMI), in which MMI agreed to design and develop software required to run a new programmable controller that Gregory was purchasing from another source. Gregory agreed to pay MMI at a rate of $40 per hour for software, $50 per hour for engineering, and $75 per hour for supervision. MMI delivered the software on the date specified and Gregory took delivery. Gregory complained that the software had not been completed to his satisfaction, but he did not permit MMI to correct any defects and in fact never indicated his specific objections.

When Gregory failed to pay, MMI sued Gregory for breach of contract. Gregory counterclaimed that the software was so defective that it constituted a breach of the implied warranty of fitness for a particular purpose.

DYKMAN, Judge

It is undisputed that this was a mixed contract, i.e. a contract for both goods and services. The issue is whether the mixed contract was predominantly for goods or for services.

"The test for inclusion or exclusion [within the UCC] is not whether [contracts] are mixed, but, granting they are mixed, whether their predominant factor, their thrust, their purpose, reasonably stated, is the rendition of service, with goods incidentally involved (e.g., contract with artist for painting) or is a transaction of sale, with labor incidentally involved (e.g. installation of a water heater in a bathroom)."[1]

Gregory cites many cases which he alleges support construing the contract as one primarily for goods. Nevertheless, we conclude that *Data Processing v. L.H. Smith Oil Corp.* is on point and more compelling. In that case, as here, the parties contracted for custom computer programming. The appellate court phrased the issue as "whether a contract to provide computer programming is a contract for the sale and purchase of goods and thus subject to the provisions of article 2 of the UCC, or one for the performance of services, and thus subject to common law principles." The court noted that "DPS was *to act* with specific regard to Smith's

need. Smith bargained for DPS's skill in developing a system to meet its specific needs." The court concluded the contract was for services, and not subject to UCC warranty provisions. The court held that the "mere means by which DPS's skills and knowledge were to be transmitted to Smith's computers was incidental."

In the present case, the contract provided that all MMI charges to Gregory would be on the basis of time, at stated rates, and materials. We must determine whether the contract's predominant factor, thrust and purpose is the rendition of a service or the transaction of a sale. We may look to evidence of billing to determine this issue. On January 18, 1983, Terry Coleman, an agent for Gregory, wrote the following in a letter to Sally Peterson, president of MMI: "3. The projected total, excluding bonus, is therefore approximately $59,828, of which $55,969 is labor." In addition, we may look to the language of the contract to determine whether it is more in accord with services instead of sales. The contract speaks in terms of "mandays," "development," "time," "design," etc. These words connote the rendition of services and not a sales transaction.

Based on this evidence, we conclude that this was primarily a service contract. The method by which MMI transmitted that service was merely incidental. Therefore the transaction is not subject to the provisions of the UCC.

---

[1]*Bonebrake v. Cox.*

Case Questions

1. Was the sale of the computer software the sale of a good covered by Article 2?

2. What test did the court use to make this determination?

3. Why did it matter whether or not the contract was covered by Article 2?

4. What impact does the designation of goods or services have on the buyer's rights?

Distinguishing Goods from Real Property

When property attached to real property is to be sold, is it goods or real property? It could be considered real property because it is attached to realty. Alternatively, it could be considered goods because it will be severed when sold and movable at the time of sale. Code treatment depends on the type of property: minerals, crops, timber, or buildings.

Minerals such as oil and gas, buildings, or other materials to be removed from real property are goods as long as they are severed *by the seller.* A contract for the sale of copper ore to be mined by the seller, then transported and delivered to the buyer, is a contract for sale under Article 2. However, the same contract is not governed by the Code if the copper ore is to be mined and removed by the buyer.

A contract for the sale of growing crops, timber, or other things attached to real property and capable of being severed without material harm to the land is a sales contract. These contracts are governed by the Code whether the goods are severed by the buyer or by the seller.

Leases

Lease contracts are governed by an article presently offered for state adoption as an addition to the UCC—Article 2A. A **lease** is a transfer of the right to possession and use of goods for a term in return for consideration. Unless otherwise agreed, possession is returned to the original owner after the lease expires. The provisions of Article 2A are substantially similar to the provisions of Article 2 discussed in this part.

General Principles under the Code

There are a number of overriding principles that apply throughout the Code.

Merchant

While the Code applies to all transactions in goods, even those between nonmerchants, it often imposes a higher standard of conduct on merchants. A **mer-**chant is one who deals in goods of the kind that are the subject matter of the contract or is represented as having skill peculiar to those goods [UCC § 2-104(1)]. Thus, a car dealer would be a merchant in a contract for the sale of a car, but not if selling a television set. Occasionally, the Code sets forth different rules for transactions **between merchants.** In a transaction between merchants, both parties are merchants. This text will note where the Code provides different rules with respect to merchants or transactions between merchants.

UCC § 2–104. Definitions

(1) "Merchant" means a person who deals in goods of the kind or otherwise by his occupation holds himself out as having knowledge or skill peculiar to the practices or goods involved in the transaction.

Good Faith

In every contract there is implied a duty to act in **good faith** [UCC § 1–203]. This duty requires that the parties to the contract act with honesty [UCC § 1-201(19)]. This is a subjective test because it focuses on whether or not an individual actually acted with honesty. This is different than questioning whether such conduct was reasonable under the circumstances. Merchants are held to both an objective and a subjective standard of good faith: honesty in fact, the subjective standard, and "the observance of reasonable commercial standards of fair dealing in the trade," the objective standard [UCC § 2–103(1)(b)].

UCC § 1–201. General Definitions

(19) "Good faith" means honesty in fact in the conduct or transaction concerned.

The following reading concerns the relationship between the covenant of good faith and ethics. Do you think that the obligation of good faith requires ethical behavior in contract performance?

*The Implied Covenant of Good Faith and Fair Dealing—Adding an Ethical Obligation**

There is implied in every contract a covenant of good faith and fair dealing, both at common law and under the Uniform Commercial Code. While there is near uniform agreement that the covenant is implied in every contract, there is, however, disagreement over what this standard entails, specifically whether a subjective or an objective standard is required. If one acts with a "pure heart" but in violation of commercial reasonableness standards, is he acting in good faith? It has been suggested that one is acting in bad faith where his conduct violates "traditional notions of accepted business ethics." *Seaman's Direct Buying Service, Inc. v. Standard Oil.*†

This could be seen as a significant departure from traditional contract theory under which the agreement of the parties typically comprises the full extent of the parties' legal obligation. It is our position, however, that this is not a departure. It is through the obligation of good faith that the ethical dimension is implied in contract formation and performance. We believe, first, that there are accepted principles of business ethics applicable to contract, and, second, that these principles are an integral part of the common law.

Certain actions, such as truthfulness, keeping promises, and fulfilling one's duties are universally recognized as ethical or good. In analyzing the ethics that underlie principles of good faith and fair dealing in the contract context, it is important to consider the concept of justice, generally, and more specifically ancillary notions of fairness, duty and honesty. The category of justice relevant to issues of good faith and fair dealing is termed commutative justice. Commutative justice is concerned with the relationships which bind individuals in their private dealings and transactions. In a typical agreement between two parties, an agreement is made to exchange goods or services. The transaction begins with both parties equal. When one party begins to perform his part of the bargain, the equality is upset and it becomes necessary for the other party to perform in order to restore the balance. To violate the terms of the agreement is a violation of the standards dictated by the principles of commutative justice. Under these principles, one acts unethically when he accepts another party's contractual performance, yet refuses to perform as promised.

Further, in many breaches of contract, the ethical duty to tell the truth is violated. The moral question of whether one is violating the ethical duty to be truthful is established by examining the intent of the party making the statement. The intention to mislead must, thus, be the focus of a discussion of good faith and fair dealing. One is morally bound to keep promises because he has intended to invoke a process — the contractual process — whose very aim is to further peoples' promises. Similarly, breaching a contract would, under certain circumstances, be morally wrong using Kant's categorical imperative, because it would give everyone the right to similarly breach contracts.‡

Not all breaches of contract, however, would be in bad faith or in violation of ethical principles. In most situations, the breaching party knows that he will compensate the other party for any damages incurred because of the breach. There is no intent to injure in such situations. On the other hand, where the circumstances are such that upon breach the injured party will not be fully compensated, and it is with such intent that the contract is breached,

---

*Source: Timothy B. Brown, S. J., and Nan S. Ellis, "Lender Liability for Tortious Breach of the Implied Covenant of Good Faith and Fair Dealing," *Selected Proceedings of the National Conference of the American Business Law Association*, p.863 (1990).

†36 Cal. 3d 752, 686 P.2d 1158, 206 Cal. Rptr. 354 (1984).

‡The categorical imperative can be stated: "I ought never to act except in such a way that I can also will that my maxim should become a universal law." [Kantian ethics are discussed in Chapter 2.]

the obligation of good faith is violated. Thus, it is only where the intent, either by adopting a ''see you in court attitude'' or because contract damages will not fully compensate the injured party, that accepted notions of business ethics would be offended by the breach.

Thought Questions

1. What is the issue addressed by the authors?
2. What do the authors see as the interrelationship between law and ethics?
3. According to the authors, why wouldn't all breaches of contract be unethical? Do you agree?
4. Should one face tort or contract liability for violating the implied covenant of good faith and fair dealing?

Unconscionability

Contractual provisions that are **unconscionable** are unenforceable under the Code [UCC § 2–302]. Although it is clear that courts will not enforce unconscionable clauses in contracts, it is less clear what exactly is meant by the term. The Code drafters define the term using the term in the definition: ''The basic test, is whether, in the light of the general commercial background and the commercial needs of the particular trade or case, the clauses involved are so one-sided as to be *unconscionable*

under the circumstances existing at the time of the making of the contract'' [UCC § 2–302, comment 1]. It is apparent from this comment that one-sidedness is somehow related to unconscionability. Unconscionability is an equitable doctrine concerned with fairness. It is intended to protect parties with unequal bargaining power against harsh provisions imposed by the stronger party. As you read the next case, ask whether it is fair for the court to enforce the challenged provisions. To what extent should the doctrine of unconscionability protect merchants?

GILLMAN v. CHASE MANHATTAN BANK
535 N.E.2d 824 (N.Y. Ct. App. 1988)

Jamaica Tobacco and Sales Corp. (Jamaica) was a wholesale distributor of tobacco products operated by Steven Frohlich. As part of this business, Jamaica purchased tax stamps from the city and state of New York. To purchase the stamps, Jamaica had to post a security bond that it could only obtain by providing a letter of credit to the bond company. Chase Manhattan (Chase) agreed with Jamaica to furnish this letter of credit. This agreement included a clause that gave Chase the right to deduct any loan amounts from all deposits held by the bank and the right to exercise this setoff ''without notice or demand'' whenever the bank felt insecure.

When Chase learned that Jamaica was experiencing financial difficulties, it transferred funds from Jamaica's checking account to a separate account. This resulted in the dishonor of several of Jamaica's checks. Jamaica argued that the setoff was unconscionable.

HANCOCK, Judge

An unconscionable contract has been defined as one that ''is so grossly unreasonable or unconscionable in the light of the mores and business practices of the time and place as to be unenforceable according to

its literal terms.'' The doctrine, which is rooted in equitable principles, is a flexible one, and the concept of unconscionability is ''intended to be sensitive to the realities and nuances of the bargaining process.'' A determination of unconscionability generally requires a showing that the contract was both procedurally and substantively unconscionable when made—that is, "some showing of an 'absence of meaningful choice on the part of one of the parties together with contract terms which are unreasonably favorable to the other party.'"

The procedural element of unconscionability requires an examination of the contract formation process and the alleged lack of meaningful choice. The focus is on such matters as the size and commercial setting of the transaction, whether deceptive or high-pressured tactics were employed, the use of fine print in the contract, the experience and education of the party claiming unconscionability and whether there was disparity in bargaining power.

Here, the claim of procedural unconscionability is based solely on Frohlich's testimony that he was unaware of the terms of the agreement, that the agreement was never called to his attention, that he never read it, that no one read it to him and that, indeed, he did not know of its existence. There is no claim of deception or that Frohlich lacked experience or expertise. Nor is there any suggestion that the application was signed as a result of high-pressured tactics. On the contrary, Frohlich signed the instrument in his own office where he had time to study it and, if necessary, discuss it with a lawyer. The contract concerned a type of commercial transaction routinely entered into in the course of Jamaica's business and one with which Frohlich was necessarily familiar from his several years of running the business.

Given the commercial setting of this transaction, Frohlich's claim that he was unaware of the agreement provisions, even if the claim were to be fully credited, could not support a determination of procedural unconscionability.

Nor are we persuaded by the argument that the security agreement was substantively unconscionable. This question entails an analysis of the substance of the bargain to determine whether the terms were unreasonably favorable to the party against whom unconscionability is urged. While ordinarily determinations of unconscionability are based on the court's conclusion that both the procedural and substantive components are present, there have been exceptional cases where the term of the contract is so outrageous as to warrant holding it unenforceable on the ground of substantive unconscionability alone. The contract term in question here would clearly not fall within this exceptional category; moreover, considering their commercial context, their purpose and their effect, we conclude, that by any reasonable standard, those terms were not so overbalanced in favor of Chase as to be substantively unconscionable.

The aim of the Uniform Commercial Code unconscionability provision (UCC § 2–302), it has been said, is to prevent oppression and unfair surprise, not to readjust the agreed allocation of the risks in the light of some perceived imbalance in the parties' bargaining power. Here, when the two commercial parties to the contract entered into the arrangement, they were aware that Jamaica would customarily be carrying a debt for credit purchases of tax stamps at a level close to the limit in the letter of credit. In return for the letter of credit, Jamaica gave Chase a security interest in its checking account. In doing so, it necessarily assumed the risk that the bank might find it necessary to take action without prior notice with respect to that account.

Case Questions

1. What provision in the contract did Jamaica challenge as unconscionable?

2. What analysis did the court adopt to determine whether or not the clause was unconscionable?

3. What is the difference between unconscionability and good faith?

4. How could a merchant ever successfully argue unconscionability?

5. Should parties to a contract be protected from harsh provisions to which they agreed?

CONTRACT FORMATION

All elements necessary to make a binding contract at common law must also be present to form a binding contract for the purchase and sale of goods. To be enforceable, a sales contract must be supported by consideration, the parties must come to mutual assent on the contract terms, the parties must have contractual capacity, and the contract objective must be legal. The Code provides some flexibility that simplifies contract formation and implements the parties' intent.

Offer and Acceptance

A contract for the sale of goods is formed when an offer is accepted. At common law, both the offer and the acceptance must be *definite* and *certain* to create an enforceable contract. By contrast, the Code permits enforcement of contracts made in any manner sufficient to show an agreement [UCC § 2–204(1)]. For example, under the Code, a contract is enforceable even if the exact point at which the deal was closed is ambiguous, so long as the actions of the parties indicate that a binding obligation was intended [UCC § 2–204(2)]. Similarly, under the Code, contracts with one or more omitted terms do not fail for indefiniteness so long as the parties intend to create a contract and there is a reasonably certain basis for giving an appropriate remedy [UCC § 2–204(3)]. There is a contract even if there is uncertainty as to nearly every detail of the contract.

Supplying Terms

Omitted or ambiguous details are supplied by the Code through one of the following means.

Course of Dealing

The terms the parties agree on govern their performance. However, additional or interpretive terms may be supplied by course of dealing, usage of the trade, and course of performance. For example, a deal for 1,000 bricks might be understood to refer to a standard weight measure rather than 1,000 bricks by count. The interpretation of a contract term such as delivery in ''June–August'' may be drawn from the industry's standards or the parties' previous dealings. For example, this could be interpreted to require deliveries to be drawn out over the two-month period if this is standard performance in the industry.

UCC § 1–205. Course of Dealing

(1) A course of dealing is a sequence of previous conduct between the parties to the transaction which . . . establish[es] a common basis of understanding for interpreting their expressions and other conduct.

Gap Fillers

The Code philosophy is that contracts will be enforced even if terms are omitted. The Code, by its **gap-filler** terms, provides methods by which omitted terms may be supplied. The most common of these provisions concern price, delivery, and payment.

UCC § 1–205. Usage of Trade

(2) A usage of trade is any practice or method of dealing having such regularity of observance in a . . . trade as to justify an expectation that it will be observed with respect to the transaction in question.

UCC § 2–208. Course of Performance

(1) Where a contract for sale involves repeated occasions for performance by either party with knowledge of the nature of the performance . . . by the other, any course of performance accepted . . . shall be relevant to determine the meaning of the agreement.

Open Price Term

For a variety of reasons, parties may wish to leave the price term open. Typically, the seller believes that the market price will rise in the future, while the buyer believes that the market price will fall. Both seek to take advantage of favorable price moves and are willing to set the price later. A contract for the sale of goods is sufficiently definite even if it lacks a precise price if the parties so intend. The price will be a reasonable price at the time for delivery if (1) nothing is said about price; (2) the price is left to be agreed by the paries later and they fail to agree; or (3) the price is to be fixed according to a market price or other standard set by a third person but it is not so set [UCC § 2–305(1)]. If the parties agree that either the seller or buyer may set the price, it must be fixed in good faith.

Where the price is not fixed and one of the parties is responsible, the other party has the option to either treat the contract as canceled or personally fix a reasonable price. For example, Alan agrees to sell Bertha a precious diamond necklace, the price to be fixed by Charles's appraisal. If Charles cannot appraise the diamond because Alan refuses to allow Charles to examine the diamond, Bertha has the option of either canceling or setting a reasonable price for the diamond herself.

The open price term provision is only applicable where the parties clearly intend a contract even though the price term is not yet settled. If the parties are still negotiating about price and have not yet agreed to a contract, the gap-filling price term provision is inapplicable. Similarly, if the parties intend to be bound only if the price is set or agreed and it is not fixed or agreed, there is no contract [UCC § 2–305(4)]. In such cases, the buyer must return any goods already received or pay their reasonable value at the time of delivery if unable to return them. The seller must return any portion of the price paid.

Open Delivery Term   The Code provides similar gap fillers for sales contracts that are silent as to delivery. The place for delivery is typically the seller's place of business [UCC § 2–308]. The time for delivery is a reasonable time after contract formation [UCC § 2–309]. For example, in the opening scenario, if no place for delivery is specified, China Chefs completes its delivery at its place of business. It is not responsible to deliver the china to The Place Downstairs.

Open Payment Term   The Code fills the gaps if the parties fail to specify procedures for payment of the price. Payment is to be made at the time and place at which the buyer is to receive the goods [UCC § 2–310(a)]. Further, payment can be made by any customary means unless the seller demands legal tender [UCC § 2–511(2)]. For example, The Place Downstairs may pay by check unless China Chefs demands cash.

Open Quantity Term   A contract term calling for a quantity tied to the output of the seller is an **output contract.** A contract setting the quantity according to the needs or requirements of the buyer is a **requirements contract.** This means such output or requirements as actually occur in good faith [UCC § 2–306]. The Code regards such contracts as sufficiently definite even though precise numbers are not specified.

Firm Offer

At common law, an offeror can revoke an offer any time prior to acceptance. This is true even if the offeror has promised to keep the offer open, unless consideration, creating an option contract, is received in return for this promise. For example, assume that on January 2, Alan offers to sell his house to Bill for $100,000, giving Bill 10 days in which to decide. If, on January 3, Alan changes his mind and revokes his offer to Bill by effectively communicating the revocation, any attempted acceptance by Bill is ineffective to create a contract.

The Code provides a limited exception to the rule requiring consideration for irrevocable offers. The **firm offer** provision permits a merchant to make a binding firm offer without consideration. An offer in a merchant's signed writing to buy or sell goods promising that it will be held open becomes irrevocable even if no consideration is paid. A firm offer is irrevocable for the period stated in the offer [UCC § 2–205]. However, no offer will be held open for longer than three months. Thus, section 2–205 applies when three requirements are met, as summarized in Figure 19–1. First, the offeror must be a merchant. Second, the promise not to revoke must be in writing and signed. Third, the offer must contain assurances that it will be held open. For example, assume that on January 2, China Chefs, from our opening scenario, offers in a writing signed by Jan to sell china to The Place Downstairs for $10,000, giving the buyer 10 days in which to decide. If, on January 3, Jan changes her mind and attempts to revoke her offer, the revocation is ineffective. The offer of January 2 is a firm offer and is irrevocable for the 10 days promised. This is true because China Chefs is a merchant, the offer is in writing and signed, and the offer contains a promise to hold the offer open.

UCC § 2–205. Firm Offers

An offer by a merchant to buy or sell goods in a signed writing which by its terms gives assurance that it will be held open is not revocable, for lack of consideration, during the time stated or if no time is stated for a reasonable time, but in no event may such period of irrevocability exceed three months.

The firm offer may be contained in forms prepared by the offeree. This could result in an unfair surprise to Jan in the above example. Therefore, if

---

Figure 19–1   Firm Offer

- Offer.
- By a merchant.
- In a signed writing.
- Gives assurances that it will remain open.
- Is not revocable.
- For time period stated, or for a reasonable time. In no event will the offer be held open for longer than 3 months.

UCC § 2–205.

The Place Downstairs' form includes a firm offer term, Jan must sign it separately to create an irrevocable offer. This affords the offeror protection against inadvertently signing a firm offer term buried in boilerplate language of an offeree's form.

The Acceptance

The Code simplifies the acceptance process, creating contracts where that is the parties' intent.

Method of Acceptance

The offer may specify the manner of acceptance necessary to create a contract. However, if the offer doesn't specify, the common law requires the offeree to match the method of communication used by the offeror: a mailed offer might invite a mailed acceptance, a face-to-face offer a face-to-face response. The Code rejects these rigid rules and permits acceptance in any manner and by any medium reasonable under the circumstances [UCC § 2–206(1)]. This flexibility allows for modern, more time-savings methods of communication. For example, it seems reasonable to fax a response to a mailed offer.

Acceptance by Performance

The buyer might offer to buy goods with an order for shipment, such as "Please ship 100 screws at $1.00 per screw." The Code allows the offeree to respond by prompt shipment of the goods or by a promise to ship the goods [UCC § 2–206(1)(b)]. Further, commencing performance is acceptance if the offeror is notified [UCC § 2–206(2)]. If the offeror is not notified of the acceptance within a reasonable period of time, the offeror may treat the offer as having lapsed. The offeror may then contract with someone else for the goods desired. For example, Ben Buyer orders 10,000 swizzle sticks from Sam Seller, requesting shipment as soon as possible. Sam begins to manufacture, package, and ship the swizzle sticks but fails to notify Ben. Because Ben did not receive an acknowledgment of his order within a reasonable time, he may justifiably order the swizzle sticks elsewhere. He has no liability to Sam Seller on the offer. By contrast, if Sam notifies Ben that performance has begun, a binding contract is created.

However, what if Sam accepts the offer by shipping nonconforming goods? In other words, what if the goods shipped were not exactly the goods ordered? At common law, shipment of nonconforming goods is a counteroffer. Acceptance of the nonconforming goods is acceptance of the counteroffer, creating a contract for delivery of the nonconforming goods. Under the Code, a nonconforming shipment is an *acceptance* of the offer–purchase order and simultaneously a *breach* that entitles the buyer to damages for the breach. The seller can avoid liability for this breach if the buyer is notified that the nonconforming goods were shipped only as an accommodation. The notification makes the nonconforming shipment a counteroffer that the offeror can either accept or reject.

Battle of the Forms

Return to our opening scenario where The Place Downstairs orders 100 place settings at $20 each from China Chefs' catalog advertising china for sale. The order is made through use of a preprinted purchase order form. The catalog advertisement is an invitation seeking offers and the purchase order form is an offer. On the back of the purchase order form are printed numerous "boilerplate" provisions that are favorable to the buyer. One of those provisions might be, for example:

> By accepting this order Seller warrants that the items furnished will be in full conformity with buyer's specifications and fit for the uses intended by buyer. This warranty is made in addition to any other warranties, express or implied, made by the Seller to the buyer.

China Chefs receives the purchase order and responds by sending The Place Downstairs an acknowledgment form purporting to accept the offer by reciting the same price, quantity, and delivery information stated in the buyer's form. However, on the back of the acknowledgment form are printed numerous boilerplate provisions favorable to the seller. For example;

> Seller makes no warranty express or implied, and any implied warranty of merchantability or fitness for a particular purpose is hereby disclaimed by the seller.

A further provision might state:

> Any controversy arising out of or relating to this contract, or the breach of this contract, shall be settled by arbitration in accordance with the Rules of the American Arbitration Association.

Does the exchange of the above forms result in the formation of a contract? If so, what are the terms of the contract? Is there a warranty? Is the contract subject to arbitration?

At common law, there would be no contract at this point. The common law requires the response to

Figure 19–2a   Purchase Order Form (front side)

THE **PLACE DOWNSTAIRS**   **Purchase Order**   NO: 63281
DATE: 12/30/92

VENDOR NO: 5479

VENDOR: China Chefs
Chicago, Illinois 60693

SHIP TO: The Place Downstairs
123 Slow Lake Dr.
Columbia, MD 21045

BUYER NAME	EXPEDITER	CONFIRMING TO	
The Place Downstairs			

F.O.B.	SHIP VIA	COL./PPD	TERMS
DESTINATION	BEST WAY	FRT PAID	NET 30

LINE NO.	PART/DESCRIPTION/QUANTITY	U/M	UNIT PRICE/DISCOUNT	EXTENDED PRICE
001	Catalog #C34589 100 place settings Royal Wedge Pattern: Heather	Each	$20.00	$2,000.00

VENDOR: REVIEW INSTRUCTIONS BELOW

- Any changes to quantity, price, terms, F.O.B., or material substitutions must be authorized by buyer.
- All shipments shall be prepaid. If F.O.B. origin, prepay freight and bill as a separate item on your invoice.
- Terms and conditions listed on reverse side apply to all orders.
- Deliveries accepted only between 8:00 A.M. and 4:00 P.M., M-F.

TOTAL AMOUNT $2,000.00

ISSUED BY

_____

VENDOR ACKNOWLEDGEMENT REQUIRED

_____

be the "mirror image" of the offer to be an acceptance; otherwise, it is a rejection and counteroffer. In the above example, the acknowledgment form contains additional and different terms from those stated in the purchase order. At common law, the acknowledgment is a counteroffer that rejects the purchase order offer. Only if China Chefs shipped the china would a contract exist. The contract is created upon shipment, with shipment of the china acting as acceptance of the counteroffer, based on the terms stated in the counteroffer.

The Code changes this rule. Contract formation typically occurs in one of two ways. Either the buyer and the seller agree orally concerning price, quantity, and delivery and follow with confirmation letters, or the buyer merely sends a purchase order, as above, in response to advertised price, quantity, and delivery information. Regardless of which way the contract formation process begins, there is ultimately an exchange of forms. The buyer's forms were prepared by a lawyer to give the buyer an advantage. The seller's forms were prepared to give the seller an advantage. Look at the purchase order in Figure 19–2. Is it likely that an acknowledgment form would coincidentally be the mirror image of this form? Unfortunately, the buyer and seller will probably not read each other's forms or notice the differences until a dispute arises. When the seller refuses to ship the goods or the buyer refuses to pay, the question of whether a contract exists or what precise terms are included in the contract must be addressed.

Figure 19–2b   Purchase Order Form (reverse side)

Buyer hereby buys and Seller hereby-sells all those items set forth on the face hereof subject to the terms set forth below, together with such additional terms and conditions as may be specified on the face of this Purchase Order.

SECTION A — INSTRUCTIONS TO SELLER — PART I

A. Purchase Order Number: Buyer's order number, including any amendment designation or controlling blanket order number, must appear on all invoices, packing lists, bills of lading, packages, containers, or correspondence processed under this order.

B. Packing List: Packing list is to accompany each shipment of goods and if such shipment completes the order, the following notation MUST appear thereon: {This shipment completes this order".

C. Packing and Insurance: No charge for packaging or insurance will be allowed unless specifically noted herein. Goods must be packaged to assure safe arrival at destination.

D. Invoices and Payment: Unless otherwise provided in this order, no invoices shall be issued nor payments made prior to delivery. Individual invoices must be issued for each shipment under this order. Unless freight or other charges are itemized, any discount will be taken on full amount of invoices. All payments are subject to adjustment for shortage or rejection.

E. Discounts: Cash discount period shall commence with the date of actual receipt of invoice or actual receipt of acceptable goods ordered herein, whichever is later.

SECTION A — PART II

Clause No. 1—Acceptance: THIS ORDER EXPRESSLY LIMITS ACCEPTANCE TO THE TERMS STATED HEREIN AND ANY ADDITIONAL OR DIFFERENT TERMS PROPOSED BY THE SELLER ARE REJECTED. THIS ORDER BECOMES A CONTRACT SUBJECT TO THE TERMS AND CONDITIONS SET FORTH AND INCORPORATED HEREIN BY REFERENCE, WHEN ACCEPTED BY ACKNOWLEDGEMENT BY SELLER OR COMMENCEMENT OF PERFORMANCE BY SELLER.

Clause No. 2—Delivery: Deliveries are to be made both in quantities and at times specified herein. If Seller's deliveries shall fail to meet schedule, Buyer, without limiting its other rights or remedies, may direct expedited routing and any excess costs incurred thereby shall be debited to Seller's account. Buyer may in accordance with Clause 5 'Default—Cancellation' cancel all or part of this order in the event Seller fails to deliver goods as scheduled herein. Buyer shall not be liable for Seller's commitments or production arrangements in excess of the amount, or in advance of the time, necessary to meet Buyer's delivery schedule. Goods which are delivered in advance of schedule may, at Buyer's option, either (i) be returned at Seller's expense for proper delivery (ii) have payment therefore withheld by Buyer until the date that goods are actually scheduled for delivery, or (iii) place goods in storage for Seller's account until delivery date specified herein.

Clause No. 3—Changes: Buyer may at any time, by a written order and without notice to the sureties, make changes within the general scope of this order, in any one or more of the following: (i) Drawings, designs or specifications, where the supplies to be furnished are to be specially manufactured for Buyer in accordance therewith; (ii) method of shipment or packing; (iii) place of delivery; and (iv) the period of performance of work, and Seller shall comply therewith.

Clause No. 4—Default Cancellation: Buyer reserves the right, by written notice of default, to cancel this order, without liability to Buyer, in the event of the happening of any of the following: Insolvency of Seller, the filing of a voluntary petition in bankruptcy by Seller, the filing of an involuntary petition to have Seller declared bankrupt, the appointment of a Receiver or Trustee for Seller, or the execution by Seller of an assignment for the benefit of creditors. If seller fails to perform as specified herein, or if Seller breaches any of the terms hereof, Buyer reserves the right, without any liability to Buyer, upon giving Seller written notice and allowing Seller reasonable time to remedy such deficiency. to (i) cancel this order in whole or in part, by written notice to Seller, and (ii) obtain the goods ordered herein from another source with any excess cost resulting therefrom, chargeable to Seller, if such deficiencies are not remedied. Buyer agrees to accept goods which were ready for shipment prior to the cancellation notification, subject to the provisions set forth in Clauses 2 and 3 hereof, and provided that such goods are free and clear of all encumbrances. If, after notice of cancellation of this order has been submitted as provided above, it is determined that the failure to perform this order is due to causes beyond Seller's control, such notice of default shall be deemed to have been issued pursuant to Clause 6—Termination and rights and obligations of the parties hereto, shall in such event, be governed by said clause, provided Seller notifies Buyer promptly of the occurence of such occasion.

Clause No. 5—Remedies: The remedies provided Buyer herein shall be cumulative and in addition to any other remedies provided by law or equity. A waiver of a breach of any provision hereof shall not constitute a waiver of any other breach. This order is governed by the laws of the state shown in the Buyer's address on the face of this order.

Clause No. 6—Assignment: This order, or any interest therein, including any such claims for monies due or to become due with respect thereto, may only be assigned upon the written consent of Buyer. Any payment to any assignee of any claim under this order, in consequence of such consent, shall be subject to set-off, recoupment or other reduction for any claim which Buyer may have against Seller.

Clause No. 7—Warranties: Seller expressly warrants that all items delivered hereunder will be free from defects, of good materials and workmanship, and will conform to applicable specifications, drawings, samples, and performance specifications whether set forth in this order or in Seller's sales literature. In the event of a conflict between the terms of this order, and such sales literature, the terms of this order shall prevail. The foregoing warranties shall survive inspection and acceptance of and payments for the items delivered hereunder and shall run to Buyer, its successors, assigns and customers. Said warranties shall not be deemed to limit any warranties of additional scope given to Buyer by Seller, nor to Buyer's rights or Seller's obligations under any other provision of this order, at law or in equity. No warranties are waived by the Buyer supplying plans, specifications or data or inspecting or accepting the goods. When Buyer furnishes specifications to the Seller, Seller shall immediately notify Buyer of any infringement claim and Buyer may defend or negotiate the disposition of any such claims.

UCC § 2–207. Additional Terms in Acceptance or Confirmation

(1) A definite and seasonable expression of acceptance or a written confirmation which is sent within a reasonable time operates as an acceptance even though it states terms additional to or different from those offered or agreed upon, unless acceptance is expressly made conditional on assent to the additional or different terms.

The three subsections of UCC section 2–207 deal with these issues. Subsection (1) addresses whether or not the writings exchanged create a contract. Subsection (2) establishes the terms of that contract. Subsection (3) preserves the deal if no contract is found from the writings, but the parties nevertheless perform as if a contract exists.

Is There a Contract?   Under the Code, an acceptance is an acceptance even though it includes terms additional to or different from those stated in the offer [UCC § 2–207(1)]. A binding contract is created by exchange of the purchase order and the acknowledgment forms as in the China Chefs example. The acknowledgment is an expression of acceptance. Even though it contains different terms (the warranties disclaimer) and new terms (the arbitration provision), the acceptance is not a counter-

Figure 19–3   Battle of the Forms: Is There a Contract?

Yes	If there is an acceptance.
Even if	There are new or different terms.
Unless	The acceptance conditions acceptance on offeror acceptance of the new or different terms.

UCC § 2–207(1).

Figure 19–4   Battle of the Forms: Do Additional Terms Become a Part of the Contract?

Yes	If both parties are merchants.
Unless	The offer limits acceptance.
	There is a material alteration.
	The offeror objects to the term.
No	If one part is not a merchant. The terms of the contract are the terms of the offer.

UCC § 2–207(2).

offer as under common law. The Code drafters reasoned that a deal that the parties believe has in fact been closed should be treated as a contract. This is consistent with commercial practice, particularly if neither party breaches or complains. Figure 19–3 summarizes this rule.

Two important provisos should be noted. First, under UCC section 2–207(1), an *acceptance* operates as an acceptance. A counteroffer or a rejection will not operate as an acceptance. For example, if Sam offers a "1980 Ford Van for sale at $5,000" and Ben responds "$5,000 is too much, I'll give you $3,000," there is no contract. The response was a rejection and a counteroffer, not an acceptance. There must be a definite acceptance before a contract is created. How much can the acceptance differ from the offer and still qualify as an acceptance? In other words, when do the different or additional terms become so important that the response is not an acceptance but rather a rejection and counteroffer? The line is easy to draw if the parties disagree over crucial terms. In the opening scenario, no contract would exist if China Chefs' acknowledgment stated a different price of $50 per place setting. Similarly, if The Place Downstairs purchase order required delivery to the buyer's place of business, while China Chefs' acknowledgment required the seller only to make the goods available at the seller's place of business, the parties have not yet reached a "meeting of the minds." The acknowledgment would be a rejection of the terms stated in the purchase order and a counteroffer. By contrast, if the forms agree on price, quantity, and delivery terms, but only disagree on preprinted terms that are generally not bargained for, the acknowledgment would be an acceptance creating a contract.

The second important proviso is that no contract is created if the acceptance is expressly made conditional on agreement by the offeror to the new or different terms contained in the acceptance. For instance, in the above example, the acknowledgment might further state that the seller agrees "only if" or "provided that" the arbitration and warranty disclaimer are included in the final contract. The acknowledgment would be a rejection and a counteroffer and there would be no contract unless these terms were accepted by The Place Downstairs.

What Are the Terms of the Contract?   The Code treats *additional* terms separately from *different* terms. The arbitration provision in the example is an additional term. The offer does not mention arbitration. It is a term added by the acceptance. By contrast, the warranty disclaimer is a different term. The offer included the warranties implied under the Code as well as an express warranty. The acceptance expressly disclaimed all warranties.

Additional Terms   Additional terms are considered proposals to modify the contract. Additional terms will *automatically* become a part of the contract if *both* parties are merchants unless (1) the offer expressly limits acceptance to the terms of the offer, (2) the additional terms materially alter the contract, or (3) the offeror objects to the additional term within a reasonable amount of time [UCC § 2-207(2)]. Figure 19–4 summarizes this rule. Applying this rule, the arbitration term in the example above will automatically become a part of the contract because both China Chefs and The Place Downstairs are merchants unless The Place Downstairs objects or arbitration materially alters the offer. The question of whether or not both parties are merchants is only relevant when considering the question of whether additional terms can automatically become part of the contract, not whether or not a contract exists. If either the buyer or seller are not merchants, a contract would still exist on The Place Downstairs' (the offeror's) terms [UCC § 2–207(1)].

UCC § 2–207. Additional Terms in Acceptance or Confirmation

(2) The additional terms are to be construed as proposals for addition to the contract. Between merchants such terms become part of the contract unless:

(a) the offer expressly limits acceptance to the terms of the offer;

(b) they materially alter it; or

(c) notification of objection to them has already been given or is given within a reasonable time after notice of them is received.

Does the arbitration provision materially alter the contract? This depends on what constitutes materiality? A material alteration results in surprise or hardship if the other party is unaware of it. What is considered standard in the business forms the basis for evaluating surprise to the offeror. Both arbitration clauses and warranty disclaimers are generally considered material alterations. However, arbitration clauses are so common in some industries that they would not be a material alteration. In the above example, the arbitration clause would probably be a material alteration that would not be part of the contract. Because material alteration is not relevant to whether or not a contract exists, a contract would still exist without the arbitration clause.

Different Terms   Contradictions between those terms offered and those accepted present a more difficult question. It is not satisfactorily answered by UCC section 2–207 or the court decisions interpreting the section. The problem stems from the fact that a contract is created when the acceptance contains additional or different terms from the offer, but the Code only specifies when additional terms become a part of that contract. There are two approaches to resolving this problem. Under one approach, clauses that disagree are each considered as objections to the different terms. Neither conflicting term becomes a part of the contract—the conflicting terms cancel each other out. Therefore, the contract consists only of the terms agreed to and terms supplied by the Code gap-filler provisions. If the first approach is applied to our example, the buyer's warranties in the purchase order and the seller's warranty disclaimer in the acceptance would cancel each other out. The Code's implied warranties would fill in the gaps. Under the second approach, the seller accepted the

Figure 19–5   Battle of the Forms: Where the Writings Do Not Establish a Contract

There can still be a contract if	The parties conduct themselves as if there were a contract.
What are the terms?	The terms on which the writings agree, plus gap-filler provisions.

UCC § 2–207(3).

buyer's terms and the seller's different terms simply do not become a part of the contract. Under this interpretation, the buyer's warranties become a part of the contract, but the seller's disclaimer would not.

Conduct of the Parties   What is the result if no contract results from the writings exchanged, but the parties never read the writings exchanged, assume they have a contract, and begin performance? The same two questions arise: Is there a contract? What are its terms? Recall that at common law, acceptance with new and different terms would be a counteroffer, and performance by the offeror would be an acceptance creating a contract containing the terms of the accepted counteroffer. Under the Code, conduct by both parties that recognizes a contract establishes a contract even if the writings are insufficient [UCC § 2–207(3)]. A contract is created by the *conduct,* not by the writings. It is unnecessary to classify either writing as an offer or acceptance. If the parties believe that there is a contract and act accordingly, the law supports this. The terms of the contract are the terms on which the writings agree along with any Code gap-filling provisions. This is illustrated in Figure 19–5.

UCC § 2–207. Additional Terms in Acceptance or Confirmation

(3) Conduct by both parties which recognizes the existence of a contract is sufficient to establish a contract for sale although the writings of the parties do not otherwise establish a contract. In such case the terms of the particular contract consist of those terms on which the writings of the parties agree, together with any supplementary terms incorporated under any other provision of this Act.

The following case tests this complex battle of the forms problem. Try to discover when the contract is created and what are its terms.

DIAMOND FRUIT GROWERS, INC. v KRACK CORP.
794 F.2d 1440 (9th Cir. 1986)

Krack is a manufacturer of cooling units that contain steel tubing it purchases from outside suppliers. Metal-Matic is one of Krack's tubing suppliers. The parties had been dealing with each other for about 10 years. At the beginning of each year, Krack sent a blanket purchase order to Metal-Matic stating how much tubing Krack would need for the year. Throughout the year, Krack sent release purchase orders to Metal-Matic. Metal-Matic sent Krack an acknowledgment form and then shipped the tubing.

Metal-Matic's acknowledgment form disclaimed all liability for consequential damages (such as lost profits) and limited Metal-Matic's liability for defects. These terms were not contained in the purchase order. Further, Metal-Matic's acceptance was "expressly made conditional to purchaser's acceptance of the terms and provisions of the acknowledgment form."

When a cooling unit sold to Diamond Fruit Growers leaked ammonia due to a leak in a Krack cooling unit, Diamond sued Krack to recover losses suffered. Kraft then sued Metal-Matic, who claimed that as part of the contract with Kraft, Metal-Matic had disclaimed all liability.

WIGGINS, Judge

If the contract between Metal-Matic and Krack contains Metal-Matic's disclaimer of liability, Metal-Matic is not liable to indemnify Krack for part of Diamond's damages. Therefore, the principal issue before us is whether Metal-Matic's disclaimer of liability became part of the contract between these parties.

Section 2–207 applies to this case. One intended application of § 2–207 is to commercial transactions in which the parties exchange printed purchase order and acknowledgment forms. The drafters of the UCC recognized that "[b]ecause the forms are oriented to the thinking of the respective drafting parties, the terms contained in them often do not correspond." Section 2–207 is an attempt to provide rules of contract formation in such cases. In this case, Krack and Metal-Matic exchanged purchase order and acknowledgment forms that contained different or additional terms. This, then, is a typical § 2–207 situation. Section 2–207 provides rules of contract formation in cases such as this one in which the parties exchange forms but do not agree on all the terms of their contract.

A brief summary of § 2–207 is necessary to an understanding of its application to this case. Section 2–207 changes the common law's mirror-image rule. At common law, an acceptance that varies the terms of the offer is a counteroffer and operates as a rejection of the original offer. If the offeror goes ahead with the contract after receiving the counteroffer, his performance is an acceptance of the terms of the counteroffer.

Generally § 2–207(1) "converts a common law counteroffer into an acceptance even though it states additional or different terms." The only requirement under § 2–207(1) is that the responding form contain a definite and seasonable expression of acceptance. The terms of the responding form that correspond to the offer constitute the contract. Under § 2–207(2), the additional terms of the responding form become proposals for additions to the contract. Between merchants the additional terms become part of the contract unless the offer is specifically limited to its terms, the offeror objects to the additional terms, or the additional terms materially alter the terms of the offer. UCC § 2–207(2).

However, § 2–207(2) is subject to a proviso. If a definite and seasonable expression of acceptance expressly conditions acceptance on the offeror's assent to additional or different terms, the parties' differing forms do not result in a contract unless the offeror assents to the additional terms. If the offeror assents, the parties have a contract and the additional terms are a part of that contract. If, however, the offeror does not assent, but the parties proceed with the transaction as if they have a contract, their performance results in a contract. UCC § 2–207(3). In that case, the terms of the contract are those on which the parties' forms agree plus any terms supplied by the UCC.

In this case, Metal-Matic expressly conditioned its acceptance on Krack's assent to the additional terms contained in Metal-Matic's acknowledgment form. Therefore, we must determine whether Krack assented to Metal-Matic's limitation of liability term.

Metal-Matic contends that Krack assented to the limitation of liability term when it continued to accept and pay for tubing after Metal-Matic insisted that the contract contain its term.

One of the principles underlying § 2–207 is neutrality. If possible, the section should be interpreted so as to give neither party to a contract an advantage simply because it happened to send the first or in some cases the last form. Section 2–207 accomplishes this result in part by doing away with the common law's "last shot" rule. At common law, the offeree/counterofferor gets all of its terms simply because it fired the last shot in the exchange of forms. Sections 2–207(3) does away with this result by giving neither party the terms it attempted to impose unilaterally on the other. Instead, all of the terms on which the parties' forms do not agree drop out, and the UCC supplies the missing terms.

With these principles in mind, we turn now to Metal-Matic's argument that Krack assented to the disclaimer when it continued to accept and pay for tubing once Metal-Matic indicated that it was willing to sell tubing only if its warranty and liability terms were part of the contract.

If we were to accept Metal-Matic's argument, we would reinstate to some extent the common law's last shot rule. That result is avoided by requiring a specific and unequivocal expression of assent on the part of the offeror when the offeree conditions its acceptance on assent to additional or different terms. If the offeror does not give specific and unequivocal assent but the parties act as if they have a contract, the provisions of § 2–207(3) apply to fill in the terms of the contract.

We hold that because Krack's conduct did not indicate unequivocally that Krack intended to assent to Metal-Matic's terms, that conduct did not amount to the assent contemplated by § 2–207(1).

Case Questions

1. Was a contract created by the writings exchanged?

2. Did the liability limitation clause become a part of the contract? Why or why not?

3. Why did the court reject Metal-Matic's argument? Compare the common law's last shot rule with the Code's approach in section 2–207(3).

4. Do you agree that policy considerations support rejecting the last shot rule?

Consideration

The Code leaves unchanged the common law rule that contracts must be supported by **consideration** to be enforceable. Under the Code, as at common law, contracts must generally involve a bargained for exchange in order to be enforceable.

Modification

At common law, contract modification requires additional consideration to be enforceable. For example, assume Beatrice Buyer contracts to buy a piece of real estate for $100,000 from Sylvia Seller, and the parties subsequently agree to a contract modification raising the price to $110,000; the contract modification is not enforceable without additional consideration because of the **preexisting duty** rule. Both parties were under a preexisting duty to purchase and sell the real estate for $100,000. Only Beatrice is promising to do something new in the second contract, pay an additional $10,000. Sylvia is doing nothing that she is not already bound to do in the first contract.

The Code changes this rule with respect to contract modification and enforces the contract as modified [UCC § 2-209(1)]. Contract modifications are necessary and desirable, so they are enforced free from the technicalities of the common law. Under the Code, if Ben Buyer contracts to buy $100,000 worth of work gloves from Sam Seller, the contract could be modified to raise the price by $10,000 without additional consideration. The need for a ready supply of goods often overrides price concerns. For example, if the parties have an ongoing commercial relationship, the buyer may pay the price increase to guarantee a future source of supply.

By contrast, the buyer could always refuse the contract modification proposal and hold the seller to the terms of the original contract.

The modification must meet the Code's good faith test. Sam Seller may seek to raise the price because market prices have risen substantially and he cannot perform without a substantial loss. In this case, Sam Seller's modification would be in good faith. By contrast, if Sam Seller knows Ben Buyer desperately needs the work gloves and they are unavailable elsewhere on short notice, Sam Seller's price gouging would be in bad faith. Such extortion would be inconsistent with the Code's good faith principle and the modification would be unenforceable.

The possibility that one party might falsely allege a contract modification is addressed by the Code's statute of frauds, discussed below. If a contract modification results in a contract for the sale of goods of $500 or more, the modification must be in writing [UCC § 2–209(3)]. This prevents Sam Seller from asserting an oral price increase to a $499 contract without a writing signed by Ben.

Writing

Often, the agreement between the parties is evidenced by a writing. Questions arise about whether a writing is required. Further questions arise when the written contract is accompanied by collateral oral agreements.

Statute of Frauds

As a general rule, contracts do not have to be in writing to be enforceable. However, the **statute of frauds** requires that some contracts be in writing to prevent fraud and perjury. Although the statute of frauds is somewhat controversial, the Code retains a writing requirement. Because the potential for fraud rises as the contract value rises, sales contracts where the price is $500 or more must be evidenced by a writing [UCC § 2–201(1)].

UCC § 2–201. Statute of Frauds

(1) . . . a contract for the sale of goods for the price of $500 or more is not enforceable . . . unless there is some writing sufficient to indicate that a contract for sale has been made between the parties and signed by the party against whom enforcement is sought.

The Writing   What kind of writing is sufficient to satisfy the writing requirement? The parties need not sign a document clearly labeled ''Contract.'' Nor are witnesses or notaries required. The writing need not be in one document; it can be pieced together from several writings. The Code's writing requirement is less restrictive than under common law. Under the Code, there must be some writing to suggest that a contract for sale has been made between the parties and signed by the party against whom enforcement is sought [UCC § 2–201(1)]. The writing must only afford a basis for believing that a purported oral contract is legitimate. The writing may even omit or incorrectly state the contract terms. The price, time, and place of payment or delivery, the quality of the goods, and warranties may all be omitted and proven by oral evidence or supplied by the Code's gap fillers. Only the quantity term must appear in the writing. If the quantity is incorrectly stated, the contract is only enforceable up to the amount stated.

There are three requirements for a writing. First, the writing must provide evidence of a contract for the sale of goods. The writing does not have to prove conclusively that a contract exists, nor provide all terms. The writing is sufficient if it verifies the oral testimony by the plaintiff.

The second requirement is a signature by the party against whom enforcement is sought. The signature requirement is liberally construed, and any symbol made with the intent to authenticate is a signature [UCC § 1–201(39)]. A signature may be printed, stamped, or made by initials. Under some circumstances, a letterhead is sufficient. The third requirement is that the writing must specify a quantity.

The Confirmation Letter   If one merchant sends another merchant a letter confirming an oral agreement, the confirmation letter can meet the writing requirement even though the letter is not signed by the receiving party as long as the receiving party has reason to know of its contents. The recipient can avoid this by making an objection within 10 days after receipt of the confirmation letter. An example will best illustrate. Mike Merchant and Dan Dealer enter into an oral contract to sell $1,000 of dish towels. Later, Mike sends a letter confirming the oral agreement, which is received by Dan on August 1. Dan never objects to the contents of the letter. When the market price of dish towels rises to $1,500, Dan refuses delivery as promised. In Mike's suit against Dan for nonperformance, Dan argues that because the contract price was greater than $500, a writing is required. When Mike offers the confirmation letter as the writing, Dan asserts that the confirmation letter is insufficient because it is not signed by Dan. However, under the ''merchant's exception,'' the confirmation letter is a sufficient writing to satisfy the statute of frauds. The following case illustrates how the merchant's exception creates a ''Merchant, read your mail'' rule.

UCC § 2–201. Formal Requirements; Statute of Frauds

(2) Between merchants if within a reasonable time a writing in confirmation of the contract and sufficient against the sender is received and the party receiving it has reason to know its contents, it satisfies the requirements of subsection (1) against such party unless written notice of objection to its contents is given within 10 days after it is received.

BAZAK INTERNATIONAL CORP. v. MAST INDUSTRIES, INC.
535 N.E.2d 633 (N.Y. Ct. App. 1989)

Bazak International (Bazak) made an oral agreement to purchase fabric centers from the seller Mast Industries (Mast). Bazak sent five purchase orders to Mast. The purchase orders never expressly alerted Mast that they were intended to confirm the previous oral agreement. Mast never objected to the terms stated in the purchase orders, but never delivered the textiles.

Bazak filed a complaint against Mast alleging breach of contract. Mast moved to have the complaint dismissed because of the statute of frauds. Mast argued that the only writings, the purchase orders, were insufficient under the Code because Mast never signed them. The court considered the question of whether the purchase orders qualified as confirmatory writings within the ''merchant's exception'' to the statute of frauds [UCC § 2-201(2)].

KAYE, Judge

UCC § 2–201(1) requires that the writing be ''sufficient to indicate'' a contract, while § 2–201(2) calls for a writing ''in confirmation of the contract.'' We see no reason for importing a more stringent requirement of explicitness to the later section, and holding merchants engaged in business dealings to a higher standard of precision in their word choices. The Official Commentary describes UCC § 2–201(1) as simply requiring ''that the writing afford a basis for believing that the offered oral evidence rests on a real transaction.'' We hold that the same standard applies under UCC § 2–201(1) and § 2–201(2).

Section 2–201(2) recognized the common practice among merchants, particularly small businesses, to enter into oral sales agreements later confirmed in writing by one of the parties. Absent such a provision, only the party receiving the confirmatory writing could invoke the statute of frauds, giving that party the option of enforcing the contract or not depending on how advantageous the transaction

proved to be. UCC § 2–201(2) was intended to address that inequity; it encourages the sending of confirmatory writings by removing the unfairness to the sender.

While we hold that explicit words of confirmation are not required, the writing still must satisfy the test articulated in UCC § 2–201(1) that it be ''sufficient to indicate that a contract for sale has been made.'' A purchase order, standing alone, is unlikely to meet this test. On the other hand, if the writing contains additional evidence that it is based upon a prior agreement, then as a policy matter it is not unfair to require the recipient to make written objection where there is an intent to disavow it.

Finally, as additional protection against abuse and inequity, we note that the consequence of a failure to give timely written notice of objection to a confirmatory writing is only to remove the bar of the Statute of Frauds. The burden of proving that a contract was indeed made remains with the plaintiff. Thus, UCC § 2–201(2) neither binds the receiving merchant to an agreement it has not made nor delivers an undeserved triumph to the sending merchant. It does no more than permit the sender to proceed with an attempt to prove its allegations.

We therefore conclude that, in determining whether writings are confirmatory documents within UCC § 2–201(2), neither explicit words of confirmation nor express references to the prior agreement are required, and the writings are sufficient as long as they afford a basis for believing that they reflect a real transaction between the parties.

It remains for us to apply this standard to the facts and determine whether the documents in issue satisfy the requirements of § 2–201(2).

Of the various requirements of § 2–201(2), four are not in controversy. There is no dispute that both parties are merchants, that the writing was sent within a reasonable time after the alleged agreement, that it was received by someone with reason to know of its contents, and that no written objection was made. If the writings can be construed as confirming the alleged oral agreement, they are sufficient under § 2–201(1) against Bazak—the sender—since Bazak signed them. Thus, the question is whether the documents here were sufficient to indicate the existence of a prior agreement.

The handwritten notations on the purchase order forms provide a basis for believing that the documents were in furtherance of a previous agreement.

The terms set forth are highly specific; precise quantities, descriptions, prices per unit and payment terms are stated. The documents refer to an earlier presentation by defendants' agent. The date April 23, 1987, is written on the forms and the date April 30 on the transmission, indicating reference to a transaction that took place a week before they were sent.

While no one of these factors would be sufficient under UCC § 2–201(2), considered together they adequately indicate confirmation of a preexisting agreement so as to permit Bazak to go forward and prove its allegation.

Case Questions

1. What is the issue the court faced in applying the merchant's exception?

2. What is the rationale for allowing a writing to be sufficient against a merchant who has not signed it?

3. Is there a danger of abuse if purchase orders, as in this case, are construed as confirmatory writings?

4. How does the merchant's exception to the statute of frauds [UCC § 2–201(2)] relate to the merchants rule in the battle of the forms [UCC § 2–207(2)]?

Exceptions   Three statutory exceptions to the writing requirement are provided: (1) specially manufactured goods, (2) admissions, and (3) part performance. Each requires initial proof of an oral contract. In each instance, ''something extra'' must be offered as additional support to verify the existence of the oral contract.

1. *Specially manufactured goods.* No writing is required for (1) goods specially manufactured for the buyer, (2) that are not suitable for sale to others in the ordinary course of the seller's business, (3) where the seller has made either a substantial beginning to manufacture or commitments for procurement, (4) before the seller received any notice of repudiation by the buyer, and (5) the circumstances indicate that the goods are for the buyer [UCC § 2–201(3)(a)]. Under these circumstances, it appears that an oral contract existed. Why else would the seller specially manufacture goods suitable only for

one buyer? Such contracts are enforced without a writing.

2. *Admissions in court.* An oral contract will be enforced if a party admits in court, pleadings, or testimony that an oral contract was made. Admitted contracts are enforced only for the quantity admitted [UCC § 2–201(3)(b)]. For example, the admission of a sale of 50 widgets does not corroborate a contract for the sale of 500 widgets.

3. *Part performance.* Partial performance may substitute for the required writing where the buyer makes the payment and the seller accepts the goods. Part performance corroborates the oral contract [UCC § 2–201(3)(c)]. Why else would the seller deliver goods and the buyer accept them unless a contract was made? Part performance makes the contract enforceable only *to the extent that* it has been partially performed. For example, Ben Buyer

Figure 19–6   Parol Evidence

Evidence is inadmissible if it contradicts:

- A later (written or oral) agreement.
- A contemporaneous oral agreement.

> **Merger Clause**
> This agreement signed by both parties constitutes a final written expression of all the terms of this agreement and is a complete and exclusive statement of those terms.

and Sam Seller enter into an oral contract for the sale of 100 garden rakes. If Sam delivers 50 garden rakes to Ben and Ben accepts them, the contract is enforceable for 50 (not 100) garden rakes.

The Parol Evidence Rule

Occasionally, one party attempts to introduce evidence of an oral agreement made separate from a written contract. The parties may have orally modified the writing, orally clarified the written terms while signing, or made collateral agreements before signing. Whether such evidence should be admitted into evidence is addressed by the **parol evidence rule.** As is illustrated in Figure 19–6, the UCC substantially codifies the common law parol evidence rule [UCC § 2–202]. Because writings are usually more reliable than the parties' memories, written terms are given preference over oral testimony. A writing intended by the parties as a final expression of their agreement cannot be contradicted by evidence of (1) any prior agreement (written or oral), or (2) a contemporaneous oral agreement. In some instances, the written agreement must be explained or supplemented by oral evidence showing a course of dealing, course of performance, usage of the trade, or by evidence of consistent additional terms. The parol evidence rule permits introduction of additional evidence that (1) does not contradict the written agreement, (2) is contained in a contemporaneous written agreement, or (3) represents an agreement made after the writing. Additionally, where the parties never intended the writing to be a final expression of their agreement, extrinsic evidence is admissible.

Therefore, an initial question in any parol evidence case is whether the parties intended the writing to be the final expression of their agreement. Such intent might be made clear if a merger clause is included in the contract. A **merger clause** specifies the parties' intent that the writing represents their final agreement and that all prior negotiations should be *merged* into the written agreement. An example of a merger clause would be:

An effective merger clause helps the trial judge infer the parties' intent and usually triggers the parol evidence exclusions.

Further, the court may declare that the writing is an **integration,** — that is, a "complete and exclusive" statement of the contract terms. Thereafter, additional terms are inadmissible even if they do not contradict the terms in the writing. Whether the writing is an integration depends on whether the additional terms are the kind that would most likely have been included in a writing *if agreed on*. Under most circumstances, a merger clause provides strong evidence that the writing constitutes the "complete and exclusive" agreement of the parties.

In spite of the parol evidence rule, parol evidence is generally considered admissible if offered to prove misrepresentation, fraud, bad faith, undue influence, duress, or mistake. A merger clause could be invalidated if it would be unconscionable to enforce it.

THE INTERNATIONAL SALES CONTRACT: THE CONVENTION ON CONTRACTS FOR THE INTERNATIONAL SALE OF GOODS

An Italian company wishes to buy handsaws from a U.S. supplier. Would the contract formation be governed by U.S. or Italian law? If the handsaws were lost in shipment, would the risk of loss be governed by U.S. or Italian law? Uncertainty as to choice of law has created problems in contracts for the international sales of goods.

Because this uncertainty is an impediment to international trade, the United Nations Commission on International Trade law (UNCITRAL) has attempted to (1) reduce legal obstacles to international trade; and (2) promote development of new legal concepts. As part of this mission, UNCITRAL adopted the Convention on Contracts for the International Sale of Goods (CISG) at the Vienna Conference in 1980. **CISG** applies only to contracts for international sales of goods, not domestic contracts. The treaty was ratified by the United States in 1986, and became effective January 1, 1988. It has at this point been ratified by only a few nations, among them Argentina, Australia, Austria, Canada, China, Egypt, Finland, France, Germany, Hungary, Italy, Mexico, Russia, Spain, Switzerland, Syria, and the United States.[2]

Scope of CISG

CISG applies to contracts for the international sale of goods.

International

A contract is international when the parties to the contract are "parties whose places of business are in different states" (countries). It is irrelevant where the goods are located, or where contract formation occurs. Further, the countries involved must have ratified the convention. For example, if a U.S. firm contracts for the sale of goods with a Japanese firm, CISG will not apply. Whether U.S. or Japanese law applies will be determined by conflict of laws provisions unless a choice of law provision is contained in the contract.

In addition, the parties to the contract may "opt out" of CISG by including in the contract, for example, "This contract shall not be governed by the United Nations Convention on Contracts for the International Sale of Goods, but shall be governed by the Maryland Uniform Commercial Code."

Goods

Although the Convention applies only to contracts for the sale of **goods,** the term is not defined. Presumably, the definition would be similar to the UCC definition. CISG excludes from Convention coverage contracts for the sale of commercial paper, investment securities, ships, aircraft, hovercraft, and electricity contracts.

Other Exclusions

To prevent conflict with the many consumer protection laws, the Convention expressly excludes from its coverage contracts for the international sale of goods to consumers [Article 2]. Further, CISG governs only the formation of the contract and the rights and obligations of the parties to the contract. It does not govern the validity of the contract or its effect on title to the goods.

General Provisions

Under the Convention, local courts must focus on international practice rather than domestic usage. For example, CISG gap-filler principles are found by reference to common international practice and law, not by reference to local law.

The obligation of good faith, which underlies UCC formation and performance, is not a part of a Convention contract. Good faith is only relevant in court interpretation of the Convention, not of the contract.

Formation: The Agreement

Drafting a statute designed to provide uniform rules to govern all contracts for the international sale of goods, regardless of the local law, is difficult. While U.S. law stems from the common law, much of the world exists under a civil law system. These differences are particularly acute in contract formation questions. While common law focuses on offer and acceptance, civil law emphasizes the agreement process.

Under CISG, a contract becomes binding "when an acceptance of an offer becomes effective" [Article 23].

Offer

An offer is (1) "a proposal for concluding a contract," which (2) indicates "an intention to be bound in case of acceptance," and which is (3) "sufficiently definite" [Article 14]. Under CISG, an advertisement in a catalog would not be an offer because it does not indicate an intention to be bound in the case of acceptance.

Definite and Certain   The offer must be definite in describing the goods, indicating their quantity and their price. Other terms can be left open.

1. *Description of the goods.* The goods do not need to be described with any particularity. It is enough if the goods are "indicated."

2. *Open price term.* The Convention allows most forms of flexible pricing, since an offer is definite if it fixes or "makes provision for" determin-

---

[2]The list of ratifying countries as of January 25, 1993, includes Argentina, Australia, Belarus, Bulgaria, Canada, Chile, Czechoslovakia, Denmark, Egypt, Finland, Germany, Ghana, Guinea, Hungary, Iraq, Italy, Lesotho, Mexico, Netherlands, Norway, Poland, Romania, Singapore, Spain, Sweden, Switzerland, Syrian Arab Republic, Ukraine, Russia, United States, Venezuela, Yugoslavia, and Zambia.

ing the price. If the price is tied to an index, includes an escalator clause, or is to be set by a third party, "provision is made" for determining the price. Even in the circumstances where a buyer orders a good with no price stated, the definiteness requirement has probably been met. Here, the buyer agrees to pay the seller's current price at the time the contract is created for such goods [Article 55].

3. *Open quantity terms.* Requirements and output contracts are sufficiently definite under the Convention because an offer is definite if it fixes or "makes provision" for determining the quantity.

Firm Offer   An offer is typically revocable any time before acceptance. However, if the offeror indicates that the offer is irrevocable, it cannot be revoked. This provision is similar to the UCC firm offer provision but applies even without a "signed writing" [Article 16].

Acceptance: Battle of the Forms

An acceptance indicates assent to the offer. The Convention rejects the UCC's approach to the battle of the forms dilemma and adopts close to the mirror-image requirement of common law. If the seller's acknowledgment differs on any material terms from the buyer's purchase order, the forms do not create a contract [Article 19]. The purchase order is an offer; the acknowledgment is a rejection and counteroffer.

If, as is typical, the parties perform believing that there is a contract, what is the result? Again, the Convention adopts the common law approach. There is a contract. The buyer's purchase order is the offer, the seller's acknowledgment is the counteroffer. Buyer's acceptance of the goods is the acceptance. The contract terms are the terms of the acknowledgment. This follows the common law "last shot" principle where the party sending the last form gets the "last shot" and those terms become a part of the contract.

Consideration

No consideration is required to make a binding contract under CISG.

Statute of Frauds

Contracts for sale are enforceable without a written contract [Article 11]. However, a country ratifying the Convention may provide, by reservation, that domestic law governs the form requirements of the contract [Article 96]. Thus, while the United States has not made this reservation, it is possible that a contract for the sale of goods between a U.S. buyer and a foreign supplier would be subject to the statute of frauds if the country of the supplier made the reservation and had a domestic statute of frauds. A telex or telegram would meet any statute of frauds requirement notwithstanding local law.

END–OF–CHAPTER QUESTIONS

1. How are merchants treated differently from nonmerchants under the UCC? What are the reasons for the different treatment? Do you agree that merchants should be held to a higher standard than nonmerchants?

2. Should the United States have ratified CISG?

3. Compare and contrast the UCC provisions for contract formation with those under CISG.

4. Explain the relationship between the statute of frauds and the parol evidence rule.

5. Evaluate: "Under the UCC, an agreement modifying a contract is unenforceable without additional consideration under the preexisting duty rule."

6. Boge, a dairy farmer, entered into a loan agreement with Bank, giving it a security interest in his cows. When Boge defaulted on the loan, Bank threatened foreclosure. Boge then entered into an agreement with Riley, the person from whom he had purchased the cows, to resell and repurchase the cows. In effect, this repurchase would refinance the sale so that Boge could pay off the bank loan. In order to finalize the deal with Riley, Boge needed information about his loan that Bank refused to furnish. The deal with Riley fell through. Bank repossessed the cows, sold them below market value, and sued Boge for the unpaid loan balance. Boge counterclaimed asserting that Bank had violated the covenant of good faith and fair dealing. Will Boge prevail? See *United States National Bank of Oregon v. Boge,* 102 Or. App. 262, 12 UCC Rep. Serv.2d 16 (1990).

7. On May 1, Mike offers in writing to sell to Ben 100 wrenches at $10.50 per wrench, ''offer to remain open until the end of the month.'' On May 15, Mike writes to Ben that the price of the wrenches has risen and that the cost is now $20. Ben accepts the original offer. When Mike refuses to ship the wrenches at $10.50, Ben initiates suit. Mike argues alternatively that (1) he revoked the offer before acceptance and there is, thus, no contract; and (2) since no consideration is required for contract modification, the contract as modified (wrenches for $20) is enforceable. Who is correct? Does it matter whether Mike is a merchant?

8. The seller offered for sale copper tubing in a telegram ''as is—where is.'' The buyer telegrammed a response accepting the offer, but included delivery terms: ''FOB our truck your plant loaded.'' Does the exchange of writings create a contract? See *Koehring Co. v. Glowacki*, 77 Wis.2d 497, 253 N.W.2d 64 (1977).

9. What if the parties in Question 8 performed? Would there be a contract? What would be the terms of the contract? See *Jones & McKnight Corp. v. Birdsboro Corp.*, 320 F. Supp. 39 (N.D. Ill. 1980).

10. Offen, Inc., entered into an oral contract to sell petroleum products with Rocky Mountain Constructors, Inc. Offen delivered the products together with delivery tickets. The delivery tickets stated that an 18 percent interest rate and attorney fees would be charged if the price remained unpaid and collection was required. The invoices mailed after delivery contained similar language. Is there a contract? Are there any additional terms? Do they become a part of the contract? Is the contract enforceable? See *Offen, Inc. v. Rocky Mountain Constructors, Inc.*, 7 UCC Rep. Serv.2d 47 (Colo. Ct. App. 1988).

Chapter 20

Performance of the Sales Contract

■

CRITICAL THINKING INQUIRIES

As you read this chapter, you should be able to address the following:

- Explain the relationship between tender and performance.
- Explain the relationship between substantial performance and perfect tender.
- What are the buyer's options upon receipt of nonconforming goods? How do they compare to the buyer's options upon receipt of conforming goods?
- Explain the relationship between rejection and revocation of acceptance.
- Evaluate the following statement: ''The buyer is never obligated to accept nonconforming tender.''

MANAGERIAL PERSPECTIVE

Michael is the owner of a dress shop. He enters into a contract to buy 1,500 clothing clips, size 0, from Clips, Inc. Nothing is said in the contract about delivery or payment terms. When the clips arrive, they are not size 0 but size 1.

- Does Michael have to accept the clips?
- Does he have to give Clips, Inc. a chance to deliver the clips promised before he orders from another supplier?
- If Michael accepts them, can he change his mind and send them back?
- What are the delivery and payment terms in this contract?

When creating contracts for the sale of goods, managers must be aware of the Code gap-filler provisions. The parties to the contract can separately negotiate and specify payment and delivery terms in the contract. However, if the parties do not specify, the Code will provide the terms. Managers who do not want these terms must be careful to override the Code provisions. Managers, whether they are managers of seller or buyer companies, must be familiar with the obligations of both parties to the sales contract. Sellers must appreciate the implications of delivering nonconforming goods and fully understand the seller's right to cure to best protect themselves. Buyers must appreciate the implications of accepting goods and the circumstances under which they might reject or revoke the acceptance. This chapter will familiarize the manager with these concepts.

INTRODUCTION

Tender

The contract for sale creates certain obligations: the seller must deliver the goods and the buyer must pay for them. However, neither party must perform until the other party **tenders** performance [UCC § 2–507]. In simple terms, tender means that one party indicates to the other party that he or she is ready, willing, and able to perform. Each party's obligation to *perform* is conditioned on the other party's *tender* of performance. For example, the seller's tender of delivery is a condition to the buyer's duty to pay for those goods. The buyer's tender of payment is a condition to the seller's duty to deliver the goods. These are concurrent conditions, which means that unless otherwise agreed, payment and delivery are due at the same time. This is illustrated in Figure 20–1. If the sale is on credit, the buyer is relieved of the duty to tender payment before the seller's duty to deliver. Tender of performance is important because it triggers the other party's obligation to perform. Performance is important because it discharges the contractual obligation.

CONFORMING GOODS

The parties' agreement on timing and form of payment and delivery controls their duties. However, if the parties have not specified the time, manner and

Figure 20–1   Tender

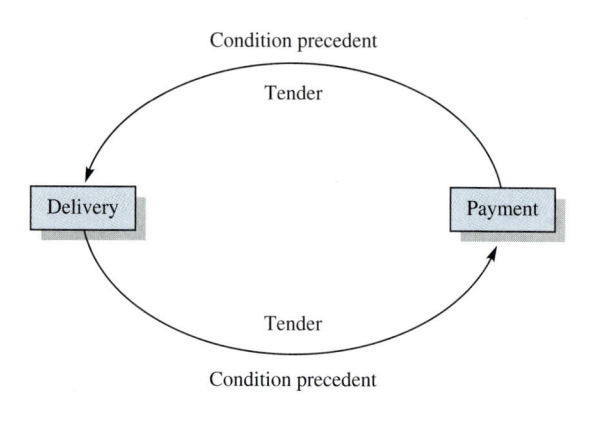

place in which payment and delivery will be made, the UCC gap-filler provisions supply these applicable terms.

Seller's Obligation to Deliver the Goods

The seller in a sales contract is obligated to deliver **conforming** goods to the buyer. This means that the seller must deliver the exact goods promised. *What* exactly must the seller do to tender delivery? *When* must the seller tender delivery of the goods? *Where* must the seller tender delivery of the goods? If the contract does not provide the answers to these questions, the UCC supplies them in its "gap-filler" sections.

Manner of Delivery

To determine what the seller must do to tender delivery, the type of contract must be determined. As is illustrated in Figure 20–2, the Code provides different treatment for three types of contracts: (1) contracts where the goods are in the possession of third parties and will not move (**bailment contracts**), (2) carrier contracts, and (3) all other contracts.

In General   To tender delivery, the seller must make conforming goods available to the buyer and notify the buyer of the delivery [UCC § 2–503]. Tender can be made at any reasonable hour. The seller must keep the goods available for a reasonable period to enable the buyer to take delivery. Thus, there are

Figure 20–2   Manner of Delivery

Type of Contract	Manner of Delivery
In general	Put and hold conforming goods at the buyer's disposition and notify buyer.
Goods in the possession of third parties	• Tender negotiable document of title; or • Obtain bailee's acknowledgment of buyer's right.
Shipment contract (FOB seller's source)	• Deliver goods to a carrier and make contract for transportation that is reasonable in light of the nature of the goods; and • Obtain and deliver documents of title; and • Notify buyer.
Destination shipment contract (FOB buyer's destination)	Put and hold conforming goods at buyer's disposition at the location.

Figure 20–3   Mercantile Terms

FOB	Free on Board (UCC § 2–319)
	     When delivery is FOB the place of shipment, the seller bears only the risk and expense of delivering the goods to the carrier.
	     When delivery is FOB the place of destination, the seller bears the expense and the risk of transporting the goods to the buyer at that destination.

CIF	Cost, Insurance, and Freight (UCC § 2–320) The sale price includes the cost of the goods, insuring the goods, and shipping them to the destination.
C & F	Cost and Freight The sale price includes the cost of the goods and freight charges to the destination, but not insurance.

two essential requirements of tender: (1) put and hold conforming goods at the buyer's disposition, and (2) notify the buyer. For example, in our opening scenario, all Clips, Inc. must do to tender delivery of the clothing clips is to make the clips available as promised and notify Michael that they are ready to be picked up. If the contract for sale is for delivery of numerous goods, all goods must be tendered in a single delivery unless otherwise specified [UCC § 2–307]. The buyer must furnish facilities reasonably suitable for receipt of the goods.

UCC § 2–503. Manner of Seller's Delivery

(1) Tender of delivery requires that the seller put and hold conforming goods at the buyer's disposition and give the buyer any notification reasonably necessary to enable him to take delivery.

Goods in the Possession of Third Parties   Where the goods are in the possession of a third party (the **bailee**) and will not be moved when sold, the manner in which the seller tenders depends on the contract terms. For example, grain stored in a grain elevator is often sold by the farmer to buyers who

continue storing at the elevator. The parties may pass title to the grain using a document of title such as a warehouse receipt. If a negotiable document of title is used, the seller tenders delivery of the goods by tendering the negotiable document to the buyer. If a negotiable document is not used, the seller tenders delivery by obtaining the bailee's acknowledgment of the buyer's right to the goods [UCC § 2–503(4)(a)]. For example, to sell grain stored in a grain elevator, the seller must either deliver a warehouse receipt to the buyer or obtain the grain elevator owner's acknowledgment of the change in ownership.

UCC § 2–503. Manner of Seller's Delivery

(4) Where the goods are in possession of a bailee and are to be delivered without being moved

(a) tender requires that the seller either tender a negotiable document of title or procure acknowledgment by the bailee of the buyer's right to possession of the goods.

Carrier Contracts   Where the goods are to be shipped by carrier, parties will create one of two types of contracts: (1) a contract that requires the seller to deliver the goods to a particular destination (a **destination contract**), or (2) a contract that does not require delivery to a particular destination (a **shipment contract**). The parties indicate their intent by "shorthand" delivery or mercantile terms such as FOB. Mercantile terms are outlined in

Figure 20–3. If a destination contract is intended, the contract will typically specify FOB buyer's destination. If a shipment contract is intended, the contract will typically specify FOB seller's source. If shipment is intended, but neither a shipment nor a destination contract is indicated, a shipment contract is presumed.

Destination Contract   Where the contract requires delivery at a particular destination, the seller must make the goods available to the buyer at that location. For example, if Betty from Baltimore contracts for the purchase of 100 pounds of crabs from Sam of San Antonio, FOB Baltimore, Sam must deliver conforming crabs in Baltimore [UCC § 2–503(3)].

Shipment Contract   Where the contract requires shipment but does not require delivery at a particular destination, the seller must (1) deliver the goods to a carrier and make a contract for their transportation that is reasonable considering the nature of the goods; (2) obtain and promptly deliver any documents, such as a bill of lading, necessary for the buyer to pick up the goods; and (3) promptly notify the buyer of the shipment [UCC § 2–504]. Assume that in the above example, the contract specified FOB San Antonio. The seller would first have to deliver the crabs to the carrier and make a contract to transport them from San Antonio to Baltimore—which is reasonable, considering the nature of the goods. For example, if crabs need to be refrigerated and the contract with the carrier did not provide for refrigeration, the tender is ineffective. Further, the seller would have to deliver to the buyer any documents needed to pick up the crabs in Baltimore. Finally, the seller would have to notify the buyer that the shipment was made and when to expect the goods.

Time for Delivery

If there is no provision in the contract about time of delivery, the seller must deliver the goods within a reasonable time after contract formation. The buyer then has a reasonable time within which to accept and pay for the goods [UCC § 2–309].

UCC § 2–309. Absence of Specific Time Provisions

(1) The time for shipment or delivery . . . shall be a reasonable time.

Figure **20–4**	Delivery and Payment
Time for delivery	Reasonable time after contracting.
Place for delivery	Seller's place of business, or seller's residence, or third location.
Payment	At time and place at which the buyer is to receive the goods.
Payment if document of title	At time and place at which the buyer receives the document.

Place for Delivery

If there is no provision in the contract for where the seller must deliver the goods, the place for delivery is the seller's place of business. For example, assume Dan Dealer enters into a contract to sell a car to Ben Buyer. Unless otherwise agreed, Dan does not have to deliver the car to Ben. Dan must only make the car available at Dan's place of business [UCC § 2–308].

There are several exceptions to this general rule. First, if the seller has no place of business, the place for delivery is the seller's residence. Second, if at the time of contracting the parties are aware that the goods are kept in another location, then that other location is the place for delivery. If, in the above example, both parties knew that the car was kept in a lot across town, that lot would be the place for delivery. Third, the general rule does not apply where delivery is to be made by carrier or where the goods are in the hands of a third party. Figure 20–4 summarizes these provisions.

UCC § 2–308. Absence of Specified Place for Delivery

Unless otherwise agreed

(a) the place for delivery of goods is the seller's place of business or if he has none his residence; but

(b) in a contract for the sale of identified goods which to the knowledge of the parties at the time of contracting are in some other place, that place is the place for their delivery;

Buyer's Obligation to Accept the Goods and Make Payment

If the seller tenders delivery of conforming goods, the buyer must **accept** them. Failure to accept or **rejection** is a breach of contract by the buyer. Acceptance occurs in one of three ways. First, the buyer can accept by indicating either that the goods are **conforming** or that they will be kept even though they are nonconforming. Second, the buyer can accept by failing to make a timely rejection. Third, the buyer can accept by treating the goods in a way that is inconsistent with an intent to reject them [UCC § 2–606(1)]. For example, the buyer's use of goods is such an acceptance. After acceptance of conforming goods, the buyer must pay the contract price, and it is too late to reject.

UCC § 2–606. What Constitutes Acceptance of Goods

(1) Acceptance of goods occurs when the buyer

(a) after a reasonable opportunity to inspect the goods signifies to the seller that the goods are conforming or that he will take . . . them in spite of their nonconformity; or

(b) fails to make an effective rejection . . . ; or

(c) does any act inconsistent with the seller's ownership;

Payment

What exactly must the buyer do to tender payment for the goods? When must the buyer tender payment for the goods? Where must the buyer tender payment for the goods? If the parties have not provided the answers to these questions in the contract, the UCC supplies answers.

Manner of Payment   The buyer must tender payment to trigger the seller's obligation to deliver the goods. The buyer's tender of payment can be made by any means acceptable in the ordinary course of business unless the seller demands legal tender, in which case the buyer must be given a reasonable period of time in which to obtain it [UCC § 2–511]. In other words, payment can be made by check if that is common in the ordinary course of business, unless the seller demands cash. If cash is demanded, the buyer is given a reasonable period of time to get the cash. If payment is made by check, it satisfies the payment obligation only if the check is paid by the buyer's bank. Payment is ineffective if the check is dishonored (bounces).

Time and Place for Payment   If there are no payment provisions in the contract, payment is due at the time and place the buyer is to receive the goods. If delivery will be made by a document of title,

Figure 20–5   Substantial Performance at Common Law

If the Seller Tenders Substantial Performance	If the Seller Does Not Tender Substantial Performance
The buyer must accept the nonconforming tender and pay seller the contract price.	The buyer does not have to accept the nonconforming tender. The buyer is not liable for the contract price or damages.
The buyer is entitled to compensatory damages from the seller.	The buyer is entitled to compensatory damages from the seller.

payment is due at the time and place the buyer is to receive the document regardless of when and where the goods are to be received [UCC § 2–310]. The buyer has a right to inspect the goods after delivery before payment is due. The parties can, of course, agree otherwise, as with a contract that specifies that the shipment is cash on delivery (COD).

Figure 20–4 summarizes the rules with respect to payment and delivery.

NONCONFORMING GOODS

Perfect Tender

At common law, substantial performance by one party triggers the other party's duty to perform. Under the **substantial performance** doctrine, performance with minor, inadvertent, unimportant, and unintentional deviations nevertheless meets the tender requirement triggering the other party's duty to perform. However, it does not fully discharge all contractual obligations. The seller remains liable for damages caused by the failure to exactly perform all promises. Figure 20–5 illustrates this principle.

The substantial performance doctrine is inapplicable to sales contracts. **Perfect tender** is required both to trigger the other party's obligation to perform and to discharge the performing party's obligations. Perfect tender or exact performance is delivery of totally conforming goods with no deviations. Figure 20–6 illustrates the perfect tender rule. Compare this figure with Figure 20–5.

Buyer's Right of Inspection

The buyer has a right to inspect the goods to determine if they are conforming [UCC § 2–511]. The

Figure 20–6   Perfect Tender under the UCC

If the Seller Tenders Substantial Performance	If the Seller Does Not Tender Substantial Performance
The buyer does not have to accept the nonconforming tender. The buyer is not liable for the contract price or damages.	The buyer does not have to accept the nonconforming tender. The buyer is not liable for the contract price or damages.
The buyer is entitled to compensatory damages from the seller.	The buyer is entitled to compensatory damages from the seller.

inspection may be at any reasonable place and time and in any reasonable manner. The buyer is responsible for any inspection expenses. However, if the goods are nonconforming, the buyer may recover inspection expenses from the seller. If the goods are delivered COD, the buyer loses this right to inspect before payment but does not lose the right to inspect before acceptance.

Buyer's Options

If conforming goods are delivered, the buyer must accept the goods and pay for them. However, where the goods are nonconforming—where they are defective even in some small detail—the buyer has three choices. First, the buyer may accept all goods even though they are nonconforming. Second, the buyer may accept any **commercial units** and reject the rest. Third, the buyer may reject all of the goods. The only limitation is that the buyer cannot break up commercial units. A commercial unit is a unit that in commercial usage would be considered a whole and that would be substantially impaired by division [UCC § 2–105(6)]. For example, if a seller contracts to deliver to a buyer 100 crochet hooks size 00, and instead delivers 50 hooks size 00 and 50 hooks size 0, the buyer can either accept all of them in spite of the nonconformity, reject all of them because of their nonconformity, or accept the 50 conforming hooks and reject the 50 nonconforming hooks. If they are packaged in packages of 10 each, the buyer would be unable to break open the packages (split the commercial unit).

Acceptance or Rejection

In order to properly reject the crochet hooks, the buyer must notify the seller of the rejection within a reasonable period of time after receipt of the goods. The rejection is effective when this notice is received by the seller [UCC § 2–602]. The buyer may not exercise any ownership over rejected goods. For example, if Irene orders a green dress from the Dresses-R-Us Company and a blue dress is delivered instead, Irene has the option of accepting or rejecting the dress. If she chooses to reject the dress, she must notify Dresses-R-Us within a reasonable period of time, and she cannot wear the dress to the office party after rejection.

Buyer's Duties toward Rejected Goods

Irene must exercise reasonable care with respect to the dress (goods in the possession of the buyer that have been rejected) for a period of time sufficient to permit Dresses-R-Us to remove it [UCC § 2–602(2)(b)]. What is reasonable depends on the circumstances and on the nature of the goods. For example, Irene's care for the dress probably would include little more than keeping it safe for the seller. By contrast, if Irene had ordered filet mignon and the seller had delivered T-Bones, Irene's duty would include refrigeration until the seller could pick up the steak.

UCC § 2–603. Merchant's Duties as to Rightfully Rejected Goods

(1) . . . when the seller has no agent or place of business at the market of rejection a merchant buyer is under a duty after rejection of goods in his possession or control to follow any reasonable instructions received . . . and in the absence of such instructions to make reasonable efforts to sell them for the seller's account if they are perishable or threaten to decline in value speedily.

Further, if Irene were a merchant, her duties with respect to the nonconforming goods would increase. The merchant-buyer must follow all reasonable instructions of the seller where the seller has no agent nor place of business in the buyer's city [UCC § 2–603]. The duty is imposed on the merchant by good faith and commercial practice. Reasonable instructions include instructions to reship, store, or deliver to a third party. The buyer is entitled to receive reimbursement for expenses incurred in following all reasonable instructions. For example, if the seller instructed the merchant-buyer to store the goods until the seller could arrange for an agent to pick them up, the buyer would be entitled to reimbursement for storage expenses from the seller.

If the seller does not give the buyer any instructions, the merchant buyer must make reasonable efforts to resell the goods for the seller's account, but only if the goods are perishable or likely to decline in value quickly. For example, assume that the merchant-buyer orders 100 pounds of oranges from Sam Seller, and Sam delivers 100 pounds of bananas, instead. The buyer rejects the bananas and receives no instructions from Sam on what to do with them. The merchant-buyer is under a duty to attempt to resell them because bananas are likely to spoil quickly. If the buyer is able to resell the bananas, the money received is the seller's, but the buyer is entitled to reimbursement for the expenses of caring for and selling the goods, including a reasonable commission.

In the following case, was the merchant-buyer following the reasonable instructions of the seller?

THE MITRAL CORP. v. VERMONT KNIVES, INC.
566 A.2d 406 (Vt. 1989)

Vermont Knives (Vermont) ordered 7,800 blade-blanks from The Mitral Corp. (Mitral), to be used to manufacture boot-knives. The first shipment contained 5,565 blade-blanks and was accepted. The second shipment contained 5,420 blade-blanks for a total of 10,985. Vermont refused to accept the second shipment.

Counsel for Mitral contacted Vermont and stated that he understood there was a dispute as to the quantity of blade-blanks but suggested that Vermont accept the shipment because storage fees were mounting and Mitral could not use the blade-blanks if they were returned. The blade-blanks were then delivered to Vermont.

After all attempts at negotiations on a price for the excess goods failed, Mitral argued that Vermont accepted the entire shipment and is obligated to pay for it. Vermont contended that it did not accept the second shipment and is, therefore, not obligated to pay for the second shipment.

ALLEN, Chief Justice

Vermont concedes on appeal that it agreed to purchase 7,800 blade-blanks. The question before us is whether it accepted the blade-blanks in excess of that number. We note at the outset that Mitral was obligated to deliver, and Vermont to accept, the quantity of blade-blanks to which the parties agreed. Delivery of too many blanks would not conform to the contract. Vermont, upon tender of the second shipment, could have rejected them, accepted them, or accepted the quantity stipulated for in the contract and rejected the remainder. The trial court concluded that Vermont initially rejected the second shipment, but that its subsequent action in picking up the blade-blanks constituted the acceptance. With this we cannot agree. The excess blade-blanks had been rightfully rejected by the defendant,[1] and it then became Vermont's duty to follow Mitral's instructions with respect to them. The only evidence regarding instructions is contained in the letter from plaintiff's counsel which, reasonably interpreted, told the defendant to pick up the blade-blanks to avoid further storage charges. A merchant buyer's retention and storage of rightfully rejected goods (goods in excess of those contracted for), at the instruction of the seller, does not violate the buyer's

---

[1] "Rejection of goods must be within a reasonable time after their delivery or tender" and "is ineffective unless the buyer seasonably notifies the seller." Here, Vermont notified Mitral that it was rejecting the shipment on the day of the second delivery. Vermont both rejected the shipment within a reasonable time and gave prompt notice to Mitral.

duty to follow reasonable instructions of the seller under § 2–603(1).

There have been no further negotiations with respect to the price for the excess, notwithstanding repeated efforts by the plaintiff to initiate such negotiations. The record does not support the finding that after negotiations the defendant accepted the second shipment, nor does the plaintiff argue an express acceptance. Instead, it contends that the retention of the blade-blanks by the defendant constitutes the acceptance. While it is true that an acceptance occurs when the buyer does any act inconsistent with the seller's ownership, there is nothing in the record before us to indicate such an act. While possession for an inordinate amount of time may be inconsistent with the seller's ownership, the possessory act here was pursuant to the seller's request after an effective and timely rejec-

tion. The trial court erred in concluding that the defendant accepted the 3,185 blade-blanks in excess of the number ordered.

Case Questions

1. In what way were the blade-blanks nonconforming?
2. Why did Vermont have a duty to follow Mitral's instructions after it rejected the blade-blanks?
3. Did Vermont accept the goods in spite of their nonconformity? Why wasn't the fact that Vermont subsequently accepted delivery and retained the blade-blanks considered an acceptance by the court?
4. Why was the question of whether or not Vermont accepted the blade-blanks important? What is the significance of the ruling?

Figure 20–7   Revocation of Acceptance: Permitted Where

1. Buyer accepted:
   - Because hidden defect not discovered; or
   - Because of reasonable assumption that defect would be cured.

   and
2. Defect substantially impaired value.

UCC § 2–608.

Buyer's Right to Revoke Acceptance

When the seller delivers nonconforming goods, the buyer has the option of accepting or rejecting the goods. If the buyer chooses to accept, any right to subsequently reject the goods is surrendered. However, the buyer might be permitted to **revoke the acceptance.** Whether or not the buyer will be permitted to revoke the acceptance depends on (1) the circumstances under which the buyer accepted and (2) the degree of nonconformity [UCC § 2–608]. See Figure 20–7.

First, the buyer can only revoke the acceptance if it was either made (1) on the reasonable assumption that the nonconformity would be cured by the seller and it was not, or (2) without discovery of the nonconformity and induced either by the difficulty of discovery before acceptance or by the seller's assurances of conformity [UCC § 2–608(1)]. For exam-

ple, assume, in our opening scenario, that Clips, Inc. delivers nonconforming clips to Michael. Michael notices the nonconformity and notifies Clips, Inc., who assures him that the nonconformity will be promptly cured. Relying on such assurances, Michael accepts the clips. Under these circumstances, Michael may revoke his acceptance if the nonconformity is not cured. Michael could similarly revoke his acceptance if the clips appeared to be conforming but had a latent defect that could not easily be discovered. Acceptances made under any other circumstances cannot be revoked.

UCC § 2–608. Revocation of Acceptance

(1) The buyer may revoke his acceptance of a . . . commercial unit whose non-conformity substantially impairs its value to him if he has accepted it

(a) on the reasonable assumption that its nonconformity would be cured and it has not been . . . ; or

(b) without discovery of such non-conformity if his acceptance was reasonably induced either by the difficulty of discovery before acceptance or by the seller's assurances.

Second, the buyer may revoke the acceptance only if the nonconformity substantially impairs the value of the goods to the buyer. At common law, tender that *substantially* conforms to the tender promised (under the substantial performance doctrine) is sufficient to trigger the buyer's obligation to perform. The substantial performance doctrine was, in part, rejected by the UCC and replaced by the perfect tender doctrine. However, where the buyer attempts to revoke acceptance, the substantial performance doctrine still applies. Performance that would qualify as substantial performance at common law is not substantial impairment under the UCC. Where goods are tendered with minor defects that would have constituted substantial performance at common law, the buyer under the Code can reject those goods. However, where the buyer accepts those goods, revocation of acceptance is not permitted because the nonconformity does not substantially impair the value of the goods to the buyer. Whether or not the buyer is permitted to revoke this acceptance, the goods are nevertheless nonconforming, so the seller is liable for contract damages because of the breach. Figure 20–8 summarizes this rule.

Figure 20–8   Revoking Acceptance under the UCC

If the Buyer Accepts Nonconforming Tender that Is

Substantial Performance	Not Substantial Performance
The buyer may *not* revoke the acceptance.	The buyer may revoke the acceptance of nonconforming tender if there was a latent defect or the goods were accepted because of the seller's assurances.
The buyer is entitled to compensatory damages from the seller.	The buyer is entitled to compensatory damages from the seller.

In the following case, ask yourself whether the buyers should be permitted to revoke their acceptance. Is there a substantial impairment?

FORTIN v. OX-BOW MARINA, INC.
557 N.E.2d 1157 (Mass. 1990)

The Fortins purchased a Bayliner, a power boat, from the Ox-Bow Marina, which promised delivery in time for the boating season. The new boat was delivered on April 23, 1985. It arrived with ill-fitting engine latches, marred gel coat in the cockpit, a missing bow eye, and numerous scrapes on the hull. The Fortins inspected the boat on May 8, 1985, and noted a number of defects. The Ox-Bow sales representative assured them that all defects would be cured by the time of closing on the boat.

On the day of closing, the Fortins noted that none of the preparation work had been started. They were reluctant to close until the boat was operational, but agreed to following assurances from Ox-Bow that the boat would be completely ready shortly.

The Fortins experienced continued difficulties with the boat. Ox-Bow repeatedly attempted repairs, but new problems were discovered. By October 1985, the hoses in the toilet system were replaced, and a new starboard engine was installed, but none of the other defects had been repaired. The Fortins notified Ox-Bow that they were revoking their acceptance and seeking a refund of the purchase price. The trial court found that the Fortins revoked their acceptance and ordered Ox-Bow to return the purchase price.

LYNCH, Judge

The Fortins' rights in this regard are governed by Art. 2 of the UCC. There is no dispute that the Fortins, having inspected the boat on several occasions earlier and after noting a number of defects, did not reject the boat, as they would have been entitled to do under § 2–602. However, a buyer may revoke an acceptance providing that he or she can show that the "nonconformity" in the goods that the buyer has purchased "substantially impairs [their] value to him [or her]," § 2–608(1); that the buyer accepted the goods on the "reasonable assumption that [their] nonconformity would be cured and it has not been seasonably cured," § 2–608(1)(A), and that he or she revoked acceptance "within a reasonable time after the buyer discovers or should have discovered the ground for it." § 2–608(2).

The issue of whether a revocation was effective, whether defects substantially impaired the value of goods, and whether notice of revocation was timely, are all matters to be resolved by the fact finder. The evidence that the starboard engine overheated twice; the bilge pump was defective; there was an array of malfunctioning electrical equipment; and the marine toilet only functioned partially—none of which alone could be characterized as minor, cosmetic, or insubstantial problems with a power boat—in concert support a finding of substantial impairment of the boat's value.

The defendant stresses the replacement of the defective starboard engine with a new engine prior to the Fortins' revocation and the Fortins' use of the boat on some six or seven weekends in the summer of 1985, to assert that the judge clearly erred in finding the boat's value had been substantially impaired.

In weighing this issue the trier of fact must decide whether the defects substantially impair the value of the goods to the revoking buyer, § 2–608(1). Most courts read this test as an objective, or common-sense, determination that the impaired value of the goods to the buyer was substantial as opposed to trivial, or easily fixed, given his subjective needs. The evaluation is made in light of the "totality of the circumstances" of each particular case, including the number of deficiencies and type of nonconformity and the time and inconvenience spent in downtime and attempts at repair. Thus, it has been said that, in the proper circumstances, even cosmetic or minor defects that go unrepaired despite a number of complaints or attempts at repair, or remaining minor defects after an earlier, serious problem has been repaired, or defects which do not totally prevent the buyer from using the goods, but circumscribe that use or warrant unusual or excessive maintenance actions in order to use, can substantially impair the goods' value to the buyer. Experiencing in a major investment a series of defects, even if some have been cured and others are curable, can shake a buyer's faith in the goods, at which point "the item not only loses its real value in the buyer's eyes, but also becomes an article whose integrity has been substantially impaired and whose operation is fraught with apprehension."

Under these principles we have no difficulty in concluding that the judge's finding of substantial impairment was not clearly erroneous, despite the fact that the Bayliner's most serious defect, the starboard engine, was rectified before the Fortins revoked acceptance. There was evidence that a number of defects, observed by the Fortins from the moment their Bayliner arrived at Ox-Bow Marina, were never repaired, despite regularly repeated complaints.

Whether notice of revocation has been made within a "reasonable time" is also a question of fact. Many courts have held that any delay on the part of the buyer in notification of revocation of acceptance is justified where the buyer is in constant communication with the seller regarding nonconformity of the goods, and "the seller makes repeated assurances that the defect or nonconformity will be cured and attempts to do so."

Beginning weeks before they accepted the Bayliner, right up through the time of revocation, the Fortins were in frequent contact with Ox-Bow Marina in an effort to have their boat repaired. That conduct was encouraged by Ox-Bow who kept assuring them that those problems would be redressed. It would be anomalous, given the UCC's purpose to encourage buyers and sellers to reach reasonable accommodations to minimize losses, to penalize buyers like the Fortins for their patience in giving sellers like Ox-Bow the opportunity to rectify nonconformities before revoking acceptance of the goods.

The findings of fact by the trial judge, not clearly erroneous, support his conclusion that the Fortins' delayed revocation of acceptance of the Bayliner was timely in the circumstances of this case.

Case Questions

1. What was the issue concerning the Fortins' revocation of acceptance?

2. Is the test for determining whether "substantial impairment" occurred an objective or subjective one?

3. Can a buyer revoke acceptance where minor problems reoccur? Can you think of any problems that this might cause buyers of consumer goods?

Lemon Laws

Because of the requirement that a buyer cannot revoke its acceptance unless the defects substantially impair the value of the good, car buyers have found it difficult to revoke their acceptance of so-called lemons — cars that have numerous problems requiring repeated and often unsuccessful repair attempts.

Often, no one defect amounts to substantial impairment. The Federal Trade Commission and many states have enacted **lemon laws** to protect consumers. However, how well these laws have worked is the subject of debate. As you read the following article, ask yourself whether the lemon laws should be reformed.

What Makes a Lemon?*

Traditionally in common law, if someone bought a product that failed to function as promised, he had but one party to gripe to — the party that sold the thing to him. In 1975 Congress changed all that with the passage of a consumerist-minded "federal warranty law" that gives aggrieved consumers rights against the manufacturers of faulty products, as distinct from sellers.

Thus began what has now become a complex tangle of federal and state laws involving the rights of car owners of poorly made or serviced vehicles. Consumer rights in the case of so-called lemon automobiles are now enshrined not only in a sub-part of the 1975 federal warranty act but in the statutes of 44 states as well. In various ways, the state and federal laws are in considerable conflict and, predictably enough, the party caught increasingly in the middle is the consumer.

At the heart of the problem is how to resolve disputes over precisely what constitutes a "lemon" automobile. Under the federal warranty law, a car that rolls off the showroom floor and instantly starts belching clouds of smoke is not necessarily a lemon at all. In many cases the car buyer must first present his complaint to an arbitration panel, usually run by none other than the manufacturer of the vehicle. Such panels are empowered to compel the manufacturer to refund the purchase price to the owner, but in practice that almost never happens. Instead, the typical adjudication boils down to, "Take it back to the shop one more time."

Because the federal procedure in effect gives the car companies so much say at the start of the complaint, many states have enacted lemon laws of their own, with specific definitions of just how many times a car needs to be fixed for the same malfunction before it becomes a certified lemon.

But car companies tend not to apply those laws in their arbitration programs. Instead, they advise their panels to resolve disputes the same way they always have. Says a General Motors spokesman, "We don't use the lemon laws in our arbitration programs. The program isn't designed to be a court system, and it should not be up to the arbitrators to interpret laws."

Thus, seven states and District of Columbia have lately passed supplementary legislation offering consumers new government-managed arbitration panels in addition to the company run programs. (Connecticut, Massachusetts, Montana, New York, Texas, Vermont and Washington.) "The primary benefit," says Stephen Mindell, an assistant attorney general in New York, "is that it provides an even playing field in a neutral forum."

This in turn has infuriated the car companies, which argue that the arrangement unconstitutionally denies them the right to a jury trial. Thus, in a case that it is likely to have an impact nationwide, the Motor Vehicle Manufacturers Association and the Automobile Importers of America have now jointly filed suit in both state and federal court in New York challenging parts of that state's program.

All of which leaves car owners pretty much lost in the shuffle. If the carmakers prevail in their attack on state lemon law panels, owners of clunkers will once again find themselves at the mercy of manufacturers in deciding when a car is a lemon.

But what if the states prevail? In that case, arbitration panels under the control of vote-hungry politicians will undoubtedly proliferate, and it will not be long before panelists discover that the surest way to get reappointed is to decide in favor of consumers, no matter what the facts of each case. Not long after that carmakers will begin recovering their costs by raising sticker prices—and guess who will wind up paying the bill.

Thought Questions

1. What does Fanning see as the result if the state laws are struck down? Do you agree?

2. Can you identify any flaws in Fanning's reasoning?

3. What does Fanning see as the result if the state laws prevail? Do you agree? Can you identify any bias in her viewpoint or flaws in her reasoning?

4. What is the value conflict presented in this article?

5. Can you offer an alternative solution to the problem?

Figure 20–9   Seller's Right to Cure

Within time for performance	Seller given absolute right to cure.
Given further reasonable time	If seller reasonably believed that the goods would be accepted in spite of nonconformity

---

UCC § 2–508. Cure by Seller

(1) Where any tender or delivery by the seller is rejected because non-conforming and the time for performance has not yet expired, the seller may seasonably notify the buyer of his intention to cure and may then within the contract time make a conforming delivery.

Seller's Right to Cure

As is illustrated in Figure 20–9, where nonconforming goods are delivered, the seller has a right to **cure** the defect in one of two situations. First, the seller is permitted to cure where the time for performance has not yet expired if it can be done within the time specified in the contract [UCC § 2–508(1)]. For example, assume Susan Seller contracts to deliver 100 lime green pillows to Butch Buyer on June 15. Susan delivers 100 forest green pillows on May 15 and Butch rejects. Susan can notify Butch that she intends to cure and deliver the lime green pillows promised by June 15.

UCC § 2–508. Cure by Seller

(2) Where the buyer rejects a non-conforming tender which the seller had reasonable grounds to believe would be acceptable with or without money allowance the seller may if he seasonably notifies the buyer have a further reasonable time to substitute a conforming tender.

Second, the seller is permitted to cure even if it cannot be done within the delivery time specified if the seller had reasonable grounds to believe that the goods would be acceptable even though nonconforming [UCC § 2–508(2)]. For example, Susan might deliver the new and improved version of the CD player ordered by the buyer. If the buyer rejects, the seller may cure because she reasonably believed that the buyer would accept the player. Prior course of dealing, course of performance, or usage of the trade are often evidence of reasonableness on the seller's part. For example, Susan might reasonably believe that nonconforming goods are acceptable if the buyer has accepted such goods in the past. The seller must notify the buyer of her intent to cure to be given a further reasonable period of time in which to cure.

Read the following case and determine the limits on the seller's right to cure.

WORLDWIDE RV SALES & SERVICES, INC. v. BROOKS

534 N.E.2d 1132 (Ind. Ct. App. 1989)

Brooks agreed to purchase a motorhome with dual roof air conditioning from Worldwide for $39,000. He made a $1,500 deposit. When Brooks arrived to pick up his motorhome as agreed on March 5, 1987, he discovered that it had only one roof air conditioner, and Brooks refused to accept the unit. He sued for the refund of his deposit.

STATON, Judge

Worldwide argues that UCC § 2−508 entitled it to cure the problem and prevent cancellation of the contract. Worldwide claims that on the same day Brooks rejected the motorhome Worldwide offered to install a second roof air conditioner at no extra charge. Our examination of the record reveals that Worldwide's representative asked if the deal could be saved if they installed a second roof air conditioner. This "offer to cure" was accompanied with the warning that this alteration would result in a hole in the center of the motorhome.[2] To benefit from the remedial effect of UCC § 2−508 the seller must "make a conforming delivery" or "substitute a conforming tender." Worldwide did not fulfill this statutory requirement.

Worldwide's brief states that Worldwide tendered conforming goods on the same day Brooks rejected them. The facts do not substantiate this claim. UCC § 2−503 states that "[t]ender of delivery requires that the seller put and hold conforming goods at the buyer's disposition and give the buyer any notification reasonably necessary to enable him to take delivery." We have already determined that Brooks rejected the goods because they were non-conforming and that Worldwide's offer to cure was inadequate.

Case Questions

1. Could Worldwide cure within the time specified in the contract? Did they reasonably believe that the nonconforming tender would be acceptable?

2. Was the offer to cure satisfactory?

3. How does the seller's right to cure mitigate the perfect tender rule?

4. What policy rationale could the drafters have for giving the seller an opportunity to cure? Does this rationale adequately support this provision? Are there alternatives that could balance the party's contractual expectations?

---

[2]It appears from the record that Brooks wanted one roof air conditioning unit near the front of the vehicle and one near the back. Instead there was one air conditioning unit in the center of the vehicle. Apparently Worldwide's offer to cure consisted of installing a front and back unit and removing the center one, leaving a hole in the roof.

Excuses

Sometimes, an excuse is provided for nonperformance. Where one party is excused from performance, the excuse provides only a defense for nonperformance, it does not substitute for performance.

Breach by One Party

In the case of installment contracts, it must frequently be determined whether breach by one party can operate as an excuse for the other party's performance. In an installment contract, the seller has agreed to deliver the goods in separate lots. What is the effect of a nonconforming delivery of one installment? In particular, what are the buyer's obligations with respect to the nonconforming shipment, and what are the buyer's obligations with respect to the undelivered installments? In other words, can the buyer reject the nonconforming installment, and can the whole contract be canceled? The buyer may reject the nonconforming shipment if the defect substantially impairs the value of that installment and cannot be cured [UCC § 2–612(2)]. For example, assume the College Bookstore contracts to purchase 500 Business Law textbooks, to be delivered in two installments of 250 each. If the first installment contains 250 books printed upside down, the Bookstore could reject the installment because the defect would substantially impair the value of the books to the Bookstore. By contrast, the Bookstore could not reject if the first installment contained 249 books instead of 250. The defect would not substantially impair the value of the installment.

After rejecting the nonconforming installment, may the buyer cancel the remaining installments? Must the Bookstore accept and pay for the next shipment of 250 textbooks, or is the Bookstore free to treat the contract as canceled and to order the books from someone else? That depends on the severity of the breach. The buyer is relieved from its obligation to accept future installments where the nonconformity with respect to the installment delivered substantially impairs the value of the *whole contract* [UCC § 2–612(3)]. However, the right to treat the entire contract as breached will be lost if the buyer either (1) accepts a nonconforming tender without notifying the seller of the cancellation, (2) brings a lawsuit only for past installments, or (3) demands performance as to future installments.

Assurance of Performance

A contract is not merely a bargained for promise. A continuing sense of reliance and confidence that the promises will be performed is an essential feature of a contract. An insecure party is given the right to demand that the other party provide assurances that performance will be forthcoming because if either the willingness or the ability of one party to perform declines, the other party is in effect deprived of a substantial part of this bargain [UCC § 2–609]. For example, a seller might be concerned about having to deliver on credit to a buyer on the verge of insolvency. Similarly, a buyer might fear that a seller's

deliveries are becoming uncertain and wonder whether it is necessary to wait for the delivery date hoping that the seller will in fact deliver.

The UCC provides three measures to help the unsure party. First, where one party has "reasonable grounds for insecurity," performance and any preparation may be suspended, as long as commercially reasonable. Second, the unsure party may demand that adequate assurances of the other party's performance be made upon request. Third, the contract may be treated as broken if the unsure party's concerns are not relieved within a reasonable period of time, not to exceed 30 days.

To illustrate, assume Horace Hammers, Inc. agrees to sell 1,000 hammers to the Happy Hardware Store on credit, delivery to be made on August 1. Before the time for shipment, Horace learns that Happy has defaulted on several loans, is in a precarious financial condition, and may be on the verge of bankruptcy. Horace is afraid if it ships the hammers on credit as promised that Happy will be unable to pay. Horace could ask Happy for assurances and delay shipment until those assurances are received. If assurances are not received within 30 days from the request, Horace could treat the contract as breached by Happy.

UCC § 2–610. Anticipatory Repudiation

When either party repudiates the contract with respect to a performance not yet due the loss of which will substantially impair the value of the contract to the other, the aggrieved party may

(a) for a commercially reasonable time await performance . . . ; or

(b) resort to any remedy for breach . . . ; and

(c) . . . suspend his own performance.

Anticipatory Repudiation

An **anticipatory repudiation** occurs where, prior to the time for performance, a party indicates an intent not to perform. For example, assume Don enters into a contract to sell Ken 400 Christmas trees to be delivered on December 1. An anticipatory repudiation occurs when Ken tells Don on October 2 that he will not accept the trees. Don is given two options because Ken's failure to perform would substantially impair the value of the contract. He can (1) wait a commercially reasonable time for performance; or (2) treat the contract as broken when notified on October 2 and immediately seek contract damages [UCC § 2–610].

If Don chooses the first option, two further questions arise. First, what if, on November 15, Ken changes his mind and tells Don that he will accept conforming Christmas trees? Ken may retract his repudiation as long as the time for performance has not yet passed, and Don has not canceled the contract or materially changed his position, such as by canceling the supplier's order or selling the Christmas trees elsewhere [UCC § 2–611(1)].

Second, what is a commercially reasonable time to wait for performance? If Don waits too long for performance, he cannot recover damages that he could have avoided. Can Don wait until December 1 to begin to look for another buyer of his Christmas trees? He probably cannot, because Christmas trees are likely to decline in value quickly (nobody buys Christmas trees on December 26). Therefore, it would be unreasonable for Don to wait so late.

UCC § 2–613. Casualty to Identified Goods

Where the contract requires for its performance goods identified when the contract is made, and the goods suffer casualty without fault of either party before the risk of loss passes to the buyer . . .

(a) if the loss is total the contract is avoided; and

(b) if the loss is partial . . . the buyer may . . . at his option either treat the contract as avoided or accept the goods with due allowance from the contract price for the deterioration . . . but without further right against the seller.

Impossibility of Performance: Casualty to Identified Goods

Where goods identified to the contract have been destroyed, both parties are excused from performance because it would be impossible for the seller to perform. If the goods have been totally destroyed, neither party is at fault, and the risk of loss has not yet passed to the buyer, both buyer and seller are relieved from their obligations under the contract [UCC § 2–613(a)]. The excuse applies only where goods identified to the contract have been destroyed. Identification occurs where goods are designated as the goods covered by the contract [UCC § 2–501(1)]. For example, if Fred Farmer contracted to deliver 100 bushels of corn, he would be excused

from performance by a drought that killed all his corn crop if the contract specified that the corn was to be grown on Fred's land. By contrast, if the crop was not identified, Fred would not be excused and would be expected to obtain comparable corn elsewhere. Identification to the contract is discussed in Chapter 21.

If the destruction is partial, the buyer is given an option. The buyer can either treat the contract as at an end, or can accept the goods with an allowance in contract price for the destruction [UCC § 2–613(b)]. Destruction is considered partial where only a portion of the identified goods are totally destroyed or where all of the goods are partially destroyed. For example, assume Sam contracts to sell Bill his car for $5,000, but before delivery can be made the car is vandalized. If the car is partially destroyed, Bill can choose to treat the contract as avoided, in which case neither Bill nor Sam have any rights or liabilities under the contract. Alternatively, he can accept the car and pay Sam $5,000 minus the amount of damages.

Commercial Impracticability

In some instances, an excuse is provided where an unforeseen circumstance falls short of impossibility of performance.

Failure of a Presupposed Condition A seller is excused from timely delivery where performance has been made **commercially impracticable** by unforeseen circumstances. The excuse arises where the nonoccurrence of the unforeseen circumstance was a *basic* assumption on which the contract was made. The seller's *delay* can be excused, and under some circumstances the seller's performance is *entirely* excused.

UCC § 2–615. Excuse by Failure of Presupposed Conditions

(a) Delay in delivery by a seller is not a breach of his duty under a contract for sale if performance as agreed has been made impracticable by the occurrence of a contingency the non-occurrence of which was a basic assumption on which the contract was made.

Whether performance will be excused depends on whether the difficulty in performance was caused by ''the occurrence of a contingency the nonoccurrence of which was a basic assumption on which the contract was made'' [UCC § 2–615(a)]. Whether this test is met generally turns on whether the parties should have been able to reasonably foresee the occurrence of the event? Only if the event was not foreseeable is performance excused. For example, assume Polynesian Fruit, Inc. agreed to deliver 100 pounds of coconuts from Pago Pago in the South Pacific to San Francisco by ocean carrier. The seller would probably be excused when the outbreak of World War II made delivery impracticable. By contrast, if the event was foreseeable, performance will generally not be excused. For example, a seller will probably not be excused from a promise to deliver oil from Saudi Arabia if continued political unrest forces closing of the oil wells. The parties should have foreseen the contingency. However, the same seller might be excused if a major earthquake forced the well closure. Increased costs, including increased costs of supplies, do not excuse performance. Such increased costs are exactly the type of business risk the parties agree to shift in their contract because they are reasonably foreseeable. Delays due to labor strikes would fall in the category of reasonably foreseeable risks. By contrast, performance may be excused by dramatic increases in cost if caused by severe shortages of raw materials due to war or embargo. In the following case, should the seller be released from its promise due to the commercial impracticability doctrine?

ARABIAN SCORE v. LASMA ARABIAN LTD.
814 F.2d 529 (8th Cir. 1987)

Arabian Score (Arabian) entered into an agreement to purchase from Lasma Arabian Ltd. (Limited) an Arabian colt named Score. The agreement provided that Arabian would pay Limited $1 million in exchange for Score and various promotion services of Score, such as advertising by Lasma Corp. (Lasma). The contract required Lasma to spend $250,000 for the performance of those services. Within the year, Score died. Arabian brought suit against Lasma and Limited seeking the money not yet spent from the $250,000 allocated for the promotion of Score on the ground of impossibility of performance.

The district court ruled that because Score's death was a foreseeable risk that was assumed by Arabian by the terms of the purchase agreement, neither the doctrine of impossibility nor of commercial frustration was applicable.

WOLLMAN, Circuit Judge

Beating dead horses is the sport of appellate judges, a generally harmless pastime painful only to the readers of appellate opinions. Paying for the promotion of dead horses can be an expensive proposition, however, as the facts of this case make abundantly clear.

In *Garner v. Ellington* the Arizona Court of Appeals defined commercial frustration as circumstances beyond the control of the parties which render performance of the contract impossible and exonerate the party failing to perform. The court did not limit the doctrine to strict impossibility but included impracticability caused by extreme or unreasonable difficulty or expense. The court did require, however, proof that the supervening frustrating event was not reasonably foreseeable.

In *Mohave County v. Mohave-Kingman Estates* the Arizona Supreme Court stated that ''while Arizona recognizes the doctrine of commercial frustration . . . we do not see fit to interpret it as a general absolution whenever performance under the contract becomes difficult or expensive. Proper application of this doctrine requires us to examine whether the allegedly frustrating event was reasonably foreseeable.'' In that case, the court refused to apply the doctrine where a zoning change had affected the economic feasibility of a contract to buy and develop land. The court reasoned that ''the doctrine of commercial frustration does not apply to the instant case because the risk of change in the zoning ordinances was an event properly foreseeable by the defendants, and one which they would have contracted against.''

Arizona rejects the application of the commercial frustration doctrine when a party assumes the risk of a frustrating event. The Arizona Supreme Court rejected a commercial frustration claim by a guarantor who had agreed to remain liable for the rent due on a liquor license "without respect to future changes in condition." A change in law made renting liquor licenses illegal, but the court required the guarantor to pay, stating: "If the parties to a contract have agreed in express or implied terms that the risk of loss shall fall upon one or the other of the parties, full effect is given to such provision."

We conclude that the trial court was correct in holding that the commercial frustration doctrine is inapplicable in this case, both because Score's death was foreseeable and because Arabian assumed the risk that Score might die prematurely.

It is with some reluctance that we affirm the district court's grant of summary judgment. That reluctance stems from the thought that spending $197,108.86 to promote a dead horse borders on the bizarre. The parties to this agreement were sophisticated and, we assume, well-heeled businesspersons, however, and that which we find to be somewhat unusual may be commonplace to those who inhabit the wealthy world of the horsey set.

Case Questions

1. What is the difference between the doctrines of impossibility and commercial frustration?

2. Why is the question of reasonable foreseeability important?

3. What happens next? What happens to the $197,108.86?

4. Why should the court consider upsetting the agreement between the parties? What are the value conflicts? Is there a better balanced resolution than the one announced by this court?

Substituted Performance   Where the agreed on manner of delivery becomes "commercially impracticable," but a commercially reasonable substitute is available, such substituted performance must be tendered and accepted [UCC § 2–614]. For example, buyer and seller contracted for delivery of wheat "FOB Kosmos Steamer at Seattle." War led to the cancellation of that line's sailing schedule after space had already been booked. The seller was entitled, and in fact required, to arrange for substituted delivery. For example, the Kosmos owner was required to contract with another steamship line to service the customer.

The difference between the two types of commercial impracticability is a matter of degree. In the first example, the unforeseen circumstance pertains to the heart of the contract, while in this instance, the impossibility of performance arises in connection with a relatively incidental matter.

THE INTERNATIONAL SALES CONTRACT

Seller's Obligation to Deliver the Goods

The seller to an international sales contract must deliver the goods and any documents necessary to transfer title [Article 30]. The seller must deliver the quantity and quality of goods promised.

Manner and Place of Delivery

Much like under the UCC, the manner of delivery is determined under CISG by the type of contract. Because delivery of goods in international sales contracts is typically accompanied by delivery of documents, CISG provides that the seller must deliver the documents promised. The seller is given a right to cure defects in the documents if cure can be obtained within the performance date provided in the contract [Article 34].

CISG recognizes three types of contracts: (1) delivery contracts, (2) shipment contracts, (3) contracts where delivery is not specified.

Delivery Contracts   A delivery contract is a contract where the seller must deliver the goods to a place specified in the contract. The seller's delivery duties in delivery contracts are excluded from CISG coverage and are governed by local law.

Shipment Contracts   A shipment contract is a contract where the seller promises to deliver the goods, the promise requires shipment by carrier, but the contract does not provide for delivery to destination. To deliver the goods in a shipment contract, the seller must, first, deliver the goods to the carrier [Article 31(a)]. Second, the seller must either provide insurance coverage for the goods or give the buyer information necessary to allow the buyer to obtain insurance [Article 32(3)]. Third, if the goods are not identified to the contract by the shipping documents, the seller must notify the buyer of the consignment specifying the goods [Article 32(1)]. Last, the seller must arrange for transportation of the goods if the contract provides. The transportation must be "appropriate" and the terms must be common [Article 32(2)].

No Delivery Contracts   Unless otherwise specified in the contract, the seller must make the goods available for the buyer [Article 31(b) and (c)]. *Where* the goods must be available depends on whether a location is specified in the contract. If the contract indicates where the goods are kept, the buyer must pick them up there. If the contract does not indicate where the goods are kept, the buyer must pick the goods up at the seller's place of business.

Time for Delivery

As under the UCC the seller must make delivery as specified in the contract or within a "reasonable" time [Article 33].

Buyer's Obligation to Accept the Goods and Make Payment

The buyer must take delivery of conforming goods and pay the contract price [Article 53]. As with the UCC, unless the contract provides for a credit sale, payment is due when the seller "hands over" the goods [Article 58(1)] and the seller need not deliver the goods until the buyer has tendered payment. Where the contract provides for shipment of the goods under negotiable documents of title, the buyer must pay upon receipt of the documents [Article 58(2)].

Typically, the place of "handing over" the goods or documents is the place for payment. Alternatively, payment may be made at the seller's place of business or another location specified in the contract. The buyer must "export" payment to the seller [Article 54]. This is important if the buyer is from a country with restrictions on the transfer of funds. In addition, the buyer must obtain whatever authorization is necessary to make payments abroad.

Nonconforming Goods

Fundamental Breach

Where the seller delivers nonconforming goods, the buyer is entitled to relief from the seller if the nonconformity is a "fundamental breach." While the concept of fundamental breach is uncertain, it is defined as a breach whose results "substantially deprive [the buyer] of what he is entitled to expect under the contract" [Article 25]. The fundamental breach standard certainly differs from the perfect tender rule of the UCC and appears to impose a stricter standard on the buyer than even the "substantial impairment" requirement for revocation of acceptance.

Buyer's Right of Inspection

The buyer is given a right to inspect the goods before payment.

Buyer's Options

The treaty did not adopt the UCC distinction between rejection, acceptance, and revocation of acceptance. In order for the buyer to be permitted to reject the goods, first, the inspection must be timely. Second, the buyer must notify the seller of the nonconformity timely. Third, the nonconformity must create a fundamental breach. Last, the seller must be permitted an opportunity to cure the breach.

Seller's Right to Cure

The seller is given a right to cure any nonconformities. The seller may cure up to the delivery date even if the nonconformity creates a fundamental breach. After the delivery date, the seller may cure if the breach can be cured without unreasonable delay or inconvenience. The cure by the seller need not be perfect but must meet the fundamental breach test.

END–OF–CHAPTER QUESTIONS

1. Why does the Code provide gap-filling provisions?
2. Compare and contrast the seller's obligations in an international contract with a contract under the UCC. The buyer's obligations?
3. Sarah Seller agrees to sell Beverly Buyer 100 pounds of hamburger. If nothing is said as to delivery or payment terms, is

the contract sufficiently definite to be enforceable? What are the seller's obligations? What are the buyer's obligations? What is the price?

4. After examining the cabinet doors on display, Cleo ordered cabinet doors from Cabinet Wholesalers. Unfortunately, the doors that were delivered did not look like the doors in the store. The doors on display were a solid color, while those delivered had shadings of red, white, and yellow, giving the doors a striped appearance. Cleo immediately went to the store and informed them that the doors received were the wrong color. Cabinet Wholesalers refused to exchange them. Cleo never installed the doors and has stored them in his basement. Has Cleo accepted or rejected the cabinet doors? See *DeLong v. Cabinet Wholesaler's Inc.*, 554 N.E.2d 574 (Ill. App. 1990).

5. In Question 4, should Cabinet Wholesalers be given an opportunity to cure?

6. In Question 4, what are Cleo's duties with respect to the doors?

7. Caldwell ordered from Mayo a magnetic sign to adhere to the door of his car, advertising his business name. The sign was picked up on January 27. Caldwell never paid for the sign and informed Mayo in May that the sign did not adhere to the door. Has Caldwell accepted the goods? See *Mayo v. Caldwell, 11 UCC rep. Serv.2d 1153 (1989)*. Can Caldwell revoke his acceptance?

8. Bob Smith ordered from Zabriskie Chevrolet a "brand new car that would operate properly." Barbara Smith took delivery of the car on February 10. About 7/10s of a mile from the dealer, on her way home, the car stalled at a light. It stalled each time the car stopped. After another mile, the car would only operate in low gear. When Barbara got home, Bob immediately called the dealer and canceled the sale. Zabriskie towed the car back to the dealership, replaced the transmission with one from another car, and attempted to redeliver the car. Do the Smiths have to accept and pay for the car? See *Zabriskie Chevrolet, Inc. v. Smith*, 240 A.2d 195 (1968).

9. Jaffe Fish Co., Inc., agrees to sell 100 pounds of jumbo shrimp to Mazur Bros. On March 1, 100 pounds of large shrimp are delivered. Mazur Bros. rejects the shrimp as nonconforming on March 6. Was this an effective rejection? See *Mazur Bros. v. Jaffe Fish Co., Inc.*, 3 UCC Rep. 419 (1965).

10. Enron Corp. entered into agreements to purchase a specified quantity of gas from Resources Investment Corp. Each agreement contained a "take-or-pay" clause in which the defendants agreed that if in any year it did not accept delivery of the specified amount, it would nevertheless pay for it. The defendants argue that their performance should be excused because of price-induced energy conservation, foreign commodity competition, abnormally warm weather, an economic recession, and an unforeseeable change in the natural gas market. Are the defendants correct? Should they be excused from their performance because of commercial impracticability?

Chapter 21

Title Concerns and Risk of Loss

■

CRITICAL THINKING INQUIRIES

As you read this chapter, you should be able to address the following:

- Explain the relationship between identification and transfer of title.
- Explain the relationship between transfer of title and transfer of risk of loss.
- Evaluate the following statement: ``The Bulk Sales Act completely protects unsecured creditors who lend in reliance upon the debtor's inventory.''
- How do conflicting policy considerations make problems with title particularly difficult to resolve?

MANAGERIAL PERSPECTIVE

Sheila is in charge of negotiating a contract for the sale of 1 million umbrellas for Clips, Inc. She enters into an agreement with the buyer for a purchase price of $100,000. After the contract is completed but before they are delivered, a fire ravages the warehouse and the umbrellas are totally destroyed. The buyer calls and wants replacement umbrellas; Sheila's boss wants the buyer to pay for the umbrellas that were destroyed.

- Did the buyer or Clips, Inc. have an insurable interest in the umbrellas?
- Does the buyer have to pay for the umbrellas?

These questions concern risk of loss. Because under the UCC the answers depend almost entirely on what the contract specifies, Sheila should have considered the risk of loss provisions before negotiating a contract. A manager of both seller and buyer companies needs to be familar with the Code rules to negotiate a beneficial risk of loss provision.

TRANSFER OF TITLE

Contrary to the common misconception about the incidents of ownership and title, transfer of title is of limited significance under the UCC. Title transfer does not determine who bears the risk of loss for damaged goods; it does not determine whether the seller can sue the buyer for the price; it does not determine whether the seller's creditors can levy on the goods. Title transfer is included in the UCC to resolve nonsales issues such as ownership of goods for criminal law or tax purposes.

Identification

Goods must be both existing and identified before title is transferred [UCC §2–401(1)]. Goods that are not both existing and identified are termed **future goods. Identification** is the manner in which the seller specifies the goods to be sold. It can be set by the parties' agreement [UCC §2–501(1)]. When the contract does not mention identification, the UCC rules govern. When the contract is for existing and specified goods, the goods are identified when the contract is made. By contrast, when the contract is for future goods, the goods are identified when they are designated by the seller as the goods covered by the contract [UCC §2–501(1)(a) and (b)].

Why is identification important? First, identification must occur before title can pass. Second, identification gives the buyer a special property interest, an insurable interest, and the right to inspect the goods [UCC §2–501.]

UCC §2–501. Manner of Identification of Goods

(1) [I]dentification can be made at any time and in any manner explicitly agreed to by the parties. In the absence of explicit agreement identification occurs

(a) when the contract is made if it is for the sale of goods already existing and identified;

(b) if the contract is for the sale of future goods . . . when the goods are shipped, marked or otherwise designated by the seller as goods to which the contract refers;

When Title Transfers

When does title to goods pass? Title can pass as provided in the contract. If title is not mentioned, it typically passes with identified goods when the

Figure 21–1   Transfer of Title

Type of Contract	When Title Transfers
Carrier contract	FOB seller's location: Title passes at the time and place of shipment. FOB buyer's location: Title passes on delivery at destination.
Goods will not move	If document of title: Title passes on delivery of the document of title. If no document of title: Title passes at the time and place of contracting.
All other cases	Title passes on delivery of the goods.

seller completes delivery of the goods. Title is generally tied to possession of the goods. As is illustrated in Figure 21–1, passage of title depends on the type of contract: (1) carrier contracts, (2) contracts where the goods will not move, and (3) all other cases.

Carrier Contracts

Where the contract authorizes shipment but does not require the seller to deliver the goods to a particular destination (a shipment contract, as in FOB seller's point of business), title passes at the time and place of shipment [UCC § 2–401(2)(a)]. By contrast, where the contract requires the seller to deliver the goods to a particular destination (a destination contract, as in FOB buyer's place of business), title passes on tender of the goods at that destination [UCC § 2–401(2)(b)]. For example, if Betty Buyer in Buffalo contracts to buy 100,000 umbrellas from Sheila in Cincinnati, FOB Cincinnati, title passes when the goods arrive in Cincinnati. By contrast, if the contract is FOB Buffalo, title passes when tendered to Betty in Buffalo.

Goods Will Not Move

Where the goods will not move at the time of sale, title passes on delivery of the document of title, or if there is no document of title, title passes at the time and place of contracting [UCC 2–401(3)]. For example, if Bill Buyer contracts to buy grain stored in a grain elevator, title passes when the warehouse receipt is delivered. If the parties have chosen not to use a document of title, title passes when the contract is made.

All Other Cases

In all other cases, title passes when and where the seller completes performance. In other words, title passes when the seller completes physical delivery of the goods [UCC § 2–401(2)]. If Sidney Seller contracts to sell Bea Buyer a living room sofa, title passes when Bea picks up the sofa or when Sid delivers it to Bea, if that is what the contract requires.

Transfer of Title Back to Seller

What if the seller delivers the goods but the buyer rejects them? Similarly, what if the seller accepts the goods, but then revokes the acceptance? A *rightful* revocation of acceptance or a rejection, even if not justified, revests title in the seller [UCC § 2–401(4)]. For example, Sam of Seattle and Ben of Boston enter into a contract for the purchase and sale of 1,000 lawn mowers, to be shipped FOB Seattle. Sam delivers 1,000 lawn mowers to the common carrier in Seattle, makes a reasonable contract for their transportation, delivers the bill of lading to the buyer, and notifies the buyer of the shipment. Thus, Sam has tendered delivery of the lawn mowers. Title passes at the time of shipment, when the lawn mowers are delivered to the carrier in Seattle. However, if Ben rejects the lawn mowers when delivered, title revests in Sam. This in no way affects imposition of the risk of loss. If the lawn mowers are destroyed on the way back to Sam, allocation of loss is determined by the risk of loss provisions discussed later in this chapter, not by who possesses title.

PROBLEMS REGARDING TITLE

This section will consider situations in which there will typically be three people involved: the true owner (O), a seller (S), and the purchaser (P). Figure 21–2 illustrates this scheme. Typically, S is in possession of something, lacks the authority to sell it, but does so anyway, to a special type of purchaser, a **bona fide purchaser** (BFP). A BFP is a good faith purchaser for value. The question addressed in this section is who has the right to the goods between the true owner (O) and the BFP (P). Although S is the party who is really at fault, by the time the sale is discovered S has typically either spent or absconded with the money. Therefore, when O finds P in possession

Figure 21–2

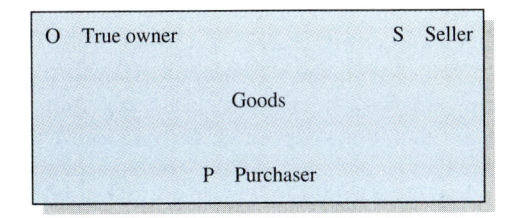

of the property, the only viable alternative is to get the property back from P. If O gets the goods back, P has a lawsuit against S; if O fails to get the goods back, O has a lawsuit against S.

Easy decisions are impossible because there are two important policies of the law that are in competition. One overriding policy is to protect owners of property. By contrast, the law also strives whenever possible to protect bona fide purchasers. Commerce is promoted by enforcing BFP's expectations. Commerce would be hindered if one buying a couch needed to verify ownership for protection. Requirements of investigating title before sale are generally limited to real estate transfers.

UCC § 2–403. Power to Transfer; Good Faith Purchase of Goods; "Entrusting"

(1) A purchaser of goods acquires all title which his transferor had. . . . A person with voidable title has power to transfer good title to a good faith purchaser for value. When goods have been delivered under a transaction of purchase the purchaser has such power even though

(a) The transferor was deceived as to the identity of the purchaser, or

(b) the delivery was in exchange for a check which is later dishonored, or

(c) it was agreed that the transaction was to be a "cash sale", or

(d) the delivery was procured through fraud.

Void versus Voidable Title

One way of dealing with these competing policies is by examining the seller's title. The BFP (P) gets title that is at least as good as the title of the seller (S). However, if the seller's title is subject to limitations, the BFP's title is subject to those same limitations. Similarly, if the seller has "void" title, the BFP also gets void title. For example, assume that in our opening scenario, one of Sheila's employees, Rob, steals an umbrella shipment. He has void title and the purchaser, even a BFP, gets only void title. Sheila can recover the stolen goods from the purchaser. Similarly, if Rob acquires the shipment through fraud in the execution, he would have void title to those goods and Sheila could recover the goods from the BFP.

The BFP can under some circumstances get even better title than the title of the seller. If S has voidable title, P can get good title [UCC § 2–403(1)]. Under these circumstances, S has the "power to transfer good title" to a BFP. For example, assume that Dan DeFrauder tricks Tom TruOwner into selling him his antique wedding ring in exchange for worthless stock in a gold-mining operation. When Tom discovers the fraud, he also discovers that Dan has sold the ring to Bertha BonaFide. If Dan attempts to get his ring back from Bertha, he will fail. Dan, S, had voidable title (title obtained by fraud in the inducement is voidable), and therefore, had the power to pass good title to Bertha, P. Bertha's title is good enough to withstand the claim by Tom. Tom is left with a lawsuit against Dan (if he can find him).

In order for the purchaser to be able to defeat the claim by the true owner, first, the seller must have voidable title, and second, the purchaser must be a BFP. Section 2–403(1) provides an illustrative list of situations in which S has voidable title. Typical examples include where S obtained the goods through fraud in the inducement, in exchange for a check that later bounced, or where S deceived O as to his or her identity. The following case illustrates how one with voidable title can pass good title.

CHARLES EVANS BMW, INC. v. WILLIAMS
196 Ga. App. 230, 396 S.E.2d 650 (Ct. App. Ga. 1990)

Williams sold his car to Hodge, accepting a cashier's check as payment. Without noting that Hodge was the buyer, Williams signed the certificate of title as seller and delivered the document and car to Hodge. The next day, Hodge, representing himself as Williams, sold the car to Evans BMW (Evans). Hodge gave Evans the certificate of title signed by Williams and Evans gave Hodge a check made payable to Williams. Hodge cashed the check at a local bank using a drivers license issued to Williams. Williams discovered that the cashier's check Hodge had given him was a forgery. By the time Evans discovered that it had purchased the car from Hodge, not Williams, it had already resold the car. At the direction of the local police, Evans repurchased the car and returned the car to Williams. Then Evans brought suit asking for return of the car from Williams.

The trial court granted summary judgment in favor of Williams. Evans appealed.

CARLEY, Chief Judge

Williams was not deprived of his car by a physical taking of which he was unaware. The undisputed evidence shows that Williams delivered his car under a transaction of purchase procured by the perpetration of a criminal fraud whereby he was deceived as to the identity of the purchaser who gave him a check which was later dishonored. In these circumstances, Williams conveyed voidable title to Hodge and Hodge, having voidable rather than void title, had the power to transfer good title to a good faith purchaser for value. UCC § 2–403 empowers a purchaser with a voidable title to confer good title upon a good faith purchaser for value where the good[s] were procured through fraud punishable as larcenous under the criminal law. The distinction between theft and fraud in this context is found in the statutory definitions of "delivery" and "purchase." Delivery concerns a voluntary transfer of possession, a purchase refers to a voluntary transaction creating an interest in property. UCC § 1–201. In the present case, Williams voluntarily relinquished possession to Hodge. As one commentator has pointed out, "[a] thief who wrongfully takes goods is not a purchaser . . . but a swindler who fraudulently induces the victim to voluntarily deliver them is a purchaser."

It follows that, if Evans was a good faith purchaser for value, it acquired good title to the car from Hodge.

" 'Good faith' means honesty in fact in the conduct or transaction concerned." UCC § 1–201. " 'Good faith' in the case of a merchant means honesty in fact and the observance of reasonable commercial standards of fair dealing in the trade." UCC § 2–103. There is ample evidence of Evans' "good faith" in its transaction with Hodge. Evans' agent who actually negotiated the purchase neither knew nor had reason to know that Hodge's representations were false.

In opposition, there was no evidence to show that, in negotiating and consummating the purchase from Hodge, Evans had been less than honest or had failed to observe reasonable commercial standards of fair dealing. Therefore, on the undisputed evidence Evans was, as a matter of law, a good faith purchaser for value when it bought the car from Hodge.

Under the undisputed evidence, Evans acquired good title to the car when it purchased it from Hodge and it retains that good title as against Williams who conveyed voidable title to Hodge. It follows that the trial court erred in granting appellee's motion for summary judgment.

Case Questions

1. Using the authors' scheme shown in Figure 21–2, identify parties O, S, and P in this case.

2. Why is one with voidable title given the power to transfer good title to a good faith purchaser?

3. What could Williams have done to protect himself? What could Evans have done to protect itself?

4. The court states that "there is ample evidence of Evans' 'good faith' in its transaction with Hodge." To what factors might the court be referring?

In addition to the seller having voidable title, P must be a good faith purchaser for value to get good title. To be a good faith purchaser one must purchase in good faith. Good faith requires "honesty in fact."

Can one be a good faith purchaser if purchasing without actual knowledge of any impropriety but under circumstances where the fraud would have been discovered if an investigation had been conducted?

JOHNSON & JOHNSON PRODUCTS, INC. v. DAL INTERNATIONAL TRADING CO. AND QUALITY KING MANUFACTURING CO., INC.
798 F.2d 100 (3d Cir. 1986)

Johnson and Johnson (J & J Ltd) sold 80,000 dozen toothbrushes and baby supplies to Dal International Trading Co. (Dal). Dal orally represented that it intended to distribute the products in Poland only. The goods instead ended up in the hands of Quality King, an independent distributor in the so-called gray market. As is a common gray market practice, when the goods arrived at Quality King's warehouse, the J & J Ltd. shipping labels had been removed from most of the shipping cartons.

Because the prices set for the Polish market were so low, Quality King distributed the products at a price lower than those set by Johnson & Johnson in the United States. Johnson & Johnson sued to prevent Quality King from distributing the products.

The district court granted the preliminary injunction because Quality King was not a good faith purchaser under Section 2–403(1) of the UCC, finding that the gray market transaction was conducted under "suspicious circumstances."

STAPLETON, Circuit Judge

We believe that Quality King subjectively suspected that appellees would not approve of its purchase of these goods. We believe the legally relevant question, however, is whether Quality King knew that the goods had been obtained from J & J Ltd. by fraud, or suspected as much and closed its eyes to the truth.

Rather than address the legally relevant question of whether Quality King subjectively knew or suspected that there was a flaw in the title of one of its predecessors, the district court found that the circumstances called for inquiry and that, if Quality King had investigated, it would have learned that it was acquiring a voidable title. We believe that the court committed an error of law when it held that Quality King had a duty to inquire and charged it with the knowledge that an investigation would have arguably disclosed.

The purpose of the good faith purchaser doctrine, codified in Sections 2–403 and 2–103 of the UCC, is to promote commerce by reducing transaction costs; it allows people safely to engage in the purchase and sale of goods without conducting a costly investigation of the conduct and rights of all previous possessors in the chain of distribution. The imposition on the purchaser of a duty to investigate is thus fundamentally at odds with the rationale underlying these two sections of the UCC.

We predict that the New Jersey Supreme Court would not impose on Quality King a duty to inquire.

This prediction is based on *Breslin v. New Jersey Investors, Inc.* We believe Breslin clearly suggests that the answer to the question of whether Quality King was honest in fact is to be "determined by looking to the mind of [Quality King]" and not to "what the state of mind of a prudent man should have been" as a result of inquiry. We also note that by adopting the subjective, "pure heart and . . . empty head" standard, the New Jersey Supreme Court would be aligning itself with the prevailing view of the good faith purchaser concept.

We hold, therefore, that the district court erred in concluding that Quality King had a duty to inquire into the chain of title of the gray market goods. Since the only inference supported by the record is that Quality King had neither knowledge nor suspicion of a fraud by Dal, appellees did not demonstrate a likelihood of ultimate success.

For the foregoing reasons, we will vacate the preliminary injunction.

Case Questions

1. Is good faith measured by an objective or a subjective test?

2. Analyze: "The purpose of the good faith purchaser doctrine, codified in section 2–403 of the UCC, is to promote commerce by reducing transaction costs."

3. How are merchants treated differently from nonmerchants in defining the concept of good faith?

Entrusting Possession to a Merchant

Assume, as is illustrated in Figure 21–3, that the cameo Enrica inherited from her grandmother cracks and she takes it to a jeweler who both sells and repairs antique jewelry. If the jeweler mistakenly sells her

Figure 21–3

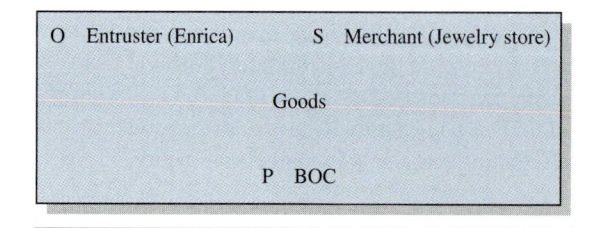

O Entruster (Enrica)	S Merchant (Jewelry store)
	Goods
	P BOC

cameo, can she recover the cameo from the hands of the purchaser? Most probably not! By "entrusting possession" to a merchant, she has given the merchant the power to pass good title to a buyer in the ordinary course. Notice that in this scenario Enrica is O, the true owner, the jeweler is S, and P is a special type of BFP, a **buyer in the ordinary course of business (BOC)**. The UCC protects the reasonable expectations of the purchaser, even at the expense of the true owner. In order for P to win, S must be a merchant and P must be a BOC [UCC § 2–403(2)].

Remember, a merchant is a dealer who deals in goods of the kind covered by the contract. A BOC is one who buys in good faith out of a merchant's inventory [UCC § 1–201(9)].

In the following case, the court examines the question of when one qualifies as a BOC.

UCC § 2–403. Power to Transfer; Good Faith Purchase of Goods; "Entrusting"

(2) Any entrusting of possession of goods to a merchant who deals in goods of that kind gives him power to transfer all rights of the entruster to a buyer in the ordinary course of business.

UCC § 1–201. General Definitions

(9) "Buyer in the ordinary course of business" means a person who in good faith and without knowledge that the sale to him is in violation of the ownership rights or security interest of a third party in the goods buys in ordinary course from a person in the business of selling goods of that kind.

RICHTER v. U.S.

663 F.Supp. 68 (S.D. Fla. 1987)

Emanuel Mikalef Jewelry Manufacturers, Inc. (Mikalef), the owner of an emerald and diamond ring, sold the ring to Morton Dock on consignment for $240,000. Dock was a dealer in goods similar to the ring. Dock neither returned the ring nor paid for it.

Dock, saying that he was a "jewelry merchant from Indianapolis," sold the ring to Richter, who paid Dock for the ring with a series of checks payable to an H. Matekunas.

Mikalef, who never received payment from Dock, brought charges with the State District Attorney's office. Richter sued to recover the ring from the United States, which was using the ring as evidence in the criminal case.

GONZALEZ, District Judge

In relinquishing possession of the ring to Dock, Mikalef entrusted the ring to Dock within the meaning of UCC § 2–403. Moreover, Dock was known to Mikalef as a merchant who dealt in goods of the same or similar kind as the ring. This imparted Dock with the "power to transfer all rights of the transferor to a buyer in the ordinary course of business." UCC § 2–403(2).

Mikalef maintains that the plaintiff was not a "buyer in the ordinary course of business." The plaintiff stated in his deposition that Dock introduced himself to the plaintiff as a merchant who dealt in goods similar to the ring in question. The plaintiff, however, had never met Dock before the transaction. Moreover, the circumstances of the sale were of such a nature as to place the plaintiff on "notice" that there might be something questionable about the transaction.

Under Florida law, "[a] person has notice of a fact when . . . (c) From all the facts and circumstances known to him at the time in question he has reason to know it exists." UCC § 1–201(25). Clearly, the method of payment in itself was sufficient to cause the plaintiff to question the circumstances of the sale. The request for payment by nine separate checks made out to an individual with whom the plaintiff had never dealt, together with the plaintiff's lack of familiarity with Dock, were sufficient suspicious circumstances to give the plaintiff "reason to know" that the sale might not be in the ordinary course of business. Subsequent purchasers are protected by the provisions of UCC § 2–403(2) when such purchasers engage in "routine business transaction[s]." The circumstances presented here do not constitute a sale to a "buyer in the ordinary course of business" as used under Florida law.

Accordingly, it is hereby ordered that the ring be returned to the third-party defendant.

Case Questions

1. Using the authors' scheme, identify the parties as O, S, and P.

2. Compare (a) the good faith purchaser for value, with (b) the buyer in the ordinary course.

3. When is a purchaser who buys from a merchant protected?

4. Why is a BFP protected only when buying from a merchant?

Figure 21–4

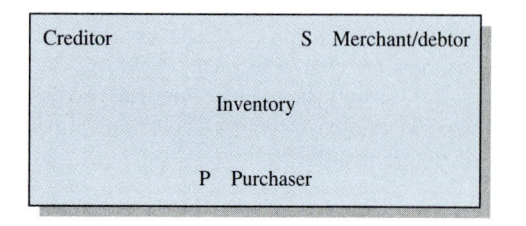

Bulk Sales

The Bulk Sales Act was enacted to protect creditors who extend unsecured credit knowing that in the event of debtor default they can levy on the debtor-merchant's inventory to pay the loan. The danger that the Bulk Sales Act is meant to address is that the debtor-merchant (S) might secretly liquidate the inventory in bulk (selling to P) and conceal the money, spend the money, or flee without paying its creditors (see Figure 21–4).

The Bulk Sales Act protects unsecured creditors by invalidating bulk sales unless certain procedures, primarily notice requirements, are followed. Because creditors' rights can be protected in other ways, the National Conference of Commissioners on Uniform State Laws and the American Law Institute (the governing bodies responsible for the UCC) recommended repeal or revision of Article 6, the Bulk Sales Act.* The revised Bulk Sales Act is considered here because, although the merchant has the power and the right to pass good title to the purchaser, the title can be invalidated if the sale is in violation of the Act.

UCC § 6–102. "Bulk Transfers"

(3) The enterprises subject to this Article are all those whose principal business is the sale of merchandise from stock, including those who manufacture what they sell.

Scope of the Act

The Act covers **bulk sales** by enterprises whose principal business is selling merchandise from inventory.

---

*The following states have repealed Article 6: Arkansas, Colorado, Illinois, Kansas, Kentucky, Louisiana, Maine, Minnesota, Montana, Nebraska, Nevada, New Mexico, Oregon, Pennsylvania, South Dakota, West Virginia, and Wyoming. The following states have revised Article 6: Arizona, California, Hawaii, Oklahoma, and Utah.

Businesses that principally offer services, such as barbershops, hotels, and restaurants, are not governed by the Bulk Sales Act. Further, only transfers in bulk are subject to the Act. In order for a transfer to be a transfer in bulk, it must either be a transfer of a *major* part of inventory or a transfer of a *substantial* part of equipment plus a transfer of a major part of inventory. For example, assume that Ben Borrower borrowed money from Chuck Creditor to finance his jewelry store. Although the loan is unsecured, Chuck is confident that in the event of default, Ben has sufficient inventory to pay the loan. Assume further that Ben has 100 gems worth $150,000 in inventory. Ninety of the gems are worth $30,000 total. Ten gems are worth $120,000 total. If Ben sells the 10 valuable gems, is this a transfer in bulk? In other words, is this a transfer of a *major* part of inventory? It seems likely that it is a bulk sale because it is a transfer of more than 50 percent of the value of the inventory.

UCC § 6–102. "Bulk Transfers"

(1) A "bulk transfer" is any transfer in bulk and not in the ordinary course of the transferor's business of a major part of the materials, supplies, merchandise or other inventory of an enterprise subject to this Article.

Compliance Procedure

There are four procedures that must be followed to comply with the Bulk Sales Act. These procedures afford creditors advance notice of the bulk sale and an opportunity to protect themselves.

List of Creditors   The transferor (S in Figure 21–4) must furnish the transferee (P) with a list of the creditors existing at the time of the transfer, including the names of the creditors, the amounts of their claims, and their business addresses [UCC § 6–104(2)]. The transferor is responsible for the accuracy of the list. If a mistake is made in compiling the list, the transfer is voided only if the transferee had actual knowledge of the mistake [UCC § 6–104(3)]. For example, if a creditor was omitted from the list, that creditor can only invalidate the transfer if the transferee actually knew of the omitted creditor.

Schedule of Property   The transferee and the transferor must prepare a schedule or list that sufficiently identifies the property transferred. Both the transferee and the transferor are responsible for the accuracy of the schedule [UCC § 6–104(1)(b)]. For example, if a valuable piece of property transferred is omitted from the schedule, there is noncompliance and the transfer can be invalidated.

Preservation of the List   The transferee must save the list of creditors and schedule of property for six months. Further, either the list must be filed in a public office or the transferee must permit inspection and copying from the list [UCC § 6–104(1)(c)].

Notice to Creditors   Last, the transferee must give notice to the creditors listed at least 10 days before the transferee takes possession of the goods or pays for them (whichever comes first). In general, the transferee must notify the creditors that a bulk transfer is about to be made. If the transferee is uncertain whether the debts of the transferor are to be paid in full, a more detailed notice is required that includes, for example, the location and description of the property and the address where the schedule and the list of creditors can be inspected [UCC § 6–107].

Additional Requirement   Some states have enacted an additional requirement, imposing on the transferee an obligation to see that the monies paid to the transferor are actually used to pay the transferor's debts [UCC § 6–106].

Effect of Noncompliance

If the procedures are not followed, the sale is "ineffective against any creditor" [UCC § 6–105]. Creditors can disregard the sale and levy on the property as if it were still in the hands of the debtor-transferor. However, the creditor can not levy on the property if it has been transferred to a bona fide purchaser by the transferee [UCC § 6–110]. Therefore, given the risks of noncompliance, the bulk purchaser should attempt to guarantee compliance.

RISK OF LOSS

Assume that Sheila from our opening scenario and Ben Buyer contract for the sale of 1,000 umbrellas for $20,000. If the umbrellas are lost, destroyed by fire, damaged by vandals, or stolen, does Sheila or Ben bear the risk of loss? If Sheila bears the risk of loss, she will not be paid for the umbrellas. If Ben

bears the risk of loss, he must pay Sheila the contract price. Obviously, Sheila has the risk of loss before contracting with the buyer. Obviously, Ben bears the risk of loss after the contract has been completely performed. The question, therefore, is when does risk of loss shift from seller to buyer? By contrast with the pre-Code treatment, shift of risk of loss under the UCC does *not* follow title transfer. Instead, the Code's risk of loss provisions depend on (1) the parties agreement, (2) breach by either party, and (3) at what point in the transaction the loss occurred [UCC § 2–509 and § 2–510]. The UCC risk of loss encourages both parties to obtain insurance when necessary.

Risk of Loss: Agreement of the Parties

The parties may agree when the risk of loss will shift as long as the agreement is made in good faith and is not unconscionable [UCC § 2–509(4)].

In some instances, the language used by the parties is evidence of an implicit agreement. For example, when the parties contract to sell goods **sale on approval,** the parties are agreeing that the goods will be delivered to the buyer to use, look at, and decide whether or not to buy. In a sale on approval situation, the risk of loss remains on the seller until the buyer accepts the goods or for a reasonable period of time. In a sale on approval contract, the seller pays any expenses in returning the goods [UCC § 2–326]. By contrast, where the parties have agreed to a **sale or return** provision, the goods are delivered to the buyer, who will either resell them or return them to the seller. In a sale or return contract, the risk of loss shifts to the buyer and remains on the buyer until the goods are delivered to the seller. The buyer pays any expenses of returning the goods. If the parties do not agree, the UCC allocates the loss depending on whether or not the parties to the contract are in breach.

UCC § 2–326. Sale of Approval and Sale or Return

(1) Unless otherwise agreed, if delivered goods may be returned by the buyer even though they conform to the contract, the transaction is,

(a) a "sale on approval" if the goods are delivered primarily for use, and

(b) a "sale or return" if the goods are delivered primarily for resale.

Risk of Loss: No Breach

Where the parties are not in breach and the loss is due to the fault of neither party, the UCC classifies sales contracts into three different categories: (1) carrier contracts, (2) contracts where the goods will not move, and (3) all other cases [UCC § 2–509]. (See Figure 21–5.)

Carrier Contracts

If the contract authorizes shipment by the seller but does not require delivery at a particular destination (a shipment contract), the risk of loss passes when the goods are delivered to the common carrier [UCC § 2–509(1)(a)]. The shipment contract is typically indicated by the use of shorthand shipment terms such as FOB seller's place of business. To shift risk of loss, the seller delivers the goods to the common carrier, makes a contract for transportation of the goods that is reasonable in light of the nature of the goods, delivers any necessary documents to the buyer, and notifies the buyer of the shipment.

By contrast, if the contract requires shipment by a carrier to a particular destination (a destination contract), risk of loss passes when the goods are tendered at that location [UCC § 2–509(1)(b)]. The

destination contract is typically indicated by the use of the shipment term FOB buyer's place of business.

To illustrate, assume that Sam Seller in Seattle contracts to sell 500 pounds of cheese to Ben Buyer in Butte, FOB Seattle. Assume further that Sam contracts for the delivery in a refrigerated truck, sends Ben the document of title (bill of lading) needed to take delivery of the shipment, and notifies Ben of the shipment. If the truck crashes between Seattle and Butte, Ben bears the risk of loss. Because the contract was a shipment contract, risk of loss passes to the buyer on delivery to the carrier. Delivery was made by Sam because the contract for transportation was reasonable and notice and the necessary documents were provided to the buyer. By contrast, if the contract had instead provided FOB Butte, the seller would bear the risk of loss. In the destination contract, the risk of loss does not pass to the buyer until the goods are actually tendered to the buyer in Butte.

UCC § 2–509. Risk of Loss in the Absence of Breach

(1) Where the contract requires or authorizes the seller to ship the goods by carrier

(a) if it does not require him to deliver them at a particular destination, the risk of loss passes to the buyer when the goods are duly delivered to the carrier . . .

(b) if it does require him to deliver them at a particular destination and the goods are there duly tendered while in the possession of the carrier, the risk of loss passes to the buyer when the goods are there duly so tendered as to enable the buyer to take delivery.

Goods Will Not Move

Where the goods are in possession of a bailee and will be delivered without being moved, risk of loss allocation depends on whether delivery is to be made by a document of title. Where delivery is to be made by a negotiable document of title such as a warehouse receipt, risk of loss passes on delivery of the document. By contrast, where there is no document of title, risk of loss passes when the bailee acknowledges the buyer's rights in the goods [UCC § 2–509(2)]. For example, assume that Beth Buyer buys corn stored in a corn silo, with title to pass when a negotiable document of title is delivered to Beth. If, the night before the document is to be delivered to Beth, the silo burns down, the seller bears the risk of loss. The risk would not shift until the document was delivered.

Figure 21–5   Risk of Loss

Type of Contract	When Risk of Loss Passes
Carrier contract	Shipment: Risk of loss passes when the goods are delivered to the carrier. Destination: Risk of loss passes when the goods are tendered to the buyer at that location.
Goods will not move	If document of title: Risk of loss passes when the document is delivered to the buyer. If no document of title: Risk of loss passes when the bailee acknowledges the buyer's rights in the goods.
All other cases	If the seller is a merchant: Risk of loss passes on delivery to the buyer. If the seller is not a merchant: Risk of loss passes on tender of delivery.

UCC § 2–509. Risk of Loss in the Absence of Breach

(2) Where the goods are held by a bailee to be delivered without being moved, the risk of loss passes to the buyer

(a) on his receipt of a negotiable document of title covering the goods; or

(b) on acknowledgment by the bailee of the buyer's right to possession of the goods;

All Other Cases

In all other cases, when risk of loss shifts depends on whether the seller is a merchant. The risk of loss passes to the buyer on *receipt* of the goods from a seller merchant. Receipt occurs when the buyer takes physical possession of the goods. If the seller is not a merchant, risk of loss passes to the buyer on *tender* of delivery within the meaning of section 2–503, as discussed in Chapter 20 [UCC § 2–509(3)]. For example, assume that Susan Seller and Barbara Buyer

---

UCC § 2–509. Risk of Loss in the Absence of Breach

(3) In any case not within subsection (1) or (2), the risk of loss passes to the buyer on his receipt of the goods if the seller is a merchant; otherwise the risk passes to the buyer on tender of delivery.

---

enter into a contract for the sale of Susan's car. Assume further that Susan calls Barbara and informs her that the car is ready to be picked up. Before Barbara arrives, the car is destroyed by a tornado. In this case, because Susan is not a merchant, Barbara bears the risk of loss. Risk shifted to Barbara when the car was tendered, when Susan indicated that the car was available for Barbara to pick it up. By contrast, if Susan were a car dealer, she would bear the risk of loss. Risk of loss would not shift if the seller were a merchant until actual delivery.

The following case illustrates the difficulty of classifying contracts for risk of loss purposes.

SILVER v. WYCOMBE, MEYER & CO., INC.
477 N.Y.S.2d 288 (N.Y. Civ. Ct. 1984)

The plaintiff, Silver, an interior decorator, ordered custom furniture from the defendant, Wycombe, Meyer & Co., Inc. (Wycombe). On about February 23, 1982, Wycombe sent invoices to Silver advising that the furniture was ready for shipment. Silver paid Wycombe in full and asked Wycombe to ship one room of furniture but to hold the other. Accordingly, one room of furniture was shipped to Silver. Before any instructions were given concerning the second room of furniture, it was destroyed in a fire. Silver's insurance company paid Silver for the loss and sued Wycombe arguing that risk of loss never passed to the buyer.

SAXE, Judge

In the absence of contrary agreement by the parties, risk of loss under the Uniform Commercial Code is determined by the manner in which delivery is to be made (UCC § 2–509). The original order, documented by defendant Wycombe's order form, indicates a price of $7,053 '' + del'y,'' and all invoices provide for shipment to plaintiff's home ''Truck prepaid.'' It is clear that the provisions of UCC § 2–509 (1) govern the issue of when risk of loss passes to the buyer ''where the contract requires or authorizes the seller to ship the goods by carrier . . .''

Under the facts of the case at bar, the terms of the contract as it regards delivery are not stated. It is

apparent, however, that regardless of the particular agreement between buyer and seller, defendants have set forth no facts sufficient to place the risk of loss upon plaintiff.

Defendants, however, advance the novel theory that, because of plaintiff's request that they hold the furniture subject to further instruction, they became mere bailees of the goods and that the provisions of UCC § 2–509(2) should govern this case. They argue that the invoices informing plaintiff that the furniture was ready for shipment constitute acknowledgment of the buyer's right to possession, transferring the risk of loss pursuant to UCC § 2–509(2)(b) to the buyer.

This position is entirely without merit. The provisions of UCC § 2–509(2) contemplate a situation in which goods are in the physical possession of a third party who will continue to hold them after consummation of the sale. Therefore, this is not a provision appropriately applied to the circumstances at bar which anticipate the passing of title and physical possession more or less simultaneously. Furthermore, bailment requires delivery of the goods to the bailee. Having concluded that defendants failed to establish delivery of the furniture to plaintiff, by no stretch of the imagination may plaintiff be said to have redelivered it to defendants for safekeeping.

Defendants cannot transform what is clearly a sale of goods into a bailment simply because they acceded to the buyer's request to postpone delivery. The agreement between buyer and seller clearly contemplates delivery at the buyer's home and, under the Uniform Commercial Code, risk of loss remains upon a merchant seller until he completes his performance with reference to the physical delivery of the goods (UCC § 2–509(3).)

Accordingly, judgment for plaintiff in the amount demanded in the complaint together with costs, disbursements and interest.

Case Questions

1. Why did the defendants argue that they were mere bailees?

2. What was the effect of the invoice advising the buyer that the furniture was ready to be shipped?

3. What type of contract was this? Shipment? Bailment? All other cases?

Risk of Loss: Breach

A major objective of the UCC risk of loss provisions is to place the loss on the party most likely to manage the risk such as by purchasing insurance. This policy is particularly apparent in the loss allocation scheme adopted where one party is in breach.

Seller's Breach

If the seller ships nonconforming goods, the risk of loss remains with the seller until the buyer accepts the goods in spite of their nonconformity or until the seller cures the breach [UCC § 2–510(1)]. For example, assume Sam Seller contracts to deliver to Bonus Bookstore 150 Business Law textbooks and instead sends 150 Principles of Accounting textbooks. Assume further that Bonus rejects the books and they are totally destroyed in a train wreck on the way back to Sam's warehouse. Sam bears the risk of loss because the goods were nonconforming and were rejected by the buyer.

In the following case, the court considers the question of risk of loss when the seller delivers nonconforming goods.

UCC § 2–510. Effect of Breach on Risk of Loss

(1) Where a tender or delivery of goods so fails to conform to the contract as to give a right of rejection the risk of their loss remains on the seller until cure or acceptance.

LYKINS OIL CO v. FEKKOS
507 N.E.2d 795 (Ohio Ct. Common Pleas 1986)

On April 20, 1985, the defendant, Fekkos, purchased from the plaintiff, Lykins Oil Company (Lykins), a 16-horsepower diesel tractor. On Saturday, April 27, the tractor was delivered to his residence. The next day, when attempting to use the tractor, Fekkos discovered that it was defective. The defects included a dead battery, overheating while pulling either the mower or tiller, missing safety shields over the muffler and the power takeoff, and a missing water pump. On Monday, Fekkos notified Lykins of the defects and was informed that Lykins would have the tractor picked up from Fekkos's residence within the next couple of days.

Because of the difficulty of getting the tractor into his garage, Fekkos placed the tractor with the tiller attached in his front yard at the edge of the lawn. No pickup was made on Tuesday. On Wednesday, Fekkos discovered that the tractor was missing.

Lykins brought this action to recover the value of the stolen tractor from Fekkos.

WATSON, Judge

Plaintiff argues that UCC § 2–602 applies to this matter. Plaintiff argues that because defendant was already in possession of the tractor at the time he rejected it, he had the duty to hold it with reasonable care for a sufficient length of time for plaintiff to remove it from defendant's premises. Plaintiff asserts that defendant breached this duty and is liable to plaintiff because the tractor was unavailable to be picked up by plaintiff on May 1, the day after the purchase order was canceled and two days after defendant rejected the tractor.

On the other hand, defendant argues that UCC 2–510 controls the matter. Defendant argues that because the tractor was of no use to him as delivered, it failed to conform to the contract so as to give him a right to reject it. Thus, defendant asserts, under UCC § 2–510 the risk of loss remained on the seller at the point of the tractor theft on May 1, because no cure or acceptance had been made at that point.

Alternatively, defendant argues that if UCC § 2–602 is applicable, he still is entitled to summary judgment because subsequent to his rejection he held the tractor with reasonable care, forced because of the necessity of jump starting, the impassibility of his driveway and inaccessibility of his garage. Defendant argues that it would be unreasonable to assume that he could have anticipated that someone would "go to the trouble of removing the tiller, and then push or winch a 1,200-plus pound tractor onto a truck."

The court is mindful that section 2–510 refers to revocation of acceptance rather than rejection prior to acceptance, but the court would note that the rationale as to rejection is similar. Thus, where a buyer has taken possession of goods prior to rejection, the goods so nonconforming that the right to reject them arises, the risk of loss remains on the seller unless through the buyer's negligence they are lost, stolen, or destroyed. The actual risk of loss never actually shifts, but liability of the buyer arises upon his failure to exercise reasonable care for the goods' preservation until such time as the seller removes the goods rightfully rejected.

As to the instant case, while it may be said that the seller retained the risk of loss of the nonconforming tractor, the liability for loss would fall on the buyer, defendant, if the facts show that the buyer breached his duty to hold the tractor with reasonable care for sufficient time for removal, after notification of rejection to seller.

On the facts, the court finds that the actions taken by the defendant were reasonable under all the circumstances and that defendant did not breach his duty to use reasonable care to hold the tractor until plaintiff would retrieve it. The court notes that there is no evidence that any of plaintiff's employees indicated their dissatisfaction with defendant's decision to park the tractor on his front lawn when told by defendant that that was where he would leave it until they came. The evidence shows that defendant acted reasonably because of the inaccessibility of his garage on account of the demolition of his driveway.

Accordingly, reasonable minds could only conclude that defendant took reasonable care to hold the tractor. Defendant is entitled to judgment as a matter of law.

Case Questions

1. Compare and contrast section 2–602 and section 2–510 of the UCC.

2. Why did the seller bear the risk of loss?

3. Why might the UCC have different risk of loss provisions when a party is in breach?

The result is a bit more complicated if the buyer accepts the nonconforming goods. Assume that in the above example where Sam promises to deliver 150 Business Law textbooks to Bonus Bookstore, Bonus accepts the textbooks unaware of the nonconformity, as would be the case if the book covers read

Business Law but the insides were Accounting. Because Bonus would be entitled to justifiably revoke its acceptance, the loss remains on the seller as if from the beginning to the extent of any deficiency in the buyer's insurance coverage. For example, assume that the contract price for the textbooks is $7,500 and that the buyer has insurance for $5,000. If the books are destroyed, the buyer's insurance company bears $5,000 of the loss and the seller bears the remaining $2,500.

UCC § 2–510. Effect of Breach on Risk of Loss

(2) Where the buyer rightfully revokes acceptance he may to the extent of any deficiency in his effective insurance coverage treat the risk of loss as having rested on the seller from the beginning.

Buyer's Breach

Similarly, where the buyer is in breach, the buyer bears the risk of loss to the extent of any deficiency in the seller's insurance coverage. Thus, as long as the loss occurs within a "commercially reasonable time," the buyer who repudiates the contract or rejects conforming goods bears a limited risk. To illustrate, assume that in the above example the textbooks were to be delivered on August 1. Assume further that conforming books were identified to the contract, and that the buyer repudiated the contract on July 25. If, on August 2, the books are destroyed in a warehouse fire, the buyer bears any uninsured loss.

UCC § 2–510. Effect of Breach on Risk of Loss

(3) Where the buyer as to conforming goods already identified to the contract for sale repudiates or is otherwise in breach before risk of their loss has passed to him, the seller may to the extent of any deficiency in his effective insurance coverage treat the risk of loss as resting on the buyer for a commercially reasonable time.

DOCUMENTS OF TITLE

Introduction

Documents of title are written instruments that permit transfer of the ownership of goods that are in shipment or storage. The document is both evidence of receipt of the goods by the bailee (**warehouse-**

man or **carrier**) and is a contract for the shipment or storage of identified goods. A document of title is a bill of lading, warehouse receipt, or other document for delivery of goods [UCC § 1–201(15)]. The two major types of documents that will be considered here are bills of lading and warehouse receipts.

A **bill of lading** is a document issued by a carrier to the shipper of goods listing the goods to be shipped, the terms of delivery, and the destination [UCC § 1–201(6)]. Bills of lading are particularly important in international sales contracts and, thus, are discussed in depth, along with letters of credit, in Chapter 34. Bills of lading used in domestic transactions are governed by UCC Article 7. See Figure 21–6 for an example of a bill of lading.

UCC § 1–201. General Definitions

(15) "Document of Title" includes bill of lading, dock warrant, dock receipt, warehouse receipt or order for the delivery of goods, and also any other document which in the regular course of business or financing is treated as adequately evidencing that the person in possession of it is entitled to receive, hold and dispose of the document and the goods it covers. To be a document of title a document must purport to be issued by or addressed to a bailee and purport to cover goods in the bailee's possession which are either identified or are fungible portions of an identified mass.

A **warehouse receipt** is a document issued by a warehouseman acknowledging receipt of the goods identified in the document. It typically specifies the terms of the contract for storage. See Figure 21–7 for an example of a warehouse receipt.

UCC § 1–201. General Definitions

(6) "Bill of lading" means a document evidencing the receipt of goods for shipment issued by a person engaged in the business of transporting or forwarding goods.

Warehouse receipts are also used to finance the sale of merchandise held in storage. The storage will be either at the warehouseman's premises or on the owner's premises (called **field warehousing**). Warehouse receipt financing is accomplished by the following procedure. The owner stores goods with the warehouseman and receives a warehouse receipt in

Figure 21–6 Bill of Lading

Bill of Lading

Shipper	
Consignee: (Complete name and address)	Forwarding agent
	Point and country or origin / Place of receipt
Notify party	Domestic routing instructions
Pier	Place of delivery
Ocean vessel / Port of landing	
Point of discharge	

CARRIER'S RECEIPT		PARTICULARS FURNISHED BY SHIPPER		
Marks and numbers	Number of packages	Description of goods	Gross weight	Measurement

• Received in apparent good order and condition except as otherwise noted hereon the goods, containers, or other packages for transportation from the place of receipt or port of loading subject to exceptions, limitations, and conditions and to be delivered to the consignee or assigns

(TERMS OF THIS BILL OF LADING CONTINUED ON REVERSE.)

TOTAL FREIGHT $____________

DATE ____________ BY ____________ (Agent)

return. The owner then takes the warehouse receipt and sells it or uses it as security for a loan. Alternatively, if the owner is the seller of goods to a buyer on credit, the goods may be shipped to a warehouse, a warehouse receipt issued in the buyer's name, and the goods to be delivered to the buyer on payment of the purchase price.

UCC § 1–201. General Defintions

(45) "Warehouse receipt" means a receipt issued by a person engaged in the business of storing goods for hire.

Several additional terms, unique to Article 7, must be defined.

Shipper: The shipper is the person who delivers the goods to the common carrier and makes the contract for their shipment. The shipper is typically the seller of the goods. The shipper is not the common carrier.

Consign: Consign means to send the goods to someone else. Thus, the **consignor** is the shipper (the person from whom the goods have been received) [UCC § 7–102(c)], and the **consignee** is the person to whom the goods will be delivered [UCC § 7–102(b)]. Often, the consignor will be the seller of goods and the consignee will be the buyer.

Issuer: The issuer of the document creates the document. Typically, the issuer will be the carrier [UCC § 7–102(g)].

Figure 21–7   Warehouse Receipt–Not Negotiable

Warehouse Receipt—Not Negotiable

Receipt and lot number _____   Vault no. ____ ____ ____ ____ ____

                                                                        ____ ____ ____ ____ ____

                                                            Date of issue _____ 19 _____

        Received for the account of and deliverable to _____
of (address) _____
    the goods enumerated on attached schedule and stored in Company warehouse, located at
_____. These goods are accepted upon
the following conditions.
        That the value of all goods stored is not over $ _____ per pound unless
a higher value is noted on the schedule, for which an additional monthly storage charge of
$ _____ on each $ _____ will be made.

Ownership. The Customer, Shipper Depositor, or Agent represents and warrants that he is lawfully possessed of goods to be stored and/or has the authority to store or ship said goods. (If the goods are mortgaged, notify The Company the name and address of the mortgagee.)
Payment of Charges. Storage bills are payable monthly in advance for each month's storage or fraction thereof. The Depositor will pay reasonable attorney's fee incurred by the Company in collecting delinquent accounts.
Liability of Company. The Company shall be liable for any loss or injury to the goods caused by its failure to exercise such care as a reasonably careful person would exercise under like circumstances. The Company will not be liable for loss or damage to fragile articles not packed, or articles packed or unpacked by other than employees of this Company.
Change of Address. Notice of change of address must be given the Company in writing, and acknowledged in writing by the Company.
Transfer or Withdrawal of Goods. The warehouse receipt is not negotiable and shall be produced and all charges must be paid before delivery to the Depositor, or transfer of goods to another person; however, a written direction to the Company to transfer the goods to another person or deliver the goods may be accepted by the Company at its option without requiring tender of the warehouse receipt.
Access to Storage, Partial Withdrawal. A signed order from the person in whose name the receipt is issued is required to enable others to remove or have access to goods. A charge is made for stacking and unstacking, and for access to stored goods.
Building—Fire—Watchman. The Company does not represent or warrant that its building cannot be destroyed by fire. The Company shall not be required to maintain a watchman or sprinkler system and its failure to do so shall not constitute negligence.
Claims or Errors. All claims for non delivery of any article or articles and for damage, breakage, etc., must be made in writing within ninety (90) days from delivery of goods stored or they are waived. Failure to return the warehouse receipt for correction within _____ (   ) days after receipt thereof by the depositor will be conclusive that it is correct and delivery will be made only in accordance therewith.
Warehouseman's Lien. The Company reserves the right to sell the goods stored, in accordance with the provisions of the Uniform Commercial Code (Business and Commerce Code if stored in Texas), for all lawful charges in arrears.
Termination of Storage. The Company reserves the right to terminate the storage of the goods at any time by giving to the Depositor thirty (30) days' written notice of its intention so to do, and, unless the Depositor removes such goods within that period, the Company is hereby empowered to have the same removed at the cost and expense of the Depositor. or the Company may sell them at auction in accordance with state law.
THIS DOCUMENT CONTAINS THE WHOLE CONTRACT BETWEEN THE PARTIES AHD THERE ARE NO OTHER TERMS, WARRANTIES, REPRESENTATIONS, OR AGREEMENTS OF EITHER DEPOSITOR OR COMPANY NOT HEREIN CONTAINED.

Storage per month or fraction thereof $ _____   Wrapping and preparing for storage $ _____
                    Warehouse labor $ _____   Charges advanced $ _____
                              Cartage $ _____   _____ $ _____
                Packing at residence $ _____   _____ $ _____
                                                            By _____

Bailee: The bailee is the person who acknowledges possession of the goods and contracts to deliver them. Again, this is typically the carrier or warehouseman [UCC § 7–102(a)].

A document of title can either be negotiable or nonnegotiable. If the document is negotiable, it is in a form that indicates that the intent of the parties is (1) that the holder of the document should have possession of the goods, and (2) that possession should be free from the normal defenses to a contract. A document is negotiable if it indicates that the goods are to be delivered to ''bearer or to the order of a named person'' [UCC § 7–104(1)(a)]. In order to be a holder of a negotiable document, one must be in possession of a bearer document or in possession of an order document properly indorsed. The concepts of negotiability and negotiation of documents of title are similar to those concepts in commercial paper, which are discussed in depth in Chapters 24 and 25.

Although the documents may differ in form and use, the issues that must be considered are typically the same. Two basic questions must be considered: (1) What are the duties of the bailee? and (2) What are the rights of a purchaser of the document? These questions are answered by Article 7 of the UCC. It should be noted that, unlike Article 2, most of Article 7 cannot be varied by agreement.

The Bailee's Obligation

There are typically two risks in document of title cases: (1) the goods are lost, destroyed, or damaged, or (2) the bailee is unable to deliver the goods as demanded. While the obligations of carriers are substantially similar to those of warehousemen, the differences warrant separate treatment.

Carrier's Obligations

The carrier has two basic obligations: (1) to exercise reasonable care with respect to the goods while they are in the carrier's possession, and (2) to deliver the goods as promised.

Reasonable Care   What if the goods are lost or damaged while in the carrier's possession? The general rule at common law is one of absolute liability. Under Article 7, however, the carrier is obligated to exercise the degree of care with respect to the goods that a "reasonably careful man would exercise under like circumstances" [UCC § 7–309]. However, Article 7 does not replace the common law rule. Thus, carriers face absolute liability for lost or damaged goods subject to certain common law exceptions such as an act of God, an act of a public enemy, or acts of the shipper.

Delivery of the Goods   The carrier must deliver the goods to the person entitled to them under the document. If the bill of lading is nonnegotiable, this means the goods must be delivered to the named consignee. If the bill is negotiable, the goods must be delivered to whomever is legally in possession of the bill. In general, the carrier faces absolute liability for misdelivery.

UCC § 7–309. Duty of Care;

(1) A carrier who issues a bill of lading whether negotiable or nonnegotiable must exercise the degree of care in relation to the goods which a reasonably careful man would exercise under like circumstances. This subsection does not repeal or change any law which imposes liability upon a common carrier for damages not caused by its negligence.

Warehouseman's Obligations

The warehouseman has three basic obligations: (1) to prepare the warehouse receipt, (2) to exercise due care with respect to the goods while they are in his or her possession, and (3) to deliver the goods as promised.

Prepare the Warehouse Receipt   The warehouseman must prepare the warehouse receipt containing certain information. If the warehouseman fails to include the specified information, he or she is liable to anyone injured by the omission [UCC § 7–202]. For example, a good faith purchaser of the document may recover damages from the issuer caused by the nonreceipt or misdescription of the goods [UCC § 7–203].

Reasonable Care   The warehouseman must exercise reasonable care with respect to the goods in its possession or face liability for damages caused by negligence [UCC § 7–204]. This duty of care contrasts with the carrier's absolute liability.

Unless otherwise agreed, the warehouseman must keep separate the goods covered by each receipt. This permits identification and delivery of those goods. An exception is made in the case of fungible goods [UCC § 7–207].

Delivery of the Goods   The warehouseman is obligated to deliver the goods to the person entitled to the goods under the document as long as (1) the holder has satisfied the bailee's lien for storage charges, (2) the holder of a negotiable document surrenders the document, and (3) the warehouseman has no excuses [UCC § 7–403(1)]. In general, the warehouseman is absolutely liable to the holder of the document for misdelivery.

Good Faith Purchasers

A negotiable document of title "duly negotiated" will pass on to certain bona fide purchasers greater rights to the document of title and the goods than the seller had, similar to the rights afforded the holder in due course in commercial paper cases.

Due Negotiation is the transfer of a negotiable document to a holder who buys in good faith and without notice of any problems. A person who takes through due negotiation gets title to the document of title and title to the goods. The holder is entitled to delivery of the goods free from any claim or defense.

THE INTERNATIONAL SALES CONTRACT

Title

The CISG (the Convention on Contracts for the International Sale of Goods) governs only the formation of the contract and the rights and duties of the parties to the contract. It does not govern title issues or the rights of purchasers. Many title questions are answered in international trade by documents of title.

Risk of Loss

Allocation of risk of loss in the international sales contract is substantially similar to domestic sales. As under the UCC, transfer of title has no bearing on imposition of risk of loss.

The CISG, much like the UCC, provides that the parties may negotiate with respect to allocation of loss [Article 67]. Similarly, CISG allocates loss depending on the type of contract involved. Under the CISG, contracts fall into two categories: (1) carrier contracts and (2) other cases.

Carrier Contracts

Carrier contracts under the CISG are either: (1) shipment contracts, (2) destination contracts, or (3) transshipment contracts.

Shipment Contracts   Where the contract provides for shipment but does not require the seller to deliver the goods to the buyer's location, risk of loss passes to the buyer when the goods are "handed over" to the *first* carrier. For example, if Sam Seller in Columbus, Ohio, USA, contracts to sell 1,000 bushels of wheat to Ben Buyer in Moscow, FOB Columbus, risk of loss passes when the goods are delivered to the trucking firm in Columbus that will take them to the international carrier in New York City.

Destination Contract   By contrast, if the contract provided FOB Moscow, risk would not pass until the goods are delivered to Moscow.

Transshipment Contract   Alternatively, if the contract provided FAS New York City, (free alongside a ship) the seller would bear the responsibility of delivering the goods to the common carrier in New York City for delivery to Moscow.

Other Cases

Where the goods will not be shipped to the buyer, the risk of loss passes when the buyer picks up the goods or they are "at the disposal" of the buyer [Article 69].

In the Event of Breach

Unlike the UCC approach, the CISG rules on risk of loss are not changed by breach of the contract.

The following article explains how important it is for one involved in international trade to appreciate the CISG.

 ### U.N. Convention Demystifies International Sales Contracts*

Put yourself in the following situation: you are a U.S. exporter who is to perform a sales contract for candy-striped barber poles, CIF Le Havre, France, with an Italian gondola company in Venice. The buyer won't pay or accept further shipments because the stripes come off in the water when the poles are used as channel markers.

Which law governs the problems created by this sale: U.S., Italian, French, or some general principles of international law?

The answer to our situation could be that the applicable law is the United Nations Convention on Contracts for the International Sale of Goods (CISG). This treaty, which became the United States Law governing export-import transactions on January 1, 1988, establishes uniform legal rules to govern the formation of international sales contracts and the rights and obligations of the buyer and seller. As a result, the CISG is expected to facilitate and stimulate international trade.

---

*Source: Mark A. Goldstein, "U.N. Convention Demystifies International Sales Contracts," *Business Credit,* November–December 1990, pp. 20–21.

The CISG applies automatically to all contracts for the sale of goods between traders from two different countries where both those countries have ratified the CISG. This automatic application will take place unless the parties to the contract expressly exclude (''opt-out'') of all or part of the CISG or expressly provide a choice of law clause stipulating a law other than that of the CISG. Parties can also expressly choose to apply the CISG when it would not automatically apply.

The United States has reserved that the CISG will only apply when the other party to the transaction also has its place of business in a contracting party or country. The Office of the Legal Adviser of the United States Department of State maintains that there will be 40 to 50 countries for which the Convention will be in force in the next four years, and that the Convention will become applicable to untold thousands of international sales contracts annually.

The CISG and the UCC: Similarities and Differences

The Scope of the CISG is similar to Article 2 of the UCC, effective in the United States except Louisiana, due largely to the fact that the United States played a very active role in the negotiation of the Convention. The CISG and the UCC allow for supplementation of agreements with agreed upon trade usages and established courses of dealing. Both legal codes give great weight to the concept that the contract governs the transaction and treat revocation of acceptance, warranties, risk or loss, notice, excuse, remedies, cover, and assurances of performance in a similar manner.

However, the following are six key areas in which the CISG and the UCC differ. U.S. traders familiar with the UCC should consider these areas carefully.

- The CISG does not have a provision similar to the Statute of Frauds. A contract, therefore, need not be in writing and other formalities need not be present for the formation or modification of a contract.
- The CISG requires that an acceptance of an offer ''mirror'' the terms of the offer for a contract to be formed. Nonmirroring acceptances will operate as counteroffers only.
- Unlike the UCC's ''mailbox rule,'' a contract is formed at the time the acceptance is received by the offeror, not when the acceptance is mailed or transmitted.
- Irrevocable offers, under the CISG, are held open without being in writing.
- Unlike under the UCC, under the CISG, it is not clear that a contract would be formed if the price is not specified.
- Finally, due to its recent passage, the CISG has not yet developed a large body of private case law to support it if parties encounter gaps in the law.

Should You Opt Out of the CISG?

The American Bar Association has provided three observations on the benefits of the CISG. First, U.S. businesses can avoid the difficulties of reaching agreement with foreign buyers on choice-of-law issues because the CISG will be readily available for compromise. Second, the use of the CISG as a body of law governing international sales of goods will decrease the time and legal costs otherwise involved in research of different unfamiliar laws. And third, the CISG will reduce the problems of proof of foreign law in domestic and foreign courts.

It is likely that application of the CISG will make sense for smaller firms and for American firms contracting with companies in countries whose laws, and whose legal interpretation of their laws, is obscure, unfamiliar, or not suited for international sales of goods. However, some larger, more experienced firms may want to continue their current practices at least with regard to parties with whom they have been doing business on a regular basis.

Most importantly, when opting out it is not sufficient to simply say, "the laws of New York apply" because CISG would be the law of the State of New York under certain circumstances. Rather one should say, "the provisions of the Uniform Commercial Code as adopted by the State of New York apply, and not the United Nations Convention on Contracts for the International Sale of Goods."

Thought Questions

1. Analyze the following statement: "CISG is expected to facilitate and stimulate international trade."

2. Analyze the following statement: "It is likely that application of the CISG will make sense for smaller firms. However, some larger, more experienced firms may want to continue their current practices."

3. List the similarities and the differences between the CISG and the UCC outlined in the article.

END–OF– CHAPTER QUESTIONS

1. Explain the relationship between (a) identification, (b) transfer of title, and (c) risk of loss.

2. Analyze the following statement: "Where the buyer is in breach, the buyer bears the risk of loss to the extent of any deficiency in the seller's insurance coverage."

3. Evaluate the following statement: "Before determining who bears the risk of loss in any transaction, it is necessary to determine who has title to the goods."

4. Fred Lane sold a new boat to a person representing himself to be John Willis in return for a check for $6,285. The check was later dishonored. Jimmy Honeycutt bought the boat for $2,500 about six months later from a man representing himself as "Garrett." Garrett indicated that he was selling the boat for someone else. When he couldn't reach the third-party seller, Garrett signed the title in the name of that third party, Patterson. Who is entitled to the boat, Lane or Honeycutt? See *Lane v. Honeycutt*, 188 S.E.2d 604 (1972).

5. Barco Auto Leasing Corp. entered into a contract with Exotic Car Leasing whereby Exotic sold a BMW to Barco and leased it back. Exotic defaulted on its lease payments, and when Barco attempted to repossess the BMW it discovered that the owners of Exotic had sold the car to Holt International and disappeared. Holt had purchased the car for $18,000. Although Exotic did not have the certificate of title at the time of the sale, it informed Holt that the document would be delivered promptly. When the title was not delivered promptly, Holt was told that the title was lost, but a duplicate certificate would be obtained. A duplicate title was eventually supplied. Who is entitled to the car, Barco Leasing or Holt International? Is Holt a buyer in the ordinary course? See *Barco Leasing Corp. v. Holt*, 548 A.2d 1161 (1988).

6. A West German corporation enters into a contract to sell wine to a North Carolina distributor to be shipped from West Germany. The shipment terms did not require any particular destination. The wine was delivered to the ocean vessel for shipment on November 29. All necessary documents were forwarded to defendant's bank in North Carolina. The documents were received on December 27. On January 24th, the buyer learned that the shipment

of wine had left Germany aboard the MS *Munchen*, which had been lost at sea with all cargo aboard. The West German seller sued the North Carolina buyer for the purchase price. Did risk of loss pass? See *Rheinberg-Kellerel GmbH v. Vineyard Wine Co.*, 281 S.E.2d 425 (1981).

7. Martin entered into a contract to purchase a new hay-mowing machine from Melland's. He traded in his old hay-mowing machine as the down payment on the new machine. He immediately mailed Melland's title to the old machine, but continued to use the old machine ''until they had the new one ready.'' Before the new one was ready, the old hay-mower was destroyed by fire. Who bears the risk of loss, Martin or Melland's? See *Martin v. Melland's, Inc.*, 283 N.W.2d 76 (1979).

8. Joseph enters into a contract to purchase video games from Andrews to be shipped from Sunnyvale, California, to Baltimore, Maryland, FOB Baltimore. The video games are delivered to the common carrier, but are stolen between Sunnyvale and Baltimore. Who bears the risk of loss, Joseph or Andrews? What recourse might that party have against the common carrier?

9. Ben Buyer buys a gold locket for his wife for their 11th anniversary. Before he can give the locket to his wife, it is stolen by Tom Thief. Tom leaves the locket with Mike Merchant for engraving. Mike is in the business of selling and repairing jewelry. Mike mistakenly sells the locket to Gilda Gullible. Ben discovers that Gilda has his locket. Can Ben get the locket back from Gilda?

10. Albert Cement Co. contracts to sell to ABC Construction Co. 1,000 bags of cement mix. ABC Co. agrees to pick up the cement mix at Albert Cement's warehouse. The cement mix is ready to be picked up and ABC is notified. Before ABC can arrange for the mix to be picked up, it is destroyed in a warehouse fire. Who bears the risk of loss? Explain.

Chapter 22

Warranties and Remedies

■

CRITICAL THINKING INQUIRIES

As you read this chapter, you should be able to address the following:

- Analyze the following statement: "It is unconscionable for a seller to disclaim liability for personal injury loss to a consumer."
- How might the implied warranties of merchantability and fitness for a particular purpose overlap? Think of a situation where an injured plaintiff might sue for both.
- How do the seller's available remedies differ depending on who has possession of the goods?
- What factors influence the buyer's decision on whether to cover or to sue for nondelivery?
- How would a seller's damages differ in an international sales contract?

MANAGERIAL PERSPECTIVE

HardYard, Inc. manufactures and sells lawn products. As part of its line of yard tools it sells a rake that has an unfortunate tendency to break off if the consumer rakes too vigorously. HardYard is concerned with potential liability.

- What is the potential liability under breach of warranty?
- How can HardYard minimize this liability? Would disclaimers or warnings be effective?
- Should HardYard discontinue marketing this product altogether? What are the ethics of marketing a product that you know has the potential for injury?
- Is your answer to this question affected by HardYard's decisions on warnings? Is it more ethical to market this product in spite of the potential for injury if the consumer is informed of the risk by an accompanying label?

A manager must be aware of these risks and the potential for legal liability. Similarly, the manager must be able to calculate potential liability where the goods delivered are not the goods promised. This chapter will acquaint you with the information needed to assess the risks and liability.

WARRANTIES

Warranties are promises made about the goods. They can be express or implied.

Warranty of Title

In every sale of goods, the seller warrants that **good title** will be conveyed and that the transfer is rightful [UCC § 2–312(1)(a)]. For example, assume that a thief steals a watch from the true owner and sells the watch to a jewelry store. Assume further that someone purchases the watch from the jewelry store. If the true owner finds out who has the watch and recovers it, the purchaser has a claim against the jewelry store for breach of the warranty of title. In addition, the seller warrants that the goods will be delivered free from any claim of the seller's creditors except those of which the buyer has knowledge. However, in some cases, circumstances indicate that the warranties of title are not made. For example, when one purchases goods sold at a sheriff's sale, the seller makes no such warranties.

Express Warranties

Products liability warranties are promises made about the nature or quality of the product sold. When a seller warrants something about the good, the seller is promising that the good will conform to the statement made. The seller may do that expressly, as in a statement such as "This table is solid oak," or the promise may be implied by law.

When Is the Warranty Created?

Express warranties are made when the seller shows the buyer a sample or model, describes the goods, or makes a statement of fact about the goods. In such circumstances, the seller warrants that the goods will match the sample or model, the description, or the statement of fact [UCC § 2–313(1)]. As long as the statement (1) relates to the goods and (2) is part of the basis of the bargain, an express warranty is made.

It is not required that the seller use magic words of warranty to create a warranty [UCC § 2–313(2)]. An express warranty is created by statements of fact ("This is a new table"), or descriptions ("This is a solid oak table), or samples ("Your table will look just like this sample") even without using the word *warranty.*

UCC § 2–313. Express Warranties

(1) Express warranties by the seller are created as follows:

(a) Any affirmation of fact or promise made by the seller to the buyer which relates to the goods and becomes part of the basis of the bargain creates an express warranty that the goods shall conform to the affirmation or promise.

(b) Any description of the goods which is made part of the basis of the bargain creates an express warranty that the goods shall conform to the description.

(c) Any sample or model which is made part of the basis of the bargain creates an express warranty that the whole of the goods shall conform to the sample or model.

The seller's intent in making the statement is immaterial. In other words, it is not necessary for the seller to intend to make an express warranty by making the statement.

UCC § 2–313. Express Warranties

(2) . . . an affirmation merely of the value of the goods or a statement purporting to be merely the seller's opinion or commendation of the goods does not create a warranty.

Fact versus Opinion

In order to create an express warranty, the seller must make a statement of *fact*. Statements of opinion do not create express warranties. **Sales puffing** by the seller does not create a warranty. Thus, statements of fact ("This is a 1991 Plymouth with only 27,000 miles") create express warranties, but statements of opinion ("This car will last 127,000 miles if it will run a day") do not.

It is not always easy to tell the difference between a statement of opinion and fact. Statements of value are generally statements of opinion; predictions of the future are generally statements of opinion. However, the same statement might be a statement of opinion if made to a knowledgeable buyer and a statement of fact if made by an expert appraiser to a buyer with no information. Similarly, the same statement might be a statement of opinion if made by an average seller, but a statement of fact if made by an expert. Read the following case and try to determine whether the statement is a statement of fact or opinion.

BALOG v. CENTER ART GALLERY
745 F.Supp. 1556 (D. Hawaii 1990)

In 1978, the plaintiffs, the Balogs, visited one of the defendant's, Center Art Gallery, art galleries where they bought several pieces of artwork purportedly by Salvador Dali for a total purchase price of $36,000. After the sale, Center Art mailed to the Balogs a ''Confidential Appraisal-Certificate of Authenticity'' for each of the artworks purchased and followed with additional mailings. In each mailing, Center Art maintained that the art was produced by Dali and that it had appreciated in value. The Balogs, private collectors without expertise regarding the authenticity of artwork, relied on the representations of Center Art. In 1988, the Balogs discovered that Center Art had been accused of false representations about artwork and sued for breach of warranty.

PENCE, Senior District Judge

Presumably, the Code would protect purchasers of counterfeit artworks, such as the plaintiffs, by means of the express warranty provisions of UCC § 2–313. It is clear that the defendants offered an express warranty to the plaintiffs, as that term is contemplated under UCC § 2–313, that all pieces of art sold to them were Dali originals.

However, the fact that a warranty was offered does not end the matter since § 2–313(2) provides that ''any affirmation merely of the value of the goods or a statement purporting to be merely the seller's opinion or commendation of the goods does not create a warranty.''

The sale of artwork presents a unique area, since a dealer's statement that a work is the product of a particular artist can never be more than an educated guess or opinion (excluding, of course, the possibility that the dealer was an eyewitness to the work's production).

This problem is not one which was created solely by the drafting and adoption of the UCC. In fact, it was the dispositive issue in the case of *Jendwine v. Slade*, decided almost 200 years ago. In deciding whether or not the act of putting the name of an artist in a catalogue as the painter of a picture created a warranty as to the painting's authorship, Lord Kenyon stated that:

[I]t was impossible to make this the case of a warranty; the pictures were the work of artists some centuries back, and there being no way of tracing the picture itself, it could only be a matter of opinion whether the picture in question was the work of the artist whose name it bore or not.

There is no basis for this court to conclude, based on the papers now before it, that the defendants made any attempt to disclaim their opinion that the works in questions were the products of Salvador Dali. Furthermore, this court is of the view that not only did the plaintiffs engage in justifiable reliance upon the defendants' expertise and superior knowledge, but that the defendants encouraged such reliance and belief in the authenticity of the artwork by continuing to solicit additional sales from the plaintiffs and by continuing to send them Certificates of Authenticity and representing that their original investments increased in value. In the face of such facts, this court is led to agree that ''the requirements of fair dealing where there is a relationship between parties in which there is a basic inequality of knowledge, expertness, or economic power'' will provide a basis for the plaintiffs to seek redress of damages based upon a violation of the express warranties provided for by § 2–313.

The defendants here are alleged to have made very strong claims with respect to the artwork sold to the plaintiffs, and to have reiterated those statements repeatedly with the intent that the plaintiffs rely upon the defendants' representations. Furthermore, given the price of the various items sold, it is clear that the plaintiffs would have been reasonable in relying upon the defendants representations as their primary, if not sole basis for information regarding the authenticity of the pieces. . . . [T]he plaintiffs were effectively precluded by the price of the pieces from undertaking an extensive investigation into the veracity of the defendants' claims that the artwork was genuine. Thus, the arguments for the imposition of the ''reasonable basis in fact'' test has even more strength when applied to the facts of this case. Where parties are in such a discrepancy as far as information, the capacity to verify that information and bargaining position, fairness dictates that representations offered by one party with the expectation that they be relied upon by another have some reasonable basis in fact. Such is the requirement of § 2–313; therefore, to the extent that the evidence indicates that such representations do not possess a reasonable basis in fact, at the time these representations were made, this court finds that the party offering those representations will have violated the express warranties provided under UCC § 2–313.

Case Questions

1. Should the amount that the buyer paid for the art be of any relevance? Would your decision be any different if the buyer paid $25,000 or $25 million for what the seller represented to be a Monet?

2. The court found the fact that Center Art Gallery continued to solicit further sales from the Balogs and continued to represent the artwork as that of Dali (increasing in value) significant. Could one argue that both actions by Center Art Gallery are irrelevant?

3. What standard did the court apply? How does this standard differ from typical express warranty cases? How does this standard differ from the common law fraud standard?

4. Evaluate the following statement: ''Given the price of the various items sold, it is clear that the plaintiffs would have been reasonable in relying upon the defendants representations as their primary, if not sole basis for information regarding the authenticity.''

Disclaimer

The seller may disclaim express warranties by clear language only if the disclaimer is reasonable and consistent with the statements made. To illustrate, a statement by a seller while showing a sample such as ''Your lawn mower would, of course, be different than this since it would not have the grass catcher'' disclaims the express warranty with respect to the catcher created when showing the sample.

Implied Warranties

In some cases, warranties are implied by law even though the seller has not made them expressly. To best understand the warranties implied under the UCC, the following questions will be asked: (1)

UCC § 2–314. Implied Warranty: Merchantability

(1) Unless excluded . . . a warranty that the goods shall be merchantable is implied in a contract for their sale if the seller is a merchant with respect to goods of that kind.

who makes the warranty and when is it made, (2) what is warranted, and (3) how can the warranty be disclaimed?

There are two warranties implied by the UCC: (1) the warranty of merchantability and (2) the warranty of fitness for a particular purpose.

Warranty of Merchantability

The warranty of merchantability is implied in UCC section 2–314.

UCC § 2–314. Implied Warranty: Merchantability

(2) Goods to be merchantable must be at least such as

(a) pass without objection in the trade under the contract description; and . . .

(c) are fit for the ordinary purposes for which such goods are used; and

(d) run . . . ; and

(e) are adequately contained, packaged, and labeled as the agreement may require; and

(f) conform to the promises or affirmations of fact made on the container or label if any.

Who Makes the Warranty? The warranty of merchantability is implied whenever the seller is a merchant [UCC § 2–314(1)]. Nonmerchants, or consumer sellers, do not make this warranty.

What Do They Warrant? Merchant-sellers warrant that the goods sold are **merchantable.** The Code supplies an illustrative list of what goods are merchantable [UCC § 2–314(2)]. To be merchantable, goods must be of average quality. They must be "fit for the ordinary purposes" for which they are intended, and they must be comparable to goods acceptable in the trade. For example, HardYard's rake would not be merchantable because it is not fit for the ordinary purpose for which it is intended — raking.

Is food merchantable when it contains glass or pits? Under the age-old distinction between "foreign" and "natural" substances, food with foreign substances in it is not merchantable (e.g., glass); food with natural substances in it is merchantable (e.g., pits). Did the court in the following case use this distinction?

WEBSTER v. BLUE SHIP TEA ROOM
347 Mass. 421, 198 N.E.2d 309 (1964)

The plaintiff, Webster, ordered fish chowder in the Blue Ship Tea Room, the defendant restaurant. While she was eating it, a fish bone became stuck in her throat. The bone had to be medically removed. Webster sued for breach of implied warranty.

REARDON, Judge

We must decide whether a fish bone lurking in a fish chowder, about the ingredients of which there is no other complaint, constitutes a breach of implied warranty under applicable provisions of the Uniform Commercial Code. The plaintiff has vigorously reminded us of the high standards imposed by this court where the sale of food is involved and has made reference to cases involving stones in beans, trichinae in pork, and to certain other cases, here and elsewhere, serving to bolster her contention of breach of warranty.

Chowder is an ancient dish preexisting even "the appetites of our seamen and fishermen." [The court outlines the manner in which chowder has been made through the years.]

Thus, we consider a dish which for many long years, if well made, has been made generally as outlined above. It is not too much to say that a person sitting down in New England to consume a good New England fish chowder embarks on gustatory adventure which may entail the removal of some fish bones from his bowl as he proceeds. We are not inclined to tamper with age old recipes by any amendment reflecting the plaintiff's view of the effect of the Uniform Commercial Code upon them. We are aware of the heavy body of case law involving foreign substances in food, but we sense a strong distinction between them and those relative to unwholesomeness of the food itself, e.g. tainted mackerel, and a fish bone in a fish chowder. In any event, we consider that the joys of life in New England include the ready availability of fresh fish chowder. We should be prepared to cope with the hazards of fish bones, the occasional presence of which in chowders is, it seems to us, to be anticipated, and which, in the light of a hallowed tradition, do not impair their fitness or merchantability. We are most impressed by *Allen v. Grafton,* where in Ohio, the Midwest, in a case where the plaintiff was injured by a piece of oyster shell in an order of fried oysters, Mr Justice Taft held that "the possible presence of a piece of oyster shell in or attached to an oyster is so well known to anyone who eats oysters that we can say as a matter of law that one who eats oysters can reasonably anticipate and guard against eating such a piece of shell." [The court dismissed the claim.]

Case Questions
1. Did the court base its decision on the distinction between foreign and natural substances or on the reasonable expectations of the plaintiff?

2. Was the plaintiff basing her claim on the warranty of merchantability or fitness for a particular purpose?

3. Would the result in this case have been any different if the restaurant was located in Iowa? Why or why not?

Warranty of Fitness for a Particular Purpose

The warranty of fitness for a particular purpose is implied in UCC section 2–315.

UCC § 2–315. Implied Warranty: Fitness for Particular Purpose

Where the seller at the time of contracting has reason to know any particular purpose for which the goods are required and that the buyer is relying on the seller's skill or judgment to select or furnish suitable goods, there is unless excluded . . . an implied warranty that the goods shall be fit for such purpose.

Who Makes the Warranty?   The warranty of fitness for a particular purpose can be made by any seller. It is not limited to merchant-sellers. However, it arises only where (1) at the time of contracting the seller has reason to know of a particular purpose, and (2) the buyer is relying on the seller's skill and judgment to furnish suitable goods [UCC § 2–315].

Thus, it arises only where the buyer has a *particular* purpose, as distinguished from the ordinary purpose for which such goods are generally intended.

What Is Warranted?   In such a case, the seller warrants that the goods furnished are suitable for the particular purpose for which such goods are sought. For example, if you buy a pair of shoes from a shoe store, the ordinary purpose for which such shoes are intended is walking on ordinary ground. Under the implied warranty of merchantability, the shoes must be fit for that ordinary purpose. By contrast, if you buy shoes for mountain climbing, that is a particular purpose. If the seller knows that particular purpose and you rely on the seller to furnish suitable shoes, the seller warrants that the shoes sold are suitable for mountain climbing (the particular purpose.) If HardYard, Inc. sells its rakes to rake the infield of a baseball diamond, the rake must be suitable for raking the infield.

Read the next case, where the plaintiff used sunglasses for the particular purpose of protecting his eyes while playing baseball.

FILLER v. RAYEX CORP.
435 F.2d 336 (7th Cir. 1970)

Filler, the plaintiff, was injured when playing baseball. Although he was wearing flipped-down "baseball sunglasses" manufactured by Rayex Corp., the defendant, he lost a fly ball in the sun and the ball struck the sunglasses, shattering the lens into sharp splinters that pierced his right eye. The eye had to be removed. Filler's coach had bought the sunglasses after seeing the following advertisement:

The package was labeled: "Simply flip for instant eye protection." The sunglasses were substantially similar to ordinary sunglasses. Filler sued Rayex for breach of the implied warranty of fitness for a particular purpose. The trial court found Rayex liable for breach of implied warranty. Rayex appealed.

CUMMINGS, Circuit Judge

We agree that defendant is liable for breach of an implied warranty of fitness for a particular purpose. Indiana has adopted the implied warranty provision of the Uniform Commercial Code dealing with fitness for a particular purpose. These sunglasses were advertised as baseball sunglasses that would give "instant eye protection." Although they were intended for use by baseball fielders, the thickness of the lenses ranges only from 1.2 mm. to 1.5 mm., so that shattering into exceedingly sharp splinters would occur on their breaking. Since they lacked the safety features of plastic or shatterproof glass, the sunglasses were in truth not fit for baseball playing, the particular purpose for which they were sold.

Therefore, breach of that implied warranty was properly found.

Judgment is affirmed.

Case Questions

1. Did the court base liability on breach of an express warranty or breach of an implied warranty?
2. If liability was predicated on breach of an implied warranty, why was the advertisement relevant?
3. Why is Filler allowed to sue for breach of contract when the baseball coach, not Filler, purchased the eyeglasses?
4. What feature did the seller probably think made the glasses suitable for baseball?

How Can These Warranties Be Disclaimed?

In order to **disclaim** the implied warranty of merchantability, the merchant-seller must expressly mention the term *merchantability*. [UCC § 2–316(2)]. Thus, a general disclaimer such as "All implied warranties are hereby disclaimed" is insufficient to disclaim the implied warranty of merchantability. The disclaimer does not have to be in writing to be effective. However, if it is in writing it must be **conspicuous**. A disclaimer is conspicuous if it is written so that a reasonable person ought to see it [UCC § 1–201(10)]. For example, a disclaimer is not conspicuous if buried in the middle of a multiparagraph document in small-sized print.

UCC § 2–316. Exclusion or Modification of Warranties

(2) Subject to subsection (3), to exclude or modify the implied warranty of merchantability or any part of it the language must mention merchantability and in case of a writing must be conspicuous.

In order to disclaim the implied warranty of fitness for a particular purpose, the disclaimer must be in writing and be conspicuous [UCC § 2–316(2)]. However, a general disclaimer is effective. For ex-

ample, a statement disclaiming "All implied warranties" is effective to disclaim the warranty of fitness. The disclaimer in Figure 22–1 would effectively disclaim both implied warranties if conspicuous.

UCC § 2–316. Exclusion or Modification of Warranties

(2) . . . to exclude or modify any implied warranty of fitness the exclusion must be by a writing and conspicuous. Language to exclude all implied warranties of fitness is sufficient if it states, for example, that "There are no warranties which extend beyond the description on the face hereof."

There are several exceptions to the general rules outlined above. First, in spite of the requirements, a disclaimer such as "AS IS" or "WITH ALL

Figure 22–1   Common Effective Warranty Disclaimer

THE SELLER HEREBY DISCLAIMS ALL WARRANTIES, EXPRESS OR IMPLIED, INCLUDING THE IMPLIED WARRANTIES OF MERCHANTABILITY AND FITNESS FOR A PARTICULAR PURPOSE.

FAULTS" is effective to disclaim both implied warranties even though it does not mention the word *merchantability* [UCC § 2–316(3)]. Second, even if a disclaimer meets the requirements of UCC section 2–316, it cannot disclaim liability for personal injury to a consumer [UCC § 2–719(3)]. It is **unconscionable** to allow the seller to disclaim such loss.

In the following case, the question of unconscionability was considered by the court.

SCHLENZ v. JOHN DEERE CO.
511 F.Supp. 224 (D. Mont. 1981)

In May 1976, the Schlenzes, the plaintiffs, purchased a round hay baler manufactured and sold by the John Deere Co., the defendants. Deere warranted that the baler was safe, merchantable, and fit for the purpose of producing round hay bales. On about June 26, 1976, LeVon Schlenz's right arm was caught in the hay baler and severed. LeVon and his wife sued Deere for breach of express and implied warranties.

HATFIELD, District Judge

II. Implied Warranties

Plaintiffs claim that defendants breached implied warranties of merchantability and fitness. See § § 2–314, 2–315. The Montana UCC, however, allows a seller to disclaim these implied warranties by means of "conspicuous" language in a writing.

In the purchase order, defendants included language which "EXPRESSLY DISCLAIMS THE IMPLIED WARRANTIES OF MERCHANTABILITY AND FITNESS." The accompanying warranty for the round hay baler specifically provided that defendants do "NOT MAKE ANY IMPLIED WARRANTY OF MERCHANTABILITY OR FITNESS." In each case, the warranty disclaimers were printed in significantly larger typeface than the other printing in the body of the text. In each case, the warranty disclaimers were the only words in the body of text printed in capital letters. The disclaimers were printed in language sufficiently conspicuous to be effective disclaimers under 2–316(2).

III. Express Warranties

Plaintiffs state that, prior to the purchase of the round hay baler, Les Candee and plaintiff LeVon Schlenz received John Deere Company advertising and promotional materials, including an operator's manual for the John Deere 500 round baler. LeVon Schlenz claims that he relied on the statements in the promotional materials in deciding with Les Candee to purchase the John Deere 500 round baler.

Manufacturers, such as defendants, create express warranties under 2–313, if they make representations in advertising brochures that the purchaser relies on as part of the basis for the bargain. Here, defendants expressly warranted the safety of the John Deere 500 round baler allegedly purchased by plaintiff LeVon Schlenz jointly with Les Candee. The John Deere 500 round baler operator's manual specifically provides that

The safety of the operator was one of the prime considerations in the minds of John Deere engineers when this baler was designed. Shielding, simple adjustments, and other safety features were built into the baler wherever possible.

Defendants, by means of conspicuous language, both in the purchase order and in the attached warranty, disclaimed all express warranties. The disclaimer, however, was ineffective to destroy the express warranty of safety made in the operator's manual.

IV. Limitation of Remedies

Defendants issued a printed warranty on the John Deere 500 round baler. The warranty limited purchaser remedies to replacement or repair of defective parts. The warranty provided that "[i]n no event will the dealer, John Deere or any company affiliated with John Deere be liable for incidental or consequential damages or injuries."

Parties are free under the Montana UCC to limit or even exclude consequential damages "unless the limitation or exclusion is unconscionable." 2–719(3).

If the remedy limitation is valid in this contract, plaintiffs' claims based on LeVon Schlenz's personal injuries would be barred.

Limitations of damages for personal injuries in the case of "consumer goods" is prima facie unconscionable under 2–719(3). Farm equipment, such as the round hay baler, however, is defined in the Montana UCC as "equipment" rather than as "consumer goods."

Although the limitation of remedy provisions is not prima facie unconscionable, this court may, as a matter of law, find the remedy limitation clauses unconscionable and refuse to enforce those clauses. See 2–201(1). This court shall therefore consider evidence on plaintiffs' claim that the remedy limitations are unconscionable.

Case Questions

1. Why are disclaimers for personal injury unenforceable against consumers?

2. If the good sold was not a consumer good, why was the court discussing the issue of unconscionability?

3. What happens next? Do you think the disclaimer is unconscionable? Explain.

4. Which warranties, express or implied, were excluded by disclaimer? How?

To Whom Do These Warranties Run?

When a seller makes the implied warranties outlined above, to whom are these promises made? This is a question of **privity.** Does the promise merely extend to the direct buyer, the person with whom the seller entered into the contract? Or does it extend to buyers down the chain of distribution? For example, if HardYard, Inc. sells a rake to a retail outlet that in turn sells the rake to Carol Consumer and Carol is injured when it breaks, can Carol sue HardYard for breach of warranty? Did the warranty of merchantability run with the product? Did HardYard make the warranty to Carol? As is illustrated in Figure 22–2, this is a question of **vertical privity.** Traditionally, the answer to this question was no. Lack of privity was an absolute defense for HardYard, Inc. in Carol's suit. The UCC fails to address this question. However, lack of privity is generally no longer a defense in breach of warranty cases.

A second privity question is addressed by the UCC. As is illustrated in Figure 22–3, the question of **horizontal privity** deals with the question of whether in the above example the retailer would face liability to Carol's daughter if she used the rake and was injured. Could Carol's daughter sue the retailer (the seller from whom Carol purchased the rake) even though she was not a party to the contract? Instead of taking a position on this question, the Code offered the states three alternatives in section 2–318. When a state adopted the Code, it adopted one of the three alternatives.

UCC § 2–318. Alternative A

A seller's warranty extends to any natural person who is in the family or household of his buyer or who is a guest in his home if it is reasonable to expect that such person may use, consume or be affected by the goods and who is injured in person by breach of the warranty.

Figure 22–2 Vertical Privity

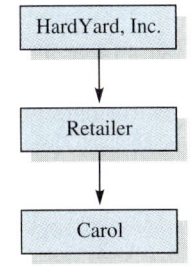

Figure 22–3 Horizontal Privity

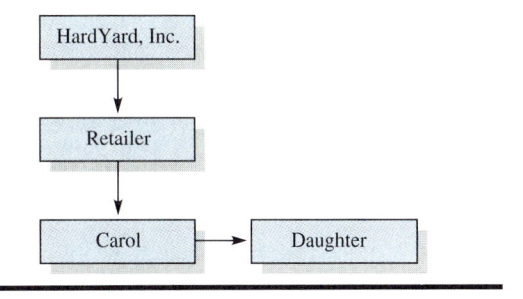

Alternative A   Alternative A is the alternative chosen in most states. Under alternative A, Carol's daughter could sue the manufacturer. She is a member of the family of the buyer and it is reasonable for the retailer to expect that she would use the product. Thus, she could recover from the retailer for her personal injury loss.

Alternative B   Alternative B removes the limitation that the plaintiff be a member of the household or guest of the buyer. Any reasonably foreseeable plaintiff may sue. Therefore, if Carol's friend borrowed the rake and was injured, she would be a permissible plaintiff even though not a member of the family or a guest. However, Alternative B applies only to natural person plaintiffs (not corporations) and only for personal injury loss (not property loss).

UCC § 2–318. Alternative B

A seller's warranty extends to any natural person who may reasonably be expected to use, consume or be affected by the goods and who is injured in person by breach of the warranty.

Alternative C   Alternative C removes the restrictions from Alternative B. Under Alternative C, the warranty runs even to corporate plaintiffs, and applies even to property damages as long as it is reasonably foreseeable that the plaintiff might be injured by the product.

UCC § 2–318. Alternative C

A seller's warranty extends to any person who may reasonably be expected to use, consume or be affected by the goods and who is injured by breach of the warranty.

Warranty as a Basis for Products Liability

As is discussed in the next chapter, warranty is one of the three bases on which products liability claims may be predicated. The following article considers whether products liability insurers that become aware of deadly products have either a moral or a legal obligation to inform consumers of such dangers. As products liability claims gain attention from the business community, such questions will become more common.

*The Dangers Insurance Companies Hide (Insurers don't have to tell you when they know you're about to be killed)**

Imagine a manufacturer who discovers that one of his products has a defect that is causing grave injuries to unsuspecting consumers. If he promptly warns them, halts production, and recalls the products, he will be obeying a moral obligation deeply rooted in our religious and ethical heritage. The obligation is expressed this way in Leviticus 19:16: ''Neither shalt thou stand idly by the blood of thy neighbor.''

■ ■ ■

In a final scenario, our manufacturer neither warns of the defect nor recalls the product. Figuratively, he lays a nearly invisible trip wire and flees. Watching him do it from the window, and then sitting in silence as consumers are ambushed, is the manufacturer's product-liability insurer. He is above it all. He sounds no warning. . . . He claims that his conduct is morally right—even though . . . he is not a ''stranger'' to [the consumer] since the insurer profits from the consumer, and even though . . . he in essence enabled [the manufacturer] to lay the trip wire by underwriting the effort. His conduct, he points out, is required by the courts. They have ruled that an insurer has no affirmative duty to warn the

---

*Source: Morton Mintz, ''The Dangers Insurance Companies Hide,'' *The Washington Monthly,* January/February 1991. Reprinted with permission.

public or to facilitate a recall of a product it insures. "Indeed, under the laws of, I think, every state," Craig A. Berrington, general counsel of the American Insurance Association, told me, "the insurer has an absolute obligation to provide a defense for that policyholder against claims that arise, and the insurer can be sued when policyholders believe that insurers are not vigorous enough in providing that defense."

Lie-Ability Insurance

"My primary concern," Berrington said, is that no standard be established under which "insurers essentially become police officers or reporting officials — an arm of the government . . . or that insurers do the work of government and be blamed when government fails in its responsibility to make judgments as to what products ought not to be on the market. . . . A legal duty to disclose with regard to a product that the insurance company has covered would be contrary to the insurer's statutory and contractual obligations today and place the insurer in a terrible bind."

Berrington has a point about the role of government, but through him the insurance industry makes an argument for preserving the confidentiality of a commercial relationship no matter the cost in human life. It's an argument that government, which has no higher mission than public safety, must not compel insurers to divulge information that would protect us from massive, continuing disease, injury, and death. It's an argument that would surely astound most Americans were they aware of it; but through a quiet accretion of court rulings, and without congressional debate, this privileged position asserted by product-liability insurers has evolved into national policy. It's an argument that in essence is an excuse for the insurance industry to stand by the blood of its neighbors.

Meanwhile, the neighbors in the marketplace and the workplace have been shedding lots of blood. Consider the dreadful catastrophes caused by only two products: the Dalkon Shield, the defective intrauterine contraceptive device (IUD), and asbestos, the deadly mineral.

New Year's Eve Irresolution

The Dalkon Shield was sold in the United States from January 1971 to June 1974, when the manufacturer, pressed by a worried Food and Drug Administration (FDA), ended domestic sales (but continued foreign sales until at least April 1975). During those three and one-half years, physicians implanted an estimated 2.2 million of the devices in the United States and 800,000 in some 100 other countries. For at least a decade after the sales halt, according to recently available court documents, the liability insurer joined the manufacturer in suppressing knowledge of the IUD's hazardous defects. The foreseeable and preventable result was that tens if not hundreds of thousands of women suffered life-threatening pelvic infections. . . . In addition, hundreds of children were born with injuries inflicted by the Dalkon Shield while it was their companion in the womb, causing blindness, cerebral palsy, and mental retardation. Eighteen deaths have been reported, but the toll is certainly much higher, if only because in the Third World countries no one was counting.

The insurer was Aetna Casualty & Surety Company. . . . In its corporate publications, Aetna acclaims itself a "good corporate citizen." Notably, it was an ACS senior claims adjuster who, on New Year's Eve of 1981, writing in the margin of a complaint filed by a Dalkon Shield victim, raised the rarely asked question: "What is the duty of an insurer to the public when it has knowledge of serious product defects which are likely to cause injury?"

■ ■ ■

[At this point the author outlines the asbestos disaster.]

Why did insurers conceal their knowledge and continue to provide coverage? Disclosure, Brodeur[1] explained, would "have encouraged claims and damage suits, and run counter to basic insurance-company practice, which is to write as much coverage as possible, and as cheaply as possible, in order to reap a rich harvest of premiums that, when invested, will return enough money to pay for future claims and make a profit for the company. . . .

■ ■ ■

Fortunately, some first break the mold. In 1970, for example, Charles K. Cox, president of the Insurance Company of North America (INA), said that INA "will no longer insure the company that knowingly dumps its wastes." . . . However admirable, such exceptions provide no clue as to how many deaths and injuries insurers could have prevented through the years, or could prevent from now on, by dedicating themselves to loss prevention and by disclosing their knowledge of dangerous defects in products and needless workplace hazards. Brodeur found that insurers could have saved the lives of tens of thousands who fell victim to only one product, asbestos. So it's a fair question: What did the insurer's know and when did they know it about hazardous defects identified after marketing in, say, automobiles? Aircraft? Athletic gear? Building materials? Butane lighters? Drugs and vaccines? Food additives? Playground equipment and toys? Toxic chemicals? No one asks the insurers to reveal everything they know. And they shouldn't, says National Insurance Consumer Organization's president Robert Hunter. "But in the case of a product that kills they have a duty to warn."

Thought Questions

1. Why do insurance companies fail to warn consumers?
2. Evaluate the following statement: "In the case of a product that kills, insurance companies have a duty to warn consumers."
3. Compare the duty of the manufacturer to warn consumers to the duty of the insurance company.
4. Are insurance companies acting ethically in concealing these dangers? How would a utilitarian thinker answer this question? A Kantian philosopher?

---

[1] Brodeur is the author of a book detailing the asbestos controversy entitled *Outrageous Misconduct*.

REMEDIES OF SELLER AND BUYER

The availability of remedies for breach of contract is what separates a contract from a mere promise; a contract is a legally enforceable promise. A promise is legally enforced by awarding damages. The remedies available under the Code for breach of the sales contract are contract damages, with the characteristics discussed in Chapter 18. For example, they are generally designed so that "the aggrieved party may be put in as good a position as if the other party had fully performed" the contract [UCC § 1–106(1)]. Second, punitive damages are not available for breach of the sales contract. Third, consequential damages are recoverable only, under the rule of *Hadley v. Baxendale*,[2] where they were reasonably anticipated at the time of contract formation as a likely result of the breach.

---

[2] 9 Exch. 341, 156 Eng. Rep. 145 (1854).

The UCC classifies the remedies depending on whether the aggrieved party is the seller or the buyer.

Seller's Remedies

Seller's Remedies on Buyer's Insolvency

Various remedies are provided to protect a seller in the case of buyer insolvency. In these cases, the buyer has not always breached the contract. These remedies are generally triggered solely by the buyer's insolvency. Buyers are **insolvent** either when unable to pay their debts when they become due or when their liabilities exceed their assets [UCC § 1–201(23)]. The Code will not force the seller to deliver the goods without protection where there is reason to believe that the buyer will not be able to pay because of insolvency. The seller may either (1) demand cash and withhold the goods, (2) stop delivery of the goods, or (3) reclaim the goods.

Demand Cash Payment and Withhold Delivery of the Goods When the seller discovers that the buyer is insolvent, the seller can demand a cash payment for the goods and can refuse to deliver the goods unless the buyer pays in cash [UCC § 2–702(1)]. For example, assume that HardYard, Inc. promises to ship 100 rakes to Ben's Landscaping Co. on credit, payment to be made within 60 days. If HardYard discovers that Ben is insolvent, it may refuse to deliver the rakes on credit in spite of its previous promise and can instead demand a cash payment.

In addition, the seller can refuse to deliver an installment promised where the buyer has wrongfully rejected, revoked acceptance, or failed to pay for a previous installment even without a showing of buyer insolvency. [UCC § 2–703(1)]. For example, assume that Stefan's Office Supply, Inc. has contracted with Ben's Printing Co. to deliver 10 cartridges per month for Ben's printers, shipment to be on the first of the month, payment on the 15th. If Stefan ships the 10 cartridges as promised in September but is not paid on the 15th, it can withhold delivery of October's shipment.

UCC § 2–702. Seller's Remedies on Discovery of Buyer's Insolvency

(1) Where the seller discovers the buyer to be insolvent he may refuse delivery except for cash, and stop delivery.

Stop Delivery of Goods When the seller discovers the buyer's insolvency after the goods are delivered to the carrier but before the goods are delivered to the buyer, the seller can stop delivery of the goods [UCC § 2–705(1)]. If the seller had learned of the buyer's insolvency before shipment, it could have refused shipment. If it learns of the insolvency after shipment, it can stop delivery.

UCC § 2–705. Seller's Stoppage of Delivery in Transit or Otherwise

(1) The seller may stop delivery of goods in the possession of a carrier when he discovers the buyer to be insolvent and may stop delivery of carload, truckload, planeload or larger shipments when the buyer repudiates or fails to make a payment due before delivery or if for any other reason the seller has a right to withhold or reclaim the goods.

In addition, the seller can stop delivery of large shipments (carloads, truckloads) where the buyer repudiated or failed to make payments due before shipment. In this case, the right to stop delivery exists whether or not the buyer is insolvent but only applies to large shipments.

In order to stop delivery, the seller must notify the carrier in a timely manner. The carrier must follow the instructions of the seller. The seller is required to reimburse the carrier for any expenses incurred in stopping delivery. The seller may stop delivery until the goods are delivered to the buyer [UCC § 2–705(2)].

Reclaim the Goods on Buyer's Insolvency When the seller discovers that the buyer is insolvent after the buyer has received the goods, the seller may reclaim the goods [UCC 2–702(2)]. However, the right to reclaim the goods is subject to a 10-day limitation. The seller can only reclaim goods in the buyer's possession if a demand is made within 10 days of their receipt. For example, assume that Snacks, Inc. promises to deliver 100 boxes of potato chips to Mom & Pop, Inc. on credit. The potato chips are delivered as promised on January 10. If, on the 19th, Snacks discovers that Mom & Pop was insolvent when the chips were delivered and demands return, it could successfully reclaim the chips. The demand for reclamation was made within 10 days of delivery of the chips. By contrast, Snacks could not recover the chips if the demand was made on the 21st. The 10-day period has expired. After 10 days, Snacks could reclaim the goods only if Mom & Pop misrepresented its financial soundness in writing within the last three months. Only then is the 10-day limit inapplicable.

UCC § 2–705. Seller's Stoppage of Delivery in Transit or Otherwise

(2) As against such buyer the seller may stop delivery until

(a) receipt of the goods by the buyer; or

(b) acknowledgment to the buyer by any bailee of the goods; or

(d) negotiation to the buyer or any negotiable document of title covering the goods.

UCC § 2–702. Seller's Remedies on Discovery of Buyer's Insolvency

(2) Where the seller discovers that the buyer received goods on credit while insolvent he may reclaim the goods upon demand made within ten days after the receipt, but if misrepresentation of solvency has been made to the particular seller in writing within three months before delivery the ten day limitation does not apply.

If the seller reclaims the goods, other existing remedies are waived. This means that a seller cannot reclaim the goods and then sue the buyer for breach of contract because the buyer is not paying the agreed-on contract price for the goods.

Seller's Remedies in General

Where the buyer breaches the contract, the seller has a choice of available remedies determined by a variety of factors, such as who has possession of the goods and whether there is a ready market for resale [UCC § 2–703]. The remedies available are summarized in Figure 22–4.

Identify Goods to the Contract Notwithstanding Breach In order for the seller to successfully sue for damages, the goods must first be identified to the contract. Where the buyer has anticipatorily breached the contract before identification, the seller may identify conforming finished goods to the contract [UCC § 2–704(1)].

Figure 22–4   Seller's Remedies in General

- Withhold delivery of the goods.
- Stop delivery.
- Identify goods to the contract.
- Resell and recover damages.
- Recover damages for nonacceptance.
- Recover the price.
- Cancel.

UCC § 2–703.

Furthermore, where the goods are not yet finished, the seller is given a choice. The seller, exercising reasonable commercial judgment, can either (1) finish unfinished goods and identify them to the contract, (2) cease manufacture of the goods and resell the unfinished goods for scrap or salvage, or (3) act in any other reasonable manner [UCC § 2–704(2)]. For example, assume that the Sidney Shirt Co. has promised to manufacture and deliver 200 shirts to the Baltimore Boutique. Before Sidney can complete manufacture of the shirts, Baltimore calls and cancels the order. Sidney can choose to either complete manufacture and resell or to sell the unfinished shirts as scrap. In this instance, Sidney could choose to finish the shirts, because in the exercise of good commercial judgment it appears that completing manufacture would increase their value and thus decrease the buyer's damages. By contrast, if the shirts were embroidered with the Baltimore Boutique crab emblem, they would be unsuitable for sale through regular retail outlets and the additional costs to finish them would not be justified.

UCC § 2–704. Seller's Right to Identify Goods to the Contract Notwithstanding Breach

(2) Where the goods are unfinished an aggrieved seller may in the exercise of reasonable commercial judgment for the purposes of avoiding loss either complete the manufacture and wholly identify the goods to the contract or cease manufacture and resell for scrap or salvage value or proceed in any other reasonable manner.

Resell the Goods When the buyer breaches the contract, the seller may resell the goods. If the resale is in good faith and in a commercially reasonable man-

Figure 22–5   Computation of Resale Damages

Contract price	($3.49 × 100)	$349
Resale price	($3.00 × 100)	300
Damages recoverable		$ 49*

*Plus incidental damages but minus expenses saved.

ner, the seller recovers the difference between the contract price and the price of resale (plus incidental damages minus expenses saved) [UCC § 2–706]. For example, assume that Gourmet Foods, Inc. contracts to sell 100 pounds of Brie Cheese to Rory's Roadside Saloon for $3.49 per pound. Rory changes his mind and before delivery calls Gourmet and cancels his order. As is illustrated in Figure 22–5, if Gourmet resells the cheese for $3.00 per pound, it can successfully sue Rory for $.49 per pound. Gourmet can recover this amount even if the fair market value of the cheese is $3.30 per pound as long as the sale was made in good faith and in a **commercially reasonable manner.**

UCC § 2–706. Seller's Resale

(1) The seller may resell the goods concerned. Where the resale is made in good faith and in a commercially reasonable manner the seller may recover the difference between the resale price and the contract price together with any incidental damages, but less expenses saved in consequence of the buyer's breach.

The sale can either be public or private, as a unit or in parcels. The main requirement is that it be ''commercially reasonable.'' Everything about the sale, including time, place, method, manner, and terms must be commercially reasonable. The court in the following case tries to determine what is meant by the term *commercially reasonable*.

APEX OIL CO. v. THE BELCHER COMPANY OF NEW YORK, INC.
855 F.2d 997 (2d Cir. 1988)

Apex entered into a contract to sell home heating oil to Belcher Co. at a price of 89.70 cents per gallon to be unloaded from the *Bordeaux*. After 141,535 barrels had been pumped into Belcher's terminal, Belcher refused to accept the remaining 48,000 barrels because its sulphur content did not conform to the contract specifications.

Because Apex had promised to deliver heating oil to Cities Services later in the month, it obtained Cities' permission to deliver the oil early. The oil was delivered on February 12, one day after it was rejected by Belcher.

Ultimately, Belcher agreed to pay for the oil accepted but refused to accept the additional 48,000 barrels at the contract price. Apex sold 48,000 barrels to Gill & Duffus Co. in April at a price of 76.25 cents (13.45 cents below the contract price) and sued for the difference between the contract price and the Gill & Duffus resale. Belcher argued that the oil identified to the contract was the oil that Apex sold to Cities Service the day after the breach, not the oil sold in March to Gill & Duffus. Apex argued that because oil is fungible, the oil sold to Gill & Duffus was identified to the contract. The District Court awarded damages to the plaintiff-seller. Belcher appealed.

WINTER, Circuit Judge

The Uniform Commercial Code provides various remedies to sellers for default by buyers. A seller may, as Apex seeks to do, fix its damages by reselling the goods and recovering from the buyer the difference between the resale price and the contract price.

Resolving the instant dispute requires us to survey various provisions of the Uniform Commercial Code. The first such provision is Section 2–501, which defines ''identification.'' Section 2–501 informs us that the *Bordeaux* oil was identified to the contract. It does not end our inquiry, however, because it does not exclude the possibility that a seller may identify goods to a contract, but then substitute, for the identified goods, identical goods that are then identified to the contract.

We agree that fungible goods resold pursuant to Section 2–706 must be goods identified to the contract, but need not always be those originally identified to the contract. In other words, at least where fungible goods are concerned, identification is not always an irrevocable act and does not foreclose the possibility of substitution. It would make no sense to hold that such replacement (that is, reidentification) can never occur after breach. For example, it serves no purpose of the Code to force an aggrieved seller to segregate goods originally identified to the contract when doing so is more costly than mixing them with other identical goods. To give a concrete example, suppose that Apex had been unable to find someone to take the *Bordeaux* oil immediately after the oil was rejected by Belcher and that the only storage tank available to Apex was already half-full of No. 2 heating oil. To mix the *Bordeaux* oil with the oil in the only available tank and to identify the first 48,000 gallons sold to the contract is the only sensible thing to do. Doing so, of course, bases the damage award on resales of different oil from that previously identified to the contract. Under a rule that prevents reidentification of goods to a contract, Apex would be forced in the hypothetical to choose between its resale remedy and a costly diversion of the *Bordeaux*.

Thus, Section 2–706 should not be construed as always proscribing the resale of goods other than those originally identified to the broken contract. Nevertheless, as that Section expressly states, "[t]he resale must be reasonably identified as referring to the broken contract," and "every aspect of the sale including the method, manner, time, place and terms must be *commercially reasonable*." § 2–706(2). [Emphasis added.] Moreover, because the purpose of remedies under the Code is to put "the aggrieved party . . . in as good a position as if the other party had fully performed," the reasonableness of the identification and of the resale must be determined by examining whether the market value of, and the price received for, the resold goods "accurately reflects the market value of the goods which are the subject of the contract."

Perhaps the most obvious example of an unreasonable identification and resale would occur when the resold goods and the originally identified goods are not fungible. Another example of an unreasonable identification and resale would be to claim as a

resale the sale of goods located where they would have a significantly lower value than the originally identified goods. For example, had Apex purported to identify and resell 48,000 barrels of No. 2 oil in a storage tank in the Virgin Islands, where heating oil is presumably less useful and valuable than in Boston, while simultaneously delivering the same amount to Cities Service in Boston, the identification and resale would be unreasonable.

The most pertinent aspect of reasonableness with regard to identification and resale involves timing. Here, Apex's delay of nearly six weeks between the breach on February 11, 1982 and the purported resale on March 23 was clearly unreasonable, even if the transfer to Cities Service had not occurred. Steven Wirkus, of Apex testified that the market price for No. 2 heating oil on February 12, when the *Bordeaux* oil was delivered to Cities Service, was "[p]robably somewhere around 88 cents a gallon or 87." (The contract price, of course, was 89.70 cents per gallon.) Wirkus also testified that the market price fluctuated throughout the next several weeks. The Gill & Duffus resale, which was for April delivery, fetched a price of 76.25 cents per gallon—some 11 or 12 cents below the market price on the day of the breach.

In view of the long delay and the apparent volatility of the market for No. 2 oil, the purported resale failed to meet the requirements of Section 2–706 as a matter of law. The delay unquestionably prevented the resale from "accurately reflect[ing] the market value of the goods."

The rule that a "resale should be made as soon as practicable after . . . breach," should be stringently applied where, as here, the resold goods are not those originally identified to the contract. In such circumstances, of course, there is a significant risk that the seller, who may perhaps have already disposed of the original goods without suffering any loss, has identified new goods for resale in order to minimize the resale and maximize damages. Because the sale of the oil identified to the contract to Cities Service on the next day fixed the value of the goods refused as a matter of law, the judgment on the breach-of-contract claim must be reversed.

Case Questions

1. How much should Apex recover in damages?
2. Was the resale commercially reasonable? What factors did the court consider in making this decision?

3. What other products have the same fungible characteristics that make identification inexact?

4. Suppose the seller's market was limited and resale forced the seller to forgo a second sale of the same commodity. Is the general measure of damages (contract price minus resale) adequate even though the seller will be denied the profit on both sales?

If the resale is by a private sale, the seller must give reasonable notice to the buyer of intent to resell the goods [UCC § 2–706(3)]. Where the resale is by a public sale, the seller must, similarly, give the buyer reasonable notice unless the goods are perishable or likely to decline in value quickly [UCC § 2–706(4)(b)]. For example, assume that Grocers Supply, Inc. contracts to deliver 100 cans of peas to the Green Giant Grocery Store. If Green Giant refuses to accept the peas, Grocers Supply, Inc. must notify Green Giant that the goods will be resold. The seller may buy at a public sale but not at a private one [UCC § 2–706(4)(d)]. If the price at resale is more than the contract price, the seller may keep the excess and does not have to turn it over to the buyer [UCC § 2–706(6)].

Recover the Price   When the seller sues to recover the contract price, to have the buyer pay as promised in the contract, specific performance is being sought. As was explained in Chapter 18, specific performance as an equitable remedy is available at common law only in limited circumstances. Similarly, the seller is only entitled to recover the price in three situations: (1) where the buyer has accepted the goods, (2) where the goods have been destroyed and the buyer has the risk of loss, and (3) where the seller is unable to resell goods identified to the contract that are reasonably priced [UCC § 2–709(1)]. If the seller elects to sue for price, the goods must be held for the buyer [UCC § 2–708(2)].

Damages for Nonacceptance or Repudiation   When the buyer has either refused to accept the goods or has anticipatorily breached the contract, the goods are in the hands of the seller. If the seller then elects not to resell the goods, damages for nonacceptance or **repudiation** are recoverable. The seller can recover the difference between the contract price and the market price at the time and place of tender (plus incidental damages, minus expenses saved) [UCC § 2–708(1)]. For example, assume that Gourmet Foods, Inc. contracts to sell 100 pounds of Brie Cheese to Rory's Roadside Saloon for $3.49 per pound. Rory changes his mind and before delivery calls Gourmet and cancels his order. As is illustrated in Figure 22–6, if the fair market value of the cheese is $3.30 per pound, Gourmet can recover $.19 per pound.

UCC § 2–708. Seller's Damages for Non-Acceptance or Repudiation

(1) . . . the measure of damages for non-acceptance or repudiation by the buyer is the difference between the market price at the time and place for tender and the unpaid contract price together with any incidental damages, but less expenses saved in consequence of the buyer's breach.

Ordinarily, these damages will put the plaintiff in the position that he or she would have been in had the contract been performed as promised. In the example, if Rory performed the contract as promised, Gourmet would have sold the cheese and had $349. Using the above formula for recovery, Gourmet has the cheese worth $330 and receives damages of $19. Thus, Gourmet, is adequately compensated.

However, sometimes the damages outlined above are inadequate to put the plaintiff in the position that he or she would have been in had the contract been performed as promised. Then, the seller may sue for the profit that he or she would have made under the broken contract [UCC § 2–708(2)]. Recovery of lost profits is frequently permitted when the goods are standard-priced goods. In such a case, profit is determined by the difference between list price and

Figure 22–6   Nonacceptance

Contract price ($3.49 × 100)	$349
Fair market value ($3.30 × 100)	330
	———
Damages recoverable	$ 19*

*Plus incidental damages but minus expenses saved.

manufacturing cost to the manufacturer [UCC § 2–708 Comment 2]. Similarly, lost profits are recoverable where the seller is a volume seller. In such cases, general damages are inadequate to compensate the seller. For example, assume that Dan Dealer promises to sell to Ernie a new 1994 Ford Truck for $20,000. Dan has 10 similar trucks on the lot and can get more from the manufacturer within a day. Ernie breaches the contract and refuses to take delivery. On that same day, Dan resells the truck to Burt for $20,000. Using the standard measure of damages, Dan would recover no damages since the resale price is the same as the contract price. It appears that Dan has suffered no loss. However, if Ernie had not breached the contract, Dan would have sold two trucks, one to Ernie and one to Burt. Because Dan makes $1,000 profit on each truck sold, and he lost one sale, he has lost $1,000. He could recover this lost profit because general contract damages would not adequately compensate him.

UCC § 2–708. Seller's Damages for Non-Acceptance or Repudiation

(2) If the measure of damages provided in subsection (1) is inadequate to put the seller in as good a position as performance would have done then the measure of damages is the profit (including reasonable overhead) which the seller would have made from full performance by the buyer.

In the following case, determine whether or not the general measure of damages would be sufficient to put the plaintiff in the position that it would have been in had there been no breach.

VAN NESS MOTORS, INC. v. VIKRAM
221 N.J. Super. 543, 535 A.2d 510 (1987)

Van Ness Motors, Inc., an automobile dealer, entered into a contract for the sale of a new 1987 Dodge pickup truck with defendant Vikram. Vikram gave a $100 deposit but refused to accept delivery. Van Ness sold the truck to another purchaser for approximately the same price and sued to recover damages. The lower court dismissed the suit because Van Ness had suffered no damages. Van Ness appealed.

LANDAU, Judge

We disagree with the trial judge's conclusion respecting the lost profit damages. This case is governed by § 2–708 of the Uniform Commercial Code. As explained in the New Jersey Study Comment, § 2–708(2) was designed to provide to a dealer-seller of standardized goods in unlimited supply the additional relief of recognizing that ''had the breaching buyer performed, the dealer would have made two sales instead of one.'' As stated in *Snyder v. Herbert Greenbaum & Assoc., Inc.*:

The whole concept of lost volume status is that the sale of the goods to the resale purchaser could have been made with other goods had there been no breach. In essence, the original sale and the second sale are independent events, becoming related only after breach, as the original sale goods are applied to the second sale. To require a credit for the proceeds of resale is to deny the essential element that entitles the lost volume seller to § 2–708(2) in the first place—the mutual independence of the contract and the resale.

In *Snyder,* it was also held that the seller must sustain the burden of establishing that he is in fact a lost volume seller, and if he fails to do so he will be deemed an ordinary seller who must give credit for the proceeds of a resale in determining lost profit damages for the breach. Recently, in *Islamic Republic of Iran v. Boeing Co.*, the 9th Circuit Court of Appeals recognized that

Most other jurisdictions have held that to qualify as a 'lost volume' seller under Section 2–708(2), the seller needs to show only that it could have supplied both the breaching purchaser and the resale purchaser.

We are in agreement with the comments of the New Jersey commission, and the rationale of the cited authorities, and conclude that it was reversible error to reject the effort by Van Ness Motors, Inc. to establish its lost profit merely because it was able to resell the truck under contract for substantially the same price.

Inasmuch as the trial judge's early ruling in this case had the effect of obviating the necessity for Vikram to present a defense, he should be afforded the opportunity to challenge the existence of the contract, its breach, or the method of computation of lost profits. Similarly, plaintiff should be allowed to demonstrate that it was a "lost volume" seller in these circumstances.

Case Questions

1. If the seller is a lost volume seller, how are the general damages inadequate compensation?

2. How will the lost profits be determined?

3. Given the opportunity cost argument of this case, is the price less resale ever a sufficient remedy? Should the court consider the dealer's additional inventory financing costs incurred because only one truck was sold?

Buyer's Remedies

Buyer's Right to Goods on Seller's Insolvency

When the seller becomes insolvent, the buyer risks injury only where payment has been made and delivery is not yet received. The Code offers limited protection in such a case.

When the buyer has paid some of the purchase price for goods not yet delivered and the seller becomes insolvent, the buyer may claim the goods under narrow circumstances [UCC § 2–502]. The buyer may receive the goods if all of the following have been met:

*   The buyer makes a tender of any unpaid portion of the purchase price.

*   The goods are identified to the contract.

*   The seller becomes insolvent within 10 days after receipt of the first installment of the price.

Buyer's Remedies in General

When the seller breaches the contract, the buyer has a choice of remedies [UCC § 2–711]. These are outlined in Figure 22–7. Much as in the instance of

Figure 22–7   Buyer's Remedies in General

*   Cover.
*   Recover damages for nondelivery.
*   Recover damages for accepted goods.
*   Specific performance.
*   Cancel.
*   To enforce a security interest.

UCC § 2–711.

seller's breach, the remedy chosen is determined by a variety of factors—for example, who has possession of the goods.

Cover   When the seller breaches the promise to deliver goods, the buyer may choose to **cover**—to buy comparable goods from someone else. If the cover is made in good faith and without unreasonable delay, the buyer recovers the difference between the contract price and the cost of cover (plus incidental damages minus expenses saved) [UCC 2–712(1)].

UCC § 2–712. "Cover"; Buyer's Procurement of Substitute Goods

(1) After a breach the buyer may "cover" by making in good faith and without unreasonable delay any reasonable purchase of or contract to purchase goods in substitution for those due from the seller.

If cover is made in good faith, the buyer recovers damages even if the cost of cover is greater than fair market value. For example, assume that Gourmet Foods, Inc. contracts to sell 100 pounds of Brie Cheese to Rory's Roadside Saloon for $3.49 per pound. Assume further that Gourmet changes its mind when the fair market value of the cheese rises to $5.00 per pound and cancels the order before delivery. As is illustrated in Figure 22–8, if Rory purchases comparable cheese in good faith and within a reasonable time of the breach for $5.49 per pound, Rory recovers $2.00 per pound.

Damages for Nondelivery or Repudiation   The buyer can choose instead to recover damages for nondelivery or repudiation [UCC § 2–713(1)]. The

Figure 22-8   Cover

Cost of cover ($5.49 × 100)	$549
Contract price ($3.49 × 100)	$349
	———
Damages recoverable	$200*

* Plus incidental damages but minus expenses saved.

Figure 22-9   Nondelivery

Fair market value ($5.00 × 100)	$500
Contract price ($3.49 × 100)	$349
	———
Damages recoverable	$151*

Plus incidental damages but minus expenses saved.

damages recoverable are the difference between contract price and market price at the time the buyer learned of the breach (plus incidental damages minus expenses saved) [UCC § 2-713(1). The market price is the price at the place where the seller promised to deliver the goods. For example, assume again that Gourmet fails to deliver the Brie cheese as promised. As is shown in Figure 22-9, if the contract price was $3.49 per pound and the fair market value on the date delivery was promised was $5.00, Rory can recover $1.51 per pound.

UCC § 2-713. Buyer's Damages for Non-Delivery or Repudiation

(1) . . . the measure of damages for non-delivery or repudiation by the seller is the difference between the market price at the time when the buyer learned of the price and the contract price together with an incidental and consequential damages, but less expenses saved.

For Breach in Regard to Accepted Goods   When the buyer accepts nonconforming goods and gives notice of their nonconformity, the buyer recovers for that nonconformity. The loss recoverable is determined in any way that is reasonable [UCC § 2-714(1)].

In the typical breach of warranty situation, the buyer recovers the difference between what the goods were worth as delivered and what they would have been worth if they were as promised [UCC § 2-714(2)]. For example, assume that Lemon Car Dealer, Inc. promised to deliver a 1990 Miata for a

Figure 22-10   Breach of Warranty

Miata would have been worth	$15,000
Miata was worth as delivered	8,000
	———
Contract damages	$ 7,000

contract price of $12,000. The car delivered had a defective transmission that rendered the car worth $8,000. At the time of delivery, the Miata would have been worth $15,000 because Miatas were virtually unobtainable. As is shown in Figure 22-10, the buyer can recover $7,000.

UCC § 2-714. Buyer's Damages for Breach in Regard to Accepted Goods

(2) The measure of damages for breach of warranty is the difference at the time and place of acceptance between the value of the goods accepted and the value they would have had if they had been as warranted, unless special circumstances show proximate damages of a different amount.

Specific Performance   The buyer may seek equitable relief where money damages would be inadequate compensation, such as where the goods promised were unique [UCC § 2-716(1)]. For example, assume that Jamie contracts to sell an antique quilt to Joy for $4,000. If Jamie refuses to deliver the quilt, money damages would not compensate Joy because she could not purchase a comparable quilt elsewhere. In such circumstances, Joy could obtain **specific performance.** In other words, she could require that Jamie deliver the quilt to her as promised for $4,000.

The buyer is also entitled to the goods where the buyer is unable, after reasonable attempts, to obtain comparable goods elsewhere [UCC § 2-716(3)]. The Code calls this **replevin.**

The Right to Enforce a Security Interest   When the buyer rejects nonconforming goods or revokes its acceptance, the buyer is given a security interest in those goods in the buyer's possession for the amount of payments made, and any expenses incurred in the inspection, receipt, care, or custody of the goods [UCC § 2-711(3)]. For example, assume that Joe's Bar & Grill orders 100 boxes of crab-flavored potato chips for a total contract price of $1,000. Joe pays the seller $500 when placing the order. Unfortunately, although the chips delivered are in cases marked ''crab-flavored,'' when the cases are opened the bags are found to be regular chips. In such a case, Joe can rightfully revoke his acceptance (the deformity was latent, and the defect substantial). If the seller refuses to take the chips back, Joe is entitled to sell them much as an aggrieved seller could (as discussed above) and use the amount of the resale to cover his payments and expenses. Any excess belongs to the seller.

Remedies Available to Both Buyers and Sellers

The Code specifies some types of damages that might be appropriate to both buyers and sellers.

Cancel

Both buyers and sellers may, in appropriate circumstances, cancel the contract. A decision to cancel the contract does not prevent that party from seeking damages in addition to cancellation [UCC § 2–710].

Incidental Damages

Incidental damages are available in addition to the standard measure of damages described above. Incidental damages are damages that are ''incidental'' to the breach but that occur because of the breach. The seller's incidental damages might include expenses incurred in stopping delivery, in transporting or caring for the goods after the buyer's breach, or other expenses in connection with the return or resale of the goods after the buyer's breach [UCC § 2–710]. The buyer's incidental damages might include expenses such as expenses incurred in inspecting the goods, transportation or care for goods rejected, and expenses in connection with cover [UCC § 2–715(1)].

Limitation on Remedies

The remedies available might be limited. In this section, a number of such limitations are discussed.

Statute of Limitations

In order to recover damages, the party seeking damages (the plaintiff or the aggrieved party) must bring suit within four years from breach of the contract [UCC § 2–725(1)]. The parties may agree to a

shorter period, but the period set may not be less than one year [UCC § 2–725(1)]. Ordinarily, breach of warranty occurs, and the four-year time period begins to run, when tender of delivery is made. However, when the warranty expressly covers future performance, the time period begins to run when the breach is or should have been discovered [UCC § 2–725(2)]. For example, assume that Hanna Homeowner purchases a new furnace. The furnace is delivered on June 18th but is not first used to heat the house until fall. The statute of limitations does not begin to run until the fall.

Liquidated Damages

The parties may agree in the contract on what damages would be recoverable in the event of breach. Such damages are termed **liquidated damages.** Under the Code, as at common law, liquidated damages are recoverable if reasonable and not penal in nature [UCC § 2–718(1)]. Thus, the amount specified in the contract will be awarded if reasonably related to the damages anticipated. Where the amount fixed is unreasonably large, it will be unenforceable as a penalty. For example, assume that Tom promised to sell timber to Ben Builder so that Ben could complete a restaurant in time for the holiday season. Tom agreed to deliver the timber by July 1 for a contract price of $200,000. The parties agreed that for each day the delivery was late, Tom would incur $50,000 in liquidated damages. Tom was three days late in delivery. The liquidated damages clause in this contract is unlikely to be enforced. The $50,000 figure is unreasonably high compared to the total contract price and is unlikely to be reasonably related to the damages anticipated from a day's delay.

UCC § 2–718. Liquidation or Limitation of Damages

(1) Damages for breach by either party may be liquidated in the agreement but only at an amount which is reasonable in the light of the anticipated or actual harm caused by the breach, the difficulties of proof of loss, and the inconvenience or nonfeasibility . . . of obtaining an adequate remedy.

Limitation of Damages

The parties may agree to limit or modify the damages available on breach. Such agreements are enforceable subject to the test of unconscionability [UCC § 2–719(1)]. For example, clauses attempting to limit the availability of consequential damages for personal injuries are unconscionable and unenforceable when applied to consumers [UCC § 2–719(3)].

THE INTERNATIONAL CONTRACT

The Convention on Contracts for the International Sales of Goods (CISG) provides for different treatment in the instance of international sales contracts.

Warranties

CISG does not use the warranty terminology. Instead, CISG imposes obligations on the seller of goods. These obligations, to a large extent, mirror the UCC warranty provisions.

Warranty of Title

Under CISG, the seller must deliver goods free from encumbrances on title and free from claims of third parties [Article 41]. Thus, the CISG obligation includes not only good title but also "quiet possession" (freedom from adverse claims). The parties are permitted to agree otherwise.

Warranty of Merchantability

The seller must deliver goods fit for the ordinary use for which such goods are intended and properly packaged [Article 35 (2)(a) and (d)]. Recall that CISG applies only to commercial contracts. Therefore, there is no need to restrict this promise to merchant-sellers as in the UCC's warranty of merchantability.

Warranty of Fitness for a Particular Purpose

The seller in an international contract must deliver goods fit for any particular purpose known to the seller [Article 35(2)(b)]. In particular, before this obligation is created (1) the buyer must rely on the seller's skill and judgment, and (2) that reliance must be reasonable. No obligation arises where the buyer was aware of the defect at the time of contract formation.

Disclaimers

The general concept of warranty disclaimer was incorporated into CISG with a recognition that the parties can exclude these obligations [Article 35(2)]. However, it is unclear how the vast differences in local law treatment of disclaimers will affect international contracts. For example, there is a spectrum from general prohibition of printed disclaimers (Germany) to general acceptance (United States). It is clear that the standard disclaimer language common in the United States must be modified to be used in international contracts.

Remedies

The CISG drafters faced perhaps the greatest challenge in the remedies sections. Most importantly, CISG had to in some way accommodate the civil law preference for specific performance over money damages with the common law preference for money damages.

Buyer's Remedies

CISG specifies four available remedies to the aggrieved buyer where the seller has breached the contract: (1) specific performance, (2) avoidance, (3) self-help, and (4) damages.

Specific Performance   Where the seller fails to deliver the goods, the buyer can demand specific performance if the buyer has not obtained an "inconsistent" remedy (such as avoidance) and as long as the action is not brought in a common law court [Article 46]. The buyer who has accepted nonconforming goods is entitled to specific performance of conforming goods only where the nonconformity is a **fundamental breach.** As discussed in Chapter 21, a fundamental breach occurs when the nonconformity would "substantially deprive" the buyer of "what he is entitled to expect under the contract" [Article 25]. This is similar to the "substantial impairment" concept of the UCC. The buyer is entitled to repair of nonconforming goods only where such repair is reasonable.

Avoidance   The buyer can avoid the contract only where there is a fundamental breach. The concept of avoidance under CISG is similar to UCC cancellation.

Self-Help   Where the buyer has accepted nonconforming goods, the buyer may reduce the price it pays the seller by an amount equal to the value of the nonconformity [Article 50]. For example, assume that William White promises to deliver to Irma Importer 100 cases of Chardonnay wine at a price of $100 per case for a total contract price of $10,000. If William delivers only 95 cases, Irma may deduct $500 from the price due and pay William only $9,500.

Damages The buyer may recover both direct and consequential damages. The measure of recovery for direct damages is similar to recovery under the UCC. The buyer recovers either (1) the difference between the contract price and the cost of cover or (2) the difference between the contract price and the fair market value. If the buyer covers, the damages are limited to the difference between the contract price and the cost of that cover.

Recovery of consequential damages is limited. This limitation does not mirror the rule of *Hadley v. Baxendale* which allows recovery only where such damages were reasonably anticipated at the time of contract formation as a likely result of the breach. See Chapter 18. Under CISG, consequential damages are recoverable as long as such damages were foreseeable as a "possible consequence of the breach."

Seller's Remedies
CISG specifies three available remedies to the aggrieved seller in the event of buyer breach: (1) price, (2) damages, and (3) reclaim the goods.

Price The preferred seller's remedy for breach of contract is an action for the price [Article 62]. While the right to recover price appears to be unqualified, it is clear that the seller must have performed and that the payment of the price must be due [Articles 30 and 58].

Damages The standard measure of damages is either (1) the difference between the contract price and resale or (2) the difference between the contract price and the fair market value of the goods [Articles 74–78]. CISG fails to provide for the lost volume seller.

Reclaim It appears likely that the seller can avoid the contract even after delivery of the goods and reclaim such goods [Article 64].

END–OF–CHAPTER QUESTIONS

1. List the seller's prelitigation remedies. List the seller's litigation remedies.
2. Why do sellers disclaim warranties? Why would a consumer buy a product with a warranty disclaimer?
3. Compare and contrast the seller's right to resell and the buyer's right to cover.
4. Analyze the following statement: "The UCC remedies are designed to put the injured party in as good a position as he would have been in had the contract been performed as promised."
5. Evaluate the following statement: "The injured party can routinely elect to seek specific performance."
6. Write a factual scenario where a consumer could successfully assert breach of *both* implied warranties of merchantability and fitness for a particular purpose. How could the seller protect itself from such potential lawsuits?
7. Joe is an avid camper. He purchased a new sleeping bag, explaining to the salesperson that he needed a bag that would keep him warm and protected in temperatures below zero. The salesperson gave him a bag guaranteed to keep him warm in temperatures 10 degrees below zero. Joe bought the bag and went camping. The temperature fell to zero degrees and Joe suffered frostbite. Could Joe sue? On what basis? What damages could Joe recover?
8. Wilson Trading Co. promised to deliver yarn to David Ferguson, Ltd. The contract provided that any claims relating to "twist, quality, or shade" must be made within 10 days of receipt of the yarn. Ferguson accepted the yarn, cut it, knitted it into sweaters, and washed it. The color then changed and Ferguson alleged breach of warranty. Is the limitation of damages provision enforceable? See *Wilson Trading Corp. v. David Ferguson, Ltd.*, 244 N.E.2d 685 (1968)).
9. Barbara Buyer entered into a contract with Sylvia Seller to buy 100 computer terminals at a contract price of $100,000. Before the time for delivery, Barbara called Sylvia and canceled the contract. Sylvia sold the terminals at a private sale for $85,000. The fair market value at the time was $90,000. Sylvia incurred extra shipping costs of $2,500 and extra storage costs of $1,500. What is the proper measure of Sylvia's recovery?

10. Tesoro Petroleum Corp. contracted to sell 10 million gallons of gasoline to Holborn Oil Company Ltd., in New York at a price of $1.30 per gallon. Holborn refused to accept delivery of the shipment. Tesoro sold the gasoline in Argentina for $1.10 per gallon. The fair market value at the time of resale was $.80 per gallon. Tesoro sued to recover the difference between fair market value and contract price. Holborn argued that the proper damages should be the difference between resale price and contract price. Who is right? Would your answer be any different if Tesoro was a lost volume seller? See *Tesoro Petroleum Corp. v. Holborn Oil Company Ltd.*, 547 N.Y.S.2d 1012 (1989).

Chapter 23

The Law of Products Liability

■

CRITICAL THINKING INQUIRIES

As you read this chapter, you should be able to address the following:

- Explain the relationship between negligence, breach of warranty, and strict liability.
- Evaluate the following statement: ''Negligence theory offers an adequate remedy to plaintiffs injured in products liability accidents. There is no reason for the continuation of strict products liability theory.''
- Analyze the following statement: ''Changes in products liability principles reflect basic shifts in the attitudes of the American economy over the past 150 years.''
- Analyze the following statement: ''The purpose of strict products liability is to ensure that the costs of injuries resulting from defective products are borne by the manufacturers that put such products on the market rather than the injured persons who are powerless to protect themselves.''
- Does the preceding statement reflect the ideas of rugged individualism, the progressive era, or the modern era?

MANAGERIAL PERSPECTIVE

Sarah is the vice president in charge of product development at Forever Fit, Inc. (FFI), a company that manufacturers exercise equipment. Sarah is very excited about a new stair-climber machine, now called the S-1. She fully expects that the S-1 will capture a 40 percent market share in its first year, at a profit of $20 million for FFI. She has already spent $1 million in product development, testing, and promotional materials.

Clyde, the engineer in charge of testing the S-1, has scheduled an emergency appointment with her for 10:00 A.M. He tells her that the latest test results have revealed a design flaw in the S-1. It seems that there is a tendency for the internal mechanism on the S-1 to dangerously speed up. When this happens, it is possible for the user to be injured either by trying to keep up or by being thrown from the machine. The probability of serious injury is 1 in 15,000.

Sarah must make a decision. The S-1 has been in testing for 6 months and there has been no indication of this danger before. Is Clyde sure of his test results? Have they been replicated? Does anyone else know of these findings? Did anyone put it in writing? What type of injuries are we talking about? Does Clyde know how much money FFI will lose if the S-1 is pulled from the market at this late date?

- What should Sarah do? What are her alternatives? What are the costs associated with each alternative? What is the potential for liability?
- What ethical issues are presented in this dilemma? Would a utilitarian thinker reach a different conclusion from a Kantian?
- What is the potential legal liability for FFI?

Products liability law governs claims for personal injury or property caused by the use of a product. Its scope is far broader than injuries caused by complex machinery or caustic chemicals. Everything from rifles to contraceptives have injured consumers. Even such seemingly harmless products as nightgowns and sunglasses have been the subject of major lawsuits. The impact of products liability is evident by considering the list of potential defendants. The product manufacturer, wholesaler, retailer, lessors, employers, and builders are common targets of product liability suits.

Each year, 110,000 Americans are permanently disabled and 30,000 are killed as a result of using consumer products. The economic losses from consumer products are difficult to calculate but are estimated to exceed $5 billion annually. In light of these staggering statistics, a concern for potential products liability must be part of the decisionmaking process for product designers, manufacturers, and marketers.

PRODUCTS LIABILITY LAW OVERVIEW

The following discussion of products liability first traces its development over the past 150 years. Second, product defects are classified. Finally, the predominate products liability theories are compared and contrasted.

The Evolution of Products Liability Law

Changes in products liability principles reflect a basic evolution in society's attitudes over the past century and a half. These shifts are roughly divided into three periods: rugged individualism, progressive era, and *Restatement (Second)* and beyond.

Period One—Rugged Individualism
From roughly 1840 to 1914, a rugged individualism dominated the American view of economic life. Business and individuals were left alone by the government to fend for themselves in the new industrial revolution. The doctrine of *caveat emptor* (let the buyer beware) summarized the view that purchasers must examine, test, and judge the quality of purchased goods for themselves.

To encourage the industrial revolution and to protect infant industries from high liability costs, courts developed barriers to injured victim's recovery. One

bar was the requirement of **privity,** or a contractual connection between the parties, as a condition to recovery. The classic English case of *Winterbottom v. Wright*[1] illustrates this privity requirement.

Coachman Winterbottom was thrown from a mail coach when its improperly bolted wheels collapsed. In denying Winterbottom any recovery from Mr. Wright (who had contracted with the Postmaster General to repair the coaches), the court declared: "There is no privity of contract between these parties; and if the plaintiff could sue, every passenger, or even any person passing along the road, who was injured by the upsetting of the coach might bring a similar action." Such expansive liability was a threatening prospect in 1840. Fear of deluging the court with products liability actions ("opening the floodgates of litigation") also led to the privity limitation.

Two other legal doctrines further barred plaintiffs' recovery in this period: the defenses of voluntary assumption of the risk and contributory negligence (see Chapter 8). These defenses were strictly applied by the courts. It was believed that people had to act competently to protect themselves and could not rely on court protection. Further, there was a general distrust of the jury—people believed that jurors would naturally sympathize with individual plaintiffs as opposed to large and emerging corporations. Thus, legal hurdles were created that blocked the early success of plaintiffs.

Period Two—The Progressive Era
As America moved into the progressive era, it became increasingly clear that individuals could not protect themselves from the massive economic power of corporations, and a rethinking of government's proper role took place. In products liability, the shift was marked by the landmark decision of *MacPherson v. Buick Motor Co.*[2] In *MacPherson*, the New York Court of Appeals held an automobile manufacturer liable to the ultimate purchaser for negligence despite the absence of privity. Thus, in the period stretching from approximately 1914 through the mid-1960s, product manufacturers had a duty of reasonable care to all users even if there was no contractual relationship between the manufacturer and user. This is particularly important today because consumers rarely deal directly with manufacturers.

---

[1] 152 Eng. Rep. 402 (1842).
[2] 11 N.E. 1050 (N.Y. Ct. App. 1919).

In this second period, then, plaintiffs not in privity were able to present their cases, typically negligence claims, to a jury. Whether they could win the case was another matter. Proving that the defendant acted unreasonably or carelessly was no easy task. It required evidence that the defendant knew or should have known that its conduct was unreasonably dangerous. Injured plaintiffs continued to lose suits because much of this evidence was controlled by the defendant, and the defendant could nearly always offer evidence it took care—for example, with quality control programs.

Period Three—The Restatement (Second) and Beyond

In the third and most recent period, the courts have developed a new rationale for imposing liability on manufacturers—shifting the loss. In *Greenman v. Yuba Power Co.*,[3] the California Supreme Court said: ''The purpose of such liability is to ensure that the costs of injuries resulting from defective products are borne by the manufacturers that put such products on the market rather than the injured persons who are powerless to protect themselves.''

Thus, today, plaintiffs in products liability cases are not limited to suits based on negligence. In shifting the loss, the manufacturer is liable for injuries resulting from any defective product even if the manufacturer is not negligent. The rationales justifying the imposition of strict (non-negligent) liability on manufacturers are:

1. The manufacturer profits from the sale of the product.
2. The manufacturer is in a better position than the plaintiff to prevent the injury and insure against any loss caused by the product's defect.
3. Plaintiffs have a difficult time proving negligence.
4. Strict liability provides an incentive to manufacturers for improving product safety.

The new rule became known as **strict liability** and was embodied in section 402A(1) of the *Restatement (Second) of Torts* in 1965.

---

[3] 377 P. 2d 897 (Cal. 1963).

Types of Defect

Defects may be classified as design, construction, or labeling defects. A **design defect** may occur even though the manufacturer provides flawless construction. Where the construction specifications are below the customary standards within the industry or are incapable of avoiding failure, they are considered a faulty design. For example, assume that an eyeglass manufacturer does not case harden or laminate its product. This would clearly be a defectively designed product because it would be below acceptable standards for eyeglasses, which should protect consumers' eyes against the hazards of breakage. A design defect may even occur when a whole industry produces shoddily designed products. Design defects may occur in the packaging of a product. For example, failure of a company to package drugs in child-safety tamper-proof containers may be the basis for a design defect.

By contrast, a **construction defect** occurs when the manufacturer of a product deviates from its construction specifications, and an otherwise well-designed product becomes faulty as a result. For example, assume that a rocket plant's engineering specifications call for workers to apply three separate welds to its booster rocket. A construction defect occurs if the plant fails to apply the three welds to any given rocket, or makes substandard welds that result in harm. Or, assume that a Coca-Cola plant places more sweetener in one of its vats than the recipe specifies. Injured consumers may have a cause of action against the producer based on a construction defect.

A **labeling or failure to warn defect** occurs when a manufacturer fails to warn of known hazards associated with its product. Illustrative cases include a pharmaceutical company's failure to attach a warning to a drug that is known to cause harm to the unborn fetus of pregnant women, a failure to label a product that emits harmful radiation, and a failure to warn of known allergic reactions to a product. Much litigation in the area of asbestos has been predicated on the failure of the manufacturer to warn of the hazards associated with asbestos exposure that could have been reduced with breathing filters.

Theories of Recovery

Broadly stated, there are three legal theories on which a products liability action may be based: warranty, negligence, and strict liability in tort. An in-

Figure 23–1   Theories of Products Liability

Focus	Contract	Tort
Defendant's product	Implied warranty of merchantability Implied warranty of fitness for a particular purpose	Strict liability for a defective product
Defendant's conduct		Negligence Negligent misrepresentation
Defendant's representation	Express warranty Magnuson-Moss	Strict liability for an innocent misrepresentation Negligent misrepresentation

jured plaintiff may base a case on one or more of these theories.

The three main theories differ in many ways. Figure 23–1 outlines these differences. The negligence theory focuses on the defendant's conduct. Implied warranty of merchantability and strict liability for a defective product focus on the defendant's product. Express warranty focuses on the defendant's representation. Warranty theories are contract-based, while negligence and strict liability are tort-based. Differences exist regarding the potential parties to the dispute, the elements of the case, the proof required, the remedies available, and the defenses available to the defendant.

WARRANTY THEORIES

Warranty claims focus on the product—specifically, whether the product conforms to the warranty (promise) made. Warranty actions are based on the agreement, express or implied, between the parties, subject to all the limitations of contracts actions. Warranties arise under Article 2 of the UCC, as discussed in Chapter 22. Warranties can be either express or implied.

Express Warranties

An express warranty is created by the product seller's statements or actions [UCC § 2–313]. Thus, if the seller promises that a product is "100% nonflammable," the seller has created an express warranty. Similarly, if the seller offers a sample, model, or technical specifications of the product, the seller is expressly warranting that the product sold will conform to the sample or specifications shown. If the product does not fulfill the promise, the buyer can sue for breach of the express warranty.

Implied Warranties

By contrast, implied warranties arise not from the seller's actions but by operation of law. In other words, the law imposes warranties automatically, adding implied promises to the parties' agreement when certain conditions are met. Implied warranties are of two types: (1) the implied warranty of merchantability and (2) the implied warranty of fitness for a particular purpose.

Warranty of Merchantability

In order for the implied warranty of merchantability to arise, the seller must be a merchant with respect to the goods sold. In other words, the seller must regularly deal in the goods sold. A seller who is only a casual or one-time seller is not a merchant of those goods.

Under the implied warranty of merchantability, the product must be **merchantable.** As is illustrated in Figure 23–2, the term has several meanings. In general, to be merchantable, a good must be fit for its ordinary purpose. To illustrate, hammers should not shatter under normal use and shotgun shells should not explode while still in the box. However, it is not enough that a product merely is designed or manufactured properly. To be fit, users must also be warned of any dangers associated with its use.

Warranty of Fitness for a Particular Purpose

The warranty of fitness for a particular purpose depends on seller knowledge. In order for the warranty to be implied, the seller must have reason to know (1)

Figure 23-2   Merchantable Goods

To be merchantable, goods must:

- Pass without objection in the trade under the contract description.
- In the case of fungible goods, be of fair average quality within the description.
- Be fit for the ordinary purposes for which such goods are used.
- Run.
- Be adequately contained, packaged, and labeled.
- Conform to the promises or affirmations of fact made on the container or label.

what the buyer intends to do with the goods (the particular purpose) and (2) that the buyer is relying on the seller's skill to select suitable goods. To illustrate, assume that the buyer tells the seller that she needs special boots to keep her feet dry and warm on an ice-fishing trip. An implied warranty of fitness for a particular purpose arises if the seller recommends a certain pair of boots and the buyer, in reliance on the seller's recommendation, purchases the pair recommended. The implied warranty is breached if the boots failed to keep the buyer's feet warm and dry during the ice-fishing trip. This is true even if the boots are fit for the ordinary use of walking.

Proving a Breach of Warranty

In order to establish a case based on breach of warranty, the following elements must be proved:

- The existence of the warranty either express or implied.
- The breach of the warranty.
- Notice of the breach to the seller.
- The breach must proximately cause the plaintiff's injury.
- The injury.

Consider these elements as you read the *Palmer* case.

PALMER v. A. H. ROBINS CO., INC.
684 P.2d 187 (Colo. 1984)

Carie Palmer, the plaintiff, was fitted by her obstetrician-gynecologist, Dr. Petri, with a Dalkon Shield intrauterine device (IUD) manufactured by Robins, the defendant. Palmer chose, and continued to use, the Dalkon Shield on the advice of her doctor and because of Robins' promotional materials. Her doctor also relied on promotional claims made by Robins as to the safety and effectiveness of the shield.

In August 1973, Palmer became pregnant. Her pregnancy progressed normally until she became violently ill, suffered a spontaneous septic abortion, went into septic shock, and developed a blood disorder that impeded natural blood clotting ability. In order to save her life, her doctor performed a total hysterectomy. It was her doctor's expert opinion that her uterine infection and the septic abortion were caused by the shield. Palmer sued A. H. Robins for breach of express and implied warranties. The trial court awarded her damages. The manufacturer appealed.

QUINN, Justice

The Warranty Claims

Robins raises three arguments in connection with Palmer's claims for breach of express warranty, implied warranty of merchantability, and implied warranty of fitness for a particular purpose. We consider these arguments separately and find them to be without merit.

Express Warranty

Palmer testified that Dr. Petri, before prescribing the shield, indicated to her that the shield was a superior IUD, safer than the birth control pill, and 98.9 percent effective in preventing pregnancy. Dr. Petri had drawn this information from a review of Robins literature, and conversations with Robins representatives. Palmer also subsequently read literature printed by the shield's manufacturer which reiterated the safety and effectiveness claims. These statements qualify under section 2–313(1) as affirmations of fact and product descriptions upon which Palmer relied in using the shield, as opposed to the birth control pill, as a method of contraception. There was sufficient evidence, in our view, to support a reasonable conclusion by the jury that Robins' representations concerning the superiority, effectiveness, and safety of the shield formed an essential part of Palmer's decision to have that device inserted in her body and to continue using it as a safe and effective method of contraception.

Implied Warranties

According to Robins, there was no evidence establishing that the particular purpose for which Palmer selected the shield was different from its ordinary purpose. Palmer rejected the pill as a contraceptive method because of her apprehensions over its safety and the serious health problems associated with it. It was at this point, according to Palmer, that Dr. Petri recommended the shield because it was safer and almost as effective as the pill. Dr. Petri's recommendation was based on Robins' representations concerning the safety features of the shield as well as the 1.1 percent pregnancy rate associated with its use. Palmer, relying on Dr. Petri's recommendation, chose the shield because she believed it would be

safer than other forms of contraception and would be almost as effective as the pill in preventing pregnancy. This evidence is sufficient to support Palmer's claim that she selected the shield not only to prevent pregnancy, the ordinary purpose for which an IUD is selected, but also for the particular purpose of providing her with a "safe" contraceptive device that averted such hazards as stroke, vascular clotting, and other harmful effects on the body. There can be no question that Robins knew or had reason to know of the special or particular safety features attributed to its product, since both Dr. Petri and Palmer premised their decisions on affirmative representations made by Robins. Nor can there be any question about Palmer's reliance upon Robins to furnish a product which would fulfill these particular purposes. Under these circumstances, the submission to the jury of the dual implied warranties of fitness for a particular purpose and merchantability was justified.

Case Questions

1. On what basis did the court find that A. H. Robins made an express warranty to Palmer?
2. On what values did A. H. Robins place priority in deciding to manufacture the Dalkon Shield?
3. How did Palmer's particular purpose differ from the ordinary purpose for IUD use?

Magnuson-Moss Warranties

Although the UCC warranties provide consumer protection, sellers have often circumvented the implied warranty protections by disclaiming those warranties, as discussed in Chapter 22. Sellers would ostensibly give consumers an express warranty while excluding implied warranties of merchantability and fitness for a particular purpose. For example, consider the language characterized as an express warranty in Figure 23–3.

Figure 23–3   Purported Express Warranty

Seller agrees to replace or repair any defective product if notified of said defect within 30 days, and if said product is sent to seller's place of business, postage prepaid within that period of time. This express warranty is in lieu of any other warranty, express or implied.

The language in Figure 23–3 purports to be an express warranty. However, it really disclaims rather than provides a warranty. Because such practices of artful warranty wording caused considerable consumer dissatisfaction and often deceived consumers, Congress passed the Magnuson-Moss Warranty Act. The act applies to **consumer goods,** those used for personal, family, or household purposes. Magnuson-Moss does not require that merchants make any warranty. However, it does limit sellers from excluding implied warranties. Further, when a seller chooses to make a warranty, the act requires certain disclosures. It also establishes standards for classifying warranties as either full or limited.

Warranty Disclaimers

Sellers of consumer goods that cost more than $10 who make a written warranty may not modify or disclaim an implied warranty. The seller may only limit the duration of the implied warranty to the written warranty's duration. Any limitation must be clearly and conspicuously displayed on the face of the warranty. Any modifications or disclaimers that are contrary to the act are ineffective.

Warranty Disclosure

The act requires warranty disclosures where the cost of goods is more than $15 to help consumers judge the warranty's value. These disclosures include:

- Warrantor's name and address.
- Product and parts covered.
- Warranty duration.
- Remedies promised in warranty for defects.
- Consumer's obligations and expenses necessary for warranty remedy.
- Names and addresses of approved warranty service centers.
- Legal remedies available to the consumer.
- Exclusions from warranty protections.

Full and Limited Warranties

All express warranties must be classified as either full or limited. A **full warranty** must satisfy the following minimum qualifications: (1) the seller agrees to repair a product defect within a reasonable time; (2) the consumer must have the option of a refund or a product replacement if the product cannot be fixed after a reasonable number of attempts; (3) the warranty must state that the consumer must only notify the warrantor to qualify for warranty repairs; and (4) the duration of any implied warranties may not be limited. Any warranty that does not provide these protections must be designated as a **limited warranty.**

Remedies

Magnuson-Moss allows the seller to establish informal dispute resolution procedures to remedy warranty claims. If such procedures are established — for example, arbitration — the consumer may be required to use them before bringing a breach of warranty suit. The Federal Trade Commission administers the Magnuson-Moss Act. Violations are considered unfair and deceptive trade practices. Successful litigants may recover damages plus reasonable attorney fees.

NEGLIGENCE

Negligence is a tort based on fault. As you probably remember from Chapter 8, negligence is not confined to products liability but is applicable to a variety of situations. The tort occurs when someone fails to exercise reasonable care and, as a result, another is injured. In the context of products liability, it is typically applicable when a manufacturer is negligent in manufacturing a product, in the design or construction of products, or as a result of a failure to warn of reasonably foreseeable dangers.

Negligence may occur when the manufacturer fails to do what a prudent manufacturer would have done under like circumstances. For example, the manufacturer of a water boiler would reasonably be expected to inspect the boiler before placing it on the market. If the inspection would have discovered a defect, then failure to do so is negligence.

Proving Negligence

Nineteenth-century plaintiffs could not recover under the negligence theory of products liability without first establishing contractual privity between the plaintiff and the defendant. While lack of privity is no longer a barrier to plaintiff recovery, serious obstacles to an injured plaintiff's recovery remain.

In order to prove negligence, a plaintiff must demonstrate:

- The defendant owed a duty of care to the plaintiff.
- Breach of the duty.
- Proximate cause.
- Injury.

Proving Unreasonable Conduct

Negligence focuses attention on the defendant's conduct. Negligence asks whether the defendant knew or should have known that the manufactured product was unreasonably dangerous or defective. This knowledge is difficult to prove.

To illustrate the difficulty of such proof, assume that a consumer becomes ill drinking soda pop from a bottle that contained a dead mouse. In order to show negligence, the consumer must prove that an employee at the manufacturer's plant failed to properly inspect that particular bottle, or that the manufacturer's quality control inspection procedures fell short of industry standards. This is an extremely difficult burden. Even if *res ipsa loquitur* (as discussed in Chapter 8) is invoked as an aid, the manufacturer can often rebut the presumption of negligence by producing quality control records.

Proving Proximate Cause

Proof of negligence requires more than evidence of the defendant's unreasonable conduct. The plaintiff must also prove that the defendant's unreasonable conduct proximately caused the plaintiff's injury. This is also difficult to prove. For example, until recently, there had never been a successful suit against tobacco companies for health damage caused by cigarette smoking. The medical proof linking cigarette smoking to a particular disease was inconclusive. Although cigarettes are statistically linked to cancer and other diseases, the medical and scientific proof necessary to establish proximate causation in a particular case is costly. Furthermore, given the current state of scientific technology, it is difficult to establish a definitive causal link.

Still another serious problem faced by consumers is the question of "who done it." Many products such as drugs are fungible or homogeneous. Do you remember who manufactured the last antibiotic you took? Or did you ever know the manufacturer? When such a drug causes injury, it becomes important for the injured party to prove exactly who manufactured the drug that caused the injury. Otherwise, the case will fail because proof that the defendant caused the injury is lacking. Some courts have adopted the **market share liability** approach, giving plaintiffs some assistance in such situations. This theory is discussed later in this chapter in the *Zafft* case.

Defenses

Further, defendants have affirmative defenses available, such as assumption of the risk or contributory negligence. Most states have replaced contributory negligence with some form of comparative negligence to avoid the "all or nothing" nature of contributory negligence. Thus, if the defendant can prove that the plaintiff's own negligence contributed to the injury, the recovery is reduced by that degree. For example, if a consumer stops in the middle of a busy highway without using the emergency flashers on the Ford Pinto being driven, the consumer will bear some of the liability if the car is hit from behind

and explodes in flames. If the consumer-plaintiff suffers $100,000 worth of damages and the jury finds that the plaintiff was 10 percent responsible for the accident, the award is reduced by 10 percent to $90,000.

STRICT LIABILITY

Due to difficulties in proving negligence, courts began to adopt a strict liability alternative. This resulted in the American Law Institute's drafting of section 402A of the *Restatement (Second) of Torts*. While section 402A, like other *Restatement* provisions, is not itself a law, it has been adopted by courts as an appropriate products liability standard in most states, making it law by case adoption. Strict products liability removes some of the hurdles of negligence.

Restatement (Second) of Torts § 402A.

(1) One who sells any product in a defective condition unreasonably dangerous to the user or consumer or to his property is subject to liability for physical harm thereby caused to the ultimate user or consumer, or to his property, if

(a) the seller is engaged in the business of selling such a product, and

(b) it is expected to and does reach the user or consumer without substantial change in the condition in which it is sold.

(2) The rule stated in Subsection (1) applies although

(a) the seller has exercised all possible care in the preparation and sale of his product, and

(b) the user or consumer has not bought the product from or entered into any contractual relation with the seller.

Basic Coverage of Strict Products Liability

Simply speaking, under 402A the merchant-seller of a **defective** product has liability for injuries caused by that product. Strict liability is product oriented rather than conduct oriented. Therefore, the relevant inquiry under section 402A is simply whether the product was unreasonably dangerous when it reached the user or consumer, not whether the manufacturer acted reasonably in manufacturing the product. In other words, the seller of a *defective* product faces liability for injuries caused by that product even if the seller acted *reasonably*.

Possible Plaintiffs

Section 402A applies to all consumers and users of the product. Courts have split on whether *business* users are covered because their level of sophistication reduces the need for special protection.

There is no privity requirement. In other words, the plaintiff need not have purchased the product from the defendant. In fact, the plaintiff does not have to have purchased the product at all. Courts have applied strict liability to innocent bystanders. For example, assume that Irene Innocent is stopped at a stop light next to a Pinto. If the Pinto is struck from behind and Irene is injured in the resulting fire, Irene can recover in strict liability from Ford even though she did not purchase the Pinto.

Possible Defendants

Section 402A imposes liability only on people engaged in the *business* of selling a product. Thus, a strict liability claim can only be made against merchant-sellers. This includes all merchant-sellers — wholesalers and retailers; it is not limited to manufacturers. Retailers are generally liable even for products such as canned beans that they could not have known were defective. Strict liability has even been extended to suppliers of defective component parts. However, casual sellers of a product, such as a one-time private seller of an automobile, would not be covered. Nor would free providers of a product be liable. Courts have, however, included professional *lessors* of products within the scope of coverage.

The Prima Facie Case

The defendant is liable when the plaintiff shows that damage was proximately caused by an unreasonably dangerous defective product. The prima facie case is summarized in Figure 23–4.

Figure 23–4   Prima Facie Case

- Defendant is a merchant-seller.
- Defective and unreasonably dangerous product.
- No substantial change.
- Proximate cause.
- Injuries.

Unreasonably Dangerous and Defective

The requirements of unreasonably dangerous and defective are generally treated as one element. A product can be defective in each of the three types of cases — construction defects, design defects, and failure to warn. A product is unreasonably dangerous and defective if it is dangerous beyond the expectation or contemplation of ordinary consumers. Thus, according to the *Restatement (Second),* ''good butter is not unreasonably dangerous if . . . it deposits cholesterol in the arteries; but bad butter, contaminated with poisonous fish oil, is unreasonably dangerous.'' A knife is not unreasonably dangerous if a consumer cuts himself; but it is unreasonably dangerous if the knife breaks because of a weakness in the metal.

Proximate Cause

The plaintiff must prove that the seller sold a defective product that caused the plaintiff injury. However, what if a dangerous product cannot be directly linked to a particular manufacturer? To illustrate, suppose a plaintiff takes a pill with dangerous side effects and gets violently ill. The plaintiff cannot recall which of the 40 manufacturers of this type of medication actually produced the pill. Years have passed and pharmacy records are unavailable. Are all of the manufacturers liable because they all produced an ''unreasonably dangerous'' product, or are none liable because the plaintiff cannot prove which manufacturer caused plaintiff an injury?

Consider this problem as you read the *Zafft* case.

ZAFFT v. ELI LILLY & CO.
676 S.W.2d 241 (Mo. 1984)

DES is a synthetic hormone that was manufactured to prevent miscarriages. The mothers of the plaintiffs took DES while pregnant with the plaintiffs. The plaintiffs, alleging that DES caused cancer in the daughters of women who took the drug, sued substantially all the known manufacturers and sellers of DES in Missouri at the time during which their mothers were prescribed the drug. The plaintiffs claim that the drug was sold without adequate warnings because the defendants, Eli Lilly & Co., represented the drug as safe when they knew or should have known of its potential carcinogenic effects. Because the plaintiffs cannot identify which manufacturer sold the drug actually taken by the mothers, they argue that the court should recognize a form of enterprise liability.

HIGGINS, Judge

Plaintiff must establish some causal relationship between the defendant and the injury-producing agent. The four theories considered by the trial court, recognized in other jurisdictions and presented by appellants for consideration either relax or dispense with the element of causation. One, alternative liability, applies when two or more defendants act tortiously toward the plaintiff who, through no fault of his own, cannot identify which one of the joined defendants caused the injury. The burden of proof shifts to each defendant to prove his innocence. In *Summers*, two hunters negligently fired in the direction of the plaintiff who was unable to determine which of the two shots hit and injured him. The uncontroverted materials filed by defendants indicate that 151 companies, some based in St. Louis, manufactured DES during the time in question. Thus, unlike the typical situation warranting application of alternative liability, all possible tortfeasors are not before the court and the actual wrongdoers may escape liability. In such a context, the possibility that any of the named defendants supplied the DES to plaintiff's mother is so remote that it would be unfair to require each defendant to exonerate itself. And although alternative liability as formulated in *Summers* does not require that defendants be in a better position to identify the source of the harm, this is important to application of the theory. Here, the passage of time impairs the efforts of respondents and appellants alike to determine which of the defendants were responsible. Indeed, the trial court found that appellants have easier access to possible sources of information than do respondents.

The concert of action theory imposes liability upon all those who, "in pursuance of a common plan or design to commit a tortious act, actively take part in it, or further it by cooperation or request, or who lend aid or encouragement to the wrongdoer, or ratify and adopt his acts done for their benefit."[4] A

frequent illustration of the theory is the automobile drag race. The element of agreement or cooperation necessary to application of this theory is lacking in this case. The history of development and marketing of DES reveals independent, albeit similar, conduct on the part of the drug companies. The only activity that resembles "concerted action" occurred in 1941 when the FDA required companies interested in manufacturing DES for non-pregnancy purposes to pool their clinical data in a master file for the agency's consideration. Further, the concert of action theory developed, not to relieve plaintiffs of the burden of identifying the wrongdoer, but to impose liability on culpable co-participants and thereby deter antisocial group conduct.

A third theory proposed as a basis for recovery against defendants here is industry-wide liability. Appellants cite *Hall v. E. I. du Pont de Nemours & Co., Inc.* The cases arose from 18 unrelated accidents in which children were injured by exploding blasting caps. The named defendants in *Hall* represented the entire blasting cap industry in the United States, along with its trade association. Plaintiffs alleged that defendants jointly delegated product safety functions to their association. The court cautioned against the application of industry-wide liability to a decentralized industry composed of numerous producers. This Court agrees with the majority of courts which reject industry-wide liability in DES cases because of the large number of drug manufacturers involved, the lack of evidence of delegation of responsibility for safety standards to a trade association, and the pervasive role of the FDA in setting industry-wide standards.

The case most often cited in reported opinions on the liability of unidentifiable manufacturers is *Sindell*. The *Sindell* majority, after considering and rejecting each of the three theories discussed above, adopted an extended version of alternative liability, since denominated "market share liability." This theory requires that plaintiffs join as defendants a number of DES manufacturers sufficient to constitute a substantial share of the market. The burden then shifts to each defendant to exonerate itself or to

---

[4]Prosser & Keeton, *The Law of Torts* (5th ed. 1984).

join, by third party petition, other drug producers not named by plaintiff. Damages would then be apportioned among the remaining defendants on the basis of the share of the market each held.

Respondents argue that market share liability is unfair, unworkable, and contrary to Missouri law, as well as unsound public policy. This Court agrees. The California court did not define the relevant market, nor did it specify what constitutes a "substantial share" of the market. Difficulties in determining market share for the purposes of apportioning damages remain. Rather than alleviate the concerns present with alternative liability, market share liability continues the risk that the actual wrongdoer is not among the named defendants, and exposes those joined to liability greater than their responsibility.

This Court acknowledges and respects the compelling reasons motivating the trial court and courts of other states to resolve the dilemma presented in these cases by straining existing law or adopting novel theories. Plaintiffs are innocent and claim serious injuries alleged to result from their mothers' use of DES. Yet simply to state, as have courts ruling in favor of plaintiffs, that as between an innocent plaintiff and negligent defendants, the latter should bear the cost of the injury, and that defendants can better absorb this cost, ignores strong countervailing considerations.

Missouri law does not guarantee relief to every deserving plaintiff. To shift the burden of proof on causation to respondents substantially alters the existing rights and liabilities of the litigants. There is insufficient justification at this time to support abandonment of so fundamental a concept of tort law as the requirement that a plaintiff prove, at a minimum, some nexus between wrongdoing and injury.

Because the theory plaintiffs urge has no support in precedent, the case presents a public policy choice, one with which legislatures, as well as courts, have struggled. Competing with the interests of appellants are legitimate concerns that liability will discourage desired pharmaceutical research and development while adding little incentive to production of safe products, for all companies face potential liability regardless of their efforts. And the consequences of imposing liability without identification extend to other areas of products liability law (Salk anti-polio vaccine; asbestos).

This Court concludes that the theories advanced by plaintiffs do not persuade the Court to abandon the Missouri tort law which requires that they establish a causal relationship between the defendants and the injury-producing agent as a precondition to maintenance of their causes of action. Strict liability in tort continues to provide a remedy to those plaintiffs who satisfy the identification requirement.

Case Questions

1. What legal hurdle faced the plaintiff in this particular case? Discuss.
2. Why did the court decide that each of the theories urged by plaintiffs should not apply in this case? Discuss.
3. What is the value conflict between the proponents and the opponents of market share liability?
4. Does Judge Higgins make any descriptive assumptions with which the market share liability proponents might disagree?
5. In your opinion, is there a just way to resolve the conflict in this case? Discuss.

Damages

Damages can be recovered for "physical harm caused to the ultimate user or consumer, or to his property." Thus, damages would be awarded for bodily injury or for emotional harm resulting in bodily injury. Physical injury of the property, such as the destruction of a truck due to a faulty axle, is typically covered. However, pure economic loss, such as lost profits resulting from the truck's destruction, are not compensable. Economic loss, if any, would have to be pursued under warranty theory.

Defenses to a Strict Products Liability Action

As under other products liability theories, a number of defenses are available to strict tort liability. These include the state-of-the-art defense, product alteration or modification, product misuse, and comparative fault.

State-of-the-Art Defense

It would seem that a manufacturer is liable even if it exercised "all possible care" in producing a product. Nevertheless, manufacturers have been permit-

Figure 23–5   State-of-the-Art Spectrum

Negligence	Defendant Manufacturers Generally Argue This Standard	Plaintiffs Generally Argue This Standard	Absolute Liability
Liability only if the defendant knew or should have known (a reasonable manufacturer would have knowledge of the risk).	Liability if defendant *could* have known of the risk because technology was available in the industry but the manufacturer did not use it.	Liability because knowledge existed somewhere (even if in a wholly unrelated discipline remote to manufacturer's business).	Liability for unknowable risks. Impute nonexistent knowledge to the defendant.

ted to raise a state-of-the-art defense when a potentially dangerous condition is not known or discoverable by currently existing scientific means. To illustrate, suppose a drug is approved for use by the FDA. Unknown to the manufacturer, the drug produces premature baldness in the male children of women who take the drug. Would the drug manufacturer be liable in this case? Figure 23–5 outlines the spectrum of alternative treatments.

As you read the *Feldman* case, consider which of the state-of-the-art standards outlined in Figure 23–5 was adopted by the court.

FELDMAN v. LEDERLE LABORATORIES
479 A.2d 374 (N.J. 1984)

Dr. Harold Feldman, the father of the plaintiff, Carol Ann Feldman, prescribed Declomycin (tetracycline) for Carol Ann approximately seven times from September 1960, when she was eight or nine months old, until the end of 1963, to prevent secondary infections from childhood diseases. Carol Ann's teeth were discolored gray from use of the tetracycline. Scientific literature existed by 1960 that related tooth staining to tetracycline use. In 1963, the defendant, Lederle Laboratories, received complaints from doctors that Declomycin was causing tooth staining and referred this information to the FDA in May 1963. Commencing in mid-December 1963, after receipt of FDA approval, it included the same warning in the Declomycin literature as in other tetracycline. The jury found for the manufacturer. Carol Ann appealed alleging that the product lacked adequate warnings.

SCHREIBER, Judge

We commence our strict liability analysis with the now familiar refrain that to establish strict liability a plaintiff must prove that the product was defective, that the defect existed when the product left the defendant's control, and that the defect caused injury to a reasonably foreseeable user. The defect may take one of three forms: a manufacturing flaw, a design defect, or an inadequate warning.

This is a strict liability warning case. The product has been made as the manufacturer intended.

The plaintiff does not contend that it contained a manufacturing defect. Declomycin's purpose was to act as did other tetracycline—as an antibiotic. However, it had several advantages over other antimicrobial therapeutics. The plaintiff does not dispute this. Indeed, there is no evidence that plaintiff's usage of Declomycin was not adequate in this respect. Nor was there any proof that it was improperly designed. The crux of the plaintiff's complaint is that her doctor should have been warned of a possible side effect of the drug in infants, discoloration of teeth.

The failure-to-warn strict liability classification is similar to the improper design category. The manufacturer is under a duty to produce and distribute a product that is reasonably fit, suitable, and safe. It has not met that obligation if it puts a defective article into the stream of commerce that causes injury or damage.

Generally, the state of the art in design defect cases and available knowledge in defect warning situations are relevant factors in measuring reasonableness of conduct. We observed that "the state of the art refers not only to the common practice and standards in the industry but also to the other design alternatives within practical and technological limits at the time of distribution."[5]

Similarly, as to warnings, generally conduct should be measured by knowledge at the time the manufacturer distributed the product. Did the defendant know, or should he have known, of the danger, given the scientific, technological, and other information available when the product was distributed; or, in other words, did he have actual or constructive knowledge of the danger?

Under this standard, negligence and strict liability in warning cases may be deemed to be functional equivalents. Constructive knowledge embraces knowledge that should have been known based on information that was reasonably available or obtainable and should have alerted a reasonably prudent person to act. Put another way, would a person of reasonable intelligence or of the superior expertise of the defendant charged with such knowledge conclude that defendant should have alerted the consuming public?

Furthermore, a reasonably prudent manufacturer will be deemed to know of reliable information generally available or reasonably obtainable in the

---

[5]*Suter v. San Angelo Foundry & Mach. Co.*, 406 A.2d 140 (1979).

industry or in the particular field involved. Such information need not be limited to that furnished by experts in the field, but may also include material provided by others. Thus, for example, if a substantial number of doctors or consumers had complained to a drug manufacturer of an untoward effect of a drug, that would have constituted sufficient information requiring an appropriate warning.

In strict liability warning cases, unlike negligence cases, however, the defendant should properly bear the burden of proving that the information was not reasonably available or obtainable and that it therefore lacked actual or constructive knowledge of the defect. The defendant is in a superior position to know the technological material or data in the particular field or specialty. The defendant is the expert, often performing self-testing. It is the defendant that injected the product in the stream of commerce for its economic gain. As a matter of policy the burden of proving the status of knowledge in the field at the time of distribution is properly placed on the defendant.

Reversed and Remanded.

Case Questions

1. What type of strict liability case was this? Why?
2. What level of knowledge is a defendant manufacturer held to according to *Feldman?* Compare this to the state-of-the-art spectrum. Where does *Feldman* end up on this spectrum?
3. Who bears the burden of proof concerning the defendant's knowledge or lack thereof? Why? Discuss.
4. How does one's position on the state-of-the-art spectrum reflect his or her value assumptions?

Product Misuse

A manufacturer is generally not liable in negligence, strict liability, or warranty if the plaintiff's injuries are caused by an abnormal or unintended use of the product. To illustrate, if a plaintiff is injured using the butt of a loaded rifle to pound in a nail, the rifle manufacturer would not be liable. However, if the misuse is foreseeable, the manufacturer might be liable for failure to warn. Consider the product misuse defense as you read the following unusual case.

DANIELL v. FORD MOTOR CO.
581 F. Supp. 728 (D. N.M. 1984)

In 1980, Daniell, the plaintiff, locked herself inside the trunk of a 1973 Ford LTD automobile in an attempt to commit suicide. She was unable to get out because the trunk lacked an internal opening release, and she remained in the trunk for nine days. Daniell argued that lack of an internal opening release was a design defect. She further claimed that the manufacturer had a duty to warn of this condition. She brought this suit to recover for psychological and physical injuries arising from that occurrence. She based her claim on: (1) strict liability; (2) negligence; and (3) breach of express and implied warranties. Ford moved for summary judgment.

BALDOCK, Judge

Three uncontroverted facts bar recovery under any of these theories. First, the plaintiff ended up in the trunk compartment of the automobile because she felt "overburdened" and was attempting to commit suicide. Second, the purposes of an automobile trunk are to transport, stow and secure the automobile spare tire, luggage and other goods and to protect those items from elements of the weather. Third, the plaintiff never considered the possibility of exit from the inside of the trunk when the automobile was purchased. Plaintiff has not set forth evidence indicating that these facts are controverted. The overriding factor barring plaintiff's recovery is that she intentionally sought to end her life by crawling into an automobile trunk from which she could not escape. This is not a case where a person inadvertently became trapped inside an automobile trunk. The plaintiff was aware of the natural and probable consequences of her perilous conduct. Not only that, the plaintiff, at least initially, sought those dreadful consequences. Plaintiff, not the manufacturer of the vehicle, is responsible for this unfortunate occurrence.

Recovery under strict products liability and negligence will be discussed first because the concept of duty owed by the manufacturer to the consumer or user is the same under both theories in this case. As a general principle, a design defect is actionable only where the condition of the product is unreasonably dangerous to the user or consumer. Under strict products liability or negligence, a manufacturer has a duty to consider only those risks of injury which are foreseeable. A risk is not foreseeable by a manufacturer where a product is used in a manner which could not reasonably be anticipated by the manufacturer and that use is the cause of the plaintiff's injury. The plaintiff's injury would not be foreseeable by the manufacturer.

The design features of an automobile trunk make it well near impossible that an adult intentionally would enter the trunk and close the lid. The dimensions of a trunk, the height of its sill and its load floor and the efforts to first lower the trunk lid and then to engage its latch, are among the design features which encourage closing and latching the trunk lid while standing outside the vehicle. The court holds that the plaintiff's use of the trunk compartment as a means to attempt suicide was an unforeseeable use as a matter of law. Therefore, the manufacturer had no duty to design an internal release or opening mechanism that might have prevented this occurrence.

Nor did the manufacturer have a duty to warn the plaintiff of the danger of her conduct, given the plaintiff's unforeseeable use of the product. Another reason why the manufacturer had no duty to warn the plaintiff of the risk inherent in crawling into an automobile trunk and closing the trunk lid is because such a risk is obvious. There is no duty to warn of known dangers in strict products liability or tort. Moreover, the potential efficacy of any warning, given the plaintiff's use of the automobile trunk compartment for a deliberate suicide attempt, is questionable.

The court notes that the automobile trunk was not defective under these circumstances.

Case Questions

1. What legal theories did Daniell use to advance her claim to relief? Discuss.

2. Why were Daniell's claims summarily dismissed?

3. Do you view this claim as frivolous or do you think it has some merit? Argue both sides.

Product Alteration or Modification

The plaintiff or some third party might alter the product's design, function, or use, or remove a warning from that originally designed by the manufacturer. To illustrate, a machine shop foreman may take a safety guard off a drill press because ''it slows the guys down.'' Suppose a machinist is injured while using the guardless drill press? Courts in alteration cases generally distinguish between an injury caused by a defect originally present in the product and an injury caused by an alteration. In the former case, the manufacturer would certainly be liable. However, if the injury is caused by the alteration, then a further question must be answered: Was the alteration foreseeable? If it was, the manufacturer may be liable if it failed to warn against the foreseen modification. For example, suppose a manufacturer was notified that machinists were regularly injured because of the removal of the drill press guard. In this case, it would have a duty to warn against such removal and/or make removal of the guard substantially more difficult. However, if the alteration was unforeseeable, the alteration defense would relieve the defendant from liability.

Comparative Negligence

In theory, the contributory negligence of the plaintiff is immaterial in a strict liability claim. Because the claim is not based on the negligence of the defendant, the contributory negligence of the plaintiff is also irrelevant. However, a number of states recognize the comparative negligence defense. The comparative responsibility of the plaintiff may diminish the award of damages proportionately according to the measure of the plaintiff's responsibility. To illustrate, if plaintiff is 30 percent responsible for plaintiff's own injury and suffers $10,000 in damages, plaintiff will be awarded only $7,000.

TORT REFORM

For the past 20 years, there has been increasing talk of tort reform, both at the federal and the state levels. The proposals vary. Whether or not reform is needed is subject to debate. The debate surrounding tort reform is briefly examined here.

Is There Need for Reform?

Arguments Favoring Tort Reform

Those in favor of tort reform assert that:

1. The size and number of damage awards are increasing.

2. Lawyers get a substantial percentage of the awards and are encouraged to bring frivolous suits by the contingency fee arrangement.

3. This has lead to increased insurance liability costs.

4. These increased costs have hurt American companies' ability to be competitive in the international market.

5. The fear of liability action (primarily products liability actions) has caused companies to act in ways that are undesirable. For example, a recent survey shows that 47 percent of those businesses surveyed have withdrawn a product from the market, that 39 percent have chosen not to introduce a new product, and that 25 percent have discontinued new product research.

6. The increasingly large awards have driven some insurance companies out of business, have severely injured others and have led to a so-called insurance crisis.

7. Other countries offer a less costly tort litigation alternative. Proponents cite that European countries typically utilize a negligence rather than a strict liability standard, impose procedural burdens on the plaintiff, limit discovery, limit punitive damages, do not use contingency fee arrangements, and the loser pays the winner's legal expenses.

Arguments Opposing Tort Reform

Those in opposition to tort reform question the basic assertions of those in favor of tort reform. They assert that:

1. Neither the size nor number of damage awards is increasing. Opponents assert that any increase is due to a few mass tort lawsuits (asbestos, Dalkon Shield).

2. The contingency fee arrangement is the only way certain people can get legal representation. Such arrangements do not encourage frivolous lawsuits since the lawyers only get paid if they win.

3. The liability costs are a true cost of doing business and should be reflected in the price of the product.

4. These liability costs add only a small percentage to the cost of products. Further, for-

eign companies doing business in this country must also consider products liability costs.

5. There is little evidence that defendants' actions are caused by the fear of products liability actions. Further, to some extent, these assertions might be evidence that the tort reform system is working. If companies are voluntarily withdrawing dangerous products from the market, the system is working.

6. The so-called insurance crisis was caused more by poor management by insurance companies and unreasonably low premiums than by a tort crisis.

7. The comparison to other countries with national health insurance programs is inappropriate.

The Proposals

There have been proposals for reform of the tort litigation system both at the federal level and in various states.

Proposed Federal Products Liability Law

Federal reform has been proposed in Congress in various forms throughout the 1980s. No legislation has passed. There is a perceived need for federal action because the present state-by-state approach lacks uniformity and consistency.

The federal proposals would generally:

1. Establish a uniform statute of limitations.
2. Allow the state-of-the art defense.
3. Enact a limit on punitive damages.
4. Eliminate joint and several liability.
5. Limit applicability of strict liability.

State Reform

A number of states have enacted some type of state tort reform. The proposals on the state level include the following:

1. Limit the statute of limitations.
2. Limit strict liability.
3. Put caps on punitive damages.
4. Put caps on pain and suffering damages.
5. Either eliminate contingency fees, cap attorney fees, or have the losers pay the winner's attorney's fees.
6. Limit discovery.
7. Limit the use of paid experts.

Consider the following questions concerning tort reform:

1. What is the value conflict in the question of tort reform?
2. What problems exist in determining who is right on the question of tort reform?
3. What changes have been made in state law so far? Can you suggest any other possible changes to improve the system?
4. How does your view of the role and effectiveness of the jury impact your position on the tort reform proposals?

All of these tort reform proposals are hotly contested. Some—for example, putting caps on pain and suffering awards—are subject to a question of constitutionality. The following debate on the question of limiting punitive damage recovery illustrates the disagreement. Read the editorial presented first and then the response that follows.

---

*Curb Civil Suit Excesses; Rein In Punitive Damages**

Editorial: Limits on Punitive Damages Will Help Restore Fairness to the Legal System

Being wronged can be extremely rewarding. Huge punitive damage awards in lawsuits make it possible.

Meant to punish wrongdoers and discourage them from doing wrong again, punitive damages are out of control.

Vice President Dan Quayle wants to rein in our litigious society. He recommended 50 legal reforms at the American Bar Association convention, including strict limits on punitive damage awards.

There's room to debate how strict the limits should be, but Quayle is headed down the right road. Twenty-eight states have laws governing punitive damage awards, but they're haphazard.

According to Quayle, we spend over $80 billion a year on litigation and insurance. Too much goes to lawyers, not victims—up to 75 percent of a $9 billion asbestos case, by one estimate.

Society pays a price. Even a few multi-million-dollar cases can encourage a lawsuit-happy citizenry to sue at the drop of a hat. They discourage businesses from developing lifesaving products—like vaccines or birth control devices.

People deserve protection from fraud and abuse, but punitive damages can be unfair. Rules for deciding wrongdoing can be confusing and lax. They can mean big damages against deep-pocket companies that may not be responsible.

A Georgia helicopter ambulance crashed while carrying a patient. Uninjured, he died later from earlier injuries. Even so, his estate got $1.3 million in punitive damages from the ambulance service and the hospital authority.

What would be fairer?

- Clear, convincing standards for proof of wrongdoing.
- Judges who know the whole case deciding punitive damages, not juries who see one victim's case.
- Paying punitive damages to courts or state governments rather than to plaintiffs to discourage frivolous or get-rich-quick suits.

Then punitive damages can do what they're meant to—make wrongdoers pay, not make lawyers rich.

Opposing View: Forget the Myths and Leave the System Alone to Protect the Public[*]

Capping punitive damages puts a cap on safety. Surely, Americans deserve better protection. Independent studies show that punitive damages are awarded rarely—and almost always in response to extremely serious misconduct. They are also carefully controlled by the courts.

Yet dialogue about punitive damages continues to be drowned in myth. How can limiting punitive damages to the actual damage caused by manufacturers give the USA a competitive boost when a just-released study documents that such awards are far too rare to impact on national competitiveness?

In over 25 years, just 208 product liability cases even touched this ratio. Many of these were later reduced. Further, as the new study by professors Michael Rustad and Thomas Koenig indicates, these infrequent awards were, in most cases, appropriately assessed because, despite clear knowledge of danger, the defendants made conscious decisions to trade safety for profit, or foster harm through extreme carelessness.

Should no one be punished for tragedies caused by exploding gas tanks, disintegrating tires, IUD-caused sterilizations, contaminated surgical bandages or purposely destroyed recall notices? The Silkwood plutonium contamination case was also factored in this study.

[*]Bob Gibbins, president, Association of Trial Lawyers of America.

Overwhelmingly, Rustad and Koenig found punitive damages to be "infrequently awarded" considering that only 355 awards were identified from a 25-year period during which the Consumer Product Safety Commission estimated 20,000 product-related injuries each year. They further found that most defendants subsequently implemented such critical safety measures as product withdrawals and improved warnings.

Making the USA competitive again is a tough problem. But watering down legal punishment for those willfully endangering the public is not an acceptable remedy. Ensuring product safety is.

Thought Questions

1. What value assumption is made by the editor?

2. What value assumption is made by Gibbins?

3. Both sides use statistical evidence to support their positions. Evaluate the use of this evidence.

4. Both sides use striking examples to support their positions. Identify one example from each position.

5. What descriptive assumptions does the editor make about how the judicial system works? Do you agree with these assumptions?

6. Are other proposals better able to deal with the alleged problems in the tort litigation system without some of the objections to limitation on punitive damage awards?

FEDERAL PRODUCT REGULATION

The federal government's involvement in consumer protection from potentially hazardous products parallels similar involvement in the areas of consumer debt, purchases of securities, and product marketing. The federal government's main responsibility here can be summed up as *prevention*. The federal law attempts to prevent injuries through standard setting and regulation. In the following materials, the three primary federal agencies involved in the regulation of potentially hazardous products are briefly reviewed: the National Highway Traffic and Motor Vehicle Safety Administration, the Food and Drug Administration, and the Consumer Product Safety Commission.

National Traffic and Motor Vehicle Safety Administration

The goal of the National Traffic and Motor Vehicle Safety Act is to reduce deaths and injuries connected with traffic accidents. The act established the National Highway Traffic and Motor Vehicle Safety Administration (NHTSA) authorizing it to establish motor vehicle standards. It is unlawful for manufacturers or dealers to sell any motor vehicle unless it conforms to these safety standards.

NHTSA's motor vehicle safety standards must be reasonable, practicable, and appropriate considering the impact on accident and injury reductions. NHTSA has issued standards for occupant protection, windshields, control panels, lights and reflectors, brake systems, fuel systems, body strength, and tires.

Food and Drug Administration

The federal Food, Drug, and Cosmetic Act, enacted in 1938, regulates the sale and distribution of food, drugs, and cosmetics to control harmful substances and to eliminate consumer deception. The act prohibits the sale or distribution of adulterated or misbranded food, drugs, or cosmetics.

The Food and Drug Administration (FDA) administers the act as well as related consumer protection acts such as the Filled Milk Act, the Federal Import Milk Act, the Tea Importation Act, the Federal Caustic Poison Act, and the Fair Packaging and Labeling Act.

The FDA has rulemaking powers and the power to investigate records of producers of food, drugs, and cosmetics, to seize products, and to grant premarket approval for the sale and distribution of new drugs. The act also regulates color additives. A color additive is deemed unsafe unless listed by the FDA. No color additive will be listed if it has been found to induce cancer in man or animal.

The act does not provide for private enforcement. However, compliance with the act is not a defense to actions in negligence. Federal courts may enjoin violations of the act. For example, they may enjoin the sale of unapproved drugs. The FDA may refer a case to the U.S. Attorney for criminal prosecution of serious violations. However, the defendant must first be given an opportunity to meet with representatives of the agency to explain why no criminal proceeding should be instituted. As is clear from the next case, some violations of the act constitute misdemeanors, while others result in felonies.

U.S. v. BRADSHAW
840F. 2d 871 (11th Cir. 1988)

Bradshaw (appellant) operated an illegal wholesale drug business selling steroid drugs to customers without prescriptions. Most of his customers were athletes who took steroids to improve athletic performance. The Food and Drug Administration has not approved the use of steroids for such purpose.

Bradshaw sold steroids to Shields and Perkins, who bought them for personal consumption and resale as willing buyers who got what they expected. Bradshaw took a variety of measures to avoid detection. He moved from state to state frequently. He used mail drops rather than his home address when mailing drugs. He used false names and mislabeled his packages as vitamins. He even discussed methods of avoiding detection with his customers. He obtained a Florida drug wholesaler's permit by misrepresenting himself to Florida state drug authorities.

Bradshaw was charged with violating the federal Food, Drug, and Cosmetic Act. Violation of the act is a felony if it is a second offense or if it is committed with "intent to defraud or mislead." Bradshaw was convicted of a felony and appealed his conviction.

ANDERSON, Judge

We must determine whether the trial judge properly submitted the government's theory to the jury. Bradshaw urges us to construe the Act strictly to limit the felony penalty to situations in which the conduct defrauds or misleads the ultimate consumer. In considering Bradshaw's argument, we are mindful that "[t]he starting point of statutory construction is the plain language of the statute itself."

We see no indication in the language of the statute or its legislative history that Congress meant to limit the felony penalty to conduct intended to defraud the ultimate consumer to the exclusion of the government enforcement agencies. To the contrary, the structure of the statutory scheme, the purpose of the statute, and the case law persuade us that Congress meant to encompass conduct intended to defraud government enforcement agencies.

As noted at the outset, the Act lists the acts which constitute criminal violations of the Act. Section 333(a) provides that anyone who violates a provision of section 331 commits a misdemeanor. Section 333(b) provides that "[n]otwithstanding the provisions of subsection (a) of this section, if any person commits . . . such a violation [i.e., a violation of section 331] with intent to defraud or mislead . . .," he commits a felony.

Several of the acts section 331 prohibits concern only the government. For example, section 331(p) prohibits the failure to permit FDA access to records and failure to make reports to the FDA and section 331(f) (refusal to permit FDA inspection). After reading these sections with section 333, it is clear that the FDA is the entity most likely to be defrauded under these provisions. Thus, we conclude that Congress intended the "intent to defraud or mislead" language of section 333(b) to extend to the FDA.

The purpose of the statute also supports our conclusion. The general scheme of the Act and its legislative history indicate that the overriding congressional purpose was consumer protection — the protection of the public against any misbranded or adulterated food, drug, device, or cosmetic. When Bradshaw misled the governmental agencies, thereby frustrating their efforts to protect the public, he indirectly misled and defrauded the public. Thus, Bradshaw's actions fell squarely within the congressional purpose. Bradshaw's arguments that the Act's goal of consumer protection somehow limits the felony penalty to conduct intended to defraud the consumer are unpersuasive. Our result is entirely consistent with that goal.

Finally, although the particular provision at issue here has not been previously interpreted, case law interpreting similar provisions in other statutes is much the same as our interpretation of the FDA Act.

Case Questions

1. Under what theory was the government pursuing a felony conviction against Bradshaw? What was Bradshaw's argument?

2. What is the value conflict evident in this case? On what basis could one argue that there should be no liability since Bradshaw sold to willing buyers who got what they expected?

3. List the support the court used to sustain the government's position.

4. Do you agree with the FDA's position of failing to approve steroids for building muscle mass? Explain.

Consumer Product Safety Commission

The Consumer Product Safety Act (1972) established the Consumer Product Safety Commission (CPSC) to protect consumers against unsafe products. The act is designed to (1) protect the public against unreasonable risks of injury associated with consumer products, (2) assist consumers in evaluating the comparative safety of consumer products, (3) develop uniform safety standards for consumer products and minimize conflicting state and local regulations, and (4) promote research and investigation into the cause and prevention of product-related deaths, illnesses, and injuries. To fulfill these purposes, the CPSC has been granted a broad range of powers to regulate **consumer products.**

Consumer Product

A consumer product is broadly defined to include any article produced or distributed for sale to a consumer, or for a consumer's personal use, consumption, or enjoyment in or around a household, residence, school, building, in recreation, or otherwise. This does not include products that are not customarily sold to or used by consumers. However, items not ordinarily produced for consumer purchase but customarily used by consumers are included within the definition. For example, a coin-operated copier machine would be covered even though it is not ordinarily sold to consumers because manufacturers produce them for consumer use.

The act specifically excludes some products from regulation — for example, tobacco, pesticides, firearms, aircraft, drugs, food, boats, and motor vehicles. These items are regulated by other laws.

Unreasonable Risks

The CPSC may issue consumer product safety rules only after finding that the rule is reasonably necessary to reduce or eliminate an unreasonable risk of injury from the product. The CPSC must consider a cost-benefit analysis, weighing the risk against the economic impact of any proposal. For example, the court overturned a CPSC rule that required labels on swimming pool slides warning of the risk of paraplegia. The court held that the probability the warning would reduce such injuries was not documented and that the cost to the manufacturers exceeded any speculative benefit.

Standards and Bans

The CPSC sets safety standards for products and may issue a product ban if no safety standard would be adequate to protect the consumer. However, voluntary safety standards are preferred over mandatory standards. Therefore, if an industry has voluntarily adopted standards to address a particular product's safety hazard, the CPSC must rely on that standard. Further, even if a voluntary standard is not in effect, the CPSC often works with the particular industries urging adoption of adequate voluntary safety standards before the CPSC seeks to implement mandatory rules.

In addition, the act permits the CPSC to promulgate a performance or labeling standard. A **performance standard** is one that may be measured by a test. For example, one performance standard adopted to reduce the risk of injury when using walk-behind lawn mowers requires that "shields used to prevent access to the blade must be capable of withstanding a static tensile force of 50 pounds without permanent separation, crack or deformation." A **labeling standard** requires that some type of marking be included on the product. For example, a CPSC standard requires a label on lawn mowers warning of the danger of inserting hands and feet into the chute.

At this point, the CPSC has only issued a few mandatory safety standards. They include regulation of swimming pool slides, architectural glazing materials, matchbooks, walk-behind lawn mowers, and omnidirectional citizen band antennas. The CPSC's largest impact is in the area of convincing industries to adopt voluntary safety standards.

Remedies and Penalties

Products that do not conform to safety standards may be seized by the government. In addition, there are both civil and criminal penalties for violating the act. Any person who knowingly violates the act is subject to a civil fine of up to $2,000 for each violation. Any person who both knowingly and willfully violates the act may suffer a $50,000 fine and/or imprisonment for up to one year.

Interested parties may sue to enforce a consumer product safety standard or certain other CPSC orders. If successful, the plaintiff may recover the costs of the suit, including attorney fees. Additionally, persons injured as a result of a knowing and willful violation may obtain damages for their injury.

END-OF-CHAPTER QUESTIONS

1. State the major economic rationale for the privity requirement in early products liability law. Is it still valid? What conditions have changed that mitigate against it?

2. Compare and contrast state products liability law and the Magnuson-Moss Act.

3. Under what circumstances would a person choose to pursue a negligence action rather than a breach of implied warranty action? How might a defendant's response to these two theories differ? Discuss fully.

4. Argue one of the opposing positions on the tort reform issue. Be prepared to support your position.

5. Think back to the FFI scenario in the chapter opener. If Sarah decides to market the S-1 anyway, what is FFI's potential legal liability? Is there any way that FFI can minimize this liability? What would be the impact of CPSC involvement?

6. What are the basic policy rationales for strict products liability law? What value conflicts are addressed in this position? What practical limitations were recognized in adopting strict products liability? What new practical impact does strict liability cause?

7. The plaintiff, Kenneth Garrison, sued the defendant, Heublein, Inc., the manufacturer and distributor of Smirnoff Vodka, for physical and mental injuries resulting from the consumption of Heublein's product over a 20-year period. What type of theory would Garrison most likely employ in this case? State the case in its strongest form for Garrison. What defense should Heublein raise? Discuss. See *Garrison v. Heublein*, 673 F.2d 189 (7th Cir. 1982).

8. George Becker, the plaintiff, was severely injured when he slipped and fell against a frosted shower door in the apartment he leased from IRM Corporation, the defendant-landlord. The door was made of untempered glass, and it is undisputed that the risk of serious injury would have been substantially reduced had the door been made of tempered glass. IRM Corporation purchased the 36-unit apartment building in 1974. It had been built in 1962. Do the policies that gave rise to strict liability make sense in this case between a plaintiff-tenant and his landlord? Thoroughly discuss the policies and apply them in this case. See *Becker v. IRM Corporation*, 669 P.2d 116 (Cal 1985).

9. The plaintiff, Shaffer, ordered a glass of wine at a restaurant operated by the defendant, Victoria Station, Inc. In the

course of taking his first or second sip of wine, the wineglass broke in Shaffer's hand, causing permanent injury. Shaffer sued Victoria Station, Inc. under theories of breach of implied warranty of merchantability and strict liability. What hurdles would Shaffer face in this case? Who should prevail? See *Shaffer v. Victoria Station. Inc.*, 588 P.2d 233 (Wash 1978).

10. Four-year-old Richard Nicholas was badly burned while playing with matches when his T-shirt caught fire. He sued Union Underwear Company, Inc., the manufacturer and seller of the shirt, using a strict liability theory. What type of product defect would be alleged here? Do you think this defect rendered the product "unreasonably dangerous"? Discuss what defenses might be raised in this case. Are there offsetting hazards from fire retardant treatment that should be considered in a cost-benefit analysis? How would the CPSC approach this problem. See *Nicholas v. Union Underwear Co.*, 602 S.W.2d 429 (Ky 1980).

11. Scandinavian Airline System (SAS) sued the manufacturer, United Aircraft Corp., for property damage resulting from the failure of two United jet aircraft engines on two different occasions. The failure of these jet engines caused damage to the engines themselves and to the two Scandinavian DC-9 aircraft on which they were installed. Do the policies that gave rise to strict liability support SAS's use of that theory in this case? Discuss fully. See *Scandinavian Airline System v. United Aircraft Corp.*, 601 F.2d 425 (9th Cir. 1979).

Part V

Commercial Paper

■

Chapter 24

Negotiability

■

CRITICAL THINKING INQUIRIES

As you read this chapter, you should be able to address the following:

- Explain the relationship between negotiable instruments and non-negotiable instruments.
- Evaluate the following statement: ''A holder of a non-negotiable instrument has no rights under the instrument.''
- Analyze the following statement: ''Given the rationale for negotiability, it should be solely a matter of form determinable from the face of the instrument.''
- Why would the holder want to know the fixed amount and the time for payment?
- Why is an instrument subject to acceleration ''payable at a definite time''? Does the holder know when payment will be made?

MANAGERIAL PERSPECTIVE

Jones is the chief financial officer of a small company, Umbroo, Inc. that manufactures umbrellas. Umbroo is considering financing its sales by accepting short-term promissory notes for payment.

Jones is concerned about default on the notes. To eliminate the risk of nonpayment, he is considering selling them at discount to the ABC Bank. He wants to structure the transaction in a way that will increase the marketability of these notes, minimize the risks to Umbroo, Inc., and get the most money possible.

- What should Jones consider in making this decision?
- What potential liability would Umbroo, Inc., have to ABC Bank?
- What factors would ABC weigh in deciding whether or not to purchase the paper at discount?

This is a classic commercial paper scenario. It illustrates both the pervasiveness of commercial paper in today's society and the benefits. Umbroo's customers will be able to purchase umbrellas on credit. Umbroo will be able to minimize the risks of nonpayment and avoid the cash flow difficulties of extending credit by selling the paper. ABC Bank will make money by buying the paper at discount and collecting the full amount.

INTRODUCTION

Money was created to eliminate the awkwardness of bartered exchanges. However, the use of money created problems of its own. For one, it was dangerous to carry large sums of money. As a result, commercial paper was developed. Commercial paper represents both money and the promise of future payment of money. For example, a check can be used as money to pay for goods, but it provides safeguards from the dangers of handling money and is in fact a promise to pay money in the future.

Commercial paper performs a crucial function in the business community, facilitating commerce and serving as the primary means of payment for goods and services. Considering the frequency of the credit transaction, the importance of commercial paper cannot be overemphasized. Commercial paper can be either negotiable or non-negotiable.

The Importance of Negotiability

Negotiability is important because it creates an instrument marketable in commerce. Jones and Umbroo, Inc. can sell their paper, rather than waiting for payment. In that way, they can finance more sales and reduce the risks of nonpayment. The ABC Bank is willing to buy **negotiable** paper (this refers to the form of the paper) properly **negotiated** (this refers to the transfer process) hoping to become a **holder in due course** (a type of superplaintiff). As we will see, the rights of a holder in due course of negotiable paper are awesome. The holder in due course of negotiable paper takes free from most claims and defenses that could have been asserted against the seller of the paper. For example, assume that Umbroo sells 100 cases of umbrellas to The Department Store, taking in return a promissory note for $10,000. Assume further that Umbroo sells the note for $9,000 to ABC Bank, who becomes a holder in due course. If the umbrellas are defective,

that defense is not good against the holder in due course, ABC Bank. The Department Store must pay the promissory note in spite of its defense. Thus, the risks of nonpayment are reduced for the holder in due course. The holder in due course is more willing to buy the paper and more willing to pay a higher price for that paper. This makes more money available for Umbroo, Inc. to finance the next sale. Commerce is facilitated. On the other hand, the rights of a purchaser of non-negotiable paper are similar to the rights of an assignee on a contract. Such a purchaser takes subject to all claims and defenses that could have been asserted against the seller of the paper. If Umbroo had merely assigned its contract right, ABC Bank would have taken subject to The Department Store's defense (see Chapter 17).

The Law

The early law governing commercial paper was created by merchants using commercial paper. Initially, this law was applied by a separate court system throughout 14th-century Europe. As these courts were absorbed into the traditional system, the courts continued in many cases to apply "the law merchant."

Today, the law of commercial paper is governed by Article 3 of the Uniform Commercial Code. Article 3 replaced the Uniform Negotiable Instruments Law (1896) and was intended to provide for changing commercial practices and uniformity. Article 3 was adopted in all 50 states. However, Article 3 recently underwent a substantial revision, its first since adoption in the early 1950s. Revised Article 3 is intended to accommodate modern technologies, in particular the advent of computer processing of a high volume of checks. Further, revised Article 3 recognizes the needs of a rapidly expanding national and international economy, the requirement for more rapid funds availability and new payment mechanisms, and the need for more clarity and certainty.

This text will consider the 1990 revisions to Article 3. At this writing, 26 states had adopted the revised Article 3.[1] Because of the significant

---

[1] The following states have adopted revised Article 3: Alaska, Arizona, Arkansas, California, Connecticut, Florida, Hawaii, Idaho, Illinois, Indiana, Kansas, Louisiana, Minnesota, Mississippi, Missouri, Montana, Nebraska, New Mexico, North Dakota, Oklahoma, Pennsylvania, Utah, Virginia, Washington, West Virginia, and Wyoming. Adoption is pending in District of Columbia, Maine, Massachusetts, New Hampshire, New York, Ohio, and Oregon.

Figure 24–1   Note

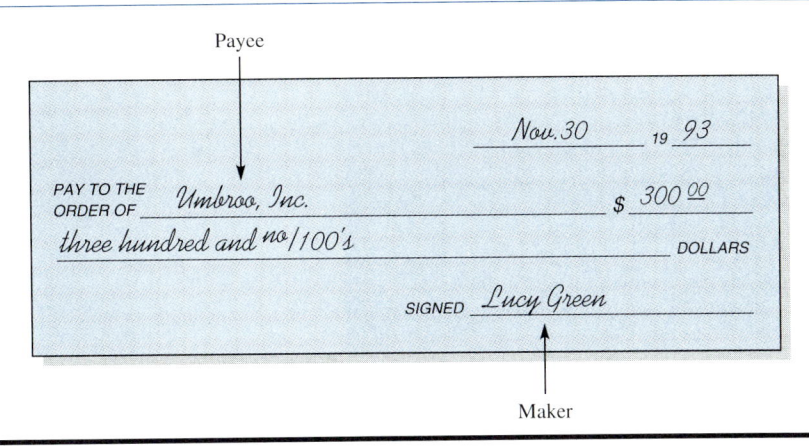

---

changes incorporated in the revisions, this part will, where relevant, indicate the changes from prior law.

Types of Negotiable Instruments and the Parties to Them

There are many types of negotiable instruments. For example, money is perhaps the most negotiable of all paper. However, the scope of Article 3 is limited to two types of instruments: notes and drafts [UCC § 3–102(1)].

Note
A **note** is a two-party instrument where one party promises to pay money to another party [UCC § 2–104(e)]. The party to pay is called the **maker.** The party to be paid is called the **payee.**

In Figure 24–1, Umbroo, Inc. is the *payee* and Lucy is the *maker* [UCC § 3–103(a)(5)]. If the maker on the note is a bank, the note is called a **certificate of deposit** [UCC § 2–104(j)]. Figure 24–2 is a sample promissory note.

Draft
A **draft** is a three-party instrument where one party orders a second party to pay money to a third party [UCC § 3–104(e)]. The one who orders payment is called the **drawer** [UCC § 3–103(a)(3)]; the one who is to pay is called the **drawee** [UCC § 3–103(a)(2)]; and the one to be paid is called the payee. In Figure 24–3, Umbroo, Inc. is the *payee*, Lucy is the *drawer* and the Last National Bank is the *drawee*.

A draft where the drawee is a bank and that is payable on demand is called a **check** [UCC § 3–104(f)]. A draft where the drawer and the drawee are the same bank is termed a **cashier's check** [UCC § 3–104(g)]. A draft drawn by one bank on another bank, or payable through another bank, is termed a **teller's check** [UCC § 3–104(h)].

REQUISITES OF NEGOTIABILITY

Because the requirements of negotiability are designed to encourage the marketability of commercial paper, it is obviously necessary for the purchaser of such paper to be able to ascertain quickly whether the paper is negotiable. Thus, as a general rule, one must be capable of determining negotiability from the face of the instrument without reference to any other source. Negotiability is a matter of *form*. If the instrument is in the proper form, it is negotiable; if the instrument is not in the proper form, it is not negotiable.

In order for an instrument to be negotiable, all requirements of negotiability stated in UCC section 3–104 must be met. In general, to be negotiable, an instrument must be:

- In writing.
- Contain a promise or order.
- Signed by the maker or drawer.
- Unconditional.
- To pay a fixed amount.
- In money.
- Contain no other undertaking.

Figure 24–2 Promissory Note

$ *$12,000* ______________________, Kansas *March 29* 19 *93* **NOTE (Time or Installment)**
(Bank Office and Location)

For Value Received, the Undersigned (whether one or more than one) promises to pay to the order of Bank ("Bank ") the sum of *twelve thousand* Dollars (the "Principal Sum") without offset with interest on the unpaid balance of the Principal Sum from the date hereof until maturity at the per annum percentage rate as indicated by the box checked below; provided that, if no box is checked, interest will be charged at a floating per annum rate at all times equal to the Bank's Prime Rate (as hereinafter defined), plus two (2%) percent.

[X] FIXED: *10* %/ [ ] VARIABLE: A rate at all times equal to the Bank's Prime Rate, as that rate changes from time to time, plus ________ % per annum (2% per annum, if blank), the rate hereon increasing or decreasing each time and as of the date the Bank's Prime Rate increases or decreases, provided that the interest rate hereon will never be lower than ________ % per annum. The term "Prime Rate," as used in this Note, means the floating and fluctuating per annum prime rate of interest of the Bank established and declared by the Bank at any time and from time to time.

Undersigned shall pay to Bank the Principal Sum, plus interest at the per annum rate indicated above, according to the schedule adjacent to the box marked below, provided that, if no box is checked below, the Note shall be payable to the Bank UPON DEMAND:

[X] TIME: The Principal Sum plus accrued interest shall be due on *September 12*, 19 *97*. Interest shall be payable whenever demanded by the Bank. (If no date is specified, the Principal Sum plus annual interest shall be due on the date thirty (30) days following the date of the Note.)

[ ] INSTALLMENT (Separate Payments of Principal and Interest): In ________ consecutive principal installments of $ ________ each, commencing on the ________ day of ________, 19 ________, and on the same day of each succeeding ________ and a final principal installment of $ ________, due and payable on ________, 19 ________, on which date the unpaid balance of the Principal Sum plus accrued and unpaid interest shall be payable in full. Interest shall be payable whenever demanded by the Bank from time to time.

[ ] INSTALLMENT (Combined Payments of Principal and Interest—Use this paragraph for FIXED-RATE loans only): In ________ consecutive installments of $ ________ commencing on the ________ day of ________, 19 ________, and on the same day of each succeeding ________ and a final installment of $ ________ due and payable on ________, 19 ________, on which date the unpaid balance of the Principal Sum plus accrued and unpaid interest shall be payable in full.

The Undersigned may prepay the Principal Sum, in whole or in part, provided that, if interest on the unpaid balance of the Principal Sum accrues at a FIXED per annum percentage rate as indicated by the box checked above, then the Undersigned may prepay the Principal Sum, in whole or in part, provided that the undersigned gives to the Bank not less than fifteen (15) days prior to the date of prepayment written notice of the amount of the prepayment and the date on which it is to be made, and the Undersigned pays to the Bank together with the prepaid Principal Sum, a prepayment fee equal to the positive remainder of:

1. the present value of a series of amounts, scheduled to be paid on the same dates upon which interest would be payable hereunder had no prepayment been made, determined by applying (A) the positive difference obtained by subtracting from the interest rate on this Note the Treasury instrument yield determined by the Bank as of the date which is three (3) banking days prior to the prepayment date, by reference to source material selected by the Bank, for an instrument of a term equivalent to the period of time from the prepayment date to the maturity date of this Note, to (B) the prepaid Principal Sum as scheduled to be outstanding from time to time for the remainder of the original term of this Note; MINUS
2. the present value of a series of amounts, scheduled to be paid on the same dates upon which interest would be payable hereunder had no prepayment been made, determined by applying (A) the positive difference obtained by subtracting from the interest rate on this Note the yield for a Treasury instrument of a term equivalent to the period of time from the date of this Note to the maturity date of this note as such yield is reported in the Federal Reserve Statistical Release H.15 (519) (the "Release") as of the date of this Note, to (B) the prepaid Principal Sum as scheduled to be outstanding from time to time for the remainder of the original term of this Note.

The present value calculations will be made by use of a discount rate equal to the Treasury instrument yield referred to in paragraph 1 immediately above. For purposes of computing the prepayment fee, the term "Treasury instrument" shall mean those designated in the Release as "Treasury bills (secondary market)" if the relevant term is six months or less, and those designated "Treasury constant maturities" if the relevant term is more than six months. In the event any time period in respect of which a percentage rate is to be determined by reference to the Release is other than a period for which the Release contains rate information, the rate to be used in calculating the prepayment fee shall be determined by interpolation of rates for Treasury instruments of relevant maturities. In the absence of manifest error, the amount of the fee as determined by the Bank shall be deemed presumptively correct.

Interest will be calculated on the basis of a 360 day year applied to the actual number of days the Principal Sum, or any portion thereof, is outstanding. After maturity (whether by acceleration, declaration, extension or otherwise), the unpaid balance of the Principal Sum plus accrued and unpaid interest thereon earned to maturity shall bear interest payable on demand at a per annum rate of interest which is equal to the rate of interest on this Note until maturity, as indicated above, plus 1% per annum. If the blank in this sentence is completed, the Bank is authorized to deduct any payment from Bank account number ________ on or after the date the payment is due.

The obligations of the Undersigned evidenced by this Note are secured by, guaranteed by, and are part of the obligations referred to in any security agreement, guaranty agreement, mortgage, deed of trust, pledge agreement, loan agreement, hypothecation agreement, indemnity agreement, letter of credit application, assignment or any other document previously, simultaneously or hereafter executed and delivered by any of the Undersigned or by any other party (collectively, the "Loan Documents") as security for, as a guaranty of, or in connection with obligations of any of the undersigned to the Bank or to any other holder, whether or not this Note is specifically referred to therein. If this Note is a renewal, extension or modification of the terms of any existing obligation of the Undersigned to the Bank, which obligation is secured by an interest in real property, Undersigned and Bank agree that this Note is not intended to be a novation but is rather intended only to renew, extend or modify the obligation to the extent applicable.

All payments of the principal of and interest on this Note shall be (a) paid in lawful money of the United States of America during regular business hours of the Bank at the office of the Bank set forth above or at such other place as the Holder may at any time or from time to time designate in writing to the Undersigned, and (b) applied first to the payment of all accrued and unpaid interest and other charges and then to the payment of principal. Any payment on this Note made by an instrument drawn on a financial institution other than the Bank shall be credited on the business day following the business day on which the Bank received the instrument. If the Undersigned does not make payment within fifteen (15) days after the date on which it is demanded or otherwise due and payable, the Undersigned agrees to pay a late charge equal to 5% of the amount of any past due interest.

Each Obligor (which term shall include the Undersigned and each endorser, guarantor, accommodation party and surety hereof) hereby waives demand, presentment for payment, protest, notice of dishonor and of protest and agrees that at any time and from time to time and with or without consideration, the Holder may, without notice to or further consent of any Obligor and without in any manner releasing, lessening or affecting the obligations of any Obligor hereunder and under any of the Loan Documents: (a) release, surrender, waive, add, substitute, settle, exchange, compromise, modify, extend or grant indulgences with respect to, (i) this Note, (ii) any of the Loan Documents, (iii) all or any part of any collateral or security for this Note, and (iv) any Obligor; (b) complete any blank space in this Note according to the terms upon which the loan evidenced hereby is made; and (c) grant any extension or other postponements of the time of payment hereof. If the Undersigned consists of two or more parties, the term "Undersigned" as used herein means each of such parties, jointly and severally, and their obligations hereunder are joint and several. The Holder may (without notice to or consent of any of the Undersigned or any other Obligor, and with or without consideration) release, compromise, settle with, or proceed against any one or more of the Undersigned or any other Obligor without releasing, lessening or affecting the obligations hereunder or under any of the Loan Documents of the other or others of the Undersigned or any other Obligor. The Undersigned promptly shall provide such financial, operational or business information in each instance and in such form as the Bank in its sole discretion shall require. The term "Holder" as used herein means the holder of this Note, including the Bank.

The occurrence of any one or more of the following events shall constitute a default under this Note: (a) failure of the Undersigned to pay when due any amount required to be paid by Undersigned hereunder; (b) the death of any Obligor; (c) the failure of any Obligor to perform or comply with any of the provisions hereof and/or of the Loan Documents; (d) the occurrence of a default under any of the Loan Documents; (e) if any information contained in any financial statement, application, schedule, report or any other document given by the Undersigned or any other party in connection with the obligations of the Undersigned evidenced by this Note or any of the Loan Documents is not in all respects true and accurate or if the Undersigned or such other party failed to state any material fact or any fact necessary to make such information not misleading; (f) the filing of any petition under the Bankruptcy Act or any similar Federal or State statute by or against any Obligor; (g) an application for the appointment of a receiver for, the making of a general assignment for the benefit of creditors by, or the insolvency of, any Obligor; (h) the dissolution, merger, consolidation, or reorganization of any Obligor; (i) the determination in good faith by the Bank that a material adverse change has occurred in the financial condition of any Obligor from the condition set forth in the most recent financial statement of such Obligor theretofore furnished to the Bank, or from the financial condition of such Obligor as theretofore most recently disclosed to the Bank in any other manner; or (j) the determination in good faith by the Bank that the prospect of payment of this Note is impaired for any reason. Whenever there is a default under this Note, the Bank may, at its option, (a) declare the unpaid balance of the Principal Sum, together with all unpaid and accrued interest thereon, to be immediately due and payable, and (b) exercise any or all rights and remedies available to it hereunder under applicable laws and under any of the Loan Documents.

If this Note is placed in the hands of an attorney for collection after maturity (whether by acceleration, declaration, extension or otherwise), the Undersigned shall pay on demand all costs and expenses of collection including an attorney's fee equal to 20% of the then outstanding unpaid balance of the Principal Sum. As security for the payment of all obligations under this Note, each Obligor hereby pledges and grants to the Holder a lien on and security interest in, and authorizes the Holder to offset such obligations of such Obligor to the Holder against, all property of such Obligor now or at any time hereafter in the possession of, in transit to, under the control of, or on deposit with, the Holder in any capacity whatsoever, including, without limitation any balance of any deposit account and any credits with the Holder.

If this Note is not paid at maturity (whether by acceleration, declaration, extension or otherwise), each Obligor who signs this Note and/or the Unconditional Guaranty of Payment set forth below, hereby authorizes and empowers any attorney of any Court of Record within the United States to appear for each such Obligor or any one or more of them in any Court in one or more proceedings or before any clerk thereof, and confess judgment against each such Obligor, without prior notice, or opportunity to prior hearing, in favor of the holder for the then unpaid balance of the Principal Sum, with interest accrued thereon and the cost of suit and an attorney's fee of 15% of such unpaid balance of the Principal Sum, hereby waiving and releasing, to the extent permitted by law, all errors and all rights of exemption, appeal, stay of execution, inquisition and extension upon any levy on real estate or personal property to which each such Obligor may otherwise be entitled under the laws of the United States or of any state or possession of the United States now in force which may hereafter be passed.

In the event any one or more of the provisions of this Note shall for any reason be held to be invalid, illegal or unenforceable, in whole or in part or in any respect, or in the event that any one or more of the provisions of this Note operate or would prospectively operate to invalidate this Note, then and in either of those events, such provision or provisions only shall be deemed null and void and shall not affect any other provision of this Note and the remaining provisions of this Note shall remain operative and in full force and effect and shall in no way be affected, prejudiced or disturbed thereby. AGREEMENT WAIVING RIGHT TO TRIAL BY JURY: Each Obligor who signs this Note hereby (i) covenants and agrees not to elect a trial by jury of any issue triable of right by a jury, and (ii) waives trial by jury in any action or proceeding to which such Obligor and/or the Bank may be parties, arising out of, in connection with, or in any way pertaining to this Note and/or the Loan Documents. This waiver of jury trial is separately given, knowingly and voluntarily, by each Obligor who signs this Note, and is intended to encompass and to constitute a waiver of trial by jury of all claims against all parties to such actions and proceedings, including claims against parties who are not parties to the Loan Documents or any of them. The Bank is hereby authorized and requested to submit this Note to any court having jurisdiction over the subject matter, such Obligor and the Bank, so as to serve as conclusive evidence of each such Obligor's waiver of right to trial by jury.

Each right, power and remedy of the Holder hereunder, under the Loan Documents or under applicable laws shall be cumulative and concurrent, and the exercise of any one or more of them shall not preclude the simultaneous or later exercise by the Holder or any or all such rights, powers or remedies. No failure or delay by the Holder to insist upon the strict performance of any one or more provisions of this Note or of the Loan Documents or to exercise any right, power or remedy consequent upon a breach thereof or default hereunder shall constitute a waiver thereof, or preclude the Holder from exercising any such right, power or remedy. By accepting full or partial payment after the due date of any amount of principal or interest, and by permitting the Undersigned to designate a Bank deposit account from which payments due hereunder may be deducted, the Holder shall not be deemed to have waived the right either to require payment when due and payable of all other amounts of principal of or interest on this Note or to exercise any rights and remedies available to it in order to collect all such other amounts due and payable under this Note. No modification, change, waiver or amendment of this Note shall be deemed to be made by the Holder unless in writing signed by the Holder, and each such waiver, if any, shall apply only with respect to the specific instance involved. This Note shall be deemed made in, and shall be governed by the laws of, the State of Kansas.

The signature(s) and seal(s) of the Undersigned is/are subscribed to this Note the day and year written above.

By: ______________________ (SEAL) By: *James C. Jones* (SEAL)

By: ______________________ (SEAL) By: *Umbroo, Inc.* (SEAL)

Figure 24–3   Draft

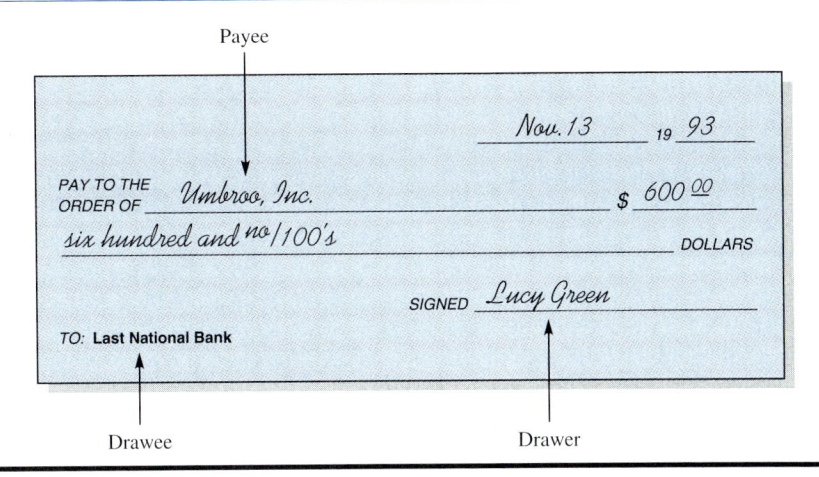

Payee

Nov. 13 19 93

PAY TO THE ORDER OF _Umbroo, Inc._ $ 600 00

six hundred and no/100's   DOLLARS

SIGNED _Lucy Green_

TO: **Last National Bank**

Drawee

Drawer

- Payable on demand or at a definite time.
- Payable to order or to bearer.

Writing

Because an intangible or oral promise cannot easily be transferred, the promise or order must be in writing to be negotiable. However, the writing requirement is liberally construed. A writing includes printing, typewriting, pen, pencil, or even paint [UCC § 1–201(46)]. In addition, there is no requirement that the writing be on paper. There is a famous article that talks of "The Negotiable Cow," and the Internal Revenue Service each year is the payee on a number of "negotiable shirts."

UCC § 1–201. General Definitions

(46) "Written" or "writing" includes printing, typewriting or any other intentional reduction to tangible form.

Promise or Order

Negotiable instruments are either promises or orders. If they are promises, they are notes. If they are orders, they are drafts. If they are neither, they are non-negotiable.

Promise

A **promise** is a commitment to pay [UCC § 3–103(9)]. Because it is merely an acknowledgment of a debt, an IOU by itself is not a promise.

UCC § 3–103. Definitions

(9) "Promise" means a written undertaking to pay money signed by the person undertaking to pay. An acknowledgment of an obligation by the obligor is not a promise.

Order

An **order** is a direction to an agent such as a bank to pay. A mere authorization, such as "This authorizes payment," is not an order. However, words of courtesy, such as "Please pay Jane Doe," do not turn an order into a mere request.

UCC § 3–103. Definitions

(6) "Order" means a written instruction to pay money signed by the person giving the instruction. . . . An authorization to pay is not an order.

Signed by the Maker or Drawer

The definitions of both promises (signed by the person undertaking to pay) and orders (signed by the person giving the instruction) make clear that in order to be negotiable, the instrument must be signed by the proper person. However, a formal **signature** is not required to meet the requirement of a signature. The test is one of "intent to *authenticate*" [§ 1–201(39)]. Authentication may be printed, stamped, or written. It may be by initials or even by thumbprint. For example, if a maker or drawer signs

Figure 24-4 Effective Signature in Body of Writing

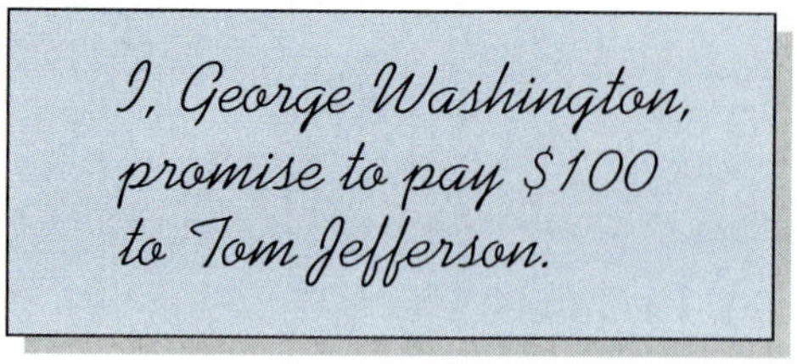

> I, George Washington, promise to pay $100 to Tom Jefferson.

the instrument with an ''X'' on the signature line, this may be a sufficient signature if made with intent to authenticate.

UCC § 1-201. General Definitions

(39) ''Signed'' includes any symbol executed or adopted by a party with present intention to authenticate a writing.

Further, the signature does not have to be at the bottom of the instrument. It may be in the body of the instrument or even in the letterhead, if used with intent to authenticate the writing. For example, the writing in Figure 24-4 contains an effective signature.

In addition, a trade name can be used as a signature [UCC § 3-401(b)]. For example, if Maria Maker operates a convenience store under the trade name ''Maria's Munchies,'' the use of the trade name ''Maria's Munchies'' as a signature binds Maria.

Unconditional

A promise or order must be unconditional if the instrument is to pass freely in commerce. A promise or order is **unconditional** unless one of the two tests set forth in UCC section 3-106 make the promise or order conditional: (1) it is subject to an express condition, or (2) it is subject to the terms in another writing.

Express Conditions

Express conditions destroy the negotiability of an instrument. For example, a note that provides that ''I, Michael Maker, promise to pay to the order of Joey Lechner $200 only if he delivers to me a bike in good working order'' is not negotiable. It is sub-

ject to an express condition. Michael is promising to pay Joey (and subsequent holders) only if a bike is delivered and it is in good working order. One contemplating buying that note has no way to determine from the face of the instrument whether or not Michael's promise to pay has been triggered— whether or not the condition has been satisfied.

UCC § 3-106. Unconditional Promise or Order

(a) . . . a promise or order is unconditional unless it states (i) an express condition to payment.

By contrast, a note that states ''I, Michael Maker, promise to pay to the order of Joey Lechner $200 for a bike'' is negotiable. It is not conditional. Although stating the consideration (the bike) might be considered an implied condition, only express conditions destroy negotiability. Implied conditions are irrelevant.

Subject to Another Writing

Executing a note ''subject to'' or ''governed by'' the provisions of the underlying contract destroys the negotiability of the note. This is true whether or not the underlying contract contains any conditions or terms that would have destroyed the negotiability. The rationale is that the holder must look off the face of the instrument to determine whether or not it is to be paid. For example, a note that states: ''This note is subject to a contract of sale dated April 19, 1993, between the parties'' is conditional and non-negotiable. Similarly, an otherwise negotiable note that provides: ''Rights and obligations of the parties with respect to this note are stated in an agreement dated June 18, 1993, between the parties'' is conditional and non-negotiable.

UCC § 3-106. Unconditional Promise or Order

(a) . . . a promise or order is unconditional unless it states . . . (ii) that the promise or order is subject to or governed by another writing, or (iii) that rights or obligations with respect to the promise or order are stated in another writing.

However, there is a distinction between making the note *subject to* the terms in another agreement and *mere reference* to another agreement. For example, language in a note that refers to the under-lying agreement and indicates that the instrument was executed "as per" or "in conjunction with" that underlying agreement does not destroy the ne-gotiability of the note. The note is merely referring to the underlying agreement. It is not subject to the terms of that agreement.

Many notes issued in commercial transactions are secured by collateral or are subject to acceleration or prepayment rights. As an exception to the above stated rule, the fact that such rights are contained in another writing will not destroy the negotiability of the note [UCC § 3–106(b)]. For example, a note is not conditional if it contains the following state-ment: "This note is secured by a security interest in collateral described in a security agreement created by the parties on today's date. Rights and obliga-tions with respect to the collateral are governed by the security agreement."

UCC § 3–106. Unconditional Promise or Order

(a) . . . A reference to another writing does not of itself make the promise or order conditional.

In the following case, the court applies old Ar-ticle 3 of the UCC to determine whether the note merely refers to another agreement or makes the note subject to the terms in the other agreement.

SOVRAN BANK, N.A. v. FRANKLIN
13 UCC Rep.Serv.2d 174 (Cir. Ct. Va. 1990)

On March 11, 1985, the plaintiff, Sovran Bank, N.A., sent a commitment letter to lend up to $812,000 to Orlando West Investor (Orlando), outlining repayment terms. The note was executed on Sovran's standard note form, with Sovran filling in specific terms. Principal was payable on demand, with interest payable quarterly. The note included the following language: "[i]f this Note is issued pursuant to a commitment letter, it shall be entitled to its benefits and subject to its terms and conditions, including any amendments thereto." Payment terms stated in the note and commitment letter conflicted. Defendant, Franklin, was a general partner of Orlando. In a suit on the note, the Court first considers the question of negotiability.

HARRISK, Judge

An initial question that must be resolved is whether this note is a negotiable instrument as defined by the Commercial Code. A note "must contain an uncondi-tional promise to pay a sum certain in money . . ." to be considered a negotiable instrument. UCC § 3–104. The Commercial Code further provides that "[a] promise or order is not unconditional if the instrument states that it is subject to or governed by any other agreement." UCC § 3–105(2)(a).

Language stating that the note is governed by another agreement renders the note non-negotiable. However, if the note merely states that it arises out of a separate agreement, it is a negotiable instru-ment. These two closely related factual situations must be analyzed with reference to the Code's in-tent: to insure that the holder can reasonably ascer-tain all essential terms of the note from its face. UCC § 3–105, Official Comment 8.

The distinction is between a mere recital of the existence of the separate agreement or a reference to it for informa-tion, which under paragraph (c) of subsection (1) will not affect negotiability, and any language which, fairly con-strued, requires the holder to look to the other agreement for the terms of payment.

The language of the note in question does not merely state that a commitment letter may exist, but clearly goes beyond that to make the grid note sub-ject to the terms of the commitment letter. This lan-guage evidences a conditional promise to pay, ren-dering the note non-negotiable.

Case Questions
1. Rewrite the note to make it negotiable.
2. Analyze: "It is the Code's intent to in-sure that the holder can reasonably ascer-tain all essential terms of the note from its face."

Particular Fund Doctrine

Under prior law, to be unconditional, the entire assets of the maker or drawer had to back up the obligation. If the instrument by its terms limited payment to only one source, the instrument was conditioned on the availability of that source and its sufficiency to meet the obligation. Thus, instruments that *limited* payment to a particular fund were conditional and non-negotiable. By contrast, instruments that merely *indicated* from which source payment was expected to be made were not conditional and were negotiable. If the fund was insufficient when payment was due, payment was made from another source.

The 1990 revisions to Article 3 reject the particular fund doctrine (see Figure 24–5). No reason was seen to require the entire assets of the obligor to back up the obligation. Market forces will determine the marketability of these limited instruments. If potential buyers are leary of instruments that are limited to particular funds, they will not buy them. Article 3 will still govern them.

UCC § 3–106. Unconditional Promise or Order

(b) A promise or order is not made conditional . . . (ii) because payment is limited to resort to a particular fund or source.

Fixed Amount

In order to be negotiable, the instrument must promise or order the payment of a **fixed amount** of money. Certain adjustments to that fixed sum are permitted, such as the addition of interest and other charges. Thus, it is clear that a note promising payment of "$1,000 with 8 percent interest" is negotiable. Similarly, a note promising payment of "$1,000 with 8 percent interest before January 1, 1993, but 10 percent after" is negotiable.

While this is similar to the "sum certain" requirement of old Article 3, the absolute prohibition against leaving the face of the instrument to determine the fixed sum is rejected. For example, a note payable at a rate of interest tied to the published prime rate, such as "$1,000 with interest at 2 points over prime," is negotiable under revised Article 3 [UCC § 3–112], but was non-negotiable under prior law (see Figure 24–6). To a large extent, this change was made because a number of notes are issued tied to the prime rate. The amount of interest must be readily ascertainable by reference to either a formula or an index described in the instrument.

UCC § 3–104. Negotiable Instrument

(a) . . . "negotiable instrument" means an unconditional promise or order to pay a fixed amount of money, with or without interest or other charges.

UCC § 3–112. Interest

(b) Interest may be stated in an instrument as a fixed or variable amount of money or it may be expressed as a fixed or a variable rate or rates. The amount or rate . . . may require reference to information not contained in the instrument.

Read the following case considering the question of variable rate notes before the revisions.

Figure 24–5   Particular Fund Doctrine in UCC Old and Revised Article 3: A Comparison

Old Article 3	Revised Article 3
Particular fund: Instruments where payment is limited to a particular fund are conditional and non-negotiable.	Particular fund: Rejected. Such instruments are negotiable.

Figure 24–6   Sum Certain (UCC Old Article 3) and Fixed Amount (UCC Revised Article 3): A Comparison

Old Article 3	Revised Article 3
Sum certain: Instruments with a variable interest rate are non-negotiable. Negotiability is destroyed if one has to leave the face of the instrument to find the rate.	Fixed amount: Variable interest rates are permitted. It does not destroy negotiability to leave the face of the instrument to refer to a described index.

GOSS, JR. v. TRINITY SAVINGS & LOAN ASSOCIATION
813 P.2d 492 (Oklahoma 1991)

In May 1982, the Gosses, the plaintiffs, obtained an adjustable rate mortgage loan from Trinity Savings & Loan (Trinity) to buy a new home. When Trinity tried to sell the note to the Federal National Mortgage Association (FNMA), it discovered that the note incorrectly showed the accrual rate of interest at 12.5 percent instead of the 16.5 percent that Trinity alleged was agreed to by the parties. The note was changed to reflect that "error" and FNMA purchased the note. The parties disagreed on whether the Gosses were aware of the alteration. The Gosses failed to make all payments. They alleged material alteration and fraud. FNMA asked for foreclosure.

LAVENDER, Justice

The question squarely presented is whether a variable interest rate note is a negotiable instrument pursuant to the Uniform Commercial Code. In the present case, the Gosses argue the note is not negotiable in that it does not satisfy the "sum certain" requirement of section 3–104(1)(b) since in order to determine what the variable interest rate is, an outside source must be consulted. The term "sum certain" is not defined in the Code. However, section 3–106 provides direction as to what a sum certain can be. Additional language concerning the sum certain requirement is found in Comment 1 of section 3–106. These comments have not been adopted as part of the official statute, however, they can be referred to when interpreting questions arising under the Code. Comment 1 reads:

It is sufficient that at any time of payment the holder is able to determine the amount then payable from the instrument itself with any necessary computation. . . . The computation must be one which can be made from the instrument itself without reference to any outside source, and this section does not make negotiable a note payable with interest "at the current rate."

We recognize the language insofar as the unofficial comment reads, would support the Gosses' contention that the note is not negotiable since an outside source must be consulted. We find, however, though there exists meritable argument on both sides of the question, we are persuaded the more rational, albeit difficult decision would hold the note is a negotiable instrument.

If the intent of the Code was to aid in the continued expansion of commercial practices, then common sense would tell us that when faced with a widespread commercial practice, such as in the present case, this court should acknowledge it.

The rule requiring certainty in commercial paper was a rule of commerce before it was a rule of law. It requires commercial, not mathematical certainty. As uncertainty which does not impair the function of negotiable instruments in the judgment of business men ought not to be regarded by the courts. . . . The whole question is, do [the provisions] render the instruments so uncertain as to destroy their fitness to pass current in the business world?

Adjustable interest rates are being routinely used in the commercial marketplace. "Since 1980, VRNs [variable rate notes] have become increasingly popular. For example, in 1984 approximately 80 percent of new mortgages and 60 percent of all mortgages had variable rates." While we are cognizant of the language of the Comment stating that it must not be necessary to refer to any outside source for the note to contain a sum certain on its face, we point to the official language of the Code which directs this court to liberally construe the act so as "to permit the continued expansion of commercial practices through custom, usage and agreement of the parties. . . ."

In the present case, the interest in this note was tied to the stated rate of interest as defined by the T-bill index. Before the advent of mass communication facilities offering ready access to such sources and the introduction of variable interest rates into the marketplace, the concern expressed by Comment 1 may have been justified, however, not so today. Any stranger to the transaction under the present set of facts, would not have been disadvantaged by the terms of the note, since the rate on the note could easily have been determined by making a simple phone call to check on the T-bill rate or refer to a published listing.

Therefore, for this court to construe the note as anything other than negotiable would in our opinion thwart the basic mandate laid down by the drafters that the Code remain flexible and responsive to the business community. Moreover, we see it as our responsibility to recognize and adopt established business practices.

On the narrow set of facts presented, we hold the note in our case negotiable. Because the business community considers such a note negotiable, it makes little sense for this court to find otherwise by focusing on a single line in the unofficial text of the code where its official reasoning and purpose would direct us to conclude otherwise.

Of final note, as of May 1990, there is a proposed final draft for revising article 3 on negotiable instruments. Section 1–112(b) of the proposed draft reads as follows:

Interest may be stated in an instrument as a fixed or variable amount of money or it may be expressed as a fixed or variable rate or rates. The amount or rate of interest may be stated or described in the instrument in any manner and may require reference to information not contained in the instrument.

As to the case at bar, we are comfortable that ours is a correct interpretation of the Code. However, we urge the legislature to review these proposed revisions and adopt such changes as would make our statutory law more responsive to current business practices.

Case Questions

1. How would the result of this case differ under revised Article 3? Would the analysis have been the same?
2. If the same result could have been reached, why was it necessary to revise the statute?
3. Is the statute still uniform if different state courts interpret it differently? Explain.
4. How could variable notes proliferate as the court states if they are not negotiable?

If an instrument provides for the payment of a stated sum "with interest" but does not specify the amount of interest, it is still negotiable. The judgment rate of interest (the rate set by statute to be added to judgments awarded) is supplied [UCC § 3–112(b)].

While revised Article 3 does not say so expressly, presumably the negotiability of a note is not lost by provisions for the addition of attorney fees or collection costs. These were permissible under prior law and are presumably what is meant by "other charges."

As was apparent from *Goss v. Trinity Savings*, the negotiability of variable rate loans has been the subject of a substantial amount of controversy. Read the following article, in which the author advocates precisely the type of reform that is contained in revised Article 3.

---

*An Argument for the Alteration of the UCC to Include Variable Rate Notes as Negotiable Instruments**

I. Introduction

With the advent of a more dynamic economy and fluctuating interest rates, variable rate notes (VRNs) have become the most predominant form of lending instrument in today's society. Borrowers as well as lenders find distinct advantages in using this form of instrument over the traditional fixed rate notes which were popular before this decade. Despite the widespread

---

*Source: Thomas B. Fiddler, "An Argument for the Alteration of the UCC to Include Variable Rate Notes as Negotiable Instruments," *Pittsburgh Journal of Law and Commerce*, 9 J.L & Com. 115 (1989) (footnotes omitted). Reprinted with permission.

commercial acceptance of VRNs, the Uniform Commercial Code (UCC) has not been altered to reflect this predominance. Thus, bound by an outdated UCC, courts have consistently interpreted these notes to be non-negotiable instruments.

■ ■ ■

V. An Argument for Making VRNs Negotiable

With narrow and explainable exceptions, courts have consistently refused to give negotiable status to VRNs. However, these instruments are widely used and accepted by both borrowers and lenders. In an economy with changing interest rates, the need for these instruments is obvious to protect the borrower and the lender. The UCC was meant to be flexible and to reflect the commercial practices of current times. Given the popularity and commercial use of VRNs, the UCC must be changed.

The logical next question is, ''Who should make the change, the legislature or the judiciary?'' Arguments can be made for both. Nonetheless, the stronger argument is that the legislature should institute the change. The clearest way to solve the uncertainty of a variable rate effect on negotiability would be by statute. A statutory amendment would give the commercial community an unambiguous standard to guide their practices.

To this point, only one state, Tennessee, has altered its version of the UCC to include VRNs as negotiable instruments. These changes should serve as models for other states in making VRNs negotiable instruments. A note is defined as negotiable under the Tennessee code if the instrument contains an unconditional promise or order to pay a sum in money which is determinable by a formula as provided in writing, whether or not such formula requires the use of extrinsic criteria. The sum certain requirement in Tennessee makes a sum payable a sum certain even though it is to be paid with a renegotiable or variable rate of interest.

The state legislatures should not be hesitant to change their versions of the UCC. The concerns of having the sum payable to be determined from a single instrument are not present in this instance. The requirement of negotiability ''demands that an instrument bear a definite sum in order that subsequent holders can take and transfer the instrument without plumbing the intricacies of individual relationships or payback schemes.''

''The sum certain requirement developed at a time when, unlike the present, there were no mass communication facilities offering ready access to such sources. When the specific source is named, one can easily ascertain the interest rate by newspapers, telephone or computer.'' So far as VRNs are concerned, modern technology has made obsolete the worries that were present when the sum certain requirement was developed.

Of course, worries still exist that a VRN refers to a specific bank's rates. For example, if the VRN does not, then the same problems exist that were always of concern, namely that a stranger cannot determine the terms of the agreement. The VRN should refer to a specific bank rate. If it does not refer to a specific bank rate, then the problems of a stranger not being able to determine the sum are once again present.

The argument has also been made for judicial change of the negotiability status of VRNs. Justice Compton in *Taylor [v. Roeder]* makes a strong argument for judicial change. Obviously, the UCC does call for liberal constructions of its provisions. The UCC also provides for the promotions of its underlying policies, one of which is to permit the continued expansion of commercial practices and uses. By recognizing those provisions the court could justify holding VRNs to be negotiable. The problem, however, with that approach is that some courts have refused outright to deem VRNs negotiable, feeling that it is the legislature's responsibility to make that change. UCC section 3–106 is unequivocal in its command that the sum certain must be determined solely from the face of the instrument.

Courts could also justify making VRNs negotiable instruments by asserting an analogy between notes calling for reference to a bank's rate with those cases calling for reference to a statutory rate. Since the reference to an outside source is permitted if the outside source is a statute, a similar exception could be created for referring to a particular bank's interest rate. A bank's rate, like the statute, is a reliable source available to the public at large.

Nonetheless, it is not the court's duty to amend unambiguous statutory laws in a political system such as ours. The job of the court is to interpret the cases in light of the statutes. When the statutes are unambiguous, no room exists for courts to decide the way laws should be. It is the legislature's duty to respond to changes in society and to ensure that the statutes fairly resolve the disputes that may arise.

For seven years, VRNs have not only been authorized by Congress, but also have been the most predominant form of lending instrument. The time has arrived for state legislatures to amend their versions of the UCC to reflect this reasonable commercial practice. All segments of our society have accepted VRNs as not only desirable, but also necessary. Furthermore, the worries that are present with other notes in which the sum certain cannot be determined without substantial difficulties are not present with VRNs. The necessary information to compute the sum can be attained with great ease.

Thought Questions

1. Analyze: "So far as VRNs are concerned, modern technology has made obsolete the worries that were present when the sum certain requirement was developed."
2. Would Fiddler think that the case of *Goss v. Trinity Savings* was correctly decided?
3. Does UCC revised Article 3 meet Fiddler's concerns?
4. Is the fact that these instruments are commercially accepted relevant?
5. Argue that courts can resolve this ambiguity and that statutory revision was unnecessary.

Money

In order to be negotiable, the promise must be to pay **money** [UCC § 3–104(a)]. The test of governmental sanction is used to define money [UCC § 1–201(24)]. While money is not limited to legal tender, money does not include a medium of exchange accepted in the community. Because such things as gold dust, subway tokens, or cigarettes, which may be accepted as a medium of exchange in a local community, are of fluctuating value and lack governmental sanction, they are not money.

UCC § 1–201. General Definitions

(24) "Money" means a medium of exchange authorized or adopted by a domestic or foreign government.

Similarly, promises to perform services or to deliver other consideration do not create negotiable instruments. For example, assume that Jerry promises to deliver to Tom "100 pounds of cheese." This promise is not negotiable.

The promise to pay money is not limited to a promise to pay in U.S. dollars. If the instrument specifies payment in foreign money, such as "I promise to pay bearer 100 Swiss francs," unless otherwise provided, payment can be made either in the foreign money or in equivalent U.S. dollars [UCC § 3–107]. If the parties choose to pay in U.S. dollars, the Code provides the conversion rate.

UCC § 3–107. Instrument Payable in Foreign Money

Unless the instrument otherwise provides, an instrument that states the amount payable in foreign money may be paid in the foreign money, or in an equivalent amount in dollars calculated by using the current bank-offered spot rate at the place of payment for the purchase of dollars on the day on which the instrument is paid.

No Other Undertaking

It has repeatedly been said that a negotiable instrument is a "courier without luggage." By this same token, a cluttered instrument is non-negotiable.

Thus, an instrument must be a simple promise or order, unburdened with additional promises, to pay money to be negotiable [UCC § 3–104(a)(3)].

However, there are three exceptions to this general rule. By and large, these additional promises are permitted because they strengthen the obligation or in some way add to the assurances that payment will be made. It is permissible for an instrument to contain (1) promises that collateral has been given, maintained, or protected; (2) authorization for a confession of judgment by the debtor, or disposal of collateral; or (3) a waiver of law provision [UCC § 3–104(a)(3)]. For example, a note that is otherwise negotiable but contains any of the clauses in Figure 24–7 would be negotiable.

UCC § 3–104. Negotiable Instrument

(a) . . . ''negotiable instrument'' means an unconditional promise or order to pay a fixed amount of money . . . if it:

(3) does not state any other undertaking or instruction by the person promising or ordering payment to do any act in addition to the payment of money.

Payable on Demand or at a Definite Time

The holder of an instrument must be able to tell when it becomes due or the instrument is not negotiable. Thus, to be negotiable, an instrument must be either payable on demand or at a definite time [UCC § 3–104(a)(2)].

Payable on Demand

An instrument is payable **on demand** when it is payable ''on demand,'' ''at sight,'' or doesn't say anything about when it is payable [UCC § 3–108(1)]. Checks with current dates are **demand in-**

Figure 24–7   Clauses that Do Not Alter Negotiability

- ''If the holder of this instrument should deem himself or herself insecure at any time, he or she may ask for and receive additional collateral.''
- ''In the event of default the maker authorizes the holder of this note to obtain judgment against the maker.''
- ''Maker hereby waives any right that he or she might have under state or federal law, including the federal Truth-in-Lending Act.''

---

struments because no time for payment is stated. If the instrument is antedated or postdated, it is not payable before the date on the instrument [UCC § 3–113].

UCC § 3–108. Payable on Demand or at Definite Time

(a) A promise or order is ''payable on demand'' if it (i) states that it is payable on demand or at sight, or otherwise indicates that it is payable at the will of the holder, or (ii) does not state any time of payment.

It is important to remember that an instrument in which no time for payment is stated is a negotiable demand instrument. Problems do not arise when no time for payment is indicated, but where instead an indefinite time is stated.

Payable at a Definite Time

An instrument is negotiable if it is payable at a certain time. The time for payment must be readily ascertainable at the time the promise or order is issued [3–108(b)]. Thus, instruments payable ''10 days after sight,'' or ''on or before February 16, 1994,'' or ''5 years after stated date'' are negotiable and payable at a definite time.

It is not entirely clear how addition of the language of UCC revised Article 3 — ''or at a time or times readily ascertainable'' — changes prior law. For example, under prior law, a dated note payable ''On the day of the next Ohio State University–University of Michigan football game'' would be non-negotiable even though that date is available. Because one would have to leave the face of the instrument to find the date, the note was not payable at a definite time and non-negotiable. While it is unclear whether the revised language would change that result, it seems likely that this is not what is meant by ''readily ascertainable.''

UCC § 3–108. Payable on Demand or at Definite Time

(b) A promise or order is ''payable at a definite time'' if it is payable on elapse of a definite period of time after sight or acceptance or at a fixed date or dates or at a time or times readily ascertainable at the time the promise or order is issued.

When payment is tied to an event of uncertain time, such as "when my corn crop harvests," "payable 10 days after my marriage," or "payable when I receive my income tax refund," the instrument is non-negotiable. This is true even if the event occurs. In the following case, to what event is payment tied?

IN RE ESTATE OF BALKUS v. SECURITY FIRST NATIONAL BANK
128 Wis.2d 246 (1985)

When James Balkus died, his sister, Vesely, discovered in his personal property six deposit slips from a savings account. On each slip was the following in handwriting: "Payable to Ann Balkus Vesely on P.O.D. [payable on death]. The full amount and other deposits." Each deposit was signed by James Balkus and dated. Vesely filed claims on the deposit slips. When the Circuit Court disallowed the claims, Vesely appealed arguing that they were negotiable instruments and that she was a holder in due course.

NETTESHEIM, Judge

We first address Vesely's contention that the endorsed deposit slips are negotiable instruments. UCC section 3–104 defines a negotiable instrument. We conclude that the endorsed deposit slips are not negotiable instruments because they fail to meet the requirement that the writing be payable at a definite time. Section 3–109(2) states that an instrument which is "payable only upon an act or event uncertain as to time of occurrence is not payable at a definite time." The 1961 Report of the Wisconsin Legislative Council indicates that section 3–109(2) "[m]akes post obituary notes non-negotiable, even after the death has occurred."

Because the "payable on death" term of the deposit slips makes the instrument payable upon an event uncertain as to the time of occurrence, i.e., the date of Balkus's death, the endorsed deposit slips are not payable at a definite time and are therefore not negotiable instruments. In order to qualify as holder in due course, Vesely must hold a negotiable instrument. Vesely thus, is not a holder in due course.

Case Questions

1. These notes are termed postobituary notes. They were quite common at one time. Could this note have been written in any way to make it negotiable? See UCC section 3–108(b).

2. Why is this note non-negotiable even after Balkus's death? Isn't the time for payment now certain?

Acceleration and Prepayment   Many notes include **acceleration clauses,** giving the holder the right to demand payment early if for any specified reason payment at the time originally stated is in doubt [UCC § 1–208]. Similarly, the maker or drawer often retains the right to pay early—to "prepay" the obligation. In both cases, the instrument is still payable at a definite time [UCC § 3–108(b)]. For example, a note otherwise negotiable that specifies "payable on January 13, 1994, but in the event that the holder shall deem himself insecure, then this note shall be immediately due at the holder's option" is negotiable. It is payable at a definite time—January 13, 1994—subject to acceleration.

UCC § 3–108. Payable on Demand or at Definite Time

(b) A promise or order is "payable at a definite time" if it is payable [at a definite time] subject to rights of (i) prepayment, (ii) acceleration.

A note that is payable at a definite time subject to acceleration or prepayment is negotiable whether the acceleration is at the option of the holder or occurs automatically upon the happening of a specified event. For example, a note otherwise negotiable that specifies "payable on November 25, 1995. But if my house is sold before that time, this note shall be immediately due and payable'' is negotiable. It is payable at a definite time—November 25, 1995—subject to acceleration.

Although the exact time for payment is unknown, a note payable at a definite time subject to acceleration or prepayment is no less certain than a note payable on demand. In fact, it is more certain because it at least states a definite time beyond which payment cannot run.

Extension An instrument may be payable at a definite time subject to certain extensions. Whether this instrument is payable at a definite time depends on what triggers the extension and whether a further definite time is specified. If the extension is at the option of the holder, the instrument is payable at a definite time and negotiable [UCC § 3–108(b)]. For example, a note otherwise negotiable that provides ''Payable on September 28, 1992, subject to extension at the option of the holder'' is negotiable.

UCC § 3–108. Payable on Demand or at Definite Time

(b) A Promise or order is ''payable at a definite time'' if it is payable [at a definite time] subject to rights of . . . (iii) extension at the option of the holder, or (iv) extension to a further definite time at the option of the maker or acceptor or automatically upon or after a specified act or event.

By contrast, if the extension is at the option of the maker, a further definite time must be stated in order for the note to be negotiable [UCC § 3–108(b)]. For example, a note that provides ''payable on September 30, 1994, subject to extension at the option of the maker'' is not negotiable, but a note that specifies ''payable on September 30, 1994, subject to extension to September 30, 1995, at the option of the maker'' is negotiable.

Similarly, if the extension occurs automatically upon the happening of some specified event, a further definite time must be stated in order for the instrument to be negotiable [UCC § 3–108(b)]. For example, a note that provides ''payable on September 12, 1990, but if my soybean crop fails, payment shall be extended until November 30, 1991'' is negotiable. It is payable at a definite time—September 12, 1990—subject to extension automatically up-

on the occurrence of a specified event—failure of the soybean crop—to a further definite time—November 30, 1991.

Payable to Order or to Bearer

In order to be negotiable, an instrument must contain special ''order'' or ''bearer'' language. The so-called **words of negotiability** put the parties on notice that they are dealing with a negotiable instrument. Clearly, the intent of the maker or drawer upon issue is that the instrument can be negotiated. Whether this requirement has been satisfied is entirely a matter of *form*. In each case, one should look for the magic words indicating either **bearer** or **order paper**. As is discussed in Chapter 25, in addition to determining whether an instrument is negotiable, classifying an instrument as either order or bearer paper determines how the instrument can be negotiated.

Bearer Paper

As a general rule, an instrument is payable to bearer when the word *bearer* appears in the paper [UCC § 3–109(a)]. Thus, an instrument ''pay to *bearer*'' or ''Pay to John Doe or *bearer*'' is negotiable bearer paper. In addition, paper that does not indicate a payee, as in ''pay to cash'' or ''pay to the order of Cash,'' is bearer paper.

UCC § 3–109. Payable to Bearer or to Order

(a) A promise or order is payable to bearer if it:

(1) states that it is payable to bearer or to the order of bearer or otherwise indicates that the person in possession of the promise or order is entitled to payment;

(2) does not state a payee; or

(3) states that it is payable to or to the order of cash or otherwise indicates that it is not payable to an identified person.

Order Paper

As a general rule, paper is order paper when the word ''order'' or ''assigns'' appears in the paper [UCC § 3–109(b)]. Thus, an instrument that is payable ''to the *order* of John Doe'' or ''payable to the *assigns* of Jane Joe'' is order paper. The instrument must be payable to the order of an ''identified person.'' That person must be identified with certainty, so that it is clear whose indorsement is needed to

Figure 24–8   Preprinted Form with Both Order and Bearer Language

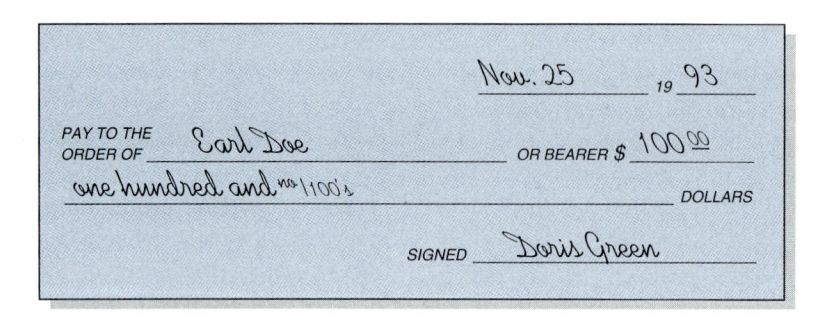

negotiate the paper (see Chapter 25). The payee can be identified in any way, including by name, identifying number, office or account number. The payee can include trusts, agents, and organizations [UCC § 3–110].

An instrument can have *both* order and bearer language. This typically occurs when the drawer or maker is using preprinted forms carelessly. Occasionally a preprinted form will have both order and bearer language preprinted. The drawer of the instrument in Figure 24–8 should have crossed out the order language or deleted the term *bearer*. When both are left—when the instrument has characteristics of both order and bearer paper—the instrument is bearer paper [UCC § 3–109(b)].

UCC § 3–109. Payable to Bearer or to Order

(b) A promise or order that is not payable to bearer is payable to order if it is payable (i) to the order of an identified person; or (ii) to an identified person or order.

A note that is payable *neither* to order nor to bearer is non-negotiable. For example, a note that specifies ''Pay John Jones'' lacks both bearer and order language. It is neither order nor bearer paper; it is non-negotiable and is not governed by UCC Article 3. Revised Article 3 creates an exception for *checks* that fail this requirement. If a check is otherwise negotiable but lacks order or bearer language, it is nevertheless fully negotiable and governed by Article 3 [UCC § 3–104(c)]. Checks are negotiable instruments even if they lack the words of negotiability because they are generally written on preprinted forms, and the occasional situation where the drawer crosses out the ''order'' language should

not exclude the check from Article 3 treatment. The public expects that they are negotiable and Article 3 will now treat them as such. Figure 24–9 illustrates how this has changed under revised Article 3.

Miscellaneous Provisions that Do Not Affect Negotiability

There are a number of provisions that are unrelated to negotiability.

Date of the Instrument
An instrument may be antedated or postdated [UCC § 3–113(a)]. An instrument may be undated. If it is undated, its date is its date of issue [UCC § 3–113(b)].

Contradictory Terms
Occasionally, an instrument contains contradictory terms. For example, if a check indicates the amount in numbers as $300 but in words as ''three hundred ten dollars,'' the words control over the numbers [UCC § 3–114]. Similarly, typewritten terms control over printed terms, and handwritten terms control over both printed and typewritten terms [UCC § 3–114].

Incomplete Instruments
When a maker or drawer signs an instrument that is not complete with the intent that it be completed, it is termed an incomplete instrument [UCC § 3–115(1)]. It may be enforced as written or as completed [UCC § 3–115(2)]. If the completion is not authorized, it is termed a material alteration [UCC § 3–115(3)]. For example, sometimes a drawer gives someone a blank check, authorizing that per-

Figure 24–9 Order and Bearer Language, UCC Old and Revised Article 3: A Comparison

Old Article 3	Revised Article 3
Both order and bearer language: Order paper unless ''bearer'' words were handwritten or typewritten.	Both order and bearer language: Bearer paper
Neither order nor bearer: Governed by UCC Article 3, but there can be no holder in due course.	Neither order nor bearer: Governed by Article 3, including holder in due course status.

son to fill in the purchase price. If the amount is completed as authorized, the check is enforceable. By contrast, if another amount is indicated, it is a material alteration and not enforceable as written.

END–OF–CHAPTER QUESTIONS

1. Explain why each party might want the instrument to be negotiable.

2. Why, as a general rule, must negotiability be determined from the face of the instrument?

3. Why was the sum certain/fixed amount requirement changed to allow variable rate notes to be negotiable? Is the fact that these notes were accepted in commerce persuasive? Is the fact that instruments that are payable in foreign money subject to the exchange rate to equivalent U.S. dollars are negotiable consistent with this reasoning?

4. What is meant by the following phrase: ''A negotiable instrument must be a *courier without luggage*''?

5. Is the following instrument negotiable? Be sure to consider all requisites.

> April 19, 1994
>
> One year from date, I promise to pay to the order of Laura Palmer the sum of $4000 plus interest at 2 points over the prime rate as set by Chase Manhattan Bank. This note is executed as per a contract for the purchase and sale of flour entered into between the parties this date. This note is subject to acceleration in the event of default by the maker. In the event of default the maker will be liable for attorney fees. This note is subject to extension at the option of the holder.
>
> Signed: *Mom Maker*
> Mom Maker

6. Charles and Alice Faulkner signed a promissory note for $25,000 payable to the order of Elmer Miller and Ronald Rotert with interest accruing at the rate of 8 percent from the date of death of Elmer Miller. Principal and interest were payable in monthly installments beginning one month after Miller's death. In the event of default, the note gave the holder the right to accelerate payment and the maker agreed to pay collection costs, including attorney's fees. Is this note negotiable? See *Rotert v. Faulkner*, 660 S.W. 2d 463 (Mo. 1983).

7. Air Terminal issued a promissory note in the amount of $125,000 made payable to Sunayers Limited Partnership. The note provided: ''This note is secured by that certain Purchase and Security Agreement dated June 18, 1984. Reference is made to the Purchase and Security Agreement for additional rights of the holder hereof.'' Is this note negotiable? See *First Federal Savings & Loan Association v. Gump & Ayers Real Estate, Inc.*, 771 P. 2d 1096 (1989).

8. Is the following note negotiable?

> Dec. 25, 1994
>
> 60 days after I receive my income tax return, I promise to pay to Joe Jones or bearer, the sum of $300 for a used motorcycle.
>
> Signed: *Mike Maker*
> Mike Maker

9. Are the following order or bearer paper?
   a. Pay to John Doe or bearer.
   b. Pay to the order of John Doe or bearer.
   c. Pay to John Doe.
   d. Pay to the assigns of John Doe.

10. Is the following instrument negotiable?

Oct. 19, 1993

I, Reva Lewis, promise to pay to the order of Vanessa Chamberlain $100,000 with interest on the date of my next birthday from the proceeds of the sale of my house. If I should die before my next birthday, this note shall become immediately due and payable.

Signed: *Reva Lewis*

Reva Lewis

Chapter 25

Transfer and Negotiation

◼

CRITICAL THINKING INQUIRIES

As you read this chapter, you should be able to address the following:

- Explain the relationship between negotiability and negotiation.
- Explain the relationship between negotiation and transfer.
- Why might one choose to use a special indorsement instead of a blank indorsement?
- What is the importance of holder status?

MANAGERIAL PERSPECTIVE

Joe is the manager of Produce-R-Us, a small grocery store. Produce accepts checks from its customers for payment and, in fact, has even accepted second party checks as a service to its customers. Joe is considering changing that policy. Produce is in possession of a check payable to Paula Peterson. A customer gave Produce the check apparently indorsed by Paula as payment for his groceries. Now Produce discovers that the indorsement by Paula is a forgery.

- Can Produce recover on this check?
- How might Produce best protect itself from situations like this in the future?

In order to answer these questions, one must first understand how a check is negotiated and the importance of holder status. This chapter begins to examine those questions.

INTRODUCTION

The previous chapter discussed negotiability of an instrument. Negotiability is solely a matter of the form of the instrument. This chapter will discuss **negotiation.** The term *negotiation* refers to the transfer process—the process by which the instrument is physically transferred from one person to another.

The first movement of an instrument between parties is called its **issue.** Issue is the initial delivery of the instrument by the maker or drawer (called the issuer), typically to the payee [UCC § 3–105(1)]. **Transfer** is the delivery of the item from that person to subsequent persons [UCC § 3–203(a)]. In any type of transfer there will be a transferor and a transferee. The **transferor** is the party who transfers. The **transferee** is the party to whom the instrument is transferred. In other words, the transferor transfers the instrument to the transferee. There are numerous transfers in the typical life of an instrument.

A negotiation is a special type of transfer. A transfer where the transferee becomes a **holder** is a negotiation [UCC § 3–201(1)]. By contrast, if the transferee of the instrument is not a holder, the transfer of the instrument is a mere transfer.

UCC § 3–201. Negotiation

(1) ''Negotiation'' means a transfer of possession, whether voluntary or involuntary, of an instrument by a person other than the issuer to a person who thereby becomes a holder.

HOLDER

The central issue in this chapter is the concept of a holder. The classification of the transferee as a holder or nonholder is what determines whether the transferee acquired the instrument by transfer or by negotiation. As we will see in Chapter 26, a holder has certain rights on the instrument that a nonholder does not have, and a special type of holder—a holder in due course—has even greater rights.

The term *holder* is a technical term. It is defined in UCC section 1–201(20), but the following definition is, perhaps, more useful: a holder of an instrument is a party who has possession of the instrument and has good title to it.

UCC § 1–201. General Definitions

(20) ''Holder'' . . . means the person in possession if the instrument is payable to bearer or, in the case of an instrument payable to an identified person, if the identified person is in possession.

Possession

Possession means the actual physical possession of the instrument. The holder can obtain possession either by voluntary delivery or by involuntary transfer [UCC § 1–201(1)]. Therefore, for example, either a thief or a finder of bearer paper is a holder of an instrument when in possession of the instrument.

Good Title

The second requirement is that a holder must have good title to the instrument. How a transferee obtains good title to the instrument depends on whether the instrument is bearer paper or order paper.

Bearer Paper

If the instrument is bearer paper, anyone in possession of the instrument has good title [UCC § 3–201(b)]. For example, if Dan Drawer draws a check payable to ''Cash'' and delivers it to Produce-R-Us, Produce is a holder. Produce is in possession of bearer paper. If Tom Thief steals the check, Tom is a holder. If Tom delivers the check to the Second Avenue Grocery Store, the Grocery Store is a holder because it is in possession of bearer paper.

UCC § 3–201. Negotiation

(b) . . . If an instrument is payable to bearer, it may be negotiated by transfer of possession alone.

Order Paper

If the instrument is order paper, the process of transferring title is a bit more involved. As was discussed in Chapter 24, an instrument payable to an identified person (the payee) is order paper. A payee in pos-

Figure 25–1   Holder—Order Paper

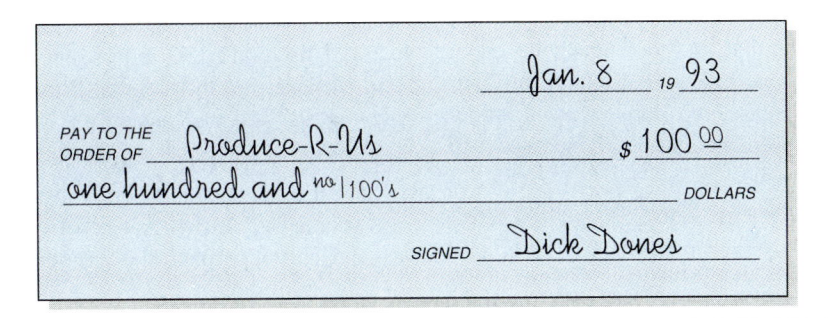

session of order paper is a holder [UCC § 1–201(19)]. In fact, only the identified person can be a holder. For example, assume that as in Figure 25–1, Dick Dones draws a note payable to the order of Produce-R-Us. If Dick delivers the note to David, David is not a holder. By contrast, if Dick delivers the note to Produce-R-Us, Produce is a holder.

In order to negotiate order paper, more than mere transfer of possession is required. The payee must also indorse the instrument [UCC § 3–201(b)]. Good title to the instrument is passed only by proper indorsement by the payee. Therefore, in order for anyone else to become a holder of the note in Figure 25–1, Produce must indorse the note. If Produce indorses the note and delivers it to Sue, Sue is a holder. She is in possession of order paper plus a proper indorsement.

UCC § 3–201. Negotiation

(b) . . . if an instrument is payable to an identified person, negotiation requires transfer of possession of the instrument and its indorsement by the holder.

As is illustrated in the following case, without the proper indorsement, no one can be a holder of order paper.

MOUNTAIN RIDGE STATE BANK v. INVESTOR FUNDING CORP.

13 U.C.C. Rep. Serv. 184 (Sup. Ct. N.J 1990)

Investors intending to invest in real estate limited partnerships issued a number of promissory notes payable to Investor Financing Corp. (IFC). IFC transferred the promissory notes to Mountain Ridge State Bank (the Bank) in exchange for $2,093,300. Unfortunately, there was no investment program. When the maker-investors discovered that they had been defrauded, they stopped making payments on the notes. The Bank sued for the unpaid balance on the notes, claiming holder in due course status.

THOMPSON, Judge

The party seeking to assert holder in due course status must first meet the preliminary requirements of being a ''holder.'' The Uniform Commercial Code defines ''holder'' as ''one who is in possession of a document of title or an instrument or an investment security drawn, issued or indorsed to him or to his order or to bearer or in blank.'' UCC § 1–201. By definition, mere ownership or possession of a note is insufficient to qualify an individual as a holder. The instrument must be obtained through the process of ''negotiation.''

The Bank clearly is not a holder as defined by the code. The notes were not issued to the Bank. No indorsement appears on the notes either to the Bank, its order or in blank. The Bank itself states that it does not allege that there is any indorsement attached to or present with each note.

The requirements that an indorsement be on or firmly affixed to a note is a settled feature of commercial law. In this case, the Bank is not a holder because the notes were not properly indorsed and therefore not negotiated.

While it is true that the indorsement requirement may be a technical one, the privileged status of a holder in due course is also a technical creation which inures only upon strict compliance with the requirements of the Code. The Bank in this case is not a holder and therefore cannot be a holder in due course.

Case Questions

1. Were the notes in this case order or bearer instruments? How can you tell?

2. Why didn't IFC indorse the notes when it transferred them to the Bank?

3. What recourse does the Bank have now?

4. The court states that "The requirements that an indorsement be on or firmly affixed to a note is a settled feature of commercial law." Can you explain the reasoning behind this requirement?

Very often, an instrument that is order paper will have multiple payees. In such a situation, if the instrument is payable to "Paula and Pete Payee," both Paula and Pete must indorse the instrument to pass title. By contrast, if the instrument is payable to "Paula or Pete Payee," either Paula or Pete may indorse the instrument to pass title. Finally, if the instrument is payable to "Paula and/or Pete Payee," either Paula or Pete may indorse the instrument to pass good title [UCC § 3–110(d)].

INDORSEMENTS

An indorsement is a signature on the instrument. Although it is usually on the back of the instrument, it is effective anywhere, even on an **allonge,** a paper firmly attached to the instrument [UCC § 3–204(a)]. An indorsement is usually made either to negotiate the instrument, restrict payment, or to in-

cur indorser's liability [UCC § 3–204(a)]. However, any ambiguous signature is construed as an indorsement.

If the instrument is payable to a name other than the name of the holder, the indorsement may be in the name as it appears on the instrument, or in the correct name, or in both. For example, the name of the payee is sometimes misspelled on the instrument. In some cases, the name on the instrument is totally different from the correct name. For example, assume that, as in Figure 25–2, Mike Maker issues the following instrument, payable to "Pete Teitel" instead of "Pete Title." In this case, Pete may properly indorse the instrument in the name as it appears on the instrument, "Pete Teitel," or in the name "Pete Title," or use both names. Because of the confusion created by using either name alone, the preferred commercial practice is to indorse in both names. Similarly, if Mike issues the instrument

---

Figure 25–2   Instrument Payable to Misspelled Name

payable to a woman in her maiden name, she could properly indorse the note in her maiden name, her married name, or both.

Types of Indorsements

There are several different types of indorsements. An indorsement can be **qualified** or unqualified, **restrictive** or nonrestrictive, and **special** or **blank.** An indorsement usually falls into more than one of these categories. For example, an indorsement can be unqualified, nonrestrictive, and blank.

Qualified Indorsements

As will be discussed in Chapter 27, the law implies that the indorser makes certain promises by indorsing an instrument. Simply put, an indorser promises to pay the instrument if it is not paid when due [UCC § 3–415(a)]. This is an *unqualified* indorsement. If the indorser does not want to make this promise, the indorsement can be made ''without recourse'' [UCC § 3–415(b)]. This is a *qualified* indorsement (see Figure 25–3).

Restrictive Indorsements

Indorsements can attempt to be restrictive or nonrestrictive. An indorsement may (1) restrict further transfer, (2) be conditional, (3) be made ''for collection only,'' or (4) be made payable to a fiduciary. An indorsement that attempts to restrict further transfer, as in Figure 25–4, is ineffective to prevent further transfer. In other words, Allan in Figure 25–4 can negotiate the instrument to subsequent holders by indorsement [UCC § 3–206(a)]. The restrictive indorsement operates as a special indorsement, as discussed below. Later holders are permitted to disregard the restrictive indorsement.

An indorsement that states a condition limiting the holder's right to receive payment, as in Figure 25–5, is ineffective to condition payment [UCC § 3–206(b)]. Allan's right to enforce the instrument is not affected by the condition. Similarly, the maker must pay the instrument regardless of whether the condition has been performed.

Most restrictive indorsements are meant to restrict negotiation of the instrument for bank collection purposes, as in Figure 25–6.

These are true restrictive indorsements because further negotiation is limited to some extent. An illustration best explains the law. Suppose that, as in

Figure 25–3   Qualified Indorsement

Figure 25–4   Limits Further Transfer

Figure 25–5   Conditional Indorsement

Figure 25–6   Restricts Negotiation

Figure 25–7   Check Payable to Xavier Doe

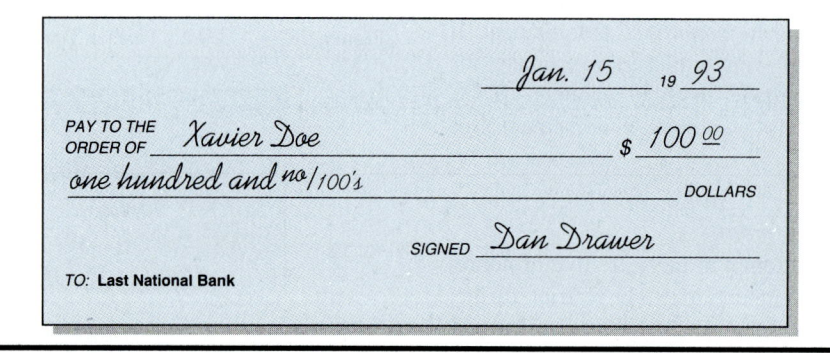

Figure 25–7, Dan Drawer draws a check payable to Xavier Doe drawn on the Last National Bank (LNB). Assume further that Xavier indorses the check, as in Figure 25–8, and writes above the signature line "For Deposit Only." The check is then stolen by Tom Thief, who cashes it at the First Avenue Grocery Store. The Grocery Store indorses the check and deposits it in its account with the Second National Bank. The account of First Avenue is credited and the check is forwarded to the Last National Bank for collection. Last National pays the check. In this example, First Avenue Grocery Store and the Second National Bank are liable for paying inconsistent with the restrictive indorsement. Transferees have liability for taking the instrument inconsistent with the restrictive indorsement. Last National Bank has no such liability because the drawee does not have the same liability where the item is paid in the bank collection process [UCC § 3–206(c) (1) (2) and (4)]. By contrast, Last National Bank would have

Figure 25–8   Check Restrictively Indorsed by Xavier Doe

liability if Tom presented the check for payment over the counter and Last National paid the check [UCC § 2–306(c)(3)].

An indorsement payable to an agent or trustee is a type of restrictive indorsement. Assume, for example, that the payee indorses a check "Pay to Tom in trust for Bob." If Tom indorses the check in blank and delivers it to Hank for value, Hank may take the instrument as long as he has no notice that Tom is committing a breach of fiduciary duty by negotiating the instrument. Similarly, if Tom deposits the check in his account with the Third National Bank, Third National is acting properly as long as it has no notice of breach of fiduciary duty. The drawee bank can properly cash the check for Tom as the bank is ignorant about Tom's breach of fiduciary duty under the trust [UCC § 3–206(d)].

Special/Blank Indorsements

An indorsement can be either special or blank. An indorsement that identifies a specific payee is a **special** indorsement [UCC § 3–205(a)]. Suppose, for example that Dan Drawer draws a check payable to the order of Pam Payee. A special indorsement is where Pam names a new payee when indorsing the instrument—for example, "Pay Mike" (see Figure 25–9). A special indorsement preserves the instrument's "order character," reducing the risk of misappropriation. The new payee is often called the **special indorsee.** In the same way that an instrument originally drawn to order can only be negotiated with the indorsement of the payee, a special indorsement limits negotiation of the paper by requiring the indorsement of the special indorsee. Thus, this instrument can only be negotiated with Mike's indorsement. In other words, without Mike's indorsement, no one can be a holder of this instrument.

An indorsement in blank is one where the payee does not name a new payee when indorsing. A blank indorsement converts order paper into bearer paper. Similarly, a blank indorsement retains the bearer status of bearer paper [UCC § 3–205(b)]. Therefore, the instrument can be negotiated by mere transfer of possession after a blank indorsement. Assume that Mike Maker issues a note payable to the order of Hank Montgomery. Hank's blank indorsement, as in Figure 25–10, converts the order paper into bearer paper. Anyone in possession of this paper after Hank's indorsement is a holder. Hank's blank indorsement effectively "orders" payment to anyone in rightful possession of the instrument.

However, it is possible to convert the bearer paper back into order paper by a special indorsement. Assume that in the above example, Hank delivers

Figure 25–9   Special Indorsement

Figure 25–10   Blank Indorsement

Figure 25–11   Indorsement Converting Bearer Paper to Order Paper

the instrument to Judy Jones. She can convert the bearer instrument back into an order instrument by adding "Pay to Judy Jones" over the blank indorsement (see Figure 25–11). This instrument cannot be further negotiated without Judy's indorsement. An alternative method is for Judy to add the "Pay Dick Thompson" below the blank indorsement, as in Figure 25–12. This instrument is now order paper that cannot be further negotiated without Dick's indorsement.

Figure 25–13 summarizes the different types of indorsements. Read the following case and determine whether the indorsement on the instrument was special or blank, restrictive or nonrestrictive, and what was the impact of these factors.

Figure 25–12 Alternative Indorsement Converting Bearer Paper to Order Paper

Figure 25–13 Types of Indorsements

Type	Example	Effect
Special	Pay to Pam Smith	Converts bearer paper to order paper; Pam Smith's indorsement is needed to negotiate
Blank	John Jones	Converts order paper to bearer paper; anyone in possession is a holder
Qualified	John Jones without recourse	John is not making any promises as an indorser to pay on the instrument
Unqualified	John Jones	John is making the promise of an indorser
Restrictive	John Jones for deposit only	Restricts further delivery
Nonrestrictive	John Jones	No attempt to restrict further negotiation

WALCOTT v. MANUFACTURERS HANOVER TRUST
507 N.Y.S.2d 961 (N.Y. Civ. Ct. 1986)

Kenneth Walcott alleged that he sent his paycheck of $359 to the Midatlantic Mortgage Co. in payment of his mortgage. He alleged that he indorsed the check and placed his mortgage number and the Midatlantic mailing sticker on the back of the check. The check never reached the Midatlantic Mortgage Co. It was deposited into the account of Bilko Check Cashing Corp. (Bilko) with Manufacturers Hanover Trust (Manufacturers Hanover). The check was finally cleared through Citibank and charged to the account of the drawer, The New York City Transit Authority. Walcott alleged that it was stolen by a thief who took it to Bilko. The issue is whether the payee's indorsement was a special or restrictive indorsement. The indorsements looked like this.

ENDORSE HERE

Kenneth Walcott

603052

Bilko Check Cashing
Manufacturers Hanover

DO NOT SIGN/WRITE/STAMP BELOW THIS LINE
FOR FINANCIAL INSTITUTION USE ONLY

HARKAVY, Judge

Special Indorsement
Examination of the back of the check reveals that Mr. Walcott did not specify any particular indorsee. In order for the alleged attached sticker to have served that purpose, it must have also complied with UCC § 3–202 subdivision (2): "An indorsement must be written by or on behalf of the holder and on the instrument or a paper so firmly affixed thereto as to become a part thereof." The back of the check shows no sticker attached at all. Even if it had originally been affixed thereto, as plaintiff claims, it obviously became detached easily, thus failing to meet the indorsement requirement under the UCC to constitute a special indorsement.

Restrictive Indorsement
As to the numbers written underneath plaintiff's signature, they did not have the effect of restricting plaintiff's indorsement. UCC § 3–205. This section of the Uniform Commercial Code is very specific. The series of numbers representing plaintiff's mortgage account was insufficient to restrict negotiation of plaintiff's check.

Blank Indorsement
Plaintiff's indorsement had the effect of converting the check into a bearer instrument. The series of numbers having no restrictive effect, Mr. Walcott indorsed the check in blank, or otherwise stated, he simply signed his name. A blank indorsement under UCC § 3–204 subdivision (2) ". . . specified no particular indorsee and may consist of a mere signature." Additionally, "An instrument payable to order and indorsed in blank becomes payable to bearer and may be negotiated by delivery alone. . . . " Consequently, since plaintiff failed to limit his blank indorsement, the check was properly negotiated by delivery to third party Bilko and properly cashed by them.

Case Questions

1. Compare and contrast a special indorsement and a restrictive indorsement.

2. What is Walcott's recourse at this point?

Forgeries

The question of holder status can arise when there has been a forgery on the instrument.

Forged Indorsements

A forged indorsement on a bearer instrument, either originally drawn as bearer paper or converted from order paper to bearer paper by a blank indorsement, does not affect the passing of title. Since no indorsement is necessary to pass title of bearer paper, a forged indorsement is mere surplus with no legal affect on the transfer. Thus, forgeries "outside of the chain of title" are irrelevant.

By contrast, because a forgery is an ineffective indorsement, a forgery of a signature necessary to pass title will affect the passing of title. A forgery of the signature of the payee or special indorsee on order paper is ineffective to pass title. Therefore, no one can be a holder after such a forgery.

An instrument can be transferred many times. During the course of these transfers, an instrument can be converted from order paper to bearer paper and back to order paper. In determining holder status, it is important to examine the instrument at each step and to determine whether at that step the instrument is order paper or bearer paper. Only if the instrument is order paper at that particular step are valid indorsements needed to pass title. If an instru-

ment is bearer paper at a particular step, no indorsements are needed to pass title. If no indorsement is required, the fact that the signature is forged is irrelevant.

An example will illustrate these principles. Assume that Bob Boron draws and delivers a check payable to the order of Charlie Chain, as in Figure 25–14. Charlie indorses the back of the instrument in blank and leaves it on his bedstand (see Figure 25–15). That night, Tom Thief creeps into Charlie's room and steals the check. Tom delivers the check to Frank Furrier. When asked to indorse the check, Tom forges the name "David Earl." Frank adds a special indorsement "Pay to Frank Furrier." Before he can deposit the check into his account, it is stolen by John Bright. John forges the name of Frank Furrier to the back of the check and delivers it to the Second Avenue Grocery Store in return for groceries. In this example, Charlie's blank indorsement converts what was initially order paper into bearer paper. After the indorsement, Tom and Frank are both holders. Both are in possession of bearer paper. Because no indorsement was needed to negotiate the bearer paper, the forged "David Earl" signature is irrelevant. By contrast, Frank's special indorsement converted the paper back into order paper. Therefore, neither John nor the Second Avenue Grocery were holders. Because Frank's indorsement was needed to negotiate the instrument after the special

---

Figure 25–14   Check Payable to Charlie Chain

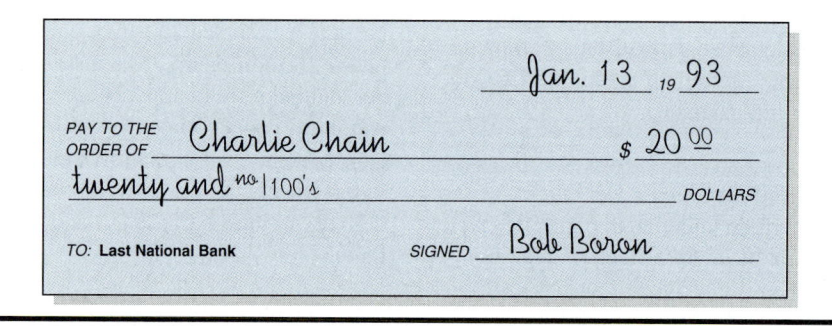

Jan. 13, 19 93

PAY TO THE ORDER OF __Charlie Chain__ $ 20 00

__twenty and no/100's__   DOLLARS

TO: Last National Bank   SIGNED __Bob Boron__

Figure 25–15   Series of Indorsements with Forgeries

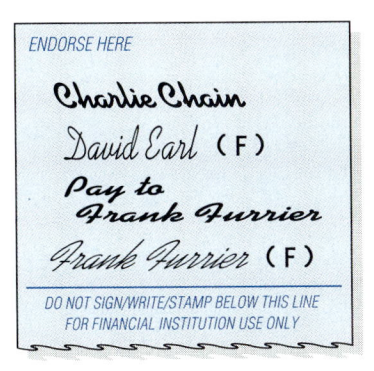

ENDORSE HERE

Charlie Chain
David Earl (F)
Pay to
Frank Furrier
Frank Furrier (F)

DO NOT SIGN/WRITE/STAMP BELOW THIS LINE
FOR FINANCIAL INSTITUTION USE ONLY

indorsement, no one can be a holder without the necessary indorsement. The forgery is ineffective as the indorsement.

Forged Drawer's Signature

A forged drawer's signature has no effect on holder status. Therefore, it is possible to be a holder of an instrument with a forged drawer's signature as long as all necessary indorsements are valid.

END–OF–CHAPTER QUESTIONS

1. Why might someone use a special indorsement to convert bearer paper into order paper?

2. An instrument "pay to the order of bearer" is in the possession of Dick Thomas. Is he a holder? Explain.

3. Classify the following indorsement: "John Jones, without recourse."

4. Dick Jones draws a check "Pay to the order of Sally Smith" and delivers it to Jill France. Is Jill a holder of the instrument?

5. Midge Myers makes a promissory note payable to the order of her niece, "Maureen Myers." She mails it to Maureen at Maureen's college dorm. Unfortunately, Maureen's roommate gets the mail and sees the check. Before Maureen comes home, her roommate steals the check and forges Maureen's signature on the back of the check. The roommate then takes the check to the bookstore where she uses it to pay for her books. The bookstore has no reason to suspect that the signature is forged. The bookstore deposits it into its account with the First National Bank. Is the bookstore a holder of this instrument? Is the First National Bank a holder of this instrument?

6. A check "pay to the order of Bill and/or Joe Doe" is in the possession of Joe. Joe indorses it in blank. A thief steals the check and forges Bill's indorsement and cashes the check at the Grocery Store. Is the Grocery Store a holder?

7. Al Joseph breaks into Jennifer Dutton's apartment and steals a pad of checks. Al forges Jennifer's signature to a check made payable to Andy Joseph. Andy indorses the check and cashes it at the Corner Liquor Store. Is Corner a holder?

8. Mitch Maples makes a promissory note "payable to Pamela Paul." Pamela indorses the instrument "pay to Jean Simmons only if she has delivered to me a stereo set in good working order. /s/ Pamela Paul" and gives the note to Jean. Jean indorses the note in blank and deposits it in her account with the Second National Bank. Is the Second National Bank a holder? Does it matter whether or not Jean has delivered a stereo to Pamela?

9. Darlene Brown draws a check "pay to the order of Ellen Harris" and delivers it to Ellen. Ellen indorses it in blank and intends to put it in her purse but instead it drops to the ground as Ellen goes to the bank. Larry finds the check on the ground and takes it to his bank, the Fourth National Bank, to cash it. Fourth requires that Larry indorse the check before it will cash it. Larry forges the name "Ike Morris" on the back and delivers it to Fourth. Is Fourth a holder of this check?

10. Andrea Pastor draws a check "pay to the order of Stefan Snyder" and delivers it to Stefan. Stefan indorses it in blank and

delivers it to Darryl Darling. Darryl writes above Stefan's signature "pay to Darryl Darling." Frank Richards steals the check, forges Darryl's signature, and cashes the check at the Corner Check Cashing Agency. Was Stefan a holder of this check? Darryl? Frank? Corner Check Cashing?

Chapter 26

Holder in Due Course

CRITICAL THINKING INQUIRIES

As you read this chapter, you should be able to address the following:

- Compare and contrast the rights of a holder in due course and an assignee on a contract.
- Analyze the following statement: "Value under UCC Article 3 does not equal consideration under contract law."
- Does the concept of a holder in due course offer any benefits to the maker or drawer?
- Analyze the following statement: "It is a basic rule at common law that whenever property is transferred, the transferee acquires at least whatever rights the transferor had in that property. Because a negotiable instrument is a type of property, this principle applies to the transfer of an instrument."
- Compare and contrast the rights of a holder in due course and a mere holder.

MANAGERIAL PERSPECTIVE

Joe Camp owns a small factory that makes hardware supplies. To speed processing of orders, he decides to upgrade his computer equipment and buys new computers from The Computer Store. Because of the expense, he finances the purchase signing a promissory note in which he promises to pay the $90,000 debt in monthly installments. Unfortunately, all computers delivered are defective. Joe refuses to pay any monthly bills until replacement computers are delivered. However, he discovers that The Computer Store negotiated the note to the First National Bank. First National Bank contends that it should be paid whether the computers work or not.

- Does Joe have to pay First National Bank?
- Does it matter whether First National is a holder in due course or not?
- How could Joe have protected himself?
- Would Joe's rights be any different if First National was an assignee of a contract right instead of a holder in due course?

A holder in due course (HDC) of a properly negotiated negotiable instrument is a type of superplaintiff. A holder in due course is permitted to enforce the instrument even where the maker or drawer has defenses. Most of these defenses are not good against the holder in due course. By contrast, remember that an assignee of a contract right takes *subject* to all claims and defenses good against the assignor. In other words, if First National in the opening scenario is a holder in due course, it will take the instrument free from most claims and defenses; Joe will have to pay First National and then sue The Computer Store. On the other hand, if First National is merely an assignee, it will take the instrument subject to all claims and defenses; Joe will not have to pay First National. This chapter will consider (1) how one becomes a holder in due course and (2) the rights of a holder in due course.

HOLDER IN DUE COURSE

The general rule for determining if someone is a **holder in due course** is found in UCC section 3–302. Basically, a holder in due course must meet nine conditions:

1. Holder.
2. Negotiable instrument.
3. No question of authenticity.
4. Value.
5. Good faith.
6. Without notice that the instrument is overdue.
7. Without notice of forgery or alteration.
8. Without notice of claim.
9. Without notice of defense.

Holder of a Negotiable Instrument

In order for someone to be a holder in due course, the instrument must be negotiable and it must have been properly negotiated into the hands of a holder.

Authenticity

No one can be a holder in due course of an instrument that is obviously a forgery, has clearly been altered, or that is so irregular that the holder should question its authenticity [UCC § 3–302(a)(1)]. There is no reason to extend holder in due course

protection to persons who take instruments under circumstances that should call into question the authenticity of the instrument. Persons who take such irregular instruments do so at their own risk.

UCC § 3–302. Holder in Due Course

(a) . . . ''holder in due course'' means the holder of an instrument if:

(1) the instrument . . . does not bear such apparent evidence of forgery or alteration or is not otherwise so irregular or incomplete as to call into question its authenticity.

Value

In order to be a holder in due course of an instrument, one must give **value** in exchange for the instrument [UCC § 3–302(a)(2)]. If the holder has not given value, there has been no out-of-pocket loss and there is no need for holder in due course protection. In general, the out-of-pocket loss required is value. The meaning of value is summarized in Figure 26–1.

To the Extent that the Promise Has Been Performed

It is important to note that value under UCC Article 3 does not equal consideration under contract law. Consideration sufficient to support a contract under contract law includes future promises of performance. However, one only gives value to the extent that those promises are *actually performed*. For example, assume that Paula is the payee on a $5,000 note and agrees to deliver the note to Hank in exchange for 100 bicycle helmets. While this is clearly a contract supported by consideration, Hank has not yet given value. He has not performed the agreed-on promise. He has no out-of-pocket loss and it is not necessary for the holder in due course doctrine to protect him. If he learns that the maker was defrauded into issuing the note, Hank can protect him-

---

Figure 26–1   Value

- Performed promise.
- Security interest acquired.
- Antecedent debt.
- Exchange for negotiable instrument.
- Irrevocable obligation.

self by rescinding the contract and refusing to deliver the helmets. Until he begins performance, he has not given value.

Furthermore, it is clear that one only becomes a holder in due course *to the extent* that the promise is performed [UCC § 3–303(a)(1)]. Assume that in the above example, Hank delivers 50 of the promised bicycle helmets. He is then a holder in due course *to the extent* that he performed his promise. Because he performed half of his promise, he is a holder in due course of one half of the note, or $2,500.

UCC § 3–303. Value and Consideration

(a) An instrument is issued or transferred for value if:

(1) the instrument is issued or transferred for a promise of performance, to the extent the promise has been performed.

Do not be surprised when a holder agrees to accept an instrument in exchange for an amount less than the face value of the instrument (a discount). If a holder agrees to accept the instrument at discount, the amount of the discount is not subtracted. For example, remember that The Computer Store in our opening scenario is the payee on a note for $90,000. If it negotiates the note to the First National Bank for $80,000, First National has given value and is a holder in due course of the full $90,000 note.

However, assume that in the above example, First National pays $70,000 of the $80,000 promised and discovers that the computers are defective (a defense). First National is a holder in due course only *to the extent* that it performed its promise before it received notice. Because First National performed only seven eighths (or 87.5 percent) of its promise, it is a holder in due course of only seven eights of the $90,000 note or $78,750. ($70,000 divided by $80,000 = .875 × $90,000 = $78,750) [UCC § 3–302(d)].

UCC § 3–302. Holder in Due Course

(d) If . . . the promise of performance that is the consideration for an instrument has been partially performed, the holder may assert rights as a holder in due course of the instrument only to the fraction of the amount payable under the instrument equal to the value of the partial performance divided by the value of the promised performance.

Security Interest

Where an instrument is taken as collateral, the holder gives value [UCC § 3–302(a)(b)]. However, value is only given to the extent of the debt secured [UCC § 3–302(e)]. For example, assume that Frank Auto Sales is the payee on a $5,000 note. Frank uses this note as collateral to obtain a $4,000 loan from the Last National Bank. Last is a holder in due course of the note, but only for $4,000, the amount of the debt secured.

UCC § 3–302. Holder in Due Course

(e) If . . . [the holder of] an instrument has only a security interest in the instrument . . . [the holder] may assert rights as a holder in due course only to an amount payable under the instrument which, at the time of enforcement of the instrument, does not exceed the amount of the unpaid obligation secured.

Antecedent Claim

If the holder takes the instrument in payment of an existing debt, the holder gives value [UCC § 3– 303(a)(3)]. For example, assume that Dolly owes Tammy $40,000. If Dolly negotiates a $40,000 note in payment of the debt, Tammy has given value.

Would it matter if Tammy reserves the right to enforce the debt until she has been paid on the note? Read the following case.

SALEMY v. DIAB

587 A.2d 305 (N.J. Super. 1991)

Diab and Golden were the makers of a $75,000 promissory note payable to Anderson. Anderson negotiated the note to Salemy in payment of a $70,000 antecedent debt. In return for the note, Salemy's attorney sent a written release to Anderson's attorney. The cover letter contained the following instruction: ''Please hold [the release] in escrow pending my client's receipt of the sum of $75,000.''

BRODY, Judge

Defendants argue that plaintiff is not a holder in due course. The precise issue they raise is whether plaintiff gave value for the note in view of the conditional nature of his release of Anderson's debt.

Defendants mistakenly direct our attention to the section 3–303(a) definition, whose wording has the effect of withholding holder-in-course status from a holder who has taken a negotiable instrument in return for making an unperformed promise. Uniform Commercial Code Comment 3 to section 3–303 explains the meaning given to the section 3–303(a) definition:

Paragraph (a) . . . requir[es] that the agreed consideration shall actually have been given. An executory promise to give value is not itself value . . . The underlying reason of policy is that when the purchaser learns of a defense against the instrument or of a defect in title he is not required to enforce the instrument, but is free to rescind the transaction for breach of the transferor's warranty. (Section 3–417). There is thus not the same necessity for giving him the status of a holder in due course, cutting off claims and defenses, as where he has actually paid value. A common illustration is the bank credit not drawn upon, which can be and is revoked when a claim or defense appears.

At first blush there appears to be little difference between a promisor's unexecuted promise of performance, such as a promise to extend credit, and a creditor's release of an antecedent debt. In both cases the holder may sustain no loss if the negotiable instrument is dishonored. But that is not always so. A holder-promisor who has not yet performed before the dishonor has lost nothing, but a holder-creditor who has released a debt before the dishonor has lost an earlier opportunity to collect it. It is difficult, if not impossible, in some cases for a creditor to measure the loss attributable to forbearance. Section 3–303 therefore protects the creditor in all cases by treating the release of an antecedent debt as the giving of value.

Another cause of confusion arises from the conditional nature of the release in this case. Section 3–303 applies when the negotiable instrument is taken ''in payment'' of an antecedent claim. Defendants contend that because the release given here expressly postpones payment of the antecedent claim until the instrument is paid, plaintiff never treated the debt as paid and therefore did not give value.

The argument is flawed because, unless the parties have otherwise agreed, whenever a holder takes a negotiable instrument in payment of an antecedent debt, the underlying obligation is restored should the instrument be dishonored. Thus the condition in the release adds nothing to the rights plaintiff had even if the release had been unconditional.

Case Questions

1. Did the plaintiff in this case suffer any out-of-pocket loss? Should he be afforded the holder in due course protection?

2. Analyze: ''A holder-promisor who has not yet performed before the dishonor has lost nothing, but a holder-creditor who has released a debt before dishonor has lost an earlier opportunity to collect it.''

In Exchange for a Negotiable Instrument

A holder who gives a negotiable instrument in return for a negotiable instrument gives value [UCC § 3–303(a)(4)]. For example, assume that Joan is the payee on a negotiable promissory note for $1,000 payable in 90 days. If Joan needs money now, she might agree to negotiate the note to Helen for $950. If Helen writes Joan a negotiable check for $950 in return for the $1,000 promissory note, Helen has given value. Giving this negotiable instrument is value because if this check were negotiated to a holder in due course, Helen would be obligated to pay.

Irrevocable Obligation

If the holder undertakes an irrevocable commitment in return for the instrument, value has been given [UCC § 3–303(a)(5)]. For example, if First

National Bank issues a letter of credit in return for the check from The Computer Store, the bank has given value.

How Can a Bank Give Value?

Assume that Alan writes a check for $1,000 to Bud. Bud indorses the check and deposits it in his account with First National Bank. If Alan stops payment on the check, First National cannot collect the check from the drawee. If Bud has no money in his account from which to subtract the $1,000, the question arises as to whether First National can qualify as a holder in due course. A bank gives value when it acquires a security interest in the instrument [UCC § 3–303(a)(2)]. A bank acquires a security interest in an instrument to the extent that the bank allows the customer to withdraw funds from a deposited check or cashes the check [UCC § 4–210(a)]. Thus, merely making a provisional credit to the customer's (Bud's) account is not giving value. The bank must allow the customer to use or withdraw those funds.

Determining whether a bank has given value can be a relatively easy matter. However, where there is an existing balance when the check is deposited and there is a flurry of activity in the account, it is not always easy to determine when the bank has allowed its customer to draw against the funds at issue. This determination is made easier by the Code's adoption of the first-in, first-out rule (FIFO) [UCC § 4–210(b)]. In other words, to determine whether the bank has allowed its customer to draw against funds deposited, any existing balances (first in) must first be withdrawn (first out). An example best illustrates. Assume that Donna writes Penny a $500 check for rent. Penny indorses the check and deposits it into her account with the Lessor's National Bank (LNB). At the time, Penny has $600 in her account. LNB provisionally credits Penny's account and forwards the check for payment to the drawee. The next day, Penny cashes a check for $300 at the bank. Later that afternoon, LNB pays two checks drawn on Penny's account, one for $250 and one for $150. The following day, LNB receives notice from the drawee that Donna's check has been dishonored because Donna stopped payment on the check. Penny has no money in her account and LNB wants to claim holder in due course status. Has LNB given value (see Figure 26–2)? The first $300 withdrawal came from the existing balance, with $300 remaining. The $250 of check 1 came from the $300 re-

Figure 26–2   Penny's Account

	+	−
Balance	$600	
Deposit—Donna's check	$500	
Withdrawals		
Penny cashes a check		$300
Check 1 Paid		$250
Check 2 Paid		$150

maining. LNB has at this point not allowed Penny to draw against Donna's $500 check. However, when LNB pays the $150 check 2, it uses up the $50 remaining from the balance and "dips into" Donna's check to the amount of $100. Therefore, LNB has given value and is a holder in due course for the amount of $100 of the $500 check deposited.

In Good Faith and without Notice

In order to be a holder in due course of an instrument, the holder must take the instrument in **good faith** and **without notice** of a number of things. Before examining exactly what the holder must not know, one must understand what is meant by the concepts of *good faith* and *without notice*. Are they the same? How does one receive notice of something?

These two requirements are not the same, although courts often treat them together. The Code's definition of good faith imposes a subjective test. Thus, it does not matter whether a reasonable person would have suspected something was wrong, or whether a reasonable person would have acted differently. The test is whether the *holder* acted with "honesty in fact" [UCC § 1–201(19) and § 3–103(4)]. The Code's definition of good faith is sometimes called the "pure heart/empty head" approach. Similarly, it is sometimes said to codify the expression "ignorance is bliss." Read the following case where the court applies this test.

UCC § 1–201. General Definitions

(19) "Good faith" means honesty in fact in the conduct or transaction concerned.

FLAGSHIP BANK v. CENTRAL FLORIDA COACH LINES, INC.
33 UCC Rep. Serv. 613 (C.P. Pa. 1981)

On about December 20, 1977, Central Florida Coach Lines, Inc. (Florida Coach), issued two checks to Thomas York. York indorsed the checks and deposited them in his account in the Flagship Bank of Orlando (the Bank). York was permitted to draw against these checks. When the checks were presented for payment, they were dishonored because Florida Coach had issued a stop payment order. The Bank sued Florida Coach, asserting holder in due course status.

TOOLE, Judge

This case was tried by the Bank on the theory that it was a holder in due course of both checks and as such took them free of any personal defenses Florida Coach may have had against the depositor, Mr. York. Florida Coach contends that the Bank is not a holder in due course because a stop order had been issued against the checks, and also because the Bank permitted the depositor to withdraw funds before allowing appropriate clearance time for the checks.

We are satisfied that the Bank took the instruments in good faith. Good faith, according to the Code, means "honesty in fact."

The proper test for determining good faith in Pennsylvania is not one of negligence or a duty to inquire, but rather it is one of willful dishonesty or actual knowledge.

In the instant case, the record reveals that the Bank acted honestly in fact in the conduct or transaction concerned. Certainly there is nothing in the record to establish any willful dishonesty or actual knowledge on the part of this Bank which would require us to deny it "holder in due course" status.

Florida Coach also contends that the Bank did not act in good faith when it permitted the payee to withdraw from the account without awaiting collection. This same argument was presented and rejected in *Mellon Bank, N.A. v. Donegal Mutual Ins. Co.*, wherein the court stated:

Defendant asserts the plaintiff's failure to credit McConnell's account with plaintiff and await collection from the drawee, rather than delivering cash to McConnell, also

involves a "bad faith" taking of the instrument. But this method of accommodating its own customer has nothing to do with "taking" an instrument. Payment by the collecting bank might be imprudent and is certainly a risk assumed by the depository-collecting bank (plaintiff) as to the drawee (Farmer's Bank), but it does not affect plaintiff's rights against defendant who by drawing the instrument and placing it in the stream of commerce has engaged to pay it to any holder.

The record also establishes that the Bank took the instruments without any notice of the stop payment order or of any defense or claim which Florida Coach may have had against the depositor. The Bank has therefore satisfied all of the statutory requirements necessary to qualify as a "holder in due course" of the instruments.

Case Questions

1. Compare an objective test for determining good faith with a subjective test. How might the result of this case have differed if the court had imposed an objective test?

2. Would the court's decision with respect to good faith change if the depositor were a new account, or one frequently overdrawn?

3. Revised Article 3 introduces a definition of good faith to apply to Articles 3 and 4 [UCC § 3–103(4)]. It provides that good faith requires not only "honesty in fact" but "the observance of reasonable commercial standards of fair dealing." If the *Flagship Bank* court were to apply this standard, would it reach a different result? Explain.

The requirement of without notice differs from the requirement of good faith. Here, the Code imposes an objective test. If a reasonable person would be suspicious under the circumstances, the holder has notice.

The Code specifies what notice is fatal to holder in due course status. One cannot be a holder in due course if the instrument is taken with notice (1) that it is overdue or has been dishonored, (2) that it contains an unauthorized signature or has been altered,

(3) of any claim described in UCC section 3–306, or (4) that a party has a defense or claim in recoupment [UCC § 3–302(a)(2)].

UCC § 1–201. General Definitions

(25) A person has ''notice'' of a fact when

(a) he has actual knowledge of it; or

(b) he has received a notice or notification of it; or

(c) from all the facts and circumstances known to him at the time in question he has reason to know that it exists.

Without Notice that Instrument Is Overdue

To be a holder in due course, one must take the instrument without notice that it is overdue or has been dishonored. This is based on the assumption that if paper is overdue, something is wrong. Section 3– 304 provides rules to determine when an instrument is overdue, treating demand instruments separately from instruments that are payable at a definite time.

UCC § 3–304. Overdue Instrument

(b) With respect to an instrument payable at a definite time the following rules apply:

(2) If the principal is not payable in installments and the due date has not been accelerated, the instrument becomes overdue on the day after the due date.

Definite Time

It is a relatively simple matter to determine when an instrument payable at a definite time is overdue. For example, one cannot be a holder in due course of an instrument payable on July 1 by buying it on July 2. It is obviously overdue. However, even instruments payable at a definite time present certain interesting questions. For example, when is an instrument payable in installments overdue? The Code distinguishes between defaults in payment of principal and interest. One who takes an instrument with notice of a missed *principal* installment cannot be a holder in due course [UCC § 3–304(b)(1)]. By contrast, one who takes an instrument with notice of a default in a purely *interest* installment can be holder in due course [UCC § 3–304(c)]. For example, remember that in the opening scenario, Joe promised

to pay a $90,000 debt in monthly installments. First National Bank could not be a holder in due course of the note if it purchased the note with a notation ''Missed April 15 payment,'' because the April 15 payment is a payment of *principal* and interest.

UCC § 3–304. Overdue Instrument

(b) With respect to an instrument payable at a definite time the following rules apply:

(1) If the principal is payable in installments . . . the instrument becomes overdue upon default . . . of an installment, and the instrument remains overdue until the default is cured.

UCC § 3–304. Overdue Instrument

(c) . . . an instrument does not become overdue if there is default in payment of interest but no default in payment of principal.

Where an installment payment is overdue, it remains overdue until the default is cured [UCC § 3– 304(b)(1)]. Cure after purchase will not improve the holder's status. To illustrate, assume that First National Bank in the above example bought the note on May 1 with the notation of a missed payment. If Joe cured the default (made up the missed payment) on May 15, this would not improve the Bank's status; it would still lack holder in due course status because it purchased the note with notice that there was a missed payment of principal.

It should also be noted that a common provision in promissory notes grants holders the right to *accelerate* payment of the instrument if they are insecure about payment. This means that a holder who in good faith fears default may ''call the loan'' and demand payment of the entire obligation immediately. No one can be a holder in due course who takes an instrument knowing that payment has been accelerated.

UCC § 3–304. Overdue Instrument

(b) With respect to an instrument payable at a definite time the following rules apply:

(3) If a due date with respect to principal has been accelerated, the instrument becomes overdue on the day after the accelerated due date.

Demand

A demand instrument is overdue on the day after demand is made [UCC § 3–304(a)(1)]. However, because it is difficult for a purchaser of a demand instrument to know whether demand has been made if it is not indicated on the instrument, no one can be a holder in due course of a demand instrument if it is purchased more than a reasonable time after issue [UCC § 3–304(a)(3)]. It is presumed that demand was made and refused. In order to determine the reasonableness of the time period, courts must look at the circumstances of the particular case, the nature of the instrument, and trade usage. Factors such as the distance between the place of issue and the place of negotiation, holidays, and special circumstances are all relevant.

---

§ 3–304. Overdue Instruments

(a) An instrument payable on demand becomes overdue at the earlier of the following times:

(3) if the instrument is not a check, when the instrument has been outstanding for a period of time after its date which is unreasonably long under the circumstances of the particular case in light of the nature of the instrument and usage of the trade.

A check (a special type of demand instrument) is overdue *90* days after its date [UCC 3–304(a)(2)]. This 90-day rule substitutes for the 30-day rule under old Article 3 (see Figure 26–3). To illustrate, assume that Joe writes The Computer Store a check for the computers on May 3, 1992. If The Computer Store negotiates the check to the Friendly Finance Company on August 5, 1992, The Computer Store cannot be a holder in due course of that instrument because it was purchased more than 90 days after its issue. The Computer Store gave value with notice that the instrument was overdue. Note that the 90-day time period affects the ability of third parties to become holders in due course; it does not affect whether or not the check is "good." A drawee bank

Figure 26–3   Rules for Overdue Checks, UCC Old and Revised Article 3

Old Article 3	Revised Article 3
Check is presumed to be overdue 30 days after issue	Check is overdue 90 days after issue

may still pay the check even though it is more than 90 days old.

Notice of Forgery or Alteration

One cannot be a holder in due course of an instrument purchased with notice of forgery or a material alteration. For example, assume that Mitch gives a promissory note to Pete for $100; Pete *crudely* raises the amount to $1,000 and negotiates it to Hank. Hank is not a holder in due course of that instrument because he purchased it with notice of a material alteration. By contrast, assume that Mitch wrote the promissory note on January 2, 1993, mistakenly dated it 1992, noticed his error, and changed the date to 1993. Because minor erasures and obvious changes in date are not suspicious, Hank is a holder in due course of this instrument.

UCC § 3–302. Holder in Due Course

(a) . . . "holder in due course" means the holder of an instrument if:

(2) the holder took the instrument . . . (iv) without notice that the instrument contains an unauthorized signature or has been altered.

Notice of a Claim

One cannot be a holder in due course if the instrument is purchased with notice of a claim [UCC § 3– 302(a)(2)(v)]. A claim is a claim to ownership of the instrument, or any other right to possession, including liens.

Notice of a Defense

One cannot be a holder in due course if the instrument is purchased with notice of a defense (called defenses in recoupment) [UCC § 3–302(a)(2)(vi)]. This is fundamental to the concept of the holder in due course as a type of bona fide purchaser deserving special protection. Obviously, one who purchases with knowledge of the obligor's defenses does not deserve special protection. For example, assume that Bob issues a promissory note payable to Lemon Auto Sales for a used car. The car is defective. If Patriots Bank buys the note knowing that the car is defective, it is not a holder in due course because it knew of Bob's defense.

Special Purchases

One cannot be a holder in due course of an instrument purchased at a judicial sale, as part of a bulk transfer, or as a successor in interest to an estate or other entity [UCC § 3–302(c)]. Thus, a purchaser of commercial paper at an execution sale or a sale in bankruptcy is not a holder in due course. A creditor who attaches commercial paper to enforce a judgment lien is not a holder in due course. Where one bank purchases the substantial part of the commercial paper held by a second bank threatened by insolvency, the bank purchasing in bulk is not a holder in due course. Where a new partnership buys all the assets of an old partnership, the new partnership is not a holder in due course of the paper acquired.

Not Fatal Knowledge

Purchasing an instrument with knowledge that it is antedated or postdated does not destroy holder in due course status. Similarly, knowledge that a party to the instrument has been discharged does not affect holder in due course status. Further, merely taking an instrument from a fiduciary is not fatal knowledge. However, taking an instrument from a fiduciary as payment for the fiduciary's personal debt, for the personal benefit of the fiduciary, or as a deposit to the fiduciary's personal account is notice of a defense that will destroy holder in due course status [UCC § 3–307(b)(2)].

Payee as a Holder in Due Course

While not typical, it is possible for the payee to qualify as a holder in due course. For example, assume that Joe Camp, in the opening scenario, pays for the computers bought from The Computer Store by giving the store a cashier's check bought from the ABC Bank. If Joe bought the cashier's check with a check that bounced, the bank may assert nonpayment as a defense to its obligation to pay the cashier's check. The Computer Store is a holder in due course entitled to payment because there is no reason for The Computer Store to be treated any differently than it would be if the cashier's check had been made payable to Joe and negotiated to The Computer Store. In both instances, The Computer Store paid value without notice of any claims or defenses.

SHELTER RULE

It is a basic rule at common law that whenever property is transferred, the transferee acquires at least whatever rights the transferor had in that property. Because a negotiable instrument is a type of property, this principle applies to the transfer of an instrument. Thus, it is possible to acquire the rights of a holder in due course without actually becoming one. This can be done by "taking shelter" in the holder in due course rights of one's transferor. The rights one acquires by the shelter rule are no different from true holder in due course rights. The shelter rule, as codified in UCC section 3–203(1), assures the holder in due course of a free market for the instrument.

UCC 3–203. Transfer of Instrument; Rights Acquired by Transfer

(b) Transfer of an instrument, whether or not the transfer is a negotiation, vests in the transferee any right of the transferor to enforce the instrument, including any right as a holder in due course.

General Rule

A general statement of the shelter rule is simple: One who takes an instrument from a holder in due course gets holder in due course rights. That is true even if the transfer is made by gift, with knowledge of claims and defenses of an obviously overdue instrument. The transferor was a holder in due course; therefore, the transferee gets holder in due course rights. An example will illustrate. As is illustrated in Figure 26–4, assume that Alan sells his car to Mike, taking as payment a promissory note made payable to Alan. Alan sells the note to Charles, who becomes a holder in due course. Charles gives the note to his daughter Diana as a birthday present. In this example, Diana is not a holder in due course because she didn't give value. However, she has the rights of a holder in due course because the transferee (Diana) gets whatever rights (holder in due course rights) her transferor (Charles) had. If Diana gave the note to her husband, Hank, he too would have holder in due course rights because his transferor (Diana) had those rights.

Figure 26–4   Shelter Rule: Illustration of General Rule

Figure 26–5   Shelter Rule: Illustration of Party to Fraud Exception

Party to the Fraud Exception

There is an important exception to the shelter rule. This rule cannot confer holder in due course protection to one who is involved in any fraud or illegality with respect to the instrument [UCC § 3–203(b)]. For example, assume that, as is illustrated in Figure 26–5, Peg Porter induces Michelle Marbles by fraud to issue a note payable to Peg. Assume further that Peg negotiates the note to Helen, who is a holder in due course, and then repurchases the note from Helen. Peg does not have the rights of a holder in due course.

UCC § 3–203. Transfer of Instrument

(b) . . . but the transferee cannot acquire rights of a holder in due course if the transferee engaged in fraud or illegality affecting the instrument.

Further, because Peg was involved in the fraud, she is not permitted to "wash" the instrument through a holder in due course to acquire holder in due course rights.

Read the following case and determine whether or not the transferee should acquire holder in due course rights.

FINALCO, INC. v. ROOSEVELT
235 Cal. App.3d 1301, 3 Cal.Rptr.2d 865 (1991)

Roosevelt purchased undivided co-ownership interests in computer equipment owned by Dover. He paid Dover $8,000 in cash and issued a promissory note for the balance. Dover negotiated the note to Finalco sometime prior to June 1986. Finalco negotiated the note to Michigan National Bank, which in turn negotiated the note to Marine Midland Bank. Finalco received notice of Roosevelt's default on January 21, 1987, and with that knowledge repurchased the note. When Finalco sued Roosevelt for default, Roosevelt asserted violations of securities laws, common law fraud, and misrepresentation. Finalco asserts holder in due course protection.

JOHNSON, Judge

We find defendant's claims fail for a fundamental reason: lack of sufficient evidence linking Finalco to any of the alleged wrongdoing on the part of Dover. There was insufficient evidence to establish Finalco engaged, with Dover, in a conspiracy to defraud Roosevelt. The evidence did establish, however, Finalco was a holder in due course of the note sued upon and, therefore, took free of any defenses Roosevelt may have had against Dover even assuming those defenses were established.

Roosevelt contends Finalco was not a holder in due course of the note because at the time it accepted assignment of the note from Dover it was on notice Roosevelt was in default on his payments. There is no evidence to support this claim. Although the record does not reflect the date Roosevelt's note was assigned from Dover to Finalco it had to have been prior to June 25, 1986, because on that date Michigan National Bank, to whom Finalco indorsed the note, in turn indorsed the note to Marine Midland. The first indication of Finalco's knowledge of Roosevelt's default is Finalco's letter of January 21, 1987.

Roosevelt next contends even if Finalco took the note from Dover as a holder in due course Finalco lost that status when it assigned the note to the Michigan National Bank because after the assignment Finalco was no longer a holder. Furthermore, when Finalco subsequently reacquired Roosevelt's note several months before trial it did not take as a holder in due course because by then Finalco clearly knew Roosevelt was in default.

Roosevelt's argument ignores § 3−201(1) of the [California] Commercial Code which provides, "Transfer of an instrument vests in the transferee such rights as the transferor has therein. . . ."

This "shelter" provision is identical to § 3−201(1) of the Uniform Commercial Code. "Its policy is to assure the holder in due course a free market for the paper." (Uniform Commercial Code Comment 3.) Thus, when a transferee takes an instrument from a holder in due course the transferee takes free from all claims and defenses to the same extent as did the holder in due course even if the transferee is aware of those claims and defenses. If this was not the rule, a holder in due course could be deprived of a market for the instrument if the obligor widely disseminated notice of a claim or defense. Such a result would not benefit the obligor, who would still be liable to the holder in due course, but it would harm the holder in due course by destroying a market for the instrument.

Under Commercial Code § 3−201(1) it is irrelevant that Finalco could not reacquire the note as a holder in due course. The shelter provision does not make the transferee a holder in due course, it transfers the freedom from claims and defenses of the original holder in due course to each succeeding transferee. Finalco was simply another transferee in a chain of transfers of the Roosevelt note. Where the transferee happens to have been a prior holder in due course, it takes back from its transferor the same rights it transferred. Here, Finalco was in no better or worse position vis a vis Roosevelt's claims and defenses against Dover than if Finalco had originally retained possession of Roosevelt's note.

Case Questions

1. Analyze: "The policy of the shelter rule is to assure the holder in due course a free market for his paper."

2. Why did Finalco need to use the shelter rule?

3. Should Finalco have been denied the benefits of the shelter rule as a party to the underlying fraud?

Transfer that Is Not a Negotiation

Under UCC old Article 3, there was confusion over whether the shelter rule could give someone holder status if there were missing indorsements. Under revised Article 3, the shelter rule clearly applies even if the transfer is not a negotiation. In other words, one can get the rights of a holder by the shelter rule. If the transferor is a holder, the transferee is entitled to enforce the instrument as a holder. However, the transferee is not given the procedural presumptions discussed later in the chapter. For example, assume that Snidley defrauds Dwight into issuing a promissory note payable to the order of Snidley. Assume further that Snidley negotiates the note to Nell, who takes as a holder in due course. If Nell transfers the note to Dudley without indorsement, Dudley is not a holder. However, he does have the rights of a holder and is entitled to enforce the instrument. He further has Nell's rights as a holder in due course. Figure 26–6 summarizes the revisions of the shelter rule.

CLAIMS AND DEFENSES

The importance of holder in due course status for the purchaser can best be understood by comparing this status with the status of an assignee of a contract right. The assignee takes subject to all claims and defenses that the obligor (maker or drawer) could have asserted against the assignor (see Chapter 17). By contrast, the holder in due course takes free from most of the claims and defenses that the maker or drawer could have asserted against the payee. The advantage of being a holder in due course is that a holder in due course takes free from most claims and defenses and a mere holder takes subject to most claims and defenses.

Rights of a Holder in Due Course

A holder in due course, and one with holder in due course rights, takes free from all claims (assertions of ownership) to an instrument [UCC § 3–306]. The holder in due course takes free from certain **personal defenses,** and subject to the so-called **real defenses.**

Figure 26–6   Shelter Rule, UCC Old and Revised Article 3

Old Article 3	Revised Article 3
A person who, as a prior holder, had notice of fraud cannot improve his or her position	Eliminates this exception
General rule was a person could not acquire holder status by shelter rule	Can acquire holder status by shelter rule

Personal Defenses

A holder in due course takes free from all personal defenses. Although the personal defenses are not listed in the Code, they include defenses to a simple contract, such as fraud in the inducement, misrepresentation, mistake, and lack of consideration [UCC § 3–305(a)(2)]. Assume, for example, that The Computer Store in our opening scenario failed to deliver the computers to Joe as promised. If the note were negotiated into the hands of First National Bank, a holder in due course, First National would take the note free from Joe's defense because the defense of failure of consideration is a personal one. In other words, Joe would have to pay First National and then sue The Computer Store for breach of contract.

UCC § 3–305. Defenses and Claims in Recoupment

(a) . . . the right to enforce the obligation of a party to pay an instrument is subject to the following:

(2) a defense . . . that would be available if the person entitled to enforce the instrument were enforcing a right to payment under a simple contract.

Alternatively, assume that the computers were delivered as promised, they were accepted by Joe, and it was subsequently discovered that the computers were defective. Joe has a defense of breach of warranty (the Code calls these claims in recoupment). It is a personal defense that cannot be asserted sucessfully against third-party holders in due course. However, it can be asserted against a payee even if that payee is a holder in due course [UCC § 3–305(b)]. Again, Joe would have to pay First National and sue The Computer Store for breach of contract.

Real Defenses

Even a holder in due course takes subject to real defenses. In other words, the maker or drawer can assert real defenses to avoid payment even against a holder in due course. The real defenses are listed in section 3–305(a)(1) and summarized in Figure 26–7.

Infancy   The defense of infancy is a real defense that can be asserted against a holder in due course even if under state law the defense makes promises voidable rather than void [UCC § 3–305(a)(1)(i)]. The intent is to protect the infant (minor) even at the expense of loss to the holder in due course.

Figure 26–7   Real Defenses

- Infancy.
- Other incapacities that render an obligation void under state law.
- Fraud in the execution.
- Discharge in insolvency.

UCC § 3–305. Defenses and Claims in Recoupment

(a) . . . the right to enforce the obligation of a party to pay an instrument is subject to the following:

(1) a defense of the obligor based on (i) infancy of the obligor to the extent it is a defense to a simple contract.

Other Defenses that Render an Obligation Void Other defenses that make obligations *void* are real defenses that are good against holders in due course

[UCC § 3–305(a)(1)(ii)]. For example, to the extent that incompetence, guardianship, illegality, and duress make an obligation *void* under state law, they are real defenses. If they make the obligation merely *voidable* under state law, they are personal defenses. For example, whether illegality, which is most frequently a question of gambling or usury statutes, is a real defense depends on whether contracts in violation of gambling statutes are void or voidable under state law. Read the following case and determine whether economic duress is a real or a personal defense under District of Columbia law.

UCC § 3–305. Defenses and Claims in Recoupment

(a) . . . the right to enforce the obligation of a party to pay an instrument is subject to the following:

(1) a defense of the obligor based on . . . (ii) duress, lack of legal capacity, or illegality of the transaction which, under other law, nullifies the obligation of the obligor.

FEDERAL DEPOSIT INSURANCE CORP v. MEYER
755 F.Supp. 10 (D.C. 1991)

Certain partners in the law firm of Finley Kumble issued promissory notes to secure loans made by the National Bank of Washington (NBW). Upon NBW insolvency, the Federal Deposit Insurance Corp. (FDIC) took over as receiver. It sued the partners as makers. Under section 1823(e) of the Federal Deposit Insurance Act of 1950, the FDIC had the rights of a holder in due course of these notes. The partners asserted the defense of economic duress against the FDIC.

PRATT, District Judge

The Finley Partners concede that 1823(e) operates to place the FDIC in the position of a holder in due course, taking promissory notes free of personal defenses. They argue, however, that § 1823(e) does not extinguish real defenses set forth in the Uniform Commercial Code ("UCC") and that their economic duress defense constitutes such a real defense.

The main legal question, then, is whether economic duress is a personal defense that rendered NBW's title to the promissory notes voidable, or a real defense that rendered its title entirely void. The Finley Partners suggest that duress of any nature constitutes a real defense, citing UCC § 3–305(2)(b) and several cases from outside the District of Columbia. A careful reading of the UCC and its Official Commentary reveals that it does not make such a blanket classification.

First, § 3–305 provides that holders in due course take free of all defenses except for "such other incapacity, or duress, or illegality of the transaction, as renders the obligation of the party a nullity." The words "such" and "as" indicate that the section is not stating that any type of duress renders an obligation to be a nullity. Rather, it suggests that only those types of duress that are so severe as to render it a nullity stand as exceptions to the rule that holders in due course take free of defenses.[1]

---

[1]Official Comment 6 supports this view of the words "such" and "as" in UCC § 3–305. The first sentences state: " Duress is a matter of degree. An instrument signed at the point of a gun is void, even in the hands of a holder in due course. One signed under threat to prosecute the son of the maker may be merely voidable, so that the defense is cut off." Clearly, the section is not placing all types of duress in the same category.

Of course, the question left open is what type of duress is severe enough to render it a nullity. Neither UCC § 3–305 nor the Official Comment attempt to establish a rule governing which types of duress render a transaction void as opposed to merely voidable. Instead, Official Comment 6 declares that "[a]ll such matters are therefore left to the local law." Further supporting this point is the Commentary of Chancellor William D. Hawkland on UCC § 3–305: "Unlike the case of infancy, these three defenses [incapacity, duress, illegality] may be raised only if state statutory or case law makes the transaction void from the outset and not merely voidable."

The Finley Partners do not cite any precedent from the District of Columbia that supports the view that economic duress renders a transaction void. In fact, they point out that in *Ozerol v. Howard University*, the D.C. Court of appeals quoted section 175 of the *Restatement (Second) of Contracts* which states that duress by threat (rather than by physical compulsion) renders a contract voidable rather than void. Although that case fails to distinguish between void and voidable contracts, it calls attention to the *Restatement*'s distinction between the two categories.

The District of Columbia explicitly followed this distinction in *Williams v. Amann*. In that case, the Municipal Court of Appeals for the District of Columbia stated that "[w]hatever duress may have existed at the time of the execution of the contract was that which operated only upon the mind of the appellant and did not involve physical compulsion.

Therefore, the contract was voidable only; not void." Given the fact that *Williams* and *Ozerol* both support the modern *Restatement* view, and that no D.C. cases have been found that hold to the contrary, the correct conclusion is that in the District of Columbia physical compulsion is the only type of duress that can render a transaction entirely void.

The Finley Partners do not allege that they were physically compelled to sign the promissory notes in question. They themselves labeled their defense as "economic" duress, and the substance of their allegations are that they signed the notes because of the threat that their wages and standing in the firm would decrease if they refused. Such economic duress does not reach the level of physical compulsion capable of rendering a transaction entirely void. Thus, NBW held at least voidable title to the promissory notes when the FDIC took over as Receiver. Thus, defendants' economic duress defense is not valid against the FDIC.

Case Questions

1. Compare and contrast infancy and duress as defenses.

2. Why didn't the court discuss whether or not the Finley Partners had a valid claim of economic duress?

3. If the Code seeks uniformity, why rely on individual state law (void versus voidable) to determine if economic duress is a real defense? Is there an alternative?

Fraud in the Execution   Fraud in the execution is a real defense and good against a holder in due course. This is by contrast to fraud in the inducement, which is a personal defense. Fraud in the execution occurs where, for example, the maker is tricked into signing a note believing that it is merely a receipt. The obligation is void because the maker never intended to sign such an instrument at all. This defense includes the situation where the maker knowingly signs a negotiable instrument but is ignorant of its essential terms. It is not enough that the maker did not know what was signed. The test of this defense is "excusable ignorance." There must have been no reasonable opportunity to obtain the knowledge [UCC § 3–305(a)(1)]. In determining what is a reasonable opportunity, all relevant factors will be considered, such as intelligence, education, business experience, ability to understand and read English, and the nature of any representations made.

UCC § 3–305. Defenses and Claims in Recoupment

(a) . . . the right to enforce the obligation of a party to pay an instrument is subject to the following:

(1) a defense of the obligor based on . . . (iii) fraud that induced the obligor to sign the instrument with neither knowledge nor reasonable opportunity to learn of its character or its essential terms.

Insolvency Proceedings   The defense of discharge in insolvency proceedings is a real defense. It is not cut off by purchase by a holder in due course. Insolvency proceedings includes bankruptcy. Therefore, if the maker's debts are discharged by a bankruptcy proceeding, the defense of discharge is good even against a holder in due course.

Other Real Defenses   There are two additional real defenses that are not listed in section 3–305: forgery and material alteration. These will both be discussed in Chapter 29.

Rights of a Non-Holder in Due Course

One who is not a holder in due course takes the instrument subject to all claims and defenses, both real and personal [UCC § 3–305 and § 3–306].

UCC § 3–305. Defenses and Claims in Recoupment

(c) . . . the obligor may not assert against the person entitled to enforce the instrument a defense, claim in recoupment or claim to the instrument of another person, but the other person's claim to the instrument may be asserted by the obligor if the other person is joined in the action and personally asserts the claim against the person entitled to enforce the instrument.

Jus Tertii

The contract of the obligor is to pay the holder. The doctrine of **jus tertii** concerns claims and defenses of a person other than the obligor. Under this doctrine, the rights of a third party cannot be used even against a mere holder [UCC § 3–305(c)]. For example, assume Joe Camp in our opening scenario delivered a cashier's check issued by the ABC Bank to The Computer Store in payment for the computers. Subsequently, Joe learns that The Computer Store had defrauded him. The Computer Store may enforce the check against ABC even though it is not a holder in due course. ABC Bank is not permitted to assert the defense of a third party (Joe) against even a nonholder in due course. ABC can only assert the defense if Joe is joined in the action. ABC is only permitted to assert a third-party defense where the instrument has been lost or stolen and the party seeking enforcement is not a holder in due course.

Procedural Matters

Section 3–301 outlines the parties entitled to enforce an instrument. Unless a defense is asserted, a holder is entitled to recover by mere production of the instrument [UCC § 3–308]. Only if the obligor has a claim or defense does the party's status as a holder in due course become relevant.

LEGISLATIVE LIMITATIONS

Because of the potential for abuse against consumers, the Federal Trade Commission (FTC) promulgated a rule that effectively abolished the holder in due course concept in consumer transactions. The FTC rule requires that the following language be included on all consumer credit paper:

NOTICE:
ANY HOLDER OF THIS CONSUMER CREDIT CONTRACT IS SUBJECT TO ALL CLAIMS AND DEFENSES WHICH THE DEBTOR COULD ASSERT AGAINST THE SELLER OF GOODS OR SERVICES OBTAINED PURSUANT HERETO OR WITH THE PROCEEDS HEREOF. RECOVERY HEREUNDER BY THE DEBTOR SHALL NOT EXCEED AMOUNTS PAID BY THE DEBTOR HEREUNDER.

It is generally accepted that the effect of this notice is to destroy the negotiability of the instrument because the instrument is clearly "subject to" any claims or defenses. Thus, parties to consumer paper are deprived of Article 3 rights and purchasers are mere assignees.

Read the following excerpt. Is abolishment of the holder in due course concept in consumer transactions a good idea? Should it be extended to commercial ventures?

---

*The Death of Contract**

The "holder in due course" concept was worked out by Lord Mansfield and his successors in the late 18th and early 19th centuries against a business background in which bills of

---

*Source: Grant Gilmore, "The Death of Contract," (Columbus, Ohio: The Ohio State University Press) n.18, at 108 (1974). Reprinted with permission.

exchange and promissory notes did in fact circulate and could be expected to pass through a number of hands before being retired. As the modern banking system developed, instruments gradually ceased to circulate. In this century nothing is rarer than a true negotiation to a third party purchaser for value—the use of negotiable notes which pass from dealer to finance company in the attempt to carry out consumer frauds is hardly a "true negotiation." The whole "holder in due course" concept could usefully have been abolished when negotiable instruments law was codified at the end of the 19th century. In fact it was preserved like a fly in amber both in the N.I.L. [Negotiable Instruments Law] and in its successor, Article 3 of the Uniform Commercial Code. Indeed our codifications typically preserve once vital but now obsolete concepts in much the same way that our museums preserve the ancient artifacts of bygone civilizations.

Thought Questions

1. Does the holder in due course concept offer any benefit to the obligor?
2. If the concept of holder in due course were eliminated, would Article 3 serve any useful purpose?
3. Evaluate: "The use of negotiable notes which pass from dealer to finance company in the attempt to carry out consumer frauds is hardly a 'true negotiation.' "

END–OF–CHAPTER QUESTIONS

1. Peter is the payee on a negotiable instrument in the amount of $10,000. He indorses it in blank and delivers it to Henrietta in exchange for Henrietta's promise to deliver an antique car. Before she can deliver the car, she learns that Peter defrauded the maker into issuing him the note. With that knowledge, she delivers the car. Is Henrietta a holder in due course? Explain.

2. The Computer Store is the payee on a promissory note for $12,000. It agrees to negotiate the note to First National Bank for $9,000. First National pays The Computer Store $6,000 and then discovers that the maker of the note has a defense. Is First National a holder in due course? If so, to what extent?

3. Paula was the payee on a $10,000 check. On June 18, she deposited it into her account with the Next National Bank. At the time she deposited the check, she had a balance of $5,000. That day, the bank paid two checks drawn on her account for $1,000 and $2,500, respectively. The next day, Paula deposited another check in the amount of $1,500. The bank paid three more checks drawn on her account in the amounts of $500, $1,000, and $150. On June 25, Next received notice that the $10,000 check would not be paid because of a stop payment order. Is Next a holder in due course of that check?

4. On May 14, 1992, John paid for his groceries with a check on which he was the payee. The check was dated December 17, 1991. The Grocery Store acted in good faith. Is the Grocery Store a holder in due course? Explain.

5. Alan induced Mike by fraud to make a note payable to Alan. Alan negotiated it to Ben, who took with notice of the fraud. Ben negotiated it to Charles, a holder in due course, and then repurchased the note. Is Ben a holder in due course? Can Ben claim the rights of a holder in due course?

6. Ralston owed Rockland Trust $125,000. South Shore National Bank lent Ralston $47,000, crediting $38,000 of the loan amount to a new checking account. Ralston drew a check on this new account for $21,000 payable to Rockland Trust with instructions to Rockland Trust to wire $21,000 to two boat companies in

Maryland. The check was deposited into Ralston's account with Rockland Trust. South Shore certified the check and charged Ralston's account. When both banks discovered that Ralston was involved in fraud, Rockland Trust refused to wire the money to Maryland and South Shore applied the remaining $17,000 against the outstanding loan balance. South Shore refused to pay the certified check. Is Rockland Trust a holder in due course? See *Rockland Trust Co. v. South Shore National Bank*, 366 Mass. 74, 314 N.E.2d 438 (1974).

7. Bennett purchased a car with money given to him by his grandparents, titling the car in the name of his mother. His mother insured the car with United States Fidelity and Guaranty Company. (USF&G). Bennett lent the car to a friend, who wrecked it. USF&G wrote his mother a check in the amount of $4,400 to settle the claim. His mother negotiated the check to Bennett. Bennett deposited the check in his checking account and waited for the check to clear. In the meantime, he agreed to purchase a new car and gave the car dealer a postdated check to pay for the new car. When USF&G discovered that his mother was not the true owner of the insured car, they stopped payment on the check. Was Bennett a holder in due course of this check? Did Bennett give value? See *Bennett v. United States Fidelity and Guaranty Co.*, 19 N.C.App. 66, 198 S.E.2d 33 (1973).

8. Wilhelm and Allen were in default to Centerre Bank in the amount of $142,000. They sold limited partnership interests to investors, taking negotiable promissory notes for $150,000 as payment. They refinanced their debt to the bank, executing a refinancing note for $150,000 and delivering the investors' promissory notes, properly indorsed, as collateral for the loan. When Wilhelm and Allen defaulted on the refinancing note, the bank attempted to collect on the investors' notes. The investors asserted that they were defrauded into issuing the notes. Centerre Bank (the bank) asserted holder in due course status. Has the bank given value? To what extent? See *Audsley v. Allen*, 774 S.W.2d 142 (Mo. 1989).

9. Defendant, Asati, Inc. (Asati), opened a business checking account with Bank of New York (BNY). On December 29, 1989, Asati indorsed a check drawn by CWM for $610,205 and deposited it in its account with BNY. The CWM check was regular in every way. BNY provisionally credited Asati's account and forwarded the check to First Union for payment. As required by its funds availability policy, BNY made the funds from the CWM check available to Asati on Wednesday, January 3. At about 3:00 P.M. on that day, the vice president of Asati requested three certified checks of $200,000 each from BNY. The teller checked Asati's account, determined that there were sufficient funds, put a $600,000 hold on the account, and issued the certified checks. The checks were issued at about 3:15. At about 3:32 P.M. BNY received notice that the drawee had dishonored the CWM check on the basis of a stop payment order. BNY sued CWM as drawer of the check. CWM asserted as a defense that the air-supported structure erected by Asati, the consideration for which the CWM check was partial payment, collapsed. Is BNY a holder in due course? Did BNY give value? Did it act in good faith? See *Bank of New York v. Asati, Inc.*, 15 U.C.C. Rep.Serv. 521 (N.Y. Sup. Ct. 1991).

10. In 1984, Culver entered into a business arrangement with Nasib Ed Kalliel under which Kalliel was to manage the financial aspects of Culver's farm while Culver managed the farm. The $30,000 borrowed from Rexford State Bank was deposited into Culver's account. Culver believed that Kalliel was responsible for repayment. About one week later, Gilbert, whom Culver believed worked for Kalliel, requested that Culver sign a document which Culver believed to be a receipt for the $30,000. The document

was a preprinted promissory note that was incomplete at the time signed. The note was subsequently completed, calling for payment of $50,000 at 14.5 percent interest. (Apparently the Bank had given Kalliel $50,000.) If the bank negotiated the note to a holder in due course, can Culver assert fraud in the execution as a defense? See *Federal Deposit Insurance Corp. v. Culver,* 640 F. Supp. 725 (D. Kansas 1986).

Chapter 27

Liability of the Parties

■

CRITICAL THINKING INQUIRIES

As you read this chapter, you should be able to address the following:

- Compare and contrast the maker's contract and the drawer's contract.
- Compare and contrast primary liability and secondary liability.
- Evaluate the following statement: "When a drawee bank dishonors a draft it has liability to holders under its drawee contract."
- Analyze the following statement: "An accommodation party is liable in the capacity in which that party signs the instrument."
- Explain the relationship between contract liability and warranty liability.

MANAGERIAL PERSPECTIVE

Andy Davids decides to sell his car to Michael Aarons. Michael makes a check payable to the order of Andy in the amount of $5,000 drawn on Second National Bank. Andy indorses the check and negotiates it to Joe Samuels as the down payment on a new car. Joe indorses it and deposits it in his account with First National Bank. First National presents it for payment to the drawee, Second National Bank. Second National dishonors the check because Michael had stopped payment on the check.

- What is Michael's liability on this check? Does it matter if Joe or First National is a holder in due course?
- Does something have to be done to trigger Michael's liability?
- What is Andy's liability on this check? Does something have to be done to trigger Andy's liability?
- What is Second National's liability on this check?

This is a typical liability scenario. A holder of an instrument in entitled to enforce the instrument. This chapter will discuss against whom the instrument can be enforced and on what basis. There are two basic ways in which one can incur liability in the commercial paper area: (1) contract liability and (2) warranty liability. Contract liability is liability "on the instrument" that stems from one's signature on the instrument. Warranty liability is liability "off the instrument" that comes from the movement of the instrument.

CONTRACT LIABILITY

Whenever one signs a negotiable instrument, contract liability is created. The capacity in which one signs (maker, drawer, indorser) determines the type of contract made. In other words, whenever one signs an instrument, certain promises are automatically made. The specifics of those promises vary depending on whether one signs as a maker, drawer, or indorser. Therefore, in any liability question, one must first identify the parties on the instrument. Label Michael, Andy, Joe, First National, and Second National in the opening scenario.

When the contract liability is absolute and unconditional, the liability is **primary.** By contrast, when the contract liability is conditioned on certain technical rights, the liability is **secondary.**

Signature by an Authorized Agent

Because contract liability on an instrument is created by signature, no one is liable on an instrument unless the person or the person's authorized agent signs the instrument [UCC § 3–401(a)]. Thus, a principal can incur contract liability on an instrument if the instrument is signed by an agent of that principal [UCC § 3–402(a)]. The liability of the principal is determined by applicable agency law, which generally provides that the principal is liable if the agent is authorized to enter into the contract on behalf of the principal. The principal is liable if the agent is authorized whether or not the principal's name appears on the instrument [UCC § 3–402(a)]. This means that an undisclosed principal incurs liability on a negotiable instrument in the same manner as under a simple contract (see Chapter 36).

Of equal importance is the question of the liability of the agent. Under general agency law, if an authorized agent enters into a contract on behalf of a

disclosed principal, the principal is liable and the agent is not. The question is a bit more complicated in the case of negotiable instruments because the instrument might end up in the hands of a third party unaware of the fact that the signature is a signature of a mere agent. The Code attempts a balance. First, an agent has no liability on an instrument if the principal is unambiguously identified as such in the instrument [UCC § 3–402(b)(1)]. For example, assume that Alicia Allen is an agent for Pauline Peters and signs a promissory note on behalf of Alicia: "Pauline Peters, by Alicia Allen, agent." Alicia is not liable on this instrument. It is clear to third parties that she signed this instrument only as the representative for Pauline.

UCC § 3–402. Signature by Representative

(b)(1) If the form of the signature shows unambiguously that the signature is made on behalf of the represented person who is identified in the instrument, the representative is not liable.

By contrast, if Alicia either fails to identify the principal or fails to indicate that she is signing only as an agent, she is liable to a holder in due course who doesn't know that she is merely signing as an agent [UCC § 3–402(b)(2)]. For example, if Alicia signs the note "Alicia Allen," she is liable to a holder in due course because this note fails to identify Pauline as the principal. Similarly, if Alicia signs "Alicia Allen, agent," Alicia is liable. Last, if Alicia signs "Pauline Peters, Alicia Allen" she is liable because she has named the principal but failed to identify herself as an agent.

UCC § 3–402. Signature by Representative

(b)(2) . . . if (i) the form of the signature does not show unambiguously that the signature is made in a representative capacity or (ii) the represented person is not identified in the instrument, the representative is liable on the instrument to a holder in due course that took the instrument without notice that the representative was not intended to be liable on the instrument.

The situation is different if the person attempting to enforce the instrument is not a holder in due course. In each example above, Pauline is liable to

Figure 27–1 Check Drawn on Principal's Account

Oakview Elementary P.T.A.
1234 Apple Road
Centerville, OH

July 8 19 93

PAY TO THE ORDER OF _School Supply_ $ _100⁰⁰_

one hundred and ⁿ°/100's DOLLARS

TO: Last National Bank   SIGNED _Ann Tyler_

---

a non-holder in due course as long as the agent is acting as authorized. However, Alicia can escape liability by proving that the original parties did not intend for her to be liable.

UCC § 3–402. Signature by Representative

(b)(2) . . . With respect to any other person, the representative is liable on the instrument unless the representative proves that the original parties did not intend the representative to be liable on the instrument.

If the instrument is a check drawn on the principal's account, the agent is not liable even if representative capacity is not indicated [UCC § 3–402(c)]. For example, assume that Ann Tyler is the treasurer of the Oakview Elementary School PTA.

Assume further that, as in Figure 27–1, Ann signs a check drawn on the PTA account. If she is authorized to issue this check, she has no personal liability. While Ann signed as drawer without any indication that she was signing merely as an agent, the check is clearly drawn on the PTA account.

UCC § 3–402. Signature by Representative

(c) If a representative signs the name of the representative as drawer of a check without indication of the representative status and the check is payable from an account of the represented person who is identified on the check, the signer is not liable on the check.

Read the following case and determine whether or not the agent has personal liability.

FINNISH FUR SALES CO., LTD. v. JULIETTE SHULOF FURS, INC.
770 F.Supp. 139 (S.D. N.Y. 1991)

Defendant Corporation, Juliette Shulof Furs (JSF), purchased fur pelts from the plaintiff, Finnish Fur Sales, Co. (FFS), at auction. JSF made a cash down payment and gave a negotiable instrument for $30,328.39. Defendant Juliette Shulof signed the instrument ''Juliette A. Shulof'' above the printed name of the corporation. The instrument was negotiated into the hands of a holder in due course, Okobank, presented for payment, and dishonored on February 7, 1989. Okobank sued both the corporation and Juliette Shulof personally.

LEISURE, District Judge

The relevant section of the Code is § 3–403, which governs signatures by authorized representatives. Under subsection (2)

An authorized representative who signs his own name to an instrument

(a) is personally obligated if the instrument neither names the person represented nor shows that the representative signed in a representative capacity;

(b) except as otherwise established between the immediate parties, is personally obligated if the instrument names the person represented but does not show that the representative signed in a representative capacity or if the instrument does not name the person represented but does show that the representative signed in a representative capacity. [UCC § 3–403(2)]

Official Comment 3 to this section offers examples of signatures and the legal implication of each type of signature. An authorized representative will not be personally bound by the following: a signature in the name of the represented party; "Peter Pringle by Arthur Adams, Agent"; or "Peter Pringle Arthur Adams," parol evidence may be offered in litigation between the immediate parties to prove representative capacity.

In the case at bar, Mrs. Shulof signed as "Juliette A. Shulof" above a typed name of "Juliette Shulof Furs, Inc.," which had been typed in by the preparer of the instrument, FFS. The cases interpreting signature of this type demonstrate the special treatment of negotiable instruments under New York law. New York has, as a general rule, a policy against imposing personal liability on corporate officers if the circumstances are ambiguous. However, this policy gives way before the policy considerations underlying UCC § 3–403, which "aims to foster certainty and definiteness in the law of commercial paper, requirements deriving from the 'necessity for takers of negotiable instruments to tell at a glance whose obligation they hold.'" *Rotuba Extruders, Inc. v. Ceppos.*

Construing Section 3–403(2), the New York Court of Appeals held that "the basic law is that resort to extrinsic proof is impermissible when the face of the instrument itself does not serve to put its holder on notice of the limited liability of the signer." In *Rotuba*, a promissory note had been signed by the chief executive officer of a corporation as "Kenneth Ceppos," on a signature line directly below the printed name of the corporation. The

court held that under Section 3–403(2)(b), the note named the corporation but did not indicate that Ceppos had signed in a representative capacity, and that only sufficient evidence establishing an agreement between the immediate parties that Ceppos would not be personally liable would excuse him from such liability.

In *Bankers Trust Co. v. Javeri,* the Appellate Division stated unequivocally that in the case of a holder in due course, the suit is not between the "immediate parties" to the negotiable instrument, and that extrinsic evidence cannot be introduced to release the signatory from his personal obligation.

The court in this District has also held, under New York law, that as to a holder in due course "the relevant inquiry is limited to whether the face of the instrument put [the holder] on notice that [the signatory] signed in his representative capacity only. This is true even though the check also bears the [corporation's] imprint." *Carador v. Sana Travel Serv., Ltd.*

The Court finds the case at bar to be analogous to the holdings in *Javeri* and *Rotuba*. It is undisputed that Okobank never dealt with either of the Shulofs or JSF. Accordingly, the Court finds that Mrs. Shulof's signature did not give notice that she signed in a representative capacity only, and therefore she is personally liable.

Case Questions

1. Why wasn't Juliette Shulof permitted to introduce parol evidence to prove that she signed merely as a representative?

2. Was the corporation jointly liable?

3. Analyze: "This decision fosters certainty and definiteness in the law of commercial paper, requirements deriving from the necessity for takers of negotiable instruments to tell at a glance whose obligation they hold."

Maker's Contract

The maker of a negotiable instrument is *primarily* liable on the instrument. In essence, the maker of a note promises to pay the holder when the instrument is due [UCC § 3–412]. This is an unconditional, absolute promise.

Joint makers are jointly and severally liable. In other words, each maker is liable for the full amount of the note. However, each is entitled to contribution from other comakers. For example, assume that, as is illustrated in Figure 27–2, Marly, Jocelyn, and Brooke act as joint makers on a promissory note for

$12,000. If, when the note becomes due, the holder of the instrument demands the full $12,000 from Marly, she must pay the full amount. However, she is entitled to contribution of $4,000 each from Jocelyn and Brooke.

UCC § 3–412. Obligation of Issuer of Note or Cashier's Check

The issuer of a note . . . is obliged to pay the instrument (i) according to its terms at the time it was issued. . . . The obligation is owed to a person entitled to enforce the instrument or to an indorser who paid the instrument under Section 3–415.

Read the following case. Should the subsequent divorce of the comakers change their liability on a promissory note?

Figure 27–2   Joint Makers of a Promissory Note

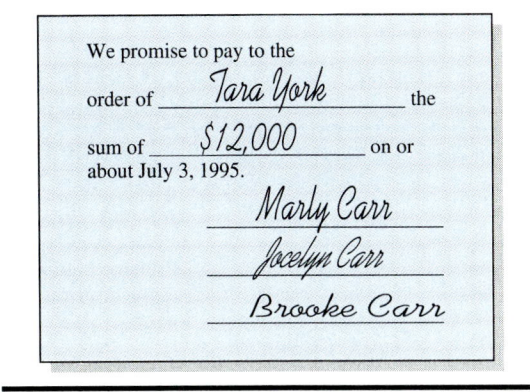

We promise to pay to the order of _Tara York_ the sum of _$12,000_ on or about July 3, 1995.

Marly Carr
Jocelyn Carr
Brooke Carr

GRIMES v. GRIMES
267 S.E.2d 372 (Ct. App. N.C. 1980)

Mr. and Mrs. Grimes executed a promissory note in the amount of $27,600 when they were separated but still married. Mr. Grimes paid the entire debt and sued Mrs. Grimes to recover her contribution.

MORRIS, Chief Judge

It is true that at common law, a note evidencing a debt executed jointly by husband and wife rendered the husband liable on the note, but not the wife. However, this rule no longer obtains. Now where the wife executes a promissory note as a co-maker, she is primarily liable thereunder. This result follows from the rule that, nothing else appearing, a person signing his or her name at the bottom of the face of a promissory note is a maker thereof, and is primarily liable thereon.

With respect to the applicability of the Uniform Commercial Code, as adopted in North Carolina, on the negotiable note in question, it is clear that the liability of a person signing a negotiable instrument is determined by the capacity in which one executes the instrument. Under [old] UCC § 3–413, the maker "engages that he will pay the instrument according to its tenor at the time of his engagement. . . ." A maker's liability is unconditional

and absolute. When two or more persons execute a note as makers, they are jointly and severally liable, unless the language of the note clearly indicates the contrary. Because of the joint and several nature of a maker's obligation under a note, when one co-maker pays the instrument he is entitled to contribution from other co-makers.

We are of the opinion that a co-maker's right to contribution is unaffected by the marital relationship of the parties to a note. This case is different from those situations to which a presumption of gift attaches, because in those cases the wife had been given merely a transfer of value from the husband. Defendant, as a co-maker, has an absolute and unconditional obligation under the note. The fact that the proceeds from the loan were used during the marriage is of no moment. At any rate, plaintiff and defendant were divorced at the time plaintiff paid the balance due under the note. No presumption of gift arises, therefore, from plaintiff retiring the debt.

Case Questions

1. Is there any way that Mrs. Grimes could have protected herself from this outcome?

2. Why did the court find that Mr. Grimes did not make Mrs. Grimes a gift when he paid the debt?

Figure 27–3   Drawer's Contract Liability, UCC Old and Revised Article 3

	Old Article 3	Revised Article 3
Drawer's contract	Secondary liability—liable only after presentment, dishonor, notice of dishonor, and protest	Primary liability—liable after dishonor

Drawer's Contract

The drawer of a draft promises to pay the holder if the draft is not paid when due [UCC § 3–414(b)]. Thus, Michael in the opening scenario has drawer's contract liability. Although the liability of the drawer is referred to as primary liability, it is only triggered by dishonor of the instrument. In other words, it is expected that the holder of the instrument will first look to the drawee for payment. Figure 27–3 summarizes how this changes prior law.

UCC § 3–414 Obligation of the Drawer

(b) If an unaccepted draft is dishonored, the drawer is obliged to pay the draft (i) according to its terms at the time it was issued. . . . This obligation is owed to a person entitled to enforce the draft or to an indorser who paid the draft.

The drawer may disclaim this liability by drawing the draft "without recourse," except that it is not possible for the drawer on a check to disclaim liability [UCC § 3–414(e)].

Indorser's Contract

When one signs as an indorser to an instrument, the contract of an indorser is automatically made. An indorser is secondarily liable, promising to pay holders only after presentment, dishonor, and notice of dishonor [UCC § 3–415(a),(c),(e)]. The indorser can avoid this contract by signing the instrument "**without recourse**" [UCC § 3–415(b)]. For example, assume that Michael in the opening scenario writes a check payable to the order of Andy Davids. Andy indorses the check "without recourse" and delivers it to Joe Samuels. Joe indorses the check and delivers it to Howard. Howard makes a timely presentment of the check to the drawee for payment. The drawee dishonors the check and Howard gives timely notice of dishonor to all parties. In this instance, Howard can enforce this check against Joe on his indorser's contract. By contrast, Howard cannot enforce the check against Andy. By signing "without recourse," Andy has disclaimed any liability as an indorser (see Figure 27–4).

Figure 27–4   Indorser's Liability

UCC § 3–415. Obligation of Indorser

(a) . . . if an instrument is dishonored, an indorser is obliged to pay the amount due on the instrument (i) according to the terms of the instrument at the time it was indorsed. . . . The obligation of the indorser is owed to a person entitled to enforce the instrument or to a subsequent indorser who paid the instrument.

Technical Rights

Because indorser's contract liability is contingent on satisfaction of the technical rights of presentment, dishonor, and notice of dishonor, it is important to understand the specifics of these rights. As a general rule, if the technical rights are not satisfied, indorsers are totally discharged from contract liability [UCC § 3–415(c)(e) and § 3–503(a)]. By contrast, the drawer is not owed notice of dishonor and is only discharged for late presentment if deprived of funds because of the delay, as illustrated in the next section [UCC § 3–414(f)].

Presentment

Presentment is a demand for payment (or acceptance). Basically, the holder **presents** the instrument to either the maker or the drawee and demands payment [UCC § 3–501(a)].

UCC § 3–501. Presentment

(a) "Presentment" means a demand made by or on behalf of a person entitled to enforce an instrument (i) to pay the instrument made to the drawee or a party obliged to pay the instrument . . . , or (ii) to accept a draft made to the drawee.

How Made   Presentment can be made in any commercially reasonable fashion, including by oral, written, or electronic means [UCC § 3–501(b)(1)].

Time of Presentment   The proper time for presentment varies depending on what type of instrument is involved. In order to trigger the contract of the indorser on a *check*, the check must be presented within 30 days from the date of indorsement. If presentment is not made timely, the indorser is totally discharged [UCC § 3–415(e)]. Further, if the check is not presented within 30 days from the date of issue, and the drawee bank goes insolvent during the delay, the drawer is discharged to the extent that the drawer suffers a loss because of the delay [UCC § 3–414(f)]. This situation is extremely rare. Not only is it unlikely that the drawee bank will go insolvent during the delay depriving the drawer of deposited funds, it is even more unlikely that the amount will not be insured by Federal Deposit Insurance.

To illustrate, assume that, as in Figure 27–5, Darlene Drawer draws a check payable to the order of Vanessa Payee on June 10, 1993. Assume further that Vanessa indorses the check and negotiates it to Frank Cooper on June 18, 1993. Frank indorses the check on July 3 and deposits it into his account with the Fifth National Bank. If Fifth National presents the check for payment on July 21, Vanessa is relieved of her indorser's contract liability because presentment was not made within 30 days from the date she indorsed the check. Frank is liable on his indorser's contract because presentment was made timely—within 30 days from the date of his indorsement. Darlene is only relieved of liability if the drawee bank became insolvent between July 10 (the

Figure 27–5   Timely Presentment on a Check

end of the 30-day period from the date of issue) and July 21 (the actual date of presentment), and to the extent that she is not protected by FDIC insurance.

Presentment of *drafts payable at a definite time* is required to trigger the liability of indorsers. Presentment can either be made on the date indicated on the draft or at a later time [UCC § 3–502(b)(3)].

Presentment on a *note* is treated differently because it is common for the technical rights, including presentment, to be waived in the case of notes and, in most instances, presentment to the maker is not contemplated. Rather, the expectation is that on the payment date, the maker will pay the note as promised. Therefore, on the typical note, presentment is not required to trigger the indorser's contract liability. (Remember, makers are primarily liable. Presentment is never required to trigger the maker's contract liability.) In other words, as is illustrated in Figure 27–6, assume that Sam Student is the maker on a promissory note payable to Lemon Auto Sales. The note is payable on July 3, 1995. Lemon indorses the note and sells it at discount to the Friendly Finance Company. Friendly buys the note in good faith and without notice. On July 3, 1995, Sam fails to pay the note because the car was defective. Friendly can sue either Sam on his maker's contract or Lemon on its indorser's contract. Sam has primary liability as a maker without technical rights. If Friendly is a holder in due course, Sam's personal defense of breach of warranty is not good. Lemon has liability as an indorser and presentment is not required to trigger that liability.

Figure 27–7 summarizes when presentment is due and how this differs from prior law.

Rights of Party to Whom Presentment Is Made   If the party to whom presentment is made (the drawee or the maker) requests it, the presenter must (1) exhibit the instrument and (2) provide reasonable identification [UCC § 3–501(b)(2)]. Similarly, without dishonoring the instrument, the party to whom presentment is made may return an instrument that lacks a proper indorsement and refuse payment or acceptance if the presentment violates the terms of the instrument, other agreement of the parties, or law [UCC § 3–501(b)(3)]. Last, the party to whom presentment is made may establish a cutoff time no earlier than 2 P.M. and treat the presentment as occurring on the next business day if the presentment is after the cutoff time [UCC § 3–501(b)(4)].

Dishonor

An instrument can be dishonored in one of three ways. First, an instrument is dishonored if payment is refused. Second, an instrument is dishonored if payment is not made within certain specified time limits. Third, in check-collection cases, an instrument must be dishonored as specified.

Refusal and Inaction   It is obvious that an instrument is dishonored when payment is requested and refused. It is just as obvious that inaction must become dishonor at some point. In other words, assume that you ask someone to pay the instrument presented and that person goes in the back room to "think about it" and never comes out. At some point "never coming out of the back room" becomes dishonor. The question is, at what point does inaction equal dishonor? The answer depends on the type of instrument and how the instrument is presented.

Where the instrument is a *note payable on demand*, it must be presented to trigger the maker's payment obligation. It is dishonored if not paid on

---

Figure 27–6   Timely Presentment on a Note

Figure 27–7   Time for Presentment, UCC Old and Revised Article 3

	Old Article 3	**Revised Article 3**
Check	Presentment due within 7 days from the date of indorsement to trigger indorser's liability	Presentment due within 30 days from the date of indorsement to trigger in-dorser's liability
Instruments Payable at a Definite Time	Presentment due on date indicated to trigger indorser's liability	*Note*: Presentment not necessary to trig-ger indorser's liability; instrument dis-honored if not paid on date indicated *Draft*: Presentment is necessary on or before the date indicated on the draft
Instruments Payable on Demand	Presentment due within a reasonable period of time after indorsement (con-sider nature of the instrument, usage of trade, and facts of particular case	*Note*: Presentment only required if note is payable through a bank; otherwise, instrument is dishonored if not paid upon demand; no time limit specified *Draft*: Presentment required; no time limit specified

the day of presentment [UCC § 3–502(a)(1)]. In other words, the maker is given until the end of the day of presentment before inaction is dishonor.

Where the instrument is a *note payable at a definite time,* presentment is not necessary. It is dishonored if it is not paid on the due date [UCC § 3–502(a)(3)]. In other words, the maker is given until the end of the due date before inaction is dishonor. Figure 27–8 summarizes dishonor of notes.

A *draft payable at a definite time* is dishonored if not paid on the date stated in the instrument or on the date of presentment, whichever is later [UCC § 3–502(b)(3)]. For example, assume that a draft payable on July 7, 1992, is presented for payment on July 10. It is dishonored if not paid on July 10 (either the day specified or the day of presentment, whichever is *later*).

Drafts payable on demand are dishonored if not paid on the day of presentment, except where pre-sented through the check-collection process [UCC § 3–502(b)(2)]. This includes checks presented for payment over the counter. In other words, assume

that Jocie Davies writes a check payable to the order of Bob York drawn on the First National Bank. If Bob takes the check to the First National Bank and presents it for payment on July 7, it is dishonored if not paid on that day. First National has time between the time of presentment and close of business on that day to inspect the instrument before payment or dis-honor. Figure 27–9 summarizes dishonor of drafts.

Action: The Check-Collection Process   In the above examples, inaction equals dishonor. If the maker or drawee does not pay the instrument within a certain amount of time, the failure to act is a dishonor. By contrast, where a check is presented through the check-collection process, inaction equals payment. While the specifics of how the check-collection process works will be explained in the next chapter, a brief explanation is required here. It is important to realize that checks presented through the check-collection process are presented in bulk. Approximately 36 billion checks are pre-sented in this manner each year, most of which are paid when presented. Rather than requiring the drawee bank to notify the presenting party of its intent to pay the item in so many cases, the Code requires notification only if the intent is *not* to pay the item. To dishonor a check presented for payment through the check-collection process, the drawee bank must make a timely return of the item or send timely notice of dishonor [UCC § 3–502(b)(1)]. The time period within which the bank must act is its **midnight deadline,** or midnight of the banking day

Figure 27–8   Dishonor of Notes

Type of Note	**When Dishonored**
Payable on demand	Dishonored if not paid on day of presentment
Other notes	Dishonored if not paid on date on which it is payable

Figure 27–9   Dishonor of Drafts

Type of Draft	When Dishonored
Checks presented over the counter	Dishonored if not paid on the day of presentment
Draft payable at a definite time	Dishonored if not paid on the day the draft becomes payable or the day of presentment, whichever is later

following presentment of the check [UCC § 4–104(a)(10)]. Failure to dishonor a check by the midnight deadline equals payment.

Notice of Dishonor

Notice of dishonor is required to trigger the contract liability of all indorsers [UCC § 3–503(a)]. This notice may be given by any person and may be made in any commercially reasonable fashion, including orally, in writing, or by electronic communication [UCC § 3–503(b)]. Regardless of the method chosen, it must reasonably identify the instrument dishonored. Where a check presented for payment through the check-collection process is dishonored, return of the check typically serves as notice of dishonor [UCC § 3–503(b)].

Notice of dishonor must be made timely to trigger indorser's liability. Where a check is presented for payment through the check-collection process, notice of dishonor must be given by any bank in the chain by its midnight deadline. Notice of dishonor must be given by other persons within 30 days [UCC § 3–503(c)].

For example, assume that, as illustrated in Figure 27–10, Michael Aarons writes a check payable to the order of Andy Davids drawn on Second National Bank. Michael negotiates the check to Joe Samuels. Assume further that instead of presenting the check directly to Second National Bank for payment, Joe deposits it into his account with First National Bank. First National forwards it for collection to the Last National Bank, which presents it for payment on Monday, July 12th. Second National has until midnight on Tuesday, July 13th, to dishonor the item. Return of the check to Last National is dishonor and notice of dishonor. Assume that Last National receives the returned check on Wednesday, July 14th. Last National has until its midnight deadline, midnight of Thursday, July 15th, to notify First National of the dishonor. This means that Last National must put the check in the mail to First National by midnight on Thursday. Assume that First National receives the check on Friday and that Saturday is not a banking day. First National has until midnight Monday to notify Joe of the dishonor. Assume that Joe receives notification of dishonor on July 20. Joe has until August 19 to notify Andy of the dishonor.

For all other instruments, notice must be given by all parties within 30 days [UCC § 3–503(c)].

Protest

Protest is a certificate of dishonor used in international transactions. It is no longer required as a condition to contract liability of secondary parties (see Figure 27–11). If requested by a holder, it is a service that can be offered by the banking system. Protest must identify the instrument and certify that presentment was made, dishonor occurred, and notice of dishonor was given [UCC § 3–505(b)].

Figure 27–10   Timely Notice of Dishonor

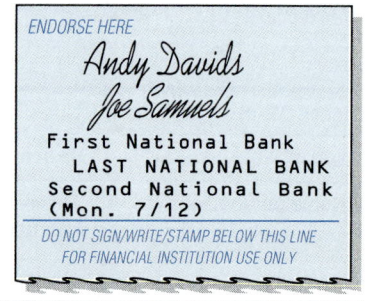

Figure 27–11 Protest, UCC Old and Revised Article 3

	Old Article 3	Revised Article 3
Protest	Required to trigger indorser and drawer's contracts on all drafts either drawn or payable outside the United States	No longer mandatory, must be requested by the holder; even if requested, protest is not a condition to the liability of either indorsers or drawers

UCC § 3–505. Evidence of Dishonor

(b) A protest is a certificate of dishonor made by a United States consul or vice consul, or a notary public or other person authorized to administer oaths by the law of the place where dishonor occurs.

Excuse

The holder may be excused from making presentment or giving notice of dishonor. The technical rights may be *entirely* excused or a *delay* may be excused.

Presentment is entirely excused in a number of situations. First, if the presenting party cannot with reasonable diligence make presentment, it is excused [UCC § 3–504(a)(i)]. For example, where the drawee cannot be found, the holder is excused from making presentment. Second, presentment is excused if the maker has repudiated the promise to pay, is dead, or is in insolvency proceedings [UCC § 3–504(a)(ii)]. Third, presentment is excused where under the terms of the instrument presentment is not required or where it has been waived [UCC § 3–504(a)(iii)(iv)]. Further, presentment is excused where the drawer or indorser has no reason to expect that the instrument will be paid [UCC § 3–504(a)(iv)]. For example, where the drawer has stopped payment on a check, the holder is entirely excused from making presentment [UCC § 3–504(a)(v)].

Notice of dishonor is entirely excused where under the terms of the instrument it is not required [UCC § 3–504(b)(i)] or where it has been waived [UCC § 3–504(b)(ii)].

Delay in giving notice of dishonor is excused where the delay is caused by an act beyond the control of the person giving the notice and that person acts reasonably [UCC § 3–504(c)]. The Supreme Court of Tennessee explained the rule in 1868, excusing the delay in presentment by a Northern holder of a promissory note signed by a Tennessee maker. The Civil War was the "circumstance beyond the control" of the holder. The Court stated:

Obstacles of the kind which will excuse, need not be of the degree or extent which make travel, intercourse, presentment, impossible. It is enough if they be of the degree and character which deter men of ordinary prudence, energy and courage, from encountering them.[1]

UCC § 3–504. Excused Presentment and Notice of Dishonor

(c) Delay in giving notice of dishonor is excused if the delay was caused by circumstances beyond the control of the person giving the notice and the person giving the notice exercised reasonable diligence after the cause of the delay ceased to operate.

Drawee's Contract

A party who takes a draft in payment of a debt expects the drawee on which it is drawn to pay it. However, the drawee does not make a contract on the draft (it has not signed the draft and no one has any liability without signing the draft). Thus, the drawee has no liability on a draft unless the drawee *accepts* it [UCC § 3–408].

Nonbank Drafts

The drawee can become liable on the draft by accepting it. **Acceptance** is the "drawee's signed agreement to pay a draft as presented" [UCC § 3–409(a)]. An acceptor has primary liability on the instrument (much like a maker) and promises to pay the draft as accepted [UCC § 3–413]. Acceptance must be written on the draft, but a signature alone is sufficient. Read the following case to see what constitutes this signed promise.

---

[1]*Polk v. Spinds*, 5 Col. (Tenn.) 431 (1868), at 433.

NORTON v. KNAPP
64 Iowa 112 (1884)

The plaintiffs sold a flaxseed-cleaner mill to the defendant. Because the sales price had not been paid, the plaintiffs drew a sight draft on the defendant, Miles Knapp. The draft stated:

"$80.   La Crosse, Wis., April 18, 1882.

"At sight pay to the order of *Exchange Bank of Nora Springs, Iowa, eighty dollars,* value received, and charge the same to the account of

"NORTON & KELLER.

"To Miles Knapp, Nora Springs, Ia."

Norton and Keller claim that Miles Knapp accepted the instrument by writing "Kiss my foot. Miles Knapp." on the back of the draft and sued on the contract of an acceptor.

SEEVERS, Judge

The amount in controversy being less than $100, the court has certified certain questions upon which the opinion of this court is desired. In substance, two of them are whether the words "kiss my foot," on the back of the draft, signed by the drawee, is a legal and valid acceptance; and whether such acceptance can be introduced in evidence without showing it was the intention to accept the draft. The rule upon this subject is thus stated in 1 Pars. Bills & Notes; 282: "If a bill is presented to a drawee for the purpose of obtaining his acceptance, and he does anything to or with it which does not distinctly indicate that he will not accept it, he is held to be an acceptor, for he has the power, and it is his duty, to put this question beyond all possibility of doubt."

The rule we understand to be, if the drawee does anything with or to the bill, or writes thereon anything, which does not clearly negative an intention to accept, then he can or will be charged as an acceptor. The question, then, is what construction should be placed on the words "kiss my foot," written on the bill and signed by him? They cannot be rejected as surplusage. Such language is not ordinarily used in business circles or polite society. But

by their use the defendant meant either to accept or refuse to accept the bill. It cannot be he meant the former; therefore, it must be the latter. It seems quite clear to us that the defendant intended, by the use of the contemptuous and vulgar words above stated, to give emphasis to his intention not to accept or have anything to do with the bill or with the plaintiff. We understand the words, in common parlance, to mean and express contempt for the person to whom the words are addressed, and when used as a reply to a request, they imply, and are understood to mean, a decided, unqualified, and contemptuous refusal to comply with such request. In such sense they were undoubtedly used when the defendant was requested to accept the bill.

Case Questions

1. Why did the court have to determine the meaning of the phrase "kiss my foot"?

2. What was the result of the holding that there was no acceptance? What would have been the result if the court had found that Miles Knapp accepted the draft?

3. Does this mean that the buyer does not have any liability to pay for the mill?

Certification of Checks

Just as in the case of a nonbank draft, a drawee bank has no liability on a check merely because it has been drawn on that bank. Therefore, the bank has no obligation to the holder to pay the check. The bank has, of course, made an agreement with its customer (the drawer) and may have liability for breach of that agreement. This will be discussed in Chapter 28.

Figure 27-12   Certified Check

Just as in the case of a nonbank draft, the drawee bank incurs liability on a check by accepting it. Acceptance of a check by a drawee bank is called **certification.** The drawee bank has no obligation to certify a check, and refusal to certify is not dishonor [UCC § 3–409(d)]. However, if the drawee bank certifies a check, it becomes primarily liable on the check [UCC § 3–413] and both the drawer [UCC § 3–414(c)] and all prior indorsers [UCC § 3–415(d)] are discharged. For example, assume that, as is illustrated in Figure 27–12, Dan draws a check to Tom for $500, drawn on the P.I. National Bank. Tom indorses the check and negotiates it to Sam. Sam takes the check to P.I National, which certifies the check. Sam negotiates it by indorsement to Humphrey. In this case, P.I. National has primary liability on the check. Both Dan and Tom are discharged (the drawer and the prior indorser). However, Sam still has liability because he indorsed after the certification (subsequent indorser).

Surety's Contract

Suretyship matters arise whenever the obligor (maker or drawer) must get others to "lend their name" to the basic obligation. Such a person is called a **surety.** The nature of the suretyship arrangement is best understood by examining the three contracts that make up the relationship. The first contract, K1 in Figure 27–13 on page 536, is the contract between the creditor and the debtor. For example, assume that Mike borrows $15,000 from the Friendly Finance Co. The agreement in which Friendly agrees to lend the money and Mike agrees to repay it is K1. The second contract, K2 in Figure 27–13, is the promise by the surety to back up the underlying obligation. For example, assume further that

Friendly was only willing to lend Mike the money if Sam promised to "lend his name" to the contract. In other words, Sam promises that if Mike does not repay the money in K1, that he will pay. This is K2. The third contract, K3 in Figure 27–13, is the promise by the debtor to reimburse the surety if the surety is forced to pay on K2. In other words, Mike promises that if Sam has to pay on K2, then he will be reimbursed. K3 is frequently implied.

Common Law Suretyship Rights

Sureties have many common law remedial rights in addition to the right of reimbursement (K3). Because these common law rights are available to sureties on commercial paper, they will be briefly outlined here.

Exoneration   The surety has an equitable right to compel the debtor to pay the creditor at maturity. This avoids the suit on K3 and might protect the surety from having to pay on K2 by forcing the debtor to pay the obligation when the debtor has the money.

Subrogation   If the surety has to pay on K2, the surety is subrogated to the rights of the creditor. In other words, the surety can "jump into the shoes" of the creditor and proceed against the debtor on K1. This may help the surety if the creditor has, for example, a security interest in collateral.

Contribution   Cosureties are given a right to a pro rata share of the amount paid out under K2. For example, assume that Curly, Larry, and Moe are cosureties on a $12,000 note. If Moe pays $12,000 on K2, he is entitled to $4,000 each from Curly and Larry as contribution. This applies to cosureties only.

Figure 27–13   Suretyship Relationship

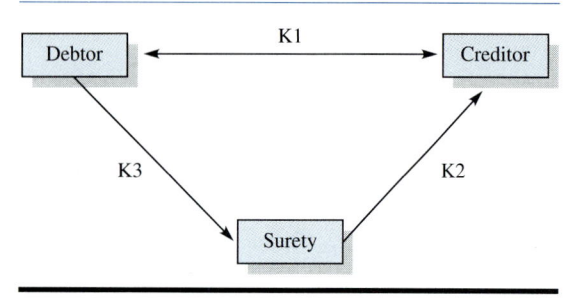

Pain v. Packard   The rule of *Pain v. Packard*,[2] gives the surety the right to demand that the creditor sue the debtor on K1. If the creditor does not sue, the surety is discharged. The rule of *Pain v. Packard* has been separately codified in over half the 50 states.

Strictissimi Juris   An agreement between the creditor and the debtor that changes K1 in any detail discharges the nonconsenting surety and releases him or her from K2. Some courts will even release the surety if the modification of K1 benefits the surety.

Suretyship under the Code

Under the Code, sureties are called **accommodation parties.** It is not necessary that the accommodation party receive consideration in return for the suretyship promise [UCC § 3–419(b)].

Accommodation parties are liable in the capacity in which they sign [UCC § 3–419(b)]. This means that accommodation parties that sign as comakers are liable as makers, with primary liability. By contrast, accommodation parties that sign as indorsers

---

[2]13 Johns. 17 (N.Y. Ct. App. 1816).

(the Code calls this an **anomalous indorsement**) are liable as indorsers. For example, assume that, as is illustrated in Figure 27–14, the Bedrock Bank agrees to lend Betty $10,000 if Wilma and Barney agree to act as sureties. Betty issues a promissory note for $12,000 payable to the Bedrock Bank. Barney signs the front of the note. Wilma indorses the note before delivery to Bedrock. Bedrock sells the note at discount ($11,000) to the Stone Age Finance Co. Barney, an accommodation maker, has the primary liability of a maker. Wilma, an accommodation indorser, has the contract liability of an indorser. If Betty fails to pay the note when due, and Wilma is given timely notice of dishonor, Wilma has liability. Even though Barney's liability is the same as a maker and Wilma's liability is the same as a regular indorser, it might be important to distinguish them as accommodation parties to take advantage of the special defenses available to sureties.

UCC § 3–419. Instruments Signed for Accommodation

(b) An accommodation party may sign the instrument as maker, drawer, acceptor, or indorser and . . . is obliged to pay the instrument in the capacity in which the accommodation party signs.

There is an exception to this general rule if the accommodation party unambiguously **guarantees collection** rather than payment of the instrument. If one guarantees collection, the **guarantor** is liable only after an execution of judgment is returned unsatisfied against the obligor, the obligor is insolvent, the obligor cannot be served with process (cannot be found), or it "is apparent that payment cannot be obtained" [UCC § 3–419(d)]. For example, if Wilma indorses "Wilma, collection guaranteed,"

Figure 27–14   Liability of Accommodation Parties

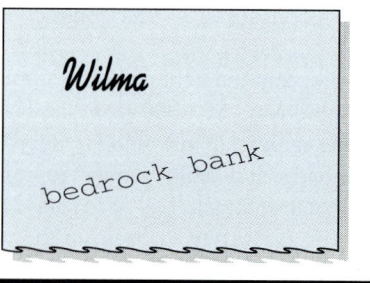

I promise to pay to the order of the Bedrock Bank the sum of $12,000 one year from date.

Barney Rock

Betty Bop

Wilma

bedrock bank

she would only be liable if Betty failed to pay the note, Stone Age successfully sued Betty, and the judgment remained unpaid.

Signing with words of guaranty or as an anomalous indorser creates a presumption that the party signing is an accommodation party. A person taking the instrument has notice of the accommodation status of the party [UCC § 3–419(c)]. Again, in Figure 27–14, Stone Age knows that Wilma is indorsing as an accommodation party because her signature is outside the chain of title. If Stone Age wants to rebut this presumption, it must produce evidence that Wilma received a direct benefit from the loan [UCC § 3–419(a)].

The accommodation party is given the common law rights as a surety plus the following special UCC rights.

UCC § 3–419. Instruments Signed for Accommodation

(e) An accommodation party who pays the instrument is entitled to reimbursement from the accommodated party.

Reimbursement   The common law right to reimbursement is codified in section 3–419(e). Thus, if either Barney or Wilma in Figure 27–14 are forced to pay Stone Age, they are entitled to be reimbursed by Betty.

Tender of Payment   The Code's answer to *Pain v. Packard* is the doctrine of **tender of payment.** The basic policy of this section is to protect the surety from increased risk. There are two provisions in section 3–603 that provide a defense to the surety where the payment due has been offered to the creditor and refused. The extent of the discharge de-

pends on who offers payment. First, if the party offering payment is one against whom the accommodation party has a right of recourse, the accommodation party is totally discharged from the contract obligation [UCC § 3–603(b)]. For example, assume that, as is illustrated in Figure 27–15, Mona Lisa borrows $120,000 from Michael Angelo on the condition that Sam Surety and Don Atello act as sureties. Don signs as an accommodation indorser on the back of the note *above* the signature of Sam, who acts as a subsurety. If Sam pays the debt, he can recover from either Mona under K3 or Don as a prior surety. Therefore, Sam has a right of recourse against both Don and Mona. If, on the date that the instrument is due, Don offers full payment and Michael refuses the payment, Sam is totally discharged from his surety liability. If Michael had accepted the payment, Sam would have been totally discharged. Therefore, he is totally discharged by Michael's refusal. Similarly, if Mona offered payment, both Sam and Don would be totally discharged because both have a right of recourse against Mona.

UCC § 3–603. Tender of Payment

(b) If tender of payment of an obligation to pay an instrument is made to a person entitled to enforce the instrument and the tender is refused, there is discharge, to the extent of the amount of the tender, of the obligation of an indorser or accommodation party having a right of recourse with respect to the obligation to which the tender relates.

Second, if Sam tenders full payment to Michael, Sam is discharged by Michael's refusal, but only to the extent of *subsequent* liability [UCC § 3–603(c)].

Figure 27–15   Tender of Payment Defense

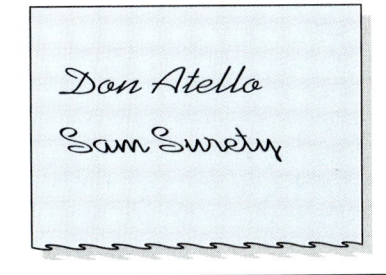

Thus, Sam still has liability for the $120,000 principal and interest that accrued before the tender of payment, but has no liability for subsequent interest.

Read the following case and determine to what extent the surety should be discharged.

UCC § 3–603. Tender of Payment

(c) If tender of payment of an amount due on an instrument is made to a person entitled to enforce the instrument, the obligation of the obligor to pay interest after the due date on the amount tendered is discharged.

JESSEE v. FIRST NATIONAL BANK
267 S.E.2d 803 (Ct. of App. Ga. 1980)

Jessee and four other sureties were cosureties on two notes held by the First National Bank of Atlanta (Bank). The contract of surety between Jessee, his cosureties, and the Bank limited the liability of each surety to 20 percent. Jessee tendered his 20 percent of the debt to the Bank and the Bank refused to accept the payment. Jessee argued (1) he is completely discharged from his obligation as surety; and alternatively (2) he is discharged for any subsequent liability.

SMITH, Judge

The present law governing the discharge of parties for liability on negotiable instruments is found in UCC § 3–601 *et seq*. The Bank's refusal of the tender did not discharge Jessee from his 20 percent liability.

Jessee further contends that the Bank's refusal of his tender increased his risk as he was no longer entitled to equitable subrogation and that he was, therefore, discharged as a matter of law. Subrogation inures only to a surety who has paid the debt of his principal. Where less than the total amount of that debt is tendered, subrogation is not permitted. As Jessee is not entitled to subrogation, this contention is without merit.

The final enumeration of error asserts that the trial court incorrectly computed the amount of Jessee's liability. We agree. Under the terms of their

contract, Jessee tendered full payment of his obligation to the Bank. Under UCC § 3–604(1), Jessee was discharged to the extent of all subsequent liability for interest, costs and attorney fees on the notes as of the date of his tender. Since Jessee is liable for no more than the amount which he tendered to the Bank, the judgment should be amended accordingly.

Case Questions
1. How does the tender of payment defense differ from *Pain v. Packard*?
2. The Court states that "The Bank's refusal of the tender did not discharge Jessee from his 20 percent liability." Why not?
3. Why is the surety only discharged for subsequent liability when a tender of full payment is made and refused?

Modifications   The Code's version of the common law doctrine of strictissimi juris is contained in section 3–605. This section can be understood best by the use of an example. Assume that Ben Casey borrows $10,000 from First National Bank, signing a note promising to repay the debt on a date stated in the note. First National insists that Dr. Kildare sign the note as an accommodation party. Assume further that the note is negotiated to the Second National

Bank. Section 3–605 is concerned with agreements between Second National and Ben and the extent to which modifications will discharge both Dr. Kildare and First National.

Assume that Second National and Ben reach an agreement under which Ben pays $3,000 on this debt and is released from liability. This is normally made as part of a settlement, because Ben is in financial difficulty. The discharge of the debtor discharges neither the accommodation party nor the indorser [UCC § 3–605(b)]. Neither has been injured by the agreement. To the extent that Ben made a $3,000 payment, the liability of the surety and indorser was reduced. This section allows the creditor to settle with the debtor without losing rights against sureties.

Alternatively, assume that Second National extends the due date of the instrument, agrees to a material modification of K1, or impairs collateral backing up K1. If the creditor and debtor agree to modify K1 in such a manner, the surety is discharged to the extent that the surety is injured by the modification [UCC § 3–605(c),(d),(e)]. However, because it is believed that rarely will an extension of time injure a surety, the surety has the burden of proving injury where there is an extension of time. By contrast, where there is a material modification or an impairment of collateral, it is more likely that the surety will be injured. Therefore, the holder has the burden of proving that the surety was not injured by the modification [UCC § 3–605, comments 4 and 5].

Any discharge under section 3–605 is applicable only if (1) the accommodation party has not consented to the modification and (2) there is no waiver. Because clauses waiving standard suretyship defenses are routinely included in notes, this section only applies in the rare case where no such waiver exists.

WARRANTY LIABILITY

It is necessary to understand the stages in the life of negotiable instruments. **Issuance** is the first delivery of the instrument to a holder [UCC § 3–105(a)]. **Presentment** is the demand for payment or acceptance (the last delivery of the instrument) [UCC § 3–501(a)]. **Transfer** is every transaction in between. The Code implies certain warranties (promises) upon presentment and transfer.

Transfer Warranties

These warranties are found in UCC sections 3–416 and 4–207. The latter controls if the instrument has entered the bank collection process. Because they are substantially the same, this chapter will focus on those found in Article 3. It is easy to understand the warranty provisions by examining a series of questions.

Who Makes Transfer Warranties?

Anyone who transfers an instrument and receives consideration makes transfer warranties [UCC § 3–416(a)]. For example, assume that, as in Figure 27–16, a check payable to the order of Joe Camp is indorsed by Joe "without recourse" and negotiated to the First Avenue Grocery Store in exchange for groceries. Assume further that the Grocery Store indorses the check and deposits it into its account with the Second National Bank, which indorses it and presents it for payment to the drawee bank, the Third National Bank. Joe and the Grocery Store both make transfer warranties. They both are transferors and both received consideration in return for the instrument. The fact that Joe indorsed this instrument "without recourse" is irrelevant for warranty liability purposes. The qualified indorser makes the same warranties as the unqualified indorser. Second National is not a transferor because presentment is not a transfer. It is important to keep the distinction between transfer and presentment clear.

Figure 27–16   Transfer Warranty Liability

To Whom Are These Warranties Made?

Transfer warranties are made to the transferee and, if the transfer is by indorsement, to subsequent transferees [UCC § 3–416(a)]. In other words, in Figure 27–16, Joe makes the transfer warranty to the Grocery Store (the transferee) and to Second National (the subsequent transferee) because the transfer was by an indorsement. This enables remote holders (Second National) to sue Joe directly and to avoid a multiplicity of lawsuits (Second suing the Grocery Store, and then the Grocery Store suing Joe).

What Is Warranted?

The transferor's promises upon transfer are summarized in Figure 27–17.

Good Title   The transferor warrants that there are no forgeries on the instrument necessary to the chain of title. In other words, the transferor warrants that the transferee can be a holder of the instrument [UCC § 3–416(a)(1)]. It is important to remember the difference between indorsements necessary to the chain of title and those that are not necessary to the chain of title. (See Chapter 25 if you do not remember this distinction.) If a forgery is of a signature not necessary to the chain of title, then the warranty of good title has not been breached. In addition, remember that a forged drawer's signature does not affect good title. In other words, even if the drawer's signature is forged, the warranty of good title has not been breached.

All Signatures Are Authentic   The warranty that all signatures are authentic is breached with any forged indorsement and with a forged drawer's signature.

Material Alterations   If there are any material alterations, the warranty has been breached.

Figure 27–17   Transfer Warranties

- Good title.
- All signatures are authentic.
- No material alteration.
- There is no claim or defense that can be asserted against the transferor.
- The warrantor has no knowledge of any insolvency proceedings of maker, acceptor, or drawer.

No Defenses   The transferor promises that the instrument is not subject to any claims or defenses. This warranty is made even to a holder in due course. Even if the transferee is a holder in due course who takes free of the claim or defense, the transferee does not buy a lawsuit. The holder in due course has the option to proceed against the transferor for breach of warranty or the obligor asserting holder in due course status.

What Is Recovered in the Event of Breach?

The person to whom transfer warranties are made may recover for the loss suffered as a result of the breach. However, the amount recovered cannot be more than the amount of the instrument plus expenses and lost interest [UCC § 3–416(b)]. In order to recover, the plaintiff must have taken the instrument in good faith.

Presentment Warranties

The presentment warranties are found in UCC sections 3–417 and 4–208.

Who Makes These Warranties?

These warranties are made by the presenter and all prior transferors [UCC § 3–417(a)]. For example, Joe, the Grocery Store, and Second National all make presentment warranties in Figure 27–16.

To Whom Are these Warranties Made?

Presentment warranties are made to either the drawee or the maker—to the party to whom presentment is made [UCC § 3–417(a)].

What Is Warranted?

Exactly what is warranted depends on the type of instrument presented. Section 3–417(a) provides that the presentment warranties for *unaccepted drafts* are:

- Good title.
- No material alteration.
- No knowledge of any forged drawer's signature.

Note that in contrast to the transfer warranties, there is no presentment warranty that all signatures are authentic.

For *all other instruments,* only good title is warranted [UCC § 3–417(d)]. Warranties, other than the warranty of good title, are not necessary for other instruments. For example, consider the maker of a $4,000 note. If the note is presented for payment, it is not necessary that the presenter warrant that there are no material alterations. The maker should know what the note promised when it was issued. Similarly, the maker should be aware of the authenticity of the maker's own signature without the need for a warranty.

What Is Recovered in the Event of Breach?

The drawee may recover from the breaching party the amount paid by the drawee less the amount that the drawee has received, or is entitled to receive, from the drawer [UCC § 3–417(b)]. In addition, the drawee may recover expenses and interest lost because of the breach [UCC § 3–417(b)]. Attorneys fees are included as expenses. The drawee's right to recover for breach of warranty is not affected by the drawee's negligence in paying the item [UCC § 3–417(b)].

Can These Warranties Be Disclaimed?

Under revised Article 3, the warranty provisions can be disclaimed by indorsing with such words as "without warranties." Warranty liability may be disclaimed on all instruments but checks—the check-collection system relies on these warranties (see Chapter 28).

END–OF–CHAPTER QUESTIONS

1. Peter decided to start a business. First State Bank agreed to loan Peter $100,000 if he would obtain two sureties to guarantee repayment. Paul and Mary agreed to cosign the note for Peter. Peter and Paul signed the front of the note and Mary signed the back. Peter issued a note to First State Bank. First State indorsed the note in blank and negotiated it to Friendly Finance at a discount. Assume that Friendly is a holder in due course.

   If Friendly demands payment from Peter, can Friendly hold him liable on his contract? If Friendly demands payment from Mary, can she force Friendly to first demand payment from either Peter or Paul? Explain.

2. Tom, Dick, and Harry are the comakers on a $30,000 note. The note is not paid when due. Hank, the holder of the note, sued Tom for $30,000. Will he be successful? Discuss.

3. Dave issued a check to Pam as payment for professional services. It was payable to the order of Pam. Frank stole the check, forged Pam's indorsement, and cashed the check at the Grocery. The Grocery indorsed and presented the check for payment to Last National Bank (LNB), the drawee. LNB paid the check out of Dave's account. Assume that the LNB has to recredit Dave's account. Can LNB recover from Grocery on a contract? Can LNB recover from Grocery on a warranty?

4. On January 3, 1993, Roger wrote a check to Holly in the amount of $1,000 as payment for a used car. Holly negotiated the check to the Springfield Deli in exchange for party supplies on January 11th. The Deli took the check in good faith and without notice. The Deli deposited the check into its account with the Springfield State Bank on January 20th. Springfield State presented it for payment to the drawee bank on January 23. Roger had stopped payment on the check because the car was defective. The drawee bank dishonored the check. Discuss the contract liability of Roger, Holly, and the Deli. Discuss the warranty liability of Roger, Holly, and the Deli.

June 18, 1993

Pay to the order of *First State Bank* one year from date. $100,000

Peter Smith

Paul Jones

Mary Brown

FIRST STATE BANK

5. Nola wrote a check to the Grocery Store on January 1, 1993. The Grocery presented the check for payment to the drawee on January 3, 1993. How much time does the drawee have to pay or return the check?

6. Tom wrote a check payable to Lisa Mitchell in exchange for a used car. The car was defective. Lisa indorsed the check "Lisa Mitchell, without recourse" and negotiated it to The Boutique. The Boutique indorsed the check and deposited it into its account with the Salem State Bank. Salem presented the check for payment to the drawee. The drawee dishonored the check because payment had been stopped on the check. Is Lisa liable on her indorser's contract? Is Lisa liable for breach of warranty?

7. Joe Nash drew a check payable to the order of Helen Brady. Tom Thief stole the check, forged Helen's name to the check, and delivered it to the Grocery Store in exchange for groceries. The Grocery Store acted in good faith and without notice of a forgery. The Grocery Store deposited the check into its account with the Sixth State Bank. Sixth presented the check for payment to the drawee. The drawee had been notified of the theft and dishonored the check. Discuss both the contract and warranty liability of all parties.

8. Pam knowingly sold defective goods to Dave. Dave gave Pam a check payable to bearer for the goods. Pam delivered the check to Bill who took it for value, in good faith, and without notice. Pam then repurchased the check from Bill and gave it to her husband, Hoover, as a gift.

Hoover took the check in good faith and without notice. Hoover presented the check to the drawee bank, but it was dishonored because Dave had issued a stop payment order. Assume that prompt notice of the dishonor was given to all parties. Is Dave liable to Hoover on a contract? Is Bill liable to Hoover on a contract? Is Pam liable to Hoover on a contract? Explain.

9. A note is signed on the bottom right as follows:

By:	/s/	Jerry B. Attkisson
		FJB Corporation
		Sec/Treas.
	/s/	Jerry B. Attkisson
		JERRY B. ATTKISSON
	/s/	Faset J. Seay
		FASET J. SEAY

Are Attkisson and Seay personally liable on this note? Explain. See *Attkisson v. Cavanagh,* 411 S.E.2d 786 (Ct. App. Ga. 1991).

10. The defendant, John R. Mott, Inc. (Mott), loaned the plaintiff, Trinity Construction, Inc. (Trinity), $120,000 at an annual interest rate of 11 3/4 percent. Trinity signed a promissory note. Trinity attempted to pay Mott the balance on the debt. Mott refused because Trinity offered only the principal balance and not the future interest. Trinity argued that it is discharged from paying additional interest by section 3–605. Is Trinity correct? Explain. See *Trinity Construction, Inc. v. John R. Mott, Inc.,* 534 N.Y.S.2d 838 (N.Y. Sup. Ct. 1988).

Chapter 28

The Bank and Its Customer

■

CRITICAL THINKING INQUIRIES

As you read this chapter, you should be able to address the following:

- Explain the relationship between wrongful dishonor and not properly payable.
- Explain the relationship between death or incompetence of a customer and forged indorsement.
- Analyze the following statement: ''Technically, the bank is not permitted to pay items over valid stop payment orders. However, the bank is unlikely to be liable for such a payment.''
- What is the ''best position'' rationale? List some examples of rules based on this rationale.

MANAGERIAL PERSPECTIVE

Mark Andrews owns a bookstore near the local college campus. He opens the store account with the Best National Bank. Tom Thief steals a check from the bookstore checkbook and writes a check for $5,000 payable to the Crooks Liquor Store. Best National pays this check when it is presented. The bookstore's check to its book supplier is returned ''not sufficient funds'' because of the $5,000 payment and the books are not shipped in time for fall classes.

- Can Mark successfully demand that Best reimburse his account for the $5,000 payment?
- Can Mark successfully demand that Best pay the book supply company?
- Can Mark recover damages for the profits lost on the books not shipped?

This scenario illustrates two of the typical issues that arise in bank deposit cases. What happens when the bank pays an item that it is not supposed to pay? In other words, can Mark get his money back? What happens when the bank fails to pay an item that it is supposed to pay? In other words, what is the Bank's liability to Mark on the returned check? These questions face anyone in a relationship with a bank.

RELATIONSHIP BETWEEN THE BANK AND ITS CUSTOMER

The relationship between the bank and its customer is a debtor-creditor relationship, with the customer-depositor as the creditor and the bank as the debtor. When a customer makes a deposit, that money is lent to the bank with the bank promising to repay it as directed by the customer. When the customer writes a check, the check is a direction to repay those funds as ordered. The specifics of repayment are outlined in the contract between the bank and customer, typically signed when the account is opened.

Scope of Article 4

The law governing this relationship is found primarily in Article 4 of the UCC. However, these rules are closely related to the rules found in Article 3. If there is a conflict between the two articles, Article 4 controls [UCC § 4–102(1)]. Both articles 3 and 4 were substantially revised in 1990.

Because Article 4 regulates the relationship between the bank and its customer, three definitions establish the scope of Article 4: bank, customer, and item.

UCC § 4–105. Bank . . .

In this Article:

(1) "**Bank**" means a person engaged in the business of banking, including a savings bank, savings and loan association, credit union, or trust company.

The drawee bank from Article 3 is referred to as the **payor bank** in Article 4 [UCC § 4–105(3)].

In this discussion, the **customer** will alternately be referred to as the customer, the drawer, or the depositor.

UCC § 4–104. Definitions

(5) "**Customer**" means a person having an account with a bank or for whom a bank has agreed to collect items.

UCC § 4–104. Definitions

(9) "**Item**" means an instrument or a promise or order to pay money handled by a bank for collection or payment.

The term **item** will be used interchangeably with the term *check*.

The Code's treatment of the relationship between a bank and its customer provides few customer rights. Moreover, the provisions of the Code can be varied by agreement between the parties as long as that agreement does not disclaim the bank's liability for lack of good faith or for failure to exercise due care or limit damages for the lack or failure [UCC § 4–103(a)]. This agreement is generally contained in the signature card signed by the customer when the bank account is opened. In addition, Federal Reserve regulations, operating letters, and clearing-house rules operate as such agreements even without customer assent [UCC § 4–103(b)]. In particular, Regulations J and CC promulgated by the Federal Reserve Board modify the provisions of Article 4 in bank-collection cases.

Duties of the Bank

Remember that the drawee bank makes no promise to third parties to pay items [UCC § 3–409]. The promise to pay a check is in the contract between the customer-drawer and the bank. As part of this contract, the bank promises to pay items that are **properly payable.** Most of the controversies in this regard arise either from the bank paying an item that is not properly payable or failing to pay an item that is properly payable.

Bank's Liability for Paying Items Not Properly Payable

The drawee bank is permitted to charge its customer's account for properly payable items [UCC § 4–401(a)]. It may not charge its customer's account for items that are not properly payable. When a bank pays an item that is not properly payable and charges its customer's account, it must recredit that account. An item is properly payable if it is authorized by the customer in the agreement between the bank and the customer [UCC § 4–401(a)].

UCC § 4–401. When Bank May Charge Customer's Account

(a) A bank may charge against the account of a customer an item that is properly payable from the account even though the charge creates an overdraft. An item is properly payable if it is authorized by the customer and is in accordance with any agreement between the customer and bank.

Forged Indorsements   A check with a forged indorsement necessary to the chain of title is not properly payable [UCC § 4–401, official comment 1]. By agreement with the drawer, the bank promises to pay whomever the drawer of the item directs the bank to pay. Where there is a forged indorsement in the chain of title, so that the instrument is not presented by a holder, the bank is not paying the person it was ordered to pay. Therefore, the bank must recredit the customer's account for the amount of the improperly paid item.

Forged Drawer's Signatures   A forgery does not operate as the signature of the drawer [UCC § 3–403(a)]. Thus, a check with a forged drawer's signature is not properly payable because the customer did not direct the payor bank to pay the item and to charge its account [UCC § 4–401, official comment 1].

Again, the bank will be required to recredit its customer's account in the absence of customer negligence, which is discussed in the following chapter. Returning to our opening scenario, the forged check drawn by Tom Thief on Mark's bookstore account is not properly payable. When Mark demands recredit, Best National Bank must recredit the bookstore account for $5,000.

Altered Items   An item that has been materially altered is not properly payable in its altered state. For example, if Wally Wrongdoer steals a check Mark has written to an employee, changes the name of the payee to his own name, and indorses the item, it is

treated as a forged indorsement case. Because of the alteration, the bank did not pay the person (employee) as directed and must recredit Mark's account for the full amount of the check.

Alternatively, assume that Mark writes a check payable to Ernie Employee for $100. Assume further that Ernie raises the amount of the check from $100 to $1,000 and transfers the item to Hank Holder, a holder in due course. Best National Bank pays the item and charges Mark's account for $1,000. Because Mark directed Best National to pay Ernie only $100, the item is properly payable only for that amount. Therefore, the bank must recredit Mark's account for $900.

Overdrafts   When presented with an item that, if paid, would create an overdraft, the drawee bank can choose either to pay the item or to dishonor it [UCC § 4–401(a)]. If it pays the item, the bank may properly charge its customer's account and recover the amount of the overdraft from the customer.

However, the drawee has no obligation to pay such an item and is not liable for failure to pay the item. To illustrate, assume that the balance in Dan Drawer's account is $100. A check in the amount of $125 is presented to the drawee bank for payment. The bank can rightfully dishonor the item. Alternatively, the bank can pay the item and charge Dan's account for $125. Because there is only $100 in the account, the bank can turn to Dan on an implied promise to reimburse the bank for the $25 shortage.

Stale Checks   A check dated more than six months before presentment is termed a **stale check.** The rules regulating stale checks reflect a general mistrust of old checks. A presumption exists that there is a defense to the obligation or the check would have been presented within a reasonable time of issue. Again, the bank is given a choice. The bank does not have to pay the stale check [UCC § 4–404]. However, it can pay the item if it does so in good faith and charge its customer's account for the amount of the item. For example, a bank might knowingly pay a stale check when it is in the position to know that the drawer wants the check paid.

However, the bank must pay *certified* checks when presented, even if stale [UCC § 4–404]. Certified checks are treated differently because the bank assumes primary liability upon certification and typically charges the customer's account at that time.

UCC § 4–404. Bank Not Obliged to Pay Check More Than Six Months Old

A bank is under no obligation to a customer having a checking account to pay a check, other than a certified check, which is presented more than six months after its date, but it may charge its customer's account for a payment made thereafter in good faith.

Death or Incompetence of the Customer   Does the death or incompetence of the customer affect the bank's ability to pay an item drawn by the customer before death or incapacity? Because the bank was considered to be an agent for the customer, and under general agency law the death or incapacity of the principal terminates the agency relationship, the common law rule was that death and incompetence automatically revoked the bank's authority to pay items. By contrast, under the Code, the bank's authority to pay an item is not automatically terminated by the death or incompetence of the customer. Given the tremendous volume of items handled daily, requiring banks to verify the continued life and competence of its drawer before paying checks would be unworkable. Therefore, a bank may pay any item until it receives knowledge of the customer's death or incompetence [UCC § 4–405(a)]. In addition, the bank is given a further reasonable opportunity to act on any knowledge acquired.

UCC § 4–405. Death or Incompetence of Customer

(a) . . . Neither death nor incompetence of a customer revokes the authority to accept, pay, collect, or account until the bank knows of the fact of death or of an adjudication of incompetence and has reasonable opportunity to act on it.

Even with knowledge of the death of the drawer, the bank may pay or certify checks for 10 days after the date of death [UCC § 4–405(b)]. Note that the 10-day provision applies only to the death of the drawer not to an adjudication of incompetence. This rule permits holders of checks drawn shortly before death to cash them without filing a claim in probate. Because most such checks are payment for immediate obligations, there is usually no reason for non-payment. For example, assume that, as in Figure 28–1, Dan Drawer draws a check on the Second National Bank payable to The Grocery Store for gro-

Figure 28–1   Payment after Drawer's Death

June 3:	Dan draws check.
June 5:	Dan dies.
June 7:	Bank learns of death.
June 10:	Check presented and payment made.

ceries purchased on June 3. On June 5, Dan dies. On June 7, Second National Bank learns of Dan's death. If the check is presented for payment on June 10, Second National may pay the check because it is within 10 days from the date of death.

UCC § 4–405. Death or Incompetence of Customer

(b) Even with knowledge, a bank may for 10 days after the date of death pay or certify checks drawn on or before that date unless ordered to stop payment by a person claiming an interest in the account.

The bank may pay checks during this 10-day period unless it is ordered to stop payment by a person claiming an interest in the account of the deceased. Assume, in the above example, that on June 9 Joe informs the bank that he claims an interest in Dan's account and that the bank should dishonor all checks subsequently presented. Even if Joe is a third party with no relationship to Dan Drawer, the check presented for payment on June 10 is not properly payable. This is true in spite of any weakness of Joe's claim. The bank has no right or responsibility to determine the validity of the claim or even whether it is colorable. The mere assertion of a claim terminates the bank's right to pay the check.

Stop Payment Orders   The customer has a right to stop payment on checks and to revoke the drawee bank's right to pay [UCC § 4–403(a)]. A stop payment order is effective if the bank has a reasonable opportunity to act on the order and it identifies the check with reasonable certainty [UCC § 4–403(a)]. Generally, any information that reasonably identifies the account and the check is sufficient.

The order may be given orally or in writing. An oral stop payment order is effective for 14 days unless confirmed in writing. A written order is binding on the bank for six months and may be renewed in writing [UCC § 4–403(b)].

Items paid over a valid stop payment order are not properly payable. However, the bank is unlikely to be liable for such payment. First, to recover, the customer must prove that the drawee bank paid over a binding stop payment and that this payment caused loss to the customer [UCC § 4–403(c)]. Second, the drawee bank may use the right of **subrogation** to avoid recredit [UCC § 4–407].

The right of subrogation allows the drawee bank to subrogate itself to the rights of, or to ''jump into the shoes of,'' anyone up the chain of title that would help the bank defeat the customer's demand for recredit. In other words, if there is anyone up the chain that could hold the customer liable on its drawer's contract, the drawee bank can assert the rights of that person and does not have to recredit the drawer's account. Several examples will illustrate how this right helps the bank.

UCC § 4–407. Payor Bank's Right to Subrogation on Improper Payment

It a payor bank has paid an item over the order of the drawer or maker to stop payment, or after an account has been closed, or otherwise under circumstances giving a basis for objection by the drawer or maker, to prevent unjust enrichment and only to the extent necessary to prevent loss to the bank by reason of its payment of the item, the payor bank is subrogated to the rights

(1) of any holder in due course on the item against the drawer.

Example 1. Mark Andrews, as in Figure 28–2, issues a check for $5,000 drawn on the Best National Bank payable to Freddy Car Dealer in exchange for a used car. When Mark discovers that he could have obtained a better car for less money elsewhere, he orders Best National to stop payment on the check to Freddy. Freddy presents the check for payment to Best National, which inadvertently pays the item over the valid stop payment order. When Mark discovers the payment, he demands that Best National recredit his account. To what extent is Best National liable for the payment?

The payment was clearly improper because it was made over a valid stop payment order. However, Mark must prove both that he suffered loss and the amount of loss because of the Bank's improper payment. In this example, Mark will be unable to do so. Because Mark has liability on his drawer's contract for $5,000 with no defense to assert against Freddy, he has suffered no loss because of Best National's improper payment. Further, Best National can subrogate itself to the rights of the payee against the drawer. The bank can assert whatever claims the payee might have asserted against the drawer. Applying this to Figure 28–2, Best National can assert whatever claims Freddy has against Mark. Freddy can hold Mark liable both on his drawer's contract and on his underlying contractual obligation. Because Mark has no defense to either claim, Best National can avoid recredit.

Example 2. Mark Andrews, as in Figure 28–3, issues a check for $5,000 drawn on Best National Bank payable to Freddy Car Dealer in exchange for a used car. Shortly after taking possession, Mark discovers that the car has a faulty transmission. He immediately stops payment on the check. Freddy cashes the check at his bank, the Citizens Bank, which presents the check for payment. Best National

Figure 28–2   Check Paid over Stop Payment: No Defense

Presents to Best National

inadvertently pays the item over the valid stop payment order. When Mark discovers the payment, he demands that Best National recredit his account. Again, Best National will not be required to recredit Mark's account. If Citizens Bank is a holder in due course, Best National can acquire this holder in due course status by subrogating itself to the rights of Citizens Bank [UCC § 4–407(1)]. Although in this case Mark has a defense against Freddy, it is a personal defense, which is not a good defense against a holder in due course. Because Citizens Bank could hold Mark liable on his drawer's contract, Best National (in Citizen Bank's place) does not have to recredit Mark's account.

Example 3. Through fraud in the execution, Freddy Car Dealer obtains a check for $5,000 drawn by Mark Andrews on Best National Bank. Shortly after issuing the check, Mark discovers the fraud and stops payment on the check. As is illustrated in Figure 28–3, Freddy cashes the check at his bank, the Citizens Bank, which presents the check for payment. Best National inadvertently pays the item over the valid stop payment order. When Mark discovers the payment, he demands that Best National recredit his account. Unlike the above examples, in this case Best National will be liable for improper payment. Although Best National can acquire the holder in due course status of Citizens Bank, Mark has a real defense to payment, a defense that will defeat even the claim of a holder in due course. Therefore, allowing Best National to assert Citizen Bank's claim will not improve Best National's position against Mark.

Postdated Checks   Occasionally, a drawer will issue a postdated check. For example, the drawer might issue a check on June 3 dated June 18. The bank may pay this item and properly charge the customer's account when the item is presented for payment, even though paid before June 18, unless the customer has notified the bank of the postdating [UCC § 4–401(c)]. An effective notice must identify the check with reasonable certainty and give the bank a reasonable opportunity to act on it [UCC § 4–401(c)]. The notice requirement recognizes the difficulty of the automated check-collection system to accommodate postdated checks. This is a change from prior law. Figure 28–4 summarizes this change.

UCC § 4–401. When Bank May Charge Customer's Account

(c) A bank may charge against the account of a customer a check that is otherwise properly payable from the account, even though payment was made before the date of the check, unless the customer has given notice to the bank of the postdating describing the check with reasonable certainty.

If the bank pays the item before the date indicated on the notice of postdating, the bank is liable for damages caused by the payment, including damages for wrongful dishonor [UCC § 4–401(c)]. For example, assume that Mark issues a check postdated to June 18 and that the drawee bank pays

Figure 28–3   Check Paid over Stop Payment Order: With Defense

Presents to Best National

Figure 28–4   Proper Payment of Postdated Check, UCC Old and Revised Article 4

Old Article 4	Revised Article 4
Postdated check is not properly payable until date that appears on check	Postdated check is properly payable before the date that appears on the check unless the customer gives notice to the drawee of postdated nature

the check on June 15. Mark discovers the improper payment on June 20 and demands that his account be recredited. Assume further that Mark gave the drawee the proper notice of postdating. The payor bank must recredit the account only if the drawer has suffered loss because of the payment.

UCC §4–401. When Bank May Charge Customer's Account

(c) . . . If a bank charges against the account of a customer a check before the date stated in the notice of postdating, the bank is liable for damages for the loss resulting from its act. The loss may include damages for dishonor of subsequent items.

Assume instead that Mark issues a check on January 1 postdated January 25. On January 17, the drawee bank pays the item over Mark's notice of postdating, and on January 18, Mark issues a stop payment order. Here, Mark was injured by the bank's actions. If the bank had not paid the item prematurely, it would have received the stop payment order in time to avoid payment. However, even when the customer gives notice of postdating, the bank is able to use the doctrine of subrogation to avoid recredit.

Bank's Liability for Wrongful Dishonor
The payor bank is liable for **wrongful dishonor** where it fails to pay an item that is properly payable [UCC § 4–402]. Typically, wrongful dishonor occurs mistakenly as the result of bookkeeping errors, computer errors, or inadvertent charges to the wrong account.

The payor bank is liable to its customer for damages proximately caused by the wrongful dishonor of an item [UCC § 4–402(b)]. Because the bank owes no obligation to third-party holders to pay an item, it is not liable to third parties for dishonor.

UCC § 4–402. Bank's Liability to Customer for Wrongful Dishonor

(a) . . . a payor bank wrongfully dishonors an item if it dishonors an item that is properly payable.

Proof of Damages   At common law, under the **trader rule,** a merchant whose check was wrongfully dishonored was entitled to substantial damages on the basis of defamation *per se* without proof that actual damage occurred. This was because dishonor of a merchant's check was presumed to reflect on the merchant's credit, to defame the merchant's character, and to injure the merchant's business. The Code rejects the trader rule and limits bank liability to actual damages proved [UCC § 4–402(b), official comment 1].

UCC § 4–402. Bank's Liability to Customer for Wrongful Dishonor

(b) A payor bank is liable to its customer for damages proximately caused by the wrongful dishonor of an item. Liability is limited to actual damages proved and may include damages for an arrest or prosecution of the customer or other consequential damages.

Damages Recoverable   The customer may recover compensatory damages. For example, if the customer was arrested or prosecuted because of the wrongful dishonor, damages proximately caused by the arrest are recoverable. Other consequential damages are also recoverable if proximately caused by the dishonor. Claims for mental distress and anxiety have not uniformly been allowed by the courts. For some courts this may depend on whether the dishonor was intentional. Whether a bank is liable for noncompensatory damages, such as punitive damages for intentional dishonor, is not addressed in section 4–402 and must be decided under other law [UCC § 4–402, official comment 1].

Read the following case and determine what damages are recoverable.

SKOV v. CHASE MANHATTAN BANK
407 F.2d 1318 (3d Cir. 1976)

Chase Manhattan Bank mistakenly dishonored Skov's check to its supplier of cleaned King-fish and dolphin. Because of the dishonor, the supplier ceased storing fish for delivery to Skov, which made it impossible for Skov to continue selling such fish. Skov sued to recover the lost profits.

PER CURIAM

After careful review of the record, we have determined that the defendant's contention that there is not substantial evidence to support the trial judge's findings that by reason of this dishonor, the supplier terminated its arrangement of storing the above-mentioned fish for future delivery to plaintiff, without payment until delivery, and that such termination made it impossible for plaintiff to continue its sales of such fish to the hotel customers who had been buying such fish from it during the first quarter of 1967, must be rejected. Also, the record discloses that there was substantial evidence in support of the amount of consequential damages which the experienced and able trial judge found had been proximately caused by the bank's mistake.

The trial judge properly relied on § 4–402 of the Uniform Commercial Code, which is not a model of clarity in its reference to "damages proximately caused," "actual damages proved," and "consequential damages." However, the statutory language used authorized the trial judge on this record to award damages by determining the annual loss of profits to plaintiff from the termination of his relationship with his supplier and to project this loss for a three-year period. The only appellate court case which counsel or the court has been able to find applying this statutory language concerning damages is fully consistent with determination made by the finder in this case. See *Louks v. Albuquerque Nat'l Bank,* 418 P.2d 191 (1966).

Case Questions

1. What were the consequential damages that the customer was trying to recover? Did the court allow recovery? Explain.

2. Why might some courts be reluctant to impose consequential damages? What is the value conflict?

3. Return to the opening scenario. Will Mark be able to recover the profits lost when the books were not shipped?

The bank is not liable to its customer for justified dishonor where, for example, there are insufficient funds in the drawer's account to cover the item. Also excluded are situations where there is a missing indorsement, an incomplete or missing signature by the drawer, a material alteration, or an improper presentment.

Duties of the Customer

The customer also has duties with respect to the bank account. In general, the customer must act reasonably (not negligently). If negligent, the customer will not be allowed to assert certain claims against the bank. For example, a person whose negligence substantially contributes to a forgery is not allowed to assert the forgery [UCC § 3–406]. (This preclusion will be discussed in detail in Chapter 29).

The Bank Statement Rule

In addition, the customer must exercise reasonable care in examining the bank statement or items to discover an unauthorized signature or alteration and must notify the bank promptly of any irregularities [UCC § 4–406(c)]. This duty, called the bank statement duty, arises when the bank complies with its duty to send or make the bank statement available to the customer [UCC § 4–406(a)]. The bank must either return or make the items paid available to the customer or provide information to allow the customer to reasonably identify the items paid [UCC § 4–406(a)].

UCC § 4–406. Customer's Duty to Discover and Report Unauthorized Signature or Alteration

(c) . . . the customer must exercise reasonable promptness in examining the statement or the items to determine whether any payment was not authorized because of an alteration or because a purported signature . . . was not authorized. If . . . the customer should reasonably have discovered the unauthorized payment, the customer must promptly notify the bank of the relevant facts.

A customer who does not act promptly cannot assert a forged drawer's signature or an alteration if the delay in reporting the wrongdoing caused the bank any loss [UCC § 4–406(d)(1)]. For example, the bank might suffer a loss where, between the time the customer should have notified the bank of a forgery and the time that notice was given, the forger fled with all assets. Here, the payor bank lost an opportunity to recover on the forged check because of the delay.

In addition, the customer is prevented from asserting subsequent unauthorized signatures or alterations by the *same wrongdoer* on items paid after the first item or statement was available to the customer for 30 days and before the customer notified the bank [UCC § 4–406(d)(2)]. Thus, the customer is given 30 days to examine its bank statement and notify the bank before this preclusion applies.

UCC § 4–406. Customer's Duty to Discover and Report Unauthorized Signature or Alteration

(d) If the bank proves that the customer failed, with respect to an item, to comply with the duties imposed on the customer by subsection (c), the customer is precluded from asserting against the bank:

(1) the customer's unauthorized signature or any alteration on the item, if the bank also proves that it suffered a loss by reason of the failure.

For example, assume that Frank Forger stole a pad of checks from Dan Drawer. As is illustrated in Figure 28–5, on January 2, the bank paid forged check 1 for $100. On January 5, the bank paid forged check 2 for $150. On January 10, Dan re-

Figure 28–5	Bank Statement Rule
1/2	Check 1: $100
1/5	Check 2: $150
1/10	Bank statement
2/2	Check 3: $500
2/15	Check 4: $100
	Check 5: $150
2/27	Bank notified

ceived his bank statement revealing the checks forged by Frank. On February 2, the bank paid check 3 forged by Frank for $500. Forged checks 4 and 5 were paid on February 15 for $100 and $150, respectively. On February 27, Dan notified the bank of the irregularities in his bank statement and demanded recredit. The bank must recredit checks 1 and 2, (unless it can demonstrate that it suffered a loss because of Dan's delay) as long as Dan reports his forgery within one year from the time that the statement was made available [UCC § 4–406(f)]. Similarly, the bank must recredit Dan's account on check 3. Although this check was paid after Dan received his bank statement, it was paid within the 30-day period allotted to Dan to review the statement. However, the bank does not have to recredit Dan's account on checks 4 and 5. Both items were paid more than 30 days after Dan received his bank statement and before Dan notified the bank of the irregularities revealed on the statement. Therefore, the customer may not assert the forgeries on checks 4 and 5. The justification for this preclusion is that if the customer had given timely notification to the bank with respect to checks 1 and 2, the bank would have known of the potential for subsequent forgeries and might have dishonored checks 4 and 5. Under these circumstances, the customer was in the best position to have prevented the loss [UCC § 4–406, comment 3].

The preclusions explained above do not apply if the customer is able to show that the bank failed to exercise ordinary care in paying the item. Revised Article 4 has adopted a comparative negligence scheme. If the customer can prove bank negligence, the loss is allocated between the parties proportionately [UCC § 4–406(e)]. In other words, if the bank's negligence in paying the item was 60 percent responsible for the loss, it will bear 60 percent of the liability. Figure 28–6 summarizes the changes from prior law.

UCC § 4–406. Customer's Duty to Discover and Report Unauthorized Signature or Alteration

(d) If the bank proves that the customer failed, with respect to an item, to comply with the duties imposed on the customer by subsection (c), the customer is precluded from asserting against the bank:

(2) the customer's unauthorized signature or alteration by the same wrongdoer on any other item paid in good faith by the bank if the payment was made before the bank received notice from the customer of the unauthorized signature or alteration and after the customer had been afforded a reasonable period of time, not exceeding 30 days, in which to examine the item or statement of account and notify the bank.

Figure 28–6   Bank Statement Rule: UCC, Old and Revised Article 4

Old Article 4	Revised Article 4
Customer given 14 days within which to examine bank statement	Customer given 30 days within which to examine bank statement
If bank failed to exercise ordinary care, the preclusion was totally eliminated (contributory negligence scheme)	If bank fails to exercise ordinary care, the loss is allocated proportionately (comparative negligence scheme)

Read the following case applying old Article 4 and the bank statement rule.

PUTNAM ROLLING LADDER CO., INC. v. MANUFACTURERS HANOVER TRUST CO.

546 N.E.2d 904 (Ct. App. N.Y. 1989)

In December 1979, Putnam Rolling Ladder Co. (Putnam) opened a checking account with Manufacturers Hanover Trust Co. (MHT). Between February and December 1980, MHT paid 37 checks totaling $48,094 over signatures that appeared to be those of Putnam officers. In reality, they were forgeries by Juanita Johnson, Putnam's assistant bookkeeper. On December 10, 1980, Putnam notified MHT of the forged checks and demanded recredit. The long delay in discovering the forgeries was due to the fact that Johnson was responsible for reconciling Putnam's bank statements. MHT asserts that Putnam violated its bank statement duty; Putnam asserts that MHT failed to exercise ordinary care in examining the checks. (A number of the checks were paid with only one signature, in spite of the fact that two were required.)

The trial court found that both parties were negligent, applied comparative negligence principles, and awarded Putnam half of its loss. Putnam appealed.

KAYE, Judge

The UCC Scheme for Loss-Shifting

Articles 3 and 4 of the UCC envision a series of shifting burdens of risk of loss with respect to forged checks. Initially, the law places the risk of forgeries on the bank. A forged signature is not "properly payable," and the bank cannot debit the depositor's account. (UCC 4–401(1)).

The UCC, however, imposes certain reciprocal duties on the customer. Failure to comply with those duties shifts the burden of loss from bank to customer. UCC 4–406 imposes upon a customer the duty to inspect its statement and canceled checks with reasonable care and promptness. Failure to do so results in preclusion of any claim against the bank

for repeated forgeries by the same wrongdoer after the first such forged check and statement reflecting it are made available to the customer. This rule reflects the fact that the customer is generally in a better position than the bank to prevent repetition of forgery. A skillful forgery may not be detected by even a careful bank inspector, but the customer to whom the canceled check and statement are returned should know whether or not it actually intended to authorize payment of its funds to the named payee. Thus, the shifting burden of loss is intended as well to encourage the parties to use reasonable care in situations where, from a systematic point of view, that is the efficient loss-avoidance mechanism.

Finally, UCC 4–406(3) shifts the loss of even repeated forgeries back to the bank when the customer, although in breach of its own duty to inspect its canceled checks and statements, is able to establish that the bank lacked ordinary care in paying the forged checks. By reallocating the burden of loss to the bank the Code thus encourages proper business practices on the part of banks as well as their customers.

Under UCC 4–406(3), the customer who wishes to invoke the exception to UCC 4–406(2) preclusion bears the burden of establishing that the bank also acted without ordinary care in paying the items. Section 4–406 does not, however, define ordinary care. Instead, ordinary care in article 4 generally is discussed in the Official Comments to section 4–103, where it is noted that "ordinary care" is used "with its normal tort meaning and not in any special sense relating to bank collections." It would appear, therefore, that the customer could prove a bank lacked ordinary care by presenting any type of proof that the bank failed to act reasonably. In this case, plaintiff adduced such proof that MHT's inspection procedures were so superficial as to offer no realistic opportunity to detect forged checks.

Comparative Negligence

The importation of comparative negligence into the UCC—which was drafted before widespread acceptance of comparative fault—is not without its advocates, but has generally been rejected by both courts and commentators. We agree. It is not for the courts to unsettle the UCC's carefully drawn balance by introducing comparative fault principles taken from tort law.

Moreover, the UCC serves an important objective not shared by the law of torts. Unlike tort law, the UCC has the objective of promoting certainty and predictability in commercial transactions. By prospectively establishing rules of liability that are generally based not on actual fault but on allocating responsibility to the party best able to prevent the loss by the exercise of care, the UCC not only guides commercial behavior but also increases certainty in the marketplace and efficiency in dispute resolution. These ends would not be furthered by the introduction of the sort of fact inquiries necessitated by comparative negligence.

In that plaintiff adduced sufficient evidence of the bank's lack of ordinary care in paying the 37 forged checks (thereby avoiding preclusion under UCC 4–406(2) for its own negligence), and the bank offered no evidence whatever of general rules or usage, judgment should have been awarded to plaintiff in the undisputed amount of its loss.

Case Questions

1. How would this case have been decided differently under revised Article 4?

2. Revised Article 3 provides that "In the case of a bank that takes an instrument for processing for collection or payment by automated means, reasonable commercial standards do not require the bank to examine the instrument if the failure to examine does not violate the bank's prescribed procedures and the bank's procedures do not vary unreasonably from general banking usage" [UCC § 3–103(7)]. How does this definition upset the balance of which the *Putnam* court speaks? Can you envision any circumstances where the payor bank might be negligent if failure to examine items for wrongdoing does not constitute negligence?

3. The court asserts that adoption of a comparative negligence scheme would mitigate promotion of certainty and predictability in commercial transactions. Do you agree?

BANK COLLECTIONS AND DEPOSITS

In addition to regulating the relationship between the bank and its customer, Article 4 governs the check-collection process. The process is also regulated by federal law, specifically by Federal Reserve Regulations CC and J.

In addition to the terminology discussed above, Article 4 offers other definitions:

Payor bank: This is another name for the drawee bank [UCC § 4–105(3)].

Depositary bank: This is the first bank to which an item is transferred for collection. The depositary bank can be the payor bank [UCC § 4–105(2)].

Intermediary bank: An intermediary bank is any bank to which an item is transferred for collection, excluding the payor or depositary bank [UCC § 4–105(4)].

Collecting bank: A collecting bank is any bank handling an item for collection except the payor bank [UCC § 4–105(5)].

Presenting bank: A presenting bank is any bank presenting an item. This obviously cannot include the payor bank [UCC § 4–105(6)].

To illustrate, assume that Mark Andrews writes a check payable to Books, Inc., drawn on the Best National Bank. Books deposits the check in its account with the First National Bank; First National transfers it to Second National Bank, who presents it for payment. In this scenario, First National is the depositary Bank and a collecting bank. Second National is an intermediary/collecting/presenting bank. Best National is the payor bank.

The Process

When the drawer issues a check to the payee, the payee needs to obtain payment on the item. The bank-collection process is the process by which the payee is able to receive such payment. Collection begins when the item is deposited in a depositary bank. The process is basically one of transferring the item from the depositary bank to the payor bank and remitting the proceeds back to the depositary bank and eventually to its customer. The complexity var-

ies with the number of banks handling the item. Whether the check will be processed through an intermediary bank, and, if so, the number of intermediary banks involved, depends primarily on the distance between the depositary bank and the payor bank.

Consider the most complex bank collection scenario—a cross-country bank collection case, illustrated in Figure 28–7. Sam, a resident of Baltimore, Maryland, writes a check for $25 drawn on his local bank, Peoples National Bank, payable to his niece, Colleen, a resident of Lorain, Ohio. Colleen deposits the check in her account with the Lorain National Bank. Lorain National Bank provisionally credits Colleen's account for the amount of the check, subject to reversal (chargeback) if the item should subsequently be dishonored by the payor bank [UCC § 4–214(a)] and debits the account of the bank to which the item will next be forwarded. The depositary bank must use ordinary care in forwarding the item toward the payor bank [UCC § 4–202]. If the bank forwards the item by its midnight deadline (midnight of the day following the day of receipt of the item), it is acting reasonably [UCC § 4–202(b)].

As the check travels to the payor bank, corresponding debits and credits accompany the physical transfer of the item until it is eventually presented for payment to Peoples National Bank.

At this point, the payor bank must decide whether to pay or dishonor the check. The payor bank may check the authenticity of the drawer's sig-

Figure 28–7   Cross-Country Collection

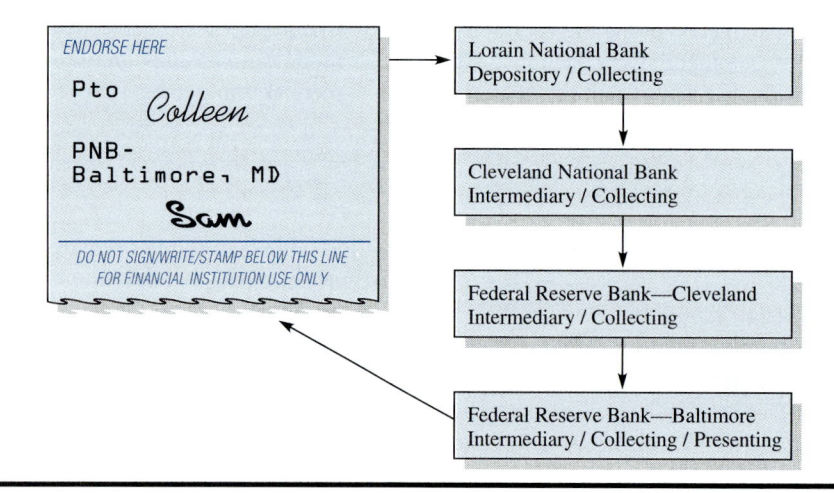

nature, may check for the presence of necessary indorsements, and may check whether the drawer's account has sufficient funds from which to pay the item. In the meantime, the payor bank will typically make provisional settlement for the item by crediting the account of the presenting bank for the amount of the item. This should be done by midnight of the banking day of receipt of the item [UCC § 4–302(a)(1)]. However, the bank may treat any item received after 2 P.M. as received on the next banking day [UCC § 4–108].

If Peoples National decides to pay the item, it will debit Sam's account and remit payment to the presenting bank, Federal Reserve Bank—Baltimore in Figure 28–7, which will make remittance eventually to the depositary bank and Colleen. This will be accomplished by bookkeeping entries.

By contrast, if Peoples National decides to dishonor the item, it will return the check to the presenting bank [UCC § 4–301(a)(1)] or directly to the depositary bank, revoking the provisional settlement [Reg. CC 229.31]. If the check is unavailable for some reason, the payor bank may instead send a written notice of dishonor [UCC § 4–301(a)(2)]. This must be accomplished by its midnight deadline to avoid final payment [UCC § 4–302].

Final Payment Rule

Upon **final payment,** all provisional settlements become final, and the right to chargeback is lost. The drawer's liability on the item and the underlying debt is discharged. In addition, once final payment occurs, a customer's stop payment order cannot be honored, and notice of death or incompetence of the drawer comes too late to affect the payor's rights on the item.

A check is typically finally paid when the payor bank pays the item in cash, or when it makes a provisional settlement and fails to dishonor the item by its midnight deadline [UCC § 4–215(a)].

Excuses in the Bank-Collection Process

Where the payor or collecting bank faces liability for failure to act timely, delay may be excused if caused by "circumstances beyond the control of the bank," including computer malfunctions, as long as the bank acts reasonably under the circumstances [UCC § 4–109(b)]. This section has been strictly applied by the courts.

Read the following case and determine whether the bank should be excused from timely dishonor.

UCC § 4–109. Delays

(b) Delay by a collecting bank or payor bank beyond time limits prescribed or permitted by this [act] . . . is excused if (i) the delay is caused by interruption of communication or computer facilities, suspension of payments by another bank, war, emergency conditions, failure of equipment, or other circumstances beyond the control of the bank, and (ii) the bank exercises such diligence as the circumstances require.

FIRST WYOMING BANK, N.A. v. CABINET CRAFT DISTRIBUTORS, INC.
624 P.2d 227 (Wyo. 1981)

Quality Kitchens issued a check payable to Cabinet Craft Distributors for $10,000 on the defendant, First Wyoming Bank, on May 6, 1978, as partial payment for cabinets. The check was deposited into the account of Cabinet Craft Distributors, Inc. (Cabinet Craft), on May 8th and presented for payment on Monday, May 22. It was sent to the computer center in Billings, Montana, that day by courier and arrived in Billings between 8 and 10 P.M. Normally, the courier would wait at the computer center until the checks were processed and return immediately with the checks and a computer printout. However, on May 22, after the courier had passed, the main road between Sheridan and Billings was closed due to flooding. Although the courier could have taken an alternate route and delivered the checks to the First Wyoming Bank by May 23, it arranged to have the checks flown to Sheridan on Western Airlines. Unfortunately, the checks were not delivered to the bank in Sheridan but were instead delivered to the First Wyoming Bank in Casper, Wyoming, and not delivered to Sheridan until May 25. On May 25, the bank dishonored the Cabinet Craft check for insufficient funds. The bank was held liable for the amount of the check and appealed asserting excuse.

ROSE, Chief Justice

It is obvious that the flooded road between Billings and Sheridan which disrupted the normal procedure for delivery of the check was a "circumstance beyond the control of the bank." Our inquiry is whether the bank used "such diligence as the circumstances required," in allowing the Montana computer center to give the check to Western Airlines for delivery and in not following up the failure of the airline to deliver the packet on schedule. In answering this question we must consider that the stipulated facts show that the bank had an alternative to using Western Airlines: its courier could have taken a different route. We are also somewhat handicapped by a lack of information. For example, although we know that the bank had previously used the airline's delivery service, we do not know what the airline's previous record for timely deliveries had been. We do not know if the computer center in turning the check over to the airline emphasized the need for a timely delivery. We do not know if the bank could have traced the checks which failed to arrive on the Western Airline flight and gotten them sooner.

We have found no case involving a claimed excuse identical to the one involved here and only a few cases involving somewhat similar excuses. The Montana case is, perhaps, most in point. A bank in Butte, Montana, had its checks processed at a computer center in Great Falls, Montana. In the usual course of business the Butte bank's checks were sent by armored car to Great Falls for processing.

Unfortunately for the Butte bank, it received some checks on May 11, 1970. That day the armored car broke down and did not reach Great Falls until 1:30 A.M., May 12. Moreover, the computer in Great Falls malfunctioned with the result that the checks were not returned to Butte until 2:30 P.M. on May 12, rather than at 7:00 A.M. on that date. The Butte bank's "midnight deadline" for dishonoring the checks was midnight of May 12.

The Montana court said:

> Under the exception . . . the bank must show: (1) a cause for the delay; (2) that the cause was beyond the control of the bank; and (3) that under the circumstances the bank exercised such diligence as required.

Along these lines our appellee urges that we note that there is no evidence in the record that the appellant bank made any efforts to trace the checks when they did not arrive in Sheridan aboard the Western Airlines flight as scheduled. Perhaps a trace started on the missing checks that morning would have enabled the bank to obtain the checks that day and meet the midnight deadline for dishonoring the insufficient-funds check which is the focus of this appeal.

In the case before us, there is no showing that defendant-appellant bank used any diligence when the packet of checks failed to arrive as scheduled on the flight from Montana.

The cases discussed above persuade us that the appellant bank has failed to prove an excuse sufficient to enable it to escape liability for its failure to dishonor the check in question by the midnight deadline imposed by the UCC.

Case Questions

1. Why might courts apply the excuse section so strictly?
2. What is the liability of the payor bank?
3. What should the payor bank have done to satisfy the court's "diligence" requirement?

Funds Availability

At what point is there a right to draw on funds deposited in a bank account? The answer to this question varies depending on a variety of factors. First, where the payee presents a check directly to the drawee bank for payment, the drawee bank has until close of business on the day of presentment to pay the item [UCC § 3–506(2)].

A second issue concerns when customers can get access to funds from their banks. Where the customer deposits money (cash) in the account, it is available at the opening of the bank's next banking day

[UCC § 4–213(f)]. A more difficult question is presented when a check drawn to the customer's order is deposited. Where the payee and the drawer maintain accounts at the same bank, the payee can withdraw funds at the opening of the bank's second banking day following the deposit [UCC § 4–215(e)(2)]. For example, if Paula deposits a check drawn on the ABC Bank into her account with the ABC Bank on Monday, she has the right to withdraw those funds Wednesday morning — unless, of course, the item is dishonored. During this time, the ABC Bank is ascertaining whether or not the item is properly payable and posting the item to the drawer's account.

Where the depositary bank is not the same bank as the payor bank, the payee can withdraw the funds when final payment occurs *and* the bank has had a reasonable time to receive a returned item and it has not [UCC § 4–215(e)(1)]. Remember, a collecting bank learns of final payment merely by not learning of dishonor within a reasonable time because final payment typically occurs when the payor bank fails to dishonor the item by its midnight deadline. Only if the payor bank actually dishonors the item will the depositary bank receive notice.

Where provisional settlements have been given to the depositor by the depositary bank, the bank is reluctant to allow its customer to withdraw those funds until it is sure that the provisional settlements have become final, that there has been no dishonor, and that there is no danger of chargeback. Therefore, it wants to wait before allowing its customer to draw on the funds and frequently imposes a delay between the time of deposit and the date of funds availability. Because of concern over this delay, Congress passed the Expedited Funds Availability Act, imposing timetables within which banks must make customer's funds available. Therefore, customers are permitted access to funds as outlined in Figure 28–8.

Figure 28–8   Permanent Funds Availability Schedules (availability of different types of checks deposited the same day)

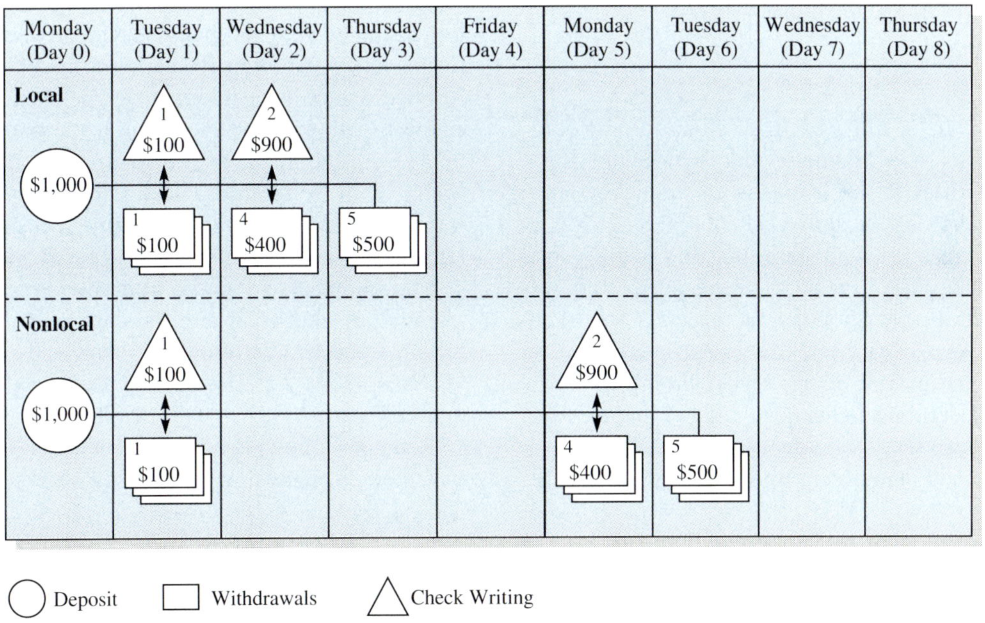

Source: Federal Register Vol. 52, No. 238 December 11, 1987, 47117.

[1]The first $100 of a day's deposit must be made available for either cash withdrawal or check writing purposes at the start of the next business day [§ 229.10(c)(1)(vii)].

[2]Local checks must be made available for check writing purposes by the second business day following deposit [§ 229.12(b)].

[3]Nonlocal checks must be made available for check writing purposes by the fifth business day following deposit [§ 229.12(c)].

[4]$400 of the deposit must be made available for cash withdrawal no later than 5:00 P.M. on the day specified in the schedule. This is in addition to the $100 that must be made available on the business day following deposit [§ 229.12(d)].

[5]The remainder of the deposit must be made available for cash withdrawal at the start of business the following day [§ 229.12(d)].

Figure 28-9   Encoded Numerals for Electronic Processing

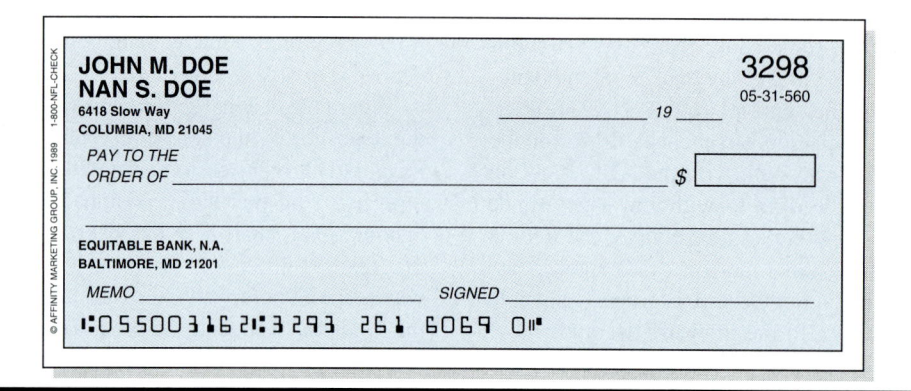

Computer Processing of Checks

As more and more banks are processing checks by computer, it becomes important for any chapter on bank collections to at least address issues raised by such processing. In large part, the revisions of Article 4 were meant to address bulk-processing concerns. There are several methods of computer processing of checks that are presently in varying degrees of use.

Magnetic Ink Character Recognition (MICR)

Most banks use **Magnetic Ink Character Recognition (MICR)** encoding to electronically process checks. As is illustrated in Figure 28-9, a check is encoded with numerals that identify the payor bank, the account to be charged, and the number of the check. When the check is deposited with the depositary bank, the check is encoded to identify the amount of the check. From this point on, it is electronically handled without the need for visual inspection. The computer reads the encoded numbers and automatically sorts and routes the check.

Check Truncation

There are currently two types of **check truncation** technologically feasible. The first type of check truncation is drawee retention of checks, where the check, deposited with the depositary bank, moves normally through the bank-collection process. The major change occurs when the drawee-payor bank receives the item. Instead of returning all items to the customer with the bank statement, the drawee retains either the original item or a microfilm copy. Revised Article 4 encourages this type of check truncation by allowing a payor bank to furnish its customer with the information that would normally be available on the returned check [UCC § 4–406(a)]. If it is the bank's policy to destroy the checks, it must retain copies for seven years [UCC § 4–406(b)].

The second type of check truncation is depositary retention of checks, where the depositary bank retains the check, microfilms the item, and sends the vital statistics by electronic impulse directly to the drawee bank.

Read the following article about check imaging, a method of processing that is becoming technologically feasible.

Check Imaging: Banks Are Getting the Picture*

Image-based systems, which reduce the physical handling of paper checks, are now becoming commercially available, and in time, they are likely to redefine check processing.

---

*Source: Mark Arend, "Check Imaging: Banks Are Getting the Picture," Reprinted with permission from *ABA Banking Journal*. May 1992. © 1992 American Bankers Association.

Eventually—probably in this decade—say industry observers, full-scale check image processing will become a reality, starting with truncation of the paper checks at the bank of first deposit. Numerous legal, technical, and financial hurdles have yet to be crossed, but the potential savings seem to justify a move in that direction.

Fed Support

Helping direct some image technology efforts is the Federal Reserve Board, which monitors costs associated with check clearing operations.

"From my own efforts to update some estimates compiled by two Federal Reserve economists a few years ago, it appears that the industry spends nearly $4 billion each year in the proof-of-deposit function," Paul Connolly, senior vice-president at the Federal Reserve Bank of Boston, said at a recent conference. "Using best estimates, the costs for payor banks to receive and process their inclearing checks, post the checks to customer accounts, prepare statements, and send statements and canceled checks to customers, are over $10 billion annually," he added. "These figures certainly suggest that new approaches to reducing the labor intensity and paper intensity of the check system could be very cost effective."

The Fed is leading efforts to establish interbank applications of check image technology, so that the industry as a whole can benefit from it. But today's image systems don't include key capabilities necessary for interbank applications, said Connolly.

For this vision to be realized even in part, said Connolly, image systems would need to include the ability to store a complete check image and to retrieve the image and deliver it to another bank's image system.

■ ■ ■

Imaging Advantages

Besides gaining operating efficiency, banks that have invested in check image technology are exploiting new marketing opportunities, such as offering new products and services to customers. For example, some banks that use the technology offer their customers image statements, which eliminate the cost of mailing multiple checks to customers each month.

"The postage savings are enough to defray the investment in the equipment," says Lindsey C. Lawrence, president of BayBanks Systems, Inc., a technology division of Bay-Banks, Inc., a $9.5 billion-assets bank holding company in Boston. A 25-cent fee for the service, which the bank calls CheckView, also helps cover the cost of the technology.

■ ■ ■

Thought Questions

1. Is this article prescriptive or descriptive?
2. The author states that "Numerous legal . . . hurdles have yet to be crossed." What are some of those hurdles? Can they be resolved? Should they be resolved? What are the value conflicts?
3. Will imaging benefit banks or customers? Why are banks pursuing this method of processing? What are the benefits to customers?
4. The article states that in order for check imaging to be successful, "image systems would need to include the ability to store a complete check image and to retrieve the image and deliver it to another bank's image system." Why? Are there any legal reasons?

ELECTRONIC FUNDS TRANSFER

Several types of electronic funds transfer systems have developed, such as FEDWIRE (an EFT network connecting the 12 Federal Reserve banks and their branches), Clearing House Interbank Payment Systems (CHIPS, an electronic funds transfer network transferring funds among member New York City banks), and automated clearinghouses (ACHs, regional associations of banks for processing electronic items such as direct deposits of social security checks).

In response to the rise in EFTS and the predictions of the future "checkless" society, Congress enacted the Electronic Fund Transfer Act (EFTA) in 1978. The EFTA governs electronic funds transfers between consumer accounts and financial institutions. It requires certain disclosures, provides for documentation of transfers, offers error-resolution procedures, imposes liability for noncompliance, and allocates liability in the event of loss or theft. Because the EFTA governs consumer transactions, it is discussed in Chapter 33 on Consumer Protection.

Article 4A

Wire transfers not regulated by the EFTA are governed by UCC Article 4A. Article 4A was added to the UCC in 1989 and has been enacted in about 30 states.

The primary focus of Article 4A is the **wholesale wire** transfer, not covered by the EFTA. Payments covered by Article 4A are generally between businesses and financial institutions. The funds transfer that is covered by Article 4A can be illustrated by the following example. Assume that Acme, a debtor, wants to pay a $10,000 debt owed to Coyote, Inc. To do this, it transmits an instruction to Acme's bank to credit $10,000 to the bank account of Coyote, Inc. If Acme's bank and Coyote's bank are different banks, Acme's bank will instruct Coyote's bank to credit Coyote's account for $10,000 [Article 4A, Prefatory Note].

Article 4A regulates these types of funds transfers, which are not governed by the EFTA. In any funds transfers, there are certain risks of loss, such as where the transfer is delayed because of insolvency, or if a bank fails to execute the payment order of its customer. There may also be an error in the payment order. A major purpose of Article 4A is to determine how risk of loss should be allocated in these cases.

END–OF–CHAPTER QUESTIONS

1. Has the UCC abandoned the "best position" rationale in incorporating comparative negligence principles into section 4–406? Is the payor bank encouraged to be careful?

2. Explain the relationship between final payment and the midnight deadline.

3. Explain the relationship between funds availability and final payment.

4. One of the motivations in revising Article 4 was to update the UCC to accommodate changes in check processing and modern technologies. Give examples of changes in the UCC that attempt to do this. Do you think they are successful? Can you think of any other statutory roadblocks to modernization.

5. Frank Forger stole a check from Michael Thomas's checkbook with the First National Bank. He wrote a check to the Campus Bookstore for $1,000. The Campus Bookstore deposited the check in its account with the Second National Bank. The check was forwarded for collection and presented for payment. First failed to detect the forgery and paid the item. When Michael discovered the forgery, he demanded recredit. Does First have to recredit Michael's account? Explain. This issue will be further developed in Chapter 29.

6. Between January 23, 1964, and March 5, 1967, Peoples National Bank paid 25 forged checks from Gennone's account. All of the checks were forged by Gennone's wife. Gennone's wife took the bank statements before Gennone saw them. In June 1965, Gennone notified Peoples that he was not receiving his canceled checks and bank statements. Gennone informed Peoples of the forgeries on March 6, 1967. Does Peoples have to recredit Gennone's account? Explain. See *Gennone v. Peoples National Bank and Trust Co.*, 9 U.C.C. Rep. Serv. 707 (Pa. Common Pleas 1971).

7. David Siegel drew a check for $20,000 on New England Merchants National Bank made payable to Peter Peters, post-

dated November 14, 1973. New England paid the check on September 17. Siegel discovered the error when another check was returned for insufficient funds. Siegel demanded recredit. Must New England recredit? Does it matter whether Massachusetts has adopted revised Article 4? See *Siegel v. New England Merchants National Bank*, 437 N.E.2d 218 (Mass. 1982).

8. Century Buick draws a check for $48,470 on the Bank of Mid-Jersey made payable to Grand Prix. It was deposited into the Bank of Leumi and routed to Mid-Jersey for collection. It was returned on October 4 for insufficient funds. On October 13, Century Buick stopped payment on the check. Then the check was redeposited. This time, Leumi made an error in encoding, crossed out the encoded sum with a lead pencil, and wrote in the corrected figure. It was presented for payment on Friday, October 20. It was dishonored on Tuesday, October 24. Was the item dishonored timely? If not, can Mid-Jersey be excused from timely dishonor because of the encoding error? Explain. See *Bank Leumi Trust Co. v. Bank of Mid-Jersey*, 499 F.Supp. 1022 (D. N.J. 1980).

9. David Dworsky owed $45,000 to Lincoln National Bank. To pay the debt, David gave Lincoln a check payable to David's partnership, drawn by a company called Agretch payable on Wells Fargo Bank. The check was presented for payment at Wells Fargo on Friday, November 29, 1985. Because the employees could not find the check, they reported the check as lost and sent a notice of dishonor to Lincoln. David contended that this was not an effective, timely dishonor because Wells Fargo did not prove that the check was lost or destroyed. Was this an effective dishonor? See *Lincoln National Bank v. Dworsky*, 267 Cal. Rptr. 361 (Cal. Ct. App. 1990).

10. Explain the relationship between subrogation under UCC section 4–407 and stop payment orders. Can you think of any reasons supporting the doctrine of subrogation?

Chapter 29

Wrongdoing and Error

■

CRITICAL THINKING INQUIRIES

As you read this chapter, you should be able to address the following:

- Explain the relationship between loss allocation for forged drawer's signatures and forged indorsements.
- Analyze the following statement: "The Code attempts to place the loss on the party best able to avoid the loss." Give examples of rules that prove this statement.
- Explain the relationship between the impostor rule, the fictitious payee rule, and negligence.
- Evaluate the following statement: "In the instance of forged drawer's signatures, the loss is always borne by the payor bank."
- Analyze the following statement: "The rules governing encoding errors encourage electronic processing of checks."

MANAGERIAL PERSPECTIVE

Tim Green is the owner of a dry cleaning store, Tim's DryCleaning. As payment for dry cleaning, he takes a check drawn on the First National Bank allegedly by "Al Brown." However, the signature was forged.

He also took a check allegedly made payable to his customer "Jane Evans." The customer indorsed the check and negotiated it to Tim. However, the indorsement was forged—the customer was not Jane Evans.

Tim has also suffered check losses caused by employee misconduct. Tim's bookkeeper has been preparing checks made payable to "Cleaning Supplies," allegedly as payment for cleaning solvents. Tim has just discovered that no such payments were ever made—the bookkeeper has himself been indorsing the checks and keeping the money.

Tim is considering changing the store's policy on accepting checks because of his fear of forgery.

- What is Tim's potential liability on the forged check? How can he minimize his potential liability?
- What is his potential liability on the forged indorsement? How can he minimize his potential liability?
- What is his potential liability on the checks drawn by his bookkeeper? How can he minimize his potential liability?

The major question in cases of wrongdoing and error is which innocent party will bear the loss from this wrongdoing. Obviously, the criminal is the one at fault. In all cases, the party who has liability has a lawsuit against the criminal. However, the criminal is a very unlikely candidate from whom to recover. Therefore, the party who is left with the lawsuit against the criminal is generally said to be the party bearing the loss.

There are a number of rationales underlying the Code's loss allocation rules. First, the Code attempts to place the loss on the party best able to avoid the loss. Thus, if one of the two innocent parties was in a position to prevent the criminal from committing the wrong, that party will most likely bear the loss. Second, the Code attempts to place the loss on the party most likely to have insurance against this type of loss. Therefore, it is useful to remember that financial institutions generally have forgery insurance to protect them from wrongdoing losses. Third, the Code attempts to encourage development of new less expensive methods of processing checks. The Code wants to support the ease of commercial transactions, not to impose obstacles.

This chapter will examine these loss allocation rules as applied to forgery, material alteration, and encoding errors.

FORGERY

Forged Drawer's Signature

Who will bear the loss in the instance of forged drawer's signatures depends on whether the payor bank pays or dishonors the item when it is presented for payment.

If the Payor Bank Pays the Item

Under the doctrine of *Price v. Neal,*[1] the payor bank that pays an item over a forged drawer's signature bears the loss. The **final payment rule,** codified in section 3–418, prevents the payor bank from recovering payments made by mistake, as over a forged drawer's signature, from a holder in due course or one who in good faith acted in reliance on the payment [UCC § 3–418(c)]. For example, assume that Mr. Crook steals one of Al Brown's checks. As in Figure 29–1, he makes it payable to Tim Green in our opening scenario for dry cleaning services and forges Al's signature. Assume further that Tim deposits it in his account with the Last National Bank. Last National presents the check to the payor First National Bank for payment. First National pays the item and charges Al's account. Al demands that First National recredit his account because the check is not properly payable [UCC § 4–401]. In the absence of customer negligence, discussed later in this chapter, the bank must recredit its customer's account.

UCC § 3–418. Payment or Acceptance by Mistake

(c) The remedies provided by subsection (a) or (b) may not be asserted against a person who took the instrument in good faith and for value or who in good faith changed position in reliance on the payment.

Moreover, First National has no recourse against prior collecting banks. This is the doctrine of *Price v. Neal.* First National cannot recover from either

---

[1] 97 Eng. Rep. 871 (K.B. 1762).

Figure 29–1   Forged Drawer's Signature, Check Paid

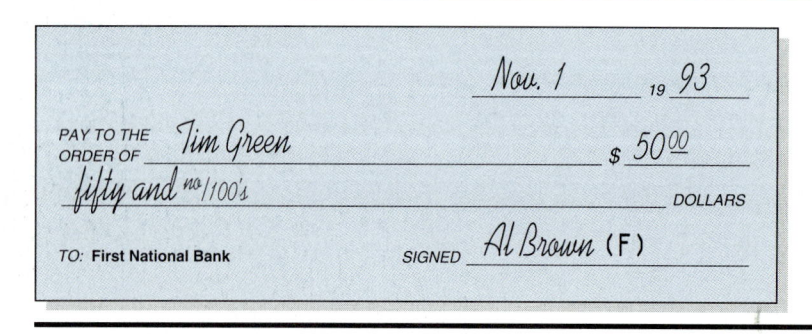

Tim or Last National on their indorser's contracts for two reasons. First, indorsers promise to pay holders and the payor bank is not a holder. Second, indorsers promise to pay only when there has been a dishonor, and there has not been a dishonor in this case. Similarly, First National cannot recover from either party for breach of warranty. First National cannot recover for breach of presentment warranties. It cannot use the warranty that all signatures are authentic because there is no presentment warranty of authentic signatures — the presenter warrants only that he has no *knowledge* of a forged drawer's signature. In the typical situation, this warranty is not breached because the presenting bank is generally unaware of the forgery. In addition, First National cannot successfully argue that the warranty of good title has been breached because good title is not affected by a forged drawer's signature. Further, First National cannot recover for breach of transfer warranties, including the transfer warranty of authentic signatures, because transfer warranties are made only to transferees, and the payor bank is not a transferee.

(One presents an item for payment — one does not transfer the item.) First National is left with a lawsuit against the forger.

UCC § 3–418. Payment or Acceptance by Mistake

(a) . . . if the drawee of a draft pays . . . the draft and the drawee acted on the mistaken belief that-
. . . the signature of the drawer of the draft was authorized, the drawee may recover the amount of the draft from the person to whom . . . payment was made.

Therefore, it is clear that when a payor bank pays an item over a forged drawer's signature, in the absence of customer negligence the payor bank bears the loss. Mistaken payments may be recovered only from a nonholder in due course or one who did not justifiably change position in reliance on the payment [UCC § 3–418(a)(b)].

Read the following case and determine whether the bank is permitted to recover the mistaken payment.

FIRST NATIONAL CITY BANK v. ALTMAN
3 U.C.C. Rep. Serv. 815 (N.Y. Sup. Ct. 1966)

The defendant, Altman, is a wholesale diamond dealer. Nieman introduced himself as a buyer for J. W. Mays, Inc., and selected a number of diamonds, which Altman kept sealed inside an envelope. A few days later, Nieman sent a check for $22,300.80 drawn on the account of J. W. Mays, Inc., at First National City Bank as payment for the diamonds. Nieman then came and selected more diamonds. The same procedure was followed, and Nieman's letter confirming the sale arrived with a check for $23,900.75 as payment for the second group of diamonds. Immediately, Altman deposited each check into his account at the Trade Bank. When Nieman requested delivery of the first envelope of diamonds, Altman contacted the Trade Bank and, before turning over the diamonds, determined that the first check had been paid by the drawee. He turned over the second selection of diamonds several days later but did not first determine that the second check had been paid. First National City Bank sued to recover the amounts of the two checks because they were forgeries paid by mistake.

TIERNEY, Judge

Payment or acceptance of any instrument is final in favor of "a person who has in good faith changed his position in reliance on the payment" (UCC § 3–418). This legal principle was long ago enunciated in *Price v. Neal*, (1762) where it was held that a drawee who pays an instrument on which the signature of the drawer is forged is bound on his accep-

tance and cannot recover back his payment from a holder in due course, or a person who had in good faith changed his position in reliance on the payment.

The facts are clear that with respect to the first packet of diamonds, defendant Altman did not make delivery thereof until he had first ascertained that the check by which payment had been made had been paid by plaintiff. Accordingly, defendant

Altman, the payee of the check, does qualify as a person who changed his position in reliance on the drawee's payment. However, in all of the circumstances, the court is of the view that the issue of his good faith presents a triable issue of fact which precludes summary dismissal of the action based on the first check. It has been held that the negligence of the purchaser, at the time he acquired title to the instrument, in not making inquiries which, if made, might reveal the fact of the forgery, releases the drawee from the rule of *Price v. Neal*, and enables the drawee to recover from the purchaser the amount paid to him on the instrument.

Inasmuch as defendant Altman did not determine that the second check had been paid by plaintiff prior to delivery of the second packet of diamonds, said defendant is not in a position to claim the status of "a person who has . . . changed his position in reliance on the payment." Therefore, the proscription against the drawee stated in the rule of *Price v. Neal* loses its impact.

Case Questions

1. Why didn't Altman argue that he was a holder in due course?

2. The court applied former UCC Article 3. Would this decision have been decided any differently under current law?

3. Did the court apply the correct test for good faith? Was Altman's negligence relevant?

If the Payor Bank Dishonors the Item

If the payor bank dishonors the item, the first person to deal with the forger will bear the loss. For example, assume again that in our opening scenario Tim deposits the check drawn by "Al Brown" into his account with the Last National Bank. Assume further that Last National negotiates the check to Second National Bank, which presents the check to the payor bank, First National Bank, and that First National dishonors the item. First National can revoke the provisional settlement given to Second National. Second National, the presenting bank, can easily pass this loss up the chain of title, suing either Last National or Tim for breach of the transfer warranty of authentic signatures. Thus, the loss will be passed up the chain, until the first person to deal with the Forger—Tim

(the one who could have most easily prevented the loss) bears the loss. Tim is left with a lawsuit against the forger. This is illustrated in Figure 29–2.

Forged Indorsement

Who bears the loss in a forged indorsement case does not depend on whether the payor bank pays the item. Regardless, the first person who deals with the forger will bear the loss. All subsequent parties can sue up the chain based on breach of warranty of (1) good title, (2) authentic signatures, and (3) no defenses. Returning to our opening scenario, as is illustrated in Figure 29–3, assume that Tim takes the check made payable to his customer "Jane Evans" and deposits it in his account with the Last National

---

Figure 29–2   Check with Forged Drawer's Signature—Check Dishonored

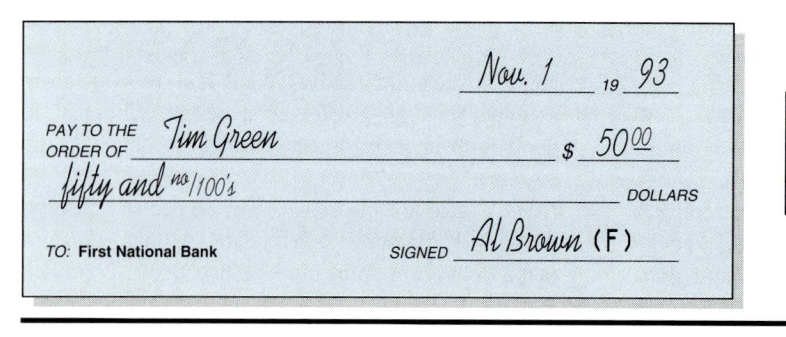

Figure 29–3 Check with Forged Indorsement

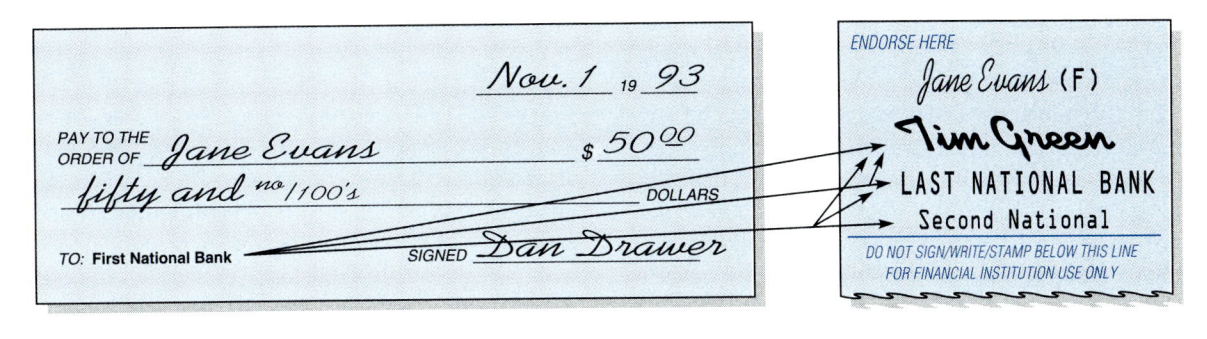

Figure 29–4 Check with Material Alteration

Bank. Remember that the indorsement was forged on the check. Assume further that Last National forwards it for collection to Second National Bank and that it is then presented for payment to First National. Assume that First National pays the item and charges the drawer's account. When the drawer discovers the improper payment, First National must recredit the account, because checks with forged indorsements are not properly payable. First National then sues either Second National, Last National, or Tim for breach of the presentment warranty of good title. If First National sues Second National, Second National sues either Last National or Tim for breach of the transfer warranty of good title. Last National can also sue Tim for breach of the transfer warranty of good title. Thus, the first person to deal with the forger—Tim—bears the ultimate loss in the case of forged indorsements. This is true whether or not the payor bank pays the item.

MATERIAL ALTERATION

An alteration is any unauthorized change in an instrument that modifies the liability of any party on that instrument or any unauthorized addition of words or numbers to an incomplete instrument [UCC § 3–407(a)]. Again, the first person to deal with the wrongdoer generally bears the loss of an alteration. For example, as is illustrated in Figure 29–4, assume that David Kayes makes a check payable to the order of Jeremy Doe in the amount of $500. Assume further that Jeremy negotiates the check to Derek Riley, who fraudulently changes the amount of the check to read $5,000 and deposits it in his account with the Columbia National Bank. Columbia National forwards it for collection to the payor, Best National Bank, which pays the item and debits David's account for $5,000. When David discovers the overpayment, he demands recredit. Best

National must recredit David's account for $4,500 because the check was only properly payable for $500. Best National can sue prior parties, including Columbia National, for breach of the presentment warranty that there are no material alterations. Columbia National cannot sue Jeremy because he has breached no warranty (there was no alteration at the time of transfer) and because under contract liability, he promised only to pay the amount due on the instrument at the time he indorsed ($500). Therefore, Columbia National is left with a lawsuit against Derek.

UCC § 3–407. Alteration

(b) . . . an alteration fraudulently made discharges a party whose obligation is affected by the alteration unless that party assents or is precluded from asserting the alteration.

Assume, instead, that the payor bank dishonored the item. In that case, Best National will revoke the provisional credits given to Columbia National. Assume further that Derek cashed the check and has no money deposited with Columbia National from which it can set off the $5,000. Columbia National cannot sue Jeremy for breach of warranty because, as outlined above, no warranties were breached. However, it can sue Jeremy for the $500 originally promised in the indorser's contract even though an alteration discharges any party whose liability is affected by the alteration [UCC § 3–407(b)]. Such discharge is not good against one who took the instrument in good faith, for value, and without notice of the alteration [UCC § 3–407(c)].

PRECLUSION FOR ASSERTING

There are several exceptions to rules discussed in the preceding sections. Basically, these involve situations where one is precluded from asserting the forgery or material alteration. These arise typically where the party precluded was in the best position to avoid the loss. Because it failed to act to avoid the loss, it will bear the loss.

Impostor Rule

The first exception is the **impostor rule.** This rule deals with a situation of *impersonation*, where an impostor appears before the person defrauded and pretends to be some other person. Where the maker or drawer (issuer) is induced by an impostor to issue the instrument, the issuer bears the loss [UCC § 3–404(a)]. The indorsement is effective to pass title and no warranties are, therefore, breached. For example, assume that a woman posing as Smith offers to sell a car titled in the name of Susan Smith. Bob accepts and issues a check in the name of Susan Smith to pay for the car. When Bob discovers that the name transferring the title was forged, that the woman with whom he dealt was not Susan Smith, and that the indorsement on his check was forged, he demands that his bank recredit his account. In this case, the bank does not have to recredit Bob's account. Because the check was issued to an *impostor*, the indorsement is effective to pass title, no warranties are breached, and the check is properly payable. It doesn't matter if the impersonation is face to face or through the mails. Similarly, the indorsement is effective if Susan impersonated the president of Smith Corporation and forged the indorsement of Smith Corporation.

UCC § 3–404. Impostors

(a) If an imposter, by use of the mails or otherwise, induces the issuer of an instrument to issue the instrument to the impostor . . . by impersonating the payee of the instrument . . . an indorsement of the instrument by any person in the name of the payee is effective . . . in favor of a person who, in good faith, pays the instrument.

Read the following case. Does the impostor rule apply?

■

MINSTER STATE BANK v. BAUERBAND
17 UCC Rep. Serv.2d 526 (Mass. App. 1992)

In November 1989, Edward Bauerband contacted the plaintiff bank, Minster State Bank, with whom he had a long-standing banking relationship. Edward requested a loan application purportedly on behalf of himself and his wife, Michelle. Upon receipt of the completed loan documents, including a promissory note, Minster issued a cashier's check for $25,000 payable to Edward and Michelle. Edward forged Michelle's name to the cashier's check and deposited it in his own business account at defendant bank, Baybank. When the forgery was discovered, Minster sued Baybank for breach of warranty.

SHERMAN, Judge

Baybank contends that it is not liable for breaching warranties because Edward's forgery of Michelle's signature constituted an effective indorsement of the check in question.

Minster argues, however, that because neither Edward Bauerband nor any other "impostor" contacted or actually appeared at the plaintiff bank impersonating Michelle Bauerband, this case entails nothing more than an ordinary forged indorsement. Minster's contention ignores, however, the critical statutory language which renders the section applicable to impersonation "by the use of the mails or otherwise." As Uniform Commercial Code Comment 2 indicates:

Subsection (1) (a) is new. It rejects decisions which distinguish between face-to-face imposture and imposture by mail. . . . The position here taken is that the loss regardless of the type of fraud which the particular impostor has committed, should fall upon the maker or drawer.

This is not restricted to situations involving the role-playing of actual, physical impostors who impersonate the individual whose signature has been forged in a face-to-face confrontation with the maker or drawer.

The essential flaw, then, in Minster's position is that it mistakenly equates the absence of a physical impostor with a lack of the kind of impersonation cognizable under the "impostor rule." It is this broader concept of impersonation undertaken to defraud the maker or drawer which is the additional element distinguishing [impostor rule] cases from ordinary forgeries. In the instant case, Edward Bauerband's actions went well beyond merely forging his wife's name on the back of Minster's check. Such forgery was indeed only the final stage of a fraudulent scheme conceived and implemented by Edward which began with creating the false impression that his wife jointly sought a bank loan and would be jointly liable; which required

forging her name on a promissory note and other loan documents; and which necessarily entailed impersonating her participation in every aspect of the transaction to insure that his scheme would culminate in his ultimate receipt of the $25,000 in question.

Such impersonation of Michelle Bauerband renders Edward's forgery of her signature an effective indorsement of the check made and drawn upon Minster. Baybank is thus excused from the customary collecting bank warranties, and the loss of the sum in question must be borne by Minster. This result is consistent with the underlying rationale of the Uniform Commercial Code "impostor rule" which encompasses the maxim "that as between two innocent [parties], the one whose act was the cause of the loss should bear the consequences." It was Minster which enjoyed a long-standing banking relationship with both Bauerbands, which was in a position to detect the initial forgery of Michelle's signature on the promissory note and loan documents, which was first deceived by Edward's impersonation of his wife's involvement and which ultimately delivered the check in question to the "impostor." It is essential to note that such analysis of Minster's position is not tantamount to a finding of negligence on its part as common law negligence is irrelevant under [the impostor rule]. Rather, the appropriate Uniform Commercial Code inquiry focuses on which party, within the Code's system for allocating risk of loss from forged instruments, was in the better position to protect itself.

Case Questions

1. Why does the court believe that Minster State Bank was in the best position to protect itself?

2. How could Minster State Bank have prevented this loss?

3. Explain how Baybank transferred good title over a forged indorsement.

Fictitious Payee

The second exception governs situations where the instrument is payable to a fictitious person or payable to a real person but the maker or drawer did not intend the payee to have any interest in the instrument [UCC § 3–404(b)]. Again, in such instances, the indorsement in the name of the named payee is effective [UCC § 3–404(b)].

UCC § 3–404. Fictitious Payees

(b) If (i) a person whose intent determines to whom an instrument is payable does not intend the person identified as payee to have any interest in the instrument, or (ii) the person identified as the payee of an instrument is a fictitious person, . . .

(2) An indorsement by any person in the name of the payee . . . is effective . . . in favor of a person who, in good faith, pays the instrument or takes it for value or for collection.

For example, recall the opening scenario, where Tim's bookkeeper has been preparing checks payable to Cleaning Supplies, a nonexistent company, forging its indorsement and cashing the checks. In this instance, Tim bears the loss. The indorsement is effective to pass title. The check is properly payable. Alternatively, assume Cleaning Supplies is an actual company that does business with Tim's dry cleaning store. If the bookkeeper intended to steal the check when it was drawn (that is, never intended Cleaning Supplies to have an interest in the check), the fictitious payee rule applies and the indorsement is effective. Further, assume that the checks of the dry cleaning store must be signed by both Tim and the bookkeeper. Assume further that the bookkeeper prepares a check to the order of Cleaning Supplies, either a fictitious company or one to whom no money is owed, and obtains Tim's signature, with Tim believing that this is a proper payment. If the bookkeeper takes the check and forges the indorsement of Cleaning Supplies, the indorsement is effective under the fictitious payee rule.

The rationale for this rule is that because the drawer or maker is in the best position to prevent the fraud, it should bear the loss rather than the customer or collecting bank. However, if the person taking or paying the check might have prevented the loss by the use of ordinary care, that person should bear the loss to the extent that this carelessness contributed to the loss [UCC § 4–404(d)].

Read the following case and determine whether or not the fictitious payee rule should apply.

UCC § 3–404. Impostors; Fictitious Payees

(d) . . . if a person paying the instrument or taking it for value or for collection fails to exercise ordinary care . . . and that failure substantially contributes to loss . . . the person bearing the loss may recover from the person failing to exercise ordinary care to the extent the failure to exercise ordinary care contributed to the loss.

■

MERRILL LYNCH, PIERCE, FENNER & SMITH, INC. v. CHEMICAL BANK
442 N.E.2d 1253 (Ct. App. N.Y. 1982)

An accounts payable employee of Merrill Lynch presented false invoices to the check-issuing department. Believing that they represented debts due suppliers, 13 checks for a total of $115,180 were issued and paid by Chemical Bank. The employee indorsed the checks in the name of the payees and deposited the checks in out-of-state bank accounts. When the wrongdoing was discovered, the drawer Merrill Lynch sued Chemical Bank for recredit.

FUCHSBERG, Judge

Our analysis may well begin with the observation that [the Code] bespeaks an exception to the general rule governing the responsibility of a bank to its customers. For it is basic that ordinarily a drawee bank may not debit its customer's account when it pays a check over a forged indorsement.

It follows that, in the typical case in which payment is made on a check that is not properly payable, the payment is deemed to have been made solely from the funds of the drawee bank rather than from those of its depositor. But, when the conditions which [the fictitious payee rule] contemplates prevail, the indorsement, though forged, is still effective, and the instrument then must be treated as "both a valuable instrument and a valid instruction to the drawee to honor the check and debit the drawer's account accordingly."

This departure from the general rule is explained by Official Comment 4, which advises, "The principle followed is that the loss should fall upon the employer as a risk of his business enterprise rather than upon the subsequent holder or drawee. The reasons are that the employer is normally in a better position to prevent such forgeries by reasonable care in the selection or supervision of his employees, or, if he is not, is at least in a better position to cover the loss by fidelity insurance; and that the cost of such insurance is properly an expense of his business rather than of the business of the holder or drawee."

Since the assumptions instinct in this rationalization are hardly indisputable, it is no surprise that the rule it supports represents a conscious choice between the traditional one, which was more protective of the bank's customer, and the one in the code, which, as some commentators have bluntly acknowledged, was "a banker's provision intended to narrow the liability of banks and broaden the responsibility of their customers." Thus, whatever, in the abstract, may have been the equities of the respective contentions of the competing commercial camps, there can be little doubt but that the outcome, so far as the code is concerned, was calculated to shift the balance in favor of the bank "in situations in which the drawer's own employee has perpetrated the fraud or committed the crime giving rise to the loss."

[T]he fact that [the fictitious payee rule] fails to delineate a standard of care, to which a bank itself must adhere if it is to advantage itself of this section,

was no oversight. In contrast are sections 3–406 and 4–406 of the Uniform Commercial Code, which, along with the "padded payroll" provision, deal with defenses which may be available to a drawee bank in forged indorsement cases.

It is fair to conclude, therefore, that, unlike cases which fall within the foregoing sections, a drawee bank's mere failure to use ordinary care in the handling of a check whose forgery has brought it within the embrace of [the fictitious payee rule] will not subject it to liability.

This is not to say that, if a check is "tainted in some other way which would put the drawee on notice, and which would make its payment unauthorized" a drawee bank may yet not be liable. For instance, a drawee bank surely is not immunized by [the fictitious payee rule] when it acts dishonestly. In short, "a basis for liability independent of any liability which might be created by payment over a forged instrument alone" may very well survive.

In contrast, without more, in the present case, it is at once clear that the irregularities on which Merrill Lynch here focuses were part and parcel of the forgeries themselves and "could not possibly have alerted the bank to the fact that the checks were tainted, indeed it would have been most remarkable if the drawee bank had even noticed them."

Case Questions

1. Was the employer in a better position to detect the fraud than the drawee or depositary banks?

2. How would this case have been resolved differently under revised Article 3? Explain. Discuss the shift in loss allocation between old and revised Article 3 evident in this section.

3. Return to the opening vignette. Who bears the loss for the checks issued by Tim's bookkeeper to Cleaning Supplies, Inc.? Explain.

Other Employee Fraud

In other cases where an employer has given responsibility with respect to instruments to an employee, the employer bears the loss. For example, where the

employee has the authority to sign or indorse instruments, to process instruments, or to list the names of potential payees and misuses this authority, the employer bears the loss [UCC § 4–405]. Again, it is believed that the employer is in a better position to avoid the loss by being careful in choosing employees, in supervising them, and in adopting other precautionary safeguards.

For example, assume that Julie Brown issues a check payable to Tim's DryCleaning. Assume further that Tim's bookkeeper, Bill, is responsible for processing checks. Bill has the authority to indorse checks and deposit them into Tim's DryCleaning's account. Bill indorses this check, but instead of depositing it into Tim's DryCleaning's account, he deposits it into an account he has opened in the name of Tim's DryCleaning. In this case, the indorsement is considered effective. Tim bears the loss.

However, if the person paying the check fails to exercise ordinary care, that person shares in the loss proportionately [UCC § 3–405(b)]. For example, a question might arise as to whether or not the depositary bank in the above example exercised ordinary care when it allowed the bookkeeper to open an account in the name of Tim's DryCleaning.

UCC § 3–405. Employer's Responsibility for Fraudulent Indorsement by Employee

(b) . . . if an employer entrusted an employee with responsibility with respect to the instrument and the employee . . . makes a fraudulent indorsement of the instrument, the indorsement is effective as an indorsement of the person to whom the instrument is payable if it is made in the name of that person.

UCC § 3–405. Employer's Responsibility for Fraudulent Indorsement by Employee

(b) . . . If the person paying the instrument or taking it for value or collection fails to exercise ordinary care in paying or taking the instrument and that failure substantially contributes to the loss resulting from the fraud, the person bearing the loss may recover from the person failing to exercise ordinary care to the extent the failure to exercise ordinary care contributed to the loss.

Negligence

Both Sections 3–406 and 4–406 provide that one may also be precluded from asserting wrongdoing if that person's negligence contributed to the forgery

or material alteration. For example, a person can contribute to a forgery by being careless in hiring employees, in the care of a signature stamp, or in the care of a checkbook. For example, a person can contribute to a material alteration by leaving blanks in an instrument or by writing the instrument using pencil. If the drawer's negligence substantially contributes to the wrongdoing, the wrongdoing may not be asserted against the payor bank. In other words, if the drawer is responsible for the wrongdoing, the drawer may not demand that the payor bank recredit its account.

However, the payor bank also has a duty of care with respect to items presented for payment. If the payor bank also fails to act carefully and the bank's negligence contributes to the wrongdoing, the loss is allocated between the parties using a comparative negligence scheme [UCC § 3–406(b)]. This is a change from prior law, which used a contributory — all or nothing — negligence scheme. Further, while revised Article 3 does not specify what exactly is required to meet the ''ordinary care'' standard, it does not require that banks processing the checks for collection visually examine the checks for forgeries [UCC § 3–103(7)].

UCC § 3–406. Negligence Contributing to Forged Signature or Alteration of Instrument

(a) A person whose failure to exercise ordinary care substantially contributes to an alteration of an instrument or to the making of a forged signature on an instrument is precluded from asserting the alteration or the forgery against a person who, in good faith, pays the instrument or takes it for value or for collection.

UCC § 3–406. Negligence Contributing to Forged Signature or Alteration of Instrument

(b) . . . if the person asserting the preclusion fails to exercise ordinary care in paying or taking the instrument and that failure substantially contributes to loss, the loss is allocated between the person precluded and the person asserting the preclusion according to the extent to which the failure of each to exercise ordinary care contributed to the loss.

Read the following case and determine the way in which the loss should be allocated.

FIREMAN'S FUND INSURANCE CO. v. BANK OF NEW YORK

539 N.Y.S.2d 339 (Sup. Ct. 1989)

Actors Equity used the services of Cris Associates, an employment agency, to hire a comptroller. Cris screened applicants and described their backgrounds to Actors Equity, who then interviewed the candidates. Actors Equity hired a ''Nicholas Scotti'' without requesting an investigative report and after calling only one reference. Scotti forged four checks totalling $100,000 and Actors Equity discovered the forgeries one year later. It also discovered that Scotti was actually named Piscotti, had a criminal record for crimes including forgery, and that his résumé was almost totally fabricated. Actors Equity sued the payor bank for recredit.

MILONAS, Justice

The law is settled that ''ordinarily a drawee bank may not debit its customer's account when it pays a check over a forged indorsement.'' As the Court of Appeals noted in *Spielman v. Chemical Bank*, ''[i]n most cases, however, the forgery is not effective to transfer the instrument and the drawee is liable because it is in a position to detect the forgery before payment. Thus, in such cases it is the drawee, as between two innocent parties, who is accountable for the loss.'' Accordingly, ''payments made on forged or unauthorized indorsements are at the peril of the bank unless it can claim protection upon some principle of estoppel.'' In that connection, section 3–406 of the Uniform Commercial Code provides

Any person who by his negligence substantially contributes to . . . the making of an unauthorized signature is precluded from asserting the . . . lack of authority against a holder in due course or against a drawee or other payor who pays the instrument in good faith and in accordance with the reasonable commercial standards of the drawee's or payor's business.

The foregoing rule is based on the doctrine of equitable estoppel that ''where one of two innocent persons must suffer by the acts of a third, he who has enabled such third person to occasion the loss, must sustain it.''

In the instant situation, the conduct of the union in retaining someone to manage many millions of dollars in funds without conducting, or insisting upon, a reasonable and trustworthy background investigation constitutes negligence substantially contributing to the making of the unauthorized signatures involved here. Certainly, Actors Equity may not avoid the consequences of its own omissions by claiming that it relied upon Cris Associates to properly screen applicants. The evidence at trial clearly demonstrates that Actors Equity never received nor even demanded a financial or security check of any of the candidates whose names were being forwarded by Cris Associates, much less of Scotti in particular, and then utterly failed to perform even the most cursory investigation of its own. Indeed, if Actors Equity had conducted even a perfunctory examination into Scotti's credentials, his deficiencies and unsavory history would have become glaringly obvious. Thus, Actors Equity basically accepted at face value an individual whom it put in charge of millions of dollars of its funds. Such conduct was clearly negligent. Since plaintiff's loss herein was proximately caused by the negligence of Actors Equity, and the bank paid on the forged instruments in good faith and in accordance with its reasonable commercial standards, defendant should not have been held liable on the four checks.

Case Questions

1. Analyze: ''Where one of two innocent persons must suffer by the acts of a third, he who has enabled such third person to occasion the loss, must sustain it.''

2. How did Actors Equity contribute to the making of a forgery? What could it have done to prevent the loss?

3. Could the payor bank have also used the bank statement rule to avoid recredit? See Chapter 28.

| Figure 29-5 | Liability for Negligence in Examining Checks for Forgeries, UCC Old and Revised Article 3 |

Old Article 3	Revised Article 3
Courts split, but a majority of courts found that payor banks had a duty to examine checks for forgeries	Banks have no duty to examine checks for forgeries
Contributory negligence	Comparative negligence

Revised Article 3 significantly changed the Code's loss allocation scheme in the event of forged checks in two significant ways: (1) by relieving the payor bank of the duty of examining signatures; and (2) by replacing the contributory negligence scheme with a comparative one (see Figure 29–5). Read the following essay, in which the authors argue that these changes shift the loss from the payor bank to the customer. Do you agree?

Banks and Their Customers under the Revisions to Uniform Commercial Code Articles 3 and 4: Allocation of Losses Resulting from Forged Drawer's Signatures*

A two-tier system of liability, recognizing the economic realities of litigating disputes over small amounts, would be a better approach than either the UCC or the Revised UCC (RUCC). Under this approach, if the amount of the forged check is less than a specified amount, for example $500, the customer would bear no loss regardless of negligence. The bank would recredit the customer's account for the item amount even if that customer's negligence contributed to the forgery. This strict liability rule for smaller items would protect the customer from the need to litigate the negligence issue because it is not cost effective to do so. Where the amount exceeds the given statutory minimum, however, the customer's negligence would become relevant. This two-tier system would allocate losses from forgeries between customers and payor banks more fairly than either the UCC or the RUCC.

Under the UCC, the payor bank often refuses to recredit a customer's account, asserting customer negligence. When the amount of the item is relatively small, even the non-negligent customer often absorbs the loss rather than litigating the negligence question because of the high cost of litigation. The revisions provide even less incentive to litigate because they lower the bank's standard of care, thus decreasing the customer's chances of recovery. If under the present law in most states (where failure on the part of the payor bank to examine items for forged signatures constitutes bank negligence) customers rarely find it cost effective to litigate the question of negligence on small items, it will be even less likely for the question of negligence to be litigated under the RUCC provisions, where the failure to examine such items on the part of the payor bank does not necessarily constitute bank negligence.

Moreover, the comparative negligence scheme further reduces the likelihood of litigation; even where the customer proves the bank's negligence, recovery may be reduced by any contributory negligence. The proposed two-tier system, however, would relieve the customer of the burden of litigating the issue of negligence where economically unfeasible. The payor bank would be able to recoup these small item losses through forgery insurance.

By comparison, the question of negligence is worth litigating where larger amounts are at stake. Accordingly, states considering this issue should combine the basic UCC approach with the proportional loss allocation scheme of the revision for amounts over $500. The

*Source: Nan S. Ellis and Steven B. Dow, "Banks and Their Customers under the Revisions to Uniform Commercial Code Articles 3 and 4: Allocation of Losses Resulting from Forged Drawer's Signatures," 25 Loyola of Los Angeles Law Review 57 (1991). Reprinted with permission of the Loyola of Los Angeles Law Review. Copyright 1991 by the Loyola of Los Angeles Law Review. All rights reserved.

customer should be able to claim the forged item was not properly payable and demand recredit. On these large items, the payor bank should be able to defend against the demand for recredit by proving customer negligence, and the customer should be able to rebut this with a showing of payor bank negligence. The payor bank, however, should not be relieved of the burden of examining items for forged signatures, as the revisions clearly propose. Such a rule would effectively relieve the payor bank from bearing any loss because in all but the most unusual cases the *only* sort of fault a payor *would ever have* is failing to examine an item. It is reasonable to impose a duty on the payor bank to check signatures on at least large checks. The RUCC fails to provide adequate incentives for the payor bank to be careful because it does not obligate the bank to check signatures on any items, even large ones.

■ ■ ■

V. Conclusion

While the present law governing loss allocation from forged drawers' signatures needs improvement, the changes proposed in the revised Article 3 fall considerably short of the mark. The combined effect of the changes—. . . the comparative negligence rule, and, most importantly, effectively relieving the payor bank of its duty to examine signatures—shifts the loss onto the customer to an even greater extent than under present law and will possibly increase overall forgery losses.

The examination of the revised Article 3 reveals an underlying effort behind the proposed changes to shift the loss resulting from forged drawers' signatures away from the payor bank. The Uniform New Payments code (NPC) drafters undertook a similar effort more than a decade ago. Under the NPC, the loss would have been shifted away from the payor bank onto prior collecting banks. That approach was severely criticized and eventually abandoned. Now the new revisions shift the loss onto the payor's customers. This approach is no more justified than the previously rejected NPC approach, and should not be adopted.

Promoting electronic processing of checks is a worthwhile goal. The resulting cost savings will surely benefit banks and, if these savings are passed on to check users, their customers as well. This goal, however, does not justify the revisions to Article 3. The banks developed and implemented electronic processing and check truncation with the current loss allocation scheme in place. This suggests that many bankers consider these measures to be cost effective under present law. The RUCC proposed changes will likely result in a more widespread use of these electronic methods, but they will burden the customers with the entire cost of forgeries. Current law . . . gives banks an incentive to verify their customer's signature on items before paying them because the banks will generally bear the loss if they pay items carrying forged drawers' signatures. It also creates an incentive to develop new technologies to diminish forgery losses, such as electronic signature verification that will remain compatible with electronic processing. Under the RUCC these important incentives would vanish.

Reducing litigation is also a worthwhile goal. The revisions will certainly have the effect of reducing litigation. Again, however, the bank's customers will bear the entire cost because it is unlikely that even non-negligent customers would litigate most cases of small forgery losses. The goal of reducing litigation should not be achieved at the expense of an equitable loss allocation scheme.

The two-tier proposal would promote electronic check processing and would reduce the amount of potential litigation, while maintaining incentives for both banks and their customers to prevent forgery. Therefore, it would reduce the overall amount of forgery losses. Under the two-tier scheme, banks would be able to use complete electronic processing on an overwhelming majority of items. Banks would continue to have an incentive to verify signatures and would likely continue to develop new technologies to reduce forgery losses even further. Customers would continue to have an incentive to be careful with their checks because of the chance that a forgery might exceed the statutory minimum.

State legislatures should not adopt the revised Article 3 unless the rules relating to loss allocation from forged drawers' signatures are reconsidered and substantially revised.

Thought Questions

1. Explain the authors' proposed two-tier system of liability. How does it differ from current statute?
2. What are the "economic realities of litigating disputes over small amounts" that the authors mention?
3. Why are the authors opposed to the RUCC relieving the payor bank from the duty to examine items for forgeries? Do you agree? What are the goals meant to be achieved by the revisions, according to the authors? In your opinion, do the goals justify the revisions?

ENCODING ERRORS

There are a number of legal problems that can arise through errors in the computer encoding used to process checks. For example, the amount of the check can be improperly encoded by the collecting bank. This type of error differs from a material alteration because it does not change the contract of any party to the instrument. Obviously, the amount can be either overencoded or underencoded.

UCC § 4–209. Encoding and Retention Warranties

   (a) A person who encodes information on . . . an item after issue warrants to any subsequent collecting bank and to the payor bank . . . that the information is correctly encoded.

Overencoding

When a check is mistakenly overencoded, the following might occur. Dan Drawer draws a check for $45 payable to Pete Payee. Pete deposits the check in his bank, where the amount is encoded as $10,045. The check is electronically processed, the payor bank debits the drawer's account for $10,045, and the depositary bank credits Pete's account for the same amount. When Dan discovers the mistake, he demands that the payor bank recredit his account for the $10,000 overcharge. Recredit is required because the item is only properly payable for $45. The payor bank recovers the $10,000 overcharge from the depositary bank for breach of the encoding warranties in revised Article 4 [UCC § 4–209(a)].

Underencoding

A somewhat different problem is presented if the error by the depositary bank is one of underencoding. For example, a check drawn for $1,000 might be improperly encoded as a check for $100. In this case, the payee-depositor's account would be credited for $100 rather than $1,000 and the drawer's account would likewise be debited. The problems arise when the depositor-payee notices the shortage in the account and demands credit. The payor bank owes the full $1,000, and if it suffers a loss (such as when the customer only had $200 in the account to be charged), it can recover from the depositary bank for breach of encoding warranties [UCC § 4–209].

END–OF–CHAPTER QUESTIONS

1. The rule of *Price v. Neal* places the loss on payor banks that pay over forged drawer's signatures. Make a list of possible policy justifications for such a rule.
2. Why are forged indorsements treated differently from forged drawer's signatures?
3. Explain why parties are precluded from asserting forgeries and material alterations in some cases. Do you agree with this shift in the risk of loss?
4. Explain the relationship between breach of warranty, contract liability, and wrongdoing and error.
5. Without the knowledge of her husband, Edmund Jezemski, Paula mortgaged property through Philadelphia Title Insurance

Company. She came to the closing with a man whom she introduced as her husband. She and this man executed the mortgage, obtaining from the Title Company a check for the mortgage loan proceeds payable to Edmund and Paula Jezemski. The check which showed the purported indorsements of all the payees was presented to and paid by the drawee bank, Fidelity-Philadelphia Trust Company, and charged against Title Company's account. Upon discovery of the existence of the mortgage, Edmund set aside the mortgage, and the repayment of the amount advanced by the mortgage. If the Title Company sues the drawee bank to recover the amount of the check, will it be successful? Explain. See *Philadelphia Title Insurance Co. v. Fidelity-Philadelphia Trust*, 212 A.2d 222 (Pa. 1965).

6. Arena Auto Auction, Inc. mailed a check dated December 17, 1963, to Plunkett Auto Sales, Rockford, Illinois. Tom Plunkett signed his name to the check and cashed it at the plaintiff-appellee Bank. On January 9, 1964, the check was returned to the plaintiff bank because of a stop payment order by the drawer. The check had been mistakenly sent to the Rockford Tom Plunkett instead of a Plunkett in Alabama. The defendant, Arena Auto Auction, Inc. issued a second check in the same amount to the same payee, and again sent the check to the Rockford Tom Plunkett. He was, however, unable to cash the second check. The plaintiff bank sued the drawer to recover the amount of the first payment. On what grounds is the plaintiff bringing this suit? Who will prevail? See *Park State Bank v. Arena Auto Auction, Inc.*, 207 N.E.2d 158 (Ill. Ct. App. 1965).

7. The computer that controled Phil's check-writing machine was programmed to issue a check to Supplier Co., a firm to which Phil owed money. The address of the Supplier Co. was changed by Darlene, an accounts payable clerk whose duties included entering information onto the computer, to her own address. When the check was issued and mailed to Darlene, she indorsed it in the name of Supplier Co. and deposited it into an account in the name of Supplier Co. that she had opened. When the fraud was discovered, Phil demanded recredit from the payor bank. Does the payor bank have to recredit the account? Explain. See UCC § 3–405, Official Comment 3 Case 5.

8. David Worth was authorized by his employer CAL to purchase 12 cashier's checks from American Bank to pay for the lease of cars. Rather than using the checks to pay for the cars, Worth had the checks totaling $146,100 made payable to Joe Lake Enterprises. Worth forged the indorsement and presented the checks to Kim, a teller at American Bank and part of the fraudulent scheme. When CAL discovered the fraud, it sued American. American asserted the "padded payroll defense." Who has liability? See *C.A.L., Inc. v. Worth*, 813 S.W.2d 12 (Mo. Ct. App. 1991).

9. In March 1984, Sue Russell began work as Bay Paper's bookkeeper, responsible for the payroll account, keeping the general ledger, and maintaining the checkbook. She was solely responsible for issuing checks and reviewing and reconciling bank statements. Bay Paper hired Sue without performing an extensive background check, nor was she bonded. Beginning in October 1985, Sue began writing duplicate payroll checks payable to existing Bay Paper employees. She forged the signature of the president of Bay Paper and then forged the indorsements on such checks. She then deposited the checks into her personal bank account maintained with the payor bank. In 1986, Bay Paper discovered the fraud and demanded recredit. Will it be successful? Is your answer affected by the double forgery? See *Southern Guaranty Ins. Co. v. First Alabama Bank*, 540 So.2d 732 (Ala. 1989).

10. Dale Brown wrote a check for $10 using a typewriter to put the figure "10" and the word "ten" in the appropriate spaces. Unfortunately, a large blank space was left after the figure and the word. The payee of the check typed the word "thousand" after the word "ten" and added a comma and three zeros after the figure "10." The payor bank in good faith paid $10,000 when the check was presented. When Dale discovered the payment, she demanded recredit. Will she be successful? See UCC § 3–406, Official Comment 3, Case 3.

Part VI

Debtor-Creditor Rights

■

Chapter 30

Creation and Perfection of a Security Interest: Introduction to Secured Transactions

■

CRITICAL THINKING INQUIRIES

As you read this chapter, you should be able to address the following:

- Analyze the following statement: ''Article 9 applies to all transactions intended to create a security interest regardless of form.''
- Explain the relationship between enforceability and perfection.
- Analyze the following statement: ''The distinctions among classes of collateral are made foremost on the basis of the *use* to which the property is being placed, rather than solely on the basis of the kind of property involved.''
- Why is classification of collateral important?

MANAGERIAL PERSPECTIVE

The Last National Bank has been approached by Tom Leary, who wants to borrow $500,000 to finance the opening of his new bookstore café. Last National is concerned about protecting itself, both in the event of Tom's default and against third parties. Tom has offered to grant Last National a security interest in the equipment that he is purchasing for the café. Tom has also offered a security interest in equipment at another one of his restaurants.

- How would a security interest protect Last National in the event of Tom's default?
- Is there a difference between the two security interests offered?
- How can Last National protect itself against third parties?

The importance of credit today cannot be overstated. Few consumers are able to purchase a car without financing. Few businesses are able to finance their operation without credit. A debtor can borrow without security merely by signing a loan contract promising to repay the funds borrowed. However, often a security interest is offered to induce the creditor to extend credit. The creditor can lend money to a debtor who provides existing assets as security, or the creditor-seller can lend money to a debtor to allow the purchase of property. The creation of the security interest makes the creditor a **secured party** [UCC § 9–105(m)]. The property in which the interest is created is **collateral** [UCC § 9–105(c)].

A security interest in the debtor's property minimizes the risks associated with the loan. It can protect the secured party against (1) the debtor in the case of default, (2) the trustee in the case of bankruptcy, (3) bona fide purchasers of the collateral, and (4) other creditors of the debtor.

SCOPE OF ARTICLE 9

Historically, a wide variety of security devices existed. Each device was governed by a separate set of rules. Differences existed in the secured party's rights against the debtor and third parties, in the debtor's rights against the secured party, and in filing requirements. This led to a system full of uncertainty and confusion.

UCC § 9–102. Policy and Subject Matter of Article

(1) . . . this Article applies

(a) to any transaction (regardless of its form) which is intended to create a security interest in personal property or fixtures including goods, documents, instruments, general intangibles, chattel paper or accounts.

Secured transactions are now governed by Article 9 of the Uniform Commercial Code (UCC). Article 9 abandons the distinctions among the various security devices. In place of the complex pre-Code system, Article 9 substitutes the single term **security interest.** Article 9 provides a scheme by which creditors, through the use of security interests, can protect themselves against the debtor and third parties. When dealing with a security interest, the cred-

itor must be careful to follow the Article 9 rules or lose this protection.

Subject to the exceptions set forth in Section 9–104, the basic test for whether a transaction is covered by Article 9 is whether it is intended to create a security interest in personal property [UCC § 9–102(a)]. Article 9 covers all consensual security interests in personal property. This excludes straightforward sales, pure credit arrangements, mortgages on real property, and nonconsensual liens such as judgment liens.

The circumstances under which a lease can be an Article 9 security interest has been the subject of much discussion. The question is whether a transaction is a true lease or a disguised installment sale with the seller retaining title until the purchase price is paid in full (a security interest).

UCC § 1–201. General Definitions

(37) . . . A transaction creates a security interest if the consideration the lessee is to pay the lessor for the right to possession and use of the goods is an obligation for the term of the lease not subject to termination . . . and . . .

(d) the lessee has an option to purchase the goods for no additional or nominal additional consideration.

A security interest is created when the lessee becomes the owner of the property in exchange for lease payments already made [UCC § 1–201(37)]. In addition, even where the lessee must pay something to purchase the property at the end of the lease term, the lease can be a security interest. The existence and details of the option to purchase after expiration of the lease term are important. If the lease agreement provides for an option to purchase at no additional charge or nominal consideration, the lease is a security interest [UCC § 1–201(37)]. For example, assume that Sam leases a piece of equipment to Ben for 3 years for $200 per month and the equipment has a useful life of 10 years. Ben has the option to purchase the equipment at the end of the lease term with all rental payments applied to the purchase price. The purchase can be accomplished for an additional payment of $100. This is a nominal payment creating a security interest because Ben could buy a machine with a useful life of seven more years for only $100. Leases are not always Article 9 security interests. Where the amount of the option equals approximately the fair market value of the asset, the transaction is a true lease.

Read the following case and ask whether the transaction is a lease or a security interest.

IN RE ROYAL FOOD MARKETS, INC. v. U.S. BERKEL FOOD MACHINES, INC.

121 B.R. 913 (Bankr.Ct. S.D. Fla. 1990)

The debtor, Royal Food Markets, Inc., and the creditor, U.S. Berkel Food Machines, Inc., entered into an "Equipment Lease" in which the creditor leased supermarket equipment to the debtor. The lease was a fixed-term lease with an option to purchase at the end of the lease for $10. Following debtor default, the creditor attempted to regain possession of the equipment. The debtor declared bankruptcy. The debtor asked the bankruptcy court for a declaratory determination of the validity of the lease.

WEAVER, Judge

Whether an agreement is a true lease or a security agreement is to be determined by the facts of each case. Most courts look to a combination of factors in determining whether an agreement is a lease or a security agreement. Whether an option to purchase is included in the agreement is one of the most often applied factors and is one which is specifically addressed by the Uniform Commercial Code.

In determining whether the consideration paid for the exercise of the option was nominal, several courts have applied the "economic realities" test which states that, "If at the end of the term of the lease, the only economically sensible course for the lessee is to exercise the option to purchase the property, then the agreement is a security agreement."

This court has previously adopted a second test which examines the relationship of the option price to the original purchase or list price and holds that if the option price is less than 25 percent of the original

purchase or list price then the consideration is regarded as nominal. In the case at bar, the option price to purchase the equipment at the expiration of the lease is $10 or approximately .000027 percent of the original equipment cost and thus meets the above cited 25 percent test. This Court finds from the evidence presented, and considering the initial down payment and the total sum of lease payments to be made under the agreement, that the only economically sensible course for the debtor to take at the end of the lease term would be to exercise the option. Having made such a finding, this Court concludes that the consideration to be paid by the debtor for the purchase option was nominal.

Case Questions

1. What is the consequence of the court's decision that this is a security interest?

2. Explain the relationship between the economic realities test and nominal consideration.

In addition to governing secured transactions, Article 9 also covers sales of accounts or chattel paper. Commercial financing on the basis of accounts and chattel paper is conducted so often that the distinction between a sale and a security interest is blurred. Therefore, under present treatment, the distinction is unnecessary. All such sales are governed by Article 9.

Exclusions from Article 9 Coverage

Section 9–104 excludes certain transactions from Article 9 coverage, such as where the transaction is governed by other law. For example, Article 9 does not apply to landlord's liens, wage assignments, security interests governed by federal law, or transfers of tort claims.

CLASSIFICATION OF COLLATERAL

The property subject to the security interest is the *collateral*. Article 9 adopts a complicated scheme by which collateral is classified into basic groups. Because many of the rules under Article 9 depend on the class of collateral involved, an understanding of this classification scheme is central to an understanding of the article. The distinctions among classes are made foremost on the basis of the *use* to which the property is being placed in the hands of the debtor, rather than solely on the basis of the kind of property involved. Collateral can be divided into three basic groups: **goods, semi-intangibles,** and **intangibles.**

Goods

Collateral that consists of tangible property is **goods.** Goods are all things that are movable, excluding primarily real estate [UCC § 9–105(h)]. Goods include standing timber to be cut, unborn young animals, and growing crops [UCC § 9–105(h)]. Goods are further subdivided into consumer goods, equipment, farm products, and inventory.

Consumer Goods

Goods that are used or bought primarily for personal, family, or household purposes are **consumer goods** [UCC § 9–109(1)]. For example, a television set used in the debtor's home is a consumer good.

UCC § 9–105. Definitions

(h) ''Goods'' includes all things which are movable at the time the security interest attaches.

UCC § 9–109. Classification of Goods

Goods are

(1) ''consumer good'' if they are used or bought for use primarily for personal, family or household purposes.

Inventory

Goods are **inventory** if they are held for sale or lease [UCC § 9–109(4)]. For example, a television set in an appliance store or appliance store warehouse is inventory. In addition, raw materials, work in progress, or materials used in a business are inventory. Thus, fuel used in manufacture, scrap metal produced in manufacture, and containers used to package the goods produced are inventory. Goods are inventory, even though not held for sale, if they are used up or consumed in a short period of time in the production of an end product. For example, pencils, paper, and typewriter ribbons are all inventory.

UCC § 9–109. Classification of Goods

Goods are

(4) ''inventory'' if they are held by a person who holds them for sale or lease . . . or if they are raw materials, work in progress or materials used or consumed in a business.

Farm Products

The category **farm products** includes goods used or produced in farming operations if they are in the possession of the farmer-debtor [UCC § 9–109(3)]. The category includes crops or livestock, as well as products of crops and livestock, as long as such products are in an unmanufactured state. Thus, maple syrup, milk, and eggs are all farm products. After farm products have been converted to a manufactured state, they cease to be farm products and become inventory if held for sale.

UCC § 9–109. Classification of Goods

Goods are

(3) ''farm products'' if they are crops or livestock or supplies used or produced in farming operations or if they are products of crops or livestock in their unmanufactured states . . . and if they are in possession of a debtor engaged in raising, fattening, grazing or other farming operations.

Equipment

Goods are categorized as **equipment** if they are used or bought for use primarily in a business [UCC § 9–109(2)]. Thus, a machine used by a debtor to manufacture goods is equipment. A television set in a doctor's office is equipment. A farmer's tractor or a law firm's books are also equipment because businesses include farming and professions [UCC § 9–

109(2)]. In the opening scenario, Tom Leary's oven is an example of equipment covered by Last National's security interest. In general, goods used in business are equipment when they are fixed assets or have relatively long useful lives. In addition, goods that do not fit into any of the other three categories of goods are equipment.

UCC § 9–109. Classification of Goods

Goods are

(2) ''equipment'' if they are used or bought for use primarily in business.

The use to which the collateral is put in the hands of the debtor determines its category. A freezer is equipment used in a restaurant, inventory in an appliance store, and consumer goods in a person's home. However, the classes of goods are mutually exclusive—the same property cannot, for example, be both equipment and inventory. In borderline cases, the *principal use* to which the property is put is determinative. Thus, a farmer's jeep might be consumer goods or equipment, depending on its principal use.

What if the principal use changes? Read the following case and ask yourself whether the airplane is a consumer good or equipment.

COMMERCIAL CREDIT EQUIPMENT CORP. v. CARTER
516 P.2d 767 (Wash. 1973)

Ray Carter bought an airplane for $23,955, securing payment with a security agreement. At the time of purchase, Carter intended to use the airplane for his own personal use only. He used the airplane as such for three months after purchase. He then used the plane in the course of business. Upon Carter's default, Commercial Credit repossessed the plane, sold it, and sued Carter for the remaining debt balance. Because consumers are protected in such cases, the question of classification is crucial.

BRACHTENBACH, Judge

First, we hold that the intent of the defendant at the time the plaintiff's security interest attached to the collateral is controlling and necessitates the conclusion that the airplane came within the code definition of consumer goods.

The plaintiff, however, urges an alternate theory, contending that the defendant, when faced with the financial inability to meet the monthly payments, rented the airplane to third parties. In fact about nine months after executing the security agreement, the defendant did make the plane available for rental. In terms of overall use of the plane from purchase until taking of possession by plaintiff, the evidence indicates more hours for rental use than for plaintiff's personal use. From these facts, the plaintiff concludes that the plane was not used primarily for personal purposes.

It is true that the cited statute refers to goods used primarily for personal, family or household purposes. Uniform Commercial Code § 9–109, Comment 2 states: ''In borderline cases—a physician's care or a farmer's jeep which might be either consumer goods or equipment—the principal use to

which the property is put should be considered determinative.'' Unfortunately neither section 9–109 nor the comment is precise in stating the point in time at which the principal use is to be measured. Conceivably it could be either the principal use at the time the security agreement attaches, such use at the time the debtor takes possession upon default, or the principal use to which the collateral has been put between the attachment of the security interest and taking of possession.

It is the underlying purpose and policy of the code to ''simplify, clarify and modernize the law governing commercial transactions.'' It is inconsistent with this declared underlying purpose and policy to require a creditor to monitor use of the collateral in order to ascertain its proper classification. The uncertainty caused by the potentially shifting status of the goods is not desirable in the commercial world. Also, there exists a potential mischief by debtors facing default who might endeavor to convert goods from the category of equipment to consumer goods to avoid a deficiency and, likewise, by creditors making the opposite claim in order to benefit from a deficiency.

We turn therefore to the second basis for the trial court's conclusion that the airplane was not "consumer goods." The trial court reasoned that the aircraft fell within the definition of "equipment" because consumer goods were not intended to cover expensive hobby items such as airplanes. We disagree since we find nothing in the statute to imply any exclusion dependent upon cost or nature of the goods. Rather, the decisive factor is whether the goods are used or bought for use primarily for personal, family or household purposes.

In accord with this interpretation is *Atlas Credit Corp. v. Dolbow,* in which the court held, without analysis, that a boat purchased for $5,980 was consumer goods. Indeed, it has been observed that

[t]he classifications of Sec 9109 are based solely on use or function and it is almost, if not impossible, to conceive of an item of tangible personal property that cannot be a

consumer goods. Even the recently retired "Queen Mary" could qualify as a consumer goods if purchased by a billionaire for his own personal use and one recalls that the late Henry Ford, at one time bought up entire factories for his personal museum. *In re Trumble.*

The finding that the defendant intended the airplane for personal use conclusively brings it within the Code definition of consumer goods.

Case Questions

1. Does a classification of collateral as consumer goods benefit the debtor or creditor?
2. Are there reasons for arguing that an expensive good should not be classified as a consumer good? For example, should a mobile home be classified as a consumer good?
3. How should collateral be classified when the debtor lies about the use?

Semi-intangibles

Semi-intangible assets include various legal rights represented by paper. These are documents, instruments, and chattel paper.

Documents

Documents of title such as warehouse receipts or bills of lading are classified as **documents** [UCC § 9–105(f)].

Instruments

Negotiable and non-negotiable instruments such as checks, promissory notes, and certificates of deposits, as well as Article 8 securities such as stock certificates and bonds are **instruments** [UCC § 9–105(1)(i)]. In addition, any other right to the payment of money evidenced by a writing is an instrument if it is of the type that is transferred by delivery in the ordinary course of business.

Chattel Paper

A writing that is evidence of both a promise to pay and a security interest in specific goods is called **chattel paper** [UCC § 9–105(b)]. A promissory note and a security agreement together are chattel paper. For example, assume that a car dealer sells a car on credit to a consumer, receiving in return a promissory note and a security interest in the car as

collateral. If the car dealer uses this contract as collateral for a bank loan, it is chattel paper.

Intangibles

This type of collateral is purely intangible, not evidenced by a writing, but it may be the subject of commercial financing transactions. There are two types of intangible collateral: accounts and general intangibles.

Accounts

An **account** is a right to payment for goods sold or leased or for services rendered, such as an ordinary account receivable [UCC § 9–106].

General Intangibles

General intangibles are any personal property, other than goods, accounts, chattel paper, documents, instruments, and money [UCC § 9–106]. This includes such property as goodwill, literary rights, copyrights, trademarks, and patents.

CREATION OF A SECURITY INTEREST

The process by which the secured party and the debtor create a security interest that is enforceable between these two parties (**attachment** and **en-**

forceability) must be distinguished from the process by which the secured party gains protection against third parties (**perfection**).

Before a security interest can attach and be enforceable against the debtor, three criteria must be met: (1) an agreement must be entered into between the debtor and creditor; (2) value must be given; and (3) the debtor must have rights in the collateral.

Security Agreement

The first requirement is an agreement between the parties granting a security interest. If the collateral is in the possession of the secured party, an oral agreement is sufficient. Thus, where a debtor borrows money from the secured party and allows the secured party to keep a coin collection as security for the loan, the first requirement has been met.

However, where the collateral is not in the possession of the secured party, a written security agreement is required. This serves a statute of frauds function facilitating proof and protecting the debtor. The **security agreement** is the agreement creating the security interest [UCC § 9–105(1)]. Figure 30–1 is a sample security agreement. A security agreement must (1) contain a description of the collateral and (2) be signed by the debtor [UCC § 9–203(1)(a)].

Description of the Collateral

The security agreement must describe the collateral. The description does not have to be extremely detailed as long as it "reasonably identifies" the collateral [UCC § 9–110]. This rejects a "serial number" test requiring an exact and detailed description. Under the Code's approach, broad descriptions of collateral, such as "All inventory used in the production of boats" or "all equipment located at . . ." are sufficient descriptions.

UCC § 9–105. Definitions

(1) "Security agreement" means an agreement which creates or provides for a security interest.

UCC § 9–110. Sufficiency of Description

For the purposes of this Article any description of personal or real property is sufficient whether or not it is specific if it reasonably identifies what is described.

Unless otherwise specified, the security interest includes proceeds [UCC § 9–306(2)]. **Proceeds** are whatever is received upon the sale or exchange of the collateral [UCC § 9–306(1)]. Thus, in our opening scenario, Last National's security interest would cover a new freezer purchased to replace a freezer already covered by the security interest.

Moreover, the security interest may apply to **after-acquired property,** property that may be acquired by the debtor in the future [UCC § 9–204]. For example, assume that Dan Debtor grants a security interest in "accounts receivable now owned or hereafter acquired" to Sam Simon. Sam's security interest attaches to accounts receivable as they are acquired by Dan. However, there is an exception to this rule for consumer goods. No security interest attaches to after-acquired consumer goods unless they are acquired within 10 days from the time the secured party gives value [UCC § 9–204(2)]. This protects the consumer from overreaching by creditors. For example, assume that Dan Debtor arranges to borrow money from First Finance Company (FFC), granting in return a security interest in "all consumer goods now owned or hereafter acquired." Dan receives $5,000 from FFC on August 1. FFC's security interest will not attach to a television set purchased on August 25 because it was acquired more than 10 days after the loan was made.

Signature by the Debtor

The security agreement must be signed by the debtor [UCC § 9–203(1)(a)]. The requirement of a signature is liberally construed, with the test being whether there is intent to authenticate [UCC § 1–202(39)]. Thus, a typewritten signature will satisfy the signature requirement if that is the intent. The debtor must sign the security agreement, but there is no corresponding requirement that the secured party sign.

Value

The second requirement that must be met before an enforceable security interest is created is that the secured party must give value. A creditor gives **value** when it takes the security interest in return for the extension of credit or a binding commitment to extend credit, for a preexisting debt, or in return for any consideration sufficient to support a contract [UCC § 1–201(44)]. Several examples will illustrate.

Figure 30–1a   Security Agreement

SECURITY AGREEMENT

For value received, the undersigned, herein called "Debtor", hereby grants to Last National Bank (The Secured Party), whose principal office is located at 123 Main Street, Columbia, Maryland, a continuing security interest in the Collateral described in Paragraph I to secure payment of any and all indebtedness of Debtor to Secured Party ("indebtedness").

I.   Collateral.   The Collateral of the Security Agreement is all equipment now owned or hereafter acquired located at _____ 4501 Silver Spring Lane, Columbia, Maryland. _____. This includes all proceeds of the foregoing.

II.   Definitions.   As used herein:

2.1   "Collateral" means and includes any and all property of Debtor in which Secured Party now has or by this Agreement now or hereafter acquires a security interest, including without limitation, Debtor's Equipment.

III.   Warranties, Covenants and Agreements: Debtor warrants and agrees as follows:

3.1   Secured Party at its option may disburse loan proceeds directly to the seller of any Collateral to be acquired by Debtor with proceeds of loans from Secured Party.

3.2   At the time any Collateral becomes subject to a security interest in favor of Secured Party, Debtor shall be deemed to have warranted that (i) Debtor is the lawful owner of such Collateral and has the right and authority to subject to any security interest other than that in favor of Secured Party; (ii) none of the collateral is subject to any security interest other than that in favor of Secured Party and there are no financing statements on file, other than in favor of Secured Party; and (iii) Debtor has acquired its rights in the Collateral in the ordinary course of its business.

3.3   Debtor will keep the Collateral free at all times from any and all liens, security interests and encumbrances other than those in favor of Secured Party. Debtor will not, without the prior written consent of Secured Party, sell or lease, or permit to be sold or leased, all or any part of the Collateral. Secured Party or its agents may at any and all reasonable times inspect the Collateral and may enter upon any and all premises where the same is kept or might be located.

3.4   Debtor will do all acts and things, and will execute all writings requested by Secured Party to establish, maintain and continue the perfected and first security interest of Secured Party in the Collateral, and will promptly on demand pay all costs and expenses of filing and recording, including the costs of any searches deemed necessary by Secured Party to establish and determine the validity and the priority of Secured Party's security interest.

3.5   Debtor will promptly and within the time that they can be paid without interest or penalty all taxes, assessments and charges which are now, or hereafter during the effective period of this Agreement may become, a lien or charge upon any of the Collateral.

IV.   Defaults

4.1   Upon the occurrence of any of the following events (an "Event of Default"), Debtor shall be in default under this Agreement:

(i)   Any failure to comply with, or breach of any of the terms, provisions, or warranties of this Agreement, or any other agreement between the Debtor and Secured Party; or

(ii)   Any failure to pay the indebtedness when due, or such portion thereof as may be due, by acceleration, or otherwise; or

(iii)   Any loss, theft, substantial damage or destruction to or of any Collateral or the issuance or filing of any attachment, levy, garnishment or the commencement of any proceeding in connection with or of any judicial process of, upon or in respect of Debtor or any of the Collateral; or

(continued on back)

Figure 30–1b Security Agreement

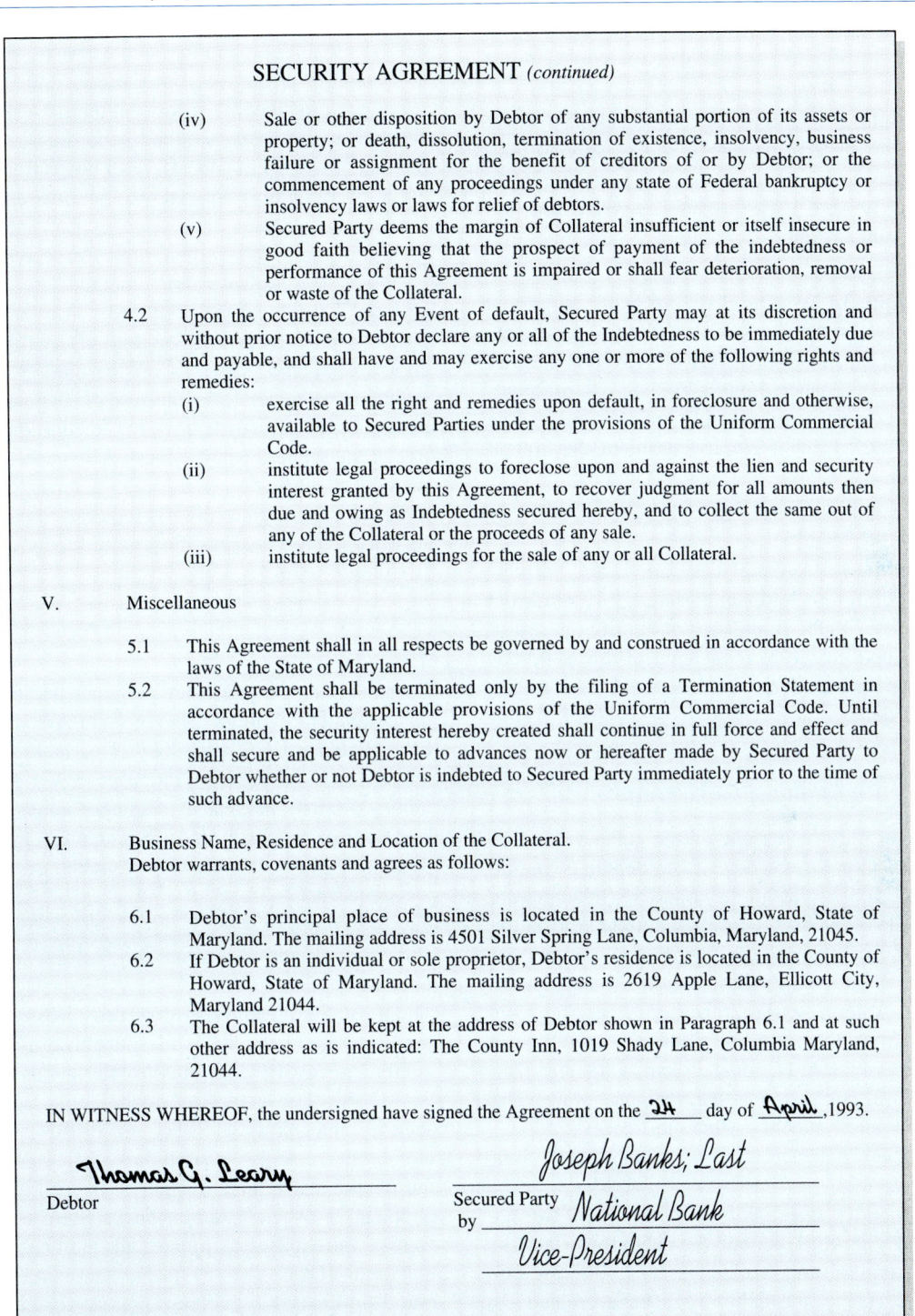

SECURITY AGREEMENT *(continued)*

(iv) Sale or other disposition by Debtor of any substantial portion of its assets or property; or death, dissolution, termination of existence, insolvency, business failure or assignment for the benefit of creditors of or by Debtor; or the commencement of any proceedings under any state of Federal bankruptcy or insolvency laws or laws for relief of debtors.

(v) Secured Party deems the margin of Collateral insufficient or itself insecure in good faith believing that the prospect of payment of the indebtedness or performance of this Agreement is impaired or shall fear deterioration, removal or waste of the Collateral.

4.2 Upon the occurrence of any Event of default, Secured Party may at its discretion and without prior notice to Debtor declare any or all of the Indebtedness to be immediately due and payable, and shall have and may exercise any one or more of the following rights and remedies:

(i) exercise all the right and remedies upon default, in foreclosure and otherwise, available to Secured Parties under the provisions of the Uniform Commercial Code.

(ii) institute legal proceedings to foreclose upon and against the lien and security interest granted by this Agreement, to recover judgment for all amounts then due and owing as Indebtedness secured hereby, and to collect the same out of any of the Collateral or the proceeds of any sale.

(iii) institute legal proceedings for the sale of any or all Collateral.

V. Miscellaneous

5.1 This Agreement shall in all respects be governed by and construed in accordance with the laws of the State of Maryland.

5.2 This Agreement shall be terminated only by the filing of a Termination Statement in accordance with the applicable provisions of the Uniform Commercial Code. Until terminated, the security interest hereby created shall continue in full force and effect and shall secure and be applicable to advances now or hereafter made by Secured Party to Debtor whether or not Debtor is indebted to Secured Party immediately prior to the time of such advance.

VI. Business Name, Residence and Location of the Collateral.
Debtor warrants, covenants and agrees as follows:

6.1 Debtor's principal place of business is located in the County of Howard, State of Maryland. The mailing address is 4501 Silver Spring Lane, Columbia, Maryland, 21045.

6.2 If Debtor is an individual or sole proprietor, Debtor's residence is located in the County of Howard, State of Maryland. The mailing address is 2619 Apple Lane, Ellicott City, Maryland 21044.

6.3 The Collateral will be kept at the address of Debtor shown in Paragraph 6.1 and at such other address as is indicated: The County Inn, 1019 Shady Lane, Columbia Maryland, 21044.

IN WITNESS WHEREOF, the undersigned have signed the Agreement on the __24__ day of __April__,1993.

Thomas G. Leary
Debtor

Joseph Banks; Last
Secured Party
by _*National Bank*_
*Vice-President*

Example 1. Assume that Tom Leary borrows $10,000 from Last National Bank, signing a security agreement to secure repayment. Last National has extended immediately available credit and has given value.

Example 2. Assume that Last National Bank contracts with Tom Leary to lend him $10,000. Tom grants a security interest to Last National to secure repayment. Last National has given value because it entered into a binding commitment to extend credit.

Example 3. Assume that Tom Leary requests a loan from Last National Bank and signs a security agreement. Last National has not given value because it has not entered into a binding commitment. Value is given when it actually extends credit. The time at which value is given determines the time at which the security interest attaches and can be very important in determining the secured party's priority against third parties.

Example 4. Assume that Tom Leary borrows $10,000 from Last National on January 1, 1992. On February 15, 1993, Tom grants a security interest to Last National to secure repayment of this $10,000. Last National has given value as security for an antecedent debt.

Debtor's Rights in the Collateral

The debtor must have rights in the collateral before a security interest attaches. If the debtor owns the collateral, it has rights in the collateral. In a contract for the sale of goods, the buyer acquires rights in the goods when the goods are identified to the contract for sale, as outlined in UCC Article 2 (see Chapter 20). For example, assume that Tom Leary borrows $5,000 from Last National Bank to purchase a freezer, giving Last National a security interest. The freezer is in possession of the appliance store. The security interest attaches when the freezer is identified by the appliance store as belonging to Tom [UCC § 2–501].

If a security agreement has been made, the secured party gives value, and the debtor has rights in the collateral, a valid Article 9 security interest, enforceable against the debtor, has been created. If these steps have not been taken, the security interest is not even enforceable against the debtor.

PERFECTION

The security agreement creates the security interest between the debtor and the secured party. However, to obtain priority over third parties, the secured party must **perfect** the security interest. A perfected security interest may still be subordinate to some claims; however, in general, after perfection the secured party is protected against creditors and transferees of the debtor and, in particular, against the trustee of the debtor in bankruptcy proceedings.

There are basically three methods by which a security interest can be perfected: (1) by automatic perfection, (2) by possession, and (3) by filing. The choice of method depends on the classification of collateral. In general, the purpose of each method of perfection is to provide a means for third-party notice of the secured party's claim. The most common method of perfection is by filing a financing statement. In fact, such a filing is required to perfect all security interests except those specifically excluded [UCC § 9–302].

Automatic Perfection

Certain security interests are perfected automatically on attachment, without filing or taking possession of the collateral [UCC § 9–302]. This includes three major types of security interests: (1) a purchase money security interest in consumer goods, (2) assignment of accounts, and (3) temporary automatic perfection in instruments, negotiable documents, and proceeds.

Purchase Money Security Interest in Consumer Goods

The most significant type of security interest that is perfected automatically is the **purchase money security interest (PMSI)** in consumer goods [UCC § 9–302(d)]. The exclusion applies only where the security interest is a PMSI. A PMSI is created either when a seller–secured party sells collateral to the debtor and retains a security interest to secure payment or when a debtor-buyer borrows money from a third party to finance the purchase of the collateral [UCC § 9–107]. For example, assume that Tom Leary buys a television set for his family from Sam Seller on credit and grants Sam a security interest in the television set to secure payment. This is a PMSI because the security interest was retained by the seller to secure payment of the purchase price. Alternatively, assume that Tom borrows the money to purchase the television set from the Last National Bank and pays Sam. If Tom grants Last National a security interest in the collateral, a PMSI is created. This is true only if Tom uses the money borrowed to finance the purchase. While in reality it is often difficult to prove how Tom actually uses the money, if he takes the money borrowed from Last National and pays off insistent creditors, buying the television set with other funds, Last National does not have a PMSI. Because the secured party in the above examples has a PMSI in consumer goods, the security interest is automatically perfected.

UCC § 9–107. Definitions: ''Purchase Money Security Interest''

A security interest is a ''purchase money security interest'' to the extent that it is

(a) taken or retained by the seller of the collateral to secure all or part of its price; or

(b) taken by a person who by making advances or incurring an obligation gives value to enable the debtor to acquire rights in or the use of the collateral if such value is in fact so used.

However, this exclusion is limited to consumer goods. Automatic perfection of consumer goods eliminates the administrative burden of filing with little danger to third persons. In the case of consumer goods, there is little need for filing to notify third parties of the interest, to some extent, because of the perception that consumer goods are of modest value and likely to decline in value rapidly. The security interest Tom Leary has offered Last National in our opening scenario in the equipment he is purchasing is not automatically perfected. Although it is a PMSI, it is not a PMSI in consumer goods.

Moreover, security interests, even PMSIs, in motor vehicles are not automatically perfected [UCC § 9–302(1)(d)]. Therefore, a filing may be required to perfect a security interest in motor vehicles, even if the motor vehicle is a consumer good. On the other hand, a filing is not required in any state that uses certificates of title as evidence of motor vehicle ownership [UCC § 9–302(3)(b)]. This excludes from the filing requirements the situation where Charlie Consumer purchases a motor vehicle from Car Dealer, Inc. on credit, granting a security interest in the car in a title state. Car Dealer, Inc.'s security interest would be perfected by compliance with the certificate of title statute. This might require the secured party to note its interest on the title or to take possession of the title. However, if Car Dealer, Inc. financed purchase of the car as inventory, granting Merchants National Bank a security interest in the inventory, a filing is required because a security interest in inventory is not exempt from the filing requirement [UCC § 9–302(3)(b)].

Assignment of Accounts

An assignment of accounts that is not an assignment of a significant part of the assignor's accounts is automatically perfected [UCC § 9–302(1)(e)]. This perfects isolated, or casual, assignments where no one would contemplate a filing.

The major difficulty in applying this provision is in determining what is a ''significant'' part of the outstanding accounts of the assignor. Courts have generally employed one of two tests to make this determination. One approach has been to question the ''casualness'' of the assignment. Casual or isolated assignments are automatically perfected. Routine assignments, or assignments to a professional lender, are not automatically perfected and a filing is required. A number of courts instead measure the significance of the portion assigned mathematically, comparing the accounts assigned to the assignor's total accounts receivable. If the percentage assigned is large, it is a significant portion of the assignor's accounts and a filing is required. Which test does the court in the following case apply?

UCC § 9–302. When Filing Is Required to Perfect Security Interest

(1) A financing statement must be filed to perfect all security interests except the following:

(e) an assignment of accounts which does not alone or in conjunction with other assignments to the same assignee transfer a significant part of the outstanding accounts of the assignor.

IN RE TRI–COUNTY MATERIALS, INC.
114 B.R. 160 (C.D. Ill. 1990)

The debtor, Tri-County Materials, Inc., operated a sand and gravel pit. Tri-County entered into an agreement to supply Ladd Construction Co. with 100,000 tons of sand and gravel at $2.50 per ton. In order to complete its contractual obligation, it leased equipment from KMB, Inc. To secure its obligation under the lease agreement, Tri-County assigned part of its account with Ladd to KMB. KMB did not file a financing statement. At the time Tri-County declared bankruptcy, Ladd owed Tri-County $43,413.71, and Tri-County owed KMB $30,484. The question discussed by the court is whether KMB had a perfected security interest in the account.

MIHM, District Judge

Although the Code does not define "significant part," case law has developed two tests.

The first test is referred to as the percentage test. This test focuses on the size of the assignment in relation to the size of outstanding accounts.

The second test is the "casual or isolated" test. This test is suggested by the language of Comment 5 to UCC § 9–302 which states that:

The purpose of the subsection (e) (1) exemption is to save from ex post facto invalidation casual or isolated assignments; some accounts receivable statutes have been so broadly drafted that all assignments, whatever their character or purpose, fall within their filing provisions. Under such statute many assignments which no one would think of filing may be subject to invalidation. The subsection (1) (e) exemptions go to that type of assignment. Any person who regularly takes assignments of any debtor's accounts should file.

The totality of circumstances surrounding the transaction determines whether an assignment was casual or isolated. If the transaction was not part of a regular course of commercial financing then under this test filing is not required. The rationale appears to be the reasonableness of requiring a secured creditor to file if assignment of debtor's accounts is a regular part of business and the corresponding unreasonableness of a filing requirement for casual or isolated transactions.

There is no authoritative determination of whether both tests must be met in order to claim the exemption or whether either by itself is sufficient. The statutory language specifically requires that the assignment be an insignificant part of the outstanding account. Thus, at the very least, this test must be met in every instance. A showing of a casual or isolated assignment of a significant part of outstanding accounts would not be entitled to the exemption given this clear statutory requirement. On the other hand, given the comments to the UCC regarding the purpose of this exemption, in a case involving the transfer of an insignificant part of outstanding accounts to a creditor whose regular business is financing, such accounts should not fall within this exemption. Thus it is a logical result of the language and purpose of this section to require that both tests be met.

Tri-County had 10 accounts at the time of the Chapter 11 filing, of which the largest by far was the Ladd contract for $250,000. It is clear that the assignment was not of the entire Ladd account but only of that portion of the account necessary to cover the balance due to KMB. At the time the parties entered into the Agreement, the total rental amount was estimated at $30,000; the actual figure turned out to be $30,484. The ratio of the amount assigned to the total account, even assuming that the Ladd contract was the only account, is approximately 12 percent.

Although there is no bright line marking the division between significant and insignificant, the 12 percent figure is surely on the "insignificant" side. Thus, the first test has been satisfied.

KMB was not in the business of accepting contract assignments, nor had either party to the assignment engaged in such a transaction at other times. The bankruptcy court found that despite the "isolated" nature of this assignment, it was "a classic secured transaction," and thus failed to fall within the "casual and isolated" exception to the filing requirement.

This Court agrees with that assessment. This is not the type of ''casual'' transaction in which reasonable parties would fail to see the importance of filing. Rather, it was evidenced by a formal, written agreement between two corporations; notice of the agreement was sent to Ladd, and other conduct engaged in by KMB indicates the degree of formality attached to it. This is the type of transaction for which the UCC requires filing in order to perfect.

Case Questions

1. What is the rationale for exempting assignments of insignificant parts of accounts from the filing requirement?

2. Explain the relationship between PMSIs in consumer goods and assignments of accounts.

3. The court finds that both tests should be met in order for the filing exemption to apply. Do you agree? Explain.

Temporary Automatic Perfection

A security interest in instruments or negotiable documents is automatically perfected for a period of 21 days from the time of attachment if it arises for new value under a written security agreement [UCC § 9–302(1)(b) and § 9–304(4)]. This allows the debtor to keep the collateral for any reason for short periods of time where commercially practicable.

Similarly, certain security interests remain perfected for a period of 21 days where the secured party allows the debtor to have possession of the collateral for certain specified reasons, including loading, storing, shipping, manufacturing, processing, and ultimate sale or exchange [UCC § 9–304(5) and § 9–304(4)(a)]. This continuous perfection applies to security interests in instruments, negotiable documents, and goods held by a bailee who has not issued a negotiable document. The 21-day period runs from the date the secured party turns over the collateral to the debtor. For example, a contract for sale might be structured so that a bank issues a letter of credit and receives a bill of lading from the seller in return for honoring drafts drawn on the letter of credit. The bank is given a perfected security interest in the document and the goods to secure payment of the sale price by the buyer. If the bank allows the buyer to have possession of the bill of lading to get possession of the goods from the carrier for ultimate resale, the security interest remains perfected for 21 days from the time the debtor acquires possession.

Last, security interests in proceeds are automatically perfected [UCC § 9–306(3)]. The security interest remains continuously perfected in proceeds where the security interest in the original collateral was perfected, as long as the proceeds are collateral in which a security interest could be perfected by filing in the same place where the original filing was made. For example, assume that a debtor grants a security interest to a secured party in a piece of machinery. The secured party properly perfects the security interest by filing. If the debtor trades the machine for a replacement, a security interest in the new machine continues to be perfected. By contrast, where the proceeds are a different type of collateral so that the original filing would either be an ineffective means of perfection or made in an improper place, the security interest continues to be perfected in the proceeds for a period of beyond 10 days. To continue perfection of the interest in proceeds beyond 10 days, the secured party must perfect the interest before the expiration of the 10-day period.

Perfection by Possession

No filing is necessary to perfect a security interest in certain types of collateral in the possession of the secured party [UCC § 9–305 and § 9–302(1)(a)]. Possession by the secured party achieves the goals of perfection by notifying third parties of the secured party's interest in the collateral. Possession is the required method of perfection of a security interest in money or instruments [UCC § 9–304(1)]. In addition, it perfects security interests in goods, negotiable documents, or chattel paper. By contrast, accounts and general intangibles cannot be perfected by possession.

The concept of possession, actual or constructive, has been an elusive concept throughout history. It is not defined in the Code. While it is easy to envision how a secured party might possess a watch, for example, it is more difficult to determine how a secured party might possess inventory or goods held by a bailee. A secured party might possess a debtor's inventory by placing the inventory in a field warehouse and obtaining possession of the warehouse receipt. Similarly, one might possess goods held by a bailee by having a document issued in the name of the secured party or by notifying the bailee of the secured party's interest.

In general, the security interest is perfected from the time possession is obtained and continues while possession is retained. If collateral, other than goods covered by a negotiable document, is held by a bailee, the security interest is perfected from the time the bailee receives notification of the secured party's interest [UCC § 9–305].

Perfection by Filing

The third method of perfecting a security interest is by filing. Filing is effective to perfect a security interest in all collateral except for money and instruments. In addition, filing is the only method of perfecting a security interest in accounts and general intangibles. Figure 30–2 summarizes and outlines the proper methods of perfection for each class of collateral.

What to File

In order to perfect a security interest by filing, the secured party must file a **financing statement,** which serves as notice to third parties of the security interest. A short financing statement is all that is required to be filed. Figure 30–3 is an example of a financing statement. The security agreement can be substituted for the financing statement if it contains the required information and is signed by the debtor [UCC § 9–408(1)]. A financing statement must [UCC § 9–402]:

- Give the names of the debtor and the secured party.
- Be signed by the debtor.
- Give an address of the secured party.
- Give a mailing address of the debtor.
- Describe the collateral.

Sufficiency of the Financing Statement　If the financing statement meets these requirements, it perfects the security interest. In addition, if the financing statement "substantially complies" with the requirements and is "not seriously misleading," it is effective to perfect the security interest, even if it contains errors or omissions [UCC § 9–402(8)]. In determining whether a financing statement substantially complies, the purpose meant to be served by the financing statement must be considered. The financing statement is intended to act as notice to third parties of the *existence* of the security interest, not of the *details* of the security agreement. An interested third party is expected to contact the secured party to ascertain any additional information needed. This can best be illustrated by examining some common errors.

Figure 30–2　Perfection of the Security Interest

Class of Collateral	How to Perfect
Accounts, general intangibles	Only by filing
Goods	Actual possession or by filing
PMSI in consumer goods	Actual possession, automatic perfection (except for motor vehicles), or filing
Money, instruments	Only by actual possession, except that a security interest is automatically perfected for 21 days to the extent that it arises for new value given under a written security agreement
Negotiable documents and chattel paper	Actual possession or by filing, except that a security interest in negotiable documents is automatically perfected for 21 days to the extent that it arises for new value under a written security agreement
Non-negotiable document	Filing as to goods, or bailee issuing document in name of secured party (possession of secured party), or secured party notifying bailee of security interest

Figure 30–3   Financing Statement

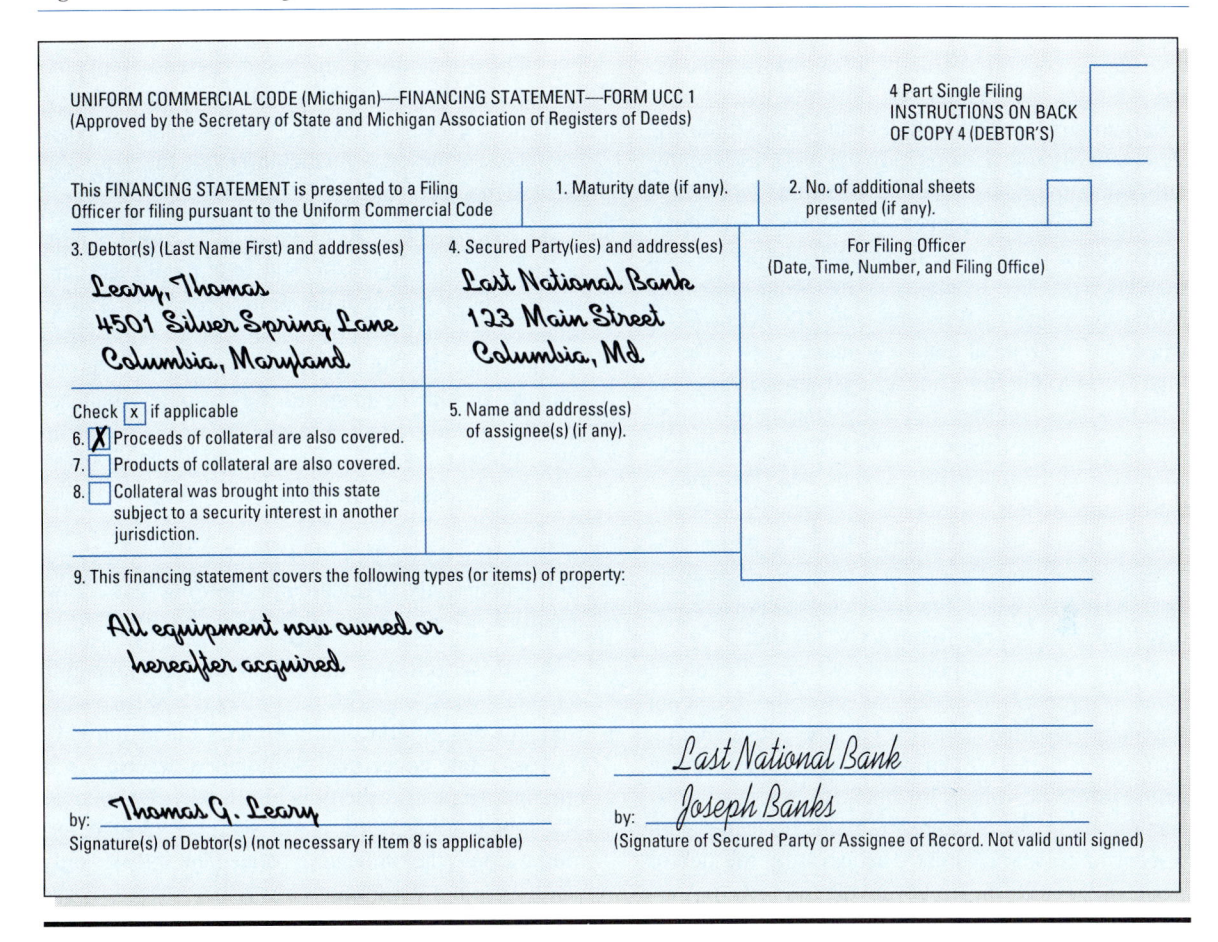

UNIFORM COMMERCIAL CODE (Michigan)—FINANCING STATEMENT—FORM UCC 1
(Approved by the Secretary of State and Michigan Association of Registers of Deeds)

4 Part Single Filing
INSTRUCTIONS ON BACK
OF COPY 4 (DEBTOR'S)

This FINANCING STATEMENT is presented to a Filing
Officer for filing pursuant to the Uniform Commercial Code

1. Maturity date (if any).

2. No. of additional sheets
presented (if any).

3. Debtor(s) (Last Name First) and address(es)

Leary, Thomas
4501 Silver Spring Lane
Columbia, Maryland

4. Secured Party(ies) and address(es)

Last National Bank
123 Main Street
Columbia, Md

For Filing Officer
(Date, Time, Number, and Filing Office)

Check [x] if applicable
6. [X] Proceeds of collateral are also covered.
7. [ ] Products of collateral are also covered.
8. [ ] Collateral was brought into this state
subject to a security interest in another
jurisdiction.

5. Name and address(es)
of assignee(s) (if any).

9. This financing statement covers the following types (or items) of property:

All equipment now owned or
hereafter acquired

Last National Bank

by: *Thomas G. Leary*

by: *Joseph Banks*

Signature(s) of Debtor(s) (not necessary if Item 8 is applicable)

(Signature of Secured Party or Assignee of Record. Not valid until signed)

UCC § 9–402. Formal Requisites of Financing Statement

(8) A financing statement *substantially* complying with the requirements of this section is effective even though it contains minor errors which are not seriously misleading. [Emphasis added.]

1. Names of the debtor and the secured party. The financing statement contains both the names of the debtor and the secured party [UCC § 9–402]. What if an error exists with respect to the name of the debtor? Because it is the debtor's name on the financing statement that is used by the filing officer to index the filing, if the debtor's name is incorrect, a third-party credit searcher might be unable to locate the filing. Therefore, errors in the debtor's name are closely examined. In general, if a **reason-ably diligent credit searcher** would most likely discover the financing statement searching under the debtor's true name, then the filing is not seriously misleading and will, most likely, be found to be effective despite the error.

Errors in this regard generally arise either where the debtor's name is misspelled or incomplete or where the debtor's name is listed by a trade name when the debtor is doing business as a sole proprietorship. The ''reasonable diligent credit searcher'' test is used to determine the validity of the financing statement. For example, financing statements listing the name of the debtor as ''Gustavson'' when the true name was ''Gustafson,'' listing the name of the debtor as ''Excell Department Stores'' when the true name was ''Excel Stores, Inc.,'' and listing the name of the debtor as ''Nara Dist., Inc.,'' when the true name was ''Nara Non Food Distributing, Inc.,'' were found to be valid because a reasonably diligent credit searcher should be able to find these statements. Omission of ''Co.'' or ''Inc.'' after an otherwise proper debtor name is not seriously misleading. Where the debtor is operating as a sole proprietorship under a trade name, the financing statement should list the individual debtor's name rather than the trade name. To determine whether or not an error in this respect is seriously misleading, again courts apply the reasonably diligent credit searcher test. For example, a financing statement listing the name of the debtor as ''Platt Fur Co.'' when the individual debtor's name was ''Henry Platt'' was found to be not seriously misleading and effective. By contrast, financing statements listing the name of the debtor as ''West Coast Avionics'' where the individual debtor's name was ''Thomas,'' listing the debtor's name as ''Carolyn's Fashion Shop'' where the individual debtor's name was ''Hill,'' and listing the debtor's name as ''Landman Dry Cleaners'' where the individual debtor's name was ''Leichter'' were found to be invalid.

An interesting question arises where the debtor's name is properly listed at the time the financing statement is filed but the debtor subsequently changes its name. Even where the name change would render the financing statement seriously misleading, the security interest remains perfected with respect to collateral already acquired by the debtor [UCC § 9–402(7)]. However, the filing is not effective with respect to collateral acquired by the debtor more than four months after the name change, unless a new financing statement is filed.

The previous discussion focused on errors in the debtor's name. The financing statement must also include the secured party's name. However, because the financing statement is not indexed by the name of the secured party, errors in this respect are generally not crucial.

2. Signature of the debtor. The debtor must sign the financing statement. The signature requirement protects the debtor against creditor overreaching. The signature of the secured party is not required. Any symbol made with present intent to authenticate is a signature. For example, a typed corporate name on a financing statement is a sufficient signature.

3. Addresses. The financing statement must contain the addresses of both the debtor and the secured party. Whether the omission of the required address or mistakes in the address destroy the effectiveness of the financing statement depends on whether or not the mistakes are seriously misleading. The deciding factor is whether or not a reasonably diligent credit searcher could find the party from the address given. Financing statements listing the address as ''Ellworth St.'' instead of ''Ellsworth St.,'' listing only a P.O. Box number in a given city, and listing only ''Coca-Cola Bottling Co., East Hartford, Conn.'' were all found to be effective.

4. Description of the collateral. The financing statement must describe the collateral. Where relevant, the description should include a description of the real estate concerned. Although a description is required, great specificity is not. Under the doctrine of ''notice filing,'' the credit searcher must determine from the financing statement itself only whether or not certain items *may* be covered by the security interest so that the credit searcher might make further inquiry. Recall that a description is sufficient if ''it reasonably identifies what is described'' [UCC § 9–110]. Descriptions such as ''all inventory of debtor'' and ''all accounts receivable'' are generally sufficient.

Read the following case and determine (1) whether the description is sufficient and (2) whether the errors made the description ''seriously misleading.''

IN RE ESQUIRE PRODUCE CO., INC.
5 U.C.C. Rep. Serv. 257 (E.D. N.Y. 1968).

In August of 1966, the debtor, Esquire Produce Co., Inc., bought a 1966 Ford Van Econoline, serial #E16AH889201, under a retail installment contract for $2,870.87, including finance charges. It made a down payment of $600 and agreed to pay the balance in monthly installments. A security interest was granted to Ford Motor Credit Corp. to secure repayment. A financing statement was filed in September that described the collateral as: "1966 Ford Serial #E16AH859201." On October 25, the debtor declared bankruptcy; on October 26, Ford Credit filed a corrected financing statement with the correct serial number.

PRICE, Referee in Bankruptcy

The trustee contends that the description of the vehicle set forth in the UCC financing statements filed by Ford on September 6, 1966, does not comply with Section 9–110. He points out that the vehicle is described in the installment contract as a 1966 Ford Van Econoline 6 cylinder serial #E16AH889201 while in the financing statement it is merely described as a "1966 Ford serial number #E16AH859201." It is his position that this description is deficient in two respects, first, that it does not adequately describe the vehicle and second that the serial number is incorrect.

It is Ford's contention that the description adequately identifies the vehicle in accordance with Section 9–110 and that the error in the serial number is a minor, typographical mistake which is not seriously misleading.

So far as the trustee's first contention, that the description of the vehicle was not sufficient is concerned, I find that the description of the vehicle as a "1966 Ford" is sufficient compliance with Section 9–110. It was the purpose of the Uniform Commercial Code to liberalize the filing requirements in secured transactions by substituting a system of notice filing for that which required the filing of the security instrument itself. It was to give notice that a chattel might be covered by a security agreement which would require further investigation to discover the actual situation.

I come now to the trustee's second contention that the error in the serial number was not immaterial but was "serious and prejudicial."

In my opinion the error in the serial number in the case at bar was a "minor error which was not seriously misleading." It was obviously a typographical error since it substituted a "5" for an "8" in the 11 digit number. It should not be difficult to the trustee to envision such a harmless error since page 2 of the memorandum submitted by him refers to the number in the UCC financing statement as "E116AH859201" instead of the correct number which it bears, namely "E16AH859201." He has inadvertently added an extra "1" to the number, clearly, not a fatal error.

I find that the UCC financing statement filed by Ford on September 6, 1966, complied with the applicable section of the New York State Uniform Commercial Code.

Case Questions
1. Explain the relationship between adoption of notice filing and the holding in this case.
2. If this error is not seriously misleading, can you imagine an error in describing collateral that would be seriously misleading?

Where to File

Where should the secured party file the financing statement? To encourage uniform adoption of the Code and as a compromise between local interest groups and those favoring central filing, the UCC offered each state three alternatives, as summarized in Figure 30–4. When individual states adopted Article 9, each choose one of the three alternatives. Under the first alternative, all filings are made in the secretary of state's office, except those that are related to real estate. Real estate–related filings are made locally, generally in the office of the County Recorder of Deeds in the county where the property is located. This alternative has been chosen by only four states.

Under the second alternative, the same provision is made with respect to real estate–related filings. In addition, local filings are required for farm-related collateral and consumer goods. Such filings are to be made either in the county of the debtor's residence or, if the debtor is not a resident of the state, in the county where the goods are kept. In the case of all other collateral, the filing is to be made centrally in the office of the secretary of state.

Under the third alternative, a variety of filings is required, depending on the collateral involved. Again, where the collateral is real estate related, farm related, or consumer goods, a local filing as in Alternatives 1 and 2 is required. However, under this alternative, in all other instances, a dual filing is

Figure 30–4   Where to File

	Type of Collateral	Where to File
First Alternative	Related to real estate All other cases	Registry of Deeds Secretary of state
Second Alternative	Farm collateral, consumer goods, and crops Related to real estate All other cases	County recorder (county of residence or county where goods kept) Registry of Deeds Secretary of state
Third Alternative	Farm collateral, consumer goods, and crops Related to real estate All other cases	County Recorder (county of residence or county where goods kept) Registry of Deeds Secretary of state and Local filing either in county in which debtor has place of business if only one or county in which debtor resides if debtor has no place of business.

required. The secured party must file in the secretary of state's office as well as locally. If the debtor has a place of business in only one county of the state, the local filing is required, generally in the County Recorder's office in such county. If the debtor has no place of business in the state but resides in the state, then the local filing should be made in the county in which the debtor resides [UCC § 9–401(1)].

A few examples will illustrate.

Example 1. A secured party seeks to perfect a security interest in equipment used in farming operations. Under Alternative 1, the financing statement should be filed in the secretary of state's office. Under Alternatives 2 and 3, a local filing is required. This filing should be made either in the county of the debtor's residence or, if the debtor is not a resident of the state, in the county where the goods are kept.

Example 2. A secured party seeks to perfect a security interest in a piano used for personal use. The piano is classified as consumer goods. Under Alternative 1, the filing should be made in the secretary of state's office. Under Alternatives 2 and 3, the filing should be made locally as outlined in Example 1.

Example 3. A secured party seeks to perfect a security interest in a piano used to give piano lessons. The piano is classified as equipment. Under Alternatives 1 and 2, the filing should be made in the secretary of state's office. Under Alternative 3, the filing should be made both in the secretary of state's office and locally. If the debtor has a place of business in only one

county in the state, the filing should be made in that county. If the debtor has no place of business in the state but resides in the state, the filing should be made in the county in which the debtor resides. If the debtor either has no place of business or has a place of business in more than one county and does not reside in the county, a local filing is not required.

UCC § 9–401. Place of Filing

(2) A filing which is made in good faith in an improper place or not in all of the places required . . . is nevertheless effective with regard to any collateral as to which the filing complies . . . and is also effective with regard to collateral covered by the financing statement against any person who has knowledge of the contents of such financing statement.

Effect of Improper Filing

If a secured party in good faith makes a filing in the wrong place, the financing statement is effective with regard to any collateral for which the filing did comply [UCC § 9–401(2)]. For example, if the secured party files a financing statement covering equipment and consumer goods where correct to perfect an interest in equipment but not consumer goods, the financing statement perfects the interest in equipment. In addition, the improperly filed financing statement is effective against any person with knowledge of the contents of the financing statement [UCC § 9–401(2)].

Mechanics of Filing

When Is the Financing Statement Effective? Presentation of the financing statement and payment of the filing fee or acceptance of the statement by the filing officer equals filing [UCC § 9–403(1)]. Even if the filing officer fails to properly index and file the financing statement, the secured party's interest is perfected.

Duration of Financing Statement The financing statement is effective for a period of five years from the date of the filing [UCC § 9–403(2)]. If a continuation statement is not filed before the expiration of the five-year period, the security interest becomes unperfected and is deemed to have been unperfected against one who became a purchaser or lien creditor before the lapse.

A secured party wishing to file a continuation statement may do so within six months of expiration of the five-year period. The continuation statement must be signed by the secured party, identify the original statement by file number, and state that the original statement is still effective.

Termination Statement When the debtor pays the debt, a termination statement can be filed to indicate the termination of the security interest. The secured party must, upon written demand by the creditor, send to the debtor a termination statement indicating that the secured party no longer claims a security interest in the collateral and identifying the financing statement by file number [UCC § 9–404(1)]. The secured party must send the termination statement within 10 days of demand. The debtor can then file the termination statement.

Additional protection is offered in the case of consumer goods. No demand is required by the debtor. The secured party must file a termination statement within one month of payment. If the secured party fails to comply, the debtor can recover $100 plus damages for actual loss [UCC § 9–404(1)].

Request for Statement of Account

The debtor can get information about the security interest by sending a statement of account to the secured party for verification [UCC § 9–208]. Typically, the debtor intends to furnish this information to third parties. The secured party must respond to the request within two weeks. If the secured party fails to respond, the debtor can recover for any loss caused by the secured party's failure to respond. In addition, if the debtor included, in good faith, a statement of the outstanding debt or a list of the collateral, the secured party's interest is limited to that shown in the statement against any person who has been misled by the failure to comply.

END–OF–CHAPTER QUESTIONS

1. What is notice filing? Give examples of instances where the Code sections adopt this concept.

2. What are the underlying policies of UCC Article 9? List some provisions that further those policies.

3. Analyze the following statement: ''In general, the purpose of each method of perfection is to provide a means for third-party notice of the secured party's claim.'' Why might a secured party choose one method of permissible perfection over another?

4. What is the effect of a financing statement signed by the secured party instead of the debtor? See UCC § 9–402(2).

5. The whole system of perfection by public filing is based on the concept of public notice to third parties of the security interest. Is any protection offered in the Code to a third party with notice of a possible outstanding security interest who questions the debtor and is told that the debt is paid and the security interest terminated? See UCC § 9–208.

6. Textron Financial Corp. leases business equipment to Village Import Enterprises. At the end of the lease term, Village Import can buy the equipment for $1. Is this a true lease or a security interest? Textron argues that it cannot be a security interest without words in the lease creating a security interest. Are they correct? Explain. See *In re Village Import Enterprises*, 126 B.R. 307 (E.D. Tenn. 1991).

7. John and Clara Lockovich purchased a 22-foot motor boat for $32,500 to be used primarily for personal purposes, granting the seller a security interest in the boat. How should this collateral be classified?

Is the value relevant? Explain. How can the secured party perfect its security interest? See *In re Lockovich*, 940 F.2d 916 (3d Cir. 1991).

8. Symons bought a Sonar Drum set with cymbals to play in a dance band, granting a security interest to the seller, Grinnell Brothers. At the time of purchase, Symons was employed as an insurance salesman. How should the drum set be classified? What should Grinnell Brothers do to perfect its interest? See *In re Symons*, 5 U.C.C. Rep. Serv. 262 (E.D. Mich. 1967).

9. Harry Swiney loaned his cousin $17,000 to buy a Cadillac DeVille, taking a security interest in the car. Harry neither filed a financing statement nor noted his interest on the vehicle's certificate of title. Does Harry have a perfected security interest? Explain. Is your answer affected by the fact that Harry is in possession of the car? See *U.S. v. One 1987 Cadillac DeVille*, 774 F.Supp. 221 (D. Del. 1991).

10. The debtor granted the secured party a security interest in four accounts receivable totaling $173,144. This was the only assignment of this type between the parties. The secured party was not in the business of accepting assignments. The accounts assigned were 14 percent of the debtor's overall accounts but 25 percent of the collectible accounts. Does the secured party have to file a financing statement to perfect its security interest? See *In re Crabtree Construction, Inc.*, 87 B.R. 212 (S.D. Fla. 1988).

Chapter 31

Enforcing the Security Interest: Priority and Default

■

CRITICAL THINKING INQUIRIES

As you read this chapter, you should be able to address the following:

- Explain the relationship between notice filing and the first in time, first in right rule.
- Analyze the following statement: "The special treatment granted PMSIs is designed to make it easier for debtors to acquire additional purchases." Give examples of this special treatment.
- Evaluate the following statement: "The secured party's rights against the debtor in the case of debtor default are strengthened by perfection."
- Explain the relationship between an action on the underlying debt, strict foreclosure, and repossession and sale of the collateral.
- Analyze the following statement: "The secured party must act commercially reasonably in all aspects of the repossession and resale of collateral."

MANAGERIAL PERSPECTIVE

Joe Banks is a commercial loan officer at the Last National Bank. Last National has loaned Tom Leary $500,000 to finance the opening of a new bookstore café. Tom granted Last National a security interest in all inventory "now owned or hereafter acquired" to secure the loan and promised to make monthly payments of $5,000.

Tom approached Joe last month for additional inventory financing. Joe refused. Tom has missed the last two monthly payments. Joe has discovered that Tom obtained financing from the supplier of the inventory, granting the seller a security interest in the inventory bought. Joe has also discovered that Tom failed to pay his federal income taxes due last month. Joe is concerned that Tom is on the verge of bankruptcy.

- What can Last National do to recover the debt owed? Should it proceed against the collateral?
- If Last National attempts to enforce its security interest, will it have priority over the other inventory financier?
- If the IRS attempts to collect the taxes due against the inventory, will Last National have priority?
- What affect will Tom's bankruptcy have on Last National's ability to collect the loan?

This chapter focuses on enforcement of the security interest against competing third parties and against the debtor. What are the rights and liabilities of the secured party and the debtor? Understanding these rights is understanding the very essence of a secured transaction. Lenders take security interests precisely because of the protections offered against the debtor and third parties.

PRIORITIES

The secured lender **perfects** its security interest to protect itself against third parties, including unsecured creditors, judgment lien creditors, the debtor's trustee in bankruptcy, purchasers of the collateral, other secured parties, and statutory lien creditors. It is important to realize that in a priorities dispute, the creditor with priority is able to recover its debt out of the collateral with typically nothing left for the subordinate party.

Article 9 priority rules are designed to protect the reliance of diligent third parties, to promote the free flow of commerce by giving protection to bona fide purchasers, and to protect purchase money secured parties whenever possible. Further, the rules promote commercial fairness and commercial certainty because parties can easily determine their priority status before entering into a transaction.

Rights of an Unperfected Secured Party

A security interest does not need to be perfected to be enforceable against the debtor. In addition, the secured creditor, even an unperfected secured creditor, has *priority over* (1) general creditors of the debtor, (2) transferees of accounts and general intangibles with knowledge of the security interest, and (3) other unperfected secured parties whose security interest attached after the first security interest [UCC § 9–201]. For example, assume that Charles Creditor sells his shoe store to Dan Debtor, retaining a security interest in inventory. Charles does not perfect the security interest. If Sam, a supplier of shoes to Dan on credit, claims priority to the inventory because Charles's security interest is unperfected, Sam will lose. Sam is a general unsecured creditor whose interest is subordinate to Charles's secured creditor rights.

However, an unperfected security interest is *subordinate to* the rights of (1) persons entitled to priority over perfected secured parties; (2) certain

lien creditors; (3) certain nonordinary course buyers of goods, instruments, documents, or chattel paper; (4) certain transferees of accounts and general intangibles; and (5) perfected secured parties [UCC § 9–301].

Persons Entitled to Priority over Perfected Secured Parties

Anyone who has priority over a perfected security interest has priority over an unperfected security interest [UCC § 9–301(1)(a)]. This is logical because the process of perfection gives the secured party greater, not lesser, protection against third parties. The parties who have priority over perfected secured parties will be discussed below.

Lien Creditors

One who becomes a **lien creditor** before a security interest is perfected has priority over the security interest. An unsecured creditor typically becomes a lien creditor upon **levy,** when the sheriff seizes the property (collateral) pursuant to a judgment [UCC § 9–301(3)]. Most importantly, the debtor's trustee in the event of bankruptcy has the status of a lien creditor who acquired the lien on the date the bankruptcy petition was filed. The judgment lien creditor and the trustee in bankruptcy have priority over prior unperfected secured parties. For example, assume that Sheila, a secured party, takes a security interest in manufacturing equipment but fails to file a financing statement. A creditor of the debtor who levies on the machinery pursuant to a judgment has priority over Sheila, an unperfected secured party. Similarly, Sheila's interest is subordinate if the debtor files a petition in bankruptcy. As a lien creditor acquiring a lien on the date the bankruptcy petition is filed, the trustee has priority over prior unperfected secured parties such as Sheila.

As a general rule, the filing of a financing statement is effective to perfect a security interest only from the time it is filed. For example, a secured party's status, as perfected or unperfected, in a dispute with a lien creditor is determined by whether or not the security interest was perfected at the time the lien creditor acquired the lien. To illustrate, if, in the above situation, Sheila failed to perfect her security interest at the time of creation but filed a financing statement after the debtor's petition in bankruptcy was filed, Sheila would be considered unperfected in a priority dispute with the trustee and would be subordinate to the trustee's claims. The security interest was unperfected *at the time* the bankruptcy petition was filed because the financing statement was not yet filed.

However, there is an exception to this rule for purchase money secured parties [UCC § 9–301(2)]. A purchase money secured party is given a 10-day grace period (from the date the debtor acquires possession of the collateral) within which to file the financing statement. If the secured party files within the 10-day grace period, it can defeat creditors who acquired their lien in the gap between the creation of the security interest and its perfection. For example, assume that on December 19, Dan Dealer sells to Debbie Debtor a piece of equipment, receiving a purchase money security interest (PMSI) in return. The property is delivered to Debbie that day. On December 25, an unsecured creditor levies on the equipment pursuant to a judgment, creating a judgment lien. On December 28, Dan files a financing statement. Dan has priority over the lien creditor. Because the financing statement was filed within the 10-day grace period, the PMSI is perfected and treated as if it were perfected all along.

UCC § 9–301. Persons Who Take Priority Over Unperfected Security Interests

(2) If the secured party files with respect to a purchase money security interest before or within ten days after the debtor receives possession of the collateral, he takes priority over the rights of a . . . lien creditor which arise[s] between the time the security interest attaches and the time of filing.

Nonordinary Course Buyers

An unperfected security interest is subordinate to the interests of nonordinary course buyers who give value and receive delivery of the collateral without knowledge of the security interest [UCC § 9–301(1)(c)]. For example, assume that Sidney obtains a security interest in a piece of equipment but fails to file a financing statement. Assume further that the debtor sells the equipment to Tom. Tom defeats the unperfected security interest if he took possession of the equipment without knowledge of the security interest. By contrast, if Tom has knowledge of the security interest at the time he takes possession of the collateral, he will not have priority.

In addition, buyers of farm products in the ordinary course of business have priority over unperfected secured parties [UCC § 9–301(1)(c)]. By contrast, buyers *in bulk* of farm products would lose to the unperfected secured party.

Transferees of Accounts and General Intangibles

Purchasers of accounts and general intangibles have a similar priority [UCC § 9–301(1)(d)]. Again, the purchaser has priority to the extent that value is given without knowledge of the security interest and before the interest is perfected.

Perfected Secured Parties

A perfected secured party has priority over an unperfected secured party regardless of the order in which the security interests attach. For example, assume that First National Bank loans Tom Leary $10,000, taking in return a security interest in a piece of equipment without filing a financing statement. Subsequently, Last National, in our opening scenario, makes a loan to Tom, taking in return a security interest in the same piece of equipment. Last National files a financing statement, perfecting its security interest. Last National has priority even if it knew of First National's security interest and even though its security interest attached after First National's interest. Perfected security interests beat unperfected security interests. First National could have easily protected itself against subsequent secured parties by filing a financing statement.

Priority among Secured Creditors

Where there is a conflict over the same collateral between two secured creditors, the general rule is that the first to file or perfect the security interest has priority [UCC § 9–312(5)]. This is often termed the "first in time, first in right" rule. If two secured parties both perfect by filing, the first to file or perfect has priority. For example, assume that Dan borrows $10,000 from Ann, granting her a security interest in a piece of equipment and filing a financing statement on March 1. On March 2, Bill loans $20,000 to Dan, taking in return a security interest in the same collateral. Bill files a financing statement that day. Ann has priority because she filed and perfected first. Bill could have protected himself by conducting a filing search and discovering Ann's competing interest.

UCC § 9–312. Priorities Among Conflicting Security Interests in the Same Collateral

(5)(a) Conflicting security interests rank according to priority in time of filing or perfection.

UCC § 9–312. Priorities Among Conflicting Security Interests in the Same Collateral

(5)(a) . . . Priority dates from the time a filing is made covering the collateral or the time the security interest is first perfected, whichever is earlier, provided that there is no period thereafter when there is neither filing nor perfection.

Conflicting security interests are ranked by the time of perfection *or* filing, *whichever comes first* [UCC § 9–312(5)(a)]. For example, assume that Amy receives a security interest in equipment from Dan and files a financing statement on March 1 but doesn't loan any money at that time. On March 15th, Betty loans Dan $10,000, taking a security interest in the same equipment. She files a financing statement that same day. On March 17th, Amy loans Dan $10,000 under the terms of the prior agreement. Amy has priority because she filed the financing statement first, in spite of the fact that Betty's security interest was perfected first. Thus, even though Amy's security interest was not perfected until money was actually loaned (value given) on March 17th, priority dates from the time of filing or perfection, "whichever is earlier." Again, Betty could have protected herself by a simple filing search.

Perfection may occur in more than one way. As long as the security interest remains continuously perfected, the time of the initial perfection is determinative. For example, assume that Last National loans $10,000 to Tom Leary on June 1, receiving in return a security interest in a negotiable document under the terms of a written security agreement. On June 6, Tom grants a security interest in the same collateral to Lenders National, which promptly files a financing statement. On June 11, Last National files a financing statement. Last National has priority. Because a security interest in a negotiable document pursuant to a written security agreement is automatically perfected for 21 days, it was automatically perfected on June 1. Therefore, Last National perfected its security interest first. Because Last Na-

tional filed the financing statement before the expiration of the 21-day period, the security interest was continuously perfected and defeats subsequent security interests.

In order to have priority, the filing must perfect the security interest. For example, if a secured party files a financing statement in the wrong place, or only in one of two places necessary, the secured party's interest is subordinate to a secured party that properly perfects its security interest. This is true even if the first secured party later properly perfects.

Purchase Money Security Interests

Purchase money security interests (PMSIs) are given a type of superpriority status to, among other things, make it easier for debtors to acquire additional purchases. Without PMSI priority, a debtor whose original creditor refused to advance further funds would effectively be denied credit to make additional purchases. The PMSI exception applies to priority disputes between PMSIs and prior perfected security interests in the same collateral. Thus, the conflict arises only when the prior perfected security interest applies to after-acquired property. Under the general rule, the prior perfected secured party would have priority with respect to the after-acquired property because it perfected first. The exception for PMSIs gives the purchase money secured party a way to obtain priority over the prior perfected secured party's after-acquired property clause. Presumably, the purchase money secured party would not make the sale on credit unless priority was available. Two categories of PMSIs are created: (1) PMSIs in collateral other than inventory and (2) PMSIs in inventory.

UCC § 9–312. Priorities Among Conflicting Security Interests in the Same Collateral

(4) A purchase money security interest in collateral other than inventory has priority over a conflicting security interest in the same collateral . . . if the purchase money security interest is perfected at the time the debtor receives possession of the collateral or within ten days.

PMSIs in Noninventory Collateral   The PMSI in noninventory collateral has priority over a conflicting security interest in the same collateral as long as the PMSI is perfected at the time the debtor receives possession of the collateral or within 10 days [UCC

§ 9–312(4)]. For example, assume that on February 1, Tom, in our opening scenario, grants Last National a security interest in ''all equipment now owned or hereafter acquired.'' Last National advances $10,000 pursuant to this agreement and files a financing statement. On March 1, Tom acquires a new freezer, granting its supplier a PMSI. The supplier files a financing statement on March 9. The supplier's PMSI has priority over Last National's after-acquired property interest because the supplier's interest was perfected before expiration of the 10-day grace period.

The purchase money secured interest has priority as long as it is perfected within the 10-day period regardless of the method of perfection. For example, assume that Dan Debtor grants Al a non-PMSI in consumer goods now owned or hereafter acquired. Subsequently, Dan acquires a new television set, granting Ben a PMSI in the consumer good. Ben has priority over Al's interest. Because Ben's PMSI is automatically perfected when Dan receives possession of the good, the perfection requirement is satisfied.

Read the following case and determine who has priority.

GREENBUSH STATE BANK v. STEPHENS
463 N.W.2d 303 (Ct. of App. Minn. 1990).

In June 1984, David Stauffenecker granted Greenbush State Bank (bank) a security interest in all livestock and farm equipment ''now owned or hereafter acquired,'' including an Oliver tractor. The bank filed a financing statement on June 19, 1984. In the fall of 1986, Stauffenecker traded the Oliver tractor and $4,500 for a John Deere tractor. Stephens provided the money for the purchase, was permitted to use the tractor, and understood that he would own the tractor until Stauffenecker paid him back. Upon Stauffenecker's default, the bank attempted to repossess the tractor from Stephens. The question is one of priority between the interests of the bank and Stephens.

DAVIES, Judge

Generally, a security interest is perfected by filing a financing statement. Here, the trial court found that the bank filed its original financing statement, with its after-acquired property clause, on or about June 19, 1984. There was no postexchange period when the bank did not have a perfected interest in Stauffenecker's equipment. That equipment included the John Deere tractor as soon as it was acquired. Thus, the bank's interest therein was immediately perfected. Even so, a purchase money security interest could defeat the bank's security interest under the code had it been perfected. UCC 9–912(4). Thus, in order to retain the benefit of his purchase money security interest against the claim

of another secured party, Stephens had to perfect within 20 days. Stephens, however, did not file within 20 days. Having failed to file, he loses to the Bank's perfected interest.

Case Questions
1. Why didn't the bank automatically have priority under the first to file rule?
2. Why is Stephens being treated as a purchase money secured party? Does Stephens have a security interest?
3. Note: The state of Minnesota gives purchase money secured parties a 20-day grace period rather than the standard 10-day period. Why didn't Stephens file within this period?

PMSIs in Inventory A PMSI in inventory has priority over a conflicting security interest in the same inventory if the purchase money secured party jumps through four hoops:

1. The PMSI must be perfected at the time the debtor receives possession of the inventory.
2. The purchase money secured party must give notice in writing to prior secured par-

ties with interests in after-acquired inventory timely perfected by filing.

3. The notice must be received within five years before the debtor receives possession of the inventory.

4. The notice must state that the person giving the notice has or expects to acquire a PMSI in inventory of the debtor and must describe the inventory [UCC § 9–312(3)].

Thus, two basic requirements must be met for priority: the perfection requirement and the notification requirement. The perfection requirement is similar to the requirement applicable to noninventory collateral except that there is no 10-day grace period. The PMSI must be perfected at the time the debtor receives possession of the collateral. Thus, modifying the example examined above to apply to inventory, a different result is reached. On February 1, Tom Leary grants Last National a security interest in ''all inventory now owned or hereafter acquired.'' Last National makes a $10,000 advance pursuant to this agreement and files a financing statement. On March 1, Tom acquires additional inventory, granting Ben a PMSI. Ben files a financing statement on March 9. In this instance, Ben's PMSI is subordinate to Last National's interest because it was not perfected at the time Tom received the inventory.

In addition, the purchase money secured party must give written notice to prior secured parties who previously filed financing statements covering the same collateral. It is not necessary to give notice to prior secured parties who have not filed financing statements, even if the purchase money secured party has actual notice of their interest. Notice must be given before the debtor receives possession of the collateral and is effective for five years. The rationale for the additional notification requirement stems from the nature of the relationship between a debtor and an inventory third party. Typically, the secured party makes periodic advances against new inventory and periodic releases of old inventory as there is inventory turnover. The notification requirement attempts to protect the inventory financier from a fraudulent debtor who seeks advances from the secured party based on inventory acquired with funds obtained in return for a PMSI in such inventory. If the secured party receives notice, most likely

there will be no further advance; if the secured party does not receive notice, the security interest has priority over subsequent purchase money secured parties.

Priority between Perfected Secured Parties and Lien Creditors

As a general rule, perfected secured parties have priority over lien creditors acquiring their lien after perfection. This includes the trustee in bankruptcy who has the rights of a lien creditor acquiring a lien on the date of bankruptcy.

State Lien Creditors

Most states have created, either by statute or by common law, liens on goods for work performed or services rendered, such as artisan's liens and repairman's liens. Such lien creditors defeat the claims of prior perfected secured parties as long as the lien creditor is in possession of the collateral (and unless the state statute provides otherwise) [UCC § 9–310]. Such liens have priority because they arise from work that enhances or preserves the value of the collateral. For example, assume that Lemon Auto Credit finances Mary's purchase of a new car, taking in return a security interest in the car and perfecting its security interest. Subsequently, Mary takes the car to Ronnie's Repair Shop for repair. She fails to pay the repair bill and defaults on the car loan. Both Ronnie and Lemon claim an interest in the car to satisfy Mary's debts. Ronnie will win as long as he retains possession of the car even if Lemon did not consent to the repair work. Ronnie can enforce his lien against the car to pay for the repairs and other necessary costs.

UCC § 9–310. Priority of Certain Liens Arising by Operation of Law

When a person in the ordinary course of business furnishes services or materials with respect to goods subject to a security interest, a lien upon goods in the possession of such person given by statute or rule of law for such materials or services takes priority over a perfected security interest unless the lien is statutory and the statute expressly provides otherwise.

Federal Tax Lien Creditors

When one fails to pay federal taxes due, the Internal Revenue Service (IRS) can claim a lien on all taxpayer property, real and personal, now owned or hereafter acquired (in all property the taxpayer owns or ever hopes to own), arising at the moment of assessment. Priority disputes that arise when the IRS attempts to enforce this lien against property covered by a perfected security interest are governed by the Federal Tax Lien Act of 1966 (FTLA).

Although the tax lien arises on assessment, it is subordinate to security interests perfected before notice of the tax lien is filed. For example, assume that Last National Bank loans $10,000 to Tom Leary, taking in return a security interest in a piece of equipment. Last National files its financing statement on February 3. Tom fails to pay his taxes and a notice of tax lien is filed on April 1. Both Last National and the IRS claim an interest in the equipment. In this instance, Last National has priority in the equipment because the security interest was perfected before notice of the tax lien was filed.

In addition, the prior perfected secured party with an after-acquired property provision has priority with respect to property acquired by the debtor within 45 days of the filing of the tax lien. By contrast, the security interest is subordinate to the IRS for property acquired after this 45-day period. The secured party's knowledge of the tax lien filing is irrelevant. For example, assume that on February 1, Midtown Bank lends money to Bob Darling, taking a security interest in all equipment now owned or hereafter acquired, and files a financing statement. On March 1, the IRS files a notice of tax lien against Bob. On April 1, and again on May 1, Bob acquires two new pieces of equipment. Midtown has priority as to the equipment acquired on April 1 (within 45 days of the tax filing), but the IRS has priority as to the equipment acquired on May 1 (acquired after expiration of the 45-day period).

Further, the perfected secured party has priority over the IRS with respect to future advances made within 45 days of the tax lien filing if they were made without actual knowledge of the tax lien, pursuant to a security interest perfected before the tax lien filing. For example, assume that New City Bank loans Delia Ryan $10,000, taking a security interest in Delia's equipment, and files a financing statement. On March 1, the IRS files a tax lien against Delia. On April 1, New City loans Delia an additional $10,000 pursuant to the original security agreement. New City's security interest in the equipment has priority over the IRS with respect to the full $20,000 as long as it did not know of the tax lien at the time of the second loan.

Judicial Lien Creditors

Although the rights of a judicial lien creditor are superior to the rights of an unperfected secured party, they are subordinate to the rights of a prior perfected secured party. The secured party's priority covers advances made after the judicial lien was acquired but pursuant to the prior security agreement as long as the advances are made within 45 days of the date on which the judicial lien is created. The secured party has priority even if the advances were made with knowledge of the judicial lien. In addition, the secured party has priority for advances made after the 45-day period if the advances were made without knowledge of the judicial lien [UCC § 9–301(4)]. For example, assume that Best Bank loans Jan Brick $5,000 pursuant to a security agreement providing for future advances and granting a security interest in Jan's equipment. Best files a financing statement perfecting the security interest. On February 1, Charlie Sanders acquires a judicial lien against Jan. Best advances Jan an additional $10,000 on March 1 and an additional $15,000 on April 1. Best has priority over Charlie as to the initial $5,000 as a prior perfected secured party, and as to the March 1 advance because the advance was made within the 45-day grace period, even if the advance was made with knowledge of the judicial lien. By contrast, Best's interest would be subordinate to the interest of Charlie as to the April 1 advance (made after the expiration of the 45-day grace period) unless the advance was made without actual notice of the judicial lien.

UCC § 9–301. Persons Who Take Priority Over Unperfected Security Interests

(4) A person who becomes a lien creditor while a security interest is perfected takes subject to the security interest only to the extent that it secures advances made before he becomes a lien creditor or within 45 days thereafter or made without knowledge of the lien or pursuant to a commitment entered into without knowledge of the lien.

Priority between Perfected Secured Parties and Purchasers

Where a debtor sells the collateral and then defaults, a dispute might arise between the prior secured party and the purchaser. In general, a security agreement is effective against third parties, including bona fide purchasers. Thus, the perfected secured party has priority [UCC § 9–201]. However, there are certain exceptions to the general rule where the purchaser is able to defeat the prior secured party. If the security interest is not perfected, the purchaser will take free from that interest [UCC § 9–301(1)(c) and (d)]. In addition, under certain circumstances, the purchaser has priority even over prior perfected secured parties.

Purchasers of Goods

Two situations in which purchasers of goods take free from the security interest are purchases from inventory [UCC § 9–307(1)] and purchases by consumer buyers from consumer sellers [UCC 9–307(2)].

Purchases from Inventory Purchasers from inventory take the collateral free from prior perfected security interests. This priority is intended to protect the retail purchaser who purchases from inventory and to encourage the marketability of goods. Several conditions must be met before the purchaser gains priority: (1) the purchaser must be a buyer in the ordinary course, (2) the purchase must not involve a sale of farm products from a person engaged in farming operations, and (3) the security interest must be "created by his seller" [UCC § 9–307(1)].

UCC § 9–307. Protection of Buyers of Goods

(1) A buyer in ordinary course of business . . . other than a person buying farm products from a person engaged in farming operations takes free of a security interest created by his seller even though the security interest is perfected and even though the buyer knows of its existence.

UCC § 1–201. General Definitions

(9) "Buyer in ordinary course of business" means a person who in good faith and without knowledge that the sale to him is in violation of the . . . security interest of a third party in the goods buys in ordinary course from a person in the business of selling goods of that kind.

1. Buyer in the ordinary course. Only special types of purchasers—**buyers in the ordinary course**—have priority over prior perfected security interests. A buyer in the ordinary course (BOC) is a person who buys from inventory, in good faith, and without knowledge that the sale is in violation of a security agreement [UCC § 1–201(9)]. For example, assume, as is illustrated in Figure 31–1, that Doris Consumer purchases a stereo from the Stereo Shop. Assume further that the ABC Bank has a security interest in all of the Stereo Shop's inventory and that it has perfected the interest by filing a financing statement. If the ABC Bank claims an interest in the stereo in the hands of Doris, it will lose as long as the other conditions are met. Doris is purchasing from a person in the business of selling

Figure 31–1   Protection for Buyer in the Ordinary Course

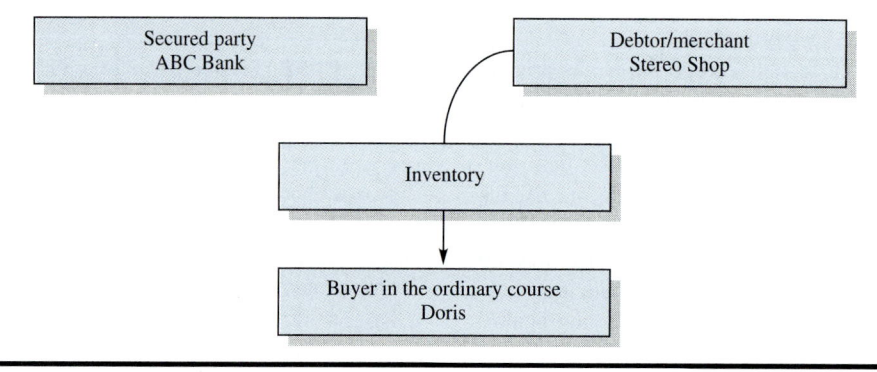

goods of that kind—in the business of selling stereos. She has priority over prior perfected secured parties.

However, in order for Doris to qualify as a buyer in the ordinary course she must be buying "in ordinary course." This excludes transfers in bulk, such as where entire businesses are sold, including inventory. In addition, she must purchase the inventory in good faith and without knowledge that the purchase was in violation of a security interest. However, she has priority even if she purchases with knowledge of the existence of the security interest. While this appears to be in conflict with the good

faith requirement, given the nature of the transaction, the apparent discrepancy is understandable. Doris has priority when she buys from inventory even with knowledge that the inventory is encumbered by a security interest because it is common for inventory to be used for financing purposes. In most cases, the debtor-seller is permitted to sell the inventory without encumbrance. Only if Doris knows that the particular sale is in violation of the security agreement will she be denied priority.

Read the following case and determine whether the purchaser, Meador, meets the buyer in the ordinary course test.

MERCHANTS AND PLANTERS BANK & TRUST v. PHOENIX HOUSING SYSTEMS, INC.

729 S.W.2d 433 (Ct. App. Ark. 1987)

On August 28, 1985, Phoenix Housing granted Merchants and Planters Bank (bank) a security interest in all inventory (modular homes) to secure repayment of a loan. Jim Meador, vice president and CEO of Phoenix, bought a home, Unit 1019, for $80,000, with a $40,000 down payment. The home was tendered to Meador before it was completed. Phoenix Housing defaulted on its loan to the bank. The issue is whether Meador was a buyer in the ordinary course.

MAYFIELD, Judge

According to UCC § 9–307(1), a buyer in the ordinary course of business takes free of a security interest created by his seller even though the security interest is perfected and even though the buyer knows of its existence.

[A]t least five conditions must be met in order for one to qualify as a buyer in the ordinary course of business under 9–307(1): (1) he must be a buyer in the ordinary course; (2) he must not take the goods in total or partial satisfaction of a preexisting debt; (3) he must have bought the goods from one who was in the business of selling goods of that kind; (4) he must buy in good faith and without knowledge that the purchase was in violation of another's security interest; and (5) the competing security interest must be one created by his or her seller.

In the present case, we do not think the evidence previously set out, will support a finding that Jim Meador was a buyer in the ordinary course of business when he purchased Unit 1019. Without restat-

ing the evidence, it is enough to say that the amount of Meador's down payment was larger than usual; the Manufacturer's Certificate of Origin was given to Meador before the unit was completed and before the purchase price was fully paid, both of which were not according to the usual way the matters were handled; after the sale to Meador, Phoenix agreed to refund Meador's money and sell the unit to Petromark, and there is no evidence that such agreement was a usual way of operating; and there was a relationship between Phoenix and Meador which was not the usual customer relationship.

By this last statement we do not mean to suggest that Meador could not make a purchase from Phoenix in the ordinary course of business. The sale to Meador, simply put, was not such a sale.

Case Questions

1. Why doesn't Meador qualify as a buyer in the ordinary course?

2. What is the policy justification for protecting buyers in the ordinary course?

2. Farm products exception. The priority given to a buyer in the ordinary course does not apply to a person buying farm products from a person engaged in farming operations. Thus, a purchaser, even in the ordinary course, of farm products from a person engaged in farming takes subject to a perfected security interest in the farm product created by the farmer. For example, assume that Fred Farmer borrows money to purchase a new tractor granting ABC Bank a security interest in all crops and livestock to finance the loan. Farmer sells several cows to a slaughterhouse. Although the slaughterhouse is a buyer in the ordinary course, it takes subject to ABC's security interest.

3. Created by his or her seller. The buyer in ordinary course takes free of security interests created by his or her seller, not by previous sellers. For example, assume that Able purchases a car, granting a security interest to ABC Bank to finance the purchase. Able sells the car to Baker Car Sales, a car dealer, as a trade-in on a second car. Baker Car Sales subsequently sells the car to Charlene. Charlene, as a buyer in the ordinary course, takes free only of security interests created by her seller—Baker. She does not take free of security interests created by Able. Therefore, Charlene takes subject to Bank's security interest.

Consumer Sales   In the case of consumer goods, a consumer buyer can get priority over prior perfected security interests [UCC § 9–307(2)]. This priority dispute typically arises when the secured party's security interest is a PMSI in consumer goods automatically perfected without filing. Several conditions must be met before the purchaser has priority:

1. The goods must be consumer goods in the seller's hands. In other words, the seller must be a consumer.
2. The buyer must buy without knowledge of the security interest.
3. The purchaser must buy for value and for personal, family, or household purposes. In other words, the buyer must be a consumer.
4. There must not be a financing statement covering the goods.

UCC § 9–307. Protection of Buyers of Goods

(2) In the case of consumer goods, a buyer takes free of a security interest even though perfected if he buys without knowledge of the security interest, for value and for his own person, family or household purposes unless prior to the purchase the secured party has filed a financing statement covering such goods.

To illustrate this exception, assume that Able purchases a television set on credit, granting the Department Store-seller a security interest (PMSI) in the television set to secure repayment. As is illustrated in Figure 31–2, assume further that Able sells the television set to her next door neighbor, Brown, as a gift for Brown's son. If the Department Store attempts to enforce its security interest against the television set in the hands of Brown, it will be unsuccessful. Although a PMSI in consumer goods is automatically perfected, Brown takes free of the Department Store's security interest because Brown is a consumer buyer purchasing from a consumer seller without notice of the security interest. If the Depart-

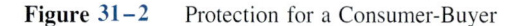

Figure 31–2   Protection for a Consumer-Buyer

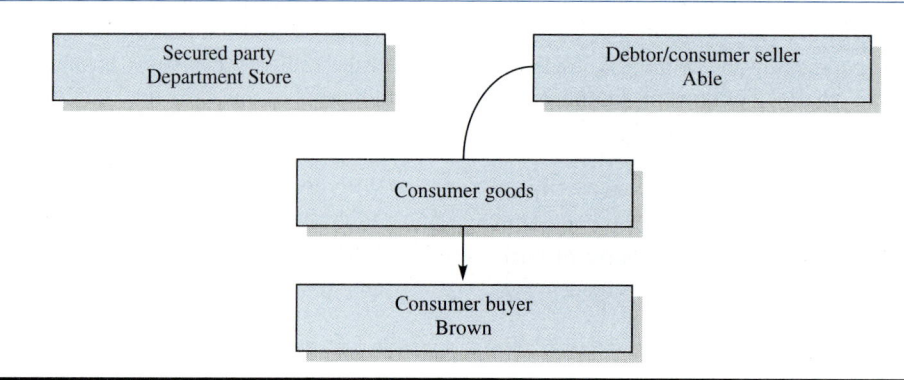

ment Store had wished to protect itself completely, it could have done so by filing a financing statement covering the collateral. Only then would Brown take subject to the Department Store's interest.

There are three situations where the purchaser will take subject to the secured party's claim. First, the purchaser with knowledge of the security interest will not have priority. Second, the purchaser who is not buying for personal, family, or household use will not have priority because the goods purchased would not be consumer goods in the buyer's hands. This occurs where, for example, the consumer seller sells consumer goods to a dealer for ultimate resale,

because the goods are inventory in the dealer (seller's) hands. Third, the purchaser takes subject to the secured party's claim where a financing statement covering the transaction has been filed. This is true even in the instance of a casual sale from a consumer seller to a consumer buyer, even in a garage sale, in spite of the fact that few consumer buyers are likely to conduct a filing search before engaging in such a transaction. Thus, the prior perfected secured party may protect itself against the possibility of unauthorized sales by its debtor by filing.

Does the purchaser in the following case have priority over the perfected secured party?

IN RE SCOTT
52 B.R. 821 (W.D. Ky. 1985)

On July 2, 1980, Scott granted the Bank a security interest in a Marquis Mercruiser boat. The Bank filed its financing statement on July 14, 1980, in the office of the county clerk, Clark County, Indiana, the county of Scott's residence. In May 1981, Scott sold the boat to Bass. Both Scott and Bass purchased the boat for their personal use. Scott then filed a petition of bankruptcy.

BROWN, Bankruptcy Judge

The Bank did properly file in the county of the debtor's residence, Clark County, Indiana on July 14, 1980, thus perfecting its security interest in the boat.

Having found that the Bank was perfected, we now turn to the issue of whether the Bank's security interest is superior to any interest of Bass. Bass argues that he is a bona fide purchaser, having bought the boat in good faith, for consideration, and without knowledge of the Bank's prior security interest. Even assuming that Bass is a bona fide purchaser, unfortunately, the law does not protect him. The Bank's interest is superior to that of Bass pursuant to Section 9–307(2).

The purchase by Bass of the boat occurred on or about May, 1981. The financing statement was filed by the Bank on July 14, 1980, clearly prior to the Bass' purchase. As to priority between these two claimants, the Bank must prevail and is entitled to immediate possession of the boat.

Case Questions
1. Analyze: "Even assuming that Bass is a bona fide purchaser, unfortunately, the law does not protect him. The Bank's interest is superior to that of Bass pursuant to Section 9–307(2)."
2. How could Bass have protected himself?

Purchasers of Chattel Paper and Instruments
Purchasers of chattel paper have priority over perfected secured parties who have allowed the debtor to keep possession of the paper [UCC § 9–308]. First, if the secured party claims the interest as mere proceeds of the security interest, the purchaser has priority over the prior perfected secured party if the

purchaser gave new value and took the collateral in the ordinary course of business, even if the purchaser knows that the specific paper or instrument is subject to the security interest [UCC § 9–308(b)].

Second, if the prior perfected secured party claims a direct interest in the chattel paper or instrument, the purchaser has priority under more limited circumstances. To achieve priority under these circumstances, the purchaser must not only give new value and take possession of the chattel paper or instrument in the ordinary course of its business, but it must do so without knowledge of the security interest. Thus, a secured party with a direct security interest in the chattel paper can completely protect itself against subsequent purchasers by stamping or noting the interest on the paper. For example, assume that Third Bank loans Lemon Auto Dealer money, taking in return a security interest in Dealer's chattel paper, allowing Lemon to retain possession of the chattel paper, and perfects by filing. Lemon wrongfully assigns the chattel paper to Friendly Finance Company in exchange for additional financing. Friendly takes possession of the paper. In this instance, Friendly has priority over Third Bank's prior perfected security interest only if it had no knowledge of the security interest when it acquired the assignment.

Purchasers of Negotiable Instruments and Documents

A purchaser who is a holder in due course of a negotiable instrument, or an analogous holder of a document or security, has priority over a prior perfected secured interest in such instruments, documents, or securities, preserving the rights of holders in due course, as discussed in Chapter 26 [UCC § 9–309]. Figure 31–3 summarizes the priority rules.

COURSES OF ACTION ON DEBTOR DEFAULT

Priority questions focus on the ability of a secured party to protect its interest against third parties. Similarly, the secured party has certain rights against the debtor in the event of debtor default and certain limitations on those rights. These rights form the very basis of the secured transaction. Possession of these rights is what separates secured lenders from unsecured lenders.

Default

In general, **default** is whatever the parties say it is, typically in the security agreement. The most common instance of default is the debtor's failure to make principal or interest payments on time. However, most security agreements include a host of

Figure 31–3   Priorities

Party	Has Priority Over
Unperfected	General unsecured creditors Later unperfected secured parties
Lien creditors	Unperfected secured parties Later perfected secured parties
Perfected	Unperfected Later lien creditors Later perfected secured parties Bona fide purchasers Later tax liens
Purchase money secured parties	
In noninventory	Prior perfected secured parties with after-acquired interests, if perfected within 10 days
In inventory	Prior perfected secured parties with after-acquired interests, if perfected when debtor acquires collateral and secured party gives notice
State statutory lien creditors	Prior perfected secured parties as long as lien creditor is in possession of collateral
Bona fide purchaser	
Buyer in the ordinary course	Prior perfected secured parties
Consumer buyer from consumer seller	Prior perfected secured parties unless purchaser knows of security interest and unless secured party perfected by filing

additional instances that can constitute default, such as (1) filing of a competing financing statement covering the collateral; (2) sale of the collateral; (3) failure to maintain adequate insurance on the collateral; (4) failure to make prompt payment of any taxes on the collateral; (5) loss, theft, or destruction of the collateral; (6) debtor's death; or (7) debtor's bankruptcy. The events that can constitute default are limited only by the creditor's imagination (and the doctrine of unconscionability in a consumer transaction). See, for example, the sample security agreement, Figure 30–1 in Chapter 30.

In addition, security agreements commonly contain **acceleration clauses.** An acceleration clause gives the secured party the right to declare the *entire* amount of the loan due on the occurrence of any provision of default. Acceleration clauses are permissible as long as the secured party acts in good faith in accelerating the loan [UCC § 1–208]. Further, security agreements typically contain **insecurity clauses**, authorizing the secured party to accelerate payment if the secured party "deems himself insecure." Although some states have enacted protective legislation restricting the use of insecurity clauses in consumer transactions, such clauses are generally enforced. Again, the secured party is under a duty to act only if the creditor "in good faith believes that the prospect of payment or performance is impaired" [UCC § 1–208].

Secured Party's Options after Default

Once default under the terms of the security agreement has occurred, the secured party has several options, including several nonlegal alternatives. This discussion focuses on judicial alternatives. The judicial remedies available to the creditor are cumulative—one does not have to select one to the exclusion of others [UCC § 9–501(1)]. These rights apply to unperfected as well as perfected security interests because perfection is relevant only against third parties. All that is necessary with regard to action against the debtor is that an enforceable security interest attach.

UCC § 9–501. Default

(1) When a debtor is in default under a security agreement, a secured party . . . may reduce his claim to judgment, foreclose or otherwise enforce the security interest by any available judicial procedure.

The secured party may either (1) bring an action on the underlying debt, (2) repossess and retain the collateral (strict foreclosure), and/or (3) repossess and resell the collateral.

Secured Party's Action on the Debt

The secured party may bring an action against the debtor personally. Upon receipt of the judgment, the secured party then levies on the collateral and any other unencumbered assets of the debtor pursuant to the judgment. To the extent that the levy is made on the collateral, the lien relates back to the date of perfection of the security interest. This may become important in the event of debtor bankruptcy, as discussed in Chapter 32.

Repossession of the Collateral

The secured party may **repossess** the collateral upon default [UCC § 9–503]. If it can be accomplished without "breach of the peace," the secured party can adopt **self-help** repossession and avoid judicial action. In general, repossession made over any protest of the debtor is a breach of the peace. Repossession using a weapon is a breach of the peace. Repossession where the secured party gains access to the collateral by unauthorized entry is a breach of the peace. For example, the secured party cannot enter the debtor's garage to repossess a car. By contrast, self-help repossession of the debtor's car parked in the driveway is permissible. Without an agreement to the contrary, the secured party is not required to give the debtor notice of intent to repossess the collateral when using self-help repossession.

UCC § 9–503. Secured Party's Right to Take Possession After Default

. . . In taking possession a secured party may proceed without judicial process if this can be done without breach of the peace or may proceed by action.

Where self-help repossession is not feasible—as where, for example, the car is routinely kept in the debtor's garage—resort to judicial process is necessary. While due process guarantees an opportunity for defense, full-fledged trials are rarely required. State statutes commonly provide for some form of "show cause hearing" where the debtor is given an opportunity to present any evidence against repossession.

Following repossession, the secured party must use reasonable care in the custody and preservation of the collateral [UCC § 9–207(1)].

Realizing upon the Collateral

Following default and repossession, the secured party may recover for the debt owed by either (1) strict foreclosure or (2) resale.

Strict Foreclosure   The secured party may elect to keep the collateral in *full* satisfaction of the debt, termed **strict foreclosure** [UCC § 9–505(2)]. While the secured party loses the right to recover any deficiencies from the debtor, high costs associated with foreclosure sales are avoided. Strict foreclosure is permitted in all cases except where the collateral is consumer goods for which the debtor has paid 60 percent of the purchase price (or 60 percent of the loan amount in the case of non-PMSIs). In the case of such consumer goods, the secured party must dispose of the collateral within 90 days from the date of repossession [UCC § 9–505(1)]. This exception offers protection to a consumer who has built up substantial equity in consumer goods. However, the consumer can authorize strict foreclosure by signing, after default, a statement renouncing rights to force a sale.

Where the secured party elects strict foreclosure, the Code imposes notice requirements [UCC § 9–505(2)]. First, notice of such intent must be sent to the debtor. In the case of consumer goods, no further notice is required. In all other cases, additional notice must be given to all secured parties with competing interests in the collateral from whom the secured party has received written notification of such interest. The debtor, or any secured party entitled to notice, may object to strict foreclosure in writing as long as it is received by the secured party within 21 days from the day the notice was sent. If the secured party receives objection, the collateral must be sold.

Sale of the Collateral   Alternatively, the secured party may choose to dispose of the collateral and to use the proceeds from the sale to satisfy the debtor's obligation [UCC § 9–504]. In general, the secured party is given a great deal of flexibility in how this is to be accomplished. The secured party may "sell, lease, or otherwise dispose of the collateral."

The collateral may be sold by public or private sale [UCC § 9–504(2)]. Private sales are encouraged because of the belief that they result in higher prices. The primary limitation on the secured party's conduct is that all aspects of the sale must be "commercially reasonable" [UCC § 9–504(3)]. The secured party must handle the collateral in a commercially reasonable manner prior to sale and must sell the collateral within a commercially reasonable time after repossession. While the Code does not define the term *commercially reasonable,* the mere fact that a better price could have been obtained if the sale had been conducted differently does not necessarily mean that it was conducted in a commercially unreasonable manner [UCC § 9–507(2)]. On the other hand, selling on a recognized market, obtaining fair market value, and selling in conformity with established commercial practices is proof of acting in a commercially reasonable manner.

Read the following case and determine whether or not the behavior by the creditor was "commercially reasonable."

UCC § 9–504. Secured Party's Right to Dispose of Collateral After Default

(3) . . . Sale or other disposition may be . . . at any time and place and on any terms but every aspect of the disposition including the method, manner, time, place and terms must be commercially reasonable.

UCC § 9–507. Secured Party's Liability for Failure to Comply with the Part

(2) . . . If the secured party either sells the collateral in the usual manner in any recognized market thereof or if he sells at the price current in such market at the time of his sale or if he has otherwise sold in conformity with reasonable commercial practices among dealers in the type of property sold he has sold in a commercially reasonable manner.

STANDARD BANK & TRUST CO. v. CALLAGHAN
532 N.E.2d 1015 (Ill. App. 1988)

Standard Bank & Trust Company foreclosed its security interest, conducted a judicial sale, and bought the collateral for a price of $221,000 based on presale appraisals. The Bank then sued for a deficiency of $292,404.70. The property was appraised after the sale at $291,600. The trial court found that the sale was commercially unreasonable because the purchase price was too low and barred recovery of the deficiency judgment. Plaintiff appealed.

INGLIS, Justice

Section 9–504(3) of the Code provides that "every aspect of the disposition including the method, manner, time, place and terms must be commercially reasonable." While price alone does not establish commercial reasonableness, this court has recently stated that price is the key component in assessing commercial reasonableness. In determining whether price is commercially reasonable, Illinois courts have long recognized that property does not bring its full value at forced sales. This is similarly recognized in section 9–507(2) of the code which provides that "[t]he fact that a better price could have been obtained by a sale at a different time or in a different method from that selected by the secured party is not of itself sufficient to establish that the sale was not made in a commercially reasonable manner." UCC 9–507(2). Thus, it has consistently been held that mere inadequacy of price in the absence of fraud or mistaken or illegal practice will not vitiate a sale. We do not depart from this well-established rule.

In the instant action, one of the debtors was present at the sale and objected to plaintiff's bid on the basis that it was too low. More importantly though, the evidentiary hearing revealed facts which rendered the appraisal relied on by plaintiff of dubious validity. Specifically, it was established that plaintiff's appraiser made his conclusion of value after one visit to the property, and subsequently used an associate to "gather data" to determine the accuracy of his conclusions. These factors led the court to conclude that plaintiff engaged in a "mistaken practice" in that it "relied upon an appraiser's report that it knew, or ought to have known was too low."

Accordingly, we conclude that the trial court, in light of its determination that the plaintiff engaged in a mistaken practice, correctly found plaintiff's bid to be commercially unreasonable.

Case Questions

1. If the purchase was at a public sale, why is the secured party liable for buying the collateral at a price that is too low? Weren't other parties free to bid a higher price?

2. What is the secured party's liability for acting unreasonably?

Further, there are notice requirements similar to the notice requirements mandated in strict foreclosure. Unless the collateral is perishable, likely to decline in value, or of the type customarily sold on a recognized market, notice of the sale must be given to the debtor [UCC § 9–504(3)]. Notice must be given of the time and place of a public sale and of the time after which a private sale will take place. This allows the debtor time to redeem the collateral prior to sale. If the collateral is consumer goods, no further notice is required. In all other cases, notice must be sent to competing secured parties from whom the secured party has received written notice of a claim in the collateral [UCC § 9–504(3)]. Notice must be sent far enough in advance of the resale to give the debtor a reasonable chance to redeem the goods or to attend the sale with the ability to repurchase the collateral.

The secured party may purchase the collateral at a public sale [UCC § 9–504(3)]. In addition, if the goods are of the type that are customarily sold on a recognized market or of the type that are subject to widely distributed standard price quotations, the secured party may purchase at private sale.

UCC § 9–504. Secured Party's Right to Dispose of Collateral After Default

(3) . . . Unless collateral is perishable or threatens to decline speedily in value or is of a type customarily sold on a recognized market, reasonable notification of the time and place of any public sale or reasonable notification of the time after which any private sale . . . is to be made shall be sent by the secured party to the debtor.

Proceeds from the sale will be applied, first, to the expenses incurred in repossession and sale, including reasonable legal expenses; second, to the debtor's debt; and third, to satisfy the security interest of subordinate secured parties who have advised the secured party of demand for a proportion of the proceeds [UCC § 9–504(1)]. Any surplus will be paid to the debtor. By contrast, if the sale is insufficient to satisfy the debtor's obligations, the debtor owes any deficiency, as long as the sale was conducted in a commercially reasonable manner even if the sale price was substantially below fair market value. For example, assume that Fifth National Bank repossesses a car with a blue book value of $5,000 and sells it for $2,000 at a public sale. If the debtor owes $6,000, Fifth National is entitled to a deficiency judgment of $4,000 as long as the sale was conducted reasonably, with the secured party making a commercially reasonable attempt to attract qualified purchasers. By contrast, if Fifth National conducted the sale fraudulently or in bad faith purposely to realize a low price, it will not be entitled to compute the deficiency based on the sale price. In the above example, if the $2,000 sale price was obtained in bad faith, the available deficiency would be calculated by comparing the fair market value to the outstanding debt, allowing the secured party to recover a deficiency of $1,000. Where there are minor flaws in the repossession or resale proceeding, some courts will deny the secured party the right to any deficiency. Other courts will presume that the collateral is worth at least as much as the amount of the debt, leaving the creditor with the task of proving that the amount realized in the sale was commercially reasonable. Still other courts hold that minor flaws do not limit the secured party's right to recover a deficiency judgment. In any case, the secured party is liable to the debtor for any damages [UCC § 9–507].

Debtor's Right of Redemption   The debtor may redeem the collateral before the secured party has disposed of it by paying the *entire* debt plus all expenses reasonably incurred in retaking, storing, and preparing the collateral for sale [UCC § 9–506]. If the security agreement includes an acceleration clause, this means that in order to redeem, the debtor must pay the entire outstanding loan amount, not just the missed installments.

Secured Party's Liability for Failure to Comply   In addition to the possibility of tort liability for creditor misconduct, the Code creates statutory liability for failure to comply with Article 9 rules [UCC § 9–507]. Because the major requirement of creditor behavior is that of commercial reasonableness, liability arises typically when the creditor acts in a commercially unreasonable fashion. In the event that the secured party is acting in an impermissible fashion, the debtor, and presumably a competing secured

party, may get an injunction [UCC § 9–507(1)]. Then the court could order disposition under appropriate terms and conditions.

If the sale has occurred, the secured party is liable for any loss caused by noncompliance [UCC § 9–507(1)]. Presumably, this is the difference between the amount actually received from the sale and the amount that would have been received had the secured party acted properly. In addition, in the case of consumer goods, the debtor has the right to recover at least "the credit service charge plus 10 percent of the principal amount of the debt or the time price differential plus 10 percent of the cash price" as minimum damages [UCC § 9–507(1)].

END–OF–CHAPTER QUESTIONS

1. A purchase money security interest in consumer goods gets priority over a bona fide purchaser only if a financing statement is filed. Can you think of any reason why the secured party might not file a financing statement?

2. List the consumer protection provisions of Article 9. Why are consumers treated differently from other debtors?

3. Why are purchase money security interests in inventory collateral treated differently from purchase money security interests in noninventory collateral?

4. Why might a secured party choose one course of action on debtor default over another?

5. Burton Rainsdon ran a cattle-raising operation. When Burton became ill, he asked his son, Robert, to care for 150 head of cattle. On March 23, 1982, Robert agreed to purchase 100 head of these cattle, with Burton retaining a purchase money security interest. Burton filed a financing statement on April 30, 1982. At the time, Valley Bank had a security interest in all of Robert's "livestock, now owned or hereafter acquired." Valley Bank filed a financing statement on January 22, 1980. Robert defaulted on both debts. Who has priority in the cows? Does it make any difference when Robert acquired possession of the cows? Explain. See *Valley Bank v. Rainsdon,* 793 P.2d 1257 (Idaho 1990).

6. In January 1984, Barry Galloway bought a car from Silver City Dodge, Inc., granting the Shawmut Bank a security interest in the car. Shawmut did not file a financing statement. In early May, Galloway sold the car to Earl Dion for $10,500. At the time, Galloway told Dion that he had bought the car for cash and explained that there was no certificate of title because the vehicle was not registered. Can Dion qualify as a good faith purchaser for value when he bought the car without receiving the certificate of title? Would it make any difference if Shawmut had properly noted its security interest on the certificate of title? Explain. See *Dion v. Silver City Dodge*, 495 N.E.2d 274 (Mass. 1986).

7. In September 1983, Northern Commercial Co. sold a Caterpillar Tractor to Les Cobb, taking a security interest to secure payment of the purchase price. Cobb defaulted on the loan. Northern Commercial repossessed the tractor and purchased the tractor itself at a private sale for $110,000 (about one third the original purchase price of the tractor). Was this purchase permissible? Explain. See *Northern Commercial Co. v. Cobb*, 778 P.2d 205 (Alaska 1989).

8. Oscar Belvin bought and took possession of a John Deere cotton picker for $35,000, borrowing the money for the purchaser from Crossroads Bank. Cross-roads filed a financing statement on February 10, 1989. On December 29, 1989, Corim brought a garnishment action against Belvin based on an April 21, 1989, judgment. Who has priority with respect to the cotton picker? See *Corim v. Belvin*, 414 S.E.2d 491 (Ct. App. Ga. 1992).

9. The First National Bank loaned Susan Carr $5,000 pursuant to a security agreement providing for future advances and granting a security interest in Susan's equipment. First National perfected its security interest by filing a financing statement. On February 1, Joe Michaels acquired a judicial lien against Susan. On March 1, First National advanced Susan an additional $10,000. On April 1, First National advanced Susan an additional $15,000. On May 1, Susan declared bankruptcy. If First National, Joe, and the trustee all claim an interest in the equipment, who has priority?

10. On March 1, Grant, a television dealer, borrowed $15,000 from Lincoln Bank and entered into a written agreement giving the bank a security interest in all Grant's television sets now owned or hereafter acquired. On that date, Lincoln filed a financing statement. On June 1, Grant borrowed $5,000 from North State Bank to buy 100 new televisions. North State filed a financing statement before Grant took possession. Grant defaulted. Which Bank has priority in the inventory?

Chapter 32

Debtor-Creditor Law

■

CRITICAL THINKING INQUIRIES

As you read this chapter, you should be able to address the following:

- Explain the relationship between state protection and bankruptcy.
- Analyze the following statement: ''The stay protects the debtor from creditor collection and gives the trustee in bankruptcy an opportunity to collect debtor property.''
- Why are preferences recoverable by the trustee?
- Explain the relationship between straight bankruptcy and reorganization.

MANAGERIAL PERSPECTIVE

Joe is the owner of a small company in the business of selling lumber supplies to construction companies. He has sold supplies on credit to A & M Construction Co. In return, Joe has taken a security interest in certain pieces of machinery owned by A & M.

Unfortunately, A & M has not repaid the loans. Joe is contemplating what action to take. He is considering enforcing his security interest, or forcing A & M into involuntary bankruptcy. A & M has offered to pay him half of the debt if he agrees to forgive the entire obligation. Joe thinks that other creditors will file bankruptcy if he doesn't.

- What are Joe's considerations if he decides to enforce the security interest?
- Should Joe take the partial payment? Are there any risks if A & M ends up in bankruptcy anyway?
- Should Joe force A & M into bankruptcy? Are there other options?

The study of debtor-creditor law is essentially a study of remedies available to the creditor and limitations on those remedies. The debtor is protected from creditor action by both state and federal law. The greatest protection is provided to the debtor in bankruptcy.

INTRODUCTION

An introduction to the study of creditor collection remedies begins with an understanding of liens. A **lien** is a legal charge on property in favor of one creditor that must be satisfied before the property is available to the debtor or other creditors. Consensual liens are created by the debtor as either UCC Article 9 security interests or real property mortgages. Nonconsensual liens are either judicial liens or statutory liens. A **judicial lien** is a general lien on all debtor property resulting from prejudgment collection efforts such as attachment or garnishment, from the judgment, or from efforts to enforce the judgment, such as by levy and execution. Other liens are created by state and federal statute. Some of the more common **statutory liens** are landlord, materialman's, mechanic's, and tax liens.

STATE COLLECTION EFFORTS

A creditor can use nonjudicial methods to collect a debt, such as a dunning letter and use of credit collection agencies. In addition, a number of judicial methods are available.

Garnishment

Garnishment is brought by the creditor (the garnishor) and directed at the property of the debtor in the hands of a third party (the garnishee). The most common garnishees are the debtor's employer, who holds wages due the debtor, and the debtor's bank, which holds the debtor's checking and savings accounts.

In many states, garnishment can be used either as a pre- or postjudgment remedy. Because due process guarantees the debtor notice and opportunity to be heard before garnishment, prejudgment garnishment is generally not allowed without a hearing. Because of the potential for extreme hardship to the debtor, wage garnishments are carefully regulated. For example, the Consumer Credit Protection Act prohib-

its an employer from discharging an employee (the debtor) because of a garnishment. Further, the amount of the permissible garnishment is also limited. See Chapter 33 for a complete discussion of the Consumer Credit Protection Act.

Attachment

Attachment is a prejudgment remedy in which the creditor seizes property in the hands of the debtor to gain priority in case a judgment is obtained. Most state statutes allow attachment upon posting of a bond, where, for example, the defendant is outside the court's jurisdiction or the plaintiff's claim is based on fraud. Again, because of due process limitations, attachment cannot be obtained without some form of preliminary hearing with notice to the defendant and opportunity for defendant input.

Repossession

As discussed in the previous chapter, secured creditors may repossess the collateral using self-help repossession without notice to the defendant if it can be accomplished without breach of the peace. If not, a judicial proceeding is required. The debtor might be given notice and an opportunity to present defenses to repossession at a show cause hearing. Alternatively, the creditor might use a **cognovit note** in which the debtor consents in advance to the holder obtaining a judgment against the debtor without notice or hearing. Statutory treatment of cognovit provisions varies substantially from state to state. Some states allow their use and some states prohibit it. Enforcement of cognovit notes is constitutional as long as the debtor voluntarily waives the debtor's rights to notice and hearing.

Levy and Execution

A judgment lien arises when the creditor obtains a judgment against the debtor. In some states, the award of the judgment itself creates a lien. In other states, the lien arises only when the judgment creditor records the judgment. In still other states, the lien arises on execution or levy.

Execution is the process by which the judgment is enforced against the property of the debtor. Most states provide for a writ of execution by which the judgment creditor has the debtor's property seized (**levy**) and sold to satisfy the judgment.

Realizing on the Collateral

The judgment creditor receives payment from the property of the debtor after levy by selling the property at auction. Satisfaction is obtained against the equitable property of the debtor by the use of a **creditor's bill** compelling the debtor to turn over equitable assets (such as intangible property) to be sold at auction.

Today, all states restrict the property that is subject to creditor action. Certain classes of property, termed **exempt property,** are not available to the creditor. Such things as the family Bible, wearing apparel, household furniture, tools used in the debtor's trade, insurance policies, and the primary residence of the debtor are generally exempt within certain monetary limits.

Nonbankruptcy Arrangements

An insolvent debtor can choose either state or federal protection. Liquidation can be accomplished either through discharge proceedings in bankruptcy, through state court receivership, or by an assignment for the benefit of creditors. Nonliquidation alternatives are common law settlements, reorganization, and wage-earner plans.

State Court Receiverships

Most states provide by statute for the creation of receiverships. Commonly, a receiver is appointed to act as trustee over the debtor's property pending liquidation.

Common Law Settlements

A common law settlement is a contract between the debtor and at least two creditors. Such contracts can be either compositions, extensions, or both. A **composition** is an agreement where creditors agree to accept specific partial payments in full satisfaction of their claims. An **extension** is a contract where creditors agree to extend the time for payment by the debtor. A settlement can be both a composition and an extension if the creditors agree to accept less at a later date.

Composition and extensions are governed by common law contract law. To be enforceable, all elements necessary to support a contract at common law must be found. Historically, the troublesome question involved the existence of consideration supporting the settlement. This is acutely true in the instance of compositions. Under contract law, an agreement by a creditor to accept a lesser sum in full satisfaction of a liquidated debt (one in which the amount in controversy is not in dispute) is not supported by consideration and is not enforceable. The debtor, after paying the agreed-on lesser sum, could be faced with a lawsuit for the rest of the original debt. However, composition agreements are generally enforceable. Courts find consideration in the agreement *between* the creditors, in effect creating an exception to the consideration requirement. Thus, as long as two or more creditors enter into a composition agreement, it is enforceable, discharging the claims of all creditors who enter into the agreement.

Assignment for the Benefit of Creditors

A general **assignment for the benefit of creditors** is an assignment of all or substantially all of the debtor's nonexempt property to a trustee to liquidate and distribute the proceeds to the creditors. In general, the trustee (assignee) takes the property subject to all liens and claims that could have been asserted against the debtor (assignor). The most important of these is the Article 9 security interest. A perfected secured party has priority over the trustee. The assignee for the benefit of the creditors has priority over an unperfected security interest unless all of the debtor's creditors had knowledge of the existence of the security interest at the time the assignment for the benefit of creditors was made [UCC § 9–301].

The purpose of an assignment for the benefit of creditors is to liquidate and distribute the debtor's estate. In this respect, an assignment for the benefit of creditors is similar to a straight bankruptcy proceeding discussed in the next section. However, in an assignment for the benefit of creditors, the debtor is not given a discharge unless the creditors agree in a composition agreement. This means that following liquidation and distribution, the debtor is liable for any deficiency owed.

STRAIGHT BANKRUPTCY

Bankruptcy is a remedy provided by the federal Bankruptcy Act (BA) as recognized in Article 1 of the U.S. Constitution. While state law generally rewards prompt action by creditors, bankruptcy attempts to achieve equality of treatment. All creditors of like class are treated similarly. Debtors may choose from a number of forms of bankruptcy relief, depending on their particular circumstances.

Chapter 7, known as straight bankruptcy or liquidation, is probably the most common form of bankruptcy. Hundreds of thousands of petitions are filed annually. In straight bankruptcy, the debtor turns all assets, excluding exempt property, over to a trustee to be sold, and the proceeds are distributed to satisfy the claims of creditors. In return, the debtor is discharged from all unsatisfied debts. This procedure gives an honest debtor a fresh start.

Commencing the Proceedings

The bankruptcy proceeding begins with the filing of either a voluntary or an involuntary **bankruptcy petition.** Any person, including corporations and partnerships, may file voluntary petitions except railroads, government institutions, banks, insurance companies, and savings and loan institutions. The debtor does not have to be **insolvent**—that is, either unable to pay debts as they become due or with liabilities greater than assets.

The filing of a voluntary petition automatically operates as an adjudication of bankruptcy. Alternatively, the bankruptcy proceeding may be commenced by the filing of an involuntary petition. Certain debtors are protected from such a filing, such as the parties excluded above. In addition, farmers and charitable corporations are protected. When there are 12 or more creditors, 3 must join the involuntary petition. If there are less than 12 creditors, only 1 must file. Regardless, as a group, the debtor must owe these creditors claims of at least $5,000.

Stay

Automatically upon the filing of a bankruptcy petition a **stay** arises that protects the debtor from creditors and gives the trustee an opportunity to collect debtor property. The stay prohibits creditors from beginning or continuing any judicial proceeding to enforce claims, including any action to enforce a judgment already obtained, any action to gain possession of property of the debtor, and any act to create, perfect, or enforce a lien against property of the debtor [BA § 362]. In short, creditors of the debtor can do nothing to attempt to collect the debt owed them after the filing of the bankruptcy petition.

Proceeding

Following the filing of the bankruptcy petition, the debtor files a schedule of assets and liabilities and a list of creditors, including a list of all debts. Creditors are then notified and asked to file proofs of claim with the court. After all proofs of claim have been filed, a first meeting of creditors occurs. At this meeting, the trustee in bankruptcy is appointed as the representative of the general unsecured creditors.

Gathering the Property

It is the job of the trustee to gather the debtor's estate, sell all property, pay expenses and priority claims, and distribute the remainder of the proceeds to the unsecured creditors. Obviously, it is in the best interest of the unsecured creditor for the trustee to gather the largest estate possible. Bankruptcy law gives the trustee certain powers to use to do that.

Debtor's Rights in the Property

The trustee is given title to all property owned by the debtor on the date of the petition filing. In general, property acquired by the debtor after the filing of the petition is not part of the estate. For example, assume that A & M Construction from our opening scenario files a bankruptcy petition on March 25. On March 26, the company builds a deck and receives a $2,000 payment. The $2,000 is not part of the estate because it did not belong to the debtor when the bankruptcy petition was filed. This rule is designed to give the debtor a "fresh start."

BA § 541. Property of the Estate

(a) . . . Such estate is comprised of all the following property . . .

(1) . . . all legal or equitable interest of the debtor in property as of the commencement of the case.

There are two situations where property acquired by the debtor after the petition is filed is part of the estate. First, property that the debtor acquires by inheritance, divorce decree, or life insurance within 180 days of the filing of the petition is part of the estate [BA § 541(a)(5)]. Second, proceeds or profits from property in the estate are included in the estate even if generated after the filing of the petition [BA

§ 541(a)(6)]. For example, assume that the debtor's estate includes an apartment building. Rent received after the filing of the bankruptcy petition is in the estate. This includes property obtained from the sale or conversion of property in the debtor's estate. Assume, for example, that the debtor owned a car that was destroyed after the filing of the petition. Insurance proceeds are automatically part of the estate.

The trustee gets whatever interest the debtor had in the property. It is often said that the trustee "steps into the shoes of the debtor." Thus, the trustee takes subject to whatever liens and encumbrances were good against the debtor. Further, the trustee may use any defense available to the debtor, such as fraud, mistake, statute of frauds, statutes of limitations, usury, or any other personal defense. For example, assume that a creditor claims money due for the purchase and sale of a car. The trustee can assert, in the debtor's place, the defense of breach of warranty if the car was not merchantable. In addition, the trustee can use this power to defeat the claims of secured parties. For example, assume that a security interest is granted but the secured party neither takes possession of the collateral nor requires the debtor to sign a security agreement, so that the security interest is not enforceable against the debtor. Therefore, the security interest is not enforceable against the debtor's trustee in bankruptcy.

The debtor may claim certain property as **exempt** and have it removed from the estate available for eventual distribution. The property that is exempt is set forth in both state and federal law. The debtor elects whether to assert the state or federal exemptions, unless the state in which the debtor resides has eliminated the federal alternative. The debtor is not permitted to choose some exemptions from the state list and some from the federal list. Basically, the exemptions allow the debtor to live, not lavishly, retaining such property as a residence, a car, household goods, and clothes within certain monetary limits [BA § 522(d)].

Avoiding Powers of the Trustee

Voiding a creditor's claim against the estate increases the amount available for distribution to other creditors. In addition, any property that the trustee is able to recover increases the estate available. Therefore, the trustee is given certain powers to avoid and disallow claims. The trustee can use these powers against secured and unsecured claims. One of the most significant trustee powers is the power to avoid transfers that were not timely recorded or perfected. The trustee has four basic avoidance powers.

Hypothetical Lien Creditor The trustee has the rights of a creditor who gets a judicial lien on the date of bankruptcy [BA § 544(a)(1)], whether or not such a creditor actually exists [BA § 544(a)(3)]. Thus, the trustee can avoid any transfer that could have been avoided by such creditor under state law. With respect to personal property, the applicable state statute is the Uniform Commercial Code (UCC). Because unperfected security interests are subordinate to the rights of lien creditors, the trustee can hypothesize a lien creditor acquiring its lien on the date the bankruptcy petition was filed and defeat any unperfected security interests [UCC § 9–301(1)(b)]. For example, assume that Joe in the opening scenario sells $10,000 worth of supplies to A & M Construction on credit on January 1, taking in return a security interest in equipment. Assume further that Joe's interest is unperfected. On April 16, A & M files a bankruptcy petition. The trustee acquires the rights of a lien creditor obtaining a lien on April 16. Because such a creditor can defeat Joe's unperfected security interest, the trustee defeats the interest.

BA § 544. Trustee as Lien Creditor

(a) The trustee shall have, as of the commencement of the case, . . . the rights and powers of, or may avoid any transfer of property of the debtor or any obligation incurred by the debtor that is voidable by—

(1) a creditor that extends credit to the debtor at the time of commencement of the case, and that obtains, at such time . . . a judicial lien on all property . . . whether or not such a creditor exists.

Alternatively, assume that Second National Bank lends A & M Construction $10,000 on January 1, taking in return a security interest in equipment. A & M files a bankruptcy petition on April 16, and Second National perfects its interest on April 20. The trustee can invalidate Second National's interest because even though the security interest was ultimately perfected, it was unperfected on the date the bankruptcy petition was filed. It is this date that determines the rights of the trustee.

Last, assume that on January 15, Joe sells equipment on credit to A & M Construction, taking in return a purchase money security interest in the equipment purchased. A & M obtains the equipment that afternoon. On January 20, A & M files a bankruptcy petition. On January 21, Joe perfects its security interest. Although Joe had not filed a financing statement on the date the bankruptcy petition was filed, the trustee may not disallow his security interest. This is true because there is a 10-day grace period (from the date the debtor took possession of the collateral) for perfection of purchase money security interests [UCC § 9–301(2)].

Actual Creditor

The trustee also has the right to avoid any transfers that an actual creditor could avoid under state law [BA § 544(b)]. In using this power, the size of the claim held by the actual creditor and asserted by the trustee is irrelevant. If an actual creditor holding a $10 claim could defeat a $10,000 security interest, the trustee "jumps into the shoes" of the actual creditor (after defeating the actual creditor's claim on some other grounds) and defeats the entire security interest.

BA § 544. Trustee as Lien Creditor

(b) The trustee may avoid any transfer of an interest of the debtor in property or any obligation incurred by the debtor that is voidable under applicable law by a creditor holding an unsecured claim that is allowable.

The trustee uses this power to invalidate interests not timely perfected by looking for a creditor who lent and obtained a lien during the gap between the security interest's creation and perfection. The trustee defeats the gap creditor's lien and asserts the rights of the lien creditor against the secured party. For example, assume that Fourth National Bank lends Dan Debtor $10,000 on March 1, taking in return a security interest in a piece of equipment. On April 1, Chuck Creditor extends credit in the amount of $50 to Dan, getting a judicial lien on the collateral equipment on April 30. On May 2, Fourth National perfects its security interest. On May 15, Dan files a bankruptcy petition. Chuck is an actual gap creditor. An unperfected security interest (Fourth National) is subordinate to the rights of a person who becomes a judicial lien creditor (Chuck) without knowledge of

the security interest and before it is perfected [UCC § 9–301]. Because Chuck became a lien creditor before Fourth National perfected its security interest, Chuck defeats Fourth National's claim. The trustee can use its actual lien creditor power to jump into Chuck's shoes (after defeating Chuck's claim on other grounds), and because Chuck can defeat Fourth National's claim, the trustee can invalidate Fourth National's interest. In addition, in spite of the fact that Chuck's claim is only $50, the trustee can defeat the entire $10,000 security interest. However, it would be very unusual for Chuck to both lend and to obtain the necessary judicial lien in the gap period. Both are required.

Preferences

The trustee has the power to void preferential payments to achieve the policy of equality of distribution among creditors [BA § 547]. Subject to certain exceptions, the trustee can avoid a **preference** if six conditions are met, as summarized in Figure 32–1.

1. Transfer. First, the debtor must make a transfer of the debtor's property. A **transfer** includes every method of disposing of property, including the granting of a security interest [BA § 101(54)]. For example, assume that A & M Construction owes Joe $20,000. On April 1, it pays Joe $2,000. The following day, A & M files a bankruptcy petition. This payment is the simplest type of transfer. Assume, instead, that A & M owes Joe $20,000 and on January 2 gives Joe a security interest in all inventory, which Joe perfects. A & M files a bankruptcy petition on January 3. A transfer was made by the granting of a security interest.

If the security interest is not perfected when it is created, the transfer occurs when the security interest is perfected rather than when it is created. For example, assume that on May 3, A & M Construction buys materials from Joe on credit and gives Joe

---

Figure 32–1   Preferences

1. Transfer of debtor property
2. To or for the benefit of a creditor
3. On account of an antecedent debt
4. While the debtor was insolvent
5. Within 90 days of the filing of the petition
6. Allows the creditor to receive a larger percentage than had the transfer not been made

a security interest in equipment. Joe perfects the security interest on November 20. A & M files a bankruptcy petition on November 21. The transfer occurred on November 20, when the security interest was perfected.

BA § 547. Preferences

(2) For the purposes of this section . . . a transfer is made—

(A) at the time such transfer takes effect between the transferor and the transferee, if such transfer is perfected at, or within 10 days after, such time.

However, the secured party has a 10-day grace period within which to file a financing statement. If the financing statement is filed within that grace period, the transfer is made when the security interest was created [BA § 547(e)((2)(A)]. For example, assume that A & M Construction buys $5,000 worth of goods on credit from Joe on January 1, granting Joe a security interest in equipment. Joe files a financing statement on January 9. A & M files a bankruptcy petition on January 15. In this instance, there was no preferential transfer. Because the financing statement was filed within the 10-day period, the perfection relates back and the transfer was made on January 1. (The transfer on January 1 would not constitute a preference because it was made in exchange for the $5,000 loan. It would, therefore, not be on account of an antecedent debt.)

When is a transfer made when a payment is made by check? On the day the check is delivered or the day on which it is honored? The following case deals with this issue.

BARNHILL v. JOHNSON
112 S.Ct. 1386 (1992)

The debtor paid Barnhill by a check dated November 19 on November 18. The check was honored by the drawee bank on November 20. The debtor later filed a bankruptcy petition. The 90th day before the filing of the petition was November 20. The trustee attempted to recover the payment as preferential. The Bankruptcy Court and the District Court did not allow recovery. The Court of Appeals reversed and certiorari was granted.

REHNQUIST, Chief Justice, delivered the opinion of the Court, in which **WHITE, O'CONNOR, SCALIA, KENNEDY, SOUTER,** and **THOMAS, JJ.,** joined; **STEVENS, Judge,** filed a dissenting opinion, in which **BLACKMUN, Judge** joined

Our task is to determine whether, under the definition of transfer provided by § 101(54), and supplemented by § 547(e), the transfer that the trustee seeks to avoid can be said to have occurred before November 20.

We begin by noting that there can be no assertion that an unconditional transfer of the debtor's interest in property had occurred before November 20. This is because receipt of a check gives the recipient no right in the funds held by the bank on the drawer's account. Myriad events can intervene between delivery and presentment of the check that would result in the check being dishonored. The drawer could choose to close the account. A third party could obtain a lien against the account by garnishment or other proceedings. The bank might mistakenly refuse to honor the check.

The import of the preceding discussion for the instant case is that no transfer of any part of the debtor's claim against the bank occurred until the bank honored the check on November 20. The drawee bank honored the check by paying it. At that time, the bank had a right to "charge" the debtor's account. Honoring the check, in short, left the debtor in the position that it would have occupied if it had withdrawn cash from its account and handed it over to petitioner. We thus believe that when the debtor has directed the drawee bank to honor the check and the bank has done so, the debtor has implemented a "mode, direct or indirect . . . of disposing of property or an interest in property." § 101(54). For the purposes of payment by ordinary check, therefore, a "transfer" as defined by

§ 101(54) occurs on the date of honor, and not before. And since it is undisputed that honor occurred within the 90-day preference period, the trustee presumptively may avoid this transfer.

Finally, we note that our conclusion that no transfer of property occurs until the time of honor is consistent with § 547(e)(2)(A). That section provides that a transfer occurs at the time the transfer "takes effect between the transferor and the transferee. . . ." For the reasons given above, and in particular because the debtor in this case retained the ability to stop payment on the check until the very last, we do not think that the transfer of funds in this case can be said to have "taken effect between the debtor and petitioner" until the moment of honor.

Case Questions

1. Why did the court find that the transfer was not made when the check was delivered? Isn't payment by check equivalent to payment in cash?

2. What is the effect of this decision?

---

2. To a creditor. Only payments to creditors are voidable as preferences. Thus, if, on the eve of bankruptcy, the debtor made a $10,000 gift to a friend, the trustee could not void it as a preference.

3. For or on account of an antecedent debt. In order to be preferential, a transfer must be made on account of a preexisting debt. For example, assume that A & M Construction buys $10,000 from Joe on credit on the eve of bankruptcy, granting in return a security interest. The transfer in this case would not be preferential because it was made in return for new credit rather than to secure a preexisting loan.

4. Made while the debtor is insolvent. In order to be preferential, the transfer must have been made while the debtor was insolvent. However, there is a rebuttable presumption of debtor insolvency within 90 days prior to the filing of the bankruptcy petition [BA § 547(f)].

5. Within 90 days of the filing of the bankruptcy petition. Payments made within 90 days prior to the filing of the bankruptcy petition are preferential and voidable by the trustee in bankruptcy. For example, assume that on February 1, A & M Construction pays Joe $2,000 and on April 10, $3,000. On July 1, A & M files a bankruptcy petition. The trustee can void the April 10 payment (within the 90-day period) but not the February 1 payment (outside the 90-day period).

In addition, the trustee may void transfers made within one year prior to the filing of the bankruptcy petition if made to **insiders** with reasonable cause to believe that the debtor was insolvent at the time of the transfer [BA § 547(b)(4)(B)]. Thus, in order to void a transfer made outside the 90-day period, the trustee must be able to show (1) the transfer was made to an insider (the term *insider* includes a relative or partner of an individual debtor or an officer or director of a corporate director) [BA § 101(31)]; (2) that the debtor was insolvent at the time the transfer was made (the presumption of insolvency exists only for the 90 days preceding the filing of the petition); and (3) that the insider had reasonable cause to believe that the debtor was insolvent. For example, assume A & M Construction pays Andy Schulman, a partner in A & M, $5,000 on an existing debt on April 10, 1992. Assume further that A & M files a bankruptcy petition on March 17, 1993. The trustee can recover the payment as preferential if A & M was insolvent when the payment was made and Andy had reason to know of the insolvency.

6. The transfer enables the creditor to receive a greater percentage than under straight bankruptcy. In order for a transfer to be preferential, it must enable the creditor to receive a larger "share of the pie" than under liquidation proceedings. For example, assume that A & M Construction owes $10,000 to Charlie Creditor, a general unsecured creditor. On May 1, A & M pays $5,000, and on May 2, it files a bankruptcy petition. If the estate is sufficient to satisfy 25 percent of unsecured claims, the payment to Charlie is a preference. The payment enabled Charlie to receive $6,250 ($5,000 ÷ 25 percent of $5,000). Without the payment, he would have received only $2,500 (25 percent of $10,000).

There are several exceptions to the above rules, such as the exclusion for substantially contemporaneous exchanges [BA § 547(c)(1)] and payments in the ordinary course [BA § 547(c)(2)]. For example, if A & M receives a utility bill from the Electric Company on May 1, pays the bill on June 1, and files for bankruptcy on July 1, the payment is not preferential.

Fraudulent Conveyances The trustee may invalidate, as fraudulent conveyances, transfers within one year of the filing of the bankruptcy petition made with actual intent to defraud creditors [BA § 548 (a)(1)]. Certain circumstances create a presumption of intent to defraud, such as transfers of all debtor assets, transfers where the debtor continues in possession of the property, secret transfers, or transfers to family members. Further, transfers made within one year of the filing of the bankruptcy petition are voidable where an insolvent debtor (or one made insolvent by the transfer) received less than a reasonably equivalent value for the property transferred [BA § 548(a)(2)].

BA § 548. Fraudulent Transfers and Obligations

(a) The trustee may avoid any transfer . . . of the debtor . . . that was made . . . within one year before the date of the filing of the petition, if the debtor—

(1) made such transfer . . . with actual intent to hinder, delay, or defraud any entity to which the debtor was . . . indebted.

As you read the following case, ask yourself whether there was actual intent to defraud.

IN RE OSBOURNE
124 B.R. 726 (W.D. Ky. 1989)

James Osbourne, doing business as Harrodsburg Ready Mix and Supply Co. and the S & M Trucking Co., incurred a secured debt of over $170,000 owed to Coplay. On March 15, 1988, Osbourne transferred his one-half interest in his home to his wife "for love and affection." Coplay Cement Co. filed suit on April 22, 1988, to repossess the collateral. Coplay received the right to repossession on June 10 but never executed it because Osbourne told him that he was selling the business and would pay him from the proceeds of the sale. The business was never sold and Osbourne filed a bankruptcy petition on February 9, 1989.

DICKINSON, Bankruptcy Judge

Under section 548(A)(1), the Trustee is entitled to avoid any transfer of the debtor's property made within one year before the filing of a petition if such transfer was made voluntarily or involuntarily with actual intent to hinder, delay or defraud creditors. To avoid a transfer pursuant to § 548(A)(1), the Trustee must prove the following: (1) a transfer of an interest of the debtor's property or the incurring of an obligation; (2) made on or within one year of petition date; and (3) with actual fraudulent intent.

In the present case, this Court has no difficulty finding that Osbourne transferred his one-half interest in the marital residence to Barbara Osbourne within one year of filing the bankruptcy petition. Hence the first two elements have been satisfied. The third element of actual fraudulent intent, however, is the crucial and questionable element in this case. The Trustee must prove by clear and convincing evidence that the debtor actually intended to defraud his creditors at the time the transfer was made. Fraudulent intent however is rarely susceptible to direct proof. Therefore the courts have developed circumstances or "badges of fraud" to establish the requisite intent. Among the "badges of fraud" from which the courts have inferred intent include the following:

a. inadequate or no consideration given for the transfer;

b. transfers made to a family member or close relation;

c. debtor's financial condition before and after the transfer;

d. conveyance made while a suit is pending or threatened by creditors against the debtor;

e. secret or concealed conveyance;

f. debtor remains in possession, reserves the right to use or benefit, or deals with the property as his own.

A combination of the above circumstantial facts generally provides reasonable grounds to find the transfer was made with actual intent to hinder, delay or defraud creditors.

A review of the facts in the present case reveals the existence of a number of "badges of fraud." On the date of the transfer between debtor and Barbara Osbourne, debtor had been substantially indebted to Coplay. In fact, the transfer occurred shortly before Coplay filed suit against Osbourne in state court and at no time prior to the transfer did Osbourne notify Coplay of the transfer. Admittedly, the transfer was made to Barbara Osbourne, debtor's wife, for little or no consideration.

Based upon our review of the undisputed facts, we conclude that the transfer of property by the debtor to his spouse for no consideration, while remaining in possession of property and at a time that his financial condition was questionable clearly indicates a scheme to defraud creditors. Accordingly the Trustee may avoid the transfer under § 548.

Case Questions

1. What is the purpose of setting aside fraudulent conveyances? To which policy underlying bankruptcy law does this relate?

2. Why do courts use "badges of fraud"? Do you think that debtors "intend" the fraud in such circumstances?

3. What happens to the house?

Distributing the Property

One in possession of property of the bankruptcy estate at the time the petition is filed must turn the property over to the trustee. Thus, even perfected secured creditors in possession of recently repossessed collateral must turn the collateral over to the trustee. In addition, because of the automatic stay, the secured party must obtain relief from the stay to either repossess or to sell the property.

Claims secured by valid liens, such as perfected Article 9 security interests and properly recorded real property mortgages, are satisfied before unsecured claims. If the property subject to the lien is worth less than the amount of the secured claims, the trustee may abandon it as of "inconsequential value" and let the lienholder keep it. By contrast, if the property is worth more than the amount of the claims asserted, the trustee will sell the property, pay lien creditors, and keep the remainder for the estate.

General Claims

All other claims constitute general claims. The bankruptcy estate has been created for eventual sale and distribution of the proceeds to general claimants.

Proof and Allowance of Claims   Creditors that wish to participate in the eventual distribution must file a **proof of claim** with the court. However, distribution is only made to allowable claims. A claim will be disallowed if it is unenforceable against the debtor for any reason.

Priorities

Typically, the estate is insufficient to pay all creditors. Therefore, to a large extent, the study of distribution of the estate concentrates on the order in which one is given access to the limited funds. This is important because if one is too far down the distribution ladder, one collects very little. There are six class of claims [BA § 507]. Each class must be paid in full before the next class is paid in part. If there is not enough money to fully pay the claimants in any one class, the funds available are prorated among the creditors in that class.

1. *Administration expenses* have the first priority, including attorney's fees; costs of repairing, storing, or selling property; and the trustee's fee.

2. Certain *unsecured claims* have second priority. In an involuntary case, a claim arising in the *ordinary course* of the debtor's business, after commencement of the case but before the appointment of a trustee or the order for relief, shall next be paid. For example, the creditors of Dan Debtor Donuts, Inc. file an involuntary petition in bankruptcy on May 30. On June 2, Xavier makes his regular delivery of powdered sugar. Xavier's claim is in this second class of claims.

3. Subject to certain specified exceptions, *wage claims* are classified third, including claims for salary, commissions, vacation, severance, and sick pay. However, only wages earned by an individual within 90 days before the filing of the bankruptcy petition fall into this category. In addition, the amount is limited to $2,000 for each employee. For example, assume that the ABC Business files a petition in bankruptcy on September 28, owing Ernie wages for the months of August and September totaling $6,000. Ernie has third priority status for $2,000 of those wages. The remaining $4,000 is a general claim without priority.

4. Claims for contributions to *employee benefit plans* have a fourth priority. The priority applies only to contributions due from services rendered within 180 days before the filing of the bankruptcy petition. The amount given priority is calculated by multiplying the number of employees times $2,000 and subtracting the total of the amount paid under the third priority above and the amount paid by the estate to other employee benefit plans.

5. *Consumers* who made a money deposit for property or services that were never provided have a fifth priority, limited to $900 per claimant. For example, assume that Charlie Consumer pays $3,000 as a deposit on Dan Debtor's car, which he has agreed to purchase. Charlie has fifth priority status for $900 of the deposit. The remaining $2,100 is a general claim without priority.

6. Certain specified *tax claims* have a sixth priority status.

Order of Distribution

The Bankruptcy Act sets forth the rules governing distribution of the estate and the order in which such distribution will be made [BA § 726]. Each creditor within a particular class must be paid in full before any claim in the next class will be paid. If there are insufficient funds to pay all claims within a particular class, the claims share pro rata in the available proceeds. The distribution is made in the following order:

1. The classes afforded priority, in the order discussed above, are paid first.
2. Allowed unsecured claims timely filed, or tardily filed if the creditor did not have notice or actual knowledge of the bankruptcy, are paid next.
3. Allowed unsecured claims tardily filed except as outlined above are paid third.
4. Fines and punitive damages are paid fourth.
5. Postpetition interest on prepetition claims are paid fifth.
6. Last, in the event that there is anything undistributed, the remainder goes to the debtor.

Discharge

In general, the goal of a debtor in bankruptcy is to achieve a *discharge* extinguishing all debt liability. In fact, bankruptcy operates to discharge *most* debtors from liability on *most* debts.

Objections to Discharge

A debtor that is denied a discharge is in a disastrous position, having given up possession of all but exempt property for distribution to creditors but still owing creditors for debts not fully paid. The 10 grounds justifying a denial of discharge are as follows [BA § 727(a)]:

1. A discharge is denied to corporations and partnerships. Only individual debtors can achieve discharge under Chapter 7.

The next six grounds require a finding of some type of improper behavior on the part of the debtor.

2. A debtor who has made a fraudulent conveyance may be denied a discharge.
3. An unjustified failure to keep or preserve necessary financial information justifies denial of discharge.
4. A discharge may be denied where the debtor knowingly and fraudulently in connection with the case:
   a. Made a false oath or account.
   b. Presented a false claim.
   c. Gave, received, or attempted to give or receive consideration for action or inaction with respect to the case; or
   d. Withheld information relating to the debtor's financial affairs.
5. A debtor who has failed to satisfactorily explain any loss of assets may be denied a discharge.
6. A debtor may be denied a discharge who has refused to testify under specified circumstances.
7. A debtor who has committed, as an insider, any of the foregoing acts in connection with another bankruptcy case may also be denied a discharge.
8. A debtor who has obtained a discharge in straight bankruptcy, or under the provisions of Chapter 11, within the last six years is denied a discharge.

9. A debtor who has obtained a discharge in a Chapter 13 proceeding within the last six years is denied a discharge unless sufficiently large payments were made under the Chapter 13 plan.

10. Where the court has approved a written waiver of discharge, executed by the debtor after the order for relief, discharge will be denied.

Exceptions to Discharge

A discharge relieves the debtor of all debts whether or not a proof of claim is filed and whether or not the claim is allowable [BA § 727(b)]. However, the following debts will not be discharged [BA § 523].

1. Taxes for the three years preceding the filing.

2. Debts that have been incurred based on false representations.

3. Debts that are neither listed nor scheduled.

4. A debt for fraud in a fiduciary capacity.

5. Alimony or child support payments.

6. Claims for willful and malicious injury by the debtor.

7. Fines or penalties owed to a governmental unit.

8. Certain debts incurred as educational loans.

9. Any debt that was or could have been listed or scheduled by the debtor in a prior bankruptcy case.

Effect of Discharge

In general, a discharge protects the debtor from future action by creditors to enforce remaining obligations. In addition to barring judicial action to collect the unpaid debt, the discharge prohibits creditor extrajudicial actions such as phone calls and dunning letters. Debtors are also protected from creditor pressure by limiting the enforceability of reaffirmation agreements. A reaffirmation agreement is an agreement by the debtor to repay a discharged debt. Under bankruptcy law, such agreements are only enforceable if the agreement was made before the discharge was granted, the court advised the debtor of its consequences, and the debtor had a right to rescind the agreement for 30 days. Further, in the case of consumer debts not secured by real property, the agreement must not impose undue hardship and

must be in the best interest of the debtor or the agreement must be a good faith settlement of dischargeability litigation [BA § 524(c) and (d)].

CHAPTER 11

As an alternative to filing for straight bankruptcy seeking liquidation and distribution under Chapter 7, a debtor might choose to file for **reorganization** under Chapter 11. A debtor filing under Chapter 11 seeks protection from creditor action while developing a plan to pay creditors.

Commencing the Case

Just as under straight bankruptcy, the Chapter 11 case begins with the filing of a bankruptcy petition. Again, the petition can be filed either by the debtor or by creditors, with the grounds for creditor action the same as discussed for Chapter 7 bankruptcy. Again, debtor insolvency is not a prerequisite to seeking protection under Chapter 11. With minor exceptions, debtors eligible to file under straight bankruptcy can file under Chapter 11.

Creditor Organization

Following the filing of the petition, the debtor files a list of creditors, who are notified of the pending case. It is not necessary for a creditor whose name appears on the schedule of creditors to file a proof of claim.

A meeting of creditors is held within a reasonable period of time following the filing of the petition. Because it is common for a debtor in Chapter 11 to have a large number of creditors, the court can appoint a committee of unsecured creditors comprised of the seven largest unsecured creditors willing to serve. This committee typically investigates the debtor's acts and financial condition and participates in the formulation of the plan.

Operation of the Business

The primary function of a Chapter 11 filing is the financial rehabilitation of the debtor. To properly achieve this rehabilitation, the continued operation of any business is required. Thus, unless extraordinary circumstances dictate otherwise, the business remains in operation, with the debtor and existing management ordinarily in control.

Alternatively, a trustee may be appointed where there has been fraud, dishonesty, and/or mismanagement by the debtor or where the appointment is in the best interests of the creditors [BA § 1104]. Where a trustee is not appointed, an examiner may instead be appointed to investigate the competence and honesty of the debtor.

Debtor Protection

In order for the debtor to be successful in operation of the business, not only must Chapter 11 provide for protection from creditor action but it must also aid the debtor in overcoming existing financial problems. One of the first problems encountered by most Chapter 11 debtors is obtaining additional credit. Several incentives are offered to potential lenders. First, unsecured creditors that extend credit after the filing of the petition in the "ordinary course of business" have administrative expense priority status. In addition, the court may, after hearing, provide this same status for nonordinary course lenders.

Second, the court may, after hearing, afford lenders priority over other administrative expenses, a lien on the debtor's unencumbered property, or a lien on the debtor's encumbered property. In fact, the court may grant to postpetition lenders a lien on already encumbered property that is equal to or has priority over existing liens, as long as it ensures "adequate protection" to existing lienholders [BA § 364(d)].

To assist the debtor in the operation of its business, the debtor may continue using and selling noncash encumbered property without court hearing [BA § 363]. For example, if Al's Appliance Store files a Chapter 11 petition and First Bank has a perfected security interest in Al's inventory, Al can continue to sell inventory in the ordinary course of business. Again, the court might require that the Bank's interest be given adequate protection. The court can, upon hearing, allow the debtor to use or sell encumbered noncash property not in the ordinary course of business. Similarly, cash collateral may be used upon court order.

Plan of Rehabilitation

It is the plan of rehabilitation—its function and effect—that distinguishes Chapter 11 from straight bankruptcy. If no trustee has been appointed, the debtor has the first opportunity to prepare and file a plan. If a trustee has been appointed, the trustee, debtor, creditors' committee, and any other interested party might prepare and file a plan. More than one plan may be filed.

Basically, the purpose is to set forth a plan for repayment to the creditors. The plan should divide creditors into classes of creditors, giving equal treatment to members of the same class. However, there will not necessarily be equal treatment between members of different classes. For example, it is common to treat creditors holding small claims differently from those holding large claims.

Acceptance of the Plan

The first step in the acceptance process is disclosure of the plan to the creditors. The bankruptcy court does not judge the fairness or appropriateness of the plan but, instead, requires full disclosure to creditors affected with the assumption that they will make this judgment. Thus, before acceptances can be sought, creditors must be provided with copies of the plan (or summaries) and a written disclosure statement approved by the court (after hearing) as containing adequate information.

Creditors with allowed claims and shareholders with allowed interests are entitled to vote on plan acceptance [BA § 1126(a)]. In spite of this provision, the votes of parties who would receive nothing under a plan do not need to be solicited. Such parties are deemed to have voted against such plan. Similarly, parties whose class is not impaired under the plan are deemed to have voted for the plan. The rights of a class are not impaired if its legal rights are not changed to a significant extent by the plan [BA § 1124]. In order for a class of claims to have accepted the plan, more than one half the number of claims and two thirds the dollar amount of the allowed claims actually voting on the plan must approve it.

Confirmation of the Plan

A hearing on confirmation is then conducted. While more than one plan can be filed and accepted, it is only possible for one plan to be confirmed by the court. Even a plan that has been accepted by every class of claims must be confirmed [BA § 1129(a)]. This ensures that the creditors of each class are treated fairly and that dissenting members of each class are treated fairly. For example, one requirement is that dissenting members of each class are to receive under the plan at least as much as they would have received under a straight bankruptcy.

If a plan has not been accepted by every class, it is still possible for it to be confirmed. Such a confirmation is sometimes referred to as a **cram down.** The court must determine whether confirmation of such a plan would be fair and equitable.

The provisions of a Chapter 11 plan are binding on the debtor, creditors, and shareholders even if such parties have not accepted the plan. In general,

confirmation of the plan operates as a discharge. For example, if, under the confirmed plan, Dan was to pay 2 percent of his outstanding debt of $10,000 to Chuck for 40 months, at the end of the 40-month period the entire debt would be discharged even though only $8,000 of the amount had been repaid.

Read the following case where the court decides whether or not a plan should be confirmed. Do you think the plan is fair and equitable?

IN RE D & F CONSTRUCTION INC., v. CLASSIC HOMES, INC.

865 F.2d 673 (5th Cir. 1989).

Cimarron Properties began a construction project financed by Mercury/Milam and evidenced by a one-year promissory note and mortgage. When Cimarron was unable to complete the project, the debtor, D & F Construction, Inc., took it over, assuming the loan and the security agreement and receiving additional financing. D & F also agreed to a net profits agreement. D & F completed the construction but failed to pay the loan, which was over $7 million on the day the bankruptcy petition was filed.

D & F proposed a Chapter 11 plan of reorganization, to which only Mercury Savings Association and Ben Milam Savings and Loan Association (Mercury/Milam) objected. The plan (1) rejected the net profits agreement and (2) provided a negative amortization plan for repayment of the debt over a 15-year period. By the terms of the plan, more than $4.7 million would still be owed by the 15th year. There would be a balloon payment of $4.7 million on April 15, 2002. Mecury/Milam challenged confirmation of the plan. When the District Court affirmed the decision of the Bankruptcy Court, Mercury/Milam appealed.

CLARK, Chief Judge

Section 1129(b)(1) of the bankruptcy code provides that a debtor may "cram down" its plan over the objection of a creditor "if the plan does not discriminate unfairly, and is fair and equitable with respect to each class of claims or interests that is impaired under, and has not accepted, the plan." Section 1129(b)(2) then sets forth requirements which must be met for a plan to be "fair and equitable." A plan which does not meet the standards set forth in § 1129(b)(2) cannot be "fair and equitable." However, technical compliance with all the requirements in § 1129(b)(2) does not assure that the plan is "fair and equitable." Section 1129(b)(2) sets minimal standards plans must meet. However, it is not to be interpreted as requiring that every plan not prohibited be approved. A court must consider the entire plan in the context of the rights of the creditors under state law and the particular facts and circumstances when determining whether a plan is "fair and equitable."

Assuming without deciding that the requirements set forth in § 1129(b)(2) are literally met, the debtor's plan is neither fair nor equitable. Mercury/Milam did not lend its credit to this project on the strength of Cimarron's fiscal integrity nor that of the debtor. It furnished funds that paid for constructing the apartments on the basis that it be given a right under Texas law to recover its funds from the land and improvements if they could not be repaid as promised. Yet, under the plan, Mercury/Milam cannot exercise the foreclosure rights it reserved. In addition, the plan's negative amortization requires that for the first 12 years Mercury/Milam increase its financing of this project and thus assume a worse financial position than it was in at the time of confirmation. The net effect of negative amortization is to force Mercury/Milam to make a post-confirmation loan to the debtor for a period of 12 years.

We do not hold there can never be an occasion when negative amortization would be fair and equitable. We do say this plan is not fair and equitable.

Negative amortization coupled with deferring substantially all repayment of principal for 15 years can only be considered reasonable if one speculates that the present condition of the Fort Worth, Texas real estate market will improve substantially.

A plan that is not fair and equitable with respect to an impaired secured creditor cannot be confirmed on the basis that such inequity is necessary to protect junior creditors. If market conditions are such that an effective plan of reorganization cannot be developed that is fair and equitable to dissenting creditors, Mercury/Milam is entitled to foreclose on its liens.

Case Questions

1. Could you change the plan in this case to be fair and equitable?

2. Why are cram downs permissible?

CHAPTER 13

Another alternative to filing for straight bankruptcy, available to individuals with regular income, is a Chapter 13 filing. It is less complicated and therefore less expensive than straight bankruptcy. Subject to few exceptions, an individual with unsecured debts of less than $100,000 and secured debts of less than $350,000 may use Chapter 13. A Chapter 13 case is initiated by the debtor filing a petition—there are no involuntary Chapter 13 cases. The filing creates an automatic stay, giving the debtor protection from creditor action while the plan for repayment is being prepared.

A trustee is appointed in every Chapter 13 case. In fact, the powers of the trustee are similar to the powers discussed in the straight bankruptcy section except that the debtor does not have to relinquish possession of all debtor property to the trustee. It is the role of the trustee to utilize avoidance powers to protect the estate of the debtor.

The debtor prepares and files the Chapter 13 plan, which provides for full payment in cash of all claims entitled to priority. The plan may provide for less than full payment of other unsecured claims. It is only important that the plan treat all unsecured claims in the same class similarly. Payment under the plan must be made within three years, or within five years if the court grants an extension. Debtor payments must begin within 30 days from the filing of the plan.

Before a Chapter 13 plan can be confirmed, the court must approve the plan. The court will approve a plan that is fair and equitable. The interests of unsecured claims are protected by the requirement that the plan cannot give them less than they would have received in a straight bankruptcy proceeding. Upon completion of the payments specified in the plan for relief, the debtor is given a complete discharge. The discharge available under Chapter 13 is sometimes referred to as a ''superdischarge'' because except for debts with priority, alimony, and child support payments, all debts are discharged without the numerous exceptions found in straight bankruptcy.

Figure 32–2 on page 638 compares the various bankruptcy alternatives.

MORALITY OF BANKRUPTCY

Is it moral to file for bankruptcy and discharge your lawful debts? Are the bankruptcy laws, because they sanction this conduct, immoral? The following article explores the moral component of the bankruptcy laws.

How to Think about Bankruptcy Ethics: Ethics in Bankruptcy*

Is bankruptcy ''wrong?'' The question as posed is too complicated. The term ''bankruptcy'' suffers, not from an insufficiency, but from an excess, of meaning. ''Bankruptcy'' is, at least, a scheme for collecting the property of the debtor; for distributing ''equally'' among

---

*Source: J. D. Ayer, ''How to Think about Bankruptcy Ethics: Ethics in Bankruptcy,'' 60 Am Bankruptcy L.J. 355 (1986). Reprinted with permission.

Figure 32–2 Comparison of Bankruptcy Alternatives

	Chapter 7	Chapter 11	Chapter 13
Goal	Liquidation and discharge	Reorganization and discharge	Adjustment and discharge
Petition	Voluntary and involuntary	Voluntary and involuntary	Voluntary
Debtor	Individuals; partnerships; corporations; excluding railroads, insurance companies, banks, savings and loans, and credit unions	Individuals; partnerships; corporations; same exclusions as for Chapter 7 except railroads	Individuals with regular income and unsecured debts of less than $100,000 or secured debts of less than $350,000
Procedure	Nonexempt property gathered, sold, and proceeds distributed	Plan submitted, approved, and followed	Plan submitted, approved, and followed
Discharge	Debts discharged after distribution; no discharge for corporations, partnerships, where debtor misconduct, and for certain debts including taxes, school loans, child support, and alimony	Confirmation and payment is discharge	Superdischarge; all debts discharged except debts with priority, alimony, and child support
Advantages	Fresh start	Debtor's business continues in operation	Debtor retains property; more debts discharged

creditors; for protecting going-concern values; for giving the debtor a discharge. Better to ask a narrower question: is it "wrong" to avoid paying one's debts? Or to put it differently, is there an obligation, independent of the law, to pay one's debts; and if so, what, if anything, can we learn about this obligation from bankruptcy law?

Certainly in times past, the law has assumed that there was an independent obligation to pay one's debts. It was once well established that a promise to pay a debt discharged in bankruptcy was enforceable on the basis of the "moral obligation" to pay one's debts, independent of the discharge. And not only the law. There is good reason to believe that this obligation was one that debtors took "to heart as well as to mind;" an "ethical" obligation, in the sense that I am using the term.

■ ■ ■

If you wanted to make a case that bankruptcy is no longer a "wrong," I suspect you could do it best through scrutinizing the history of the bankruptcy discharge. If you want to make clear your disapproval of people who do not pay their debts, one way to do it is simply to refuse to release them from liability: to provide that the debtor remains liable until the debt is paid notwithstanding his present or prospective ability to pay. *Granting* a discharge does not, of itself say that it is "right" to avoid paying one's debts. But if the state has any role as teacher, then granting the discharge is at least consistent with an attitude of tolerance towards not paying one's debts. And indeed, I think the development of the discharge over the past several centuries gives vivid evidence of our changed attitudes toward the place of bankruptcy in our law.

■ ■ ■

Thus, if the law is a teacher, then the law's attitude to paying one's debts is in some sense a lesson to the debtor as to what should be the debtor's attitude towards paying his debts. But on closer scrutiny, I think the history and place of the discharge is more complicated than it appears at first blush.

This is true, first, because of the great diversity of motives that lie behind the discharge. We are well aware that the idea of legislative "intent" in any case is at best something of a heroic fiction. But not even heroic fiction is enough to deal with the diversity of motives for the discharge. Thus for example, it seems clear that the purpose of including a discharge in the 1705 Act was not to relieve the debtor from his debts. Rather, the purpose was to induce the debtor's cooperation: if creditors may grant, or deny, the discharge, the debtor will have to be alert to stay in their good graces. While the original "cooperation" policy has receded, it remains in present law. It is found in the provisions mandating that the debtor's discharge be denied if he conceals property of the estate or business records, or if he makes a false oath, or refuses to obey a lawful order. That is, the Code today provides that the debtor will be denied his discharge if he does *not* cooperate with the administration.

In any event, by 1898, the stated purpose of the discharge had changed. Thus it has been conventional since 1898 to say that the purpose of the discharge is to give the debtor a "fresh start."

■ ■ ■

1. BANKRUPTCY AS A PLANNING TOOL

I want to approach my next point through a sharp, but I trust a sufficiently brief, detour. In the handbooks of Seneca the Elder, there are a number of rhetorical exercises that pose problems in political and moral thought. One such exercise tells the story of 10 young men who have dissipated their fortunes. They learn of a rule which provides that a blind man is entitled to 1,000 *denarii* from the state. They agree to draw lots; the loser will be blinded and take the award. The "successful" contestant is indeed blinded, and applies for the 1,000 *denarii*. But on these facts, the state refuses to give the money.

What is going on here? Without making too much of it, I suppose the point is that the young men misunderstood the purpose of the rule. The 1,000 *denarii* was supposed to be an instance of compassion for misfortune: it wasn't something you could bring about by choice. And I think the same kind of problem underlies bankruptcy law. The question is: whether and to what extent is it proper to use bankruptcy as a "planning tool"? . . . I don't think we have any clear consensus on this issue. But I do think our decision on this issue implies some particular notions about the question whether bankruptcy is "wrong."

a. Exemption Planning

I know of no issue that better typifies our confusion over the moral content of bankruptcy law than the matter of "exemption planning." Here is the classic example: Debtor, a resident of the state of Magenta, has $5,000 in cash, and owes claims in the amount of $100,000. Debtor consults Leonard Lawyer to assist Debtor in dealing with his creditors. Leonard Lawyer advises Debtor to file for bankruptcy. Under the law of Magenta, cash is vulnerable to creditor execution; but Magenta permits the debtor to exempt $5,000 in an account in a Savings and Loan Association. Is it proper for Debtor, on the eve of bankruptcy, to protect money by putting the cash in a Savings and Loan account? More pointedly, suppose Debtor knows nothing about the exemption laws of Magenta. Is it proper for Leonard Lawyer to advise him to do so?

■ ■ ■

c. Bankruptcy in Business Planning

Business bankruptcy (including reorganization) has achieved a notoriety of late unknown since the Great Depression. In the process it has sustained an onslaught of criticism alleging that managers or entrepreneurs are manipulating the bankruptcy process to evade just debts. The criticism is broad-ranging, and much of it is too abstract to permit coherent comment . . . . [C]onsider these facts: Buyer is considering the purchase of a piece of property. The price is $1 million: $200,000 down, plus the assumption of a 10-year $800,000 mortgage at 12 percent—payments of $11,477.68 per month. Buyer doesn't have the cash to meet the mortgage payments, but he feels he could do it if he could extend the term to 20 years, giving him a monthly payment of $8,808.69—a saving of $2,668.99 per month. Without making any effort to refinance, Buyer pays the $200,000 and takes title to the property. Before the first payment is due, Buyer asks Seller to accept the 20-year stretchout. Seller refuses. Buyer immediately files for relief under chapter 11. Clearly, chapter 11 offers opportunities that would allow him to save the property: he might be able to stall the Seller long enough to get new financing from a third party, or he might simply wear Seller down to the point where he accepts the 20-year stretchout that he previously rejected. Failing that, he may even be able to confirm a plan over Seller's objection.

■ ■ ■

What adds bite to the hypothetical is the very strong suggestion that Buyer had this plan in mind *all along*, from the moment he began negotiations: in other words, that he used the possibility of bankruptcy as a business planning device. . . .

d. Summary

In this section, I have been trying to isolate an ''ethical'' component in bankruptcy law. I considered the nature and scope of the discharge; the law of fraudulent transfer, and the matter of bankruptcy as a ''business planning'' device. I suggested that policies underlying the discharge for the most part do not consider whether a debtor ought, or ought not, to pay his just debts. . . . Finally, I suggested that there is evidence, although fragmentary and incomplete, to suggest that bankruptcy should be regarded as a remedy for unanticipated misfortune, but not as a planning device.

Thought Questions

1. Do you think that the history of bankruptcy suggests a weakening today in the perception of what is morally wrong? Explain.
2. Select some provisions in the bankruptcy laws that suggest a moral component.
3. Do you agree that bankruptcy should not be used as a planning device?

END–OF–CHAPTER QUESTIONS

1. What factors do you think have contributed to making us a debt-oriented society?
2. What would influence a debtor's decision whether to file for straight bankruptcy, reorganization, or Chapter 13? Explain.
3. Are the debtor-creditor laws balanced in favor of creditors? Explain.
4. Explain the relationship between preferences and fraudulent conveyances.
5. Analyze the following statement: ''The trustee has the power to void preferential

payments to achieve the policy of equality of distribution among creditors.''

6. Christy Baker borrows $5,000 from John York on January 1, granting John a security interest in equipment to secure repayment. John files the financing statement on January 12. Christy files a bankruptcy petition on January 15. Upon what basis might the trustee invalidate this security interest? Explain.

7. Compare the confirmation of a plan of reorganization with liquidation. Does a cram down plan have more in common with liquidation?

8. On June 25, 1982, the Rockport National Bank lent David Crowley $6,500 to buy a Mercedes sedan, taking in return a security interest. The bank failed to file a financing statement but repeatedly asked Crowley for the title so that it could note its interest on the certificate of title. Crowley failed to furnish the title. Under Massachusetts law, the certificate of title statute did not apply because the car was over 10 years old. When Crowley filed for bankruptcy, the trustee attempted to void the security interest. Who has priority, the trustee or Rockport? Explain. See *In re Crowley*, 42 B.R. 603 (D. Maine 1984).

9. In 1982, a construction enterprise was organized. A parent corporation was created as a holding company with stock in four subsidiaries, one of which was Jobst & Sons. By early 1984, the parent company was in financial difficulties. On May 3, Jobst borrowed $250,000 from Commercial National Bank to continue the operations. In exchange, Jobst guaranteed the parent's debt to the bank (approximately $7.4 million) and granted the bank a security interest in all of its assets. Ten months later, Jobst filed for bankruptcy. The bank enforced its security interest, selling the collateral. If the trustee attempts to recover the collateral as preferential, will it be successful? If the trustee attempts to recover the collateral as a fraudulent conveyance, will it be successful? Explain. See *Covey v. Commercial National Bank*, 960 F.2d 657 (7th Cir. 1992).

10. Bildisco, a company in the business of distributing building supplies, filed for reorganization under Chapter 11 of the bankruptcy laws. Bildisco had a three-year collective bargaining agreement with a union. Bildisco was having financial trouble paying health and pension obligations under the contract. It requested, as part of the debtor's reorganization, permission to reject the collective bargaining agreement. The rejection would save the company $100,000 and help it to survive. Do you think the court should grant the request? Explain. See *N.L.R.B. v. Bildisco*, 104 S. Ct. 1188 (1984).

Chapter 33

Consumer Protection

■

CRITICAL THINKING INQUIRIES

As you read this chapter, you should be able to address the following:

- Identify any gaps in the federal laws that relate to credit extension and/or collection.
- Compare and contrast nonjudicial and judicial debt collection.
- Contrast secured and unsecured debts in relationship to the consequences of each.
- Analyze: ``The nature of credit collection is such that there is no ethical way to collect debt.``
- How will the trend toward lender liability affect consumers?

MANAGERIAL PERSPECTIVE

Adrian Rye was hired as a senior manager of Ethical Debt Collectors, a collection agency that handles business accounts. After just one month on the job, Rye wonders whether the company name is an oxymoron. He is constantly confronted with moral questions and ethical dilemmas concerning debt collection, even though the company complies with the laws. Additionally, he is confused by the morass of laws governing debtor/creditor relations and their apparent overlappage. Nonetheless, he is determined to work through the problems and manage an ethical credit collection company.

Ethical Debt Collectors received an account from Honest John's Pawn Shop for collection. Honest John's extended a loan to a debtor at an interest rate higher than legally permissible.

- What policies should Rye establish to ensure compliance with the law?
- What policies should Rye establish to ensure his desire to manage an ethical credit collection company?
- Should Ethical Debt Collectors collect Honest John's account?

Had society heeded Shakespeare's admonition "neither a borrower nor a lender be," Adrian Rye would not have a problem and we could have dispensed with this chapter. However, this is not the case. Managers, such as Rye, will have to face law and ethics in the management of debt.

The average American family owes $40,000. And the average consumer continues to be willing to go further in debt to accumulate more "things." The essence of this attitude is summed up well by a bumpersticker that reads, "He who dies with the most toys wins."

This chapter is about those who owe money—**debtors**—and those to whom money is owed—**creditors.** The chapter first takes a historical perspective and then examines the incurrence of debt through borrowing and the laws that apply. Next, the chapter delves into the debt collection process and the applicable laws. Finally, the chapter treats lender liability.

HISTORICAL PERSPECTIVE

The debtor/creditor relationship is not new. Back in the middle ages under feudal rule in England, creditors were ordinarily the landholding class, while debtors were lowly servants who worked the land. These debtor-servants were locked in an impasse. They needed to live on the land and work it for survival. Yet it was the very land that drove them deeper into debt, because of the financial requirements of their landlords, which they ordinarily were not able to meet. Held in bondage to the land, these serfs became resigned to their plight.

This type of indentureship did not escape this country. The need for landowners to work the land resulted in a demand for slaves—involuntary servants. Enslavement in the United States was abolished in 1863; however, remnants of the system have continued down through the 20th century under different guises. Today, for example, many farmers are heavily in debt due to the purchase of high-tech machinery and other farm-related items. This, coupled with bad farm years, have indentured them to their creditors. For many of them, working the farm is not an option but the only foreseeable way of eventually extricating themselves from indebtedness.

The law has evolved over the centuries in the area of debtor/creditor relations. Everyone has heard of debtor prisons where those who could not afford to pay their creditors spent sleepless nights in damp dungeons. Debtors' prisons are only of historical interest now, yet the pain of debt continues to be a real threat. One of the biggest causes of divorce today is debt. One of the significant causes of suicide is financial distress. Debt takes its toll. How true is the saying, "you either pay me now or pay me later."

INCURRING THE DEBT

There are two major ways in which debt can be incurred. First, one can borrow money from a lender. The lender may be a bank, another financial institute, or even a friend. This is normally referred to as a **closed-end credit** transaction since it is a "one shot deal" in which a sum certain is borrowed and the details of the repayment are specified.

Another method by which the debtor/creditor relationship arises is by the use of credit cards such as Visa, Discover, and American Express. This is normally referred to as an **open-end credit** transaction since the extension of credit is repeated and the specific amounts charged are not definitively specified beforehand. The amounts of the periodic repayments are not ordinarily specified, either. Both of these loan extension transactions are governed by federal statutes: the Equal Credit Opportunity Act (ECOA), the Truth in Lending Act (TILA), and the Fair Credit Reporting Act (FCRA) (see Figure 33–1).

Figure 33–1   Federal Consumer Legislation

Act	Description
Equal Credit Opportunity Act	Requires nondiscrimination in extension of credit
Truth in Lending Act	Requires disclosures to consumer regarding credit extension
Fair Credit Reporting Act	Regulates credit bureaus and their reporting
Electronic Funds Transfer Act	Regulates electronic funds transfers
Fair Debt Collection Practices Act	Restricts practices of third-party debt collectors

Equal Credit Opportunity Act

Congress passed the Equal Credit Opportunity Act in 1975. It prohibits creditors from discriminating against credit applicants on the basis of sex, marital status, race, color, religion, national origin, and age. Additionally, creditors may not discriminate against an applicant because of public dependency or because he or she exercised a right under the act. The plan of the act is to keep lenders focused on creditworthiness rather than on subjective considerations that have the effect of excluding minorities from credit with no rational basis.

The ECOA commits to the Federal Home Loan Board (FHLB) the authority to prescribe regulations to carry out the purposes of the act. The FHLB has promulgated regulations to fulfill that prescription. These regulations, known as Regulation B, are the heart of the law's requirements.

ECOA applies to all persons who regularly participate in the decision to extend **consumer** credit — primarily for personal, family, or household purposes — and most of its provisions are applicable to transactions involving **commercial** credit as well.

Generally, Regulation B prohibits creditors from making statements to applicants that would discourage them from pursuing an application. And a creditor may not use any of the information to discriminate against the applicant on the basis of any of the protected classes. To help ensure against such practices, the Regulation contains some absolute no-nos that include a prohibition against asking:

- Whether any of the income stated in the application is derived from alimony or child support (unless it is made clear that the applicant does not have to answer).

- About the sex, race, color, religion, or national origin of the applicant (except for purposes of monitoring).

- About the applicant's birth control practices.

- About intentions concerning the bearing, rearing, or capacity to have children.

Model application forms provided by the FHLB aid credit extenders in complying with the act.

In most cases, the act requires a creditor to notify an applicant within 30 days of any favorable or adverse action taken on a credit application. The notification must be in writing and include a statement of the specific reasons for the adverse decision or a disclosure of the applicant's right to receive such a statement upon request. Statements that the applicant was "deemed noncreditworthy," failed to pass the "minimum internal standards," or achieved "too low a score on a creditworthiness point scale" are too vague to meet the "specific reasons" requirement.

The act specifically delegates the authority to enforce the act to a variety of agencies. The Federal Trade Commission has responsibility for enforcing the act with respect to businesses that are not specifically under the enforcement domain of another agency.

There are no criminal sanctions for violating the ECOA. However, the civil sanctions may be harsh. A creditor who violates the act may be liable for actual damages plus $10,000 in punitive damages. In a class action suit, the total recovery may be much more. Additionally, plaintiffs who are successful are entitled to attorney fees, and a creditor who loses pays the court costs. The next case involving the cancellation of a credit card involves equal credit opportunity issues.

MILLER v. AMERICAN EXPRESS CO.
688 F. 2d 1235 (9th Cir. 1982)

Maurice Miller applied for and received an American Express (Amex) credit card (designated a basic card). His wife applied for and was granted a supplementary card signed by both her and her husband. Mr. Miller died. Pursuant to company policy, American Express canceled Mrs. Miller's supplementary card and invited her to apply for a basic account. She applied and was issued a new card.

Mrs. Miller brought suit against Amex for violation of the ECOA based on Amex's cancellation of her supplementary card. The district court awarded summary judgment to Amex and Mrs. Miller appealed to the Ninth Circuit Court of Appeals.

BOOCHEVER, Judge

The issues on this appeal are whether Amex's policy of [canceling] a spouse's supplementary account upon the death of the basic cardholder violated the ECOA and whether a plaintiff must always show discriminatory intent or effect to establish an ECOA violation. . . . We hold that there has been credit discrimination within the meaning of the ECOA and that . . . judgment on the issue of liability should have been granted to Mrs. Miller, rather than to Amex.

The ECOA makes it unlawful for any creditor to discriminate with respect to any credit transaction on the basis of marital status. It also authorizes the Board of Governors of the Federal Reserve System (Board) to prescribe regulations and creates a private right of action for . . . actual and punitive damages.

In order to carry out the purposes of the ECOA, the Board promulgated . . . regulations. . . . Section 202.7(c)(1) provides that a creditor shall not terminate the account of a person who is contractually liable on an existing open-end account on the basis of a change in marital status in the absence of evidence of inability or unwillingness to repay. . . .

By its terms, section 202.7(c) reaches only terminations of existing open-end accounts on which the credit holder is contractually liable. . . . "Contractually liable" means "expressly obligated to repay all debts arising on an account by reason of an agreement to that effect." Amex has argued that the reference to persons "contractually liable" was meant to exclude spouses who are only "users" of accounts. . . .

Mrs. Miller was not, however, merely a user of her husband's basic account. She was personally liable under the contract creating her supplementary account for all debts charged on her card by any person. . . .

Other differences between Mrs. Miller's card and her husband's also persuade us that her supplementary account was in substance a separate account from her husband's basic one. Her card was issued in her own name, carried an additional issuance fee, and had a different account number and expiration date from Mr. Miller's card.

Mrs. Miller's account was terminated in response to her husband's death and without reference to or even inquiry regarding her creditworthiness. It is undisputed that the death of her husband was the sole reason for Amex's termination of Mrs. Miller's credit. Amex contends that its automatic cancellation policy was necessary to protect it from noncreditworthy supplementary cardholders. The regulations, however, prohibit termination based on a spouse's death in the absence of evidence of inability or unwillingness to repay. Amex has never contended in this action that the death of her husband rendered Mrs. Miller unable or unwilling to pay charges made on her card. The fact that the cancellation policy could also result in the termination of a supplemental cardholder who was not protected by the ECOA, such as a sibling or friend of the basic cardholder, does not change the essential fact that Mrs. Miller's account was terminated solely because of her husband's death. The interruption of Mrs. Miller's credit on the basis of the change in her marital status is precisely the type of occurrence that the ECOA and regulations thereunder are designed to prevent.

We hold that the undisputed facts show, as a matter of law, that Amex violated the ECOA and regulations thereunder in its termination of Mrs. Miller's supplementary card. For this reason, we reverse the district court's grant of summary judgment for Amex and instruct that . . . judgment should be awarded to Mrs. Miller on the issue of liability.

Case Questions

1. Was Mrs. Miller contractually liable under the terms of the agreement? Why or why not? Does this make a difference? Explain.

2. Was it Amex's intent to discriminate on the basis of marital status? What is the support for your answer? Should it make any difference under the act?

3. Assume that Amex had a policy of canceling supplementary cards on the death of a basic cardholder who is not a spouse. Would this violate the ECOA? Explain.

Truth in Lending Act

We are a credit-oriented society. Every American — adult and child — owns an average of one credit card. There are a variety of types of credit cards on the market. Some are store-specific — that is, they can only be used at one store. An example is a Sears credit card. Others are national — for example, MasterCard and Visa, which may be tied to a local bank.

Additionally, a variety of institutes, from banks to credit unions, loan money to consumers who desire to realize their "dreams." Each credit card or loan comes with its own credit terms. To help the consumer compare the various credit terms available, the Truth in Lending Act (TILA) was enacted to ensure meaningful disclosure of these terms. By such disclosure, the consumer is in a better position to make informed decisions on the use of credit.

TILA authorizes the Federal Reserve Board (FRB) to enact regulations implementing the act. The FRB has enacted a number of regulations, known collectively as Regulation Z, to adapt TILA to a variety of circumstances.

Coverage

TILA only applies to consumer credit. TILA is not applicable to commercial credit. Hence, a loan to purchase a home, an automobile for personal use, or an appliance for household use would trigger the requirements of TILA. However, a loan to erect a shopping center or to purchase an automobile or an appliance for business use would not be governed by TILA.

TILA applies when the extension of credit is to a natural person. Hence, credit extension to corporations, partnerships, trusts, governments, and charitable organizations is not covered by TILA. Apparently, Congress was principally concerned about the individual consumer and believed that business organizations and government were sufficiently astute to fend for themselves.

Under TILA, creditors must make certain prescribed disclosures to the debtor. A creditor, as defined in the act, is one who regularly extends credit. Assume Sarah loaned money to her friend, Barb. Unless Sarah was in the business of regularly extending credit, she would not have any obligation under TILA to make the required disclosures.

TILA applies to real estate transactions. However, it only applies to other consumer credit transactions when the amount of the loan is $25,000 or less. Finally, the act is only applicable when the credit extension is (1) subject to a finance charge or (2) repayable in more than four installments.

Disclosure

Regulation Z requires that certain disclosures be made for both open-end and closed-end credit transactions. Generally, with open-end credit, the terms of the plan must be disclosed beforehand to the cus-

tomer and periodically thereafter on each billing statement. With other than open-end credit, the customer is afforded all the disclosures before entering into the contract for credit.

All required disclosures must be clear and conspicuous, so that they may be readily observable to the consumer. Small print or terms buried in lengthy documents do not satisfy the "clear and conspicuous" requirement. The FRB has prepared model forms for common credit transactions. Those who adopt these model forms will be assured that they will not violate the clear and conspicuous requirement. Those who opt to use their own forms proceed at their own risk.

One of the key disclosures that a creditor is required to make is the **finance charge.** The finance charge is the cost of the loan and includes the interest charges, service charges, loan and credit report fees, all which must be disclosed. Another key item that TILA requires to be disclosed is the **annual percentage rate (APR).** The APR is a uniform way of calculating the interest rate so that it may be used to compare the costs of financing. It is an expression of the relationship of (1) the amount financed, (2) the finance charge, and (3) the rate of repayment. There are formulae and tables (and, of course, computer programs) for figuring out the APR.

Rescission

Under TILA, the consumer may cancel certain credit transactions within three days. This right of rescission applies when an interest is acquired in real property (used as a principal dwelling) to secure repayment of the loan (security interest). The right, however, does not apply when a first mortgage is given to secure the financing of a home.

Contractors who install major appliances or who do repairs on a consumer's home will be hesitant to start work until more than three days after a contract for the work is signed. However, in an emergency, such as a broken furnace in the winter or a cracked pipe cutting off the water supply, the consumer may effectively waive the right of rescission in writing.

Credit Cards

TILA regulates the use of credit cards. No credit cards may be issued that are not requested. Under TILA, a credit cardholder's liability is limited to $50 for any charges incurred as a result of unauthorized use. Unauthorized use may occur when the card is lost or stolen. In such event, a cardholder may prevent all liability by notifying the issuer that the card was lost or stolen before any charges occur. However, if the cardholder permits another to use the card, expressly or impliedly, any use is considered authorized.

Administrative Enforcement

Several administrative agencies are given the responsibility of enforcing TILA. For example, the Federal Reserve Bank enforces TILA among its state member banks. The comptroller of the currency is charged with enforcing its provisions among National Banks. The Federal Trade Commission enforces its provisions where a creditor has not been assigned to another agency. Enforcement includes, in proper cases, requiring restitution, an adjustment to the consumer's account, and an order requiring a creditor to cease and desist from violating the act.

Remedies

Consumers who are injured as a result of a violation of the act are entitled to actual damages. In addition, the creditor may be liable for up to twice the finance charge. The maximum liability is capped at $1,000 for individual actions. Class actions, however, may result in much greater liability; and, those consumers who are successful may also recover court costs and attorney fees.

Creditors may avoid liability by adjusting an error within 60 days after discovery. Also, creditors may escape liability if the error was made in good faith, such as a clerical error or an error resulting from a computer malfunction. Creditors who willfully and knowingly violate the act are subject to criminal penalties, which carry a fine and imprisonment.

Fair Credit Reporting Act

Creditors need information when considering whether to extend credit. Some of the information is contained within the borrower's application. Other information is supplied by the consumer credit reporting industry. This industry consists of businesses, referred to as credit bureaus and investigative reporting companies, which gather information about people for use by credit extenders. Such information may also be helpful to insurance companies and employers when making decisions to insure and employ. These companies provide a worthwhile and needed service. But, when the information is incomplete and inaccurate, decisions are made based on a distorted profile. Because these inaccuracies were commonplace, Congress passed the Fair Credit Reporting Act (FCRA) in an attempt to reduce their incidence. The FCRA regulates the gathering, maintenance and dissemination of information used to determine a person's eligibility for credit, insurance, or employment.

Coverage

The act imposes on consumer reporting agencies the obligation to adopt reasonable procedures to ensure confidential and accurate consumer reporting. A **consumer reporting agency** is defined as an entity that ''regularly engages . . . in the practice of assembling or evaluating consumer credit information or other information on consumers for the purpose of furnishing consumer reports to third parties.''

Included within this definition are **credit bureaus** and **investigative reporting companies.** Credit bureaus assemble and disseminate existing information. Investigative reporting companies compile information from questioning friends, neighbors, and acquaintances of the person.

The act does not cover the exchange of business credit reports. It covers only consumer information—that which is related to personal and household affairs. And it does not cover reports that are made by a business based on that business's *experience* with the consumer. For example, assume that a bank was investigating the creditworthiness of an applicant. It contacted the applicant's employer, who released information concerning the applicant's employment record. This release of information would not be covered. Now assume that the bank contacted the local credit bureau and requested credit information the bureau had compiled. This is the type of information that is covered by the act.

Permissible Purposes

Consumer reporting agencies may furnish consumer reports to those it has reason to believe intend to use the information for the purpose of making decisions regarding credit extension, employment, or insurance, or otherwise have a legitimate business need for the information. The agency may furnish information even though the consumer has not consented to (or may even have objected to) the disclosure. Reporting agencies must maintain reasonable procedures to ensure that the information is not released for purposes not permitted under the act. It must do this by ascertaining the identity of the user and verifying the use. The user must also certify the purposes for which the information will be used.

Accurate Reporting

Reporting agencies must follow reasonable procedures to ensure accurate information about consumers. No specific requirements exist for this compliance, but courts have been called on to determine what is reasonable compliance, as the next case illustrates.

WOOD v. HOLIDAY INNS, INC.
508 F.2d 167 (5th Cir. 1975)

Glen Wood, an executive vice president of SAR Manufacturing, checked into the Holiday Inn at Phenix City, Alabama. At the time of check-in he tendered payment by using his Gulf Oil credit card. The clerk returned his credit card after making an imprint of it.

Gulf furnishes to National Data Corporation a list of all credit cancellations. Holiday Inns are authorized to contact National Data to ascertain credit approval or denial.

Gulf maintained a file on Wood. The credit manager had noticed that there were large amounts of charges in comparison to Wood's income. He was unaware that Wood was using the credit card for business as well as personal expenses. Gulf directed National to inform those seeking credit approval, not to extend credit, and to pick up Wood's credit card.

Goynes, the night auditor of the Holiday Inn, called National Data during the early morning to confirm Wood's credit card number and to receive authorization to extend credit. He received the following communication:

Do not honor this sale. Pick up the credit card and send it in for reward.

According to Wood, at 5:00 A.M., Goynes awakened him by telephone and falsely informed him that Goynes needed the credit card to make another imprint. Goynes then went to Wood's room, secured the credit card, and promised to return it in a few minutes. When Goynes failed to return, Wood dressed and went down to the front desk where Goynes told him that the card had been "seized," and that cash payment was required. Goynes refused to call Gulf Oil at Wood's request. Wood then paid cash and left the motel.

Wood was so angry and frustrated that three days later, when relating the incident to a friend, he had a heart attack. Wood sued Gulf, Holiday Inn, and others. The jury returned a verdict in favor of Wood. The district court then granted Gulf and Holiday Inn's motions for judgments notwithstanding the verdict. Wood appealed to the 5th Circuit Court of Appeals.

MORGAN, Judge

Wood's primary claim against Gulf is based upon the Fair Credit Reporting Act. . . . The Act charges "consumer reporting agencies" and users of "consumer credit reports" with various responsibilities. Failure to discharge these duties appropriately may give rise to civil liability.

Wood alleged that Gulf negligently failed to comply with the provisions of the Fair Credit Reporting Act as both a consumer reporting agency and a user of a consumer report. Gulf argues that it was not a consumer reporting agency as defined in [the act], and the district court so held, apparently as a matter of law.

The Act defines a consumer reporting agency as:

[A]ny person which, for monetary fees, dues or on a cooperative nonprofit basis, regularly engages in whole or in part in the practice of assembling or evaluating consumer credit information or other information on consumers for the purpose of furnishing consumer reports to third parties.

Gulf vigorously asserts that . . . no third party was furnished a report. In essence, Gulf contends, and the district court held, that the credit in this case was to be extended only by Gulf, not by [Holiday Inn].

Much of the confusion in this case stems from the multifaceted position of the Phenix City facility, the recipient of Gulf's communication. The Phenix City Holiday Inn accepted the Gulf credit card and was therefore Gulf's representative in facilitating the extension of Gulf's credit. But the Phenix City facility also honored a number of major credit cards and in fact, nothing prevented the Phenix City Inn from extending credit on its own account.

The communication by Gulf to the Phenix City Inn was made to a separate business entity. However, the credit to be extended was Gulf's, and the Phenix City facility was merely acting as Gulf's representative in extending the credit. Hence, the communication was not "for the purpose of furnishing consumer reports to third parties." It was merely directed from Gulf to its local representative, made for the purpose of protecting Gulf rather than for the purpose of influencing the Phenix City Inn's own credit decision.

Wood next maintained that Gulf is liable . . . as a user of a credit report. . . .

Whenever credit or insurance for personal, family, or household purposes, or employment involving a consumer is denied or the charge for such credit or insurance is increased either wholly or partly because of information contained in a consumer report from a consumer reporting agency, the user of the consumer report shall so advise the consumer against whom such adverse action has been taken and supply the name and address of the consumer reporting agency making the report.

The district court held that there was no evidence that Wood was damaged by Gulf's failure to report the name and address of the reporting agency. Wood renews his argument on appeal, contending that if Gulf had informed him promptly of its decision to terminate his credit, the incident at the Holiday Inn would have been avoided.

Apparently, the only requirement placed upon a "user" of a credit report is the duty to disclose the name and address of the reporting agency when

credit is denied. There is no evidence that the actions of Goynes or the reaction of Wood would have been any different if Wood had been told at the time his credit card was withdrawn . . . that Gulf held a favorable credit report. . . .

We need not base our decision upon the timing of the notification, however, for there is no indication that Gulf relied upon this report in making its decision to revoke Wood's credit. Gulf certainly had a credit report in its possession, but there is uncontradicted testimony that this report played no part in Gulf's decision. Of course, the jury would normally be free to disregard the denials of a company holding a credit report that it used the report in evaluating a consumer.

Here, however, there was simply nothing in the consumer report which could have caused Gulf to terminate Wood's credit. Not only was all of the information contained in the report already in Gulf's possession, but the only inference that one could draw from the report was favorable to Wood. Indeed the condition which caused the termination of credit—Wood's monthly income in relation to the charges on his account—was in no way conveyed by the report. Hence, we feel that the district judge properly dismissed the cause of action based upon the "user" provision of the Fair Credit Reporting Act. [The case was remanded to the lower court for other reasons not relevant to this discussion.]

Case Questions

1. What are the issues in this case?
2. Why did the court determine that Gulf was not a "consumer reporting agency" under the Fair Credit Reporting Act? Analyze the court's reasoning.
3. Why did the court hold that Gulf did not violate any of the user requirements under the FCRA? Do you agree with this approach? Explain.
4. Does Wood have any other theory of recovery against Gulf? Does he have any other causes of action against anyone else? Explain.

Obsolete Information

Consumer reporting agencies must purge their files of obsolete information. Generally, obsolete information is that which is older than seven years. It includes information about suits and judgments and records of arrest and conviction. There are exceptions to this rule. Information about bankruptcies may remain for 10 years. And none of these limitations apply if the consumer credit report is to be used in connection with (1) a credit transaction involving $50,000 or more, (2) the underwriting of life insurance involving $50,000 or more, or (3) the employment of an individual at an annual salary of $20,000 or more.

More stringent requirements are placed on investigative reports. Any adverse information contained in such a report that is over three months old must be reverified before it can be used.

Notice of Reports

Consumers are entitled to notice of the fact or content of reports under three circumstances. The first circumstance occurs when a consumer reporting agency furnishes a report for employment purposes that is based on public information (e.g., criminal records and civil litigation history) and that may likely have an adverse effect on the consumer's ability to obtain employment. Here, the consumer is entitled to know that public information is being reported and the name and address of the user. The reporting agency, however, may avoid this requirement if it maintains strict procedures to ensure that the public information is complete and current.

The second circumstance that triggers notice obligations is when a consumer is denied credit, insurance (or the charges increased), or employment because of information supplied by a consumer reporting agency. Here, the user of the report is obligated to inform the consumer of the adverse action and the name and address of the agency that supplied the report. When there is a denial of credit or the charge for credit is increased based on information other than that supplied by a reporting agency, the consumer is entitled to the reasons (though not the source) for the adverse action.

Third, stringent notification rules apply when an investigative report is requested. The requestor is required to inform the consumer in writing of such request. Within three days after the investigative report is ordered, the consumer must be informed that the report contains information regarding the consumer's character, general reputation, personal characteristics, and/or mode of living. Additionally, the business requesting the investigative report must inform the consumer of his or her right to a full disclosure of the nature and scope of the investigation requested. An exception to the notification exists when an investigative report is to be used for employment purposes for a position for which the consumer did not specifically apply—for example, when employees are being considered for promotion.

Disputed Information

Information is always subject to dispute. The FCRA affords a consumer an opportunity to effectively dispute information. When the consumer disputes information, the credit reporting agency is required to reinvestigate the information "unless it has reasonable grounds to believe that the dispute by the consumer is frivolous or irrelevant." After the reinvestigation, inaccurate information must be deleted. In the event the reinvestigation fails to resolve the dispute, the consumer is entitled to have placed in the agency's files a statement of his or her version of the dispute. This statement, or a summary, must be included in any subsequent consumer report. Additionally, the consumer may require that notice of any inaccurate or disputed information be sent to all prior users.

Remedies and Enforcement

Remedies for violation of the provisions of the FCRA include criminal and civil penalties. Consumers who are harmed as a result of a violation of the act may recover actual damages, court costs, and reasonable attorney fees. If the violation is willful as opposed to negligent, the consumer may also recover punitive damages. A reporting agency or a user of the information that can demonstrate that it maintained reasonable procedures to ensure compliance with the act will be free from liability.

The Federal Trade Commission enforces the FCRA to the extent that enforcement is not specifically delegated to another agency. A violation of the act is deemed to be an "unfair or deceptive act or practice" in violation of the Federal Trade Commission Act. As such, the FTC has the power to investigate activities, issue rules to enforce compliance, require companies to file reports, and compel the production of documents and the appearance of witnesses.

ELECTRONIC FUNDS TRANSFER ACT

The traditional bank collection process involves "float" and generates lots of paper. In order to reduce float and paper, several types of electronic funds transfer systems (EFTS) have arisen. In response to the rise in EFTS and the predictions of the future "checkless" society, Congress enacted the Electronic Funds Transfer Act in 1978 (EFTA). EFTA establishes rights and liabilities of consumers, financial institutions, and intermediaries in electronic funds transfers (EFTs).

The EFTA governs electronic funds transfers between consumers' accounts that were established primarily for personal, family, or household purposes. Thus, it does not cover EFTs among financial institutions.

The primary EFTs covered are point-of-sale transfers (POS), automated teller machine transactions (ATMs), direct deposits or withdrawals, and transfers initiated by telephone.

The EFTA requires certain disclosures, provides for documentation of transfers, offers error-resolution procedures, and imposes liability for noncompliance.

Disclosure Requirements

Certain terms and conditions involving the consumer's account must be disclosed at the time the consumer enters into the contract for EFT service. If there are any changes that would result in greater cost or liability for the consumer or decreased access to the consumer's account, the financial institution must notify the consumer of any such change in writing at least 21 days before the effective date.

Documentation of Transfers

Financial institutions must provide documentation to the consumer. For each EFT initiated from an electronic terminal, such as an ATM or POS, the financial institution must provide a receipt at the time the transfer is made. These receipts operate as canceled checks or credit card bills might, as both proof of payment and as an aid to the consumer in the discovery and resolution of any errors. In addition, the financial institution must provide the consumer with periodic statements for each account that may be accessed by an EFT (see Figure 33–2).

Figure 33–2   EFTA Information Contained on Periodic Statements

- Amount and date of the transfer.
- Type of transfer.
- Identity of the account.
- Identity of any third party involved.
- Location or identification of the electronic terminal.

Stopping Preauthorized Transfers

The consumer may stop payment of a preauthorized EFT (such as payment of a utility bill or insurance premium) by notifying the financial institution orally or in writing. The notification can be made at any time up to three business days before the scheduled date of such transfer. The financial institution may require written confirmation within 14 days of the oral stop payment.

The consumer is not given the right to reverse a POS or ATM transaction. Unlike a check, an ATM or POS transaction is the equivalent of a cash transaction.

Error Resolution

A consumer who believes that an error has occurred must notify the financial institution within 60 days of transmission of the EFT documentation. The institution must then conduct an investigation of the alleged error, determine whether an error has occurred, and notify the consumer of the results of the investigation within 10 business days. Alternatively, the financial institution may provisionally recredit the consumer's account within 10 business days of notification and complete its investigation and determine whether or not an error occurred within 45 days.

If the financial institution determines that an error did occur, it must correct the error within one business day from the determination. If the financial institution determines that an error did not occur, it must notify the consumer within three business days of its decision along with the reasons for its findings. The consumer may then request reproductions of all documents on which the financial institution relied. Treble damages against the financial institution are awardable for certain violations.

Consumer Liability

An authorized transfer includes transfers voluntarily initiated by the consumer, as well as transfers by those with actual authority to initiate the transfer. A consumer's liability for unauthorized transfers is no more than $50 or the amount obtained in the transfer, whichever is less. Even this liability may be avoided if the consumer promptly notifies the financial institution of the danger of unauthorized transfer. Thus, if Tom's access card is stolen, he will not have any liability for transfers made after he notifies the financial institution of the theft, and he would be liable for a maximum of $50 for transfers made before the notification was given.

If the consumer fails to notify the financial institution of the loss or theft of the access device within two business days from the time the consumer learns of the loss or theft, the consumer is liable for losses up to $500 (see Figure 33–3).

Financial Institution Liability

A financial institution is liable for failure to make an EFT or failure to stop payment of a preauthorized transfer from a consumer's account in accordance with proper customer instructions. However, there is no liability for failure to make an EFT if the consumer's account has insufficient funds from which to make the transfer, if the funds are subject to legal process, if the transfer would exceed a credit limit, or if the electronic terminal has insufficient cash to complete the transaction. Where the action by the financial institution was not intentional and was the result of a bona fide (good faith) error, damages will be limited to actual damages proved, as long as the institution has maintained procedures reasonably adapted to avoid such error.

Financial institutions are also liable for "any actual damage sustained" for violations of other provisions of the EFTA, including failure to properly disclose, failure to provide the required documentation, and improper issuance of access cards. Violations also carry civil penalty of not less than $100 nor greater than $1,000. Here, the bona de error defense is also available to the financial institution.

Figure 33–3 Consumer Liability under EFTA

Consumer Liability	Circumstances
No Liability	After notification to bank
No more than $50	Before notification within two-day period
No more than $500	If consumer fails to notify bank of loss within two days from consumer's knowledge of loss of card

Criminal Liability

Anyone who knowingly and willfully gives false or inaccurate information, fails to provide information required to be disclosed, or fails to comply with any provision of the EFTA is liable for a fine of up to $5,000, or up to one year in prison, or both. This includes consumers who fraudulently report EFT losses. In addition, liability of up to $10,000 and/or imprisonment of up to 10 years is possible for acts such as use of counterfeit, fictitious, altered, forged, lost, or fraudulently obtained debit cards.

Floating and Shifting: The Evolution of Debtor-Creditor Relations and Law*

Originally, the barter method of transfer was used to meet the needs of society. The relationship was based on the immediate exchange of value, and the opportunity for underhandedness was minimal. From the barter system, which had definite limitations, society moved to a cash system. Here again the transfer was immediate and the contemporaneous inspections and exchanges minimized fraud. . . . Because of advancements in technology, and in order to meet the requirements of demand and convenience, checks and charges became the principal form of payment for goods and services. The institution of the checking system introduced the concept of "float" or the period that intervenes between the time a check is given as payment and the time the check clears the bank. Float gives consumers who are dissatisfied with the product or service purchased an opportunity to stop payment on their checks before these clear the bank. When credit extension and credit cards were widely

*Source Adapted from John Blackburn, Elliot Klayman, and Martin Malin, *The Legal Environment of Business* (Burr Ridge, Ill.: Richard D. Irwin, 1979). Reprinted with permission.

introduced, the float period was increased and consumers enjoyed the additional advantage of "buying now and paying later." Along with these advantages the credit system opened the way for various debtor and creditor abuses.

In the 1960s the consumers' cause, championed by consumer advocates and groups, made great strides as legislation to protect consumers was introduced and passed. The spirit of consumerism moved into the 1970s as the momentum for additional consumer protection continued. . . .

The decade of the 1980s signalled retreat from the consumer oriented wave of legislation. The credit system and governmental regulation of debtor-creditor relations were targeted as a prime cause of spiralling inflation of that era. Amendments to Truth in Lending legislation were a retreat from the fuller disclosure requirements required by its predecessor. There was a definite move to permit the normal market forces to regulate debtor-creditor relations, and the spirit of deregulation drove consumer legislation. Many feared that this move would work to the severe disadvantage of the consumer. . . .

Once again the sands are shifting, as we move deeper into the 90s. The lesson and heartache of the savings and loan crisis is a fresh wound. The demand for ethics in government is spilling over to the private sector. Consciousness about the national debt, deficit spending, fiscal responsibility and the environment are all driving protectionist attitudes that indicate a renewed wave of consumer-oriented legislation, and case law. With all of this the trend is towards fuller disclosure, and truthfulness in consumer-debtor relations. At the same time, there is a technological move to electronic funds transfer systems, such as automatic teller machines and debit transaction cards, which threaten to move us back to a type of cashless society where there was no float and consumer-debtor relations were less problematic. . . . Debtor-creditor relations and its laws [are] "seasonal" and will undoubtedly not stop here, but will continue cycling.

Thought Questions

1. Summarize the point that the author is attempting to make. Do you agree with it? Explain.
2. Does the title of the article give you a clue as to the content of the article? Explain.
3. What do the authors mean by the last sentence? Is there a way of predicting the cycles?

COLLECTING THE DEBT

Debt collection methods can be divided into two categories. Creditors may seek the help of the courts to collect delinquent debts. This method of judicial enforcement is normally reserved for cases where nonjudicial debt collection procedures fail.

Nonjudicial methods of debt collection are varied. They range from the sublime to the ridiculous. Debt collectors have demonstrated a penchant for creativity. Sometimes their approaches offend traditional standards of fair play. For this reason, Congress passed legislation to curb abusive practices.

Fair Credit Billing Act

One of the first stages in collecting a debt is to bill the debtor. Because of the increased use of computerized posting and billing and the frailty of human beings, errors and disputes often arise. It was the awareness of these problems that gave rise to the Fair Credit Billing Act (FCBA). The FCBA covers consumer credit transactions where a credit card is used. The act prescribes billing disclosure and dispute resolution requirements for creditors.

Under the act, prior to the issuance of a credit card, a creditor must make certain disclosures to the consumer. These disclosures include the amount of the finance charge and how it is computed, the amount of the minimum periodic payment, and a notice of the procedures to follow should there be a billing error. The act also imposes on creditors the obligation of making disclosures to their customers in periodic statements. The act establishes procedures for consumer complaints and creditors' responses to billing errors. To facilitate the process, the creditor must inform the consumer, in billing statements, of the address to send billing inquiries. The consumer must then notify the creditor at that address of any billing error. Upon receipt of the notice, the creditor must resolve the dispute within two billing cycles by correcting the consumer's account or supplying the consumer with a written clarification, including documentation if requested, stating reasons why the creditor believes the statement is accurate. Any creditor who violates the act will not be permitted to collect the disputed amount or finance charges (not exceeding $50) for each disputed item.

Fair Debt Collection Practices Act

The Fair Debt Collection Practices Act (FDCPA) regulates the collection of consumer debt—that which arises for personal, family, or household purposes. Debt that arises due to a commercial purpose—for example, purchasing a business or buying inventory—is not covered.

The act places restrictions on debt collectors. Debt collectors are defined as those who regularly collect debts for others. Hence, it does not cover businesses that collect their own debts unless they give the impression that they are a separate debt collection entity.

The FDCPA, primarily enforced by the Federal Trade Commission, establishes certain prohibitions against communications and practices by debt collectors and certain rights for consumers.

Communication

Under the act, a debt collector is limited in its communications when attempting to collect the debt. First, it may not contact the consumer at an unusual or inconvenient time or place. Hours between 8:00 A.M. and 9:00 P.M. are presumptively convenient; however, even here, if the debt collector knows that the consumer works third shift and sleeps in the morning, a call during that time would violate the act. In such a case, a call at 10:00 P.M. would probably not violate the act.

Second, a debt collector is not permitted to contact a consumer who is represented by an attorney, unless the attorney does not respond or the consumer consents to the direct communication. Third, the debt collector may not contact the consumer at the consumer's place of employment if the debt collector knows that the employer has a policy of not permitting such communications.

Fourth, under the act, a consumer may cause collection communications to cease by notifying the debt collector in writing of this desire. Fifth, the act generally prohibits the debt collector from communicating with third parties about the debt. Third parties include neighbors, friends, and employers. They do not include the consumer's spouse, parents of a minor, and attorneys. The one exception to this prohibition is that the debt collector may contact third parties to obtain location information. Of course, if the debt collector knows the whereabouts of the debtor, then it is unlawful to contact a third party. When communicating with a third party for the purpose of acquiring location information, the debt collector must be careful not to violate the detailed provisions of the act. These provisions are designed to protect the privacy of the debtor by prohibiting the collector from (1) informing the third party that the consumer owes a debt, (2) communicating by postcard, (3) using any language or symbol on correspondence to the third party that would indicate that the sender is in the debt collection business, and (4) identifying the debt collector's employer unless expressly requested.

Practices

The act prohibits the debt collector from harassing, abusing, or oppressing any person in connection with the debt collection. Such unlawful practices include, for example, the use of obscene language, repeatedly causing a telephone to ring, and the publicizing of a list of consumers who refuse to pay debts.

The act also prohibits a debt collector from making false or misleading misrepresentations to persons in connection with the collection of any debt. Such unlawful practices include falsely representing that the debt collector (1) is affiliated with the government, (2) is an attorney, (3) has sold the accounts to another, or (4) is representing that the collector will take certain action that it does not intend to take or is not lawfully entitled to take.

Finally, the act prohibits a debt collector from using unfair or unconscionable means to collect the debt. Some unlawful practices are listed in Figure 33–4.

Consumer Rights

The FDCPA recognizes that debts may be disputed. Consequently, under the act, the debtor must be notified that he or she may notify the debt collector in writing within 30 days that all or a part of the debt is disputed. If, in fact, the debtor so notifies, the debt collector must cease all further collection efforts until it supplies the debtor with a verification of the indebtedness. Verification is satisfied when the debt collector receives a judgment evidencing the debt or a statement, itemizing the debt still owed by the consumer, stating the consideration the debtor received for the debt.

Remedies

Those who are aggrieved as a result of a violation of the FDCPA may recover for the actual damages suffered. The court is also authorized to award additional damages up to $1,000, the amount determined by the severity of the violation. And attorney fees and court costs will be awarded against the debt collector who violates the act.

The Federal Trade Commission is the primary enforcer of the act. It may seek civil penalties against violators for each violation. In a proper case, the FTC may institute a civil action on behalf of consumers injured by a violator.

JUDICIAL REMEDIES

When nonjudicial debt collection fails, it is not unusual for a creditor to institute judicial action in an effort to collect the debt. There are a variety of judicial actions that may facilitate debt collection.

Figure 33–4   Unfair Debt Collection Practices

- Accepting a check from the debtor postmarked by more than five days (with some exceptions).
- Depositing any postdated check prior to the date on the check.
- Communicating with the consumer by postcard containing information about the debt.
- Collecting additional amounts on a debt not provided for by agreement.

Normally, a creditor must first obtain a court judgment. This process, involving a civil suit, was discussed in Chapter 3. After a judgment is obtained, the creditor may invoke court actions to collect on the judgment. But before discussing those actions, it is necessary to consider prejudgment remedies.

Prejudgment Remedies

Obtaining a judgment often involves a lengthy process and much expense. And during the process, the debtor may dispose of property or other creditors may seize the debtor's property to satisfy their own claims. For this reason, it is often desirable to take advantage of state statutes that provide for judicial prejudgment remedies. The most common prejudgment remedy of this kind is attachment—the seizure of property by a court officer, ordinarily a sheriff's deputy. Attachment is not available in every case but only under extraordinary circumstances. Although state statutes differ as to when attachment is available, they normally permit it when the defendant is willfully avoiding service of process, or where the defendant is likely to hide assets with the intent to defraud creditors.

When a complaint for attachment is granted, specific property is seized and held pending the judgment. In the event that the judgment is granted in favor of the plaintiff, the property may be sold to satisfy the judgment. If the judgment is rendered in favor of the defendant, then the defendant is entitled to a return of the property. Additionally, in most jurisdictions, the defendant would be entitled to any damages that had been caused by the attachment. Assume, for example, that the defendant's storefront business was attached. In such a case, the sheriff would probably accomplish the attachment by padlocking the store. Should a judgment on the alleged debt be rendered in favor of the debtor, the creditor would be liable to the store owner for the loss of profits and other damages.

Several U.S. Supreme Court decisions have made it clear that due process must be afforded in prejudgment remedies. In most instances, this means that the debtor must be afforded notice of the prejudgment proceeding and an opportunity for an adversarial hearing to determine whether the remedy is proper.

Oftentimes, the use of attachment as a prejudgment remedy strengthens the creditor's bargaining position. A debtor deprived of specific property may be more willing to talk terms of a settlement.

Postjudgment Remedies

Once a plaintiff obtains a court judgment ordering the defendant to pay a sum of money, the defendant may voluntarily do so. However, in some cases, the defendant still refuses to pay the judgment. In such a case, the plaintiff has a variety of remedies, including (1) judgment-debtor examination, (2) execution, and (3) garnishment.

Judgment-Debtor Examination

Once a judgment attaches, the creditor may seize the debtor's property, force a sale of it, and apply the proceeds of that sale to satisfy the judgment. However, in order to do this, the creditor needs to discover the property the debtor owns and its location. To facilitate this discovery, the creditor may subject the debtor to a **judgment-debtor examination.** The debtor is given notice to appear in court on a date and time certain to answer questions pertaining to his or her assets. Additionally, the creditor may issue a subpoena to the debtor requiring that he or she bring specific documents, such as deeds, vehicle registration titles, and financial statements. Once property is located, the creditor may execute on it or garnishee it.

Execution

Execution is the process whereby the judgment debtor's property is seized and sold to satisfy the judgment. Procedures vary from state to state. Generally, the clerk of courts issues a writ of execution that directs an official (such as a sheriff) to seize described property and sell it at a public auction.

It is important to note the difference between the prejudgment attachment and the postjudgment execution. Property seized in connection with an execution results in a sale to satisfy the judgment. Property seized in connection with an attachment is held pending the outcome of a lawsuit.

Garnishment

Garnishment is a seizure of property owned by the debtor that is in the hands of a third party. The most common type of garnishment is the garnishment of wages. Garnishment of a debtor's money held in a bank account is also common.

In a typical garnishment proceeding, the creditor files an affidavit declaring that there is an unsatisfied judgment and that the third party (garnishee) is holding property owned by the debtor. The court then issues a writ of garnishment and serves it on the garnishee. The garnishee must then answer by describing the nature and the amount of the debtor's property being held by the garnishee. Any property so held must be turned over to the court, which will then use it to satisfy the creditor's judgment.

Title III of the Consumer Credit Protection Act regulates wage garnishments. Under the act, a creditor may not garnishee more than 25 percent of the debtor's "disposable earnings." Disposable earnings are defined as the wage earner's salary less deductions "required by law." Generally, it is equivalent to a person's take-home pay. Disposable earnings includes saving plan deductions but would not include deductions for taxes, alimony, and child support payments.

The federal statute also prohibits an employer from discharging an employee because of a garnishment for any "one indebtedness." Assume that Early Jones owes Finance Credit Corporation $1,000 on a loan. Finance Credit Corporation obtains a judgment against Jones and garnishees Jones's wages once a month until the judgment is satisfied. Since the garnishment is for only one debt, Jones's employer may not fire him because of the repetitive garnishments.

LENDER LIABILITY

Recently, a fertile area of liability favoring third parties has opened up against lenders. In the past, lenders' biggest headache was debtor default. Now they have to concern themselves with potential liability as well. With the savings and loan crisis and the fall of a number of savings institutions due to reasons ranging from negligence to criminal conduct, lending institutions are no longer "sacred cows." They are potentially liable under contract, tort, and statutory laws for a wide range of activities.

Contracts

The process of banks loaning money starts with a loan application filled out by the borrower. A lender must process a loan application in good faith and abide by its own representations and policies. Any breach may result in liability for damages to the borrower. For example, assume that the lender's policy as communicated to the customer is that the lender will inform the applicant of the decision on the loan application within three business days. However, the bank sits on the application for 10 days and then approves the loan. Because of the delay, the applicant loses the benefit of a contract on a house. The bank may be liable for breach of contract.

A **loan commitment** is an agreement to extend a loan under the terms contained in the agreement. Any deviation from the terms constitutes a breach for which the borrower may be entitled to damages. For example, if the lender increases the interest rate charged, decreases the amount of the loan, or adds unfavorable terms contrary to the commitment, the borrower may be successful in a suit for breach of contract.

Some loans are given as a lump sum; others are periodic, such as a **line of credit.** Under a line of credit, the lender preapproves the limits on which the borrower may draw. Should the lender alter that commitment without a justifiable reason, the lender would be in breach.

When a borrower is in default, the lender may, under the terms of the loan agreement, accelerate the loan so that the full amount of the loan becomes due. Sometimes, however, under the circumstances, the lending institution agrees to not accelerate and to work out a plan for repayment. The **workout plan** may consist of extension of the time for payment, or the payment of interest only for a specified time before resuming regular payments. Even if there is a lack of consideration for the workout, the doctrine of promissory estoppel would probably preclude the lender from reneging on the agreement not to accelerate as long as the borrower was in compliance (see Chapter 14).

Remedies such as damages and specific performance are available on breach of a contract. Consult Chapter 18 for a discussion of the various remedies available.

Torts

A tort, as discussed in Chapters 7 and 8, is a civil wrong against another. Lenders commit intentional torts when engaging in deceit or fraud. Fraud occurs when there is a material misrepresentation that is calculated to induce reliance, and is justifiably relied on to a party's detriment. Fraud may occur when, for example, a lending institute gives false information to a borrower about the loan or the institution. Or should a bank knowingly disclose false information to a third party about a customer, liability for damages results. When the tortious conduct is intentional, punitive damages are awardable.

Negligence is another basis of lender liability. Lenders must act reasonably and prudently to avoid liability. In one case, a lending institute was held liable when it approved a loan for an amount less than the amount requested on the application.[1] The court found that the bank did not act as a reasonably prudent banker under the circumstances, since it failed to adhere to the industry standards in evaluating the loan application.

Statutory Laws

Banking is a regulated industry. Violation of state or federal banking regulations may result in liability. In addition, the entanglement in the affairs of the borrower's business may expose the lender to liability under the environmental laws as discussed in Chapter 51 and in the next case.

---

[1]*Jacques v. First Nat'l Bank,* 515 A.2d 756 (Md 1986).

UNITED STATES v. FLEET FACTORS CORP.
901 F. 2d 1550 (11th Cir. 1990)

Fleet Factors advanced funds to Swainsboro Print Works (SPW), a cloth-printing facility. To secure the loans, Fleet took an assignment of SPW's accounts receivable and also took a security interest in its textile facility, equipment, inventory, and fixtures. Thereafter, SPW was adjudicated bankrupt and a trustee took control of the facility. Fleet Factors foreclosed on some of the inventory and equipment and hired a company to auction it. Fleet then contracted with a company to remove the unsold items and to leave the facility "broom clean."

The Environmental Protection Agency, upon inspection, found 700 55-gallon drums containing toxic chemicals and 44 truckloads of material containing asbestos left at the facility. At a cost of about $400,000, the EPA responded to the environmental threat, and then it sued SPW's two principal officer-stockholders and Fleet for recovery of the costs.

Fleet's motion for summary judgment was denied by the federal district court. It appealed to the Court of Appeals.

KRAVITCH, Judge

The Comprehensive Environmental Response Compensation and Liability Act [CERCLA] was enacted by Congress in response to the environmental and public health hazards caused by the improper disposal of hazardous wastes. The essential policy underlying CERCLA is to place the ultimate responsibility for cleaning up hazardous waste on "those responsible for problems caused by the disposal of chemical poison." Accordingly, CERCLA authorizes the federal government to clean up hazardous waste dump sites and recover the cost of the effort from certain categories of responsible parties.

The parties liable for costs incurred by the government in responding to an environmental hazard are: (1) the present owners and operators of a facility where hazardous wastes were released or are in danger of being released; (2) the owners or operators of a facility at the time the hazardous wastes were disposed. . . . The government contends that Fleet is liable for the response costs associated with the waste at the SPW facility as either a present owner and operator of the facility . . . or the owner or operator of the facility at the time the wastes were disposed. . . .

CERCLA . . . imposes liability on "any person who at the time of disposal of any hazardous substance owned or operated any . . . facility at which such hazardous substances were disposed of. . . ." CERCLA excludes from the definition of "owner or operator" any "person, who, without participating in the management of a . . . facility, holds indicia of ownership primarily to protect his security interest in the . . . facility." Fleet has the burden of establishing its entitlement to this exemption. There is no dispute that Fleet held an "indicia of ownership" in the facility . . . and that this interest was held primarily to protect its security interest in the facility. The critical issue is whether Fleet participated in management sufficiently to incur liability under the statute.

. . . The government urges us to adopt a narrow and strictly literal interpretation of the exemption that excludes from its protection any secured creditor that participates in any manner in the management of a facility. We decline the government's suggestion because it would largely eviscerate the exemption Congress intended to afford to secured creditors. Secured lenders frequently have some involvement in the financial affairs of their debtors in order to insure that their interests are being adequately protected. To adopt the government's interpretation of the secured creditor exemption could expose all such lenders to CERCLA liability for engaging in their normal course of business.

Fleet, in turn, suggests that we adopt the distinction delineated by some district courts between permissible participation in the financial management of the facility and impermissible participation in the day-to-day or operational management of a facility.

. . . In order to achieve the "overwhelmingly remedial" goal of the CERCLA statutory scheme, ambiguous statutory terms should be construed to favor liability for the costs incurred by the government in responding to the hazards at such facilities. The district court's broad interpretation of the exemption would essentially require a secured creditor to be involved in the operations of a facility in order to incur liability. This construction ignores the plain language of the exemption and essentially renders it meaningless. Individuals and entities involved in the operations of a facility are already liable as operators under the express language [of the statute]. Had Congress intended to absolve secured creditors from ownership liability, it would have done so. Instead, the statutory language chosen by Congress explicitly holds secured creditors liable if they participate in the management of a facility.

This construction of the secured creditor exemption . . . should give lenders some latitude in their dealings with debtors without exposing themselves to potential liability. Nothing in our discussion should preclude a secured creditor from monitoring any aspect of a debtor's business. Likewise, a secured creditor can become involved in occasional and discrete financial decisions relating to the protection of its security interest without incurring liability.

Our ruling today should encourage potential creditors to investigate thoroughly the waste treatment systems and policies of potential debtors. If the treatment systems seem inadequate, the risk of CERCLA liability will be weighed into the terms of the loan agreement. Creditors, therefore, will incur no greater risk than they bargained for and debtors, aware that inadequate hazardous waste treatment will have a significant adverse impact on their loan terms, will have powerful incentives to improve their handling of hazardous wastes.

Similarly, creditors' awareness that they are potentially liable under CERCLA will encourage them to monitor the hazardous waste treatment systems and policies of their debtors and insist upon compliance with acceptable treatment standards as a prerequisite to continued and future financial support. Once a secured creditor's involvement with a facility becomes sufficiently broad that it can anticipate losing its exemption from CERCLA liability, it will have a strong incentive to address hazardous waste problems at the facility rather than studiously avoiding the investigation and amelioration of the hazard.

Fleet's involvement with SPW, according to the government, increased substantially after SPW ceased printing operations . . . and began to wind down its affairs. Fleet required SPW to seek its approval before shipping its goods to customers, established the price for excess inventory, dictated when and to whom the finished goods should be shipped, determined when employees should be laid off, supervised the activity of the office administrator at the site, received and processed SPW's employment and tax forms, controlled access to the facility, and contracted . . . to dispose of the fixtures and equipment at SPW. These facts, if proved, are sufficient to remove Fleet from the protection of the secured creditor exemption. Fleet's involvement in the financial management of the facility was pervasive, if not complete. Furthermore, the government's allegations indicate that Fleet was also involved in the operational management of the facility. Either of these allegations is sufficient as a matter of law to impose CERCLA liability on a secured creditor. AFFIRMED and REMANDED.

Case Questions

1. What issue does this case present?
2. Comment: "[A]mbiguous, statutory terms should be construed to favor liability."
3. How could Fleet have protected its interest without running the risk of losing the statutory exemption?
4. What is the impact of this case upon lenders?

END–OF–CHAPTER QUESTIONS

1. What factors do you think have contributed to making us a debt-oriented society?
2. Do you believe that the ECOA has resulted in attitudinal changes in our society? Explain.
3. Develop an ethical strategy for a creditor to collect a debt.
4. Are the debtor/creditor laws balanced in favor of creditors? Explain.
5. The Shirkers applied for a $100,000 loan to finance the purchase of a house. Three days later, they were informed that the loan was approved; however, they were also informed that based on their credit record, the interest rate was 2 percent higher than had their credit record been unblemished. Because of the higher interest rate, the Shirkers could not afford the loan and they lost the house. What must the Shirkers prove in order to recover for the loss against the lending institute? What facts would support the lending institute's decision?
6. Amoco uses a complex computerized system to evaluate credit card applicants. Thirty-eight factors are considered. One factor is ZIP codes. The system assigns a low rating to those ZIP code areas where it has had an unfavorable delinquency rating. Cherry, a white woman, resides in a predominantly black neighborhood that has been assigned a low rating. She was refused a credit card in part because of her ZIP code rating. Has Amoco violated the Equal Credit Opportunity Act? Explain. See *Cherry v. Amoco Oil Co.*, 490 F. Supp. 1026 (N.D. Ga. 1980).

7. Ben's Auto Sales is engaged in the retail sale of used cars. Most of its sales are installment transactions providing for four or more payments. Ben's Autos sells at a cash price and at a ''deferred payment price.'' The prices are, however, the same. It discloses the finance charge and the annual percentage rate as zero. What is the argument that Ben's Auto Sales is in violation of the Truth in Lending Act? See *Hazzie v. Reynolds*, 623 F.2d 638 (10th Cir. 1980).

8. SARMA provides a computerized credit reporting service that utilizes a computerized ''automatic capture'' feature. Subscribers feed specific identifying information into SARMA's central computer to gain access to a consumer's credit history. SARMA's computer then displays the credit history file that matches the consumer. When the subscriber accepts a given file as the consumer's, the computer automatically captures any information that its central file did not have. Do you see any potential legal problems with such a credit-gathering and -reporting system? Explain. See *Thompson v. San Antonio Merchants Ass'n*, 682 F.2d 509 (5th Cir. 1982).

9. Turner defaulted on his obligation to make payments to Impala Motors. A term in the contract read that upon ''default of payment of this note, or any part of it, Impala may take possession of said property in any manner it may elect.'' Comment on the contractual provision. See *Turner v. Impala Motors*, 503 F.2d 607 (6th Cir. 1974).

10. Credit Bureau operates a debt collection agency. It collects money on behalf of creditors. Associated Consumers is one of its customers. It referred a debt owed by Jeter to Credit Bureau. Credit Bureau sent a letter to Jeter containing the following:

> This is our final notice to you before recommending that our client give the account to their attorney for legal action.
>
> Although it may cause you embarrassment, inconvenience and further expense, we will do so if the entire balance is not in this office within the next five days.

Jeter did not respond. Thereafter, Credit Bureau determined that further collection efforts were impractical and it closed its file. Jeter contemplated suing Bureau for violation of the Fair Debt Collection Practices Act. Do you believe Credit Bureau has violated the act? Analyze. See *Jeter v. Credit Bureau, Inc.*, 760 F.2d 1168 (11th Cir. 1985).

Chapter 34

International Sales Transactions

■

CRITICAL THINKING INQUIRIES

As you read this chapter, you should be able to address the following:

- What are the major risk issues in making payment for and delivery of goods sold in international commerce?
- What are the ambiguities in international sales law and how are they resolved by practices prevailing in systems of international sales and payments?
- What issues of performing international trade contracts may be resolved by advances in electronic communications?
- What are the reasons that noncurrency payment or exchange systems such as countertrade are proliferating for international trade relations with developing nations?

MANAGERIAL PERSPECTIVE

A.B.Corp., a U.S.-based importer, is beginning to make purchases of foreign-made goods for resale in the United States. D.E.F.GmBH, an export seller in Germany, has negotiated a contract with A.B.Corp. to make several shipments of specified goods from Germany to the United States. A.B.Corp. is obligated to pay when the goods arrive. However, after A.B.Corp. received delivery of the first shipment and made payment, the delivery was inspected, revealing that it did not meet the contract specifications and was also short the required quantity. A.B.Corp. sought to stop payment of the funds its bank had wired to D.E.F.GmBH. However, the electronic payment was made so quickly that D.E.F.GmBH's bank received and credited its account before A.B.Corp complained.

- What payment and delivery issues are worsened as the distance grows between buyer and seller or if they are situated in different nations?
- What ambiguities in various nations' laws complicate contract negotiations, performance, payments, and deliveries?
- What is the incentive for intermediaries such as banks, carriers, export/import brokers, or inspectors to participate in international sales transactions?

The *transaction anxiety* expressed in the opening scenario has existed since trade began. It has always been caused by traders' concerns over the many risks of contracting. The seller is apprehensive as to whether the buyer's check will be honored, payment will be stopped, installment payments will be made when promised, or that payment will be made at all. Buyers worry that the seller may never ship the goods or will otherwise cheat the buyer. There are risks of transportation delay, damage, or shipments short of the promised quantity. The goods may never arrive, may not meet specifications, or may not meet the buyer's expectations of quality, durability, or timely delivery.

As the distance increases between traders, they tend to become increasingly unfamiliar with each other's commercial and financial reputations. Transaction anxiety becomes particularly acute in international transactions for several additional reasons. Sudden currency fluctuations can eliminate profits. Governments may threaten to expropriate foreigner's assets, nationalize whole industries, or bar future foreign business. The perils of overseas navigation and the longer transport distances increase the risks of loss, damage, or delay. Finally, contract enforcement can be different and uncertain in foreign nations, possibly forcing the innocent party into a hostile forum.

Several of the chapters preceding this one discussed the domestic and international legal problems involved in commercial contracting and performance through the making of payments and deliveries. This chapter discusses some related matters, some of which are peculiar to the unique risks of international sales transactions. The first section discusses *documentary sales* that can reduce many of these risks. The second section covers various payment options for the buyer. The final section discusses alternatives to international documentary transactions. Before proceeding, it might be useful to review several foundational matters discussed in Chapters 19 through 29, including the role of documents in sales transactions, documents of title, title and risk of loss problems, and the process of negotiating commercial paper.

DOCUMENTARY DELIVERIES

The seller has significant risk that the buyer will not adequately pay for the goods, and the seller often has limited recourse against the buyer. However, this risk can be reduced in a documentary sale by the use of documents of title, as discussed in Chapter

21. International documentary sales were first developed as commercial customs during medieval times but have survived evolving through the law merchant into modern statutory law. **Documents of title** are legal instruments used in both domestic and international goods shipments that are evidence of the good's ownership. They include a variety of documents commonly used in domestic and international commerce, such as bills of lading, warehouse receipts, air waybills, and dock receipts.

Documents of title are necessary in international documentary transactions to ensure that the seller receives payment and the buyer receives rightful ownership of the goods sold. They facilitate trade in cargoes that are still in transit. For example, commodities such as grains or petroleum products can change hands several times during the several weeks of transit. Documents of title are governed by Article 7 of the UCC, the Federal Bills of Lading Act (U.S. exports), and various treaties and customs in foreign nations.

Documents of title are issued by a party receiving goods, the *bailee,* specifying who holds legal title to goods physically held by the bailee. For example, a carrier issues a bill of lading and a warehouse operator issues a warehouse receipt indicating its responsibilities as bailee in the transport and holding of *consigned* goods for the seller's benefit. The buyer may rightfully claim the goods from the carrier or warehouse by presenting the document of title in exchange for the goods. The documentary sale is effected by endorsement and transfer of a document of title that is exchanged for the payment usually made by negotiation of a draft or letter of credit. Documents of title can be *straight,* that is non-negotiable, which restricts their transfer. However, documents of title are often more useful if made negotiable. Negotiability facilitates trade between parties contracting at long distance because they can use third-party intermediaries (e.g., banks) to withhold rightful transfer of goods until payment is adequately made.

Bills of Lading

Bills of lading are documents of title a carrier issues showing the consigned goods belong to the seller. Title is transferred to the buyer by the seller's indorsement and negotiation through the banking system. Bills of lading generally serve two purposes: (1) they represent the carrier's contract to transport the goods, and (2) they constitute title to the goods that is transferable on indorsement and/or physical transfer of the document. After the seller releases the goods to the carrier, having loaded them on a truck, train, ship, barge, or airplane, the seller retains rightful ownership by retaining the bill of lading. The seller can then transmit the bill of lading along with other shipping documents through the banking system until exchanged with the buyer for payment. Alternatively, the seller may divert a shipment in transit, if necessary, to another buyer or pledge the bill of lading as collateral on a loan.

Negotiable bills of lading are similar to checks, notes, and drafts because they can be made negotiable to bearer or to order. Rightful ownership of goods held under a *bearer bill of lading* is transferred by simply delivering the document itself, without the additional safeguard of requiring an indorsement. Bearer documents of title involve considerable risk of loss if stolen, making them unsuitable for most international documentary sales. Bearer instruments are most useful in domestic freight where the carrier makes direct delivery to the buyer's premises because payment is not directly connected to delivery, as necessary in the international transactions discussed in this chapter.

Order bills of lading are made out "to the order of" a named person, usually the shipper, carrier, or a bank. The named party can transfer ownership and the right to receive delivery of the goods after the named person indorses the bill of lading over to another person. The indorsement is the act of making the "order." After a carrier issues a bill of lading, the document is transferred through the seller's agents (e.g., a bank) and finally delivered to the buyer, usually as payment is made. The carrier may rightfully release the goods only to the holder of the bill of lading, usually the buyer. *Misdelivery* of the goods to some other party without receiving the properly negotiated bill of lading obligates the carrier for any resulting damages the buyer suffers. The rightful holder of the bill of lading may reclaim the goods from any party who wrongfully received the delivery. Carriers are given a lien for goods rightfully in their possession to secure the payment of freight and associated fees. If the carrier remains unpaid, the goods may be sold at auction to pay these expenses. Of course, any balance in the sale proceeds must be paid to the rightful holder of the bill of lading. The *Barclays Bank* case illustrates this problem.

BARCLAYS BANK, LTD. v. COMMISSIONERS OF CUSTOMS AND EXCISE
Queen's Bench Div., 1963 [1963] 1 Lloyd's Rep. 81.

Bruitrix Electric Co., Ltd., purchased 100 cartons of washing machines from Hudig & Pieters, a Dutch supplier. The shipping terms were CIF, delivered to Cardiff, United Kingdom. Delivery was conditioned against acceptance of a bill of exchange (letter of credit) payable 37 days after shipment. The shipment was made from Rotterdam on February 15, 1961, under a bill of lading made out to the shipper's order. The bill of exchange, invoice, and bill of lading were exchanged without objection. The goods were unloaded at Cardiff, United Kingdom, on February 18, 1961, and stored before passing through customs in a warehouse of the British Transport Commission. After payment of freight charges, the goods were to be released on the order of the carrier, Bristol Steam Navigation Co., Ltd. Bruitrix executed a written pledge of the bill of lading to Barclays Bank as security for advances the bank made to Bruitrix.

The Customs and Excise Commission obtained a judgment against Bruitrix for unpaid purchase tax in August 1961. The sheriff of Glamorgan took possession of the goods on September 29 to satisfy the customs and excise tax lien. Barclays and Bristol Steam exchanged the bill of lading for delivery orders that the British Transport Commission used to issue dock warrants, as substitute documents of title for the goods. Barclays claims that Bruitrix's pledge of the bill of lading document also effectively pledged the goods themselves to Barclays for the loan advances to Bruitrix. This would preclude the sheriff's later execution against the goods themselves for the unpaid custom's tax.

DIPLOCK, Lord Justice

The contract for the carriage of goods by sea, which is evidenced by a bill of lading, is a combined contract of bailment and transportation under which the shipowner undertakes to accept possession of the goods from the shipper, to carry them to their contractual destination and there to surrender possession of them to the person who, under the terms of the contract, is entitled to obtain possession of them from the shipowners. Such a contract is not discharged by performance until the shipowner has actually surrendered possession (that is, has divested himself of all powers to control any physical dealing in the goods) to the person entitled under the terms of the contract to obtain possession of them.

So long as the contract is not discharged, the bill of lading, in my view, remains a document of title by endorsement and delivery of which the rights of property in the goods can be transferred. It is clear law that where a bill of lading or order is issued in respect of the contract of carriage by sea, the shipowner is not bound to surrender possession of the goods to any person whether named as consignee or not, except on production of the bill of lading. Until the bill of lading is produced to him, unless its absence has been satisfactorily accounted for, he is entitled to retain possession of the goods and if he does part with possession he does so at his own risk if the person to whom he surrenders possession is not in fact entitled to the goods.

In the present case, the contract of carriage evidenced by the bills of lading, had not been discharged on June 2, 1961, when Bruitrix purported to pledge the goods to the Bank by deposit of the bills of lading as security for advancement of money to them. The goods were in the constructive possession of the shipowner being held in the physical possession of the British Transport Commission on behalf of and to the order of the shipowner who had power to control any physical dealing with them.

In my opinion the pledge made on June 2, by deposit of the bill of lading was a valid pledge and as a consequence I think that I can give judgment for the plaintiffs in this case.

Case Questions

1. What is the issue concerning the priority of claims on the goods of the bank, carrier, Customs and Excise Commission, and the sheriff?

2. What reasons support the bank's claim it had superior rights in the goods as well as the documents representing the goods?

Rights of Holders of Bills of Lading

The law governing negotiable documents of title parallels negotiable instrument law discussed in Chapters 24 through 29. There is a good faith purchaser for value concept similar to the holder in due course (HDC) concept. This creates a special status for **holders by due negotiation** who purchase the document for value, in good faith, without notice of adverse claims against the document, and take the document in the ordinary course of their business. Such holders take free of adverse claims against the goods. For example, assume D.E.F.GmBH delivers goods to a trucking carrier for delivery to the ship at the port. The trucker obtains a bill of lading from the ship and negotiates it to a bank for cash but then misappropriates the cash. The bank is a good faith purchaser taking paramount title to both the goods and the bill of lading itself because the holder gave value without notice of the trucker's theft. The law of negotiable documents creates this special status of holder by due negotiation to encourage intermediaries to participate in the negotiation of documents of title without risking losses if the documents are dishonored.

Carrier Responsibility for Damage

The parties' allocation of risk of loss to goods during long shipments is a complex problem, as originally discussed in Chapter 21. Under the customs and regulations applicable in the United States, the carrier has nearly absolute liability to the party burdened by risk of loss throughout transport. However, this American rule is substantially limited for international carrier liability.

Various legislation, treaties, and international agreements over the last century have significantly reduced international carrier liability, forcing shippers to insure international shipments. Shippers and importers must generally prove the carrier's negligence before they can collect any damages from an international carrier. There are 17 *exemptions* (e.g., act of God, perils of the sea, crew negligence) that shield international carriers from most liabilities. Additionally, there are rather low monetary limits on carrier liability. However, the **Hamburg rules** are quickly being adopted by many nations; the United States has signed but not yet ratified the Hamburg rules. They shift the burden of proof to carriers, eliminating the 17 exemptions, and raising the monetary limits. The Hamburg rules express the monetary limits in **special drawing rights (SDRs),** a composite or pool of five major currencies: U.S. dollars, British pounds, Japanese yen, German deutsch marks, and French francs.

Both buyers and sellers in international sales transactions need to undertake careful risk management to minimize risk exposure throughout the sale transaction and during its performance. Competent *risk management* requires cost-benefit analyses of several factors. First, the costs of such risk is embedded into delivered prices because the seller retains risk of loss in a *destination* contract. Alternatively, in a *shipment* contract, the price should theoretically be reduced to reflect the buyer's responsibility for freight charges and the associated assumption of risk of loss during transport. Second, carrier liability for loss or damage during transit is usually reflected in freight rates. Ultimately, the price depends on whether the goods sale contract explicitly or impliedly calls for the price to include shipping charges. Third, additional uninsured risks may arise during loading and unloading, transport by inland carriers (e.g., truck, train, river barge, pipeline), or intermediate storage and warehousing. This risk analysis can avoid costly and inefficient purchase of double coverage. However, multiple payments from multiple sources usually cannot be collected. Risk management fundamentally helps avoid uncompensated losses.

Carriers have a responsibility to make notations directly on the bill of lading indicating any obvious damage to the goods. The carrier's representative usually makes a visual inspection of the goods' external appearance as received from the seller. Sometimes, obvious damage is noted during onloading, transport, or offloading. However, such cursory examination is likely to reveal only the most obvious problems (e.g., leaks, discoloration,

insect infestation, mold or mildew, broken packaging). Any condition of the goods about which the carrier knows or should know must be noted, resulting in a **foul bill of lading.** By contrast, a **clean bill of lading** lacks any such notation of obvious defects. In the goods sale contract, the buyer often requires a clean bill and therefore need not pay against a foul bill. Of course, the carrier's damage notations on the bill guarantee neither the goods' quality nor their conformance with the contract description.

Buyers often insist that the goods sale contract call for preshipment inspections by independent third parties. The inspector can take samples or make a chemical analysis of raw materials to issue a *certificate of analysis,* weigh a sample or the whole to issue a *certificate of weight,* or otherwise inspect finished goods issuing a **certificate of inspection.** While preshipment inspection does not ensure against theft, damage, or contamination during transit, it can provide near conclusive evidence of the seller's full and satisfactory performance under the goods sale contract description. *Inspection on arrival* can further satisfy the buyer that the goods conform to the contract description.

Carrier Storage

Goods are not always loaded aboard ship or other carrier's vehicle immediately upon arrival at the dock or freight terminal. Sometimes the goods may be stored in the carrier's port warehouse, terminal, or with a nearby independent warehouse operator. Such delays are often necessary until the next ship, trailer, boxcar, or container arrives that is destined for the importer's port. Occasionally, a carrier may bump a shipment sent by a small shipper, giving priority to the carrier's better customers. Such delaying practices are not always harmful to the seller or buyer. However, if the goods are perishable, the buyer has an immediate need, or the seller needs immediate payment, such delays can be costly. Goods sale contracts often call for an **on board bill of lading** requiring actual loading on the designated vessel or vehicle before payment may be made. If the goods are temporarily stored by the carrier, a **received-for-shipment bill of lading** is issued. After the goods are actually loaded, the carrier may convert a received-for-shipment bill into an on board bill by simply recording the date and the vessel's name directly on the document.

Intermodal Transport

The typical international sales transaction necessarily involves at least one segment of domestic or **inland freight.** This is transportation between the seller's premises and the port or between the receiving port and the buyer's premises. The seller is often required to use its own trucks or contract with an independent motor carrier, rail carrier, barge line, pipeline, or other carrier for the inland freight segments. While the buyer's truck might reclaim the imported goods at the port, quite often the buyer must contract for inland freight by an independent inland carrier. In many parts of the world, the inland freight shipments may cross borders of nations neighboring the seller's or buyer's nation. The use of inland freight complicates the documentary transfer, requiring successive indorsements and transfers of the shipping documents and ostensibly requires separate contracts for each segment of transport. For example, either trucks belonging to D.E.F.GmBH or an independent German motor carrier could deliver export goods to an independent steamship carrier at the nearby port.

The complexities of inland freight are reduced somewhat by two factors. First, there is a trend toward **containerization**, where freight is usually loaded inside standard-sized metal boxes that are more easily loaded, unloaded, and transferred between tractor trailers, flatbed railcars, and aboard special freighter vessels or as airfreight. The use of containers reduces the need to *break bulk* by parceling out large sea shipments into smaller units to make them more easily handled and loaded on trucks. Second, shippers can do "one-stop shopping" with large carriers who use their connections in the transportation industry to subcontract the inland freight segments. These *combined transport operators* use a **combined transport document** in place of a standard bill of lading. The combined transport operator usually assumes liability for losses of goods in transit. An inland freight carrier directly responsible for any damage occurring on that segment is usually contractually bound to indemnify the combined transport operator for any damages paid to shippers. Sometimes the seller or buyer can more efficiently arrange inland freight from a local carrier. Because **straight bills of lading** are non-negotiable, their use is largely relegated to domestic and inland freight where the goods are loaded directly from the seller to the carrier and are then delivered directly to the buyer's premises.

FINANCING INTERNATIONAL SALES: COLLECTING THE BUYER'S PAYMENT

The seller's transaction anxiety over the risks of the buyer's nonpayment is greatly alleviated in domestic trade. Buyers and sellers in the same nation usually enjoy generally reliable payment systems—the buyer risks greater reputational damage if payments become unreliable, and access to the legal system is more predictable and usually less costly. Nearly all these risks are greater in international commerce. Therefore, international traders usually structure their transactions to have interdependent payments and deliveries. This practice minimizes these considerable risks and attendant uncertainties. This section discusses the major methods used to finance international sales and adequately make the buyer's payment. In competitive international markets, sellers must explore using traditional financing alternatives or create innovative solutions.

Open Accounts

The simplest payment method places considerable risk on the seller: The seller ships goods simply on the promise that the buyer will make payment. In an **open account,** the seller must trust that the buyer will pay and not use this considerable bargaining position to exact concessions. Nevertheless, open accounts are useful to win the buyer's trust, and the buyer may agree to pay a higher price. Open accounts can help win sales in highly competitive markets. They are often quite safe if the traders have had long and successful relations.

Prepayment

Sellers concerned with the buyer's creditworthiness may reverse the risks of open accounts by instead requiring the buyer to prepay in advance. This method shifts the greatest uncertainty to the buyer that the goods will not be delivered. When market forces favor sellers, buyers may be unable to refuse making prepayment. Some traders compromise by making mutual showings of good faith: The buyer makes a partial down payment and the seller ships without receiving full payment. The risks of such good faith can be further reduced where the parties agree to installment payments and deliveries.

In markets with excess supply, is it ethical for the buyer to exact favorable open account terms from the seller? When demand outstrips supply, is it ethical for sellers to exact more favorable prepayment terms? Clearly, price is not the only term on which the balance of market power is focused. Given the market's acceptance of the various traditional payment methods and the demand by both sides to create new payment options, the pressures on either trading partner to shift profits and transaction risks becomes the "ethics of the market."

Payment by Draft

The buyer's payment can be made by check, draft, or other *bill of exchange* representing a transfer of funds to the seller when honored by the buyer's bank after negotiation through the banking system. A **clean collection** occurs when the seller's bank receives payment on the draft after the buyer has received the goods. This imposes greater risks on the seller if the buyer becomes insolvent or stops payment on the draft. The seller can reduce this risk by insisting on a documentary collection. Review the form and negotiability of drafts, which were discussed in Chapters 24 to 29.

Sight Drafts

The seller initiates a documentary collection in a *cash against documents* transaction by preparing the other required shipping documents and making a **sight draft** payable to itself and drawn on the buyer. The seller is simultaneously the drawer and payee on a sight draft, while the buyer is the drawee. If the seller were to attempt making an unauthorized draft, the buyer's bank would simply dishonor the draft and refuse payment. However, in an authorized transaction where the seller's shipping documents are in order, the buyer's bank will usually honor the draft, transferring payment to the seller's bank and crediting the seller's account. The bank is then authorized to transfer the shipping documents to the buyer, enabling the buyer to rightfully claim the goods from the carrier or warehouse.

Payment against the documents on a sight draft splits the risks between buyer and seller. The seller is paid only if the documents are in order, and the buyer receives no documentary rights to the goods until payment is made. The seller still risks incurring the transportation costs and losing the sale if the buyer dishonors the draft. The buyer still has the risks that the documents are forgeries, the goods were damaged in transit, or the goods do not conform to the documents' description as inspected. However, unlike some other payment forms, payment by sight draft balances these risks.

Time Drafts

A similar process is used when the buyer's bank honors a **time draft** payable at some time in the future. The documents are released to the buyer when the buyer signs a time draft obligating future payment from the buyer or from its bank account. The time draft then becomes a **trade acceptance** and effectively extends the buyer credit. If the bank accepts, the draft becomes a **banker's acceptance** obligating the bank. In addition to the seller's risks in using a sight draft, the time draft transaction further risks the seller's payment if the buyer later becomes insolvent. Acceptances are often traded in the secondary market, depending on the creditworthiness of the buyer or its bank. Sellers may insist on the bank following certain contingency plans if the buyer dishonors a draft, such as storing, insuring, and warehousing the goods until another buyer is found.

Letters of Credit

The buyer's risk of the goods' nondelivery or nonconformance and the seller's risk of nonpayment for goods shipped in international commerce are reduced significantly by the use of letters of credit. The **letter of credit** (L/C) is a bank's documentary assurance to the seller that payment for the goods will be made when certain delivery documents are presented. A contract for the international sale of goods may obligate the seller to deliver goods only if the buyer acquires an L/C from a large, reputable bank. The buyer makes a contract for the L/C and pays the bank a fee for this service, usually a percentage of the face amount (1/8 to 1 percent). The L/C substitutes or adds the bank's known credit reputation for the buyer's and the bank becomes the primary obligor to pay the purchase price.

To facilitate such international sales transactions, banks active in L/C services usually work through their own foreign branches or have a working relationship with other major banks in the seller's country. L/Cs are made *negotiable*, permitting their transfer through the banking system or to other parties. They can also be made non-negotiable in favor of only one party. L/Cs are also called *credits, documentary credits,* or *bills of exchange.*

Evolution of Letters of Credit

Letters of credit evolved as a merchantile speciality entirely separate from common law contract concepts. Completely absorbed into the English common law by the 1700s along with the Law Merchant, letter of credit law found its way into American jurisprudence where it flourishes today. Its origins may be traced more deeply into history. There is evidence letters of credit were used by bankers in Renaissance Europe, Imperial Rome, ancient Greece, Phoenicia, and even early Egypt. These simple instruments survived despite their nearly 3,000 year old lineage because of their inherent reliability, convenience, economy, and flexibility.[1]

Applicable Law

While many nations' law may apply to L/Cs, two sources are important. First, Article 5 of the UCC on letters of credit, codified in the United States, applies to L/C transactions between two U.S. businesses. Second, in the 1930s, the International Chamber of Commerce compiled the accepted customs used by merchants and bankers in international transactions into the **Uniform Customs and Practices for Documentary Credits (UCP).** The UCP's latest 1983 revision is used throughout the world as the primary reference for interpreting L/Cs. International L/Cs often specifically elect to apply the UCP, so U.S. and foreign courts usually cite the UCP as definitive authority. The discussion in this chapter combines these two complementary sources of L/C law. Figure 34–1 illustrates the form of a letter of credit.

Parties to the Letter of Credit

There are usually at least four parties involved with the payment side of an L/C transaction: (1) buyer (account party), (2) L/C issuing bank, (3) seller (L/C beneficiary), and (4) seller's correspondent bank. The L/C obligates the issuing bank to accept or negotiate a draft that makes a payment to a specified beneficiary. Such "payable to" L/Cs are non-

transferable. All L/Cs must be written as a binding promise to pay an amount of money up to a sum certain in a stated currency, payable only up to a stated maturity date, and only on the seller's presentation of specified documents.

Conditions of Payment

Payment can be conditioned only on the presentation of satisfactory documents and not on the occurrence of any other events. For example, the issuing bank's obligation to pay on an L/C can be made conditional only on satisfactory and strict compliance in terms among all the documents. This leaves no room for conditions such as the issuing bank obtaining a lien on the goods or the bank inspecting the goods for defects. L/C transactions involve at least three primary sets of contracts and documents: (1) the contract of sale for goods, (2) the L/C, and (3) the bill of lading, which may be accompanied by other documents.

Primary Documents Required in Letter of Credit Transactions

1. Goods sale contract.
2. Letter of credit.
3. Bill of lading.

Initiating Letter of Credit Transactions

The letter of credit process is usually initiated when the goods sale contract obligates the buyer to obtain the L/C. The buyer makes an L/C application to the issuing bank. An L/C is issued only after the bank is satisfied with the buyer's creditworthiness. The application specifies the conditions of the seller's *full performance,* which must be satisfied before the issuing bank may rightfully forward the payment. For example, D.E.F.GmBH's documents must precisely describe the goods, the quantity, inspection standards, and various shipping terms, such as the shipping date, packaging, handling, carrier descriptions, freight costs, and insurance requirements. There can be no discrepancy on these terms when compared with A.B.Corp's L/C.

Unconfirmed and Confirmed Letters of Credit

The issuing bank's L/C is usually forwarded to the seller through the seller's bank. The latter acts as a correspondent of the issuing bank. The seller's bank, known as an **advising bank,** has no legal

---

[1]*Voest-Alpine Int. Corp. v. Chase Manhattan Bank,* 707 F.2d 680 (2d Cir. 1983).

Chapter 34 International Sales Transactions 671

Figure 34–1   Letter of Credit

Specimen

Homewood International Bank
1234 Burr Ridge Rd.
Chicago, IL 60606
Telex. 555-1221

IRREVOCABLE DOCUMENTARY LETTER OF CREDIT

☐ This is a confirmation of our letter of credit opened by Fax

☒ This credit is forwarded to the advising bank by Air Mail

Date of Issue
June 6, 1994

Advising Bank
Bundes Bank, A.G.
Leifostrasse 17
8000 Meuchen
Germany

LETTER OF CREDIT NUMBER

Of Issuing Bank	Of Advising Bank
XXX	XX

Amount
U.S. $15,947.00

Applicant
A.B. Corp.
456 Monroe
Chicago, IL 60646

Beneficiary
D.E.F. GmBh
Industrass 7
7000 Meuchen am Main
Germany

Latest Date for Negotiation	Latest Date for Shipment
Aug. 15, 1994	Aug. 1, 1994

Dear Sirs:

We hereby issue in your favor this documentary letter of credit, which is available ☐ against presentation of the following documents

☒ against beneficiaries draft at   sight   drawn on ourselves

accompanied by the following documents (*in duplicate* unless otherwise specified):

☒ Commercial Invoice and two copies

☒ Packing List

☒ Special U.S. Customs Invoice

☒ Negotiable Marine/AK Insurance Policy or Certificate covering: ☐ All Risks   ☒ War Risks

☐ Other Risks (please specify)

☒ Full set of clean on board ocean bills of Lading issued to order of shipper, endorsed in blank, marked "Freight Prepaid"

☐ Clean Air Waybill in   consigned to

Notify   J.D. Broker, Customs Agent, 9879 Commerce Ave.,
         Chicago, IL 60611

Evidencing shipment of: One Milling Machine, Model SX-586

F.O.B. Chicago

Shipment From
Germany to Chicago, Illinois

| Partial Shipments: | ☐ Permitted | ☒ Prohibited |
| Transshipments: | ☐ Permitted | ☒ Prohibited |

Special Conditions

ALL DOCUMENTS TO BE SENT IN ONE AIR MAILING
UNLESS OTHERWISE EXPRESSLY STATED ON THIS CREDIT ALL BANKING CHARGES EXCEPT ISSUING BANK CHARGES ARE FOR THE ACCOUNT OF THE BENEFICIARY

WE HEREBY ENGAGE WITH THE BONAFIDE HOLDERS OF ALL DRAFTS DRAWN AND/OR DOCUMENTS PRESENTED UNDER AND IN COMPLIANCE WITH THE TERMS OF THE LETTER OF CREDIT THAT SUCH DRAFTS AND/OR DOCUMENTS WILL BE DULY HONORED UPON PRESENTATION TO US.

THE AMOUNT OF EACH DRAWING MUST BE ENDORSED ON THE REVERSE SIDE OF THIS LETTER OF CREDIT BY THE NEGOTIATING BANK.

DRAFTS MUST BE MARKED AS DRAWN UNDER THIS CREDIT.

Homewood International Bank

Signature

Authorized Signature   *ISSUING BANK*

Advising Bank's Notification

Aug. 12, 1994
Bundes Bank, A.G.

Place, Date, Name, and Signature of Advising Bank

obligation to pay the seller if the transaction is an **unconfirmed letter of credit.** The advising bank must usually transmit the L/C, verify the authenticity of the documents prepared by the seller, and compare the issuing bank's signature with a specimen in the advising bank's files.

If the seller cannot rely solely on the security of the issuing bank's reputation to ensure payment, the seller may insist on a term in the goods sale contract requiring a **confirmed letter of credit.** In such cases, the seller's bank acts as a **confirming bank.** In addition to providing the services of an advising bank, the confirming bank becomes obligated to pay the seller when adequate documents are provided, even if the buyer or issuing bank defaults.

Confirmed L/Cs give the seller a double security: promises to pay by both the issuing bank and the confirming bank. Such extra assurance is more costly, possibly raising the buyer's price, cutting the seller's profit, or both. However, when shipments are made to nations with currency controls or poor debt ratings, the seller may be justified in demanding a confirmed L/C. The buyer's government may impose currency or payment restrictions after the goods sale contract is made or after the goods are shipped but before the seller receives payment. The seller's insistence on a confirmed L/C helps avoid payment delays, nonpayment, or some of the risks of currency devaluation. Additionally, it is usually easier and cheaper to enforce payment on the L/C from a domestic bank than from a foreign bank.

Seller's Document Preparation

The seller should carefully examine all the conditions in the L/C before identifying the goods to the contract or assembling the shipment. The seller, also known as the shipper, may not be obligated to ship unless the L/C exactly conforms to the conditions stated in the goods sale contract. For example, if the sizes and colors of goods stated in the L/C do not match these terms as stated in the goods sale contract, the issuing bank may have made an error or the buyer may have changed its order. If the seller does not carefully verify the L/C against the goods sale contract, the seller could forfeit a profitable sale, ship goods unpaid for, or otherwise breach the goods sale contract. In cases of such *discrepancies* among the documents, the seller should contact the buyer immediately to modify the goods sale contract or obtain an amended L/C.

After the seller verifies it can comply with the conditions stated in the L/C, the seller must prepare the required documents. Many transactions require a bill of lading, a commercial invoice listing the terms of the goods sale contract, an insurance policy covering risks during shipment, an inspection certificate or certificates confirming the goods shipped meet the contract specifications, and any necessary clearances, export licenses, or certificates of origin necessary for government or customs officials. Most of these documents must be compared with the L/C and all must conform with the description in the goods sale contract.

Documents Typically Compared against the Letter of Credit

- Bill of lading.
- Commercial invoice.
- Inspection certificate or certificates.
- Insurance policy or policies.
- Governmental clearance/export license.
- Certificate of origin.

Duties of Issuing Banks

The issuing bank must make **payment against the documents** by paying the seller directly or by reimbursing the confirming bank when the required documents are forwarded that indicate satisfaction of the specified *full performance* standards. The buyer is not obligated to pay unless the issuing bank ensures that the documents clearly comply exactly with the L/C's conditions. For example, A.B.Corp's. L/C application may require the issuing bank to pay only if D.E.F.GmBH's documents list the precise goods ordered. The carrier's bill of lading and separate inspections must show the goods actually shipped exactly meet the full performance requirements required under the goods sale contract.

If all is in order, the issuing bank pays on the L/C, the buyer pays or becomes legally obligated to pay the issuing bank, and the issuing bank indorses the documents over to the buyer. This gives the buyer the right to claim the goods from the carrier upon arrival. At this point, the buyer is commonly known as the *consignee*. Sellers should always specifically insist on receiving an *irrevocable letter of credit*. Unless specifically made irrevocable, an L/C is revocable, permitting the issuing bank to unilaterally cancel or modify its obligation to pay. The parties to an L/C are willing to take on these risks only if the L/C is an obligation independent of the goods sale contract. Therefore, the buyer cannot cancel payment if the goods can be found more cheaply elsewhere or arrive defective. In such cases, the buyer must pursue the seller on breach of contract independently of the payment process if the L/C is irrevocable. Figure 34–2 illustrates the flow of documents and funds in an L/C transaction.

Duties of Advising and Confirming Banks

The seller indorses and forwards all the required documents to its advising bank. The advising bank is given a reasonable time to verify the documents' authenticity and accuracy. UCC Article 5 limits this to three days before the documents must be forwarded to the issuing bank. The seller must redraft nonconforming documents when rejected by the advising bank if there are discrepancies between the L/C and the goods sale contract if there is still time before the L/C expires. The seller's lateness may breach the goods sale contract, if it so provides.

A confirming bank must usually pay ''against the documents,'' so the seller immediately receives cash or a credit balance at the confirming bank. This involves payment on a sight draft or bill of exchange initiated by the seller, which is drawn on the issuing bank's L/C. However, the seller must await payment on the draft in an unconfirmed L/C because the seller's bank acts only as an advising bank. Even in such cases, if the seller receives a *banker's acceptance* draft, the seller can immediately sell the draft at discount on the commercial paper market to raise funds.

Strict Compliance Rule

L/Cs arose to reduce the risks inherent in long-distance transactions between contracting parties in different legal systems and with various cultural customs. Long experience showed such transactions could become unprofitable if either party varied their performance even slightly. For this reason, the customs, practices, and case law surrounding L/Cs insist on **strict compliance** between the seller's documents and the *full performance* standards as specified by the buyer in the L/C. The risks of international documentary sales leave no room for the tolerance for variations inherent in the common law concept of *substantial performance*. Therefore, the seller is not entitled to payment unless the documents are in strict compliance with the L/C terms. For example, A.B.Corp.'s bank need not negotiate its L/C to the correspondent bank representing D.E.F.GmBH if the bill of lading, invoice, and inspection certificates are not in exact compliance with the specifications A.B.Corp. made in its L/C application.

The strict compliance rule permits the issuing bank to avoid payment if demanded by someone who is not the designated beneficiary or if the documents do not exactly conform. Even misspellings can excuse payment, although some courts ignore immaterial typographical errors. Issuing, confirming, and advising banks are required to carefully inspect all documents for such discrepancies. The UCP relieves banks of liability when the bank introduces errors in transmitting L/Cs and shipping documents. When time permits, banks often allow buyers the opportunity to give written waivers if the discrepancies are immaterial. Where the discrepancies are not waived and the issuing bank refuses to honor payment on the L/C, it must immediately notify the seller's bank of the dishonor and either return the documents or hold them for other disposition. The seller is entitled to a return of the goods but may decide to resell them to another buyer to preserve their value or avoid prohibitive reshipment charges.

The Strict Compliance Principle

There is no room for documents which are almost the same or which will do just as well.[2]

Strict compliance can also present ethical dilemmas. Assume the issuing bank refuses to pay on documents with immaterial differences. The buyer is the bank's major customer and just purchased the goods more cheaply elsewhere. Is it ethical for the issuing bank to refuse this payment when it had previously made payment on this seller's previous installment deliveries despite such trivial inconsistencies? Assume a buyer includes L/C terms it suspects the seller will neglect to include in the docu-

---

[2]*Equitable Trust Co. v. Dawson Partners*, 27 Lloyd's L.R. 49, 52 (1927).

Figure 34–2 Flow of Documents and Funds in a Letter of Credit Transaction

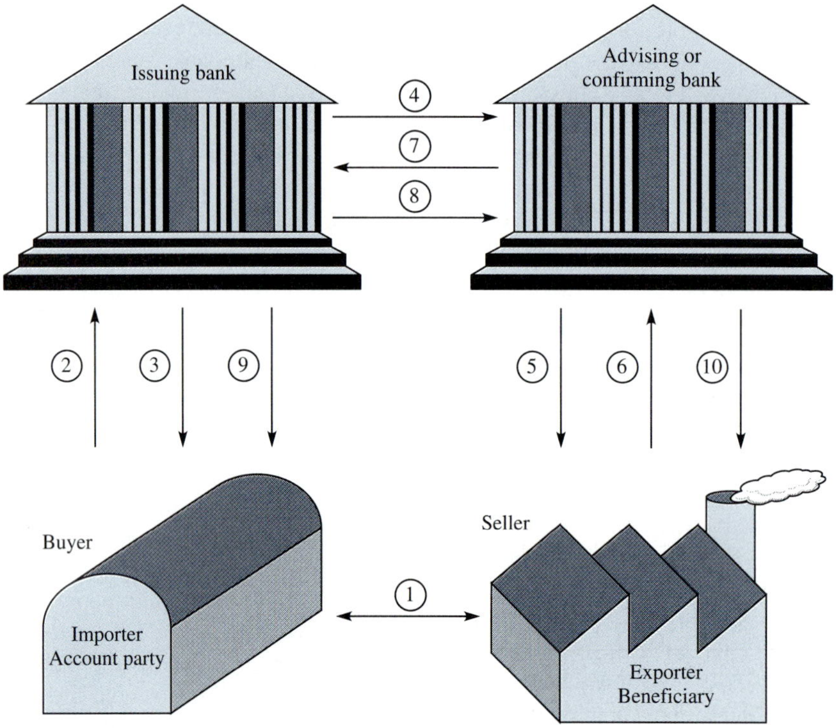

1. Contract for the international sale of goods.
2. Buyer (account party) applies to the issuing bank for an L/C designating the seller as beneficiary.
3. Issuing bank makes commitment to buyer to issue L/C specifying buyer's terms of full performance.
4. L/C is forwarded from issuing bank to the seller's advising or confirming bank.
5. Advising or confirming bank forwards buyer's L/C to seller for seller's preparation of documents in conformance with L/C.
6. Seller forwards documents (e.g., bill of lading, inspection certificates, export license, customs clearance) to advising or confirming bank.
7. Advising or confirming bank carefully checks documents, advises seller to make any necessary revisions, and forwards documents to issuing bank.
8. Issuing bank carefully checks documents for discrepancies and either (a) honors L/C by paying seller, confirming bank, or bank issuing back-to-back L/C; otherwise, (b) bank dishonors L/C if there are discrepancies or bank revokes a revocable L/C.
9. Issuing bank forwards bill of lading and any other documents to buyer as necessary to claim goods from carrier.
10. Advising bank pays seller, credits seller's account, or pays transferee if beneficiary negotiated L/C.

ments. Is it ethical for the buyer to waive these discrepancies when the issuing bank dishonors only if the seller accepts a major price concession after the goods are shipped?

A few U.S. courts have permitted exceptions to strict compliance, suggesting that a *substantial compliance rule* is developing. Under such a standard, banks may be required to look beyond the documents by investigating facts relating to the parties' true intent. For example, some courts may ignore either misspellings or slightly mistaken names of the beneficiary if no confusion is likely to result. There is a trend to apply this rule only in cases where the buyer alleges the issuing bank wrongfully honored documents but the documents were really in substantial compliance. This rule can place hardship on banks, so it applies neither in suits by the seller for wrongful dishonor nor in suits by the buyer to enjoin payment. The strict compliance standard is still applicable in these latter two cases.

Fraud Exception

International trade depends on the unwavering obligation of issuing banks to pay on an irrevocable and conforming L/C. However, there have developed instances where the L/C beneficiary (seller) has com-

mitted such serious fraud that a court may enjoin the issuing bank from making payment. An injunction preserves the issuing bank's international reputation for honoring its credits while preventing the seller from abusing the L/C process.

Two types of fraud are recognized: (1) forged or altered documents, and (2) the beneficiary's **fraud in the transaction.** These exceptions are limited to intentional and active frauds and not to mere breach of warranty by the seller. Breach of warranty is of lesser seriousness, and the buyer should reduce these risks by requiring pre- and postshipment inspections. If the buyer fails to obtain sufficient inspections or an inspection fails to uncover the breach, the buyer is not entitled to an injunction restraining payment on the L/C. Instead, the buyer must pursue the seller for breach of contract. The following classic case illustrates fraud in the transaction.

SZTEJN v. J. HENRY SCHRODER BANKING CO.

31 N.Y.S.2d 631 (N.Y. App. Div. 1941)

Sztejn entered into a goods sale contract with an Indian corporation, Transea Traders, Ltd., for the purchase of hog bristles. J. Henry Schroder issued an irrevocable L/C to Transea for the purchase price. Transea shipped 50 cases of cowhair and other rubbish to Sztejn under a bill of lading that erroneously conformed to the L/C by listing the contents as hog bristles. Transea's advising bank, the Chartered Bank of India, forwarded Transea's draft to Schroder for payment under the L/C. Sztejn sought to enjoin Schroder from honoring the draft claiming fraud in the transaction.

SHIENTAG, Justice

It is well established that a letter of credit is independent of the primary contract of sale between the buyer and the seller. The issuing bank agrees to pay upon presentation of documents, not goods. This rule is necessary to preserve the efficiency of the letter of credit as an instrument for the financing of trade. One of the chief purposes of the letter of credit is to furnish the seller with a ready means of obtaining prompt payment for his merchandise. It would be a most unfortunate interference with business transactions if a bank before honoring drafts drawn upon it was obliged or even allowed to go behind the documents, at the request of the buyer and enter into controversies between the buyer and the seller regarding the quality of the merchandise shipped. If the buyer and the seller intended the

bank to do this they could have so provided in the letter of credit itself, and in the absence of such a provision, the court will not demand or even permit the bank to delay paying drafts which are proper in form. Of course, the application of this doctrine presupposes that the documents accompanying the draft are genuine and conform in terms to the requirements of the letter of credit.

This is not a controversy between the buyer and seller concerning a mere breach of warranty regarding the quality of the merchandise. It must be assumed that the seller has intentionally failed to ship any goods ordered by the buyer. In such a situation, where the seller's fraud has been called to the bank's attention before the drafts and documents have been presented for payment, the principle of the independence of the bank's obligation under the letter of credit should not be extended to protect the unscrupulous seller. It is true that even though the documents are forged or fraudulent, if the issuing bank has already paid the draft before receiving notice of the seller's fraud, it will be protected if it exercised reasonable diligence before making such payment. However, in the instant action Schroder has received notice of Transea's active fraud before it accepted or paid the draft.

The distinction between a breach of warranty and active fraud on the part of the seller is supported by authority and reason. As one court has stated:

> Obviously, when the issuer of a letter of credit knows that a document, although correct in form, is, in point of fact, false or illegal, he cannot be called upon to recognize such a document as complying with the terms of a letter of credit.

While the primary factor in the issuance of the letter of credit is the credit standing of the buyer, the security afforded by the merchandise is also taken into account. In fact, the letter of credit requires a bill of lading made out to the order of the bank and not the buyer. Although the bank is not interested in the exact detailed performance of the sales contract, it is vitally interested in assuring itself that there are some goods represented by the documents. Accordingly, the defendant's motion to dismiss the supplemental complaint is denied.

Case Questions

1. What is the primary issue in cases seeking the invalidation of an L/C?
2. For what reasons do the courts attempt to enforce L/Cs whenever possible?

Standby Letters of Credit

The L/Cs discussed above are called *straight letters of credit*. However, L/Cs are not only used as the buyer's payment mechanism. **Standby letters of credit** are used to guarantee the account party's performance of a service contract, construction contract, loan, or other obligation under a sales contract. For example, the buyer might require that the seller provide a standby L/C to ensure that the seller will perform any warranty promised. If the seller failed to repair or replace the goods after a specified notice period, the buyer, as a standby L/C beneficiary, would receive a prearranged payment. The seller would then be liable to reimburse the issuing bank.

The bank issuing the standby L/C must pay when presented with the documents required in the standby L/C. For example, the L/C usually requires a letter from a designated independent third party or some other previously agreed-to certification document indicating the account party has breached the guaranteed obligation. Standby L/Cs are unenforceable if the bank is required to pay on anything other than a presentation of documents. This would effectively become a performance bond requiring the issuing bank to make a determination of "questions of fact or law at issue between the account party and the beneficiary."[3] U.S. banks are prohibited from making such performance bonds. The following case illustrates some of the political problems with standby L/Cs and the reluctance of courts to enjoin the honor of any L/C.

---

[3]Opinions of the U.S. Comptroller of the Currency, Interpretive Ruling No. 7.7016.

AMERICAN BELL INTERNATIONAL v. ISLAMIC REPUBLIC OF IRAN
474 F.Supp. 420 (S.D.N.Y. 1979)

American Bell, a subsidiary of AT&T, contracted with the Iranian government, then controlled by the Shah, to provide telecommunications equipment and consulting services to improve Iran's international communications. Iran made a $38 million down payment toward the $280 million contract price. Iran required American Bell to provide a standby L/C as a bond for Bell's performance of the contract. After the Shah was overthrown in 1979, Bell discontinued these operations because invoices went unpaid. Bell sought to enjoin Manufacturers, the issuing bank, from honoring the L/C payment to the subsequent Islamic Republic government.

MACMAHON, District Judge

To be sure, Bell faces substantial hardships upon denial of its motion. Should Manufacturers pay the demand, Bell will immediately become liable to Manufacturers for $30.2 million, with no assurance of recouping those funds from Iran for the services performed. While counsel represented in graphic detail the other losses Bell faces at the hands of the current Iranian government, these would flow regardless of whether we ordered the relief sought. The hardship imposed from a denial of relief is limited to the admittedly substantial sum of $30.2 million.

But Manufacturers would face at least as great a loss, and perhaps a greater one, were we to grant relief. Upon Manufacturers' failure to pay, Bank Iranshahr could initiate a suit on the Letter of Credit and attach $30.2 million of Manufacturers' assets in Iran. In addition, it could seek to hold Manufacturers liable for consequential damages beyond that sum resulting from the failure to make timely payment. Finally, there is no guarantee that Bank Iranshahr or the government, in retaliation for Manufacturers' recalcitrance, will not nationalize additional Manufacturers' assets in Iran in amounts which counsel, at oral argument, represented to be far in excess of the amount in controversy here.

Apart from a greater monetary exposure flowing from an adverse decision, Manufacturers faces a loss of credibility in the international banking community that could result from its failure to make good on a letter of credit.

Bell, a sophisticated multinational enterprise well advised by competent counsel, entered into these arrangements with its corporate eyes open. It knowingly and voluntarily signed a contract allowing the Iranian government to recoup its down payment on demand, without regard to cause. It caused Manufacturers to enter into an arrangement whereby Manufacturers became obligated to pay Bank Iranshahr the unamortized down payment balance upon receipt of conforming documents, again without regard to cause.

Both of these arrangements redounded tangibly to the benefit of Bell. The contract with Iran, with its prospect of designing and installing from scratch a nationwide and international communications system, was certain to bring to Bell both monetary profit and prestige and good will in the global communications industry. The agreement to indemnify Manufacturers on its Letter of Credit provided the means by which these benefits could be achieved. One who reaps the rewards of commercial arrangements must also accept their burdens. One such burden in this case, voluntarily accepted by Bell, was the risk that demand might be made on the funds constituting the down payment. To be sure, the sequence of events that led up to that demand may well have been unforeseeable when the contracts were signed. To this extent, both Bell and Manufacturers have been made the unwitting and innocent victims of tumultuous events beyond their control. But, as between two innocents, the party who undertakes by contract the risk of political uncertainty and governmental caprice must bear the consequences when the risk comes home to roost. So ordered.

Case Questions
1. What political issue is Bell attempting to raise in seeking to enjoin Manufacturers' payment on the standby L/C?
2. What reasons support rejecting Bell's plea for an injunction?

Transferable Letters of Credit
Most L/Cs are nontransferable because they are specifically made payable to only one named beneficiary, normally the goods seller. However, the named seller may be acting only in the capacity of a reseller, wholesaler, export trading company, middleman, or other broker. The reseller simply arranges for the sale between the buyer and a manufacturer or other supplier. The wholesaler may have limited capital or seek to avoid the personal financial risk of advancing payment to the supplier with the reseller's own cash or credit. A transferable or *negotiable letter of credit* can facilitate this transaction.

The L/C can be made transferable to the supplier. Thereby, the reseller need only indorse the L/C over to the supplier to make the payment. The issuing bank must agree to the additional transferability risk and may therefore receive additional fees. The supplier also must agree to accept the L/C as payment. The supplier might be willing to accept transfer of the L/C based on the strength of the issuing bank's reputation, on the reseller's broader business contacts, or on the lack of hard currencies to effect the transaction. The transferee must comply with all the L/C terms before the issuing or confirming bank will disburse the funds. For example, crude oil produced in a developing country might be sold through a reseller to a buyer in an industrialized nation. If the developing nation has currency controls and/or shortages of hard currencies, the transferable L/C may be the only way to effect the sale. *General letters of credit* have no transfer restrictions, while *special letters of credit* prohibit transferability or limit transfer to one or more banks.

Back-to-Back Letters of Credit

Another form of financing for resellers with minimal capital involves two L/Cs, with the second L/C depending on the first. The reseller uses the first L/C issued by the buyer's bank, called a *countercredit*, as collateral for obtaining a second L/C, the **back-to-back letter of credit,** issued by the reseller's bank. The second L/C is used to finance the reseller's acquisition of raw materials, unfinished goods, or finished goods from a supplier.

In a back-to-back L/C, the second L/C is made payable to the supplier and the first L/C is usually assigned over to the supplier's issuing bank. This permits the reseller to use the buyer's creditworthiness in acquiring the supplier's goods. For example, the crude oil exporter in the preceding example could have financed the transaction differently. The exporter could assign the buyer's L/C to the reseller's bank, using the buyer's credit as collateral to obtain a second L/C payable to the crude oil supplier. The reseller's issuing bank usually requires the documents in both L/C transactions to be identical. The complexities of back-to-back L/Cs are reduced somewhat when the same bank issues both L/Cs.

Red Clauses

Partial payments under an L/C may be made to various suppliers, intermediaries, or other consultants until the ceiling amount of the credit is fully exhausted.

Red clauses are generally noted on the L/C in red ink. They represent the issuing bank's promise to reimburse an advising or confirming bank that has advanced a partial payment on the L/C. These payments are usually characterized as loans made to the exporting manufacturer or reseller. The funds advanced are usually limited to making payments for raw materials, down payments, or other costs of acquisition, shipping, and manufacturing. When the issuing bank makes final payment on its honor of the L/C, this repays the loan made by the advising or confirming bank. Loan advances under red clauses present somewhat greater risks for the buyer and its issuing bank. If the seller defaults, the issuing bank and ultimately the buyer may be liable for the loan amounts advanced. The buyer's ability to gain satisfaction from the defaulting seller are obviously limited.

Revolving Letters of Credit

Under long-term contracts to supply goods or services over several years in numerous installments, it can be convenient to use a single umbrella L/C to finance all the installment transactions. A **revolving letter of credit** is like a revolving line of credit. As funds are advanced, drawing down the L/C face amount, the face amount can be raised as the buyer repays the earlier advances. The revolving L/C entitles the seller to make a series of drafts over a fixed time period against the ceiling amount on the L/C as the seller makes installment shipments. The buyer's installment payments periodically replenish the L/C credit line back upward toward its face amount so the seller can draw against the L/C for future shipments.

Revolving L/Cs can also be used for large construction projects where services are supplied by foreign contractors and building materials are supplied by foreign suppliers. These parties may draw against the L/C and receive periodic progress payments from the L/C until it is fully exhausted. Documentation required for payments under a revolving L/C may include inspection certificates indicating the contractor's successful partial completion or traditional sale documents showing delivery of the goods.

ALTERNATIVES TO TRADITIONAL DOCUMENTARY SALES

The costs and delays of documentary transfers and collections have combined with technological advances, foreign exchange problems, and politics to inspire innovations in trade exchange and finance.

International sales are becoming increasingly competitive, while traditional documentary exchanges are politically impossible for much of the world's population. As a result, innovative order and payment processing is evolving, private and public institutions are participating, and age-old barter systems reemerge and are evolving into complex systems of exchange.

Computerized Contracting, Documentation, and Payments

Computerized telecommunications promises to preclude many of the parties' transaction anxieties and eventually replace the physical transmittal of documents. Computers are becoming linked worldwide by modem, direct telecommunications connections, and other forms of E-mail. Orders, confirmations, documents of title, payments, and inspection and other certificates can be transmitted electronically. In the future, all primary, secondary, and third parties will be able to participate in this grand electronic communications system, including seller-shippers, consignee-buyers, carriers, warehouse operators, insurers, customs officials, inspectors, banks, and other financial intermediaries. However, questions remain about computer security and which institutions will provide these services.

Electronic Data Interchange (EDI)

The beginning point for computerized order processing innovations is **electronic data interchange (EDI).** Computer technology has the capacity to transmit price quotes, negotiations, orders, and transfer documents, and to make payments instantly and with fewer errors. This can contribute to achieving inventory cost savings under **just-in-time inventory (JIT)** techniques and more accurately match suppliers with customers.

EDI transmittal of bills of lading and other transport documents require some modification to the traditional method of physical indorsement and transfer of paper-based documents. The Comite Maritime International adopted the **CMI Rules for Electronic Bills of Lading** in 1990 to facilitate development of EDI. If all parties agree to use EDI transmittals, the carrier's computerized records may actually become the official documents. The party indicated on the carrier's computer becomes the *holder* of the document as updated throughout transit. Other intermediaries, such as large international banks, may

be expected to compete to become the *electronic repository* for domestic and international EFT/EDI documents.

As EDI systems become widely accepted as more reliable than physical documentary exchanges, the risks of delay and lost or altered documents will be minimized. At this writing, partial pilot EDI systems are in use, primarily in domestic U.S. transactions. The American Bar Association's ad hoc committee on EDI is drafting protocols for EDI use that may become the model for both domestic and international EDI. Large banks with substantial domestic and international documentary trade business are becoming central computerized clearinghouses for EDI and the electronic payments discussed next. Of course, the threat of computer security breaches may plague EDI systems, particularly as nonfinancial system users come *on-line*, opening the system to many more users and the attendant increase in the number of incidents of access. Nevertheless, such problems are probably not insurmountable, so electronic systems will continue developing.

Electronic Funds Transfer (EFT)

As discussed in Chapter 28, EFT systems are becoming well developed in domestic commerce. Wire funds transfers have a long history in domestic and international banking. Combining such systems with electronic documentary sales should be a simple step. International payment systems are frequently made a part of goods transactions when payments are transferred between foreign and domestic banks. Domestic EFT is replacing the physical movement of checks and drafts through the banking system. The Society for World-Wide Interbank Financial Telecommunication (SWIFT) provides an international interbank network to facilitate payments between banks. SWIFT is in use in over 50 nations worldwide, including the United States, Canada, and many European nations. SWIFT transfers are replacing telex and mail for international funds transfers, further entrenching the banks as the central processing facilities for EFT/EDI.

Secondary Markets for Payments

Secondary markets have developed to help sellers convert their international receivables into cash. Use of these alternatives may reduce the seller's proceeds as compensation to these secondary market counterparties. Similar transactions costs and quantifiable risks are common in other widely used payment alternatives. **Factoring** of international open accounts receivables is effected through a global network of factors. Typically, a U.S. seller contracts with a U.S. factor who finds a foreign factor through the network located in the buyer's home nation. If the buyer is found creditworthy, the foreign factor and then the U.S. factor guarantee the buyer's payment. Factor guaranties are usually sufficient collateral for the U.S. seller's bank to advance trade financing to the seller for acquisition or commencement of manufacturing the goods. Collection of the buyer's payments are made by the foreign factor and forwarded through the domestic factor to the seller or directly to the seller's bank.

Forfait financing developed during the post–World War II reconstruction of Europe to aid financing the Europeans' purchases of foreign goods. Typically, the goods sale contract requires the buyer to give a promissory note or time draft in exchange for the delivery documents. The seller then sells this negotiable instrument, indorsing it over to a bank at a discount. The bank assumes the risk of the buyer's nonpayment unless the buyer's bank also guarantees the buyer's payment. Forfait financing is growing, particularly in Europe and Asia, but the traditionally large minimum transaction size has restricted its wider acceptance in the United States.

The market for bankers and trade acceptances discussed earlier are typical. The buyer can issue a sight or time draft in exchange for an advance of the purchase price that the buyer receives as proceeds from reselling imported goods. Acceptances are usually paid at a discounted amount representing the bank's compensation for the advance financing. Bankers and trade acceptances can be sold at further discount to short-term investors on the secondary market and often make up substantial holdings of mutual funds.

Public Institutional Finance Assistance

Public agencies, governments, and intergovernmental agencies often have a political mandate to finance domestic construction projects by foreign companies and suppliers or to encourage exports. Typically, the public agency guarantees an L/C issued by the buyer's bank. For example, the **Agency for International Development (AID)** might make a commitment to a U.S. bank to facilitate a U.S. exporter to sell goods to an overseas buyer requiring credit. The

U.S. Eximbank also finances exports of U.S. products by making or guaranteeing either the exporter's working capital or the buyer's purchase money loan or L/C. Many other nations have similar agencies providing a variety of financial assistance. The **Foreign Credit Insurance Corporation** is a subdivision of Eximbank. It assembles a consortium of private insurance companies to insure exports from losses due to commercial and political risks. The **Commodity Credit Corporation** provides payment assurances to U.S. sellers of surplus agricultural goods.

Countertrade

This section explores the buyer's payment for goods or services by means other than the direct payment with hard currency, drafts, or letters of credit. Most of the world's developing nations suffer unfavorable balances of trade, have large debt burdens to foreign banks, and/or have a shortage of *hard currency* that can be easily and reliably convertible to other currencies. Such nations often limit their citizens' purchases of foreign goods and services, usually through government restrictions on the outflow of currency. In many such nations, citizens may legally purchase only those imported products that the government considers are essential. This often precludes the direct purchase of most foreign-produced consumer goods and even precludes the purchase of foreign-produced capital goods if destined for industries the government decrees are less essential. Such restrictions leave a tremendous gap in satisfying these nations' demand and probably limit the marketability of their raw materials and products.

Countertrade, which includes various forms of barterlike, product-for-product exchanges, has increased steadily in recent years to bridge this gap. Countertrade functions as a primary method to increase these nations' imports and expand the foreign markets for their products. By some accounts, the various forms of countertrade may account for up to 40 percent of all world trade, a substantial share. In the 1980s, the U.S. government quietly chose not to encourage countertrade, insisting that it was contrary to an efficient and free-market trading system. However, the Omnibus Trade and Competitiveness Act of 1988 required the president to establish an *Interagency Group on Countertrade*, which is only now expected to begin encouraging U.S. firms' use of countertrade. The act also established the *Office* *of Barter* within the International Trade Commission of the Department of Commerce to monitor international barter and provide information useful to the expansion of transactions beneficial to U.S. business.

Numerous industrialized nations require or encourage countertrade, including Canada, Australia, Norway, Greece, and Austria. Many industrialized nations encourage countertrade to expand their exports by creating new markets and exploiting their technologies and advanced manufacturing processes through licensing. Many nations require countertrade when their governments purchase expensive military hardware.

The Commerce Department lists at least 67 developing nations that actively encourage or require at least some countertrade relations.[4] These nations comprise the majority of the world's population and lie primarily within the former communist bloc, Latin America, Africa, the Middle East, and Asia. The governments of most developing nations view countertrade as a primary method to finance large public works projects (e.g., water projects, power plants), increase exports, realize the benefits of industrialization, raise their citizens' quality of life, and create economic expansion. With the collapse of the planned economies of the communist world and the increasing desire of developing nations to increase their productive and industrial bases, countertrade will probably continue to flourish in the 1990s and beyond. Countertrade is most active in the aerospace industry, military equipment, construction projects, chemicals, agriculture, and minerals.

What Is Countertrade?

Countertrade is a general term encompassing several forms of compensatory trade that involve reciprocal exchanges of goods and/or services that link two or more cross-border trade exchanges. Countertrade typically involves little or no payment in currency for goods or services. An elementary form of countertrade is a simple contractual link between

transactions by two enterprises in two different nations. For example, a U.S. computer maker might trade 100 486-based PCs to a firm in a southeast Asian nation in exchange for 600 hard disk drives assembled or manufactured in that nation. Little cash changes hands, and the goods traded have roughly equivalent values. As will become evident in the sections below, countertrade is often complex, awkward, and risky. Therefore, successful countertrade requires careful analysis and sometimes rather protracted negotiations. The various prevailing forms of countertrade permit the parties to individualize their unique transactions by utilizing one or more countertrading techniques.

Barter

Barter is the oldest and simplest form of countertrade: Two trading partners engage in a one-time direct exchange of goods with approximately equal value. Manhattan Island was reputedly bartered from local Indians for $24 of goods. Although pure barter is declining in favor of other forms of countertrade, the OPEC nations have used barter extensively, trading oil for other needed products and services. Barter requires no financial transfers, financial valuations, or the intervention of other countertrading parties. However, today, the greater sophistication of trading parties, the limited flexibility of barter, and the difficulties of equalizing value may require assistance from third parties to dispose of unwanted goods taken in barter.

Swaps are a form of barter where the trading parties swap their delivery responsibilities for equivalent commodities to each other's clients to save transportation costs (e.g., crude oil, chemicals, minerals, raw materials). For example, a Swiss exporter may have a contract to deliver certain minerals to Mexico. In a separate transaction, a U.S. firm has agreed to sell similar minerals to Spain. The Swiss and U.S. firm might barter to swap their obligations, reaping considerable savings by reducing their transportation costs.

Counterpurchase

Counterpurchase is probably the most common form of countertrade. The seller agrees to accept other goods in full or partial payment rather than cash. These goods may be produced by the importer or by another entity in the importing nation. In the example concerning the U.S. PC manufacturer's exchange, the U.S. computer manufacturer agreed to

---

[4]See Pompiliu Verzariu, "International Countertrade: A Guide for Managers and Executives" (U.S. Department of Commerce, International Trade Administration, Washington, D.C.: August 1992), and Pompiliu Verzariu and Paula Mitchell, "International Countertrade: Individual Country Practices," (U.S. Department of Commerce, International Trade Administration, Washington, D.C.: August 1992).

counterpurchase disk drives rather than receive cash. Counterpurchase differs from traditional barter because all the goods or services exchanged are given an ostensible value in currency. These values are then equalized so the consideration given and received by both sides is balanced, although little or no currency changes hands.

Goods traditionally exported by the countertrading nation are most commonly offered in counterpurchase—for example, raw materials, agricultural commodities, minerals, or chemicals. Additionally, surplus goods and low-technology products are also given in exchange for the products desired from the industrialized trading partner. Figure 34–3 illustrates a counterpurchase transaction.

Buybacks

Buybacks or *compensation* is becoming a common form of countertrade in which the goods seller agrees to accept payment in the form of products derived from the original goods sold. Buybacks were used extensively in international trade with the former communist world. For example, a U.S. machine tool seller might agree to be compensated with the finished goods output from the importing nation's factory that was outfitted with the U.S. machine tools. The buyback contributes to expansion and modernization of the importing nation's indus-

trial base. Some exporters sell turnkey projects by building, outfitting, and managing production facilities in foreign nations. They can be compensated through buyback with a portion of the plant's output. However, such larger projects are complex, must be composed of several related countertrade contracts, and the turnkey supplier must defer receipt of payment for a considerable time. Buyback transactions are illustrated in Figure 34–4.

Legal Aspects of Countertrade

Countertrade fundamentally involves political and legal issues in nearly all participating nations for at least three reasons. First, countertrade is generally triggered by currency or trade restriction laws in at least one of the nations involved. These regulations may also (1) specify the form of countertrade taken by their own government's extensive foreign procurement programs, (2) restrict private sector imports to countertrade, and/or (3) require government approval of particular countertrade deals. Second, the impact of countertrade may be restricted by other laws in many industrialized nations, such as the U.S. antitrust laws, trade restrictions, antibribery restrictions, and health and safety regulations. Third, countertrade often requires complex negotiations and raises unique problems of contract enforcement.

Figure 34–3   Counterpurchase

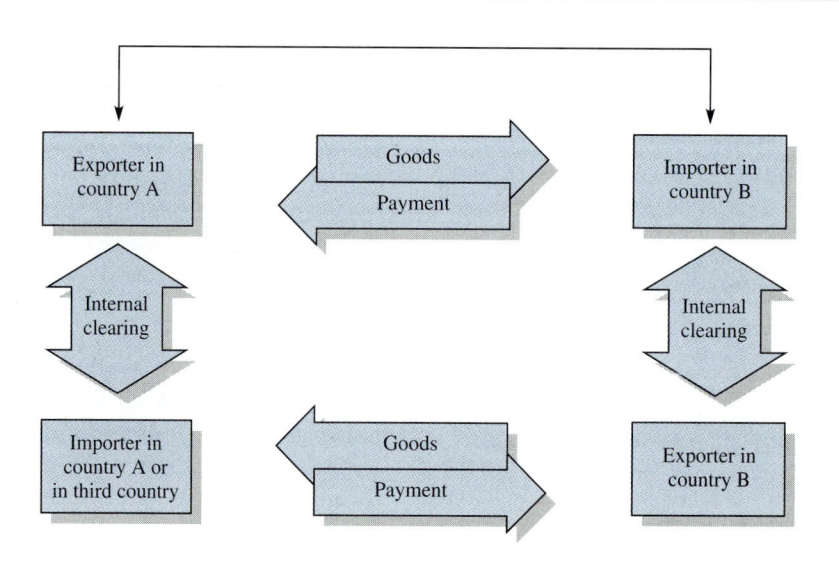

Figure 34–4   Buyback

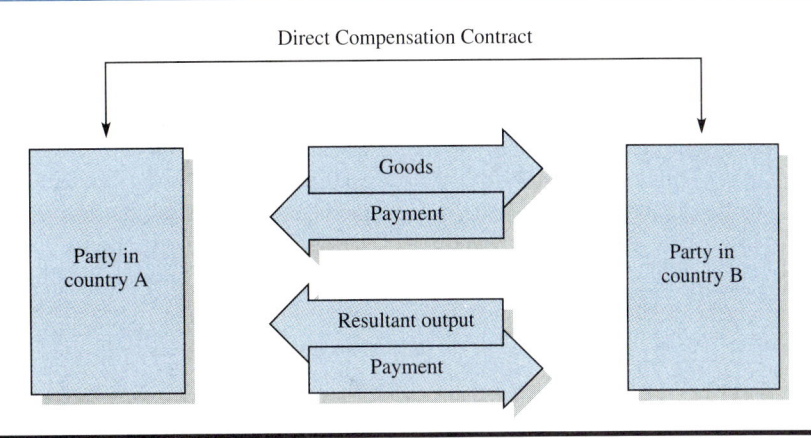

The antitrust laws in the United States, the EC, and some other, mainly industrialized, nations may be triggered by some countertrade deals if that nation can assert jurisdiction. In some counterpurchase deals, the exporter must take back products that it can only dispose of in a distressed market. Any *refusal to deal* with suppliers or customers unless they help dispose of these goods may be illegal under the Clayton Act. The very nature of countertrade is a form of *forced reciprocity* that could be illegal as an unfair method of competition under the Clayton Act or an unreasonable restraint of trade under the Federal Trade Commission Act. These laws are detailed further in Chapters 46 and 47.

Most nations have import restrictions and customs laws designed to protect domestic industry. The United States has a wide array of protections from "unfair" foreign competition. Countertrade contracts are inherently suspect because the goods or services exchanged for U.S. exports are difficult to value. U.S. exporters who regularly resell such foreign goods may be in violation of one or more laws. The antidumping laws restrict the import of goods the foreign exporter sells in the United States at prices lower than in their home market. Dumping laws are intended to protect U.S. competitors when they cause a form of price discrimination injury. *Countervailing duties* are levied on imported goods subsidized by a foreign government. Various provisions of the Tariff Act of 1930, the Trade Expansion Act of 1961, and the Trade Act of 1974 prohibit imports that constitute unfair methods of competition, threaten national security, disrupt domestic

U.S. markets, or violate international trade agreements. Various powers exist in federal agencies, the U.S. Trade Representative, and the president to halt such sales or retaliate, under Super 301 powers, against the offending foreign government. Such trade restrictions are discussed further in Chapter 52.

The Foreign Corrupt Practices Act, discussed in Chapter 44, may be violated if the countertrade agreement involves bribery of foreign officials by a domestic U.S. concern (firm or other entity). Given that countertrade fundamentally involves valuation problems that can hide profit margins and broker's fees, the pricing could also conceal bribes made to foreign officials. Allegations that the potentially large profit margins in countertrade conceal such hidden payments are difficult to disprove, particularly long after the fact. U.S. health and safety laws are far more restrictive than in most nations with which the U.S. exporter will be conducting countertrade. The foreign goods taken in exchange must satisfy these standards unless the U.S. firm disposes of the counterpurchased goods in other nations that have less restrictive regulations.

Contracting Aspects of Countertrade

While many countertrade contracts in the past were probably simple documents, today they are becoming increasingly complex. Countertrade transactions can initially be based on fairly standard goods sale contracts. It is paramount to ensure that quality specifications are carefully stipulated, delivery schedules are narrowed, restrictions are minimized on where the exporter may dispose of the counter-purchased goods, and force majeure and penalty provisions are carefully stated and understood. Many of the standard international sale contract terms are usually present but must be specially negotiated for a countertrade deal (e.g., currency, penalties, carrier specifications, and document requirements).

It is advisable to have a separate contract for the counterpurchase or buyback of goods or services. Additionally, there should be a separate *protocol*

contract (e.g., link contract, countertrade agreement, frame agreement, or letter of undertaking) tying together the primary sale (export) contract with the counterpurchase or buyback contract. Thereby, if one of the underlying contracts is breached, the other contract can be rescinded. Clearly, experienced and competent legal counsel and countertrade assistance is advisable to navigate the peculiarities of all nations involved in the linked countertrade transaction.

Controversy over the Inefficiencies of Countertrade*

While countertrade would always seem to generate win-win outcomes for experienced and willing participants, the practice is not without its detractors. Some economists argue countertrade distorts the world's markets for goods, currencies, and labor so is therefore inherently inefficient. They believe that encouraging countertrade slows the market's natural clearance and correction mechanisms that should weed out inefficient producers of obsolete or poor quality goods. Countertrade opponents were successful in leading GATT and the Reagan and Bush administrations to quiet opposition against promoting countertrade during the late 1980s.

The perfect competition model predicts that competitive forces in large and atomized markets will force down prices as producers implement efficiencies and are encouraged to innovate. At this equilibrium, inefficient producers are deterred and only more efficient producers are attracted into that industry. However, countertrade arguably perpetuates inefficient producers unable to directly compete effectively in the world's currency-based markets. For example, two inefficient producers may bypass the world's currency-based market for their goods to derive greater value in return for their exports. Therefore, countertrade is inherently inefficient because it causes considerable frictions in transactions. Countertraders can earn potentially high and abnormal profit margins, sometimes derived from a lack of information about the value of goods received in counterpurchase payments and sometimes derived from production inefficiencies. Countertrade fundamentally disrupts efficient markets by perpetuating inefficient producers, it sends incorrect signals to producers, it tolerates excessive supply of unneeded goods, and it causes sluggish market clearance at inefficient prices.

Countertrade critics also suggest that the practice generates no new demand; one source of supply is simply exchanged for another. This erects barriers to entry into world markets for those nations and firms not participating in countertrade. The inefficiencies of countertrade create dead-weight loss on world economies. This falls most heavily on the developing nation which must pay a premium for the industrialized nation's goods. The premium covers excessive inefficiencies and abnormally high transactions costs paid to the intermediaries needed to effect successful countertrade sales. Countertrade also burdens efficient producers of the goods sold by the developing nation because the efficient producers must compete with an essentially subsidized producer. Finally, countertrade encourages overproduction of less desirable, inferior, and obsolete goods thereby diverting financial resources away from more worthy investments.

---

*Source: "Controversy over the Inefficiencies of Countertrade," by John W. Bagby ©1993.

Despite these potent free-market arguments against countertrade, the practice is also viewed in political terms. Countertrade proponents argue that the practice opens world markets to developing nations, which is better than the more limited trade these nations would have without countertrade. The developing nations which are forced to use countertrade have numerous capability and technological barriers to becoming world-class competitors within any reasonable time frame. Buyback transactions may actually serve to speed these nations toward industrialization. Additionally, the goods purchased with countertrade improve their citizens' quality of life. This probably helps developing nations avoid divisive political and social unrest that could be externalized to other nations. For example, if Western industrialized nations refuse to countertrade with the Commonwealth of Independent States (former Soviet Union), the social and economic chaos could bring back the cold war. Finally, industrialized nations that use countertrade may have a comparative advantage over nations with an ideological bias against countertrade.

Thought Questions

1. What is the main issue in encouraging countertrade? What is the issue that countertrade opponents argue?

2. What biases are there when governments support countertrade? What are the biases among countertrade opponents?

3. What might be the eventual resolution of these apparently contradictory positions?

In the future, there will probably be even more effective countertrading. Successful countertrade clearinghouses are emerging with extensive worldwide contacts to match the sources and the demand for countertraded products and services. Computerization will speed the search for and matching of countertrading opportunities. Optimization techniques may make this matching more efficient, reducing the inefficiencies and potential legal problems of countertrade. A world of opportunity awaits the technologically driven and ingenious agents of countertrade.

END–OF–CHAPTER QUESTIONS

1. What are the transaction anxiety issues confronting an exporter-seller dealing in international commerce? What are the transaction anxiety issues confronting an importer-buyer dealing in international commerce?

2. What are the issues involved in the transition from the physical exchange of documents in international transactions to the electronic transmission and archiving of this information?

3. What are the major legal issues under U.S. law that could taint a countertrade deal?

4. Advocates of using countertrade as an important alternative to traditional documentary payments argue that the practice is necessary for certain types of international trade. However, opponents argue that countertrade should be discouraged. What are the central issues separating these two groups? What reasons do they use to support their positions? What biases are revealed in analyzing these two positions?

5. Bozel, a Brazilian exporter in Rio de Janeiro, made shipment of calcium silicon under separate bills of lading to three U.S. buyers, shipped to a Louisiana port. Banque de Depots, a Swiss bank, sought to enforce a judgment it won against Bozel for allegedly misapplying the bank's funds. A U.S. correspondent bank held the bills of lading for the buyers. A court order was issued to the bank authorizing the seizure of 1,300 metric tons of the mineral located in Louisiana. Should the court of appeals permit the buyers to receive the bills of lading and delivery of the minerals? What issues arise in preserving the policy of strict respect for the

transferability of documents of title? See *Banque de Depots v. Feroligas,* 569 So.2d 40 (La. 1990).

6. Springfield, an English importer of wines, purchased wine on open account from Pfeiffer, a German wine exporter. The contract required Springfield to immediately collect payments on the wine it resold and apply those funds to the open Pfeiffer account payable. However, in a separate factoring agreement with Springfield, Arbuthnot advanced funds to Springfield conditioned on Springfield's assignment of the same accounts receivables to Arbuthnot. Springfield's customers were then required to make payments directly to Arbuthnot. Can Pfeiffer collect Springfield's delinquent payments directly from Arbuthnot? See *Pfeiffer GmBH v. Arbuthnot Factors,* [1988] 1 W.L.R. 150 (Q.B.D.).

7. North Carolina National Bank issued an irrevocable L/C for Adastra Knitting Mills' purchase of up to $135,000 worth of "100% Acrylic Yarn." Courtaulds, the seller, presented a draft to draw on the L/C accompanied by a commercial invoice describing the goods as "Imported Acrylic Yarns" and packing lists with a description as "Cartons marked:—100% Acrylic." The bank dishonored the draft based on these discrepancies, the goods were returned, and the seller sued for payment on the draft from the bank. What is the issue presented by this case? Should the appellate court order the bank to pay? What reasons support your answer? See *Courtaulds North America, Inc. v. North Carolina National Bank,* 528 F.2d 802 (4th Cir. 1975).

8. Banco de Guatemala issued a standby L/C naming Rumex and Bell (a Chicago commodities broker) as beneficiaries. The L/C was used to finance the purchase of 6,000 metric tons of black beans by Indeca for the Guatemalan people. Continental bank

confirmed the L/C, agreeing to pay Rumex when documents were presented showing the beans were loaded aboard ship in Hong Kong. Continental initially dishonored the credit because the documents contained substantial discrepancies: no draft was included, the bill of lading misidentified the shipper, the insurance certificate was unsatisfactory, and the certificate of origin was not legalized. Although some of the corrected documents were suspect, Continental finally paid on the documents. Bell absconded with the money and the beans never arrived. Even though Continental had no knowledge of the fraud, should it be held liable under the tort of negligent misrepresentation for not uncovering the fraud? See *Instituto Nacional de Commercializacion Agricola (Indeca) v. Continental Illinois National Bank,* 858 F.2d 1264 (7th Cir. 1988).

9. When an issuing bank uses language declaring the L/C will "remain in force for a period of 6 months," can the L/C be revoked in a shorter time? What is the issue in such a case? What is the apparent contract interpretation problem at issue here? See *Conoco, Inc. v. Norwest Bank Mason City,* 767 F.2d 470 (8th Cir. 1985).

10. Under separate contracts, Pagnan was due 65,000 tons of Thai tapioca and Granaria was due 21,000 tons of Chinese manioc, a plant from which slightly higher quality tapioca is derived out of the plant's starchy roots. Pagnan and Granaria negotiated an agreement in which Granaria would sell the manioc to Pagnan for eventual delivery to Italy, and Pagnan would sell to Granaria an equivalent amount of Thai tapioca to be delivered to a northern European port. What type of transaction is this? Is it a breach of contract for either party to renege on this obligation? See *Pagnan SpA v. Granaria BV,* [1986] 2 Lloyd's Rep. 547 (C.A.).

Unit III

Business Organizations

■

PART 7   AGENCY
PART 8   PARTNERSHIPS
PART 9   CORPORATIONS

UNIT III OVERVIEW: INTRODUCTION TO BUSINESS ORGANIZATIONS

This unit presents the legal aspects of American and international business organizations. All businesses must adopt some legal configuration that defines the rights and liabilities of participants in the firm's ownership, control, personal liability, life span, and financial structure. Entrepreneurs involved in business startups need to understand the different characteristics of business organizations. This enables them to balance constituents' needs and later upgrade from one form of business organization to another. This Overview surveys the predominant types of business organizations and facilitates a comparison of sole proprietorships, agency, partnerships, limited liability companies, and corporations.

SOLE PROPRIETORSHIPS

Sole proprietorships are the easiest form of business to establish—the owner simply starts operations. Millions of sole owners in the United States manage and own their own businesses as proprietorships. There is no separation between the individual and the business, so the owner has unlimited liability for the business's contracts, debts, and torts. Financing is limited to the owner's personal resources and bank loans, as enhanced by the business's reputation. Sole proprietors directly pay individual income tax on their Form 1040, computed on the profits of the business net of allowable costs, deductions, credits, and exclusions as filed on IRS Schedule C. Many sole proprietorships are sufficiently large to hire employees, use agents, adopt unique business names, and otherwise "organize" their businesses.

AGENCY

The *agency* is a consensual relationship between the *principal* (employer) and agent (employee) arising automatically when the two parties consent to the agent acting for the principal. Strictly speaking, an agency is not a separate form of business organization. However, all but the smallest sole proprietorship businesses are organized to use agents as employees and independent contractors. All general partners are agents of the partnership. As artificial entities, corporations must use agents. Agency law, as generally stated in the *Restatement (Second) of Agency*, defines the relationships among principals, agents, and outside third parties. Most businesses make and perform their contracts through their agents.

GENERAL PARTNERSHIPS

The *general partnership* is an association of two or more persons who carry on a business for profit. Partnerships are created by simply commencing operations. Partners generally contribute capital, property, and services to the partnership, share equal voice in management, and equally share profits and losses. These rights and duties are automatically defined under law, usually the *Uniform Partnership Act*. However, the partners can fine-tune their arrangement with a formal partnership agreement. Partners generally share personal unlimited liability for partnership debts. Partners are individually taxed on their proportionate share of partnership income, or they deduct their proportionate share of partnership loss. Under the partnership flow-through tax treatment, the partnership is not a separate taxable entity so it files only an information tax return. The law presumes that associates operating a business together are partners unless they carefully characterize their relationship as something else such as a limited partnership, corporation, or limited liability company.

LIMITED PARTNERSHIPS

Limited partnerships are treated much like general partnerships. However, they are only created under statute, usually the *Revised Uniform Limited Partnership Act*. In order for passive investors to become limited partners and have their liability limited to their initial investment, the limited partnership must satisfy the statutory creation process, limited partners cannot become excessively entangled in management, and they cannot use their surnames in the business name. There must be at least one general partner with managerial control and unlimited liability. Limited partnerships may generally use the partnership flow-through tax treatment.

LIMITED LIABILITY COMPANIES

There has been continued demand for a business organization form that resembles a corporation, including limited liability and a centralized management structure, while still receiving the partnership flow-through tax treatment. Subchapter S corporations and limited partnerships are often too restrictive or cumbersome. In 1977, a Wyoming statute was passed that emulated a hybrid organization form used extensively in Europe and Latin America, the **limited liability company (LLC).** The IRS has ruled that LLCs may have the favorable flow-through tax treatment so long as the LLC does not show the two clearest indicia of a corporation—that is, the LLC can have no continuity of life and its ownership interests can not be freely transferable. Nearly 20 states have passed LLC laws, over 16 other states have similar bills pending in their legislatures, and the remaining states show strong interest in adopting LLC legislation. There are some differences among the various states' LLC laws, so a *Model Limited Liability Company Act* is under development by the American Bar Association.

LLCs are generally formed and owned by *members,* not shareholders, under a document filed with the state known as the *articles of organization,* not a charter. Rather than bylaws, the LLC has an *operating agreement.* No shares are issued because members hold *units* or *interests* in the LLC. No board of directors governs the LLC—centralized control is given to its *managers*. While some LLCs may be expected to operate much like partnerships, others can emulate the corporate form in most respects. However, they cannot be publicly traded and must automatically terminate after some event (e.g., death of a member or accomplishment of a stated purpose) or have a fixed duration. For example, Minnesota limits LLCs to 30 years, after which they are reformed or liquidated. LLCs should flourish during the 1990s, particularly if corporate tax rates rise.

CORPORATIONS

The *corporation* is an artificial entity, separate from its owners or operators. Like limited partnerships, the corporation must be specifically created under a special law that grants limited liability to investors. All states and most nations have such business incorporation statutes. Corporations separately own their property, can sue or be sued, are separately liable on contracts they make, and are liable for the torts of their agents. Corporations must pay a separate income tax. Corporations can have perpetual life, and owners can freely transfer their ownership shares.

Corporations are *publicly traded* if they have numerous shareholders or bondholders who trade these securities on a national securities exchange. Generally, publicly traded corporations are registered with the Securities and Exchange Commission or other similar government agency in foreign nations. By contrast, *closely held corporations* have few security holders, and these securities are not traded on an exchange. Typically, a small, family, or close-knit group owns a privately held corporation and seeks to exclude outsider participation and avoid the costs of publicly disclosing their finances and operations. Shareholders in the special form of *Subchapter S corporation* may use the partnership flow-through taxation treatment if certain restrictions are satisfied. The profits of all other corporations are first taxed at the corporate level, then each shareholder is taxed again when the corporate profits are distributed as dividends. This constitutes the so-called double tax on dividends.

MISCELLANEOUS FORMS OF BUSINESS ORGANIZATION

There are a number of less common forms of business organization that have gained popularity from time to time. To circumvent the 19th-century prohibition against corporate ownership of real estate, the *Massachusetts Trust* was developed. Today, owners can transfer title to their real estate, securities, or other property to a trustee, who manages the property for the beneficiaries. The beneficiaries can have limited liability if they refrain from exercising extensive control over the trustee. Tax treatment varies between the corporate, partnership, and trust tax method, depending on various factors. A **real estate investment trust (REIT)** provides similar benefits when it primarily holds real estate. REITs can avoid the corporate double tax if most income is regularly distributed to beneficiaries. **Real estate limited partnerships** were a common form of tax shelter before the 1986 Tax Reform Act. **Cooperatives** may operate as nonprofit unincorporated associations if tax rules are carefully followed. *Joint ventures* are like partnerships and are organized for limited purposes and continue only for a limited duration. *International joint ventures* are usually limited alliances between corporations from different nations. They are typically organized as corporations in the host nation.

FACTORS AFFECTING CHOICE OF ORGANIZATION FORM

As suggested above, several key variables are customized to tailor the business organization to its constituent's needs. Corporations and LLCs are *separate entities* from their participants. By contrast, sole proprietorships and partnerships are not strictly separate entities. This affects the owners' tax liability, limited liability, and transferability of ownership. It also impacts the organization's continuity of life, form of property ownership, and contracting, management, and litigation responsibilities. *Limited liability* is the key feature necessary to attract risk capital.

Passive investors are encouraged to trust in professional managers when the investors' potential liability is limited to their initial capital contribution. Constraints on the *transferability of interest* also affects capital raising. Ownership is more difficult to transfer in partnerships, limited partnerships, LLCs, and closely held corporations. Only corporations, as separate entities, can have perpetual *continuity of existence*. All other organization forms are somehow limited in duration. For example, partnerships dissolve if any partner dies or goes bankrupt, and sole proprietorships are similarly terminated.

Tax law has such a profound impact on the choice of business organization form that it often overshadows all other considerations. Sole proprietors, most partners, LLC members, and Subchapter S shareholders are taxed only once on the profits of their organizations. The organizations themselves are not separately taxed. Participants pay individual income tax on their proportionate share of taxable income at their individual marginal rates of 15, 28, or 33 percent, the rates prevailing at this writing. This avoids the *double tax* levied on corporate profits before they are distributed and taxed to the participants. At this writing, there are corporate marginal tax rates of 15, 25, 34, and 39 percent, although some tax increase proposals could raise both corporate and individual tax rates. Entrepreneurs considering the choice of business organization form should seek competent and current tax advice and competent legal counsel in forming most types of organizations. The relevant factors are captured in the following concept summary.

Comparison of Business Organization Forms

Characteristics	Type of Business Organization				
	Sole Proprietorship	General Partnership	Limited Partnership	Limited Liability Company	Corporation
Formation	No formalities	No formalities	Statutory formation	Statutory formation	Statutory formation
Separate Entity	No	No	No	Yes	Yes
Continuity of Existence	Dissolves on owner's death or bankruptcy	Dissolves on partner's death, withdrawal, or bankruptcy	Dissolves on general partner's death, withdrawal, or bankruptcy, not on limited partner's	Dissolves according to statute or according to articles of organization	Perpetual life or term fixed in articles of incorporation
Limited Liability	Owner has unlimited liability	Partners have unlimited liability	General partners have unlimited liability; limited partners have limited liability	Members have limited liability	Shareholders have limited liability
Management and Control	Owner has complete control	Partners share control unless otherwise agreed	General partners have control; limited partners must avoid excessive entanglement in management	Managers have control	Shareholders delegate control to board, then to management
Transferability of Ownership	Owner may sell business or assets	Partner status nontransferable without other partners' consent	Transfer usually restricted	Transfer usually restricted	Freely transferable unless otherwise agreed
Taxation	Ordinary income to owner	Partnership flow-through treatment	Partnership flow-through treatment	Partnership flow-through treatment	Corporate double tax except Subchapter S

Part VII

Agency

■

Chapter 35

Agency Relationships

■

CRITICAL THINKING INQUIRIES

As you read this chapter, you should be able to address the following:

- What issues are raised when an individual entrepreneur chooses to expand the business when more activity is required than one person can do comfortably?
- How should an employee be held responsible when negotiating or performing contracts for the employer?
- What ambiguities in employment contracts are clarified by agency law? What assumptions are made when the law is designed to form a standardized employment contract?
- What opposing forces are balanced between the employer's interest in maintaining confidentiality and the employee's desire for the flexibility to change jobs?
- What reasons support the law balancing rules or contract terms that encourage loyal and efficient employees against rules providing employees with job security?

MANAGERIAL PERSPECTIVE

Running his business consumed most of Perry's time. His expertise was limited to the design and production of the widgets he sells to retailers. Eventually, Perry realized he could expand the business by hiring employees and outside consultants to cover several key functions for which he had little time and limited skills—sales, accounting, and legal advice. Consequently, Perry hired Alma, an experienced salesperson in the wholesale widget business, and Allen, an experienced maintenance engineer. Additionally, Perry retained two consulting firms to provide accounting, tax, and management consulting services — the law firm of Allen and Applebee and Art and Andy's Accounting Service.

- What issues arise when employees are given authority to make contracts for the employer?
- What duties do employees owe their employer? What reasons support the law imposing these duties?
- What ambiguities are present when independent consultants are hired to provide services to an employing firm?
- What issues arise when an agent is terminated? What reasons make termination so critical to the employer?

Sole proprietors seldom have enough time or expertise to perform all the necessary duties of their businesses. Therefore, growing firms must usually hire employees and retain outside consultants. As artificial entities, corporations can conduct business only through agents, giving most managers some authority to contract with suppliers, customers, and employees. Because agents have widely varying levels of authority, it is a fundamental managerial concern to know precisely when an agent becomes authorized and how to limit agents' powers. A proliferation of agents can expose the employer to broad and sometimes unexpected liability. Additionally, managers need to understand the extent of their personal agency responsibilities to their employer.

The laissez-faire freedom of contract principle permits a principal and an agent to specify their relationship in great detail. However, they can simply rely on agency law and customs, developed over centuries of experience, to supply a standardized set of contract terms. Employers want contract terms providing flexibility and profitability, expense reduction, and protection of their assets. Employees seek stable work environments, fair treatment, and ever increasing compensation. These incentives are often in conflict, suggesting employment is a ''zero sum'' game to allocate limited stakes between employer and employee. The law of agency and employment, discussed in this chapter, balances the parties' self-interests, although employees' rights have expanded significantly in recent years, a matter of great concern to managers. The liabilities of the various parties in tort and contract are discussed in Chapter 36.

NATURE OF AGENCY

An agency is a relationship between two persons. Either can be natural human beings, artificial entities (e.g., corporations, governments, or associations), or a combination of natural and artificial persons. An **agency** is defined as a fiduciary relationship that results when one person, the **principal**, consents that another person, the **agent**, shall act on behalf of the principal. The agent must also consent to the agency and thereby becomes subject to the principal's control. Agents are usually employees appointed by the principal/employer. However, all employees may not be agents if they have no authority to contract for or change the employer's legal relationships. For example, in the opening scenario,

Alma is an employee of Perry who would probably have authority to negotiate contracts of sale for Perry's widgets. Allen, also an employee, might have no authority since he does physical labor using Perry's machinery. Similarly, all agents need not be employees. For example, Perry's accountant and lawyer may have certain authority to represent Perry's business, but they are not employees because their firms are independent and represent other clients. Figure 35–1 illustrates the basic relationships among principal, agent, and third parties.

Types of Agencies

As suggested above, the terms *employment* and *agency* are often used rather loosely to describe several different relationships. An employment relationship arises when an employer hires another person, an employee. Employment is also called the **master-servant** relationship, an anachronism useful mostly to analyze tort liability for the employee's actions. An **independent contractor** may be hired by an employer so long as the employer retains no right to exercise close control over the independent contractor's actual performance. The distinction between a servant and an independent contractor is discussed further in Chapter 36. The distinction is critical to several matters: the resolution of tort liability, the collection of employment taxes, the computation of wages, workers', and employment compensation, and the allocation of responsibility for safety in the workplace. An agency is distinguished from a **bailment**, which is a relationship created when a property owner merely transfers rightful possession of the property to a bailee. The bailee is neither an employee nor an agent. For example, if Perry stores widget inventory in an independent warehouse, the warehouse operator is neither Perry's employee nor his agent, unless they agree otherwise.

Agents may be classified in many ways. **General agents** are granted broad powers by the principal to negotiate a broad range of transactions. **Special agents** have much narrower power and typically only execute specific transactions or several related transactions. For example, corporate presidents are usually general agents because they have broad management powers. By contrast, a stockbroker is usually a special agent because the broker is typically authorized only to buy or sell specific securities. **Subagents** are agents hired by the agent. The questions that arise about subagents' authority, their du-

Figure 35–1   Agency Relationships

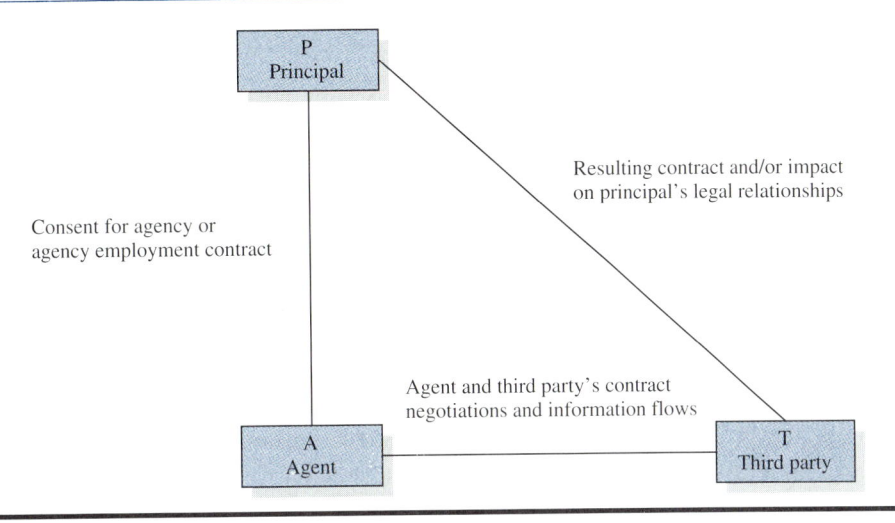

ties, and their responsibilities under tort law are discussed later. **Gratuitous agents** serve without compensation.

FORMATION OF AGENCY

An agency arises whenever the principal and agent consent that the agent may act for the principal. An agency is often created by an employment contract in which both principal and agent consent that the agent is authorized to act for the principal and the contract states a purpose for the agency. In most instances, such employment contracts may be expressed either orally or in writing. Written agency contracts are only required when the contract the agent will negotiate for the principal must be in writing under the statute of frauds. This is known as the **equal dignities rule** because an equal level of formality or dignity is necessary to authorize an agent as is necessary for the underlying transaction the agent negotiates. For example, if Perry seeks to sell his factory, then his real estate agent's listing contract must also be in writing because the statute of frauds requires written land sale contracts.

Written contracts are advisable even if the law does not require them. The parties are more likely to consider the potential pitfalls of their arrangement when forced to prepare a written contract. This process focuses both parties' attention on alternatives and projects the risks before actual performance. The **power of attorney** is a formalized written

agency contract that can grant narrow or broad powers to an agent. The agent becomes an **attorney in fact,** which is really another term for agent and should not be confused with an attorney-at-law.

Capacity

Contract law requires that all contracting parties have contractual capacity, as discussed in Chapter 13. The law protects certain incapacitated persons who are typically underage, drunken, drugged, or insane, considering them incapable of giving genuine contractual consent. In the agency setting, this rule requires that the principal have contractual capacity before becoming irrevocably bound in a contract negotiated by the agent. However, an agent need not have contractual capacity so long as the agent has the minimum ability to act for another person. For example, very young or mentally incompetent persons may be incompetent to act as agents particularly if they cannot understand the consequences of the transaction. By contrast, teenagers are minors with no contractual capacity but are nevertheless generally qualified to act as agents.

Agent's Authority

Although the agent's authority is discussed more fully in Chapter 36, it is useful to understand the role of authority in the formation of an agency. An agency relationship becomes effective only after the principal grants the agent authority to act and the agent accepts the appointment. The principal may grant authority in several ways. First, where the principal and agent expressly agree, an actual express authority arises. Second, an agent's powers can be expanded beyond those expressly granted when needed due to the surrounding circumstances, such as an emergency, under actual implied authority. Third, the principal who leads a third party to reasonably believe the agent is authorized creates an apparent authority or an agency by estoppel. Finally, even where no authority exists or the agent's power is limited, the agent's voluntary unauthorized act can be retroactively authorized if the principal later ratifies. Without authority from some source, an agent has no power to bind the principal in contract. Therefore, third parties must satisfactorily determine an agent's authority or find themselves without an enforceable contract with the principal.

Nondelegable Duties

Principals generally may delegate any act to an agent. However, the principal's personal performance may be required in certain instances, effectively prohibiting the agent's performance of such personal duties. Under contract law, a personal service contract is nondelegable without the permission of the party expecting performance. Additionally, society has an interest in verifying the principal's identity, so an agent may not sign a testator's will, attest to another person's statements under oath, or cast the principal's vote in a public election. For example, Perry cannot appoint a lawyer or accountant to sign his will or vote for him in a political election.

DUTIES OF AGENT TOWARD PRINCIPAL

The law of agency provides an efficient set of rights and duties between the principal and the agent. These are derived from centuries of experience. Agency law holds the agent to significant responsibilities to balance the significant powers conferred by the principal. The principal also has significant responsibility when employing agents. Freedom of contract gives the parties great latitude to add, subtract, or change the rights and duties implied by law. Agency law is read in conjunction with the employment contract and other related documents, such as the principal firm's code of conduct, to define for-

mation of the agency, interpret the agent's duties, assess the adequacy of the agent's performance, and make available the parties' remedies.

Agency law is derived from the legal precedents set by case law. These have been consolidated into the *Restatement (Second) of Agency*. This law is supplemented by other state and federal regulations covering worker safety, equal employment opportunity, and employment security matters. The basic principles discussed in the following sections form the basis for regulating many professionals. For example, the duties owed to clients by attorneys, accountants, investment advisers, securities and commodities brokers, real estate brokers, corporate officers, and business consultants are largely the specific application of the various agency duties discussed below.

Fiduciary Duty of Loyalty

In return for the agent's broad powers to affect the principal's relationships, the agent owes a fiduciary duty of good faith and utmost loyalty to the principal. The agent must conduct the principal's business with integrity. Therefore, the agent may not have any adverse personal financial interest in the principal's transactions during the agency. Some aspects of this duty persist even after the agency is terminated. Although the duty of loyalty may seem vague, it becomes more precise as it is applied to more specific situations. The fiduciary duty is a most basic ethical matter applicable to nearly all persons in business and government. Violation of this duty suggests the abuse of position and trust, condemned by nearly all ethical theories except perhaps certain conceptions of egoism or Machiavellianism.

Conflicts of Interest

The ancient proviso that no person can serve two masters is at the heart of the prohibition against an agent simultaneously serving two principals in the same transaction. This would be a **dual** or **double agency,** and the agent would be unable to serve either principal fully. If the agent negotiates gains for one principal, the gains necessarily come as losses to the other. For example, a stockbroker representing both the buyer and the seller of securities cannot maximize the selling price while simultaneously minimizing the purchase price. Dual agents are often given confidential information by either or both principals concerning key terms and the principals' willingness to sell or buy at the maximum or minimum price stated. Usually, one principal receives slightly better service than the other. Double agents violate ethical norms under the conception of loyalty held by most people. Even if the agent scrupulously attempts to "split the difference" by negotiating fair terms on some middle ground, neither principal receives the quality of service expected of an independent and loyal agent.

Conflicts of interest are not always so obvious. Sometimes a full-time agent for one party may be paid a secret bribe, gratuity, gift, or kickback by the other party. The law presumes these payments exert some influence on the agent's judgment and thereby harm the principal. For example, a supplier's sales personnel may treat the customers' purchasing agent to entertainment, travel, or other gifts. The law presumes these benefits are intended to influence purchasing decisions made by the purchasing agent. Therefore, either the agent's solicitation or receipt of such benefits creates a conflict of interest and is generally considered unethical.

Dual agency is not always unlawful. It may be legitimized where the agent fully discloses all matters that might impact the agent's judgment and both principals consent. This **fully informed consent** from both principals is necessary for the agent to fulfill the fiduciary duty to both principals and be entitled to compensation. Full disclosure often diffuses an emerging ethical dilemma if all parties involved are given the opportunity to consider the potential conflict before proceeding.

Some agents do not actually engage in negotiations for either principal but simply bring them together to let them negotiate independently. This is not a dual agency, so it does not violate fiduciary duties or ethical norms. For example, if neither principal entrusts confidential information to a "go-between" who gives neither party advice in the transaction, the finder may collect a **finder's fee.** The following case illustrates the kind of unethical pressure a double agent exercised on a trusting principal. The court permitted the aggrieved principal to rescind the contract and refuse to pay the agent's compensation.

ADAMS v. KERR
655 S.W. 2d 49 (Mo. App. 1983)

The Kerrs, an elderly couple, listed their four-unit apartment with Red Carpet Realty for $118,000. The broker, Richard Birner, persuaded the Kerrs to accept $110,000 and finance the sale to Robert Adams. Adams and Donald Earhardt managed and sold real estate through a separate partnership, A & E Associates. Red Carpet never revealed to the Kerrs that Kathryn Brethold, a Red Carpet Agent, had represented A & E Associates for several years in other transactions. The Kerrs accepted Adams's offer.

The purchase contract required the buyer to provide a credit report to the seller's satisfaction. Adams furnished the Kerrs with a perfunctory one-page net worth analysis of A & E Associates. There were no phone numbers, account numbers, or other specific identifying details about the partnership. This was the first time the Kerrs had heard of A & E Associates. The Kerrs then asked for but did not receive a credit report. Mr. Kerr and his son Leland informed Red Carpet that the Kerrs would not go through with the contract. Red Carpet's attorney wrote the Kerrs a letter threatening suit by Red Carpet and the purchasers. When the Kerrs arrived at the closing to sign the relevant transfer papers, they again requested a credit report but were told by Red Carpet's agent "you don't need one." The Kerrs refused to transfer the property without an adequate credit report and Red Carpet brought suit.

KARONI, Judge

The credit report is a material part of the contract, as the Kerrs were taking a sizable purchase money note secured by a first deed of trust. The purchaser's credit was a significant factor in the contract. When the Kerrs told Birner they did not wish to go through with the contract, Birner did not ask why. Moreover, when the Kerrs asked for a satisfactory credit report at the closing, Brethold refused, telling them it was not necessary. Adams thus refused to comply with the contract provision. Defendants allege that Red Carpet and the agents breached their fiduciary duty by (1) divulging confidential information concerning terms of sale to prospective purchasers and (2) representing both parties without full disclosure or consent to their dual capacity.

The broker is the agent of the seller unless it is otherwise understood and provided for and therefore owes the seller undivided loyalty and is required to exercise the utmost fidelity and good faith. It is the broker's duty to keep the principal fully informed, to make full disclosure of all facts and to exercise reasonable care and diligence in the performance of his duty. The broker must not do anything which makes the transaction more difficult or burdensome for his principal or which endangers the transaction. Moreover, "there is scarcely a rule of law which has received more uniform approval than that an agent cannot serve the opposing party without the knowledge and consent of his principal." A broker that represents both seller and purchaser without disclosing forfeits his commission. Further, after the broker finds a buyer, he must not take any action that hinders or prejudices his principal.

Case Questions

1. What issue is raised by the Red Carpet agent's former dealings for A & E Associates?

2. What reasons support the court's application of the conflict of interest rule?

3. What factor might legitimize Red Carpet's activities in this case?

4. What alternative hypothesis could explain the Kerrs' decision to rescind the sale?

Self-Dealing

Self-dealing is another type of unethical conflict of interest in which the agent's own personal financial interests directly conflict with the principal's financial interests. Agents may not have any undisclosed, unapproved personal financial interest in a transaction in which the principal has a financial interest. For example, the law firm representing Perry negotiates a sale of Perry's business to a buyer without revealing that the purchaser is a friend or family member of Perry's attorney. This would violate the attorney's fiduciary duty to Perry. Such adverse interests must be fully disclosed and receive the principal's consent to avoid the agent's violation of the fiduciary duty.

The self-dealing prohibition also requires agents to refrain from competing directly with the principal while the agency is in effect. Most firms' employees are prohibited from working for competing firms or personally competing against the principal during their employment. For example, a tax accountant would be prohibited from moonlighting by taking on tax clients personally even if the work was performed on the accountant's own time. However, this prohibition is relaxed after the agency is terminated. Generally, an agent may compete against the principal after the agency is terminated unless the agent signs a valid covenant not to compete or the agent improperly solicits co-workers or clients before leaving the former employer. Many businesspersons consider such solicitation to be another unethical abuse of position and trust.

Some agents act on a nonexclusive basis, permitting them to represent many principals. If the agent clearly communicates this fact to all principals, and they consent, there is no conflict of interest. For example, theatrical agents typically represent numerous performing acts and personalities. This provides flexibility to select a suitable performer for a particular role. The following case illustrates an unethical conflict of interest when a nonexclusive agent failed to adequately inform the client about the agent's various adverse and competing interests.

DETROIT LIONS, INC. v. ARGOVITZ
580 F.Supp. 542 (E.D.Mich. 1984)

Billy Sims was a professional football player. He first signed a contract with the Houston Gamblers of the U.S. Football League and later signed a second contract with the Detroit Lions of the National Football League. Jerry Argovitz represented Billy Sims in the early stages of contract negotiations. Although Sims was informed that Argovitz sought to personally acquire a U.S. Football League franchise for Houston, it became evident that Sims was unaware of Argovitz's substantial financial interest in the Houston Gamblers. Argovitz failed to inform Sims that a deal between Sims and the Detroit Lions was very close. Sims's ego had been bruised by the slow pace of negotiations and the one-sided information Argovitz provided about the pace of negotiations.

Despite Argovitz's clear conflict of interest, he offered Sims a $3.5 million a year contract that included skill and injury guaranties as well as a $500,000 a year loan at 1 percent over prime rate. Argovitz planned to receive his $100,000 agency fee out of Sims's loan. Argovitz failed to inform Sims that the Lions would probably match the Gamblers' financial package. Sims incorrectly believed the Lions were not that interested in him. Thereafter, Argovitz made no effort to secure an equal or better offer from the Lions. After Sims signed with the Gamblers, Argovitz insisted that Sims sign some ''overlooked'' paperwork including a document in which Sims surrendered any claim against Argovitz for breach of fiduciary duty or conflict of interest. Even though Argovitz's negotiations with the Lions were still ongoing, Argovitz failed to inform Sims because he knew Sims might then be lost to the Houston Gamblers, the team Argovitz owned.

DEMASCIO, District Judge

An agent's duty of loyalty requires that he not have a personal stake that conflicts with the principal's interest in a transaction. The principal is entitled to the best efforts and unbiased judgment of his agent. The law denies the right of an agent to assume any relationship that is antagonistic to this duty to his principal, and it has many times been held that the agent cannot be both buyer and seller at the same time or connect his own interest with property involved in his dealings with another.

A fiduciary violates the prohibition against self-dealing not only by dealing with himself on his principal's behalf, but also by dealing on his principal's behalf with a third party in which he has an interest such as a partnership in which he is a member. The transaction is voidable by the principal unless the agent disclosed all material facts in the agent's knowledge that might affect the principal's judgment. The mere fact that the contract is fair to the principal does not deny the principal the right to end the contract when it was negotiated by an agent in violation of the prohibition against self-dealing. Fraud on the part of the agent is presumed. The burden of proof then rests upon the agent to show that his principal had full knowledge, not only of the fact the agent was interested, but also of every material fact known to the agent which might affect the principal and that having such knowledge, the principal freely consented to the transaction.

It is not sufficient for the agent to inform the principal that he has an interest that conflicts with the principal's interest. Rather, he must inform the principal ''of facts that come to his knowledge that are or may be material that affect his principal's rights, interests, or influence the action he takes.''

Argovitz clearly had a personal interest in signing Sims with the Gamblers that was adverse to Sims' interest—he would profit if the Gamblers were profitable, and would incur substantial personal liabilities should the Gamblers not be financially successful. Since this showing has been made, fraud on Argovitz's part is presumed and the Gamblers' contract must be rescinded.

As a court sitting in equity, we are dismayed by Argovitz's egregious conduct. The careless fashion in which Argovitz went about ascertaining the highest price for Sims' service convinces us of the wisdom of the maxim: No man can serve two masters whose interests are in conflict.

Case Questions

1. What is the main issue confronting the court concerning Argovitz's alleged breach of fiduciary duty?
2. What does the court conclude about Argovitz's conduct concerning Sims?
3. What reasons support the court's finding?
4. What are the legal and ethical assumptions or analogies used as precedent and applied to the facts of this case?

Confidentiality

Confidentiality, the third aspect of the fiduciary duty, becomes necessary because principals often provide confidential information to their agents for the effective conduct of the principal's business. The agent would be ineffective without knowing special facts about the principal's trade secrets, business plans, financial plans, customer lists, sales tactics, manufacturing technologies, and/or new product information. The principal intends this information to be used only to further the principal's business. However, it is subject to abuse if the agent competes with the principal or communicates the valuable private information to a competitor. The fiduciary duty prohibits all agents and employees from misusing the principal's confidential information. It is usually unethical to reveal an employer's confidences unless compelled by law.

The principal has a property right in information produced by all its employees and agents. Generalized knowledge of a trade or profession that the agent gains while in the principal's service is not the principal's exclusive property. Any intellectual property produced by the agent during employment may be used by either party after the agency is terminated unless otherwise provided by contract. These matters are discussed more fully later in this chapter in the section on innovations.

The problem of confidentiality raises an important bargaining point in negotiating the agency contract. Many employment contracts include clauses called **covenants not to compete.** These are restrictive provisions that limit the agent's right to work for a competing firm or personally compete with the principal after the agency is terminated. If these clauses are unreasonably broad, they will be ruled unenforceable as an illegal restraint of trade under contract law. Employers must be careful to restrict the geographic scope and duration of such clauses to reasonable proportions (e.g., one or two years). An ethical dilemma may arise when employers attempt to restrict an employee's freedom to work for a competitor after termination if the employee is exposed to limited confidential information. Increasingly, the courts are refusing to enforce overbroad covenants not to compete because they excessively burden an employee's mobility.

The trend toward stricter treatment of these non-competition clauses reinforces another trend—the use of confidentiality clauses. Many employees and agents exposed to significant confidential information must promise in the employment contract to refrain from revealing or using confidential information learned in the course of their employment after the employment is terminated.

Duty of Care

Agents must use reasonable skill and care in conducting the principals' business. They must use all the skill they possess plus any skills the agent claims and any additional skills specified in the employment contract. It is probably unethical for an agent to claim skills he or she does not really possess. Such false bravado is often the basis for liability and ethical abuse. For example, résumé falsification eventually catches up to job applicants when they are called on to use the skills expected from the experience or degrees they falsely claimed.

Restatement (Second) of Agency § 379, Comment C

A paid agent represents that he had at least the skill and undertakes to exercise the care which is standard for that kind of employment in the community. A business agent represents that he understands the usages [and customs] of the business.

Professional agents such as accountants, brokers, or attorneys must exercise skill equal to other similar professionals in that region. However, the law does not imply that the agent guarantees success unless the agent specifically makes that promise. However, when an agent's negligent performance causes damage to the principal, liability questions arise. An agent may be released from liability for negligence in the employment contract.

Gratuitous Agents

Gratuitous agents serve without compensation and often argue they should be held to a lower standard of care because they receive no financial rewards. However, the law does not usually adjust an agent's standard of care by the amount of compensation received. The principal is entitled to money damages for injuries from torts such as negligence, willful misconduct, or fraudulent damages even against a gratuitous agent. For example, if the principal's friend is a stockbroker and promises to sell the principal's stock gratuitously, there is no liability for breach of contract. However, the gratuitous agent would be liable in tort for the principal's losses if the stock was sold very late after the sale order was made and a market decline caused the principal to receive far less in proceeds. This negligent failure to act is a wrongful and disobedient act.

Obedience

Agents must generally obey any reasonable directions the principal provides that will impact the principal's business. Even agents given broad discretion must obey the principal's directives. Of course, an agent need not obey orders that are illegal, immoral, or unreasonable. That would probably be unethical. The agent may in good faith interpret vague commands or be disobedient during an emergency if obedience would damage the principal. For example, the owner or principal of an apartment complex might direct the agent (superintendent) to seek permission before repairing an individual apartment's heating unit. However, in an emergency during which the principal is unavailable for consultation, the agent could disobey this directive and order repairs of the heating unit if cold weather would damage pipes and breach the tenant's lease.

Accounting

The agent's fiduciary duty requires that all property and funds belonging to the principal be accounted for adequately. This is the **duty to account** or provide an **accounting.** It requires the agent to keep accurate records and keep the agent's individual property separate from the principal's property. Upon demand, the agent must produce accurate records of receipts and disbursements to the principal. Any commingling of funds belonging to the

principal and agent makes it difficult to determine the true ownership. Commingling is a fundamental ethical abuse discovered among professional agents such as accountants, real estate brokers, investment professionals, and attorneys. To avoid even the appearance of unethical behavior in handling client funds, attorneys are generally required by the disciplinary rules of their state bar associations to hold all client funds in bank accounts separate from their personal funds. Any doubts about the true ownership of property held by an agent are resolved in the principal's favor.

Communication

Agents must communicate to the principal all relevant information and notices they receive in the course of performing the principal's business. Agents are often the principal's most visible communicator because they regularly receive or provide information to third parties about the principal's business. For example, an apartment manager usually has the responsibility of receiving tenant notices concerning termination of the tenant's lease. As agent, the manager must communicate this notice and any other relevant information to the principal. Additionally, information the manager learns, such as a tenant's misconduct, is relevant because it may signal that the tenant has breached the lease covenants. Such information must also be communicated to the principal. It is probably unethical for an agent to withhold information from the principal either in sympathy for the third party or to conceal the agent's poor performance. The following case indicates that the agent's duty to disclose is modified when it is reasonable to presume the principal should understand the customs and usages of the business.

F. W. MYERS AND CO. v. HUNTER FARMS
319 N.W.2d 186 (Iowa 1982)

Hunter Farms was involved in farming and in the resale of farm chemicals. It initiated negotiations for a supply of Sencore, a farm herbicide that was not readily available in the United States, from Petrolia Grain and Feed Co. in Canada. Hunter learned through an import specialist with the U.S. Customs Service that a 5 percent duty would initially be imposed on the herbicide, but the amount of the duty could be revised when the herbicide arrived and Customs could see an actual ingredients list. Hunter hired Myers to help move the herbicide through U.S. Customs. When the Customs Service discovered there were chemicals in the herbicide not listed on the label, the import duty was raised from $30,000 to over $128,000. Myers paid the additional amount but Hunter refused to reimburse Myers, claiming Myers had breached the duty of care as an import broker by failing to advise Hunter that the duty was tentative until the actual importation.

LARSON, Justice

An agent is required to exercise such skill as required to accomplish the object of his appointment. If he fails to exercise reasonable care, diligence, and judgment under the circumstances, he is liable to the principal for any loss or damage.

There was substantial evidence to support the trial court's finding that there was no breach of duty by Myers. Evidence was presented that the standard of care for import brokers did not include a special duty to render advice to the importer unless requested to do so. Expert testimony showed such brokers basically draft the necessary papers, arrange for the necessary bonds, and actually forward the duty payment. There was no evidence of a request to advise Hunter on import law nor was there any evidence that Myers was advised that Hunter was new in the import business.

The scope of an agent's duty to disclose is explained in the *Restatement*, section 381:

Unless otherwise agreed, an agent is subject to a duty to use reasonable efforts to get his principal information which is relevant to affairs entrusted to him and which the agent has noticed, the principal would desire to have and which can be communicated without violating a superior duty to a third person.

This statement requires that the agent have notice the principal would desire to have the relevant information. In this case there was evidence of the open ended nature of an initial duty assessment and this was widely understood by importers. Myers was never informed of the need to convey this information to Hunter which, it could reasonably presume was fundamental knowledge of that importer. Myers was never advised of Hunter's lack of experience in the business, nor was it aware of the labeling of the herbicide which caused the increase in the duty charge. Absent knowledge of Hunter's special need for advice and for the circumstances which give rise to the additional importation fees, there was no special duty of Myers to advise Hunter of the tentative nature of the assessment.

Case Questions

1. What was the issue concerning Myers's alleged duty toward Hunter Farms?
2. What reasons support Myers's allegation that it did not breach its duty to Hunter Farms?
3. Is there a reasoning error, bias, or assumption in Hunter Farms' position concerning the knowledge about the tentative assessment of import duties?

Imputation of Knowledge or Notice

An agent authorized to transact the principal's business generally has authority to receive information from third parties. When third parties provide information to the agent, the law presumes the agent will comply with the duty to communicate. Knowledge or notice received by the agent is therefore imputed to the principal. After the third party gives notice to the agent, the third party is relieved from repeating the communication to the principal or to any other agent who might later replace the original agent. The principal and agent are treated as one party after information is communicated to the agent. For example, if the IRS notifies Perry's accountant of the need to provide documentation to support a tax deduction Perry took, agency law presumes that the IRS need not recommunicate this to Perry even if the accountant never tells Perry about the IRS request.

The **imputation rule** does not apply if the agent acts in bad faith or deliberately fails to communicate notice or knowledge to the principal. If the third party and agent conspire to harm the principal, then the imputation doctrine is inapplicable. In such cases, the principal is not charged with the knowledge nor presumed to have received the information. The agent may also be liable for breach of fiduciary duty and for failing to adequately communicate material information to the principal.

Principal's Rights and Remedies

The law gives a choice of remedies to an injured principal for the agent's breach of duty. Principals are generally entitled to sue the agent for breach of contract, sue in tort for lost profits, or sue for judgments paid to a third party. Any secret profits a disloyal agent obtains are unethical and may be recovered by the principal. Any bribe, gift, or kickback received by the agent must be turned over to the principal. Agents guilty of disloyalty are not entitled to *any* compensation. Double agents are denied payment if either principal is uninformed about the relationship. Agents must indemnify (repay) their principals for losses paid to third parties that were necessitated by the agent's tortious conduct. Any property wrongfully retained by the agent is held in a constructive trust for the principal's benefit. Before any of these monetary remedies are ordered, there must be an accounting, the comprehensive financial review of transactions, payments, and disbursements discussed above. For example, Perry's accountant or attorney must provide records showing the disposition of all Perry's transactions, funds, and property handled on Perry's behalf.

Innovations

An agent may not use a principal's confidential information for personal gain. The employer may reinforce this right to have exclusive ownership of information produced by the employee by stating this in the employment contract. For example, a contractual term that specifies that the employee is required to perform specific research or develop a particular technology vests the principal with exclusive ownership to the specified innovation. This arrangement would be considered a **work for hire** because the employment contract would be sufficient to transfer all rights in the information or intellectual property developed by the employee to the employer.

Employment contracts that do not specify that any particular design, research, or innovations are expected as part of the employee's duties do not vest exclusive ownership of the technology in the employer. Inventions developed on the employer's time belong to both parties. The employer has a **shop right,** a nonexclusive right to use in the innovation, without any obligation to pay the employee royalties. The employee's compensation is sufficient consideration for the employer to enjoy the shop right, even after the employee is terminated. However, the employee may continue to use or license the innovation separately after termination of employment. Additionally, the employee may retain exclusive ownership without any employer shop right if the invention was not a work for hire and was developed by the employee's own effort and personal investment and on the employee's own time.

The ownership of intellectual property raises ethical dilemmas for several reasons. First, intellectual property is intangible and susceptible to duplication often without detection. Second, the employer makes investments in facilities, research, and employee education essential to the development of intellectual property. Third, employees often believe they should be able to use the fruits of their own ingenuity for personal gain even if developed for their employer. As a result, employees may not realize the misappropriation of intellectual property is wrongful or unethical.

Assignments

Assignments are possible for all types of intellectual property: patents, copyrights, trademarks, trade secrets, and know-how. An employee may transfer exclusive rights to any innovation in a separate **patent assignment** that may be part of the original employment contract, an amendment signed later, or (as illustrated in *Aetna Standard Engineering Company v. Rowland,* which follows) even after termination. The assignment may be broadly worded to include any innovations developed while under contract to the employer or specific as to a particular development, as in the *Aetna* case. *Aetna* illustrates ethical tensions concerning intellectual property and the costs of a stubborn impasse that results in both parties' loss of exclusive rights over the innovation.

AETNA STANDARD ENGINEERING COMPANY v. ROWLAND

493 A.2d 1375 (Pa. 1985)

Rowland was hired as a general staff engineer under an oral contract with Aetna. He signed no written contract or agreement nor did he make any oral agreement to assign to Aetna inventions he designed during his employment. Before employment, Rowland was never informed that his duties would include inventing, and he never received any pay increase after he was designated to join the IHI project. Both Rowland and Remmer, his supervisor, signed a disclosure document after designing the plug mill receiving table for IHI so that Aetna could apply for a patent. Rowland and Remmer signed the application as joint inventors. After Rowland was laid off from Aetna, he refused to assign his patent interest in the receiving table as requested by Aetna. Remmer assigned his interest but was no longer employed at Aetna.

CIRILLIO, Judge

The mere existence of employer-employee relationship does not of itself entitle the employer to an assignment of any inventions which the employee devises during the employment. However, the absence from the employment contract of an express agreement to assign will not preclude the employer as a matter of law from asserting a claim to the employee's invention. Instead, a court must closely scrutinize the employment contract, so that, absent an express contrary agreement, an employee must assign his invention to his employer if he was hired for the purpose of using his inventive ability to solve a specific problem or to design a procedure or device for the employer; in such a case the invention is the precise subject of the employment contract.

Although an employer might not be entitled to an assignment of the employee's invention, the employer will likely have a license or "shop right" to use the invention without paying the employee any additional compensation as royalties; the shop right rule thus creates an exception from the employee's patent right to exclude others from making or using his invention. A **shop right** will arise where the employee devises the invention on the employer's time, at the employer's expense, and using the employer's materials and facilities. The shop right allows the employer to use the invention without any additional or special compensation.

Where an employee by contract is hired to make a particular invention or solve a specific problem for the employer the property inventions of the employee belongs to the employer. The employee has sold in advance the fruit of his talent, skills, and knowledge to his employer who is entitled to it; in making such inventions or solving such problems the employee is merely doing what he was hired to do.[1]

Rowland received no special compensation for his work on the IHI contract; however, that work was simply within the normal scope of his duties as an Aetna engineer. More importantly, he had no express agreement with the appellant, written or oral, to assign to it any invention he created during his employment. Aetna asked Rowland to assign the disclosure document and patent application as a joint inventor with Remmer; Aetna made no claims to the patent until after it had discharged Rowland. On these facts we cannot imply an agreement in Rowland's employment contract to assign his invention to Aetna.

However, Aetna has a shop right to use the patented table. Rowland testified that he assumed Aetna would own any inventions he designed. The table was designed at Aetna's place of business and with its resources for the IHI contract. While Aetna has no right to Rowland's patent interest, it is entitled to the royalty-free, non-exclusive use of the table in its IHI project.

Case Questions

1. What is the issue concerning ownership of innovations as expressed in the *Aetna* case?

2. In what three ways can an employer have rights to use an employee's innovation or invention?

3. What three conditions entitle an employee to retain a right to use an innovation invented while employed? What reasons justify the employer's claim to an employee's innovation? What reasons justify an employee's exclusive claim to owning an invention?

---

[1] *Quaker State Oil Refining Co. v. Talbot,* 174 A. 99, 101 (Pa. 1936).

The uncertainties illustrated in the *Aetna* case are often addressed with a specific term in the employment contract that requires the employee to assign all patents, inventions, or trade secrets developed on the employer's time to the employer. Employers often include the patent assignment clauses to clarify the employer's ownership of the innovation and to require the employee to assist in procuring a patent. A few state statutes and many courts would limit the enforceability of patent assignment clauses to inno-

Figure 35-2   Special Terms in Agency and Employment Relations

Special Term	Duty	Rationale or Practical Effect
Covenant Not to Compete	Prohibits employee/agent from competing with employer/principal after termination	Protects employer/principal's confidences and trade secrets; unenforceable if too broad
Confidentiality Clause	Prohibits employee/agent from using or divulging employer/principal's confidences or trade secrets	Protects employer/principal's confidences and trade secrets; must be specific, does not cover generalized professional knowledge
Work for Hire	Employment contract specifying project or development expected from employee/agent	Vests exclusive ownership to intellectual property in employer/principal
Shop Right	Employer/principal's common law right to nonexclusive use of developments made by employees while on job	Assures employer/principal of right to use developments by employees/agents; employee/agent retains nonexclusive right to sell and use discovery independently or in competition with employer/principal
Patent Assignment Clause	Transfers ownership of patentable developments from employee/agent to employer/principal	Assures employer of exclusive ownership of discoveries made by employees/agents while in employ
Force Majeure	Contract clause releasing a contract obligation due to a listed and unforeseen event or condition	Discharges duty of contracting party to perform if the event occurs (e.g., act of God, labor strike, failure of supply)
Preparatory Steps	Employee/agent's acts in preparation to quit that optimize competition with former employer/principal	Violates employee/agent's fiduciary duty to employer/principal if confidential information stolen or other employees/agents actively solicited while still employed
Co-Worker Solicitation Prohibition	Employment/agency contract term prohibiting solicitation of co-workers to compete against employer/principal	Restrains employees/agents from quitting and taking co-workers to compete against employer/principal
Termination Notice	Requires employer/principal and/or employee/agent to notify of termination	Allows time for replacement of employee/agent or opportunity to find employment

vations that are developed on the employer's premises. These statutes give the employee exclusive ownership over developments made entirely off the employer's premises and financed by the employee. However, the ownership issue may remain clouded where an employee is hired to do research and development and is exposed to confidential information about technologies that contribute at least in part to the employee's individual invention. Figure 35-2 summarizes some special terms in agency and employment contracts and Figure 35-3 summarizes the agent's duties to the principal.

Subagents

Agents can be liable for the unlawful or negligent acts of a subagent if this causes harm to the principal. If the principal authorizes the agent to appoint a subagent, then the subagent owes all the traditional agency duties to both the principal and to the agent who hired the subagent. However, if the agent was not authorized to hire a subagent, the subagent has no authority to bind the principal. The principal cannot enforce duties against an unauthorized subagent, and the subagent is not entitled to compensation from the principal. Therefore, only authorized subagents stand in a fiduciary relationship to the principal. Unauthorized subagents owe fiduciary duties only to the agent. Even when a subagent's appointment is clearly authorized, there can be ambiguity and widespread misunderstanding on who should benefit from the subagent's duties. The following article illustrates the risks of using subagents and the ambiguity created.

Figure 35–3   Duties of Agent to Principal

Agent's Duties	Summary
Fiduciary duty of loyalty	Refrain from conflicts of interest and self-dealing Maintain principal's confidences No dual agency without both principals' fully informed consent
Duty of care	Use reasonable skill and care judged by professional and community standards Level of compensation is irrelevant

Obedience	Obey all reasonable directives
	Exceptions:
	    Illegal or immoral command
	    Emergency situations

Accounting	Keep accurate books and records Provide comprehensive summary of receipts and disbursements No commingling of principal's funds with agent's funds
Communication	Communicate to principal all relevant notices and information concerning principal's business Notice/knowledge imputed to principal
Contract performance	Perform duties specifically assumed in agency employment contract

*Home Buyers' Agents Threaten Brokers**

Renee Talley winces when she recalls the 18 months she wasted with a succession of real-estate agents shopping for a new home for her family of five.

"I'd get dressed in the morning thinking I was going to spend the whole day looking at houses," she says. "The agent would show me one house, and I'd say, 'That's it?' " Another agent said her offer for one house was "insulting" and refused to present it to the seller.

Only when the Talleys retained their own real-estate broker—a tactic almost unheard of until recently—did they finally make some progress. Soon Mrs. Talley was seeing scores of houses. When she found one she liked in the Dallas suburb of Highland Park, the sale closed in a week and a half, despite a flurry of negotiations over concessions that the Talley's broker, Erle Rawlins III, urged them to seek from the seller.

"I'll never buy a house any other way," Mrs. Talley vows.

Quiet Revolution

Experiences like the Talleys' are helping to ignite a quiet revolution in the way U.S. homes are bought and sold. Until recently, all residential real-estate agents and brokers represented the sellers, a fact lost on many home buyers. Now, arguing that the traditional arrangement does buyers a tremendous disservice—by, for example, jacking up prices and limiting selection—a new breed of brokers has emerged to fend for them.

*Source: Christi Harlan, *The Wall Street Journal*, February 5, 1991, p. B1.

The old order "is a true 'buyer beware' situation if there ever was one," says Luke Graves, an Austin, Texas, broker who started Buyers 1 three years ago to represent home purchasers. "It's like working with an attorney who represents the defendant, and you're the plaintiff."

Many traditional brokers and agents disagree. They say buyers' brokers have just as much incentive to make a sale as sellers' brokers, because both generally rely on commissions. And they bristle at the notion of sharing commissions with buyers' agents, sometimes freezing out the newcomers.

Traditionalists further argue that buyer representation isn't necessary, because Realtors' code of ethics calls for them to treat both seller and buyer fairly. To do otherwise would be self-destructive, they add, because today's buyer may someday be a seller.

"We're going to treat everybody fairly and equally," says Mary Frances Burleson, president-elect of the Dallas Association of Realtors. "It's the code of ethics, and it's the golden rule."

Despite such resistance, buyer advocacy appears to be taking off. Barry Miller, president of Buyer's Resource in Denver and a leader of the movement, says 30,000 to 38,000 buyer representatives are operating in the residential real-estate business today, compared with "not even five" in 1983. (So far, they are concentrated in the West and Southwest, but they are starting to appear in the East as well.) The National Association of Realtors, dominated by traditional agents and brokers, counts 800,000 members.

Recent changes in state real-estate regulations may accelerate the trend. In recent years, 43 states have adopted rules aimed at making home buyers aware of agents' and brokers' true clients. New York requires oral disclosure of a broker's client, and has drafted rules that will call for written disclosure. Texas and California already require written disclosure. New Jersey, which doesn't have a disclosure rule, is considering one.

Consumer advocates say such rules will prompt more home buyers to retain their own brokers by illuminating the one-sided nature of the traditional process. It's all too easy, the advocates argue, for first-time home purchasers to believe that sellers' agents are working for them, especially when a buyer and agent spend a lot of time together, looking at houses and discussing the buyer's wants and needs.

In a survey last year, the Consumer Federation of America concluded that "there is widespread ignorance about how to buy a house efficiently" because just 33 percent of respondents knew that real-estate agents represent only sellers.

The lines can become fuzzy for traditional agents, too, because they typically spend more time with buyers than with sellers. "I feel more comfortable with the people in the car knowing I work for them," says Don Difiore, a Realtor in Aurora, Colorado, who has begun representing buyers as well as sellers.

Free Agents

Buyer representatives—who make themselves known through radio advertising and word-of-mouth, and hope one day to have their own Yellow Page category—say the first service they give house hunters is a wider selection of homes. Many buyers' advocates are Realtors (though few ever represent sellers). So, they can offer buyers homes from the Realtors' Multiple Listing Service (usually splitting a sales commission with the listing broker, just as conventional agents do), as well as point buyers to homes for sale by owners (negotiating a fee beforehand with sellers). Without listings of their own to profit from selling, buyers' brokers are freer to discuss the merits of one house over another, they say.

At the sales stage, buyers' brokers hammer for concessions from the seller. Scott Gratrix, a construction contractor in Denver, worked with Mr. Miller to buy a home two years ago in a suburban country-club community. Mr. Gratrix says he paid 25 percent less than the listed price for the house and, despite extensive renovations, still has the lowest cost per square foot of any home in the area.

In many states, buyers using a traditional agent can have their attorney negotiate concessions after a home inspection has been conducted. But Mr. Rawlins, the buyers' broker in Dallas, says most lawyers aren't in a position to offer guidance on a property's market value, point out shortcomings and suggest an offering price.

Moreover, buyers' brokers can provide a purchaser with financial and personal information about the seller, giving the buyer potential negotiating leverage. By contrast, sellers' representatives are prohibited by law from divulging such information. In the past, this has often meant information traveled a one-way street from buyer to seller.

But there are still some hitches in this bold new real-estate world—and most of them, predictably, revolve around money. Especially in areas where the move to buyers' brokers is just getting started, traditional brokers say sellers shouldn't have to pay part of their commission to someone who is presumably working against their interests.

The issue became so heated in Milwaukee that an early buyers' broker there sought bankruptcy court protection in 1988 after sellers' brokers reduced his share of sales commissions or refused outright to share commissions. Some buyers' brokers protect themselves by making sure before they show a house that the listing agent will share the commission.

Commissions also raise another nettlesome issue for buyers' brokers. Some critics wonder whether buyers' advocates have an incentive to negotiate the best deal on a home if their paycheck is a percentage of the sales price.

Some buyers' brokers say they've found a solution to this potential conflict of interest—and also a way to avoid commission squabbles with sellers' brokers: request a retainer fee up front from clients, generally 1 percent to 4 percent of what a buyer is willing to pay for a home. If the selling broker won't share the commission with the buyers' broker, the retainer isn't refunded.

The commission tug of war is "the natural enemy" of the buyer-representation movement, says Laurene Janik, general counsel of the National Association of Realtors. "If there weren't the compensation issue," she says, "there wouldn't be an issue."

Thought Questions

1. What issue confronts the real estate profession about the allegiance of the buyer's agent? How could this relationship harm an unsuspecting buyer?

2. What are the reasons that the law presumes the buyer's broker owes a fiduciary duty only to the seller unless the buyer has a separate contract?

3. What alternative methods of compensation are there to splitting the commission in order to preserve incentives for the seller's broker while more closely aligning the buyer's broker's interests with the buyer?

DUTIES OF PRINCIPAL TOWARD AGENT

Most duties in the agency relationship flow from the agent to the principal because the agent is delegated special powers that can profoundly affect the principal's business and financial affairs. There are only a few duties the principal owes to the agent. As with any contract, the principal must perform the terms specified in the agency or employment contract. For example, a real estate sales agent's listing contract often provides the agent with a minimum time period to attempt making the sale. If the home seller (principal) terminates the agent before this time has elapsed, this would constitute a breach of contract.

Some agency relationships are established without a specific agency employment contract, so agency law establishes the principal's duties to protect the agent's interests in (1) receiving the promised compensation and (2) reasonable facilitation of the agent's safe performance.

Compensation

The principal must compensate the agent for successful accomplishment of services. Compensation is generally based on a term in the agency or employment contract that sets an hourly, weekly, monthly, or annual salary rate. Alternatively, compensation might be stated as a specified dollar amount for a quantity of work performed, a percentage commission based on sales, or a combination of several compensation methods. If the agency is clearly gratuitous, the principal has no duty to compensate the agent.

The principal is required to keep accurate records of all business activity the agent conducts if necessary to compute the agent's compensation. For example, manufacturing and shipping records may be necessary to compute a field sales agent's commission. The agent's compensation may be triggered by the mere passage of time, as with a salary, a volume of business or production activity, as with a commission, or the achievement of an objective. For example, an attorney on a **contingency fee** compensation contract will be entitled to receive attorneys fees only if the client's case is won or settled favorably. Similarly, real estate agents are usually entitled to a commission only when the agent is a "procuring cause" of finding a "ready, willing, and able buyer." However, even where the agent's compensation is well specified, there may still be ambiguity over the principal's obligation to compensate, as illustrated in the following case.

HECHT v. MELLER
244 N.E.2d 77 (N.Y. Ct. App. 1968)

Helen Hecht had a written real estate listing contract with Herbert and Joyce Meller to find a buyer for their personal residence and an adjacent lot for $75,000. The Meller's accepted an offer from a ready, willing, and able buyer for $60,000. Before the parties could close the sale with full payment and a transfer of title, the house was substantially destroyed by fire. An applicable New York statute permits buyers to rescind a home sale contract if the premises are destroyed before closing. Helen Hecht sued the Mellers for her $3,600 brokerage commission, which they refused to pay because the buyer had rescinded the sale under the statute.

KEATING, Judge

A New York statue does not render real estate contracts unenforceable but, rather, simply bestows a privilege on vendees to rescind the contract. This court has consistently stated that a real estate broker's right to commissions attaches when he procures a buyer who meets the requirements established by the seller. At the juncture that the broker produces an acceptable buyer he has fully performed his part of the agreement with the vendor and his right to commission becomes enforceable. The brokers' ultimate right to compensation has never been held to depend on the performance of their realty contract or the receipt by the seller of the selling price unless the brokerage agreement with the vendors specifically so conditioned payment. As the court stated in *Guilder v. Davis:*

> Even from a defect in the title of the vendor, or a refusal to consummate the contract on the part of the purchaser for any reason in no way attributable to the broker, the sale falls through, nevertheless the broker is entitled to his commissions, for the simple reason that he has performed his contract.[2]

---

[2] *Guilder v. Davis,* 33 N.E. 599, 600 (N.Y. 1893).

At the time the contract is rescinded the broker and the seller are equally blameless. When it is realized that the seller has the contractual flexibility to allocate the possible risk of having to pay the brokerage commission, it creates no inequity to apply our constantly announced rule. The vendor can protect against the risk by either conditioning the brokerage contract so that commissions would only be paid out of the proceeds of the sale, or contracting with the vendee that he would either have to purchase the property irrespective of its condition or pay the broker's earned commission if he elected to rescind the contract.

Even though the property is destroyed, the performance of the contract may in some instances still be advantageous to the vendee. The vendee may choose to perform because the contract permits an abatement in the purchase price or requires insurance proceeds received by the vendor to be credited towards the purchase price of the property. Insurance proceeds will be credited if either the vendee contracts for the vendor to insure the property or the vendee pays the premiums for the vendor.

Even though the contingency foreseen by the statute has occurred, the possibility the buyer will opt out of the contract is even more remote. Neither the section's legislative history nor its language support a privilege to the seller not to pay an earned brokerage commission. The expense of the brokerage commission must be paid by the vendor who has contracted for the brokers services, even though the legislature has given the vendee the privilege of rescinding the contract which the broker helped to bring about.

Case Questions

1. What is the issue the court confronted concerning Helen Hecht's compensation?

2. What is the conclusion about a real estate agent's entitlement to compensation if the sale falls through? What reasons support this?

3. Apart from the purchase price adjustment or an insurance settlement, what other protections might exist for the purchaser if the building or other structures are destroyed before the closing date?

Some agency relationships do not specify the agent's compensation yet are clearly not gratuitous. In these instances, the law will infer a fair compensation implied from the circumstances. This is a contractual remedy, **quantum meruit,** used to measure an agent's compensation in these instances. Typically, the usages of trade in the agent's profession can provide evidence of the ''going rate'' that other principals generally pay for similar services. In computing a fair compensation, courts often consider such factors as (1) the amount of work provided, (2) the agent's skill or reputation, and (3) the agent's success. Quantum meruit may be the only basis for compensation if the agent had only apparent authority or authority was given retroactively by ratification.

Reimbursement and Indemnity

The principal must reimburse an authorized agent's expenses and indemnify losses reasonably related to the agent's operation of the principal's business. Unless the agency employment contract provides otherwise, the principal must usually pay for down payments, interest payments, deposits, rents, taxes, fees charged by lawyers, accountants, or consultants, damage awards paid to third parties, or any other expense necessary to conduct the principal's business. For example, Perry must reimburse Alma, his sales agent, for her travel expenses while authorized to make customer calls. If Perry's attorney and accountant operate the business while Perry is on an extended vacation, Perry must indemnify any losses they suffer.

Noninterference

Unless the agency or employment contract requires the principal to actively assist with the agent's performance, there is no duty on the principal to actively provide assistance. However, the principal must make it possible for the agent to reasonably complete the services required. The principal may not prevent the agent's performance or make it difficult to perform successfully. The agent must be given access to buildings, offices, files, equipment, and other facilities where the agent's work must be performed. For example, Perry must provide access to his books and records for the accountant's preparation of income tax returns or to documents the attorney needs for Perry's litigation. The principal may not appoint another agent to sell within an exclusive territory if the agent is granted an exclusive right in the contract to sell there. However, the principal may appoint other agents if no exclusive rights are provided in their contracts.

Increasingly, tort law requires the principal to disclose the risks involved with performance of an agency. For example, if Perry hires an agent to collect debt payments from a violent debtor, Perry must inform the agent of any dangerous tendencies known about the debtor. Increasingly, the occupational safety and health laws require the principal to provide a safe working environment free from workplace hazards and toxins. This creates an ethical dilemma for employers if they fail to adequately warn or safeguard employees about known risks.

Agent's Rights and Remedies

Agents typically have a narrower choice of remedies than the principal because the principal owes a narrower range of duties to the agent. Of course, the principal is responsible for any damages arising from the principal's breach of a specific term in the agency employment contract. Additionally, the agency or employment contract may provide for remedies such as indemnity, reimbursement, and/or liquidated damages or provide a security interest. Agents may sue for damages if they do not receive their rightful compensation. Sometimes it may be necessary for the principal to conduct an accounting to determine the level of business used to compute a commission.

The law may automatically provide the agent with a lien against any of the principal's property rightfully held in the agent's possession. Some statutes specify the agent's right to a lien. For example, an attorney has an automatic lien on workpapers prepared for a client to ensure payment for services. Accountants are usually presumed to own client workpapers, so a lien is often unnecessary. For most other agents, liens arise only when specifically stated in the employment contract. The principal's duties to the agent are summarized in Figure 35–4.

TERMINATION OF AGENCY

From the principal's perspective, the termination of an agency is of critical importance. Once authorized, an agent may change the principal's relationships with third parties, which represents a very

Figure 35–4 Duties of Principal to Agent

Principal's Duties	Summary
Compensation	Pay agent compensation required in agency employment contract
	Keep accurate records to permit computation of compensation
Reimbursement/ indemnity	Repay agent's expenses paid or losses from operating principal's business
Noninterference	May not interfere with agent's performance
	Facilitate agent's access to principal's property
	Notify agent of unsafe conditions
	Exclusive agency: May not appoint competing agent
Contract performance	Perform duties specifically assumed in agency employment contract

great power. The principal must be capable of easily terminating the agent's broad power, particularly if the agent becomes incompetent, inefficient, or untrustworthy. After either party stops consenting, the basis for the agency is lost.

Power versus Right

Generally, agencies are terminable at will when either the principal or agent wants the relationship to cease. This means either party has the *power* to terminate unless the agency is irrevocable or coupled with an interest, as discussed below. This result follows logically from the mutuality concept of contract law. If the agent could not renounce authority and was forced to work for the principal, this would amount to involuntary servitude. A correlative right exists for the principal to fire the agent at will because the principal should not be required to accept the services of an untrustworthy or unnecessary employee. Employment at will is a controversial subject of employment relations and is discussed further in Chapter 49.

While the power to terminate an agency nearly always exists, the *right* to terminate the agency may be limited in the agency employment contract. For example, consider a contract with a provision requiring that employment be maintained for a minimum time period to adequately fulfill its purpose (e.g., a real estate sale). Any premature termination breaches this contract provision. Therefore, even though either party has the *power* to terminate the relationship, the parties may give up their *rights* to terminate when the employment contract restricts the right to terminate. Where such provision exists, yet one party nevertheless terminates prematurely, the innocent party may sue the terminating party for damages due to the wrongful termination.

Some agency employment contracts include special terms addressing the termination process or events permitting termination. For example, labor union collective bargaining agreements often require the employer to prove some **just cause** before an employee may be fired. Some contracts contain **force majeure** provisions that permit termination when performance becomes permanently difficult. Force majeure provisions often list numerous unforeseeable events that relieve either party's duty to perform, including strikes, war, weather conditions, regulatory changes, acts of God, or failure of supply. Some agency and employment contracts include a **severance pay** or **liquidated damage** provision calling for payment of a termination penalty that entitles one of the parties to certain monies.

Irrevocable Agency

In some situations, the principal may not have the power or right to unilaterally revoke the agency. The agent's authority becomes irrevocable if the agent has a personal financial interest in the subject matter of the agency that is independent of the principal's interest. For example, as security for a loan, Perry might grant authority in the loan documents that appoints Perry's bank as his agent, permitting the bank to repossess and sell the collateral if Perry defaults on the loan. This is an **irrevocable agency** because it is an **agency coupled with an interest.** The bank's security interest in the property is the interest that makes the agency irrevocable. To create an agency coupled with an interest, the agency agreement or loan documentation must clearly establish this form of security interest. There are other limitations on the principal's power to terminate certain agencies, as discussed below.

Terminating Foreign Sales Agents and Distributors
Many foreign nations, including most of the developing world and Latin American countries, have special laws to protect the employment of local agents hired by firms from other nations. For example, an American firm doing business in South America through a local distributor or sales agent is probably prohibited from terminating the agent at will. Usually, these statutes require some notification before the termination becomes effective. Some nations require as much as one year's lead time before the agent may be terminated. It is an open question whether these statues simply provide for severance pay equivalent to the notice or actually require the foreign firm to continue using an untrustworthy agent until the period of notice lapses. Firms doing business in international commerce must carefully consider the use of foreign agents by screening them and monitoring their progress carefully to avoid the hardships if termination becomes necessary.

Uniform Durable Power of Attorney Act
Almost one third of the United States have passed the Uniform Durable Power of Attorney Act (UDPAA). This law permits a principal to provide a written power of attorney to an agent that cannot be terminated at the principal's will. Such a power of attorney usually becomes effective when the principal becomes disabled or incapacitated by illness or mental incompetence. The power of attorney must clearly state that the principal intends the authority to persist after the principal becomes disabled or incapacitated. A principal should carefully select an agent designated to receive this irrevocable power because it confers power that is difficult to cancel except by court decree for the agent's breach of duty.

Act of the Parties

Principals or agents may personally or jointly terminate agencies either through provisions in the agency employment contract or by their own, unilateral actions. Terminations by virtue of contract provisions can include the accomplishment of the contract purpose, the happening of an event, or the lapse of a prescribed time period. The parties may agree in a later contract to rescind the agency employment contract, the principal may revoke the agency authority, or the agent may renounce authority. The unilateral act of either party raises questions about the power or the right to terminate the agency, as previously discussed. Additionally, notice of the termination may be required so that the party notified is able to make alternative arrangements.

Accomplishment of Contract Purpose/ Occurrence of Events

Where the agency relationship has a single purpose or is intended to accomplish only one event, the agency is automatically terminated with the accomplishment of the event. For example, after Perry's successful collection suit against a defaulting debtor, the attorney's contract for legal services typically terminates.

An event or condition may trigger termination of the agency even if there is no successful fulfillment of the agency's purpose. For example, disastrous economic conditions, the failing financial position of the agent or principal, or drastic changes in the marketability of the principal's products could become an event or condition terminating the agency without any successful fulfillment of purpose. The agency employment contract may specify nearly any event or condition terminating the agent's authority.

Lapse of Time

After the passage of a specified number of days, months, or years, a contractual provision may specify termination. An agency or employment contract terminates by its own terms when the specified time period lapses. For example, it is common for real estate listing contracts to state a minimum term, such as six months, to enable the selling agent sufficient time to develop a successful marketing plan. Any unauthorized act by the agent after the contractual time has lapsed is ineffective to bind the principal unless the principal fails to notify third parties. However, the principal and agent often both ignore the lapse of a time specified in their contract by voluntarily continuing the relationship. This creates an **agency at will.**

Mutual Agreement

As a consensual or contractual relationship, an agency gives the parties the power to rescind the consent or contract. A mutual agreement by both the principal and the agent relieves them both of future performance obligations. However, the mutual rescission contract must also relieve the parties of their past responsibilities or they will remain liable for them. For example, an agent may remain liable for damages due to disloyal acts before the rescission. Similarly, the principal must make payments of any unpaid compensation, indemnity, or reimbursement that was still due to the agent for services performed before mutual rescission.

Unilateral Termination: Revocation or Renunciation

Except where an agency is irrevocable or coupled with an interest, either party can unilaterally terminate the agency. This illustrates the parties' *power* to terminate. However, the *right* to terminate may be limited by contractual terms. The principal's unilateral termination is referred to as a **revocation.** The agent's unilateral termination is a **renunciation** of the authority. Damages may be due to the innocent party if the terminating party has no right to terminate.

Operation of Law

Under certain circumstances, the agency employment contract may be automatically terminated. Most parties would want the agency to terminate if significant events occur that frustrate the agency's purpose. These events closely parallel the events that terminate an unaccepted offer under contract law: either party's death, incapacity, or bankruptcy, and destruction of the subject matter. In these situations, contracts with an unexpired term or unfulfilled purpose are terminated by operation of law and neither party is liable for wrongful termination of future services. However, death or bankruptcy of either the principal or the agent does not terminate an agent's irrevocable authority that is coupled with an interest.

Incapacity, Bankruptcy, Death

An agency is such a personal relationship that the death or insanity of either party terminates the agent's authority. The agent's authority is also terminated automatically if the principal goes bankrupt, because this severely limits the principal's ability to conduct business through the agent's new contracts in the future. By contrast, the agent's bankruptcy terminates authority only if the agent's solvency is necessary to effectively represent the principal.

Illegality

An agency will automatically terminate if its objective becomes illegal. As under contract law, the law presumes the principal would prefer termination of the agent's authority if the business activity becomes illegal. The same holds true where the principal's business must be conducted under a professional license. For example, an agent's authority to sell liquor or firearms is terminated if the principal's license to sell these goods is revoked. Where the agent's professional license is necessary to conduct business for the principal, the agent's loss of license also terminates authority. For example, Perry's accountant and attorney may not practice these professions if they are temporarily or permanently disbarred. An agent's authority is automatically terminated if the professional license becomes suspended or revoked.

Impossibility or Impracticality

Where an agent's authority is limited to contracts involving a particular subject matter, the agent's authority automatically terminates if the subject matter is destroyed. For example, a real estate agent's authority to sell the principal's home automatically terminates if the home is destroyed by fire. By contrast, a general agent's authority or power of attorney to deal in many areas for the principal does not terminate if a single or only a few items at issue are destroyed or lost.

An agency automatically terminates by operation of law if war breaks out between the different nations of the principal and the agent. If both principal and agent are citizens of the same nation, a war terminates authority only if the business activity becomes illegal, unexpectedly impractical, or hazardous.

In unusual situations, the agent's authority is terminated by operation of the law if performance becomes impractical or there is such a significant change in business conditions that reasonable parties would expect authority to terminate. For example, significant changes in the marketability of the subject matter terminates the agency. If a farmer had authorized an agent to sell the farm and soon thereafter oil was discovered under the farmland, the agent's authority would automatically terminate by operation of law because an oil discovery constitutes a significant change in business conditions.

Post-Termination Relationships

The termination of an agent's authority by an act of the parties or operation of law does not terminate all of the parties' duties to each other or toward third parties. After the agency has terminated, the agent's fiduciary duty may continue, the principal's duty to compensate or facilitate the agent's removal of property may continue, the principal may be required to give notice of termination to third parties, and either the principal or agent may still be responsible for torts committed to third parties.

Continuing Fiduciary Duty

When an agency is terminated, there is often close scrutiny of both parties' conduct immediately before and after the termination. The principal may have treated the agent unfairly or terminated without good cause. The agent may have become disloyal before leaving the principal's employment, perhaps by making preparations to compete with the principal after leaving. The agent is prohibited from taking any **preparatory steps** to compete with the former employer in a new business venture if this violates the fiduciary duty. Before termination, the former employee may legitimately make contracts essential to starting the new business: lining up suppliers, negotiating leases, establishing a new corporation, or soliciting prospective customers and clients. However, some preparatory steps are a conflict of interest, particularly if the agent solicits the principal's former employees or clients. The agent may not photocopy the principal's documents nor misappropriate the principal's trade secrets.

Employers may reinforce this duty by including a separate contractual provision, a **co-worker employment prohibition,** that prohibits the agent from hiring co-workers after the agent terminates. If the agent solicits the principal's other employees working under a fixed-term employment contract, the agent may be liable for tortious interference with these contractual relations. Agents may not take client lists, trade secrets, or other confidential information belonging to the principal for use in the agent's competing business. Of course, any generalized business knowledge the agent learned while in the principal's employment may be used without restriction.

END–OF–CHAPTER QUESTIONS

1. Integrate, compare, and contrast the agent's two primary duties of care and loyalty. Where do they overlap? How are they different? What similar and different purposes do they serve?

2. Big Motors Corp. hired Ralph to join its staff of automotive engineers under an oral employment-at-will contract. Ralph was attached to an emissions design team

along with several other mechanical and chemical engineers. The team developed designs for several engine emissions systems before Big Motors assigned the team to develop a more effective catalytic converter that would reduce exhaust emissions immediately after an engine is started. Just as the team finished the project, Ralph persuaded several team members to join him in quitting Big Motors so they could start their own consulting firm. Ralph intended to design a competing catalytic converter using several technologies the team developed and learned while working at Big Motors. What are the issues in a suit that Big Motors might bring against Ralph? What conclusions are likely in Big Motors' suit against Ralph?

3. Consider the problem stated in Question 2. How could Big Motors rewrite its engineers' employment contracts to eliminate the ambiguities in its rights to innovations and thereby protect its investment in the design team if another engineer quits to compete like Ralph did?

4. Stokely-Van Camp, a food processor, hired an advertising firm, Lennen & Newell, to develop advertising campaigns for the food processor's various lines of consumer goods. As part of the mix of print, direct mail, coupon, and media advertising designed by Lennen & Newell, the advertising firm contracted with CBS, a major TV and radio network, to place numerous advertisements. What are the issues CBS must argue if it is not paid for the Stokely-Van Camp advertisements it ran? What reasons support not holding Stokely-Van Camp liable? What reasons support holding Stokely-Van Camp liable? See *CBS v. Stokely-Van Camp*, 456 F.Supp. 539 (1977).

5. The Hagues listed their farm for sale with Harvey Hilgendorf, a licensed broker. However, the Hagues terminated the listing before it expired. Due to their financial difficulties, the Hagues decided to sell all their land holdings at one time through another broker. What reasons would the Hagues use to justify the termination? What reasons support the original agent's claim that the Hagues breached the contract? What would be the agent's remedy? See *Hilgendorf v. Hague*, 293 N.W.2d 272 (Iowa 1980).

6. Gordon listed his land (approximately 181 acres) for sale with Ramsey, a licensed real estate broker. Ramsey offered to purchase the land personally at $800 per acre, and Gordon agreed. Before they could transfer the property, Gordon sold the land to another person for $800 per acre. In the interim, Ramsey had found another buyer willing to pay $1,250 per acre. Ramsey claims Gordon's sale cost him a $90,000 profit. What reasons support Ramsey's claim? What reasons support Gordon's refusal to pay? See *Ramsey v. Gordon*, 567 S.W.2d 868 (Tex. Civ. App. 1978).

7. Carr shipped goods on the Maine Central Ry. but paid prices in excess of the standard charges. When Carr discovered the overcharge, he insisted Maine Central Ry. process a request required by the Interstate Commerce Commission for permission to validate the rebate. Maine Central Ry. failed to process the request within the required time period. Carr sued Maine Central Ry. for failure to perform under its duty of care. Is a gratuitous agent held to the same standard of care as a compensated agent? See *Carr v. Maine Central Ry.*, 102 A. 532 (N.H. 1917).

8. Gray died shortly after granting Tylle in writing a 20 percent interest in his half of a government petroleum lease. Tylle agreed to pay Gray $10,000 and appointed Gray as agent and operator of the lease until further notice to develop and operate the petroleum extraction from the leased property. Tylle claimed a return of his $10,000 from Gray's estate and declared the agency terminated. What reasons would Gray's estate administrator use to argue that Tylle's claim was invalid so the estate could retain the $10,000? See *In re Estate of Gray*, 541 P.2d 336 (Colo. App. 1975).

9. Penny authorized Arnold to acquire certain goods from particular vendors and contract to have them shipped to Penny's warehouse on the ABC AirCarrier Co., an airline specified by Penny. She believed these were the best companies with which to do business considering their reputations for price, quality, and delivery time. After the first installment of goods was shipped, Arnold discovered that the ABC AirCarrier Co. was in financial trouble and might forfeit to lenders several of its freighter airplanes that were collateral for loans made to ABC. Further business news reports reasonably led Arnold to believe ABC's bankruptcy was imminent, and this threatened a cessation of operations while Penny's goods were in transit. Arnold was unable to contact Penny with his suggestion to substitute a new carrier, so Arnold took it upon himself to cancel the carriage contract with ABC AirCarrier and directed the shipper to use the XYZ AirCargo Co. instead. The XYZ AirCargo Co. filed for bankruptcy while Penny's goods were in transit and the goods were not delivered until months later. Is Arnold liable to Penny for damages from the late shipments due to Arnold's disobedience to Penny's specification of an air carrier?

10. Consider the facts in Question 9. Assume that ABC AirCarrier had informed Arnold of its financial troubles before the date for shipping, giving him the option to cancel Penny's contract. However, Arnold had heard rumors about XYZ AirCargo's financial problems and, without consulting Penny, made a choice not to cancel the ABC contract. What issue would Penny raise in a suit against Arnold if Penny's goods shipment was delayed if ABC went bankrupt rather than XYZ?

Chapter 36

Agency: Third-Party Relations

■

CRITICAL THINKING INQUIRIES

As you read this chapter, you should be able to address the following:

- What risks do principals bear in using agents to negotiate business contracts? Why does the law protect third parties' expectations when dealing with authorized agents?

- How much responsibility does an outside third party have to voluntarily discover whether the principal's agent is authorized to negotiate a contract for the principal? Who is in the best position to investigate that the agent has sufficient power to negotiate contracts?

- What ambiguity does the third party confront when an agent does not voluntarily divulge the principal's identity? What reasons might justify the principal's confidentiality? Do these reasons overcome the agent's duty to act in a forthright and honest manner with third parties?

- When a firm's economic activity affects outsiders, who should bear the costs? Why should costs be allocated?

- Must employers be responsible for preventing the harmful side effects of their employees' acts in case damage is caused to outsiders? What reasons support holding the employer liable? What would be the most effective and efficient method to reduce injuries?

MANAGERIAL PERSPECTIVE

Perry's widget manufacturing firm was attaining some success, so he authorized the hiring of more sales staff, supervised by Alma, his lone former salesperson. The five new recruits signed employment contracts with Alma as Perry's representative. They were specifically granted authority to make wholesale widget sales to industrial customers. However, the contract was silent on whether they could offer discounts, warranties, credit, or arrange shipping. Some sales personnel were involved in an automobile accident while attending a widget trade show in a distant city.

- What are the issues that may arise when potential customers request the sales personnel to modify the standard terms of sale?

- What reasons support limiting the employer-principal's risk exposure to matters specifically authorized? What reasons support expanding the employer-principal's risk exposure beyond matters specifically authorized?

- What assumptions are made in holding the employer/master liable for damages in the automobile accident if the sales personnel were at fault?

The actions of agents are involved in the conduct of nearly all businesses (sole proprietorships, partnerships, and corporations) and most activities of governments and unincorporated associations (e.g., labor unions). An understanding of how an agent's activities impact the principal is fundamental to the manager's effective use of agents. This chapter discusses the impact agents have on the principal's contract and tort responsibilities. There are limits on the use of agents. These limits concern (1) the direct monitoring of agents' activities, (2) the suboptimal contracts and performances they occasionally make, and (3) the possibility that an employee or agent may injure an outsider. Managers of all agents should undertake risk management techniques to reduce the firm's exposure from their agents' torts, including purchasing insurance, ensuring agent competence, training and licensing employees, and periodic monitoring. This is facilitated where all agents and employees know the applicable law and are instructed to avoid damaging others. The principal needs to balance the perceived benefits of extending its reach through use of agents against the costs of monitoring and misbehavior.

CONTRACT LIABILITY OF THE PRINCIPAL

The effectiveness of using agents to conduct business is largely dependent on the agent's authority. Contracts enforceable against the principal result when an agent is authorized to conduct preliminary negotiations, make offers or counteroffers, and/or accept third parties' offers. For example, when Perry's purchasing agent is authorized to acquire vehicles for the company's fleet, the agent may validly negotiate the sale contract with the manufacturer or dealers. Perry's firm thereby becomes bound in contract to pay for these vehicles. This a form of vicarious liability because the principal's contract responsibilities are derived from the acts of another person, the agent. The principal's contract liability is derived from three basic forms of authority: actual authority (express and implied), apparent authority, and ratification.

Express Authority

The analysis of an agent's authority begins by focusing on the precise power that a principal actually confers on the agent. **Actual authority** is composed of express authority and implied authority. An agent is authorized by the principal's directions, written or

oral, to negotiate contracts or to otherwise have an affect on the principal's legal relationships. Express authority is often granted in a document such as an employment contract, a resolution of the board of directors, an advisory memorandum, or a special document known as a **power of attorney**, illustrated in Figure 36-1. Additionally, the corporation's bylaws typically grant express authority to the president, and sometimes to other officers, to take actions affecting the corporation's legal relationships.

Implied Authority

In addition to all the actual authority expressly granted by a principal, agents usually possess supplemental implied authority. **Implied authority** includes additional authority that an agent may reasonably assume exists to implement the express authority. Implied authority is a *penumbra* around a central grant of express authority that arises as necessary to carry out and implement an express grant. This means that it is legitimate to "read between the lines" of the agent's express authorization to infer additional details of the authority. There can be no implied authority unless first there is express authority upon which to base the implied authority.

Most often, a principal expressly grants an actual express authority. This is so general that it fails to itemize the specifics of the agent's powers, particularly in unusual or unforeseen situations. Most principals and agents expect that the agent will fill in the details with reasonable actions that carry out the principal's main objective. For example, the superintendent of an apartment building might simply be granted the power to "manage" the building. Unless the apartment owner specifically limits the super's power, additional authority is implied to facilitate successful management. Does this include authority to hire employees, sign leases with new tenants, evict unworthy tenants, repair appliances in an apartment unit, or make capital improvements? The concept of implied authority usually answers these questions.

An agent generally has implied authority to make contracts reasonably necessary to conduct the business in the customary fashion. The apartment superintendent would usually have authority to do any of the acts listed above but not the authority to make capital improvements. Implied authority generally does not include the power to borrow money, issue negotiable instruments, sell capital assets, or create a security interest on the principal's property (mort-

Figure 36–1   Power of Attorney

Know by these presents: I, _____ herein, and appoint _____ my true and lawful attorney in fact for me to act in my name, for my use and my benefit. This grant includes the following powers:

1. Agent may demand, recover, collect, receive, and litigate every debt, bequest, interest, dividend, annuity, and other amount owing to me currently due or which shall become due to me or claimed by me. The appointed agent may also execute releases of the satisfaction of payment of these sums and enter into compromise or settlement of these claims.

2. This appointed agent may exercise all powers regarding real property or any interest in real property including: contracts for purchase, taking possession, granting or receiving title, execution of leases for any term or purpose, sell, exchange, convey with or without warranty, mortgage, transfer in trust, or otherwise encumber real property to secure payment of negotiable or non-negotiable debts, notes, or performance obligations.

3. The named agent is authorized to exercise powers over personal property and goods, merchandise, choses in action, including: contracts to sell, buy, exchange, transfer title in any legal manner, mortgage, transfer in trust, encumber or secure payment of negotiable or non-negotiable debt or note or other obligation.

4. The named agent is entitled to borrow money and execute and deliver negotiable or non-negotiable debts, transfer notes with or without security.

5. The named agent may make loans of money and receive negotiable or non-negotiable notes for repayment.

6. The named agent may create, amend, or terminate any trust for which I am trustor or beneficiary.

7. The named agent may vote stock, exercise any stock right, accept dividend payments, participate in any corporate financing, reorganization, merger, liquidation, consolidation, or other fundamental corporate change, or participate in restructuring or adjustment of any corporate security.

8. The named agent may transact any legal business including execution, signature, acknowledgment, delivery, or receipt of any deed, lease, assignment of lease, indenture, indemnity, agreement, mortgage, deed of trust, extension, renewal, waiver, negotiable document, non-negotiable document, or other signed instrument. I, the undersigned, give and grant to this agent as attorney in fact the full power and authority to do and perform all and every act and thing whatever necessary and appropriate to fulfill the above intents and purposes that I could lawfully do or cause to be done myself. My said attorney has sole discretion to exercise these powers for any purpose, at any time, and in any manner and to fix terms for cash, credit, and forms of property.

Signatures below witnessed on _____ day of _____ , 19 _____ .

_____

_____

gage or lien). These latter actions are more extraordinary, so they are implied only if the nature of the principal's business suggests that the agent should do them. For example, an agent of a banking or financial firm who regularly borrows, lends, or issues negotiable instruments would be expected to have the implied authority to perform these acts. An agent's authority may also be implied from a course of conduct or implied out of necessity, such as in an emergency.

Course of Conduct

Business customs are precedents followed in commercial settings. Customs create expectations among commercial parties as they deal through agents. Business customs differ among industries and within an industry among geographic regions. Third parties who deal through another firm's agent may usually presume the agent has a level of authority similar to most agents in that region and industry. Customs developed between the principal and a third party are called a **course of conduct**. Customs developed in an entire industry or a region are recognized as a **usage of trade**. The following case illustrates usages in an industry that authorize an agent even if contradictory to a specific limitation the principal placed on the agent.

JACKSON v. GOODMAN
244 N.W.2d 423 (1976)

During a robbery of the St. Regis Hotel, a hotel employee was murdered. This prompted the hotel's general manager, Frank Bromer, to offer a $1,000 reward to anyone providing information that would lead to the arrest and conviction of the murderer. Jackson claimed the reward after the information he furnished led to an arrest and subsequent conviction. The hotel owners, including Goodman, refused to pay the reward, claiming that Bromer had no authority to spend hotel funds in an amount over $50 without their approval. Jackson appealed the trial judge's decision to overrule the jury's verdict giving the reward to Jackson.

KAUFMAN, J.

There was sufficient evidence to present jury questions concerning the presence of either inherent authority or ratification. An individual with the authority to make a contract may offer a reward. The authority to contract may be inferred from the authority to manage the business. Such authority is limited to making "contracts which are incidental to making such business, are usually made in it, or are reasonably necessary in conducting it." One of the factors to be considered to the extent of authority is the custom of similar businesses at the same time and place.

Other courts have presumed authority in the president of a bank to offer, on behalf of the bank, a reward for information leading to the arrest of a defaulting teller. Similarly, the authority to offer a reward for the arrest of persons maliciously destroying railroad tracks has been held to be within the implied authority of the railroad's superintendent.

The dissent views the question of implied authority of the business. We view this question from the perspective of the plaintiff.

Where the specific business exhibits a general course of behavior relative to the questioned acts, the inquiry generally will give greater focus to the specific concern than the course of conduct in similar businesses. Where, as here, the transaction is one unusual to the specific business affected, the emphasis must differ. In such case, significant emphasis must be put on the course of business conduct in the community at large concerning rewards and on whether the recipient party reasonably believes that the agent is authorized . . . and has no notice that he is not so authorized [*Restatement of Agency, Second*, Section 161]. A jury, as the repository of "community sense" is in a unique position to decide questions of unusual course of conduct and reasonable reliance in such unusual cases.

MCGREGOR, J., dissenting

In the present case, Bromer cannot be said to have been authorized to offer the reward. Nor do I find any evidence presented at trial which justify the jury in concluding that Bromer had either the apparent or inherent authority to offer the reward.

A general manager can only have the apparent or inherent authority to do those things which managers at that business at that time and place customarily do. As such, contracts entered into by general managers are only binding on the principal if they are incidental to a business such as the principal's, are usually made in such a business or are reasonably necessary in conducting in such business. I do not think it can be reasonably said that the reward in the present case is either incidental or reasonably necessary in conducting the hotel business. Nor do I think in the absence of any evidence to the contrary, that it can be assumed that such rewards are usually made in the hotel business. I conclude that there was no evidence presented that Bromer had the apparent authority to offer the reward in the instant case.

Case Questions

1. On what issue do the majority justice (Kaufman) and the dissenting justice (McGregor) have differing opinions?

2. What is the ambiguity in the phrase "industry custom" that can cause the two opposing judges to take different approaches?

3. If you were to decide this case, what analogous situations might be used to provide precedents or guidance to solve the issue in this case?

4. Discuss and critique the reasons used by both judges to support their view of implied authority. Critique their attack of each others' views.

Emergencies

In some instances, it is necessary for an agent to use implied authority in unforeseen situations such as where the agent's employment contract fails to specify how the agent should react in an emergency. In an emergency, unless specifically limited, the agent has additional authority reasonably necessary to prevent the principal from sustaining substantial losses. For example, in one case, a train owned by the principal railroad injured a passenger. The railroad's stationmaster transported the injured passenger to a physician for treatment. The passenger's legs were amputated and the passenger sued the railroad. Although the railroad denied liability, the court held that its agent, the stationmaster, had implied authority arising from an emergency to secure the aid of a physician. The court stated "when an employee is injured by a railroad train, and immediate attention is demanded in order to save life, or prevent great injury, in this pressing and imperious need it is held that when the highest officer of the corporation engages a physician, the emergency has created in him authority on the company to pay such services."[1]

Emergency implied authority expands an agent's power beyond the agent's usual sphere of authority. Typically, the principal is unavailable for quick consultation needed for the extension of the agent's ex-

press authority to deal with the emergency need. Additional emergency authority is implied because some factor beyond the principal's or agent's control is likely to damage or cause the principal a loss. For example, the authority of Perry's agent might be expanded if drastic market price changes occur in the raw materials used to make widgets. A resort manager usually forbidden from making changes in capital assets would probably have emergency authority to repair a boat dock if it became detached from its mooring and floated into the water. Figure 36–2 illustrates actual authority.

Apparent Authority and Estoppel

In some situations, an agent's powers are expanded neither by agreement with the principal nor by custom or emergency. Under the doctrine of **apparent authority** or **ostensible authority**, authority may be created or expanded when the principal causes third parties to reasonably believe the agent has authority. Even a volunteer nonagent may be authorized if the principal holds out the purported agent as having authority. In such cases, the agent has this *power* to contract but has no legal *right* to affect the principal's legal relationships.

Where a principal's words or inaction makes it appear to reasonably acting third parties that the purported agent has authority, the agent will be authorized. This *holding-out* is effective to authorize the agent but only in contracts with third parties who

---

[1] *Vandalia Railroad Co. v. Bryan*, 110 N.E. 218 (1950).

Figure 36–2   Agent's Actual Authority

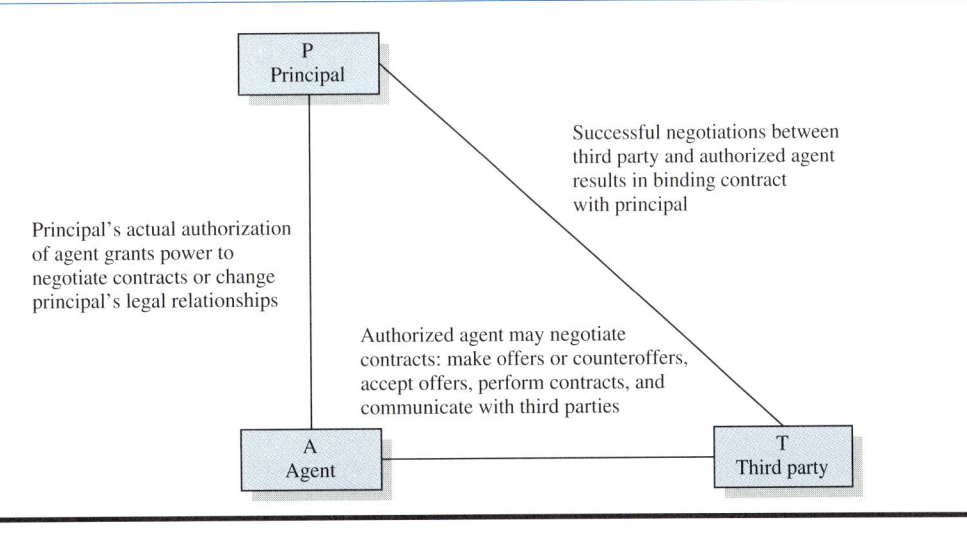

Figure 36–3   Agent's Apparent Authority

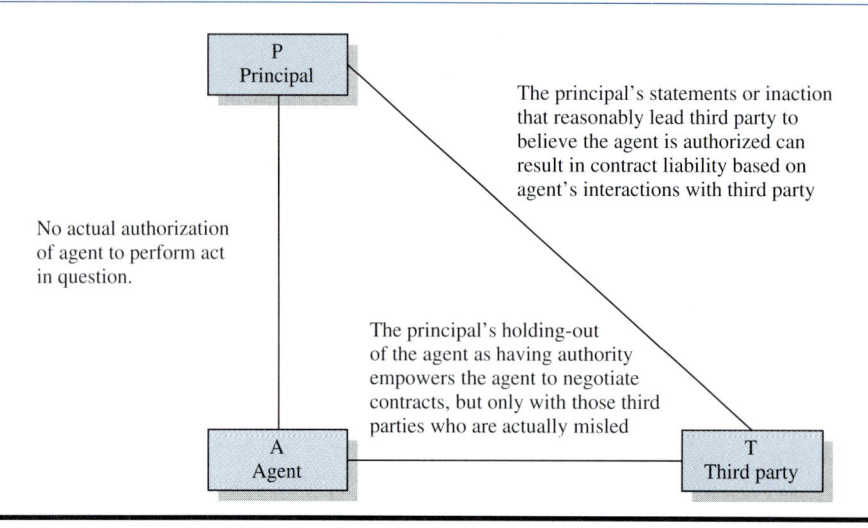

are aware of the principal's holding-out. For example, assume a jewelry store owner requests the accounting clerk to watch the store while the owner temporarily leaves. Although the clerk usually had no sales authority, the owner's action cloaks the clerk with the authority of an agent, thereby authorizing the clerk's sales. The store may be bound by the apparent agent's sales if such circumstances lead customers to reasonably believe the clerk was authorized. Apparent authority is created by the principal's actions and is implemented by the agent's voluntary action. Figure 36–3 illustrates apparent authority.

Agents may also be empowered by a theory similar to apparent authority. The doctrine of **estoppel** applies where the principal's words, conduct, or lack of action makes it appear to reasonable third parties that the purported agent has authority. For estoppel to apply, the third party (or parties) must know of the principal's representations and change his or her position in reliance on these appearances. Estoppel requires proof that the third party took some action in reliance on the principal's representations. For example, assume a supplier negotiated a contract to sell parts to Perry's company with Andrew, Perry's accountant. Although Andrew was not actually authorized to negotiate supply contracts, Perry's statements to the supplier could be reasonably believed by the supplier as authorizing Andrew. If the supplier ceased looking for other customers for these parts and Perry disavowed Andrew's contract, the supplier's reliance on Perry's representations was reasonable. The supplier's failure to shop elsewhere constituted a change of position, so that Perry would nevertheless be bound in contract with the supplier under agency by estoppel. A third party's change in position may result from the payment of money, the expenditure of labor, the third party's termination of negotiations with other customers or vendors, the third party's suffering of a loss, or any other action that subjects the third party to legal liability.[2] What did the principal do in the following case to lead third parties to believe the agent had authority?

---

[2] *Restatement (Second) of Agency* § 8.

LUNDBERG v. CHURCH FARMS INC.
502 N.E.2d 806 (Ill. App. 1986)

Church Farms of Manteno, Illinois, was owned by Gilbert Church. Advertisements to sell breeding rights in Church's stallion, Imperial Guard, advised third parties to inquire with Herb Bagley, the manager of Church Farms who lived at Church Farms. Vern Lundberg contacted Bagley because Herb was the only employee available at the Church Farms premises. Lundberg negotiated a contract with Church Farms through Bagley for a two-year breeding right including a syndication agreement covering Imperial Guard. During the contract performance, Gilbert Church moved Imperial Guard away from the Church Farms location. Lundberg sued Church Farms for this breach of contract and Church responded that Bagley was unauthorized to sign breeding contracts in the name of Church Farms. Church appealed from a trial court judgment for Lundberg.

UNVERZAGI, J.

The party asserting an agency has the burden of proving its existence, but may do so by inference and circumstantial evidence. Additionally, an agent may bind his principal by acts which the principal has not given him actual authority to perform, but which he appears authorized to perform. An agent's apparent authority is that authority which "the principal knowingly permits the agent to assume or which he holds his agent as possessing. It is the authority that a reasonably prudent man, exercising diligence and discretion, in view of the principal's conduct, would naturally suppose the agent to possess." The agent's authority must be derived from some act or statement of the principal. Defendant argues that plaintiffs' proof is based on Bagley's own assertion of authority rather than the acts or statements of Church Farms or Gil Church. We disagree.

The plaintiffs produced evidence at trial that Gil Church approved the Imperial Guard advertisement listing Herb Bagley as Church Farms' manager, and directing all inquiries to him. Church also permitted Bagley to live on the farm and to handle its daily operations. Bagley was the only person available to visitors to the farm. Bagley answered Church Farms' phone calls, and there was a pre-printed signature line for him on the breeding rights package.

The conclusion is inescapable that Gil Church affirmatively placed Bagley in a managerial position giving him complete control of Church Farms in its dealing with the public. We believe that this is just the sort of "holding out" of an agent by a principal that justifies a third person's reliance on the agent's authority. We cannot accept defendants contention that the Lundbergs were affirmatively obligated to seek out Church to ascertain the actual extent of Bagley's authority.

Case Questions

1. What is the issue about the conduct of Church Farms and Gilbert Church concerning Herb Bagley's authority?

2. What reasons support the law recognizing apparent authority or estoppel?

3. What assumptions are made by the court's application of the apparent authority doctrine concerning third parties' expectations (such as those of the Lundbergs) in dealing with a person such as Herb Bagley?

4. How can a principal prevent the extension of additional authority such as Church Farms suffered in the preceding case?

Secret Limitations

The doctrines of apparent authority or inherent authority may apply where an agent is clothed with apparent general authority but the principal has secretly specified limitations on the agent's authority. In such situations, if a third party can reasonably infer the agent would have authority to do a particular act, then the secret limitation is ineffective if the third party is unaware and the contracts negotiated by that agent are nevertheless enforceable. Assume in the jewelry store example that the store owner secretly prohibited the clerk from making any sales and the clerk was always on duty during operating hours. The clerk would have apparent or inherent authority to make sales, at least for stock on hand at listed prices.

Lingering Apparent Authority and Notice

As discussed in Chapter 35, an agent's actual authority is extinguished when the principal terminates the agency relationship. However, this may not completely terminate the principal's exposure to risk particularly if the agent has further contacts or negotiations with third parties. The agent's apparent authority continues after the termination of actual authority until the principal notifies third parties of the termination. This continuing authority is known as **lingering apparent authority**. Direct personal notice must be given to all third parties with whom the agent directly dealt during the term of the agency. However, persons who may have known of the agency but who never actually contracted nor extended credit to the principal through the agent are not entitled to direct personal notice. **Public notice** given by the principal to the general public is sufficient if announced in a newspaper of general circulation in all the areas in which the agent acted for the principal.

Persons unaware of the agency are usually not entitled to notice. No notice is required when the principal dies. Perhaps the principal's death is such a notorious event that most everyone in a small community learns of it. A few states have passed statutes preserving the notice requirement when the principal dies. Before notice is given, the principal's breach of the former agent's unauthorized contract can be satisfied out of the principal's estate. Most states also dispense with the notice requirement where the principal becomes insane or bankrupt or when war breaks out between the nations of principal and agent.

Ratification

While actual authority is usually given before the agent acts, it may also be conferred afterwards. **Ratification** is the principal's adoption of the agent's previously unauthorized act. Ratification arises in two general situations: (1) an agent exceeds the lim-ited authority granted, or (2) a nonagent purports to act as agent for another. In these situations, a principal may supply the needed authority afterwards.

Relation Back

Authority by ratification is actually a legal fiction because the third party is bound to a contract made when the agent had no authority. For example, if an unauthorized agent negotiates a contract on July 1 and the principal ratifies the contract on July 15, after ratification, the law presumes the transaction was originally authorized on July 1. However, fairness dictates that the third party may withdraw from the contract at any time after it is made and before the principal ratifies. This prevents the principal from ratifying after the third party withdraws so any attempted ratification has no retroactive effect. Figure 36–4 illustrates this.

Requirements for Ratification

The principal's retroactive authorization is effective only when the requirements for ratification are satisfied. First, the agent's action must be one that the principal could have done lawfully. For example, while it may appear that an unauthorized agent's forged signature on a document appears illegal, the act could be ratified because the principal is legally entitled to sign. Of course, the purported agent could be held liable for criminal forgery and liable in tort for the principal's losses. Second, the purported agent's act must be intended to benefit the principal. Third, the third party must have a reasonable belief that the agent is authorized to act for the principal's benefit. Fourth, the principal may ratify an act only if the principal has full knowledge of the facts and

Figure 36–4   Ratification: Relation-Back Doctrine

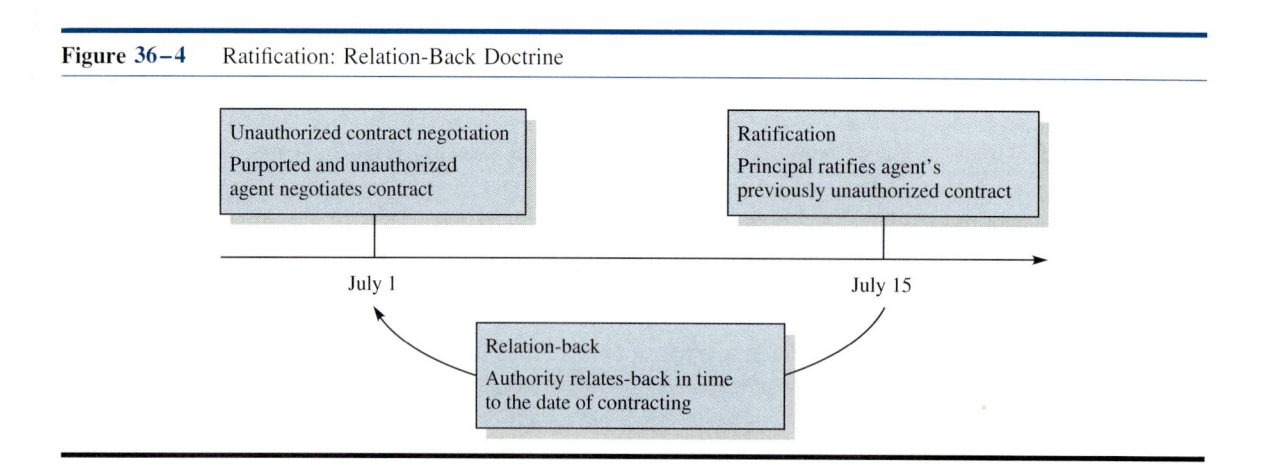

circumstances. Finally, a ratification is effective only if the principal approves the entire transaction, not just the most favorable parts. Ratification of a portion of the agent's contract is ineffective. If the statute of frauds applies to the contract negotiated by the agent, ratification must also be in writing under the equal dignities rule.

Requirements for Ratification

1. Agent's act must be one the principal could have done personally.
2. Agent's act must be intended to benefit the principal.
3. Third party must reasonably believe agent is authorized.
4. Principal's ratification must be based on full knowledge of the circumstances.
5. Principal must approve entire transaction.

Implied Ratification

A principal's ratification may be made by express verbal or written conduct, or it may be inferred from the principal's conduct. Ratification is implied from the principal's silence or retention of benefits. For example, the principal will have ratified the unauthorized agent's order of goods if the principal accepts and uses them. The principal is not required to disavow an agent's purported contract unless the principal uses the goods. One person cannot force another person to act. Therefore, the agent's unauthorized contracting cannot force the principal to renounce the contract unless the principal exercises control over the goods.

Restatement (Second) of Agency § 94b

[A]cquiescence can be inferred from silence even though the purported agent had theretofore been a stranger to the purported principal. Nevertheless, the latter's silence is usually more significant if an agent has exceeded his powers in the particular transaction.

A more common form of implied ratification occurs where the principal receives and retains benefits from the third party's contract with full knowledge of the transaction. A ratification is implied if the principal receives the delivery of goods or services, knows they came from the third party, and knowingly uses them. However, if the principal is physically unable to return the benefits, then no ratification will be implied. For example, if, unknown to Perry, one of his employees engages a cleaning service to provide maintenance on Perry's property while Perry is absent, Perry cannot return these benefits after later discovering them. A principal who innocently receives property that has become an inseparable part of the principal's property, such as a fixture built into real estate, is also free to retain these benefits; no ratification is implied.

BRADSHAW v. MCBRIDE
649 P.2d 784 (Utah Sup. Ct. 1982)

Aretta Parkinson transferred the Parkinson farm to her eight children. Roma Funk, one of Parkinson's daughters, orally negotiated to sell the Parkinson farm to Barbara Bradshaw. Thereafter, Funk hired a real estate broker to close the transaction by preparing an earnest money agreement and warranty deeds to convey the Parkinson farm. None of the Parkinson children signed the earnest money agreement and only three of the eight children signed the warranty deed. Thereafter, the Bradshaws took possession of the farm but most of the Parkinson children refused to convey their interests in the farm. The children appealed from a trial court decision granting specific performance of the oral sale contract holding that the children ratified Roma Funk's oral contract by failing to repudiate it.

STEWART, J.

A principal may impliedly or expressly ratify an agreement made by an unauthorized agent. Ratifi cation of an agent's acts relates back to the time the unauthorized act occurred and is sufficient to create a relationship of principal and agent. A deliberate and valid ratification with full knowledge of all the material facts is binding and cannot afterward be revoked or recalled. However, a ratification requires the principal to have knowledge of all material facts and intent to ratify. Under some circumstances, failure to disaffirm may constitute ratification of the agent's acts. Quoting Williston on contracts:

> Ratification like original authority [need] not be expressed. Any conduct which indicates assent by the purported principal to become a party to the transaction is sufficient. Even silence with full knowledge of the facts may manifest affirmance and thus operate as ratification. The person with whom the agent dealt will so obviously be deceived by assuming the professed agent was authorized to act as such that the principal is under a duty to undeceive him. So a purported principal may not be willfully ignorant nor may he purposely shut his eyes to means of information within his possession and control and thereby escape ratification.

The trial court found that the defendants other than Funk had ratified the Funk-Bradshaw agreement in part, by their knowledge and acceptance of the agreement. This finding, however, is not clearly supported by the evidence in the record as to defendants who were not notified of the agreement until receipt of the warranty deeds prepared by [the real estate agent]. Funk testified that she did not contact her brother Foch or John Lister [administrator of one of Parkinson's children's estate]. Foch testified that when he first learned of the agreement he was opposed to it, but was willing to go along with the agreement only if the court found it enforceable. He continually stated his objection to the agreement, and his actions cannot be interpreted as ratification. John Lister testified that he did not become aware of the agreement until he received the real estate doc-

uments from Hansen. Lister did not sign the documents and did nothing to ratify the agreement between Funk and Bradshaw. When presented with a writing to convey ownership and property, Lister had no duty to disavow any putative agreement. On the contrary, his failure to sign is evidence of rejection. It is clear that neither Foch nor Lister in fact ratified the agreement.

Furthermore, there was no ratification as a matter of law because the Utah statute of frauds requires that any agent executing an agreement conveying an interest in land on behalf of his principal must be authorized in writing. In order to enforce an oral agreement, the same kind of authorization that is required to clothe an agent initially with authority with contract must be given by the principal to constitute a ratification of an unauthorized act. Where the law requires the authority to be given in writing, the ratification must also be in writing. [The Bradshaw's possession of the Parkinson farm did not satisfy the part performance doctrine under the statute of frauds, so a written contract and ratification were necessary. Because there was no ratification in this case, judgment for the Bradshaws is reversed in favor of the Parkinson children.]

Case Questions

1. What is the issue in the preceding case? What critical facts were missing in the allegation that the Parkinson children authorized the sale of the farm?

2. What reasons support the court's finding? Are these convincing?

3. What other facts might be necessary to change the outcome?

An agent whose authority is specifically limited by the principal may not disregard this limitation except in an emergency. As discussed in Chapter 35, the agent is liable for disobedience to the principal's directives. The third parties are also bound by limitations on an agent's authority if they know of the limitation. For example, assume the principal specifies in writing that the agent may not convey the principal's real estate to a buyer until the buyer successfully produces a good credit report. Assume the third party knows of this limitation. If the third party has poor credit but the agent nevertheless conveys

the property, the principal is not bound and may rescind the sale. Third parties are generally expected to recognize the apparent limitations of corporate officers or government officials because they ordinarily have only limited authority.

Third Party's Duty to Determine Authority

Usually, a third party cannot simply rely on the agent's claim of authority to represent a principal. Principals are not liable on contracts negotiated by an unauthorized agent unless an apparent authority or ratification occurs. This usually means that third parties must inquire into the agent's authority or run the risk that the agent is unauthorized and the contract will be unenforceable. For example, when a home owner lists the residence for sale with a real estate broker, the broker is usually authorized only to communicate offers and acceptances between the buyer and the seller. If the real estate agent purports to have authority to sell the house at a price lower than the listing price, the home seller will usually not be bound on a contract with a third-party purchaser. Therefore, third parties should inquire into an agent's authority and may need to demand written assurances or speak directly with the principal to eliminate this risk.

Soliciting Agent

A question often arises whether sales personnel have authority to contract for the principal by negotiating the terms of sale. Generally, a retail salesperson has authority only to sell goods out of inventory at the listed price and has no additional authority to negotiate lower prices, to agree to unusual terms, or to sell more than the number of goods held in inventory. Traveling field personnel are further limited in most situations to simply soliciting orders. They cannot bind their principal to contract on any terms. Such limitations are often evident on the order form the salesperson uses, which may include a disclaimer reserving power to the principal to approve the order.

Common Disclaimer in Order Forms

Customer orders not binding until the offer is accepted at the home office.

The authority of sales personnel is often limited for two reasons. First, where sales involve extending credit to the third-party purchaser, the principal prefers to conduct a credit investigation before completing the sale. Second, the principal may wish to avoid a stockout that could arise if field sales personnel oversold the principal's inventory. This could damage the principal if replacement inventory was unavailable or had higher cost. By reserving the power to accept the contract, the principal ensures that goods sold or services promised will be available in sufficient quantities and at reasonable cost to have profitable business. Therefore, when a soliciting sales agent receives a third party's buyers order, this generally constitutes an offer. Before the principal accepts this offer, the third party may generally withdraw or revoke the offer unless it is a firm offer or the principal has an option contract.

Authority to Hire Subagent

Generally, an agent may not delegate the authority granted by the principal unless special circumstances exist. In most instances, the agent's services are considered unique and therefore nondelegable under contract law. The agent's personal characteristics, skills, integrity, and financial condition are essential in the parties' relationship. However, in many situations, the principal may tolerate or even encourage the agent to hire subagents. **Subagents** are agents of the principal appointed by the first agent. Both the agent and the principal can ratify any contract made by a subagent. The subagent owes fiduciary duties to both the principal and the agent.

Agents can be authorized to hire subagents in several situations. First, the principal can expressly authorize the appointment of a subagent. For example, when a homeowner lists the residence with a real estate agency, the listing contract commonly permits any licensed broker working for the agency to represent the homeowner in a home sale. Second, in emergency situations, the agent may appoint a subagent. For example, if the agent becomes ill and the principal's business begins to deteriorate, a subagent may be hired. Third, usages in the principal's trade or prior conduct between the principal and the agent may have permitted the agent to hire subagents in the past. This authorizes the agent to hire subagents in the future unless the principal specifically withdraws this right in the future. For example, an attorney in fact with the power of attorney to generally represent the principal's business may hire a real estate agent to sell property for the principal. Fourth, the character of the business may suggest that certain nondiscretionary, mechanical, or ministerial duties can be delegated to a subagent. For example, an independent agent representing numerous principals can be expected to hire employees to conduct nondiscretionary activities.

CONTRACT LIABILITY OF AGENT

The agent's contract liability is determined largely by analyzing the same authorization questions discussed above in the principal's contract liability. The primary inquiry is whether the agent had authority to contract for the principal. The next inquiry may focus on the agent's implied warranty of authority. Regardless of these inquiries, the agent may separately assume liability apart from the principal's liability. A few limited circumstances give the third party a choice to hold either the principal or the agent liable.

Conduit Theory

In most situations, the agent acts primarily to extend the principal's reach by directly affecting the principal's business. Most agents do not want personal liability on contracts negotiated for the principal. Usually, all three parties — principal, agent, and third party — fully understand that the agent assumes only a representative status. The **conduit theory** explains how authorized agents avoid contract liability to the third party. When the principal authorizes an agent to negotiate contracts, the agent simply acts as a conduit through whom the principal communicates with third parties.

For example, when a corporate purchasing agent negotiates contracts with a supplier to acquire component parts, only the purchasing corporation and the outside supplier are bound together in contract. The purchasing agent will have no personal contract liability because the agent acts only as a conduit through whom communications flow between the supplier and the customer. Typically, none of the three parties expects the agent to be liable if the customer corporation fails to pay its bill. The purchasing agent usually has no rights against the supplier should it fail to make timely and conforming deliveries. The following sections discuss the agent's liability under the conduit theory and limited exceptions when the agent has personal liability.

Unauthorized Contracts

Agents expect third parties to believe two things: (1) the agent works for an existing principal, and (2) the principal authorized the agent to act. If the principal truly exists and has authorized the agent's conduct, the third party suffers no harm. However, if the agent is unauthorized or no principal exists, the third party may suffer damage. In other words, the third party is misled by the agent's representations or appearances and the contract is negotiated for the principal when the agent is really unauthorized.

The third party may reveal confidential information to the agent during negotiations. If no principal exists, the agent could misuse this information. If the third party believes the agent is authorized, negotiations with other principals may be discontinued. In either case, the purported agent misrepresents that a principal exists and this may injure the third party. Therefore, the law usually gives the third party a remedy against the agent if there is no principal or the agent is unauthorized. Similar problems arise if an agent exceeds a limited grant of authority.

Implied Warranty of Authority

The principal has no contract liability for acts of an unauthorized agent unless an apparent authority or ratification occurs. No act by an unauthorized agent can bind the principal. Because of this, the law has developed two theories to protect third-party expectations in such situations. First, most states imply that agents make a warranty of authority. If the agent has sufficient authority, the implied warranty of authority is superfluous. However, if the agent is totally unauthorized or has only limited authority, the third party has a basis to seek damages from the purported agent.

An alternative theory exists in many states permitting the third party to sue the purported agent for damages: the tort of fraud or deceit. The third party must prove that the purported agent claimed to represent a principal and the third party relied on those representations. Under either theory, the third party may win damages if confidences are revealed to an unauthorized agent or contract negotiations with another principal were terminated.

Nonexistent Principal

Agents are typically liable whenever they purport to act for a principal who does not actually exist at the time of negotiations. Of course, in such situations, the purported agent is not actually an agent at all but only claims to be an agent. This situation is known as a **nonexistent principal** situation.

A common class of nonexistent principals includes situations in which the agent purports to act for an organization that has no recognized legal status. For example, agents of unincorporated associations such as some charities, religious organizations and churches, labor unions, clubs, fraternities, and the like are not separate legal entities unless they are organized as a corporation, or a special statute recognizes them as unincorporated associations. The purported agent is personally liable for contracts made for the benefit of an unincorporated association because they are not legal entities. Organizations can overcome this problem by establishing a ''building corporation'' or other special organization under state law. This permits the conduit theory to apply so that the members or agents who contract for construction, maintenance, repair, and operation of these facilities have no personal liability. For example, most college fraternities are unincorporated associations but have a building corporation operated by their alumni to hold legal title to the fraternity house and operate the fraternity or sorority.

Purported agents also represent nonexistent principals during the creation of new corporations. **Corporate promoters** initially organize corporations by making various contracts to raise capital, hire lawyers, accountants, and other consultants, purchase and lease real estate, and acquire inventory. Promoters represent a nonexistent principal until the corporation is formally organized. Even thereafter, the promoter retains personal liability on preincorporation contracts until the corporation adopts or ratifies the promotion contracts. This subject is discussed in greater detail in Chapter 40.

The third party and the purported agent may discuss such problems during negotiations. If the third party understands and accepts the agent's tenuous status, this may release the agent from liability. When the third party understands that no principal exists, there can be no reliance necessary for the third party's claim of damages. There are even a few states where the agent is not liable if the third party can easily discover that the principal is nonexistent.

Authorized Contracts

In most situations, the third party knows that the agent is merely a representative of a known principal. Commonly, the third party is interested in contracting through the agent because of the principal's reputation for reliable service and/or quality products. Many agents use letterhead, brochures, business cards, or verbal representations identifying the principal to take advantage of the principal's goodwill and reputation.

However, in limited situations, the principal or agent may find it advantageous not to reveal the principal's identity. For example, the principal may desire anonymity. Agents are not generally required to identify their principal, so they sometimes purport to act personally. For example, the principal may insist the agent keep the principal's identity confidential. Some agents go even further and negotiate contracts as if no principal exists at all. However, so long as the agent is authorized, a binding contract results between the third party and the unknown principal. The third party's knowledge about the principal's existence or identity may take three forms: disclosed principal, partially disclosed principal, and undisclosed principal.

Disclosed Principal

A principal whose existence and identity are known to the third party is a **disclosed principal**. In such cases, the agent acts as a mere conduit and has no contract liability unless the agent cosigns or co-makes the contract. The disclosed principal is liable on authorized contracts even if the agent does not communicate the precise terms or the third party's identity to the principal. In most situations, the agent has a duty to inform the principal of material matters affecting the agency. However, the agent's failure to inform does not affect the enforceability of the contract between the principal and the third party. This rule applies even if the agent is unauthorized and the principal later ratifies. Of course, either the principal or the third party may withdraw before ratification.

Partially Disclosed Principal

In some unusual situations, the agent may concede that a principal exists but refuse to divulge the principal's identity. The law does not require the agent to identify a principal even if the third party requests it. While the agent may be liable for misrepresenting the principal's identity, the agent is free to maintain confidentiality. For example, an expert real estate agent may be hired by a principal to acquire land secretly. A principal may desire confidentiality to avoid the third party's heightened expectations about the purchase price.

From the third party's perspective, the identity of the principal may have little significance in many situations. Most contracting parties are indifferent about the other party's identity unless the principal's personal characteristics are important for performance. For example, the principal's creditworthiness or reputation would be important in a personal service contract. By contrast, if there are adequate assurances of reliable performance, the principal's identity is usually irrelevant. For example, a third-party supplier would usually be satisfied dealing with an unidentified principal if the whole purchase price was placed in escrow. However, the third party could suffer damage if it halted advertising to sell property because it believed a sale was completed to an unidentified principal but the principal later breached the contract. In these situations, the third party may need additional assurance of performance. The agent might be coaxed to cosign the contract to provide assurance to the third party, and some states hold the agent liable while the principal remains partially disclosed.

Undisclosed Principal

Both the identity and existence of an **undisclosed principal** is unknown by the third party. This means the third party believes only the agent is the other party to the contract. Typically, the agent never even suggests that a principal exists by acting as if the agent will perform personally. An undisclosed principal, like a partially disclosed principal, often seeks anonymity to guard against the third party's heightened hopes in negotiations over price. Financially well-to-do principals generally believe that if third parties know the principal's identity, they will inflate the purchase price.

Election between Principal or Agent Liability

The third party's expectations are protected by the election doctrine. The principal is bound in contract to the third party even though the principal's existence and identity are undisclosed so long as the agent is authorized. To protect the third party's expectations, the third party may elect to hold either the principal or the agent liable for breach of contract. However, the third party may not hold both principal and agent liable. This rule has caused some procedural difficulties because initially, the third party only knows the agent's identity. Sometimes during pretrial discovery the third party may compel the agent to reveal the principal's identity or the third party's investigator discovers the principal's identity. Thereafter, the third party can assess whether the principal or the agent is financially better able to satisfy a judgment. To further protect the third party, courts typically permit the third party to add or substitute the principal to the suit after the principal is identified. However, when the third party learns of the principal's identity and takes the suit to judgment, the suit itself constitutes an election and the third party is barred from later suing the other party.

VAN D. COSTAS INC. v. ROSENBERG
432 So.2d 656 (Fla. Ct. App. 1983)

The Magic Moment Restaurant contracted with Van D. Costas, Inc., to provide construction services on the Magic Moment Restaurant building. Magic Moment Restaurant was owned by Seascape Restaurants, Inc., of which Rosenberg was president and a part owner. The construction contract was signed by Rosenberg, and "Jeff Rosenberg, The Magic Moment" was typed under his signature. The parties disputed both the performance by Van D. Costas and payment by Seascape Restaurants. Van D. Costas sued Rosenberg for the breach of construction contract. Rosenberg defended that as an agent, he was a mere conduit so only Seascape was liable as owner of the Magic Moment Restaurant. Van D. Costas contends Seascape was an undisclosed principal, so Rosenberg may be held individually liable. Van D. Costas appealed from a trial court ruling that Rosenberg was not liable.

GRIMES, Judge

It is well settled that where one enters into a contract as agent for an undisclosed principal, he may be held liable on the contract.

In order for an agent to avoid personal liability on a contract negotiated in his principal's behalf, he must disclose not only he is an agent but also the identity of his principal, regardless of whether the third party knows he was acting in a representative capacity. It is not the third person's duty to seek out the identity of the principal; rather, the duty to disclose the identity of the principal is on the agent. The use of a trade name is not necessarily an official disclosure of the identity of the principal and the fact of agency so as to protect the agent against personal liability.[3]

[The following quote] discusses the liability of the agent under circumstances in which it appears that he is acting for someone else but the identity of his principal is unknown to the other party.

Principal Partially Disclosed

Unless otherwise agreed, a person purporting to make a contract with another for a partially disclosed principal is a party to the contract.

COMMENT: A. A principal is a partially disclosed principal when, at the time of making the contract in question, the other party thereto has noticed that the agent is acting for a principal but has no notice of the principal's identity. The fact that, to the knowledge of the agent, the other party does not know the identity of the principal is of great weight in ascribing to the other party the intention to hold the agent liable either solely or as a surety or co-promisor with the principal. The inference of an understanding that the agent is a party to the contract exists unless the agent gives such complete information concerning his principal's identity that he can be readily distinguished. If the other party has no reasonable means of ascertaining the principal, the inference is almost irresistible and prevails in the absence of agreement to the contrary.[4]

---

[3] 3 Am.Jr.2d Agency § 320 (1962).

[4] *Restatement (Second) of Agency* § 321.

Of course, if the contracting party knows the identity of the principal, the principal is deemed to be disclosed. A dispute concerning such knowledge presents an issue of fact. Here, however, nothing indicates that appellant had ever heard of Seascape at the time the contract was signed. Subsequent knowledge of the true principal is irrelevant where performance of an indivisible contract has commenced. The trial court emphasized that Costas drafted the contract. However, it was not incumbent upon him to ferret out the record ownership of Magic Moment when he had every reason to believe that one of the owners was signing the contract. Rosenberg knew that the owner was Seascape, and he had it within his power to avoid personal liability by properly disclosing his principal. The law holds Rosenberg legally responsible.

Case Questions

1. Identify the agent, the principal, its owner, and the trade name referred to in the preceding case.

2. What assumption underlies the rule that the use of a trademark or trade name in a contract negotiated or signed by the agent does not sufficiently give the third party notice of the principal's identity? Why should this provide a reason to make the agent liable to the third party?

3. Under what circumstances should the law find it wrongful for the agent to conceal the principal's identity from the third party? How should the law deal with such situations?

Agent's Assumption of Liability

While the third party may elect to hold either the principal or agent liable if the principal's existence is undisclosed, the agent's potential liability can be made explicit in the contract. A contract negotiated by the agent may specifically state that the agent is also liable as a cosigner or comaker. For example, it may become necessary for Perry's agent to guarantee Perry's performance before a third party would willingly contract. Banks often require a close corporation's officer or president to cosign a loan made to the corporation. Whenever an agent cosigns or comakes a contract with an outsider, the agent actually becomes a coprincipal. Courts generally require clear proof that the agent intended to be primarily liable before the agent will be held liable as a comaker.

Third-Party Liability Where Principal Undisclosed

Third parties are bound in contract to the undisclosed principal unless the contract requires the agent to perform personal services or the third party's assent rests on special confidence placed in the agent. The agent of an undisclosed principal may usually enforce the principal's contract against the third party. However, the agent must relinquish this right to the principal because the principal's rights are superior to the agent's rights.

The agent is entitled to indemnification from the principal for the costs of defending suits brought by a third party. However, the agent's indemnification right may be of little value if the principal becomes insolvent or disappears. The agent may reduce this risk by taking possession of the principal's property, by acquiring a security interest (lien), or by requiring a performance bond. Third parties may reduce their risk of dealing with an undisclosed principal by including language in the contract in which the agent is verified as the principal in the transaction.

The principal's identity may also be significant to the third party if the third party has strong animosity toward the principal. In certain situations, the law permits the third party to rescind a contract authorized by an unidentified principal if the third party shows that ill will, hatred, or mistrust would be fundamental to the third party's decision not to contract. However, this third-party right to rescind may be avoided if the agent simply assigns the contract to the principal thereafter. Of course, the contract of sale can also specifically be made nonassignable. Figure 36–5 illustrates the agent's liability on contracts.

TORT LIABILITY

Although contract liability has thus far been the primary focus in agency law, tort liability also demands close attention. A principal risks tort liability for the acts of agents and other employees. The concept of **vicarious liability** places ultimate responsibility for an agent's torts on the principal.

The analysis of tort liability typically designates the principal as the **master** and the employee or agent as a **servant**. The risks inherent in using agents leads to three types of liability. First, the master's direct liability results from the master's own intentional or negligent conduct that harms the servant or third parties. Second, the servant's negligent or intentional misconduct leads to the servant's direct liability. Third, the law has developed vicarious liability under the doctrine of respondeat superior, which holds the master indirectly liable for torts committed by the servant.

Master's Direct Liability

Every person is personally and directly responsible for his or her own torts. A master who personally commits negligent or intentional harm to third parties has **direct liability**. Masters must supervise their servants, agents, and employees or face direct liability for negligent supervision.

The master's direct liability can arise from conduct beyond the master's personal misdoings. Liability for third parties' injuries increases when the master hires incompetents or criminals. The master

must give servants proper instructions, provide safe and sufficient work facilities, and supervise servants to ensure that they perform competent and quality work. A **negligent entrustment** arises when a firm permits its employees to use defective equipment that injures third parties. Liability directly results from a firm's insufficient instruction to employees on the use of the firm's equipment. All persons, both employees and third parties, must be supervised and safeguarded from improper use of equipment or facilities.

Restatement (Second) of Agency § 213

A person conducting activities through servants or other agents is subject to liability for harm resulting from his conduct if he is negligent or reckless:

(a) in giving improper or ambiguous orders or in failing to make regulations or

(b) in the employment of improper persons or instrumentalities in work involving risk or harm to others:

i. in the supervision of the activities; or

ii. permitting or failing to prevent, negligent or other tortious conduct by persons whether or not his servants or agents upon premises or with instrumentalities under his control.

The master is also directly liable for authorizing the servant's tortious activity. For example, a tavern owner has direct liability for injuries resulting from instructing the "bouncer" to physically remove a rowdy patron. Similarly, a firm that instructs its employees to make false representations in negotiating contracts has direct tort liability for fraud.

Servant's Direct Liability

Agents are ultimately liable for their own torts: All persons must act responsibly. There is direct liability for servants who fail to act with due care or who make intentional aggressions. Servants have direct liability even if acting for or under the direction of the employer. For example, an agent who falsely represents the principal's business is liable for fraud even if the master is also liable directly or vicariously. However, agents are not directly liable for intentional torts unless the agent intended the misrepresentation.

An agent is not liable for failing to exercise special privileges that belong to the principal. These might include defending the principal's property or using the principal's right of entry on the land of

Figure 36–5   Agency Authority and Contract Liability

Agent's Authority	Disclosed Principal	Partially Disclosed Principal	Undisclosed Principal
Actual Authority: Express	Principal and third party liable. Agent not liable unless otherwise agreed.	Third party's election to hold either principal or agent liable. Third party liable unless personal services or ill will between third party and principal.	Third party's election to hold either principal or agent liable. Third party liable unless personal services or ill will between third party and principal.
Actual Authority: Implied	Principal and third party liable. Agent not liable unless otherwise agreed.	Third party's election to hold either principal or agent liable. Third party liable unless personal services or ill will between third party and principal.	Third party's election to hold either principal or agent liable. Third party liable unless personal services or ill will between third party and principal.
Apparent Authority	Principal and third party liable. Agent not liable unless otherwise agreed.	Third party's election to hold either principal or agent liable. Third party liable unless personal services or ill will between third party and principal.	Impossible.
Ratification	Agent liable until ratification. Third party may rescind before ratification. After ratification, third party bound unless personal services or ill will with principal.	Agent liable until ratification. Third party may rescind before ratification. After ratification, third party bound unless personal services or ill will with principal. Principal or agent liable by third party's election.	Agent liable until ratification. Third party may rescind before ratification. After ratification, third party bound unless personal services or ill will with principal. Principal or agent liable by third party's election.
Unauthorized Agent	Principal not liable. Agent liable for third party's damages. Third party may rescind contract.	Principal not liable. Agent liable for third party's damages. Third party may rescind contract.	Principal not liable. Agent liable for third party's damages. Third party may rescind contract.

another. Many courts hold both the master and servant **jointly and severally** liable for torts committed by the servant. This means the third party is entitled to collect the entire judgment from either or both the master and/or the servant. However, only one recovery is permitted. If either the master or the servant must pay a judgment, the right of indemnity may permit contribution from the other.

Respondeat Superior

The doctrine of vicarious liability is one of the most important elements of agency law. It holds that the master or employer will be held liable for torts committed by the servant or employee when acting within the scope of the servant's employment. When a master chooses to expand its business by employing others, its responsibility is also expanded. The term **respondeat superior** makes the master liable for the servant's misdeeds. While the servant has the direct liability described above for torts the servant commits, the respondeat superior doctrine shifts the risk of loss from the third party to either the master or the servant. The law usually requires the servant to indemnify the master for tort judgments the master is required to pay to third parties that result from the servant's torts. Of course, much of this problem is reduced by the availability of liability insurance, used extensively for vehicles driven in the master's business. Third parties who sue the master for the servant's torts generally must prove two elements: (1) that there was a master-servant relationship and (2) that the servant's tort was committed within the scope of employment.

*The Rationales for Vicarious Tort Liability: Respondeat Superior**

Since the late 17th century, the common law has recognized the master's financial responsibility for torts committed by its servants.[†] This is a form of vicarious liability known as *respondeat superior*, a term that literally means "let the superior respond." Employers, known as masters in the language of tort liability analysis, are liable for the torts their servants commit while acting within the scope of their employment. This rule of law shifts the risk of harm to the employer so it raises controversial economic and ethical issues that deserve close examination.

Vicarious tort liability is a public policy intended to protect the outside third parties who are affected by a business' activities when conducted through its agents. Several social and economic arguments are often cited to support vicarious liability. First, as the primary beneficiary of a servant's acts, the master's business should also accept all the burdens. Similarly, economists often argue that to obtain the goal of true efficiency, every economic actor must internalize, that is accept personally the whole burden of all costs generated by their activity. Economic actors who *externalize* their costs cause side effects that can harm some or all of society. Tort and economic theory provide that such losses should not be borne by a single victim who had no control or benefit from another's activity. When someone fails to bear the "wealth effects" of their activity they have less incentive to act innovatively, carefully, or efficiently. Respondeat superior motivates careful administration by placing the economic burden of servants' activities on their employers.

A second argument is that the person who is in the best position to select, train, monitor, and supervise their servants' activities should be responsible for the impact of that activity. This is the issue of "control" or fault that is fundamental to most notions of justice. It holds that responsibility rests on the person with the preponderance of authority and influence over whether and how an activity is conducted. Respondeat superior deters masters from permitting their servants to act irresponsibly. Economists recognize this principle by arguing that financial responsibility should fall on the "least-cost provider" of supervision. Thereby, society is burdened with the lowest costs of engaging in that economic activity. The master also benefits when servants are carefully selected, trained, and supervised because a productive workforce raises the efficiency and effectiveness of the master's business. Of course, the servant's direct liability for torts they commit motivates servants to act carefully.

A third rationale for vicarious liability is the *deep pocket theory*. Under it, the person who is in the best position to absorb the loss should pay for harm caused by the activity. Servants typically have fewer resources than their masters so this theory suggests the master should pay for damages the servant causes to outsiders. The master can pass on these costs to customers by raising the price of their products or services. This "socializes" the risk of the servant's activity. The master's products or services will therefore be more accurately priced by including a "premium" to cover losses from the dangerous activity. If this premium becomes too large, other, less costly forms of achieving the activities' objectives will arise

---

*Copyright ©1993 by John W. Bagby.
[†]*Jones v. Hart*, K.B. 642, 90 Eng.Rep. 1255 (1698).

to displace the more costly activity. Today, most masters purchase liability insurance as the method of spreading this risk among all those insured. In addition, conscientious insurers pressure masters and servants to reduce risks and lower the social costs of the activity.

Employers are usually not liable for damages caused by independent contractors. Employers have no right to directly supervise or control an independent contractor's activities. This lack of contact makes it difficult for employers to carefully administer the independent contractor's methods. Therefore, the employer's liability would be far less effective making independent contractor responsibility for their own employees more efficient. Additionally, independent contractors generally have financial depth so they can provide a more direct deep pocket. Independent contractors are most effectively used where they have special expertise which the employer lacks. The employer must be careful not to take too much control over independent contractor activities to avoid unintended vicarious liability.

Thought Questions

1. What reasons support vicarious liability for a servant's torts? Can good criticism be made against any of these reasons? Are there hidden descriptive or value assumptions underlying the justifications for respondeat superior?

2. What reasons support eliminating vicarious liability for servant's torts? What criticism can be made against these reasons?

3. Are there some situations in which the third-party victim should bear some of the loss caused by the servant? In what situations should this be true, and how would you distinguish these situations from those in which the master should be solely liable?

Master-Servant Relationship

The first step in analyzing a respondeat superior problem is to determine whether there is a relationship between the tortfeasor and the alleged master. In other words, is the purported agent a servant of the master or principal? This is the **master-servant relationship,** which must be distinguished from contract relations between an employer and an independent contractor. Independent contractors are solely responsible for their own torts, so their employers usually have no vicarious liability for their torts.

The most fundamental factor in a master-servant relationship is the master's **right of control** over the servant's activities. Employers typically have the right to control both the means a servant uses on the job to carry out the assigned tasks and the end result of the service activity. Employers have no right to control the means used by an independent contractor although the end result is controlled by the contract hiring the independent contractor. Unfortunately, the right to control factor is not as clear-cut as it may seem. It is often complicated by the fact that many servant employees are given broad freedom to execute their job responsibilities. Additionally, some independent contractors obey the dictates of their employer. These facts often make a determination of the right to control elusive, so the law must also look to other factors to define the master-servant relationship.

A preliminary factor is the intent of the employer and the employee. Second, courts examine how much supervision is usually necessary for the type of work performed. Where employees generally receive little supervision, they look more like independent contractors. However, if the employer commonly provides extensive supervision, then employees look like servants. A third factor focuses on the employee's level of skill. Typically, servants have rather generic skills possessed by many people, while independent contractors have professional or high levels of skill. Clearly, skills are related to supervision: lower skilled employees generally require more supervision, while experienced employees with a recognized profession generally need less supervision.

The next factor focuses on the employee's contract. The independence factor usually suggests that an independent contractor works for many employ-

Figure 36–6   Factors Distinguishing Servants from Independent Contractors

	Right to Control		Parties' Intent			Skills		Number of Employers		Payment by		Tools Owned By		Customs/Usages	
	Means	Outcome	Servant	IC	Extensive Supervision	High	Low	One	Several	Wages/Salary	Job	Employer	Employee	Servant	IC
Servant	Yes	Yes	Yes	No	Yes	No	Yes	Yes	No	Yes	No	Yes	No	Yes	No
Independent Contractor (IC)	No	Yes	No	Yes	No	Yes	No	No	Yes	No	Yes	No	Yes	No	Yes

ers on an irregular basis. Independent contractors accept or reject new engagements when they have sufficient additional capacity. By contrast, a servant tends to work regularly and exclusively for a single employer. The fifth factor focuses on how the employee is paid: independent contractors are usually paid to complete a defined set of tasks, while servants are paid by pay periods (e.g., hourly, piecework, weekly, biweekly, monthly, or annual salary). The sixth factor concerns tools of the trade and is related to the skills factor. Independent contractors usually bring their own tools of trade and work at many different premises. By contrast, a servant usually uses both the facilities and tools of the employer. The final factor focuses on customs and usages of the trade in the locality and for that type of work performed.

These master-servant definition factors become quite useful in determining close cases. For example, consider two methods of hiring an accountant. Accountants often operate in private practice and are retained by many clients. This gives the accountant the right to supervise his or her own work, render highly specialized professional services, and be paid for a particular job (e.g., preparation of a tax return or an audit). Additionally, the accountant may do much of the work at numerous sites or at the accountant's own office. All of these factors suggest that the accountant is an independent contractor. However, an accountant may be hired exclusively by a firm, be paid a salary, be subordinate to a corporate officer such as the vice president of finance, work exclusively at the employer's premises, and use the employer's tools. The accountant in this latter example is most likely a servant. These master-servant factors are summarized in Figure 36–6. They are also becoming increasingly important under tax law to determine when an employer is obligated to withhold taxes. These factors must be carefully assessed and the preponderance of them used to designate an employee as an independent contractor or a servant, as illustrated in the following case.

MASSEY v. TUBE ART DISPLAY, INC.
551 P.2d 1387 (Wash. App. 1976)

The McPherson Realty Company hired Tube Art Display to move a sign from its previous location to a new site. Tube Art's service manager and employees photographed the site and provided measurements for an excavation necessary to install the sign. Tube Art then hired defendant Richard F. Redford, a backhoe operator, to dig the hole. Redford began digging in the early evening hours, and later that evening the backhoe bucket struck a small natural gas pipeline. Redford examined the pipe and believed there was no leak, so he left the site. Around 2 A.M. the following morning, there was an explosion and fire in the building serviced by the gas pipeline. This accident killed two people and destroyed most of the building's contents. Massey, as tenant of that building, sued Tube Art, alleging total destruction of its valuable property. Tube Art defended that because Redford was an independent contractor, Tube Art should not be liable.

SWANSON, Judge

An independent contractor is generally found as one who contracts services for another but, who is not controlled by the other nor subject to the others right to control with respect to his physical conduct in performing the services. Whether one acting for another is a servant or an independent contractor, several factors must be taken into consideration.

In *Jackson v. Standard Oil Company* [this court held] the plaintiff need not show that the principal controlled or had the right to control every aspect of the agent's operation in order to incur vicarious liability. Rather,

> it should be sufficient that the plaintiff presents substantial evidence of control or right of control for those activities from whence the actionable negligence flowed. If the rule were otherwise, then a person wishing to accomplish a certain result through another could declare the other to be an independent contractor generally, and yet retain control over a particularly hazardous undertaking without incurring liability for acts arising out of that part. Such a result would effectively thwart the purpose of the rule of vicarious liability.

In this regard, it may be emphasized that it is not de facto control nor actual exercise of a right to interfere with or direct the work which constitutes the test, but rather, the *right to control* the negligent actor's physical conduct in the performance of the service. The trial judge stated,

> I think that under the undisputed evidence in this case they not only had the right to control, but they did control. They controlled the location of the spot to dig. They controlled the dimensions. They controlled the excavation and they got the building permits. They did all of the discretionary work that was necessary before he started to operate. They knew that the method of excavation was going to be by use of a backhoe rather than a pick and shovel which might have made a little difference on the exposure on this situation. They in effect created the whole atmosphere in which he worked. And the fact that even though he did not work for them all of the time and they paid him on a piecework basis for the individual job didn't impress me particularly when they used him the number of times they did. Most of the time they used him for this type of work.

Redford had been essentially self-employed for about five years at the time of trial, was free to work for other contractors, select the time of day to perform the work assigned, paid his own income and business taxes and did not participate in any of Tube Art's employee programs. [However] during the previous three years Redford worked exclusively for sign companies and 90 percent of his time for Tube Art. He had no employees, was not registered as a contractor or subcontractor, was not bonded, did not himself obtain permits or licenses for his jobs, and dug the holes at locations and in dimensions in exact accordance with instructions of his employer. In fact, Redford was left no discretion with regard to the placement of the excavations that he dug. Rather, it was his skill in digging holes pursuant to the exact dimensions prescribed that caused him to be preferred over other backhoe operators.

In the present case, Tube Art can exercise control over where the hole can be dug, the day it was to be dug, and how deep the hole should be. Moreover, it was not unreasonable to expect Tube Art to know that gas pipes might very well be lurking in the vicinity of the proposed excavation. In such a case it was incumbent upon Tube Art to ascertain where other service pipes might be. Tube Art cannot disclaim liability. Rather, where the danger to others is great, a duty is imposed upon an employer to make such provision against negligence as may be commensurate with the obvious danger. It is a duty which cannot be delegated to another source to avoid liability for its neglect.

Case Questions

1. What is the issue in the *Massey* case and in other cases involving alleged use of independent contractors when the master is sued by an outsider harmed by the employee?

2. What is the ambiguity in resolving this question?

3. What reasons are used to hold Redford was a servant of Tube Art Display, Inc.? Describe the reasons used to argue that Redford was an independent contractor. Which reasons do you believe should be given priority in balancing this controversy?

Independent Contractor Liability

There are some exceptions to the independent contractor's sole liability for its tortious acts. The employer has direct liability for the wrongful acts of an independent contractor if the employer provides negligent instructions, supervision, tools, or if the employer chooses an irresponsible independent contractor. Employers are responsible for the torts of an independent contractor where the employer has a **nondelegable duty**. These are special statutory responsibilities owed to the public by landlords, municipalities, railroads, and common carriers to maintain safe conditions. An employer is also strictly liable for damages caused by an independent contractor doing inherently dangerous activities.

Scope of Employment

The analysis of respondeat superior cases also focuses on a second element. The master is held responsible only for the torts the servant commits while going "about the master's business." When the servant is "off duty," the master is unable to supervise the servant's activities. The master has no responsibility for the servant's personal activities. Therefore, the third party must also prove the servant's tort was performed within the **scope of employment** for the master.

While this may seem another easy question to answer, in practice it has proved to be ambiguous and sometimes unpredictable. There is rather voluminous case law on this point focusing on two main inquiries: (1) the servant's pursuit of the master's business objectives and (2) the foreseeability of the servant's negligent act. Potential conflicts between these two inquiries are addressed in the Restatement (Second) of Agency.

Most of the scope of employment cases center around two major issues. First, masters usually argue that the servant's wrongful act was unauthorized. Therefore, there should be no respondeat superior liability because that authority should define the scope of employment. Second, many cases have concerned the servant's negligent driving of a motor vehicle. Although driving generally places the servant within the scope of employment, there may be some deviation from the most direct travel route. Many courts have become entangled in distinguishing between a mere detour from the master's business and extensive deviations, sometimes considering them as independent frolics. Figure 36–7 diagrams the respondeat superior relationship.

Restatement (Second) of Agency § 228

1. Conduct of a servant is within the scope of employment if, but only if:
   a. it is of the kind he is employed to perform;
   b. it occurs substantially within the authorized time and space limits;
   c. it is actuated, at least in part, by a purpose to serve the master; and
   d. if force is intentionally used by the servant against another, the use of force is not unexpected by the master.

Unauthorized Acts

The scope of employment and the extent of servant's authority are closely related concepts. However, most courts recognize that some unauthorized acts fall within the scope of employment. For example, unauthorized contracting that is later ratified is within the scope of employment. Many servants are specifically given broad discretion to implement the master's business, while other masters tolerate the servant's voluntary assumption of broad authority. Therefore, some unauthorized acts are nevertheless within the servant's scope of employment.

Some servants provide physical protection services for their master's business. For example, a security guard, vehicle driver, or repossession agent usually engages in physical activities that occasionally result in assaults, batteries, false imprisonment, or other personal aggressive torts. The law usually considers that such activities should be reasonably foreseeable by the master, so they are within the scope of employment. However, this rule does not apply to the servant's violent actions against coworkers based on a personal grudge. Third parties may rescind contracts the servant negotiates if fraudulent misrepresentations are made.

Detour versus Frolic

Early cases held that any departure the servant made from the most direct manner of performing the master's business was outside the scope of employment. However, the law has evolved and tolerates minor deviations from the master's business. This inquiry now focuses on the degree of deviation. Slight deviations are within the scope of employment; gross deviations are outside the scope of employment.

Some courts use the distinction between a detour and a frolic to characterize the degree of deviation.

Figure 36-7   Respondeat Superior: Vicarious Tort Liability

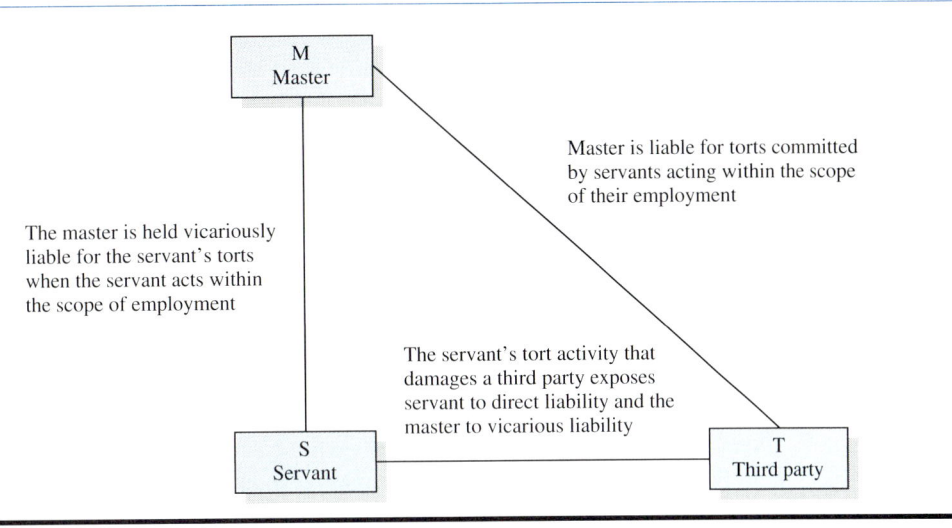

Considerable case law concerns delivery drivers who negligently injure bystanders while traveling their routes. In some cases, the servant may select a longer or alternate route rather than the most direct route between two delivery points. This is considered a "mere detour," so they remain within the scope of employment because an employee is given some discretion to make route decisions. However, if a significant side trip is taken for personal reasons, the diversion is designated an independent frolic, so the master is not responsible for torts committed. The detour versus frolic distinction is explored in the following classic case.

RILEY v. STANDARD OIL COMPANY OF NEW YORK
132 N.E. 97 (N.Y. Ct. App. 1921)

Million, a chauffeur employed by the defendant, was directed to pick up some barrels of paint at the Long Island Railroad yard about 2 1/2 miles away and return with them to his master's premises. However, after loading the truck, Million discovered some waste pieces of wood that he threw onto the truck and took to his sister's house. This deviation caused Million to turn in the opposite direction when leaving the yard away from his master's mill and toward his sister's house about four blocks away. After unloading the wood, Million began his return to the mill on a route that passed by the freight yard entrance. Before he reached the entrance, Million had an accident, injuring the plaintiff.

ANDREWS, Judge

A master is liable for the result of a servant's negligence when the servant is acting in his business; when he is still engaged in the course of his employment. It is not the rule itself but its application that ever causes a doubt. The servant may be acting for himself. He may be engaged in an independent errand of his own. He may abandon his master's service permanently or temporarily. While still doing his master's work, he may also be serving a purpose of his own. He may be performing his master's work but in a forbidden manner.

No formula can be stated that will enable us to solve the problem whether at a particular moment a particular servant is engaged in his master's business. We recognize that the precise facts before the court will vary the result. We realize that differences of degree may produce unlike effects. But, whatever the facts, the answer depends on a consideration of what the servant was doing, and why, when, where, and how he was doing it.

A servant may be ''going on a frolic of his own, without being at all on his master's business.'' He may be so distant from the proper scene of his labor, or he may have left his work for such a length of time, to evidence a relinquishment of his employment. Or the circumstances may have a more doubtful meaning. That the servant is where he would not be had he obeyed his master's orders in itself is immaterial, as it may tend to show a permanent or temporary abandonment of his master's service. Should there be such a temporary abandonment the master again becomes liable for the servant's acts when the latter once more begins to act in his business. Such a re-entry is not affected merely by the mental attitude of the servant. There must be that attitude coupled with a reasonable connection in time and space with the work in which he should be engaged. No hard and fast rule on the subject either of space or time can be applied. It cannot be said of a servant in charge of his master's vehicle who temporarily abandons his line of travel for a purpose of his own that he again becomes a servant only when he reaches a point on his route which he necessarily would have passed had he obeyed his orders. He may use a different way back. Doubtless the circumstance may be considered in connection with the other facts involved.

We are not called upon to decide whether the defendant might not have been responsible while this accident had occurred while Million was on his way to his sister's house. That would depend whether this trip would be regarded as a new and independent journey on his own business, distinct from that of his master or a mere deviation of the general route from the mill and back. Considering the short distance and the little time involved, considering that the truck when it left the yard was loaded with the defendant's goods for delivery to its mill and it was the general purpose of Million to return there, it is quite possible a question of fact would be presented to be decided by a jury. At least, however, with the wood delivered, with the journey back to the mill begun at some point in the route Million again engaged in the defendant's business. That point, in view of all the circumstances we think he had reached.

Case Questions

1. What does the New York Court of Appeals conclude in the preceding case concerning the servant's scope of employment?

2. What reasons would support the argument that Million was not within the scope of his employment? What reasons would support the argument that Million was within the scope of his employment?

3. Should Million's master be held liable for damages caused by Million's tort while detouring from the master's business? Why?

Misrepresentation

A third party injured by the servant's false claims or misrepresentations generally has remedies in either contract or tort. The master has direct liability for false claims it encourages the servant to make to third parties. In some states, the master has direct liability for negligently permitting the servant's misrepresentations. The master will have vicarious liability whenever the servant is cloaked in actual or apparent authority to make representations concerning the master's business. Even if the master is blameless and ignorant of the servant's misrepresentations, the master is liable to third parties harmed by the servant's false claims. Where the third party cannot prove that either the master or the servant knew the misrepresentations were false, the contract may nevertheless be rescinded under

contract law. For example, assume Perry's sales agent Alma falsely claims that Perry's widgets have high tensile strength. Perry may be held liable for any intentional fraud and is always subject to the buyer's rescission of the contract if the misrepresentation is innocent.

Servant's Intentional Torts

The common intentional torts such as assault, battery, defamation, fraud, or trespass can be performed by servants for their own personal purposes. The master is often not liable for the servant's intentional torts. Intentional torts are analyzed in the same manner as negligence cases. First, the master-servant relationship must be determined and second, the master is liable if the act occurred within the servant's scope of employment.

The third party's proof of an intentional tort requires that the master must have intended the servant to undertake the wrongful act in question. This often requires proof similar to a conspiracy. A master's intentional tort liability has occurred in a few situations. First, the master is liable for tortious acts caused by a servant with a known tendency to commit torts. For example, if the employer has observed the servant acting recklessly in the past, the master's failure to supervise future acts exposes the master to intentional tort liability. Second, where force is common in the performance of the master's business, the master may be liable for excessive use of force. The barroom bouncer, debt collector, and others engaged in similar trades are examples. Third, the master is liable for the servant's intentionally wrongful acts done to promote the master's business.

Subagents

Both principals and their agents may be held liable for the torts of subagents. Where the agent is authorized to hire a subagent, the master may be held vicariously liable for the subagent's torts. The same master-servant and scope of employment analysis must be performed. Where the agent is not authorized to hire subagents, only the agent is vicariously liable for subagent torts. This liability holds true for negligence, intentional torts, and misrepresentation.

Borrowed Servants

A **borrowed servant** is the agent of one employer whose services are loaned to another employer. Questions often arise as to which employer is responsible under respondeat superior for a borrowed servant's torts. The employer who has the primary right to control the agent's activities is generally held liable for the agent's torts. Borrowed servants who perform services for only a short time usually expose their original masters to vicarious liability. Borrowed servants who work for the borrowing master for a longer time expose the borrowing master to vicarious liability.

CRIMINAL LIABILITY

Any person who personally commits criminal activities is personally liable for the consequences of his or her own act. Therefore, an agent is directly liable

for criminal activities conducted both within and without the scope of employment, whether authorized or unauthorized. However, questions often arise as to the master's criminal liability for a servant's acts. Where there is evidence of a traditional multiparty criminal activity, the master and other participating parties may be held criminally liable. For example, where the master coplans the crime with the servant, the master may be liable as a **coconspirator**. Where the master facilitates the servant's criminal activity before its commission, the master may be criminally liable as an **accessory before the fact**. Assistance given during the criminal act is **aiding and abetting**. Assistance after commission of the crime exposes the master to liability as an **accessory after the fact**.

There are some crimes that do not require proof of criminal intent (*mens rea*). This makes the crime prosecutable against the master even if the master does not participate or intend the servant's criminal act. For example, criminal penalties apply to a business for antitrust violations even though only a corporation's agents can have criminal intent. Some other statutes assign criminal liability under a strict liability theory, so proof of intent is unnecessary. Numerous courts apply the respondeat superior doctrine from tort law to the criminal activities of servants, requiring analysis of the master-servant and scope of employment questions.

END–OF–CHAPTER QUESTIONS

1. Albert, as sales representative for the Principle Implement Company, regularly assisted potential customers in determining suitability of equipment sold by Principle Implement. Theodore, a customer, was interested in purchasing a specialized frandibulator that would satisfy Theodore's specifications. Albert falsely represented that a frandibulator sold by Principle Implement had the characteristics Theodore needed. Albert was authorized only to correctly represent the capabilities of products. Theodore purchased a frandibulator from Albert that was unsuitable and caused damage to Theodore. Describe the legal analysis of Theodore's suit against Principle Implement based on contract. Describe the legal analysis of Theodore's suit against Principle Imple-

ment based on tort. How can a principal avoid liability under either contract or tort theories in this type of situation?

2. Art and Andy's Accounting Service was traditionally engaged in audit services for its numerous clients. Due to intense competition among accounting firms, Art and Andy's firm was only marginally profitable in its auditing services. Art and Andy agreed to expand into providing tax services for its current and new clients. Several new associates were hired to prepare both individual and business tax returns. Unknown to Art and Andy, two new associates solicited clients for other types of management consulting engagements, services well beyond the audit or tax lines of business that Art and Andy had authorized. Art and Andy had specifically limited all associates to work on audit and tax engagements. When Art and Andy discovered the management consulting contracts, they advised these clients that this service would not be provided. What rights do the clients have against Art and Andy's Accounting Services? What ambiguities are there in Art and Andy's directives to the new associates?

3. The Perry Company, a securities brokerage firm, commonly permitted its retail sales agents and brokers to handle much of its client paperwork for the firm's trading activities. Thomas, a customer, had customarily dealt with a sales broker who had left the firm. Perry Company hired a new broker, Angela, who was specifically instructed not to handle customer's paperwork. Thomas asked Angela to purchase a block of stock for Thomas's account. Angela was aware of the firm's prior policy permitting brokers to handle the paperwork, and she told Thomas to pay for the shares in cash. Thomas met Angela one afternoon at a location away from the Perry Company office. Angela gave Thomas an invoice showing the purchase of the shares and took Thomas's cash. Angela never executed Thomas's trade and absconded with his cash. If Thomas sues either Angela or Perry Company for de-

livery of his stock or the return of his cash, what must he prove about the Perry Company's authorization of Angela?

4. Fred, a field supervisor for Van Stavern Construction Company, ordered construction materials from Sutton's Steel and Supply. Fred's order was made in the name of D. B. Van Stavern, the owner and president of the construction company, rather than in the construction company's name. Invoices for several loads that Sutton delivered to the construction company were paid by the company's employees based on invoices showing D. B. Stavern's name. All payments were made by employees of the company with corporate checks. However, over $40,000 worth of unpaid debts for Sutton's deliveries to Van Stavern Construction remain unpaid. D. B. Van Stavern denied personal liability on these debts. Sutton claims the construction company's payments on previous invoices ratify the contract with D. B. Van Stavern as principal. D. B. Van Stavern claimed that he had no knowledge of the unauthorized contracts. Should D. B. Van Stavern be held personally liable as having ratified contracts made by Fred? See *Sutton Steel and Supply, Inc. v. Van Stavern,* 496 So.2d 1360 (La. App. 1986).

5. John was the pastor of a church that had bylaws vesting general charge of the church's business affairs and property transactions to a committee of church members. Over time, John asserted greater control over the church business matters, including borrowing large sums from local financial institutions and mortgaging church property as collateral. He never sought the committee's permission before initiating these transactions. John used these funds to build a church swimming pool, renovate the church, construct parking lots, and revise the church landscaping. Eventually, the debt burden caused the church to default on these loans. A new property committee sued the minister and the banks. The new property committee claimed that John had

no authority for the contracts, so the church should not be liable. What theories might be argued by the church and how might the pastor and banks respond? See *Perkins v. Rich,* 415 N.E.2d 895 (1981).

6. J.R. was widely known as a distrusted and hated individual in his home town. J.R. had conducted his ranching and oil businesses in a ruthlessly ambitious manner, earning him a deserved reputation for opportunism, intolerance, and for preying on others' misfortunes. Eventually, many townfolk shunned J.R. by intentionally avoiding any contracting or other business relations for fear they might be personally damaged. As J.R. became aware of the townfolk's concerted effort to avoid dealing with him, he sought other methods of contracting locally. J.R. often hired out-of-town attorneys or other agents to purchase farmland and commercial buildings. One such attorney negotiated the purchase of Clayton's farm at a fair market price. This attorney never acted as if he represented J.R., or any other principal, for that matter. Explain what type of principal J.R. is in this transaction and the liability of J.R., Clayton, and the attorney? How could Clayton rescind the sale of this farm to J.R., and how might J.R. characterize the sale differently to avoid such an action by Clayton?

7. A school district contracted with L.N.T. Steel Products, Inc., to install room partitions in the school. Webster was contracted by L.N.T. to make the installations. Webster's contract provided for payment according to the number of partitions installed. Webster was not an L.N.T. employee. Webster had no contractor's license and hired other workers to do the installation. Webster's workers were paid directly by L.N.T. L.N.T. also provided Webster with blueprints. At no time was Webster supervised by L.N.T. officials on the job. During the installation, Webster left the job site one day in his own vehicle to find a public telephone to call L.N.T. about the job. Webster in-jured Peirson while negligently driving his car to make the call. Discuss the arguments Peirson might use in claiming Webster was a servant of L.N.T. as master. Discuss the arguments L.N.T. would use to characterize Webster as an independent contractor. What is the impact of this characterization on L.N.T. or Webster's liability? See *L.N.T. Steel Products, Inc. v. Peirson,* 425 A.2d 242 (1981).

8. Lano worked as project engineer for Thermal Equipment Company. He commonly drove the company van, which held company tools he used, directly from home to work sites and occasionally ran errands for Thermal after work hours. Lano's van collided with Lazar one night while Lano drove home from work. Lano had followed a longer route home than usual to make personal purchases at a store. Lazar claimed thermal equipment was liable because Lano was a servant and was acting within the scope of his employment. What arguments might Lazar make that Lano was within the scope of his employment? What arguments would Thermal Equipment use that Lano was on a frolic and on his own time? See *Lazar v. Thermal Equipment Co.,* 195 Cal.Rptr. 890 (Cal. App. 1983).

9. Federal government officials from the Federal Home Loan Bank Board persuaded Thomas Gaubert, the chairman and largest shareholder of the Independent American Savings Association (IASA), to merge his savings and loan association into Investex, a failing Texas thrift. This caused IASA's financial conditions to deteriorate. Federal officials pressured Gaubert to quit his presidency and permit federally designated personnel to continue managing the firm. Within two years, IASA was considered financially insolvent and Gaubert lost $75 million of share value and $25 million in personal real estate holdings pledged to guarantee IASA finances. Discuss the analysis of a tort claim against the U.S. government based on negligent supervision of IASA by federal officials from the Federal

Home Loan Bank Board. What national policies might be affected by this decision, and what reasons would be used to argue those conclusions? See *United States v. Gaubert*, 111 S.Ct. 1267 (1991).

10. As an employee of a large management consulting firm, Andrew was assigned to a project at the Trident Corporation. While reviewing confidential files, Andrew discovered that Trident was considering an acquisition of an unnamed competitor. Andrew remembered certain characteristics of a competing firm he learned while on a previous consulting engagement for another firm. Discuss the management consulting firm's potential liability if Andrew uses this inside information for criminal insider trading in the shares of the competing firm, which is later acquired by the Trident Corporation.

Part VIII

Partnerships

■

Chapter 37

Partnership: Creation and Duties

■

CRITICAL THINKING INQUIRIES

As you read this chapter, you should be able to address the following:

- Compare and contrast the reasoning underlying the two theories of partnerships: (1) a partnership should be treated as an entity separate from its constituent partners, and (2) a partnership is simply an aggregation of its members.
- Why should the business activities of several people acting together be designated a partnership? What is the impact on the individual participants if their operation is considered a partnership?
- What ambiguities arise about the ownership of property used in a partnership's business?
- Why do partnership business activities have a direct financial impact on all partners? How could partners avoid the negative personal impact of poor managerial decisions made by their copartners?
- How does the unlimited liability of partners affect the selection of the partnership form for a new business?

MANAGERIAL PERSPECTIVE

After graduation from business school, Pam, Paul, and Peter started a management consulting business. They offered to advise other businesses about contemporary management problems in marketing, accounting, finance, and regulatory compliance. However, none of them had a clear understanding of how to form their business, nor did they understand the legal impact of simply beginning to operate a business for profit as co-owners. After only a short time, expenses for their rent, office furniture, computers, and company cars grew larger than their income. Eventually, several lenders forced them into involuntary bankruptcy.

The three were surprised to find their business was actually a partnership and this meant each had personal liability for all business expenses. This problem was magnified because of Paul's efforts to get the firm some quick name recognition and a favorable reputation. Paul had obligated the business to provide numerous clients with consulting services at prices too low to cover direct costs. Pam had negotiated on a large line of credit for their firm and the other partners were now required to personally repay advances the firm had taken.

- How would an understanding of partnerships and their formation assist business planning for similar new ventures?
- Ignorance of what key factors may raise difficulties for these partners in their business?

The law of partnerships addresses the fundamental questions of business organization. Persons acting together often form a partnership, with unexpected impact. For example, it is particularly important for entrepreneurs to understand that their copartners' activities may affect each other copartner financially. Partners owe duties to each other derived from the basic law of agency. Partners should carefully consider how they order their affairs or risk the standardized terms imposed by partnership law. The ambiguities of partnership property will have an effect on outside creditors who are also well advised to understand the risks of dealing with partnerships. Partners should be aware of the special impact of tort and criminal law on the partnership form. This chapter provides critical insight into the creation of partnerships and the various duties owed by all participants.

INTRODUCTION

Partnerships arise naturally whenever associates fail to organize their business firm in some other form, such as a corporation. Partners have unlimited liability for the debts of their business, and all partners are automatically considered agents of the business. Therefore, before commencing business in any form, it is advisable to consider the form of organization that is best suited for the business and establish operational plans consistent with their objectives.

Partnership law provides an automatic scheme for the operation of partnerships even when the parties have not planned their business form. Partnership law reflects an evolution of rules derived from precedents that settled real disputes among partners and with outsiders. It draws a balance between the various parties' needs and expectations. Generally, having "default" partnership rules is more efficient than requiring all partnerships to fully define their relationship by contract. Partnership law provides a framework to resolve disputes and define rights and duties encountered by the "typical" partnership. However, the laissez-faire freedom of contract theory permits partnerships to vary most partnership rules to suit their particular needs.

Partnership Law

Partnerships have existed for centuries. Modern partnership law has evolved from common law developed in England and in the states during the 19th century. The Uniform Partnership Act (UPA) was drafted in 1914 by the National Conference of Commissioners on Uniform State Laws (NCCUSL). The UPA was first adopted by Pennsylvania in 1915. The UPA has become the primary law governing partnerships in all the states except one: Louisiana retains its civil law drawn from its continental European roots. The Commissioners have proposed a revision, the Revised Uniform Partnership Act (RUPA), which is roughly based on a revision in partnership law by the state of Georgia. RUPA is introduced later and discussed throughout Chapters 37 and 38.

PARTNERSHIP DEFINITION

Business associates need to be mindful of the UPA definition of a partnership. Whenever two or more persons associate and operate as co-owners of a business for profit, their relationship is automatically designated a **partnership**. Of course, it is possible to associate in some other way, such as in the corporate form, in a limited partnership, under a lease, in a franchise relationship, in an employment relationship, or merely in contract. However, unless the parties are careful to characterize the association as one of these or some other relationship, it may be considered a partnership. All copartners have authority to contract for the partnership, and each individually has unlimited liability for partnership debts.

UPA § 6. Partnership Defined

. . . an association of two or more persons to carry on . . . a business for profit.

A partnership is a voluntary grouping of *two or more persons*, either individuals or a combination of legal entities. Each participant must have capacity to contract. Corporations may combine with persons to form a partnership or with other corporations, or persons may combine with other persons. Consent by all persons involved is necessary. Therefore, every member must approve of all others' membership, both when the partnership is first formed and later on when new partners are admitted. However, the partners may agree that new partners are admitted by a membership committee, which is the practice in many large law and accounting firms.

A partnership exists only when the partners conduct a *business for profit*. This does not mean that the partnership must be "profitable" but only that the partners have a profit motive for their undertaking. However, the mere sharing of gross returns by joint property owners does not in itself establish a partnership. For example, Pam, Paul, and Peter could have organized their business as independent contractors to avoid partnership liability for any of their acts. Joint tenancies, common property ownership, tenancies by the entirety, or other forms of joint or common co-ownership are not partnerships. With some exceptions, the UPA Section 7 treats the receipt of a share of business profits by a participant as evidence of a partnership.

Profit Distribution *Not* Indicating Partnership

- Installment payment on debt.
- Wages or compensation paid to an employee or agent.
- Rent paid to a landlord.
- Annuity payments to widow(er) or personal representative of deceased partner.
- Interest payment on loan; may be variable with business' profits.
- Consideration paid for sale of goodwill.

UPA § 7.

In the UPA Section 7 exceptions noted in the list, none of the individuals receiving payments are receiving profits as *co-owners*. Therefore, it is possible to characterize multiparty relationships as loans, leases, property co-ownership, consignment, or agency/employment without incurring partnership unlimited liability or extending general agency authority. The co-owner of a business shares the risks of conducting a business enterprise, which are different from the risks between debtor and creditor, property co-owners, les-sor and lessee, or agent and employee. A business co-owner also shares management functions with the other partners. Of course, passive co-owners of an apartment building who are not partners could alternatively establish a partnership engaged in the business of owning and managing apartment building(s) for profit. Similar relationships may be characterized either as partnerships or as other types of relationships (e.g., property co-owners), so care must be taken to choose only the particular form desired.

Partners usually contribute money as capital, property essential for operating the business, and their personal services to manage and operate the business. However, the UPA permits flexibility in the various partners' contributions. Some may contribute money or property, while others contribute only services. Any combination of contributions the partners agree to is permissible. Often, financial partners intend to be inactive in management, so they combine with expert professionals who provide critical management skills. Partnerships may be formed with each partner contributing in varying amounts as they mutually agree. The UPA assumes that profits and losses will be shared equally. If profits are shared unequally, the UPA presumes that losses are shared in the same proportion as profits. However, the partners may specify different percentages for sharing profits and/or losses. Pam, Paul, and Peter contributed primarily services, but probably needed some capital. The following case illustrates how an ethical dilemma can arise for partners who understand the impact of the partnership relationship and thereby take advantage of their associates. If other participants are ignorant of partnership law and the formalities it requires, this can create confusion and conflicting claims.

MILLER v. CITY BANK & TRUST
266 N.W.2nd 687 (Mich. App. 1978)

Mr. and Mrs. Miller married in 1959. Thereafter, Mrs. Miller joined Mr. Miller in running his nursery business, which had been operating for some time but was in financial distress. By 1974, when Mr. Miller died, the business had become prosperous.

Mrs. Miller made no capital contributions to the business but held a management position. She kept all the books, hired and fired employees, and performed physical labor. Periodically, both the Millers received equal payments from the business. Household expenses were taken out of the business account.

In separate transactions, Mr. Miller subdivided some land adjoining the nursery that he had owned separately before the marriage. Mrs. Miller's signature was necessary to convey these lots. A business registration certificate was filed in 1960 indicating that the business was operated as a partnership. A similar certificate was filed for the subdivision project in 1966, but it expired in 1971. Checking accounts, vehicles, and other equipment were bought and held under the assumed business name. However, annual tax forms and schedules listed the business as a sole proprietorship and Mrs. Miller's occupation was listed as housewife. Additionally, Michigan business activity forms and Mr. Miller's self-employed pension and profit sharing plan documents indicated the business was a sole proprietorship. The Millers never executed any formal written partnership agreement. Mrs. Miller testified that Mr. Miller had described their relationship as that of partners, telling her ''She was the best partner he ever had.'' Mrs. Miller appealed from a trial court decision holding there was no partnership between the Millers effectively denying her full ownership of the subdivided land as a surviving partner.

DANHOF, Chief Judge

The determination of whether a partnership exists is a question of fact. The burden of proof to show a partnership is on the one alleging the partnership, and the burden is stricter when relatives are the alleged partners.

The elements of a partnership are generally considered to include a volunteer association of two or more people with legal capacity in order to carry on, via co-ownership, a business for profit. Co-ownership of the business requires more than merely joint ownership of the property and is usually evidenced by joint control and the sharing of profits and losses.

It is not disputed that the parties were involved in a business venture for profit and had the legal capacity to form a partnership. However, the evidence relating to co-ownership does not indicate that a legal partnership was contemplated. Prior to the marriage, Mr. Miller operated the business and owned all the property. Mrs. Miller made no capital contribution except her services. Even though plaintiff worked long and hard hours, this does not establish a partnership. This evidence could also be viewed as consistent with an employer-employee relationship or that of a helpful wife who assisted her husband without them intending a legal partnership. Co-ownership is also indicated by profit sharing. In fact, profit sharing is prima facie evidence of a partnership. However, the court did not find an agreement to share the profits and we cannot say that this was clearly erroneous. Mr. and Mrs. Miller's receipt of monthly payments from the nursery checking account does not necessarily establish profit sharing. The payments could also be reasonably viewed as salary or wages. Another possible interpretation would be that Mr. Miller was withdrawing money from his sole proprietorship and was dividing it equally because he felt an obligation to share equally with his wife, as a wife rather than with a business partner.

Another indicia of co-ownership is mutual agency and control. That Mrs. Miller kept the books, wrote checks, and hired and fired, does not necessarily establish any control other than that which might be given to a trusted employee. No evidence of an agreement with respect to mutual control was presented.

The intention of the parties who enter into a partnership comprising the above mentioned elements is the controlling issue in this case. The filing of the business registration papers listing the business as a partnership gives support to plaintiff's claim. As long as the registration was effective, it raised a presumption of a partnership, but this can be overcome by competent evidence. Since the registration certificate filed for the subdivision operation expired in 1971, it does not raise a presumption of a partnership.

The other evidence supporting plaintiff's claim is that plaintiff testified that the parties entered into an oral agreement and that Mr. Miller told her ''She was the best partner he ever had.'' The use of the term partner is one factor to be considered in analyzing whether a partnership exists, but is not controlling. Mrs. Miller seemed to consider the whole marriage as a partnership and Mr. Miller could have meant that she was the best partner in marriage rather than in business.

The evidence introduced against these claims indicated that the deceased did not intend to form a legal partnership with his wife. First, there is no written agreement and there is only plaintiff's testimony in support of an oral one. The income tax returns and schedules listed the business as sole proprietorship, listed Mr. Miller's income as wages and

Mrs. Miller's occupation as a housewife. [Other forms] listed the business as a sole proprietorship. All the capital contributions came from Mr. Miller and the property remained in his name and none was transferred to the partnership. Although none of these facts are conclusive, they are all factors to be weighed in the decision. Affirmed.

Case Questions

1. What reasons support the court classifying the Millers' business as a sole proprietorship owned by Mr. Miller? What reasons would support classifying the business as a partnership owned by both the Millers?

2. What is the rival hypothesis the court looks for to counter Mrs. Miller's assertion that the business was a partnership? What evidence is used to support this rival hypothesis?

3. State the value assumption underlying the court's view of whether partnerships arise automatically in a marriage. State the value assumptions underlying the court's view of a partnership asserted by any relative.

Entity versus Aggregate Theory of Partnerships

Legal scholars have had some difficulty classifying the fundamental form of partnerships. Are partnerships legal entities separate from their constituent partners, or are partnerships simply aggregations of their members? This dilemma is discussed because it has important legal ramifications; it is not just another academic discourse. The outcome of the debate is unclear because certain partnership attributes indicate the aggregate form, while others indicate the entity form. Partnerships are often referred to as "the" business entity, yet partnerships clearly exist only while the individual partners are willing to aggregate together.

The UPA and legal history in the United States treat partnerships as *aggregates* for several purposes. A few states still require all partners to be joined together in partnership litigation and to hold joint title to partnership property. Partnerships are dissolved automatically when any partner becomes disassociated with the firm. Partners have joint and several liability for partnership debts. All partners owe fiduciary duties to each individual copartner. Tax law generally makes each partner individually liable for tax liability on his or her allocable share of partnership gains or losses. Each of these factors makes the partnership appear to be an aggregate.

There are also *entity* aspects to tax law and to each partner's fiduciary duties. The partnership must file an information tax return showing the firm's gross receipts, expenses, depreciation deductions, income or loss, and each individual partner's percentage share. This permits the IRS to cross-reference the income or loss claimed on each individual's Form 1040 tax return. Partners also owe a fiduciary duty to the partnership as an entity. Today, most states permit partnerships to hold property in the partnership name, sue or be sued in the partnership name even if individual partners are not named, and maintain partnership books and records at the firm's place of business. Finally, partnership creditors have priority over partnership assets in relation to the individual partner's creditors if they all become insolvent.

There is a clear trend in the 20th century towards treating partnerships as entities. This is reinforced by the proposed RUPA revision that retains aggregate status only as necessary to maintain the favorable partnership "flow through" tax treatment. The impact of these attributes becomes clearer in the RUPA commentary that follows and with further study of partnerships.

*Revision of the Uniform Partnership Act**

Between 1902 and 1914, the National Conference of Commissioners on Uniform State Laws (NCCUSL) struck a balance between two competing forces in drafting the original UPA. One group initially offered mercantilist versions in which partnerships were viewed as entities

*Source: "Revision of the Uniform Partnership Act" by John W. Bagby ©1993.

separate from their member partners. The other group based the later revisions on the common law aggregate theory. The resulting UPA became a compromise between these forces.

While the UPA has been in effect for nearly 80 years, with remarkably few amendments, attitudes have changed toward some UPA provisions. Recommendations have surfaced to amend the law consistent with evolutions in the case law, difficulties with the old-UPA, and simplifications reflecting common practice found in well-planned partnership agreements. After Georgia made substantial revision to its UPA in 1984, an American Bar Association committee recommended similar revisions for the UPA. A NCCUSL drafting committee appointed in 1987 produced the RUPA in 1991. RUPA is now becoming available for the states' adoption. However, the process of replacement by all the states may take several years, during which time both the UPA and the RUPA will be important.

RUPA proposes three fundamental changes and numerous minor and technical changes. First, the entity theory is adopted except where aggregate theory is still necessary. For example, the partnership ''flow-through'' tax treatment under the Internal Revenue Code is an incident of aggregate status. The NCCUSL drafters worked closely with the Internal Revenue Service to assure partners would be taxed on their allocable share of profits (losses) avoiding the corporate double-tax.

The second major change concerns new rules on partnership breakups because many commentators found the UPA concept of dissolution was confusing. After a partner withdraws, the surviving partners are sometimes forced to discontinue (wind-up) the business or continue it only with great difficulty. RUPA establishes two tracks for breakups: continuation or discontinuation. The new rules integrate the three major breakup problems in both tracks: (1) the subsequent obligations of withdrawing and continuing partners, (2) the buyout of a withdrawing or expelled partner, and (3) winding-up a partnership that will be discontinued.

There is a third major change to partners' rights and duties *inter se* (among themselves). RUPA replaces many mandatory rules with default rules so problems are resolved by RUPA unless the partners otherwise agree. This means that most RUPA provisions can be varied in the partnership agreement to achieve the desired governance structure. RUPA clarifies a partner's duties as agent: care, loyalty, good faith and fair dealing, and RUPA retains each partner's designation as a fiduciary. Partnerships may file a ''Statement of Authority'' with a government office to expand or restrict any individual partner's authority to make particular types of contracts on behalf of the partnership. This can eliminate some uncertainty about whether the partnership is liable on a particular contract made with outsiders.

Thought Questions

1. Why is it now advisable to amend the UPA? Would it be sufficient to simply permit the courts to clarify partnership relations, and also let partnership agreements customize the partnership's governance?

2. What concepts are ambiguous in the UPA? How does the proposed RUPA clarify these ambiguities?

3. What biases were present in the original UPA drafting effort? How were these resolved? How does the proposed RUPA resolve these biases?

Joint Ventures

Joint ventures are similar to general partnerships: They involve the operation and co-ownership of a business for profit. However, joint ventures are usually conducted for narrower, more limited purposes and usually continue for shorter durations than most general partnerships. Of course, some general partnerships have similar limitations, so the two organizational forms may be difficult to distinguish in practice.

Joint ventures are generally governed by partnership law.[1] For example, joint adventurers owe each other fiduciary duties, a principle established in the leading case defining that duty, *Meinhard v. Salmon*.[2] Joint adventurers must have equal rights to control the enterprise and they must share a community of interest. However, joint adventurers may agree to delegate control to one participant or hire an independent manager. The duration of a joint venture is usually fixed in an agreement governing the relationship, although it may be defined by the completion of a single project. For example, joint ventures are often found among the members of an underwriting syndicate, the purchasers and developers of a tract of land, or the joint research and development efforts of manufacturing corporations. Joint ventures may also be terminable at will.

Joint ventures are distinguishable from general partnerships in a few additional ways. Members of a joint venture do not generally have the same broad implied or apparent authority of a general agent as partners in a general partnership possess. Broad authority may nevertheless be specifically granted. Although participants in a joint venture have the same unlimited liability as general partners, the limit on their authority also limits the participants' potential liability. Death of a joint adventurer does not automatically dissolve the joint venture. Joint ventures are carefully scrutinized under the antitrust laws because they may become a convenient conduit for monopolization, price-fixing, or other anticompetitive activity.

International Joint Ventures

International joint ventures are emerging as a predominant form of business organization between cooperating firms from different nations. They are similar to domestic joint ventures to the extent that they involve participation by two or more firms collaborating on narrow business ventures for profit. However, international joint ventures are typically organized under detailed contracts and usually take the form of a limited liability corporation chartered in the host nation.

The international joint venture agreement typically specifies the scope of the parties' cooperation; their respective contributions, control, and profit sharing; the venture's duration, and the parties' rights to continue or be bought out after the venture terminates. There may be additional provisions on intellectual property licensing, confidentiality, expertise, and royalty payments. These provisions are needed because international joint ventures often involve participation between two firms from different nations. One firm is often regarded as a technological leader from an industrial nation. The other firm is usually a local firm in the host nation that desires a transfer of technology, management assistance, or a unique product supplied from the other firm. International joint ventures have been necessary to do business in many socialist and developing countries. Broader affiliations are often termed **global strategic alliances**.

The European Economic Community (EC) has established a new form of business organization under EC law for participating firms based only in the various EC member nations.[3] The European Economic Interest Grouping (EEIG) has some characteristics of both corporations and partnerships. The EC regulation establishes the basic structure for the EEIG, and regulations are provided by the nation in which the EEIG is organized. Like joint ventures, the EEIG must define the member firms' relative cooperation and must apportion its profits and losses among the participants. While EEIGs may be used for research and development, production, purchasing, and marketing, the participants must remain autonomous, so the EEIG may not manage the participants' separate activities involving their separate personnel, finance, and other investments. Firms from nations outside the EC may only participate in an EEIG indirectly through a subsidiary or affiliate if organized in an EC nation.

Mining Partnerships

The **mining partnership** is treated like a general partnership, but some differences apply in a few states. These partnerships involve an association

---

[1]See Taubman, *What Constitutes a Joint Venture?* vol. 41, Cornell Law Quarterly, p. 640 (1956); *Parks v. Riverside Insurance Co.*, 308 F.2d 175 (10th Cir. 1962); and *Burruss v. Green Auction & Realty Co. Inc.*, 319 S.E.2d 725 (Va. 1984).

[2]*Meinhard v. Salmon*, 249 N.Y. 458, 164 N.E. 545 (N.Y. Ct. App. 1928).

[3]EEC Council Regulation No. 2137/85.

among two or more owners of oil and gas or mineral rights where the partners operate a joint operation to extract the minerals and share the profits. The partners may delegate operations to one participant or to a subcontractor. Mining partnerships need not automatically dissolve when one partner dies. Generally, ownership is freely transferable unless otherwise agreed.

PARTNERSHIP FORMATION

Partnerships are formed quite easily; no particular formalities are necessary. There are no particular qualifications for partners except that partners must have capacity to contract. Therefore, partnerships with minors are voidable under contract law. Today, if a corporation's charter empowers it to be a general partner, the corporation is permitted by partnership law to become a partner, either with other corporations or with individuals. For example, corporations are often the general partner in modern limited partnerships.

When two or more persons associate to co-own and operate a business for profit, the business is automatically designated a partnership unless the participants carefully characterize the relationship as something else (e.g., employment, lease, passive co-ownership). The unwitting operation as a partnership poses problems in two instances: (1) the enterprise becomes insolvent and outsiders seek unlimited liability for all participants, or (2) the enterprise is successful and one or more participants seek to share in the profits or exercise control. For example, Pam, Paul, and Peter were ignorant that in simply commencing their consultation operations they had formed a partnership. As a partner, each had unlimited liability for Paul's loss leader consulting engagements negotiated with prospective clients. The following case illustrates the financial incentive to designate the business as a partnership. It also reinforces the uncertainty about whether many business firms are in reality partnerships, suggesting the need for more careful planning.

CUTLER v. BOWEN
543 P.2d 1349 (Utah 1975)

The Havana Club, a tavern owned by Dale Bowen, operated in a rented building. Frances Cutler was hired as a bartender and manager of the business. Bowen and Cutler agreed to receive $100 per week plus one half the net profits. However, the business was terminated four years later after the city redevelopment agency took over the building. Bowen retained the $10,000 damage payment made by the redevelopment agency. Cutler sued to receive half the former firm's going concern value, claiming she and Bowen were partners. Bowen appealed from a judgment in favor of Cutler.

CROCKETT, Justice

A basic principle of partnership law is set forth in our uniform partnership act:

Rules for determining the existence of a partnership.
    In determining whether a partnership exists these rules shall apply: (4) the receipt by a person of a share of the profits of a business is prima facie evidence that he is a partner in the business, but no such inference shall be drawn if such profits were received in payment:
    (b) as wages of an employee or rent to a landlord.

On the question whether profit sharing should be regarded simply as wages, it is important to consider the degree to which a party participates in the man-

agement of the enterprise and whether the relationship is such that the party shares generally in the potential profits or advantages and thus should be held responsible for losses or liability incurred therein.

    It is not shown here that any occasion arose where the plaintiff's responsibility for debts or other liabilities of the business was tested. However, throughout the four years in which she operated and managed the club, apparently with competence and efficiency, it was her responsibility to see that all bills were paid, including the rental on the lease, employees' salaries, the cost of all purchases, licenses and other expenses of the business. During that time she saw the defendant Bowen only infrequently for the purpose of rendering an accounting and dividing the profits. It is further pertinent that the parties reported their income tax as a partnership.

Under the arrangement as shown and as found by the trial court, a good case can be made out that it was largely through the capability, experience, and efforts of the plaintiff that, in addition to the physical plant, there existed a separate asset in the value of the "going concern and good will" of the business, which was being lost by its displacement. The plaintiff's involvement in this business was such that she would have been liable for any losses that might have occurred in its operations; she was entitled to participate in any profits or advantages that inured to it.

The cessation of operation of the Havana Club, was properly regarded as a termination of the partnership. The rule governing the rights of the parties in such circumstances is that after all debts and liabilities of the partnership have been satisfied, each partner should be repaid his contributions thereto and any remainder allocated as their interests appear. Except for the physical assets, which belong to the defendant and to which the plaintiff makes no claim, the further asset of the business; that is, the value of what is called going concern and goodwill belong to the two of them as partners in the enterprise; and that when the business could not be relocated, the $10,000 should probably be regarded as compensation for the loss by the forced relocation of the business; and that the parties having lost the respective equal shares in the going business operation, they should also share equally in the compensation for its loss. [Judgment Affirmed.]

Case Questions

1. What reasons support the plaintiff's claim that the Havana Club was operated as a partnership? What reasons support the defendant's claim it was not a partnership?

2. What rival hypothesis are there to the plaintiff's claim that sharing profits was evidence that a partnership existed?

3. What ambiguities existed in the relationship between Cutler and Bowen concerning the Havana Club? How could the parties have made this clearer?

Articles of Partnership

Oral partnership agreements are generally valid unless their relationship is governed by the statute of frauds, discussed in Chapter 16. However, it is always advisable to establish and clarify the partners' relationships with a written partnership agreement, often called the **articles of partnership**. By going through the motions of drafting the document, the parties can better consider their business purpose and establish their expectations. The drafting exercise permits the design of a suitable business structure and helps minimize fraud and surprise. Typically, the partnership agreement allocates the partners' relative participation in management, profits, and losses under various scenarios. A description and format for typical articles of partnership terms appears in Figure 37–1.

The Partnership's Firm Name

Partners often name their firm by combining all their surnames. However, this may be impractical if the partnership has too many partners or they prefer a name that suggests the firm's business activity—for example, "Acme Accounting Service." Any firm name that is other than the surnames of all the partners is considered a **fictitious name** because it does not accurately reflect all the participants. Partnerships with fictitious names must register the name in all states it does business. Registration must generally include the partners' names and addresses, the partnership's fictitious name and its address, and the partnership's business. To avoid confusion, partnerships are often prohibited from using names that are deceptively similar to other firms' names. Registration provides individuals and businesses in the state with the information needed to assert their rights against the partnership. Partnerships failing to comply are subject to fine and may be denied access to the state's courts until the name is registered.

Partnership by Estoppel

There can be unlimited personal liability for persons who give the appearance that they are acting like a partnership. A **partnership by estoppel** arises if an outside third party is led to reasonably believe a

Figure 37–1   Partnership Agreement/Articles of Partnership (common provisions)

I. BASIC PARTNERSHIP STRUCTURE

FIRM NAME: Usually, the surnames of all partners or the founders; alternatively, a fictitious name must be registered in all states in which the partnership is "doing business."

DATE: Date of initial agreement; dates of revisions, amendments, or addenda are also desirable.

PARTNERS' NAMES: Founding partners' names listed; provision may be made for the names and dates new partners are admitted and the dates founders retire.

PLACE OF BUSINESS: Address of the partnership's principal place of business and the state under which the partnership is formed.

FORM AND TYPE OF BUSINESS: Statement that the firm is a general (or limited) partnership; description of its business operations and purpose (e.g., retail sales, accounting services, manufacturing).

TERM: Statement of the date business was initially started and the duration; events may be listed that trigger termination (e.g., death, incapacity, or bankruptcy of a named partner or any partner; completion of purpose; illegality of partnership purpose).

II. FINANCIAL ARRANGEMENTS

PARTNERS' INITIAL CAPITAL CONTRIBUTIONS: Founders' initial investment in money or property value listed or referenced in an attachment.

CHANGES IN CAPITAL: Governance process to require additional contributions, whether interest accrues on capital, time allowed to make contributions, definition and limitation on rights to demand return of capital, and whether priorities exist between partners over capital. Definition and listing of partnership versus individual partner property.

SHARES OF PROFITS (LOSSES): List of partners' names and their initial percentage share of profits and separately of losses if different from profits. Definition of profits and loss, reference to accounting methods if different from GAAP, and the fiscal year if different from the calendar year, including special reserves, drawing rights, distributions, and if compensation is limited to winding up.

FINANCIAL INFORMATION: Partners' rights to inspect books and records, place for keeping partnership books, duty to prepare financial statements and tax filings, maintenance of bank and brokerage accounts, and responsibility for negotiable instruments (e.g., checks, notes).

III. MANAGEMENT

MANAGING PARTNER(S): Name(s) of managing partner(s), selection and replacement process, and managing partner's rights and authority.

PARTNERS' VOTING RIGHTS: List partners' names and voting weights, and situations requiring majority vote and unanimous decisions.

PARTNERS' INDIVIDUAL AUTHORITIES: Grant and limitation on particular powers of particular partners and/or managing partners to bind the partnership in contract (e.g., borrow, settlement of partnership claims by arbitration, confess a judgment, purchase material and inventory, sell stock in trade, negotiate service and employment contracts, and/or sell partnership real estate).

ADMISSION OF NEW PARTNERS: Process of admitting new partners, determining and/or financing their capital contributions, and subcommittee for sponsoring and approving new partners.

DISPUTES AMONG PARTNERS: Partner deadlock will be resolved using mediation unless conflicting claims are made to assets or distributions. In the latter case the dispute will be submitted to binding arbitration. Arbitrators and procedures will be used according to rules set by the American Arbitration Association.

IV. DISSOLUTION

CAUSES OF DISSOLUTION: Events or circumstances permitting rightful dissolution, winding up, liquidation, and termination of the partnership.

WRONGFUL DISSOLUTION: Causes of wrongful dissolution, valuation of outgoing partner's financial interests, limitation on wrongfully dissolving partner's financial rights (e.g., no share in goodwill, long-term payout of partnership share, and/or damages owed to surviving partners).

DUTIES TO WIND UP: Duties of winding-up partner to discharge partnership debts and liabilities, creditor notification, conduct of liquidation, valuation of partnership property, financial settlements with other partners, rights to property in kind, distribution of surplus in accordance with capital accounts and percentage of profits, and rights to continue business.

V. SIGNATURES

EXECUTION: Signatures of witnesses, partners, dates, and notaries; matters of formal execution.

---

partnership exists. Partnership by estoppel is neither a real partnership nor is it a separate form of business organization. It arises under equitable principles to protect the reasonable expectations of third parties by creating partnershiplike liability for contracts made by an alleged partner.

Two elements are required for a partnership by estoppel: (1) words or conduct that claim a partnership exists, and (2) third parties rely to their detriment, reasonably believing in the partnership and changing their position in reliance. Once a partnership by estoppel is established, all the partners by estoppel are authorized to the same extent as partners in real partnerships. For example, if Smith pretends Jones is her partner and Jones does not complain, Smith becomes authorized as a partner by estoppel to bind herself and Jones to contracts giving them both unlimited liability.

UPA § 16.   Partner by Estoppel

(1) When a person, by words spoken or written or by conduct, represents himself, or consents to another representing him to anyone, as a partner in an existing partnership or with one or more persons not actual partners, he is liable to any such person . . . and if he has made such representation . . . in a public manner he is liable to such person. . . .

(a) When a partnership liability results, he is liable as though he were an actual member of the partnership.

(b) When no partnership liability results, he is liable jointly with the other persons . . . so consenting to the contract or representation.

Representations made in private should result in only limited potential for partnership liability. However, a public representation can expose the partners by estoppel to unlimited partnership liability to anyone in the public who heard and reasonably relied on the representation of partnership. In *Reisen Lumber & Millwork v. Simonelli*,[4] Simonelli and Millinger operated the Yorke Investment Co. as a partnership. They filed a business name certificate showing their individual involvement. In 1964, the partnership was dissolved and Simonelli continued operating the business alone under the Yorke name. No certificate of dissolution was ever filed, so Millinger's name was still on the public record as a partner in Yorke. Reisen Lumber extended credit to Yorke but never knew of Millinger's former involvement. Millinger was not held liable for Yorke's unpaid debts to Reisen as a partner by estoppel because Millinger's name on the certificate was unknown to Reisen when it extended credit to Simonelli.

---

[4]*Reisen Lumber & Millwork v. Simonelli*, 237 A.2d 303 (N.J. Super. 1967).

PARTNERSHIP PROPERTY

Partnerships, like most business firms, must use property for their operations: real estate and buildings to house their facilities, machinery for manufacturing, office equipment for administration, inventory for sale or works in progress, and capital to operate. Issues may arise concerning the nature of partnership property, the rights of partners and the partnership in partnership property, how to distinguish partnership property from the partners' individual property, and the nature of a partner's ownership interest in the partnership. This section discusses these issues.

Tenancy in Partnership

The UPA established a new form of co-ownership for property belonging to a partnership. **Tenancy in partnership** grants equal property rights for all partners to use partnership property for partnership purposes unless all partners consent to some personal use. Like joint tenancy or tenancy by the entireties discussed in Chapter 9, the tenancy in partnership includes the right of **survivorship**. The share a deceased partner had in specific partnership property vests immediately in the copartner(s). Of course, the decedent partner's heirs inherit the decedent's partnership interest but are not substituted as partners.

Unlike ownership under joint tenancy, a partner may not transfer or assign his or her interest in specific partnership property in a sale, by will or intestate succession, nor can a partner encumber it with a mortgage or other security interest. Partnership property is not subject to attachment or execution by an individual partner's creditor. However, as described below, an individual partner's creditor with an unsatisfied charging order may sometimes foreclose against the ***partner's interest***. This protects the ongoing partnership business from losing rights to particular partnership assets if one partner defaults on a personal loan. Of course, a partnership creditor may execute against or attach partnership property if the partnership granted a security interest in such property, as when a partnership mortgages partnership property.

Individual versus Partnership Property

There is often uncertainty about the ownership of partnership property because partnerships are formed informally. This raises ambiguities arising from the

Figure 37–2   Partnership versus Individual Partner Property: Intent Factors

	Tends to Support as Either:	
Factor	**Partnership Property**	**Individual Property**
Property tax payments	Partnership pays	Individual partner pays
Insurance premiums	Partnership pays	Individual partner pays
Financial records	Recorded as partnership asset	Unrecorded on partnership books; or Recorded on individual partner's books
Income tax returns	Recorded as partnership asset	Unrecorded on partnership books; or Recorded on individual partner's books
Rent paid on property	No rent paid to individual partner	Rent paid by partnership to individual partner
Maintenance and repair expenses	Partnership pays	Individual partner pays

characteristics of a partnership's entity versus aggregate status. Partnership property may be held in the name of the partnership, in a single partner's name, in the name of some but not all partners, or in the name of all partners individually. Therefore, ownership is not determined simply by the record title holder. This may lead to questions concerning the true ownership of alleged partnership property. Individual partners may legitimately claim they own particular property used in the partnership business because they simply loaned the property to the partnership. Individual partners may claim ownership of property contributed as capital to the partnership. At the same time, the other partners or the partnership's creditors have conflicting incentives to claim that such property is partnership property because this may increase their share if the partnership assets are later liquidated. This ambiguity raises considerable ethical questions, particularly for the partner entrusted with recordkeeping and management.

The partners' *intent* concerning the ownership of any piece of property is the most influential factor. The intent concerning ownership may be apparent from the title, who pays the property taxes, who pays the insurance premiums, how the property is recorded on the partnership books or on partnership tax returns, separate oral or written agreements between the partners, whether the partnership paid rent on the property, or who pays the maintenance and repair expenses for the property. When disputes arise about the true ownership of alleged partnership property, the courts will consider the preponderance of these factors to determine the parties' intent. This intent may be reflected in several ways, as summarized in Figure 37–2.

Is it ethical for the partnership to appropriate an individual partner's property for partnership use? Conversely, is it ethical for a single partner to take advantage of poorly kept partnership records and appropriate partnership property for personal use? As the following case illustrates, these questions arise all too often when partnerships dissolve.

UPA § 8. Partnership Property

(1) All property originally brought into the partnership stock or subsequently acquired by purchase or otherwise, on account of the partnership, is partnership property.

(2) Unless the contrary intention appears, property acquired with partnership funds is partnership property.

GUALDIN v. CORN
595 S. W. 2nd 329 (Mo. App. 1980)

Corn entered into a partnership with Gualdin on land Corn inherited from his parents. They agreed to share all costs, labor, losses, and profits equally without paying rent on Corn's land. The parties used partnership funds to clear the land, maintain fences, and cultivate crops. Two buildings were erected on Corn's land at partnership expense. After the partnership dissolved, Gualdin took the "removable" assets from Corn's land and paid Corn $7,500 for them. Gualdin sued Corn for one half the interest in the value of the "nonremovable" buildings. Gualdin appealed from a trial court judgment for Corn.

GREEN, Justice

The rule is well established that improvements made upon lands owned by one partner, if made with partnership funds for purposes of partnership business, are the personal property of the partnership, and a non-landowning partner is entitled to his proportionate share of their value. [Under the Uniform Partnership Act § 8]:

1. All property originally brought into the partnership stock or subsequently acquired by purchase or otherwise, on account of the partnership is partnership property.
2. Unless the contrary intention appears, property acquired with partnership funds is partnership property.

The general rule [above] is activated only where, as here, there is no agreement between the parties which controls such disposition. It matters not that the landowning partner contributed the use of his land to the partnership, that the non-landowning partner knew that the improvements, when made, could not be removed from the land, or that a joint owner with the landowning partner was not joined in this suit for dissolution and accounting for the partnership. The trial court should have awarded plaintiff his proportionate share of the value of the improvements at the time of the dissolution of the partnership. Reversed.

Case Questions

1. What is the issue the court confronted about the ownership of property? How are the improvements classified — individual or partnership property?
2. What reasons support the court's holding that the improvements are the individual property of the partner Corn? What reasons support holding that the improvements belong to the partnership?
3. What alternative hypotheses are there to explain how these partners handled the ownership of the land and the rights to the improvements?

The RUPA resolves some of the ambiguity about property under the UPA and the case law. The vague term *stock* as a reference to general partnership property is eliminated because it is often used to refer only to inventory, is sometimes expanded to all assets, and could be misinterpreted as an investment security — for example, "capital stock." Anything acquired in the partnership name or acquired in the partners' individual names with an indication they do business as a partnership is designated as partnership property. RUPA presumes property purchased with partnership funds belongs to the partnership and property acquired in an individual partner's name without the use of partnership funds belongs to the individual partner. This RUPA presumption can be overcome with convincing contrary evidence.

Partner's Interest

The property right each partner has in ownership of the partnership itself is known as the **partner's interest**. This includes a share of the profits and surplus. The traditional rights of a partner also include the right to participate in management, demand an accounting, inspect partnership books, and cause dissolution. While a partner's property right is considered an intangible personal property right, it cannot be transferred intact to an outsider. Partnership membership requires unanimous consent of all partners. Full transfer would be permitted only where it was equivalent to the transferring partner's withdrawal and the other partners' unanimous approval to admit the transferee.

The transfer or assignment of a partner's interest does not automatically dissolve the partnership. The partner(s) remaining after assignment may continue operations without winding up the business. Further, the transferee has none of the traditional partner rights of participating in management, requiring an accounting, inspection of records, or causing dissolution. However, the transferee may receive the assigning partner's share of profits as defined in the partnership agreement and may share in any surplus remaining after dissolution.

When a partner dies, the partner's interest passes to the deceased partner's personal representative (e.g., administrator or executor). The death triggers a dissolution. Partnerships that have not planned how to provide funding for a deceased partner's share may be forced into liquidation. Many well-planned partnerships have provisions in their partnership agreements to value the deceased partner's interests. For example, an alternative partnership agreement between Pam, Peter, and Paul could have provided for payment to the partnership from life insurance policies; annuities could have provided periodic payments to a surviving spouse; and goodwill could have been excluded from the valuation process.

CREDITORS' RIGHTS

Creditors of a partnership have different rights and difficulties than do the creditors of a corporation. All partners have unlimited individual liability for the debts of the partnership. Shareholders of a corporation generally have their liability limited to their initial capital contribution. The UPA provides that partners have **joint liability** for contracts. This effectively requires creditors to sue all partners together in a single suit for an effective judgment against the partnership. Partners have **joint and several liability** for the partnership's torts, permitting an effective suit against fewer than all partners. For example, if a client sues a law partnership for malpractice, any or all the partners are liable for the whole judgment amount. However, due process requires every defendant must be given a "day in court," so judgments are generally ineffective against partners' personal assets unless they are individually served with process (summons). Therefore, only the partners named as defendants are individually responsible for an adverse judgment.

Three developments diminish these procedural difficulties: (1) most states have separate statutes providing for each partner's joint and several liability for breach of contract damages, (2) **common-name statutes** validate suits brought against the partnership as an entity, and (3) experienced and powerful creditors (e.g., commercial lenders) often demand some or all the partners sign the loan notes in both their individual and partner capacities. RUPA would make partners jointly and severally liable for all partnership debts.

Partner's Individual Liability

It would be easiest for a creditor to satisfy an adverse judgment against the partnership by going after the most valuable or visible assets, whether they belong to the partnership or to an individual partner(s). However, generally, creditors must exhaust partnership assets before going after the individual partners' assets to satisfy judgments. The individual assets of partners unnamed in the litigation are liable for partnership debts only after insolvency. Partners required to pay more than their proportional share of a partnership debt may generally seek contribution from the unnamed partners. Additionally, a term in the partnership agreement may allocate losses or liability and would be enforceable, but only as between the partners.

Consider the example of the ABC partnership that breached a contract to Acme Corp. Only the partnership and A were named as defendants in the suit. If partnership assets are insufficient to pay the judgment, Acme may not proceed against B & C personally unless ABC is in insolvency. A's personal assets are liable to pay the deficiency after the ABC assets are exhausted. A could seek to have two thirds of the damages A was required to pay to Acme contributed one third by B and one third by C. However, if the ABC partnership agreement provided for B to bear all losses, A could recover the entire amount of the judgment from B, both for the value of partnership assets and A's personal assets paid to Acme. The agreement would not shield A's interest in partnership assets nor A's personal assets from liability to Acme because the partnership agreement cannot adversely affect third parties. However, it can affect the partners' relations among themselves, (*inter se*) requiring the loss sharing among A, B, and C.

Creditors of Individual Partners: Charging Order

Individual partners may have a large proportion of their individual assets tied up in the partnership. This encourages each partner's individual creditors to view each partner's interest in partnership assets as an important source to satisfy the partner's individual debts (e.g., home mortgage, car loan, and personal credit line). However, if it were easy for creditors of individual partners to attach partnership assets for individual partner debts, this would compromise the partnership operations and the livelihood of other partners. The UPA has drawn a balance in this area by developing a multistep process for individual creditors. A **charging order** permits the partnership to maintain its assets, redeem the defaulting partner's debt, and reduce the adverse impact of individual creditor claims on the partnership's business.

The charging order resembles a garnishment order. The creditor may petition the court for an order to receive the defaulting partner's share of partnership profits until the debt is satisfied. If a projection of the debtor-partner's share of profits shows it is unlikely to satisfy the individual creditor's claim within a reasonable time, the creditor may again go to court to apply for a foreclosure of the debtor-partner's interest in the partnership. These delays provide the other partners with time to redeem, or pay off, the defaulting partner's debt and thereby save the partnership from liquidation. In the worst case, the foreclosure could require liquidation of the partnership assets, effectively putting the partnership out of business. Because foreclosure puts such a strain on the other innocent partners, courts seldom order a foreclosure unless the defaulting partner's projected flow of profits is clearly insufficient to satisfy the debt.

RUPA Approach

RUPA extends its entity theory approach to creditor's rights problems by permitting suit by or against the partnership. RUPA generally shields individual partner's assets from creditor's claims until after partnership assets are first exhausted. A creditor may proceed directly against an individual partner's assets without first obtaining a judgment against the partnership in five major instances. First, where the creditor also wins a judgment against the individual

partner. Second, where the partnership is in bankruptcy. Third, the partner may agree that partnership assets need not be exhausted first. Fourth, a court may permit individual partner liability when it would be equitable, when partnership assets are clearly insufficient, or when exhausting partnership assets would be excessively burdensome. Fifth, the partner may be obligated by law or contract to pay independently of the partnership's existence. Under RUPA, partners are more like guarantors; they are not primarily responsible for unsatisfied partnership debts.

Under RUPA, the charging order more closely resembles a lien. RUPA would permit an unpaid creditor holding a charging order to foreclose. However, normally, no dissolution and liquidation of the partnership would be required unless the partnership was at will when the charging order was issued. Under RUPA, charging order foreclosures generally would require only the sale of the debtor-partner's partnership interest. The purchaser at such a sale would not become a partner unless the other partners unanimously approved. The proceeds from the foreclosure sale would go to the unpaid creditor.

PARTNERS' RIGHTS AND DUTIES AMONG THEMSELVES

A partner's interest includes a ''bundle of rights'' considered fundamental to the partner's status. Partners may choose their associates, veto fundamental changes in the business form, participate in management, limit the extent of authority and permissible activities of their copartners, and they are entitled to their share in financial rights. The rights held by each partner create duties on the other partners. The partner's duties to each other arise under the UPA and the case law interpreting partners' rights. These rights and duties arise automatically. However, the partners may vary or eliminate some of them either with provisions in the articles of partnership or by separate agreement. The RUPA would expand the partners' ability to vary statutory rules by contract to achieve their objectives.

Partners must generally be obedient to partnership votes, enter contracts only when authorized, and provide services to the partnership. However, **silent partners** are expected only to contribute capital. The partnership's expectations for any partner's individual efforts may also vary. The partnership may be entitled to damages if a partner's inactivity requires hiring a replacement.

Partner Fiduciary Duties

Each partner is considered an agent of the partnership and of each other partner to the extent necessary to accomplish the partnership business purpose. Therefore, each partner owes a fiduciary duty of care, good faith, and loyalty both to the partnership and to the other partners. These duties are generally enforceable in equity, but only after an **accounting**, a comprehensive financial review of transactions and cash flows. This accounting prerequisite is also known as the **exclusivity** rule. It permits a more accurate depiction of the partner's activities before these matters become issues in a breach of duty suit.

RUPA would eliminate exclusivity and the need to dissolve the partnership before a suit is brought between partners. RUPA would grant courts more flexibility to fashion equitable remedies or order a wrongful partner to pay damages to the other partners.

Duty of Care

Partners must conduct the partnership business with care. Partners are not responsible for partnership losses due to honest errors in judgment, the lack of ordinary care, or for external factors beyond their control. This is like the business judgment rule in corporate law, which protects officers and directors from shareholder suits for simple negligence. However, partners can be held liable for acts beyond simple negligence: culpable negligence, recklessness, gross negligence, or wanton and willful misconduct. RUPA retains these concepts by making a partner liable for lack of due care only when it constitutes gross negligence or willful misconduct. Consider whether Paul was exercising due care in negotiating so many loss leader consulting engagements for the management consulting business discussed in the opening scenario. Were these simple lapses in judgment or gross negligence?

Duty of Loyalty

The essence of an agent's fiduciary duty is the duty of loyalty requiring the utmost good faith and fair dealing with the other partners. A classic expression of this duty was written by Judge Benjamin Cardozo, indicating its importance among joint adventurers who are like partners.

Fiduciary Duty of Partners

Joint adventurers, like copartners, owe to one another, while the enterprise continues, the duty of the finest loyalty. Many forms of conduct permissible in a workaday world for those acting at arm's length, are forbidden to those bound by fiduciary ties. A trustee is held to something stricter than the morals of the marketplace. Not honesty alone, but the punctilio of an honor the most sensitive, is the standard of behavior. . . . Only thus has the level of conduct for fiduciaries been kept at a level higher than that trodden by the crowd.[5]

UPA § 21. Partner Accountable as a Fiduciary

(1) Every partner must account to the partnership for any benefit, and hold as a trustee for it any profits derived by him without the consent of the other partners from any transaction connected with the formation, conduct, or liquidation of the partnership or from any use by him of its property.

Each partner's fiduciary duties have been interpreted to prohibit a partner's secret profits, a partner's competition with the partnership, and a partner's breach of confidentiality. As in any agency relationship, the fiduciary duty of loyalty is the most fundamental ethical concern in partnerships. The abuse of position when a partner owes a duty of loyalty presents the most recurrent of ethical dilemmas in partnership relations.

The UPA specifically forbids any partner from making a **secret profit** from transactions for the partnership. This generally prohibits a partner from personally receiving a kickback or rebate from an outsider who contracted with the partnership. The secret payment is like a bribe to encourage the partner to grant the contract to the outsider. The rule also forbids a partner from making a secret profit in a transaction the partner makes directly between himself and the partnership. This rule does not forbid contracts between a partner and the partnership. However, the potential for conflicts of interest require a **fully informed consent**—that is, approval by the other partners after full disclosure of the partner's adverse interest. Any partner breaching this

---

[5]*Meinhard v. Salmon*, 249 N.Y. 458, 164 N.E. 545 (N.Y. Ct. App. 1928).

duty is liable to the partnership for the secret profit. The law confronts this recurring ethical dilemma by requiring the other partners' approval before such suspect transactions can be legitimized.

Partners are forbidden from competing with the partnership. This means no partner may independently enter the same line of business as the partnership. However, the partnership may make explicit exceptions to this general rule. Some partners are so valuable to the partnership that it is better to have them join as a competing partner than to lose that partner's contribution altogether. It is also a breach of a partner's fiduciary duty to misuse confidential partnership or trade secret information. For example, if a partner used client lists or new product information for personal purposes or shared this information with an outsider, this would breach the partner's fiduciary duty.

RUPA recognizes that partners should be able to pursue their own self-interest without always seeking their copartners' permission first or risk a fiduciary breach. While RUPA prohibits the partners from eliminating altogether the duty of good faith and fair dealing, it permits the partnership to specify permissible outside business interests or other conduct.

Financial Rights

Membership in a partnership automatically involves several financial rights and correlative duties. First, partners are entitled to their proportionate share of profits (losses), capital gains on partnership prop-erty sold, and the surplus remaining after liquidation. Unless otherwise agreed, profits and losses are shared equally and in the same proportion. Second, partners are each entitled to a return of their capital investments(s), adjusted for later contributions or withdrawals. Third, partners are entitled to *reimbursement* for expenses they personally advance for the partnership business. When a partner operates the partnership business over a long period of time, the net losses suffered by the partner must be indemnified. Additionally, this right of *indemnification* includes the right to receive repayment for sums paid by a partner to settle judgments against the partnership. Fourth, these financial rights would be difficult to enforce unless each partner were required to *account* for their receipt, use, or disbursement of partnership funds or other assets. Adequate records must be kept and each partner has the right to *inspect the partnership books and records*. Generally, the partnership books must be kept at the principal place of business.

Unless otherwise agreed, partners generally have no right to receive compensation beyond their share of profits. Of course, partners must receive periodic payments to meet their own personal living expenses. These are called **advances** or **draws**. Partners are entitled to interest and principal payments only on legitimate loans made to the partnership, not their capital contributions, unless otherwise agreed. The last surviving partner is usually entitled to compensation for winding up the partnership business. However, this raises ethical questions and fairness, as indicated in the following case.

ALTMAN v. ALTMAN
653 F.2d 755 (3rd Cir. 1981)

Between 1952 and 1973, Sidney and Ashley Altman operated real estate construction partnerships in Pennsylvania. They shared equally in management and control of the partnerships, received identical salaries, and charged equal amounts of personal expenses to the partnerships. After Sidney moved to Florida in 1973 he began withdrawing from active management of the partnerships, returning to Pennsylvania only occasionally. However, soon thereafter, the brothers began negotiating Sidney's eventual retirement from the business. Ashley claimed the retirement was implemented on the partnership books by the end of 1973, but Sidney claimed they came to no agreement on his retirement.

Sidney brought suit to dissolve the partnership, alleging Ashley violated the partnership agreement, misappropriated partnership assets, and generally excluded Sidney from the business. Ashley appealed the trial court's judgment that no dissolution had occurred and sought compensation beyond his share of the profits for his management efforts between 1973 and 1977.

SITZ, Chief Judge

The Pennsylvania Supreme Court has emphasized that ''In the absence of an agreement to the contrary, a partner is not entitled to compensation beyond his share of the profits, for services rendered by him in performing partnership matters. [The] right to compensation arises only where the services rendered extend beyond normal partnership functions.''

Ashley emphasizes that after August 1973 the entire management and supervision of the partnerships were left to him. He asserts that he not only preserved the partnerships' properties but also maximized the profits during this period. Ashley apparently is contending that compensation is awarded under Pennsylvania Law whenever it would be highly inequitable not to do so. However, such services must extend beyond normal partnership functions. Thus, Ashley must show more than the fact that a failure to award compensation would be highly inequitable; he must also show that his services extended beyond normal partnership function.

The services rendered by Ashley maintained the operation of existing business in the same manner as they had been before Sydney's departure. The lack of participation in the partnerships by Sydney was with the consent of Ashley. Thus, we conclude that the district court did not commit error when it awarded Sydney an amount equal to one half of the personal expenses charged to the business partnerships by Ashley. The judgment of the district court will be affirmed.

Case Questions

1. Under what conditions should a continuing partner be awarded compensation for running the business?

2. What reasons were used to deny Ashley additional compensation for continuing the partnership?

3. What assumptions are made about the relative contributions of services by partners and how these may change over time if compensation is denied? What are the assumptions if compensation is granted?

When the partnership business is left in the hands of a single managing partner or in the hands of a single surviving partner, ethical problems arise. During such times, there is a strong temptation to take excessive salary and make excessive and unconsented personal use of partnership assets. While partnership law provides for the other partners' vindication of these rights, such transgressions often go undetected. Therefore, it ultimately becomes an ethical dilemma for the managing or surviving partner.

Rights in Dissolution

Unlike corporations that have perpetual life, partnerships can exist only with the consent of all partners. In a partnership at will, any partner has the unqualified right to retire or withdraw. The other partners may expel any partner by simply dissolving and then reform the partnership excluding the expelled partner. Of course, the participants in an ongoing business may desire more certainty than this provides. The articles of partnership or other agreement may establish special termination procedures and provide for rightful dissolution such as after the passage of time or the happening of an event. For

example, a partnership formed to develop a tract of land would be severely compromised if one partner withdrew before all the lots were sold because this could force the partnership to sell the whole tract at a wholesale price, frustrating the partnership's efforts to profit through sales at retail prices.

Where a partner withdraws or is expelled in violation of established procedures, the dissolution is wrongful, triggering the liability for damages. The wrongfully withdrawing partner may be liable to the partnership or the remaining partners may be liable to the wrongfully expelled partner. An effective **continuation agreement** usually limits the outgoing partner's rights to require a winding up with its attendant liquidation of partnership assets. Typically, the outgoing partner has no right to receive a portion of goodwill, the payout of the outgoing partner's financial interests is delayed, and the remaining partners may reform and continue the business. Winding up is discussed further in Chapter 38.

RUPA effectively abandons the dissolution regime of the UPA in favor of the new partnership breakup concept called **partner dissociation**. RUPA provides supplementary provisions on wrongful dissociation, establishes the right to continue business, and provides procedures for the **buyout of a partner**. RUPA dissolutions are discussed more fully in Chapter 38.

PARTNERS' TORT LIABILITY

Partners are liable for the torts committed by their copartners, other agents, and employees just like any other principal. The respondeat superior doctrine permits the victim of a servant's tortious act to recover damages from either party if the servant was acting within the scope of employment for the master. Just as under respondeat superior, the wrongful partner or employee must indemnify the partnership for payments made to such injured victims.

UPA § 13 Partnership Bound by Partner's Wrongful Act

Where, by any wrongful act or omission of any partner acting in the ordinary course of the business of the partnership or with the authority of his co-partners, loss or injury is caused to any person, not being a partner . . . the partnership is liable therefor.

The partnership is usually liable for the negligent torts of its servants or partners if conducted while pursuing the partnership business. However, a partnership is usually not liable for intentional torts committed by its servants or copartners. A partnership seldom intends or authorizes the tortious act. The commission of intentional torts is seldom within the scope of the partnership business. For example, the partners in a barroom business would not be liable for one partner's unprovoked attack of a peaceable patron.[6]

The partnership may be liable for tortious acts of servants or copartners where these acts were either authorized or were an incidental part of conducting partnership business. For example, there may be partnership liability for the intentional tort of fraud. Misstatements may occur in connection with authorized partnership business because partners often make representations to customers. Therefore, partnership liability for intentional torts often depends on how closely the intentional act falls within the scope of the partnership business.

---

[6]*Vrabal v. Acri*, 103 N.E.2d 564 (Ohio 1952).

PARTNERS' CRIMINAL LIABILITY

Partners are generally not liable for the criminal acts of their servants or copartners. A copartner's criminal liability presents similar intent problems as discussed above in the vicarious liability of masters and for partners' intentional torts. It is difficult to hold partners criminally liable unless they participate or authorize the criminal act. Additionally, the aggregate theory of partnerships has insulated them from liability because a partnership has not been considered a type of entity that can be held criminally liable. Therefore, only the servant or copartner who committed the criminal act is usually criminally liable.

Increasingly, criminal statutes recognize that partnerships are entities that may be criminally liable. For example, the Foreign Corrupt Practices Act, which outlaws foreign bribes to gain business, applies to all *domestic concerns*, including partnerships. The Racketeer Influenced and Corrupt Organizations law (RICO) prohibits the use of racketeering profits to finance any *enterprise*, which includes partnerships. These laws address ethical matters and are addressed more fully in Chapter 44. Partners may be held criminally liable for other forms of participation in criminal activities such as conspiracy or assisting the criminal as an accessory, before or after the fact.

END–OF–CHAPTER QUESTIONS

1. The debate between observers claiming partnerships are aggregates and those who claim partnerships are entities causes some confusion. Explain what reasons support designating partnerships as aggregates. Explain the reasons that support designating a partnership as an entity. What impact would the RUPA have on this debate?

2. Discuss the problems with holding a partnership liable for the intentional torts or criminal activities committed by an employee or copartner. What reasons support holding the partnership liable? What reasons support insulating the partnership or other partners from liability?

3. Acme Mfg. is a manufacturing partnership among Peter, Allen, and Charles created under written articles of partnership showing their business purpose and mu-

tual assent. After several years of break-even operations, Acme hired Arthur, an outsider, to provide accounting and management consulting services. Arthur established Acme's accounting system, improved the internal control system, and advised Peter, the managing partner, on several major decisions about employees and new product development. Despite these efforts, Acme's product market eventually fell, forcing Acme into insolvency. SupplyCo., one of Acme's long-time suppliers, sued Arthur for part of the unpaid Acme debt, claiming he was a partner. What issue will arise concerning Arthur's potential liability? What reasons would SupplyCo. need to prove to hold Arthur liable?

4. The Outrigger West Hotel was operated by two companies, with 73 percent of gross receipts going to OWLP, a limited partnership, and 27 percent to Hawaii Hotels Operating Co. (HHOC). OWLP owned the Outrigger and paid its 73 percent share of Hawaii excise taxes. The Hawaii director of taxes claimed OWLP owed 100 percent of the Outrigger's excise taxes. The director conceded that if the Outrigger was considered a partnership, each partner would owe the excise taxes separately, not jointly. The director claimed HHOC was not a partner liable for its 26 percent share of excise taxes because HHOC only operated the Outrigger under contract to OWLP. Should partnership law apply to the Outrigger joint venture? What reasons support the director's argument that HHOC was not a partner? See *In re O. W. Ltd. Partnership*, 668 P.2d 56 (Ha. Ct. App. 1983).

5. Two recent business school graduates, Tom and Paula, agreed to begin a consulting business after they graduate. After graduation, they began business operations. Both used their automobiles to call on clients and their personal computers to provide accounting services, financial analysis, and memos advising clients. They eventually leased office space and borrowed from the bank to purchase of-

fice furniture. However, within a few months, a recession began and their clients terminated their consulting contracts. Tom and Paula eventually defaulted on their lease and loan. Tom was penniless but Paula had a substantial inheritance. What must the landlord and bank prove to hold Paula liable for all of the defaulted payments? If Paula pays these judgments, what must she prove to get Tom's contribution to these expenses?

6. C & F Trucking was a partnership owned by Carroll and Fulton. Carroll purchased a trailer for use in the business, using his own money. The seller's invoice showed C & F as the purchaser and the title certificate listed C & F as owner. After Fulton filed for bankruptcy, the bankruptcy trustee claimed the trailer was Fulton's individual property. Is the trailer Fulton's or Carroll's individual property, or is it a partnership asset? See *In re Fulton*, 43 B.R. 273 (M.D. Tenn. 1984).

7. Eugene and Marlowe operated the family farm known as the Mehl Brothers Farms as a partnership but without a written agreement. The brothers operated very informally; each usually informed the other before withdrawing funds from the partnership account to pay personal expenses. Eugene withdrew partnership funds and purchased a tavern, the Dagmar Bar. Bonnie received the tavern in a property settlement after their divorce. The title and liquor license were held in the name of Eugene and his wife Bonnie. However, tax records and the divorce settlement papers show the partnership owned the tavern. Marlowe claimed the tavern was partnership property after the farm partnership was dissolved. What reasons support designating the tavern as partnership property? What reasons support holding the tavern as Eugene's and then Bonnie's individual property? See *Mehl v. Mehl*, 786 P.2d 1173 (Mont. 1990).

8. Dr. Antenucci and Dr. Pena were partners in medical practice. Both doctors had treated Elaine Zuckerman while she was pregnant with her son Daniel. Elaine won

a judgment against Pena for malpractice, but Antenucci was found not liable. Nevertheless, Elaine sought to hold Antenucci liable as a partner to Pena. Should Dr. Antenucci's liability hinge on the fact that Elaine failed to name the partnership as defendant in the suit and that the doctors were partners? See *Zuckerman v. Antenucci*, 478 N.Y.S.2d 578 (1984).

9. Steve and Jim were partners in the firm Locus Development, a software manufacturer. Each had substantial business interests outside Locus. Steve, a big risk taker, eventually became insolvent and was hounded by creditors of his other businesses. These creditors sought to levy against Steve's interest in Locus to satisfy their claims. What device is available for the creditors to make their claims? What could happen if this device is insufficient to pay their claims? How could Jim have avoided the worst-case outcome?

10. The Paul G. Veale & Co. was an accounting partnership with an agreement permitting the partners to pursue other business interests. However, partners were specifically prohibited from competing directly with the firm in its business of accounting services without the other partners' unanimous approval. Rose, a partner, performed accounting services for outside clients. The other partners sought their share of Rose's profits. What is the issue in this case? What reasons support holding Rose liable? See *Veale v. Rose*, 657 S.W.2d 834 (Tex. Ct. App. 1983).

Chapter 38

Partnership: Operation and Termination

■

CRITICAL THINKING INQUIRIES

As you read this chapter, you should be able to address the following:

- Compare and contrast the reasons used to justify granting or limiting individual partners' authority to bind the partnership in contracts with outsiders. What ambiguities are there to outsiders dealing with a partner?
- What assumptions are made when partnership law automatically grants individual partners the power to manage, share in financial gains, contribute to financial losses, and have access to partnership records? How can the partnership customize individual partner rights?
- Why can incoming and outgoing partners be held liable for matters beyond their control, such as contractual or tort duties incurred before or after their association with the partnership?
- What issues are raised when a partner departs from the partnership?
- What ambiguity is there about a partnership's continuing business when one partner is expelled, dies, or quits? Why is dissolution necessary?

MANAGERIAL PERSPECTIVE

The Triple-P partnership of Pam, Paul, and Peter, a management consulting firm, became financially distressed. This caused their creditors to examine the firm's business activities, immediately raising questions about how the firm was managed. Partnership law presumes the partners actively participate equally in a democratic decisionmaking process. Further, the law presumes that any partner may conduct business with outsiders in the usual way of doing business. Paul's initial efforts to give the firm visibility were unsuccessful. Pam's excessive borrowing was not carefully considered by all three partners.

- How could these three partners have prevented the bankruptcy and dissolution of their partnership?
- What issues of risk exposure arise for third-party creditors in contracting with individual partners acting for the partnership?

This chapter discusses several issues of partnership operation, partnership management, the turnover of individual partners, and the continuation or termination of partnerships after dissolution. Creditors and suppliers may have particularly acute problems when dealing with partners. Additionally, the partners themselves should understand the legal ramifications of their personal and firm-related actions because these actions can become a pitfall for the unwary.

INTRODUCTION

This chapter focuses on the partnership governance process, the partnership's relations with outside suppliers or customers, and the process for orderly satisfaction of claims made by creditors and owners. Partnership law is based on the laissez-faire principle, so partners are permitted considerable flexibility to alter their legal relationships in the operation and dissolution of their partnership. It is of critical importance to newly formed partnerships that the participants consider their likely future roles in operating the firm. For example, the partners should consider limiting the contractual authority of those partners lacking managerial expertise.

Some partnerships are also well advised to limit the voting rights and managerial decisionmaking powers of inexperienced or passive partners. Partners should plan for the inevitable dissolution of the partnership that is triggered when any partner becomes dissociated with the firm through death, illness, expulsion, retirement, or loss of enthusiastic or competent participation. Provisions in the articles of partnership or in separate agreements among partners can also address questions about authority, management powers, and dissolution rights permitting the partnership to reduce the negative impact of doing business or unforeseen dissolution.

INDIVIDUAL PARTNER'S AUTHORITY

In the absence of an agreement to the contrary, each partner has authority to make contracts that bind the partnership in carrying out partnership affairs in the usual way it does business. This means each partner is a general agent of each other partner and of the partnership, but only for partnership business. This also means that each partner is a principal to each other partner when acting as agents of the partnership. Under UPA Section 9, this is considered **implied authority** granting agency power to each partner to carry out the partnership's ordinary business affairs. Authority can also be implied as reasonably necessary to carry out an express grant. For example, a partner with express authority to operate a television repair business would have additional implied authority to purchase replacement parts because stocking parts is necessary to operate the business.

Partners must have the power or authority to act for the partnership before the partnership is held contractually bound to an outsider. Partners acting without the power conferred by some form of authority are liable to outsiders under the **implied warranty of authority**, similar to that made by any purported agent who simply pretends to be authorized. Sometimes a partner has the *power* to act for the partnership but lacks any *right* conferred by the partnership. For example, a partnership may forbid a particular partner from making sales from inventory without the other partners' approval. The unauthorized partner may still be cloaked with apparent authority or appear to be carrying on partnership business in the usual way. Therefore, the partnership will be bound to the outsider by the unauthorized partner's act. In such a case, the unauthorized partner has the power but not the right to contract. An unauthorized partner may be held liable to the copartners for breach of the partnership agreement, disobedience with a partnership resolution, or violation of some other limit on his or her authority by making the unauthorized contract. For example, Peter could be liable to the other partners for the unauthorized contracts he made that exposed the Triple-P partnership to losses.

UPA § 9. Partner Agent . . . as to Partnership Business

(1) Every partner is an agent of the partnership for the purpose of its business, and the act of every partner . . . for apparently carrying on in the usual way the business of the partnership . . . binds the partnership unless the partner so acting has no authority to act for the partnership in the particular matter, and the person with whom he is dealing has knowledge of the fact.

When a particular partner's contract is authorized, each partner has *joint liability* on the contract. This traditionally required that an outsider claiming that the partnership breached the contract must join all partners in any suit seeking performance or a remedy. No single individual partner could be held liable for the entire breach of contract judgment against the partnership. However, a few states became dissatisfied with this rule and now impose *joint and several liability* on partners for authorized contract duties. Other states permit suit against the partnership as an entity, so collection can be made against partnership assets. Many states require exhaustion of partnership assets before bringing suit against individual partners on breach of contract damages. RUPA would impose joint and several liability on all partners for all liabilities, tort and contract.

Carrying on Partnership Business in the Usual Way

A crucial provision in UPA Section 9 automatically implies that each partner has authority to conduct partnership business in the usual way that the particular partnership in question has been previously operated. Such evidence might come from the previous business practices of that partnership. Alternatively, evidence of other similarly situated partnership businesses might be used to indicate a usage of trade. However, if the third party knows that the particular partner has no authority to bind the partnership, then only the unauthorized partner and not the partnership is liable. For example, assume that Paul and Peter denied Pam the authority to purchase computer software for the firm's clients even though it was typical for individual partners in similar consulting businesses to make such purchases. The partnership and all partners would be liable on Pam's purchases unless the software seller knew of Pam's limited authority. Pam would then be liable based on an implied warranty that she had authority, the same presumption as under agency law. Pam's disobedient conduct would also pose an ethical dilemma. The following case illustrates the problem of a partner's implied authority.

SCHNUCKS MARKETS INC. v. CASSILLY
724 S. W. 2nd 644 (Mo. App. 1987)

Glenn Parks Properties was a real estate development business operated as a partnership by David Cassilly and Joseph Masson. Cassilly had contracted with Schnucks to split the costs of extending a sewer line to the Schnucks market. Schnucks sued Glenn Park when the partnership failed to pay its share of the approximately $25,000. Glenn Park claimed Cassilly had no authority to contract. The partnership appealed the trial court judgment for Schnucks.

PUDLOWSKI, Justice

[The Uniform Partnership Act provides in Section 9, as paraphrased]:

1. Every partner is an agent of the partnership for the purpose of its business and the act of every partner, for apparently carrying on in usual way the business of the partnership binds the partnership unless the partner so acting has in fact no other authority to act for the partnership in the particular matter, and the person with whom he is dealing has knowledge of the fact that he has no such authority.

The act of the partner must be ''for the purpose of its business'' and in ''carrying on in the usual way the business of the partnership.'' Negotiating at conventions and elsewhere an oral contract to divide the cost of the sewer installation necessary for develop-

ment of the property certainly fits these requirements. [However] Glenn Park contends that negotiating the installation of sewer lines is a one time deal and thus not in the course of partnership business. This is clearly refuted by the record.

Glenn Park argues that since Cassilly denied agency, there arose a disputed issue of material facts [requiring jury consideration. However] Cassilly's denial of agency did not elevate this to a legally material issue for even if Cassilly did not possess ability, Glenn Park would still be bound. [The Uniform Partnership Act] requires that if the partner in fact has no authority, ''the person with whom he is dealing must have knowledge that he has no such authority.'' Glenn Park presented no evidence that Schnuck had knowledge of Cassilly's supposedly limited status. Judgment affirmed.

Case Questions

1. What are the two issues concerning Cassilly's authority to negotiate contracts to split the costs of extending a sewer line?
2. Would the provision of utilities to development land be considered a "usual way" to operate a real estate development partnership?
3. What is the impact of expanding the implied authority of partners to the usual way of doing business? How can this implied authority be limited?

Express Authority

Partnerships may extend express authority to particular partners, employees, or outsiders in the same manner as done under agency law. *Express authority* may be set forth in the articles of partnership, in an agreement among partners, by a resolution passed by a majority of partners, or by managing partner(s) authorized to delegate such power to another partner, to an employee, or to an outsider.

Some partnership activities are considered so fundamental to the firm's existence that a simple majority vote by partners is not sufficient to authorize the act. For example, all partners must vote unanimously to assign partnership property to satisfy creditor claims, sell the partnership goodwill, do any act that would make it impossible to conduct ordinary business, or commit a partnership claim to arbitration. Given that arbitration is more acceptable now than when the UPA was first drafted, the decision to arbitrate should not be treated differently than a decision to litigate. RUPA leaves it to the courts to enumerate when unanimous partner consent is necessary.

Apparent Authority

Under the circumstances of a partnership's operations, it may appear that a partner has authority for a particular act. If it is reasonable for an outsider to presume from appearances that the partnership has given the partner specific authority, then contracts made by that partner are binding on the partnership. For example, if Pam, Peter, and Paul advertise that prospective clients may "talk to any partner" about hiring the firm, then any secret limitations on Paul's authority to contract must be communicated to clients. Paul would have apparent authority to obligate the firm to service a new client. However, if an outsider knows Paul's authority is limited, Paul has no apparent authority to contract with that outsider. Of course, Paul could be held personally liable un-

der the implied warranty of authority for an unauthorized contract if the outsider knew of Paul's limited authority. Is it ethical for an outsider to contract with Paul knowing he was unauthorized?

Ratification

The partnership can *ratify* unauthorized acts of partners, employees, or outside agents in the same way any other principal may retroactively authorize a previously unauthorized act. For example, one of Pam's unauthorized borrowings may later appear advantageous to Peter and Paul. The other partners can ratify Pam's loan so long as the creditor does not rescind before Peter and Paul can ratify the entire transaction. If the partnership ratifies an unauthorized contract after circumstances change to the outsider's disadvantage, is this ethical conduct? For example, in some states a partnership can ratify one partner's unauthorized purchase of fire insurance even after a fire destroys the insured premises. Despite the legality of a ratification after fire loss, is it ethical to take advantage of the insurer's ignorance of the partner's lack of authority? Partners' various bases for authority are summarized in Figure 38–1.

Authority in Particular Transactions

Partners customarily have authority to bind the partnership to several recurring types of transactions under the doctrines of apparent authority, implied authority, and under the UPA Section 9 concept of carrying out the partnership in the usual way. Such circumstantial authority may vary with the circumstances. Nevertheless, a partner usually has authority to make contracts necessary to operate the partnership business, purchase or sell partnership inventory in the ordinary course of business, give standard warranties on goods sold at retail, borrow money or execute commercial paper for a trading firm, purchase necessary business insurance, hire employees, or settle claims the firm has against outsiders and claims

Figure 38–1   Authority of Partners and Partnerships

Type of Authority	Definition	Part-nership Bound	Partner Bound	Third Party Bound
Express Authority	Actual authority expressed orally or in writing	Yes	No	Yes
Implied Authority	Actual authority necessary to accomplish express grant; additional power needed to detail vague express grant	Yes	No	Yes
Apparent Authority	Authority reasonably perceived by outsiders, appearances made by partnership	Yes	No	Yes
Carrying on Partnership Business in the Usual Way	Authority implied from UPA and reasonably made apparent by this partnership or other similar business consistent with outsider's expectations	Yes	No	Yes
Ratification	Retroactive authorization granted after partner contracts but before outsider rescinds	Yes	No	Yes
Unauthorized	Partner not empowered but nevertheless volunteers, purporting to have partnership authorization	No	Yes, implied warranty of authority	No

outsiders have against the firm. However, certain fundamental acts affecting the partnership require unanimous partner consent. In most cases, to avoid dissatisfaction, an outsider is always best advised to seek assurances of a partner's authority.

The courts have developed a distinction between trading and nontrading partnerships that never appeared in the UPA. **Trading partnerships** are engaged in the regular business of farming, manufacturing, and buying and selling goods, whether at retail or wholesale. The law presumes trading partnerships need working capital, so courts are more likely to presume any partner has authority to borrow or execute negotiable instruments. **Nontrading partnerships** have no substantial inventory. Usually, they provide services (e.g., law firms, accounting firms, and consultants), so courts have presumed they have lower borrowing needs. Many courts would require actual evidence of a partner's authority to borrow before holding the partnership liable. Nevertheless, if a loan was unauthorized, the creditor could probably still recover if the partnership used the loan proceeds for partnership purposes.

Similar distinctions are made when a partner attempts to sell partnership real estate. Circumstantial authority is more readily presumed if real estate sales are part of the partnership's usual course of business. Unanimous consent would probably be required to authorize sale of the sole premises on which partnership business is conducted. The partnership can recover title to real estate that was transferred without authority unless the property is thereafter resold to a bona fide purchaser for value who has no notice of the unauthorized transfer.

RUPA Statement of Partnership Authority

The proposed RUPA retains the concept of implying authority for "carrying on partnership in the usual way" and explicitly extends this to the usual way that other businesses "of the kind" are operated. RUPA treats authority for transfer of any property with a recorded title (e.g., vehicles) the same as for real estate. RUPA permits, but does not require, the partnership to file a **statement of authority** in a manner similar to filing under fictitious name notification statutes. This filing facilitates transfer of real estate and other record title property because it lists the particular authorized partners who are necessary to execute a transaction. It places outsiders on constructive notice of which partners are necessary for authorized transfers. However, statements restricting a particular partner's authority would bind outsiders only if they actually know of the limitation. Statements of authority would be valid for five years and must list the partnership name and address and names and addresses of all partners or of an appointed agent. It must be signed by all or at least 10 partners, whichever is fewer. Such statements are already used in Georgia and California.

MANAGEMENT OF THE PARTNERSHIP

Partnership law presumes that all partners participate fully and equally in partnership business. Although equality is presumed, variations in the partners' management rights may appear in the articles of partnership or in a separate agreement between the partners. The laissez-faire principle permits these varied responsibilities and powers to achieve the partners' desires. Unless otherwise agreed, all partners have an equal voice or vote in the management of the partnership's affairs.

There are three levels of approval necessary to effective partnership management. First, unanimity is required for *fundamental* decisions affecting the partnership's essential character. This includes choosing or changing the partnership's usual course or line of business, admitting new partner(s), assigning partnership property to creditors or entering voluntary bankruptcy, disposing of partnership goodwill, confessing a judgment against the partnership, submitting partnership claims to arbitration, or doing any other act that would make it impossible to carry on the ordinary business of the partnership. Of course, if any of these fundamental acts is performed

by a single unauthorized partner, the others may ratify it with a unanimous vote.

A second level of *operational* partnership decisionmaking requires majority rule so long as it does not violate an existing partnership agreement or some provision in the articles of partnership. These are policy decisions made within the partnership's basic line(s) of business. For example, decisions concerning the particular brands of products carried, the pricing of products for resale, advertising, hiring and firing employees, borrowing, and the amount of effort each partner must apply to the business are all operational matters subject to majority rule. Some partnerships assign some or all of these tasks to managing partner(s) or to a managing committee.

A third category of matters includes day-to-day or *ordinary business decisions*. The partner making such decisions must have authority, as discussed in the previous section. For example, the actual purchase of approved goods for resale, the disciplining of an errant employee, or the amount of discount negotiated with a particular customer are day-to-day ordinary business decisions. Partners are permitted to make these decisions if authorized.

The articles of partnership or a separate partnership agreement may override any of these three governance matters. For example, common ways that partnerships change the trilogy of unanimity—majority rule—authority are with a managing partner or managing committee or deadlock resolution methods, as discussed next. Large accounting and law partnerships often include partnership agreement provisions that permit the admission of new partners with less than a unanimous partner vote, usually by a vote of a membership committee. Some partnerships classify partners (e.g., senior partners, junior partners) in a hierarchy, giving stronger powers and perhaps a larger allocation of profits to partners that are more senior or more productive. The following case illustrates the distinction between fundamental changes and ordinary business decisions.

PATEL v. PATEL
260 Cal. Rptr. 255 (Cal. Ct. App. 1989)

Mr. and Mrs. Patel formed a partnership with their son Raj to own and operate the City Center Motel in Urika, California. The motel had previously been owned by Mr. and Mrs. Patel. The motel property was held in the name of Mr. and Mrs. Patel. However, the partnership agreement required approval by Raj before the property could be sold. Raj later refused to approve the sale of the motel property and the buyers sought specific performance of his parents' contract to sell. The buyers appealed from a judgment that the sale contract was unenforceable.

CHANNEL, Associate Justice

Every partner is an agent of the partnership for the purpose of its business, and the act of every partner to carry on the business of the partnership binds the partnership. However, partners acting without the authority of the remaining partners may not do any act that would make it impossible to carry on the ordinary business of the partnership. In the case of a commercial or trading partnership in which the usual partnership business is to hold and sell real property, a contract such as that involved in this case—to sell the sole partnership assets—would be enforceable. By contrast, when—as in the present case—the usual partnership business is to run a business, rather than to hold it in anticipation of its eventual sale, the partnership is not bound by a contract selling that business without the approval of all the partners. Under these circumstances the trial court properly denied specific performance of the unauthorized contract in order to prevent destruction of the partnership.

[The Uniform Partnership Act Section 10 states, as paraphrased]:

Where title to a real property is in the name of one or more of the partners, whether or not the record discloses the right of the partnership, the partners in whose name

the title stands may convey title to such property, but the partnership may recover such property unless the property has been conveyed to a bonafide purchaser for value without knowledge that the partner executing the conveyance has exceeded his authority.

[Despite the purchasers' contention the sale was effective because they were bonafide purchasers for value without knowledge of Raj's interest,] to enforce the contract of sale without Raj's approval would frustrate the purpose of the UPA by making it impossible for the partnership to continue. As the purpose of the partnership is to operate the motel, rather than to hold it for eventual sale, we believe that the better result would be to preserve the partnership and hold the contract unenforceable. Judgment affirmed.

Case Questions

1. Why is the rule of partner unanimity applied in the *Patel* case?

2. What ambiguity in ownership and approval of the sale led to the dispute in this case?

3. What is assumed about individual partner ownership and partnership authority in UPA Section 10?

Managing Partner or Committee

Many large partnerships could not be efficiently managed if the unanimity or majority rule decision-making criteria were always required. Additionally, some partnerships are not confident that newly admitted partners should be given voting rights equal to the more experienced and senior partners. As a result, it is quite common for large accounting, law, investment banking, and consulting partnerships to provide for a management hierarchy. This may take one or a combination of forms including a managing partner, committee of managing partners, separate junior and senior partner status, variable voting powers, and a managing partner(s) review and removal process. Managing partner responsibilities

are usually defined in a partnership agreement or in the articles of partnership.

It is not usually advisable for the partnership agreement to permit the managing partner(s) to change the partnership line of business without the other partners' consent. For example, a large accounting firm accustomed to practicing external auditing would be best advised to secure broad-based consent among most partners before adding new lines of services such as management consulting or tax preparation. On the other hand, an excessively stringent grant of power to the managing partner(s) could hamstring the business from making needed quick adaptations, particularly if the managing partner(s) alone were reluctant to expand the business.

Such problems suggest the partnership might consider a provision to add new lines of business without unanimous approval but with supermajority vote. Provisions requiring periodic review and possible removal of the managing partner(s) are also advisable. Partners unwilling to enter a risky new business may always dissolve the partnership before much headway is made. However, if their partnership agreement imposed penalties for a premature retirement or wrongful dissolution, this would not be a reasonable course. To prevent injustice, such provisions should be made inapplicable to a dissenting partner's withdrawal or dissolution when the partnership changes its line of business.

Partner Deadlock

A partnership can be brought to a standstill of indecision when a partnership vote is taken on policy matters and the outcome is equally split. This can happen when a partnership has just two partners, when there are an even number of partners, or when there is an odd number of partners but an odd number abstain or are not voting. Although such divided votes are unusual, they can impose a paralyzing deadlock if ordinary business decisions are stymied. However, such indecision is not really a deadlock in votes taken over fundamental partnership matters. The unanimity requirement presumes that it is difficult to win votes on fundamental changes, so the partnership retains authority to engage in its previous lines of business. It may be unethical to consciously impose deadlock to coerce other partners into some action.

One solution is to dissolve the partnership, but this is a drastic measure and it may trigger penalties for wrongful dissolution. Some states permit the partner dissenting from a contracting decision to make a personal disclaimer of liability for the other partner's contracts. The dissenter must notify third parties of this disclaimer to be free from their claims. Of course, if the partnership retains the benefits of the unauthorized contract, this may constitute an implied ratification. Alternatively, the third party could claim quasi-contract damages. As discussed later in this chapter, courts may consider a petition to dissolve the partnership involuntarily without penalty if the deadlock reflects irreconcilable differences and bad will.

INCOMING AND OUTGOING PARTNERS

Most successful partnerships experience changes in personnel over the firm's life. Partners may be expelled for incompatibility or technical incompetence, they may retire or move on to other work, or they may become legally incompetent or may die. The remaining partners may seek to fill these voids with "new blood," and many partnerships must admit new partners when the firm experiences growth. In all these instances, there are complex questions about the firm's financial responsibility to the departing partner. To what extent may partnership creditors lay claim to the incoming or outgoing partner's capital contribution? Can outsiders make claims against that partner's unlimited personal liability for debts that arose while that partner was associated with the firm? Is there liability for debts arising before a new partner's association began? For example, if Paul quits the Triple-P partnership, creditors who made loans to the firm or sold goods on credit during his membership could legitimately claim that his creditworthiness was a factor used to extend the partnership credit. This usually means a retiring partner in a position like Paul's could retain unlimited liability for partnership debts even after retirement.

Incoming Partner's Liability

An incoming partner's creditworthiness was probably unavailable for consideration by creditors whose loans were made to the partnership before the new partner joined. This theory supports the UPA rule in Section 17 limiting incoming partners' liability to their capital contribution for debts arising before they joined the firm. Of course, an incoming partner could knowingly accept responsibility for preexisting partnership debts as a condition of membership or capital contribution. Incoming partners have unlimited liability for debts arising after they join. RUPA retains this rule because it flows naturally from the entity theory that RUPA adopts. In the next case, a limitation is placed on incoming partner liability for past partnership debts.

KALICHMAN v. BEVERLY HOLDING CO.
520 N.Y.S. 2nd 255 (N.Y. App. Div. 1987)

Kalichman and Kline were partners in a business that owned and managed an apartment building. Kline died before the partnership repaid a $189,000 loan. Kline's sons, Jack and Frank, were heirs to Kline's share of the partnership but never participated in managing the partnership business. Kalichman settled a suit by the lender, Beverly Holding Co., for $100,000 after the partnership defaulted on the loan. Jack and Frank were sued by Beverly, which alleged that they had to pay a share of the liability. Jack and Frank appealed a judgment against them requiring payment on the loan.

CASEY, Justice

The existence of a partnership arrangement does not demonstrate or indicate [Jack and Frank's] assumption of a preexisting obligation on the loan. [UPA § 41(7) provides:]

> The liability of a third person becoming a partner in the partnership continuing the business . . . to the creditors of the dissolved partnership shall be satisfied out of the partnership property only.

[The UPA] limits incoming partners' liability to the partnership property unless personal liability is expressly assumed through the partnership agreement or otherwise. Joseph Kline's death dissolved his partnership with Kalichman by operation of law. Kalichman then had the right to possess the property for a partnership purpose, as well as the duty to wind up the affairs of the partnership and to pay Joseph Kline's legal representative a proportionate share in partnership surplus. These events did not occur here, however, since Kalichman continued the partnership business with Jack and Frank's consent. Having continued to carry on the partnership business after Joseph Kline's death, Kalichman must bear all the losses, while the UPA limits Jack and Frank's liability to their interest in the property. Jack and Frank's association with the partnership was to receive income. While this fact might evidence the formation of a partnership between Jack and Frank and Kalichman, it does not evidence that Jack and Frank ever assumed personal liability for preexisting loans incurred by Joseph Kline. Judgment reversed.

Case Questions
1. What is the issue in determining an incoming partner's liability for preexisting partnership debts?

2. What reasons support reversing the decision in favor of the lender?

3. Would the answer be different if Jack and Frank had assumed their father's management role in the partnership after his death?

Outgoing Partner's Financial Rights

The departure of a partner from the partnership causes the technical dissolution of the partnership. Unless otherwise agreed, the surviving partners may thereafter choose to discontinue or continue the partnership business. UPA Section 42 gives outgoing partners or the estate of a deceased partner the right to receive their proportionate share of the partnership's value if the surviving partners continue the business. On the other hand, if the partnership is terminated, each outgoing partner has the right to a proportionate share of the partnership's liquidation value. Unless the partnership is insolvent, payments are due to all outgoing partner(s) or to a deceased partner's estate. The outgoing partner or estate then becomes a creditor of the partnership that is subordinate to outside creditors.

Valuing the Departing Partner's Interest
Section 42 of the UPA gives an outgoing partner or a deceased partner's estate the right to receive the value of the partner's interest in the partnership as of

the date of dissolution. Going concern value is the proper measure unless the partnership is terminated and liquidated. Until this is paid, the obligation includes interest at the legal rate or a share of the profits in proportion to the departing partner's share of partnership capital. This choice encourages the continuing partners to settle up more quickly. The share of profits option need not equal the departing partner's former regular share of profits. For example, after retirement, Paul is entitled to receive his share of the partnership's value as a return of capital with either interest or a share of subsequent profits. Peter and Pam, as continuing partners, must bear all subsequent partnership losses before they complete making payment to Paul because he is no longer responsible for managing Triple-P's decisions.

The value of a partner's interest usually includes a component of **goodwill**—that is, the reasonable projection that existing customers will continue patronizing the firm and the firm's reputation will attract new business. Goodwill is usually computed as the excess of going concern value over the liquidation value of partnership assets. However, goodwill often represents the personal expertise and reputation of particular partners and adds to partnership value only while those partners continue working. It is often difficult to accurately value goodwill due to many uncertainties. When goodwill is personal to some partners, its value is lost when the firm is liquidated. Then it usually becomes impossible to receive any goodwill value. Therefore, the allocation of goodwill among departing and continuing partners is imprecise and may trigger resentment, particularly if the departing partner receives any goodwill attributable to the continuing partners. The articles of partnership in many well-planned and successful partnerships include provisions that establish a valuation method for a departing partner's interests that often specifically ignores and effectively eliminates goodwill from the departing partner's share. Valuation is discussed later in the section on continuation agreements.

RUPA Buyouts

RUPA retains the basic principles described in the preceding section. RUPA considers the payment of a departing partner's interest to be the **buyout** of a person dissociating with the partnership. Payments are treated similarly to distributing a departing partner's share. RUPA permits the continuing partner-

ship to withhold this payment until the expiration of a specified term or until the accomplishment of an undertaking, if either are specified in the partnership agreement.

Outgoing Partner's Liability: Preexisting Debts

Generally, a retiring partner retains unlimited liability after departing for credit extended to the firm during that partner's membership. However, most courts imply that partnership assets must first be exhausted to satisfy such debts before the departing partner is held liable. Continuing partners make an implied promise to release the departing partner from liability unless the partners have otherwise allocated liability in the articles of partnership or in a separate agreement. Usually, the continuing partners agree to pay preexisting debts and indemnify the departing partner if partnership creditors win a judgment against the departing partner.

Creditors are not bound by these agreements unless the departing partner is released by creditors in a **novation**, an agreement substituting the continuing partners for the previous partners' liability. This release may be implied if the creditor knows of the dissolution and consents to altering the debt. For example, assume a supplier received notice that Pam was retiring from Triple-P and Peter and Paul would continue the business thereafter. Pam would be released from the claim if the supplier accepted Peter and Paul's note (IOU) for repayment of the outstanding debt. A departing partner retains liability for preexisting partnership debts if the partnership is insolvent at the time of dissolution. RUPA basically retains these rules. A partnership is an entity under RUPA, so the dissociation of a particular partner does not change the continuing partners' liability on preexisting partnership debts.

Outgoing Partner's Liability: New Debts

Departing partners are not liable for new debts incurred after dissolution unless the creditor had no notice of the dissolution. However, under the partnership by estoppel theory, a departing partner may be liable for an outsider's extension of credit to the partnership after dissolution if the creditor believed in good faith that the departing partner was still a partner. To avoid such liability, actual notice must be given to all creditors who knew of the departing partner's association with the partnership. Constructive notice is sufficient for creditors who knew of the partnership but never previously extended credit. For example, publication of the dissolving partner's departure in a newspaper of general circulation in the area the partnership operated would be sufficient to constitute constructive notice.

A **dormant partner**, a partner unknown to creditors, is excused from giving any notice because creditors could never have relied on the dormant partner's creditworthiness. From the departing partner's perspective, it is clearly advisable to give actual notice of dissolution to all known creditors, publish a general or constructive notice to the public, and seek release or a novation from all substantial creditors. RUPA retains these rules. RUPA would expose dissociating partners to liability on debts incurred only within the two years following the partner's departure. If actual notice is given to former creditors or constructive notice by publication is given to potential creditors who knew of that partner's association with the partnership, then RUPA would hold that the dissociating partner has no liability.

Is it ethical for continuing partners to withhold notice so that the departing partner will retain secondary liability for the partnership's debts? Where the retiring partner wrongfully dissolves or admits fault in overborrowing, the retiring partner may still have a moral obligation to contribute to paying these debts, at least out of his or her partnership share. However, consider the example of a successful partnership in which the continuing partners withhold notice of dissolution triggered by the retirement of a well-known but senile partner. The continuing partners may know that because of the departing partner's senility, he will not monitor the notification of creditors. If the partnership receives loans from creditors who wrongly assume the departing partner is still associated with the firm, this activity is prob-

ably unethical. It might constitute illegal fraud for continuing partners to expose the departing partner to the added liability.

DISSOLUTION

A partnership ends after an event triggering **dissolution**. This is the first of a string of events along one of two tracks: one is the end stage terminating the business, and the other is only a temporary dissolution, followed by continuation as a new partnership.

UPA § 29. Dissolution Defined

The dissolution of a partnership is the change in the relation of the partners caused by any partner ceasing to be associated in the carrying on . . . of the partnership business.

Dissolution is triggered by one of several acts of the partner(s) or by an event specified in UPA Sections 31 or 32. There is no automatic dissolution where a partner assigns his or her partnership interest, when a partner's creditor obtains a charging order against that partner's interest, when a new partner is admitted, or simple dissension arises among partners that can be resolved. Dissolution may be rightful or wrongful, which can affect the various parties' rights and liabilities. The following sections discuss what causes dissolution, the alternatives of winding up or continuing a dissolved partnership business, the various parties' rights and duties accompanying dissolution, and how partnership assets are distributed to partners and creditors after liquidation. The following article illustrates the importance of careful business planning and thoughtful drafting of a partnership agreement to avoid the many pitfalls of operating as co-owners.

---

*How to Cut Losses, Avoid Fights When Partners Are Breaking Up**

When one of five partners in Vahl Inc. died unexpectedly, the small Brooklyn airplane-parts maker faced its first major threat in more than a decade. The death of the partner, who held

---

a large chunk of stock and helped manage the company, ''was a terrible blow to us,'' says partner Henry Dieken.

Hours before the burial, the surviving owners sat down for a meeting. After hard negotiations, they accomplished a feat rare among entrepreneurial partnerships. Instead of squabbling over how to settle the dead partner's estate and at what price, they agreed to buy out the heirs according to a buy-sell pact the partners had signed. Then they promised in a second accord not to cash out for at least three years.

''It would have been easy at that point to let things go sour,'' Mr. Dieken says. Instead, ''we resolved it right then.''

Every year, thousands of partnerships face crushing blows like the one sustained by Vahl. In the best of times, partnerships are fragile. But in the current recession, the breakup rate has worsened as cost-cutting and other pressures heighten tensions between partners, says Keith Irwin, a San Jose, California, management consultant.

A breakup can taint the lives of partners for years, miring them in litigation and claiming numerous innocent victims, from employees to entire companies. Two entrepreneurs in the southwestern U.S. watched the value of their successful waterbed-sheet start-up, Hydro-Dynamics Inc., plunge after a dispute over strategy. With bigger competitors threatening their markets, the former college friends couldn't agree on whether to diversify. The ensuing fight over buy-out terms drained their resources, and the business finally had to be sold at a fire-sale price.

Many breakups are unavoidable. But frequent meetings, candid talks, written agreements and attention to trouble signs can help partners avoid disputes and cut losses in the event of a fight.

Warning signs are often subtle. ''Partners begin to notice that it's harder to talk over problems,'' says Albert A. Murphy, a San Diego consultant. ''They begin withholding information from each other.''

Differences in philosophy usually deepen over time and should be addressed quickly. Two years after Michael Macco brought a law school friend into his Huntington, New York, law partnership, serious differences in philosophy and work habits surfaced. While the founding partners were on Easy Street by our 50s,'' Mr. Macco says, the new partner's ''attitude was, 'Why kill yourself now when you're going to be working until you're 65?' ''

Although discussing the problem was uncomfortable, the men managed to end the partnership without wrecking the friendship. ''We didn't want to invest 10 years in something that was going to break up eventually anyway,'' Mr. Macco says.

Restless or Greedy

Other times, a partner may grow restless, resentful or simply greedy. The majority owner of a fast-growing semiconductor start-up was stunned when a big customer told him, ''You know, we have been approached by one of your competitors, and the senior partner has the same name as one of your partners.'' When the owner investigated, he found his two partners had set up a competing 50-employee firm in Japan, using his manufacturing process to steal business. The partners split and are still mired in hostile buy-out talks.

Unexpected changes in a partner's life circumstances can wreak havoc. When another of Mr. Macco's partners decided to run for public office and won, the partners ended up revising the terms of their partnership three times before they found a suitable way of divvying up revenue to reflect the partner's new, shortened work schedule at the firm. In their meetings, the partners—who are also friends—were blunt. ''Maybe your future is to be governor or president some day,'' Mr. Macco said. ''But this firm is my meal ticket.''

Partnerships that survive spend time striving for consensus. When one of five partners in Mostly Handmade Inc. asked to take charge of buying merchandise, a task long shared by all the owners of the 20-year-old specialty retailer in Evanston, Illinois, the partners "talked late into the night" about the issue, says Rita Allison, one of the owners. Although the partner eventually decided to leave the business, the time spent talking preserved peace and renewed the remaining partners' commitment to their strategy.

Committing the business's philosophy and goals to a written statement can help avert blowups. While it isn't often possible to set specific objectives, a general statement by each partner of his or her vision for the company—whether it will become a giant corporation or remain a tightly run, successful small business, for instance—can reveal potential problems.

Many successful partners also forge a written partnership agreement at the outset. "If everybody is happy on Day One, it ought to be easy to record that sense of harmony and agreement," says Anthony Walters, a partner with Ernst & Young in Chicago. "And if you can't agree on something, what better time to find out than before it becomes an issue—before there are dollars riding on the decision?"

Seeking Guidance

A trusted consultant, lawyer or accountant can help guide those discussions. "The written agreement has to be a good one. And producing it can create some ill feeling," says George Hamman, a Chicago attorney who works with partnerships.

Terms for buying out one or more partners should be set down in writing, consultants say. Managing the death, disability or retirement of a partner; bringing children into the business; and raising capital are other areas for discussion.

Some partnerships write rules for charging expenses to the business—a seemingly minor issue that can spark major blowups. When an owner of a successful office-design firm discovered that his partner had been renovating his house at the expense of the company, he ordered an audit that revealed other questionable practices. Enraged, he began an effort to dissolve the partnership, which is continuing amid threats of litigation.

Dennis Dalton, a Fremont, California, consultant, also recommends that partners sign agreements identifying products or ideas that are the property of the company and agreeing not to appropriate them for a specified period.

Airtight copyright documents can be crucial, as a partner in one software start-up discovered the hard way. The partner, who was also the sales manager, blamed soft sales on competition from industry giants. He never dreamed that his partner, a software engineer, had quietly formed a new company to field competing products. Worse yet, when the salesman tried to salvage the firm, he discovered that the copyright documents developed by the engineer were full of loopholes. The salesman lost $500,000 trying to save the company, which went under anyway.

Even with firm written agreements, regular meetings and lots of good will, preserving a partnership often demands personal sacrifice. The buy-out agreement that saved Vahl set a stock price well below the firm's market value. "We priced it at a level where if something happened, we could pay it," Mr. Dieken says.

The partners' discussion on such issues "hasn't always been beautiful boardroom meetings. There has been some shouting," Mr. Dieken says. "But it has only lasted one day. If we hadn't gotten it off our chests, we would have been unhappy."

Thought Questions

1. For what major reasons do partners often have disputes with each other that can threaten the continuation of their business?

2. What is a common issue that can lead to dissension in those partnerships dependent on unique technology to be competitive?

3. How can partners avoid the seemingly inevitable pitfalls of discord and lost expectations?

Dissolution by Act of Parties

Under the aggregate theory, a partnership is a consensual relationship that can exist only so long as all partners agree to participate. A partnership is dissolved by an agreement made at any time by all the partners. This agreement may look forward to dissolution after a specified period of time lapses, such as 10 years, or dissolution may not be permitted until after a specific undertaking is achieved, such as the construction and sale of a building. A unanimous partner agreement to dissolve during its specified term or undertaking is also enforceable.

In a **partnership at will,** there is no obligation to remain joined in partnership for any period of time. Any individual or subgroup of partners may withdraw from a partnership at will without incurring liability. However, in partnerships with a specified term or undertaking, no individual or subgroup of partners may rightfully dissolve without violating the partnership agreement. In such cases, an individual partner has only the *power* but not the *right* to dissolve. Thus, an individual partner who wrongfully dissolves in violation of the partnership agreement is liable to the remaining partners for damages. This gives the other partners the right to continue operating the partnership business. A valid expulsion provision permits rightful dissolution without violating the partnership agreement.

Dissolution by Operation of Law

Partnership law parallels agency and contract law in the presumption that the partners would dissolve the partnership under certain conditions. Under UPA Section 31, a partnership automatically dissolves when (1) any partner dies, (2) there is a bankruptcy of any partner or the partnership, (3) an event makes it unlawful for any partner to participate in the business, or (4) the partnership business itself becomes unlawful. For example, a partnership that operated a cocktail lounge would dissolve if the partnership lost its liquor license. A law firm partnership would dissolve if any partner was disbarred from practicing

law. Of course, partnerships dissolved by operation of law may reform later and continue in the same or another legal business activity.

Dissolution by Court Decree

In several circumstances, the courts have the power to dissolve a partnership on application by or for a partner. First, dissolution can be ordered when a partner is declared legally insane or when a partner becomes incompetent, defined as permanently "incapable of performing his part of the partnership contract." While an illness of short duration must generally be tolerated by copartners, a long-term illness incapacitating the partner for a substantial portion of a fixed-term partnership would probably be a sufficient incapacity for court-ordered dissolution. Second, analogous to commercial impracticability, a court may order dissolution if the partnership business can be run only at a loss. Short-term unprofitability is probably an insufficient basis for dissolution, but when there is no reasonable expectation of profit, a court-ordered dissolution may be appropriate.

Court-ordered dissolution is also appropriate if a partner's misconduct is so severe that it permanently interferes with the conduct of partnership business. For example, courts have ordered dissolution where there was a willful breach of the partnership agreement, exclusion of copartners from management, hiding or misrepresenting business information from copartners, diversion of partnership funds to the wrongful partner's separate corporation, and incessant bickering and lawsuits. However, minor misconduct or temporary dissension is not a sufficient basis. For example, disagreements over bookkeeping, temper flare-ups, rudeness to customers, and minor judgment errors have been held insufficient to order dissolution. A court will not order dissolution if the partner requesting dissolution does not have **clean hands**— that is, he or she is personally blameless. UPA Section 32 includes an equitable catchall provision permitting dissolution in other circumstances such as disloyalty or deep-rooted distrust.

Postdissolution Options

The term *dissolution* in the common vernacular is believed to encompass several separate events and processes that signify cessation of partnership business and the end stages of the partnership itself. However, dissolution has only one technical and legal meaning: an event in which the partners' relationship changes. Dissolution does not immediately conclude all partnership activities. It simply prompts one of two alternative processes: (1) permanent dissolution, requiring a winding-up process and eventual termination of the partnership, or (2) settlement with a departing partner by paying off his or her partnership interest and the continuation of the partnership business. This choice has developed largely because some agreements among partners permit or require continuation after dissolution. For example, a partnership for a specified term or undertaking may be continued after technical dissolution. Some partnerships establish procedures to expel a partner and continue thereafter. Additionally, an agreement to continue a partnership after dissolution may appear in the articles of partnership or in a separate agreement.

Under the partnership entity theory of RUPA, these two tracks of dissolution would be codified, permitting partners to avoid dissolution even without an agreement permitting continuation. When a partner becomes dissociated with the partnership, the remaining partners would usually have the choice of either buying out that partner and continuing their business or dissolving the partnership and winding up the business. RUPA would require dissolution less often than under the current UPA. The two tracks are illustrated in Figure 38–2 and discussed in the sections that follow.

The Winding-Up Alternative

If the remaining partners have no right to continue the partnership business, the event causing technical dissolution starts the **winding-up** process that concludes existing business. Unless otherwise agreed, any partner not guilty of wrongful dissolution may wind up the partnership. However, if several partners start conflicting processes to wind up the business, votes by majority rule must settle the conflicts. Unanimity may be required to do extraordinary acts such as continue the business for a long time. Any partner may petition for court supervision of the winding up. An independent receiver may be appointed if the previous partnership operations were characterized by fraud, mismanagement, or waste. The last surviving partner who winds up the partnership generally has a right to receive compensation for overseeing the process, an exception to the general rule restricting partners' compensation to their share of profits.

An **accounting** must be performed to determine several matters important to liquidation: each partner's financial position, the partnership's liabilities to outsiders, outsiders' liabilities to the partnership, and the whereabouts and value of partnership assets. The partnership must pay its outstanding debts, deliver goods already promised to customers, and provide services owed to clients. The winding-up partners must assess existing partnership liabilities with a view to satisfying or settling them effectively. For example, it would be appropriate for the winding-up partners to finish work on a nearly completed service engagement. By contrast, it might be best to negotiate the delegation of a long-term executory contract so that winding up may be completed more quickly. Contract law permits a partnership's clients to reject the delegation of unique partnership personal service contracts to other firms. Of course, any false claims against the partnership should be challenged to avoid making unnecessary payment.

The winding-up process requires the dissolved partnership to convert its assets to cash as part of the liquidation process. The winding-up partner must locate partnership assets and determine their value to facilitate **liquidation**. For example, accounts receivables should be collected or assigned to a factor. Outsiders' contract performances due to the partnership should be received unless they are long-term contracts that can be settled or assigned to another buyer for the best price available. Partnership assets should be sold to acquire a cash fund to pay off partnership creditors. The remainder is distributed to the partners.

The liquidation value of assets should be maximized to benefit partners and ensure that creditors are fully paid. The proceeds of some assets sales are maximized only when sold piecemeal, such as in the ordinary course of business. However, a large inventory of goods may not sell off quickly, so it may be less costly to sell them on the wholesale market. Of course, the highest return often comes from selling the partnership business as a going concern. The

Figure 38–2   Two Tracks of Partnership Dissolution

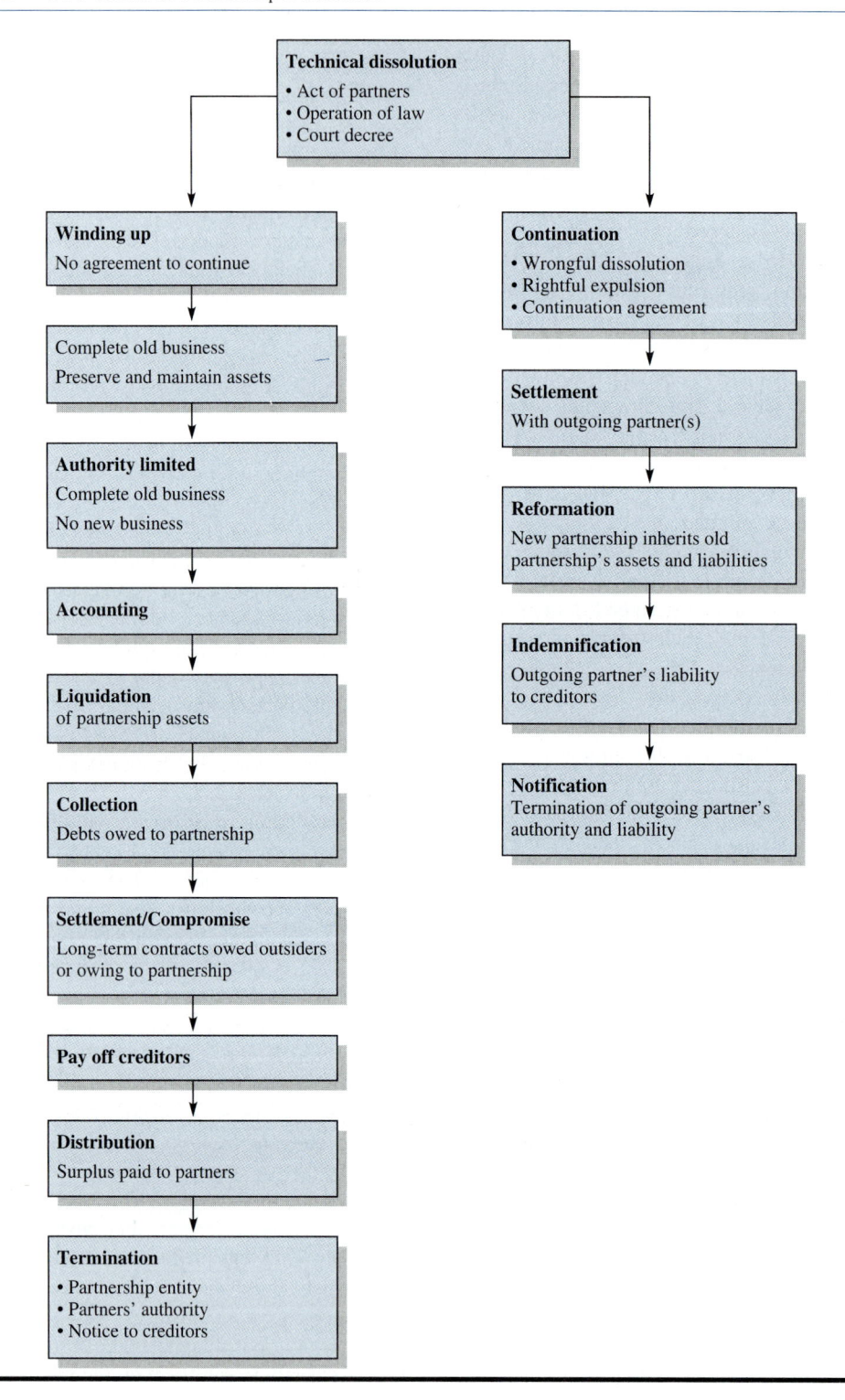

winding-up partners continue to owe a fiduciary duty to make such decisions, liquidate promptly, and maximize the liquidation proceeds.

After liquidation, the proceeds must be **distributed**, first to outside creditors, second to partner creditors, third to repay partners' capital contributions, and finally, the balance, constituting profits, to the partners and any deceased partner's estate. Unless otherwise agreed, partners have no rights to receive particular assets. However, occasionally the partners may agree that some assets will be subject to a **distribution in kind** in satisfaction of the partners' claims. However, this is unusual due to inevitable disagreements over which partner is entitled to particular assets and how to value them. Following distribution, the winding up is complete and the partnership is terminated. **Termination** discontinues any further partner authority to bind the partnership or other partners in contract.

Authority during Winding Up

Partners' authority is limited during winding up. UPA Section 35 permits a partner to bind the partnership in contract "by any act appropriate for winding up partnership affairs or completing transactions unfinished at dissolution." As discussed above, the winding-up partner has considerable flexibility to settle existing contracts, and this authority extends over to that partner's decisions to enter new contracts that are necessary to close out business. The only new contracts authorized are those necessary to facilitate the completion of old business. For example, the winding-up partner would probably lack the authority to take new customer orders for goods the firm does not already have in inventory. By contrast, there would be authority to enter new contracts to sell goods already in the partnership's inventory.

Authority also exists to preserve and maintain assets or prepare them for liquidation. For example, to maximize the sale price of a partnership vehicle it might be necessary to contract for body repairs, new tires, or a new paint job. Similar contracts may be needed to enhance the value of a partnership's real estate. Works in progress inventory often needs additional work to assemble finished products and maximize their value. Partnership machinery might need refurbishing before sale. During winding up, the borrowing of money would usually be considered an unauthorized act of new business unless funds were needed to preserve, maintain, repair, or prepare assets for liquidation. While many of these contracts may appear on first glance to be unauthorized because they are "new contracts," they are authorized as a legitimate part of the winding-up process.

The partnership by estoppel theory protects the reasonable expectations of outsiders who previously dealt with the partnership or knew of the partnership's existence. To be sure there is no *lingering apparent authority*, the winding-up partner must give actual notice to outsiders who extended credit to the partnership in the past. Such creditors include those who directly loaned money to the partnership in the past, as well as those who deliver goods or services to the partnership on credit. For example, because the phone company extends credit for local dialing privileges and long-distance services, it deserves actual notice. Anyone who entrusted money to a partner for the partnership's benefit deserves actual notice.

The notice requirements illustrate the importance of archiving all transactions and keeping accurate records. Constructive notice of the partnership's termination is sufficient for outsiders who previously knew of the partnership but never extended credit. Outsiders who never previously knew of the partnership need not receive either type of notice. Notice may be unnecessary if the partnership business becomes illegal or the unauthorized partner with whom the outsider is dealing has gone into bankruptcy. These latter matters are considered sufficiently notorious to inform creditors. Unauthorized contracts made by partners during winding up can nevertheless expose the other partners to liability. These innocent partners must be indemnified if the wrongful partner knew of the dissolution before making an unauthorized contract. The following case illustrates how authority is limited during winding up.

KING v. STODDARD
104 Cal. Rptr. 903 (Cal. Ct. App. 1972)

The *Walnut Kernel* was a newspaper operated by the Stoddard family. The Stoddard's son, Limon, continued operating the newspaper after his mother and father died. King, an accountant who provided accounting services during wind up, was not paid. He sued both the son and the estates of the deceased parents. Executors of the parents' estates argued that Limon's authority to hire an accountant was limited to only the wind-up process of the partnership business. The accountant argued his services were necessary to continue operating the paper after the Stoddards' death triggered dissolution so that the newspaper could be sold as a going concern. The executors appealed from a judgment granting payment to the accountant.

BROWN, Judge

A dissolution operates only with respect of future transactions; as to everything past the partnership continues until all pre-existing matters are terminated. After dissolution a partner can bind the partnership by any act appropriate for winding up the partnership affairs. It is this latter provision upon which the court based its decision that the estates of the deceased partners were liable for the accounting services performed after dissolution. The court found that Limon Stoddard, Jr.'s continuation of the *Walnut Kernel* business was an appropriate act for winding up the partnership, since the assets of the business would have substantial value only if it was a going concern business.

We disagree with this finding. It is probably true that there might have been advantages to the partnership to sell the business as a going business, but the indefinite continuation of the partnership business is contrary to the requirement for winding up the affairs of dissolution. The record reflects the fact that the surviving partner was not taking action to wind up the partnership as was his duty nor did the estates consent in any way to a delay. Rather, their insistence on winding up took the form of an effort

to sell the business and a suit to require an accounting. There is nothing in the record upon which to base the argument made by the respondent that appellants consented to his continued employment. The fact that they did not object is of no relevance. They had no right to direct and did not participate in the operation of the business. The determination that the acts of the accountants were rendered during a winding up process is not based upon substantial evidence. We conclude that the services of respondent's were rendered after dissolution resulting from the deaths of the partners and do not constitute services during the winding up process of the partnership. Judgment reversed.

Case Questions

1. What was the issue about the authority of Limon Stoddard, Jr., to retain an accountant in the *King* case?

2. Why was the going concern business argument rejected by the court?

3. How could a winding-up partner temporarily continue operating the partnership business if the objective was to maximize its value and resell it as a going concern given the problems in the *King* case?

Continuation of Partnership Business

Many successful partnerships choose to continue their business after dissolution. The departure of one partner, particularly in large service firms, does not usually eliminate the firm's goodwill, so surviving partners typically seek to maintain their employment. Surviving partners may continue a dissolved business without liquidating assets if the dissolution was wrongful, a partner is rightfully expelled, or there is a continuation agreement. Recall the discussion of incoming and outgoing partners. Continuing partners must indemnify outgoing partners for pre-

existing partnership debts, and notice must be given to terminate the outgoing partner's authority and liability for new debts. Additionally, the new partnership inherits all the assets and liabilities of the dissolved partnership. RUPA presumes that the rights and duties among continuing partners remain the same as before dissolution.

Wrongful Dissolution

Many partnership agreements specify a minimum fixed term, such as 10 years, for the partnership or that it should continue until a particular objective is attained, such as the building, development, and sale of a fully occupied shopping center. A partnership agreement will often place a fixed term or specify an objective because this better ensures the new partners' commitment to make financial and work contributions. Many partners are unwilling to join a new venture without assurances that the capital needed and the other partners' participation critical to success will be present throughout the expected minimum time believed necessary to develop a new product, see a business strategy through to completion, or permit the full development of goodwill. **Wrongful dissolution** occurs when a partner's retirement causes dissolution in breach of a fixed or specified term. Wrongful dissolution also arises where a partner petitions a court for dissolution either due to another partner's conduct that prejudices the carrying on of the business or due to a partner's willful or persistent breach of the partnership agreement.

Continuing partners are permitted to use partnership property after wrongful dissolution only if they pay the value of the wrongful partner's interest. This amount may be reduced by the value of goodwill and by any damages caused by the wrongful dissolution. For example, assume Paul dissolved Triple-P before its five-year term ended, permitting Peter and Pam to continue the business. At dissolution, the partnership business must be appraised to compute Paul's share. This amount may be reduced by his share of goodwill and by any damages the dissolution caused to Peter and Pam, such as the legal expenses of dissolution and any fees paid to replace Paul's special expertise. Peter and Pam need not actually settle with Paul until after the fixed term expires or after the specified objective is attained. Continuing partners may use the wrongfully dissolving partner's capital contribution until the partnership agreement's specified terms are fulfilled. However, the continuing partners must indemnify the wrongfully departing partner for existing and future partnership liabilities.

Expulsion

The partnership is dissolved when a partner is expelled. **Expulsion** is the involuntary retirement or dismissal of a partner according to a basis established in the partnership agreement. These bases may include matters such as professional incompetence, negligence, shirking, low productivity, legal incompetence, or simple incompatibility as deter-

mined by a vote of the other partners. Only a few states require that the expulsion meet any fairness standard, good faith duty, particular procedures, notice, or include a specification of charges leading to expulsion. An expelled partner is entitled to all the rights of a deceased partner's estate: payment of his or her partnership interest including goodwill within a reasonable time and indemnification against partnership liabilities. The expelled partner has no right to cause liquidation, so the remaining partners may continue the business. While some partnership agreements alter these rights, a partner is entitled to damages if expelled in violation of the expulsion agreement.

Even without an expulsion provision, all the other partners could achieve a similar result by simply dissolving the partnership and reforming without the partner they seek to expel. However, this **reformation** would necessitate winding up and liquidation or it might breach a partnership agreement containing a specified term or undertaking. Therefore, drafters of a partnership agreement should carefully consider whether it is advisable to include an expulsion provision and how it should operate to maintain fairness, particularly if necessary to attract and retain competent partners.

Continuation Agreement

The partners in many successful partnerships seek to preserve their business by entering a **continuation agreement**. This may be memorialized in the partnership agreement, in a separate agreement by all the partners, or in an agreement made by some or all of the partners at the time of dissolution. A continuation agreement usually permits the surviving partners to continue the business while requiring them to settle the outgoing partner's share. The settlement amount may be agreed to at dissolution or specified in the agreement in a number of ways: a specified dollar amount, a formula, or a proportion of value established by independent appraisal or through arbitration. The amount specified may be partially or fully funded by life insurance proceeds payable to the firm for that purpose.

Continuation agreements may take the form of a **buy-sell** agreement obligating the continuing partners to purchase and the outgoing partner to sell his or her interest. An agreement may give surviving partners the option to purchase a deceased partner's share or even obligate them to purchase. Without a properly drawn continuation agreement, the surviving partners may be required to bargain with a deceased partner's estate over the settlement value, the timing of the payments, or their right to continue the business. The estate's bargaining power is increased where the partnership holds a single asset and liquidation could effectively put the partnership out of business. For similar reasons, the continuing partners should carefully consider alternatives to liquidating considerable amounts of partnership property to purchase an outgoing partner's share. Surviving partners may have insufficient resources or borrow-

ing power to pay a deceased partner's share. For these reasons, continuation agreements, fair valuation formulae, life insurance policies, limitations on goodwill in valuing a retiring partner's interest, and specified term provisions that trigger wrongful dissolution must be orchestrated to prevent financial hardship on the continuing partners. The following case illustrates that the incorporation of a partnership is a hybrid form of dissolution that includes some aspects of winding up and some aspects of continuing the underlying business.

HOOPER v. YODER
732 P. 2nd 852 (Colo. 1987)

David Yoder and Steven Hooper operated Beautiful Daydreams, a partnership for the manufacture and sale of frozen yogurt bars. Eventually, the partnership was incorporated and suit arose because Yoder alleged Hooper caused all the corporate stock to be issued to Hooper and none to Yoder. Yoder also claimed Hooper drew a salary from the business without Yoder's consent. The trial court found for Yoder, ordering Hooper to transfer half of his stock and half of the salary Hooper wrongfully paid to Yoder.

LOHR, Justice

As a general rule, when partners organize a corporation to operate the business of the partnership and transfer the assets to the corporation, the partnership is dissolved. This is so because such action usually reflects the express will of the parties that the partnership be dissolved. We find no support in the record for a finding that the parties intended that the partnership would continue after the corporation was organized. The partnership between Hooper and Yoder was dissolved upon the incorporation of Beautiful Daydreams.

The dissolution of a partnership does not automatically terminate the existence of a partnership. On dissolution the partnership is not terminated but continues until the winding up of the partnership affairs is completed. The winding up includes the entire process of settling the partnership affairs after dissolution. When partners organize a corporation to continue the business of the firm, the winding up of the partnership includes transfer of the partnership assets to the corporation in exchange for corporate stock.

Here, the winding up of the partnership remained incomplete pending issuance of corporate stock to Hooper and Yoder in equal amounts pursuant to the agreement they made as partners prior to incorporation. The winding up of the partnership was not

accomplished upon incorporation and the partnership continued to exist . . . [therefore] so did the fiduciary duties that one partner owes to another. Partners in a business enterprise owe to one another the highest duty of loyalty; they stand in a relationship of trust and confidence to each other and are bound by standards of good conduct and square dealing. Each partner has the right to demand and expect from the other a full, fair, open and honest disclosure of everything effecting the relationship.

Hooper's action in causing the issuance of 95 shares of stock to himself and none to Yoder and drawing his salary from the business without the assent or knowledge of Yoder are the very antithesis of the type of fair dealing required between partners in winding up a partnership. A partner is not entitled to salary or other compensation for services in conducting the partnership business. This is true even if the services rendered by one partner are disproportionately valuable to any services performed by the others. However, the Uniform Partnership law does recognize a surviving partner's right to "reasonable compensation" for those services necessary to the winding up of partnership affairs after its dissolution. Any such entitlement to compensation during the winding up period is tempered by equitable considerations. The trial court's decision to deny compensation to Hooper for his services was proper. Judgment affirmed.

Case Questions

1. What is the issue concerning Hooper's conduct during winding up?

2. What reasons support the application of the fiduciary rule applied to a winding-up partner?

3. What assumption is the court making about Hooper's intent in issuing the stock? Is there an alternative hypothesis to explain his behavior?

Distribution of Assets

During wind up, the partnership must settle all financial claims against it held by both outsiders and by the partners. The liquidation of assets converts partnership property to cash that is more easily used to satisfy creditor claims. When this cash is insufficient to fully satisfy creditors, the partnership's assets also include any partner contributions necessary to make up the difference. Distribution is fairly simple for solvent partnerships, becomes more problematic in partnership insolvency, and is quite complex when some or all partners are also insolvent.

Rules for Distribution

1. Outside creditors' claims.
2. Partner claims as creditors (advances).
3. Partners' capital contributions.
4. Partners' profits.

UPA § 40(b).

Solvency

The winding-up partner has an obligation to discharge all claims against a dissolved but solvent partnership out of partnership assets. UPA Section 40(b) requires the full payment of outside creditors before any distribution is made to partners. Next, partners' loans or advances made to the partnership must be fully paid. Third, each partner's capital contribution must be fully returned. Finally, any surplus remaining is profit shared equally among the partners unless they have an agreement to share profits in some other proportion (see Distribution Example 1).

Distribution Example 1   The Triple-P partnership of Peter, Paul, and Pam is rightfully dissolved. When Triple-P was started, Peter and Pam each made a $10,000 capital contribution and Paul contributed $15,000. After Paul wound up the partnership and liquidated all partnership assets, this produced a fund of $50,000. Paul paid off creditors as follows:

1. Rent for the remaining term of their office lease was settled by paying the landlord a lump sum of $3,500.

2. Unpaid employee salaries, withholding taxes, and pension contributions amounted to $2,500.

3. Utility, phone, and janitorial bills amounted to $1,500.

Paul had never been repaid a $1,000 advancement he made for Triple-P as a down payment on the firm's computer. Triple-P was a solvent partnership because the $50,000 in assets was sufficient to first pay off outside creditors ($3,500 + $2,500 + $1,500 = $7,500), inside creditors ($1,000), and the partners' capital contributions ($10,000 + $10,000 + $15,000 = $35,000). The surplus remaining was partnership profit ($50,000 − $7,500 − $1,000 − $35,000 = $6,500) shared equally by Peter, Pam, and Paul unless their agreement required a different profit sharing ratio. Therefore, Peter and Pam each received $12,166.66 ($10,000 capital and $2,166.66 profit) and Paul received $18,166.66 ($15,000 capital, $1,000 loan repayment, and $2,166.66 profit).

LANGNESS v. "O" STREET CARPET SHOP
353 N.W. 2nd 709 (Neb. 1984)

The partnership NFL Associates was formed by Langness, Freedman, and the "O" Street Carpet Shop, Inc., by its president, Gerald Neva, to invest in real estate. "O" Street contributed a purchase contract valued at $5,000. Langness contributed $14,000 cash. Freedman contributed legal services, although no value was placed on them in the articles of partnership. "O" Street Carpet received $8,000 worth of Langness's $14,000 contribution, with the remaining $6,000 used a down payment to purchase the rental property. The articles of partnership permitted Langness to receive payments of $116.66 per month, which was considered as a return of Langness capital. Five years later, the partnership sold the rental property, realizing $52,001.20. Thereafter, the partnership was dissolved and wound up by Neva and Freedman, who calculated the remaining assets valued at $48,824.41 after paying a partnership debt of $3,176.79. Langness would receive $16,792.01, "O" Street would receive $26,808.58, and Freedman $5,223.82. Langness sued, claiming a right to a larger share of the partnership assets.

PER CURIAM

$8,000 of the $14,000 contributed by Langness went to "O" Street Carpet, thereby reducing its capital contribution at the time to $1,000. During the life of the partnership, "O" Street Carpet contributed an additional $4,005 in capital. Thus, "O" Street Carpet's total capital contribution is $5,005.00.

Freedman contributed no money or property. It is the general rule that a partner who contributes only services to the partnership is not deemed to have made a capital contribution to the partnership such as to require capital repayment upon dissolution unless the parties have agreed to the contrary.

Langness was issued 47 checks for $116.66, 3 checks for $33.32, and 1 check for $117.32. We calculate her total capital withdrawals as $6,300.30 which reduced her capital in the partnership to $7,699.70.

We now reach the question of the appropriate amounts of the distribution to each of the partners. The partnership agreement provides: "Upon dissolution of the partnership after settlement of all of its debts, liabilities, and other obligations, the partners are entitled to all remaining assets of the partnership in equal proportions in liquidation of all their respective interests in the partnership." Amounts owing to partners to reimburse them for capital contributions are liabilities of the partnership and take priority over amounts owing to partners in respect to profits.

Of the $48,824.41 in assets remaining after payment of the partnership debts, $7,099.70 is to be paid to Langness for capital contribution and $5,005.00 to "O" Street Carpet for its capital contribution. The remaining $36,119.71 is to be divided according to the partners' share in the profits, which is on a 45–45–10 basis. This calculation requires $16,253.87 to be paid to "O" Street Carpet and $3,611.97 to Freedman. At the time of the winding up of the partnership the distribution should have been as . . . [shown in the accompanying table]: Since Langness was paid only $16,792.01 she is entitled to an additional $7,161.56.

Upon dissolution each partner impliedly consents that his co-partners receive their appropriate shares of the partnership assets. Anything one partner receives over his appropriate share is obtained without the consent of the other partners. Therefore, Freedman holds any amount he received over his appropriate share in trust for the partnership, which in turn owes it to Langness. The same is true for the excess amount received by "O" Street Carpet. We know that this is not a case where it was plead

	Return of Capital	Share of Profits	Total
Langness	$ 7,699.70	$16,253.87	$23,963.57
"O" St. Carpet	5,005.00	16,253.87	21,258.87
Freedman	0.00	3,611.97	3,611.97
TOTAL	$12,704.70	$36,119.71	$48,824.41

or proved that Freedman and "O" Street Carpet engaged in a concerted fraud upon their partner Langness.

Case Questions

1. What is the issue that determines a partner's responsibility to repay money received during the dissolution?

2. Why were "O" Street and Freedman required to repay amounts they received back to the partnership and ultimately to Langness?

3. What is the assumption about partners who receive excess amounts of distribution after dissolution concerning their obligation to their copartners?

Insolvency

Insolvent partnership distributions are more complex because it becomes necessary for individual partners' unlimited liability to cover the excess of partnership liabilities over assets. Insolvency is not equivalent to bankruptcy because an insolvent firm may be able to continue operating for some time even with a negative capital balance as long as it is not yet in default on its current debt payments. By contrast, a partnership may enter bankruptcy voluntarily by unanimous consent of all partners or involuntarily when two or more creditors "throw the partnership into bankruptcy." Bankruptcy provides more equal protection for all creditors by making fair distribution of the debtor's assets among all creditors. Secured creditors with a lien on collateral have priority over the liquidation proceeds derived from the liquidation of the collateral. A dissolved partnership is insolvent if it cannot pay all its liabilities to outside or inside creditors and return each partners' capital (see Distribution Example 2).

Distribution Example 2 Consider the following change in Distribution Example 1. Paul raised only $40,000 in liquidation proceeds, enough to pay off all Triple-P's outside and inside creditors, but repayment of partners' capital contributions is $3,500 short. The partners will receive a pro rata share of the remaining capital according to the ratio of their original capital contributions: Peter: 2/7 ($9,000); Pam: 2/7 ($9,000); and Paul: 3/7 ($13,500) of the remaining $31,500. Unless otherwise agreed, no partner has any priority to receive a greater percentage share return of his or her capital than as represented by the proportions contributed.

When the partnership's insolvency is so serious that outside creditors' claims cannot be satisfied from the liquidation proceeds, the partners must make additional contributions from their individual

property. Of course, the partnership agreement may change the general rule that each partner shares losses in the same proportion as profits are shared. For example, in the ABC partnership, A and B's substantial capital contributions put them at much greater financial risk than C, who had made no contribution. Because C had so little financial risk and stood to gain from the other partners' risking their own capital, C was willing to agree to accept half the losses even though A, B, and C shared profits equally (see Distribution Example 3).

Distribution Example 3 Consider the following change in Distribution Examples 1 and 2. Paul raised only $5,000 by liquidating partnership assets, leaving $2,500 of outside creditors' claims unpaid, Paul's $1,000 loan unpaid, and no capital or profits left for the partners. Each partner must contribute 1/3 of the loss: $3,500/3 = $1,166.66. However, Paul will pay out only $166.66 after his $1,000 loan is netted against his $1,166.66 payment. Initially, each partner owes an equal share of losses before partner loan repayments are deducted if the partners share losses in the same proportion as profits and the profits are shared equally, unless otherwise agreed.

Individual versus Partnership Creditors

Distribution in an insolvent partnership is further complicated when one or more partners are also insolvent. The creditors of the partnership have competing claims against the individual partner's creditors, each seeking to receive a share of the individual property belonging to insolvent partners. Conversely, individual partner's creditors must compete with partnership creditors for a share of the partnership liquidation proceeds. UPA Section 40(h) applies a **marshaling of assets** concept, sometimes called the **jingle rule**. This gives partnership creditors absolute priority over individual creditors with respect to partnership assets, meaning partnership creditors are paid completely before individual creditors can receive anything. Contrarily, individual partner's creditors have absolute priority over partnership creditors with respect to individual partner assets. Today, the jingle rule applies only in state courts sitting in equity.

The Bankruptcy Reform Act of 1978 eliminated the jingle rule when either the partnership or an individual partner is in federal bankruptcy court. Partnership creditors retain absolute priority over partnership assets but they now share equal status with individual creditors with respect to individual partner's assets. The trustee administering a bankrupt partnership may extend its power over solvent individual partners as needed to satisfy partnership creditor claims. The trustee of a bankrupt individual partner has the power to foreclose that partner's partnership interest to accumulate proceeds to pay off individual partner's creditor claims. RUPA would abandon the jingle rule and make no distinction between a partner's interest in capital and profits.

END–OF–CHAPTER QUESTIONS

1. What reasons support the UPA requirement that an accounting is required whenever the partnership is dissolved? What argument might be made to avoid an accounting if the partnership was wrongly dissolved by a partner retiring before the end of a specified term?

2. The ABC partnership owned a single parcel of real estate, an apartment building that produced significant income. After a favorable upsurge in the real estate market, A and B started talking about a sale of the building to release funds for other investments. What are the issues confronting a potential buyer when A and B begin negotiations to sell the building? Why does partnership law address these issues?

3. Consider how the answer to Question 2 changes if the partnership owned numerous tracts of land held for speculation. C had told a real estate agent that A and B were authorized to negotiate to sell a large parcel of development land. However, when a contract of sale was made, C sued to stop the sale. C claims that unanimity is required for sale of the land. Alternatively, C argues that the sale would represent an unauthorized disposal of the partnership's goodwill. Are A and B authorized to make the sale? Based on *Owens v. Palos Verdes Monaco,* 191 Cal. Rptr. 381 (1983).

4. D and N owned a real estate partnership called D/N Realty. Each had general authority to deposit checks in the partnership's bank account for matters related to the partnership business. N deposited two large checks in this account that N received from K. Soon thereafter, N withdrew an amount equal to these two checks from the D/N account. The checks from K bounced, leaving insufficient funds in the D/N account for which the bank seeks reimbursement from D and N. On what theory should N be liable for the overdraft? On what theory could D argue against personal liability for the overdraft? See *Bank of Commerce v. DeSanis,* 451 N.Y.S.2d 974 (1982).

5. X, Y, and Z are partners at will in XYZ Plumbing Supply, largely selling to building contractors. XYZ had no partnership agreement and had accumulated $100,000 in debts outstanding to one large plumbing equipment manufacturer. When XYZ began experiencing cash flow problems, the firm attracted A to join as a silent partner to provide needed capital. A contributed $50,000 and was given an equal share of the profits but did not participate in management. Financial problems worsened and the major supplier sued the partnership for the $100,000 owed. The XYZ firm and the three original partners, X, Y, and Z, had no liquid assets, so the supplier sued A for the whole amount. What is the extent of A's liability on the supplier's bill? What reasons support A's denial of liability?

6. The Alex Company, a partnership between Alex, Lawrence, and Jacob, owned and operated apartment buildings beginning in 1964. In 1974, Jacob retired but the parties failed to agree on the firm's value until 1976. During that two-year

period, the apartment buildings appreciated greatly in value. Jacob sued for an accounting and to require a winding up and a determination of his share valued as of the date of suit. What reasons support the date Jacob asserts is proper for valuation? What alternate argument will Alex and Lawrence probably make? See *Oliker v. Gershunoff*, 241 Cal.Rptr. 415 (1987).

7. Four individuals entered a written partnership agreement with the stated purpose of leasing various real estate holdings for profit. R was obligated to manage the properties, and the other three partners agreed to service the properties with their physical labors. R gave the other three notice of dissolution a year later and demanded an immediate accounting, winding up, and determination of R's partnership share. On what basis may the other partners continue the business? May R participate in the winding up if the other partners fail to do so, arguing R's dissolution was wrongful? See *Girard Bank v. Haley*, 332 A.2d 443 (Pa. 1975).

8. Assume each of the following involves a valid partnership. Explain whether there is a dissolution and, if so, what the grounds are for dissolution.

a. The only two partners, A and B, agree that each will work at least 40 hours each week for partnership business, except for sick days and vacation. B constantly shirks by leaving work early.

b. A and B operate a partnership under an agreement to continue the business until they build, substantially lease, and sell an office building. After three years, the building is 95 percent leased but a depressed real estate market lowers the building's appraisal. A retires, demanding a dissolution, and B claims damages.

c. In Question 8(b), assume that A died instead of retiring and before dissolution, B claims damages.

d. Would the answer to Question 8(c) be different if A filed for bankruptcy?

9. A supplier had sold goods to the H and H partnership for several years. T, one of the two partners, purchased the whole partnership business after dissolution by the other partner. T continued the business under the H and H name as a sole proprietorship. The supplier's salesman was notified of the change in ownership and business form. Thereafter, T continued to purchase goods from the supplier on credit but eventually defaulted. The supplier sued the retired partner for the unpaid balance. On what theory would the supplier argue it should collect from the retired partner? On what theory would the retired partner disclaim any liability? See *Sta-Rite Indus., Inc. v. Taylor*, 492 P.2d 726 (Ariz. 1972).

10. The XYZ partnership is dissolved but insolvent. Partner X is also individually insolvent. The financial position of the partnership is as follows:

Bank loan (unsecured):	$30,000
Capital contributions:	
X	$10,000
Y	10,000
Z	10,000
Total capital	$30,000
Assets' liquidation value:	
Inventory	$ 4,000
Machinery	2,500
Bank account	500
Total assets	$ 7,000

How will the excess of liabilities over assets be made up under the jingle rule? How are matters treated differently under federal bankruptcy law?

Chapter 39

Limited Partnerships

■

CRITICAL THINKING INQUIRIES

As you read this chapter, you should be able to address the following:

- What reasons support the statutory creation of a form of partnership in which the liability of some members is limited to their initial contributions?
- What are the issues underlying the legal rule that holds limited partners to unlimited personal liability for defective formation or excessive entanglement in limited partnership management?
- Why should limited partners be given a status equivalent to a shareholder's status in a corporation? Is the analogy between limited partnerships and corporations flawed?
- What reasons, aside from tax treatment, are there to explain the current preference for limited partnerships over closely held or publicly traded corporations for some types of ventures?

MANAGERIAL PERSPECTIVE

Peter, Pam, and Paul proposed to become general partners in a limited partnership. The three approached Lem and Patricia, two wealthy investors, seeking their passive participation as limited partners in the new firm, Triple-LP. This is the first limited partnership that Peter, Pam, and Paul's attorney and tax adviser have ever formed. The limited partnership certificate was never filed with the state. After several months of operations, Patricia insisted on participating in voting on daily managerial decisions made by Peter, Pam, and Paul. As Triple-LP's financial performance worsened, Lem's interest was sold through his regular stockbroker to another broker's customer by using a national screen-based telecommunications system.

- How could Triple-LP or the individual investors have avoided problems that will arise due to these events?
- What issues arise for Peter, Pam, and Paul regarding their promotion of Triple-LP?

This chapter focuses on the formation, operation, dissolution, and risks of using limited partnerships. While similar to general partnerships, the **limited partnership** can only be created under a statute. One or more general partners must have unlimited liability. There must be at least one or more limited partners who remain passive in partnership management before they can limit their financial liability to the capital contribution.

The law of limited partnerships is based on both common law and statutory concepts: contracts, agency, partnerships, limited partnerships, taxes, and securities regulations. This chapter first explores the risks of investing in defectively formed limited partnerships, and then turns to the extent of a limited partner's participation in managerial decisions. It is important to use only competent and experienced legal and tax counsel in the formation of limited partnerships and in investigating their investment risks. For most participants in limited partnerships, the partnership flow-through tax treatment is an essential feature that may be lost if the limited partner's interests are publicly traded in the securities markets. Many factors heighten the risks of using limited partnerships for the unwary and inexperienced.

JUSTIFICATIONS FOR LIMITED PARTNERSHIPS

Deeply rooted in Western culture and the common law is the concept of personal responsibility for the consequences of one's activities. This underlies the unlimited liability concept applied to sole proprietorships and general partnerships as well as to separate legal entities such as business corporations themselves. Unlimited liability is most appropriate where the owners directly participate in business operations. It sets incentives for the participants to act carefully and apply their deliberate attention to conducting the business's affairs. The law presumes that decisionmakers understand the impact of their decisions because they are in the best position to evaluate the risks that follow. However, experience during the early Industrial Revolution showed that unlimited liability constrained growth. The growing enterprises sought to pursue economies of large-scale production but found it too cumbersome to assemble sufficient capital from direct owners and managers.

Limited liability developed as an exception to the personal responsibility rule intended to permit passive investors to participate financially but without any direct involvement in business decisionmaking. By breaking these investors' passive participation from their unlimited responsibility, entrepreneurs were enabled to attract sufficient capital for industrial expansion. The development of limited liability is often cited as the primary reason for the development of other business organization forms: trusts, limited partnerships, corporations, and franchises. Generally, all these forms shield inactive participants from liability.

Limited partnerships originally developed in medieval Europe as **commenda** and were codified in the French Commercial Code, which eventually became the model for the modern law of Louisiana. Limited partnerships flourished under the civil law in European nations for many years before gaining success in the United States. Today, many German firms are formed as limited partnerships, called *Kommanditgesellschaft,* which display the more familiar abbreviation *KG*. In the United States, statutes authorized limited partnerships as early as the 1820s, long before corporations were widely used. Their early acceptance in the United States probably reflects three factors: (1) the long history of successful limited partnership use in Europe, (2) the requirement for at least one general partner's unlimited liability in every limited partnership, and (3) the limited partner's resemblance to a passive lender.

Uses for Limited Partnerships

The corporate form became more readily acceptable at the turn of the 20th century. Sources of business financing broadened through the commercial banks and the securities markets, permitting corporations to flourish as the predominate business form used by larger industrial firms. This probably diminished the importance of limited partnerships. However, by World War II, corporations were taxed more heavily than other business forms, encouraging a resurgence of limited partnerships that still persists today.

Like general partnerships, most limited partnerships use the *flow-through* partnership method of federal taxation to avoid the *double tax* on corporate dividends. Unlike corporations, limited partnerships are not taxed a first time on the firm's profits and then a second time when profits are eventually distributed to the owners. Instead, most general and limited partnerships are not taxed at all as entities. Tax liability flows through to the individual partners as their own individual tax liability. Therefore, the total federal tax liability on limited partnership participants is usually significantly less than on similarly situated corporate owners.

The favorable tax treatment stimulated the proliferation of limited partnerships as **tax shelters** during the post–World War II period. However, the 1986 Tax Reform Act reduced some of the popularity of limited partnerships as tax shelters. For example, the act eliminated the attraction of using tax shelters by lowering the high marginal individual tax brackets, although at the time of this writing there are proposals to raise the marginal tax rates on the highest brackets. The act also prohibited most individuals from offsetting their regular income against passive tax shelter losses, the primary inducement of tax sheltering income.

Today, limited partnerships are most popular in high-risk enterprises such as oil well drilling ventures, Broadway shows, movie productions, research and development ventures, amusement parks, commercial real estate developments, heavy construction equipment leasing, mortgage loan pools, and some agricultural ventures (e.g., orchards, cattle operations). Most often, the general partner in these ventures performs all management and development activities and is organized as a corporate general partner with unlimited liability. Corporate general partners are still permitted to offset passive limited partnership losses against the corporation's ordinary income. Most states permit a limited partner to simultaneously be a shareholder, officer, and/or director of the corporate general partner. They view corporate shareholding as a legitimate method to limit one's personal liability. However, some view this as a subterfuge to avoid unlimited personal liability.

LAW APPLICABLE TO LIMITED PARTNERSHIPS

The limited liability concept is a legal fiction created only by statute because it alters the common law rule of unlimited responsibility of participants in a venture. Therefore, limited partnerships in the United States are created only by statute. After experiments with varying limited partnership statutes during the 19th century, in 1916 the National Conference on Uniform State Laws reported out the first limited partnership act intended for usage in all states. This **Uniform Limited Partnership Act (ULPA)** is still the law in about a quarter of the states. Since that time there have been two modernization efforts: the 1976 **Revised Uniform Partnership Act (RULPA)** and some minor revisions made to RULPA in 1985. This chapter focuses on all three laws. As with other uniform and model acts, some states have modified their ULPA or RULPA and their courts' interpretations may differ. A few states, such as Delaware, California, and Louisiana, have somewhat unique limited partnership laws. ULPA or RULPA are not the exclusive laws applicable to limited partnerships in any particular state. Gaps in the limited partnership law are filled in by the applicable law of contracts, agency, the UPA, tax law, and occasionally the securities laws.

LIMITED PARTNERSHIP FORMATION

Limited partnerships are formed with a similar level of formality as needed to form corporations. For both forms, the failure to substantially comply can subject the participants to unlimited liability. The noncomplying group is viewed as an association of partners who failed to secure their limited liability. This results in their joint and several liability as general partners. Therefore, care must be taken to ensure adequate compliance with the applicable ULPA or RULPA.

Before beginning operations, the law generally requires that a **certificate of limited partnership** containing specified information be filed with the secretary of state in the state of creation. RULPA eliminated the ULPA requirement of local or county filing. The filing is public information permitting outsiders to discover the limited partnership's purpose and firm name, the identity of the individual limited and general partners, and the firm's initial financial structure. Amendments must be filed when a partner withdraws, a new partner is admitted, or there are changes in the partners' capital contribution. RULPA assumes the existence of a separate document—a limited partnership agreement—that

Figure 39–1   Certificate of Limited Partnership

The undersigned, desiring to form a Limited Partnership under the Revised Uniform Limited Partnership Act of the State of _____, make this certificate for that purpose.

1   **NAME**. The name of the Limited Partnership shall be "_____."

2   **PURPOSE**. The business of the Limited Partnership shall be to [describe].

3   **LOCATION**. The location of the Limited Partnership's principal place of business is _____ County, _____.

4   **AGENT FOR SERVICE OF PROCESS**. The agent for service of process on the Limited Partnership in the State of _____ shall be _____, whose address is _____.

5   **MEMBERS AND DESIGNATION**. The names, business addresses, and designation of the members as General or Limited Partners, are as follows:

_____	[address]	General Partner
_____	[address]	Limited Partner
_____	[address]	Limited Partner

6   **TERM**. The term for which the limited partnership is to exist is _____.

7   **INITIAL CONTRIBUTION OF PARTNERS**. The amount of cash, a description, and statement of the agreed value of other property or services contributed by each partner are as follows:

[name]   [describe]
[name]   [describe]
[name]   [describe]

8   **SUBSEQUENT CONTRIBUTIONS OF PARTNERS**. Each partner may (but shall not be obliged to) make additional contributions to the capital of the Limited Partnership as agreed or as follows:

[name]   [describe]
[name]   [describe]
[name]   [describe]

9   **PROFIT SHARES OF PARTNERS**. The share of profits that each Partner shall receive by reason of his or her contribution is as follows:

[name]   _____%
[name]   _____%
[name]   _____%

Signed _____, 19_____

_____

_____

_____

Signed and sworn before me, the undersigned authority, this ___ Day, 19___.
        Notary Public _____ County, _____.

---

further details the parties' various rights and liabilities. Figure 39–1 illustrates a certificate of limited partnership under RULPA.

RULPA substantially duplicated ULPA's required items of disclosure for the public filing of a certificate of limited partnership. RULPA further requires the disclosure of the name of the agent who is designated to receive service of process. RULPA requires disclosure of general and limited partners' financial shares and requires that the designation *Limited Partnership,* or an abbreviation such as *L.P.,* must appear as part of the firm's name. Neither ULPA nor RULPA provide much privacy, particularly for limited partners. However, there have been pressures to give limited partners the similar level of privacy and other privileges that corporate shareholders enjoy. This has led to some changes in the 1985 RULPA. For ex-

ample, certificates may omit any reference to financial contributions or shares and limited partners need not be listed nor must they sign the certificate.

Defective Formation

When a limited partnership is defectively formed, not all limited partners are held to the unlimited liability of a general partner. The ULPA makes a vague exception where there was substantial compliance with the statutory formation requirements. For example, assume that Peter, Pam, and Paul failed to properly file the Triple-LP certificate of limited partnership. Lem or Patricia would have unlimited liability unless they could show that Triple-LP made a substantial compliance in good faith with the formation requirements.

What constitutes *substantial compliance*? Filing delays, incomplete or erroneous information, or missing signatures are defects in filings that would probably permit the filing to remain in substantial compliance if Triple-LP was acting in good faith. RULPA eliminates the good faith language under the theory that filing is the minimum notice needed to qualify limited partners for limited liability. Does this mean RULPA enforces a higher ethical standard than ULPA to prevent bad faith? Perhaps there was experience with limited partnership promoters who intentionally ignored the required formation formalities to share unlimited liability with unsuspecting limited partners. By intentionally disregarding the limited partners' expectations, are these promoters' acts in bad faith and unethical in breaching a trust relationship?

Reliance

Early cases under ULPA made another exception to limited partners' unlimited liability for defective formation. Based on the estoppel principle, before holding the limited partner liable, many courts require proof of the outsider's **reliance** on the good faith belief that the limited partner was actually a general partner. RULPA codifies the reliance element, making a limited partner liable "only if the third party actually believed in good faith that the person was a general partner at the time of the transaction." However, outsiders cannot recover damages for defective formation beyond the limited partners' capital contributions if the outsider knew the firm was a limited partnership. The following case illustrates reliance.

GARRETT v. KOEPKE

569 S.W.2d 568 (Tex. Civ. App. 1978)

A limited partnership was formed to operate the Continental Longview Motor Inn in Longview, Texas. The partnership agreed to make lease payments on an advertising sign that Garrett and Henson were previously obligated to pay. After the partnership defaulted on these payments, Garrett and Henson sued for reimbursement of its expenses in paying damages for the breach of the sign lease. Although the limited partners were identified as such in the partnership agreement, the agreement was never filed with the secretary of state. However, Garrett knew he was dealing with a limited partnership and understood the consequences. The limited partners assumed control to wind up the business and distribute its assets after the general partner's resignation. Garrett and Henson sued the limited partners, claiming their unlimited liability as general partners.

AKIN, Justice

We see no logical reason to strip appellees of their limited liability under their partnership agreement merely because they failed to comply. The purpose of the filing requirements under the act is to provide notice to third persons dealing with the partrership of the essential features of the partnership agreement. Since appellees knew that the entity with which they were dealing was a limited partnership, as well as the consequences of dealing with such an entity, they were in no way prejudiced by the failure to comply with the statute. We see no compelling policy reason here for holding that appellees became general partners by requiring technical compliance with these notice provisions. Indeed, such was not the intent of the legislature in enacting the statute; instead, its intent was to provide notice of limited liability of certain partners to third parties dealing with the partnership. The nature of the legal existence of a partnership does not depend upon filing required by a stature. We hold, therefore, that where a party has acknowledged the entity with which he is dealing is a limited partnership that status is not changed for failing to file.

Appellants next contend that some of the limited partners lost their shield of limited liability when they took a controlling position in the business of the partnership. We cannot agree. The debt upon which appellants are suing arose when the general partner controlled the motel. The alleged participation of appellees in the business that may jeopardize their limited liability occurred after this debt was incurred. Thus, assuming that they participated in the management and control of the limited partnership so as to make them liable as general partners, their liability for obligations incurred before they were general partners can only be satisfied out of partnership property. Consequently, they cannot be held liable for this debt. Affirmed.

Case Questions

1. What is the issue concerning the effectiveness of the limited liability of the limited partnership in the *Garrett* case?

2. Why were the appellants' claims for unlimited liability denied in this case?

3. What ambiguity is created when a limited partnership certificate is not filed?

Misstatements in Certificate

Any known false statements in a limited partnership certificate expose all partners to unlimited liability for damages caused by the fraud. Limited partners are required to amend the certificate immediately on discovering such misstatements. For example, Lem or Patricia would be liable for falsely stating an inflated value on property they contributed as capital to the Triple-LP limited partnership. Such misrepresentations may mislead outsiders to believe Triple-LP has a minimum amount of assets to cover loan repayments. Therefore, the overvaluation contributes to the extension of credit based on the misstatement. This causes damage to the creditor if the limited partnership defaults. Intentional misrepresentations constitute fraud, an unethical act. The 1985 RULPA amendments would release limited partners from this liability if they are not listed in and did not sign the certificate of limited partnership. This release clearly tolerates unethical conduct by limited partners who knowingly permit the use of such misstatements.

Renunciation

Limited partners can avoid unlimited liability for defective formation if they "erroneously" believe they are limited partners and file a **renunciation** after discovering the defect. The limited partner may not exercise the rights of a general partner and must immediately disclaim any interest in future profits. Profits already distributed may be retained and the former limited partner's capital contribution must be returned. Only creditors relying on the limited partner's participation before the renunciation may hold them to unlimited liability. Assume Patricia renounces her limited partnership interest after discovering Triple-LP was defectively formed. If no creditor can prove reliance on Patricia's finances in loaning money or advancing goods on credit before

renunciation, Patricia retains full limited liability. Does renunciation signal that the limited partner may know about the promoter's potential unethical conduct?

Assurances

How do successful limited partnerships attract limited partner investors if defective formation or misrepresentations threaten them with unlimited liability? Fundamentally, it is the limited partners' duty to carefully review and monitor the formation process. However, in the marketing of investment-grade limited partnerships, assurances are usually provided by independent outside attorneys, investment bankers, appraisers, and accountants each who write **comfort letters** to provide assurances to potential limited partners. These consultants are subject to potential malpractice liability for contributing to the defective formation or the making of false claims in the limited partnership certificate. Of course, the general partner also has unlimited liability. A large, well-respected, and financially stable corporate general partner has primary unlimited liability. However, there are fewer protections for investors in small limited partnerships. This forces potential investors to retain reliable counsel to review the transaction before investing, to monitor the formation, and to help the limited partner consider making any necessary renunciation.

Partner Capacity

Limited partnerships must have at least one general partner with unlimited liability and one limited partner. There is no upper limit on the number of general or limited partners. However, there can be adverse tax and securities regulations consequences if limited partners are too numerous. Any person with legal capacity may become a general or limited partner, so a natural person, corporation, partnership, another limited partnership, a trust, or an estate may participate.

It is possible to be both a general and a limited partner simultaneously. For what reason would a general partner also become a limited partner? As a general partner, there would still be unlimited liability. Modern limited partnerships formed under RULPA may give limited partners some governance powers that the general partner may not share. When a general partner also becomes a limited partner, this entitles the general partner to share these powers with limited partners. Additionally, a general partner holding a limited partnership interest would share with other limited partners in financial rights (e.g., profit sharing, return of capital contribution) and in the assignability of their interests. The capital contribution of a general partner may be small as compared with limited partners. The general partner might have a larger profit participation by also holding a limited partnership interest.

Foreign Limited Partnership Registration

Any artificial entity such as a corporation or a limited partnership exists only to the extent recognized under the applicable local law. A limited partnership is usually created or "domesticated" only in one state. It is not qualified to be **doing business** in another state until separately registered in that foreign jurisdiction. The term *foreign* refers to limited partnerships formed outside the state, whether formed in another state or in another nation. This concept is similar to foreign corporations discussed in the next chapter.

Qualification to do business generally means filing an *application for registration* with the secretary of state in each state where minimum business contacts are made or planned. Registration must include the foreign limited partnership's name and address, general partners' names and addresses, name and address of a local agent to receive service of process, and a statement of the limited partnership's general business purpose. ULPA made no provision for registration of foreign limited partnerships, so most ULPA states have separate statutes requiring registration. RULPA requires foreign limited partnership registration.

Failure to file prohibits the limited partnership from suing others in that state's courts but does not invalidate the foreign limited partnership's contracts or the limited partners' limited liability. For exam-

ple, if Triple-LP is organized in Pennsylvania, it is a foreign limited partnership even in the border states of Ohio and Maryland. Registration in these foreign states is necessary before Triple-LP is permitted to sue others in these foreign states' courts. However, an unregistered foreign limited partnership could still defend suits brought in other states. Most of the internal affairs of a foreign limited partnership are governed by the law of their home state of organization. However, relations with outsiders may be governed by other states where the limited partnership operates as a foreign entity.

LIABILITIES OF LIMITED PARTNERS

The most fundamental feature of the limited partnership is that passive investors are exposed to liability only to the extent of their capital contributions so long as they do not act like general partners. The key to their limited liability is remaining passive. As ULPA Section 7 suggests, active participation accompanies the general partner's role.

ULPA § 7. Limited Partner Not Liable to Creditors

A limited partner shall not become liable as a general partner unless, in addition to his exercise of his rights and powers as a limited partner, he takes part in the control of the business.

A limited partner may cross the line between passivity and into the risks of greater activity in two ways. First, the use of the limited partner's surname as part of the firm's business name suggests an active involvement. Second, the limited partner may be involved in "excessive entanglement" in managing the limited partnership.

Use of Limited Partner's Name

The limited partner's name in the business suggests strongly to outsiders that the limited partner's financial resources are available to satisfy the firm's liabilities. Third parties relying on a limited partner's financial capacity may hold the limited partner to unlimited liability for the firm's debts. This is similar to a holding out or estoppel theory because the outsider is led to believe the limited partner has financial responsibility. This causes a detriment to the outsider triggering the liability. For example, assume Patricia's surname was included in the firm name. If an outside creditor expected that Patricia's personal finances were available to pay firm debts, Patricia could be held to unlimited liability.

RULPA requires the term *limited partnership* or an acceptable abbreviation to clearly appear in the firm name. Under RULPA, limited partners who knowingly permit the use of their surnames in the firm name are liable to creditors who have no knowledge that the limited partner is not a general partner. Where a limited partner shares a surname with a general partner, there is no liability. This surname liability rule also sets an ethical standard. When a limited partner knowingly permits the use of his or her name in the firm name, it is equivalent to an unethical misrepresentation.

Limited Partner's Control

Because management and control are responsibilities usually associated with liability, ULPA makes limited partners liable who take part in the control of the business. This represents the more restrictive *control* test. It holds limited partners to unlimited liability for their control activities irrespective of the extent of entanglement in management or the outsider's knowledge and reliance on this activity.

Is the logic of limited partner liability sound? Corporate shareholders may participate in management and exercise control without automatic exposure to unlimited liability. Additionally, there may be important reasons to permit some limited partner involvement. For example, a limited partner may have valuable and unique expertise. Most passive business owners desire at least some voice in decisions that fundamentally affect their investments. Nevertheless, the drafters of ULPA specifically restricted control to the general partner, leaving no room for limited partners' active participation. The following classic case illustrates the limited partner's exposure to unlimited liability from excessive entanglement and control.

HOLZMAN v. DE ESCAMILLA
195 P.2d 833 (Cal. Ct. App. 1948)

Hacienda Farms, Ltd., was a limited partnership in which De Escamilla was the general partner and Russell and Andrews were limited partners. After the partnership went bankrupt, Holzman, a third party, sued Russell and Andrews, claiming they became general partners by taking part in control of the partnership business. Hacienda Farms produced vegetables and truck crops that were marketed principally by Andrews and cultivated by De Escamilla. The limited partners' control is revealed by De Escamilla's trial testimony:

Q. Did you have a conversation or conversations with Mr. Andrews or Mr. Russell before planting the tomatoes?

A. We always conferred and agreed as to what crops we would put in.

Q. Who determined that it was advisable to plant watermelons?

A. Mr. Andrews.

Q. Who determined that string beans should be planted?

A. All of us, there was never any planting done except the first crop that was put into the partnership as an asset by myself, there was never any crop that was planted or contemplated in planting that was not thoroughly discussed and agreed upon by the three of us; particularly Andrews and myself.

De Escamilla was consulted by Russell and Andrews on a regular basis and occasionally they overruled his choice of crops to plant for Hacienda Farms. Eventually, Andrews and Russell forced De Escamilla to resign as manager. At no time could De Escamilla write checks on the limited partnership account without a countersignature by either Russell or Andrews.

MARKS, Justice

Section 2483 of the civil code provides as follows:

A limited partner shall not become liable as a general partner, unless, in addition to the exercise of his rights and powers as a limited partner, he takes part in control of the business.

Russell and Andrews both took part in the control of the business. The manner of withdrawing money from the bank accounts is particularly illuminating. The two men had absolute power to withdraw all the partnership funds in the bank without the knowledge or consent of the general partner. Either Russell or Andrews could take control of the business from De Escamilla by refusing to sign checks for bills contracted by him and thus limiting his activities in the management of the business. They required him to resign as manager and selected his successor. They were active in dictating the crops to be planted, some of them against the wish of De Escamilla. This clearly shows that they took part in control of the business of the partnerships and became liable as general partners. Judgment affirmed.

Case Questions

1. What is the issue in the *Holzman* case in holding a limited partner liable beyond the capital contributions for the debts of the limited partnership?
2. What reasons justify using the control element as an indicator of limited partner liability?
3. How could the limited partners have avoided liability in *Holzman*?

While nothing prohibits a limited partner's involvement in management, the exposure to unlimited liability probably deters many legitimate limited partner activities. ULPA provides no guidance on what constitutes control, so the control test may be an unreasonable restriction deterring justifiable activities by limited partners. As a result, four adaptations have developed: (1) the reliance test, (2) case law exceptions to the control test, (3) the initial RULPA safe harbor exceptions, and (4) additional exceptions added by the 1985 RULPA's safe harbor.

Reliance Test

Many states have interpreted ULPA to prevent a limited partner's unlimited liability unless the third party had knowledge and relied on the limited partner's control. Thus, a limited partner would be personally liable only where the outsider legitimately expected the limited partner's financial resources were available to satisfy the firm's liabilities because the limited partner openly exercised substantially the same powers as a general partner. For example, Patricia could be liable for debts unpaid by Triple-LP if not satisfied out of the firm's assets or from Peter, Pam, and Paul's personal assets. However, Patricia would be liable only if the creditor knew of Patricia's managerial involvement, so she could exercise hidden control and not be personally liable.

Many courts have also chipped away at the ULPA control test when the limited partner exercises no control but only becomes involved in some other capacity. Many ULPA states permit limited partners to communicate their views or give advice to the general partner, work for the limited partnership as employees if supervised under the general partner's control, or nominate key employees. In all these exceptions, the limited partner's involvement is permissible if the general partner has ultimate authority to veto the limited partner's decision. An ethical question is raised when an outsider brings suit against a limited partner. Should the outsider's attorney continue the litigation when it becomes clear the outsider never relied on the limited partner's finances in extending credit?

RULPA § 303(a). Liability to Third Parties

[I]f the limited partner participates in the control of the business, he [or she] is liable only to persons who transact business with the limited partnership reasonably believing, based on the limited partner's conduct, that the limited partner is a general partner.

RULPA Safe Harbors

RULPA Section 303 codifies the ULPA control test but modifies it with a form of reliance. A limited partner's participation that is substantially equivalent to a general partner's control retains unlimited liability. A concealed limited partner exercising a general partner's control would still have unlimited liability.

RULPA codified the case law exceptions by providing a list of statutory liability exceptions: the RULPA **safe harbor** exceptions. A limited partner retains limited liability even when participating in a listed protected activity. The list includes various limited partnership employment, consultation, and surety activities. The safe harbor also includes many shareholderlike rights and permits participation in the firm's fundamental governance process: bringing derivative suits, requesting or attending partner meetings, and casting votes on fundamental firm matters like dissolution, substantial asset sales, basic changes in the firm's business, general partner conflict of interest transactions, or making amendments to the limited partnership agreement.

RULPA Safe Harbors

The term *participation in control* triggering unlimited liability for a limited partner does not include participation in one or more of the following:

- Acting as contractor, agent, or employee of a limited partnership.
- Consulting or advising the general partner on limited partnership business.
- Acting as surety for a limited partnership.
- Voting, proposing, approving, or disapproving fundamental limited partnership action on:
  (i)   Dissolution and winding up.
  (ii) Sale, exchange, mortgage, pledge, or lease of substantially all limited partnership assets.
  (iii) Incurring a limited partnership debt outside the ordinary course of business.
  (iv) A change in the nature of the limited partnership's business.
  (v)   Removal of a general partner.

RULPA § 303(b)

The RULPA safe harbor list is not exclusive, so other "control-like" acts may become permissible as encountered by the courts without the limited partner incurring unlimited liability. The 1985 RULPA amendments expand this safe harbor list to include additional shareholderlike rights.

1985 RULPA Safe Harbors

- Act as an officer, director, or shareholder of the corporate general partner.
- Bring a derivative action for the limited partnership's benefit.
- Request or attend a partners' meeting.
- Vote on:
  (i)   Admission of general partner.
  (ii) Admission or removal of a limited partner.
  (iii) General partner's conflict of interest transaction.
  (iv) Amendment of partnership agreement or certificate of limited partnership.
- Wind up limited partnership business.

RULPA § 303(b)

Corporate Limited Partners

Should a limited partner be permitted affiliation with a corporate general partner such as by owning its shares, participating in its management, or serving as its officer or director? A few states under ULPA held such affiliation was deceptive because it let the limited partners exercise the forbidden control over the limited partnership. Therfore, such limited partners were held to unlimited liability. Today, most states resolve this dilemma by preferring the limited liability rule of corporate law, permitting the limited partners to retain their limited liability. For example, assume that Peter, Pam, and Paul are not personally general partners but control the T-P Corp., the corporate general partner in Triple-LP. Each of the three also owns limited partner interests in Triple-LP. RULPA gives the three limited liability despite their participation in managing Triple-LP through T-P Corp., as illustrated in the following case.

FRIGIDAIRE SALES CORP. v. UNION PROPERTIES, INC.
562 P 2nd 244 (Wash. 1977)

Leonard Mannon and Raleigh Baxter were limited partners of Commercial Investors while they were simultaneously officers, directors, and shareholders of Union Properties, the sole general partner of Commercial Investors. Mannon and Baxter controlled the Union Properties Corporation and thereby were able to control the day-to-day management of Commercial Investors. Frigidaire sued Commercial and Mannon and Baxter for breach of contract. The court of appeals affirmed the trial court's decision that Mannon and Baxter were not liable beyond their capital contribution.

HAMILTON, Associate Justice

We find the Texas Supreme Court's decision [in *Dahlany v. Fidelity Lease Limited* is] distinguishable from the present case. In *Dahlany,* the corporation and the limited partnership were set up contemporaneously, and the sole purpose of the corporation was to operate the limited partnership. The Texas Supreme Court found that the limited partners who controlled the corporation were obligated to their other limited partners to operate the corporation for the benefit of the partnership. "Each act was done then, not for the corporation, but for the partnership." This is not the case here. The pattern of operation of Union Properties was to investigate and conceive of real estate investment opportunities and, when it found such opportunities, to cause the creation of limited partnerships with Union Properties acting as the general partner. Commercial was only one of several limited partnerships so conceived and created. Respondents did not form Union Properties for the sole purpose of operating Commercial. Hence, their acts on behalf of Union Properties were not performed merely for the benefit of Commercial.

We agree with our court of appeals analysis that this concern with minimum capitalization is not peculiar to limited partnerships with corporate general partners, but may arise anytime a creditor deals with a corporation. Because our limited partnerships statutes permit parties to form a limited partnership with a corporation as the sole general partner, this concern about minimal capitalization, standing by itself, does not justify a finding that the limited partners incurred general liability for their control of the corporate general partner.

Petitioner was never led to believe that respondents were acting in any capacities other than in their corporate capacities. When the shareholders of a corporation, who are also the corporations officers and directors, conscientiously keep the affairs of the corporation separate from their personal affairs, and no fraud or manifest injustice is perpetrated upon third persons who deal with the corporation, the corporation's separate entity should be respected.

For us to find the respondents incurred general liability for the general partnership's obligations would require us to apply a literal interpretation of the statute and totally ignore the corporate entity of Union Properties, when petitioner never knew it was dealing with a corporate entity. There can be no doubt that respondents controlled the corporation. However, they did so only in their capacities as agents for their principal, the corporate general partner.

Petitioner entered into the contract with Commercial. Respondents signed the contract in their capacities as President and Secretary-Treasurer of Union Properties, the general partner of Commercial. In the eyes of the law it was Union Properties, as a separate entity which entered into the contract with petitioner and controlled the limited partnership. Because respondents scrupulously separated their actions on behalf of the corporation from their personal actions, petitioner never mistakenly assumed that respondents were general partners with general liability. Petitioner knew Union Properties was the sole general partner and did not rely on respondents' control by assuming that they were also general partners. If petitioner had not wished to rely on the solvency of Union Properties as the only general partner it could have insisted that respondents personally guarantee contractual performance. The decision of the court of appeals is affirmed.

Case Questions

1. What is the issue Frigidaire is alleging should cause the limited partners Mannon and Baxter to lose their limited liability?

2. What reasons did the court use to support the conclusion that the limited partners retain their limited liability? What factor would need to be changed in order to find Baxter and Mannon liable and not protected by their limited partnership limited liability?

3. From the limited partnership's creditors' perspective, what would be the difference between Mannon and Baxter's participation in the limited partnership managed by the Union

Properties Corporation they controlled and their participation if the limited partnership were instead a subsidiary corporation of Union Properties?

PARTNERS' RIGHTS IN LIMITED PARTNERSHIPS

Limited partners have many rights similar to the general partners in an ordinary general partnership. For example, ULPA prohibits the general partner from doing acts that would change the fundamental nature of the limited partnership without first obtaining unanimous partner consent. Limited partners may not cause dissolution unless otherwise agreed or when dissolution is sought by court decree, as discussed later in this chapter. All participants in a limited partnership must comply with the applicable ULPA or RULPA, the federal tax laws, and any applicable securities laws to retain the favorable partnership flow-through tax treatment. Most limited partner rights are derived from the applicable ULPA or RULPA, although additional rights are often specified in the limited partnership agreement. These rights can be classified as (1) contract rights derived from the limited partnership agreement, (2) financial rights, (3) membership rights, and (4) partnership governance rights.

Limited Partnership Agreement

The trend in limited partnership law is away from the general partner's absolute control and toward the definition of greater limited partner rights in the partnership agreement. Both RULPA and the 1985 amendments open the door to significantly greater limited partner involvement without risking the exercise of forbidden control that abrogates limited liability. This trend is bringing the limited partner's status closer to that of corporate shareholders. Further expansion of contractual limited partner rights will require a more precise specification of the control problem discussed in the preceding section. It may eventually lead to a merger of the reliance theory and partnership by estoppel as the threshold for a limited partner's unlimited liability. This trend also suggests that many terms contained in complex modern general partnership agreements may eventually become part of limited partnership agreements.

There is an impression that the general partner dominates the limited partnership and limited partners have little power. This is probably true with the larger, limited partnerships that develop a specific project and are managed by an expert corporate general partner. For example, limited partner rights are generally more limited in oil well drilling ventures or movie productions because the corporate general partner is large, prosperous, and experienced. However, in many other cases, the general partner is viewed as a managing partner who must be subject to monitoring and replacement as necessary to protect the limited partners' investment.

Under RULPA, limited partners may be given governance rights much as in general partnerships, including some of the following rights: continuation of the business after dissolution, oversight or expulsion of the general (managing) partner, veto and revision of the partnership line of business and strategy, and consultation into the general partner's policy decisions. Limited partnership agreements often limit the partnership to a fixed term or to the attainment of a particular objective. Goodwill is often excluded from the distributed share of a prematurely departing partner. The general partner is often limited to conducting activities directly relevant to the business.

Due to the special relationship among parties in a limited partnership, some matters are treated differently than in a general partnership. For example, financial matters such as profit or loss sharing, capital contributions, distributions, and salaries are often specified with greater precision than in simple general partnerships. Accounting treatment for a limited partnership's specific projects is sometimes different and written in greater detail because most limited partners are passive investors while general partners in traditional partnerships look to the firm as their primary livelihood. The general partner is typically the only person competent or inclined to do the work of the limited partnership. Therefore, his or her withdrawal or expulsion requires a longer period of notice than is required for many general partnerships because in the latter, all partners are assumed to contribute services or expertise. Finally, changes in a limited partnership's membership are often less significant than changes in a general partnership's membership. A limited partners' expertise, creditworthiness, agency authority, and fiduciary duties are immaterial. This stands in contrast to the importance of these matters for any general partner. Therefore, the limited partnership agreement often makes it unnecessary to have unanimous consent for a limited partner to assign his or her interest or to admit a new limited partner. The clear trend is to expand the rights of limited partners while recognizing the practical limitations of their passive role as investors.

Financial Rights

Financial rights are usually the most important feature to a limited partner. While many well-designed limited partnership agreements specify financial rights in great detail, the rudiments are defined in both ULPA and RULPA. Distributions of profits and losses are shared in proportion to each partner's capital contribution. However, the limited partnership agreement often provides for some other allocation. This differs from the presumption of an equal profit division in general partnerships. For example, in recognition of the risk inherent in Peter, Pam, and Paul's unlimited liability and their active participation in management, it would be justifiable for the Triple-LP agreement to allocate greater profits to them because they made only nominal capital contributions compared with the limited partners. An allocation based on capital contributions would probably be unacceptable to the general partners. Before the 1986 Tax Act, many tax shelter limited partnerships allocated a larger portion of losses to limited partners than to general partners.

Some limited partnerships provide for general partners to take salaries rather than a share of profits. This recognizes their need to receive payment for their efforts particularly in a tax shelter limited partnership that is expected to experience losses. By contrast, limited partners usually do not receive salaries because it could signal excessive entanglement in control.

The limited partnership agreement may require periodic distributions of capital. For example, limited partners may receive payments before the project is completed, such as where a real estate venture begins selling some units of a completed project (e.g., condominiums). Limited partners withdrawing before the term ends or before a specified objective is attained are entitled to a distribution. They must be paid the fair value of their interest in the partnership or some other amount if specified in the limited partnership agreement, less any damages caused if the withdrawal is wrongful. Once a distribution becomes vested, the partner(s) become creditors of the limited partnership until the distribution is paid.

Unless otherwise agreed, all partners, including limited partners, may inspect and copy partnership books and records. This permits them to monitor the general partner's fiduciary and stewardship responsibilities and determine the accuracy of financial statements and distributions. RULPA specifically requires the limited partnership to maintain records at an office within the state. The records must include the partners' names and addresses, the limited partnership certificate and agreement, tax returns for the past three years, financial statements, and records showing each partners' contributions and their valuations. These records are subject to reasonable inspection and copying by limited partners at reasonable hours. RULPA permits contributions of cash, property, or services to be performed in the future. Each partner's obligation to contribute is enforceable by the limited partnership.

Membership Rights

As in general partnerships, all members of a limited partnership have the right to choose their associates. Unanimous written consent of all partners is required to start the partnership and to admit any new partner, including both limited partners and general partners. Changes in membership are not effective until an amended certificate of limited partnership is filed reflecting the change. RULPA permits the partnership agreement to modify this requirement with a less formal *admission* procedure used widely in investment-grade and master limited partnerships. For example, the Triple-LP agreement could authorize any two of the three general partners to admit new limited partners without the limited partners' consent. This would enable the firm to expand without Lem or Patricia's approval because they are passive investors who might not adequately appreciate the firm's capital needs.

Limited partnership interests are assignable, and like general partnership assignments, the assignee becomes a substitute partner only by complying with the partnership's admission procedures. The outgoing partner retains liability for unpaid contributions and misstatements in the limited partnership certificate. The assignee receives only the assignor's rights to share in profits, losses, and return of capital; no other rights are transferred. Although the assignor's partnership status ceases, the limited partnership is not dissolved.

An assignee can become a substitute partner entitled to all limited partner rights only if the remaining partners unanimously consent or the assignment complies with the substitute partner procedures in the limited partnership's agreement. Limited partnerships may not prohibit assignments but may restrict them. For example, an outsider could become a limited partner in Triple-LP by purchasing Lem's assignment of his interest if the other partners approve. The Triple-LP agreement cannot make it impossible to assign but could give the remaining partners a right of first refusal or provide for some other substitute partner approval procedure. As with the admission of a new partner, the certificate must be amended to reflect the assignment. RULPA abandons the term *substitute limited partner* but retains the concept.

Limited partners may withdraw from the limited partnership in accordance with the limited partnership agreement, which may specify a particular event permitting rightful withdrawal. Withdrawing limited partners are entitled to the fair value of their interests as evaluated on the date of their departure. In the absence of a withdrawal provision, the limited partner must give at least six months' notice to the general partner before withdrawing. Notice is necessary because many limited partnerships need the combined contributions of all limited partners to achieve their specified objective. The agreement may restrict a limited partner from withdrawing prematurely and from collecting the full fair value until the stated event happens. For example, assume Triple-LP has a business objective to develop a shopping center. The agreement could specify that completing construction and obtaining leases for 80 percent of the center's space are prerequisites to any partner's withdrawal. This objective would be frustrated if any partner withdrew capital prematurely, so the agreement may limit payment of fair value until after these events occur.

Partnership Governance Rights

For many years, there has been controversy over the level of control a limited partner can exercise before losing limited liability. Under ULPA, considerable partnership governance rights are forfeited by limited partners. However, the impact of this mechanical trade-off has diminished with the realization that no one is injured if limited partners are treated more like shareholders. Adaptations of the reliance on control, partnership by estoppel doctrines, and the RULPA safe harbors are probably sufficient to protect outsiders from deception. As discussed previously, limited partners may vote on many matters or veto the general partner's activities when these rights are specified in the partnership agreement or RULPA. Some participation rights are more limited under ULPA. A limited partner's involvement does not extend to control or rights to use limited partnership property for any purpose.

Derivative Actions

RULPA gives limited partners a right equivalent to the corporate shareholder's right to bring derivative suits. Limited partners may sue to vindicate a limited partnership right and recover a judgment that benefits the limited partnership if the general partner refuses to do so and efforts fail to encourage the general partner to sue. Derivative litigation vindicates legal interests of the limited partnership in suits against either an outsider or insider who has allegedly damaged the partnership. Any damages recovered belong to the limited partnership because the limited partner acts only as a representative to vindicate the limited partnership's interests. The rationale, mechanics, and limitations on derivative suits are discussed further in Chapter 41. Of course, limited partners may sue directly to vindicate their contract and statutory rights (e.g., profit distribution and dissolution after the term expires). There may be other rights for limited partners in publicly traded limited partnerships under the securities laws.

GENERAL PARTNER RIGHTS AND DUTIES

General partner rights and duties closely parallel those of an ordinary partnership. They stem from the general partner's status as an agent of the limited partnership, from the UPA, and from the applicable version of ULPA or RULPA. These can be modified by the partnership agreement. General partners may manage the partnership business, vote on partnership governance matters, use partnership property for partnership business, receive a share of profits, receive a return of their capital on withdrawal or dissolution, and participate in winding up and dissolution.

General partners have the authority of a general agent to carry on the partnership business in the usual way. These rights can be expanded or restricted in the partnership agreement. For example, the Triple-LP partnership agreement may give Peter, Pam, and Paul the right to manage the partnership and its property. However, the agreement might replace their share of profits with a salary, particularly if Triple-LP is a tax shelter. General partners may have less authority to make fundamental changes in the partnership business where limited partners have a vote or veto power over such extraordinary actions. General partners may withdraw after giving notice, if consistent with the partnership agreement. However, they may be liable for damages if withdrawal is premature.

The duties of general partners are also derived from the law of agency, general partnership law, the applicable ULPA or RULPA, and the limited partnership agreement. General partners are fiduciaries who must refrain from conflicts of interest and from self-dealing. This raises significant ethical questions similar to those applicable to agents and managing partners of a general partnership.

General partners may vary their liabilities among themselves by agreement. However, they cannot eliminate their unlimited liability to outsiders. Various management duties must actually be performed or at least overseen by general partners: maintenance of partnership books and records, preparation and archiving of tax returns, preparing and amending the partnership certificate and agreement, and registering as a foreign limited partnership, as necessary. General partners must obtain the limited partners' approval for fundamental partnership changes. As the next case illustrates, although general partners owe a duty of due care in operating the partnership business, they are protected by a form of the *business judgment rule* that parallels the analogous rule in corporate law.

WYLER v. FEUER

149 Cal. Rptr. 626 (Cal. Ct. App. 1978)

Feuer and Martin Productions, Inc., formed a limited partnership with Wyler to finance a movie version of a best-selling book by Simone Berteaut. Feuer and Martin were quite successful in producing broadway musicals. They had produced the successful motion picture *Cabaret*. The limited partnership agreement with Wyler provided interest-free financing for a $1.6 million project, and Wyler would receive up to 50 percent of the profits. Feuer and Martin were required to raise $850,000 in production financing by September 30, 1973, or they would be in breach of the contract. The motion picture produced cost $1.5 million but took in total receipts of only $478,000. Because Wyler received only $313,500 for his $1.5 million investment, he sued Feuer and Martin for mismanaging the limited partnership. Wyler appealed from a judgment in favor of Feuer and Martin.

FLEMING, Justice

A limited partnership affords a vehicle for capital investment whereby the limited partner restricts his liability to the amount of his investment in return for surrender of any right to manage and control the partnership business. In a limited partnership, the general partner manages and controls the partnership business. In exercising his management functions the general partner comes under a fiduciary duty of good faith and fair dealing towards other members of the partnership.

These characteristics—limited investor liability, delegation of authority to management, and fiduciary duty owed by management to investors—are similar to those existing in corporate investment, where it has long been the rule that directors are not liable to stockholders for mistakes made in the exercise of honest business judgment, or for losses incurred in the good faith performance of their duties when they used such care as an ordinarily prudent person would use. By this standard a general partner may not be held liable for mistakes made or losses incurred in the good faith exercise of reasonable business judgment.

The plaintiff did not produce sufficient evidence to hold the defendants liable for bad business management. Plaintiff's evidence showed that the picture did not make money, was not sought after by distributors, and did not live up to its producers' expectation. The same could be said of the majority of motion pictures made since the invention of cinematography. No evidence showed that defendant's decisions and efforts failed to conform to the general

duty of care demanded of an ordinarily prudent person in like position under similar circumstances. The good faith business judgment and management of a general partner need only satisfy the standard of care demanded of an ordinarily prudent person, and will not be scrutinized by the courts with cold clarity of hindsight.

Case Questions

1. What is the issue that Wyler contends could make Feuer and Martin liable?

2. What reasons support holding Feuer and Martin liable? What reasons are used to hold Feuer and Martin not liable?

3. What is the value assumption inherent in the business judgment rule concerning the activities of a corporate officer or director or a general partner in the operation of the business?

DISSOLUTION

The dissolution and winding-up process for limited partnerships parallels the process for general partnerships with some notable exceptions. Most importantly, unless otherwise agreed, the departure of a limited partner does not dissolve the firm, and the order of distribution priorities is different.

The passage of a fixed term or happening of an event specified in the agreement dissolves a limited partnership. The death, incapacity, insanity, or withdrawal of a general partner dissolves the limited partnership unless a continuation agreement or unanimous consent of remaining partners is given. This may require admitting an additional limited or general partner to maintain the minimum of one of each. Bankruptcy or insolvency of any partner does not cause dissolution, except under RULPA where a general partner's insolvency dissolves the limited partnership unless an explicit agreement to the contrary is made. Limited partners may force court-ordered dissolution if wrongfully denied a return of their capital, partnership liabilities remain unpaid or partnership property is insufficient for repayment, or the general partner fails to dissolve as required in the partnership agreement. RULPA adds the following bases for dissolution: unanimous written consent of all partners and the withdrawal of a general partner in the absence of a continuation agree-

ment. RULPA requires the filing of a **cancellation certificate** on dissolution and when winding up is started.

Winding Up

The multistage winding up, liquidation, and termination process discussed for general partnerships in Chapter 38 is generally applicable to limited partnerships. Because neither the ULPA nor the RULPA provide many precise guidelines, the UPA process is followed. The winding-up partner has the same narrower authority during winding up as in a general partnership. RULPA permits winding up by general partners who have not wrongfully dissolved (e.g., violated the agreement), by a limited partner if there is no general partner, or by a court on application of a limited partner. A winding-up limited partner does not have unlimited liability unless the business is continued. This effectively transforms the limited partner into a general partner with unlimited liability.

Distribution of Assets

After liquidation of limited partnership assets, the various claims of creditors, general partners, and limited partners must be satisfied out of the proceeds. This parallels the distribution process for general partnerships discussed in Chapter 38. However, the order of priorities differs between the UPA, ULPA, and RULPA.

Order of Distribution of Assets

1. Outside creditors and limited partner creditors.
2. Limited partners' profits.
3. Limited partner capital.
4. General partner creditors.
5. General partner profits.
6. General partner capital.

ULPA § 23.

Order of Distribution of Assets

1. All creditors: Outsiders and limited and general partners.
2. Unpaid distributions, all partners.
3. Capital contributions, all partners.
4. Profits, all partners.

RULPA § 804.

RULPA simplified the ULPA order of distribution by giving general partners equal status with limited partners for loans. Under either ULPA or RULPA, the limited partnership agreement may change priorities among partners. For example, the general partners, Peter, Pam, and Paul, may have priority in receiving repayment of their loans over the return of limited partner capital to Lem and Patricia. However, an outside creditor's claims cannot be subordinated to partner claims without the outsider's consent. If the liquidating limited partnership is insolvent, the limited partners cannot force general partners to repay lost capital contributions unless the partnership agreement provides otherwise. Unless otherwise agreed, no partner is entitled or required to receive distributions in kind of particular assets. As in general partnerships, the distribution of liquidation proceeds envisions all assets will be sold, converting them to cash for distribution to all claimants.

TAXATION OF LIMITED PARTNERSHIPS

Not all limited partnerships may receive the favorable partnership flow-through tax treatment. If the Treasury Department determines that a limited part-

nership really operates as a corporation and uses the limited partnership form as a subterfuge, it may be subject to the corporate double tax. If a limited partnership has five or more of the six predominant characteristics of a corporation, it will be taxed as a corporation.

Characteristics Triggering Corporate Tax Liability

1. Association of owners operating together.
2. Carrying on a business.
3. Continuity of life.
4. Separation of ownership and management.
5. Limited liability.
6. Free transferability of ownership interests.

Most limited partnerships share at least four of the corporate characteristics listed above. Therefore, to maintain the favorable partnership flow-through tax treatment, the well-designed limited partnership must have an agreement with provisions that fix a finite life for the venture and restrict transferability of limited partnership interests. Most successful limited partnerships are intended to last only for a fixed term or until a specified objective is attained. Additionally, a provision requiring the right of first refusal or permitting the general partner to veto assignments would probably satisfy the federal tax rule (see Figure 39–2).

PUBLICLY TRADED LIMITED PARTNERSHIPS

Under both the federal securities laws and most state blue sky securities laws discussed in Chapter 44, limited partnership interests are considered securities because they involve the investment of money into a common enterprise where the promise of profits is derived from the efforts of others. This often requires the registration of limited partnership interests unless they are exempt as intrastate offerings, small offerings, or private placements. Various state exemptions may apply specifically to limited partners involved in the initial startup of a limited partnership. Generally, the resale of limited partnership interests are restricted.

The resale market for limited partnership interests is a small, informal, and dispersed market. Resale restrictions are necessary to maintain the limited

Figure 39–2   Comparison of General and Limited Partnerships

Feature	General Partnership	ULPA Limited Partnership	RULPA Limited Partnership	RULPA Limited Partnership (1985)
Creation	Two or more persons to carry on a business for profit; no formalities	Two or more persons to carry on a business for profit; one limited and one general partner required; file certificate locally	Two or more persons to carry on a business for profit; one limited and one general partner required; file certificate with secretary of state	Two or more persons to carry on a business for profit; one limited and one general partner required; file certificate with secretary of state
Management and Control	Equal vote by general partners unless otherwise agreed	Equal vote by general partners unless otherwise agreed; no control by limited partners	Equal vote by general partners unless otherwise agreed; no control by limited partners; unlimited liability if third party knows of involvement; safe harbor activities permitted	Equal vote by general partners unless otherwise agreed; no control by limited partners; unlimited liability if third party knows of involvement; expanded safe harbor activities permitted
Liability	Unlimited for general partners	Unlimited for general partners; limited for limited partners to capital contribution unless name used or control exercised	Unlimited for general partners; limited for limited partners to capital contribution unless name used or control exercised; safe harbor activities	Unlimited for general partners; limited for limited partners to capital contribution unless name used or control exercised; safe harbor activities expanded
Agency Authority	General partner is general agent	General partner is general agent; limited partner has no authority	General partner is general agent; limited partner has no authority except for safe harbor activities	General partner is general agent; limited partner has no authority except for safe harbor activities
Fiduciary Duty	General partner owes duty	General partner owes duty; limited partner owes no duty	General partner owes duty; limited partner owes no duty unless as employee	General partner owes duty; limited partner owes no duty unless as employee or other consultant
Duty of Care	General partner owes duty	General partner owes duty; limited partner owes no duty	General partner owes duty; limited partner owes no duty unless as employee	General partner owes duty; limited partner owes no duty unless as employee or other consultant
Assignment of Interest	Assignable; not substitute partner without unanimous consent	Assignable; not substitute partner without unanimous consent	Assignable; not substitute partner without unanimous consent or compliance with agreement and amended certificate	Assignable; not substitute partner without unanimous consent or compliance with agreement and amended certificate
Dissolution	Partner action; operation of law; court decree	Agreement; continuation unless general partner not replaceable; court decree; death of last surviving limited partner	Agreement; continuation unless general partner not replaceable or is bankrupt; court decree; death of last surviving limited partner	Agreement; continuation unless general partner not replaceable or is bankrupt; court decree; death of last surviving limited partner
Liquidation Priority	Outside creditors Partner creditors Partner capital Partner profits	Creditors: Outsiders and limited partner Profits: Limited partner Capital: Limited partner Creditors: General partner Profits: General partner	Creditors: All Unpaid distributions: All partners Capital: All partners Profits: All partners	Creditors: All Unpaid distributions: All partners Capital: All partners Profits: All partners

partnership's favorable tax treatment and continue the exemption of limited partnership offerings from costly securities registration. General partnership interests are usually not securities because the general partners' personal efforts are required for the firm's operations.

Some limited partnership interests that were originally exempt may later become subject to the securities laws. For example, **roll-up** transactions restructure privately held limited partnership interests by consolidating them into another limited partnership, into a publicly traded corporation, or into a Real Estate Investment Trust (REIT). As the following commentary suggests, the process of trading limited partnership interests and roll-ups has created some controversy about the misuse of this market.

*Problems of Enhancing Limited Partnership Resale Liquidity**

Most limited partnerships are initially designed to restrict the transferability of their ownership interests to qualify for the favorable partnership pass-through tax treatment. However, the general decline in limited partnership values encourages the development of a more active resale market. Four factors have conspired to depress the value of limited partnerships. First, in the 1980s, there was a general decline in the value of the predominant limited partnership assets: oil and gas ventures and real estate. Second, the 1986 Tax Act made limited partnership tax shelters less attractive. Third, some of the few limited partnership brokers which help match buyers and sellers have withdrawn from making a market, further depressing liquidity and prices. Fourth, news about the first three problems decreases the number of willing buyers for limited partnership interests and this further decreases liquidity and prices.

Limited partnership ventures are difficult for investors to evaluate because there is insufficient periodic financial reporting. Analysts must individually appraise the cash flow and fair market value of the commercial real estate or oil and gas assets. Allegedly, some participants in the secondary resale market have made excessive price markups (sometimes over 15 percent) and excessive commissions, charged improper fees, and sold risky limited partnerships unsuitable for a particular investor's needs.

The National Association of Securities Dealers (NASD), a private regulator of brokers, may enforce a 5 percent limit on the markup in resales of limited partnerships. Another NASD recommendation would require limited partnership dealers to present at least three price quotes to its customer as evidence of efforts to find a "best execution" price for each customer. Standardizing the processing of limited partnership trades would reduce uncertainty by shortening the settlement process: e.g., payment, delivery, and registration of the new owner. Some limited partnership industry groups are trying to establish a disclosure system for collection of objective limited partnership performance measures.

Roll-up transactions generally combine the assets formerly belonging to several limited partnerships into a single corporation. This creates greater liquidity. However, the roll-up practice of combining troubled limited partnerships with financially healthy ones has combined with other factors to make huge losses for shareholders in the new roll-up. For example, some limited partners have been pressured by the roll-up sponsor or its sponsoring brokerages into approving unfavorable transactions. Critics charge that roll-up sponsors receive excessively high fees to convert limited partnerships into public corporations.

The Securities and Exchange Commission (SEC) has issued new rules to require disclosure of the risks that the value of a roll-up may decline. The sponsors of roll-ups must also disclose their compensation, other expected personal benefits, and any potential conflicts of

*Source: "Problems of Enhancing Limited Partnership Resale Liquidity," by John W. Bagby ©1993.

interest. Limited partners must be given a minimum of 60 days to evaluate the roll-up disclosures which are often difficult to comprehend and are full of jargon. Reform legislation has been introduced into Congress to clarify the roll-up process, require independent evaluation of the transaction's fairness, and permit limited partners to communicate together without violating the SEC's proxy solicitation rules. The secondary market for resale of limited partnership interests is undergoing fundamental changes to better serve investors' needs. However, the steps taken should not detract from the willingness of market participants to provide the needed liquidity.

Thought Questions

1. What are the legal and ethical issues involved with the limited partnership liquidity problems?

2. What are the reasons that new industry standards, regulation, or legislation are urged for the limited partnership resale market?

3. What alternative hypotheses are there for the loss of limited partnership values and their liquidity problems?

END–OF–CHAPTER PROBLEMS

1. For what reasons did the limited partnership develop as an alternative to the sole proprietorship, general partnership, or corporation?

2. Under RULPA and its 1985 amendments, what additional limited partner involvement in partnership activities are permitted? Contrast how these limited partner rights compare to the rights of a shareholder. What reasons support this trend?

3. What is the premise for the theory that limited partner involvement should lead to unlimited liability? How has this premise evolved and what part of the theory remains under the most liberal RULPA amendments and the case law?

4. What arguments justify the differing distribution priorities under ULPA and RULPA?

5. Discuss the problems encountered in recent years in the secondary trading of limited partnership interests and in restructured limited partnerships, called roll-up corporations.

6. G, W, and Mr. & Mrs. L commenced a business to develop real estate and filed a limited partnership certificate in Virginia under the ULPA. W was the general partner and the others were limited partners.

Mr. and Mrs. J won a judgment against all the partners for breach of warranty. Should the limited partners lose their limited liability because they failed to "swear" to the statements in the certificate? See *Wisniewski v. Johnson*, 286 S.E.2d 223 (Va. 1982).

7. B, S, and R purchased land to build an apartment building under the name EA, Ltd. B promised to pay a finder's fee to M for finding DSG to finance EA, Ltd., as a limited partner. EA, Ltd., refused to pay M, claiming the limited partnership was not officially formed by filing until after M's work was performed. Under ULPA, is the limited partnership liable for M's fee? See *Shindler v. Marr & Assoc.*, 695 S.W.2d 699 (Tex. App. 1985).

8. W, the sole general partner, properly formed the DP limited partnership to manage apartments and other real estate investments in the District of Columbia. After financial difficulties, the limited partners replaced W with two new general partners, R & T. W remained a general partner but left to work for another real estate firm. Partnership creditors sued W, who defended that the limited partners gave R & T orders on management decisions and W's orders were ignored. Are

the limited partners' exercise of control sufficient to insulate an inactive general partner from liability? See *Weil v. Diversified Indus.*, 319 F.Supp. 778 (D.C.D C. 1970).

9. MHM, a limited partnership organized to build and operate recreational facilities, reinvested half of the firm's profits annually. The limited partners were required by federal tax law to pay their share of tax liability on all profits, whether distributed or retained in the business. Should a court order the general partner to distribute all profits rather than reinvest them? On what premise do the general partners base their suit? See *Brooke v. Mt. Hood Meadows Oregon, Ltd.*, 725 P.2d 925 (Or. App. 1986).

10. The sole general partner made extensive loans to the limited partnership; the loans were recorded as debts owed to the general partner; written notes were executed by the general partner to herself as creditor; and all these facts were known to the limited partner. After the general partner's death, the limited partner argued the loans were instead the general partner's capital contribution. What arguments are there to support the limited partner's contention, and what counterarguments could be made? See *Park Cities Corp. v. Byrd*, 522 S.W.2d 572 (Tex. Civ. App. 1975).

Part IX

Corporations

■

Chapter 40

Corporate Formation and Capital Structure

■

CRITICAL THINKING INQUIRIES

As you read this chapter, you should be able to address the following:

- For what reasons do the states create artificial entities such as corporations and limited partnerships that grant their participants limited liability?
- What is the issue in the precise timing of forming a corporation that determines the promoters' legal responsibilities?
- For what purpose is there a distinction between domestic corporations and out-of-state or foreign corporations? How and why does this impact the corporation?
- What are the basic issues that separate the two major types of corporate securities: equity and debt?
- What principles of agency law are analogous to the corporate law problems involving corporate promoters and the sale of stock subscriptions?

MANAGERIAL PERSPECTIVE

Carl and Claudia had successfully operated their private investigation business as a partnership for several years. They were impressed with the prospect of becoming a corporation because of the prestige and power implicit in the corporate form. They also believed a corporation would shield their personal and individual assets from business risks because of corporate limited liability. This prompted them to reorganize their partnership into a corporation they called InvestigatCo. During the promotion stage, each of them made preincorporation contracts with lenders, landlords, prospective employees, consultants, suppliers, and customers without first acquiring the other's consent. Considerable common stock in InvestigatCo was sold to outsiders before incorporation, but neither Carl nor Claudia paid as much per share as did the outsiders for the majority of voting shares they retained. They incorporated without the assistance of an experienced attorney, so their certificate of incorporation contained numerous errors and omissions. It was not filed until long after corporate operations commenced. Carl continued to use the firm's bank account for personal purposes, and they failed to conduct meetings for the board of directors and shareholders.

- What legal issues are raised by Carl and Claudia's activities?
- What alternative actions could have been taken to avoid the problems raised?

As was important for proper partnership planning, promoters should consider how to best satisfy the needs of various corporate participants during the corporate formation process. This careful planning permits the design of corporate governance provisions in the charter and bylaws to reflect the expectations of the likely constituents. The following material on the nature of corporations, limited liability, incorporation, and the design of capital structure is essential in planning for a variety of likely contingencies.

NATURE OF CORPORATIONS

Corporations have fast become the predominant business organization form in the United States and in most other nations. During the mid-19th century, there were few corporations. Most economic activity was conducted by sole proprietorships and partnerships. Today, while corporations represent only about a quarter of the total number of business organizations, they generate about 90 percent of gross business receipts. By contrast, sole proprietorships today account for nearly two thirds of business organizations but generate only about 6 percent of gross receipts. Partnerships comprise about a tenth of business organizations and generate less than 5 percent of gross receipts. These market share statistics suggest that the creation, governance, operation, and termination of corporations are very significant issues for business. Most Americans are affected directly by corporations as employees, investors, pensioners, and customers.

Characteristics of Corporations

Critical inquiry has sought to explain the success of the corporate form. Commonly, corporate characteristics are cited as primary reasons for the success. Corporations are *legal entities* separate from their participants and owners. Since there is no basis for the existence of artificial entities, they must be created under authority granted by state legislatures. This gives corporations the legal status of artificial persons, making them capable of owning, selling, or purchasing property, giving them standing to bring or defend suits, and entitling them to constitutional rights such as due process, equal protection, security from unreasonable searches and seizures, and the privileges and immunities of other citizens.

The entity status of corporations implies several other important corporate characteristics. Because owners are separate, the corporation can exist independently and survive the death of an owner or owners. This suggests a corporation can have *perpetual existence*. Unless restricted by contract or regulation, there can be *free transferability of corporate ownership*. Perpetual existence and free transferability probably contribute to the vitality of the public financial markets because corporate ownership, represented by stock and other securities, trades freely. Such liquidity of ownership is difficult with most partnerships because they dissolve so easily and are inseparable from their participants for many purposes. Corporations often have *separate ownership and control*. Owners are often passive investors who delegate management powers through the board of directors to officers and ultimately to professional managers.

These characteristics combine to permit the most attractive and often cited corporate feature: *limited liability*. Shareholders are ordinarily shielded from unlimited personal liability for corporate debts. Shareholder liability is limited to the initial capital contribution for claims unsatisfied out of corporate assets. This feature is often cited as the main reason passive investors are willing to risk their capital in remote ventures. Before they agree to contribute their capital, passive investors demand to be isolated from unlimited liability for risks of failure from the decisions made by distant managers.

The American corporate form flourished during the Industrial Revolution enabling productive capacity in the United States to expand as risk-averse investors became able to invest in ventures beyond their expertise and geographic reach. The limited liability of corporations and limited partnerships was probably the primary structure necessary for the vast improvement in living standards in the industrial world later experienced during the 20th century.

Theory of the Firm

Economists theorize that large firms are actually just a "bundle of contracts."[1] Corporations have emerged as the predominant economic force because they have some cost advantages in bringing functions in-house over individual entrepreneurs who

---

[1] See Ronald H. Coase, *The Nature of the Firm*, 4 Economica 386 (1937).

must subcontract many details of production. There are substantial *transactions costs* for sole proprietor entrepreneurs because they must separately subcontract so many of their contracts for research, design, parts fabrication, assembly, transportation, accounting, legal services, advertising, warehousing, and marketing. As firms grow, they bring these functions in-house to gain cost savings.

Larger firms can exercise greater control over operations and reduce transactions costs through *form contracting*. For example, the standardized purchase order and the collective bargaining agreement with labor unions are less costly forms of contracting than are involved with the separate negotiation of each individual supply or employment contract. Additionally, firms reduce costs by monitoring shirkers, they gain consistency in quality control, they maintain sufficient capacity to meet unexpected demand, their size and diversity can enhance goodwill—and all this helps attract capital. These are part of the *economies of scale* that also explain the tendency for firms to organize as corporations. As greater efficiencies are found in firms of increasing size, the limited liability feature reinforces this growth by attracting passive capital, reinforcing the choice of the corporate form.

Classification of Corporations

Corporations are commonly classified according to several attributes. **Public corporations** are generally governmental or quasi-governmental units designed to administer public affairs. For example, many municipalities (cities, towns, boroughs, and townships) are organized as municipal corporations under state statutes establishing their purpose and granting them certain powers. **Private corporations** are organized for business purposes. They are owned by individuals and generally have a profit motive, although some are **not-for-profit organizations** with charitable or community benefit purposes—for example, major charities, fraternal societies, the scouts, and some hospitals. Nonprofit corporations may not distribute their surpluses to participants or they risk losing their special tax-exempt status.

Publicly traded corporations are generally private, for-profit corporations that have some class of securities (e.g., stocks, bonds) trading on a national securities exchange. This exposes them to the disclosure and corporate democracy regulations imposed by the securities exchanges and under the securities laws. Publicly traded corporations are contrasted with **closely held corporations**, also called *close corporations, closed corporations,* or *privately held corporations.* Close corporations operate similarly to incorporated partnerships because they are managed by the owners and ownership is restricted to a small group of close associates and their relatives. Close corporations are of all sizes and can be governed by the same general corporation law as publicly traded corporations in many states. However, some states provide special close corporation statutes or at least some special provisions applicable to close corporations, permitting them to operate more informally. For example, these laws may authorize shareholder agreements and permit exclusive control to remain within a group of insiders. The favorable partnership flow-through tax treatment is available to certain close corporations that also qualify under the federal Internal Revenue Code as **Subchapter S corporations,** discussed in the overview to Unit III.[2]

Corporations are considered **domestic corporations** in the state where they are incorporated and **foreign corporations** in all other states. Nearly half the publicly traded corporations are incorporated in Delaware. Nevertheless, most Delaware corporations have the preponderance of their assets and facilities situated in other states. They are considered domestic corporations in Delaware and foreign corporations in the other states despite having their headquarters and major facilities located outside Delaware. The impact of foreign corporation status is discussed more fully later in this chapter. **Professional corporations (PC)** became popular in the 1970s among firms practicing accounting, law, engineering, and other recognized professions. PC status permitted these firms to take advantage of the favorable taxation of corporate pension funds. However, the expansion and liberalization of alternative pension plans has slowed the trend toward using the PC form.

---

[2]Subchapter S corporations permit use of the partnership flow-through form of taxation, thus avoiding the double tax on dividends. Shareholders in a Subchapter S corporation must unanimously elect the treatment. Subchapter S corporations are limited to 35 shareholders, none of whom may be another corporation. No less than 75 percent of gross revenues may be derived from active operations, effectively limiting passive investment income from dividends, rents, or bond interest to 25 percent. Only one class of shares is permissible.

Corporations are established by the states. Each state may have different corporation laws. Delaware's corporate law is the most influential because so many publicly traded corporations are chartered there. The Revised Model Business Corporation Act (RMBCA) is a model act adopted by over 30 states in its original form or in one of several revised forms. The corporation laws and court interpretations in several large states are also influential on the development of corporate law, including New York, Pennsylvania, California, Illinois, New Jersey, North Carolina, and Texas. This text focuses primarily on the RMBCA while occasionally indicating significant differences in other states' laws.

Naderite Mossbacks Lose Control over Corporate Law*

The American Law Institute (ALI), perhaps the most elite group of lawyers in the U.S., finally approved its massive analysis of U.S. corporate law last month. When the ALI set to work on the proposal 14 years ago, it hoped to transform corporate law radically. In the end, it succeeded only in transforming itself. As adherents of the new law and economics movement struggled with devotees of old fears of corporate power, the ALI was transmuted from a quiet enclave into a very public, quasi-legislative body, subject to all the usual controversy and intrigue.

Selected from the ranks of distinguished scholars and practitioners, the ALI is best known for drafting "Restatements" of the law in various areas. These restatements, notably of tort and contract law, serve as authoritative guides for both legal briefs and judicial opinions.

When the ALI embarked on a restatement of corporate law in 1978, some of the institute's members viewed the project as a useful strategy for heading off an effort by Ralph Nader and his allies to inject the federal government even further into corporate governance. Others, sympathetic to Mr. Nader, thought that a properly drafted restatement would have a good chance of achieving Mr. Nader's goal of displacing the diverse corporate law of the 50 states with a centralized regulatory system. However, there was never a consensus within the ALI about what was wrong with corporate law or exactly why the ALI needed to spend energy changing it.

1978 was almost exactly the moment when the law and economics movement began to replace the New Deal view of corporate law—which held that shareholders were pawns ruthlessly exploited by management—with the more emiprically grounded view that the market operates, albeit imperfectly, to cause corporate management to maximize profits. Traditional thinking about corporate law favors encouraging lawsuits by shareholders against managers and directors as a means of preventing abuses by corporate insiders. The new perspective was that the best way to protect shareholders was by enforcing the contracts among the company's officers and directors, and by fashioning legal rules that encourage the operation of market forces to constrain the worst instincts of management.

Unfortunately, this new perspective was "astonishingly unrepresented" in the early days of the ALI project, as Ralph Winter, a federal judge who is closely associated with the law and economics movement, pointed out at the time. Judge Winter observed that of the four reporters, 10 consultants and 45 advisers to the ALI's Corporate Governance Project in the early days, only one adviser was affiliated with the law and economics approach. More than anything else, it was the attempt to exclude market-oriented thinking from the ALI's project that blew up the ALI's old ways of doing business.

*Source: Jonathan R. Macey, "Naderite Mossbacks Lose Control over Corporate Law," *The Wall Street Journal*, June 24, 1992, p. A19.

As a result, much to the shock of the distinguished older scholars at the helm of the project, who were used to going about their business in a discreet hush, prominent young scholars vehemently criticized the ALI. In 1983, Henry Manne, now the dean of the George Mason law school and a prominent member of the law and economics movement, called the ALI's early recommendations "a new threat to the corporate free enterprise system" because they would have removed authority from directors and markets and given it to courts and lawyers.

Corporate lawyers in private practice now joined the market-oriented academics. Charles Hansen, a prominent corporate lawyer and a member of the ALI wrote in 1990 that the ALI's positions "do not reflect current law but rather call for fundamental and unwarranted changes in existing law." As such, they went far beyond the ALI's mandate to "restate" the law; they actually were rewriting it.

Soon corporate America was adding its voice to that of the scholars and practitioners. The American Corporate Counsel Association, the American Society of Corporate Secretaries, the Business Roundtable and the National Association of Manufacturers all acted in various ways, quiet and not so quiet, to influence the ALI's deliberations.

Members of the ALI angrily complained that corporate America was engaging in a brazen attempt to influence the law that governed it. There were accusations that corporations were hiring members of the ALI to represent their interests in that body's deliberations and that they were removing their legal business from law firms with partners who were sympathetic to the ALI's pro-litigation outlook.

The ALI reacted to this lobbying with outrage and dismay. Members of the ALI were told that the interests of their clients "should be left outside the door." One ALI member was requested to disclose the fact that he represented a group of corporate executives before expressing his views at ALI meetings. In theory, members of the ALI should be impartial policy makers. In actuality, if they are not influenced by their clients, they are at risk of being influenced by their own interests as lawyers—interests that favor more litigation.

Given a choice between a corporate law that reflected only lawyers' interests and one that reflected the interests of both lawyers and their clients, it seemed clear to all but the most shortsighted ALI officials that the interests of corporate clients should be taken into account. The stakes, after all, were very high: Even before the final report was approved, courts in nine jurisdictions had adopted pronouncements in preliminary drafts as law.

In the end, the views of corporate executives and market-oriented economists had a strong salutary impact on the ALI lawyers, even if the final result was often an ideologically inconsistent compromise. For instance, the corporate executives wanted strong rules discouraging takeovers, while the law and economics group favored an unfettered market for corporate control. The final report is somewhere in between.

The push and pull of competing interests created a more honest report. The ALI dropped the misleading term "restatement" from its reform project. And the controversy surrounding the project forced more democracy upon the ALI. Attendance at ALI meetings discussing corporate governance issues tripled. Over time, the law and economics movement obtained greater representation among the reporters, consultants and advisers to the project. The hundreds of scholarly articles and conferences devoted to the ALI's proposals had an influence on the final outcome, even though many of these articles and conferences enjoyed corporate sponsorship.

Gradually, even some of the old-line scholars associated with the project began to see the merit of the younger generation's law and economics perspective. By the time the ALI membership approved the 1,068-page final draft at its annual meeting last month, even Henry Manne and Charles Hansen had few complaints.

Thought Questions

1. What is the issue separating the old school of corporate law drafters from the newer school?
2. What reasons support the old school's formula for corporation laws?
3. What reasons support the new school's criticism of the old school?

LIMITED LIABILITY: PIERCING THE CORPORATE VEIL

Limited liability is the predominant corporate feature sought through incorporation. However, there are limits to how this concept shields shareholders' personal assets from liability. For example, many lenders insist that close corporate shareholders and/ or officers cosign or comake loans. This makes them personally liable as equal obligors with the corporation. In these situations, only weak creditors are prevented from seeking full satisfaction of their debts from such managing shareholders. Trade creditors or judgment creditors are often considered weak creditors because they have only limited repayment assurances—for example, collateral or surety.

Where the corporate form is used improperly or fraudulently, the courts may disregard the legal separateness between shareholders and their corporation, holding the shareholders to unlimited liability for corporate debts. Is it ethical for shareholders to undercapitalize the corporation, ignore corporate formalities, and use the corporation as an ''incorporated pocketbook'' for their personal business and financial affairs? This ethical dilemma constantly aggravates public policymaking because there are legitimate uses of the corporate form. The doctrine of piercing the corporate veil draws an ethical balance between defensible uses and corrupt misuse of the corporate form.

The limited liability concept is widely accepted in most Western nations as necessary for raising capital and permitting the attainment of economies of scale. However, many former communist nations and some third-world nations find inequities in corporate limited liability. The Bhopal chemical disaster in 1985 posed such a clash in the acceptability of limited liability. Union Carbide created a local Indian subsidiary to operate local chemical production and to make sales. Indian law required that the plant must be operated mostly by Indian nationals. There

was some evidence of operational incompetence and even sabotage that could have contributed to the 1985 accident that released cyanide gas, injuring thousands. After the disaster, public sentiment in India turned to ignoring the corporate separateness between the Union Carbide parent corporation and the Indian subsidiary. To compensate the victims, Union Carbide established a trust fund for injury payments that would have been unnecessary in most Western nations without proof Union Carbide used the corporate form improperly. The threat of bad publicity and nationalization (confiscation) of the subsidiary's assets may have played a role in Union Carbide's decision to compensate the Bhopal victims. Limited liability receives varied treatment worldwide.

Limited liability is probably most useful for large, publicly traded corporations with numerous shareholders. Creditors would have great procedural difficulty suing such geographically dispersed defendants. Highly visible large investors, parent corporations, and institutional investors with ''deep pockets'' would be the most vulnerable, giving them an incentive to characterize their corporation investments as debt or other nonequity holdings. This would ultimately deter shareholder liability suits. Additionally, many creditors have other methods to ensure repayment of debts. Creditworthiness, investigations, collateral and security arrangements, sinking funds, contractual restrictions on managerial decisions, dividend payout restrictions, and financial responsibility arrangements (e.g., liability insurance) all provide creditors with some safety from nonpayment. These devices also protect shareholders from unlimited liability because debts are more likely to be paid. Of course, shareholders can lose their investments if the corporation is liquidated in bankruptcy. Despite the numerous creditor protections in corporate and commercial law, the doctrine of piercing the corporate veil has arisen, restricting the limited liability concept somewhat (see Figure 40–1).

Figure 40–1   Piercing the Corporate Veil

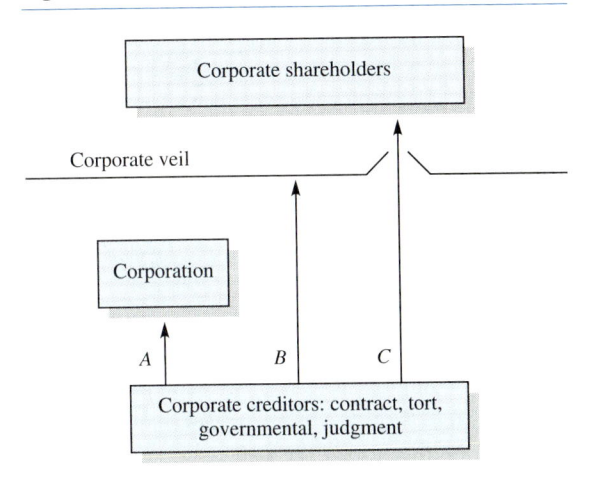

A   Normally, corporations are solely liable for liabilities in contract, tort, after judgments, and to governments (taxes, penalties)

B   Limited liability usually shields shareholders from liability to their initial investment for corporate debts

C   Corporate creditors can pierce the corporate veil, exposing shareholders to unlimited liability under the theories of alter ego, undercapitalization, or fraud

Alter Ego

Shareholders may be sued directly for corporate liabilities beyond the shareholders' initial investment in exceptional circumstances. This exception to limited liability is intended to prevent injustice, fraud, violation of the law, or public losses. In one case, a corporation was formed to produce neon lights that infringed on the inventor's patent. Limited liability was ignored because it would violate the spirit of the patent laws to shield the two shareholders who violated the patent holder's intellectual property rights. The corporate form should not be used to "defeat public convenience, justify wrong, protect fraud, or defend crime, [otherwise] the law will regard the corporation as an association of persons."[3] Of course, it is legitimate for controlling shareholders to limit their liability by operating a business organized in the corporate form. Just because a corporation has insufficient assets to pay its debts, standing alone, does not justify holding shareholders to

unlimited liability. However, the corporate veil may be pierced where shareholders dominate corporate activities to carry out an improper purpose.

The **alter ego theory** of piercing the corporate veil applies where shareholders hold extensive control over the corporation and effectively maintain no real separateness from the corporate entity; hence the term *alter ego,* which literally means "other self." Corporations used as mere instrumentalities for dominant shareholders' personal affairs are prime targets. Courts look for a combination of several factors: shares owned by a few shareholders, failure to issue stock, corporate assets commingled with shareholders' personal assets, and the failure to maintain sufficient corporate formalities. Corporations must keep books and records separate from the records of their shareholders or affiliated corporations. A shareholder's payment of personal debts with corporate funds and extensive use of corporate assets for personal purposes is evidence of an alter ego situation. If corporate and shareholder assets cannot be readily differentiated, there may be an alter ego.

The shareholder's failure to observe traditional required corporate formalities is another factor. The maintenance of separate corporate records, board and shareholder meetings, minutes of corporate meetings, and the holding of elections are all necessary to avoid alter ego claims. However, states are increasingly adopting special close corporation statutes that relax certain corporate formalities. Most of these statutes require incorporators' or shareholders' intentional designation of the corporation as a "statutory close corporation." Some states further require the shareholders to agree in writing to permit this relaxation of corporate formality. For example, shareholders of a close corporation incorporated under the Statutory Close Corporation Supplement to the MBCA would not have unlimited liability for relaxed corporate formalities. However, there could still be unlimited liability under alter ego if other such factors were proven.

Inadequate Capitalization

Corporations with inadequate or "thin financing" may expose their shareholders to unlimited liability under piercing the corporate veil. The test examines the adequacy of assets and capital contributed to the corporation *when it is initially formed* to carry on normal business operations and pay reasonably fore-

---

[3]*United States v. Milwaukee Refrigerated Transit Co.,* 142 F. 247 (E.D. Wis. 1905). In this case, the parent brewery was held liable for the illegal rebates made by its subsidiary.

seeable future liabilities. This theory assumes that shareholders must place sufficient capital at risk in good faith to cover the corporation's likely prospective liabilities. Corporations that are adequately financed initially but that later suffer losses are not inadequately capitalized. Additional capital contributions are not required later if the business is adequately financed initially.

Shell corporations, with few or no assets, that are organized only to avoid liability are typical of inadequately capitalized corporations. Creditors in many states cannot pierce the corporate veil for inadequate capitalization if they knew the shell was thinly financed. By contrast, inadequate capitalization is a *per se* (automatic) basis for piercing in California.

Inadequate financing can raise tax liability questions. For example, corporations with excessively high debt-to-equity ratios (over 4 to 1 is often suggested) whose shareholders hold the debt in roughly equal proportions to their equity holdings are candidates. The IRS views these as thinly financed corporations seeking to avoid the double tax on dividends through the disguise of shareholders' equity as debt. Interest payments on debt are tax deductible, so the IRS may redesignate these payments as **disguised dividends** to assess additional tax liability. Some state courts also treat this excessive shareholder-held debt as disguised equity and subordinate the insiders' creditor claims to outside creditors, as discussed next.

Deep Rock Doctrine

The resolution of creditors' claims against a bankrupt corporation is a complex process. As discussed in Chapter 33, priority claimants in several different classes are satisfied first, then secured creditors receive the liquidation value of their collateral, and finally unsecured debt by all other creditors is joined together and such creditors split up the liquidation value of whatever assets remain in proportion to the debt they held. Because creditors under a piercing theory are usually in this last class, they may not receive full repayment.

The major shareholders of some corporations make secured loans in the same proportion as they hold equity. The **Deep Rock doctrine** is an *equitable subordination* of both secured and unsecured claims of such major shareholder-creditors.[4] Courts consider several factors in subordinating these shareholders' claims: fraud, mismanagement, undercapitalization, commingling of assets, lack of independence, excessive control, and whether the debt was bargained for at arm's length. Deep Rock subordination is distinguished from piercing liability because these shareholders are not held to unlimited liability without the creditor's satisfaction of a piercing theory.

Parent-Subsidiary Corporations

It is legitimate to form affiliated corporate groups of parent corporations or holding companies that wholly own or hold a majority of the shares in subsidiaries. This organization can result from an acquisition or initial subsidiary incorporation. It permits parent and brother-sister corporations to avoid the liabilities of an affiliate. Even if the group has common directors, officers, and managers, limited liability remains effective. However, piercing theories are employed if one member uses excessive control over an affiliate in a corporate structure to externalize the costs of operations on outsiders. In parent-subsidiary relations, courts apply the various piercing theories: alter ego, corporate formalities, and undercapitalization. Generally, the plaintiff must prove that the parent had nearly complete control of the subsidiary or affiliate, the control was used for fraud or wrong, and this caused direct injury to the plaintiff.

Fraud is a factor considered in parent-subsidiary cases where creditors are reasonably led to believe the resources of the whole affiliated group are available to satisfy the liabilities of any other member. This represents the *instrumentality rule,* applicable where the affiliated group is organized to expose the subsidiary to the risks but is controlled by the parent or affiliate that dominates the subsidiary so that it has no separate mind of its own.

The instrumentality rule was applied to the Pennsylvania Railroad, which owned and operated the West Jersey and Seashore Railroad Company as a part of the larger Pennsylvania Railroad System. The Pennsylvania Railroad logo appeared on the West Jersey's rolling stock, on its timetables, and on its conductors' uniforms.[5] The parent was held liable for injuries to the occupants of a car hit by the

---

[4]*Taylor v. Standard Gas & Electric Co.,* 306 U.S. 307 (1939).

[5]*Ross v. Pennsylvania Railroad Co.,* 148 A.741 (N.J. 1930).

subsidiary's train because the West Jersey subsidiary was a mere instrumentality of the Pennsylvania Railroad parent corporation. Some courts would hold liable any member of an affiliated corporate group, including brother-sister corporations, under the more expansive theory of **enterprise liability**. The next case illustrates how the enterprise liability question of affiliated corporate groups arises.

BERGER v. COLUMBIA BROADCASTING SYSTEM, INC.
433 F.2d 991 (5th Cir. 1972)

CBS Films was a wholly owned subsidiary of the Columbia Broadcasting System (CBS). CBS considered CBS Films to be a division of CBS—the firm's organization chart showed CBS Films as deriving its authority from various CBS employees. Jerome Berger negotiated a contract with CBS Films to provide film footage for the 1965 International Fashion Festival to be licensed to CBS Films. Digges, the administrative vice president of CBS Films, negotiated the contract for CBS Films. CBS Films also obtained a right of first refusal to broadcast further such films produced by Berger from 1966 through 1974.

Later that year, CBS Director of Special Events Paul Levitan negotiated a separate contract with another party, Crowley, to broadcast a fashion show that Berger claimed was similar to the Berger film. Berger sued CBS for breach of contract, claiming the Crowley show was substantially similar to Berger's. Berger alleged that CBS should be responsible for the breach of contract by CBS Films because CBS Films was the alter ego of CBS. CBS appealed a lower court verdict in favor of Berger for $200,000.

GOLDBERG, Circuit Judge

A corporation is a creature of the law, endowed with a personality separate and distinct from that of its owners. The principle purpose of which is to accord stockholders an opportunity to limit their personal liability. However, the separateness of corporate entity has been disregarded and a parent corporation held liable for the acts of its subsidiary because the subsidiary's affairs had been so controlled as to render it merely an instrument or agent of its parent. An aggrieved party must prove something more than a parent's mere ownership of a majority or even all of the capital stock and the parent's use of its power to elect officers and directors of the subsidiary.

Courts have developed various legal theories and descriptive terms to explain the relationship between a subsidiary and its dominating parent. A dominated subsidiary has been labeled an instrument, agent, adjunct, branch, dummy, department, or tool of the parent corporation. In *Lowendahl v. Baltimore and Ohio Ry.* the court postulated the following three elements necessary to sustain application of the instrumentality rule:

(1) Control, not merely majority or complete stock control, but complete domination, not only of finances, but of policy and business practice in respect to the transaction attacked so that the corporate entity as to this transaction had at the time no separate mind, will or existence of its own; (2) Such control must have been used by the defendant to commit fraud or wrong, to perpetuate the violation of a statutory or other positive legal duty or a dishonest or unjust act in contravention of plaintiff's legal rights; (3) The control and breach of duty must proximately cause the injury or unjust loss.

The trial court held that at all relevant times CBS Films was merely an instrumentality of the defendant based on the following findings: (1) the board of films consisted solely of CBS employees, (2) the organization chart of CBS included CBS Films, (3) all authority for CBS Films passed through employees of CBS. We think that it is obvious that these factual determinations, standing alone, are insufficient to sustain application of the instrumentality rule. The evidence concerning the relationship between CBS and CBS Films could not sustain any finding that CBS completely dominated not only the finances, but the policy and business practice of CBS Films.

Complete stock ownership, common officers and directors, and the use of organizational charts illustrating lines of authority are all business practices common to most parent-subsidiary relationships. Proof of a parent's potential to dominate its subsidiary is precisely the kind of evidence consistently rejected as insufficient in proving a community of management between corporations. Affixing labels to corporate relationships for purposes of showing a parent's complete domination of a subsidiary is a dangerous business. This court has no alternative but to reverse the decision of the district court on the simple basis that plaintiff has failed to prove, in accordance with New York law, that CBS Films was the alter ego of the defendant. The judgment of the district court is reversed.

Case Questions

1. What is the issue in piercing the corporate veil of a subsidiary to hold its parent liable for subsidiary debts?

2. What reasons support Berger's argument that CBS Films was merely an instrumentality of CBS?

3. What reasons support the CBS argument that CBS should not be liable for CBS Films' debts? What assumption about management, policy, and finances underlie the limited liability rule of parent-subsidiary relationships?

Some commentators argue that piercing the corporate veil is more compelling in cases of fraud and other torts than in contract cases.[6] Contract creditors have the opportunity to evaluate the corporation's creditworthiness before the debt is created, enabling them to impose special protections and improve the probability of repayment. By contrast, tort and fraud victims are usually unable to negotiate protection before the debt is incurred. For example, a bank can easily investigate the corporation's debt repayment history before making a new loan, but a bystander can hardly investigate a taxi company's finances before being accidentally hit by one of its taxis. Tort victims often exhaust liability insurance first, then go after corporate assets before pursuing individual shareholders. Inadequate capitalization seems most compelling in tort cases. Therefore, more stringent standards apply to contract claimants than to tort claimants in piercing cases.

INCORPORATION PROCESS

As with limited partnerships, the corporate form changes the fundamental common law rule that owners and participants are responsible for their actions. As artificial creatures of state law, corporations cannot exist without specific authorization from state legislatures. From time to time, social activists like Ralph Nader advocate federal chartering of corporations to make corporate law uniform throughout the nation. However, there is pervasive federal regulation with direct impact on corporations. The tra-

dition of federalism makes the elimination of state corporation chartering unlikely. However, in nearly every other nation in the world, the central or national government is responsible for corporation chartering.

Incorporation should not be excessively time-consuming or expensive. An experienced attorney should be consulted to ensure satisfactory compliance with applicable incorporation statutes. An accountant should also be retained to establish financial records and controls as well as help optimize the new organization's tax status. Incorporators should select the proper state for incorporation. Privately held close corporations are probably best advised to incorporate in the state where their primary business activities are conducted. Out-of-state incorporation should be considered only for larger, multistate businesses with complex capital structures or other special needs. Corporate law in many states favors management freedom of action. For example, Delaware's well-developed law is most suitable for large, publicly traded corporations. Choice of the state of incorporation may also be affected by tax rates, particularly the **franchise tax** or **capital stock tax** levied on the number of shares issued or the shares' par value.

The advantages of incorporation in foreign nations varies widely. However, special restrictions on foreign ownership, local participation, and taxation make it difficult to generalize. Therefore, competent counsel is always necessary to select among alternate business organization forms in foreign nations. Large *multinational enterprises* comprised of various branches, joint ventures, global strategic alliances, and subsidiaries operate throughout the world. Many dominate international commerce.

---

[6]See e.g., Easterbrook and Fischel, *Limited Liability and the Corporation*, 52 Univ.of Chic.L.Rev. 89 (1985).

Their growing economic and political powers may make them the target of restrictive legislation, particularly in the developing countries. Many industrialized nations target them with protectionist trade restrictions.

Corporate Charter

The incorporation process is one of the last steps in the broader process known as *promotion*, which is discussed later in this chapter. Incorporation is commenced by the corporate promoters or incorporators, who must file a **certificate of incorporation**, also variously known as the **corporate charter** or the **articles of incorporation**. The articles are filed with a designated state agency, usually the secretary of state. Upon acceptance, the articles become a charter that effectively grants the corporation "personhood" or entity status. This accords limited liability on shareholders and gives the corporation a license to operate.

Although state requirements vary, under the RMBCA, certain information is *mandatory*: a unique corporate name must be chosen that is not confusingly similar to any other name; the number of authorized shares must be stated; the name and address of the principal place of business must be stated; the corporation's registered agent designated to receive service of process must be named; and each incorporator's name and address must be listed.

Additional information is optional or *permissible*: initial directors' names and addresses, a corporate purpose ("any lawful purpose" is acceptable), the corporate duration ("perpetual" is acceptable), the par value of shares, and special corporate governance matters such as cumulative voting, preemptive rights, staggering of directors, quorum and special requirements for shareholder and/or director meetings, officer and director indemnification, bylaw revision process, share transfer restrictions, close corporation designation, and antitakeover provisions. The certificate or a later amendment must describe any complex capital structures, detailing each separate class: the relative rights, special dividend, or liquidation preferences, voting privileges, and limitations, as illustrated in Figure 40–2.

Organizational Meeting

Corporate existence commences only after the articles are filed and the incorporators hold two meetings, often held back to back in the law offices of the

Figure 40–2 Articles of Incorporation

Art. I:	The name of the corporation is the KBE Corp.
Art. II:	The address of the corporation's registered office in the state of Illinois is 1234 Homewood Place, Schaumburg, Illinois. The registered agent of the corporations in Karen Craig at said address of the corporation.
Art. III:	The duration of the corporation is perpetual.
Art. IV:	The purpose of the corporation is to engage in any lawful purpose for which a corporation can be formed in the state of Illinois.
Art. V:	The corporation is authorized to issue 1,000,000 shares of class A common stock with no par value, 100,000 shares of class B common stock with par value of $10 per share, and 15,000 shares of preferred stock with par value of $25 per share.
Art. VI:	Business affairs of the corporation shall be managed by the board of directors.
Art. VII:	The board of directors is empowered to adopt, amend, or repeal such bylaws of the corporation as it sees fit.
Art. VIII:	The Incorporator is Jack J. Roberts, 456 Ridge Road, Schaumburg, Illinois.

Attestation:

I, the undersigned, make, file, and record these Articles of Incorporation to form a corporation under the laws of the state of Illinois, and certify the facts listed herein are true, so accordingly I set my hand and seal this ___ day of ___ , 19___ .

_____
Jack J. Roberts

promoter's attorney. First, many states require an **organizational meeting** of the incorporators, each of whom must be natural persons. Incorporators are often surrogates called **dummy incorporators**, such as members of the law office staff, whose only purpose is to create the new corporation. Typically, they have no financial interest in the new organization. The provisional incorporators elect the initial directors and then promptly resign. Second, the new directors convene the first directors' meeting to adopt bylaws and ratify or adopt promoters' preincorporation contracts. **Preincorporation contracts**, discussed in the next section, are made with investors, consultants, suppliers, customers, and employees as needed for corporate operations. Additionally, corporate officers are usually elected and other resolutions passed to commence normal operations by opening bank accounts, issuing stock, and setting the initial stock price.

Bylaws

The corporate charter functions like a constitution for the corporation by defining broad structural matters. Corporate **bylaws** are more like statutes supplementing the charter with more detailed rules governing corporate governance and operational matters. Shareholders inherently have the power to adopt, amend, or repeal both charter and bylaw provisions. However, many corporate charters delegate the authority over bylaws to the board. Bylaws address matters such as officer duties, director and shareholder meeting formalities (frequency, notice, quorum, and location), director powers, share transfer procedures, and officer and director compensation and indemnification. The bylaws must be consistent with the charter and the law. Bylaws need not be filed with the state, so they can remain confidential. Some close corporation statutes permit shareholder agreements to substitute for the bylaws of close corporations.

Defective Incorporation

Another area of unlimited liability concern to shareholders is defective incorporation. Although the incorporation process is relatively straightforward, failure to comply may bar the corporation from exercising its rights as a separate entity, suing, owning, or conveying property, and providing shareholders with limited liability. Defective incorporation may result from a failure to sign the articles,

the nonpayment of applicable fees, insufficient capitalization, or insufficient information in the articles. There are three classifications of imperfect incorporation: de facto, de jure, and defective corporations. However, these classifications are becoming obsolete as the RMBCA and other state statutes more precisely define when the corporate form is attained.

Insignificant defects can render an incorporation as a **de jure corporation**. Substantial compliance with the incorporation statutes ensures effective incorporation when there are only minor errors in the charter (e.g., wrong addresses, misspellings). However, a few states require perfect compliance with mandatory requirements, leaving de jure status only for problems with permissible charter provisions. The **de facto corporation** status arises with somewhat more serious errors or omissions. Incorporators may prove that they nevertheless made a colorable (seemingly valid), good faith attempt at compliance with a valid incorporation statute and then made actual use of this corporate form. For example, nonpayment of corporate franchise fees or incorporation taxes would probably result in a de facto incorporation. De facto status protects the shareholders with limited liability from suits by third parties that contracted with the de facto corporation. However, the state may bring a **quo warranto** (on what authority) action to cancel the defective incorporation. The next case illustrates the de facto doctrine.

CLINTON INVESTORS CO. v. WATKINS
536 N.Y.S.2d 270 (N.Y. App. 1989)

Vern Watkins, claiming to be the treasurer of the Clifton Park Learning Center, negotiated a three-year lease with Clinton Investors Co. for space in a building to be occupied by the Learning Center. Just before the lease commenced, Watkins and Clinton signed a rider (amendment) to the lease, this time identifying the tenant as the Clifton Park Learning Center, Inc. Watkins had not properly formed the corporation, nor used an attorney in the incorporation process, and did not otherwise satisfy the incorporation statutes. However, Watkins had reserved use of the name "Clifton Park Learning Center" in a document filed with the secretary of state. Clifton Park Learning Center was not formally incorporated until a year later. Within the next year, its lease payments were in default, and Clinton Investors sued Clifton Park Learning Center and Watkins to recover the amounts due. Clinton appealed the trial court's dismissal of the suit against Watkins.

VESAWICH, Justice

No corporation existed when Watkins signed the lease with plaintiff. His legal status was that of a promoter of Clifton Park Learning Center. A promoter that executes a preincorporation contract in the name of a proposed corporation is personally liable unless the other parties otherwise agree. Watkins asserts that because the Learning Center Corporation subsequently adopted the lease, he is no longer liable. However, corporate adoption of a contract gives rise to corporate liability in addition to any individual liability. The promoter nevertheless remains obligated unless there has been a novation between the corporation and the plaintiff. There is no explicit or implicit agreement by plaintiff not to hold Watkins personally liable on the lease.

Watkins also argues that because the Learning Center conducted its affairs with plaintiff as a corporation it should be treated as a de facto corporation. A pivotal element of a de facto corporation is a colorable attempt to comply with the statutes governing incorporation. The only activity approaching colorable compliance is an alleged name reservation. The action of a subsequently formed corporation to adopt the lease is an acknowledgment that Watkins had signed as a promoter of a proposed corporation. Judgment reversed and entered against Watkins.

Case Questions
1. What is the issue in determining the liability of a resulting corporation from preincorporation contracts made by its promoters? What is the issue in holding the promoters personally liable?
2. What reasons support holding a corporate promoter liable on preincorporation contracts? What assumption does this make about the parties' activities after the preincorporation contract is accepted?
3. What weight should be given to the fact that the landlord accepted payments from the later incorporated Clifton Park Learning Center before it became insolvent?

Wholly defective incorporation exposes the promoters, incorporators, and shareholders to unlimited liability. Such participants are considered partners or joint adventurers personally sharing unlimited joint and several liability. However, in some states, there is a trend to hold only the active shareholders to unlimited liability, thereby shielding passive shareholders. Several states and the RMBCA eliminate these defective incorporation classifications. Most states now make the secretary of state's issuance of the corporate certificate the definitive moment at which corporate existence commences, so the limited liability privilege is not conferred on shareholders until then. The RMBCA holds only the participants who operate the defective corporation while knowing of its insufficient formation to be jointly and severally liable.

A **corporation by estoppel** is similar to estoppel in the agency or partnership context. The doctrine generally estops third parties from denying the existence of a corporation if it relied on the fact of incorporation when this matter was "held out" to outsiders. This usually arises when a third party seeks to hold an incorporator or promoter personally liable on a contract with a defectively formed corporation. For example, IBM sued Cranson, who defectively formed the Real Estate Service Bureau, because it failed to file its certificate. However, IBM relied on Cranson's representation that the purchase contract for IBM typewriters was made directly with the corporation. This estopped IBM from holding Cranson personally liable.[7]

CORPORATE PROMOTERS

Promoters are the guiding force in the creation of new corporations, fulfilling an essential economic and societal objective. **Promoters** initially form corporations by procuring rights and capital with a view to the incorporation of an ongoing business. Under the corporation law of promotion, charlatans can be held responsible for forming bogus businesses to deceive unsuspecting investors. This section discusses the functions, duties, and compensation surrounding the preincorporation contracting of corporate promoters.

---

[7]*Cranson v. International Business Machines Corp.*, 200 A.2d 33 (Md. 1964).

Figure 40–3   Stages of Corporate Promotion

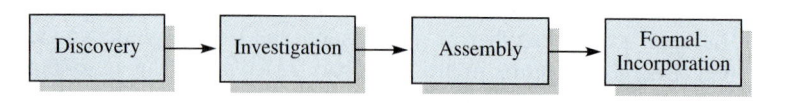

Promoters generally follow four major steps in creating new businesses as corporations. First, during the *discovery* stage, the promoter develops or discovers someone who has a new product or process. Alternatively, the promoter plans the reorganization into a corporation of an old proprietorship or partnership business that has already discovered an exploitable idea. Second, the promoter undertakes *investigation,* collecting information to analyze financial, human resource, and technological feasibility to justify the project. Third, the promoter undertakes *assembly,* procuring resources and making commitments necessary to run an ongoing business. Finally, the promoter undertakes *incorporation* by engaging counsel to prepare and file incorporation documents, and holding organiza-tional meetings, electing directors, selling stock, and commencing operations. These steps are depicted in Figure 40–3.

Promoters' Duties

Promoters have an unusual position under agency law. They are considered fiduciaries toward each other consistent with partnership law. This rule recognizes that the promotion project is a joint venture for the limited purpose of incorporation. Some courts require a written contract of promotion that constitutes more than a proposal before implying partnershiplike liability. The law also holds promoters to fiduciary duties to the corporation and to subscribers for shares, who become the future shareholders. This assumes a fiction, because the promoter is an agent for a nonexistent principal (the corporation) during most promotion activities. Therefore, promoters must act in good faith, avoid conflicts of interest, and renounce secret profits. **Secret profits** are unethical kickbacks or the unconsented receipt of special fees for awarding a corporate contract to a third party. Promoters' contracts with the corporation should be fully disclosed to the board or to shareholders for their approval to avoid the appearance that the promoters received any secret profits. A promoter's fiduciary duty can be enforced by copromoters, subscribers for shares, the resulting corporation, and the shareholders. The following case illustrates this duty.

GOLDEN v. OAHE ENTERPRISES, INC.
295 N.W.2d 270 (N.Y. App. 1989)

Emmick promoted the formation of Oahe Enterprises, with himself and others as investors. Emmick contributed certain stock in Colonial Manors, Inc., as his contribution. Colonial Manors' board had valued that stock at $19 per share for internal stock option purposes. However, a month before Oahe was incorporated, the Colonial Manors board lowered that stock value to $9.50 per share. Emmick failed to disclose this value reduction to other Oahe investors. Oahe sued Emmick for the diminished value, but the trial court found in Emmick's favor.

WOLMAN, Chief Justice

When a promoter benefits from a violation of his fiduciary duty at the expense of the corporation or its members this is often characterized as the promoter's secret profit. Such profit is not secret if all interested parties know of and assent to it. Where a promoter through overvaluation of property exchanged for stock and failure to disclose all material facts regarding such a change, takes more from the corporation than he transfers in, he is held liable for what courts term secret profit.

As a promoter, Emmick stood in a fiduciary relationship to both the corporation and its stockholders and was bound to deal with them in the utmost good faith. The valuation of the Colonial Manor stock was based on Emmick's self-serving estimate of matters well known to him as a Colonial Manor insider and warped by Emmick's self-interest. Emmick was not trading stock that had an easily ascertainable value, he was not dealing with people experienced in transactions of this type. Emmick was the controlling member of the Oahe board and in possession of information pertinent to the value of his Colonial Manor stock not generally available to the public or to the other Oahe board members. He failed in his duty to the corporation to disclose information regarding stock he intended to transfer into Oahe for Oahe shares and is therefore liable for the shortfall to the corporation. This difference can be equalized by canceling the number of Oahe shares held by Emmick that is proportional to the overvaluation. This court has upheld the cancellation of stock under circumstances where original issue stock was transferred for the worthless stock of another corporation or for services to be performed in the future. Judgment reversed.

Case Questions

1. What is the issue regarding the fairness of transactions by a corporate promoter?

2. What reasons support the corporation's recovery of any shortfall in value from property transferred to it for its stock?

3. What is the ambiguity in using noncash property to pay for stock in a new corporation? What ambiguity is there in using stock option valuation formulae as the value of the stock to the recipient?

Promoters need compensation to have adequate incentive to undertake the risks of promotion activities. The secret profit prohibition restricts legitimate compensation choices to the receipt of stock, commissions on stock sales, fees for their services, and/or employment by the resulting corporation. However, promoters are not automatically entitled to such compensation—it must be approved by the resulting corporation pursuant to a contract. Where promoters are uneasy about this uncertainty, they may assume control of the initial board to ensure that the corporation adopts their promotion contracts. For example, Carl and Claudia, from the chapter opening scenario, would be expected to control the initial and subsequent boards to control a sufficient block of stock and thereby the corporation. Occasionally, the courts are asked to grant compensation on a quantum meruit basis.

Liability on Preincorporation Contracts

There is significant ambiguity to promotion contract liability because the prospective corporation is a nonexistent principal at the time when preincorporation contracts are negotiated. How can a promoter purport to represent a nonexistent principal? Should the contractual liability of the promoter and third parties be conditional on successful corporate formation, followed by the corporation's deliberate approval of such contracts? This section discusses these and other related problems involved with preincorporation contract enforceability by and against (1) the corporation, (2) the promoter(s), and (3) third parties.

Corporation Liability

When a promoter lines up investors, suppliers, and customers, there is no existing corporation to be bound until after the formalities of creation are completed and the new corporation takes deliberate action to acknowledge responsibility for its promoters' contracts. A few states follow the English rule requiring the corporation to enter a *novation* agreement. This substitutes the corporation for the promoter as obligor in a new contract, replacing the preincorporation contract. However, the majority American rule holds the newly incorporated entity to preincorporation contracts after it either *ratifies* or *adopts* them.

The newly elected board of directors typically reviews the promoters' preincorporation contracts and then by resolution accepts those deemed advantageous to the emerging new business. Experienced promoters usually ensure this acceptance by personally holding sufficient stock and/or directorships to win the necessary votes. However, the board is not obligated to adopt any particular preincorporation contract. Indeed, the board is required by its fiduciary duty to refuse disadvantageous or conflict-of-interest transactions. As stated above, promoters must also observe the fiduciary duty in negotiating preincorporation contracts.

Ratification may be implied by the corporation's conduct where it accepts the benefits of a preincorporation contract. For example, there is an *implied ratification* where the corporation retains or uses land, goods, or services purchased in a promoter's preincorporation contract. In some states, ratification could also be implied if the promoters become the initial directors or the preincorporation contract expenses were essential to corporate formation. For example, the attorney fees to pay for InvestigatCo's incorporation or the financial printer's fees needed to issue stock certificates are essential to formation. A few states specifically require payment for these essential expenses, but most states would impose quasi-contractual liability on the new corporation for the benefits received.

Promoter Liability

The promoter may be personally liable on preincorporation contracts if the corporation rejects the contract or the corporation is never actually formed. Promoters can avoid this liability by stating clearly in negotiations and/or written contracts that the contract only obligates the third party and the prospective corporation. Some courts view the preincorporation contract as a continuing offer from the third party to the corporation that becomes binding only after ratification or adoption. This underscores the promoter's representative capacity. The third party's right to withdraw before ratification may be limited, particularly in preincorporation stock subscriptions, as discussed later in this chapter.

Where the negotiation or contract is unclear on whether the corporation is bound, the third party can hold the promoter liable. For example, the promoter is liable if the corporation is never formed or never ratifies. Courts use several theories to hold promoters liable: the promoter's implied warranty of authority, an implied warranty of formation and ratification, the promoter is equivalent to a surety or guarantor, or the promoter is the only other party named in the contract. However, the corporation must indemnify or reimburse the promoter for contract benefits the corporation retains if the promoter is held liable. The following case illustrates how the promoter's liability is contingent on the third party's understanding of the obligation.

COOPERS & LYBRAND v. FOX
758 P.2d 683 (Colo. Ct. App. 1988)

Gary Fox was in the process of promoting a corporation, to be named G. Fox and Partners. Before the formal incorporation, Gary negotiated a tax and accounting services contract with Coopers & Lybrand, a national accounting firm. Coopers understood that the corporation was not yet in existence. There was no specific agreement between Coopers and Fox concerning Fox's personal liability to pay Coopers for the services. After Coopers completed its work on the Fox contract, it billed ''Mr. Gary Fox, Fox and Partners, Inc.'' Coopers sued Gary Fox individually after neither he nor the corporation paid the Coopers bill. Coopers appealed a trial court finding that Fox had no personal promoter liability to pay Coopers its fee.

KELLEY, Chief Judge

The uncontroverted facts placed Fox squarely within the definition of a promoter. A promoter is one who alone or with others, undertakes to form a corporation and to procure for it the rights, instrumentalities, and capital to enable it to conduct business. As a general rule, promoters are personally liable for the contract they make, although made on behalf of a corporation yet to be formed. A well recognized exception to the general rule of promoter liability is that if the contracting party knows the corporation is not in existence but nevertheless agrees to look solely to the corporation and not to the promoter for payment, then the promoter incurs no personal liability. The existence of an agreement to release the promoter from liability may also be shown by circumstances making it reasonably certain that the parties intended to and did enter into the agreement. Release of the promoter depends on the intent of the parties. The promoter has the burden of proving an alleged agreement to release.

Fox seeks to bring himself within the exception of the general rule of promoter liability. However, as the proponent of the exception, he must bear the burden of proving the existence of the alleged agreement releasing him from liability. There was no agreement regarding Fox's liability. Thus, Fox failed to sustain his burden of proof, and the trial court erred in granting judgment in his favor. The judgment is reversed.

Case Questions

1. What is the primary issue in determining a promoter's personal liability on preincorporation contracts?

2. What reasons support holding the promoter liable for preincorporation contracts for which no release has been given?

3. What fact in the *Coopers* case might support Fox's argument of an implied release from the activities of Coopers?

Third-Party Liability

Third parties are generally bound on preincorporation contracts even before the corporation ratifies. If the corporation is never formed or it rejects the contract, the third party is seldom held liable directly to the promoter. Generally, the corporation alone has the right to enforce preincorporation contracts. However, if the corporation is never formed, some courts permit the promoter to enforce a contract that was not clearly made directly with the prospective corporation. For example, Carl could enforce a lease negotiated with the landlord if Carl signed the lease individually, not as a promoter, and InvestigatCo was never formed.

CORPORATE POWERS

The charter defines the breadth of activities that a corporation may undertake. **Corporate powers** define the corporation's allowable purposes that can limit or enable the corporation to undertake activities. It defines the methods the corporation may use to implement these purposes. The corporate purpose clause was used quite extensively in the 19th century to *limit* corporate powers. At that time, society generally distrusted large aggregations of capital, such as corporations. Until the New Deal, the laissez-faire theory effectively limited the states from closely regulating business. The U.S. Constitution was strictly interpreted to deny states much power to regulate commerce. State regulation was viewed both as a taking of private property without just compensation and as an undue interference with the freedom of contract.

Eventually the federal government and the states began to regulate corporations. Coincidentally, the more ''liberal'' states passed incorporation statutes that authorized incorporation for ''any lawful purpose.'' Corporate charters may be worded to either broaden or narrow corporate powers. When the corporation acts within its express or implied powers, the action is permitted and deemed **intra vires**. Corporate actions outside the permissible range are unlawful and **ultra vires**. Most corporate statutes automatically grant numerous powers the corporation may exercise unless limited in the charter.

In addition to the powers expressed in the charter and/or corporate statutes, the courts have added powers that are implied as necessary to implement powers expressed or as necessary to accomplish the corporation's goals. This implication is similar to the implication of additional powers for an agent. Most modern corporations were incorporated after the liberalization of corporate purposes, making implied corporate powers important only for corporations with older or intentionally restrictive charters.

Ultra Vires

Before the states liberalized the grants of corporate power, the corporation could escape liability for crimes, torts, or contracts under the ultra vires doctrine if the act was not authorized in the corporate charter. Some decisions permitted third parties to renege on a contract if the subject matter was beyond the corporation's specifically granted powers. However, modern decisions and corporation statutes now restrict the ultra vires doctrine to shareholder suits brought to enjoin a corporation from the imminent commission of an ultra vires act. Neither the corporation nor the third party may raise ultra vires as a defense to a breach of contract. The ultra vires doctrine also retains some vitality for close corporations with charters that impose restrictions on lawful activities. Such restrictions may be designed to keep a close corporation's operations within a narrow range of activities. The law today generally permits corporations to participate in what was formerly ultra vires: the guarantee of the debts of others, making charitable contributions, and participating in joint ventures or partnerships.

Permissible Corporate Powers

Perpetual duration.

Sue and be sued.

Use corporate seal.

Adopt and amend bylaws.

Purchase, receive, lease, and use property.

Sell, mortgage, lease, and dispose of property.

Purchase, hold, sell, and so on investment securities.

Make and enforce contracts.

Borrow money and incur liabilities.

Lend money and invest.

Receive and hold personal property as collateral security.

Participate as promoter, partner, member, or associate.

Conduct business within or without the state.

Elect directors and appoint officers, employees, and agents.

Pay pensions and operate profit sharing plans.

Make donations for public welfare, charitable, scientific, and educational purposes.

Transact business to aid governmental policy.

Make payments or donations to further the business.

RMBCA § 3.02.

FOREIGN CORPORATIONS

Domestic corporations are at home in the state that chartered them. **Foreign corporations** are chartered in another state; **alien corporations** are chartered in another nation. For example, a Pennsylvania corporation is domestic while operating in Pennsylvania, it is a foreign corporation when operating in Maryland, Ohio, or Illinois, and it is an alien corporation when operating in France. Since the 1839 Supreme Court case of *Bank of Augusta v. Earle*,[8] a corporation has had "no existence out of the boundaries of the sovereignty by which it was created." Because corporations are artificial entities created by law, they can exist only where that law operates. Outside that state, they have no legal existence. Of course, strict adherence to this principle would impose costly duplication of incorporations in all the states where a multistate business operated. The Commerce Clause of the U.S. Constitution prohibits state laws from unduly burdening interstate commerce. Therefore, to avoid this burden, the states must license out-of-state corporations, permitting these foreign corporations to "qualify," become "domesticated," and thereby legally "do business."

Doing Business

The U.S. Constitution's Due Process Clause forbids states from imposing its laws and jurisdiction over out-of-state persons or corporations unless there were sufficient **minimum contacts** within the state. The prominent case of *International Shoe v. State of Washington*[9] requires a balancing of the inconvenience in being subjected to another state's law with the amount of contact the corporation had within that state. Jurisdiction is imposed on the corporation only when this does not "offend traditional notions of fair play and substantial justice." Before a state's so-called long-arm statute may be validly used to exercise jurisdiction over a defendant corporation, it must have purposefully availed itself of the privilege of conducting activities within the state, thus evoking the benefits and protections of that state's law. Additionally, domesticated corporations must have agents located within the state who are designated to receive service of process. Many corporations have assets located within the state that can be attached to satisfy money judgments against the corporation. Corporations doing business within the state must be domesticated.

Many domestication statutes do not directly define **doing business**. Rather, doing business is defined negatively in statutory lists and court decisions saying what is *not* considered doing business. In

[8]*Bank of Augusta v. Earle,* 38 U.S. 519 (1839).

[9]*International Shoe v. State of Washington,* 326 U.S. 310 (1945).

most states, a foreign corporation may do the following activities without requiring domestication: bring or defend suit or arbitration, hold shareholder or director meetings, maintain bank accounts, process transfers or make deposits of its corporate securities, sell goods through local independent contractors, solicit purchases of goods by phone or mail, solicit purchases of goods by traveling sales agents if the order is accepted outside the state, collect or secure debts, passively own real estate, or conduct isolated transactions. Case law has generally established that a foreign corporation is doing business in another state where it maintains permanent offices and facilities, warehouses goods, accepts contracts, performs contracts, ships goods from or to its location within that state, builds, installs, or repairs property within the state, or where it purchases, operates, and sells real estate within the state. The following case illustrates how doing business is negatively defined.

HERVISH v. GROWABLES, INC.
449 So.2d 684 (La. Ct. App. 1984)

Deborah Hervish was a resident of Florida until August 1982, when she moved to Louisiana. Prior to her departure, Hervish became interested in a line of children's furniture manufactured by Growables, Inc., a Florida corporation. Before leaving Florida, Hervish placed an order for approximately $2,600 worth of Growables furniture and left a $2,000 deposit toward the total purchase price. Growables agreed to ship the furniture to Louisiana, although delivery was delayed. When the furniture eventually arrived, Hervish paid the Ryder truck driver the balance she owed plus shipping charges totalling almost $900. Nearly all the furniture had been damaged and Hervish was unsuccessful in getting resolution either from Ryder or Growables. Hervish sued Growables in Louisiana courts, but the trial court granted Growables' motion to dismiss the suit.

CHEHARDY, Judge

A court may exercise personal jurisdiction over a nonresident, who acts directly or by an agent, as to a cause of action arising from the nonresident's:

(a) Transacting any business in the state;
(b) Contracting or to supply services or things in the state;
(c) Causing injury or damage by an offense or quasi-offense committed through an act or omission in this state;
(d) Causing injury or damage in this state by an offense or quasi-offense committed through an act or omission outside of this state, if he regularly does or solicits business, or engages in any other persistent course of conduct, or derives substantial revenue from goods used or consumed or services rendered in this state.

In order for the proper exercise of jurisdiction over a nonresident, there must be sufficient minimum contacts between the nonresident defendant and the forum state to satisfy due process and traditional notions or fair play and substantial justice. It is essential in each case that there be some act by which the defendant purposefully avails itself of the privilege of conducting activities within the state, thus evoking the benefits and protections of its law. Knowledge alone or foreseeability that property will come to rest in a particular state is insufficient to subject a defendant to jurisdiction, unless the facts or circumstances lead to a conclusion that a defendant purposefully availed itself of the privilege of conducting activities with clear notice that it would be subject to suit there.

At the time Ms. Hervish ordered the furniture, she was a Florida resident. She obtained a brochure advertising the furniture in Florida; she went personally to the Growables office in Florida to place the order. The only incidents that took place in Louisiana are Ms. Hervish's calls to Growables to question the delay in shipment, the delivery — through a third party truck — of the furniture into the state, and Ms. Hervish's payment of the balance of the purchase price to the truck driver upon delivery.

There is no evidence that Growables transacts any business in Louisiana, that its representatives or agents travel to Louisiana for business purposes, or that it advertises or otherwise solicits business in Louisiana or from Louisiana residents, either directly or by mail. There is no evidence that Growables derives any substantial revenue from business in Louisiana, or ''engages in any persistent course of conduct'' in this state. We can find no other case in which a Louisiana court has found an isolated incident of delivery, without other affiliating circumstances, sufficient to provoke long arm jurisdiction to a foreign corporation. This single transaction would not justify our concluding that Growables purposely availed itself of the privilege of conducting activities within Louisiana. Judgment affirmed.

Case Questions

1. What is the issue in finding that a foreign corporation is doing business in another state?
2. What reasons support Louisiana withholding its jurisdiction over a foreign corporation that arguably damaged one of Louisiana's citizens?
3. What ambiguities in interstate commerce reinforce this doing business problem?

Under the domestication requirement, foreign corporations must register in all states in which they intend to be doing business to enjoy the same rights as domestic corporations to have access to their courts and the protections of all their laws. The corporation must apply for a **certificate of authority** issued by the secretary of state, register and maintain an office and agent in the state, pay annual fees, and file an annual report in many states. Unregistered foreign corporations doing business in another state may be assessed penalties, their officers may be separately assessed penalties, and shareholders may lose their limited liability. A few states deny enforcement to contracts made by an undomesticated corporation.

The taxation of a foreign corporation's profits derived from in-state activities presents a related question of each state's jurisdictional powers. This is a highly controversial issue because corporations locate production facilities to minimize taxes, while state governments seek to collect every legitimate tax dollar. It is often difficult to separate the precise proportion of value added to products partially produced in foreign states from the value added in some other taxing state. Multinational corporations raise similar problems when they spread activities in various nations: design, component part manufacture, final assembly, administration, advertising, and marketing. Critics allege that Japanese transplant auto manufacturing subsidiaries pay little or no income tax in the United States because they willingly pay high component part prices to the parent firm's foreign suppliers. This effectively transfers taxable profits out of the United States and back to Japan. Is this ethical or politically advisable?

CAPITAL STRUCTURE

Corporations must finance the acquisition of productive assets and the firm's continuing operations. The firm's securities, usually comprised of stocks and bonds, usually represent the initial financing, and these are used episodically for extraordinary financing. However, more broadly considered, the mix of a firm's ownership, control, and financial rights represents its **capital structure**. This can be composed of various sources of funds and credit: publicly offered stocks and bonds, privately placed securities, loans and lines of credit from banks, trade credits, accounts receivable financing (factoring), field warehousing, inventory financing, leasing, installment purchases, sales and leasebacks, profits from investments and speculation, and self-financing through retained earnings.

Corporations often select their mix of financing by historical accident, market conditions, the availability of collateral, and tax incentives. So long as debt interest payments remain tax deductible to the corporation and are taxed only when paid to the creditor, the optimization of capital structure suggests holding at least some debt. Dividend distributions on equity are subject to the so-called double tax on dividends. Corporate income from operations is taxed first as corporate profit, then a second time when distributed to shareholders as their individual income. The IRS assumes corporations that retain ''excessive'' earnings are attempting to avoid this double tax. Therefore, the IRS can penalize excessive retentions with a third retained earnings tax on these undistributed retentions. This is intended to provide an incentive to raise dividend payouts.

Stock

Corporate **stock** is the quintessential security, representing a contract between the corporation and its owners, who are called **stockholders** or **shareholders**. Shares of stock represent a bundle of rights to own, vote, receive dividends, and claim the residual value of the corporation after liquidation. Stock is intangible personal property that can be bought and sold, used as collateral for loans, or transferred by gift, will, or descent. The shareholder's specific mix of preferences in voting, dividends, and liquidation value can be varied to create several different classes of stock.

Common Stock

Common stock is the most universal type, because all corporations must have at least one class of stock with unlimited voting privileges. Common stock is junior to other more senior securities because other securities usually have preferences over common in dividends or interest and in liquidation. Common shares may be issued in several classes, each having a separate bundle of rights. For example, General Motors created Class E common stock to exchange for Electronic Data Systems (EDS) stock held by EDS's former shareholders. Series E dividends are tied to profits made solely by GM's EDS division. Within any class of security, there can be different **series** typically issued at different times. Series are distinguished by only minor variations in the dividend or interest rate, sinking funds, or redemption or conversion privileges.

Fractional shares, or **scrip**, are less than a whole share and usually result from reverse stock splits. For example, if Carl and Claudia recapitalize the 1,000 InvestigatCo shares in a 1 for 2 reverse stock split, there may be some former holders of an odd number of shares who receive only 1/2 share for their odd shares. Corporations usually have the power to repurchase scrip because the scrip imposes administrative burdens. Scrip holders must combine their fractional shares to exercise a vote or receive dividends.

Preferred Stock

Stock issued with preferences over common stock is called **preferred stock**. Unlike common stock, there are no inherent rights in preferred stock except as stated on the certificates, in offering documents (e.g., a prospectus), in the corporate charter or bylaws, and in board resolutions authorizing the issue. Preferred stock has only the preferences specifically stated, usually a preference over common stock to receive a specified dividend and a preference in liquidation or bankruptcy. Preferred dividends are usually stated as a dollar amount or a percentage of the preferred's stated value per share. However, preferred dividends could be computed under more complex formulae such as a percentage of profits above some level and possibly some portion paid from a particular source. **Participating preferred** can be designed to receive variable income from the surplus remaining after or with payment of common dividends.

Preferred dividends are generally discretionary by vote of the board, although there can be mandatory preferred dividends. Preferred can be designated as **cumulative preferred,** entitling the shareholder to receive all dividends missed in prior years before common shareholders are paid anything. **Noncumulative preferred** shareholders forfeit the dividends omitted in prior years. **Cumulative if earned preferred stock** entitles each shareholder to dividend priority only if earnings were sufficient to pay the dividend in the prior year but the board failed to declare dividends.

Redemption and Convertibility

Some classes of preferred stock or bonds may have special provisions that permit the exchange of the shares for cash or other securities. **Convertible** securities give the security holder the right to exchange the security for some other security. Many issues of preferred stock and debenture bonds include a conversion privilege permitting holders to exchange their senior securities for common stock. This privilege may be triggered by an event or may exist only during a specified time period. Conversion is advantageous when the price of common rises above the senior security price or a corporate control contest is expected and the voting power of common stock is desired to approve or oppose a takeover. The price of convertible securities often closely parallels the converted security.

The corporation may have a **redemption** right to convert an outstanding security into cash or into some other security. This requires that a **call** provision be included in the bylaws or articles and stated directly on the security certificates. For example, many corporations paid high interest rates on their junk (high yield) bonds. Most such corporations were well advised to reserve a right to recall them by prepaying the principal and terminating the high associated interest expense. Preferred stock may also be redeemable, convertible, neither, or both.

Bonds

Bonds are debt securities evidencing the obligation to repay the principal at a fixed future date and pay interest for the use of the principal. Bonds are classified by their income, term structure, purpose, and collateral. **Variable rate bonds** have an interest rate pegged to some index of market rates. **Participating bonds** permit bondholders a variable return depending on the corporation's income. **Commercial paper** is short-term debt usually maturing within 90 days; the proceeds are used for commercial purposes (cash flow), and issuance is usually exempt from SEC registration. **Purchase money** securities are usually issued for funds used to purchase significant assets, such as machinery, a plant, or particular equipment (railroad cars or airliners). The proceeds from **refunding securities** are used to roll over old debt.

Debentures are unsecured bonds without any provision to create any lien to secure the loan with particular collateral. By contrast, **mortgage bonds** are typically secured with collateral. Even if the bonds are not protected by collateral, there are often other security provisions in the **trust indenture**, the master debt contract administered by an independent third party, the **indenture trustee**.

In addition to bondholders' contractual senior status ahead of stockholders for repayment in liquidation or bankruptcy, the bond indenture typically includes other repayment assurances such as sinking fund provisions and dividend restrictions. A **sinking fund** requires the corporation to make periodic partial principal payments into the sinking fund to accumulate a source for repayment of the bond principal at the maturity date. Other restrictions may prohibit the payment of dividends if bond interest payments are in default or if the corporation gets into precarious financial condition. The indenture trustee is responsible to ensure that the corporation obeys these indenture requirements. Some bonds receive additional security from independent guarantors such as a government, another corporation, or an insurer.

Stocks and Bonds Compared

Most corporations have some mix of both stock and bonds in their capital structure. However, the line separating the two is not always clear, particularly as financial engineers invent new and innovative securities. The difference emerges primarily when stock-like securities are designated as bonds to avoid the double tax on dividends. The following case illustrates this dilemma. Consider the court's discussion that a primary feature of equity is voting. Some observers note that the voting control aspects of equity and debt are reversed in some other nations. For example, in Japan, major creditors exert considerable control over management and often tolerate default on payments, while Japanese equityholders are typically inactive in management. Figure 40–4 summarizes the differences between stock and bonds.

JOHN KELLEY CO. v. COMMISSIONER
326 U.S.521 (1946)

Two cases, *Kelley* and *Talbot Mills,* are consolidated here to explore the difference between debt and equity under the Internal Revenue Code. In *Kelley,* the family-owned corporation was reorganized when $250,000 of income debenture bearer bonds were offered only to existing shareholders. These debentures were payable in 20 years, with interest at 8 percent noncumulative; interest payments could be missed if net income was insufficient. The debenture holders had priority over stockholders but were subordinated to other creditors. The bonds were redeemable at the corporation's option and the holders had no voting rights. The majority of debentures were issued in exchange for the original preferred stock. Common stock was owned in the same proportion by the same stockholders before and after the recapitalization.

Figure 40–4   Debt versus Equity

Characteristic	Common Stock	Preferred Stock	Bonds
Type of Claim	Equity	Equity	Debt
Security Holder's Status	Owner	Owner	Creditor
Taxable as Corporate Income	Yes	Yes	No
Corporate Duty to Pay Income	Only after board vote	If stipulated, otherwise after board vote	Yes, unless stipulated otherwise
Fixed or Variable Income Payments	Variable	Generally, fixed but variable portion possible if stipulated	Generally, fixed but variable if stipulated
Fixed Maturity Date	No	Generally, no	Yes
Right to Vote	Yes	No unless stipulated or extraordinary event	No
Preference: Income	No	Yes, over common	Yes, over equity
Preference: Liquidation and Bankruptcy	No	Yes, over common	Yes, over equity
Cumulative Payments Missed in Prior Year	No	Yes, if specified	Yes
Lien on Collateral	No	No	If stipulated
Preemptive Rights	If stipulated	Generally, no	No

The *Talbot Mills* case involved a corporation that recapitalized its 5,000 shares of common stock, which were mostly held by members of the Talbot family. Stockholders surrendered four fifths of their stock and took registered notes in exchange. Four hundred thousand dollars in notes were issued to existing shareholders, bearing annual interest at rates not to exceed 10 percent and not to fall under 2 percent. The actual interest rate was subject to net earnings in the previous year. These notes could not be transferred except to the company, interest was cumulative, and dividends could not be paid on the remaining stock until interest on the notes was first paid. The note indenture limited the corporation right to mortgage its assets, but the notes could be subordinated by the corporate board.

Opinion of the court by REED, Justice

The corporations in both cases deducted the payments as interest from their reports of gross income. The commissioner of the IRS asserted deficiencies because the payments were considered dividends and not interest. It is reasonably possible to conclude that the secured annual payments were interest to creditors in one case and dividends to stockholders in the other case. In the *Kelley* case, there were sales of the debentures as well as the exchanges of preferred stock for debentures, a promise to pay a certain annual amount, if earned, a priority for the debentures over common stock, the debentures were assignable without regard to any transfer of stock, and a definite maturity date in the reasonable future was stated. These are indicia of indebtedness and support the tax court conclusion that the annual payments were interest on indebtedness. On the other hand, in *Talbot Mills* case, the tax court found the factors were present of fluctuating annual payments with a 2 percent minimum, the limitation of the issue of notes [only] to stockholders in exchange only for stock, to be characteristics which distinguish the *Talbot Mills* notes from the *Kelley* debentures. The tax court reached the conclusion that the annual payments by *Talbot Mills* were in reality dividends and not interest.

The documents under consideration embody elements of obligations and elements of stock. There is no one characteristic, not even exclusion from management, which can be said to be decisive in the determination of whether the obligations are risk investments in the corporations or debts. So-called stock certificates may be authorized by corporations which are really debts, and promises to pay may be executed which have incidents of stock. This leads us to affirm the *Talbot Mills* decree and to reverse the *Kelley* judgment.

Case Questions

1. What is the central issue in distinguishing debt from equity?
2. What reasons were used to find that the *Talbot Mills* notes were disguised equity?
3. What features of the *Kelley* debentures made them legitimate debt?

Other Securities

The investment markets have seen a proliferation of new investment vehicles in recent years. Generally, those issued by corporations are classified as securities and are regulated by the SEC. Securities may represent the right to buy or sell another "underlying" security some time in the future or after an event occurs. These are generally referred to as **options**. **Puts** permit the option holder to sell (or *put*) a security to the put issuer at a specified price. **Call** options permit the holder to purchase a specified security (or *call* it) from the issuer in the future at a specified price. For example, an XYZ Corp. call might entitle the holder to purchase 100 shares of XYZ Corp. from the option issuer at $50 per share some time within the next year. The issuer stands to profit by the call fee if XYZ stays below $50 but stands to lose an unlimited amount if XYZ rises above $50 within a year. Corporations often issue **stock options** to their upper management as part of incentive or deferred compensation plans. Separate securities firms issue standardized stock options that trade on the securities exchanges to enable other investors to speculate in the price movements of a corporation's stock without actually owning the underlying corporate stock.

Warrants are a type of certificated option that are often included as part of a package of other securities used in merger and acquisition transactions. They are usually issued by the corporation issuing the underlying security and trade on the public securities markets. **Rights** generally refer to short-term options that may be transferable in the public securities markets.

Specialized securities with profitability tied to macroeconomic factors, indexes, commodities or futures prices, or baskets of securities are usually not considered securities. These are often called **derivatives**. Derivatives may be separately regulated by the commodities regulators. Problems of differentiating securities and derivatives are detailed in Chapter 44.

Stock Subscriptions

When a corporation plans to sell stock for the first time, it enters into contracts with prospective investors to issue them the stock in the future. These prospective contracts are usually made in writing and are called **stock subscriptions**. Promoters sell **preincorporation subscriptions,** which are stock subscriptions used for the initial financing of a new incorporation. These create special obligations, which are discussed in the next section. Subscriptions are also made by existing corporations to provide new financing. These are **postincorporation subscriptions,** which are governed by traditional principles of offer and acceptance under contract law. When an enforceable postincorporation subscription contract is accepted, the subscriber becomes a shareholder with all the attendant rights even if the corporation fails to actually issue the stock as promised.

Preincorporation Subscriptions

For the incorporation to be successful, the promoter must assemble a sufficient amount of enforceable commitments from share subscribers to accumulate the minimum funds the new business needs to start operations. The subscriber becomes a shareholder only after the corporation is validly formed, the board accepts the subscription authorizing the issuance of the shares, and the subscriber pays for the new shares. Even if the corporation thereafter fails to actually issue the stock, the subscriber obtains the rights of a shareholder.

The prospective corporation would have great difficulty forming if numerous subscribers pulled out before the minimally sufficient capital was assembled. Therefore, most states' corporation statutes make stock subscriptions irrevocable for six months, although the time varies in some states between three months and one year. There is a similar outcome in a few states under a cross-consideration theory that assumes all subscribers make their investment in reliance on each other, so each promise is enforceable. A subscriber may be held liable for any unpaid portion if the subscription is breached. By contrast, the corporation is not bound to issue stock to subscribers until after formation, when the board deliberately sets the subscription price and adopts the preincorporation subscriptions. Subscribers obtain the rights of shareholders only after full payment for the shares.

Authorization and Issuance

Corporations may validly issue new stock only if there are **authorized shares** in the charter. When first incorporated, the new charter must state the total amount of authorized stock. Later in a corporation's life, further stock sales may be contemplated, but an insufficient number of shares may still be authorized if most are already issued. A charter amendment requiring shareholder approval is necessary to increase the number of authorized shares. Unauthorized stock sales are considered void. Many incorporators predict the corporation may have later financing needs, so they authorize more shares than needed at first. This provides flexibility for later financing needs, declaration of stock dividends, issuing stock options, the conversion of other securities, or the making of acquisitions.

After authorized shares are sold to investors, they become **issued**. Shares repurchased by the corporation from shareholders are called **treasury shares**. These cannot be voted by management nor are dividends paid on treasury shares. However, like authorized shares, treasury shares may be sold without shareholder reauthorization. **Outstanding shares** are those held by shareholders. Therefore, treasury shares are authorized, issued, but not currently outstanding. **Unissued shares** are authorized but have never been sold to investors a first time. Treasury stock may be canceled, whereupon it again becomes authorized but unissued stock. The distinction between treasury stock and authorized but unissued stock is eliminated in the RMBCA. Corporations usually retain a bank or stock registrar to oversee stock issuance to prevent any overissue.

Consideration for Shares

Corporation law has historically regulated the consideration paid for shares, both in form and amount. These laws were intended to set some minimum corporate capital to protect creditors by requiring maintenance of a minimum of valuable assets. Most states required the corporation to establish a minimum **par value** per share that aggregates to become the corporation's **stated capital** (Stated capital = Issued shares × Par value). The par value is fixed in the charter and printed on the stock certificates. Any change requires a shareholder vote. Most corporations sell stock for more than par. The excess received is recorded in an account called either **capital surplus** or **capital contributed in excess of par**. Shares may not be sold for less than par, and no dividends may be paid out of stated capital.

The par value concept is an anachronism. Many corporations spend all the capital raised by issuing shares, so the fiction that some minimum capital was lying around at the corporation to satisfy creditors was an illusion. Stated capital really only states a historical event. Today, most states permit issuance of low par or **no-par stock,** eliminating par as a restriction on corporate financial management. Delaware and a few other states require the corporate board to fix a **stated value** that aggregates to the stated capital account. Stated value must reflect the value of consideration received for no-par shares.

Watered Stock

Stock may be paid for with money, labor performed, personal property, real property, or intangibles (registered patent, trademark, or copyright). Issued shares must be fully paid for. Unsecured promissory notes or promises of future services are illegal as consideration. Shares are void and may be canceled if paid for with an illegal consideration. However, promoters who performed legitimate preincorporation activities may receive stock for their services. While stock may not be issued as a gift, employee stock ownership plans (ESOPs) and executive stock options are permissible.

Shares sold below par or for an inadequate consideration are considered **watered stock** because they dilute the corporation's capital. The initial shareholder-subscriber who purchased the shares is liable for the watered stock as if it were an unpaid subscription. Creditors may sue shareholders participating in the watering based on the theory that the consideration for shares constitutes a *trust fund* for creditors. Alternatively, creditors who relied on the corporation's stated capital in making loans may sue shareholders under a *misrepresentation theory.* Shareholders who purchase their shares later are not liable unless they knew of the watering or participated in it.

Nonmonetary property used to pay for shares must be valued in good faith. Although most states presume the board acts in good faith in valuing property exchanged for shares, there is liability if the property is intentionally overvalued. In some states, shareholders are liable for any watered value if the property is worth less than the value stated when that shareholder transferred the property for shares. With the predominance of no-par stock, these matters are of decreasing importance. Shares may be sold for the best price obtainable, and expenses for underwriting and promotion may be deducted.

Stock Transfers

In addition to the state and federal securities laws discussed in Chapter 44, there are two major state laws that govern the issuance and transfer of the actual stock certificates of publicly traded and closely held corporations. The state corporate law that governs enforceability of transfer restrictions is discussed in the next section. This section discusses Article 8 of the UCC, effective in all states.

Article 8 has a parallel structure to Articles 3 and 4, which govern commercial paper and bank deposits. Article 8 establishes the regime for negotiation, indorsement, and transfer of stock certificates. Securities may be either **certificated,** if evidenced by a written instrument, or **uncertificated,** if represented by a book entry maintained by the issuer or by its separate transfer agent. **Registered** securities name the owner specifically. **Bearer securities** are transferred without indorsement by transfer of possession, so they are always certificated. In some European nations, bearer bonds are still a popular investment device. They are now illegal in the United States because of the difficulties in tracing and taxing them.

Article 8 requires a corporation to transfer the record ownership of securities when sold by a former security holder. If the corporation overissued shares beyond its authorized capitalization, it must either purchase similar shares or pay their value plus interest to the aggrieved shareholder. Security certificates are *negotiated* either by *indorsement* to the buyer or *in blank* when held in a **street name** by a brokerage or its agent. This latter option facilitates collateralizing margin loans, permits loaning the securities to short sellers, and facilitates quick trading by speculators.

Shares must be registered if transferred to a **bona fide purchaser (BFP)** who received them in good faith and without notice of adverse claims. An adverse claim might be that the shares were wrongfully transferred out of a trust operated for the claimant's benefit or were transferred in violation of a transfer restriction. The corporation must replace securities that the registered owner has lost or that were damaged or stolen unless a bona fide purchaser requests registration first. Article 8 provides for reclamation of securities wrongfully transferred. It also implies warranties by all intermediate transferees that the transferor rightfully transferred the securities, each was a BFP, and no forged endorsements were made. Uncertificated securities are used increasingly to reduce the costs of negotiation and the risks of holding the actual certificates.

Transfer Restrictions

The free transferability of investment securities may be limited by a **transfer restriction** if valid under state law. Transfer restrictions serve several purposes: (1) they help maintain control within a small group of owner-managers in a closely held corporation and thereby exclude outsiders, (2) they help maintain an election to be treated as a statutory close corporation, (3) they help maintain a Subchapter S election for favorable partnership income taxation treatment, and (4) they help preserve a transaction exemption from registration under the Securities Act of 1933 (e.g., private placement). Additionally, some transfer restrictions obligate the corporation or other shareholders to purchase the seller's shares, enhancing the shares' marketability. Transfer restrictions are generally valid if imposed before the stock is issued. In addition, they must be reasonable, and they must be printed conspicuously on the security certificate.

There are several types of transfer restrictions. The **right of first refusal** prohibits the holder from reselling the shares without first making them available to the corporation or to other shareholders. The price is usually one offered to the shareholder or is mutually negotiated. A purchase price may be fixed in advance by an **option agreement** or defined in a pricing formula reflecting such measures as book value, capitalized expected future earnings, an independent appraisal, and/or other measures. A **consent restraint** requires permission of the board or other shareholders before the sale. Specific persons may be restricted from purchase, such as competitors. The **buy-sell** agreement obligates the corporation or other shareholders to purchase at a predefined or formula price after a specified event occurs (e.g., death of shareholder, employee termination). The following case illustrates that courts enforce transfer restrictions only as far as clearly indicated.

IN RE ESTATE OF SPAZIANI
480 N.Y.S.2d 854 (N.Y. Surr. Ct. 1984)

The heirs of Vincent Spaziani demanded that the administrator of Spaziani's estate distribute to them in equal shares the stock he held in the corporation Spaziani Bakeries, Inc. When initially incorporated, Spaziani Bakeries had five original subscriber shareholders, who each took stock certificates with the following transfer restriction printed thereon: "No certificate of stock or any interest therein in this corporation shall be transferred . . . until it has first been offered for sale . . . to this corporation." Spaziani Bakeries, Inc., argued the stock transfer restriction should be enforced, thereby requiring the estate administrator to first offer the stock for sale back to the corporation. The trial court denied the request of Spaziani Bakeries, Inc., and distributed the stock to the heirs. Spaziani Bakeries, Inc., appealed.

GILBERT, Judge

A common objective of incorporation is to guarantee and define the continuation of a family business, including the parties who are to be shareholders. Clauses are inserted into the certificate of incorporation to accomplish this objective. However, draftsmen must pay particular attention to the language used if it is to be binding upon the estate of deceased shareholder.

Stockholders have basic ownership rights to stock, including the right to dispose of it as self-interest dictates. A closed corporation generally will seek to define or limit such right of disposition in its certificate of incorporation. One of the common methods of limiting such right of disposition is by requiring stockholders to offer the stock first to the corporation or by giving it a right of refusal, before transferring the stock to another party. Therefore, there has evolved in the law a general principle that the courts will uphold and enforce restrictions on a stockholder's right of disposition of his stock, if reasonable and for a valid business purpose. A first option restricting, or right of first refusal, on behalf of the corporation or other stockholders has been determined to be a reasonable and valid business purpose. Consequently, such a clause has been adopted by the incorporators of Spaziani Bakeries, Inc., herein, and is valid and enforceable.

The draftsmen of such a clause must be very careful if it is the intention of the incorporators to bind the estate of a stockholder with such a clause. In order to bind the estate the restriction must not only be reasonable but must also be clearly expressed as intended to bind the estate. Such restrictions are limited by the principle "that death would not be presumed to trigger the operation of a repurchase option which did not mention death as a specified contingency." If the certificate of incorporation specifically excludes stock passing by will or intestacy, the restrictive clause will not be applicable by such passage by will or intestacy. If silent as to the contingency of death such a restrictive clause is not valid and enforceable against the estate.

Therefore, the administratrix herein is not required to offer the stock back to the corporation. She may distribute it in kind to the distributee of Vincent Spaziani, since the contingency of death was not specifically referred to in a certificate of incorporation.

Case Questions

1. What is the issue in holding stock transfer restrictions applicable to the estate of a deceased shareholder?

2. Are there other transferees of corporate stock restricted by a transfer restriction who might not be subject to the restriction unless the restriction is worded broadly enough to include them?

3. What is assumed by the rule announced in the *Spaziani* case concerning the incorporators' intent, and can they include stock transfer restrictions in the certificate of incorporation?

END–OF–CHAPTER PROBLEMS

1. Compare and contrast all the situations under corporate law when there may be liability of corporate participants beyond their initial investment.

2. What was the rationale underlying the limitation of corporate powers in their charters? Why has this rationale evolved and what is the resulting situation concerning the breadth of corporate powers today?

3. Compare and contrast the two major types of corporate securities used in the capital structure of most corporations: debt versus equity. What is a major reason corporations use both types of financing?

4. There is a general theory in the common law that restrictions against alienation (restricting sales) are disfavored. Generally, a restriction will be enforced only where it is justified by some more pressing purpose. Transfer restrictions limiting the sale of stock have been prohibited for this reason. What reasons might justify the enforceability of stock transfer restrictions?

5. Carlton owned the stock in 10 corporations, each of which owned two taxi cabs operating in the New York City area. Each taxi had only the minimum $10,000 liability insurance. Walkovsky sued Carlton when injured by a taxi owned by Seon Cab, one of Carlton's companies. Walkovsky sought to pierce the corporate veil to hold Carlton personally liable for the amount of Walkovsky's injuries that exceeded the minimum liability insurance coverage. What decision and what reasons support recognizing corporate separateness? What reasons support piercing the corporate veil? See *Walkovsky v. Carlton*, 223 N.E.2d 6 (N.Y. 1968).

6. John Thomas owned Jon-T Chemicals, Inc., which incorporated a wholly owned subsidiary, Jon-T Farms, Inc., with $10,000 of capital to lease land and operate farms. Officers, directors, administrative offices, and consultants were shared by both of the Jon-T corporations. The government sued Jon-T Chemicals to recover fraudulent agricultural subsidies

received by Jon-T Farms of over $2 million and drafts converted from the federal Commodity Credit Corporation of over a quarter million dollars. Both John Thomas and Jon-T Farms were insolvent. Should the corporate parent be liable for the liabilities of its subsidiary? What reasons would support piercing the parent corporation's veil? See *United States v. Jon-T Chemicals, Inc.*, 768 F.2d 686 (5th Cir. 1985).

7. Robertson made a contract obligating Levy to incorporate Penn. Ave. Record Shack to purchase Robertson's ongoing business. The assets were transferred but Levy's articles of incorporation were rejected by the secretary of state. Nevertheless, Levy commenced business as Penn. Ave. Record Shack and paid Robertson with a note Levy signed as president of the Penn. Ave. Record Shack. The corporation was finally formed more than a week later. Penn. Ave. discontinued business six months later after making only one payment on the debt to Robertson. Is Levy personally liable for the debts incurred when the corporate form was defective? What ambiguities are presented by situations like this? See *Robertson v. Levy*, 197 A.2d 443 (D.C. 1964).

8. The RKO company contracted to sell the Kent Theatre to Jenofsky and Graziano, the promoters of a prospective corporation to be known as Kent Enterprises, Inc. The contract stated the parties' understanding that the corporation would be formed, and if completed by the date the theatre was transferred, the parties would consider the corporation substituted for Jenofsky and Graziano. The articles of incorporation were filed before the transfer date, but RKO sought to hold the promoters personally liable. Were the promoters released from personal liability?

Under what conditions are promoters not liable for contracts they made in anticipation of incorporation? See *RKO-Stanley Warner Theatres, Inc. v. Graziano*, 355 A.2d 830 (Pa. 1976).

9. The C.C.Nut Corp., with all its facilities and its charter in Pennsylvania, conducted a direct marketing business. C.C.Nut distributed its colorful catalog of ''outdoor/woodsey'' clothing throughout the United States by mail, and customers filled orders in three ways: orders phoned in over its 800 number, orders sent by mail to the Pennsylvania warehouse, or sales made over the counter at its outlet mall store in State College, Pennsylvania. C.C.Nut had cultivated an enviable reputation nationwide for customer satisfaction, quick shipments, cheerful returns, and quality merchandise. Discuss the legal risks inherent in the following two business plans presented by the aggressive new president, Michael Craig: (1) expand operations to retail sales locations at mall stores all over the nation, (2) save costs and increase sales volume by purchasing less expensive, less durable clothing.

10. The stock of a corporation owning a fast-food restaurant was owned equally by three individuals who operated the restaurant. After a management dispute, one was ousted from employment by the other two. Thereafter, the remaining two shareholders caused the corporation to issue to themselves and to several active employees an amount of authorized but unissued new shares for $100 per share. The ousted shareholder claimed this diluted the corporate value because book value was over $250 per share and market value was over $500 per share. Was the consideration received for these shares insufficient? See *Gazda v. Kolinski*, 458 N.Y.S.2d 387 (1982).

Chapter 41

Shareholder Rights

■

CRITICAL THINKING INQUIRIES

As you read this chapter, you should be able to address the following:

- What reasons support the corporate democracy model in which shareholders, as owners of the corporation, delegate the power to manage the day-to-day corporate affairs by electing the board of directors, which in turn appoints the corporate officers who supervise the professional managers?

- How does the proxy system give corporate managers an advantage in conducting shareholder meetings through mail absentee balloting rather than permitting voting only in person? What are the advantages to shareholders of this proxy system?

- Why is the board rather than shareholders given broad discretion in declaring dividends?

- What arguments support empowering shareholders to bring litigation for the corporation's benefit? What are the opposing rival hypotheses?

- How do the assumptions about how corporate governance works differ between publicly traded and closely held corporations?

MANAGERIAL PERSPECTIVE

Carl and Claudia sold a minority interest in InvestigatCo shares to numerous outsiders. Thereafter the firm's operations changed significantly. For example, Carl and Claudia can no longer operate the corporation informally. Regular shareholder and director meetings are required, and the managing officers are then required to consider the new shareholders' opinions. Carl and Claudia recognize that having outside shareholders also requires a dispersal of the financial resources that they alone shared previously. For example, the payment of dividends and distribution of liquidation proceeds are shared pro rata. However, Carl and Claudia also now find that all shareholders equally share certain rights in common, irrespective of the proportion of their ownership in the firm. For example, any other shareholder may now inspect corporate records to ensure that Carl and Claudia are adequate stewards of corporate assets. Additionally, Carl and Claudia are exposed to shareholder derivative suits for mismanagement. These pressures now force Carl and Claudia to operate the firm to optimize additional interests other than their own personal interests.

Of course, this new focus of responsibility is not enough, standing alone, to completely alter the balance of power. Even though the minority shareholders have votes, receive dividend payments, and claim assets after liquidation in proportion to their shareholdings, Carl and Claudia's majority position still gives them the largest claim to corporate cash flow. Other shareholders who are not directors and officers may be deprived of corporate employment and its compensation. This tension sets up the potential for the oppression of minority shareholders.

- What can Carl and Claudia do to maintain power as majority shareholders, directors, and officers of InvestigatCo?

- What corporate structure, governance, and contractual arrangements could minority shareholders employ to avoid oppression by Carl and Claudia?

This chapter discusses the shareholder's "bundle of rights" represented by governance power, financial claims, and litigation preference. A balance is often drawn by law and contract between these competing interests in close corporations.

CORPORATE DEMOCRACY MODEL

The governance of all corporations, large or small, publicly traded or closely held, is based on a single corporate governance model. While this model differs somewhat by agreement and in reality, it is useful to examine its characteristics. As owners, shareholders possess a *bundle of rights* to vote, receive dividends, participate in liquidation, and monitor managers' performance. Corporate law presumes that shareholders delegate managerial control that an owner usually possesses to the board by the election of individual directors. Shareholders retain their bundle of other rights.

The board further delegates its powers to officers to manage the day-to-day corporate activities through election or selection by the board. The board retains the power to supervise and replace officers and other managers. The board also declares dividends and determines the corporation's major policies, including the proposal of any fundamental corporate changes. Officers are responsible to select, monitor, and supervise managers. Managers oversee all the remaining personnel in the conduct of corporate operations. This statutory corporate governance model is illustrated in Figure 41–1.

The corporate governance model raises numerous ethical questions for all these participants. Majority shareholders can use their position of control to exact concessions from management, force management to accept the shareholder's policies, or to grant favors to other firms related to the majority shareholder. During merger and acquisition activities, large shareholders may demand a premium value for their controlling position, at other shareholders' expense. Except when there is poor or scandalous corporate performance, management can often get away with using corporate assets for personal gain. This includes creating the appearance of pursuing corporate goals while management actually enlarges its empire and gives only mediocre performance.

The corporate governance model is intended to prevent misuses of power and breaches of fiduciary duty. An ethical analysis theme runs throughout corporate governance because it impacts shareholder rights so profoundly. However, the system may not be working so well. The American Law Institute has completed a long study of corporate governance resulting in the final report of the *Corporate Governance Project*. This document may affect management's accountability and corporate governance in the 1990s and beyond.

*Management Control Reality**

The statutory corporate governance model does not accurately reflect reality. While the more obvious formalities of this model are usually followed, the actual behavior of closely held and publicly traded corporations differ quite widely. Most close corporate shareholders are active participants on the board, in management, and in day-to-day operations. Some minority shareholders are squeezed out of any participation in control and receive minimal financial rewards. The formalities of the statutory model are a burden on many smaller close corporations, prompting some states to pass separate close corporate law provisions that relax many burdensome formalities.

The close corporate governance reality contrasts sharply with the larger publicly traded corporations. The latter have thousands of geographically dispersed shareholders. Few public shareholders also participate on the board or in management except for a few top executives through their employee stock incentive compensation plans. Sometimes, the largest blocks

*"Management Control Realty," © 1993 by John W. Bagby.

Figure 41-1   Corporate Governance Model

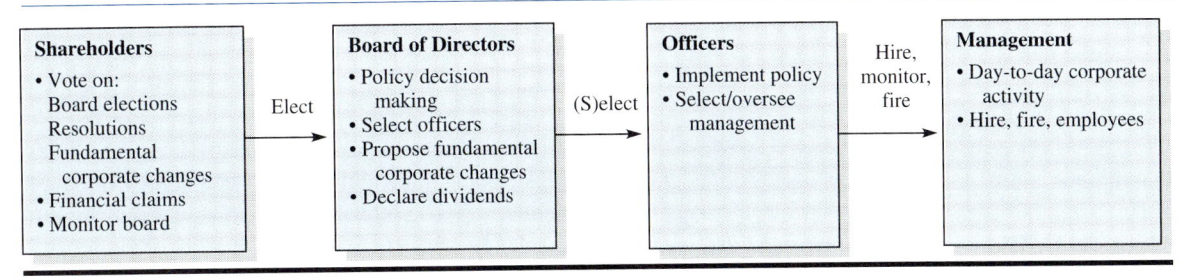

of stock are held by a few founding families, takeover financiers, and institutional investors (e.g., mutual funds, pension plans, insurance companies, and trusts).

Most corporate election decisions are made by the thousands of individual shareholders who routinely vote by proxy in favor of managements' candidates and proposals. This has permitted officers and management to perpetuate themselves in office in the overwhelming majority of cases. However, there is a trend among institutional investors to more actively monitor corporate performance by pressuring management and the board to change policies. More activist institutional investors are beginning to coordinate their proxy voting because they have threatened management with adverse votes.

Critics charge that the reality of managerial control contradicts the corporate democracy model. They argue that recent corporate scandals suggest that some modification is needed. By contrast, other observers resist changing the system, citing the **Wall Street rule**: Disgruntled shareholders should just "vote with their feet" by selling their shares. Corporate laws and the newfound shareholder activism will probably change the management control reality as dissident shareholders assemble potent groups of shareholder votes to influence management.

Thought Questions

1. Does the Wall Street rule imply that shareholder activism is misdirected?
2. What reasons support a new direction for corporate governance?

SHAREHOLDER MEETINGS

Shareholders' limited role in corporate governance is largely implemented through democratic participation and voting at annual or special shareholder meetings. Shareholders have no other control powers unless specified in the charter, bylaws, or shareholder agreements, or when shareholders act in their capacity as authorized corporate officers, employees, or agents. Shareholders may vote for directors at **regular shareholder meetings** held annually on a date fixed in the bylaws. Some states require an annual meeting at least every 13 months. State laws and stock exchange rules often require regular annual meetings.

Shareholders also occasionally approve extraordinary and fundamental corporate changes, often at a **special shareholder meeting** held infrequently, only when extraordinary votes are needed. Special meetings are called by the board or by holders of a specified minimum percentage of voting shares (e.g., 10 or 25 percent). For example, corporations like InvestigatCo must usually hold regular annual meetings to elect directors. As majority shareholders, Carl and Claudia will probably reelect themselves as directors, even over the dissent of minority shareholders. If a merger is negotiated with another corporation, Carl and Claudia can vote their shares to approve this fundamental change at a special shareholder meeting. Shareholders are inherently entitled to vote on charter amendments and bylaw changes and shareholders may propose resolutions for corporate action. However, many charters reserve the power to amend bylaws to the board.

Notice and Quorum

Shareholder and board meetings must be conducted with procedural safeguards to ensure a fair consideration of the issues and candidates and permit all to prepare for meaningful debate. The Revised Model Business Corporation Act (RMBCA) requires that notice be given between 10 and 60 days before the meeting. The notice must state the place, date, time, and purpose for the meeting. A more specific agenda is usually not required. Notice may be waived by any shareholder showing acquiescence in the failure of notice. For example, attendance at the meeting is a **waiver of notice** in some states although most states recognize that attendance without an adequate opportunity to prepare frustrates the purpose of notice.

Corporate bylaws must generally contain a **quorum** requirement representing the minimum number of shares or votes actually present at the meeting or represented by proxy that are necessary to conduct valid business. Although the corporation generally sets its own quorum in the articles or bylaws, some states set minimum requirements. Delaware prohibits a quorum of less than one third of voting shares. Unless the corporate articles provide otherwise, the RMBCA sets the quorum at half the voting shares.

Notice and quorum requirements are designed to prevent tyranny by the minority. If unannounced meetings were held by management or other small groups of shareholders, resolutions might be passed or board members elected contrary to the interests of an uninformed majority. This could effectively disenfranchise most shareholders. Of course, quorum requirements do not completely prevent tyranny. A large or well-organized minority could win elections where only a ''bare quorum'' is present or after many shareholders have left the meeting when the quorum was determined. A resolution could pass by a bare majority of the minimal one-third quorum: one sixth of all outstanding shares plus one share. Assume InvestigatCo articles set the quorum at one third, Carl and Claudia each hold 17 percent of the voting stock, and no other shareholders send proxies or attend the meeting. Carl's resolutions could win over Claudia's objections with just one additional voting share. Alternatively, Carl's votes alone could

pass resolutions if Claudia left the meeting before voting. A few states invalidate resolutions taken after the quorum is lost.

Open Forum Concept

Open meetings are fundamental to effective shareholder democracy and to board democracy in board meetings. Good attendance permits an **open forum** to nurture constructive debate by encouraging opposing views and challenges to particular viewpoints. All this can lead to better-reasoned judgments. Without an open forum, *groupthink* may dominate, permitting factions to force through their agenda unchecked by careful reason, deliberation, or diversity. The open forum is particularly important at board meetings because board members must represent shareholders' interests to the best of their ability and loyalty. Diverse viewpoints, particularly from nonmanagement outsiders, reduces management directors' tendency to vote together as a block. Others' views help shape better corporate policy.

Shareholder meetings have historically been rather uneventful scripted affairs closely following the distributed agenda. Officers and directors sit atop a stage in front of a theater full of shareholders. Reports prepared by public affairs personnel are proofed by legal counsel, then presented to polish the corporate image. The passage of management's resolutions are strongly urged. Occasionally, an individual corporate *gadfly* complains about management performance or corporate finances. A few shareholders may speak against management's resolution proposals, ask questions about corporate performance, or offer their own proposals. Minutes are kept, elections are held, and votes taken on special resolutions. Very seldom are *insurgent* groups successful in unseating management's slate of director candidates or in winning a resolution to curb management's discretion. A resurgence of shareholder activism in the early 1990s has produced some contested proxy fights that are beginning to curb unbridled management power, as discussed further in Chapter 45.

Shareholder Consents

Some states permit shareholder action without a formally convened meeting. Meetings may be impossible on short notice yet shareholders need to take quick action. **Shareholder consents** under the

RMBCA, in Delaware, and California permit action without a meeting. A separate written shareholder consent to the proposed action substitutes for a vote taken at a shareholder meeting.

Delaware permits shareholder consents if they satisfy the corporation's own minimum voting requirements. However, the RMBCA validates only unanimous shareholder consents. Under the RMBCA, if one shareholder revokes consent before all shareholders deliver their written consent, the approval becomes invalid. The information technology revolution of fax machines and E-mail would seem to make shareholder consents a more promising method of corporate governance, particularly for close corporations. However, unanimous consents are cumbersome for large, publicly traded corporations. The deliberation advantages of the open forum are frustrated by the communication difficulties for anyone other than the consent's solicitor. Shareholder consents are not generally replacing annual meetings so proxies remain effective and annual meetings are still required.

SHAREHOLDER VOTING

The corporate governance model gives shareholders only a limited level of control absent some contrary provision in the charter, bylaws, or a shareholder agreement. Shareholder voting is the major remnant of direct democracy in the corporate governance model. Most shareholder power is exercised through representative democracy accomplished by the elected corporate board.

Shareholders' *voting eligibility* is limited to **shareholders of record** holding stock on the **record date.** This is a date set in the charter or bylaws. It cannot be more that 70 days prior to the shareholder meeting under the RMBCA. This time period varies by state. The stock transfer books are closed on the record day so a list of eligible shareholder voters can be prepared. Alternatively, the board may set the record day, although some states fix it as the last day when notice of the meeting may be sent to shareholders.

Do purchasers of stock after the record day have the right to vote? The corporation must allow the legal title holder on the record day to vote. When a new stock owner is not yet registered on the corporation's books, the seller must provide the buyer with a proxy. Trustees hold legal title but must vote consistent with the best interests of a beneficiary.

Co-owners of stock must all vote together. Much stock is held in **street name,** indorsed in blank or to the broker's nominee. As discussed further in Chapter 45, the securities laws require the broker to provide the beneficial owner with a proxy.

Voting Mechanics

Shareholder votes on resolutions follow the traditional **straight voting** system, in which each share has one vote and a *simple majority* of a quorum wins. In director elections, there are usually several directors' seats up for election at one time, making it unlikely that any one candidate will receive a majority of votes unless the candidate is immensely popular. Numerous successive votes might be necessary to eventually fill all seats, prolonging the meeting excessively. Therefore, board candidates win with a **plurality** of votes—the greatest number cast. The candidates receiving the greatest number of votes are elected until all of the several open seats are filled. For example, if 100,000 shares are present at the annual meeting of InvestigatCo, 50,001 are necessary to approve a resolution. If five director candidates—A, B, C, D, and E—run to fill three vacant board seats, the three receiving the highest votes would be elected: A with 25,000, B with 24,000, and C with 23,000—but not D who received 14,500, nor E with only 13,500 votes.

The charter or bylaws may establish some other voting system. **Supermajority voting** requirements are a common variant, in which a higher percentage than a simple majority is needed to pass resolutions. Commonly, a supermajority is necessary to approve fundamental corporate changes such as mergers or a charter amendment. Supermajority votes are useful in close corporations to protect minority shareholders from oppression. Most states permit the articles to establish a different minimum *required vote* for winning resolutions or elections. Of course, a larger required vote or higher quorum may actually encourage impasse if shareholders are apathetic. Therefore, the charter and bylaws must balance minority rights with potential voter apathy, given the adverse effect of gridlock on policymaking.

Some states and some corporations provide for special voting groups, also known as **class voting.** Shareholders of nonvoting classes or series (e.g., preferred) are given limited voting rights in certain situations. For example, preferred may be given voting rights over certain designated seats on the board.

Class votes on resolutions effectively give that class a veto privilege and create specified *contingent voting*. For example, the charter might permit typically nonvoting preferred to vote only so long as there are *dividend arrearages* — that is, mandatory cumulative dividends that remain unpaid. All classes of securities have the contingent right to approve or reject a plan of reorganization proposed in Chapter 11 bankruptcy or in a voluntary recapitalization. Any senior class of securities has the right to vote as a class to veto a resolution that would eliminate the vested rights of that class, create a new class with rights superior to the class, or subordinate the class's rights to another class of securities.

One-Share, One-Vote

In traditional American politics and corporate governance, the equal protection concept has spawned an expectation of one-person, one-vote. However, state corporate law has always permitted varying voting privileges: common voting rights, limited preferred voting rights, and even **supervoting shares** with more than one vote per share. A New York Stock Exchange (NYSE) rule required the *one-share, one-vote rule* for the common stock of listed companies until the 1980s, when takeovers proliferated. The National Association of Securities Dealers (NASD), which regulates the over-the-counter (OTC) stock market, began attracting the listings of takeover target corporations that formerly traded on the NYSE. The OTC had no one-share, one-vote rule. Some corporations began to create new classes of stock with supervoting powers that were sold primarily to management and its allies as a means to consolidate control by voting against a takeover. Even if a hostile takeover bidder bought over 50 percent of the outstanding voting common shares, managements' supermajority voting power could be cast to reject any merger or fundamental corporate change or vote for its director candidates.

The SEC entered the fray with Rule 19c-4, which prohibited any new supervoting classes of stock, effectively grandfathering about 350 corporations with existing supervoting shares. However, Rule 19c-4 was later invalidated because the SEC had overstepped its proxy authority: the SEC had ventured into shareholder voting rules, an area traditionally left to state law regulation. The importance of this controversy is diminished now that the hostile takeovers have subsided.

Cumulative Voting

Straight voting often inhibits minority shareholders' representation on the board, thereby limiting benefits from the open forum. Some states and many corporations institute **cumulative voting,** giving each share one vote for every director vacancy. Supervoting shares have one vote for every director vacancy for which they are entitled to vote multiplied by the number of votes to which they are entitled per share. This permits all shareholders to accumulate votes for any number of director candidates. Minority shareholders may concentrate votes on one or a few candidates to improve their chances of electing at least one or a few directors. While majority shareholders also have proportionately more votes, their votes must be spread over a majority of candidates to control the board. Cumulative voting is applicable only in directors' elections.

Most states have **permissive cumulative voting,** so the practice is followed only if required by the corporate charter. For example, cumulative voting is permissive in Delaware and under the RMBCA. Many states require the shareholder meeting notice to state conspicuously that cumulative voting is authorized; otherwise, cumulative voting cannot be used at that meeting. A few states require cumulative voting unless it is specifically denied in the articles. California and a few other states have **mandatory cumulative voting,** requiring its use in most instances. Cumulative voting is also required under several federal statutes for nationally chartered banks, public utility holding companies, investment companies (e.g., mutual funds), and some corporations reorganized under the bankruptcy laws. Mandatory cumulative voting may not be barred in the charter or bylaws of these corporations. Figure 41–2 illustrates the mechanics of cumulative voting. Four scenarios show effective and ineffective uses.

Circumventing Cumulative Voting

Majority shareholders may try one or more of five methods to weaken the effect of cumulative voting. First, the smaller percentage of shares held by the minority lessens the number of minority directors electable under cumulative voting. If minority shareholders are disillusioned or apathetic and refrain from voting, they lose power to elect minority directors. Second, incorporation in states with only permissive cumulative voting allows the majority to

Figure 41–2   Cumulative Voting Example

$$MinSh = \frac{VotSh}{TotDir + 1} + 1$$

where:

  MinSh $=$ Minimum number of shares needed to elect **one** director
  VotSh $=$ Number of voting shares present or represented at the election
  TotDir $=$ Total number of director vacancies to be filled at the election

Example

Of the 1,000 outstanding shares for InvestigatCo, Claudia holds 400 shares and Carl holds 600 shares. Six board vacancies are to be filled at an election. Claudia needs 144 shares to elect one director and 288 shares to elect two directors, as computed below:

$$MinSh = \frac{1,000}{6 + 1} + 1 = \frac{1,000}{7} + 1 = 143 + 1 = 144$$

Claudia's total possible votes are 400 shares $\times$ 6 vacancies $= 2,400$ votes. Carl's total possible votes are 600 shares $\times$ 6 vacancies $= 3,600$ votes. At most, Claudia can elect two of her favored director candidates, G and H, if she accumulates at least 864 votes for each and Carl accumulates his 3,600 votes, 600 for each of his favored candidates: A, B, C, D, E, and F, as indicated on Ballot 1.

However, if Claudia foolishly spreads her 2,400 votes evenly over all 6 of her favored candidates ($2,400/6 = 400$ votes each for G, H, I, J, K, and L), she may not elect any director if Carl spreads his votes evenly, as indicated on Ballot 2.

If Carl foolishly accumulates his 3,600 votes evenly for three candidates, 1,200 each for A, B, and C, and Claudia discovers this and accumulates her votes for J, K, and L, he could lose control of the board, as indicated in Ballot 3.

Carl can avoid losing control by simply accumulating all his votes for his favored candidates A, B, C, and D as indicated in Ballot 4.

	Carl's Votes						Claudia's Votes						Directors Elected
Ballot	A	B	C	D	E	F	G	H	I	J	K	L	
1	600	600	600	600	600	600	864	864	168	168	168	168	C, D, E, F, G, H
2	600	600	600	600	600	600	400	400	400	400	400	400	A, B, C, D, E, F
3	1,200	1,200	1,200	0	0	0	0	0	0	800	800	800	A, B, C, J, K, L
4	900	900	900	900	0	0	0	0	0	800	800	800	A, B, C, D, K, L

eliminate the cumulative voting right altogether. However, a large minority or supermajority requirement for amending the articles can make it difficult to eliminate cumulative voting.

The third method might find the majority simply casting its votes to remove the minority director or directors right after election. Experience with this tactic has led most states to require that a director cannot be removed, except for cause, if the number of votes cast against removal would be sufficient to elect that director initially. Directors may usually be removed *for cause* such as for dereliction of duty or disloyalty. Fourth, reducing the size of the board reduces the minority's prospects of electing even

one minority director. For example, there would be little chance for a 5 percent minority shareholder to elect even one director if there are only five board seats.

The final tactic is used by many corporations — dividing boards into two or more subgroups, with each group running for election in a different year. This tactic is known as a **classified board** with **staggered directors terms.** Each subgroup has a term of office that overlaps other subgroups. For example, a 12-director board could be classified into three subgroups, each with four members holding office for three years. Only four vacancies would be filled in any one year, reducing the number to be filled and thwarting cumulative voting except for a large and well-organized minority. States with mandatory cumulative voting generally prohibit staggered terms. There is some regulatory effort to prohibit staggered terms, and some recent shareholder proposals are eliminating them. However, it is often argued that staggered terms provide continuity, preventing an all-new and inexperienced board from ever taking over. As the number of directors to be elected is reduced and/or the size of the minority decreases, the majority can shut out minority representation on the board even under cumulative voting.

Proxy Voting

Apathethic and dispersed shareholders frustrate the participative goals of the corporate governance model. Shareholder majorities typically attend only the meetings of closely held corporations. Few shareholders in publicly traded corporations attend meetings in person, so without absentee balloting, many publicly traded corporations could not attract a quorum and would never conduct valid business. Eventually quorum requirements would be lowered further, frustrating the participative democracy goal.

The solution to this problem is the proxy absentee shareholder balloting system. The term **proxy** variously refers to (1) the shareholder's intangible power of attorney transferring voting power to another, (2) the individual agent who actually votes the shares, or (3) a formal written absentee ballot conferring voting power. State corporation laws permit any shareholder of record with voting rights to vote by proxy in an election or on resolutions. The federal securities law has largely supplanted state law in the proxy solicitations of publicly traded corporations, as discussed in Chapter 45.

Type of Proxy

Shareholders may grant various degrees of authority in a proxy. Minimal proxies delegate only the right to vote as the shareholder specifies. For example, Claudia might grant a limited proxy to vote only for her favored director candidates. Proxies are liable for failure to vote as directed. Management often seeks broader discretion to vote as it best sees fit in a **general proxy.** The proxy must always be voted in the shareholder's best interests. Power to vote for an extraordinary or fundamental corporate change must be stated specifically and cannot be inferred from a general proxy.

Proxies are terminable by the shareholder at will, by execution of a substitute proxy, later appointment of another individual as proxy, attendance at the shareholders' meeting if intending to vote personally, or by the subsequent sale of the stock. Many proxies are limited in time by their terms. Proxies can be made irrevocable if the vote is transferred for a consideration. A **proxy coupled with an interest** is given by a shareholder to secure the creditor's loan for purchase of the stock. The creditor might require an irrevocable proxy until the loan is fully paid. Stock sold after the record day is usually accompanied by an irrevocable proxy granted to the purchaser.

Under state law, there is generally no particular form or wording necessary to validate a proxy. Valid proxies have been written in letters, telegrams, faxes, carbon or photocopies, in handwriting, and if signed or initialed. Computer E-mail messages could be validated under some circumstances. However, a few state statutes require written proxies. Corporate election inspectors verify whether the proxies received are genuine, although there is a presumption of validity if they are properly filed with the corporate secretary of the meeting. The federal proxy rules impose several formalities such as a uniform ballotlike format and a solicitation package meeting rigid requirements. Proxy contests for the control of publicly traded corporations are an evolving problem, as discussed in Chapter 45.

International Shareholder Voting

Shareholder voting in various nations does not receive consistent treatment. Some nations, like the United States and the United Kingdom, openly welcome foreign investors to own any type of security, voting and nonvoting alike. However, other nations severely restrict or prohibit foreign shareholder voting outright. For example, the Swiss have historically prohibited foreigners from owning any voting stock. Swiss companies generally have dual equity capitalization: voting stock only for Swiss nationals and nonvoting for foreigners.

The Japanese effectively reverse the roles of debt and equity; creditors exercise control over corporate debtors through the **keiretsu** or vertical cartels of related firms. Equity is traditionally nonactivist, acquiescing in management's selection of directors and corporate policies. Therefore, shareholder voting in Japan is of little consequence, a reality that

Boone Pickens discovered after acquiring a substantial block of Koito, a Japanese electrical parts manufacturer. Pickens could not elect even one seat on Koito's board. Even the United States restricts the ownership or voting control by aliens in certain U.S. industries such as airlines and defense contractors.

The future for more international shareholder democracy is uncertain. Some nations — for example, Switzerland and Mexico — are beginning to permit at least token foreign shareholder voting to encourage foreign investment. Nations with emerging stock markets are likewise recognizing they must deregulate foreign shareholder voting to attract new capital. However, many nations still view foreign shareholder voting as impinging on their sovereignty, perhaps seeing it as equivalent to foreigners voting in their political elections. Forms of legal, contractual, and cultural barriers to foreign shareholder voting will probably continue in many nations. Particularly those nations with smaller economies, protectionist industrial policies, and cultural biases against foreign influence should be expected to restrict foreign shareholder voting.

FINANCIAL RIGHTS

The shareholder's bundle of rights includes financial rights affecting cash flow, financial performance, and distributions. This section discusses the shareholder's right to purchase newly issued shares, receive dividends, redemptions, and repurchases of outstanding securities, and the privilege to inspect corporate books and records.

Preemptive Rights

The board has discretion over the timing of new sales of previously authorized stock or treasury stock. New stock authorizations require shareholder approval because the charter must be amended. A majority faction could pass this amendment over the minority's dissent and then selectively buy the stock itself or sell it to designated outsiders. This could dilute the minority's voting power, decrease its access to dividends, and reduce its return after liquidation. Of course, management will probably invest the new issue's proceeds. Investments yielding equal or higher returns than from current corporate assets would not dilute the minority's financial claims. Only the minority's control would be di-

luted. **Preemptive rights** permit existing shareholders to preserve their *proportional interests* in newly authorized issues of stock.

Preemptive rights give existing shareholders a *right of first refusal* to purchase newly issued shares in proportion to their current shareholdings. Existing shareholders are not obligated to purchase. Preemptive rights are not generally granted for sales of previously authorized shares, whether unissued or repurchased as treasury shares. Shareholders are presumably already on notice of the potential dilution from previously authorized shares, although a few states allow preemptive rights for sales made long after the previous authorization. For example, New York restores preemptive rights for issuances made two years or more after the original authorization. Only shares issued for cash are subject to preemptive rights; no rights exist for stock issued to purchase specific property, as part of an acquisition or share exchange in a takeover, or as part of an ESOP.

Preemptive Rights Procedures

Existing shareholders' preemptive rights originate when new stock is authorized. The corporation must notify shareholders before preemptive rights expire and before selling the new shares to others. Sale prices may not be set by auction, include a premium for exercise of the preemptive right, or fall below par. Unless market conditions change drastically, the preemptive price should be close to any price obtained in subsequent sales. Shareholders may enforce their preemptive rights by specific performance to compel issuance, by seeking damages or an injunction against sales to outsiders, or by suit to cancel any shares sold.

Preemptive rights are no longer required by most states because they often frustrate financing. New York requires preemptive rights unless the articles provide otherwise. The RMBCA, California, and Delaware law do not require but permit the charter to provide for preemptive rights. Preemptive rights are difficult to apportion precisely in complex capital structures that include various classes and/or series of stock with differing bundles of voting, dividend, and liquidation rights. Some states require the board to attempt preserving the relative rights of existing classes. Preemptive rights are difficult to administer in publicly traded corporations because new shares are sold through underwriting syndicates. The uncertainties and delay of first offering shares to existing shareholders is usually prohibitive. Courts sometimes declare a **fraudulent dilution** if management insiders are favored in new share offerings. *Quasi-preemptive rights* are occasionally inferred based on the managers' fiduciary duty even if not required by law or the charter.

Distributions

The primary purpose of corporations is to generate financial returns for shareholders. Distributions to shareholders are paid regularly and pro rata with dividends, irregularly when the corporation selectively buys back stock in a redemption or repurchase, and one final time upon liquidation. Distributions are normally made in cash, but property in kind and stock or other securities of that or another corporation may also be distributed. Distributions raise conflicts among management, creditors, and shareholders. The board must regularly seek reelection from the very shareholders who receive these distributions. Large distributions can imperil the corporation's ability to repay creditors so distribution law addresses these conflicts.

Types of Dividends

Dividends are periodic distributions of corporate property to shareholders made *pro rata*—that is, in proportion to the number of shares held. Dividends are not tax deductible to the corporation, creating the so-called double tax on corporate profits: Profits are taxed as corporate income, then again as individual income when received by shareholders. Most profitable corporations have *regular dividends,* paid quarterly out of corporate profits to avoid a penalty tax on excessive retentions. The board sets the dividend depending on the availability of corporate earnings for the period, other sources of cash, the need to generate working capital internally, and the market's expectations for regular payouts. **Preferred dividends** are often a dollar amount fixed in the charter or bylaws or set at a percentage of par. **Special dividends** are paid irregularly, if the board finds a sufficient surplus.

Stock dividends are paid in stock, usually of the same class and series as the shareholder already holds. However, some stock dividends are distributed from stock of a subsidiary or another corporation. **Stock splits** are distinguishable from stock dividends primarily in form rather than in substance. When stock is split, a prescribed number of shares is divided into a different number of the same shares. For example, when Carl and Claudia cause InvestigatCo stock to split two for one, Carl's 600 shares will increase to 1,200 shares and Claudia's 400 shares will split into 800 shares. Unlike with a stock dividend, InvestigatCo need not make a transfer of funds on its books from any surplus account for a stock split. Shareholder approval is required if additional shares must be authorized for the stock split.

In a **reverse stock split,** the corporation exchanges fewer shares for each shareholder's former holdings. For example, a 1 for 500 reverse stock split would result in Claudia holding only scrip, four fifths of one share. Claudia would then forfeit her voting and dividend rights, permitting Carl to cause the corporation to repurchase Claudia's scrip, effectively squeezing her out.

Available Sources for Distributions

The corporation may pay dividends or make redemptions and repurchases only out of a "legitimate source" of funds. These legal restrictions developed to prevent the shareholder-controlled board from dissipating corporate assets, impairing the ability to repay creditors. These legal restrictions are often drawn in terms of anachronistic par values. The advent of bond indenture provisions and independent indenture trustees to monitor the corporation's debt repayment has alleviated much of the need for dividends restrictions. Underwriters and long-term creditors are strong enough to negotiate **negative covenants** in loan documents or bond indentures. These are contractual dividend restrictions that prohibit dividend payments when the corporation is in a weak financial condition as determined by various complex formulae.

It is illegal for corporations to pay dividends while insolvent or from any source not permitted by state corporation law. **Nimble dividends** are illegal dividends paid from stated capital. Most states require that dividends be paid only from a *surplus* account. Dividends are universally permitted from **earned surplus,** the total of accumulated profits from the corporation's conception reduced by all losses and all dividends ever paid out. Many states permit dividend payments from *paid-in surplus* or *capital surplus,* the excess price paid for stock over par or stated value. Preferred dividend arrearages must often be fully paid before any common dividends are paid from capital surplus.

A few states permit the corporation to pay dividends from a reduction in stated capital creating a **capital reduction surplus.** Few states permit the corporation to reappraise assets upward to create a **revaluation surplus** for dividends. For example, assume an oil company's petroleum reserves were acquired for $100 million when oil was priced at $11 per barrel. Later, the company's geologists double their estimates of these petroleum reserves, and oil prices quadruple to $44 per barrel. A few states would permit the corporation to revalue its petroleum reserves upwards by 800 percent to $800 million, permitting a substantial dividend even if there were no earned surplus. The foolishness of this approach is evident: The estimated petroleum reserves are uncertain, and oil prices can easily plummet, eliminating the temporary appearance of a surplus. By contrast, if the oil field was sold at a high of $800 million in cash, the seller could record $700 million in earned surplus and legitimately pay dividends from this source.

Illegal Dividends

Directors are jointly and severally liable for the full amount of illegal dividends if suit is brought by the corporation or its creditors. Directors may defend against these claims if they did not participate in the unlawful declaration, voted against it, relied in good faith on inaccurate financial reports showing a legal surplus, or were absent from the board meeting. Directors may seek contribution from other directors if ordered to repay illegally declared dividends. Shareholders may also be liable to return dividends, particularly when the declaration renders the corporation insolvent. However, shareholders are not liable if the corporation is still solvent and shareholders had no knowledge that the dividend was unlawful.

Dividend Declaration

Dividend declarations are totally within the discretionary business judgment of the board to determine. Shareholders have no inherent right to a particular dividend declaration even if surpluses exist. Of course, some preferred dividends are *mandatory* if surpluses exists. The board typically meets quarterly to review financial performance and future plans, then passes a resolution declaring the dividend payable to shareholders of record on a certain day in the near future. After declaration, the dividend becomes a debt owed by the corporation to shareholders.

Identifying which shareholders are entitled to the dividend is troublesome, particularly when the corporation's shares are actively traded near the record date. Stock sold after the fourth day preceding the record date are **ex-dividend** — the seller receives the dividend and the buyer receives only subsequent dividends. Stock prices do not always fall by the whole amount of the dividend after the declaration, permitting *dividend capture plays*.

Compelling Dividend Payments

Infrequently, shareholders have sued the board to compel the declaration of a dividend. Most board dividend decisions are protected from such suits by the business judgment rule. However, where the board acts unreasonably by withholding dividends in bad faith, arbitrarily, and in abuse of its discretion, the courts may invoke equitable powers to order a dividend declaration. In the leading case of *Dodge v. Ford Motor Co.,*[1] Henry Ford terminated large special dividends earned from the Model T's huge success. Henry publicly stated he would reinvest these funds to broaden the benefits of industrialization. The Dodge brothers successfully won a dividend payment because this was an arbitrary decision inconsistent with maximizing shareholder wealth. Ironically, the proceeds were used to establish the Dodge Motor Co.

Shareholders disgruntled about low dividend payments have few options. First, there is the Wall Street rule — vote with your feet. However, this is often futile in close corporations because there is no liquid market. Second, the shareholder may negotiate with management, perhaps threatening IRS imposition of a "triple tax" on excessive retentions unless dividends are paid.

The third option is to bring a suit in equity and meet a difficult burden of proving bad faith. *Bad faith* may arise from intense hostility between the ruling majority factions and the minority, evidence of the majority's attempt to freeze out the minority. This can be reinforced with evidence of conflict of interest, excessive perks and salaries, or the majority's intentional avoidance of income taxes on dividend payouts. For example, in *Cole Real Estate Corp. v. Peoples Bank & Trust,*[2] Helen Cole used

---

[1]*Dodge v. Ford Motor Co.,* 170 N.W. 668 (Mich. 1919).
[2]*Cole Real Estate Corp. v. Peoples Bank & Trust,* 310 N.E.2d 275 (Ind. Ct. App. 1974).

the Cole Real Estate Corporation business as her personal entitlement. Helen appropriated all corporate profits as personal compensation and perks. No dividends were paid to the bank-trustee, which held a minority block of stock. The court ordered a dividend because Helen's domination of corporate dividend payouts was arbitrary and a conflict of interest.

Shareholders seeking to compel dividend payments must first exhaust intracorporate remedies by "making a demand" on the board. Although this is often futile, it permits the board to correct its own misbehavior avoiding litigation costs. There must be a sufficient legal surplus. The legitimacy of the earnings retention is considered, as evidenced by an audit, expansion plans, or industry averages supporting large working capital needs. Conflicts of interest are also relevant. Finally, a special shareholder status may be persuasive to compel a dividend: a minority shareholder, a passive acquisition of shares (e.g., inheritance), or a preferred shareholder. Most dividend suits occur in closely held corporations because bad faith is not well policed by a stock market. Low payouts in publicly traded corporations arguably reduce stock price, making management vulnerable to replacement or the corporation susceptible to a hostile takeover. The next case is one of the few examples of such dividend cases.

SMITH v. ATLANTIC PROPERTIES, INC.
422 N.E. 2d 798 (Mass. 1981)

Atlantic Properties, Inc., was a closely held real estate investment corporation held in equal share by four persons: Louis E. Welfson, Paul T. Smith, Abraham Zimbel, and William H. Burke. Both the articles and bylaws required an 80 percent affirmative vote of outstanding shares to make major corporate decisions. Atlantic was profitable for many years and by 1961 had accumulated about $172,000 in retained earnings, with more than half held in cash. Dividends were paid only in 1964 and 1970 for about $10,000 each year. Considerable disagreement and ill will arose between Welfson and other shareholders. Welfson wanted Atlantic's earnings spent on repairs and improvements in existing buildings and facilities on the Norwood land. While other stockholders wanted dividends, Welfson regularly voted against dividend payments, and the 80 percent provision gave him this veto power.

The Internal Revenue Service assessed penalty taxes on the unreasonable accumulation of undistributed corporate earnings and profits under IRC Section 541 in every year between 1962 and 1968. Atlantic incurred the substantial penalties and legal expenses largely because of Welfson's dividend votes. The other shareholders sued to have a court declare a dividend. The trial court ordered Atlantic directors to declare a reasonable dividend, and it retained jurisdiction for five years to ensure compliance. Both parties appealed.

CUTTERS, Justice

With respect to the past damage to Atantic caused by Dr. Welfson's refusal to vote in favor of any dividends, the trial judge was justified in finding that his conduct went beyond what was reasonable. Dr. Welfson had been warned of the dangers of an assessment. He had refused to vote dividends in any amount adequate to minimize that danger and had failed to bring forward a convincing, definitive program of appropriate improvements which could withstand scrutiny by the IRS. He recklessly ran serious and unjustified risks on precisely what the penalty taxes were eventually assessed, risks which were inconsistent with any reasonable interpretation of a duty of "utmost good faith and loyalty."

Although the trial court's reservation of jurisdiction is appropriate in this case, its purpose should be stated more affirmatively and revised to provide: (a) a direction that Atlantic's directors prepare promptly financial statements of state and federal income and excise tax returns for the five most recent calendar years, (b) an instruction that they confer with one another with a view to stipulating a general dividend and capital improvements policy for the next ensuing three fiscal years. Thereafter, the court may direct the adoption in carrying out of a specific dividend and capital improvement policy adequate to minimize the risk of further penalty tax assessments. So ordered.

Case Questions

1. What is the issue in ordering a corporation to declare dividends?
2. For what reason did Welfson refuse to declare a dividend?
3. What ambiguities must be clarified when the trial court orders declaration of a dividend?

Redemptions and Repurchases

The creditor protections from dividend abuses — for example, sufficient surplus and corporate solvency — also apply to redemption or repurchase distributions. Dividends, redemptions, and repurchases are indistinguishable from a creditor protection perspective. However, these distributions are fundamentally different: Only dividends must be paid pro rata, both redemptions and repurchases are inherently discriminatory because only some shareholders are bought out. Shareholders surrender nothing in receiving a dividend, yet lose all or part of their securities in a redemption or repurchase. Tax treatment also differs: Dividends trigger the double tax, while redemptions and repurchases are partly a nontaxable "return of capital," so only capital gains tax is owed on the appreciation.

A **redemption** results from a contractual provision giving the corporation a **call privilege** or option. When exercised, the corporation alone decides whether a security holder must return the security to the corporation for cancellation in exchange for a previously specified price. For example, because junk bonds have such high interest rates and some preferred stock has high dividend payment requirements, the corporation often reserves the right to redeem these securities. If interest rates fall, the corporation can refinance at lower rates, lowering the firm's cost of capital. Nearly any type of security can be made redeemable.

The redemption price and privilege are commonly granted in the charter, bylaws, indenture, or on the security certificates. There is no power to redeem unless granted in some such document. Redemptions could be misused to eliminate disruptive shareholders or perpetuate management in power. Therefore, redemptions may not be done selectively but can be done pro rata or randomly by lot. Unless a particular event or condition makes for a *mandatory redemption*, the board has discretion to decide when and how much of any redeemable class of securities is called. However, a single class of common stock is not redeemable.

Repurchases differ from redemptions. Repurchases are mutually agreed on by both the corporation and shareholder. Repurchases may be privately negotiated, consummated confidentially over the securities exchanges, or made in a self-tender offer. Corporations inherently have the power to repurchase their own shares, because most state corporation laws authorize the practice. As the next case illustrates, state law does not require that repurchases be made ratably or randomly selected by lot.

UNOCAL CORP. v. MESA PETROLEUM CO.
493 A.2d 946 (Del. 1985)

Mesa Petroleum Co. owned about 13 percent of Unocal's stock. To gain further control, Mesa made a front-loaded two-tier cash tender offer for about 37 percent of Unocal's stock at $54 per share. Mesa planned to acquire the other 49 percent of Unocal's stock by paying with highly subordinated high-yield (junk) bonds that Mesa claimed were worth $54 per share. Unocal's board responded with a self-tender to repurchase the remaining 49 percent of its own shares by giving senior nonjunk securities worth approximately $72 per share.

Mesa challenged the Unocal defensive maneuver as unjustified by the business judgment rule. The trial court's vice chancellor temporarily restrained Unocal from proceeding with the self-tender, then certified this case for appeal.

MOORE, Justice

It is now well established that in the acquisition of its shares, a Delaware corporation may deal selectively with its stockholders, provided the directors have not acted out of a sole or primary purpose to entrench themselves into office. The board's power to act derives from its fundamental duty and obligation to protect the corporate enterprise, which includes stockholders, from harm reasonably perceived, irrespective of its source. The business judgment rule, including the standards by which director conduct is judged, is applicable in the context of a takeover. A court will not substitute its judgment for that of the board if the latter's decision can be attributed to any rational business purpose.

Because of the omnipresent specter that a board may be acting primarily in its own interests, rather than those of the corporation and its shareholders, there is an enhanced duty that calls for judicial examination at the threshold before the protection of the business judgment rule may be conferred. The directors must show that they had reasonable grounds for believing that a danger to corporate policy and effectiveness existed because of another person's stock ownership. Such proof is materially enhanced, as here, by the approval of a board comprised of a majority of outside independent directors who have acted in accordance with the foregoing standards. The restriction placed upon a selective stock repurchase is that the directors may not have acted solely or primarily out of a desire to perpetuate themselves in office. The defensive measures to thwart or impede a takeover must be motivated by a good faith concern for the welfare of the corporation and its stockholders, which in all circumstances must be free of any fraud or any misconduct.

A further aspect is the element of balance. A defensive measure must be reasonable to the threat posed. This entails an analysis by the director of the nature of the takeover bid and its effect on the corporate enterprise. Examples include: inadequacy of the price, nature and timing of the offer, questions of legality, the impact on constituencies other than the shareholders (i.e. creditors, customers, employees, and perhaps even the community), the risk of non-consummation and the quality of the securities being offered in the exchange.

It is now well recognized that two-tiered tender offers are a classic coercive measure designed to stampede shareholders into tendering at the first tier, even if the price is inadequate, out of fear of what they will receive at the back end. The board's objective was either to defeat the inadequate Mesa offer or provide the other 49 percent of shareholders with $72 worth of senior debt. We find that both purposes are valid. However, such efforts would have been thwarted by Mesa's participation in the exchange offer. Thus, we are satisfied that the selective exchange offer is reasonably related to the threats posed. There is no support in Delaware law for the proposition that when responding to a perceived harm, a corporation must guarantee a benefit to a stockholder who is deliberately provoking the danger being addressed. There is no obligation of self-sacrifice by a corporation and its shareholders in the face of such a challenge. The decision of the court of chancery is therefore reversed and the preliminary injunction is vacated.

Case Questions

1. What is the issue in the takeover defensive tactic adopted by Unocal?
2. For what reasons or under what conditions may a corporate board repurchase its shares? Is the standard more stringent if the repurchase is discriminatory and defensive in a hostile takeover?
3. What ambiguities were there in the Unocal board's decision to repurchase, and how was this ambiguity resolved?

The SEC has prohibited the type of takeover defensive discriminatory repurchase Unocal made. All tender offers and self-tenders must be open to *all holders* of the class of security. The rule exempts discriminatory redemptions, repurchases of scrip, repurchases of dissenter's stock, odd lot purchases (blocks of less than 100 shares), and discriminatory repurchases of closely held corporate securities.

Inspection of Corporate Records

Shareholders have the right to examine corporate information to monitor management. The right of **inspection of corporate books and records** provides access to financial statements to verify financial performance and responsible voting, to minutes of corporate meetings (shareholder, board, and board committees), and to shareholder lists facilitating shareholder communications. Initially, the inspection right was inferred under the common law but today is supplemented with a statutory inspection privilege and SEC disclosures. Usually, the shareholder must notify the corporation of the inspection request. The corporation must then permit the shareholder to examine and copy corporate records at reasonable times even if accompanied by the shareholder's agent, attorney, or accountant.

Limitations on Inspection

The inspection right is not unlimited. Competitors could use it to misappropriate trade secrets, or it could be used used vindictively to harass or extort from the corporation. Management tends to oppose inspection because it often arises in an air of hostility. Therefore, the courts look closely at all the surrounding circumstances, including the parties' potential conflicts of interest or ulterior motives. The shareholder's request must be motivated by good faith, be in the corporation's best interests, or seek to protect shareholder rights. The shareholder must have a *proper purpose:* A close connection must exist between a legitimate shareholder concern and the information sought. For example, If Carl obstructs Claudia's participation in InvestigatCo corporate activities, there is a close connection between her inspection request and any oppression she may suffer as a minority shareholder. However, if she merely seeks to embarrass Carl or misappropriate InvestigatCo confidences to start a competing business, her inspection should be denied as having an improper purpose.

The shareholder's primary purpose satisfies this limitation even if the shareholder has another, illegitimate purpose. Inspection will usually be denied if the shareholder's predominant intent is corporate extortion or to advance personal grievances, or present personal political or social views. Is it ethical for a competitor to purchase a small block of shares to access a corporation's confidential information for a competitive advantage? There are many types of "right to know" laws that may interfere with confidentiality, among them laws requiring notices of toxic substances used around employees, the Freedom of Information Act, financial disclosures, and the shareholder's inspection right. The perfect competition model assumes competitors and customers have "perfect information" about processes, products, and markets. Therefore, the ethical problems of industrial espionage are unclear without solid evidence of misappropriation or bribery. The following case illustrates a competitor's request for inspection.

CARTER v. WILSON CONSTRUCTION COMPANY, INC.
348 S.E.2d 830 (N.C. Ct. App. 1986)

William Carter was a shareholder and former officer and employee of the Wilson Construction Company, Inc. After leaving Wilson Construction, he became a part owner and employee of a competitor, C&L Contracting Company. Wilson refused to purchase Carter's stock, and Wilson's net worth declined, prompting Carter to request Wilson grant Carter access to inspect the books and records of Wilson Construction Company. After Wilson refused, Carter won a trial court judgment granting access and assessing penalties against both Wilson Construction Company and its president. Wilson appealed.

JOHNSON, Judge

Wilson contends that plaintiff's stated purpose was "a mask for more illegitimate purposes that would damage Wilson's ability to compete." The pertinent portion of the North Carolina statutes section 55–38 provides:

A qualified shareholder, upon written demands stating the purpose thereof, shall have the right, in person, or by attorney, accountant or other agent, at any reasonable time or times, for any purpose, to examine at the place where they are kept and make extracts from, the books and records of account, minutes and record of shareholders of a domestic corporation.

It is undisputed by the parties that plaintiff is a qualified shareholder. The issue is whether plaintiff's request to examine the corporate records was for "any proper purpose." After a statutory restriction, a shareholder has a common law right to inspect and examine the books and records of the corporation, given to him for the protection of his interest. The statute quoted above does not give a qualified shareholder an absolute right of inspection and examination for a mere fishing expedition, or for a purpose not germane to the protection of his economic interest as a shareholder in the corporation. For a shareholder to have the right to actually visit a corporation's office and possibly dispute its normal operation in order to inspect corporate books and records of account, his motives must be "proper." Purposes which have previously been deemed proper are the shareholder's good faith desire to (1) determine the value of his stock, (2) investigate the conduct of the management, and (3) determine the financial condition of the corporation. The burden of proof rests upon the defense, if they wish to defeat the shareholder's demand, to allege and show by facts, if they can, that the shareholder is motivated by some improper purpose.

Here, plaintiff stated a proper purpose in his complaint. Defendants must overcome the presumption of good faith in plaintiff's favor by showing that plaintiff's purpose is improper. [The evidence of Carter's conflict of interest] is insufficient to override the presumption that plaintiff is acting in good faith. The mere possibility that a shareholder may abuse his right to gain access to corporate information will not be held to justify a denial of a legal right. Judgment is affirmed.

Case Questions
1. What is the issue in establishing a proper purpose for shareholder inspection of corporate records?
2. What kind of activities would make Carter's motive improper?
3. What are the reasons that shareholders have no absolute right to inspect corporate records?

Some states make the inspection right absolute irrespective of motive. For example, California permits unrestricted shareholder access to records but would enjoin an *improper use* of the information obtained. A few states limit inspection to "serious" shareholders who hold a minimum number of shares (e.g., 5 percent) or shareholders who have owned shares for a minimum time (e.g., six months). For example, the New York inspection law is limited to such serious shareholders. In *Sadler v. NCR Corp.*,[3] a shareholder was permitted to examine the shareholder list to facilitate a tender offer and proxy fight to replace the board of NCR Corp. The fact that NCR was incorporated in Maryland, which restricts the inspection right, did not invalidate application of the New York inspection law under the commerce clause. Limitations vary among the states as to the type of information sought—for example, shareholder lists, correspondence, trade secrets, or only excerpts of specified records.

Financial Statements
The RMBCA and some other state statutes require corporate annual reports be distributed to shareholders and include a balance sheet, income statement, and statement of changes in shareholders' equity. This right is most important in close corporations because the SEC periodic disclosure requirements are inapplicable. While close corporate shareholders who have corporate employment may periodically see some records, minority shareholders may be squeezed out of any corporate financial information.

SHAREHOLDER SUITS

The shareholder's bundle of rights would be an illusion without some mechanism to vindicate them. A few close corporate charters or shareholder agreements require shareholders to arbitrate disputes. This can maintain confidentiality and reduce litigation costs. However, most shareholders' only option is to sue the corporation, the board, managers, or an outsider who wronged the shareholder or the corpo-

[3]*Sadler v. NCR Corp.,* 928 F.2d 48 (2nd Cir. 1991).

ration. Shareholders have three basic forms of suit available: (1) direct suits against the corporation for violating a shareholder's personal right, (2) a class action combining numerous shareholders' direct actions, or (3) a shareholder derivative suit claiming the corporation suffered a wrong.

Shareholder Direct Suits

Shareholders may vindicate any violation of right in the shareholders' bundle: voting, inspection, dividends, liquidation priority, preemptive rights, or any other specified in the charter, bylaws, stock certificates, or contract. In a **shareholder direct action,** the shareholder is the aggrieved party seeking a personal remedy. When several similarly situated shareholders suffer identical wrongs, they may band together in a **class action shareholder direct suit.** Typically, a single shareholder or small group of shareholders brings suit as representatives of all shareholders' collective interests. The following case illustrates the important difference between the two major types of collective shareholder suits: class actions and derivative suits.

RICHARDSON v. ARIZONA FUELS CORPORATION

614 p.2d 636 (Utah 1980)

The plaintiffs, Richardson and two other stockholders of the Major Oil Company, brought a class action lawsuit on behalf of themselves and all other Major shareholders against Arizona Fuels Corporation and Eugene and Deanna Dalton. Arizona Fuels allegedly owned 47 percent of the outstanding stock of Major, either directly or indirectly. The Daltons were allegedly controlling stockholders of Arizona Fuels and officers and directors of both Major oil company and Arizona Fuels. The plaintiffs alleged that Arizona Fuels and the Daltons breached their fiduciary duties to Major Oil Company and its stockholders and had mismanaged Major Oil's business. The trial court certified this suit as a class action, and Arizona Fuels appealed.

STEWART, Justice

A class action and a derivative action rest upon fundamentally different principles of substantive law. A derivative action must necessarily be based on a claim for relief which is owned by the stockholders' corporation. The stockholder, as a nominal party, has no right, title or interest whatsoever in the claim itself.

A class action, on the other hand, is predicated on ownership of the claim for relief sued upon by the representative of the class and all other class members in their capacity as individuals. Shareholders of the corporation may have claims for relief directly against their corporation because the corporation itself has violated rights possessed by the shareholders and a class action would be an appropriate means for enforcing their claims. A recovery in a class action is a recovery which belongs directly to the shareholders. However, in a derivative action, the plaintiff shareholder recovers nothing and the judgment runs in favor of the corporation.

There is no doubt that the first 8 of 11 causes of action [stated in the plaintiff's complaint] allege injury to the corporation only. The injury alleged can be asserted by plaintiffs derivatively as stockholders on behalf of corporation.

The ninth cause of action alleges initially that the defendants "breach their fiduciary duties to Major Oil and to its stockholders." The distinction between a fiduciary duty owed to the corporation as a whole as opposed to the stockholders collectively does not appear to be one of substance. Although plaintiff frames this claim in the alternative as one belonging to the shareholders, the claim for relief belongs to the corporation. Any compensatory damages which may be recovered on account of breach by defendants of their fiduciary duty as directors and officers are arising as a result of mismanagement of the corporation by defendants [and] belong to the corporation and not to the stockholders individually.

The 10th cause of action alleges that defendants defrauded the stockholders of Major Oil Company. Each of the six alleged defalcations states a claim belonging to the corporation and not to the stock-holders and not to any of them individually. In no regard can the 10th cause of action be interpreted as stating a claim belonging to the stockholders indi-vidually, and therefore that claim for relief will not support a class action.

The 11th cause of action alleges the possibility of other conversions of Major's assets and alleges that the defendants should be required to account to the stockholders for all of the assets of Major and dis-gorge themselves of any assets so converted. This claim also clearly belongs to the corporation.

The class action device, if used inappropriately and in lieu of a derivative action, is likely to result in grave injustices, not the least of which is the diversion of assets recovered in a lawsuit from cred-itors of a corporation to stockholders, thereby re-versing long established substantive rules of law as

to the relative priorities of the claims of creditors and stockholders. We therefore reverse the district court's certification of this suit as a class action and remand for further proceedings.

Case Questions

1. What is the central issue that separates the two types of collective suits: shareholder de-rivative suits and shareholder class action suits.

2. What reasons support the court's reclassifica-tion of Richardson's suit as a shareholder de-rivative suit and not as a class action?

3. What ambiguities were there in Richardson's claims of shareholder personal wrongs that the court clarified in reclassifying this suit as a shareholder derivative suit?

Shareholder Derivative Litigation

As the *Arizona Fuels* case illustrates, shareholders have standing to vindicate the corporations' rights as well as their personal rights under certain circum-stances. Experience shows that some corporate man-agements' breach of fiduciary duties are simply not pursued by the corporation. Particularly if the wrongdoers are top corporate officers, they are un-likely to cease their unlawful activity unless threat-ened by shareholder litigation. Courts of equity first devised the **shareholder derivative suit** to give management an incentive to remain loyal and avoid conflicts of interest. Shareholders may sue for the corporation's benefit, and any recovery or remedy be-longs directly to the corporation. Shareholders are only indirectly or "derivatively" benefited by such litigation due to their ownership in the corporation. The threat that shareholders will monitor manage-ment behavior is a primary deterrent to management conflicts of interest, particularly in close corpora-tions where there is no stock market discipline. De-rivative suits also pursue claims the corporation de-clines to assert against outsiders.

Derivative suits are subject to misuse by unscru-pulous shareholders who are not really protecting corporate interests. Instead, some shareholders use the threat of costly litigation to exact a *settlement value*. **Strike suits** are unfounded intimidation suits brought only to secure a personal settlement and/or

attorneys fees. The threat of extensive discovery and the disruption of normal business activity accompa-nying a groundless lawsuit involves such a settle-ment value.

Derivative litigation almost always raises ethical questions about one of the participants. Manage-ment may be acting irresponsibly if the shareholders honestly and accurately pursue management's fraud. By contrast, shareholders act irresponsibly if they threaten derivative litigation just to receive the set-tlement value. Plaintiff's attorneys act unethically when they encourage unfounded strike suits simply to generate attorney's fees. These problems have led to restrictions on derivative suits that balance the legitimate role of shareholders as police against their illegitimate role as burglars.

The *contemporaneous ownership rule* requires the derivative plaintiff to have been a shareholder of the corporation when the alleged wrongdoing took place. The shareholder-plaintiff must fairly and ad-equately represent all other shareholders' interests in the litigation. Before filing the suit, the shareholder must *make a demand* in writing on the board to correct the wrong. The RMBCA gives the board at least 90 days thereafter to "mend its ways" and accommodate the shareholders before derivative lit-igation can proceed. Demand is excused if it would be futile, such as where all board members are al-leged wrongdoers or the corporation will suffer irreparable harm if the demand is made. This *demand futility* rule is controversial and is nearly eliminated in the RMBCA and the ALI Corporate Governance Project. However, the recent Supreme Court case of *Kamen v. Kemper Financial Services, Inc.*[4] declined to institute a federal *universal demand rule* deferring to state regulation of derivative litigation.

Many states also require that the derivative plaintiff make a demand on shareholders, but this may be excused if the shareholders are not empowered to ratify the alleged wrongdoing. For example, demand on shareholders is unnecessary for allegations of management fraud, unlawful acts, negligent acts, or if notifying numerous shareholders would be prohibitively costly. The derivative litigation may be dismissed for failure to make a demand on the board or shareholders when demand is not excused.

Litigation Expenses

The reasons for and potential misuse of derivative litigation deeply involves the expenses of litigating and settling these suits. Because strike suits can be so costly to the corporation, restrictions have developed to minimize expenses. Most states require the derivative plaintiff to post a *bond* or other security to cover the corporation's litigation expenses (e.g., attorney's and witness fees) should the litigation eventually be proved unfounded. Judges often have discretion to require *security for expenses*, and it may be required only for smaller or ''nonserious'' shareholders. The victorious derivative plaintiff is usually

entitled to reimbursement for litigation expenses if the corporation recovers a *common fund* monetary recovery or obtains a *substantial benefit* such as ousting wrongdoing directors. Most states require that the corporation reimburse winning officers and directors in derivative litigation, although some states give corporate boards discretion to award expenses to these individuals. Losing officers and directors may not collect in many states and are usually denied reimbursement for deliberate dishonesty or unjustifiable personal gain. Officer and director indemnification and insurance are discussed further in Chapter 42.

Derivative Suit Dismissal

Corporations can avoid unfounded or harassing derivative suits if a board subcommittee of directors independent from management reviews the suit's merits and dismisses the litigation. The board's *special litigation committee (SLC)* may evaluate whether derivative suits are strike suits by investigating the allegations and recommending dismissal. An issue in reviewing such dismissals may concern the SLC's independence from management. If the SLC members have conflicts of interest or fail to adequately investigate the allegations, a court may overrule the SLC dismissal. When the SLC process works, it provides a corporate policymaker's insights into whether the corporation may suffer more goodwill loss from the negative publicity surrounding a divisive derivative suit than it could hope to gain even if the derivative suit was successful. The following case illustrates court review of an SLC dismissal.

---

[4] *Kamen v. Kemper Financial Services, Inc.*, 111 S.Ct. 1711 (1991).

ZAPATA CORPORATION v. MALDONADO
430 A.2d 779 (Del. 1981)

William Maldonado, a Zapata Corporation stockholder, brought a derivative action against 10 officers and directors of Zapata, alleging breach of fiduciary duty. Maldonado failed to make a demand on the board of directors to bring the suit, claiming that the demand would be futile because all directors were named defendants and allegedly participated in the wrongdoing. Thereafter, four directors resigned and two new outside directors were added to the board and appointed to an independent investigation committee (an SLC) to determine whether the derivative litigation should continue. The committee concluded that the suit should be dismissed forthwith as inimical to the company's best interest. Zapata appealed a trial court determination that Maldonado could proceed with the derivative suit.

QUILLEN, Justice

The law of the state of incorporation determines whether the directors have the power of dismissal. Directors of Delaware corporations derive their managerial decision making power, which encompasses decisions to litigate, from Delaware statutes. As a general rule, a stockholder cannot be permitted to invade the discretionary field committed to the judgment of the directors and sue in the corporation's behalf when the managing body refuses. Board members will not be allowed to cause a derivative suit to be dismissed when it would be a breach of their fiduciary duty. A board decision to cause a derivative suit to be dismissed as detrimental to the company after demand has been made and refused, will be respected unless it is wrongful.

The demand requirement itself evidences that the managerial power is retained by the board. When a derivative plaintiff is allowed to bring suit after a wrongful refusal, the board authority to choose whether to pursue the litigation is not challenged although its conclusion — reached through the exercise of that authority — is not respected since it is wrongful. This merely saves the plaintiff the expense and delay of making a futile demand resulting in a probable tainted exercise of that authority in a refusal by the board or giving control of litigation to the opposing side. But the board entity remains in power to make decisions regarding litigation. The problem is one of member disqualification, not the absence of power in the board.

The corporate power inquiry then focuses on whether the board tainted by the self-interest of a majority of its members, can legally delegate its authority to a committee of two disinterested members. We find our statute clearly requires an affirmative answer to this question.

If corporations can consistently wrest bonafide derivative actions away from well meaning derivative plaintiffs through the use of the committee mechanism, the derivative suit will lose much, if not all, of its generally recognized effectiveness as an intra-corporate means of policing boards. If, on the other hand, corporations are unable to rid themselves of meritless or harmful litigation and strike suits, the derivative action, created to benefit the corporation, will produce the opposite, unintended result.

If a committee composed of independent and disinterested directors, conducted a proper review of the matters before it, considered a variety of factors and reached, in good faith, a business judgment that the action was not in the best interest of the corporation, the action must be dismissed. The issue becomes solely independence, good faith, and reasonable investigation.

The final substantive judgment, whether a particular lawsuit should be maintained requires a balance of many factors — ethical, commercial, promotional, public relations, employee relations, fiscal as well as legal.

After an objective and thorough investigation of a derivative suit, an independent committee may cause its corporation to file a pretrial motion to dismiss. The basis of the motion is the best interest of the corporation, as determined by the committee. This should include a thorough written record of the investigation and its findings and recommendations.

First, the court should inquire into the independence and good faith of the committee and the basis supporting its conclusions. The corporation should have the burden of proving independence, good faith, and a reasonable investigation. If the court determines either that the committee is not independent or has not shown reasonable basis for its conclusions, the court shall deny the corporation's motion.

The second step provides the essential key to striking a balance between legitimate corporate claims as expressed in derivative stockholders' suits and a corporation's best interest as expressed by an independent investigating committee. The court should determine, applying its own independent business judgment, whether the motion should be granted. The court of chancery should give special consideration to matters of law and public policy in addition to the corporation's best interests. If the court's independent business judgment is satisfied, the court may proceed to grant the motion. Judgment reversed and remanded.

Case Questions

1. What is the issue surrounding the question of permitting shareholder derivative suits? What is the issue in permitting a special litigation committee of the board to dismiss derivative suits?

2. What reasons support permitting shareholder derivative suits? What reasons support permitting board oversight of corporate litigation?

3. What factors should be considered in a corporation's maintenance of litigation?

SHAREHOLDER RIGHTS IN CLOSE CORPORATIONS

The corporation statutes applicable to large, publicly traded corporations are not always well suited to closely held corporations because the latter are really hybrid *incorporated partnerships*. Many close corporation shareholders are employees, officers, and directors. There are far fewer passive investors than in public corporations. This integration of ownership and control in the hands of a few shareholders suggests why close corporations are often treated differently. However, experience has shown that minority shareholders are particularly vulnerable to

freezeouts or **squeezeouts,** an oppressive misappropriation of the minority's participation and property rights. Controlling shareholders often pay themselves the bulk of corporate profits through high salaries and perks, leaving the minority with poor dividend returns. Minority shareholders' inspection and litigation rights are often too costly to balance the majority's power effectively. Because few outsiders are willing to accept such risks of oppression, close corporate shares are not very marketable, further isolating the minority. Therefore, the courts often entertain minority shareholder oppression suits, fashioning appropriate remedies, as in the next case.

BALVIK v. SYLVESTER
411 N.W.2d 383 (N.D. 1987)

Elmer Balvik and Thomas Sylvester converted their electrical contracting partnership into the newly formed Weldon Corporation. The partners retained their portion of control in the new corporation, with Sylvester receiving 70 percent of the Weldon shares and Balvik receiving 30 percent. Soon after incorporation, a fundamental policy dispute arose in which Sylvester desired to reinvest corporate profits in Weldon and Balvik sought to withdraw these profits either as dividends or as bonus compensation. Eventually, Balvik was fired, allegedly for poor performance. This also ended his receipt of financial benefits: his salary was discontinued, dividends were insufficient, and his capital contribution remained with Weldon. Balvik sought court dissolution of Weldon Corporation claiming Sylvester committed an illegal, oppressive, and fraudulent act. Sylvester appealed the trial court–ordered dissolution.

VANDE WALLE, Justice

The word "oppressive" can contemplate a continuing course of conduct. The absence of mismanagement or misapplication of assets does not prevent a finding that the conduct of the dominant directors or officers has been oppressive.

The limited market for stock in a close corporation and the natural reluctance for potential investors to purchase a noncontrolling interest in a closed corporation that has been marked by dissension can result in a minority shareholder's interest being held

"hostage" by the controlling interest, and can lead to situations where the majority "freezes out" minority shareholders by use of oppressive tactics. Courts have analyzed alleged "oppressive" conduct by those in control in terms of "fiduciary duties" owed by the majority shareholders to the minority and to the "reasonable expectations" held by the minority shareholders in committing their capital and labor.

Balvik clearly has been "frozen out" of a business in which he reasonably expected to participate. As a result, Balvik is entitled to relief. We recognize that forced dissolution of a corporation is a drastic remedy which should be invoked with extreme caution and only when justice requires it. In a sense, a forced dissolution allows minority shareholders to exercise retaliatory "oppression" against a majority.

We believe that the trial court abused its discretion in ordering the extreme remedy of dissolution. Weldon is apparently an ongoing business, ordering its dissolution and liquidation is unduly harsh. Balvik sought as an alternative remedy that "the defendant pay to the plaintiff the true value of his stock." We believe that this is the appropriate remedy here. Consequently, we remand this case for the entry

order requiring either Weldon or Sylvester to purchase Balvik's stock at a price determined by the court to be the fair value thereof.

Case Questions

1. What is the issue in court intervention into the oppression of a minority shareholder through a freezeout or squeezeout?

2. For what reasons was Sylvester's conduct considered oppressive?

3. Is there any plausible rival hypothesis to explain Sylvester's activities in the *Balvik* case other than to oppress Balvik?

The RMBCA and several states, notably Delaware and New York, have special close corporation provisions, statutes, or supplements to better conform the law to the reality of close corporation governance problems. For example, the RMBCA's *Model Statutory Close Corporate Supplement* is available for adoption by any RMBCA state. These laws generally enable close corporations to operate informally like partnerships and authorize the special shareholder agreements and control devices discussed next. However, these laws vary widely in defining close corporations. Recall that federal tax law eliminates the double tax on dividends of Subchapter S Corporations with 35 or fewer shareholders. Delaware limits close corporation status to corporations with fewer than 30 shareholders; California limits it to 10 shareholders. Many statutes require the corporation to specifically elect to be treated as a close corporation.

Shareholder Voting Arrangements

Planning to prevent oppression before dissension arises in a close corporation is wise. The firm can adopt the statutory close corporation form, adopt special charter and bylaw provisions, enter shareholder or voting arrangements. Control can be held by a group of shareholders who contract together to vote their shares in a particular way. The **voting pool** requires all pool members to vote in a specified way, usually as the majority decides. Voting pools are enforceable if they have a proper purpose, such as to elect pool members to the board, but they cannot be designed to defraud creditors. Defectors breaching

the agreement may be ordered by specific performance to vote as agreed or submit to any binding arbitration provided in the *pooling agreement*. An **irrevocable proxy** may provide for an even stronger consolidation of votes, possibly avoiding litigation.

Voting trusts provide a still stronger and more formal consolidation of voting powers. A trustee is appointed to vote shares transferred into a trust that is governed by provisions to which the participating shareholders agree. Voting trusts must usually be written, filed with the corporation, hold legal title to the transferred shares, issue **voting trust certificates**—a security evidencing the former shareholder's financial but not control rights—and are limited to a 10-year duration. The voting trustee owes a fiduciary duty to the former shareholders, who become beneficiaries of the trust. For example, shares must be voted in the former shareholders' best interests. Voting trusts consolidate control in the trustee, who can be selected beforehand by beneficiary vote or some other criteria. They are useful where passive investors are unfamiliar with the business, or creditors require more security when loans are made to financially troubled corporations. Voting trusts were used widely to create monopolies in the late 19th century and were the original object of the federal anti*trust* laws.

Other devices mentioned previously are also used in close corporations. Certain classes of stock may have special voting privileges and preferential financial rights. Supervoting shares may be used to consolidate power in experienced insiders. Stock transfer restrictions are often used to exclude outsiders from participation. Supermajority votes may be required for fundamental corporate changes minimizing victimization of the minority. Special bylaw or articles provisions may abolish the board or permit shareholders to control the board's discretion in setting corporate policies, salaries, or dividends. Finally, agreements may establish preemptive rights, require arbitration, or resolve deadlocks.

END–OF–CHAPTER QUESTIONS

1. Explain the assumptions and operation of the corporate governance model currently in effect in most states' corporation law. How is this different from how corporate governance actually works in closely held and publicly traded corporations?

2. What are the assumptions underlying the open forum concept presumed for shareholder and board meetings? What are the alleged advantages to decisionmaking from this ideal? What alternate hypotheses are there for corporate governance under the open forum?

3. Why are proxies necessary? What could happen to corporate governance without the proxy system?

4. Jim has approximately 2,500 of the 10,000 outstanding shares in the XYZ Corp. There are seven directors to be elected at the next shareholders' meeting. Jim seeks to elect some representation to the board. Explain the shareholder voting device that might help Jim secure that voice on the board. Does Jim have sufficient shares to secure a seat?

5. What are the arguments in support of preemptive rights? What arguments can be used against the practice?

6. Magline stock was held by eight individuals, most of whom were employed by the corporation. Managers had low base salaries and potentially high incentive bonuses. Substantial earnings were retained in Magline for working capital, and no dividends were paid. After Miller, one of the principal shareholders, was injured, his participation and compensation were reduced while at the same time Magline became highly profitable. Should a court

of equity order Magline to pay dividends? See *Miller v. Magline, Inc.*, 256 N.W.2d 761 (Mich. 1977).

7. The petitioner bought shares in Honeywell, Inc., after learning it produced antipersonnel fragmentation bombs for use in the Vietnam war. Thereafter, the petitioner made unsuccessful attempts to examine Honeywell's shareholder list to electioneer for directors who would pledge to oppose the corporation's production of war munitions. Does the petitioner have a proper purpose for inspecting Honeywell's books and records? What is the impact of the determination of a proper purpose? See *State Ex Rel. Pillsbury v. Honeywell, Inc.*, 191 N.W.2d 406 (Minn. 1971).

8. The board of City Investing Co. rejected a tender offer from Tamco Ent., allegedly because it would have adversely impacted management's compensation. The derivative plaintiffs contended that the board breached its fiduciary duty in not permitting shareholders the advantage of the large tender offer premium Tamco offered. Are the derivative plaintiffs required to make a demand on the board before proceeding with the suit? See *Pogostin v. Rice*, 480 A.2d 619 (Del. Supr. 1984).

9. Rodd and his family held the majority of shares, board seats, and officerships in Rodd Electrotype Co. Rodd caused the corporation to repurchase some of his shares at a favorable price but denied this to Donahue, a minority shareholder. Must a corporation treat all shareholders equally when shares are redeemed? See *Donahue v. Rodd Electrotype Co.*, 228 N.E.2d 505 (Mass. 1975).

10. The two equal shareholders in the Certified Moving Corp. had a written agreement to arbitrate disputes in governing corporate matters. One party voted for and the other against a board resolution to purchase a warehouse. Should their agreement requiring arbitration of the board decision to purchase the warehouse be enforced? See *Application of Vogel*, 19 N.Y.S.2d 589 (Ct. App. 1967).

Chapter 42

Officers and Directors: Management Powers and Duties

■

CRITICAL THINKING INQUIRIES

As you read this chapter, you should be able to address the following:

- What reasons under the corporate governance model support giving management power over corporate affairs?
- What assumptions about inside directors' behavior suggest that the board of directors needs subcommittees composed of outsiders who are independent of corporate management? What evidence is there that boards perform better with at least some independent directors?
- What assumptions are made about the courts' competence to second-guess management's reasonable business judgment? What is the conclusion about the role of judicial review of managerial decisions?
- What are the value assumptions concerning the loyalties of corporate management? If there is evidence contradicting this assumption, how could legal rules constrain corporate officers' and directors' conflicts of interest?

MANAGERIAL PERSPECTIVE

The ABC Corp. is controlled by its board and the officers elected by the board. The ABC board is composed of all the ABC officers and a few prominent outsiders representing ABC's main suppliers, bankers, and customers. The outsiders recognize their lack of familiarity with ABC's operations, so they generally defer to the inside directors' judgments because the insiders have intimate knowledge of corporate operations. ABC has recently witnessed an eroding market share. Securities analysts have downgraded their forecasts of ABC's earnings, making the stock price decline. Most inside directors and officers own large blocks of ABC stock purchased through the company's stock option plan.

- What problems are presented when the ABC board negotiates its takeover by a large company?
- What special duties do the outside directors have in such a transaction?
- What benefits are there in the board's understanding of management's duties of care and loyalty in a takeover?

BOARD OF DIRECTORS

The powers of corporate boards flow from their election by shareholders and from corporation law granting the board "all corporate powers."[1] The board typically delegates the day-to-day decisionmaking responsibilities to officers (s)elected by the board. Officers, in turn, select managers to run the business. There are exceptions such as where the officers also constitute a majority on the board or where close corporate shareholders retain policymaking or even managerial powers. These relationships arise from corporation law, although they may be varied by private agreement (e.g., charter, bylaws, shareholder resolutions or agreements, board resolutions, voting trust, and/or bond indentures).

The board generally represents three constituencies: insiders, outsiders, and nonmanagement affiliates. **Insider board members** are regular employees, typically upper level managers and officers of the corporation, its subsidiaries, affiliates, or parent. They traditionally dominate board deliberations. **Outside directors** are not employees but are usually from other corporations or institutions, with no direct contractual relations with the corporation. Recent pressure by stock exchange rules, regulations, the SEC, and investors has increased the number of outside directors, arguably expanding the board's objectivity. Outsiders may have less direct financial and organizational ties to management. Their diversity can balance management by challenging unreasonable management policies when discussed in an open forum. **Nonmanagement affiliate directors** are recruited from other firms with which the corporation contracts: suppliers, major customers, investment bankers, law firms, past employees, employees' relatives, and consultants. The importance of corporate boards has increased in recent years. Directors' compensation has also increased significantly. Median board compensation was $47,000 per year in 1992 excluding expenses to attend meetings, liability insurance premiums, and sometimes substantial perks.

Director Qualifications

At the turn of the century, corporate law imposed stringent director qualifications: residence, shareholding, minimum age, and citizenship. However, modern corporation statutes leave such qualifications to the charter or bylaws. The bylaws often specify the number of board members, the minimum board quorum, and meeting notice requirements. Some laws and professional standards prohibit government officials, regulators, judges, and independent auditors from board membership to avoid conflicts of interest. Board members improperly elected or violating any applicable qualifications may be disqualified in a legal proceeding. These **de facto directors** must abide by the same fiduciary duties as properly elected and qualified **de jure directors.** Any board action taken with a de facto director vote is valid so long as the de facto director acts in good faith.

In some other industrialized nations, the corporate board composition is more rigidly regulated. For example, **codetermination** under German law requires representation by the corporation's labor union or unions on corporate boards to reinforce labor harmony. German corporations have two boards, a **supervisory board** with 5 union representatives, 5 representatives elected by shareholders, and 1 "public interest" representative elected by the 10 other board members. A second **managing board** has three members representing labor, sales, and production. Given Germany's rather tranquil labor environment and its traditionally strong competitive economy, critics often argue that the United States should adopt some variation of the codetermination model. United Steelworkers' president was admitted to the Chrysler board during that company's financial rehabilitation in the early 1980s. However, few other U.S. corporations have labor representation on their boards unless the corporation is employee-owned (e.g., Avis and Weirton Steel).

Board Elections

The corporation's initial board is named in the articles or elected by incorporators, usually at a meeting just following the corporation's initial organizational meeting. These *initial directors* are often called "dummy directors," particularly when they are law firm employees simply assisting the incorporation. Dummy directors are intended only to serve until replaced by shareholder vote after stock is issued. Regular directors are elected thereafter at regularly held annual shareholder meetings. Directors hold office for the period stipulated in the articles, typically one year, unless longer, staggered terms are required. Directors serve for their elected

---

[1]RMBCA §8.01(b).

term or longer, until validly replaced. Directors elected to replace a deceased or retiring director serve only the balance of that unfilled term. Most state corporation laws permit the board to vote for a replacement to serve for the remainder of an unfilled term, unless the charter or bylaws reserve that power to shareholders.

Classified Boards

Many corporations have **classified boards** with staggered terms lasting for several years. This permits continuity because only a portion of the board is replaced at any particular annual shareholder meeting. For example, assume ABC Corp. has a 12-member board classified into three groups of four directors each. Each year, only one group is elected to three-year terms. Four of the other eight directors hold over to the following year, and the other four hold office until they are up for re-election two years later. Classified boards have other purposes and effects: (1) they may specifically represent different classes of securities, (2) they impede takeovers because the bidder cannot replace a board majority for at least two years, and (3) they dilute the effect of cumulative voting, as discussed in Chapter 41. There is some pressure from regulators to restrict classified boards to prevent the practice from entrenching unresponsive management. Classified boards are summarized in Figure 42–1.

Removal

At one time, directors were removable only *for cause* after a hearing. Today, most states permit removal by a majority shareholder vote, but some states still require a showing of cause. If cumulative voting is used, no director can be removed if the number of votes cast against removal exceeds the number of votes needed to elect that director ini-

tially. If the charter or bylaws permit, a director may be removed without cause or by a vote of the board for cause. Minority directors would not be useful to ensure an open forum if they could be removed too easily by an antagonistic opposition.

During the 1980s, many corporations vulnerable to takeovers granted their top executives and board members quite favorable severance pay. These termination contracts are often called **golden parachutes** because the executive continues receiving high salary levels for several years after a hostile takeover, even if the executive is fired. After takeovers, managers in many acquired corporations are fired because of duplication or their alleged incompetence. Some observers argue golden parachutes amount to an unethical *waste* of corporate assets and a flagrant betrayal of management's fiduciary duties.[2] However, if an officer or director is unconcerned about continued pay after a takeover, the decision to merge may not be tainted with self-interest. The controversy is diminished somewhat where shareholders approve the golden parachute. Golden parachutes may contribute to managements' greater independence, permitting more forthright consideration of a takeover offer. A takeover target's stock price generally rises after golden parachutes are instituted. This suggests the market agrees that they neutralize management's conflicts of interest.

DIRECTOR MEETINGS

The board exercises powers specified by statute, the charter, the bylaws, and board resolutions. The predominate policy choices usually concern what prod-

[2]Philip Cochran and Stephen Wartik, "Golden Parachutes: A Closer Look," 26 *California Management Review* (1984), p. 111.

Figure 42–1 Board of Directors Classification

Board Type	Election Frequency	Effect on Takeover	Effect on Cumulative Voting	Representation of Classes of Securities	Board Continuity
Classified	Every year	Slows takeover	Tends to frustrate cumulative voting	Facilitates class representation	Preserves continuity
Unclassified	Every second or third year	Takeover bidder can replace board immediately	Full effect of cumulative voting	Class representation difficult	Uncertain continuity

ucts and services to provide, pricing, oversight of management, declaring dividends, setting compensation, and recommending fundamental corporate changes to shareholders.

Most board powers are exercised after deliberation and consensus. This may follow the formal process of voting on resolutions offered at meetings convened with a quorum after directors receive reasonable notice. The open forum deliberations at board meetings are even more critical than at shareholder meetings because directors are expected to exercise more business sophistication than shareholders.

Most corporations are required to hold **regular board meetings** at fixed intervals such as quarterly, semiannually, or annually. Notice of **special director meetings** must precede any meeting held at irregular or extraordinary times—for example, to consider an extraordinary action such as a merger. *Notice* to directors must be a reasonable advance announcement stating any extraordinary matters scheduled for deliberation. General statements about routine matters are usually sufficient. If notice is inadequate, shareholders could vote to invalidate the board's action. A director's attendance without receiving notice may constitute a **waiver of notice** unless the director specifically objects to the lost opportunity to prepare.

Valid action at board meetings, as at shareholder meetings, depends on the presence of a **quorum** to prevent tyranny by the minority. Many state laws, including the RMBCA, set the quorum at a majority of the directors. The charter or bylaws may vary this. The minimum quorum under the RMBCA, New York, and Delaware cannot be set below one third. New Jersey and Delaware permit members who are physically absent but are included through conference call or video conferencing to vote and be part of the quorum.

Board election and meeting requirements impact corporate ethics and operational efficiency. Election procedures that conceal the board's performance from open view and from more direct democratic shareholder choice may insulate the board from the shareholders' will. For example, inadequate notice requirements, a low minimum quorum, and classified boards make it difficult for shareholders to replace the board when the corporation performs badly. Nevertheless, these same policies can make corporate operations more efficient. Matters requiring quick action would be impeded by long notice

periods or a large quorum. Continuity and "institutional memory" of classified boards can facilitate better-reasoned decisions. Corporate governance design choices represent a trade-off between the perhaps fairer but somewhat inefficient outcomes of "pure democracy" as compared to the possibly less fair but more efficient outcomes if the board is somewhat more insulated from shareholders. Corporate governance is a continuing ethical debate balancing expediency against shareholder activism.

Action without Meetings

Takeover activities and emergencies occur suddenly and unexpectedly yet require quick responses, usually before the next regularly scheduled board meeting. Even special board meetings are impractical if long notice requirements and the geographical dispersion of outside directors cause delays. Outside directors are the most inconvenient members to attract in an emergency, yet their participation is the most crucial to well-reasoned decisions made without the appearance of conflicts of interest.

Corporate law permits a limited use of a more spontaneous method for consultation, deliberation, and consent. The RMBCA **director consent** procedure validates actions or resolutions made by the board in conference calls or in separate contacts. A unanimous written consent must describe the action taken, be signed by each director, and be reflected in the board minutes and corporate records.[3] A few states permit board action even without unanimous consent.

States generally prohibit directors from making agreements to limit their decisionmaking discretion. Directors are fiduciaries who must carefully consider their decisions without any constraint that might adversely impact the corporation. Agreements limiting directors' voting discretion frustrate the corporate governance model. For example, a contract might purport to prohibit the board from declaring a dividend, or it might purport to transfer individual director's voting rights to a controlling director. While most courts hold these agreements invalid, there is a trend to enforce them. This is particularly true for closely held corporations, where board contracts are more acceptable. Delaware and California make such agreements enforceable, although directors may not generally vote by proxy.

---

[3]RMBCA §8.21.

Board Deadlock

A corporate board risks **deadlock** whenever an even number of directors split their votes equally. It is clearly best to have an odd number of directors because unless an odd number of directors is absent or abstains from voting, deadlock is impossible. Some charters now provide for arbitration of deadlocked disputes. Without deadlock-breaking provisions, the courts may intervene in Delaware, New Jersey, and Pennsylvania, by appointing a custodian to exercise complete power over corporate decisions. For example, in *Wollman v. Littman*,[4] a temporary receiver was appointed to ensure the orderly functioning of the regular course of business until a dispute between two board factions was reconciled. However, if deadlock will irreparably harm the corporation it may be dissolved, liquidated, and the assets distributed to shareholders under a court order.

A few states, such as California, New Jersey, New York, Pennsylvania, and Texas, permit a court to appoint an impartial outsider as a **provisional director** to cast deadlock-breaking votes. Such extraordinary action is proper usually in close corporations where the continued deadlock would result in an impairment of the corporation's business. Therefore, the provisional director serves only during the deadlock or until removed by a court order or by a shareholder majority's written consent.

COMMITTEES OF THE BOARD

The division of responsibility between the board and management is most clear for outside directors because they run their own separate businesses. Some corporations even delegate day-to-day corporate management to outside professional management companies. For example, mutual funds hire independent professional investment managers. A corporation owning rental property could validly delegate the responsibility to rent its apartments to an independent property management company. Even where corporate employees manage the corporation, board oversight is so extensive and time-consuming that some tasks must be delegated to subgroups of the board. These **committees of the board** often research particular matters and report the findings to the whole board for possible action.

The actual decisionmaking on certain basic policy matters cannot be delegated to board committees, matters such as dividend declaration, bylaw amendments, filling board vacancies, or initiating mergers and acquisitions. Board committees may study these matters first and then recommend approval by the whole board. However, with few exceptions, the board can decline any board committee recommendation.

Types of Board Committees

The boards of most large corporations have an **executive committee** composed of the chairman of the board (COB), chief executive officer (CEO), and other specified executives and officers. Executive committees are provided for by corporate statute, charter provision, or the bylaws. Historically, the executive committee exercised many of the whole board's operational powers. However, this is diminishing as other special-purpose committees emerge.

Increasingly, special-purpose board committees are created by law, private standards, or custom. They are staffed largely with independent, outside directors to avoid insiders' conflicts of interest. For example, the New York Stock Exchange requires all listed corporations to have an **audit committee** composed solely of outsiders to monitor the corporation's accounting and auditing process, assess internal control, interact with independent auditors, and oversee the general audit program.[5] The audit committee must be independent of the CEO to prevent any authority or financial link that might bias the audit committee's work. Independence may prevent a self-interested management from falsifying accounting records or misappropriating corporate assets.

A **nominating committee** selects director candidates for shareholder vote. The SEC encourages the use of outside directors to enhance the unbiased selection of candidates. The **compensation committee** evaluates compensation packages (salary, bonuses, and stock options) approved by the board for management and for board members. However, conflict of interest questions would arise if the board

---

[4]*Wollman v. Littman*, 316 N.Y.S.2d 526 (N.Y. App. Div. 1970).

[5]*New York Stock Exchange Company Manual*, pp. A23–A30. Audit committees proliferated after the questionable payments scandals during the late 1970s following the Watergate era. This led to passage of the Foreign Corrupt Practices Act in 1977, which had a considerable impact on accounting.

set its own compensation. Use of an independent compensation committee that evaluates pay issues can reduce any perceived conflict. In some larger corporations, the pay of top managers often reflects recommendations by independent consultants who compare compensation levels of managers at similarly sized and/or competitor corporations. However, this process may be tainted because corporate CEO compensation seems uncorrelated with corporate performance, and CEO pay has risen much faster than inflation or other employees' pay.

Chapter 41 introduced the **special litigation committee,** composed of independent directors necessary to dismiss shareholder derivative litigation. When disinterested directors review any corporate litigation, the prospect of managements' conflict of interest is diminished. Additional types of committees reflect constant innovation. For example, an SEC Compliance Oversight Committee was developed in the SEC's 1989 settlement with Drexel Burnham Lambert, the junk bond underwriter. Significant SEC violations were found, suggesting the need for specialized oversight beyond what the audit committee could apparently provide. Board committees are summarized in Figure 42–2.

POWERS OF THE BOARD

The board is empowered to set corporate policy through analysis and resolution. It implements this power by selecting, monitoring, supervising, and dismissing corporate officers. Most corporate charters empower the board to amend bylaws unless this power is specifically reserved to shareholders. This power sharing is analogous to the narrower consensus needed to change the statutes of a political entity. Amendments to corporate charters, like constitutional changes in government, require broader consensus.

The board is responsible for evaluating and initiating **fundamental corporate changes**: charter amendments, mergers, sale of substantially all corporate assets, or dissolution. The board usually assesses fundamental changes and then negotiates with appropriate parties before seeking final shareholder

Figure 42–2   Board Committees

Committee Type	Committee Function	Inside versus Outside Directors	Comments
Executive	Oversees board's operations	Mostly insiders	CEO, COB, CFO, other major officers usually members
Audit	Prepares audit plan, Monitors auditing	Mostly outsiders	NYSE required
Nominating	Reviews director performance, Identifies candidates	Mostly outsiders (trend)	Intended to objectively evaluate management and directors
Compensation	Reviews management compensation and stock options	Mostly outsiders (trend)	Controversial Potential conflicts of interest
Special Litigation	Reviews shareholder derivative suits, Can dismiss suits	Mostly outsiders	Averts damaging litigation
SEC Compliance Oversight	Oversees compliance with SEC regulations	Mostly outsiders	May be SEC required

approval. Thereafter, shareholders are usually entitled to approve or reject the proposal. For example, ABC Corp's. board must first initiate merger negotiations with a large takeover bidder. If the board resolves to proceed, shareholder approval is required before the transaction is effective.

The board's fiduciary oversight duties often require the inspection of corporate records. Competent decisionmaking assumes each director has access to corporate books, records, financial statements, correspondence, memoranda, and minutes. This **director's inspection right** is superior to shareholders' inspection rights because it is unqualified in many states. On the other hand, Delaware permits the corporation to deny a director access unless a court verifies that the director has no adverse personal interest. The director may generally be accompanied by an attorney or accountant for advice and make reasonable extracts of the documents inspected. Former directors may be denied access to records unless the inspection is necessary to vindicate their personal responsibility as former directors.

Directors may bring **director derivative suits** similar to shareholder derivative suits. These may become necessary if a conflict of interest by other directors prevents the corporation from vindicating corporate rights. The director sues only in a representative capacity; as in shareholder derivative suits, any recovery belongs to the corporation and not to the director individually.

CORPORATE OFFICERS

Corporations typically have *officers* selected by the board to carry out the board's policy directives and operate the business. All corporate employees are hired by officers or under their direction. Some closely held corporation bylaws reserve the election of officers to the shareholders. Officers are usually agents of the corporation, so they owe the duties of care and loyalty. Many officers also serve on the board. Most state laws permit corporations to have fewer or more than the traditional officer positions: chief executive officer (CEO), chief financial officer (CFO), chairman of the board, president, several vice presidents, secretary, and treasurer.

Officers must conform to any officer requirements stipulated in corporate law, charter, or bylaws. For example, the ABC Corp. bylaws might require the COB to also serve as a director, the chief legal counsel to be a licensed attorney, and the CFO to be a CPA. While one person may usually hold more than one office simultaneously, some states prohibit holding two offices with incompatible functions, such as secretary and president. Officers are agents, so the corporation always has the *power* of removal with or without cause unless dismissal procedures are specified in the charter or bylaws. However, the corporation may not have the *right* to remove officers working under a long-term employment contract. If an officer is dismissed without the right to do so, the corporation is liable for salary for the remainder of the contract term, although the officer must usually try to mitigate damages.

Officer Power and Authority

Each particular officer's authority is derived from state law, the charter, bylaws, board resolutions, or from custom. Some corporations grant particular officers rather specific *express authority*. Many corporations grant higher ranking officers more general powers that are stated in vague terms, permitting *implied authority* to expand the more general express authority granted. When a particular officer's power to make a contract is questioned, it may be necessary to show proof of authority, such as a bylaw provision or board resolution. Unauthorized officers do not bind the corporation and may be personally liable for such acts the corporation later gives it's *ratification*.

A particular officer's authority to act for the corporation in a particular way raises the question of inherent powers. This is a form of implied authority combined with apparent authority, custom, and precedent. **Inherent authority** may be presumed to reside with a particular type of office. Traditional express authority and inherent authority of each type of officer are discussed in the following sections and are summarized in Figure 42–3 on page 884.

President

Traditionally, the president is a director and the principal corporate officer empowered to preside over officer meetings with no inherent authority except as stated in law or the bylaws. However, there is a trend to presume that the president is a more general corporate agent possessing broader powers. This is reinforced where the president also holds the title of *general manager* or *CEO*. Such a principal officer has authority to conduct the corporate business by making many employment, production, marketing, and financial decisions. The next case illustrates how a president might seek to act outside the traditional boundaries of the office.

LEE v. JENKINS BROTHERS
268 F.2d 357 (2d Cir. 1959)

Jenkins was given charge of the Bridgeport plant after Jenkins Brothers purchased it from the Crane Company. Yardley, as president of Jenkins Brothers, approached Lee, a former employee at the Bridgeport plant when under Crane control, offering Lee a pension of $1,500 per year starting in 1950 if Lee would remain at the Bridgeport plant. However, Lee was discharged in 1945, and no further pension payments were made pursuant to Lee's contract with Yardley. Lee sued Jenkins Brothers and Yardley for the unpaid pension.

MEDINA, Circuit Judge

The rule most widely stated is that the President only has authority to bind his company by acts arising in the usual and regular course of business but not for contracts of an "extraordinary nature." As the corporation became more common it became increasingly evident that many corporations, particularly small closely held ones, did not normally function in the formal ritualistic manner. While the board of directors still nominally controlled corporate affairs, in reality, officers and managers frequently ran the business with little, if any, board supervision. The natural consequence of such a development was that third parties commonly relied on the authority of such officials in almost all such transactions. The pace of modern business life was too swift to insist on the approval by the board of every transaction that was in any way "unusual."

It is generally settled that the president, as part of the regular course of business, has authority to hire and discharge employees and fix their compensation. In doing so he may agree to hire them for a specific number of years if the term selected is deemed reasonable. But employment contracts for life or on a permanent basis are generally regarded as extraordinary and beyond the authority of any corporate executive. Jenkins would have us analogize the pension agreement involved herein to these generally condemned lifetime employment contracts because it extends over a long period of time, is of indefinite duration, and involves an indefinite liability on the part of the corporation. It is said that

[lifetime employment contracts] unduly restrict the power of the shareholders and future boards of directors on questions of managerial policy; they subject the corporation to an inordinately substantial amount of liability; they run for long and indefinite periods of time. Of these reasons the only one applicable to pension agreements is that they run for long and indefinite periods of time. There the likeness stops. Future director or shareholder control is in no way impeded; the amount of liability is not disproportioned; the agreement was not only reasonable but beneficial and necessary to the corporation; pension contracts are commonly used fringe benefits in employment contracts. Moreover, unlike the case with life employment contracts, courts have often gone out of their way to find pension promises binding and definite even when labeled gratuitous by the employer.

Apparent authority is essentially a question of fact. It depends not only on the nature of the contract involved, but the officer negotiating it, the corporation's usual manner of conducting business, the size of the corporation and number of stockholders, the circumstances that give rise to the contract, the reasonableness of the contract, the amounts involved, and who the contracting third party is.

Assuming there was sufficient proof of the making of the pension agreement, reasonable men could differ on the subject of whether or not Yardley had apparent authority to make the contract, and that the trial court erred in deciding the question is a matter of law. [The pension's enforceability becomes a jury question.]

Case Questions

1. What is the primary issue in determining the breadth of the apparent authority of a corporate president?
2. What reasons support expanding the authority of a corporate president beyond traditional justifications for an apparent authority that arises for any other agent?
3. What assumptions have changed from the early days of corporate law concerning the inherent powers of the corporate president's office?

As the *Jenkins Brothers* case illustrates, there is growing recognition that corporate presidents and CEOs possess authority to hire and fire employees but not to promise lifetime employment, which must be deliberately approved by the board. The board must also approve extraordinary salaries, bonuses, and stock options for other officers and directors. Many corporations seek shareholder approval for ESOP and stock option plans when they become expensive. The SEC now requires disclosure of the projected value of all compensation, including stock option plans, for the top five officers. This permits shareholders to raise objections to management compensation at annual shareholder meetings. This regulation was prompted by the perception that top corporate executives' salaries were excessive and uncorrelated to performance.

Chairman of the Board (COB)

The principal director who presides over board meetings is the **chairman of the board.** This office was traditionally combined with the president and/or CEO. However, there is a trend to split up the COB and the CEO to permit a balance between two powerful leaders by granting different types of influence. The COB in many corporations is an older senior executive who retains an advisory and policymaking role and relinquishes authority over operational matters to a younger CEO or president. This emerging bifurcated leadership model suggests that there may be some incompatible functions between these two positions, reinforcing the split.

Vice President

The position of vice president has evolved somewhat from the single person who often acted as "second in command." Increasingly, numerous vice presidents head various distinct corporate functions (e.g., finance, operations, design, and sales). In many corporations, the title vice president may be attached to distinct divisions, lines of business, or product lines. For example, assume ABC Corp. is a large automobile manufacturer with a vice president for each of three major car brands, one for trucks, and one for component and replacement parts. Traditionally, vice presidents had no inherent powers; they derived authority only from the bylaws and board resolutions. However, increasingly these various specialized vice presidents have more general authority within their functions or divisions, particularly over employment and production decisions. The senior vice president traditionally has direct succession to the presidency, although many bylaws specify succession when the president or CEO is unable to perform.

Secretary-Treasurer

Secretary and treasurer are two officerships with minimal inherent powers, so bylaws or board resolutions often give them specific powers. The **treasurer** oversees the corporate treasury and receives funds paid to the corporation. Disbursements must usually be authorized by board resolution. The **secretary** keeps corporate records and minutes of corporate meetings (e.g., board, officer, shareholder). The secretary is custodian of the **corporate seal,** a stamp affixed to authenticate corporate documents by making an impression in wax or stamped into paper. Some states still permit the seal to be used as a corporate agent's signature on corporate contracts or legal instruments. Secretaries in these states must carefully guard against unauthorized access to the corporate seal.

Some corporations appoint the same person as secretary and treasurer. The chief financial officer (CFO) may be variously designated as the vice president of finance, vice president of accounting, comptroller, or treasurer. Some corporations have more than one of these offices to split up financial policymaking and financial operations among two or more individuals.

Figure 42–3   Corporate Officers' Powers and Authority

Officer	Function	Typical Authority	Inherent Authority
Chairman of the Board (COB)	Presides over board meetings	Votes and deliberates	None
Chief Executive Officer (CEO)*	Presides over officer meetings, general agent over operations	General authority over operations	Broad
President	Presides over officer meetings, general agent over operations	General authority over operations	Broad
Vice President(s)	Operates assigned division or function	General authority within function or division	Within line of succession to presidency in emergency
Chief Financial Officer (CFO)	Controls financial operations	General authority over finance	None
Secretary-Treasurer	Keeps corporate records, guards financial assets	General authority over finance and corporate records	Holds corporate seal, Deposits checks payable to corporation

*Also known as general manager.

DUTY OF CARE

All corporate employees are fiduciaries; this includes directors, officers, managers, and employees. Traditions from tort and agency law require all members of management to act with due care and loyalty in the activities undertaken for the corporation. This responsibility often exposes management to scrutiny over the outcomes of their decisions and their underlying state of mind in acting. Accountability varies with management's intent; a stronger mindset produces more severe sanction than simple or ordinary negligence. Recklessness or gross negligence lies somewhere in between. This section explores management's duty of care, essentially a standard of negligence.

Three general matters are important in determining management's care. The first focus is on the type of act in question. Management may be liable for *omissions* in negligently failing to act when it should have or for *commissions* of acts that directly damage the corporation or shareholders. Next, management decisions are reviewed against standards of care

stated in statutes, case law precedents, and the judge or jury's personal expectations for managerial performance. Finally, the business judgment rule gives management significant latitude in decisionmaking. Management may be absolved from liability for alleged harm if decisions are made in good faith. Management must generally act with ordinary reasonable prudence and with reasonable diligence, a standard set through comparison with other similarly situated managers. Most state corporation laws provide a formulation for this duty similar to RMBCA §8.30.

RMBCA §8.30 General Standards for Directors

(a) A director shall discharge his duties as a director, including his duties as a member of a committee:

(1) in good faith;

(2) with the care an ordinarily prudent person in a like position would exercise under similar circumstances; and

(3) in a manner he reasonably believes to be in the best interests of the corporation.

Duty of Attention

Directors must give at least a minimum of attention to the corporate matters before them. Some corporate statutes and case law require directors to make "reasonable inquiry" into matters presented or coming to the board's attention. Directors must generally attend meetings, gain knowledge about the corporation's operations and markets, and monitor its financial condition. Directors must record their dissent to decisions believed unlawful or unauthorized. They must seek expert advice for corporate decisions involving significant aspects of law, regulation, accounting, or investment banking. Directors should resign if unable to meet this minimum burden.

Many older cases recognized no difference among directors, holding all to the same standard of due care. However, some more recent cases have held *inside directors* to a more thorough understanding of corporate matters than *outsiders* because insiders have constant exposure and participate in corporate tasks, presumably giving them an advantage. Outsiders naturally have less familiarity with corporate affairs due to other demands on their time.

In closely held corporations, directorships are often held by spouses and other family members of the principals. These may be **nominal directors,** mere figureheads who serve gratuitously and without any real expectation of taking responsibility. Many courts hold them to a lesser expectation of performance. However, the majority rule remains that *all* directors are held to the same *objective* standard of conduct. By contrast, the directors of financial institutions (e.g., banks or investment companies) make decisions that not only affect their own shareholders but also directly impact customers' assets. Confidence is critical in the safety of the financial system that in turn impacts all sectors of the economy. Therefore, such directors are often held to a higher standard of care than the directors of nonfinancial corporations.

Right to Rely

Directors' duty of care may intimidate many outsiders from joining corporate boards just as their objective influence is needed most. However, the duty of care does not effectively require full-time "hands-on" exposure to all internal corporate workings. Directors' decisionmaking may be legitimately based on information and reports prepared by management. Even inside directors are unable to directly observe all relevant corporate details. Directors may rely on the reports, information, statements, or decisions supplied by officers, employees, outside consultants, independent auditors, and board committees, if made in good faith.

This **right to rely** is limited where suspicious circumstances would lead a reasonably acting director to independently investigate and verify the report. When incorrect information is supplied, the board may believe it unless circumstances suggest otherwise. For example, directors of the ABC Corp. are entitled to believe the value a professional appraiser gives a corporate asset unless the appraiser's conflict of interest becomes evident. The RMBCA §8.30 (b) is typical in permitting reliance.

RMBCA §8.30 (b) General Standards for Directors

(b) In discharging his duties a director is entitled to rely on information, opinions, reports, or statements, including financial statements and other financial data, if prepared or presented by:

(1) one or more officers or employees of the corporation whom the director reasonably believes to be reliable and competent in the matters presented;

(2) legal counsel, public accountants, or other persons as to matters the director reasonably believes are within the person's expert or professional competence; or

(3) a committee of the board of directors of which he is not a member if the director reasonably believes the committee merits confidence.

Business Judgment Rule

The duty of care seems to permit the courts to regularly second-guess director decisions. However, this could potentially deter many qualified board candidates, particularly outsiders. The courts shield directors from such extensive liability under the **business judgment rule,** which recognizes that business decisions involve the deliberate balancing of potential risks and rewards. Directors are not personally liable even if later events produce losses so long as they make informed decisions with a rational basis, within their authority, in good faith, and without conflicts of interest. Acts motivated by personal self-interest are disloyal. This breaches the fiduciary duty of loyalty, as discussed later in this chapter.

The business judgment rule gives the board a qualified immunity from shareholder suit to encourage innovation and calculated risk-taking. The courts recognize it would be inappropriate to use hindsight to second-guess complex decisionmaking by managers using their professional intuition and experience. A trial held long after the events in question cannot accurately recreate the pressured environment in which the decisions were made. As the following case illustrates, shareholders must prove serious and gross negligence or recklessness before a business judgment is deemed unreasonable.

SHELENSKY v. WRIGLEY
237 N.E.2d 776 (Ill. App. Ct. 1968)

The plaintiff minority shareholder, Shelensky, brought a derivative suit against the directors of the Chicago Cubs, alleging negligence and mismanagement. The corporation owned and operated the Chicago Cubs and operated Wrigley Field, the Cubs' home ballpark. Philip K. Wrigley, corporate president, owned approximately 80 percent of the stock. The Cubs were the only major league baseball team with no lights at their home field. In 1966, 932 of the total 1,620 major league games were played at night. Shelensky alleged that night games can maximize attendance, revenue, and income.

From 1961 to 1965, the Cubs sustained operating losses from baseball operation, which Shelensky attributed to inadequate Cubs' home game attendance. The director's refusal to install lights at Wrigley Field and schedule night games allegedly contributed to further deterioration in the Cubs' financial condition. Cubs daytime home games had substantially lower attendance than road games. Comparisons with the Chicago White Sox showed higher attendance and revenue with night games. Wrigley allegedly refused to install lights because of his personal opinion "that baseball is a day time sport and the installation of lights and night baseball will have a deteriorating affect on the surrounding neighborhood." Wrigley allegedly admitted that he is not interested in whether the Cubs would benefit financially from installing lights because of his concern for the neighborhood but would consider night games with a new stadium in Chicago. Shelensky also alleged that the other directors had acquiesced in Wrigley's policy, permitting him to dominate the board. Shelensky alleged that Wrigley's attitude was arbitrary and capricious and constituted mismanagement and waste of corporate assets and sought the liability of Wrigley and the other directors for negligence and failure to exercise reasonable care in managing corporate affairs.

SULLIVAN, Justice

We are not satisfied that the motives assigned to Philip K. Wrigley and through him to the other directors are contrary to the best interest of the corporation and the stockholders. For example, it appears to us that the affect on the surrounding neighborhood might well be considered by a director who is considering the patrons who would or would not attend if the park were in a poor neighborhood. Furthermore, the long run interest in the corporation and its property value at Wrigley Field might demand all efforts to keep the neighborhood from deteriorating. By these thoughts we do not mean to say that we have decided that the decision of the directors' was a correct one. That is beyond our jurisdiction and ability. We are merely saying that the decision is one properly before the directors and the motives alleged in the amended complaint showed no fraud.

Plaintiff claims that the losses of defendant corporation are due to poor attendance at home games. However, factors other than attendance may affect the earnings or losses. For example, in 1962, attendance at home and road games decreased appreciably compared with 1961, and yet the loss from direct baseball operation and of the whole corporation was considerably less.

The record shows the plaintiff did not feel that he could allege that the increased revenues would be sufficient to cure the corporate deficit. The only cost plaintiff was at all concerned with was that of installation of lights. No mention was made of operation and maintenance of the lights or other possible increases in operating costs in night games and we cannot speculate as to what other factors might influence the increase or decrease if the Cubs were to play night home games.

Finally, we do not agree with plaintiff's contention that failure to follow the example of the other major league clubs in scheduling night games constituted negligence. Plaintiff made no allegations that these teams' night games were profitable or that the purpose for which night baseball had been undertaken was fulfilled. Furthermore, it cannot be said that directors, even those of corporations that are losing money, must follow the lead of the other corporations in the field. Directors are elected for their business capabilities and judgment and the courts cannot require them to forgo their judgment because of the decisions of directors of other companies. Courts may not decide these questions in the absence of a clear showing of dereliction of duty on the part of the specific directors and mere failure to follow the crowd is not such a dereliction. For the foregoing reasons the order of dismissal entered by the trial court is affirmed.

Case Questions

1. What is the issue in an alleged director negligence and mismanagement suit?

2. What reasons support the business judgment rule that prohibits courts from second-guessing managerial decisions unless there is fraud or arbitrary or unreasonable conduct?

3. What other hypothesis might be consistent with the Cubs' poor financial performance other than the potential for higher revenues with the larger attendance at night games?

The business judgment rule received wide attention during the takeover boom of the 1980s. Poorly managed corporations became vulnerable to takeovers challenging the board to act in the best interests of shareholders, employees, suppliers, customers, and the communities surrounding corporate facilities. Mergers were feared because some corporate raiders were widely known to replace the target management after the takeover. As the *TransUnion* case that follows illustrates, corporate boards have no immunity if they rely on insufficient information or management succumbs to an obvious conflict of interest. The business judgment rule requires the board to act with diligence in creating a rational basis for decisions to accept or oppose a takeover. Defensive tactics must be reasonable, considering any threat posed by the hostile bidder.

SMITH v. VANGORKOM
488 A.2d 858 (Del. 1985)

VanGorkom was chairman and CEO of TransUnion Corporation, owning approximately 75,000 shares. He was approaching retirement. TransUnion had considerable investment tax credits but was unable to use them because of insufficient income, making TransUnion worth more merged into a profitable company than left independent. VanGorkom agreed with members of the Pritzker family to merge TransUnion into the Marmon Group, Inc., controlled by the Pritzkers. TransUnion stock was then trading in the $30 per share range, and the Pritzker offer of $55 per share represented a substantial premium. VanGorkom proceeded to ramrod the merger proposal through the TransUnion board with only a short undocumented presentation summarizing the Pritzkers' offer.

None of the TransUnion directors was a trained financial expert. The board included outside directors with strong business credentials—four were chief executives of major publicly traded companies. After a short (two-hour) discussion, the board approved the merger without examining any merger documents or receiving any expert financial advice. Shareholders approved the merger with a nearly 80 percent margin. Thereafter, suit was brought by some TransUnion shareholders alleging that the directors acted unreasonably and abused their business judgment. The shareholders appealed an adverse ruling by the trial court in favor of TransUnion's Board.

HORSEY, Justice

Directors are charged with an unyielding fiduciary duty to the corporation and its shareholders. The business judgment rule exists to protect and promote the full and free exercise of the managerial power granted. The party attacking a board decision as uninformed must rebut the presumption that its business judgment was an informed one; turning on whether the directors have informed themselves "prior to making a business decision, of all material information reasonably available to them." There is no protection for directors who have made "unintelligent or unadvised judgment." A director's duty to exercise an informed business judgment is in the nature of a duty of care, as distinguished from a duty of loyalty.

In a specific context of a proposed merger, a director has a duty to act in an informed and deliberate manner in determining whether to approve an agreement of merger before submitting a proposal to the stockholders. The TransUnion board did not reach an informed business judgment in voting to sell the company for $55 per share pursuant to the Pritzker cashout merger proposal. The directors (1) did not adequately inform themselves as to VanGorkom's role in forcing the sale of the company and in establishing the purchase price; (2) were uninformed as to the intrinsic value of the company; and (3) given the circumstances, were grossly negligent in approving the sale of the company upon two hours' consideration without prior notice and without the exigency of a crisis or emergency.

Without any documents before them concerning the proposed transaction, the members of the board were required to rely entirely upon VanGorkom's 20-minute oral presentation of the proposal. No written summary of the terms of the merger was presented; the directors were given no documentation to support the adequacy of a $55 price per share; and the board had before it nothing more than VanGorkom's statement of his understanding of the substance of the agreement.

Directors are fully protected in relying in good faith on reports made by officers. There is no evidence that any report concerning the Pritzker pro-

posal was presented to the board. VanGorkom's oral presentation of the terms which he had not seen and a brief oral statement regarding the feasibility of leveraged buyout do not qualify as reports. VanGorkom was basically uninformed as to the essential provisions of the very merger document about which he was talking. At a minimum, a report must be pertinent to the subject matter upon which the board is called to act. Considering all of the surrounding circumstances—hastily calling the meeting without prior notice, the proposed sale without any prior consideration of the issue or necessity, the urgent time constraint imposed by Pritzker, and the total absence of any documentation whatsoever—the directors were duty bound to make reasonable inquiry and the inadequacy of that upon which they now claim to have relied would have been apparent.

A substantial premium may provide one reason to recommend a merger, but in the absence of other sound valuation information, the fact of a premium alone does not provide an adequate basis upon which to assess fairness of an offering price. Counsel advised the board it would be subject to lawsuits if it rejected the $55 per share offer. It is of course a fact of corporate life that today when faced with difficult or sensitive issues, directors are often subject to suit, irrespective of the decisions they make. However, counsel's mere acknowledgment of this circumstance cannot be rationally translated into a justification for a board permitting itself to be stampeded into a patently unadvised act. The defendants contend that the stockholders' overwhelming vote approving the Pritzker merger agreement had the legal effect of curing any failure of the board to reach an informed business judgment in its approval of the merger. However, TransUnion's stockholders were not fully informed of all facts material to their vote on the Pritzker merger. The director defendants breached their fiduciary duty of candor by their failure to make true and correct disclosures of all information they had, or should have had, material to the transactions submitted for stockholder approval.

We hold, therefore, that the trial court committed reversible error in applying the business judgment rule in favor of the director defendants in this case. Reversed and remanded.

Case Questions

1. What is the issue in the case that would permit directors to take advantage of the business judgment rule?

2. For what purpose did the defendant-directors argue that a fairness opinion was unnecessary and that they were subject to suit for rejecting the Pritzkers' $55 offer? Are these relevant to the question of whether the board was adequately informed?

3. Given the holding in the *TransUnion* case, what steps must be taken by corporate boards of target corporations before approving a merger proposal?

Following the *TransUnion* case, apprehension about potential liability spread among the boards of many vulnerable potential target corporations, making it more difficult to recruit competent outside directors. Thereafter, most states, including Delaware, enacted laws permitting corporations to indemnify their boards for breach of the duty of care as discussed later in this chapter.

FIDUCIARY DUTY OF LOYALTY

The fiduciary duty of loyalty is the most fundamental aspect of an agent's responsibilities to the principal. For corporate employees, officers, and directors, the fiduciary duty requires the highest of fidelity and trust in all activities affecting the corporation and sometimes in actions directly affecting shareholders. The board, officers, and management must devote undivided allegiance to the corporation in all corporate decisions. Management must avoid all conflicting interests and secret profits if gained at the corporation's expense.

Although the fiduciary duty of corporate employees is necessarily written in vague terms to capture many types of disloyal acts, it is not so ambiguous in application. Several recurring types of conflict of interest transactions may attract managers but are forbidden by the fiduciary duty of loyalty: (1) conflicts of interest, (2) transactions with the corporation, (3) interlocking directorates, (4) competition with the corporation, (5) usurpation of corporate opportunities, and (6) establishing compensation for the board and management.

Conflicts of Interest

Corporate managers may be tempted to accept bribes, kickbacks, secret payments, or "gifts" from suppliers or customers to direct corporate business to a particular outsider. For example, assume the ABC Corp. purchasing manager is invited to spend a complimentary week at a SupplyCo's north-woods hunting lodge. After attending, ABC's purchasing manager subsequently cancels a competing supplier's contract and grants the new contract to SupplyCo. This suggests a conflict of interest because it appears that the purchasing manager yielded to a personal and conflicting interest—his best judgment on ABC's optimal supplier was affected by the SupplyCo "gift." Employees representing both sides in a transaction breach the fiduciary duty to one or both corporations. As discussed in Chapter 35, independent agents can represent two principals only if both principals give their fully informed consent.

Transactions with the Corporation

Another conflict of interest arises where the corporate employee enters a transaction with the corporation. The corporation may invalidate an unfair contract made with a director. Most corporation laws provide a special approval process for such *conflict of interest transactions* between an *interested director* and the corporation. Typically, a transaction is not voidable if the corporation makes a fully informed consent through approval with a board or shareholder resolution or if the transaction is intrinsically fair to the corporation. Board ratification is usually valid if a majority of the board members voting in favor of the transaction are **disinterested directors,** who have no interest in the transaction and are not under the employment control of any interested director. A compensation or audit committee of the board composed of outside directors is particularly well suited to approve such transactions because of its independence.

Interlocking Directorates

Director conflicts of interest can arise between the corporation and some other corporation in which a director has a financial interest. There is an **interlocking directorate** where a director holds seats on two corporate boards. Such connections exist quite frequently because there is a limited pool of talented directors from which the thousands of publicly traded corporations can choose, creating demand for the more skillful directors. Additionally, outside directors with experience at other corporations provide critical competence to improve the board's decisions. The Clayton antitrust law prohibits interlocking directorates between two competing corporations because of the natural temptation to make collusive communications or fix prices through that director. However, interlocks between suppliers and customers or between totally unaffiliated corporations are generally not illegal.

A director sitting on the boards of two corporations that contract together can create a conflict of interest. The director could influence one corporation to accept an unfavorable transaction with the other corporation. The **intrinsic fairness** test applies to transactions between corporations with interlocking directorates. Approval by the board or shareholders based on disclosure of full material information is necessary unless the transaction passes the intrinsic fairness test.

Subsidiaries not wholly owned by the parent corporation often confront this problem when transactions occur between the corporations. Minority shareholders may validly question whether the parent's influence on the subsidiary's board causes the subsidiary's acquiescence to unfavorable contracts or the loss of valuable governmental advantages damaging minority shareholders' interests. The parent corporation has the burden of proving such transactions are fair to the subsidiary. This is seldom a problem if the subsidiary is wholly owned because no outside interest will be damaged if the intracorporate transaction is made at ''nonmarket'' prices.

Vertical integration is used quite extensively in Japan. Most Japanese corporations are organized into vertical ''trading groups'' called *keiretsu*. Large Japanese industrial firms solidify their relationships with suppliers, customers, banks, and investment bankers through *cross-shareholdings*, interlocking directorates, and supply contracts for a substantial amount of their output and requirements.

Pressure is allegedly communicated in the keiretsu through interlocking directors coaxing smaller suppliers to lower prices, improve quality or service, and abstain from supplying competitors. Such pressure may violate the director's fiduciary duty under U.S. law.

Competing with the Corporation

Managers are forbidden by the fiduciary duty from competing with the corporation. While corporate employees may ''moonlight'' during their off-duty time, they may not compete directly with the corporation's business. Of course, many employees learn new skills while working for one business and then leave to start their own competing businesses. While this does not directly violate the fiduciary duty, it raises fiduciary issues. For example, if Smith quits the ABC Corp. to start or join a competing firm, Smith's fiduciary duty to ABC forbids certain preparatory activities. Smith may not use ABC's facilities or confidential information and may not lure away other ABC employees or its customers before leaving ABC. As discussed in Chapter 35, employers can use employment contracts that include confidentiality and noncompetition clauses to protect their trade secrets and investment in employees.

Corporate Opportunity Doctrine

A variation of the prohibition against competing with the corporation is the **corporate opportunity doctrine.** Employees are forbidden from diverting or usurping for personal benefit any expectancy the corporation has in business opportunities or other properties. The employment contract implies that each employee will devote full and undivided time to corporate business, so on-duty time cannot be used for building up a personal business. This doctrine has two aspects: (1) the forbidden use of company assets (time, facilities, staff, and/or resources) to run a personal business, and (2) the forbidden diversion of a business opportunity the corporation might expect. The positions managers hold, particularly senior officers and inside directors, exposes them to business opportunities intended for the corporation. Managers use their positions to develop contacts and gain visibility. This constitutes a corporate asset. It violates the fiduciary duty and the corporate opportunity doctrine for managers to usurp opportunities for personal gain identified through their managerial positions if the corporation loses the profit potential.

Guth v. Loft[6] is the classic case of a diverted corporate opportunity. Guth was president of Loft, a confectioner, fountain syrup manufacturer, and candy retailer. Guth's position enabled him to discover that the Pepsi-Cola formula and franchise system was available for purchase out of its 1931 bankruptcy. Loft had been unable to receive cost reductions from Coke, its main cola supplier. Rather than offer the advantageous purchase of the Pepsi business to Loft, Guth used Loft's resources, his work time at Loft, and the discovery of Pepsi to take the Pepsi opportunity for himself, through a corporation he secretly formed. The diversion of Pepsi for Guth's personal and selfish purposes breached his fiduciary duty to Loft and put Guth in direct competition with Loft.

Identifying Corporate Opportunities

If corporate employees are permitted to have employment or financial interests outside work, what principle distinguishes these activities from prohibited corporate opportunities? Generally, management may cultivate personal business opportunities that have no close similarity with the corporation's existing or planned lines of business. The *expectancy theory* forbids managers from pursuing corporate opportunities where the corporation has an interest or expectancy arising from some previous corporate right or relationship. A more restrictive model is applied in New York and Delaware, the *line of business* test. Employees' personal business activities are forbidden if they lie in the same line of business as the corporation's existing or prospective range of activities. A few states apply the *intrinsic fairness* test, declaring an employee's activity as a corporate opportunity on an ad hoc basis. These three tests often overlap.

After the corporation or shareholders suing derivatively establish that the employee's activity is a forbidden corporate opportunity, the burden of proof shifts, requiring the employee to justify the activity. Evidence that the opportunity was presented to the corporation first and then rejected by the board is helpful. It is always safest to fully disclose the opportunity and receive approval from a disinterested majority of the board before personally pursuing any corporate opportunity. An employee's activities may fall under an exception, such as the permissible personal investment portfolio of managers in financial firms and exceptions negotiated in the manager's employment contract. The insider trading prohibition discussed in Chapter 45 is essentially a variation of the corporate opportunity doctrine and an extension of the confidentiality aspect of the fiduciary duty.

Management Compensation

Management compensation is an increasingly controversial and complex matter. Income tax considerations, pension regulations, and the labor markets complicate management compensation. For example, funds flow through the corporation as tax deductible corporate expenses but later become taxable to employees as salary. There are numerous taxability issues for deferred compensation (e.g., pensions) and for an employees' receipt of nontaxable benefits (e.g., perks, fringe benefits, company cars, insurance). Salaries may appear excessive in some close corporations if dividends are disguised as compensation or as tax-free perks to avoid the double tax on dividends. Management, particularly officers and directors, are in a position to control their own compensation, triggering conflict of interest questions. This section discusses how corporate law constrains management compensation.

Variable elements of compensation are used increasingly to motivate employees by correlating compensation to the corporation's performance: ESOPs, bonuses, and stock options. Most ESOPs are approved by shareholders, particularly when additional shares must be authorized.

Directors receive increasing amounts of compensation and other benefits. To avoid conflicts of interest, the board's compensation committee should be composed of outside directors who set compensation for board members, officers, and upper-tier managers. Generally, this compensation must be reasonable, considering the services performed and the pressures of the labor markets. Unreasonably high pay may be challenged in a shareholder derivative suit as a conflict of interest and a waste of corporate assets. There are proposals to deny corporate tax deductions for compensation over $1 million if the compensation is not tied to corporate

---

[6]*Guth v. Loft,* 5 A.2d 503 (Del. 1939).

performance. A few cases have invalidated compensation paid for past services, presuming that undue influence inspired the decision.

Loans to employees or officers may appear as a conflict of interest, particularly when made to less-creditworthy employees or at below-market interest rates. Many states require board or shareholder approval of such insider loans and also require that the loan must benefit the corporation. For example, it might be improper for ABC Corp. to offer a large loan at below-market rates to facilitate a newly hired executive to purchase a new home. However, if the board determined that hiring the new executive was essential but the executive would not accept the position without the assurance of a new home, then the insider loan might be validated.

The Burgeoning Growth in Executive Compensation*

Top executives' compensation grew at alarmingly fast rates through the 1980s as corporate profits and stock prices rose. However, the bubble burst, stock prices fell, layoffs abounded, and a recession hit yet executive pay continued increasing at many companies. Sometimes their pay increased at triple the rate of other employees. Graef Crystal, a former management compensation consultant turned critic, argues that top management pay at many companies rises when the corporation is either successful or unsuccessful frustrating the incentive theory of executive compensation.

Experts often disagree widely on the precise compensation received by any particular executive of a publicly-traded corporation. Standards for disclosing compensation in past years' annual reports and in proxy statements have permitted significant elements of executive pay to become buried in financial footnotes. For example, stock options are often granted to top executives at prices reflecting a significant discount over the current market prices. The executive may be given several months to exercise the options, reaping an instant profit of the difference between the exercise price and the current market value. These matters have been decipherable by only a few experts because boards may later adjust the ''exercise prices'' of stock options to further favor the executive. This problem helps explain the vast differences between news reports of executives' pay and the ''salary'' figure as disclosed.

Independent compensation consulting firms are usually retained by the board's compensation committee to survey similar executives at competing firms to formulate a recommendation. The consultants' advice often suggests raising the top executives' pay to prevent other firms from hiring the executives away. This has led to steadily escalating executive pay at rates much higher than measures such as inflation, earnings growth, or other employees' pay. As corporate performance deteriorated in the early 1990s, executive pay continued to soar. This prompted critics' pressure on the SEC to permit non-binding shareholder votes on executive pay matters. Then the SEC required new disclosures showing clear comparisons between executive pay and corporate performance. One proposal would permit shareholder votes on the selection of compensation consultants which are allegedly beholden to top management. Another proposal would limit tax deductibility of excessive salaries.

A predictable outcome to this brewing controversy has been shareholder activism in the design of incentive pay plans. Some plans more closely link executive compensation to stock price, earnings per share, or other financial performance measures. However, such systems can have unintended and undesirable consequences. For example, a CEO might reduce R&D or advertising expenditures to temporarily raise earnings, stock price, and the CEO's pay.

*''The Burgeoning Growth in Executive Compensation,'' © 1993 by John W. Bagby,

Such action would compromise the corporation's ability to immediately compete or innovate in the future. Some CEOs' pensions are linked to corporate earnings in the last few years before their retirement giving an incentive to manipulate gross income and cut expenses. The temporary boost in earnings or the use of corporate cash flow to buy back stock that temporarily boosts stock price directly benefits the CEO. While all these actions arguably breach the CEO's fiduciary duty, the CEO may offer plausible alternate explanations, clouding the issue. Nevertheless, the once secret decisions on executive compensation are now being thrust into public scrutiny assuring somewhat closer monitoring of the fiduciary duty.

Thought Questions

1. What are the reasons that executive compensation has been rising at rates unconnected to corporate performance?
2. What assumptions are made in expanding shareholder activism to executive compensation matters?

Indemnification of Managers

Management is often exposed to suit by shareholders, regulators, and outsiders. Corporations may generally make advance payments or later **indemnify** an employee who incurred litigation expenses or paid a money judgment if the employee acted with reasonable business judgment and in good faith. Indemnification of certain expenses is prohibited because it reduces the executive's incentive to act carefully. However, as suits against management have proliferated, the states increasingly permit indemnification for litigation, irrespective of a favorable or unfavorable outcome of the litigation.

Following the *TransUnion* case discussed earlier in this chapter, most states have modified their corporation statutes. Some *require* corporations to indemnify management when it successfully defends a suit. Most states now clearly *permit* indemnification of managers unsuccessful in their litigation. There is some variation among the statutes: Some permit indemnification only of litigation expenses, not judgments, while others permit indemnification of court-approved settlements. Indemnification rights are usually stated in the charter, bylaws, or a separate agreement. A few states limit director liability for breach of the duty of care, some permit the corporation to alter the level of care expected, and some statutes set dollar limits on director liability. Shareholder approval for some changes is necessary in some states. Many of these expenses may be insured with directors and officers

(D&O) insurance, shifting the risk to an insurance carrier. However, some states still prohibit insuring deliberate acts of dishonesty.

TORTS AND CRIMES

Torts and crimes committed by corporate employees or for the benefit of the corporation present complex problems of responsibility. The direct and vicarious liability problems discussed in Chapter 36 are generally applicable to corporations. Corporations are liable for torts committed by servants acting within the scope of their employment. Conviction for many types of crimes requires proof of the actor's intent. Courts have traditionally refused to hold corporations liable because they had no mind to form this requisite criminal intent. Additionally, when corporate crimes occur only partial knowledge of the scheme is held by different employees, few understand the whole picture.

The attitude toward punishing corporations for corporate crime is changing. The federal government and most states now impose liability for criminal acts authorized by the board, an officer, or a supervising manager possessing authority. Additionally, there are an increasing number of crimes with broad public impact for which no proof of intent is required. For example, Ford was prosecuted for criminal negligent homicide for its Pinto design under an Indiana statute requiring no proof of intent. The next case illustrates how criminal responsibility can rise up the corporate hierarchy.

UNITED STATES v. PARK

421 U.S. 720 (1975)

Acme Markets was a national retail grocery chain with headquarters in Philadelphia, Pennsylvania. Acme's wholesale and retail distribution network employed over 36,000 employees responsible for moving food stored in 12 warehouses out to nearly 900 retail outlets. Acme was charged numerous times for violations of the federal Food, Drug, and Cosmetic Act in its failure to maintain sanitary conditions at some warehouses. Rodent infestation in its Baltimore warehouse was discovered by federal inspectors. Evidence showed that the rodent activity persisted in the warehouse and some lots of food had rodent contamination.

The U.S. attorney concluded that these repeated violations necessitated bringing criminal charges against Acme's chief executive officer, Park. Park admitted in testimony that Acme employees were theoretically under his control but that the company's organizational structure delegated food safety assignments to individuals who in turn had staff and departments under them. Park merely conferred with Acme personnel responsible for sanitation when receiving FDA inspection notices. Park testified that delegating this responsibility was all he could do to remedy these problems. Park appealed his conviction under the federal Food, Drug, and Cosmetic Act.

BERGER, Chief Justice

Cases under the Federal Food, Drug, and Cosmetic Act of 1906 reflected the view both that knowledge or intent were not required to be proved in prosecutions under its criminal provisions, and that responsible corporate agents could be subjected to the liability thereby imposed. A corporate agent, through whose act, default, or omission the corporation committed a crime, was himself guilty individually of that crime. The principle had been applied whether or not the crime required ''consciousness of wrongdoing,'' and it had been applied not only to those corporate agents who themselves committed the criminal act, but also to those who by virtue of their managerial positions or other similar relation to the actor could be deemed responsible for its commission.

In providing sanctions which will reach and touch the individuals who execute the corporate mission — and this is by no means necessarily confined to a single corporate agent or employee — the act imposes not only a positive duty to seek out and remedy violations when they occur but also, and primarily, a duty to implement measures that will ensure that violations will not occur. The theory upon which responsible corporate agents are held criminally accountable for ''causing'' violations of the act permits a claim that a defendant was ''powerless'' to prevent or correct the violation to ''be raised defensively at trial on the merits.''

The government establishes a prima facie case when it introduced evidence sufficient to warrant a finding by the trier of the facts that the defendant had, by reason of his position in the corporation, responsibility and authority either to prevent in the first instance, or promptly to correct, the violation complained of, and that he failed to do so. The failure thus to fulfill the duty imposed by the interaction of the corporate agent's authority and the statute furnishes a sufficient causal link.

We conclude that viewed as a whole in the context of the trial, the charge was not misleading and contained an adequate statement of the law to guide the jury's determination. Judgment affirmed.

Case Questions

1. What is the issue in *United States v. Park* concerning the personal liability of corporate officers for criminal violations committed by the corporation?

2. Many other crimes require that the prosecution prove specific intent by a particular individual before conviction. What ambiguities would exist in proving specific intent by individuals in a large organization?

3. What assumptions are made in *United States v. Park* concerning the power, authority, and understanding of a business's diverse parts by the CEO?

END–OF–CHAPTER QUESTIONS

1. What reasons are there to set qualifications for board members?

2. The XYZ Corp. is considering a charter amendment to classify its board of directors, staggering their terms. The XYZ board will then have nine members, in three classified groups consisting of three members each. Only one class of directors will be elected in each year to serve three-year terms that overlap the other two classes. What are the arguments that favor this approach? What are the arguments against classification?

3. TargetCo, an underperforming discount retail department store, had 11 board members, 6 of whom were outsiders residing in geographically dispersed cities. Fred Rated, the CEO of Campow stores, made a takeover overture to the CEO of TargetCo, James Hunker. James immediately phoned all TargetCo. board members separately, arguing that the takeover should be vigorously opposed. Discuss the legality of the board contact method James used. What reasons justify using such a method? What problems could arise if all board members are not willing to accept James' strategy?

4. What are the options confronting a corporation in which two equal factions of directors are deadlocked in their decision-making? What assumptions underlie these remedies?

5. PubCo is a publicly traded corporation with its stock trading on the New York Stock Exchange. Describe the type of board committee structure that PubCo will likely have, the committees' functions, and the character of each committee's membership.

6. Kanavos had borrowed money from Hancock Bank on numerous occasions, always dealing with Brown at the bank. Brown's responsibilities at the bank increased during this period, until he was promoted to executive vice president. Kelly, the bank's president, always approved Brown's loans. After Kanavos experienced financial difficulties, the bank's board approved a workout agreement. Unknown to the bank, Brown amended the agreement and Kanavos sued the bank when the board refused to honor Brown's amendment, claiming he was unauthorized. What reasons would support Brown's authority? What reasons would contradict his authority? See *Kanavos v. Hancock Bank & Trust*, 439 N.E.2d 311 (Mass. App. 1982).

7. Henry Ford's Model T was wildly successful, permitting the Ford Motor Co. to pay shareholders high regular and special dividends. As majority shareholder and in control of the board, Henry decided to discontinue the special dividend payments so he could achieve his avowed purpose of spreading the benefits of his industrial process invention, the assembly line, and spread the benefits of industrialized capitalism thereby enhancing the U.S. economy. He plowed these earnings back into Ford and vertically integrated the Ford Corporation. The Dodge brothers complained that his purpose was improper. What theory supports Henry Ford in his decision to discontinue dividends to invest in plant and equipment? What theory supports the Dodges' in their seeking a return of the missed special dividends? See *Dodge v. Ford Motor Co.*, 170 N.W. 668 (Mich. 1919).

8. Officers and key employees of Duane Jones, an advertising agency, quit Duane Jones to join a competitor, claiming that the work atmosphere had become intolerable. Before leaving, these personnel used corporate assets of Duane Jones to plan their move, took corporate files, and lured other employees and customers to the new firm. What are the issues arising in this case, and for what reasons should the court decide in favor of either party? See *Duane Jones Co. v. Burke*, 306 N.Y. 172 (1954).

9. Getty Oil owned or controlled 71 percent of the common stock of Skelly Oil; the remaining 29 percent was traded on the New York Stock Exchange. During the

federal government's mandatory oil import program, each oil company was given a quota on oil imports, effectively limiting their rights to import oil. The program administrator required Skelly to share in Getty's quota because it was a subsidiary. Getty sued for a declaration that it need not share its allocation with Skelly. Should the presence of common directors on the boards of Getty and Skelly determine how Getty allocates its import quotas between itself and its subsidiary Skelly? Explain. See *Getty Oil Co. v. Skelly Oil Co.*, 267 A.2d 883, (Del. 1970).

10. As founder, officer, and major shareholder of Cattle King Co., Inc., Stanko set the firm's policies and monitored operations from his home in a distant city. Stanko directed employees to violate the Federal Meat Inspection Act when federal inspectors were absent, rebox and resell meat rejected by retailers, misbrand and post-date meat shipments, and conceal evidence that returned meat was spoiled. Can Stanko or Cattle King be held liable for criminal violations of the federal meat inspection law? See *United States v. Cattle King Packing Co. Inc.*, 793 F.2d 232 (10th Cir. 1986).

Chapter 43

Fundamental Corporate Changes

■

CRITICAL THINKING INQUIRIES

As you read this chapter, you should be able to address the following:

- What is the issue in certain corporate transactions that make them so "fundamental" to the corporation's existence?
- What reasons support the minimum legal steps necessary for the approval of fundamental corporate changes?
- What assumptions are made about the behavior of management and controlling shareholders underlying their duties of care and loyalty during fundamental corporate changes?
- For what reasons do the managements of potential takeover target corporations install defensive devices to deter takeovers?

MANAGERIAL PERSPECTIVE

The ABC Corp. has a significant cash surplus. The ABC board has designated this cash for use in reinforcing ABC's existing lines of business and in expanding into related industries. The ABC vice president of finance has finished a study of potential investment targets. The study strongly recommends the acquisition of XYZ, a publicly traded corporation that manufactures component parts such as those used by ABC. After some preliminary negotiations between the two corporations' presidents, the XYZ president proposes to take XYZ private in a management buyout (MBO). After the MBO, the XYZ management team members will own the corporation and promise to exchange their XYZ shares for ABC shares. This will consummate ABC's acquisition of XYZ.

- Are there are management liability problems in the XYZ management's pursuit of this acquisition by cashing out XYZ's former public shareholders?
- Do ABC shareholders have any right to oppose the transaction?
- What must management do to accommodate dissenting shareholders — those who oppose the acquisition?

INTRODUCTION

The relationship between shareholders, the corporation, and the chartering state represents a contract that establishes a fundamental framework for the corporation's form and activities. The corporate governance model gives shareholders the right to veto fundamental corporate changes that would alter the corporation's basic nature and affect their *vested rights*. Permanent and significant alterations in the corporate structure are **fundamental corporate changes.** These include the amendment of the corporate charter, some types of merger, the sale of substantially all corporate assets, recapitalizations, and the dissolution of the corporation.

Most states require the board to initiate fundamental corporate changes by first studying the proposal before passing a board resolution. Next, the proposal must usually receive a larger majority of shareholder votes than is normally required. Some states and some corporate chargers require supermajority approval, such as by a two thirds shareholder vote. The RMBCA and Delaware require approval by a majority of outstanding shares, usually more than a simple majority of the votes cast. The RMBCA and a few other states permit minor charter amendments such as a corporate name change, extension of the corporate duration, and some expansion of capitalization without shareholder approval. Shareholders dissatisfied with such changes because they fundamentally alter the enterprise may dissent and receive *appraisal rights;* the corporation must then purchase their shares at fair value.

Fundamental corporate changes are also regulated by other major laws. For example, favorable federal tax treatment is a practical necessity for mergers or sales of assets. Mergers between publicly traded corporations usually require proxy solicitations; takeovers accomplished through tender offers are regulated under the federal securities laws. These federal securities law aspects are covered more fully in Chapter 45.

All types of business combinations potentially alter the competitive structure of their industries. Federal and state antitrust laws impact many business combinations, particularly mergers that tend toward a monopoly. This chapter discusses only the corporate law impinging on the attendant negotiation, approval, and corporate structure changes. Also, state antitakeover laws are discussed because they have been critically important since the takeover boom of the 1980s.

Fundamental corporate changes nearly always raise ethical questions because they impact the rights of shareholders and the expectations of other corporate constituencies (e.g., suppliers, customers, employees, and surrounding communities). Fundamental corporate transactions abruptly alter control over large blocks of corporate assets, change security holders' claims, and modify the established financial expectations of management. Therefore, conflicts of interest inevitably arise, particularly between the board, officers, shareholders, and other constituents. Much of the corporate law studied here addresses these conflicts by establishing minimum standards for management's behavior and the approval process.

Fundamental corporate changes are not easily consummated in most foreign nations. Takeovers have been prevalent in the United States, Great Britain, and Canada. However, Japan and most European nations have cultural aversions to takeovers, friendly or hostile, particularly by foreign firms. These cultural structures are often reflected in the corporation and securities laws of these nations. It may be difficult, sometimes impossible, to merge corporations without procuring significant consensus among most of these foreign corporations' constituencies and the host government. For example, Swiss law prohibited foreigners from holding voting shares in Swiss corporations until 1992, when the Swiss government gave mere symbolic permission for only small foreign holdings of Swiss voting shares.

Cultural aversions to takeovers are also reflected in unyielding attitudes that create nonlegal barriers to acquisitions. For example, T. Boone Pickens acquired nearly 30 percent of Koito, a publicly traded Japanese automotive electrical supplier that mainly serves Toyota. However, Pickens failed to win even one seat of Koito's board, allegedly because of Japanese cultural aversion to outsiders' interference with corporate governance. The Japanese may have viewed Pickens as a disruptive force seeking to disturb the corporate governance harmony that the Japanese prize so highly.

Many Third World nations prohibit takeovers allegedly out of fear that foreign control of their productive capacity will deplete their natural resources.

Even the United States erects barriers to foreign takeovers in some sensitive industries, particularly U.S. defense contractors and U.S. airlines. This is apparently intended to prevent adverse foreign influence on matters of national security. While corporate mergers and acquisitions receive varied treatment worldwide, the trend toward global financial markets may inevitably dismantle these barriers.[1] The trend toward privatization may provide a unique opportunity to reconfigure state-owned businesses through acquisitions by private corporations, some by foreigners.

CHARTER AMENDMENTS

Amendment to a corporation's charter fundamentally changes the corporation's "constitution," thereby altering the relative rights and liabilities among corporate constituencies. **Charter amendments** are permissible only if they could lawfully be contained in the original charter. Frequent amendments include a change in the corporation name, change in the authorized stock, amendment to the bundle of rights of particular classes of stock, creation of new classes of stock, classification of the board, changing the board's size, or extension of the corporation's life. During the 1980s takeover boom, many charter amendments established takeover defenses, some permitted indemnification of directors for breach of the duty of care, and others established employee stock ownership plans (ESOPs).

An amendment must begin as a board resolution and then receive shareholder approval. Successful amendments are then filed with the secretary of state in the state of incorporation, becoming effective only after a new certificate of incorporation is issued. Some states permit a state official—for example, the Corporation Commissioner in California—to review amendments to ensure that they are "fair, just and reasonable." Any amendment that would materially or adversely affect some class of shareholders may be disapproved unless the securities are publicly traded. The more extraordinary charter amendments trigger shareholder appraisal rights; minor amendments do not.

---

[1]See "Fear of Finance," *The Economist*, September 19, 1992, pp. 5–48.

Class Voting

If the charter amendment would adversely affect the vested rights of a particular shareholder class, that class may be given a **class vote.** For example, XYZ Corp. might defend against ABC's takeover attempt with an XYZ charter amendment. XYZ could reclassify XYZ common shares controlled by management to have supervoting powers, which would enable management votes to block a merger and dilute the voting power of all other common shareholders. Such a subordination would trigger a right by other common shareholders to veto the charter amendment. Even if the affected class was normally nonvoting, it would be given temporary voting rights.

The veto power is permitted to any class that would suffer adverse impact through a recapitalization or reclassification, changes in par value, number of authorized shares, or ownership benefits (e.g., liquidation or dividend preference, voting privileges, or preemptive rights). For example, an XYZ charter amendment might seek to cancel the accumulated but unpaid dividend arrearages of preferred shareholders. The normally nonvoting XYZ preferred shareholders could nevertheless veto the amendment. For what reasons would these preferred shareholders ever consider approving such an amendment? Perhaps a financially troubled corporation could avoid bankruptcy only if all classes of security holders gave up something, effectively "hunkering down" by restructuring its equity and debt.

CORPORATE COMBINATIONS: TAKEOVERS AND ACQUISITIONS

Fundamental changes occur with corporate combinations such as takeovers, mergers, consolidations, acquisitions, and purchases or sales of substantially all corporate assets. Merger and acquisition (M&A) activity is often explained by one or more theories. *Synergism* suggests that a combination of two or more corporations or parts are worth more together than separated due to *economies of scale* in operations and finances. For example, ABC and XYZ may have excessive administrative capacity while they are independent, but achieve economies when unnecessary services are combined. The merged corporation could eliminate duplicate layers of man-

Figure 43–1   Merger

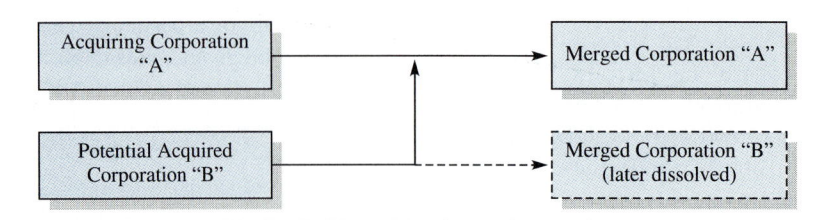

agement, accounting and legal staff, and executives, permitting significant cost savings. Some independent firms have complementary technologies or product lines that could be more effective when shared after a merger. Expertise in basic technologies could be applied to diverse manufacturing processes. XYZ might share its manufacturing know-how—for example, a similar "coatings" technology used in the production of such diverse products as photographic film, dry cell batteries, recording tape, and computer disks. Such operational synergies are often cited as a major justification for mergers.

Financial synergies are also cited to justify some corporate combinations. One firm's unused tax benefits (e.g., loss carryforwards) might be better used by the merged firm. Conglomerates have often resulted from such alleged financial synergies. When one division is in recession, another division's successes may smooth the combined firm's cash flows; cyclical successes by one corporation can fill in cyclical losses of another when merged. However, such financial synergies produce dubious benefits for shareholders, who are probably better able to diversify their own investments.

Takeover targets are often considered "undervalued" if the stock market is unwilling to bid up the stock price of a poorly managed firm. Takeover bidders often identify such targets to acquire them more cheaply than purchasing similar assets outright. The combined firm may be better managed and any unprofitable divisions spun off to reduce the financial drag on the combined new firm. However, the experience of the 1980s suggests that there is little profit from such takeovers. Once such targets are put "in play," the undervaluation evaporates as their price is bid up. This primarily benefits the target's shareholders. Takeover consultants such as investment bankers and lawyers charge high fees, further reducing potential profitability. Many takeovers

have been financed with junk bonds (high yield debt). However, such overleverage often imperils the merged firms' cash flow during recession, as evidenced by the numerous bankruptcies of firms merged in the early 1990s.

Mergers and Consolidations

Merger is a predominant corporate combination method—the acquired firm is absorbed by the acquiring firm. The surviving firm inherits all the assets and liabilities of the acquired firm, so the latter may be dissolved. Shareholders of the acquired firm are paid for their shares with cash, securities in the acquiring firm, debt, or some combination. Most mergers result from some negotiations among both corporations' managers that results in an *agreement in principle* specifying the terms of exchange. "Out" clauses often permit either or both parties to cancel if significant changes occur before the final consummation. For example, ABC might retain the right to abandon the merger if too many of ABC's shareholders exercised their dissenters' appraisal rights. The boards and shareholders of both corporations must approve the transaction, including the terms of exchange—the price or the package of consideration paid for the acquired corporation's shares. This classic merger form is illustrated in Figure 43–1.

Another form of combination, the **consolidation,** combines two or more acquired corporations, all of which may be dissolved after the combination. A new corporation is formed that inherits all the rights and liabilities of the consolidating corporations. The same approval process described for mergers is followed. Figure 43–2 illustrates the classic consolidation.

In a *cash for stock* merger or consolidation, shareholders in the acquired corporation are paid with cash. In a *stock for stock* transaction, the ac-

Figure 43-2   Consolidation

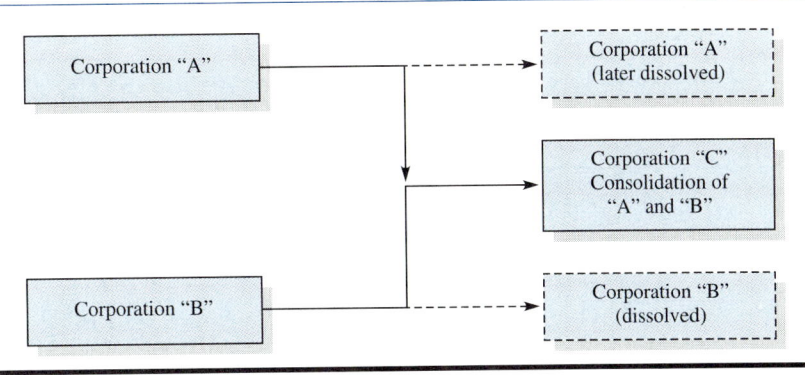

quired corporation's shareholders receive stock, often equity shares in the surviving corporation. Other packages of compensation, including some cash, junk bonds, equity, and special "rights," may also be used. The *compulsory share exchange*, discussed later in this chapter, is a form of stock for stock transaction requiring participation by the acquired corporation's shareholders.

Small-Scale Merger

Several states, including Delaware and California, permit *small-scale mergers* without the acquiring corporation's shareholders' approval, dissenters' appraisal rights, or any issuance of new securities to pay off the acquired corporation's shareholders. Typically, a large corporation acquires a small corporation, using its own previously authorized shares or treasury stock. Some stock exchanges require approval by the acquiring corporation's shareholders if the acquiring corporation's outstanding common stock will increase substantially, even if the shares were previously authorized. The acquired corporation's shareholders must approve unless they tendered their stock previously.

Short-Form Merger

Some states, including Delaware, permit a parent corporation to merge a subsidiary without any shareholder approval if the parent holds such a large majority of the subsidiary's shares that shareholder approval is assured. Some of these states require 100 percent ownership of the subsidiary, but Delaware permits **short-form mergers** for subsidiaries owned 90 percent or more. Both boards must pass identical merger resolutions. This is a form of cashout

merger, with no appraisal rights for the acquiring corporation's shareholders. It enables the parent to more easily eliminate its 10 percent or less minority shareholders.

Triangular Mergers

An increasingly popular combination involves merging the acquired corporation into a subsidiary of the acquiring corporation. These **triangular mergers** can avoid problems with traditional mergers. For example, the acquiring corporation can avoid inheriting the acquired corporation's liabilities and need not seek the approval of its shareholders. In a **forward triangular merger,** a subsidiary is formed by the acquiring corporation that is then merged with the acquired corporation. Delaware permits the acquiring corporation to pay the acquired corporation's shareholders with an exchange of shares in either the parent or its subsidiary. Approval by the acquired corporation's shareholders is still necessary and their dissenter's rights are preserved. Figure 43–3 illustrates a forward triangular merger.

A **reverse triangular merger** simply reverses the form of the forward triangular merger. The acquired corporation survives and the acquiring corporation's subsidiary is merged into the acquired corporation. The former subsidiary may then be dissolved. The subsidiary's shares held by the acquiring parent may automatically be converted into shares of the acquired corporation. The acquired corporation's shares are simultaneously converted into shares of the parent. After consummation, the parent's shares are held by the acquired corporation's former shareholders.

Figure 43–3   Triangular Merger

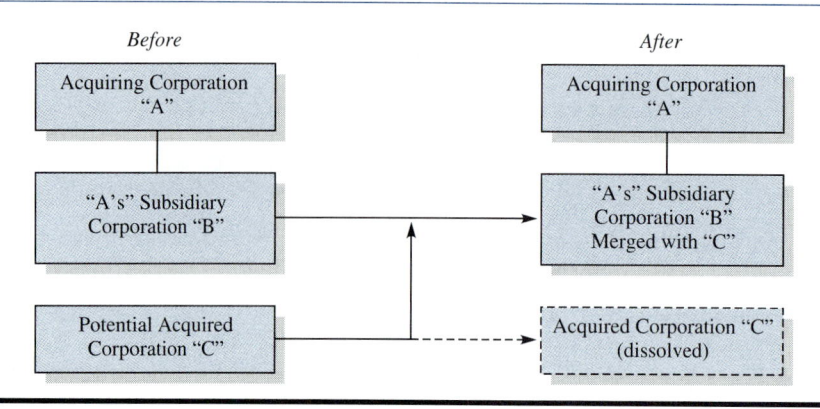

Reverse triangular mergers preserve the acquired corporation's legal existence to retain some valuable contract rights, franchises, intellectual property rights (e.g., patents, copyrights, and/or trademarks), or licenses that are restricted from transfer to the acquired corporation. Some states, such as California, use the de facto merger doctrine described later in this chapter to ignore that a triangular merger seeks to isolate the acquiring parent from the acquired corporation's liabilities or eliminate shareholder approval and dissenters' rights. Reverse triangular mergers are illustrated in Figure 43–4.

Acquisitions or Exchanges of Stock

Acquisitions need not trigger a fundamental corporate change. Combinations similar to mergers or consolidations are accomplished when the acquiring corporation purchases a controlling interest or all the stock of the acquired corporation. The separate existence of both corporations is retained, the acquired corporation has limited liability, and ownership and control transfers to the acquiring corporation. Between the 1960s and 1980s, open stock market purchases and tender offers were widely used to buy out the acquired corporation's shareholders individually. Where the acquired corporation is purchased with a significant amount of debt, it is generally referred to as a *leveraged buyout (LBO)*. If the corporation's management makes the purchase, the transaction is known as a *management buyout (MBO)*.

The mandatory or **compulsory share exchange,** permissible under the RMBCA, must be approved by both corporations' boards. After majority approval by the acquired corporation's shareholders, they must exchange their shares in the acquired corporation for shares in the acquiring corporation. This technique removes these shareholders' discretion to refuse participation in the exchange, as can shareholders in stock market or tender offer acquisitions. Shareholders may still dissent from the transaction.

SALE OF SUBSTANTIALLY ALL CORPORATE ASSETS

Many acquiring corporations seek to avoid merger safeguards: approval by shareholders, dissenters' appraisal rights, and inheriting the acquired corporation's liabilities. Some acquiring corporations attempt to acquire all of the other corporation's assets and specifically exclude any assumption of liabilities. However, most states treat a sale of substantial corporate assets as the functional equivalent of a merger to retain these procedural safeguards. Delaware requires no dissenters' appraisal rights in substantial asset sales.

A recurring problem for any corporate restructuring is legal compliance when assets are sold. How much of a selling corporation's assets constitute "substantially *all* corporate assets"? First, examine whether operating assets are sold on such a large scale that the sale effectively places the corporation out of business. By contrast, if significant assets are sold but the corporation effectively continues in its former operations, the sale is not substantial. Sales out of inventory are usually not "substantial," so no shareholder approval is needed. However, an inventory sale that departs from past practice by effec-

Figure 43-4   Reverse Triangular Merger

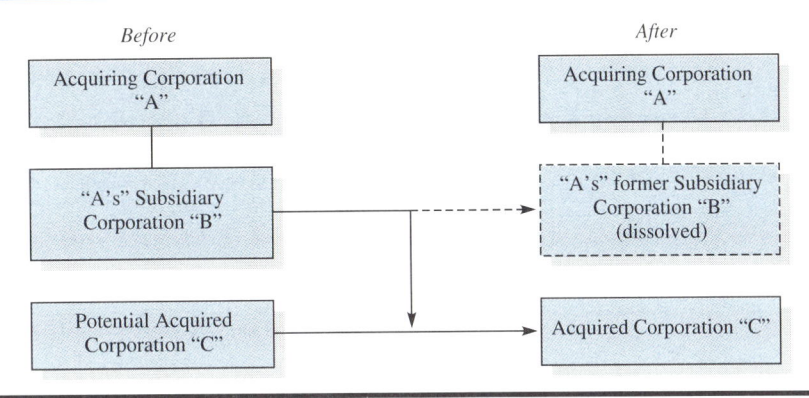

tively depleting the corporation's whole stock in just a few transactions would probably be substantial because it is out of the ordinary course of business.

A corporation originally organized to develop, build, or acquire a single asset for eventual sale need not seek shareholder approval when the asset is finally sold. For example, assume XYZ Corp. was originally organized to build, lease, and then sell an apartment complex. While the apartment sale would be substantial in relation to the corporation's operating assets, the sale would be in the ordinary course of the business as originally envisioned because the corporation originally limited its purpose. The sale of substantially all corporate assets is illustrated in Figure 43-5.

After a corporation makes a substantial asset sale and it distributes the sale proceeds to shareholders, unsecured creditors may be left with impaired claims, particularly if the acquiring corporation does not assume the liabilities. For this reason, courts sometimes apply the de facto merger doctrine discussed next, requiring the acquiring corporation to assume the liabilities. Some courts apply equitable principles, imposing a constructive trust on the sale proceeds to create a fund to satisfy creditors' claims.

Commercial law may separately require the acquiring corporation to help protect creditors. The *bulk sales* provisions of UCC Article 6 require the purchaser to notify all known creditors before the sale. State *fraudulent conveyance* laws require the acquiring corporation to satisfy creditors' claims if the sale renders the selling corporation insolvent or leaves it a financially empty shell. These legal restrictions on asset sales may frustrate some ''quick turnaround'' corporate restructuring plans.

DE FACTO MERGERS

The preceding discussion illustrates that different forms of corporate combinations can have some similar economic effects but impact corporate constituents differently. Shareholders' voting rights may differ, they may or may not have appraisal rights, creditors' protections vary, and the tax impact may differ. However, most states protect the vulnerable rights of shareholders and creditors by ignoring the transaction's particular form and recognizing its substance. The **de facto merger** doctrine gives courts equitable powers to imply special rights if these rights are denied because of the transaction's form. Courts have unwound a few transactions in extreme cases to avoid unfairness.

If the practical effect of the transaction is similar to a merger, similar procedural safeguards are implied in the de facto merger. Courts consider whether the transaction (1) effectively allows an uninterrupted continuation of the acquired corporation's business, management, facilities, and product lines, (2) fails to transfer its liabilities to the acquiring corporation, and (3) continues the acquired corporation's shareholders as owners in the acquiring corporation. The theory underlying de facto mergers is generally applied to the sale of substantially all corporate assets, thereby requiring that dissenters' appraisal rights be implied.

Successor Liability

Acquiring corporations generally inherit all the acquired corporation's liabilities, including potentially risky product liability claims that consumers have

Figure 43–5   Sale of Substantially All Corporate Assets

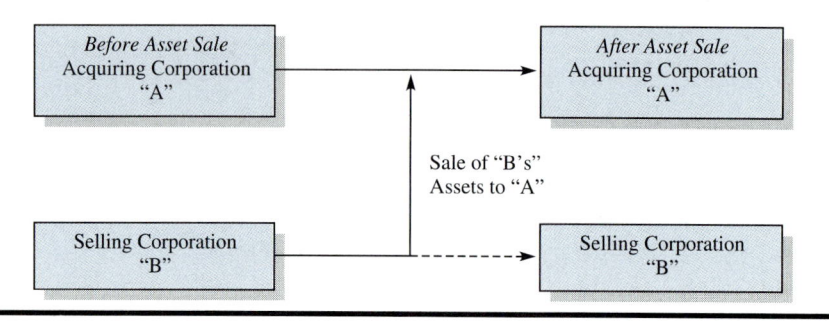

against the acquired corporation. Some acquiring corporations have sought to avoid these or other potentially large contingent liabilities by characterizing the transaction as a sale of assets or a triangular merger. The courts generally apply the de facto merger doctrine, holding the acquiring corporation liable for the acquired corporation's liabilities. However, if the selling corporation continues to exist and the consideration paid for its assets is not quickly distributed to its former shareholders, the de facto merger doctrine may be inapplicable. If only certain products or lines of business are acquired and the selling corporation continues thereafter, the acquiring corporation may not be liable on any product lines it did not purchase. The following case illustrates the difficulties of successor liability.

MARKS v. MINNESOTA MINING & MANUFACTURING CO.
232 Cal. Rptr. 594 (Cal. Ct. App. 1986)

Minnesota Mining & Manufacturing Company (3M) formed a subsidiary called McGahn/Del. that purchased all the assets of an independent company, McGahn/Cal., Inc., a manufacturer of breast implants. Mary Marks underwent breast augmentation surgery in which two defective McGahn implants were used. The defects required Marks to undergo several additional operations until implants from another manufacturer were substituted. Eventually, McGahn/Del. removed the breast implants from the market due to numerous consumer complaints and an FDA investigation. Thereafter, 3M dissolved McGahn/Del., Inc., and reorganized it as a division within 3M. Marks sued 3M on a product liability claim for the defective breast implants. Both parties appealed a jury verdict of $25,850 compensatory damages and $75,000 punitive damages, although the punitives were deleted by the trial judge.

NEWSOM, Judge

A purchaser of assets for cash generally does not assume the seller's liabilities. However, a de facto merger has occurred where the assets of one corporation are transferred without consideration which can be made available to satisfy claims or where the consideration consists wholly of shares of the purchaser's stock which are promptly distributed to the seller's shareholders. The agreement here provided for the assumption by 3M of specified liabilities shown on the McGahn balance sheets.

In the *Shannon* case, Harris Intertype Corporation entered into an agreement with Samuel M. Langston Company to purchase assets in exchange for Harris stock. Langston was required to change its name. It was subsequently dissolved and the Harris stock distributed to its shareholders. Harris assumed all obligations which were necessary for the uninterrupted continuation of normal business operations. A Harris subsidiary took over and continued the operations of Langston under the name, the Langston Company. The subsidiary was merged into Harris the year after the plaintiff was injured by a product manufactured by the first Langston Corporation. The court characterized this transaction as a de facto merger, and on that basis found Harris liable for the damages due to the defective product. ''Public policy requires that Harris Intertype, having received the benefits of a going concern, should also assume the cost which all other going concerns must ordinarily bear.'' The court added that ''solvent corporations, going concerns, should not be permitted to discharge their liabilities to injured persons simply by shuffling paper and manipulating corporate entities.''

Here, as in *Shannon*, the result of the transaction was exactly that which would have occurred had a statutory merger taken place, and we are accordingly convinced of the necessity and fairness of transferring liability from McGahn/Cal. to McGahn/Del. We therefore find that the reorganization

amounted to a continuation and a de facto merger. Thus, when McGahn/Del. became a part of its parent, as a matter of corporate law it carried with it all of its liabilities. The critical fact is that while there was more than one merger or reorganization, an analysis of each transaction discloses to us that its intrinsic structure and nature, unlike a sale of assets for cash, was of a type in which the corporate entity was continued and all liability was transferred. All of the indicia of a merger are present. The judgment is reversed with instructions to reinstate the judgment including the award of punitive damages.

Case Questions

1. What is the issue in determining the successor liability of the purchaser of corporate assets?

2. What ambiguity does the court in the preceding case note in the two ''reorganization'' transactions from McGahn/Cal. to McGahn/Del. and then to the 3M division?

3. What was the value assumption the court used in ignoring the form of the transaction and focusing on its substance?

DISSENTING SHAREHOLDERS' APPRAISAL RIGHTS

The strict unanimity rule required for partners' approval of fundamental changes would be impractical for corporations. Shareholders are not generally agents that expose other shareholders to unlimited liability as are partners. The large number of corporate shareholders would give those opposing fundamental changes extortionate power to threaten vetoing the proposal. This tyranny of the minority could damage the corporation's attempt to achieve reasonable corporate reformation goals. Corporate law strikes a balance between the need for broad consensus to approve fundamental organic changes in corporate structure, the protection of minority rights, and the avoidance of a tyranny by either the majority or minority. This balance has produced a ''safety valve,'' the **dissenting shareholders' appraisal right.**

The appraisal remedy gives shareholders the right to receive payment for their shares if they oppose a fundamental corporate change. Dissenters must be

paid ''fair value'' for their shares as appraised before the fundamental change has any impact on share price or marketability. Dissenters' rights are particularly important in close corporations where there is no readily available or liquid stock market through which shares can be sold. Several states, including Delaware, deny appraisal rights for exchange-traded securities or those held by more than 2,000 shareholders assuming liquidity provides a fair price. However, there is some evidence that big-block sales of stock may themselves affect price, often artificially lowering the price below fair value.

Dissenters' Appraisal Process

Dissenters must precisely follow the statutory appraisal process, which is generalized as follows. The corporation first notifies shareholders of the right to dissent. Dissenters must file a written objection to the proposal before the election and then may not vote in favor of it. Within a short time after the resolution passes, typically 10 days, the dissenter must make a written demand on the corporation to pay fair value and physically submit the shares within one month. Early notice permits the corporation to determine if sufficient cash exists to pay all dissenters. If too many shareholders dissent, the fundamental corporate change may become impractical.

After notice, the dissenter loses any further shareholder rights — for example, voting or receiving dividends. The dissent may be revoked within the next 60 days. The corporation must respond with a written offer to all dissenters, offering to pay fair value, as established by the corporation. The corporation's response must be mailed within 7 to 10 days following either the merger or the expiration of the dissenting period, whichever is later. Some states require that this communication must include recent financial statements. The dissenter's acceptance constitutes a contract for the repurchase of the dissenter's shares at the price indicated.

Fair Value Determination

Although most shareholders accept the corporation's offer, some dissenters may feel the corporation tried to save money by undervaluing their shares. A **judicial appraisal procedure** may be brought by dissatisfied shareholders. Some states permit the corporation to initiate this to consolidate all appraisals into a single lawsuit. Most statutes require determination of **fair value,** although other similar terms are used in some states: value, fair cash value, market value, or full market value. The Delaware appraisal statute requires that fair value must be determined "exclusive of any element of value arising from the accomplishment or expectation of the merger or consolidation, together with a fair rate of interest . . . [taking] into account all relevant factors."[2] Generally, there are no more specific statutory procedures, so courts define fair value with the factors identified in the Delaware block method, discussed shortly.

Many courts appoint appraisers with wide latitude to employ appropriate valuation factors. A few states permit jury evaluation of fair value, although only limited appeal is usually permitted. The court may apportion costs of the appraisal proceeding as it sees fit. For example, if XYZ's offer is close to the judicial appraisal, then dissenters may be assessed court costs because their suit appears arbitrary or vexatious. However, if XYZ's offer is substantially undervalued, then both attorney's fees and costs could be assessed against the corporation because its offer appears to be a "low ball."

The **Delaware block method** is the most widely used valuation method, employing a weighted average of four elements: (1) market value, (2) net asset value, (3) capitalized dividends, and (4) capitalized earnings. Great weight is usually accorded to market value where the corporation's shares are widely held and freely trade on a liquid market. However, lesser weight is accorded when markets are thin, infrequently traded, or nonexistent. Net asset value is the aggregate of all corporate assets' liquidation value as reduced by corporate liabilities. However, when asset values reflect historical cost, depreciated book value, or replacement values of assets, they include artificial discounts or premiums such as unrealized appreciation, inaccurate depreciation, or extra service life. Net asset value is given great weight only when the corporation is not a going concern or is likely to liquidate.

The valuation of most nonpublic, going-concern corporations heavily weight one or a combination of cash flow measures: earnings and dividends. Typically, the preceding five years' earnings (or dividends) are averaged and a capitalization ratio is applied or multiplied by its reciprocal, the *earnings multiplier*. The multiplier is the average price-earnings multiplier derived from other firms in the corporation's industry. For example, if ABC's annual earnings per share (EPS) averaged $5 and its stock price averaged $75 for the past five years, it would have a multiplier of 15. If XYZ's value depended on its competitors' multiplier, which is 17, then XYZ's $4 EPS would be capitalized by that 17 multiplier, resulting in a valuation of $68 per share. This process is conjectural at best, reflecting the assumption that all firms in the industry perform similarly. The use of capitalized dividends to evaluate a corporation has similar flaws but is further obscured because dividends are declared at the board's discretion and often do not correlate directly with earnings.

The Delaware block method is best illustrated by an example, here the often cited case *Application of Delaware Racing Association.*[3] Delaware Park was

---

[2]Delaware General Corporation Law §262(h).

[3]*Application of Delaware Racing Association,* 213 A.2d 203 (Del. 1965).

a thoroughbred horse racing track owned by Steeplechase and later by its successor, Racing. Earnings were reinvested in the business between 1937 and 1963, so no dividends were ever paid. As the track's business began to decline, William Du Pont suggested all shareholders should donate their shares to Delaware Park, Inc., a charitable corporation. Alternatively, Du Pont would pay the other shareholders $1,530 per share based on a professional appraisal and then Du Pont would donate the shares. Du Pont and other shareholders donated 1,390 shares, giving Delaware Park, Inc., ownership of over 90 percent of Racing. This permitted a Delaware short-form merger between Racing and Delaware Park, Inc. Dissenting shareholders brought an appraisal proceeding, claiming the valuation should be based on liquidation value, but the Delaware court used going-concern value instead. The four factors were evaluated, acknowledging fundamental errors in the appraiser's improper reconstruction of market value, use of an excessive multiplier, and improper weighting of factors. The stock was revalued at $2,321.30, a 52 percent increase over the value fixed by Du Pont's appraiser.

The following case illustrates the beginnings of a trend to supplement the Delaware block method with valuation methods based on modern theories of financial economics.

WEINBERGER v. U.O.P., INC.
457 A.2d 701 (Del. 1983)

The Signal Company had a controlling interest (50.5 percent) in U.O.P., Inc. Five of U.O.P.'s directors were Signal employees. Signal's internal financial analysis reports showed that it would be a good investment to purchase the remainder of U.O.P. at up to $24 per share. Meetings were held between the executive committee of Signal's board, U.O.P.'s President Crawford, and Signal's officers. Signal proposed to pay between $20 and $21 per share for the remainder of U.O.P.'s shares, a range they concluded was fair to both Signal and U.O.P.'s minority shareholders. Lehman Brothers issued a favorable fairness opinion at the $21 price and both corporations' boards approved the cash merger. U.O.P.'s management and board urged its minority shareholders to approve the merger, and only 2.2 percent of the minority shares voted against the merger. However, some U.O.P. shareholders challenged the merger's fairness and the price and then appealed from a judgment in favor of the defendants U.O.P. management.

MOORE, Justice

Material information, necessary to acquaint the U.O.P. shareholders with the bargaining positions of Signal and U.O.P. was withheld under circumstances amounting to a breach of fiduciary duty. We therefore conclude that this merger does not meet the test of fairness. We adopt a more liberal, less rigid and stylized, approach to the valuation process than has heretofore been permitted by our courts.

A primary issue mandating reversal is the preparation by two U.O.P. directors, Arledge and Chitiea, of their feasibility study for the exclusive use and benefit of Signal. Using U.O.P. data, it described the advantages to Signal of ousting the minority at a price range $21 to $24 per share. It shows that a return on the investment on $21 would be 15.7 percent versus 15.5 percent at $24 per share. This was a difference of only two-tenths of 1 percent, while it meant over $17 million to the minority. Certainly, this was a matter of material significance to U.O.P. and its shareholders.

The concept of fairness has two basic aspects: fair dealing and fair price. The former embraces questions of when the transaction was timed, how it was initiated, structured, negotiated, disclosed to the directors, and how the approvals of the directors and the stockholders were obtained. The latter aspect of fairness relates to the economic and financial considerations of the proposed merger, including all relevant factors: assets, market value, earnings, future prospects, and any other elements that effect the intrinsic or inherent value of a company's stock.

Plaintiff's evidence was that on the date that the merger was approved the stock was worth at least $26 per share. In support, he offered the testimony of a chartered investment analyst who used two basic approaches to valuation: a comparative analysis of the premium paid over market in 10 other tender offer merger combinations, and a discounted cash flow analysis.

The chancellor perceived that the approach to valuation was the same as that in an appraisal proceeding. Consistent with precedent, he rejected plaintiff's method of proof and accepted defendant's evidence of value as being in accord with practice under prior case law. This means that the so-called "Delaware block" or weighted average method was employed wherein the elements of value, i.e., assets, market price, earnings, etc. were assigned a particular weight and the resulting amounts added to determine the value share. This procedure has been in use for decades. However, to the extent that it excludes other generally accepted techniques used in the financial community and the courts it is now clearly outmoded.

The standard Delaware block weighted average method of valuation, merely employed in appraisal and other stock valuation cases, shall no longer exclusively control such proceedings. We believe that a more liberal approach must include proof of value by any techniques or methods which are generally considered acceptable in the financial community and otherwise admissible in court.

It is significant that the determination of "fair value must be based upon all relevant factors." Only the speculative elements of value that may arise from the "accomplishment or expectation" of the merger are excluded. We take this to be a very narrow exception to the appraisal process, "designed to eliminate use of pro forma data and projections of a speculative variety relating to the completion of a merger. But elements of future value, including the nature of the enterprise, which are known or susceptible of proof as of the date of the merger and not the product of speculation, may be considered. When the trial court deems it appropriate, fair value also includes any damages, resulting from the taking, which the stockholders sustain as a class.

The appraisal remedy that we approve may not be adequate in certain cases, particularly where fraud, misrepresentation, self dealing, deliberate waste of corporate assets, or gross and palpable over reaching are involved. Under such circumstances, the chancellor's powers are complete to fashion any form of equitable and monetary relief as may be appropriate, including rescissory damages. Since it is apparent that this long completed transaction is too involved to undo, and in view of the chancellor's discretion, the award, if any, should be in the form of monetary damages based upon entire fairness standards, i.e., fair dealing and fair price. The judgment of the court of chancery finding the merger fair is reversed.

Case Questions

1. What is the issue in a valuation proceeding for appraisal rights of dissenting shareholders?
2. Does the new valuation method announced in the *Weinberger v. U.O.P.* case introduce any ambiguities into the valuation process?
3. What assumptions are made about the valuation process used in modern financial theory when that theory is incorporated into the law?

SPECIAL PROBLEMS IN CORPORATE CONTROL BATTLES

Changes in corporate control usually require transactions in securities that have voting privileges needed for approval. Shareowners are usually left to buy, sell, or vote their shares in their own self-interest, even if this exploits minority shareholders' interests. However, controlling shareholders are sometimes subject to the same fiduciary duties as management owes to the corporation and its other shareholders. Subordinating shareholders' self-interest also raises ethical issues. These problems are acute in the squeezeout of minority shareholders, shifts in corporate control, and management-inspired takeover defensive tactics.

Squeezeouts of Minority Shareholders

Minority shareholders in closely held corporations are particularly vulnerable to be squeezed out or frozen out. This is a structural problem for minority shareholders that is manifest as losses in fundamental corporate changes. Squeezeouts emerge from hostility, competition, and jealousy among close corporate shareholders. The majority may actively seek to eliminate the minority to selfishly monopolize the corporation's success.[4]

Close corporate shareholders often fail to design their relationship to avert such conflicts. They act more like partners regulated under corporate governance principles so corporate formalities, bylaws, and recordkeeping may be ignored and corporate assets commingled with personal assets. Closely held corporations are further complicated by family or marital antagonism, rivalry over inherited corporate participation, and resentment at sharing benefits with counterproductive or uncreative members, who are often considered unwelcome intruders. Open hostility may be suppressed until a domineering and controlling matriarch or patriarch retires or dies or a central managing figure loses power. Such events may launch the squeezeout.

[4]See F. Hodge O'Neal, *Oppression of Minority Shareholders,* rev. ed. (Wilmette, Il.: Callaghan, 1990).

*Minority Shareholder Squeezeout Techniques and Responses**

Minority shareholders in close corporations are often under intense threat of being frozen out of corporate affairs. The majority may legally use various techniques to oppress the minority and eventually pressure them to sell out. There is usually a limited market for close corporation shares because outsiders astutely avoid becoming substitute victims. Also, many close corporations impose share transfer restrictions. Corporate democracy renders the minority relatively powerless to challenge the majority's decisions to change bylaws, make fundamental corporate changes, or further reduce the minority's participation. For example, the majority may eliminate cumulative voting, stagger or reduce the board's size, or eliminate other shareholder rights.

A squeeze typically entails the curtailment of financial rights and information to pressure the minority to sell out at low prices. Controlling shareholders may divert corporate cash flow to themselves as high salaries, thereby excluding minority shareholders from employment. Dividends are often eliminated, depriving the minority of any financial return. Cash flow is also siphoned off through the majority's excessive perks, favorable contracts with outside corporations owned by the majority, and as loan repayment with high interest rates paid to the majority. Except in egregious cases, the majority is usually protected by the business judgment rule in making these decisions. Derivative litigation is costly and difficult. The minority is often intentionally isolated from information about corporate operations and finances. Mandatory disclosure under the securities laws lessens this problem somewhat in publicly traded corporations.

Three constraints may restrict the majority's unbridled oppression: the fiduciary duty of loyalty, the minority's vigilant monitoring of corporate activities, and effective preplanning. Courts increasingly recognize unfairness if the majority acts in bad faith. Shareholders should be alert to sudden changes in corporate finances or management's performance. Information may be available from government regulators, through the shareholder's inspection privilege, and ultimately through pretrial discovery. Minority protections may be installed before the oppression commences with provisions placed in the corporate charter or bylaws and by privately negotiated contracts. For example, the bylaws may include alternative dispute resolution methods (e.g., deadlock arbitration), long-term employment contracts including ''for cause'' dismissal provisions, supermajority voting for fundamental corporate

*Source: ''Minority Shareholder Squeeze-Out Techniques and Responses'' © 1993 by John W. Bagby.

changes, mandatory dividend provisions, and dissolution provisions that can help protect minority rights. Of course, such restrictions can hamstring the corporation's flexibility. Minority protections must be continually balanced against the corporation's legitimate need to adapt.

Thought Questions

1. What issues arise in the minority's claim of oppression by the majority?
2. In analyzing freezeouts, what assumptions are made concerning the activities and intentions of the relevant parties?
3. What are plausible alternative hypotheses to explain the evidence a minority shareholder uses to show oppression?

Fiduciary Duties of Controlling Shareholders

A *controlling shareholder's* influence in many corporate governance matters may be exercised by a single shareholder or group of shareholders combining to form a simple majority. *Working control* may be effected with less than 50 percent in publicly traded corporations. Voting blocks as small as 10 or 20 percent are sometimes sufficient control because the other shareholders are geographically dispersed, disorganized, and apathetic. However, smaller blocks in closely held corporations are the epitome of an oppressed minority. A fiduciary duty is increasingly implied regarding the actions of controlling shareholders when they cause corporate action that unfairly prejudices nonparticipating shareholders. Transactions must be made in good faith and be free from fraud.

The particular aspects of controlling shareholders' fiduciary duties varies with the circumstances, the degree of control exercised, and the personal benefits derived, permitting the courts to balance controlling shareholder power with the impact on other shareholders. Controlling shareholders may be liable in damages, and some courts may rescind and reverse any transaction found unfair to the other shareholders. However, the business judgment rule protects controlling shareholder action unless it is arbitrary, unreasonable, an abuse of discretion, or in bad faith.

Parent-Subsidiary Relations

Parent corporations owe a duty of good faith to the minority shareholders in their subsidiaries. Transactions between the parent and subsidiary must be fair to the subsidiary and its minority shareholders. Controlling shareholders have the burden of proving the **intrinsic fairness** of the transaction to the corporation. Although controlling shareholders may validly enter contracts with a subsidiary, there are inherently conflicting incentives. For example, sales to the parent at below market prices shift the subsidiary's profits to the parent, damaging the subsidiary's minority shareholders. In *Sinclair Oil Co. v. Levien,*[5] Sinclair, the parent of Sinven, breached its fiduciary duty to Sinven's minority shareholders when Sinclair breached a contract with Sinven and then prevented Sinven from vindicating its rights.

Restructuring

Fiduciary duty questions also arise when controlling shareholders change the corporation's capital structure and this intentionally damages the minority. Acts that siphon off corporate assets to the controlling shareholder, through dividend reductions combined with high-paying employment for the controlling group, can freeze out the minority. The controlling block's purchase of a new stock offering intended to consolidate its control may violate the block's fiduciary duty to the minority. Corporate share repurchases and redemptions may wrongfully freeze out the minority or siphon off assets to the minority's disadvantage, as alleged in *Donahue v. Rodd Electrotype Co.*[6] In *Zahn v. Transamerica Corp.,*[7] a mandatory redemption of certain shares

[5]*Sinclair Oil Co. v. Levien,* 280 A.2d 717 (Del. 1971).
[6]*Donahue v. Rodd Electrotype Co.,* 228 N.E.2d 505 (Mass. 1975).
[7]*Zahn v. Transamerica Corp.,* 162 F.2d36 (3d. Cir. 1947).

permitted controlling shareholders to appropriate a highly appreciated corporate asset and freeze the redeemed shareholders out of participation. This violated the controlling faction's fiduciary duty.

Control Transactions

Controlling shareholders generally are free to sell their shares and thereby pass control to the purchaser. However, if they procure other benefits not shared with the minority, the fiduciary duty may be violated.[8] In *Jones v. H.F. Ahmanson & Co.*,[9] the controlling shareholders sold their stock in United Savings and Loan to a public holding company they created primarily to increase the liquidity of their own United stock. This breached a fiduciary duty to the minority because the minority was locked out of this liquidity opportunity. The fiduciary duty may be breached when a control premium accompanies a *sale of office* held by the controlling shareholder. A sale of control is unlawful if the seller knows or has reason to know the purchaser will mismanage or loot the corporation. **Looting** includes acts that deprive the corporation of its assets' value. The seller may be liable for the losses for failing to investigate a buyer notorious for fraud, for causing the business to fail, or there are other grounds for suspicion.

Takeover Tactics

Corporations on both sides have employed numerous devices during takeover activities. Bidders make surprise tender offers for a controlling block or for all a target's shares. Sometimes they make confidential purchases of a potential target's stock in public stock market purchases, in privately negotiated purchases, or from professional arbitrageurs who accumulate stocks they believe will be "in play." Increasingly, these methods are considered hostile in that the target's management are certain to oppose any fundamental corporate change following the acquisition. Sometimes the target management argues that the takeover bidder will loot or mismanage the target, dissipating employees and harming the communities surrounding the target's facilities. However, observers suggest that target corporations are undervalued because their managements are under-

productive. The management allegedly opposes takeovers to preserve its own employment and perks. State antitakeover laws and takeover defensive tactics contributed to the end of hostile takeovers in the late 1980s. Today, most mergers and acquisitions are negotiated directly between the takeover bidder and the target's management.

Takeover Defenses

Takeover targets have used the ingenuity of their investment bankers and lawyers to devise **takeover defenses.** Defenses usually take the form of new securities issues, repurchase of outstanding securities, contingent asset sales, and other contracts and charter amendments that make the target unattractive when the takeover commences. Some potential targets make capital structure changes in anticipation of a takeover. A *recapitalization* restructures the target's assets or capital structure. For example, XYZ Corp. might seek to avert ABC Corp.'s takeover by issuing new debt or preferred stock in exchange for outstanding common stock. Alternatively, it might give certain shareholders supervoting privileges. These actions could cause XYZ's debt-equity ratio to deteriorate. **Golden parachutes**—large severance pay contracts for top executives displaced after a takeover—may be offered. Some target managements have pursued *scorched earth* policies that sell off the corporation's *crown jewels* or other prized and most valuable assets.

The simple repurchase of some outstanding stock can act as a takeover barrier. After the purchase, the voting power of existing shareholders is raised and the distribution of the target's cash to former shareholders makes the corporation less attractive. Repurchases have been made at premium prices to deter potential hostile bidders, the so-called **greenmail** payments. Greenmail is controversial; some theorists and state laws consider that it violates management's fiduciary duty. The stock price of corporations paying greenmail usually drops after the payment is widely publicized. The target expects the bidder to terminate further takeover attempts in return for the premium paid. The bidder must usually sign a **standstill** agreement promising not to purchase target shares for some time.

Management Duties in Takeovers

Management's efforts to defend against hostile takeovers is judged by the duty of care and fiduciary duty of loyalty. Recall that *Unocal v. Mesa Petro-*

---

[8]See Andrews, *The Stockholders' Right to Equal Opportunity in the Sale of Shares*, vol. 78, Harvard Law Review p. 505 (1965).

[9]*Jones v. H.F. Ahmanson & Co.*, 460 P.2d 464 (Cal. 1969).

leum Co., discussed in Chapter 41, permitted management's defensive self-tender. Management may not use "unbridled discretion to defeat any perceived threat by [using] any Draconian means available." *Smith v. VanGorkom*, discussed in Chapter 42, established a heightened duty of care for directors during takeovers. The business judgment rule insulates management from liability for decisions to install defensive tactics unless management acts arbitrarily, in bad faith, oppressively, or with a conflict of interest.

Particular takeover defenses are justified so long as necessary to achieve a valid corporate purpose that is reasonably related to the takeover's threat to shareholders' interests. For example, XYZ management might validly install a defensive device to oppose a hostile takeover threat if ABC made a deficient bid, the defense contributed to XYZ's strategy to increase its value, better bids were induced, corporate constituencies were threatened (e.g., stockholders, employees, suppliers, customers, and/or surrounding communities), or the bidder would destroy an advantageous and distinctive corporate culture. Courts must also consider the target management's potential conflict of interest in defending against takeovers. However, this is but one of several factors. The following case explains the **poison pill** takeover defense and illustrates its justification in light of management's duties.

MORAN v. HOUSEHOLD INTERNATIONAL, INC.
500 A.2d 1356 (Del. 1985)

Household International's board formulated a takeover defense with the advice of investment bankers. Household adopted a so-called poison pill rights plan as a preventive mechanism to ward off future hostile takeovers. The poison pill had two triggering events: a "30 percent trigger," activated by a tender offer for 30 percent or more of Household shares, and "20 percent trigger," activated by the actual acquisition of 20 percent of Household's shares by any single group or entity. If the 30 percent provision was triggered, Household was required to issue immediately exercisable rights to each existing shareholder to purchase 1/100th of a new share of preferred stock for $100. If the 20 percent provision was triggered, each holder could purchase 1/100th of a preferred share, but if the preferred was not purchased and a merger or consolidation occurred thereafter, the rights holder could then purchase $200 worth of the common stock of the tender offeror for $100. This latter "flipover" provision is the controversy in this suit. Moran challenged the Household board's decision to institute the rights plan.

MCNEILLY, Justice

This case is distinguishable from others cited since here we have a defensive mechanism adopted to ward off all possible future advances and not a mechanism adopted in reaction to a specific threat. This distinguishing factor does not result in the directors' losing the protection of the business judgment rule. To the contrary, preplanning for the contingency of a hostile takeover might reduce the risks that, under the pressure of a takeover bid, management will fail to exercise reasonable judgment. Therefore, in reviewing a preplanned defensive mechanism it seems even more appropriate to apply the business judgment rule.

Appellants contend that the Delaware statute does not authorize the issuance of sham rights such as the rights plan here. They contend that the rights were designed never to be exercised, and that the plan has no economic value. Appellants sham contention fails. As to the rights, they can and will be exercised upon the happening of a triggering mechanism as we have observed during the current struggle of Sir James Goldsmith to take control of Crown Zellerbach. Appellants also contend that the Delaware statute authorizes the issuance of rights "holders thereof to purchase from the corporation any shares of *its* capital stock of any class." Therefore, their contention continues, the plain language of the statute does not authorize Household to issue rights to purchase another's capital stock upon a merger.

The fact that the rights here have as their purpose the prevention of coercive two-tier tender offers does not invalidate them. We conclude that the rights plan does not prevent stockholders from receiving tender offers, and that the change of Household's structure was less than . . . results from the implementation of other defensive mechanisms upheld by various courts.

The rights plan will result in no more of a structural change than any other defensive mechanism adopted by a board of directors. The rights plan does not destroy the assets of the corporation. The implementation of the plan neither results in any outflow of money from the corporation nor impairs its financial flexibility. It does not dilute earnings per share and does not have any adverse tax consequences for the corporation or its stockholders. The plan has not adversely affected the market price of Household's stock. Comparing the rights plan with other defensive mechanisms, it does less harm to the value structure of the corporation than do the other mechanisms. Other mechanisms result in increased debt of the corporation.

Appellants contend that the board was unauthorized to fundamentally restrict stockholders rights to conduct a proxy contest. Appellants contend that the 20 percent trigger effectively prevents any stockholder from first acquiring 20 percent or more shares before conducting a proxy contest and further it prevents stockholders from banding together in a group to solicit proxies. The effect upon proxy contests will be minimal. Many proxy contests are won with an insurgent ownership of less than 20 percent and very large holdings are no guarantee of success.

There are no allegations here of any bad faith on the part of the directors' action in the adoption of the rights plan. The adoption of the rights plan was in reaction to what is perceived to be the threat in the market place of coercive two-tier tender offers. We conclude the directors were not grossly negligent. The directors were given beforehand a notebook which introduced a three page summary of the plan along with articles on the current takeover environment. The extended discussion between the board and representatives of the law and investment banking firms before approval of the plan reflected a full and candid evaluation of the plan. The directors reasonably believed that Household was vulnerable to coercive acquisition techniques and adopted a reasonable defensive mechanism to protect itself. Affirmed.

Case Questions

1. What issues are presented in judging the validity of a poison pill rights plan as discussed in the preceding case?

2. Poison pills generally deter takeover threats so completely that they are never exercised. What assumption does the court make concerning the potential use of the poison pill rights?

3. What reasons support the finding that the Household board acted with good business judgment?

Several influential management takeover duty cases emerged from Delaware in the 1980s. In *Revlon, Inc. v. MacAndrews & Forbes Holdings, Inc.,*[10] Revlon's management granted a lockup option to Forstmann Little & Co., a white knight, to avert a hostile takeover by Pantry Pride. In several successive rounds, Pantry Pride raised its bid for Revlon. However, this upward bidding was interrupted when Revlon signed the lockup with Forstmann Little. When a takeover by someone becomes "inevitable," the target's management must conduct an auction to sell off the corporation and maximize the price that shareholders receive. There is still some ambiguity on exactly when a takeover becomes inevitable. The target management cannot lawfully retain a poison pill or negotiate a lockup if this would end an auction prematurely or shield management's MBO. Favoritism for one particular bidder over others is condemned in *Mills Acquisition Co. v. MacMillan, Inc.*[11]

---

[10]*Revlon, Inc. v. MacAndrews & Forbes Holdings, Inc.,* 506 A.2d 173 (Del. 1986).

[11]*Mills Acquisition Co. v. MacMillan, Inc.,* 559 A.2d 1261 (Del. 1989).

Figure 43-6   Takeover Tactics

Tactic	Definition	Effect or Use
Crown Jewels	Prized and most valuable assets of potential takeover target corporation	Target management averts takeover threat by selling crown jewels, making target unattractive
Golden Parachutes	Favorable severance pay contracts for top management; triggered by hostile takeover	Deters hostile takeover or cushions top executives if terminated after takeover
Greenmail	Premium paid over market price by target to repurchase a block of stock from hostile bidder; usually accompanied by a standstill agreement	Hostile bidder accumulates target shares to extort greenmail premiums; occasionally consummates takeovers to make takeover threats credible
Lockup Option	Target's contract to sell crown jewels cheaply to a white knight only if hostile bidder is successful	Deters hostile takeover much like sale of crown jewels
Pac-Man Defense	Target attempts takeover of the hostile bidder; named for the once popular video game	Both target and hostile bidder become locked in tender offers for each other
Poison Pill Rights	Large potential liability triggered by takeover; usually gives target's shareholders rights to buy stock cheaply or sell their stock to merged corporation at a large premium	Deters hostile takeover; target is made financially unattractive
Standstill Agreement	Hostile bidder agrees with target to refrain from another accumulation of target's shares for a specified time period	Averts takeover by hostile bidder for specified time; usually given in consideration for greenmail payment
White Knight	Friendly merger partner located by target to avoid takeover by hostile bidder	Rescues target from hostile takeover by offering higher takeover price

Shareholders often believe management's takeover defenses cost them extra value that could be derived from a takeover and has led to significant litigation. In *Paramount Communications, Inc. v. Time*,[12] the target's management was permitted to install takeover defenses if this furthered an established strategy to maximize the corporation's long-term value. Additionally, the target's management may validly consider the impact of a hostile takeover on all corporate constituencies, including stockholders, employees, suppliers, customers, surrounding communities, and others. Some takeover tactics are summarized in Figure 43-6.

STATE TAKEOVER LEGISLATION

Nearly all states now have statutes restricting takeovers of targets either incorporated in the state or that have their principal place of business or substantial business facilities within the state. State takeover laws may encourage corporations to locate there to avert hostile takeovers. Some observers be-

---

[12]*Paramount Communications, Inc. v. Time*, 571 A.2d 1140 (Del. 1989).

lieve this enables the state to retain local employment. First generation state antitakeover efforts placed a burden on interstate commerce and conflicted with the Williams Act's evenhanded tender offer rules. For example, in *Edgar v. Mite Corp.*,[13] the Supreme Court held that the Williams Act preempted an Illinois antitakeover law that allowed state regulators to block takeovers. The waiting periods in the law conflicted with the Williams Act's ordering of tender offer events.

Second generation state takeover statutes have generally been held constitutional because they concern traditional state shareholder democracy and internal corporate governance. These are matters not

---

[13]*Edgar v. Mite Corp.*, 457 U.S. 624 (1982).

directly addressed by the Williams Act. Many such laws include **shareholder protection** provisions requiring that shareholders receive a "fair price" in a takeover. Another derivation imposes a **merger moratorium** prohibiting a takeover bidder from merging the target until other shareholders or the target's management approve or several years pass. Pennsylvania also prohibits greenmail.

The following case illustrates the Supreme Court's approval of state antitakeover **control share acquisition** provisions. Such provisions generally allow the other shareholders to grant or deny voting rights to a takeover bidder. This effectively requires the bidder to negotiate with the target management and convince other shareholders that the takeover is more advantageous than under current management's version of the status quo.

CTS CORP. v. DYNAMICS CORP. OF AMERICA
481 U.S. 69 (1987)

Indiana enacted antitakeover provisions, including a control share acquisitions provision applicable to Indiana corporations. The act sets three thresholds—20, 331/3, and 50 percent—that trigger particular rights to deter hostile takeovers. Takeover bidders acquiring control shares above these thresholds may not also acquire voting rights unless specially granted by other shareholders. This provision practically requires majority approval by the preexisting disinterested shareholders before a takeover bidder may take control of a corporation. The question is decided at the next regularly scheduled shareholder meeting or at a special shareholder meeting that the acquirer may require. The corporation may redeem the bidder's control shares at fair market value if it desires to do so after the shareholders refuse to grant voting rights to the takeover bidder.

Dynamics Corporation of America owned 9.6 percent of C.T.S. common stock when it announced a tender offer for up to 271/2 percent of C.T.S. stock. Dynamics challenged the Indiana control share act, claiming that it is preempted by the federal Williams Act.

POWELL, Justice

The Indiana Act operates on the assumption that independent shareholders faced with tender offers are at a disadvantage. By allowing such shareholders to vote as a group, the Act protects them from the coercive aspects of some tender offers. If, for example, shareholders believe that a successful tender offer will be followed by a purchase of nontendering shares at a depressed price, individual shareholders may tender their shares even if they doubt the tender offer is in the corporation's best interest to protect themselves from being forced to sell at a depressed price.

In such a situation under the Indiana Act, the shareholders as a group, could reject the offer. It furthers the federal policy of investor protection. The Indiana Act does not give either management or the offeror an advantage in communicating with the shareholders about the impending offer. The Act also does not impose an indefinite delay on tender offers. Nor does the Act allow the state government to interpose its views of fairness between willing buyers and sellers of shares of the target company. Rather the Act allows shareholders to evaluate the fairness of the offer collectively. If the offeror fears an adverse shareholder vote under the Act, it can make a conditional tender offer, offering to accept shares on the condition that the shares receive voting rights within a certain period of time.

Dynamics contends that the statute is discriminatory because it will apply most often to out-of-state entities. As a practical matter, most hostile tender offers are launched by offerors outside Indiana. "The fact that the burden of a state regulation falls on some interstate companies does not, by itself, establish a claim of discrimination against interstate commerce." So long as each state regulates voting rights only in the corporations it has created, each corporation will be subject to the law of only one state. No principle of corporation law and practice is more firmly established than a state's authority to regulate domestic corporations, including the authority to define the voting rights of shareholders. Accordingly, we conclude that the Indiana Act does not create an impermissible risk of inconsistent regulations by different states. It is an accepted part of business landscape in this country for states to create corporations, to prescribe their powers, and to define the rights that are acquired by purchasing their shares. A state has an interest in promoting stable relationships among parties involved in the corporation it charters, as well as insuring that investors of such corporations have an effective voice in corporate affairs. There can be no doubt that the Act reflects these concerns. A change of management may have important effects on the shareholders interest, it is well within the state's role as overseer of corporate governance to offer this opportunity.

Whether the control share statute protects shareholders of Indiana corporations or protects incumbent management seems to be a highly debatable question, but it is extraordinary to think that the constitutionality of the Act should depend on the answer. Nothing in the constitution says that the protection of entrenched management is any less important a "putative local benefit" than the protection of entrenched shareholders, and I do not know what qualifies us to make that judgment. As long as the state's corporation law governs only its own corporations and does not discriminate against out-of-state interests, it should survive this court's scrutiny under the commerce clause.

SCALIA, Justice, Concurring in Part and Concurring in the Judgment

I do not share the courts apparent high estimation of the benefits of the state's statute at issue here. But a law can be both economic folly and constitutional. The Indiana control share acquisition chapter is at least the latter.

Case Questions

1. What is the central issue in determining the validity of a state law affecting tender offers?
2. What reasons support state regulation of shareholder voting?
3. What types of state law antitakeover provisions might conflict more directly with the Williams Act?

DISSOLUTION, WINDING UP, AND LIQUIDATION

The final and most fundamental corporate action is to end its existence. Although some corporations are intended to terminate automatically after a specified event or particular date, corporations are capable of perpetual life. Therefore, a board resolution and shareholder approval is usually necessary to dissolve the corporation voluntarily without judicial intervention. Notice is required and nonvoting shares are given a class veto. Alternatively, a unanimous shareholder consent may also be used. Newly incorporated corporations that remain inactive within the first two years may be dissolved simply by the in-

corporators or the board. Under these dissolution methods, articles of dissolution must be filed with the secretary of state. Some states permit charter provisions calling for dissolution by less than a majority in close corporations, equivalent to partnerships.

There are usually no appraisal rights because the corporation will be liquidated to distribute proceeds. Therefore, dissenters suffer only if the corporation would have been worth more as a going concern than its breakup value in liquidation. Known creditors must be given individual notice, and notice by publication is also required. This process usually takes about six months, allowing creditors to make their claims before the final distribution is made to shareholders. A few states require longer periods such as up to three years to wind up corporate business and better facilitate filing creditors' claims. The RMBCA gives unnotified corporate creditors up to five years to file claims against directors, officers, or shareholders if the liquidation proceeds are distributed.

Involuntary Dissolution

A corporation may be dissolved without its consent in an **involuntary dissolution** action brought by the state, creditors, or shareholders. Administrative dissolution by the secretary of state or state attorney general may be brought for violation of mandatory compliance with the corporation law. For example, the state may seek to dissolve the corporation for failure to file the annual report, nonpayment of the franchise tax, failure to maintain a registered office or agent, continual violation of its charter, or because the charter was procured by fraud. However, judicial dissolution is quite a severe action, so it is seldom undertaken. Dissolution is reserved for flagrant and excessive violations. Creditors may seek involuntary dissolution or involuntary bankruptcy if the corporation is insolvent.

Shareholder suits for involuntary dissolution may be based on irreconcilable board or shareholder deadlock that threatens to cause irreparable injury; illegal, oppressive, or fraudulent activities of those in control; *waste* of corporate assets; or expiration of a fixed corporate term. Minority shareholders in closely held corporations may seek dissolution if they are defrauded, oppressed, or intentionally frozen out. Some courts have enjoined a voluntary dissolution where the majority attempts to dissolve as a freezeout technique when they intend to reform immediately thereafter without the minority shareholder.

Winding Up, Liquidation, and Termination

Corporate dissolution is only the first of several steps leading to "the end." Dissolution terminates the corporation's right to conduct ongoing business as a separate entity, shielding shareholders with limited liability. Thereafter, the existing corporate affairs must be wound up through completion of existing contracts, assignment and delegation of contracts not susceptible to completion in a short time, debts paid, accounts collected, and assets sold or liquidated to create a fund to distribute to creditors and shareholders. The corporation may sue on obligations owed to it and be sued for creditors' claims it challenges.

The board may wind up, acting as trustees. A trustee is appointed by the court if the corporation's board or shareholders are deadlocked or its management is guilty of fraud or mismanagement; a receiver is appointed if dissolution is involuntary. As in partnership law, after dissolution the corporation must wind up existing business and may make new contracts only as necessary to finish old business. The trustee pays taxes and dissolution expenses first; next, the secured value of creditors' claims is paid; next, the unsecured claims of creditors are satisfied; next, liquidation preferences are accommodated and accrued dividend arrearages of preferred shareholders are distributed. If anything remains, this "residual value" is distributed pro rata to common shareholders.

The final act of ending corporate existence is **termination** of the corporate charter. Any agent purporting to act for a terminated corporation has personal liability for representing a nonexistent principal. There is no lingering apparent authority if proper notice is given.

The parties' rights in fundamental corporate changes are summarized in Figure 43–7.

END–OF–CHAPTER QUESTIONS

1. Describe the approval process for fundamental corporate changes such as a material charter amendment, merger, or sale of substantially all corporate assets. For what reasons do some shareholders have opposing rights in fundamental corporate changes?

2. Distinguish between triangular mergers and sales of substantially all corporate assets. What assumptions are made in using one method over the other?

3. Corporate combinations can be intended to squeeze out minority shareholders from the fundamentally changed corporation. What are the reasons and assumptions underlying the economic forces and legal rules addressing squeezeouts, particularly in closely held corporations?

Figure 43–7   Fundamental Corporate Changes

Fundamental Corporate Change	Acquirer-Bidder-Purchaser			Acquired-Target-Seller		
	Board Approval	Shareholder Approval	Dissenters' Appraisal	Board Approval	Shareholder Approval	Dissenters' Appraisal
Charter amendment	Yes	Yes	Yes, unless immaterial	N/A	N/A	N/A
Merger	Yes	Yes	Yes	Yes	Yes	Yes
Consolidation	Yes	Yes	Yes	Yes	Yes	Yes
Triangular merger	Yes	No	No	Yes	Yes	Yes
Reverse triangular merger	Yes	No	No	Yes	Yes	Yes
Sale of substantially all corporate assets	Yes	No	No	Yes	Yes	Yes, except in Delaware
Mandatory share exchange	Yes	No, unless charter amendment necessary	No, unless charter amendment necessary	Yes	Yes	Yes
Share acquisition or tender offer	Yes	No	No	No, management gives opinion	No, each individual shareholder has choice to sell	No
Going private transaction	N/A	N/A	N/A	Yes	No, individual shareholder's choice to sell	No, unless merger
Dissolution	Yes	Yes	Usually no	N/A	N/A	N/A

4. What are the reasons that hostile takeovers produce so much shareholder litigation? What are the underlying assumptions made in assessing the various parties' behaviors? What ambiguities produce some of the uncertainty?

5. Discuss the issues and the underlying rationale in two controlling shareholder situations: sale of control and control share acquisition acts. What is the requirement that selling shareholders share the control premium received from an acquiring bidder? Is "control" a corporate asset to be shared among all shareholders when an exiting controlling shareholder sells control? How does this underlying theory compare to the right created by state "control share acquisition" antitakeover laws giving nonacquiring shareholders the right to grant the acquiring shareholder voting rights?

6. Alad Corp. manufactured ladders. It eventually sold its whole business to another corporation, Alad II, including Alad's plant, equipment, inventory, trademarks, and goodwill. It continued to produce the same line of ladders under the Alad name, and Alad II sold them through the same sales force. There was no assumption of Alad's liabilities. Ray was injured on a defective ladder purchased by his employer from Alad. The change in

ownership was not publicly evident. Aside from proof of the product liability theory, what would Ray need to prove to hold Alad II liable for the injury? See *Ray v. Alad Corp.*, 560 P.2d 3 (Cal.1977).

7. McLoon Oil and other corporations merged into the Lido Corporation in 1976, leaving two dissenting shareholders demanding appraisal rights. The dissenting shareholders rejected Lido's offer. The trial court accepted a referee's valuation of the merged corporations' stock that included no discount for the lesser value for a minority block of stock due to its nonmarketability. Should the appraisal process for a dissenter from a fundamental corporate change be penalized for holding a minority interest that makes the stock less marketable and hence less valuable? See *In re McLoon Oil Co.*, 565 A.2d 997 (Maine 1989).

8. Alpert and others held 28 percent of the common stock in 79 Realty Corp., which owned a valuable building in New York City. A limited partnership, Madison 28 Associates, formed a corporation, 28 Williams St., to purchase the building by using a two-step merger between the two corporations — 79 Realty and 28 Williams St. This effectively squeezed out Alpert and others, who were required to take cash in the merger. The 28 Williams St. Corp. then transferred the building to the limited partnership, Madison 28, and the corporation was dissolved. What is the central issue here, and what reasons support the two opposing sides? Should the merger be rescinded for unfairness to the minority shareholders? See *Alpert v. 28 Williams St. Corp.*, 473 N.E.2d 19 (N.Y. Ct. App. 1984).

9. Amanda Acquisition Corp. was incorporated by its parent, High Voltage Engineering Corp., to acquire Universal Foods Corp., a Wisconsin corporation, by undertaking a tender offer. The Wisconsin antitakeover law forbids an acquiring corporation from merging with an acquired corporation for three years after the acquisition unless the target's management approved the transaction in advance. Even then, the control share acquisition provision requires that the minority shareholders must approve the merger. Wisconsin corporations are not permitted to opt out of the law's protection as in other states with similar provisions. Is the Wisconsin law unconstitutional as preempted by the Williams Act covering tender offers? What reasons support both sides in this controversy? See *Amanda Acquisition Corp. v. Universal Foods Corp.*, 877 F.2d 496 (7th Cir. 1989).

10. Balvik and Sylvester incorporated their electrical contracting partnership into the Weldon Corporation. Each was hired as a principal employee and each became an officer and director. However, Balvik received 30 percent of the voting stock and Sylvester received 70 percent, consistent with the value of their former partnership shares. This left Balvik only a minority voice in the corporation and their dispute over reinvesting or paying out earnings caused disharmony. Although they had good relations as partners, after incorporation a feud soon erupted and Balvik was fired, ostensibly for poor performance. Should Balvik be granted a dissolution because Sylvester caused Balvik to be squeezed out? See *Balvik v. Sylvester*, 411 N.W.2d 383 (N.D. 1987).

Unit IV

Regulation of Business

■

OVERVIEW: THE REASONS FOR REGULATION

Unit IV addresses a broad range of legal environmental and regulatory concerns for business. Today, business is broadly regulated by local, state, and federal governments as well as by private professional associations and foreign governments. However, the manager's range of decisionmaking was not always so constrained. Before the New Deal era, Supreme Court interpretations of the U.S. Constitution reinforced this country's historical preference for free-market decisionmaking. This philosophy was founded on the colonists' contempt for the British crown's authoritarian rule and the economic restraint imposed by British mercantilism.

The Constitution framers included provisions in the Constitution and in the Bill of Rights pronouncing broad social, political, and economic freedoms to encourage **laissez-faire** free markets and other libertarian ideals. These principles limited the role of federal, state, and local governments in the economy and thereby minimized governments' intrusion on business. For example, the *Contracts Clause* prohibited states from impairing the obligations of contracts. Regulation diminished the value of private property, so it was generally limited by the *economic due process* concept. Even today, U.S. economic

freedom stands in stark contrast to the intrusive government decisionmaking historically prevailing throughout the world's developed and developing economies.

The best-known statement of this laissez-faire preference was made in Adam Smith's 1776 publication *The Wealth of Nations*. He predicted that the ''invisible hand'' of capitalism implemented through self-interested economic actors would ''naturally'' drive the market to optimize social welfare. Private property would provide incentives to take risks and innovate as long as actors were entitled to the profits of their effort. Competition would discipline participants to become efficient, attracting new competitors as abnormally high profits become available. The primary economic questions would be answered with *allocative efficiency:* what is produced, how is it produced, who receives that production, and how is production changed.

Adam Smith's model makes further assumptions such as those underlying the **perfect competition model**: markets must have numerous rational buyers and sellers, all market participants have perfect information, there are no barriers restricting new firms' entry into markets, only standardized products are sold, and no participant possesses market power (e.g., no monopoly power). The market "clears" for quantities and at prices that form an *equilibrium*. Adam Smith believed there is only limited justification for government intervention in free markets because government intrusion is "unnatural." In his view, government has only three legitimate duties: (1) provide for national defense, (2) administer the justice system to preserve property rights and facilitate enforcement of transactions, and (3) establish public works or other public goods that are valuable throughout society but that private enterprise might neglect (e.g., roads, dams, and parks).

MARKET FAILURES

There has been considerable experience with the operation of markets illustrating that Adam Smith's assumptions are difficult to achieve in the real world. The market seldom operates just as Adam Smith predicted; sometimes it produces market inefficiencies or *market failures*. Many observers argue that market failure suboptimizes society's welfare, emphasizing the injurious side of self-interest. For example, polluters can often hide the side effects of their industrial processes, eventually harming society. While democratic market economies such as that in the United States prefer market systems, critics often justify government intervention to correct market failures through regulation. Additionally, some observers argue that a competitive market system is incapable of addressing many social and public policy preferences generated by a pluralistic democracy. Public consensus often pressures government to more equitably distribute income, conserve natural resources, eliminate minority discrimination, pursue nationalistic goals, stabilize economic volatility, and instigate various other social policies.

Monopoly Power

The perfect competition model operates well by allocating scarce resources efficiently but only when no seller possesses monopoly power and no buyer possesses monopsony buying power. Monopolies are the antithesis of perfect competition because the monopolist has power to set high prices, reduce the quantity produced, and become slow to innovate. The resulting artificial equilibrium provides excessively high monopoly profits to the monopolist and a suboptimally low level of products for consumers. The burden of this *dead-weight loss* transfers wealth from society to the monopolist. Competition is further deterred where the monopoly is reinforced by *barriers to entry,* conditions making it difficult to compete with the monopolist (e.g., patents, high fixed production start up costs, and legal or trade barriers).

Numerous regulatory policies have been introduced to limit monopoly power and force the market back toward the benefits of more perfect competition. The U.S. antitrust laws and the antimonopoly laws in the EC and many other nations are intended to correct for the market failure that permits monopolies to form. Interestingly, GATT and other "free trade" agreements between most nations are designed to serve the same purpose. Trade barriers erect monopolistic barriers to entering foreign markets. They tend to preserve market power for each nations' domestic producers at the expense of more perfect competition.

A form of monopolization occurs when one or a few sellers of scarce commodities can supply far less than the market demands. This permits the seller or sellers to earn large *windfall profits* until additional supplies or substitutes materialize. While this would seem to be the essence of careful business forecasting that the market model rewards, there can be political pressures to regulate and tax them. Windfall profits have occasionally been viewed as a form of monopoly power if no particular skill or ingenuity was involved in generating them and the windfall profits are very large. Windfall profit taxes transfer the undue windfall from producers to consumers. For example, the Arab oil embargo raised energy prices nearly 20-fold during the 1970s. As the oil crisis began to unfold, Congress regulated pricing by taxing the oil and gas industry's windfall profits. A similar theory has led to rationing scarce commodities during wartime and price controls to control inflation. President Nixon imposed such a price control program in the early 1970s. Cornering a market in commodities by buying or tying up all the available supply is an illegal form of monopoly under the commodities laws.

Monopsony, a *buyer's* market power, creates unequal bargaining power, a particular problem in the labor markets. Employees negotiate from a weak position because they are dispersed and unconnected as individuals. By contrast, most employers have monopsony (or oligopsony) powers in buying the services of employees. Some economists argue that the labor markets can never efficiently allocate labor resources because of employers' inherent bargaining advantage. There is considerable experience with employers that actively used their monopsony powers, particularly during the Industrial Revolution. This provoked the unionization movement in most industrialized nations. It also inspired a more severe backlash of workers who experimented with the political and economic ideologies of socialism and communism developed by Marx and Lenin. Political reaction to the unequal bargaining powers of farmers contributed to the regulation of railroad freight rates, creating a special status for agricultural cooperatives and the pervasive farm subsidy programs.

Natural Monopolies and Destructive Competition

A *natural monopoly* is inevitable in some industries because monopoly is a more efficient form than competition. Industries with declining long-run average costs can provide services more cheaply if granted a monopoly than under direct competition. For example, it would be foolish to have numerous competing utilities (e.g., electricity, natural gas, waterworks) serving the same customers. Such firms have high fixed generation, pumping, and transport costs to establish their generation capacity and to create and maintain their distribution networks composed of miles of wires or pipe. Turn-of-the-century experience with the fledgling electric power industry revealed another form of market failure, **destructive competition.** These early electric companies engaged in rampant price-cutting until they were forced to sell below cost. Eventually, most went bankrupt, leaving an unregulated monopoly for the lone survivor. After the deregulation of U.S. airlines in 1980, the airlines entered a period of destructive competition because they had more capacity than demand. Several U.S. airlines eventually went bankrupt.

There is an inefficient waste of societal resources when competition arises in a natural monopoly and the competitors duplicate their networks. If all these competitors have at least some business, none can offer prices as low as could a single monopolist. Therefore, governments usually grant an exclusive franchise creating the monopoly for each utility. Public utility commissions regulate prices and profits to avert the natural monopolist's tendency to raise price and cut output. Over time, technology may be expected to eliminate the cost advantages of a natural monopoly. For example, deregulation of long-distance telephone service, local cellular phone service, and cable television occurred after competition became a more efficient way to discipline these markets than regulation. The railroads' natural monopoly eventually disappeared as motor transport and airlines became more acceptable, reliable, and cost effective.

Externalities

Individuals' pursuit of self-interest through competitive markets often has side effects that impact others. **Externalities** are by-products of an individual's economic activities that impose costs or bestow benefits on others. Externalities are a form of market failure because the bargained-for exchange in the market does not include all the costs of that activity. For example, consider a manufacturing process that produces waste water that is dumped into local streams and gives off particulates and toxic gases into the air. There are limited incentives to control such pollution because abatement equipment is costly. Instead, the polluter can impose these costs on the environment, defiling a type of *public good*, as discussed in the next section. Polluters produce the classic *negative externality* because they ride free on others who actually bear the costs of pollution. The free market may actually encourage pollution, particularly when it is difficult to detect or the harms cannot be discovered immediately, a *delayed manifestation*. A *free rider* can take advantage of the situation by shifting some of the costs of production to others.

Political pressure often mounts to regulate externalities and thereby make everyone *internalize* the costs of their economic activity. Regulation and tax policies have been directed toward overcoming the market's failure to discipline those producing negative externalities. Public policies have also encouraged the production of *positive externalities*, the beneficial outgrowth of economic activity. For example, tax and industrial policy may create incentives to attract new industry. This benefits local merchants and employment, the surrounding community, and the tax base for local governments.

There are critics of using externalities to justify regulation. The well-known economist Ronald Coase has suggested that bystanders may already be compensated for externalities through cheaper land purchases or higher wages for employees in dangerous industries. The costs of controlling externalities must be weighed against the benefits expected before society implements any costly regulatory policy.

Public Goods

Markets fail to provide some goods or services efficiently or in sufficient quantities for society. **Public goods** are goods and services that are usually provided by government. Generally, there is no additional or *marginal cost* in providing public goods to an additional person and it is *nonrival* or difficult to exclude anyone from consuming them. For example, private enterprise is unlikely to provide the sea navigational assistance of a lighthouse. Shipowners, consumers, and suppliers share the benefit of safe and reliable trade when government provides lighthouse safety services, a classic public good. Government provides tax-financed public goods or regulation to cure the market's failure to supply them.

Garrett Hardin illustrates the public goods problem in his famous narrative on the *Tragedy of the Commons*. Consider the capacity problem of the U.S. open range in the late 1800s. Each cattle rancher had an incentive to expand his herd, conceivably maximizing his gain. Feeding cattle on the public open range appeared to be costless. However, as the number of ranchers and their herds grew, the range could not feed all the cattle. Eventually, the range grass on which the herds foraged was stripped away and did not regenerate. Most ranchers' herds became malnourished, and many died off.

Hardin commented that "ruin is the destination toward which all men rush, each pursuing his own best interest in a society that believes in the freedom of the commons. Freedom in a commons brings ruin to all." Advocates of laissez-faire economics and libertarianism cite this story of the Tragedy of the Commons to justify converting public lands into private property. They argue that individual ranchers are far less likely to overgraze if they must personally bear the negative "wealth effects" of overusing land they own. However, air and water resources are often cited as commons subject to a similar tragic destruction. Regulation theorists cite the tragedy as evidence of the impending destruction of public goods without regulation. The debate between free marketers and regulators reinforces the significance of distinguishing between private and public goods. Society has experimented with privatizing several theretofore public goods: (1) police and fire protection, (2) roads and turnpikes, and (3) mail service. Many governments still own their nations' telephone service. There are few "pure" public goods because most goods and services have some aspect of rivalness or excludability. The "goods" listed in the accompanying table are often underproduced by private enterprise and therefore share some characteristics of public goods.

Potential Public Goods the Market Allegedly Fails to Produce Sufficiently

Civil defense	Justice system	Industrial policy
Utilities	Waterworks	Sanitation
Public markets	Mail services	Grain elevators
Scenic views	Harbors	Locks and dams
Train stations	Bus terminals	Airports
Communications	Universities	Basic research
Parks and public land	Roads and streets	Docks and wharves
Public education	Public broadcasting	Fireworks displays
National defense	Law enforcement	Emergency services

Asymmetric Information

Free-market economists predict that the market will operate efficiently when buyers and sellers are well informed. However, information is costly in the real world, and par-

ticipants have varying abilities to effectively process and use their information. For example, employees often have incomplete information about workplace hazards or pollution. With more perfect information, employees might demand higher wages or pressure politicians for enhanced safety protection. This reality of imperfect information in most markets has triggered political pressures for disclosure regulations such as the food and drug labeling laws. The securities and franchising laws are intended to improve consumers' information. Many observers argue that financial disclosure laws in the United States make the U.S. securities markets the most efficient of all the world's markets. The more dominant market failures are summarized in the concept summary.

EVALUATING REGULATORY JUSTIFICATIONS

Regulatory programs are usually established when social and political pressures are exerted. Many regulatory programs are evaluated by the fairness of redistributing income or wealth that market forces have consolidated. However, regulation is also evaluated by economic analysis when invoked to correct market failures and force the market mechanism to work as predicted. Economic efficiency is cited to justify those regulations that arguably reduce the waste of societal resources for a given level of economic activity. Another economic measure of the efficiency of regulation is *pareto optimality*. Under this model, a regulation or any other action produces optimal efficiency when it causes society to become better off while no one is made worse off. Pareto efficiency is used to protect some faction of the economy from carrying the whole burden of the change.

Multiple Regulatory Explanations

Few regulatory programs are based on a single justification. Sometimes the market failure explanation is weak but there are persistent political pressures on regulators. For example, there were political pressures to continue the regulation of transportation rates long after motor trucks offered an alternative transport mode that eliminated the railroads' natural monopoly. In other instances, a regulatory program may be rationalized as correcting multiple market failures. For example, product liability laws attempt to correct the market's failure to supply consumers with more perfect information about products. Additionally, product liability laws are explained as a method to prevent manufacturers from externalizing their costs of defective design or negligent production techniques.

Concept Summary: Market Failures Justifying Regulation

Type of Market Failure	Definition	Examples	Regulatory Program
Monopoly/Market Power	Market power held by a single or a few producers enabling their reduction of quantity produced and increases in price to maximize profits	Utilities, goods manufactured under patents, windfall profits for 1970s oil industry, late-18th-century U.S. railroads	Antitrust laws, rate regulation of natural monopolies, price regulation
Unequal Bargaining Power	Market power permitting one party to set the terms of trade	Employer monopsony, buying power for labor and services	Labor-management laws requiring collective bargaining
Destructive Competition	Excessive price-cutting, forcing competitors to sell below cost, causing bankruptcy of all competitors, leaving one a monopoly	Turn-of-the-century electric utilities, contemporary U.S. airlines, Depression era U.S. trucking	Exclusive utility franchises, rate regulation for natural monopolies
Externalities	Side effects or by-products of economic activity that impose costs or bestow benefits on others	Pollution and workplace dangers	Environmental and occupational safety regulation
Public Goods	Goods and services that are underproduced by private enterprise that are nonrival and nonexcludable	Public roads, air and water resources, national defense, law enforcement	Environmental law, taxes funding public works and government programs
Asymmetric Information	Buyers and sellers do not share equal information because of its costs or efforts to hide information	Insufficient information about corporate financial performance	Financial disclosure under securities laws, workplace hazard warnings
Barriers to Entry	Conditions deterring new competitors or development of new substitute products	Patents, high startup costs, large economies of scale and density	Antitrust laws, treaties lifting trade barriers, industrial policy

Part X

Securities Law

■

Chapter 44

Regulation of the Investment Markets:
Public Offerings and Private Placements

Chapter 45

Securities Market Regulation: Insider
Trading, Proxies, Tender Offers, and
Securities Professionals

Regulation of the Investment Markets: Public Offerings and Private Placements

■

CRITICAL THINKING INQUIRIES

As you read this chapter, you should be able to address the following:

- What issues arise in regulating the ''free markets'' for securities?
- What reasons support the U.S. prohibition of foreign bribery if some other nations ignore or condone the practice?
- What assumptions underlie requiring registration of new securities issues and financial disclosures provided to prospective investors?
- What legal ambiguities arise in financing new business operations with participations sold to investors?

MANAGERIAL PERSPECTIVE

The ABC Corp. is a privately held close corporation. Potentially profitable new business opportunities will require substantial capital infusion for success. ABC's banks are reluctant to lend the needed capital. Venture capitalists will take too much control from the existing owners. ABC's vice president of finance suggests that the board should consider either a private placement of securities or ''going public.''

- What confidential revelations are necessary for these financing alternatives?
- Compare ABC's cost burden for a private placement or going public.
- What types of financing contracts trigger the federal securities laws, and which do not?
- What regulators might then become involved with ABC's management and corporate governance?
- What liability risks are raised by such financing?

INTRODUCTION TO THE INVESTMENT MARKETS

The term *laissez-faire* economics was generally applied to the securities and investments markets before the Great Depression. However, the 1929 stock market crash triggered passage of federal and state regulations. Government addressed fraud and coercive pressure rampant during the Roaring Twenties. Such abuses undermine the *integrity of the market*, which is considered essential to keeping the U.S. securities markets the most liquid and efficient in the world. Ethical considerations permeate the securities laws — they were passed primarily to address fraud, self-interest, and fiduciary problems. Many other nations with established and emerging securities markets pattern their regulations on the U.S. system. Eventually, borderless capital markets will make financing from anywhere readily available to the most deserving firms anywhere in the world. This chapter primarily discusses U.S. regulation, comparing it with some regulatory schemes used in other nations.

Investment and capital raising are opposite sides of the same markets. These markets are regulated because they are "impersonal." Most investors and capital users are detached from each other — professional intermediaries act for them. The varying objectives and needs of these parties have spawned a wide diversity in investment vehicles tailored to the type of assets represented, the investment's duration, claims against collateral, tax treatment, intermediary expertise, and the parties' personal responsibilities. Diverse investments are produced by changing some of these factors: securities, commodities, futures, options, swaps, and loans, among others. Some investments are regulated only by the law of contracts and torts. However, bad experiences with some investments led to special regulation of specific investments: banking regulation by the states and the Federal Reserve Board (Fed), securities markets regulation by the states and the Securities and Exchange Commission (SEC), and commodities and futures market regulation by the Commodities Futures Trading Commission (CFTC).

Underwriting, Investment, and Commercial Banking

The underwriting of an *initial public offering (IPO)* is the accepted U.S. process for the first distribution of a new security before it begins to trade on a "sec-

ondary" stock exchange market. **Underwriting** is the *primary* marketing of a new security through a network of independent intermediaries — an **underwriting syndicate.** A *lead underwriter* organizes this group of wholesale dealers and advises the issuer. Each syndicate member agrees to distribute a portion of the new issue, sometimes through other retail dealers, then ultimately to public investors. These large groups spread the risk that some of the securities will remain unsold or the market price might fall before the public offering is complete. *Firm commitment* underwriters commit to pay the issuer a specified amount of proceeds. They profit by the *spread* between the sale price to investors and the proceeds given to the issuer. Underwriters are only willing to promise their *best efforts* to less well-established issuers; they make a commission rather than a wholesale profit on the spread. *Competitive bidding* among underwriters is necessary for some municipal and government bonds and for public utility holding companies. The *Dutch auction* uses competitive bidding for several separate portions of some new issues.

The underwriting practice was first used in the United States to retire the civil war debt pioneered by famous financiers such as J. P. Morgan and Jay Cooke. Their monopoly powers over capital formation in both investment and commercial banking prompted regulatory reactions — for example, the Glass-Stegall Act of 1933, separating investment banking companies from the commercial banks (e.g., customer deposits and checking and savings accounts). However, most nations have not separated these banking functions. For example, *universal banking* in Germany combines commercial with investment banking. Japanese and U.S. banks are beginning to blur the distinction between commercial and investment banking. Commercial banks may sell securities through their underwriting and brokerage subsidiaries, and some brokers offer check-writing privileges on mutual funds or brokerage accounts.

The British *queue* system empowers the Bank of England to select an *impact day* on which public subscriptions for the securities are accepted or offers are solicited from the public. Underwriters have less risk, largely providing administrative services in soliciting, processing, and distributing the new securities offering. The EC has issued directives resembling the U.S. prospectus registration process. However, exemptions will probably allow continued universal banking, permitting the German banks to sell unregistered securities directly to their customers.

In the United States, **underwriters** are broadly defined to include any person who has either purchased from an issuer with a view to reselling securities or provides assistance in distributing the securities. Underwriters have special responsibilities and potential liabilities: (1) they ensure the accuracy of disclosures that the issuer makes in the prospectus and registration statement, (2) only underwriters may negotiate with the issuer before the public offering is made, and (3) certain security sales during the offering period may not be made by the issuer or its underwriters. Care must be taken when any consultant becomes involved with a firm's financing to avoid unintentionally becoming an underwriter. For example, any assistance ABC Corp. might receive from a venture capitalist, law firm, or auditor in assembling an underwriting syndicate or convincing investors to purchase the securities constitutes underwriting, exposing that consultant to legal responsibility. Figure 44–1 illustrates the chain of distribution for new securities issues.

Securities Exchanges

The markets for existing securities are composed of stock exchanges, investment bankers, and broker-dealers who help firms raise capital by selling securities and facilitating investors' trading. There is a similar structure for the commodities markets. **Securities exchanges** are facilities that permit the organized sale and purchase of securities. Sales are often made in an auctionlike atmosphere among the floor brokers who execute trades for affiliated brokerage houses that in turn represent investor-clients.

The **New York Stock Exchange (NYSE)** trades securities in the largest U.S. corporations and in some foreign corporations. The securities of somewhat smaller corporate issuers are listed to trade on the **American Stock Exchange (AMEX).** The **Over-the-Counter (OTC)** market has grown rapidly, listing securities of both large and small issuers. The **National Association of Securities Dealers (NASD)** has established telephone and computer

Figure 44–1   Underwriting and Distribution of Securities

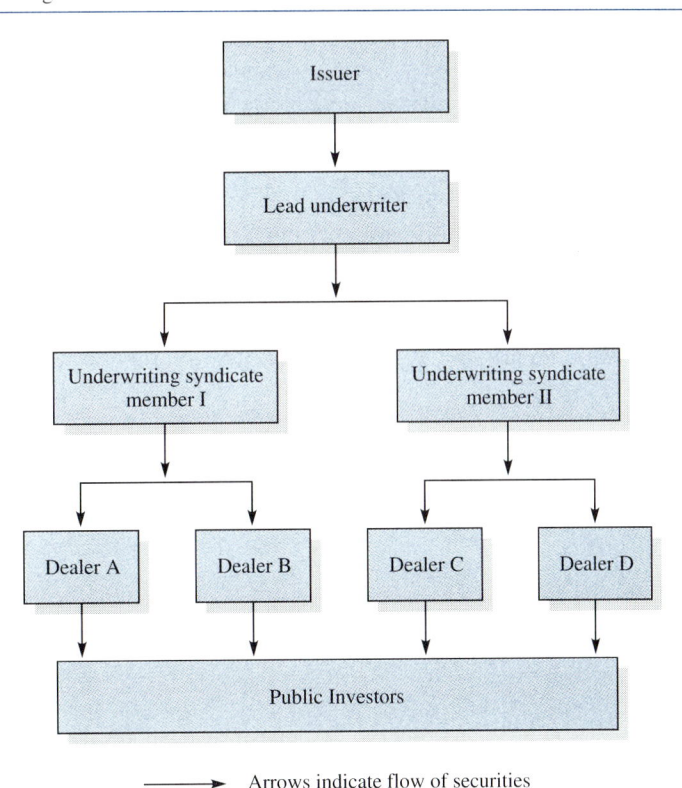

Arrows indicate flow of securities

terminal connections among thousands of geographically dispersed OTC broker-dealers. This electronic network is the **National Association of Securities Dealers' Automated Quotation (NASDAQ)** service. The NASDAQ constitutes an exchange facility. There are numerous other regional securities exchanges within the United States, and important exchanges in many of the world's major cities. For example, major international exchanges exist in Toronto, Hong Kong, London, Sydney, Montreal, Frankfurt, Paris, Brussels, Milan, Zurich, and Amsterdam. Important securities exchanges are emerging in Singapore, Seoul, Madrid, Taiwan, Indonesia, Mexico City, Kingston, and many Eastern European capitals.

Stock exchange floor brokers trade for clients for a fee, and some trade personally as investors or speculators for their own accounts. Some brokerages satisfy customer orders out of securities already held in the broker's inventory. Other times, the customer's local broker transmits an order to buy or sell through the main office in New York and to representatives in the exchange, who signal floor brokers to execute the trade. Orders are executed at the market price then prevailing, although some customers require a favorable price movement before trading. A **limit order** postpones the transaction until the price moves to the customer's desired price.

Floor brokers may trade with other floor brokers, but it is often more reliable to trade directly with **specialists** who occupy well-known positions on the exchange floor. They regularly buy and sell (specialize) in only one or a few securities. Specialists are obligated to *make a market* in their chosen securities. This provides *liquidity,* creating a reliable market by purchasing from ready sellers and selling to ready buyers. Specialists profit from the spread, and must compile a **specialist's book** of all the limit orders that cannot immediately be executed until the price moves. The specialist acts as the floor broker's agent by completing the transaction for the floor broker's customer after the price moves. OTC specialists are called **market makers.**

Increasingly, the world's issuers have their securities *listed* or registered for official trading on numerous nation's exchanges. For example, U.S. law facilitates the listing of Canadian issuers on U.S. exchanges. However, cross-border trading in foreign securities is still somewhat risky and difficult. First, there are frequent and sometimes significant exchange rate fluctuations between the customer's national currency and the currency in the stock exchange's host nation. Second, most nations have different securities regulations and exchange listing requirements that can impede cross-border trading.

Some foreign firms' securities trade on U.S. exchanges as **American Depository Receipts (ADR).** A foreign bank holds the actual foreign securities and issues ADR certificates to represent the underlying foreign securities, so only the ADR actually trades on U.S. exchanges. Foreign issuers may also have their shares actually trade on U.S. exchanges under relaxed SEC registration. The disclosure requirements for foreign issuers are somewhat less burdensome and reveal less information about their management than U.S. firms must. This is consistent with the additional secrecy many foreign nations permit to their publicly traded firms.

Brokerages are increasingly affiliating with foreign brokers, or they establish foreign branches to trade legally on foreign securities exchanges. Exchanges in two nations may establish **electronic trading links** to facilitate foreign trading. The floor broker representing a domestic customer may receive price quotes, recent sales timing, and sales volume information for the foreign securities. For example, a trading link exists between the NASDAQ and the London Stock Exchange. Links may soon be used to transmit orders for immediate execution on the other nation's exchange floor.

The Federal Securities Laws

Since 1933, the federal government has enacted seven major securities laws, numerous amendments, and other laws applicable to investment-related transactions. The **Securities Act of 1933 (1933 Act)** was the first of President Franklin D. Roosevelt's *New Deal* legislation to address the problems believed to have caused the 1929 stock market crash. The 1933 Act requires issuers of new securities to make extensive financial and operational disclosures and register new securities issues with the SEC. There are *transaction exemptions* for small offerings, intrastate sales, some foreign issues, and private placements. Exemptions reduce the registration burden and compliance costs.

The **Securities Exchange Act of 1934 (1934 Act)** regulates the secondary trading markets, the exchanges, broker-dealers, insider trading, proxy solicitations, and tender offers. It requires publicly traded issuers to periodically disclose their finances and other matters. The 1933 Act, its amendments, disclosure standards, and interpretive SEC rules, are detailed in this chapter, and the 1934 Act is covered in Chapter 45.

There are five other major securities laws. The **Public Utility Holding Company Act of 1935** was intended to correct abusive pyramid-style capital structures of public utilities. The **Trust Indenture Act of 1939** prohibits conflicts of interest that harm bondholders by prohibiting management-hired indenture trustees. The **Investment Company Act of 1940** requires special SEC registration and oversight of mutual funds and money market funds. The **Investment Advisor Act of 1940,** which requires the licensing of persons who provide security investment advice for a fee, is discussed in Chapter 45. The **Securities Investor Protection Act of 1970** created the Securities Investor Protection Corporation to insure customer accounts against losses when a brokerage becomes insolvent. Other laws relevant to securities transactions and investment professionals that are discussed in this chapter include racketeering laws, commodity exchange laws, and foreign bribery laws.

The American Bar Association Committee on Federal Regulation of Securities has urged the American Law Institute to rewrite the federal securities laws and eliminate inconsistent definitions, procedures, and costly duplication. This effort produced the **Federal Securities Code,** but it is unlikely to pass through Congress. Nevertheless, the Code has prompted the SEC to revise the disclosure system, making it more cost efficient, and some courts cite the Code as if it were a *Restatement*.

Most nations have similar securities laws, although few are enforced as vigorously as in the United States. During the post–World War II occupation of Japan, U.S.-style securities laws were "installed" in Japan. However, the Japanese have given variable enforcement to these laws, and the insider trading law has been largely ignored. Apparently, U.S.-style securities laws are culturally incompatible with some nations. Some critics argue that the U.S. securities markets will ultimately lose out to the laissez-faire markets in other nations such as Hong Kong. However, many Eastern European stock markets are beginning to follow the U.S. system. The United States's extensive capital market experience has produced fair trading rules, making U.S. markets the envy of the world. Investors are attracted to markets perceived as providing a *fair*

game, relatively free of fraud and insider trading abuses. "Harmonization" of diverse international securities institutions will probably occur as nations coalesce toward a regulatory equilibrium.

State Blue Sky Laws

The 1933 and 1934 acts were not the first securities laws. Kansas first experimented with a **blue sky law** in 1911. This term grew out of the extravagant claims made by securities promoters that critics compared to "selling building lots in the blue sky in fee simple." Blue sky laws have roots in the law of contracts and the tort of fraud. Common law remedies became ineffective when the securities markets went interstate. Early securities laws also arose in some foreign nations. Laws addressing speculation were initiated well before the 20th century after the Dutch speculative frenzy over tulip bulbs and the English investors' disastrous experience with exploiting the "South Sea Bubble."

The **Uniform Securities Act** provides for registration of securities, licensing of broker-dealers, antifraud protections for investors, and enforcement powers somewhat similar to the SEC's powers. Securities registered under the 1933 Act may be easily registered concurrently with most states. However, New York's blue sky law is sufficiently different to require significant separate *qualification* of new issues. Intrastate and privately placed issues that are exempt under federal law may still require state blue sky registration. All the states have also adopted UCC Article 8 which governs the transfer process for securities and enforces transfer restrictions, as previously introduced in Chapter 40 and discussed later in this chapter.

RACKETEER INFLUENCED AND CORRUPT ORGANIZATIONS

The 1970 **Organized Crime Control Act** contains the federal racketeering laws. Their potential impact is significant for those involved in securities transactions. The **Racketeer Influenced and Corrupt Organizations (RICO)** provisions establish criminal violations and treble damage civil liability for persons who use the profits from certain repeated criminal acts to subsidize an organization. This law was originally intended to assist government enforcers' criminal prosecution of organized crime by encouraging private damage suits by victims. However, it has been aggressively used against the securities industry, usually unconnected with organized crime. As a compound or "supercrime," RICO is violated when two or more related crimes, known as **predicate offenses,** are committed as part of a pattern of racketeering activity. Numerous states have separate racketeering laws with widely variable provisions.

RICO Elements

The RICO claim must prove (1) the commission of at least two acts within 10 years, (2) that constitutes a pattern, (3) of racketeering activity, (4) by which the defendant, (5) invests in, maintains an interest in, or participates in, (6) an enterprise, (7) affecting interstate or foreign commerce. The underlying crimes or predicate offenses include traditional activities of organized crime, both federal and state crimes, such as murder, arson, drug dealing, extortion, gambling, bribery, counterfeiting, white slave trafficking, labor union–related crimes, and loan sharking. RICO has a significant impact in securities law because securities fraud and mail and wire fraud are also predicate offenses. For example, RICO would be violated if ABC Corp.'s investment banker made numerous purchases of ABC's shares just before ABC's next public offering to temporarily boost ABC's price and make the IPO successful. As discussed in Chapter 45, such market manipulation is a form of securities fraud. These numerous transactions would clearly constitute a pattern of activity intended to assist ABC in selling its shares for an artificially high price, thus actionable under RICO.

Controversy over RICO

There is considerable controversy over the alleged misuse of RICO by private plaintiffs and zealous federal prosecutors. The treble damage remedy encourages many private plaintiffs to allege RICO claims in nearly every securities fraud suit. RICO claims have allegedly coerced many defendants into paying a "settlement value" just to minimize their RICO defense costs and reduce uncertainty from RICO interpretations. Criminal RICO is also subject to misuse because the law contains extensive pretrial forfeiture provisions permitting prosecutors to seize assets allegedly tainted as racketeering profits. For example, the U.S. Attorney for New York City used the threat of a RICO forfeiture to bring down "junk bond king" Michael Milken for securities fraud. Milken and his employer, Drexel Burnham Lambert, were charged with numerous counts of securities fraud. This eventually led to the firm's bankruptcy. Of course, most criminal laws permit pretrial seizures from individuals and small or large companies to deter defendants from fleeing or hiding stolen property. Forfeitures become permanent only after conviction. The Comprehensive Crime Control Act of 1984 permits seizure and sale of vehicles, boats, or houses used in drug dealing.

Should RICO's ambiguities and the alleged abuses by plaintiffs and prosecutors prompt the courts to restrain RICO's potential misuse by changing RICO requirements? The following case illustrates why such changes in RICO will probably come only from the Congress.

SEDIMA v. IMREX COMPANY, INC.
473 U.S.479 (1985)

RICO provides a private civil action to recover treble damages for injury "by reason of a violation of" its substantive provisions. The initial dormancy of this provision and its recent greatly increased utilization are now familiar history. Sedima, a Belgian corporation, entered into a joint venture with respondent Imrex Co. to sell electronic components to other Belgian buyers, who would order parts through Sedima. Imrex would obtain the parts in the United States for shipment to Europe. Sedima and Imrex were to split the net proceeds. Sedima became convinced Imrex presented inflated bills and cheated Sedima out of a portion of its proceeds by allegedly collecting for nonexistent expenses. Sedima sued Imrex, claiming RICO violations, and Imrex appealed, arguing that a criminal RICO conviction is a prerequisite to proof of a predicate offense and that the civil plaintiff must suffer a special "racketeering injury" before a civil RICO action may be commenced.

WHITE, Justice

The language of RICO gives no obvious indication that a civil action can proceed only after a criminal conviction. The word "conviction" does not appear in any relevant portion of the statute. To the contrary, the predicate acts involve conduct that is "chargeable" or "indictable," and "offense(s)" that are "punishable," under various criminal statutes. As defined in the statute, racketeering activity consists not of acts for which the defendant has been convicted, but of acts for which he could be. Thus, a prior conviction requirement cannot be found in the definition of "racketeering activity." We can find no support in the statute's history, its language, or considerations of policy for a requirement that a private treble damages action under RICO can proceed only against a defendant who has already been criminally convicted. To the contrary, every indication is that no such requirement exists. Accordingly, the fact that Imrex and the individual defendants have not been convicted under [RICO] or the federal mail and wire fraud statutes does not bar Sedima's action.

[We] perceive no distinct "racketeering injury" requirement. Given that "racketeering activity" consists of no more and no less than commission of a predicate act, we are initially doubtful about a requirement of a "racketeering injury" separate from the harm from the predicate acts. Section 1964(c) authorizes a private suit by "[a]ny person injured in his business or property by reason of a violation of §1962" [that] in turn makes it unlawful for "any person," not just mobsters, to use money derived from a pattern of racketeering activity to invest in an enterprise, to acquire control of an enterprise through a pattern of racketeering activity, or to conduct an enterprise through a pattern of racketeering activity. If the defendant engages in a pattern of racketeering activity in a manner forbidden by these provisions, and the racketeering activities injure the plaintiff in his business or property, the plaintiff has a claim. There is no room in the statutory language for an additional, amorphous "racketeering injury" requirement.

This less restrictive reading is amply supported by our prior cases and the general principles surrounding this statute. RICO is to be read broadly.

This is the lesson not only of Congress' self-consciously expansive language and overall approach, but also of its express admonition that RICO is to "be liberally construed to effectuate its remedial purposes."

It is so ordered.

POWELL, Justice, Dissenting

The legislative history makes clear that the statute was intended to be applied to organized crime, and an influential sponsor of the bill emphasized that any effect it had beyond such crime was meant to be only incidental.

Senator McClellan, a leading sponsor of the bill, stated that "proof of two acts of racketeering activity, without more, does not establish a pattern." The bill was not aimed at sporadic activity, but that the "infiltration of legitimate business normally requires more than one 'racketeering activity' and the threat of continuing activity to be effective. It is this factor of continuity plus relationship which combines to produce a pattern." The ABA Report suggests that to effectuate this legislative intent, "pattern" should be interpreted as requiring that (i) the racketeering acts be related to each other, (ii) they be part of some common scheme, and (iii) some sort of continuity between the acts or a threat of continuing criminal activity must be shown. By construing "pattern" to focus on the manner in which the crime was perpetrated, courts could go a long way toward limiting the reach of the statute to its intended target—organized crime.

Today's opinion inevitably will encourage continued expansion of resort to RICO in cases of alleged fraud or contract violation rather than to the traditional remedies available in state court. It defies rational belief, particularly in light of the legislative history, that Congress intended this far-reaching result.

Case Questions

1. What is the issue in expanding RICO to securities activities?

2. What assumptions are made by the dissent in advocating a "mobsters only" limitation on civil RICO suits?

Four years after *Sedima*, the Supreme Court in *H. J. Inc. v. Northwestern Bell Telephone Co.*,[1] restricted the ''pattern'' requirement as Justice Powell suggested. Proof of a RICO pattern must be based on some relationship between the predicate offenses, such as the same or similar purpose, results, participants, victims, or methods of committing the predicate offenses. Two isolated predicate acts that pose no threat of continuity do not form a pattern. RICO is not reserved only for mobsters. It impacts lawyers, investment bankers, arbitrageurs, securities professionals, and the auditors of publicly traded companies. However, the Supreme Court's 1993 decision in *Reves v. Ernst & Young*[2] relieved auditors of RICO liability unless they actively and knowingly participate in a securities fraud.

RICO is also subject to some ethical abuse, such as when a civil plaintiff misuses the treble damage threat to reach settlement or a zealous prosecutor uses it for political publicity. RICO claims have been brought in such diverse areas as contract disputes, religious protests, retirement village mismanagement, commodities speculation, and against tele-evangelists. The criminal penalties are potentially severe: up to a $25,000 fine and 20 years' imprisonment per violation. RICO strikes an ethical balance because legitimate competitors of enterprises financed by illegal racketeering activities are placed at a significant disadvantage.

FOREIGN CORRUPT PRACTICES ACT

Reactions to the illegal use of corporate funds during the Watergate era prompted Congress to pass the **Foreign Corrupt Practices Act (FCPA)** in 1977. The FCPA prohibits bribery of foreign officials in order to gain foreign business. Separate accounting standards provisions require careful recordkeeping and financial controls to help publicly traded corporations prevent bribery. However, controversy over the 1977 law's ambiguities led to clarification in the *Foreign Corrupt Practices Act Amendments of 1988*, passed as part of the Omnibus Trade Bill to encourage U.S. exports. Foreign bribery by all U.S. **domestic concerns** is prohibited.

---

[1]*H. J. Inc. v. Northwestern Bell Telephone Co.*, 492 U.S. 229 (1989).

[2]*Reves v. Ernst & Young*, 113 S.Ct. 1163 (1993).

Domestic Concerns Prohibited by FCPA from Foreign Bribery

. . . any individual who is a citizen, national, or resident of the U.S.; and any corporation, partnership, association, joint-stock company, business trust, unincorporated association, or sole proprietorship which has its principal place of business in the U.S., or which is organized under the laws of a state of the U.S.

Domestic concerns are prohibited from making corrupt payments, offers to pay, or offers to give anything of value to foreign officials to influence a decision to grant business. Under the FCPA, **foreign officials** are persons with discretionary powers to grant or assist in granting business to the domestic concern. This includes members of foreign political parties, foreign political candidates, or officials of foreign firms. Foreign personnel with merely ministerial or clerical responsibilities are exempt. This provision has been used to define allowable **grease payments** made to lower-echelon employees without discretionary authority. Such payments are used merely to facilitate the clearance of previously contracted for goods or services. Facilitating payments are not illegal bribery so long as they are legal in the host nation. For example, a customs official at a foreign border might request a ''gratuity'' from ABC Corp.'s delivery driver. If this payment is routine in the host nation, ABC is not liable for illegal foreign bribery. Bona fide promotional expenses, contract performance expenses, and lodging for foreign officials during sales presentations are not illegal.

Accounting Standards Provisions

The SEC oversees the FCPA accounting standards provisions for publicly traded domestic concerns. Accurate recordkeeping and maintenance of internal accounting controls is required. Separate SEC rules prohibit falsification of records or lying to accountants. **Internal accounting controls** are systems and procedures for the production of accurate financial statements that permit reconciliation of assets and records and safeguard corporate assets. Such controls help supervise employees, reducing the possibility they might use corporate assets to make a bribe. What types of internal controls are necessary in most publicly traded corporations? The following case illustrates a complete lack of controls, illegal under the FCPA.

S.E.C. v. WORLD-WIDE COIN INVESTMENTS, LTD.

567 F. Supp. 724 (N.D. Ga. 1983)

World-Wide Coin Investments was a publicly traded company listed on the Boston Exchange and engaged primarily in wholesale and retail sales of rare coins, precious metals, gold and silver coins, and bullion. Inventory was purchased as collections from estates and private individuals, from dealers, on domestic commodities exchanges, and at coin shows. Prior to July 1979, the company's assets totaled over $2 million and it had over 40 employees. By August 1981, the company's assets amounted to less than $500,000, and it had only three employees. The SEC sought an injunction against the corporation and its directors, an accounting, and a return of misappropriated assets.

VINING, Judge

The safeguarding of World-Wide's physical inventory was one of its most severe problems; the company's vault, where most of the rare coins were kept, was unguarded and left open all day to all employees. Furthermore, no one employee was responsible for the issuance of coins from the vault. Scrap silver and bags of silver coins were left unattended in the hallways and in several cluttered, unlocked rooms at World-Wide's offices.

Hale [the president] also failed to initiate an adequate system of itemizing World-Wide's physical inventory. Rather than maintaining a perpetual inventory system, the company relied on a manual quarterly system, which was not effective in safeguarding the assets or in keeping an accurate account of the inventory. World-Wide's system made it relatively simple for an employee to improperly value and/or misappropriate large items of inventory. [The auditor] testified that he could not determine how much was actually paid for the coins in World-Wide's inventory, since there were no backup documents and only a few coins were cost-coded.

This court has noted the lack of supervision over the accounting department and the lack of expertise in the area. World-Wide maintains no separation of duties in the area of purchase and sales transactions, and valuation procedures for ending inventory. For instance, a single salesperson can do all the following tasks without supervision or review by another employer or officer: appraise a particular coin offered for purchase by a customer, purchase that coin with a check that the salesperson alone has drawn, count that same coin into inventory, value the coin for inventory purposes, and sell the coin to another purchaser.

Employees, none of whom was bonded, were also allowed to take large amounts of inventory off the company's premises for purposes of effecting a sale without giving a receipt, as well as being given cash to purchase the precious metals and coins at various locations, also without giving a receipt. Nor were employees required to write source documents relating to the purchase and sale of coins, bullion, and other inventory, making it impossible to ascertain whether a particular inventory item had been sold at a profit or loss, or whether it had even been sold. Although pre-numbered invoices could have been used to help alleviate this problem, they were not.

There were no procedures enforced with respect to writing checks. Since employees have been allowed to write checks without noting the purpose of the transaction on the instrument or on any other document, source documents for most checks do not exist. All employees have had access to presigned checks, and there had been no dollar limit over which an employee cannot write a check. Furthermore, employees have not been required to get approval before writing a check. These policies have caused World-Wide to bounce over 100 checks since Hale took over the management of the company.

Approximately $1.7 million worth of checks were written to Hale, his affiliates, or to cash, all without supporting documentation or any indication of the purpose of the checks. Hale testified that approximately $250,000 worth of these checks were repayments of loans he had personally made to the company, but he failed to introduce any executed promissory notes or any document to support that claim. The SEC also introduced various checks to and/or bills from local bars and restaurants written by Hale and reimbursed by either World-Wide or

East Coast Coin. Numerous checks written to Hale on World-Wide's account were superimposed over purchase orders, supposedly as source documentation for the transactions.

The FCPA was enacted on the principle that accurate recordkeeping is an essential ingredient in promoting management responsibility and is an affirmative requirement for publicly held American corporations to strengthen the accuracy of corporate books and records, which are "the bedrock elements of our system of corporate disclosure and accountability." A motivating factor in the enactment of the FCPA was a desire to protect the investor.

In order to maintain accountability for the disposition of its assets, a business must attempt to make it difficult for its assets to be misappropriated. Internal accounting controls [must be] specifically designed to provide reasonable, cost-effective safeguards against the unauthorized use or disposition of company assets and reasonable assurances that financial records and accounts are sufficiently reliable for purposes of external reporting. Internal accounting controls are basic indicators of the reliability of the financial statements and the accounting system and records from which financial statements are prepared.

The definition of accounting controls does comprehend reasonable, but not absolute, assurances that the objectives expressed in it will be accomplished by the system. The concept of "reasonable assurances" recognizes that the costs of internal controls should not exceed the benefits expected to be derived. Congress was fully cognizant of the cost-effective considerations which confront companies as they consider the institution of accounting controls and of the subjective elements which may lead reasonable individuals to arrive at different conclusions. Congress has demanded only that judgment be exercised in applying the standard of reasonableness. The size of the business, diversity of operations, degree of centralization of financial and operating management, amount of contact by top management with day-to-day operations, and numerous other circumstances are factors which management must consider in establishing and maintaining an internal accounting controls system. However, an issuer would probably not be successful in arguing a cost-benefit defense in circumstances [as here] where the management, despite warnings by its auditors of significant weaknesses of its accounting control system, had decided, after a cost benefit analysis, not to strengthen them, and then the internal accounting controls proved to be so inadequate that the company was virtually destroyed.

The evidence is this case reveals that World-Wide, aided and abetted by Hale and Seibert, violated the FCPA. The internal recordkeeping and accounting controls of World-Wide have been sheer chaos since Hale took over control of the company. [Judgment for the SEC.]

Case Questions

1. In FCPA enforcement actions, what is the issue about the impact of internal accounting controls on foreign bribery?

2. What ambiguities are created when there is poor recordkeeping and insufficient internal controls?

Enforcement and Administrative Process

The FCPA splits enforcement powers between the SEC and the Justice Department. The SEC has civil powers over publicly traded companies and enforces the accounting standards provisions. The Justice Department may bring criminal cases against any domestic concern and has civil powers like the SEC's over nonpublicly traded domestic concerns. Fines for violation of the bribery provisions of up to $2 million may be levied against publicly traded corporations. Individuals may be fined up to $100,000 and/or imprisoned up to five years. The SEC may also levy civil penalties. The U.S. Attorney General's office is empowered to issue guidelines to domestic concerns seeking approval of specific proposed conduct.

The FCPA is a fundamental ethical code for international business. It becomes problematic when other nations view the United States as imperialistic in exporting its values. This may intensify the clash of cultures. However, this ethical export has been effective where U.S.-trained auditors carry their expectations and judgments with them on audits of foreign issuers. Bribery undermines the perfect competition model, permitting foreign officials to profiteer at the expense of their own nations. FCPA critics have charged that the law is self-defeating. If U.S. firms refuse to bribe foreign officials, then firms from other nations without antibribery laws will just fill in the gap. However, the evidence is mixed. U.S. exports grew steadily since the FCPA's passage, although possibly at a lower rate than if bribery were permitted. Meanwhile, FCPA enforcement has been rather lax since the mid-1980s.

The FCPA has also been used to resolve another ethical dilemma: to restrict excessive *perks* that management can too easily control without adequate oversight. This was a predictable problem at Playboy Enterprises, which for years lavished Hugh Hefner, his family, and friends with extensive and undisclosed perks and services at the numerous Playboy mansions, estates, and other facilities.[3]

COMMODITY FUTURES REGULATION

Commodities and commodity futures are areas of investment outside the SEC's jurisdiction. The **Commodity Futures Trading Commission (CFTC)** has authority over contracts for future delivery of some underlying asset, traditionally an agricultural product, raw material, or precious metal. Today, there are futures contracts covering various financial products used by speculators, investors, and users of such assets to *hedge*. New forms of futures and derivative investment contracts that impact securities markets are continually under development. This trend has more clearly linked the commodities futures markets and the securities markets.

Commodity Futures Markets

Futures contracts are standardized commitments to deliver or take delivery of a specified quantity and quality of a commodity at a previously specified price, obligating the seller to deliver the commodity sometime within the specified future delivery month. These contracts are traded on commodities exchanges resembling the securities exchanges. The best-known futures exchanges include the *Chicago Board of Trade (CBOT)*, the *Chicago Mercantile Exchange (Merc)*, the *New York Mercantile Exchange*

(NY Merc), and the *Commodity Exchange Corp. (COMEX)*. Other futures exchanges include the Kansas City Board of Trade, the Coffee, Sugar and Cocoa Exchange, the Mid-America Commodity Exchange, the New York Cotton Exchange, the New York Futures Exchange, the Minneapolis Grain Exchange, the London International Financial Futures Exchange, and the Chicago Rice and Cotton Exchange. Most futures trading activity is centered in Chicago, while most securities trading is centered in New York. This creates some interesting financial rivalries.

A futures contract typically entitles one side of the transaction to receive some specified amount of the underlying asset or commodity at a future specified date. Futures permit users of the underlying commodity to hedge against the price prevailing today for a commodity the user will need in several months. For example, the ABC meat-packing firm might find it advantageous to purchase pork belly futures to lock in a currently favorable price for the meat it needs to make hot dogs within six months. If prices in the pork market rise during the following six months, ABC's profits on the futures contracts make up for any higher prices paid for pork in the future. This is **hedging,** effectively permitting ABC to lock in a currently favorable price for the pork that is its primary raw material. ABC can then avoid raising its hot dog prices and avoid risking the loss of profits when pork prices rise. Few futures investors ever intend to take actual physical delivery of the underlying commodity so most are settled in cash a few hours or days before the specified delivery date. A speculator taking physical delivery has a difficult task of finding an end user to take the commodities.

Futures contracts cover a wide range of *agricultural products*—wheat, corn, oats, soybeans, barley, flaxseed, rapeseed, rye, and cotton; *livestock products*—cattle, hogs, pork bellies, and (chicken) broilers; *processed agricultural products*—soybean meal, soybean oil, cocoa, coffee, orange juice, and sugar; *building materials*—lumber and plywood; *precious and other metals*—gold, silver, platinum, palladium, copper, and aluminum; and *petroleum products*—crude oil, gasoline, and heating oil. The popular new derivations are **financial futures** primarily based on underlying financial assets or indicators such as various *foreign currencies*—British pound, German deutsch mark, Swiss franc, Japanese yen, Canadian dollar, and Eurodollars; *government*

---

[3]*In re Playboy Enterprises, Inc.*, S.E.C. Admin.Proc.File No.3–5931 (1980).

securities — treasury bonds, treasury notes, treasury bills, and GNMA bonds; and *market indexes* — S&P 100 and S&P 500 stock indexes, Major Market Index, Value Line index, NYSE Composite index, and an increasing number of others. The futures markets consist of users of these commodities and speculators willing to provide liquidity by contracting on the other side of these transactions.

Futures contracts evolved from the *cash forward* contracts used to mitigate the illiquidity when a deluge of harvested grain simultaneously hit the market. This glut usually lowered prices, caused delivery delays, and led to crop spoilage. Cash forward contracts negotiated at planting time obligated the farmer to sell a specified quantity and the grain merchant or food processor to buy it after the future harvest time for a predetermined price. Farmers were provided with up-front cash for planting and an assured market. Price fluctuations during the contract period naturally provoked some parties to breach. There came pressure to standardize cash forward contracts, converting these sometimes unreliable contracts into futures contracts. Trading on more liquid and impersonal futures exchange markets discouraged breach, and the contracts became more reliable for hedging and speculating. Today, nonstandard cash forward contracts are generally exempt from futures regulation. The following passage from Justice Stevens' opinion in *Merrill Lynch, Pierce, Fenner & Smith, Inc. v. Curran*[4] illustrates how the futures market functions and its problems.

The Commodity Exchange Act (CEA), has been aptly characterized as ''a comprehensive regulatory structure to oversee the volatile and esoteric futures trading complex.'' When buyers and sellers entered into contracts for the future delivery of an agricultural product, they arrived at an agreed price on the basis of their judgment about expected market conditions at the time of delivery. Because the weather and other imponderables affected supply and demand, normally the market price would fluctuate before the contract was performed. A declining market meant that the executory agreement was more valuable to the seller than the commodity covered by the contract; conversely, in a rising market the executory contract had a special value for the buyer, who not only was assured of delivery of the commodity but also could derive a profit from the price increase.

A speculator who owned no present interest in a commodity but anticipated a price decline might agree to a future sale at the current market price, intending to purchase the commodity at a reduced price on or before the delivery date. A ''short'' sale of that kind would result in a loss if the price went up instead of down. On the other hand, a price increase would produce a gain for a ''long'' speculator who had acquired a contract to purchase the same commodity with no intent to take delivery but merely for the purpose of reselling the futures contract at an enhanced price.

The advent of speculation in futures markets produced well-recognized benefits for producers and processors of agricultural commodities. A farmer who takes a ''short'' position in the futures market is protected against a price decline; a processor who takes a ''long'' position is protected against a price increase. Such ''hedging'' is facilitated by the availability of speculators willing to assume the market risk that the hedging farmer or processor wants to avoid. The speculators' participation in the market substantially enlarges the number of potential buyers and sellers of executory contracts and therefore makes it easier for farmers and processors to make firm commitments for future delivery at a fixed price. The liquidity of a futures contract, upon which hedging depends, is directly related to the amount of speculation that takes place.

Futures Regulation

The commodities markets were first federally regulated under the Futures Trading Act of 1922, later renamed the **Commodity Exchange Act (CEA)** in the 1936 revision. Several revisions have followed. The CFTC was established by the CEA as a quasi-independent regulatory commission similar to the SEC. The five CFTC commissioners are appointed by the president with Senate confirmation and serve staggered, five-year terms. There must be political balance: No more than three commissioners may be from any political party. Unlike the SEC, the CFTC is created under **sunset legislation,** requiring Congressional reauthorization every five years.

The proliferation of financial futures products that often behave like securities or impact the securities markets has caused a jurisdictional dispute between the CFTC and the SEC. Agreements between the agencies, court cases,[5] and congressional action

---

[4]*Merrill, Lynch, Pierce, Fenner & Smith, Inc. v. Curran,* 456 U.S. 353 (1982).

[5]See *American Stock Exchange v. Chicago Mercantile Exchange,* 883 F.2d 537 (7th Cir. 1989) (''Stock basket'' instruments are similar to futures contracts so are regulated by the CFTC; case discusses derivative product regulation and the jurisdictional boundary between the SEC and the CFTC.)

have split powers between the two agencies. The SEC regulates securities and derivative instruments based on securities unless they resemble futures contracts. The CFTC regulates forward and futures contracts that resemble futures or have no underlying asset that is a security. This segregation has been important to futures market participants because the CFTC has traditionally exercised only relaxed regulation. The lower margin loan requirements for commodities investments contributes to this. Proponents justify the CFTC's permissive regulation because most participants are professional traders or affluent investors with lesser need for government protection. Proponents argue that strict regulation of futures markets will drive the trading overseas. However, the futures and securities markets are becoming more closely linked, causing pressure to increase and coordinate these two regulators.

The CFTC is responsible for licensing commodities exchanges, called *contract markets*, standardizing futures contract terms (type, quantity, quality, delivery time and place), and regulating commodities professionals, including floor brokers and traders, *futures commission merchants* (customer's brokers), and *commodity pool operators*, who operate syndicates or trusts for portfolios of futures. The CFTC has enforcement powers over futures price manipulation, fraud, and deception through investigation and bringing administrative or civil enforcement proceedings. Serious violations may be referred to the Justice Department for criminal prosecution, which can carry fines up to $500,000 and imprisonment up to five years. Less serious futures market disputes are increasingly resolved by arbitration.

SECURITIES AND EXCHANGE COMMISSION

The federal securities laws are primarily enforced by the SEC and private parties. The SEC is a quasi-independent regulatory agency headed by five presidentially appointed commissioners who must be confirmed by the Senate and represent political balance. SEC commissioners serve staggered, five-year terms. One is designated the chairperson, spokesperson and figurehead leader.

SEC enforcement is implemented through its nine regional and several branch offices located in major financial centers nationwide. The SEC's major divisions concentrate on specialized subareas of securities regulations and provide expertise to the commissioners. The *Division of Corporation Finance* helps establish disclosure standards and reviews registration statements, prospectuses, proxy solicitations, and periodic reports to shareholders. The *Division of Market Regulation* oversees exchanges, brokers, and dealers. The *Division of Enforcement* investigates and prosecutes violations of SEC administrative actions and civil suits brought in federal district court. The *Division of Investment Management Regulation* oversees investment advisors and regulates investment companies (mutual funds). The *Division of Corporate Regulation* regulates public utility holding companies. Other special offices provide consultation on accounting standards issues (Office of the Chief Accountant), economic studies (Directorate of Economic and Policy Analysis), appellate activities (Office of the General Counsel), and international agreements and enforcement (Office of International Affairs). Other offices support different aspects of the SEC's internal activities.

Investigatory and Enforcement Powers

The SEC has authority to investigate and prosecute violations of the securities laws in the federal courts, promulgate substantive and interpretive rules, adjudicate administrative controversies within the agency, and provide advice to Congress, the courts, and other regulators on matters that impact the securities markets. Investigations are generally conducted by studying the markets' behavior and monitoring trading activities. More specific inquiry is also made into specific allegations of wrongdoing. Investigations often begin after an individual's complaint or when the exchange's computer detects unusual trading. Sometimes, surprise inspections are made at securities firms, or information filed at the SEC triggers a suspicion of lawbreaking. Informal and private inquiries are then made by interviewing potential witnesses, examining brokerage records, and evaluating trading data.

After the informal investigation produces adequate information to show the likelihood of a securities violation (*administrative probable cause*), the commissioners may vote to issue a **Formal Order of Investigation (FOI).** The FOI permits SEC enforcement personnel to use the subpoena power to question witnesses under oath and require them to produce documents. If a witness is reluctant to testify, the SEC must enforce the subpoena in federal court. Further silence by the witness is punishable by contempt of court unless the SEC investigation is unauthorized or the SEC acts in bad faith and without a reasonable basis. Many SEC investigatory targets are the clients of brokers, accountants, lawyers, or investment bankers. The target need not be notified before such consultants are required to answer the subpoena.

After sufficient information is gathered, personnel from the Division of Enforcement decide whether to proceed against the alleged violator in a variety of ways. An administrative hearing may be held before an SEC administrative law judge (ALJ). The ALJ may deny, suspend, or revoke a broker's license to trade, issue a public censure of certain individuals, issue cease and desist orders for repeat offenders, debar officers and directors from practice before the SEC, effectively banning their office as a publicly traded issuer, order civil money penalties, or require **disgorgement**—a return of illegally obtained funds. The SEC received some of this stronger enforcement authority in the *Enforcement Remedies Act of 1990*.

Stronger actions are also pursued through federal district court, which may order civil penalties, enjoin the violator's activities, and optionally provide **ancillary relief.** Such creative remedies are often part of a **consent decree** in which the defendant typically neither admits nor denies the wrongdoing but consents to the injunction and agrees to undertake other remedial action. For example, ABC could consent to an injunction against future violations of the FCPA accounting standards provisions while agreeing to hire new accountants, add outside directors, revamp its internal control system, and change its business practices to prevent future FCPA violations. Consent decrees are used extensively by many other federal regulators.

Serious violations are referred to the Department of Justice (DOJ), which has parallel investigatory powers. The DOJ may bring criminal prosecutions in federal courts seeking fines and/or imprisonment. Private plaintiffs injured by securities violations have the right to bring private civil damage suits. This is a phenomenon largely restricted to the United States because most civil law nations relegate law enforcement to government regulators. There is pressure to shrink individuals' rights to sue in the United States due to the liability crisis. However, relegating all enforcement to government raises the costs of government, reduces the deterrence of the laws, and engenders disrespect for the law when enforcement is lax. Nevertheless, tort reform pressures will probably continue for some time, eventually constricting some private rights.

SEC Rulemaking

Like other quasi-legislative federal administrative agencies, the SEC has rulemaking powers. The SEC studies a problem, solicits comments, and proposes, promulgates, rescinds, and enforces its own rules. Such rules provide significant regulatory detail in the areas of periodic disclosure, proxy solicitation, tender offer, insider trading, and broker-dealer oversight. The informal notice and comment rulemaking process is followed for substantive rules. Notice of a proposed rulemaking is published in the Federal Register, providing affected parties an opportunity to comment. Comments often convince the SEC to modify the rule proposal. The SEC must justify the cost effectiveness of its substantive rules. Formal rulemaking derived from adversarial hearings is used to grant authority to exchanges to trade particular new securities.

The SEC also has significant powers of persuasion. Almost from the beginning, the SEC has enjoyed an outstanding reputation for its expertise, independence, efficiency, and performance. The SEC capitalizes on this respect by authoring studies, filing *amicus curie* (friend of the court) briefs to influence the decisions of various courts, and proposing legislation to Congress. Successes in these efforts are a tribute to the SEC's credibility.

REGISTRATION OF SECURITIES ISSUES

The securities laws are intended to ensure fair treatment to investors by improving the available information about firms that issue securities. The 1933 Act was intended to break the ''reckless practices of the Roaring Twenties,'' when less accurate information was disclosed than today. Investors were pressured into subscribing to new securities offerings, called **initial public offerings (IPO),** before much was known about the issuer's finances or prospects. Today, more accurate financial, operational, and forecast information is distributed to prospective investors before sales commence. Dealers were also pressured to make blind resale commitments for securities from unknown issuers. A cooling-off period is now required, the *waiting period,* during which SEC reviews the IPO disclosures. Of course, SEC review does not constitute any verification of the prospectus's accuracy, provides no analysis of the securities as an investment, and represents no legal audit of the IPO process.

The issuer in an IPO must register new securities with two documents: the **registration statement,** filed with the SEC, and the **prospectus,** distributed to potential investors, the **offerees.** Both documents contain roughly the same information: the issuer's *basic information package,* including audited financial statements, five years of comparative financial information, management's discussion and analysis (MD&A), a description of the issuer's management, a description of the new security and its terms, the intended use of the IPO proceeds, and a listing of the securities' risk factors. Well-established issuers need not duplicate information such as the financials if they are contained in a current annual report to shareholders. The term *prospectus* is given a broad meaning to ensure that the issuer takes full responsibility for the accuracy of all disclosures. Any person associated with its production, such as the issuer, its investment bankers, auditors, the board, or management may be held responsible for inaccuracies or misstatements in the prospectus.

Prospectus

Any notice, circular, advertisement, letter, or communication, written or by radio or television, which offers any security for sale or confirms the sale of any security.

Three types of prospectus may be used at different times during the registration process. The **formal prospectus** or *statutory prospectus* is the definitive disclosure and sales device used during IPO sales. Before sales may commence, a draft form of prospectus is used, the **preliminary prospectus** or **red herring,** illustrated in Figure 44–2. The red herring may not state the IPO offering price, may not be used after sales begin, and must be replaced by the formal prospectus. A *summary prospectus* may be distributed during the waiting period, and **supplemental sales materials** may be distributed

after sales commence. Numerous SEC registration forms are available; each is tailored to particular types of offerings and issuers.

Pre-Filing, Waiting, and Post-Effective Periods

SEC rules divide the IPO process into three periods. The **pre-filing period** constitutes all the time before a registration statement is filed with the SEC. For this four- to six-month period prior to filing, the issuer decides to make the IPO, negotiates to assemble the investment banking syndicate, and prepares the registration statement and prospectus. No sales may occur during the pre-filing period.

Neither the issuer nor its investment bankers may "jump the gun" or **precondition** the market by hinting that the IPO is coming or issuing favorable reports to spark interest in the IPO. This prohibition is a reaction to the Roaring Twenties practice of publicizing the IPO before sales without providing much financial information. For example, ABC Corp. and its investment bankers are prohibited from intentionally timing favorable news releases, analysts reports, projections, market letters, speeches, or new product announcements to coincide with an expected IPO during the pre-filing period. Such publicity prompts demand before investors evaluate the issuer or the IPO. However, ABC should continue its ordinary advertising and must respond truthfully to legitimate and unsolicited inquiries from the press, financial analysts, and shareholders.

The 20-day **waiting period** begins after the issuer files its registration statement with the SEC. During this time prospectus amendments are made in response to SEC review and criticism and the underwriting syndicate is more formally organized. No securities sales are allowed, but four types of statutory offers or preliminary negotiations are permitted: (1) **tombstone ads,** the stark, boxed financial press announcements stating the price, as illustrated in Figure 44–3, (2) red herring prospectuses, (3) unaccepted *oral offers,* and (4) **summary prospectuses** containing only condensed information. All other communications during the waiting period are illegal. The 20-day period is restarted with each amendment, unless the SEC clears the IPO for final sales through *acceleration* of registration. The waiting period is a form of cooling-off period, to permit investors to assimilate the red herring prospectus information.

Figure 44–2 Red Herring Prospectus

NUVEEN
PROSPECTUS

Subject to Completion
May 3, 1989

10,000,000 Shares

Nuveen Performance Plus Municipal Fund, Inc.

Common Stock

Nuveen Performance Plus Municipal Fund, Inc. (the "Fund") is a newly organized, closed-end, diversified management investment company. The Fund's primary investment objective is current income exempt from Federal income tax, and its secondary objective is the enhancement of portfolio value through the selection of tax-exempt bonds and municipal market sectors that, in the opinion of the Fund's investment adviser, are undervalued. *See* "Investment Objectives and Policies." The Fund will seek to achieve its investment objectives by investing in a diversified portfolio of investment grade quality tax-exempt Municipal Obligations (as defined herein). No assurances can be given that the Fund's investment objectives will be achieved. The Fund's principal office is located at 333 West Wacker Drive, Chicago, Illinois 60606, and its telephone number is (312) 917-7825. Investors are advised to read the Prospectus and retain it for future reference.

The Fund's Board of Directors may in the future authorize the issuance of shares of preferred stock in order to provide leverage to the Common Stock, if the Board should determine that such leverage would be advantageous to the Common Shareholders under then existing and projected market conditions. No decision has yet been made by the Board to issue preferred stock, and the Fund does not anticipate the issuance of preferred stock under current market conditions. *See* "Special Leverage Considerations" and "Description of Capital Stock."

Prior to this offering, there has been no public market for the Common Stock. Application will be made to list the Common Stock on the New York Stock Exchange.

THESE SECURITIES HAVE NOT BEEN APPROVED OR DISAPPROVED BY THE SECURITIES AND EXCHANGE COMMISSION NOR HAS THE COMMISSION PASSED UPON THE ACCURACY OR ADEQUACY OF THIS PROSPECTUS. ANY REPRESENTATION TO THE CONTRARY IS A CRIMINAL OFFENSE.

	Price to Public	Underwriting Discounts and Commissions	Proceeds to the Fund (1)
Per Share	$15.00	$	$
Total (2)	$150.000.000	$	$

(a)

(1) Before deduction of expenses payable by the Fund, estimated at $

(2) The Fund has granted to the Underwriters an option, exercisable for 30 days from the date of this Prospectus, to purchase up to 1,500,000 additional shares to cover over-allotments, if any. To the extent that such option is exercised in full, the total Price to Public will be $172,500,000 total Underwriting Discounts and Commissions will be $, and total Proceeds to the Fund will be $. *See* "Underwriting."

The Common Stock is offered by the several Underwriters, subject to prior sale, when, as and if delivered to and accepted by them, and subject to the right of the Underwriters to reject any order in whole or in part. It is expected that delivery of the shares will be made at the offices of Alex. Brown & Sons Incorporated, Baltimore, Maryland, on or about , 1989.

Alex, Brown & Sons
Incorporated

John Nuveen & Co.
Incorporated

A. G. Edwards & Sons, Inc.

Blunt Ellis & Loewi
Incorporated

Dain Bosworth
Incorporated

Legg Mason Wood Walker
Incorporated

The date of this Prospectus is , 1989.

(b) Information contained herein is subject to completion or amendment. A registration statement relating to these securities has been filed with the Securities and Exchange Commission. these securities may not be sold nor may offers to buy be accepted prior to the time the registration statement becomes effective. This prospectus shall not constitute an offer to sell or tr the solicitation of an offer to buy nor shall there be any sale of these securities in any State in which such offer, solicitation or sale would be unlawful prior to registration or qualification under the securities laws of any such State.

The preliminary (red herring) prospectus is identical to the formal prospectus except (a) the price and date are omitted, (b) a red-colored warning (here colored blue) is printed in the margins, and the final prospectus may be corrected or updated.

When the waiting period ends, the **post-effective period** begins. Sales of securities may commence when the 20-day period expires or the SEC accelerates the registration's effective date. Registration statements are subject to varying levels of SEC review, depending on the issuer's financial reputation. New, unknown, and privately held issuers are closely reviewed, while filings of only a small sam-

Figure 44-3 Tombstone Ad

ADVERTISEMENT

This announcement is not an offer to sell or a solicitation of an offer to buy any of these securities. The offering is made only by the Prospectus.

600,000 Shares
First Financial Caribbean Corporation
Common Stock

Price $18.50 Per Share

Copies of the Prospectus may be obtained in any State in which this announcement is circulated only from such of the Underwriters as are qualified to act as dealers in securities in such State.

Brean Murray, Foster Securities Inc.

Bear, Stearns & Co. Inc.	The First Boston Corporation
A.G. Edwards & Sons, Inc.	Kidder, Peabody & Co. Incorporated	Lehman Brothers
Oppenheimer & Co., Inc.	PaineWebber Incorporated
Prudential Securities Incorporated	Smith Barney, Harris Upham & Co. Incorporated
Allen & Company Incorporated	Kemper Securities, Inc.
Advest, Inc. Clark Melvin Securities Corporation	Cowen & Company
Dominick & Dominick Incorporated	First Albany Corporation	Foley Mufson Howe & Company
Johnston, Lemon & Co. Incorporated	Laidlaw Equities, Inc.	Ladenburg, Thalmann & Co. Inc.
Legg Mason Wood Walker	Morgan Keegan & Company, Inc.
Needham & Company, Inc.	Parket/Hunter Incorporated	Pennsylvania Merchant Group Ltd
The Robinson-Humphrey Company, Inc.	Robotti & Eng Incorporated
Scott & Stringfellow Investment Corp.	Stephens Inc.	Tucker Anthony Incorporated
Unterberg Harris H.G. Wellington & Co. Inc.	Wheat First Butcher & Singer Capital Markets

November 9, 1992

---

pling of well-established issuers are reviewed. The issuer may receive an SEC letter pinpointing omissions or inaccuracies and ''encouraging'' conforming amendments. This review is enforced by a threatened SEC **refusal order** preventing sales or a **stop order** halting sales. The SEC commonly accelerates the effective date after the price amendment is filed. This permits sales shortly thereafter to take advantage of a favorable ''market window of opportunity.'' Prospectus amendments must be filed immediately during the post-effective period and stickers attached to existing prospectuses for minor amendments.

The post-effective sales period lasts for at least 40 days or until all securities are sold to buyers with investment intent. Speculators and arbitrageurs who intend to profit from a quick resale do not have investment intent. A final prospectus must be delivered prior to or with all supplemental sales materials, written offers, confirmations of sale, or actual deliveries of the securities. Some *secondary* reselling of the IPO securities may commence immediately on the exchange. Additionally, some issuers make IPOs of the same securities they already had trading on the exchange. Confusion about whether a particular customer purchased new IPO securities or bought existing shares on the exchange has led to the practice of forwarding a prospectus to all buyers during this IPO period. However, broker-dealers not part of the underwriting syndicate and dealers sold out of their original allotment need not forward a prospectus with sales executed on the exchange. The requirements of the three time periods of the IPO are illustrated in Figure 44–4.

Shelf Offerings

In the traditional IPO registration, the issuer and underwriting syndicate are expected to use good faith efforts to sell out the whole issue immediately.

The securities laws restrict underwriters' **stabilization** of market prices only to the post-effective period. Underwriters often make exchange purchases of excess shares offered for sale to maintain a minimum floor price. This discourages uncertain investors from panicking during the IPO. However, stabilization becomes illegal after the post-effective period, at which time it would be considered a form of price *manipulation*. This obligation to sell quickly frustrates some issuers' desire to satisfy the costly and time-consuming registration process without having to sell the securities immediately because market conditions may be suboptimal or the issuer may not yet need the proceeds.

In 1981, the SEC expanded the use of **shelf registration,** an alternative process not requiring the issuer to immediately sell the securities. Well-established and reliable issuers may comply with the complex registration process many months before the securities are actually sold. Thereafter, the issuer may sell the securities as new funds are needed. Registered securities are held in inventory "on the shelf" and sold only as needed. For example, ABC

Figure 44–4   Registration Process

	Pre-Filing Period	F i l e	**Waiting Period**	R e g i s t r a t i o n	**Post-Effective Period**
			20 days or until SEC accelerates effective date of registration statement		40 days or until all the securities have been sold to investors
Prohibited Actions	No contracts to sell securities No announcements conditioning the market (gun jumping)	w i t h	No contracts to sell securities		No preliminary or red herring prospectuses

Permitted/ Required Actions	Can contact investment bankers for advice
	Can negotiate with underwriters for possible participation in underwriting syndicate
	Must prepare registration statement, preliminary prospectus, and supporting documents for SEC filing
	Must maintain "business as usual" communications with security holders, customers, suppliers, the press, and securities analysts
		S E C	Can publish or distribute statutory offers to buy or sell securities, including:
			    Tombstone ads
			    Preliminary prospectus
			    Formal oral offers
			    Summary prospectuses
			Distribution of preliminary red herring prospectus
				o n e f f e c t i v e	Must forward formal prospectus before or with all confirmations of sales, deliveries of securities
					Must attempt to sell all of the newly registered securities unless registered as a shelf offering

Finance Corp., ABC's financing subsidiary, may register bonds and retain them on the shelf until it needs the proceeds to make loans to customers who want ABC's products. The shelf has reduced registration costs and may dispense with costly investment banking fees in some instances.

WHAT IS A SECURITY?

The securities laws apply only to transactions in a certain type of investment: The security. Other types of financing, ownership, and participation transactions are not covered by the complex, costly, and sometimes perplexing securities laws. Therefore, fitting an investment into the definition of a security is critical to establishing the jurisdictional boundary of the securities laws and thereby confines the SEC's strict regulation.

Security

The term **security** means any note, stock, treasury stock, bond, debenture, evidence of indebtedness, transferable share, *investment contract*, voting trust certificate, certificate of deposit for a security, fractional undivided interest in oil, gas, or other mineral rights, any put, call, straddle, stock option, warrant, or in general, any interest or instrument commonly known as a *security*.

Any contract right or instrument on the statutory list is automatically covered by the securities laws unless exempt. Purely commercial, consumption, and consumer transactions are exempt. For example, corporate *commercial paper* maturing in nine months or less, consumer loans, and trade credits need not be registered. Bonds, notes, and bills of the federal government, state bonds, municipal bonds (munis), and government-guaranteed industrial revenue bonds are exempt. While most insurance policies and annuities are exempt, *variable* and *universal life* insurance are considered securities because they are marketed as having variable returns. The securities of many charitable institutions, banks, and securities issued in a bankruptcy reorganization are exempt from registration, although they may be regulated later and are regulated by other agencies such as the Federal Reserve Board.

Notes have been particularly problematic. Demand notes that bear no "family resemblance" to exempt notes are securities. The courts will consider whether (1) the notes are sold to raise cash, (2) they earn the creditor a profit, (3) they are offered to the public and commonly traded, (4) their investors expect securities law protections, and (5) other factors replace the protections of the securities laws and reduce the risk to investors.

Investment Contracts

In addition to stocks and bonds, the term *security* usually includes limited partnership interests, equipment trust certificates, some franchises and pyramid selling schemes, options, voting trust certificates, and some forms of condominium ownership such as *time shares*. The statutory definition's catchall phrase **investment contract** includes any new and innovative contract rights resembling traditional securities. As the following famous case illustrates, an innovative investment contract involves the following four elements: (1) an investment of money, (2) in a common enterprise or scheme, (3) from which the investor has the expectation of profits, (4) that are derived from the efforts of others (promoter).

SECURITIES AND EXCHANGE COMMISSION v. HOWEY CO.
328 U.S. 293 (1946)

The W. J. Howey Co. solicited mostly nonresident Florida hotel guests vacationing near Howey's orange groves to purchase parcels of its producing orange groves. It also offered the services of Howey's affiliate, Howey-in-the-Hills, Co., to cultivate, harvest, and market the oranges. Most investors purchased both a land sale contract and the separate 10-year service contract. All parcels were contiguous, with no fences or field markers to divide the land. The harvested crop was pooled and investors shared profits based on their proportional ownership of land irrespective of their trees' actual production or quality. The SEC challenged these contracts as actually a sale of unregistered securities.

MURPHY, Justice

Section 2 (1) of the Act defines the term "security" to include the commonly known documents traded for speculation or investment. This definition also includes "securities" of a more variable character, designated by such descriptive terms as "certificate of interest or participation in any profit-sharing agreement," "investment contract." The legal issue in this case turns upon a determination of whether, under the circumstances, the land sales contract, the warranty deed and the service contract together constitute an "investment contract" within the meaning of Section 2 (1).

An investment contract for purposes of the Securities Act means a contract, transaction or scheme whereby a person invests his money in a common enterprise and is led to expect profits solely from the efforts of the promoter or a third party, it being immaterial whether the shares in the enterprise are evidenced by formal certificates or by nominal interests in the physical assets employed in the enterprise. It embodies a flexible rather than a static principle, one that is capable of adaptation to meet the countless and variable schemes devised by those who seek the use of the money of others on the promise of profits.

The transactions in this case clearly involve investment contracts as so defined. The respondent companies are offering something more than fee simple interests in land, something different from a farm or orchard coupled with management services. They are offering an opportunity to contribute money and to share in the profits of a large citrus fruit enterprise managed and partly owned by respondents. They are offering this opportunity to persons who reside in distant localities and who lack the equipment and experience requisite to the cultivation, harvesting and marketing of the citrus products. Such persons have no desire to occupy the land or to develop it themselves; they are attracted solely by the prospects of a return on their investment. Indeed, individual development of the plots of land that are offered and sold would seldom be economically feasible due to their small size. Such tracts gain utility as citrus groves only when cultivated and developed as component parts of a larger area. A common enterprise managed by respondents or third parties with adequate personnel and equipment is therefore essential if the investors are to achieve their paramount aim of a return on their investments. Their respective shares in this enterprise are evidenced by land sales contracts and warranty deeds, which serve as a convenient method of determining the investors' allocable shares of the profits. The resulting transfer of rights in land is purely incidental.

Thus, all elements of a profit-seeking business venture are present here. The investors provide the capital and share in the earnings and profits; the promoters manage, control and operate the enterprise. It follows that the arrangements whereby the investors' interests are made manifest involve investment contracts, regardless of the legal terminology in which such contracts are clothed. The investment contracts in this instance take the form of land sales contracts, warranty deeds and service contracts which respondents offer to prospective investors. And respondents' failure to abide by the statutory and administrative rules in making such offerings, even though the failure result from a bona fide mistake as to the law, cannot be sanctioned under the Act. The test is whether the scheme involves an investment of money in a common enterprise with profits to come solely from the efforts of others. If that test is satisfied, it is immaterial whether the enterprise is speculative or non-speculative or whether there is a sale of property with or without intrinsic value. The statutory policy of affording broad protection to investors is not to be thwarted by unrealistic and irrelevant formulae. Reversed.

Case Questions
1. What is the issue in applying the securities laws to new investments? What assumptions are made about the characteristics common to all "securities"?

2. What ambiguities are there in any financial design or "financial engineering" tailored to investors' and promoters' needs?

Numerous cases have refined the four *Howey* elements as new financial contracts have arisen. An investment of money was lacking in *Teamsters v. Daniel*[6] because employees made no direct contribution of their money into the union's compulsory, noncontributory pension plan. There is a common enterprise whenever a pooling of investors' funds is used by the enterprise. Investors' fortunes rise and fall together *(horizontal commonality)* in most securities. Usually, investors' fortunes are also correlated with the issuer's success *(vertical commonality)*. A repurchase agreement covering numerous separate casks of scotch whiskey the distiller expected to blend provided sufficient pooling of investors' interests to constitute a common enterprise in *SEC v. Haffenden-Rimar Int'l.*[7]

The courts have not required that an investor's profits come only from the efforts of others. Some securities perform partly from the investors' own efforts. For example, an executive's ESOP stock may rise due to that executive's own efforts but the stock is nevertheless a security. The Supreme Court rejected the **sale of business doctrine** as an exception to the definition of a security despite the theory that profitability was largely based on the buyer's own efforts. In *Landreth Timber Co. v. Landreth*,[8] the former owner of a sawmill sold all the stock in Landreth Timber Co., effectively selling the whole business. This constituted the sale of a security even though profitability depended on the purchaser's success in operating the business. A few financial contracts that were on the statutory list have been nevertheless exempted. In *United Housing Foundation v. Forman*,[9] the "stock" tenants bought entitling them to lease an apartment in New York City's publicly subsidized Co-Op city had none of the usual incidents of stock—for example, profit sharing, transferability, voting rights, or dividends.

EXEMPT TRANSACTIONS

Some issuers can avoid or significantly reduce the costs of IPO registration for securities sold wholly intrastate, in small offerings, or private placements. These *transactions exemptions* were originally part of the 1933 Act implemented under SEC regulations. The public's pressure on Congress and the SEC to improve access to capital markets for small business has increased the popularity of these transaction exemptions. The *exempt securities* that were discussed earlier in this chapter are different from these transaction exemptions because the sale of unregistered securities is permitted under special circumstances. Care must be taken to conscientiously comply with the transaction exemption requirements or the issuer and underwriters will be liable for selling unregistered securities.

Securities exchanged by the issuer for securities held by current security holders are often exempt. No commissions may be paid to broker-dealers because of the pressure they traditionally exert. No new funds can be raised from the existing security holders, but funds can flow from the issuer out to security holders, effectively a partial liquidation. Such voluntary exchanges are part of voluntary recapitalizations, reorganizations in the federal courts or by authorized government agencies, and for securities issued in mergers. However, most mergers require additional disclosures.

Intrastate Offerings

Deference to the *federalism* principal that divides governmental powers between the federal government and the states lies at the heart of the **intrastate offerings** exemption. When local investors finance local firms that do mostly local business, the participants' close proximity may substitute for federal regulation. Intrastate offerings involve a complete relaxation of SEC registration. Issuers may attempt to comply directly with the intrastate exemption provision Section 3(a)(11) of the 1933 Act. However, most find it easier to follow SEC Rule 147, a *safe harbor* for intrastate sales. All purchasers must be residents of the state, and no resales may be made to out-of-state investors for at least nine months. A restrictive legend must be placed directly on the security certificates banning transfer within the restricted period. The issuer must be domiciled and *doing business*, defined in Chapter 40, within the state.

Rule 147 also requires the issuer to satisfy three *80 percent tests* signifying that the issuer's predominant economic effects are within the state: (1) at least 80 percent of the issuer's *gross revenues* are derived from within the state, (2) at least 80 percent of the issuer's *assets* are located within the state, and

---

[6]*Int'l B'hd of Teamsters v. Daniel*, 439 U.S. 551 (1979).

[7]*SEC v. Haffenden-Rimar Int'l.*, 496 F.2d 516 (5th Cir. 1974).

[8]*Landreth Timber Co. v. Landreth*, 471 U.S. 681 (1985).

[9]*United Housing Foundation v. Forman*, 421 U.S. 837 (1975).

(3) at least 80 percent of the issue's *proceeds* are spent within the state. Of course, customers may come from out of state, and the proceeds spent largely at in-state suppliers eventually flow out of state. Nevertheless, the 80 percent tests are designed to see that the dominant contracting parties with the issuer do business locally so that local pressures, oversight, and laws are applicable. Rule 147 defers to any applicable state registration under the blue sky laws.

Small Issues

Small business has chronically suffered from difficulties in raising capital. In recent years, bank loans are reportedly more difficult to obtain, venture capitalists demand control and huge profit sharing, and federally guaranteed small-business loans have diminished. Since 1933, Congress and from time to time the SEC have struggled to make small-business financing more readily available through the securities markets. The **small-issue** exemption balances the capital needs of small business with investor protection. There is considerable history of fraudulent and high-pressure sales tactics in small-business financing.

Regulation A permits relaxed registration on the "short form" for U.S. and Canadian issuers of up to $5 million in new securities issued within any 12-month period. The issuer must file an **offering statement** notice with the SEC describing the issuer and the securities, including unaudited financial statements. All offerees (potential investors) must receive an **offering circular** containing roughly the same information. The SEC has oversight powers to police the small-issue market. The SEC's 1992 *small-business initiatives* permit *testing the waters* by Regulation A issuers relaxing the prohibition against preregistration conditioning. The jumping the gun prohibition is relaxed, permitting communications with potential offerees to evaluate market demand for the issue. The issuer can reprice or withdraw a planned issue if the market is not interested in the proposed issue.

Small-Business Issuers

The SEC created a new small-business exemption in 1992 for **small-business issuers** with annual revenues of less than $25 million. The SEC estimated that approximately 3,000 U.S. or Canadian public reporting companies could qualify for this less costly registration under an *integrated small-business disclo-sure/registration* system. *Form SB-2* must include a description of the securities, the issuer, its investments, and its securities markets, and include audited financial statements. SEC Rule 175 applies, permitting small-business issuers to disclose projections made in good faith and on a reasonable basis without incurring liability for fraud or misstatements.

Private Placements

The market for securities placed privately, largely with institutional investors, has grown rapidly. Traditionally, only mostly small or risky firms made such **private placements.** However, today, many larger and financially stable issuers sell new issues privately. This permits them to maintain confidentiality and avoid the costs of registration. This system is justified where there are few investors. Most offerees must be sophisticated investors considered able to fend for themselves by demanding that the issuer provide sufficient information and permitting them to monitor the risks of default. Many private placement *institutional investors* are sophisticated investors such as pension funds or insurance companies.

Regulation D

The SEC's **Regulation D** implements Section 4(2) of the 1933 Act. It permits relaxed registration for "transactions by an issuer not involving a public offering." These offerings are used widely today. For example, if ABC's management were to make an LBO to take ABC private, it might sell some "high-yield debt" to institutional investors to provide funds to cash out the remaining public shareholders. Over three quarters of the $25 billion used in the 1989 takeover of RJR Nabisco was privately placed junk bond debt. Another common use of private placements is by blue chip issuers such as the GMAC finance subsidiary of GM. GMAC periodically makes private placements of securitized CAR (certificates of automobile receivables) loans to fund its financing of new automobile sales through GM dealers.

Regulation D is a combination of the small-issue and private placement exemption. Sales are generally limited to no more than 35 unsophisticated investors but to an unlimited number of **accredited investors,** parties with sufficient financial sophistication, net worth, experience, and knowledge to minimize and withstand the securities' risk. Accredited investors include certain pension funds, most banks, institutional investors, corporations, employee benefit plans, pension funds, the issuer's upper-level managers, and well-to-do individuals. No particular disclosures are needed for accredited investors except what the issuer negotiates. All disclosures must be delivered to all other buyers. Nonaccredited investors must receive information similar to a registration statement. Publicly traded issuers must use their current annual reports. Issuers must file *Form D* with the SEC, a simple notification listing minimal information. Regulation D has three thresholds with different requirements for each: Rules 504, 505, and 506.

Rule 504 is limited to $500,000 for unregistered sales and up to $1 million within any 12-month period if registered under state blue sky laws. There are no restrictions on the number of offerees, on their investment sophistication, or on resale of their securities. No disclosure is required if at least one state blue sky law requires some form of disclosure and all public offerees receive the document.

Rule 505 is limited to $5 million within any 12-month period, with sales to nonaccredited investors limited to 35. Unlimited numbers of accredited investors are permitted. No specific disclosures are required in sales to accredited investors, but the issuer must respond to their questions. In offerings below $2 million, sales to nonaccredited investors must include the information in a Regulation A offering circular. If sales are between $2 million and $5 million, the disclosures must resemble Form SB-2. Publicly traded issuers may use their most recent annual report as supplemented with a proxy statement, quarterly reports, and current reports, as discussed later in this chapter.

Rule 506 has no upper dollar limitation and requirements similar to Rule 505 on disclosures and nonaccredited/accredited investor limits. However, the issuer must reasonably believe that all nonaccredited investors are somewhat sophisticated, meaning they "have such knowledge and experience in financial and business matters [to be] capable of evaluating the merits and risks." Resale of all the 500 series securities is restricted.

Integration and Resale Restriction

The SEC has developed two concepts to prevent issuers from misusing these transaction exemptions as a pretext to make an unregistered public offering. **Integration** combines several supposedly separate exempt offerings into one if they are made too close in time and the proceeds are used for the same general purpose in a single plan of financing. When an issuer's exempt offerings are integrated, the SEC then applies its dollar and investor limits to the combined financing. The exemption is lost if the totals violate these limitations. For example, assume ABC made a Rule 505 offering of $5 million in preferred stock to 33 nonaccredited investors and numerous accredited investors in January and in August sold $500,000 in debentures to 3 nonaccredited investors as a Regulation A small offering. The SEC could integrate these two seemingly separate offerings if all the proceeds were used to renovate ABC's factory. ABC would fail both the $5 million limitation of either Regulation D or Regulation A and would exceed the 35 nonaccredited shareholder limit for Regulation D.

All the transaction exemptions except Regulation A impose **resale restrictions** forbidding initial purchasers from immediately reselling the securities. This discourages the issuer from evading registration by selling first to investors who immediately intend to resell to the public, profiting on the spread between the acquisition cost and the resale price. This first group of purchasers might seemingly satisfy the transaction exemption limits but would in reality be acting like underwriters of an unregistered public offering. Such sales would deprive ultimate investors of disclosure and the other protections of registration. **Rule 144** prohibits resale by the initial purchasers unless they have **investment intent,** a genuine objective to hold the securities for longer-term investment purposes. Initial purchasers must hold the securities for a minimum time period, typically two years, and thereafter sell only small amounts, such as no more than 1 percent in any quarter. Boldface legends must appear on all transaction exempt securities warning of any resale restriction and that some other restrictions apply.

The SEC's efforts at internationalization of the securities markets has resulted in **Rule 144A**. This is actually an exception to the resale restrictions for private placement securities issued by domestic or foreign issuers that are to be sold only among **qualified institutional investors (QIB)**. The QIB requirement is analogous to the sophisticated and accredited investors discussed earlier. However, QIBs are limited to only institutional investors with securities investments in excess of $100 million. Issuers must first satisfy some transaction exemption, need disclose only as much information as required in their home nation, and must restrict resale to only QIBs. Thereafter, trading may proceed unrestricted, but only among QIBs. QIBs effectively become a smaller second market tier for private placements. The transaction exemption requirements are compared in Figure 44–5.

SECURITIES ACT LIABILITIES

The 1933 Act provides remedies for investors damaged by material misstatements in the registration statement or prospectus. *Materiality,* discussed more fully in Chapter 45, is the importance of statements or conditions that would affect a reasonable investor's decision. Investors may return the securities under Section 12. In private damage actions under Sections 11 or 12(2), the investor may sue those responsible for the omission or misstatements. This can include the issuer, its board and officers who signed the registration statement, control persons, auditors, and investment bankers. Willful violators are subject to criminal liability under Sections 17 or 24 of the 1933 Act. Criminal cases are referred to the Justice Department for prosecution.

The responsible parties may assert the defense of **due diligence** against such suits. If the defendants reasonably believed that the registration statement disclosures were true and there was no negligence, they are not liable. Must all these potential defendants conduct an independent investigation into the truth of disclosures? The following classic case illustrates the tough burden these parties have in establishing their due diligence.

ESCOTT v. BARCHRIS CONSTRUCTION CORP.
283 F.Supp.643 (S.D.N.Y. 1968)

The purchasers of BarChris Construction Corp.'s convertible debentures sued several persons involved in the IPO, claiming the registration statement was false and misleading. BarChris built bowling alleys during the bowling industries' expansion. However, the IPO coincided with the industry's saturation. BarChris's bookings of new orders began to fall, and many of its receivables became uncollectable as numerous bowling alleys defaulted. Significant errors and omissions in BarChris's financial statements concerned cash flow, sales, income, earnings per share, assets, and liabilities. The plaintiffs alleged that the defendants failed to meet their "due diligence" and "adequate investigation" duties before signing the registration statement.

McLEAN, District Judge

Russo

Russo was, to all intents and purposes, the chief executive officer of BarChris. He was a member of the executive committee. He was familiar with all aspects of the business. He was personally in charge of dealings with the factors. He acted on BarChris's behalf in making the financing agreements. Russo knew all the relevant facts. He could not have believed that there were no untrue statements or material omissions in the prospectus. Russo has no due diligence defenses.

Vitolo and Pugliese

They were the founders of the business who stuck with it to the end. Vitolo was president and Pugliese was vice-president. Pugliese in particular appears to have limited his activities to supervising the actual construction work. Vitolo and Pugliese are each men of limited education. It is not hard to believe that for them the prospectus was difficult reading, if indeed they read it at all. But whether it was or not is irrelevant. The liability of a director who signs a registration statement does not depend upon whether or not he read it or, if he did, whether or not he understood what he was reading. Vitolo and Pugliese were not as naive as they claim to be. They were members of BarChris's executive committee. At meetings of that committee BarChris's affairs were discussed at length. They must have known what was going on. Certainly they knew of the inadequacy of cash in 1961. They knew of their own large advances to the company which remained unpaid. They knew that they had agreed not to deposit their checks until the financing proceeds were received. They knew and intended that part of the proceeds were to be used to pay their own loans.

Figure 44-5 Exempt Transactions

	Ceiling Price	Number of Investors	Investor Qualification	Solicitation	Resale Restriction	Disclosure
Exchange	No new funds Old for new securities	Only existing security holders	Existing security holders	No commissioned brokers used	Control persons and underwriters restricted	Prospectus
Intrastate Rule 147	Unlimited	Unlimited	All state residents	Offerees Residents	No sale to out-of-state residents for first nine months	None
Regulation A	$5 million	Unlimited	None	None	None	Offering circular
Private Placement	Unlimited	Few offers	Sophisticated investors	No public solicitation	None unless by contract	Investor material information
Regulation D Rule 504	$1 million within 12 months	Unlimited	None	No public solicitation Blue Sky disclosure to all	Restricted Rule 144	None
Regulation D Rule 505	$5 million within 12 months	35 nonaccredited investors Unlimited accredited investors	None	No public solicitation	Restricted Rule 144	None if sold only to accredited investors; nonaccredited investors' sales under $2 million S-18 information must be made available if given to accredited investors
Regulation D Rule 506	Unlimited	35 nonaccredited investors Unlimited accredited investors	None	No public solicitation	Restricted Rule 144	

Kircher

Kircher was treasurer of BarChris and its chief financial officer. He is a certified public accountant and an intelligent man. He was thoroughly familiar with BarChris's financial affairs. He knew of the customers' delinquency problem. He knew how the financing proceeds were to be applied and he saw to it that they were so applied. He arranged the officers' loans and he knew all the facts concerning them.

Kircher's contention is that he had never before dealt with a registration statement, that he did not know what it should contain, and that he relied wholly on Grant, Ballard and Peat, Marwick to guide him. He claims that it was their fault, not his, if there was anything wrong with it. He says that all the facts were recorded in BarChris's books where these experts could have seen them if they had looked. Kircher has not proved his due diligence defenses.

Birnbaum

Birnbaum was a young lawyer, admitted to the bar in 1957, who, after brief periods of employment by two different law firms and an equally brief period of practicing in his own firm, was employed by BarChris as house counsel and assistant secretary in October 1960. Unfortunately for him, he became secretary and a director of BarChris on April 17, 1961, after the first version of the registration statement had been filed with the Securities and Exchange Commission. He signed the later amendments, thereby becoming responsible for the accuracy of the prospectus in its final form.

Although the prospectus, in its description of "management," lists Birnbaum among the "executive officers" and devotes several sentences to a recital of his career, the fact seems to be that he was not an executive officer in any real sense. He did not participate in the management of the company. As house counsel, he attended to legal matters of a routine nature. Among other things, he incorporated subsidiaries, with which BarChris was plentifully supplied.

It seems probable that Birnbaum did not know of many of the inaccuracies in the prospectus. He must, however, have appreciated some of them. In any case, he made no investigation and relied on the others to get it right. As a lawyer, he should have known his obligations under the statute. He should

have known that he was required to make a reasonable investigation of the truth of all the statements in the unexpertised portion. Having failed to make such an investigation, he did not have reasonable ground to believe that all these statements were true. Birnbaum has not established his due diligence defenses except as to the audited 1960 figures.

Auslander

Auslander was an "outside" director, i.e., one who was not an officer of BarChris. He was chairman of the board of Valley Stream National Bank in Valley Stream, Long Island. In February and early March 1961, before accepting Vitolo's invitation, Auslander made some investigation of BarChris. He obtained Dun & Bradstreet reports which contained sales and earnings figures for periods earlier than December 31, 1960. He caused inquiry to be made of certain of BarChris's banks and was advised that they regarded BarChris favorably.

Auslander was elected a director on April 17, 1961. The registration statement in its original form had already been filed, of course without his signature. On May 10, 1961, he signed a signature page for the first amendment to the registration statement which was filed on May 11, 1961. This was a separate sheet without any document attached. Auslander did not know that it was a signature page for a registration statement. He vaguely understood that it was something "for the SEC." At the May 15 directors' meeting, however, Auslander did realize that what he was signing was a signature sheet to a registration statement. A copy of the registration statement in its earlier form as amended on May 11, 1961 was passed around at the meeting. Auslander glanced at it briefly. He did not read it thoroughly.

In considering Auslander's due diligence defenses, a distinction is to be drawn between the expertised and non-expertised portions of the prospectus. As to the former, Auslander knew that Peat, Marwick had audited the 1960 figures. He believed them to be correct because he had confidence in Peat, Marwick. He had no reasonable ground to believe otherwise.

As to the non-expertised portions, however, Auslander is in a different position. He seems to have been under the impression that Peat, Marwick was responsible for all the figures. This impression was not correct, as he would have realized if he had read the prospectus carefully. Auslander made no investigation of the accuracy of the prospectus. He relied on the assurance of Vitolo and Russo, and upon the information he had received in answer to his inquiries back in February and early March. These inquiries were general ones, in the nature of a credit check.

Section 11 imposes liability in the first instance upon a director, no matter how new he is. He is presumed to know his responsibility when he becomes a director. He can escape liability only by using that reasonable care to investigate the facts which a prudent man would employ in the management of his own property. In my opinion, a prudent man would not act in an important matter without any knowledge of the relevant facts, in sole reliance upon representations of persons who are comparative strangers and upon general information which does not purport to cover the particular case. Auslander has not established his due diligence defense with respect to the misstatements and omissions in those portions of the prospectus other than the audited 1960 figures.

The Underwriters and Coleman

The underwriters other than Drexel made no investigation of the accuracy of the prospectus. They all relied upon Drexel as the "lead" underwriter. Drexel did make an investigation. Drexel's employee Coleman was first introduced to BarChris on September 15, 1960. Thereafter, he familiarized himself with general conditions in the industry, primarily by reading reports and prospectuses of the two leading bowling alley builders, American Machine & Foundry Company and Brunswick. These indicated that the industry was still growing. He also acquired general information on BarChris by reading the 1959 stock prospectus, annual reports for prior years, and an unaudited statement for the first half of 1960. He obtained a Dun & Bradstreet report on BarChris and read BarChris's annual report for 1960 which was available in March. [However] after Coleman was elected a director on April 17, 1961,

he made no further independent investigation of the accuracy of the prospectus.

It is clear that no effectual attempt at verification was made. The question is whether due diligence required that it be made. Stated another way, is it sufficient to ask questions, to obtain answers which, if true, would be thought satisfactory, and to let it go at that, without seeking to ascertain from the records whether the answers in fact are true and complete?

The purpose of Section 11 is to protect investors. To that end the underwriters are made responsible for the truth of the prospectus. If they may escape that responsibility by taking at face value representations made to them by the company's management, then the inclusion of underwriters among those liable under Section 11 affords the investors no additional protection.

In order to make the underwriters' participation in this enterprise of any value to the investors, the underwriters must make some reasonable attempt to verify the data submitted to them. They may not rely solely on the company's officers or on the company's counsel. A prudent man in the management of his own property would not rely on them.

It is impossible to lay down a rigid rule suitable for every case defining the extent to which such verification must go. It is a question of degree, a matter of judgment in each case. In the present case, the underwriters' counsel made almost no attempt to verify management's representations. I hold that that was insufficient.

Case Questions

1. What is the issue in determining whether an insider has done enough to investigate the issuer's financial position? What is this issue for an outside director? What is this issue for the underwriters?

2. What evidence is used to find the underwriters liable for the misstatements in the registration statement?

FINANCIAL REPORTING AND DISCLOSURE

Financial disclosure is the centerpiece of both the 1933 and 1934 acts. The 1933 Act registration and prospectus disclosures are episodic occurring only once, at the beginning of a security's life. By contrast, the 1934 Act disclosures are periodic, continuously issued at quarterly and annual intervals. The SEC has integrated these two disclosure systems to reduce costly duplication. **Regulation S-X** specifies the format for financial statements, while **Regulation S-K** prescribes the content and format for nonfinancial disclosures. These regulations are the primary source of regulatory accounting standards. *Generally accepted accounting principles (GAAP),* as announced by the *Financial Accounting Standards Board (FASB),* must also be followed. The SEC periodically supplements GAAP with **Financial Reporting Releases.** SEC accounting violations and case law interpretations, which appear as *Accounting and Auditing Enforcement Releases,* are also influential.

The basic philosophy of the securities acts is that the market can function reasonably well when economic actors have adequate information. Disclosure is the key to equalizing the inevitable *information asymmetries* when critical data is held only by insiders. Without mandatory disclosures to ''level the playing field,'' issuers would be expected to disclose primarily favorable information, hide unfavorable information, and negotiate selective disclosures to a favored few. Empirical studies show that mandatory disclosure significantly reduces the risk of new issues.

There are huge costs in recordkeeping, design of accounting systems, internal controls, auditing, financial statement preparation, and disclosure distribution, particularly for large, publicly traded companies. Because of these costs, disclosure probably deters some companies from going public. Efficient-market ideologues argue that disclosure is irrelevant to market efficiency because information is so widely available that prices already reflect it even before disclosure. However, in the real world, there is considerable information asymmetry. For example, European investors must rely on informal communications because disclosure is much less detailed than in the United States. European investors are often surprised when adverse information suddenly lowers market prices.

Under the 1934 Act, issuers with a class of securities traded on an exchange or the OTC market must register with the SEC as **registrants.** Registrants must make *periodic disclosures* that are intended to keep security holders, analysts, and the markets reasonably current with the issuer's financial performance. Annual reports must be distributed to shareholders and the similar *Form 10K* filed with the SEC. These must include extensive audited *financials,* including a balance sheet, income statement, funds flow statement, and accompanying notes, some comparative past financial information, the **management discussion and analysis (MD&A),** and other information describing the issuer, its securities, lines of business, executive compensation, and securities markets. Unaudited quarterly reports showing abbreviated financials and discussions must be sent to shareholders and filed with the SEC on *Form 10Q. Current reports,* filed on *Form 8K,* are required after extraordinary events: changes in control, acquisition of significant assets, bankruptcy, change in auditors, resignation of directors in dispute over policy, or any event the issuer desires.

The SEC's long-developing pilot computerization project is now becoming operational. **EDGAR,** the Electronic Data Gathering Analysis and Retrieval system, will make on-line access possible to all SEC financial filings, including registration statements, 10Ks, 10Qs, and others. This may reduce the costly paperwork of the over 5 million paper filings made annually by issuers. Eventually, anyone with a computer and a modem will be able to log on EDGAR and browse or download data for personal analysis.

The MD&A has become an important signal of management's insider interpretation of how events and significant financial conditions impact the issuer. The following subjects must be discussed candidly and without withholding management's material assessment: liquidity, capital resources, results of operations, and the impact of changing price levels (inflation). This narrative of ''soft information'' has taken on new importance. The SEC has disciplined issuers that have withheld material interpretations, particularly of financial risks that are not readily detectable from the financial statements.[10] As the following article suggests, an understanding of the theoretical nature of information helps illuminate the relationship between mandatory and discretionary disclosures.

---

[10]See *In re Caterpillar,* SEC Rel.No.34-30532 (3/31/92).

Management Discussion of Business Performance: An Analytical and Empirical Evaluation

The Theoretical Nature of Mandatory Information Disclosure

The issue of mandatory disclosure can be broken down into six basic elements: (1) impetus, (2) content, (3) form, (4) timing, (5) value to users, and (6) cost of production. The *impetus* for disclosure of information is largely determined by SEC disclosure obligations and generally accepted accounting principles (GAAP) established by the accounting profession. Certain strictly quantitative elements and particular events or occurrences must be reported if particular "litmus paper" tests are met. For example, such accounting concepts as accrual, matching, "placed in service," irrescindable obligation, and right to receive payments define points in time when the certainty of a transaction is sufficient to trigger a particular accounting treatment and then disclosure. These established conditions permit very little discretion for the registrant, which must record these events and later report them, usually in summary form. Independent auditors verify that published financial statements appear to accurately reflect these record-keeping conventions. However, the impetus for disclosure of extraordinary or adverse conditions is not well defined by GAAP or by SEC disclosure obligations. Indeed, registrants may volunteer information even when no requirement exists in disclosure standards. Extraordinary events may also trigger the need for a discussion of trends or events.

The *content* of financial disclosures is well established by the disclosure standards of GAAP and the securities laws. Generally, these content reporting standards have evolved from the apparent needs of investors as determined by the SEC and the accounting profession and from the demands of financial statement users. By contrast, the standards for the content of nonfinancial disclosures are only beginning to evolve.

The *form* of financial disclosures has evolved into a mechanistic portrayal of quantitative information and supporting explanations or footnotes. Registrants have little discretion in formatting their financial statements. For example, periodic financial disclosures must meet the highly formalized format of Regulation S-X. Little deviation from SEC forms is permitted. By contrast, the disclosure of nonfinancial information permits management to exercise a considerable level of formatting discretion. In the MD&A, for example, management should use a textual format to discuss the results of operations, the firm's liquidity and capital resources, the performance of its business segments, or the impact of inflation. Adverse or extraordinary events with a financial impact are usually reported even more flexibly in press releases or as responses to analysts' questions.

The *timing* of disclosures is also subject to standards that have both precise and vague characteristics. The securities laws generally require disclosure of financial information in periodic reports within 45 days after the close of each fiscal quarter, within 90 days following the close of the fiscal annual period, and within 15 days following the occurrence of specified extraordinary events (the form 8-K current report). While the registrant's discretion in the timing of disclosures is constrained by these regulations, there may be considerably more

Source: John W. Bagby, Marilyn R. Kintzele, and Philip L. Kintzele, "Management Discussion of Business Performance: An Analytical and Empirical Evaluation," 26 Am.Bus.L.J. 57 (1988), pp. 61–66, reprinted with permission of the American Business Law Journal.

discretion in the reporting of unspecified extraordinary and adverse conditions arising between periodic reports.

Disclosure standards are often changed when financial statement users persuade the Financial Accounting Standards Board (FASB), Congress, or the SEC that additional disclosure is of *value to users*. Occasionally, the SEC or the FASB initiates refinements or additions to disclosure requirements because of the well-publicized fraudulent behavior or financial failure of particular registrants. Typically, it is argued that the value of new information to users is necessary to remove asymmetric information imbalances between registrants and investors. This results in better informed markets that are more likely to be efficient in the sense that security prices closely approximate the underlying value of the registered firm.

The concept of materiality has been considered the trigger of relevance and therefore for the value of disclosures. Unfortunately, there is a gap between the courts' "reasonable investor" materiality standard and the SEC's "quantitative materiality test." Under the less precise "reasonable investor" standard, "an omitted fact is material if there is a substantial likelihood that reasonable shareholders would consider it important. . . ." This test permits the judge or jury to subjectively judge whether an undisclosed fact would have been part of the total mix of information used to buy or sell the registrant's securities. By contrast, the SEC, the accounting profession, and a few courts apply a more objective test, suggesting that it improves predictability and is therefore necessary to guide disclosure decisions. This test involves a balancing of both the indicated probability that the event will occur and the anticipated magnitude of the event in light of the totality of the company's activity. Ultimately, one good measure of materiality is whether the registrant's market price is affected by disclosure of the information in question.

Increasingly, the SEC and FASB are also considering the *registrant's costs* in producing the information disclosed. Issuers are usually the least-cost producer of financial and internal information due to their proximity to the source. In most nondisclosure enforcement cases, complaining investors need only demonstrate a prima facie need for material information to convince the SEC that the registrant should undertake the cost of producing it. Increasingly, however, the SEC and FASB recognize that the production and reporting information may involve three types of costs. First, information may include private trade secrets, disclosure of which would impede the registrant's competitive ability. Second, short-term financial fluctuations are too easily misinterpreted. Third, registrants may not currently be collecting certain types of information. Therefore, the additional collection and reporting burden might outweigh the usefulness of the new information.

Classification of Information

The six information criteria just discussed suggest several dichotomies that distinguish important features of information. This permits broad classification of information for the purposes of mandatory disclosure. Initially, it seems obvious to focus on *nonpublic* rather than *publicly known* information. Public information is already in the hands of the market and presumably investors' actions are based on it, while nonpublic information is more likely to require disclosure.

Also, information may be generated *internally* to the registrant or may arise *externally*. For example, the results of operations, employee behavior, or the registrant's efforts at innovation and production are internal matters. Some of these may justifiably be kept private, for their disclosure could cause the loss of a competitive advantage. By contrast, external market conditions involve matters like the firm's contracts with outsiders (e.g., suppliers, customers, security holders, financiers, government entities), the condition of the registrant's industry, or the state of the economy in general. Increasingly, registrants are expected to correlate internal and external events and conditions to present a broader understanding of the firm's future prospects.

Another interesting dichotomy separates the *operational* and *financial* conditions of the registrant. Operational information involves events and conditions concerning the registrant's lines of business and the performance of assets deployed for those purposes. Industry segment disclosures, for example, concern the status and performance of a business's divisions, subsidiaries, or lines of business. These new requirements illustrate the evolution of disclosure standards to include an evaluation of internal operational issues. By contrast, financial information concerns the results of transactions between the registrant and outsiders in raising capital for investment. Financial information about the firm's transactions in disposing of productive assets may affect the firm's securities prices as investors and analysts revise their estimates of future earnings prospects.

The form and timing of disclosures also lead to additional information dichotomies. The information disclosed may be largely numerical aggregations of transaction information; these are commonly recognized as *quantitative disclosures*. The balance sheet, income statement, and statement of changes in financial conditions reflect amounts of assets and liabilities, expenses and revenues, and the flow of transactions during an accounting period. Quantitative disclosures of historical information have long been the real substance of financial disclosure. However, there is now a trend to increase *qualitative information*. These disclosures are largely verbal descriptions of the events and conditions underlying the quantitative financial disclosures, including interpretations of these events' impact on future performance. The management report, management discussion and analysis, description of the securities and the registrant's business, and explanatory footnotes to financial statements provide understanding of the events or conditions described in those statements as well as the implications derived therefrom. Qualitative disclosures increase the financial statement user's understanding of accounting methods and financial reporting conventions used by the registrant. Generally, quantitative financial reporting is governed by Regulation S-X and qualitative disclosures are governed by Regulation S-K of the SEC rules.

Registrants often choose to make voluntary disclosures that are not specifically mandated by the securities laws. The SEC urges, but does not require, many of these disclosures. This results in an additional information dichotomy: some disclosures are mandated while others are made at the discretion of management. *Discretionary disclosures* are those in which one or more of the six criteria previously mentioned (impetus, content, form, timing, materiality, and cost of production) are not precisely structured by the SEC or FASB. Also, a discretionary impetus for disclosure arises where the registrant may exercise judgment as to the need for disclosure. Discretion as to *content* suggests that the specific level of detail or type of format is not mandated or structured. Discretion as to *form* indicates that the registrant may have great flexibility in the size, shape, placement, and format of presentation. Finally, discretionary *timing* indicates that the registrant may make the disclosure at any time within the constraints imposed by the mandated disclosure. It would appear that registrants have the greatest discretion with respect to qualitative information disclosed in press releases or in the management discussion and analysis.

Thought Questions

1. How are the main issues in corporate disclosure related in the regulator's decision to mandate financial reporting?
2. For what reasons are discretionary disclosures made by firms?

END–OF–CHAPTER QUESTIONS

1. What reasons support abandoning laissez-faire to regulate the investment and securities markets? What reasons support easing regulation?

2. What is the issue in the U.S. fixation on separating commercial from investment banking? For what reasons should universal banking be permitted?

3. What is the theory and evidence supporting the need for the foreign bribery prohibition under the FCPA? What reasons are used to attack the FCPA?

4. What is the issue inherent in the SEC's powers to combine several seemingly separate exempt offerings for testing against the maximum limitations for dollar amount and nonaccredited investors? What are the assumptions made when the SEC makes this combination? Compare and contrast this theory with the issue and assumptions underlying the resale restrictions for exempt offerings.

5. What are the main issues in designing a disclosure system? What reasons support the considerations in any particular disclosure?

6. A brokerage client's account was suddenly declared as having insufficient equity against the client's margin loan. The brokerage liquidated the client's securities holdings. Is there a sufficient pattern of illegal activities in the liquidation to permit the client to sue under RICO? See *Modern Settings, Inc. v. Prudential-Bache Securities, Inc.* 629 F.Supp. 860 (S.D.N.Y. 1986).

7. Manor Nursing Centers, Inc., registered 450,000 common shares with the SEC for sale to the public at $10 per share. The prospectus declared the sale was "all or nothing," so no shares would be sold unless all 450,000 were sold. Subscribers' funds were to be held in a bank in escrow, but no mention was made that brokers were paid a commission to help sell. Even though all 450,000 shares were not sold, Manor kept the proceeds, no escrow was ever established, and brokers received special commissions. Must the prospectus be amended to reflect changes in conditions such as these or does the issuer risk liability for omissions? See *SEC v. Manor Nursing Centers, Inc.*, 458 F.2d 1082 (2d Cir. 1972).

8. A client invested $50,000 in a discretionary commodity futures trading account with Merrill, Lynch. The client alleged the brokers so mishandled these funds that losses reduced the account balance to just over $16,000. Should the client be able to characterize the trading account as a security to take advantage of the more favorable securities antifraud remedies instead of the commodity broker laws? See *Silverstein v. Merrill, Lynch, Pierce, Fenner & Smith*, 618 F.Supp. 436 (S.D.N.Y. 1985).

9. Dare To Be Great, Inc., was a wholly owned subsidiary of Glen W. Turner Enterprises, Inc. Self-improvement programs were offered, the Adventure I for $300 and Adventure II for $700, which included self-motivation tapes and seminars. Adventures III and IV cost between $2,000 and $5,000 and in addition included rights to become "independent sales trainees" authorized to sell Adventures to others, netting up to $900 for each new Adventure sold. Adventures were generally sold at "Adventure Meetings" conducted like old-time revivals emphasizing making easy money. Trainees need only lure prospects to these meetings. Are the Adventure III and IV packages securities? What form of analysis is used and what is the key ambiguity? See *SEC v. Glen Turner Ent.*, 474 F.2d 476 (9th Cir. 1973).

10. Mac Donald Investment Co., a Minnesota corporation, registered $4 million of unsecured promissory notes with the Minnesota securities division but relied on the intrastate exemption to avoid federal SEC registration. Sales were made principally to Minnesota residents. The proceeds were used to make secured loans to out-of-state land developers. Should the SEC issue a stop order to halt sales as violating the intrastate exemption or Rule 147 thereunder? See *SEC v. Mac Donald Investment Co.*, 343 F.Supp. 343 (D.Minn. 1972).

Chapter 45

Securities Market Regulation: Insider Trading, Proxies, Tender Offers, and Securities Professionals

CRITICAL THINKING INQUIRIES

As you read this chapter, you should be able to address the following:

- What is the issue in restricting insider trading for executives, employees, and consultants of a publicly traded corporation?
- What is the assumption underlying the designation of particular officers, directors, and large shareholders as insiders? What is assumed about their purchases and sales of shares within a short time period?
- For what reason is insider trading considered a form of securities fraud?
- What is assumed about management's influence over corporate governance in the SEC's proxy regulations?
- What assumptions underlie the Williams Act's regulation of tender offers?
- What are the alternate hypotheses for the behavior expected of securities professionals in dealing with their clients?

MANAGERIAL PERSPECTIVE

Upper management at the XYZ Corp. has become interested in expanding XYZ's product lines by acquiring an existing widget manufacturer. Two major firms in the widget industry were identified by XYZ's financial staff, including ABC Corp., a privately held corporation manufacturing widgets using advanced widget-processing technology. Although, ABC's technologies are secret, non-public information, XYZ discovered some details as ABC's supplier of machinery. Disclosure was necessary for XYZ to effectively fabricate the new widget-processing equipment ABC needed. The other widget manufacturer, DEF Corp., is approximately the same size as ABC and is publicly traded.

Personal use of confidential information and the communications with shareholders in corporate control contests pose significant fiduciary questions under state corporate law and intimately involve the securities laws. This chapter discusses the responsibilities of corporate employees and outsiders in tender offers, proxy contests, and any other situation where nonpublic information has value in insider trading.

- What legal and ethical problems are there for XYZ engineers who worked closely with ABC's production and operations engineers to design and install the new equipment?
- Would XYZ, its financial analysts, or its engineers be liable for insider trading if the proposed acquisition was tipped to friends and family?
- What types of internal control or ethical codes might discourage leaks of this information to XYZ?

INSIDER TRADING

Insider trading inspires considerable controversy. Its definition is vague, it is difficult to detect, and many nations ignore the practice—though most nations restrict it. Insider trading deserves careful study because most managers are eventually exposed to confidential, nonpublic information that could impact security prices. Many corporate employees are tempted by the prospect of making "easy money" on inside information; many receive "tips" from insiders. Initially, **insider trading** can be defined as an unfair advantage taken by persons exposed to confidential, nonpublic information about an issuer when they tip or trade with uninformed shareholders.

In the United States, insider trading is made unlawful as a civil, regulatory, and criminal wrong under several sources of law. Initially, insider trading was not generally prohibited under the state common law, particularly where an insider with confidential information purchased shares on the impersonal stock exchanges.[1] However, insider trading was declared an unlawful form of fraud by omission and a breach of the manager's fiduciary duty in *Strong v. Repide*.[2] When the **special circumstances** of the manager's secret knowledge provide a trading advantage in face-to-face transactions, shareholders can expect management to assume a trusteeship role. Congress reacted to rampant insider trading during the Roaring Twenties by passing the Securities and Exchange Act of 1934. Section 16 of the 1934 Act restricts short-swing profits. Eventually, the SEC designated insider trading as a form of fraud by omission. The SEC promulgated SEC Rule 10b-5, the predominant contemporary basis for the insider trading prohibition.

Insider Trading in International Markets

U.S. insider trading laws are more stringent than those in other nations. For many years, most nations found the practice to be a victimless crime, considering it to be part of a manager's **perks,** benefits usually expected by an insider, close friends, and relatives. Insider trading was considered, at most, "just unethical." Today, most nations are beginning to restrict insider trading in some way. The EC issued a directive in 1989 prohibiting insider trading by primary and secondary insiders based on nonpublic information likely to have a significant impact on securities' prices. However, the extensive U.S. civil and criminal sanctions and the private right to sue for damages have still not been adopted worldwide. For example, only a nongovernmental board in Germany regulates insider trading. The Japanese have generally ignored their insider trading prohibition even though it is patterned after U.S. law.

Numerous insider trading scandals in Europe and the Far East have caused many nations to recognize that without insider trading restrictions, their markets may be perceived as unfair. For example, there were major insider trading scandals in the late 1980s and early 1990s in the United Kingdom, Ireland, France, Germany, and Japan. However, investors can more easily trade in other nations' markets, perceived as a "fair game." The more mobile capital will leave the "rigged" markets with active insider trading. This has led to an equilibrium in insider trading regulation.

Regulators in the world's securities markets are also beginning to cooperate together. At one time, insiders and tippees used Switzerland and other foreign havens to trade in the U.S. markets. Foreign governments generally ignored the stricter U.S. definition of insider trading, considering it inconsistent with their concept of fiduciary duties.[3] Some enacted **blocking** laws to prevent pretrial discovery or the questioning of overseas witnesses. The SEC has negotiated over 20 separate **memoranda of understanding,** essentially bilateral agreements with other nations' regulators to cooperate in enforcing each other's securities laws. Nevertheless, some U.S. citizens and many foreigners cannot understand the U.S. fascination with insider trading enforcement. Some critics argue that the costs of enforcement outweigh the benefits. This continuing controversy suggests a critical analysis of arguments for insider trading enforcement.

---

[1]*Goodwin v. Agassiz,* 186 N.E. 659 (Mass. 1933).
[2]*Strong v. Repide,* 213 U.S. 419 (1909).

[3]*The Sante Fe Case,* 22 Int'l.Leg.Mat. 785 (1985) (Swiss S. Ct.).

The Evolving Controversy over Insider Trading

The Insider Trading Theoretical Controversy

There is considerable debate among economists, lawyers, and securities professionals over the efficacy of restricting insider trading. Those opposing the restriction argue that the incentives and results from certain insider trading are beneficial. The theorists who support the restriction allege that the practice is unfair, contravenes basic fiduciary standards, and undermines investor confidence in the capital markets. The recent trading restriction legislation and early court opinions argue principally that insider trading is unfair. Indeed, Congress's original trading restriction in section 16(b) was designed to prevent "the most vicious practices . . . [in] the flagrant betrayal of their fiduciary duties by officers and directors." Although investors expect fairness in the markets, proponents of this view contend, insiders' informational advantages cannot be overcome through competition. As the public perceives unfairness in the capital markets, investors will retreat and invest in alternatives to securities, thereby impeding the formation of capital. Confidence in the capital markets is fragile, so trading restriction is necessary to maintain investors' confidence and ultimately, the integrity of the securities markets.

Opponents of trading restrictions view insider trading as a victimless crime and restricting it as a waste of enforcement resources. It has been argued that investors trade on "fundamental" considerations or for personal financial needs independent of short-term inside information. The opponents' argument notwithstanding, however, disclosure of the inside information would probably induce the transaction at some other price reflecting inside information. Rational traders would not simply "take" the market price if the inside information reflected a better assessment of intrinsic value. Disclosure of adverse information would result in lower prices and disclosure of favorable information would result in higher prices. Losses attending nondisclosure is one type of injury the trading restriction is intended to prevent.

Opponents of the trading restriction also argue that any loss in confidence affects only the issuer whose shares are traded, not the markets generally. As a result, insider trading has no negative affect on the securities markets. Therefore, insider trading restrictions should be left to private contracting by shareholders who can respond by simply prohibiting insider trading, perhaps through corporate charter amendments or by passage of a shareholder resolution. However, this argument fails to recognize that a general disenchantment with the securities markets could arise if insider trading is perceived as widespread. Firms in volatile industries are more susceptible to insider trading than are firms with stable markets. Moreover, it is unlikely that shareholders could detect, monitor, or effectively remedy insider trading. Indeed, prior to the recent wave of prosecutions, the SEC had great difficulty discovering insider trades.

In addition, a few commentators have argued that insider trading is beneficial to the issuer. First, since the issuer's management produces the confidential information, management has a greater claim to it than do outside traders. However, this argument ignores the claim that corporate confidences belong only to the corporation and its shareholders. Management has no secondary right in the information it produces; there is no authority for the suggestion that a hierarchy of claims over inside information exists after the corporation's rights, unless a contract creates one. Second, the *emolument* theory suggests that "profits from sure thing

Source: John W. Bagby, "The Evolving Controversy over Insider Trading," 24 Am. Bus. L.J. (1987), pp. 561–620, reprinted with permission of the American Business Law Journal.

speculation in the stocks of their corporations were more or less generally accepted by the financial community as part of the emolument for serving as a corporate officer or director. . . . '' One version of this theory actually encourages the use of inside information by those ''entrepreneurs'' who fail to receive compensation for their talents in direct relation to the successes they produce. If entrepreneurs who are the insiders responsible for new developments fail to perceive a connection between their creativity and the sufficiency of their rewards, the incentive to produce creative development is diminished. Therefore, insider trading should be permitted to link the entrepreneur's creativity to his rewards when the market produces price fluctuations commensurate with the issuer's gains from the creative projects. Trading thus allegedly benefits the issuer as well, since the insider's official compensation may be reduced, providing corresponding benefit to shareholders.

The emolument theory fails to recognize several difficulties. First, there are incentive reward systems that can approximate the positive motivation of entrepreneurial insider trading.* Second, insiders will have an incentive to manipulate the timing and accuracy of the information disseminated. Third, unproductive insiders will have many of the same opportunities to trade as do creative insiders. Fourth, insider trading opportunities also exist in adverse situations and would reward poor performance, an outcome at odds with the entrepreneurial theory. Fifth, the emolument theory allows for trading by insiders unassociated with the creative ventures. Sixth, there will be incentives to select higher-risk investments producing wider stock price fluctuations that provide more opportunities for trading profits. These shortcomings illustrate that emolument theory of insider trading has significant flaws.

Finally, opponents of the trading restriction argue that efficiency is enhanced with unrestricted trading. When insiders trade, the amount of available information increases, enabling the market to *infer* fundamental information about the firm's prospects. Consequently, insider trading ''signals'' the market to move in the correct direction more quickly. Several studies of insider trading based on SEC filings by statutory insiders under section 16(a) tend to support the ''signalling'' theory. The evidence indicates that insiders consistently outperform the market by correctly predicting the direction of their issuer's future stock price movements. In contrast, proponents of restrictions on insider trading claim that the market will become more efficient if trading is restricted. Information will flow to the market as it is produced rather than as it is manipulated by inside traders. Indeed, internal corporate efficiency is enhanced because decision-making is more accurate and timely if insiders do not manipulate the flow of information within the firm to enhance their personal trading opportunities. This theoretical controversy has been important for courts and the SEC because the unfairness and market integrity arguments underlie the misappropriation theory. Additionally, congressional intent supporting the Insider Trading Sanctions Act illustrates the predominance of the unfairness and market integrity arguments in the continuing development of insider trading jurisprudence.

Thought Questions

1. What reasons support the prohibition of insider trading? What reasons support eliminating the prohibition of insider trading?

2. What reasoning errors or fallacies are evident in critics' arguments against insider trading restrictions? What biases might be introduced in managers' decisionmaking if they are permitted to appropriate inside information for personal gain?

---

*For example, stock options, bonuses, promotions, fringe benefits and special project evaluations can provide a more direct reward link than insider trading without the associated loss of market confidence or the damaging trading by ''non-entrepreneurial'' insiders and tippees.

3. Compare and contrast the path of confidential information flow under the signaling theory argued by insider trading enforcement critics versus the information path suggested by proponents of insider trading enforcement.

Short-Swing Profits: Section 16

The original federal restriction of insider trading is contained in Section 16 of the 1934 Act. This provision restricts **short-swing profits,** a purchase and sale of the issuer's registered equity securities within six months, by **statutory insiders** who include officers, directors, and 10 percent shareholders. Section 16 permits the corporation to recover short-swing profits in suits brought by the corporation or by a shareholder suing derivatively. The Section 16 concept that short-swing insider profits belong to the corporation codifies the corporate opportunity doctrine: Personal profits derived from confidential corporate information harm the corporation.

Statutory Insiders' Section 16(a) Reporting

Section 16 has two basic provisions: Section 16(a) requires statutory insiders to disclose trades, and Section 16(b) restricts short-swing profits. The disclosure rules require a public SEC filing and a separate notice to all exchanges on which the securities trade. Notice must be within the 10 days following any month that a purchase or sale occurs. Newly elected officers and directors must report their existing holdings right after their election. For example, XYZ's officers, directors, and 10 percent shareholders must disclose their trading in XYZ stock. They are presumed to know about XYZ's plans to acquire a widget manufacturer. The 10 percent shareholder disclosure rules are separate from the disclosure by 5 percent shareholders under the tender offer rules discussed later in this chapter. The SEC strengthened enforcement in 1991 because Section 16(a) reporting violations were so widespread.

All members of the issuer's board of directors must comply with Section 16. The reporting duties also apply to substitutes who perform the director's duties, such as an aide or an administrative assistant. An interlocking director serving on two issuers' boards may be considered a deputy working for either corporation. Interlocking directors are presumed to communicate confidential information between corporations. In such cases, each corporation assumes the individual director's Section 16 disclosure and trading responsibilities.[4]

The law presumes that officers and directors are regularly exposed to significant confidential policymaking of the type insiders could exploit for personal trading advantages. However, many firms have bestowed officerlike titles on middle managers who have no significant policymaking responsibility or exposure. For example, one stock brokerage company gave the title "executive vice president" to its more productive sales representatives. Banks generally designate as officers the employees with titles of assistant cashiers. Some early cases focused on an officer's duties rather than title by recognizing that stock trading by such "titled middle managers" was exempt from Section 16. A 1991 SEC rule reinforces this view: **officers** now include only "executive officers" who perform significant policymaking. Persons holding mere honorary titles are exempt.

Officers Under Section 16

- Issuer's president.
- Vice presidents in charge of principal business units, divisions, or functions.
- Officers of the issuer's parent or subsidiaries who perform policymaking for the issuer.
- Principal financial officer.
- Principal accounting officer.

The 10 percent shareholder duties are also subject to some ambiguity. Shareholdings could be apportioned among family members: spouse, minor children, and live-in relatives. If no single person officially holds over 10 percent but the group's holdings aggregate to 10 percent or more, the issuer might confide in the group's leader just like any other 10 percent shareholder. The SEC has developed the **beneficial ownership** concept to combine all the

---

[4]*Feder v. Martin Marietta Corp.*, 406 F.2d 260 (2d Cir. 1969).

shares of such related groups. However, reasonable proof that no control was exercised over the group's holdings could rebut this. The 1991 SEC rules clarified how these and other cooperating groups among relatives, friends, business associates, and firms may be subject to the beneficial ownership rules.

Section 16 applies to statutory insiders' trades in any class of equity security, whether or not registered with the SEC. However, only registered equity securities are used to qualify 10 percent shareholders as statutory insiders. Registered equity securities include common stock, preferred stock, preincorporation subscriptions, transferable shares, voting trust certificates, limited partnership interests, and most securities convertible into common (e.g., convertible debentures, warrants, and rights). Classes are determined by the preponderance of similarities in voting and other preferences. Minor differences dictated by market pressures at the time of issue, such as different preferred dividend rates between different series, still constitute a single class of equity securities.

Congress gave the SEC enhanced civil powers under the Enforcement Remedies Act of 1990. New sanctions may be applied to late or omitted filings of statutory insiders. For example, officers, directors, and all other signatories of SEC filings may be debarred from practice before the SEC. Additionally, the SEC may seek money penalties and cease and desist orders in SEC administrative hearings without going to federal court. The SEC's 1991 revision of Section 16(a) now requires issuers to disclose statutory insiders' late filings in their annual report. Issuers failing to accurately disclose late filers are subject to antifraud liability, pressuring statutory insiders to correctly disclose their trades.

Short-Swing Damages: Section 16(b)
Statutory insiders are liable to repay short-swing profits to the corporation as damages. To compute these insider profits, a sliding six-month scale is used to capture any *purchase and sale* or *sale and purchase* made within any six-month period. A purchase or sale is triggered by an executory contract to sell or by the actual transfer of shares. Derivative securities such as convertibles, options, warrants, or stock appreciation rights are considered purchased when the derivative is acquired. Such derivatives are not considered sold until the derivative or converted security is sold. The SEC's new 1991 rule reversed the old treatment of derivatives by exempting the exercise or

conversion of the derivative, effectively lengthening the holding period for the six-month test. The corporation or any shareholder may sue derivatively for short-swing profiteering by statutory insiders. The the recovery belongs to the corporation, not individually to any shareholder. A shareholder may continue pursuing a Section 16(b) suit even after exchanging the equity securities in question for securities in the corporation's merger partner.[5]

Short-swing damages are computed by netting the lowest purchase price and highest sale price within any six-month period. No FIFO (first-in, first-out) method of matching securities purchased against securities sold is used. Instead, the lowest purchase and highest sale price are netted until all securities transactions are exhausted. Netting between the next lowest purchase and next highest sale continues until the total short-swing profit potential is maximized. This method is used to hold statutory insiders to a high standard of conduct and to impose a stronger deterrent. Short-swing profits include sales made at high prices first netted against later purchases at low prices because insiders may also profit from confidential bad news by selling short.

An example illustrating Section 16(b) liability is depicted in Figure 45–1. Assume a statutory insider at XYZ sells 100 shares of XYZ common stock at $100 per share in January and purchases 100 shares at $50 per share in March. Another 100 shares are purchased in April for $40 per share. Even though the January sale occurred first, the short-swing profit realized is $6,000 ($100 − $40 = $60 per share × 100 shares). No netting is made between the $50 purchase and the $100 sale because the $40 purchase price was lower, occurred within six months of the $100 sale, and maximizes the short-swing damages.

Section 16 and SEC rules exempt certain transactions by persons presumed not to trade on confidential information. Market makers and specialists must file Section 16(a) reports but only incur Section 16(b) short-swing liability when trading for their own accounts—their market-making activities are exempt. Dealers and underwriters in an initial public offering (IPO) are generally not considered statutory insiders. Arbitrageurs making near simultaneous purchases and trades are exempt if they satisfy SEC rules. However, other institutional inves-

---

[5]*Gollust v. Mendell,* 111 S.Ct. 2173 (1991).

Figure 45–1   Short-Swing Profit Liability

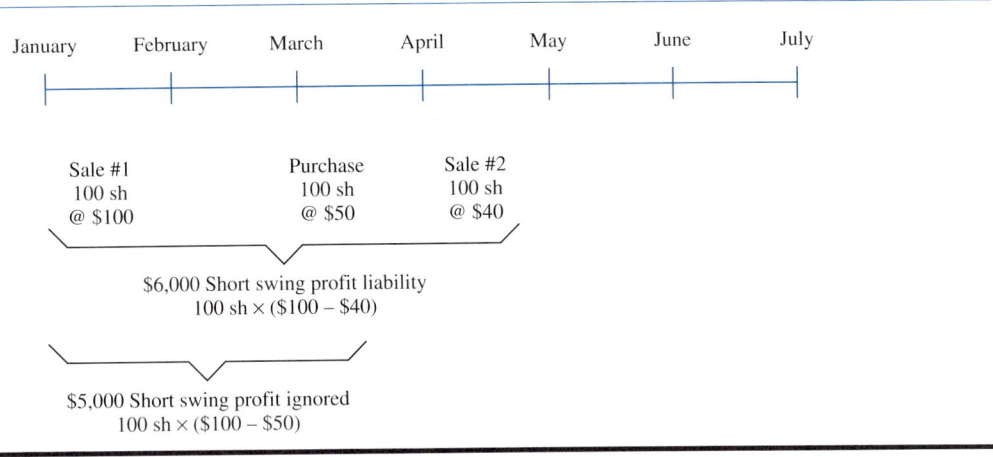

tors, mutual funds, pension funds, and insurance companies are not generally exempt from the Section 16 reporting and trading restrictions. While Section 16 is the original insider trading restriction and the primary source of insider trading information, most contemporary insider trading enforcement is brought under the 1934 Act's general antifraud provision Section 10(b) and SEC Rule 10b-5.

Rule 10b-5 and Insider Trading

Neither Section 16 nor state laws were considered sufficient to deter the rather widespread insider trading. For example, the fraud concept of misrepresentation is largely inapplicable to *omissions*, a failure to reveal material facts, and to *half-truths*, partially true but misleading statements requiring clarification. The **reliance** element is difficult to prove. In 1942, the SEC recognized these shortcomings when it became aware that the president of some company in Boston was going around buying up the corporations stock from shareholders at $4 per share telling them that the company is doing very badly, whereas in fact the earnings are going to be quadrupled and will be $2 per share.[6] This story prompted the SEC to enliven dormant Section 10(b), implementing it with SEC Rule 10b-5, the most pervasive antifraud provision in the securities laws.

[6]Statement of Milton Friedman in American Bar Association, Section of Corporation, Banking, and Business Law, Conference on Codification of the Federal Securities Laws, 22 Bus. Law. 793, 921–23 (1967).

SEC Rule 10b-5

It shall be unlawful for any person, directly or indirectly, by the use of any means or instrumentality of interstate commerce, or of the mails, or of any facility of a national securities exchange,

(1) to employ any device, scheme, or artifice to defraud,

(2) to make any untrue statement of a material fact or to omit to state a material fact necessary in order to make the statements made, in the light of the circumstances under which they were made, not misleading, or

(3) to engage in any act, practice or course of business which operates or would operate as a fraud or deceit upon any person, in connection with the purchase or sale of any security.

When applied to insider trading, Rule 10b-5 imposes the **disclose or abstain** rule: Insiders at all levels within the issuer must *disclose* the confidential information to the market or their trading partner before trading or *abstain* altogether from trading until the confidential information becomes public. Disclose or abstain is often a Hobson's choice, because disclosure would prevent the insider from profiting on the information and usually violates the insider's fiduciary duties. This is the fundamental ethical dilemma posed by insider trading: It is unethical to disclose an employer's confidences, and it is also unethical to breach one's fiduciary duty to shareholders by converting confidential corporate information for personal gain.

The disclose or abstain rule was clearly applied in the oft-cited case of *SEC v. Texas Gulf Sulphur Co.*[7] Texas Gulf Sulphur (TGS) kept confidential its substantial mineral discovery to acquire mineral leases surrounding the Timmons, Ontario, drilling site more cheaply. TGS falsely denied rumors of the discovery while numerous TGS employees purchased TGS stock before the public disclosure raised TGS's stock price. If TGS employees disclosed the discovery before trading, this would violate their fiduciary duty of confidentiality. The only viable choice was to abstain, making insider trading illegal. While TGS owed surrounding landowners no duty to disclose the mineral discovery, TGS employees' fiduciary duty required them to volunteer the information before trading with shareholders. TGS's false denial of rumors also violated Rule 10b-5 as a form of disclosure fraud.

Who Is an "Insider"?

Rule 10b-5 restricts more insiders than the upper level officers, directors, and big-block shareholders restrained by Section 16. Employees at any level can have access to confidential, nonpublic information. Rule 10b-5 requires no public disclosure of an insider's trading as does Section 16(a). Rule 10b-5 is violated when an insider or a **tippee** who receives inside information from an insider makes *either* a purchase *or* sale of the issuer's securities while in possession of confidential, nonpublic information. Rule 10b-5 applies to both registered and unregistered securities.

In re Cady, Roberts & Co.[8] first established the trading restriction when (1) a relationship gives access to information, (2) that is intended only for a corporate purpose, and (3) is used unfairly for the insider's personal benefit. However, the mere possession of confidential information while trading is not unlawful. The insider must have acquired the information *improperly,* a point made in *Chiarella v. U.S.*[9] This case rejected the SEC's **parity of information rule** or **possession theory** that purported to outlaw trading while in the mere possession of nonpublic information. Analysts' diligent research often produces nonpublic information that they must be permitted to use to advise clients or trade on personally without incurring liability. Otherwise, analysts would have no incentive to provide their essential services.

Outsider liability for insider trading has posed recurring difficulties. Under what circumstances does an outsider inherit the disclose or abstain duty from an inside tipper? What other outsiders are constrained if they originate or are exposed to nonpublic confidences about the issuer whose shares are traded? The following classic case established the "no tipping" rule.

---

[7]*SEC v. Texas Gulf Sulphur Co.,* 401 F.2d 833 (2d Cir.) *cert denied* 394 U.S. 976 (1969).

[8]*In re Cady, Roberts & Co.,* 40 SEC 907 (1961).
[9]*Chiarella v. U.S.,* 445 U.S. 222 (1980).

DIRKS v. SEC
463 U.S. 646 (1983)

As a New York securities analyst, Dirks received information from Secrist, a former officer of Equity Funding of America. Equity Funding's financials vastly overstated its assets. Corruption and fraud were rife. Dirks investigated by questioning numerous employees. He then discussed his findings openly with his firm's brokers and advised several clients to liquidate nearly $16 million in Equity Funding holdings. Over this period, Equity Funding's stock price plunged from $26 to $15 before the NYSE halted trading. Eventually, the SEC filed a complaint against Equity Funding and it went into receivership. The SEC censured Dirks for communicating the nonpublic information he discovered about the fraud but did not discipline him more severely because of his assistance in uncovering the fraud. Dirks appealed his censure.

POWELL, Justice

In the seminal case of *In re Cady, Roberts & Co.*, the SEC recognized that the common law in some jurisdictions imposes on "corporate 'insiders,' particularly officers, directors, or controlling stockholders" an "affirmative duty of disclosure . . . when dealing in securities." Unlike insiders who have independent fiduciary duties to both the corporation and its shareholders, the typical tippee has no such relationship.[10] In view of this absence it has been unclear how a tippee acquires the *Cady, Roberts* duty to refrain from trading on inside information.

The SEC's position as stated in its opinion in this case, is that a tippee "inherits" the *Cady, Roberts* obligation to shareholders whenever he receives inside information from an insider. This view differs little from the view that we rejected as inconsistent with congressional intent in *Chiarella*. Imposing a duty to disclose or abstain solely because a person knowingly receives material non-public information from an insider and trades on it could have an inhibiting influence on the role of market analysts, which the SEC itself recognizes is necessary to the preservation of a healthy market. It is commonplace for analysts to "ferret out and analyze information," and this often is done by meeting with and questioning corporate officers and others who are insiders. And information that the analysts obtain normally may be the basis for judgments as to the market worth of a corporation's securities. The analyst's judgment in this respect is made available in market letters or otherwise to clients of the firm. It is the nature of this type of information, and indeed of the

markets themselves, that such information cannot be made simultaneously available to all of the corporation's stockholders or the public generally.

The need for a ban on some tippee trading is clear. Not only are insiders forbidden by their fiduciary relationship from personally using undisclosed corporate information to their advantage, but they may not give such information to an outsider for the same improper purpose of exploiting the information for their personal gain.

Thus, some tippees must assume an insider's duty to the shareholders not because they receive inside information, but rather because it has been made available to them *improperly*. The insider's disclosure is improper only where it would violate his *Cady, Roberts* duty. Thus, a tippee assumes a fiduciary duty to the shareholders of a corporation not to trade on material non-public information only when the insider has breached his fiduciary duty to the shareholders by disclosing the information to the tippee and the tippee knows or should know that there has been a breach. As Commissioner Smith perceptively observed in *Investors Management Co.*: "[T]ippee responsibility must be related back to insider responsibility by a necessary finding that the tippee knew the information was given to him in breach of a duty by a person having a special relationship to the issuer not to disclose the information."

In determining whether a tippee is under an obligation to disclose or abstain, it thus is necessary to determine whether the insider's "tip" constituted a breach of the insider's fiduciary duty. All disclosures of confidential corporate information are not inconsistent with the duty insiders owe to shareholders. In some situations, the insider will act consistently with his fiduciary duty to shareholders, and yet release of the information may affect the market. For example, it may not be clear—either to the corporate insider or to the recipient analyst—whether the information will be viewed as material non-public information. Corporate officials may mistakenly think the information already has been disclosed or that it is not material enough to affect the market. Whether disclosure is a breach of duty therefore depends in large part on the purpose of the disclosure. This standard was identified by the SEC itself in *Cady, Roberts*: a purpose of the securities laws was to eliminate "use of inside information for personal advantage." Thus, the test is whether the insider

---

[10][Renumbered—originally footnote 14 in *Dirks*] Under certain circumstances, such as where corporate information is revealed legitimately to an underwriter, accountant, lawyer, or a consultant working for the corporation, these outsiders may become fiduciaries of the shareholders. The basis for recognizing this fiduciary duty is not simply that such persons acquired nonpublic corporate information, but rather that they have entered into a special confidential relationship in the conduct of the business of the enterprise and are given access to information solely for corporate purposes. When such a person breaches his fiduciary relationship, he may be treated more properly as a tipper than a tippee. For such a duty to be imposed, however, the corporation must expect the outsider to keep the disclosed nonpublic information confidential, and the relationship at least must imply such a duty.

personally will benefit, directly or indirectly, from his disclosure. Absent some personal gain, there has been no breach of duty to stockholders. And absent a breach by the insider, there is no derivative breach. As Commissioner Smith stated in *Investors Management Co.*: "It is important in this type of case to focus on policing insiders and what they do . . . rather than on policing information per se and its possession. . . ."

As the facts of this case clearly indicate, the tippers were motivated by a desire to expose the fraud. In the absence of a breach of duty to shareholders by the insiders, there was no derivative breach by Dirks. Dirks therefore could not have been "a participant after the fact in [an] insider's breach of a fiduciary duty." We conclude that Dirks, in the circumstances of this case, had no duty to abstain from use of the inside information that he obtained. The judgment of the Court of Appeals therefore is Reversed.

Case Questions

1. What is the issue in determining whether a tippee inherits the insider's disclose or abstain duty?

2. What is assumed about the workings of analysts and their contribution to fair and efficient securities markets?

3. What ambiguities are there for tippees in trading on inside information?

The "no tipping" rule of *Dirks* prohibits a tippee's trading if the tippee knows or has reason to know that the insider breached a fiduciary duty in tipping. The Equity Funding insiders breached no fiduciary duty in revealing the fraud to Dirks. The disclose or abstain rule is inherited by tippees only when the confidence is revealed *improperly,* such as when the insider expects a personal benefit, payment, or a return favor for the tip. The famous *Dirks* footnote 14 (renumbered as footnote 10 in the *Dirks* case presented here) created another class of **temporary insiders** who are bound by the disclose or abstain rule when exposed to confidences while working in a consulting capacity for the issuer. Their fiduciary duty is directly owed to their immediate employer, who expressly or impliedly pledges confidentiality to the issuer as part of the consultation engagement. These temporary insiders must avoid both personal insider trading and avoid tipping others about confidential nonpublic information they discover or receive in consulting.

Misappropriation Theory

The *Chiarella* decision prompted the SEC to develop a new insider trading theory based on information misappropriation. This theory substantially broadens an outsider's potential liability for insider trading. It is a common misconception that only traditional insiders employed by the issuer can be liable and that the confidential, nonpublic information must come from within the issuer whose shares are traded. Secret information about takeovers often originates with an outside bidder and may be communicated to the bidder's employees and to the bidder's consultants and employees, including investment bankers, law firms, financial printers, and auditors. Therefore, the **misappropriation theory** restricts insider trading by anyone who misappropriates confidential, nonpublic information from a confidential source for use in personal trading or tipping. It is commonly believed that tender offer insider trading by outsiders is harmful.

The Value of Confidential Takeover Information

In a tender offer situation, the effect of increased activity in purchases of the target company's shares is to drive up the price of the target company's shares, but this effect is damaging to the offering company because the tender offer will appear commensurately less attractive and the activity may cause it to abort. The deceitful misappropriation of confidential information by a fiduciary, whether described as theft, conversion, or breach of trust, has consistently been held to be unlawful[11]

For example, XYZ might retain a financial printer to produce SEC filings and documents for distribution to shareholders. These consultants' employees, like *Chiarella* the markup man are prohibited from misappropriating for personal use any confidences revealed by XYZ or other clients because the information is intended only for corporate pur-

---

[11]*U.S. v. Newman,* 664 F.2d 12 (2d Cir. 1981).

poses. Similar prohibitions exist for the employees of Wall Street law firms and underwriters. Misappropriation is a form of theft that violates the outsider's fiduciary duty to the employer.

Outsider trading is an illegal form of insider trading even though there may be no direct fiduciary duty owed to the issuer whose shares are traded. A misappropriation occurs where there is a confidential *source* for information, with superior *rights* to keep it confidential, and the source has *intent* to keep it confidential, by making *efforts* to do so. This is consistent with a common understanding that insider trading is illegal whenever a confidant steals information for personal benefit. The case of *Carpenter v. U.S.* affirms the misappropriation theory of insider trading enforcement under the mail and wire fraud statute but only mildly supports misappropriation as a theory under the securities laws.

CARPENTER v. U.S.
484 U.S. 19 (1987)

The Wall Street Journal's "Heard on the Street" column was researched and written by R. Foster Winans. It purported to reveal theretofore secret rumors and other information about certain stocks or groups of stocks that Winans researched with interviews with insiders, analysts, and other efforts. Winans and his friends Brant and Felis traded in advance of Winan's often market-moving stories. This violated *The Journal*'s employee manual. The three were convicted of securities fraud and violating the federal mail and wire fraud statute. These trading patterns were discovered by Brant's and Felis's former employer, an investment bank. Carpenter and Winans separately revealed the scheme to the SEC. The defendants appealed their conviction.

WHITE, Justice

The Court is evenly divided with respect to the convictions under the securities laws and for that reason affirms the judgment below on those counts. For the reasons that follow, we also affirm the judgment with respect to the mail and wire fraud convictions.

The Journal as Winans' employer, was defrauded of much more than its contractual right to his honest and faithful service. Here, the object of the scheme was to take *The Journal*'s confidential business information—the publication schedule and contents of the "Heard" column—and its intangible nature does not make it any less "property" protected by the mail and wire fraud statutes.

"Confidential information acquired or compiled by a corporation in the course and conduct of its business is a species of property to which the corporation has the exclusive right and benefit, and which a court of equity will protect through the injunction process or other appropriate remedy." *The Journal* had a property right in keeping confidential and making exclusive use, prior to publication of the schedule and contents of the "Heard" columns. As the Court has observed before:

[N]ews matter, however little susceptible of ownership or dominion in the absolute sense, is stock in trade, to be gathered at the cost of enterprise, organization, skill, labor, and money, and to be distributed and sold to those who will pay money for it, as for any other merchandise.

[I]t is sufficient that *The Journal* has been deprived of its right to exclusive use of the information, for exclusivity is an important aspect of confidential business information and most private property for that matter.

We cannot accept petitioners' further argument that Winans' conduct in revealing prepublication information was no more than a violation of workplace rules and did not amount to fraudulent activity. The concept of "fraud" includes the act of embezzlement, which is "the fraudulent appropriation to one's own use of the money or goods entrusted to one's care by another."

We have noted "even in the absence of a written contract, an employee has a fiduciary obligation to protect confidential information obtained during the course of his employment." As the New York courts have recognized, "It is well established, as a general proposition, that a person who acquires special knowledge or information by virtue of a confidential or fiduciary relationship with another is not free to exploit that knowledge or information for his own personal benefit but must account to his principal for any profits derived.''

We have little trouble in holding that the conspiracy here to trade on *The Journal*'s confidential information is not outside the reach of the mail and wire fraud statutes, provided the other elements of the offenses are satisfied. *The Journal*'s business information that it intended to be kept confidential was its property; the declaration to that effect in the employee manual merely removed any doubts on that score and made the finding of specific intent to defraud that much easier. Winans continued in the employ of *The Journal*, appropriating its confidential business information for his own use, all the while pretending to perform his duty of safeguarding it. In fact, he told his editors twice about leaks of

confidential information not related to the stock-trading scheme, demonstrating both his knowledge that *The Journal* viewed information concerning the ''Heard'' column as confidential and his deceit as he played the role of a loyal employee. [Defendants' conviction in the] judgment below is Affirmed.

Case Questions

1. What is the issue in making it illegal for outsiders to trade in the shares of an unrelated issuer?

2. What reasons make the misappropriation of information equivalent to misappropriating tangible property?

3. What is the insider trading issue in establishing employee rules of confidentiality as a term of the employment?

Enforcement of Insider Trading and Securities Fraud

Insider trading became rampant during the 1980s, triggering public pressure and congressional action to curb the practice. Three new laws and numerous SEC rules and enforcement actions strengthen the penalties and disincentives for insider trading and other securities frauds. The **Insider Trading Sanctions Act** of 1984 **(ITSA)** permits the SEC to seek up to a triple penalty in enforcement suits brought in federal court. ITSA suits are tried only to a judge, never a jury. ITSA damages are computed as ''the profit gained or loss avoided,'' calculated as the difference between the insider's purchase price and the market trading price right after public disclosure of the inside information.

In 1988, Congress passed the **Insider Trading and Securities Fraud Enforcement Act (ITSFEA)**, further strengthening enforcement powers, establishing a statutory private right of action for insider trading damages, and increasing criminal penalties. ITSFEA permits the payment of **bounties** to informants in securities fraud cases. Brokerage firms are required to more closely supervise employee activities to prevent tipping and insider trading. ITSFEA gave the SEC authority to assist foreign securities regulators in enforcing insider trading laws and to negotiate assistance agreements.

The **Enforcement Remedies and Penny Stock Reform Act (ERPSRA)** of 1990 substantially increased the SEC's internal enforcement powers, precluding the necessity of federal district court litigation in all cases. New SEC powers include debarment, disgorgement, cease and desist orders, and money penalties. The SEC's additional powers over penny stock reform, program trading, and market emergencies are discussed later in this chapter.

The various penalties under the ITSA, ITSFEA, RICO, and ERPSRA are cumulative with other penalties. In particularly serious cases, an inside trader could conceivably be required to (1) pay an ITSA triple penalty, (2) make **disgorgement** of insider trading profits to repay aggrieved investors, (3) repay Section 16(b) short-swing profits to the corporation, (4) pay civil money penalties to the SEC, (5) pay treble damages under RICO, and (6) be subject to criminal fines and imprisonment in a Justice Department prosecution under the securities laws, RICO, and/or the mail and wire fraud statutes. Penalties under state blue sky and state RICO laws are also cumulative. The very different aspects of the short-swing profit rules under Section 16(b) and insider trading prohibited under Rule 10b-5 are illustrated in Figure 45-2.

The elements of a 10b-5 case alleging insider trading or securities fraud must be proved by the government or by private litigants in addition to the

Figure 45–2 Insider Trading Theories Compared

	SEC Act Section 16(b)	SEC Rule 10b-5
Potential Plaintiffs	Issuer or shareholder suing derivatively for short-swing profits; SEC to enforce §16(a) insider reports	SEC, Justice Department, and shareholders who trade contemporaneously with insider
Potential Defendants	Statutory insiders: officers, directors, and 10 percent shareholders and deputies, nominees, or others performing policy-making activities	Any employee of the issuer, temporary insider, or misappropriator and certain tippees
Proof of Access to and Use of Inside Information	No proof required: access and use presumed for statutory insiders	Proof required: misappropriation or tipee status
Securities Covered	Any registered equity security	Any security, registered or not
Disclosure Required	Statutory insiders must report all changes in shareholdings within 10 days after any month in which a purchase or sale transaction occurs	Insider must publicly disclose inside information or abstain from trading
Tipee Liability	No tipee liability	Tipee liable for insider trading if: Tippee knows or has reason to know that the tipper (insider) breached a fiduciary duty in tipping; and Tipper transferred tip for an improper purpose (i.e., personal benefit)
Damages Recoverable	Match highest sale and purchase or purchase and sale within any six-month period	Disgorge illegal insider trading profit; SEC actions: ITSA treble penalty paid to U.S. Treasury; damages held in escrow for victims, claimants
Criminal Penalties	No criminal penalties; SEC may refer insider trading evidence to Justice Department	Justice Department may prosecute under Rule 10b-5 or mail and wire fraud statutes; penalties of up to 10 years' imprisonment and $1 million fine for individuals, $2.5 fine for firms
Civil Penalties	SEC has enhanced civil powers under Enforcement Remedies Act for §16(a) filing violations: debarment, cease and desist orders, money penalties, and sanctions against issuers failing to disclose §16(a) filing violations	SEC has enhanced civil powers under Enforcement Remedies Act for illegal insider trading: debarment, cease and desist orders, money penalties, and disgorgement

misappropriation, deception, or other fraudulent scheme at issue. The defendant must have acted with **scienter** or intent. The fraud must be made *in connection with the purchase or sale of securities*. The misrepresentation or omission must be *material*, as illustrated in *TSC Industries Inc. v. Northway, Inc.,* presented later in this chapter. Rule 10b-5 private litigants must commence their suits within one year following discovery of facts constituting the violation and within three years after the occurrence.[12] In civil enforcement and private damage suits, the case must be proved by a **preponderance of the evidence.** The Justice Department must prove any criminal case **beyond a reasonable doubt.**

Rule 10b-5 cases require proof of **reliance,** an element of causation focusing on the defrauded victim's belief and consequent action based on the trust given to the misrepresentor's false statement. Reli-

---

[12]*Lampf, Pleva, Lipkind, Prupis & Petigrow v. Gilberton,* 111 S.Ct. 2773 *reh'g. denied* 112 S.Ct. 27 (1991).

ance is fairly easy to prove in disclosure fraud cases. For example, in *SEC v. Texas Gulf,* discussed earlier in this chapter, it was reasonable for investors to directly believe Texas Gulf's false denial of the mineral discovery, causing them to trade at artificially lower prices. However, reliance is difficult to prove in insider trading and disclosure omission cases. No information flows directly from the defendant for the plaintiff to rely on.

The next case illustrates that modern financial economics has contributed the **efficient capital markets hypothesis** to insider trading enforcement. Application of this theory to disclosure fraud cases suggests a presumption that all publicly available information becomes quickly embedded in stock prices. Using this hypothesis, the Supreme Court developed a legal rule, the **fraud on the market** theory, permitting investors to prove reliance by showing they merely relied on posted market prices as an effective conduit for true, false, and omitted information from the issuer or its insiders.

BASIC, INC. v. LEVINSON
485 U.S. 224 (1988)

Basic, Inc., manufactured refractories, the nonstick lining for industrial furnaces. Combustion Engineering discussed acquiring Basic in 1976, but Basic denied such rumors in 1977 and 1978. Finally, in December 1978, Basic requested that the NYSE suspend trading in Basic stock pending its first public announcement of takeover negotiations. The next day, Basic's board accepted Combustion's $46 per share offer and announced its approval of Combustion's tender offer. A class action of investors who sold their Basic stock before the public announcement at lower prices was brought against Basic for disclosure fraud. Basic argued these investors failed to prove reliance on any misstatements in trading on the anonymous stock exchange.

BLACKMUN, Justice

Succinctly put: The fraud on the market theory is based on the hypothesis that, in an open and developed securities market, the price of a company's stock is determined by the available material information regarding the company and its business. . . . Misleading statements will therefore defraud purchasers of stock even if the purchasers do not directly rely on the misstatements. . . . The causal connection between the defendants' fraud and the plaintiffs' purchase of stock in such a case is no less significant than in a case of direct reliance on misrepresentations.

The modern securities markets, literally involving millions of shares changing hands daily, differ from the face-to-face transactions contemplated by early fraud cases, and our understanding of Rule 10b-5 reliance requirement must encompass these differences.

In face-to-face transactions, the inquiry into an investor's reliance upon information is into the subjective pricing of that information by that investor. With the presence of a market, the market is interposed between seller and buyer and, ideally, transmits information to the investor in the processed form of a market price. Thus, the market is performing a substantial part of the valuation process performed by the investor in a face-to-face transaction. The market is acting as the unpaid agent of the investor, informing him that given all the information available to it, the value of the stock is worth the market price.

Presumptions typically serve to assist courts in managing circumstances in which direct proof, for one reason or another, is rendered difficult. The courts below accepted a presumption, created by the fraud-on-the-market theory and subject to rebuttal by petitioners, that persons who had traded Basic shares had done so in reliance on the integrity of the price set by the market, but because of petitioners' material misrepresentations that price had been fraudulently depressed. Requiring a plaintiff to show a speculative state of facts, i.e., how he would have acted if omitted material information had been disclosed, or if the misrepresentation had not been made, would place an unnecessarily unrealistic evidentiary burden on the rule 10b-5 plaintiff who has traded on an impersonal market.

Congress expressly relied on the premise that securities markets are affected by information, and enacted legislation to facilitate an investor's reliance on the integrity of those markets:

> No investor, no speculator, can safely buy and sell securities upon the exchanges without having an intelligent basis for forming his judgment as to the value of the securities he buys or sells. The idea of a free and open public market is built upon the theory that competing judgments of buyers and sellers as to the fair price of a security bring about a situation where the market price reflects as nearly as possible a just price. Just as artificial manipulation tends to upset the true function of an open market, so the hiding and secreting of important information obstructs the operation of the markets as indices of real value.

The presumption is also supported by common sense and probability. Recent empirical studies have tended to confirm Congress' premise that the market price of shares traded on well-developed markets reflects all publicly available information, and, hence, any material misrepresentations. It has been noted that ''it is hard to imagine that there ever is a buyer or seller who does not rely on market integrity. Who would knowingly roll the dice in a crooked crap game?'' Because most publicly available information is reflected in market price, an investor's reliance on any public material misrepresentations, therefore, may be presumed for purposes of a Rule 10b-5 action.

Any showing that severs the link between the alleged misrepresentation and either the price received (or paid) by the plaintiff, or his decision to trade at a fair market price, will be sufficient to rebut the presumption of reliance. For example, if petitioners could show that the ''market makers'' were privy to the truth about the merger discussions here with Combustion, and thus that the market price would not have been affected by their misrepresentations, the causal connection could be broken: the basis for finding that the fraud had been transmitted through market price would be gone. Similarly, if, despite petitioners' allegedly fraudulent attempt to manipulate market price, news of the merger discussions credibly entered the market and dissipated the effects of the misstatements, those who traded Basic shares after the corrective statements would have no direct or indirect connection with the fraud. Petitioners also could rebut the presumption of reliance as to plaintiffs who would have divested themselves of their Basic shares without relying on the integrity of the market. For example, a plaintiff who believed that Basic's statements were false and that Basic was indeed engaged in merger discussions, and who consequently believed that Basic stock was artificially underpriced, but sold his shares nevertheless because of other unrelated concerns, e.g., potential antitrust problems, or political pressures to divest from shares of certain business, could not be said to have relied on the integrity of a price he knew had been manipulated.

The judgment of the Court of Appeals is vacated and the case is remanded for further proceedings consistent with this opinion. It is so ordered.

WHITE, Justice, with Whom Justice O'CONNOR Joins, Concurring in Part and Dissenting in Part

The federal courts have proved adept at developing an evolving jurisprudence of Rule 10b-5 in such a manner. But with no staff economists, no experts schooled in the ''efficient-capital-market hypothesis,'' no ability to test the validity of empirical market studies, we are not well equipped to embrace novel constructions of a statute based on contemporary microeconomic theory. The Congress with its superior resources and expertise, is far better equipped than the federal courts for the task of determining how modern economic theory and global financial markets require that established legal notions of fraud be modified. For while the economists' theories which underpin the fraud-on-the-market presumption may have the appeal of mathematical exactitude and scientific certainty, they are—in the end—nothing more than theories which may or may not prove accurate upon further consideration. Even the most earnest advocates of economic analysis of the law recognize this.

Even if I was prepared to accept (as a matter of common sense or general understanding) the assumption that most persons buying or selling stock do so in response to the market price, the fraud-on-the-market theory goes further. For in adopting a "presumption of reliance," the Court also assumes that buyers and sellers rely—not just on the market price—but on the "integrity" of that price. It is this aspect of the fraud-on-the-market hypothesis which most mystified me. To define the term "integrity of the market price," the majority quotes approvingly from cases which suggest that investors are entitled to "rely on the price of a stock as a reflection of its value." But the meaning of this phrase eludes me, for it implicitly suggests that stocks have some "true value" that is measurable by a standard other than their market price. While the Scholastics of medieval times professed a means to make such a valuation of a commodity's "worth," I doubt that the federal courts of our day are similarly equipped.

Even if securities had some "value"—knowable and distinct from the market price of a stock—investors do not always share the Court's presumption that a stock's price is a "reflection of [this] value." Indeed, "many investors purchase or sell stock because they believe the price inaccurately reflects the corporation's worth." As we recognized: "[I]nvestors act on inevitably incomplete or inaccurate information, [consequently] there are always winners and losers; but those who have 'lost' have not necessarily been defrauded."

Case Questions

1. In Rule 10b-5 disclosure fraud cases, what is the issue concerning the causal connection between disclosure misstatement or omission and an investor's decision to trade?

2. What reasons support adoption of the fraud on the market rule? What reasons support rejecting fraud on the market as proof of reliance?

3. What alternate hypotheses and reasons to explain investor behavior are consistent with their reliance on the market's integrity?

THE MARKET FOR CORPORATE CONTROL

The securities markets are actually a market for the purchase and sale of voting rights that can shift corporate control from one group to another. Arbitrageurs, individual financiers, dissident shareholders, institutional investors, existing shareholders, other corporations, and the issuer's management can participate in this market. Prior to the 1990s, hostile takeovers were the predominant form of corporate control transaction. Some well-financed individual corporate raiders made tender offers to purchase the shares of takeover target corporations by offering to pay a premium price for their "undervalued" stock. In response, many corporations instituted takeover defenses, and most states enacted antitakeover statutes that eventually slowed hostile takeovers.

The 1990s are witnessing a shift in corporate control contests away from hostile takeovers by tender offer to corporate control battles within the corporation. Proxy contests are a primary tool in modern corporate control battles. Pressure on management to restructure, sell unprofitable units, reorganize administration, or replace upper management is felt increasingly through threats of adverse shareholder voting. Insurgent shareholder groups are increasingly led by activist institutional investors that hold large blocks of voting stock. They coerce incumbent management to change policies or they replace upper managers by threatening to oust management's candidates for the board. Such **proxy settlements** will probably characterize the new form of corporate governance during the 1990s.

For most of the modern era, management has controlled the machinery of corporate democracy. Shareholders in most publicly traded corporations are geographically dispersed and incapable of concerted collective action. The costs of shareholder activism are sufficiently high as to deter all but the biggest shareholders. Management can satisfy quorum requirements for shareholder meetings by soliciting **proxies**—shareholder absentee ballots. Management can restrict the resolutions put before shareholders, pay its proxy solicitation expenses from the corporate treasury, and generally examine the voted ballots before the election. This enables management to resolicit large-block voters to vote in management's favor. In Delaware, management can count abstentions for its side. These structures give a substantial advantage to management in corporate governance and control contests.

The corporate control process is susceptible to considerable ethical abuse by management and sometimes by minority shareholders. Management has an incentive to expend excessive corporate resources to win elections. Dissident shareholders are restricted by several factors: (1) activism is futile if their costs rise above the stock's appreciation potential after they restructure or install more efficient management, and (2) institutional investors' special duties to shareholders, policyholders, and retirees prohibit endangering these interests.

Managers have a personal conflict of interest in denying dissidents access to the shareholder list. This self-preservation motive arises from their fear of losing influence or employment. They are inspired to oppose dissident proxy solicitors or tender offerors. It is probably unethical for management to yield to this self-interest at shareholders' expense. By contrast, some corporate managements oppose takeovers by corporate raiders known for their own selfish motives. For example, numerous corporate managements have been confronted by greenmailers and the market's ignorance of long-range plans. The proxy and tender offer rules are designed to balance the selfish motives of all participants in corporate control battles. This ethical dilemma is a complex interplay between corporate democracy, fiduciary duties, and secret information.

PROXY CONTESTS

Corporate democracy is generally implemented at annual or special shareholder meetings. Most votes are cast with absentee or *proxy* ballots. As discussed in Chapter 41, the proxy system is necessary to prevent tyranny by the minority, such as when management casts votes to perpetuate itself. Quorum requirements could make it difficult to pass effective resolutions without proxy solicitations. Therefore, the quorum and proxy solicitation rules help to maximize voter turnout to effectuate the benefits of broad-based consensus and shareholder democracy.

While state corporation law generally governs the form, validity, and process of proxy solicitations, SEC rules govern most of the proxy process for publicly traded issuers. The SEC has promulgated the **proxy rules** to conduct corporate governance truthfully and in the open. Section 14 of the 1934 Act and SEC proxy rules require full disclosure by management and dissident proxy solicitors, prohibit fraud, and facilitate individual shareholder proxy proposals.

Proxy solicitations involve electioneering and the facilitation of balloting to convince shareholders to vote for particular board candidates or for or against particular proposals. Solicitations are made by management every year for annual shareholder meetings and occasionally by dissident or insurgent shareholders seeking to oust or better control management. Proxy solicitations include a wide variety of communications among shareholders that trigger special duties. A **proxy solicitation** includes *any* request to give or revoke a proxy, the furnishing of a proxy form, and electioneering by advertisement, direct mail, direct telephone contact, and contact by professional proxy solicitors. For example, if ABC's board proposes a merger with XYZ, the ABC board must solicit proxies from ABC shareholders.

Care must be taken by management and dissident shareholders because nearly any communication with other shareholders may constitute a solicitation, triggering the special duties discussed in the following sections. For example, a proxy solicitation occurred when information about a refinancing plan was sent in a letter to shareholders and when blank proxy forms were mailed along with the annual meeting announcement to shareholders.

All proxy solicitations must comply with the complex SEC proxy rules. However, there is no solicitation in management's routine mailing of periodic disclosures, such as annual or quarterly reports, or when there is coverage of proxy fights by the press—it is protected by the First Amendment. Compliance is required for solicitations of all exchange-listed equity and for exchange-listed debt when bondholders are entitled to vote—for example, in reorganization plans. The SEC revised the proxy rules in 1992, substantially reducing the regulatory compliance burden on dissident or insurgent solicitors.[13] Now, presolicitation dialogue is permitted that strengthens the powers of institutional and other large-block, nonmanagement shareholders.

---

[13]See SEC Securities Exchange Act Release No. 31,326 (November 16, 1992).

Proxy Statements

Special disclosures must be filed by any person engaged in a proxy solicitation to inform shareholders of the solicitor's motives and permit informed voting. The **proxy statement** is the primary communication used by management and also by insurgents. Preliminary copies must be filed with the SEC at least 10 days before distribution of the final proxy statement to shareholders. Final revised copies are typically filed concurrently with mailing. Copies must be sent to all exchanges trading the issuer's voting securities. **Schedule 14A,** filed with the SEC, duplicates this information.

Information Required in a Proxy Statement

- Solicitor's identity.
- Payor of solicitor's proxy solicitation expenses.
- Legal terms of proxy.
- Director election information.
- Details on fundamental corporate change proposals.
- Issuer's financials.

Management must disclose additional information when it solicits proxies for board elections. The 1992 SEC rule revision requires more details on the compensation paid to the top five senior executives, including the CEO. An aggregate figure of all executives' compensation is no longer required. The top five executives' compensation must appear in chart form, showing regular pay, deferred compensation, bonuses, and the value of stock options under various hypothetical scenarios. To highlight management's successes or failures, the SEC now requires juxtaposing management's compensation for the past three years alongside the total of shareholder return and the returns for an industry index such as the S&P 500 or some other recognized market and industry indexes. The board's compensation committee must disclose how corporate performance measures are used to determine CEO pay. Even if management does not solicit proxies, most of this information must be disclosed in an **information statement,** preventing management from concealing its compensation and performance.

Proxy Form

Proxies must be printed in a ballotlike format. A blank date line must be included so that only the shareholder's latest proxy is counted. Boxes alongside the names of particular candidates or for particular resolutions (e.g., merger) must be provided to facilitate shareholder approval, disapproval, or abstention from voting. Proxies solicited by management or permitting management to vote incomplete ballots must conspicuously state these facts. Space must be provided for write-in candidates. Figure 45–3 illustrates the SEC's sample form of proxy.

As discussed in Chapters 41 and 44, many shareholders never receive stock certificates, so their shares are held in a **street name,** registered to their broker or some nominee. Although this facilitates quicker settlement of trades and provides collateral for the investor's margin loans, it means that many investors' names are absent from the corporation's record books. SEC rules require the corporation to provide sufficient proxy materials to brokers to ensure full participation by all these investors. Brokers must forward proxy solicitations to all investors beneficially owning shares held in street name at the corporation's expense. The Independent Election Corporation of America provides assistance to brokers by compiling lists of beneficial shareholders for use by corporations and insurgent proxy solicitors.

Proxy Contest Mechanics

An increasing number of battles for corporate control occur between management and independent proxy solicitors. During such intense conflicts, shareholders are best served with complete and accurate information for intelligent voting decisions. Dissidents generally pay their own expenses. Sometimes, the dissident wins the proxy solicitation and is directly reimbursed by the corporation.

Management's decided advantage extends to its unlimited access to lists of eligible shareholders. The proxy rules give management a choice of providing the list to the dissident or withholding the list to keep it confidential. In the latter case, management must mail the dissident's proxy statements at the dissident's expense. This tactic can frustrate the dissident's resolicitation and intense electioneering on selected large-block shareholders. Many corporations have no confidential voting policy. Management can resolicit proxies initially cast for the dissident, giving management an advantage over dissidents. The 1992 SEC proxy rule revision requires management to make the shareholder list

Figure 45–3   Proxy Form

Proxy

P

R

O

X

Y

This Proxy is Solicited on Behalf of the Board of Directors

The undersigned hereby appoints   and   and each of them, with full power of substitution, the proxies of the undersigned to vote all shares of Common stock of   which the undersigned is entitled to vote at the Annual Meeting of Stockholders of the corporation to be held at the principal corporate office,   , on April   ,19   , at 10:00 A.M. and at any adjournments or postponements thereof, with the same force and effect as the undersigned might or could do if personally present thereat.

1. ELECTION OF DIRECTORS ☐ FOR all nominees listed below   ☐ WITHHOLD AUTHORITY
        (except as marked to the contrary below)   to vote for all nominees listed below

(The Board of Directors recommends a vote FOR.)

This proxy will be voted in the Election of Directors in the manner described in the Proxy Statement for the Annual Meeting of Stockholders
(INSTRUCTION: To withhold authority to vote for one or more individual members, write such
                name or names in the space provided below.)

2. PROPOSAL TO AMEND THE CERTIFICATE OF INCORPORATION of the Company to increase the authorized number of shares of Preferred Stock, $ 01 par value, from 1,000,000 to 10,000,000. (The Board of Directors recommends a vote FOR.)
                ☐ FOR   ☐ AGAINST   ☐ ABSTAIN

3. PROPOSAL TO RATIFY THE SELECTION OF   ,as independent public accountants for the corporation for the fiscal year ending December   , 19 (The Board of Directors recommends a vote FOR.)
                ☐ FOR   ☐ AGAINST   ☐ ABSTAIN

4. In their discretion, the Proxies are authorized to vote upon much other business as may properly come before the meeting.

- -

This proxy when properly executed will be voted in the manner directed herein by the undersigned stockholder. If no direction is made, this proxy will be voted FOR Proposals 1, 2 and 3.

Please sign exactly as name appears below. When shares are held by joint tenants, both should sign. When signing as attorney, executor, administrator, trustee or guardian please give full title as such. If a corporation, please sign in corporate name by President or other authorized person. If a partnership, please sign in full partnership name by authorized person.

DATED ——————————————— 19

———————————————————
Signature

———————————————————
Signature if held jointly

PLEASE MARK, SIGN, DATE AND RETURN THE PROXY CARD PROMPTLY
USING THE ENCLOSED ENVELOPE

available to dissidents in situations that usually benefit management: going private and partnership roll-up transactions.

The 1992 SEC proxy revision relaxed a prohibition on presolicitation communications that deterred formation of many dissident groups. Formerly, mere contacts among 10 or more shareholders constituted a proxy solicitation, even if the "solicitor" did not request that the others grant any voting authority. However, this rule intimidated big-block institutional investors, which feared their contacts might violate the proxy rules. Such contacts are now permitted without any requirement to disclose which other shareholders were contacted so long as voting authority is not solicited. Additionally, anyone may now announce his or her own voting intent publicly without an SEC filing. Media solicitations are also exempt if the written solicitation is filed.

The SEC's liberalization of institutional shareholder communications and executive compensation disclosures shifts some of the balance of power back to shareholders. The free exchange of views are permitted and coalitions can be formed to more effectively challenge management. However, management still has structural advantages that make insurgent proxy solicitations difficult for all but the most affluent, powerful, and well-connected dissidents. In recognition of this continuing imbalance in shareholder democracy, the SEC has established the mandatory small shareholder proposal process discussed next.

Mandatory Shareholder Proposals

An alternate shareholder solicitation method is available to small shareholders, who are usually unable to afford an independent proxy solicitation. The corporation must include certain reasonable shareholder proposals along with management's proxy solicitation at the corporation's expense. This alternative gives small shareholders at least some voice in corporate governance. However, the process was criticized in the 1960s because of harassment and grandstanding. Apparently, some small shareholders' proposals simply aired their personal political and social views. This led to significant SEC restriction of the process to only "serious" proposals. Shareholders using the process must have a serious financial interest in the corporation, such as owning a minimum of 1 percent or $1,000 worth of shares, and have held the shares for at least one year. Small shareholders are permitted only one proposal per year.

If management desires, it may limit shareholder proposals to only 500 words, including the proposal itself with all the supporting advocacy. Rebuttal by management to such shareholder proposals must be included in the proxy statement and forwarded promptly to the shareholder. Proposals that duplicate independent proposals or that have attracted weak support in prior years may be excluded. Shareholders must deliver their proposals more than 120 days before the date of the prior year's proxy release to permit management's analysis and the SEC's review if management excludes the proposal. Management may exclude a shareholder proposal under guidelines of SEC Rule 14a-8(c). Either the SEC or the shareholder may appeal management's exclusion.

SEC Guidelines: Rule 14a-8(c) Management Exclusion of Shareholder Proposals

1. Improper under state law (e.g., mandatory board directive).
2. Illegal.
3. Violates SEC rules.
4. Furthers personal grievance or pecuniary interest.
5. Unrelated to issuer's business.
6. Beyond issuer's power to implement.
7. Relates to ordinary business operations.
8. Relates to board election or censure of particular director.
9. Runs counter to another proposal.
10. Is moot.
11. Substantially duplicates another proposal.
12. Requires specific dividend declaration.

The SEC will no longer routinely designate shareholder proposals addressing executive compensation as "ordinary business decisions." In the past, management usually excluded such proposals, leaving executive compensation decisions to board subcommittees and outside pay consultants. This controversy, introduced in Chapter 42, erupted in the early 1990s over excessive top-management pay. Pressure is expected on many poorly performing corporations with rising and ambiguous executive compensation. There was criticism that this SEC rule encourages shareholder "micromanagement" of corporate affairs. However, SEC rules should not obstruct reasonable shareholder efforts to more closely tie executive compensation to investors' financial fortunes.

Institutional shareholders are becoming much more activist in proxy contests. This may be a reaction to the perceptions that (1) management has become isolated from market incentives, and (2) shareholder democracy and corporate performance diminishes while executive compensation continues rising. Independent and small shareholder proxy proposals have recently addressed corporate governance issues such as confidential shareholder voting, cumulative voting, staggered directors' terms, poison pills and other takeover defenses, shareholder voting equality, golden parachutes, and management compensation. Social issues have also been popular, including continued business with South Africa, Northern Ireland, and other nations perceived to have human rights violations, military issues, animal rights, and discontinuation of corporate political action committees (PACs).

Some proxy issues are resolved through **proxy settlements** made between management and insurgent solicitors who threaten divisive proxy contests. While settlements may resolve issues more efficiently, they are clouded in secrecy. This may actually pervert shareholder democracy if management uses corporate resources to pay off dissidents with greenmail and silence them with **standstill** agreements. All of this occurs outside shareholder scrutiny. Nevertheless, many recent settlements seem advantageous to all parties by avoiding the cost of protracted proxy campaigns.

Proxy Rule Enforcement

Participants in proxy contests may be held liable under SEC proxy rules and for proxy fraud. SEC Rule 14a-9 generally prohibits false and misleading statements in proxy materials and in the "total mix" of communications made to shareholders. The solicitations of proxy contestants imply a form of trust, leading shareholders to expect that their best interests are represented.[14] Therefore, there is liability for negligent and intentional misrepresentations made in proxy statements, SEC filings, or other communications, creating great potential liability. This liability extends to negligent disclosures in the annual report, which is considered part of management's proxy statement. Certain foreign issuers, public utility holding companies, and issuers in bankruptcy reorganization are exempt. The courts are continuing to reinforce the point made in the following classic case that only material misrepresentations are actionable as proxy fraud.[15] The standard of **materiality** announced here is applicable in all other securities law contexts: registration statement misstatements, periodic disclosure fraud, and extraordinary disclosures of tender offers, merger negotiations, or other matters.

---

[14]See *Virginia Bankshares, Inc. v. Sandberg,* 111 S.Ct. 2749 (1991). (Board's qualitative and conclusory recommendation to approve freezeout merger in proxy solicitation actionable as proxy fraud; no private right of action where definite causation lacking.)

[15]See *Mendell v. Greenberg,* 927 F.2d 667 (2d Cir. 1990). (Failure to disclose speculative tax impact of merger on selling shareholder not proxy fraud.)

TSC INDUSTRIES, INC., v. NORTHWAY, INC.
426 U.S. 438 (1976)

National Industries acquired 34 percent of TSC Industries' voting shares and then placed five of National's nominees on TSC's board. The new board proposed a sale of all TSC's assets to National. The buyout of remaining TSC shareholders would be made with National preferred stock and warrants. Both corporations issued a joint proxy statement urging shareholder approval. TSC was liquidated and dissolved after shareholder approval.

Northway sued, claiming that the TSC proxy statement was false and misleading in several respects. It failed to state that National's president was on the TSC board when proxies were solicited and that National might be deemed a parent of TSC under SEC rules. It failed to note some "bad news" in a letter from an investment banker concerning the size of the premium that TSC shareholders would receive in the exchange transaction. A final omission was that a mutual fund, on whose board a National employee sat, made large purchases of National before the exchange transaction. However, the TSC proxy statements admitted National's substantial influence over TSC. Northway alleged that disclosure of these factors might have indicated a conspiracy to manipulate National's price upward to make the transaction appear favorable to TSC shareholders. The Court of Appeals found the omissions were material.

MARSHALL, Justice

The question of materiality, it is universally agreed, is an objective one, involving the significance of an omitted or misrepresented fact to a reasonable investor. Variations in the formulation of a general test of materiality occur in the articulation of just how significant a fact must be or, put another way, how certain it must be that the fact would affect a reasonable investor's judgment.

The disclosure policy embodied in the proxy regulations is not without limit. Some information is of such dubious significance that insistence on its disclosure may accomplish more harm than good. The potential liability for a Rule 14a-9 violation can be great indeed, and if the standard of materiality is unnecessarily low, not only may the corporation and its management be subjected to liability for insignificant omissions or misstatements, but also management's fear of exposing itself to substantial liability may cause it simply to bury the shareholders in an avalanche of trivial information.

The general standard of materiality that we think best comports with the policies of Rule 14a-9 is as follows: An omitted fact is material if there is a substantial likelihood that a reasonable shareholder would consider it important in deciding how to vote. This standard is fully consistent with Mill's general description of materiality as a requirement that "the defect have a significant propensity to affect the voting process." It does not require proof of a substantial likelihood that disclosure of the omitted fact would have caused the reasonable investor to change his vote. What the standard does contemplate is a substantial likelihood that, under all the circumstances, the omitted fact would have assumed actual significance in the deliberations of the reasonable shareholder. Put another way, there must be a substantial likelihood that the disclosure of the omitted fact would have been viewed by the reasonable investor as having significantly altered the "total mix" of information made available.

Rule 14a-9 is concerned only with whether a proxy statement is misleading with respect to its presentation of material facts. If there was no collusion or manipulation whatsoever in the National and Madison purchases—that is, if the purchases were made wholly independently for proper corporate and investment purposes, then by Northway's implicit acknowledgment they had no bearing on the soundness and reliability of the market prices listed in the proxy statement, and it cannot have been materially misleading to fail to disclose them.

Case Questions

1. What is the issue in determining whether a fact is material for purposes of the antifraud provisions of the securities laws?

2. For what reasons does liability under the antifraud provisions arise only when misstatements or omissions are material? What danger is there if misstatements appear in a proxy statement?

3. What other standards of materiality may be used in related fields such as in auditing? In what ways do these standards differ?

TENDER OFFERS

There was a wave of conglomerate mergers in the 1960s that prompted U.S. financiers to adapt the British "takeover bid" to become the U.S. tender offer. **Tender offers** are not well defined but typically involve a publicly announced offer to purchase a large stake, often a controlling interest, in a target issuer in exchange for cash, securities, or a combination of consideration. If the bidder is successful, the target can be merged into the bidder, operated as a subsidiary, restructured, or sold off in pieces to pay for the acquisition. For example, Chevron (Standard Oil of California) merged with Gulf Oil Co. after Chevron's successful tender offer for Gulf shares. Tender offers were used in hostile takeovers because they are generally made without the support of the target's management. As discussed in Chapter

43, with the exceptions of Great Britain, Canada, and the United States, laws and cultural practices in most foreign nations view hostile takeovers negatively. For example, most European and Japanese laws impede takeovers and mergers that are not amicably negotiated.

Tender offers occur very quickly, affording little time for careful evaluation by target shareholders. Before Congress regulated tender offers in 1968, shareholders were often stampeded into tendering without due consideration. This largely favors Wall Street arbitrageurs and seriously disadvantages individual shareholders living outside the financial centers. The **Williams Act** amended the 1934 Act to improve tender offer disclosure and slow the process so all shareholders can better assess it. Tender offers are one of the several corporate acquisition methods discussed in Chapter 43 that enable participation in the market for corporate control.

Williams Act Notification

The Williams Act balances incumbent management's power with a bidder's natural advantage. Quick tender offers have panicked shareholders to accept a partial tender offer. Tender offer bidders are usually willing to pay a premium for a bare controlling block in the first round of a two-tier tender offer. Nontendering shareholders realize they may be forced later to participate in a lower-priced merger or second-tier tender offer. Therefore, shareholders tender quickly to avoid receiving lower compensation paid on the ''back end.'' After considerable experience in the 1960s with this technique, Congress passed the Williams Act to slow this process and require equal treatment of all shareholders.

The Williams Act requires two disclosures by tender offerors. **Schedule 13D** provides an early warning to management and the market that a potential bidder has accumulated the target's shares. All shareholders holding 5 percent of any equity security after they acquire 2 percent or more of any registered equity security if the purchase results in the ownership of 5 percent or more must disclose this fact. The purchaser's identity and background must be disclosed, including the source and amounts of funds used, the number of shares owned, any contracts concerning the issuer's securities (e.g., options), and any present or likely future plans to control the target. Inadvertent or unintentional non-

compliance is not improper if the 5 percent shareholder notifies the SEC and refrains from making a tender offer.[16] The EC has an *antiraider* directive requiring disclosure of stock transfers equal to 10 percent or more of publicly listed companies.

When a bidder begins a tender offer, a **Schedule 14D-1** ''tender offer statement'' must be filed with the SEC, telephoned to the exchanges, and hand-delivered to the issuer. In addition to information contained in a Schedule 13D, the tender offer bidder must describe any negotiations with the issuer (e.g., takeover overtures), state the bidder's purpose and plans for the target, fully describe the tender offer terms, include copies of related letters to shareholders or press releases, and include certain bidders' financial statements. The target's management must respond quickly with its own **Schedule 14D-9** advising shareholders of management's evaluation of the tender offer. The market was often volatile during the takeover boom of the 1980s, bidding up prices of potential takeover targets right after 5 percent shareholders first appeared.

What Is a Tender Offer?

Both the Williams Act and the SEC have failed to define tender offers precisely. Nevertheless, some sense of the term can be derived from cases and SEC interpretations.[17] A **tender offer** generally involves a widespread public announcement and solicitation of shareholders; it is not privately negotiated. Tender offer bidders usually attempt to acquire a large block of shares quickly by paying a non-negotiable premium over the prevailing market price. Tender offers remain open for only a short time and create some pressure on shareholders to sell. The block sought need not be a majority, although it often constitutes effective control.

The tender offer bidder may make an offer contingent on receiving sufficient shares tendered to constitute control. If less than the desired number are tendered, the bidder may terminate the tender offer and refuse to purchase any shares tendered. In a few cases, a tender offeror has immediately negotiated private purchases without further Williams Act compliance. For example, this tactic was ap-

---

[16]*Rondeau v. Mosinee Paper Corp.,* 422 U.S. 49 (1975).

[17]*Wellman v. Dickinson,* 475 F.Supp. 783 (S.D.N.Y. 1979) *aff'd* 682 F.2d 355 (2d Cir. 1982) *cert. denied* 460 U.S. 1069 (1983).

proved in *Hanson Trust PLC v. SCM Corp.*,[18] effectively exempting these so-called **street sweeps** from the Williams Act tender offer rules. However, the SEC opposes street sweeps, believing that they exert pressures on shareholders similar to tender offers.

Tender Offer Mechanics

Although the press eagerly reports tender offers, the tender offeror must also file Schedule 14D-1 with the SEC and personally communicate the offer to all shareholders. The proxy rules are adapted to require the target corporation's management to either provide a list of shareholder names and addresses to the tender offeror or distribute the tender offer notice at the tender offeror's expense. If a list is provided, the number or percentage of shares held may not be disclosed or the bidder might concentrate efforts on large-block holders, frustrating the Williams Act's equal opportunity principle.

While most Williams Act regulations are disclosures, a few have substantive requirements. Tender offers must remain open for a minimum of 20 days. If more shares are tendered than requested, they must be purchased on a pro rata basis. This may result in some shares being held by all tendering shareholders after the purchase. If insufficient shares are tendered, the offeror can withdraw the offer or raise the price to entice more shareholders to tender. However, all tendering shareholders must receive any such price increase. The tender offer rules are designed to prevent shareholder haste or any preference given to early tenderors or big-block holders friendly to the offeror. Tendering shareholders may withdraw their shares, effectively *revoking acceptance* of the tender offer, during the 15 days following their tender or until the offeror accepts the tendered shares for payment.

Tender Offer Restrictions

Numerous activities are prohibited during a tender offer. It is illegal for the bidder to trade in the target's securities during a tender offer. Such trading could pressure the target's stock price and constitute illegal manipulation. Tender offer insider trading is made illegal by SEC Rule 14e-3. However, this rule is worded to prohibit trading during a tender offer while merely possessing nonpublic information. The validity of prohibiting tender offer insider trading under SEC Rule 14e-3 was confirmed in *U.S. v. Chestman*,[19] even if the practice is not based on the misappropriation theory. It is also illegal to **short tender** shares borrowed by the tenderor. This is considered a manipulative device probably intended to yield a profit from the difference between a lower price when purchased later and the higher tender offer price.

Parking

It is illegal to engage in **stock parking,** where one party intentionally disguises stock beneficially owned by encouraging an accomplice to make the actual purchase. For example, a potential bidder interested in a takeover might hide its substantial stock ownership by holding less than 5 percent while other individuals hold large blocks for the potential bidder. The bidder avoids filing a Schedule 13D until the tender offer is made, which signals the accomplices to tender their parked shares. The parking bidder may expect such assistance from accomplices as repayment for prior favors, or the parker may implicitly promise to reimburse stock losses while the stock is parked.

Some critics view stock parking as a mere "technical violation" of the 13D reporting rule. However, it constitutes manipulation and fraud when done intentionally to conceal the potential bidder's takeover intentions from the target and from the market. Parking artificially depresses prices enabling the bidder to control a large block before the market can bid up the target's price after it is "in play." Clearly, the intent to conduct stock parking is difficult to prove unless someone admits to the scheme. Parking is also illegal to create bogus tax losses, evade broker's net capital requirements, or manipulate prices by creating the appearance of trading activity.

Tender Offer Liability

Violators of the tender offer rules may be held liable for fraud, failure to file schedules when required, and manipulative acts. The SEC, shareholders, tar-

---

[18]*Hanson Trust PLC v. SCM Corp.*, 774 F.2d 47 (2d Cir. 1985).

[19]*U.S. v. Chestman,* 947 F.2d 551 (2d Cir. 1991) in banc, *cert. denied* 112 S.Ct. 1759 (1992).

get corporation, competing bidders, or the tender offeror may have the right to enforce the tender offer rules. Injunctions and damage actions may be appropriate. Section 14(c) imposes antifraud rules similar to SEC Rule 10b-5. The SEC has expanded enforcement authority and power to refer egregious cases to the Justice Department for criminal prosecution.

Going Private

There are special duties on management when it makes a tender offer for outstanding shares to take the issuer private in a LBO or MBO. Management must disclose if it intends to make its own tender offer to compete with an outsider's tender offer. Going private may permit management to suspend public financial reporting and compliance with the 1934 Act and proxy rules, thereby reducing its costs and blocking public scrutiny of the corporation's confidential activities. The going private corporation will seek **delisting** from all exchanges on which its securities traded. Delisting requires notice and sometimes a hearing because it clearly reduces shareholder liquidity. A different matter arises when the SEC issues a **temporary suspension of trading.** This may be necessary when an orderly market cannot be maintained pending an announcement of important news if unverified rumors are affecting prices.

The final step in going private is the **termination of SEC registration,** permitted only after the number of security holders falls below 300. Termination occurs 90 days after notice to the SEC. Financial reporting may be discontinued only if the issuer has no outstanding class of publicly traded securities, debt or equity. There has been considerable controversy over the potential breach of fiduciary duty when managers take their firms private. Allegedly, the management group has an incentive to withhold disclosure of favorable plans, thereby keeping stock price low during the going private buyout. This may permit it to profit by going public again a few years later at higher prices.

REGULATION OF THE SECURITIES BUSINESS

The securities laws impact more than issuers, investors, and underwriters. There are substantial regulations on market operations and trading practices applicable to market intermediaries such as brokers, dealers, investment advisers, and financial planners. This section discusses these public and private regulatory schemes.

Broker-Dealer Regulation

All brokers and dealers must be registered, either with the SEC for the securities business or with the CFTC in the commodity futures business. **Brokers** are agents who effect transactions on the exchanges or the OTC market for client-customers. Brokers are compensated by commission. Commodity brokers are called **futures commission merchants.** By contrast, **dealers** trade ''for their own account,'' making a wholesaler's profit on the *spread* between acquisition and resale prices. **Floor traders** at the exchanges are also registered. Brokers in municipal securities are regulated by the **Municipal Securities Rulemaking Board.** The primary dealers in U.S. government securities are selected and monitored by the Treasury Department, although their activities came under SEC scrutiny after a 1991 scandal.

The various exchanges are also regulated by the SEC and CFTC. The exchanges participate in regulating their member firms, floor traders, and brokers. The exchanges, NASD, FASB, state CPA societies, and state bar associations are considered **self-regulatory organizations (SRO).** SROs are responsible for much of their members' licensing and oversight. SROs license, discipline, and debar members for inappropriate behavior or negligent client service. The SROs have an intimate understanding of their professions, making them particularly appropriate self-regulators. The securities markets have had much success with *private self-regulation* such as in other professions (e.g., medicine, law, accounting, engineering, and architecture). However, critics suggest discipline is lax, so self-interested professional regulation must be balanced by government.

Financial Condition

Brokers and dealers are somewhat like banks — they cannot successfully operate without considerable working capital. Customers' assets should not be jeopardized while held by brokers as collateral or for customers' convenience. The 1934 Act requires accurate recordkeeping, filing annual financial reports (FOCUS reports) with the SEC, and maintenance of the minimum **net capital requirements.** These are minimum net worth measures comparable to bank reserves. **Hypothecation** is a pledge of securities held in street name to a lender for loans made to the broker. This practice is permissible when the broker loans the customer funds to purchase the securities. However, it is illegal without the customer's permission. Hypothecation endangers the broker's financial condition, and the customer loses priority for return of the hypothecated securities if the broker becomes insolvent.

Conflicts of Interest

Brokers act as agents to their customers. Brokers owe fiduciary duties in executing securities transactions, giving investment advice, and safeguarding customers' securities. The securities laws specifically address several natural broker conflicts of interest. The **shingle theory** sets minimum standards for brokers' fair treatment of customers. When the broker commences business by "hanging out the shingle," the broker impliedly warrants fair dealing, the disclosure of conflicts, and relevant information, and must make forthright truthful statements and provide competent service.

The **know thy customer rule** requires the broker to fully assess each customer's financial condition and investment objectives so that only uniquely suitable recommendations are made. This duty has prompted most brokers to complete rather extensive questionnaires providing financial profiles of new customers before a new account is opened. The **suitability** duty is violated by "boiler room" operations involving high-pressure direct-mail or brokers' "cold calls," when inadequate or false information is provided about investments.

Congress reacted to similar marketing abuses in the penny stock market by passing the **Penny Stock Reform Act** in 1990. There were many high-pressure sales of cheap stocks (under $5) by dealers who made excessive markups even by those who already charged a commission. Additionally, inadequate information was often given and unsuitable recommendations made for these largely unknown and risky penny stocks. The act gives the SEC power to bar penny stock brokers from the business, prohibits brokerage firms from hiring barred brokers, and requires disclosure of bid/ask prices and penny stock risks. Disciplinary histories of penny stock brokers must be made available to investors via 800 numbers. Many observers believe this law effectively kills the penny stock market, depriving risky startup firms of an important capital source. The Vancouver Stock Exchange in Canada has just such a reputation for risky, cheap, startup stocks.

A recurring broker conflict involves the incentive to encourage customers' habitual trading just to generate commission income. **Churning** is excessive trading in a discretionary trading account in which the customer trusts the broker to trade whenever and whatever is "needed." Courts examine the number and frequency of trades, repeated transaction in the same security, short holding periods, numerous unprofitable or unauthorized trades, unsophisticated customers, and trading between various customer accounts. Another method of churning is the broker's issuance of **false confirmations,** written billings showing unordered trades. Inattentive customers unwittingly accept the unwanted trading activity. Churning is illegal and an ethical issue because the broker controls the customer's financial fortunes and stands to profit personally from the trading authority entrusted to the broker.

Broker-Dealer Insider Trading

Broker-dealers have numerous insider trading and tipping opportunities. Sometimes, brokers are tempted to label their recommendations to customers as "privileged" or as coming from an "inside track." There is extensive experience with insider trading prosecutions against multiservice financial institutions that include separate divisions for broker-dealers and investment banking. This experience has led to specific regulations requiring adequate supervision of brokers.

The **supervision** duty requires the superiors of broker-dealers to establish oversight and control procedures that (1) ensure compliance with the securities laws, (2) enforce the broker's shingle duty, (3) prohibit the quotation of prices for unregistered securities and (4) minimize the opportunities for insider trading and tipping. For example, the brokerage sales staff must learn the securities laws, management may need to periodically review broker correspondence, codes of conduct must be installed and actively enforced, and Chinese walls must be installed at multiservice financial institutions.

A **Chinese wall** includes control procedures to prevent dissemination of inside information from departments that create or access inside information to the broker-dealers who might trade on or tip confidential information. The term is derived from the "Great Wall of China" which so effectively separated China from outside influences. Internal policies and procedures should be installed to prevent trading or making customer recommendations based on confidential information. For example, the identities of takeover targets generated by the investment banking unit of a multiservice financial institution are regularly placed on **restricted lists,** prohibiting broker-dealers from recommending listed securities to customers. Physical isolation of these different divisions into different locations and different cities helps inhibit tipping conversations among employees.

Securities Arbitration

The securities laws and SRO disciplinary rules permit SEC administrative discipline of broker-dealers, including censure, suspension, debarment, civil penalties, and imprisonment in egregious cases. Additionally, there are private rights of action awarding damages to customers injured by a broker-dealer's violation of the antifraud rules or other restrictions discussed above. However, two trends are limiting customers' rights to sue. First, the courts are narrowing the scope of private remedies except where the law clearly protects individual customers by permitting private suits. Second, most brokerage account agreements include arbitration clauses for customer disputes. Early courts permitted suit despite these arbitration clauses. However, *Shearson/American Express v. McMahon*[20] implemented Congress's intent to encourage arbitration as an alternative dispute resolution method.

The SEC oversees the SROs' operation of securities arbitration. Arbitration panels conduct trial-like hearings but with fewer costly legal safeguards than in litigation. Both parties may be represented by counsel. Arbitration generally is less public, nonappealable, and less costly than litigation. However, there is a trend to increase prearbitration discovery, raising costs closer to litigation. Arbitrators are only beginning to disclose their decisionmaking reasoning. Arbitration panels are generally composed of three members, one representing the securities industry and the other two representing the general public. Arbitration clauses must be clearly highlighted and their impact explained to customers. Despite these safeguards, there is significant evidence that arbitration favors broker-dealers when compared with litigation. Nevertheless, arbitrators generally have professional expertise in the brokerage business and arbitration has reduced the costs of customer disputes dramatically.

Investment Advisors

The Investment Advisor Act of 1940 was intended to correct the abuse of client-advisees by the "unscrupulous tipsters and touts" who stigmatized that profession in the past. **Investment advisors** are persons who charge a fee to advise others, directly or through published analyses and reports, on the value of securities or on the advisability of investing in, purchasing, or selling securities. Investment advisors must register with the SEC and disclose certain information about their background and business practices. Investment advisors are fiduciaries who must follow minimum standards of conduct, refrain from conflicts of interest, and may only recommend securities suitable for clients' individual circumstances. **Scalping** is an advisors recommendation of securities the advisor owns. It can move the price upward, permitting the advisor to make a personal profit. Scalping is an illegal form of market manipulation.

The act exempts the advisory services of broker-dealers, bank recommendations to trust customers, and the advice of lawyers, accountants, engineers, and teachers when given incidentally to other services. Also exempt are wholly intrastate advisories, advisories made to only insurance companies, and advisors with less than 15 clients. The First Amendment protects investment advisory newsletters if published regularly and given general circulation.[21]

Financial planners are generally exempt from investment advisor regulation as long as they make no particular securities investment recommendations. Many financial planners provide other services (e.g., personal budgeting, asset management) and recommendations (e.g., purchases of insurance and annuities), so they can remain exempt from registration under the act. However, care must be taken to avoid making securities recommendations unless the financial planner is also a registered investment advisor. There are pressures to regulate financial planning by requiring disclosure of conflicts, compensation, and experience; testing and certification

---

[20]*Shearson/American Express v. McMahon*, 482 U.S. 220 (1987).

[21]*Lowe v. SEC*, 472 U.S. 181 (1985).

of professional skills; and periodic inspections. Numerous SROs are emerging to certify and regulate financial planning.

Trading Practices and Irregularities

The securities markets are evolving towards Congress's grand vision of a **national market system.** Indeed, an even broader ''international market system'' is permitting near unconstrained flows of capital over national boundaries. These trends are accelerated by the reduction of national barriers to broker-dealer operations, the proliferation of computerized 24-hour cross-border screen-based quotation and order execution systems, and securities trading by the world's largest firms on other nations' exchanges. Another trend is the *institutionalization* of the markets by large institutional investors: pension funds, mutual funds, insurance companies, and investment banks. Over half of corporate securities are held by institutions that conduct over two thirds of all trades. Of course, individuals participate indirectly through their interests in financial institutions. However, in this changing environment, securities regulators are reexamining the regulation of trading practices and manipulation to harmonize the world's securities markets.

The Enforcement Remedies and Penny Stock Reform Act of 1990 empowered the president to close down the markets in emergencies. Many observers convinced Congress that this power and the restriction of program trading could prevent another sharp market decline such as occurred in October 1987. **Program trading** takes many forms; the best known is *index arbitrage.* Trades are made in a group of individual stocks that comprise some stock index on the New York exchange. Simultaneously, offsetting trades are made in that index's futures contract on the Chicago futures exchange. Small differences in their comparative prices give risk-free profits. The large size of such transactions arguably distorts the market. The exchanges have introduced **circuit breakers** to prohibit program trading if market prices make significant moves within any one day.

Market Manipulation
Prevention of market manipulation was a major purpose of the original securities laws. The practice reportedly occurred quite frequently during the Roaring Twenties. Manipulation undermines the free-market forces of supply and demand, weakening the market's integrity as a fair place for investment and capital raising. **Market manipulation** includes various forms of intentional interference with free markets. Typically, the manipulator attempts to set, stabilize, raise, or lower the market price prevailing for single stocks or for groups of securities, or intentionally affects trading volume. Manipulation is an ethical dilemma because investors are intentionally misled that the market price represents the true indication of value.

Enforcement efforts directed at manipulation suffer from some obvious difficulties in distinguishing legitimate trades from prohibited trades intended solely to influence price, volume, or the appearance of trading. Several provisions of the 1933 and 1934 acts prohibit market manipulation, including SEC Rule 10b-5. Enforcement against manipulative schemes is often based on stock exchange computers tracking unusual trading activities, FBI wiretaps, long-distance and cellular phone records, trading records, testimony of witnesses, and participants' confessions. Additionally, SROs and various enforcement agencies exchange investigatory leads and evidence to enhance their efforts.

There are simple and complex methods of manipulation. Large, single trades give the appearance of heightened supply or demand. Series of trades at successively higher or lower prices give the appearance of genuine price movements and enhanced demand. Transactions in options and derivative securities may also reinforce the manipulators' illegal scheme. False disclosures or rumors reinforce investors' perceptions. Combinations of several such devices and coordinated activities by groups of coconspirators enhance manipulation. However, such conspiracies are more easily detected.

Fictitious transactions are sometimes made with **matched orders:** The manipulator makes near simultaneous purchase and sale orders of the same size and price. Such sales are often hidden through different brokers as prearranged **wash sales. Marking the close** is a trade made higher or lower than the prevailing price near the close of daily trading. It gives an appearance of late price movement and can affect the following day's trading prices or volumes. A series of trades made by conspirators at successively higher prices is **bull raiding. Bear raiding** is the opposite—prearranged transactions at successively lower prices. Raiding is intensified by rumors that reinforce the appearance that the price movements are legitimate.

Frontrunning includes a group of manipulative schemes similar to insider trading. For example, a broker-dealer may purchase stock for its own account just before executing a large customer order that is expected to move the price upward. Another form of frontrunning is the broker-dealer's trade just before announcing a market-moving buy or sell recommendation in that stock. The practice is similar to an investment adviser's scalping.

Stabilization includes efforts to prevent price movements. It is illegal except during an IPO, where it is considered ''necessary to prevent a decline in the open market price of the security being distributed'' and thereby make the IPO a success, the preeminent goal. Stabilization occurs daily in many European markets, where it is justified to prevent panic. The central banks of many nations regularly ''intervene'' in the currency markets to ''prop up'' a declining currency's value, another form of stabilization. Stabilization is still manipulation because it disguises the market's true sentiment. Some investment banking syndicate members withhold portions of a popular-selling IPO, called **hot issues.** As demand for the artificially constrained volume of shares inflates the price, syndicate members trickle out sales, making higher profits on the spread. This practice is manipulative and illegal.

Commodity Futures Manipulation

It is also illegal to manipulate the commodity futures markets. The CEA prohibits manipulation of commodity prices, cornering a commodity, or causing false rumors or crop reports that affect the price of commodities. Manipulation includes intentional schemes to profit primarily from the market impact of the trader's own actions that induce an ''artificial price'' not reflecting market forces. False rumors and matched transactions are also illegal under the CEA.

An illegal **corner** involves gaining control over substantially all the deliverable supply of the commodity or asset underlying a futures contract to force others to purchase at inflated prices. Many futures investors have *short positions* and usually close out their futures contracts just before the expiration date approaches. However, if there are *squeeze conditions*, the shorts must scramble to arrange for actual physical delivery of the underlying commodity. It is illegal to squeeze the shorts by buying up deliverable supply or take other manipulative actions that cause the price of the futures or underlying com-

modities to rise with a view to extracting higher prices. As the securities and commodities markets become linked through derivative instruments, these unique features of commodities manipulation are also becoming manipulative schemes in the securities markets.

END–OF–CHAPTER QUESTIONS

1. There is significant controversy over the value of insider trading enforcement. What reasons support enforcement efforts against insider trading? What reasons support reducing enforcement efforts against insider trading? Reconcile these arguments and synthesize the remaining unresolved issue.

2. Explain what is meant by the ''market for corporate control.'' For what reasons are corporate managements apprehensive about this market?

3. Foremost-McKesson purchased the assets of Provident Securities Co. with over $4 million in cash and nearly $50 million in convertible debentures. Half the debentures were registered for public sale, with the proceeds paid to Provident, and the other half were distributed directly to Provident shareholders in exchange for their Provident stock. If all Provident's debentures were converted, Provident would become a 10 percent shareholder under Section 16. What constitutes the purchase of equity shares by Provident? What constitutes the sale? Must Provident be a 10 percent shareholder at both the time of purchase and sale to be restricted by the Section 16 short-swing profit rule? See *Foremost-McKesson, Inc. v. Provident Securities Co.*, 423 U.S. 232 (1976).

4. Chestman, a stockbroker, received a tip that A&P would make a tender offer for Waldbaum stock. The tip was originally transferred from the CEO of Waldbaum through the CEO's sister, to her daughter, through her daughter's husband, and ultimately to Chestman. The husband sought Chestman's advice on whether to make the tender. The sister and daughter agreed to secrecy but the husband never accepted

any duty of confidentiality. Is Chestman liable for misappropriation of inside information in trading on the tip? See *U.S. v. Chestman*, 947 F.2d 551 (2d Cir. 1991) in banc, *cert.denied* 112 S.Ct. 1759 (1992).

5. Discuss the issue, underlying reasons, and assumptions used in adopting the fraud on the market theory. What is the primary ambiguity in its implementation? See *Basic v. Levinson*, 485 U.S. 224 (1988).

6. Courtois and Antoniu worked at two different Wall Street investment banking firms in merger and acquisition advisory work for takeover bidder clients. Newman received numerous tips of impending takeover bids from these two individuals, transferred these tips to two others, and all three made secretive trades in numerous takeover targets. All three profited after public announcement of the takeovers, selling their stock in the targets. What are the issues in an insider trading case against Newman? For what reason is Newman liable for illegal insider trading? See *U.S. v. Newman*, 664 F.2d 12 (2d Cir. 1981).

7. Assume the facts in Question 6 except that Newman's tippees already held stock in some of the takeover targets. The tips caused them to refrain from selling before the takeover announcements. Comment on the insider trading liability of Newman and the two other tippees.

8. Consider each of the following shareholder proposals a small shareholder seeks to include with management's proxy solicitation. What general reasons could management use to exclude any of these proposals? Next, comment on the specific reasons management might use to exclude the particular proposal.
   a. Management must begin disclosing the substance of its negotiations with this shareholder's affiliated personal business; the corporation granted the contract to a competitor of the shareholder's business.
   b. Management must cease doing its small amount of business with Yugoslavia because of that nation's alleged human rights violations. See *In re Mobil Corp.*, [1981 Transfer Binder] Fed.Sec.L.Rep. (CCH) para.76,832 (1981).
   c. The board must declare special dividends in addition to the current level of regular dividends.
   d. The board's compensation committee must immediately undertake a study of CEO salaries at competitors. Excessive portions of the officers' salaries at the corporation must be refunded to the corporation. A new by law requiring shareholder approval of executive compensation must be approved each year.

If any of the above are excluded, what alternative actions can the shareholder take?

9. An unsophisticated investor was lured into frequent trades in OTC stocks by the broker. The broker would regularly mark up the securities 15 to 40 percent over its acquisition costs and additionally charge a commission on the sale. These stocks posed excessive risks for the customer and the frequent trading wiped out any potential profitability. Does this violate any broker-dealer duties? Explain. See *Charles Hughes & Co. v. SEC*, 139 F.2d 434 (2d Cir. 1943).

10. A well-known financier is secretly accumulating stock in ABCorp. not quite up to the 5 percent limit. The financier encouraged several associated Wall Street arbitrageurs to do likewise. During this period, the group spread false rumors that ABCorp. had lost a key defense contract to its rivals. This news artificially depressed ABCorp.'s price, enabling the group to accumulate a controlling block more cheaply. What securities laws have been violated? For what reasons are these laws in existence?

Part XI

Trade Regulation

■

Chapter 46

Restraints of Trade and Monopolies

■

CRITICAL THINKING INQUIRIES

As you read this chapter, you should be able to address the following:

- How does antitrust legislation impact business and our economy?
- Distinguish between the rule of reason and per se violations.
- What do unreasonable restraints of trade and monopolies have in common?
- Analyze the tests for unlawful monopolization.
- Examine a world without antitrust legislation.

MANAGERIAL PERSPECTIVE

Benton Hauser, the new territorial division manager of Computer Graphics of America, will be attending the Computer Trade Association convention, of which Computer Graphics is a member. On the Association's agenda are such topics as pricing, new products, demographic information, and licensing agreements.

Additionally, Computer Graphics has a virtual monopoly on a computer-enhanced animated graphic system it developed for use in the building industry. Computer Graphics is expanding its operations and desires to set up dealer outlets and franchising operations in an effort to discourage other companies from entering this market.

- How far can the association go before violating laws against unreasonable restraints of trade?
- How far can Computer Graphics go before it is in violation of laws against monopolies?

The maxim "Ignorance of the law is no excuse" certainly holds true in this area of restraints of trade and monopolies. Reliance on legal counsel in this "sophisticated" realm is, of course, important. Yet, it is no substitute for a solid understanding of those activities that may cause antitrust problems to the firm.

The economic systems of most modern societies are organized around one of two basic models: the state-planned economy and free enterprise. A **state-planned economy** is one based on public ownership of property with centralized production and distribution of goods. Under this system, the allocation of resources is planned by the state, or a small group of people, which makes economic choices for the masses. This is the system that is adopted in one form or another in communist countries.

The American economic system is based on **free enterprise.** The prevailing economic philosophy in this country, and in many others, is that freedom to compete in the market results in operating efficiencies and consumer welfare. Antitrust legislation, the subject of this chapter, is aimed at safeguarding free enterprise by punishing firms and individuals whose business practices undermine the freedom to enter and compete in American markets.

In the last half of the 19th century, the American public became enraged at business practices that led to the concentration of power in the hands of a few elite industrialists. Large corporations were using the trust as a secret device to control the oil, sugar, cotton, and whiskey industries, and thus eliminate competition. A **trust** is an arrangement whereby owners of stock in a company transfer their interests to trustees who are granted the right of management control. Concentrating control of an industry's major corporations in trustees gave the trustees the power to fix prices, divvy up territories, and, in essence, engage in anticompetitive practices. This they did with zeal, and because of coercive practices directed toward smaller businesses, the public's outcry for reform was pronounced.

State antitrust regulation proved ineffective to mitigate the power of the trusts. Congress, therefore, responded by passing legislation designed to curb the trust and preserve free competition. In 1890, Congress enacted the Sherman Antitrust Act (often referred to as the Sherman Act), and in 1914, the Clayton Act. The Clayton Act is the subject of the next chapter. This chapter explores the Sherman

Antitrust Act. Section 1 of the act restricts unreasonable restraints of trade. Section 2 prohibits monopolization and attempts to monopolize.

UNREASONABLE RESTRAINTS

> Every contract, combination . . . or conspiracy, in restraint of trade or commerce among the several states . . . is declared to be illegal. . . .

Section 1 of the Sherman Act requires a contract, combination, or conspiracy. The phrase *contract, combination, or conspiracy* involves joint and concerted action. Therefore, two or more offenders must be present to violate this section of the act. There must be joint or concerted action; unilateral action will not constitute a violation. A corporation cannot conspire with itself. Neither can a company conspire with its wholly owned subsidiary because they actually have a "unity of purpose or a common design."[1]

A strict, literal interpretation of section 1 would lead to the conclusion that every contract is illegal. In essence, every contract restrains trade. Assume, for example, that Jim enters into a contractual agreement with Computer Graphics to purchase a system. Now Jim is no longer in the market for a computer graphics system. The price and terms of the sale between Jim and Computer Graphics are legally fixed. However, Congress obviously did not intend this type of contract to be a violation of section 1. Not every contract in restraint of trade is a violation of section 1 — only unreasonable restraints of trade.

Rule of Reason

Common law prohibitions against restraints of trade existed even before the enactment of the federal antitrust acts. Actions restraining competition constituted torts, and certain agreements in restraint of trade were unenforceable.

The **covenant not to compete** (discussed in Chapter 15) was a common form of restraint of trade courts considered under common law principles. A

---

[1]*Copperweld Corp. v. Independence Tube Corp.*, 467 U.S. 752 (1984).

Figure 46−1 Rule of Reason Acronym

Rule of Reason Elements	Rule of Reason Explanation
Purpose	Desired end
Intent	Motivation
Power	Market power
Effect	Economic impact

Figure 46−2 Horizontal and Vertical Relationships

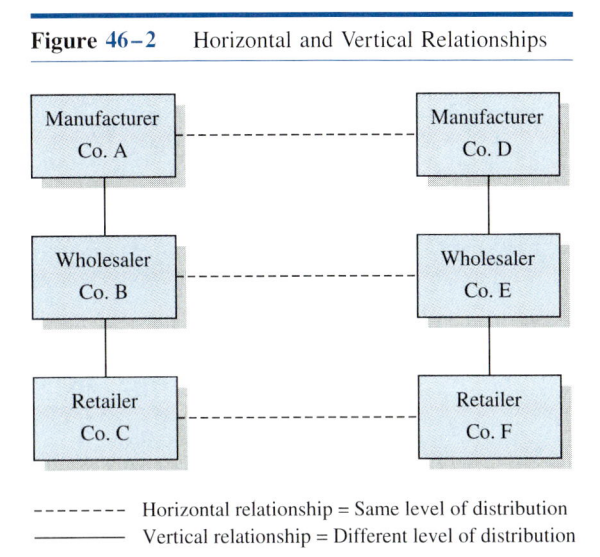

------- Horizontal relationship = Same level of distribution
———— Vertical relationship = Different level of distribution

covenant not to compete is an agreement whereby one person agrees not to compete against another. These covenants are often found in contracts involving the sale of a business. For example, assume that Lil Buyer desires to purchase a beauty shop owned by Frank Seller. Lil wants to ensure that after the sale Frank will not open up a competing beauty shop and draw away all of the customers. Therefore, she negotiates the contract to include a clause whereby Frank agrees not to open up a competing shop.

Under the common law, courts were prone to enforce a provision such as the one between Frank and Lil as long as the restriction was reasonable as to geographics and time. For example, a clause prohibiting Frank from competing anywhere in the United States for life would clearly be unreasonable. It would be broader than necessary to protect the legitimate business purpose. On the other hand, a restriction confined to three years within a 10-mile radius of the shop would probably be deemed reasonable and enforceable. In essence, the courts applied a rule of reason to determine whether the restriction was necessary to protect a legitimate business purpose, or was overly broad and thereby anticompetitive.

Covenant not to compete clauses are still common in employment contracts, where employers seek to protect themselves from competition from employees who leave the company. Courts apply the rule of reason to these covenants.

Courts examine the purpose, intent, power and effect of the restraint when determining the reasonableness of a firm's action. (This may be remembered by its acronym—PIPE. See Figure 46−1.) A restraint would be considered reasonable if (1) the

firm's *purpose* and the *intent* for the activity is not anticompetitive, (2) the firm's market *power* is not dominant, and (3) the restraint does not have a pernicious *effect* on competition.

When the courts first began to interpret section 1 to determine what constituted a violation of the Sherman Act, they were prone to borrow from the common law and apply the rule of reason. They interpreted "every restraint of trade" as being every *unreasonable* restraint of trade. Courts examined suspect business practices by balancing their business purpose and their competitive effect. After analyses, some business practices were deemed to be violative *per se* (in and of themself) without the necessity of any economic analyses. These per se violations involve those practices that lack a legitimate business purpose and whose impact on the market is anticompetitive.

Vertical Territorial Division

A **vertical division** of the market results when two companies at different levels of distribution agree to limit distribution or location to defined geographical areas (see Figure 46−2). The U.S. Supreme Court, in *United States v. Arnold Schwinn & Co.*[2] ruled this

---

[2] 388 U.S. 365 (1967).

arrangement to be a per se violation of section 1 of the Sherman Act if the supplier of the goods relinquished ownership to the distributor, as opposed to consigning[3] the goods to the distributor. In the following case, the U.S. Supreme Court reevaluated the *Schwinn* rule and considered whether vertical geographic allocations should instead be evaluated under a rule of reason approach.

---

[3]Consignment is a transaction where goods are ''loaned'' to a vendor, and payment is not expected and title does not pass until the vendor sells the goods.

CONTINENTAL T.V., INC. v. GTE SYLVANIA, INC.
433 U.S. 36 (1977)

GTE Sylvania, Inc. (respondent), manufactures and distributes television sets. It sold directly to a select group of retailers. Sylvania controlled the number of retailer-distributors within geographical areas and required them to sell exclusively from specified locations.

One of GTE's retail distributors, Continental T.V., Inc. (appellant), unhappy with Sylvania's decision to enlist another distributor in Continental's area, informed Sylvania that it was relocating Sylvania merchandise outside its approved location. Sylvania terminated Continental's dealership. Litigation followed. Continental claimed that Sylvania violated section 1 of the Sherman Act by prohibiting the sale of Sylvania goods in areas outside specified locations. A jury found for Continental and awarded damages. The Court of Appeals reversed and the U.S. Supreme Court granted certiorari.

POWELL, Justice

The traditional framework of analysis under section 1 of the Sherman Act is familiar and does not require extended discussion. Section 1 prohibits ''[e]very contract, combination . . . or conspiracy, in restraint of trade or commerce.'' Since the early years of this century a judicial gloss on this statutory language has established the ''rule of reason'' as the prevailing standard of analysis. Under this rule, the factfinder weighs all of the circumstances of a case in deciding whether a restrictive practice should be prohibited as imposing an unreasonable restraint on competition. *Per se* rules of illegality are appropriate only when they relate to conduct that is manifestly anticompetitive. . . .

In essence, the issue before us is whether *Schwinn's per se* rule can be justified. . . .

The market impact of vertical restrictions is complex because of their potential for a simultaneous reduction of intrabrand competition and stimulation of interbrand competition. Significantly, the Court in *Schwinn* did not distinguish among the challenged restrictions on the basis of their individual potential for intrabrand harm or interbrand benefit. Restrictions that completely eliminated intrabrand competition among Schwinn distributors were analyzed no differently from those that merely moderated intrabrand competition among retailers. The pivotal factor was the passage of title: All restrictions were held to be *per se* illegal where title had passed, and all were evaluated and sustained under the rule of reason where it had not. The location restriction at issue here would be subject to the same pattern of analysis under *Schwinn*.

Vertical restrictions reduce intrabrand competition by limiting the number of sellers of a particular product competing for the business of a given group of buyers. Location restrictions have this effect because of practical constraints on the effective marketing area of retail outlets. Although intrabrand competition may be reduced, the ability of retailers to exploit the resulting market may be limited both by the ability of consumers to travel to other franchised locations and, perhaps more importantly, to purchase the competing products of other manufacturers. None of these key variables, however, is affected by the form of the transaction by which a manufacturer conveys his products to the retailers.

Vertical restrictions promote interbrand competition by allowing the manufacturer to achieve certain efficiencies in the distribution of his products. These "redeeming virtues" are implicit in every decision sustaining vertical restrictions under the rule of reason. Economists have identified a number of ways in which manufacturers can use such restrictions to compete more effectively against other manufacturers. For example, new manufacturers and manufacturers entering new markets can use the restrictions in order to induce competent and aggressive retailers to make the kind of investment of capital and labor that is often required in the distribution of products unknown to the consumer. Established manufacturers can use them to induce retailers to engage in promotional activities or to provide service and repair facilities necessary to the efficient marketing of their products. Service and repair are vital for many products, such as automobiles and major household appliances. The availability and quality of such services affect a manufacturer's goodwill and competitiveness of his product. Because of market imperfections such as the so-called "free rider" effect, these services might not be provided by retailers in a purely competitive situation, despite the fact that each retailer's benefit would be greater if all provided the services than if none did.

Accordingly, we conclude that the *per se* rule stated in *Schwinn* must be overruled. In so holding we do not foreclose the possibility that particular applications of vertical restrictions might justify *per se* prohibition. . . . But we do make clear that departure from the rule-of-reason standard must be based upon demonstrable economic effect rather than—as in *Schwinn*—upon formalistic line drawing.

In sum, we conclude that the appropriate decision is to return to the rule of reason that governed vertical restrictions prior to *Schwinn*. When anticompetitive effects are shown to result from particular vertical restrictions, they can be adequately policed under the rule of reason, the standard traditionally applied for the majority of anticompetitive practices challenged under section 1 of the Act. Accordingly, the decision of the Court of Appeals is Affirmed.

Case Questions

1. What was the holding in *Schwinn*? How did it affect dealerships?

2. What are the economic justifications for permitting vertical territorial restrictions? What are the counterarguments?

3. Analyze: "The restraint posed by vertical territorial restrictions is really no different than vertical price fixing." (See the *Monsanto* case, presented later in this chapter.)

4. What effect do you think this decision has on manufacturers? Distributors? Consumers?

5. Under what circumstances would a vertical geographical restriction be a violation of Sherman Act section 1?

Exclusive Dealing

Exclusive dealing contracts are subject to the rule of reason. An **exclusive dealing contract** exists when a buyer agrees to purchase all of its requirements needs from a seller. Exclusive dealing contracts may be desirable from the buyer's and seller's perspectives. Buyers have a sure source of supply; sellers have a sure source of outlet. In some cases, an exclusive dealing contract is, however, unwanted and thrust on the buyer as a precondition to any dealing.

Section 1 of the Sherman Act makes an exclusive dealing contract illegal when it unreasonably restrains trade. Section 3 of the Clayton Act makes such a contract illegal if its effect may substantially lessen competition or tend to create a monopoly in any line of commerce. Clayton Act section 3 only applies to goods, whereas, Sherman Act section 1 applies to services as well as goods.

An exclusive dealing contract results in a restraint of trade because the buyer is foreclosed from the seller's competitors. Whether a particular exclusive dealing contract violates Clayton Act section 3 or Sherman Act section 1 depends on several factors: the degree of market foreclosure, the extent of the disparity of bargaining strength between the buyer and seller, and the extent of exclusive dealing within the industry.

Per Se Standard

Courts have ruled that some business practices lack any redeeming value. They are deemed to have a pernicious effect on competition and are classified as *per se* violations of Sherman Act section 1. Once a business practice is classified as per se, the courts are not apt to engage in a detailed economic analysis of the purpose and effect of the practice. Presumably, that analysis was done by earlier courts considering similar cases, and businesses are on advance notice that the practice is illegal per se. Those practices that fall within the per se category include (1) horizontal agreements to divide the market, (2) horizontal and vertical price-fixing, (3) tie-ins, and (4) group boycotts.

Horizontal Division of Market

Agreements to divide the market between companies at the same level of distribution are per se violations of section 1 of the Sherman Act (see Figure 46–2). For example, Company A and Company B are retail distributors of mattresses. Under section 1, it is unlawful for them to agree to restrict their distribution to particular geographic areas. Suppose they divided their market so that Company A took the north and west side of the city while Company B took the south and east sides. By doing this, they would avoid competing with each other. This agreement obviously restrains trade and is deemed illegal per se. This is also the case when companies distribute the same branded product, even though such an agreement may actually tend to promote interbrand competition, as illustrated in the next case.

UNITED STATES v. TOPCO
405 U.S. 596 (1972)

Topco is a trade association comprised of about 25 independent regional supermarket chains. The chains operate in 33 states. Topco serves as a purchasing agent for its members. Its primary purpose is "to obtain high quality merchandise under private labels in order to compete more effectively with larger national and regional chains." Topco members are prohibited from distributing Topco-controlled brands outside of their designated territories.

The United States brought an action against Topco charging it with unreasonable restraint of trade in violation of section 1 of the Sherman Act. The district court held that Topco's actions were procompetitive and found in favor of Topco. The government appealed directly to the U.S. Supreme Court.

MARSHALL, Justice

. . . While the Court has utilized the "rule of reason" in evaluating the legality of most restraints alleged to be violative of the Sherman Act, it has also developed the doctrine that certain business relationships are per se violations of the Act without regard to a consideration of their reasonableness. One of the classic examples of a per se violation of section 1 is an agreement between competitors at the same level of the market structure to allocate territories in order to minimize competition. Such concerted action is usually termed a "horizontal" restraint, in contradistinction to combinations of persons at different levels of the market structure, e.g., manufacturers and distributors, which are termed "vertical" restraints. This Court has reiterated time and time again that "[h]orizontal territorial limitations . . . are naked restraints of trade with no purpose except stifling of competition."

We think that it is clear that the restraint in this case is a horizontal one, and, therefore, a per se violation of section 1. . . .

In applying these rigid rules, the Court has consistently rejected the notion that naked restraints of trade are to be tolerated because they are well intended or because they are allegedly developed to increase competition.

Antitrust laws in general, and the Sherman Act in particular, are the Magna Charta of free enterprise. They are as important to the preservation of economic freedom and our free-enterprise system as the Bill of Rights is to the protection of our fundamental personal freedoms. And the freedom guaranteed each and every business, no matter how small, is the freedom to compete—to assert with vigor, imagination, devotion, and ingenuity whatever economic muscle it can muster. Implicit in such freedom is the notion that it cannot be foreclosed with respect to one sector of the economy because certain private citizens or groups believe that such foreclosure might promote greater competition in a more important sector of the economy.

The District Court determined that by limiting the freedom of its individual members to compete with each other, Topco was doing a greater good by fostering competition between members and other large supermarket chains. But, the fallacy in this is that Topco has no authority under the Sherman Act to determine the respective values of competition in various sectors of the economy. On the contrary, the Sherman Act gives to each Topco member and to each prospective member the right to ascertain for itself whether or not competition with other supermarket chains is more desirable than competition in the sale of Topco-brand products. Without territorial restrictions, Topco members may indeed "[cut] each other's throats." But, we have never found this possibility sufficient to warrant condoning horizontal restraints of trade.

BURGER, Chief Justice, Dissenting

With all respect, I believe that there are two basic fallacies in the Court's approach. . . . First, while I would not characterize our role under the Sherman Act as one of "rambl[ing] through the wilds," it is indeed one that requires our "examin[ation of] difficult economic problems." We can undoubtedly ease our task, but we should not abdicate that role by formulation of *per se* rules with no justification other than the enhancement of predictability and the reduction of judicial investigation. Second, from the general proposition that *per se* rules play a necessary role in antitrust law, it does not follow that the particular *per se* rule promulgated today is an appropriate one. Although it might well be desirable in a proper case for this Court to formulate a *per se* rule dealing with horizontal territorial limitations, it would not necessarily be appropriate for such a rule to amount to a blanket prohibition against all such limitations. More specifically, it is far from clear to me why such a rule should cover those division-of-market agreements that involve no price fixing and which are concerned only with trademarked products that are not in a monopoly or near-monopoly position with respect to competing brands. The instant case presents such an agreement; I would not decide it upon the basis of a *per se* rule.

The District Court specifically found that the horizontal restraints involved here tend positively to promote competition in the supermarket field and to produce lower costs for the consumer. The Court seems implicitly to accept this determination, but says that the Sherman Act does not give Topco the authority to determine for itself "whether or not competition with other supermarket chains is more desirable than competition in the sale of Topco-brand products." But the majority overlooks a further specific determination of the District Court, namely, that the invalidation of the restraints here at issue "would not increase competition in Topco private label brands." Indeed, the District Court seemed to believe that it would, on the contrary, lead to the likely demise of those brands in time. And the evidence before the District Court would appear to justify that conclusion.

There is no national demand for Topco brands, nor has there ever been any national advertising of those brands. It would be impracticable for Topco, with its limited financial resources, to convert itself into a national brand distributor in competition with distributors of existing national brands. Furthermore, without the right to grant exclusive licenses, it could not attract and hold new members as replacements for those of its present members who, following the pattern of the past, eventually grow sufficiently in size to be able to leave the cooperative organization and develop their own individual private-label brands. Moreover, Topco's present members, once today's decision has had its full impact over the course of time, will have no more reason to promote Topco products through local advertising and merchandising efforts than they will have such reason to promote any other generally available brands. . . .

Indeed, the economic effect of the new rule laid down by the Court today seems clear: unless Congress intervenes, grocery staples marketed under private-label brands with their lower consumer prices will soon be available only to those who patronize the large national chains.

Case Questions

1. Why did Topco assign territories? Why did the court characterize the allocation of territories as a horizontal restraint?

2. Note that this case was decided before *GTE Sylvania*. Do you think that the same rationale in *Sylvania* could be applied to support Chief Justice Burger's dissent? Explain.

3. How could Topco change its organizational structure to avoid a Sherman violation and yet continue to be competitive with the national chains?

4. Compare and contrast the approaches of the majority and dissent.

Price-Fixing

Price-fixing agreements are illegal per se, whether they be horizontal or vertical. Price is the "guts" of free market competition, and a price fix quite necessarily eliminates competition. Once a price fix is found, the courts will not inquire into the reasonableness of the price. The reasonable price of today may become the unreasonable price of tomorrow. Consequently, fixing maximum prices is just as violative of the Sherman Act as fixing minimum prices.

Illegal price-fixing arrangements include nonprice agreements that tend to result in price uniformity. Nonprice violations may be agreements concerning delivery prices, trade-ins, sales returns, trading stamps, and credit terms. For example, beer wholesalers agreed to sell beer to retailers only on condition that payment be made by the time of delivery. The U.S. Supreme Court found this agreement to be an illegal price fix and held that credit terms are an inseparable part of the price.[4] Not every agreement, however, that has an incidental effect on price is deemed a price fix. In *Chicago Board of Trade v. U.S.*, a commodity exchange adopted a rule that prohibited brokers from selling grain "to arrive" (during hours the exchange was closed) for a price different than the last quoted price when the exchange was open. The U.S. Supreme Court held that although the incidental impact of the rule was the fixing of prices

for grain to arrive, the practice was a "time fix" properly analyzed under the rule of reason.[5]

Vertical price fixes ordinarily occur when a manufacturer and its distributor agree that a product will be sold for a designated price. Manufacturers may want their products sold at a minimum price in order to maintain a quality image. Or, they may desire to avoid price slashing among their distributors and thus enhance their distributors' chances for survival. In any case, the parties' motivation is irrelevant. Such an agreement has been a per se violation of section 1 of the Sherman Antitrust Act since Congress repealed the Miller-Tydings Amendment in 1975. That amendment had exempted resale price maintenance agreements sanctioned by state law from Sherman's reach.

It is not illegal for a manufacturer to suggest the product be sold at a designated price. A manufacturer may choose to deal with whom it will. Consequently, it may refuse to deal with those who do not adhere to its suggested price. However, certain conduct raises a presumption that "suggested prices" really amount to a concerted agreement to fix prices. If, for example, a manufacturer terminates a dealer for noncompliance, and then receives that person back into the "fold" and the dealer now complies, a presumption is raised that the "prodigal" *agreed* to maintain the manufacturer's price. The following case illustrates the facts necessary to raise a presumption of an illegal resale price maintenance agreement.

---

[4]*Catalano, Inc. v. Target Sales, Inc.*, 446 U.S. 643 (1980).

[5]*Chicago Board of Trade v. U.S.*, 246 U.S. 231 (1918).

MONSANTO COMPANY v. SPRAY-RITE SERVICE CORP.
466 U.S. 752 (1984)

Monsanto Company manufactures agricultural herbicides. Spray-Rite Service Corporation was a wholesale distributor of agricultural chemicals and an authorized distributor of Monsanto herbicides. Monsanto refused to renew Spray-Rite's distributorship.

Spray-Rite brought suit against Monsanto, alleging that it violated section 1 of the Sherman Act by conspiring to fix the resale prices of Monsanto herbicides. It further maintained that Monsanto terminated Spray-Rite's dealership in furtherance of the conspiracy. The district court found for Spray-Rite and awarded $10.5 million in damages. The Seventh Circuit Court of Appeals affirmed the decision. The U.S. Supreme Court granted certiorari.

POWELL, Justice

This Court has drawn two important distinctions that are at the center of this and any other distributor-termination case. First, there is the basic distinction between concerted and independent action—a distinction not always clearly drawn by parties and courts. Section 1 of the Sherman Act requires that there be a ''contract, combination . . . or conspiracy'' between the manufacturer and other distributors in order to establish a violation. Independent action is not proscribed. A manufacturer of course generally has a right to deal, or refuse to deal, with whomever it likes, as long as it does so independently. . . . [T]he manufacturer can announce its resale prices in advance and refuse to deal with those who fail to comply. And a distributor is free to acquiesce in the manufacturer's demand in order to avoid termination.

The second important distinction in distributor-termination cases is that between concerted action to set prices and concerted actions on nonprice restrictions. The former have been *per se* illegal since the early years of national antitrust enforcement. The latter are judged under the rule of reason, which requires a weighing of the relevant circumstances of a case to decide whether a restrictive practice constitutes an unreasonable restraint on competition.

. . . For example, the fact that a manufacturer and its distributors are in constant communication about prices and marketing strategy does not alone show that the distributors are not making independent pricing decisions. A manufacturer and its distributors have legitimate reasons to exchange information about the prices and the reception of their products in the market. Moreover, it is precisely in cases in which the manufacturer attempts to further a particular marketing strategy by means of agreements on often costly nonprice restrictions that it will have the most interest in the distributor's resale prices. The manufacturer often will want to ensure that its distributors earn sufficient profit to pay for programs such as hiring and training additional salesmen or demonstrating the technical features of the product, and will want to see that ''free-riders'' do not interfere. . . . Nevertheless, it is of consid-

erable importance that independent action by the manufacturer, and concerted action on nonprice restrictions, be distinguished from price-fixing agreements, since under present law the latter are subject to *per se* treatment and treble [triple] damages. Permitting an agreement to be inferred merely from the existence of complaints, or even from the fact that termination came about ''in response to'' complaints, could deter or penalize perfectly legitimate conduct. As Monsanto points out, complaints about price-cutters ''are natural—and from the manufacturer's perspective, unavoidable—reactions by distributors to the activities of their rivals. . . . ''

. . . There must be evidence that tends to exclude the possibility that the manufacturer and nonterminated distributors were acting independently. . . . [T]he antitrust plaintiff should present direct or circumstantial evidence that reasonably tends to prove that the manufacturer and others ''had a conscious commitment to a common scheme designed to achieve an unlawful objective.'' . . . Applying this standard to the facts of this case, we believe there was sufficient evidence for the jury reasonably to have concluded that Monsanto and some of its distributors were parties to an ''agreement'' or ''conspiracy'' to maintain resale prices and terminate price-cutters. There was testimony from a Monsanto district manager, for example, that Monsanto on at least two occasions . . . about five months after Spray-Rite was terminated, approached price-cutting distributors and advised that if they did not maintain the suggested resale price, they would not receive adequate supplies of Monsanto's new corn herbicide. When one of the distributors did not assent, this information was referred to the Monsanto regional office, and it complained to the distributor's parent company. There was evidence that the parent instructed its subsidiary to comply, and the distributor informed Monsanto that it would charge the suggested price. Evidence of this kind plainly is relevant and persuasive as to a meeting of minds.

An arguably more ambiguous example is a newsletter from one of the distributors to his dealer-customers. The newsletter is dated . . . just four weeks before Spray-Rite was terminated. It was written after a meeting between the author and several Monsanto officials, and discusses Monsanto's efforts to "get the 'market place in order.' " The newsletter reviews some of Monsanto's incentive and shipping policies, and then states that in addition "every effort will be made to maintain a minimum market price level." . . .

If, as the courts below reasonably could have found, there was evidence of an agreement with one or more distributors to maintain prices, the remaining question is whether the termination of Spray-Rite was part of or pursuant to that agreement. It would be reasonable to find that it was, since it is necessary for competing distributors contemplating compliance with suggested prices to know that those who do not comply will be terminated. Moreover, there is some circumstantial evidence of such a link. Following the termination, there was a meeting between Spray-Rite's president and a Monsanto official. There was testimony that the first thing the official mentioned was the many complaints Monsanto had received about Spray-Rite's prices. In addition, there was reliable testimony that Monsanto never discussed with Spray-Rite prior to the termination the distributorship criteria that were the alleged basis for the action. By contrast, a former Monsanto salesman for Spray-Rite's area testified that Monsanto representatives on several occasions . . . approached Spray-Rite, informed the distributor of complaints from other distributors—including one major and influential one, and requested that prices be maintained. Later that same year, Spray-Rite's president testified, Monsanto officials made explicit threats to terminate Spray-Rite unless it raised its prices.

. . . [T]he evidence in this case created a jury issue as to whether Spray-Rite was terminated pursuant to a price-fixing conspiracy between Monsanto and its distributors. The judgment of the court below is affirmed.

Case Questions

1. What was the issue in this case?
2. What was the evidentiary standard adopted by the Court of Appeals to support a claim of concerted price-fixing? What evidentiary standard did the Supreme Court adopt? Which serves the purposes of the antitrust laws best?
3. What facts support the claim that Monsanto conspired to fix prices?
4. What can Monsanto and other dealers do to avoid the inference of concerted price-fixing?

Circumstantial evidence of a price fix may be sufficient proof of a violation. It is unlikely that a firm would admit to conspiring to fix prices, and equally unlikely that a firm would generate any writings in evidence of a price fix. Meetings between competitors or systematic release of pricing data by one firm to another coupled with identical prices raise a presumption of illegal price-fixing.

In contrast to price-fixing, which is illegal, price leadership is not. In an **oligopolistic market,** where few firms dominate a concentrated market, the smaller firms are often prone to follow the lead of the "big guys" on pricing strategy. One day a leader announces a new price, and shortly thereafter other firms in the industry follow. This is not illegal as long as the pricing decisions are made independently.

Tying Arrangements

A tying arrangement occurs when a buyer is not permitted to purchase one item without purchasing another item also. From a seller's perspective, tying arrangements may be desirable. Where, for example, the seller has a unique item that has a large demand, the seller may increase its profits by tying the sale of the desirable product to a less desirable one. Assume, for example, that IBM has a deluxe model copier that has unique features not duplicable because of patent rights. If IBM sold the machine subject to the purchaser buying all the copying paper from IBM, this would be a tie-in, which could greatly benefit IBM. The copier is the tying product, and the paper is the tied product.

A tying arrangement may restrain competition. It inhibits free choice in the tied product market by forcing the purchaser to buy the seller's product. And, it creates an artificial restraint on the forces of supply and demand by creating a greater demand for a product than would otherwise exist. For these reasons, tying arrangements are per se illegal under section 1 of the Sherman Act (products or services) and section 3 of the Clayton Act (products only) when three prerequisites are met: (1) a significant amount of commerce is affected, (2) two separate products are involved, and (3) the seller has sufficient economic power in the tying product to enforce the tie-in.

In *Jefferson Parish Hospital District v. Hyde*, the U.S. Supreme Court faced the question of whether a hospital that conditioned patient operations to required use of a preselected anesthesiologist service was guilty of violating Sherman Act section 1. The court found that two separate products were linked—anesthesiological services and other patient care. However, the court found that the hospital did not possess sufficient forcing power since 70 percent of the patients residing in the geographical area entered other hospitals where they were able to select their anesthesiologists.[6]

---

[6]110 F. Supp. 295 (D. Mass. 1953).

Group Boycotts

The antitrust laws do not interfere with a company's right to refuse to deal with another firm. However, Sherman Act section 1 prohibits two or more firms from agreeing to refuse to deal with another firm. These unreasonably restrain trade by forcing business closures or by interfering with a firm's judgment and ability to transact business. As such, these agreements constitute per se violations of section 1 of the Sherman Act.

The following article presents a Japanese form of business that presents serious antitrust concerns in the United States.

Reflections of Keiretsu*

Keiretsu is a Japanese industrial organization form that has been both praised and criticized in recent years. Firms within a Keiretsu share links among firms in different industries and between firms that stand in vertical relationships. Japanese firms within a Keiretsu tend to solidify their relationships through various links and affiliations such as: cross shareholding, interlocking directorates, social structures among top management, financial commitments, joint affiliation within commercial and investment banks, joint R & D activities, technology transfers, primary or exclusive customer supplier relationships, and unspoken social norms creating expectations for all employees to concentrate their personal purchases only from Keiretsu members.

Significant legal questions arise in the United States about the operation of Keiretsu. . . . Keiretsu structures arguably violate the prohibitions against restraints of trade under the antitrust laws of the U.S. . . .

■ ■ ■

Antitrust Barriers to Keiretsu

Western critics commonly allege that Japanese style Keiretsu behave like cartels. This strongly suggests that illegal restraints of trade . . . accompany some aspects of Keiretsu relationships. On its face, the description of common Keiretsu relations suggests that threats and intimidation by lead industrial firms are anticompetitive practices that exert monopolization pressures on Keiretsu members. Contracts and practices that prohibit suppliers from selling outside their Keiretsu channel or boycott outside suppliers potentially violate U.S. and Japanese antitrust law.

As the Japanese economy has grown and there are numerous viable competitors in each industry, the Keiretsu has evolved from horizontal or intermarket Keiretsu into vertical structures. . . . Keiretsu are probably most vulnerable to allegations of vertical restraints of trade, up and down the chain of distribution. Under U.S. law, the classic analysis of prohibited

---

*Source: John Bagby, "Reflections of Keiretsu," Working Paper 92-1, The Mary Jean and Frank P. Smeal College, Pennsylvania State University. Reprinted with permission.

vertical restraints of trade focus on a lead firm and its downstream pressures on distributors. While such pressures exist in Japanese style Keiretsu relationships, it is alleged the greater pressures are focused upstream towards suppliers. Therefore, the traditional U.S. vertical restraint of trade analysis is somewhat inappropriate to applications on Japanese Keiretsu.

■ ■ ■

Exclusive Distributorships

Exclusive distributorships invert the coercion upstream from distributor or other reseller to a supplier. When the retailer has the sole right to sell goods produced by a particular manufacturer or sold through a particular distributor, this is known as an "exclusive distributorship." Effectively this grants a geographic monopoly over that manufacturer's brand. Exclusive distributorships are often promoted as essential to prevent free riding. For example, low priced discounters with thin profit margins are less able to provide expensive technical expertise in sales or service and hold smaller inventories of parts or new products. By contrast, the high priced, high cost, service-oriented retailer can afford these services because their higher profit margins permit larger expenses for promotion, service, adequate inventories, parts, and hiring trained sales personnel. If low priced discounters proliferate in selling the same products as the high priced retailers, consumers tend to use the expertise of the high priced retailer but make actual purchases from the discounter eventually forcing the high priced retailers out of business. Exclusive distributorships are justified on an elimination of the low priced discounters "free riding" on the sales expenditures of high priced retailers.

Exclusive distributorships, however, eliminate intrabrand competition within a geographic region in favor of interbrand competition. Eventually, the price structure of all competitors in the industry may rise higher than if price competition, both within and among brands, remains vigorous. Japanese style Keiretsu can be enhanced by exclusive distributorships because this reinforces the community of interest within the Keiretsu chain of distribution and it enhances competition only with the Keiretsu.

Customer or Territorial Restrictions

A suppliers' restriction on which resellers may sell to particular customers or within particular regions are considered customer or territorial restrictions. Such restrictions also reduce intrabrand competition, allegedly strengthening interbrand competition. They provide a minimum incentive to other resellers by permitting oligopoly profits and they tend to favor some distribution channels over others. They are considered illegal when they tend to limit competition and have no legitimate economic or business objective. Therefore, the rule of reason applies to customer territorial restrictions. . . . In Japanese style Keiretsu, such restrictions probably proliferate. The continuation of relations with a particular supplier are threatened unless certain customers or territories are ignored by the reseller. This permits the distribution network for the lead industrial firm to be strengthened in pieces and prevents the growth of large and powerful potentially insurgent retailers or distributors downstream from the lead industrial firm.

Concerted Refusal to Deal

U.S. antitrust laws prohibit a concerted refusal to deal as a method to enforce other vertical price and nonprice restrictions. This discipline assists in maintaining resale price maintenance. However, it is illegal to actively harass downstream resellers into following a resale price maintenance scheme. Any illegal monitoring, rather than a simple refusal to deal, is prohibited. The shunning activity of Keiretsu members against disruptive suppliers or distributors is similar to a concerted refusal to deal. Concerted refusals to deal in Keiretsu generally force compliance with exclusive dealing, exclusive distributorship, and price discrimination schemes. They are not usually intended to support a price floor, as is typical in U.S. violations.

Thought Questions

1. Analyze whether the concept of Keiretsu would be workable in this country.
2. Argue that Keiretsu does not violate antitrust laws.
3. Analyze: ''The U.S. should outright ban Japanese firms that employ Keiretsu from doing business in the United States.''

MONOPOLIES

Section 2 of the Sherman Antitrust Act makes monopolizing or attempting to monopolize any part of interstate or foreign trade or commerce unlawful. Unlike section 1, which takes two parties for violation, one party may be guilty of a section 2 violation. The section does not make it unlawful to simply be too big. *Monopolize* is a verb, and so when identifying violations, size must be combined with an assessment of what the corporation did to become or maintain a monopoly. A violation of section 2 turns on an analysis of three factors: (1) relevant market, (2) market power, and (3) intent.

Relevant Market

The relevant market is the sphere within which a firm's monopoly power is measured. It includes the market sector where a dominant firm may exercise anticompetitive practices such as raising prices and excluding competition. The relevant market generally identifies those firms that possess the ability to operate independent of market competition. The relevant market is broken down into product and geographic markets.

Product Market

The relevant product market is determined by assessing what goods are substitutable. Coca Cola Company has a 100 percent share of the market in Coke. However, the relevant product market is broader than Coke because other products influence Coca Cola's pricing and other competitive practices. Should Coca Cola raise its prices substantially, even its most loyal customers would switch to a reasonable substitute, such as Pepsi Cola or another similar but more reasonably priced cola. These cola substitutes are deemed to be within the same relevant product market.

Economists measure substitutability by a concept called cross-elasticity of demand. **Elasticity of demand** measures the relationship between the change of demand for a product and the change of price for that product. **Cross-elasticity of demand** measures the effect a price change on one good has on the relationship between the demand for that good and another good.

Assume that table salt is selling for $3 per pound, and that the price is increased 25 cents per pound. Will that affect the demand for salt and the demand for pepper? Probably not. The demand for salt will not be reduced, nor will the demand for pepper increase. Therefore, there is no cross-elasticity of demand between salt and pepper. They are not substitutable and consequently, are not within the same relevant product market. Consider, however, the impact of an increase in Coca Cola prices on the demand for Coke and Pepsi. In contrast, here we have close substitutes and consequently a high cross-elasticity of demand. As the price of Coke is raised, the demand for Coke will decrease, and the demand for Pepsi will increase. The higher the cross-elasticity of demand, the more apt a product is to be considered within the relevant product market. The following U.S. Supreme Court landmark case involving flexible packaging materials illustrates well the concept of substitutability as it applies to identification of the relevant product market.

UNITED STATES v. DU PONT & CO.
351 U.S. 377 (1956)

The United States charged E. I. du Pont de Nemours & Co., Inc., with monopolizing the cellophane market in violation of section 2 of the Sherman Antitrust Act. Du Pont produced about 75 percent of the cellophane sold in the United States. Cellophane constituted less than 20 percent of all flexible packaging materials sold.

The U.S. district court found the relevant product market to be flexible packaging materials and found for Du Pont. The government appealed directly to the U.S. Supreme Court, contending that the relevant product market was cellophane.

REED, Justice

If cellophane is the ''market'' that du Pont is found to dominate, it may be assumed it does have monopoly power over that ''market.'' Monopoly power is the power to control prices or exclude competition. It seems apparent that du Pont's power to set the price of cellophane has been limited only by the competition afforded by other flexible packaging materials. Moreover, it may be practically impossible for anyone to commence manufacturing cellophane without full access to du Pont's technique. However, du Pont has no power to prevent competition from other wrapping materials. . . . Price and competition are so intimately entwined that any discussion of theory must treat them as one. It is inconceivable that price could be controlled without power over competition or vice versa. . . .

Determination of the competitive market for commodities depends on how different from one another are the offered commodities in character or use, how far buyers will go to substitute one commodity for another. For example, one can think of building materials as in commodity competition but one could hardly say that brick competed with steel or wood or cement or stone in the meaning of Sherman Act litigation; the products are too different. . . . Whatever the market may be, we hold that control of price or competition establishes the existence of monopoly power under section 2. Our next step is to determine whether du Pont has monopoly power over cellophane: that is, power over its price in relation to or competition with other commodities. The charge was monopolization of cellophane. The defense, that cellophane was merely a part of the relevant market for flexible packaging materials.

But where there are market alternatives that buyers may readily use for their purposes, illegal monopoly does not exist merely because the product said to be monopolized differs from others. If it were not so, only physically identical products would be a part of the market. To accept the Government's argument, we would have to conclude that the manufacturers of plain as well as moisture-proof cellophane were monopolists, and so with films such as Pliofilm, foil, glassine, polyethylene, and Saran, for each of these wrapping materials is distinguishable. . . . What is called for is an appraisal of the ''cross-elasticity'' of demand in the trade. The varying circumstances of each case determine the result. In considering what is the relevant market for determining the control of price and competition, no more definite rule can be declared than that commodities reasonably interchangeable by consumers for the same purposes make up that ''part of the trade or commerce,'' monopolization of which may be illegal. . . . In determining the market under the Sherman Act, it is the use or uses to which the commodity is put that control. The selling price between commodities with similar uses and different characteristics may vary, so that the cheaper product can drive out the more expensive. Or, the superior quality of higher priced articles may make dominant the more desirable. Cellophane costs more than many competing products and less than a few. But whatever the price, there are various flexible wrapping materials that are bought by manufacturers for packaging their goods in their own plants or are sold to converters who shape and print them for use in the packaging of the commodities to be wrapped.

It may be admitted that cellophane combines the desirable elements of transparency, strength and cheapness more definitely than any of the others. . . . But, despite cellophane's advantages, it has to meet competition from other materials in every one of its uses. . . . Food products are the chief outlet, with cigarettes next. The Government makes no challenge . . . that cellophane furnishes less than 7 percent of wrappings for bakery products, 25 percent for candy, 32 percent for snacks, 35 percent for meats and poultry, 27 percent for crackers and biscuits, 47 percent for fresh produce, and 34 percent for frozen foods. Seventy-five to 80 percent of cigarettes are wrapped in cellophane. Thus, cellophane shares the packaging market with others. The overall result is that cellophane accounts for 17.9 percent of flexible wrapping materials, measured by the wrapping surface.

Moreover a very considerable degree of functional interchangeability exists between these products. . . . It will be noted . . . that except as to permeability to gases, cellophane has no qualities that are not possessed by a number of other materials. . . .

We conclude that cellophane's interchangeability with the other materials mentioned suffices to make it a part of this flexible packaging material market. . . . That market is composed of products that have reasonable interchangeability for the purposes for which they are produced — price, use and qualities considered. While the application of the tests remains uncertain, it seems to us that du Pont should not be found to monopolize cellophane when

that product has the competition and interchangeability with other wrappings that this record shows. [Affirmed]

Case Questions

1. What is the issue this case presents? What did Du Pont contend was the appropriate relevant product market? What did the government contend was the appropriate relevant product market? Why does it make a difference?

2. Identify the factors necessary to determine the relevant product market.

3. What is the strong argument for rejecting the government's argument? Are there any weak arguments?

4. Change the facts in this case to achieve a different result.

Geographic Market

The relevant geographic market consists of the area within which the company competes. In *du Pont,* the relevant geographical market was the United States, since its distribution was national. However, consider an independent local grocery store on the north end of a city. It probably only attracts customers from that sector of the city and, consequently, the relevant geographic market is the north end of the city. Relevant geographic markets may consist of the United States, regions of the country, states, cities, and local sectors.

Market Power

Market power is assessed by determining a firm's power to raise prices and exclude competition within a given relevant product and geographic market. One way of assessing this market power is to determine the firm's share of the market. Share of the market may be based on the number of units sold or sales revenue. While these figures may not always be clear, they may be derived from market surveys, trade association reports, or economists.

There is no "crystal clear" test for what share of the market constitutes an illegal monopoly. Courts approach each case individually. However, there are some guidelines derived from case law:

85 to 100 percent = Monopoly

51 to 84 percent = Gray area

 0 to 50 percent = No monopoly

In the gray area, courts examine factors other than market share to assess market power. Industry structure, market concentration, height of barriers to entry, and nature of the competitive environment are all relevant.

Intent

Size alone is insufficient to constitute a violation of section 2 of the Sherman Act. Power within a defined relevant market must be coupled with an intent to monopolize before a violation occurs. The intent does not have to be specific but may be inferred from certain improper conduct. The type of conduct that satisfies the intent requirement involves activity designed to acquire or maintain a monopoly. This may take the form of illegal conduct such as price-fixing, concerted refusals to deal, or other unreasonable restraints of trade. However, the intent requirement may be met by more subtle behavior, such as sustained pricing below cost.

Presumably, a firm will not continue to price below cost and lose money unless its motives are to drive a competitor out of business and thus profit in the long run. Consequently, continued below-cost pricing is the type of predatory conduct that meets the intent requirement. Other normally legal conduct raises suspicion when committed by a firm possessing monopoly power. In *United States v. United Shoe Machinery Corp.*, United Shoe was charged with monopolizing shoe machines.[7] It possessed 75 percent of the market of shoe machines. It refused to sell its machines; instead, the company leased them under 10-year leases and provided free maintenance and repair service. The court found requisite intent to monopolize, holding that United's leasing system was conduct that excluded competition by cementing relationships with customers and ensuring closer and more frequent contacts with them.

Attempts to Monopolize

Section 2 of the Sherman Antitrust Act makes it unlawful to attempt to monopolize. Three ingredients are necessary to establish an unlawful attempt to monopolize: (1) specific intent to control prices or destroy competition, (2) predatory conduct directed to accomplishing the unlawful purpose, and (3) a dangerous probability of success.

Unlike the case of monopolization, where only a general intent is needed, specific intent must be found in attempt to monopolize cases. There must be evidence of a specific intent to control prices or exclude competition. This may be gleaned from internal company memoranda or conduct such as below-cost pricing.

Intent alone is insufficient. As with cases of monopolizing, there must be some unfair conduct. Unfair conduct may consist of predatory pricing or excluding competition.

And finally, the firm must be in a position to accomplish its desired end. If there is no dangerous probability of the firm succeeding, it cannot be found "attempting to monopolize" in violation of Sherman Act section 2. Assessment of the dangerous probability criterion involves an analysis of the market—the industry and the firm—to determine whether the firm has the probability, given its conduct, to monopolize a relevant market.

Lawful Monopolies

Not every monopoly is unlawful. For example, patents are legal monopolies. The government confers patents for new inventions. The patent holder has the right to exclude others from manufacturing and selling a product covered by the patent. However, even patent holders must be careful not to engage in conduct intended to monopolize beyond the purview of the lawfully granted patent.

Public utilities are another example of legal monopolies. They, however, are not beyond the reach of monopolization. In *MCI Communications Corp. v. American Telephone & Telegraph Co.*, MCI accused AT&T of Sherman Antitrust Act section 2 violations.[8] AT&T was a regulated monopoly of telecommunications. Nonetheless, the court found that under the **essential facilities doctrine**, AT&T's refusal to interconnect MCI with local distribution facilities constituted an unlawful willful extension of a lawful monopoly. Under the essential facilities doctrine, liability under Sherman Act section 2 occurs when (1) there is control of an essential facility by a monopolist, (2) the competitor is unable to duplicate the essential facility, and (3) the monopolist denies the use of the facility to the competitor (4) even though it is feasible to make the facility available.

A monopolist may have acquired monopoly power through natural forces or through superior skill, foresight, and industry. Some geographical areas cannot support more than one laundromat or one movie theater. Often, one firm may become the sole survivor in a market because of superior skill. The distinction between superior skill and unlawful intent in violation of Sherman Act section 2 may be a very thin one, however.

EXEMPTIONS

Some organizations and activities enjoy an exemption from the federal antitrust acts by statute (see Figure 46–3). Some of these exemptions exist because the organizations or activities are subject to other regulation. For example, the insurance business is exempt by statute from the federal antitrust laws. Insurance activities are highly regulated by state insurance commissioners, and this regulation is deemed to be sufficient. Similarly, public utilities, which are closely regulated by other agencies, are exempt from the antitrust laws. Banking, exporting, securities, trucking, railroad, airline, and energy in-

---

[7] 110 F. Supp. 205 (D. Mass. 1953).

[8] 708 F.2d 1081 (7th Cir. 1983).

dustries possess at least limited immunity from antitrust violations for the same reason.

Other activities are exempt by statute for practical reasons. Labor unions, for example, are exempt from the antitrust laws. Otherwise, the existence of unions, which monopolize the supply of labor, would be threatened. Farmers and fishermen, by statute, do not violate the antitrust laws when they form cooperative marketing associations. Some activities are the beneficiaries of antitrust exemption by judicial decision. Baseball is one such activity, although no other sport has been able to win immunity from the courts. Another judicially im-

Figure 46–3   Antitrust Exemptions

Airlines	Insurance
Banking	Labor unions
Baseball	Public utilities
Energy	Railroads
Exporting	Securities
Farmers	Trucking
Fishermen	

posed exemption is the state action exemption. The following case sets out the requirements for this exemption.

TOWN OF HALLIE v. CITY OF EAU CLAIRE
471 U.S. 34 (1985)

The town of Hallie and three other towns (the Towns) are located adjacent to the City of Eau Claire (the City). The City obtained federal funds to help build a sewage treatment facility. The facility is the only one in the market available to the Towns. The City refused to supply sewage treatment services to the Towns. It does supply its sewage facilities to individuals within the Town's areas if a majority of individuals within the area vote to have their homes annexed into the City and to use the City's sewage collection and transportation services.

The Towns sued the City, alleging that the City used its monopoly power over sewage treatment to gain an unlawful monopoly over sewage collection and transportation services; and that this constituted an illegal tie-in and an unlawful refusal to deal with the Towns.

The district court found in favor of the City, holding that its activities fell within the state action exemption to the antitrust laws. The United States Court of Appeals for the Seventh Circuit affirmed. The U.S. Supreme Court granted certiorari.

POWELL, Justice

The starting point in any analysis involving the state action doctrine is the reasoning of *Parker v. Brown*. In *Parker*, relying on principles of federalism and state sovereignty, the Court refused to construe the Sherman Act as applying to the anticompetitive conduct of a State acting through its legislature. Rather, it ruled that the Sherman Act was intended to prohibit *private* restraints on trade, and it refused to infer an intent to "nullify a state's control over its officers and agents" in activities directed by the legislature.

Municipalities, on the other hand, are not beyond the reach of the antitrust laws by virtue of their status because they are not themselves sovereign. Rather, to obtain exemption, municipalities must demonstrate that their anticompetitive activities

were authorized by the State "pursuant to state policy to displace competition with regulation or monopoly public service."

The determination that a municipality's anticompetitive activities constitute state action is not a purely formalistic inquiry; the State may not validate a municipality's anticompetitive conduct simply by declaring it to be lawful. On the other hand, in proving that a state policy to displace competition exists, the municipality need not "be able to point to a specific, detailed legislative authorization" in order to assert a successful *Parker* defense to an antitrust suit. Rather . . . it would be sufficient to obtain *Parker* immunity for a municipality to show that it acted pursuant to a "clearly articulated and affirmatively expressed . . . state policy" that was "actively supervised" by the State.

The City cites several provisions of the Wisconsin code to support its claim that its allegedly anticompetitive activity constitutes state action. We therefore examine the statutory structure in some detail.

Wisconsin Stat. section 62.18(1) (1982) grants authority to cities to construct, add to, alter, and repair sewerage systems. The authority includes the power to "describe with reasonable particularity the district to be [served]." This grant of authority is supplemented by Wis. Stat. Ann. section 66.069(2)(c) (Supp. 1984), providing that a city operating a public utility

may by ordinance fix the limits of such service in unincorporated areas. Such ordinance shall delineate the area within which service will be provided and the municipal utility shall have no obligation to serve beyond the area so delineated.

With respect to joint sewerage systems, section 144.07(1) provides that the State's Department of Natural Resources may require a city's sewerage system to be constructed so that other cities, towns, or areas may connect to the system, and the Department may order that such connections be made. Subsection (1m) provides, however, that an order by the Department of Natural Resources for the connection of unincorporated territory to a city system shall be void if that territory refuses to become annexed to the city.

The Towns contend that these statutory provisions do not evidence a state policy to displace competition in the provision of sewage services because they make no express mention of anticompetitive conduct. As discussed above, the statutes clearly contemplate that a city may engage in anticompetitive conduct. Such conduct is a foreseeable result of empowering the City to refuse to serve unannexed areas. It is not necessary, as the Towns contend, for the state legislature to have stated explicitly that it expected the City to engage in conduct that would

have anticompetitive effects. . . . [I]t is sufficient that the statutes authorized the City to provide sewage services and also to determine the areas to be served. We think it is clear that anticompetitive effects logically would result from this broad authority to regulate.

The Towns' argument amounts to a contention that to pass the "clear articulation" test, a legislature must expressly state in a statute or its legislative history that it intends for the delegated action to have anticompetitive effects. This contention embodies an unrealistic view of how legislatures work and of how statutes are written. No legislature can be expected to catalog all of the anticipated effects of a statute of this kind.

In sum, we conclude that the Wisconsin statutes evidence a "clearly articulated and affirmatively expressed" state policy to displace competition with regulation in the area of municipal provision of sewerage services. These statutory provisions plainly show that "the legislature contemplated the kind of action complained of." This is sufficient to satisfy the clear articulation requirement of the state action test.

We conclude that the actions of the City of Eau Claire in this case are exempt from the Sherman Act. . . . We accordingly affirm the judgment of the Court of Appeals for the Seventh Circuit.

Case Questions

1. What is the issue?
2. Compare and contrast the parties' legal positions.
3. Is the *Parker* doctrine rational? Analyze.
4. In what way did the state of Wisconsin articulate a policy to displace competition with regulation in the area of municipal provision of sewerage services? Should it make any difference that the state did not *compel* the city to act?

REMEDIES

Violations of the Sherman Antitrust Act constitute a crime. The U.S. Department of Justice has the power to criminally prosecute offenders. Criminal convictions may result in large fines, and imprisonment for individuals.

Sherman Act violations also result in civil offenses. The Justice Department has the power to seek injunctions against violators. Many antitrust

complaints filed against companies result in consent decrees. A **consent decree** is not an admission of wrongdoing by the firm but an agreement to abide by the decree that prohibits certain conduct or requires specific action.

Private parties and companies injured as a result of antitrust violations may sue and recover treble damages. Some of these suits have ended in huge judgments. For example, Berkey Photo obtained a $77 million judgment against Eastman Kodak for antitrust violation; Telex obtained a $259.5 million judgment against IBM for antitrust violations, but the judgment was eventually vacated and settled by agreement of the parties. Finally, state attorney generals are authorized to sue antitrust offenders on behalf of injured citizens.

Antitrust actions are among the most complex suits, often involving thousands of exhibits, scores of witnesses, months of trials, and reams of trial transcripts. Many firms, in an effort to prevent antitrust offenses and costly litigation, periodically audit their procedures, policies, and practices.

END–OF–CHAPTER QUESTIONS

1. Compare and contrast the system of free enterprise with a system based on communism.

2. State and analyze the benefits and detriments that would result from abolishing the per se category under Sherman Act section 1.

3. Comment on the difference in proof requirements between an attempt to monopolize and a monopolization case. Is the difference justified? Analyze.

4. Lear Siegler, Inc. purchased Regal Tube Company and operated it as an unincorporated division. Thereafter, Copperweld Corp. purchased the Regal division. The purchase agreement contained a clause prohibiting Siegler and its subsidiaries from competing in the United States with Regal for five years. Copperweld transferred Regal's assets to a newly formed, wholly owned subsidiary corporation. A former officer of Lear Siegler, Inc., set out to establish a steel tubing business in competition with Regal and formed Independence Tube Corp. Independence made an offer to Yoder Company to supply a tubing mill. After Yoder accepted the offer, Copperweld sent Yoder a letter stating that it would be ''greatly concerned if [the former Lear Siegler officer] contemplates entering the structural tube market . . . in competition with Regal Tube.'' The letter further stated that Copperweld would take ''any and all steps which are necessary to protect our rights under the terms of our purchase agreement. . . .'' Yoder canceled its acceptance. Can Independence Tube Corp. successfully charge Copperweld and Regal Tube with conspiring to violate section 1 of the Sherman Act? Analyze. See *Copperweld Corporation v. Independence Tube Corporation*, 467 U.S. 752 (1984).

5. The Maricopa Foundation for Medical Care (Foundation), a nonprofit corporation, is composed of licensed doctors engaged in private practice. The Foundation was designed to promote fee-for-service medicine as an alternative to the existing health insurance plans. The Foundation establishes the schedule of maximum fees that participating doctors agree to accept as payment in full for services for patients insured under the plan. Fee schedules limit the amount that a member doctor may recover for services performed for patients insured under plans approved by the Foundation. To obtain approval, insurers agree to pay doctors' charges up to the scheduled amounts. Does the Sherman Act prohibit this practice? Analyze. See *Arizona v. Maricopa County Medical Society*, 457 U.S. 332 (1982).

6. The National Collegiate Athletic Association (NCAA) adopted a plan for televising college football games. The plan limited the total number of televised collegiate football games overall and for any one team. It also prohibited the sale of any television rights to intercollegiate games. ABC and CBS have agreements with the NCAA to abide by the plan. The College Football Association (CFA) is composed of NCAA member universities. The CFA negotiated a contract with NBC that would have allowed a greater number of televised appearances for its member colleges than permitted under the NCAA plan. Does the NCAA television plan unlawfully restrain trade in violation of the Sherman Act? Explain. See *National Collegiate Athletic Association v. Board of Regents of the University of Oklahoma and University of Georgia Athletic Association*, 468 U.S. 85 (1984).

7. Fortner Enterprises, Inc., buys and improves residential lots. U.S. Steel Corporation operates a division that manufactures and assembles components of prefabricated houses. Credit Corporation is a wholly owned subsidiary of U.S. Steel. Fortner borrowed over $2 million from Credit Corporation to purchase vacant land and erect prefabricated houses on it. As a precondition of the loan Fortner was required to agree to buy the houses from U.S. Steel. What additional information would you like to determine whether this action constitutes an illegal tie-in? See *United States Steel Corp. v. Fortner Enterprises, Inc.*, 429 U.S. 610 (1977).

8. Kodak manufactures and sells photocopiers and micrographic equipment. It also sells service and replacement parts for its equipment. Kodak has adopted policies to limit the availability of parts to independent service organizations (ISOs). It sells replacement parts only to buyers of Kodak equipment who use Kodak service or repair their own machines. Additionally, Kodak contracts for the manufacture of its parts with independent original equipment manufacturers (OEMs). As part of the agreement, the OEMs are not permitted to sell to ISOs. As a result, many ISOs have been forced out of business. Formulate at least six questions, the answers to which would help you answer the question: Has Kodak violated the Sherman Act? See *Eastman Kodak Co. v. Image Technical Services, Inc.*, 112 Sup. Ct. 2072 (1992).

9. Grinnell Corporation controls three companies that have over 87 percent of the accredited central station protection business. This type of business protects homes from fire and burglary by hazard-detecting devices installed on the premises. Accreditation results from the ability to meet the standards of a rating bureau and is recognized by insurance carriers who often require accreditation as a precondition to writing insurance. Grinnell argues that the relevant service market should also include watchman service, services that set off an audible alarm, and unaccredited central station services. Do you agree? Explain. Why is Grinnell making the argument? See *United States v. Grinnell Corp.*, 384 U.S. 563 (1966).

10. SMCRC and NCMCA are rate bureaus composed of common carriers operating in four states. On behalf of their members, these rate bureaus submit joint rate proposals for approval or rejection by the Public Service Commissions in each state. This rate-making procedure is authorized but not compelled by the states within which the rate bureaus operate. Are these activities entitled to immunity under the state action doctrine? Explain. See *Southern Motor Carriers Rate Conference, Inc. v. United States*, 471 U.S. 48 (1985).

Chapter 47

Mergers and Price Discrimination

■

CRITICAL THINKING INQUIRIES

As you read this chapter, you should be able to address the following:

- Distinguish between relevant product markets and relevant geographic markets.
- Analyze: ''Merger activity is healthy for the economy.''
- Identify the factors that are relevant in determining whether a merger is lawful or unlawful.
- Distinguish between lawful and unlawful price discrimination.
- How does the Robinson-Patman Act differ from other antitrust laws?

MANAGERIAL PERSPECTIVE

Olivant, Inc. is in the business of providing computerized travel information to travel agencies. It has about 40 percent of the market within a three-state area. It has adopted a goal of increasing its market share within the next five years so that it is clearly the leader in that market. The new chief executive officer (CEO) of the company has proposed a strategy of accomplishing this goal by mergers and acquisitions of competitors. In addition to this strategy, the CEO desires to reexamine the pricing structure whereby higher fees would be charged to agencies in areas where there is less competition and lower fees in areas where there is more competition. Admittedly, the CEO knows very little about the laws in this area and is interested in knowing the potential legal pitfalls of his strategy.

- What should the CEO know to determine whether particular mergers will violate the antimerger laws?
- What should the CEO know to determine whether her strategy will violate the Robinson-Patman Act?

Antitrust enforcement policy changes with the political climate. Companies that are safe one day from antitrust prosecution may find that a different climate exists tomorrow. And, there is always the potential threat of private treble damage suits by injured competitors. For these reasons, officers and managers at Olivant, Inc., and others need to be familiar with the antitrust aspects contained in this chapter—mergers and price discrimination.

The Sherman Antitrust Act, treated in Chapter 46, examined unreasonable restraints of trade and monopolies. Still, that act did not effectively curb all activities that undermined free competition. In 1914, 24 years after enacting the Sherman Act, Congress passed the Clayton Act. This chapter examines section 7, the antimerger provision, and section 2, the anti–price discrimination provision, of the Clayton Act. Both these sections are designed to complement the Sherman Antitrust Act and thereby promote competition.

Section 7 of the Clayton Act is aimed at mergers that tend to lessen competition or create a monopoly. Section 2 of the Clayton Act prohibits **price discrimination**, whereby a seller gives a more favorable price treatment to one buyer than another, when that practice threatens to undermine competition.

MERGERS

A **merger** occurs when one company acquires another company. Mergers come in all shapes and forms. For example, Company A may acquire Company B by purchasing Company B's stock. That is called merger by stock acquisition. Or Company A may acquire Company B by purchasing Company B's assets. This is referred to as merger by asset acquisition. Sometimes, the acquired firm is subsumed within the acquiring firm's enterprise: A + B = A. Other times, the acquired firm may maintain a distinct identity: A + B = A and B. Here, both companies survive the merger. The company that acquires the other company may be referred to as a parent company and the acquired company, a subsidiary. Still other times, two firms may merge and form a third company: A + B = C (see Figure 47–1).

Some mergers are friendly and some are not. In a friendly merger, the acquired company desires the merger, and the merger is often preceded by negotiation and agreement. In an unfriendly merger, an acquired firm (target) is reluctantly taken over by a

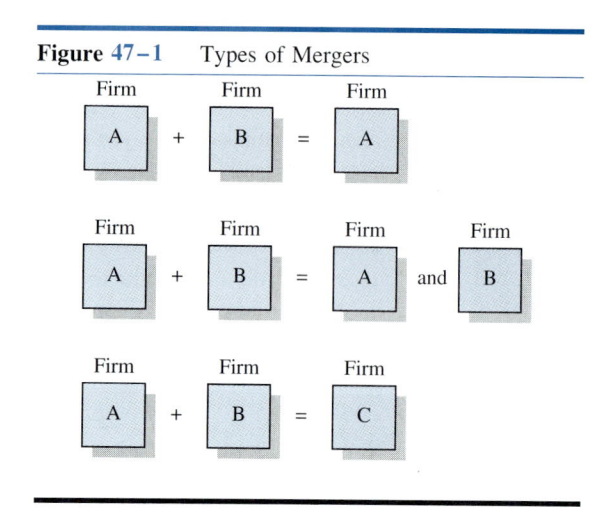

Figure 47–1   Types of Mergers

"raider" company (see Figure 47–2). This is often accomplished by a **tender offer**—offering to purchase a controlling interest in the stock from the shareholders at an above-market price. (Tender offers are regulated by the Securities and Exchange Commission and are discussed more fully in Chapter 45.)

A raider corporation might seek to take over another company for many reasons. The target company may have excess cash or attractive raw materials. Acquisition might strengthen the raider's overall earnings. Perhaps acquisition would result in a fuller product line. Not to be discounted are the ego rewards the raider might enjoy from a takeover.

A target company need not sit back and allow the raider to succeed. Various techniques can help fend off the attacker. Shareholders can be dissuaded from selling their shares to the raider, especially if they are convinced that the new management would not act in the company's best interest. Also, the target may engage in a bidding war by offering shareholders more money for their stock. Sometimes a target company will seek to merge with a **white knight**—a company that will favor existing management and leave the target basically undisturbed. Another tactic is the **shark repellant** defense. Here, the target attempts to thwart the raid by making itself undesirable. For example, it may acquire a company in the raider's same product line, and thus raise antitrust objections to the raid. A few companies have successfully invoked the **Pac Man** defense. This is where the target launches a counterattack and attempts to take over its raider. More and more companies are realizing the necessity of having a pre-

Figure 47–2   Unfriendly Merger

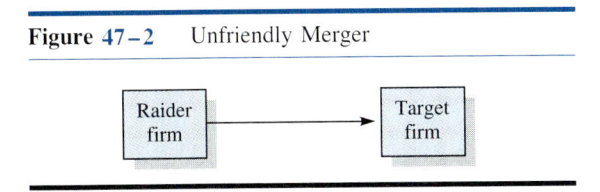

planned strategy to counter takeover threats. Many companies have emergency crisis teams and takeover manuals to respond to such threats.

The Clayton Act regulates merger activity. Section 7 of the act prohibits mergers when the effect of the merger "may be substantially to lessen competition, or to tend to create a monopoly." To violate section 7, the merger activity need not actually lessen competition or result in a monopoly. It need only pose such a threat. In this respect, section 7 is intended to nip anticompetitive activity in the bud. A threefold analysis helps determine whether a merger violates the act. Each of these components should be included in a merger analysis:

- Determine the relevant market.
- Prepare a premerger profile.
- Do a postmerger prognosis.

Relevant Market

The concept of relevant market was discussed in Chapter 46 under monopolization. The relevant market is the competitive market within which the merger is analyzed. When evaluating a merger under Clayton Act section 7, this relevant market—product and geographic—must be defined.

Relevant Product Market

Cross-elasticity of demand and substitutability, as under Sherman Act section 2, are essential considerations for determining the relevant product market. Under Clayton Act section 7, however, courts are apt to divide the markets into submarkets. This is because section 7 is concerned not only with actual monopolization but also the protection of potential competition. As a result, the courts often narrowly define the product market, even to the extent in one case where retail frozen pies were designated as an appropriate submarket.

The U.S. Supreme Court has cited several criteria germane to the determination of the relevant product market. They are listed in the following case involving a merger of lead smelters.

RSR CORP. v. FTC
602 F.2d 1317 (9th Cir. 1979)

RSR Corporation operated lead smelting plants in Dallas and Newark, N.J. These two plants produced secondary lead. Secondary lead is recycled from other lead products. Primary lead is processed from raw lead ore. RSR was the country's second largest producer of secondary lead, producing 12.16 percent.

Quemetco operated lead smelting plants in Seattle, Indianapolis, and City of Industry, California, and was completing a plant in Walkill, N.Y. Quemetco produced 7.02 percent of the secondary lead in the United States, ranking it fifth among secondary lead producers. RSR Corporation acquired Quemetco and the merger resulted in RSR maintaining its second position in the market with an increased share of 19.18 percent.

The Federal Trade Commission (FTC) found that the merger violated section 7 of the Clayton Act and ordered RSR to divest itself of all premerger Quemetco assets except the Seattle plant. The case was appealed. Set out here is the portion of the opinion dealing with the determination of the relevant product market.

PREGERSON, Judge

The parties first disagree over whether the overall lead market (including both primary and secondary lead) or the secondary lead market alone is the relevant product market for testing the RSR/Quemetco merger under Section 7. RSR contends that substantial competition exists between primary and secondary producers in the production of soft lead; thus, the overall lead market must be considered. The

FTC, relying on distinctions between the primary and secondary lead markets, argues that the secondary lead market alone is the relevant product market.

The factors used to determine the relevant product market in an antitrust case were set out by the Supreme Court in *Brown Shoe Co. v. United States* . . . . The Court stated that the outer boundaries of a product market can be determined by the ''reasonable interchangeability of use or the cross-elasticity of demand between the product itself and substitutes for it.'' The Court observed that well-defined submarkets may also exist which, in themselves, can constitute product markets for antitrust purposes, and suggested that determining the boundaries of such a submarket could be done ''by examining such practical indicia as industry or public recognition of the submarket as a separate economic entity, the product's peculiar characteristics and uses, unique production facilities, distinct customers, distinct prices, sensitivity to price changes, and specialized vendors.'' The Court then explained that, since Section 7 prohibits any merger that may substantially lessen competition in *any* line of commerce, the effects of a merger must be examined in each economically-significant submarket to determine if there is a reasonable possibility that the merger will substantially lessen competition in that submarket. . . .

We have considered each of the *Brown Shoe* indicia separately and find that substantial evidence supports the FTC's determination that the secondary lead market is the relevant product market for testing the RSR/Quemetco merger. We have briefly summarized some of this evidence below.

Industry or public recognition of the submarket as a separate economic entity: Evidence was presented to show that the lead industry distinguished between primary and secondary lead in terms of the products and their producers. RSR contends that this recognition signifies only that the industry is aware of the different raw material source for each type of lead. Nevertheless, evidence indicated that consumers and lead producers, as well as national production reports, distinguish between the two types of lead.

Product's peculiar characteristics: Secondary lead is derived from recycling other lead products [e.g., scrap automobile batteries], not from smelting raw lead ore. As a result, secondary lead as a rule contains impurities (primarily metals) not found in primary lead. Secondary lead, although it can be purified almost to the degree of pure lead, is generally used as hard or metallic lead. Primary lead, since it is pure and free of hardening metals, is generally used as soft lead. Soft lead and hard lead are generally not used for the same purposes. Primary and secondary soft lead can sometimes be interchanged, as can primary and secondary hard lead, but certain uses require . . . primary lead, while other uses require secondary lead. Moreover, it is usually not economical for a primary producer to manufacture hard lead. Secondary producers obtain some soft lead as a by-product of the manufacture of antimonial lead; due to impurities, this soft lead is generally not suitable for most industrial soft lead uses.

Distinct customers: At the time of the FTC hearing, hard lead was chiefly used for automobile battery posts and grids, while soft lead was used for battery oxides and tetraethyl lead, an antiknock additive to gasoline. Battery manufacturers were thus the major customers of both primary and secondary lead producers. Evidence was presented to show that some customers specify not only that they require hard or soft lead but also that they want primary or secondary lead.

Distinct vendors: Most of the lead produced by primary producers is pure or soft lead. Although metal can be added to the pure lead to harden it, the evidence shows that it is not economical to do so. Moreover, casting characteristics of artificially-hardened lead make it unsuitable for battery grids and posts. Thus, primary producers generally restrict their production to soft lead. Secondary producers, on the other hand, chiefly produce hard lead. During the production of antimonial lead, a hard lead, some soft lead is also produced. At the time of the merger, secondary producers were using most of this soft lead in their internal operations rather than selling it to manufacturers of battery oxides.

Distinct prices: RSR presented evidence that only one worldwide price is set for lead: no distinctions between primary and secondary lead are made on the London Exchange. But the evidence showed and the FTC found that, although both primary and secondary producers discount the price of lead, secondary lead customarily sells for about 10 percent less than primary lead.

Sensitivity to price changes: Because secondary lead is generally shipped over shorter distances than primary lead, secondary producers customarily ship by truck while primary producers ship by rail. Evidence was presented to show that trucking costs vary more widely than rail costs, causing secondary lead prices to vary accordingly.

Although some of the evidence presented to the FTC was open to differing interpretations, we are not permitted to second-guess its findings if supported by substantial evidence. We hold that the findings were so supported and that the FTC correctly applied the law in making its findings on relevant product market.

Affirmed.

Case Questions

1. What is the issue in this case?

2. Compare and contrast RSR Corporation and Quemetco.

3. How would you list, in order of importance, the *Brown Shoe* criteria for determining submarkets?

4. Compare and contrast the parties' positions. Why would RSR Corporation want primary and secondary lead to be within the same relevant product market?

Relevant Geographical Market

Section 7 of the Clayton Act prohibits mergers that may substantially lessen competition "in any line of commerce in any section of the country." Hence, it is necessary to determine the relevant geographic market. The **relevant geographic market** is the particular area where the acquired firm is a significant competitor. It may encompass an area such as the entire United States or a single city. There are two approaches to defining the relevant geographic market. One approach defines the market by identifying the points where the acquired firm makes significant sales. The second approach includes all points where the acquired firm's activities competitively affect other firms. For example, assume that Olivant, Inc., acquired by Computer Graphics, markets its computer programs in Ohio, Indiana, and Illinois. It is very possible that Olivant affects firms marketing computers in Michigan. If so, these firms will have to price their computer programs with sensitivity to Olivant as a potential competitor. If the price is high enough, Olivant could enter the Michigan market. Hence, under the second approach, Michigan would be included within the relevant geographic market. Under the first, of course, it would not.

Premerger Profile

Determining the relevant product and geographic markets completes the first step of a merger analysis. We now have a framework for the next step: developing a premerger profile. The premerger profile requires determining the type of merger, the size of the companies, and the concentration of the industry. Analysis of this information enables us to do

a postmerger prognosis. But first, each aspect of the premerger profile is examined more closely.

Type of Merger

Mergers may be classified into one of four categories for Clayton Act Section 7 analysis: horizontal, vertical, product extension, and conglomerate (see Figure 47–3).

A **horizontal merger** occurs when two competitive firms at the same level of distribution merge. Level of distribution refers to where the company operates in the marketing chain—for example, manufacturing, wholesaling, or retailing. A merger between two clothing wholesalers, then, would be horizontal. Of the four types of mergers, the horizontal merger poses the greatest immediate threat to competition; those firms that were once competing against each other no longer do so.

The **vertical merger** occurs when two firms at different levels of competition that deal in the same products merge. An example would be a merger between a clothing wholesaler and retailer. The impact on competition from this type of merger, while more subtle than that of a horizontal merger, definitely exists. For example, assume that a manufacturer of sporting goods acquires retail sporting goods stores. Competition will be affected in two ways. The acquirer obviously will supply the retail sporting goods stores. Consequently, no other sporting goods manufacturer can successfully compete for the stores' business. A second likely result is that the retail sporting goods competitors can no longer obtain their goods from the acquiring firm.

The third type of merger, the **extension merger,** occurs when two firms at the same level of compe-

Figure 47–3   Classification of Mergers

Class of Merger	Characteristic	Likelihood of Antitrust Violation (rank order)	Example
Horizontal	Same product among competitors	1	Merger between two manufacturers of computer chips
Vertical	Same product among noncompetitors	2	Merger between manufacturer and distributor of building supplies
Product Extension	Related product among noncompetitors	3	Merger between paperclip and rubberband firms
Conglomerate	Different products among noncompetitors	4	Merger between office equipment firm and sporting goods firm

tition, but in different geographical markets, merge. Or such a merger occurs between two firms operating in the same geographical relevant markets but selling different though related products. These types of mergers are ordinarily not a great threat to competition. However, consider the following case involving an attempted merger between a firm dealing in household bleach and a firm dealing in detergents.

FTC v. PROCTER & GAMBLE CO.
386 U.S. 568 (1967)

Procter & Gamble (P&G) acquired the assets of Clorox Chemical Co. Clorox was the leading manufacturer of household liquid bleach, a whitening agent used in washing clothes and fabrics. Clorox sold nationally, having 13 plants throughout the United States. It had 48.8 percent of the market or about $40 million in annual sales. Its largest competitor, Purex, had 15.7 percent of the liquid bleach market. The top four firms accounted for almost 80 percent of the market. The remaining 20 percent was spread among 200 small producers. Clorox had assets of $12 million.

P&G manufactures household products. Before its acquisition, it did not produce household liquid bleach. Its main products are soaps, detergents, and cleansers.

P&G has sales exceeding $1 billion and assets over $500 million. P&G was the nation's largest advertiser, spending over $125 million for advertising and sales promotions.

The FTC charged P&G with violation of section 7 of the Clayton Act. It concluded that P&G violated the act and ordered P&G be divested of Clorox. The Court of Appeals reversed. The U.S. Supreme Court granted certiorari.

DOUGLAS, Justice

Section 7 of the Clayton Act was intended to arrest the anticompetitive effects of market power in their incipiency. The core question is whether a merger may substantially lessen competition, and necessar- ily requires a prediction of the merger's impact on competition, present and future. The section can deal only with probabilities, not with certainties. And there is certainly no requirement that the anti- competitive power manifest itself in anticompetitive action before section 7 can be called into play. If the enforcement of section 7 turned on the existence of actual anticompetitive practices, the congressional policy of thwarting such practices in their incipiency would be frustrated.

All mergers are within the reach of section 7, and all must be tested by the same standard, whether they are classified as horizontal, vertical, conglomerate or other. As noted by the Commission, this merger is neither horizontal, vertical, nor conglomerate. Since the products of the acquired company are complementary to those of the acquiring company and may be produced with similar facilities, marketed through the same channels and in the same manner, and advertised by the same media, the Commission aptly called this acquisition a "product-extension merger." . . .

The anticompetitive effects with which this product-extension merger is fraught can easily be seen: (1) the substitution of the powerful acquiring firm for the smaller, but already dominant, firm may substantially reduce the competitive structure of the industry by raising entry barriers and by dissuading the smaller firms from aggressively competing; (2) the acquisition eliminates the potential competition of the acquiring firm.

The liquid bleach industry was already oligopolistic before the acquisition, and price competition was certainly not as vigorous as it would have been if the industry were competitive. Clorox enjoyed a dominant position nationally, and its position approached monopoly proportions in certain areas. The existence of some 200 fringe firms certainly does not belie that fact. Nor does the fact, relied upon by the court below, that, after the merger, producers other than Clorox "were selling more bleach for more money than ever before." In the same period, Clorox increased its share from 48.8 percent to 52 percent. The interjection of Procter into the market considerably changed the situation. There is every reason to assume that the smaller firms would become more cautious in competing due to their fear of retaliation by Procter. It is probable that Procter would become the price leader and that oligopoly would become more rigid.

The acquisition may also have the tendency of raising the barriers to new entry. The major competitive weapon in the successful marketing of bleach is advertising. Clorox was limited in this area by its relatively small budget and its inability to obtain substantial discounts. By contrast, Procter's budget was much larger; and, although it would not devote its entire budget to advertising Clorox, it could divert a large portion to meet the short-term threat of a new entrant. Procter would be able to use its volume discounts to advantage in advertising Clorox. Thus, a new entrant would be much more reluctant to face the giant Procter than it would have been to face the smaller Clorox.

The Commission also found that the acquisition of Clorox by Procter eliminated Procter as a potential competitor. The Court of Appeals declared that this finding was not supported by evidence because there was no evidence that Procter's management had ever intended to enter the industry independently and that Procter had never attempted to enter. The evidence, however, clearly shows that Procter was the most likely entrant. Procter had recently launched a new abrasive cleaner in an industry similar to the liquid bleach industry, and had wrested leadership from a brand that had enjoyed even a larger market share than had Clorox. Procter was engaged in a vigorous program of diversifying into product lines closely related to its basic products. Liquid bleach was a natural avenue of diversification since it is complementary to Procter's products, is sold to the same customers through the same channels, and is advertised and merchandised in the same manner. Procter had substantial advantages in advertising and sales promotion, which, as we have seen, are vital to the success of liquid bleach. No manufacturer had a patent on the product or its manufacture, necessary information relating to manufacturing methods and processes was readily available, there was no shortage of raw material, and the machinery and equipment required for a plant of efficient capacity were available at reasonable cost. Procter's management was experienced in producing and marketing goods similar to liquid bleach. Procter had considered the possibility of independently entering but decided against it because the acquisition of Clorox would enable Procter to capture a more commanding share of the market.

It is clear that the existence of Procter at the edge of the industry exerted considerable influence on the market. First, the market behavior of the liquid bleach industry was influenced by each firm's predictions of the market behavior of its competitors, actual and potential. Second, the barriers to entry by a firm of Procter's size and with its advantages were not significant. There is no indication that the barriers were so high that the price Procter would have to charge would be above the price that would maximize the profits of the existing firms. Third, the number of potential entrants was not so large that the elimination of one would be insignificant. Few firms would have the temerity to challenge a firm as solidly entrenched as Clorox. Fourth, Procter was found by the Commission to be the most likely entrant. These findings of the Commission were amply supported by the evidence.

The judgment of the Court of Appeals is reversed and remanded with instructions to affirm and enforce the Commission's order.

Case Questions

1. What is the issue in this case?

2. What is the strongest argument for holding that this merger violates the Clayton Act? What is the weakest argument?

3. What counterarguments could you make in support of the lawfulness of the merger?

4. As P&G's chief executive officer, formulate strategy for lawfully entering the liquid bleach industry after this case.

The fourth type of merger poses the least threat to competition. Called the **conglomerate merger,** it involves two firms that deal in totally unrelated products. For example, a rubberband manufacturer's buyout of a soft drink producer would be a conglomerate merger. Even here, however, as in *Procter & Gamble Co.,* there is a possibility that the merger would be deemed illegal under Clayton Act section 7. A court's ruling will depend on the size of the company and the market structure.

Size of Companies

The larger the acquiring company, the greater a merger's impact on competition. In one case, *Brown Shoe,* the 3rd largest retail shoe seller and the 4th largest shoe manufacturer, acquired Kinney, the 8th largest retail seller and the 12th largest shoe manufacturer.[1] The sheer size of these two firms contributed to the ultimate holding that the merger violated Clayton Act section 7. As this example implies, each company's market share becomes a factor in predicting the effects of the merger. The larger the firms' postmerger combined market share, the more likely the merger will violate Clayton Act section 7.

Concentration

A third facet of the premerger profile requires an examination of the structure of the industry, the concentration of firms, and emerging trends within it. Here, we ask how many firms are in the relevant market and what percentage of the market is attributed to the leading firms. If thousands of firms compete within an industry, each with 1 percent or less of the market, the industry would be considered unconcentrated. In an unconcentrated industry, mergers are not highly suspect. If, however, a few firms within an industry dominate a large share of the market, mergers between top firms would be highly suspect. The trend of concentration—whether the makeup of the industry is moving toward greater or lesser concentration—is also important.

Postmerger Prognosis

After identifying the relevant market and preparing a premerger profile, the next step is to determine whether the merger is violative of Clayton Act section 7. The postmerger prognosis seeks to answer the question: Is it probable that the merger will substantially lessen competition or tend to create a monopoly? There is no clear numerical formula for that determination. The following case, however, is a helpful guide.

---

[1] *Brown Shoe Co. v. United States,* 370 U.S. 294 (1961).

UNITED STATES v. VON'S GROCERY CO.

384 U.S. 270 (1966)

Von's Grocery Company acquired its direct competitor, Shopping Bag Food Stores, both retail grocery companies in Los Angeles, California. The United States brought an action charging that the acquisition violated section 7 of the Clayton Act. The U.S. District Court concluded that there was no reasonable probability that the merger would substantially lessen competition or tend to create a monopoly. The government appealed directly to the U.S. Supreme Court.

BLACK, Justice

The market involved here is the retail grocery market in the Los Angeles area. In 1958 Von's retail sales ranked third in the area and Shopping Bag's ranked sixth. In 1960 their sales together were 7.5 percent of the total $2.5 billion of retail groceries sold in the Los Angeles market each year. For many years before the merger both companies had enjoyed great success as rapidly growing companies. From 1948 to 1958 the number of Von's stores in the Los Angeles area practically doubled from 14 to 27, while at the same time the number of Shopping Bag's stores jumped from 15 to 34. During that same decade, Von's sales increased fourfold and its share of the market tripled. The merger of these two highly successful, expanding and aggressive competitors created the second largest grocery chain in Los Angeles with sales of almost $172,488,000 annually. In addition the findings of the District Court show that the number of owners operating single stores in the Los Angeles retail grocery market decreased from 5,365 in 1950 to 3,818 in 1961. By 1963, three years after the merger, the number of single-store owners had dropped still further to 3,590. During roughly the same period, from 1953 to 1962, the number of chains with two or more grocery stores increased from 96 to 150. While the grocery business was being concentrated into the hands of fewer and fewer owners, the small companies were continually being absorbed by the larger firms through mergers. According to an exhibit prepared by one of the Government's expert witnesses, in the period from 1949 to 1958 nine of the top 20 chains acquired 126 stores from their smaller competitors. . . . Moreover . . . acquisitions and mergers in the Los Angeles retail grocery market have continued at a rapid rate since the merger.

The facts of this case present exactly the threatening trend toward concentration which Congress wanted to halt. The number of small grocery companies in the Los Angeles retail grocery market had been declining rapidly before the merger and continued to decline rapidly afterwards. This rapid decline in the number of grocery store owners moved hand in hand with a large number of significant absorptions of the small companies by the larger ones.

In the midst of this steadfast trend toward concentration, Von's and Shopping Bag, two of the most successful and largest companies in the area, jointly owning 66 grocery stores merged to become the second largest chain in Los Angeles. This merger cannot be defended on the ground that one of the companies was about to fail or that the two had to merge to save themselves from destruction by some larger and more powerful competitor. What we have on the contrary is simply the case of two already powerful companies merging in a way which makes them even more powerful than they were before. If ever such a merger would not violate section 7, certainly it does when it takes place in a market characterized by a long and continuous trend toward fewer and fewer owner-competitors which is exactly the sort of trend which Congress, with power to do so, declared must be arrested.

Appellees' primary argument is that the merger between Von's and Shopping Bag is not prohibited by section 7 because the Los Angeles grocery market was competitive before the merger, has been since, and may continue to be in the future. Even so, section 7 ''requires not merely an appraisal of the immediate impact of the merger upon competition, but a prediction of its impact upon competitive conditions in the future; this is what is meant when it is said that the amended section 7 was intended to arrest anticompetitive tendencies in their 'incipiency.' '' It is enough for us that Congress feared that a market marked at the same time by both a continuous decline in the number of small businesses and a large number of mergers would slowly but inevitably gravitate from a market of many small competitors to one dominated by one or a few giants, and competition would thereby be destroyed. Congress passed the Celler-Kefauver Act to prevent such a destruction of competition. Our cases since the passage of that Act have faithfully endeavored to enforce this congressional command. We adhere to them now.

Reversed and remanded.

Case Questions

1. What is the issue this case presents?
2. Could you define the relevant product market in a different way than the court does? The relevant geographic market?

3. Prepare a premerger profile of both companies.

4. Do you agree that the merger would probably lessen competition? Analyze.

5. Change the profile of the companies such that the merger would clearly not violate the Clayton Act.

Defenses

The plaintiff in a Clayton Act section 7 case must prove that the merger may substantially lessen competition or tend to result in a monopoly. One defense to the charge is for the defendant to muster evidence attacking that conclusion. For example, in *United States v. General Dynamics Corporation,* the government complained that General Dynamics' acquisition of another coal producer, United Electric Coal Companies, violated section 7 of the Clayton Act. The coal-producing industry was found to be very concentrated. General Dynamics was able to rebut the presumption of illegality by a showing that United Electric's long-term coal reserves were almost depleted and that the merger would not substantially lessen competition.[2]

Section 7 is inapplicable to corporations that purchase stock "solely for investment" purposes. This is an absolute defense if proved by the defendant. Also, the failing company defense provides that a merger that is a last resort to save a dying company will be excused from section 7 compliance.

Enforcement

Violation of section 7 constitutes a civil offense. Private parties who have been injured as a result of a section 7 violation may recover treble damages. The Justice Department and the Federal Trade Commission may also enforce the act by seeking divestiture of a merger already accomplished. **Divestiture** is the unraveling of a merger by returning the firms to their status before the merger. It is often very difficult and complicated, as exemplified by the divestiture of AT&T which took two years to accomplish.

The Hart-Scott-Rodino Antitrust Improvements Act was enacted to reduce the incidence of postmerger divestitures. The act, an amendment to the Clayton Act, requires that a 30-day premerger notice be given to the FTC of the firm's intent to merge.

The act applies when the acquiring company has at least $100 million of sales or assets, and the company to be acquired has at least $10 million. The FTC and the Justice Department are empowered to enjoin mergers that would violate section 7.

Since 1968, the Justice Department has issued guidelines on its enforcement policy regarding mergers. These guidelines have been revised periodically. Designed to inform business about which mergers will be challenged and which will go unchallenged, the guidelines lack the effect of law, and courts are not bound by them. Still, they enable businesses to conduct themselves in a manner that will be a "safe harbor" from government challenge.

The guidelines are based on a formula known as the Herfindahl-Hirschman Index (HHI). The HHI measures concentration within the industry. It is calculated by summing the square of the market shares of each firm and is illustrated in Figure 47–4. The HHI in the Widget industry equals 1,018. Should any two firms merge, the HHI would change. For example, if Firms 1 and 4 merged, the HHI would change to 1,378. The net change as a result of the

Figure 47–4   Calculation of HHI in the Widget Industry

Firm	Market Share	Market Share Squared
1	20	400
2	17	289
3	12	144
4	9	81
5	6	36
6	5	25
7	3	9
8	3	9
9–33	1 each	25
Total	100	1,018 (HHI)

[2] 415 U.S. 486 (1974).

merger would be 360. However, the merger of Firms 7 and 8 would result in an HHI of 1,036, an increase of only 18.

Under the merger guidelines, any industry having an HHI below 1,000 is deemed unconcentrated; an HHI between 1,000 and 1,800 is moderately concentrated; and an industry above 1,800 is highly concentrated. Thus, the widget industry in Figure 47–4, with an HHI of 1,018, would be considered moderately concentrated. Mergers among competitors in highly concentrated industries will more likely be challenged than those in unconcentrated industries. Most recently, the Justice Department and the Federal Trade Commission have issued new joint guidelines for antitrust enforcement that is explored in the following article.

*A Merging of the Minds on Antitrust Policy**

. . . The apparent difference between the new and old guidelines arguably reflects a shift away from the . . . focus on economic theory to the . . . more pragmatic enforcement policy.

Defining the Market

To understand [the] . . . changes, it would be helpful to describe how the agencies will apply the new guidelines in working through some of the basic steps of merger analysis: defining the market, calculating concentration levels, and assessing factors other than concentration that could bear on the merger's competitive impact.

The new guidelines use essentially the same approach to product and geographic market definition that the agencies have relied on since at least the early 1980s. . . .

After the relevant market has been defined, the next step in merger analysis is to identify the firms participating in the market to calculate the increase in market concentration as a result of the merger. Firms that currently sell in a market, of course, are considered "in the market" for the purpose of calculating concentration.

In addition, the agencies will include in the market those firms . . . [that] enter and exit relatively quickly and at little expense in response to competitive conditions.

■ ■ ■

Concentrating on Competition

Having identified the relevant market and the firms that participate within that market, the agencies then calculate how much concentration will increase as a result of the merger. Concentration was once deemed the most important factor in merger analysis. The traditional presumption was that, everything else being equal, a larger number of competitors leads to more vigorous competition, i.e., a market with 100 firms, each of which has only a 1 percent share of the market, is likely to be more competitive than a market with four firms, each of which has a 25 percent share of the market. The old guidelines justified this presumption primarily on the grounds that successful collusion was more likely as a market concentration increased—small cartels are easier to form and maintain than large cartels.

Experience has shown, however, that there is no necessary relationship between concentration and competition. Some industries with only few competitors are intensely competitive, while many industries with a large number of firms are competitively sluggish. The new guidelines acknowledge this difficulty by adopting a broader and more theoretical approach to evaluating the competitive consequences of mergers that increase concentration.

*Source: John Magney, Steve MacIssac, and Patrick J. McDermott, "A Merging of the Minds on Antitrust Policy," American Lawyer Newspaper's Group, Inc. 1992, *Conn. Law Tribune,* August 3, 1992. Reprinted with permission.

■ ■ ■

Policy Conforms to Practice

The principal change under the new guidelines is the characterization of the agencies' likely reaction to various changes in concentration in moderately concentrated and highly concentrated markets. Under the old guidelines, the government was "likely to challenge" mergers that increased the HHI more than 100 points in moderately concentrated markets. The new guidelines simply state that mergers in this HHI range "potentially raise significant competitive concerns," and leave the determination whether enforcement action is warranted to an analysis of a host of other factors. In fact, as the agencies themselves have candidly acknowledged, this change simply reflects the fact that the government has in recent years rarely challenged mergers in this HHI range.

The new guidelines also treat mergers in concentrated markets (i.e., HHI above 1,800) somewhat differently from the old guidelines. While the old guidelines stated that a government challenge was "likely" in such markets if the merger increased the HHI more than 50 points and was virtually certain if the HHI increased by 100 points or more, the new guidelines take the position that an HHI increase of between 50 and 100 points will only "raise significant competitive concerns" requiring further analysis and an increase of 100 points or more only establishes a presumption, rebuttable by the parties, that the merger will harm competition.

In Defense of Mergers

The new guidelines give fairly extensive treatment to the countervailing factors merger proponents will rely on in urging the agencies to look beyond the HHI. The most important arguments merger supporters are likely to make are that the merger will make possible certain "efficiencies" that will benefit consumers and that large customers (so-called power buyers) and new entrants will exert enough market discipline to keep merging firms (and their rivals) from raising prices after a merger.

Too Rigorous a Test?

The same can be said of the competitive analysis of "entry"—the emergence of a new competitor in response to a price increase or other factors. . . .

The new guidelines set forth a three-prong entry test. For the agencies to consider the defense, entry must be "timely, likely and sufficient in its magnitude, character and scope" to prevent or counteract a merger's anti-competitive effects. . . .

■ ■ ■

In sum, the new guidelines approach the entry questions from a far more rigorous analytical perspective than that employed by the courts in the past decade. Indeed, it is questionable whether the agencies themselves will be able, given the time constraints and data limitations they face in a typical merger investigation, to sort through the new guidelines' complex entry analysis.

A Successful Synthesis?

By recognizing the importance of actors other than concentration—countervailing buyer power, efficiencies, and entry—the new guidelines in many respects reflect the evolution of the agencies' merger analysis and enforcement policies over the past decade. That evolution has been driven to a large extent by economic theories and empirical insights that have seriously eroded the force of the traditional presumption of a close relationship between concentration and competition.

At the same time, the new guidelines advance new theories based on modern economics to justify looking to concentration as a starting point for merger analysis. Whether this effort at synthesis will succeed will ultimately depend, of course, not on economics or agency policy, but on the courts.

Thought Questions

1. Will the new approach result in more or fewer antitrust challenges? Explain.

2. How would you rank order the importance of the following when considering a merger's effect on competition: concentration, buyer power, efficiencies, and entry.

3. Criticize the new approach.

4. Analyze: "Whether this effort at synthesis will succeed will ultimately depend, of course, not on economics or agency policy, but on the courts."

PRICE DISCRIMINATION

Section 2 of the Clayton Act prohibits discrimination "where the effect of such discrimination may be substantially to lessen competition or tend to create a monopoly. . . ." The section was intended to eliminate sellers' practice of treating one customer more favorably than another pricewise in an effort to eliminate competition. For example, assume that Knit Wit Corporation, a manufacturer and supplier of sporting clothes, sells its clothing to customers in Montana and to customers in New York (see Figure 47–5). Herring Bone competes directly for the sporting clothes business in New York. In the absence of a law to the contrary, Knit Wit could slash its price to New York customers below its charge to Montana customers in an attempt to remove Herring Bone, its main competitor. Knit Wit might even price its goods below cost, until its motive was accomplished — the removal of Herring Bone from the competitive market. In the meantime, in Montana, where competition is minimal, Knit Wit could

keep its prices to customers high and thus make up for losses in the New York market. The favorable treatment to New York customers would result in a type of competitive injury to Herring Bone referred to as **primary-line injury.** Section 2 of the Clayton Act was designed to prohibit this type of competitive practice.

In the 1920s, large chain stores arrived in the market. Because of their size, they were able to command lower prices from their suppliers. Independent stores, particularly grocers, were disappearing from the competitive market because of these discriminatory practices. For example, assume that Cooperative Grocery Association (CGA) purchased large quantities of groceries. It could extract great discounts from, for example, Wholesale Grocers, which enabled CGA to sell its goods cheaper than its Ma and Pa competitors. This practice caused injury to these independent buyers. This situation is referred to as **secondary-line injury,** because the injury occurs at the buyer's level (see Figure 47–6). However, because of the restrictive application of

Figure 47–5   Price Discrimination—Primary-Line Injury

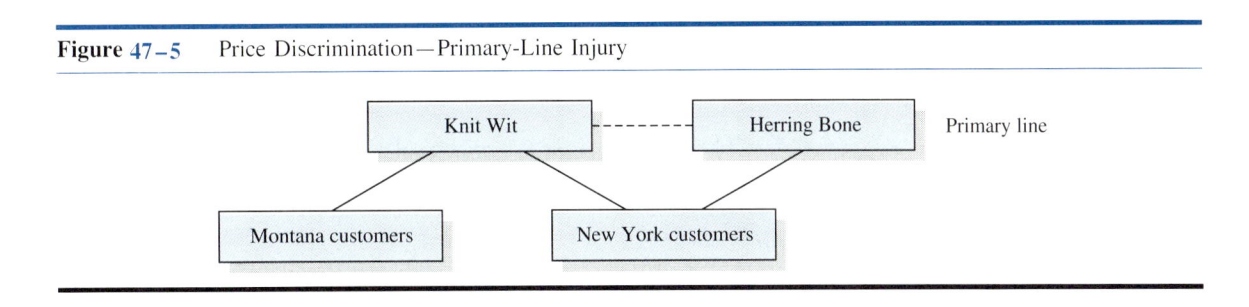

section 2, the courts interpreted it not to reach this secondary-line injury. To provide a remedy, the act was amended in 1937 by the Robinson-Patman Act. As amended, the act prohibits (1) sellers from discriminating in price in the sale of commodities that are of like grade and quality when it results in competitive injury, (2) buyers from knowingly inducing or receiving a price discrimination, and (3) other discriminatory practices accomplished by brokerage payments and promotional allowances and services.

Seller Discrimination

The heart of the Robinson-Patman Act is section 2(a), which prohibits unjustifiable price discrimination in interstate commerce. In order to meet the interstate commerce requirement, the violator must be engaged in interstate commerce, the price discrimination must occur in interstate commerce, and at least one of the purchases must be made in interstate commerce. Violation of the act occurs when there is a (1) price difference, (2) involving two sales of, (3) commodities, (4) of like grade and quality, (5) that results in competitive injury.

Price Difference
Discrimination in price occurs when a seller charges two customers different prices. Price is based on the actual cost to the buyer. Therefore, to determine if there has been a difference in price, adjustments may have to be made. Assume that Olivant, Inc., sells 100 megabytes of computerized travel service to Customer 1 at $100 a megabyte payable cash on delivery. Orange Crate delivers 100 megabytes of computerized travel services to customer 2 at $100 a megabyte with terms of payment including a 2 percent discount if paid within 10 days. Customer 2 has actually received a more favorable price treatment than customer 1. This constitutes a price difference.

Two Sales
Price discrimination only occurs when there have been two actual completed sales. A completed sale occurs when there is a contract for the sale of the goods. Gifts or consignments are not covered under the act. Sales that are disguised as gifts or consignments are, however, subject to the act. For example, assume Tires of Tomorrow sells one tire to a customer for $60 on the terms that the customer gets another tire free. For purposes of price discrimination, the transaction would be considered a sale of two tires for $60.

Commodities
The act only applies to tangible goods that are movable. It does not apply to real estate, services, leases, or loans. When a sale involves both commodities and services, the essential nature of the contract controls. For example, a contract for the sale of a refrigerator coupled with a service contract on the refrigerator would probably be considered a sale of a commodity within the Robinson-Patman act. In one case, however, where bricks were sold to a buyer along with a contract to construct housing facilities, the court found the whole arrangement to be a construction service contract not covered by the act.

Like Grade and Quality
Goods that are the subject of unjustified price discrimination must be of like grade and quality. Basketballs and tennis balls are obviously not of like grade and quality. Gloves made of leather are not of the same grade and quality as gloves made of vinyl. Consequently, a price difference in those cases is justified. Some manufacturers produce a product that they will sell in two different markets. Some will be imprinted with a national brand while others

Figure 47–6   Price Discrimination—Secondary-Line Injury

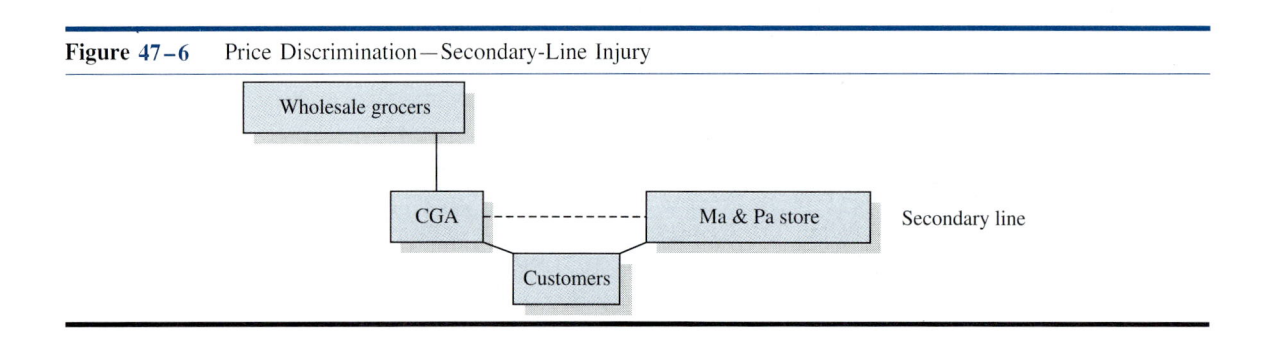

will be stamped with a private brand. Customer preference is normally greater for the nationally branded item than the private branded one. The two products are nonetheless considered as like grade and quality. Customer preference and psychological motivation are not taken into account for purposes of "like grade and quality."

Injury to Competition

Still another ingredient that must be present in a Robinson-Patman violation is competitive injury. Price discrimination in the sale of commodities of like grade and quality does not constitute a violation of section 2 of the Clayton Act in the absence of competitive injury. For example, in *FTC v. Borden*, the Supreme Court remanded the case to the Court of Appeals to determine whether anyone suffered competitive injury. In holding that there was no competitive injury, that court stated:

We are of the firm view that where a price differential between a premium and nonpremium brand reflects no more than a consumer preference for the premium brand, the price difference creates no competitive advantage to the recipient of the cheaper private brand product on which injury could be predicated. . . .

The price difference does not create a competitive advantage by which competition could be injured, and, furthermore, no customer has been favored over another.[3]

Competitive injury may occur at the seller's level as in the case of primary-line injury or at the buyer's level as in the case of secondary-line injury. The injury does not have to be actual, only potential. Injury may be presumed from circumstantial evidence such as **predatory pricing**—lowering prices solely to put a competitor out of business. This is illustrated by the next case.

---

[3] *Borden v. F.T.C.*, 381 F.2d 175 (5th Cir. 1967).

CONTINENTAL BAKING CO. v. OLD HOMESTEAD BREAD CO.
476 F.2d 97 (10th Cir. 1973)

Four principal wholesale bakeries sold bread to independent grocery stores in Denver and southeastern Wyoming: Continental Baking Co., Rainbo, Old Homestead, and Interstate Brands. Each operated large modern bakeries in Denver. In 1962, Continental built a new large bakery in Denver. When completed, it was able to serve its customers by operating the plant at 50 percent capacity. It could not, however, operate profitably at this level.

In the Denver–southeast Wyoming area, the greater number of independent grocery stores were members of Associated Growers (AG). They formed "Five States Supply Company," which provided bread labeled Tender Crust to members. Continental agreed to furnish the Tender Crust bread. The agreement between Five States and Continental was that the Tender Crust would be sold to the grocers for at least 1 cent less than Continental's nationally branded Wonder Bread, which was of "like grade and quality."

Old Homestead, the appellee, sued Continental (appellant), Rainbo, and Interstate alleging unlawful price discrimination. Interstate, the plaintiff, cross-claimed against Continental. A jury returned in favor of Old Homestead against Continental in the amount of $1,048,500 and for Interstate against Continental in the amount of $200,000. Continental appealed to the 10th Circuit Court of Appeals.

SETH, Judge

The terms "price discrimination" means no more than price differentiation, or the charging of different prices to different customers for goods of like grade and quality. It is undisputed that Continental charged one price per loaf for its product labeled "Wonder Bread" and a different price for its product labeled "Tender Crust Bread." It is also uncontroverted that both of these brands were of like grade and quality. Since the goods are of like grade and quality, the fact that they are sold under different labels will not justify . . . price discrimination under section 2(a).

Price discrimination is, of course, not illegal per se. Plaintiffs . . . must have shown that the effect of the price discrimination "may be substantially to lessen competition or tend to create a monopoly in any line of commerce, or to injure, destroy, or prevent competition with any person who either grants or knowingly receives the benefit of such discrimination. . . ." The courts and the FTC have established several methods of proof directed to this injury to competition requirement.

Growth Tending to Monopoly

If plaintiffs here can show that this price discrimination had a tendency to create a monopoly in their "line of commerce," then this injury to competition requirement has been satisfied. . . . [D]uring the four-year period 1964–1967, inclusive, Continental's market share went from about 35 percent to 51 percent. Also, the number of competitors went from four to three when Old Homestead dropped out.

Under the monopoly cases (Sherman Act section 2), it is fairly clear that a market share of 51 percent would not constitute monopoly power. . . . However, the question here is whether a four-year growth from 35 percent to 51 percent is growth *tending to create* a monopoly.

Predatory Intent

There are several significant but isolated facts in the case before us which could support a finding of predatory intent. For example, in 1962, Continental built a bakery which was the largest in the Rocky Mountain Area but which at its opening operated at 33 million pounds, or 50 percent of its capacity. The vice president testified that he knew that it could not be operated profitably until it reached 75 percent capacity, or 52 million pounds. From 1963 to 1967, Continental increased its production by 50 percent or from 33 million pounds to 52 million pounds and at the end of the period was for the first time in the black. The seemingly impossible goal Continental set for itself in 1963 and, in view of the existing suppliers, the achievement of that goal would indicate that Continental's operations were based on something more than "fierce competitive instincts." The record also shows that the plaintiff Old Homestead ceased to do business on December 31, 1967, and on January 2, 1968, Continental raised its prices and did away with all discounts. . . .

The record clearly shows that both plaintiffs suffered some injury during the complaint period. . . . [T]aking the record as a whole, the jury could easily infer that Continental's price discrimination incorporated in the Tender Crust program was the proximate cause of the price declines and of fluctuations during the period which resulted in lost profits and in a decline in sales actually made by appellees with a diversion of business from appellees to appellant.

An analysis of the exhibits covering the years 1963 and 1967 permits the tabulation [in the following table] to be made.

1963	Sales in Dollars	Pounds of Bread
Continental	$ 5,100,875	27,739,659
Rainbo	2,559,039	14,938,838
Interstate	2,314,000	12,850,000
Old Homestead	4,118,938	22,850,000
Total	$14,092,852	78,378,497
1967		
Continental	$ 7,319,792	40,850,512
Rainbo	3,186,818	17,521,511
Interstate	2,879,000	16,000,000
Old Homestead	906,445	5,030,000
Total	$14,292,055	79,402,023

In comparing the sales in dollars for the years 1963 and 1967, assuming that these four companies represent the total independent wholesale bread market, then Continental's sales represented $5,100,875 of the total $14,092,852 or 36.2 percent of the dollar volume of sales in 1963. In 1967, Continental's sales represented $7,319,792 of approximately the same total volume or 51.2 percent. Also, these figures show that Old Homestead's losses during these years were not redistributed evenly over the remainder of the market but the relatively greatest amount went to Continental.

Comparing the sales in pounds, Continental's sales volume in 1963 was 27,739,659 of a total market of 78,378,497 or 35.4 percent. In 1967, Continental's sales volume was 40,850,512 of a total market of 79,402,023 or 51.5 percent.

The record contains substantial evidence of the injury to competition to support the finding of the jury. [Affirmed.]

Case Questions

1. What is the issue this case presents?
2. What type of competitive injury must the plaintiffs show to prevail?
3. Analyze the evidence for predatory intent in this case. Do you agree it supports a case for competitive injury? Explain.
4. Do you agree that the injury was related to the Ten-der Crust program? Explain. Explain why Old Home stead and Interstate may have suffered injury.
5. In retrospect, what should Continental have done to avoid Robinson-Patman problems?

Price Discrimination Defenses

The Robinson-Patman Act prohibits unjustified price discrimination. Some price discrimination is deemed justified. The two main defenses to an alleged Robinson-Patman Act violation are meeting competition and cost justification.

Meeting Competition

Sellers are entitled to lower their prices to meet competition without running afoul of the Robinson-Patman Act. Under this defense, the seller must prove that the lower price ''was made in good faith to meet an equally low price of a competitor.''

Good faith involves honest intentions. A seller must be careful to verify the prices charged by its competitors before reducing its price. By acting prudently, the seller will avoid a violation even if it turns out that the seller was mistaken.

Sellers may not beat competition under the guise of meeting it. And, after it has lowered its price to meet competition, a seller must continue to monitor its competition. When its competitor raises the price, the seller can no longer continue to discriminate in price.

The following case involving beer prices illustrates the difficulty of applying the meeting competition defense.

FALLS CITY INDUSTRIES, INC. v. VANCO BEVERAGE, INC.
460 U.S. 428 (1983)

Falls City Industries, Inc. (petitioner) sold beer at its Louisville, Kentucky, brewery to wholesalers in Indiana, Kentucky and 11 other states. Vanco Beverage, Inc. (respondent) was the only wholesale distributor of Falls City beer in Vanderburgh County, Indiana, which includes the city of Evansville. Across from Vanderburgh County is Henderson County, Kentucky, where Falls City Beer is distributed by Dawson Springs, Inc. Kentucky is less than 10 miles from Evansville, and they are within the same metropolitan area. Falls City raised its prices to Vanco. Vanco sued Falls City, alleging price discrimination in violation of the Robinson-Patman Act. The district court rejected Falls City's meeting competition defense. It found that ''Falls City had created the price disparity by raising its prices to Indiana wholesalers more than it had raised its Kentucky prices.'' Rather than adjusting its prices to meet customer competition, it charged a uniform price in each state. The district court's finding was affirmed by the Seventh Circuit Court of Appeals. The U.S. Supreme Court granted certiorari.

BLACKMUN, Justice

On its face, section 2(b) requires more than a showing of facts that would have led a reasonable person to believe that a lower price was available to the favored purchaser from a competitor. The showing required is that the ''lower price . . . *was made* in good faith *to meet*'' the competitor's low price. Thus, the defense requires that the seller offer the lower price in good faith *for the purpose* of meeting the competitor's price, that is, the lower price must actually have been a good-faith response to that competing low price. In most situations, a showing of facts giving rise to a reasonable belief that equally low prices were available to the favored purchaser from a competitor will be sufficient to establish that the seller's lower price was offered in good faith to meet that price. . . .

. . . Although the District Court characterized the Indiana prices charged by Falls City and its competitors as "artificially high," there is no evidence that Falls City's lower prices in Kentucky were set as part of a plan to obtain artificially high profits in Indiana rather than in response to competitive conditions in Kentucky. Falls City did not adopt an illegal system of prices maintained by its competitors. The District Court found that Falls City's prices rose in Indiana in response to competitors' price increases there; it did not address the crucial questions whether Falls City's Kentucky prices remained lower in response to competitors' prices in that State.

. . . [T]he persistent interstate price difference could well have been attributable, not to Falls City, but to extensive state regulation of the sale of beer. Indiana required each brewer to charge a single price for its beer throughout the State, and barred direct competition between Indiana and Kentucky distributors for sales to retailers. In these unusual circumstances, the prices charged to Vanco and other wholesalers in Vanderburgh County may have been influenced more by market conditions in distant Gary and Fort Wayne than by conditions in nearby Henderson County, Ky. Moreover, wholesalers in Henderson County competed directly, and attempted to price competitively, with wholesalers in neighboring Kentucky counties. A separate pricing structure might well have evolved in the two States without collusion, notwithstanding the existence of a common retail market along the border. Thus, the sustained price discrimination does not itself demonstrate that Falls City's Kentucky prices were not a good-faith response to competitors' prices there.

The Court of Appeals explicitly relied on two other factors in rejecting Falls City's meeting-competition defense: the price discrimination was created by raising rather than lowering prices, and Falls City raised its prices in order to increase its profits. Neither of these factors is controlling. Nothing in section 2(b) requires a seller to *lower* its price in order to meet competition. On the contrary, section 2(b) requires the defendant to show only that its

"lower price . . . was made in good faith to meet an equally low price of a competitor." A seller is required to justify a price difference by showing that it reasonably believed that an equally low price was available to the purchaser and that it offered the lower price for that reason; the seller is not required to show that the difference resulted from subtraction rather than addition.

Nor is the good faith with which the lower price is offered impugned if the prices raised, like those kept lower, respond to competitors' prices and are set with the goal of increasing the seller's profits. . . . A seller is permitted "to retain a customer by realistically meeting in good faith the price offered to that customer, without necessarily changing the seller's price to its other customers." The plain language of section 2(b) also permits a seller to retain a customer by realistically meeting in good faith the price offered to that customer, without necessarily freezing his price to his other customers.

Section 2(b) specifically allows a "lower price . . . to any purchaser or purchasers" made in good faith to meet a competitor's equally low price. A single low price surely may be extended to numerous purchasers if the seller has a reasonable basis for believing that the competitor's lower price is available to them. Beyond the requirement that the lower price be reasonably calculated to "meet not beat" the competition, Congress intended to leave it a "question of fact . . . whether the way in which the competition was met lies within the latitude allowed." Once again, this inquiry is guided by the standard of the prudent businessman responding fairly to what he reasonably believes are the competitive necessities.

A seller may have good reason to believe that a competitor or competitors are charging lower prices throughout a particular region. In such circumstances, customer-by-customer negotiations would be unlikely to result in prices different from those set according to information relating to competitors' territorial prices. A customer-by-customer requirement might also make meaningful price competition unrealistically expensive for smaller firms such as Falls City, which was attempting to compete with larger national breweries in 13 separate States. . . .

. . . The District Court and the Court of Appeals did not decide whether Falls City had shown facts that would have led a reasonable and prudent person to conclude that its lower price would meet the equally low price of its competitors in Kentucky throughout the period at issue in this suit. Nor did they apply the proper standards to the question whether Falls City's decision to set a single statewide price in Kentucky was a good-faith, well-tailored response to the competitive circumstances prevailing there. The absence of allegations to the contrary is not controlling; the statute places the burden of establishing the defense on Falls City, not Vanco. There is evidence in the record that might support an inference that these requirements were met, but whether to draw that inference is a question for the trier of fact, not this Court. [Reversed and Remanded.]

Case Questions

1. What is the issue this case presents?

2. Diagram the facts of this case. Do you believe the legislature contemplated such a fact scenario when it passed the Robinson-Patman Act? Explain.

3. Analyze the three reasons the Court of Appeals used to reject Falls City's meeting competition defense.

4. Do we have a final decision in this case? Explain.

Cost Justification

As originally enacted, section 2 of the Clayton Act permitted price discrimination based on volume discounts. The rationale behind this exemption was that it is "cheaper to sell by the dozen." Presumably, all sellers would experience a reduction in costs on volume sales and there would be no competitive edge by one over another because each could reduce their prices to the extent of the cost savings. Under the act, however, a small-volume sale justified a large discount. Consequently, large chain stores were able to command disproportionately large discounts based on volume sales.

The Robinson-Patman Act amended the language of the Clayton Act to permit price differentials only where the price difference is likened to differences "in the cost of manufacture, sale, or delivery." Under this proviso, the seller has the burden of justifying a cost break based on an equal cost savings. Volume sales may, for example, result in transportation savings, a savings in storage expenses, or even lower personnel and administrative costs. A seller does not have to give a cost reduction based on quantity sales. However, if it does, it must make it equally available to all purchasers.

Buyer Discrimination

The Robinson-Patman Act applies with equal force to buyer-induced discrimination. It makes it unlawful for a buyer to knowingly receive a discrimination in price.

The U.S. Supreme Court decided a case clarifying the buyer discrimination section. A&P was a customer of Borden. A&P was thinking of purchasing its milk elsewhere and communicated that to Borden. A&P sought offers from other dairies and received a more favorable bid from Bowman, another dairy. Borden, in response to the competitive pressures, responded with a bid that undercut Bowman. Although Borden thought it was meeting competition, A&P knew that Borden's bid actually undercut Bowman. Charged with buyer discrimination, the U.S. Supreme Court held that A&P could not be in violation since Borden had a good meeting competition defense against price discrimination.[4]

Nonprice Discrimination

Price discrimination is not the only way to violate the Robinson-Patman Act. Congress recognized that other discriminatory practices might similarly result in competitive injury. The act therefore prohibits the payment of brokerage fees except for services actually performed. This provision was intended to eliminate the practice of extracting "dummy" brokerage. Assume that a large retail grocery chain sought favorable treatment from its supplier that was neither cost justified nor within the meeting competition defense. One way to disguise a price discrimination would be for the buyer's agent to receive a broker's fee for arranging the sale. This, however, would be unlawful under the act since the buyer's broker renders services to the buyer and not the seller.

Another antidiscriminatory section of the Robinson-Patman Act requires that any payment by the seller to the buyer for promotions or merchandising

---

[4]*Great Atlantic & Pacific Tea Co., Inc. v. FTC,* 440 U.S. 69 (1979).

services be made proportionally available to competing customers. Similarly, another section prohibits the seller from furnishing services to its customer unless the services are made available on proportionally equal terms to competing customers.

Courts are prone to scrutinize the "proportionally equal terms" requirement. Assume that a seller of designer jeans offers "display services" to customers who purchase at least 10,000 pairs of its jeans per month. Only one customer fulfills this condition. A court might very well find that the condition was a pretext for discrimination against competing customers in violation of the "proportionally equal terms" requirement. It would be wiser for the seller to offer some services to those who purchase lesser quantities as well, perhaps increasingly greater services for quantities such as 2,000, 5,000, 7,500, and 10,000 pairs of jeans, respectively. Or a seller may base the value of the services contributed on a percentage of the dollar amount of monthly purchases. For example, the seller could offer an allowance for display services of 1 percent of the dollar amount of the customer's monthly purchases without violating the "proportionally equal terms" requirement.

END–OF–CHAPTER QUESTIONS

1. Compare and contrast the Clayton Act and the Sherman Antitrust Act.

2. Compare and contrast horizontal, vertical, conglomerate, and product extension mergers. Which is the most likely to violate the Clayton Act? Why?

3. What are the weaknesses of the Herfindahl-Hirschman Index? Analyze.

4. In what way does the Robinson-Patman Act protect competition? Would competition be better served without it? Explain.

5. The Philadelphia National Bank (PNB) is the second largest commercial bank in Pennsylvania and the 21st largest in the nation. Girard Trust Corn Exchange Bank (Girard) is the third largest commercial bank in Pennsylvania. Both banks operate in the same four-county area. Girard has assets of about $750 million, and PNB has assets of $1 billion. In Philadelphia, the number of banks has declined from 108 to 42 in the last 16 years. PNB and

Girard have proposed a merger. The resulting bank would be the largest in the four-county area. It would have over 30 percent of the total assets, deposits, and net loans. What is the relevant product market? Would the merger violate the Clayton Act? Explain. What additional information would you like to analyze to make that determination? *United States v. Philadelphia National Bank*, 374 U.S. 321 (1963).

6. General Motors accounts for 40 percent of the total automotive sales. It ranked first in sales and second in assets of all corporations in 1955. General Motors produces one half of the industry's automobiles. Du Pont is a supplier of automotive finishes and fabrics. It acquired 23 percent of General Motors' stock. Since then, it supplies General Motors with 67 percent of its automotive finishes and 52 percent of its fabrics. What type of merger was involved? How might the merger violate Clayton Act section 7? See *United States v. du Pont & Co.*, 353 U.S. 586 (1957).

7. Assume that the Stonehinge Industry is structured as follows:

Firm	Share of Market (percent)
A	20%
B	15
C	13
D	11
E	9
F	8
G	5
H	5
I	5
J–R	1 each
Total	100%

Would a merger between Firms A and B likely be challenged by the Justice Department? Explain. Would a merger between Firms A and F likely result in a Justice Department challenge? Explain. How about a merger between D and H? What further information would be helpful to consider?

8. The *Bismarck Tribune* is a newspaper distributed in Bismarck, North Dakota. The *Morning Pioneer* is a newspaper distributed in Mandan, North Dakota. Until recently, the papers did not compete. However, the *Tribune* has entered Mandan, and in an attempt to capture a market share, has lowered its price below the price it charges Bismarck customers. The *Tribune*'s news contained in its paper delivered to Mandan is older than its news contained in its paper delivered to Bismarck. Also, the advertisements in both newspapers are geared towards the Bismarck shopper. Has the *Tribune* violated the Robinson-Patman Act? Analyze. *Morning Pioneer, Inc. v. Bismarck Tribune Co.*, 342 F. Supp. 1138 (D.N.D. 1972).

9. Utah Pie sold frozen pies in Salt Lake City. One competitor, who also sold frozen pies in other markets, attempted to challenge Utah Pie in Salt Lake City. It cut the price of its frozen pies in Salt Lake City while maintaining higher prices in other markets. In response, Utah Pie dropped the price of its pies from $4.15 per dozen to $2.75 per dozen. The competitor had an industrial spy in Utah's plant who knew that on several occasions, Utah Pie had sold its pies below actual cost. Nevertheless, Utah Pie increased its sales volume and continued to earn a profit. Has Utah Pie's competitor violated the Robinson-Patman Act? Explain. What possible defenses are available to Utah Pie's competitor? See *Utah Pie v. Continental Baking Co.*, 386 U.S. 685 (1967).

10. Winesaps sells grape juice and distributes it through wholesalers throughout the United States. It also sells an unbranded grape juice that is physically identical in chemistry as the branded grape juice except for a different food color additive that makes the unbranded juice burgundy

in color. Winesaps sells the unbranded juice directly to retail supermarket chains. There is a decisive consumer preference for the branded Winesaps over the unbranded due in large part to the national advertising associated with the branded juice. Winesaps sells its branded juice to wholesalers for $36 per carton (each carton contains 12 64-oz. containers). Winesaps sells its unbranded juice to retail supermarket chains for $33 a carton. Machos also sells grape juice and is competing for A&P, a supermarket chain, which is one of Winesaps' unbranded customers. Ron Balk, the vice president in charge of purchases at A&P, called Winesaps' sales representative, Jim Martin, and indicated that A&P was thinking about switching its business to Machos. The phone conversation went like this:

Balk: You know, there are a lot of competitors out there and your unbranded juice is the best but not the only . . .

Martin: What are you saying—that you can get a better deal?

Balk: Well, we have been talking to Machos and they can guarantee us faster delivery.

Martin: Can they do better than $33 a carton?

Balk: We are going to talk once again with them and come to a final decision Monday. It would be helpful if you could give us your bottom line.

Martin: We can do better than any of our competitors.

■ ■ ■

Monday Morning

Balk: Jim, we are going with Machos unless you save us some money.

Martin: You name it. How much do you want our juice for?

Balk: $31.50 a carton.

Martin: You got it.

Winesaps continued to sell its unbranded juice for $33 a carton to other retail chains, including Fazios and Krogers, who operated chain stores in direct competition with A&P. Fazios' sales declined in the year following the price concession to Machos, while Kroger's and A&P's sales increased as reflected in the following chart.

Is A&P in violation of the Robinson-Patman act? Explain. Is Winesaps in violation of the act? Explain.

Company	Sales	
	Year 1	Year 2
Fazios	686,000 quarts	420,000 quarts
Krogers	512,000 quarts	532,000 quarts
A&P	432,000 quarts	705,000 quarts

Chapter 48

Regulation of Product Marketing

■

CRITICAL THINKING INQUIRIES

As you read this chapter, you should be able to address the following:

- What are the advantages and disadvantages of various ways to protect a product idea?
- Why register a trademark?
- Compare and contrast the laws that protect against trade identity confusion.
- Analyze the remedies available in the case of deceptive advertising.
- Analyze the sufficiency of the laws against deceptive and unfair selling practices.

MANAGERIAL PERSPECTIVE

The Research and Development division of Molger Company has developed an inexpensive process to freeze-dry coffee. This process preserves a unique taste. The company executives are very aware that this will give it a competitive advantage over other coffee manufacturers. The company executives come together to discuss how to protect their idea from being disclosed to a competitor by a member of the company, by outright theft through corporate espionage, or by a third party with whom Molger is doing business.

Molger Company also desires to choose an exclusive product name for their product that they can protect. Molger intends to do widespread advertising. Its marketing department has produced some advertising copy, which includes the claim: ''Our freeze-dried coffee is fresher and tastier.''

- How can Molger adequately protect the idea?
- How can Molger protect a brand name?
- What advertising laws circumscribe Molger's advertising plans?

Molger Company will soon find out that the law affects marketing decisions — from product planning to distribution. Federal and state statutes protect consumers and competitors. Administrative law also affects product marketing, particularly through the regulatory involvement of the Federal Trade Commission (FTC). Additionally, certain tort law proscribes some marketing practices. This chapter discusses the legal environment of marketing decisionmaking from idea protection to product distribution (see Figure 48–1).

PROTECTING THE PRODUCT IDEA

In the past few decades, American society has added information and innovation to the formula for producing wealth. Now, knowledge is considered every bit as much a factor in making money as labor, capital, land, plant, and equipment. Moreover, ideas are important "assets" of a company. Consequently, the law affords ideas protection.

The U.S. Constitution, in Article I, section 8, clause 8, authorizes Congress "to promote the progress of science and useful arts by securing for limited times to authors and inventors the exclusive right to their respective writings and discoveries."

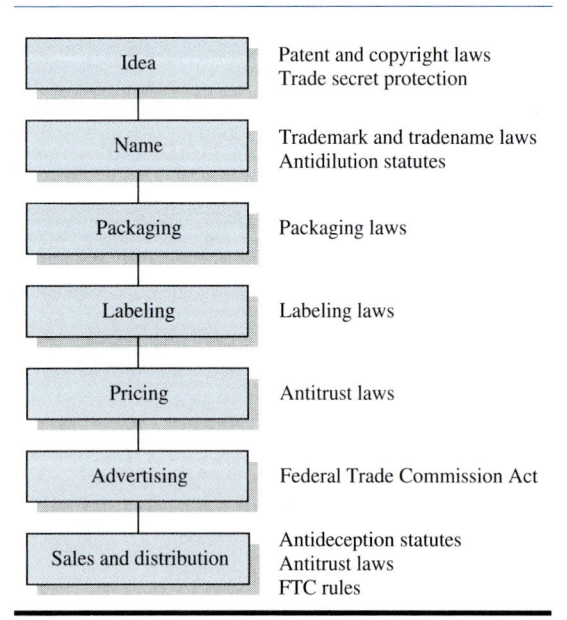

Figure 48–1   Chain of Marketing Decisions and Laws Affecting Those Decisions

Idea	Patent and copyright laws Trade secret protection
Name	Trademark and tradename laws Antidilution statutes
Packaging	Packaging laws
Labeling	Labeling laws
Pricing	Antitrust laws
Advertising	Federal Trade Commission Act
Sales and distribution	Antideception statutes Antitrust laws FTC rules

Pursuant to this provision, Congress passed a series of both patent and copyright acts. The law of trade secrets affords additional protection to ideas.

Patent Protection

A **patent** may be granted on a process, a chemical, a machine, a design, or a plant. To be patentable, the invention must be novel, useful, and nonobvious. By *novel*, the law requires that the invention not be known by others or described in a printed publication before the patent application is made. To be *useful*, an invention must be concretely embodied or applied in a nonfrivolous way. The Supreme Court defined *nonobviousness* as demanding a difference between the subject matter sought to be patented and the prior art so that the subject matter would not be obvious to a person experienced in the area. What is required is a "substantial degree of technical advance" according to congressional statutes.

Suppose Molger's freeze-drying is patentable as a novel, useful, nonobvious process. How would Molger obtain a patent? Obtaining a patent typically involves consulting with a patent attorney since the application process is very technical. Essentially, a patent application would be filed with the Commissioner of Patents and Trademarks. A patent examination would then be conducted by an examiner at that office to determine if the freeze-drying process has already been patented. If not, and the process is patentable, Molger would have exclusive rights to the process for 17 years from the date of issuance of the patent.

Protection through patents, however, is often unwise from a marketing perspective. First, the patent application often takes years to approve. By that time, the innovation may become obsolete. Second, if the patent application is granted, the innovation, including its complete design, becomes public information. Molger's competitors now would be fully apprised of the discovery. A competitor may employ an improved freeze-drying process (working off Molger's design) without violating the patent and hence obtain an advantage. But even if the patent is obviously infringed, Molger must prove that in court after expensive litigation.

Copyright Protection

Any tangible medium of expression, such as writings, sound recordings, motion pictures, sculptures, notated choreographic works, or maps and charts, are copyrightable. If Molger's new process involves the creation of a computer program, the program is copyrightable. Even microchip design is given copyright protection pursuant to the Semiconductor-Chip Protection Act of 1984.

To obtain **copyright** protection, the word *copyright* (or its abbreviation) or the symbol © must be on copies of the program along with Molger's name and the year of copyright, any time the program is distributed (see Figure 48–2). In addition, Molger would need to *register* the copyright by applying to the Office of Copyright at the Library of Congress and sending it two copies of the program. Molger's copyright would last for 75 years from the date of its publication or 100 years from its creation, whichever expires first. If Molger were a natural person and not a corporation, the duration of copyright protection would be the life of the author plus 50 years. The weakness of the copyright system to Molger is that, as with the patent system, copyrighted mate-

Figure 48–2   Copyright and Trademark Protection

rial, like patents, immediately becomes public information available to Molger's competitors.

There are exemptions under the copyright laws that give a person the right to use copyrighted materials without securing permission. The following case discusses the ''fair use'' exemption.

BASIC BOOKS, INC. v. KINKO'S GRAPHICS CORP.
758 F.Supp 1522 (SDNY 1991)

Kinko's, under its Professor Publishing program, photocopied pages from books previously published by the plaintiffs (Basic Books, Harper & Row, John Wiley & Sons, McGraw-Hill, Penguin Books, Prentice Hall, Richard D. Irwin, and Morrow & Co.). It compiled them in numbered packets and distributed them for profit without seeking permission from the publishers.

The plaintiffs, all major publishing houses, brought suit against Kinko's in federal district court alleging copyright infringement. Kinko's defended on the grounds that the copying constituted fair use.

MOTLEY, Judge

I. Fair Use
Coined as an ''equitable rule of reason,'' the fair use doctrine has existed for as long as the copyright law. It was codified in [Sec] 107 of the Copyright Act of 1976. . . . [See Figure 48–3.]

[T]his court has the task of evaluating the copying under the fair use doctrine. . . .

A. The Four Factors of Fair Use
1. Purpose and Character of the Use Section 107 specifically provides that under this factor we consider ''whether [the] use is of a commercial nature or is for nonprofit educational purposes.'' The Su-

preme Court has held that ''commerical use of copyrighted material is presumptively an unfair exploitation of the monopoly privilege that belongs to the owner of the copyright.'' . . .

It has been argued that the essence of ''character and purpose'' is the transformative value, that is, productive use, of the secondary work compared to the original. . . . ''A quotation of copyrighted material that merely repackages or republishes the original is unlikely to pass the test.'' . . . Kinko's work cannot be categorized as anything other than a mere repackaging.

The use of the Kinko's packets, in the hands of the students, was no doubt educational. However, the use in the hands of Kinko's employees is commercial. . . .

Figure 48–3   Fair Use Statutory Excerpt

Notwithstanding the provisions of section 106, the fair use of copyrighted work, including such use by reproduction in copies or phonorecords or by any other means specified by that section, for purposes such as criticism, comment, news reporting, teaching (including multiple copies for classroom use), scholarship, or research, is not an infringement of copyright. In determining whether the use made of a work in any particular case is a fair use the factors to be considered shall include—(1) the purpose and character of the use, including whether such use is of a commercial nature or is for nonprofit educational purposes; (2) the nature of the copyright work; (3) the amount and substantiality of the portion used in relation to the copyrighted work as a whole; and (4) the effect of the use upon the potential market for or value of the copyrighted work.

Source: Copyright Act of 1976, section 107.

Kinko's has not disputed that it receives a profit component from the revenue it collects for its anthologies. The amount of that profit is unclear; however, we need only find that Kinko's had the intention of making profits. Its Professor Publishing promotional materials clearly indicate that Kinko's recognized and sought a segment of a profitable market, admitting that "tremendous sales and profit potential arise from this program."

2. The Nature of the Copyrighted Work   The second factor concerns the nature of the copyrighted work. Courts generally hold that "the scope of fair use is greater with respect to factual than non-factual works." Factual works, such as biographies, reviews, criticism and commentary, are believed to have a greater public value and, therefore, uses of them may be better tolerated by the copyright law. Works containing information in the public interest may require less protection. Fictional works, on the other hand, are often based closely on the author's subjective impressions and therefore, require more protection. . . . The books infringed . . . were factual in nature. This factor weighs in favor of defendant.

3. The Amount and Substantiality of the Portion Used   "There are no absolute rules as to how much of a copyrighted work may be copied and still be considered a fair use." This third factor considers not only the percentage of the original used but also the "substantiality" of that portion to the whole of the work; that is, courts must evaluate the qualitative aspects as well as the quantity of material copied. A short piece which is "the heart of" a work may not be fair use and a longer piece which is pedestrian in nature may be fair use. The balancing of the four factors must be complete, relying solely upon no one factor. The purpose of the use may be balanced against the amount and substantiality of the use. For example, "even substantial quotations might qualify as fair use in a review of a published work."

Courts have found relatively small quantitative uses to be fair use. . . .

This factor, amount and substantiality of the portions appropriated, weighs against defendant. In this case, the passages copied ranged from 14 to 110 pages, representing 5.2 percent to 25.1 percent of the works. In one case Kinko's copied 110 pages of someone's work and sold it to 132 students. Even for an out-of-print book, this amount is grossly out of line with accepted fair use principles.

4. The Effect of the Use on Potential Markets for or Value of the Copyrighted Work   The fourth factor, market effect, also fails the defendant. This factor has been held to be "undoubtedly the single most important element of fair use." . . . "To negate fair use one need only show that if the challenged use 'should become widespread, it would adversely affect the potential market for the copyrighted work.'"

Kinko's confirms that it has 200 stores nationwide, servicing hundreds of colleges and universities which enroll thousands of students. The potential for widespread copyright infringement by defendant and other commercial copiers is great. In this case, Kinko's has admitted that its market for these anthologies or packets is college students. The packets were compiled as a result of orders placed by professors at Columbia University, New York University and the New School for Social research as to what readings they needed to supply their courses. In this case, the competition for "student dollars" is easily won by Kinko's which produced 300- to 400-page packets including substantial portions of copyrighted books at a cost of $24 to the student. . . .

This court finds the excerpts copied by defendant Kinko's are not a fair use of plaintiffs' copyrights and, therefore, constitute infringement. . . . Plaintiff is granted . . . damages [$510,000], injunctive relief and attorneys' fees and costs.

Case Questions

1. What is the issue in this case?

2. Analyze whether the defendant met any of the factors considered fair use.

3. What specific facts were most damaging to Kinko's?

4. What policies could Kinko's institute to ensure compliance with copyright law while still maintaining its Professor Publishing program?

Figure 48–4   Classroom Guidelines for Fair Use Exemption

- Brevity—only excerpts, selections, or individual articles or chapters are to be copied.
- Spontaneity—constraints make it unreasonable to expect a timely request for permissions and a reply to such request.
- Cumulative effect—copying shall not substitute for purchase of books, periodicals, or publisher's reprints.

Guidelines have been adopted to determine fair use for scholarly photocopying of printed matters. These guidelines are part of the legislative history of the Copyright Act. They attempt to give a brighter line indicator for fair use for distributing material in the classroom. The guidelines are summarized in Figure 48–4.

Trade Secret Protection

It is often wisest to protect a new idea through the law of trade secrets, rather than patent or copyright registration. A **trade secret** is defined by the Uniform Trade Secrets Act and by case law development. Both under the act and as a result of case law development, a trade secret is information that:

1. Is not generally known.
2. Is protected through some security measures to maintain its secrecy.
3. Is valuable.
4. Requires a substantial expenditure of time, money, or labor to develop.

To illustrate, product ideas such as making a cigarette 100 millimeters long or making a stainless steel razor blade would not be entitled to trade secret protection since they would fail to meet criteria 1, 2, and 4 above. In contrast, the formula to make Coca Cola, the ingredients in Kentucky Fried Chicken, or a new freeze-drying process would all be considered trade secrets.

Trade secrets require no registration or expensive fees, as are often incurred in obtaining a patent. Trade secrets are *not* disclosed to the public. A further benefit of trade secrets law is that trade secrets, unlike patents and copyrights, may be protected forever.

The tort of *misappropriation* protects the owner of a trade secret from wrongful disclosure of that secret to another. (See Chapter 7 for a discussion of misappropriation.)

Protection from Employee Disclosure

A contract is the best way to protect trade secrets from employee disclosure. Molger's employees could be asked to agree to keep confidential certain categories of information such as innovations, customer lists, and financial and marketing information. In return for an employee's promise of confidentiality, Molger could give some consideration such as a stock option or sum of money. Many of these agreements contain restrictions on an employee's right to use trade secrets after terminating employment. In addition, many confidentiality agreements also contain a clause assigning all innovations and inventions to the employer during the employment term.

Protection from Competitor Espionage

Competitive espionage has become increasingly common. The following article describes legal as well as illegal methods of gathering intelligence from the opposition.

*Snooping on Your Competitor**

While illegal corporate espionage makes headlines occasionally, it probably accounts for only a small fraction of corporate intelligence-gathering. There are many other ways you can find out what your competitors are up to that are completely legal, if sometimes ethically questionable.

The legal use of intelligence-gathering techniques has increased dramatically as more and more companies learn how cheap and effective it is. . . . Nor is snooping limited to companies that make highly engineered hardware. Enterprises such as Chemical Bank, the USV Laboratories subsidiary of Revlon, the specialty grocery products group of Del Monte, General Foods, Kraft, and J. C. Penney are all busy monitoring what the other guy is doing.

■ ■ ■

The techniques fall into four broad categories. The first covers ways of getting information from competitors' employees, past or present.

Milking Potential Recruits

When they interview students for jobs, some companies pay special attention to those who have worked for competitors, even temporarily. Job seekers are eager to impress and often have not been warned about divulging what is proprietary. They sometimes volunteer valuable information.

■ ■ ■

Picking Brains at Conferences

Companies send engineers to conferences and trade shows to question competitors' technical people. Often conversations start innocently—just a few fellow technicians discussing processes and problems that seemingly do not relate to trade secrets. Yet even though they are aware of the value of proprietary information, engineers and scientists often brag about surmounting technical challenges, in the process divulging sensitive information. . . .

Conducting Phony Job Interviews

Companies sometimes advertise and hold interviews for jobs that don't exist in order to entice competitors' employees to spill the beans. The practice is legal, provided the interviewer doesn't explicitly ask for trade secrets. Often applicants have toiled in obscurity or feel that their careers have stalled. They're dying to impress somebody. . . .

■ ■ ■

Debriefing Design Consultants

In certain industries—computers, for example—competitors frequently use the same design consultants. While conferring with a consultant it has hired to help it with a new product, a company can sometimes learn confidential information about products competitors are developing.

Debriefing Competitors' Former Employees

They will often supply damaging information about the company they used to work for, especially if they left on bad terms. If they are leaving the industry and have remained friendly with salespeople they competed against, they just might reveal how they were able to, say, crack an account.

The second general category consists of techniques to get information from people who do business with competitors.

Encouraging Key Customers to Talk

In every industry companies show new products to certain key customers because their willingness to buy the product is considered indispensable for success. These customers are sometimes loyal to a competitor, however, and will get on the phone to it as soon as a competing salesman has left the office.

For example, a while back Gillette told a large Canadian account the date on which it planned to begin selling its Good News disposable razor in the U.S. The date was six months before Bic Corp. was scheduled to introduce its own disposable razor in America. The Canadian distributor promptly called Bic and told it about the impending product launch. Bic put on a crash program and was able to start selling its razor shortly after Gillette did.

■ ■ ■

The third general category consists of ways to find out what a competitor is up to from published material and documents often available from public sources.

Analyzing Help-Wanted Ads

Help-wanted ads are in effect press releases. Months before MCI Communications Corp. announced its electronic mail service, it ran ads recruiting technicians and engineers trained in the kind of data communications used in such a service. A competitor following these ads could have figured out months in advance that MCI might be planning to offer electronic mail. Marke Track Inc., of Bloomfield, New Jersey, provides ad monitoring of clients' competitors on a regular basis.

■ ■ ■

Studying Aerial Photographs

Although it is often illegal for a company to photograph a competitor's plant from the air . . . there are legitimate ways to get the photos. If a competitor's plant is near a waterway or was the subject of an environmental impact study, aerial photos often are on file with the U.S. Geological Survey or Environmental Protection Agency. These are public documents, available for a nominal charge. Obtaining these photos from time to time will reveal plant expansions, the layout of a competitor's manufacturing facility (often a clue to the processes being used), and inventory buildups (a tip-off to upcoming sales drives).

Obtaining Freedom of Information Act Filings

Thank you, Big Brother. Companies can get information about competitors from government agencies by asking for it under the Freedom of Information Act [FOIA]. But such requests are themselves public documents and could be obtained by the competitor by using the FOIA. This could tip him off about your hopes to, say, copy his new product. If you wish to make your inquiry discreetly, a company dedicated exclusively to that task, FOI Services Inc. of Rockville, Maryland, will make the request for you.

■ ■ ■

The fourth category embraces techniques for directly observing competitors or analyzing physical evidence of their activities.

■ ■ ■

Taking Plant Tours

. . . Under a chief executive who has since died, Avalon Industries Inc., a crayon and toy manufacturer in Brooklyn, New York, encouraged its salespeople to make tours of competitors' plants under assumed identities. Posing as potential distributors or potential customers who had just invented a game that required crayons easily got Avalon's salespeople inside plants where they obtained sensitive information about the competitors' manufacturing processes. To make sure they could do this, Avalon trained its salespeople in the different types of machinery used in the industry. Color me dirty.

Doing Reverse-Engineering

Companies increasingly buy competitors' products and take them apart to examine their components. From such analysis they can determine costs of production and sometimes even manufacturing methods.

Advanced Energy Technology Inc. of Boulder, Colorado, learned first-hand of such tactics. No sooner had it announced a patented new product, a type of speed-reduction gear, than it received 50 orders. About half of the requests were from competitors asking for only one or two of the gears.

Buying Competitors' Garbage

While it is illegal for a company's personnel or its agents to enter a competitor's premises to collect his leavings, it is legitimate to obtain them from a trash hauler. Once it has left the competitor's premises, refuse is legally considered abandoned property. While some companies now shred the paper coming out of their design labs, they often neglect to do this for almost-as-revealing refuse from the marketing or public relations departments.

Thought Questions

1. What separates ethical from unethical intelligence-gathering efforts?
2. What can a company do to protect itself from competitive espionage?

Preventing Disclosure by a Third Party

Molger, like many companies, may not have the physical or economic capability to distribute its product in a foreign or domestic market. It may therefore decide to **license** (permit by contract) another manufacturer to produce or sell its product using its secret process. Typically, a licensing agreement will provide for royalties to be paid to the licensor (Molger) from the sale of its product. **Royalties** are simply a percentage share of the profit, payable to the creator of the work. The agreement also might have a confidentiality clause protecting Molger from the licensee's disclosure of its secret.

CHOOSING A PRODUCT NAME

Choosing a new name for a product is no easy task since there are about 1 million brand names already employed in the United States alone. Marketing impact is not the only consideration in the naming of a product. The scheme of laws surrounding product names and symbols must be consulted before selecting a new name.

Trademarks and Trade Names

Product names and symbols may be protected by registering a trademark or trade name with the U.S. Patent and Trademark Office pursuant to the Lanham Act of 1946. A **trademark** is used to distinguish a certain product such as "Wheaties" or a "Big Mac" from other similar products. Consumers can thus be assured of consistency between their expectations and the product purchased. A **trade name** identifies the particular company manufacturing the product, such as General Mills or McDonald's — or Molger Company.

To obtain a registered trademark or trade name, an application is filed with the Patent Office. A drawing of the mark or name must accompany the application. One prerequisite for the grant of registration is that the mark, name, or symbol be previously *used* by the company. The effect of registering a trademark is discussed in the following case.

PARK 'N FLY, INC. v. DOLLAR PARK AND FLY, INC.
469 U.S. 189 (1985)

Park 'N Fly, Inc., the petitioner, operates long-term parking lots near airports. The petitioner opened facilities in Cleveland, Houston, Boston, Memphis, and San Francisco. It applied to the U.S. Patent and Trademark Office (Patent Office) to register a service mark consisting of the logo of an airplane and the words "Park 'N Fly." The registration was issued. Almost six years later, the petitioner filed an affidavit with the Patent Office to establish the incontestable status of the mark. As required by section 15 of the Trademark Act of 1946 . . . (Lanham Act), the affidavit stated that the mark had been registered and in continuous use for five consecutive years, that there had been no final adverse decision to petitioner's claim of ownership or right to registration, and that no proceedings involving such rights were pending.

The respondent, Dollar Park and Fly, Inc., also provides long-term airport parking services, but only has operations in Portland, Oregon. The respondent calls its business "Dollar Park and Fly." The petitioner filed an infringement action in the U.S. District Court for the District of Oregon and requested that the court permanently enjoin the respondent from using the words "Park and Fly" in connection with its business. Respondent contended that petitioner's mark was unenforceable because it is merely descriptive. (A descriptive mark is a mark that merely describes a characteristic or function of the good or service without identifying its source or distinguishing it from similar goods or services. For example, "Eat here" is descriptive; "McDonald's" is not.)

The District Court permanently enjoined the respondent from using the words "Park and Fly" and any other mark confusingly similar to "Park 'N Fly." The Court of Appeals for the Ninth Circuit reversed, determining that petitioner's mark is in fact merely descriptive, and therefore respondent should not be enjoined from using the name "Park and Fly." The U.S. Supreme Court granted certiorari.

O'CONNOR, Judge

This case requires us to consider the effect of the incontestability provisions of the Lanham Act in the context of an infringement action defended on the grounds that the mark is merely descriptive. Statutory construction must begin with the language employed by Congress and the assumption that the ordinary meaning of that language accurately expresses the legislative purpose. With respect to incontestable trade or service marks, [section] 33(b) of the Lanham Act states that "registration shall be conclusive evidence of the registrant's exclusive right to use the registered mark" subject to the conditions of [section] 15 and certain enumerated defenses.

. . . The Lanham Act expressly provides that before a mark becomes incontestable an opposing party may prove any legal or equitable defense which might have been asserted if the mark had not been registered. Thus, [section] 33(a) would have allowed respondent to challenge petitioner's mark as merely descriptive if the mark had not become incontestable. With respect to incontestable marks, however, [section] 33(b) provides that registration is *conclusive* evidence of the registrant's exclusive right to use the mark, subject to the conditions of [section] 15 and the seven defenses enumerated in [section] 33(b) itself. Mere descriptiveness is not recognized by either [section] 15 or [section] 33(b) as a basis for challenging an incontestable mark. The incontestability provisions, as the proponents of

the Lanham Act emphasized, provide a means for the registrant to quiet title in the ownership of his mark. The opportunity to obtain incontestable status by satisfying the requirements of [section] 15 thus encourages producers to cultivate the goodwill associated with a particular mark. This function of the incontestability provisions would be utterly frustrated if the holder of an incontestable mark could not enjoin infringement by others so long as they established that the mark would not be registrable but for its incontestable status.

The judgment of the Court of Appeals is reversed and the case is remanded for further proceedings consistent with this opinion.

Case Questions

1. What is the issue this case presents?
2. What is the shortcoming of the incontestability provisions? What are the benefits?
3. Is "Park 'N Fly" descriptive or nondescriptive? Explain.

Denying and Challenging Registration

The Patent Office may deny registration for a number of reasons. A common reason for denying registration is that the mark or name is simply *generic*—that is, a common name such as *fried potatoes* or *ice cream*. To permit registration of common names would be to deny their usage to other producers of the product. Another reason for denying registration is that, as was suggested in *Park 'N Fly,* the mark is merely descriptive and has no **secondary meaning.** Secondary meaning pertains to the association of a term with a particular product over a period of time so that the public consciously associates the term with the product.

Primary meaning involves a term that the public does not identify with any manufacturer or product. Thus, geographic terms, surnames, or descriptive names must have a secondary meaning to be registrable. To illustrate, *ebony* has the primary meaning of a type of wood. But it has a secondary meaning pertaining to a magazine and would therefore be registrable. The same would apply to geographic terms such as Nantucket—the name of an island community primarily, and the name of a shirt, secondarily.

Notice of an application is published in the Patent Office's Official Gazette. In addition to the Patent Office's own evaluation of a registration application, interested parties may challenge the application and raise objections. A common reason for objecting to an application is that there is a "likelihood of confusion" between the requested trademark and a trademark previously registered. For example, a cola-flavored drink Koka Kola would be confusingly similar to Coca Cola (see the next section, Trade Identity Confusion).

After a trademark is registered, it may be challenged by other companies in a court proceeding if the mark later becomes a generic or common name for an item. Thus, Donald F. Duncan, Inc., lost its right to register the word *yo-yo,* and King-Seeley Co. lost its right to register the word *Thermos.* Other valuable marks lost in this way include cellophane, aspirin, linoleum, shredded wheat, and milk of magnesia. "Xerox," "Kleenex," and "Band-Aid" have carried on extensive advertising and policing campaigns to prevent their marks from becoming generic. Some companies, such as Jello and 3-M (Scotch), have inserted the word *brand* in their advertising to inform the public that the gelatin and tape are produced by those companies.

Another test of a trademark's validity is the significance of a mark. If the trademark's significance in the minds of the consuming public is the producer, the mark is valid; if it is the product then the mark is invalid.

Apart from a term becoming the popular or generic way to refer to an item, there are other ways for a producer to lose trademark rights. If a producer has discontinued use of the trademark without an intention to resume use, the mark is considered *abandoned*. When abandonment occurs, the mark may be used by other producers. Further, if the holder of the trademark or trade name ceases to do business, the rights in the mark or name cease. They have no independent existence.

Trade Identity Confusion

A variety of laws, including federal and state statutes and the common law, protect against trade identity confusion resulting from competitors' activities. These laws protect the goodwill that a producer has in its name or product. Trademark infringement, state antidilution statutes, and the Lanham Act are such laws and are the subject of the following materials.

Trademark Infringement

Under the Lanham Act, there is a **trademark infringement** if a competitor's mark is "likely to cause confusion or mistake or to deceive as to the source or origin of such goods or services." There are many ways that confusion may occur. Certainly, a similar appearance in the marks or a similarity in sound would cause confusion. Thus, Vornado company was held to have infringed the trademark of Tornado company (both made vacuums).

To prove confusion, surveys will often be used to provide proof of consumer reactions. Courts scrutinize the surveys to make sure they constitute a representative sample, contain unbiased questions, and are verified and tabulated by an expert.

If registration is infringed, a victim will typically first seek an injunction to stop the infringement. Beyond this, if the infringement is shown to be intentional, the victim may recover for damages resulting from its lost sales and any profits gained by the infringer from its wrongful activity.

State Antidilution Statutes

The main idea behind state **antidilution statutes** is that use of a mark similar to that of the plaintiff will, over a period of time, dilute the distinctiveness of the plaintiff's mark. Dilution differs from trademark infringement since dilution involves a "watering down" of a mark's distinctiveness over a long period of time. Trademark infringement requires immediate product confusion. To illustrate, people are not likely to be confused by the use of "Polaroid" as a name for refrigerators. Thus, there probably would be no trademark infringement action. Yet, a court has held that Polaroid's distinctive name was diluted by a refrigeration company's usage and therefore enjoined the company from using the name "Polaroid" under a state antidilution statute.

Palming Off and the Lanham Act

Palming off is a common law tort. It involves the substitution of one's own product for that of another. Palming off can occur in many ways. For example, a cola maker may copy a nonfunctional feature of a product, such as the distinctive shape of a Coca Cola bottle, and deceive the public. Or a competitor may sell his or her goods or services under the trademark of another, such as sewing "London Fog" labels in the competitor's own trenchcoats. Both cases would involve palming off.

Section 43(a) of the Lanham Act permits a company to sue a competitor for a false description or representation of the competitor's product. This includes palming off. The following case involving the game Trivial Pursuit discusses liability under section 43(a) for causing trade identity confusion through a kind of palming off.

SELCHOW & RIGHTER CO. v. DECIPHER, INC.

598 F.Supp. 1489 (E.D.Va. 1984)

Trivial Pursuit, produced by a plaintiff, Selchow & Righter Co., is a board game that has achieved commercial success in the United States. After frequent play of the Master Game, questions will inevitably be repeated. Therefore, there is a substantial demand for replacement cards containing new questions that can be used with the Master Game. To address this demand, Selchow manufactures and sells subsidiary card sets to use with the Master Game.

The defendant, Decipher, Inc. (Decipher), is a Virginia corporation that manufactures and sells games. Decipher's chief executive officer and primary shareholder, Warren L. Holland, Jr., created and designed Forte Trivia Cards—Volume One. Holland first produced a prototype design of the outside box, the cards, and the inside boxes that would hold the cards. Both the prototype and the actual product Forte Trivial Cards bear a strong resemblance to the Trivial Pursuit subsidiary sets. Even the order of the color code on the Forte Trivia Cards mimics Trivial Pursuit's question and answer cards. Selchow sued Decipher, Inc., to enjoin it from continuing its practice.

DOUMAR, Judge

Reduced to its essentials, the plaintiffs claim that the defendant has violated the prohibition against unfair competition by marketing FORTE in such a manner that its card and packaging mimic the trade dress of TRIVIAL PURSUIT in violation of 15 U.S.C. [section] 1125(a). . . .

The Lanham Act was designed, in part, to curb deceptive and misleading uses of trademarks and to provide protection against unfair competition. The statute was designed to protect not only business but also the general public from the use of false trade descriptions. Section 1125(a) prohibits a competitor from deceiving buyers into believing that its product is that of another. This is sometimes referred to as "palming off."

The key issue in this case is whether it is likely that the public will be confused so as to believe that FORTE Trivia Cards emanate from the makers of TRIVIAL PURSUIT. Although mere possibility of confusion is not sufficient, a showing of actual confusion is not required; only a likelihood of confusion need be shown. In the instant case, evidence of the likelihood of confusion is found from four independent sources: (1) the Court's own viewing of the products; (2) the defendant's intent to confuse the public; (3) a department store display investigation; and (4) a statistical survey.

The Court finds that the defendant, except for getting new questions, changing the predominant color and using the term TRIVIAL PURSUIT more frequently, copied the TRIVIAL PURSUIT subsidiary card set product. The Court, therefore, based upon its own inspection, must, and does, reach the inescapable conclusion that the public is likely to be confused by the overwhelming similarities between FORTE's product and TRIVIAL PURSUIT's.

Additional evidence that the public is likely to be confused as to the origin of FORTE trivia cards is department store display investigation. A private investigator randomly selected stores that sold both TRIVIAL PURSUIT– brand games and card sets, and FORTE trivia card sets. The investigator found and visited 10 stores that marketed both plaintiffs' and defendant's products in the Washington, Baltimore and New York City areas. The investigator took photographs of the displays of trivia games in the stores. In many of the displays the FORTE card sets and the TRIVIAL PURSUIT card sets were side-by-side. . . . The investigator picked up a FORTE card set and asked a salesperson "Are these made by the people who make TRIVIAL PURSUIT?" Approximately 7 out of the 10 sales clerks answered in the affirmative. The investigation is certainly not a scientific survey but, nevertheless, it seems to indicate that both the plaintiffs' and defendant's products are displayed together, just as the defendant had desired. . . .

Lastly, the Court finds evidence of likelihood of confusion in a statistical survey presented by the plaintiffs. The survey was conducted by a survey expert who has worked in the area of market research for the past 30 years. The survey consisted of two research studies. One hundred persons were interviewed in each study. The participants were evenly divided between males and females and five age groups. An interest in trivia games was established prior to any respondent's participation in the survey. . . . [In] [t]he first study . . . respondents were shown a FORTE trivia card package. Respondents were asked to look at the package as they would if they were thinking of buying such a product. The respondents were then asked a series of questions regarding who they thought made the trivia cards in the package they had just seen. The results of the package study indicated that 28 percent of the persons interviewed identified the FORTE trivia card package as a product of the company that made the TRIVIAL PURSUIT game. The second study was a display study in which respondents were shown a display of TRIVIAL PURSUIT products with the FORTE trivia card set. After viewing the display, 45 percent of the respondents identified FORTE as a product of TRIVIAL PURSUIT. The expert's conclusion was that the results indicate that sizable proportions of consumers identify FORTE trivia cards as made by the makers of the TRIVIAL PURSUIT game.

The Court, therefore, concludes that, based upon a statistical survey, a department store display investigation, its own inspection of both products and the finding that the defendant intended to confuse the public as to its product's origin, there is a likelihood that the public is confused as to the origin of the FORTE product.

. . . FORTE may, on its own package, state that it can be used for play with TRIVIAL PURSUIT. The Court, however, is of the opinion that the phrase "Real Questions For Your TRIVIAL PURSUIT Game" in large prominent letters on the top of outside box and the phrase "6,000 Real Questions for your TRIVIAL PURSUIT Game" in prominent letters on all four side panels of the outside box goes further than describing a use of the FORTE product. . . .

. . . In conclusion, the Court finds that the defendant in designing its product intended to trade off of the plaintiffs' trademark and to confuse the public. [The court ordered the defendant to remove the Forte Trivia cards from public sale.]

Case Questions

1. With what legal devices might Trivial Pursuit's manufacturer have further protected the game, its design, the game board, and its manufacturer's right to sell the game?

2. What other theories could have been used in a case against Decipher?

3. Attack the plaintiff's surveys.

4. If you were Warren Holland (the originator of the idea to manufacture replacement sets for Trivial Pursuit), what sort of marketing plan could you have used to deter "palming off"?

PACKAGING AND LABELING LAWS

Apart from laws governing the choice of a product name or symbol, many other laws govern the labeling and packaging of products (see Figure 48–5). They include such items as drugs, fabrics, hazardous substances, and cigarettes. A multitude of other products including such diverse items as oral contraceptives, color additives, and automobiles are also required to carry labels conveying important information to consumers.

PRODUCT PRICING

Pricing is a complex mix of a number of factors. Costs must be determined. These include fixed costs that do not change as output changes, such as land; and variable costs, such as materials and labor that do change as output rises or falls. A second factor is demand that concerns consumers' sensitivity to price changes. A third factor is what the competition is charging for the product. A fourth factor concerns the marketing objective, which might be to increase a product's market share through pricing below the market or to maximize short-term profits by pricing above the market. All of the above are legitimate market factors influencing the determination of a product's price.

There are, however, illegal pricing practices. These include *price-fixing*, *price discrimination*, and *deceptive pricing*. As Chapter 46 indicated, price-fixing is a per se violation of section 1 of the Sherman Antitrust Act. Chapter 47 discussed the concept of price discrimination as it arises under the Robinson-Patman Act.

Although the matter of deceptive advertising will be more fully covered in the next section, one pricing practice that is proscribed by law is the *phony special price*. This may take various forms, such as an alleged reduction in price or "sale price" without any actual reduction. Or the item may be "preticketed" by a manufacturer's markup in price and then a retailer's markdown. The Federal Trade Commission under section 5 of the Federal Trade Commission Act has the power to prohibit phony special

Figure 48–5   Federal Laws Governing Labeling and Packaging

Statute	Features
Federal Food, Drug, and Cosmetic Act (1938)	Prohibits misbranding of food, drugs, and cosmetics; requires additive labeling; authorizes FDA to administer
Wool Products Labeling Act (1939)	Requires fabric labeling indicating percentages of new wool, reprocessed wool, and other fabrics; authorizes FTC to administer
Fur Products Labeling Act (1951)	Requires labeling of fur content, including types of animals and country of origin; authorizes FTC to administer
Textile Fiber Products Identification Act (1958)	Governs labeling of man-made fiber content not covered by Wool or Fur Products Acts; authorizes FTC to administer
Hazardous Substance Labeling Act (1960)	Requires warning labels on products containing dangerous household chemicals; authorizes Consumer Product Safety Commission to administer
Fair Packaging and Labeling Act (1966)	A truth-in-packaging act; requires basic information, including origin of product, quantity, number of servings, and product usage; authorizes FTC to administer
Cigarette Labeling Act (1966)	Requires cigarette manufacturers to label cigarettes with health warnings; authorizes FTC to administer
Poison Prevention Packaging Act (1970)	Requires childproof caps on products that are dangerous to children; authorizes secretary of Health and Human Services to administer
Energy Conservation Act (1975)	Requires operating-cost and energy consumption labels for 13 major household appliances; authorizes FTC to administer
Nutrition Labeling and Education Act (1990)	Requires detailed uniform labeling of food products

prices. The FTC has also issued guidelines for pricing, including showing the regular and sale prices, the elimination of misleading bargain offers, and truthfulness.

PRODUCT ADVERTISING

Advertising is a huge business. The average consumer is exposed to several hundred advertisements each day. To accomplish this, companies are spending upward of $60 billion a year for ads in various media.

Chapter 12 expressed the general rule of contract law concerning advertisements. Advertisements are generally not considered offers. As a result, no contract is formed when a customer wishes to "accept" an advertised product or price since one cannot accept nonoffers. And if there is no contract, a customer may not sue for breach of contract if a seller violates a promise made in an advertisement. Other avenues of action are, of course, open to the customer for rep-

resentations made in advertisements. These include an action for fraud (see Chapter 13) and an action for breach of express warranties (see Chapter 22).

Advertisements are entitled to First Amendment protection as commercial speech (see Chapter 4). But the commercial speech doctrine does not protect deceptive advertisements. Original or unique advertisements are also entitled to copyright protection. Thus, brochures, newspaper ads, drawings, music, and jingles, for example, are copyrightable. In the case of a copyright infringement by a competitor, the victim would be entitled to an injunction stopping the infringement and damages, including the infringer's profits.

Deceptive Advertising

Advertising wields tremendous power both to inform the public about products and services and to shape public demand. Implicit in advertising's power is the possibility of abuse through deceptive claims. Deceptive claims misallocate resources by skewing market demands.

Congress, through the Wheeler-Lea Amendment of 1938, gave the FTC jurisdiction to guard against *deceptive* advertising. Actual deception was not required, nor was it necessary to show that an average or reasonable consumer would be deceived. In one case, the FTC challenged a GM advertised quotation of *Road and Track Magazine* saying that the Vega was the best-handling passenger car ever built in the United States. The FTC claimed that consumers might actually believe that the Vega was *in fact* the best-handling car in the U.S.[1]

Statements that are factually accurate still may leave a deceptive overall impression according to the FTC. For example, an Old Gold cigarette advertisement claimed to have the lowest nicotine levels of seven tested brands. This was true. The FTC claimed however, that the ad left a false *overall impression* that Old Golds were low in nicotine.

FTC Remedies

If the FTC believes that a company has engaged in deceptive advertisement, it may seek various remedies. These include consent decrees, cease and desist orders, civil penalties, affirmative disclosures, corrective advertising, and injunctions.

Consent Decrees

A **consent decree** is simply a voluntary agreement to stop a certain type of advertising in the future. There is no admission of guilt in the consent decree. The company, in effect, is saying, ''We do not admit doing anything wrong in the past, but we will not do it in the future.'' The FTC saves the expense of litigation by obtaining a consent decree.

Cease and Desist Orders

A **cease and desist order** is obtained after a hearing on an FTC complaint before an administrative law judge. The judge's opinion can be appealed to the full Commission and appealed further to the U.S. Court of Appeals. The order, like a consent decree,

simply requires the company to stop a certain advertising practice.

Civil Penalties

Civil penalties, including fines, the return of property, or the rescission of contracts, can be sought by the FTC in federal district court if a company violates a cease and desist order. In one case, the Readers Digest Association, Inc., violated an order to stop simulating valuable items in their mailings. A federal district court held the Digest Association liable in the amount of $7.75 million for its continued violation of the order.[2]

Affirmative Disclosures

If a statement is misleading due to omitted facts, courts have required companies to make **affirmative disclosures** of the omissions if they choose to continue to run the ad. In one case against Geritol,[3] the U.S. Court of Appeals required the statement that ''in the great majority of persons . . . *this preparation will be of no benefit*'' in relieving deficiency anemia. Most companies, including Geritol in this case, simply choose to stop the old advertising campaign, rather than continue the campaign and make the disclosures.

Corrective Advertising

A more drastic remedy, from a company's perspective, is **corrective advertising**, which mandates future advertising expenditures to correct a former misleading impression. In a case involving Listerine, a mouthwash, the Warner-Lambert Co. was required by the U.S. Court of Appeals to correct the impression that Listerine could prevent colds, by running $10 million of ads stating, ''Listerine will not help prevent colds or sore throats or lessen their severity.''[4]

Preliminary Injunctions

The following case involves another remedy available to the FTC, the power to seek a **preliminary injunction** to stop deceptive advertisements.

---

[1]*General Motors Corp.,* 85 F.T.C. 17 (1975).

[2]*United States v. Readers Digest Ass'n, Inc.,* 662 F.2d 995 (3rd Cir. 1981).

[3]*J.B. Williams Co. v. F.T.C.,* 381 F.2d 884 (6th Cir. 1967).

[4]*Warner-Lambert Co. v. F.T.C.,* 562 F.2d 749 (D.C. Cir. 1977).

FEDERAL TRADE COMMISSION v. PHARMTECH RESEARCH, INC.

576 F.Supp 294 (D.D.C. 1983)

The defendant, Pharmtech, a California corporation, manufactures Daily Greens, a food supplement in tablet form. The label affixed to the Daily Greens bottle indicated that the tablets contain vitamins A, C, and E, the mineral selenium, beta carotene, and dehydrated vegetables. Pharmtech placed advertisements for Daily Greens in various magazines and newspapers and disseminated similar television advertising.

Each advertisement claimed that the consumption of Daily Greens was associated with a reduction in the risk of certain cancers. The claim was also made that Daily Greens would contribute to certain biological defenses.

The FTC sought an injunction restraining Pharmtech from disseminating the challenged advertisements pending the outcome of administrative proceedings before the Commission.

PARKER, Judge

In making these claims, defendant relies solely on a report published by the National Academy of Sciences, entitled Diet, Nutrition and Cancer. That publication (the Report) presents the results of a comprehensive study conducted by a 13-member committee of the National Research Council, the Committee on Diet, Nutrition and Cancer (Committee) on the relationship between eating habits and cancer. The Committee concluded that frequent consumption of certain fruits and vegetables is associated with a reduction in the incidence of cancer in human beings, and found that carotene-rich vegetables, such as carrots, and cruciferous vegetables, such as broccoli, cabbage and brussels sprouts, provide this benefit. Thus, it recommended that people consume carotene-rich and cruciferous vegetables daily.

The Report, however, limited the application of its findings by several specific and cautionary warnings. First, the Committee stated that scientists have not identified the specific compounds responsible for the reduced incidence of cancer . . . in fact, this benefit may be completely unrelated to the chemical composition of the vegetables studied. Instead, the benefit may be due to the fact that people who eat vegetables eat fewer foods that cause cancer.

Second, the Report also warned that:

[t]hese recommendations apply only to foods as sources of nutrients—not to dietary supplements of individual nutrients.

It further elaborated on the potential hazards of supplementation with vitamin A and selenium . . . and drew no firm conclusions about the effect of vitamin E and selenium on cancer in human beings. These warnings are relevant because they emphasize that the findings apply to foods as people typically consume them, not to dietary supplements.

Lastly, the Report relied on studies of the consumption of raw or whole vegetables. The Report cautioned that the removal of water which occurs during dehydration may alter the protective effect of nutrients and other compounds. The Committee admonished that dehydrated foods are ''processed'' foods which ''produce significant structural and possibly major chemical changes including nutrient loss.''

Unfair or Deceptive Acts and Practices

Section 5 of the Act declares that unfair or deceptive acts or practices in or affecting commerce are unlawful. Under section 5, the capacity of an advertisement to deceive consumers is judged by the impression conveyed by the entire advertisement, and not by the impact of isolated words and phrases. An advertisement may be deceptive if it has a tendency to convey a misleading impression, even if an alternative nonmisleading impression might also be conveyed.

Moreover, an advertisement's reference to a public issue as a means to induce consumer purchases is relevant to whether the advertisement is misleading or deceptive. . . . This is because ''the representations which bear on the characteristics of the product may take on increased importance in the mind of the public." The advertiser's good faith or absence of intent to deceive is irrelevant.

Pharmtech's representations that the Report supports a finding that Daily Greens reduces the risk of cancer are unfair and deceptive because they convey a misleading impression. Pharmtech has played on the average consumer's well-founded fear of cancer as a vehicle for the sale of its product . . . and has used the findings of the Report to create the impression that Daily Greens will reduce the risk of cancer. Since there are no findings concerning the beneficial cancer effects of products like Daily Greens, and the Report in fact disclaims such a conclusion, Pharmtech's claims are misleading.

In this case, the FTC has clearly demonstrated that Pharmtech's representations that the use of Daily Greens reduces the risk of cancer are false, misleading and deceptive. This deception is especially harmful because it preys on consumers' fears about a health issue which has generated public concern. In addition, people who use Daily Greens as a substitute for whole vegetables may more likely than not neglect to eat those vegetables. This is a very real harm in view of the Report's findings that the consumption of whole vegetables has a positive effect on the reduction of cancer in humans.

The availability of whole vegetables also indicates that consumers do not have an overriding need for Daily Greens. A consumer who desires the protective benefit of vegetables is able to purchase and consume these vegetables in a nondehydrated form. Moreover, the evidence indicates that Daily Greens are not inexpensive. [The injunction was granted.]

Case Questions

1. "We should leave this area of health food products to the consumer to decide whether such claims are true or false." Comment.

2. Should courts be more strict in judging health claims than nonhealth claims? Explain.

3. Can you think of any other ways in which the advertisement may have been misleading?

4. How do you suggest Daily Greens be advertised in the future?

FTC Policy

Currently, the FTC will not find an advertisement to be deceptive unless it would mislead a "reasonable" person. Thus, the standard is what a reasonable person would believe. Second, the deception must be *material* — that is, an important factor in the purchasing decision from the perspective of that reasonable person. Third, the deception must cause a significant degree of public injury. Essentially, under the FTC's free-market approach, the FTC engages in a cost-benefit analysis of its enforcement practices. This approach involves the value of protecting the public weighed against the cost of requiring more substantiation, the degree of injury to the public, and the cost of enforcement.

DECEPTIVE AND UNFAIR SALES PRACTICES

Earlier in this chapter, we discussed deceptive practices that caused confusion concerning *the identity* of a product's producer. These included trademark infringement, palming off, and name dilution. There are numerous other practices that do not confuse the public concerning a product's identity or source but are nevertheless considered to be deceptive.

In a book detailing abuses in the marketplace, former Senator Warren Magnuson wrote: "If one were writing a textbook on deceptive selling, these schemes — . . . bait and switch, referral selling, the free gimmick, and the fear sell could be described as the basics of the course."[5]

Bait and switch occurs when an advertised low-priced item is never intended to be sold. Instead, the buyer is switched to a higher priced item after entering the store. For example, a store might advertise "Prescription Eyeglasses, $5 a pair." After consumer inquiry, the $5 eyeglasses are disparaged by a salesperson who, after explaining the benefits of a higher priced pair, switches the consumer to a $50 pair.

---

[5]W. Magnuson and J. Carper, *The Dark Side of the Marketplace* (Englewood Cliffs, N.J.: Prentice-Hall, 1968), p. 23.

Referral selling is a scheme involving a promise of free merchandise to a buyer who finds a certain number of friends who will buy the merchandise. Pots and pans and aluminum siding have been sold this way to consumers. The catch is that buyers must sign a purchase contract agreeing to pay for the merchandise if their friends do not purchase the product.

The **free gimmick** involves the promise of free goods if the buyer agrees to purchase other items over a long period of time. Record and book clubs often use this approach to selling.[6]

The **fear sell** is perhaps the most sinister of the deceptive schemes. To illustrate this technique, a salesperson, perhaps dressed in an official-looking uniform, tells a homeowner that a large maple tree in that person's front yard is dangerously infested with termites and must be removed before it falls. Before long, the maple tree is cut down and the consumer is charged an exorbitant fee for this unneeded service.

Antideception Statutes

Every state in the country and the District of Columbia have enacted statutes designed to prevent consumer deception and abuse. Most of these are patterned on section 5(a)(1) of the Federal Trade Commission Act, which prohibits "unfair or deceptive acts and practices."[7] These state antideception laws are often called, among other things, consumer sales acts, consumer protection laws, consumer fraud acts, and deceptive trade practices acts.

A number of state statutes make the fear sell, bait and switch, and referral sales schemes per se violations of their antideception statute. The FTC, in addition to forbidding these practices, prohibits the use of the word *free* if items the consumer must purchase are marked up to recover costs.

---

[6]The FTC promulgated a rule concerning negative option plans that requires a buyer to affirmatively reject unwanted goods. Under the rule, the seller must clearly describe the plan's terms, the purchase requirements, and the right of the buyer to terminate plan membership.

[7]In addition to following section 5(a)(1), the Federal Trade Commission drafted an Unfair Trade Practices and Consumer Protection Act in 1967. Most state statutes are patterned in part on this model act.

The major advantage to consumers of the state statutes over the FTC Act is that they generally permit a private enforcement action by the aggrieved consumer. Under the statutes, a consumer may sue not only the corporation who engages in the deceptive practice but also its agents, including any ad agency who knowingly participates in the deception. Damages almost always include actual out-of-pocket losses and attorney fees to the successful consumer litigant. Some statutes also authorize minimum damage awards greater than the actual loss. The statutes also allow for punitive damages designed to punish the defendant.

In addition to the private right of action, the state statutes typically provide for an enforcement action by the state's attorney general's office or the state consumer agency. Both civil and criminal penalties may be sought by the state. In contrast to state antideception statutes, the FTC Act can be enforced only by the Federal Trade Commission, which, due to limited resources, must obviously be very selective in choosing enforcement targets.

Unfair Acts and Practices

Section 5(a)(1) of the FTC Act prohibits not only deception but also "*unfair* . . . acts and practices."

As a result of serious business opposition and lobbying efforts in the late 1970s, Congress prohibited the FTC from promulgating any legislative rules based on its authority to police *unfair* acts. However, the FTC still may apply this doctrine against targeted businesses on a case-by-case basis through adjudication.

PRODUCT DISTRIBUTION

The marketing distribution system is designed to place goods where they are needed and wanted. Concerning consumer goods, *distribution* involves a series of contracts as the goods move from the manufacturer to the wholesale middleman, the retailer, and ultimately, the consumer.

Beginning with the manufacturer, a variety of legal limitations exist on its contracts with wholesale middlemen or retailers. These limits were discussed in Chapter 46. They include the prohibition of tying contracts and resale price maintenance contracts.

In addition to the schemes mentioned in the previous section, several other distribution practices are carefully regulated by FTC rules and/or state law. These rules, it should be noted, apply only to transactions between a seller and a *consumer*. These include the regulation of door-to-door sales, mail-order sales, pyramid sales, and other regulated practices.

Door-to-Door Sales

Since high-pressure tactics are commonplace in door-to-door sales, the FTC promulgated a Trade Regulation Rule concerning a cooling-off period for door-to-door sales.[8] Essentially, this rule (and state antideception statutes that have incorporated its language) permits the buyer to cancel a home solicitation sale for over $25 with no penalty within three days. Notice of this right to cancel must be given near the buyer's signature and in a detachable form that the consumer can mail to the seller. Further, the seller must return any funds taken from the consumer within 10 business days.

Mail-Order Sales

Mail-order sales often result in consumer complaints and dissatisfaction. To deal with these problems, the FTC promulgated a rule concerning mail-order merchandise.[9] Many state statutes have incorporated this rule in some form. Under the rule, sellers must be able to deliver the consumer goods within 30 days or offer the consumer the option of either consenting to the delay or receiving a refund and canceling the contract.

Pyramid Sales

Nutritional additives, beauty aids, soaps, and other consumer products are often sold through **pyramid sales** schemes. Simply stated, the scheme involves in reality not the sale of a product but the sale of the right to sell the product. To illustrate, A sells the right to sell Nutro-Herb to B, C, and D and collects a percentage of all their sales. B sells the right to sell

Nutro-Herb to E, F, and G, who in turn seek to sell this right to others. This scheme is a per se violation of many state antideception statutes since, in practice, only the first few layers of participants ever recoup their initial investment. The rest find it mathematically more difficult to the point of impossibility to sell the right.[10]

Other Practices

A variety of industries have also been the subject of regulation by FTC rules. Specific rules cover used car sales, funeral home services, home insulation sales, correspondence schools, and hearing aids sales. State consumer protection statutes have gone much further. Many specifically cover, in addition to the above, automobile repairs and estimates, entertainment clubs, health spas, dance studios, real estate, insurance, home improvement, and encyclopedia sales.

END–OF–CHAPTER QUESTIONS

1. Are the protections against deceptive sales practices adequate? Analyze.

2. What are the chief differences between the FTC Act and state antideception statutes? Discuss.

3. Compare and contrast antidilution statutes and trademark protection.

4. For what sorts of words or names will one be unable to obtain a registered trademark or trade name?

5. Doctors took a spleen out of a cancer patient with consent in hopes of improving the patient's condition. Without the consent of the patient, the doctors used the excised spleen to manufacture certain human cells that were particularly immune from certain types of cancer. The doctors sought to patent their find. Comment on the patentability of such a process. Com-

---

[8]16 C.F.R. Part 429 (1973).
[9]16 C.F.R. Part 435 (1975).

[10]A scheme requiring each person to sell only three memberships to recoup their investment would sign up every person in the world after a mere 21 layers of the pyramid.

ment on the ethics of the procedure. See *Moore v. Regents of the University of California*, 793 P. 2d 479 (Cal. 1990).

6. Many manufacturers of beer have begun selling low-calorie beer called light or "lite." Is the term *lite* as applied to a low-calorie beer registrable as a trademark? Discuss. See *Miller Brewing Company v. G. Heilemann Brewing Co.*, 561 F.2d 75 (7th Cir. 1977).

7. W.S.M. was the holder of several trademarks, including one for "Opry" as operators of the Grand Ole Opry and Opryland U.S.A. W.S.M. sued Dennis Hilton for violating its trademark in the operation of his Country Shindig Opry. Is *Opry* a generic term, so that W.S.M. is not entitled to the exclusive use of this name? How is trademark genericism tested? See *W.S.M., Inc. v. Hilton*, 724 F.2d 1320 (8th Cir. 1984).

8. On August 14, 1983, the defendant, Dave Towel Cadillac, Inc., advertised a Fleetwood automobile for $20,450. When the plaintiff, Gaylan, went to purchase the car two weeks later, its selling price was $23,216. What deceptive practice is Dave Towel Cadillac engaged in? Does Gaylan have any remedies for common law breach of contract or fraud? What reme-

dies are available under the FTC Act or a state antideception act? See *Gaylan v. Dave Towel Cadillac, Inc.*, 473 N.E.2d 64 (Ohio Mun. 1984).

9. American Home Products advertised that its drug product, Anacin, contained a unique pain-killing formula that has been conclusively proven to be superior in effectiveness to all other nonprescription analgesics. What test would be employed in determining whether this contention is deceptive? What type of evidence should American Home Products have to substantiate its claim? See *American Home Products Corp. v. F.T.C.* 695 F.2d 681 (3d Cir. 1982).

10. The defendant, Floyd, admitted in a deposition that he purchased 10,000 "alligator" logos with the belief they were originals or imitations of the plaintiff's IZOD trademark. Floyd also admitted that he personally sewed these logos on garments and that he sold the garments at a flea market booth. Has Floyd violated any laws? If so, in what way? Fully discuss. What remedy, if any, should be granted Lacoste Alligator, S.A., the holder of the alligator trademark? See *Lacoste Alligator, S.A. v. Bluesteen's Men's Wear, Inc.*, 569 F.Supp 491 (D.S.C. 1983).

Part XII

Labor Law

■

Chapter 49

Employment Relations

Chapter 50

Equal Employment

Chapter 49

Employment Relations

■

CRITICAL THINKING INQUIRIES

As you read this chapter, you should be able to address the following:

- What is the reason for the employment-at-will rule?
- What are the legal, ethical, and practical concerns that must be balanced by employers when deciding whether to institute a drug-detection program?
- Are the statutory protections for workers in the area of minimum wages, unemployment compensation, pensions, and disability adequate?
- Under what circumstances should a union consider seeking representation status in a company?
- Analyze: ''The union and management are equal in negotiating power.''
- Analyze: ''Federal and state laws are sufficient to encourage worker safety.''

MANAGERIAL PERSPECTIVE

Alaska Oil, an oil rig company, is considering implementation of a drug-testing program for its oil rig workers. The company is concerned about the threat of unionization should such a program be implemented. The company is also concerned about lawsuits by workers who are fired as a result of refusing to take the test or failing the test. Additionally, Alaska Oil desires to implement a private pension program and to establish tighter safety controls over its operations in response to employee discontent. Alaska Oil seeks advice on whether to implement such programs and, if so, the specifics of the program.

- What are some guidelines that Alaska Oil should consider if it decides to implement a drug-testing program? Safety and pension programs?
- How does the concept of employment at will relate to Alaska Oil's concerns?
- What can Alaska Oil lawfully do to thwart unionization?
- What must the workers do in order to unionize?

Today, Alaska Oil and other companies must be aware of the limits on discharging an employee, the characteristics of a lawful drug-testing program, the need for safety concern and other employee protections, and the whole unionization process. These are very common issues facing employers.

In the 19th and early 20th centuries, the workplace was by and large free from any legal regulation or interference. Employers were free to create and terminate employment at the employer's will. Employers were also free from any legal obligation to recognize or bargain with any union representing a group of workers. In fact, in many cases, union activity was deemed to be illegal altogether.

The philosophic milieu of this period was so consistently antiregulation that the free-market theory was raised to constitutional status by the Supreme Court. Thus, the Court found that many governmental attempts to regulate businesses were a denial of businesses' due process right to property. As we shall see in this chapter, times have changed. This chapter will familiarize the student with the status of employment at will, the issue of drug testing in the workplace, statutory benefits for employees, federal labor law applicable to the employer and employee, and worker safety and compensation statutes.

EMPLOYMENT-AT-WILL

Until recently, in every state in the United States, in the absence of a formal employment contract, an employer could discharge an employee for a good cause, a bad cause, or no cause at all, without legal liability. This principle is called **employment-at-will** employment. An at-will employee could thus be discharged without notice for any reason and correspondingly could leave without notice for any reason.

Laws Affecting the at-Will Employment Rule

A wide variety of federal and state laws have chipped away at the employment-at-will rule. For example, the Lloyd-Lafollete Act of 1912 protected federal employees from removal except for cause. This civil service protection was gradually extended to state and municipal employees through state and local laws. The job security of government workers was further strengthened by several U.S. Supreme

Court cases holding government employees to be vested with property rights in their employment. These rights to continued employment could not be denied to an employee without procedural due process (see Chapter 4).

In the private sector, a major legislative assault on the employment-at-will rule occurred through the passage of the **Wagner Act** in 1935 (more fully discussed later in this chapter). Under this federal law, employers were prohibited from discharging employees because of their union affiliation or activity. Employees dismissed in violation of the Wagner Act were often entitled to reinstatement and back pay.

In addition, in the 1960s and 1970s, a wide variety of federal and state civil rights laws were passed protecting workers from discriminatory discharge on the basis of the employee's race, religion, sex, national origin, age, handicap, and other causes (see Chapter 50).

Erosion of the Employment-at-Will Rule

Employment at will is still the basic presumption of the law for about half of all U.S. employees (subject to the statutes mentioned above). However, in the past 15 years, courts in over 40 states have carved out exceptions to this rule. The three most often cited exceptions to the employment-at-will rule are the public policy exception, the implied contract exception, and the good faith exception (see Figure 49–1).

Public Policy Exception

The **public policy exception** is actually a form of tort action that permits discharged employees to sue for damages if their dismissal violates a firmly established principle of public policy. Along with protection for the discharged employee, the major beneficiary of this exception is society, in whose interest the public policy was enacted.

Figure 49–1   Exceptions to the Employment-at-Will Doctrine

- Express contract
- Public policy
- Implied contract
- Good faith
- Antidiscrimination laws
- Collective bargaining agreement

Perhaps the best and most interesting discussion of the sources of public policy is found in the Arizona Supreme Court case of *Wagenseller v. Scottsdale Memorial Hospital*[1] (commonly known as the *Moon River* case). The plaintiff, Catherine Sue Wagenseller, was a nurse who refused to bare her bottom along with other employees in a staged parody of the song *Moon River* during a group camping trip. Immediately after this refusal, her employment relationship soured and she was fired from her job, just three months after being promoted. She sued, alleging that she was wrongfully discharged in violation of public policy.

The Arizona Supreme Court looked to the state constitution, state legislation, and court pronouncements to discover the state's public policy. In this case, an indecent exposure criminal statute embodied the relevant public policy. The court therefore found that the plaintiff was wrongfully discharged.

Other well-known violations of public policy include discharge due to refusing to give perjured testimony, serving on a jury, filing a workers' compensation claim, and demanding at least state minimum wages. In a Texas case, a sailor was discharged for refusing to dump oily bilge water into a river. The Texas Supreme Court held that his discharge violated public policy embodied in a federal law, the Water Pollution Control Act.[2]

Courts more recently have been confronted with cases involving discharges due to **whistleblowing**—that is, a discharge resulting from an employee's protest of employer action to a government agency. Typically, the whistle is blown on employer violations of governmentally required safety standards. The trend is that such discharges violate public policy.

Implied Contract Exception

Under the **implied contract exception,** employers remove themselves from the at-will presumption by making a promise to an employee of job tenure or when failing to follow company procedures before discharging the employee. Consider these exceptions as you read the following case.

[1]710 P.2d 1025 (Ariz. 1985).

[2]687 S.W.2d 733 (Tex. 1985).

WOOLLEY v. HOFFMANN-LA ROCHE, INC.
491 A.2d 1257 (N.J. 1985)

Richard Woolley, the plaintiff, was hired by the defendant, Hoffmann-La Roche, Inc., as an engineering section head in Hoffmann-La Roche's Central Engineering Department. There was no written employment contract. After starting to work, Woolley received and read the personnel manual. Thereafter, Woolley was formally asked to resign. He refused, and he was fired.

Woolley sued for breach of contract. The gist of his breach of contract claim was that the express and implied promises in Hoffmann-La Roche's employment manual created a contract under which he could not be fired at will.

Hoffmann-La Roche's motion for summary judgment was granted by the trial court. The Appellate Division affirmed. The New Jersey Supreme Court granted certiorari.

WILENTZ, Judge

The issue before us is whether certain terms in a company's employment manual may contractually bind the company. We hold that absent a clear and prominent disclaimer, an implied promise contained in an employment manual that an employee will be fired only for cause may be enforceable against an employer even when the employment is for an indefinite term and would otherwise be terminable at will.

The employer's contention here is that the distribution of the manual was simply an expression of the company's ''philosophy'' and therefore free of any possible contractual consequences. The former employee claims it could reasonably be read as an explicit statement of company policies intended to be followed by the company in the same manner as if they were expressed in an agreement signed by both employer and employees. From the analysis that follows we conclude that a jury, properly instructed, could find, in strict contract terms, that the manual constituted an offer; put differently, it could find that this portion of the manual (concerning job security) set forth terms and conditions of employment.

In determining the manual's meaning and effect, we must consider the probable context in which it was disseminated and the environment surrounding its continued existence. The manual, though apparently not distributed to all employees ("in general, distribution will be provided to supervisory personnel . . ."), covers all of them. Its terms are of such importance to all employees that in the absence of contradicting evidence, it would seem clear that it was intended by Hoffmann-La Roche that all employees be advised of the benefits it confers.

. . . Without minimizing the importance of its specific provisions, the context of the manual's preparation and distribution is, to us, the most persuasive proof that it would be almost inevitable for an employee to regard it as a binding commitment, legally enforceable, concerning the terms and conditions of . . . employment. . . . If there were any doubt about it . . . the name of the manual dispels it, for it is nothing short of the official *policy* of the company, it is the Personnel *Policy* Manual. As every employee knows, when superiors tell you "it's company policy," they mean business.

In order for an offer in the form of a promise to become enforceable, it must be accepted. . . . In most of the cases involving an employer's personnel policy manual, the document is prepared without any negotiations and is voluntarily distributed to the workforce by the employer. It seeks no return promise from the employees. It is reasonable to interpret it as seeking continued work from the employees, who, in most cases, are free to quit since they are almost always employees at will, not simply in the sense that the employer can fire them without cause, but in the sense that they can quit without breaching any obligation. Thus analyzed, the manual is an offer that seeks the formation of a unilateral contract—

the employees' bargained-for action needed to make the offer binding being their continued work when they have no obligation to continue.

All that this opinion requires of an employer is that it be fair. It would be unfair to allow an employer to distribute a policy manual that makes the workforce believe that certain promises have been made and then to allow the employer to renege on those promises. What is sought here is basic honesty: if the employer, for whatever reason, does not want the manual to be capable of being construed by the court as a binding contract, there are simple ways to attain that goal. All that need be done is the inclusion in a very prominent position of an appropriate statement that there is no promise of any kind by the employer contained in the manual; that regardless of what the manual says or provides, the employer promises nothing and remains free to change wages and all other working conditions without having to consult anyone and without anyone's agreement; and that the employer continues to have the absolute power to fire anyone with or without good cause.

Reversed and remanded for trial.

Case Questions

1. What issue does this case present?
2. How have workplace changes in the past century produced a need for a change in the employment-at-will rule? Discuss.
3. Does this case mean that the company cannot alter the policies contained in the manual? Explain.
4. Is it fair to permit the employee the right to quit but not permit the employer the right to fire? Explain.
5. How may future employers in New Jersey avoid having a policy manual construed to be a binding promise? Might this be against public policy? How practical is the court's solution? Explain.

Good Faith Exception

A third exception to the employment-at-will rule is the rule that employers act fairly and in good faith. Some courts have suggested that the requirement of good faith is implied in employment contracts in

much the same way as good faith is implied in contracts for the sale of goods. It requires honesty and fair dealing. It is thus considered a contract-type doctrine. Other courts have suggested that it arises as a matter of tort law to prevent malicious injury or fraudulent behavior. The difference between the two is relevant only with respect to damages (see Chapter 18).

Essentially, the **good faith exception** is designed to bring ethical principles to bear in the employment relationship. It operates to exclude a wide range of behaviors such as discharging a long-time employee without cause in order to avoid paying a pension, or discharging an employee who has just been diagnosed as having terminal cancer. ''Good faith''

cases often overlap with either the public policy or implied contract cases.

Supporting the Employment-at-Will Rule

The vast majority of legal scholars have supported the trend toward limiting or eliminating the employment-at-will rule. At least a few writers have protested, as indicated by the following law journal excerpt.

---

*A Defense of the Employment at Will Rule**

Indeed, the employment relationship has much in common with the marriage relationship. Both function well only so long as consensus continues. Both often start with a probationary period. If the relationship survives this, a honeymoon period ensues; in both employment and marriage the parties contemplate, if not a lifelong relationship, at least one that each thinks of as permanent. The passage of time brings problems that put strains on the relationship, but consensus survives the strains in the good employment relationship, as in the good marriage. The abiding feature of consensus remains despite occasional and normal blips of discord. In an unsatisfactory employment relationship the employee either quits or is fired because he is, in the employer's judgment, in some way irremediably unsatisfactory: he cannot do his job well enough, or is unreliable, too often absent, a troublemaker, dishonest, or drinks on the job. Likewise, in an unsatisfactory marriage one spouse seeks to be free of the other when he or she believes the relationship is irremediably unsatisfactory. . . .

It is perhaps curious that the marriage relationship and the employment relationship are moving in opposite directions with regard to the legal effects of dissolution. During most of the past century marriage was dissoluble only through a finding of fault of one party, whereas an employment relationship, unless otherwise expressly agreed, was terminable without liability at the will of either party. As to the employment relationship, the law has recently moved toward the position that the relationship cannot be terminated without liability at the will of the employer unless the employee is at fault, whereas marriage can now be dissolved without a finding of fault. Stated otherwise, the rule struggling to emerge is that the employer is relieved of liability only when he in good faith terminates the employee for sufficient cause, either the employee's failure to perform the job satisfactorily or a bona fide decision in regard to the business which involves eliminating or reducing a particular category of employee. . . .

Thought Questions

1. The author analogizes the employment relationship to a marriage. What are the flaws in this analogy?

2. Has the author overstated the law? Explain.

---

*Source: Richard Power, ''A Defense of the Employment at Will Rule,'' 27 St. Louis U. L. J. 881 (1983). Copyright 1983 Saint Louis University Law Journal. Reprinted with permission.

DRUG TESTING IN THE WORKPLACE

A host of new legal issues has confronted the court system in recent years. Employers face an upsurge in cases involving more traditional theories of liability, including defamation, invasion of privacy, and the intentional or negligent infliction of emotional distress. In addition employers must grapple with the legitimacy of employee drug, AIDS, and polygraph tests. Since drug testing contains many of the difficult legal, moral, and practical issues that face employers, it will be used as a model for emerging issues of employer liability.

Drug Abuse: The Problem

Drug and alcohol abuse on the job is an enormous drain on the American economy and results in the death and personal injury of myriads of people. Studies indicate that drug and alcohol abuse cost the U.S. economy $60 billion a year. In comparison to their co-workers, drug abusers miss 10 times as many workdays, are much less productive, and are far more likely to steal. In a recent 10-year period, 50 train accidents were due to drug or alcohol-impaired workers, and in those, 37 people were killed, 80 were injured, and more than $34 million dollars worth of property was destroyed. In 1987, a tragic train wreck involving the collision of an Amtrak passenger train and a Conrail train was due at least in part to drug use by the Conrail engineer.

Drug Testing: The Employer's Motive

Under the doctrine of **respondeat superior,** employers may be liable for the torts of their employees committed during the course of employment. Since drug- and alcohol-impaired workers are far more likely to commit torts than their co-workers, potential employer liability resulting from substance-abusing workers also increases. In addition, employer expense may result from the loss of business, goodwill, increased costs of health care and insurance premiums, liability under the federal Occupational Safety and Health Act (OSHA) for failure to maintain a workplace "free from recognized hazards that are causing or are likely to cause death or serious physical harm to its employees," and liability from product liability suits due to poorly made products. Hence, it is not surprising that employers desire to curb drug abuse in the workplace.

Employer Response: Drug Screening

Many employers have reacted to the drug and alcohol abuse crisis by implementing some form of drug testing. The predominant issues involved in the employment of drug tests include the following:

- Many tests are not trustworthy. This may result in the wrongful disclosure of nondrug-abusing employees and their wrongful discipline.
- Privacy may be invaded by compelling employees to turn over bodily fluids to the employer and by detecting off-hours drug usage.
- The scope of the drug-screening program may be overbroad and encompass employees in nonjob-related activities.

Legal Implications of Drug Screening

Constitutional, statutory, and common law principles are involved in any drug-screening program. First, the U.S. Constitution's Fourth Amendment protects government employees from unreasonable searches and seizures (recall the state action requirement of government action before the Constitution applies). Most courts have declared blanket plans for drug screening of government employees to be unconstitutional unless there is either probable cause or a reasonable suspicion of an individual's drug use. Other constitutional issues may include the right to privacy, equal protection, and due process.

Second, the Federal Civil Rights Act Title VII prohibits discrimination based on "race, color, religion, sex, or national origin" (see Chapter 50). If a drug test disproportionately penalizes a protected group, this may violate Title VII.

Third, the National Labor Relations Act (NLRA) prohibits a unilateral change in certain subjects of bargaining between a firm and a union (discussed later in this chapter). Drug testing may thus require the consent of the union representing a firm's workers.

Fourth, common law rights that may be violated include a wrongful discharge action (under some exception to the employment-at-will rule), an invasion of privacy action for disclosure or intrusion, and defamation for falsely charging an employee with drug use. Maintaining the accuracy and confidentiality of all records is therefore essential. In addition, no disclosure of potentially negative information about an employee should ever be made without a legitimate interest by the requesting party.

Fifth, a few state statutes and municipal ordinances prohibit drug testing except under very limited circumstances. Some state laws strictly regulate or prohibit various forms of polygraph and AIDS testing as well.

Finally, the Federal Rehabilitation Act of 1973 and the Americans with Disability Act of 1991 prohibit the denial of employment opportunities to certain people on the basis of drug or alcohol abuse except where current abuse poses a direct threat to property or the safety of others. In the following case, a drug-abusing employee sued for the violation of a state "handicap" antidiscrimination statute after his firing.

HAZLETT v. MARTIN CHEVROLET, INC.
496 N.E.3d 478 (Ohio 1986)

James T. Hazlett, the appellee, was employed by Martin Chevrolet, Inc., the appellant, as a finance insurance manager. His responsibilities included the sale and implementation of dealer financing for Martin Chevrolet's new car customers. Hazlett did not report to work one week because he was suffering from hepatitis and having drug-withdrawal symptoms. Hazlett was an alcoholic and used other chemicals, including cocaine. He was summarily terminated when he asked for a leave of absence for 28 days in order to obtain care for his addiction.

Hazlett filed a complaint with the Ohio Civil Rights Commission (OCRC). After a hearing, the OCRC found that Martin Chevrolet discriminated against Hazlett in violation of R.C. 4112.02(A) and ordered reinstatement and back pay. Martin Chevrolet filed a petition for judicial review. The court affirmed the OCRC decision. On appeal, the court of appeals affirmed. The case was appealed to the Supreme Court of Ohio.

LOCHER, Judge

The issue before us is whether drug addiction and alcoholism are handicaps as defined in R.C. 4112.01(A)(13). Pursuant to the discussion that follows we find for appellee and hold that drug addiction and alcoholism are handicaps as defined by R.C. 4112.01(A)(13).

R.C. 4112.01(A)(13) states that " '[h]andicap' means a medically diagnosable, abnormal condition which is expected to continue for a considerable length of time, whether correctable or uncorrectable by good medical practice, which can reasonably be expected to limit the person's functional ability, including, but not limited to, seeing, hearing, thinking, ambulating, climbing, descending, lifting, grasping, sitting, rising, any related function, or any limitation due to weakness and significantly decreased endurance, so that he can not perform his everyday routine living and working without significantly increased hardship and vulnerability to what are considered the everyday obstacles and hazards encountered by the nonhandicapped." R.C. 4112.02 indicates that "it shall be an unlawful discriminatory practice" to discharge, without just cause, an individual on the basis of . . . a handicap.

In the course of the evidence adduced below, the unrebutted deposition of Dr. Edward Novasel, a physician in general practice, indicated that drug addiction creates in its victims a debilitating chemical imbalance that is an abnormal physical condition. Such condition limits the user's functional ability, including physical endurance, mental capacity and judgment. While treatment of a drug addiction may cause the condition to go into remission, the effects of the drug may remain for a considerable period of time. It is clear to us that alcohol and/or drug addiction falls within the ambit of R.C. 4112.01(A)(13).

A number of courts have reviewed this issue and have come to the conclusion that drug and/or alcohol addiction is a handicap. . . .

The threads that run through these cases are first, that alcoholism and/or drug addiction is a handicap and second, if an individual, because of alcoholism and/or drug addiction is unable to perform his or her responsibilities, he or she may be lawfully discharged. We do not depart from these rules today.

In the present case evidence demonstrated that on several occasions appellant had granted disability or sick leave for employees. In one instance three or four weeks' leave was granted for phlebitis; in another, four weeks' leave was allowed for a heart attack. Most importantly, the unrebutted testimony of appellant's own witness, general manager Arthur Sweet, indicated that appellee was doing a good job. . . . Moreover, when appellant was notified by the OCRC that drug addiction was a handicap, Sweet asked appellee if he could come back to work. Appellee testified that when he spoke with Sweet he asked for leave of "28 days or a month. And at that time Mr. Sweet expressed what I determined was concern. . . . And I told him at that time that I had problems with drugs and alcohol. And it was at that time that he told me that . . . hit him like a ton of bricks. And he'd have to terminate me. They'd have to replace me." In contrast, Sweet testified that the reason for termination was that appellant could not do without appellee for the requested length of time.

Some additional observations are in order to insure that our decision herein is not misconstrued. Today, we have not endorsed drug addiction or alcoholism. Where chemical dependency adversely affects job performance an employer is clearly within its rights to discharge the employee. Where, as in the instant case, an employee is discharged in contravention of statute on the basis of a handicap, the consequence of such action resulting in a judgment for the employee is appropriate.

To prove a prima facie case of handicap discrimination the commission must show not only that the complainant was handicapped and that the action was taken by the employer, at least in part, because the complainant was handicapped, but, further, that the complainant, though handicapped, can safely and substantially perform the essential function of the job in question. . . .

One measure of a culture's viability and maturity is established by how well it addresses its problems. We gain nothing by pretending alcoholics and drug addicts can solve their problems without help or that substance abuse problems do not exist. By affirming that alcoholics and drug addicts are handicapped, to the extent that a dependency exists and has not yet compromised work skills, we seek to deal with a problem at a point where these individuals are still productive members of society, can still be helped, and still have the incentive to help themselves. Beyond this point the statute does not protect the chemically dependent individual. It is with these considerations in mind that we hold that drug addiction and alcoholism are handicaps as defined in R.C. 4112.01(A)(13) and affirm the judgment of the court below.

Judgment affirmed.

Case Questions

1. What issue does this case present?
2. What are the arguments against drug or alcohol addiction being considered a handicap?
3. How would an employee or the Ohio Civil Rights Commission make out a case of handicap discrimination based on alcohol or drug addiction? Discuss.
4. Select the key facts that influenced the court's decision.
5. As an employer faced with the various legal and practical problems associated with drug screening, what would you do?

STATUTORY BENEFITS FOR WORKERS

The law provides employees with certain minimum-based securities (see Figure 49–2). These include minimum wages, unemployment compensation, and disability and retirement benefits. In addition, employers may opt to establish private pensions for their employees under the regulatory eye of the federal government.

Minimum Wages

The **Fair Labor Standards Act (FLSA)** regulates child's work. It prohibits the employment of children under age 14 and regulates the time and type of work for those aged 14 to 17. The FLSA is administered by the Wage and Hour division of the Labor Department, which regulates, in addition, employee wages and hours. Currently, the **minimum wage** is $4.25 per hour, and a standard workweek is 40

Figure 49–2   Statutory Employee Benefits

Act	Employee Benefits
Fair Labor Standards Act	Child labor restrictions Minimum wages
Unemployment Compensation Acts	Wage benefits
Social Security Act	Pension income Disability income Medical coverage
Employee Retirement Income Security Act	Private pension Fringe benefits
Occupational Safety and Health Act	Imposes safety and health requirements on employers
Workers Compensation Acts	Benefits for workers injured or killed on job
Worker Adjustment and Retraining Notification Act	Requires advance notice to employee of plant closure

hours, beyond which an employee is entitled to at least time and one-half wages.

Certain occupations are exempt from the wage and hour requirements. They include agriculture, fishing, casual domestic service, outside salespersons, and child actors. In addition, executive, administrative, and professional personnel, who ordinarily receive a salary not tied to the number of hours worked, are exempt.

Unemployment Compensation

All states have **unemployment compensation** insurance. Covered employers pay a federal unemployment tax. This tax would essentially be required even if a state did not have an unemployment compensation system.

Those who have worked for a minimum specified period within the past 52 weeks are eligible for unemployment benefits, which are a percentage of the worker's pay. Workers, however, are not eligible if they quit the job, are fired for just cause, or are not working due to a labor stoppage. Workers must be capable of work, be actively looking for work, and accept suitable work.

Social Security

The **Social Security Act** established the **Social Security Administration,** which administers a federal social safety net program for the elderly and disabled, known as **Old-Age, Survivors, and Disability Insurance (OASDI).** Employees are required to contribute to the social security fund over their working lives. Employers are also obligated to contribute a portion to the fund. At retirement, benefits are based on a formula determined by a number of factors, including the number of quarters that the employee has paid and the age at retirement. Generally, an employee is first eligible to retire at age 62; however, retirement at a later age results in greater benefits. Under the OASDI, disability benefits may accrue. In order to be eligible for disability benefits, an employee must have contributed for a minimum number of quarters and be disabled—unable to work for at least 12 months.

Medicare is administered by the Social Security Administration under the act. It provides health and medical care benefits. Everyone who is eligible for OASDI and is at least 65 years old receives Hospital Insurance (HI) under the plan. Those who elect Supplementary Medical Insurance (SMI) receive physician and related medical benefits. The beneficiary must pay for SMI; the premiums are partially subsidized by the government and so the rates are lower than market.

ERISA

The **Employee Retirement Income Security Act (ERISA)** regulates employer private benefit plans, including medical, disability, and pension. It is primarily concerned with private pension plans established by the employer. ERISA has a wide array of reporting and disclosure requirements. It requires that a company have a plan administrator who is responsible for complying with the ERISA requirements.

ERISA established the **Pension Benefit Guaranty Corporation (PBGC)** within the Department of Labor. Employers who have established pension plans pay for termination insurance, which protects those employees whose retirement benefits are vested.

FEDERAL LABOR LAW

This section deals with the federal law of labor relations, and in particular, the National Labor Relations Act of 1935 (NLRA) and its subsequent amendments. Before the particular provisions of the NLRA are discussed, a brief history of the American union movement will be recounted.

History of the Union Movement

The American union movement has had a varied and sometimes troubled history. The history may be divided into three periods.

Rise and Opposition of the Union Movement (1865–1920s)

After the Civil War, American corporations experienced phenomenal growth. By the turn of the century, U.S. Steel (under Andrew Carnegie) was the world's largest corporation. The employment of huge work forces by their corporations radically changed the nature of the employment relationship from a personal relationship to one almost entirely economic in nature.

Workers began to band together for mutual aid and assistance. At first, worker organizations were devoted to social betterment, stressing such matters as improved education, housing, and language training for recently arrived immigrants. With the founding of the American Federation of Labor (AFL) by Samuel Gompers in 1886, workers' concerns turned to the "bread and butter" issues of wages, hours, and working conditions.

Unions were met with formidable obstacles to their legal recognition. Some employers hired the infamous Pinkerton guards to harass and even kill workers. After the passage of the Sherman Act in 1890 (see Chapter 46), courts held union activities to be an illegal combination in restraint of trade. Employers also forced prospective employees to sign **yellow dog contracts** in which the employee promised never to join a union while employed. In addition, federal courts frequently issued injunctions barring labor activity, and state and federal courts imposed vicarious liability on unions for the torts of their members, thereby bankrupting many unions. It was, in short, a period of great tribulation for the union movement.

Legitimacy and Growth of the Union Movement (1930s–1970s)

In 1932, Congress passed the **Norris-LaGuardia Act.** The act prohibited yellow dog contracts, federal court injunctions barring unions, and the vicar-

ious liability of unions. In 1935, the **National Labor Relations Act (NLRA**—also known as the Wagner Act) was passed by Congress. Along with other matters, section 7 of the NLRA gave workers three basic rights: the right to organize, the right to bargain collectively, and the right to engage in other concerted activities for the purpose of collective bargaining or other mutual aid or protection. The NLRA also created the **National Labor Relations Board (NLRB)** as the administrative body to develop and apply the NLRA. A list of unfair employer practices was made part of federal law as well (see Figure 49–3). Union strength reached its zenith in the early 1950s, when over 30 percent of the American labor force was unionized.

Decline of the Union Movement (1970s to present)

Following World War II and some crippling union strikes, the legislative pendulum began to swing in an antiunion direction. Unions began to be perceived as somewhat unpatriotic, communistic, and at times mob-dominated.

In 1947, Congress passed the **Taft-Hartley Act,** designed to protect employees who did not wish to join unions. A list of unfair union practices was made a part of federal law. In the wake of Congressional investigation of mob activity, Congress passed the **Landrum-Griffin Act** in 1959 to govern the operation of internal union affairs.

The greatest blow to unions' strength was not legislative, however, but economic. In the mid-1980s, just 18 percent of all workers belonged to unions, roughly half the percentage of three decades earlier. Among other factors, this was due to:

- A major shift in the employment patterns of Americans away from manufacturing (the backbone of union strength) toward the service and financial sectors.

- Women and minorities who have been traditionally resistant to trade unionism constitute a growing percentage of the labor force.

- Employment shifting from the predominantly unionized north and east to the relatively non-unionized south and west.

- Global trade patterns, including the huge American trade deficit, increased foreign competition, relatively low foreign wages, and the export of jobs overseas, which has contributed to union pressure to accept wage and noneconomic concessions in the 1980s and 1990s.

The future of the union movement, if it is to continue to be a major factor in American life, appears to be in its ability to attract service and government workers as well as part-time and nontraditional workers — for example, the elderly and homemakers. In addition, unions must broaden their emphasis to include such matters as child care, pay equity, workplace stress, and sexual harassment to attract the new breed of American worker.

National Labor Relations Board

The National Labor Relations Board has authority to prevent unfair labor practices and resolve representation questions "affecting commerce." Commerce includes anything beyond a minimum amount of trade, traffic, commerce, transportation, or communication.

Exempt Employers

The NLRA specifically exempts certain employers from Board supervision. Exempted employers are generally employers who are covered by some other statute, such as:

- The U.S. government (the U.S. Postal Service is covered).
- Federal Reserve banks.
- Municipal, county, or state employers.
- Employers subject to the Railway Labor Act.
- Labor organizations not acting as employers.

The NLRA permits the Board to decline jurisdiction over otherwise covered employers. Generally, the Board declines to exercise jurisdiction over employers who have a minimal impact on interstate commerce. In addition, the Board generally declines to exercise jurisdiction over religious and charitable institutions.

Exempt Employees

The NLRA specifically exempts certain employees from Board jurisdiction. Those include

- Agricultural laborers.
- Household domestics.
- Independent contractors defined in accordance with agency law.
- Individuals employed by parents or spouse.
- Individuals employed by an exempt employer.
- Supervisors, whose authority requires independent judgment.

Figure 49–3   Employer Unfair Labor Practices

- Restraining or coercing employees in the exercise of their rights under the act
- Dominating or interfering with formation or administration of labor organizations
- Discriminating to encourage or discourage union membership in any labor organization in regard to hiring, discharging, or terms of employment
- Discriminating against employees who file charges or testify under the act in good faith
- Refusing to bargain with employees' representatives

Board Organization

The Board is divided administratively into two distinct functions. The Board is a five-member panel appointed by the president and located in Washington, D.C. It exercises a judicial function by deciding labor cases on appeal after these have been tried before an administrative law judge. In contrast, the general counsel's office exercises a prosecutorial function by investigating and issuing complaints against persons who engage in illegal labor practices. The Board has regional offices around the United States that exercise these functions.

Representation and Unfair Labor Practices

The NLRB conducts elections under section 9 of the NLRA to determine whether a union will represent employees as their collective bargaining agent. When the Board determines, for example, that a bargaining unit does not adequately represent employees, or that an election must be set aside because of improprieties, the Board's decision is generally not appealable. These types of cases are called **representation cases.**

The Board also may investigate, prosecute, and determine **unfair labor practices (ULP)** by either the employer or a union. Section 8(a) of the NLRA lists *employer* ULPs (see Figure 49–3). Section 8(b) lists *union* ULPs (see Figure 49–4). The final resolution of either a representation or a ULP case is made by the five-member Board. In contrast to representation cases, however, Board decisions and orders in ULP cases are generally appealable to the U.S. Court of Appeals.

Figure 49–4   Union Unfair Labor Practices

- Restraining or coercing employees in the exercise of their rights under the act
- Coercing employers to discriminate to encourage or discourage union membership
- Refusing to collectively bargain in good faith with an employer
- Engaging in secondary boycotts requiring excessive membership dues
- Requiring employers to pay for services that are not to be performed
- Picketing for union recognition under specified conditions

Establishing the Collective Bargaining Relationship

Under Section 7, employees must have a free choice to determine whether to be represented by a union. Any restraint via employer threats or intimidation with respect to the exercise of this choice is considered an employer ULP.

Targeting a Company

Generally, a union is contacted by an unhappy employee or may on its own determine that a company is a good target for organization. A union representative will then visit the company and attempt to locate employees who might lead a union recognition campaign. If sufficient employee interest exists, an organizing committee is established to educate employees about the benefits of the union and the legal procedures necessary for recognizing the union.

Solicitation

Before the NLRB regional offices hold a representation election, sufficient employee interest in the union must be proven. Employee interest is demonstrated when at least 30 percent of the employees sign cards authorizing the union to act as their bargaining agent.

Generally, employers may limit the solicitation of employee signatures by other employees, via handbills and signs, to nonwork times (e.g., coffee breaks, lunch hours) and to nonwork areas (e.g., the cafeteria). The rule ''work time is for work'' is the law. Nonemployees may be barred from solicitation on the employer's property even during nonwork times and in nonwork areas so long as there are other means available to reach the employees. However, all no-solicitation rules must be applied evenhandedly to union and nonunion solicitation alike.

Election Petition

Once a union gets at least 30 percent of the employees to sign authorization cards, it may demand employer recognition as the employees' bargaining representative. An employer may then choose to recognize the union and begin to bargain with it. More often, however, the employer will assert that it has a ''good faith doubt'' concerning whether the majority of employees really want this union. The union must then file a petition with the NLRB demanding a representation election that will certify the union as the employees' representative.

The NLRB may deny the union's election petition for a variety of reasons. The bargaining unit established for the employees may be inappropriate. This may be due to the union's mixing together professional and nonprofessional employees or because the unit contains employees with radically different interests or job functions.

If a recognition election was held during the preceding 12-month period and the union seeking recognition lost, the NLRB will deny the petition. This **election bar rule** for 12 months assures employers of industrial peace for a time after an election. Or, the election petition will be barred if another union currently represents the employees and a collective bargaining agreement with that union is in force. This **contract bar rule** prohibits rival unions from petitioning for an election unless the agreement has been in force for more than three years.

Assuming the NLRB grants the union's petition, it will order an election to be held by secret ballot of the employees within 30 days of the NLRB's order. Notices of the time and place of the election must be posted by the employer.

Election Campaign

The period before the election is used by both union and management to campaign. The union's traditional campaign themes include higher compensation and benefits, greater job security, less subjectivity in wages and promotions, and greater worker control. The employer's traditional campaign themes include the high membership dues of unions, the union's strike record resulting in a loss of employee income, a threat to existing benefits due to a toughening of management's bargaining posture, and the employees' general distaste for change.

The election must be conducted under **laboratory conditions.** This means that the uninhibited wishes of the employees must not be interfered with in an undue manner. Violations of the laboratory condition standard include, for example, captive-audience meetings by employers within 24 hours of an election. Unfair labor practices by either the employer or the prospective union also violate laboratory conditions. If the Board determines that these conditions were violated, it will set aside the election and order a new election upon the filing of an objection by the aggrieved party.

Negotiating the Collective Bargaining Agreement

Once a union is recognized by either an employer's voluntary choice or by Board certification, two re-

sults follow. The union becomes the exclusive bargaining agent of the employees, and the union and employer have a duty to bargain in good faith.

Doctrine of Exclusivity

Under section 7, employees have protection in several circumstances. One protected right is "the right to bargain collectively through representatives of their own choosing." This means that once a union is chosen, it becomes the *exclusive* bargaining agent of the employees. All negotiations between the employer and its employees must go through the union.

Another protected right under section 7 is "the right to engage in concerted activities for the purpose of collective bargaining or other mutual aid or protection." The meaning of **concerted activities** is discussed in the following case.

MEYERS INDUSTRY, INC.
281 NLRB No. 118 (1986)

Kenneth Prill, an employee who drove a tractor-trailer truck, encountered brake problems with a truck. He informed his employer that he would not drive the truck and also informed state officials, who, upon inspecting the truck, issued a citation to the employer. As a result, Prill was discharged. He claimed that the discharge was an employer ULP. The Board in Meyers I rejected his claim. Prill appealed. The D.C. Circuit Court of Appeals remanded the case back to the Board "to particularize more fully the Board's rationale for its decision in Meyers I." What follows is the Board's decision on remand—Meyers II.

DECISION

In Meyers I, the Board adopted the following definition of the term "concerted activities": "In general, to find an employee's activity to be 'concerted,' we shall require that it be engaged in with or on the authority of other employees, and not solely by and on behalf of the employee himself." The Meyers I definition expressly distinguishes between an employee's activities engaged in "with or on the authority of other employees" (concerted) and an employee's activities engaged in "solely by and on behalf of the employee himself" (not concerted). There is nothing in the Meyers I definition which states that conduct engaged in by a single employee at one point in time can never constitute concerted activity within the meaning of Section 7.

The court [of appeals] queried whether Meyers I is consistent with *NLRB v. LLoyd A. Fry Roofing Co.*, . . . "a case quite similar on its facts to Meyers." We respectfully point out that *Lloyd A. Fry* and the instant [case] are factually distinguishable in a critical respect. In *Lloyd A. Fry*, where concerted activity was established, the record was replete with instances in which the discharged employee (Varney) acted on a collective basis with other employees preceding his discharge. Thus, . . . Varney engaged in "numerous discussions" with his fellow drivers regarding the safety of the employer's trucks and Varney and a fellow employee . . . collectively met with management representatives specifically to discuss solutions to truck maintenance problems that had engendered numerous complaints by other employees. In the instant case, there is no record evidence whatsoever that employee Prill at any relevant time or in any manner joined forces with any other employee, or by his activities intended to enlist the support of other employees in a common endeavor.

Finally, because the *Alleluia Cushion* doctrine at its origin and in its most appealing form concerns a single employee's invocation of a statute enacted for the protection of employees generally, we must consider whether any linkages to concerted activity may be discerned in such an individual employee act or whether overall public policy considerations should move us to protect even purely individual activity that is aimed at securing employer compliance with other statutes that benefit employees.

As explained in our discussion of *City Disposal . . .* the Supreme Court regarded proof that an employee action inures to the benefit of all simply as proof that the action comes within the "mutual aid or protection" clause of Section 7. It found "concerted" activity because the employee's invocation of the contract was an extension of the collective employee activity that produced the contract. . . . Can an employee's invocation of a statute be regarded as the extension of "concerted activity" in any realistic sense? Certainly the activity of the legislators themselves cannot be said to be concerted activity within the contemplation of the Wagner Act. And while there may be concerted activity in the lobbying process preceding the passage of such legislation, the linkage is attenuated; any such activity is far removed from the particular workplace, and the critical link between lobbying and enforcement of the law is the legislative process itself, which is not a part of any ongoing employee-generated process such as the negotiation and administration of collective-bargaining agreements. . . . Furthermore, a doctrine that rested on the presence of concerted employee activity prior to passage of a particular law would require a choice between two unattractive positions: either we would have to indulge in a presumption that all statutes that benefit employees are the product of concerted employee activity or we would have to make factual inquiries into who had worked for passage of the law in question.

In short, in construing Section 7 we are not holding that employee contract rights are more appropriate subjects for joint employee action than are rights granted by Federal and state legislation concerning such matters as employee safety. We merely find that invocation of employee contract rights is a continuation of an ongoing process of employee concerted activity, whereas employee invocation of statutory rights is not. We believe that we best effectuate the policies of the Act when we focus our resources on the protection of actions taken pursuant to that process.

With respect to the public policy question, we must simply note that, although it is our duty to construe the labor laws so as to accommodate the purposes of other Federal laws, this is quite a different matter from taking it upon ourselves to assist in the enforcement of other statutes. The Board was not intended to be a forum in which to rectify all the injustices of the workplace. In Meyers I, the Board noted that although we may be outraged by a respondent who may have imperiled public safety, we are not empowered to correct all immorality or illegality arising under all Federal and state laws.

Accordingly, [a]s we find that employee Prill acted alone and did not engage in concerted activities within the meaning of Section 7, we shall dismiss the complaint.

Case Questions

1. Analyze the circumstances under which individual activities are protected by section 7.

2. Why does the Board distinguish an individual's assertion of contract rights under a collective bargaining agreement from an individual's assertion of statutory rights? Is it a logical distinction?

3. What could Prill have done in this case to *both* protect his job under section 7 and to protect his life (by not driving an unsafe truck)? Discuss.

4. How should a union respond to this case in future collective bargaining negotiations?

Duty to Bargain in Good Faith

Once a union is certified, the employer and the union also have a duty to bargain in good faith. In

general, the principle of **voluntarism** dominates the good faith bargaining process. Voluntarism means that both parties are given the freedom to work out their agreement based on their own relative power. The state's role is limited to a referee's role, ensuring that the rules of the game are followed.

Good faith bargaining means more than going through the motions. It is a ULP to initially present the other side with a "take it or leave it" proposal. While bargaining can proceed to an impasse, and there is no duty to reach an agreement, some flexibility must be demonstrated to bargain in good faith.

Generally, both the union and the employer must furnish requested data relevant to the bargaining process. Such data includes wage rates, insurance coverage, job classifications, and seniority lists. If an employer claims that it is *unable* to afford a union's demand, it must back up that claim with hard economic data on profits and losses. Companies usually do not make this claim so that the company's financial picture remains private.

The act distinguishes between three subjects of bargaining. *Mandatory subjects* include "wages, hours, and conditions of employment." Both parties must bargain about these, although they may bargain to an impasse.

Illegal subjects of bargaining are subjects that the law prohibits the parties from bargaining about. For example, while it is legal to bargain for a **union shop,** in which employees are required to join a union within some period after being hired (often 30 days), bargaining to set up a **closed shop** is illegal. A closed shop is one in which the employer agrees to hire only union members. An **agency shop,** in which an employee need not join a union but must pay union dues and fees in any case, is legal.[3]

Permissive subjects of bargaining are legal, nonstatutory subjects. These may include subjects normally within the employer's complete prerogative, such as the employer's decision to sell or close all or part of its business. Employers may also choose to relocate union work to a nonunion facility so long as the change is due to sound economic reasons other than labor costs — for example, a more efficient plant, or tax abatements — and is not motivated by antiunion purposes. Unlike mandatory subjects, a party may not insist on a permissive subject as a precondition for reaching an agreement. In other words, parties may not bargain to an impasse on a permissive subject.

One area that has generated much litigation concerns plant closings. As stated, an employer's decision to wholly or partly close or even relocate its operation is not a mandatory subject of bargaining. However, the effects of the employer's decision on employees, such as severance pay and transfer rights, is a mandatory subject of bargaining. Refusal to bargain about the effects of a plant closing with a union before the closing is considered an employer ULP.

Under the **Worker Adjustment and Retraining Notification Act (WARN),** employers of more than 100 employees must give 60 days notice of a plant closing or mass layoff. Notice is required for a plant closing when 50 or more full-time employees will lose their jobs, or for mass layoffs, when at least one third of the employees or 500 employees at a single site will lose their jobs. Violations carry stiff fines.

Strikes, Lockouts, and Boycotts

The employee's ultimate weapon is the **strike** — work stoppage. Under the NLRA, employees who strike due to an employer ULP are entitled to reinstatement on termination of the strike. However, if the strikers have engaged in violence or have threatened other employees who may wish to cross the picket line, they are not entitled to reinstatement.

In contrast, economic strikers — for example, those that strike for higher wages — are not entitled to reinstatement. An employer who replaces the economic strikers during the strike need not rehire the strikers. But when new jobs do become available, it is generally considered a ULP not to rehire the economic strikers.

The **lockout** is the employer's counterpart to an employee strike. In a lockout, the employer simply refuses to allow the employees into its plant to work.

If a lockout's purpose is to discourage union organizational efforts, it is a ULP. In contrast, if the lockout's design is simply to bring economic pressure on a union during collective bargaining negotiations, it is lawful.

Secondary Pressure

A **secondary boycott** occurs when a union pressures a neutral third party to stop handling another employer's products or services. This form of pressure

---

[3]Under state "right to work" laws adopted in many southern and western states, any form of mandatory union membership is illegal. In these states, even the union or agency shop is prohibited.

is also called a **hot cargo** agreement. Hot cargo refers to goods made or handled by an employer with whom the union has a dispute. The aim of this boycott is to force the employer into making concessions with the union by involving third parties. However, the NLRA's purpose is to confine disputes to the parties — the union and the employer with whom the union has a dispute. Consequently, secondary boycotts that pull in third persons who are not part of the disagreement are illegal.

There are two exceptions to the secondary boycott prohibition. Third parties in the construction industry may agree with a union to pressure another employer at the job site of the construction. Thus, an agreement by an electrical subcontractor and a union that seeks to pressure the plumbing subcontractor at the same job site into hiring union employees is legal. Agreements in the garment industry are also legal exceptions to the secondary boycott prohibition.

Union Membership Rights

In response to concerns about the way unions were treating their members, Congress in 1959 passed an amendment (known as the Landrum-Griffin Act) to the NLRA that included a ''Bill of Rights'' for union members. These rights include the right to vote in union elections, the right to assemble with other members, freedom of speech at union meetings, and the right not to have dues or fees increased except by majority vote. The act also prohibits the discipline of union members or their fining, suspension, or expulsion without notice of the charges and a full hearing on the charges. In addition, under the act, various reports, such as the union's constitution, bylaws, and annual financial reports, are required to be filed by the union with the Secretary of Labor.

WORKERS' SAFETY

Both the federal and state governments are concerned with worker safety. The following discussion focuses on the federal OSH Act designed to improve safety conditions, and the states' workers' compensation acts designed to compensate workers for on-the-job injuries.

OSH Act

The **Occupational Health and Safety Act (OSH Act)** established three related federal administrative agencies. The **National Institute of Occupational Safety and Health (NIOSH)** conducts studies on occupational health concerns. The **Occupational Safety and Health Review Commission (OSHRC)** adjudicates violations of the act. The **Occupational Safety and Health Administration (OSHA)** enforces the act.

The act requires employers to provide a place of employment free from recognized hazards that cause or are likely to cause serious injury or death. In addition to this general duty, employers must also comply with specific occupational health standards imposed by OSHA pursuant to the act. These standards are derived from NIOSH recommendations and other sources.

OSHA discovers violations of the general and specific duty requirements by information from employers and employees and by inspections. Employers are under a duty to disclose injuries and deaths. The act prohibits employer retaliation against employees who blow the whistle on the employer for violations. The area of inspections is treated in Chapter 5. Violations are punishable by fines and jail for willful violations. An employer may contest an alleged violation, and the issue will be heard by an administrative law judge. That decision is appealable to OSHRC, whose decision is in turn appealable to the federal Court of Appeals.

Workers' Compensation

Every state has a **workers' compensation statute.** These statutes provide benefits to those employees who are injured on the job and survivor benefits to those killed on the job. Employees may not ordinarily sue employers for on-the-job injuries. However, benefits are payable from a state-administered workers' compensation fund regardless of fault. The injury or death must arise out of the employment and occur in the course of employment. Injuries arise out of employment when they are peculiarly related to the job. They occur within the course of employment when they are within the time, location, and circumstances of employment. Benefits under the typical statute include compensation for medical expenses, loss of wages, and disability.

The source of the benefits is from a tax on employers. The tax varies depending on the type of work, the size of the company, and the experience factor of the company regarding claims. For this reason, employers are motivated to employ and enforce safety standards and policies.

END–OF–CHAPTER QUESTIONS

1. Discuss the arguments pro and con for the erosion of employment at will.

2. What concerns must be balanced in determining whether and how to institute a drug-detection program?

3. What is the doctrine of exclusivity? How does it affect safety concerns of an employee?

4. How do mandatory and permissive subjects of bargaining differ concerning the parties' duty to bargain? Provide examples of each.

5. Specify the statutory benefits for employees, and identify any gaps in the "safety net."

6. The plaintiff, Buethe, a part-time copilot, alleged that he was terminated for refusing to fly an unsafe airplane. Indiana law requires aircraft to conform to federal standards of airworthiness. The two aircraft that Buethe balked at flying arguably did not conform to standards. Is Buethe protected from discharge under an exception to the employment-at-will rule? Discuss. Is Buethe protected from discharge if he was a member of a union and a collective bargaining agreement was in place? See *Buethe v. Britt Airlines, Inc.*, 787 F.2d 1184 (7th Cir. 1980).

7. The state of New Jersey instituted a random, mandatory program of drug testing for jockeys at state race tracks. What arguments may be offered in favor of the program? Against? Discuss. See *Shoe-*

maker v. Handel, 619 F.Supp 1089 (D. N.J. 1985), *aff'd* 795 F.2d 1136 (3d Cir. 1986).

8. A company had a work rule prohibiting "solicitation for any cause, or distribution of literature of any kind during working time. . . . Whether on working time or not, no employee may distribute literature of any kind in any working areas of the plant." Are these no-solicitation rules, which would prohibit employees from distributing literature or soliciting support for a union, valid? Discuss. What if the rules were limited to union solicitation alone? See, *Our Way, Inc.,* 268 NLRB No. 61 (1983).

9. Metropolitan Teletronics Corp. operated two facilities, one in New York City and one in New Jersey. It opened a new facility in New Jersey and transferred union workers there. Many New York City workers lost their jobs. Its decision to move was motivated by a foreclosure action on its New York City facility and the offer of financial assistance by the state of New Jersey. Must the employer bargain with the union over its decision to relocate? Discuss. Must it bargain with the union on any other matters? Discuss. See *Metropolitan Teletronics Corp.,* 279 NLRB No. 134 (1986).

10. Plywood Industries manufactures furniture. It uses various automated cutting machines. The company is aware that there are some very dangerous conditions in the factory that involve general safety hazards and also violations of specific OSHA standards. Several employees have complained, and their managers have told them that conditions will be remedied soon. The employees have threatened to blow the whistle. What are the obligations of the employer? How might OSHA discover the violations?

Chapter 50

Equal Employment

■

CRITICAL THINKING INQUIRIES

As you read this chapter, you should be able to address the following:

- What is the issue in public policy legislation that equalizes pay among all persons holding the same job?
- What reasons support and oppose legislation prohibiting discrimination?
- What is ambiguous about the use of ''protected classes'' to define those minorities disadvantaged by unlawful discrimination?
- What is the fallacy in using circumstantial evidence that compares the proportion of a protected class in an employer's work force with the proportion of that group in the whole population? Are there other plausible hypotheses to explain the disparity?
- What is ambiguous about the common interaction among males and females that may trigger the perception of sexual harassment?

MANAGERIAL PERSPECTIVE

ABCorp. has traditionally provided engineering services and construction contracting for the commercial building industry. ABC's operations are composed of three divisions: (1) field construction crews, (2) professional engineering design and drafting, and (3) support office personnel for administration and management. Construction crews are composed of unionized tradespersons, engineering services are nonunion professional engineers and drafting personnel, and administrative and managerial personnel include management and nonunion clerical staff. The field construction crews have historically attracted men, the engineers are mainly men, and the clerical workers are mostly women. There has been some sexual diversity among the drafting personnel and the management team in recent years. Originally, these positions were held mostly by men, though recent hires have included women.

Many of the male construction workers are openly hostile to hiring women for positions requiring extensive physical labor. Some openly allege women are less physically capable to justify not hiring them. The very few women hired have quit after a short time. Several macho male workers have conspired to make the work environment uncomfortable for women construction workers. Although ABC has tried to hire women engineers at several local engineering colleges, the few women engineering graduates can demand much higher salaries than ABC would pay.

ABC has started hiring women art school graduates as drafting personnel at much lower salaries than many of the ABC's male drafting personnel. All the managers are white males, having worked their way up through the ranks—most managers were formerly foremen in the construction division. There have been no black male foremen because ABCorp. management believes that the predominantly white labor force would not show black foremen sufficient respect. The chief clerical administrator is a woman who worked her way up through the secretarial ranks. She has never hired any of the qualified males applying for clerical jobs.

- What issues will arise if internal applicants are overlooked and external applicants are deterred from applying for particular ABC jobs because they were historically held by persons of the opposite sex or another race?
- What reasons might ABC offer to justify its ''promotion from within'' policy for upper managers that appears to favor males?
- What issue does this raise for outside female candidates experienced in construction management?

This chapter focuses on the application of a variety of constitutional, legislative, and regulatory laws prohibiting employment discrimination. The United States has experienced considerable conflict throughout its history, including the divisive Civil War, over the role that culture plays in inspiring discrimination. There is controversy over the role law enforcement should play in limiting discrimination based on a person's race, sex, religion, national origin, age, or disabilities. Considerable empirical evidence and litigation suggests that discrimination continues, particularly against women, minorities, older workers, and the disabled.

The failure of employers to hire and reward based solely on merit misallocates resources. The labor markets are thereby made imperfect because qualified applicants are relegated to lower-skilled jobs, leaving a pool of competent workers underutilized. The equal opportunity laws discussed here were passed to correct these market imperfections and thereby establish antidiscrimination as a legal and ethical principle. This chapter reviews the impact of several laws and regulatory structures administered by the Equal Employment Opportunity Commission (EEOC) and state agencies on employment decisions to hire, fire, promote, or set terms and conditions of employment. The major laws include the Equal Pay Act of 1963, Title VII of the Civil Rights Act of 1964, the Vocational Rehabilitation Act of 1973, the Age Discrimination in Employment Act of 1967, the Americans with Disabilities Act of 1990, the Civil Rights Act of 1991, and various state laws.

Few nations show the level of concern for equal employment and discrimination matters as does the United States. Cultural diversity and a varied immigrant ancestry probably contribute to U.S. economic and social successes. Part of the attraction to early colonists and to the subsequent ''waves'' of immigrants has been the U.S. promise of religious and political freedom for persons from nearly every other nation. This tradition of mixing peoples of disparate national origins stands in stark contrast to most other nations' factional violence and their pressures to maintain ''ethnic purity.'' For example, some critics charge that the undesirable, low-paying, and menial jobs in Japan are reserved for immigrants from other Asian nations.

Some observers claim that many nations presume their economic successes are due to their racial and religious homogeneity because this limits how alter-native value systems or lifestyles might undermine their values. During economic downturns, discrimination may seem an easy way to limit competition from recognizable ethnic groups. Periodically, grassroots discriminatory movements gain strength in many nations, such as ethnic violence among the former Yugoslavian provinces, the resurgence of Nazi-inspired racism in Germany, and the ethnic genocide of the Kurds in Iraq. Other nations are more active in pursuing discriminatory governmental policies. For example, there is still no comprehensive prohibition of religious discrimination in Northern Ireland, Israel permits only Jews to vote in elections, and the role of women in the Moslem world is officially restricted. When compared with the United States, certain groups in most nations endure considerably more discrimination than any particular group does in the United States.

A few nations are beginning to adopt antidiscrimination laws, although most such laws are poorly enforced. For example, a larger role for women is opening up in some Asian nations. The EC has adopted an equal pay policy and will soon permit somewhat unrestricted movement of workers, licensed professionals, and the self-employed throughout Europe. It is difficult to enforce antidiscriminatory policies, but the United States's experience illustrates the potential for success. The following sections examine discrimination on the basis of a person's membership in particular **protected classes.** These are demographic classifications of particular characteristics of human populations (e.g., race, color, religion, sex, age, national origin, and disability).

EQUAL PAY ACT

The **Equal Pay Act** was passed in 1963, amending the **Fair Labor Standards Act (FLSA).** It prohibits unequal pay for work requiring ''equal skill, effort, and responsibility . . . under similar working conditions'' performed by either sex. When two substantially similar jobs are held by a male and a female, the employer must generally pay them equally. The act requires employers to specify a **job description** for all jobs. This is a content analysis compiling the skills needed and tasks required for each job. The availability of job descriptions permits the comparison of any two jobs to determine their similarity and how they compare for the required equality in pay rates.

Pay differentials for the same job classification are permitted in a few instances but cannot be based on sex. Bona fide seniority and merit systems are permissible. For example, ABCorp. may have company productivity policies applicable to managers and union contract seniority provisions applicable to production workers. Seniority provisions may legitimately form the basis for varying pay rates in favor of the more senior or more productive employees. However, such policies must be nondiscriminatory on the basis of sex.

Shift differentials in payrates based on the time of a work shift are usually valid if rotation among shifts is open to both sexes. However, shift differentials may be invalid if there are no differences in working conditions between shifts and one shift is staffed predominantly by one sex. Management training programs often rotate newly hired employees through different jobs to provide them with broad, companywide experience. Trainees may be paid at different rates than permanent employees in comparable jobs so long as the training programs are open equally to both sexes.

Comparable Worth

Comparable worth was originally developed during World War II as a more expansive interpretation of the equal pay theory. Comparable worth would extend the pay equity requirement beyond two jobs with near identical tasks to any two jobs, even if not substantially equal, but which require similar levels of skill, effort, and responsibility under similar working conditions. For example, a female administrative assistant to ABCorp.'s top manager and a male middle manager might do quite different job tasks yet face roughly equal levels of difficulty and responsibility. Recurrent pressures to adopt comparable worth arise to adjust pay rates equalizing pay for two jobs. Females traditionally occupy lower-paying clerical and service jobs while higher-paying positions seem to be reserved for males. The comparable worth theory is sometimes championed as the only way to correct injustices of sexual stereotyping and eliminate the ''glass ceiling'' that allegedly holds female pay below the level of males.

Critics of comparable worth argue that it limits the operation of free labor markets. It creates an artificial price equilibrium because the labor market would no longer be cleared by matching the demand for particular skills with the supply of qualified applicants. Equalizing pay under comparable worth incorrectly signals individuals to enter trades or professions that have an excessive supply of workers and a lower demand because they can expect to receive pay equal to other professions. A simultaneous signal deters individuals' entry into trades or professions that the market finds more valuable because pay is ''equalized'' with other, lower-priced skills. Pay equalization under comparable worth arguably distorts the allocation of resources, resulting in a net wealth transfer from a scarce group of persons with more valuable skills to a more abundant group with less valuable skills.

The lower federal courts have not required application of comparable worth in Equal Pay Act cases. However, in *County of Washington v. Gunther*,[1] the Supreme Court suggested comparable worth might be applicable under Title VII of the Civil Rights Act of 1964 as a remedy for intentional, gender-based discrimination. Some states and local governments have instituted comparable worth pay scales for state government employees. Canada requires comparable worth in both its public and private sectors.

Employers must monitor the development of comparable worth for two reasons. First, comparable worth would radically alter the labor markets. Second, it could also apply beyond gender-based pay discrimination into pay discrimination on the basis of other classifications such as race, color, national origin, age, and religion.

CIVIL RIGHTS ACT OF 1964

The most important U.S. antidiscrimination law is Title VII of the Civil Rights Act of 1964. It applies to employers of 15 or more employees, unions representing employees of such employers, unions operating hiring halls, and to employment agencies. Title VII prohibits discrimination in employment decisions: hiring, firing, promotion, compensation, or setting terms and conditions of employment if based on race, color, religion, national origin, or sex. These classifications are known as **protected classes** or **suspect classes.** Employers may be liable if illegal discrimination is proved under any one of three antidiscrimination theories discussed in the next sections: (1) disparate treatment, (2) disparate impact, or (3) a pattern or practice of discrimination.

---

[1]*County of Washington v. Gunther*, 452 U.S. 161 (1981).

Discrimination is the practice of choosing or differentiating among alternatives based on some distinguishable characteristic. Discrimination is generally a fundamental part of decisionmaking. Discrimination in employment decisions should be based on objective and measurable differences in a person's qualifications that are directly related to job performance. Discrimination becomes unlawful if employment decisions disregard such objective job performance measures but instead are based on bias or prejudice against an applicant because of membership in a protected class. For example, ABCorp.'s preference for male construction workers prejudices women as a class.

Illegal discrimination may occur in the hiring process, in constructive discrimination (resignation prompted by harassment), and by implementing differences between protected classes in the terms of employment, compensation, or working conditions. While Title VII never requires hiring any particular person, it prohibits discrimination in employment decisions based on the person's membership in a protected class.

Disparate Treatment

Disparate treatment is any direct action to favor one group or disfavor another group by outright discrimination in hiring, promotion, or firing. An-nounced policies or actual use of discriminatory policies favoring one group over another group are illegal. For example, statements like "blacks need not apply" or "this is a man's job" are evidence of disparate treatment. Such overt practices are rare today, so the courts accept proof by inference from circumstantial evidence. The plaintiff must prove the basic elements of a prima facie case of disparate treatment.

Prima Facie Case: Disparate Treatment

1. Applicant is a member of a protected class.
2. Applicant is qualified for the job.
3. Applicant is rejected
4. Position remained open after applicant's rejection.

After the plaintiff's prima facie case is made, the burden of proof shifts to the employer to show that there was a legitimate reason for the disparate treatment. Even this justification may be rebutted if the plaintiff has statistical evidence of the employer's pattern of past discrimination. The following case illustrates illegal discrimination when the employer intermixes legal reasons with prohibited discriminatory reasons.

■

PRICE WATERHOUSE v. HOPKINS
490 U.S. 228 (1989)

Ann Hopkins was a senior manager at the Washington, D.C., office of the public accounting firm Price Waterhouse. Her candidacy for promotion to partner in 1982 was held over for reconsideration to the following year and thereafter dropped. Only 7 of the 662 Price Waterhouse partners were women. Hopkins was the only woman of 88 partner candidates in 1982. Although her supporters and opponents conceded her strong professional accounting skills, Hopkins was characterized as "overly aggressive, unduly harsh, difficult to work with, and impatient with staff." She was also described as "macho" and "overcompensating for being a woman." She was advised to take a "course at charm school" and to walk, talk, and dress "more femininely, wear makeup, have her hair styled, and wear jewelry." Price Waterhouse claimed the negative decision was based primarily on legitimate factors— Hopkins' interpersonal skills. The trial court held Price Waterhouse unlawfully discriminated against her on the basis of sex by consciously considering sexual stereotypes and Hopkins appealed.

BRENNAN, Justice

In passing Title VII, Congress made the simple but momentous announcement that sex, race, and national origin are not relevant to the selection, evaluation, or compensation of employees. The statute does not purport to limit the other qualities and characteristics that employers may take into account in making employment decisions. The critical inquiry is whether gender was a factor in the employment decision at the moment it was made. Title VII was meant to condemn even those decisions based on a mixture of legitimate and illegitimate considerations.

To say that an employer may not take gender into account is not the end of the matter. Title VII preserves the employer's remaining freedom of choice. The employer shall not be liable if it can prove that, even if it had not taken gender into account, it would have come to the same decision. In saying that gender played a motivating part in an employment decision, we mean that, if we asked the employer at the moment of the decision what the reasons were and if we received a truthful response, one of those reasons would be that the applicant or employee was a woman. An employer who acts on the basis of the belief that a woman cannot be aggressive has acted on the basis of gender. We are beyond the day when an employer could evaluate employees by assuming or insisting that they matched the stereotype associated with their group.

An employer who objects to aggressiveness in women but whose positions require this trait places women in an intolerable and impermissible Catch-22: out of a job if they behave aggressively and out of a job if they don't. Title VII lifts women out of this bind. Price Waterhouse invited partners to submit comments; some of the comments stemmed from sex stereotypes; the Policy Board's decision on Hopkins was an assessment of the submitted comments; and Price Waterhouse in no way disclaimed reliance on the sex-linked evaluations. The defendant may avoid a finding of liability only by proving by a preponderance of the evidence that it would have made the same decision even if it had not taken the plaintiff's gender into account. [On remand to determine whether Price Waterhouse would have made the same decision without considering sex stereotyping, the trial court ordered she be made a partner].

Case Questions

1. What is the issue in this case? How can an employer avoid liability in mixed-motive decisions? What is the apparent ambiguity in the decision?

2. What would be the effect if *client* comments indicated that Hopkin's aggressive behavior was inappropriate and requested she be replaced?

Disparate Impact

After Title VII was passed, most employers removed disparate treatment language from their employment policies and discouraged disparate treatment in making employment decisions. The **disparate impact** theory arose to prove that hiring standards and employment practices may nevertheless fail to adequately protect suspect classes. The employer's use of apparently neutral employment practices may have hidden biases that adversely impact a protected class. For example, while height restrictions may appear appropriate and unbiased, they adversely impact females and some Asians if unnecessary to job performance. General intelligence tests such as the SAT allegedly favor the groups whose backgrounds are used to develop the tests when these groups are tested for jobs. Consider ABCorp.'s insistence on promoting managers from within. Although this employment policy appears justified by emphasizing the experience factor, it adversely impacts women and black males. There probably are alternate selection criteria available that would not always disqualify females and black men for ABCorp. management jobs.

Physical requirements and intelligence tests must be directly related to necessary job performance or they may cause a disparate impact. Plaintiffs alleging discrimination may offer statistical evidence comparing the demographic profile of the employer's work force with the available pool of qualified applicants. If certain minorities are underrepresented in the employer's work force, this provides circumstantial evidence of a disparate impact on those groups. However, the next case illustrates how faulty comparisons may unfairly persecute employers if the classifications used for statistical comparison are overinclusive or underinclusive.

WARDS COVE PACKING CO. INC. v. ANTONIO
490 U.S. 642 (1989)

Wards Cove Packing operates Alaskan salmon canneries with two basic groups of employees: (1) nonwhites in lower paid and unskilled "cannery jobs," and (2) whites holding higher paid and skilled "noncannery jobs." Certain "cannery" employees claimed Ward's Cove Packing violated Title VII by discriminating in hiring and promotions, causing a disparate impact on nonwhites. The alleged discriminatory acts included nepotism, rehire preferences, lack of objective hiring practices, separate hiring channels, and the practice of not promoting from within. Allegedly, these practices caused racial stratification and denied nonwhite employees employment opportunities on the basis of race. The employer appealed an appeals court holding that once employees make out a prima facie case of disparate impact, the burden shifts to the employer to prove that no discrimination occurred.

WHITE, Justice

In holding that respondents (employees) had made out a prima facie case of disparate impact, the court of appeals relied solely on respondents' statistics showing a higher percentage of nonwhite workers in the cannery jobs and a lower percentage of such workers in the noncannery positions. Although statistical proof can alone make out a prima facie case, the Court of Appeals' ruling here misapprehends our precedents and the purposes of Title VII, and we therefore reverse.

The "proper comparison (is) between the racial composition of (the at-issue jobs) and the racial composition of the qualified . . . population in the relevant labor market." With respect to the skilled noncannery jobs at issue here, the cannery work force in no way reflected "the pool of qualified job applicants" or the "qualified population in the labor force." Measuring alleged discrimination in the selection of accountants, managers, boat captains, electricians, doctors, and engineers—and the long list of other "skilled" noncannery positions found to exist by the District Court by comparing the number of nonwhites occupying these jobs to the number of nonwhites filling cannery worker positions is nonsensical. If the absence of minorities holding such skilled positions is due to a dearth of qualified nonwhite applicants (for reasons that are not petitioners'

fault), petitioners' selection methods or employment practices cannot be said to have had a "disparate impact" on nonwhites.

The Court of Appeals' theory, at the very least, would mean that any employer who had a segment of his work force that was—for some reason—racially imbalanced, could be hauled into court and forced to engage in the expensive and time-consuming task of defending the "business necessity" of the methods used to select the members of his work force. The only practical option for many employers will be to adopt racial quotas, insuring that no portion of his work force deviates in racial composition from the other portions thereof, this is a result that Congress expressly rejected in drafting Title VII.

The Court of Appeals also erred with respect to the unskilled noncannery positions. Racial imbalance in one segment of an employer's work force does not, without more, establish a prima facie case of disparate impact with respect to the selection of workers for the employer's other positions, even where workers for the different positions may have somewhat fungible skills (as is arguably the case for cannery and unskilled noncannery workers). As long as there are no barriers or practices deterring qualified nonwhites from applying for noncannery positions, if the percentage of selected applicants who are nonwhite is not significantly less than the percentage of qualified applicants who are non-white, the employer's selection mechanism probably does not operate with a disparate impact on minorities. Where this is the case, the percentage of nonwhite workers found in other positions in the employer's labor force is irrelevant to the question of a prima facie statistical case of disparate impact.

Moreover, isolating the cannery workers as the potential "labor force" for skilled noncannery positions is at once both too broad and too narrow in its focus. Too broad because the vast majority of these cannery workers did not seek jobs in skilled non-cannery positions; there is no showing that many of them would have done so even if none of the arguable "deterring" practices existed. Thus, the pool of cannery workers cannot be used as a surrogate for the class of qualified job applicants because it contains many persons who have not (and would not) be noncannery job applicants. Conversely, if respon-dents propose to use the cannery workers for comparison purposes because they represent the "qualified labor population" generally, the group is too narrow because there are obviously many qualified persons in the labor market for noncannery jobs who are not cannery workers. The judgment of the Court of Appeals is reversed, and the case is remanded.

Case Questions

1. What statistical comparison error was made by the lower court? What is the problem in comparing minority participation in the employer's work force with minority presence in the population at large? With what population should the employer's work force be compared?

2. What is the impact of making the erroneous comparison as done by the lower court in this case?

The faulty comparison discussed in the *Wards Cove Packing* case deserves some clarification. Consider the example of ABCorp.'s use of women in engineering positions. It is invalid to compare the proportion of women engineers at ABCorp. with the proportion of women in the outer population. The comparison should be with the number of available and qualified women engineers in the population. The lower court's comparison is faulty because it would create a quota system forcing the hiring of unqualified persons.

The *Wards Cove Packing* case also placed the burden of proving a disparate impact from the employer's employment practice on the employee. However, the Civil Rights Act of 1991, discussed later in this chapter, shifts the burden of proof to the employer. After the plaintiff alleging a disparate impact proves a prima facie case, the burden then shifts to the employer to prove there was no disparate impact from the alleged discrimination under the revised law.

Pattern or Practice of Discrimination

The **pattern or practice** theory of discrimination expands on the disparate impact that affects one individual to a pattern or practice that affects a whole protected class. Statistical evidence comparing the employer's work force with the outer population illustrated in *Wards Cove Packing* may establish that employment policies created a pattern or practice of discrimination. When such broad systematic discrimination occurs, other employers may mimic this discrimination, further broadening the discrimination. The developing reputation then further deters qualified minorities from applying for any jobs. Circumstantial evidence of the employer's underutilization of qualified minorities creates a presumption of discrimination against all job applicants from the affected protected class. Such evidence may come from low utilization of available minorities and disparate pay for minorities holding similar jobs. The three discrimination theories are summarized in Figure 50–1.

PROTECTED CLASSES

Discrimination in employment practices is prohibited by Title VII on the basis of a person's membership in a **protected class**—a demographic classification of persons who have been historically subjected to discrimination. Employment practices that discriminate against or in favor of persons because of their membership in a protected class are illegal under the three theories discussed above. Title VII originally defined protected class to include

Figure 50–1   Discrimination Theories

	Disparate Treatment Theory	**Disparate Impact Theory**	**Pattern or Practice Theory**
Statement of Theory	Employer, union, or employment agency announces and/or uses intentional discriminatory policies that are more favorable to one group than to a protected class	Employer, union, or employment agency uses job selection standards that appear neutral; yet result in a disparate impact on a protected class	Employer, union, or employment agency's track record reveals a pattern or practice of discrimination affecting a protected class of persons rather than a specific individual
Proof Required	Intent to discriminate Inferences are allowed from circumstantial evidence Employment of a qualified applicant from a protected class is rejected, and job remains unfilled afterward Burden of proof shifts to employer to justify actions	No proof of discriminatory intent required Adverse effect on protected class; statistical proof may be used Employer unable to justify the employment practice as job related Evidence of disparate treatment unavailable	No proof of discriminatory motive required Inference from statistical analysis: Compare the percentage of suspect class members in the employer's work force with its percentage in job applications and among the general public; employer's work force contains a substantially lower percentage of suspect class members than of members of other groups
Examples	Biased hiring, firing, and promotion practices ''Blacks need not apply'' ''This is a man's job''	General intelligence or achievement tests covering background rather than specified job skills Unjustified height restrictions or high school diploma requirement	Qualified persons in the protected class deterred from applying due to employer's reputation for discrimination Low utilization of protected class applicants Pay differences between members of protected class and members of other groups in comparable jobs Similar pattern or practice of discrimination by other employers

race, religion, national origin, and sex. Age and disability were added by later legislation. From time to time, there are pressures to add others, such as sexual preference, HIV infection, and obesity.

Race

Racial discrimination has been specifically outlawed by numerous laws, including the Thirteenth, Fourteenth, and Fifteenth Amendments to the U.S. Constitution, the Civil Rights Act of 1866, and the Civil Rights Act of 1964. These laws were originally enacted to reverse the incidents of slavery for blacks. However, they apply to all persons because everyone is a member of a particular race. This means that **reverse discrimination** is also prohibited — for

example, when preference is given to members of a protected class historically subjected to discrimination.[2] Reverse discrimination is discussed later.

Religion

A fundamental reason for the founding of the American colonies was religious freedom. The constitutional founders prohibited religious discrimination in the First Amendment's bar on federal legislation that either restricts the free exercise of religion or establishes a religion. The Fourteenth Amendment's absorption principle applies this First Amendment

---

[2]*Regents of the University of California v. Bakke*, 438 U.S. 265 (1978).

bar to religious discrimination in state legislation. Title VII prohibits employment discrimination on the basis of religion. The term **religion** includes standard denominations and other sincerely held ethical or moral-based belief systems. Traditional religions such as Christianity, Judaism, Islam, Buddhism, and Hinduism are protected as well as beliefs such as atheism and agnosticism.

The major problem area in religious discrimination is the extent to which an employer must make **reasonable accommodation** for employees' religious observances. An employee's religious practices such as the observance of sabbath or religious holidays may conflict with the employer's work schedule. The courts balance the hardships of requiring employers to permit observance against the hardship on the employee's beliefs. Religious discrimination is permitted where the employer's accommodation of employees' beliefs would impose an undue hardship on the business. The following classic case illustrates this balance in the observation of the sabbath.

TRANS WORLD AIRLINES, INC. v. HARDISON
432 U.S. 63 (1977)

Hardison worked in TWA aircraft maintenance, which operated 24 hours a day. The union's collective bargaining agreement gave employees some choice of job and shift assignments based on seniority. Hardison used his seniority to avoid work on Saturday, his Sabbath. However, his seniority dropped when he was transferred to another department. Hardison was discharged after his refusal to work on Saturdays. He sued for an injunction under Title VII, claiming an unlawful religious discrimination. Both the trial court and the Court of Appeals agreed with Hardison that TWA had not made reasonable efforts to accommodate Hardison's religious needs. The Court of Appeals suggested that TWA could have permitted Hardison to work a four-day week, using a supervisor or another worker in his place, or filled Hardison's Saturday shift from other available competent personnel, or arranged a ''swap between Hardison and another employee either for another shift or for the Sabbath days.'' TWA appealed the decision to the Supreme Court.

WHITE, Justice

We disagree with the Court of Appeals in all relevant respects. It is our view that TWA made reasonable efforts to accommodate and that each of the Court of Appeals' suggested alternatives would have been an undue hardship within the meaning of the statute as construed by the EEOC guidelines.

It appears to us that the (seniority) system itself represented a significant accommodation to the needs, both religious and secular, of all of TWA's employees. The seniority system represents a neutral way of minimizing the number of occasions when an employee must work on a day that he would prefer to have off. Additionally, recognizing that weekend work schedules are the least popular, the company made further accommodation by reducing its work force to a bare minimum on those days.

Any employer who, like TWA, conducts an around-the-clock operation is presented with the choice of allocating work schedules either in accordance with the preferences of its employees or by involuntary assignment. Insofar as the varying shift preferences of its employees complement each other, TWA could meet its manpower needs through voluntary work scheduling.

It was essential to TWA's business to require Saturday and Sunday work for at least a few employees even though most employees preferred those days off. Allocating the burdens of weekend work was a matter for collective bargaining. In considering criteria to govern this allocation, TWA and the union had two alternatives: adopt a neutral system, such as seniority, a lottery, or rotating shifts, or allocate days off in accordance with the religious needs of its employees. TWA would have had to adopt the latter in order to assure Hardison and others like him of getting the days off necessary for strict observance of their religion, but it could have done so only at the expense of others who had strong, but perhaps nonreligious, reasons for not working on weekends. There were no volunteers to relieve Hardison on Saturdays, and to give Hardison Saturdays off, TWA would have had to deprive another employee of his shift preference at least in part because he did not adhere to a religion that observed the Saturday Sabbath.

Title VII does not contemplate such unequal treatment. The repeated, unequivocal emphasis of both the language and the legislative history of Title VII is on eliminating discrimination in employment, and such discrimination is proscribed when it is directed against majorities as well as minorities.

To require TWA to bear more than a de minimis cost in order to give Hardison Saturdays off is an undue hardship. Like abandonment of the seniority system, to require TWA to bear additional costs when no such costs are incurred to give other employees the days off that they want would involve unequal treatment of employees on the basis of their religious belief. By suggesting that TWA should incur certain

costs in order to give Hardison Saturdays off, the Court of Appeals would in effect require TWA to finance an additional Saturday off and then to choose the employee who will enjoy it on the basis of his religious beliefs. While incurring extra costs to secure a replacement for Hardison might remove the necessity of compelling another employee to work involuntarily in Hardison's place, it would not change the fact that the privilege of having Saturdays off would be allocated according to religious beliefs.

Case Questions

1. What is the religious discrimination issue in scheduling work in a round-the-clock workplace?
2. For what reasons are employers not always required to make accommodation to the varying range of religious observances?

National Origin

Discrimination based on **national origin** focuses on the country from which a person's forebears emigrated. This type of discrimination often arises when an employer refuses to hire persons with surnames typical of a particular national origin or requires fluency in English. National origin discrimination is usually proved under disparate impact or pattern or practice theories. For example, ABCorp. might require English fluency for all employees. However, if only the sales staff, purchasing managers, and supervisors regularly communicate with customers, suppliers, and co-workers, the English fluency requirement may discriminate against persons of particular national origin, such as Hispanics. Language fluency requirements must be a business necessity or they will unlawfully and adversely impact certain groups.

Immigration Reform

The 1986 Immigration Reform Act prohibits the employment of illegal aliens and requires employers to verify the work eligibility of all new hires. Form I-9 must be filed with the Immigration and Naturalization Service (INS) after a reasonable examination of documents (e.g., birth certificate or a green card). The **Frank Amendment** prohibits employers from accomplishing compliance by discriminating on the

basis of national origin, citizenship, English fluency, appearance, or tests revealing national origin. For example, if ABCorp. avoided hiring persons with Hispanic accents to reduce the possibility of hiring an illegal alien, this would be a prohibited selection criteria if the employer has over three employees.

Sex

Discrimination on the basis of gender is prohibited by numerous laws: the Nineteenth Amendment granting women's suffrage, the Equal Pay Act, Title VII, and the Pregnancy Discrimination Act. Society has stereotyped many jobs according to gender, relegating many women to clerical positions and often dissuading women from jobs with physical labor. Women are beginning to receive fairer treatment in employment as sex roles blur and the economy increasingly evolves toward services. Today, women represent over 40 percent of the employed work force. The prohibition protects both women and men of all races, national origins, religions, and ages. Sexual harassment may be considered a form of sexual discrimination, as discussed later in this chapter.

Pregnancy Discrimination

Employment discrimination against pregnant women is prohibited by the Pregnancy Discrimination Act of 1978. Nearly three fourths of all pregnant women were employed when they became pregnant. Over half return to work after their newborn reaches three months of age, and nearly three fourths return to work by the child's first birthday. Employers are prohibited from forcing pregnant employees to take leaves of absence while they are still qualified to work. Pregnancy leaves must be handled like any other temporary disability leave and employers may not specify the length of postdelivery leave period. Promotions or job assignments may not be denied on the basis of pregnancy. These protections extend to both married and unmarried women and also to men. For example, an employer that provides family medical benefits and pregnancy coverage for female employees cannot deny these benefits to the spouses of male employees if spouses are covered in the plan.

Fetal Protections

Employers are becoming concerned that exposure to hazardous working conditions for pregnant workers or for those of childbearing age could cause liability for infertility, miscarriage, or birth defects. Medical science has yet to provide conclusive evidence on the effects of exposure to many toxic substances, radiation, or other dangerous conditions. Some employers have reacted defensively by refusing employment or terminating jobs of women of childbearing age. Some other employers have required such women to sign waivers purporting to release the employer from liability. *International Union v. Johnson Controls*[3] held that many such practices are discriminatory on the basis of sex. This decision leaves a considerable and indeterminate burden on employers to discover and monitor workplace conditions, interpret early, perhaps inconclusive signals from medical research, install costly protections, and inform employees. The problem may not be limited to women—research is beginning to link birth defects to the toxic exposures experienced by males.

Sex-Plus Discrimination

It is prohibited for employers to require additional qualifications of one sex while tolerating noncompliance by the other sex. For example, one airline practiced illegal **sex-plus discrimination** when it prohibited female flight attendants from being married while permitting married male flight attendants.

Similar sex-plus discrimination occurs when only one sex is permitted to retire early, smoke on the job, or receive desirable overseas assignments. The *Hopkins* case discussed earlier in this chapter illustrates sex-plus discrimination because male accountants could be rewarded for acting aggressively while an aggressive woman was not promoted.

Sexual Preference

No federal law protects employees from discrimination based on sexual preference. However, over 100 municipalities have passed antidiscrimination laws to protect homosexuals from various types of discrimination. Only a few such laws are comprehensive in prohibiting discrimination in the granting of credit, renting or selling housing, education, access to public facilities, and employment decisions. Conversely, a few states have considered passing statutes to ban such municipal ordinances. For example, Colorado voters amended the state's constitution in 1992 to overturn homosexual protection ordinances previously enacted by several Colorado cities. Such bans against protection ordinances may violate the Equal Protection Clause.

Age

Although Title VII does not prohibit discrimination on the basis of age, the Age Discrimination in Employment Act was passed in 1967 and was amended in 1978 and 1990. Persons between 40 and 70 years of age are protected from some forms of age discrimination. The Act has triggered numerous private suits by middle-aged white male employees allegedly displaced by lower-paid, younger workers. Additionally, the EEOC enforces the law, and employers with 20 or more employees must comply.

An employer may impose physical fitness requirements that are directly related to job performance even if this forms a pattern or practice discrimination against workers within certain age groups. For example, public safety concerns may permit physical tests of visual acuity, reaction time, and physical strength for bus drivers, train engineers, airplane pilots, firefighters, or police officers even if fewer persons over 40 are hired. Since 1991, forced retirement at an arbitrary age is prohibited except for upper managers with policymaking authority with substantial employer-financed retirement benefits. Some of these problems are discussed in the reading that follows.

---

[3]*International Union v. Johnson Controls*, 111 S.Ct. 1196 (1991).

*Cause and Effects of Age Discrimination**

Claims of age discrimination skyrocketed during the recession of the early 1990s; an annual rate of nearly 50,000 claims per year were filed in 1992. More suits will probably accompany the aging of the huge postwar baby boom population. This poses costly litigation and settlement expense for both large and small companies. Observers charge that employers camouflage age discrimination by making mass layoffs that include a larger proportion of older workers. Many are allegedly replaced with younger, less-qualified workers paid at lower rates. Middle managers are frequent litigants when employers restructure and down-size their work forces. Some employers prefer younger employees because seniority systems tend to raise wage costs with an employee's age. Other employers insist on the perceived strength and appearance of younger employees. The problem is most acute in service in-dustries, sales functions, and advertising, which often emphasize youthfulness. Opponents argue that older workers have more experience, greater loyalty, and make longer commit-ments because of their need to support more mature families.

Some employers frustrate their cases in dismissing older workers by making derogatory statements about older employees' productivity, pay, or appearance. This can reveal dis-criminatory purposes. For example, making statements like ''new blood'' or a ''younger and more attractive'' image is needed can provide the evidence of discriminatory intent. Most cases are settled out of court, sometimes for several hundred thousand dollars for each employee fired.

Employers can improve their chances of defending such suits by avoiding discriminatory comments, basing termination on relevant factors other than age, avoiding large-scale ter-minations of older workers, and replacing fired employees with more qualified recruits. The **Older Workers' Benefit Protection Act** of 1990 permits employers to give a separate component of severance pay in exchange for the employee's waiver of right to sue for age discrimination. Such agreements must be written in plain language, provide several weeks for the employee's decision, notify the employee of rights under the act, suggest analysis by the employee's own attorney, and provide additional compensation beyond the severance to which employees are normally entitled.

Thought Questions

1. For what reasons are younger employees considered superior to older employees? For what reasons are older employees considered superior to younger employees?

2. What assumptions are made by employers who discriminate against older workers about younger employees' expectations as they grow older?

*Source: ''Cause and Effects of Age Discrimination,'' © 1993 by John W. Bagby.

Handicaps and Disabilities

Title VII did not originally protect handicapped or disabled workers. However, the **Vocational Reha-bilitation Act of 1973** and the **Americans with Dis-abilities Act of 1990 (ADA)** make this a new pro-tected class. The 1973 act required federal contractors to consider hiring handicapped workers if the job could be performed after a **reasonable accommodation** is made. **Handicaps** include phys-ical or mental impairments that substantially limit a person's major life activities. For example, the act protects handicaps that result from diabetes, epilepsy, deafness, disfigurement, heart disease, cancer, retardation, blindness, paraplegia, quadriplegia, alcoholism, and drug abuse. If such handicaps do not impact job performance, they cannot be considered in employment decisions. Even communicable diseases must be disregarded if the risk of transmission is slight.[4] Courts are only beginning to deal with the many difficult questions posed by HIV-infected employees.

The ADA expanded this coverage to nearly all private employers and broadened the term **disability** to include additional handicaps. All Title VII remedies and procedures apply to disabled workers. Employers may use only valid screening devices that measure abilities relevant to the particular job tasks. Discrimination on the basis of an applicant's disability unconnected with job performance is prohibited. The ADA also requires significant modification of facilities to make reasonable accommodation for access and use by the disabled. For example, workstations must be accessible for disabled employees and public facilities must be modified to accommodate the disabled, such as by widening doors and making curb cuts to accommodate wheel chairs. While many critics charge that the ADA's accommodation modifications impose massive societal costs, there is significant evidence that many modifications have been made rather cheaply. New facility designs should include easy access for the disabled because this is less costly than retrofitting older facilities.

Employment discrimination decisions pose significant ethical dilemmas. Managers ignore some of the best talent when their personal prejudices influence promotion or hiring decisions. Managers indulging in their personal preferences subjugate their employer's productivity and externalize the costs of discrimination onto otherwise qualified applicants who lose important opportunities. Equality of opportunity, not equality of result, is the essence of the U.S. Declaration of Independence, the Bill of Rights, the Constitution, and the equal opportunity laws. Employment discrimination is not morally justified even to satisfy widespread prejudice among customers or existing employees.

---

[4]*School Board of Nassau County Florida v. Arline,* 480 U.S. 273 (1987).

STATUTORY EXCEPTIONS TO TITLE VII

Employment discrimination is permitted in three narrowly defined exceptions: (1) bona fide occupational qualifications, (2) professionally developed aptitude tests, and (3) valid nondiscriminatory seniority systems. These permit limited discrimination based on an applicant's age, national origin, sex, religion, disability, and occasionally race.

Bona Fide Occupational Qualification

Where the employer's business necessity requires that hirees have a particular religion, sex, or national origin, the requirement may be a permissible **bona fide occupational qualification (BFOQ).** Where employment of persons from other groups would undermine the business' success, applicants may be required to satisfy a BFOQ. For example, churches may validly require candidates for certain jobs (e.g., clergy) be ordained and belong to that religion. Kosher butcheries may hire only Jewish butchers. Female models may be required to display women's fashions. Language fluency is necessary for tour guides or for co-worker communication. Race is never a BFOQ.

BFOQs are not granted easily by the courts. Maximizing co-worker or customer satisfaction or avoiding minor inconvenience does not justify a BFOQ. For example, ABCorp. cannot insist on hiring only male construction workers to please the existing male work force. Airlines may not insist on using only female flight attendants even if there is evidence females are better than males at calming anxious passengers. Gourmet restaurant patrons' preference for male waiters over females does not justify a BFOQ for male waiters only. Similarly, ethnic restaurants may not insist on waiters of a particular ethnic background or appearance even to achieve the desired ambience.

There is an interesting paradox in requiring a particular sex in locker room jobs. A legitimate BFOQ exists requiring female locker room attendants in female exercise clubs. By contrast, it is discriminatory to exclude female sportswriters from the male locker rooms of professional sports teams. This might be explained by comparing the short time sportswriters spend in the locker room with the full time spent by locker room attendants. Are there additional plausible explanations illustrating this business necessity?

Professionally Developed Ability Tests

Employers may validly test the education, skills, knowledge, and performance potential of job applicants with **professionally developed aptitude tests.** Any qualifications tested must be directly related to the successful performance of job tasks and must constitute a business necessity. The qualifications and tests must be validated as accurate and reliable predictors of job performance. Employers have difficulty using anything but reliable and scientifically designed tests that predict successful job performance.

The famous case of *Griggs v. Duke Power Co.*[5] first established the process of disparate impact analysis and required test validation. Candidates for janitorial jobs were required to possess a high school diploma or pass the Wonderlick aptitude test. However, this test tended to reward whites' experiences over blacks' without any relationship to the expected job tasks. Tests may not be used if they disqualify members of a protected class at higher rates than other persons are disqualified unless the test is validated, a task usually performed by industrial psychologists.

EEOC guidelines require employers to publish **job descriptions** cataloging the qualifications and job tasks expected for each job. Tests must be validated that discriminate only between applicants with the required skills and candidates without the skills. EEOC guidelines permit test validation by one of three methods. **Criterion validity** of a test is demonstrated by a strong statistical relationship between test results and observed job performance. **Content validity** exists when the test measures actual characteristics or skills used on the job. **Construct validity** exists if the test measures characteristics considered useful on the job. For example, ABCorp. might use a typing test to qualify candidates for a secretarial job. The test includes a sample of typing (content validity), and there is strong statistical evidence that good typists perform well as secretaries (criterion validity). Construct validity is used when the job description includes more ambiguous characteristics. For example, a psychological test of bravery, emotional stability, or leadership might be validly used for a police officer in addition to a marksmanship test that has content validity.

Seniority Systems

Bona fide seniority systems are permitted if not intended to discriminate unlawfully. Employers often install seniority policies and unions often demand that collective bargaining agreements include **seniority system** provisions. Seniority favors employees with higher rank, longer spans of service, or other priorities in their position. Employers may validly favor more senior employees in decisions to lay off, promote, or give merit raises or grant other privileges. Seniority arguably engenders loyalty, permits retention of experienced and productive employees, and eliminates favoritism.

Seniority may tend to perpetuate the effects of past discrimination, frustrating the equal opportunity laws. For example, when economic downturns force layoffs, the seniority system first requires the layoff of more recently hired employees who were probably employed under less discriminatory conditions. Nevertheless, bona fide nondiscriminatory seniority systems prevail over the strict application of equal employment laws.[6]

SEXUAL HARASSMENT

Although Title VII does not specifically prohibit sexual harassment, when a supervisor makes submission to unwelcome advances of a sexual nature a condition of employment, this may be prohibited as discriminatory. This area has gained significant notoriety in recent years as many victims divulged mistreatment through sexual harassment by famous persons. However, this area is filled with ambiguity due to the difficulties in distinguishing between nonoffensive social gestures and unlawful sexual harassment. Additionally, the two sexes may misunderstand the differences between their sensitivities to horseplay and the use of or response to sexual innuendo as a source of power.

Sexual harassment most clearly occurs when an employee is hired, promoted, or given raises on the basis of submitting to sexual relations with a supervisor to gain the new job. This is unlawful discrimination on the basis of sex because other applicants may be better qualified yet the person harassed is rewarded for submission. Employees

---

[5]*Griggs v. Duke Power Co.,* 401 U.S. 424 (1971).

[6]*International B'hd of Teamsters v. United States,* 431 U.S. 324 (1977).

who quit a job because of unwanted sexual harassment can maintain an action for **constructive discharge.**

To clarify the area, the EEOC has issued guidelines that apply general Title VII principles to co-workers, supervisors, and employers whether or not the harassment was authorized. **Sexual harassment** can occur when a job applicant or an employee receives unwelcome sexual advances, requests for sexual favors, or verbal or physical contact of a sexual nature. Such actions are illegal when the surrounding circumstances make submission to the sexual advance a term or condition of employment, the so-called **quid pro quo** harassment. The law punishes the perpetrators and grants a right of action to victims passed over for a new job, a promotion, or raise that was given to a less qualified person who submitted to the harassment.

Sexual harassment also arises when a **hostile working environment** is created. Sexual innuendo, off-color remarks, and demeaning jokes can create an intimidating or offensive work environment. For example, in *Meritor Savings Bank v. Vinson*,[7] a sexually harassing environment was created when a bank employee repeatedly submitted to the supervisor's sexual advances out of fear of losing the job. The employer had grievance procedures but failed to adequately enforce its sexual harassment prohibition. Employers and supervisors may be held liable for damages for failing to take appropriate corrective action against the sexually harassing acts of employees. Harassing co-workers should be disciplined. Prevention is an acceptable method to sensitize all employees. For example, exposure to examples at seminars or viewing videos depicting possible harassment can inspire discussion that clarifies the sensibilities of both sexes. The following case illustrates a poisoned work atmosphere and the employer's duty to remedy the situation.

---

[7]*Meritor Savings Bank v. Vinson*, 477 U.S. 57 (1986).

BUNDY v. JACKSON
641 F.2d 934 (D.C. Cir. 1981)

Sandra Bundy was a vocational rehabilitation specialist finding jobs for former criminal offenders in the District of Columbia Department of Corrections. Bundy received numerous sexual advances from co-workers. Burton continually called her into his office requesting that she spend workday afternoons with him at his apartment. He asked about her sexual interests. Gainey made sexual advances and asked her to join him at a motel and in the Bahamas. Swain, her supervisor, dismissed her complaints, saying, "Any man in his right mind would want to rape you." Although she never received poor performance ratings, Bundy's supervisors thereafter began to criticize her. Jackson, the Director, failed to correct the situation. This behavior led her to believe her supervisors were impeding her promotion because she had offended them in resisting their advances.

WRIGHT, Chief Judge

We thus have no difficulty inferring that Bundy suffered discrimination on the basis of sex. Moreover, we have no difficulty ascribing the harassment—the "standard operating procedure"—to Bundy's employer, the agency. Although Delbert Jackson himself appears not to have used his position as Director to harass Bundy, an employer is liable for discriminatory acts committed by supervisory personnel. However, officials in the agency who had some control over employment and promotion decisions had full notice of harassment committed by agency supervisors and did virtually nothing to stop or even investigate the practice.

We thus readily conclude that Bundy's employer discriminated against her on the basis of sex. What remains is the novel question whether the sexual harassment of the sort Bundy suffered amounted by itself to sex discrimination with respect to the "terms, conditions, or privileges of employment." Numerous cases find Title VII violations where an employer created or condoned a substantially discriminatory work environment, regardless of whether the complaining employees lost tangible job benefits as a result of the discrimination.

Bundy's claim on this score is essentially that "conditions of employment" include the psychological and emotional work environment—that the sexually stereotyped insults and demeaning propositions to which she was indisputably subjected and which caused her anxiety and debilitation, illegally poisoned that environment. The relevance of these "discriminatory environment" cases to sexual harassment is beyond serious dispute.

The employer can thus implicitly and effectively make the employee's endurance of sexual intimidation a "condition" of her employment. The woman then faces a "cruel trilemma." She can endure the harassment. She can attempt to oppose it, with little hope of success, either legal or practical, but with every prospect of making the job even less tolerable for her. Or she can leave her job, with little hope of legal relief and the likely prospect of another job where she will face harassment anew.

The final Guidelines of Sexual Harassment in the Workplace (Guidelines) issued by the Equal Employment Opportunity Commission on November 10, 1980, offer a useful basis for injunctive relief in this case. Those Guidelines define sexual harassment broadly:

> Unwelcome sexual advances, requests for sexual favors, and other verbal or physical conduct of a sexual nature constitute sexual harassment when (1) submission to such conduct is made either explicitly or implicitly a term or condition of an individual's employment, (2) submission to or rejection of such conduct by an individual is used as the basis for employment decisions affecting such individual, or (3) such conduct has the purpose or effect of unreasonably interfering with an individual's work performance or creating an intimidating, hostile, or offensive work environment.

Applying these Guidelines to the present case, we believe that the Director of the agency should be ordered to raise affirmatively the subject of sexual harassment with all his employees and inform all employees that sexual harassment violates Title VII of the Civil rights Act of 1964, the Guidelines of the EEOC, the express orders of the Mayor of the District of Columbia, and the policy of the agency itself. The Director should also establish and publicize a scheme whereby harassed employees may complain to the Director immediately and confidentially. The Director should promptly take all necessary steps to investigate and correct any harassment, including warnings and appropriate discipline directed at the offending party, and should generally develop other means of preventing harassment within the agency.

Case Questions

1. What is the issue in designating as sexual harassment behaviors that do not exactly require submission to sexual advances?
2. What reasons support holding that a harassing work atmosphere is equivalent to sexual harassment?

Sexual harassment poses an ethical dilemma when supervisors use their power to extract sexual favors from subordinates. The supervisor uses an implied threat of an adverse employment decision unless the subordinate submits. There is a large disparity between males' and females' perception of sexual harassment. Even less blatant forms of sexual harassment can tip the balance of office political power toward the harasser. Does this mean that co-workers' tasteless sexual joking is unethical? This ambiguity will clear up but only slowly as all employees become aware of just exactly when playful behavior degrades into sexual harassment.

EQUAL EMPLOYMENT ENFORCEMENT

The antidiscrimination laws are enforced by many entities: private suits by discrimination victims, internal employer enforcement, local and state fair employment practices agencies, and the federal EEOC under powers granted by various federal, state, and local laws. Most state agencies and the EEOC may investigate, conciliate, and litigate grievances by bringing enforcement actions when grievances are filed by prospective or existing employees. The EEOC and most state agencies have rulemaking powers to implement these laws.

Recordkeeping

The EEOC and some states require recordkeeping and disclosure of certain information that provides comparative statistical data for disparate impact and pattern or practice theory suits. Employers, unions, and employment agencies must keep biographical and demographic records about all job applicants and information used in making other employment decisions (e.g., promotions, demotions, transfers, layoffs, and pay changes). Records must be made available whenever discrimination or enforcement actions are filed. Employers must post notices of employees' rights under the antidiscrimination laws.

Agency Investigations

State agency and EEOC intervention begins when an aggrieved employee perceives an unlawful discrimination. Charges are initially filed with the state agency if covered by state law to permit resolution at the state level. If the state agency takes no action within 60 days, charges may be filed with the EEOC if this is within 180 days after the alleged discrimination or within 300 days if state law requires local filing first. Some critics believe this statute of limitations is too short when compared with most other legal rights. Others argue that short limitations periods are needed because the failings of memory are more pronounced in employment discrimination situations and the potential for emotionally inspired reprisal is so great.

The EEOC must notify the employer of the charges and investigate the incident, often by visiting the employer to question supervisors, co-workers, and the alleged wrongdoer. Employer records are examined and subpoenas issued for confidential documents and to question witnesses. The EEOC may inform the employer of intent to seek conciliation, a form of mediated settlement, if there is reasonable cause that a Title VII violation occurred. If the EEOC finds insufficient cause, it must inform the employee by sending a **right to sue letter** advising that the employee may proceed individually if desired. The employee then has only 90 days to file suit in a state or federal court.

Conciliation

The EEOC settles most complaints through alternative dispute resolution by **conciliation.** This is typically a confidential proceeding between the EEOC and the employer without the alleged victim present. If the EEOC's evidence of wrongdoing is compelling, the employer usually agrees voluntarily to a remedy. The conciliation agreement is binding on both parties and enforceable in the courts if the employer disobeys it or the EEOC attempts other enforcement actions. If conciliation is not reached, the EEOC may proceed with an enforcement action in federal district court. Both conciliation and court remedies often include a package of employer-reimbursed back pay, litigation costs, job reinstatement, attorney's fees, and affirmative action, which is discussed next. Private litigants may receive compensatory and punitive damages for intentional discrimination. Figure 50–2 illustrates the EEOC process.

Affirmative Action

Some courts have implied additional remedies permitting proactive plans to avoid future discrimination. **Affirmative action** programs include active recruiting for minorities through the establishment of goals and timetables to secure greater participation in the employer's work force by members of protected classes. Affirmative action plans are adopted in some union collective bargaining agreements and are required for most federal contractors.

Affirmative action plans risk charges of reverse discrimination. For example, if qualified white male applicants are displaced by less qualified minorities or women, this constitutes a preference that may be reverse discrimination. Some affirmative action plans have unnecessarily ''trammeled'' nonminority employees' rights, such as where a union contract gave minorities a preference to avoid layoffs. This violates the Fourteenth Amendment's Equal Protection Clause. While a hiring preference closes off only one of many employment opportunities, a layoff preference places the entire burden of achieving equal employment opportunity on those individuals laid off. Such disruption is unreasonable as an affirmative action plan.

Is it ethical to correct the discriminatory abuses of many years in a short time on the backs of innocent job applicants? Critics charge affirmative action plans attempt to redress past wrongs by unfairly treating qualified applicants passed over in preference to favored minorities. The following case illustrates the courts' general endorsement of privately negotiated affirmative action plans.

Figure 50–2   EEOC Procedures

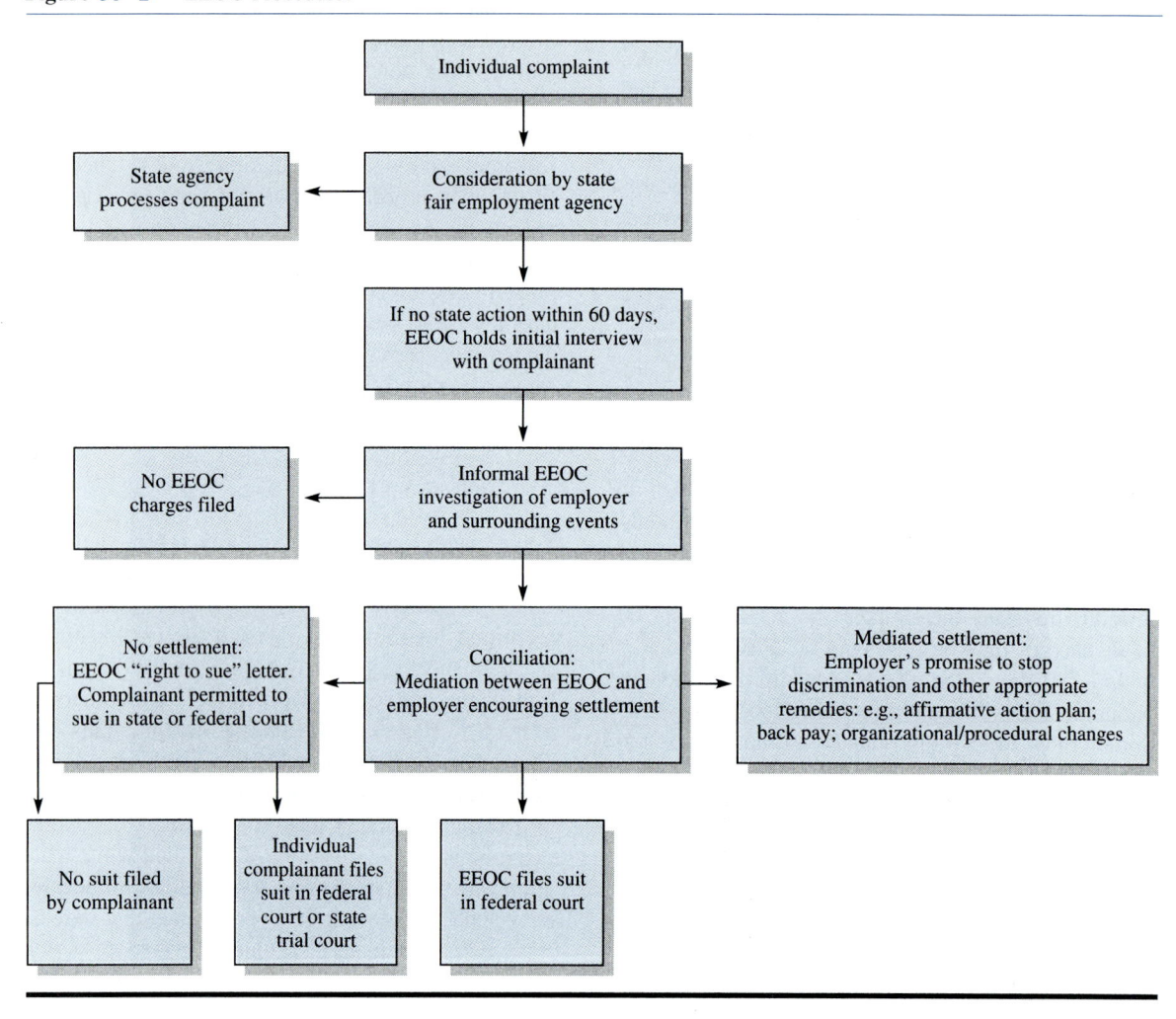

UNITED STEELWORKERS OF AMERICA v. WEBER
443 U.S. 193 (1979)

The 1974 master collective bargaining agreement between Kaiser Aluminum & Chemical Corp. and the United Steelworkers of America (USWA) required implementation of an affirmative action plan to eliminate conspicuous racial imbalance. Kaiser's in-plant craft-training programs were nearly exclusively populated by whites. The affirmative action plan required Kaiser to reserve 50 percent of the openings in these programs for blacks until the percentage of black craftworkers in the Kaiser work force came up to the percentage of blacks in the local labor force. In the first year, seven blacks and six whites were selected for the training program at one plant on the basis of seniority. The most senior black selected had less seniority than several white workers rejected for the program, including Weber. Weber claimed reverse racial discrimination when he was rejected. The USWA appealed a finding of reverse discrimination in the affirmative action plan.

BRENNAN, Justice

Respondent (Weber) argues that Congress intended in Title VII to prohibit all race-conscious affirmative action plans. Respondent's argument rests upon a literal interpretation of 703(a) and (d) of the Act. Those sections made it unlawful to "discriminate . . . because of . . . race" in hiring and in the selection of apprentices for training programs.

Respondent's argument is not without force. But it overlooks the significance of the fact that the Kaiser-USWA plan is an affirmative action plan voluntarily adopted by private parties to eliminate traditional patterns of racial segregation.

Congress' primary concern in enacting the prohibition against racial discrimination in Title VII of the Civil Rights Act of 1964 was with "the plight of the Negro in our economy." Before 1964, blacks were largely relegated to "unskilled and semiskilled jobs." Because of automation the number of such jobs was rapidly decreasing.

As a consequence, "the relative position of the Negro worker (was) steadily worsening. In 1947 the nonwhite unemployment rate was only 64 percent higher than the white rate; in 1962 it was 124 percent higher." Integration of blacks into the mainstream of American society could not be achieved unless this trend were reversed.

Given this legislative history, we cannot agree with respondent that Congress intended to prohibit the private sector from taking effective steps to accomplish the goal that Congress designed Title VII to achieve. The very statutory words intended as a spur or catalyst to cause "employers and unions to self-examine and to self-evaluate their employment practices and to endeavor to eliminate, so far as possible, the last vestiges of an unfortunate and ignominious page in this country's history," cannot be interpreted as an absolute prohibition against all private, voluntary, race-conscious affirmative action efforts to hasten the elimination of such vestiges. Nothing contained in Title VII "shall be interpreted to require any employer . . . to grant preferential treatment . . . to any group on account of" a de facto racial imbalance in the employer's work force. The section does not state that "nothing in Title VII shall be interpreted to permit" voluntary affirmative efforts to correct racial imbalances. The natural inference is that Congress chose not to forbid all voluntary race-conscious affirmative action.

[This] plan does not unnecessarily trammel the interests of the white employees. The plan does not require the discharge of white workers and their replacement with new black hirees. Nor does the plan create an absolute bar to the advancement of white employees; half of those trained in the program will be white. Moreover, the plan is a temporary measure; it is not intended to maintain racial balance, but simply to eliminate a manifest racial imbalance. Preferential selection of craft trainees at the Gramercy plan will end as soon as the percentage of black skilled craftworkers in the Gramercy plan approximates the percentage of blacks in the local labor force.

Case Questions

1. For what reasons was this affirmative action plan initiated?

2. Do the arguments in this case also support affirmative action plans for minorities other than blacks?

Affirmative action plans impose the least burden on qualified nonminorities when they are reviewed periodically and are discontinued as soon as balance for the affected protected class or classes is achieved. *Johnson v. Transportation Agency, Santa Clara California*[8] held that such plans should be limited to "attaining" balance and are not intended to become permanent quotas for "maintaining" balance. Neutral alternative remedies should be used and quotas waived when there are no qualified minority applicants. **Minority setasides** reserve a minimum number of government contracts or privileges for minorities, but have been challenged as reverse discrimination. While some setaside programs have been found constitutional,[9] the future of FCC license preferences for females is uncertain.[10]

[8]*Johnson v. Transportation Agency, Santa Clara, California,* 480 U.S. 616 (1987).

[9]*Fullilove v. Klutznick,* 448 U.S. 448 (1980); *Metro Broadcasting, Inc. v. F.C.C.,* 497 U.S. 547 (1990).
[10]*Lamprecht v. F.C.C.,* 958 F.2d 382 (D.C. Cir. 1992).

Executive Order Program

Several U.S. presidents have implemented Title VII with executive orders prohibiting discrimination and requiring affirmative action plans by federal contractors. Executive Order No. 11,246 requires all federal contracts to include a provision prohibiting discrimination. This applies to the protected classes of race, color, creed, national origin, age, and sex. Federal contracts must also contain a provision requiring nondiscriminatory hiring practices. Federal contracts may be canceled for violation of these terms. Executive Orders No. 11,246 and 11,375 created the Office of Federal Contract Compliance Programs to oversee most federal contractors' equal employment practices and affirmative action programs that include goals and timetables to achieve minority balance.

Other Remedies

Additional remedies exist under state and local laws, and some have been fashioned by the courts. The EEOC often negotiates court-approved **consent decrees** with employers charged with widespread discriminatory practices. Typically, the employer agrees to adopt new practices and/or affirmative action plans and promises to refrain from future discrimination. **Reinstatement** may be ordered for wrongly fired or constructively discharged individuals, **back pay** (with interest) ordered to compensate for earnings lost while the unlawful discrimination denied the applicant the job or promotion, and **retroactive seniority** given from the time of the discrimination.

Civil Rights Act of 1991

The **Civil Rights Act of 1991** authorized recovery of punitive damages for intentional, malicious, or reckless discrimination. Compensatory damages are recoverable for lost future wages, pain and suffering, mental anguish, and other noneconomic damages. However, the 1991 law imposes **damage caps** limiting the total dollar amount recoverable in all but race discrimination cases. Critics plan to challenge the damage caps because they discriminate in favor of race and against other protected classes. The sliding scale damage caps rise with the number of employees, as illustrated in Figure 50–3.

Figure 50–3   Discrimination Damage Caps

Number of Employees	Upper Limit on Damages (compensatory and punitive)
0–14	No damages allowed
15–100	$ 50,000
101–200	100,000
201–500	200,000
over 500	300,000

The 1991 law reversed several aspects of discrimination law imposed by the courts. For example, while the burden of proof was placed on the discrimination victim by the *Wards Cove Packing* case discussed earlier, the 1991 law shifts it back to the employer after the victim establishes a prima facie case. The employer's claim that a particular employment practice is a business necessity is not a defense to intentional discrimination. Either party may request a jury trial, which often favors the alleged victim. **Test norming** by which test scores are adjusted to favor certain protected classes is prohibited. There was much rhetoric surrounding passage of the 1991 law, particularly that it was essentially a ''quota bill'' despite its explicit prohibition of quotas. Critics claimed that it made private suits so easy that employers would probably adopt quotas to avoid costly litigation. However, a real danger of this law may be to discourage employers from using aptitude tests, which are proven to be better predictors of future performance than interviews, references, educational credentials, or experience.

END–OF–CHAPTER QUESTIONS

1. What is the issue in requiring comparable worth to adjust the pay scales of different workers? For what reason is comparable worth urged on the courts and legislatures? What reasons are used to criticize comparable worth? What plausible alternate hypothesis to the discrimination theory might be given for the pronounced differences in pay rates between males and females?

2. World Am Airlines requires pilots to hold college degrees. Arlene, a licensed female pilot without a college degree, was turned down for a World Am pilot opening. World Am's personnel officer testified at Arlene's EEOC hearing that "all pilots are rigorously trained and receive periodic refresher courses. The college degree ensures efficient performance of all pilots in this training." What theory of discrimination will Arlene use in her claim against World Am? What other issues arise?

3. Some plaintiffs have introduced statistical flaws in the comparisons used to prove discrimination suits based on the disparate impact or pattern or practice theories. Explain a faulty comparison and then change the example to cure this reasoning error.

4. What is the discrimination issue under Title VII for blatant sexual harassment? What are the reasons this theory is expanded to less blatant sexual innuendo and off-color jokes of a sexual nature?

5. A teacher's religious beliefs required observance of six religious holidays annually. The board of education permitted him to use three paid personal leave days for these holidays but required him to take unpaid and unauthorized leaves for the remaining three. The school board denied his request to cease docking his pay in exchange for his offer to pay for a substitute on these three days. Was the school board providing reasonable accommodation for the teacher's religious observances? See *Ansonia Board of Education v. Philbrook*, 479 U.S. 60 (1986).

6. The Los Angeles Water Department's pension program computed employee contributions to the plan based on standard mortality tables showing that women live longer than men. This would permit women, on average, to draw benefits longer and in greater amounts than males. Therefore, the pension plan required female employees to contribute nearly 15 percent more to the plan than males. Is this program discriminatory on the basis

of sex? What alternative conclusions would be consistent with these reasons? What would be the impact of ignoring sex in actuarial decisions to set premiums in insurance where claims histories differ between the sexes, such as automobile liability insurance that typically charges more for young male drivers, medical insurance, or life insurance? See *Los Angeles Department of Water and Power v. Manhart*, 435 U.S. 702 (1978).

7. Pan Am discharged a 43-year-old employee with 17 years of service as part of a work force reduction that laid off other employees. The process was allegedly a rigorous, fair, and nondiscriminatory evaluation of productivity applied uniformly. The process found the 43-year-old to be the least productive of his peer group. Was there discrimination on the basis of age? See *Coburn v. Pan American World Airways*, 711 F.2d 339 (D.C. Cir. 1983).

8. A female phone company employee with 19 years' service was turned down for promotion to switchman. The phone company justified the refusal on the basis that women were not eligible because the job was too strenuous and switchmen were on 24-hour call. A state statute prohibited the employment of women in jobs requiring lifting of over 30 pounds. Is sex a BFOQ for the switchman position? See *Weeks v. Southern Bell & Telephone Co.*, 408 F.2d 228 (5th Cir. 1969).

9. A female applicant was turned down for the position of correctional counselor at the Alabama maximum security prison. The state board of corrections prohibited hiring females for "contact" positions requiring close physical proximity with male inmates. Is sex a valid BFOQ for correctional counselor? See *Dothard v. Rawlinson*, 433 U.S. 321 (1977).

10. A minority setaside program in the city of Richmond required that minority subcontractors receive 30 percent of the dollar amount of each city construction project. Minority subcontractors were defined as businesses owned or controlled 51 percent

by "blacks, Spanish speaking, Orientals, Indians, Eskimos or Aleuts." Although 50 percent of Richmond's population was black, only 0.67 percent of contracts were awarded to minority subcontractors in the prior five years. A nonminority plumbing contractor was unable to find minority subcontractors to include in its bid to refit the jailhouse and sought a waiver from the setaside requirements. The city reopened the bidding after a minority contractor filed a late bid even though made at a higher price. Is the city's setaside ordinance illegal as discriminatory? See *City of Richmond v. J.A. Croson*, 488 U.S. 469 (1989).

Part XIII

Corporate Social Responsibility

■

Chapter 51

Environmental Law

■

CRITICAL THINKING INQUIRIES

As you read this chapter, you should be able to address the following:

- What is the proper relationship between federal and state governments regarding the regulation of the environment?
- Compare and contrast the various federal laws designed to protect the environment.
- Articulate a comprehensive environmental national policy.
- What are the major obstacles preventing us from winning the war on pollution?

MANAGERIAL PERSPECTIVE

Chemical Management obtained a loan from First Federal Bank to build a hazardous waste burning plant at a site located on the banks of the Ohio River. First Federal loaned the money on condition that it have a management voice in the construction of the plant. The county Port Authority owns the land and Chemical Management leases from it.

Chemical Management is required to comply with all regulatory air, water, and solid waste pollution standards. However, it is very concerned about the liability it may incur as a result of emissions and spills.

- What federal acts must Chemical Management be concerned about?
- Who is potentially liable in the event of a spill?
- Who may pursue claims against Chemical Management in the event of an accident?

In the past, companies could disregard the environment with impunity. Today, however, it is economically prudent for companies and managers to be environmentally conscious. The statutory schemes are such that the incentives are too strong and the sanctions too great to ignore the environmental impact of business operations. Moreover, society's future existence and quality of life depend upon environmental consciousness and conservation.

Environmental law initially was a specific application of tort and property law. Later, Congress (and state legislatures) passed statutes to deal with particular pollution problems. Environmental statutes are now highly complex and detailed and apply to many aspects of the conduct of a business. This chapter first touches on the common law and then turns its attention to key federal statutory laws designed to regulate our environment (see Figure 51–1).

COMMON LAW

The common law developed methods of resolving disputes over disposal of wastes. Negligence, strict liability, and trespass are causes of action available to defeat environmental wrongdoing. However, these methods are not without their problems (see Chapters 7 and 8). Another common tool to remedy individual and community harm is the tort, nuisance.

Figure 51–1   Federal Environmental Statutes

Statute	Description
National Environmental Policy Act (NEPA)	Requires preparation of an environmental impact statement (EIS) for federal actions that may significantly affect the quality of the environment
Clean Air Act (CAA)	Regulates emissions and establishes standards and licensing to meet clean air requirements
Clean Water Act (CWA)	Regulates the nation's water to make it safe for swimming and fishing and eliminates discharge of pollutants into navigable waters
Safe Drinking Water Act (SDWA)	Establishes minimum standards for drinking water
Resource Conservation and Recovery Act (RCRA)	Regulates hazardous waste sites and handlers
Toxic Substances Control Act (TSCA)	Regulates hazardous chemical substances
Endangered Species Act (ESA)	Protects endangered species and their habitats from harm
Federal Environmental Pesticide Control Act	Regulates pesticides
Nuclear Waste Policy Act (NWPA)	Established a national plan for disposal of nuclear wastes
Price-Anderson Act (PAA)	Protects nuclear licensees from risk of liability above $560 billion
Comprehensive Environmental Response, Compensation and Liability Act (CERCLA)	Regulates and identifies hazardous sites and specifies liability for responsible parties
Superfund Amendments and Reauthorization Act (SARA)	Establishes a superfund to clean up hazardous waste spills
Federal Land Policy and Management Act (FLPMA)	Provides that Bureau of Land Management identify and protect critical environmental areas
Coastal Zone Management Act (CZMA)	Establishes a uniform system of state controls for coastal lands

In addition, a body of law, referred to as toxic torts, has grown up in response to mass impact by pollution activities. Both nuisance law and toxic torts are highlighted below.

Nuisance

A nuisance may be either private or public. A **private nuisance** is anything that unreasonably disturbs, damages, or interferes with the use of land. A private nuisance affects one or a few persons. A **public nuisance** is an unreasonable interference of the use of land that affects a large number of people. Private nuisance actions are brought by individuals, whereas public nuisance actions are brought by the government.

Even as late as the 1970s, private nuisance law was one of the principal methods available to individuals for combating pollution. Its effectiveness in dealing with pollution problems is limited, however. Only landowners or other persons in possession of an interest in land can sue in private nuisance. In addition, many common law rules further limit the circumstances in which a private landowner can sue in private nuisance to stop a polluter from harming the landowner. For example, under the common law, the pollution must be an *unreasonable* interference with the landowner's use of land. Determining unreasonableness necessarily requires that the land-owner's interest be balanced against the utility of the conduct alleged to cause the nuisance. The courts typically decide that the conduct is unreasonable if the harm outweighs the utility of the activity. Thus, it is difficult to determine in advance what will be unreasonable. In addition, the pollution must interfere with the landowner's *use* of land. A variety of activities, including noxious odors and unsightly disturbances, have been considered interferences with the use of land. Nonetheless, the connection to land requirement limits the types of problems that private nuisance can remedy.

Even where the harm to the landowner is severe, courts may find that there is no nuisance. If the landowner comes onto the scene after the activity alleged to cause the nuisance is already established, then courts are likely to hold that the landowner "came to the nuisance," and therefore cannot complain of the activity.

Courts have broad powers to remedy a nuisance. The court may order the person causing the nuisance to pay money damages to compensate the landowner for the interference with the use and enjoyment of the land. The court may also issue an injunction prohibiting the defendant from continuing the nuisance. The following case illustrates problems that the courts face in applying common law nuisance to industrial pollution.

BOOMER v. ATLANTIC CEMENT CO.
257 N.E.2d 870 (N.Y. 1970)

Atlantic operated a large cement plant near Albany, New York. Several nearby landowners, including Boomer, sued Atlantic, seeking damages and an injunction prohibiting Atlantic from continuing to injure their property with the dirt, smoke, and vibrations coming from the plant.

The trial court found that there was a nuisance but denied the injunction. It did award the plaintiffs temporary damages for the harm already caused to their property and allowed them to sue in the future for further damages. It denied the injunction because the plant contributed 300 jobs to the local economy and represented an investment of $45 million. Also, the trial court noted that Atlantic was unlikely to be able to develop techniques to eliminate its pollution in the near future. An intermediate appellate court affirmed the denial of the injunction and the landowners appealed to New York's highest court.

BERGAN, Judge

The public concern with air pollution arising from many sources in industry and in transportation is currently accorded ever wider recognition accompanied by a growing sense of responsibility in State and Federal Governments to control it. Cement plants are obvious sources of air pollution in the neighborhoods where they operate.

It seems apparent that the amelioration of air pollution will depend on technical research in great depth; on a carefully balanced consideration of the economic impact of close regulation; and of the actual effect on public health. It is likely to require massive public expenditure and to demand more than any local community can accomplish and to depend on regional and interstate controls.

A court should not try to do this on its own as a by-product of private litigation and it seems manifest that the judicial establishment is neither equipped in the limited nature of any judgment it can pronounce nor prepared to lay down and implement an effective policy for the elimination of air pollution. This is an area beyond the circumference of one private lawsuit. It is a direct responsibility for government and should not thus be undertaken as an incident to solving a dispute between property owners and a single cement plant—one of many—in the Hudson River valley.

The ground for the denial of injunction, notwithstanding the finding both that there is a nuisance and that plaintiffs have been damaged substantially, is the large disparity in economic consequences of the nuisance and of the injunction. This theory cannot, however, be sustained without overruling a doctrine which has been consistently reaffirmed in several leading cases in this court and which has never been disavowed here, namely that where a nuisance has been found and where there has been any substantial damage shown by the party complaining an injunction will be granted.

This result [awarding temporary damages but denying the injunction] is a departure from a rule that has become settled; but to follow the rule literally in these cases would be to close down the plant at once. This court is fully agreed to avoid that . . . drastic remedy; the difference in view is how best to avoid it.

One alternative is to grant the injunction but postpone its effect to a specified future date to give opportunity for technical advances to permit defendant to eliminate the nuisance; another is to grant the injunction [unless defendant pays] permanent damages to plaintiffs which would compensate them for the total economic loss to their property present and future caused by defendant's operations. For reasons which will be developed the court chooses the latter alternative.

If the injunction were to be granted unless within a short period—e.g., 18 months—the nuisance be abated by improved methods, there would be no assurance that any significant technical improvement would occur.

The parties could settle this private litigation at any time if defendant paid enough money and the imminent threat of closing the plant would build up the pressure on defendant. If there were no improved techniques found, there would inevitably be applications to the court . . . for extensions of time to perform on showing of good faith efforts to find such techniques.

Moreover, techniques to eliminate dust and other annoying by-products of cement making are unlikely to be developed by any research the defendant can undertake within any short period, but will depend on the total resources of the cement industry nationwide and throughout the world. The problem is universal wherever cement is made.

For obvious reasons the rate of the research is beyond [the] control of defendant. If at the end of 18 months the whole industry has not found a technical solution a court would be hard put to close down this one cement plant if due regard be given to equitable principles.

On the other hand, to grant the injunction unless defendant pays plaintiffs such permanent damages as may be fixed by the court seems to do justice between the contending parties. All of the attributions of economic loss to the properties on which plaintiffs' complaints are based will have been redressed.

It seems reasonable to think that the risk of being required to pay permanent damages to injured property owners by cement plant owners would itself be a reasonable effective spur to research for improved techniques to minimize nuisance.

Thus it seems fair to both sides to grant permanent damages to plaintiffs which will terminate this private litigation. . . . [Judgment denying the injunction affirmed.]

Case Questions

1. What is the issue?
2. What would have been the impact had the court not changed the rule of law granting injunctions?
3. What role should the court play in making decisions about how much pollution should be allowed in general?
4. How effective would nuisance law be in preventing or abating nationwide pollution problems? What is the solution?

Toxic Torts

Although the common law has not been considered adequate to deal with most pollution problems, one area where the common law still has potential for a significant role is compensation of individual victims for what has become known as **toxic torts.** Toxic torts generally involve injuries to a class of people exposed to, and caused by, a harmful substance. The full extent of the injuries is often not known because of long latency periods for diseases associated with toxic agents — for example, cancer. The connection between the exposure and the in-jury is usually unclear because the injuries often have multiple potential causes, and science rarely can establish with certainty that exposure to a specific amount of a substance will cause a particular injury.

The courts have applied traditional common law principles of negligence, strict liability, and products liability (discussed in Chapters 7, 8, and 23) to decide cases where individuals' health has been damaged by such toxic substances as Agent Orange, asbestos, dioxin, and radioactive substances. Victims face difficulties in recovering for their injuries, as discussed in the following reading.

The Causal Connection in Mass Exposure Cases: A "Public Law" Vision of the Tort System*

Accidents in the course of the production, distribution, marketing, consumption, and disposal of toxic agents can have catastrophic consequences. Even a single instance of product defect, carelessness, or risk-taking may increase for thousands or even millions of people of one or more generations the danger of contracting cancer or some other insidious disease. Ultimately, after a latency period that usually spans two or more decades, this disease risk will materialize and cause the disability or death of a significant portion of the exposed population. If the resulting complex damage actions against manufacturers of toxic agents are tried under traditional methods of case-by-case adjudication, they will likely consume hundreds of millions of dollars' worth of public and private resources. These expenditures will dwarf the compensation recovered by victims.

■ ■ ■

Current criticism of the tort system as a scheme too cumbersome, costly, and haphazard to accomplish its accident prevention and compensation objectives suggests that our reliance on private damage actions is misplaced. This criticism may come close to the mark in connection with sporadic accidents such as automobile collisions — accidents of the sort that Holmes termed "isolated, ungeneralized wrongs." Ironically, however, it is the wholesale character of mass exposure risks and the profitmaking context in which they occur that should inspire a degree of optimism about the tort system's capacity to control mass accidents and redress their victims. For in contrast to sporadic accidents, which generally result from all-too-human individual lapses of attention, mass exposure torts are frequently products of the deliberate policies of businesses that tailor safety investments to profit margins. Such risk-taking policies should be especially amenable to control through threats of liability.

■ ■ ■

The Causal Connection Problem

The question that plagues mass exposure cases is specific causation: when there are alter-native possible sources of the plaintiff's injury, which source is actually responsible?

*Source: David Rosenberg, "The Causal Connection in Mass Exposure Cases: A 'Public Law' Vision of the Tort System," 97 Harv. L. Rev. 849 (1984). Reprinted with permission.

Mass exposure cases present two distinct varieties of specific-causation questions. First, it is often unclear which one of several manufacturers of a given toxic agent produced the particular unit of the substance that harmed the plaintiff. The generic character of the product, the inconspicuousness of the exposure event, and the long latency period frequently prevent identification of the responsible manufacturer.

Second and far more common is the problem of determining the origin of the victim's disease. Rarely is any particular toxic agent the exclusive source of a given disease. Insidious diseases generally have several sources, each of which may by itself be sufficient to bring about the condition. Epidemiological statistics, which constitute the best (if not the sole) available evidence in mass exposure cases, can only attribute a proportion of the disease incidence in the population to each potential source. Epidemiologists can estimate the proportion of disease incidence attributable to the "excess risk" created by the toxic agent and the proportion attributable to the "background risk"—the cumulative risk attributable to all other factors. But given current limits on our knowledge of the etiology of insidious diseases, and given the generality of statistical data, it is impossible to pinpoint the actual source of the disease afflicting any specific member of the exposed population.

■ ■ ■

The "Public Law" Proposal

. . . [A] public law approach would enable courts to overcome the problems posed by systematic causal indeterminacy. Accordingly, the central component of this public law approach is the replacement of the preponderance rule by a standard of proportional liability. Under such a standard, courts would impose liability and distribute compensation in proportion to the probability of causation assigned to the excess disease risk in the exposed population . . . despite the absence of individualized proof of the causal connection.

■ ■ ■

Corrective Justice and Rights-Based Deterrence

Systems of rights are premised on the concept of individual entitlement to personal security and autonomy—entitlement that may not usually be overridden or compromised for the good of society. Tortious conduct, whether defined by moral, political, or economic criteria, constitutes a wrongful infringement of those entitlements. From a rights-oriented standpoint, then, the role of the tort system is to perform "corrective justice" in order to preserve entitlements against wrongful infringement. The fundamental tenet of such corrective justice is that wrongdoers should make their victims whole.

Yet the idea that tort liability can provide full compensation for losses resulting from personal injury is dubious indeed.

■ ■ ■

The Proportionality Rule

From the standpoint of corrective justice, the proportionality rule . . . achiev[es] the tort system's goal of preserving the value of entitlement. The proportionality rule discounts recovery by the probability that the plaintiff's loss was caused by some other wrongdoer, by a nonculpable source, or by the plaintiff. Thus, the proportionality rule holds the wrongdoer accountable for neither more nor less than the injury losses fairly attributable to the wrongdoer's conduct.

Thought Questions

1. What is the policy issue presented by this article?
2. What are the weaknesses of a proportionality rule of liability and compensation?
3. Do you think the author's proportionality rule is likely to be adopted by the legal system in this country? Why or why not?

FEDERAL LEGISLATIVE SOLUTIONS TO ENVIRONMENTAL PROBLEMS

The common law has largely been supplanted by statutes as a method of controlling pollution and remedying environmental problems. An explosion of public concern over environmental issues occurred in the 1960s and 1970s. Congress responded to this outpouring of concern with the passage of several key pieces of environmental legislation. The cornerstones of federal efforts to reduce pollution and halt the degradation of the environment were passed between 1969 and 1972. Such statutes depend on government agencies staffed by experts to implement their provisions.

Federal Agencies

The **Environmental Protection Agency (EPA),** created in 1970, is the federal agency that deals with most forms of pollution (see Figure 51–2). Congress delegated to the EPA the authority to establish and enforce standards governing pollution of particular parts of the environment such as air and water. Congress has also made the EPA responsible for regulating particular types of pollution such as pesticides, solid wastes, hazardous wastes, toxic substances, and noise.

The EPA is not, however, the only federal agency that regulates pollution or has authority over environmental problems. The Department of Transportation regulates transportation of hazardous wastes. The Department of the Interior regulates the environmental effects of coal mining and activities on federally owned lands. The Nuclear Regulatory Commission regulates the use and effects of radioactive materials. The Department of Agriculture regulates logging in the National Forests.

The remainder of this chapter discusses the substantive provisions of several of the key federal environmental statutes. Many aspects of pollution control and environmental protection are regulated by state and local governments. These controls are not discussed.

National Environmental Policy Act

Congress first established a national policy to prevent damage to the environment when it passed the **National Environmental Policy Act** of 1969 **(NEPA).** Congress declared that as far as possible, it would be:

the continuing policy of the Federal Government, in cooperation with State and local governments, and other concerned public and private organizations, to use all practicable means and measures . . . to foster and promote the general welfare, to create and maintain conditions under which man and nature can exist in productive harmony, and fulfill the social, economic and other requirements of present and future generations of Americans.[1]

NEPA requires federal agencies proposing to take ''major federal actions significantly affecting the quality of the human environment'' to prepare a detailed statement on the environmental impact of the proposed action. This statement, known as the **environmental impact statement (EIS),** requires the disclosure of any:

- Adverse environmental effects that could not be avoided.
- Alternatives to the proposal.
- Relationship between short-term uses of the environment and maintenance and enhancement of long-term productivity.
- Irreversible and irretrievable commitments of resources that the proposed action would require if it were implemented.[2]

---

[1] 42 U.S.C. § 4331.
[2] 42 U.S.C. § 4332.

Figure 51–2   Environmental Protection Agency

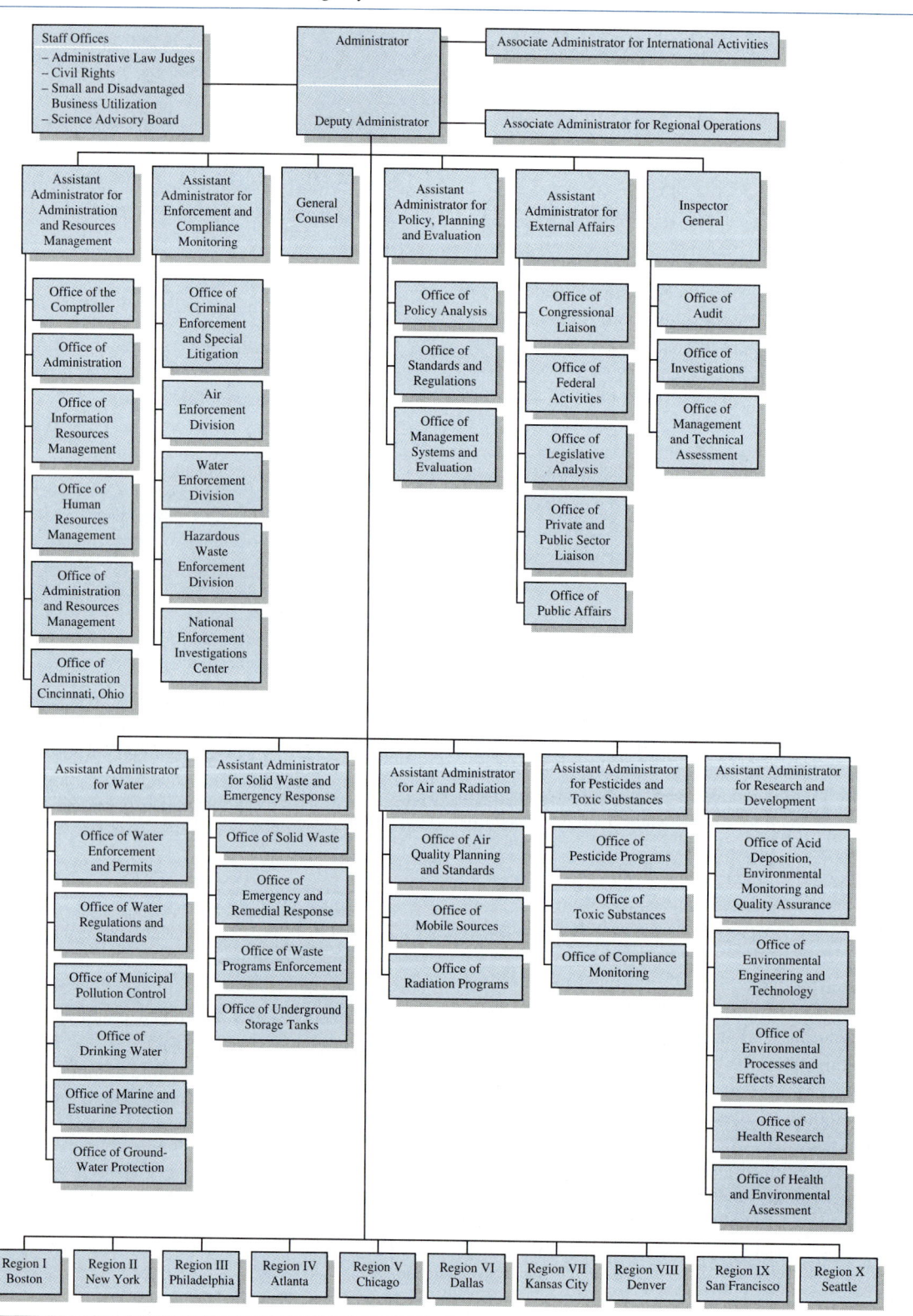

Source: *U.S. Governmental Manual 1986–87* (Washington, D.C.: U.S. Government Printing Office, 1986), p. 865.

The term *major federal action* was construed rather broadly in order to further Congress's policy of improving the environment. Hence, NEPA has affected a wide range of actions beyond those that are purely federal. It applies to actions by private entities that require approval, in the form of permits or licenses, by an agency of the federal government. For example, construction and operation of a nuclear power plant requires a license from the Nuclear Regulatory Commission (NRC). Thus, the NRC must prepare an EIS on its decision to approve a construction or operating license. NEPA also applies when a federal agency leases land to a private person for activities such as grazing, oil and gas production, coal mining, or timber cutting.

Agencies may not go forward with proposed actions if they have not prepared an EIS that complies with the statute. Thus, EIS requirements have been used by environmental groups, property owners, state and local governments, and even business groups to oppose actions by the federal government. This is what happened in the following case involving tuna fisheries.

CENTER FOR MARINE CONSERVATION v. BROWN
LEXIS 3801 (D.D.C. 1993)

The spawning stock and biomass of the Western Atlantic bluefin tuna has been in constant decline since the 1970s. To counter the decline, the United States and 21 other nations entered into the International Convention for the Conservation of Atlantic Tunas (ICCAT), which established the ICCAT commission (Commission). The Commission formulates recommended harvest levels of tuna. The United States enacted the Atlantic Tunas Convention Act (ATCA), which makes the quotas proposed by the Commission binding on the United States.

The Commission recommended its first tuna catch reduction in 1981, and at that time the National Marine Fisheries Service (NMFS) issued an environmental impact statement (EIS) in conjunction with the implementation of the recommended quota reduction. In 1991, ICCAT recommended a 10 percent tuna reduction and NMFS held meetings and solicited public comment to determine how that reduction would be implemented in the United States. A final environmental assessment (EA) issued by the NMFS stated that reduction of the fishing quota would not create any significant environmental impact, and it did not file a new EIS. The plaintiff, the Center for Marine Conservation, sued, alleging that failure to file an EIS violated NEPA.

GREEN, Judge

To determine whether an EIS is necessary, that is, whether a proposed action will have a "significant impact" on the human environment, an agency considering a rulemaking must prepare an environmental assessment (EA). The EA, described by the applicable regulations as a "concise public document," must "include brief discussions of the need for the proposal, of alternatives of the environmental impacts of the proposed action and alternatives, and a listing of agencies and persons consulted." The regulations provide a list of numerous factors to be considered when determining whether an impact will be "significant."

There is a four-part test when examining an agency's conclusion of no significant impact. The factors to be considered are:

1. whether the agency took a "hard look" at the problem;

2. whether the agency identified the relevant areas of environmental concern;

3. . . . whether the agency made a convincing case that the impact was insignificant; and

4. . . . whether the agency convincingly established that changes in the project sufficiently reduced it to a minimum.

A thorough review of the administrative record reveals that each of the four prongs of the test are satisfied and that the agency's conclusion that a new EIS was not required in conjunction with defendants' 1992 rulemaking was not arbitrary and capricious. The EA as well as other portions of the administrative record clearly evidence that the defendants took a hard look at the problems of the declining tuna population and the need to implement ICCAT's recommendation that the United States' 1992–93 quota be reduced by 10 percent. In addition, the defendants properly identified the relevant areas of environmental concern as the impact of the rulemaking on the tuna fishery.

With respect to the third and fourth prongs of the requested inquiry, the defendants have made a convincing case that the environmental impact of the rulemaking is "insignificant" for purposes of NEPA. In short, review of the administrative record reveals that it was clearly rational for the agency to conclude that a 10 percent reduction in the 1992–1993 harvests was "not expected to jeopardize the long-term productive capability of the stock, but rather to slightly improve stock condition compared with no action."

The defendants' conclusion of no significant impact also withstands scrutiny under the specific elements of consideration delineated in the CEQ [Council on Environmental Quality] regulations. Those regulations provide that an agency should look at both "context" and "intensity" when determining the significance of an environmental impact. Specific factors of consideration include the degree to which the proposed action affects public health or welfare, unique characteristics of the geographical area where action will be taken, the degree to which the effects on the quality of the human environment are likely to be highly controversial, the degree to which possible effects are highly uncertain or involve unique or unknown risks, and the degree to which the action may establish a precedent for future actions. Other specified factors are

whether the legislation or agency action is related to other actions with cumulatively significant impacts, the degree to which the action may cause loss or destruction of significant scientific, cultural, or historical resources, the degree to which the action may adversely affect endangered or threatened species or its habitat that has been determined to be critical under the Endangered Species Act of 1973, and whether the action threatens violations of other laws enacted for the protection of the environment.

As illustrated by the administrative record, the 10 percent quota reduction for the 1992–93 fishery is unlikely to affect the public health or welfare, will not impact a unique geographic location, will not destroy significant scientific, cultural, or historical resources, and will slightly benefit the tuna population. Though the record does indicate that the quota reduction would cause some controversy between certain sectors of the fishing industry and conservation groups, the reduction's effects on the human environment do not appear to be so "highly controversial" as to require an EIS. In addition, while plaintiffs allege that "methods of monitoring the bluefin fishery are uncertain," the degree of the possible effects of the quota reduction on the human environment have not been shown to be "highly uncertain" or to involve "unique or unknown risks."

For the reasons stated . . . judgment is hereby entered in favor of defendants, and against plaintiffs.

Case Questions

1. What is the issue this case presents?
2. List the possible impacts of the tuna reduction rule. Do you think these are significant? Who would be most affected? Explain.
3. What questions would you like to pose to the judge who wrote this opinion?
4. Why do you think the agency would resist filing an EIS?

Clean Air Act

Shortly after the passage of NEPA, Congress completely revised its strategy for dealing with air pollution. Previous federal air pollution statutes had

given the federal government little enforcement or regulatory authority (see Figure 51–3). And NEPA was only a directive to federal agencies—not companies. This changed with passage of the **Clean Air Act** of 1970 **(CAA).** The Clean Air Act is the most

Figure 51–3   Top 10 Air Polluters

Company	Activity	Annual Percentage of All Toxic Chemicals Total = 2,427,695,968 lbs. Emitted into Air
Renco Holdings	Iron and steel processing	4.91
3M	Chemicals Tapes Automotive products	2.99
Eastman Kodak	Photographic chemicals Household products	2.85
Du Pont	Petroleum Coal-refining chemicals	2.20
General Motors	Autos Engines Military weapons	1.93
Courtaulds Fibers	Synthetic fibers Autos Trucks and tractors	1.84
Ford	Autos Trucks and tractors	1.31
Hoechst Celanese	Chemicals Plastics Agricultural products	1.23
BASF	Agricultural and industrial chemicals	1.19
General Electric	Engines Electronics Electrical equipment	1.19
Other		78.36

Source: John Holusha, "The Nation's Polluters—Who Emits What, and Where," *The New York Times,* October 13, 1991, sec. 3, col. 1, p. 10.

extensive of the federal environmental regulatory statutes. Congress has used it as the model for other environmental regulatory statutes.

Standards

Under the CAA, Congress for the first time put the federal government in the business of setting specific limits on pollutants in the atmosphere. The statute requires the EPA to set the maximum amounts of pollutants allowed in the atmosphere, referred to as **national ambient air quality standards (NAAQS).** Pollutants covered by NAAQS include particulates, sulfur oxides, carbon monoxide, nitrogen dioxide, ozone, hydrocarbons, and lead. There are currently 189 substances that are covered. The statute places emission limits on existing sources, both mobile sources—for example, automobile emissions—and stationary sources. The statute also introduced the concept of new source performance standards (NSPS) for categories of new stationary sources. Sources covered by NSPS are required to install the best system of emissions reduction that has been "adequately demonstrated." These standards apply to newly constructed sources and to major modifications of existing sources.

Another significant addition was the national emission standards for hazardous air pollutants (NESHAP). This section establishes emission standards for hazardous pollutants, defined as those that would cause an increase in death rates or an increase in serious irreversible, or incapacitating reversible, illnesses.

The final type of emissions standards that Congress established in 1970 was "reasonably available control technology" (RACT) for existing sources in areas that did not meet the NAAQS, called *nonattainment areas*. RACT, like the NSPS, requires the source to install a certain level of technology or meet the levels of emissions attainable through the use of that technology.

To deal with the problem of allocating the cleanup burden between existing sources and new sources, a "market" in air emissions was created. Thus, a new source may be required to purchase or otherwise obtain from an existing source sufficient emissions reductions to more than offset the new emissions from the new facility.

Amended recently, the Clean Air Act tightened pollution controls for coal-burning electric power plants, a chief source of dangerous pollutants. Coal burning causes the formation of sulfuric and nitric acids, which contribute to the "greenhouse effect" (global warming) and produce acid rain. In addition, the amendments require states to develop and periodically revise their plans for meeting national ambient air quality standards. (The plans are subject to EPA approval.) Approximately 100 cities have been designated as not complying with the smog standard established by the EPA.

Many facilities that were not previously subject to the Clean Air Act have been brought into the regulatory framework by the amendments. Under this regulatory scheme, states are required to develop programs for EPA approval. Following EPA approval, a large number of facilities will be required to submit detailed permit applications to the states. Operating permits will then be issued to companies by the state, subject to EPA veto. These operating permits specify the applicable emission limits, fees, and monitoring, recording, and reporting requirements.

Prevention of Significant Deterioration

Although the CAA stated that its purpose was to protect and enhance the nation's air, there were no provisions specifying how much dirtier the air could get in areas that were cleaner than the NAAQS. Therefore, amendments to the act created the prevention of significant deterioration (PSD) program, which requires detailed review of proposed major

new stationary sources in clean air areas. Such sources are required to install the "best available control technology" (BACT) if they are to locate in clean air areas. Finally, such sources are required to show that the ambient air would not be significantly degraded by their emissions. The cleaner the air is in the area where the new source proposes to build, the less the source would be allowed to emit. Thus, the cleanest air is protected the most.

State-Federal Cooperative Program

The structure of the CAA was radically different from past federal pollution laws, which basically left control with the states and made the federal government a cheerleader and source of money. Under the CAA, the federal government sets uniform standards for ambient air quality and emissions, but the states are allowed to implement these standards if they demonstrate to the EPA that they possess the authority and ability to enforce the national standards. Thus, the CAA follows a model of federal-state cooperation. This approach is particularly appropriate in attacking pollution problems that cross state lines and clearly affect the nation as a whole while also having a particular impact in local areas.

The principal method of state involvement is through **state implementation plans (SIPs).** The states are given primary responsibility for designing and implementing plans to achieve the NAAQS within their boundaries. Thus, they have wide latitude in choosing among the various control methods and technologies to achieve the ambient air quality standards. These include transportation control plans (TCPs), new source performance standards, controls on existing stationary sources, and siting or zoning requirements for new sources. The SIP must be approved by the EPA. When it is, it has the force of state and federal law and is thus enforceable by the federal and state governments.

Enforcement

The CAA provides for direct federal enforcement of the clean air provisions. If the government brings a lawsuit to force compliance, it may also seek civil penalties of up to $25,000 per day per violation. The statute also allows for criminal penalties, including stiff fines and possible imprisonment. The federal government is also given the power to enforce a state's SIP if it determines that the state is not adequately enforcing the SIP.

Finally, to provide a further method of enforcement and a check on state and federal enforcement, Congress allowed any person to file suit to enforce provisions of the act. Such "citizen suits" may be brought against the source and the federal or state government agency. To further encourage such suits, citizens or any party to a suit may be awarded reasonable attorneys' fees if the suit is successful.

Clean Water Act

The federal government first recognized and dealt with water pollution in the Rivers and Harbors Act of 1899. However, this statute was primarily aimed at keeping the nation's waterways open for navigation. In 1965, Congress required states to establish goals and uses of its waterways and a plan to achieve these.

In 1972, however, Congress radically changed the regulatory scheme when it passed the **Clean Water Act (CWA).** It added a completely new system of effluent limitations, limiting pollutants contained in the water discharged from a plant and issuing permits for individual discharges. The role of the federal government was greatly increased so that it had primary responsibility for setting policy and standards, while, as under the CAA, looking to the states for implementation.

Effluent Limitations

Effluent limitations are specific numerical limits on particular substances that are applied to each source that discharges pollutants (the effluent) into the water. The effluent limitations are imposed through a system of permits under the **National Pollutant Discharge Elimination System (NPDES).** No point source, such as a pipe, may discharge any liquid unless it obtains a permit.

The CWA established goals of zero discharges. The act also established an interim goal that waters were to be fishable and swimmable. Given the current technology, it seems that these goals will not be met for a long time (see Figure 51–4).

Technology-Based Standards

The NPDES permit sets the effluent limitations for a particular plant. Those effluent limitations are based on several technological standards specified in the statute. Congress has followed a policy of "ratcheting" to achieve these standards. Thus, all indus-

trial plants were first required to install the best practicable control technology currently available (BPT) by 1977. Such plants were then required to meet a more stringent standard of best available technology economically achievable (BAT) by 1984, but this has since been extended.

Additional Standards for Industrial Sources

The act contains a number of other effluent limitations. It provides for new source performance standards (NSPS) similar to those contained in the CAA. Industrial point sources that discharge into sewage treatment plants must also meet pretreatment standards. These standards require that the industrial point source pretreat its discharge to remove toxic pollutants so that it will not interfere with the treatment technology used in the sewage treatment plant. This was intended to prevent industrial discharges from contaminating or killing the biological processes used to treat organic pollution.

Solid and Hazardous Wastes

Congress first dealt with toxic substances in 1976 when it passed two statutes: the **Toxic Substances Control Act (TSCA)** and the **Resource Conservation and Recovery Act (RCRA).** TSCA regulates the production and manufacture of toxic chemicals other than pesticides. RCRA regulates hazardous wastes produced by industry.

The EPA has promulgated regulations defining hazardous waste to include (1) specifically listed substances or constituents, (2) wastes that meet one or more of four criteria of ignitability, corrosivity, reactivity, or toxicity, or (3) substances that are determined through testing to possess dangerous characteristics.

RCRA has been described as a "cradle to grave" regulatory scheme for hazardous waste. Thus, it covers generators and transporters of hazardous waste as well as operators of treatment, storage, or disposal facilities. The cradle to grave description is in many ways, however, a misnomer. The "cradle" merely starts at the point that a substance is determined to be a "waste," even though that substance may have had a long history as a potentially toxic or hazardous substance. Nor is it really accurate to say there is a "grave" for hazardous wastes, since most such wastes retain their hazardous characteristics after storage or disposal. No currently used method of disposal can guarantee that the waste remains iso-

Figure 51–4   Top 10 Water Polluters

Company	Activity	Annual Percentatge of All Toxic Chemicals Discharged into Water Total = 88,994,123 lbs.
Arcadian	Liquid nitrogen phosphates	11.86
3M	Chemical tapes Auto products	8.20
Freeport McMoran	Mineral oil Gas refining	7.75
ITT	Automotive electronics Timber products	6.05
Allied Signal	Aerospace products Automotive products	5.19
Louisiana Pacific	Lumber Aluminum windows and doors	4.86
Weyerhaeuser	Wood products Shipping containers	4.47
Strategic Minerals	Processing nonferrous materials	4.13
Monsanto	Industrial and household chemicals	2.71
Simpson Holdings	Holding company	2.39
Other		42.40

Source: John Holusha, "The Nation's Polluters," *The New York Times,* October 13, 1991, sec. 3, col. 1, p. 10.

lated from the environment forever. Chemical conversion to nontoxic substances or complete destruction are the only truly permanent solutions.

Manifests and Labels

RCRA is an ambitious attempt to identify, track, and ensure the safe treatment and disposal of all hazardous wastes. This is accomplished by requiring that detailed records be kept of all such wastes from the time they are determined to be hazardous. These records include labeling requirements for waste containers and manifests that must accompany wastes when they are transported.

Generators are responsible for where the wastes are sent. Thus, transporters are required to take hazardous wastes only to the treatment, storage, or disposal facility designated by the generator. These provisions, along with the manifest and labeling requirements, were intended to help stop the practice of "midnight dumping."

Treatment, Storage, and Disposal Facilities

Probably the most important aspect of RCRA is its regulation of treatment, storage, and disposal facilities. RCRA requires operators of facilities that treat, store, or dispose of hazardous wastes to obtain a permit. To obtain a permit, the facility must meet design, operation, performance, insurance, and financial responsibility standards issued by the EPA. The statute authorizes EPA to issue standards that are "necessary to protect human health and the environment."

RCRA also imposes specific design standards. For example, it requires all new landfills and surface impoundments to have double liners. Liners are either thick sheets of plastic or several feet of packed clay.

In addition, RCRA requires treatment, storage, and disposal facilities to comply with operation standards. For example, landfills and surface impoundments must continually monitor the quality of any **leachate** (liquid that percolates through the fill, picking up toxic chemicals) from the facility and the quality of the groundwater surrounding the facility. If the level of a suspect chemical exceeds background levels, then corrective action may be required. In most cases, RCRA requires the operator to be responsible for the facility, including groundwater monitoring, for 30 years after the facility is closed. In addition, the operator must place a restriction on the deed for the property containing the facility. The restriction informs all potential purchasers that the land includes a treatment, storage, or disposal facility that is covered by RCRA standards. Finally, the operator is required to have insurance that covers potential claims due to contaminated groundwater.

Superfund

In the late 1970s, the public became aware of the risks inherent in the uncontrolled and undocumented methods that had for decades been used to dispose of hazardous waste. In response to the public uproar, Congress, in 1980, enacted the Comprehensive Environmental Response Compensation and Liability Act (CERCLA), known as **Superfund**. It addresses a very serious problem—the cleanup of sites where hazardous waste was treated or disposed of in an unsafe manner.

Pursuant to CERCLA 30,000 inactive waste sites were identified. From that list the EPA identified sites that merited remedial action, and which were eligible for Superfund cleanup monies.

Superfund takes its name from the fund set up to finance hazardous waste site cleanups. The money for the fund derives partly from a tax on chemical feedstock manufacturers and petroleum companies and partly from general revenues. Congress has pumped about $10 billion into the fund. Congress envisioned that money from the fund would be used to clean up some sites but that the government would recover most of those funds from the parties responsible for the hazardous wastes at the sites. This was accomplished by including a strict liability provision—those responsible for hazardous waste spills were made strictly liable for the cost of the cleanup.

Liability

CERCLA authorizes the EPA to remove wastes or take other remedial action whenever there is a release, or a substantial threat of a release, into the environment of any hazardous substance or any pollutant or contaminant that may present an imminent and substantial danger to the public health and welfare. In connection with the strict liability provision, the government is permitted to sue **potentially responsible parties** for the government's costs of cleanup. The government is also authorized to order potentially responsible parties to clean up the site themselves or to sue them to force them to perform the cleanup. Potentially responsible parties are owners and operators of waste sites, lessees and lessors, generators and transporters of the wastes, and those who have a managerial voice in the operations, as does First Federal Bank in our opening scenario.

There are limited defenses to the strict liability standard. Owners or operators may avoid liability if the spill was caused by an act of God, an act of war, or an act or omission by a third party. If the discharge was caused solely by the act or omission of a third party that has no relationship with the owner, then the third party, rather than the owner or operator of the facility or vessel, is liable for the cost of the cleanup. There is also an innocent purchaser defense available to owners, who, after diligent investigation, had no knowledge that the wastes were on the premises before purchase.

Each party who contributes waste to a site that is subject to a cleanup action is jointly and severally liable for the cost of the cleanup. This means that each party that contributes any amount of waste to the site is potentially liable for the entire cost of the cleanup of that site. This seemingly harsh standard, which could place a crushing financial burden on parties that contribute relatively small amounts of waste, is based on traditional common law rules of liability. Furthermore, that a party is potentially liable for the entire cost does not preclude it from obtaining a contribution toward that liability from the other parties that contributed waste to the site. The imposition of the joint and several liability standard simply is intended to leave it to the responsible party, rather than to the government, to find those other responsible parties and to obtain contributions from them.

The following case illustrates some of the issues courts are faced with in interpreting the Superfund statute.

NEW YORK v. SHORE REALTY CORP.
759 F.2d 1032 (2d Cir. 1985).

Donald LeoGrande was the sole officer and stockholder of Shore Realty Corp. (Shore). In July 1983, Shore purchased land on a small peninsula jutting into Hempstead Harbor. A number of tanks on the property contained 700,000 gallons of hazardous chemicals. The site also had over 400 drums of chemicals as well as other containers of waste. The substances on the site were toxic, some were carcinogenic, and many were combined in ways that may have increased their toxic effects. Shore was incorporated solely to purchase the site for development into condominiums.

In February 1984, the state of New York sued LeoGrande and Shore to clean up the site, citing CERCLA and state nuisance law. The district court found the defendants liable for the state's costs of cleaning up the site, basing its decision in part on CERCLA. The case was appealed.

OAKES, Circuit Judge

CERCLA authorizes the federal government to respond in several ways. EPA can use Superfund resources to clean up hazardous waste sites and spills. . . . At the same time, EPA can sue for reimbursement of cleanup costs from any responsible parties it can locate, allowing the federal government to respond immediately while later trying to shift financial responsibility to others. . . . In addition, CERCLA authorizes EPA to seek an injunction in federal district court to force a responsible party to clean up any site or spill that presents an imminent and substantial danger to public health or welfare or the environment. . . .

Congress clearly did not intend, however, to leave cleanup under CERCLA solely in the hands of the federal government. [S]tates, like EPA, can sue responsible parties for remedial and removal costs if such efforts are "not inconsistent with" the NCP [standards set by EPA to govern cleanups]. While CERCLA expressly does not preempt state law, it precludes "recovering compensation for the same removal costs or damages or claims" under both CERCLA and state or other federal laws. . . .

A. Liability for Response Costs under CERCLA
We hold that the district court properly awarded the State response costs under [the liability section of Superfund]. *Covered Persons.* CERCLA holds liable . . . classes of persons:

(1) the owner and operator of a vessel . . . or a facility, [or] (2) any person who at the time of disposal of any hazardous substance owned or operated any facility at which such hazardous substances were disposed of. . . .

Shore argues that it is not covered by [1] because it neither owned the site at the time of disposal nor caused the presence or the release of the hazardous waste at the facility. While section [1] appears to cover Shore, Shore attempts to infuse ambiguity into the statutory scheme, claiming that [1] could not have been intended to include all owners, because the word "owned" in section [2] would be unnecessary since an owner "at the time of disposal" would necessarily be included in [1]. Shore claims that Congress intended that the scope of [1] be no greater than that of section [2] and that both should be limited by the "at the time of disposal" language. By extension, Shore argues that both provisions should be interpreted as requiring a showing of causation. We agree with the State, however, that [1] unequivocally imposes strict liability on the current owner of a facility from which there is a release or threat of release, without regard to causation.

Shore's claims of ambiguity are illusory; section 9607(a)'s structure is clear. Congress intended to cover different classes of persons differently. Section [1] applies to all current owners and operators, while section [2] primarily covers prior owners and operators. Moreover, [2]'s scope is more limited than that of section [1]. Prior owners and operators are liable only if they owned or operated the facility "at the time of disposal of any hazardous substance"; this limitation does not apply to current owners, like Shore. . . .

Shore's causation argument is also at odds with the structure of the statute. Interpreting [1] as including a causation requirement makes superfluous the affirmative defenses provided in section

9607(b), each of which carves out from liability an exception based on causation. Without a clear congressional command otherwise, we will not construe a statute in any way that makes some of its provisions surplusage.

Furthermore, as the State points out, accepting Shore's arguments would open a huge loophole in CERCLA's coverage. It is quite clear that if the current owner of a site could avoid liability merely by having purchased the site after chemical dumping had ceased, waste sites certainly would be sold, following a cessation of dumping, to new owners who could avoid the liability otherwise required by CERCLA. . . . We will not interpret section 9607(a) in any way that apparently frustrates the statute's goals, in the absence of a specific congressional intention otherwise.

D. LeoGrande's Personal Liability

We hold LeoGrande liable as an "operator" under CERCLA, for the State's response costs. Under CERCLA "owner or operator" is defined to mean "any person owning or operating" an onshore facility, and "person" includes individuals as well as corporations. More important, the definition of "owner or operator" excludes "a person, who, without participating in the management of a . . . facility, holds indicia of ownership primarily to protect his security interest in the facility." The use of this exception implies that an owning stockholder who manages the corporation, such as LeoGrande, is liable under CERCLA as an "owner or operator." That conclusion is consistent with that of other courts that have addressed the issue. In any event, LeoGrande is in charge of the operation of the facility in question, and as such is an "operator" within the meaning of CERCLA.

Judgment affirmed.

Case Questions

1. What is the issue in this case?
2. Assuming that Shore was certain to be found liable as a current owner, why did the state seek to have LeoGrande held personally liable as a operator?
3. Is it fair to hold landowners liable for cleanup of toxic spills that they do not cause? Explain.
4. Why is the common law of nuisance not an effective way to deal with leaking hazardous waste dumps? Explain.

Community Right to Know

Superfund amendments require companies that use hazardous substances to notify the communities surrounding their operations about any hazardous substances used or stored on the site. This program dovetails with a regulation under the Occupational Safety and Health Act requiring companies using hazardous substances to inform their workers of the hazards associated with those substances and of safety information. Companies are also required to tell local authorities what those substances are and to provide **material safety data sheets (MSDSs)** that contain safety and treatment information. The act also requires companies to immediately notify the local authorities whenever there is a release of an extremely hazardous substance. To make proper use of this information, the statute also requires the local authorities to make emergency plans that designate who would respond to a particular emergency and how they would respond.

END–OF–CHAPTER QUESTIONS

1. Is tort law an effective method of combating pollution? Of compensating victims? Why or why not?
2. Compare and contrast the policies behind the Clean Air Act, Clean Water Act, and RCRA.
3. Describe the state-federal cooperative model of implementing pollution control laws. Can you suggest another model?
4. Critique the cradle to grave regulatory scheme for hazardous wastes.
5. Who ultimately pays for a Superfund cleanup? Explain.
6. Spur Industries operated a large cattle feedlot on farmland west of Phoenix. Years after Spur had established its operation, Webb Development began building retirement homes north of the feedlot.

The development expanded southward until it came so close to the feedlot that some 1,300 lots closest to the feedlot were unfit for homes because of the odor and fly problems. The feedlot admittedly used the best management practices. The developer chose the area because the farmland cost much less than land closer to Phoenix. Would the homeowners have a claim for nuisance? Does the developer have a claim for nuisance? What remedy would be appropriate? See *Spur Industries Inc. v. Del E. Webb Development Co.,* 494 P.2d 700 (Ariz. 1972).

7. The Atomic Energy Commission produced a 10-volume plan advocating a program to develop a liquid metal fast breeder reactor. The program plan called for test facilities and demonstration plants and the AEC conceded that an EIS would be required before those facilities could be built. The AEC claimed, however, that no EIS was required for the research and development program itself. Is this research and development plan a ''major federal action''? If so, when should an EIS be prepared? At the very start of research when little is known? Or later, when commercial feasibility has been demonstrated? See *Scientists' Institute for Public Information v. Atomic Energy Commission,* 481 F.2d 1079 (D.C. Cir. 1973).

8. Narragansett operated an asphalt concrete plant. The company renovated its air pollution control devices by replacing the existing fabric filter dust collector with an electrostatic precipitator. New source performance standards (NSPS) apply to any facility that ''constructed'' a new source or ''modified'' an old source. Is replacement of old pollution equipment with new equipment that does not emit more pollutants ''construction'' of a new source or ''modification'' of an old source? See *United States v. Narragansett Improvement Co.,* 571 F.Supp. 688 (D.R.I. 1983).

9. A psychotic vagrant opened a valve on the bottom of one of Southern Pacific's railroad tank cars, releasing 21,000 gallons of formaldehyde. Formaldehyde is classified by EPA as a hazardous substance. The spill flowed into a nearby culvert and from there into a small creek and then into a navigable river. The tank car was a standard design commonly used for this purpose. The car was standing in a switching yard in an unfenced, unlighted, and unpatrolled area. The track on which the car stood was accessible by footpaths and was across a field from a bus station.

A 38-year-old vagrant, who had a history of psychotic illness, admitted having been under the tank car, but his testimony was only partially coherent. The valve required two separate steps to be opened, but the evidence indicated that the plug on the valve had come loose during transportation, so that it was easy to open when it normally would have been impossible without special tools.

The Clean Water Act absolves the owner of a facility from responsibility for spills of hazardous substances into navigable waters if the spill was caused solely by a third party. Does Southern Pacific meet the test for the third-party defense? Explain. See *Southern Pacific Transportation Co. v. United States,* 13 Ct.Cl. 402 (1987).

10. Hayes refurbishes airplanes, including repainting them. Repainting the planes with spray guns generated a waste mixture of paint and solvents. This waste is defined as a hazardous waste due to its ignitability. Hayes contracted with Performance Advantage to dispose of this waste, but Performance dumped it illegally in unpermitted disposal sites. Hayes claimed that it did not know the waste was classified as hazardous or that Performance was dumping it at a site without a permit. Is knowledge that the waste was hazardous or that a permit was needed required to assess civil penalties? Criminal penalties? See *United States v. Hayes International Corp.,* 786 F.2d 1499 (11th Cir. 1986).

Chapter 52

International Business Law

■

CRITICAL THINKING INQUIRIES

As you read this chapter, you should be able to address the following:

- Define international law and identify its sources.
- Compare and contrast the advantages and disadvantages of various means of carrying on international business.
- Analyze the regulatory environment of a multinational enterprise.
- Evaluate remedies available to U.S. firms in response to unfairly traded imports.
- Compare the relative advantages of arbitration and litigation as international dispute resolution mechanisms.

MANAGERIAL PERSPECTIVE

Plain-Grinder, Inc. (PGI) is a Delaware corporation that manufactures high-quality machine tool equipment. At a recent trade show in New York, PGI's marketing director learned of a very substantial interest in its products from several companies based in Southeast Asia. PGI has never sold its products outside the United States. At a high-level meeting of PGI's executives two camps emerged, one favorably and the other unfavorably disposed to doing business in Southeast Asia.

- What are PGI's options for entering foreign markets in Southeast Asia?
- What are the legal implications of doing business overseas?
- What are the potential problems and how might disputes be resolved?

The essential nature of the law of international business transactions is indicated by the rate at which business is being globalized. Approximately $25 trillion in capital is transferred across national boundaries each year. In addition, political solutions are increasingly being proposed in response to the United States's burgeoning trade deficit (the amount that imports exceed exports) and the negative economic consequences to the United States of local businesses moving their operations across the border and overseas.

Opportunities abound for companies doing business in foreign countries. In order to operate successfully in today's global legal environment, businesses need some understanding of the law of international business transactions. (Chapter 34 treated international sales transactions.) This chapter introduces the business student to the principles of international business law. It is chiefly concerned with the legal environment in which international business operates.

INTERNATIONAL LAW

Traditionally, **international law** has been defined as the law governing relations among nations. Thus, international law governs boundary disputes between nations. Likewise, international diplomacy, negotiations, and treaty relations are subjects of this traditional definition. Communications, aviation, transportation, and commerce are also affected by international law principles.

A broader definition of international law includes **comparative law**—a comparison of two different legal systems. Thus, the American approach to contract law might be compared to a similar approach—the British, for example—or a dissimilar approach such as the Hindu or communist approaches. Comparisons may yield valuable insights not only about what the law is, but also what it ought to be.

International law includes the law governing international organizations, such as the United Nations, or the law governing **supranational organizations**— nations that cooperate together above and beyond national limitations— such as the European Economic Community[1] (EC) commonly known as the Common Market. Rules of supranational organizations affect individuals directly without further action by any country. In contrast, the rules of international organizations must be adopted by a country before they affect an individual.

International law also includes the law governing entities that do business in different countries. The applicable law might be the domestic law of one of the countries where its business transactions are performed. The particular domestic law to be applied is the subject of rules called conflict of laws rules. Another source of law governing relations among entities of different countries are treaties or international agreements.

History of International Law

International law, as traditionally defined (the law governing relations between nations), was derived from Roman law and church canon law. Initially, international law was viewed as being based on natural or a "higher" law. Gradually, as positivism began to shape legal thinking in the 19th century, international law emphasized the need for a nation's consent to a rule of international law (see Chapter 2 for more on natural law and positivism). Thus, many international law cases today turn on the ability to prove a nation's consent to some legal obligation.

Domestic and International Lawmaking

In **domestic law,** legislatures enact statutes, courts generally make binding precedents,[2] and administrative agencies issue regulations. Limited comparisons may be drawn between domestic and international lawmaking.

For example, the European Economic Community has legislative, judicial, and administrative powers that are similar to a nation's. ANCOM, the Andean Common Market,[3] also exercises these powers to a lesser extent. Other looser regional federations, such as the Association of Southeast Asian Nations (ASEAN), exercise even fewer lawmaking powers.

---

[1]The EC was created by the Treaty of Rome in 1957. Consisting of 12 member nations, the EC has served to harmonize and coordinate the economic policies of its members. Its legal authority is exercised through four institutes—the Commission, the Council, the European Parliament, and the Court of Justice.

[2]Many countries do not recognize the principle of *stare decisis* and so do not view court decisions as a source of law in the common law sense.

[3]ANCOM was founded in 1969 by the Cartegena Agreement. Consisting of four South American member nations, it has achieved far less economic or legal integration than the EC.

The United Nations has an international court called the International Court of Justice (ICJ). The ICJ has 15 judges, no 2 of whom may be from the same country. Located at The Hague in the Netherlands, the ICJ has two basic sources of jurisdiction. The first is **advisory jurisdiction,** in which the UN or its organs (such as the Security Council) may request an opinion on a legal matter. These advisory opinions are nonbinding on the requesting agency.

The second basis of jurisdiction is called **contentious jurisdiction,** in which one state can bring a dispute against another state as long as both have accepted the ICJ's jurisdiction. Individuals and businesses may not resolve their disputes before the ICJ—only nations. In the following case, the United States claimed that the ICJ had no contentious jurisdiction to decide a case filed against it by Nicaragua.

NICARAGUA v. UNITED STATES
I.C.J. Reports 392 (1984)

Nicaragua contended that the United States violated international law by certain military and paramilitary activities conducted in Nicaragua and in the waters off Nicaragua's coast. Nicaragua filed a case against the United States in the ICJ. The United States claimed that the ICJ had no jurisdiction to decide this case.

The United States had, in 1946, recognized the jurisdiction of the ICJ subject to the right to modify this recognition by giving a six-month notice. On April 6, 1984, the United States sought to withdraw this recognition immediately with respect to any dispute arising between it and a Central American country. Three days later, Nicaragua filed this application with the ICJ.

OPINION

The most important question relating to the effect of the 1984 notification is whether the United States was free to disregard the clause of six months' notice which, freely and by its own choice, it had appended to its 1946 Declaration. In so doing the United States entered into an obligation which is binding upon it vis-a-vis other States. . . . Although the United States retained the right to modify the contents of the 1946 Declaration or to terminate it, a power which is inherent in any unilateral act of a State, it has, nevertheless assumed an inescapable obligation towards other States . . . by stating formally and solemnly that any such change should take effect only after six months have elapsed as from the date of notice.

In sum, the six months' notice clause forms an important integral part of the United States Declaration and it is a condition that must be complied with in case of either termination or modification. Consequently, the 1984 notification, in the present case, cannot override the obligation of the United States to submit to the compulsory jurisdiction of the Court vis-a-vis Nicaragua, a State accepting the same obligation.

The first ground of inadmissibility relied on by the United States is that Nicaragua has failed to bring before the Court parties whose presence and participation is necessary for the rights of those parties to be protected and for the adjudication of the issues raised in the Application. The United States first asserts that adjudication of Nicaragua's claim would necessarily implicate the rights and obligations of other States, in particular those of Honduras, since it is alleged that Honduras has allowed its territory to be used as a staging ground for unlawful uses of force against Nicaragua and the adjudication of Nicaragua's claims would necessarily involve the adjudication of the rights of [these other] States.

[The ICJ rejected this contention, claiming that third parties were free to intervene in this case if they wished, or institute separate proceedings to protect their rights.]

Secondly, the United States regards the Application as inadmissible because each of Nicaragua's allegations constitutes no more than . . . a single fundamental claim, that the United States is engaged in an unlawful use of armed force, or breach of the peace, or acts of aggression against Nicaragua, a matter which is committed by the Charter and by practice to the competence of other organs, in particular the United Nations Security Council. All allegations of this kind are confided to the political organs of the Organization for consideration and determination; the United States quotes Article 24 of the Charter, which confers upon the Security Council "primary responsibility for the maintenance of international peace and security."

. . . The Charter accordingly does not confer *exclusive* responsibility upon the Security Council . . . . While in Article 12 there is a provision for a clear demarcation of functions between the General Assembly and the Security Council, in respect of any dispute or situation, that the former should not make any recommendation with regard to that dispute or situation unless the Security Council so requires, there is no similar provision anywhere in the Charter with respect to the Security Council and the Court. The Council has functions of a political nature assigned to it, whereas the Court exercises purely judicial functions. Both organs can therefore perform their separate but complementary functions with respect to the same events.

The [next] ground of inadmissibility put forward by the United States is that the Application should be held inadmissible in consideration of the inability of the judicial function to deal with situations involving ongoing conflict. The allegation, attributed by the United States to Nicaragua, of an ongoing conflict involving the use of armed force contrary to the Charter is said to be central to, and inseparable from, the Application as a whole, and is one which a court cannot deal effectively without overstepping proper judicial bounds. The resort to force during ongoing armed conflict lacks the attributes necessary for the application of the judicial process, namely a pattern of legally relevant facts discernible by the means available to the adjudicating tribunal, establishable in conformity with applicable norms of evidence and proof, and not subject to further material evolution during the course of, or subsequent to, the judicial proceedings. It is for reasons of this nature that ongoing armed conflict must be entrusted to resolution by political processes.

. . . A situation of armed conflict is not the only one in which evidence of fact may be difficult to come by. . . . Ultimately, however, it is the litigant seeking to establish a fact who bears the burden of proving it; and in cases where evidence may not be forthcoming, a submission may in the judgment be rejected as unproved, but is not to be ruled out as inadmissible [at the outset] on the basis of an anticipated lack of proof. As to the [difficulty] of implementation of the judgment . . . [i]t should be observed that the Court "neither can nor should contemplate the contingency of the judgment not being complied with." Both the Parties have undertaken to comply with the decisions of the Court. [This contention by the U.S. was therefore rejected.]

The Court unanimously found that Nicaragua's Application was admissible.

Case Questions

1. What are the issues in this case?
2. Analyze the decision and rationale for each contention.
3. Less than two months after this ruling by the ICJ, the United States unilaterally announced that it was withdrawing from any further proceedings in this case. What is the international impact of a withdrawal of this nature?

Sources of International Law

When no exact analogy to domestic lawmaking can be found on the international plane, international law must look to other sources. The charter of the ICJ lists sources of international law (see Figure 52–1). They are treaties, international custom, general principles of law recognized by civilized nations, and judicial decisions and opinions of legal scholars.

Treaties

Treaties function like contracts between two or more nations. Treaties can affect political issues, such as boundary disputes or nuclear tests. They may also cover such matters as international trade, tariffs, taxation, aviation, and human rights.

International Custom

International custom is a widely accepted official practice by many nations over a long period of time.

Figure 52–1 Article 38 of the Statute of the International Court of Justice

1. The Court, whose function is to decide in accordance with international law such disputes as are submitted to it, shall apply:
(a) international conventions . . . establishing rules expressly recognized by the contesting states;
(b) international custom, as evidence of a general practice accepted as law;
(c) the general principles of law recognized by civilized nations;
(d) . . . judicial decisions and the teachings of the most highly qualified publicists of the various nations, as subsidiary means for the determination of rules of law.

Figure 52–2 Options for Entering a Foreign Market

Indirect export sales → Direct export sales → Foreign agent → Foreign distributor → Licensing → Foreign branch

Since international law is based on a nation's consent, if a nation has consistently rejected a custom, the custom is not binding on that nation. To illustrate, the international custom of not prosecuting a foreign diplomat either civilly or criminally is now a well-settled principle of international law.

General Principles of Law

General principles of law recognized by civilized nations are found by examining domestic legal systems. To illustrate, most nations, as a matter of domestic law, do not admit coerced confessions into evidence.

Judicial Decisions and the Opinions of Legal Scholars

In the strict sense, judicial decisions and the opinions of legal scholars are not actually international law, but evidence what an international law principle might be. Thus, a decision by the ICJ or a scholarly opinion by the International Law Commission (a UN commission made up of international legal scholars to assist in the development of international law) carries great weight. In contrast, a domestic court decision from the U.S. Supreme Court or the opinion of one scholar would carry much less weight before an international court or between countries.

ENTERING A FOREIGN MARKET

Plain-Grinder, Inc. (PGI), from the opening scenario, is considering entering a foreign market. At a meeting of PGI's corporate board, several ideas were tossed out by board members concerning how best to do business overseas.

The average American lawyer is probably unversed in advising PGI about the legal issues involved in entering a foreign market. Nevertheless, good legal advice may be obtained from many sources. Some very large law firms have foreign branch offices or arrangements with legal advisers in other countries. Thus, these firms may be consulted for help. Names of legal advisers actually residing in another country may be gleaned from large accounting firms, banks, and businesses with overseas operations. U.S. embassies can also supply names, as can the Department of Commerce.

Some of the best business help may be obtained from the numerous trade associations that are present in almost all state capitals and in most large cities. States also have many services for overseas trade development, including seminars, counseling, handbooks, and referrals. Likewise, the federal government, through the Department of Commerce and the International Trade Administration, to select just two examples, can offer a wealth of information. One government printing office publication, "A Basic Guide to Exporting,"[4] contains literally thousands of sources of overseas information along with addresses and phone numbers. Chambers of Commerce are also extremely helpful.

Options in Doing Business Overseas

PGI will find that the available options open for selling its equipment may be viewed along a spectrum. The spectrum ranges from very simple to very complex legal transactions, depending on the degree of PGI's foreign presence (see Figure 52–2). Frequently, a company begins its foreign business activity on the left side of the spectrum and evolves over time to more complex commitments.

---

[4]This publication can be obtained from the U.S. Government Printing Office, Washington, D.C., and is published by the Department of Commerce's International Trade Administration.

Indirect Export Sales

Many U.S. companies act as intermediaries to help export products from an American firm to foreign buyers. For example, PGI could employ an export management company (EMC) and market a product overseas through the EMC's network of contacts in the foreign market. Likewise, Export Trading Companies (ETC) may assist in marketing products overseas. An ETC takes title to the goods in the United States. A seller retains title when selling through an EMC. ETCs usually provide a range of financial services and are generally larger than an EMC. A federal statute, the Export Trading Company Act, encourages the formation of ETCs by removing antitrust liability and by permitting banks to set up ETCs.

Direct Export Sales

In the event PGI decides to sell its machine tool equipment without the use of an intermediary, it would have to address several issues before entering a contract with a Southeast Asian buyer. These include the method of resolving disputes, discussed at the end of this chapter, and the risk of loss or destruction of the equipment in shipping, discussed in Chapter 34. Other concerns include:

- The language to be used in the contract.
- The law that will govern the contract.
- U.S. export and foreign import regulations.

PGI must make sure that one particular language (preferably English for an American firm) is the official language for the final draft of the contract. A choice of language clause within the contract accomplishes this purpose. Particularly when very technical legal terms and product descriptions are used, language differences, if unresolved, may create many disputes in interpretation.

A choice of law clause simply selects the law that will be used to govern the contract. Parties are generally free to select the governing law so long as the law chosen has a substantial relationship to the contract. U.S. law would have such a relationship to PGI's contract. The law of Madagascar would not.

The United Nations Convention on Contracts for the International Sale of Goods (CISG) provides for a law of international sales of goods and resembles UCC Article 2. (See Chapter 19.) The CISG has been ratified by the United States and many other countries, including several Southeast Asian nations with whom PGI might be dealing. A choice of forum clause designates the particular country where any disputes will be resolved. PGI would most likely wish to have the United States be the selected forum. The Hague Convention on the Choice of Court and a similar convention on choice of law encourages judicial respect for choice of forum and choice of law clauses.

To export goods from the United States, PGI may need to obtain an export license. Different types of licenses are required, depending on the destination of the goods, the type of goods, and any specific export restrictions applying to certain countries. The Export Administration Regulations promulgated by the Department of Commerce govern the type of license required. Violation of U.S. export laws may result in either civil or criminal penalties.

The United States, in addition to requiring a license, also prohibits the diversion of products to unauthorized countries or the participation in a boycott of any friendly country under the Export Administration Act. PGI thus could not agree to stop doing business with Singapore in order to get a more favorable contract from a Hong Kong company.

Specific foreign import requirements, including documentation requirements, are listed in a guide published by the Bureau of National Affairs called *The Export Shipping Manual*.

Foreign Agents and Distributorships

Two common ways available to PGI to market products in Southeast Asia would be through Southeast Asian agents or distributors. There are a number of basic differences between agents and distributors.

As a general rule, foreign agents do not buy or sell products for their own accounts, but simply collect orders and forward them to the principal (e.g., PGI). The agent's payment for its services would be a commission—that is, a percentage of the sales price. The sales contract thus directly links PGI with a Southeast Asian buyer.

In contrast, the foreign distributor buys or sells the product for its own account. The Southeast Asian distributor's payment is therefore the difference between the purchase price from PGI and the selling price to Southeast Asian buyers. There is no direct contractual link between PGI and the ultimate buyer.

American sellers (principals) cannot assume that the agency rules learned here in the United States apply worldwide. In some countries, principals have more limited liability for the acts of their agents—in others, more expanded liability. Obviously, local law must be consulted. This is particularly so since in many countries, this local law of agency or distributorship may not be varied by contract. The reason for the choice of agency or distributorships are complex. They include possible differences in tax treatment both here and abroad, reporting requirements, standards of liability, antitrust concerns, and local laws protecting one of the parties (typically, an agent).

Licensing

Perhaps high tariffs (import fees) or shipping costs make a direct or indirect sale to Southeast Asian buyers by PGI noncompetitive. On the other hand, a direct manufacturing presence by a PGI-controlled company has other drawbacks. The Southeast Asian government may be very inhospitable to foreign-controlled companies. There may also be a risk of **expropriation**—that is, the seizure of PGI's assets by that government.

A middle ground between direct and indirect sales and actual production abroad is **licensing.** Licensing is a contractual arrangement in which a licensee (a Southeast Asian company) pays royalties (compensation) to a licensor (PGI) for the right to use the licensor's property. That property may include PGI's trademarks, patents, copyrights, trade secrets, or manufacturing and marketing know-how.

Of course, licensing is not without risks. Since PGI loses some control over its property, PGI must be concerned with the misuse of its property by the licensee. For example, the licensee may disclose PGI's secrets to a third party. Or the licensee may produce inferior products, harming PGI's reputation for quality.

Significant legal concerns in licensing agreements include taxes, antitrust laws, particularly in the European Economic Community, and U.S. export restrictions on the transfer of technical data. Further, many countries, particularly in the third world, have laws prohibiting restrictions on the licensee's use of the licensed technology.

Foreign Branches and Subsidiaries

PGI may decide to open a branch of its operation in Southeast Asia. A branch is simply PGI's direct legal presence in another country. The advantage of a branch over licensing, for example, is that PGI maintains total control of the business operation of the branch.

The major disadvantage of a branch is that the total assets of PGI, not only in Southeast Asia but in the United States as well, are exposed to liability in a Southeast Asian lawsuit. In addition, certain countries prohibit the creation of a foreign branch. In contrast, Mexico offers economic and regulatory incentives for companies to locate in that country. As a result, there are almost 2,000 assembly plants on the Mexican-U.S. border. This **maquiladora** (border plant) industry employs 500,000 workers.

A subsidiary, in contrast, is a separate legal corporation, set up by a parent corporation (e.g., PGI) under the laws of the foreign country. There are a number of advantages of a subsidiary over a branch. These advantages include the shielding of assets of the parent corporation outside of that foreign country from legal judgments, a better corporate image in the foreign country, the ability to apply for governmental grants in the foreign country, and better access to security markets and courts in the foreign country. The major disadvantages compared to branches include possible negative tax consequences and the cost and legal difficulty of establishing a subsidiary abroad.

A joint venture may be a method for establishing a direct presence in a foreign country. A joint venture is a cooperative arrangement between two or more firms to do business for profit. Through joint ventures, which may be organized as partnerships or even corporations, a company may do business in another country. Some countries require that one of the joint venturers be a host nation resident.

MULTINATIONAL ENTERPRISES

A **multinational enterprise (MNE)** is a business enterprise with several unique traits. First, the business operates some commercial enterprise—for example, a subsidiary, a branch, or an unincorporated association—in two or more countries. Second, there is common ownership of the enterprises through some stock or contractual linkage. Third, the entire organization has a common purpose that is achieved through its overall management. Within this broad definition, one can place such corporate giants as IBM, General Electric, and McDonald's, as well as corporate midgets operating a single foreign subsidiary.

MNEs are not creatures of international law. They are created by national law and, currently, only national law controls them. In recent years, there has been a push toward some kind of international control of MNE behavior due to the concerns about MNEs summarized in Figure 52–3.

Regulating the Multinational Enterprise

The chief means of regulating MNEs is the nation's own domestic law. Because MNEs are not subject to any one nation's laws, there is a perceived need to regulate MNEs on the international level.

Various international codes of conduct are specifically aimed at MNEs. At the present time, these codes are not legally enforceable but rather require voluntary compliance. Of course, courts or legislatures may adopt one of the voluntary codes as a model for domestic law.

The major voluntary codes have been primarily published by various United Nations agencies. One very important non-UN code, however, is published by the Organization for Economic Cooperation and Development (OECD). The OECD is an organization made up of the major market economies such as the United States, Japan, France, and Great Britain and is designed to promote economic growth. With this constituency, the OECD guidelines have had a major impact on MNEs, most of whose headquarters are in OECD member nations.

Figure 52–3   Host Government Concerns about MNEs

- Intrusion on the political environment of the local host government.
- Introduction of values that are inimical or at least insensitive to local cultural concerns such as consumerism.
- Freedom from accountability to any one legal system due to an MNE's ability to limit regulation of its affairs by restructuring its form and by using choice of forum clauses and tax havens.
- Securing a monopolistic or oligopolistic position in a local economy, displacing local businesses.
- Decapitalizing a host country by withdrawing royalties and dividends from the host country.
- Lacking loyalty to any particular government or people.
- Unwillingness to disseminate technology or information to the host country.
- Possessing unfair negotiating advantages with labor by its ability to relocate its facilities.

Problem of Expropriation

Expropriation (or nationalization) is the taking of a foreign national's property for a public purpose. The rate of such takings rapidly accelerated after World War II as the result of revolutions and the elimination of colonial rule; however, expropriations have more recently subsided.

The major issue in most expropriation cases is the extent of compensation. The U.S. State Department has traditionally called for ''prompt, adequate, and effective'' compensation. This standard has been rejected by the UN General Assembly's Declaration on the Establishment of a New International Economic Order (NIEO). A major aim of the NIEO declaration was to redistribute global wealth from industrialized to developing nations. The NIEO supports the view that only ''appropriate'' levels of compensation should be paid, the amount to be determined solely by the law and courts of the nationalizing country. Appropriate compensation rarely, if ever, includes amounts for natural resources such as oil or gas. In addition, subtractions are contemplated for such things as environmental damage or any unjust circumstances surrounding the initial foreign investment.

The United States has set up the Overseas Private Investment Corporation (OPIC) to protect American corporations from the risk of expropriation. OPIC is a quasi-governmental agency that, for an annual premium, insures foreign investments. Some private insurance companies also insure against the risk of expropriation.

If an expropriation occurs, a foreign nation might not be subject to suit in U.S. courts under two doctrines: the **act of state doctrine** and **sovereign immunity.** The act of state doctrine arises from the reluctance of U.S. courts to judge the validity of acts of foreign countries within their own territory. At least a part of this judicial reluctance springs from a desire to avoid interfering with the executive branch's conduct of foreign relations. Thus, the act of state doctrine relates to the constitutional idea of separation of powers by keeping the courts out of a foreign country's executive branch business.

Sovereign immunity relates not to the acts of a foreign country but to its status as a sovereign state. Simply being a foreign state makes it immune from suit in the United States in certain limited circumstances under the Foreign Sovereign Immunities Act (FSIA). Basic exceptions to immunity from suit under the FSIA include claims based on a foreign state's:

- Expropriation of property located in the United States.

- Rights in real property located in the United States.

- Torts occurring within the United States.

- Commercial activities carried on in the United States or that cause a direct effect in the United States.

The following case discusses the commercial activity exception to the FSIA.

TEXAS TRADING & MILLING CORP. v. FEDERAL REPUBLIC

647 F.2d 300 (2d Cir. 1981)

Nigeria, an African nation that exports considerable amounts of high-grade oil, contracted to buy huge quantities of Portland cement. It overbought. The country's docks and harbors became clogged with ships waiting to unload. As a result, imports of other goods ground to a halt. The nation repudiated its contracts.

Disgruntled suppliers sued, and Nigeria sought to insulate itself from liability under the doctrine of sovereign immunity. The cases were ultimately consolidated on appeal to the Second Circuit Court of Appeals.

KAUFMAN, Judge

. . . [T]he section most frequently relevant, and the one applicable here, is [section] 1605 [of the Foreign Sovereign Immunities Act of 1976]. It provides, in part:

(a) A foreign state shall not be immune from the jurisdiction of courts of the United States or of the States in any case—

(2) in which the action is based upon a commercial activity carried on in the United States by the foreign state; or upon an act performed in the United States in connection with a commercial activity of the foreign state elsewhere; or upon an act outside the territory of the United States in connection with a commercial activity of the foreign state elsewhere and that act causes a direct effect in the United States.

Crucial to each of the three clauses of [section] 1605(a)(2) is the phrase "commercial activity." . . . If the activity is not "commercial," but, rather, is "governmental," then the foreign state is entitled to immunity. . . .

. . . We are referred to no less than three separate sources of authority to resolve this fundamental definitional question [i.e., the meaning of the phrase "commercial activity"].

The first source is statements contained in the legislative history itself. Perhaps the clearest of them was made by Brunn Rawest, then Chief of the Foreign Litigation Section of the Civil Division, Department of Justice. Rawest stated: "[I]f a government enters into a contract to purchase goods and services, that is considered a commercial activity. It avails itself of the ordinary contract machinery. It bargains and negotiates. It accepts an offer. It enters into a written contract and the contract is to be performed." The House Report seems to conclude that a contract or series of contracts for the purchase of goods would be *per se* a "commercial activity" . . . and the illustrations cited by experts who testified on the bill . . . support such a rule. Or, put another way, if the activity is one in which a private person could engage, it is not entitled to immunity.

The second source for interpreting the phrase "commercial activity" is the "very large body of case law which exist[ed]" in American law upon passage of the Act in 1976. Testifying on an earlier version of the bill, Charles N. Blower, then Legal Adviser of the Department of State, stated:

[T]he restrictive theory of sovereign immunity . . . which has been followed by the Department of State and the courts since it was articulated in the familiar letter of Acting Legal Adviser Jack B. Tate . . . would be incorporated into statutory law. This theory limits immunity to public acts, leaving so-called private acts subject to suit. The proposed legislation would make it clear that immunity cannot be claimed with respect to acts or transactions that are commercial in nature, regardless of their underlying purpose.

Finally, current standards of international law concerning sovereign immunity add content to the "commercial activity" phrase of the FSIA. . . . The legislative history states that the Act "incorporates standards recognized under international law," and the drafters seem to have intended rather generally to bring American sovereign immunity practice into line with that of other nations. At this point, there can be little doubt that international law follows the restrictive theory of sovereign immunity.

Under each of these three standards, Nigeria's . . . contracts . . . qualify as "commercial activity." . . . Nigeria's activity here is in the nature of a private contract for the purchase of goods. Its purpose—to build roads, army barracks, whatever—is irrelevant. . . . We find defendants' activity here to constitute "commercial activity," . . . .

. . . [T]he relevant inquiry under the direct effect clause when plaintiff is a corporation is whether the corporation has suffered a "direct" financial loss. To discover whether breach of a contract causes this type of loss, we look to *Carey v. National Oil Corp.* . . . In *Carey,* we decided that a direct effect can

arise not only from a tort, but from cancellation of a contract for the sale of oil as well. Here, the effect of the suppliers was "direct." They were beneficiaries of the contracts that were breached.

Finally, the most difficult aspect of the direct effect clause concerns its phrase, "in the United States" . . . [T]he financial loss in these cases occurred "in the United States." First, the cement suppliers were to present documents and collect money in the United States, and the breaches precluded their doing so. Second, each of the plaintiffs is an American corporation. . . . [The court found sovereign immunity was inapplicable.]

Case Questions

1. What two issues did the court analyze here to find an exception to Nigeria's sovereign immunity?

2. What is the "restrictive theory" of sovereign immunity found in the Tate letter?

3. Analyze "Direct effect in the United States is shown."

4. Is the claim of sovereign immunity appropriate to commercial activities? Analyze.

International Ethical Codes of Conduct

To date, two groups have established ethical codes of conduct for MNEs. However, neither code has been formally adopted—they serve as voluntary guidelines. The United Nations Center for Transnational Corporations and the Organization for Cooperation and Development (OECD) established codes designed to ensure that MNEs respect and serve the goals of the host nation and that the MNEs are fairly treated. The codes set ethical codes for the MNEs and the host country and cover such issues as technology transfer, international financial transfers, labor relations, and nationalization.

There are specialized codes of conduct and guidelines as well. For example, the Sullivan Principles were designed to guide corporations who wanted to act responsibly in their business dealings with South Africa. The Sullivan Principles embrace nonsegregation within the work force and equal employment opportunity. The author of the Sullivan Principles later repudiated them and called for a complete boycott of business with South African companies. However, because of more recent com-

mitments on the part of the South African government to end apartheid, the United States lifted certain sanctions, thus setting an example for other nations.

The Valdez Principles, promulgated by the Coalition for Environmentally Responsible Economics, are directed toward environmental concerns and arose when the *Exxon Valdez* tanker steered off course and spilled millions of tons of oil off the coast of Alaska. The damages to the environment are enormous and continue to be assessed. At last count, fewer than 30 corporations had adopted the Valdez Principles (see Figure 52–4).

INTERNATIONAL TRADE REGULATION — GATT

In order to promote world trade, a framework for removing trade barriers and protectionist policies was constructed. That framework is called the General Agreement of Tariffs and Trade (GATT). GATT resulted from a series of meetings between countries from 1946 to 1948. GATT has been amended from time to time through multilateral negotiations.

Figure 52-4   Summary of the Valdez Principles

1. Protection of the biosphere by controlling the release of pollutants that cause environmental damage to the air, water, earth, and its inhabitants.
2. Conservation of natural resources.
3. Reduction and disposal of waste with a preference for recycling.
4. Wise use of energy.
5. Minimization of environmental and safety risks to employees and communities by employing safe technology and preparedness for emergencies.
6. Marketing of safe products and services and informing consumers of the environmental impact of such products and services.
7. Damage compensation for the environmental harm we cause.
8. Full disclosure to employees and to the public of environmental harm our operations pose or cause.
9. The employment on the board of directors of at least one person qualified to represent environmental interests.
10. Conducting an annual self-evaluation and working toward independent environmental audits to be made available to the public.

Currently, over 110 nations are members of GATT. The United States has adopted GATT by way of presidential executive order. Although many of its provisions have been enacted by statute, GATT as a whole has never been adopted by Congress nor by a treaty.

The principle of nondiscrimination is at the heart of GATT. This means that GATT members agree to unconditionally grant the same rate of duty and treatment to other GATT members, regardless of the country of origin. For example, the United States may not charge higher tariff rates for imported coffee from Brazil than it charges to Colombia or Nigeria for coffee.

This nondiscrimination principle is expressed through a Most Favored Nation Clause (MFN). MFN treatment is the normal or general treatment given to a product. GATT does permit numerous exceptions to MFN treatment. For example, a country may depart from this treatment to protect its national security. In addition, nations may grant preference to less-developed countries in the form of lower tariffs.

U.S. Trade Remedies

Both GATT and U.S. statutes permit remedies to be imposed on unfairly traded imports. These remedies include antidumping duties, countervailing duties, section 337 remedies, and escape clause proceedings.

GATT has been fairly successful at reducing tariff barriers. However, there are a number of problems that continue to hamper the efficiency of GATT. GATT really has no effective enforcement structure and depends upon voluntariness. Nor does GATT have the extensive resources necessary to monitor trade regulations and breaches. Also GATT is focused on the traditional exchange of currency for goods and has not directed attention to trade in services or **countertrade.** Countertrade occurs when multinationals, for example, agree to an arrangement other than the sale and purchase of products, as for example, a bartering arrangement.

Antidumping Duties

Dumping is the practice of selling goods in a foreign market at a price lower than in the home market. Selective, predatory dumping may drive competitors in the foreign market out of business. To illustrate, assume that a Korean-manufactured sneaker is sold in the Korean market for $45 (U.S.) but is dumped in the United States at a price of $25. The Korean manufacturer, if successful in eliminating U.S. competition, would be left in a monopolistic or oligopolistic position in the United States.

Antidumping duties (ADs) are imposed on unfairly priced imports to reflect the import's true—as opposed to dumped—price if the price in the home market is higher than in the U.S. market and the dumped import is causing a material injury to a domestic industry. Typically, a petition is filed by an affected domestic industry (although the U.S. government may initiate the proceedings as well) with the Department of Commerce's International Trade Administration (ITA). The ITA determines the comparative prices. The International Trade Commission (ITC), an independent federal agency, then determines whether the dumped imports are causing a material injury to that domestic industry. The Department of Commerce's issuance of a final antidumping order (appealable to the Court of International Trade) terminates the antidumping procedure.

Countervailing Duties

Governments frequently pay bounties or give grants to manufacturers to encourage exports. These subsidized goods can then be sold for a lower price in the foreign market.

Countervailing duties (CVDs) may be imposed on the imported goods to counteract these subsidies. The procedure for imposing CVDs parallels the antidumping procedure. First, the ITA determines the existence and amount of the subsidy. Second, the ITC determines whether the subsidized imports are causing a material injury to a domestic industry. The Department of Commerce's issuance of a final CVD order terminates the procedure.

Section 337 Remedies

Section 337 of the Tariff Act is directed at unfair methods of import competition other than dumping or subsidies. These unfair methods include patent, copyright, and trademark infringement, as well as such anticompetitive activities as palming off, false advertising, and misappropriating trade secrets.

U.S. companies or the ITC may initiate an action against a section 337 violator. To win, an industry must show, in addition to unfair competition, that it has been or likely will be substantially injured by the practices.

The major drawback to a section 337 action is that the ITC has no power to grant damages, which is the typical remedy imposed by district courts in these cases. In addition, the president, in his discretion, may veto any relief granted by the ITC.

Sometimes goods with a U.S. trademark are manufactured overseas under a U.S. license. A businessperson will then buy these goods and ship them to the United States in an attempt to undercut the U.S. trademark holder's selling price in the United States. This practice is possible when the dollar strengthens against foreign currencies. This entire practice is called **gray market** importing and has been, on occasion, held to be illegal by the ITC.

Escape Clause Proceedings

The U.S. Trade Act of 1974 (section 201) permits the president, on the recommendation of the ITC, to impose remedies on any product whose importation is causing serious injury to domestic industry. These remedies may include import quotas or supplemental duties on the products. These are called **escape clause** proceedings, since by them a country may escape tariff concessions granted under GATT.

The escape clause proceeding takes place before the ITC on the filing of a petition by an affected industry. The ITC determines whether that industry is suffering, or is threatened with, a serious injury substantially caused by increasing imports. Any rec-

ommendation of a remedy is forwarded to the president, who has 60 days to grant or deny relief. Under this power, the president has restricted the import of motorcycles, oil, and stainless steel flatware.

IMPORTS

The U.S. Customs Service is primarily responsible for administering the Tariff Act, the U.S.'s principal law covering imports. One of the Service's major responsibilities is to assess and collect duties on imported goods. The Service also protects American health, safety, and welfare by banning, for example, illegal drugs or weapons from entry. Finally, the Service enforces customs laws and agency or court-ordered remedies for trade problems.

Tariff rates or duties on imported goods are set by tariff schedules. The schedules classify items first by product category. The United States and other countries are moving toward a uniform system of classifying products.

Once a product category is determined, the rate of tariff is determined by the product's country of origin. There are typically three different tariff rates in the United States: the lowest rate or duty-free rate for products from the least developed countries, the normal or most favored nation rate (MFN), and the full rate to non-MFN countries.

The third step in calculating the applicable duty is the dollar valuation of the item by the Customs Service. Disputes between the Service's determination and an importer on any one of these three steps are appealable to the Court of International Trade (CIT). The CIT is an American court located in Washington, D.C. Decisions of the CIT are appealable to the U.S. Court of Appeals for the Federal Circuit and ultimately to the U.S. Supreme Court.

North American Free Trade Agreement

The North American Free Trade Agreement (NAFTA) was signed by Canada, the United States, and Mexico in 1992, and on legislative approval in those countries will be effective. The agreement is designed to reduce tariffs (on about 20,000 products) and trade barriers. When fully operational it will create the largest free trade area in the world — 360 million consumers and a $6.5 trillion gross domestic product.

NAFTA also deals with copyright and trademark protection, environmental protection, and the creation of special panels to resolve disputes among the three countries.

There is concern in the United States that the agreement will result in the loss of U.S. jobs to cheaper Mexican labor and that it will encourage U.S. companies to relocate to Mexico to avoid stringent health, safety, and environmental laws. Others fear that it will put Caribbean nations at a competitive disadvantage and that NAFTA should be expanded to include the Western Hemisphere. The following article suggests the complexity that relates to the determination of tariffs on imported automobiles and NAFTA's impact.

Nationality of Autos Big Trade Issue*

In a factory covering the area of 19 football fields Honda is making engines with American and Japanese parts that will be put into Civics assembled in Canada. Question: what nationality is the engine, and, ultimately, the car?

■ ■ ■

Under the rules of a 1988 trade agreement between the United States and Canada, the engines and cars were considered to be Japanese—at least by the Customs Service, which says that as a result Honda owes $17 million in duties on cars that came across the border from Canada in 1989 and 1990.

But [a] new trade agreement [NAFTA] . . . treats the cars as Canadian, free from import duties. And the Canadians successfully insisted that the treaty apply retroactively, which means Honda, which has yet to pay its Customs Service debt because of legal wrangling, will not have to, thereby making it the only large beneficiary of the provision for determining a car's nationality.

■ ■ ■

Canada had feared that the customs audit, released last spring, would discourage Asian and European companies from building factories in Canada to supply the American market.

■ ■ ■

From the 75 tons of 25-pound aluminum ingots that arrive here every day, wrapped in dishwasher-size bales with thick plastic bands, to the sand used to mold iron-alloy piston cylinder sleeves, many of the materials and virtually all of the labor here is as American as the cornfield outside.

As it happens, the president of the company, the money to build the factory and some engine parts assembled here, such as the camshafts, come straight from Japan.

Many additional parts come from the American subsidiaries of Japanese companies, although the Customs Service counted them as American in its audit.

It Gets Confusing

So how did Customs determine the cars were Japanese? The old rules involved rounding off a lot of figures, since car makers were allowed to calculate the nationality of each major part, like the top and bottom of the engine, and then take the average of all the major systems to determine the overall nationality.

The Customs Service calculated, with unusual reasoning, that the top halves of the engines were American and the bottom halves were American, but that when put together, the entire engine was 100 percent Japanese. Customs officials reached this conclusion by rounding down the weight of the American content of the top halves of the engines. Once one of the halves was counted as less than American the entire engine counted as Japanese.

The American content of the top half of the engine, known as the engine head, could be rounded down because of another unusual interpretation by the Customs Service. The 1988 pact specified that only the "direct costs of assembly" should be included, so the service excluded the cost of molding and polishing engine parts here.

■ ■ ■

Engines are the guts of cars, and once the Customs Service had deemed the engine to be Japanese, the entire Civic was labeled as Japanese, making it subject to the 2.5 percent tax on cars imported to the United States.

Over all, the interpretations reduced the American and Canadian content of the Civic to 48 percent, from the figure of 69 percent asserted by Honda. To qualify for duty-free treatment, at least 50 percent of a car's value must be made in the two countries.

■ ■ ■

Since Government auditors left its plant in 1990, Honda has increased the North American content of its engines. For example, the engine bolts that hold the bearing cap and the crankshaft casing were imported then and now are bought from an American company. . . .

The new trade rules [NAFTA] will resolve some of the confusion by eliminating rounding. The nationality of each car will depend on the number of domestically produced parts, weighted by the price of each part. That means, of course, that each car maker will have to create a remarkable bureaucracy to keep track of the nationality of most of the 5,000 or more parts that go into each car.

To qualify for duty-free treatment, a car maker will initially have to spend as much money on North American parts as on imported parts. Over the next eight years [under NAFTA] . . . auto makers will . . . have to increase the North American content to 62.5 percent of the total . . . [in order to be free of import taxes].

Thought Questions

1. How large a part does politics play in customs calculations? Explain.
2. Why do you think Canada negotiated the new trade agreement [NAFTA] with the United States making the cars import tax free?
3. What is the motivation and hope of the United States? Explain.

RESOLVING INTERNATIONAL DISPUTES

Despite parties' attempts to resolve disputes through preventive means such as contract drafting, or such means as negotiations, differences may be irreconcilable. This section briefly discusses two basic international dispute resolution devices: arbitration and litigation.

Arbitration

Arbitration was discussed in Chapter 3. It has enormous advantages as an international dispute resolu-

tion mechanism. Arbitration addresses the following issues: parties may be unfamiliar with any selected country's laws, publicity from litigation may be unwanted, a particular court system may decline jurisdiction, judgments may be difficult to enforce. In addition, a commercial relationship typically continues even while a dispute is being arbitrated.

Through a contractual arbitration clause, parties to an agreement may provide that arbitration will be the exclusive remedy for any disputes arising between them. A well-drafted arbitration clause includes a mechanism for selecting an arbitrator, the governing rules of procedure, the place, the language, the substantive law, the division of expenses, the time in which arbitration is to be held, and a waiver of any judicial review of the arbitration award.

Various treaties, including the United Nations Convention on the Recognition of Foreign Arbitral Awards (which the United States has signed), encourage American recognition of international arbitration agreements and awards. Model rules for arbitration have been issued by the United Nations, the World Bank, the International Chamber of Commerce (ICC), and many nations, including the United States. The ICC has a permanent and busy court of arbitration established to handle international disputes.

Litigation

At times, arbitration may not be possible because a court has struck down an arbitration clause within the contract, there is no arbitration clause in the contract, or a court will not enforce an arbitration award. Issues that must be determined concerning litigation include the law that applies and the place for the lawsuit. The issues may be resolved through choice of law and choice of forum clauses, as previously mentioned.

Service of a complaint may be accomplished in many countries through a procedure outlined in The Hague Convention on the Service Abroad of Judicial and Extrajudicial Documents. The United States is a member of the Convention. The Hague Convention Taking Evidence Abroad governs discovery procedures in signatory nations. The United States is also a member of this Convention.

The following case concerns the enforceability of a foreign judgment in an American court.

TAHAN v. HODGSON
662 F.2d 862 (D.C. Cir. 1981)

The plaintiff, Chamis Tahan, operates a travel agency in Jerusalem that acted as agent for the travel agency of the defendant, Sir John G. Hodgson. A dispute arose and the relationship ended. Tahan claimed that Hodgson owed him money for past services. Hodgson denied the debt.

Tahan filed suit in Israel. Tahan's attorney served Hodgson personally in Jerusalem, but Hodgson refused to acknowledge service on the grounds that the papers were drawn in Hebrew, a language he did not read. Hodgson subsequently returned the papers to Tahan's attorney's office. Tahan then obtained a default judgment against Hodgson in the amount of $54,114.40, plus legal fees in the amount of $3,870.00. It is this default judgment in Israel that Tahan now seeks to have enforced by the courts of the United States. The district court refused to enforce the Israeli judgment. Tahan appealed.

WILKEY, Judge

The seminal case in the area of enforcement of foreign judgments is *Hilton v. Guyot*. *Hilton* found that "the merits of the case should not, in an action brought in this country upon the judgment, be tried afresh, as on a new trial or on appeal, upon the mere assertion of the party that the judgment was erroneous in law or in fact" if

there has been opportunity for a full and fair trial abroad before a court of competent jurisdiction, conducting the trial upon regular proceedings, after *due citation* or voluntary appearance of the defendant, and under a system of jurisprudence likely to secure an impartial administration of justice between the citizens of its own country and those of other countries, and there is nothing to show either prejudice in the court, or in the system of laws under which it was sitting, or fraud in procuring the judgment, or any other special reason why the comity [respect for other countries' laws] of this nation should not allow it full effect. . . .

. . . [T]he legal issues raised in this case reduce to three. First, was there "due citation" of defendant? That is, was there effective service of process? Second, would enforcement of this default judgment be "repugnant to fundamental notions of what is decent and just" in the United States? And, third, what applicability does the doctrine of reciprocity have to this case?

A. Effective Service of Process
Even if defendant were unable to read Hebrew, he should have surmised that the papers being served upon him were legal in nature, and that he could

ignore them only at his peril. In fact, it is certain that he *was* cognizant of the fact that the papers served upon him were legal in nature. The parties had, after all, been involved in a heated legal dispute for several months, making charges and countercharges against one another and rendering accounts and counteraccounts.

. . . As a man who had done business in Israel for some years, he seems to have been singularly insensitive to the problem he faced by means of his having been personally served with process in Israel. He showed bad judgment in not putting the matter in the hands of an Israeli lawyer. It would be insulting were we to require that the Israeli legal machinery adapt itself by translating the official language of that country, Hebrew, into any defendant's language.

B. Public Policy

. . . We believe that American public policy will not be violated by enforcement of the Israeli judgment.

C. The Reciprocity Requirement

It is unlikely that reciprocity is any longer a federally mandated requirement for enforcement of foreign judgments or that the District of Columbia itself has such a requirement that this court is obliged to follow.

The logical rule would seem to be that, in the absence of an action by the legislature, the courts should refrain from creating or resurrecting a reciprocity doctrine. The issue of how best to respond to a foreign nation's scrutinization of an American judgment is, after all, a political one. . . .

Even assuming that reciprocity is required by either the federal government or the District of Columbia, we would still enforce the Israeli judgment since Israel in all probability *would* enforce a similar American judgment and thus meets the reciprocity

criterion. Israel provides for enforcement of foreign judgments by a statute. . . . Israeli courts have indeed ruled that a party with a foreign judgment may, if it wishes, bring suit on the foreign judgment in a local Israeli court and obtain an Israeli judgment.

As commerce becomes increasingly international in character, it is essential that businessmen recognize and respect the laws of those foreign nations in which they do business. They cannot expect foreign tribunals to have one set of laws for their own citizens and another, more favorable, set for the citizens of other countries. It is also essential that American courts recognize and respect the judgments entered by foreign courts to the greatest extent consistent with our own ideals of justice and fair play. Unfettered trade, good will among nations, and a vigorous and stable international—and national—economy demand no less.

We find enforcement of the Israeli judgment to be required by these goals and American precedent. The judgment of the district court is accordingly *Reversed and Remanded*.

Case Questions

1. What is the issue in this case?

2. Summarize the requirements the Supreme Court case of *Hilton v. Guyot* sets out as prerequisites for the enforcement of a foreign judgment in this country. What is the reason for each? Analyze.

3. What if the service was in a rare language not easily translatable? Should the result be different?

4. Analyze: "Comity is the most important factor in this case."

5. What are the practical problems of collecting a judgment in another country?

END–OF–CHAPTER QUESTIONS

1. How has international law changed in the past 30 years? Point out specific evidences of shifts in recent years.

2. Should the ICJ have greater enforcement powers in regard to its judgments? Why or why not? If so, what would these powers look like?

3. How might intellectual property be protected internationally? Suggest various possibilities.

4. What positive aspects can you list concerning MNEs? What aspects are negative?

5. Compare the advantages and disadvantages of international arbitration.

6. Cuba retaliated against the U.S. reduction of imports by nationalizing many U.S. companies in Cuba. Cuba's seizure of sugar contracted for by a U.S. company was challenged in U.S. courts. Should U.S. courts determine the legitimacy of the Cuban seizure? Analyze. Assume that a statute was passed that prohibited U.S. courts from declining to exercise jurisdiction based on the act of state doctrine. How would this affect your answer? See *Banco Nacional de Cuba v. Sabbatino*, 376 U.S. 398 (1964).

7. A sales contract was entered between an American importer and the manufacturer of Swiss typewriters. Nothing in the contract specified currency of payment. After the contract was entered, the exchange rate of dollars to Swiss francs changed so radically that the American importer's costs doubled. What law is applicable to this contract? Why? Is the contract subject to any escape routes? What kinds of clauses ought to have been in this contract to protect the American importer?

8. Imported embroidered pillowcases were classified as a product of the People's Republic of China rather than as a product of Hong Kong. The cloth was manufactured in China, but it was cut and assembled in Hong Kong. How should the proper country of origin be determined in this case? Why would importers challenge a customs determination that these pillowcases were the product of China? Ana-

lyze. See *Belcrest Linens v. United States*, 573 F.Supp. 1149 (C.I.T. 1983).

9. Rhone Poulenc, S.A., a French company, produced ASM, a chemical used in the manufacture of detergents. The ITC determined that Rhone Poulenc was selling ASM at less than its fair value and assessed duties. Rhone Poulenc challenged the ITC's determination, claiming that there was no threat of material damage to any domestic industry from its exports. What sorts of data would be useful in determining whether an import materially threatens domestic industry? See *Rhone Poulenc, S.A. v. United States*, 592 F.Supp. 1318 (C.I.T. 1984).

10. Nelson Bunker Hunt entered a contract with British Petroleum (B.P.) to convey half of his interests in a Libyan oil field in exchange for certain production and other payments by B.P. Hunt also was to have no personal liability to B.P. under this contract. After Libya nationalized this oil field, B.P. sought and obtained a British court's judgment that B.P.'s contract with Hunt was frustrated and that Hunt owed B.P. $35 million dollars. Hunt declined to accept service in this British suit but he did file suit in the United States to have the contractual ''no liability'' provision enforced. Is the British court's judgment entitled to recognition in this U.S. proceeding? Why or why not? Analyze. See *Hunt v. B.P. Exploration Co.*, 492 F.Supp 885 (N.D. Tex. 1980).

Chapter 53

The Liability of Accountants and Auditors

■

CRITICAL THINKING INQUIRIES

As you read this chapter, you should be able to address the following:

- Compare and contrast the ordinary professional standard of care with the fiduciary standard.
- Analyze the defenses to negligence available to an accountant.
- Evaluate the evolution of the accountant's liability to third parties.
- Criticize an accountant's potential liability under federal securities law.
- Analyze: ''The SEC process of enforcement against an accountant is efficient and effective.''
- Create alternatives for deterring accountant misconduct.

MANAGERIAL PERSPECTIVE

McKenzie, Howell, and Sensenig is an accounting firm that has been rising in stature, adding partners and expanding its client base rapidly. There is no policy manual in place in the firm that informs the accountants of legal requirements and responsibilities and warns them of potential pitfalls.

Rhesa Rowen, a new partner, raised concerns at the monthly partnership meeting about the emerging higher standards required by accountants, their potential liability to nonclients that rely on their audits, and the maze of securities and other laws that may pose difficulties for accountants. She suggested a committee be formed to construct a detailed manual covering these matters. Randall Ross, a senior partner, responded to Rowen, ''We do not need a manual to tell us what we already know. There is just one simple rule at McKenzie, Howell, and Sensenig: Be honest.''

- Who is right—Rowen or Ross?
- What would you advise Rowen to include in such a manual?
- How could the firm ensure that the manual is accurately updated?

The liability of the accountant is a topic about which McKenzie, Howell, and Sensenig and all accountants should be informed. Accountants have been facing increasing legal liability. In a recent four-year period, ''Big 8'' accounting firms alone paid out at least $179 million in settlements and judgments.[1] Part of this liability springs from a growing recognition of the accountant's responsibility to the investing public at large. Moreover, accountants, like other professionals, are perceived as having ''deep pockets'' due to their insurance coverage.

Accountants play several important roles in our economic life. Our complex economy requires the activities of accountants to check and verify that individuals and businesses act as good stewards of other people's capital. In a free-market economy, which relies heavily on investments through financial markets, accountants also provide the information for directing investments in the most efficient manner.

This chapter brings together some of the areas already studied in various parts of this text. The chapter covers the common law liability of accountants with reference to contract and tort law principles. Further, accountants' liability intersects with public law—in this case, for example, the law regulating securities. Here, both civil and criminal liability must also be addressed. Finally, the chapter briefly examines the law of accountants' working papers and the accountant-client privilege.

COMMON LAW LIABILITY OF ACCOUNTANTS

Common law theories of accountant liability include contract and tort. In these areas, the law has evolved from a protectionism mode to a liberal extension of liability. Also relevant to this section are defenses to liability, to be discussed later in this chapter.

Contract Liability

The basic principles of contract discussed earlier in this book also apply to contracts for an accountant's services. For example, there must be a valid offer containing definite terms, and an acceptance (see

Chapter 12). If no fee is stated, a reasonable fee will be implied by the court. Contingent fee arrangements, in which an accountant charges on a percentage basis for work done, are prohibited by the ethical rules of the American Institute of Certified Public Accountants (AICPA),[2] except with respect to tax matters pending before a government agency. In tax cases, an accountant may charge a percentage of any amount saved by his or her services.

Rules concerning illegal contracts apply as well to accountants. Thus, an unlicensed accountant will not be able to collect a fee since the licensing statute is regulatory in nature (see Chapter 15).

Other basic rules of contract law also apply to accountants. The statute of frauds applies to contracts for accounting services not performable within a year (see Chapter 16). Since the contract for accounting services is personal in nature, it may not be assigned without both parties' consent (see Chapter 17). An accountant's obligations are discharged due to impossibility, disability, or death (see Chapter 18).

An accountant who fails to perform according to the terms of a contract is liable for breach of contract. Damages are measured by the client's loss (see Chapter 18).

Tort Liability

An accountant who fails to properly perform the services agreed to may also be liable under tort principles. The most common tort theory creating liability for the accountant is negligence. Negligence is defined as a departure from the standard of care of an ordinary prudent member of the accounting profession that causes injury to the client.

Ordinary Standard of Care

The accountant is not an insurer of work nor is the accountant expected to perform services perfectly. Rather, the accountant is held to the ordinary professional standards applied to persons performing that type of work (see Figure 53–1). Concerning

---

[1]The ''Big 8'' are the eight largest accounting firms in the country.

[2]The AICPA is a national professional organization of CPAs whose membership is made up of those possessing certified public accounting certificates issued by their state boards of accountancy. The Financial Accounting Standards Board (FASB) is a committee set up by the AICPA to establish accounting standards.

Figure 53–1 Good Accountants' Practices

- Use office standards and professional practice manual.
- Use and maintain working papers.
- Keep records and files well organized.
- Establish an internal system to notify clients of relevant changes in the law, deadlines, and filings.
- Computerize records with adequate backups.
- Continue education.
- Hold frequent partnership meetings to discuss ethical issues.
- Review liability insurance policies periodically.

Figure 53–2 Auditors' Opinions

Type of Opinion	Description
Unqualified	The financial statements are free from any material misstatement and accurately reflect the financial position of the company
Qualified	The financial statements are fairly presented except for departures that are set out in the auditor's explanatory paragraphs
Adverse	Financial statements do not fairly present the financial position of the company
Disclaimer	Insufficient evidence to form an opinion on the fairness of the financial statements

audits, there are fundamental requirements of care codified in the *Statement on Auditing Standards No. 1* issued by the AICPA. These are further elaborated on in other sections of the AICPA Professional Standards. While these, of course, must be studied in detail, courts generally hold that an auditor who complies with generally accepted accounting principles (GAAP)[3] or generally accepted auditing standards (GAAS)[4] and AICPA professional standards exercises the required standard of reasonable care. When auditing an accountant's financial statements, an auditor may give any one of four types of opinions: unqualified, qualified, adverse, and disclaimer (no opinion) (see Figure 53–2).

Illustrations of a breach of the standard of care of an ordinary prudent accountant or auditor include failing to render a proper opinion based on the evidence (see *In the Matter of Greenspan*, presented later in this chapter), failing to adequately train or supervise junior personnel, failing to discover embezzlement achieved through check lapping,[5] weak internal controls, or kiting,[6] and losing the client's books or records.

Fiduciary Standard of Care

On occasion, an accounting firm is held to a standard of care higher than reasonable professional care. Although the ordinary engagement to audit is tested by a negligence standard, special circumstances may create a fiduciary relationship. A **fiduciary** is someone in a position of trust who must exercise the highest degree of candor and honesty. Accountants who perform investment-advisory services for a client, serve on the board of directors, or prosecute claims for tax refunds are fiduciaries.

Liability to Nonclients

Accounting reports and auditors' opinions are examined and relied on by third parties, such as potential creditors of a business, who have *no* contractual relationship with the maker of the report. (A sample auditor's opinion letter is illustrated in Figure 53–3). These persons are not in **privity** with the accountant—that is, they are not parties to the auditing contract between the accountant and the client. Virtually every case that has considered the matter of an accountant's liability to a nonclient third party begins with a discussion of Justice Cardozo's landmark decision in *Ultramares Corp. v. Touche*.[7]

---

[3]GAAP is a "technical accounting term which encompasses the conventions, rules, and procedures necessary to define accepted accounting practice at a particular time" [AICPA, Professional Standards, *Auditing* ¶ 150.02, at 82 (CCH 1985).]

[4]GAAS includes *Statements on Auditing Standards (SAS)* promulgated by the AICPA.

[5]Lapping is the misappropriation of a customer's payment. The customer's account is credited when another customer pays at a later date.

[6]Kiting is the creation of bank balances that are false. An employer uses the period necessary to clear checks to conceal a cash shortage or to prevent overdrafts.

[7]174 N.E. 441 (N.Y. 1931).

> **Figure 53–3**   Auditor's Opinion Letter
>
> **McKenzie, Howell, & Sensensig, C.P.A.s**
> **247 Shorward Dr.**
> **Great Neck, N.Y. 11027**
>
> June 9, 1995
>
> To the Board of Directors:
>
> We have audited the accompanying balance sheet of Creative Graphics Company as of December 31, 1994, and the related statements of income, retained earnings, and cash flows for the year then ended. Our responsibility is to express an opinion on these financial statements based on our audit.
>
> We conducted our audit in accordance with generally accepted auditing standards. Those standards require that we plan and perform the audit to obtain reasonable assurance that the financial statements are free of material misstatement. An audit includes examining, on a test basis, evidence supporting the amounts and disclosures in the financial statements. An audit also includes assessing the accounting principles used and significant estimates made by management, as well as evaluating the overall financial statement presentation. We believe that our audit provides a reasonable basis for our opinion.
>
> In our opinion, the financial statements referred to above represent fairly, in all material respects, the financial position of Creative Graphics company as of December 31, 1994, and the results of its operations and its cash flows for the year then ended, in conformity with generally accepted accounting principles.
>
> McKenzie, Howell, & Sensenig
> Great Neck, N.Y.

In *Ultramares,* Touche Niven & Co. was hired to prepare and certify the 1923 balance sheet of Fred Stern & Co. Touche knew that these balance sheets would be distributed to Stern's present and future creditors, who would loan money to Stern on the basis of these reports (plaintiff Ultramares was not one of Stern's creditors in 1923). Touche certified that Stern had a net worth of over $1 million when Stern was, in fact, insolvent. The following year Stern went bankrupt and Ultramares, one of Stern's creditors, sued Touche for the loans it made to Stern that were now unrecoverable.

The court held that Touche could not be liable to a third party such as Ultramares for *ordinary negligence* since:

> If liability for negligence exists, a thoughtless slip or blunder, the failure to detect a theft or forgery beneath the cover of deceptive entries, may expose accountants to a liability in an indeterminate amount for an indeterminate time to an indeterminate class.[8]

It was a fear of imposing potentially unlimited liability on the accounting profession, then, that led the court in *Ultramares* to exempt accountants from liability to nonclients for ordinary negligence.

Departure from Ultramares

In the years after *Ultramares,* many courts across the country grappled with the holding of that case. Some agreed that an accountant could not be liable to nonclients, except for intentional fraud or gross negligence. "Honest belief" by the accountant was sufficient in certain cases to exempt the accountant from liability. Other courts, troubled with the broad exemption given to accountants by *Ultramares,* distinguished their holdings from the *Ultramares* decision. For example, in a New York high court case,[9] where the particular third parties who would rely on the audit were identified before the audit was made, the accountant was held liable to the third party for ordinary negligence. Here, the users of the financial report were an identifiable group of limited partners of the accountant's client.

A further extension of *Ultramares* held an accountant liable for ordinary negligence if the *class of persons* using the financial report was foreseen, even if the *particular* user was not foreseen. A class of persons might be "all commercial banks," as opposed to a particular user such as "Chase Manhattan Bank." Thus, in one case,[10] the accountant prepared financial statements knowing that the statements were to be used by its client to procure a loan. The accountant, who did not know the identity of the potential third-party lender, was held liable to the eventual lender for injuries resulting from the

---

[8]174 N.E. at 444.
[9]*White v. Guarente,* 372 N.E.2d 315 (N.Y. 1977).
[10]*Rusch Factors, Inc. v. Levin,* 284 F.Supp 85 (D.R.I. 1968).

accountant's ordinary negligence. This extension of liability for negligence to a known *class* of third parties is called the *Restatement rule* since it was proposed by the *Restatement (Second) of Torts*.

The following case expands an accountant's liability even beyond a foreseen *class* of third parties or a *particular* foreseen user, to *all* foreseeable potential users of a financial statement.

ROSENBLUM v. ADLER
461 A.2d 138 (N.J. 1983)

The plaintiffs, Harry and Barry Rosenblum, brought this action against Touche Ross & Co. (Touche), a partnership, and the individual partners. Touche, a prominent accounting firm, had audited the financial statements of Giant Stores Corporation (Giant). The Rosenblums, allegedly relying on the correctness of the audits, acquired Giant common stock in conjunction with the sale of their business to Giant. That stock proved to be worthless after the financial statements were found to be fraudulent. The Rosenblums claimed that Touche negligently conducted the audits and that Touche's negligence was a proximate cause of their loss. The case rose to the Supreme Court of New Jersey.

SCHREIBER, Judge

We have never passed upon the problem of an accountant's liability to third persons who have relied on negligently audited statements to their economic detriment. Many other jurisdictions have limited an accountant's liability to those with whom the accountant is in privity. . . . The leading opinion is that of Chief Judge Cardozo in *Ultramares v. Touche*. . . .

Chief Judge Cardozo . . . believed that imposition of this type of exposure would be an undue burden upon the [accountants], when balanced against the functions they performed.

We long ago discarded the requirement of privity in a products liability case based on negligence. . . . It is interesting to compare [Justice Cardozo's] language in *MacPherson* [a products liability case] with his position in *Ultramares*.

[*MacPherson*] demonstrate[s] that negligent misrepresentations referring to products may be the basis of liability irrespective of privity. . . .

Why should a claim of negligent misrepresentation [of accountants] be barred in the absence of privity when no such limit is imposed where the plaintiff's claim . . . is based on liability for defects in products arising out of a negligent misrepresentation? If recovery for defective products may include economic loss, why should such loss not be compensable if caused by negligent misrepresentation? The maker of the product and the person mak-

ing a written representation with intent that it be relied upon are, respectively, impliedly holding out that the product is reasonably fit, suitable and safe and that the representation is reasonably sufficient, suitable and accurate.

The fairness of the imposition of a duty on accountants cannot be appraised without an understanding of the independent accountant's auditing function. It is particularly important to be aware of the independent auditor's role in order to assess the propriety of imposing any duty to those who may rely on the audit.

At one time the audit was made primarily to inform management of irregularities and inefficiencies in the business. . . . That function remains one of the principal reasons for the audit. Gradually a need for independent audits was generated by public ownership of business enterprises and by requirements of the stock exchanges and the Securities and Exchange Commission (SEC). Institutional investors, investment specialists, stockholders, and lenders demanded more and reliable information. It is now well recognized that the audited statements are made for the use of third parties who have no contractual relationship with the auditor. Moreover, it is common knowledge that companies use audits for many proper business purposes, such as submission to banks and other lending institutions that might advance funds and to suppliers of services and goods that might advance credit. . . . Government has increasingly utilized accounting as a means to control business activities. Some examples of such use are public utility rate regulation and regulation of bank and insurance companies.

The auditor's function has expanded from that of a watchdog for management to an independent evaluator of the adequacy and fairness of financial statements issued by management to stockholders, creditors, and others.

The objection to imposing a duty on accountants to third persons to whom the statements have been given by the company for proper business purposes is the specter of financial catastrophe. It is feared that the unknown costs will be so severe that accounting firms will not be able to absorb the losses that will be visited upon them, particularly because in all likelihood the audited clients will be judgment proof or unable to satisfy their share of the indebtedness due. The reasonableness of this concern is questionable.

Independent auditors have apparently been able to obtain liability insurance covering these risks or otherwise to satisfy their financial obligations. We have no reason to believe that they may not purchase malpractice insurance policies that cover their negligent acts leading to misstatements relied upon by persons who receive the audit from the company pursuant to a proper business purpose.

The extent of financial exposure has certain built-in limits. The plaintiffs would have to establish that they received the audited statements from the company pursuant to a proper company purpose, that they, in accordance with that purpose, relied on the statements and that the misstatements therein were due to the auditor's negligence and were a proximate cause of the plaintiff's damage. The in-

jured party would be limited to recovery of actual losses due to reliance on the misstatement. Negligence of the injured party could bar or limit the amount of recovery under [contributory negligence]. The accounting firm could seek indemnification or contribution from the company and those blameworthy officers or employees. The auditors could in some circumstances, such as when auditing a privately owned company, expressly limit in their certificates the persons or class of persons who would be entitled to rely upon the audit. Some commentators recognize that a "factor which may limit the foresight of reasonable reliance is the presence of a disclaimer of responsibility attached to the information."

. . . The cause is remanded to the trial court for further proceedings consistent with this opinion.

Case Questions

1. Why did Chief Justice Cardozo limit an accountant's liability for negligence to cases involving privity? Analyze.

2. Are the cases of liability for negligent misrepresentations concerning manufactured products distinguishable from negligent misrepresentations concerning accounting services? What did the court think?

3. As a policy matter, is it wise to hold auditors liable for their errors that were relied upon by nonclients? Why or why not? Does the availability of liability insurance affect your answer?

4. Analyze the factors that limit an auditor's exposure to nonclient third parties.

Discovery of Fraud

One duty owed by auditors to third parties is the discovery of employee or management fraud. It was the failure of the auditors, as part of their annual investigation, to discover management fraud that contributed to the massive fraud in the *Equity Funding* case.[11]

---

[11]The failure of Equity Funding Corp. of America involved the gross inflation of net income and assets through the issuance of fictitious life insurance policies, fictitious sales commissions, and failure to record borrowings as liabilities.

As a result of their participation in the fraud, three former auditors served time in prison. Other accounting firms paid almost $44 million settling claims resulting from the *Equity Funding* litigation.

Likewise, the failure of E.S.M. Government Securities in 1985 and the failure of Fund of Funds, both allegedly due to management fraud, led to liability suits in the $100 million range. Investors of Miniscribe Corp. won a $200 million judgment against Coopers & Lybrand because a jury concluded that the firm was at fault for failing to discover falsified financial records of the company. Recent failures of thrift institutions such as Lincoln Savings and Loan and Silverado Banking, Savings and Loan Association, have resulted in large settlements by big accounting firms for their involvement in the collapse of those financial institutions. The following article discusses various fraudulent schemes and methods to ferret out fraud.

Financial Fraud: Schemes and Indicia*

Fraud is a familiar topic in today's financial news. Traveling under such aliases as "white collar crime," "defalcation," "irregularities," and "embezzlement," the problem's apparent ubiquity in recent years has made it a major focus of the business community.

■ ■ ■

Various recurring fraudulent schemes and some methods of detection are outlined below.

Petty Cash

Employee embezzlement of petty cash often is camouflaged by false or inadequate documentation. Petty cash disbursements tend to be categorized as either expendable items, like meals and taxi rides, or as items of a more physical nature, such as office supplies. Most petty cash schemes center on expendables. As a result, those searching for fraud should try to chart the relationship of the two disbursement categories over an extended period of time and watch for signs of a dramatic rise in expendables in relation to goods. If such a rise coincides with a personnel change, it becomes more significant and warrants follow-up.

One technique for uncovering fraud is to compare the dates on which employees received advances or disbursements from . . . funds with the sick leaves, vacation time or other absences of the approving supervisors. . . .

Another technique is to vary the usual pattern of counting petty cash. For example, it should first be counted early in the morning, preferably on a Friday since it is believed that most borrowings take place on that day of the week. Later that day—after lunch but before the first petty cash clerk leaves for the day—it should be counted a second time. Many employees who borrow from petty cash replace the money before the next count, never expecting that the money will be counted twice the same day. Use of this technique will reveal not only the shortages but the identities of the employees responsible for the embezzlement as well.

Accounts Payable

In its simplest form, accounts payable fraud involves the formation of a dummy corporation to invoice the payer and receive the funds. However, some payable frauds manipulate valid invoices from existing companies. As with petty cash frauds, more sophisticated accounts payable schemes manipulate services rather than assets.

■ ■ ■

Government contracts that are awarded on a "cost plus" basis are particularly susceptible to accounts payable schemes. In such contracts, fictitious invoices are merely passed along as costs to the purchaser.

*Source: Marvin Levy, "Financial Fraud: Schemes and Indicia," *Journal of Accountancy,* August 1985. Reprinted with permission.

Cash Inventory

In cash inventory schemes, inventory is purchased with cash or its equivalent, rather than by check, and is not placed on the books. . . .

This fraud may be detected by identifying ratios between inventory components that are out of proportion with each other after adjusting for beginning and ending balances. If, for example, one X and one Y are used to make one item Z, which is sold, then the use of 3,000 units of X and 1,000 units of Y might indicate a cash inventory scheme relative to the purchase of Y. High beginning or ending levels of either component also must be taken into consideration.

■ ■ ■

In addition to inventory components, freight expenses often are out of proportion when a cash inventory fraud is perpetrated. . . .

■ ■ ■

Cash inventory schemes are not uncommon among franchisees and managements reporting to absentee owners. Managements or owners do this to avoid paying taxes or to pay a smaller royalty to the franchiser, since both the tax due and the royalty are based on sales.

False Payroll

The false-payroll scheme involves the creation of a fictitious employee, with management cashing . . . spurious payroll checks. Such checks most often bear a second endorsement, indicating that the person to whom the check is payable was not the one who cashed it. Canceled checks play an important role in many schemes because a cursory examination seems to indicate payment to the original payee.

■ ■ ■

One technique that is useful in detecting false-payroll fraud is the preparation of a list of all employees who have failed to elect life or medical insurance. Ghosts seldom do so, since it is a waste of money. Preparing this list is a cost-effective technique because legitimate exceptions, such as coverage by a spouse, can be verified easily. . . .

Another method of exposing a ghost is to examine Social Security numbers. Numbers assigned to a ghost often are numbers not issued by the government. The creator of the ghost may not be aware of this.

■ ■ ■

. . . Sometimes the perpetrator unwittingly establishes a trail that leads to himself by using the first three digits of his own number. . . .

Lapping Schemes

In lapping schemes, employees steal from one customer's account and attempt to cover the theft by applying to that account later collections from another customer. These embezzlements are most likely to occur when a company's poor internal controls do not provide for different employees to open the mail and schedule receipts, prepare deposit slips, go to the bank and post to the books.

Lapping schemes can become extremely difficult for perpetrators to control because they can grow to involve hundreds of accounts. For this reason, many lapping schemes perpetrators cannot take much time off from their jobs. Some are now putting their data on disks and tracking their schemes by micro-computer.

■ ■ ■

A review of retrieved customer checks will lead to the identification of deposits made in the company's name in a bank with which the company doesn't do business. An increase in customer complaints that accounts are being billed for amounts previously paid are often the first clue that lapping is taking place. Customers should be asked to submit these checks so that they may be examined for deposit data. Companies can sometimes benefit from implementing a sampling program whereby customers are offered a coupon of some specified value in return for copies of their canceled checks.

■ ■ ■

In the end, it should be remembered that businesses exist to make a profit—and any finding not in concert with this basic premise should be viewed with suspicion.

Thought Questions

1. Fraud is a composite of motive, method, and opportunity. How can management take away one or more of these necessary ingredients?

2. Explain why the following would be an indication of possible fraud:
   a. A high rate of employee turnover in the accounting or bookkeeping departments.
   b. The failure of an employee to take a leave.
   c. Photocopies of invoices in the files.

3. What can industries do to police themselves in order to reduce financial fraud?

Defenses to Negligence

In an action based on negligence, the accountant may raise various defenses. Common defenses are contributory negligence and the statute of limitations.

Contributory Negligence

As was stated in Chapter 8, a tortfeasor may escape liability for negligence if the plaintiff was contributorily negligent. In most states, the plaintiff's contributory negligence is no longer an absolute defense. Instead, under modern comparative negligence principles, the plaintiff's damages are reduced by his or her relative fault. In general, accountants have not fared well in raising the contributory negligence defense.

For example, in one case,[12] Ernst & Ernst was sued by a trustee in bankruptcy. The trustee alleged that the debtor's financial condition was aggravated by Ernst & Ernst's negligent audit. Contributory negligence was raised as a defense since the presi-

dent of the bankrupt company knew the financial condition was much worse than reported. The court stated that it was the duty of auditors to ferret out such knowledge and ''[contributory] negligence . . . is a defense only when it has contributed to the accountant's failure to perform his contract and to report the truth.''

There are cases in which contributory negligence has been accepted as a defense. Thus, where a client rejects an auditor's recommendation or, in contrast, realizes that the auditor's advice is wrong and still follows that advice, the auditor has successfully invoked the contributory negligence defense. The auditor's success may be due to the plaintiff's failure to prove a prima facie case. Thus, if the plaintiff cannot show reliance on the auditor's advice since the plaintiff rejected it, for example, there is no causation. And, if causation is not proven, there is no negligence.

Statute of Limitations

The lapse of the period during which suit may be brought is a defense to a liability suit. After that period, known as the **statute of limitations**, suits

[12]*Shapiro v. Glekel,* 380 F. Supp. 1053 (S.D.N.Y. 1974).

are barred. State statutes regarding the length of time in which a suit may be brought vary widely. In general, a suit based on a contract claim is measured from the date the contract is entered. Suits based on negligence are measured from a date no later than when the negligence should have been discovered.

FEDERAL SECURITIES LAWS AND ACCOUNTANT'S LIABILITY

The securities laws provide for both an accountant's civil liability to third parties and Securities and Exchange Commission (SEC) administrative proceedings against an accountant.

Liability to Third Parties under the Securities Act of 1933

Subject to a number of exemptions described in Chapter 44, the Securities Act of 1933 makes it unlawful to sell or deliver a security "unless a registration statement is in effect." These registration statements are filed with the Securities and Exchange Commission and contain a thorough analysis of a company's business, including product lines, divisions, marketing strategies, contracts, major customers, and the like. The controlling idea behind the Securities Act of 1933 is to ensure that an investor has adequate information on which to make an investment decision.

Accountants are part of a team that includes attorneys, underwriters, financial institutions, and other experts who help to prepare the registration statement and prospectus under the 1933 Act.

Liability under Section 11

Section 11 of the 1933 Act provides that any person acquiring a security may sue any person (including an accountant) who has prepared or certified the registration statement that contains a false statement or omission of material fact. Damages are calculated by the difference between the amount paid for the securities and (1) their value at the time of suit, or (2) the selling price of the securities before suit was brought, or (3) the selling price of the securities after suit was brought if this is less than (1). The following case discusses both an accountant's liability under Section 11 and defenses to Section 11 liability.

ESCOTT v. BARCHRIS CONSTRUCTION CORP.
283 F.Supp. 643 (S.D.N.Y. 1968)

BarChris Construction Corp. was primarily engaged in the business of building bowling alleys. In 1961, BarChris filed a registration statement with the SEC that covered a $3.5 million issuance of securities. The next year, due to a downturn in public interest, business waned, then collapsed. BarChris filed for bankruptcy in October 1962. The purchasers of the securities brought suit under Section 11, claiming damages due to misrepresentations and material omissions in the filed registration statements. Among the various defendants were BarChris's auditors, Peat, Marwick, Mitchell & Co.

MCCLEAN, Judge

It is a prerequisite to liability under Section 11 of the Act that the fact which is falsely stated in a registration statement, or the fact that is omitted when it should have been stated to avoid misleading, be "material." A material fact [is] defined as:

> a fact which if it had been correctly stated or disclosed would have deterred or tended to deter the average prudent investor from purchasing the securities in question.

The average prudent investor is not concerned with minor inaccuracies or with errors as to matters which are of no interest to him. The facts which tend to deter him from purchasing a security are facts which have an important bearing upon the nature or condition of the issuing corporation or its business.

Judged by this test, there is no doubt that many of the misstatements and omissions in this prospectus were material. This is true of all of them which relate to the state of affairs in 1961, i.e., the overstatement of sales and gross profit for the first quarter, the understatement of contingent liabilities as of April 30, the overstatement of orders on hand and the failure to disclose the true facts with respect to officers' loans, customers' delinquencies, application of proceeds and the prospective operation of several alleys.

The Due Diligence Defense

Section 11(b) provides:

Notwithstanding the provisions of subsection (a) no person . . . shall be liable as provided therein who shall sustain the burden of proof—

(3) that . . . (B) as regards any part of the registration statement purporting to be made upon his authority as an expert . . . (i) he had, after reasonable investigation, reasonable ground to believe and did believe, at the time such part of the registration statement became effective, that the statements therein were true and that there was no omission to state a material fact . . .

This [is commonly referred to as] the due diligence defense for an expert. Peat, Marwick has pleaded it.

Most of [Peat, Marwick's] actual work was performed by a senior accountant, Berardi, who had junior assistants, one of whom was Kennedy.

Berardi was then about 30 years old. He was not yet a CPA. He had had no previous experience with the bowling industry. This was his first job as a senior accountant. He could hardly have been given a more difficult assignment.

The purpose of reviewing events subsequent to the date of a certified balance sheet (referred to as an S-1 review when made with reference to a registration statement) is to ascertain whether any material change has occurred in the company's financial position which should be disclosed in order to prevent the balance sheet figures from being misleading. The scope of such a review, under generally accepted auditing standards, is limited. It does not amount to a complete audit.

Berardi made the S-1 review in May 1961. He devoted a little over two days to it, a total of 20 1/2 hours. He did not discover any of the errors or omissions pertaining to the state of affairs in 1961 . . . , all of which were material. The question is whether, despite his failure to find out anything, his investigation was reasonable within the meaning of the statute['s due diligence defense].

In substance, what Berardi did is similar to what [the directors] did. He asked questions, he got answers which he considered satisfactory, and he did

nothing to verify them. For example, he obtained from Trilling [BarChris' comptroller] a list of contracts. The list included Yonkers and Bridge. Since Berardi did not look at any contract documents, and since he was unaware of the executive committee minutes . . . , he did not learn that BarChris had no contracts for these jobs. Trilling's list did not set forth contract prices for them. . . .

Berardi noticed that there had been an increase in notes payable by BarChris. Trilling admitted to him that BarChris was "a bit slow" in paying its bills. Berardi recorded in his notes of his review that BarChris was in a "tight cash position." Trilling's explanation was that BarChris was experiencing "some temporary difficulty."

Berardi had no conception of how tight the cash position was. He did not discover that BarChris was holding up checks in substantial amounts because there was no money in the bank to cover them. He did not know of the loan from Manufacturers Trust Company or of the officers' loans. Since he never read the prospectus, he was not even aware that there had ever been any problem about loans from officers.

During the 1960 audit Berardi had obtained some information . . . , not sufficiently detailed even then, as to delinquent notes. He made no inquiry . . . about this in his S-1 review. Since he knew nothing about [BarChris' treasurer's] notes of the executive committee meetings, he did not learn that the delinquency situation had grown worse. . . .

There had been a material change for the worse in BarChris's financial position. That change was sufficiently serious so that the failure to disclose it made the 1960 figures misleading. As far as results were concerned, his S-1 review was useless.

Accountants should not be held to a standard higher than that recognized in their profession. I do not do so here. Berardi's review did not come up to that standard. He did not take some of the steps which Peat, Marwick's written program prescribed. He did not spend an adequate amount of time on a task of this magnitude. Most important of all, he was too easily satisfied with glib answers to his inquiries.

This is not to say that he should have made a complete audit. But there were enough danger signals in the materials which he did examine to require some further investigation on his part. Generally accepted accounting standards required such further investigation under these circumstances. It is not always sufficient merely to ask questions.

Here again, the burden of proof is on Peat, Marwick. I find that that burden has not been satisfied. I conclude that Peat, Marwick has not established its due diligence defense.

Case Questions

1. Isolate the ethical components behind the law in this case and explain.

2. Why was Peat, Marwick unable to show due diligence?

3. Identify Berardi's major failure in this case.

4. Imagine that you are a young, inexperienced auditor like Berardi and are suddenly given a major responsibility. What should you do?

Liability under Section 12(2)

Section 12(2) imposes liability on a seller of securities if there were material omissions or misstatements in the seller's oral or written communications with the purchaser. Thus, the misrepresentation may occur in something other than a registration statement. Although reliance by the purchaser is required, reliance is presumed once the materiality of the omission or misstatement is proven. **Materiality** is a fact that would be considered important to the reasonable investor. In addition, unlike Section 11, the purchaser must be in privity with the seller.

Since accountants are normally not sellers of securities, courts have generally held accountants not to be liable under this section. Other courts have held, however, that accountants will be liable if they have "aided and abetted" the seller in the misrepresentation. Although Section 12(2) liability is normally based on a showing of a seller's negligence, liability through "aiding and abetting" requires a showing of *knowledge* of the misrepresentation.

Damages are more limited under Section 12(2) than under Section 11. Here, a purchaser may only sue for rescission and the return of the purchase price, or damages based on the purchase price if the purchaser no longer owns the security. Both Section 11 and Section 12(2) suits must be brought within one year of discovery of the misrepresentation but in no event more than three years after the securities were publicly offered for sale.

Liability to Third Parties under the Securities and Exchange Act of 1934

While the 1933 Act regulates the initial issuance and distribution of securities, the Exchange Act of 1934 regulates the trading of those securities on national security exchanges. As Chapter 45 indicated, once a security is registered under the 1934 Act, annual reports (known as Form 10-K), quarterly reports (Form 10-Q), and a number of other reports must be periodically filed with the SEC. In addition, a copy of a company's annual report must be given to all shareholders as well as detailed information about the company before any shareholders' vote.

Accountants play a large role in the preparation of all of these materials. In fact, the SEC has prescribed a specific regulation that contains the SEC's rules concerning the application of accounting principles to all statements made under the 1933 and 1934 Acts.

An accountant's liability under the 1934 Act chiefly arises from a violation of the antifraud provisions of that act, namely, Section 10(b) and Rule 10b-5 (see Chapter 45). These provisions permit a plaintiff to sue an accountant for making a fraudulent or misleading statement in connection with the purchase or sale of any security. The misrepresentation must be material, but direct reliance on the misrepresentation by the purchaser is not a requirement. To establish a claim for damages, the plaintiff must also prove that the accountant acted with **scienter** — that is, with knowledge or intent. Most courts agree that a reckless disregard for the truth, even in the absence of actual intent to deceive, satisfies the scienter requirement. As with Section 11, privity under this section is not required.

SEC Enforcement

The SEC has broad regulatory powers over the accounting profession. As stated above, the SEC has the power to prescribe forms for financial disclosure filings. Two other powers must also be stated — the power of the SEC to conduct investigations and its power to administratively discipline an accountant.

Concerning investigations, the SEC generally begins with an informal inquiry. In this informal inquiry, based on possible statutory or rule violations, the SEC often requests the accountant to produce documents. (See the section Accountants' Working

Papers and the Accountant-Client Privilege, later in this chapter.) If the SEC proceeds to a formal inquiry, it may issue a **subpoena duces tecum** requiring the submission of records and papers. Further, the SEC has power to hear sworn testimony and to take written depositions.

After an inquiry, the SEC may take one of several actions. It may negotiate a settlement with an accountant. It may sue for an injunction in federal court to bar any continuing violation of the law. Or it may proceed administratively against an accountant.

Under SEC Rule 2(e), the SEC may deny, temporarily or permanently, the authority of an accountant to practice or appear before the SEC. The SEC may also decide to publicly censure an accountant or impose a suspension from specific categories of practice. Many of these proceedings are settled by the agreement of the accountant. The basis for sanctions under Rule 2(e) is contained in Figure 53–4.

Figure 53–4   SEC Rule 2(e) Basis for Sanctions

- Lacks the qualifications to represent others
- Lacks character of integrity
- Engaged in unethical or improper professional conduct
- Willfully violated or aided and abetted in the violation of federal securities laws.

It should be noted that an accountant will not be censured for mistakes but only for acting in bad faith under Rule 2(e). The term **bad faith** is designed to cover a broad range of unfair and unethical practices. In many cases, private litigants use information gathered by an SEC investigation and administrative proceedings to bring a civil action against an accountant.

The SEC administrative ruling in the following case illustrates the gravity of the 2(e) proceeding.

IN THE MATTER OF GREENSPAN
LEXIS 1687 (S.E.C. 1991)

ZZZZ Best Co. (Z Best) is in the business of providing residential and commercial carpet, upholstery, and drapery cleaning services. In December 1986, it raised $15 million in a public offering. It registered the securities with the SEC. Shortly thereafter, Z Best filed for bankruptcy protection. Minkow, the company's chief executive officer, president, and chairman of the board, and others were convicted of crimes and securities fraud in connection with company activities.

Greenspan was retained by Z Best to audit its balance sheet, as of April 30, 1986, and related financial statements. He issued an unqualified report, which was included within the SEC registration statements. The SEC commenced a 2(e) proceeding against Greenspan, alleging unethical and improper conduct and willful violation of the Securities Acts.

COMMISSION

Contrary to Greenspan's representation in his audit report, he failed to audit Z Best's fiscal 1986 fiscal balance sheet and fiscal 1985 financial statements in accordance with GAAS. Greenspan knew or, but for his reckless conduct, should have known, that his representations and that his examinations were made in accordance with GAAS and that the financial statements were fairly presented in conformity with GAAP and were materially false and misleading.

In the performance of his audit of Z Best's financial statements, Greenspan failed to comply with several major GAAS provisions. Specifically, Greenspan failed to:

1. Obtain sufficient competent evidential matter.

2. Adequately plan the audit and consider audit risk.

3. Act with due professional care; and

4. Conduct his examinations as an independent auditor.

In addition, Greenspan failed to ensure that the financial statements disclosed, in conformity with GAAP, the nature of certain transactions between Z Best and individuals or companies that were ''related parties'' to Z Best even though Greenspan had knowledge that the transactions were related party transactions.

Greenspan Failed to Obtain Sufficient Competent Evidential Matter

Evidential matter supporting the financial statements consists of the underlying accounting data and all corroborating information available to the auditor. By itself, however, accounting data (i.e., general ledgers and returns), cannot be considered sufficient support for financial statements. When evidential matter can be obtained from independent sources outside an entity, it provides greater assurance of reliability for purposes of an independent audit than that secured solely within the entity. In addition, GAAS states that representations from management cannot be substituted for the application of auditing procedures necessary to afford a reasonable basis for the opinion on the financial statements.

1. Z Best's Fiscal 1985 Balance Sheet Was Not Audited in Accordance with GAAS

Greenspan's representation in his audit report that he had examined Z Best's fiscal 1985 balance sheet in accordance with GAAS was completely false. In fact, Greenspan simply relied on a purported audit report signed by a "Richard Evans," provided to him by Z Best management, which unqualified audit report stated that Richard Evans ("Evans") had audited Z Best's fiscal 1985 balance sheet in accordance with GAAS and that the balance sheet was presented in conformity with GAAP. In fact, Evans did not exist. Rather, both the balance sheet and Evans' purported audit report were fabricated. . . .

. . . A successor auditor is required to obtain sufficient competent evidential matter to afford a reasonable basis for expressing an opinion on the financial statements he has been engaged to audit, as well as for evaluating the consistency of the application of accounting principles in that year as compared to the preceding year. Greenspan failed to gather such sufficient competent evidential matter and to follow procedures required by GAAS to be performed by successor auditors. Specifically, Greenspan failed to:

1. Attempt to communicate with Evans prior to accepting the audit engagement.
2. Request Z Best's consent for him to review Evans' work paper.
3. Attempt to visit Evans and discuss the audit procedures followed by Evans and the results thereof and to review Evans' audit program.

Greenspan's failure to follow the above procedures in relying on Evans' audit report prevented him from discovering that Evans did not exist and that Evans therefore could not have audited Z Best's fiscal 1985 balance sheet or any portion of its fiscal 1985 financial statements, facts which would have raised substantial doubt as to the integrity of Z Best's management and the authenticity of its fiscal 1985 balance sheet.

2. Z Best's Fiscal 1986 Financial Statements Were Not Audited in Accordance with GAAS Because Sufficient Competent Evidential Matter Was Not Obtained

The broad objectives of internal accounting control are to provide management with reasonable assurance that assets are safeguarded from unauthorized use or disposition and that financial records are sufficiently reliable to permit the preparation of the company's financial statements in conformity with GAAP.

During Z Best's fiscal year 1986, it had material weaknesses in its internal controls, including but not limited to:

1. Excessive use of cashier's checks and checks made out to cash, which rendered it virtually impossible to trace to whom payments were made or what they were for.
2. The control of cash receipts by Minkow. and
3. Minkow's overriding or existing internal controls.

Greenspan knew of each of these material weaknesses.

When the auditor considers the internal control systems to be weak, the auditor must perform substantive tests of transactions and balances. . . . Greenspan failed to obtain sufficient competent evidential matter and failed to perform necessary substantive tests, notwithstanding Z Best's material weaknesses in internal controls and his knowledge thereof.

Greenspan Failed to Adequately Plan His Fiscal 1986 Audit and to Assess Audit Risk

GAAS requires that an auditor, when planning the audit, obtain knowledge of matters that relate to the nature of the entity's business, and consider matters affecting the industry in which the entity operates.

Prior to conducting his audit of Z Best's fiscal 1986 financial statements, Greenspan had no experience with auditing entities involved in the insurance restoration industry.

Greenspan Failed to Exercise Due Professional Care

Greenspan unduly relied on representations of Z Best management without obtaining sufficient competent evidential matter from third parties. This undue reliance included Greenspan's acceptance of copies instead of original documents. Many of these copies were documents fabricated. . . . Greenspan's undue reliance on management representations did not constitute the proper degree of professional skepticism required and had a direct adverse impact upon his ability to search for irregularities in Z Best's financial statements. Greenspan's undue reliance on representations of Z Best management constitutes a failure to act with due professional care.

Accordingly, IT IS HEREBY ORDERED that Samuel George Greenspan is permanently denied the privilege of appearing or practicing before the Commission as an accountant from the date of this Opinion and Order. [Greenspan consented to the Opinion and Order.]

Case Questions

1. What is the issue in this case?

2. Analyze: "Greenspan should not be punished for negligent and inadvertent acts. The penalty in this case does not fit the offense."

3. Identify what you think to be Greenspan's worst offense. Why?

4. Assume that Greenspan would have pursued the "Trail of Evans" and that the company had someone pose as Evans and Greenspan was duped. Would this have made a difference? Explain.

CRIMINAL LIABILITY OF ACCOUNTANTS

Accountants may be criminally liable for various violations of federal and state laws. The main sources of criminal liability are the violations of the Federal Mail Fraud Statute, the Federal False Statements Statute, the Securities Acts of 1933, and the Securities and Exchange Act of 1934.

Mail fraud occurs when a person perpetrates a scheme to defraud another of money or property using the mails. Mailing a false financial statement with an intent to defraud a third party may render an accountant criminally liable under the Federal Mail Fraud Statute. Its violation carries a maximum penalty of imprisonment and a fine.

The Federal False Statements Statute prohibits knowingly making any false statement to any federal agency or department. This can occur by filing a knowingly false securities statement. It can also occur by knowingly making a false statement in response to a government inquiry. Its violation carries a maximum penalty of imprisonment and a fine.

It is also a felony to knowingly make a false statement or willfully overvalue any property to secure a loan from federal banks, agencies, credit unions, savings and loans, and federally insured banks. Such false statements carry a penalty of a fine and imprisonment.

The Securities Act of 1933 contains section 24, which prohibits willful misstatements or omissions of material fact in a registration statement. (Note that for criminal liability to be imposed, a misstatement must be *willful*. Civil liability under Section 11 may be imposed without respect to willfulness.) Its violation carries a maximum penalty of imprisonment and a fine.

Section 32(a) of the Securities and Exchange Act of 1934 prohibits the willful filing of false or misleading SEC statements or the willful violation of the Exchange Act's antifraud provisions (found in Section 10(b)). In one well-known case,[13] the court found the defendant to have acted "willfully" if "he deliberately closed his eyes to the obvious" or if "he recklessly stated as facts matters of which he knew he was ignorant." Its violation carries a maximum penalty of imprisonment and a fine.

ACCOUNTANTS' WORKING PAPERS AND THE ACCOUNTANT–CLIENT PRIVILEGE

Papers given to an accountant by a client belong to the client and must be returned. Papers produced by the accountant to accomplish an audit are owned by

---

[13] *U.S. v. Natelli*, 527 F.2d 311 (2d Cir. 1975).

the accountant. These products of an accountant's activity are called the accountant's **working papers** and embrace the accountant's written thought processes in an audit.

The accountant's ownership rights to working papers is limited. The major limitation is that accountants must prevent any confidential information in the papers from being communicated to third persons such as other accountants, the government, or other clients. In general, an accountant should procure a client's consent before releasing any working papers. Subpoenas in a criminal case may, however, require accountants to turn over their working papers even without client consent. In addition, clients generally have a right of access to the papers.

The claim of the **accountant-client privilege** can be asserted to resist discovery requests or as a ground for refusing to testify in court. At common law, there was no privilege between accountants and their clients such as that existing between attorneys and their clients.

State statutes in many states have enacted an accountant-client privilege. Since these are *state* statutes, they only apply to state matters. Thus, concerning federal securities claims, federal tax claims, or federal antitrust matters, no privilege exists. Since privileges are created for the benefit of the client, however, only the client may waive the privilege in cases where it does exist.

END–OF–CHAPTER QUESTIONS

1. Compare and contrast the areas of accountants' potential common law liability.

2. Distinguish between an action against an accountant under SEC Sections 11 and 12(2).

3. Distinguish between an action against an accountant under SEC Sections 11 and 10(b).

4. Under what circumstances would the SEC publicly censure or otherwise discipline an accountant?

5. Analyze: "The AICPA should work for legislative changes in the law." If so, where should it concentrate its efforts?

6. The widow of a decedent brought suit against an accountant for professional negligence. The complaint alleged that he had failed to advise her to disclaim her inherited interest in an estate within the applicable period so as to avoid payment of gift taxes. What elements must be proven by the widow to maintain an action for negligence? See *Link v. Barokas & Martin,* 667 P.2d 171 (Alaska 1983).

7. The accountants in this case advised their clients to invest in a truck purchase and leasing venture. The investment involved the purchase and lease of a new $60,000 truck. The accountants in fact purchased a used truck and trailer. The accountants further signed the client's name to documents twice although they had no power to do so, and combined their clients' money with that of other investors without informing their clients. No registration statement with the SEC was ever filed on this investment. What civil and statutory duties did the accountants breach with their client? See *En Yun Hsu v. Leaseway Transportation Corp.,* Fed Sec. L. Rep. (CCH) ¶ 92043 (N.D. Cal. March 29, 1985).

8. An accounting firm, Timm, Schmidt and Company, prepared financial statements for Clintonville Fire Apparatus, Inc. (C.F.A.). The statements were accompanied by an opinion letter expressing that the statements fairly presented the financial condition of C.F.A. and were prepared in accordance with GAAP. C.F.A. obtained credit from Citizens Bank in the amount of $380,000 based on the statement. The following year Timm discovered an error in the statements in the amount of $400,000 and had to send out corrected statements. C.F.A. went bankrupt and Citizens sued Timm for accountant malpractice. What is the result under *Ultramares?* Under *Rosenblum?* See *Citizens State Bank v. Timm, Schmidt and Co.,* 335 N.W.2d 361 (Wis. 1983).

9. Devco served clients who could not afford to pay the initial lump-sum premium to purchase insurance policies. Timely monthly payments to Devco, in return for its payment of the lump-sum premium, were crucial to Devco's success. When Devco converted to an in-house computer system, it soon experienced severe prob-

lems in checking delinquent accounts. The problem was compounded by the failure of Devco's president to look at computer printouts of the delinquent accounts. An accounting firm was hired to audit Devco's records. It employed a proper statistical test and determined that an inordinate number of accounts were in arrears, but it ignored the result of the tests in issuing its financial statement. A bank relied on the audited financial statements and extended a line of credit to Devco. When it learned of the delinquent accounts, it withdrew its line of credit, causing Devco to liquidate. Devco sued its auditors for negligence. Were they negligent? What defenses can be raised in this action? See *Devco Premium Finance v. North River Ins.*, 450 So.2d 1216 (Fla. App. 1984).

10. To make a public offering of its stock, a corporation filed a registration statement and issued a prospectus. An accounting firm certified the value of the corporation's assets and its net worth. One month after the registration statement was filed, the plaintiff, Ackerman, purchased the corporation's stock. A year later, the corporation announced a huge reduction in its assets and an increase in its bad debt reserves. After Ackerman's stock significantly declined in value, Ackerman sued, claiming there were misrepresentations in the registration statement and prospectus. What securities law provisions might the accountants have violated? What would their best defense be? See *Ackerman v. Clinical Data, Inc.*, 1985 Fed Sec.L.Rep (CCH) ¶ 92,207 (S.D.N.Y. July 8, 1985).

Chapter 54

The Corporate Culture: Corporate Social Responsibility

■

CRITICAL THINKING INQUIRIES

As you read this chapter, you should be able to address the following:

- What is meant by corporate social responsibility?
- How do one's views on the efficiency of markets affect one's views on corporate social responsibility?
- Lord Chancellor Edward Thurlow said, ''Did you ever expect a corporation to have a conscience, when it has no soul to be damned and no body to be kicked?'' Do you agree?
- What is the obligation of upper management in a corporation with respect to corporate social responsibility? How does this differ from the general obligation of employees?
- Why can't the market, in conjunction with the law, ensure socially responsible behavior by corporations?

MANAGERIAL PERSPECTIVE

Adele has just been promoted to vice president of human resource management at Acme, Inc. She has worked at Acme for five years and is proud of the ''socially responsible'' nature of the firm. However, her first week in the new job she is faced with several upsetting issues. She discovers that Louise has applied for and been denied Adele's old job as director of human resource management. Apparently, it was thought that because Adele was a woman, ''it wouldn't look good'' for another woman to be hired. In addition, Sandra comes into Adele's office and tells her that she (Sandra) has been the object of sexual harassment for a period of six months and that nothing has been done about it. The person to whom she registered the formal complaint told Sandra that ''she must have misunderstood'' the actions.

Adele is upset. She didn't think that Acme was the kind of company to treat its employees with so little caring.

- What should Adele do to deal with the immediate problems?
- What should Adele do to offer a more long-term solution?
- Is Adele's obligation any different now that she is a part of top management than it was before?
- Why do you think Adele didn't notice Acme's attitude earlier?

This example illustrates the two related ethical issues presented in this text: individual ethics and corporate ethics. First, Adele must, as an individual, decide what is the "right" action. She can use any of the various theories of normative philosophy discussed in Chapter 2 to make this decision. However, her decisionmaking is complicated by the fact that she is operating within a corporate organization. While there is not one set of rules for what is morally right in one's personal life and another set for what is right in business activities, the organizational environment creates a unique set of challenges for one seeking to make the right decision within a business. Further, what can Adele, as a member of top management, do to create the environment in which ethical decisions by others take place?

Second, Acme, Inc., as an organization, must respond. This is a question of ethical behavior by corporations, often termed corporate social responsibility. If one decides that corporations should act in a socially responsible manner, what does this mean? These questions will be addressed in this chapter.

INTRODUCTION

Adele's decision is not an easy one. While she can use philosophy to help her decide the proper course of action, she must be aware that her decision is being made within the context of an organization. She must consider the personal consequences of her decision.

In the Introduction to his book *Moral Mazes: The World of Corporate Managers*, sociologist Robert Jackall suggested that business ethics must do more than apply traditional philosophy to standard case studies. He examined what he termed the "organizational ethics" of corporations — the moral rules in use and how the organizational ethics influenced individual action. Read the following excerpt from his book and ask yourself what within the corporation influences people to utilize one set of ethics for personal decisions and another for corporate action.

*Moral Mazes: The World of Corporate Managers**

Only an understanding of how men and women in business actually experience their work enables one to grasp its moral salience for them. Bureaucratic work shapes people's consciousness in decisive ways. Among other things, it regularizes people's experiences of time and indeed routinizes their lives by engaging them on a daily basis in rational, socially approved, purposive action; it brings them into daily proximity with and subordination to authority, creating in the process upward-looking stances that have decisive social and psychological consequences; it places a premium on a functionally rational, pragmatic habit of mind that seeks specific goals; and it creates subtle measures of prestige and an elaborate status hierarchy that, in addition to fostering an intense competition for status, also makes the rules, procedures, social contexts, and protocol of an organization paramount psychological and behavioral guides. In fact, bureaucratic contexts typically bring together men and women who initially have little in common with each other except the impersonal frameworks of their organizations. Indeed, the enduring genius of the organizational form is that it allows individuals to retain bewilderingly diverse private motives and meanings for action as long as they adhere publicly to agreed-upon rules. . . . As a result, bureaucratic work causes people to bracket, while at work, the moralities that they might hold outside the workplace or that they might adhere to privately and to follow instead the prevailing morality of their particular organizational situation. As a former vice-president of a large firm says: "What is right in the corporation is not what is right in a man's home or in his church. *What is right in the corporation is what the guy above you wants from you.* That's what morality is in the corporation." Of course, since public legitimacy and respectability depend, in part, on

Source: Robert Jackall, *Moral Mazes: The World of Corporate Managers* (New York: Oxford Univ. Press, 1988), pp. 5–6, 193. Reprinted with permission.

perceptions of one's moral probity, one cannot admit to such a bracketing of one's conventional moralities except, usually indirectly, within one's managerial circles where such verities are widely recognized to be inapplicable except as public relations stances.

■ ■ ■

[Jackall concludes his book with a chapter entitled "Invitations to Jeopardy," where he states:]

In short, bureaucracy creates for managers a Calvinist world without a Calvinist God, a world marked by the same profound anxiety that characterized the old Protestant ethic but one stripped of that ideology's comforting illusions. Bureaucracy poses for managers an intricate set of moral mazes that are paradigmatic of the quandaries of public life in our social order. Within this framework, the puzzle for many individual managers becomes: How does one act in such a world and maintain a sense of personal integrity?

Thought Questions

1. Analyze: "Bureaucratic work causes people to bracket, while at work, the moralities that they might hold outside the workplace or that they might adhere to privately and to follow instead the prevailing morality of their particular organizational situation."

2. Do you have any anecdotal evidence to support Jackall's thesis that corporate bureaucracy creates a series of moral mazes that make it difficult to succeed and maintain personal integrity?

3. What can be done to eliminate this bracketing? Make some suggestions.

WHY THE MARKET CAN'T DO IT

The conservative economic paradigm rests on the assumption that the free market promotes social utility and justice by ensuring that the economy is producing what consumers want, that prices are at the lowest levels, and that resources are efficiently used. Adam Smith, one of the fathers of this paradigm, believed that when individuals act in their own self-interest, guided by the invisible hand of the market, social good is achieved.[1] This paradigm does not advocate unethical behavior. Instead, it is based on the belief that good consequences are achieved by individual pursuit of happiness. Under this theory corporations are encouraged to act responsibly to maximize long-term profits.

Read the following excerpt where Milton Friedman, a conservative economist, advocates this view. Socially responsible behavior is a part of the pursuit of profits.

[1] Adam Smith, *An Inquiry into the Nature and Causes of the Wealth of Nations* (1776).

*The Social Responsibility of Business**

The view has been gaining widespread acceptance that corporate officials and labor leaders have a "social responsibility" that goes beyond serving the interest of their stockholders or their members. This view shows a fundamental misconception of the character and nature of

*Source: Milton Friedman, *Capitalism and Freedom* (Chicago: University of Chicago Press, 1962), pp. 133–36. © 1962 by the University of Chicago; all rights reserved. Reprinted by permission of the publisher.

a free economy. In such an economy, there is one and only one social responsibility of business — to use its resources and engage in activities designed to increase its profits so long as it stays within the rules of the game, which is to say, engages in open and free competition, without deception or fraud. Similarly, the ''social responsibility'' of labor leaders is to serve the interests of the members of their unions. It is the responsibility of the rest of us to establish a framework of law such that an individual in pursuing his own interest is, to quote Adam Smith again, ''led by an invisible hand to promote an end which was no part of his intention. Nor is it always the worse for the society that was no part of it. By pursuing his own interest, he frequently promotes that of the society more effectually than when he really intends to promote it. I have never known much good done by those who affected to trade for the public good.''[†]

Few trends could so thoroughly undermine the very foundations of our free society as the acceptance by corporate officials of a social responsibility other than to make as much money for their stockholders as possible. This is a fundamentally subversive doctrine. If businessmen do have a social responsibility other than making maximum profits for stockholders, how are they to know what it is? Can self-selected private individuals decide what the social interest is? Can they decide how great a burden they are justified in placing on themselves or their stockholders to serve that social interest? Is it tolerable that these public functions of taxation, expenditure, and control be exercised by the people who happen at the moment to be in charge of particular enterprises, chosen for those posts by strictly private groups? If businessmen are civil servants rather than the employees of their stockholders, then in a democracy they will, sooner or later, be chosen by the public techniques of election and appointment.

Thought Questions

1. How does asking corporations to be socially responsible ''show a fundamental misconception of the character and nature of a free economy''? Explain.

2. Friedman states that corporate executives should try to maximize profits ''within the rules of the game.'' What does this mean? Do the rules of the game mean ''within the law,'' or might they include ethical custom?

3. If shareholder-owners of the company do not approve of the way in which the corporate executives are running the company, theoretically they can remove the executives. However, as is pointed out in Chapter 41, because most voting is done by the use of proxies, rarely is a director removed. Does this affect your evaluation of Friedman's position?

[†]Adam Smith, *The Wealth of Nations* (1776), book IV, Chapter ii (London: Cannon, 1930), p. 421.

Market Imperfections

Conservative economists believe that a free market itself leads to socially desired decisions. Under this view, the benefits and burdens of society are allocated in a just manner, and allocated efficiently. However, this theory is based on the assumptions of **a perfectly competitive market.** The characteristics of a perfectly competitive market are outlined in Figure 54–1. However, markets are not perfectly

Figure 54–1   Perfectly Competitive Market

- Many buyers and sellers
- No barriers to entry or exit
- Perfect information
- No buyer or seller has substantial market share
- Homogeneous product
- Costs of production paid by each seller

Figure 54–2   Flaws in Market Decisionmaking

- Producers and consumers lie
- Perfect rationality, perfect information, and perfect mobility do not exist
- Individuals and corporations may have goals other than profit maximization
- External costs (e.g., pollution) are not included in market costs
- Corporations get confused about short- and long-run profits
- Goods carry secondary needs
- Markets do not respond to need or justice
- Markets may violate rights

Figure 54–3   Limits of the Law

- Time-lag problem
- Making of the law
  —Lack of value consensus
  —Social minimums
- Implementing the law
  —Inadequacy of measures aimed at corporation
  —Inadequacy of measures aimed at individuals

competitive. As is outlined in Figure 54–2 and was discussed in the Unit IV Overview, the assumptions of perfect competition are flawed. For example, the model of a perfectly competitive market assumes perfect information. However, often people do not know that they are being injured (asbestos injuries to workers), or know where to apply pressure (if you want to withdraw your support from a company making soap, you might switch brands of soap from one brand to another; however, both brands might be made by the same company).

As was pointed out in the Unit IV Overview, the acceptance of market failures has justified governmental regulation. Further, such acceptance explains why Friedman's position has been rejected by many. It has been suggested that because "the market can't do it," corporate social responsibility is required.

WHY THE LAW CAN'T DO IT

If one accepts the position that the free market alone cannot ensure socially desired results, it might be suggested that the market in conjunction with the law (regulation) can ensure these results. By contrast, many believe that law is inadequate to ensure ethical behavior for a number of reasons, as outlined in Figure 54–3.

Time-Lag Problem

Law is basically reactive. In other words, the law *responds* to socially undesirable behavior. The law is often changed after injury. For example, only after a drug has been found to have dangerous side effects

will it be removed from the market. The legal response takes time and allows injury to continue while the law is being made.

Making the Law

It has been suggested that relying solely on governmental regulation to require ethical behavior forgets the role that business plays in making the very laws that regulate them. It is not uncommon for the law to incorporate industry standards. For example, the Uniform Commercial Code typically allows banks to act in accordance with general banking custom. Further, while limits have been imposed on business influence by such things as the campaign contribution and political action committee regulations, business plays a role in lobbying for law that is desirable to business.

In addition, regulatory agencies and the companies they regulate "share" employees; that is, regulators frequently leave government service and are hired by the industries that they regulated.

Moreover, the corporations often know more about their industry than the regulatory agencies. For example, the drug company marketing the product with harmful side effects is likely to know about those side effects before the Food and Drug Administration. If corporations fail to furnish administrative agencies with complete and accurate information, regulation is ineffective.

Most importantly, law is ineffective if society lacks "consensus as to the values we want to advance."[2] For example, as a society, we are in favor of environmental protection. Therefore, one might oppose driving the spotted owl to extinction by overlogging. However, as a society we are also in favor of employment. Where do we strike the balance when protection of the spotted owl potentially costs jobs? Which value has priority for society?

---

[2]Christopher D. Stone, *Where the Law Ends* (New York: Harper Collins, 1975), p. 97.

Last, laws are most commonly of the "thou shalt not" variety rather than the "thou shalt" type. In other words, the law typically prohibits "bad" behavior rather than mandating "good" behavior. The law sets a floor below which people should not fall—it does not require that one "be all that one can be." To some extent, this is the role of ethics.

Implementing the Law

Even if laws are adopted on which there is consensus and that are reasonably clear, they are not always effective deterrents to unethical corporate behavior.

Corporate Deterrent

The law does not always effectively deter unethical corporate behavior because it fails to recognize that the corporation is not an individual. For example, individuals are deterred from illegal behavior by internalized restraints such as guilt, shame, and conscience. None of these are applicable to the corporate individual.

Further, some of the major sanctions that are imposed against individuals—imprisonment and the death penalty—are inapplicable to corporations. Moreover, corporate fines are often inadequate to control corporate misconduct. Such fines are often insignificant when compared with corporate profits, they are calculated as costs of doing business, and they are uncertain. Perhaps most importantly, the benefits to the person within the organization making the decisions often outweigh any potential corporate fine. For example, legal liabilities are not always attached to the person or department that made the decision that caused the fine. Therefore, it is often unlikely that corporate legal liability will translate into individual loss, such as lost promotions or salary.

Individual Deterrent

Furthermore, legal sanctions are not always an effective deterrent even when aimed at key individuals

Figure 54–4   Philosophy of Milton Friedman

A Duty to maximize profits: To make as much money as possible while conforming to the basic rules of the society, both those embodied in law and those embodied in ethical custom.

within the organization primarily because they fail to recognize that individual decisionmaking is different within an organization. For example, in a corporation, responsibility for any one decision is widespread—those at the top are often insulated from "bad news." Further, when responsibility can be attached to one key individual, the penalties imposed by juries in so-called white-collar crime cases have typically been light.

CORPORATE SOCIAL RESPONSIBILITY

Because of the perceived inadequacies in relying on both market decisionmaking and legal constraints as the sole impetus for ethical corporate behavior, it has been suggested that corporations must act pursuant to corporate social responsibility goals. If one accepts the position that corporations should act in a socially responsible manner, there are many different views of how a corporation should behave to act socially responsibly.

Friedman: Make Profits

Recall Milton Friedman's position, set out earlier in this chapter. Friedman believes that what is best for society is achieved when individuals act in their own self-interest within the free-market context. Friedman, as summarized in Figure 54–4, represents the school of belief that corporations, in order to be socially responsible, should act in their own self-interest—in the pursuit of profits.

*The Social Responsibility of Business Is to Increase Its Profits**

The discussions of the "social responsibilities of business" are notable for their analytical looseness and lack of rigor. What does it mean to say that "business" has responsibilities? Only people can have responsibilities. A corporation is an artificial person and in this sense

*Source: Milton Friedman, "The Social Responsibility of Business Is to Increase Its Profits," *New York Times Magazine,* September 13, 1970. Reprinted with permission.

may have some artificial responsibilities, but "business" as a whole cannot be said to have responsibilities, even in this vague sense. The first step toward clarity in examining the doctrine of the social responsibility of business is to ask precisely what it implies for whom.

■ ■ ■

In a free-enterprise, private-property system, a corporate executive is an employee of the owners of the business. He has direct responsibility to his employers. That responsibility is to conduct the business in accordance with their desires, which generally will be to make as much money as possible while conforming to the basic rules of the society, both those embodied in law and those embodied in ethical custom. . . . The key point is that, in his capacity as corporate executive, the manager is the agent of the individuals who own the corporation . . . and his primary responsibility is to them.

■ ■ ■

What does it mean to say that the corporate executive has a "social responsibility" in his capacity as a businessman? If this statement is not pure rhetoric, it must mean that he is to act in some way that is not in the interest of his employers.

Thought Questions

1. Does Friedman believe that corporations owe no ethical obligations to society?
2. What should the corporate executive do when his or her obligation to maximize profits conflicts with ethical custom?

Goodpaster and Matthews: Moral Projection

Friedman asserted in the preceding essay that "Only people can have responsibilities." Another view is presented in the following essay by Professors Kenneth Goodpaster and John Matthews. As outlined in Figure 54–5, Goodpaster and Matthews believe that corporations can have moral responsibility. Goodpaster and Matthews suggest that by viewing the group as if it were an individual—moral projection—one can conclude that "a corporation can have a conscience." The authors believe that to

Figure 54–5   Philosophy of Kenneth E. Goodpaster and John E. Matthews, Jr.

A Duty to have a strong corporate conscience: Moral Projection: Rationality and Respect

judge responsible behavior, we should project onto the corporation the qualities of rationality and respect. In their article, the authors imagine the possible objections to the concept of moral projection and rebut them.

Can a Corporation Have a Conscience?*

Objection 1 to the Analogy

Corporations are not persons. They are artificial legal constructions, machines for mobilizing economic investments toward the efficient production of goods and services. We cannot hold a corporation responsible. We can only hold individuals responsible.

---

*Source: Kenneth E. Goodpaster and John B. Matthews, Jr., "Can a Corporation Have a Conscience?" January-February 1982. Reprinted by permission of *Harvard Business Review.* Copyright © 1982 by the President and Fellows of Harvard College; all rights reserved.

Reply

Our frame of reference does not imply that corporations are persons in the literal sense. It simply means that in certain respects concepts and functions normally attributed to persons can also be attributed to organizations made up of persons. Goals, economic values, strategies, and other such personal attributes are often usefully projected to the corporate level by managers and researchers. Why should we not project the functions of conscience in the same way? . . .

Objection 2

A corporation cannot be held responsible at the sacrifice of profit. Profitability and financial health have always been and should continue to be the "categorical imperative" of a business operation.

Reply

We must of course acknowledge the imperatives of survival, stability, and growth when we discuss corporations, as indeed we must acknowledge them when we discuss the life of an individual. Self-sacrifice has been identified with moral responsibility in only the most extreme cases. The pursuit of profit and self-interest need not be pitted against the demands of moral responsibility. Moral demands are best viewed as containments—not replacements—for self-interest.

This is not to say that profit maximization never conflicts with morality. But profit maximization conflicts with other managerial values as well. The point is to coordinate imperatives, not to deny their validity.

Objection 3

Corporate executives are not elected representatives of the people, nor are they anointed or appointed as social guardians. They therefore lack the social mandate that a democratic society rightly demands of those who would pursue ethically or socially motivated policies. By keeping corporate policies confined to economic motivations, we keep the power of corporate executives in the proper place.

Reply

The objection betrays an oversimplified view of the relationship between the public and the private sector. Neither private individuals nor private corporations that guide their conduct by ethical or social values beyond the demands of law should be constrained merely because they are not elected to do so. The demands of moral responsibility are independent of the demands of political legitimacy and are in fact presupposed by them.

To be sure, the state and the political process will and must remain the primary mechanisms for protecting the public interest, but one might be forgiven the hope that the political process will not substitute for the moral judgment of the citizenry or other components of society such as corporations.

■ ■ ■

Objection 7

Why is it necessary to project moral responsibility to the level of the organization? Isn't the task of defining corporate responsibility and business ethics sufficiently discharged if we clarify the responsibilities of men and women in business as individuals? Doesn't ethics finally rest on the honesty and integrity of the individual in the business world?

Reply

Yes and no. Yes, in the sense that the control of large organizations does finally rest in the hands of managers, of men and women. No, in the sense that what is being controlled is a cooperative system for a cooperative purpose. The projection of responsibility to the organization is simply an acknowledgment of the fact that the whole is more than the sum of its parts. . . .

Studies of management have long shown that the attributes, successes, and failures of organizations are phenomena that emerge from the coordination of persons' attributes and that explanations of such phenomena require categories of analysis and description beyond the level of the individual. Moral responsibility is an attribute that can manifest itself in organizations as surely as competence or efficiency.

Objection 8

Is the frame of reference here proposed intended to replace or undercut the relevance of the "invisible hand" and the "government hand" views, which depend on external controls?

Reply

No. Just as regulation and economic competition are not substitutes for corporate responsibility, so corporate responsibility is not a substitute for law and the market. The imperatives of ethics cannot be relied on—nor have they ever been relied on—without a context of external sanctions. And this is true as much for individuals as for organizations.

This frame of reference takes us beneath, but not beyond, the realm of external systems of rules and incentives and into the thought processes that interpret and respond to the corporation's environment. Morality is more than merely part of that environment. It aims at the projection of conscience, not the enthronement of it in either the state or the competitive process.

The rise of the modern large corporation and the concomitant rise of the professional manager demand a conceptual framework in which these phenomena can be accommodated to moral thought. The principle of moral projection furthers such accommodation by recognizing a new level of agency in society and thus a new level of responsibility.

Objection 9

Corporations have always taken the interests of those outside the corporation into account in the sense that customer relations and public relations generally are an integral part of rational economic decision making. Market signals and social signals that filter through the market mechanism inevitably represent the interests of parties affected by the behavior of the company. What then, is the point of adding respect to rationality?

Reply

Representing the affected parties solely as economic variables in the environment of the company is treating them as means or resources and not as ends in themselves. It implies that the only voice which affected parties should have in organizational decision making is that of potential buyers, sellers, regulators, or boycotters. Besides, many affected parties may not occupy such roles, and those who do may not be able to signal the organization with messages that effectively represent their stakes in its actions.

To be sure, classical economic theory would have us believe that perfect competition in free markets (with modest adjustments from the state) will result in all relevant signals being "heard," but the abstractions from reality implicit in such theory make it insufficient as a frame of reference for moral responsibility. In a world in which strict self-interest was congruent with the common good, moral responsibility might be unnecessary. We do not, alas, live in such a world.

The element of respect in our analysis of responsibility plays an essential role in ensuring the recognition of unrepresented or underrepresented voices in the decision-making of organizations as agents. Showing respect for persons as ends and not mere means to organizational purposes is central to the concept of corporate responsibility.

Thought Questions

1. Do the authors suggest that corporate social responsibility replace the market or legal restraints imposed on corporations? Explain.

2. Do you see any problems with treating organizations as individuals? Explain.

Stone: A Reflective Process

As outlined in Figure 54–6, Christopher D. Stone asserts that corporate social responsibility requires a thoughtful, deliberative process of decisionmaking. Read the following excerpt on Stone's concept of corporate responsibility.

Figure 54–6   Philosophy of Christopher D. Stone

A Duty to engage in a reflective process prior to making decisions

What "Corporate Responsibility" Might Really Mean*

If people are going to adopt the terminology of "responsibility" (with its allied concepts of corporate conscience) to suggest new, improved ways of dealing with corporations, then they ought to go back and examine in detail what "being responsible" entails—in the ordinary case of the responsible human being. Only after we have considered what being responsible calls for in general does it make sense to develop the notion of a corporation being responsible.

To begin with, for want of any real model of responsibility, the proponents of corporate responsibility all too often seem to identify it with corporate giving to charity—a sort of questionable copout, both theoretically and practically. But responsibility should not be confused with altruism. In the case of human beings it is to meet far more complex and subtle needs that responsibility is developed and nurtured.

We know that it is futile to hope that all socially undesirable behavior can be anticipated by legal rule-makers. We know that attempts to enforce all social desiderata by law would be more costly than it would be worth. We fear, too, that such attempts would unsatisfactorily

*Source: Christopher D. Stone, *Where the Law Ends,* Chapter 12, "What 'Corporate Responsiblity' Might Really Mean" (New York City: Harper Collins, 1975). Copyright © 1975 by Christopher D. Stone. Reprinted by permission of Harper Collins Publishers, Inc.

enlarge the role of government while severely diminishing personal freedom. There are thus certain virtues, both to the individuals and to the society at large, of encouraging people to act in socially appropriate ways because they believe it the "right thing" to do, rather than because (and thus, perhaps only to the extent that) they are ordered to do so. Trusting to responsible behavior through some measure of self-control is often a preferable solution to some of the most difficult and perhaps otherwise insoluble problems of social organization.

Why these observations are important is that when we look back now on the unsatisfactoriness of present measures for controlling corporations, we can identify the very sorts of problems that have led to the nurturing of responsibility in human beings. . . . Thus, the functions for which we need responsibility in human beings have distinct counterparts in the realm of corporate behavior. But what does it mean to be responsible? What does being responsible involve?

Once we start to examine what responsibility consists of in an ordinary person, we can see more clearly why there is something so unsatisfactory about current discussions of corporate responsibility. . . .

The problem is that judgments of responsibility can be ascribed according to two schemes that are superficially distinct, if not in outright opposition. The first sense of responsibility, Responsibility 1, emphasizes following the law. . . . The second sense, Responsibility 2, emphasizes cognitive process, and, in a way almost diametrically opposed to Responsibility 1, puts a premium on autonomy, rather than rule obedience. Specifically, responsibility in the second sense emphasizes that a person's deliberations include the following elements:

- . . . Reflection is always an ingredient of responsibility in this sense.
- Responsible behavior begins with perception. . . .
- A responsible person . . . acts with an awareness that he will be accountable for what happens.
- To be responsible in this sense emphasizes a person's taking into account the consequences and repercussions of his actions. . . .
- He must consider and weigh alternatives.
- . . . The reflection must be structured by reference to the society's moral vocabulary—that is, by characterizations in terms of "good," "bad," "just," and so forth, by thinking of "obligations," "rights," and "duties."
- One must have, in addition to a moral vocabulary, a moral inclination—a desire, probably as much internalized as conscious, to "do the right thing."
- Closely related is the fact that one must be prepared to give some justification for what he is doing. Overlooking for a moment the variation among traditional ethical theories, by and large they hold in common the view that to be responsible involves being prepared to explain, to give good reasons for one's actions; the responsible actor is willing to generalize the grounds for what he has done. This preparedness to justify, and especially the preparedness to do so in terms that admit of generalization (the Golden Rule, Kant's Categorical Imperative), is an important step toward the socialization of one's actions, inasmuch as it forces awareness of the social setting and the socially sanctified grounds of behavior.

■ ■ ■

Which of these two notions of responsibility—that which emphasizes following rules or that which emphasizes cognitive process, with some allowance for autonomy—would we ideally want to implant into corporations? The answer is both. For where it *is* feasible to design relatively unambiguous rules for corporate behavior—not to include nonskeletal meats in frankfurters—all we want is the responsibility of the rule-following, role-adhering sort.

But as I have stressed throughout, there is also a large range of cases where rigid rules are increasingly ineffective, and perhaps even counterproductive, as instruments of corporate control. To meet the problems in those areas the responsibility that is needed—whether we are talking about corporations or persons—is a responsibility of the "mature" sort, emphasizing cognitive process, rather than blind rule obedience.

Thought Questions

1. In Stone's opinion, how does corporate social responsibility differ from corporate altruism?
2. What, in Stone's view, is meant by a "responsible corporation"?

CORPORATE CULTURE

If one accepts an obligation for socially responsible behavior beyond making profits, the corporation needs to recognize the various social roles that it plays: It is a citizen, an employer, a producer. In other words, it has been suggested that the corporation owes an obligation to various stakeholders, of which shareholders are only one. In order for a corporation to act responsibly, the people within that organization must act responsibly. The culture within a corporation must be one in which ethical decision-making is not only condoned but encouraged.

The U.S. Sentencing Commission, in a major initiative against white-collar crime, issued federal sentencing guidelines effective November 1, 1991. These guidelines cover most federal crimes and relate to corporate liability for a whole host of crimes committed by employees. By adopting a "carrot and stick" approach, these guidelines encourage corporate management to create an ethical corporate culture. The "stick" is corporate fines of up to $290 million. The "carrot" dramatically reduces these fines for corporations with "an effective program to prevent and detect violations of the law" [United States Sentencing Guidelines § 8C 2.5(f)].

An "effective compliance" program requires a strong institutional response but leaves specifics up to the corporation.

Who Creates the Corporate Culture?

It is the obligation of upper management to establish an effective corporate culture. Read the following excerpt from "The Parable of the Sadhu" in which the author writes about the obligation of the leader. The author, Buzz McCoy, while mountain climbing in Nepal, came across a sadhu dying of exposure. Instead of assuming responsibility for rescuing him, his group merely carried the sadhu to the next group down the mountain. They believe that the Sadhu most probably died.

*The Parable of the Sadhu**

■ ■ ■

One of our problems was that as a group we had no process for developing a consensus. We had no sense of purpose or plan. The difficulties of dealing with the sadhu were so complex that no one person could handle it. Because it did not have a set of preconditions that could guide its action to an acceptable resolution, the group reacted instinctively as individuals. The cross-cultural nature of the group added a further layer of complexity. We had no leader

---

*Souce: Buzz McCoy, "The Parable of the Sadhu," *Harvard Business Review,* September–October 1983, pp. 103–8. Mr. Mccoy is managing director of Morgan Stanley & Co., Inc., and president of Morgan Stanley Realty, Inc. He is also an ordained ruling elder of the United Presbyterian Church. Reprinted with permission of *Harvard Business Review.*

with whom we could all identify and in whose purpose we believed. Only Stephen was willing to take charge, but he could not gain adequate support to care for the sadhu.

Some organizations do have a value system that transcends the personal values of the managers. Such values, which go beyond profitability, are usually revealed when the organization is under stress.

■ ■ ■

The word "ethics" turns off many and confuses more. Yet the notions of shared values and an agreed-on process for dealing with adversity and change—what many people mean when they talk about corporate culture—seem to be at the heart of the ethical issue. People who are in touch with their own core beliefs and the beliefs of others and are sustained by them can be more comfortable living on the cutting edge. At times, taking a tough line or a decisive stand in a muddle of ambiguity is the only ethical thing to do. If a manager is indecisive and spends time trying to figure out the "good" thing to do, the enterprise may be lost.

Business ethics, then, has to do with the authenticity and integrity of the enterprise. To be ethical is to follow the business as well as the cultural goals of the corporation, its owners, its employees, and its customers. Those who cannot serve the corporate vision are not authentic business people and, therefore, are not ethical in the business sense.

Thought Questions

1. What does McCoy mean when he says: "To be ethical is to follow the business as well as the cultural goals of the corporation, its owners, its employees, and its customers"? Do you agree?

2. If a part of business ethics is to follow the "core beliefs" of the leaders, what do you do if your core beliefs differ from those of corporate management?

3. The author talks of the shared values of the corporation. How do you think that Robert Jackall, the author of *Moral Mazes* presented in the beginning of this chapter, would respond to this excerpt?

How to Set the Corporate Culture

How does one, as a manager, set a corporate culture in which ethical decisionmaking is encouraged? A number of ways have been suggested, ranging from corporate audits (an internal examination of the ethics of the organization, comparable to the way a financial audit examines the financial activities of the organization), ethics training sessions, and mechanisms to encourage employee reporting of violation.

One of the more common ways in which upper management attempts to encourage ethical behavior is by adopting a corporate codes of ethics. In corporate codes, upper management sets forth guidelines for ethical behavior. Examples of two corporate codes are found in the following essay, where the author argues that corporate codes are not very useful.

*Ethical Codes**

Ethical codes are statements of the norms and beliefs of an organization. These norms and beliefs are generally proposed, discussed, and defined by the senior executives in the firm

---

*Source: LaRue Tone Hosmer, *The Ethics of Management* (Homewood, Ill.: Richard D. Irwin, 1987), pp. 153–57. Copyright © 1987 by Richard D. Irwin. Reprinted by permission.

and then published and distributed to all of the members. Norms, of course, are standards of behavior; they are the ways the senior people in the organization want the others to act when confronted with a given situation. An example of a norm in a code of ethics would be, "Employees of this company will not accept personal gifts with a monetary value over $25 in total from any friend or associate, and they are expected to pay their full share of the costs for meals or other entertainment (concerts, the theatre, sporting events, etc.) that have a value above $25 per person." The norms in an ethical code are generally expressed as a series of negative statements, for it is easier to list the things a person should not do than to be precise about the things a person should do.

The beliefs in an ethical code are standards of thought; they are the ways that the senior people in the organization want others to think. This is not censorship. Instead, the intent is to encourage ways of thinking and patterns of attitudes that will lead towards the wanted behavior. Consequently, the beliefs in an ethical code are generally expressed in a positive form. "Our first responsibility is to our customer" is an example of a positive belief that commonly appears in codes of ethics; another would be "We wish to be good citizens of every community in which we operate." Some company codes of ethics appear in Figures 1 and 2.

Figure 1   The Ethics Code of Borg-Warner Corporation: "To Reach beyond the Minimal"

Any business is a member of a social system, entitled to the rights and bound by the responsibilities of that membership. Its freedom to pursue economic goals is constrained by law and channeled by the forces of a free market. But these demands are minimal, requiring only that a business provide wanted goods and services, compete fairly, and cause no obvious harm.

For some companies that is enough. It is not enough for Borg-Warner. We impose upon ourselves an obligation to reach beyond the minimal. We do so convinced that by making a larger contribution to the society that sustains us, we best assure not only its future vitality, but our own.

This is what we believe. . . .

We believe in the dignity of the individual. However large and complex a business may be, its work is still done by people dealing with people. Each person involved is a unique human being, with pride, needs, values and innate personal worth. For Borg-Warner to succeed we must operate in a climate of openness and trust, in which each of us freely grants others the same respect, cooperation and decency we seek for ourselves.

We believe in our responsibility to the common good. Because Borg-Warner is both an economic and social force, our responsibilities to the public are large. The spur of competition and the sanctions of the law give strong guidance to our behavior, but alone do not inspire our best. For that we must heed the voice of our natural concern for others. Our challenge is to supply goods and services that are of superior value to those who use them; to create jobs that provide meaning for those who do them; to honor and enhance human life, and to offer our talents and our wealth to help improve the world we share.

We believe in the endless quest for excellence. Though we may be better today than we were yesterday, we are not as good as we must become. Borg-Warner chooses to be a leader—in serving our customers, advancing our technologies, and rewarding all who invest in us their time, money, and trust. None of us can settle for doing less than our best, and we can never stop trying to surpass what already has been achieved.

We believe in continuous renewal. A corporation endures and prospers only by moving forward. The past has given us the present to build on. But to follow our visions to the future, we must see the difference between traditions that give us continuity and strength, and conventions that no longer serve us—and have the course to act on that knowledge. Most can adapt after change has occurred; we must be among the few who anticipate change, shape it to our purpose, and act as its agents.

We believe in the commonwealth of Borg-Warner and its people. Borg-Warner is both a federation of businesses and a community of people. Our goal is to preserve the freedom each of us needs to find personal satisfaction while building the strength that comes from unity. True unity is more than a melding of self-interests; it results when values and ideals are also shared. Some of ours are spelled out in these statements of belief. Others include faith in our political, economic and spiritual heritage; pride in our work and our company; the knowledge that loyalty must flow in many directions; and a conviction that ownership is strongest when shared. We look to the unifying force of these beliefs as a source of energy to brighten the future of our company and all who depend on it.

Source: Borg-Warner Corporation booklet, 1982.

Do ethical codes work? Are they helpful in conveying to all employees the moral standards selected by the board of directors and president? Not really. The problem is that it is not possible to state the norms and beliefs of an organization relative to the various constituent groups—employees, customers, suppliers, distributors, stockholders, and the general public—clearly and explicitly, without offending at least one of those groups. It is not possible to say, for example, that a company considers its employees to be more important to the success of the firm than its stockholders, without putting the stockholders on notice that profits and dividends come second. Stockholders, and their agents at trust departments and mutual funds, tend to resent that, just as the employees would if the conditions were reversed. Consequently codes of ethics are usually written in general terms, noting obligations to each of the groups but not stating which takes precedence in any given situation.

The basic difficulty with codes of ethics is that they do not establish priorities between the norms and beliefs. The priorities are the true values of a firm, and they are not included. As an example, let us say that one division in a firm is faced with declining sales and profits; the question is whether to reduce middle-management employment and cut overhead costs—the classic downsizing decision—but the code of ethics says in one section that we respect our employees and in another section that we expect ''fair'' profits. How do we decide? What is ''fair'' in this instance? The code of ethics does not tell us.

■ ■ ■

Ethical dilemmas are conflicts between economic performance and social performance, with the social performance being expressed as obligations to employees, customers, suppliers, distributors, and the general public. Ethical codes can express a general sense of the

---

Figure 2   The Ethics Code of Johnson & Johnson: ''Our Credo''

We believe our first responsibility is to the doctors, nurses, and patients, to mothers and all others who use our products and services.
In meeting their needs everything we do must be of high quality.
We must constantly strive to reduce our costs in order to maintain reasonable prices.
Customers' orders must be serviced promptly and accurately.
Our suppliers and distributors must have an opportunity to make a fair profit.
We are responsible to our employees, the men and women who work with us throughout the world.
Everyone must be considered as an individual.
We must respect their dignity and recognize their merit.
They must have a sense of security in their jobs.
Compensation must be fair and adequate, and working conditions clean, orderly and safe.
Employees must feel free to make suggestions and complaints.
There must be equal opportunity for employment, development and advancement for those qualified.
We must provide competent management, and their actions must be just and ethical.
We are responsible to the communities in which we live and work and to the world community as well.
We must be good citizens—support good works and charities and bear our fair share of taxes.
We must encourage civic improvements and better health and education.
We must maintain in good order the property we are privileged to use, protecting the environment and natural resources.
Our final responsibility is to our stockholders.
Business must make a sound profit.
We must experiment with new ideas.
Research must be carried on, innovative programs developed and mistakes paid for.
New equipment must be purchased, new facilities provided and new products launched.
Reserves must be created to provide for adverse times.
When we operate according to these principles, the stockholders should realize a fair return.

Source: Johnson & Johnson annual report, 1982, p. 5.

obligation members of senior management feel towards those groups, but the codes cannot help a middle- or lower-level manager choose between the groups, or between economic and social performance.

Thought Questions

1. Look at Johnson & Johnson's code of ethics. Did the credo require that the company remove Tylenol from the shelves of every store after it discovered that some bottles had been tampered with and deaths had resulted?

2. Does Hosmer assert that corporations should not adopt codes of ethics?

3. If codes of ethics are not sufficient to set the culture of the corporation, what else should management do?

END–OF–CHAPTER QUESTIONS

1. Analyze the following statement: "The market is like a tool: designed to do certain jobs but unsuited for others" [Lindbloom, "The Limited Competence of Markets"].

2. Make a list of market imperfections. Give an example of each.

3. Analyze the following statement: "The extent to which one views markets as flawed affects one's view on corporate social responsibility."

4. Analyze the following statement: "Law seems most appropriate where it is used to enforce acceptable minimums, rather than to force from each person what he is fully capable of" [Stone, *Where the Law Ends*, p. 101].

5. What attitudes create the corporate culture?

6. It was suggested that one reason that the law is inadequate as the sole guide for corporate behavior is because of the lack of societal consensus regarding which values should be considered. If that is true, how can corporate executives better know what to do?

7. If the law is inadequate to regulate corporate behavior, is deregulation the answer?

8. How should Acme, Inc., in the opening scenario respond to the issue presented? Does your view of social responsibility affect your answer?

9. Compare and contrast the views of (a) Milton Friedman, (b) Goodpaster and Matthews, and (c) Christopher Stone.

10. Are corporations well suited to creating and implementing social programs? Does this affect your position on corporate social responsibility? Does your answer depend on whether you view corporate social responsibility as mandating "good deeds" or prohibiting "bad deeds"?

Appendixes

■

Appendix A

The Constitution of the United States of America

PREAMBLE

We the People of the United States, in Order to form a more perfect Union, establish Justice, insure domestic Tranquility, provide for the common defense, promote the general Welfare, and secure the Blessings of Liberty to ourselves and our Posterity, do ordain and establish this Constitution for the United States of America.

ARTICLE I

Section 1 All legislative Powers herein granted shall be vested in a Congress of the United States, which shall consist of a Senate and House of Representatives.

Section 2 The House of Representatives shall be composed of Members chosen every second Year by the People of the several States, and the Electors in each State shall have the Qualifications requisite for Electors of the most numerous Branch of the State Legislature.

No Person shall be a Representative who shall not have attained to the age of twenty five Years, and been seven Years a Citizen of the United States, and who shall not, when elected, be an Inhabitant of that State in which he shall be chosen.

Representatives and direct Taxes shall be apportioned among the several States which may be included within this Union, according to their respective Numbers, which shall be determined by adding to the whole Number of free Persons, including those bound to Service for a Term of Years, and excluding Indians not taxed, three fifths of all other Persons.[1] The actual Enumeration shall be made within three Years after the first Meeting of the Congress of the United States, and within every subsequent Term of ten Years, in such Manner as they shall by Law direct. The Number of Representatives shall not exceed one for every thirty Thousand, but each State shall have at Least one Representative, and until such enumeration shall be made, the State of New Hampshire shall be entitled to choose three, Massachusetts eight, Rhode-Island and Providence Plantations one, Connecticut five, New York six, New Jersey four, Pennsylvania eight, Delaware one, Maryland six, Virginia ten, North Carolina five, South Carolina five, and Georgia three.

When vacancies happen in the Representation from any State, the Executive Authority thereof shall issue Writs of Election to fill such Vacancies.

The House of Representatives shall chuse their Speaker and other Officers; and shall have the sole Power of Impeachment.

Section 3 The Senate of the United States shall be composed of two Senators from each State, chosen by the Legislature thereof,[2] for six Years; and each Senator shall have one Vote.

Immediately after they shall be assembled in Consequence of the first Election, they shall be divided as equally as may be into three Classes. The Seats of the Senators of the first Class shall be vacated at the Expiration of the second Year, of the second Class at the Expiration of the fourth Year, and of the third Class at the Expiration of the sixth Year, so that one third may be chosen every second Year; and if Vacancies happen by Resignation, or otherwise, during the Recess of the Legislature of any State, the Executive thereof may make temporary Appointments until the next Meeting of the Legislature, which shall then fill such Vacancies.[3]

No Person shall be a Senator who shall not have attained to the Age of thirty Years, and been nine Years a Citizen of the United States, and who shall not, when elected, be an Inhabitant of that State for which he shall be chosen.

The Vice President of the United States shall be President of the Senate, but shall have no Vote, unless they be equally divided.

The Senate shall chuse their other Officers, and also a President pro tempore, in the Absence of the Vice President, or when he shall exercise the Office of President of the United States.

---

[1]Changed by the Fourteenth Amendment.

[2]Changed by the Seventeenth Amendment.
[3]Changed by the Seventeenth Amendment.

The Senate shall have the sole Power to try all Impeachments. When sitting for that Purpose, they shall be on Oath or Affirmation. When the President of the United States is tried, the Chief Justice shall preside: And no Person shall be convicted without the Concurrence of two thirds of the Members present.

Judgment in Cases of Impeachment shall not extend further than to removal from Office, and disqualification to hold and enjoy any Office of honor, Trust or Profit under the United States: but the Party convicted shall nevertheless be liable and subject to Indictment, Trial, Judgment and Punishment, according to Law.

Section 4   The Times, Places and Manner of holding Elections for Senators and Representatives, shall be prescribed in each State by the Legislature thereof; but the Congress may at any time by Law make or alter such Regulations, except as to the Places of chusing Senators.

The Congress shall assemble at least once in every Year, and such Meeting shall be on the first Monday in December, unless they shall by Law appoint a different Day.[4]

Section 5   Each House shall be the Judge of the Elections, Returns and Qualifications of its own Members, and a Majority of each shall constitute a Quorum to do Business; but a smaller Number may adjourn from day to day, and may be authorized to compel the Attendance of absent Members, in such Manner, and under such Penalties as each House may provide.

Each House may determine the Rules of its Proceedings, punish its Members for disorderly Behaviour, and, with the Concurrence of two thirds, expel a Member.

Each House shall keep a Journal of its Proceedings, and from time to time publish the same, excepting such Parts as may in their Judgment require Secrecy; and the Yeas and Nays of the Members of either House on any question shall, at the Desire of one fifth of those Present, be entered on the Journal.

Neither House, during the Session of Congress, shall, without the Consent of the other, adjourn for more than three days, nor to any other Place than that in which the two Houses shall be sitting.

Section 6   The Senators and Representatives shall receive a Compensation for their Services, to be ascertained by Law, and paid out of the Treasury of the United States. They shall in all Cases, except Treason, Felony and Breach of the Peace, be privileged from Arrest during their Attendance at the Session of their respective Houses, and in going to and returning from the same; and for any Speech or Debate in either House, they shall not be questioned in any other Place.

No Senator or Representative shall, during the Time for which he was elected, be appointed to any civil Office under the Authority of the United States, which shall have been created, or the Emoluments whereof shall have been encreased during such time; and no Person holding any Office under the United States, shall be a Member of either House during his Continuance in Office.

Section 7   All Bills for raising Revenue shall originate in the House of Representatives; but the Senate may propose or concur with Amendments as on other Bills.

Every Bill which shall have passed the House of Representatives and the Senate, shall, before it becomes a Law, be presented to the President of the United States; If he approves he shall sign it, but if not he shall return it, with his Objections to that House in which it shall have originated, who shall enter the Objections at large on their Journal, and proceed to reconsider it. If after such Reconsideration two thirds of that House shall agree to pass the Bill, it shall be sent, together with the Objections, to the other House, by which it shall likewise be reconsidered, and if approved by two thirds of that House, it shall become a Law. But in all such Cases the Votes of both Houses shall be determined by yeas and Nays, and the Names of the Persons voting for and against the Bill shall be entered on the Journal of each House respectively. If any Bill shall not be returned by the President within ten Days (Sundays excepted) after it shall have been presented to him, the Same shall be a Law, in like Manner as if he had signed it, unless the Congress by their Adjournment prevent its Return, in which Case it shall not be a Law.

Every Order, Resolution, or Vote to which the Concurrence of the Senate and House of Representatives may be necessary (except on a question of Adjournment) shall be presented to the President of the United States; and before the Same shall take Effect, shall be approved by him, or being disapproved by him, shall be repassed by two thirds of the Senate and House of Representatives, according to the Rules and Limitations prescribed in the Case of a Bill.

Section 8   The Congress shall have Power To lay and collect Taxes, Duties, Imposts and Excises, to pay the Debts and provide for the common Defence and general Welfare of the United States; but all Duties, Imposts and Excises shall be uniform throughout the United States.

To borrow Money on the credit of the United States;

To regulate Commerce with foreign Nations, and among the several States, and with the Indian Tribes;

To establish an uniform Rule of Naturalization, and uniform Laws on the subject of Bankruptcies throughout the United States;

To coin Money, regulate the Value thereof, and of foreign Coin, and fix the Standard of Weights and Measures;

To provide for the Punishment of counterfeiting the Securities and current Coin of the United States;

To establish Post Offices and post Roads;

To promote the Progress of Science and useful Arts, by securing for limited Times to Authors and Inventors the exclusive Right to their respective Writings and Discoveries;

---

[4]Changed by the Twentieth Amendment.

To constitute Tribunals inferior to the supreme Court;

To define and punish Piracies and Felonies committed on the high Seas, and Offences against the Law of Nations;

To declare War, grant Letters of Marque and Reprisal, and make Rules concerning Captures on Land and Water;

To raise and support Armies, but no Appropriation of Money to that Use shall be for a longer Term than two Years;

To provide and maintain a Navy;

To make Rules for the Government and Regulation of the land and naval Forces;

To provide for calling forth the Militia to execute the Laws of the Union, suppress Insurrections and repel Invasions;

To provide for organizing, arming, and disciplining, the Militia, and for governing such Part of them as may be employed in the Service of the United States, reserving to the States respectively, the Appointment of the Officers, and the Authority of training the Militia according to the discipline prescribed by Congress;

To exercise exclusive Legislation in all Cases whatsoever, over such District (not exceeding ten Miles square) as may, by Cession of particular States, and the Acceptance of Congress, become the Seat of the Government of the United States, and to exercise like Authority over all Places purchased by the Consent of the Legislature of the State in which the Same shall be, for the Erection of Forts, Magazines, Arsenals, dock-Yards, and other needful Buildings;—And

To make all Laws which shall be necessary and proper for carrying into Execution the foregoing Powers, and all other Powers vested by this Constitution in the Government of the United States, or in any Department or Officer thereof.

Section 9　The Migration or Importation of such Persons as any of the States now existing shall think proper to admit, shall not be prohibited by the Congress prior to the Year one thousand eight hundred and eight, but a Tax or duty may be imposed on such Importation, not exceeding ten dollars for each Person.

The Privilege of the Writ of Habeas Corpus shall not be suspended, unless when in Cases of Rebellion or Invasion the public Safety may require it.

No Bill of Attainder or ex post facto Law shall be passed.

No Capitation, or other direct, Tax shall be laid, unless in Proportion to the Census of Enumeration herein before directed to be taken.[5]

No Tax or Duty shall be laid on Articles exported from any State.

No Preference shall be given by any Regulation of Commerce or Revenue to the Ports of one State over those of another: nor shall Vessels bound to, or from, one State, be obliged to enter, clear, or pay Duties in another.

No Money shall be drawn from the Treasury, but in Consequence of Appropriations made by Law; and a regular Statement and Account of the Receipts and Expenditures of all public Money shall be published from time to time.

No Title of Nobility shall be granted by the United States: And no Person holding any Office of Profit or Trust under them, shall, without the Consent of the Congress, accept of any present, Emolument, Office, or Title, of any kind whatever, from any King, Prince, or foreign State.

Section 10　No State shall enter into any Treaty, Alliance, or Confederation; grant Letters of Marque and Reprisal; coin Money; emit Bills of Credit; make any Thing but gold and silver coin a Tender in Payment of Debts; pass any Bill of Attainder, ex post facto Law, or Law impairing the Obligation of Contracts, or grant any Title of Nobility.

No State shall, without the Consent of the Congress, lay any Imposts or Duties on Imports or Exports, except what may be absolutely necessary for executing its inspection Laws: and the net Produce of all Duties and Imposts, laid by any State on Imports or Exports, shall be for the Use of the Treasury of the United States; and all such Laws shall be subject to the Revision and Controul of the Congress.

No State shall, without the consent of Congress, lay any Duty of Tonnage, keep Troops, or Ships of War in time of Peace, enter into any Agreement or Compact with another State, or with a foreign Power, or engage in War, unless actually invaded, or in such imminent Danger as will not admit of delay.

ARTICLE II

Section 1　The executive Power shall be vested in a President of the United States of America. He shall hold his Office during the Term of four Years, and, together with the Vice President, chosen for the same Term, be elected, as follows

Each state shall appoint, in such Manner as the Legislature thereof may direct, a Number of Electors, equal to the whole Number of Senators and Representatives to which the State may be entitled in Congress: but no Senator or Representative, or Person holding an Office of Trust or Profit under the United States, shall be appointed an Elector.

The Electors shall meet in their respective States, and vote by Ballot for two Persons, of whom one at least shall not be an inhabitant of the same State with themselves. And they shall make a List of all the Persons voted for,

---

[5]Changed by the Sixteenth Amendment.

and of the Number of Votes for each; which List they shall sign and certify, and transmit sealed to the Seat of the Government of the United States, directed to the President of the Senate. The President of the Senate shall, in the Presence of the Senate and House of Representatives, open all the Certificates, and the Votes shall then be counted. The Person having the greatest Number of Votes shall be the President, if such Number be a Majority of the whole Number of Electors appointed; and if there be more than one who have such Majority, and have an equal Number of Votes, then the House of Representatives shall immediately chuse by Ballot one of them for President; and if no Person have a Majority, then from the five highest on the List the said House shall in like Manner chuse the President. But in chusing the President, the Votes shall be taken by States, the Representation from each State having one Vote; A quorum for this purpose shall consist of a Member or Members from two thirds of the States, and a Majority of all the States shall be necessary to a Choice. In every Case, after the Choice of the President, the Person having the greatest Number of Votes of the Electors shall be the Vice President. But if there should remain two or more who have equal Votes, the Senate shall chuse from them by Ballot the Vice President.[6]

The Congress may determine the Time of chusing the Electors, and the Day on which they shall give their Votes; which Day shall be the same throughout the United States.

No Person except a natural born Citizen, or a Citizen of the United States, at the time of the Adoption of this Constitution, shall be eligible to the Office of President; neither shall any Person be eligible to that Office who shall not have attained to the Age of thirty five Years, and been fourteen Years a Resident within the United States.

In Case of the Removal of the President from Office, or of his Death, Resignation, or Inability to discharge the Powers and Duties of the said Office, the Same shall devolve on the Vice President, and the Congress may by Law provide for the Case of Removal, Death, Resignation or Inability, both of the President and Vice President, declaring what Officer shall then act as President, and such Officer shall act accordingly, until the Disability be removed, or a President shall be elected.[7]

The President shall, at stated Times, receive for his Services, a Compensation, which shall neither be encreased nor diminished during the Period for which he shall have been elected, and he shall not receive within that Period any other Emolument from the United States, or any of them.

Before he enter on the Execution of his Office, he shall take the following Oath or Affirmation: — "I do solemnly swear (or affirm) that I will faithfully execute the Office of President of the United States, and will to the best of my Ability, preserve, protect, and defend the Constitution of the United States."

Section 2 The President shall be Commander in Chief of the Army and Navy of the United States, and of the Militia of the several States, when called into the actual Service of the United States; he may require the Opinion, in writing, of the principal Officer in each of the executive Departments, upon any Subject relating to the Duties of their respective Offices, and he shall have Power to grant Reprieves and Pardons for Offences against the United States, except in Cases of Impeachment.

He shall have Power, by and with the Advice and Consent of the Senate, to make Treaties, provided two thirds of the Senators present concur; and he shall nominate, and by and with the Advice and Consent of the Senate, shall appoint Ambassadors, other public Ministers and Consuls, Judges of the supreme Court, and all other Officers of the United States, whose Appointments are not herein otherwise provided for, and which shall be established by Law; but the Congress may by Law vest the Appointment of such inferior Officers, as they think proper, in the President alone, in the Courts of Law, or in the Heads of Departments.

The President shall have Power to fill up all Vacancies that may happen during the Recess of the Senate, by granting Commissions which shall expire at the End of their next Session.

Section 3 He shall from time to time give to the Congress Information of the State of the Union, and recommend to their Consideration such Measures as he shall judge necessary and expedient; he may, on extraordinary Occasions, convene both Houses, or either of them, and in Case of Disagreement between them, with Respect to the Time of Adjournment, he may adjourn them to such Time as he shall think proper; he shall receive Ambassadors and other public Ministers; he shall take Care that the Laws be faithfully executed, and shall Commission all the Officers of the United States.

Section 4 The President, Vice President and all civil Officers of the United States, shall be removed from Office on Impeachment for, and Conviction of, Treason, Bribery, or other high Crimes and Misdemeanors.

ARTICLE III

Section 1 The judicial Power of the United States, shall be vested in one supreme Court, and in such inferior Courts as the Congress may from time to time ordain and establish. The Judges, both of the supreme and inferior Courts, shall hold their Offices during good Behaviour, and shall, at stated Times, receive for their Services, a Compensation, which shall not be diminished during their Continuance in Office.

---

[6]Changed by the Twelfth Amendment.

[7]Changed by the Twenty-fifth Amendment.

Section 2   The judicial Power shall extend to all Cases, in Law and Equity, arising under this Constitution, the Laws of the United States, and Treaties made, or which shall be made, under their Authority;— to all Cases affecting Ambassadors. other public Ministers and Consuls;— to all Cases of admiralty and maritime Jurisdiction;— to Controversies to which the United States shall be a party;— to Controversies between two or more States;— between a State and Citizens of another State;[8] — between Citizens of different States;— between Citizens of the same State claiming Lands under Grants of different States, and between a State, or the Citizens thereof, and foreign States, Citizens or Subjects.

In all Cases affecting Ambassadors, other public Ministers and Consuls, and those in which a State shall be Party, the supreme Court shall have original Jurisdiction. In all the other Cases before mentioned, the supreme Court shall have appellate Jurisdiction, both as to Law and Fact, with such Exceptions, and under such Regulations as the Congress shall make.

The Trial of all Crimes, except in Cases of Impeachment, shall be by Jury: and such Trial shall be held in the State where the said Crimes shall have been committed; but when not committed within any State, the Trial shall be at such Place or Places as the Congress may by Law have directed.

Section 3   Treason against the United States, shall consist only in levying War against them, or in adhering to their Enemies, giving them Aid and Comfort. No Person shall be convicted of Treason unless on the Testimony of two Witnesses to the same overt Act, or on Confession in open Court.

The Congress shall have Power to declare the Punishment of Treason, but no Attainder of Treason shall work Corruption of Blood, or Forfeiture except during the Life of the Person attainted.

ARTICLE IV

Section 1   Full Faith and Credit shall be given in each State to the public Acts, Records, and judicial Proceedings of every other State. And the Congress may by general Laws prescribe the Manner in which such Acts, Records and Proceedings shall be proved, and the Effect thereof.

Section 2   The Citizens of each State shall be entitled to all Privileges and Immunities of Citizens in the several States.

A Person charged in any State with Treason, Felony, or other Crime, who shall flee from Justice, and be found in another State, shall on Demand of the executive Authority of the State from which he fled, be delivered up, to be removed to the State having Jurisdiction of the Crime.

No Person held to Service or Labour in one State, under the Laws thereof, escaping into another, shall, in Consequence of any Law or Regulation therein, be discharged from such Service or Labour, but shall be delivered up on Claim of the Party to whom such Service or Labour may be due.[9]

Section 3   New States may be admitted by the Congress into this Union; but no new State shall be formed or erected within the Jurisdiction of any other State; nor any State be formed by the Junction of two or more States, or Parts of States, without the Consent of the Legislatures of the States concerned as well as of the Congress.

The Congress shall have Power to dispose of and make all needful Rules and Regulations respecting the Territory or other Property belonging to the United States; and nothing in this Constitution shall be so construed as to Prejudice any Claims of the United States, or of any particular State.

Section 4   The United States shall guarantee to every State in this Union a Republican Form of Government, and shall protect each of them against Invasion; and on Application of the Legislature, or of the Executive (when the Legislature cannot be convened) against domestic Violence.

ARTICLE V

The Congress, whenever two thirds of both Houses shall deem it necessary, shall propose Amendments to this Constitution, or, on the Application of the Legislatures of two thirds of the several States, shall call a Convention for proposing Amendments, which, in either Case, shall be valid to all Intents and Purposes, as Part of this Constitution, when ratified by the legislatures of three fourths of the several States, or by Conventions in three fourths thereof, as the one or the other Mode of Ratification may be proposed by the Congress; Provided that no Amendment which may be made prior to the Year One thousand eight hundred and eight shall in any Manner affect the first and fourth Clauses in the Ninth Section of the first Article; and that no State, without its Consent, shall be deprived of its equal Suffrage in the Senate.

ARTICLE VI

All Debts contracted and Engagements entered into, before the Adoption of this Constitution, shall be as valid against the United States under this Constitution, as under the Confederation.

The Constitution, and the Laws of the United States which shall be made in Pursuance thereof; and all Treaties made, or which shall be made, under the Authority of the

---

[8]Changed by the Eleventh Amendment.

[9]Changed by the Thirteenth Amendment.

United States, shall be the supreme Law of the Land; and the Judges in every State shall be bound thereby, any Thing in the Constitution or Laws of any State to the Contrary notwithstanding.

The Senators and Representatives before mentioned, and the Members of the several State Legislatures, and all executive and judicial Officers, both of the United States and of the several States, shall be bound by Oath or Affirmation, to support this Constitution; but no religious Test shall ever be required as a Qualification to any Office or public Trust under the United States.

ARTICLE VII

The Ratification of the Conventions of nine States, shall be sufficient for the Establishment of this Constitution between the States so ratifying the Same.

Done in Convention by the Unanimous Consent of the States present the Seventeenth Day of September in the Year of our Lord one thousand seven hundred and eighty seven and of the Independance of the United States of America the Twelfth. In witness whereof We have hereunto subscribed our Names.

■ ■ ■

[The first 10 amendments are known as the ''Bill of Rights.'']

Amendment I (Ratified 1791)

Congress shall make no law respecting an establishment of religion, or prohibiting the free exercise thereof; or abridging the freedom of speech, or of the press; or the right of the people peaceably to assemble, and to petition the Government for a redress of grievances.

Amendment 2 (Ratified 1791)

A well regulated Militia, being necessary to the security of a free State, the right of the people to keep and bear Arms, shall not be infringed.

Amendment 3 (Ratified 1791)

No Soldier shall, in time of peace be quartered in any house, without the consent of the Owner, nor in time of war, but in a manner to be prescribed by law.

Amendment 4 (Ratified 1791)

The right of the people to be secure in their persons, houses, papers, and effects, against unreasonable searches and seizures, shall not be violated, and no Warrants shall issue, but upon probable cause, supported by Oath or affirmation, and particularly describing the place to be searched, and the persons or things to be seized.

Amendment 5 (Ratified 1791)

No person shall be held to answer for a capital, or otherwise infamous crime, unless on a presentment or indictment of a Grand Jury, except in cases arising in the land or naval forces, or in the Militia, when in actual service in time of War or public danger; nor shall any person be subject for the same offence to be twice put in jeopardy of life or limb; nor shall be compelled in any criminal case to be a witness against himself, nor be deprived of life, liberty, or property, without due process of law; nor shall private property be taken for public use, without just compensation.

Amendment 6 (Ratified 1791)

In all criminal prosecutions, the accused shall enjoy the right to a speedy and public trial, by an impartial jury of the State and district wherein the crime shall have been committed, which district shall have been previously ascertained by law, and to be informed of the nature and cause of the accusation; to be confronted with the witnesses against him; to have compulsory process for obtaining Witnesses in his favor, and to have assistance of counsel for his defence.

Amendment 7 (Ratified 1791)

In Suits at common law, where the value in controversy shall exceed twenty dollars, the right of trial by jury shall be preserved, and no fact tried by a jury, shall be otherwise re-examined in any Court of the United States, than according to the rules of the common law.

Amendment 8 (Ratified 1791)

Excessive bail shall not be required, nor excessive fines imposed, nor cruel and unusual punishments inflicted.

Amendment 9 (Ratified 1791)

The enumeration in the Constitution, of certain rights, shall not be construed to deny or disparage others retained by the people.

Amendment 10 (Ratified 1791)

The powers not delegated to the United States by the Constitution, nor prohibited by it to the States, are reserved to the States respectively, or to the people.

Amendment 11 (Ratified 1795)

The Judicial power of the United States shall not be construed to extend to any suit in law or equity, commenced or prosecuted against one of the United States by Citizens of another State, or by Citizens or Subjects of any Foreign State.

Amendment 12 (Ratified 1804)

The Electors shall meet in their respective states, and vote by ballot for President and Vice-President, one of whom, at least, shall not be an inhabitant of the same state with themselves; they shall name in their ballots the person voted for as President, and in distinct ballots the person voted for as Vice-President, and they shall make distinct lists of all persons voted for as President, and of all persons voted for as Vice-President, and of the number of votes for each, which lists they shall sign and certify, and transmit sealed to the seat of the government of the United States, directed to the President of the Senate;—The President of the Senate shall, in the presence of the Senate and House of Representatives, open all the certificates and the votes shall then be counted;—The person having the greatest number of votes for President, shall be the President, if such number be a majority of the whole number of Electors appointed; and if no person have such majority, then from the persons having the highest numbers not exceeding three on the list of those voted for as President, the House of Representatives shall choose immediately, by ballot, the President. But in choosing the President, the votes shall be taken by states, the representation from each state having one vote; a quorum for this purpose shall consist of a member or members from two-thirds of the states, and a majority of all the states shall be necessary to a choice. And if the House of Representatives shall not choose a President whenever the right of choice shall devolve upon them, before the fourth day of March next following, then the Vice-President shall act as president, as in the case of the death or other constitutional disability of the President.[10]—The person having the greatest number of votes as Vice-President, shall be the Vice-President, if such number be a majority of the whole number of Electors appointed, and if no person have a majority, then from the two highest numbers on the list, the Senate shall choose the Vice-President; a quorum for the purpose shall consist of two-thirds of the whole number of Senators, and a majority of the whole number shall be necessary to a choice. But no person constitutionally ineligible to the office of President shall be eligible to that of Vice-President of the United States.

Amendment 13 (Ratified 1865)

Section 1   Neither slavery nor involuntary servitude, except as a punishment for crime whereof the party shall have been duly convicted, shall exist within the United States, or any place subject to their jurisdiction.

Section 2   Congress shall have power to enforce this article by appropriate legislation.

Amendment 14 (Ratified 1868)

Section 1   All persons born or naturalized in the United States, and subject to the jurisdiction thereof, are citizens of the United States and of the State wherein they reside. No State shall make or enforce any law which shall abridge the privileges or immunities of citizens of the United States; nor shall any State deprive any person of life, liberty, or property, without due process of law; nor deny to any person within its jurisdiction the equal protection of the laws.

Section 2   Representatives shall be apportioned among the several States according to their respective numbers, counting the whole number of persons in each State, excluding Indians not taxed. But when the right to vote at any election for the choice of electors for President and Vice President of the United States, Representatives in Congress, the Executive and Judicial officers of a State, or the members of the Legislature thereof, is denied to any of the male inhabitants of such State, being twenty-one[11] years of age, and citizens of the United States, or in any way abridged except for participation in rebellion, or other crime, the basis of representation therein shall be reduced in the proportion which the number of such male citizens shall bear to the whole number of male citizens twenty-one years of age in such State.

Section 3   No person shall be a Senator or Representative in Congress, or elector of President and Vice President, or hold any office, civil or military, under the United States, or under any State, who, having previously taken an oath, as a member of Congress, or as an officer of the United States, or as a member of any State legislature, or as an executive or judicial officer of any State, to support the Constitution of the United States, shall have engaged in insurrection or rebellion against the same, or given aid or comfort to the enemies thereof. But Congress may by a vote of two-thirds of each House, remove such disability.

Section 4   The validity of the public debt of the United States, authorized by law, including debts incurred for payment of pensions and bounties for services in suppressing insurrection or rebellion, shall not be questioned. But neither the United States nor any State shall assume or

---

[10]Changed by the Twentieth Amendment.

[11]Changed by the Twenty-sixth Amendment.

pay any debt or obligation incurred in aid of insurrection or rebellion against the United States, or any claim for the loss or emancipation of any slave; but all such debts, obligations and claims shall be held illegal and void.

Section 5   The Congress shall have power to enforce, by appropriate legislation, the provisions of this article.

Amendment 15 (Ratified 1870)

Section 1   The right of citizens of the United States to vote shall not be denied or abridged by the United States or by any State on account of race, color, or previous condition of servitude.

Section 2   The Congress shall have power to enforce this article by appropriate legislation.

Amendment 16 (Ratified 1913)

The Congress shall have power to lay and collect taxes on incomes, from whatever source derived, without apportionment among the several States, and without regard to any census or enumeration.

Amendment 17 (Ratified 1913)

The Senate of the United States shall be composed of two Senators from each State, elected by the people thereof, for six years; and each Senator shall have one vote. The electors in each State shall have the qualifications requisite for electors of the most numerous branch of the State legislatures.

When vacancies happen in the representation of any State in the Senate, the executive authority of such State shall issue writs of election to fill such vacancies: *Provided,* That the legislature of any State may empower the executive thereof to make temporary appointments until the people fill the vacancies by election as the legislature may direct.

This amendment shall not be so construed as to affect the election or term of any Senator chosen before it becomes valid as part of the Constitution.

Amendment 18 (Ratified 1919; Repealed 1933)

Section 1   After one year from the ratification of this article the manufacture, sale, or transportation of intoxicating liquors within, the importation thereof into, or the exportation thereof from the United States and all territory subject to the jurisdiction thereof for beverage purposes is hereby prohibited.

Section 2   The Congress and the several States shall have concurrent power to enforce this article by appropriate legislation.

Section 3   This article shall be inoperative unless it shall have been ratified as an amendment to the Constitution by the legislatures of the several States, as provided in the Constitution, within seven years from the date of the submission hereof to the States by the Congress.[12]

Amendment 19 (Ratified 1920)

The right of citizens of the United States to vote shall not be denied or abridged by the United States or by any State on account of sex.

Congress shall have power to enforce this article by appropriate legislation.

Amendment 20 (Ratified 1933)

Section 1   The terms of the President and Vice President shall end at noon on the 20th day of January, and the terms of Senators and Representatives at noon on the 3d day of January, of the years in which such terms would have ended if this article had not been ratified; and the terms of their successors shall then begin.

Section 2   The Congress shall assemble at least once in every year, and such meeting shall begin at noon on the 3d day of January, unless they shall by law appoint a different day.

Section 3   If, at the time fixed for the beginning of the term of the President, the President elect shall have died, the Vice President elect shall become President. If a President shall not have been chosen before the time fixed for the beginning of his term, or if the President elect shall have failed to qualify, then the Vice President elect shall act as President until a President shall have qualified; and the Congress may by law provide for the case wherein neither a President elect nor a Vice President elect shall have qualified, declaring who shall then act as President, or the manner in which one who is to act shall be selected, and such person shall act accordingly until a President or Vice President shall have qualified.

Section 4   The Congress may by law provide for the case of the death of any of the persons from whom the House of Representatives may choose a President whenever the right of choice shall have devolved upon them, and for the case of the death of any of the persons from whom the Senate may choose a Vice President whenever the right of choice shall have devolved upon them.

Section 5   Sections 1 and 2 shall take effect on the 15th day of October following the ratification of this article.

Section 6   This article shall be inoperative unless it shall have been ratified as an amendment to the Constitu-

---

[12]Repealed by the Twenty-first Amendment.

tion by the legislatures of three-fourths of the several States within seven years from the date of its submission.

Amendment 21 (Ratified 1933)

Section 1   The eighteenth article of amendment to the Constitution of the United States is hereby repealed.

Section 2   The transportation or importation into any State, Territory, or possession of the United States for delivery or use therein of intoxicating liquors, in violation of the laws thereof, is hereby prohibited.

Section 3   This article shall be inoperative unless it shall have been ratified as an amendment to the Constitution by conventions in the several States, as provided in the Constitution, within seven years from the date of the submission hereof to the States by the Congress.

Amendment 22 (Ratified 1951)

Section 1   No person shall be elected to the office of the President more than twice, and no person who has held the office of President, or acted as President, for more than two years of a term to which some other person was elected President shall be elected to the office of the President more than once. But this Article shall not apply to any person holding the office of President when this Article was proposed by the Congress, and shall not prevent any person who may be holding the office of President, or acting as President, during the term within which this Article becomes operative from holding the office of President or acting as President during the remainder of such term.

Section 1   This Article shall be inoperative unless it shall have been ratified as an amendment to the Constitution by the legislatures of three-fourths of the several States within seven years from the date of its submission to the States by the Congress.

Amendment 23 (Ratified 1961)

Section 1   The District constituting the seat of Government of the United States shall appoint in such manner as the Congress may direct:

A number of electors of President and Vice President equal to the whole number of Senators and Representatives in Congress to which the District would be entitled if it were a State, but in no event more than the least populous State; they shall be in addition to those appointed by the States, but they shall be considered, for the purposes of the election of President and Vice President, to be electors appointed by a State; and they shall meet in the District and perform such duties as provided by the twelfth article of amendment.

Section 2   The Congress shall have power to enforce this article by appropriate legislation.

Amendment 24 (Ratified 1964)

Section 1   The right of citizens of the United States to vote in any primary or other election for President or Vice President, for electors for President or Vice President, or for Senator or Representative in Congress, shall not be denied or abridged by the United States or any State by reason of failure to pay any poll tax or other tax.

Section 2   The Congress shall have power to enforce this article by appropriate legislation.

Amendment 25 (Ratified 1967)

Section 1   In case of the removal of the President from office or of his death or resignation, the Vice President shall become President.

Section 2   Whenever there is a vacancy in the office of the Vice President, the President shall nominate a Vice President who shall take office upon confirmation by a majority vote of both Houses of Congress.

Section 3   Whenever the President transmits to the President pro tempore of the Senate and the Speaker of the House of Representatives his written declaration that he is unable to discharge the powers and duties of his office, and until he transmits to them a written declaration to the contrary, such powers and duties shall be discharged by the Vice President as Acting President.

Section 4   Whenever the Vice President and a majority of either the principal officers of the executive departments or of such other body as Congress may by law provide, transmit to the President pro tempore of the Senate and the Speaker of the House of Representatives their written declaration that the President is unable to discharge the powers and duties of his office, the Vice President shall immediately assume the powers and duties of the office as Acting President.

Thereafter, when the President transmits to the President pro tempore of the Senate and the Speaker of the House of Representatives his written declaration that no inability exists, he shall resume the powers and duties of his office unless the Vice President and a majority of either the principal officers of the executive department or of such other body as Congress may by law provide, transmit within four days to the President pro tempore of the Senate and the Speaker of the House of Representatives their written declaration that the President is unable to discharge the powers and duties of his office. Thereupon Congress shall decide the issue, assembling within forty-eight hours for that purpose if not in session. If the Congress, within twenty-one days after receipt of the latter written declaration, or, if Congress is not in session, within twenty-one days after Congress is required to assemble, determines by two-thirds vote of both Houses that the President is unable to discharge the powers and duties of his office, the Vice President shall continue to discharge the same as Acting President; otherwise, the President shall resume the powers and duties of his office.

Amendment 26 (Ratified 1971)

Section 1   The right of citizens of the United States, who are eighteen years of age or older, to vote shall not be denied or abridged by the United States or by any State on account of age.

Section 2   The Congress shall have power to enforce this article by appropriate legislation.

Amendment 27 (Ratified 1992)

No law, varying the compensation for the services of the Senators and Representatives, shall take effect, until an election of Representatives shall have intervened.

Appendix B

Uniform Commercial Code (Excerpts from the Official Text–1990)*

Title

An Act

To be known as the Uniform Commercial Code, Relating to Certain Commercial Transactions in or regarding Personal Property and Contracts and other Documents concerning them, including Sales, Commercial Paper, Bank Deposits and Collections, Letters of Credit, Bulk Transfers, Warehouse Receipts, Bills of Lading, other Documents of Title, Investment Securities, and Secured Transactions, including certain Sales of Accounts, Chattel Paper, and Contract Rights; Providing for Public Notice to Third Parties in Certain Circumstances; Regulating Procedure, Evidence and Damages in Certain Court Actions Involving such Transactions, Contracts or Documents; to Make Uniform the Law with Respect Thereto; and Repealing Inconsistent Legislation.

ARTICLE 1   GENERAL PROVISIONS

Part 1   Short Title, Construction, Application and Subject Matter of the Act

§1–101.   Short Title

This Act shall be known and may be cited as Uniform Commercial Code.

§1–102.   Purposes; Rules of Construction; Variation by Agreement

(1) This Act shall be liberally construed and applied to promote its underlying purposes and policies.

(2) Underlying purposes and policies of this Act are

(a) to simplify, clarify and modernize the law governing commercial transactions;

(b) to permit the continued expansion of commercial practices through custom, usage and agreement of the parties;

(c) to make uniform the law among the various jurisdictions.

(3) The effect of provisions of this Act may be varied by agreement, except as otherwise provided in this Act and except that the obligations of good faith, diligence, reasonableness and care prescribed by this Act may not be disclaimed by agreement but the parties may by agreement determine the standards by which the performance of such obligations is to be measured if such standards are not manifestly unreasonable.

(4) The presence in certain provisions of this Act of the words "unless otherwise agreed" or words of similar import does not imply that the effect of other provisions may not be varied by agreement under subsection (3).

(5) In this Act unless the context otherwise requires

(a) words in the singular number include the plural, and in the plural include the singular;

(b) words of the masculine gender include the feminine and the neuter, and when the sense so indicates words of the neuter gender may refer to any gender.

§1–103.   Supplementary General Principles of Law Applicable

Unless displaced by the particular provisions of this Act, the principles of law and equity, including the law merchant and the law relative to capacity to contract, principal and agent, estoppel, fraud, misrepresentation, duress, coercion, mistake, bankruptcy, or other validating or invalidating cause shall supplement its provisions.

§1–104.   Construction Against Implicit Repeal

This Act being a general act intended as a unified coverage of its subject matter, no part of it shall be deemed to be impliedly repealed by subsequent legislation if such construction can reasonably be avoided.

§1–105.   Territorial Application of the Act; Parties' Power to Choose Applicable Law

(1) Except as provided hereafter in this section, when a transaction bears a reasonable relation to this state and also to another state or nation the parties may agree that the law either of this state or of such other state or nation

shall govern their rights and duties. Failing such agreement this Act applies to transactions bearing an appropriate relation to this state.

(2) Where one of the following provisions of this Act specifies the applicable law, that provision governs and a contrary agreement is effective only to the extent permitted by law (including the conflict of laws rules) so specified:

Rights of creditors against sold goods. Section 2–402.

Applicability of the Article on Leases. Sections 2A–105 and 2A–106.

Applicability of the Article on Bank Deposits and Collections. Section 4–102.

Governing Law in the Article on Funds Transfers. Section 4A–507.

Bulk transfers subject to the Article on Bulk Transfers. Section 6–103.

Applicability of the Article on Investment Securities. Section 8–106.

Perfection provisions of the Article on Secured Transactions. Section 9–103.

§1–106. Remedies to Be Liberally Administered

(1) The remedies provided by this Act shall be liberally administered to the end that the aggrieved party may be put in as good a position as if the other party had fully performed but neither consequential or special nor penal damages may be had except as specifically provided in this Act or by other rule of law.

(2) Any right or obligation declared by this Act is enforceable by action unless the provision declaring it specifies a different and limited effect.

§1–107. Waiver or Renunciation of Claim or Right After Breach

Any claim or right arising out of an alleged breach can be discharged in whole or in part without consideration by a written waiver or renunciation signed and delivered by the aggrieved party.

§1–108. Severability

If any provision or clause of this Act or application thereof to any person or circumstances is held invalid, such invalidity shall not affect other provisions or applications of the Act which can be given effect without the invalid provision or application, and to this end the provisions of this Act are declared to be severable.

§1–109. Section Captions

Section captions are parts of this Act.

Part 2 General Definitions and Principles of Interpretation

§1–201. General Definitions

Subject to additional definitions contained in the subsequent Articles of this Act which are applicable to specific Articles or Parts thereof, and unless the context otherwise requires, in this Act:

(1) ''Action'' in the sense of a judicial proceeding includes recoupment, counterclaim, set-off, suit in equity and any other proceedings in which rights are determined.

(2) ''Aggrieved party'' means a party entitled to resort to a remedy.

(3) ''Agreement'' means the bargain of the parties in fact as found in their language or by implication from other circumstances including course of dealing or usage of trade or course of performance as provided in this Act (Sections 1–205 and 2–208). Whether an agreement has legal consequences is determined by the provisions of this Act, if applicable; otherwise by the law of contracts (Section 1–103). (Compare ''Contract.'')

(4) ''Bank'' means any person engaged in the business of banking.

(5) ''Bearer'' means the person in possession of an instrument, document of title, or certificated security payable to bearer or indorsed in blank.

(6) ''Bill of lading'' means a document evidencing the receipt of goods for shipment issued by a person engaged in the business of transporting or forwarding goods, and includes an airbill. ''Airbill'' means a document serving for air transportation as a bill of lading does for marine or rail transportation, and includes an air consignment note or air waybill.

(7) ''Branch'' includes a separately incorporated foreign branch of a bank.

(8) ''Burden of establishing'' a fact means the burden of persuading the triers of fact that the existence of the fact is more probable than its nonexistence.

(9) ''Buyer in ordinary course of business'' means a person who in good faith and without knowledge that the sale to him is in violation of the ownership rights or security interest of a third party in the goods buys in ordinary course from a person in the business of selling goods of that kind but does not include a pawnbroker. All persons who sell minerals or the like (including oil and gas) at wellhead or minehead shall be deemed to be persons in the business of selling goods of that kind. ''Buying'' may be for cash or by exchange of other property or on secured or unsecured credit and includes receiving goods or documents of title under a pre-existing contract for sale but does not include a transfer in bulk or as security for or in total or partial satisfaction of a money debt.

(10) ''Conspicuous'': A term or clause is conspicuous when it is so written that a reasonable person against whom it is to operate ought to have noticed it. A printed heading in capitals (as: NON-NEGOTIABLE BILL OF LADING) is conspicuous. Language in the body of a form is ''conspicuous'' if it is in larger or other contrasting type or color. But in a telegram any stated term is ''conspicuous.'' Whether a term or clause is ''conspicuous'' or not is for decision by the court.

(11) ''Contract'' means the total legal obligation which results from the parties' agreement as affected by this Act and any other applicable rules of law. (Compare ''Agreement.'')

(12) ''Creditor'' includes a general creditor, a secured creditor, a lien creditor and any representative of creditors, including an assignee for the benefit of creditors, a trustee in bankruptcy, a receiver in equity and an executor or administrator of an insolvent debtor's or assignor's estate.

(13) ''Defendant'' includes a person in the position of defendant in a cross-action or counterclaim.

(14) ''Delivery'' with respect to instruments, documents of title, chattel paper, or certificated securities means voluntary transfer of possession.

(15) ''Document of title'' includes bill of lading, dock warrant, dock receipt, warehouse receipt or order for the delivery of goods, and also any other document which in the regular course of business or financing is treated as adequately evidencing that the person in possession of it is entitled to receive, hold and dispose of the document and the goods it covers. To be a document of title a document must purport to be issued by or addressed to a bailee and purport to cover goods in the bailee's possession which are either identified or are fungible portions of an identified mass.

(16) ''Fault'' means wrongful act, omission or breach.

(17) ''Fungible'' with respect to goods or securities means goods or securities of which any unit is, by nature or usage of trade, the equivalent of any other like unit. Goods which are not fungible shall be deemed fungible for the purposes of this Act to the extent that under a particular agreement or document unlike units are treated as equivalents.

(18) ''Genuine'' means free of forgery or counterfeiting.

(19) ''Good faith'' means honesty in fact in the conduct or transaction concerned.

(20) ''Holder,'' with respect to a negotiable instrument, means the person in possession if the instrument is payable to bearer, or in the case of an instrument payable to an identified person, if the identified person is in possession. ''Holder'' with respect to a document of title means the person in possession of the goods are deliverable to bearer or to the order of the person in possession.

(21) To ''honor'' is to pay or to accept and pay, or where a credit so engages to purchase or discount a draft complying with the terms of credit.

(22) ''Insolvency proceedings'' includes any assignment for the benefit of creditors or other proceedings intended to liquidate or rehabilitate the estate of the person involved.

(23) A person is ''insolvent'' who either has ceased to pay his debts in the ordinary course of business or cannot pay his debts as they become due or is insolvent within the meaning of the federal bankruptcy law.

(24) ''Money'' means a medium of exchange authorized or adopted by a domestic or foreign government as a part of its currency.

(25) A person has ''notice'' of a fact when

(a) he has actual knowledge of it; or

(b) he has received a notice or notification of it; or

(c) from all the facts and circumstances known to him at the time in question he has reason to know that it exists.

A person ''knows'' or has ''knowledge'' of a fact when he has actual knowledge of it. ''Discover'' or ''learn'' or a word or phrase of similar import refers to knowledge rather than to reason to know. The time and circumstances under which a notice or notification may cease to be effective are not determined by this Act.

(26) A person ''notifies'' or ''gives'' a notice or notification to another by taking such steps as may be reasonably required to inform the other in ordinary course whether or not such other actually comes to know of it. A person ''receives'' a notice or notification when

(a) it comes to his attention; or

(b) it is duly delivered at the place of business through which the contract was made or at any other place held out by him as the place for receipt of such communications.

(27) Notice, knowledge or a notice or notification received by an organization is effective for a particular transaction from the time when it is brought to the attention of the individual conducting that transaction, and in any event from the time when it would have been brought to his attention if the organization had exercised due diligence. An organization exercises due diligence if it maintains reasonable routines for communicating significant information to the person conducting the transaction and there is reasonable compliance with the routines. Due diligence does not require an individual acting for the organization to communicate information unless such communication is part of his regular duties or unless he has reason to know of the transaction and that the transaction would be materially affected by the information.

(28) ''Organization'' includes a corporation, government or governmental subdivision or agency, business trust, estate, trust, partnership or association, two or more persons having a joint or common interest, or any other legal or commercial entity.

(29) ''Party,'' as distinct from ''third party,'' means a person who has engaged in a transaction or made an agreement within this Act.

(30) ''Person'' includes an individual or an organization (See Section 1–102).

(31) ''Presumption'' or ''presumed'' means that the trier of fact must find the existence of the fact presumed unless and until evidence is introduced which would support a finding of its nonexistence.

(32) ''Purchase'' includes taking by sale, discount, negotiation, mortgage, pledge, lien, issue or reissue, gift or any other voluntary transaction creating an interest in property.

(33) ''Purchaser'' means a person who takes by purchase.

(34) ''Remedy'' means any remedial right to which an aggrieved party is entitled with or without resort to a tribunal.

(35) ''Representative'' includes an agent, an officer of a corporation or association, and a trustee, executor or administrator of an estate, or any other person empowered to act for another.

(36) ''Rights'' includes remedies.

(37) ''Security interest'' means an interest in personal property or fixtures which secures payment or performance of an obligation. The retention or reservation of title by a seller of goods notwithstanding shipment or delivery to the buyer (Section 2–401) is limited in effect to a reservation of a ''security interest''. The term also includes any interest of a buyer of accounts or chattel paper which is subject to Article 9. The special property interest of a buyer of goods on identification of those goods to a contract for sale under Section 2–401 is not a ''security interest'', but a buyer may also acquire a ''security interest'' by complying with Article 9. Unless a consignment is intended as security, reservation of title thereunder is not a ''security interest'', but a consignment in any event is subject to the provisions on consignment sales (Section 2–326).

Whether a transaction creates a lease or security interest is determined by the facts of each case; however, a transaction creates a security interest if the consideration the lessee is to pay the lessor for the right to possession and use of the goods is an obligation for the term of the lease not subject to termination by the lessee, and

(a) the original term of the lease is equal to or greater than the remaining economic life of the goods, (b) the lessee is bound to renew the lease for the remaining economic life of the goods or is bound to become the owner of the goods, (c) the lessee has an option to renew the lease for the remaining economic life of the goods for no additional consideration or nominal additional consideration upon compliance with the lease agreement, or

(d) the lessee has an option to become the owner of the goods for no additional consideration or nominal additional consideration upon compliance with the lease agreement.

A transaction does not create a security interest merely because it provides that

(a) the present value of the consideration the lessee is obligated to pay the lessor for the right to possession and use of the goods is substantially equal to or is greater than the fair market value of the goods at the time the lease is entered into, (b) the lessee assumes risk of loss of the goods, or agrees to pay taxes, insurance, filing, recording, or registration fees, or service or maintenance costs with respect to the goods, (c) the lessee has an option to renew the lease or to become the owner of the goods, (d) the lessee has an option to renew the lease for a fixed rent that is equal to or greater than the reasonably predictable fair market rent for the use of the goods for the

term of the renewal at the time the option is to be performed, or (e) the lessee has an option to become the owner of the goods for a fixed price that is equal to or greater than the reasonably predictable fair market value of the goods at the time the option is to be performed.

For purposes of this subsection (37):

(x) Additional consideration is not nominal if (i) when the option to renew the lease is granted to the lessee the rent is stated to be the fair market rent for the use of the goods for the term of the renewal determined at the time the option is to be performed, or (ii) when the option to become the owner of the goods is granted to the lessee the price is stated to be the fair market value of the goods determined at the time the option is to be performed. Additional consideration is nominal if it is less than the lessee's reasonably predictable cost of performing under the lease agreement if the option is not exercised;

(y) ''Reasonably predictable'' and ''remaining economic life of the goods'' are to be determined with reference to the facts and circumstances at the time the transaction is entered into; and (z) ''Present value'' means the amount as of a date certain of one or more sums payable in the future, discounted to the date certain. The discount is determined by the interest rate specified by the parties if the rate is not manifestly unreasonable at the time the transaction is entered into; otherwise, the discount is determined by a commercially reasonable rate that takes into account the facts and circumstances of each case at the time the transaction was entered into.

(38) ''Send'' in connection with any writing or notice means to deposit in the mail or deliver for transmission by any other usual means of communication with postage or cost of transmission provided for and properly addressed and in the case of an instrument to an address specified thereon or otherwise agreed, or if there be none to any address reasonable under the circumstances. The receipt of any writing or notice within the time at which it would have arrived if properly sent has the effect of a proper sending.

(39) ''Signed'' includes any symbol executed or adopted by a party with present intention to authenticate a writing.

(40) ''Surety'' includes guarantor.

(41) ''Telegram'' includes a message transmitted by radio, teletype, cable, any mechanical method of transmission, or the like.

(42) ''Term'' means that portion of an agreement which relates to a particular matter.

(43) ''Unauthorized'' signature or indorsement means one made without actual, implied or apparent authority and includes a forgery.

(44) ''Value.'' Except as otherwise provided with respect to negotiable instruments and bank collections (Sections 3–303, 4–208 and 4–209) a person gives ''value'' for rights if he acquires them

(a) in return for a binding commitment to extend credit or for the extension of immediately available credit whether or not drawn upon and whether or not a charge-back is provided for in the event of difficulties in collection; or

(b) as security for or in total or partial satisfaction of a preexisting claim; or

(c) by accepting delivery pursuant to a preexisting contract for purchase; or

(d) generally, in return for any consideration sufficient to support a simple contract.

(45) "Warehouse receipt" means a receipt issued by a person engaged in the business of storing goods for hire.

(46) "Written" or "writing" includes printing, typewriting or any other intentional reduction to tangible form.

§1–202. Prima Facie Evidence by Third Party Documents

A document in due form purporting to be a bill of lading, policy or certificate of insurance, official weigher's or inspector's certificate, consular invoice, or any other document authorized or required by the contract to be issued by a third party shall be prima facie evidence of its own authenticity and genuineness and of the facts stated in the document by the third party.

§1–203. Obligation of Good Faith

Every contract or duty within this Act imposes an obligation of good faith in its performance or enforcement.

§1–204. Time; Reasonable Time; "Seasonably"

(1) Whenever this Act requires any action to be taken within a reasonable time, any time which is not manifestly unreasonable may be fixed by agreement.

(2) What is a reasonable time for taking any action depends on the nature, purpose and circumstances of such action.

(3) An action is taken "seasonably" when it is taken at or within the time agreed or if no time is agreed at or within a reasonable time.

§1–205. Course of Dealing and Usage of Trade

(1) A course of dealing is a sequence of previous conduct between the parties to a particular transaction which is fairly to be regarded as establishing a common basis of understanding for interpreting their expressions and other conduct.

(2) A usage of trade is any practice or method of dealing having such regularity of observance in a place, vocation or trade as to justify an expectation that it will be observed with respect to the transaction in question. The existence and scope of such a usage are to be proved as facts. If it is established that such a usage is embodied in a written trade code or similar writing the interpretation of the writing is for the court.

(3) A course of dealing between parties and any usage of trade in the vocation or trade in which they are engaged or of which they are or should be aware give particular meaning to and supplement or qualify terms of an agreement.

(4) The express terms of an agreement and an applicable course of dealing or usage of trade shall be construed wherever reasonable as consistent with each other; but when such construction is unreasonable express terms control both course of dealing and usage of trade and course of dealing controls usage of trade.

(5) An applicable usage of trade in the place where any part of performance is to occur shall be used in interpreting the agreement as to that part of the performance.

(6) Evidence of a relevant usage of trade offered by one party is not admissible unless and until he has given the other party such notice as the court finds sufficient to prevent unfair surprise to the latter.

§1–206. Statute of Frauds for Kinds of Personal Property Not Otherwise Covered

(1) Except in the cases described in subsection (2) of this section a contract for the sale of personal property is not enforceable by way of action or defense beyond five thousand dollars in amount or value of remedy unless there is some writing which indicates that a contract for sale has been made between the parties at a defined or stated price, reasonably identifies the subject matter, and is signed by the party against whom enforcement is sought or by his authorized agent.

(2) Subsection (1) of this section does not apply to contracts for the sale of goods (Section 2–201) nor of securities (Section 8–319) nor to security agreements (Section 9–203).

§1–207. Performance or Acceptance Under Reservation of Rights

(1) A party who with explicit reservation of rights performs or promises performance or assents to performance in a manner demanded or offered by the other party does not thereby prejudice the rights reserved. Such words as "without prejudice," "under protest" or the like are sufficient.

(2) Subsection (1) does not apply to an accord and satisfaction.

§1–208. Option to Accelerate at Will

A term providing that one party or his successor in interest may accelerate payment or performance or require collateral or additional collateral "at will" or "when he deems himself insecure" or in words of similar import shall be construed to mean that he shall have power to do so only if he in good faith believes that the prospect of payment or performance is impaired. The burden of establishing lack of good faith is on the party against whom the power has been exercised.

§1–209. Subordinated Obligations

An obligation may be issued as subordinated to payment of another obligation of the person obligated, or a creditor may subordinate his right to payment of an obligation by agreement with either the person obligated or another creditor of the person obligated. Such a subordination does not create a security interest as against either the common debtor or a subordinated creditor. This section shall be construed as declaring the law as it existed prior to the enactment of this section and not as modifying it.

Note: This new section is proposed as an optional provision to make it clear that a subordination agreement does not create a security interest unless so intended.

ARTICLE 2 SALES

Part 1   Short Title, General Construction and Subject Matter

§2–101.   Short Title

This Article shall be known and may be cited as Uniform Commercial Code—Sales.

§2–102.   Scope; Certain Security and Other Transactions Excluded From This Article

Unless the context otherwise requires, this Article applies to transactions in goods; it does not apply to any transaction which although in the form of an unconditional contract to sell or present sale is intended to operate only as a security transaction nor does this Article impair or repeal any statute regulating sales to consumers, farmers or other specified classes of buyers.

§2–103.   Definitions and Index of Definitions

(1) In this Article unless the context otherwise requires
    (a) "Buyer" means a person who buys or contracts to buy goods.
    (b) "Good faith" in the case of a merchant means honesty in fact and the observance of reasonable commercial standards of fair dealing in the trade.
    (c) "Receipt" of goods means taking physical possession of them.
    (d) "Seller" means a person who sells or contracts to sell goods.
(2) Other definitions applying to this Article or to specified Parts thereof, and the sections in which they appear are:
    "Acceptance." Section 2–606.
    "Banker's credit." Section 2–325.
    "Between merchants." Section 2–104.
    "Cancellation." Section 2–106(4).
    "Commercial unit." Section 2–105.
    "Confirmed credit." Section 2–325.
    "Conforming to contract." Section 2–106.
    "Contract for sale." Section 2–106.
    "Cover." Section 2–712.
    "Entrusting." Section 2–403.
    "Financing agency." Section 2–104.

    "Future goods." Section 2–105.
    "Goods." Section 2–105.
    "Identification." Section 2–501.
    "Installment contract." Section 2–612.
    "Letter of Credit." Section 2–325.
    "Lot." Section 2–105.
    "Merchant." Section 2–104.
    "Overseas." Section 2–323.
    "Person in position of seller." Section 2–707.
    "Present sale." Section 2–106.
    "Sale." Section 2–106.
    "Sale on approval." Section 2–326.
    "Sale or return." Section 2–326.
    "Termination." Section 2–106.
(3) The following definitions in other Articles apply to this Article:
    "Check." Section 3–104.
    "Consignee." Section 7–102.
    "Consignor." Section 7–102.
    "Consumer goods." Section 9–109.
    "Dishonor." Section 3–507.
    "Draft." Section 3–104.
(4) In addition Article 1 contains general definitions and principles of construction and interpretation applicable throughout this Article.

§2–104.   Definitions: "Merchant"; "Between Merchants"; "Financing Agency"

(1) "Merchant" means a person who deals in goods of the kind or otherwise by his occupation holds himself out as having knowledge or skill peculiar to the practices or goods involved in the transaction or to whom such knowledge or skill may be attributed by his employment of an agent or broker or other intermediary who by his occupation holds himself out as having such knowledge or skill.
(2) "Financing agency" means a bank, finance company or other person who in the ordinary course of business makes advances against goods or documents of title or who by arrangement with either the seller or the buyer intervenes in ordinary course to make or collect payment due or claimed under the contract for sale, as by purchasing or paying the seller's draft or making advances against it or by merely taking it for collection whether or not documents of title accompany the draft. "Financing agency" includes also a bank or other person who similarly intervenes between persons who are in the position of seller and buyer in respect to the goods (Section 2–707).
(3) "Between merchants" means in any transaction with respect to which both parties are chargeable with the knowledge or skill of merchants.

§2–105.   Definitions: Transferability; "Goods"; "Future Goods"; "Lot"; "Commercial Unit"

(1) "Goods" means all things (including specially manufactured goods) which are moveable at the time of iden-

tification to the contract for sale other than the money in which the price is to be paid, investment securities (Article 8) and things in action. ''Goods'' also includes the unborn young of animals and growing crops and other identified things attached to realty as described in the section on goods to be severed from realty (Section 2–107).

(2) Goods must be both existing and identified before any interest in them can pass. Goods which are not both existing and identified are ''future'' goods. A purported present sale of future goods or of any interest therein operates as a contract to sell.

(3) There may be a sale of a part interest in existing identified goods.

(4) An undivided share in an identified bulk of fungible goods is sufficiently identified to be sold although the quantity of the bulk is not determined. Any agreed proportion of such a bulk or any quantity thereof agreed upon by number, weight or other measure may to the extent of the seller's interest in the bulk be sold to the buyer who then becomes an owner in common.

(5) ''Lot'' means a parcel or a single article which is the subject matter of a separate sale or delivery, whether or not it is sufficient to perform the contract.

(6) ''Commercial unit'' means such a unit of goods as by commercial usage is a single whole for purposes of sale and division of which materially impairs its character or value on the market or in use. A commercial unit may be a single article (as a machine) or a set of articles (as a suite of furniture or an assortment of sizes) or a quantity (as a bale, gross, or carload) or any other unit treated in use or in the relevant market as a single whole.

§2–106.   Definitions: ''Contract''; ''Agreement''; ''Contract for Sale''; ''Sale''; ''Present Sale''; ''Conforming to Contract''; ''Termination''; ''Cancellation''

(1) In this Article unless the context otherwise requires ''contract'' and ''agreement'' are limited to those relating to the present or future sale of goods. ''Contract for sale'' includes both a present sale of goods and a contract to sell goods at a future time. A ''sale'' consists in the passing of title from the seller to the buyer for a price (Section 2–401). A ''present sale'' means a sale which is accomplished by the making of the contract.

(2) Goods or conduct including any part of a performance are ''conforming'' or conform to the contract when they are in accordance with the obligations under the contract.

(3) ''Termination'' occurs when either party pursuant to a power created by agreement or law puts an end to the contract otherwise than for its breach. On ''termination'' all obligations which are still executory on both sides are discharged but any right based on prior breach or performance survives.

(4) ''Cancellation'' occurs when either party puts an end to the contract for breach by the other and its effect is the same as that of ''termination'' except that the cancelling

party also retains any remedy for breach of the whole contract or any unperformed balance.

§2–107.   Goods to Be Severed From Realty: Recording

(1) A contract for the sale of minerals or the like (including oil and gas) or a structure or its materials to be removed from realty is a contract for the sale of goods within this Article if they are to be severed by the seller but until severance a purported present sale thereof which is not effective as a transfer of an interest in land is effective only as a contract to sell.

(2) A contract for the sale apart from the land of growing crops or other things attached to realty and capable of severance without material harm thereto but not described in subsection (1) or of timber to be cut is a contract for the sale of goods within this Article whether the subject matter is to be severed by the buyer or by the seller even though it forms part of the realty at the time of contracting, and the parties can by identification effect a present sale before severance.

(3) The provisions of this section are subject to any third party rights provided by the law relating to realty records, and the contract for sale may be executed and recorded as a document transferring an interest in land and shall then constitute notice to third parties of the buyer's rights under the contract for sale.

Part 2   Form, Formation and Readjustment of Contract

§2–201.   Formal Requirements; Statute of Frauds

(1) Except as otherwise provided in this section a contract for the sale of goods for the price of $500 or more is not enforceable by way of action or defense unless there is some writing sufficient to indicate that a contract for sale has been made between the parties and signed by the party against whom enforcement is sought or by his authorized agent or broker. A writing is not insufficient because it omits or incorrectly states a term agreed upon but the contract is not enforceable under this paragraph beyond the quantity of goods shown in such writing.

(2) Between merchants if within a reasonable time a writing in confirmation of the contract and sufficient against the sender is received and the party receiving it has reason to know its contents, it satisfies the requirements of subsection (1) against such party unless written notice of objection to its contents is given within 10 days after it is received.

(3) A contract which does not satisfy the requirements of subsection (1) but which is valid in other respects is enforceable

   (a) if the goods are to be specially manufactured for the buyer and are not suitable for sale to others in the ordinary course of the seller's business and the seller, before notice of repudiation is received and under circumstances which reasonably indicate that the goods are for the buyer, has made either a substantial beginning of their manufacture or commitments for their procurement; or

(b) if the party against whom enforcement is sought admits in his pleading, testimony or otherwise in court that a contract for sale was made, but the contract is not enforceable under this provision beyond the quantity of goods admitted; or

(c) with respect to goods for which payment has been made and accepted or which have been received and accepted (Section 2–606).

§2–202.   Final Written Expression: Parol or Extrinsic Evidence

Terms with respect to which the confirmatory memoranda of the parties agree or which are otherwise set forth in a writing intended by the parties as a final expression of their agreement with respect to such terms as are included therein may not be contradicted by evidence of any prior agreement or of a contemporaneous oral agreement but may be explained or supplemented

(a) by course of dealing or usage of trade (Section 1–205) or by course of performance (Section 2–208); and

(b) by evidence of consistent additional terms unless the court finds the writing to have been intended also as a complete and exclusive statement of the terms of the agreement.

§2–203.   Seals Inoperative

The affixing of a seal to a writing evidencing a contract for sale or an offer to buy or sell goods does not constitute the writing a sealed instrument and the law with respect to sealed instruments does not apply to such a contract or offer.

§2–204.   Formation in General

(1) A contract for sale of goods may be made in any manner sufficient to show agreement, including conduct by both parties which recognizes the existence of such a contract.

(2) An agreement sufficient to constitute a contract for sale may be found even though the moment of its making is undetermined.

(3) Even though one or more terms are left open a contract for sale does not fail for indefiniteness if the parties have intended to make a contract and there is a reasonably certain basis for giving an appropriate remedy.

§2–205.   Firm Offers

An offer by a merchant to buy or sell goods in a signed writing which by its terms gives assurance that it will be held open is not revocable, for lack of consideration, during the time stated or if no time is stated for a reasonable time, but in no event may such period of irrevocability exceed three months; but any such term of assurance on a form supplied by the offeree must be separately signed by the offeror.

§2–206.   Offer and Acceptance in Formation of Contract

(1) Unless otherwise unambiguously indicated by the language or circumstances

(a) an offer to make a contract shall be construed as inviting acceptance in any manner and by any medium reasonable in the circumstances;

(b) an order or other offer to buy goods for prompt or current shipment shall be construed as inviting acceptance either by a prompt promise to ship or by the prompt or current shipment of conforming or nonconforming goods, but such a shipment of nonconforming goods does not constitute an acceptance if the seller seasonably notifies the buyer that the shipment is offered only as an accommodation to the buyer.

(2) Where the beginning of a requested performance is a reasonable mode of acceptance an offeror who is not notified of acceptance within a reasonable time may treat the offer as having lapsed before acceptance.

§2–207.   Additional Terms in Acceptance or Confirmation

(1) A definite and seasonable expression of acceptance or a written confirmation which is sent within a reasonable time operates as an acceptance even though it states terms additional to or different from those offered or agreed upon, unless acceptance is expressly made conditional on assent to the additional or different terms.

(2) The additional terms are to be construed as proposals for addition to the contract. Between merchants such terms become part of the contract unless:

(a) the offer expressly limits acceptance to the terms of the offer;

(b) they materially alter it; or

(c) notification of objection to them has already been given or is given within a reasonable time after notice of them is received.

(3) Conduct by both parties which recognizes the existence of a contract is sufficient to establish a contract for sale although the writings of the parties do not otherwise establish a contract. In such case the terms of the particular contract consist of those terms on which the writings of the parties agree, together with any supplementary terms incorporated under any other provisions of this Act.

§2–208.   Course of Performance or Practical Construction

(1) Where the contract for sale involves repeated occasions for performance by either party with knowledge of the nature of the performance and opportunity for objection to it by the other, any course of performance accepted or acquiesced in without objection shall be relevant to determine the meaning of the agreement.

(2) The express terms of the agreement and any such course of performance, as well as any course of dealing

and usage of trade, shall be construed whenever reasonable as consistent with each other; but when such construction is unreasonable, express terms shall control course of performance and course of performance shall control both course of dealing and usage of trade (Section 1–205).

(3) Subject to the provisions of the next section on modification and waiver, such course of performance shall be relevant to show a waiver or modification of any term inconsistent with such course of performance.

§2–209. Modification, Rescission and Waiver

(1) An agreement modifying a contract within this Article needs no consideration to be binding.

(2) A signed agreement which excludes modification or rescission except by a signed writing cannot be otherwise modified or rescinded, but except as between merchants such a requirement on a form supplied by the merchant must be separately signed by the other party.

(3) The requirements of the statute of frauds section of this Article (Section 2–201) must be satisfied if the contract as modified is within its provisions.

(4) Although an attempt at modification or rescission does not satisfy the requirements of subsection (2) or (3) it can operate as a waiver.

(5) A party who has made a waiver affecting an executory portion of the contract may retract the waiver by reasonable notification received by the other party that strict performance will be required of any term waived, unless the retraction would be unjust in view of a material change of position in reliance on the waiver.

§2–210. Delegation of Performance; Assignment of Rights

(1) A party may perform his duty through a delegate unless otherwise agreed or unless the other party has a substantial interest in having his original promisor perform or control the acts required by the contract. No delegation of performance relieves the party delegating of any duty to perform or any liability for breach.

(2) Unless otherwise agreed all rights of either seller or buyer can be assigned except where the assignment would materially change the duty of the other party, or increase materially the burden or risk imposed on him by his contract, or impair materially his chance of obtaining return performance. A right to damages for breach of the whole contract or a right arising out of the assignor's due performance of his entire obligation can be assigned despite agreement otherwise.

(3) Unless the circumstances indicate the contrary a prohibition of assignment of ''the contract'' is to be construed as barring only the delegation to the assignee of the assignor's performance.

(4) An assignment of ''the contract'' or of ''all my rights under the contract'' or an assignment in similar general terms is an assignment of rights and unless the language or the circumstances (as in an assignment for security) indicate the contrary, it is a delegation of performance of the duties of the assignor and its acceptance by the assignee constitutes a promise by him to perform those duties. This promise is enforceable by either the assignor or the other party to the original contract.

(5) The other party may treat any assignment which delegates performance as creating reasonable grounds for insecurity and may without prejudice to his rights against the assignor demand assurances from the assignee (Section 2–609).

Part 3   General Obligation and Construction of Contract

§2–301. General Obligations of Parties

The obligation of the seller is to transfer and deliver and that of the buyer is to accept and pay in accordance with the contract.

§2–302. Unconscionable Contract or Clause

(1) If the court as a matter of law finds the contract or any clause of the contract to have been unconscionable at the time it was made the court may refuse to enforce the contract, or it may enforce the remainder of the contract without the unconscionable clause, or it may so limit the application of any unconscionable clause as to avoid any unconscionable result.

(2) When it is claimed or appears to the court that the contract or any clause thereof may be unconscionable the parties shall be afforded a reasonable opportunity to present evidence as to its commercial setting, purpose and effect to aid the court in making the determination.

§2–303. Allocation or Division of Risks

Where this Article allocates a risk or a burden as between the parties ''unless otherwise agreed,'' the agreement may not only shift the allocation but may also divide the risk or burden.

§2–304. Price Payable in Money, Goods, Realty, or Otherwise

(1) The price can be made payable in money or otherwise. If it is payable in whole or in part in goods each party is a seller of the goods which he is to transfer.

(2) Even though all or part of the price is payable in an interest in realty the transfer of the goods and the seller's obligations with reference to them are subject to this Article, but not the transfer of the interest in realty or the transferor's obligations in connection therewith.

§2–305. Open Price Term

(1) The parties if they so intend can conclude a contract for sale even though the price is not settled. In such case the price is a reasonable price at the time for delivery if

(a) nothing is said as to price; or

(b) the price is left to be agreed by the parties and they fail to agree; or

(c) the price is to be fixed in terms of some agreed market or other standard as set or recorded by a third person or agency and it is not so set or recorded.

(2) A price to be fixed by the seller or by the buyer means a price for him to fix in good faith.

(3) When a price left to be fixed otherwise than by agreement of the parties fails to be fixed through fault of one party the other may at his option treat the contract as cancelled or himself fix a reasonable price.

(4) Where, however, the parties intend not to be bound unless the price be fixed or agreed and it is not fixed or agreed there is no contract. In such a case the buyer must return any goods already received or if unable so to do must pay their reasonable value at the time of delivery and the seller must return any portion of the price paid on account.

§2–306.   Output, Requirements and Exclusive Dealings

(1) A term which measures the quantity by the output of the seller or the requirements of the buyer means such actual output or requirements as may occur in good faith, except that no quantity unreasonably disproportionate to any stated estimate or in the absence of a stated estimate to any normal or otherwise comparable prior output or requirements may be tendered or demanded.

(2) A lawful agreement by either the seller or the buyer for exclusive dealing in the kind of goods concerned imposes unless otherwise agreed an obligation by the seller to use best efforts to supply the goods and by the buyer to use best efforts to promote their sale.

§2–307.   Delivery in Single Lot or Several Lots

Unless otherwise agreed all goods called for by a contract for sale must be tendered in a single delivery and payment is due only on such tender but where the circumstances give either party the right to make or demand delivery in lots the price if it can be apportioned may be demanded for each lot.

§2–308.   Absence of Specified Place for Delivery

Unless otherwise agreed

(a) the place for delivery of goods is the seller's place of business or if he has none his residence; but

(b) in a contract for sale of identified goods which to the knowledge of the parties at the time of contracting are in some other place, that place is the place for their delivery; and

(c) documents of title may be delivered through customary banking channels.

§2–309.   Absence of Specific Time Provisions; Notice of Termination

(1) The time for shipment or delivery or any other action under a contract if not provided in this Article or agreed upon shall be a reasonable time.

(2) Where the contract provides for successive performances but is indefinite in duration it is valid for a reasonable time but unless otherwise agreed may be terminated at any time by either party.

(3) Termination of a contract by one party except on the happening of an agreed event requires that reasonable notification be received by the other party and an agreement dispensing with notification is invalid if its operation would be unconscionable.

§2–310.   Open Time for Payment or Running of Credit: Authority to Ship Under Reservation

Unless otherwise agreed

(a) payment is due at the time and place at which the buyer is to receive the goods even though the place of shipment is the place of delivery; and

(b) if the seller is authorized to send the goods he may ship them under reservation, and may tender the documents of title, but the buyer may inspect the goods after their arrival before payment is due unless such inspection is inconsistent with the terms of the contract (Section 2–513); and

(c) if delivery is authorized and made by way of documents of title otherwise than by subsection (b) then payment is due at the time and place at which the buyer is to receive the documents regardless of where the goods are to be received; and

(d) where the seller is required or authorized to ship the goods on credit the credit period runs from the time of shipment but post-dating the invoice or delaying its dispatch will correspondingly delay the starting of the credit period.

§2–311.   Options and Cooperation Respecting Performance

(1) An agreement for sale which is otherwise sufficiently definite (subsection (3) of Section 2–204) to be a contract is not made invalid by the fact that it leaves particulars of performance to be specified by one of the parties. Any such specification must be made in good faith and within limits set by commercial reasonableness.

(2) Unless otherwise agreed specifications relating to assortment of the goods are at the buyer's option and except as otherwise provided in subsection (1)(c) and (3) of Section 2–319 specifications or arrangements relating to shipment are at the seller's option.

(3) Where such specification would materially affect the other party's performance but is not seasonably made or where one party's cooperation is necessary to the agreed

performance of the other but is not seasonably forthcoming, the other party in addition to all other remedies

(a) is excused for any resulting delay in his own performance; and

(b) may also either proceed to perform in any reasonable manner or after the time for a material part of his own performance treat the failure to specify or to cooperate as a breach by failure to deliver or accept the goods.

§2–312. Warranty of Title and Against Infringement; Buyer's Obligation Against Infringement

(1) Subject to subsection (2) there is in a contract for sale a warranty by the seller that

(a) the title conveyed shall be good, and its transfer rightful; and

(b) the goods shall be delivered free from any security interest or other lien or encumbrance of which the buyer at the time of contracting has no knowledge.

(2) A warranty under subsection (1) will be excluded or modified only by specific language or by circumstances which give the buyer reason to know that the person selling does not claim title in himself or that he is purporting to sell only such right or title as he or a third person may have.

(3) Unless otherwise agreed a seller who is a merchant regularly dealing in goods of the kind warrants that the goods shall be delivered free of the rightful claim of any third person by way of infringement or the like but a buyer who furnishes specifications to the seller must hold the seller harmless against any such claim which arises out of compliance with the specifications.

§2–313. Express Warranties by Affirmation, Promise, Description, Sample

(1) Express warranties by the seller are created as follows:

(a) Any affirmation of fact or promise made by the seller to the buyer which relates to the goods and becomes part of the basis of the bargain creates an express warranty that the goods shall conform to the affirmation or promise.

(b) Any description of the goods which is made part of the basis of the bargain creates an express warranty that the goods shall conform to the description.

(c) Any sample or model which is made part of the basis of the bargain creates an express warranty that the whole of the goods shall conform to the sample or model.

(2) It is not necessary to the creation of an express warranty that the seller use formal words such as ''warrant'' or ''guarantee'' or that he have a specific intention to make a warranty, but an affirmation merely of the value of the goods or a statement purporting to be merely the seller's opinion or commendation of the goods does not create a warranty.

§2–314. Implied Warranty: Merchantability; Usage of Trade

(1) Unless excluded or modified (Section 2–316), a warranty that the goods shall be merchantable is implied in a contract for their sale if the seller is a merchant with respect to goods of that kind. Under this section the serving for value of food or drink to be consumed either on the premises or elsewhere is a sale.

(2) Goods to be merchantable must be at least such as

(a) pass without objection in the trade under the contract description; and

(b) in the case of fungible goods, are of fair average quality within the description; and

(c) are fit for the ordinary purposes for which such goods are used; and

(d) run, within the variations permitted by the agreement, of even kind, quality and quantity within each unit and among all units involved; and

(e) are adequately contained, packaged, and labeled as the agreement may require; and

(f) conform to the promises or affirmations of fact made on the container or label if any.

(3) Unless excluded or modified (Section 2–316) other implied warranties may arise from course of dealing or usage of trade.

§2–315. Implied Warranty: Fitness for Particular Purpose

Where the seller at the time of contracting has reason to know any particular purpose for which the goods are required and that the buyer is relying on the seller's skill or judgment to select or furnish suitable goods, there is unless excluded or modified under the next section an implied warranty that the goods shall be fit for such purpose.

§2–316. Exclusion or Modification of Warranties

(1) Words or conduct relevant to the creation of an express warranty and words or conduct tending to negate or limit warranty shall be construed wherever reasonable as consistent with each other; but subject to the provisions of this Article on parol or extrinsic evidence (Section 2–202) negation or limitation is inoperative to the extent that such construction is unreasonable.

(2) Subject to subsection (3), to exclude or modify the implied warranty of merchantability or any part of it the language must mention merchantability and in case of a writing must be conspicuous, and to exclude or modify any implied warranty of fitness the exclusion must be by a writing and conspicuous. Language to exclude all implied warranties of fitness is sufficient if it states, for example, that ''There are no warranties which extend beyond the description on the face hereof.''

(3) Notwithstanding subsection (2)

(a) unless the circumstances indicate otherwise, all implied warranties are excluded by expressions like ''as is,'' ''with all faults'' or other languages which in common understanding calls the buyer's attention to the exclusion of warranties and makes plain that there is no implied warranty; and

(b) when the buyer before entering into the contract has examined the goods or the sample or model as fully as he desired or has refused to examine the goods there is no implied warranty with regard to defects which an examination ought in the circumstances to have revealed to him; and

(c) an implied warranty can also be excluded or modified by course of dealing or course of performance or usage of trade.

(4) Remedies for breach of warranty can be limited in accordance with the provisions of this Article on liquidation or limitation of damages and on contractual modification of remedy (Section 2–718 and 2–719).

§2–317. Cumulation and Conflict of Warranties Express or Implied

Warranties whether express or implied shall be construed as consistent with each other and as cumulative, but if such construction is unreasonable the intention of the parties shall determine which warranty is dominant. In ascertaining that intention the following rules apply:

(a) Exact or technical specifications displace an inconsistent sample or model or general language of description.

(b) A sample from an existing bulk displaces inconsistent general language of description.

(c) Express warranties displace inconsistent implied warranties other than an implied warranty of fitness for a particular purpose.

§2–318. Third Party Beneficiaries of Warranties Express or Implied

Note: If this Act is introduced in the Congress of the United States this Section should be omitted. (States to select one alternative.)

Alternative A

A seller's warranty whether express or implied extends to any natural person who is in the family or household of his buyer or who is a guest in his home if it is reasonable to expect that such person may use, consume or be affected by the goods and who is injured in person by breach of the warranty. A seller may not exclude or limit the operation of this section.

Alternative B

A seller's warranty whether express or implied extends to any natural person who may reasonably be expected to use, consume or be affected by the goods and who is injured in person by breach of the warranty. A seller may not exclude or limit the operation of this section.

Alternative C

A seller's warranty whether express or implied extends to any person who may reasonably be expected to use, consume or be affected by the goods and who is injured by breach of the warranty. A seller may not exclude or

limit the operation of this section with respect to injury to the person of an individual to whom the warranty extends.

§2–319. F.O.B. and F.A.S. Terms

(1) Unless otherwise agreed the term F.O.B. (which means "free on board") at a named place, even though used only in connection with the stated price, is a delivery term under which

(a) when the term is F.O.B. the place of shipment, the seller must at that place ship the goods in the manner provided in this Article (Section 2–504) and bear the expense and risk of putting them into the possession of the carrier; or

(b) when the term is F.O.B. the place of destination, the seller must at his own expense and risk transport the goods to that place and there tender delivery of them in the manner provided in this Article (Section 2–503);

(c) when under either (a) or (b) the term is also F.O.B. vessel, car or other vehicle, the seller must in addition at his own expense and risk load the goods on board. If the term is F.O.B. vessel the buyer must name the vessel and in an appropriate case the seller must comply with the provisions of this Article on the form of bill of lading (Section 2–323).

(2) Unless otherwise agreed the term F.A.S. vessel (which means "free alongside") at a named port, even though used only in connection with the stated price, is a delivery term under which the seller must

(a) at his own expense and risk deliver the goods alongside the vessel in the manner usual in that port or on a dock designated and provided by the buyer; and

(b) obtain and tender a receipt for the goods in exchange for which the carrier is under a duty to issue a bill of lading.

(3) Unless otherwise agreed in any case falling within subsection (1)(a) or (c) or subsection (2) the buyer must seasonally give any needed instructions for making delivery, including when the term is F.A.S. or F.O.B. the loading berth of the vessel and in an appropriate case its name and sailing date. The seller may treat the failure of needed instructions as a failure of cooperation under this Article (Section 2–311). He may also at his option move the goods in any reasonable manner preparatory to delivery or shipment.

(4) Under the term F.O.B. vessel or F.A.S. unless otherwise agreed the buyer must make payment against tender of the required documents and the seller may not tender nor the buyer demand delivery of the goods in substitution for the documents.

§2–320. C.I.F. and C. & F. Terms

(1) The term C.I.F. means that the price includes in a lump sum the cost of the goods and the insurance and freight to the named destination. The term C. & F. or C.F. means that the price so includes cost and freight to the named destination.

(2) Unless otherwise agreed and even though used only in connection with the stated price and destination, the term C.I.F. destination or its equivalent requires the seller at his own expense and risk to

(a) put the goods into the possession of a carrier at the port for shipment and obtain a negotiable bill or bills of lading covering the entire transportation to the named destination; and

(b) load the goods and obtain a receipt from the carrier (which may be contained in the bill of lading) showing that the freight has been paid or provided for; and

(c) obtain a policy or certificate of insurance, including any war risk insurance, of a kind and on terms then current at the port of shipment in the usual amount, in the currency of the contract, shown to cover the same goods covered by the bill of lading and providing for payment of loss to the order of the buyer or for the account of whom it may concern; but the seller may add to the price the amount of the premium for any such war risk insurance; and

(d) prepare an invoice of the goods and procure any other documents required to effect shipment or to comply with the contract; and

(e) forward and tender with commercial promptness all the documents in due form and with any indorsement necessary to perfect the buyer's rights.

(3) Unless otherwise agreed the term C. & F. or its equivalent has the same effect and imposes upon the seller the same obligations and risks as a C.I.F. term except the obligation as to insurance.

(4) Under the term C.I.F. & C. & F. unless otherwise agreed the buyer must make payment against tender of the required documents and the seller may not tender nor the buyer demand delivery of the goods in substitution for the documents.

§2–321.   C.I.F. or C. & F.: "Net Landed Weights"; "Payment on Arrival"; Warranty of Condition on Arrival

Under a contract containing a term C.I.F. or C. & F.

(1) Where the price is based on or is to be adjusted according to "net landed weights," "delivered weights," "out turn" quantity or quality or the like, unless otherwise agreed the seller must reasonably estimate the price. The payment due on tender of the documents called for by the contract is the amount so estimated, but after final adjustment of the price a settlement must be made with commercial promptness.

(2) An agreement described in subsection (1) or any warranty of quality or condition of the goods on arrival places upon the seller the risk of ordinary deterioration, shrinkage and the like in transportation but has no effect on the place or time of identification to the contract for sale or delivery or on the passing of the risk of loss.

(3) Unless otherwise agreed where the contract provides for payment on or after arrival of the goods the seller must before payment allow such preliminary inspection as is

feasible; but if the goods are lost delivery of the documents and payment are due when the goods should have arrived.

§2–322.   Delivery "Ex-Ship"

(1) Unless otherwise agreed a term for delivery of goods "ex-ship" (which means from the carrying vessel) or in equivalent language is not restricted to a particular ship and requires delivery from a ship which has reached a place at the named port of destination where goods of the kind are usually discharged.

(2) Under such a term unless otherwise agreed

(a) the seller must discharge all liens arising out of the carriage and furnish the buyer with a direction which puts the carrier under a duty to deliver the goods; and

(b) the risk of loss does not pass to the buyer until the goods leave the ship's tackle or are otherwise properly unloaded.

§2–323.   Form of Bill of Lading Required in Overseas Shipment; "Overseas"

(1) Where the contract contemplates overseas shipment and contains a term C.I.F. or C. & F. or F.O.B. vessel, the seller unless otherwise agreed must obtain a negotiable bill of lading stating that the goods have been loaded on board or, in the case of a term C.I.F. or C. & F., received for shipment.

(2) Where in a case within subsection (1) a bill of lading has been issued in a set of parts, unless otherwise agreed if the documents are not to be sent from abroad the buyer may demand tender of the full set; otherwise only one part of the bill of lading need be tendered. Even if the agreement expressly requires a full set

(a) due tender of a single part is acceptable within the provisions of this Article on cure of improper delivery (subsection (1) of Section 2–508); and

(b) even though the full set is demanded, if the documents are sent from abroad the person tendering an incomplete set may nevertheless require payment upon furnishing an indemnity which the buyer in good faith deems adequate.

(3) A shipment by water or by air or a contract contemplating such shipment is "overseas" insofar as by usage of trade or agreement it is subject to the commercial, financing or shipping practices characteristic of international deep water commerce.

§2–324.   "No Arrival, No Sale" Term

Under a term "no arrival, no sale" or terms of like meaning, unless otherwise agreed,

(a) the seller must properly ship conforming goods and if they arrive by any means he must tender them on arrival but he assumes no obligation that the goods will arrive unless he has caused the nonarrival; and

(b) where without fault of the seller the goods are in part lost or have so deteriorated as no longer to conform to the contract or arrive after the contract time, the buyer may proceed as if there had been casualty to identified goods (Section 2–613).

§2–325. "Letter of Credit" Term; "Confirmed Credit"

(1) Failure of the buyer seasonably to furnish an agreed letter of credit is a breach of the contract for sale.

(2) The delivery to seller of a proper letter of credit suspends the buyer's obligation to pay. If the letter of credit is dishonored, the seller may on seasonable notification to the buyer require payment directly from him.

(3) Unless otherwise agreed the term "letter of credit" or "banker's credit" in a contract for sale means an irrevocable credit issued by a financing agency of good repute and, where the shipment is overseas, of good international repute. The term "confirmed credit" means that the credit must also carry the direct obligation of such an agency which does business in the seller's financial market.

§2–326. Sale on Approval and Sale or Return; Consignment Sales and Rights of Creditors

(1) Unless otherwise agreed, if delivered goods may be returned by the buyer even though they conform to the contract, the transaction is

(a) a "sale on approval" if the goods are delivered primarily for use, and

(b) a "sale or return" if the goods are delivered primarily for resale.

(2) Except as provided in subsection (3), goods held on approval are not subject to the claims of the buyer's creditors until acceptance; goods held on sale or return are subject to such claims while in the buyer's possession.

(3) Where goods are delivered to a person for sale and such person maintains a place of business at which he deals in goods of the kind involved, under a name other than the name of the person making delivery, then with respect to claims of creditors of the person conducting the business the goods are deemed to be on sale or return. The provisions of this subsection are applicable even though an agreement purports to reserve title to the person making delivery until payment or resale or uses such words as "on consignment" or "on memorandum." However, this subsection is not applicable if the person making delivery

(a) complies with an applicable law providing for a consignor's interest or the like to be evidenced by a sign, or

(b) establishes that the person conducting the business is generally known by his creditors to be substantially engaged in selling the goods of others, or

(c) complies with the filing provisions of the Article on Secured Transactions (Article 9).

(4) Any "or return" term of a contract for sale is to be treated as a separate contract for sale within the statute of frauds section of this Article (Section 2–201) and as contradicting the sale aspect of the contract within the provisions of this Article on parol or extrinsic evidence (Section 2–202).

§2–327. Special Incidents of Sale on Approval and Sale or Return

(1) Under a sale on approval unless otherwise agreed

(a) although the goods are identified to the contract the risk of loss and the title do not pass to the buyer until acceptance; and

(b) use of the goods consistent with the purpose of trial is not acceptance but failure seasonably to notify the seller of election to return the goods is acceptance, and if the goods conform to the contract acceptance of any part is acceptance of the whole; and

(c) after due notification of election to return, the return is at the seller's risk and expense but a merchant buyer must follow any reasonable instructions.

(2) Under a sale or return unless otherwise agreed

(a) the option to return extends to the whole or any commercial unit of the goods while in substantially their original condition, but must be exercised seasonably; and

(b) the return is at the buyer's risk and expense.

§2–328. Sale by Auction

(1) In a sale by auction if goods are put up in lots each lot is the subject of a separate sale.

(2) A sale by auction is complete when the auctioneer so announces by the fall of the hammer or in other customary manner. Where a bid is made while the hammer is falling in acceptance of a prior bid the auctioneer may in his discretion reopen the bidding or declare the goods sold under the bid on which the hammer was falling.

(3) Such a sale is with reserve unless the goods are in explicit terms put up without reserve. In an auction with reserve the auctioneer may withdraw the goods at any time until he announces completion of the sale. In an auction without reserve, after the auctioneer calls for bids on an article or lot, that article or lot cannot be withdrawn unless no bid is made within a reasonable time. In either case a bidder may retract his bid until the auctioneer's announcement of completion of sale, but a bidder's retraction does not revive any previous bid.

(4) If the auctioneer knowingly receives a bid on the seller's behalf or the seller makes or procures such a bid, and notice has not been given that liberty for such bidding is reserved, the buyer may at his option avoid the sale or take the goods at the price of the last good faith bid prior to the completion of the sale. This subsection shall not apply to any bid at a forced sale.

Part 4 Title, Creditors and Good Faith Purchasers

§2–401. Passing of Title; Reservation for Security; Limited Application of This Section

Each provision of this Article with regard to the rights, obligations and remedies of the seller, the buyer, purchasers or other third parties applies irrespective of title to the goods except where the provision refers to such title. Insofar as situations are not covered by the other provisions of this Article and matters concerning title become material the following rules apply:

(1) Title to goods cannot pass under a contract for sale prior to their identification to the contract (Section 2–501), and unless otherwise explicitly agreed the buyer acquires by their identification a special property as limited by this Act. Any retention or reservation by the seller of the title (property) in goods shipped or delivered to the buyer is limited in effect to a reservation of a security interest. Subject to these provisions and to the provisions of the Article on Secured Transactions (Article 9), title to goods passes from the seller to the buyer in any manner and on any conditions explicitly agreed on by the parties.

(2) Unless otherwise explicitly agreed title passes to the buyer at the time and place at which the seller completes his performance with reference to the physical delivery of the goods, despite any reservation of a security interest and even though a document of title is to be delivered at a different time or place; and in particular and despite any reservation of a security interest by the bill of lading

(a) if the contract requires or authorizes the seller to send the goods to the buyer but does not require him to deliver them at destination, title passes to the buyer at the time and place of shipment; but

(b) if the contract requires delivery at destination, title passes on tender there.

(3) Unless otherwise explicitly agreed where delivery is to be made without moving the goods,

(a) if the seller is to deliver a document of title, title passes at the time when and the place where he delivers such documents; or

(b) if the goods are at the time of contracting already identified and no documents are to be delivered, title passes at the time and place of contracting.

(4) A rejection or other refusal by the buyer to receive or retain the goods, whether or not justified, or a justified revocation of acceptance revests title to the goods in the seller. Such revesting occurs by operation of law and is not a "sale."

§2–402. Rights of Seller's Creditors Against Sold Goods

(1) Except as provided in subsections (2) and (3), rights of unsecured creditors of the seller with respect to goods which have been identified to a contract for sale are subject to the buyer's rights to recover the goods under this Article (Section 2–502 and 2–716).

(2) A creditor of the seller may treat a sale or an identification of goods to a contract for sale as void if as against him a retention of possession by the seller is fraudulent under any rule of law of the state where the goods are situated, except that retention of possession in good faith and current course of trade by a merchant-seller for a

commercially reasonable time after a sale or identification is not fraudulent.

(3) Nothing in this Article shall be deemed to impair the rights of creditors of the seller

(a) under the provisions of the Article on Secured Transactions (Article 9); or

(b) where identification to the contract or delivery is made not in current course of trade but in satisfaction of or as security for a pre-existing claim for money, security or the like and is made under circumstances which under any rule of law of the state where the goods are situated would apart from this Article constitute the transaction a fraudulent transfer or voidable preference.

§2–403. Power to Transfer; Good Faith Purchase of Goods; "Entrusting"

(1) A purchaser of goods acquires all title which his transferor had or had power to transfer except that a purchaser of a limited interest acquires rights only to the extent of the interest purchased. A person with voidable title has power to transfer a good title to a good faith purchaser for value. When goods have been delivered under a transaction of purchase the purchaser has such power even though

(a) the transferor was deceived as to the identity of the purchaser, or

(b) the delivery was in exchange for a check which is later dishonored, or

(c) it was agreed that the transaction was to be a "cash sale," or

(d) the delivery was procured through fraud punishable as larcenous under the criminal law.

(2) Any entrusting of possession of goods to a merchant who deals in goods of that kind gives him power to transfer all rights of the entruster to a buyer in ordinary course of business.

(3) "Entrusting" includes any delivery and any acquiescence in retention of possession regardless of any condition expressed between the parties to the delivery or acquiescence and regardless of whether the procurement of the entrusting or the possessor's disposition of the goods have been such as to be larcenous under the criminal law.

(4) The rights of other purchasers of goods and of lien creditors are governed by the Articles on Secured Transactions (Article 9), Bulk Transfers (Article 6) and Documents of Title (Article 7).

Part 5 Performance

§2–501. Insurable Interest in Goods; Manner of Identification of Goods

(1) The buyer obtains a special property and an insurable interest in goods by identification of existing goods as goods to which the contract refers even though the goods so identified are nonconforming and he has an option to return or reject them. Such identification can be made at

any time and in any manner explicitly agreed to by the parties. In the absence of explicit agreement identification occurs

(a) when the contract is made if it is for the sale of goods already existing and identified;

(b) if the contract is for the sale of future goods other than those described in paragraph (c), when goods are shipped, marked or otherwise designated by the seller as goods to which the contract refers;

(c) when the crops are planted or otherwise become growing crops or the young are conceived if the contract is for the sale of unborn young to be born within twelve months after contracting or for the sale of crops to be harvested within twelve months or the next normal harvest season after contracting whichever is longer.

(2) The seller retains an insurable interest in goods so long as title to or any security interest in the goods remains in him and where the identification is by the seller alone he may until default or insolvency or notification to the buyer that the identification is final substitute other goods for those identified.

(3) Nothing in this section impairs any insurable interest recognized under any other statute or rule or law.

§2–502. Buyer's Right to Goods on Seller's Insolvency

(1) Subject to subsection (2) and even though the goods have not been shipped a buyer who has paid a part or all of the price of goods in which he has a special property under the provisions of the immediately preceding section may on making and keeping good a tender of any unpaid portion of their price recover them from the seller if the seller becomes insolvent within ten days after receipt of the first installment on their price.

(2) If the identification creating his special property has been made by the buyer he acquires the right to recover the goods only if they conform to the contract for sale.

§2–503. Manner of Seller's Tender of Delivery

(1) Tender of delivery requires that the seller put and hold conforming goods at the buyer's disposition and give the buyer any notification reasonably necessary to enable him to take delivery. The manner, time and place for tender are determined by the agreement and this Article, and in particular

(a) tender must be at a reasonable hour, and if it is of goods they must be kept available for the period reasonably necessary to enable the buyer to take possession; but

(b) unless otherwise agreed the buyer must furnish facilities reasonably suited to the receipt of the goods.

(2) Where the case is within the next section respecting shipment tender requires that the seller comply with its provisions.

(3) Where the seller is required to deliver at a particular destination tender requires that he comply with subsection

(1) and also in any appropriate case tender documents as described in subsections (4) and (5) of this section.

(4) Where goods are in the possession of a bailee and are to be delivered without being moved

(a) tender requires that the seller either tender a negotiable document of title covering such goods or procure acknowledgment by the bailee of the buyer's right to possession of the goods; but

(b) tender to the buyer of a non-negotiable document of title or of a written direction to the bailee to deliver is sufficient tender unless the buyer seasonably objects, and receipt by the bailee of notification of the buyer's rights fixes those rights as against the bailee and all third persons; but risk of loss of the goods and of any failure by the bailee to honor the non-negotiable document of title or to obey the direction remains on the seller until the buyer has had a reasonable time to present the document or direction, and a refusal by the bailee to honor the document or to obey the direction defeats the tender.

(5) Where the contract requires the seller to deliver documents

(a) he must tender all such documents in correct form, except as provided in this Article with respect to bills of lading in a set (subsection (2) of Section 2–323); and

(b) tender through customary banking channels is sufficient and dishonor of a draft accompanying the documents constitutes non-acceptance or rejection.

§2–504. Shipment by Seller

Where the seller is required or authorized to send the goods to the buyer and the contract does not require him to deliver them at a particular destination, then unless otherwise agreed he must

(a) put the goods in the possession of such a carrier and make such a contract for their transportation as may be reasonable having regard to the nature of the goods and other circumstances of the case; and

(b) obtain and promptly deliver or tender in due form any document necessary to enable the buyer to obtain possession of the goods or otherwise required by the agreement or by usage of trade; and

(c) promptly notify the buyer of the shipment. Failure to notify the buyer under paragraph (c) or to make a proper contract under paragraph (a) is a ground for rejection only if material delay or loss ensues.

§2–505. Seller's Shipment Under Reservation

(1) Where the seller has identified goods to the contract by or before shipment:

(a) his procurement of a negotiable bill of lading to his own order or otherwise reserves in him a security interest in the goods. His procurement of the bill to the order of a financing agency or of the buyer indicates in addition only the seller's expectation of transferring that interest to the person named.

(b) a non-negotiable bill of lading to himself or his nominee reserves possession of the goods as security but except in a case of conditional delivery (subsection (2) of Section 2–507) a non-negotiable bill of lading naming the buyer as consignee reserves no security interest even though the seller retains possession of the bill of lading.

(2) When shipment by the seller with reservation of a security interest is in violation of the contract for sale it constitutes an improper contract for transportation within the preceding section but impairs neither the rights given to the buyer by shipment and identification of the goods to the contract nor the seller's powers as a holder of a negotiable document.

§2–506.   Rights of Financing Agency

(1) A financing agency by paying or purchasing for value a draft which relates to a shipment of goods acquires to the extent of the payment or purchase and in addition to its own rights under the draft and any document of title securing it any rights of the shipper in the goods including the right to stop delivery and the shipper's right to have the draft honored by the buyer.

(2) The right to reimbursement of a financing agency which has in good faith honored or purchased the draft under commitment to or authority from the buyer is not impaired by subsequent discovery of defects with reference to any relevant document which was apparently regular on its face.

§2–507.   Effect of Seller's Tender; Delivery on Condition

(1) Tender of delivery is a condition to the buyer's duty to accept the goods and, unless otherwise agreed, to his duty to pay for them. Tender entitles the seller to acceptance of the goods and to payment according to the contract.

(2) Where payment is due and demanded on the delivery to the buyer of goods or documents of title, his right as against the seller to retain or dispose of them is conditional upon his making the payment due.

§2–508.   Cure by Seller of Improper Tender or Delivery; Replacement

(1) Where any tender or delivery by the seller is rejected because non-conforming and the time for performance has not yet expired, the seller may seasonably notify the buyer of his intention to cure and may then within the contract time make a conforming delivery.

(2) Where the buyer rejects a non-conforming tender which the seller had reasonable grounds to believe would be acceptable with or without money allowance the seller may if he seasonably notifies the buyer have a further reasonable time to substitute a conforming tender.

§2–509.   Risk of Loss in the Absence of Breach

(1) Where the contract requires or authorizes the seller to ship the good by carrier

(a) if it does not require him to deliver them at a particular destination, the risk of loss passes to the buyer when the goods are duly delivered to the carrier even though the shipment is under reservation (Section 2–505); but

(b) if it does require him to deliver them at a particular destination and the goods are there duly tendered while in the possession of the carrier, the risk of loss passes to the buyer when the goods are there duly so tendered as to enable the buyer to take delivery.

(2) Where the goods are held by a bailee to be delivered without being moved, the risk of loss passes to the buyer.

(a) on his receipt of a negotiable document of title covering the goods; or

(b) on acknowledgment by the bailee of the buyer's right to possession of the goods; or

(c) after his receipt of a non-negotiable document of title or other written direction to deliver, as provided in subsection (4)(b) of Section 2–503.

(3) In any case not within subsection (1) or (2), the risk of loss passes to the buyer on his receipt of the goods if the seller is a merchant; otherwise the risk passes to the buyer on tender of delivery.

(4) The provisions of this section are subject to contrary agreement of the parties and to the provisions of this Article on sale on approval (Section 2–327) and on effect of breach on risk of loss (Section 2–510).

§2–510.   Effect of Breach on Risk of Loss

(1) Where a tender or delivery of goods so fails to conform to the contract as to give a right of rejection the risk of their loss remains on the seller until cure or acceptance.

(2) Where the buyer rightfully revokes acceptance he may to the extent of any deficiency in his effective insurance coverage treat the risk of loss as having rested on the seller from the beginning.

(3) Where the buyer as to conforming goods already identified to the contract for sale repudiates or is otherwise in breach before risk of their loss has passed to him, the seller may to the extent of any deficiency in his effective insurance coverage treat the risk of loss as resting on the buyer for a commercially reasonable time.

§2–511.   Tender of Payment by Buyer; Payment by Check

(1) Unless otherwise agreed tender of payment is a condition to the seller's duty to tender and complete any delivery.

(2) Tender of payment is sufficient when made by any means or in any manner current in the ordinary course of business unless the seller demands payment in legal tender and gives any extension of time reasonably necessary to procure it.

(3) Subject to the provisions of this Act on the effect of an instrument on an obligation (Section 3–802), payment by check is conditional and is defeated as between the parties by dishonor of the check on due presentment.

§2–512.   Payment by Buyer Before Inspection

(1) Where the contract requires payment before inspection non-conformity of the goods does not excuse the buyer from so making payment unless

(a) the non-conformity appears without inspection; or

(b) despite tender of the required documents the circumstances would justify injunction against honor under the provisions of this Act (Section 5–114).

(2) Payment pursuant to subsection (1) does not constitute an acceptance of goods or impair the buyer's right to inspect or any of his remedies.

§2–513.   Buyer's Right to Inspection of Goods

(1) Unless otherwise agreed and subject to subsection (3), where goods are tendered or delivered or identified to the contract for sale, the buyer has a right before payment or acceptance to inspect them at any reasonable place and time and in any reasonable manner. When the seller is required and authorized to send the goods to the buyer, the inspection may be after their arrival.

(2) Expenses of inspection must be borne by the buyer but may be recovered from the seller if the goods do not conform and are rejected.

(3) Unless otherwise agreed and subject to the provisions of this Article on C.I.F. contracts (subsection (3) of Section 2–321), the buyer is not entitled to inspect the goods before payment of the price when the contract provides

(a) for delivery ''C.O.D.'' or on other like terms; or

(b) for payment against documents of title, except where such payment is due only after the goods are to become available for inspection.

(4) A place or method of inspection fixed by the parties is presumed to be exclusive but unless otherwise expressly agreed it does not postpone identification or shift the place for delivery or for passing the risk of loss. If compliance becomes impossible, inspection shall be as provided in this section unless the place or method fixed was clearly intended as an indispensable condition failure of which avoids the contract.

§2–514.   When Documents Deliverable on Acceptance; When on Payment

Unless otherwise agreed documents against which a draft is drawn are to be delivered to the drawee on acceptance of the draft if it is payable more than three days after presentment; otherwise, only on payment.

§2–515.   Preserving Evidence of Goods in Dispute

In furtherance of the adjustment of any claim or dispute

(a) either party on reasonable notification to the other and for the purpose of ascertaining the facts and preserving evidence has the right to inspect, test and sample the goods including such of them as may be in the possession or control of the other; and

(b) the parties may agree to a third party inspection or survey to determine the conformity or condition of the goods and may agree that the findings shall be binding upon them in any subsequent litigation or adjustment.

Part 6   Breach, Repudiation and Excuse

§2–601.   Buyer's Rights on Improper Delivery

Subject to the provisions of this Article on breach in installment contracts (Section 2–612) and unless otherwise agreed under the sections on contractual limitations of remedy (Sections 2–718 and 2–719), if the goods or the tender of delivery fail in any respect to conform to the contract, the buyer may

(a) reject the whole; or

(b) accept the whole; or

(c) accept any commercial unit or units and reject the rest.

§2–602.   Manner and Effect of Rightful Rejection

(1) Rejection of goods must be within a reasonable time after their delivery or tender. It is ineffective unless the buyer seasonably notifies the seller.

(2) Subject to the provisions of the two following sections on rejected goods (Sections 2–603 and 2–604),

(a) after rejection any exercise of ownership by the buyer with respect to any commercial unit is wrongful as against the seller; and

(b) if the buyer has before rejection taken physical possession of goods in which he does not have a security interest under the provisions of this Article (subsection (3) of Section 2–711), he is under a duty after rejection to hold them with reasonable care at the seller's disposition for a time sufficient to permit the seller to remove them; but

(c) the buyer has no further obligations with regard to goods rightfully rejected.

(3) The seller's rights with respect to goods wrongfully rejected are governed by the provisions of this Article on Seller's remedies in general (Section 2–703).

§2–603.   Merchant Buyer's Duties as to Rightfully Rejected Goods

(1) Subject to any security interest in the buyer (subsection (3) of Section 2–711), when the seller has no agent or place of business at the market of rejection a merchant buyer is under a duty after rejection of goods in his possession or control to follow any reasonable instructions received from the seller with respect to the goods and in the absence of such instructions to make reasonable efforts to sell them for the seller's account if they are perishable or threaten to decline in value speedily. Instructions are not reasonable if on demand indemnity for expense is not forthcoming.

(2) When the buyer sells goods under subsection (1), he is entitled to reimbursement from the seller or out of the proceeds for reasonable expenses of caring for and selling them, and if the expenses include no selling commission then to such commission as is usual in the trade or if there is none to a reasonable sum not exceeding ten per cent on the gross proceeds.

(3) In complying with this section the buyer is held only to good faith and good faith conduct hereunder is neither acceptance nor conversion nor the basis of an action for damages.

§2–604.   Buyer's Options as to Salvage of Rightfully Rejected Goods

Subject to the provisions of the immediately preceding section on perishables if the seller gives no instructions within a reasonable time after notification of rejection the buyer may store the rejected goods for the seller's account or reship them to him or resell them for the seller's account with reimbursement as provided in the preceding section. Such action is not acceptance or conversion.

§2–605.   Waiver of Buyer's Objections by Failure to Particularize

(1) The buyer's failure to state in connection with rejection a particular defect which is ascertainable by reasonable inspection precludes him from relying on the unstated defect to justify rejection or to establish breach

    (a) where the seller could have cured it if stated seasonably; or

    (b) between merchants when the seller has after rejection made a request in writing for a full and final written statement of all defects on which the buyer proposes to rely.

(2) Payment against documents made without reservation of rights precludes recovery of the payment for defects apparent on the face of the documents.

§2–606.   What Constitutes Acceptance of Goods

(1) Acceptance of goods occurs when the buyer

    (a) after a reasonable opportunity to inspect the goods signifies to the seller that the goods are conforming or that he will take or retain them in spite of their nonconformity; or

    (b) fails to make an effective rejection (subsection (1) of Section 2–602), but such acceptance does not occur until the buyer has had a reasonable opportunity to inspect them; or

    (c) does any act inconsistent with the seller's ownership; but if such act is wrongful as against the seller it is an acceptance only if ratified by him.

(2) Acceptance of a part of any commercial unit is acceptance of that entire unit.

§2–607.   Effect of Acceptance; Notice of Breach; Burden of Establishing Breach After Acceptance; Notice of Claim or Litigation to Person Answerable Over

(1) The buyer must pay at the contract rate for any goods accepted.

(2) Acceptance of goods by the buyer precludes rejection of the goods accepted and if made with knowledge of a nonconformity cannot be revoked because of it unless the acceptance was on the reasonable assumption that the non-conformity would be seasonably cured but acceptance does not of itself impair any other remedy provided by this Article for non-conformity.

(3) Where a tender has been accepted

    (a) the buyer must within a reasonable time after he discovers or should have discovered any breach notify the seller of breach or be barred from any remedy; and

    (b) if the claim is one for infringement or the like (subsection (3) of Section 2–312) and the buyer is sued as a result of such a breach he must so notify the seller within a reasonable time after he receives notice of the litigation or be barred from any remedy over for liability established by the litigation.

(4) The burden is on the buyer to establish any breach with respect to the goods accepted.

(5) Where the buyer is sued for breach of a warranty or other obligation for which his seller is answerable over

    (a) he may give his seller written notice of the litigation. If the notice states that the seller may come in and defend and that if the seller does not do so he will be bound in any action against him by his buyer by any determination of fact common to the two litigations, then unless the seller after seasonable receipt of the notice does come in and defend he is so bound.

    (b) if the claim is one for infringement or the like (subsection (3) of Section 2–312) the original seller may demand in writing that his buyer turn over to him control of the litigation including settlement or else be barred from any remedy over and if he also agrees to bear all expense and to satisfy any adverse judgment, then unless the buyer after seasonable receipt of the demand does turn over control the buyer is so barred.

(6) The provisions of subsections (3), (4) and (5) apply to any obligation of a buyer to hold the seller harmless against infringement or the like (subsection (3) of Section 2–312).

§2–608.   Revocation of Acceptance in Whole or in Part

(1) The buyer may revoke his acceptance of a lot or commercial unit whose non-conformity substantially impairs its value to him if he has accepted it

    (a) on the reasonable assumption that its non-conformity would be cured and it has not been seasonably cured; or

(b) without discovery of such non-conformity if his acceptance was reasonably induced either by the difficulty of discovery before acceptance or by the seller's assurances.

(2) Revocation of acceptance must occur within a reasonable time after the buyer discovers or should have discovered the ground for it and before any substantial change in condition of the goods which is not caused by their own defects. It is not effective until the buyer notifies the seller of it.

(3) A buyer who so revokes has the same rights and duties with regard to the goods involved as if he had rejected them.

§2–609.   Right to Adequate Assurance of Performance

(1) A contract for sale imposes an obligation on each party that the other's expectation of receiving due performance will not be impaired. When reasonable grounds for insecurity arise with respect to the performance of either party the other may in writing demand adequate assurance of due performance and until he receives such assurance may if commercially reasonable suspend any performance for which he has not already received the agreed return.

(2) Between merchants the reasonableness of grounds for insecurity and the adequacy of any assurance offered shall be determined according to commercial standards.

(3) Acceptance of any improper delivery or payment does not prejudice the aggrieved party's right to demand adequate assurance of future performance.

(4) After receipt of a justified demand failure to provide within a reasonable time not exceeding thirty days such assurance of due performance as is adequate under the circumstances of the particular case is a repudiation of the contract.

§2–610.   Anticipatory Repudiation

When either party repudiates the contract with respect to a performance not yet due the loss of which will substantially impair the value of the contract to the other, the aggrieved party may

(a) for a commercially reasonable time await performance by the repudiating party; or

(b) resort to any remedy for breach (Section 2–703 or Section 2–711), even though he has notified the repudiating party that he would await the latter's performance and has urged retraction; and

(c) in either case suspended his own performance or proceed in accordance with the provisions of this Article on the seller's right to identify goods to the contract notwithstanding breach or to salvage unfinished goods (Section 2–704).

§2–611.   Retraction of Anticipatory Repudiation

(1) Until the repudiating party's next performance is due he can retract his repudiation unless the aggrieved party

has since the repudiation cancelled or materially changed his position or otherwise indicated that he considers the repudiation final.

(2) Retraction may be by any method which clearly indicates to the aggrieved party that the repudiating party intends to perform, but must include any assurance justifiably demanded under the provisions of this Article (Section 2–609).

(3) Retraction reinstates the repudiating party's right under the contract with due excuse and allowance to the aggrieved party for any delay occasioned by the repudiation.

§2–612.   "Installment Contract"; Breach

(1) An "installment contract" is one which requires or authorizes the delivery of goods in separate lots to be separately accepted, even though the contract contains a clause "each delivery is a separate contract" or its equivalent.

(2) The buyer may reject any installment which is nonconforming if the non-conformity substantially impairs the value of that installment and cannot be cured or if the non-conformity is a defect in the required documents; but if the non-conformity does not fall within subsection (3) and the seller gives adequate assurance of its cure the buyer must accept that installment.

(3) Whenever non-conformity or default with respect to one or more installments substantially impairs the value of the whole contract there is a breach of the whole. But the aggrieved party reinstates the contract if he accepts a nonconforming installment without seasonably notifying of cancellation or if he brings an action with respect only to past installments or demands performance as to future installments.

§2–613.   Casualty to Identified Goods

Where the contract requires for its performance goods identified when the contract is made, and the goods suffer casualty without fault of either party before the risk of loss passes to the buyer, or in a proper case under a "no arrival, no sale" term (Section 2–324) then

(a) if the loss is total the contract is avoided; and

(b) if the loss is partial or the goods have so deteriorated as no longer to conform to the contract the buyer may nevertheless demand inspection and at his option either treat the contract as avoided or accept the goods with due allowance from the contract price for the deterioration or the deficiency in quantity but without further right against the seller.

§2–614.   Substituted Performance

(1) Where without fault of either party the agreed berthing, loading, or unloading facilities fail or an agreed type of carrier becomes unavailable or the agreed manner of delivery otherwise becomes commercially impracticable but a commercially reasonable substitute is available, such substitute performance must be tendered and accepted.

(2) If the agreed means or manner of payment fails because of domestic or foreign governmental regulation, the seller may withhold or stop delivery unless the buyer provides a means or manner of payment which is commercially a substantial equivalent. If delivery has already been taken, payment by the means or in the manner provided by the regulation discharges the buyer's obligation unless the regulation is discriminatory, oppressive or predatory.

§2–615. Excuse by Failure of Presupposed Conditions

Except so far as a seller may have assumed a greater obligation and subject to the preceding section on substituted performance:

(a) Delay in delivery or non-delivery in whole or in part by a seller who complies with paragraphs (b) and (c) is not a breach of his duty under a contract for sale if performance as agreed has been made impracticable by the occurrence of a contingency the nonoccurrence of which was a basic assumption on which the contract was made or by compliance in good faith with any applicable foreign or domestic governmental regulation or order whether or not it later proves to be invalid.

(b) Where the causes mentioned in paragraph (a) affect only a part of the seller's capacity to perform, he must allocate production and deliveries among his customers but may at his option include regular customers not then under contract as well as his own requirements for further manufacture. He may so allocate in any manner which is fair and reasonable.

(c) The seller must notify the buyer seasonably that there will be delay or non-delivery and, when allocation is required under paragraph (b), of the estimated quota thus made available for the buyer.

§2–616. Procedure on Notice Claiming Excuse

(1) Where the buyer receives notification of a material or indefinite delay or an allocation justified under the preceding section he may by written notification to the seller as to any delivery concerned, and where the prospective deficiency substantially impairs the value of the whole contract under the provisions of this Article relating to breach of installment contracts (Section 2–612), then also as to the whole,

(a) terminate and thereby discharge any unexecuted portion of the contract; or

(b) modify the contract by agreeing to take his available quota in substitution.

(2) If after receipt of such notification from the seller the buyer fails so to modify the contract within a reasonable time not exceeding thirty days the contract lapses with respect to any deliveries affected.

(3) The provisions of this section may not be negated by agreement except in so far as the seller has assumed a greater obligation under the preceding section.

Part 7 Remedies

§2–701. Remedies for Breach of Collateral Contracts Not Impaired

Remedies for breach of any obligation or promise collateral or ancillary to a contract for sale are not impaired by the provisions of this Article.

§2–702. Seller's Remedies on Discovery of Buyer's Insolvency

(1) Where the seller discovers the buyer to be insolvent he may refuse delivery except for cash including payment for all goods theretofore delivered under the contract, and stop delivery under this Article (Section 2–705).

(2) Where the seller discovers that the buyer has received goods on credit while insolvent he may reclaim the goods upon demand made within ten days after the receipt, but if misrepresentation of solvency has been made to the particular seller in writing within three months before delivery the ten day limitation does not apply. Except as provided in this subsection the seller may not base a right to reclaim goods on the buyer's fraudulent or innocent misrepresentation of solvency or of intent to pay.

(3) The seller's right to reclaim under subsection (2) is subject to the rights of a buyer in ordinary course or other good faith purchaser under this Article (Section 2–403). Successful reclamation of goods excludes all other remedies with respect to them.

§2–703. Seller's Remedies in General

Where the buyer wrongfully rejects or revokes acceptance of goods or fails to make a payment due on or before delivery or repudiates with respect to a part or the whole, then with respect to any goods directly affected and, if the breach is of the whole contract (Section 2–612), then also with respect to the whole undelivered balance, the aggrieved seller may

(a) withhold delivery of such goods;

(b) stop delivery by any bailee as hereafter provided (Section 2–705);

(c) proceed under the next section respecting goods still unidentified to the contract:

(d) resell and recover damages as hereafter provided (Section 2–706);

(e) recover damages for non-acceptance (Section 2–708) or in a proper case the price (Section 2–709);

(f) cancel.

§2–704. Seller's Right to Identify Goods to the Contract Notwithstanding Breach or to Salvage Unfinished Goods

(1) An aggreviated seller under the preceding section may

(a) identify to the contract conforming goods not already identified if at the time he learned of the breach they are in his possession or control;

(b) treat as the subject of resale goods which have demonstrably been intended for the particular contract even though those goods are unfinished.

(2) Where the goods are unfinished an aggrieved seller may in the exercise of reasonable commercial judgment for the purposes of avoiding loss and of effective realization either complete the manufacture and wholly identify the goods to the contract or cease manufacture and resell for scrap or salvage value or proceed in any other reasonable manner.

§2–705.   Seller's Stoppage of Delivery in Transit or Otherwise

(1) The seller may stop delivery of goods in the possession of a carrier or other bailee when he discovers the buyer to be insolvent (Section 2–702) and may stop delivery of carload, truckload, planeload or larger shipments of express or freight when the buyer repudiates or fails to make a payment due before delivery or if for any other reason the seller has a right to withhold or reclaim the goods.

(2) As against such buyer the seller may stop delivery until

(a) receipt of the goods by the buyer; or

(b) acknowledgment to the buyer by any bailee of the goods except a carrier that the bailee holds the goods for the buyer; or

(c) such acknowledgment to the buyer by a carrier by reshipment or as warehouseman; or

(d) negotiation to the buyer of any negotiable document of title covering the goods.

(3)(a) To stop delivery the seller must so notify as to enable the bailee by reasonable diligence to prevent delivery of the goods.

(b) After such notification the bailee must hold and deliver the goods according to the directions of the seller but the seller is liable to the bailee for any ensuing charges or damages.

(c) If a negotiable document of title has been issued for goods the bailee is not obliged to obey a notification to stop until surrender of the document.

(d) A carrier who has issued a non-negotiable bill of lading is not obliged to obey a notification to stop received from a person other than the consignor.

§2–706.   Seller's Resale Including Contract for Resale

(1) Under the conditions stated in Section 2–703 on seller's remedies, the seller may resell the goods concerned or the undelivered balance thereof. Where the resale is made in good faith and in a commercially reasonable manner the seller may recover the difference between the resale price and the contract price together with any incidental damages allowed under the provisions of this Article (Section 2–710), but less expenses saved in consequence of the buyer's breach.

(2) Except as otherwise provided in subsection (3) or unless otherwise agreed resale may be at public or private sale including sale by way of one or more contracts to sell or of identification to an existing contract of the seller. Sale may be as a unit or in parcels and at any time and place and on any terms but every aspect of the sale including the method, manner, time, place and terms must be commercially reasonable. The resale must be reasonably identified as referring to the broken contract, but it is not necessary that the goods be in existence or that any or all of them have been identified to the contract before the breach.

(3) Where the resale is at private sale the seller must give the buyer reasonable notification of his intention to resell.

(4) Where the resale is at public sale

(a) only identified goods can be sold except where there is a recognized market for a public sale of futures in goods of the kind; and

(b) it must be made at a usual place or market for public sale if one is reasonably available and except in the case of goods which are perishable or threaten to decline in value speedily the seller must give the buyer reasonable notice of the time and place of the resale; and

(c) if the goods are not to be within the view of those attending the sale the notification of sale must state the place where the goods are located and provide for their reasonable inspection by prospective bidders; and

(d) the seller may buy.

(5) A purchaser who buys in good faith at a resale takes the goods free of any rights of the original buyer even though the seller fails to comply with one or more of the requirements of this section.

(6) The seller is not accountable to the buyer for any profit made on any resale. A person in the position of a seller (Section 2–707) or a buyer who has rightfully rejected or justifiably revoked acceptance must account for any excess over the amount of his security interest, as hereinafter defined (subsection (3) of Section 2–711).

§2–707.   "Person in the Position of a Seller"

(1) A "person in the position of a seller" includes as against a principal an agent who has paid or become responsible for the price of goods on behalf of his principal or anyone who otherwise holds a security interest or other right in goods similar to that of a seller.

(2) A person in the position of a seller may as provided in this Article withhold or stop delivery (Section 2–706) and recover incidental damages (Section 2–710).

§2–708.   Seller's Damages for Non-Acceptance or Repudiation

(1) Subject to subsection (2) and to the provisions of this Article with respect to proof of market price (Section 2–723), the measure of damages for non-acceptance or repudiation by the buyer is the difference between the

market price at the time and place for tender and the unpaid contract price together with any incidental damages provided in this Article (Section 2–710), but less expenses saved in consequence of the buyer's breach.

(2) If the measure of damages provided in subsection (1) is inadequate to put the seller in as good a position as performance would have done then the measure of damages is the profit (including reasonable overhead) which the seller would have made from full performance by the buyer, together with any incidental damages provided in this Article (Section 2–710), due allowance for costs reasonably incurred and due credit for payments or proceeds of resale.

§2–709. Action for the Price

(1) When the buyer fails to pay the price as it becomes due the seller may recover, together with any incidental damages under the next section, the price

(a) of goods accepted or of conforming goods lost or damaged within a commercially reasonable time after risk of their loss has passed to the buyer; and

(b) of goods identified to the contract if the seller is unable after reasonable effort to resell them at a reasonable price or the circumstances reasonably indicate that such effort will be unavailing.

(2) Where the seller sues for the price he must hold for the buyer any goods which have been identified to the contract and are still in his control except that if resale becomes possible he may resell them at any time prior to the collection of the judgment. The net proceeds of any such resale must be credited to the buyer and payment of the judgment entitles him to any goods not resold.

(3) After the buyer has wrongfully rejected or revoked acceptance of the goods or has failed to make a payment due or has repudiated (Section 2–610), a seller who is held not entitled to the price under this section shall nevertheless be awarded damages for non-acceptance under the preceding section.

§2–710. Seller's Incidental Damages

Incidental damages to an aggrieved seller include any commercially reasonable charges, expenses or commissions incurred in stopping delivery, in the transportation, care and custody of goods after the buyer's breach, in connection with return or resale of the goods or otherwise resulting from the breach.

§2–711. Buyer's Remedies in General; Buyer's Security Interest in Rejected Goods

(1) Where the seller fails to make delivery or repudiates or the buyer rightfully rejects or justifiably revokes acceptance then with respect to any goods involved, and with respect to the whole if the breach goes to the whole contract (Section 2–612), the buyer may cancel and whether or not he has done so may in addition to recovering so much of the price as has been paid

(a) "cover" and have damages under the next section as to all the goods affected whether or not they have been identified to the contract; or

(b) recover damages for non-delivery as provided in this Article (Section 2–713).

(2) Where the seller fails to deliver or repudiates the buyer may also

(a) if the goods have been identified recover them as provided in this Article (Section 2–502); or

(b) in a proper case obtain specific performance or replevy the goods as provided in this Article (Section 2–716).

(3) On rightful rejection or justifiable revocation of acceptance a buyer has a security interest in goods in his possession or control for any payments made on their price and any expenses reasonably incurred in their inspection, receipt, transportation, care and custody and may hold such goods and resell them in like manner as an aggrieved seller (Section 2–706).

§2–712. "Cover"; Buyer's Procurement of Substitute Goods

(1) After a breach within the preceding section the buyer may "cover" by making in good faith and without unreasonable delay any reasonable purchase of or contract to purchase goods in substitution for those due from the seller.

(2) The buyer may recover from the seller as damages the difference between the cost of cover and the contract price together with any incidental or consequential damages as hereinafter defined (Section 2–715), but less expenses saved in consequence of the seller's breach.

(3) Failure of the buyer to effect cover within this section does not bar him from any other remedy.

§2–713. Buyer's Damages for Non-Delivery or Repudiation

(1) Subject to the provisions of this Article with respect to proof of market price (Section 2–723), the measure of damages for non-delivery or repudiation by the seller is the difference between the market price at the time when the buyer learned of the breach and the contract price together with any incidental and consequential damages provided in this Article (Section 2–715), but less expenses saved in consequence of the seller's breach.

(2) Market price is to be determined as of the place for tender or, in cases of rejection after arrival or revocation of acceptance, as of the place of arrival.

§2–714. Buyer's Damages for Breach in Regard to Accepted Goods

(1) Where the buyer has accepted goods and given notification (subsection (3) of Section 2–607) he may recover as damages for any non-conformity of tender the loss resulting in the ordinary course of events from the seller's breach as determined in any manner which is reasonable.

(2) The measure of damages for breach of warranty is the difference at the time and place of acceptance between the

value of the goods accepted and the value they would have had if they had been as warranted, unless special circumstances show proximate damages of a different amount.

(3) In a proper case any incidental and consequential damages under the next section may also be recovered.

§2-715.   Buyer's Incidental and Consequential Damages

(1) Incidental damages resulting from the seller's breach include expenses reasonably incurred in inspection, receipt, transportation and care and custody of goods rightfully rejected, any commercially reasonable charges, expenses or commissions in connection with effecting over and any other reasonable expense incident to the delay or other breach.

(2) Consequential damages resulting from the seller's breach include

(a) any loss resulting from general or particular requirements and needs of which the seller at the time of contracting had reason to know and which could not reasonably be prevented by cover or otherwise; and

(b) injury to person or property proximately resulting from any breach of warranty.

§2-716.   Buyer's Right to Specific Performance or Replevin

(1) Specific performance may be decreed where the goods are unique or in other proper circumstances.

(2) The decree for specific performance may include such terms and conditions as to payment of the price, damages, or other relief as the court may deem just.

(3) The buyer has a right of replevin for goods identified to the contract if after reasonable effort he is unable to effect cover for such goods or the circumstances reasonably indicate that such effort will be unavailing or if the goods have been shipped under reservation and satisfaction of the security interest in them has been made or tendered.

§2-717.   Deduction of Damages From the Price

The buyer on notifying the seller of his intention to do so may deduct all or any part of the damages resulting from any breach of the contract from any part of the price still due under the same contract.

§2-718.   Liquidation or Limitation of Damages; Deposits

(1) Damages for breach by either party may be liquidated in the agreement but only at an amount which is reasonable in the light of the anticipated or actual harm caused by the breach, the difficulties of proof of loss, and the inconvenience or nonfeasibility of otherwise obtaining an adequate remedy. A term fixing unreasonably large liquidated damages is void as a penalty.

(2) Where the seller justifiably withholds delivery of goods because of the buyer's breach, the buyer is entitled to restitution of any amount by which the sum of his payments exceeds

(a) the amount to which the seller is entitled by virtue of terms liquidating the seller's damages in accordance with subsection (1), or

(b) in the absence of such terms, twenty percent of the value of the total performance for which the buyer is obligated under the contract or $500, whichever is smaller.

(3) The buyer's right to restitution under subsection (2) is subject to offset to the extent that the seller establishes

(a) a right to recover damages under the provisions of this Article other than subsection (1), and

(b) the amount or value of any benefits received by the buyer directly or indirectly by reason of the contract.

(4) Where a seller has received payment in goods their reasonable value or the proceeds of their resale shall be treated as payments for the purposes of subsection (2); but if the seller has notice of the buyer's breach before reselling goods received in part performance, his resale is subject to the conditions laid down in this Article on resale by an aggrieved seller (Section 2-706).

§2-719.   Contractual Modification or Limitation of Remedy

(1) Subject to the provisions of subsections (2) and (3) of this section and of the preceding section on liquidation and limitation of damages,

(a) the agreement may provide for remedies in addition to or in substitution for those provided in this Article and may limit or alter the measure of damages recoverable under this Article, as by limiting the buyer's remedies to return of the goods and repayment of the price or to repair and replacement of non-conforming goods or parts; and

(b) resort to a remedy as provided is optional unless the remedy is expressly agreed to be exclusive, in which case it is the sole remedy.

(2) Where circumstances cause an exclusive or limited remedy to fail of its essential purpose, remedy may be had as provided in this Act.

(3) Consequential damages may be limited or excluded unless the limitation or exclusion is unconscionable. Limitation of consequential damages for injury to the person in the case of consumer goods is prima facie unconscionable but limitation of damages where the loss is commercial is not.

§2-720.   Effect of "Cancellation" or "Rescission" on Claims for Antecedent Breach

Unless the contrary intention clearly appears, expressions of "cancellation" or "rescission" of the contract or the like shall not be construed as a renunciation or discharge of any claim in damages for an antecedent breach.

§2-721.   Remedies for Fraud

Remedies for material misrepresentation or fraud include all remedies available under this Article for nonfraudulent breach. Neither rescission or a claim for rescission of the contract for sale nor rejection or return of the goods shall bar or be deemed inconsistent with a claim for damages or other remedy.

§2–722. Who Can Sue Third Parties for Injury to Goods

Where a third party so deals with goods which have been identified to a contract for sale as to cause actionable injury to a party to that contract

(a) a right of action against the third party is in either party to the contract for sale who has title to or a security interest or a special property or an insurable interest in the goods; and if the goods have been destroyed or converted a right of action is also in the party who either bore the risk of loss under the contract for sale or has since the injury assumed that risk as against the other;

(b) if at the time of the injury the party plaintiff did not bear the risk of loss as against the other party to the contract for sale and there is no arrangement between them for disposition of the recovery, his suit or settlement is, subject to his own interest, as a fiduciary for the other party to the contract;

(c) either party may with the consent of the other sue for the benefit of whom it may concern.

§2–723. Proof of Market Price: Time and Place

(1) If an action based on anticipatory repudiation comes to trial before the time for performance with respect to some or all of the goods, any damages based on market price (Section 2–708 or Section 2–713) shall be determined according to the price of such goods prevailing at the time when the aggrieved party learned of the repudiation.

(2) If evidence of a price prevailing at the times or places described in this Article is not readily available the price prevailing within any reasonable time before or after the time described or at any other place which in commercial judgment or under usage of trade would serve as a reasonable substitute for the one described may be used, making any proper allowance for the cost of transporting the goods to or from such other place.

(3) Evidence of a relevant price prevailing at a time or place other than the one described in this Article offered by one party is not admissible unless and until he has given the other party such notice as the court finds sufficient to prevent unfair surprise.

§2–724. Admissibility of Market Quotations

Whenever the prevailing price or value of any goods regularly bought and sold in any established commodity market is in issue, reports in official publications or trade journals or in newspapers or periodicals of general circulation published as the reports of such market shall be admissible in evidence. The circumstances of the preparation of such a report may be shown to affect its weight but not its admissibility.

§ 2–725. Statute of Limitations in Contracts for Sale

(1) An action for breach of any contract for sale must be commenced within four years after the cause of action has accrued. By the original agreement the parties may reduce the period of limitation to not less than one year but may not extend it.

(2) A cause of action accrues when the breach occurs, regardless of the aggrieved party's lack of knowledge of the breach. A breach of warranty occurs when tender of delivery is made, except that where a warranty explicitly extends to future performance of the goods and discovery of the breach must await the time of such performance the cause of action accrues when the breach is or should have been discovered.

(3) Where an action commenced within the time limited by subsection (1) is so terminated as to leave available a remedy by another action for the same breach such other action may be commenced after the expiration of the time limited and within six months after the termination of the first action unless the termination resulted from voluntary discontinuance or from dismissal for failure or neglect to prosecute.

(4) This section does not alter the law on tolling of the statute of limitations nor does it apply to causes of action which have accrued before this Act becomes effective.

[REVISED] ARTICLE 3 NEGOTIABLE INSTRUMENTS

Part 1 General Provisions and Definitions

§ 3–101. Short Title

This Article may be cited as Uniform Commercial Code-Negotiable Instruments.

§ 3–102. Subject Matter

(a) This Article applies to negotiable instruments. It does not apply to money, to payment orders governed by Article 4A, or to securities governed by Article 8.

(b) If there is conflict between this Article and Article 4 or 9, Articles 4 and 9 govern.

(c) Regulations of the Board of Governors of the Federal Reserve System and operating circulars of the Federal Reserve Banks supersede any inconsistent provision of this Article to the extent of the inconsistency.

§ 3–103. Definitions

(a) In this Article:

(1) "Acceptor" means a drawee who has accepted a draft.

(2) "Drawee" means a person ordered in a draft to make payment.

(3) "Drawer" means a person who signs or is identified in a draft as a person ordering payment.

(4) "Good faith" means honesty in fact and the observance of reasonable commercial standards of fair dealing.

(5) ''Maker'' means a person who signs or is identified in a note as a person undertaking to pay.

(6) ''Order'' means a written instruction to pay money signed by the person giving the instruction. The instruction may be addressed to any person, including the person giving the instruction, or to one or more persons jointly or in the alternative but not in succession. An authorization to pay is not an order unless the person authorized to pay is also instructed to pay.

(7) ''Ordinary care'' in the case of a person engaged in business means observance of reasonable commercial standards, prevailing in the area in which the person is located, with respect to the business in which the person is engaged. In the case of a bank that takes an instrument for processing for collection or payment by automated means, reasonable commercial standards do not require the bank to examine the instrument if the failure to examine does not violate the bank's prescribed procedures and the bank's procedures do not vary unreasonably from general banking usage not disapproved by this Article or Article 4.

(8) ''Party'' means a party to an instrument.

(9) ''Promise'' means a written undertaking to pay money signed by the person undertaking to pay. An acknowledgment of an obligation by the obligor is not a promise unless the obligor also undertakes to pay the obligation.

(10) ''Prove'' with respect to a fact means to meet the burden of establishing the fact (Section 1-201(8)).

(11) ''Remitter'' means a person who purchases an instrument from its issuer if the instrument is payable to an identified person other than the purchaser.

(b) Other definitions applying to this Article and the sections in which they appear are:

''Acceptance''	Section 3–409
''Accommodated party''	Section 3–419
''Accommodation party''	Section 3–419
''Alteration''	Section 3–407
''Anomalous indorsement''	Section 3–205
''Blank indorsement''	Section 3–205
''Cashier's check''	Section 3–104
''Certificate of Deposit''	Section 3–104
''Certified check''	Section 3–409
''Check''	Section 3–104
''Consideration''	Section 3–303
''Draft''	Section 3–104
''Holder in due course''	Section 3–302
''Incomplete instrument''	Section 3–115
''Indorsement''	Section 3–204
''Indorser''	Section 3–204
''Instrument''	Section 3–104
''Issue''	Section 3–105
''Issuer''	Section 3–105

''Negotiable instrument''	Section 3–104
''Negotiation''	Section 3–201
''Note''	Section 3–104
''Payable at a definite time''	Section 3–108
''Payable on demand''	Section 3–108
''Payable to bearer''	Section 3–109
''Payable to order''	Section 3–109
''Payment''	Section 3–602
''Person entitled to enforce''	Section 3–301
''Presentment''	Section 3–501
''Reacquisition''	Section 3–207
''Special indorsement''	Section 3–205
''Teller's check''	Section 3–104
''Transfer of instrument''	Section 3–203
''Traveler's check''	Section 3–104
''Value''	Section 3–303

(c) The following definitions in other Articles apply to this Article:

''Bank''	Section 4–105
''Banking day''	Section 4–104
''Clearing house''	Section 4–104
''Collecting bank''	Section 4–105
''Depositary bank''	Section 4–105
''Documentary draft''	Section 4–104
''Intermediary bank''	Section 4–105
''Item''	Section 4–104
''Payor bank''	Section 4–105
''Suspends payments''	Section 4–104

(d) In addition, Article 1 contains general definitions and principles of construction and interpretation applicable throughout this Article.

§ 3–104. Negotiable Instrument

(a) Except as provided in subsections (c) and (d), ''negotiable instrument'' means an unconditional promise or order to pay a fixed amount of money, with or without interest or other charges described in the promise or order, if it:

(1) is payable to bearer or to order at the time it is issued or first comes into possession of a holder;

(2) is payable on demand or at a definite time; and

(3) does not state any other undertaking or instruction by the person promising or ordering payment to do any act in addition to the payment of money, but the promise or order may contain (i) an undertaking or power to give, maintain, or protect collateral to secure payment, (ii) an authorization or power to the holder to confess judgment or realize on or dispose of collateral, or (iii) a waiver of the benefit of any law intended for the advantage or protection of an obligor.

(b) ''Instrument'' means a negotiable instrument.

(c) An order that meets all of the requirements of subsection (a), except paragraph (1), and otherwise falls within the definition of ''check'' in subsection (f) is a negotiable instrument and a check.

(d) A promise or order other than a check is not an instrument if, at the time it is issued or first comes into possession of a holder, it contains a conspicuous statement, however expressed, to the effect that the promise or order is not negotiable or is not an instrument governed by this Article.

(e) An instrument is a ''note'' if it is a promise and is a ''draft'' if it is an order. If an instrument falls within the definition of both ''note'' and ''draft,'' a person entitled to enforce the instrument may treat it as either.

(f) ''Check'' means (i) a draft, other than a documentary draft, payable on demand and drawn on a bank or (ii) a cashier's check or teller's check. An instrument may be a check even though it is described on its face by another term, such as ''money order.''

(g) ''Cashier's check'' means a draft with respect to which the drawer and drawee are the same bank or branches of the same bank.

(h) ''Teller's check'' means a draft drawn by a bank (i) on another bank, or (ii) payable at or through a bank.

(i) ''Traveler's check'' means an instrument that (i) is payable on demand, (ii) is drawn on or payable at or through a bank, (iii) is designated by the term ''traveler's check'' or by a substantially similar term, and (iv) requires, as a condition to payment, a countersignature by a person whose specimen signature appears on the instrument.

(j) ''Certificate of deposit'' means an instrument containing an acknowledgment by a bank that a sum of money has been received by the bank and a promise by the bank to repay the sum of money. A certificate of deposit is a note of the bank.

§ 3–105.   Issue of Instrument

(a) ''Issue'' means the first delivery of an instrument by the maker or drawer, whether to a holder or nonholder, for the purpose of giving rights on the instrument to any person.

(b) An unissued instrument, or an unissued incomplete instrument that is completed, is binding on the maker or drawer, but nonissuance is a defense. An instrument that is conditionally issued or is issued for a special purpose is binding on the maker or drawer, but failure of the condition or special purpose to be fulfilled is a defense.

(c) ''Issuer'' applies to issued and unissued instruments and means a maker or drawer of an instrument.

§ 3–106.   Unconditional Promise or Order

(a) Except as provided in this section, for the purposes of Section 3-104(a), a promise or order is unconditional unless it states (i) an express condition to payment, (ii) that the promise or order is subject to or governed by another writing, or (iii) that rights or obligations with respect to the promise or order are stated in another writing. A reference to another writing does not of itself make the promise or order conditional.

(b) A promise or order is not made conditional (i) by a reference to another writing for a statement of rights with respect to collateral, prepayment, or acceleration, or

(ii) because payment is limited to resort to a particular fund or source.

(c) If a promise or order requires, as a condition to payment, a countersignature by a person whose specimen signature appears on the promise or order, the condition does not make the promise or order conditional for the purposes of Section 3-104(a). If the person whose specimen signature appears on an instrument fails to countersign the instrument, the failure to countersign is a defense to the obligation of the issuer, but the failure does not prevent a transferee of the instrument from becoming a holder of the instrument.

(d) If a promise or order at the time it is issued or first comes into possession of a holder contains a statement, required by applicable statutory or administrative law, to the effect that the rights of a holder or transferee are subject to claims or defenses that the issuer could assert against the original payee, the promise or order is not thereby made conditional for the purposes of Section 3-104(a); but if the promise or order is an instrument, there cannot be a holder in due course of the instrument.

§ 3–107.   Instrument Payable in Foreign Money

Unless the instrument otherwise provides, an instrument that states the amount payable in foreign money may be paid in the foreign money or in an equivalent amount in dollars calculated by using the current bank-offered spot rate at the place of payment for the purchase of dollars on the day on which the instrument is paid.

§ 3–108.   Payable on Demand or at Definite Time

(a) A promise or order is ''payable on demand'' if it (i) states that it is payable on demand or at sight, or otherwise indicates that it is payable at the will of the holder, or (ii) does not state any time of payment.

(b) A promise or order is ''payable at a definite time'' if it is payable on elapse of a definite period of time after sight or acceptance or at a fixed date or dates or at a time or times readily ascertainable at the time the promise or order is issued, subject to rights of (i) prepayment, (ii) acceleration, (iii) extension at the option of the holder, or (iv) extension to a further definite time at the option of the maker or acceptor or automatically upon or after a specified act or event.

(c) If an instrument, payable at a fixed date, is also payable upon demand made before the fixed date, the instrument is payable on demand until the fixed date and, if demand for payment is not made before that date, becomes payable at a definite time on the fixed date.

§ 3–109.   Payable to Bearer or to Order

(a) A promise or order is payable to bearer if it:

(1)   states that it is payable to bearer or to the order of bearer or otherwise indicates that the person in

possession of the promise or order is entitled to payment;

(2) does not state a payee; or

(3) states that it is payable to or to the order of cash or otherwise indicates that it is not payable to an identified person.

(b) A promise or order that is not payable to bearer is payable to order if it is payable (i) to the order of an identified person or (ii) to an identified person or order. A promise or order that is payable to order is payable to the identified person.

(c) An instrument payable to bearer may become payable to an identified person if it is specially indorsed pursuant to Section 3-205(a). An instrument payable to an identified person may become payable to bearer if it is indorsed in blank pursuant to Section 3-205(b).

§ 3–110. Identification of Person to Whom Instrument Is Payable

(a) The person to whom an instrument is initially payable is determined by the intent of the person, whether or not authorized, signing as, or in the name or behalf of, the issuer of the instrument. The instrument is payable to the person intended by the signer even if that person is identified in the instrument by a name or other identification that is not that of the intended person. If more than one person signs in the name or behalf of the issuer of an instrument and all the signers do not intend the same person as payee, the instrument is payable to any person intended by one or more of the signers.

(b) If the signature of the issuer of an instrument is made by automated means, such as a check-writing machine, the payee of the instrument is determined by the intent of the person who supplied the name or identification of the payee, whether or not authorized to do so.

(c) A person to whom an instrument is payable may be identified in any way, including by name, identifying number, office, or account number. For the purpose of determining the holder of an instrument, the following rules apply:

(1) If an instrument is payable to an account and the account is identified only by number, the instrument is payable to the person to whom the account is payable. If an instrument is payable to an account identified by number and by the name of a person, the instrument is payable to the named person, whether or not that person is the owner of the account identified by number.

(2) If an instrument is payable to:

(i) a trust, an estate, or a person described as trustee or representative of a trust or estate, the instrument is payable to the trustee, the representative, or a successor of either, whether or not the beneficiary or estate is also named;

(ii) a person described as agent or similar representative of a named or identified person, the instrument is payable to the represented person, the representative, or a successor of the representative;

(iii) a fund or organization that is not a legal entity, the instrument is payable to a representative of the members of the fund or organization; or

(iv) an office or to a person described as holding an office, the instrument is payable to the named person, the incumbent of the office, or a successor to the incumbent.

(d) If an instrument is payable to two or more persons alternatively, it is payable to any of them and may be negotiated, discharged, or enforced by any or all of them in possession of the instrument. If an instrument is payable to two or more persons not alternatively, it is payable to all of them and may be negotiated, discharged, or enforced only by all of them. If an instrument payable to two or more persons is ambiguous as to whether it is payable to the persons alternatively, the instrument is payable to the persons alternatively.

§ 3–111. Place of Payment

Except as otherwise provided for items in Article 4, an instrument is payable at the place of payment stated in the instrument. If no place of payment is stated, an instrument is payable at the address of the drawee or maker stated in the instrument. If no address is stated, the place of payment is the place of business of the drawee or maker. If a drawee or maker has more than one place of business, the place of payment is any place of business of the drawee or maker chosen by the person entitled to enforce the instrument. If the drawee or maker has no place of business, the place of payment is the residence of the drawee or maker.

§ 3–112. Interest

(a) Unless otherwise provided in the instrument, (i) an instrument is not payable with interest, and (ii) interest on an interest-bearing instrument is payable from the date of the instrument.

(b) Interest may be stated in an instrument as a fixed or variable amount of money or it may be expressed as a fixed or variable rate or rates. The amount or rate of interest may be stated or described in the instrument in any manner and may require reference to information not contained in the instrument. If an instrument provides for interest, but the amount of interest payable cannot be ascertained from the description, interest is payable at the judgment rate in effect at the place of payment of the instrument and at the time interest first accrues.

§ 3–113. Date of Instrument

(a) An instrument may be antedated or postdated. The date stated determines the time of payment if the instrument is payable at a fixed period after date. Except as provided in Section 4-401(c), an instrument payable on demand is not payable before the date of the instrument.

(b) If an instrument is undated, its date is the date of its issue or, in the case of an unissued instrument, the date it first comes into possession of a holder.

§ 3−114.   Contradictory Terms of Instrument
If an instrument contains contradictory terms, typewritten terms prevail over printed terms, handwritten terms prevail over both, and words prevail over numbers.

§ 3−115.   Incomplete Instrument
(a) ''Incomplete instrument'' means a signed writing, whether or not issued by the signer, the contents of which show at the time of signing that it is incomplete but that the signer intended it to be completed by the addition of words or numbers.

(b) Subject to subsection (c), if an incomplete instrument is an instrument under Section 3-104, it may be enforced according to its terms if it is not completed, or according to its terms as augmented by completion. If an incomplete instrument is not an instrument under Section 3-104, but, after completion, the requirements of Section 3-104 are met, the instrument may be enforced according to its terms as augmented by completion.

(c) If words or numbers are added to an incomplete instrument without authority of the signer, there is an alteration of the incomplete instrument under Section 3-407.

(d) The burden of establishing that words or numbers were added to an incomplete instrument without authority of the signer is on the person asserting the lack of authority.

§ 3−116.   Joint and Several Liability; Contribution
(a) Except as otherwise provided in the instrument, two or more persons who have the same liability on an instrument as makers, drawers, acceptors, indorsers who indorse as joint payees, or anomalous indorsers are jointly and severally liable in the capacity in which they sign.

(b) Except as provided in Section 3-419(e) or by agreement of the affected parties, a party having joint and several liability who pays the instrument is entitled to receive from any party having the same joint and several liability contribution in accordance with applicable law.

(c) Discharge of one party having joint and several liability by a person entitled to enforce the instrument does not affect the right under subsection (b) of a party having the same joint and several liability to receive contribution from the party discharged.

§ 3−117.   Other Agreements Affecting Instrument
Subject to applicable law regarding exclusion of proof of contemporaneous or previous agreements, the obligation of a party to an instrument to pay the instrument may be modified, supplemented, or nullified by a separate agreement of the obligor and a person entitled to enforce the instrument, if the instrument is issued or the obligation is incurred in reliance on the agreement or as part of the same transaction giving rise to the agreement. To the extent an obligation is modified, supplemented, or nullified by an agreement under this section, the agreement is a defense to the obligation.

§ 3−118.   Statute of Limitations
(a) Except as provided in subsection (e), an action to enforce the obligation of a party to pay a note payable at a definite time must be commenced within six years after the due date or dates stated in the note or, if a due date is accelerated, within six years after the accelerated due date.

(b) Except as provided in subsection (d) or (e), if demand for payment is made to the maker of a note payable on demand, an action to enforce the obligation of a party to pay the note must be commenced within six years after the demand. If no demand for payment is made to the maker, an action to enforce the note is barred if neither principal nor interest on the note has been paid for a continuous period of 10 years.

(c) Except as provided in subsection (d), an action to enforce the obligation of a party to an unaccepted draft to pay the draft must be commenced within three years after dishonor of the draft or 10 years after the date of the draft, whichever period expires first.

(d) An action to enforce the obligation of the acceptor of a certified check or the issuer of a teller's check, cashier's check, or traveler's check must be commenced within three years after demand for payment is made to the acceptor or issuer, as the case may be.

(e) An action to enforce the obligation of a party to a certificate of deposit to pay the instrument must be commenced within six years after demand for payment is made to the maker, but if the instrument states a due date and the maker is not required to pay before that date, the six-year period begins when a demand for payment is in effect and the due date has passed.

(f) An action to enforce the obligation of a party to pay an accepted draft, other than a certified check, must be commenced (i) within six years after the due date or dates stated in the draft or acceptance if the obligation of the acceptor is payable at a definite time, or (ii) within six years after the date of the acceptance if the obligation of the acceptor is payable on demand.

(g) Unless governed by other law regarding claims for indemnity or contribution, an action (i) for conversion of an instrument, for money had and received, or like action based on conversion, (ii) for breach of warranty, or (iii) to enforce an obligation, duty, or right arising under this Article and not governed by this section must be commenced within three years after the [cause of action] accrues.

§ 3−119.   Notice of Right to Defend Action
In an action for breach of an obligation for which a third person is answerable over pursuant to this Article or Article 4, the defendant may give the third person written

notice of the litigation, and the person notified may then give similar notice to any other person who is answerable over. If the notice states (i) that the person notified may come in and defend and (ii) that failure to do so will bind the person notified in an action later brought by the person giving the notice as to any determination of fact common to the two litigations, the person notified is so bound unless after seasonable receipt of the notice the person notified does come in and defend.

Part 2   Negotiation, Transfer, and Indorsement

§ 3–201.   Negotiation

(a) "Negotiation" means a transfer of possession, whether voluntary or involuntary, of an instrument by a person other than the issuer to a person who thereby becomes its holder.

(b) Except for negotiation by a remitter, if an instrument is payable to an identified person, negotiation requires transfer of possession of the instrument and its indorsement by the holder. If an instrument is payable to bearer, it may be negotiated by transfer of possession alone.

§ 3–202.   Negotiation Subject to Rescission

(a) Negotiation is effective even if obtained (i) from an infant, a corporation exceeding its powers, or a person without capacity, (ii) by fraud, duress, or mistake, or (iii) in breach of duty or as part of an illegal transaction.

(b) To the extent permitted by other law, negotiation may be rescinded or may be subject to other remedies, but those remedies may not be asserted against a subsequent holder in due course or a person paying the instrument in good faith and without knowledge of facts that are a basis for rescission or other remedy.

§ 3–203.   Transfer of Instrument; Rights Acquired by Transfer

(a) An instrument is transferred when it is delivered by a person other than its issuer for the purpose of giving to the person receiving delivery the right to enforce the instrument.

(b) Transfer of an instrument, whether or not the transfer is a negotiation, vests in the transferee any right of the transferor to enforce the instrument, including any right as a holder in due course, but the transferee cannot acquire rights of a holder in due course by a transfer, directly or indirectly, from a holder in due course if the transferee engaged in fraud or illegality affecting the instrument.

(c) Unless otherwise agreed, if an instrument is transferred for value and the transferee does not become a holder because of lack of indorsement by the transferor, the transferee has a specifically enforceable right to the unqualified indorsement of the transferor, but negotiation of the instrument does not occur until the indorsement is made.

(d) If a transferor purports to transfer less than the entire instrument, negotiation of the instrument does not occur. The transferee obtains no rights under this Article and has only the rights of a partial assignee.

§ 3–204.   Indorsement

(a) "Indorsement" means a signature, other than that of a signer as maker, drawer, or acceptor, that alone or accompanied by other words is made on an instrument for the purpose of (i) negotiating the instrument, (ii) restricting payment of the instrument, or (iii) incurring indorser's liability on the instrument, but regardless of the intent of the signer, a signature and its accompanying words is an indorsement unless the accompanying words, terms of the instrument, place of the signature, or other circumstances unambiguously indicate that the signature was made for a purpose other than indorsement. For the purpose of determining whether a signature is made on an instrument, a paper affixed to the instrument is a part of the instrument.

(b) "Indorser" means a person who makes an indorsement.

(c) For the purpose of determining whether the transferee of an instrument is a holder, an indorsement that transfers a security interest in the instrument is effective as an unqualified indorsement of the instrument.

(d) If an instrument is payable to a holder under a name that is not the name of the holder, indorsement may be made by the holder in the name stated in the instrument or in the holder's name or both, but signature in both names may be required by a person paying or taking the instrument for value or collection.

§ 3–205.   Special Indorsement; Blank Indorsement; Anomalous Indorsement

(a) If an indorsement is made by the holder of an instrument, whether payable to an identified person or payable to bearer, and the indorsement identifies a person to whom it makes the instrument payable, it is a "special indorsement." When specially indorsed, an instrument becomes payable to the identified person and may be negotiated only by the indorsement of that person. The principles stated in Section 3-110 apply to special indorsements.

(b) If an indorsement is made by the holder of an instrument and it is not a special indorsement, it is a "blank indorsement." When indorsed in blank, an instrument becomes payable to bearer and may be negotiated by transfer of possession alone until specially indorsed.

(c) The holder may convert a blank indorsement that consists only of a signature into a special indorsement by writing, above the signature of the indorser, words identifying the person to whom the instrument is made payable.

(d) "Anomalous indorsement" means an indorsement made by a person who is not the holder of the instrument. An anomalous indorsement does not affect the manner in which the instrument may be negotiated.

§ 3–206.   Restrictive Indorsement

(a) An indorsement limiting payment to a particular person or otherwise prohibiting further transfer or negotiation of the instrument is not effective to prevent further transfer or negotiation of the instrument.

(b) An indorsement stating a condition to the right of the indorsee to receive payment does not affect the right of the indorsee to enforce the instrument. A person paying the instrument or taking it for value or collection may disregard the condition, and the rights and liabilities of that person are not affected by whether the condition has been fulfilled.

(c) If an instrument bears an indorsement (i) described in Section 4-201(b), or (ii) in blank or to a particular bank using the words ''for deposit,'' ''for collection,'' or other words indicating a purpose of having the instrument collected by a bank for the indorser or for a particular account, the following rules apply:

(1)   A person, other than a bank, who purchases the instrument when so indorsed converts the instrument unless the amount paid for the instrument is received by the indorser or applied consistently with the indorsement.

(2)   A depositary bank that purchases the instrument or takes it for collection when so indorsed converts the instrument unless the amount paid by the bank with respect to the instrument is received by the indorser or applied consistently with the indorsement.

(3)   A payor bank that is also the depositary bank or that takes the instrument for immediate payment over the counter from a person other than a collecting bank converts the instrument unless the proceeds of the instrument are received by the indorser or applied consistently with the indorsement.

(4)   Except as otherwise provided in paragraph (3), a payor bank or intermediary bank may disregard the indorsement and is not liable if the proceeds of the instrument are not received by the indorser or applied consistently with the indorsement.

(d) Except for an indorsement covered by subsection (c), if an instrument bears an indorsement using words to the effect that payment is to be made to the indorsee as agent, trustee, or other fiduciary for the benefit of the indorser or another person, the following rules apply:

(1) Unless there is notice of breach of fiduciary duty as provided in Section 3-307, a person who purchases the instrument from the indorsee or takes the instrument from the indorsee for collection or payment may pay the proceeds of payment or the value given for the instrument to the indorsee without regard to whether the indorsee violates a fiduciary duty to the indorser.

(2) A subsequent transferee of the instrument or person who pays the instrument is neither given notice nor otherwise affected by the restriction in the indorsement unless the transferee or payor knows that the fiduciary dealt with the instrument or its proceeds in breach of fiduciary duty.

(e) The presence on an instrument of an indorsement to which this section applies does not prevent a purchaser of the instrument from becoming a holder in due course of the instrument unless the purchaser is a converter under subsection (c) or has notice or knowledge of breach of fiduciary duty as stated in subsection (d).

(f) In an action to enforce the obligation of a party to pay the instrument, the obligor has a defense if payment would violate an indorsement to which this section applies and the payment is not permitted by this section.

§ 3–207.   Reacquisition

Reacquisition of an instrument occurs if it is transferred to a former holder, by negotiation or otherwise. A former holder who reacquires the instrument may cancel indorsements made after the reacquirer first became a holder of the instrument. If the cancellation causes the instrument to be payable to the reacquirer or to bearer, the reacquirer may negotiate the instrument. An indorser whose indorsement is canceled is discharged, and the discharge is effective against any subsequent holder.

Part 3   Enforcement of Instruments

§ 3–301.   Person Entitled to Enforce Instrument

''Person entitled to enforce'' an instrument means (i) the holder of the instrument, (ii) a nonholder in possession of the instrument who has the rights of a holder, or (iii) a person not in possession of the instrument who is entitled to enforce the instrument pursuant to Section 3-309 or 3-418(d). A person may be a person entitled to enforce the instrument even though the person is not the owner of the instrument or is in wrongful possession of the instrument.

§ 3–302.   Holder in Due Course

(a) Subject to subsection (c) and Section 3-106(d), ''holder in due course'' means the holder of an instrument if:

(1)   the instrument when issued or negotiated to the holder does not bear such apparent evidence of forgery or alteration or is not otherwise so irregular or incomplete as to call into question its authenticity; and

(2)   the holder took the instrument (i) for value, (ii) in good faith, (iii) without notice that the instrument is overdue or has been dishonored or that there is an uncured default with respect to payment of another instrument issued as part of the same series, (iv) without notice that the instrument contains an unauthorized signature or has been altered, (v) without notice of any claim

to the instrument described in Section 3-306, and (vi) without notice that any party has a defense or claim in recoupment described in Section 3-305(a).

(b) Notice of discharge of a party, other than discharge in an insolvency proceeding, is not notice of a defense under subsection (a), but discharge is effective against a person who became a holder in due course with notice of the discharge. Public filing or recording of a document does not of itself constitute notice of a defense, claim in recoupment, or claim to the instrument.

(c) Except to the extent a transferor or predecessor in interest has rights as a holder in due course, a person does not acquire rights of a holder in due course of an instrument taken (i) by legal process or by purchase in an execution, bankruptcy, or creditor's sale or similar proceeding, (ii) by purchase as part of a bulk transaction not in ordinary course of business of the transferor, or (iii) as the successor in interest to an estate or other organization.

(d) If, under Section 3-303(a)(1), the promise of performance that is the consideration for an instrument has been partially performed, the holder may assert rights as a holder in due course of the instrument only to the fraction of the amount payable under the instrument equal to the value of the partial performance divided by the value of the promised performance.

(e) If (i) the person entitled to enforce an instrument has only a security interest in the instrument and (ii) the person obliged to pay the instrument has a defense, claim in recoupment, or claim to the instrument that may be asserted against the person who granted the security interest, the person entitled to enforce the instrument may assert rights as a holder in due course only to an amount payable under the instrument which, at the time of enforcement of the instrument, does not exceed the amount of the unpaid obligation secured.

(f) To be effective, notice must be received at a time and in a manner that gives a reasonable opportunity to act on it.

(g) This section is subject to any law limiting status as a holder in due course in particular classes of transactions.

§ 3-303. Value and Consideration

(a) An instrument is issued or transferred for value if:

(1) the instrument is issued or transferred for a promise of performance, to the extent the promise has been performed;

(2) the transferee acquires a security interest or other lien in the instrument other than a lien obtained by judicial proceeding;

(3) the instrument is issued or transferred as payment of, or as security for, an antecedent claim against any person, whether or not the claim is due;

(4) the instrument is issued or transferred in exchange for a negotiable instrument; or

(5) the instrument is issued or transferred in exchange for the incurring of an irrevocable obligation to a third party by the person taking the instrument.

(b) "Consideration" means any consideration sufficient to support a simple contract. The drawer or maker of an instrument has a defense if the instrument is issued without consideration. If an instrument is issued for a promise of performance, the issuer has a defense to the extent performance of the promise is due and the promise has not been performed. If an instrument is issued for value as stated in subsection (a), the instrument is also issued for consideration.

§ 3-304. Overdue Instrument

(a) An instrument payable on demand becomes overdue at the earliest of the following times:

(1) on the day after the day demand for payment is duly made;

(2) if the instrument is a check, 90 days after its date; or

(3) if the instrument is not a check, when the instrument has been outstanding for a period of time after its date which is unreasonably long under the circumstances of the particular case in light of the nature of the instrument and usage of the trade.

(b) With respect to an instrument payable at a definite time the following rules apply:

(1) If the principal is payable in installments and a due date has not been accelerated, the instrument becomes overdue upon default under the instrument for nonpayment of an installment, and the instrument remains overdue until the default is cured.

(2) If the principal is not payable in installments and the due date has not been accelerated, the instrument becomes overdue on the day after the due date.

(3) If a due date with respect to principal has been accelerated, the instrument becomes overdue on the day after the accelerated due date.

(c) Unless the due date of principal has been accelerated, an instrument does not become overdue if there is default in payment of interest but no default in payment of principal.

§ 3-305. Defenses and Claims in Recoupment

(a) Except as stated in subsection (b), the right to enforce the obligation of a party to pay an instrument is subject to the following:

(1) a defense of the obligor based on (i) infancy of the obligor to the extent it is a defense to a simple contract, (ii) duress, lack of legal capacity, or

illegality of the transaction which, under other law, nullifies the obligation of the obligor, (iii) fraud that induced the obligor to sign the instrument with neither knowledge nor reasonable opportunity to learn of its character or its essential terms, or (iv) discharge of the obligor in insolvency proceedings;

(2) a defense of the obligor stated in another section of this Article or a defense of the obligor that would be available if the person entitled to enforce the instrument were enforcing a right to payment under a simple contract; and

(3) a claim in recoupment of the obligor against the original payee of the instrument if the claim arose from the transaction that gave rise to the instrument; but the claim of the obligor may be asserted against a transferee of the instrument only to reduce the amount owing on the instrument at the time the action is brought.

(b) The right of a holder in due course to enforce the obligation of a party to pay the instrument is subject to defenses of the obligor stated in subsection (a)(1), but is not subject to defenses of the obligor stated in subsection (a)(2) or claims in recoupment stated in subsection (a)(3) against a person other than the holder.

(c) Except as stated in subsection (d), in an action to enforce the obligation of a party to pay the instrument, the obligor may not assert against the person entitled to enforce the instrument a defense, claim in recoupment, or claim to the instrument (Section 3-306) of another person, but the other person's claim to the instrument may be asserted by the obligor if the other person is joined in the action and personally asserts the claim against the person entitled to enforce the instrument. An obligor is not obliged to pay the instrument if the person seeking enforcement of the instrument does not have rights of a holder in due course and the obligor proves that the instrument is a lost or stolen instrument.

(d) In an action to enforce the obligation of an accommodation party to pay an instrument, the accommodation party may assert against the person entitled to enforce the instrument any defense or claim in recoupment under subsection (a) that the accommodated party could assert against the person entitled to enforce the instrument, except the defenses of discharge in insolvency proceedings, infancy, and lack of legal capacity.

§ 3–306.   Claims to an Instrument

A person taking an instrument, other than a person having rights of a holder in due course, is subject to a claim of a property or possessory right in the instrument or its proceeds, including a claim to rescind a negotiation and to recover the instrument or its proceeds. A person having rights of a holder in due course takes free of the claim to the instrument.

§ 3–307.   Notice of Breach of Fiduciary Duty

(a) In this section:

(1) "Fiduciary" means an agent, trustee, partner, corporate officer or director, or other representative owing a fiduciary duty with respect to an instrument.

(2) "Represented person" means the principal, beneficiary, partnership, corporation, or other person to whom the duty stated in paragraph (1) is owed.

(b) If (i) an instrument is taken from a fiduciary for payment or collection or for value, (ii) the taker has knowledge of the fiduciary status of the fiduciary, and (iii) the represented person makes a claim to the instrument or its proceeds on the basis that the transaction of the fiduciary is a breach of fiduciary duty, the following rules apply:

(1) Notice of breach of fiduciary duty by the fiduciary is notice of the claim of the represented person.

(2) In the case of an instrument payable to the represented person or the fiduciary as such, the taker has notice of the breach of fiduciary duty if the instrument is (i) taken in payment of or as security for a debt known by the taker to be the personal debt of the fiduciary, (ii) taken in a transaction known by the taker to be for the personal benefit of the fiduciary, or (iii) deposited to an account other than an account of the fiduciary, as such, or an account of the represented person.

(3) If an instrument is issued by the represented person or the fiduciary as such, and made payable to the fiduciary personally, the taker does not have notice of the breach of fiduciary duty unless the taker knows of the breach of fiduciary duty.

(4) If an instrument is issued by the represented person or the fiduciary as such, to the taker as payee, the taker has notice of the breach of fiduciary duty if the instrument is (i) taken in payment of or as security for a debt known by the taker to be the personal debt of the fiduciary, (ii) taken in a transaction known by the taker to be for the personal benefit of the fiduciary, or (iii) deposited to an account other than an account of the fiduciary, as such, or an account of the represented person.

§ 3–308.   Proof of Signatures and Status as Holder in Due Course

(a) In an action with respect to an instrument, the authenticity of, and authority to make, each signature on the instrument is admitted unless specifically denied in the pleadings. If the validity of a signature is denied in the pleadings, the burden of establishing validity is on the person claiming validity, but the signature is presumed to be authentic and authorized unless the action is to enforce the liability of the purported signer and the signer is dead or incompetent at the time of trial of the issue of validity of the signature. If an action to enforce the instrument is brought against a person as the undisclosed principal of a person who signed the instrument as a party to the instrument, the plaintiff has the burden of establishing that the defendant is liable on the instrument as a represented person under Section 3-402(a).

(b) If the validity of signatures is admitted or proved and there is compliance with subsection (a), a plaintiff producing the instrument is entitled to payment if the plaintiff proves entitlement to enforce the instrument under Section 3-301, unless the defendant proves a defense or claim in recoupment. If a defense or claim in recoupment is proved, the right to payment of the plaintiff is subject to the defense or claim, except to the extent the plaintiff proves that the plaintiff has rights of a holder in due course which are not subject to the defense or claim.

§ 3–309.   Enforcement of Lost, Destroyed, or Stolen Instrument

(a) A person not in possession of an instrument is entitled to enforce the instrument if (i) the person was in possession of the instrument and entitled to enforce it when loss of possession occurred, (ii) the loss of possession was not the result of a transfer by the person or a lawful seizure, and (iii) the person cannot reasonably obtain possession of the instrument because the instrument was destroyed, its whereabouts cannot be determined, or it is in the wrongful possession of an unknown person or a person that cannot be found or is not amenable to service of process.

(b) A person seeking enforcement of an instrument under subsection (a) must prove the terms of the instrument and the person's right to enforce the instrument. If that proof is made, Section 3-308 applies to the case as if the person seeking enforcement had produced the instrument. The court may not enter judgment in favor of the person seeking enforcement unless it finds that the person required to pay the instrument is adequately protected against loss that might occur by reason of a claim by another person to enforce the instrument. Adequate protection may be provided by any reasonable means.

§ 3–310.   Effect of Instrument on Obligation for Which Taken

(a) Unless otherwise agreed, if a certified check, cashier's check, or teller's check is taken for an obligation, the obligation is discharged to the same extent discharge would result if an amount of money equal to the amount of the instrument were taken in payment of the obligation. Discharge of the obligation does not affect any liability that the obligor may have as an indorser of the instrument.

(b) Unless otherwise agreed and except as provided in subsection (a), if a note or an uncertified check is taken for an obligation, the obligation is suspended to the same extent the obligation would be discharged if an amount of

money equal to the amount of the instrument were taken, and the following rules apply:

(1)   In the case of an uncertified check, suspension of the obligation continues until dishonor of the check or until it is paid or certified. Payment or certification of the check results in discharge of the obligation to the extent of the amount of the check.

(2)   In the case of a note, suspension of the obligation continues until dishonor of the note or until it is paid. Payment of the note results in discharge of the obligation to the extent of the payment.

(3)   Except as provided in paragraph (4), if the check or note is dishonored and the obligee of the obligation for which the instrument was taken is the person entitled to enforce the instrument, the obligee may enforce either the instrument or the obligation. In the case of an instrument of a third person which is negotiated to the obligee by the obligor, discharge of the obligor on the instrument also discharges the obligation.

(4)   If the person entitled to enforce the instrument taken for an obligation is a person other than the obligee, the obligee may not enforce the obligation to the extent the obligation is suspended. If the obligee is the person entitled to enforce the instrument but no longer has possession of it because it was lost, stolen, or destroyed, the obligation may not be enforced to the extent of the amount payable on the instrument, and to that extent the obligee's rights against the obligor are limited to enforcement of the instrument.

(c) If an instrument other than one described in subsection (a) or (b) is taken for an obligation, the effect is (i) that stated in subsection (a) if the instrument is one on which a bank is liable as maker or acceptor, or (ii) that stated in subsection (b) in any other case.

§ 3–311.   Accord and Satisfaction by Use of Instrument

(a) If a person against whom a claim is asserted proves that (i) that person in good faith tendered an instrument to the claimant as full satisfaction of the claim, (ii) the amount of the claim was unliquidated or subject to a bona fide dispute, and (iii) the claimant obtained payment of the instrument, the following subsections apply.

(b) Unless subsection (c) applies, the claim is discharged if the person against whom the claim is asserted proves that the instrument or an accompanying written communication contained a conspicuous statement to the effect that the instrument was tendered as full satisfaction of the claim.

(c) Subject to subsection (d), a claim is not discharged under subsection (b) if either of the following applies:

(1)   The claimant, if an organization, proves that

(i) within a reasonable time before the tender, the claimant sent a conspicuous statement to the person against whom the claim is asserted that communications concerning disputed debts, including an instrument tendered as full satisfaction of a debt, are to be sent to a designated person, office, or place, and (ii) the instrument or accompanying communication was not received by that designated person, office, or place.

(2) The claimant, whether or not an organization, proves that within 90 days after payment of the instrument, the claimant tendered repayment of the amount of the instrument to the person against whom the claim is asserted. This paragraph does not apply if the claimant is an organization that sent a statement complying with paragraph (1)(i).

(d) A claim is discharged if the person against whom the claim is asserted proves that within a reasonable time before collection of the instrument was initiated, the claimant, or an agent of the claimant having direct responsibility with respect to the disputed obligation, knew that the instrument was tendered in full satisfaction of the claim.

§ 3–312.   Lost, Destroyed, or Stolen Cashier's Check, Teller's Check, or Certified Check*

(a) In this section:

(1) "Check" means a cashier's check, teller's check, or certified check.

(2) "Claimant" means a person who claims the right to receive the amount of a cashier's check, teller's check, or certified check that was lost, destroyed, or stolen.

(3) "Declaration of loss" means a written statement, made under penalty of perjury, to the effect that (i) the declarer lost possession of a check, (ii) the declarer is the drawer or payee of the check, in the case of a certified check, or the remitter or payee of the check, in the case of a cashier's check or teller's check, (iii) the loss of possession was not the result of a transfer by the declarer or a lawful seizure, and (iv) the declarer cannot reasonably obtain possession of the check because the check was destroyed, its whereabouts cannot be determined, or it is in the wrongful possession of an unknown person or a person that cannot be found or is not amenable to service of process.

(4) "Obligated bank" means the issuer of a cashier's check or teller's check or the acceptor of a certified check.

(b) A claimant may assert a claim to the amount of a check by a communication to the obligated bank describing the check with reasonable certainty and requesting payment of the amount of the check, if (i) the claimant is the drawer or payee of a certified check or the remitter or payee of a cashier's check or teller's check, (ii) the communication contains or is accompanied by a declaration of loss of the claimant with respect to the check, (iii) the communication is received at a time and in a manner affording the bank a reasonable time to act on it before the check is paid, and (iv) the claimant provides reasonable identification if requested by the obligated bank. Delivery of a declaration of loss is a warranty of the truth of the statements made in the declaration. The warranty is made to the obligated bank and any person entitled to enforce the check. If a claim is asserted in compliance with this subsection, the following rules apply:

(1) The claim becomes enforceable at the later of (i) the time the claim is asserted, or (ii) the 90th day following the date of the check, in the case of a cashier's check or teller's check, or the 90th day following the date of the acceptance, in the case of a certified check.

(2) Until the claim becomes enforceable, it has no legal effect and the obligated bank may pay the check or, in the case of a teller's check, may permit the drawee to pay the check. Payment to a person entitled to enforce the check discharges all liability of the obligated bank with respect to the check.

(3) If the claim becomes enforceable before the check is presented for payment, the obligated bank is not obligated to pay the check.

(4) When the claim becomes enforceable, the obligated bank becomes obliged to pay the amount of the check to the claimant if payment of the check has not been made to a person entitled to enforce the check. Subject to Section 4-302(a)(1), payment to the claimant discharges all liability of the obligated bank with respect to the check.

(c) If the obligated bank pays the amount of a check to a claimant under subsection (b)(4) and, after the claim became enforceable, the check is presented for payment by a person having rights of a holder in due course, the claimant is obliged to (i) refund the payment to the obligated bank if the check is paid, or (ii) pay the amount of the check to the person having rights of a holder in due course if the check is dishonored.

(d) If a claimant has the right to assert a claim under subsection (b) and is also a person entitled to enforce a cashier's check, teller's check, or certified check which is lost, destroyed, or stolen, the claimant may assert rights with respect to the check either under this section or Section 3-309.

Part 4   Liability of Parties

§ 3–401.   Signature

(a) A person is not liable on an instrument unless (i) the person signed the instrument, or (ii) the person is represented by an agent or representative who signed the instrument and the signature is binding on the represented person under Section 3-402.

(b) A signature may be made (i) manually or by means of a device or machine, and (ii) by the use of any name, including a trade or assumed name, or by a word, mark, or symbol executed or adopted by a person with present intention to authenticate a writing.

§ 3–402.   Signature by Representative

(a) If a person acting, or purporting to act, as a representative signs an instrument by signing either the name of the represented person or the name of the signer, the represented person is bound by the signature to the same extent the represented person would be bound if the signature were on a simple contract. If the represented person is bound, the signature of the representative is the "authorized signature of the represented person" and the represented person is liable on the instrument, whether or not identified in the instrument.

(b) If a representative signs the name of the representative to an instrument and the signature is an authorized signature of the represented person, the following rules apply:

(1) If the form of the signature shows unambiguously that the signature is made on behalf of the represented person who is identified in the instrument, the representative is not liable on the instrument.

(2) Subject to subsection (c), if (i) the form of the signature does not show unambiguously that the signature is made in a representative capacity or (ii) the represented person is not identified in the instrument, the representative is liable on the instrument to a holder in due course that took the instrument without notice that the representative was not intended to be liable on the instrument. With respect to any other person, the representative is liable on the instrument unless the representative proves that the original parties did not intend the representative to be liable on the instrument.

(c) If a representative signs the name of the representative as drawer of a check without indication of the representative status and the check is payable from an account of the represented person who is identified on the check, the signer is not liable on the check if the signature is an authorized signature of the represented person.

§ 3–403.   Unauthorized Signature

(a) Unless otherwise provided in this Article or Article 4, an unauthorized signature is ineffective except as the signature of the unauthorized signer in favor of a person who in good faith pays the instrument or takes it for value. An unauthorized signature may be ratified for all purposes of this Article.

(b) If the signature of more than one person is required to constitute the authorized signature of an organization, the signature of the organization is unauthorized if one of the required signatures is lacking.

(c) The civil or criminal liability of a person who makes an unauthorized signature is not affected by any provision of this Article which makes the unauthorized signature effective for the purposes of this Article.

§ 3–404.   Impostors; Fictitious Payees

(a) If an imposter, by use of the mails or otherwise, induces the issuer of an instrument to issue the instrument to the imposter, or to a person acting in concert with the imposter, by impersonating the payee of the instrument or a person authorized to act for the payee, an indorsement of the instrument by any person in the name of the payee is effective as the indorsement of the payee in favor of a person who, in good faith, pays the instrument or takes it for value or for collection.

(b) If (i) a person whose intent determines to whom an instrument is payable (Section 3-110(a) or (b)) does not intend the person identified as payee to have any interest in the instrument, or (ii) the person identified as payee of an instrument is a fictitious person, the following rules apply until the instrument is negotiated by special indorsement:

(1) Any person in possession of the instrument is its holder.

(2) An indorsement by any person in the name of the payee stated in the instrument is effective as the indorsement of the payee in favor of a person who, in good faith, pays the instrument or takes it for value or for collection.

(c) Under subsection (a) or (b), an indorsement is made in the name of a payee if (i) it is made in a name substantially similar to that of the payee or (ii) the instrument, whether or not indorsed, is deposited in a depositary bank to an account in a name substantially similar to that of the payee.

(d) With respect to an instrument to which subsection (a) or (b) applies, if a person paying the instrument or taking it for value or for collection fails to exercise ordinary care in paying or taking the instrument and that failure substantially contributes to loss resulting from payment of the instrument, the person bearing the loss may recover from the person failing to exercise ordinary care to the extent the failure to exercise ordinary care contributed to the loss.

§ 3–405.   Employer's Responsibility for Fraudulent Indorsement by Employee

(a) In this section:

(1) "Employee" includes an independent contractor and employee of an independent contractor retained by the employer.

(2) ''Fraudulent indorsement'' means (i) in the case of an instrument payable to the employer, a forged indorsement purporting to be that of the employer, or (ii) in the case of an instrument with respect to which the employer is the issuer, a forged indorsement purporting to be that of the person identified as payee.

(3) ''Responsibility'' with respect to instruments means authority (i) to sign or indorse instruments on behalf of the employer, (ii) to process instruments received by the employer for bookkeeping purposes, for deposit to an account, or for other disposition, (iii) to prepare or process instruments for issue in the name of the employer, (iv) to supply information determining the names or addresses of payees of instruments to be issued in the name of the employer, (v) to control the disposition of instruments to be issued in the name of the employer, or (vi) to act otherwise with respect to instruments in a responsible capacity. ''Responsibility'' does not include authority that merely allows an employee to have access to instruments or blank or incomplete instrument forms that are being stored or transported or are part of incoming or outgoing mail, or similar access.

(b) For the purpose of determining the rights and liabilities of a person who, in good faith, pays an instrument or takes it for value or for collection, if an employer entrusted an employee with responsibility with respect to the instrument and the employee or a person acting in concert with the employee makes a fraudulent indorsement of the instrument, the indorsement is effective as the indorsement of the person to whom the instrument is payable if it is made in the name of that person. If the person paying the instrument or taking it for value or for collection fails to exercise ordinary care in paying or taking the instrument and that failure substantially contributes to loss resulting from the fraud, the person bearing the loss may recover from the person failing to exercise ordinary care to the extent the failure to exercise ordinary care contributed to the loss.

(c) Under subsection (b), an indorsement is made in the name of the person to whom an instrument is payable if (i) it is made in a name substantially similar to the name of that person or (ii) the instrument, whether or not indorsed, is deposited in a depository bank to an account in a name substantially similar to the name of that person.

§ 3–406. Negligence Contributing to Forged Signature or Alteration of Instrument

(a) A person whose failure to exercise ordinary care substantially contributes to an alteration of an instrument or to the making of a forged signature on an instrument is precluded from asserting the alteration or the forgery against a person who, in good faith, pays the instrument or takes it for value or for collection.

(b) Under subsection (a), if the person asserting the preclusion fails to exercise ordinary care in paying or taking the instrument and that failure substantially contributes to loss, the loss is allocated between the person precluded and the person asserting the preclusion according to the extent to which the failure of each to exercise ordinary care contributed to the loss.

(c) Under subsection (a), the burden of proving failure to exercise ordinary care is on the person asserting the preclusion. Under subsection (b), the burden of proving failure to exercise ordinary care is on the person precluded.

§ 3–407. Alteration

(a) ''Alteration'' means (i) an unauthorized change in an instrument that purports to modify in any respect the obligation of a party, or (ii) an unauthorized addition of words or numbers or other change to an incomplete instrument relating to the obligation of a party.

(b) Except as provided in subsection (c), an alteration fraudulently made discharges a party whose obligation is affected by the alteration unless that party assents or is precluded from asserting the alteration. No other alteration discharges a party, and the instrument may be enforced according to its original terms.

(c) A payor bank or drawee paying a fraudulently altered instrument or a person taking it for value, in good faith and without notice of the alteration, may enforce rights with respect to the instrument (i) according to its original terms, or (ii) in the case of an incomplete instrument altered by unauthorized completion, according to its terms as completed.

§ 3–408. Drawee Not Liable on Unaccepted Draft

A check or other draft does not of itself operate as an assignment of funds in the hands of the drawee available for its payment, and the drawee is not liable on the instrument until the drawee accepts it.

§ 3–409. Acceptance of Draft; Certified Check

(a) ''Acceptance'' means the drawee's signed agreement to pay a draft as presented. It must be written on the draft and may consist of the drawee's signature alone. Acceptance may be made at any time and becomes effective when notification pursuant to instructions is given or the accepted draft is delivered for the purpose of giving rights on the acceptance to any person.

(b) A draft may be accepted although it has not been signed by the drawer, is otherwise incomplete, is overdue, or has been dishonored.

(c) If a draft is payable at a fixed period after sight and the acceptor fails to date the acceptance, the holder may complete the acceptance by supplying a date in good faith.

(d) ''Certified check'' means a check accepted by the bank on which it is drawn. Acceptance may be made as stated in subsection (a) or by a writing on the check which indicates that the check is certified. The drawee of a check has no obligation to certify the check, and refusal to certify is not dishonor of the check.

§ 3–410.   Acceptance Varying Draft

(a) If the terms of a drawee's acceptance vary from the terms of the draft as presented, the holder may refuse the acceptance and treat the draft as dishonored. In that case, the drawee may cancel the acceptance.

(b) The terms of a draft are not varied by an acceptance to pay at a particular bank or place in the United States, unless the acceptance states that the draft is to be paid only at that bank or place.

(c) If the holder assents to an acceptance varying the terms of a draft, the obligation of each drawer and indorser that does not expressly assent to the acceptance is discharged.

§ 3–411.   Refusal to Pay Cashier's Checks, Teller's Checks, and Certified Checks

(a) In this section, "obligated bank" means the acceptor of a certified check or the issuer of a cashier's check or teller's check bought from the issuer.

(b) If the obligated bank wrongfully (i) refuses to pay a cashier's check or certified check, (ii) stops payment of a teller's check, or (iii) refuses to pay a dishonored teller's check, the person asserting the right to enforce the check is entitled to compensation for expenses and loss of interest resulting from the nonpayment and may recover consequential damages if the obligated bank refuses to pay after receiving notice of particular circumstances giving rise to the damages.

(c) Expenses or consequential damages under subsection (b) are not recoverable if the refusal of the obligated bank to pay occurs because (i) the bank suspends payments, (ii) the obligated bank asserts a claim or defense of the bank that it has reasonable grounds to believe is available against the person entitled to enforce the instrument, (iii) the obligated bank has a reasonable doubt whether the person demanding payment is the person entitled to enforce the instrument, or (iv) payment is prohibited by law.

§ 3–412.   Obligation of Issuer of Note or Cashier's Check

The issuer of a note or cashier's check or other draft drawn on the drawer is obliged to pay the instrument (i) according to its terms at the time it was issued or, if not issued, at the time it first came into possession of a holder, or (ii) if the issuer signed an incomplete instrument, according to its terms when completed, to the extent stated in Sections 3-115 and 3-407. The obligation is owed to a person entitled to enforce the instrument or to an indorser who paid the instrument under Section 3-415.

§ 3–413.   Obligation of Acceptor

(a) The acceptor of a draft is obliged to pay the draft (i) according to its terms at the time it was accepted, even though the acceptance states that the draft is payable "as

originally drawn" or equivalent terms, (ii) if the acceptance varies the terms of the draft, according to the terms of the draft as varied, or (iii) if the acceptance is of a draft that is an incomplete instrument, according to its terms when completed, to the extent stated in Sections 3-115 and 3-407. The obligation is owed to a person entitled to enforce the draft or to the drawer or an indorser who paid the draft under Section 3-414 or 3-415.

(b) If the certification of a check or other acceptance of a draft states the amount certified or accepted, the obligation of the acceptor is that amount. If (i) the certification or acceptance does not state an amount, (ii) the amount of the instrument is subsequently raised, and (iii) the instrument is then negotiated to a holder in due course, the obligation of the acceptor is the amount of the instrument at the time it was taken by the holder in due course.

§ 3–414.   Obligation of Drawer

(a) This section does not apply to cashier's checks or other drafts drawn on the drawer.

(b) If an unaccepted draft is dishonored, the drawer is obliged to pay the draft (i) according to its terms at the time it was issued or, if not issued, at the time it first came into possession of a holder, or (ii) if the drawer signed an incomplete instrument, according to its terms when completed, to the extent stated in Sections 3-115 and 3-407. The obligation is owed to a person entitled to enforce the draft or to an indorser who paid the draft under Section 3-415.

(c) If a draft is accepted by a bank, the drawer is discharged, regardless of when or by whom acceptance was obtained.

(d) If a draft is accepted and the acceptor is not a bank, the obligation of the drawer to pay the draft if the draft is dishonored by the acceptor is the same as the obligation of an indorser under Section 3-415(a) and (c).

(e) If a draft states that it is drawn "without recourse" or otherwise disclaims liability of the drawer to pay the draft, the drawer is not liable under subsection (b) to pay the draft if the draft is not a check. A disclaimer of the liability stated in subsection (b) is not effective if the draft is a check.

(f) If (i) a check is not presented for payment or given to a depositary bank for collection within 30 days after its date, (ii) the drawee suspends payments after expiration of the 30-day period without paying the check, and (iii) because of the suspension of payments, the drawer is deprived of funds maintained with the drawee to cover payment of the check, the drawer to the extent deprived of funds may discharge its obligation to pay the check by assigning to the person entitled to enforce the check the rights of the drawer against the drawee with respect to the funds.

§ 3–415.   Obligation of Indorser

(a) Subject to subsections (b), (c), and (d) and to Section 3-419(d), if an instrument is dishonored, an indorser is obliged to pay the amount due on the instrument (i) according to the terms of the instrument at the time it was indorsed, or (ii) if the indorser indorsed an incomplete instrument, according to its terms when completed, to the extent stated in Section 3-115 and 3-407. The obligation of the indorser is owed to a person entitled to enforce the instrument or to a subsequent indorser who paid the instrument under this section.

(b) If an indorsement states that it is made "without recourse" or otherwise disclaims liability of the indorser, the indorser is not liable under subsection (a) to pay the instrument.

(c) If notice of dishonor of an instrument is required by Section 3-503 and notice of dishonor complying with that section is not given to an indorser, the liability of the indorser under subsection (a) is discharged.

(d) If a draft is accepted by a bank after an indorsement is made, the liability of the indorser under subsection (a) is discharged.

(e) If an indorser of a check is liable under subsection (a) and the check is not presented for payment, or given to a depositary bank for collection, within 30 days after the day the indorsement was made, the liability of the indorser under subsection (a) is discharged.

§ 3–416.   Transfer Warranties

(a) A person who transfers an instrument for consideration warrants to the transferee and, if the transfer is by indorsement, to any subsequent transferee that:

(1)   the warrantor is a person entitled to enforce the instrument;

(2)   all signatures on the instrument are authentic and authorized;

(3)   the instrument has not been altered;

(4)   the instrument is not subject to a defense or claim in recoupment of any party which can be asserted against the warrantor; and

(5)   the warrantor has no knowledge of any insolvency proceeding commenced with respect to the maker or acceptor or, in the case of an unaccepted draft, the drawer.

(b) A person to whom the warranties under subsection (a) are made and who took the instrument in good faith may recover from the warrantor as damages for breach of warranty an amount equal to the loss suffered as a result of the breach, but not more than the amount of the instrument plus expenses and loss of interest incurred as a result of the breach.

(c) The warranties stated in subsection (a) cannot be disclaimed with respect to checks. Unless notice of a claim for breach of warranty is given to the warrantor within 30 days after the claimant has reason to know of the breach and the identity of the warrantor, the liability of the warrantor under subsection (b) is discharged to the extent of any loss caused by the delay in giving notice of the claim.

(d) A [cause of action] for breach of warranty under this section accrues when the claimant has reason to know of the breach.

§ 3–417.   Presentment Warranties

(a) If an unaccepted draft is presented to the drawee for payment or acceptance and the drawee pays or accepts the draft, (i) the person obtaining payment or acceptance, at the time of presentment, and (ii) a previous transferor of the draft, at the time of transfer, warrant to the drawee making payment or accepting the draft in good faith that:

(1)   the warrantor is, or was, at the time the warrantor transferred the draft, a person entitled to enforce the draft or authorized to obtain payment or acceptance of the draft on behalf of a person entitled to enforce the draft;

(2)   the draft has not been altered; and

(3)   the warrantor has no knowledge that the signature of the drawer of the draft is unauthorized.

(b) A drawee making payment may recover from any warrantor damages for breach of warranty equal to the amount paid by the drawee less the amount the drawee received or is entitled to receive from the drawer because of the payment. In addition, the drawee is entitled to compensation for expenses and loss of interest resulting from the breach. The right of the drawee to recover damages under this subsection is not affected by any failure of the drawee to exercise ordinary care in making payment. If the drawee accepts the draft, breach of warranty is a defense to the obligation of the acceptor. If the acceptor makes payment with respect to the draft, the acceptor is entitled to recover from any warrantor for breach of warranty the amounts stated in this subsection.

(c) If a drawee asserts a claim for breach of warranty under subsection (a) based on an unauthorized indorsement of the draft or an alteration of the draft, the warrantor may defend by proving that the indorsement is effective under Section 3-404 or 3-405 or the drawer is precluded under Section 3-406 or 4-406 from asserting against the drawee the unauthorized indorsement or alteration.

(d) If (i) a dishonored draft is presented for payment to the drawer or an indorser or (ii) any other instrument is presented for payment to a party obliged to pay the instrument, and (iii) payment is received, the following rules apply:

(1)   The person obtaining payment and a prior transferor of the instrument warrant to the person making payment in good faith that the warrantor is, or was, at the time the warrantor transferred the instrument, a person entitled to enforce the instrument or authorized to obtain payment on behalf of a person entitled to enforce the instrument.

(2)   The person making payment may recover from any warrantor for breach of warranty an amount equal to the amount paid plus expenses and loss of interest resulting from the breach.

(e) The warranties stated in subsections (a) and (d) cannot be disclaimed with respect to checks. Unless notice of a claim for breach of warranty is given to the warrantor within 30 days after the claimant has reason to know of the breach and the identity of the warrantor, the liability of the warrantor under subsection (b) or (d) is discharged to the extent of any loss caused by the delay in giving notice of the claim.

(f)A [cause of action] for breach of warranty under this section accrues when the claimant has reason to know of the breach.

§ 3–418.   *Payment or Acceptance by Mistake*

(a) Except as provided in subsection (c), if the drawee of a draft pays or accepts the draft and the drawee acted on the mistaken belief that (i) payment of the draft had not been stopped pursuant to Section 4-403 or (ii) the signature of the drawer of the draft was authorized, the drawee may recover the amount of the draft from the person to whom or for whose benefit payment was made or, in the case of acceptance, may revoke the acceptance. Rights of the drawee under this subsection are not affected by failure of the drawee to exercise ordinary care in paying or accepting the draft.

(b) Except as provided in subsection (c), if an instrument has been paid or accepted by mistake and the case is not covered by subsection (a), the person paying or accepting may, to the extent permitted by the law governing mistake and restitution, (i) recover the payment from the person to whom or for whose benefit payment was made or (ii) in the case of acceptance, may revoke the acceptance.

(c) The remedies provided by subsection (a) or (b) may not be asserted against a person who took the instrument in good faith and for value or who in good faith changed position in reliance on the payment or acceptance. This subsection does not limit remedies provided by Section 3-417 and 4-407.

(d) Notwithstanding Section 4-215, if an instrument is paid or accepted by mistake and the payor or acceptor recovers payment or revokes acceptance under subsection (a) or (b), the instrument is deemed not to have been paid or accepted and is treated as dishonored, and the person from whom payment is recovered has rights as a person entitled to enforce the dishonored instrument.

§ 3–419.   *Instruments Signed for Accommodation*

(a) If an instrument is issued for value given for the benefit of a party to the instrument (''accommodated party'') and another party to the instrument (''accommodation party'') signs the instrument for the purpose of incurring liability on the instrument without being a direct beneficiary of the value given for the instrument, the instrument is signed by the accommodation party ''for accommodation.''

(b) An accommodation party may sign the instrument as maker, drawer, acceptor, or indorser and, subject to subsection (d), is obliged to pay the instrument in the capacity in which the accommodation party signs. The obligation of an accommodation party may be enforced notwithstanding any statute of frauds and whether or not the accommodation party receives consideration for the accommodation.

(c) A person signing an instrument is presumed to be an accommodation party and there is notice that the instrument is signed for accommodation if the signature is an anomalous indorsement or is accompanied by words indicating that the signer is acting as surety or guarantor with respect to the obligation of another party to the instrument. Except as provided in Section 3-605, the obligation of an accommodation party to pay the instrument is not affected by the fact that the person enforcing the obligation had notice when the instrument was taken by that person that the accommodation party signed the instrument for accommodation.

(d) If the signature of a party to an instrument is accompanied by words indicating unambiguously that the party is guaranteeing collection rather than payment of the obligation of another party to the instrument, the signer is obliged to pay the amount due on the instrument to a person entitled to enforce the instrument only if (i) execution of judgment against the other party has been returned unsatisfied, (ii) the other party is insolvent or in an insolvency proceeding, (iii) the other party cannot be served with process, or (iv) it is otherwise apparent that payment cannot be obtained from the other party.

(e) An accommodation party who pays the instrument is entitled to reimbursement from the accommodated party and is entitled to enforce the instrument against the accommodated party. An accommodated party who pays the instrument has no right of recourse against, and is not entitled to contribution from, an accommodation party.

§ 3–420.   *Conversion of Instrument*

(a) The law applicable to conversion of personal property applies to instruments. An instrument is also converted if it is taken by transfer, other than a negotiation, from a person not entitled to enforce the instrument or a bank makes or obtains payment with respect to the instrument for a person not entitled to enforce the instrument or receive payment. An action for conversion of an instrument may not be brought by (i) the issuer or acceptor of the instrument or (ii) a payee or indorsee who did not receive delivery of the instrument either directly or through delivery to an agent or a co-payee.

(b) In an action under subsection (a), the measure of liability is presumed to be the amount payable on the instrument, but recovery may not exceed the amount of the plaintiff's interest in the instrument.

(c) A representative, other than a depositary bank, who has in good faith dealt with an instrument or its proceeds on behalf of one who was not the person entitled to enforce the instrument is not liable in conversion to that person beyond the amount of any proceeds that it has not paid out.

Part 5   Dishonor

§ 3–501.   *Presentment*

(a) ''Presentment'' means a demand made by or on behalf of a person entitled to enforce an instrument (i) to pay the instrument made to the drawee or a party obliged to pay the instrument or, in the case of a note or accepted draft payable at a bank, to the bank, or (ii) to accept a draft made to the drawee.

(b) The following rules are subject to Article 4, agreement of the parties, and clearing-house rules and the like:

(1) Presentment may be made at the place of payment of the instrument and must be made at the place of payment if the instrument is payable at a bank in the United States; may be made by any commercially reasonable means, including an oral, written, or electronic communication; is effective when the demand for payment or acceptance is received by the person to whom presentment is made; and is effective if made to any one of two or more makers, acceptors, drawees, or other payors.

(2) Upon demand of the person to whom presentment is made, the person making presentment must (i) exhibit the instrument, (ii) give reasonable identification and, if presentment is made on behalf of another person, reasonable evidence of authority to do so, and (. . .) sign a receipt on the instrument for any payment made or surrender the instrument if full payment is made.

(3) Without dishonoring the instrument, the party to whom presentment is made may (i) return the instrument for lack of a necessary indorsement, or (ii) refuse payment or acceptance for failure of the presentment to comply with the terms of the instrument, an agreement of the parties, or other applicable law or rule.

(4) The party to whom presentment is made may treat presentment as occurring on the next business day after the day of presentment if the party to whom presentment is made has established a cut-off hour not earlier than 2 p.m. for the receipt and processing of instruments presented for payment or acceptance and presentment is made after the cut-off hour.

§ 3–502.   *Dishonor*

(a) Dishonor of a note is governed by the following rules:

(1) If the note is payable on demand, the note is dishonored if presentment is duly made to the maker and the note is not paid on the day of presentment.

(2) If the note is not payable on demand and is payable at or through a bank or the terms of the note require presentment, the note is dishonored if presentment is duly made and the note is not paid on the day it becomes payable or the day of presentment, whichever is later.

(3) If the note is not payable on demand and paragraph (2) does not apply, the note is dishonored if it is not paid on the day it becomes payable.

(b) Dishonor of an unaccepted draft other than a documentary draft is governed by the following rules:

(1) If a check is duly presented for payment to the payor bank otherwise than for immediate payment over the counter, the check is dishonored if the payor bank makes timely return of the check or sends timely notice of dishonor or nonpayment under Section 4-301 or 4-302, or becomes accountable for the amount of the check under Section 4-302.

(2) If a draft is payable on demand and paragraph (1) does not apply, the draft is dishonored if presentment for payment is duly made to the drawee and the draft is not paid on the day of presentment.

(3) If a draft is payable on a date stated in the draft, the draft is dishonored if (i) presentment for payment is duly made to the drawee and payment is not made on the day the draft becomes payable or the day of presentment, whichever is later, or (ii) presentment for acceptance is duly made before the day the draft becomes payable and the draft is not accepted on the day of presentment.

(4) If a draft is payable on elapse of a period of time after sight or acceptance, the draft is dishonored if presentment for acceptance is duly made and the draft is not accepted on the day of presentment.

(c) Dishonor of an unaccepted documentary draft occurs according to the rules stated in subsection (b)(2), (3), and (4), except that payment or acceptance may be delayed without dishonor until no later than the close of the third business day of the drawee following the day on which payment or acceptance is required by those paragraphs.

(d) Dishonor of an accepted draft is governed by the following rules:

(1) If the draft is payable on demand, the draft is dishonored if presentment for payment is duly made to the acceptor and the draft is not paid on the day of presentment.

(2) If the draft is not payable on demand, the draft is dishonored if presentment for payment is duly made to the acceptor and payment is not made on the day it becomes payable or the day of presentment, whichever is later.

(e) In any case in which presentment is otherwise required for dishonor under this section and presentment is excused under Section 3-504, dishonor occurs without presentment if the instrument is not duly accepted or paid.

(f) If a draft is dishonored because timely acceptance of the draft was not made and the person entitled to demand acceptance consents to a late acceptance, from the time of acceptance the draft is treated as never having been dishonored.

§ 3–503.   Notice of Dishonor

(a) The obligation of an indorser stated in Section 3-415(a) and the obligation of a drawer stated in Section 3-414(d) may not be enforced unless (i) the indorser or drawer is given notice of dishonor of the instrument complying with this section or (ii) notice of dishonor is excused under Section 3-504(b).

(b) Notice of dishonor may be given by any person; may be given by any commercially reasonable means, including an oral, written, or electronic communication; and is sufficient if it reasonably identifies the instrument and indicates that the instrument has been dishonored or has not been paid or accepted. Return of an instrument given to a bank for collection is sufficient notice of dishonor.

(c) Subject to Section 3-504(c), with respect to an instrument taken for collection by a collecting bank, notice of dishonor must be given (i) by the bank before midnight of the next banking day following the banking day on which the bank receives notice of dishonor of the instrument, or (ii) by any other person within 30 days following the day on which the person receives notice of dishonor. With respect to any other instrument, notice of dishonor must be given within 30 days following the day on which dishonor occurs.

§ 3–504.   Excused Presentment and Notice of Dishonor

(a) Presentment for payment or acceptance of an instrument is excused if (i) the person entitled to present the instrument cannot with reasonable diligence make presentment, (ii) the maker or acceptor has repudiated an obligation to pay the instrument or is dead or in insolvency proceedings, (iii) by the terms of the instrument presentment is not necessary to enforce the obligation of indorsers or the drawer, (iv) the drawer or indorser whose obligation is being enforced has waived presentment or otherwise has no reason to expect or right to require that the instrument be paid or accepted, or (v) the drawer instructed the drawee not to pay or accept the draft or the drawee was not obligated to the drawer to pay the draft.

(b) Notice of dishonor is excused if (i) by the terms of the instrument notice of dishonor is not necessary to enforce the obligation of a party to pay the instrument, or (ii) the party whose obligation is being enforced waived notice of dishonor. A waiver of presentment is also a waiver of notice of dishonor.

(c) Delay in giving notice of dishonor is excused if the delay was caused by circumstances beyond the control of the person giving the notice and the person giving the notice exercised reasonable diligence after the cause of the delay ceased to operate.

§ 3–505.   Evidence of Dishonor

(a) The following are admissible as evidence and create a presumption of dishonor and of any notice of dishonor stated:

(1) a document regular in form as provided in subsection (b) which purports to be a protest;

(2) a purported stamp or writing of the drawee, payor bank, or presenting bank on or accompanying the instrument stating that acceptance or payment has been refused unless reasons for the refusal are stated and the reasons are not consistent with dishonor;

(3) a book or record of the drawee, payor bank, or collecting bank, kept in the usual course of business which shows dishonor, even if there is no evidence of who made the entry.

(b) A protest is a certificate of dishonor made by a United States consul or vice consul, or a notary public or other person authorized to administer oaths by the law of the place where dishonor occurs. It may be made upon information satisfactory to that person. The protest must identify the instrument and certify either that presentment has been made or, if not made, the reason why it was not made, and that the instrument has been dishonored by nonacceptance or nonpayment. The protest may also certify that notice of dishonor has been given to some or all parties.

Part 6   Discharge and Payment

§ 3–601.   Discharge and Effect of Discharge

(a) The obligation of a party to pay the instrument is discharged as stated in this Article or by an act or agreement with the party which would discharge an obligation to pay money under a simple contract.

(b) Discharge of the obligation of a party is not effective against a person acquiring rights of a holder in due course of the instrument without notice of the discharge.

§ 3–602.   Payment

(a) Subject to subsection (b), an instrument is paid to the extent payment is made (i) by or on behalf of a party obliged to pay the instrument, and (ii) to a person entitled to enforce the instrument. To the extent of the payment, the obligation of the party obliged to pay the instrument is discharged even though payment is made with knowledge of a claim to the instrument under Section 3-306 by another person.

(b) The obligation of a party to pay the instrument is not discharged under subsection (a) if:

(1) a claim to the instrument under Section 3-306 is enforceable against the party receiving payment and (i) payment is made with knowledge by the payor that payment is prohibited by injunction or similar process of a court of competent jurisdic-

tion, or (ii) in the case of an instrument other than a cashier's check, teller's check, or certified check, the party making payment accepted, from the person having a claim to the instrument, indemnity against loss resulting from refusal to pay the person entitled to enforce the instrument; or

(2)   the person making payment knows that the instrument is a stolen instrument and pays a person it knows is in wrongful possession of the instrument.

§ 3–603.   *Tender of Payment*

(a) If tender of payment of an obligation to pay an instrument is made to a person entitled to enforce the instrument, the effect of tender is governed by principles of law applicable to tender of payment under a simple contract.

(b) If tender of payment of an obligation to pay an instrument is made to a person entitled to enforce the instrument and the tender is refused, there is discharge, to the extent of the amount of the tender, of the obligation of an indorser or accommodation party having a right of recourse with respect to the obligation to which the tender relates.

(c) If tender of payment of an amount due on an instrument is made to a person entitled to enforce the instrument, the obligation of the obligor to pay interest after the due date on the amount tendered is discharged. If presentment is required with respect to an instrument and the obligor is able and ready to pay on the due date at every place of payment stated in the instrument, the obligor is deemed to have made tender of payment on the due date to the person entitled to enforce the instrument.

§ 3–604.   *Discharge by Cancellation or Renunciation*

(a) A person entitled to enforce an instrument, with or without consideration, may discharge the obligation of a party to pay the instrument (i) by an intentional voluntary act, such as surrender of the instrument to the party, destruction, mutilation, or cancellation of the instrument, cancellation or striking out of the party's signature, or the addition of words to the instrument indicating discharge, or (ii) by agreeing not to sue or otherwise renouncing rights against the party by a signed writing.

(b) Cancellation or striking out of an indorsement pursuant to subsection (a) does not affect the status and rights of a party derived from the indorsement.

§ 3–605.   *Discharge of Indorsers and Accommodation Parties*

(a) In this section, the term ''indorser'' includes a drawer having the obligation described in Section 3-414(d).

(b) Discharge, under Section 3-604, of the obligation of a party to pay an instrument does not discharge the obligation of an indorser or accommodation party having a right of recourse against the discharged party.

(c) If a person entitled to enforce an instrument agrees, with or without consideration, to an extension of the due date of the obligation of a party to pay the instrument, the extension discharges an indorser or accommodation party having a right of recourse against the party whose obligation is extended to the extent the indorser or accommodation party proves that the extension caused loss to the indorser or accommodation party with respect to the right of recourse.

(d) If a person entitled to enforce an instrument agrees, with or without consideration, to a material modification of the obligation of a party other than an extension of the due date, the modification discharges the obligation of an indorser or accommodation party having a right of recourse against the person whose obligation is modified to the extent the modification causes loss to the indorser or accommodation party with respect to the right of recourse. The loss suffered by the indorser or accommodation party as a result of the modification is equal to the amount of the right of recourse unless the person enforcing the instrument proves that no loss was caused by the modification or that the loss caused by the modification was an amount less than the amount of the right of recourse.

(e) If the obligation of a party to pay an instrument is secured by an interest in collateral and a person entitled to enforce the instrument impairs the value of the interest in collateral, the obligation of an indorser or accommodation party having a right of recourse against the obligor is discharged to the extent of the impairment. The value of an interest in collateral is impaired to the extent (i) the value of the interest is reduced to an amount less than the amount of the right of recourse of the party asserting discharge, or (ii) the reduction in value of the interest causes an increase in the amount by which the amount of the right of recourse exceeds the value of the interest. The burden of proving impairment is on the party asserting discharge.

(f) If the obligation of a party is secured by an interest in collateral not provided by an accommodation party and a person entitled to enforce the instrument impairs the value of the interest in collateral, the obligation of any party who is jointly and severally liable with respect to the secured obligation is discharged to the extent the impairment causes the party asserting discharge to pay more than that party would have been obliged to pay, taking into account rights of contribution, if impairment had not occurred. If the party asserting discharge is an accommodation party not entitled to discharge under subsection (e), the party is deemed to have a right to contribution based on joint and several liability rather than a right to reimbursement. The burden of proving impairment is on the party asserting discharge.

(g) Under subsection (e) or (f), impairing value of an interest in collateral includes (i) failure to obtain or maintain perfection or recordation of the interest in collateral,

(ii) release of collateral without substitution of collateral of equal value, (iii) failure to perform a duty to preserve the value of collateral owed, under Article 9 or other law, to a debtor or surety or other person secondarily liable, or (iv) failure to comply with applicable law in disposing of collateral.

(h) An accommodation party is not discharged under subsection (c), (d), or (e) unless the person entitled to enforce the instrument knows of the accommodation or has notice under Section 3-419(c) that the instrument was signed for accommodation.

(i) A party is not discharged under this section if (i) the party asserting discharge consents to the event or conduct that is the basis of the discharge, or (ii) the instrument or a separate agreement of the party provides for waiver of discharge under this section either specifically or by general language indicating that parties waive defenses based on suretyship or impairment of collateral.

ARTICLE 4   BANK DEPOSITS AND COLLECTIONS

Part 1   General Provisions and Definitions

§ 4–101.   Short Title

This Article may be cited as Uniform Commercial Code— Bank Deposits and Collections.
As amended in 1990.

§ 4–102.   Applicability

(a) To the extent that items within this Article are also within Articles 3 and 8, they are subject to those Articles. If there is conflict, this Article governs Article 3, but Article 8 governs this Article.

(b) The liability of a bank for action or non-action with respect to an item handled by it for purposes of presentment, payment, or collection is governed by the law of the place where the bank is located. In the case of action or non-action by or at a branch or separate office of a bank, its liability is governed by the law of the place where the branch or separate office is located.
As amended in 1990.

§ 4–103.   Variation by Agreement; Measure of Damages; Action Constituting Ordinary Care

(a) The effect of the provisions of this Article may be varied by agreement, but the parties to the agreement cannot disclaim a bank's responsibility for its lack of good faith or failure to exercise ordinary care or limit the measure of damages for the lack or failure. However, the parties may determine by agreement the standards by which the bank's responsibility is to be measured if those standards are not manifestly unreasonable.

(b) Federal Reserve regulations and operating circulars, clearing-house rules, and the like have the effect of agreements under subsection (a), whether or not specifically assented to by all parties interested in items handled.

(c) Action or non-action approved by this Article or pursuant to Federal Reserve regulations or operating circulars is the exercise of ordinary care and, in the absence of special instructions, action or non-action consistent with clearing-house rules and the like or with a general banking usage not disapproved by this Article, is prima facie the exercise of ordinary care.

(d) The specification or approval of certain procedures by this Article is not disapproval of other procedures that may be reasonable under the circumstances.

(e) The measure of damages for failure to exercise ordinary care in handling an item is the amount of the item reduced by an amount that could not have been realized by the exercise of ordinary care. If there is also bad faith it includes any other damages the party suffered as a proximate consequence.
As amended in 1990.

§ 4–104.   Definitions and Index of Definitions

(a) In this Article, unless the context otherwise requires:

(1) "Account" means any deposit or credit account with a bank, including a demand, time, savings, passbook, share draft, or like account, other than an account evidenced by a certificate of deposit;

(2) "Afternoon" means the period of day between noon and midnight;

(3) "Banking day" means the part of a day on which a bank is open to the public for carrying on substantially all of its banking functions;

(4) "Clearing house" means an association of banks or other payors regularly clearing items;

(5) "Customer" means a person having an account with a bank or for whom a bank has agreed to collect items, including a bank that maintains an account at another bank;

(6) "Documentary draft" means a draft to be presented for acceptance or payment if specified documents, certificated securities (Section 8–102) or instructions for uncertificated securities (Section 8–308), or other certificates, statements, or the like are to be received by the drawee or other payor before acceptance or payment of the draft;

(7) "Draft" means a draft as defined in Section 3–104 or an item, other than an instrument, that is an order;

(8) ''Drawee'' means a person ordered in a draft to make payment;

(9) ''Item'' means an instrument or a promise or order to pay money handled by a bank for collection or payment. The term does not include a payment order governed by Article 4A or a credit or debit card slip;

(10) ''Midnight deadline'' with respect to a bank is midnight on its next banking day following the banking day on which it receives the relevant item or notice or from which the time for taking action commences to run, whichever is later;

(11) ''Settle'' means to pay in cash, by clearing-house settlement, in a charge or credit or by remittance, or otherwise as agreed. A settlement may be either provisional or final;

(12) ''Suspends payments'' with respect to a bank means that it has been closed by order of the supervisory authorities, that a public officer has been appointed to take it over, or that it ceases or refuses to make payments in the ordinary course of business.

(b) Other definitions applying to this Article and the sections in which they appear are:

''Agreement for electronic presentment''	Section 4−110.
''Bank''	Section 4−105.
''Collecting bank''	Section 4−105.
''Depositary bank''	Section 4−105.
''Intermediary bank''	Section 4−105.
''Payor bank''	Section 4−105.
''Presenting bank''	Section 4−105.
''Presentment notice''	Section 4−110.

§ 4−105.   ''Bank''; ''Depositary Bank''; ''Payor Bank''; ''Intermediary Bank''; ''Collecting Bank''; ''Presenting Bank''

In this Article:

(1) ''Bank'' means a person engaged in the business of banking, including a savings bank, savings and loan association, credit union, or trust company;

(2) ''Depositary bank'' means the first bank to take an item even though it is also the payor bank, unless the item is presented for immediate payment over the counter;

(3) ''Payor bank'' means a bank that is the drawee of a draft;

(4) ''Intermediary bank'' means a bank to which an item is transferred in course of collection except the depositary or payor bank;

(5) ''Collecting bank'' means a bank handling an item for collection except the payor bank;

(6) ''Presenting bank'' means a bank presenting an item except a payor bank.

As amended in 1990.

§ 4−106.   Payable Through or Payable at Bank: Collecting Bank

(a) If an item states that it is ''payable through'' a bank identified in the item, (i) the item designates the bank as a collecting bank and does not by itself authorize the bank to pay the item, and (ii) the item may be presented for payment only by or through the bank.

Alternative A

(b) If an item states that it is ''payable at'' a bank identified in the item, the item is equivalent to a draft drawn on the bank.

Alternative B

(b) If an item states that it is ''payable at'' a bank identified in the item, (i) the item designates the bank as a collecting bank and does not by itself authorize the bank to pay the item, and (ii) the item may be presented for payment only by or through the bank.

(c) If a draft means a nonbank drawee and it is unclear whether a bank named in the draft is a co-drawee or a collecting bank, the bank is a collecting bank.

As added in 1990.

§ 4−107.   Separate Office of Bank

A branch or separate office of a bank is a separate bank for the purpose of computing the time within which and determining the place at or to which action may be taken or notices or orders shall be given under this Article and under Article 3.

As amended in 1962 and 1990.

§ 4−108.   Time of Receipt of Items

(a) For the purpose of allowing time to process items, prove balances, and make the necessary entries on its books to determine its position for the day, a bank may fix an afternoon hour of 2 P.M. or later as a cutoff hour for the handling of money and items and the making of entries on its books.

(b) An item or deposit of money received on any day after a cutoff hour so fixed or after the close of the banking day may be treated as being received at the opening of the next banking day.

As amended in 1990.

§ 4−109.   Delays

(a) Unless otherwise instructed, a collecting bank in a good faith effort to secure payment of a specific item drawn on a payor other than a bank, and with or without the approval of any person involved, may waive, modify, or extend time limits imposed or permitted by this [Act] for a period not exceeding two additional banking days without discharge of drawers or indorsers or liability to its transferor or a prior party.

(b) Delay by a collecting bank or payor bank beyond time limits prescribed or permitted by this [Act] or by

instructions is excused if (i) the delay is caused by interruption of communication or computer facilities, suspension of payments by another bank, war, emergency conditions, failure of equipment, or other circumstances beyond the control of the bank, and (ii) the bank exercises such diligence as the circumstances require.
As amended in 1990.

§ 4–110.   Electronic Presentment

(a) "Agreement for electronic presentment" means an agreement, clearing-house rule, or Federal Reserve regulation or operating circular, providing that presentment of an item may be made by transmission of an image of an item or information describing the item ("presentment notice") rather than delivery of the item itself. The agreement may provide for procedures governing retention, presentment, payment, dishonor, and other matters concerning items subject to the agreement.

(b) Presentment of an item pursuant to an agreement for presentment is made when the presentment notice is received.

(c) If presentment is made by presentment notice, a reference to "item" or "check" in this Article means the presentment notice unless the context otherwise indicates.
As added in 1990.

4–111.   Statute of Limitations

An action to enforce an obligation, duty, or right arising under this Article must be commenced within three years after the [cause of action] accrues.
As added in 1990.

Part 2   Collection of Items: Depositary and Collecting Banks

§ 4–201.   Status of Collecting Bank as Agent and Provisional Status of Credits; Applicability of Article; Item Indorsed "Pay Any Bank"

(a) Unless a contrary intent clearly appears and before the time that a settlement given by a collecting bank for an item is or becomes final, the bank, with respect to an item, is an agent or sub-agent of the owner of the item and any settlement given for the item is provisional. This provision applies regardless of the form of indorsement or lack of indorsement and even though credit given for the item is subject to immediate withdrawal as of right or is in fact withdrawn; but the continuance of ownership of an item by its owner and any rights of the owner to proceeds of the item are subject to rights of a collecting bank, such as those resulting from outstanding advances on the item and rights of recoupment or setoff. If an item is handled by banks for purposes of presentment, payment, collection, or return, the relevant provisions of this Article apply even though action of the parties clearly establishes that a particular bank has purchased the item and is the owner of it.

(b) After an item has been indorsed with the words "pay any bank" or the like, only a bank may acquire the rights of a holder until the item has been:
(1) returned to the customer initiating collection; or
(2) specially indorsed by a bank to a person who is not a bank.
As amended in 1990.

§ 4–202.   Responsibility for Collection or Return; When Action Timely

(a) A collecting bank must exercise ordinary care in:
(1) presenting an item or sending it for presentment;
(2) sending notice of dishonor or nonpayment or returning an item other than a documentary draft to the bank's transferor after learning that the item has not been paid or accepted, as the case may be;
(3) settling for an item when the bank receives final settlement; and
(4) notifying its transferor of any loss or delay in transit within a reasonable time after discovery thereof.

(b) A collecting bank exercises ordinary care under subsection (a) by taking proper action before its midnight deadline following receipt of an item, notice, or settlement. Taking proper action within a reasonably longer time may constitute the exercise of ordinary care, but the bank has the burden of establishing timeliness.

(c) Subject to subsection (a)(1), a bank is not liable for the insolvency, neglect, misconduct, mistake, or default of another bank or person or for loss or destruction of an item in the possession of others or in transit.
As amended in 1990.

§ 4–203.   Effect of Instructions

Subject to Article 3 concerning conversion of instruments (Section 3–420) and restrictive indorsements (Section 3–206), only a collecting bank's transferor can give instructions that affect the bank or constitute notice to it, and a collecting bank is not liable to prior parties for any action taken pursuant to the instructions or in accordance with any agreement with its transferor.
As amended in 1990.

§ 4–204.   Methods of Sending and Presenting; Sending Directly to Payor Bank

(a) A collecting bank shall send items by a reasonably prompt method, taking into consideration relevant instructions, the nature of the item, the number of those items on hand, the cost of collection involved, and the method generally used by it or others to present those items.

(b) A collecting bank may send:
(1) an item directly to the payor bank;
(2) an item to a nonbank payor if authorized by its transferor; and

(3) an item other than documentary drafts to a non-bank payor, if authorized by Federal Reserve regulation or operating circular, clearing-house rule, or the like.

(c) Presentment may be made by a presenting bank at a place where the payor bank or other payor has requested that presentment be made.

As amended in 1962 and 1990.

§ 4–205. Depositary Bank Holder of Unindorsed Item

If a customer delivers an item to a depositary bank for collection:

(1) the depositary bank becomes a holder of the item at the time it receives the item for collection if the customer at the time of delivery was a holder of the item, whether or not the customer indorses the item, and, if the bank satisfies the other requirements of Section 3–302, it is a holder in due course; and

(2) the depositary bank warrants to collecting banks, the payor bank or other payor, and the drawer that the amount of the item was paid to the customer or deposited to the customer's account.

As amended in 1990.

§ 4–206. Transfer Between Banks

Any agreed method that identifies the transferor bank is sufficient for the item's further transfer to another bank.

As amended in 1990.

§ 4–207. Transfer Warranties

(a) A customer or collecting bank that transfers an item and receives a settlement or other consideration warrants to the transferee and to any subsequent collecting bank that:

(1) the warrantor is a person entitled to enforce the item;

(2) all signatures on the item are authentic and authorized;

(3) the item has not been altered;

(4) the item is not subject to a defense or claim in recoupment (Section 3–305(a)) of any party that can be asserted against the warrantor; and

(5) the warrantor has no knowledge of any insolvency proceeding commenced with respect to the maker or acceptor or, in the case of an unaccepted draft, the drawer.

(b) If an item is dishonored, a customer or collecting bank transferring the item and receiving settlement or other consideration is obliged to pay the amount due on the item (i) according to the terms of the item at the time it was transferred, or (ii) if the transfer was of an incomplete item, according to its terms when completed as stated in Sections 3–115 and 3–407. The obligation of a transferor is owed to the transferee and to any subsequent collecting bank that takes the item in good faith. A transferor cannot disclaim its obligation under this subsection

by an indorsement stating that it is made ''without recourse'' or otherwise disclaiming liability.

(c) A person to whom the warranties under subsection (a) are made and who took the item in good faith may recover from the warrantor as damages for breach of warranty an amount equal to the loss suffered as a result of the breach, but not more than the amount of the item plus expenses and loss of interest incurred as a result of the breach.

(d) The warranties stated in subsection (a) cannot be disclaimed with respect to checks. Unless notice of a claim for breach of warranty is given to the warrantor within 30 days after the claimant has reason to know of the breach and the identity of the warrantor, the warrantor is discharged to the extent of any loss caused by the delay in giving notice of the claim.

(e) A cause of action for breach of warranty under this section accrues when the claimant has reason to know of the breach.

As added in 1990.

§ 4–208. Presentment Warranties

(a) If an unaccepted draft is presented to the drawee for payment or acceptance and the drawee pays or accepts the draft, (i) the person obtaining payment or acceptance, at the time of presentment, and (ii) a previous transferor of the draft, at the time of transfer, warrant to the drawee that pays or accepts the draft in good faith that:

(1) the warrantor is, or was, at the time the warrantor transferred the draft, a person entitled to enforce the draft or authorized to obtain payment or acceptance of the draft on behalf of a person entitled to enforce the draft;

(2) the draft has not been altered; and

(3) the warrantor has no knowledge that the signature of the purported drawer of the draft is unauthorized.

(b) A drawee making payment may recover from a warrantor damages for breach of warranty equal to the amount paid by the drawee less the amount the drawee received or is entitled to receive from the drawer because of the payment. In addition, the drawee is entitled to compensation for expenses and loss of interest resulting from the breach. The right of the drawee to recover damages under this subsection is not affected by any failure of the drawee to exercise ordinary care in making payment. If the drawee accepts the draft (i) breach of warranty is a defense to the obligation of the acceptor, and (ii) if the acceptor makes payment with respect to the draft, the acceptor is entitled to recover from a warrantor for breach of warranty the amounts stated in this subsection.

(c) If a drawee asserts a claim for breach of warranty under subsection (a) based on an unauthorized indorsement of the draft or an alteration of the draft, the warrantor may defend by proving that the indorsement is effective under Section 3–404 or 3–405 or the drawer is precluded under Section 3–406 or 4–406 from asserting against the drawee the unauthorized indorsement or alteration.

(d) If (i) a dishonored draft is presented for payment to the drawer or an indorser or (ii) any other item is presented for payment to a party obliged to pay the item, and the item is paid, the person obtaining payment and a prior transferor of the item warrant to the person making payment in good faith that the warrantor is, or was, at the time the warrantor transferred the item, a person entitled to enforce the item or authorized to obtain payment on behalf of a person entitled to enforce the item. The person making payment may recover from any warrantor for breach of warranty an amount equal to the amount paid plus expenses and loss of interest resulting from the breach.

(e) The warranties stated in subsections (a) and (d) cannot be disclaimed with respect to checks. Unless notice of a claim for breach of warranty is given to the warrantor within 30 days after the claimant has reason to know of the breach and the identity of the warrantor, the warrantor is discharged to the extent of any loss caused by the delay in giving notice of the claim.

(f) A cause of action for breach of warranty under this section accrues when the claimant has reason to know of the breach.

As added in 1990.

§ 4–209.   Encoding and Retention Warranties

(a) A person who encodes information on or with respect to an item after issue warrants to any subsequent collecting bank and to the payor bank or other payor that the infor mation is correctly encoded. If the customer of a deposi-

tary bank encodes, that bank also makes the warranty.

(b) A person who undertakes to retain an item pursuant to an agreement for electronic presentment warrants to any subsequent collecting bank and to the payor bank or other payor that retention and presentment of the item comply with the agreement. If a customer of a depositary bank undertakes to retain an item, that bank also makes this warranty.

(c) A person to whom warranties are made under this section and who took the item in good faith may recover from the warrantor as damages for breach of warranty an amount equal to the loss suffered as a result of the breach, plus expenses and loss of interest incurred as a result of the breach.

As added in 1990.

§ 4–210.   Security Interest of Collecting Bank in Items, Accompanying Documents and Proceeds

(a) A collecting bank has a security interest in an item and any accompanying documents or the proceeds of either:

    (1)   in case of an item deposited in an account, to the extent to which credit given for the item has been withdrawn or applied;

    (2)   in case of an item for which it has given credit available for withdrawal as of right, to the extent of the credit given, whether or not the credit is drawn upon or there is a right of charge-back; or

    (3)   if it makes an advance on or against the item.

(b) If credit given for several items received at one time or pursuant to a single agreement is withdrawn or applied in part, the security interest remains upon all the items, any accompanying documents or the proceeds of either. For the purpose of this section, credits first given are first withdrawn.

(c) Receipt by a collecting bank of a final settlement for an item is a realization on its security interest in the item, accompanying documents, and proceeds. So long as the bank does not receive final settlement for the item or give up possession of the item or accompanying documents for purposes other than collection, the security interest continues to that extent and is subject to Article 9, but:

    (1)   no security agreement is necessary to make the security interest enforceable (Section 9–203(1)(a));

    (2)   no filing is required to perfect the security interest; and

    (3)   the security interest has priority over conflicting perfected security interests in the item, accompanying documents, or proceeds.

As amended in 1990.

§ 4–211.   When Bank Gives Value for Purposes of Holder in Due Course

For purposes of determining its status as a holder in due course, a bank has given value to the extent it has a security interest in an item, if the bank otherwise complies with the requirements of Section 3–302 on what constitutes a holder in due course.

As amended in 1990.

§ 4–212.   Presentment by Notice of Item Not Payable by, Through, or at Bank; Liability of Drawer or Indorser

(a) Unless otherwise instructed, a collecting bank may present an item not payable by, through, or at a bank by sending to the party to accept or pay a written notice that the bank holds the item for acceptance or payment. The notice must be sent in time to be received on or before the day when presentment is due and the bank must meet any requirement of the party to accept or pay under Section 3–501 by the close of the bank's next banking day after it knows of the requirement.

(b) If presentment is made by notice and payment, acceptance, or request for compliance with a requirement under Section 3–501 is not received by the close of business on the day after maturity or, in the case of demand items, by the close of business on the third banking day after notice was sent, the presenting bank may treat the

item as dishonored and charge any drawer or indorser by sending it notice of the facts.
As amended in 1990.

§ 4–213.   Medium and Time of Settlement by Bank

(a) With respect to settlement by a bank, the medium and time of settlement may be prescribed by Federal Reserve regulations or circulars, clearing-house rules, and the like, or agreement. In the absence of such prescription:

(1)   the medium or settlement is cash or credit to an account in a Federal Reserve bank of or specified by the person to receive settlement; and

(2)   the time of settlement, is:

(i)   with respect to tender of settlement by cash, a cashier's check, or teller's check, when the cash or check is sent or delivered;

(ii)   with respect to tender of settlement by credit in an account in a Federal Reserve Bank, when the credit is made;

(iii)   with respect to tender of settlement by a credit or debit to an account in a bank, when the credit or debit is made or, in the case of tender of settlement by authority to charge an account, when the authority is sent or delivered; or

(iv)   with respect to tender of settlement by a funds transfer, when payment is made pursuant to Section 4A–406(a) to the person receiving settlement.

(b) If the tender of settlement is not by a medium authorized by subsection (a) or the time of settlement is not fixed by subsection (a), no settlement occurs until the tender of settlement is accepted by the person receiving settlement.

(c) If settlement for an item is made by cashier's check or teller's check and the person receiving settlement, before its midnight deadline:

(1)   presents or forwards the check for collection, settlement is final when the check is finally paid; or

(2)   fails to present or forward the check for collection, settlement is final at the midnight deadline of the person receiving settlement.

(d) If settlement for an item is made by giving authority to charge the account of the bank giving settlement in the bank receiving settlement, settlement is final when the charge is made by the bank receiving settlement if there are funds available in the account for the amount of the item.
As amended in 1990.

§ 4–214.   Right of Charge-Back or Refund; Liability of Collecting Bank: Return of Item

(a) If a collecting bank has made provisional settlement with its customer for an item and fails by reason of dishonor, suspension of payments by a bank, or otherwise to receive settlement for the item which is or becomes final, the bank may revoke the settlement given by it, charge back the amount of any credit given for the item to its customer's account, or obtain refund from its customer, whether or not it is able to return the item, if by its midnight deadline or within a longer reasonable time after it learns the facts it returns the item or sends notification of the facts. If the return or notice is delayed beyond the bank's midnight deadline or a longer reasonable time after it learns the facts, the bank may revoke the settlement, charge back the credit, or obtain refund from its customer, but it is liable for any loss resulting from the delay. These rights to revoke, charge back, and obtain refund terminate if and when a settlement for the item received by the bank is or becomes final.

(b) A collecting bank returns an item when it is sent or delivered to the bank's customer or transferor or pursuant to its instructions.

(c) A depositary bank that is also the payor may charge back the amount of an item to its customer's account or obtain refund in accordance with the section governing return of an item received by a payor bank for credit on its books (Section 4–301).

(d) The right to charge back is not affected by:

(1)   previous use of a credit given for the item; or

(2)   failure by any bank to exercise ordinary care with respect to the item, but a bank so failing remains liable.

(e) A failure to charge back or claim refund does not affect other rights of the bank against the customer or any other party.

(f) If credit is given in dollars as the equivalent of the value of an item payable in foreign money, the dollar amount of any charge-back or refund must be calculated on the basis of the bank-offered spot rate for the foreign money prevailing on the day when the person entitled to the charge-back or refund learns that it will not receive payment in ordinary course.
As amended in 1990.

§ 4–215.   Final Payment of Item by Payor Bank; When Provisional Debits and Credits Become Final; When Certain Credits Become Available for Withdrawal

(a) An item is finally paid by a payor bank when the bank has first done any of the following:

(1)   paid the item in cash;

(2)   settled for the item without having a right to revoke the settlement under statute, clearing-house rule, or agreement; or

(3)   made a provisional settlement for the item and failed to revoke the settlement in the time and manner permitted by statute, clearing-house rule, or agreement.

(b) If provisional settlement for an item does not become final, the item is not finally paid.

(c) If provisional settlement for an item between the presenting and payor banks is made through a clearing house or by debits or credits in an account between them, then to the extent that provisional debits or credits for the item are entered in accounts between the presenting and payor banks or between the presenting and successive prior collecting banks seriatim, they become final upon final payment of the item by the payor bank.

(d) If a collecting bank receives a settlement for an item which is or becomes final, the bank is accountable to its customer for the amount of the item and any provisional credit given for the item in an account with its customer becomes final.

(e) Subject to (i) applicable law stating a time for availability of funds and (ii) any right of the bank to apply the credit to an obligation of the customer, credit given by a bank for an item in a customer's account becomes available for withdrawal as of right:

(1) if the bank has received a provisional settlement for the item, when the settlement becomes final and the bank has had a reasonable time to receive return of the item and the item has not been received within that time;

(2) if the bank is both the depositary bank and the payor bank, and the item is finally paid, at the opening of the bank's second banking day following receipt of the item.

(f) Subject to applicable law stating a time for availability of funds and any right of a bank to apply a deposit to an obligation of the depositor, a deposit of money becomes available for withdrawal as of right at the opening of the bank's next banking day after receipt of the deposit. As amended in 1990.

§ 4–216.   *Insolvency and Preferences*

(a) If an item is in or comes into the possession of a payor or collecting bank that suspends payment and the item has not been finally paid, the item must be returned by the receiver, trustee, or agent in charge of the closed bank to the presenting bank or the closed bank's customer.

(b) If a payor bank finally pays an item and suspends payments without making a settlement for the item with its customer or the presenting bank which settlement is or becomes final, the owner of the item has a preferred claim against the payor bank.

(c) If a payor bank gives or a collecting bank gives or receives a provisional settlement for an item and thereafter suspends payments, the suspension does not prevent or interfere with the settlement's becoming final if the finality occurs automatically upon the lapse of certain time or the happening of certain events.

(d) If a collecting bank receives from subsequent parties settlement for an item, which settlement is or becomes final and the bank suspends payments without making a settlement for the item with its customer which settlement is or becomes final, the owner of the item has a preferred

claim against the collecting bank. As amended in 1990.

Part 3   Collection of Items: Payor Banks

§ 4–301.   *Deferred Posting; Recovery of Payment by Return of Items; Time of Dishonor; Return of Items by Payor Bank*

(a) If a payor bank settles for a demand item other than a documentary draft presented otherwise than for immediate payment over the counter before midnight of the banking day of receipt, the payor bank may revoke the settlement and recover the settlement if, before it has made final payment and before its midnight deadline, it

(1) returns the item; or

(2) sends written notice of dishonor or nonpayment if the item is unavailable for return.

(b) If a demand item is received by a payor bank for credit on its books, it may return the item or send notice of dishonor and may revoke any credit given or recover the amount thereof withdrawn by its customer, if it acts within the time limit and in the manner specified in subsection (a).

(c) Unless previous notice of dishonor has been sent, an item is dishonored at the time when for purposes of dishonor it is returned or notice sent in accordance with this section.

(d) An item is returned:

(1) as to an item presented through a clearing house, when it is delivered to the presenting or last collecting bank or to the clearing house or is sent or delivered in accordance with clearing-house rules; or

(2) in all other cases, when it is sent or delivered to the bank's customer or transferor or pursuant to instructions.

As amended in 1990.

§ 4–302.   *Payor Bank's Responsibility for Late Return of Item*

(a) If an item is presented to and received by a payor bank, the bank is accountable for the amount of:

(1) a demand item, other than a documentary draft, whether properly payable or not, if the bank, in any case in which it is not also the depositary bank, retains the item beyond midnight of the banking day of receipt without settling for it or, whether or not it is also the depositary bank, does not pay or return the item or send notice of dishonor until after its midnight deadline; or

(2) any other properly payable item unless, within the time allowed for acceptance or payment of that item, the bank either accepts or pays the item or returns it and accompanying documents.

(b) The liability of a payor bank to pay an item pursuant to subsection (a) is subject to defenses based on breach of a presentment warranty (Section 4–208) or proof that the person seeking enforcement of the liability presented or transferred the item for the purpose of defrauding the payor bank.

As amended in 1990.

§ 4–303.   When Items Subject to Notice, Stop-Payment Order, Legal Process, or Setoff; Order in Which Items May Be Charged or Certified

(a) Any knowledge, notice, or stop-payment order received by, legal process served upon, or setoff exercised by a payor bank comes too late to terminate, suspend, or modify the bank's right or duty to pay an item or to charge its customer's account for the item if the knowledge, notice, stop-payment order, or legal process is received or served and a reasonable time for the bank to act thereon expires or the setoff is exercised after the earliest of the following:

(1)   the bank accepts or certifies the item;

(2)   the bank pays the item in cash;

(3)   the bank settles for the item without having a right to revoke the settlement under statute, clearinghouse rule, or agreement;

(4)   the bank becomes accountable for the amount of the item under Section 4–302 dealing with the payor bank's responsibility for late return of items; or

(5)   with respect to checks, a cutoff hour no earlier than one hour after the opening of the next banking day after the banking day on which the bank received the check and no later than the close of that next banking day or, if no cutoff hour is fixed, the close of the next banking day after the banking day on which the bank received the check.

(b) Subject to subsection (a), items may be accepted, paid, certified, or charged to the indicated account of its customer in any order.

As amended in 1990.

Part 4   Relationship Between Payor Bank and Its Customer

§ 4–401.   When Bank May Charge Customer's Account

(a) A bank may charge against the account of a customer an item that is properly payable from the account even though the charge creates an overdraft. An item is properly payable if it is authorized by the customer and is in accordance with any agreement between the customer and bank.

(b) A customer is not liable for the amount of an overdraft if the customer neither signed the item nor benefited from the proceeds of the item.

(c) A bank may charge against the account of a customer a check that is otherwise properly payable from the account, even though payment was made before the date of the check, unless the customer has given notice to the bank of the postdating describing the check with reasonable certainty. The notice is effective for the period stated in Section 4–403(b) for stop-payment orders, and must be received at such time and in such manner as to afford the bank a reasonable opportunity to act on it before the bank takes any action with respect to the check described in Section 4–303. If a bank charges against the account of a customer a check before the date stated in the notice of postdating, the bank is liable for damages for the loss resulting from its act. The loss may include damages for dishonor of subsequent items under Section 4–402.

(d) A bank that in good faith makes payment to a holder may charge the indicated account of its customer according to:

(1)   the original terms of the altered item; or

(2)   the terms of the completed item, even though the bank knows the item has been completed unless the bank has notice that the completion was improper.

As amended in 1990.

§ 4–402.   Bank's Liability to Customer for Wrongful Dishonor; Time of Determining Insufficiency of Account

(a) Except as otherwise provided in this Article, a payor bank wrongfully dishonors an item if it dishonors an item that is properly payable, but a bank may dishonor an item that would create an overdraft unless it has agreed to pay the overdraft.

(b) A payor bank is liable to its customer for damages proximately caused by the wrongful dishonor of an item. Liability is limited to actual damages proved and may include damages for an arrest or prosecution of the customer or other consequential damages. Whether any consequential damages are proximately caused by the wrongful dishonor is a question of fact to be determined in each case.

(c) A payor bank's determination of the customer's account balance on which a decision to dishonor for insufficiency of available funds is based may be made at any time between the time the item is received by the payor bank and the time that the payor bank returns the item or gives notice in lieu of return, and no more than one determination need be made. If, at the election of the payor bank, a subsequent balance determination is made for the purpose of reevaluating the bank's decision to dishonor the item, the account balance at that time is determinative of whether a dishonor for insufficiency of available funds is wrongful.

As amended in 1990.

§ 4–403.   Customer's Right to Stop Payment; Burden of Proof of Loss

(a) A customer or any person authorized to draw on the account if there is more than one person may stop payment of any item drawn on the customer's account or close the account by an order to the bank describing the item or account with reasonable certainty received at a time and in a manner that affords the bank a reasonable opportunity to act on it before any action by the bank with respect to the item described in Section 4–303. If the signature of more than one person is required to draw on an account, any of these persons may stop payment or close the account.

(b) A stop-payment order is effective for six months, but it lapses after 14 calendar days if the original order was oral and was not confirmed in writing within that period. A stop-payment order may be renewed for additional six-month periods by a writing given to the bank within a period during which the stop-payment order is effective.

(c) The burden of establishing the fact and amount of loss resulting from the payment of an item contrary to a stop-payment order or order to close an account is on the customer. The loss from payment of an item contrary to a stop-payment order may include damages for dishonor of subsequent items under Section 4–402.
As amended in 1990.

§ 4–404. Bank Not Obliged to Pay Check More Than Six Months Old

A bank is under no obligation to a customer having a checking account to pay a check, other than a certified check, which is presented more than six months after its date, but it may charge its customer's account for a payment made thereafter in good faith.

§ 4–405. Death or Incompetence of Customer

(a) A payor or collecting bank's authority to accept, pay, or collect an item or to account for proceeds of its collection, if otherwise effective, is not rendered ineffective by incompetence of a customer of either bank existing at the time the item is issued or its collection is undertaken if the bank does not know of an adjudication of incompetence. Neither death nor incompetence of a customer revokes the authority to accept, pay, collect, or account until the bank knows of the fact of death or of an adjudication of incompetence and has reasonable opportunity to act on it.

(b) Even with knowledge, a bank may for 10 days after the date of death pay or certify checks drawn on or before that date unless ordered to stop payment by a person claiming an interest in the account.
As amended in 1990.

§ 4–406. Customer's Duty to Discover and Report Unauthorized Signature or Alteration

(a) A bank that sends or makes available to a customer a statement of account showing payment of items for the account shall either return or make available to the customer the items paid or provide information in the statement of account sufficient to allow the customer reasonably to identify the items paid. The statement of account provides sufficient information if the item is described by item number, amount, and date of payment.

(b) If the items are not returned to the customer, the person retaining the items shall either retain the items or, if the items are destroyed, maintain the capacity to furnish legible copies of the items until the expiration of seven years after receipt of the items. A customer may request an item from the bank that paid the item, and that bank must provide in a reasonable time either the item or, if the item has been destroyed or is not otherwise obtainable, a legible copy of the item.

(c) If a bank sends or makes available a statement of account or items pursuant to subsection (a), the customer must exercise reasonable promptness in examining the statement or the items to determine whether any payment was not authorized because of an alternation of an item or because a purported signature by or on behalf of the customer was not authorized. If, based on the statement or items provided, the customer should reasonably have discovered the unauthorized payment, the customer must promptly notify the bank of the relevant facts.

(d) If the bank proves that the customer failed, with respect to an item, to comply with the duties imposed on the customer by subsection (c), the customer is precluded from asserting against the bank:

(1) the customer's unauthorized signature or any alteration on the item, if the bank also proves that it suffered a loss by reason of the failure; and

(2) the customer's unauthorized signature or alteration by the same wrongdoer on any other item paid in good faith by the bank if the payment was made before the bank received notice from the customer of the unauthorized signature or alteration and after the customer had been afforded a reasonable period of time, not exceeding 30 days, in which to examine the item or statement of account and notify the bank.

(e) If subsection (d) applies and the customer proves that the bank failed to exercise ordinary care in paying the item and that the failure substantially contributed to loss, the loss is allocated between the customer precluded and the bank asserting the preclusion according to the extent to which the failure of the customer to comply with subsection (c) and the failure of the bank to exercise ordinary care contributed to the loss. If the customer proves that the bank did not pay the item in good faith, the preclusion under subsection (d) does not apply.

(f) Without regard to care or lack of care of either the customer or the bank, a customer who does not within one year after the statement or items are made available to the customer (subsection (a)) discover and report the customer's unauthorized signature on or any alteration on the item is precluded from asserting against the bank the unauthorized signature or alteration. If there is a preclusion under this subsection, the payor bank may not recover for

breach or warranty under Section 4–208 with respect to the unauthorized signature or alteration to which the preclusion applies.
As amended in 1990.

§ 4–407. Payor Bank's Right to Subrogation on Improper Payment

If a payor bank has paid an item over the order of the drawer or maker to stop payment, or after an account has been closed, or otherwise under circumstances giving a basis for objection by the drawer or maker, to prevent unjust enrichment and only to the extent necessary to prevent loss to the bank by reason of its payment of the item, the payor bank is subrogated to the rights

 (1) of any holder in due course on the item against the drawer or maker;

 (2) of the payee or any other holder of the item against the drawer or maker either on the item or under the transaction out of which the item arose; and

 (3) of the drawer or maker against the payee or any other holder of the item with respect to the transaction out of which the item arose.

As amended in 1990.

Part 5 Collection of Documentary Drafts

§ 4–501. Handling of Documentary Drafts; Duty to Send for Presentment and to Notify Customer of Dishonor

A bank that takes a documentary draft for collection shall present or send the draft and accompanying documents for presentment and, upon learning that the draft has not been paid or accepted in due course, shall seasonably notify its customer of the fact even though it may have discounted or bought the draft or extended credit available for withdrawal as of right.
As amended in 1990.

§ 4–502. Presentment of ''On Arrival'' Drafts

If a draft or the relevant instructions require presentment ''on arrival'', ''when goods arrive'' or the like, the collecting bank need not present until in its judgment a reasonable time for arrival of the goods has expired. Refusal to pay or accept because the goods have not arrived is not dishonor; the bank must notify its transferor of the refusal but need not present the draft again until it is instructed to do so or learns of the arrival of the goods.
As amended in 1990.

§ 4–503. Responsibility of Presenting Bank for Documents and Goods; Report of Reasons for Dishonor; Referee in Case of Need

Unless otherwise instructed and except as provided in Article 5, a bank presenting a documentary draft:

 (1) must deliver the documents to the drawee on acceptance of the draft if it is payable more than three days after presentment; otherwise, only on payment; and

 (2) upon dishonor, either in the case of presentment for acceptance or presentment for payment, may seek and follow instructions from any referee in case of need designated in the draft or, if the presenting bank does not choose to utilize the referee's services, it must use diligence and good faith to ascertain the reason for dishonor, must notify its transferor of the dishonor and of the results of its effort to ascertain the reasons therefor, and must request instructions.

However the presenting bank is under no obligation with respect to goods represented by the documents except to follow any reasonable instructions seasonably received; it has a right to reimbursement for any expense incurred in following instructions and to prepayment of or indemnity for those expenses.
As amended in 1990.

§ 4–504. Privilege of Presenting Bank to Deal With Goods; Security Interest for Expenses

(a) A presenting bank that, following the dishonor of a documentary draft, has seasonably requested instructions but does not receive them within a reasonable time may store, sell, or otherwise deal with the goods in any reasonable manner.

(b) For its reasonable expenses incurred by action under subsection (a) the presenting bank has a lien upon the goods or their proceeds, which may be foreclosed in the same manner as an unpaid seller's lien.
As amended in 1990.

ARTICLE 5 LETTERS OF CREDIT

§ 5–101. Short Title

This Article shall be known and may be cited as Uniform Commercial Code—Letters of Credit.

§ 5–102. Scope

(1) This Article applies

 (a) to a credit issued by a bank if the credit requires a documentary draft or a documentary demand for payment; and

 (b) to a credit issued by a person other than a bank if the credit requires that the draft or demand for payment be accompanied by a document of title; and

 (c) to a credit issued by a bank or other person if the credit is not within subparagraphs (a) or (b) but conspicuously states that it is a letter of credit or is conspicuously so entitled.

(2) Unless the engagement meets the requirements of subsection (1), this Article does not apply to engagements to

make advances or to honor drafts or demands for payment, to authorities to pay or purchase, to guarantees or to general agreements.

(3) This Article deals with some but not all of the rules and concepts of letters of credit as such rules or concepts have developed prior to this act or may hereafter develop. The fact that this Article states a rule does not by itself require, imply or negate application of the same or a converse rule to a situation not provided for or to a person not specified by this Article.

§ 5–103.   *Definitions*

(1) In this Article unless the context otherwise requires

(a) ''Credit'' or ''letter of credit'' means an engagement by a bank or other person made at the request of a customer and of a kind within the scope of this Article (Section 5–102) that the issuer will honor drafts or other demands for payment upon compliance with the conditions specified in the credit. A credit may be either revocable or irrevocable. The engagement may be either an agreement to honor or a statement that the bank or other person is authorized to honor.

(b) A ''documentary draft'' or a ''documentary demand for payment'' is one honor of which is conditioned upon the presentation of a document or documents. ''Document'' means any paper including document of title, security, invoice, certificate, notice of default and the like.

(c) An ''issuer'' is a bank or other person issuing a credit.

(d) A ''beneficiary'' of a credit is a person who is entitled under its terms to draw or demand payment.

(e) An ''advising bank'' is a bank which gives notification of the issuance of a credit by another bank.

(f) A ''confirming bank'' is a bank which engages either that it will itself honor a credit already issued by another bank or that such a credit will be honored by the issuer or a third bank.

(g) A ''customer'' is a buyer or other person who causes an issuer to issue a credit. The term also includes a bank which procures issuance or confirmation on behalf of that bank's customer.

(2) Other definitions applying to this Article and the sections in which they appear are:

''Notation of Credit.'' Section 5–108.

''Presenter.'' Section 5–112(3).

(3) Definitions in other Articles applying to this Article and the sections in which they appear are:

''Accept'' or ''Acceptance.'' Section 3–410.

''Contract for sale.'' Section 2–106.

''Draft.'' Section 3–104.

''Holder in due course.'' Section 3–302.

''Midnight deadline.'' Section 4–104.

''Security.'' Section 8–102.

(4) In addition, Article 1 contains general definitions and principles of construction and interpretation applicable throughout this Article.

§ 5–104.   *Formal Requirements; Signing*

(1) Except as otherwise required in subsection (1)(c) of Section 5–102 on scope, no particular form of phrasing is required for a credit. A credit must be in writing and signed by the issuer and a confirmation must be in writing and signed by the confirming bank. A modification of the terms of a credit or confirmation must be signed by the issuer or confirming bank.

(2) A telegram may be a sufficient signed writing if it identifies its sender by an authorized authentication. The authentication may be in code and the authorized naming of the issuer in an advance of credit is a sufficient signing.

§ 5–105.   *Consideration*

No consideration is necessary to establish a credit or to enlarge or otherwise modify its terms.

§ 5–106.   *Time and Effect of Establishment of Credit*

(1) Unless otherwise agreed a credit is established

(a) as regards the customer as soon as a letter of credit is sent to him or the letter of credit or an authorized written advice of its issuance is sent to the beneficiary: and

(b) as regards the beneficiary when he receives a letter of credit or an authorized written advice of its issuance.

(2) Unless otherwise agreed once an irrevocable credit is established as regards the customer it can be modified or revoked only with the consent of the customer and once it is established as regards the beneficiary it can be modified or revoked only with his consent.

(3) Unless otherwise agreed after a revocable credit is established it may be modified or revoked by the issuer without notice to or consent from the customer or beneficiary.

(4) Notwithstanding any modification or revocation of a revocable credit any person authorized to honor or negotiate under the terms of the original credit is entitled to reimbursement for or honor of any draft or demand for payment duly honored or negotiated before receipt of notice of the modification or revocation and the issuer in turn is entitled to reimbursement from its customer.

§ 5–107.   *Advice of Credit; Confirmation; Error in Statement of Terms*

(1) Unless otherwise specified an advising bank by advising a credit issued by another bank does not assume any obligation to honor drafts drawn or demands for payment made under the credit but it does assume obligation for the accuracy of its own statement.

(2) A confirming bank by confirming a credit becomes directly obligated on the credit to the extent of its confirmation as though it were its issuer and acquires the rights of an issuer.

(3) Even though an advising bank incorrectly advises the terms of a credit it has been authorized to advise the credit is established as against the issuer to the extent of its original terms.

(4) Unless otherwise specified the customer bears as against the issuer all risks of transmissions and reasonable translation or interpretation of any message relating to a credit.

§ 5–108.   ''Notation Credit''; Exhaustion of Credit

(1) A credit which specifies that any person purchasing or paying drafts drawn or demands for payment made under it must note the amount of the draft or demand on the letter or advice of credit is a ''notation credit.''

(2) Under a notation credit

(a) a person paying the beneficiary or purchasing a draft or demand for payment from him acquires a right to honor only if the appropriate notation is made and by transferring or forwarding for honor the documents under the credit such a person warrants to the issuer that the notation has been made; and

(b) unless the credit or a signed statement that an appropriate notation has been made accompanies the draft or demand for payment the issuer may delay honor until evidence of notation has been procured which is satisfactory to it but its obligation and that of its customer continue for a reasonable time not exceeding thirty days to obtain such evidence.

(3) If the credit is not a notation credit

(a) the issuer may honor complying drafts or demands for payment presented to it in the order in which they are presented and is discharged pro tanto by honor of any such draft or demand;

(b) as between competing good faith purchasers of complying drafts or demands the person first purchasing has priority over a subsequent purchaser even though the later purchased draft or demand has been first honored.

§ 5–109.   Issuer's Obligation to Its Customer

(1) An issuer's obligation to its customer includes good faith and observance of any general banking usage but unless otherwise agreed does not include liability or responsibility

(a) for performance of the underlying contract for sale or other transaction between the customer and the beneficiary; or

(b) for any act or omission of any person other than itself or its own branch or for loss or destruction of a draft, demand or document in transit or in the possession of others; or

(c) based on knowledge or lack of knowledge of any usage of any particular trade.

(2) An issuer must examine documents with care so as to ascertain that on their face they appear to comply with the terms of the credit but unless otherwise agreed assumes no liability or responsibility for the genuineness, falsification or effect of any document which appears on such examination to be regular on its face.

(3) A non-bank issuer is not bound by any banking usage of which it has no knowledge.

§ 5–110.   Availability of Credit in Portions; Presenter's Reservation of Lien or Claim

(1) Unless otherwise specified a credit may be used in portions in the discretion of the beneficiary.

(2) Unless otherwise specified a person by presenting a documentary draft or demand for payment under a credit relinquishes upon its honor all claims to the documents and a person by transferring such draft or demand or causing such presentment authorizes such relinquishment. An explicit reservation of claim makes the draft or demand noncomplying.

§ 5–111.   Warranties on Transfer and Presentment

(1) Unless otherwise agreed the beneficiary by transferring or presenting a documentary draft or demand for payment warrants to all interested parties that the necessary conditions of the credit have been complied with. This is in addition to any warranties arising under Articles 3, 4, 7 and 8.

(2) Unless otherwise agreed a negotiating, advising, confirming, collecting or issuing bank presenting or transferring a draft or demand for payment under a credit warrants only the matters warranted by a collecting bank under Article 4 and any such bank transferring a document warrants only the matters warranted by an intermediary under Articles 7 and 8.

§ 5–112.   Time Allowed for Honor or Rejection; Withholding Honor or Rejection by Consent; ''Presenter''

(1) A bank to which a documentary draft or demand for payment is presented under a credit may without dishonor of the draft, demand or credit

(a) defer honor until the close of the third banking day following receipt of the documents; and

(b) further defer honor if the presenter has expressly or impliedly consented thereto. Failure to honor within the time here specified constitutes dishonor of the draft or demand and of the credit [except as otherwise provided in subsection (4) of Section 5–114 on conditional payment].

Note: The bracketed language in the last sentence of subsection (1) should be included only if the optional provisions of Section 5–114(4) and (5) are included.

(2) Upon dishonor the bank may unless otherwise instructed fulfill its duty to return the draft or demand and the documents by holding them at the disposal of the presenter and sending him an advice to that effect.

(3) ''Presenter'' means any person presenting a draft or demand for payment for honor under a credit even though that person is a confirming bank or other correspondent which is acting under an issuer's authorization.

§ 5–113.   Indemnities

(1) A bank seeking to obtain (whether for itself or another) honor, negotiation or reimbursement under a credit may give an indemnity to induce such honor, negotiation or reimbursement.

(2) An indemnity agreement inducing honor, negotiation or reimbursement

(a) unless otherwise explicitly agreed applies to defects in the documents but not in the goods; and

(b) unless a longer time is explicitly agreed expires at the end of ten business days following receipt of the documents by the ultimate customer unless notice of objection is sent before such expiration date. The ultimate customer may send notice of objection to the person from whom he received the documents and any bank receiving such notice is under a duty to send notice to its transferor before its midnight deadline.

§ 5–114.   Issuer's Duty and Privilege to Honor; Right to Reimbursement

(1) An issuer must honor a draft or demand for payment which complies with the terms of the relevant credit regardless of whether the goods or documents conform to the underlying contract for sale or other contract between the customer and the beneficiary. The issuer is not excused from honor of such a draft or demand by reason of an additional general term that all documents must be satisfactory to the issuer, but an issuer may require that specified documents must be satisfactory to it.

(2) Unless otherwise agreed when documents appear on their face to comply with the terms of a credit but a required document does not in fact conform to the warranties made on negotiations or transfer of a document of title (Section 7–507) or of a certified security (Section 8–306) or is forged or fraudulent or there is fraud in the transaction:

(a) the issuer must honor the draft or demand for payment if honor is demanded by a negotiating bank or other holder of the draft or demand which has taken the draft or demand under the credit and under circumstances which would make it a holder in due course (Section 3–302) and in an appropriate case would make it a person to whom a document of title has been duly negotiated (Section 7–502) or a bona fide purchaser of a certificated security (Section 8–302); and

(b) in all other cases as against its customer, an issuer acting in good faith may honor the draft or demand for payment despite notification from the customer of fraud, forgery or other defect not apparent on the face of the document but a court of appropriate jurisdiction may enjoin such honor.

(3) Unless otherwise agreed an issuer which has duly honored a draft or demand for payment is entitled to immediate reimbursement of any payment made under the credit and to be put in effectively available funds not later than the day before maturity of any acceptance made under the credit.

[(4) When a credit provides for payment by the issuer on receipt of notice that the required documents are in the possession of a correspondent or other agent of the issuer

(a) any payment made on receipt of such notice is conditional; and

(b) the issuer may reject documents which do not comply with the credit if it does so within three banking days following its receipt of the documents; and

(c) in the event of such rejection, the issuer is entitled by charge back or otherwise to return of the payment made.]

[(5) In the case covered by subsection (4) failure to reject documents within the time specified in subparagraph (b) constitutes acceptance of the documents and makes the payment final in favor of the beneficiary.]

Note: Subsections (4) and (5) are bracketed as optional. If they are included the bracketed language in that last sentence of Section 5–112(1) should also be included.

§ 5–115.   Remedy for Improper Dishonor or Anticipatory Repudiation

(1) When an issuer wrongfully dishonors a draft or demand for payment presented under a credit the person entitled to honor has with respect to any documents the rights of a person in the position of a seller (Section 2–707) and may recover from the issuer the face amount of the draft or demand together with incidental damages under Section 7–710 on seller's incidental damages and interest but less any amount realized by resale or other use or disposition of the subject matter of the transaction. In the event no resale or other utilization is made the documents, goods or other subject matter involved in the transaction must be turned over to the issuer on payment of judgment.

(2) When an issuer wrongfully cancels or otherwise repudiates a credit before presentment of a draft or demands for payment drawn under it the beneficiary has the rights of a seller after anticipatory repudiation by the buyer under Section 2–610 if he learns of the repudiation in time reasonably to avoid procurement of the required documents. Otherwise the beneficiary has an immediate right of action for wrongful dishonor.

§ 5–116.   Transfer and Assignment

(1) The right to draw under a credit can be transferred or assigned only when the credit is expressly designated as transferable or assignable.

(2) Even though the credit specifically states that it is nontransferable or nonassignable the beneficiary may before performance of the conditions of the credit assign his right to proceeds. Such an assignment is an assignment of an account under Article 9 on Secured Transactions and is governed by that Article except that

(a) the assignment is ineffective until the letter of credit or advice of credit is delivered to the assignee which delivery constitutes perfection of the security interest under Article 9; and

(b) the issuer may honor drafts or demands for payment drawn under the credit until it receives a notification of the assignment signed by the beneficiary which reasonably identifies the credit involved in the assignment and contains a request to pay the assignee; and

(c) after what reasonably appears to be such a notification has been received the issuer may without dishonor refuse to accept or pay even to a person otherwise entitled to honor until the letter of credit or advice of credit is exhibited to the issuer.

(3) Except where the beneficiary has effectively assigned his right to draw or his right to proceeds, nothing in this section limits his right to transfer or negotiate drafts or demands drawn under the credit.

§ 5–117.   Insolvency of Bank Holding Funds for Documentary Credit

(1) Where an issuer or an advising or confirming bank or a bank which has for a customer procured issuance of a credit by another bank becomes insolvent before final payment under the credit and the credit is one to which this Article is made applicable by paragraphs (a) or (b) of Section 5–102(1) on scope, the receipt or allocation of funds or collateral to secure or meet obligations under the credit shall have the following results;

(a) to the extent of any funds or collateral turned over after or before the insolvency as indemnity against or specifically for the purpose of payment of drafts or demands for payment drawn under the designated credit, the drafts or demands are entitled to payment in preference over depositors or other general creditors of the issuer or bank; and

(b) on expiration of the credit or surrender of the beneficiary's rights under it unused any person who has given such funds or collateral is similarly entitled to return thereof; and

(c) a charge to a general or current account with a bank if specifically consented to for the purpose of indemnity against or payment of drafts or demands for payment drawn under the designated credit falls under the same rules as if the funds had been drawn out in cash and then turned over with specific instructions.

(2) After honor or reimbursement under this section the customer or other person for whose account the insolvent bank has acted is entitled to receive the documents involved.

ARTICLE 6   BULK TRANSFERS

§ 6–101.   Short Title

This Article shall be known and may be cited as Uniform Commercial Code—Bulk Sales.

§ 6–102.   Definitions and Index of Definitions

(1) In this Article, unless the context otherwise requires:

(a) "Assets" means the inventory that is the subject of a bulk sale and any tangible and intangible personal property used or held for use primarily in, or arising from, the seller's business and sold in connection with that inventory, but the term does not include:

(i) fixtures (Section 9–313(1)(a)) other than readily removable factory and office machines;

(ii) the lessee's interest in a lease of real property; or

(iii) property to the extent it is generally exempt from creditor process under nonbankruptcy law.

(b) "Auctioneer" means a person whom the seller engages to direct, conduct, control, or be responsible for a sale by auction.

(c) "Bulk sale" means:

(i) in the case of a sale by auction or a sale or series of sales conducted by a liquidator on the seller's behalf, a sale or series of sales not in the ordinary course of the seller's business of more than half of the seller's inventory, as measured by value on the date of the bulk-sale agreement, if on that date the auctioneer or liquidator has notice, or after reasonable inquiry would have had notice, that the seller will not continue to operate the same or a similar kind of business after the sale or series of sales; and

(ii) in all other cases, a sale not in the ordinary course of the seller's business of more than half the seller's inventory, as measured by value on the date of the bulk-sale agreement, if on that date the buyer has notice, or after reasonable inquiry would have had notice, that the seller will not continue to operate the same or a similar kind of business after the sale.

(d) "Claim" means a right to payment from the seller, whether or not the right is reduced to judgment, liquidated, fixed, matured, disputed, secured, legal, or equitable. The term includes costs of collection and attorney's fees only to the extent that the laws of this state permit the holder of the claim to recover them in an action against the obligor.

(e) "Claimant" means a person holding a claim incurred in the seller's business other than:

(i) an unsecured and unmatured claim for employment compensation and benefits, including commissions and vacation, severance, and sick-leave pay;

(ii) a claim for injury to an individual or to property, or for breach of warranty, unless:

(A) a right of action for the claim has accrued;

(B) the claim has been asserted against the seller; and

(C) the seller knows the identity of the person asserting the claim and the basis upon which the person has asserted it; and

(States To Select One Alternative)

ALTERNATIVE A

[(iii) a claim for taxes owing to a governmental unit.]

ALTERNATIVE B

[(iii) a claim for taxes owing to a governmental unit, if:

(A)   a statute governing the enforcement of the claim permits or requires notice of the bulk sale to be given to the governmental unit in a manner other than by compliance with the requirements of this Article; and

(B)   notice is given in accordance with the statute.]

(f) ''Creditor'' means a claimant or other person holding a claim.

(g) (i) ''Date of the bulk sale'' means:

(A)   if the sale is by auction or is conducted by a liquidator on the seller's behalf, the date on which more than ten percent of the net proceeds is paid to or for the benefit of the seller; and

(B)   in all other cases, the later of the date on which:
(I) more than ten percent of the net contract price is paid to or for the benefit of the seller; or
(II) more than ten percent of the assets, as measured by value, are transferred to the buyer.

(ii)   For purposes of this subsection:

(A)   Delivery of a negotiable instrument (Section 3-104(1)) to or for the benefit of the seller in exchange for assets constitutes payment of the contract price pro tanto;

(B)   To the extent that the contract price is deposited in an escrow, the contract price is paid to or for the benefit of the seller when the seller acquires the unconditional right to receive the deposit or when the deposit is delivered to the seller or for the benefit of the seller, whichever is earlier; and

(C)   An asset is transferred when a person holding an unsecured claim can no longer obtain through judicial proceedings rights to the asset that are superior to those of the buyer arising as a result of the bulk sale. A person holding an unsecured claim can obtain those superior rights to a tangible asset at least until the buyer has an unconditional right, under the bulk-sale agreement, to possess the asset, and a person holding an unsecured claim can obtain those superior rights to an intangible asset at least until the buyer has an unconditional right, under the bulk-sale agreement, to use the asset.

(h) ''Date of the bulk-sale agreement'' means:

(i)   in the case of a sale by auction or conducted by a liquidator (subsection (c)(i)), the date on which the seller engages the auctioneer or liquidator; and

(ii)   in all other cases, the date on which a bulk-sale agreement becomes enforceable between the buyer and the seller.

(i) ''Debt'' means liability on a claim.

(j) ''Liquidator'' means a person who is regularly engaged in the business of disposing of assets for businesses contemplating liquidation or dissolution.

(k) ''Net contract price'' means the new consideration the buyer is obligated to pay for the assets less:

(i)   the amount of any proceeds of the sale of an asset, to the extent the proceeds are applied in partial or total satisfaction of a debt secured by the asset; and

(ii)   the amount of any debt to the extent it is secured by a security interest or lien that is enforceable against the asset before and after it has been sold to a buyer. If a debt is secured by an asset and other property of the seller, the amount of the debt secured by a security interest or lien that is enforceable against the asset is determined by multiplying the debt by a fraction, the numerator of which is the value of the new consideration for the asset on the date of the bulk sale and the denominator of which is the value of all property securing the debt on the date of the bulk sale.

(l) ''Net proceeds'' means the new consideration received for assets sold at a sale by auction or a sale conducted by a liquidator on the seller's behalf less:

(i)   commissions and reasonable expenses of the sale;

(ii)   the amount of any proceeds of the sale of an asset, to the extent the proceeds are applied in partial or total satisfaction of a debt secured by the asset; and

(iii)   the amount of any debt to the extent it is secured by a security interest or lien that is enforceable against the asset before and after it has been sold to a buyer. If a debt is secured by an asset and other property of the seller, the amount of the debt secured by a security interest or lien that is enforceable against the asset is determined by multiplying the debt by a fraction, the numerator of which is the value of the new consideration for the asset on the date of the bulk sale and the denominator of which is the value of all property securing the debt on the date of the bulk sale.

(m) A sale is ''in the ordinary course of the seller's business'' if the sale comports with usual or customary practices in the kind of business in which the seller is engaged or with the seller's own usual or customary practices.

(n) ''United States'' includes its territories and possessions and the Commonwealth of Puerto Rico.

(o) ''Value'' means fair market value.

(p) ''Verified'' means signed and sworn to or affirmed.

(2) The following definitions in other Articles apply to this Article:

(a) ''Buyer.''	Section 2–103(1)(a).
(b) ''Equipment.''	Section 9–109(2).
(c) ''Inventory.''	Section 9–109(4).
(d) ''Sale.''	Section 2–106(1).
(e) ''Seller.''	Section 2–103(1)(d).

(3) In addition, Article 1 contains general definitions and principles of construction and interpretation applicable throughout this Article.

§ 6–103.   Applicability of Article

(1) Except as otherwise provided in subsection (3), this Article applies to a bulk sale if:

(a) the seller's principal business is the sale of inventory from stock; and

(b) on the date of the bulk-sale agreement the seller is located in this state or, if the seller is located in a jurisdiction that is not a part of the United Stated, the seller's major executive office in the United States is in this state.

(2) A seller is deemed to be located at his [or her] place of business. If a seller has more than one place of business, the seller is deemed located at his [or her] chief executive office.

(3) This Article does not apply to:

(a) a transfer made to secure payment or performance of an obligation;

(b) a transfer of collateral to a secured party pursuant to Section 9–503;

(c) a sale of collateral pursuant to Section 9–504;

(d) retention of collateral pursuant to Section 9–505;

(e) a sale of an asset encumbered by a security interest or lien if (i) all the proceeds of the sale are applied in partial or total satisfaction of the debt secured by the security interest or lien or (ii) the security interest or lien is enforceable against the asset after it has been sold to the buyer and the net contract price is zero;

(f) a general assignment for the benefit of creditors or to a subsequent transfer by the assignee;

(g) a sale by an executor, administrator, receiver, trustee in bankruptcy, or any public officer under judicial process;

(h) a sale made in the course of judicial or administrative proceedings for the dissolution or reorganization of an organization;

(i) a sale to a buyer whose principal place of business is in the United States and who:

   (i) not earlier than 21 days before the date of the bulk sale, (A) obtains from the seller a verified and dated list of claimants of whom the seller has notice three days before the seller sends or delivers the list to the buyer or (B) conducts a reasonable inquiry to discover the claimants;

   (ii) assumes in full the debts owed to claimants of whom the buyer has knowledge on the date the buyer receives the list of claimants from the seller or on the date the buyer completes the reasonable inquiry, as the case may be;

   (iii) is not insolvent after the assumption; and

   (iv) gives written notice of the assumption not later than 30 days after the date of the bulk sale by sending or delivering a notice to the claimants identified in subparagraph (ii) or by filing a notice in the office of the [Secretary of State];

(j) a sale to a buyer whose principal place of business is in the United States and who:

   (i) assumes in full the debts that were incurred in the seller's business before the date of the bulk sale;

   (ii) is not insolvent after the assumption; and

   (iii) gives written notice of the assumption not later than 30 days after the date of the bulk sale by sending or delivering a notice to each creditor whose debt is assumed or by filing a notice in the office of the [Secretary of State];

(k) a sale to a new organization that is organized to take over and continue the business of the seller and that has its principal place of business in the United States if:

   (i) the buyer assumes in full the debts that were incurred in the seller's business before the date of the bulk sale;

   (ii) the seller receives nothing from the sale except an interest in the new organization that is subordinate to the claims against the organization arising from the assumption; and

   (iii) the buyer gives written notice of the assumption not later than 30 days after the date of the bulk sale by sending or delivering a notice to each creditor whose debt is assumed or by filing a notice in the office of the [Secretary of State];

(l) a sale of assets having:

   (i) a value, net of liens and security interests, of less than $10,000. If a debt is secured by assets and other property of the seller, the new value of the assets is determined by subtracting from their value an amount equal to the product of the debt multiplied by a fraction, the numerator of which is the value of the assets on the date of the bulk sale and the denominator of which is the value of all property securing the debt on the date of the bulk sale; or

   (ii) a value of more then $25,000,000 on the date of the bulk-sale agreement; or

(m) a sale required by, and made pursuant to, statute.

(4) The notice under subsection (3)(i)(iv) must state: (i) that a sale that may constitute a bulk sale has been or will be made; (ii) the date or prospective date of the bulk sale; (iii) the individual, partnership, or corporate names and the addresses of the seller and buyer; (iv) the address to which inquiries about the sale may be made, if different from the seller's address; and (v) that the buyer assumed or will assume in full the debts owed to claimants of whom the buyer has knowledge on the date the buyer receives the list of claimants from the seller or completes a reasonable inquiry to discover the claimants.

(5) The notice under subsections (3)(j)(iii) and (3)(k)(iii) must state: (i) that a sale that may constitute a bulk sale has been or will be made; (ii) the date or prospective date of the bulk sale; (iii) the individual, partnership, or corporate names and the addresses of the seller and buyer; (iv) the address to which inquiries about the sale may be made, if different from the seller's address; and (v) that the buyer has assumed or will assume the debts that were incurred in the seller's business before the date of the bulk sale.

(6) For purposes of subsection (3)(l), the value of assets is presumed to be equal to the price the buyer agrees to pay for the assets. However, in a sale by auction or a sale conducted by a liquidator on the seller's behalf, the value of assets is presumed to be the amount the auctioneer or liquidator reasonably estimates the assets will bring at auction or upon liquidation.

§ 6–104.   Obligations of Buyer

(1) In a bulk sale as defined in Section 6–102(1)(c)(ii) the buyer shall:

(a) obtain from the seller a list of all business names and addresses used by the seller within three years before the date the list is sent or delivered to the buyer;

(b) unless excused under subsection (2), obtain from the seller a verified and dated list of claimants of whom the seller has notice three days before the seller sends or delivers the list to the buyer and including, to the extent known by the seller, the address of and the amount claimed by each claimant;

(c) obtain from the seller or prepare a schedule of distribution (Section 6–106(1));

(d) give notice of the bulk sale in accordance with Section 6-105;

(e) unless excused under Section 6–106(4), distribute the net contract price in accordance with the undertakings of the buyer in the schedule of distribution; and

(f) unless excused under subsection (2), make available the list of claimants (subsection (1)(b)) by:

(i) promptly sending or delivering a copy of the list without charge to any claimant whose written request is received by the buyer no later than six months after the date of the bulk sale;

(ii) permitting any claimant to inspect and copy the list at any reasonable hour upon request

received by the buyer no later than six months after the date of the bulk sale; or

(iii) filing a copy of the list in the office of the [Secretary of State] no later than the time for giving a notice of the bulk sale (Section 6–105(5)). A list filed in accordance with this subparagraph must state the individual, partnership, or corporate name and a mailing address of the seller.

(2) A buyer who gives notice in accordance with Section 6–105(2) is excused from complying with the requirements of subsections (1)(b) and (1)(f).

§ 6–105.   Notice to Claimants

(1) Except as otherwise provided in subsection (2), to comply with Section 6–104(1)(d), the buyer shall send or deliver a written notice of the bulk sale to each claimant on the list of claimants (Section 6–104(1)(b)) and to any other claimant of whom the buyer has knowledge at the time the notice of the bulk sale is sent or delivered.

(2) A buyer may comply with Section 6–104(1)(d) by filing a written notice of the bulk sale in the office of the [Secretary of State] if:

(a) on the date of the bulk-sale agreement the seller has 200 or more claimants, exclusive of claimants holding secured or matured claims for employment compensation and benefits, including commissions and vacation, severance, and sick-leave pay; or

(b) the buyer has received a verified statement from the seller stating that, as of the date of the bulk-sale agreement, the number of claimants, exclusive of claimants holding secured or matured claims for employment compensation and benefits, including commissions and vacation, severance, and sick-leave pay, is 200 or more.

(3) The written notice of the bulk sale must be accompanied by a copy of the schedule of distribution (Section 6–106(1)) and state at least:

(a) that the seller and buyer have entered into an agreement for a sale that may constitute a bulk sale under the laws of the State of _____ ;

(b) the date of the agreement;

(c) the date on or after which more than ten percent of the assets were or will be transferred;

(d) the date on or after which more than ten percent of the net contract price was or will be paid, if the date is not stated in the schedule of distribution;

(e) the name and a mailing address of the seller;

(f) any other business name and address listed by the seller pursuant to Section 6–104(1)(a);

(g) the name of the buyer and an address of the buyer from which information concerning the sale can be obtained;

(h) a statement indicating the type of assets or describing the assets item by item;

(i) the manner in which the buyer will make available the list of claimants (Section 6–104(1)(f)), if applicable; and

(j) if the sale is in total or partial satisfaction of an antecedent debt owed by the seller, the amount of the debt to be satisfied and the name of the person to whom it is owed.

(4) For purposes of subsections (3)(e) and (3)(g), the name of a person is the person's individual, partnership, or corporate name.

(5) The buyer shall give notice of the bulk sale not less than 45 days before the date of the bulk sale and, if the buyer gives notice in accordance with subsection (1), not more than 30 days after obtaining the list of claimants.

(6) A written notice substantially complying with the requirements of subsection (3) is effective even though it contains minor errors that are not seriously misleading.

(7) A form substantially as follows is sufficient to comply with subsection (3):

Notice of Sale

(1)_____ , whose address is _____ , is described in this notice as the "seller."

(2) _____ , whose address is _____ , is described in this notice as the "buyer."

(3) The seller has disclosed to the buyer that within the past three years the seller has used other business names, operated at other addresses, or both, as follows: _____ .

(4) The seller and the buyer have entered into an agreement dated _____ , for a sale that may constitute a bulk sale under the laws of the state of _____ .

(5) The date on or after which more than ten percent of the assets that are the subject of the sale were or will be transferred is _____ , and [if not stated in the schedule of distribution] the date on or after which more than ten percent of the net contract price was or will be paid is _____ .

(6) The following assets are the subject of the sale: _____ .

(7) [If applicable] The buyer will make available to claimants of the seller a list of the seller's claimants in the following manner: _____ .

(8) [If applicable] The sale is to satisfy $_____ of an antecedent debt owed by the seller to _____ .

(9) A copy of the schedule of distribution of the net contract price accompanies this notice.

§ 6–106.   Schedule of Distribution

(1) The seller and buyer shall agree on how the net contract price is to be distributed and set forth their agreement in a written schedule of distribution.

(2) The schedule of distribution may provide for distribution to any person at any time, including distribution of the entire net contract price to the seller.

(3) The buyer's undertakings in the schedule of distribution run only to the seller. However, a buyer who fails to distribute the net contract price in accordance with the buyer's undertakings in the schedule of distribution is liable to a creditor only as provided in Section 6–107(1).

(4) If the buyer undertakes in the schedule of distribution to distribute any part of the net contract price to a person other than the seller, and, after the buyer has given notice in accordance with Section 6–105, some or all of the anticipated net contract price is or becomes unavailable for distribution as a consequence of the buyer's or seller's having complied with an order of court, legal process, statute, or rule of law, the buyer is excused from any obligation arising under this Article or under any contract with the seller to distribute the net contract price in accordance with the buyer's undertakings in the schedule if the buyer:

(a) distributes the net contract price remaining available in accordance with any priorities for payment stated in the schedule of distribution and, to the extent that the price is insufficient to pay all the debts having a given priority, distributes the price pro rata among those debts shown in the schedule as having the same priority;

(b) distributes the net contract price remaining available in accordance with an order of court;

(c) commences a proceeding for interpleader in a court of competent jurisdiction and is discharged from the proceeding; or

(d) reaches a new agreement with the seller for the distribution of the net contract price remaining available, sets forth the new agreement in an amended schedule of distribution, gives notice of the amended schedule, and distributes the net contract price remaining available in accordance with the buyer's undertakings in the amended schedule.

(5) The notice under subsection (4)(d) must identify the buyer and the seller, state the filing number, if any, of the original notice, set forth the amended schedule, and be given in accordance with subsection (1) or (2) of Section 6–105, whichever is applicable, at least 14 days before the buyer distributes any part of the net contract price remaining available.

(6) If the seller undertakes in the schedule of distribution to distribute any part of the net contract price, and, after the buyer has given notice in accordance with Section 6–105, some or all of the anticipated net contract price is or becomes unavailable for distribution as a consequence of the buyer's or seller's having complied with an order of court, legal process, statute, or rule of law, the seller and any person in control of the seller are excused from any obligation arising under this Article or under any agreement with the buyer to distribute the net contract price in accordance with the seller's undertakings in the schedule if the seller:

(a) distributes the net contract price remaining available in accordance with any priorities for payment stated in the schedule of distribution and, to the extent that the price is insufficient to pay all the debts having a given priority, distributes the price pro rata among those debts shown in the schedule as having the same priority;

(b) distributes the net contract price remaining available in accordance with an order of court;

(c) commences a proceeding for interpleader in a court of competent jurisdiction and is discharged from the proceeding; or

(d) prepares a written amended schedule of distribution of the net contract price remaining available for distribution, gives notice of the amended schedule, and distributes the net contract price remaining available in accordance with the amended schedule.

(7) The notice under subsection (6)(d) must identify the buyer and the seller, state the filing number, if any, of the original notice, set forth the amended schedule, and be given in accordance with subsection (1) or (2) of Section 6–105, whichever is applicable, at least 14 days before the seller distributes any part of the net contract price remaining available.

§ 6–107.   Liability for Noncompliance

(1) Except as provided in subsection (3), and subject to the limitation in subsection (4):

(a) a buyer who fails to comply with the requirements of Section 6–104(1)(e) with respect to a creditor is liable to the creditor for damages in the amount of the claim, reduced by any amount that the creditor would not have realized if the buyer had complied; and

(b) a buyer who fails to comply with the requirements of any other subsection of Section 6–104 with respect to a claimant is liable to the claimant for damages in the amount of the claim, reduced by any amount that the claimant would not have realized if the buyer had complied.

(2) In an action under subsection (1), the creditor has the burden of establishing the validity and amount of the claim, and the buyer has the burden of establishing the amount that the creditor would not have realized if the buyer had complied.

(3) A buyer who:

(a) made a good faith and commercially reasonable effort to comply with the requirements of Section 6–104(1) or to exclude the sale from the application of this Article under Section 6–103(3); or

(b) on or after the date of the bulk-sale agreement, but before the date of the bulk sale, held a good faith and commercially reasonable belief that this Article does not apply to the particular sale is not liable to creditors for failure to comply with the requirements of Section 6–104. The buyer has the burden of establishing the good faith and commercial reasonableness of the effort or belief.

(4) In a single bulk sale the cumulative liability of the buyer for failure to comply with the requirements of Section 6–104(1) may not exceed an amount equal to:

(a) if the assets consist only of inventory and equipment, twice the net contract price, less the amount of any part of the net contract price paid to or applied for the benefit of the seller or a creditor; or

(b) if the assets include property other than inventory and equipment, twice the net value of the inventory and

equipment less the amount of the portion of any part of the net contract price paid to or applied for the benefit of the seller or a creditor which is allocable to the inventory and equipment.

(5) For the purposes of subsection (4)(b), the "net value" of an asset is the value of the asset less (i) the amount of any proceeds of the sale of an asset, to the extent the proceeds are applied in partial or total satisfaction of a debt secured by the asset and (ii) the amount of any debt to the extent it is secured by a security interest or lien that is enforceable against the asset before and after it has been sold to a buyer. If a debt is secured by an asset and other property of the seller, the amount of the debt secured by a security interest or lien that is enforceable against the asset is determined by multiplying the debt by a fraction, the numerator of which is the value of the asset on the date of the bulk sale and the denominator of which is the value of all property securing the debt on the date of the bulk sale. The portion of a part of the net contract price paid to or applied for the benefit of the seller or a creditor that is "allocable to the inventory and equipment" is the portion that bears the same ratio to that part of the net contract price as the net value of the inventory and equipment bears to the net value of all of the assets.

(6) A payment made by the buyer to a person to whom the buyer is, or believes he [or she] is, liable under subsection (1) reduces pro tanto the buyer's cumulative liability under subsection (4).

(7) No action may be brought under subsection (1)(b) by or on behalf of a claimant whose claim is unliquidated or contingent.

(8) A buyer's failure to comply with the requirements of Section 6–104(1) does not (i) impair the buyer's rights in or title to the assets, (ii) render the sale ineffective, void, or voidable, (iii) entitle a creditor to more than a single satisfaction of his [or her] claim, or (iv) create liability other than as provided in this Article.

(9) Payment of the buyer's liability under subsection (1) discharges pro tanto the seller's debt to the creditor.

(10) Unless otherwise agreed, a buyer has an immediate right of reimbursement from the seller for any amount paid to a creditor in partial or total satisfaction of the buyer's liability under subsection (1).

(11) If the seller is an organization, a person who is in direct or indirect control of the seller, and who knowingly, intentionally, and without legal justification fails, or causes the seller to fail, to distribute the net contract price in accordance with the schedule of distribution is liable to any creditor to whom the seller undertook to make payment under the schedule for damages caused by the failure.

§ 6–108.   Bulk Sales by Auction; Bulk Sales Conducted by Liquidator

(1) Sections 6–104, 6–105, 6–106, and 6–107 apply to a bulk sale by auction and a bulk sale conducted by a

liquidator on the seller's behalf with the following modifications:

(a) "buyer" refers to auctioneer or liquidator, as the case may be;

(b) "net contract price" refers to net proceeds of the auction or net proceeds of the sale, as the case may be;

(c) the written notice required under Section 6–105(3) must be accompanied by a copy of the schedule of distribution (Section 6–106(1)) and state at least:

    (i)   that the seller and the auctioneer or liquidator have entered into an agreement for auction or liquidation services that may constitute an agreement to make a bulk sale under the laws of the State of _____ ;

   (ii)   the date of the agreement;

  (iii)   the date on or after which the auction began or will begin or the date on or after which the liquidator began or will begin to sell assets on the seller's behalf;

  (iv)   the date on or after which more than ten percent of the net proceeds of the sale were or will be paid, if the date is not stated in the schedule of distribution;

   (v)   the name and a mailing address of the seller;

  (vi)   any other business name and address listed by the seller pursuant to Section 6–104(1)(a);

 (vii)   the name of the auctioneer or liquidator and an address of the auctioneer or liquidator from which information concerning the sale can be obtained;

(viii)   a statement indicating the type of assets or describing the assets item by item;

  (ix)   the manner in which the auctioneer or liquidator will make available the list of claimants (Section 6–104(1)(f)), if applicable; and

   (x)   if the sale is in total or partial satisfaction of an antecedent debt owed by the seller, the amount of the debt to be satisfied and the name of the person to whom it is owed; and

(d) in a single bulk sale the cumulative liability of the auctioneer or liquidator for failure to comply with the requirements of this section may not exceed the amount of the net proceeds of the sale allocable to inventory and equipment sold less the amount of the portion of any part of the net proceeds paid to or applied for the benefit of a creditor which is allocable to the inventory and equipment.

(2) A payment made by the auctioneer or liquidator to a person to whom the auctioneer or liquidator is, or believes he [or she] is, liable under this section reduces pro tanto the auctioneer's or liquidator's cumulative liability under subsection (1)(d).

(3) A form substantially as follows is sufficient to comply with subsection (1)(c):

Notice of Sale

(1) _____ , whose address is _____ , is described in this notice as the "seller."

(2) _____ , whose address is _____ , is described in this notice as the "auctioneer" or "liquidator."

(3) The seller has disclosed to the auctioneer or liquidator that within the past three years the seller has used other business names, operated at other addresses, or both, as follows: _____ .

(4) The seller and the auctioneer or liquidator have entered into an agreement dated _____ for auction or liquidation services that may constitute an agreement to make a bulk sale under the laws of the State of _____ .

(5) The date on or after which the auction began or will begin or the date on or after which the liquidator began or will begin to sell assets on the seller's behalf is _____ , and [if not stated in the schedule of distribution] the date on or after which more than ten percent of the net proceeds of the sale were or will be paid is _____ .

(6) The following assets are the subject of the sale: _____ .

(7) [If applicable] The auctioneer or liquidator will make available to claimants of the seller a list of the seller's claimants in the following manner: _____ .

(8) [If applicable] The sale is to satisfy $_____ of an antecedent debt owed by the seller to _____ .

(9) A copy of the schedule of distribution of the net proceeds accompanies this notice.

   [End of Notice]

(4) A person who buys at a bulk sale by auction or conducted by a liquidator need not comply with the requirements of Section 6–104(1) and is not liable for the failure of an auctioneer or liquidator to comply with the requirements of this section.

§ 6–109.   *What Constitutes Filing; Duties of Filing Officer; Information From Filing Officer*

(1) Presentation of a notice or list of claimants for filing and tender of the filing fee or acceptance of the notice or list by the filing officer constitutes filing under this Article.

(2) The filing officer shall:

   (a) mark each notice or list with a file number and with the date and hour of filing;

   (b) hold the notice or list or a copy for public inspection;

   (c) index the notice or list according to each name given for the seller and for the buyer; and

   (d) note in the index the file number and the addresses of the seller and buyer given in the notice or list.

(3) If the person filing a notice or list furnishes the filing officer with a copy, the filing officer upon request shall note upon the copy the file number and date and hour of the filing of the original and send or deliver the copy to the person.

(4) The fee for filing and indexing and for stamping a copy furnished by the person filing to show the date and place of filing is $_____ for the first page and $_____ for each additional page. The fee for indexing each name more than two is $_____.

(5) Upon request of any person, the filing officer shall issue a certificate showing whether any notice or list with respect to a particular seller or buyer is on file on the date and hour stated in the certificate. If a notice or list is on file, the certificate must give the date and hour of filing of each notice or list and the name and address of each seller, buyer, auctioneer, or liquidator. The fee for the certificate is $_____ if the request for the certificate is in the standard form prescribed by the [Secretary of State] and otherwise is $_____ . Upon request of any person, the filing officer shall furnish a copy of any filed notice or list for a fee of $_____.

(6) The filing officer shall keep each notice or list for two years after it is filed.

§ 6–110. *Limitation of Actions*

(1) Except as provided in subsection (2), an action under this Article against a buyer, auctioneer, or liquidator must be commenced within one year after the date of the bulk sale.

(2) If the buyer, auctioneer, or liquidator conceals the fact that the sale has occurred, the limitation is tolled and an action under this Article may be commenced within the earlier of (i) one year after the person bringing the action discovers that the sale has occurred or (ii) one year after the person bringing the action should have discovered that the sale has occurred, but no later than two years after the date of the bulk sale. Complete noncompliance with the requirements of this Article does not of itself constitute concealment.

(3) An action under Section 6–107(11) must be commenced within one year after the alleged violation occurs.

[End of Alternative B]

ARTICLE 7   WAREHOUSE RECEIPTS, BILLS OF LADING AND OTHER DOCUMENTS OF TITLE

Part 1   General

§ 7–101. *Short Title*

This article shall be known and may be cited as Uniform Commercial Code—Documents of Title.

§ 7–102. *Definitions and Index of Definitions*

(1) In this Article, unless the context otherwise requires:

(a) "Bailee" means the person who by a warehouse receipt, bill of lading or other document of title acknowledges possession of goods and contracts to deliver them.

(b) "Consignee" means the person named in a bill to whom or to whose order the bill promises delivery.

(c) "Consignor" means the person named in a bill as the person from whom the goods have been received for shipment.

(d) "Delivery order" means a written order to deliver goods directed to a warehouseman, carrier or other person who in the ordinary course of business issues warehouse receipts or bills of lading.

(e) "Document" means document of title as defined in the general definitions in Article 1 (Section 1–201).

(f) "Goods" means all things which are treated as movable for the purposes of a contract of storage or transportation.

(g) "Issuer" means a bailee who issues a document except that in relation to an unaccepted delivery order it means the person who orders the possessor of goods to deliver. Issuer includes any person for whom an agent or employee purports to act in issuing a document if the agent or employee has real or apparent authority to issue documents, notwithstanding that the issuer received no goods or that the goods were misdescribed or that in any other respect the agent or employee violated his instructions.

(h) "Warehouseman" is a person engaged in the business of storing goods for hire.

(2) Other definitions applying to this Article or to specified Parts thereof, and the sections in which they appear are:

"Duly negotiate." Section 7–501.

"Person entitled under the document." Section 7–403(4).

(3) Definitions in other Articles applying to this Article and the sections in which they appear are:

"Contract for sale." Section 2–106.

"Overseas." Section 2–323.

"Receipt" of goods. Section 2–103.

(4) In addition Article 1 contains general definitions and principles of construction and interpretation applicable throughout this Article.

§ 7–103. *Relation of Article to Treaty, Statute, Tariff, Classification or Regulation*

To the extent that any treaty or statute of the United States, regulatory statute of this State or tariff, classification or regulation filed or issued pursuant thereto is applicable, the provisions of this Article are subject thereto.

§ 7–104. *Negotiable and Non-Negotiable Warehouse Receipt, Bill of Lading or Other Document of Title*

(1) A warehouse receipt, bill of lading or other document of title is negotiable

(a) if by its terms the goods are to be delivered to bearer or to the order of a named person; or

(b) where recognized in overseas trade, if it runs to a named person or assigns.

(2) Any other documents are non-negotiable. A bill of lading in which it is stated that the goods are consigned to a named person is not made negotiable by a provision that the goods are to be delivered only against a written order signed by the same or another named person.

§ 7–105.   Construction Against Negative Implication

The omission from either Part 2 or Part 3 of this Article of a provision corresponding to a provision made in the other Part does not imply that a corresponding rule of law is not applicable.

Part 2   Warehouse Receipts: Special Provisions

§ 7–201.   Who May Issue a Warehouse Receipt; Storage Under Government Bond

(1) A warehouse receipt may be issued by any warehouseman.

(2) Where goods including distilled spirits and agricultural commodities are stored under a statute requiring a bond against withdrawal or a license for the issuance of receipts in the nature of warehouse receipt, a receipt issued for the goods has like effect as a warehouse receipt even though issued by a person who is the owner of the goods and is not a warehouseman.

§ 7–202.   Forms of Warehouse Receipt; Essential Terms; Optional Terms

(1) A warehouse receipt need not be in any particular form.

(2) Unless a warehouse receipt embodies within its written or printed terms each of the following, the warehouseman is liable for damages caused by the omission to a person injured thereby:

(a) the location of the warehouse where the goods are stored;

(b) the date of issue of the receipt;

(c) the consecutive number of the receipt;

(d) a statement whether the goods received will be delivered to the bearer, to a specified person, or to a specified person or his order;

(e) the rate of storage and handling charges, except that where goods are stored under a field warehousing arrangement a statement of that fact is sufficient on a non-negotiable receipt;

(f) a description of the goods or of the packages containing them;

(g) the signature of the warehouseman, which may be made by his authorized agent;

(h) if the receipt is issued for goods of which the warehouseman is owner, either solely or jointly or in common with others, the fact of such ownership; and

(i) a statement of the amount of advances made and of liabilities incurred for which the warehouseman claims a lien or security interest (Section 7–209). If the precise amount of such advances made or of such liabilities incurred is, at the time of the issue of the receipt, unknown to the warehouseman or to his agent who issues it, a statement of the fact that advances have been made or liabilities incurred and the purpose thereof is sufficient.

(3) A warehouseman may insert in his receipt any other terms which are not contrary to the provisions of this Act and do not impair his obligation of delivery (Section 7–403) or his duty of care (Section 7–204). Any contrary provisions shall be ineffective.

§ 7–203.   Liability for Non-Receipt or Misdescription

A party to or purchaser for value in good faith of a document of title other than a bill of lading relying in either case upon the description therein of the goods may recover from the issuer damages caused by the non-receipt or misdescription of the goods, except to the extent that the document conspicuously indicates that the issuer does not know whether any part or all of the goods in fact were received or conform to the description, as where the description is in terms of marks or labels or kind, quantity or condition, or the receipt or description is qualified by ''contents, condition and quality unknown,'' ''said to contain'' or the like, if such indication be true, or the party or purchaser otherwise has notice.

§ 7–204.   Duty of Care; Contractual Limitation of Warehouseman's Liability

(1) A warehouseman is liable for damages for loss of or injury to the goods caused by his failure to exercise such care in regard to them as a reasonably careful man would exercise under like circumstances but unless otherwise agreed he is not liable for damages which could not have been avoided by the exercise of such care.

(2) Damages may be limited by a term in the warehouse receipt or storage agreement limiting the amount of liability in case of loss or damage, and setting forth a specific liability per article or item, or value per unit of weight, beyond which the warehouseman shall not be liable; provided, however, that such liability may on written request of the bailor at the time of signing such storage agreement or within a reasonable time after receipt of the warehouse receipt be increased on part or all of the goods thereunder, in which event increased rates may be charged based on such increased valuation, but that no such increase shall be permitted contrary to a lawful limitation of liability contained in the warehouseman's tariff, if any. No such limitation is effective with respect to the warehouseman's liability for conversion to his own use.

(3) Reasonable provisions as to the time and manner of presenting claims and instituting actions based on the bail-

ment may be included in the warehouse receipt or tariff.
(4) This section does not impair or repeal . . .

Note: Insert in subsection (4) a reference to any statute which imposes a higher responsibility upon the warehouseman or invalidates contractual limitations which would be permissible under this Article.

§ 7–205. Title under Warehouse Receipt Defeated in Certain Cases

A buyer in the ordinary course of business of fungible goods sold and delivered by a warehouseman who is also in the business of buying and selling such goods takes free of any claim under a warehouse receipt even though it has been duly negotiated.

§ 7–206. Termination of Storage at Warehouseman's Option

(1) A warehouseman may on notifying the person on whose account the goods are held and any other person known to claim an interest in the goods require payment of any charges and removal of the goods from the warehouse at the termination of the period of storage fixed by the document, or, if no period is fixed, within a stated period not less than thirty days after the notification. If the goods are not removed before the date specified in the notification, the warehouseman may sell them in accordance with the provisions of the section on enforcement of a warehouseman's lien (Section 7–210).

(2) If a warehouseman in good faith believes that the goods are about to deteriorate or decline in value to less than the amount of his lien within the time prescribed in subsection (1) for notification, advertisement and sale, the warehouseman may specify in the notification any reasonable shorter time for removal of the goods and in case the goods are not removed, may sell them at public sale held not less than one week after a single advertisement or posting.

(3) If as a result of a quality or condition of the goods of which the warehouseman had no notice at the time of deposit the goods are a hazard to other property or to the warehouse or to persons, the warehouseman may sell the goods at public or private sale without advertisement on reasonable notification to all persons known to claim an interest in the goods. If the warehouseman after a reasonable effort is unable to sell the goods he may dispose of them in any lawful manner and shall incur no liability by reason of such disposition.

(4) The warehouseman must deliver the goods to any person entitled to them under this Article upon due demand made at any time prior to sale or other disposition under this section.

(5) The warehouseman may satisfy his lien from the proceeds of any sale or disposition under this section but must hold the balance for delivery on the demand of any person to whom he would have been bound to deliver the goods.

§ 7–207. Goods Must Be Kept Separate; Fungible Goods

(1) Unless the warehouse receipt otherwise provides, a warehouseman must keep separate the goods covered by each receipt so as to permit at all times identification and delivery of those goods except that different lots of fungible goods may be commingled.

(2) Fungible goods so commingled are owned in common by the persons entitled thereto and the warehouseman is severally liable to each owner for that owner's share. Where because of overissue a mass of fungible goods is insufficient to meet all the receipts which the warehouseman has issued against it, the persons entitled include all holders to whom overissued receipts have been duly negotiated.

§ 7–208. Altered Warehouse Receipts

Where a blank in a negotiable warehouse receipt has been filled in without authority, a purchaser for value and without notice of the want of authority may treat the insertion as authorized. Any other unauthorized alteration leaves any receipt enforceable against the issuer according to its original tenor.

§ 7–209. Lien of Warehouseman

(1) A warehouseman has a lien against the bailor on the goods covered by a warehouse receipt or on the proceeds thereof in his possession for charges for storage or transportation (including demurrage and terminal charges), insurance, labor, or charges present or future in relation to the goods, and for expenses necessary for preservation of the goods or reasonably incurred in their sale pursuant to law. If the person on whose account the goods are held is liable for like charges or expenses in relation to other goods whenever deposited and it is stated in the receipt that a lien is claimed for charges and expenses in relation to other goods, the warehouseman also has a lien against him for such charges and expenses whether or not the other goods have been delivered by the warehouseman. But against a person to whom a negotiable warehouse receipt is duly negotiated a warehouseman's lien is limited to charges in an amount or at a rate specified on the receipt or if no charges are so specified then to a reasonable charge for storage of the goods covered by the receipt subsequent to the date of receipt.

(2) The warehouseman may also reserve a security interest against the bailor for a maximum amount specified on the receipt for charges other than those specified in subsection (1), such as for money advanced and interest. Such a security interest is governed by the Article on Secured Transactions (Article 9).

(3)(a) A warehouseman's lien for charges and expenses under subsection (1) or a security interest under subsection

(2) is also effective against any person who so entrusted the bailor with possession of the goods that a pledge of them by him to a good faith purchaser for value would have been valid but is not effective against a person as to whom the document confers no right in the goods covered by it under Section 7–503.

(b) A warehouseman's lien on household goods for charges and expenses in relation to the goods under subsection (1) is also effective against all persons if the depositor was the legal possessor of the goods at the time of deposit. ''Household goods'' means furniture, furnishings, and personal effects used by the depositor in a dwelling.

(4) A warehouseman loses his lien on any goods which he voluntarily delivers or which he unjustifiably refuses to deliver.

§ 7–210.   Enforcement of Warehouseman's Lien

(1) Except as provided in subsection (2), a warehouseman's lien may be enforced by public or private sale of the goods in block or in parcels, at any time or place and on any terms which are commercially reasonable, after notifying all persons known to claim an interest in the goods. Such notification must include a statement of the amount due, the nature of the proposed sale and the time and place of any public sale. The fact that a better price could have been obtained by a sale at a different time or in a different method from that selected by the warehouseman is not of itself sufficient to establish that the sale was not made in a commercially reasonable manner. If the warehouseman either sells the goods in the usual manner in any recognized market therefor, or if he sells at the price current in such market at the time of his sale, or if he has otherwise sold in conformity with commercially reasonable practices among dealers in the type of goods sold, he has sold in a commercially reasonable manner. A sale of more goods than apparently necessary to be offered to insure satisfaction of the obligation is not commercially reasonable except in cases covered by the preceding sentence.

(2) A warehouseman's lien on goods other than goods stored by a merchant in the course of his business may be enforced only as follows:

(a) All persons known to claim an interest in the goods must be notified.

(b) The notification must be delivered in person or sent by registered or certified letter to the last known address of any person to be notified.

(c) The notification must include an itemized statement of the claim, a description of the goods subject to the lien, a demand for payment within a specified time not less than ten days after receipt of the notification, and a conspicuous statement that unless the claim is paid within that time the goods will be advertised for sale and sold by auction at a specified time and place.

(d) The sale must conform to the terms of the notification.

(e) The sale must be held at the nearest suitable place to that where the goods are held or stored.

(f) After the expiration of the time given in the notification, an advertisement of the sale must be published once a week for two weeks consecutively in a newspaper of general circulation where the sale is to be held. The advertisement must include a description of the goods, the name of the person on whose account they are being held, and the time and place of the sale. The sale must take place at least fifteen days after the first publication. If there is no newspaper of general circulation where the sale is to be held, the advertisement must be posted at least ten days before the sale in not less than six conspicuous places in the neighborhood of the proposed sale.

(3) Before any sale pursuant to this section any person claiming a right in the goods may pay the amount necessary to satisfy the lien and the reasonable expenses incurred under this section. In that event the goods must not be sold, but must be retained by the warehouseman subject to the terms of the receipt and this Article.

(4) The warehouseman may buy at any public sale pursuant to this section.

(5) A purchaser in good faith of goods sold to enforce a warehouseman's lien takes the goods free of any rights of persons against whom the lien was valid, despite noncompliance by the warehouseman with the requirements of this section.

(6) The warehouseman may satisfy his lien from the proceeds of any sale pursuant to this section but must hold the balance, if any, for delivery on demand to any person to whom he would have been bound to deliver the goods.

(7) The rights provided by this section shall be in addition to all other rights allowed by law to a creditor against his debtor.

(8) Where a lien is on goods stored by a merchant in the course of his business the lien may be enforced in accordance with either subsection (1) or (2).

(9) The warehouseman is liable for damages caused by failure to comply with the requirements for sale under this section and in case of willful violation is liable for conversion.

Part 3   Bills of Lading: Special Provisions

§ 7–301.   Liability for Non-Receipt or Misdescription; ''Said to Contain''; ''Shipper's Load and Count''; Improper Handling

(1) A consignee of a non-negotiable bill who has given value in good faith or a holder to whom a negotiable bill

has been duly negotiated relying in either case upon the description therein of the goods, or upon the date therein shown, may recover from the issuer damages caused by the misdating of the bill or the non-receipt or misdescription of the goods, except to the extent that the document indicates that the issuer does not know whether any part or all of the goods in fact were received or conform to the description, as where the description is in terms of marks or labels or kind, quantity, or condition or the receipt or description is qualified by ''contents or condition of contents of packages unknown,'' ''said to contain,'' ''shipper's weight, load and count'' or the like, if such indication be true.

(2) When goods are loaded by an issuer who is a common carrier, the issuer must count the packages of goods if package freight and ascertain the kind and quantity if bulk freight. In such cases ''shipper's weight, load and count'' or other words indicating that the description was made by the shipper are ineffective except as to freight concealed by packages.

(3) When bulk freight is loaded by a shipper who makes available to the issuer adequate facilities for weighing such freight, an issuer who is a common carrier must ascertain the kind and quantity within a reasonable time after receiving the written request of the shipper to do so. In such cases ''shipper's weight'' or other words of like purport are ineffective.

(4) The issuer may by inserting in the bill the words ''shipper's weight, load and count'' or other words of like purport indicate that the goods were loaded by the shipper; and if such statement be true the issuer shall not be liable for damages caused by the improper loading. But their omission does not imply liability for such damages.

(5) The shipper shall be deemed to have guaranteed to the issuer the accuracy at the time of shipment of the description, marks, labels, number, kind, quantity, condition and weight, as furnished by him; and the shipper shall indemnify the issuer against damage caused by inaccuracies in such particulars. The right of the issuer to such indemnity shall in no way limit his responsibility and liability under the contract of carriage to any person other than the shipper.

§ 7–302.   Through Bills of Lading and Similar Documents

(1) The issuer of a through bill of lading or other document embodying an undertaking to be performed in part by persons acting as its agents or by connecting carriers is liable to anyone entitled to recover on the document for any breach by such other persons or by a connecting carrier of its obligation under the document but to the extent that the bill covers an undertaking to be performed overseas or in territory not contiguous to the continental United States or an undertaking including matters other

than transportation this liability may be varied by agreement of the parties.

(2) Where goods covered by a through bill of lading or other document embodying an undertaking to be performed in part by persons other than the issuer are received by any such person, he is subject with respect to his own performance while the goods are in his possession to the obligation of the issuer. His obligation is discharged by delivery of the goods to another such person pursuant to the document, and does not include liability for breach by any other such persons or by the issuer.

(3) The issuer of such through bill of lading or other document shall be entitled to recover from the connecting carrier or such other person in possession of the goods when the breach of the obligation under the document occurred, the amount it may be required to pay to anyone entitled to recover on the document therefor, as may be evidenced by any receipt, judgment, or transcript thereof, and the amount of any expense reasonably incurred by it in defending any action brought by anyone entitled to recover on the document therefor.

§ 7–303.   Diversion; Reconsignment; Change of Instructions

(1) Unless the bill of lading otherwise provides, the carrier may deliver the goods to a person or destination other than that stated in the bill or may otherwise dispose of the goods on instructions from

    (a) the holder of a negotiable bill; or

    (b) the consignor on a non-negotiable bill notwithstanding contrary instructions from the consignee; or

    (c) the consignee on a non-negotiable bill in the absence of contrary instructions from the consignor, if the goods have arrived at the billed destination or if the consignee is in possession of the bill; or

    (d) the consignee on a non-negotiable bill if he is entitled as against the consignor to dispose of them.

(2) Unless such instructions are noted on a negotiable bill of lading, a person to whom the bill is duly negotiated can hold the bailee according to the original terms.

§ 7–304.   Bills of Lading in a Set

(1) Except where customary in overseas transportation, a bill of lading must not be issued in a set of parts. The issuer is liable for damages caused by violation of this subsection.

(2) Where a bill of lading is lawfully drawn in a set of parts, each of which is numbered and expressed to be valid only if the goods have not been delivered against any other part, the whole of the parts constitute one bill.

(3) Where a bill of lading is lawfully issued in a set of parts and different parts are negotiated to different persons, the title of the holder to whom the first due negotiation is made prevails as to both the document and the

goods even though any later holder may have received the goods from the carrier in good faith and discharged the carrier's obligation by surrender of his part.

(4) Any person who negotiates or transfers a single part of a bill of lading drawn in a set is liable to holders of that part as if it were the whole set.

(5) The bailee is obliged to deliver in accordance with Part 4 of this Article against the first presented part of a bill of lading lawfully drawn in a set. Such delivery discharges the bailee's obligation on the whole bill.

§ 7–305. Destination Bills

(1) Instead of issuing a bill of lading to the consignor at the place of shipment a carrier may at the request of the consignor procure the bill to be issued at destination or at any other place designated in the request.

(2) Upon request of anyone entitled as against the carrier to control the goods while in transit and on surrender of any outstanding bill of lading or other receipt covering such goods, the issuer may procure a substitute bill to be issued at any place designated in the request.

§ 7–306. Altered Bills of Lading

An unauthorized alteration or filling in of a blank in a bill of lading leaves the bill enforceable according to its original tenor.

§ 7–307. Lien of Carrier

(1) A carrier has a lien on the goods covered by a bill of lading for charges subsequent to the date of its receipt of the goods for storage or transportation (including demurrage and terminal charges) and for expenses necessary for preservation of the goods incident to their transportation or reasonably incurred in their sale pursuant to law. But against a purchaser for value of a negotiable bill of lading a carrier's lien is limited to charges stated in the bill or the applicable tariffs, or if no charges are stated then to a reasonable charge.

(2) A lien for charges and expenses under subsection (1) on goods which the carrier was required by law to receive for transportation is effective against the consignor or any person entitled to the goods unless the carrier had notice that the consignor lacked authority to subject the goods to such charges and expenses. Any other lien under subsection (1) is effective against the consignor and any person who permitted the bailor to have control or possession of the goods unless the carrier had notice that the bailor lacked such authority.

(3) A carrier loses his lien on any goods which he voluntarily delivers or which he unjustifiably refuses to deliver.

§ 7–308. Enforcement of Carrier's Lien

(1) A carrier's lien may be enforced by public or private sale of the goods, in block or in parcels, at any time or place and on any terms which are commercially reasonable, after notifying all persons known to claim an interest in the goods. Such notification must include a statement of the amount due, the nature of the proposed sale and the time and place of any public sale. The fact that a better price could have been obtained by a sale at a different time or in a different method from that selected by the carrier is not of itself sufficient to establish that the sale was not made in a commercially reasonable manner. If the carrier either sells the goods in the usual manner in any recognized market therefor or if he sells at the price current in such market at the time of his sale or if he has otherwise sold in conformity with commercially reasonable practices among dealers in the type of goods sold he has sold in a commercially reasonable manner. A sale of more goods than apparently necessary to be offered to ensure satisfaction of the obligation is not commercially reasonable except in cases covered by the preceding sentence.

(2) Before any sale pursuant to this section any person claiming a right in the goods may pay the amount necessary to satisfy the lien and the reasonable expenses incurred under this section. In that event the goods must not be sold, but must be retained by the carrier subject to the terms of the bill and this Article.

(3) The carrier may buy at any public sale pursuant to this section.

(4) A purchaser in good faith of goods sold to enforce a carrier's lien takes the goods free of any rights of persons against whom the lien was valid, despite noncompliance by the carrier with the requirements of this section.

(5) The carrier may satisfy his lien from the proceeds of any sale pursuant to this section but must hold the balance, if any, for delivery on demand to any person to whom he would have been bound to deliver the goods.

(6) The rights provided by this section shall be in addition to all other rights allowed by law to a creditor against his debtor.

(7) A carrier's lien may be enforced in accordance with either subsection (1) or the procedure set forth in subsection (2) of Section 7–210.

(8) The carrier is liable for damages caused by failure to comply with the requirements for sale under this section and in case of willful violation is liable for conversion.

§ 7–309. Duty of Care; Contractual Limitation of Carrier's Liability

(1) A carrier who issues a bill of lading whether negotiable or non-negotiable must exercise the degree of care in relation to the goods which a reasonably careful man would exercise under like circumstances. This subsection does not repeal or change any law or rule of law which imposes liability upon a common carrier for damages not caused by its negligence.

(2) Damages may be limited by a provision that the carrier's liability shall not exceed a value stated in the doc-

ument if the carrier's rates are dependent upon value and the consignor by the carrier's tariff is afforded an opportunity to declare a higher value or a value as lawfully provided in the tariff, or where no tariff is filed he is otherwise advised of such opportunity; but no such limitation is effective with respect to the carrier's liability for conversion to its own use.

(3) Reasonable provisions as to the time and manner of presenting claims and instituting actions based on the shipment may be included in a bill of lading or tariff.

Part 4   Warehouse Receipts and Bills of Lading: General Obligations

§ 7–401.   Irregularities in Issue of Receipt or Bill or Conduct of Issuer

The obligations imposed by this Article on an issuer apply to a document of title regardless of the fact that

(a) the document may not comply with the requirements of this Article or of any other law or regulation regarding its issue, form or content; or

(b) the issuer may have violated laws regulating the conduct of his business; or

(c) the goods covered by the document were owned by the bailee at the time the document was issued; or

(d) the person issuing the document does not come within the definition of warehouseman if it purports to be a warehouse receipt.

§ 7–402.   Duplicate Receipt or Bill; Overissue

Neither a duplicate nor any other document of title purporting to cover goods already represented by an outstanding document of the same issuer confers any right in the goods, except as provided in the case of bills in a set, overissue of documents for fungible goods and substitutes for lost, stolen or destroyed documents. But the issuer is liable for damages caused by his overissue or failure to identify a duplicate document as such by conspicuous notation on its face.

§ 7–403.   Obligation of Warehouseman or Carrier to Deliver; Excuse

(1) The bailee must deliver the goods to a person entitled under the document who complies with subsections (2) and (3), unless and to the extent that the bailee establishes any of the following:

(a) delivery of the goods to a person whose receipt was rightful as against the claimant;

(b) damage to or delay, loss or destruction of the goods for which the bailee is not liable[, but the burden of establishing negligence in such cases is on the person entitled under the document];

Note: The brackets in (1)(b) indicate that State enactments may differ on this point without serious damage to the principle of uniformity.

(c) previous sale or other disposition of the goods in lawful enforcement of a lien or on warehouseman's lawful termination of storage;

(d) the exercise by a seller of his right to stop delivery pursuant to the provisions of the Article on Sales (Section 2–705);

(e) a diversion, reconsignment or other disposition pursuant to the provisions of this Article (Section 7–303) or tariff regulating such right;

(f) release, satisfaction or any other fact affording a personal defense against the claimant;

(g) any other lawful excuse

(2) A person claiming goods covered by a document of title must satisfy the bailee's lien where the bailee so requests or where the bailee is prohibited by law from delivering the goods until the charges are paid.

(3) Unless the person claiming is one against whom the document confers no right under Sec. 7–503(1), he must surrender for cancellation or notation of partial deliveries any outstanding negotiable document covering the goods, and the bailee must cancel the document or conspicuously note the partial delivery thereon or be liable to any person to whom the document is duly negotiated.

(4) "Person entitled under the document" means holder in the case of a negotiable document, or the person to whom delivery is to be made by the terms of or pursuant to written instructions under a non-negotiable document.

§ 7–404.   No Liability for Good Faith Delivery Pursuant to Receipt or Bill

A bailee who in good faith including observance of reasonable commercial standards has received goods and delivered or otherwise disposed of them according to the terms of the document of title or pursuant to this Article is not liable therefor. This rule applies even though the person from whom he received the goods has no authority to procure the document or to dispose of the goods and even though the person to whom he delivered the goods had no authority to receive them.

Part 5   Warehouse Receipts and Bills of Lading: Negotiation and Transfer

§ 7–501.   Form of Negotiation and Requirements of "Due Negotiation"

(1) A negotiable document of title running to the order of a named person is negotiated by his indorsement and delivery. After his indorsement in blank or to bearer any person can negotiate it by delivery alone.

(2)(a) A negotiable document of title is also negotiated by delivery alone when by its original terms it runs to bearer.

(b) When a document running to the order of a named person is delivered to him the effect is the same as if the document had been negotiated.

(3) Negotiation of a negotiable document of title after it has been indorsed to a specified person requires indorsement by the special indorsee as well as delivery.

(4) A negotiable document of title is "duly negotiated" when it is negotiated in the manner stated in this section to a holder who purchases it in good faith without notice of any defense against or claim to it on the part of any person and for value, unless it is established that the negotiation is not in the regular course of business or financing or involves receiving the document in settlement or payment of a money obligation.

(5) Indorsement of a non-negotiable document neither makes it negotiable nor adds to the transferee's rights.

(6) The naming in a negotiable bill of a person to be notified of the arrival of the goods does not limit the negotiability of the bill nor constitute notice to a purchaser thereof of any interest of such person in the goods.

§ 7–502.   Rights Acquired by Due Negotiation

(1) Subject to the following section and to the provisions of Section 7–205 on fungible goods, a holder to whom a negotiable document of title has been duly negotiated acquires thereby:

(a) title to the document;

(b) title to the goods;

(c) all rights accruing under the law of agency or estoppel, including rights to goods delivered to the bailee after the document was issued; and

(d) the direct obligation of the issuer to hold or deliver the goods according to the terms of the document free of any defense or claim by him except those arising under the terms of the document or under this Article. In the case of a delivery order the bailee's obligation accrues only upon acceptance and the obligation acquired by the holder is that the issuer and any indorser will procure the acceptance of the bailee.

(2) Subject to the following section, title and rights so acquired are not defeated by any stoppage of the goods represented by the document or by surrender of such goods by the bailee, and are not impaired even though the negotiation or any prior negotiation constituted a breach of duty or even though any person has been deprived of possession of the document by misrepresentation, fraud, accident, mistake, duress, loss, theft or conversion, or even though a previous sale or other transfer of the goods or document has been made to a third person.

§ 7–503.   Document of Title to Goods Defeated in Certain Cases

(1) A document of title confers no right in goods against a person who before issuance of the document had a legal interest or a perfected security interest in them and who neither

(a) delivered or entrusted them or any document of title covering them to the bailor or his nominee with actual or apparent authority to ship, store or sell or with power to obtain delivery under this Article (Section 7–403) or with power of disposition under this Act (Section 2–403 and 9–307) or other statute or rule of law; nor

(b) acquiesced in the procurement by the bailor or his nominee of any document of title.

(2) Title to goods based upon an unaccepted delivery order is subject to the rights of anyone to whom a negotiable warehouse receipt or bill of lading covering the goods has been duly negotiated. Such a title may be defeated under the next section to the same extent as the rights of the issuer or a transferee from the issuer.

(3) Title to goods based upon a bill of lading issued to a freight forwarder is subject to the rights of anyone to whom a bill issued by the freight forwarder is duly negotiated; but delivery by the carrier in accordance with Part 4 of this Article pursuant to its own bill of lading discharges the carrier's obligation to deliver.

§ 7–504.   Rights Acquired in the Absence of Due Negotiation; Effect of Diversion; Seller's Stoppage of Delivery

(1) A transferee of a document, whether negotiable or non-negotiable, to whom the document has been delivered but not duly negotiated, acquires the title and rights which his transferor had or had actual authority to convey.

(2) In the case of a non-negotiable document, until but not after the bailee receives notification of the transfer, the rights of the transferee may be defeated

(a) by those creditors of the transferor who could treat the sale as void under Section 2–402; or

(b) by a buyer from the transferor in ordinary course of business if the bailee has delivered the goods to the buyer or received notification of his rights; or

(c) as against the bailee by good faith dealings of the bailee with the transferor.

(3) A diversion or other change of shipping instructions by the consignor in a non-negotiable bill of lading which causes the bailee not to deliver to the consignee defeats the consignee's title to the goods if they have been delivered to a buyer in ordinary course of business and in any event defeats the consignee's rights against the bailee.

(4) Delivery pursuant to a non-negotiable document may be stopped by a seller under Section 2–705, and subject to the requirement of due notification there provided. A bailee honoring the seller's instructions is entitled to be indemnified by the seller against any resulting loss or expense.

§ 7–505. Indorser Not a Guarantor for Other Parties

The indorsement of a document of title issued by a bailee does not make the indorser liable for any default by the bailee or by previous indorsers.

§ 7–506. Delivery without Indorsement: Right to Compel Indorsement

The transferee of a negotiable document of title has a specifically enforceable right to have his transferor supply any necessary indorsement but the transfer becomes a negotiation only as of the time the indorsement is supplied.

§ 7–507. Warranties on Negotiation or Transfer of Receipt or Bill

Where a person negotiates or transfers a document of title for value otherwise than as a mere intermediary under the next following section, then unless otherwise agreed he warrants to his immediate purchaser only in addition to any warranty made in selling the goods

(a) that the document is genuine; and

(b) that he has no knowledge of any fact which would impair its validity or worth; and

(c) that his negotiation or transfer is rightful and fully effective with respect to the title to the document and the goods it represents.

§ 7–508. Warranties of Collecting Bank as to Documents

A collecting bank or other intermediary known to be entrusted with documents on behalf of another or with collection of a draft or other claim against delivery of documents warrants by such delivery of the documents only its own good faith and authority. This rule applies even though the intermediary has purchased or made advances against the claim or draft to be collected.

§ 7–509. Receipt or Bill: When Adequate Compliance with Commercial Contract

The question whether a document is adequate to fulfill the obligations of a contract for sale or the conditions of a credit is governed by the Articles on Sales (Article 2) and on Letters of Credit (Article 5).

Part 6   Warehouse Receipts and Bills of Lading: Miscellaneous Provisions

§ 7–601. Lost and Missing Documents

(1) If a document has been lost, stolen or destroyed, a court may order delivery of the goods or issuance of a substitute document and the bailee may without liability to any person comply with such order. If the document was negotiable the claimant must post security approved by the court to idemnify any person who may suffer loss as a result of non-surrender of the document. If the document was not negotiable, such security may be required at the discretion of the court. The court may also in its discretion order payment of the bailee's reasonable costs and counsel fees.

(2) A bailee who without court order delivers goods to a person claiming under a missing negotiable document is liable to any person injured thereby, and if the delivery is not in good faith becomes liable for conversion. Delivery in good faith is not conversion if made in accordance with a filed classification or tariff or, where no classification or tariff is filed, if the claimant posts security with the bailee if an amount at least double the value of the goods at the time of posting to indemnify any person injured by the delivery who files a notice of claim within one year after the delivery.

§ 7–602. Attachment of Goods Covered by a Negotiable Document

Except where the document was originally issued upon delivery of the goods by a person who had no power to dispose of them, no lien attaches by virtue of any judicial process to goods in the possession of a bailee for which a negotiable document of title is outstanding unless the document be first surrendered to the bailee or its negotiation enjoined, and the bailee shall not be compelled to deliver the goods pursuant to process until the document is surrendered to him or impounded by the court. One who purchases the document for value without notice of the process or injunction takes free of the lien imposed by judicial process.

§ 7–603. Conflicting Claims; Interpleader

If more than one person claims title or possession of the goods, the bailee is excused from delivery until he has had a reasonable time to ascertain the validity of the adverse claims or to bring an action to compel all claimants to interplead and may compel such interpleader, either in defending an action for non-delivery of the goods, or by original action, whichever is appropriate.

ARTICLE 8   INVESTMENT SECURITIES

Part 1   Short Title and General Matters

§8–101.   Short Title

This Article shall be known and may be cited as Uniform Commercial Code—Investment Securities

§8–102.   Definitions and Index of Definitions

(1) In this Article, unless the context otherwise requires:

(a) A "certified security" is a share, participation, or other interest in property of or an enterprise of the issuer or an obligation of the issuer which is

(i) represented by an instrument issued in bearer or registered form;

(ii) of a type commonly dealt in on securities exchanges or markets or commonly recognized in any area in which it is issued or dealt in as a medium for investment; and

(iii) either one of a class or series or by its terms divisible into a class or series of shares, participations, interests, or obligations.

(b) An "uncertificated security" is a share, participation, or other interest in property or an enterprise of the issuer or an obligation of the issuer which is

(i) not represented by an instrument and the transfer of which is registered upon books maintained for that purpose by or on behalf of the issuer;

(ii) of a type commonly dealt in on securities exchanges or markets; and

(iii) either one of a class or series or by its terms divisible into a class or series of shares, participations, interests, or obligations.

(c) A "security" is either a certificated or an uncertificated security. If a security is certificated, the terms "security" and "certificated security" may mean either the intangible interest, the instrument representing that interest, or both, as the context requires. A writing that is a certificated security is governed by this Article and not by Article 3, even though it also meets the requirements of that Article. This Article does not apply to money. If a certificated security has been retained by or surrendered to the issuer or its transfer agent for reasons other than registration of transfer, other temporary purpose, payment, exchange, or acquisition by the issuer, that security shall be treated as an uncertificated security for purposes of this Article.

(d) A certificated security is in "registered form" if

(i) it specifies a person entitled to the security or the rights it represents; and

(ii) its transfer may be registered upon books maintained for that purpose by or on behalf of the issuer, or the security so states.

(e) A certificated security is in "bearer form" if it runs to bearer according to its terms and not by reason of any indorsement.

(2) A "subsequent purchaser" is a person who takes other than by original issue.

(3) A "clearing corporation" is a corporation registered as a "clearing agency" under the federal securities laws or a corporation:

(a) at least 90 percent of whose capital stock is held by or for one or more organizations, none of which, other than a national securities exchange or association, holds in excess of 20 percent of the capital stock of the corporation, and each of which is

(i) subject to supervision or regulation pursuant to the provisions of federal or state banking laws or state insurance laws,

(ii) a broker or dealer or investment company registered under the federal securities laws, or

(iii) a national securities exchange or association registered under the federal securities laws; and

(b) any remaining capital stock of which is held by individuals who have purchased it at or prior to the time of their taking office as directors of the corporation and who have purchased only so much of the capital stock as is necessary to permit them to qualify as directors.

(4) A "custodian bank" is a bank or trust company that is supervised and examined by state or federal authority having supervision over banks and is acting as custodian for a clearing corporation.

(5) Other definitions applying to this Article or to specified Parts thereof and the sections in which they appear are:

"Adverse claim." Section 8–302.
"Bona fide purchaser." Section 8–302.
"Broker." Section 8–303.
"Debtor." Section 9–105.
"Financial intermediary." Section 8–313.
"Guarantee of the signature." Section 8–402.
"Initial transaction statement." Section 8–408.
"Instruction." Section 8–308.
"Intermediary bank." Section 4–105.
"Issuer." Section 8–201.
"Overissue." Section 8–104.
"Secured Party." Section 9–105.
"Security Agreement." Section 9–105.

(6) In addition, Article 1 contains general definitions and principles of construction and interpretation applicable throughout this Article.

§8–103.   Issuer's Lien

A lien upon a security in favor of an issuer thereof is valid against a purchaser only if:

(a) the security is certificated and the right of the issuer to the lien is noted conspicuously thereon; or

(b) the security is uncertificated and a notation of the right of the issuer to the lien is contained in the initial transaction statement sent to the purchaser or, if his interest is transferred to him other than by registration of transfer, pledge, or release, the initial transaction statement sent to the registered owner or the registered pledgee.

§8–104.   Effect of Overissue; "Overissue"

(1) The provisions of this Article which validate a security or compel its issue or reissue do not apply to the extent that validation, issue, or reissue would result in overissue; but if:

(a) an identical security which does not constitute an overissue is reasonably available for purchase, the person entitled to issue or validation may compel the issuer to purchase the security for him and either to deliver a certificated security or to register the transfer of an uncertificated security to him, against surrender of any certificated security he holds; or

(b) a security is not so available for purchase, the person entitled to issue or validation may recover from the issuer the price he or the last purchaser for value paid for it with interest from the date of his demand.

(2) "Overissue" means the issue of securities in excess of the amount the issuer has corporate power to issue.

§8–105.   Certificated Securities Negotiable; Statements and Instructions Not Negotiable; Presumptions

(1) Certificated securities governed by this Article are negotiable instruments.

(2) Statements (Section 8–408), notices, or the like, sent by the issuer of uncertificated securities and instructions (Section 8–308) are neither negotiable instruments nor certificated securities.

(3) In any action on a security:

(a) unless specifically denied in the pleadings, each signature on a certificated security, in a necessary indorsement, on an initial transaction statement, or on an instruction, is admitted;

(b) if the effectiveness of a signature is put in issue, the burden of establishing it is on the party claiming under the signature, but the signature is presumed to be genuine or authorized.

(c) if signatures on a certificated security are admitted or established, production of the security entitles a holder to recover on it unless the defendant establishes a defense or a defect going to the validity of the security;

(d) if signatures on an initial transaction statement are admitted or established, the facts stated in the statement are presumed to be true as of the time of its issuance; and

(e) after it is shown that a defense or defect exists, the plaintiff has the burden of establishing that he or some person under whom he claims is a person against whom the defense or defect is ineffective (Section 8–202).

§8–106.   Applicability

The law (including the conflict of laws rules) of the jurisdiction of organization of the issuer governs the validity of a security, the effectiveness of registration by the issuer, and the rights and duties of the issuer with respect to:

(a) registration of transfer of a certificated security;

(b) registration of transfer, pledge, or release of an uncertificated security; and

(c) sending of statements of uncertificated securities.

§8–107.   Securities Transferable; Action for Price

(1) Unless otherwise agreed and subject to any applicable law or regulation respecting short sales, a person obligated to transfer securities may transfer any certificated security of the specified issue in bearer form or registered in the name of the transferee, or indorsed to him or in blank, or he may transfer an equivalent uncertificated security to the transferee or a person designated by the transferee.

(2) If the buyer fails to pay the price as it comes due under a contract of sale, the seller may recover the price of:

(a) certificated securities accepted by the buyer;

(b) uncertificated securities that have been transferred to the buyer or a person designated by the buyer; and

(c) other securities if efforts at their resale would be unduly burdensome or if there is no readily available market for their resale.

§8–108.   Registration of Pledge and Release of Uncertificated Securities

A security interest in an uncertificated security may be evidenced by the registration of pledge to the secured party or a person designated by him. There can be no more than one registered pledge of an uncertificated security at any time. The registered owner of an uncertified security is the person in whose name the security is registered, even if the security is subject to a registered pledge. The rights of a registered pledgee of an uncertified security under this Article are terminated by the registration of release.

Part 2   Issue—Issuer

§ 8–201.   Issuer

(1) With respect to obligations on or defenses to a security, "issuer" includes a person who:

(a) places or authorizes the placing of his name on a certificated security (otherwise than as authenticating trustee, registrar, transfer agent, or the like) to evidence that it represents a share, participation, or other interest in his property or in an enterprise, or to evidence his duty to perform an obligation represented by the certificated security;

(b) creates shares, participations, or other interests in his property or in an enterprise or undertakes obligations, which shares, participations, interests, or obligations are uncertificated securities;

(c) directly or indirectly creates fractional interests in his rights or property, which fractional interests are represented by certificated securities; or

(d) becomes responsible for or in place of any other person described as an issuer in this section.

(2) With respect to obligations on or defenses to a security, a guarantor is an issuer to the extent of his guaranty, whether or not his obligation is noted on a certificated security or on statements of uncertificated securities sent pursuant to Section 8–408.

(3) With respect to registration of transfer, pledge, or release (Part 4 of this Article), "issuer" means a person on whose behalf transfer books are maintained.

§8–202.   Issuer's Responsibility and Defenses; Notice of Defect or Defense

(1) Even against a purchaser for value and without notice, the terms of a security include:

(a) if the security is certificated, those stated on the security;

(b) if the security is uncertificated, those contained in the initial transaction statement sent to such purchaser, or, if his interest is transferred to him other than by registration of transfer, pledge, or release, the initial transaction statement sent to the registered owner or registered pledgee; and

(c) those made part of the security by reference, on the certificated security or in the initial transaction statement, to another instrument, indenture, or document or to a constitution, statute, ordinance, rule, regulation, order or the like, to the extent that the terms referred to do not conflict with the terms stated on the certificated security or contained in the statement. A reference under this paragraph does not of itself charge a purchaser for value with notice of a defect going to the validity of the security, even though the certificated security or statement expressly states that a person accepting it admits notice.

(2) A certificated security in the hands of a purchaser for value or an uncertificated security as to which an initial transaction statement has been sent to a purchaser for value, other than a security issued by a government or governmental agency or unit, even though issued with a defect going to its validity, is valid with respect to the purchaser if he is without notice of the particular defect unless the defect involves a violation of constitutional provisions, in which case the security is valid with respect to a subsequent purchaser for value and without notice of the defect. This subsection applies to an issuer that is a government or governmental agency or unit only if either there has been substantial compliance with the legal requirements governing the issue or the issuer has received a substantial consideration for the issue as a whole or for the particular security and a stated purpose of the issue is one for which the issuer has power to borrow money or issue the security.

(3) Except as provided in the case of certain unauthorized signatures (Section 8–205), lack of genuineness of a certificated security or an initial transaction statement is a complete defense, even against a purchaser for value and without notice.

(4) All other defenses of the issuer of a certificated or uncertificated security, including nondelivery and conditional delivery of a certificated security, are ineffective against a purchaser for value who has taken without notice of the particular defense.

(5) Nothing in this section shall be construed to affect the right of a party to a ''when, as and if issued'' or a ''when distributed'' contract to cancel the contract in the event of a material change in the character of the security that is the subject of the contract or in the plan or arrangement pursuant to which the security is to be issued or distributed.

§8–203.   Staleness as Notice of Defects or Defenses

(1) After an act or event creating a right to immediate performance of the principal obligation represented by a certificated security or that sets a date on or after which the security is to be presented or surrendered for redemption or exchange, a purchaser is charged with notice of any defect in its issue or defense of the issuer if:

(a) the act or event is one requiring the payment of money, the delivery of certificated securities, the registration of transfer of uncertificated securities, or any of these on presentation or surrender of the certificated security, the funds or securities are available on the date set for payment or exchange, and he takes the security more than one year after that date; and

(b) the act or event is not covered by paragraph (a) and he takes the security more than 2 years after the date set for surrender or presentation or the date on which performance became due.

(2) A call that has been revoked is not within subsection (1).

§8–204.   Effect of Issuer's Restrictions on Transfer

A restriction on transfer of a security imposed by the issuer, even if otherwise lawful, is ineffective against any person without actual knowledge of it unless:

(a) the security is certificated and the restriction is noted conspicuously thereon; or

(b) the security is uncertificated and a notation of the restriction is contained in the initial transaction statement sent to the person or, if his interest is transferred to him other than by registration of transfer, pledge, or release, the initial transaction statement sent to the registered owner or the registered pledgee.

§8–205.   Effect of Unauthorized Signature on Certificated Security or Initial Transaction Statement

An unauthorized signature placed on a certificated security prior to or in the course of issue or placed on an initial transaction statement is ineffective, but the signature is effective in favor of a purchaser for value of the certificated security or a purchaser for value of an uncertificated security to whom the initial transaction statement has been sent, if the purchaser is without notice of the lack of authority and the signing has been done by:

(a) an authenticating trustee, registrar, transfer agent, or other person entrusted by the issuer with the signing of the security, or similar securities, or of initial transaction statements or the immediate preparation of signing of any of them; or

(b) an employee of the issuer, or of any of the foregoing, entrusted with responsible handling of the security or initial transaction statement.

§8–206.   Completion or Alteration of Certificated Security or Initial Transaction Statement

(1) If a certificated security contains the signatures necessary to its issue or transfer but is incomplete in any other respect:

(a) any person may complete it by filling in the blanks as authorized: and

(b) even though the blanks are incorrectly filled in, the security as completed is enforceable by a purchaser who took it for value and without notice of the incorrectness.

(2) A complete certificated security that has been improperly altered, even though fraudulently, remains enforceable, but only according to its original terms.

(3) If an initial transaction statement contains the signatures necessary to its validity but is incomplete in any other respect:

(a) any person may complete it by filling in the blanks as authorized: and

(b) even though the blanks are incorrectly filled in, the statement as completed is effective in favor of the person to whom it is sent if he purchased the security referred to therein for value and without notice of the incorrectness.

(4) A complete initial transaction statement that has been improperly altered, even though fraudulently, is effective in favor of a purchaser to whom it has been sent, but only according to its original terms

§8–207. Rights and Duties of Issuer With Respect to Registered Owners and Registered Pledges

(1) Prior to due presentment for registration of transfer of a certificated security in registered form, the issuer or indenture trustee may treat the registered owner as the person exclusively entitled to vote, to receive notifications, and otherwise to exercise all rights and powers of an owner.

(2) Subject to the provisions of subsections (3), (4), and (6), the issuer or indenture trustee may treat the registered owner of an uncertificated security as the person exclusively entitled to vote, to receive notifications, and otherwise to exercise all the rights and powers of an owner.

(3) The registered owner of an uncertificated security that is subject to a registered pledge is not entitled to registration of transfer prior to the due presentment to the issuer of a release instruction. The exercise of conversion rights with respect to a convertible uncertificated security is a transfer within the meaning of this section.

(4) Upon due presentment of a transfer instruction from the registered pledgee of an uncertificated security, the issuer shall:

(a) register the transfer of the security to the new owner free of pledge, if the instruction specifies a new owner (who may be the registered pledgee) and does not specify a pledgee:

(b) register the transfer of the security to the new owner subject to the interest of the existing pledgee, if the instruction specifies new owner and the existing pledgee: or

(c) register the release of the security from the existing pledge and register the pledge of the security to the other pledgee, if the instruction specifies the existing owner and another pledgee.

(5) Continuity of perfection of a security interest is not broken by registration of transfer under subsection (4) (b) or by registration of release and pledge under subsection (4) (c), if the security interest is assigned.

(6) If an uncertificated security is subject to a registered pledge:

(a) any uncertificated securities issued in exchange for or distributed with respect to the pledged security shall be registered subject to the pledge;

(b) any certificated securities issued in exchange for or distributed with respect to the pledged security shall be delivered to the registered pledgee; and

(c) any money paid in exchange for or in redemption of part or all of the security shall be paid to the registered pledgee.

(7) Nothing in this Article shall be construed to affect the liability of the registered owner of a security for calls, assessments, or the like.

§8–208. Effect of Signature of Authenticating Trustee, Registrar, or Transfer Agent

(1) A person placing his signature upon a certificated security or an initial transaction statement as authenticating trustee, registrar, transfer agent, or the like, warrants to a purchaser for value of the certificated security or a purchaser for value of an uncertificated security to whom the initial transaction statement has been sent, if the purchaser is without notice of the particular defect, that:

(a) the certificated security or initial transaction statement is genuine;

(b) his own participation in the issue or registration of the transfer, pledge, or release of the security is within his capacity and within the scope of the authority received by him from the issuer: and

(c) he has reasonable grounds to believe the security is in the form and within the amount the issuer is authorized to issue.

(2) Unless otherwise agreed, a person by so placing his signature does not assume responsibility for the validity of the security in other respects.

Part 3   Transfer

§8–301.   Rights Acquired by Purchaser

(1) Upon transfer of a security to a purchaser (Section 8–313), the purchaser acquires the rights in the security which his transferor had or had actual authority to convey unless the purchaser's rights are limited by Section 8–302(4).

(2) A transferee of a limited interest acquires rights only to the extent of the interest transferred. The creation or release of a security interest in a security is the transfer of a limited interest in that security.

§8–302. "Bona Fide Purchaser"; "Adverse Claim"; Title Acquired by Bona Fide Purchaser

(1) A "bona fide purchaser" is a purchaser for value in good faith and without notice of any adverse claim:

(a) who takes delivery of a certificated security in bearer form or in registered form, issued or indorsed to him or in blank;

(b) to whom the transfer, pledge, or release of an uncertificated security is registered on the books of the issuer; or

(c) to whom a security is transferred under the provisions of paragraph (c), (d) (i), or (g) of Section 8–313(1).

(2) "Adverse claim" includes a claim that a transfer was or would be wrongful or that a particular adverse person is the owner of or has an interest in the security.

(3) A bona fide purchaser in addition to acquiring the rights of a purchaser (Section 8–301) also acquires his interest in the security free of any adverse claim.

(4) Notwithstanding Section 8–301(1), the transferee of a particular certificated security who has been a party to any fraud or illegality affecting the security, or who as a prior holder of that certificated security had notice of an adverse claim, cannot improve his position by taking from a bona fide purchaser.

§8–303. "Broker"

"Broker" means a person engaged for all or part of his time in the business of buying and selling securities, who in the transaction concerned acts for, buys a security from, or sells a security to, a customer. Nothing in this Article determines the capacity in which a person acts for purposes of any other statute or rule to which the person is subject.

§8–304. Notice to Purchaser of Adverse Claims

(1) A purchaser (including a broker for the seller or buyer, but excluding an intermediary bank) of a certificated security is charged with notice of adverse claims if:

(a) the security, whether in bearer or registered form, has been indorsed "for collection" or "for surrender" or for some other purpose not involving transfer; or

(b) the security is in bearer form and has on it an unambiguous statement that it is the property of a person other than the transferor. The mere writing of a name on a security is not such a statement.

(2) A purchaser (including a broker for the seller or buyer, but excluding an intermediary bank) to whom the transfer, pledge, or release of an uncertificated security is registered is charged with notice of adverse claims as to which the issuer has a duty under Section 8–403(4) at the time of registration and which are noted in the initial transaction statement sent to the purchaser or, if his interest is transferred to him other than by registration of transfer, pledge,

or release, the initial transaction statement sent to the registered owner or the registered pledgee.

(3) The fact that the purchaser (including a broker for the seller or buyer) or a certificated or uncertificated security has notice that the security is held for a third person or is registered in the name of or indorsed by a fiduciary does not create a duty of inquiry into the rightfulness of the transfer or constitute constructive notice of adverse claims. However, if the purchaser (excluding an intermediary bank) has knowledge that the proceeds are being used or that the transaction is for the individual benefit of the fiduciary or otherwise in breach of duty, the purchaser is charged with notice of adverse claims.

§8–305. Staleness as Notice of Adverse Claims

An act or event that creates a right to immediate performance of the principal obligation represented by a certificated security or sets a date on or after which a certificated security is to be presented or surrendered for redemption or exchange does not itself constitute any notice of adverse claims except in the case of a transfer:

(a) after one year from any date set for presentment or surrender for redemption or exchange; or

(b) after 6 months from any date set for payment of money against presentation or surrender of the security if funds are available for payment on that date.

§8–306. Warranties on Presentment and Transfer of Certificated Securities; Warranties of Originators of Instructions

(1) A person who presents a certificated security for registration of transfer or for payment or exchange warrants to the issuer that he is entitled to the registration, payment, or exchange. But, a purchaser for value and without notice of adverse claims who receives a new, reissued, or reregistered certificated security on registration of transfer or receives an initial transaction statement confirming the registration of transfer of an equivalent uncertificated security to him warrants only that he has no knowledge of any unauthorized signature (Section 8–311) in a necessary indorsement.

(2) A person by transferring a certificated security to a purchaser for value warrants only that:

(a) his transfer is effective and rightful;

(b) the security is genuine and has not been materially altered; and

(c) he knows of no fact which might impair the validity of the security.

(3) If a certificated security is delivered by an intermediary known to be entrusted with delivery of the security on behalf of another or with collection of a draft or other claim against delivery, the intermediary by delivery warrants only his own good faith and authority even though he

has purchased or made advances against the claim to be collected against the delivery.

(4) A pledgee or other holder for security who redelivers a certificated security received, or after payment and on order of the debtor delivers that security to a third person, makes only the warranties of an intermediary under subsection (3).

(5) A person who originates an instruction warrants to the issuer that:

(a) he is an appropriate person to originate the instruction; and

(b) at the time the instruction is presented to the issuer he will be entitled to the registration of transfer, pledge, or release. (6) A person who originates an instruction warrants to any person specially guaranteeing his signature (subsection 8–312(3))that:

(a) he is an appropriate person to originate the instruction; and

(b) at the time the instruction is presented to the issuer

(i) he will be entitled to the registration of transfer, pledge, or release; and

(ii) the transfer, pledge, or release requested in the instruction will be registered by the issuer free from all liens, security interests, restrictions, and claims other than those specified in the instruction.

(7) A person who originates an instruction warrants to a purchaser for value and to any person guaranteeing the instruction (Section 8–312(6) that:

(a) he is an appropriate person to originate the instruction;

(b) the uncertificated security referred to therein is valid; and

(c) at the time the instruction is presented to the issuer

(i) the transferor will be entitled to the registration of transfer, pledge, or release;

(ii) the transfer, pledge, or release requested in the instruction will be registered by the issuer free from all liens, security interests, restrictions, and claims other than those specified in the instruction; and

(iii) the requested transfer, pledge, or release will be rightful.

(8) If a secured party is the registered pledgee or the registered owner of an uncertificated security, a person who originates an instruction of release or transfer to the debtor or, after payment and on order of the debtor, a transfer instruction to a third person, warrants to the debtor or the third person only that he is an appropriate person to originate the instruction and, at the time the instruction is presented to the issuer, the transferor will be entitled to the registration of release or transfer. If a transfer instruction to a third person who is a purchaser for value is originated on order of the debtor, the debtor makes to the purchaser the warranties of paragraphs (b), (c) (ii) and (c) (iii) of subsection (7).

(9) A person who transfers an uncertificated security to a purchaser for value and does not originate an instruction in connection with the transfer warrants only that:

(a) his transfer is effective and rightful; and

(b) the uncertificated security is valid.

(10) A broker gives to his customer and to the issuer and a purchaser the applicable warranties provided in this section and has the rights and privileges of a purchaser under this section. The warranties of and in favor of the broker, acting as an agent are in addition to applicable warranties given by and in favor of his customer.

§8–307.   Effect of Delivery Without Indorsement; Right to Compel Indorsement

If a certificated security in registered form has been delivered to a purchaser without a necessary indorsement he may become a bona fide purchaser only as of the time the indorsement is supplied; but against the transferor, the transfer is complete upon delivery and the purchaser has a specifically enforceable right to have any necessary indorsement supplied.

§8–308.   Indorsements; Instructions

(1) An indorsement of a certificated security in registered form is made when an appropriate person signs on it or on a separate document an assignment or transfer of the security or a power to assign or transfer it or his signature is written without more upon the back of the security.

(2) An indorsement may be in blank or special. An indorsement in blank includes an indorsement to bearer. A special indorsement specifies to whom the security is to be transferred, or who has power to transfer it. A holder may convert a blank indorsement into a special indorsement.

(3) An indorsement purporting to be only of part of a certificated security representing units intended by the issuer to be separately transferable is effective to the extent of the indorsement.

(4) An ''instruction'' is an order to the issuer of an uncertificated security requesting that the transfer, pledge, or release from pledge of the uncertificated security specified therein be registered.

(5) An instruction originated by an appropriate person is:

(a) a writing signed by an appropriate person; or

(b) a communication to the issuer in any form agreed upon in a writing signed by the issuer and an appropriate person. If an instruction has been originated by an appropriate person but is incomplete in any other respect, any person may complete it as authorized and the issuer may rely on it as completed even though it has been completed incorrectly.

(6) ''An appropriate person'' in subsection (1) means the person specified by the certificated security or by special indorsement to be entitled to the security.

(7) ''An appropriate person'' in subsection (5) means:

(a) for an instruction to transfer or pledge an uncertificated security which is then not subject to a registered pledge, the registered owner; or

(b) for an instruction to transfer or release an uncertificated security which is then subject to a registered pledge, the registered pledgee.

(8) In addition to the persons designated in subsections (6) and (7), ''an appropriate person'' in subsections (1) and (5) includes:

(a) if the person designated is described as a fiduciary but is no longer serving in the described capacity, either that person or his successor;

(b) if the persons designated are described as more than one person as fiduciaries and one or more are no longer serving in the described capacity, the remaining fiduciary or fiduciaries, whether or not a successor has been appointed or qualified.

(c) if the person designated is an individual and is without capacity to act by virtue of death, incompetence, infancy, or otherwise, his executor, administrator, guardian, or like fiduciary;

(d) if the persons designated are described as more than one person as tenants by the entirety or with right of survivorship and by reason of death all cannot sign, the survivor or survivors;

(e) a person having power to sign under applicable law or controlling instrument; and

(f) to the extent that the person designated or any of the foregoing persons may act through an agent, his authorized agent.

(9) Unless otherwise agreed, the indorser of a certificated security by his indorsement or the originator of an instruction by his origination assumes no obligation that the security will be honored by the issuer but only the obligations provided in Section 8–306.

(10) Whether the person signing is appropriate is determined as of the date of signing and an indorsement made by or an instruction originated by him does not become unauthorized for the purposes of this Article by virtue of any subsequent change of circumstances.

(11) Failure of a fiduciary to comply with a controlling instrument or with the law of the state having jurisdiction of the fiduciary relationship, including any law requiring the fiduciary to obtain court approval of the transfer, pledge, or release, does not render his indorsement or an instruction originated by him unauthorized for the purposes of this Article.

§8–309. Effect of Indorsement Without Delivery

An indorsement of a certificated security, whether special or in blank, does not constitute a transfer until delivery of the certificated security on which it appears or, if the indorsement is on a separate document, until delivery of both the document and the certificated security.

§8–310. Indorsement of Certificated Security in Bearer Form

An indorsement of a certificated security in bearer form may give notice of adverse claims (Section 8–304) but does not otherwise affect any right to registration the holder possesses.

§8–311. Effect of Unauthorized Indorsement or Instruction

Unless the owner or pledgee has ratified an unauthorized indorsement or instruction or is otherwise precluded from asserting its ineffectiveness:

(a) he may assert its ineffectiveness against the issuer or any purchaser, other than a purchaser for value and without notice of adverse claims, who has in good faith received a new, reissued, or reregistered certificated security on registration of transfer or received an initial transaction statement confirming the registration of transfer, pledge, or release of an equivalent uncertificated security to him; and

(b) an issuer who registers the transfer of a certificated security upon the unauthorized indorsement or who registers the transfer, pledge, or release of an uncertificated security upon the unauthorized instruction is subject to liability for improper registration (Section 8–404).

§8–312. Effect of Guaranteeing Signature, Indorsement or Instruction

(1) Any person guaranteeing a signature of an indorser of a certificated security warrants that at the time of signing:

(a) the signature was genuine;

(b) the signer was an appropriate person to indorse (Section 8–308); and

(c) the signer had legal capacity to sign.

(2) Any person guaranteeing a signature of the originator of an instruction warrants that at the time of signing:

(a) the signature was genuine;

(b) the signer was an appropriate person to originate the instruction (Section 8–308) if the person specified in the instruction as the registered owner or registered pledgee of the uncertificated security was, in fact, the registered owner or registered pledgee of the security, as to which fact the signature guarantor makes no warranty;

(c) the signer had legal capacity to sign; and

(d) the taxpayer identification number, if any, appearing on the instruction as that of the registered owner or registered pledgee was the taxpayer identification number of the signer or of the owner or pledgee for whom the signer was acting.

(3) Any person specially guaranteeing the signature of the originator of an instruction makes not only the warranties of a signature guarantor (subsection (2) but also warrants that at the time the instruction is presented to the issuer:

(a) the person specified in the instruction as the registered owner or registered pledgee of the uncertificated security will be the registered owner or registered pledgee; and

(b) the transfer, pledge, or release of the uncertificated security requested in the instruction will be registered by the issuer free from all liens, security interests, restrictions, and claims other than those specified in the instruction.

(4) The guarantor under subsections (1) and (2) or the special guarantor under subsection (3) does not otherwise warrant the rightfulness of the particular transfer, pledge, or release.

(5) Any person guaranteeing an indorsement of a certificated security makes not only the warranties of a signature guarantor under subsection (1) but also warrants the rightfulness of the particular transfer in all respects.

(6) Any person guaranteeing an instruction requesting the transfer, pledge, or release of an uncertificated security makes not only the warranties of a special signature guarantor under subsection (3) but also warrants the rightfulness of the particular transfer, pledge, or release in all respects.

(7) No issuer may require a special guarantee of signature (subsection (3)), a guarantee of indorsement (subsection (5)), or a guarantee of instruction (subsection (6)) as a condition to registration of transfer, pledge, or release.

(8) The foregoing warranties are made to any person taking or dealing with the security in reliance on the guarantee, and the guarantor is liable to the person for any loss resulting from breach of the warranties.

§8–313.   When Transfer to Purchaser Occurs; Financial Intermediary as Bona Fide Purchaser; ''Financial Intermediary''

(1) Transfer of a security or a limited interest (including a security interest) therein to a purchaser occurs only:

(a) at the time he or a person designated by him acquires possession of a certificated security;

(b) at the time the transfer, pledge, or release of an uncertificated security is registered to him or a person designated by him;

(c) at the time his financial intermediary acquires possession of a certificated security specially indorsed to or issued in the name of the purchaser;

(d) at the time a financial intermediary, not a clearing corporation, sends him confirmation of the purchase and also by book entry or otherwise identifies as belonging to the purchaser

(i) a specific certificated security in the financial intermediary's possession;

(ii) a quantity of securities that constitute or are part of a fungible bulk of certificated securities in the financial intermediary's possession or of uncertificated securities registered in the name of the financial intermediary; or

(iii) a quantity of securities that constitute or are part of a fungible bulk of securities shown on the account of the financial intermediary on the books of another financial intermediary;

(e) with respect to an identified certificated security to be delivered while still in the possession of a third person, not a financial intermediary, at the time that person acknowledges that he holds for the purchaser;

(f) with respect to a specific uncertificated security the pledge or transfer of which has been registered to a third person, not a financial intermediary, at the time that person acknowledges that he holds for the purchaser;

(g) at the time appropriate entries to the account of the purchaser or a person designated by him on the books of a clearing corporation are made under Section 8–320;

(h) with respect to the transfer of a security interest where the debtor has signed a security agreement containing a description of the security, at the time a written notification, which, in the case of the creation of the security interest, is signed by the debtor (which may be a copy of the security agreement) or which, in the case of the release or assignment of the security interest created pursuant to this paragraph, is signed by the secured party, is received by

(i) a financial intermediary on whose books the interest of the transferor in the security appears;

(ii) a third person, not a financial intermediary, in possession of the security, if it is certificated;

(iii) a third person, not a financial intermediary, who is the registered owner of the security, if it is uncertificated and not subject to a registered pledge; or

(iv) a third person, not a financial intermediary, who is the registered pledgee of the security, if it is uncertificated and subject to a registered pledge;

(i) with respect to the transfer of a security interest where the transferor has signed a security agreement containing a description of the security, at the time new value is given by the secured party; or

(j) with respect to the transfer of a security interest where the secured party is a financial intermediary and the security has already been transferred to the financial intermediary under paragraphs (a), (b), (c), (d), or (g), at the time the transferor has signed a security agreement containing a description of the security and value is given by the secured party.

(2) The purchaser is the owner of a security held for him by a financial intermediary, but cannot be a bona fide purchaser of a security so held except in the circumstances specified in paragraphs (c), (d)(i), and (g) of subsection (1). If a security so held is part of a fungible bulk, as in the circumstances specified in paragraphs (d)(ii) and (d)(iii) of subsection (1), the purchaser is the owner of a proportionate property interest in the fungible bulk.

(3) Notice of an adverse claim received by the financial intermediary or by the purchaser after the financial intermediary takes delivery of a certificated security as a holder for value or after the transfer, pledge, or release of an uncertificated security has been registered free of the claim to a financial intermediary who has given value is not effective either as to the financial intermediary or as to

the purchaser. However, as between the financial intermediary and the purchaser the purchaser may demand transfer of an equivalent security as to which no notice of adverse claim has been received.

(4) A "financial intermediary" is a bank, broker, clearing corporation, or other person (or the nominee of any of them) which in the ordinary course of its business maintains security accounts for its customers and is acting in that capacity. A financial intermediary may have a security interest in securities held in account for its customer.

§8–314. Duty to Transfer, When Completed

(1) Unless otherwise agreed, if a sale of a security is made on an exchange or otherwise through brokers:

(a) the selling customer fulfills his duty to transfer at the time he:

(i) places a certificated security in the possession of the selling broker or a person designated by the broker;

(ii) causes an uncertificated security to be registered in the name of the selling broker or a person designated by the broker;

(iii) if requested, causes an acknowledgment to be made to the selling broker that a certificated or uncertificated security is held for the broker; or

(iv) places in the possession of the selling broker or of a person designated by the broker a transfer instruction for an uncertificated security, providing the issuer does not refuse to register the requested transfer if the instruction is presented to the issuer for registration within 30 days thereafter; and

(b) the selling broker, including a correspondent broker acting for a selling customer, fulfills his duty to transfer at the time he:

(i) places a certificated security in the possession of the buying broker or a person designated by the buying broker;

(ii) causes an uncertificated security to be registered in the name of the buying broker;

(iii) places in the possession of the buying broker or of a person designated by the buying broker a transfer instruction for an uncertificated security, providing the issuer does not refuse to register the requested transfer if the instruction is presented to the issuer for registration within 30 days thereafter; or

(iv) effects clearance of the sale in accordance with the rules of the exchange on which the transaction took place.

(2) Except as provided in this section or unless otherwise agreed, a transferor's duty to transfer a security under a contract of purchase is not fulfilled until he:

(a) places a certificated security in form to be negotiated by the purchaser in the possession of the purchaser or of a person designated by the purchaser;

(b) causes an uncertificated security to be registered in the name of the purchaser or a person designated by the purchaser; or

(c) if the purchaser requests, causes an acknowledgment to be made to the purchaser that a certificated or uncertificated security is held for the purchaser.

(3) Unless made on an exchange, a sale to a broker purchasing for his own account is within subsection (2) and not within subsection (1).

§8–315. Action Against Transferee Based upon Wrongful Transfer

(1) Any person against whom the transfer of a security is wrongful for any reason, including his incapacity, as against anyone except a bona fide purchaser, may:

(a) reclaim possession of the certificated security wrongfully transferred;

(b) obtain possession of any new certificated security representing all or part of the same rights;

(c) compel the origination of an instruction to transfer to him or a person designated by him an uncertificated security constituting all or part of the same rights; or

(d) have damages.

(2) If the transfer is wrongful because of an unauthorized indorsement of a certificated security, the owner may also reclaim or obtain possession of the security or a new certificated security, even from a bona fide purchaser, if the ineffectiveness of the purported indorsement can be asserted against him under the provisions of this Article on unauthorized indorsements (Section 8–311).

(3) The right to obtain or reclaim possession of a certificated security or to compel the origination of a transfer instruction may be specifically enforced and the transfer of a certificated or uncertificated security enjoined and a certificated security impounded pending the litigation.

§8–316. Purchaser's Right to Requisites for Registration of Transfer, Pledge, or Release on Books

Unless otherwise agreed, the transferor of a certificated security or the transferor, pledgor, or pledgee of an uncertificated security on due demand must supply his purchaser with any proof of his authority to transfer, pledge, or release or with any other requisite necessary to obtain registration of the transfer, pledge, or release of the security; but if the transfer, pledge or release is not for value, a transferor, pledgor, or pledgee need not do so unless the purchaser furnishes the necessary expenses. Failure within a reasonable time to comply with a demand made gives the purchaser the right to reject or rescind the transfer, pledge, or release.

§8–317. Creditor's Rights

(1) Subject to the exceptions in subsections (3) and (4), no attachment or levy upon a certificated security or any share or other interest represented thereby which is outstanding is valid until the security is actually seized by the officer making the attachment or levy, but a certificated security which has been surrendered to the issuer may be

reached by a creditor by legal process at the issuer's chief executive office in the United States.

(2) An uncertificated security registered in the name of the debtor may not be reached by a creditor except by legal process at the issuer's chief executive office in the United States.

(3) The interest of a debtor in a certificated security that is in the possession of a secured party not a financial intermediary or in an uncertificated security registered in the name of a secured party not a financial intermediary (or in the name of a nominee of the secured party) may be reached by a creditor by legal process upon the secured party.

(4) The interest of a debtor in a certificated security that is in the possession of or registered in the name of a financial intermediary or in an uncertificated security registered in the name of a financial intermediary may by reached by a creditor by legal process upon the financial intermediary on whose books the interest of the debtor appears.

(5) Unless otherwise provided by law, a creditor's lien upon the interest of a debtor in a security obtained pursuant to subsection (3) or (4) is not a restraint on the transfer of the security, free of the lien, to a third party for new value; but in the event of a transfer, the lien applies to the proceeds of the transfer in the hands of the secured party or financial intermediary, subject to any claims having priority.

(6) A creditor whose debtor is the owner of a security is entitled to aid from courts of appropriate jurisdiction, by injunction or otherwise, in reaching the security or in satisfying the claim by means allowed at law or in equity in regard to property that cannot readily be reached by ordinary legal process.

§8–318.　No Conversion by Good Faith Conduct

An agent or bailee who in good faith (including observance of reasonable commercial standards if he is in the business of buying, selling, or otherwise dealing with securities) has received certificated securities and sold, pledged, or delivered them or has sold or caused the transfer or pledge of uncertificated securities over which he had control according to the instructions of his principal, is not liable for conversion or for participation in breach of fiduciary duty although the principal had no right so to deal with the securities.

§8–319.　Statute of Frauds

A contract for the sale of securities is not enforceable by way of action or defense unless:

(a) there is some writing signed by the party against whom enforcement is sought or by his authorized agent or broker, sufficient to indicate that a contract has been made for sale of a stated quantity of described securities at a defined or stated price;

(b) delivery of a certificated security or transfer instruction has been accepted, or transfer of an uncertificated security has been registered and the transferee has failed to send written objection to the issuer within 10 days after receipt of the initial transaction statement confirming the registration, or payment has been made, but the contract is enforceable under this provision only to the extent of the delivery, registration, or payment;

(c) within a reasonable time a writing in confirmation of the sale or purchase and sufficient against the sender under paragraph (a) has been received by the party against whom enforcement is sought and he has failed to send written objection to its contents within 10 days after its receipt; or

(d) the party against whom enforcement is sought admits in his pleading, testimony, or otherwise in court that a contract was made for the sale of a stated quantity of described securities at a defined or stated price.

§8–320.　Transfer or Pledge Within Central Depositary System

(1) In addition to other methods, a transfer, pledge, or release of a security or any interest therein may be effected by the making of appropriate entries on the books of a clearing corporation reducing the account of the transferor, pledgor, or pledgee and increasing the account of the transferee, pledgee, or pledgor by the amount of the obligation or the number of shares or rights transferred, pledged, or released, if the security is shown on the account of a transferor, pledgor, or pledgee on the books of the clearing corporation; is subject to the control of the clearing corporation; and

(a) if certificated,

(i) is in the custody of the clearing corporation, another clearing corporation, a custodian bank, or a nominee of any of them; and

(ii) is in bearer form or indorsed in blank by an appropriate person or registered in the name of the clearing corporation, a custodian bank, or a nominee of any of them; or

(b) if uncertificated, is registered in the name of the clearing corporation, another clearing corporation, a custodian bank, or a nominee of any of them.

(2) Under this section entries may be made with respect to like securities or interests therein as a part of a fungible bulk and may refer merely to a quantity of a particular security without reference to the name of the registered owner, certificate or bond number, or the like, and, in appropriate cases, may be on a net basis taking into account other transfers, pledges, or releases of the same security.

(3) A transfer under this section is effective (Section 8–313) and the purchaser acquires the rights of the transferor (Section 8–301). A pledge or release under this section is the transfer of a limited interest. If a pledge or the creation of a security interest is intended, the security interest is perfected at the time when both value is given by the pledgee and the appropriate entries are made (Sec-

tion 8–321). A transferee or pledgee under this section may be a bona fide purchaser (Section 8–302).

(4) A transfer or pledge under this section is not a registration of transfer under Part 4.

(5) That entries made on the books of the clearing corporation as provided in subsection (1) are not appropriate does not affect the validity or effect of the entries or the liabilities or obligations of the clearing corporation to any person adversely affected thereby.

§ 8–321. Enforceability, Attachment, Perfection and Termination of Security Interests

(1) A security interest in a security is enforceable and can attach only if it is transferred to the secured party or a person designated by him pursuant to a provision of Section 8–313(1).

(2) A security interest so transferred pursuant to agreement by a transferor who has rights in the security to a transferee who has given value is a perfected security interest, but a security interest that has been transferred solely under paragraph (i) of Section 8–313(1) becomes unperfected after 21 days unless within that time, the requirements for transfer under any other provision of Section 8–313(1) are satisfied.

(3) A security interest in a security is subject to the provisions of Article 9, but:

(a) no filing is required to perfect the security interest; and

(b) no written security agreement signed by the debtor is necessary to make the security interest enforceable, except as provided in paragraph (h), (i), or (j) of Section 8–313(1). The secured party has the rights and duties provided under Section 9–207, to the extent they are applicable, whether or not the security is certificated, and, if certificated, whether or not it is in his possession.

(4) Unless otherwise agreed, a security interest in a security is terminated by transfer to the debtor or a person designated by him pursuant to a provision of Section 8–313(1). If a security is thus transferred, the security interest, if not terminated, becomes unperfected unless the security is certificated and is delivered to the debtor for the purpose of ultimate sale or exchange or presentation, collection, renewal, or registration of transfer. In that case, the security interest becomes unperfected after 21 days unless, within that time the security (or securities for which it has been exchanged) is transferred to the secured party or a person designated by him pursuant to a provision of Section 8–313(1).

Part 4 Registration

§ 8–401. Duty of Issuer to Register Transfer, Pledge, or Release

(1) If a certificated security in registered form is presented to the issuer with a request to register transfer or an in-

struction is presented to the issuer with a request to register transfer, pledge, or release, the issuer shall register the transfer, pledge, or release as requested if:

(a) the security is indorsed or the instruction was originated by the appropriate person or persons (Section 8–308);

(b) reasonable assurance is given that those indorsements or instructions are genuine and effective (Section 8–402);

(c) the issuer has no duty as to adverse claims or has discharged the duty (Section 8–403);

(d) any applicable law relating to the collection of taxes has been complied with; and

(e) the transfer, pledge, or release is in fact rightful or is to a bona fide purchaser.

(2) If an issuer is under a duty to register a transfer, pledge, or release of a security, the issuer is also liable to the person presenting a certificated security or an instruction for registration or his principal for loss resulting from any unreasonable delay in registration or from failure or refusal to register the transfer, pledge, or release.

§ 8–402. Assurance that Indorsements and Instructions Are Effective

(1) The issuer may require the following assurance that each necessary indorsement of a certified security or each instruction (Section 8–308) is genuine and effective:

(a) in all cases, a guarantee of the signature (Section 8–312(1) or (2)) of the person indorsing a certificated security or originating an instruction including, in the case of an instruction, a warranty of the taxpayer identification number or, in the absence thereof, other reasonable assurance of identity;

(b) if the indorsement is made or the instruction is originated by an agent, appropriate assurance of authority to sign;

(c) if the indorsement is made or the instruction is originated by a fiduciary, appropriate evidence of appointment or incumbency;

(d) if there is more than one fiduciary, reasonable assurance that all who are required to sign have done so; and

(e) if the indorsement is made or the instruction is originated by a person not covered by any of the foregoing, assurance appropriate to the case corresponding as nearly as may be to the foregoing.

(2) A ''guarantee of the signature'' in subsection (1) means a guarantee signed by or on behalf of a person reasonably believed by the issuer to be responsible. The issue may adopt standards with respect to responsibility if they are not manifestly unreasonable.

(3) ''Appropriate evidence of appointment or incumbency'' in subsection (1) means:

(a) in the case of a fiduciary appointed or qualified by a court, a certificate issued by or under the direction or supervision of that court or an officer thereof and dated within 60 days before the date of presentation for transfer, pledge, or release; or

(b) in any other case, a copy of a document showing the appointment or a certificate issued by or on behalf of a person reasonably believed by the issuer to be responsible or, in the absence of that document or certificate, other evidence reasonably deemed by the issuer to be appropriate. The issuer may adopt standards with respect to the evidence if they are not manifestly unreasonable. The issuer is not charged with notice of the contents of any document obtained pursuant to this paragraph (b) except to the extent that the contents relate directly to the appointment or incumbency.

(4) The issuer may elect to require reasonable assurance beyond that specified in this section, but if it does so and, for a purpose other than that specified in subsection (3)(b), both requires and obtains a copy of a will, trust, in den-ture, articles of co-partnership, by-laws, or other controlling instrument, it is charged with notice of all matters contained therein affecting the transfer, pledge, or release.

§ 8–403.   Issuer's Duty as to Adverse Claims

(1) An issuer to whom a certificated security is presented for registration shall inquire into adverse claims if:

(a) a written notification of an adverse claim is received at a time and in a manner affording the issuer a reasonable opportunity to act on it prior to the issuance of a new, reissued, or reregistered certificated security, and the notification identifies the claimant, the registered owner, and the issue of which the security is a part, and provides an address for communications directed to the claimant; or

(b) the issuer is charged with notice of an adverse claim from a controlling instrument it has elected to require under Section 8–402(4).

(2) The issuer may discharge any duty of inquiry by any reasonable means, including notifying an adverse claimant by registered or certified mail at the address furnished by him or, if there be no such address, at his residence or regular place of business that the certificated security has been presented for registration of transfer by a named person, and that the transfer will be registered unless within 30 days from the date of mailing the notification, either:

(a) an appropriate restraining order, injunction, or other process issues from a court of competent jurisdiction; or

(b) there is filed with the issuer an indemnity bond, sufficient in the issuer's judgment to protect the issuer and any transfer agent, registrar, or other agent of the issuer involved from any loss it or they may suffer by complying with the adverse claim.

(3) Unless an issuer is charged with notice of an adverse claim from a controlling instrument which it has elected to require under Section 8–402(4) or receives notification of an adverse claim under subsection (1), if a certificated security presented for registration is indorsed by the ap-

propriate person or persons the issuer is under no duty to inquire into adverse claims. In particular:

(a) an issuer registering a certificated security in the name of a person who is a fiduciary or who is described as a fiduciary is not bound to inquire into the existence, extent, or correct description of the fiduciary relationship; and thereafter the issuer may assume without inquiry that the newly registered owner continues to be the fiduciary until the issuer receives written notice that the fiduciary is no longer acting as such with respect to the particular security;

(b) an issuer registering transfer on an indorsement by a fiduciary is not bound to inquire whether the transfer is made in compliance with a controlling instrument or with the law of the state having jurisdiction of the fiduciary relationship, including any law requiring the fiduciary to obtain court approval of the transfer; and

(c) the issuer is not charged with notice of the contents of any court record or file or other recorded or unrecorded document even though the document is in its possession and even though the transfer is made on the indorsement of a fiduciary to the fiduciary himself or to his nominee.

(4) An issuer is under no duty as to adverse claims with respect to an uncertificated security except:

(a) claims embodied in a restraining order, injunction, or other legal process served upon the issuer if the process was served at a time and in a manner affording the issuer a reasonable opportunity to act on it in accordance with the requirements of subsection (5);

(b) claims of which the issuer has received a written notification from the registered owner or the registered pledgee if the notification was received at a time and in a manner affording the issuer a reasonable opportunity to act on it in accordance with the requirements of subsection (5);

(c) claims (including restrictions on transfer not imposed by the issuer) to which the registration of transfer to the present registered owner was subject and were so noted in the initial transaction statement sent to him; and

(d) claims as to which an issuer is charged with notice from a controlling instrument it has elected to require under Section 8–402(4).

(5) If the issuer of an uncertificated security is under a duty to an adverse claim, he discharges that duty by:

(a) including a notation of the claim in any statements sent with respect to the security under Sections 8–408(3), (6), and (7), and

(b) refusing to register the transfer or pledge of the security unless the nature of the claim does not preclude transfer or pledge subject thereto.

(6) If the transfer of pledge of the security is registered subject to an adverse claim, a notation of the claim must be included in the initial transaction statement and all subsequent statements sent to the transferee and pledgee under Section 8–408.

(7) Notwithstanding subsections (4) and (5), if an uncertificated security was subject to a registered pledge at the time the issuer first came under a duty as to a particular adverse claim, the issuer has no duty as to that claim if transfer of the security is requested by the registered pledgee or an appropriate person acting for the registered pledgee unless:

(a) the claim was embodied in legal process which expressly provides otherwise;

(b) the claim was asserted in a written notification from the registered pledgee;

(c) the claim was one as to which the issuer was charged with notice from a controlling instrument it required under Section 8–402(4) in connection with the pledgee's request for transfer; or

(d) the transfer requested is to the registered owner.

§ 8–404.   *Liability and Non-Liability for Registration*

(1) Except as provided in any law relating to the collection of taxes, the issuer is not liable to the owner, pledgee, or any other person suffering loss as a result of the registration of a transfer, pledge, or release of a security if:

(a) there were on or with a certificated security the necessary indorsements or the issuer had received an instruction originated by an appropriate person (Section 8–308); and

(b) the issuer had no duty as to adverse claims or has discharged the duty (Section 8–403).

(2) If an issuer has registered a transfer of a certificated security to a person not entitled to it, the issuer on demand shall deliver a like security to the true owner unless:

(a) the registration was pursuant to subsection (1);

(b) the owner is precluded from asserting any claim for registering the transfer under Section 8–405(1); or

(c) the delivery would result in overissue, in which case the issuer's liability is governed by Section 8–104.

(3) If an issuer has improperly registered a transfer, pledge, or release of an uncertificated security, the issuer on demand from the injured party shall restore the records as to the injured party to the condition that would have obtained if the improper registration had not been made unless:

(a) the registration was pursuant to subsection (1); or

(b) the registration would result in overissue, in which case the issuer's liability is governed by Section 8–104.

§ 8–405.   *Lost, Destroyed, and Stolen Certificated Securities*

(1) If a certificated security has been lost, apparently destroyed, or wrongfully taken, and the owner fails to notify the issuer of that fact within a reasonable time after he has notice of it and the issuer registers a transfer of the security before receiving notification, the owner is precluded from asserting against the issuer any claim for registering the transfer under Section 8–404 or any claim to a new security under this section.

(2) If the owner of a certificated security claims that the security has been lost, destroyed, or wrongfully taken, the issuer shall issue a new certificated security or, at the option of the issuer, an equivalent uncertificated security in place of the original security if the owner:

(a) so requests before the issuer has notice that the security has been acquired by a bona fide purchaser;

(b) files with the issuer a sufficient indemnity bond; and

(c) satisfies any other reasonable requirements imposed by the issuer.

(3) If, after the issue of a new certificated or uncertificated security, a bona fide purchaser of the original certificated security presents it for registration of transfer, the issuer shall register the transfer unless registration would result in overissue, in which event the issuer's liability is governed by Section 8–104. In addition to any rights on the indemnity bond, the issuer may recover the new certificated security from the person to whom it was issued or any person taking under him except a bona fide purchaser or may cancel the uncertificated security unless a bona fide purchaser or any person taking under a bona fide purchaser is then the registered owner or registered pledgee thereof.

§ 8–406.   *Duty of Authenticating Trustee, Transfer Agent, or Registrar*

(1) If a person acts as authenticating trustee, transfer agent, registrar, or other agent for an issuer in the registration of transfers of its certificated securities or in the registration of transfers, pledges, and releases of its uncertificated securities, in the issue of new securities, or in the cancellation of surrendered securities:

(a) he is under a duty to the issuer to exercise good faith and due diligence in performing his functions; and

(b) with regard to the particular functions he performs, he has the same obligation to the holder or owner of a certificated security or to the owner or pledgee of an uncertificated security and has the same rights and privileges as the issuer has in regard to those functions.

(2) Notice to an authenticating trustee, transfer agent, registrar or other agent is notice to the issuer with respect to the functions performed by the agent.

§ 8–407.   *Exchangeability of Securities*

(1) No issuer is subject to the requirements of this section unless it regularly maintains a system for issuing the class of securities involved under which both certificated and uncertificated securities are regularly issued to the category of owners, which includes the person in whose name the new security is to be registered.

(2) Upon surrender of a certificated security with all necessary indorsements and presentation of a written request by the person surrendering the security, the issuer, if he has no duty as to adverse claims or has discharged the duty (Section 8–403), shall issue to the person or a person

designated by him an equivalent uncertificated security subject to all liens, restrictions, and claims that were noted on the certificated security.

(3) Upon receipt of a transfer instruction originated by an appropriate person who so requests, the issuer of an uncertificated security shall cancel the uncertificated security and issue an equivalent certificated security on which must be noted conspicuously any liens and restrictions of the issuer and any adverse claims (as to which the issuer has a duty under Section 8– 403(4)) to which the uncertificated security was subject. The certificated security shall be registered in the name of and delivered to:

(a) the registered owner, if the uncertificated security was not subject to a registered pledge; or

(b) the registered pledgee, if the uncertificated security was subject to a registered pledge.

§ 8–408.   Statements of Uncertificated Securities

(1) Within 2 business days after the transfer of an uncertificated security has been registered, the issuer shall send to the new registered owner and, if the security has been transferred subject to a registered pledge, to the registered pledgee, a written statement containing:

(a) a description of the issue of which the uncertificated security is a part;

(b) the number of shares or units transferred;

(c) the name and address and any taxpayer identification number of the new registered owner and, if the security has been transferred subject to a registered pledge, the name and address and any taxpayer identification number of the registered pledgee;

(d) a notation of any liens and restrictions of the issuer and any adverse claims (as to which the issuer has a duty under Section 8–403(4)) to which the uncertificated security is or may be subject at the time of registration or a statement that there are none of those liens, restrictions, or adverse claims; and

(e) the date the transfer was registered.

(2) Within 2 business days after the pledge of an uncertificated security has been registered, the issuer shall send to the registered owner and the registered pledgee a written statement containing:

(a) a description of the issue of which the uncertificated security is a part;

(b) the number of shares or units pledged;

(c) the name and address and any taxpayer identification number of the registered owner and the registered pledgee;

(d) a notation of any liens and restrictions of the issuer and any adverse claims (as to which the issuer has a duty under Section 8–403(4)) to which the uncertificated security is or may be subject at the time of registration or a statement that there are none of those liens, restrictions, or adverse claims; and

(e) the date the pledge was registered.

(3) Within 2 business days after the release from pledge of an uncertificated security has been registered, the issuer shall send to the registered owner and the pledgee whose interest was released a written statement containing:

(a) a description of the issue of which the uncertificated security is a part;

(b) the number of shares or units released from pledge;

(c) the name and address and any taxpayer identification number of the registered owner and the pledgee whose interest was released;

(d) a notation of any liens and restrictions of the issuer and any adverse claims (as to which the issuer has a duty under Section 8–403(4)) to which the uncertificated security is or may be subject at the time of registration or a statement that there are none of those liens, restrictions, or adverse claims; and

(e) the date the release was registered.

(4) An ''initial transaction statement'' is the statement sent to:

(a) the new registered owner and, if applicable, to the registered pledgee pursuant to subsection (1);

(b) the registered pledgee pursuant to subsection (2); or

(c) the registered owner pursuant to subsection (3).

Each initial transaction statement shall be signed by or on behalf of the issuer and must be identified as ''Initial Transaction Statement.''

(5) Within 2 business days after the transfer of an uncertificated security has been registered, the issuer shall send to the former registered owner and the former registered pledgee, if any, a written statement containing:

(a) a description of the issue of which the uncertificated security is a part;

(b) the number of shares or units transferred;

(c) the name and address and any taxpayer identification number of the former registered owner and of any former registered pledgee; and

(d) the date the transfer was registered.

(6) At periodic intervals no less frequent than annually and at any time upon the reasonable written request of the registered owner, the issuer shall send to the registered owner of each uncertificated security a dated written statement containing:

(a) a description of the issue of which the uncertificated security is a part;

(b) the name and address and any taxpayer identification number of the registered owner;

(c) the number of shares or units of the uncertificated security registered in the name of the registered owner on the date of the statement;

(d) the name and address and any taxpayer identification number of any registered pledgee and the number of shares of units subject to the pledge; and

(e) a notation of any liens and restrictions of the issuer and any adverse claims (as to which the issuer has a duty under Section 8–403(4)) to which the uncertificated security is or may be subject or a statement that there are none of those liens, restrictions, or adverse claims.

(7) At periodic intervals no less frequent than annually and at any time upon the reasonable written request of the registered pledgee, the issuer shall send to the registered pledgee of each uncertificated security a dated written statement containing:

(a) a description of the issue of which the uncertificated security is a part;

(b) the name and address and any taxpayer identification number of the registered owner;

(c) the name and address and any taxpayer identification number of the registered pledgee;

(d) the number of shares or units subject to the pledge; and

(e) a notation of any liens and restrictions of the issuer and any adverse claims (as to which the issuer has a duty under Section 8–403(4)) to which the uncertificated security is or may be subject or a statement that there are none of those liens, restrictions, or adverse claims.

(8) If the issuer sends the statements described in subsections (6) and (7) at periodic intervals no less frequent than quarterly, the issuer is not obliged to send additional statements upon request unless the owner or pledgee requesting them pays to the issuer the reasonable cost of furnishing them.

(9) Each statement sent pursuant to this section must bear a conspicuous legend reading substantially as follows: "This statement is merely a record of the rights of the addressee as of the time of its issuance. Delivery of this statement, of itself, confers no rights on the recipient. This statement is neither a negotiable instrument nor a security."

ARTICLE 9   SECURED TRANSACTIONS; SALES OF ACCOUNTS AND CHATTEL PAPER

Part 1   Short Title, Applicability and Definitions

§ 9–101.   Short Title

This Article shall be known and may be cited as Uniform Commercial Code—Secured Transactions.

§ 9–102.   Policy and Subject Matter of Article

(1) Except as otherwise provided in Section 9–104 on excluded transactions, this Article applies

(a) to any transaction (regardless of its form) which is intended to create a security interest in personal property or fixtures including goods, documents, instruments, general intangibles, chattel paper or accounts; and also

(b) to any sale of accounts or chattel paper.

(2) This Article applies to security interests created by contract including pledge, assignment, chattel mortgage, chattel trust, trust deed, factor's lien, equipment trust, conditional sale, trust receipt, other lien or title retention contract and lease or consignment intended as security. This Article does not apply to statutory liens except as provided in Section 9–310.

(3) The application of this Article to a security interest in a secured obligation is not affected by the fact that the obligation is itself secured by a transaction or interest to which this Article does not apply.

§ 9–103.   Perfection of Security Interest in Multiple State Transactions

(1) Documents, instruments and ordinary goods.

(a) This subsection applies to documents and instruments and to goods other than those covered by a certificate of title described in subsection (2), mobile goods described in subsection (3), and minerals described in subsection (5).

(b) Except as otherwise provided in this subsection, perfection and the effect of perfection or non-perfection of a security interest in collateral are governed by the law of the jurisdiction where the collateral is when the last event occurs on which is based the assertion that the security interest is perfected or unperfected.

(c) If the parties to a transaction creating a purchase money security interest in goods in one jurisdiction understand at the time that the security interest attaches that the goods will be kept in another jurisdiction, then the law of the other jurisdiction governs the perfection and the effect of perfection or nonperfection of the security interest from the time it attaches until thirty days after the debtor receives possession of the goods and thereafter if the goods are taken to the other jurisdiction before the end of the thirty-day period.

(d) When collateral is brought into and kept in this state while subject to a security interest perfected under the law of the jurisdiction from which the collateral was removed, the security interest remains perfected, but if action is required by Part 3 of this Article to perfect the security interest,

(i) if the action is not taken before the expiration of the period of perfection in the other jurisdiction or the end of four months after the collateral is brought into this state, whichever period first expires, the security interest becomes unperfected at the end of that period and is thereafter deemed to have been unperfected as against a person who became a purchaser after removal;

(ii) if the action is taken before the expiration of the period specified in subparagraph (i), the security interest continues perfected thereafter;

(iii) for the purpose of priority over a buyer of consumer goods (subsection (2) of Section 9–307), the period of the effectiveness of a filing in the jurisdiction from which the collateral is removed is governed by the rules with respect to perfection in subparagraphs (i) and (ii).

(2) Certificate of title.

(a) This subsection applies to goods covered by a certificate of title issued under a statute of this state or of another jurisdiction under the law of which indication of a security interest on the certificate is required as a condition of perfection.

(b) Except as otherwise provided in this subsection, perfection and the effect of perfection or non-perfection of the security interest are governed by the law (including the conflict of law rules) of the jurisdiction issuing the certificate until four months after the goods are removed from that jurisdiction and thereafter until the goods are registered in another jurisdiction, but in any event not beyond surrender of the certificate. After the expiration of that period, the goods are not covered by the certificate of title within the meaning of this section.

(c) Except with respect to the rights of a buyer described in the next paragraph, a security interest, perfected in another jurisdiction otherwise than by notation on a certificate of title, in goods brought into this state and thereafter covered by a certificate of title issued by this state is subject to the rules stated in paragraph (d) of subsection (1).

(d) If goods are brought into this state while a security interest therein is perfected in any manner under the law of the jurisdiction from which the goods are removed and a certificate of title is issued by this state and the certificate does not show that the goods are subject to the security interest or that they may be subject to security interests not shown on the certificate, the security interest is subordinate to the rights of a buyer of the goods who is not in the business of selling goods of that kind to the extent that he gives value and receives delivery of the goods after issuance of the certificate and without knowledge of the security interest.

(3) Accounts, general intangibles and mobile goods.

(a) This subsection applies to accounts (other than an account described in subsection (5) on minerals) and general intangibles (other than uncertificated securities) and to goods which are mobile and which are of a type normally used in more than one jurisdiction, such as motor vehicles, trailers, rolling stock, airplanes, shipping containers, road building and construction machinery and commercial harvesting machinery and the like, if the goods are equipment or are inventory leased or held for lease by the debtor to others, and are not covered by a certificate of title described in subsection (2).

(b) The law (including the conflict of laws rules) of the jurisdiction in which the debtor is located governs the perfection and the effect of perfection or non-perfection of the security interest.

(c) If, however, the debtor is located in a jurisdiction which is not a part of the United States, and which does not provide for perfection of the security interest by filing or recording in that jurisdiction, the law of the jurisdiction in the United States in which the debtor has its major

executive office governs the perfection and the effect of perfection or non-perfection of the security interest through filing. In the alternative, if the debtor is located in a jurisdiction which is not a part of the United States or Canada and the collateral is accounts or general intangibles for money due or to become due, the security interest may be perfected by notification to the account debtor. As used in this paragraph, ''United States'' includes its territories and possessions and the Commonwealth of Puerto Rico.

(d) A debtor shall be deemed located at his place of business if he has one, at his chief executive office if he has more than one place of business, otherwise at his residence. If, however, the debtor is a foreign air carrier under the Federal Aviation Act of 1958, as amended, it shall be deemed located at the designated office of the agent upon whom service of process may be made on behalf of the foreign air carrier.

(e) A security interest perfected under the law of the jurisdiction of the location of the debtor is perfected until the expiration of four months after a change of the debtor's location to another jurisdiction, or until perfection would have ceased by the law of the first jurisdiction, whichever period first expires. Unless perfected in the new jurisdiction before the end of that period, it becomes unperfected thereafter and is deemed to have been unperfected as against a person who became a purchaser after the change.

(4) Chattel paper. The rules stated for goods in subsection (1) apply to a possessory security interest in chattel paper. The rules stated for accounts in subsection (3) apply to a non-possessory security interest in chattel paper, but the security interest may not be perfected by notification to the account debtor.

(5) Minerals. Perfection and the effect of perfection or nonperfection of a security interest which is created by a debtor who has an interest in minerals or the like (including oil and gas) before extraction and which attaches thereto as extracted, or which attaches to an account resulting from the sale thereof at the wellhead or minehead are governed by the law (including the conflict of laws rules) of the jurisdiction wherein the wellhead or minehead is located.

(6) Uncertificated securities. The law (including the conflict of laws rules) of the jurisdiction or organization of the issuer governs the perfection and the effect of perfection or nonperfection of a security interest in uncertificated securities.

§ 9–104. *Transactions Excluded From Article*

This Articles does not apply.

(a) to a security interest subject to any statute of the United States, to the extent that such statute governs the rights of parties to and third parties affected by transactions in particular types of property; or

(b) to a landlord's lien; or

(c) to a lien given by statute or other rule of law for services or materials except as provided in Section 9–310 on priority of such liens; or

(d) to a transfer of a claim for wages, salary or other compensation of an employee; or

(e) to a transfer by a government or governmental sub-division or agency; or

(f) to a sale of accounts or chattel paper as part of a sale of the business out of which they arose, or an assign-ment of accounts or chattel paper which is for the purpose of collection only, or a transfer of a right to payment under a contract to an assignee who is also to do the performance under the contract or a transfer of a single account to an assignee in whole or partial satisfaction of a preexisting indebtedness; or

(g) to a transfer of an interest in or claim in or under any policy of insurance, except as provided with respect to proceeds (Section 9–306) and priorities in proceeds (Sec-tion 9–312); or

(h) to a right represented by a judgment (other than a judgment taken on a right to payment which was collat-eral); or

(i) to any right of set-off; or

(j) except to the extent that provision is made for fix-tures to Section 9–313, to the creation or transfer of an interest in or lien on real estate, including a lease or rents thereunder; or

(k) to a transfer in whole or in part of any claim arising out of tort; or

(l) to a transfer of an interest in any deposit account (subsection (1) of Section 9–105), except as provided with respect to proceeds (Section 9–306) and priorities in proceeds (Section 9–312).

§ 9–105.   Definitions and Index of Definitions

(1) In this Articles unless the context otherwise requires:

(a) "Account debtor" means the person who is obli-gated on an account, chattel paper or general intangible;

(b) "Chattel paper" means a writing or writings which evidence both a monetary obligation and a security inter-est in or a lease of specific goods, but a charter or other contract involving the use or hire of a vessel is not chattel paper. When a transaction is evidenced both by such a security agreement or a lease and by an instrument or a series of instruments, the group of writings taken together constitutes chattel paper;

(c) "Collateral" means the property subject to a secu-rity interest, and includes accounts and chattel paper which have been sold;

(d) "Debtor" means the person who owes payment or other performance of the obligation secured, whether or not he owns or has rights in the collateral, and includes the seller of accounts or chattel paper. Where the debtor and the owner of the collateral are not the same person, the term "debtor" means the owner of the collateral in any provision of the Article dealing with the collateral, the obligor in any provision dealing with the obligation, and may include both where the context so requires;

(e) "Deposit account" means a demand, time, sav-ings, passbook or like account maintained with a bank, savings and loan association, credit union or like organi-zation, other than an account evidenced by a certificate of deposit;

(f) "Document" means document of title as defined in the general definitions of Article 1 (Section 1–201), and a receipt of the kind described in subsection (2) of Section 7–201;

(g) "Encumbrance" includes real estate mortgages and other liens on real estate and all other rights in real estate that are not ownership interests;

(h) "Goods" includes all things which are movable at the time the security interest attaches or which are fixtures (Section 9–313), but does not include money, documents, instruments, accounts, chattel paper, general intangibles, or minerals or the like (including oil and gas) before ex-traction. "Goods" also includes standing timber which is to be cut and removed under a conveyance or contract for sale, the unborn young of animals, and growing crops;

(i) "Instrument" means a negotiable instrument (de-fined in Section 3–104), or a certificated security (defined in Section 8–102) or any other writing which evidences a right to the payment of money and is not itself a security agreement or lease and is of a type which is in ordinary course of business transferred by delivery with any nec-essary indorsement or assignment;

(j) "Mortgage" means a consensual interest created by a real estate mortgage, a trust deed on real estate, or the like;

(k) An advance is made "pursuant to commitment" if the secured party has bound himself to make it, whether or not a subsequent event of default or other event not within his control has relieved or may relieve him from his ob-ligation;

(l) "Security agreement" means an agreement which creates or provides for a security interest;

(m) "Secured party" means a lender, seller or other person in whose favor there is a security interest, includ-ing a person to whom accounts or chattel paper have been sold. When the holders of obligations issued under an indenture of trust, equipment trust agreement or the like are represented by a trustee or other person, the represen-tative is the secured party;

(n) "Transmitting utility" means any person primarily engaged in the railroad, street railway or trolley bus busi-ness, the electric or electronics communications transmis-sion business, the transmission of goods or pipeline, or the transmission or the production and transmission of elec-tricity, steam, gas or water, or the provision of sewer service.

(2) Other definitions applying to this Article and the sections in which they appear are:

"Account."	Section 9–106.
"Attach."	Section 9–203.
"Construction mortgage."	Section 9–313(1).
"Consumer goods."	Section 9–109(1).
"Equipment."	Section 9–109(2).
"Farm products."	Section 9–109(3).
"Fixture."	Section 9–313(1).
"Fixture filing."	Section 9–313(1).
"General intangibles."	Section 9–106.
"Inventory."	Section 9–109(4).
"Lien creditor."	Section 9–301(3).
"Proceeds."	Section 9–306(1).
"Purchase money security interest."	Section 9–107.
"United States."	Section 9–103.

(3) The following definitions in other Articles apply to this Article:

"Check."	Section 3–104.
"Contract for sale."	Section 2–106.
"Holder in due course."	Section 3–302.
"Note."	Section 3–104.
"Sale."	Section 2–106.

(4) In addition Article 1 contains general definitions and principles of construction and interpretation applicable throughout this Article.

§ 9–106.   Definitions: "Account"; "General Intangibles"

"Account" means any right to payment for goods sold or leased or for services rendered which is not evidenced by an instrument or chattel paper, whether or not it has been earned by performance. "General intangibles" means any personal property (including things in action) other than goods, accounts, chattel paper, documents, instruments, and money. All rights to payment earned or unearned under a charter or other contract involving the use or hire of a vessel and all rights incident to the charter or contract are accounts.

§ 9–107.   Definitions: "Purchase Money Security Interest"

A security interest is a "purchase money security interest" to the extent that it is

(a) taken or retained by the seller of the collateral to secure all or part of its price; or

(b) taken by a person who by making advances or incurring an obligation gives value to enable the debtor to acquire rights in or the use of collateral if such value is in fact so used.

§ 9–108.   When After-Acquired Collateral Not Security for Antecedent Debt

Where a secured party makes an advance, incurs an obligation, releases a perfected security interest, or otherwise gives new value which is to be secured in whole or in part by after-acquired property his security interest in the after-acquired collateral shall be deemed to be taken for new value and not as security for an antecedent debt if the debtor acquires his rights in such collateral either in the ordinary course of his business or under a contract of purchase made pursuant to the security agreement within a reasonable time after new value is given.

§ 9–109.   Classification of Goods; "Consumer Goods"; "Equipment"; "Farm Products"; "Inventory"

Goods are

(1) "consumer goods" if they are used or bought for use primarily for personal, family or household purposes;

(2) "equipment" if they are used or bought for use primarily in business (including farming or a profession) or by a debtor who is a non-profit organization or a governmental subdivision or agency or if the goods are not included in the definitions of inventory, farm products or consumer goods;

(3) "farm products" if they are crops or livestock or supplies used or produced in farming operations or if they are products of crops or livestock in their unmanufactured states (such as ginned cotton, wool-clip, maple syrup, milk and eggs), and if they are in the possession of a debtor engaged in raising, fattening, grazing or other farming operations. If goods are farm products they are neither equipment nor inventory;

(4) "inventory" if they are held by a person who holds them for sale or lease or to be furnished under contracts of service or if he has so furnished them, or if they are raw materials, work in process or materials used or consumed in a business. Inventory of a person is not to be classified as his equipment.

§ 9–110.   Sufficiency of Description

For the purposes of this Article any description of personal property or real estate is sufficient whether or not it is specific if it reasonably identifies what is described.

§ 9–111.   Applicability of Bulk Transfer Laws

The creation of a security interest is not a bulk transfer under Article 6 (see Section 6–103).

§ 9–112.   Where Collateral Is Not Owned by Debtor

Unless otherwise agreed, when a secured party knows that collateral is owned by a person who is not the debtor, the owner of the collateral is entitled to receive from the secured party any surplus under Section 9–502(2) or under Section 9–504(1), and is not liable for the debt or for any deficiency after resale, and he has the same right as the debtor

(a) to receive statements under Section 9–208;

(b) to receive notice of and to object to a secured party's proposal to retain the collateral in satisfaction of the indebtedness under Section 9–505;

(c) to redeem the collateral under Section 9–506;

(d) to obtain injunctive or other relief under Section 9–507(1); and

(e) to recover losses caused to him under Section 9–208(2).

§ 9–113.   Security Interests Arising under Article on Sales

A security interest arising solely under the Article on Sales (Article 2) or the Article on Leases (Article 2A) is subject to the provisions of this Article except that to the extent that and so long as the debtor does not have or does not lawfully obtain possession of the goods

(a) no security agreement is necessary to make the security interest enforceable; and

(b) no filing is required to perfect the security interest; and

(c) the rights of the secured party on default by the debtor are governed (i) by the Article on Sales (Article 2) in the case of a security interest arising solely under such Article or (ii) by the Article on Leases (Article 2A) in the case of a security interest arising solely under such Article.

§ 9–114.   Consignment

(1) A person who delivers goods under a consignment which is not a security interest and who would be required to file under this Article by paragraph (3)(c) of Section 2–326 has priority over a secured party who is or becomes a creditor of the consignee and who would have a perfected security interest in the goods if they were the property of the consignee, and also has priority with respect to identifiable cash proceeds received on or before delivery of the goods to a buyer, if

(a) the consignor complies with the filing provision of the Article on Sales with respect to consignments (paragraph (3)(c) of Section 2–326) before the consignee receives possession of the goods; and

(b) the consignor gives notification in writing to the holder of the security interest if the holder has filed a financing statement covering the same types of goods before the date of the filing made by the consignor; and

(c) the holder of the security interest receives the notification within five years before the consignee receives possession of the goods; and

(d) the notification states that the consignor expects to deliver goods on consignment to the consignee, describing the goods by item or type.

(2) In the case of a consignment which is not a security interest and in which the requirements of the preceding subsection have not been met, a person who delivers goods to another is subordinate to a person who would have a perfected security interest in the goods if they were the property of the debtor.

Part 2   Validity of Security Agreement and Rights of Parties Thereto

§ 9–201.   General Validity of Security Agreement

Except as otherwise provided by this Act a security agreement is effective according to its terms between the parties, against purchasers of the collateral and against creditors. Nothing in this Article validates any charge or practice illegal under any statute or regulation thereunder governing usury, small loans, retail installment sales, or the like, or extends the application of any such statute or regulation to any transaction not otherwise subject thereto.

§ 9–202.   Title to Collateral Immaterial

Each provision of this Article with regard to rights, obligations and remedies applies whether title to collateral is in the secured party or in the debtor.

§ 9–203.   Attachment and Enforceability of Security Interest; Proceeds; Formal Requisites

(1) Subject to the provisions of Section 4–208 on the security interest of a collecting bank, Section 8–321 on security interests in securities and Section 9–113 on a security interest arising under the Article on Sales, a security interest is not enforceable against the debtor or third parties with respect to the collateral and does not attach unless:

(a) the collateral is in the possession of the secured party pursuant to agreement, or the debtor has signed a security agreement which contains a description of the collateral and in addition, when the security interest covers crops growing or to be grown or timber to be cut, a description of the land concerned;

(b) value has been given; and

(c) the debtor has rights in the collateral.

(2) A security interest attaches when it becomes enforceable against the debtor with respect to the collateral. Attachment occurs as soon as all of the events specified in subsection (1) have taken place unless explicit agreement postpones the time of attaching.

(3) Unless otherwise agreed a security agreement gives the secured party the rights to proceeds provided by Section 9–306.

(4) A transaction, although subject to this Article, is also subject to . . . .*, and in the case of conflict

---

Note: At * in subsection (4) insert reference to any local statute regulating small loans, retail installment sales and the like.

The foregoing subsection (4) is designed to make it clear that certain transactions, although subject to this Article, must also comply with other applicable legislation.

This Article is designed to regulate all the ''security'' aspects of transactions within its scope. There is, however, much regulatory legislation, particularly in the consumer field, which sup-between the provisions of this Article and any such statute, the provisions of such statute control. Failure to comply with any applicable statute has only the effect which is specified therein.

§ 9–204.   After-Acquired Property; Future Advances

(1) Except as provided in subsection (2), a security agreement may provide that any or all obligations covered by the security agreement are to be secured by after-acquired collateral.

(2) No security interest attaches under an after-acquired property clause to consumer goods other than accessions (Section 9–314) when given as additional security unless the debtor acquires rights in them within ten days after the secured party gives value.

(3) Obligations covered by a security agreement may include future advances or other value whether or not the advances or value are given pursuant to commitment (subsection (1) of Section 9–105).

§ 9–205.   Use or Disposition of Collateral without Accounting Permissible

A security interest is not invalid or fraudulent against creditors by reason of liberty in the debtor to use, commingle or dispose of all or part of the collateral (including returned or repossessed goods) or to collect or compromise accounts or chattel paper, or to accept the return of goods or make repossessions, or to use, commingle or dispose of proceeds, or by reason of the failure of the secured party to require the debtor to account for proceeds or replace collateral. This section does not relax the requirements of possession where perfection of a security interest depends upon possession of the collateral by the secured party or by a bailee.

§ 9–206.   Agreement Not to Assert Defenses against Assignee; Modification of Sales Warranties Where Security Agreement Exists

(1) Subject to any statute or decision which establishes a different rule for buyers or lessees of consumer goods, an agreement by a buyer or lessee that he will not assert against an assignee any claim or defense which he may have against the seller or lessor is enforceable by an as-

signee who takes his assignment for value, in good faith and without notice of a claim or defense, except as to defenses of a type which may be asserted against a holder in due course of a negotiable instrument under the Article on Commercial Paper (Article 3). A buyer who as part of one transaction signs both a negotiable instrument and a security agreement makes such an agreement.

(2) When a seller retains a purchase money security interest in goods the Article on Sales (Article 2) governs the sale and any disclaimer, limitation or modification of the seller's warranties.

§ 9–207.   Rights and Duties When Collateral Is in Secured Party's Possession

(1) A secured party must use reasonable care in the custody and preservation of collateral in his possession. In the case of an instrument or chattel paper reasonable care includes taking necessary steps to preserve rights against prior parties unless otherwise agreed.

(2) Unless otherwise agreed, when collateral is in the secured party's possession

   (a) reasonable expenses (including the cost of any insurance and payment of taxes or other charges) incurred in the custody, preservation, use or operation of the collateral are chargeable to the debtor and are secured by the collateral;

   (b) the risk of accidental loss or damage is on the debtor to the extent of any deficiency in any effective insurance coverage;

   (c) the secured party may hold as additional security any increase or profits (except money) received from the collateral, but money so received, unless remitted to the debtor, shall be applied in reduction of the secured obligation;

   (d) the secured party must keep the collateral identifiable but fungible collateral may be commingled;

   (e) the secured party may repledge the collateral upon terms which do not impair the debtor's right to redeem it.

(3) a secured party is liable for any loss caused by his failure to meet any obligation imposed by the preceding subsections but does not lose his security interest.

(4) A secured party may use or operate the collateral for the purpose of preserving the collateral or its value or pursuant to the order of a court of appropriate jurisdiction or, except in the case of consumer goods, in the manner and to the extent provided in the security agreement.

§ 9–208.   Request for Statement of Account or List of Collateral

(1) A debtor may sign a statement indicating what he believes tc be the aggregate amount of unpaid indebtedness as of a specified date and may send it to the secured party with a request that the statement be approved or corrected and returned to the debtor. When the security agreement or any other record kept by the secured party identifies the collateral a debtor may similarly request the

---

plements this Article and should not be repealed by its enactment. Examples are small loan acts, retail installment selling acts and the like. Such acts may provide for licensing and rate regulation and may prescribe particular forms of contract. Such provisions should remain in force despite the enactment of this Article. On the other hand if a retail installment selling act contains provisions on filing, rights on default, etc., such provisions should be repealed as inconsistent with this Article except that inconsistent provisions as to deficiencies, penalties, etc., in the Uniform Consumer Credit Code and other recent related legislation should remain because those statutes were drafted after the substantial enactment of the Article and with the intention of modifying certain provisions of this Article as to consumer credit.

secured party to approve or correct a list of the collateral. (2) The secured party must comply with such a request within two weeks after receipt by sending a written correction or approval. If the secured party claims a security interest in all of a particular type of collateral owned by the debtor he may indicate that fact in his reply and need not approve or correct an itemized list of such collateral. If the secured party without reasonable excuse fails to comply he is liable for any loss caused to the debtor thereby; and if the debtor has properly included in his request a good faith statement of the obligation or a list of the collateral or both the secured party may claim a security interest only as shown in the statement against persons misled by his failure to comply. If he no longer has an interest in the obligation or collateral at the time the request is received he must disclose the name and address of any successor in interest known to him and he is liable for any loss caused to the debtor as a result of failure to disclose. A successor in interest is not subject to this section until a request is received by him.

(3) A debtor is entitled to such a statement once every six months without charge. The secured party may require payment of a charge not exceeding $10 for each additional statement furnished.

Part 3 Rights of Third Parties; Perfected and Unperfected Security Interests; Rules of Priority

§ 9–301. Persons Who Take Priority over Unperfected Security Interests; Rights of ''Lien Creditor''

(1) Except as otherwise provided in subsection (2), an unperfected security interest is subordinate to the rights of

(a) persons entitled to priority under Section 9–312;

(b) a person who becomes a lien creditor before the security interest is perfected;

(c) in the case of goods, instruments, documents, and chattel paper, a person who is not a secured party and who is a transferee in bulk or other buyer not in ordinary course of business or is a buyer of farm products in ordinary course of business, to the extent that he gives value and receives delivery of the collateral without knowledge of the security interest and before it is perfected;

(d) in the case of accounts and general intangibles, a person who is not a secured party and who is a transferee to the extent that he gives value without knowledge of the security interest and before it is perfected.

(2) If the secured party files with respect to a purchase money security interest before or within ten days after the debtor receives possession of the collateral, he takes priority over the rights of a transferee in bulk or of a lien creditor which arise between the time the security interest attaches and the time of filing.

(3) A ''lien creditor'' means a creditor who has acquired a lien on the property involved by attachment, levy or the like and includes an assignee for benefit of creditors from the time of assignment, and a trustee in bankruptcy from the date of the filing of the petition or a receiver in equity from the time of appointment.

(4) A person who becomes a lien creditor while a security interest is perfected takes subject to the security interest only to the extent that it secures advances made before he becomes a lien creditor or within 45 days thereafter or made without knowledge of the lien or pursuant to a commitment entered into without knowledge of the lien.

§ 9–302. When Filing Is Required to Perfect Security Interest; Security Interests to Which Filing Provisions of This Article Do Not Apply

(1) A financing statement must be filed to perfect all security interests except the following:

(a) a security interest in collateral in possession of the secured party under Section 9–305;

(b) a security interest temporarily perfected in instruments or documents without delivery under Section 9–304 or in proceeds for a 10 day period under Section 9–306;

(c) a security interest created by an assignment of a beneficial interest in a trust or a decedent's estate;

(d) a purchase money security interest in consumer goods; but filing is required for a motor vehicle required to be registered; and fixture filing is required for priority over conflicting interests in fixtures to the extent provided in Section 9–313;

(e) an assignment of accounts which does not alone or in conjunction with other assignments to the same assignee transfer a significant part of the outstanding accounts of the assignor;

(f) a security interest of a collecting bank (Section 4–208) or in securities (Section 8–321) or arising under the Article on Sales (see Section 9–113) or covered in subsection (3) of this section;

(g) an assignment for the benefit of all the creditors of the transferor, and subsequent transfers by the assignee thereunder.

(2) If a secured party assigns a perfected security interest, no filing under this Article is required in order to continue the perfected status of the security interest against creditors of the transferees from the original debtor.

(3) The filing of a financing statement otherwise required by this Article is not necessary or effective to perfect a security interest in property subject to

(a) a statute or treaty of the United States which provides for a national or international registration or a national or international certificate of title or which specifies a place of filing different from that specified in this Article for filing of the security interest; or

(b) the following statutes of this state; [list any certificate of title statute covering automobiles, trailers, mobile homes, boats, farm tractors, or the like, and any central filing statute*]; but during any period in which collateral is inventory held for sale by a person who is in the business of selling goods of that kind, the filing provisions of this Article (Part 4) apply to a security interest in that collateral created by him as debtor; or

(c) a certificate of title statute of another jurisdiction under the law of which indication of a security interest on the certificate is required as a condition of perfection (subsection (2) of Section 9–103).

(4) Compliance with a statute or treaty described in subsection (3) is equivalent to the filing of a financing statement under this Article, and a security interest in property subject to the statute or treaty can be perfected only by compliance therewith except as provided in Section 9–103 on multiple state transactions. Duration and renewal of perfection of a security interest perfected by compliance with the statute or treaty are governed by the provisions of the statute or treaty; in other respects the security interest is subject to this Article.

Note: *It is recommended that the provisions of certificate of title acts for perfection of security interests by notation on the certificates should be amended to exclude coverage of inventory held for sale.

§ 9–303. When Security Interest Is Perfected; Continuity of Perfection

(1) A security interest is perfected when it has attached and when all of the applicable steps required for perfection have been taken. Such steps are specified in Section 9–302, 9–304, 9–305 and 9–306. If such steps are taken before the security interest attaches, it is perfected at the time when it attaches.

(2) If a security interest is originally perfected in any way permitted under this Article and is subsequently perfected in some other way under this Article, without an intermediate period when it was unperfected, the security interest shall be deemed to be perfected continuously for the purposes of this Article.

§ 9–304. Perfection of Security Interest in Instruments, Documents, and Goods Covered by Documents; Perfection by Permissive Filing; Temporary Perfection Without Filing or Transfer of Possession

(1) A security interest in chattel paper or negotiable documents may be perfected by filing. A security interest in money or instruments (other than certificated securities or instruments which constitute part of chattel paper) can be perfected only by the secured party's taking possession, except as provided in subsections (4) and (5) of this section and subsections (2) and (3) of Section 9–306 on proceeds.

(2) During the period that goods are in the possession of the issuer of a negotiable document therefor, a security interest in the goods is perfected by perfecting a security interest in the document, and any security interest in the goods otherwise perfected during such period is subject thereto.

(3) A security interest in goods in the possession of a bailee other than one who has issued a negotiable document therefor is perfected by issuance of a document in the name of the secured party or by the bailee's receipt of notification of the secured party's interest or by filing as to the goods.

(4) A security interest in instruments (other than certificated securities) or negotiable documents is perfected without filing or the taking of possession for a period of 21 days from the time it attaches to the extent that it arises from new value given under a written security agreement.

(5) A security interest remains perfected for a period of 21 days without filing where a secured party having a perfected security interest in an instrument (other than a certificated security), a negotiable document or goods in possession of a bailee other than one who has issued a negotiable document therefor

(a) makes available to the debtor the goods or documents representing the goods for the purpose of ultimate sale or exchange or for the purpose of loading, unloading, storing, shipping, transshipping, manufacturing, processing or otherwise dealing with them in a manner preliminary to their sale or exchange, but priority between conflicting security interests in the goods is subject to subsection (3) of Section 9–312; or

(b) delivers the instrument to the debtor for the purpose of ultimate sale or exchange or of presentation, collection, renewal or registration of transfer.

(6) After the 21 day period in subsections (4) and (5) perfection depends upon compliance with applicable provisions of this Article.

§ 9–305. When Possession by Secured Party Perfects Security Interest Without Filing

A security interest in letters of credit and advices of credit (subsection (2)(a) of Section 5–116), goods, instruments (other than certificated securities), money, negotiable documents, or chattel paper may be perfected by the secured party's taking possession of the collateral. If such collateral other than goods covered by a negotiable document is held by a bailee, the secured party is deemed to have possession from the time the bailee receives notification of the secured party's interest. A security interest is perfected by possession from the time possession is taken without a relation back and continues only so long as possession is retained, unless otherwise specified in this Article. The security interest may be otherwise perfected as provided in this Article before or after the period of possession by the secured party.

§ 9–306.   "Proceeds"; Secured Party's Rights on Disposition of Collateral

(1) "Proceeds" includes whatever is received upon the sale, exchange, collection or other disposition of collateral or proceeds. Insurance payable by reason of loss or damage to the collateral is proceeds, except to the extent that it is payable to a person other than a party to the security agreement. Money, checks, deposit accounts, and the like are "cash proceeds." All other proceeds are "non-cash proceeds."

(2) Except where this Article otherwise provides, a security interest continues in collateral notwithstanding sale, exchange or other disposition thereof unless the disposition was authorized by the secured party in the security agreement or otherwise, and also continues in any identifiable proceeds including collections received by the debtor.

(3) The security interest in proceeds is a continuously perfected security interest if the interest in the original collateral was perfected but it ceases to be a perfected security interest and becomes unperfected ten days after receipt of the proceeds by the debtor unless

(a) a filed financing statement covers the original collateral and the proceeds are collateral in which a security interest may be perfected by filing in the office or offices where the financing statement has been filed and, if the proceeds are acquired with cash proceeds, the description of collateral in the financing statement indicates the types of property constituting the proceeds; or

(b) a filed financing statement covers the original collateral and the proceeds are identifiable cash proceeds; or

(c) the security interest in the proceeds is perfected before the expiration of the ten day period. Except as provided in this section, a security interest in proceeds can be perfected only by the methods or under the circumstances permitted in this Article for original collateral of the same type.

(4) In the event of insolvency proceedings instituted by or against a debtor, a secured party with a perfected security interest in proceeds has a perfected security interest only in the following proceeds:

(a) in identifiable non-cash proceeds and in separate deposit accounts containing only proceeds;

(b) in identifiable cash proceeds in the form of money which is neither commingled with other money nor deposited in a deposit account prior to the insolvency proceedings;

(c) in identifiable cash proceeds in the form of checks and the like which are not deposited in a deposit account prior to the insolvency proceedings; and

(d) in all cash and deposit accounts of the debtor in which proceeds have been commingled with other funds, but the perfected security interest under this paragraph (d) is

(i) subject to any right to setoff; and

(ii) limited to an amount not greater than the amount of any cash proceeds received by the debtor within ten days before the institution of the insolvency proceedings less the sum of (I) the payments to the secured party on account of cash proceeds received by the debtor during such period and (II) the cash proceeds received by the debtor during such period to which the secured party is entitled under paragraph (a) through (c) of this subsection (4).

(5) If a sale of goods results in an account or chattel paper which is transferred by the seller to a secured party, and if the goods are returned to or are repossessed by the seller or the secured party, the following rules determine priorities:

(a) If the goods were collateral at the time of sale, for an indebtedness of the seller which is still unpaid, the original security interest attaches again to the goods and continues as a perfected security interest if it was perfected at the time when the goods were sold. If the security interest was originally perfected by a filing which is still effective, nothing further is required to continue the perfected status; in any other case, the secured party must take possession of the returned or repossessed goods or must file.

(b) An unpaid transferee of the chattel paper has a security interest in the goods against the transferor. Such security interest is prior to a security interest asserted under paragraph (a) to the extent that the transferee of the chattel paper was entitled to priority under Section 9–308.

(c) An unpaid transferee of the account has a security interest in the goods against the transferor. Such security interest is subordinate to a security interest asserted under paragraph (a).

(d) A security interest of an unpaid transferee asserted under paragraph (b) or (c) must be perfected for protection against creditors of the transferor and purchasers of the returned or repossessed goods.

§ 9–307.   Protection of Buyers of Goods

(1) A buyer in ordinary course of business (subsection (9) of Section 1–201) other than a person buying farm products from a person engaged in farming operations takes free of a security interest created by his seller even though the security interest is perfected and even though the buyer knows of its existence.

(2) In a case of consumer goods, a buyer takes free of a security interest even though perfected if he buys without knowledge of the security interest, for value and for his own personal, family or household purposes unless prior to the purchase the secured party has filed a financing statement covering such goods.

(3) A buyer other than a buyer in ordinary course of business (subsection (1) of this section) takes free of a security interest to the extent that it secures future advances made after the secured party acquires knowledge of the pur-

chase, or more than 45 days after the purchase, whichever first occurs, unless made pursuant to a commitment entered into without knowledge of the purchase and before the expiration of the 45 day period.

§ 9–308.   Purchase of Chattel Paper and Instruments

A purchaser of chattel paper or an instrument who gives new value and takes possession of it in the ordinary course of his business has priority over a security interest in the chattel paper or instrument

(a) which is perfected under Section 9–304 (permissive filing and temporary perfection) or under Section 9–306 (perfection as to proceeds) if he acts without knowledge that the specific paper or instrument is subject to a security interest; or

(b) which is claimed merely as proceeds of inventory subject to a security interest (Section 9–306) even though he knows that the specific paper or instrument is subject to the security interest.

§ 9–309.   Protection of Purchasers of Instruments, Documents and Securities

Nothing in this Article limits the rights of a holder in due course of a negotiable instrument (Section 3–302) or a holder to whom a negotiable document of title has been duly negotiated (Section 7–501) or a bona fide purchaser of a security (Section 8–302) and the holders or purchasers take priority over an earlier security interest even though perfected. Filing under this Article does not constitute notice of the security interest to such holders or purchasers.

§ 9–310.   Priority of Certain Liens Arising by Operation of Law

When a person in the ordinary course of his business furnishes services or materials with respect to goods subject to a security interest, a lien upon goods in the possession of such person given by statute or rule of law for such materials or services takes priority over a perfected security interest unless the lien is statutory and the statute expressly provides otherwise.

§ 9–311.   Alienability of Debtor's Rights: Judicial Process

The debtor's rights in collateral may be voluntarily or involuntarily transferred (by way of sale, creation of a security interest, attachment, levy, garnishment or other judicial process) notwithstanding a provision in the security agreement prohibiting any transfer or making the transfer constitute a default.

§ 9–312.   Priorities among Conflicting Security Interests in the Same Collateral

(1) The rules of priority stated in other sections of this Part and in the following sections shall govern when applicable; Section 4–208 with respect to the security interests of collecting banks in items being collected, accompanying documents and proceeds; Section 9–103 on security interests related to other jurisdictions; Section 9–114 on consignments.

(2) A perfected security interest in crops for new value given to enable the debtor to produce the crops during the production season and given not more than three months before the crops become growing crops by planting or otherwise takes priority over an earlier perfected security interest to the extent that such earlier interest secures obligations due more than six months before the crops become growing crops by planting or otherwise, even though the person giving new value had knowledge of the earlier security interest.

(3) A perfected purchase money security interest in inventory has priority over a conflicting security interest in the same inventory and also has priority in identifiable cash proceeds received on or before the delivery of the inventory to a buyer if

(a) the purchase money security interest is perfected at the time the debtor receives possession of the inventory; and

(b) the purchase money secured party gives notification in writing to the holder of the conflicting security interest if the holder had filed a financing statement covering the same types of inventory (i) before the date of filing made by the purchase money secured party, or (ii) before the beginning of the 21 day period where the purchase money security interest is temporarily perfected without filing or possession (subsection (5) of Section 9–304); and

(c) the holder of the conflicting security interest receives the notification within five years before the debtor receives possession of the inventory; and

(d) the notification states that the person giving the notice has or expects to acquire a purchase money security interest in inventory of the debtor, describing such inventory by item or type.

(4) A purchase money security interest in collateral other than inventory has priority over a conflicting security interest in the same collateral or its proceeds if the purchase money security interest is perfected at the time the debtor receives possession of the collateral or within ten days thereafter.

(5) In all cases not governed by other rules stated in this section (including cases of purchase money security interests which do not qualify for the special priorities set forth in subsections (3) and (4) of this section), priority between conflicting security interests in the same collateral shall be determined according to the following rules:

(a) Conflicting security interests rank according to priority in time of filing or perfection. Priority dates from the time a filing is first made covering the collateral or the time the security interest is first perfected, whichever is earlier, provided that there is no period thereafter when there is neither filing nor perfection.

(b) So long as conflicting security interests are unperfected, the first to attach has priority.

(6) For the purposes of subsection (5) a date of filing or perfection as to collateral is also a date of filing or perfection as to proceeds.

(7) If future advances are made while a security interest is perfected by filing, the taking of possession, or under Section 8–321 on securities, the security interest has the same priority for the purposes of subsection (5) with respect to the future advances as it does with respect to the first advance. If a commitment is made before or while the security interest is so perfected, the security interest has the same priority with respect to advances made pursuant thereto. In other cases a perfected security interest has priority from the date the advance is made.

§ 9–313. Priority of Security Interests in Fixtures

(1) In this section and in the provisions of Part 4 of this Article referring to fixture filing, unless the context otherwise requires

(a) goods are ''fixtures'' when they become so related to particular real estate that an interest in them arises under real estate law

(b) a ''fixture filing'' is the filing in the office where a mortgage on the real estate would be filed or recorded of a financing statement covering goods which are or are to become fixtures and conforming to the requirements of subsection (5) of Section 9–402

(c) a mortgage is a ''construction mortgage'' to the extent that it secures an obligation incurred for the construction of an improvement on land including the acquisition cost of the land, if the recorded writing so indicates.

(2) A security interest under this Article may be created in goods which are fixtures or may continue in goods which become fixtures, but no security interest exists under this Article in ordinary building materials incorporated into an improvement on land.

(3) This Article does not prevent creation of an encumbrance upon fixtures pursuant to real estate law.

(4) A perfected security interest in fixtures has priority over the conflicting interest of an encumbrancer or owner of the real estate where

(a) the security interest is a purchase money security interest, the interest of the encumbrancer or owner arises before the goods become fixtures, the security interest is perfected by a fixture filing before the goods become fixtures or within ten days thereafter, and the debtor has an interest of record in the real estate or is in possession of the real estate; or

(b) the security interest is perfected by a fixture filing before the interest of the encumbrancer or owner is of record, the security interest has priority over any conflicting interest of a predecessor in title of the encumbrancer or owner, and the debtor has an interest of record in the real estate or is in possession of the real estate; or

(c) the fixtures are readily removable factory or office machines or readily removable replacements of domestic appliances which are consumer goods, and before the goods become fixtures the security interest is perfected by any method permitted by this Article; or

(d) the conflicting interest is a lien on the real estate obtained by legal or equitable proceedings after the security interest was perfected by any method permitted by this Article.

(5) A security interest in fixtures, whether or not perfected, has priority over the conflicting interest of an encumbrancer or owner of the real estate where

(a) the encumbrancer or owner has consented in writing to the security interest or has disclaimed an interest in the goods as fixtures; or

(b) the debtor has a right to remove the goods as against the encumbrancer or owner. If the debtor's right terminates, the priority of the security interest continues for a reasonable time.

(6) Notwithstanding paragraph (a) of subsection (4) but otherwise subject to subsections (4) and (5), a security interest in fixtures is subordinate to a construction mortgage recorded before the goods become fixtures if the goods become fixtures before the completion of the construction. To the extent that it is given to refinance a construction mortgage, a mortgage has this priority to the same extent as the construction mortgage.

(7) In cases not within the preceding subsections, a security interest in fixtures is subordinate to the conflicting interest of an encumbrancer or owner of the related real estate who is not the debtor.

(8) When the secured party has priority over all owners and encumbrancers of the real estate, he may, on default, subject to the provisions of Part 5, remove his collateral from the real estate but he must reimburse any encumbrancer or owner of the real estate who is not the debtor and who has not otherwise agreed for the cost of repair of any physical injury, but not for any diminution in value of the real estate caused by the absence of the goods removed or by any necessity of replacing them. A person entitled to reimbursement may refuse permission to remove until the secured party gives adequate security for the performance of this obligation.

§ 9–314. Accessions

(1) A security interest in goods which attaches before they are installed in or affixed to other goods takes priority as to the goods installed or affixed (called in this section ''accessions'') over the claims of all persons to the whole except as stated in subsection (3) and subject to Section 9–315(1).

(2) A security interest which attaches to goods after they become part of a whole is valid against all persons subsequently acquiring interests in the whole except as stated in subsection (3) but is invalid against any person with an interest in the whole at the time the security interests attaches to the goods who has not in writing consented to the secur-

ity interest or disclaimed an interest in the goods as part of the whole.

(3) The security interests described in subsections (1) and (2) do not take priority over

(a) a subsequent purchaser for value of any interest in the whole; or

(b) a creditor with a lien on the whole subsequently obtained by judicial proceedings; or

(c) a creditor with a prior perfected security interest in the whole to the extent that he makes subsequent advances if the subsequent purchase is made, the lien by judicial proceedings obtained or the subsequent advance under the prior perfected security interest is made or contracted for without knowledge of the security interest and before it is perfected. A purchaser of the whole at a foreclosure sale other than the holder of a perfected security interest purchasing at his own foreclosure sale is a subsequent purchaser within this section.

(4) When under subsections (1) and (2) and (3) a secured party has an interest in accessions which has priority over the claims of all persons who have interests in the whole, he may on default subject to the provisions of Part 5 remove his collateral from the whole but he must reimburse any encumbrancer or owner of the whole who is not the debtor and who has not otherwise agreed for the cost of repair of any physical injury but not for any diminution in value of the whole caused by the absence of the goods removed or by any necessity for replacing them. A person entitled to reimbursement may refuse permission to remove until the secured party gives adequate security for the performance of this obligation.

§ 9–315.   Priority When Goods Are Commingled or Processed

(1) If a security interest in goods was perfected and subsequently the goods or a part thereof have become part of a product or mass, the security interest continues in the product or mass if

(a) the goods are so manufactured, processed, assembled or commingled that their identity is lost in the product or mass; or

(b) a financing statement covering the original goods also covers the product into which the goods have been manufactured, processed or assembled. In a case to which paragraph (b) applies, no separate security interest in that part of the original goods which have been manufactured, processed or assembled into the product may be claimed under Section 9–314.

(2) When under subsection (1) more than one security interest attaches to the product or mass, they rank equally according to the ratio that the cost of the goods to which each interest originally attached bears to the cost of the total product or mass.

§ 9–316.   Priority Subject to Subordination

Nothing in this Article prevents subordination by agreement by any person entitled to priority.

§ 9–317.   Secured Party Not Obligated on Contract of Debtor

The mere existence of a security interest or authority given to the debtor to dispose of or use collateral does not impose contract or tort liability upon the secured party for the debtor's acts or omissions.

§ 9–318.   Defenses against Assignee; Modification of Contract after Notification of Assignment; Term Prohibiting Assignment Ineffective; Identification and Proof of Assignment

(1) Unless an account debtor has made an enforceable agreement not to assert defenses or claims arising out of a sale as provided in Section 9–206 the rights of an assignee are subject to

(a) all the terms of the contract between the account debtor and assignor and any defense or claim arising therefrom; and

(b) any other defense or claim of the account debtor against the assignor which accrues before the account debtor receives notification of the assignment.

(2) So far as the right to payment or a part thereof under an assigned contract has not been fully earned by performance, and notwithstanding notification of the assignment, any modification of or substitution for the contract made in good faith and in accordance with reasonable commercial standards is effective against an assignee unless the account debtor has otherwise agreed but the assignee acquires corresponding rights under the modified or substituted contract. The assignment may provide that such modification or substitution is a breach by the assignor.

(3) The account debtor is authorized to pay the assignor until the account debtor receives notification that the amount due or to become due has been assigned and that payment is to be made to the assignee. A notification which does not reasonably identify the rights assigned is ineffective. If requested by the account debtor, the assignee must seasonably furnish reasonable proof that the assignment has been made and unless he does so the account debtor may pay the assignor.

(4) A term in any contract between an account debtor and an assignor is ineffective if it prohibits assignment of an account or prohibits creation of a security interest in a general intangible for money due or to become due or requires the account debtor's consent to such assignment or security interest.

Part 4   Filing

§ 9–401.   Place of Filing; Erroneous Filing; Removal of Collateral

First Alternative Subsection (1)

(1) The proper place to file in order to perfect a security interest is as follows:

(a) when the collateral is timber to be cut or is minerals or the like (including oil and gas) or accounts subject to subsection (5) of Section 9–103, or when the financing statement is filed as a fixture filing (Section 9–313) and the collateral is goods which are or are to become fixtures, then in the office where a mortgage on the real estate would be filed or recorded;

(b) in all other cases, in the office of the [Secretary of State].

Second Alternative Subsection (1)

(1) The proper place to file in order to perfect a security interest is as follows:

(a) when the collateral is equipment used in farming operations, or farm products, or accounts or general intangibles arising from or relating to the sale of farm products by a farmer, or consumer goods, then in the office of the . . . . in the county of the debtor's residence or if the debtor is not a resident of this state then in the office of the . . . . in the county where the goods are kept, and in addition when the collateral is crops growing or to be grown in the office of the . . . . in the county where the land is located;

(b) when the collateral is timber to be cut or is minerals or the like (including oil and gas) or accounts subject to subsection (5) of Section 9–103, or when the financing statement is filed as a fixture filing (Section 9–313) and the collateral is goods which are or are to become fixtures, then in the office where a mortgage on the real estate would be filed or recorded;

(c) in all other cases, in the office of the [Secretary of State].

Third Alternative Subsection (1)

(1) The proper place to file in order to perfect a security interest is as follows:

(a) when the collateral is equipment used in farming operations, or farm products, or accounts or general intangibles arising from or relating to the sale of farm products by a farmer, or consumer goods, then in the office of the . . . . in the county of the debtor's residence or if the debtor is not a resident of this state then in office of the . . . . in the county where the goods are kept, and in addition when the collateral is crops growing or to be grown in the office of the . . . . in the county where the land is located;

(b) when the collateral is timber to be cut or is minerals or the like (including oil and gas) or accounts subject to subsection (5) of Section 9–103, or when the financing statement is filed as a fixture filing (Section 9–313) and the collateral is goods which are or are to become fixtures, then in the office where a mortgage on the real estate would be filed or recorded;

(c) in all other cases, in the office of the [Secretary of State] and in addition, if the debtor has a place of business in only one county of this state, also in the office of

. . . . of such county, or, if the debtor has no place of business in this state, but resides in the state, also in the office of . . . . of the county in which he resides.

Note: One of the three alternatives should be selected as subsection (1).

(2) A filing which is made in good faith in an improper place or not in all of the places required by this section is nevertheless effective with regard to any collateral as to which the filing complied with the requirements of this Article and is also effective with regard to collateral covered by the financing statement against any person who has knowledge of the contents of such financing statement.

(3) A filing which is made in the proper place in this state continues effective even though the debtor's residence or place of business or the location of the collateral or its use, whichever controlled the original filing, is thereafter changed.

Alternative to Subsection (3)

[(3) A filing which is made in the proper county continues effective for four months after a change to another county of the debtor's residence or place of business or the location of the collateral, whichever controlled the original filing. It becomes ineffective thereafter unless a copy of the financing statement signed by the secured party is filed in the new county within said period. The security interest may also be perfected in the new county after the expiration of the four-month period; in such case perfection dates from the time of perfection in the new county. A change in the use of the collateral does not impair the effectiveness of the original filing.]

(4) The rules stated in Section 9–103 determine whether filing is necessary in this state.

(5) Notwithstanding the preceding subsections, and subject to subsection (3) of Section 9–302, the proper place to file in order to perfect a security interest in collateral, including fixtures, of a transmitting utility is the office of the [Secretary of State]. This filing constitutes a fixture filing (Section 9–313) as to the collateral described therein which is or is to become fixtures.

(6) For the purposes of this section, the residence of an organization is its place of business if it has one or its chief executive office if it has more than one place of business.

Note: Subsection (6) should be used only if the state chooses the Second or Third Alternative Subsection (1).

§ 9–402.   Formal Requisites of Financing Statement; Amendments; Mortgage as Financing Statement

(1) A financing statement is sufficient if it gives the names of the debtor and the secured party, is signed by the debtor, gives an address of the secured party from which information concerning the security interest may be ob-

tained, gives a mailing address of the debtor and contains a statement indicating the types, or describing the items, of collateral. A financing statement may be filed before a security agreement is made or a security interest otherwise attaches. When the financing statement covers crops growing or to be grown, the statement must also contain a description of the real estate concerned. When the financing statement covers timber to be cut or covers minerals or the like (including oil and gas) or accounts subject to subsection (5) of Section 9–103, or when the financing statement is filed as a fixture filing (Section 9–313) and the collateral is goods which are or are to become fixtures, the statement must also comply with subsection (5). A copy of the security agreement is sufficient as a financing statement if it contains the above information and is signed by the debtor. A carbon, photographic or other reproduction of a security agreement or a financing statement is sufficient as a financing statement if the security agreement so provides or if the original has been filed in this state.

(2) A financing statement which otherwise complies with subsection (1) is sufficient when it is signed by the secured party instead of the debtor if it is filed to perfect a security interest in

(a) collateral already subject to a security interest in another jurisdiction when it is brought into this state, or when the debtor's location is changed to this state. Such a financing statement must state that the collateral was brought into this state or that the debtor's location was changed to this state under such circumstances; or

(b) proceeds under Section 9–306 if the security interest in the original collateral was perfected. Such a financing statement must describe the original collateral; or

(c) collateral as to which the filing has lapsed; or

(d) collateral acquired after a change of name, identity or corporate structure of the debtor (subsection (7)).

(3) A form substantially as follows is sufficient to comply with subsection (1):

Name of debtor (or assignor) ....
Address ....
Name of secured party (or assignee) ....
Address ....

1. This financing statement covers the following types (or items) of property:
    (Describe): ....

2. (If collateral is crops) The above described crops are growing or are to be grown on:
    (Describe Real Estate) ....

3. (If applicable) The above goods are to become fixtures on:*

---

*Where appropriate substitute either "The above timber is standing on . . ." or "The above minerals or the like (including oil and gas) or accounts will be financed at the wellhead or minehead of the well or mine located on . . ."

(Describe Real Estate) ....
and this financing statement is to be filed [for record] in the real estate records. (If the debtor does not have an interest of record) The name of a record owner is ....

4. (If products of collateral are claimed) Products of the collateral are also covered.
    (Use whichever is applicable) ....
    Signature of Debtor (or Assignor) ....
    Signature of Secured Party (or Assignee)

Note: Language in brackets is optional.

(4) A financing statement may be amended by filing a writing signed by both the debtor and the secured party. An amendment does not extend the period of effectiveness of a financing statement. If any amendment adds collateral, it is effective as to the added collateral only from the filing date of the amendment. In this Article, unless the context otherwise requires, the term "financing statement" means the original financing statement and any amendments.

(5) A financing statement covering timber to be cut or covering minerals or the like (including oil and gas) or accounts subject to subsection (5) of Section 9–103, or a financing statement filed as a fixture filing (Section 9–313) where the debtor is not a transmitting utility, must show that it covers this type of collateral, must recite that it is to be filed [for record] in the real estate records, and the financing statement must contain a description of the real estate [sufficient if it were contained in a mortgage of the real estate to give constructive notice of the mortgage under the law of this state]. If the debtor does not have an interest of record in the real estate, the financing statement must show the name of a record owner.

(6) A mortgage is effective as a financing statement filed as a fixture filing from the date of its recording if

(a) the goods are described in the mortgage by item or type; and

(b) the goods are or are to become fixtures related to the real estate described in the mortgage; and

(c) the mortgage complies with the requirements for a financing statement in this section other than a recital that it is to be filed in the real estate records; and

(d) the mortgage is duly recorded.

No fee with reference to the financing statement is required other than the regular recording and satisfaction fees with respect to the mortgage.

(7) A financing statement sufficiently shows the name of the debtor if it gives the individual, partnership or corporate name of the debtor, whether or not it adds other trade names or names of partners. Where the debtor so changes his name or in the case of an organization its name, identity or corporate structure that a filed financing statement becomes seriously misleading, the filing is not effective to perfect a security interest in collateral acquired by the

debtor more than four months after the change, unless a new appropriate financing statement is filed before the expiration of that time. A filed financing statement remains effective with respect to collateral transferred by the debtor even though the secured party knows of or consents to the transfer.

(8) A financing statement substantially complying with the requirements of this section is effective even though it contains minor errors which are not seriously misleading.

Note: Where the state has any special recording system for real estate other than the usual grantor-grantee index (as, for instance, a tract system or a title registration or Torrens system) local adaptations of subsection (5) and Section 9–403(7) may be necessary. See Mass. Gen. Laws Chapter 106, Section 9–409.

§ 9–403. What Constitutes Filing; Duration of Filing; Effect of Lapsed Filing; Duties of Filing Officer

(1) Presentation for filing of a financing statement and tender of the filing fee or acceptance of the statement by the filing officer constitutes filing under this Article.

(2) Except as provided in subsection (6) a filed financing statement is effective for a period of five years from the date of filing. The effectiveness of a filed financing statement lapses on the expiration of the five year period unless a continuation statement is filed prior to the lapse. If a security interest perfected by filing exists at the time insolvency proceedings are commenced by or against the debtor, the security interest remains perfected until termination of the insolvency proceedings and thereafter for a period of sixty days or until expiration of the five year period, whichever occurs later. Upon lapse the security interest becomes unperfected, unless it is perfected without filing. If the security interest becomes unperfected upon lapse, it is deemed to have been unperfected as against a person who became a purchaser or lien creditor before lapse.

(3) A continuation statement may be filed by the secured party within six months prior to the expiration of the five year period specified in subsection (2). Any such continuation statement must be signed by the secured party, identify the original statement by file number and state that the original statement is still effective. A continuation statement signed by a person other than the secured party of record must be accompanied by a separate written statement of assignment signed by the secured party of record and complying with subsection (2) of Section 9–405, including payment of the required fee. Upon timely filing of the continuation statement, the effectiveness of the original statement is continued for five years after the last date to which the filing was effective whereupon it lapses in the same manner as provided in subsection (2) unless another continuation statement is filed prior to such lapse. Succeeding continuation statements may be filed in the same manner to continue the effectiveness of the original statement. Unless a statute on disposition of public records provides otherwise, the filing officer may remove a lapsed statement from the files and destroy it immediately if he has retained a microfilm or other photographic record, or in other cases after one year after the lapse. The filing officer shall so arrange matters by physical annexation of financing statements to continuation statements or other related filings, or by other means, that if he physically destroys the financing statements of a period more than five years past, those which have been continued by a continuation statement or which are still effective under subsection (6) shall be retained.

(4) Except as provided in subsection (7) a filing officer shall mark each statement with a file number and with the date and hour of filing and shall hold the statement or a microfilm or other photographic copy thereof for public inspection. In addition the filing officer shall index the statement according to the name of the debtor and shall note in the index the file number and the address of the debtor given in the statement.

(5) The uniform fee for filing and indexing and for stamping a copy furnished by the secured party to show the date and place of filing for an original financing statement or for a continuation statement shall be $. . . . . . if the statement is in the standard form prescribed by the [Secretary of State] and otherwise shall be $. . . . . ., plus in each case, if the financing statement is subject to subsection (5) of Section 9–402, $. . . . . . The uniform fee for each name more than one required to be indexed shall be $. . . . . The secured party may at his option show a trade name for any person and an extra uniform indexing fee of $. . . . . shall be paid with respect thereto.

(6) If the debtor is a transmitting utility (subsection (5) of Section 9–401) and a filed financing statement so states, it is effective until a termination statement is filed. A real estate mortgage which is effective as a fixture filing under subsection (6) of Section 9–402 remains effective as a fixture filing until the mortgage is released or satisfied of record or its effectiveness otherwise terminates as to the real estate.

(7) When a financing statement covers timber to be cut or covers minerals or the like (including oil and gas) or accounts subject to subsection (5) of Section 9–103, or is filed as a fixture filing, [it shall be filed for record and] the filing officer shall index it under the names of the debtor and any owner of record shown on the financing statement in the same fashion as if they were the mortgagors in a mortgage of the real estate described, and, to the extent that the law of this state provides for the indexing of mortgages under the name of the mortgagee, under the name of the secured party as if he were the mortgagee thereunder, or where indexing is by description in the same fashion as if the financing statement were a mortgage of the real estate described.

Note: In states in which writings will not appear in the real estate records and indices unless actually recorded the bracketed language in subsection (7) should be used.

§ 9–404.   Termination Statement

(1) If a financing statement covering consumer goods is filed on or after . . . . . . , then within one month or within ten days following written demand by the debtor after there is no outstanding secured obligation and no commitment to make advances, incur obligations or otherwise give value, the secured party must file with each filing officer with whom the financing statement was filed, a termination statement to the effect that he no longer claims a security interest under the financing statement, which shall be identified by file number. In other cases whenever there is no outstanding secured obligation and no commitment to make advances, incur obligations or otherwise give value, the secured party must on written demand by the debtor send the debtor, for each filing officer with whom the financing statement was filed, a termination statement to the effect that he no longer claims a security interest under the financing statement, which shall be identified by file number. A termination statement signed by a person other than the secured party of record must be accompanied by a separate written statement of assignment signed by the secured party of record complying with subsection (2) of Section 9–405, including payment of the required fee. If the affected secured party fails to file such a termination statement as required by this subsection, or to send such a termination statement within ten days after proper demand therefor, he shall be liable to the debtor for one hundred dollars, and in addition for any loss caused to the debtor by such failure.

(2) On presentation to the filing officer of such a termination statement he must note it in the index. If he has received the termination statement in duplicate, he shall return one copy of the termination statement to the secured party stamped to show the time of receipt thereof. If the filing officer has a microfilm or other photographic record of the financing statement, and of any related continuation statement, statement of assignment and statement of release, he may remove the originals from the files at any time after receipt of the termination statement, or if he has no such record, he may remove them from the files at any time after one year after receipt of the termination statement.

(3) If the termination statement is in the standard form prescribed by the [Secretary of State], the uniform fee for filing and indexing the termination statement shall be $. . . . . ., and otherwise shall be $. . . . . ., plus in each case an additional fee of $. . . . . for each name more than one against which the termination statement is required to be indexed.

Note: The date to be inserted should be the effective date of the revised Article 9.

§ 9–405.   Assignment of Security Interest; Duties of Filing Officer; Fees

(1) A financing statement may disclose an assignment of a security interest in the collateral described in the financing statement by indication in the financing statement of the name and address of the assignee or by an assignment itself or a copy thereof on the face or back of the statement. On presentation to the filing officer of such a financing statement the filing officer shall mark the same as provided in Section 9–403(4). The uniform fee for filing, indexing and furnishing filing data for a financing statement so indicating an assignment shall be $. . . . . if the statement is in the standard form prescribed by the [Secretary of State] and otherwise shall be $. . . . . ., plus in each case an additional fee of $. . . . . for each name more than one against which the financing statement is required to be indexed.

(2) A secured party may assign of record all or part of his rights under a financing statement by the filing in the place where the original financing statement was filed of a separate written statement of assignment signed by the secured party of record and setting forth the name of the secured party of record and the debtor, the file number and the date of filing of the financing statement and the name and address of the assignee and containing a description of the collateral assigned. A copy of the assignment is sufficient as a separate statement if it complies with the preceding sentence. On presentation to the filing officer of such a separate statement, the filing officer shall mark such separate statement with the date and hour of the filing. He shall note the assignment on the index of the financing statement, or in the case of a fixture filing, or a filing covering timber to be cut, or covering minerals or the like (including oil and gas) or accounts subject to subsection (5) of Section 9–103, he shall index the assignment under the name of the assignor as grantor and, to the extent that the law of this state provides for indexing the assignment of a mortgage under the name of the assignee, he shall index the assignment of the financing statement under the name of the assignee. The uniform fee for filing, indexing and furnishing filing data about such a separate statement of assignment shall be $. . . . . . if the statement is in the standard form prescribed by the [Secretary of State] and otherwise shall be $. . . . . ., plus in each case an additional fee of $. . . . . for each name more than one against which the statement of assignment is required to be indexed. Notwithstanding the provisions of this subsection, an assignment of record of a security interest in a fixture contained in a mortgage effective as a fixture filing (subsection (6) of Section 9–402) may be made only by an assignment of the mortgage in the manner provided by the law of this state other than this Act.

(3) After the disclosure or filing of an assignment under this section, the assignee is the secured party of record.

§ 9–406.   Release of Collateral; Duties of Filing Officer; Fees

A secured party of record may by his signed statement release all or a part of any collateral described in a filed financing statement. The statement of release is sufficient if it contains a description of the collateral being released, the name and address of the debtor, the name and address of the secured party, and the file number of the financing statement. A statement of release signed by a person other than the secured party of record must be accompanied by a separate written statement of assignment signed by the secured party of record and complying with subsection (2) of Section 9–405, including payment of the required fee. Upon presentation of such a statement of release to the filing officer he shall mark the statement with the hour and date of filing and shall note the same upon the margin of the index of the filing of the financing statement. The uniform fee for filing and noting such a statement of release shall be $. . . . . . if the statement is in the standard form prescribed by the [Secretary of State] and otherwise shall be $. . . . . ., plus in each case an additional fee of $. . . . . for each name more than one against which the statement of release is required to be indexed.

[§ 9–407.   Information from Filing Officer]

[(1) If the person filing any financing statement, termination statement, statement of assignment, or statement of release, furnishes the filing officer a copy thereof, the filing officer shall upon request note upon the copy the file number and date and hour of the filing of the original and deliver or send the copy to such person.]

    [(2) Upon request of any person, the filing officer shall issue his certificate showing whether there is on file on the date and hour stated therein, any presently effective financing statement naming a particular debtor and any statement of assignment thereof and if there is, giving the date and hour of filing of each such statement and the names and addresses of each secured party therein. The uniform fee for such a certificate shall be $. . . . . if the request for the certificate is in the standard form prescribed by the [Secretary of State] and otherwise shall be $. . . . . Upon request the filing officer shall furnish a copy of any filed financing statement or statement of assignment for a uniform fee of $. . . . . per page.]

Note: This section is proposed as an optional provision to require filing officers to furnish certificates. Local law and practices should be consulted with regard to the advisability of adoption.

§ 9–408.   Financing Statements Covering Consigned or Leased Goods

A consignor or lessor of goods may file a financing statement using the terms "consignor," "consignee," "lessor," "lessee" or the like instead of the terms specified in Section 9–402. The provisions of this Part shall apply as appropriate to such a financing statement but its filing shall not of itself be a factor in determining whether or not the consignment or lease is intended as security (Section 1–201(37)). However, if it is determined for other reasons that the consignment or lease is so intended, a security interest of the consignor or lessor which attaches to the consigned or leased goods is perfected by such filing.

Part 5   Default

§ 9–501.   Default; Procedure When Security Agreement Covers Both Real and Personal Property

(1) When a debtor is in default under a security agreement, a secured party has the rights and remedies provided in this Part and except as limited by subsection (3) those provided in the security agreement. He may reduce his claim to judgment, foreclose or otherwise enforce the security interest by an available judicial procedure. If the collateral is documents the secured party may proceed either as to the documents or as to the goods covered thereby. A secured party in possession has the rights, remedies and duties provided in Section 9–207. The rights and remedies referred to in this subsection are cumulative.

(2) After default, the debtor has the rights and remedies provided in this Part, those provided in the security agreement and those provided in Section 9–207.

(3) To the extent that they give rights to the debtor and impose duties on the secured party, the rules stated in the subsections referred to below may not be waived or varied except as provided with respect to compulsory disposition of collateral (subsection (3) of Section 9–504 and Section 9–505) and with respect to redemption of collateral (Section 9–506) but the parties may by agreement determine the standard by which the fulfillment of these rights and duties is to be measured if such standards are not manifestly unreasonable:

    (a) subsection (2) of Section 9–502 and subsection (2) of Section 9–504 insofar as they require accounting for surplus proceeds of collateral;

    (b) subsection (3) of Section 9–504 and subsection (1) of Section 9–505 which deal with disposition of collateral;

    (c) subsection (2) of Section 9–505 which deals with acceptance of collateral as discharge of obligation;

    (d) Section 9–506 which deals with redemption of collateral; and

    (e) subsection (1) of Section 9–507 which deals with the secured party's liability for failure to comply with this Part.

(4) If the security agreement covers both real and personal property, the secured party may proceed under this Part as to the personal property or he may proceed as to both the real and the personal property in accordance with his rights and remedies in respect of the real property in which case the provisions of this Part do not apply.

(5) When a secured party has reduced his claim to judgment the lien of any levy which may be made upon his collateral by virtue of any execution based upon the judgment shall relate back to the date of the perfection of the security interest in such collateral. A judicial sale, pursuant to such execution, is a foreclosure of the security interest by judicial procedure within the meaning of this

section, and the secured party may purchase at the sale and thereafter hold the collateral free of any other requirements of this Article.

§ 9–502.   *Collection Rights of Secured Party*

(1) When so agreed and in any event on default the secured party is entitled to notify an account debtor or the obligor on an instrument to make payment to him whether or not the assignor was theretofore making collections on the collateral, and also to take control of any proceeds to which he is entitled under Section 9–306.

(2) A secured party who by agreement is entitled to charge back uncollected collateral or otherwise to full or limited recourse against the debtor and who undertakes to collect from the account debtors or obligors must proceed in a commercially reasonable manner and may deduct his reasonable expenses of realization from the collections. If the security agreement secures an indebtedness, the secured party must account to the debtor for any surplus, and unless otherwise agreed, the debtor is liable for any deficiency. But, if the underlying transaction was a sale of accounts or chattel paper, the debtor is entitled to any surplus or is liable for any deficiency only if the security agreement so provides.

§ 9–503.   *Secured Party's Rights to Take Possession After Default*

Unless otherwise agreed a secured party has on default the right to take possession of the collateral. In taking possession a secured party may proceed without judicial process if this can be done without breach of the peace or may proceed by action. If the security agreement so provides the secured party may require the debtor to assemble the collateral and make it available to the secured party at a place to be designated by the secured party which is reasonably convenient to both parties. Without removal a secured party may render equipment unusable, and may dispose of collateral on the debtor's premises under Section 9–504.

§ 9–504.   *Secured Party's Right to Dispose of Collateral After Default; Effect of Disposition*

(1) A secured party after default may sell, lease or otherwise dispose of any or all of the collateral in its then condition or following any commercially reasonable preparation or processing. Any sale of goods is subject to the Article on Sales (Article 2). The proceeds of disposition shall be applied in the order following to

    (a) the reasonable expenses of retaking, holding, preparing for sale or lease, selling, leasing and the like and, to the extent provided for in the agreement and not prohibited by law, the reasonable attorney's fees and legal expenses incurred by the secured party;

    (b) the satisfaction of indebtedness secured by the security interest under which the disposition is made;

    (c) the satisfaction of indebtedness secured by any subordinate security interest in the collateral if written notification of demand therefor is received before distribution of the proceeds is completed. If requested by the secured party, the holder of a subordinate security interest must reasonably furnish reasonable proof of his interest, and unless he does so, the secured party need not comply with his demand.

(2) If the security interest secures an indebtedness, the secured party must account to the debtor for any surplus, and, unless otherwise agreed, the debtor is liable for any deficiency. But if the underlying transaction was a sale of accounts or chattel paper, the debtor is entitled to any surplus or is liable for any deficiency only if the security agreement so provides.

(3) Disposition of the collateral may be by public or private proceedings and may be made by way of one or more contracts. Sale or other disposition may be as a unit or in parcels and at any time and place and on any terms but every aspect of the disposition including the method, manner, time, place and terms must be commercially reasonable. Unless collateral is perishable or threatens to decline speedily in value or is of a type customarily sold on a recognized market, reasonable notification of the time and place of any public sale or reasonable notification of the time after which any private sale or other intended disposition is to be made shall be sent by the secured party to the debtor, if he has not signed after default a statement renouncing or modifying his right to notification of sale. In the case of consumer goods no other notification need be sent. In other cases notification shall be sent to any other secured party from whom the secured party has received (before sending his notification to the debtor or before the debtor's renunciation of his rights) written notice of a claim of an interest in the collateral. The secured party may buy at any public sale and if the collateral is of a type customarily sold in a recognized market or is of a type which is the subject of widely distributed standard price quotations he may buy at private sale.

(4) When collateral is disposed of by a secured party after default, the disposition transfers to a purchaser for value all of the debtor's rights therein, discharges the security interest under which it is made and any security interest or lien subordinate thereto. The purchaser takes free of all such rights and interests even though the secured party fails to comply with the requirements of this Part or of any judicial proceedings

    (a) in the case of a public sale, if the purchaser has no knowledge of any defects in the sale and if he does not buy in collusion with the secured party, other bidders or the person conducting the sale; or

    (b) in any other case, if the purchaser acts in good faith.

(5) A person who is liable to a secured party under a guaranty, indorsement, repurchase agreement or the like

and who receives a transfer of collateral from the secured party or is subrogated to his rights has thereafter the rights and duties of the secured party. Such a transfer of collateral is not a sale or disposition of the collateral under this Article.

§ 9–505.   Compulsory Disposition of Collateral; Acceptance of the Collateral as Discharge of Obligation

(1) If the debtor has paid sixty per cent of the cash price in the case of a purchase money security interest in consumer goods or sixty per cent of the loan in the case of another security interest in consumer goods, and has not signed after default a statement renouncing or modifying his rights under this Part a secured party who has taken possession of collateral must dispose of it under Section 9–504 and if he fails to do so within ninety days after he takes possession the debtor at his option may recover in conversion or under Section 9–507(1) on secured party's liability.

(2) In any other case involving consumer goods or any other collateral a secured party in possession may, after default, propose to retain the collateral in satisfaction of the obligation. Written notice of such proposal shall be sent to the debtor if he has not signed after default a statement renouncing or modifying his rights under this subsection. In the case of consumer goods no other notice need be given. In other cases notice shall be sent to any other secured party from whom the secured party has received (before sending his notice to the debtor or before the debtor's renunciation of his rights) written notice of a claim of an interest in the collateral. If the secured party receives objection in writing from a person entitled to receive notification within twenty-one days after the notice was sent, the secured party must dispose of the collateral under Section 9–504. In the absence of such written objection the secured party may retain the collateral in satisfaction of the debtor's obligation.

§ 9–506.   Debtor's Right to Redeem Collateral

At any time before the secured party has disposed of collateral or entered into a contract for its disposition under Section 9–504 or before the obligation has been discharged under Section 9–505(2) the debtor or any other secured party may unless otherwise agreed in writing after default redeem the collateral by tendering fulfillment of all obligations secured by the collateral as well as the expenses reasonably incurred by the secured party in retaking, holding and preparing the collateral for disposition, in arranging for the sale, and to the extent provided in the agreement and not prohibited by law, his reasonable attorney's fees and legal expenses.

§ 9–507.   Secured Party's Liability for Failure to Comply with This Part

(1) If it is established that the secured party is not proceeding in accordance with the provisions of this Part disposition may be ordered or restrained on appropriate terms and conditions. If the disposition has occurred the debtor or any person entitled to notification or whose security interest has been made known to the secured party prior to the disposition has a right to recover from the secured party any loss caused by a failure to comply with the provisions of this Part. If the collateral is consumer goods, the debtor has a right to recover in any event an amount not less than the credit service charge plus ten per cent of the principal amount of the debt or the time price differential plus 10 per cent of the cash price.

(2) The fact that a better price could have been obtained by a sale at a different time or in a different method from that selected by the secured party is not of itself sufficient to establish that the sale was not made in a commercially reasonable manner. If the secured party either sells the collateral in the usual manner in any recognized market therefor or if he sells at the price current in such market at the time of his sale or if he has otherwise sold in conformity with reasonable commercial practices among dealers in the type of property sold he has sold in a commercially reasonable manner. The principles stated in the two preceding sentences with respect to sales also apply as may be appropriate to other types of disposition. A disposition which has been approved in any judicial proceeding or by any bona fide creditors' committee or representative of creditors shall conclusively be deemed to be commercially reasonable, but this sentence does not indicate that any such approval must be obtained in any case nor does it indicate that any disposition not so approved is not commercially reasonable.

[**Author's note:** Articles 2A, 4A, 10 and 11 have been omitted as unnecessary for the purposes of this text.]

Glossary

Abandoned property Property that is discarded with no intent to retrieve.

Acceleration clause Clause in an instrument that gives the holder the right to demand payment early if for any specified reason payment at the time originally stated is in doubt [UCC § 1–208].

Acceptance Agreement to what is offered or tendered; acceptance of goods obligates the buyer to pay for the goods. Acceptance occurs when the buyer, after reasonable opportunity to inspect the goods, indicates either that they are conforming or that buyer will accept them in spite of the nonconformity or fails to make an effective rejection [UCC § 2–606]. Acceptance of commercial paper is the ''drawee's signed agreement to pay a draft as presented'' [UCC § 3–409(a)]. An acceptor has primary liability on the instrument and promises to pay the draft as accepted [UCC § 3–413].

Accommodation party Person who signs a negotiable instrument for the purpose of lending his or her name to the instrument; a surety [UCC § 3–419(a)]. Accommodation parties are liable on the instrument in the capacity in which they sign. [UCC § 3–419(b)].

Accord and satisfaction Agreement to accept a different performance from that which was originally agreed on (accord) and the rendering of that performance (satisfaction).

Account Right to payment for goods sold or leased or for services rendered, such as an ordinary account receivable. [UCC § 9–106].

Accountant-client privilege Right and duty of an accountant to keep communications with a client confidential and to refuse to release information to third parties unless required by court order.

Accounting Comprehensive review of financial records required of agents and copartners.

Accredited investors Exempt offerees in Regulation D private placement offering who have sufficient financial sophistication, net worth, experience, and knowledge to minimize and assume the securities' risk, including certain pension funds, most banks, institutional investors, corporations, employee benefit plans, pension funds, the issuer's upper-level managers, and many well-to-do individuals.

Actual authority Precise power that the principal confers on the agent; composed of express and implied authority.

Actual malice Ill will.

Ad hominem abusive Fallacious argument attacking positions taken by particular person or group.

Ad populum argument Fallacious reasoning encouraging acceptance of attitudes held by group, reader may wish to emulate or please.

Adjudicated insane Act of a court determining formally that a person is incompetent.

Adjudication Process of trying and deciding a case.

Administrator Person named by the court to administer an estate.

Advances/draws Periodic payments to partners to meet personal living expenses.

Adversary system System of law in the United States where the judge acts as a neutral decisionmaker between advocates.

Adverse possession Involuntary transfer of real property accomplished by open, continuous, and hostile possession.

Advising bank Seller's bank in letter of credit transaction, which promises to pay when satisfactory documents are presented.

Advisory jurisdiction Power that the International Court of Justice has to render advisory opinions to nations in dispute.

Affirmative action Proactive plans to avoid future discrimination—for example, active recruiting for minorities, goals, and timetables to secure greater participation in employer's work force by protected classes.

Affirmative disclosures Remedy that requires an advertiser who has omitted certain material facts to reveal the omissions in future advertising.

After-acquired property Property that may be acquired by the debtor in the future [UCC § 9–204].

Agency Fiduciary relationship resulting from principal's consent that agent will act on principal's behalf.

Agency coupled with an interest Principal's power to unilaterally revoke agent's authority limited if agent has personal financial interest in subject matter.

Agency at will Principal and agent ignore lapse of time specified in employment contract, voluntarily continuing their relationship.

Agency by estoppel   Principal's words, conduct, or lack of action creates appearance of authority in purported agent.

Agency for International Development (AID)   U.S. agency guaranteeing foreign buyer's payment to U.S. seller.

Allonge   Paper firmly attached to an instrument [UCC § 3–204(a)].

Alter ego   Theory of piercing the corporate veil where shareholders hold too extensive control over corporation such that they are indistinguishable from corporation.

Ambiguous words   Words critical to author's argument with potentially different meanings so that they create misunderstanding.

American Depository Receipts (ADR)   Securities trading on U.S. markets issued representing actual foreign securities held by foreign bank.

American Stock Exchange (AMEX)   Securities exchange in New York trading securities of somewhat smaller U.S. companies than on the NYSE.

Americans with Disabilities Act (ADA)   1990 federal legislation extending Title VII protections to the disabled, defining additional disabilities, and requiring that facilities make adaptations to promote work by the disabled.

Analogy   Reasoning method comparing two things to generalize about their shared characteristics.

Ancillary restraints   Those restraints of trade that are collateral to the main purpose of a contract and that are generally held to be lawful.

Anecdotes   Unscientifically gathered personal experiences providing only weak evidence.

Annual percentage rate   Uniform way of calculating the interest rate so that it may be used to compare the costs of financing; designed to closely approximate the actual use of the money.

Anomalous endorsement   Endorsement made by a person who is not a holder of the instrument [UCC § 3–205(d)].

Answer   Pleading filed by the defendant that responds to the plaintiff's complaint.

Anticipatory repudiation   Indication by one party to a contract of his or her intent not to perform a contractual obligation some time in the future.

Anticorrupt practices acts   Statutes that prohibit certain types of wrongful political and business practices.

Antidilution statutes   Legislation that protects against the watering down of a company's trademark.

Apparent or ostensible authority   Agent powers expanded when principal causes third parties to reasonably believe agent has additional authority.

Appeal to authority   Fallacious reasoning technique urging acceptance of respected person's views.

Appropriation   Wrongful taking of another's property.

Arbitration clause   Clause that appears in a contract that requires a dispute to be submitted to arbitration.

Arbitrator   Neutral third party often chosen by the parties to resolve a dispute by deciding the case without being bound by formal rules of law.

Articles of partnership   Written partnership agreement specifying rights and liabilities among partners.

Articles of incorporation/charter   Document creating basic corporate governance structure.

Assault   Tort of placing another in apprehension of a battery.

Assignment   Transfer of property rights to another.

Assignment for the benefit of creditors   Type of state debtor protection; an assignment of all or substantially all of the debtor's nonexempt property to the trustee to liquidate and distribute the proceeds to the creditors.

Assumption of the risk   Defense that negates liability that occurs when the plaintiff voluntarily and knowingly exposes him- or herself to the danger that caused the injury.

Assurance of performance   Upon demand, one party to a contract guarantees to the other party that performance will be forthcoming.

Attachment   Prejudgment remedy in which a creditor seizes property in the hands of a debtor to gain priority in case a judgment is obtained.

Attachment and enforceability   Process by which a secured party creates a security interest that is good against the debtor.

Attorney in fact   Another term for agent—not attorney-at-law.

Audit committee   Board committee usually composed solely of outsiders to monitor corporate accounting and auditing process, assess internal control, interact with independent auditors, and oversee the general audit program.

Authorized shares   Amount of stock specifically designated in a corporate charter.

Back-to-back letter of credit   First letter of credit issued by the buyer's bank as collateral for second letter of credit issued by the reseller's bank to finance reseller's acquisition of raw materials, unfinished goods, or finished goods from supplier.

Bad faith   Dishonesty.

Bailee   Person who acknowledges possession of the goods and contracts to deliver them; typically, the carrier or warehouseman [UCC § 7–102(a)].

Bailment Relationship created when property owner transfers possession of property to bailee for some purpose—for example, storage, repair, or transport.

Bailment contract Contract where a bailee agrees to keep possession of personal property for another for the purpose specified, generally either transportation or storage.

Bait and switch Unfair practice where a seller lures customers into a store to buy an advertised product (bait) that it has no intention of selling, in order to sell a higher-priced item (switch).

Banker Person engaged in the business of banking, including a savings bank, savings and loan association, credit union, or trust company [UCC § 4–105(1)].

Banker's acceptance Draft accepted by buyer's bank obligating bank to make payment, often in the future.

Bankruptcy petition Paper that is filed initiating the bankruptcy proceeding.

Bank statement duty Customer's duty to exercise reasonable care in examining the bank statement or items to discover an unauthorized signature or alteration and to notify the bank promptly of any irregularities [UCC § 4–406(c)].

Barter Oldest and simplest countertrade; two trading partners engage in a one-time direct goods exchange of approximately equal value.

Battery Intentional unwanted touching of another.

Bear raiding Series of conspirators' trades at successively lower prices.

Bearer Person in possession of an instrument or document of title payable to bearer or indorsed in blank [UCC § 1–201(5)].

Bearer paper Instrument payable to ''bearer,'' to ''the order of bearer,'' or that does not indicate a specific payee, like ''pay to cash''; bearer paper can be negotiated by delivery alone.

Bearer securities Securities not registered in the owner's name, payable to bearer.

Beneficial ownership SEC's combination of all shares held by related groups for determining 10 percent shareholder status under Section 16 of the 1934 Act.

Beneficiaries Those for whose benefit a trust is established or that inherit under a will or take under an insurance policy.

Between merchants Transaction in which both parties meet the Code definition of merchants [UCC § 2–104(3)].

Beyond a reasonable doubt Proof that is necessary in a criminal case to convict a defendant.

Bilateral contract Contract that involves mutual promises.

Bill Proposed piece of legislation.

Bill of lading Document of title evidencing the receipt of goods for shipment issued by a carrier to the shipper of goods listing the goods to be shipped, the terms of delivery, and the destination [UCC § 1–201(6)].

Blank indorsement Indorsement that does not name a new payee; converts order paper into bearer paper or retains the bearer status of bearer paper [UCC § 3–205(b)]. The instrument can be negotiated by mere transfer of possession after a blank indorsement.

Blind trust Trust where the settlor neither has control over the res nor is aware of the specific investments.

Blocking law Foreign legal prohibition against providing pretrial discovery to overseas litigation.

Blue pencil test Act of a judge excising a portion of the contract or reforming it to avoid unconscionability.

Blue sky law State securities laws; term is derived from securities promoters' extravagant claims compared to ''selling building lots in the blue sky in fee simple.''

Bona fide occupational qualification (BFOQ) Employer's business necessity requires hirees have particular religion, sex, or national origin; never includes race.

Bona fide purchaser Good faith purchaser for value; one who purchases without notice of any wrongdoing.

Borrowed servant Agent of another employer on loan to an employer; employer with primary right to control agent's activities generally liable for agent's torts.

Bribery Offering of something of value in order to influence a public official.

Broad constructionists School of constitutional interpretation that liberally interprets the document.

Brokers Agents effecting transactions on exchanges or the OTC market for customers; compensated by commission.

Bulk sale Transfer in bulk and not in the ordinary course of business of a major part of inventory; or a transfer of a substantial part of the equipment made in connection with a bulk transfer or inventory [UCC § 6–102 (1)(2)].

Bull raiding Series of conspirators' trades at successively higher prices.

Business judgment rule Defense of management, officers, and directors to charges of negligence if the decisions made are authorized, made in good faith, not arbitrary, and do not abuse the discretion of the decisionmakers.

Buy-sell agreement Partners continuing after dissolution obligation to purchase outgoing partner's interest.

Buybacks Goods seller accepts payment (compensation) in products derived from the original goods sold—for example, factory output from machines traded.

Buyer in the ordinary course Person who in good faith and without knowledge that the sale to him or her is in violation of the ownership rights or security interest of a third party in the goods buys in ordinary course from a person in the business of selling goods of that kind; one who purchases in good faith from inventory [UCC § 1–201(9)].

Buyer's right of inspection   Buyer's right to inspect goods subject to a contract for purchase to determine if they are conforming [UCC § 2–511].

Buyout of a partner   RUPA alternative to dissolution and reformation excluding the partner bought out by remaining partners.

C&F   Mercantile term meaning that the sale price includes the cost of goods and freight charges but not insurance.

Call option   Security representing right to purchase underlying security from another at specified price.

Capital reduction surplus   Dividend source from reduction in stated capital; permitted in some states.

Capital structure   Mix of corporate securities providing corporate capital.

Capital surplus/capital contributed in excess of par   Aggregate of value received for shares above stated or par value.

Case law   Judge-made law.

Case of first impression   Novel case that has no precedent on which to rely.

Cashier's check   Draft where the drawer and the drawee are the same bank [UCC § 3–104(g)].

Casualty to identified goods   Where goods identified to the contract have been destroyed, both parties are excused from performance because it would be impossible for the seller to perform [UCC § 2–613(a)].

Categorical imperatives   Duties that underlie the theory of Immanuel Kant.

Causation   Relationship between reasons given and author's conclusion.

Cease and desist order   Command, usually by an administrative agency, that is similar to an injunction.

Certificate of authority   Document issued by secretary of state in foreign state entitling foreign corporation to operate in that state.

Certificate of deposit   Note where the maker is a bank [UCC § 2–104(j)].

Certificate of incorporation   Certificate issued by secretary of state authorizing commencement of operations in corporate form.

Certificate of inspection   Transit document certifying goods in shipment meet sale contract specifications.

Certificated securities   Securities evidenced by written instruments.

Certification   Acceptance of a check by a drawee bank; when a drawee bank certifies a check, it becomes primarily liable on the check and both the drawer and all prior indorsers are discharged [UCC § 3–413(j)].

Certiorari   Writ from a higher court to a lower court for the record of the case; a type of appeal.

Chairman of the board   Principal director presiding over board meetings.

Challenge for cause   Attack on a juror by a party seeking removal of the juror for a statutory reason.

Charging order   Like garnishment, permits creditor to receive funds flow from partners interest to repay debt.

Charitable trust   Trust established for a charitable purpose—for example, a church or school.

Charter amendment   Changes in the corporate charter requiring shareholder approval, as fundamentally altering the corporate form.

Chattel paper   Writing that is evidence of both a promise to pay and a security interest in specific goods [UCC § 9–105(b)].

Check   Draft where the drawee is a bank and that is payable on demand [UCC § 3–104(f)].

Check truncation   Methods of check collection where either the drawee or the depositary bank retains the checks.

Chinese wall   Control procedures to prevent dissemination of inside information within full-service securities firm among departments creating or accessing inside information and broker-dealers able to trade or tip the confidences.

Churning   Excessive, unwanted trading in discretionary trading account to generate commission income, considering number and frequency of trades, repeated transactions in identical securities, length of holding periods, unprofitable or unauthorized trades, unsophisticated customers, and trading among various customer accounts.

CIF   Mercantile term meaning that the sale price includes the cost of goods, insurance, and shipping.

Circuit breakers   Trading exchange prohibitions against program trading after market prices make significant moves within any one day.

Circular reasoning   "Begging the question"; fallacious reasoning by supporting conclusion through restating it as evidence.

Civil law   Law that is based on a code derived from old Roman law.

Civil penalties   Penalties that are imposed as a result of violation of law that does not stigmatize the offender as a criminal.

Claim in recoupment Personal defense that cannot be asserted successfully against third-party holders in due course; however, it can be asserted against a payee even if that payee is a holder in due course [UCC § 3–305(b)].

Class voting Limited voting rights given to normally nonvoting shares in specified situations—for example, class director election, reorganization plan.

Class action shareholder direct suit Shareholder suit for benefit of all similarly situated shareholders collectively seeking personal remedies; brought by representative(s).

Classified board/staggered directors terms Staggered terms for different board member groups lasting several years and overlapping terms.

Clean Air Act Federal legislation that authorized the Environmental Protection Agency to develop national ambient air quality standards, develop emission standards for new sources, and monitor the enforcement of state implementation plans.

Clean collection Seller's bank receives payment on draft after buyer receives goods.

Clean bill of lading Bill of lading lacking any notation of obvious defects.

Clean Water Act Federal leglislation that authorizes the Environmental Protection Agency to develop and enforce water quality standards and effluent limitations and to issue permits for point source discharges.

Closed-end-credit Type of credit where a sum certain is borrowed, usually with a specific repayment plan.

Closed shop Company where only members of a specific union may be employed.

Closely held corporation Private, for-profit corporation with no registered securities traded on a national securities exchange, generally excluding outsiders' participation.

CMI Rules for Electronic Bills of Lading Conventions for transmitting EDI bills of lading.

Codes Compilation of laws arranged in some logical order.

Codetermination German corporate governance and labor law system in which board representation by labor union(s) is required.

Codicil Addition to a will executed with statutory formalities.

Cognovit note Note containing a clause in which the debtor consents in advance to the holder obtaining a judgment against the debtor without notice or hearing.

Collateral Property in which a security interest is created [UCC § 9–105(c)].

Collection guaranteed Guaranty where the guarantor is liable after an execution of judgment is returned unsatisfied against the obligor, the obligor is insolvent, the obli-

gor cannot be served with process, or it "is apparent that payment cannot be obtained" [UCC § 3–419(d)].

Collecting bank Any bank handling an item for collection except the payor bank [UCC § 4–105(5)].

Combined transport document Replaces standard bill of lading on all segments of freight shipped with combined transport operator.

Comaker Person who, with another, makes the contract of absolute liability of a maker. Comakers are jointly and severally liable.

Comfort letter Assurances from investment bankers, attorneys, accountants, and/or appraisers concerning a public offering, private placement, or limited partnership offering.

Commerce clause Provision within the U.S. Constitution that permits Congress to regulate trade among the several states and with foreign countries.

Commercial bribery Offering of something of value in order to influence a company.

Commercial credit Credit that is extended primarily for business purposes.

Commercial impracticability Excuse for performance of a contract because of unforeseen circumstances.

Commercial speech Expressions that are advertisements.

Commercial unit Such unit of goods as by commercial usage is a single whole for purposes of sale and division of which materially impairs its character or value on the market or in use [UCC § 2–105(6)].

Commodity Futures Trading Commission (CFTC) U.S. federal regulatory agency responsible for futures markets.

Commodity Credit Corporation Provides payment assurances to U.S. sellers of surplus agricultural goods.

Commodity Exchange Act (CEA) Federal legislation regulating commodity futures markets.

Common carrier One who agrees to transport goods for hire.

Common law Judge-made law.

Common law marriage Marriage recognized at the common law when man and woman intend to remain together as husband and wife, hold themselves out to the community as married, and are accepted as husband and wife by the couple's peers.

Common-name statutes Validate suits brought against partnership as entity.

Common stock Most universal type of corporate stock.

Community property Property that is owned in common by both husband and wife in states that recognize this form of interest.

Comparable worth Theory extending equal pay requirement beyond two jobs with near identical tasks to any two jobs arguably requiring similar levels of skill, effort, and responsibility under similar working conditions.

Comparative law Study of law by contrasting one country's law in a particular area with another's.

Comparative negligence Defense to the tort of negligence that reduces recovery by the plaintiff's percentage of negligence contributing to the injury.

Compensation committee Board committee that evaluates compensation (e.g., salary, bonuses, and stock options) for board approval.

Compensatory damages Damages necessary to make a victim whole by awarding damages to compensate for actual injury, including pain and suffering in a tort case.

Complaint Pleading filed by the plaintiff that concisely states facts that constitute a cause of action against the defendant.

Composition Agreement where creditors agree to accept specific partial payments in full satisfaction of their claims.

Compulsory share exchange After approval by both corporate boards and majority approval by acquired corporation's shareholders, the latter must exchange acquired corporation shares for acquiring corporation shares.

Computer crimes Crimes that are directed at a computer or that use a computer to commit a crime such as theft.

Concerte activities Actions that are planned by those acting together in pursuit of an unlawful objective.

Conciliation EEOC confidential alternative dispute resolution proceeding between EEOC and employer without alleged victim present.

Conclusion Author's judgment about controversial issue based on author's evidence.

Concurrent condition When each party's obligation to perform under a contract is dependent on the other party's performance.

Concurrent jurisdiction Where more than one court has the power to hear and decide the same case; the plaintiff must elect only one court.

Condition Future event that creates or destroys obligations under a contract.

Condition precedent When a fact or event must occur before a contractual duty arises.

Condition subsequent When a fact or event occurs that discharges a party's obligation under a contract.

Conduit theory Authorized agent avoids contract liability to third party; agent is mere conduit through whom principal communicates with third parties.

Confirmed letter of credit Confirming bank (seller's bank) adds its creditworthiness to letter of credit.

Confirming bank Seller's advising bank also obligated to pay seller upon adequacy of documents even if issuing bank defaults.

Conforming goods Exact goods promised.

Conglomerate merger Merger between companies that do not compete but instead deal in unrelated products or services.

Consent Voluntary agreement, express or implied.

Consent restraint Transfer restriction on security requiring board approval.

Consequentialist Theory of normative philosophy where the rightness of actions are judged by their consequences; teleological.

Consideration Element of a contract that requires a benefit to the promisor or a detriment to the promisee bargained for and given over in exchange for a promise or an act.

Consign To deliver goods for sale or storage.

Consignee Person to whom goods are delivered for sale or storage [UCC § 7–102(b)].

Consignor Shipper; the person from whom goods have been received for sale or storage [UCC § 7–102(c)].

Consolidation Combination of two or more corporations in which combining firms are dissolved and new corporation is formed to inherit all rights and liabilities of combining corporations.

Conspicuous Written so that a reasonable person ought to see it [UCC § 1–201(10)].

Constitution Document that sets out the basic structure of a country's government—for example, the U.S. Constitution.

Construct validity EEOC-sanctioned test-validation method; demonstrated if test measures characteristics considered useful on the job.

Constructive condition Condition precedent or subsequent that is imposed on the parties by operation of law.

Constructive discharge Employees quit because of illegal, discriminatory, or harassing environment.

Constructive trust Trust that is imposed on someone by law—for example, when a person who holds legal title to property is required to hold it for another because fairness demands such.

Construction defect Defect that occurs when the manufacturer of a product deviates from its construction specifications and an otherwise well-designed product becomes faulty as a result.

Consumer credit Credit that is extended primarily for personal, family, or household purposes.

Consumer goods Goods used for personal, family, or household purposes [UCC § 9–109(1)].

Consumer reporting agency Business that regularly engages in the practice of assembling or evaluating consumer credit information or other information on consumers for the purpose of furnishing consumer reports to third parties.

Containerization Freight loaded inside standard-sized metal boxes that facilitate loading, unloading, and transfer between tractor trailers, flatbed railcars, and special freighter vessels.

Content validity EEOC-sanctioned test-validation method; demonstrated with measures of actual job characteristics or skills.

Contentious jurisdiction Power that the International Court of Justice has to render decisions over countries who accept that court's jurisdiction.

Contingency fee Contractual compensation provision conditional on specified event or condition.

Continuation agreement Term in partnership agreement or articles of partnership limiting outgoing partner's right to require wind up and liquidation of partnership assets.

Contract Agreement that the courts will enforce.

Contract bar rule Prohibition of a union election as long as another union is currently representing the employees and a collective bargaining agreement with that union has not been in force for more than three years.

Contribution Common law suretyship right under which co-sureties are given a right to a pro rata share of any amount paid to the creditor.

Contributory negligence Defense to the tort of negligence that results when the plaintiff's negligence contributes to the injury.

Control share acquisition State antitakeover provision allowing other shareholders to grant or deny voting rights to takeover bidder.

Conversion Tort of wrongfully appropriating another's property.

Co-obligor One who is obligated on a debt along with another.

Cooperatives Nonprofit unincorporated associations given special benefits under tax and antitrust laws.

Copyright Governmental grant of a right to the exclusive control of an author's or artist's creations.

Corner Gaining control over substantial deliverable supply of a commodity or other asset to force others to purchase at inflated prices.

Corporate opportunity doctrine Prohibition against fiduciary's competing with corporation by diverting corporate expectancy for personal benefit.

Corporate powers Statements in charter or corporation statutes defining permissible activities for corporation.

Corporate seal Stamp affixed to authenticate corporate documents by making impression in wax or stamped onto paper.

Corporation Artificial legal entity separating control from ownership and possessing limited liability.

Corporation by estoppel Status of defective corporation to retain limited liability as to third parties who treated business as a corporation.

Corrective advertising Remedy that requires an advertiser who has engaged in false advertising to neutralize the damage by engaging in advertising that repudiates the earlier advertising.

Counterclaim Claim made in a defendant's answer that essentially amounts to a suit against the plaintiff.

Counteroffer New offer that constitutes a rejection of the original offer.

Counterpurchase Most common countertrade; seller accepts goods rather than cash in full or partial payment.

Countertrade Compensatory trade involving reciprocal exchanges of goods and/or services linking two or more cross-border trade exchanges.

Course of conduct Customs developed between principal and agent or third party.

Course of dealing Sequence of previous conduct between the parties to a particular transaction that is useful for interpreting their expressions and other conduct [UCC § 1−205(1)].

Covenant not to compete Restrictive provision limiting agent's right to personally compete with former principal or work for competing firm.

Cover To buy comparable goods from someone else after breach of contract by the seller.

Cram down Plan for repayment of creditors under Chapter 11 of the Bankruptcy Act that has not been accepted by every class but where the court has determined that the plan is fair and equitable.

Credit bureaus Businesses that assemble and disseminate existing credit information about consumers.

Creditor beneficiary Person who has given consideration, who is an intended beneficiary of a contract though not a party, and thus is entitled to enforce the contract.

Creditors Those to whom money is owed.

Creditor's bill Court order used against the equitable property of a debtor compelling the debtor to turn over equitable assets (such as intangible property) to be sold at auction.

Criminal action Procedure by which a person is charged with a crime and brought to trial.

Criterion validity EEOC-sanctioned test-validation method; demonstrated by strong statistical relationship between test results and observed job performance.

Cultural relativism Belief that there is no universal standard by which to judge morality; under this theory, actions are moral if they are in conformity with the mores of a culture.

Cumulative-if-earned preferred stock Preferred stock entitling shareholder to receive dividends missed in prior years before declaration of common dividends if sufficient earnings existed in that prior year.

Cumulative preferred stock Preferred stock entitling shareholder to receive dividends missed in prior years before declaration of common dividends.

Cumulative voting Each share has one vote for every director vacancy.

Customer Person having an account with a bank or for whom a bank has agreed to collect items [UCC § 4–104(5)].

Cy Pres **doctrine** French: ''as near as possible''; doctrine where a charitable gift fails—for example, when the charity is no longer in existence, the court may order the gift to another charity that is as near as possible to the failed charity.

Damage Money designed to compensate a person for injury.

De facto corporation Corporation with errors in incorporation process but whose shareholders are nevertheless permitted limited liability.

De facto directors Improperly selected or qualified directors.

De facto merger Courts ignore a transaction's particular form, recognizing its substance as a merger.

De jure corporation Corporation with insignificant defects in its incorporation process.

De jure directors Properly selected and qualified directors.

De novo review Review by a court that results in a completely new consideration of the decision reviewed.

Deadlock Even number of partners or directors equally splitting their votes.

Dealers Securities professionals who trade ''for their own account,'' making wholesaler's profit on the spread between acquisition and resale prices.

Debentures Unsecured corporate debt (bonds).

Debtors Those who owe money.

Deed Instrument used to transfer title of real estate.

Deep Rock doctrine Equitable subordination of shareholders' debt to outsider's debt in bankruptcy.

Defamation Tort of injuring another's reputation by oral or written statements.

Default Failure to comply with the provisions of a contract.

Default judgment Judgment entered against a person for failure to respond or appear.

Defeasible fee Fee simple estate that is conditional—subject to being defeated on a future event or nonoccurrence.

Defective Product is defective if it is unreasonably dangerous beyond the expectation or contemplation of ordinary consumers.

Delaware block method Dominant dissenter's appraisal method, weighted average of (1) market value, (2) net asset value, (3) capitalized dividends, and (4) capitalized earnings.

Delisting Removal of issuer from all exchanges on which its securities trade.

Delivery Surrender of control of a document, instrument, or property without the right to retrieve it.

Demand instrument Instrument payable ''on demand,'' ''at sight,'' or where no time for payment is stated [UCC § 3–108(1)].

Deontological Theories of normative philosophy where the rightness or wrongness of an action is determined by the intentions of the person making the decisions, not by the consequences of the action—for example, Kantian philosophy.

Depositary bank First bank to which an item is transferred for collection; the depositary bank can be the payor bank [UCC § 4–105(2)].

Deposition Questions propounded to party or a witness face-to-face under oath before trial.

Derivative Specialized securities tied to economic factors, futures, options, or other securities.

Descriptive Explanations about the state or condition of the world.

Descriptive assumptions Author's unstated factual beliefs; hidden facts that must be true before the reasons stated can support the author's conclusion.

Design defect Defect in a product where the construction specifications are below the customary standards within the industry or are otherwise defective.

Destination contract Contract that requires the seller to deliver the goods to a particular destination.

Destructive competition Market failure through price-cutting until all competitors but one go bankrupt.

Dicta Reasoning not necessary to decide the case.

Difference principle Part of John Rawls's theory of distributive justice under which people ignorant of their position would accept social and economic inequalities only if they benefit all, especially the least advantaged. This principle stresses the importance of equal opportunities in training and education.

Direct liability Personally and directly responsible for one's own torts; master's liability for personally committing negligent or intentional harms and for negligent supervision or employees or agents.

Direct revocation Express withdrawal of an offer before it is accepted.

Directed verdict Verdict that is directed in favor of a person by the judge when reasonable minds cannot differ.

Director consent RMBCA procedure validating board action or resolution made in conference calls or separate contacts.

Director derivative suits Board right to initiate derivative suits to vindicate corporate rights; recovery or remedy belongs to the corporation.

Director's inspection right Board member's right to examine corporate records.

Disability Physical or mental handicaps that impair major life functions.

Disaffirmance Right of a minor or incompetent to avoid a contract up to a reasonable time after gaining majority age or sanity.

Discharge Release from further obligation.

Disclaimer Term in a contract where one party attempts to limit liability — for example, a statement by a seller that clearly indicates the intent not to make a warranty.

Disclose or abstain rule Insider's choice to reveal confidential information before trading or refrain from trading altogether.

Disclosed principal Existence and identity of principal known to third party.

Discrimination Choosing or differentiating among alternatives based on some distinguishable characteristic(s); illegal when employment decisions are based on a person's membership in a protected class.

Disgorgement Court-ordered return of illegally obtained funds.

Disguised dividends Corporate payments to shareholders who are also employees (e.g., excessive salary, perks) or creditors (interest); considered hidden dividend payments made to avoid the corporate double tax on dividends.

Dishonor Failure to pay or accept a negotiable instrument when properly payable.

Disinterested directors Board members without personal financial conflict of interest in transaction under review and not under direct control of an interested party.

Disparate impact Theory of illegal employment discrimination where employer's use of apparently neutral employment practices has hidden biases adversely impacting a protected class.

Disparate treatment Theory of illegal employment discrimination when direct action favors one group or disfavors another group through announced policies or actual use of discriminatory policies.

Dissenter's appraisal right/remedy Shareholder right to payment for shares if opposed to fundamental corporate change.

Dissolution Change in relation among partners after any partner ceases to be associated in carrying on partnership business.

Distribution in kind Payment of partner's share in specific assets rather than money after liquidation.

Distributive justice Theories that consider the distribution of limited commodities and burdens; similar individuals should be treated similarly. Various theories of distributive justice include egalitarian, capitalism, socialism, fairness, and entitlement.

Diversion Author's manipulative argument drawing reader's attention away from real issues or the author's weaker arguments, assumptions, or logic.

Diversity of citizenship Case where a citizen of one state is suing a citizen of another state where the amount in controversy exceeds $50,000.

Divestiture Court order to a company to eliminate a division or some other aspect of the company, usually because of antitrust violations.

Dividends Periodic distributions of corporate property to shareholders made pro rata.

Divisible Contract that can be logically separated into legal parts and illegal parts.

Document of title Written instrument that permits transfer of the ownership of goods that are in shipment or storage. The document is both evidence of receipt of the goods by the bailee and is a contract for the shipment or storage of identified goods [UCC § 1–201(15)].

Documents of title Legal instruments used in domestic and international goods shipments evidencing ownership of goods — for example, bills of lading, warehouse receipts, air waybills, and dock receipts.

Doing business Condition of a corporation's sufficient minimum contacts within a state to require qualification and appointment of agent within that foreign state.

Domestic concerns Individual, corporation, partnership, association, joint-stock company, business trust, unincorporated association, or sole proprietorship with principal place of business in the United States or organized under U.S. laws subject to FCPA foreign bribery prohibition.

Domestic corporation Business firm with major facilities in the state of its incorporation.

Dominant estate Estate that is benefited in an easement appurtenant.

Donative intent   Voluntary intent to make a gift.

Donee beneficiary   Person who has not given consideration, but is an intended beneficiary of a contract, though not a party, and is entitled to enforce the contract.

Dormant partner   Partner unknown to creditors excused from giving notice of dissociation or partnership termination.

Double agency/dual agency   Agent simultaneously serving two principals in the same transaction; potential conflict of interest unless fully informed consent by both principals.

Dower   Spousal interest of one third of a life interest in real property possessed by a decedent spouse during the marriage that was conveyed out by deed or mortgage or otherwise without the signature of the surviving spouse.

Draft   Three-party instrument where one party orders a second party to pay money to a third party; for example, a check [UCC § 3–104(e)].

Drawee   Party ordered in the draft to make payment [UCC § 3–103(a)(2)].

Drawer   Obligor on a draft. The party who orders the drawee to pay the payee [UCC § 3–103(a)(3)].

Due diligence   Measure of non-negligence among parties involved in IPO insulating them from 1933 Act liability.

Due negotiation   Transfer of a negotiable document to a holder who buys in good faith and without notice of any problems. A person who takes through due negotiation gets title to the document of title and title to the goods.

Dumping   Practice of selling products in other countries for less than they are sold at home.

Durable power of attorney   Written power of attorney that authorizes an agent to act in the stead of the principal under conditions specific in the instrument; can only be revoked by a similar writing or death.

Durable power of attorney for health care   Power of attorney entrusting to a person the power to make health care decisions in the event the principal becomes incompetent.

Duress   Coercion that results in a right to rescind a contract or grounds for a will contest.

Duty to account   Agent's fiduciary duty to reconcile status or disposition of principal's property and funds.

Earned surplus   Total of accumulated profits from a corporation reduced by losses and dividends paid.

Easement   Right of way across another's property.

Easement appurtenant   Easement over an adjacent landowner's property that benefits the dominant estate and burdens the servient estate.

Easement in gross   Personal right of way to make use of another's land.

Economic duress   Economic pressure placed on a person or company forcing something to be done that otherwise would not be done.

Economic waste   Substantial destruction of property; depreciation beyond normal wear and tear.

EDGAR   Electronic Data Gathering Analysis and Retrieval system offering on-line access to SEC financial filings.

Efficient capital markets hypothesis   Theory of financial economics stating that markets quickly and accurately incorporate new information into market prices whether or not such information is released publicly.

Effluent limitations   Emissions that are legally dischargeable from a particular source.

Ejusdem generis   Latin term that provides a rule for statutory interpretation; general words within a listing are controlled by the specific terms that precede those general words.

Election bar rule   Prohibition of a union certification election within 12 months of an election.

Elective share   Share of an estate that the surviving spouse may choose in lieu of the share given under the will.

Electronic data interchange (EDI)   Computer transmittal of price quotes, negotiations, orders, transfer documents, and payments.

Electronic trading links   Facilities on the exchanges of two different nations permitting foreign trading.

Embezzlement   Taking of money or property by someone who has been entrusted with that property.

Eminent domain   Sovereign's constitutional taking of private property for public use with just compensation.

Employee Retirement Income Security Act (ERISA)   Federal act that regulates employer private benefit plans, including medical, disability, and pension, requiring reporting and disclosure.

Employment at will   Rule that employers and employees are free to sever the relationship at any time for most any reason.

Enabling legislation   Law that establishes an administrative agency and grants power to that agency.

Enforcement   Execution of the law.

Enforcement Remedies and Penny Stock Reform Act (ERPSRA)   1990 federal securities legislation increasing SEC's internal enforcement powers, including debarment, disgorgement, cease and desist orders, and money penalties.

Enterprise liability   Unlimited liability under piercing the corporate veil among members of affiliated corporate groups.

Environmental impact statement Statement detailing the impact of proposed administrative action that must be prepared whenever an agency engages in major federal actions significantly affecting the quality of the human environment.

Environmental Protection Agency Federal agency that administers many of the pollution and environmental laws.

Equal dignities rule Agent's authority must be in writing if writing required under statute of frauds for contracts negotiated for principal.

Equal Pay Act 1963 federal legislation amending Fair Labor Standards Act (FLSA) prohibiting unequal pay for work requiring ''equal skill, effort, and responsibility . . . under similar working conditions'' performed by either sex.

Equal principle Part of John Rawls's theory of distributive justice under which each person's civil liberties, such as the right to vote and free speech, must be equal and protected from invasion by others; also called the liberty principle.

Equipment Goods used or bought for use primarily in a business, including farming and professions [UCC § 9–109(2)].

Equitable title Ownership that is recognized by a court of equity even though legal title is vested in another.

Equity Fairness; a system of courts that developed in England whereby a chancellor presided to meet out fairness in cases that were not traditionally assigned to the law courts headed by the king.

Escheat Reversion of property to the state when no heirs exist.

Ethics Principles of conduct that enable one to decide whether an activity is morally right or wrong.

Ethical dilemma Clash of beliefs or values involving questions of how people should live their lives and how they should treat others.

Ethical egoism Theory that people should act only in their own self-interest, to maximize pleasure and minimize pain.

Ex parte One-sided.

Exculpatory clause Clause in a contract that relieves a person of liability.

Ex-dividend Stock sold after the fourth day preceding record date for dividends; buyer does not receive the dividend.

Exclusive jurisdiction Where only one court has the power to hear and decide a case.

Excusable ignorance Doctrine that permits a promisee to recover damages even though the contract is illegal, when the promisor knows of the illegality, the promisee is ignorant, and the violation is technical.

Executed contract Contract that has been performed.

Execution Process by which a judgment is enforced against the property of the debtor, commonly with a writ of execution by which the judgment creditor has the debtor's property seized and sold to satisfy the judgment.

Executive committee Committee of the board usually composed of chairman, chief executive officer, and other specified executives and officers, usually empowered to exercise board powers.

Executor One named in the will to fulfill the intent of the testator as specified in the will.

Executory contract Contract that has not been performed.

Exempt property Certain classes of property unavailable to the creditor upon debtor default.

Exoneration Common law suretyship right under which the surety has the equitable right to compel the debtor to pay the creditor at maturity.

Express conditions Conditions within contracts that are clear from the language.

Express contract Contract whose terms are clear from the language.

Express trusts Trusts that are established in explicit terms.

Expressio unius exclusius alterius Latin term that expresses a method of interpreting a document; expression within the document of one thing impliedly excludes other things.

Expulsion Involuntary retirement or dismissal of partner according to partnership agreement—for example, for professional incompetence, negligence, shirking, low productivity, legal incompetence, or incompatibility.

Extension Contract where creditors agree to extend the time for payment by the debtor.

Extension merger Merger with a company that deals in related goods or services.

Externalities Side effects or by-products of one's economic activities imposing costs or bestowing benefits on others—for example, pollution.

Facts Descriptive statements about past events or current conditions from examples, empirical research, analogies, metaphors, or appeals to authority.

Fair Labor Standards Act Federal statute, administered by the Wage and Hour division of the Labor Department, that prohibits the employment of children under age 14, and regulates the time and type of work for those aged 14–17 and employees' wages and hours.

False confirmations Bogus written billings showing unordered trades to churn customer accounts.

False dilemma Irreconcilable conflicts made between author's argument and author's opposition to force reader's acceptance of author's argument.

False imprisonment   Tort of intentionally restricting another's movement.

False light   Prong of the tort invasion of privacy that is based on publication of information about a person, true or false, that makes the person appear other than as he or she really is.

Farm products   Goods used or produced in farming operations in the possession of the farmer-debtor, including crops and livestock, as well as products of crops and livestock in an unmanufactured state [UCC § 9-109(3)].

Fear sell   Inducing a sale by scaring the customer into buying.

Federal Securities Code   Consolidation and clarification of federal securities laws proposed by the American Bar Association Committee on Federal Regulation of Securities.

Federal questions   Cases that involve the U.S. Constitution, treaties, and federal statutes.

Fee simple absolute   Greatest quantum of interest that one can own in real property.

Fee tail   Estate that continues in the family to lineal descendants.

Fictitious name   Firm name other than surnames of all partners; state registration usually required.

Fictitious payee rule   Rule that places the loss on the maker or drawer when a negotiable instrument is issued to a fictitious person or to a real person with no intent for that person to have any interest in the instrument [UCC 3-404(b)].

Fictitious transactions   Market manipulation through false indication of trading.

Fiduciary   One who is in a relationship of trust—for example, a doctor or a trustee.

Final payment   Point in the collection of a check where all provisional settlements become final; occurs either when the payor bank pays cash for the check or fails to revoke provisional settlements by its midnight deadline [UCC § 4-215(a)].

Final payment rule   Rule that prevents the payor bank from recovering payments from a holder in due course or one who in good faith acted in reliance on the payment [UCC § 3-418(c)].

Finance charge   Cost of a loan.

Financial futures   Derivative investments primarily based on underlying financial assets or indicators—for example, foreign currencies, government securities, market index.

Financial planner   Professionals who provide financial planning advice—for example, personal budgeting, asset management, recommendation purchases of insurance, annuities.

Financial reporting releases   SEC accounting standards determinations.

Financing statement   Document that must be filed in order to perfect a security interest by filing; it notifies third parties of the security interest.

Finder's fee   Compensation for locating contracting parties but not for negotiating contract.

Finding statutes   Legislative enactments that specify the rights and obligations on a person who finds property that has been lost or mislaid.

Firm offer   Offer by a merchant to buy or sell goods in a signed writing that by its terms gives assurances that it will be held open. Such an offer is not revocable for lack of consideration. The offer is irrevocable for the period stated in the offer, or if no period is stated, for a reasonable time, never longer than three months [UCC § 2-205].

Fixed amount   One of the requisites for negotiability. In order for an instrument to be negotiable, it must be possible to calculate the sum of money to be paid.

Fixtures   Personal property that by reason of its annexation, character, or otherwise has become part of the real property.

Floor traders   Registered broker-dealers with seats on securities or commodities exchanges.

FOB   Mercantile term; abbreviation for "free on board."

Force majeure   Termination provisions defining when performance becomes impractical, impossible, or permanently difficult.

Foreign corporation   Corporation while not within its state of incorporation.

Foreign Corrupt Practices Act   Federal statute that prohibits the bribing of foreign officials and establishes accounting and reporting standards designed to discover such bribes.

Foreign Credit Insurance Corporation   U.S. Eximbank subdivision that assembles private insurance company consortium to insure exports against commercial and political losses.

Forfait financing   Buyer's promissory note or time draft indorsed and sold by goods seller to bank at a discount.

Formal contracts   Contracts under seal, recognizances, or negotiable instruments.

Formal Order of Investigation (FOI)   SEC action permitting SEC enforcement personnel's use of subpoena power.

Formal prospectus/statutory prospectus   Definitive disclosure and sales device used in IPO sales.

Formal rulemaking   Power of agencies to promulgate rules and regulations after notice and the opportunity for a hearing before the final rule takes effect.

Forward triangular merger   Acquired corporation is merged into subsidiary formed by acquiring corporation.

Foul bill of lading   Bill of lading with notations made during transit showing obvious damage.

Franchise tax/capital stock tax   State tax levied on number of shares issued or on shares' par value.

Fraud   Intentional misrepresentation of a material fact that induces reliance and causes injury.

Fraud in the transaction   Intentional and active fraud, not mere breach of warranty; sufficient basis for nonpayment on a letter of credit.

Fraud on the market theory   Application of efficient capital market hypothesis permitting proof of reliance through investor's awareness of posted market prices as conduit for true, false, and omitted information concerning an issuer; confers legal presumption that all publicly available information is quickly embedded in stock prices.

Fraudulent conveyance   Transfers within one year of the filing of the bankruptcy petition made with actual intent to defraud creditors, such as transfers of all debtor assets, transfers with the debtor continuing in possession of the property, secret transfers, or transfers to family members [Bankruptcy Act § 548 (a)(1)].

Fraudulent dilution   Management insiders' purchase preference over other shareholders in new share offerings.

Free enterprise   Type of economy that permits open competition and allows the market to establish supply, demand, and prices.

Free gimmick   Promise of free goods if the buyer agrees to purchase other items over a long period of time.

Freedom of Information Act   Federal statute that permits a person to request and receive information from federal administrative agencies and departments.

Freehold estates   Estates that have an indefinite duration.

Freeze-out/squeeze-out   Oppressive misappropriation of minority's participation and investment value, usually in closely held corporation.

Frontrunning   Manipulative insider schemes trading in advance of market-moving information given by the manipulator.

Full warranty   Warranty under the Magnuson-Moss Act in which the seller agrees to repair a product defect within a reasonable time, the consumer has the option of a refund or a product replacement if the product cannot be fixed after a reasonable number of attempts, the consumer must only notify the warrantor to qualify for warranty repairs, and the duration of implied warranties is not limited.

Fully informed consent   Authorization after full disclosure of partner's or double agent's potential conflict of interest.

Fundamental breach   Term used in the Convention for International Sale of Goods; a nonconformity that would "substantially deprive" the buyer of "what he is entitled to expect under the contract" [Article 25].

Fundamental corporate changes   Corporate charter amendments, merger, sale of substantially all corporate assets, or dissolution.

Fungible   Things whose units are the same or equivalent to any other unit—for example, grain.

Future goods   Goods that are not both existing and identified.

Futures commission merchants   Commodity brokers.

Futures contract   Standardized commitments to deliver or take delivery of specified quantity and quality of commodity at previously specified price; traded on commodities exchanges.

Garnishee   Third party who holds property of the debtor subject to garnishment.

Garnishor   Creditor who institutes the process of garnishment to collect a debt.

Garnishment   Action brought by the creditor and directed at the property of the debtor in the hands of a third party.

General agent   Agent with power to negotiate broad range of transactions for principal's benefit.

General intangibles   Any personal property, other than goods, accounts, chattel paper, document, instruments, and money—for example, goodwill, literary rights, copyrights, trademarks, and patents [UCC § 9–106].

General proxy   Shareholder's agent with discretion to vote in shareholder's best interest.

General verdict   Verdict where the jury pronounces who wins and how much.

General warranty deed   Deed that includes warranties assuring ownership in the grantee.

General will   Will that is executed according to the formalities of the state statute.

Gift   Transfer of property without consideration.

Glittering generality   Glib expression evoking emotional response to divert reader's attention.

Global strategic alliances   Long-term and broad international joint ventures among participants in different nations, often in multiple fields.

Golden parachutes   Favorable top-management severance pay contracts paying high salary levels for several years after a takeover.

Good faith   Honesty in fact in the conduct or transaction concerned [UCC § 1–201(19)]; obligation to act in good faith is implied in every contract under the Uniform Commercial Code.

Good faith bargaining Negotiation by union and management that is required by labor law.

Good faith exception Exception to the employment-at-will doctrine that occurs when an employer discharges an employee unfairly or with bad motive.

Goodwill Reputational value of a business.

Goods All things that are movable at the time of identification to the contract for sale or when the security interest attaches, including standing timber to be cut, unborn young animals, and growing crops [UCC § 2–105(1) and § 9–105(h)].

Government in Sunshine Act Federal statute requiring that, with some exemptions, all meetings of an independent agency be open to the public.

Gratuitous agent Agent serving without compensation.

Grease payments Facilitating payments made to lower-echelon employees without discretionary authority; not considered illegal bribery under the FCPA if legal in host nation.

Greenmail Corporate repurchase of takeover raider's stock at premium not offered to other shareholders.

Guarantor Person who promises to pay the debt of another if it is not paid when due; a surety.

Hamburg rules International risk of loss rules shifting burden of proof to carriers; eliminates traditional 17 exemptions and raises monetary limits on carrier liability for losses during shipment.

Hasty generalization Author seeks to have listener ''jump to the author's conclusion'' based on thin, biased, or still incomplete evidence.

Health care proxys Instruments designating a person empowered to make health care decisions for another.

Hearsay evidence Extrajudicial declarations, usually not under oath or subject to cross-examination, that are offered to prove the truth of the matter asserted.

Hedging Act of reducing risk by diversification or making counterbalancing deals to offset potential losses in other deals.

Holder Person in possession of an instrument that is either drawn, issued, or indorsed to his or her order or to bearer or in blank [UCC § 1–201(20)].

Holder in due course Person who is a holder of a negotiable instrument that bears no visible evidence of irregularity, and that was taken in good faith and without notice that the instrument was overdue or had been dishonored, without notice that the instrument contained an unauthorized signature or had been altered, and without notice of any claim or defense [UCC § 3–302].

Holders by due negotiation Persons who take free of adverse claims against the goods, similar to holder in due course; creates special status for purchaser of document for value, in good faith without notice of adverse claims against the document, and who takes document in the ordinary course of their business.

Holding Core of the court decision that acts as precedent.

Holographic will Will that is written solely in the handwriting of the testator and signed.

Homestead exemption Statutory exemption that is free from creditor attachment.

Horizontal merger Merger between companies that compete.

Hostile working environment Unwelcome activities of a sexual nature, innuendoes, off-color remarks, or demeaning jokes creating an intimidating or offensive work environment.

Hot issues New initial public offerings where demand outstrips supply, forcing prices upward quickly.

Household exemptions State laws that permit a head of a family to keep a portion of his or her estate free of creditor attachment; state statutes that permit certain persons to avoid paying real estate taxes.

Hybrid rulemaking Involves a blend of informal and formal rulemaking where a hearing, not as extensive as that provided in formal rulemaking, is required.

Hypothecation Pledge of street name securities to a lender to secure loans made through a broker to finance a customer's investments.

Hypothesis Projection of a chain of reasoning expected in research.

Ideology Value system, a coherent, systematic statement of values.

Identification Manner in which the seller specifies the goods to be sold. It can be set by the parties' agreement. When the contract is for future goods, the goods are identified when they are designated by the seller as the goods covered by the contract [UCC § 2–501(1)(a) and (b)].

Illegal dividends Dividends paid when no legal source exists.

Illusory promise Promise that gives an appearance of a genuine promise but really results in no legal commitment, usually because it lacks consideration.

Implied authority Supplemental authority reasonably necessary to implement express authority.

Implied contract Contract whose terms are implicitly understood.

Implied contract exception Exception to the employment-at-will doctrine when employers make a promise to an employee of job tenure or when they fail to follow company procedures before discharging the employee.

Implied in fact That which can be naturally inferred from an expression.

Implied in law That which though not express or implied nonetheless is constructed by a court.

Implied trust Trust that is established by inference.

Implied warranties Promises about goods that become part of the contract for sale even though the seller has not made them expressly.

Implied warranty of authority Partner or agent acting without authority.

Impostor rule Rule that precludes the maker or drawer from asserting any unauthorized signatures where a party issues a negotiable instrument to someone impersonating another party [UCC § 3–404(a)].

In rem jurisdiction Power of a court to enforce rights over property.

Inadequate capitalization Theory of piercing the corporate veil for corporations with thin financing when originally incorporated.

Incidental beneficiary Person who is not a party to a contract, who benefits indirectly from the contract, who was not contemplated by the parties, and who may not enforce the contract.

Incidental damages To a seller, any commercially reasonable charges, expenses, or commissions incurred in stopping delivery, in the transportation or storage of the goods after buyer's breach, or in connection with the resale of goods; to a buyer, expenses reasonably incurred in inspection, receipt, transportation, and storage of goods rightfully rejected, any commercially reasonable charges incurred while effecting cover, and other reasonable expenses related to the breach.

Incompetency Inability to manage one's affairs; lacking the requisite mental soundness to enter contracts and/or make wills.

Incorporation Process of initiating a new corporation.

Indemnification Corporate power or contract duty to advance payments or repay employee's litigation expenses or judgments owed by employee held liable but who acted with reasonable business judgment and in good faith.

Indemnity contract Agreement to compensate the indemnitee for any loss.

Indenture trustee Trustee responsible to administer bond indenture owing fiduciary duty to bondholders.

Independent contractor Employment relationship giving employer right to control only end—independent contractor controls the means of accomplishment.

Indirect revocation Implied withdrawal of an offer before it is accepted.

Individuation Process by which individuals see themselves separate from the beliefs and values of an organization.

Indorsement Signature on an instrument normally made for the purpose of either negotiating the instrument, restricting payment, or incurring indorser's liability [UCC § 3–204(a)].

Infants Minors.

Informal contracts Contracts that are not under seal, recognizances, or negotiable instruments.

Informal rulemaking Power of agencies to promulgate rules and regulations after notice and the opportunity for interested parties to make written comments before the final rule takes effect.

Information statement SEC form containing information in a proxy statement if management does not solicit proxies.

Inherent authority Authority implied for particular corporate officers derived from apparent authority, custom, and precedent.

In-house counsel Lawyer who acts as legal counsel for a company and who is an employee of that company.

Initial public offerings (IPO) New securities offerings.

Injunction Order by a court commanding one to refrain from doing something.

Injurious falsehood Intentional tort based on a false statement made with malice that tends to disparage the plaintiff's property.

Injury Wrong, hurt, or damage committed to a person's person or property.

Inland freight Transportation between seller's premises and port or between receiving port and buyer's premises.

Inquisitorial system System of law where the judge acts as both investigator and decisionmaker.

Insecurity clauses Clause in a contract authorizing a secured party to accelerate payment if the secured party "deems himself insecure."

Inside directors Board members taken from regular employees, upper-level managers, or officers of the corporation, subsidiaries, affiliates, or parent.

Insider trading Unfair advantage taken by persons exposed to confidential, nonpublic information about an issuer when tipping others or trading with uninformed shareholders.

Insider Trading Sanctions Act (ITSA) 1984 federal securities legislation permitting triple penalties in SEC insider trading enforcement suits.

Insider Trading and Securities Fraud Enforcement Act (ITSFEA) 1988 federal insider trading legislation establishing statutory private right of action for damages, increasing criminal penalties, authorizing payment of bounties to informants, and requiring brokers to supervise employee activities to prevent tipping and insider trading.

Insiders In bankruptcy, relative or partner of an individual debtor, or an officer or director of a corporate director [Bankruptcy Act § 101(31)].

Insolvent Either when unable to pay one's debts when they become due or when one's liabilities exceed one's assets [UCC § 1–201(23)].

Installment contract Contract that requires or authorizes delivery of goods in separate lots to be separately accepted [UCC § 2–612 (1)].

Instruments Negotiable and non-negotiable instruments, Article 8 securities, and any other right to the payment of money evidenced by a writing and of the type that is transferred by delivery in the ordinary course of business [UCC § 9–105(1)(i)].

Intangible personal property Personal property that cannot be touched—for example, stocks and patents.

Integration Combination of several allegedly separate exempt offerings into a single ''integrated'' offering if made too close in time and proceeds raised in a single financing plan.

Intentional infliction of emotional distress Intentional tort based on defendant's outrageous conduct that inflicts severe distress on the plaintiff.

Intentional torts Torts that are committed with consciousness of wrongdoing.

Interlocking directorate Director holds seats on two different corporate boards.

Intermediary bank Intermediary bank is any bank to which an item is transferred for collection, excluding the payor or depositary bank [UCC § 4–105(4)].

Intermediate test Test applied to gender regulation that determines whether the legislation violates the Equal Protection clause, by assessing whether the classifications substantially relate to an important government objective.

Internal accounting controls Systems and procedures for production of accurate financial statements permitting reconciliation of assets and records and safeguarding corporate assets.

International law Law that applies to the relationship between countries; law that determines where a dispute should be heard and what country's laws should apply.

Interpretation Method of reconciling terms and provisions in a contract.

Interrogatories Written questions propounded by one party to the other, who must respond in writing under oath.

Intestate Act of dying without a will.

Intrastate offerings Securities registration exemption for local issuers in close proximity to its investors, suppliers, and customers.

Intrinsic fairness Test of fairness in conflict of interest transactions is inherent fairness to corporation; may require approval by board or shareholders based on full disclosure.

Intrusion Prong of the tort invasion of privacy predicated on the unreasonable interference with another's privacy.

Inventory Goods held for sale or lease; raw materials, work in process, or materials used or consumed in a business [UCC § 9–109(4)].

Investigative reporting companies Businesses that compile information from questioning friends, neighbors, and acquaintances of a consumer.

Investment Advisor Act of 1940 Federal securities law requiring licensing of persons who provide advice in security investments for a fee.

Investment advisers Persons charging fee to advise others on value of securities or advisability of securities investments directly or through published analyses and reports.

Investment contract New, innovative contract rights resembling traditional securities involving investment of money, in common enterprise or scheme, from which investor is led to expect profits, derived from the efforts of others (promoter).

Investment Company Act of 1940 Federal securities law requiring special SEC registration and oversight of mutual funds and money market funds.

Investment intent Test of initial purchaser's genuine objective to hold securities for longer-term investment purpose.

Involuntary dissolution Administrative dissolution of corporation without its consent by state, creditor(s), or shareholder(s).

IPO See *initial public offerings*.

Irrevocable agency/agency coupled with an interest Principal's power to unilaterally revoke agent's authority; limited if agent has personal financial interest in subject matter.

Irrevocable trusts Trusts that may not be revoked by the settlor.

Issue Initial delivery of the instrument by the maker or drawer, typically to the payee [UCC § 3–105(1)].

Issues Primary subjects of a controversy.

Issued shares Amount of authorized stock actually issued and sold to shareholders.

Issuer Person who creates a document of title—for example, on a bill of lading, the issuer will be the carrier [UCC § 7–102(g)].

Item Instrument or a promise or order to pay money handled by a bank for collection; a check.

Job description Content analysis compiling tasks required and skills needed for each job, permitting comparison of two jobs for similarity.

Joint and several liability Liability of master and servant or copartners for torts of servant, employee, agent, or copartner.

Joint tenancy Concurrent estate that involves the unities of title, interest, possession, and time.

Judgment Determination of a court pronouncing its decision.

Judgment-debtor examination Interrogation of a debtor after a judgment to determine the extent and location of the debtor's property.

Judgment notwithstanding the verdict Judgment that revises the jury's verdict under circumstances where reasonable minds cannot differ and the case should have not gone to the jury.

Judicial appraisal procedure Dissenter's judicial review of allegedly insufficient corporate offer of "fair value."

Judicial lien General lien on all debtor property resulting from prejudgment collection efforts such as attachment or garnishment, from the judgment, or from efforts to enforce the judgment, such as by levy and execution.

Jurisprudence Philosophy of the law; various schools such as natural law, positivism, historical, sociological, and legal realism.

Jus tertii Doctrine under which the rights of a third party cannot be used against a nonholder in due course.

Just cause termination Agency or employment contract terms constraining termination process or events to those listed or traditional factors such as insubordination, malfeasance, and/or gross negligence.

Just compensation Amount of money that a sovereign must give to the owner of property that it takes by eminent domain.

Just-in-time inventory (JIT) Timely and accurate matching of supplies with customers' needs.

Keiretsu Japanese vertical cartels of related firms.

Know thy customer rule Requires securities broker's full assessment of customer's financial condition and investment objectives so only uniquely suitable recommendations are made.

Knowledge or notice imputation Agents authorized to receive information from third parties; agent's communication to principal presumed.

Labeling defect Defect that occurs when a manufacturer fails to warn of known hazards associated with its product.

Labeling standard Type of standard promulgated by the Consumer Products Safety Commission requiring that some type of marking be included on the product.

Laboratory conditions Neutral conditions that make it possible to determine the uninhibited wishes of employees with respect to union representation.

Laissez-faire Free-market, libertarian, economic ideology encouraging limited role for government.

Landrum-Griffin Act Federal labor law that governs the internal operation of union affairs.

Larceny Taking of another's property with intent to permanently deprive that person of that property.

Leachate Liquid that percolates through landfill, picking up toxic chemicals.

Lease Transfer of the right to possession and use of goods for a term in return for consideration.

Legal audit Process of thoroughly examining and assessing a company's legal situation.

Legal realism Theory of jurisprudence that views law as what officials do about a dispute.

Lessee One to whom property is leased.

Lessor One who leases property.

Letter of credit Bank's documentary assurance of payment for goods upon satisfactory presentation of specified delivery documents.

Levy When the sheriff seizes property pursuant to a judgment [UCC § 9-301(3)].

Libel Tort of defaming another by making written statements.

License Permission given by a licensor to a licensee to manufacture or distribute a product that is owned by the licensor.

Licensing Permitting a business to sell or manufacture the licensor's patented product.

Lien Legal charge on property in favor of one creditor that must be satisfied before the property is available to the debtor or other creditors.

Lien creditor Creditor who acquires a lien on a piece of property, generally by attachment or levy [UCC § 9-301(3)].

Life estate Estate that endures for the life of a person.

Limit order Customer restriction on price at which broker may execute order until price moves to customer's desired price.

Limited liability Special legal status for passive owners of a business: shareholders, limited partners.

Limited liability company (LLC) Hybrid of limited partnership and corporation receiving partnership flow-through tax treatment.

Limited partnership Form of partnership created under statute with at least one general partner with unlimited liability and one or more limited partners with limited liability.

Line of credit Preapproved extension of credit on which the borrower may draw.

Lingering apparent authority Apparent authority continues until principal notifies third parties of termination.

Liquidated damages Amount of money stipulated in a contract that will be awarded in the case of a breach, which amounts are reasonably calculated to approximate the actual damages.

Liquidated debt Debt that is not in dispute.

Liquidation Collection and payment of partnership debts; sale of partnership property for final distribution to partners after dissolution.

Living will statutes Legislative enactments that give effect to documents that express a person's will not to have heroic means used to save the person's life when in an irreversible terminal condition.

Living trusts Trust established to take effect while the person establishing it is still alive.

Loan committment Agreement to extend a loan under the terms contained in the agreement.

Lobbyists Those who attempt to influence governmental officials and actions.

Long-arm statutes State statutes that empower a court to assert personal jurisdiction over out-of-state defendants when defendants have committed a wrong within the state, are doing business within the state, or otherwise have sufficient minimum contacts within the state.

Looting Acts depriving a corporation of its assets' value.

Loss of consortium Loss of sex, society, and services suffered by a spouse as a result of his or her spouse's injury caused by a third party's tortious conduct.

Lost property Property that is involuntarily parted with by the owner due to neglect or carelessness.

Magnetic ink character recognition Encoding used to electronically process checks.

Magnuson-Moss Warranty Act Federal consumer protection statute that limits sellers from excluding implied warranties.

Mail fraud Federal crime of using the mails to deliberately cheat others.

Mail-order sales Sales that are regulated by some states involving purchase of items through the mails.

Mailbox rule Rule holding that the mailing of an acceptance is effective upon mailing when the offeror has used the mail to invite acceptance; the rule has been expanded to include the use of any reasonable manner of acceptance.

Main purpose doctrine Principle that takes a case outside of the statute of frauds when the main purpose of the person's promise to pay another's debt was for a personal benefit.

Maker Obligor on a note; the party who promises to pay.

Management discussion and analysis (MD&A) Textual, descriptive information about an issuer, its securities, lines of business, executive compensation, and securities markets required in periodic financial statements, prospectuses, and registration statements.

Managing board German operations board with three members representing labor, sales, and production.

Mandatory cumulative voting Cumulative voting required under state incorporation statute even if it was renounced in the corporate charter.

Mansion rights Right of the surviving spouse to remain in the family home for a period of time rent free after the death of the spouse.

Market failure By-product of markets, producing inefficiencies and failing to allocate resources as predicted.

Market makers Over-the-counter specialists available by phone or computer.

Market manipulation Various intentional interferences with free markets in an attempt to set, stabilize, raise, or lower market prices.

Market share liability Recovery against a defendant calculated on the basis of the defendant's share of the market of the product that caused injury to plaintiff.

Marking the close Trade made higher or lower than prevailing price near close of daily trading to leave the appearance of a late price movement and to affect the following day's trading prices or volume.

Marshalling of assets/jingle rule Partnership creditors have absolute priority over individual partners' creditors over partnership assets in insolvency proceedings outside federal bankruptcy court.

Master-servant Employment relationship giving the employer the right to control the end and means of the employee's activities.

Matched orders/wash sales Market manipulation through near-simultaneous purchase and sale orders of equivalent size and price.

Material alteration Any unauthorized change in an instrument that modifies the liability of any party on thatinstrument, or any unauthorized addition of words or numbers to an incomplete instrument [UCC § 3–407(a)].

Material safety data sheets   Safety and treatment information that companies must supply about hazardous wastes.

Materiality   That which is essential or makes a difference.

Mediator   Third party who attempts to facilitate settlement of a dispute.

Medicare   Program administered by the Social Security Administration under the act that provides health and medical care benefits to the elderly.

Memoranda of understanding   Treaty-like bilateral agreements among regulators in various nations for enforcing cooperation.

Memorandum   Writing necessary to satisfy the statute of frauds consisting of the names of the parties, the subject matter, the price, and the signature of the party against whom enforcement is sought.

Mentally incompetent   One who lacks the necessary mental state necessary to legally enter into contracts and make a will.

Merchant   One who deals in goods of the kind that are the subject matter of the contract or who otherwise represents him- or herself as having knowledge or skill peculiar to the practices or goods involved in the transaction [UCC § 2–104].

Merchantable   Fit for the ordinary purpose for which such goods are used; of at least fair, average, or medium quality [UCC § 2–314(2)].

Merger   Combination of two or more corporations in which acquired firm is absorbed by acquiring firm and inherits all rights and liabilities of both firms.

Merger moratorium   State antitakeover provision prohibiting target's merger with takeover bidder until approved by other shareholders or target's management or the passage of several years.

Midnight deadline   Midnight of the banking day following the banking day on which a bank receives presentment of a check or notice of dishonor [UCC § 4–104(a)(10)].

Minimum wage   Pay below which employers may not pay employees; established by states and the federal government.

Mining partnership   Association among two or more owners of oil and gas or mineral rights under joint operation to share profits.

Minority set-asides   Affirmative action quotas reserving minimum number of government contracts or privileges for minorities.

Minors   Those who are under a minimum age, usually 18 years.

Misappropriation theory   Theory restricting insider trading by anyone who misappropriates confidential, non-public information from a confidential source for personal trading or tipping.

Mislaid property   Property that is put somewhere and forgotten.

Mistake   Unintentional error that may justify rescission of a contract; defense to an intentional tort.

Mitigation of damages   Obligation of a person who has been injured by a breach of a contract to attempt to reduce the damages.

Model Business Corporation Act (MBCA)   Original model incorporation act.

Money   Medium of exchange sanctioned by a government [UCC § 1–201(24)].

Mores   Traditions and customs of a culture.

Mortgage   Instrument that uses real property to secure repayment of a debt.

Mortgage bonds   Secured corporate debt (bonds).

Motion to dismiss   Request that the court throw a case out and give victory to the movant.

Motion for judgment non obstante verdicto (n.o.v.)   Motion seeking a court's judgment that is contrary to the jury verdict on the basis that reasonable minds cannot differ and that the case should not have been decided by the jury.

Motion for judgment on the pleadings   Application to the court by a party seeking victory on consideration of the pleadings on the basis that reasonable minds cannot differ.

Motion to strike   Motion made by a party seeking a court to excise language in the party's pleading on the grounds that it is scandalous, scurrilous, obscene, or irrelevant.

Movant   One who makes a motion.

Multinational enterprise   Company that does business in more than one country.

Municipal Securities Rulemaking Board   Quasi-governmental regulator of market in tax-exempt securities issued by municipalities, state governments, and industrial revenue authorities.

Mutual rescission   Agreement by the parties to a contract to rescind the contract.

Mutual mistake   Where both parties to the contract are in error about a material fact; this usually affords either party to the contract the right to rescind the contract.

National ambient air quality standards   Atmospheric air quality standards established by the EPA for regions in the United States.

National Association of Securities Dealers (NASD)   Self-regulatory organization of securities brokers and dealers.

National Association of Securities Dealers' Automated Quotation (NASDAQ)   Telephone/computer terminal connections among geographically dispersed OTC broker-dealers constituting an exchange facility.

National Environmental Policy Act   Federal statute that declared the national environmental policy of supporting harmony between humans and their environment and the goal of ensuring that environmental information is made available to governmental officials and the public before environmental decisions are made.

National Labor Relations Act   Federal legislation administered by the NLRB and designed to prevent and remedy unfair labor practices.

National Labor Relations Board   Administrative body that administers the National Labor Relations Act and is involved in the certification of union elections.

National origin   Title VII–protected class focusing on nation from which a person's forebears emigrated.

National pollutant discharge elimination system   Environmental scheme that imposes effluent limitations through a system of permits.

Natural law   Theory of jurisprudence universally binding on all that rests on a belief in an immutable ''higher law,'' either God, human reason, or human nature.

Necessary   Good or service that is essential—for example, food, housing, and medical care.

Negative covenants   Agreement in loan or bond indenture restricting dividend payments during a corporation's weak financial position condition.

Negligence   Tort that arises as a result of a person's failure to exercise the standard of care of an ordinary prudent person under the circumstances.

Negligence per se   ''Negligence in and of itself''; negligence as a matter of law that is found when the defendant's violation of a statute results in injury to a person who is within the class of persons the statute was intended to protect and who suffers the type of harm the statute was intended to prevent.

Negligent entrustment   Master's direct liability for hiring incompetents, or providing improper instructions, supervision, or unsafe or insufficient work facilities.

Negligent torts   Torts that are committed as a result of carelessness—for example, the tort of negligence.

Negotiable   Capable of being transferred to a holder.

Negotiable instrument   Instrument that contains an unconditional promise or order to pay a fixed amount of money, is payable to bearer or order, is payable on demand or at a definite time, and does not state any other undertaking [UCC § 3–104(a)].

Negotiation   Process by which an instrument is physically transferred from one person to another so that the transferee is a holder [UCC § 3–201(1)].

Net capital requirements   Minimum net worth measures comparable to bank reserves providing financial cushion for securities firms.

New York Stock Exchange (NYSE)   Largest U.S. securities exchange listing the largest U.S. corporations.

Nimble dividends   Illegal dividends paid from stated capital.

Nominal damages   Small damages, oftentimes $1, awarded to show that there was a legal wrong even though the damages were very slight or nonexistent.

Nominating committee   Board committee that selects director and officer candidates for election.

Noncumulative preferred stock   Preferred stock not entitling the shareholder to receive dividends missed in prior years.

Noncupative will   Oral will.

Nondelegable duty   Employer's liability to the public under special statutes to maintain safe conditions; usually applicable to landlords, municipalities, railroads, and common carriers.

Nonexistent principal   Agents liable if falsely purporting to act for a nonexisting principal at the time of negotiations.

Nonfreehold estates   Estates that have a definite duration; leases.

Nonmanagement affiliate directors   Board members from other firms contracting with the corporation: suppliers, major customers, investment bankers, law firms, past employees, employees' relatives, and consultants.

Nonownership theory   Theory of property law recognizing that migratory minerals such as oil and gas are not owned until they are extracted.

Nontrading partnership   Partnership without substantial inventory, usually in services; law presumes lower borrowing needs than for a trading partnership and requires actual evidence of partner's authority to borrow.

Norris-LaGuardia Act   Federal labor law that prohibits yellow dog contracts, federal court injunctions barring unions, and the vicarious liability of unions.

Not-for-profit corporation   Corporations organized for charitable or community benefit purposes.

Note   Two-party instrument where one party promises to pay money to another party [UCC § 2–104(e)].

Notice and comment rulemaking   Informal rulemaking.

Novation   Agreement by the parties substituting a new contract for an old contract and/or new obligations for old obligations.

Novel case   Case of first impression.

Nuisance   Unreasonable interference with another's right to enjoyment of real property.

Objections Claims that an action by an opponent at trial is improper, unfair, incompetent, or irrelevant.

Obligor Promisor; one who is bound on a contract.

Offeree One to whom an offer to enter a contract is made.

Offering circular Regulation A form of shortened prospectus.

Offering statement Regulation A form of shortened registration statement.

Offeror One who makes an offer to enter a contract.

Old-Age, Survivors, and Disability Insurance Social security system whereby employees are required to contribute to a fund over their working lives, and employers are obligated to contribute a portion to the fund.

Older Workers' Benefit Protection Act 1990 federal age discrimination legislation.

On-board bill of lading Requires that goods be actually loaded on the designated vessel or vehicle before payment is made.

Open account Buyer pays for goods after delivery.

Open-end credit Type of credit extension that is not a lump sum but repeated borrowing at the option of the borrower where the amounts of periodic repayments are not specifically established.

Open forum Governance model requiring notice, open presentations, presentation of opposing views, and challenges to particular viewpoints to encourage better-reasoned decisionmaking.

Opening statements Presentation to the jury at the beginning of the case that tells the jury what the party intends to prove and what the evidence will show.

Option Contract whereby one person pays money for the right to purchase something for a specific price, which right is held open for a specified period of time.

Oral will "Foxhole" will; one that is made when death is imminent in the presence of disinterested witnesses.

Order Written instruction to pay money. It must be more than a mere authorization [UCC § 3–103(6)].

Order paper Instrument payable to the "order" or the "assigns" of a specified person. Order paper is negotiated by delivery and indorsement.

Ordinances Local or city laws or regulations.

Organizational meeting Initial meeting of incorporators to establish the corporate form.

Organized Crime Control Act of 1970 Federal law containing RICO racketeering provisions.

Original position Position in nature under John Rawls's theory of distributive justice in which people would choose fair principles if they were ignorant of their position.

OTC See Over-the-counter.

Output contract Contract in which the seller agrees to sell and the buyer agrees to buy all the output of a particular product manufactured by the seller, which will not fail for indefiniteness [UCC § 2–306]; nor will it lack mutuality of obligation; an obligation of good faith performance is implied.

Outside counsel Lawyer who is not an employee of the company that retains him or her to represent the company.

Outside directors Board members from other corporations or institutions with no direct contractual relations with corporation.

Outstanding shares Amount of authorized stock actually issued, sold, and still in the shareholders' hands.

Over-the-counter (OTC) Telecommunication-based trading facility approximating a securities exchange traditionally used by smaller and emerging companies.

Ownership theory Theory of property law recognizing that hard subsurface minerals such as coal may be owned separate and apart from the land.

Pac-Man defense Defense technique to avert a merger where the target takes over the attacker.

Palming off Deceptive passing off of a product as another product.

Pareto optimality Model of optimal efficiency for evaluating regulation or any other action that causes society to become better off while no one is made worse off.

Pari delicto At equal fault; a doctrine that protects a party to an illegal agreement who is not at equal fault with the perpetrator of the illegality.

Parity of information/possession theory SEC's attempt to outlaw trading while in mere possession of non-public information even if no breach of fiduciary duty or misappropriation of confidential information occurred.

Participating bonds Bonds permitted variable return depending on earnings.

Parol evidence Evidence that is oral or extraneous to a written agreement.

Partial integration Agreement that may be modified by parol evidence that is not inconsistent with the writing.

Partner dissociation RUPA concept of simple partnership breakup often substituted for dissolution; permits remaining partners to continue business.

Partner's interest Each partner's ownership right in partnership, including share of profits, governance, and portion upon dissolution.

Partnership Association of two or more persons to carry on a business for profit.

Partnership at will Partnership without binding obligation to continue business, permitting partners to dissociate without incurring liability.

Partnership by estoppel Unlimited personal liability for nonpartners creating the impression that they act like a partnership.

Partnership property All property originally brought into the partnership stock or subsequently acquired by purchase or otherwise with partnership funds on account of the partnership.

Past consideration Promise that is not bargained for and that occurs after the event.

Patent Governmental grant of right to the exclusive use of an invention.

Patent assignment Inventor, owner, or employee's contractual transfer of patent rights to employer or another.

Pattern or practice Theory of illegal employment discrimination where broad, systematic discrimination deters qualified minorities from applying.

Payee Party to be paid on a negotiable instrument.

Payment against the documents Issuing or confirming bank's duty to pay on letter of credit conditioned on fully satisfactory required documents.

Payor bank Drawee bank [UCC § 4–105(3)].

Penalty clauses Liquidated damage clauses within contracts that are unenforceable because they are unreasonably disproportional to any anticipated loss.

Pension Benefit Guaranty Corporation Entity established by ERISA within the Department of Labor whereby employers who have established pension plans pay for termination insurance, which protects those employees whose retirement benefits are vested under a pension plan.

Per capita "By heads"; sharing equally under an estate.

Per stirpes Form of distribution under an estate whereby a successor takes the portion of his or her deceased ancestor.

Peremptory challenges Absolute right to cause a specified number of prospective jurors to be excused, though not for cause.

Perfect competition model Markets with numerous rational buyers and sellers, all market participants have perfect information, no barriers restrict new firms' entry into markets, only standardized products sold, and no participant possesses market power (e.g., no monopoly power).

Perfection Process by which a secured party makes the security interest good against third parties.

Perfectly competitive market Market with many buyers and sellers, without barriers to entry or leaving, with perfect information, where no buyer or seller has substantial market share, where all products are homogeneous, and where the costs of production are paid by each seller; the theory of capitalism is that perfectly competitive markets achieve distributive justice.

Performance bond Suretyship agreement that guarantees a sum of money in the event performance does not occur.

Performance standard Type of standard promulgated by the Consumer Products Safety Commission; a performance standard is one that can be measured by a test.

Periodic tenancy Lease that endures from period to period until terminated by proper notice.

Perks Expected noncash employment benefits for insider.

Permissive cumulative voting Cumulative voting optional under state incorporation statute, required only if provided for in corporate charter.

Personal defenses Holder in due course takes free from all personal defenses, including such defenses as fraud in the inducement, misrepresentation, mistake, and lack of consideration.

Personal jurisdiction Right that the court has to adjudicate a case and bind persons to its judgment.

Personal property All property that is not real property; movable property.

Piercing the corporate veil Theory of unlimited liability for shareholders with excessive entanglement in the corporation.

Planned unit developments Area of land developed as one unit that includes residential, industrial, commercial, and recreational structures and land, all as part of a comprehensive scheme.

Plurality Greatest number of votes cast wins even without a majority.

Pocket veto Act of the president witholding signature on a bill at the adjournment of the legislative session.

Poison pill Takeover defense granting existing shareholders rights to sell their stock to the corporation at relatively high prices or purchase new shares at low prices, diluting the bidder's holdings; triggered by potential bidder's accumulation of a significant block.

Positivism Theory of jurisprudence that rests on the belief of law as rules prescribed by a sovereign.

Post-effective period Period after effective date of IPO registration during which sales occur.

Postincorporation subscription Stock subscription issued after incorporation.

Postjudgment examinations Creditor's examinations of judgment debtors under oath to determine what property the debtor owns that is available to satisfy the debt.

Potentially responsible parties Those who under the Superfund law are strictly liable for response costs for cleanups; generators and transporters of hazardous substances and past and present owners and operators of hazardous waste sites.

Power of attorney Formalized written agency contract.

Power to overrule Authority that a judge has to depart from stare decisis under limited circumstances — for example, when the precedent is outmoded or was decided wrong.

Preconditioning market/jumping the gun Hints of impending IPO through favorable reports to spark interest in IPO.

Predicate offenses Underlying RICO crimes constituting a pattern of racketeering activity.

Preemption doctrine Constitutional doctrine holding that a state may not pass a law inconsistent with a federal law when the subject of the area is of such a national character that the federal law should take precedence over state laws.

Preemptive rights Existing shareholder right to preserve existing proportional interests in newly authorized stock.

Pre-filing period Time preceding filing of registration statement with the SEC.

Precedent Previous case that has a binding effect on future cases.

Predatory pricing Act of pricing below cost with the intent to drive a competitor out of business.

Preference Act by a debtor of favoring one creditor over another; in bankruptcy, a transfer to a creditor on account of an antecedent debt made while the debtor was insolvent within 90 days of the filing of the bankruptcy petition that enables the creditor to receive a greater percentage than under straight bankruptcy; preferences are voidable by the trustee in bankruptcy.

Preferred stock Stock issued with preferences in liquidation and dividends.

Preincorporation contracts Contracts made by corporate promoters to initiate corporate business.

Preincorporation subscription Stock subscription issued before incorporation.

Preliminary injunction Injunction that is issued pending a full hearing on the complaint for a permanent injunction.

Preliminary prospectus/red herring Draft form of prospectus used only during the waiting period.

Preparatory steps Agent's preliminary acts to compete with the principal after termination; conflict of interest if the agent solicits the principal's former employees or clients, photocopies the principal's documents, or misappropriates the principal's trade secrets.

Preponderance By the greater weight.

Preponderance of the evidence Burden of persuasion in civil suits.

Prescriptive/normative Advocacy about how the world ought to be.

Prescriptive easements Right of way across another's land that is acquired by open, continuous, and hostile use.

Presenting bank Presenting bank is any bank presenting an item, obviously not including the payor bank [UCC § 4–105(6)].

Presentment Demand for payment or acceptance generally made to either the maker or the drawee [UCC § 3–501(a)]. It can be made in any commercially reasonable fashion [UCC § 3–501(b)(1)]; one of the technical rights that must be satisfied to trigger the contract liability of secondary parties to a negotiable instrument.

Presentment warranties Warranties made upon presentment including the warranty of good title, no knowledge of a forged maker of drawer's signature, and no material alteration.

Pretermitted heirs Heirs that are not named in the will but who take anyway because they were unknown to the testator at the time of making the will, and had the testator known of the existence of them he or she would have included them.

Preventive law Portion of the practice of law that is focused on the avoidance of legal problems.

Price discrimination Price difference; selling to one customer at one price and to another at a different price.

Primary liability Contract liability on a negotiable instrument that is absolute and unconditional; the liability of a maker or an acceptor is primary.

Primary-line injury Injury occurring when a seller suffers damages as a result of a competitor's price discrimination.

Primary meaning Term that the public does not identify with any particular manufacturer or product.

Primary restraint Restraints of trade that are purposeful and central to an agreement and that are held to be unlawful.

Primary sources Statements of the various governmental units that have the power to make law.

Prior appropriation Doctrine regarding the allocation of water rights that prefers those who claim and use the water first.

Privacy Act Federal act that protects the confidentiality of ''private'' information accumulated by federal government agencies.

Private corporation Corporation organized for business purposes having private ownership.

Private nuisance   Unreasonable interference with a person's private use and enjoyment of land.

Private placements   Transaction exemption from SEC IPO registration for nonpublic offerings under Regulation D and 500-series rules.

Privity   Direct contractual relationship between the parties.

Probate   To prove a will; to administer an estate.

Procedural due process   Requirement that the government execute laws with procedural safeguards in accord with fundamental concepts of ordered liberty.

Procedural law   Portion of the law that specifies the manner in which substantive law is enforced — for example, the law of pleading.

Proceeds   Whatever is received upon the sale or exchange of the collateral [UCC § 9–306(1)].

Professional corporation   Special private corporation organized for practice of a profession (e.g., law, accounting, or medicine) to take advantage of federal tax breaks for corporate pension funds.

Professionally developed aptitude tests   Tests for job applicant's knowledge and performance potential; must be validated as directly related to successful performance job tasks and must constitute a business necessity.

Program trading   Computer-executed investment trading.

Promise   Written commitment to pay money [UCC § 3–103(9)].

Promisee   Person to whom a promise is made.

Promisor   Person who makes a promise.

Promissory estoppel   Equitable doctrine that results in enforcement of a promise even if not supported by consideration if the promisee justifiably relies on the promise, injury results, and justice may not be avoided except by enforcing the promise.

Promoters   Persons initially procuring rights for corporation to be formed.

Proof of claim   Paper filed by creditors that wish to participate in the eventual distribution of the bankruptcy estate.

Properly payable   Test for whether a payor bank may pay and charge its customer's account.

Prospectus   Any notice, circular, advertisement, letter, or communication, written or by radio or television, that offers any security for sale or confirms the sale of any security.

Protected classes   Classifications of human population characteristics such as race, color, religion, sex, age, national origin, and disability, protected by constitution or statute.

Protest   Certificate of dishonor used in international transactions. Protest must identify the instrument and certify that presentment was made, dishonor occurred, and notice of dishonor was given [UCC § 3–505(b)].

Provisional director   Court-appointed, impartial outsider to cast deadlock-breaking votes.

Proximate cause   Direct or foreseeable cause necessary for the tort of negligence to be proved.

Proxy   Absentee shareholder balloting; shareholder's intangible power of attorney transferring voting power; individual agent actually voting for shareholder; formal written absentee ballot conferring voting power.

Proxy coupled with an interest   Irrevocable proxy transferred for consideration; often given to creditor as security for loan of funds to purchase stock.

Proxy rules   SEC procedures for truthful and open conduct of corporate governance in proxy solicitations.

Proxy settlements   Compromise between insurgent proxy solicitor and management.

Proxy solicitations   Facilitation of balloting by shareholders in board and other elections; includes any request to give or revoke a proxy, furnishing proxy form, and electioneering by advertisement, direct mail, direct telephone contact, and contact by professional proxy solicitors.

Proxy statement   Primary communication used by management and insurgents to communicate with shareholders in a proxy solicitation.

Psychological egoism   Theory that people are motivated solely by a desire to maximize pleasure and minimize pain; that people act only in their own self-interest.

Public disclosure of private facts   Prong of the tort invasion of privacy predicated on the publication of private facts about an individual that would be offensive to a reasonable person.

Public function doctrine   Constitutional principle that where a private actor exercises a power traditionally reserved to the government, the private actor's conduct is considered state action.

Public goods   Goods or services usually provided by government when underproduced by markets.

Public nuisance   Unreasonable interference with the general community's health, safety, or welfare.

Public policy   That which is good for the general public, as gleaned from a state's constitution, statutes, and case law.

Public policy exception   Exception to the employment-at-will doctrine prohibiting a discharge of an employee for reasons contrary to public policy.

Public Utility Holding Company Act of 1935   Federal securities law intended to correct abusive pyramid-style capital structures of public utilities.

Publicly traded corporation Private, for-profit corporation with a class of registered securities traded on a national exchange.

Punitive damages Damages awarded in addition to compensatory damages for the purpose of punishing and making an example of the defendant and for compensating the plaintiff additionally for the defendant's egregious conduct and the plaintiff's wounded sensibilities.

Purchase money security interest Security interest created either when a seller-secured party sells collateral to the debtor and retains a security interest to secure payment or when a debtor-buyer borrows money from a third party to finance the purchase of the collateral [UCC § 9–107].

Put option Security representing the right to sell the underlying security to another at a specified price.

Pyramid sales Also known as a chain referral plan, a type of selling where once the buyer purchases an item he or she gets paid for each additional sale for which the buyer is responsible.

Qualified indorsement Indorsement on an instrument where the indorser disclaims secondary liability on the instrument; the most common qualified indorsement is "without recourse" [UCC § 3–415(b)].

Qualified institutional buyer (QIB) Sophisticated institutional investor with securities investments over $100 million permitted to trade in the SEC Rule 144A market.

Quantum meruit Law infers fair compensation at the "going rate," implied from circumstances.

Quasi-contract Contract constructed by the courts where a benefit is conferred on another with that person's knowledge under circumstances that would be inequitable for the party not to pay for the benefit.

Quid pro quo Employment benefits conditioned on victims submission to sexual harassment.

Quitclaim deed Deed without warranties that passes title to the interest in the property that is owned by the seller—no more and no less.

Quo warranto "By what authority"; legal action by the state to cancel defective incorporation.

Quorum requirement Minimum number of shares or votes actually present at a meeting or represented by proxy to conduct valid business.

Racketeer Influenced and Corrupt Organizations (RICO) Federal racketeering provisions of the Organized Crime Control Act of 1970 making it illegal to acquire or operate an enterprise by a pattern of racketeering and imposing treble damages in private suits and other extraordinary remedies in federal criminal prosecutions.

Ratification Act of affirming a contract such as a minor may do upon becoming an adult.

Rational basis test Test applied to economic regulation that determines whether the legislation violates the Equal Protection Clause by assessing whether there is any rational basis for the legislation.

Real defense Defense that is good against a holder in due course, including infancy, certain defenses that render an obligation void, fraud in the execution, insolvency proceedings, forgery, and material alteration.

Real estate investment trust (REIT) Trust holding portfolio of real estate investments with diffused beneficial ownership by trust beneficiaries.

Real estate limited partnership Common form of tax shelter holding portfolio of real estate for investors enjoying limited liability.

Real property Land, buildings, and things permanently attached to land and buildings.

Reasonable accommodation Employer's duty to adjust employment standards to satisfy employees' religious observances.

Reasonable person Fictitious person the law constructs to determine whether a person has exercised conduct short of what a "reasonable person" might do and thus is negligent.

Reasonably diligent credit search Test used to determine whether mistakes in a financing statement render it ineffective.

Reasons Statements given in support of a conclusion represented by facts, examples, evidence, analogies, or beliefs.

Received-for-shipment bill of lading Bill of lading for goods in temporary storage by a carrier.

Record date Date set in charter or bylaws to determine shareholder voting eligibility.

Red clauses Red ink notation by issuing bank promising reimbursement to advising or confirming bank for previous partial payment advancement.

Redemption Contractual right of corporation to call specified security requiring holder's return of security to corporation for cancellation in exchange for previously specified price.

Redemption right Corporation's "call" privilege to convert outstanding security into cash or another security.

Referral selling Scheme involving a promise of free merchandise to a buyer who finds a certain number of friends who will buy the merchandise.

Reformation Remedy where a contract is altered by the court to conform to the original intent of the parties or to law.

Refusal order SEC prevention of IPO sales due to some registration defect.

Registered securities Securities with owner's name registered on corporate books.

Registrants Issuers of securities with a class of securities traded on a national securities exchange or the OTC market, registered with the SEC.

Registration statement IPO registration document filed with the SEC.

Regular board meetings Board meetings held at fixed intervals — for example, quarterly, semiannually, or annually.

Regular shareholder meetings Recurring shareholder meetings held annually on date fixed in the bylaws.

Regulation D SEC implementation of the 1933 Act section 4(2) permitting relaxed registration for private placements.

Regulation S-K SEC regulation prescribing content and format for nonfinancial disclosures.

Regulation S-X SEC regulation specifying format for financial statements.

Regulatory statute Statute enacted for the primary purpose of regulating an activity, trade, or profession — for example, the requirement that a vendor pay a sum of money to obtain a vendor's license.

Rejection Repudiation of the terms of an offer.

Relevant geographic market Physical market within which sellers or companies that are merging compete.

Reliance Element of causation focusing on the defrauded victim's belief and consequent action based on the trust given to the misrepresentor's false statement or omission.

Religion Title VII–protected class; standard denominations and other sincerely held ethical or moral-based belief systems.

Remedies Ways in which the violation of rights are redressed.

Removal jurisdiction Right of a defendant to remove a case from a state court to the federal court when the case could have been brought in the federal district court initially and when the defendant is a citizen of a different state than that in which the suit was instituted.

Renunciation Agent's unilateral termination of agency authority.

Reorganization Chapter 11; type of bankruptcy giving the debtor protection from creditor action while developing a plan to pay creditors.

Replevin Common law action by an owner to recover possession of goods.

Reply Pleading filed by a plaintiff in response to the defendant's answer that contains new matter such as a counterclaim.

Reporters Published decisions of a court or a group of courts arranged in volumes.

Repossess Action by a secured party to take possession of the collateral upon debtor default [UCC § 9–403].

Representation cases Actions that involve the certification of labor unions.

Representative sample Test group sufficiently large, broad, and random to permit generalizations about a larger population from which the sample is taken.

Repudiation Action of one party to a contract notifying the other of his or her intent to breach.

Repurchase Mutually agreed-on purchase of an outstanding security by a corporation.

Requirements contract Contract whereby the seller agrees to sell and the buyer agrees to buy all that the buyer might require of a particular product; such contracts will not fail for indefiniteness [UCC § 2–306]; nor will they lack mutuality of obligation; an obligation of good faith performance is implied.

Res Thing; contents of a trust or estate.

Res ipsa loquitur ''The thing speaks for itself''; rule of evidence that establishes a presumption of negligence if the instrumentality causing the injury was within the exclusive control of the defendant and the injury would not ordinarily occur unless someone was negligent.

Resale restrictions Prohibition against exempt securities resale by initial purchasers to discourage issuer evasion of registration.

Resource Conservation and Recovery Act Federal statute that regulates handlers of hazardous wastes.

Respondeat superior ''Let the master respond''; doctrine that holds the master (employer) liable for the negligent acts of the servant (employee) committed within the course of employment.

***Restatements* of the Law** Works produced by the American Law Institute that compile and synthesize the law into categorical statements.

Restitution Amount of money necessary to put the plaintiff back in the position he or she was in before the contract was entered.

Restricted lists Lists of securities circulated within full service securities firm prohibiting recommendation to customers of securities listed.

Restrictive covenants Clauses within landowners' deeds that prohibit certain things — for example, constructing fences that do not conform to certain specifications.

Restrictive indorsement Indorsement that either restricts further transfer, is conditional, is made ''for collection only,'' or is payable to a fiduciary [UCC § 3–206].

Revaluation surplus Dividend source from upward reappraisal of assets; permitted in some states.

Revenue raising statute Statute enacted for the primary purpose of raising revenue—for example, a regulation requiring a vendor to purchase a license in order to do business.

Reverse discrimination Prohibited preference given to members of a protected class historically subjected to discrimination.

Reverse stock split Corporation exchanges fewer shares for each of shareholders' former holdings.

Reverse triangular merger Reverses of forward triangular merger; acquired corporation survives and acquiring corporation's subsidiary merged into acquired corporation.

Revised Model Business Corporation Act (RMBCA) Revised model incorporation act.

Revised Uniform Limited Partnership Act (RULPA) Revised (1976) uniform act for the creation and operation of limited partnerships.

Revocable trusts Trusts that may be revoked by the settlor.

Revocation Principal's unilateral termination of agent's authority; the withdrawal of an offer before acceptance.

Revolving letter of credit Seller can make series of drafts over a fixed time period against the letter of credit maximum as seller makes installment shipments; replenished as form of "credit line" as buyer makes payments.

RICO See *Racketeer Influenced and Corrupt Practices Act.*

Right of first refusal Transfer restriction on security giving holder the first option to purchase or decline purchase of the securities.

Right to cure Seller's right to deliver a conforming tender; seller has this right automatically where the time for performance has not yet expired if it can be done within the time specified in the contract and is given a further reasonable time where there was no reason to believe that the tender would be refused [UCC § 2–508(1)].

Right to sue letter EEOC advice to employment discrimination victim if EEOC finds insufficient cause to sue.

Rights Transferable short-term options.

Riparian Related to the banks of a waterway—for example, a river or stream.

Riparianism Doctrine that gives people owning property adjacent to waterways certain rights and obligations with respect to the water.

Rival conclusions Alternative conclusion consistent with author's evidence.

Rival hypotheses Alternative hypothesis consistent with author's reasons.

Royalties Payments made to authors or inventors or to owners of minerals for the use of their property.

Rule 504 SEC Regulation D private placement limited to $500,000 for unregistered sales and up to $1 million within any 12-month period if registered under state blue sky laws.

Rule 505 SEC Regulation D private placement limited to $5 million within any 12-month period, sales to non-accredited investors limited to 35 and permitting sales to unlimited numbers of accredited investors.

Rule 506 SEC Regulation D private placement with no upper-dollar limitation and requirements similar to Rule 505 on disclosures and nonaccredited/accredited investor limits.

Rule of capture Rule adopted by some states that the one who brings minerals to the surface is the one who owns those minerals.

Rules of evidence Principles that govern the admissibility of evidence at a trial.

Rulemaking Power of administrative agencies to promulgate rules and regulations that are given the effect of law.

Safe harbor Statutory or regulatory assurance of compliance when specified procedures are followed exactly.

Sale Passing in title from the seller to the buyer for a price [UCC § 2–106(1)].

Sale of business doctrine Fictitious exception to security definition for security sales made to a buyer who would directly operate the issuer.

Sale on approval Contract in which the parties agree that the goods may be returned by the buyer even if conforming and the goods are delivered primarily for sale; the buyer examines them and decides whether or not to keep them.

Sale or return Contract in which the parties agree that the goods may be returned by the buyer even if conforming and the goods are delivered for sale; the buyer will either resell them or return them to the seller.

Sales puffing Statements of opinion about the quality of goods made to create an impression of quality; they do not create express warranties.

Scalping Investment adviser's recommendation of securities the adviser owns.

Schedule 13D SEC disclosure form providing early warning that the potential bidder has accumulated 5 percent or more of a target's shares.

Schedule 14A Proxy solicitation form filed with the SEC.

Schedule 14D-1 SEC disclosure form "tender offer statement," announcing a tender offer, stating tender offer terms, describing any negotiations between tender offeror and target, and stating bidder's purpose and plans for the target.

Schedule 14D-9   SEC disclosure form advising shareholders of management's views of tender offer.

Scienter   Intent to commit a legal violation; guilty knowledge or mind.

Scope of employment   Limitation on master's liability to only those torts that a servant commits while "about the master's business."

SEC Rule 10b-5   General antifraud provision of the 1934 Act.

SEC Rule 144   General resale restriction.

SEC Rule 144A   Exemption from SEC Rule 144 resale restriction for private placement securities issued by domestic or foreign issuers sold only among qualified institutional buyers.

Secondary liability   Contract liability on a negotiable instrument that is conditioned on the technical rights of presentment, dishonor, and notice of dishonor; the liability of an indorser is secondary.

Secondary-line injury   Injury occurring when a seller discriminates in price among competing buyers.

Secondary meaning   Association of a name of a product over time such that the public associates the product with the name—for example, Kleenex.

Secondary sources   Writings of legal experts, religious or philosophical ideas, moral principles, social customs, and laws from other countries and states that, though not authoritative, may nonetheless influence law.

Secret profits   Unethical kickbacks or unconsented fees made by an agent or corporate promoter.

Secretary   Corporate officer responsible for keeping corporate records and minutes of corporate meetings (e.g., board, officer, and shareholder meetings).

Secured party   Creditor in a secured transaction [UCC § 9-105(m)].

Securities Act of 1933 (1933 Act)   First of President Franklin D. Roosevelt's New Deal securities legislation; requires registration and disclosure of new securities issues.

Securities and Exchange Commission (SEC)   U.S. federal regulatory agency responsible for securities markets.

Securities Exchange Act of 1934 (1934 Act)   Second of President Franklin D. Roosevelt's New Deal securities legislation; regulates secondary trading markets, exchanges, broker-dealers, insider trading, proxy solicitations, tender offers, and requires periodical disclosure by public corporations.

Securities exchanges   Facilities permitting organized sale and purchase of securities.

Securities Investor Protection Act of 1970   Federal securities law creating Securities Investor Protection Corporation to insure customer account losses against brokerage insolvency.

Security   Means any note, stock, treasury stock, bond, debenture, evidence of indebtedness, transferable share, investment contract, voting trust certificate, certificate of deposit for a security, fractional undivided interest in oil, gas, or other mineral rights, any put, call, straddle, stock option, warrant, or in general, any interest or instrument commonly known as a "security."

Security agreement   Agreement creating a security interest that describes the collateral and is signed by the debtor [UCC § 9-203(1)(a)].

Security interest   Consensual lien on personal property granted by a debtor to a creditor to secure payment of a debtor [UCC § 1-201(37)].

Self-help repossession   Repossession by the secured party without judicial action; permissible if it can be made without a breach of the peace.

Self-regulatory organizations (SRO)   Exchanges, NASD, FASB, state CPA societies, or state bar associations responsible for licensing, oversight, and discipline of professionals in the securities industry.

Seniority system   Employment terms favoring employees with higher rank, longer spans of service, or other priorities in their position.

Servient estate   Estate that is burdened in an easement appurtenant.

Settlor   Person who establishes a trust by supplying money or property for it.

Severability   Division of provisions in a contract between those that are enforceable and those that are not.

Severance   Act of separating.

Severance pay   Payment of termination penalty entitling a party to certain moneys.

Sex-plus discrimination   Additional qualifications required of one sex while tolerating noncompliance by the other sex.

Sexual harassment   Job applicant or employee receives unwelcome sexual advances, requests for sexual favors, or verbal or physical contact of a sexual nature.

Shareholder consents   Valid action without shareholder meeting evidenced by separate written shareholder approvals for proposed action.

Shareholder derivative suit   Shareholder suit for the corporation's benefit; recovery or remedy belongs to the corporation.

Shareholder direct action   Shareholder suit seeking personal remedy.

Shareholder inspection privilege   Shareholder right to examine corporate financial statements, minutes, and shareholder lists.

Shareholder protection statute State antitakeover provision requiring that shareholders receive ''fair price'' in takeover.

Shareholders of record Shareholders are entitled to vote if they are holding stock on the record date.

Shareholders/stockholders Owners of a corporation through ownership of stock certificates.

Shark repellant Provision inserted in a company's corporate documents that discourages a takeover by making it difficult to accomplish.

Shelf registration SEC IPO registration issuer permitting issuer to wait to sell securities until the market conditions become optimal and/or the issuer needs the proceeds.

Shell corporation Corporation with little or no assets organized to avoid liability.

Shelter rule Doctrine under which a transferee from a holder in due course acquires holder in due course rights [UCC § 3–203(1)].

Shift differentials Pay differences based on time of work shift.

Shingle theory Minimum standards of brokers' fiduciary duty requiring fair treatment of customers, implied warranty of fair dealing, disclosure of conflicts and relevant information, truthful statements, and competent service.

Shipment contract Contract that does not require delivery to a particular destination.

Shipper Person who delivers the goods to the common carrier and makes the contract for their shipment; typically, the seller of the goods.

Shop right Employer's nonexclusive right to use inventions developed on employer's time without further payment.

Short-form merger Merger of 90 percent or more of an owned subsidiary into the parent without holding an election.

Short-swing profits Purchase and sale or sale and purchase of issuer's registered equity securities within six months by statutory insiders.

Short tender Illegal and manipulative tender of shares borrowed by tenderor.

Sight draft Draft immediately payable, drawn on buyer, payable to seller.

Signature Mark made with present intent to authenticate [UCC § 1–201(39)].

Silent partner Passive investor in general partnership who exercises no management control nor uses surname in the firm name.

Sinking fund Bond repayment assurance composed of periodic payments for partial repayment of principal on maturity.

Slander Tort of defaming another by making oral statements.

Slander per se Type of oral defamation that does not require proof of actual pecuniary loss in order to recover; the plaintiff must prove that the defendant's statement accused the plaintiff of (1) an act that undermined the plaintiff's business, profession, or occupation, or (2) a crime of moral turpitude, or (3) a loathsome disease, or (4) being unchaste.

Small-business issuers Small businesses with annual revenues of less than $25 million entitled to use SEC shortened disclosure system.

Small issues Securities registration exemption for small business under Regulation A or Regulation D.

Social Security Act Federal act that establishes a federal social safety net program for the elderly and disabled, known as Old-Age, Survivors, and Disability Insurance (OASDI).

Social Security Administration Federal administrative agency that administers a federal social safety net program for the elderly and disabled.

Sociological jurisprudence Theory of jurisprudence that rests on the view of law as an attempt to balance competing social interests.

Sole proprietorships Individual owns business.

Sophistry Intentional use of fallacious reasoning through the art of using superficially plausible but fallacious argument to deceive listeners.

Special agents Agent with only narrow power, usually to execute only specific transactions.

Special circumstances Shareholders' expectation that management assumes ''trusteeship'' role not to misuse manager's secret knowledge for personal gain in trading face-to-face with shareholders.

Special director meetings Board meetings held at irregular or extraordinary times—for example, for extraordinary actions or a merger.

Special dividends Dividends paid irregularly.

Special drawing rights Expression of value of goods damaged or loss during carriage under Hamburg rules based on composite or pool of five major currencies: U.S. dollar, British pound, Japanese yen, German mark, and French franc.

Special indorsee New payee after a special indorsement.

Special indorsement Indorsement that identifies a specific payee [UCC § 3–205(a)]; a special indorsement preserves the order character of the instrument and limits negotiation of the paper by requiring the indorsement of a special indorsee.

Special interrogatories Written questions the judge asks the jury regarding the verdict.

Special litigation committee Board committee composed of independent directors to evaluate advisability of litigation or to dismiss shareholder derivative litigation.

Special shareholder meetings Infrequent shareholder meetings held only for extraordinary votes.

Specialists Exchange floor brokers occupying well-known positions on an exchange floor to regularly buy and sell only one or a few securities.

Specialist's book Each specialist's listing of all unfilled limit orders awaiting price movement.

Specially manufactured goods Exception to the statute of frauds under the Uniform Commercial Code where a contract is for goods that are specially ordered and/or made for the customer.

Specific performance Contract remedy where the breaching party is ordered to perform his or her contractual obligation; a form of equitable relief.

Spendthrift trust Trust that is exempt from creditors.

Stabilization Market manipulation to prevent price movements.

Stale check Check dated more than six months before presentment.

Standby letter of credit Contingent letter of credit used as performance guaranty on another contract.

Standstill agreement Corporate raider's promise not to purchase target shares for a fixed time.

Stare decisis "Let the decision stand"; doctrine that compels a judge to apply precedent.

State action Involvement of the sovereign necessary before the Bill of Rights or the Due Process or Equal Protection clauses are applicable.

State implementation plans (SIPS) Plans instituted by states to achieve federal air and water quality standards.

State-of-the-art defense Defense asserted to products liability claims by manufacturers when a potentially dangerous condition is not known or discoverable by currently existing scientific means.

State planned economy Type of central planning economy that exists in communist countries.

Stated capital Issued shares multiplied by par or stated value per share.

Stated value Fixed value for shares in lieu of par value.

Statement of authority RUPA partnership filing providing constructive notice of particular partners' authority to transfer real estate.

Status quo The way things are at any particular time.

Statute of limitations Time limit after which a person is barred from suing.

Statutes Laws passed by the legislative branch of government.

Statutes of descent and distribution Legislative acts that order the distribution of the estate of a decedent who dies without a will.

statutory insiders Officers, directors, and 10 percent shareholders prohibited from making short-swing profits under Section 16 of the 1934 Act.

Statutory lien Lien created by state or federal statute—for example, landlord, materialman's, mechanic's, or tax liens.

Statutory will Will that is executed according to the formalities of the state legislation.

Stay Arises automatically upon the filing of a bankruptcy petition and prohibits creditors from beginning or continuing judicial proceeding to enforce claims, including any action to enforce a judgment already obtained, any action to gain possession of property of the debtor, and any act to create, perfect, or enforce a lien against property of the debtor [Bankruptcy Act § 362]; protects debtor pending adjudication of bankruptcy.

Stock Security representing ownership in corporation.

Stock dividends Dividends paid in stock, usually the same class and series as held by shareholder.

Stock parking Evasion of Williams Act Schedule 13D disclosure by intentionally disguising stock beneficially owned as owned by accomplice who holds only record title.

Stock splits Prescribed number of shares held by stockholders divided into a different number of that class.

Stock subscription Corporation's executory contract to sell new stock issue.

Stockholders/shareholders Owners of a corporation through ownership of stock certificates.

Stop order SEC halt in IPO sales due to some registration defect.

Straight bill of lading Non-negotiable bill of lading used largely in inland freight and in direct deliveries to buyer's premises.

Straight voting Each share has one vote, and a simple majority of the quorum wins the election.

Street name Securities held and indorsed to brokerage or its nominee, not registered in beneficial owner's name, to facilitate margin loans or quick transfer.

Street sweeps Privately negotiated purchase of shares after aborted tender offer from arbitrageurs and other large block holders.

Strict compliance Buyer not obligated to pay unless issuing bank assures that documents comply exactly with conditions stated in the letter of credit.

Strict constructionists School of constitutional interpretation that conservatively interprets the document.

Strict foreclosure Election by the secured party to keep the collateral in full satisfaction of the debt [UCC § 9–505(2)].

Strict liability Tort that holds a person liable regardless of fault for injuries caused by defective products, ultrahazardous activities, or harboring vicious animals.

Strictissimi juris Common law doctrine under which any agreement between the creditor and the debtor that changes the debt agreement in any detail discharges the nonconsenting surety from the suretyship promise.

Strict products liability Doctrine under which the seller of defective goods is liable to people injured by those goods.

Strict scrutiny test Test applied to race regulation that determines whether the legislation violates the Equal Protection Clause by assessing whether the government's purposes are overriding and compelling.

Strike suits Unfounded intimidation suits for settlement value and/or attorneys fees.

Subagent Agent hired by the agent.

Subchapter S corporation Essentially, incorporated partnership given favorable partnership flow-through tax treatment.

Subject matter jurisdiction Power of a court to hear a particular type of case.

Subpoena duces tecum Court order to a person requiring that person to bring documents to court or an administrative hearing.

Substantial evidence on the record review Type of review of an administrative agency decison where the court examines the record to determine if substantial evidence exists to support the administrative agency decision.

Substantial performance Performance with minor, inadvertent, unimportant, and unintentional deviation; substantial performance is sufficient at common law to trigger the other party's obligation to perform a contract.

Substantive due process Requirement that a statute be reasonably related to a legitimate governmental purpose and that the statute be fair.

Substantive law Portion of the law that specifies rights and duties.

Successor liability Acquiring corporation in a merger generally inherits all the acquired corporation's liabilities, including product liability claims against the acquired corporation.

Suitability Broker's duty to recommend only appropriate investments based on analysis of investor's financial condition and objectives.

Summary prospectus IPO sales device containing only condensed information.

Summons Notice that informs a person that he or she has been sued and tells what must be done to avoid a default judgment.

Sunset legislation Legislation requiring reauthorization of specified administrative agencies.

Superfund Synonym for the Comprehensive Environmental Response, Compensation, and Liability Act, which established a fund to clean up hazardous waste sites.

Supermajority voting Greater than majority vote required to pass a resolution or win an election.

Supervision Duty requiring superiors of broker-dealers to establish oversight and control procedures for compliance with securities laws, to enforce shingle duty, prevent quotation of unregistered security prices, and minimize insider trading and tipping.

Supervisory board German oversight board of directors composed of 5 union representatives, 5 shareholder-elected representatives, and 1 "public interest" representative elected by the 10 other board members.

Supervoting shares Stock with more than one vote per share.

Supranational rules Laws governing regional organizations such as the European Community.

Supremacy clause Clause within the U.S. Constitution that makes the constitution, treaties, and laws of the United States the supreme law of the land.

Surety Person who promises to back up the obligation of another; called an accommodation party under the Uniform Commercial Code.

Suretyship agreement Agreement whereby a third party agrees to answer for the debt of another.

Swaps Form of barter; delivery responsibilities in equivalent commodities to each others' clients swapped, saving transportation costs.

Taft-Hartley Act Federal labor law that protects employees that do not desire to join a union and prohibits unfair union practices.

Takeover defenses Corporate charter amendments, contracts, and contingent rights making corporation unattractive to takeover bidder.

Tangible personal property Personal property that can be touched—for example, clothing and furniture.

Tax shelters Business organizations usually formed as limited partnerships providing loss write-offs for owners.

Teleological Theory of normative philosophy where the rightness of actions are judged by their consequences; consequentialist.

Teller's check   Draft drawn by one bank on another bank, or payable through another bank [UCC § 3–104(h)].

Temporary insiders   Outsider, nonemployees exposed to confidences while working in a consulting capacity.

Tenancy at sufferance   Holdover tenancy; a tenancy that arises when a lease has expired and the tenant remains, contrary to the desire of the landlord.

Tenancy at will   Tenancy that is terminable on the desire of the lessor.

Tenancy by the entirety   Concurrent indivisible ownership interest held by husband and wife involving the unities of title, interest, possession, and time.

Tenancy in partnership   Form of co-ownership for property belonging to a partnership, granting all partners equal rights for partnership purposes.

Tender   Offer of payment or performance of a contractual obligation.

Tender of payment   Doctrine that discharges accommodation parties where the payment due has been offered to the creditor and refused. If the party offering payment is one against whom the accommodation party has a right of recourse, the accommodation party is totally discharged from the contract obligation [UCC § 3–603(b)]; otherwise, the accommodation party is discharged for all subsequent liability [UCC § 3–603(c)].

Tender offers   Widespread public announcement and solicitation of shareholders (not privately negotiated) to purchase large, often controlling interest, in target issuer in exchange for cash, securities, or a combination of consideration.

Term tenancy   Lease that endures for a specified period of time.

Termination   Discontinuation of partner authority to bind partnership in contract.

Termination statement   Statement filed to indicate termination of a security interest [UCC § 9–404(1)].

Testamentary trusts   Trusts established in a will.

Testator   One who dies with a will.

Third party   Person who is not a party to a contract.

Third-party beneficiary   Person (beneficiary), though not a party to the original contract, who is nonetheless benefited by the contract.

Time draft   Draft payable at some time in the future.

Tippee   Recipient of inside information from an insider.

Tombstone ads   Stark, boxed financial press announcements stating IPO price.

Tort   "Twisted wrong"; civil wrong other than a breach of a contract.

Total integration   Agreement that is the final and complete expression of the party's intentions.

Totten trust   Trust that results when a person places money into a bank account naming him- or herself as trustee for another person (beneficiary); it is withdrawable by the trustee but on death it passes to the named beneficiary.

Toxic Substances Control Act   Federal statute that regulates hazardous chemical substances.

Toxic torts   Wrongs that involve injuries, or a risk of injury, to a class of people as a result of exposure to a harmful substance.

Trade acceptance   Acceptance of time draft.

Trade fixtures   Property annexed to leased premises that is used to further a business purpose; this property may be removed by the tenant, who must repair any damage caused by such removal.

Trade name   Name of a business that is protected for exclusive use.

Trade secret   Formula or process that is valuable and obviously intended as a secret of a business.

Trademark   Distinctive mark or symbol that a company can register and use exclusively.

Trademark infringement   Act of using another's trademark without authorization.

Trader rule   Common law rule by which a merchant whose check was wrongfully dishonored was entitled to substantial damages on the basis of defamation per se without proof that actual damage occurred.

Trading partnership   Partnership regularly engaged in farming, manufacturing, buying and selling goods, at retail or wholesale; law presumes it has working capital needs, so borrowing and negotiable instruments authority is more readily inferred than for a nontrading partnership.

Transfer   In commercial paper, the delivery of the item from the payee to subsequent persons; every physical movement of a negotiable instrument between issue and presentment [UCC § 3–203(a)]. In bankruptcy, every method of disposing of property, including the granting of a security interest [Bankruptcy Act § 101(54)].

Transfer restriction   Constraint on sale of securities by agreement or printed on the face of security.

Transferee   Party to whom an instrument is transferred.

Transferor   Party who transfers an instrument.

Transfer warranties   Warranties that arise on the transfer of a negotiable instrument for consideration, including good title, authentic signatures, no defenses, no material alteration, and no knowledge of insolvency proceedings.

Transferred intent   Doctrine that imputes to a wrongdoer the intent to injure another when the wrongdoer, although not intending to injure that person, nevertheless intended to injure another.

Treasurer Corporate officer overseeing corporate treasury; handles receipt of corporate funds.

Treasury stock Authorized and issued stock later repurchased so it is not outstanding.

Trespass Wrongful entry on another's land.

Triangular merger Corporate combination merging acquired corporation into subsidiary of acquiring corporation.

Trust Arrangement where property is placed in the hands of a trustee to administer according to the terms of an instrument for the benefit of beneficiaries; a method where dominant companies came together and placed their management in the hands of trustees who exercised monopoly-type power over the market.

Trust indenture Master bond contract specifying corporation's duties and bondholder rights.

Trust Indenture Act of 1939 Federal securities law prohibiting conflicts of interest toward bondholders; prohibits management-hired indenture trustees.

Trustee Person who by virtue of holding money or property in trust for a beneficiary stands in a fiduciary relationship to the beneficiary.

U.S. Eximbank Finances U.S. exports by making or guaranteeing exporter's working capital or buyer's purchase money loan or letter of credit.

Ultra vires Corporate activities not permissible under the charter or corporation statutes.

Uncertificated securities Securities evidenced by book entry, not by written instruments.

Unconditional One of the requisites for negotiability; a promise or order is unconditional unless it is subject to an express condition or it is subject to the terms in another writing [UCC § 3–105].

Unconfirmed letter of credit Letter of credit without advising bank's responsibility to pay; bank must transmit the letter of credit, verify authenticity of the seller's documents, and compare the issuing bank's signature with specimen in files.

Unconscionable Contract that is so one-sided as to be grossly unfair.

Underwriters Person who either purchased from an issuer with a view to resell securities or assists in distributing the securities.

Underwriting Primary marketing of new securities through an independent intermediary network.

Underwriting syndicate Underwriting group assembled to market the IPO.

Undisclosed principal Identity and existence of the principal is unknown to a third party.

Undue influence Dominion that results in a right to rescind a contract; grounds for a will contest.

Unemployment compensation State-administered system whereby an employee who has been laid off or discharged unjustly has a right to compensation from a fund.

Unenforceability Contract that cannot be enforced by a court because of some technicality.

Unenforceable contract Contract that will not be enforced by a court even though the essential elements of a contract are present because of a defense such as the failure to comply with the statute of frauds.

Unfair labor practices Actions by unions or employers prohibited by the National Labor Relations Act.

Unified tax credit Credit against the unified transfer tax, affording one a $600,000 lifetime exemption for gifts and transfers on death.

Uniform Customs and Practices for Documentary Credits (UCP) Accepted customs for letters of credit among merchants and bankers in international transactions, as compiled by the International Chamber of Commerce.

Uniform Securities Act Uniform state blue sky law.

Uniform Limited Partnership Act (ULPA) Original uniform act for creation and operation of limited partnerships.

Unilateral contract Contract that involves one promise.

Unilateral mistake Where one party to a contract is in error about a fact; this usually does not afford the person a right of rescission of the contract.

Union shop Company in which all employees must join a particular union.

Unliquidated debt Debt that is in dispute.

Unissued shares Authorized but unissued shares.

Universalizability and reversibility First formulation of Kant's categorical imperative; actions are right only if individuals would be willing to be treated as they are treating others (reversibility); actions are right only if the motives for the action are motives that we would be willing to have all act on (universalizability).

Usage of trade Practice or method of dealing having such regularity of observance in a place, vocation, or trade as to justify an expectation that it will be observed with respect to the transaction in question [UCC § 1–205(2)].

Usury Excessive interest.

Utilitarianism Theory of normative philosophy where actions are judged to be right if they tend to promote happiness; actions are wrong if they tend to promote unhappiness; a good action achieves the greatest good for the greatest number.

Valid Type of contract that is enforceable.

Value system Ideology; a coherent, systematic statement of values.

Values   Ideas of importance to individuals, such as freedom of choice, tradition, order, honesty, harmony, individualism, excellence, justice, competition, cooperation, and productivity.

Venue   Local area within which a case may be tried.

Variance   Disparity or spread between the top and the bottom values used to create an average.

Vertical division   When a manufacturer or supplier and a distributor enter into an exclusive dealership.

Vertical merger   Merger between companies that are on different levels of distribution.

Vicarious liability   Principal risks tort liability for agents' and other employees' acts.

Vocational Rehabilitation Act   1973 federal legislation defining handicapped persons and providing some equal employment protections.

Void contract   Agreement that the courts will not enforce because it fails to contain all the necessary elements of a contract.

Voidable contract   Contract that a party may elect to treat as void.

Voidable title   Title that can be set aside on such grounds as mistake, fraud in the inducement, or infancy.

Voir dire   Latin for "seek and speak"; process of examining prospective jurors to determine their acceptability to sit on the jury.

Voluntarism   Labor law principle that both union and management are given the freedom to work out bargaining agreements based on their own relative power, as long as each side bargains in good faith in accord with law.

Voting pool   Contract among shareholders requiring them to vote their shares in a specified way.

Voting trust certificates   Security evidencing shareholder's financial rights in stock transferred into voting trust.

Voting trusts   Trust empowering trustee to vote shares transferred into trust as governed by trust terms.

Wagers   Gambling; creating risks for the purpose of bearing them.

Wagner Act   Federal act that prohibits employers from discharging employees due to union affiliation or activity.

Waiting period   Period beginning after issuer files registration statement at SEC but before effective date.

Waiver of notice   Right to require omitted notice forfeited if shareholder attends shareholder meeting or director attends director's meeting.

Wall Street rule   Normative observation that disgruntled shareholders should just "vote with their feet," selling their shares when disappointed with corporate management performance.

Warehouse receipt   Document of title issued by a warehouseman acknowledging receipt of the goods identified in the document [UCC § 1–201(45)]; typically specifies the terms of the contract for storage.

Warrant   Certificated option usually part of compensation package in merger or acquisition.

Warranties   Promises; in a contract for sale of goods, they are generally made about the goods; express or implied.

Warranty of fitness for a particular purpose   Warranty implied in contracts for the sale of goods where the buyer relies on the seller's skill and expertise in furnishing goods suitable for a particular purpose known to the seller.

Warranty of merchantability   Warranty implied in certain contracts for the sale of goods; merchant's promise that the goods sold will be fit for the ordinary purpose for which they are intended.

Warranty of title   Warranty by the seller in a contract for the sale of goods that good title will be conveyed and that the transfer is rightful [UCC § 2–312(1)(a)].

Waste   Depreciation beyond normal wear and tear.

Watered stock   Inadequate consideration below par or stated value received for stock.

Whistle-blowing   Act of informing a governmental agency of a company violation of law.

Whistle-blowers   Those who disclose violations of the law to government officials.

White knight   Voluntary merger with a friendly company in order to avert an unfriendly takeover.

Widow's allowance   That part of a decedent's estate that the widow may receive free of creditor's claims.

Will   Document that satisfies the requirements of law and tells how the maker's property is to descend on death.

Williams Act   1968 federal securities legislation amending the 1934 Act to govern tender offer disclosure and regulate the process.

Winding up   Process after partnership dissolution to conclude partnership business.

With reserve   Taking an assignment with the right to reimbursement from the assignor in the event that the obligor defaults.

Without reserve   Taking an assignment without the right to reimbursement from the assignor in the event the obligor defaults.

Words of negotiability   "Order" or "bearer" language in a negotiable instrument.

Work for hire   Employment term specifying employer's exclusive ownership of information produced by employee.

Working papers   Writings that reflect the work done by an attorney or accountant.

Workout plan   Agreement between a debtor and creditor, when the debtor is in default, that the creditor will not accelerate payment and the debtor will make payments in accord with an adjusted payment schedule.

Writ of execution   Judge's order requiring the seizure and sale of a debtor's property.

Wrongful discharge   Tort based on the abusive discharge of an employee for reasons that are against public policy.

Wrongful dishonor   Liability of the payor bank that fails to pay an item that is properly payable [UCC § 4–402].

Wrongful dissolution   Partner's retirement causes dissolution in breach of fixed or specified term; nonretiring partner's misconduct or willful and persistent breach of partnership agreement.

Yellow dog contract   Illegal contract in which an employee agrees not to join a union.

Zoning   Division of a city or a county into geographical areas of restriction—for example, an area zoned R would only permit residential housing.

Table of Cases

Index

A

Abandoned property, 173
Abolishing the Statute of Frauds, 306–7
Absence of precedent, 119–21
Acceleration of negotiable instruments, 482–83
Acceptance, 362–68
  additional terms, 363–66
  common law, 363
  different terms, 366
  forms, 362–68
  method of, 362
  nonbank draft, 533–34
  by performance, 362
  revocation of, 384–88
  under Uniform Commercial Code, 363–68
Acceptance of goods, sales contracts, 380–81, 382
Acceptance of offer
  assent, manifestation of, 239–41
  communication of, 243–45
  defined, 239
  by proper offeree, 243
  time when effective, 243–45
  Uniform Commercial Code and, 242–43
  variation in terms of offer, 242–43
Accepted goods, damages for non-delivery of, 438–39
Accession, personal property, 175
Accessory after fact, 743
Accessory before fact, 743
Accord and satisfaction, 343
Account, security interest, 588
Accountant-client privilege, 1160
Accountants and auditors
  accountant-client privilege, 1160
  common law liability of, 1146–54
  contract liability, 1146
  criminal liability of, 1159
  discovery of fraud, 1150–53
  federal securities laws, effect on liability of, 1154–59
  fiduciary standard of care, 1147
  negligence, defenses to, 1153–54
  nonclients, liability to, 1147–53
  ordinary standard of care, 1146–47
  SEC enforcement, 1156–59

Accountants and auditors—*Cont.*
  tort liability, 1146–47
  Ultramares Corp. v. Touche, 1147–50
  working papers, 1159–60
Accounting
  by agent, 701
  in winding-up of partnership, 785
Acquittal, 16
Actual authority, 720
Actual malice, 140
Ad hominem argument, 4–5
Adjudication, by administrative agencies; *See* Agency adjudication
Administrative agencies
  adjudication, 100–102
  constitutional background of, 94–95
  creation of, 95
  enforcement, 102–4
  function and power of, 98–104
  judicial review of agency action, 104–7
  rulemaking, 98–100
Administrative Procedure Act, 95
Administrative regulations, 14
Admission, request for, 63
Admissions, 306
Ad populum argument, 4
Adversary system, 52
Adverse possession, 182–83
Advertisement, as offer, 234
Advertising, 1056–59
Advising bank, 670, 673
Advocate, lawyer as, 24
Affirmative action, 1099–1101
Affirmative disclosures, deceptive advertising, 1057
Age, as protected class, 1093–94
Agency adjudication, 100
  formal, 100
  informal, 100–102
Agency for International Development (AID), 680
Agency(ies)
  agent's duties, 696–708
  authority, role in formation of, 695–96
  capacity of contracting parties, 695
  delegation, 696
  formation of, 695–96

Agency(ies)—*Cont.*
  general agent, 694
  irrevocable, 712
  nature of, 694–95
  nondelegable duties, 696
  operation of law, termination by, 713
  post-termination relationships, 714
  power versus right to terminate, 711–12
  principal's duties toward agent, 708–11
  ratification of agent's authority, 726–28
  rights and remedies of agent, 711
  rights and remedies of principal, 703–8
  special agent, 694
  subagent, 694–95, 705
  termination of, 711–14
  terminology, 705
  third party relations; *See* Third party agency relations
  types of, 694–95
Agent
  accounting, duty of, 701
  assumption of liability by, 733
  communication, duty of, 701–2
  contract liability of, 730–34
  duties toward principal, 696–708
  duty of care, 700–701
  election between principal or agent liability, 732–33
  fiduciary duty of loyalty, 696–700
  foreign, 1132–33
  gratuitous agents, 700–701
  knowledge or notice, imputation of, 702
  obedience, duty of, 701
  partner as, 772
  principal's duties toward, 708–11
  ratification of authority, 726–28
  rights and remedies, 711
Aggregate theory of partnership, 753
Agreed damages, 347
Air, ownership interest in, 183–85
Alexander, G., 254n
Allonge, 492
Alteration, defined, 569
Alteration of instrument, 547, 552–55
  loss allocation, 569–78